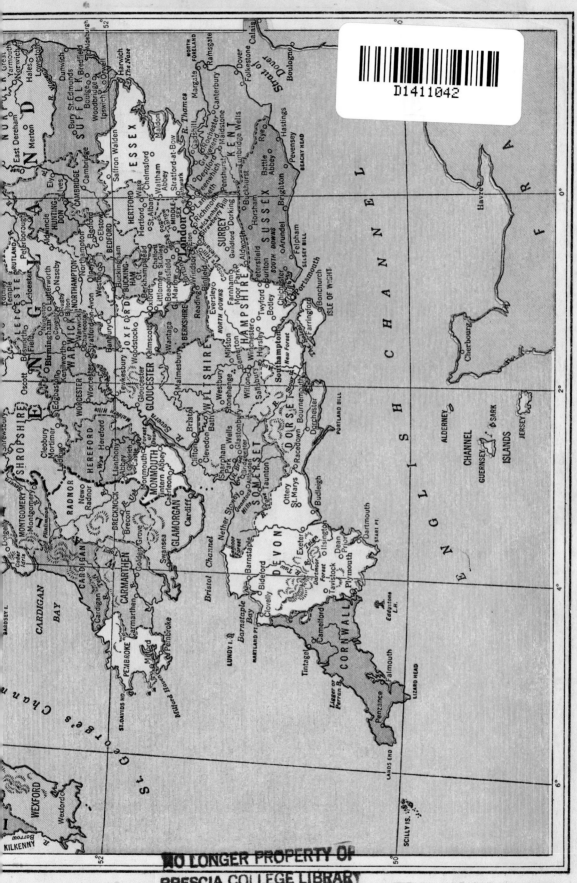

D1411042

NO LONGER PROPERTY OF
BRESCIA COLLEGE LIBRARY

FROM BEOWULF TO THOMAS HARDY

VOLUME II

HEERE BIGYNNETH THE PRIORESSES TALE

A litel scole of cristen folk ther stood
Doun at the ferther ende, in which ther were
Children an heepe, ycomen of cristen blood,
That lerned in that scole yeer by yere
Swich manere doctrine as men used there,
This is to seyn, to syngen and to rede,
As smale children doon in hire childhede.

AMONG thise children was a wydwes
sone,
A litel clergeon, seven yeer of age,
That day by day to scole was his wone,
And eek also, whereas he saugh thymage
Of Cristes mooder, hadde he in usage,
As hym was taught, to knele adoun and seye,
His Ave Marie, as he goth by the weye.

Thus hath this wydwe hir litel sone ytaught
Oure blisful lady, Cristes mooder deere,
To worshipe ay, and he forgate it naught,
For sely child wol alday soone leere;
But ay, whan I remembre on this mateere,
Seint Nicholas stant evere in my presence,
For he so yong to Crist dide reverence.

This litel child, his litel book lernynge,
As he sat in the scole at his prymer,

WAS IN ASYE, IN A GREET CITEE,
Amonges cristene folk, a Jewerye,
Sustened by a lord of that contree,
For foule usure, and lucre of vileynye,
Hateful to Crist and to his compaignye;
And thurgh the strete men myghte ride or
wende,
For it was free, and open at eyther ende.

Page 58 of the famous Kelmscott *Chaucer* (1893) printed by William Morris (see page 481), who also designed and cut the type used, and designed the borders and initials. The illustrations were drawn by Sir Edward Burne-Jones (1833–1898). Morris brought the spirit of fine craftsmanship into modern printing, and the *Chaucer* is his crowning achievement. Compare this page with the frontispiece in Volume I of this anthology. (Courtesy of the Pierpont Morgan Library.)

FROM BEOWULF TO THOMAS HARDY

NEW EDITION WITH PERIOD INTRODUCTIONS

ROBERT SHAFER

*Professor of Literature and Fellow
of the Graduate School
University of Cincinnati*

VOLUME II

THE ODYSSEY PRESS · NEW YORK

BRESCIA LIBRARY
OWENSBORO, KY.

COPYRIGHT, 1940
BY THE ODYSSEY PRESS, INC.
COPYRIGHT, 1924, 1931
BY DOUBLEDAY, DORAN AND COMPANY, INC.

ALL RIGHTS RESERVED
PRINTED IN THE U. S. A.

EIGHTH PRINTING OF THE NEW EDITION

820.8
S525

BRESCIA LIBRARY
OWENSBORO, KY.

Preface

In preparing the present new edition of *From Beowulf to Thomas Hardy* I have reconsidered the question of texts to be presented, much as if I were now compiling the work for the first time. The Revised Edition of 1931 included a number of writers not represented in the original edition. Expansion of this kind is tempting, and is always being suggested; nevertheless, it cannot continue without either increasing the size of the work beyond manageable proportions or causing me to abandon my first intention. I wished in 1924 to provide an acceptable book which would make possible a well-rounded survey of English literature without sacrifice of concentration. I then wrote, in the Preface to the first edition:

"These volumes are designed primarily for the introductory course in the general history of English literature given in many colleges and universities. The plan they follow is based on the conviction, gained from my own experience and that of many other teachers, that anthologies and collections of extracts are more useful to those who know literature than to those who are just learning to know it. It is of little permanent use for the learner to read a few pages of fragments from the work of an important writer; it may even do him harm rather than good. These volumes represent an effort to consult the learner's actual needs; and to this end not only have writers of minor importance, and works which can profitably be studied only by the mature student, been excluded, but the writers who are represented are, I hope, adequately represented."

The aim thus expressed still seems to me decidedly the most important one of such a textbook as *From Beowulf to Thomas Hardy*. Hence in the present edition I have not only refrained from increasing the number of writers included, but have actually reduced the number below the total in the Revised Edition of 1931; although eight writers or sections now first appear in the work and a great deal of new matter, including three additional plays, the passages from Bede and Pepys, letters by Gray, Cowper, Lamb, and FitzGerald, and some important poems—in particular the long narrative poem which in 1911 made Mr. John Masefield internationally famous. Even so, every teacher will miss some cherished writer or some favorite poem; I do myself, and regret, as much as anyone else, that we cannot have everything all of us would like. I hope, however, the book does now contain all that is needed for a solid foundation in the historical study of English literature.

To this end, moreover, I have for the first time divided the contents into sections, and have written a commentary on the several periods, including a final chapter on English literature of the present day. I cannot claim that these chapters constitute a "history of English literature," much less a "complete" one. I have never, indeed, been able to decide just what would constitute a "history of literature." Most books ostensibly falling in this category are not "histories" as the word is used in the field of social institutions. My own aim has been simply

6037

to provide a running commentary, designed to give students an adequate background for intelligent study of the texts, and thus to make it unnecessary to use, in connection with this new edition, any supplementary handbook. I should be inclined to call the chapters, taken by themselves, a "Preface to English Literature." I have made a strenuous effort to coördinate the commentary and the short introductions to the writers included, and hope the two kinds of introductory matter usefully complement each other throughout. Some small amount of repetition has seemed unavoidable, but this may serve the purpose of stressing matters that need to be firmly grasped. For the sake of precision in that skeleton of hard fact which is indispensable in historical study, I have added to this edition also a Chronological Outline. It may not be amiss to state here that I have, with the most recent writers on the period, accepted the corrected date for the death of Alfred which appears to be finally established; and that I have also, in both commentary and Outline, given the actual dates of publication of certain books, when known, even though the years given differ from those on the title pages of the books in question.

As in the Revised Edition, editorial omissions are indicated by asterisks (*) and, in one or two cases, by footnotes. One short passage omitted by Skeat in his translation of *Piers Plowman,* which has been used in the present edition, has not been supplied in a note, because it was thought best not to give possible occasion for scandal. For the same reason a single sentence has, with reluctance, been omitted from Dekker's *Shoemakers' Holiday.*

In the work of revision and change I have been assisted by Dr. Rudolf B. Gottfried. Dr. Gottfried is responsible for the completely revised glossary at the end of Volume I, for the modernized version of *The Second Shepherds' Play* here presented, for introductions to texts, such as this play and *The Shoemakers' Holiday,* now first included, for the Chronological Outline (in the main), and for many new footnotes. Besides acknowledging Dr. Gottfried's assistance, I must give hearty thanks to Dr. Siegmund A. E. Betz for some useful suggestions and for help with proofs. I wish also to thank Mr. Brett and Mr. Morehouse of The Macmillan Company for the unusual measures they kindly took to enable me to reprint Mr. Masefield's *Everlasting Mercy,* and to thank Mr. Masefield himself for his part in this matter. I wish further to express grateful appreciation to The Pierpont Morgan Library, The New York Public Library, and The Metropolitan Museum of Art for the use of their facilities and the generous help extended by their staffs in securing the illustrations included.

Other debts inevitably, in a work of this kind, are many, and important, and I am sorry that I cannot acknowledge them severally. It is not possible; and I must be content with a general expression of gratitude to the critics and scholars from whom I have learned.

R. S.

1 June, 1939.

Contents

V. THE ROMANTIC REACTION AND TRIUMPH, 1784–1837

VI. THE VICTORIAN ERA AND AFTER, 1837–1914

Contents

VII. THE PRESENT TIME, 1914–

Descriptive and Critical Essay 1046

Illustrations

FROM SHERIDAN TO THOMAS HARDY

The Romantic Reaction and Triumph, 1784–1837

No IMPORTANT literary change takes place overnight. We are not to suppose that a reaction against eighteenth-century standards occurred instantly upon the death of Dr. Johnson in 1784. The rise of Romanticism was, like other significant alterations in outlook, thought, and feeling, a gradual development. If we follow the course of a great river from the mountain springs and brooks which feed it in its highest reaches until finally it empties itself in the ocean, we see it first as a tiny stream, slowly enlarged as tributary streams flow into it; we may travel many miles along its course with our consciousness of its growth lulled almost to forgetfulness because that growth is indeed almost imperceptible; yet sooner or later a time comes when we suddenly realize that our hillside brook has been transformed into a vast waterway, capable of bearing large ships, and dominating not only the landscape but the life of the people along its shores.

Great literary movements usually grow in a manner not dissimilar. Men in after-ages can discern a moment when an important change has definitely taken place, a moment when a new outlook or attitude has come to the front; but it is not usually possible to determine precisely when several streams of influence united to form a great dominating movement. Hence those engaged in the historical study of literature have to keep it in mind that the dividing lines drawn between periods are no more than convenient approximations. The periods do exist, and

are clearly distinguishable from one another; yet at the same time they merge into one another, overlap, and refuse to lend themselves to the demands of an exact chronology.

The year in which Dr. Johnson died offers itself as a convenient point of division because Johnson was the last of the three acknowledged rulers of the literary world of England who successively "reigned" in the years from 1660 to 1784. The earlier two had been Dryden and Pope. Dr. Johnson was no mere upholder of tradition; he possessed courage and independence, and knew that men of genius could not finally be judged by any rule or standard except effectiveness. He did on the whole, however, share the literary faith of the eighteenth century—for example, its reliance on common sense and its distrust of the free imagination—and hence threw the massive weight of his judgments nearly always on the side of accepted standards. Thus as long as he lived, the forces of rebellion against eighteenth-century rules had a powerful foe, and the unity of the period from 1660 to 1784 was substantially maintained.

Scientific Rationalism and Human Nature

Dr. Johnson had no successor. The rationalistic impulse which had produced the characteristic literature of the Restoration and the eighteenth century was, by 1784, dead or dying, as a literary motive and as a source of critical standards. Rationalism had been a legacy of the humanism of the Renaissance. When humanism had destroyed the medieval culture based on tradition, it had slowly been forced into reliance on reason as a new source of social, intellectual, and artistic order. And as long as the seventeenth-century background of anarchic disorder had remained vivid, rationalism had been able to inspire a significant literature, chiefly satirical. But rationalism encouraged above all the desire for ordered, demonstrable knowledge, and turned the energies of men specially towards scientific discovery. As we all know, moreover, the progressive development of science from the latter part of the seventeenth century to the present time has been continuous; and from Sir Isaac Newton on, the discoveries of men of science have been so impressive as to exercise a profound influence upon the whole life and outlook of the successive generations. No one has really wanted to quarrel with science, which is only another name for exact knowledge, or with reason; nevertheless, eighteenth-century rationalism was drying up the springs of literary endeavor, and Romanticism was first of all a protest against the current rationalistic view of human nature and of imagination.

If we recall the attitude and outlook encouraged by scientific rationalism in the eighteenth century we can see at once what this means. Verifiable knowledge— as against conjecture, faith, or superstition —had been the aim of European man since the Renaissance. Prosecution of this aim necessitated a skeptical attitude towards traditional beliefs, and the elaboration of right methods of inquiry. But no limits were set to the amount and kinds of exact knowledge attainable by man, once humanity undertook the effort in the right way. And spectacular success in scientific discovery led men to believe that only time and further effort were needed in order to bring the whole realm open to human observation within the sphere of science. There were to be sciences of life, of human nature, of society, as well as physical science, chemistry, astronomy, and the like. Further, knowledge was power, as Francis Bacon had

said. Hence in proportion as the field of exact knowledge was extended, man would be able to alter and control not only his material environment, but his social organization and his behavior, for the better satisfaction of his desires; and in time earthly life would be perfectly happy for everybody.

Men, however, could not passively wait until science should be complete. Old beliefs had been undermined, and in some instances proved false. By way of anticipation, to fill an imperative need of human understanding, a new conception of the universe began to be formed in the light of what was already discovered. The early triumphs of science were secured in the field of mechanics. The universe, accordingly, came to be conceived as a vast and complex mechanical contrivance, wherein every smallest part had its appointed place and function, the whole moving in obedience to inexorable, unvarying laws discoverable by man. The logical inference from this was that man himself must be a mere machine, or small mechanical contrivance, playing a predetermined part in the precisely ordered whole.

The trouble with these hopes and inferences was not chiefly that they were contradictory. That was a difficulty which might be surmounted. The trouble went deeper. The new outlook afforded small scope for man's emotional nature, and none for his intuitions, instinctive sympathies, and kindly impulses. Observation and reason were not merely exalted; they were also placed in opposition to the rest of man's nature. Using a political analogy, we may say that they were made joint tyrants. Thus man was reduced to a kind of calculating machine, with the prospect of earthly satisfactions supplying the motive power. At the same time art was reduced practically to ornamentation, and writing tended to become a pastime of cultivated people, rather like a game played according to elaborate and strict rules. So far as poetry was anything better than this, it was still severely restricted, being confined more and more to careful observation and description.

Religion suffered no less. The new outlook was not inconsistent with the idea of a Divine Creator, but the idea suggested was merely that of a remote incomprehensible First Cause. God indeed was actually likened to a watchmaker : He had cleverly fashioned the universe as a piece of mechanism which, when He had wound it up and set it in motion, required no further attention. Such a conception obviously removed the life and substance from religion, and made Christianity seem what the historian Edward Gibbon, for example, thought it—a superstitious belief which could be imposed on ignorant barbarians, but which an enlightened humanity could no longer take seriously. Furthermore, once men had placed God completely outside the universe, and had begun to think of the latter as a self-contained mechanism, it was only a short step, and one which was soon taken, to atheistic materialism.

It was not science, but this mechanistic philosophy derived from science, against which the romantic reaction was primarily directed. A century and a half ago men could not see as clearly as we can now that the conception of mechanism derived from physical science has only a very limited usefulness as an aid towards a right understanding of the world in which we live, and of ourselves; they could not see this clearly, but some men began to feel it strongly. A few men, indeed, practically from the beginning of the eighteenth century, felt that human nature was not so much interpreted as dogmatically denied by scientific rationalism. It was evident also that the crude utilitarianism, which seemed to be the only system of conduct sanctioned by this rationalism, neglected or denied important motives that do animate human beings in their social life. These denials caused a growing protest which finally, at the end of the century, culminated in the Romantic Movement.

The Romantic Reaction Not a Concerted Movement

The Romantic Movement was not an organized campaign. No committee drew up a set of principles to which literary men were asked to subscribe. The one thing that can be said of the movement as a whole is that it was a reaction; and a reaction is, in itself,

negative. On the positive side almost any kind of effort might be made to rescue humanity from the deadening effects of eighteenth-century formalism, shallowness, incurious complacency, and materialism; and, as we shall see, efforts of very different kinds were made, not all with the conscious purpose just stated, and some of them not logically related to one another. The consequence is that we find amongst romantic writers men of opposed political beliefs, both conservatives and radicals; and men of opposed religious beliefs, both orthodox Christians and militant atheists, and also, somewhere between, men apparently indifferent to religious problems or men with new religions to propose. We find, too, men who believed themselves to be strict rationalists; philosophical critics who desired, not to attack reason, but to bring in a new conception of it; and others whom men of the early eighteenth century would have called "enthusiasts," who based their beliefs upon direct intuitions which, they asserted, gave them knowledge above the reach of reason. We find some who regarded Pope as the arch-enemy of true poetry, and others who defended him as a great poet, and modeled work of their own upon his. Moreover, we find these oppositions not only as we pass from one romantic writer to another, but occasionally within one and the same person.

The picture is one of confusion; and our sense of confusion may be deepened when we realize that, though Romanticism had a widespreading and varied background, still, the full romantic impulse was felt by only a small number of people. Nor is this all; for, as the nineteenth century advanced, and romantic poetry and prose were more and more widely recognized as great achievements, the new literature remained none the less something apart from the main stream of English life. In the early years of the nineteenth century the energies of the people were largely absorbed by the long war against revolutionary and imperial France which ended in the defeat of Napoleon at Waterloo in 1815 ; and then and later their attention was closely concentrated on those applications of science to industry which were bringing in the factory system, mass production, and the prodigious increase in trade and wealth that accompanied the growth of the British overseas empire throughout the century. Scientific rationalism, in other words, was the constructive force really in control of English life and English practical thought from the middle of the eighteenth century on; and no reaction, no protest, seriously menaced that control or interrupted the steady processes of change which were materializing English life.

The Romantic Movement, then, was not the expression in literature of a change in outlook which the English nation underwent, or even of a change which overtook a certain class. It was not a social or political movement. It was personal, and in a sense private. Its importance arises from the fact that it gave freedom of development and expression, and inspiration, to half a dozen men of remarkable genius who, with others possessed of real though slighter gifts, in the space of a few years enriched English literature almost immeasurably. In so doing, moreover, certain of the romantic writers kept men awake to the fact, whether it was seriously heeded or not, that the spirit or soul has its own needs distinct from those of the body. Romanticism, in short, revitalized not only the artistic impulse, but also spiritual aspiration and religious faith.

When, however, we contemplate the diversity of outlook, interest, talent, and aim which separates the romantic writers from one another, we may be tempted to exclaim that only the accident of time unites them, that there was no real "movement," and that the word Romanticism is indefinable. Yet it is not so. There is a real, even though loose, unity of temper holding the romantic writers together. We do not find in their work logical consistency, but we do find emotional consistency, and from this we can satisfy ourselves that the use of "Romanticism" to denominate the movement as a whole is not arbitrary, but reasonable and informative. It is always true that general terms can be applied to literature for historical purposes in only a loose and approximative fashion, just as literature can be divided off into periods in only a loose way. In England there are important differences between the literature of the Middle Ages, that of the sixteenth century, and that of the early nineteenth—differences which make it impossible to call these three periods "romantic" without distinction. But there is continuity also which demands recognition, and "romantic" is an indispensable term for the description of this common element, just as Romanticism usefully indicates that which unites an otherwise very diverse group of writers of the early nineteenth century.

The Rationalistic Attitude towards Romance

We can best perceive the continuity mentioned above, and at the same time lay a foundation for defining the Romanticism of the early nineteenth century, if we glance at the history of the word's uses. It was remarked in an earlier chapter that Pepys in his *Diary* speaks of certain things which were, he says, "almost romantic, and yet true." For Pepys, then, a "romance" was a lying tale; and the word had been used in this sense for a hundred and fifty years before the Restoration, though after 1650 its use as a term of condemnation had increased. Rationalism by then was in the ascendant, and the Middle Ages were regarded as a time of Gothic barbarism and ignorance, when the ability to distinguish between truth and falsehood was almost nonexistent. Persons of that rude time, it was supposed, could readily be taken in by tales of "impenetrable armors, enchanted castles, invulnerable bodies, iron men, flying horses, and a thousand other such things, which are easily feigned," as Thomas Hobbes contemptuously wrote in 1650. The medieval romances of love and chivalry had in truth been written by men who believed that almost anything was possible. They knew well enough the prosaic limits of possibility in their own time and land, but, as was said in Chapter II, they felt that the world was large and strange, and that it was not at all unlikely that just around the corner the oddest things might happen. It was not in the least difficult to suppose that in some less degenerate age or country men really had been braver, stronger, and more single-hearted in devotion than were such knights and barons as the poet actually knew. And why should there not be somewhere, beyond the horizon, enchanted castles, horses that could fly, and a thousand other things equal to the wayward heart's desire?

The medieval imagination, thus set free, had worked sometimes nobly, sometimes irresponsibly, but in both cases had habitually exceeded "the possibility of nature." And this was just what Hobbes and others following him in the age of rationalism condemned, because the progress of rational knowledge had shown that by no means everything was possible. On the contrary, man and the world of nature were rigidly limited in a universe of law; and it was now believed that it was the function of literary art to "imitate" or follow Nature faithfully. Man, moreover, it was also believed, was most truly himself, most fully human, when he was in a condition of balance, with reason at the helm. And because medieval romances, and seventeenth-century heroic romances as well, conspicuously violated this rationalistic canon, "romantic" became a convenient term signifying everything that violated common sense. To be "romantic" was to be childish, ridiculous, unnatural, and even profane, impious, and vile.

Sentimentalism the First Stage of Reaction

In the eighteenth century, as we have already noticed, some men began to feel that rational knowledge was not a sufficient basis for human life. Everything said in favor of balance might sound excellent, yet in practice it appeared to produce complacent stagnation, shallowness, and the calm acceptance of the extraordinary doctrine that "whatever is, is right." Similarly, realistic common sense turned out in practice to be a justification of social abuses and of a life spent in mean-spirited calculations for selfish advantage. Excitement, generous hope, worship, *interest* were removed from life. Man was found to be a great deal less than man if he no longer had some object beyond himself to which he could passionately devote his energies. Man had feelings as well

as powers of observation and thought; and an early consequence of the rationalistic attempt to banish feeling was a species of revengeful reaction, wherein the feelings reasserted themselves as something to be encouraged, if for no other reason, then for their own sake. Thus appeared sentimentalism, a new disease whose symptoms were mentioned in Chapter IV.

Sentimentalism, however, cannot be dismissed with a smile at its absurdities and a frown at its evils. Emotional susceptibility encouraged a growing interest in *persons*. Rationalism had subordinated the individual at every point to impersonal law. Awakened sensibility now led the way to a reassertion of the dignity, the worth, the importance, the rights of the individual. It began to be felt that instead of distrusting and subordinating himself, man should cherish his individuality, cultivate it, and assert it boldly, in the full confidence that his native instincts and the inward motions of his heart were his surest guides to truth and the good life.

The New Meaning of Romanticism

In the new individualism that was asserting itself we have the foundation of the Romantic Movement of the early nineteenth century. The word "romantic" can be applied to the movement as a whole because the writers who participated in it were all engaged, in one way or another, in violating common sense. To this extent the meaning of the word remained unchanged. In effect, however, its meaning was profoundly altered by the success with which rebellion against eighteenth-century rationalism was vindicated. Henceforth "romantic" became a term of praise. And in the last half-century or more many critics and historians have been tending to use the word vaguely to denote whatever they think original, vivid, and powerful in art and literature, as opposed to what is abstract, artificial, and lifeless.

We are on safer ground if we take "romantic" to mean simply the kind of thing which the unimaginative and balanced mind rejects as a contradiction of common sense or of rational knowledge. Thus a consuming love drawing two persons together irresistibly despite every obstacle, causing them to give up friends, social position, and every worldly advantage—this is "romantic." Such love is felt to be more than human, and those who exhibit it are for the time being "beside themselves," or are at any rate drawn out of themselves by overmastering attraction. Romantic lovers are commonly derided by mercantile people who have some vulgar shrewdness, and, in general, by men supposed to have their feet planted firmly on the ground. In turn we find it laughable when some plumber or bank clerk blossoms out into a romantic lover. But the spectacle of an all-conquering love between two people who can sustain the role without any intrusion of the incongruous catches at the hearts of most of us, and makes us wish ourselves in their place. We are lifted for a moment out of the dull round of daily tasks, the confined space, the dreary outlook which is our usual portion in life. We feel ourselves enlarged and renewed by the reminder that deep joyous feeling is possible and that bold action against odds may be successful. We are awakened to the perception of life as something that does after all include the unexpected, the gambling chance, perhaps even the miraculous. Anything, then, which takes us beyond the bounds of accustomed experience, and makes us feel that life can be an adventurous encounter with the unknown; anything which breaks the prison bars of supposed necessity, and brings it home to us that life is a mystery and that we are surrounded by mysteries; any vision which causes us even momentarily to suspend our usual skepticism and disbelief is "romantic."

The New Romanticism and the Middle Ages

We have now taken a general view of the cause of the romantic reaction, and have seen why the new literature which issued from it is called "romantic." Our next step must be a review of the varied developments in the latter half of the eighteenth century which constitute the reaction, and which historically led to the triumph of Romanticism in

the work of Wordsworth, Coleridge, Scott, Byron, Shelley, and Keats. These developments have an interest of their own, apart from the fact that we cannot properly understand the eighteenth century without becoming acquainted with them; but our fundamental reason for glancing at them here is that intelligent study of the great romantic writers is not possible without some knowledge of their immediate literary, political, and religious background.

We may conveniently begin by noticing that one of the earliest achievements of awakened sensibility in the eighteenth century was the stimulation of a new interest in the Middle Ages, and especially in the old heroic poetry of the Germanic and Celtic peoples. This interest was gratified astonishingly by a Scottish school teacher, James Macpherson, who in the 1760's published several volumes which purported to be translations of early Celtic poems discovered by him in the Highlands. Some contemporaries promptly doubted the genuineness of these alleged translations, and today it is accepted as certain that they were mostly forgeries, though Macpherson did have some genuine fragments which served him as a point of departure. The significant thing, however, is that the poems of Ossian—the legendary Gaelic bard to whom Macpherson attributed *Fingal, Temora,* and other "translations"—were immediately popular. Readers wanted to believe in them, despite evidence. The poet Gray, who himself paraphrased some Northern poems, was enraptured, and exclaimed that the Ossianic pieces were "full of nature and noble wild imagination."

The truth is that Macpherson's earliest readers had begun to entertain sentimental notions about the virtues of primitive people living in a simple way under the benign influence of unspoiled natural scenery; and Macpherson gave them just what they wanted. He made no attempt at a faithful representation of "barbaric" life, warfare, or even poetry as he knew it from such fragments of Gaelic verse as were accessible to him. Using the language and cadences of the English Bible, and deriving from Homer some hints concerning heroic life and character, he made a series of fancy pictures, representing ancient Northern life, not as it was, but as his contemporaries wanted to imagine it. His heroes are elaborately polite, full of tender feeling, generous, and brave; and are in all these qualities, as he pointed out, superior to the Homeric heroes. In moments of inactivity they readily drop into a vein of melancholy reflectiveness, very like that of certain eighteenth-century poets who had taken to reflecting with pleasing melancholy on graveyard scenes, moldering ruins, and other reminders of the transitory nature of life. The scenic background of the poems, too, is appropriately elemental and awe-inspiring. Macpherson, in short, succeeded in being both "noble" and "wild," and succeeded so well that his "translations" became a major influence, not only in England but also on the Continent, in awakening romantic feeling.

Another series of forgeries, the *Rowley Poems* of Thomas Chatterton, had a temporary vogue for reasons much the same as those which raised the Ossianic poems to fame. Chatterton was hailed as "the marvelous boy," and not unjustly, because all his poetry was written while he was in his teens. Made desperate by poverty, he poisoned himself with arsenic in his eighteenth year (1770). His early miserable death has kept his name alive, but not his poetry, which had some plausibility and interest only so long as the Middle Ages were still the object of enthusiastic but ignorant curiosity.

Chatterton's "wild" inventions were modeled chiefly on the traditional ballads collected by Bishop Thomas Percy and published in three volumes in 1765 as *Reliques of Ancient English Poetry*. Percy differed widely from Macpherson in that he really had a large quantity of popular poetry, some of it dating from early in the fifteenth century; and he did reproduce it, but, like Macpherson, he dressed up his "relics," freely altering and falsifying them to suit contemporary taste. Though Percy's collection did not cause the sensation that the Ossianic poems did, interest in the old English and Scottish ballads has never waned from Percy's time to ours; and the ballads not

only helped to awaken romantic feeling but served as a direct inspiration to Coleridge and Keats, and later on to Tennyson, Swinburne, Rossetti, and others.

Percy was no more interested than Macpherson in attempting to understand the Middle Ages, or the life of early peoples. Indeed, it probably did not occur to either of them, or to others, that there was anything in these fields to be learned. There was no effort at this time to challenge the long-established view of the Middle Ages as a period of barbaric rudeness, ignorance, and superstition. What was happening was simply that the relics of "barbarism" were beginning to seem interesting and charming to men who felt secure in their own civilization, politeness, and rational knowledge, but who were finding their orderly lives and conceptions tame. They wanted some excitement and novel amusement.

Hurd's "Letters on Chivalry and Romance"

Richard Hurd in his *Letters on Chivalry and Romance* (1762) makes clear the reason for the reviving interest in medieval tales. Hurd was a clergyman and became a bishop; he was also something of a classical scholar, and an admirer of Pope and Addison. He was not by intention a rebel, but he felt that since Ariosto and Tasso in Italy, and Spenser and Milton in England, had been charmed by the "Gothic" romances, it was possible that men of the eighteenth century had gone too far "in their perpetual ridicule and contempt" of medieval tales of love and chivalry. He himself, he confessed, had not read the "barbarous volumes" containing the old romances, because he had learned all that one could want to know about them from a book by a learned Frenchman. But he had been struck, in reading this book, by a surprising likeness between the manners of the Greek heroes of Homer's *Iliad* and the manners of the Gothic barbarians of the age of chivalry, and this revelation led him on to some novel conclusions.

In so far, Hurd wrote, as the heroic and the Gothic manners are identical, "the pictures of each, if well taken, must be equally entertaining." This was, in 1762, an audacious statement, but he went further and maintained that where the two ages differed the advantage lay with the Gothic period:

Much has been said, and with great truth, of the felicity of Homer's age for poetical manners. But as Homer was a citizen of the world, when he had seen in Greece, on the one hand, the manners he has described, could he, on the other hand, have seen in the west the manners of the feudal ages, I make no doubt but he would certainly have preferred the latter. And the grounds of this preference would, I suppose, have been *the improved gallantry of the feudal times, and the superior solemnity of their superstitions.*

Hurd went on to explain just what he meant. In the *Iliad,* he thought, the chief entertainment arose from the delineation of boisterous passions, provoked and kept alive from one end of the poem to the other "by every imaginable scene of rage, revenge, and slaughter." But in the romances, besides rage and slaughter, we find "the most interesting displays of love and friendship—of love elevated to its noblest heights, and of friendship operating on the purest motives." These displays awaken in us "the gentler and more humane affections," and their "beauty, novelty, and pathos" give the romances a vast advantage, in his opinion, over the Homeric poems. Similarly he thought that the religious machinery of Homer and of the Gothic poets was equally irrational, but that medieval use of the supernatural was "more amusing, as well as more awakening to the imagination."

Having concluded on these grounds for the superiority of the Middle Ages to the ancient or heroic time, Hurd went on to discuss the poetry of Milton, Spenser, and Tasso, and finally to explain how in his politer age the "growing splendor" of reason had put all the "portentous specters" of the medieval imagination to flight, with a great gain on the side of good sense, but a corresponding loss of "fine fabling." He considered this loss lamentable and unnecessary, and proceeded to attack the rationalistic requirements of verisimilitude and truth to Nature. Poets, he declared, are not so unreasonable as to expect to have their lies believed; "they think it enough if they can but bring you to *imagine* the possibility of them." There is, he insisted, another kind of truth beside philosophical or historical truth—there is also *poetical* truth, which the poet discovers in "a world of his own, where experience has less to do than consistent imagination." He admitted that poetical truth is "almost as severe a thing as historical" in those kinds of poetry which address themselves, not to the imagination, but to the heart, through the passions. But, he added,

The case is different with the more sublime and creative poetry. This species, addressing itself solely or principally to the imagination—a young and credulous faculty, which loves to admire and to be deceived—has no need to observe those cautions of credibility so necessary to be followed by him who would touch the affections and interest the heart.

Hurd was seeking entertainment, and found a threefold attraction in things "Gothic": they had the charm of novelty, they opened up scenes which were striking and "wild," and they had a sentimental appeal lacking in the heroic poetry of ancient Greece. In addition Hurd felt, somewhat obscurely, that the literary standards of the age of rationalism had stifled the imagination; and he lighted upon several considerations, into which he did not go deeply, to justify and encourage freedom in imaginative creation. In none of this was he alone. The historical value of his *Letters* lies in the fact that he gave clear expression to a general tendency, in itself rather frivolous, but significant too, in that it was a movement towards freedom.

Gothic Tales of Terror

One immediate consequence of the trend towards imaginative freedom was the "Gothic" tale of mystery and terror which flourished in the latter part of the eighteenth century. In these tales medieval settings served as an excuse for sensational action. The earliest of them was written by Horace Walpole, and was entitled *The Castle of Otranto* (1764). The species reached its culmination in *The Romance of the Forest* (1791), *The Mysteries of Udolpho* (1794), and *The Italian* (1797) of Mrs. Ann Radcliffe; and in *The Monk* (1796) of Matthew Gregory Lewis. The prime requisite for this kind of fiction was a setting distant in time or place, which by its strangeness could lend plausibility to supernatural interventions, horrible conspiracies, fiendish abductions or murders, cruel tortures, and, in general, whatever might make the fascinated reader's hair stand on end. For the purpose in view, an oriental setting could be just as effective as one full of medieval trappings, as was proved by William Beckford in his celebrated *History of the Caliph Vathek* (1786).

Though several of them can still be read with pleasure, this crop of "thrillers," taken as a whole, seems absurd and trivial. Yet the "Gothic" tales have real historical importance. They are the literary counterparts of Strawberry Hill and Fonthill Abbey, the two flimsy and pretentious Gothic edifices built, respectively, by Walpole and Beckford, in which the impressiveness of medieval architecture was reduced to the quality of stage properties. But Gothic tale and Gothic castle alike ministered to something more than the idle amusement of Walpole and of other sophisticated and bored people. In them the creative imagination was set free; and this in itself was important, even though it did not instantly work to any serious purpose. Moreover, these tales presented a world in which the passions ruled and excitement prevailed, and so prepared the way for Walter Scott; and in addition they did something to nourish a growing love of the picturesque.

Growth of Interest in Wild Natural Scenery

Thomas Gray was as ready to welcome a "noble wild" scene as a "noble wild imagination," and for the same reason. He found such a scene pleasurably stimulating to poetic emotion, primarily to the feeling of awe. This was a discovery, but Gray soon had company. At first, appreciation of natural scenery was very like the dawning interest in things "Gothic," in that nature's theatrical aspects were sought and admired. Lovers of the Middle Ages were thrilled by towering battlements, dungeons, secret passages, and the like; and now "the sounding cataract," "the tall rock, the mountains, and the deep and gloomy wood" were found to be also thrilling. Nature in her wilder aspects had from time immemorial been disliked and feared. Dislike had been inevitable as long as men had felt that they had only a precarious foothold on earth, and were able barely to win a living from a hostile land, controlled by mysterious forces which might crush or rend them without warning at any moment. And this had been the lot of most men in most places. It was the achievement, by the middle of the eighteenth century, of the feeling of security and of some power to control nature which made possible the discovery of a new pleasure. It was a pleasure akin to that which the Latin poet Lucretius describes in the famous opening lines of the second book of his *De Rerum Natura,* where he observes how sweet it is to be standing in safety on a promontory during a mighty storm at sea, while a frail ship is being tossed on the waves below, its crew helpless to avert disaster. The pleasure does not arise, Lucretius adds, from the sight of others' misery, but from the heightened consciousness of our own safety.

In similar fashion eighteenth-century Englishmen began to derive pleasure from forcible reminders of the vastness and terrifying power of nature. The search for picturesque scenery became a pastime of men of taste, and the more tremendous or "horrid" the features of a landscape were, the keener the thrill it gave. But gradually the entertainment derived from the spectacular in nature was metamorphosed. Modern readers have been apt to find the passage from Lucretius which has just been cited rather shocking, because of its lack of sentiment. Sentiment, however, was just what the eighteenth-century Englishman was full of, and presently he began to attribute to nature qualities suggested by his own feelings when in the presence of lofty crags, sylvan dells, serried banks of wooded hills, and the like. In such moments it seemed to him that he was lifted out of his ordinary cares, above life's trivialities, and not only breathed a purer air but was himself purified in spirit. Thus began to dawn a conviction that somehow nature spoke to man directly through the feelings; and, what was more, that the closer man's contact with nature the closer he would come to true wisdom.

Growing Belief in Man's Natural Goodness: Humanitarianism

The transition just outlined from the search for amusement and thrills to the search for wisdom and truth was momentous. But it was not effected exclusively through devotion to picturesque scenery. Along with the new conception of nature there was developing a new conception of man. For the purpose of discussion, we have to separate the various strands of a complex process and look at them one by one, remembering meanwhile that the new interest in the Middle Ages, the new conception of nature, and the new conception of man all went together and helped one another forward to the full romantic outlook.

The keystone of the new conception of man was simply the belief that man is by nature good. The first steps in the inculcation of this belief had been taken in England by the Earl of Shaftesbury in his *Characteristics* (1711). Shaftesbury has been discussed in Chapter IV, but it is now necessary to recall that he ascribed to man certain "natural affections," because of which men derive true satisfaction from acts promoting the welfare of society. Altruism, in other words, he held to be a part of man's inborn constitution. He also held that along with instinctive altruism, man is endowed with self-regarding impulses, such as the love of life and of the means to well-being, the love of praise, and the love of ease; but he thought that these two sets of impulses do not really conflict with one another. That which conduces to the welfare of society, he said, on the whole conduces to the happiness of the individual, and *vice versa*.

Here we have a system of morality founded on sentiment. The claim is made that man has instinctive sympathies impelling him to activity which is at once moral

and productive of his own happiness. This led on to the doctrine of man's natural goodness, which came to be widely accepted as the eighteenth century advanced. The doctrine, as it was generally understood, can be stated in a few words: Man is born with a good nature; his instinctive sympathies and impulses guide him in the right directions, towards morally good activities and also towards personal happiness; he has, in addition, the powers requisite to carry out his impulses; therefore man can, in his present life on earth, fulfill his nature and enjoy a perfectly happy existence. All that is needful to this end is that men should *just be themselves,* unafraid, trusting their spontaneous impulses.

This doctrine immeasurably sharpened the contrast, which men had always been aware of, between what should be and what is. If men are born good, why do most men behave badly and live miserably? The answer which suggested itself was that their original goodness had been corrupted by evil influences playing upon them from the surrounding world. Men themselves, consequently, could not be held responsible for their evil acts. Environment was the responsible agent. Hence if environmental influences could be altered, if men could be set free from depraving external compulsions, an idyllic existence for all would follow.

At this point the new confidence that nature and society might be controlled to serve beneficent human purposes, came into play. Social ills in particular became the subject of anxious consideration. Awakened moral sensibility expressed itself in sympathy for the unfortunate and in the determination to aid them. Alike the helpless foundling, deposited on a doorstep and left to its fate, and the murderer began to be regarded as the victims of an ill-organized society. And since society itself was the real criminal, the murderer as much as the foundling deserved pity and aid rather than punishment. In the middle and later years of the eighteenth century a multitude of proposals and efforts were made for the alleviation of human ills by a new species of being—the consecrated philanthropist or friend of mankind.

Thus humanitarianism appeared. It was

in effect a new religion, based on faith in man's natural goodness and on the confident belief that, in proportion as the external conditions of social life could be improved, humanity would be virtuous and happy. The humanitarian spirit manifested itself most notably, in the later eighteenth century, in efforts to reform English prisons and to abolish the slave trade and slavery itself. These and other efforts, however, barely scratched the surface of what was seen to be needed, as men's eyes were gradually opened, for the perfect regeneration of society. It became apparent, indeed, that nothing less than a revolution would suffice.

Political and Social Theory Based on the Doctrine of Man's Natural Goodness

In England there had existed since the end of the seventeenth century a body of political theory elaborated to justify revolution, and this now began to be studied and restated, more particularly in France than in England. The theory in question had been needed as a sanction for the English Revolution of 1688–1689, and the need had been met by the philosopher John Locke. The crucial difficulty in that revolution had been that James II, a sovereign acknowledged by everybody to hold the throne by hereditary right, had been displaced in favor of William and Mary, neither of whom had any recognized claim to the position. Either this was wholly unjustifiable and illegal, as many Englishmen believed, or the theory of the state which had hitherto been accepted was mistaken. According to long-established belief, society was divinely ordered in terms of inherited status, and the individual could only accept the position into which he was born. Some exceptions to this rule had always been recognized, and the system itself was breaking down in the seventeenth century, but it remained until 1688 the basis of sovereignty. And as long as it remained, there remained with it a lingering belief that the structure of society was not man-made, but was divinely ordained or was at least fixed by some natural necessity.

This notion was destroyed by the Revolution. William and Mary were man-made

sovereigns, inasmuch as their authority was conferred by Parliament. Clearly also what the people of England through Parliament could give, they could, if necessary, take away. Once this radical proposition had been tacitly accepted, it could only be justified on the ground that sovereignty really inhered in the people and was inalienable. Authority could be conferred or delegated for a purpose—the general welfare—but it remained at the same time with the people, who could accordingly withdraw their support from a ruler whose exercise of authority was not serving the general welfare. Locke thought that the validity of popular sovereignty could be rationally demonstrated, and in his *Two Treatises of Government* (1690) he laid the foundation of the political thought of the eighteenth century.

That thought became democratic in character and revolutionary in its implications. Locke himself had aimed, as was said above, only to give theoretic justification to a bloodless revolution already accomplished. But he could not do this without pointing the way to further developments. And when his lead was followed up in France, Shaftesbury's doctrine of man's natural goodness came in also as a formative influence. We cannot here trace out this progression or take account of ambiguities arising from use of the treacherous word "nature." It will be enough for our purpose to state the outcome in general terms.

Reason was held to have discovered that all men by nature are free, equal, and endowed with inalienable rights—the right to life and to the free pursuit of happiness, the right to control and dispose of their own persons and property, the right to think and speak as they please, and the right to oppose tyranny by force. These rights, however, were subject to the important qualification that reason, which vindicates them, must be recognized as the final arbiter of every question arising in the conduct of life. Hence no law or custom violating the dictates of reason could be accepted as binding. Of course the reason thus placed at the helm must *be* reason, clear and resplendent, and not any false appearance colored by prejudice or superstition. Everybody believed that reason was an intellectual faculty through which man was enabled to discover absolute or universal truth. Nobody doubted that man by nature possessed this faculty. It followed that men in the state of nature would all think alike, and would all act morally in accordance with reason, whose dictates must be always and everywhere the same. The state of nature, then, was a state wherein all men lived in complete freedom from external government or rule, each perfectly governed from within by reason.

We now can see how the same conclusion was being reached by different routes. Those who based man's native goodness on his possession of reason ended, exactly like those who founded it on sentiment or "natural affections," by sharply underlining the contrast between conditions as they were and conditions as they should be. Jean Jacques Rousseau exclaimed that man had been born free, yet was everywhere in chains. The popular explanation paralleled that offered by the sentimental humanitarians. It was said that "somehow" corruption had attacked a few men with the slow growth of luxury, that love of luxury had promoted unequal accumulations of property, and that thus ambition and greed had been brought into the world. A handful of unscrupulous men had obtained power over their fellows, and then had entrenched themselves firmly with the aid of prejudice and superstition. Kings and priests, in other words, upheld by irrational creeds, were at once the effect and cause of corruption—of all the pernicious social, political, and religious institutions which have enslaved man and darkened his reason.

Hence arose the belief that the progress of humanity would be forwarded by destruction. Humanity had gone off on a wrong course; if kingship and priestcraft were once rooted out, if men's chains were struck off and their eyes opened to reason, humanity could be trusted to take care of itself. With freedom once gained, everything good would follow. Experience, however, strongly suggested that freedom could not be maintained without safeguards. The problem therefore presented itself of devising a method of government completely responsible to the citizenry. The ideal was a government whose sphere and powers should be restricted to the smallest practicable proportions, and whose officers should be the servants of the people, subject to recall if they showed the slightest tendency to grasp at arbitrary power.

Consistently with the ideas which have been under discussion, a new attitude towards civilization began to appear in both England and France. In proportion as the state of nature was accepted as an ideal from which man had departed, and in proportion as contact with unspoiled natural surroundings was believed to be a source of wisdom, men began to turn in revulsion from civilization and all its works. Everything artificial became suspect, and everything natural began to be idealized. The polished sophisticated gentleman became an object of aversion. Under his fine appearance he concealed corruption, and true manhood was to be found in remote country cottages rather than in cities or royal courts. Indeed, whatever was man-made was to be condemned and shunned as the product of pride or greed, and the nursing-ground of vice; and whatever was untouched, unimproved, uncultivated on earth was to be contemplated reverently as the nursing-ground of virtue. Hence, examples of true manhood were sought in remote antiquity, and equally in remote parts of the earth where primitive conditions of life still obtained. The generous and polite Ossianic heroes rewarded the first search, and Omai, a South Sea Islander who was brought to London, most conspicuously rewarded the second. Omai captivated everybody by his dignity and gentleness, and only one or two people noticed that he became attached to civilization while he was serving as a demonstration of its evils.

The practical working conclusion to which the sentimental friends of humanity came was that true manhood was most likely to be found amongst untutored country folk living close to the soil. In time, the circle of "good men and true" was enlarged to embrace all who worked with their hands, and so came to include the mass of so-called common people, whom democratic politicians learned to flatter as "the backbone of the nation."

The French Revolution

In England, as we have been seeing, there was during the eighteenth century a steady growth of belief in the natural goodness of man and an impressive growth of humanitarianism, with accompanying interest in "noble wild" scenery and in "noble wild" man. But the development of political thought which has just been sketched took place in France. The reason for this difference is that Englishmen through the greater part of the century believed themselves to have, since the "glorious Revolution" of 1688–1689, the substantial blessings of order, security of life and property, free speech, religious toleration, and self-government by laws (as against arbitrary government by tyrants). English "liberty" was accordingly a subject of self-congratulation amongst Englishmen; and, more than that, it was recognized and acclaimed abroad as an example to Europe. Only as the century drew to a close did social discontent become at all active in England; and then it was confined to a small minority, in part because of the influence of Methodism, a religious development at which we shall presently glance.

In France, however, conditions were grievously bad. There, monarchy was absolute and was becoming decadent; the system of administration was corrupt and oppressive; public finances were in hopeless disorder; a privileged nobility was absorbing the lion's share of the national income and doing nothing useful in return; and those who worked the land were condemned to an indescribably miserable existence. No reasonable defense of the state of the nation was possible; and as the eighteenth century advanced, and some attempted reforms failed, conditions grew so flagrantly atrocious that the old monarchy and the whole social structure were ready to collapse at the first show of determined opposition.

Nevertheless, until the end, opposition remained dangerous; and was so far outlawed that political thinking was doctrinaire, and subversive criticism was in its temper desperate. Under such circumstances, no moderate solution was possible. And in fact the French Revolution, once it got under way, became a violent and embittered struggle to root out every institution which had been identified with the "unnatural" reign of prejudice and superstition. This was a large order, but the revolutionists were filled with a sacred rage, and the capacity of the guillotine was unlimited. We have already seen, moreover, why the French were confident that they had only to overturn the existing order, and to secure to themselves personal freedom, to bring in the beneficent reign of reason.

It is a disputed question how far the eloquent and passionate utopianism of Jean Jacques Rousseau was responsible for the beginning of the Revolution. Most questions concerning Rousseau are disputed. But one of the least doubtful things said of him is that, though he originated nothing, he set everything on fire. And there is no doubt that it was primarily he who charged with energizing emotion the cause of equalitarianism, freedom, and the life according to nature. From his writings, too, better than from any other source, one can see how eighteenth-century rationalism was transformed into a species of sentimental dogmatism which became a powerful engine of political and social change. The form of rationalism was preserved, but the "self-evident truths" from which reasoning was to proceed were not really self-evident at all. They were passionate aspirations which flew in the face of objective fact. The famous French rallying cry, "Liberty, Equality, Fraternity," represented, not a set of conditions which anywhere obtained, but the substance of things hoped for, from which, it was believed, earthly happiness for all men would issue.

In recognizing that a new dogmatism, with Rousseau's powerful help, arose under the cover of rationalism, we must be on our guard against supposing that Rousseau or others of his time were merely engaged in wishful thinking. They were inspired by an overwhelming conviction that human nature had noble possibilities not only unrealized in the characteristic life of the eighteenth century, but perverted or corrupted by that life and actually denied by the dominant "mechanical" philosophy, which sought truth through scientific observation, and wisdom in common sense. In bearing witness to this conviction they did not want to make a stand against "reason." The conviction was itself a kind of knowledge, born of immediate feeling; and "reason," as we have observed, was the accepted organ of knowledge. Therefore, inevitably, the party of rebellion wanted to keep "reason" on their side, though what they were determined "reason" should support was a thoroughly romantic conception of human nature.

Effect of the French Revolution in England

The American Revolution had been welcomed by some liberty-loving Englishmen as a triumphant assertion of human rights against the oppressor, even though the tyrant overthrown in this instance was their own sovereign. When, a few years afterwards, the French Revolution came, it was welcomed very generally on the same ground. The French, it was supposed, were at last striking for the freedom which Englishmen had enjoyed for a century, and of course they deserved success. Upon some, especially upon hopeful young men who had been growing up along with the growth of humanitarian sympathy, the impression made was far stronger. Their response can still best be seen from what Wordsworth wrote about his own feelings and faith at the time, in his autobiographical poem, *The Prelude*. "In the People," he says, "was my trust." As a youth he had seen only the golden side of human nature and had been ready to fight, "even to the death," to vindicate his confidence in the virtues of simple lowly people. The spectacle of human worth downtrodden had led him, like others, "to meditate with ardor on the rule and management of nations." "O" he then says,

O pleasant exercise of hope and joy!
For mighty were the auxiliars which then stood
Upon our side, us who were strong in love!
Bliss was it in that dawn to be alive,

But to be young was very Heaven! O times,
In which the meager, stale, forbidding ways
Of custom, law, and statute, took at once
The attraction of a country in romance!
When Reason seemed the most to assert her
　　rights
When most intent on making of herself
A prime enchantress—to assist the work,
Which then was going forward in her name!
Not favored spots alone, but the whole Earth,
The beauty wore of promise—that which sets
(As at some moments might not be unfelt
Among the bowers of Paradise itself)
The budding rose above the rose full blown.
What temper at the prospect did not wake
To happiness unthought of? The inert
Were roused, and lively natures rapt away!
They who had fed their childhood upon dreams,
The play-fellows of fancy, who had made
All powers of swiftness, subtlety, and strength
Their ministers—who in lordly wise had stirred
Among the grandest objects of the sense,
And dealt with whatsoever they found there
As if they had within some lurking right
To wield it;—they, too, who of gentle mood
Had watched all gentle motions, and to these
Had fitted their own thoughts, schemers more
　　mild,
And in the region of their peaceful selves;—
Now was it that both found, the meek and lofty
Did both find helpers to their heart's desire,
And stuff at hand, plastic as they could wish—
Were called upon to exercise their skill,
Not in Utopia—subterranean fields—
Or some secreted island, Heaven knows where!
But in the very world, which is the world
Of all of us—the place where, in the end,
We find our happiness, or not at all!

In these celebrated lines we have the classic expression of the joyous hope which the French Revolution aroused in the minds of some young men. They were ready to welcome with feverish excitement just such an uprising. They were ready—yet until the Revolution burst upon them they had not really believed that so good a thing could happen. Generous aspiration had led them to ardent dreams of an Earthly Paradise, when at one blow the Revolution transformed romantic visions into waking reality. All that the soaring spirit wanted to believe, and all that men of the world cynically disbelieved, was true! "Time was ready to set all things right"; and "the multitude, so long oppressed," had overnight felled tyranny and gained the power to become all that human nature ought to be.

This was the first impression. There followed a period of dismay, anger, and almost inexpressible disappointment as Wordsworth and other glad young men saw that, after all, the revolution in France was not bringing about the regeneration of humanity. The revolutionary leaders presently became "oppressors in their turn," and "changed a war of self-defense" to "one of conquest, losing sight of all which they had struggled for." Bitterly disillusioned, Wordsworth, Coleridge, and others had to readjust their outlook as best they could. Some men of their generation remained steadfast believers in an approaching perfect state of society despite all disheartening evidence; but the very great majority of Englishmen were thrown, because of their horror at the bloody excesses of the French Terror and at the appearance of military tyranny under Napoleon, into political conservatism. Wordsworth and Coleridge went with this majority, yet preserved unshaken their romantic faith in man. Henceforth it became their problem to vindicate that faith philosophically and poetically in ways consistent with social and political conservatism.

The effect of the French Revolution on English Romanticism does not, however, end here. The Revolution was the most profound upheaval which Europe had experienced since the Protestant Reformation in the sixteenth century, and, howsoever far it departed from the course its friends had anticipated, it left permanent marks. Nothing, indeed, could be quite the same after it, as time was to show. Moreover, to the generation born around 1789 or 1790 the great uprising was almost a legend by the time of their young manhood; and the early horror and disillusion felt by Wordsworth and others of his age was fading, while the social and political aspirations of the masses everywhere, once kindled by the Revolution, remained active. Hence members of the second generation of romantic writers—Byron, Shelley, and others of their age—were scarcely less affected by the Revolution than their predecessors.

So much can be said in general of the

effect of the French Revolution in England, but we can better understand its effect if we now consider briefly the work of two men whose immediate reactions to the upheaval were strikingly different.

William Godwin

We turn first to William Godwin as the English prophet and architect of a perfected free society. In 1789 Godwin was thirty-three years old and had given no sign of being marked out for fame; but four years later he published a book which became instantly famous, and then, in a little while, as British opinion swung overwhelmingly towards conservatism, infamous. The book was entitled *An Enquiry into the Principles of Political Justice; and Its Influence on General Virtue and Happiness*. Godwin had been stimulated to undertake it by the revolution in France, and was engaged in its composition for nearly two years. His intention was to make it a classic exposition of the immutable truth concerning human nature, the right ordering of human life on earth, and the happiness towards which humanity could look forward; and he did in fact succeed in making his *Enquiry* the classic English statement of French radical thought of the eighteenth century, in which he was widely read. In so doing, moreover, he produced a document of cardinal importance for the understanding of some aspects of English Romanticism.

Not long after the appearance of the *Enquiry* Godwin, answering an attack, exclaimed: "What the heart of man is able to conceive, the hand of man is strong enough to perform. . . . For myself I firmly believe that days of greater virtue and more ample justice will descend upon the earth." This sufficiently indicates his temper and the character of his aspirations. He was one of the early believers in progress, and was confident that humanity would some day attain a state of perfection on earth. That obviously was a romantic belief, to the extent that it soared beyond the common-sense view of life's possibilities. And in general Godwin's thinking was controlled by optimistic beliefs whose real warrant was that they

6037   820.8 S525   BRESCIA LIBRARY OWENSBORO, KY.

were "strong inward persuasions." The man was, in other words, an "enthusiast" in the eighteenth-century sense; and we feel that it was just what we should have expected when we learn, from his own candid admission, that his heart was beating high "with great swelling sentiments of Liberty" while he was writing the *Enquiry.*

Godwin was, however, an enthusiast of a peculiar kind. When his wife, Mary Wollstonecraft, was dying, and had been given an opiate to lessen her pain, she presently murmured, "Oh, Godwin, I am in Heaven!" But he immediately corrected her: "You mean, my dear, that your physical sensations are somewhat easier." This interchange speaks volumes. On the surface Godwin was as far from anything romantic as possible. He meant to be nothing if not exact in speech and rigorously logical in thought. Truth was precious, and would admit of no concessions, even at a death-bed. Similarly in his book, when he had laid down his premises he followed them out logically whithersoever the argument appeared to lead, undismayed by any conclusions, no matter how extravagant. And once his mind was made up, he never changed in any essential particular so long as he lived. He did confess that he had made one mistake in the *Enquiry,* but towards the end of his life he said over again, in his *Thoughts on Man* (1831), practically everything that he had set forth in the earlier treatise.

In sum, Godwin contended that all men are endowed with reason, though that faculty is not at present equally developed in all men. Men, however, of necessity act on the basis of such reason as they have. Reason is simply a power to perceive cause and effect, and so to reduce to order the impressions passively received through the senses; but what reason concludes, man must do, with no more choice than has a ten-pin when it is hit by a bowler. In order, therefore, that everybody may be equally virtuous and happy, only one thing ultimately is requisite. Happiness results from virtue; virtue results from the exercise of right reason; right reason results from life in a society politically organized in accordance with the immutable laws both of human nature and of the universe. Properly order man's social environment, consequently, and then, as one of Godwin's radical friends said, "Hey for the millennium!"

Godwin's notion on the subject of political organization was simply that the less of it we have, the better. Government depends on the exercise of force, but this directly conflicts with each man's government of himself by his own reason. Law is the imposition of punishment, but this implies free will, which we do not have. Private property is an institution even more pernicious than governmental coercion, and must be abolished. In addition, he called for the banishment of all sentiment, which only clouds and perverts reason, and for the abolition of marriage and of all contracts or promises of any kind.

The goal which Godwin envisaged, when these barriers to perfect reasonableness were swept away, was complete individual freedom, or anarchy. He recognized that the goal could not be attained simply by violent destruction, and he outlined a gradual approach. But millennial existence would be anarchical. When it came, freedom would be so complete that even actors would not sully their individualities by speaking any words but their own, musicians would not subordinate themselves to concerted orchestral performance, and ultimately the supremacy of reason would produce a race of immortal gods, each perfect and perfectly self-sufficient.

What we have particularly to notice in Godwin is that, though he preserves the form of eighteenth-century rationalism and appears to make the individual the passive creation of environing influences, still, his animating motive is faith in individual human beings and, what is more, faith in their positive creative powers. Those powers needed, he was convinced, only liberation for development and extraordinary achievement. And it was this faith, this trust in the sound "heart" of man and belief in human perfectibility, that made Godwin a prophet of coming Romanticism.

When Wordsworth faced the ruin of the hopes raised in him by the French Revolution he turned to Godwin's *Enquiry* for support, and for a few months was wholly cap-

BRESCIA LIBRARY
OWENSBORO, KY.

tivated. "Throw aside your books of chemistry," he is said to have exclaimed to one young man, "and read Godwin on Necessity!" Denial of free will impressed him because it gave rational ground for the sentimental view that crime was forced upon naturally good persons by their evil environment; but what impressed Wordsworth most deeply and lastingly was Godwin's faith in human perfectibility. After a short time he shook himself free of Godwinian radicalism, but he never ceased to feel the "noble aspiration" to individual liberty which was really the all-pervasive ground note of the *Enquiry*. *There* was something to which his north-country heart could always respond—the conception of the individual standing on his own feet, guiding himself, controlling himself, thinking for himself, sufficient in his native integrity for the ends of personal and of social well-being. And this vision was Godwin's contribution to the growth of Romanticism.

Edmund Burke

From Godwin we turn to Edmund Burke, who also was stimulated to literary activity by the French Revolution, but was roused to indignant opposition. Yet Burke was, in this, no less a forerunner and herald of Romanticism than was Godwin. We must therefore inquire briefly into the grounds of his passionate hostility to the Revolution; and at the same time we will be aided in seeing why it is impossible to tie Romanticism to any political attitude or aim. This fact itself is indisputable, but puzzling, because it appears to contradict another undoubted fact —that Romanticism by and large was really on the side of freedom against tyranny. Because of the latter fact some students have been misled into identifying Romanticism with political radicalism, and then have got into inextricable difficulties over the conservatism of Wordsworth, Coleridge, and Scott, to mention no others.

The resolution of the difficulty, however, is simple. Nobody with whom we are concerned defended tyranny. Everybody was on the side of liberty against arbitrary government and oppression. The differences which seemed to put romantic writers and their forerunners on opposite sides of the fence were merely differences concerning the means most likely to conserve or nourish human values.

On this point Burke's position is not only instructive but conclusive. Burke was a practical politician, and therefore a party man. Throughout his career he had been a Whig, and had shown at times so partisan a spirit that he had been accused of giving up to party what was meant for mankind; but from the outset of the French Revolution he was in disagreement with his fellow leaders of the Whigs, Charles James Fox and Richard Brinsley Sheridan, both of whom, as champions of liberty, welcomed the Revolution enthusiastically. In the spring of 1790 he broke with them openly and soon afterwards joined the Tory opposition, taking with him a number of followers and thereby wrecking the Whig party. During most of 1790 he was at work on a pamphlet which was both an explanation of his change to conservatism and a warning to Englishmen against what he conceived to be the wanton destruction not merely of the state, but of civilized society itself, threatened from France. This pamphlet was his famous *Reflections on the Revolution in France,* published in the autumn of 1790.

The *Reflections* were written with heat. A contemporary critic elegantly observed that Burke was a master in the composition of "virulent encomiums on urbanity and inflammatory harangues against violence." He was led, indeed, both by imperfect knowledge of conditions in France and by the vehemence of his emotion, into some indefensible claims and extravagant statements which opened him to effective retort; but what is really significant is his quick insight into the completeness of the overturn threatened and his accurate prophecy of the outcome. He was horrified by the Revolution because, in the name of the general welfare, the French people were being incited to destroy, root and branch, the institutions which gave not only form but life to the state, and thus to effect a violent and complete breach with the past. He felt that this would be an irremediable disaster which would bring greater evils in its train than any present abuses from which the French suffered. And while Louis XVI still reigned he prophesied the vain attempt to erect a republic upon the ruins of the old order, the bloody conflict between factions, the succeeding anarchy, the war of conquest, and the final collapse into a military dictatorship.

But Burke was not only concerned for the life of the French nation; he felt that all Europe would be drawn into the conflict and that European civilization itself and the Christian religion were threatened. He was convinced that the cry for justice and for abstract rights masked a vicious assault on all that had been achieved in Europe in the long struggle against barbarism and the dominance of brute force. And it was because of the magnitude and gravity of the emergency that he put mankind above party and turned to warn his countrymen. In his most important activities hitherto he had been a reformer and a champion of the oppressed. He did not in 1790 turn suddenly and wickedly into an apologist for social abuses and a defender of tyranny. On the contrary, he conceived, as John Morley said of him, that he was forced by circumstances to change his front in order not to change his ground. He judged, in other words, that even a very imperfect civilization was better than none, and that he was on the side of light and the well-being of humanity in trying to save England and Europe from a reign of barbaric force.

If now we ask what conception of the state guided Burke, equally before and after 1790, we shall at once see how he helped to prepare the way for the Romantic Movement. He consistently believed that "there's a Divinity that shapes our ends, rough-hew them how we will." He was convinced that civil society could not be constituted or upheld by man alone, that it could be accounted for only as a spiritual reality and as an expression of the Divine will. This placed him in complete opposition to the mechanistic philosophy of his century, because it meant that human beings are not actually or potentially self-sufficient, but are creatures dependent on God, directed by God's providence, and blessed with bounties which they

can destroy, but which they cannot fashion with their own unaided powers. Civilization he considered to be a slow growth requiring centuries for even a semblance of maturity, yet a growth so precarious that a single rebellious generation might destroy it. Hence he steadfastly opposed sudden or violent change, contemptuously derided paper schemes for "ideal" societies and appeals to immutable abstract principles, and strove to preserve continuity between the past and the present. Hence, too, believing that we are guided creatures, he distrusted reason and was always more ready to accept the guidance of the affections, the passions, and even prejudice. He judged that the instinctive motions of the heart might express the will of God, but that the voice of reason, as he heard it in his generation, could not possibly express more than the weak and erring mind of man. He went so far as to consider society a religious institution, nothing less, in which the Church and the civil power "are one and the same thing, being different integral parts of the same whole."

Thus Burke was in full revolt against the scientific rationalism of his century, which, as we have seen, conceived the universe as a mass of material substances moving in accordance with mechanical law, and which consequently tended to dissolve both human nature and religion and to issue in atheistic materialism. Against this, Burke insisted that we live surrounded by mystery which the mere reason cannot fathom, and that human nature is the active instrument of transcendental powers which we can only call divine. In so doing he went straight towards the center of the romantic reaction, for which others were groping in much uncertainty. Further, he helped to liberate the imagination and to broaden its field by his comparisons of society to a developing organism whose past always remains a vital conditioning part of its present. Eighteenth-century rationalism looked at the past with supercilious indifference, as a dark expanse of barbarism well over and done with. We have seen how this indifference had begun to give way to the discovery that entertainment was to be derived from the relics of Europe's Gothic Dark Ages. Burke's organic conception of life and society was more important than sentimental idealization of the life according to nature in transforming frivolous antiquarian studies into history, as that word has been understood since his day —the past regarded as a continuing process of development in vital relation to ourselves, and hence at every point relevant and significant.

Burke's attitude towards the past, however, is not so fundamentally significant as his conception of man. And his insistence that man is a religious being was strikingly supported by the rise and spread of Methodism in the eighteenth century. This revival of religion was, in effect, a reaction against scientific rationalism as pronounced as was Burke's in the field of politics, and it pointed as unmistakably as Burke's towards the growth of Romanticism. As we shall see, it is not likely that the Methodist revival had any important connection with the romantic literary renewal of the 1790's and the early nineteenth century; nevertheless, some knowledge of it is indispensable for our purposes. The Romantic Movement was the literary expression of a general reaction, against eighteenth-century "enlightenment" and rationalistic standardization, which extended beyond literature and embraced the whole of life. Some of those who participated in the literary movement did not fully understand its bearings, or came only gradually to understand them, though they gave their aid in liberating the human spirit from one or another form of tyrannical repression. Today it is possible to see the meaning of the whole reaction, as well as the need for it, more clearly than could some of the participants; but we can, of course, only do so by looking at all its aspects. When we attempt this, we discover that it was indeed a converging advance on several fronts, unplanned, apparently disconnected, yet having a common object.

John Wesley and Methodism

Practically speaking, the Methodist Church is the creation of one man, John Wesley, probably the most extraordinary Englishman of the whole eighteenth century. Not

even Wesley, however, could have succeeded in effecting a great revival of religion had his work not met a vital need. We have seen in an early section of this chapter why Christianity in the eighteenth century sank into lifeless formalism. In France, the leaders of opinion who prepared the way for the Revolution not only were unbelievers but were as hostile to Christianity and the Roman Catholic Church as they were to royalty. Priests and kings, as we have noticed, were accused of making up an evil partnership for the oppression of mankind, and of maintaining their ascendancy by fostering superstition and prejudice. In England the situation was different, but not more favorable to Christian faith. There, rationalism penetrated the Church and went far to destroy Christianity by sweeping away its personal and historic elements, and putting in their place an abstract theism which seemed inoffensive to enlightened people but which could not engage the affections of anyone or arouse a confirming voice from within the heart. The consequence was that educated people and fashionable people either were not Christians or were Christians only in name, and that ignorant people were becoming not only irreligious but brutal.

There were exceptions to this rule. Christianity was being kept alive in England; but it was carrying on an underground existence. It persisted outside of the Anglican Church in societies of Presbyterians, Baptists, Independents, Quakers, and the like, and also in the homes of some Anglicans, chiefly the families of clergymen who refused to swear allegiance to William and Mary after the Revolution of 1688–1689. These groups were small, obscure, and weak. The population of England, moreover, was both growing and shifting, and in the 1740's there were thousands of Englishmen who had no opportunity even to hear Christian teaching of any kind.

These, briefly, were the conditions amidst which John Wesley appeared. He was born in 1703, into a family where undiluted Christianity remained a living force; nevertheless, he was slow in making up his mind to a life of religious ministry, and he was not finally converted to what he conceived to be the state of a Christian until he was thirty-five. Before that he had been drawn into methodical religious observances, partly sacramental and partly the performance of good works. He was affected by the rising wave of sentimentalism, and promised to be a shining early ornament of the new humanitarianism. He became convinced, however, that neither ceremonial observances nor good works were enough. The mark of a Christian, he concluded, was to be discerned in one thing only: the assurance of the individual that he had experienced a direct act of supernatural grace in being born again of the Holy Spirit at some time following his first or natural birth. The natural man, Wesley said in one of his sermons,

. . . has scarce any knowledge of the invisible world, as he has scarce any intercourse with it. Not that it is afar off: no, he is in the midst of it; it encompasses him around about. The other world, as we usually term it, is not far from every one of us; it is above, and beneath, and on every side. Only the natural man discerneth it not; partly, because he has no spiritual senses, whereby alone we can discern the things of God; partly, because so thick a veil is interposed as he knows not how to penetrate.

But when he is born of God, born of the Spirit, how is the manner of his existence changed! His whole soul is now sensible of God, and he can say, by sure experience, "Thou art about my bed, and about my path"; I feel thee in all my ways; "Thou besettest me behind and before, and layest thy hand upon me." The spirit or breath of God is immediately inspired, breathed into the newborn soul; and the same breath which comes from, returns to, God: as it is continually received by faith, so it is continually rendered back by love, by prayer, and praise, and thanksgiving; love, and praise, and prayer being the breath of every soul which is truly born of God, and by this new kind of spiritual respiration spiritual life is not only sustained but increased day by day. . . .

His ears are now opened, and the voice of God no longer calls in vain. He hears and obeys the heavenly calling; he knows the voice of his Shepherd. All his spiritual sense being now awakened, he has a clear intercourse with the invisible world; and hence he knows more and more of the things which, before, it could not "enter into his heart to conceive." He now knows what the peace of God is; what is joy in

the Holy Ghost; what the love of God which is shed abroad in the hearts of them that believe in Him through Christ Jesus. Thus the veil being removed which before intercepted the light and voice, the knowledge and love of God, he who is born of the spirit dwelleth in love, "dwelleth in God, and God in him."

Wesley was rigorous in his insistence that the New Birth or conversion must be attested by fruits as well as by inward assurance. The natural man was made, by the New Birth, a saint, and must act like a saint—or rather he would, not from any strength or merit of his own, but because of the indwelling spirit of God, perforce act like one. Wesley himself did. And by the power of his saintliness he brought thousands to do likewise. The reader of his sermons, and journal, and letters, can come to only one conclusion, confirmed by what biographers tell of him: He was extraordinary in his energy, in his administrative ability and genius for organization, in his shrewd practical insight; he was fortunate in his long life of eighty-eight years which enabled him to round out his work; he was wholly sincere and single-hearted; and yet none of these things can explain his success. Only his saintliness, or what he regarded as supernatural grace working through him, can explain that. He said nothing new; his manner of speaking was restrained, even dry; his literary gifts shown in his sermons were not at all remarkable; but somehow he struck home to the hearts of those who heard him and made them too feel an assured confidence of the workings of supernatural grace within them. They discovered that they were religious beings, that they had been spiritually starved without knowing it, and that Christian faith could verily transform their lives. They were born again into a better nature; for whatever else Wesley accomplished, he certainly humanized thousands of people who had sunk into an almost unbelievable brutality.

For us the important thing in the Methodist Awakening is the Doctrine of the New Birth, and the fact that living belief in it spread rapidly over England, and was not confined to one sect or to one class. After Wesley's death, indeed, there came a formal separation between the Anglican Church and Methodism; but then there had sprung up within the Church of England the Evangelical Party, as it was called, which carried on in that communion the vital work of the Methodists. Hence no definite limit to Wesley's transforming power can be fixed. But its secret can be understood. The doctrine of the New Birth shattered, for believers, the conception of a self-contained universe of mechanical law, and made the mystery, indeed the miracle, of divine grace once again a living reality. God was again proclaimed not merely the creator of the universe, but a loving Father watching over His children, entering into their lives, holding out a hand to aid and save them. God was no longer an impassive First Cause speaking through inexorable law, but an illimitable Spirit of Love to Whom all things were possible.

Wesley in this fashion revived amongst his followers the sense that life's real issues and rewards are not confined to earth but are spread out to eternity. In so doing, incidentally he made his converts feel that squabbles over political rights or other worldly affairs were of no importance in comparison with the virtuous activity demanded of the twice-born for heavenly life; and thus he contributed in no small measure to the social stability of England in the years after the French Revolution. But, beyond this, he brought back into life the unexpected possibility, the unlooked-for transformation of prospects, in the operations of Grace, and the consciousness of mystery permeating life. Further, he reasserted the rights of direct individual experience against formalism, and taught men to trust their own intuitions and to back them against all odds.

The most significant feature of the romantic reaction was precisely the renewed conviction that human nature contains a daemonic element which expresses itself in sure intuitions, through the passions, and that such intuitions are to be trusted in preference to any conclusions of the mere reasoning intellect. At the point of sharpest opposition, then, to scientific, rationalism, Wesley and the romantic writers were united. But to say this without adding that the broad implications of the Methodist reaction against formalism were not realized, by Wesley himself or by his followers, would be to give a false impression. Wesley was thoroughly practical and, as was said above, single-hearted. He liberated the emotions strictly for one purpose—salvation. He believed, in effect, that human nature was a paradoxical complex of natural and supernatural elements; and he believed this because of direct experience. When he saw that, after conversion, he and others were lifted above what mere nature was capable of, he felt that he had a complete demonstration of the mingling of the divine and the human within man. But the meaning of this, to him and to his followers, was simply and narrowly religious. The early Methodists were "enthusiasts," in the eighteenth-century sense of the word, but they did not carry their "enthusiasm" into the realms of philosophy, poetry, or fiction.

William Cowper

Cowper is sometimes instanced as a link between Methodism and rising Romanticism, but not very plausibly. Cowper for a while was strongly under the influence of Evangelical Anglicanism, and wrote many hymns, some of them beautiful and all full of sincere feeling. Through the greater part of his life he was haunted by desperate religious fears, and resorted to various expedients to distract his attention and keep himself busy. The composition of poetry was one of these expedients. And, as might be expected from this, his most characteristic and important verse exhibits no distinctively Evangelical qualities.

Cowper was a cultivated gentleman, sensitive, kindly, observant, reflective, who loved simplicity and quiet. He was in touch with his times, and felt complete sympathy with the new humanitarianism. Like many another who enjoyed English freedom, too, he applauded the first efforts of the French to shake off ancient tyranny. In addition, he loved country scenes and hated the sophistication and corruption of cities. Thus his poetry brings one agreeably into contact with some of the modes of feeling and thought which were leading on to Romanticism. He was not carried off his feet, however, by any of the dogmas of Romanticism. These he encountered with an alert critical eye.

We can usefully notice some instances. Cowper hated cities and loved natural scenery, but not wild nature. The nature which appealed to him was a land trimmed, ordered, and cultivated by intelligent husbandry—a mean between the extremes of untouched wilderness and complete artificiality. So also he hated the degradation and vice which seemed inseparable from the life of great cities, but he was under no delusion concerning the lives of humble country folk. He would not for himself choose either the close infected air of cities or a peasant's hut exposed to every blast, but a life and abode like his own, midway between. In short, Cowper was full of moderate good sense; and his poetry is very different in tone from anything that savors of "enthusiasm." He is pleasantly companionable, in *The Task* as well as in his delightful letters, and invites his readers to pure enjoyment. But the companionship he affords is that of an eighteenth-century gentleman, and not the disturbing, though stimulating, company of a romantic or even "pre-romantic" soul.

Cowper's moderation and balance can be seen especially well in the quality of his humanitarianism. He was capable of strong feeling, and had a horror of needless suffering inflicted on man or beast. This horror arose from sympathetic kindliness. It was direct, untheoretic, personal. Experience of such feeling would appear to be just the thing to convince one that there must be substantial truth in the doctrine that the passions rising spontaneously from the untutored heart are to be trusted against the conclusions of the mere reasoning intellect. And to be convinced of this would be to travel along one of the paths leading to Romanticism. But Cowper was not convinced. He did not accept the sharp opposition between reason and sentiment which had long been accepted both by rationalists and by sentimentalists. His eyes were not closed by excess of feeling. He was not led on from humanitarian sympathy to belief in

"noble" equalitarian doctrines, or to acceptance of a mythical "natural" man or "noble savage" as the ideal exemplar of humanity; nor was he led to believe that spontaneous sentiment was humanity's one and sufficient source of wisdom. And this means, precisely, that he was a humanitarian without being romantic.

George Crabbe

We have now seen why Romanticism cannot be tied to any political attitude, and that there is no necessary connection between humanitarianism and Romanticism. But the latter truth can be seen even more clearly in the poetry of Cowper's younger contemporary, George Crabbe, whose testimony deserves our attention. Brought up in poverty, largely self-made, and tried by every kind of hardship, Crabbe was on the verge of desperation when he managed to win the attention, friendship, and aid of Edmund Burke. He then won the attention of the public by his treatment of the theme he knew best from personal experience—the miseries and degradation of the simple life according to nature.

Goldsmith had ostensibly treated the same theme in *The Deserted Village;* but the part of this poem on which Goldsmith had lavished his care and skill, and the part which has stuck in the minds of readers, is that depicting the former idyllic existence of the villagers. Goldsmith, with no thought of abandoning the poetic style, the manners, or the balanced good sense of the eighteenth century, had thrown himself into the oncoming current of sentimentalism and had drawn a romantically "idealistic" picture of the beauty and goodness of village life, before the advent of the land-grabbing oppressor. His essential point was that until then, contentment and the simple natural virtues had flourished upon poverty.

Crabbe wrote his first notable poem, *The Village* (1783), in conscious profound reaction against such falsehood. Rustic life as he knew it was full of wretchedness and vice; and elemental human nature as he knew it was hard, selfish, calculating, sordid. Indignantly he sought to discredit poetic "idealism" by picturing country life as it actually was, and showing the real effects of simplicity and poverty. He was moved by pity, and we can see the difference between pity and sentimentalism in the difference between his *Village* and Goldsmith's. He felt that if the lot of poor country folk was ever to be bettered, the public must be aroused by methods of unsparing realism and so be made, in effect, to share its wretchedness.

In Crabbe's later work—he lived until 1832 and wrote industriously to the end—the pictures of rustic life are not uniformly dark and grim. Once his protest had been vigorously made, he could afford to admit that even amongst the common people there was some good mixed with evil, and that gleams of happiness did occasionally light up the general blackness. But he never abandoned his realism, or his aim of destroying poetic illusion for the sake of truth, just as he also stuck to the couplets of Pope which he had learned to use as a young man. And from beginning to end he was consistently humanitarian and consistently unromantic.

Robert Burns

With Burns, we come to something different. Burns was born five years later than Crabbe, and died thirty-six years earlier. He was a peasant, and knew the life of poor country folk as intimately as Crabbe and at approximately the same time. Mostly self-educated, he was widely read in eighteenth-century literature; and, again like Crabbe, he acknowledged respectful allegiance to Pope and his school and wrote English poems in what may be called the orthodox style of the day. But these were imitative and lifeless; and he is remembered, read, and loved because he discovered that his genius lay elsewhere. He studied not only English literature, but also the popular poetry of his own Scotland, and in the latter he found an inspiration and a technique which liberated his full powers. The songs he then wrote, using his native Scots dialect, really sing themselves, and appear to be the spontaneous overflow of simple emotions with an universal appeal. Such expressive-

ness, we feel, must come straight from the heart; and in fact Burns did learn to express his own personality and sentiments perfectly, not alone in song, but also in satire and realistic tale. And though his medium was traditional in Scotland he made it wholly his own. In its homeliness, raciness, and informality, moreover, it offered a startling contrast to the abstract and comparatively cold formal diction currently regarded as the correct language of poetry.

Thus Burns found himself master of a style which implied revolt from accepted standards; and at the same time he learned to trust himself, and to consult his own feelings and reactions for his themes. His reactions were clear-cut and his feelings intense even when not deep or lasting. He was eminently the kind of man who throws himself heart and soul, impulsively, into the face of any kind of danger, into a desperate love-affair, into a forlorn cause; who may do things he is bound to be sorry for, and who may equally, the next moment, stand forth a hero. The prime difference, then, between him and Crabbe was one of temper. Crabbe was disillusioned, pessimistic, steady, persistent, and objective. Burns was joyful, optimistic, sentimental when not passionate, frank, convivial, and unstable. He was quickly plunged into depths of grief or remorse, but as quickly rose again on a new wave of hopeful feeling. He was, indeed, an "enthusiast," which is to say that he possessed the romantic temper.

Burns as well as Crabbe read Goldsmith's *Deserted Village,* but Burns accepted it with delight, and wrote his own version of idyllic peasant life in *The Cotter's Saturday Night.* It is quite true that in this poem, and in general in his treatment of "honest poverty," he had a basis of experience materially different from Crabbe's. The Scottish peasant often had a conscious integrity, a spirit of independence and self-reliance, and an iron will which promoted a stiff reaction to hardship. Nevertheless, Burns "idealized" his picture, under the influence of sentimentalism.

When he first appeared before the public, Burns himself was sentimentally "idealized." He was presented as a "heaven-sent plowman," "humble and unlettered," whose genius, in accordance with the theory of natural goodness, was the result of ignorance, unworldliness, plain living, and instinctively right feelings. He was regarded as a species of "noble savage." This was a piece of make-believe. The "unlettered plowboy" was steeped in two literatures, as has been said above, and learned his art from one and drew his ideas from the other. Yet it is true that he was significantly original. He took up pretty sentiments and charged them with passion which transformed them; he broke with established conventions and wrote the better poetry for it; he not only celebrated freedom but did a great deal, poetically, to vindicate it. In all this he pointed more directly than anyone before him to Romanticism.

William Blake

There was a contemporary of Burns, unknown to the public, living obscurely on the outermost borders of the literary and artistic world, who not only pointed directly to Romanticism, but in his convictions and work exemplified almost everything that was to enter into the Romantic Movement and almost everything that was to issue from it to our own day. This extraordinary genius was William Blake. He exerted no literary influence on contemporaries. English Romanticism would have taken exactly the same course had he never lived. Yet in the historical study of the movement he is of the first importance, both because he puts its fundamental character in a bright light, and also just because he was an isolated figure. His isolation compels us to infer that the Romantic Movement was something bound to come, if not through one man or group, then through another. For if a profound discontent with the dehumanizing limitations of scientific rationalism had not been in the air men were breathing, bound to express itself somehow, we could hardly have had the Blake whom everybody today knows and wonders at, and many struggle to understand.

Scholars and critics struggle because, as we shall see, Blake resorted in his longer

pieces to a hieroglyphic kind of writing which is dark indeed to common minds. But fortunately there is no difficulty in understanding his controlling ideas. Most of these are set forth in a little book called *The Marriage of Heaven and Hell* (1790). By this title Blake meant to assert that reality is made up of contraries, such as love and hate, neither of which can be denied in favor of the other without falsehood which brings disastrous consequences. He was trying to say that the universe is an organic whole, and that though hate considered by itself may seem extremely naughty, without it we could not have love. He therefore thought nothing but harm was done by analyzing the whole into its parts and then commanding people to cherish one part and avoid another. He thought all negation evil, and especially the negations which, as he supposed, crafty priests had foisted on mankind in the name of Christianity. He regarded Reason and Energy as contraries like love and hate, and believed that rationalists and priests had joined to repress energy, calling it "evil," in favor of passive obedience to reason, calling that "good." Against them he insisted that "energy is the only life" and is "eternal delight"; and declared, in effect, that he would rather live in Hell, if that was the abode of energy, than in Heaven, if that was the home of passive obedience. As this makes evident, he was really so anxious to exalt energy and to belittle reason that he violated his own plea for acceptance of contraries as necessary parts of an organic whole. Yet the plea had been sincere, and one has to remember that failure of logical consistency, even conscious failure, can scarcely have troubled him.

For Blake was a mystic. The mystic believes that he has achieved direct contact with ultimate or absolute reality wherein all our earthly distinctions are confounded, and our limitations transcended. But no mystic can put directly into words the truth he has learned, because speech partakes of our human limitations, and is, indeed, a medium of communication developed largely for the purposes of the knowing intellect, on the level of systematic reasoning. Hence the mystic's vision can only be hinted at or suggested in one way or another. In *The Marriage of Heaven and Hell* Blake sought to convey his mystical sense of the organic wholeness of reality and his confidence that energy is divine by shocking the reader's mind so as to rouse it to thoughtfulness, and then by giving a series of hints, as startling and dagger-like as possible. Some of the hints are conveyed in short statements, proverbial in form, and some in a few imaginative scenes. He imagines himself, for example, "walking amongst the fires of Hell, delighted with the enjoyments of genius, which to angels look like torment and insanity." He means, of course, that he was walking in a place where energy was unbounded and active, and that such a place would falsely be called Hell by the crafty priests and rulers of this world who have contrived thus to chain up the energies of men. Similarly, the "angels" are not truly angels, but beings of the kind angels would have to be if passive obedience and repression of impulses to action were really angelic.

The upshot of Blake's message is simply that energy, spontaneous energy, is life and truth and goodness—is divine. He was supremely confident of this because he had seen it, in mystical vision. He imagined that the prophets Isaiah and Ezekiel were dining with him and that he asked them how they had dared "so roundly to assert that God spoke to them." Isaiah answered, Blake tells us, that he never literally saw or heard God, but that his "senses discovered the infinite in everything," and since he was firmly persuaded that the voice of honest indignation was the voice of God, he felt justified in asserting that God had spoken to him. Then Blake asked the prophet, "Does a firm persuasion that a thing is so, make it so?" And Isaiah replied, "All poets believe that it does, and in ages of imagination this firm persuasion removed mountains; but many are not capable of a firm persuasion of anything."

Here we have the secret of Blake's confidence. A "firm persuasion" was enough. Whatever was real and true for him *must* be Truth Itself. And, since it was Truth, it must be equally truth for everybody else. Hence those who did not agree with him

must be fools, idiots, outrageous demons, cunning knaves, pale priests, insolent reasoners, or sneaking reptiles. These are his own descriptive terms for those who differed from him; and he included "reasoners" because, as we have seen, he regarded reason and energy as contraries. In this, moreover, he was only carrying on what had come to be, as we have also seen, the traditional opposition of reason and sentiment. Truth for him, as indeed for all mystics, was something above reason. It could only be discovered by imaginative vision, and *not* by observation through the eye and other senses, with the aid of reason.

The consequence, however, was that Blake repudiated what to science and to most of us is the real world. The repudiation was neither complete nor consistent; nevertheless, the poet tended to regard this earth as a veritable prison-house, because he enjoyed a visionary apprehension of another world, larger, better, and finer, to which he felt he really belonged. He could almost see this other world; at moments he did catch tantalizing glimpses of it and was enraptured; but he only achieved the vision in proportion as he emancipated himself from the tyranny of the bodily senses and of commonly accepted beliefs. He saw clearly where this placed him, and regarded it as an essential part of his mission to discredit Bacon, Locke, and Newton as "the three great teachers of atheism," or, in other words, of scientific rationalism.

Blake also realized that his visionary "real" world was in most respects a contradiction of the world of our everyday experience, though the visionary world corresponded to human aspirations, or was the fulfillment of them. His explanation was that divine energy is not simply incarnated or given bodily form in human beings, but is rather imprisoned and more or less stifled within us, and needs only liberation in order to carry us away from illusion and falsehood towards the heavenly world. His practical conclusion was that every impulse, every stir of imprisoned energy, should be carried into instant action without regard for consequences. Everything spontaneous he held to be good, and all calculation bad.

The promptings of energy, he said, were the promptings of genius; and to give one's genius scope one had only to let one's self go, with perfect trustfulness. Hence the man who is all impulse transcends the limits of earthly existence, and partakes of the happiness of the heavenly or infinite world. If this does not seem to make sense, Blake's reply is that you are lacking in faith. A firm persuasion that a thing is so, makes it so. All truths, he says, were at one time only imagined, and the only nonsensical or vain imagination is imagination without conviction.

Here at one bound we are within the guarded portals of romance, the land of dreams, the land of the heart's desire. True wisdom is to know that nothing is impossible, and that each of us can live, and does live, in whatever kind of world he chooses. The inspired man chooses eternal beauty and loveliness, and does really create what he chooses, in poetry, painting, music, or some handicraft. He is the true alchemist, transmuting lifeless sounds or inert matter into golden living forms of timeless perfection. The outrageous demon or sneaking reptile, on the contrary, chooses iron bands of law and logic and dead fact. And when the insolent atheist sees a yellow primrose, it is only a yellow primrose to him.

Blake pushed the antithesis between the two worlds, or between the literal eye and the visionary eye, as far as it would go. And one result was that some contemporaries thought him insane, and that, as was said above, he thought many of them to be fools, knaves, or demons. Another result was that, as one of his critics has said, Blake was terrific without knowing what to be terrific about. He had the fires, the creative energy, of genius, but after casting aside our everyday world he lacked substance with which to work. Retreating within himself, he lived more and more exclusively in a private world of phantoms. This private world is the scene of his prophetic poetry. And the very serious disadvantage from which that poetry suffers is unintelligibility. One cannot without long and painful study make head or tail out of most of it, and even the special student cannot give convincing

assurance that this poetry is worth a tithe of the effort it requires.

Some poetry of imperishable loveliness, however, Blake did write. There is only a little of it, but what we have is precious. It is true that as painter and engraver Blake worked more steadily to great ends, and this should be remembered, though with his designs we cannot here concern ourselves. His successful poems are lyrics; and, like other romantic writers a few years later, he went back for inspiration to the great Elizabethan age. He was drawn thither for the same reason that eighteenth-century writers and readers had neglected that period. Exuberance is barbaric, the latter had felt. Yes indeed, Blake replied, exuberance is barbaric *and beautiful*—beautiful as are all spontaneous outpourings of unsophisticated men. Similarly Blake loved the Ossianic poems and Chatterton's, and, when he heard that they were forgeries, refused to believe it. His own emotional response was to him a more important piece of evidence than any objective facts.

Blake may fairly be called a sublime crank, and he clearly illustrates the romantic temper and its workings just because he was an extremist of genius. Looking at him we can see instantly what is meant when we are told that the romantic temper is unqualifiedly individualistic, that it turns men's eyes inward upon themselves, and that it relies on "firm persuasion" as its criterion of truth. The romantic reaction was a many-sided rebellion against restrictions, most of which had once seemed rational and all of which had come to seem arbitrary. The rebels broke their chains, and walked about amidst celebrations of the beneficence of freedom. Blake shows us some of the rewards of freedom, and equally shows us its perils. Freedom to be utterly one's self should, of course, encourage the virtue of sincerity; but neither this nor any other good personal quality is in itself enough. We do not look only to personal qualities in deciding whether a man is a hero or a fanatic or a crank; we look also at his goal. It is not grand and noble to be terrific unless one is terrific to some grand and noble end. Blake thought, like others in his day, that whatever might be discovered through a life of pure spontaneity would be wisdom. His own experiments, however, come sadly close to suggesting that unchartered freedom may finally issue in gibberish.

Freedom, then, is rather a door opened to opportunity than an end in itself; and the high importance of the Romantic Movement arises from the significant uses made of freedom by the great men who converted the romantic reaction into a romantic triumph. To them we now turn, and first to Wordsworth, who stands earliest in time as he also stands first in importance.

William Wordsworth

Lyrical Ballads, with a Few Other Poems was published in 1798. No one, save perhaps its two authors, regarded the book's appearance as an epoch-making event. Reviewers were on the whole unfavorable, and the general public was scarcely aware of the book's existence. Yet this volume contained *The Ancient Mariner* and three other poems by Coleridge, and the rest of the poems in it were written by Wordsworth! Wordsworth's contributions, moreover, included such characteristic pieces as "Lines Left upon a Seat in a Yew-Tree," "We Are Seven," "Goody Blake and Harry Gill," "Simon Lee," "Expostulation and Reply," and "Lines Composed a Few Miles above Tintern Abbey."

The public of 1798 need not be harshly condemned for its failure to recognize that *Lyrical Ballads* was to stand out, more and more clearly as time passed, as one of the most important landmarks in the annals of English literature. The book's contents were, certainly, remarkable, but the book would never have attained its present historical position had its authors not gone on to become the two greatest figures in the English Romantic Movement. And Wordsworth himself realized that those who attempt something new must, if they are to succeed, slowly educate readers and thus in time create their own public. His poems constituted a deliberate challenge to existing standards and so invited controversy. Critical condemnation, when it came, did not

unsettle him. In 1800 he republished his poems with additions, and introduced them with a Preface in which he explained and defended his aims. He felt compelled, the Preface tells us, to attack the artificiality of eighteenth-century poetic style and also the sensational extravagance of the popular fiction of the 1790's. He wanted to bring in a kind of poetry which should be simple, natural, and direct, as the old ballads were, and which should express the universal passions of humanity in the language of real men. Controversy hinged chiefly on this matter of the language proper to poetry; and Coleridge, though he fully shared Wordsworth's desire for simplicity, naturalness, and directness, felt that Wordsworth had pushed too far his demand for the language actually spoken by men, and had in fact in his poems practiced better than he preached. Coleridge published his own account of the genesis of *Lyrical Ballads* and his own opinions on the subject of poetic diction in his *Biographia Literaria* (1817).

From what has just been said it could be inferred that both poets were making a stand against artificial style and false sentiment in favor of realism. But this is not the whole story. They did want to get back to reality as they understood it, and for this they needed to free themselves from eighteenth-century formalism. Equally, moreover, they wanted to discredit the notion that any true emotional pleasure could be achieved by turning one's back on the real world and escaping to the realm of irresponsible fancy with the author of some gaudy tale of terror. They were wholly convinced that we can find true pleasure, true happiness, in this "very world, which is the world of all of us," and only in this world. They were wholly convinced that even the meanest and commonest objects around us can stir us to the depths of our souls and can be sources of genuine, abiding happiness if only we see them aright. In this they were startlingly close to some things Blake had felt and said. He had written in *The Marriage of Heaven and Hell,* "A fool sees not the same tree that a wise man sees"; and he had also written, "If the doors of perception were cleansed everything would appear to man as it is, infinite." Both sentences express perfectly what Wordsworth and Coleridge had come to believe, and what they were endeavoring to show in *Lyrical Ballads*. But the identity between Blake and these poets accentuates sharply a significant difference. Blake's imaginative vision, as we have observed, carried him to a phantom world where all *was* infinity. "England's green and pleasant land" became for him only a point of departure. On Wordsworth and Coleridge spiritual perception had the opposite effect; it riveted their attention to natural scenery, to people, to the visible surrounding world in all its particularity, because there, in what was actually present, they saw intimations of eternity.

Yet their aim was no less romantic than Blake's. The real world of our daily lives, they were trying to say, is not that which appears to the dull eye of common sense or to the mere reasoning intellect, which can only argue from signs of order that the earth is a material structure whose parts interact in accordance with the laws of mechanics. The real world, they believed, is not drab, is not a mass of dead matter mechanically propelled; it is instinct with life and therefore penetrated through and through by spiritual power, creative, immortal, infinite. The things of sense speak not simply to eye and ear, but *through* eye and ear to the responding heart, spirit to spirit. And indeed no reader of Wordsworth's Preface can fail to perceive that the beliefs therein expressed issue out of the romantic reaction whose development has been traced in this chapter, and culminate in the romantic assertion that spontaneous feeling is the source of wisdom.

On this also Blake, Wordsworth, and Coleridge were in agreement. But Wordsworth and Coleridge vindicated their romantic confidence as Blake, despite brilliant promise and superb artistic powers, could not. We must now inquire how they succeeded; and since Wordsworth and Coleridge, after appearing together in *Lyrical Ballads,* carried on their work predominantly in different fields, we will postpone consideration of Coleridge until we have reviewed Wordsworth's achievement.

Wordsworth from childhood was formed by impressions of extraordinary intensity received from the world of nature, from "the sounding cataract, the tall rock, the mountain, and the deep and gloomy wood." Out of these impressions arose the conviction that he was a "dedicated spirit," and his later thought and work were centered in the effort to explore and set forth poetically the meaning of the revelation that had come to him through "nature and the language of the sense." The revelation came before he had any sort of contact with eighteenth-century philosophical thought or with the romantic reaction. When he reached manhood he found that natural scenery could no longer give him the transcendent joy, or mood of mystical insight, that formerly it had; and at the same time he encountered skeptical philosophy to make him ask if he had been the victim of a delusion. He did not think so; he had not embraced a theory which might be exploded, but had undergone a transforming experience which nothing could efface or explain away. Henceforth he sought to understand life in terms of that experience, welcoming help from any likely quarter, turning from some sources that failed him to others, but remaining true to his early impressions.

One of these impressions he thus recorded in the earliest version of *The Prelude:*

I love a public road: few sights there are
That please me more; such object hath had
  power
O'er my imagination since the dawn
Of childhood, when its disappearing line,
Seen daily afar off, on one bare steep
Beyond the limits which my feet had trod
Was like a guide into eternity,
At least to things unknown and without bound.

His love arose from the suggestion of guidance into eternity, but his imagination did not, like Blake's, leap ahead to construct symbolic representations of things unknown and without bound. He held fast to the road and to his own feeling, and tried resolutely to pierce the mystery of this and other responses elicited from him by the surrounding world. So trying, he came to see reality as something half-created, half-perceived; not just an object seen, lying wholly outside of the perceiving mind, but a union of mind and object in which each actively brought something to the whole. Reality thus conceived was alive with feeling, and perception was not a dispassionate intellectual act, but an induced mood which on occasion rose into mystical ecstasy. Wordsworth felt that life reached its consummation in such a mood of harmony and fruitful union between man and nature, as he said in a passage in the Preface to his long poem, *The Excursion,* which must be read and reread by anyone who is to understand him:

Paradise, and groves
Elysian, Fortunate Fields—like those of old
Sought in the Atlantic Main—why should they
    be
A history only of departed things,
Or a mere fiction of what never was?
For the discerning intellect of Man,
When wedded to this goodly universe
In love and holy passion, shall find these
A simple produce of the common day.
—I, long before the blissful hour arrives,
Would chant, in lonely peace, the spousal verse
Of this great consummation :—and, by words
Which speak of nothing more than what we
    are,
Would I arouse the sensual from their sleep
Of Death, and win the vacant and the vain
To noble raptures; while my voice proclaims
How exquisitely the individual Mind
(And the progressive powers perhaps no less
Of the whole species) to the external World
Is fitted :—and how exquisitely, too—
Theme this but little heard of among men—
The external World is fitted to the Mind;
And the creation (by no lower name
Can it be called) which they with blended might
Accomplish :—this is our high argument.

The "high argument" carries us to Wordsworth's conviction that Reality is a poetical mood of rapture which all may experience. The poet is the man exceptionally gifted with the shaping power of imagination which enables him to translate the mood into words and rhythms which we recognize as saying for us what we could not have expressed for ourselves, and even what we could not have felt distinctly without his guidance. Poetry, Wordsworth logically says, is "the breath and finer spirit of all knowledge." The poet, then, is a teacher, and a teacher of the

highest knowledge—which is wisdom, or the key to fullness of life. We gain fullness of life in so far as, with the poet's help, we learn for ourselves that Reality is not something objectively given, existing independently of us, to be discovered through the senses, but is *a state of feeling created through the union of man and his surrounding world.*

Howsoever far from common sense we have traveled in reaching this point, we must realize that at any rate there was nothing exclusive or fanatical in Wordsworth's transcendental belief. He had no notion of denying the validity, for practical purposes, of what passes for science amongst us. He was trying to solve a twofold problem. He had ineffaceable experience of his own to account for somehow; and he saw that actually the attempt to gain knowledge by impersonal observation, in distrust of subjective reactions and individual differences, led only to a science of inert matter moving in accordance with the laws of mechanics. A science of dead objects was useful, and he had no desire to attack it; but what he wanted was a science of life. And he was reverently moved by signs of life in the world of nature, and signs also of beautiful and beneficent design; and he found in the quality of his response something that lifted him out of dullness and inner emptiness to a better selfhood.

In trying to give form to the wisdom revealed to him, Wordsworth gathered into his poetry a great deal from the romantic reaction as it has been reviewed in this chapter. Like others before him and contemporary with him, he backed the individual and "enthusiasm" against common sense, turning from the abstract or general to the concrete and even the unique, from the external to the inward or subjective, from the seen to the unseen, from the mechanical to the dynamic, and, philosophically, from scientific rationalism to romantic faith in human goodness. In these and other ways he remains typical of his age; but he swings free of the limitations of time sufficiently to be regarded, by many today, as the greatest of the English poets after Shakespeare and Milton. And he does so despite serious per-

sonal limitations. Many in his own lifetime and since have been unable to restrain
amusement or annoyance at certain idiosyncrasies of this "dedicated spirit," and particularly at his self-importance. Moreover,
his poetry is markedly uneven, is very limited
in range, and makes rather heavy demands
on readers.

Nevertheless, Wordsworth out-tops even
the most brilliant and attractive of his contemporaries. And the fundamental reason
is that he inspires confidence, and actually
does reveal to others what was revealed to
him. The Utilitarian philosopher, John
Stuart Mill, has borne remarkable witness
to this quality of Wordsworth's genius. In
his *Autobiography* Mill has told how in 1828
he fell into a state of complete dejection,
wherein all his aims in life seemed empty,
the springs of interest drying up. He was
experiencing, as he recognized, the aridity of
an exclusively intellectual existence; and at
this juncture he took up the two-volume collection of Wordsworth's shorter poems published in 1815, and found them a source of
revelation. He says:

What made Wordsworth's poems a medicine
for my state of mind was that they expressed,
not outward beauty, but states of feeling, and
of thought colored by feeling, under the excitement of beauty. They seemed to be the very
culture of the feelings, which I was in quest of.
In them I seemed to draw from a source of inward joy, of sympathetic and imaginative pleasure, which could be shared in by all human
beings; which had no connection with struggle
or imperfection, but would be made richer by
every improvement in the physical or social condition of mankind. From them I seemed to
learn what would be the perennial sources of
happiness. . . . And I felt myself at once better and happier as I came under their influence.
. . . I needed to be made to feel that there was
real, permanent happiness in tranquil contemplation. Wordsworth taught me this, not only
without turning away from, but with a greatly
increased interest in the common feelings and
common destiny of human beings. And the delight which these poems gave me proved that
with culture of this sort there was nothing to
dread from the most confirmed habit of analysis.
. . . The result was that I gradually, but completely, emerged from my habitual depression,
and was never again subject to it.

What Wordsworth did for Mill he has
done for many another, and can still do.
There is such a thing as the education, the
culture, of the feelings. Perhaps it is the
most important part of education, and it is
always neglected. It comes, if it comes
at all, through personal associations and
through our responses to beauty. Wordsworth is content with nothing less than the
highest and the purest. He was himself
extraordinarily awake to the mysterious harmonies between man and nature, to the beauties of personal character, to the golden (not
the merely gilded) opportunities of freedom,
to the grandeur of manly independence, individual and national, to the real values of
earthly life. He did not merely see them,
he *felt* them, and drew strength and joy
from them. He did not, for joy and
strength, fly off on the wings of fancy to
"groves Elysian," or to any Utopia, but kept
his eyes fixed upon this very world of our
daily lives and found it instinct with goodness and beauty.

And what Wordsworth found, and what
he was, he still communicates to his readers
with unique directness and fullness, "from
everyday forms educing the unknown and
the uncommon." No other poet of modern
times makes us feel with equal force that "a
good book is the precious life-blood of a
master-spirit" ordained to a life beyond life.
Wordsworth achieves this because we find,
after we have discarded all in him that belongs only to an age now dead and gone, that
he did penetrate below ephemeral theory to
imperishable truths of human nature, to which
he can recall men today no less certainly
than he recalled John Stuart Mill. Time
has justified his brave confidence that he was
dedicated to the part of a teacher, and it is as
a source of one solid kind of wisdom that he
securely lives. Faith in our human nature
has never been easy, but Wordsworth, even
today, can give us unchallengeable grounds
for it and can make it live again.

Coleridge and Romantic Criticism

Coleridge and Wordsworth, as has been
said above, began their real work together
in *Lyrical Ballads,* and they must always be

spoken of together. Neither of them could have accomplished what he did without the friendship and stimulus of the other. But for the most part their fields of activity were different. Coleridge wrote a few poems supremely good of their kind; but of these one was only a short fragment ("Kubla Khan") and another, *Christabel,* was never completed. No praise is too high for these poems; nevertheless, Coleridge's own first wish was to be a philosopher, and his chief work was done in the field of criticism—philosophical, religious, political, and literary.

Inevitably, the romantic reaction brought in a new criticism along with a new imaginative literature, and Coleridge is the founder of romantic criticism. In considering his work we must first get clearly in mind the nature of the problem he faced. The conflict between Romanticism and the eighteenth century was at bottom one between two philosophies or "wisdoms"—the wisdom to be gained from dispassionate observation through the senses and generalization therefrom, and the wisdom to be gained from our emotional responses to life. Criticism is judgment, and judgment is impossible without standards. Whatever the value of the effort made in England in the seventeenth and eighteenth centuries to formulate rational standards, the romantic writers were bound to attack those standards and, indeed, the effort itself. If emotional responses, direct intuitions, were really a source of wisdom and beauty, writers needed freedom to express them in whatever form and style seemed best for the particular goal in view. Further, if direct intuition was the foundation of a sonnet or an ode, its only appeal was to the reader's intuitional appreciation. Hence a criticism founded on intuition, to replace the objective method of eighteenth-century criticism, was a cardinal need of the Romantic Movement.

Coleridge clearly saw the need and the difficulty it presented. In trying to meet the need, furthermore, he enlarged the place of criticism in English literature and, in truth, made criticism itself a creative process. The difficulty he encountered was this: emotion is individual and subjective, and consequently if emotional responses—called "firm persuasions," "sure intuitions," or what not —are made the criterion of judgment, every man at once becomes his own critic, or final authority, not only in the field of literature but in every field where evaluations are to be made. Mary knows what she likes, and that is that. John knows what he likes, and that also is that. When there is no objective standard accepted by both Mary and John to which appeal can be made, there is no basis for a meeting of minds, rational discussion, and a social judgment. Society is dissolved into its personal units, and every individual becomes a law unto himself. This is precisely the freedom set up as a goal by Godwin and by many others who contributed to the romantic reaction, and its name is anarchy.

We dread anarchy because we think of it as a collapse into chaotic disorder which would make civilized life impossible. Coleridge, however, was perfectly confident that it was possible to construct an idealistic philosophy on a basis of intuition which, when it had displaced the false rationalism of the eighteenth century, would afford sound critical standards. He was encouraged in this belief by the new literature and philosophy coming into existence by the end of the eighteenth century in Germany. There, largely under the influence of English sentimental writers and critics of rationalism, Romanticism was already flourishing, and developing a new philosophy. And there Coleridge went in 1798, with Wordsworth and Wordsworth's sister Dorothy, to learn something about the new wisdom. He came back in the following year with a competent knowledge of German and with a good many volumes of German philosophy. No certain answer can be given to the question how much he learned from Kant, Schelling, August Wilhelm von Schlegel, and others. He has been accused of plagiarizing them, but probably there is substantial truth in his own contention that what he learned from the Germans merely confirmed his own thinking, or confirmed and supplemented it. At any rate, Coleridge did a great deal to open the eyes of Englishmen to German romantic literature, criticism, and philosophy;

and in his own critical and philosophical writings and lectures he prepared the way for the decisive influence in the nineteenth century of German idealism on English thought, besides opening up a new era in literary criticism.

Nothing like an examination of Coleridge's philosophy is possible here. We must, nevertheless, see for ourselves how he proposed to close the door against chaos while accepting "firm persuasion" as the source of knowledge. For this we may glance at his own example, drawn from mathematical demonstrations. We say that in all triangles the sum of any two sides must be greater than the third, though this is a conclusion we cannot legitimately reach on the basis merely of experience, no matter how many different triangles we measure. From measurement of an indefinitely large number we can only establish a strong probability. But we do in fact feel absolute assurance "that in all possible triangles any two of the enclosing lines *will* and *must* be greater than the third." Here, then, is an universal truth, universally acknowledged by sane human beings able to understand the proposition. Yet it goes beyond objective evidence presented through the senses, and is therefore a proof that absolute knowledge of ideal reality is accessible to human beings.

Coleridge explains that though experience is our necessary starting-point, the knowledge attained can only be described as an intuition or "immediate beholding" which carries complete conviction. Here, consequently, we have a case of something intuitionally grasped which is and must be the same whenever and wherever it is grasped by a human being. We need not ask how far Coleridge could legitimately go on this basis. We are only concerned to see how he tackled the problem of establishing the necessity and universality of intuitions which, in their origin, are subjective and individual. In so far as he could succeed, he would unite all men through their common possession of a body of absolute universal truth, the evidence for which came to each man directly from within himself.

A serious problem, Coleridge recognized, was created by the freedom of the will. If the will is not free, men have no choice in their actions, and we cannot call a man moral or immoral. But if the will is, even to a limited extent, free, men have within them not only a power to discover eternal truth, but also a power of origination, even of creation. A moral standard is a predication, not of something which universally and necessarily *is*, but of what *ought* to be. Coleridge was as sure as most of us usually are that self-improvement was possible, that he could do better if he would, and that he knew the better thing to do even when he did not do it. Hence he knew from direct internal evidence that the will is free; and, since a free will is a power of origination, he also knew that the will must be a supernatural power implanted in us. This might be all very well, but it merely brought into clearer relief the fact that disagreement concerning the good, or what ought to be, does exist. Coleridge, however, was not troubled by this, because he was confident that no disagreement exists amongst those who are themselves good. What he said was that there is only one difference between mathematical science and moral science: "The postulates of geometry no man *can* deny," whereas "those of moral science are such as no good man *will* deny."

It has been necessary to go this far with Coleridge to show how he attempted to lay a solid philosophical foundation for romantic criticism. In a word, he tried to prove that by direct intuition we are in contact with eternal verities, the same always and for all men, or at least for all good men. Imagination he then defined as the power to give organic form and substance to that which is revealed to the poet or artist intuitionally. This is a power of true creation. The poet is not, as men of the eighteenth century supposed, a craftsman skilfully working according to rule. He is a god-like creator, and the form of his work issues as naturally and inevitably out of his moral intuition as the form of a tree issues out of its nature. It follows that when we are confronted by a work of true creative genius we cannot judge it by any external standard. There is no one right way of constructing a tragedy, or a comedy, or any other work of art. Every true work of art is unique and has the one form it can have to express what it does express.

Coleridge's great example was Shakespeare. To read him was to recognize, directly or intuitively, that here was a supreme creative genius. Hence his plays must have the one form right in every way for their purpose. Consequently the critic's business was to study him reverently. He could not be judged by any established standard, because the only standard applicable was implicit in his unique inspiration which dictated the form and style of the plays. Shakespeare, by the very nature of creative genius, was a law unto himself. What the critic could do was to discover the law inherent in the plays and explain Shakespeare's perfect adaptation of means to ends. This is the nature of Coleridge's own criticism of Shakespeare, and the method is applied not only to the plays but also to the characters appearing in them. The characters, in other words, are regarded as having a life of their own, as if they were real human beings, impelled by the motives of real persons, and not by a playwright's practical needs.

The net outcome was that the work of the critic was to be confined to interpretation and appreciation. All of the romantic critics lavished attention on Shakespeare, whose plays seemed providentially adapted to the new method of treatment. The consequence, however, was something which has since been called Shakespeare idolatry. The idolatrous attitude reached a climax in 1823 in the apostrophe at the close of De Quincey's celebrated essay "On the Knocking at the Gate in *Macbeth*":

O mighty poet! Thy works are not as those of other men, simply and merely great works of art, but are also like the phenomena of nature, like the sun and the sea, the stars and the flowers, like frost and snow, rain and dew, hailstorm and thunder, which are to be studied with entire submission of our own faculties, and in the perfect faith that in them there can be no too much or too little, nothing useless or inert, but that, the farther we press in our discoveries, the more we shall see proofs of design and self-supporting arrangement where the careless eye had seen nothing but accident!

Everybody nowadays would agree that De Quincey carried reverence too far. And he was not alone; Coleridge himself, after assuming that Shakespeare was perfect, got into the habit of asserting that imperfect passages in the plays could not have been written by Shakespeare and were inserted by someone else. Both Coleridge and De Quincey remind one of William Blake's insistence that the Ossianic poems of Macpherson and the Rowley poems of Chatterton must be genuine, whatever the objective evidence to the contrary, simply because he liked them.

But though Coleridge encouraged an attitude towards imaginative writers which was really uncritical and was bound to provoke a reaction in time, he also did much that was needed and fruitful. In particular, he deserves gratitude for his contention that there is an organic relation between form and meaning in works of art. In addition, he contributed materially to that revival of interest in older English literature which was a marked characteristic of the Romantic Movement and has remained one of its permanent legacies. And thus also he led the way towards another new thing, the rise of what is called the historical method in criticism. Neither he nor any of his contemporaries really used this method in the field of literature; though Coleridge came close to it, and did in fact use it in a strikingly valuable way in the field of social institutions, in his book *On the Constitution of Church and State* (1830). In this book he enforced the lesson that an institution is a product of what we now call evolution, and that it cannot be understood except in the light of its history. Thus he developed a conception whose origins we associate with Burke, and one which was soon to become indispensable in the study of every kind of human activity, and in other studies as well. And it seems scarcely doubtful that he would have applied this historical method of interpretation to literature, had he not been impelled by other considerations to insist on the transcendent, timeless perfection of Shakespeare.

As it was, Coleridge not only encouraged uncritical reverence for imaginative writers, but also encouraged a chaotic diversity of critical evaluations based on emotional responses. He vindicated impressively the "right" of the man of genius to artistic freedom. He exerted an influence which was to deepen and enrich later criticism when he insisted that the critic must endeavor to enter sympathetically into the mind and heart of the poet or artist and, in effect, re-create interpretatively the work of art under discussion. But time alone, not Coleridge or anyone else, could show whether or not such a treatment of literature would reveal a common intuitive wisdom holding free men together in a "natural" society. Coleridge himself could only help to liberate emotion, and hope for the best. Time, however, quickly showed that when critics were encouraged to rely on their instinctive responses they differed, just as imaginative writers also differed. And time quickly showed, in addition, that when critics were turned to writing about literature in terms of their own responses, or "reactions," they would begin to use literature as a point of departure for writing about themselves.

Hazlitt, Lamb, and De Quincey

The trend towards the subjective in literary criticism is seen clearly in the essays of William Hazlitt, the most important of the romantic critics after Coleridge. Hazlitt declaimed against the indulgence of idiosyncrasy but indulged his own, and believed, too, that we come closest to ideal truth in extreme individual embodiments. Hence he was always searching for and marking the *characteristic* trait or style, and so laying bare the peculiar, differentiating, personal qualities in literature and art. His approach to his subjects was of course also personal, through the emotions. His essays are a chronicle of loves and hates; and, as we should expect from this, he wrote best about his contemporaries, though he also wrote about older literature, and inevitably about Shakespeare. He discusses Shakespeare's characters in the romantic way, as if they were people. Throughout, one finds that Hazlitt's criticism is personal in some fashion. This has the very real advantage that

it adds variety, liveliness, and human interest to his essays, and gives criticism in his hands a literary importance and a life of its own which critical writings previously had not attained. The advantage arises, however, from Hazlitt's success in making criticism a means of self-expression, and thus to some extent a kind of creative writing. The result, too, is that the criticism of literature and art merges, not only into the criticism of life, but into the frankly personal essay.

What Hazlitt inaugurated, Charles Lamb delightfully completed. The difference between the two is strictly one of degree. Both continually express themselves, whatever their subjects of discourse. Both consult their feelings and instinctive responses without regard for tradition or social standards. And both engage our interest because we are glad to know them, personally, aside from what they may have to tell us about the ignorance of the learned, or the fear of death, or disagreeable people, or chimney-sweepers, or roast pig; or, on subjects literary, wit and humor, or the prose style of poets, or Restoration drama. Hazlitt significantly entitled one of his volumes *Table Talk.* And we are in fact, when we read him, really listening to the discursive conversation of a talented man, eminently worth knowing, whose like we shall never meet face to face, or outside of his own books.

Lamb's supreme advantage over Hazlitt is that the same thing is true of him, with the addition that to know him is to love him. It should be no recommendation of a critic that the first word on the lips of every reader who attempts to characterize him is "whimsical," but what reader of Lamb cares? It is true enough that he was a man of exquisite taste who savored English literature of the seventeenth century much as some men savor vintage wines, and we may be glad to recognize that his taste entered vitally into his idiosyncrasy. The fact remains, however, that we love Lamb precisely on account of his unique personality, without distinction of traits, and would not for the world, much less for criticism, have him other than he is.

No more would we have De Quincey other than he is, though for a very different reason. De Quincey irresistibly prompts one to exclaim that he is a museum-piece, in the sense that without unimpeachable testimony one could not have believed humanity capable of producing a "specimen" so rare—at once so curious, so remote, so highly individualized, and so typical. For he *is* typical. His essay "On the Knocking at the Gate in *Macbeth*" has already been quoted for a classic illustration of a tendency in which he fully participated; and in the same brief piece there occurs another typically romantic utterance. "Here," says De Quincey,

I pause for one moment to exhort the reader never to pay any attention to his understanding when it stands in opposition to any other faculty of his mind. The mere understanding, however useful and indispensable, is the meanest faculty in the human mind and the most to be distrusted; and yet the great majority of people trust to nothing else—which may do for ordinary life, but not for philosophical purposes.

This might be Coleridge speaking, or one of the German philosophical critics whom Coleridge studied. And in fact De Quincey was of their firm persuasion, and helped to make Kant familiar to the English. Further, he was at his best when writing about himself, and he developed, for this purpose, a prose style which is the principal basis of his fame. It is almost musical, in that its expressiveness seems to arise out of pure sound and rhythm, independently of words and their meanings. What can be thus expressed is a mood, a state of the emotions; and this is usually accomplished by lyric poetry. De Quincey here again was typically romantic, in breaking down the distinction between prose and verse, and also in going back for inspiration to some of the seventeenth-century masters of learned eloquence, such as Jeremy Taylor and Sir Thomas Browne. Like Lamb, too, he was capable of impish tricks. His papers "On Murder Considered as One of the Fine Arts" are his best known examples. In the second of these, speaking as a connoisseur to a man desirous of becoming his servant, who, however, was reputed to have dabbled a little in murder, he said:

If once a man indulges himself in murder, very soon he comes to think little of robbing,

and from robbing he comes next to drinking and Sabbath-breaking, and from that to incivility and procrastination. Once begin upon this downward path, you never know where you are to stop. Many a man dated his ruin from some murder or other that perhaps he thought little of at the time.

De Quincey's life is no longer the mystery it was to his contemporaries, but increased knowledge has not served to make him seem less extraordinary. He was in many respects closer to our common humanity than used to be supposed, but he was also just as wayward as we would infer when we learn that, having stayed at a dinner-party one night beyond the hour when he was safe from seizure for debt, he remained in the house of his host for a whole year. Waywardness, no doubt, was really one side of De Quincey's unique and splendid genius; nevertheless, it is not, any more than whimsicality, a characteristic appropriate to a critic. But the romantic critics, after Coleridge's attempt, did not wrestle with the thorny problem of social standards. It was not in them to fight against what John Stuart Mill called "the natural tendency of mankind to anarchy." They themselves were individualists and did not care, as Hazlitt said, to tire readers or puzzle themselves "with pedantic rules and pragmatical formulas of criticism that can do no good to anybody." None of them perceived that though genius may indeed require freedom, criticism must somehow work in terms of standards, or suffer extinction.

Yet this does not mean that the romantic critics failed. The best of them—those here under discussion—are, as we have seen, people worth knowing; and, in revealing themselves frankly in personal talk, often not even ostensibly critical, they have given us a new kind of literature which we would not be without and would not have other than it is. Many would unhesitatingly declare that if they have done this only at the sacrifice of what is properly called criticism, so much the worse for criticism. But, even strictly as critics, they accomplished much which leaves posterity in their debt. They opened up the riches of English literature before 1660, which, with the exception of

Shakespeare's plays, had been condemned and neglected; and in the case of Shakespeare, though they went to extremes, they did bring about a better understanding of his greatness. They also broadened the literary outlook by bringing the new literature and philosophy of Germany to England.

These in themselves were considerable and lasting achievements. But the romantic critics did more; they deepened criticism, made it flexible, and made it broadly significant by joining the discussion of literature with the discussion of life. Finally, they placed some critical standards on the scrap heap where they belonged, and, though they failed to place criticism on a new foundation, they did stimulate interest in literature and continue still to do so. It has been said of De Quincey that if you look to him for facts, you find, instead, "gross inaccuracies," and that if you look to him for judgment, you find, instead, "effeminate prejudices and mere flippancies draped in elaborate rhetoric." But if we are on our guard, and do not expect to find accuracy, sound judgment, or even criticism in the full sense of the word, we can still find in the romantic critics something invaluable and rare: we can find personal friends to whom literature is an absorbing delight, not a thing set apart, but something inseparably bound up with life, and indeed a consummate expression and concentration of life at its richest and best. After all else has been said about the romantic critics, everyone who reads them knows that they loved literature. Hence they remain their own best advocates; for we can still feel the freshness, the glow and ardor, of their discoveries and of their absorption in the life of the imagination.

Sir Walter Scott

At the beginning of the nineteenth century no one saw that Wordsworth and Coleridge were turning the romantic reaction into a romantic triumph. While the authors of *Lyrical Ballads* were being reproved by critics and were still unknown to most readers, the earliest popular triumphs in the romantic way of writing were achieved by Walter Scott.

Born in Edinburgh, Scott was a scion of a distinguished family of the once turbulent border country—the picturesque hilly region just north of the boundary between Scotland and England. He was bred to the law, and from early manhood practically to the end of his life he was a court officer and also a county sheriff. Furthermore, even after he had become prodigiously successful and famous as a writer, he looked upon literature as almost a side-issue, placing it far below the life of action. In later life his hero was no man of letters, but Wellington, the conqueror of Napoleon. And he took more pleasure in the building of castellated Abbotsford, and in the gradual increase of his land around it, than in his literary successes. This suggests Shakespeare, who also, as far as we know, appears to have regarded writing not as an end, but as a means to establish himself in a good position. Moreover, just as Shakespeare, whatever his conscious attitude, was a born writer who threw himself wholly into his work, so Scott, though he wrote as a means to a romantic way of life, threw himself into his literary tasks with delight, and indeed got into writing because he was born to it.

As a youth Scott was set upon a long course of reading by an illness which kept him inactive. Without method but with eager interest he read every kind of fiction, from the French heroic romances of the seventeenth century down to the tales of terror and sentiment of his own time. He then "began, by degrees, to seek in histories, memoirs, voyages, and travels, and the like, events nearly as wonderful as those which were the work of imagination, with the additional advantage that they were at least in a great measure true." In periods when activity was possible, he learned from one of his early friends the joys of antiquarianism, and particularly the pleasure to be got from collecting popular ballads of the border country which had been transmitted orally from one generation to another. In his ballad hunts, too, he became intimately acquainted with the country and with many a strongly marked local character. Always sociable, he was able to meet every kind of person on his own ground; and instinctively his keen eye took in every trait of individuality. As he grew older he became acquainted with some of the new romantic literature of Germany, and was attracted but not overwhelmed by it.

Briefly, this is the foundation of Scott's great career. He became sufficiently an antiquarian to edit the ballads he collected, and published them under the title, *The Minstrelsy of the Scottish Border* (1802–1803). Then, saturated with the old traditional narratives, he wrote some new ballads, and out of one of these attempts grew *The Lay of the Last Minstrel* (1805), a metrical romance based on a border legend concerning a feud of the mid-sixteenth century. It was immediately so successful that he was bound to write other metrical romances; and *Marmion* followed in 1808, and *The Lady of the Lake* in 1810. Still others appeared in the next couple of years, but in 1812 Lord Byron published the first two cantos of *Childe Harold's Pilgrimage,* and in the following year the first two of his romantic tales of the orient, *The Bride of Abydos* and *The Giaur;* and it became clear at once that Scott was outdistanced. His younger rival, whatever the defects of his poems, was better able to excite a thrilling interest in "strange fits of passion," whether his own passionate responses to picturesque scenery and to noble unspoiled children of nature—whom he saw or thought he saw in the wilds of Albania—or the uncontrolled passions and headlong acts of his oriental heroes and heroines. By comparison Scott seemed pale. But he had tasted blood, in the form of popular success, and was already counting heavily on the money which it had appeared he could earn from writing. Hence he determined not to be thrust aside without a struggle. As early as 1805 he had written a couple of chapters of an attempt at a novel, and several years later he had again been fiddling with it, but had been discouraged by friends who thought it dull. He now pulled out the manuscript and began to work in earnest. The result was *Waverley,* which was published anonymously in 1814. It is a romantic tale centered about the Stuart rebellion of 1745.

The book's success was instantaneous, and left no room for doubt that in the novel Scott had found a better medium for his genius than he had had in the metrical romance. From this first triumph he went on to produce *Guy Mannering* (1815), *The Antiquary* (1816), *Old Mortality* (1816), *Rob Roy* (1818), *The Heart of Midlothian* (1818), *The Bride of Lammermoor* (1819), *Ivanhoe* (1820), *Kenilworth* (1821), *The Fortunes of Nigel* (1822), *Redgauntlet* (1824), and in all some twenty novels between 1814 and 1825. These were identified on their title-pages only as "by the author of *Waverley*"; and "the Great Unknown," as he came to be called, did not publicly admit his authorship until 1827, though long before that everybody who cared to was able to learn the secret.

The Great Unknown was amused by mystification, but he had other reasons for anonymity. It gave him a valuable freedom. He was forced to write rapidly for money because, despite the consistent and phenomenal success of his novels, his expenses continued to outrun his income, and he was always gambling on his future capacity to earn still more. He did not want to cheapen his name, or appear to be a mere publisher's hack, and he was almost certainly right in thinking that the public would absorb more books by the Great Unknown than they would have welcomed under the name of Walter Scott, antiquarian, poet, and Clerk of Session of Edinburgh. The fact, too, that he was a responsible officer of a law court had something to do with the matter. It was not beneath the position he held to appear publicly as a critic or a poet, but when *Waverley* appeared, novel-writing was an undignified, if not disreputable, kind of activity.

The art of prose fiction had had a bad name at the beginning of the eighteenth century. Defoe had smuggled his tales of adventure into the homes of decent people on the pretense that they were edifying histories. Richardson towards the middle of the century had appeared as a grave moralist with a mission to banish false and corrupting romances in favor of sober truth. He, Fielding, Smollet, and even Sterne with all his fantastic whimsies, had together lifted the novel to great heights as a flexible medium for the interpretation of life and character, with a field as broad as the whole of English society. They had won their success as realists, or as delineators of character and manners. But Fanny Burney's *Evelina* (1778) had been the last considerable achievement of the eighteenth-century school of novelists. And meanwhile popular craving for the marvelous, the sensational, the crudely sentimental thing, had begun to be fed by the new Gothic romances discussed earlier in this chapter. In the years from about 1790 to about 1810 many trivial and childish, though by no means always innocent, tales of sentiment or terror were devoured by an eager public. They provided coarse food for the imagination, but to some thousands of readers they seemed better than nothing. In the years when Scott was succeeding as a poet, Jane Porter had proved that the fiction-reading public might heartily welcome what purported to be historical romance; but her *Thaddeus of Warsaw* (1803) and *Scottish Chiefs* (1810) had not appreciably helped to make the writing of popular fiction a reputable pursuit.

What Scott accomplished under the cover of anonymity was an organic union of romance and realism. He used most of the stage properties of the lesser writers whom he supplanted, and gave readers their fill of strange and colorful pageantry, dangerous escapes, resounding battles, picturesque scenes, necromancy, and indeed every kind of thrill save that to be got from the presentation of passionate love. But in his hands the setting and trappings of romance ceased to be stage properties. He carried his readers to distant scenes, not to give them a cheap escape from reality, but to drive home the truth which he, as well as Burke and Coleridge, saw—that the present is continuous with the past, that society is an organic growth, that people are interdependent and the product in large measure of environing conditions, and that reverence for tradition is the cornerstone of culture, or, as Scott himself would have said, of all manliness. Scott's own reverence for the past did not save him from anachronism and other inaccuracies, but in general he succeeded admirably in creating true and right pictures of past social conditions and in catching the temper and outlook of the periods he dealt with.

But Scott never lost sight of the fact that whatever serious purposes his revival of the past might serve, he was writing to entertain. He had stories to tell, of which history was only the scene; and exciting stories he told, with moving power, because he saw to it that the actors should be real personalities, capable of engaging the affections. His characters are not puppets who exist for the sake of the action. He had an inexhaustible interest in people, and brought to the creation of his actors a wealth of realistic observation which enabled him to make them live as credible and genuine personalities, howsoever extraordinarily individualized. In this part of his work he kept his feet firmly on the ground, and we see all his practical shrewdness, his direct confrontation of reality, and his frank delighted acceptance of people as they are and life as it has to be lived.

Yet Scott *was* a romantic dreamer, and we can best see the quality of his romantic strain, underlying his objective practical sense, when we remember that the living romance of his own life was Abbotsford. He wanted to dwell there as a feudal lord, a benevolent father as well as lawgiver to his retainers, the founder (since he was not born the inheritor) of a great landed family, living with dignity in a mansion hospitably open to all. The dream was not idle; it rested on a sound perception of realities to which the growing individualism of the time was blind. Scott looked back to the Middle Ages as a time when human interdependence was recognized and embodied in noble theory, of which chivalry and the chivalrous code were the flowers. He looked to the theory, however, rather than to the actual practice of the Middle Ages, and so was tempted into false idealization, despite his firm grasp on persistent qualities of human nature. The truth is, he did build upon noble medieval theory a vision of what might be and in his opinion should be, but a vision of what *could* be only if most men and women were all that they might be and should be. This visionary scene was his real habitation and home—"an inner world of dream and memory," it has been well said, "from which he brought great treasures, but which now and then to his undoing invaded the world of facts."

Abbotsford was a sustained and disastrous projection of a dream into the world of facts. For it, Scott wrote the novels; yet despite large profits he was continually behind, as has been mentioned above, in his race with expenses, and was finally forced into bankruptcy in 1825. "Scott's ruin" is a famous and complicated affair, but we need not review its details. Having gambled boldly and lost, he took his medicine, not with the romantic heroism that used to be ascribed to him, yet in manly enough fashion. He had known, not always and not completely perhaps, but still on the whole clearly, what he was doing, and he was equal to the consequence. His sanguine hope that he could single-handed, at the beginning of the nineteenth century, return to feudal conditions of life was absurd. Nevertheless, he did build Abbotsford and, what is more, he rehabilitated the novel as a serious form of art, extended its range indefinitely, and impressed on the minds of thousands some of the simpler articles of romantic belief. His romanticism consists essentially in his optimistic faith in human nature and in "firm persuasions," and in his attempted projection of an "ideal" world—his own "inner world of dream and memory"—into "the world of facts." This in his novels he did under the guise of history, and so became the originator of the modern historical novel which flourished for half a century or more after his death in England, in the United States, and all over Europe; and everywhere it helped to enlarge the field of men's sympathetic comprehension and also to inspire patriotic loyalties founded upon the supposedly heroic past.

Lord Byron

Byron, in driving Scott from poetry to prose, was an unconscious benefactor, because, as was said above, Scott's genius did not have full scope in his metrical romances. The younger poet, however, could say everything he had to say in verse of one kind or another, with unfailing verve and superb effect; and presently his fashionable successes in England were followed by international renown. The English lord was accepted everywhere as the classic personification of the new romantic spirit; or rather what was so accepted was his own magnificent, reckless dramatization of himself in that role. He appeared undisguised in *Childe Harold,* and thinly disguised in tales of passion with exotic settings, and in poetic dramas, of which the "satanic" *Manfred* and *Cain* are the most impressive examples. He was well endowed by nature and upbringing for the role, and did his best to live up to it, just as Scott did his best to act out in real life his own very different romantic dream. Indeed, these two titans had several points of significant contact, and themselves recognized their kinship and came in time to respect each other. But that which inevitably strikes readers is the difference between them.

Byron's was the role of the proud and noble spirit, who has tasted all the pleasures and glories of life, has found them empty and mankind despicable, and has contemptuously withdrawn himself from society. He remains in the world but not of it. He is an outlaw, self-sentenced to a station *above* the world. He is remorseful over darkly hinted crimes, yet at the same time defiantly scornful of those who venture to condemn him. This seeming paradox arises from the conviction that though he is guilty of the blackest sin, still, he *is* what he is. Born under a fatal star, he does act consistently his destined part, and is superior in honesty to the weaklings, turn-coats, hypocrites, and pious snufflers who band themselves together to set the tone of respectable society. To be disreputable in the eyes of a set of canting "pillars of society" is true glory and true honor. He therefore stands above all social judgment, and is the champion of Liberty. Beyond this point he is not a little confused. Goethe said that when Byron paused to reflect he seemed to be only a child; and in truth he does often appear to be rather a volcanic force of nature than a man capable of reason, and it is impossible to harmonize all the ideas about himself and about his loyalties which he entertained.

At times, on the basis of the doctrine of natural goodness, he conceived himself as a virtuous being, depraved by the evil deeds of others; and in agreement with this he tended to find people good in proportion as they were barbaric and "natural," or were the creatures of spontaneous impulse. On this basis he became a political liberal, the foe of tyrants and friend of the People. Yet he remained a proud patrician, hardly less repelled by the People when he came into actual contact with them than by "pillars of society." "What is (in fact) democracy?" he once asked; and answered, "an Aristocracy of Blackguards." Indeed, he frankly said, in one of the later cantos of *Don Juan,* that he "was born for opposition" and verily believed that if kings were overthrown he would become "an ultra-royalist in loyalty."

It is tempting to make this a key to Byron —to say that romantic liberation simply gave scope to a full-blown perversity, now impish, now Satanic, and set him on an endless search for piquancy. And without doubt this does explain much in his personal life and in his poetry, yet not the most important things. For Byron, underneath his morbid desire to pluck forbidden fruit, underneath his puerile vanity, false heroics, and shallow sentimentalism, did have integrity and a large capacity for right feeling. He had a soul not only of generous kindness, but of sanity.

Scott once referred to his poem *Rokeby* as a "pseudo-romance of pseudo-chivalry." Byron was capable of a similar detachment, could stand off and poke fun at his romantic pseudo-self, and managed in this and other ways to keep a firm hold on objective reality. He was never quite seduced into slavery, whether to a person, to his own dramatization of himself, to a cause, or to some "better world" existing only in the realm of imagination. As a result he grew, within limits, and matured through experience. And finally, throwing off the disguises with which he had thrilled himself and others, he wrote those satirical master-pieces which constitute his surest claim to immortality—*Beppo, The Vision of Judgment,* and *Don Juan.*

Percy Bysshe Shelley

Both Byron and his younger contemporary Shelley did nearly all that was humanly possible to justify the worst fears of those who felt that an ordered society, whatever its defects, was a safer basis for civilized life than romantic emancipation and individualism. The indictment of Shelley drawn by an English critic does not make a pretty picture: He was "an unfilial son, a professed atheist, unhonored by his school, rejected by his university, an adulterer, and the deserter, if not the murderer of his wife —the avowed enemy of all constituted power, in state, church, and family—advocate, it was reported, of a polygamous and godless Arcadia."

Now of course such an indictment is open to question. It is by no means completely true of Byron that he lived in the sanctified conviction that he was right, and the world wrong, but this is strictly and unqualifiedly true of Shelley. And he did not merely talk; he had the courage of his convictions, and attempted to live what he believed, or to believe what he lived. "At the moment of doing a thing," said Mary Shelley, he "always thought himself right." But this is an understatement; he *knew* he was right, and never admitted that he could have been wrong, whatever the consequences of his acts. Such a man, we feel, must have been something more or less than human— he must have been a monster, or a saint. And if he was a saint, we need not take seriously any indictment, however damaging in appearance a devil's advocate may contrive to make it. While he lived he was regarded, save by a small band of personal friends, as a monster; after his early death he began to be regarded by an increasing number as a saint. There have been very few, from his day to ours, who could regard him with indifference or could hold towards him any middle position between these extremes.

Obviously in Shelley, then, Romanticism

reaches a climax, in the sense that we do not find, even in Blake, a stronger inward assurance at work, and that we do not find, even in Byron, a rebellious spirit making so strong an impact on the world. It is true that upon contemporaries Byron made incomparably the stronger impression—Byron and Scott being the only romantic writers who won immediate fame. But while Shelley's fame has been of relatively slow growth and his influence more confined than Byron's, or Scott's, he has today apostles who appear to regard him almost as a messiah; and nothing like this is now true of any of the other English romantic writers.

Shelley lives, both because his poetical gifts enabled him to give perfect expression to the lyrical rapture he felt when contemplating the world of his imagination, and, perhaps even more, because his visionary world was a direct outgrowth from social and personal discontents which disturb humanity as deeply today as they did in the late eighteenth century and throughout the nineteenth century. The motive-force which roused Shelley to unique transports, expressed in song which has spontaneity and yet exhibits a consummate mastery of the rhythmical resources of the language, was love. If we ask, not unnaturally, love of what? it appears that Shelley's final answer was, Love Itself, just Love. This is baffling to the mind unattuned to romantic visions, transcending the sorry scheme of earthly things, and demands some explanation.

When Shelley announced that he had become an atheist, he meant that he had accepted the logical conclusion of eighteenth-century deism and had renounced historic Christianity. He meant also that he saw the incongruity between the eighteenth-century conception of a Universe of Law and faith in any personal God. He was still a youth at Eton when he was impelled to these sweeping repudiations; and at about the same time he encountered Godwin's *Political Justice,* which he swallowed whole. Unlike Wordsworth, he remained a Godwinian for the rest of his short life, though, under the influence of further reading and thought, he did depart from the Master's

metaphysical beliefs. At first he accepted, in place of a personal God, Necessity as the ruling force of the universe; but in time, partly to make room for human freedom, partly in obedience to his own perception of beauty pervading the world, and partly from his Greek studies, he began to think of Intellectual Beauty as the power which the created world yearningly obeyed. This is Shelley's "Platonism," derived principally from Plato's *Symposium;* but it does not mean that he became a disciple of Plato. He grew to be a devoted reader of the Greek classics, and took from them what appealed to him or what he found he could use; but he remained essentially a Godwinian, and his view of the relation between Intellectual Beauty and the universe was expressed in terms of sympathy, or temperamental longing. Hence it finally appeared to him that the real power which controls all things, animate and inanimate, was a universal sympathy, or the principle of Love itself.

Byron derisively asked Coleridge to "explain his explanation" of metaphysics, and it may be felt that the above explanation of Shelley's worship of Love is also in need of elucidation. That is because Shelley's worship arose out of one of those "firm persuasions" which are beyond the reach of the mere reasoning intellect, and can only be apprehended intuitively, and expressed symbolically—the office of poetry which, Shelley said, "turns all things to loveliness." In practice he attempted to express the beauty of ideal reality, leaving it, especially in his later poetry, to those inspired by the vision to determine how ideal beauty might be more fully realized in actual life. He had convictions on this subject, but they were simply those of eighteenth-century humanitarianism with Godwinian additions. He accepted the doctrine of natural goodness and believed human nature capable of perfection. What was needed for progress towards perfection was freedom—freedom to follow the spontaneous impulses of our naturally good natures. Hence priests, kings, and indeed all agents of constituted authority were wicked monsters who should be trampled under foot. Here he was inconsistent. He firmly insisted, like Godwin, that he was against all violence, even for the sake of freedom or reform, and desired slow peaceful change. Yet in fact, not only in his days of youthful bravado, but also later, he was enthusiastic over every armed revolt that occurred in Europe. He was as logical and thorough as Godwin in carrying his demand for personal freedom to the utmost lengths, advocating in effect the abolition of marriage, and also the abolition of poverty. This most desirable change was to be brought about by destroying the existing social system, based on selfishness, and replacing it by one based on brotherly love. Meanwhile, he believed that those in need had a right to any surplus of goods held by others.

Hazlitt asserted, shortly after Shelley's death in 1822, that Godwin had sunk into general discredit simply because he had conceived too nobly of his fellow men, and he continued:

He raised the standard of morality above the reach of humanity, and by directing virtue to the most airy and romantic heights, made her path dangerous, solitary, and impracticable. The author of the *Political Justice* took abstract reason for the rule of conduct and abstract good for its end. He places the human mind on an elevation, from which it commands a view of the whole line of moral consequences; and requires it to conform its acts to the larger and more enlightened conscience which it has thus acquired. He absolves man from the gross and narrow ties of sense, custom, authority, private and local attachment, in order that he may devote himself to the boundless pursuit of universal benevolence.

Shelley *was* what Godwin merely preached. He appeals particularly, of course, to youthful enthusiasts who have not yet learned from experience that good intentions will not suffice to reform human nature or the social structure. But by many he has been accepted as a saint of modern humanitarianism because they feel as Hazlitt did about Godwin—that it is inspiring and heartening to see a man cherishing absolute faith in humanity.

At the close of his high-flying, romantic *Defense of Poetry* Shelley exclaimed, "Poets are the unacknowledged legislators of the world," and expressed a revealing wish rather than a truth. But this and similar statements are primarily interesting because they show how he was, in his way, animated by the conviction which we have already seen at work in Blake, Wordsworth, and Coleridge—the conviction that the poetic imagination can discover ultimate truth inaccessible to the mere reasoning intellect.

John Keats

Keats, like Shelley, was convinced of the power of the poetic imagination; he went, in fact, quite as far as Blake, and held not only that ultimate truth can be discovered through the imagination but that the imagination can really create essential reality. In a letter of the autumn of 1817 Keats wrote:

I am certain of nothing but of the holiness of the Heart's affections, and the truth of Imagination. What the Imagination seizes as Beauty must be Truth—whether it existed before or not—for I have the same idea of all our passions as of Love: they are all, in their sublime, creative of essential Beauty. . . . The Imagination may be compared to Adam's dream—he awoke and found it truth:—I am more zealous in this affair, because I have never yet been able to perceive how anything can be known for truth by consecutive reasoning—and yet it must be. Can it be that even the greatest Philosopher ever arrived at his Goal without putting aside numerous objections? However it may be, O for a life of Sensations rather than of Thoughts!

Keats's life was even briefer than Shelley's, and falls within the span of Shelley's, just as Shelley's in turn falls within the span of Byron's. But his life was not too short for growth and change, and at the time of his death, early in his twenty-sixth year, he was not only discontented with the poetry he had written, but was forming new designs of the highest promise. Hence critical discussion is beset by a serious difficulty. The critic sees change and growth in the poetry Keats did write, and equally in his letters; and finds that his critical and reflective powers were constantly outrunning his poetical performance. Justice, then, pushes the critic forward, and causes him to qualify what he must say of the poetry by reference to the letters, and to qualify what he must say of the letters by consideration of what Keats would have achieved, or at any rate would have become, had he not been cut down in early manhood.

Nevertheless, whatever Keats was becoming, he did write certain imperishable poems; and those poems had a determining influence upon the course of English poetry during the remainder of the nineteenth century. We must therefore mark their quality and distinguish the kind of inspiration from which they issued, without entering further than can be helped into larger and more difficult questions. And for this purpose the passage quoted above, though written when Keats was just over twenty-two, is of central importance. In 1818 Keats wavered in the faith he had announced; but in general it is fair to say that his confidence in the passions as sources of ultimate truth revealed through the imagination remained firm. In asking for "a life of Sensations" he obviously meant a life of direct intuitions, of sharp spontaneous reactions to visual, auditory, tactual, or even olfactory impressions; and his belief was that if he could catch the concrete impression in its unspoiled essence, he would have hold of absolute truth, which is also absolute beauty. Doubtless the kind of experience which prompted this belief comes only to poets, painters, and sculptors; but what they mean by purity of sensation is that they see through the object before their eyes what it is trying to be, or what it essentially is. They *see* it; it forms itself as an image, or they form an image of it, and this is what is meant by the activity of creative imagination.

The artist, of whatever kind, has, of course, a twofold problem; he must not only be able to see, but to express through his medium what he has seen. Keats discovered himself poetically through the excitement he felt when reading Spenser's *Faerie Queene* and Chapman's translation of Homer. He was transported on fairy wings to other worlds; magic casements were opened, through which he saw the glories of chivalry and the gods and goddesses of the ancient heroic age, shining in a light that never was on land or sea. And to his wondering mind the fables of old poets seemed more real than any of the sights or sounds of his own contemporary London. His brain "new-stuffed with triumphs gay of old romance," he bent himself to the study of poetic words and images, savoring them, intoxicating himself with their sensuous charm, and in effect losing himself delightedly in golden realms. He began to love words and images for their own sake, with the pure craftsman's pleasure in the materials of his craft, and he continued his reading with the eye of a craftsman. He went on from Spenser and Chapman to other Elizabethan writers, and, above all, to Shakespeare. He also read Milton and, from amongst his contemporaries, Wordsworth. He was soaking himself in figurative and sensuous language, and asking himself what it was to be a poet. In a letter of 27 October, 1818, he gave an answer to this question, based on one thing that deeply impressed him in Shakespeare:

As to the poetical character itself (I mean that sort of which, if I am anything, I am a member; that sort distinguished from the Wordsworthian, or egotistical Sublime, which is a thing *per se* and stands alone), it is not itself —it has no self—it is everything and nothing. It has no character—it enjoys light and shade; it lives in gusto, be it foul or fair, high or low, rich or poor, mean or elevated. It has as much delight in conceiving an Iago as an Imogen. What shocks the virtuous philosopher delights the chameleon poet. It does no harm from its relish of the dark side of things, any more than from its taste for the bright one, because they both end in speculation. A poet is the most unpoetical of anything in existence, because he has no Identity—he is continually in for and filling some other body.

Shakespeare had supremely the quality which Keats here defines—a dramatic imagination enabling him so to enter into his characters that he seems to lose his own identity and become for the moment now this one, now that one. Keats, however, does not enter into the characters who appear in his poems, but only into the atmosphere surrounding them, and into the imagery, the coloring, or what he himself called "the drapery." And even here his range is limited. Distance lent enchantment to his view, and his settings were medieval or Greek, far off enough to permit the free entrance of magic, of the supernatural, and of nameless graces—far off enough, in a word, to set free an imagination eager for sensuous beauty but able to envisage it only beyond the horizon.

This, indeed, was his instinctive way of breaking the bonds of the "mechanical philosophy," and he was as consciously in revolt against prescriptive rule, and as consciously set upon proving the reality of things not dreamed of by the mere reasoning intellect, as were other romantic writers of his generation. But here also he was first of all the craftsman, and a rebel against eighteenth-century poetic diction and versification; and he fought shy of committing himself to any new positive views of man's nature or destiny, just as he put to one side Wordsworthian introspection, because he wanted to keep himself free, disinterested, impartially receptive to intimations of beauty upon which his imagination might work creatively.

The consequence was, however, that when Keats had to find something to say *through* the mythological or other machinery in which he delighted, he was at a loss. Only helplessness could have led him into the impossible dilemma around which he wrote *Lamia,* and we are pleased by this poem in spite of its meaning, which almost spoils it. Again, in *Hyperion,* he weakly fell back on notions, current in liberal circles, of the upward progress of the race. He fell back on these notions weakly because, though the romantic faith in humanity which they express can be related to his own belief in the passions and in the authenticity of the imagination, still, he made no effort such as Wordsworth made and Coleridge made to justify his faith, and ended by conveying the impression that he had seized upon the readiest meaning at hand for the sake of his machinery.

This is known as putting the cart before the horse; and Keats was led into it because

he discovered the cart first. We have just noticed how, when he read Spenser, he was attracted instinctively as a fellow-craftsman, delighting in rhythms, words, and images, and in their evocative power. Here was beauty of form and color revealed through the imagination, and not the less real because the world of Spenser's dream had no objective existence. The passions, in Spenser, were "creative of essential Beauty" embodied in the *Faerie Queene;* and Spenser, moreover, had subdued the most diverse matter to the patterns of loveliness—creatures horrible and loathsome, appearing as congruous parts of a whole which was itself triumphant Beauty. Having made this discovery once, Keats made it again when he turned to Shakespeare; and it was with reference to Shakespeare that he wrote, at the end of 1817, that the "excellence of every art is its intensity, capable of making all disagreeables evaporate from their being in close relationship with Beauty and Truth."

Keats was genuinely concerned over Truth, but it is significant that, in the famous concluding lines of the "Ode on a Grecian Urn" as well as in earlier writings, Beauty always comes first. And, furthermore, the formulas "Beauty must be Truth" and "Beauty is Truth" encouraged Keats to drift into a kind of romanticism which is a retreat from the hard, ugly world of objective fact to a dream-world where the imagination is free to create a species of beauty sufficient unto itself. An attempt has been made in these pages to show how plausible is the beginning of such a retreat; but it ends in the view that life is one thing, and art another. And from this view springs the doctrine of art for art's sake. Keats was not alone and not earliest in planting the seeds from which, in England, this doctrine was later to grow. They are clearly present in Blake; and Coleridge, in *Christabel* and "Kubla Khan," gave as much encouragement as Keats to the separation of art and life.

Those who study Keats's letters are convinced that his influence in the nineteenth century rested upon misunderstanding; and they are right to this extent, that he did grow dissatisfied with his work and did feel, at the time of his death, that his name had only been "writ in water." But the misunderstanding for which the nineteenth century is blamed is not really a misunderstanding of his poems as they are. It is something quite different; it is a failure to take into account his changing aims and hopes, and consequently a failure to understand Keats himself. The study of his development is interesting and illuminating. Nevertheless, we today, like men of the last century, remember Keats for what he wrote, and not because he came to feel that his poems betrayed immaturity. Even *Lamia,* moreover, and *Isabella, The Eve of St. Agnes, La Belle Dame sans Merci,* and *The Eve of St. Mark* are not in the least immature; they are unsurpassed masterpieces of one kind of romantic literature. And the "kind" to which they belong was bound to appear. Escape on the wings of imagination is the most obvious of retorts to the tyranny of brute fact. Blake, Coleridge, and Keats all bear witness that such escape can be made memorable; and there is no good reason why anyone should feel uneasy over the pleasure given him by these poets, simply because the path they trod led ultimately to some foolishness and mischief.

The trouble with the literature of escape is that it is insubstantial, and that it may easily become trivial, or even unintelligible. And apparently the fascination of Keats for some people today does lie in the fact that, despite the wealth of beauty he discovered and captured, he himself finally concluded that he had gone off on a wrong track. He had followed an instinctive bent, and had been encouraged so to do by the very nature of the Romantic Movement. As time passed, however, he became aware that he might have gone in a different direction. Then, gradually and uncertainly, he perceived that he could no longer devote himself to visionary glimpses of the land of faery. Self-knowledge became knowledge of a division between his own art and his own life. He became conscious of an insufficiency, for the needs of life, in the contemplation of "cold pastorals" or other cold dreams of timeless perfection; and it was this inward conflict which gave vitality to the series of great odes he wrote in 1819.

The Romantic Movement as a Whole

The writers at whose careers we have now glanced were certainly not aware that a time would come when they would all be called romantic together. The common impulse they felt was one of rebellion against scientific rationalism, and this was negative. On the positive side there was a general conviction that intuition was a sure guide to the human wisdom which the mere reasoning intellect had not only failed to achieve, but had obscured. Some held that men, once set free, would live in harmony under the guidance of intuition, held together by common beliefs and aims. They were wrong. It was immediately proved, not for the first time, that men set free will go off in all directions. Free men in France appeared unable to achieve anything between the two extremes of anarchy and despotism. The spectacle drove Burke, and then Wordsworth and Coleridge, to become politically conservative. And, in general, the strongly marked line of cleavage felt in the early nineteenth century was political. There was also, of course, a literary line of cleavage, but the two lines of division crossed each other in an irregular way. The romantic writers, moreover, would have been divided against themselves in any event, just because the movement as a whole, despite Burke and Scott, was a reassertion of individualism. Faith in the individual must live first of all as faith in one's self; if need be, against the world. And such faith must be a "firm persuasion" that one has hold of the tail of truth. Notoriously, however, a passionate conviction of this kind sets a man apart from his fellows, even though it does not always carry him to another world as it carried Blake.

An indefinite amount of evidence exists to show how far the romantic writers were, in fact, from forming a conscious "school" or united front. Wordsworth, as we have seen, thought of himself as leading a return to sanity and reality; and generally he used "romantic" in its eighteenth-century meaning, to condemn something as fantastic, wildly improbable, or extravagant. Likewise Coleridge in his *Biographia Literaria* mentions an occasion when he told Francis Jeffrey, then the editor and principal critical writer of *The Edinburgh Review,* "how utterly unfounded was the supposition that we"—*i.e.,* Coleridge, Wordsworth, and Southey—"considered ourselves as belonging to any common school but that of good sense confirmed by the long-established models of the best times of Greece, Rome, Italy and England." And Shelley wrote to Godwin, some time after reading his *Political Justice:* "I was no longer the votary of romance; till then I had lived in an ideal world."

Much has been written about the abusive persecution of the new romantic writers by the orthodox critics of the early nineteenth century, but the criticism most often cited was inspired by political considerations. Shelley was attacked as a dangerous enemy of Christianity and of constituted authority; and a determined enemy he was, at a time when most Englishmen were convinced that civilization itself was threatened with destruction by political radicalism. This in no way excuses the language used against him; but it is just as well to remember that the romantic writers were sometimes praised by so-called orthodox critics when political considerations did not compel attack, and also that the romantic writers freely attacked one another. Consider, for instance, Hazlitt on Wordsworth:

He tolerates nothing but what he himself creates; he sympathizes only with what can enter into no competition with him, with "the bare earth and mountains bare, and grass in the green field." He sees nothing but himself and the universe. He hates all greatness, and all pretensions to it but his own. His egotism is in this respect a madness; for he scorns even the admiration of himself, thinking it a presumption in anyone to suppose that he has taste or sense enough to understand him. He hates all science and all art; he hates chemistry, he hates conchology; he hates Sir Isaac Newton; he hates logic, he hates metaphysics, which he says are unintelligible, and yet he would be thought to understand them; he hates prose, he hates all poetry but his own; he hates Shakespeare, or what he calls "those interlocutions between Lucius and Caius," because he would have all the talk to himself, and considers the movements of passion in *Lear, Othello,* or *Macbeth*

as impertinent, compared with the moods of his own mind; he thinks everything good is contained in the *Lyrical Ballads,* or, if it is not contained there, it is good for nothing; he hates music, dancing, and painting; he hates Rubens, he hates Rembrandt, he hates Raphael, he hates Titian, he hates Vandyke; he hates the antique; he hates the Apollo Belvedere; he hates the Venus de Medicis. He hates all that others love and admire but himself. He is glad that Bonaparte is sent to St. Helena, and that the Louvre is dispersed, for the same reason—to get rid of the idea of anything greater, or thought greater, than himself.

Hazlitt does not say that Wordsworth is the incarnation of "rottenness, reptilism, and corruption"—the words used by one critic to describe Shelley—but it will be agreed that he succeeds in expressing vigorously a hearty dislike. And the truth is that the romantic writers, once they had asserted their freedom from whatever restrictions they hated, went their own several ways with intense conviction, each man for himself.

Yet they were held together more closely than they realized, more closely than anyone could realize until time had passed, and men could begin to look back on the first third of the nineteenth century as a whole. Today we can see clearly that in some way, not wholly explicable, the romantic writers were inspired by a common assurance which has been well expressed by Walter Bagehot. He is speaking of the sermons of one of the last expounders of the worldly prudential religion of the eighteenth century. The sermons of Sydney Smith, he says,

. . . are sensible and well-intentioned, but they have the defects of his school. With misdirected energy these divines have labored after a plain religion; they have forgotten that religion has its essence in awe, its charm in infinity, its sanction in dread; that its dominion is an inexplicable dominion; that mystery is its power.

The Methodists of the eighteenth century had regained this sense of life as a calling made sacred by the insistent demand of the spirit for infinity, and by the felt, though inexplicable, presence of God's grace. Experience, which was its own sufficient evidence, had shown them that life was shot through with infinite possibilities; and in this there was the keenest stimulus to feelings of hope and dread, both mixed with awe—and the issues of life became exciting.

The romantic writers, with the exception of Scott, were "emancipated" from Christianity; and Scott, though a loyal and sincere believer, found no excitement in religion. We have already noticed that there was in this age no direct connection between Methodism or Evangelicalism and the Romantic Movement. What happened was that some men outside of those folds became convinced, from one cause or another, that the spiritual demand for infinity was not a delusion, that human nature could not be explained on the basis of mechanical laws of cause and effect, that the age-long human dream of perfection did somehow answer to the real nature of things. They became convinced; but the Christian solution of the problem of life was not open to them, with the consequence that they were forced to search for some other, experimentally, each according to his own bent. There is a sense, therefore, in which it is misleading to speak of a romantic triumph; for though the movement did bring forth triumphant manifestations of human genius and creative power, it did not turn up any solution of its problem which found general acceptance. Wordsworth, Coleridge, Byron, Keats, and even Shelley—not to speak of lesser men—all turned first in one direction and then in another. Wordsworth and Coleridge both returned to Christianity, though not at all in a spirit of inward submission to authority.

Byron, the least genuinely romantic of the lot, came to the conclusion that all of them, including himself, had gone off "upon a wrong revolutionary" course which had brought about "the very uttermost decline and degradation of literature." He thought the poetry of Pope "ineffably" superior to anything his own age had produced, and turned to satire himself, with wonderful zest and success. We may be grateful that he thus discovered his bent; but no one would accept the conclusions which led him to self-discovery, because the romantic literature of this age is still vitally alive. It lives for two reasons: The movement of liberation found

a group of extraordinary men who themselves remain interesting personalities, fully revealed in a literature of great variety and beauty; and, further, whatever we may think today of this or that solution proposed in the generation of Wordsworth and Coleridge, these romantic writers brought literature back to vital issues, and issues with which not only the next age was to struggle; we still perplexedly face them in our own divided and distraught time.

But it was said at the beginning of this chapter that though the dominant literature of the early nineteenth century was romantic, the age itself was not. The romantic writers were a small minority engaged in rebellion, and though several of them gained enormous popularity, none of them had any great immediate effect on the national life or though⁺ It is, indeed, by no means always true—at any rate not true in any simple or obvious sense—that literature expresses the spirit of the age in which it is written. Of course it always has a relation of some kind to contemporary conditions, but that relation may be, as in this instance, one of reaction and revolt which makes an impression but does not convince. And in the romantic era it is not even true that all of the significant and still living literature of the time is romantic.

Drama at the End of the Eighteenth Century

In emphasizing the fact that not all of the living literature of the time is romantic we scarcely have occasion to speak of the drama, any more than we have spoken of it in connection with the romantic writers. They, to be sure, engaged in dramatic composition, but they produced nothing which could live upon the stage. Indeed, with two notable exceptions, no dramatic writer in England from the beginning of the eighteenth century to the end of the nineteenth produced plays which could live upon the stage. The reasons were different in the two centuries. The romantic and Victorian eras gave us dramas which do live as literature, so-called closet-dramas, some of which, like Byron's and Shelley's in the present period, are of very great interest; but these poetic plays could not success-fully be acted. Many plays of the eight-eenth century were successfully acted, but they proved ephemeral. In both centuries the stage thrived rather because of a series of talented actors than because of help given by English writers. But to this there is an important exception—the group of plays written by Goldsmith and Sheridan in the years from 1768 to 1779. Goldsmith wrote *The Good Natured Man* (1768) and *She Stoops to Conquer* (1773) as a protest against sentimentalism and false gentility; and Sheridan continued the protest, with more wit, in *The Rivals* (1775), *The School for Scandal* (1777), and *The Critic* (1779). Significantly, both had to go back to the play-wrights of the Restoration for their models in achieving an effective form and style.

Jane Austen

But though it deserves to be remembered that a reaction against high-flying gentility and the extravagances of sentimentalism gave us these delightful and witty plays at the close of the era of Good Sense, it is more important, and more to our present purpose, to recall that Jane Austen wrote her famous novels in the very midst of the romantic age. *Sense and Sensibility, Pride and Prejudice, Mansfield Park, Emma, Northanger Abbey,* and *Persuasion* were all published between 1811 and 1818, and Jane Austen was at work on them from about 1795 until within less than a year of her death in 1817. She once told a correspondent that she was "the most unlearned and uninformed female who ever dared to be an authoress"; but this was a mixture of truth and falsehood which natu-rally suggested itself as an inoffensive way out of a difficulty. The fact is that she had a pair of keen eyes, a finely balanced nature, and a quiet ubiquitous perception of the ridiculous which was the bright side of her imperturbable good sense; and that these qualities were more important to her than anything in her reading which may have helped to form her mind and character. She lived in a small world which was perfectly formed, in the sense that its ways seemed fixed, its life settled, and its people calcu-

lable. Its center was the country town, and its inhabitants the provincial and rural gen-try. Jane Austen knew this small world, in which she was born and brought up, inside and out. What was more, she liked it thor-oughly, just as it was, and saw it just as it was. Her novels are a singularly clear re-flection of her own world, contrived with the most discriminating and delicate art. Her characters are minutely and sympatheti-cally observed, and at first sight it might ap-pear that all one gets is observation from the outside—and, someone might add, observa-tion of people without much to be discovered inside. But Jane Austen did penetrate with-in her characters; and it is one of the signs of her genius that she got beyond the deline-ation of manners and built up fully rounded persons by showing them as acted upon, and acting upon, one another.

One could carry this description further, but the further one went the more insistent would become the question, How did Jane Austen manage to make the commonplace activities of a small set of very ordinary comfortable people interesting? The an-swer brings in her reading; for of course she did read, incessantly. With her clear intel-ligence and keen eyes she might have seen everything we find in her novels even if she had been as "unlearned and uninformed" as she once found it convenient to say; and in fact she did have very little formal educa-tion, and knew almost nothing of the world at first hand outside of her own small circle. And even her reading, as far as we know, was very restricted in scope. Practically, it was confined to the century of her birth, and even to contemporaries. The two writers of serious literature who meant most to her were Dr. Johnson and Cowper. Apparently next came Goldsmith and Crabbe, and Scott. The books she read incessantly were the lat-est novels from the circulating library. She read older novels too, particularly Richard-son's, and Fanny Burney's *Evelina* (1778), and later the same author's *Camilla* (1796), and Maria Edgeworth's *Castle Rackrent* (1800) and *Belinda* (1801). Her debt to Fanny Burney is large, and historically she carries on the eighteenth-century tradition of the novel of manners as she received it from *Evelina*. But her direct stimulus came from the ephemeral novels of the circulating library; and it was these which suggested her way of dealing with the apparently commonplace, if not insipid, matter of her own observation, and which consequently give us the answer to our question, How did she make her little country world interesting?

Earlier in this chapter we have glanced at the best known representatives of the art of popular fiction at the end of the eighteenth century, and in discussing Scott we have noticed that popular fiction was not in good repute at the beginning of the nineteenth century. Thrillers were the order of the day, and in them, as we have seen, readers were transported to imaginary worlds where the most sensational events were continually enacted in an atmosphere of frightful agitation. Every emotion was raised to its highest intensity, and, in particular, love was exalted as "the ruling principle of the world" which "caused all the happiness and miseries of life." Jane Austen read these romances with delight, not because her feelings were harrowed as were those of more credulous readers, but because she found them hilariously funny. She did not need the warning which Walter Scott himself addressed to a correspondent, telling her that "the world we actually live in is not that of poetry and romance." She knew what kind of world we actually live in; and in the light of the "thrilling" unrealities of shoddy romance her perceptions of its solid and enduring interest were quickened and heightened and sharpened. She began as a mere girl to write burlesque tales in which the absurdities of romantic novels were made fun of; and from this beginning she went on in her mature work to satirize what Scott in a candid moment would have called the pseudo-romantic view of life, with its overwrought emotionalism, its sentimentalism, its fanciful medievalism, and its sensationalism. It is this satirical undercurrent which fills her novels with humor, and which gives sharpness, importance, and endless interest to her characters and their lives.

Jane Austen was not alone in perceiving, and not the first to satirize, the absurdities of false romance. As early as 1752 Charlotte Lennox had published *The Female Quixote*, in which the old heroic romance, eagerly read in the seventeenth century, was burlesqued. Its exposure of falsity continued to seem relevant as the new wave of Gothic and sentimental romances rose in the second half of the eighteenth century, and Jane Austen read *The Female Quixote* with enjoyment. In her own time this burlesque was followed by others directed against the misrepresentations of romantic fiction—Maria Edgeworth's *Angelina* (in her Moral Tales, 1801), Sarah Green's *Romance Readers and Romance Writers* (1810), and Eaton Stannard Barrett's *The Heroine* (1814). But in all of these books the view taken was that the minds of readers, especially of innocent young female readers, were in danger of being poisoned by romances, and that it was a duty to warn such readers: In the real world, love was not so all-important, so intense, so careless of consequences; and, in general, real life did not afford the soul-shaking thrills of the world of romance; the real world, in sober fact, was comparatively barren, bleak, harsh, and arid. There was, therefore, a fundamental difference between these writers and Jane Austen. She was incomparably superior as an artist; but, beyond this, she thought, as we have seen, that real life and real people were better, more interesting, more delightful than the monsters—whether sentimental or villainous—of fiction and their blood-curdling and blood-kindling deeds. Real life was good enough for her, and might be shown to have its own vivid and lasting interest.

Tory England and the Industrial Revolution

Readers from those of her own day to E. M. Forster in ours have heartily agreed with Jane Austen and have fairly worshiped her. And for those engaged in historical study she has this value as a witness: She may be taken as the accomplished representative of the prevailing temper of her generation. Englishmen by and large in the romantic era felt as they had through most of the eighteenth century, that their country was a good and comfortable place to live in;

and they were not torn by romantic discontents. Scott and Byron were, as has been said, the only romantic writers who, following in the wake of the writers of "Gothic" and sentimental romances which have been discussed, achieved widespread popularity amongst their contemporaries; and they obviously did so because they gratified in a superior way an already existing popular taste for exciting entertainment. The progress of the French Revolution confirmed the average Englishman in his feeling of satisfaction with things as they were, and made him anxious only to keep them as they were. Those actively concerned with politics, indeed, got into a state of panic, saw a Jacobin (as political radicals were called) behind every moving bush, and hardened themselves against every sign of demand for even moderate reform.

But the effort to keep steady in a changing world is one thing, and the effort to keep change itself from occurring is another—is, indeed, bound to be wholly unsuccessful. Changes were taking place in England in these years, even more momentous than the long struggle against Napoleon, and a quite new economic and social alignment was coming into existence, which had not been designed or foreseen by anybody. This great internal change is called the Industrial Revolution. It was brought about by the discovery of the steam-engine, perfected by the Scotchman, James Watt, in the later years of the eighteenth century. Watt's engine made it possible to use steam power in industry, which brought about mass production of consumable goods in factories, at a great saving in labor, and caused the rapid decay of home industry. The transformation of England from an agricultural to an industrial country caused widespread and most acute hardship in the sections of the population immediately concerned, which provoked disorders terrifying to the conservative or Tory government. And the Tories were in power almost continuously from 1783 until 1830.

William Cobbett

No person, party, or earthly force could have stopped the Industrial Revolution; and the Tories were only concerned to stamp out disorder amongst the victims of the new dispensation. But they were asked to do more by one notable figure of the time, William Cobbett. Cobbett was, said a younger contemporary who knew him and observed him in action, almost a great man; and "as it was he made a great noise." He was a talented and vigorous journalist, and for the rest has been called by everybody who has written about him the very incarnation of the traditional John Bull. He was a constitutional individualist and rebel, and could not subdue himself to work with his fellow Tories, but what he wanted was identical with that which some of them would also have liked. He summed up his position when he wrote: "We want nothing new; we want only what our forefathers enjoyed, what the stock-jobbers and the place-hunters and the Pittites and the cotton lords have taken away."

Inevitably such conservatism was doomed to defeat. The good old times can never be recaptured. Yet Cobbett has not only left a name; some of his books still live and are affectionately read, because he infused everything he wrote with his own manly and very English personality, and because his antipathies are engaging, whether or not his aims are practicable. He is, moreover, the classical representative of an enduring type—the embattled countryman storming helplessly against the clever, ignoble city-chap who hoodwinks him out of his land and livelihood.

Jeremy Bentham and Utilitarianism

Cobbett represents only a class, a section, and a lost cause. If we look for a more generally representative figure who stood in the early years of the nineteenth century for what that century as a whole was predominantly to be, we have to turn to a voluminous writer whose works in our day lie dead, and heavy, on the library shelves. We must turn to Jeremy Bentham, legal reformer, founder of Utilitarianism, and heir to eighteenth-century humanitarianism, whose motto was "the greatest happiness of the greatest number." Bentham wanted change, reform, improvement, and was supremely confident that he could aid the cause of social progress. But he did not want violence or revolution. He was contemptuous of the doctrine of the abstract rights of man, and convinced that social order and the security of property were more important than any other good things a society might enjoy. He was an individualist, and believed every man to be the only qualified judge of his own interests; and accordingly wanted the utmost individual freedom consistent with order and security. He did not originate, but did give currency to, the economic doctrine of individualism known as *laissez-faire,* which means "let each man act as he pleases." He was nothing if not thoroughgoing, and contended in support of this doctrine that if gambling gave as much pleasure as poetry, then gambling was just as good as poetry.

In general, what is most interesting in Bentham, and typical of the new outlook which was coming to prevail, is his fundamental conviction that human happiness can be secured by changes in the machinery and accessories of life—by legislation and by the mass production of useful gadgets. He was responsible for many salutary reforms in English law, and he was in many ways not only well-intentioned but sensible. Nevertheless, his design for a model prison and his claims for its benefits in all their absurdity are too characteristic of him and of the outlook he typifies to be omitted from even our brief glance at him, though he should not be judged by this particular improvement he advocated. The perfect prison was to be a circular building, with the cells arranged around the outer wall in such fashion that an inspector, stationed in an apartment in the center, could at all times see everything done by every prisoner. An arrangement of blinds, however, was to keep the prisoners

from seeing the inspector, though they were to know they were being spied on, and this knowledge was to beget in them "the sentiment of an invisible omniscience." The building, called the Panopticon, was designed by Bentham's brother Samuel, and came near to being erected. One actually was built in St. Petersburg (Leningrad). In his enthusiasm for all that he fancied the governor of such a prison could accomplish, as absolute master of the environment and social life of the convicts, Bentham looked forward to see "morals reformed, health preserved, industry invigorated, instruction diffused, public burdens lightened, economy seated as it were upon a rock, the Gordian knot of the Poor Law not cut but untied [for he proposed that the same kind of building should be used also as a poorhouse]—all by a simple idea in architecture."

There we are! Salvation by machinery, the machinery of legislation and that of industry, was the appealing dream which was beginning to animate well-nigh the whole people of England during the period which students of literature call "romantic." Bentham and his disciples carried on through that period, and projected into the future, the "enlightenment" of the eighteenth century, modified by changing circumstances, but not changed in spirit. We get a not unfair notion of Bentham's position in the onward march of progress, against which the romantic writers rebelled, from the words written about him in 1806 by the Russian Admiral Mordvinoff: "He is, in my eyes, one of the four geniuses who have done, and will do most for the happiness of the human race—Bacon, Newton, Adam Smith, and Bentham: each founder of a new science, each a creator."

RICHARD BRINSLEY SHERIDAN

1751–1816

Sheridan's father was an actor and theater-manager in Dublin when the future dramatist and statesman was born there on 30 October, 1751. In 1758, the Dublin Theater Royal no longer prospering in the hands of the elder Sheridan, he went to England, where he became a teacher of elocution. His son was left at school in Dublin, and only joined his parents a year and a half later. He never returned to the city of his birth. In 1762 he entered Harrow, and remained there until 1768. His further education was received from a private tutor, and he also was taught fencing and riding. In 1770 the Sheridans settled in Bath, where Richard became busy with varied and lighthearted efforts to make his way in literature. He also became attached to Elizabeth Linley who, young though she was, had already become well known as a concert-singer, and was besieged by many admirers. To escape the attentions and threats of a disgraceful rake, whose pursuit of her was becoming notorious, she now determined to go secretly to France and take refuge, at least for the time being, in a convent. Sheridan undertook to see her safely into France, and off they went;—but, reaching an understanding with each other, instead of proceeding to a convent they went through a form of marriage before a French priest. They themselves seem to have understood this as a solemn betrothal rather than as a marriage, and what really it was nobody knows. Meanwhile, however, the families of both parties to this escapade were excited, and Miss Linley's father hastened after his daughter and brought her back to England. Upon his return Sheridan fought two duels with her persecutor, being seriously wounded at the second encounter. And his family, in an unsuccessful effort to break Miss Linley's spell, sent him off to Waltham Abbey in Essex, where he spent the winter of 1772–1773 in retirement and study. In April, 1773, he entered the Middle Temple, and in the same month he married Miss Linley with her father's consent.

Money now became an imperative need, and Sheridan wrote much, though he published nothing over his own name. He also turned his thoughts towards the theater, and in 1774 rapidly composed The Rivals, which was accepted at Covent Garden. It was performed on 17 January, 1775—and was an evident failure. The trouble lay partly in the acting, and it was decided that with some revision of the text and a change in one of the parts it might yet succeed. Accordingly it was revised, and then performed again on 28 January, this time with complete success. It has remained to the present day one of the most popular of English comedies, and one of the most discussed, so that a large literature has grown around it. The play, composed with a remarkable mastery of stagecraft, was an attack upon the weakly sentimental comedy which flourished in the eighteenth century. With this aim, Sheridan looked to the comedy of manners as it had been developed in the last quarter of the seventeenth century by Etheredge, Farquhar, Congreve, and others, and benefited largely by their example. Efforts, however, to trace his sources exactly have resulted in so many and such divergent suggestions that only one conclusion may be regarded as definitely established—the conclusion that, while Sheridan made use of types which have had a long history on the stage, and succeeded in converting much traditional matter into a brilliantly satirical comedy of the manners of his own day, still, he was on the whole very little indebted to his predecessors for the actual details of his plot and characterization.

Spurred on by his great success in his first venture, Sheridan next wrote a farce, St. Patrick's Day, for the benefit of the actor who had done most for The Rivals; and immediately proceeded to compose a comic opera, The Duenna, which was performed at Covent Garden on 21 November, 1775. Its popularity was unprecedented on the English stage, and Sheridan not unreasonably thought that his fortune was as good as made. In 1776 he became the manager of Drury Lane Theater in succession to David

Garrick; but, though he continued for many years to control the play-house, he proved incompetent to succeed with the venture, and in the end found it a source of misfortune. There *The School for Scandal*—more finished, though less sympathetic than *The Rivals*—was performed on 8 May, 1777; and there also was performed his witty farce, *The Critic,* on 29 October, 1779. In addition to these plays, Sheridan compiled several adaptations from older English or foreign originals, the last of which, *Pizarro,* was performed in May, 1779. Meanwhile he had become a social favorite. In 1777 he had been admitted to the Literary Club, and in 1780 he was elected to the House of Commons (pledged to support Charles James Fox) by Stafford. In the House he won a high reputation as an orator, and steadily supported what would now be called liberalism—opposing the war against the American colonies, defending the freedom of the press, and aiding various reforms such as the abatement of the severity of the game laws. He also became the friend and adviser of the Prince of Wales; and was one of the managers of the impeachment of Warren Hastings. It was in the course of one of his great speeches on this occasion that he referred to Gibbon's "luminous page." Report had it that afterwards, when reminded of this, he explained that he must have intended to say "voluminous." His wife died in June, 1792, while the trial of Hastings was still in progress. He married a second time in April, 1795. His misfortunes with Drury Lane and his own extravagance finally so lowered his income that in 1812 he could not bear the expense of an election, and so lost his seat in Parliament. He was then a broken man, and was, indeed, imprisoned for debt in 1813. He died in London on 7 July, 1816, and was buried in the poet's corner in Westminster Abbey.

The standard edition of *The Plays & Poems of Richard Brinsley Sheridan* is that edited by R. Crompton Rhodes (Oxford, 1928). Rhodes is also the author of a biography, *Harlequin Sheridan* (Oxford, 1933), which is superior to all its predecessors. Of great interest to a student of *The Rivals* is the text of that play as it was first performed, recently edited by Richard L. Purdy and published for the first time (Oxford, 1935). A competent general account of the drama in Sheridan's day and before is to be found in G. H. Nettleton's *English Drama of the Restoration and Eighteenth Century* (1914).

THE RIVALS
A Comedy (1775)

PREFACE

A PREFACE to a play seems generally to be considered as a kind of closet-prologue, in which—if his piece has been successful—the 5 author solicits that indulgence from the reader which he had before experienced from the audience. But as the scope and immediate object of a play is to please a mixed assembly in representation (whose judgment 10 in the theater at least is decisive), its degree of reputation is usually as determined by the public before it can be prepared for the cooler tribunal of the study. Thus any farther solicitude on the part of the writer becomes 15 unnecessary at least, if not an intrusion; and if the piece has been condemned in the performance, I fear an address to the closet, like an appeal to posterity, is constantly regarded as the procrastination of a suit from a con- 20 sciousness of the weakness of the cause. From these considerations, the following comedy would certainly have been submitted to the reader without any further introduction than what it had in the representation, but that its success has probably been founded on a circumstance which the author is informed has not before attended a theatrical trial, and which consequently ought not to pass unnoticed.

I need scarcely add that the circumstance alluded to was the withdrawing of the piece, to remove those imperfections in the first representation which were too obvious to escape reprehension and too numerous to admit of a hasty correction. There are few writers, I believe, who, even in the fullest consciousness of error, do not wish to palliate the faults which they acknowledge; and, however trifling the performance, to second their confession of its deficiencies by whatever plea seems least disgraceful to their ability. In the present instance, it cannot be said to amount either to candor or modesty in me, to acknowledge an extreme inexperience and want of judgment on matters in which, without guidance from practice or spur from success, a young man should scarcely boast of being an adept. If it be said that under such disadvantages no one should attempt to write a play, I must beg leave to dissent from the position, while the first point of experience that I have gained on the subject is a knowledge of the candor and judgment with which an impartial public distinguishes between the errors of inexperience and incapacity, and the indulgence which it shows even to a disposition to remedy the defects of either.

It were unnecessary to enter into any farther extenuation of what was thought exceptionable in this play, but that it has been said that the managers should have prevented some of the defects before its appearance to the public—and in particular the uncommon length of the piece as represented the first night. It were an ill return for the most liberal and gentlemanly conduct on their side, to suffer any censure to rest where none was deserved. Hurry in writing has long been exploded as an excuse for an author; however, in the dramatic line, it may happen that both an author and a manager may wish to fill a chasm in the entertainment of the public with a hastiness not altogether culpable. The season was advanced when I first put the play into Mr. Harris's[1] hands: it was at that time at least double the length of any acting comedy. I profited by his judgment and experience in the curtailing of it—till, I believe, his feeling for the vanity of a young author got the better of his desire for correctness, and he left many excrescences remaining because he had assisted in pruning so many more. Hence, though I was not uninformed that the acts were still too long, I flattered myself that, after the first trial, I might with safer judgment proceed to remove what should appear to have been most dissatisfactory. Many other errors there were which might in part have arisen from my being by no means conversant with plays in general, either in reading or at the theater. Yet I own that, in one respect, I did not regret my ignorance; for as my first wish in attempting a play was to avoid every appearance of plagiary, I thought I should stand a better chance of effecting this from being in a walk which I had not frequented, and where consequently the progress of invention was less likely to be interrupted by starts of recollection. For on subjects on which the mind has been much informed, invention is slow of exerting itself. Faded ideas float in the fancy like half-forgotten dreams, and the imagination in its fullest enjoyments becomes suspicious of its offspring and doubts whether it has created or adopted.

With regard to some particular passages which on the first night's representation seemed generally disliked, I confess that if I felt any emotion of surprise at the disapprobation, it was not that they were disapproved of, but that I had not before perceived that they deserved it. As some part of the attack on the piece was begun too early to pass for the sentence of *judgment,* which is ever tardy in condemning, it has been suggested to me that much of the disapprobation must have arisen from virulence of malice rather than severity of criticism; but as I was more apprehensive of there being just grounds to excite the latter than conscious of having deserved the former, I continue not to believe that probable which I am sure must have been unprovoked. However, if it was so and I could even mark the quarter from whence it came, it would be ungenerous to retort; for no passion suffers more than malice from disappointment. For my own part, I see no reason why the author of a play should not regard a first night's audience as a candid and judicious friend attending, in behalf of the public, at his last rehearsal. If he can dispense with flattery, he is sure at least of sincerity, and even though the annotation be rude, he may rely upon the justness of the comment. Considered in this light, that audience, whose *fiat* is essential to the poet's claim whether his object be fame or profit, has surely a right to expect some deference to its opinion, from principles of politeness at least, if not from gratitude.

As for the little puny critics, who scatter their peevish strictures in private circles, and scribble at every author who has the eminence of being unconnected with them, as

---

[1]Thomas Harris, manager of Covent Garden Theater.

they are usually spleen-swoln from a vain idea of increasing their consequence, there will always be found a petulance and illiberality in their remarks which should place them as far beneath the notice of a gentleman as their original dullness had sunk them from the level of the most unsuccessful author.

It is not without pleasure that I catch at an opportunity of justifying myself from the charge of intending any national reflection in the character of Sir Lucius O'Trigger. If any gentlemen opposed the piece from that idea, I thank them sincerely for their opposition; and if the condemnation of this comedy (however misconceived the provocation) could have added one spark to the decaying flame of national attachment to the country supposed to be reflected on, I should have been happy in its fate and might with truth have boasted that it had done more real service in its failure than the successful morality of a thousand stage-novels will ever effect.

It is usual, I believe, to thank the performers in a new play for the exertion of their several abilities. But where (as in this instance) their merit has been so striking and uncontroverted as to call for the warmest and truest applause from a number of judicious audiences, the poet's after-praise comes like the feeble acclamation of a child to close the shouts of a multitude. The conduct, however, of the principals in a theater cannot be so apparent to the public.—I think it therefore but justice to declare that from this theater (the only one I can speak of from experience) those writers who wish to try the dramatic line will meet with that candor and liberal attention which are generally allowed to be better calculated to lead genius into excellence than either the precepts of judgment or the guidance of experience.

THE AUTHOR

PROLOGUE

Enter SERGEANT-AT-LAW, *and* ATTORNEY *following, and giving a paper.*

SERGEANT. What's here!—a vile cramp
    hand! I cannot see
Without my spectacles.

ATTORNEY.   He means his fee.
Nay, Mr. Sergeant, good sir, try again.
        (*Gives money*)
SERGEANT. The scrawl i m p r o v e s !
    ([*Gives*] *more*) Oh, come, 'tis pretty
    plain.
Hey! how's this? The Poet's Brief *again.*
O ho!   5
Cast,[1] I suppose?
    ATTORNEY.   O pardon me—No—No—
We found the court, o'erlooking stricter laws,
Indulgent to the merits of the Cause;
By Judges mild, unused to harsh denial,
A rule was granted for another trial.   10
    SERGEANT. Then heark'ee, Dibble, did you
    mend your pleadings,
Errors, no few, we've found in our proceedings.
    ATTORNEY. Come, courage, sir, we did
    amend our plea,
Hence your new brief, and this refreshing
    fee.
Some sons of Phœbus in the courts we
    meet,   15
    SERGEANT. And fifty sons of Phœbus in
    the Fleet![2]
    ATTORNEY. Nor pleads he worse, who
    with a decent sprig
Of bays adorns his legal waste of wig.
    SERGEANT. Full-bottomed heroes thus, on
    signs, unfurl
A leaf of laurel in a grove of curl!   20
Yet tell your client that, in adverse days,
This wig is warmer than a bush of bays.
    ATTORNEY. Do you, then, sir, my client's
    place supply,
Profuse of robe and prodigal of tie—
Do you, with all those blushing powers of
    face,   25
And wonted bashful hesitating grace,
Rise in the court and flourish on the case.
                            [*Exit.*
    SERGEANT. For practice then suppose—
    this brief will show it,—
Me, Sergeant Woodward,—council for the
    poet.
Used to the ground—I know 'tis hard to
    deal   30
With this dread court, from whence there's
    no appeal;
No tricking here, to blunt the edge of law,
Or, damned in equity, escape by flaw:
But judgment given—your sentence must
    remain;
No writ of error lies—to Drury Lane!   35

[1] Found guilty.

[2] I. e., fifty poets in the debtors' prison.

Yet when so kind you seem—'tis past dis-
  pute
We gain some favor if not costs of suit.
No spleen is here! I see no hoarded fury—
I think I never faced a milder jury!
Sad else our plight! where frowns are trans-
  portation,
A hiss the gallows, and a groan—damnation!
But such the public candor, without fear
My client waives all right of challenge here. 10
No newsman from *our* session is dismissed,
Nor wit nor critic *we* scratch off the list;
His faults can never hurt another's ease,
His crime at worst—a bad attempt to please:
Thus, all respecting, he appeals to all,
And by the general voice will stand or fall.

DRAMATIS PERSONAE

Sir Anthony Absolute
Captain Absolute
Faulkland
Acres
Sir Lucius O'Trigger
Fag
David
Thomas, *a Coachman*
Mrs. Malaprop
Lydia Languish
Julia
Lucy
Maid, Boy, Servants, etc.
SCENE: *BATH*
TIME OF ACTION: *FIVE HOURS*

ACT I

Scene I. *A Street in Bath*

Coachman *crosses the stage; enter* Fag,
  looking after him

Fag. What! Thomas! sure 'tis he?—
What! Thomas! Thomas!
  Coachman. Hey!—Odds life! Mr. Fag!
—give us your hand, my old fellow-servant.
  Fag. Excuse my glove, Thomas.—I'm
devilish glad to see you, my lad. Why, my
prince of charioteers, you look as hearty!—
but who the deuce thought of seeing you in
Bath!
  Coachman. Sure, Master, Madam Julia,
Harry, Mrs. Kate, and the postilion be all
come.
  Fag. Indeed!
  Coachman. Aye, Master thought another 55
fit of the gout was coming to make him a
visit; so he'd a mind to gi't the slip, and

whip! we were all off at an hour's warning.
  Fag. Aye, aye, hasty in everything or it
would not be Sir Anthony Absolute!
  Coachman. But tell us, Mr. Fag, how
does young Master? Odd! Sir Anthony
will stare to see the captain here!
  Fag. I do not serve Captain Absolute
now.
  Coachman. Why, sure!
  Fag. At present I am employed by Ensign
Beverley.
  Coachman. I doubt, Mr. Fag, you ha'n't
changed for the better.
  Fag. I have not changed, Thomas.
  Coachman. No! Why, didn't you say
you had left young Master?
  Fag. No.—Well, honest Thomas, I must
puzzle you no farther:—briefly then—Cap-
tain Absolute and Ensign Beverley are one
and the same person.
  Coachman. The devil they are!
  Fag. So it is indeed, Thomas; and the
ensign half of my master being on guard at
present—the *captain* has nothing to do with
me.
  Coachman. So, so!—What, this is some
freak, I warrant!—Do tell us, Mr. Fag, the
meaning o't—you know I ha' trusted you.
  Fag. You'll be secret, Thomas?
  Coachman. As a coach-horse.
  Fag. Why, then, the cause of all this is—
Love,—Love, Thomas, who (as you may get
read to you) has been a masquerader ever
since the days of Jupiter.
  Coachman. Aye, aye;—I guessed there
was a lady in the case.—But pray, why does
your Master pass only for *ensign?*—now if
he had shammed *general* indeed—
  Fag. Ah! Thomas, there lies the mystery
o' the matter. Hark'ee, Thomas, my Master
is in love with a lady of a very singular taste:
a lady who likes him better as a *half-pay
ensign* than if she knew he was son and heir
to Sir Anthony Absolute, a baronet with
three thousand a year.
  Coachman. That is an odd taste indeed!
—But has she got the stuff, Mr. Fag? Is
she rich, hey?
  Fag. Rich!—Why, I believe she owns
half the stocks! Zounds! Thomas, she
could pay the national debt as easily as I
could my washerwoman! She has a lapdog
that eats out of gold,—she feeds her parrot
with small pearls,—and all her thread-
papers[1] are made of bank-notes!

----
[1] Papers folded in creases so as to form separate
divisions for different skeins of thread.

COACHMAN. Bravo! faith!—Odd! I warrant she has a set of thousands[2] at least;—but does she draw kindly with the captain?

FAG. As fond as pigeons.

COACHMAN. May one hear her name?

FAG. Miss Lydia Languish.—But there is an old tough aunt in the way—though, by-the-bye, she has never seen my Master—for we got acquainted with Miss while on a visit in Gloucestershire.

COACHMAN. Well—I wish they were once harnessed together in matrimony.—But pray, Mr. Fag, what kind of a place is this Bath? —I ha' heard a deal of it—here's a mort[3] o' merry-making, hey?

FAG. Pretty well, Thomas, pretty well— 'tis a good lounge.[4] Though at present we are, like other great assemblies, divided into parties—High-roomians and Low-roomians; however, for my part, I have resolved to stand neuter, and so I told Bob Brush at our last committee.

COACHMAN. But what do the folks do here?

FAG. Oh! there are little amusements enough; in the morning we go to the pump-room (though neither my Master nor I drink the waters); after breakfast we saunter on the parades or play a game at billiards; at night we dance. But damn the place, I'm tired of it; their regular hours stupefy me— not a fiddle nor a card after eleven!—However, Mr. Faulkland's gentleman and I keep it up a little in private parties. I'll introduce you there, Thomas—you'll like him much.

COACHMAN. Sure I know Mr. Du-Peigne —you know his Master is to marry Madam Julia.

FAG. I had forgot.—But, Thomas, you must polish a little—indeed you must.— Here now—this wig! What the devil do you do with a *wig*, Thomas?—None of the London whips of any degree of *ton*[5] wear wigs now.

COACHMAN. More's the pity! more's the pity, I say.—Odds life! when I heard how the lawyers and doctors had took to their own hair, I thought how 'twould go next.— Odd rabbit it! when the fashion had got foot on the Bar, I guessed 'twould mount to the Box!—but 'tis all out of character, believe me, Mr. Fag; and look'ee, I'll never gi' up mine—the lawyers and doctors may do as they will.

FAG. Well, Thomas, we'll not quarrel about that.

COACHMAN. Why, bless you, the gentlemen of they professions ben't all of a mind— for in our village now thoff[6] Jack Gauge, the exciseman, has ta'en to his carrots,[7] there's little Dick the farrier swears he'll never forsake his bob,[8] tho' all the college should appear with their own heads!

FAG. Indeed! well said, Dick!—But hold —mark! mark! Thomas.

COACHMAN. Zooks! 'tis the captain.—Is that the lady with him?

FAG. No! no! that is Madam Lucy, my Master's mistress's maid. They lodge at that house—but I must after him to tell him the news.

COACHMAN. Odd! he's giving her money! —Well, Mr. Fag—

FAG. Good-bye, Thomas. I have an appointment in Gydes' Porch[9] this evening at eight; meet me there, and we'll make a little party. [*Exeunt severally.*

SCENE II. A *Dressing-Room in* MRS. MALAPROP'S *Lodgings*

LYDIA *sitting on a sofa, with a book in her hand.*

LUCY, *as just returned from a message*

LUCY. Indeed, ma'am, I traversed half the town in search of it! I don't believe there's a circulating library in Bath I ha'n't been at.

LYDIA. And could not you get *The Reward of Constancy?*[10]

LUCY. No, indeed, ma'am.

LYDIA. Nor *The Fatal Connection?*

LUCY. No, indeed, ma'am.

LYDIA. Nor *The Mistakes of the Heart?*

LUCY. Ma'am, as ill luck would have it, Mr. Bull said Miss Sukey Saunter had just fetched it away.

LYDIA. Heigh-ho! Did you inquire for *The Delicate Distress?*

LUCY. Or, *The Memoirs of Lady Wood-*

---

[2]A team of six horses, of high value, running into thousands of pounds.

[3]Great deal.   [4]Good place for idlers.   [5]Style.

[6]Though.

[7]Has taken to his own (carrot-colored) hair.

[8]Wig.

[9]The so-called Lower Rooms, giving on the Walks, were kept by a Mr. Gyde.

[10]The novels mentioned in this scene, in satirical allusion to the sentimental fiction of the day, have been identified and discussed by Professor G. H. Nettleton in the Introduction to his edition of Sheridan's *Major Dramas* ("Athenaeum Press Series," Ginn).

ford? Yes, indeed, ma'am. I asked everywhere for it; and I might have brought it from Mr. Frederick's, but Lady Slattern Lounger, who had just sent it home, had so soiled and dog's-eared it, it wa'n't fit for a Christian to read.

LYDIA. Heigh-ho! Yes, I always know when Lady Slattern has been before me. She has a most observing thumb and I believe cherishes her nails for the convenience of making marginal notes.—Well, child, what *have* you brought me?

LUCY. Oh! here, ma'am.—(*Taking books from under her cloak and from her pockets*) This is *The Gordian Knot,*—and this *Peregrine Pickle.* Here are *The Tears of Sensibility* and *Humphry Clinker.* This is *The Memoirs of a Lady of Quality, written by herself,* and here the second volume of *The Sentimental Journey.*

LYDIA. Heigh-ho!—What are those books by the glass?

LUCY. The great one is only *The Whole Duty of Man,* where I press a few blonds,[11] ma'am.

LYDIA. Very well—give me the *sal volatile.*

LUCY. Is it in a blue cover, ma'am?

LYDIA. My smelling-bottle, you simpleton!

LUCY. Oh, the drops!—here, ma'am.

LYDIA. No note, Lucy?

LUCY. No, indeed, ma'am—but I have seen a certain person—

LYDIA. What, my Beverley!—Well, Lucy?

LUCY. O ma'am, he looks so desponding and melancholic!

LYDIA. Hold! Lucy—here's someone coming—quick! see who it is.   [*Exit* LUCY.
—Surely I heard my cousin Julia's voice.

Re-enter LUCY

LUCY. Lud! ma'am, here is Miss Melville.

LYDIA. Is it possible!—   [*Exit* LUCY.

Enter JULIA

My dearest Julia, how delighted am I!—(*Embrace*) How unexpected was this happiness!

JULIA. True, Lydia—and our pleasure is the greater.—But what has been the matter?—you were denied to me at first!

LYDIA. Ah, Julia, I have a thousand things

to tell you!—But first inform me what has conjured you to Bath—is Sir Anthony here?

JULIA. He is—we are arrived within this hour—and I suppose he will be here to wait on Mrs. Malaprop as soon as he is dressed.

LYDIA. Then before we are interrupted, let me impart to you some of my distress! I know your gentle nature will sympathize with me, though your prudence may condemn me! My letters have informed you of my whole connection with Beverley, but I have lost him, Julia! My aunt has discovered our intercourse by a note she intercepted and has confined me ever since! Yet, would you believe it? she has absolutely fallen in love with a tall Irish baronet she met one night since she has been here, at Lady Macshuffle's rout.[12]

JULIA. You jest, Lydia!

LYDIA. No, upon my word.—She really carries on a kind of correspondence with him, under a feigned name though, till she chooses to be known to him;—but it is a *Delia* or a *Celia,* I assure you.

JULIA. Then, surely, she is now more indulgent to her niece.

LYDIA. Quite the contrary. Since she has discovered her own frailty, she is become more suspicious of mine.—Then I must inform you of another plague! That odious Acres is to be in Bath to-day; so that I protest I shall be teased out of all spirits!

JULIA. Come, come, Lydia, hope the best —Sir Anthony shall use his interest with Mrs. Malaprop.

LYDIA. But you have not heard the worst. Unfortunately I had quarreled with my poor Beverley just before my aunt made the discovery, and I have not seen him since to make it up.

JULIA. What was his offense?

LYDIA. Nothing at all!—But, I don't know how it was, as often as we had been together, we had never had a quarrel! And somehow I was afraid he would never give me an opportunity.—So, last Thursday, I wrote a letter to myself, to inform myself that Beverley was at that time paying his addresses to another woman.—I signed it *your Friend unknown,* showed it to Beverley, charged him with his falsehood, put myself in a violent passion, and vowed I'd never see him more.

JULIA. And you let him depart so, and have not seen him since?

LYDIA. 'Twas the next day my aunt

---

[11]Silk laces of two threads, twisted and formed in hexagonal meshes. *The Whole Duty of Man* was a serious devotional work, more than a century old.

[12]Large social gathering, assembly.

found the matter out. I intended only to have teased him three days and a half, and now I've lost him for ever.

JULIA. If he is as deserving and sincere as you have represented him to me, he will never give you up so. Yet consider, Lydia, you tell me he is but an ensign, and you have thirty thousand pounds!

LYDIA. But you know I lose most of my fortune if I marry without my aunt's con- 10 sent till of age, and that is what I have determined to do ever since I knew the penalty. Nor could I love the man who would wish to wait a day for the alternative.

JULIA. Nay, this is caprice! 15

LYDIA. What, does Julia tax me with caprice?—I thought her lover Faulkland had inured her to it.

JULIA. I do not love even *his* faults.

LYDIA. But apropos—you have sent to 20 him, I suppose?

JULIA. Not yet, upon my word—nor has he the least idea of my being in Bath.—Sir Anthony's resolution was so sudden I could not inform him of it. 25

LYDIA. Well, Julia, you are your own mistress (though under the protection of Sir Anthony); yet have you, for this long year, been the slave to the caprice, the whim, the jealousy of this ungrateful Faulkland, who 30 will ever delay assuming the right of a husband while you suffer him to be equally imperious as a lover.

JULIA. Nay, you are wrong entirely. We were contracted before my father's death.— 35 *That,* and some consequent embarrassments, have delayed what I know to be my Faulkland's most ardent wish.—He is too generous to trifle on such a point—and for his character, you wrong him there, too.—No, Lydia, 40 he is too proud, too noble to be jealous; if he is captious, 'tis without dissembling; if fretful, without rudeness.—Unused to the foppery of love, he is negligent of the little duties expected from a lover—but being 45 unhackneyed in the passion, his love is ardent and sincere; and as it engrosses his whole soul, he expects every thought and emotion of his mistress to move in unison with his.— Yet, though his pride calls for this full 50 return—his humility makes him undervalue those qualities in him which should entitle him to it; and not feeling why he should be loved to the degree he wishes, he still suspects that he is not loved enough.—This 55 temper, I must own, has cost me many unhappy hours, but I have learned to think myself his debtor for those imperfections which arise from the ardor of his love.

LYDIA. Well, I cannot blame you for defending him.—But tell me candidly, Julia, had he never saved your life, do you think you should have been attached to him as you are?—Believe me, the rude blast that overset your boat was a prosperous gale of love to him.

JULIA. Gratitude may have strengthened my attachment to Mr. Faulkland, but I loved him before he had preserved me; yet surely that alone were an obligation sufficient.

LYDIA. Obligation!—why, a water spaniel would have done as much!—Well, I should never think of giving my heart to a man because he could swim!

JULIA. Come, Lydia, you are too inconsiderate.

LYDIA. Nay, I do but jest—What's here?

Enter LUCY *in a hurry*

LUCY. O ma'am, here is Sir Anthony Absolute just come home with your aunt.

LYLIA. They'll not come here.—Lucy, do you watch. [*Exit* LUCY.

JULIA. Yet I must go.—Sir Anthony does not know I am here, and if we meet, he'll detain me to show me the town. I'll take another opportunity of paying my respects to Mrs. Malaprop, when she shall treat me as long as she chooses with her select words so ingeniously *misapplied,* without being *mispronounced.*

Re-enter LUCY

LUCY. O lud! ma'am, they are both coming upstairs.

LYDIA. Well, I'll not detain you, coz.— Adieu, my dear Julia; I'm sure you are in haste to send to Faulkland.—There— through my room you'll find another staircase.

JULIA. Adieu! (*Embrace*) [*Exit.*

LYDIA. Here, my dear Lucy, hide these books. Quick, quick!—Fling *Peregrine Pickle* under the toilet—throw *Roderick Random* into the closet—put *The Innocent Adultery* into *The Whole Duty of Man*— thrust *Lord Aimworth* under the sofa—cram *Ovid* behind the bolster—there—put *The Man of Feeling* into your pocket—so, so— now lay *Mrs. Chapone* in sight, and leave Fordyce's *Sermons* open on the table.

LUCY. Oh, burn it, ma'am! the hairdresser has torn away as far as *Proper Pride.*

LYDIA. Never mind—open at *Sobriety*.—
Fling me Lord Chesterfield's *Letters*.—Now
for 'em!   [*Exit* LUCY.

Enter MRS. MALAPROP, *and* SIR ANTHONY
ABSOLUTE

MRS. MALAPROP. There, Sir Anthony,
there sits the deliberate simpleton who wants
to disgrace her family and lavish herself on
a fellow not worth a shilling.

LYDIA. Madam, I thought you once—

MRS. MALAPROP. You thought, miss!—I
don't know any business you have to think at
all—thought does not become a young
woman; the point we would request of you
is that you will promise to forget this fellow
—to illiterate him, I say, quite from your
memory.

LYDIA. Ah, madam! our memories are independent of our wills. It is not so easy to
forget.

MRS. MALAPROP. But I say it is, miss;
there is nothing on earth so easy as to *forget*
if a person chooses to set about it.—I'm sure
I have as much forgot your poor dear uncle
as if he had never existed—and I thought it
my duty so to do; and let me tell you, Lydia,
these violent memories don't become a young
woman.

SIR ANTHONY. Why, sure she won't pretend to remember what she's ordered not!
—aye, this comes of her reading!

LYDIA. What crime, madam, have I committed, to be treated thus?

MRS. MALAPROP. Now don't attempt to
extirpate yourself from the matter; you
know I have proof controvertible of it.—
But tell me, will you promise to do as you're
bid?—Will you take a husband of your
friends' choosing?

LYDIA. Madam, I must tell you plainly
that had I no preference for anyone else,
the choice you have made would be my
aversion.

MRS. MALAPROP. What business have you,
miss, with *preference* and *aversion?* They
don't become a young woman; and you
ought to know that as both always wear off,
'tis safest in matrimony to begin with a little
aversion. I am sure I hated your poor dear
uncle before marriage as if he'd been a
black-a-moor—and yet, miss, you are sensible
what a wife I made!—and when it pleased
Heaven to release me from him, 'tis unknown what tears I shed!—But suppose
we were going to give you another choice,
will you promise us to give up this Beverley?

LYDIA. Could I belie my thoughts so far
as to give that promise, my actions would
certainly as far belie my words.

MRS. MALAPROP. Take yourself to your
room.—You are fit company for nothing but
your own ill-humors.

LYDIA. Willingly, ma'am—I cannot change
for the worse.   [*Exit.*

MRS. MALAPROP. There's a little intricate
hussy for you!

SIR ANTHONY. It is not to be wondered
at, ma'am,—all this is the natural consequence of teaching girls to read. Had I a
thousand daughters, by heavens! I'd as soon
have them taught the black art as their
alphabet!

MRS. MALAPROP. Nay, nay, Sir Anthony,
you are an absolute misanthropy.

SIR ANTHONY. In my way hither, Mrs.
Malaprop, I observed your niece's maid
coming forth from a circulating library!—
She had a book in each hand—they were
half-bound volumes with marbled covers!—
From that moment I guessed how full of
duty I should see her mistress!

MRS. MALAPROP. Those are vile places,
indeed!

SIR ANTHONY. Madam, a circulating library in a town is as an evergreen tree of
diabolical knowledge!—It blossoms through
the year!—And depend on it, Mrs. Malaprop, that they who are so fond of handling
the leaves, will long for the fruit at last.

MRS. MALAPROP. Well, but Sir Anthony,
your wife, Lady Absolute, was fond of
books.

SIR ANTHONY. Aye—and injury sufficient
they were to her, madam—but were I to
choose another helpmate, the extent of her
erudition should consist in knowing her
simple letters, without their mischievous
combinations;—and the summit of her
science be—her ability to count as far as
twenty.—The first, Mrs. Malaprop, would
enable her to work *A. A.* upon my linen;—
and the latter would be quite sufficient to
prevent her giving me a shirt No. 1, and a
stock[13] No. 2.

MRS. MALAPROP. Fie, fie, Sir Anthony!
you surely speak laconically!

SIR ANTHONY. Why, Mrs. Malaprop, in
moderation now, what would you have a
woman know?

MRS. MALAPROP. Observe me, Sir Anthony. I would by no means wish a
daughter of mine to be a progeny of learn-

[13]Neckcloth.

ing; I don't think so much learning becomes a young woman. For instance, I would never let her meddle with Greek, or Hebrew, or Algebra, or simony, or fluxions, or paradoxes, or such inflammatory branches of learning—neither would it be necessary for her to handle any of your mathematical, astronomical, diabolical instruments.—But, Sir Anthony, I would send her, at nine years old, to a boarding-school in order to learn a little ingenuity and artifice. Then, sir, she should have a supercilious knowledge in accounts;—and as she grew up, I would have her instructed in geometry, that she might know something of the contagious countries;—but above all, Sir Anthony, she should be mistress of orthodoxy, that she might not misspell and mispronounce words so shamefully as girls usually do; and likewise that she might reprehend the true meaning of what she is saying.—This, Sir Anthony, is what I would have a woman know; —and I don't think there is a superstitious article in it.

Sir Anthony. Well, well, Mrs. Malaprop, I will dispute the point no further with you, though I must confess that you are a truly moderate and polite arguer, for almost every third word you say is on my side of the question.—But, Mrs. Malaprop, to the more important point in debate—you say you have no objection to my proposal?

Mrs. Malaprop. None, I assure you.—I am under no positive engagement with Mr. Acres, and as Lydia is so obstinate against him, perhaps your son may have better success.

Sir Anthony. Well, madam, I will write for the boy directly.—He knows not a syllable of this yet, though I have for some time had the proposal in my head. He is at present with his regiment.

Mrs. Malaprop. We have never seen your son, Sir Anthony; but I hope no objection on his side.

Sir Anthony. Objection!—let him object if he dare!—No, no, Mrs. Malaprop, Jack knows that the least demur puts me in a frenzy directly. My process was always very simple—in their younger days, 'twas "Jack do this";—if he demurred, I knocked him down—and if he grumbled at that, I always sent him out of the room.

Mrs. Malaprop. Tye, and the properest way, o' my conscience!—nothing is so conciliating to young people as severity.—Well, Sir Anthony, I shall give Mr. Acres his discharge, and prepare Lydia to receive your son's invocations;—and I hope you will represent *her* to the Captain as an object not altogether illegible.

Sir Anthony. Madam, I will handle the subject prudently.—Well, I must leave you; and let me beg you, Mrs. Malaprop, to enforce this matter roundly to the girl.— Take my advice—keep a tight hand; if she rejects this proposal, clap her under lock and key; and if you were just to let the servants forget to bring her dinner for three or four days, you can't conceive how she'd come about. [*Exit.*

Mrs. Malaprop. Well, at any rate I shall be glad to get her from under my intuition. —She has somehow discovered my partiality for Sir Lucius O'Trigger—sure, Lucy can't have betrayed me!—No, the girl is such a simpleton I should have made her confess it. —(*Calls*) Lucy!—Lucy!—Had she been one of your artificial ones, I should never have trusted her.

Enter Lucy

Lucy. Did you call, ma'am?

Mrs. Malaprop. Yes, girl.—Did you see Sir Lucius while you was out?

Lucy. No, indeed, ma'am, not a glimpse of him.

Mrs. Malaprop. You are sure, Lucy, that you never mentioned—

Lucy. O Gemini! I'd sooner cut my tongue out.

Mrs. Malaprop. Well, don't let your simplicity be imposed on.

Lucy. No, ma'am.

Mrs. Malaprop. So! come to me presently, and I'll give you another letter to Sir Lucius;—but mind, Lucy—if ever you betray what you are entrusted with—(unless it be other people's secrets to me) you forfeit my malevolence forever:—and your being a simpleton shall be no excuse for your locality. [*Exit.*

Lucy. Ha! ha! ha!—So, my dear *simplicity,* let me give you a little respite.— (*Altering her manner*) Let girls in my station be as fond as they please of appearing expert and knowing in their trusts;—commend me to a mask of *silliness,* and a pair of sharp eyes for my own interest under it!—Let me see to what account have I turned my *simplicity* lately.—(*Looks at a paper*) For "abetting Miss Lydia Languish in a design of running away with an ensign! —in money, sundry times, twelve pound twelve; gowns, five; hats, ruffles, caps, *etc.,* *etc.,* numberless!—From the said ensign, within this last month, six guineas and a half."—About a quarter's pay!—Item, "from Mrs. Malaprop, for betraying the young people to her"—when I found matters were likely to be discovered—"two guineas, and a black paduasoy."[14]—Item, "from Mr. Acres, for carrying divers letters"—which I never delivered—"two guineas and a pair of buckles."—Item, "from Sir Lucius O'Trigger, three crowns, two gold pocket-pieces, and a silver snuff-box!"—Well done, *simplicity!*—Yet I was forced to make my Hibernian believe that he was corresponding, not with the *Aunt,* but with the *Niece;* for though not over rich, I found he had too much pride and delicacy to sacrifice the feelings of a gentleman to the necessities of his fortune.   [*Exit.*

ACT II

Scene i.   Captain Absolute's *Lodgings*

Captain Absolute *and* Fag

Fag. Sir, while I was there, Sir Anthony came in. I told him you had sent me to inquire after his health, and to know if he was at leisure to see you.

Absolute. And what did he say on hearing I was at Bath?

Fag. Sir, in my life I never saw an elderly gentleman more astonished! He started back two or three paces, rapped out a dozen interjectoral oaths, and asked what the devil had brought you here!

Absolute. Well, sir, and what did you say?

Fag. Oh, I lied, sir—I forget the precise lie; but you may depend on't, he got no truth from me. Yet, with submission, for fear of blunders in future, I should be glad to fix what *has* brought us to Bath, in order that we may lie a little consistently. Sir Anthony's servants were curious, sir, very curious indeed.

Absolute. You have said nothing to them—?

Fag. Oh, not a word, sir,—not a word! Mr. Thomas, indeed, the coachman (whom I take to be the discreetest of whips)—

Absolute. 'Sdeath!—you rascal! you have not trusted him!

Fag. Oh, *no,* sir—no—no—not a syllable, upon my veracity!—He was, indeed, a little inquisitive; but I was sly, sir—devilish sly! "My master" (said I), "honest Thomas" (you know, sir, one says *honest* to one's inferiors), "is come to Bath to *recruit.*"—Yes, sir, I said to *recruit*—and whether for men, money, or constitution, you know, sir, is nothing to him, nor anyone else.

Absolute. Well, *recruit* will do—let it be so.

Fag. Oh, sir, recruit will do surprisingly—indeed, to give the thing an air, I told Thomas that your honor had already enlisted five disbanded chairman,[1] seven minority waiters,[2] and thirteen billiard-markers.

Absolute. You blockhead, never say more than is necessary.

Fag. I beg pardon, sir—I beg pardon.—But, with submission, a lie is nothing unless one supports it. Sir, whenever I draw on my invention for a good current lie, I always forge *indorsements* as well as the bill.

Absolute. Well, take care you don't hurt your credit by offering too much security.—Is Mr. Faulkland returned?

Fag. He is above, sir, changing his dress.

Absolute. Can you tell whether he has been informed of Sir Anthony's and Miss Melville's arrival?

Fag. I fancy not, sir; he has seen no one since he came in but his gentleman who was with him at Bristol.—I think, sir, I hear Mr. Faulkland coming down.

Absolute. Go, tell him I am here.

Fag. Yes, sir.—(*Going*) I beg pardon, sir, but should Sir Anthony call, you will do me the favor to remember that we are *recruiting,* if you please.

Absolute. Well, well.

Fag. And, in tenderness to my character, if your honor could bring in the chairman and waiters, I should esteem it as an obligation; for though I never scruple a lie to serve my master, yet it *hurts* one's conscience to be found out.   [*Exit.*

Absolute. Now for my whimsical friend—if he does not know that his mistress is here, I'll tease him a little before I tell him—

Enter Faulkland

—Faulkland, you're welcome to Bath again; you are punctual in your return.

Faulkland. Yes; I had nothing to detain me when I had finished the business I went on. Well, what news since I left you? How stand matters between you and Lydia?

Absolute. Faith, much as they were. I

---

[14] A silk, originally made at Padua.

[1] Bearers of sedan chairs.   [2] Waiters out of place.

have not seen her since our quarrel; however, I expect to be recalled every hour.

FAULKLAND. Why don't you persuade her to go off with you at once?

ABSOLUTE. What, and lose two-thirds of her fortune? You forget that, my friend.—No, no, I could have brought her to that long ago.

FAULKLAND. Nay, then, you trifle too long—if you are sure of *her,* propose to the aunt *in your own character,* and write to Sir Anthony for his consent.

ABSOLUTE. Softly, softly; for though I am convinced my little Lydia would elope with me as Ensign Beverley, yet am I by no means certain that she would take me with the impediment of our friends' consent, a regular humdrum wedding, and a reversion[3] of a good fortune on my side. No, no; I must prepare her gradually for the discovery and make myself necessary to her before I risk it.—Well, but Faulkland, you'll dine with us to-day at the hotel?

FAULKLAND. Indeed, I cannot; I am not in spirits to be of such a party.

ABSOLUTE. By heavens! I shall forswear your company. You are the most teasing, captious, incorrigible lover!—Do love like a man!

FAULKLAND. I own I am unfit for company.

ABSOLUTE. Am *I* not a lover; aye, and a romantic one too? Yet do I carry everywhere with me such a confounded farrago of doubts, fears, hopes, wishes, and all the flimsy furniture of a country miss's brain!

FAULKLAND. Ah! Jack, your heart and soul are not, like mine, fixed immutably on one only object.—You throw for a large stake, but losing—you could stake, and throw again;—but I have set my sum of happiness on this cast, and not to succeed were to be stripped of all.

ABSOLUTE. But, for Heaven's sake! what grounds for apprehension can your whimsical brain conjure up at present? Has Julia missed writing this last post? or was her last too tender, or too cool; or too grave, or too gay; or—

FAULKLAND. Nay, nay, Jack.

ABSOLUTE. Why, her love—her honor—her prudence, you cannot doubt.

FAULKLAND. O! upon my soul, I never have;—but what grounds for apprehension, did you say? Heavens! are there not a thousand! I fear for her spirits—her health—

[3] A right or hope of future possession.

her life.—My absence may fret her; her anxiety for my return, her fears for me, may oppress her gentle temper. And for her health—does not every hour bring me cause to be alarmed? If it rains, some shower may even then have chilled her delicate frame!—If the wind be keen, some rude blast may have affected her! The heat of noon, the dews of the evening, may endanger the life of her for whom only I value mine. O Jack! when delicate and feeling souls are separated, there is not a feature in the sky, not a movement of the elements, not an aspiration of the breeze, but hints some cause for a lover's apprehension!

ABSOLUTE. Aye, but we may choose whether we will take the hint or no.—Well then, Faulkland, if you were convinced that Julia was well and in spirits, you would be entirely content.

FAULKLAND. I should be happy beyond measure—I am anxious only for that.

ABSOLUTE. Then to cure your anxiety at once—Miss Melville is in perfect health, and is at this moment in Bath.

FAULKLAND. Nay, Jack—don't trifle with me.

ABSOLUTE. She is arrived here with my father within this hour.

FAULKLAND. Can you be serious?

ABSOLUTE. I thought you knew Sir Anthony better than to be surprised at a sudden whim of this kind.—Seriously, then, it is as I tell you—upon my honor.

FAULKLAND. My dear friend!—[*Calls*] Hollo, Du-Peigne! my hat!—My dear Jack —*now nothing on earth can give me a moment's uneasiness.*

Enter FAG

FAG. Sir, Mr. Acres just arrived is below.

ABSOLUTE. Stay, Faulkland; this Acres lives within a mile of Sir Anthony, and he shall tell you how your mistress has been ever since you left her.—Fag, show the gentleman up. [*Exit* FAG.

FAULKLAND. What, is he much acquainted in the family?

ABSOLUTE. Oh, very intimate. I insist on your not going; besides, his character will divert you.

FAULKLAND. Well, I should like to ask him a few questions.

ABSOLUTE. He is likewise a rival of mine —that is of my *other self's,* for he does not think his friend Captain Absolute ever saw the lady in question;—and it is ridiculous enough to hear him complain to me of *one Beverley,* a concealed skulking rival, who—

FAULKLAND. Hush!—He's here.

Enter ACRES

ACRES. Hah! my dear friend, noble captain, and honest Jack, how do'st thou? just arrived, faith, as you see.—Sir, your humble servant. Warm work on the roads, Jack!— Odds whips and wheels! I've traveled like a comet, with a tail of dust all the way as long as the Mall.

ABSOLUTE. Ah! Bob, you are indeed an eccentric planet, but we know your attraction hither.—Give me leave to introduce Mr. Faulkland to you; Mr. Faulkland, Mr. Acres.

ACRES. Sir, I am most heartily glad to see you: sir, I solicit your connections.—Hey, Jack—what, this is Mr. Faulkland, who—

ABSOLUTE. Aye, Bob, Miss Melville's Mr. Faulkland.

ACRES. Odd so! she and your father can be but just arrived before me—I suppose you have seen them.—Ah! Mr. Faulkland, you are indeed a happy man.

FAULKLAND. I have not seen Miss Melville yet, sir.—I hope she enjoyed full health and spirits in Devonshire?

ACRES. Never knew her better in my life, sir,—never better. Odds blushes and blooms! she has been as healthy as the German Spa.

FAULKLAND. Indeed!—I did hear that she had been a little indisposed.

ACRES. False, false, sir—only said to vex you; quite the reverse, I assure you.

FAULKLAND. There, Jack, you see she has the advantage of me; I had almost fretted myself ill.

ABSOLUTE. Now are you angry with your mistress for not having been sick?

FAULKLAND. No, no, you misunderstand me;—yet surely a little trifling indisposition is not an unnatural consequence of absence from those we love.—Now confess—isn't there something unkind in this violent, robust, unfeeling health?

ABSOLUTE. Oh, it was very unkind of her to be well in your absence, to be sure!

ACRES. Good apartments, Jack.

FAULKLAND. Well, sir, but you were saying that Miss Melville has been so *exceedingly* well—what then, she has been merry and gay I suppose?—Always in spirits—hey?

ACRES. Merry? Odds crickets! she has been the belle and spirit of the company wherever she has been—so lively and entertaining! so full of wit and humor!

FAULKLAND. There, Jack, there.—Oh, by my soul! there is an innate levity in woman that nothing can overcome.—What! happy and I away!

ABSOLUTE. Have done. How foolish this is! just now you were only apprehensive for your mistress's *spirits.*

FAULKLAND. Why, Jack, have I been the joy and spirit of the company?

ABSOLUTE. No, indeed, you have not.

FAULKLAND. Have I been lively and entertaining?

ABSOLUTE. Oh! upon my word, I acquit you.

FAULKLAND. Have I been full of wit and humor?

ABSOLUTE. No, faith, to do you justice, you have been confoundedly stupid, indeed.

ACRES. What's the matter with the gentleman?

ABSOLUTE. He is only expressing his great satisfaction at hearing that Julia has been so well and happy—that's all—hey, Faulkland?

FAULKLAND. Oh! I am rejoiced to hear it—yes, yes, she has a *happy* disposition!

ACRES. That she has, indeed—then she is so accomplished—so sweet a voice—so expert at her harpsichord—such a mistress of flat and sharp, squallante, rumblante, and quiverante!—There was this time month—Odds minims and crotchets![4] how she did chirrup at Mrs. Piano's concert!

FAULKLAND. There again, what say you to this? you see she has been all mirth and song—not a thought of me!

ABSOLUTE. Pho! man, is not music the food of love?

FAULKLAND. Well, well, it may be so.— Pray, Mr.——, what's his damned name?— Do you remember what songs Miss Melville sung?

ACRES. Not I, indeed.

ABSOLUTE. Stay, now, they were some pretty melancholy, purling-stream airs, I warrant. Perhaps you may recollect;—did she sing, *When absent from my Soul's Delight?*

ACRES. No, that wa'n't it.

ABSOLUTE. Or *Go, gentle Gales?* (*Sings*) "Go, gentle gales!"

ACRES. O no! nothing like it. Odds slips! now I recollect one of them—(*Sings*) "My heart's my own, my will is free."

FAULKLAND. Fool! fool that I am to fix all my happiness upon such a trifler!

[4]Half-notes and quarter-notes (music).

'Sdeath! to make herself the pipe and ballad-monger of a circle! to soothe her light heart with catches and glees![5]—What can you say to this, sir?

ABSOLUTE. Why, that I should be glad to hear my mistress had been so merry, sir.

FAULKLAND. Nay, nay, nay—I'm not sorry that she has been happy—no, no, I am glad of that—I would not have had her sad or sick;—yet surely a sympathetic heart would have shown itself even in the choice of a song—she might have been temperately healthy and somehow, plaintively gay.—But she has been dancing too, I doubt not!

ACRES. What does the gentleman say about dancing?

ABSOLUTE. He says the lady we speak of dances as well as she sings.

ACRES. Aye, truly, does she!—There was at our last race ball—

FAULKLAND. Hell and the devil!—There! —there—I told you so! Oh! she thrives in my absence!—Dancing! But her whole feelings have been in opposition with mine!— I have been anxious, silent, pensive, seden-tary—my days have been hours of care, my nights of watchfulness.—She has been all health! spirit! laugh! song! dance!—Oh! damned, damned levity!

ABSOLUTE. For Heaven's sake, Faulkland, don't expose yourself so!—Suppose she has danced, what then?—does not the ceremony of society often oblige—

FAULKLAND. Well, well, I'll contain my-self—perhaps, as you say—for form's sake. —What, Mr. Acres, you were praising Miss Melville's manner of dancing a *minuet*—hey?

ACRES. Oh, I dare insure her for that—but what I was going to speak of was her *country-dancing*. Odds swimmings! she has such an air with her!

FAULKLAND. Now, disappointment on her!—Defend this, Absolute; why don't you defend this?—Country-dances! jigs and reels —am I to blame now? A minuet I could have forgiven—I should not have minded that—I say, I should not have regarded a minuet—but *country-dances!*—Zounds! had she made one in a *cotillion*—I believe I could have forgiven even that.—But to be monkey-led for a night!—to run the gauntlet through a string of amorous, palming puppies!—to show paces like a managed filly!—O Jack, there never can be but *one* man in the world

whom a truly modest and delicate woman ought to pair with in a *country-dance;* and, even then, the rest of the couples should be her great-uncles and aunts!

ABSOLUTE. Aye, to be sure!—grandfath-ers and grandmothers!

FAULKLAND. If there be but one vicious mind in the set, 'twill spread like a contagion —the action of their pulse beats to the lascivi-ous movement of the jig—their quivering, warm-breathed sighs impregnate the very air —the atmosphere becomes electrical to love, and each amorous spark darts through every link of the chain!—I must leave you—I own I am somewhat flurried—and that con-founded looby[6] has perceived it.   [*Going.*

ABSOLUTE. Aye, aye, you are in a hurry to throw yourself at Julia's feet.

FAULKLAND. I'm not in a humor to be trifled with—I shall see her only to upbraid her.

ABSOLUTE. Nay, but stay, Faulkland, and thank Mr. Acres for his good news.

FAULKLAND. Damn his news!   [*Exit.*

ABSOLUTE. Ha! ha! ha! poor Faulkland five minutes since, "nothing on earth could give him a moment's uneasiness"!

ACRES. The gentleman wa'n't angry at my praising his mistress, was he?

ABSOLUTE. A little jealous, I believe, Bob.

ACRES. You don't say so? Ha! ha! jeal-ous of me—that's a good joke.

ABSOLUTE. There's nothing strange in that, Bob; let me tell you, that sprightly grace and insinuating manner of yours will do some mischief among the girls here.

ACRES. Ah! you joke—ha! ha! mischief— ha! ha! But you know I am not my own property; my dear Lydia has forestalled me. She could never abide me in the country, be-cause I used to dress so badly—but odds frogs and tambours![7] I shan't take matters so here, now ancient Madam has no voice in it—I'll make my old clothes know who's mas-ter. I shall straightway cashier the hunting-frock—and render my leather breeches in-capable. My hair has been in training some time.

ABSOLUTE. Indeed!

ACRES. Aye—and thoff the side curls are a little restive, my hind-part takes to it very kindly.

ABSOLUTE. Oh, you'll polish, I doubt not.

---

[5]Both catches and glees are sung by several sing-ers.

[6]Lubber.

[7]Braided loops to secure the coat or cloak, and frames used in embroidering (or fabrics so embroid-ered).

ACRES. Absolutely I propose so—then if I can find out this Ensign Beverley, odds triggers and flints! I'll make him know the difference o't.

ABSOLUTE. Spoke like a man! But pray, Bob, I observe you have got an odd kind of a new method of swearing—

ACRES. Ha! ha! you've taken notice of it —'tis genteel, isn't it?—I didn't invent it myself though; but a commander in our militia—a great scholar, I assure you—says that there is no meaning in the common oaths, and that nothing but their antiquity makes them respectable; because, he says, the ancients would never stick to an oath or two, but would say, "By Jove!" or "By Bacchus!" or "By Mars!" or "By Venus!" or "By Pallas," according to the sentiment—so that to swear with propriety, says my little Major, the "oath should be an echo to the sense";[8] and this we call the "oath referential," or "sentimental swearing"—ha! ha! ha! 'tis genteel, isn't it?

ABSOLUTE. Very genteel, and very new, indeed—and I dare say will supplant all other figures of imprecation.

ACRES. Aye, aye, the best terms will grow obsolete.—Damns have had their day.

Enter FAG

FAG. Sir, there is a gentleman below desires to see you.—Shall I show him into the parlor?

ABSOLUTE. Aye—you may.

ACRES. Well, I must be gone—

ABSOLUTE. Stay; who is it, Fag?

FAG. Your father, sir.

ABSOLUTE. You puppy, why didn't you show him up directly?   [*Exit* FAG.

ACRES. You have business with Sir Anthony.—I expect a message from Mrs. Malaprop at my lodgings. I have sent also to my dear friend, Sir Lucius O'Trigger. Adieu, Jack! we must meet at night. Odds bottles and glasses! you shall give me a dozen bumpers to little Lydia.

ABSOLUTE. That I will with all my heart.
    [*Exit* ACRES.
Now for a parental lecture! I hope he has heard nothing of the business that brought me here—I wish the gout had held him fast in Devonshire, with all my soul!

Enter SIR ANTHONY

ABSOLUTE. Sir, I am delighted to see you here, looking so well! your sudden arrival at Bath made me apprehensive for your health.

SIR ANTHONY. Very apprehensive, I dare say, Jack.—What, you are recruiting here, hey?

ABSOLUTE. Yes, sir, I am on duty.

SIR ANTHONY. Well, Jack, I am glad to see you, though I did not expect it, for I was going to write to you on a little matter of business.—Jack, I have been considering that I grow old and infirm, and shall probably not trouble you long.

ABSOLUTE. Pardon me, sir, I never saw you look more strong and hearty, and I pray frequently that you may continue so.

SIR ANTHONY. I hope your prayers may be heard, with all my heart. Well, then, Jack, I have been considering that I am so strong and hearty, I may continue to plague you a long time. Now, Jack, I am sensible that the income of your commission and what I have hitherto allowed you is but a small pittance for a lad of your spirit.

ABSOLUTE. Sir, you are very good.

SIR ANTHONY. And it is my wish, while yet I live, to have my boy make some figure in the world.—I have resolved, therefore, to fix you at once in a noble independence.

ABSOLUTE. Sir, your kindness overpowers me—such generosity makes the gratitude of reason more lively than the sensations even of filial affection.

SIR ANTHONY. I am glad you are so sensible of my attention—and you shall be master of a large estate in a few weeks.

ABSOLUTE. Let my future life, sir, speak my gratitude; I cannot express the sense I have of your munificence.—Yet, sir, I presume you would not wish me to quit the army?

SIR ANTHONY. Oh, that shall be as your wife chooses.

ABSOLUTE. My wife, sir!

SIR ANTHONY. Aye, aye, settle that between you—settle that between you.

ABSOLUTE. A *wife,* sir, did you say?

SIR ANTHONY. Aye, a wife.—Why, did not I mention her before?

ABSOLUTE. Not a word of it, sir.

SIR ANTHONY. Odd so!—I mus'n't forget *her* though.—Yes, Jack, the independence I was talking of is by a marriage—the fortune is saddled with a wife; but I suppose that makes no difference.

ABSOLUTE. Sir! sir!—you amaze me!

SIR ANTHONY. Why, what the devil's the matter with the fool? Just now you were all gratitude and duty.

---

[8] See Pope's *Essay on Criticism,* II, 165.

ABSOLUTE. I was, sir—you talked to me of independence and a fortune, but not a word of a wife.

SIR ANTHONY. Why—what difference does that make? Odds life, sir! if you have the estate, you must take it with the live stock on it, as it stands.

ABSOLUTE. If my happiness is to be the price, I must beg leave to decline the purchase.—Pray, sir, who is the lady?

SIR ANTHONY. What's that to you, sir?— Come, give me your promise to love and to marry her directly.

ABSOLUTE. Sure, sir, this is not very reasonable, to summon my affections for a lady I know nothing of!

SIR ANTHONY. I am sure, sir, 'tis more unreasonable in you *to object* to a lady you know nothing of.

ABSOLUTE. Then, sir, I must tell you plainly that my inclinations are fixed on another.

SIR ANTHONY. They are, are they? Well that's lucky—because you will have more merit in your obedience to me.

ABSOLUTE. Sir, my heart is engaged to an angel.

SIR ANTHONY. Then pray, let it send an excuse. It is very sorry—but *business* prevents its waiting on her.

ABSOLUTE. But my vows are pledged to her.

SIR ANTHONY. Let her foreclose, Jack— let her foreclose; they are not worth redeeming. Besides, you have the angel's vows in exchange, I suppose; so there can be no loss there.

ABSOLUTE. You must excuse me, sir, if I tell you once for all that in this point I cannot obey you.

SIR ANTHONY. Hark'ee, Jack.—I have heard you for some time with patience—I have been cool—quite cool; but take care— you know I am compliance itself—when I am not thwarted;—no one more easily led— when I have my own way;—but don't put me in a frenzy.

ABSOLUTE. Sir, I must repeat—in this I cannot obey you.

SIR ANTHONY. Now damn me! if ever I call you *Jack* again while I live!

ABSOLUTE. Nay, sir, but hear me.

SIR ANTHONY. Sir, I won't hear a word —not a word! not one word! So give me your promise by a nod—and I'll tell you what, Jack—I mean, you dog!—if you don't, by—

ABSOLUTE. What, sir, promise to link myself to some mass of ugliness? to—

SIR ANTHONY. Zounds! sirrah! the lady shall be as ugly as I choose: she shall have a hump on each shoulder; she shall be as crooked as the Crescent;[9] her one eye shall roll like the Bull's in Cox's Museum,[10] she shall have a skin like a mummy, and the beard of a Jew—she shall be all this, sirrah! —yet I'll make you ogle her all day, and sit up all night to write sonnets on her beauty.

ABSOLUTE. This is reason and moderation, indeed!

SIR ANTHONY. None of your sneering, puppy! no grinning, jackanapes!

ABSOLUTE. Indeed, sir, I never was in a worse humor for mirth in my life.

SIR ANTHONY. 'Tis false, sir! I know you are laughing in your sleeve; I know you will grin when I am gone, sirrah!

ABSOLUTE. Sir, I hope I know my duty better.

SIR ANTHONY. None of your passion, sir! none of your violence, if you please!—It won't do with me, I promise you.

ABSOLUTE. Indeed, sir, I never was cooler in my life.

SIR ANTHONY. 'Tis a confounded lie!—I know you are in a passion in your heart; I know you are, you hypocritical young dog! but it won't do.

ABSOLUTE. Nay, sir, upon my word.

SIR ANTHONY. So you will fly out! Can't you be cool, like me? What the devil good can *passion* do?—*passion* is of no service, you impudent, insolent, overbearing reprobate!—There, you sneer again! don't provoke me!—but you rely upon the mildness of my temper—you do, you dog! you play upon the weakness of my disposition!— Yet take care—the patience of a saint may be overcome at last!—But mark! I give you six hours and a half to consider of this: if you then agree, without any condition, to do everything on earth that I choose, why— confound you! I may in time forgive you. —If not, zounds! don't enter the same hemisphere with me! don't dare to breathe the same air, or use the same light with me; but get an atmosphere and a sun of your own! I'll strip you of your commission; I'll lodge a five-and-threepence in the hands

---

[9] A street of that shape in Bath.

[10] James Cox was a jeweler and maker of mechanical toys of great value. Of these he had a remarkable collection which he exhibited in London in 1773 and 1774.

of trustees, and you shall live on the interest. —I'll disown you, I'll disinherit you, I'll unget you! and damn me, if ever I call you Jack again! [*Exit.*

ABSOLUTE, *solus*

ABSOLUTE. Mild, gentle, considerate father—I kiss your hands!—What a tender method of giving his opinion in these matters Sir Anthony has! I dare not trust him with the truth.—I wonder what old, wealthy hag it is that he wants to bestow on me!— Yet he married himself for love, and was in his youth a bold intriguer and a gay companion!

Enter FAG

FAG. Assuredly, sir, our father is wrath to a degree; he comes down stairs eight or ten steps at a time—muttering, growling, and thumping the banisters all the way. I and the cook's dog stand bowing at the door—rap! he gives me a stroke on the head with his cane, bids me carry that to my master, then kicking the poor Turnspit into the area, damns us all, for a puppy triumvirate!—Upon my credit, sir, were I in your place and found my father such very bad company, I should certainly drop his acquaintance.

ABSOLUTE. Cease your impertinence, sir, at present.—Did you come in for nothing more?—Stand out of the way!

[*Pushes him aside, and exit.*

FAG, *solus*

FAG. Soh! Sir Anthony trims my master; he is afraid to reply to his father— then vents his spleen on poor Fag!—When one is vexed by one person, to revenge one's self on another who happens to come in the way, is the vilest injustice! Ah! it shows the worst temper—the basest—

Enter ERRAND-BOY

BOY. Mr. Fag! Mr. Fag! your master calls you.

FAG. Well, you little dirty puppy, you need not bawl so!—The meanest disposition! the—

BOY. Quick, quick, Mr. Fag!

FAG. *Quick! quick!* you impudent jackanapes! Am I to be commanded by you too? you little, impertinent, insolent, kitchenbred— [*Exit, kicking and beating him.*

SCENE II.   *The North Parade*

Enter LUCY

LUCY. So—I shall have another rival to add to my mistress's list—Captain Absolute. However, I shall not enter his name till my purse has received notice in form. Poor Acres is dismissed!—Well, I have done him a last friendly office, in letting him know that Beverley was here before him.—Sir Lucius is generally more punctual when he expects to hear from his "dear Dalia," as he calls her; I wonder he's not here!—I have a little scruple of conscience from this deceit, though I should not be paid so well if my hero knew that Delia was near fifty, and her own mistress.—I could not have thought he would have been so nice, when there's a golden egg in the case, as to care whether he has it from a pullet or an old hen.

Enter SIR LUCIUS O'TRIGGER

SIR LUCIUS. Hah! my little ambassadress! —upon my conscience, I have been looking for you; I have been on the South Parade this half hour.

LUCY. (*Speaking simply*) O gemini! and I have been waiting for your worship here on the North.

SIR LUCIUS. Faith!—maybe that was the reason we did not meet; and it is very comical too, how you could go out and I not see you—for I was only taking a nap at the Parade Coffee-House, and I chose the *window* on purpose that I might not miss you.

LUCY. My stars! Now I'd wager a sixpence I went by while you were asleep.

SIR LUCIUS. Sure enough it must have been so—and I never dreamed it was so late, till I waked. Well, but my little girl, have you got nothing for me?

LUCY. Yes, but I have; I've got a letter for you in my pocket.

SIR LUCIUS. Oh, faith! I guessed you weren't come empty-handed.—Well—let me see what the dear creature says.

LUCY. There, Sir Lucius.

(*Gives him a letter*)

SIR LUCIUS. (*Reads*) "Sir—there is often a sudden incentive impulse in love, that has a greater induction than years of domestic combination; such was the commotion I felt at the first superfluous view of Sir Lucius O'Trigger."—Very pretty, upon my word.— "As my motive is interested, you may be assured my love shall never be miscellaneous." Very well.

"Female punctuation forbids me to say more; yet let me add that it will give me joy infallible to find Sir Lucius worthy the 5 last criterion of my affections. Yours, while meretricious.—·Delia." Upon my conscience! Lucy, your lady is a great mistress of language.—Faith, she's quite the queen of the dictionary!—for the devil a word 10 dare refuse coming at her call—though one would think it was quite out of hearing.

LUCY. Aye, sir, a lady of her experience—

SIR LUCIUS. Experience! What, at seventeen?

LUCY. Oh, true, sir—but then she reads 15 so—my stars! how she will read off-hand!

SIR LUCIUS. Faith, she must be very deep read to write this way—though she is rather an arbitrary writer too; for here are a great 20 many poor words pressed into the service of this note that would get their *habeas corpus* from any court in Christendom.— However, when affection guides the pen, Lucy, he must be a brute who finds fault 25 with the style.

LUCY. Ah! Sir Lucius, if you were to hear how she talks of you!

SIR LUCIUS. Oh, tell her I'll make her the best husband in the world, and Lady 30 O'Trigger into the bargain!—But we must get the old gentlewoman's consent—and do everything fairly.

LUCY. Nay, Sir Lucius, I thought you wa'n't rich enough to be so nice. 35

SIR LUCIUS. Upon my word, young woman, you have hit it!—I am so poor that I can't afford to do a dirty action.—If I did not want money, I'd steal your mistress and her fortune with a great deal of pleas- 40 ure.—However, my pretty girl, (*Gives her money*) here's a little something to buy you a riband; and meet me in the evening and I'll give you an answer to this. So, hussy, (*Kisses her*) take a kiss beforehand to put 45 you in mind.

LUCY. O lud! Sir Lucius—I never seed such a gemman! My lady won't like you if you're so impudent.

SIR LUCIUS. Faith, she will, Lucy!—That 50 same—pho! what's the name of it?—modesty—is a quality in a lover more praised by the women than liked; so, if your mistress asks you whether Sir Lucius ever gave you a kiss, tell her *fifty*—my dear. 55

LUCY. What, would you have me tell her a lie?

SIR LUCIUS. (*Approaches her*) Ah, then, you baggage! I'll make it a truth presently.

LUCY. For shame now; here is someone coming.

SIR LUCIUS. Oh, faith, I'll quiet your conscience!

[*Sees* FAG.—*Exit, humming a tune.*

Enter FAG

FAG. So, so, ma'am! I humbly beg pardon.

LUCY. O lud! now, Mr. Fag, you flurry one so.

FAG. Come, come, Lucy, here's no one by—so a little less simplicity, with a grain or two more sincerity, if you please.—You play false with us, madam.—I saw you give the baronet a letter.—My master shall know this—and if he don't call him out, I will.

LUCY. Ha! ha! ha! you gentlemen's gentlemen are so hasty.—That letter was from Mrs. Malaprop, simpleton.—She is taken with Sir Lucius's address.

FAG. What tastes some people have!— Why, I suppose I have walked by her window an hundred times.—But what says our young lady? any message to my master?

LUCY. Sad news, Mr. Fag.—A worse rival than Acres! Sir Anthony Absolute has proposed his son.

FAG. What, Captain Absolute?

LUCY. Even so—I overheard it all.

FAG. Ha! ha! ha! very good, faith! Good-bye, Lucy, I must away with this news.

LUCY. Well—you may laugh—but it is true, I assure you.—(*Going*) But—Mr. Fag—tell your master not to be cast down by this.

FAG. Oh, he'll be so disconsolate!

LUCY. And charge him not to think of quarreling with young Absolute.

FAG. Never fear!—never fear!

LUCY. Be sure—bid him keep up his spirits.

FAG. We will—we will.

[*Exeunt severally.*

ACT III

SCENE I. *The North Parade*

Enter ABSOLUTE

ABSOLUTE. 'Tis just as Fag told me, indeed.—Whimsical enough, faith! My father wants to *force* me to marry the very girl I am plotting to run away with!—He must not know of my connection with her yet a while.—He has too summary a method of proceeding in these matters, and Lydia shall not yet lose her hopes of an elopement. —However, I'll read my recantation instantly.—My conversion is something sudden, indeed, but I can assure him it is very *sincere.* So, so!—here he comes. He looks plaguy gruff.

(*Steps aside*)

Enter SIR ANTHONY

SIR ANTHONY. No, I'll die sooner than forgive him—*Die,* did I say? I'll live these fifty years to plague him.—At our last meeting his impudence had almost put me out of temper—an obstinate, passionate, self-willed boy!—Who can he take after? This is my return for getting him before all his brothers and sisters!—for putting him at twelve years old into a marching regiment and allowing him fifty pounds a year, beside his pay, ever since!—But I have done with him; he's anybody's son, for me.—I never will see him more, never—never—never—never!

ABSOLUTE. (*Approaching*) Now for a penitential face.

SIR ANTHONY. Fellow, get out of my way!

ABSOLUTE. Sir, you see a penitent before you.

SIR ANTHONY. I see an impudent scoundrel before me.

ABSOLUTE. A sincere penitent.—I am come, sir, to acknowledge my error and to submit entirely to your will.

SIR ANTHONY. What's that?

ABSOLUTE. I have been revolving and reflecting and considering on your past goodness and kindness and condescension to me.

SIR ANTHONY. Well, sir?

ABSOLUTE. I have been likewise weighing and balancing what you were pleased to mention concerning duty and obedience and authority.

SIR ANTHONY. Well, puppy?

ABSOLUTE. Why then, sir, the result of my reflections is—a resolution to sacrifice every inclination of my own to your satisfaction.

SIR ANTHONY. Why, now you talk sense —absolute sense. I never heard anything more sensible in my life.—Confound you; you shall be *Jack* again!

ABSOLUTE. I am happy in the appellation.

SIR ANTHONY. Why, then, Jack, my dear Jack, I will now inform you—who the lady really is. Nothing but your passion and violence, you silly fellow, prevented my telling you at first. Prepare, Jack, for wonder and rapture—prepare!—What think you of Miss Lydia Languish?

ABSOLUTE. Languish! What, the Languishes of Worcestershire?

SIR ANTHONY. Worcestershire? No. Did you never meet Mrs. Malaprop and her niece, Miss Languish, who came into our country just before you were last ordered to your regiment?

ABSOLUTE. Malaprop! Languish! I don't remember ever to have heard the names before. Yet, stay—I think I do recollect something.—*Languish! Languish!* She squints, don't she?—a little, red-haired girl?

SIR ANTHONY. Squints?—A red-haired girl!—Zounds! no.

ABSOLUTE. Then I must have forgot; it can't be the same person.

SIR ANTHONY. Jack! Jack! what think you of blooming, love-breathing seventeen?

ABSOLUTE. As to that, sir, I am quite indifferent.—If I can please you in the matter, 'tis all I desire.

SIR ANTHONY. Nay, but Jack, such eyes —such eyes! so innocently wild! so bashfully irresolute! not a glance but speaks and kindles some thought of love! Then, Jack, her cheeks—her cheeks, Jack! so deeply blushing at the insinuations of her tell-tale eyes! Then, Jack, her lips!—O Jack, lips smiling at their own discretion; and if not smiling, more sweetly pouting, more lovely in sullenness.

ABSOLUTE. That's she, indeed.—Well done, old gentleman.

SIR ANTHONY. Then, Jack, her neck!— O Jack! Jack!

ABSOLUTE. And which is to be mine, sir— the niece or the aunt?

SIR ANTHONY. Why, you unfeeling, insensible puppy, I despise you! When I was of your age, such a description would have made me fly like a rocket! The *aunt,* indeed! Odds life! when I ran away with your mother, I would not have touched anything old or ugly to gain an empire.

ABSOLUTE. Not to please your father, sir?

SIR ANTHONY. To please my father! zounds! not to please—Oh, my father—odd so!—yes—yes; if my father, indeed, had desired—that's quite another matter. Though he wa'n't the indulgent father that I am, Jack.

ABSOLUTE. I dare say not, sir.

SIR ANTHONY. But, Jack, you are not sorry to find your mistress is so beautiful?

ABSOLUTE. Sir, I repeat it; if I please you in this affair, 'tis all I desire. Not that I think a woman the worse for being hand- 5 some; but, sir, if you please to recollect, you before hinted something about a hump or two, one eye, and a few more graces of that kind—now, without being very nice, I own I should rather choose a wife of mine to 10 have the usual number of limbs, and a limited quantity of back: and though *one* eye may be very agreeable, yet as the prejudice has always run in favor of *two*, I would not wish to affect a singularity in 15 that article.

SIR ANTHONY. What a phlegmatic sot it is! Why, sirrah, you're an anchorite!—a vile, insensible stock. You a soldier?— you're a walking block, fit only to dust the 20 company's regimentals on!—Odds life! I have a great mind to marry the girl myself!

ABSOLUTE. I am entirely at your disposal, sir. If you should think of addressing Miss Languish yourself, I suppose you would have 25 me marry the *aunt;* or, if you should change your mind, and take the old lady—'tis the same to me—I'll marry the *niece.*

SIR ANTHONY. Upon my word, Jack, thou'rt either a very great hypocrite, or— 30 but come, I know your indifference on such a subject must be all a lie—I'm sure it must! —Come, now—damn your demure face!— come, confess, Jack—you have been lying, ha'n't you! You have been lying, hey? 35 —I'll never forgive you if you ha'n't.—So now; own, my dear Jack, you have been playing the hypocrite—hey? I'll never forgive you if you ha'n't been lying and playing the hypocrite. 40

ABSOLUTE. I'm sorry, sir, that the respect and duty which I bear to you should be so mistaken.

SIR ANTHONY. Hang your respect and duty! But come along with me; I'll write a 45 note to Mrs. Malaprop, and you shall visit the lady directly.

ABSOLUTE. Where does she lodge, sir?

SIR ANTHONY. What a dull question! Only on the Grove[1] here. 50

ABSOLUTE. Oh! then I can call on her in my way to the coffee-house.

SIR ANTHONY. In your way to the coffee-house! You'll set your heart down in your

___

[1] The Orange Grove (named for the Prince of Orange), a fashionable resort near the North Parade.

way to the coffee-house, hey? Ah! you leaden-nerved, wooden-hearted dolt! But come along, you shall see her directly; her eyes shall be the Promethean torch to you— come along! I'll never forgive you if you don't come back stark mad with rapture and impatience—if you don't, egad, I'll marry the girl myself!

[*Exeunt.*

SCENE II. JULIA'S *Dressing-Room*

FAULKLAND, *solus*

FAULKLAND. They told me Julia would return directly; I wonder she is not yet come!—How mean does this captious, unsatisfied temper of mine appear to my cooler judgment! Yet I know not that I indulge it in any other point; but on this one subject, and to this one object, whom I think I love beyond my life, I am ever ungenerously fretful and madly capricious! I am conscious of it—yet I cannot correct myself! What tender, honest joy sparkled in her eyes when we met! How delicate was the warmth of her expression!—I was ashamed to appear less happy—though I had come resolved to wear a face of coolness and upbraiding. Sir Anthony's presence prevented my proposed expostulations; yet I must be satisfied that she has not been so *very* happy in my absence. She is coming! Yes, I know the nimbleness of her tread when she thinks her impatient Faulkland counts the moments of her stay.

Enter JULIA

JULIA. I had not hoped to see you again so soon.

FAULKLAND. Could I, Julia, be contented with my first welcome—restrained as we were by the presence of a third person?

JULIA. O Faulkland, when your kindness can make me thus happy, let me not think that I discovered more coolness in your first salutation than my long-hoarded joy could have presaged.

FAULKLAND. 'Twas but your fancy, Julia. I *was* rejoiced to see you—to see you in such health. Sure I had no cause for coldness?

JULIA. Nay then, I see you have taken something ill. You must not conceal from me what it is.

FAULKLAND. Well, then—shall I own to you—but you will despise me, Julia—nay, I despise myself for it.—Yet I *will* own that my joy at hearing of your health and arrival here, by your neighbor Acres, was somewhat damped by his dwelling much on the high spirits you had enjoyed in Devonshire—on your mirth—your singing—dancing, and I know not what! For such is my temper, Julia, that I should regard every mirthful moment in your absence as a treason to constancy. The mutual tear that steals down the cheek of parting lovers is a compact that no smile shall live there till they meet again.

JULIA. Must I never cease to tax my Faulkland with this teasing, minute caprice? Can the idle reports of a silly boor weigh in your breast against my tried affection?

FAULKLAND. They have no weight with me, Julia—No, no! I am happy if you have been so—yet only say that you did not sing with *mirth*—say that you *thought* of Faulkland in the dance.

JULIA. I never can be happy in your absence.—If I wear a countenance of content, it is to show that my mind holds no doubt of my Faulkland's truth. If I seemed sad, it were to make malice triumph and say that I fixed my heart on one who left me to lament his roving and my own credulity. —Believe me, Faulkland, I mean not to upbraid you when I say that I have often dressed sorrow in smiles, lest my friends should guess whose unkindness had caused my tears.

FAULKLAND. You were ever all goodness to me. Oh, I am a brute when I but admit a doubt of your true constancy!

JULIA. If ever, without such cause from you as I will not suppose possible, you find my affections veering but a point, may I become a proverbial scoff for levity and base ingratitude.

FAULKLAND. Ah! Julia, that *last* word is grating to me. I would I had no title to your *gratitude!* Search your heart, Julia; perhaps what you have mistaken for love, is but the warm effusion of a too thankful heart.

JULIA. For what quality must I love you?

FAULKLAND. For no quality! To regard me for any quality of mind or understanding, were only to *esteem* me. And for person—I have often wished myself deformed, to be convinced that I owed no obligation *there* for any part of your affection.

JULIA. Where Nature has bestowed a show of nice attention in the features of a man, he should laugh at it, as misplaced. I have seen men who in *this* vain article per-

haps might rank above you, but my heart has never asked my eyes if it were so or not.

FAULKLAND. Now this is not well from *you,* Julia—I despise person in a man; yet if you loved me as I wish, though I were an Ethiop, you'd think none so fair.

JULIA. I see you are determined to be unkind! The *contract* which my poor father bound us in gives you more than a lover's privilege.

FAULKLAND. Again, Julia, you raise ideas that feed and justify my doubts. I would not have been more free—no, I am proud of my restraint. Yet—yet—perhaps your high respect alone for this solemn compact has fettered your inclinations, which else had made a worthier choice. How shall I be sure, had you remained unbound in thought and promise, that I should still have been the object of your persevering love?

JULIA. Then, try me now. Let us be free as strangers as to what is past; *my* heart will not feel more liberty!

FAULKLAND. There now! So hasty, Julia? so anxious to be free? If your love for me were fixed and ardent, you would not lose your hold, even though I wished it!

JULIA. Oh, you torture me to the heart! I cannot bear it.

FAULKLAND. I do not mean to distress you. If I loved you less, I should never give you an uneasy moment.—But hear me! All my fretful doubts arise from this— Women are not used to weigh and separate the motives of their affections. The cold dictates of prudence, gratitude, or filial duty may sometimes be mistaken for the pleadings of the heart. I would not boast—yet let me say that I have neither age, person, or character, to found dislike on; my fortune, such as few ladies could be charged with *indiscretion* in the match. O Julia! when *Love* receives such countenance from *Prudence,* nice[2] minds will be suspicious of its *birth.*

JULIA. I know not whither your insinuations would tend; but as they seem pressing to insult me, I will spare you the regret of having done so.—I have given you no cause for this!   [*Exit in tears.*

FAULKLAND. In tears! Stay, Julia—stay but for a moment!—The door is fastened!— Julia!—my soul—but for one moment!— I hear her sobbing!—'Sdeath! what a brute am I to use her thus! Yet stay! Aye—she is coming now;—how little resolution there

[2]Discriminating.

is in women!—how a few soft words can turn them!—No, faith,—she is *not* coming either!—Why, Julia—my love—say but that you forgive me—come but to tell me that.—Now this is being *too* resentful. Stay! she is coming too—I thought she would—no *steadiness* in anything! her going away must have been a mere trick then—she sha'n't see that I was hurt by it.—I'll affect indifference—(*Hums a tune; then listens*) No, zounds! she's *not* coming!—nor don't intend it, I suppose.—This is not *steadiness, but obstinacy!*—Yet I deserve it. What, after so long an absence to quarrel with her tenderness?—'twas barbarous and unmanly!—I should be ashamed to see her now.—I'll wait till her just resentment is abated—and when I distress her so again, may I lose her forever! and be linked instead to some antique virago, whose gnawing passions and long-hoarded spleen shall make me curse my folly half the day and all the night.

[*Exit.*

SCENE III. MRS. MALAPROP'S *Lodgings*

MRS. MALAPROP *and* CAPTAIN ABSOLUTE

MRS. MALAPROP. Your being Sir Anthony's son, captain, would itself be a sufficient accommodation, but from the ingenuity of your appearance I am convinced you deserve the character here given of you.

ABSOLUTE. Permit me to say, madam, that as I never yet have had the pleasure of seeing Miss Languish, my principal inducement in this affair at present is the honor of being allied to Mrs. Malaprop, of whose intellectual accomplishments, elegant manners, and unaffected learning, no tongue is silent.

MRS. MALAPROP. Sir, you do me infinite honor! I beg, captain, you'll be seated.—[*He sits*] Ah! few gentlemen, now-a-days, know how to value the ineffectual qualities in a woman!—few think how a little knowledge becomes a gentlewoman. Men have no sense now but for the worthless flower—beauty!

ABSOLUTE. It is but too true, indeed, ma'am; yet I fear our ladies should share the blame—they think our admiration of *beauty* so great, that *knowledge* in *them* would be superfluous. Thus, like garden-trees, they seldom show fruits till time has robbed them of more specious blossom.—Few, like Mrs. Malaprop and the orange-tree, are rich in both at once!

MRS. MALAPROP. Sir, you overpower me

with good-breeding.—He is the very pine-apple of politeness!—You are not ignorant, captain, that this giddy girl has somehow contrived to fix he affections on a beggarly, strolling, eavesdropping ensign, whom none of us have seen and nobody knows anything of?

ABSOLUTE. Oh, I have heard the silly affair before.—I'm not at all prejudiced against her on *that* account.

MRS. MALAPROP. You are very good and very considerate, captain. I am sure I have done everything in my power since I exploded the affair; long ago I laid my positive conjunction on her, never to think on the fellow again.—I have since laid Sir Anthony's preposition before her; but, I am sorry to say, she seems resolved to decline every particle that I enjoin her.

ABSOLUTELY. It must be very distressing, indeed, ma'am.

MRS. MALAPROP. Oh, it gives me the hydrostatics to such a degree!—I thought she had persisted from corresponding with him, but behold! this very day I have interceded another letter from the fellow! I believe I have it in my pocket.

ABSOLUTE. (*Aside*) Oh, the devil! my last note.

MRS. MALAPROP. Aye, here it is.

ABSOLUTE. (*Aside*) Aye, my note indeed!—Oh, the little traitress, Lucy!

MRS. MALAPROP. There, perhaps you may know the writing. (*Gives him the letter*)

ABSOLUTE. I think I have seen the hand before—yes, I *certainly must* have seen this hand before—

MRS. MALAPROP. Nay, but read it, captain.

ABSOLUTE. (*Reads*) "My soul's idol, my adored Lydia!"—Very tender, indeed!

MRS. MALAPROP. Tender! aye, and profane too, o' my conscience.

ABSOLUTE. (*Reads*) "I am excessively alarmed at the intelligence you send me, the more so as my new rival"—

MRS. MALAPROP. That's *you,* sir.

ABSOLUTE. "Has universally the character of being an accomplished gentleman, and a man of honor."—Well, that's handsome enough.

MRS. MALAPROP. Oh, the fellow has some design in writing so.

ABSOLUTE. That he had, I'll answer for him, ma'am.

MRS. MALAPROP. But go on, sir—you'll see presently.

ABSOLUTE. "As for the old weather-beaten she-dragon who guards you"—Who can he mean by that?

MRS. MALAPROP. *Me,* sir! — *me!* — he means *me* there—what do you think now?—but go on a little further.

ABSOLUTE. Impudent scoundrel! — "it shall go hard but I will elude her vigilance, as I am told that the same ridiculous vanity which makes her dress up her coarse features and deck her dull chat with hard words which she don't understand"—

MRS. MALAPROP. There, sir! an attack upon my language! What do you think of that?—an aspersion upon my parts of speech! Was ever such a brute! sure if I reprehend anything in this world, it is the use of my oracular tongue and a nice derangement of epitaphs!

ABSOLUTE. He deserves to be hanged and quartered! let me see—"same ridiculous vanity"—

MRS. MALAPROP. You need not read it again, sir.

ABSOLUTE. I beg pardon, ma'am—"does also lay her open to the grossest deceptions from flattery and pretended admiration"—an impudent coxcomb!—"so that I have a scheme to see you shortly with the old harridan's consent, and even to make her a go-between in our interviews."—Was ever such assurance!

MRS. MALAPROP. Did you ever hear anything like it?—he'll elude my vigilance, will he?—Yes, yes! ha! ha! he's very likely to enter these doors;—we'll try who can plot best!

ABSOLUTE. So we will, ma'am—so we will.—Ha! ha! ha! a conceited puppy; ha! ha! ha!—Well, but Mrs. Malaprop, as the girl seems so infatuated by this fellow, suppose you were to wink at her corresponding with him for a little time—let her even plot an elopement with him; then do you connive at her escape—while *I,* just in the nick[3] will have the fellow laid by the heels, and fairly contrive to carry her off in his stead.

MRS. MALAPROP. I am delighted with the scheme; never was anything better perpetrated!

ABSOLUTE. But, pray, could not I see the lady for a few minutes now?—I should like to try her temper a little.

MRS. MALAPROP. Why, I don't know—I doubt she is not prepared for a first visit of this kind. There is a decorum in these matters.

---
[3]Nick of time.

ABSOLUTE. O Lord! she won't mind **me** —only tell her Beverley—

MRS. MALAPROP. Sir!

ABSOLUTE. (*Aside*) Gently, good tongue.

MRS. MALAPROP. What did you say of Beverley?

ABSOLUTE. Oh, I was going to propose that you should tell her, by way of jest, that it was Beverley who was below! she'd come down fast enough then—ha! ha! ha!

MRS. MALAPROP. 'Twould be a trick she well deserves; besides, you know the fellow tells her he'll get my consent to see her—ha! ha! Let him if he can, I say again: (*Calling*) Lydia, come down here!—He'll make me a "go-between in their interviews"! —ha! ha! ha!—Come down, I say, Lydia!—I don't wonder at your laughing, ha! ha! ha! —his impudence is truly ridiculous.

ABSOLUTE. 'Tis very ridiculous, upon my soul, ma'am, ha! ha! ha!

MRS. MALAPROP. The little hussy won't hear. Well, I'll go and tell her at once who it is—she shall know that Captain Absolute is come to wait on her. And I'll make her behave as becomes a young woman.

ABSOLUTE. As you please, ma'am.

MRS. MALAPROP. For the present, captain, your servant. Ah! you've not done laughing yet, I see—"elude my vigilance"; yes, yes; ha! ha! ha!   [*Exit.*

ABSOLUTE. Ha! ha! ha! one would think now that I might throw off all disguise at once and seize my prize with security; but such is Lydia's caprice that to undeceive were probably to lose her. I'll see whether she knows me.

(*Walks aside, and seems engaged in looking at the pictures*)

Enter LYDIA

LYDIA. What a scene am I now to go through! surely nothing can be more dreadful than to be obliged to listen to the loathsome addresses of a stranger to one's heart. I have heard of girls, persecuted as I am, who have appealed in behalf of their favored lover to the generosity of his rival; suppose I were to try it.—There stands the hated rival—an officer too!—but oh, how unlike my Beverley! I wonder he don't begin—truly he seems a very negligent wooer!—Quite at his ease, upon my word!—I'll speak first.—Mr. Absolute.

ABSOLUTE. (*Turns round*) Madam.

LYDIA. O heav'ns!—Beverley!

ABSOLUTE. Hush!—hush, my life! softly! be not surprised!

LYDIA. I am so astonished! and so terrified! and so overjoyed!—for heav'n's sake! how came you here?

ABSOLUTE. Briefly, I have deceived your aunt—I was informed that my new rival was to visit here this evening, and contriving to have him kept away have passed myself on *her* for Captain Absolute.

LYDIA. Oh, charming! And she really takes you for young Absolute?

ABSOLUTE. Oh, she's convinced of it.

LYDIA. Ha! ha! ha! I can't forbear laughing to think how her sagacity is overreached!

ABSOLUTE. But we trifle with our precious moments—such another opportunity may not occur; then let me conjure my kind, my condescending angel, to fix the time when I may rescue her from undeserved persecution and with a licensed warmth plead for my reward.

LYDIA. Will you then, Beverley, consent to forfeit that portion of my paltry wealth—that burden on the wings of love?

ABSOLUTE. Oh, come to me, rich only thus —in loveliness! Bring no portion to me but thy love—'twill be generous in you, Lydia,—for well you know it is the only dower your poor Beverley can repay.

LYDIA. (*Aside*) How persuasive are his words!—how charming will poverty be with him!

ABSOLUTE. Ah! my soul, what a life will we then live! Love shall be our idol and support! we will worship him with a monastic strictness, abjuring all worldly toys, to center every thought and action there.—Proud of calamity, we will enjoy the wreck of wealth, while the surrounding gloom of adversity shall make the flame of our pure love show doubly bright. By heav'ns! I would fling all goods of fortune from me with a prodigal hand, to enjoy the scene where I might clasp my Lydia to my bosom and say, The world affords no smile to me—but here—(*Embracing her*).—(*Aside*) If she holds out now, the devil is in it!

LYDIA. (*Aside*) Now could I fly with him to the Antipodes! but my persecution is not yet come to a crisis.

Re-enter MRS. MALAPROP, *listening*

MRS. MALAPROP. (*Aside*) I am impatient to know how the little hussy deports herself.

ABSOLUTE. So pensive, Lydia!—is then your warmth abated?

MRS. MALAPROP. (*Aside*) *Warmth abated!*—so!—she has been in a passion, I suppose.

LYDIA. No—nor ever can while I have life.

MRS. MALAPROP. (*Aside*) An ill-tempered little devil! She'll be *in a passion all her life*—will she?

LYDIA. Think not the idle threats of my ridiculous aunt can ever have any weight with me.

MRS. MALAPROP. (*Aside*) Very dutiful. upon my word!

LYDIA. Let her choice be Captain Absolute, but Beverley is mine.

MRS. MALAPROP. (*Aside*) I am astonished at her assurance!—*to his face—this to his face!*

ABSOLUTE. (*Kneeling*) Thus then let me enforce my suit.

MRS. MALAPROP. (*Aside*) Aye, poor young man!—down on his knees entreating for pity! I can contain no longer.—Why, hussy! hussy!—I have overheard you.

ABSOLUTE. (*Aside*) Oh, confound her vigilance!

MRS. MALAPROP. Captain Absolute,—I know not how to apologize for her shocking rudeness.

ABSOLUTE. (*Aside*) So! all's safe, I find. —I have hopes, madam, that time will bring the young lady—

MRS. MALAPROP. Oh, there's nothing to be hoped for from her! she's as headstrong as an allegory on the banks of Nile.

LYDIA. Nay, madam, what do you charge me with now?

MRS. MALAPROP. Why, thou unblushing rebel—didn't you tell this gentleman to his face that you loved another better?—didn't you say you never would be his?

LYDIA. No, madam—I did not.

MRS. MALAPROP. Good heav'ns! what assurance!—Lydia, Lydia, you ought to know that lying don't become a young woman!—Didn't you boast that Beverley, that stroller Beverley, possessed your heart?—Tell me that, I say.

LYDIA. 'Tis true, ma'am, and none but Beverley—

MRS. MALAPROP. Hold, hold, Assurance! —you shall not be so rude.

ABSOLUTE. Nay, pray, Mrs. Malaprop, don't stop the young lady's speech; she's very welcome to talk thus—it does not hurt *me* in the least, I assure you.

MRS. MALAPROP. You are *too* good, captain—*too* amiably patient—but come with me, miss.—Let us see you again soon, captain—remember what we have fixed.

ABSOLUTE. I shall, ma'am.

MRS. MALAPROP. Come, take a graceful leave of the gentleman.

LYDIA. May every blessing wait on my Beverley, my loved Bev—

MRS. MALAPROP. Hussy! I'll choke the word in your throat!—come along—come along.

[*Exeunt severally,* CAPTAIN ABSOLUTE *kissing his hand to* LYDIA, MRS. MALAPROP *stopping her from speaking.*

SCENE IV. ACRES' *Lodgings*

ACRES *and* DAVID, ACRES
as just dressed

ACRES. Indeed, David—do you think I become it so?

DAVID. You are quite another creature, believe me, master, by the mass! an'[4] we've any luck, we shall see the Devon monkey-roni[5] in all the print-shops in Bath!

ACRES. Dress *does* make a difference, David.

DAVID. 'Tis all in all, I think.—Difference! why, an' you were to go now to Clod Hall, I am certain the old lady wouldn't know you. Master Butler wouldn't believe his own eyes, and Mrs. Pickle would cry, "Lard presarve me!" our dairy-maid would come giggling to the door, and I warrant Dolly Tester, your honor's favorite, would blush like my waistcoat.—Oons! I'll hold a gallon, there an't a dog in the house but would bark, and I question whether Phillis would wag a hair of her tail!

ACRES. Aye, David, there's nothing like polishing.

DAVID. So I says of your honor's boots; but the boy never heeds me!

ACRES. But, David, has Mr. De-la-Grace been here? I must rub up my balancing and chasing and boring.[6]

DAVID. I'll call again, sir.

ACRES. Do—and see if there are any letters for me at the post-office.

DAVID. I will.—By the mass, I can't help looking at your head!—if I hadn't been by at the cooking, I wish I may die if I should have known the dish again myself. [*Exit.*

ACRES. (*Comes forward, practicing a dancing-step*) Sink, slide—coupee.[7]—Con-

found the first inventors of cotillions! say I —they are as bad as algebra to us country gentlemen.—I can walk a minuet easy enough when I am forced!—and I have been accounted a good stick in a country-dance.— Odds jigs and tabors! I never valued your cross-over two couple—figure in—right and left—and I'd foot it with e'er a captain in the county!—but these outlandish heathen allemandes[8] and cotillions are quite beyond me!—I shall never prosper at 'em, that's sure; mine are true-born English legs—they don't understand their curst French lingo!— their *pas*[9] this, and *pas* that, and *pas* t'other! —damn me! my feet don't like to be called paws! no, 'tis certain I have most antigallican toes!

Enter SERVANT

SERVANT. Here is Sir Lucius O'Trigger to wait on you, sir.

ACRES. Show him in.

Enter SIR LUCIUS

SIR LUCIUS. Mr. Acres, I am delighted to embrace you.

ACRES. My dear Sir Lucius, I kiss your hands.

SIR LUCIUS. Pray, my friend, what has brought you so suddenly to Bath?

ACRES. Faith! I have followed Cupid's jack-a-lantern, and find myself in a quagmire at last.—In short, I have been very ill-used, Sir Lucius.—I don't choose to mention names, but look on me as on a very ill-used gentleman.

SIR LUCIUS. Pray, what is the case?—I ask no names.

ACRES. Mark me, Sir Lucius, I falls as deep as need be in love with a young lady— her friends take my part—I follow her to Bath—send word of my arrival, and receive answer that the lady is to be otherwise disposed of.—This, Sir Lucius, I call being ill-used.

SIR LUCIUS. Very ill, upon my conscience. —Pray, can you divine the cause of it?

ACRES. Why, there's the matter; she has another lover, one Beverley, who, I am told, is now in Bath.—Odds slanders and lies! he must be at the bottom of it.

SIR LUCIUS. A rival in the case, is there? —and you think he has supplanted you unfairly?

ACRES. *Unfairly?*—to be sure he has. He never could have done *it* fairly.

---

[4]If.   [5]Macaroni, i. e., dandy.

[6]Terms of dancing.   [7]Name for a dance-step.

[8]German dances.   [9]Step.

SIR LUCIUS. Then, sure you know what is to be done!

ACRES. Not I, upon my soul!

SIR LUCIUS. We wear no swords here, but you understand me.

ACRES. What! fight him?

SIR LUCIUS. Aye, to be sure; what can I mean else?

ACRES. But he has given me no provocation.

SIR LUCIUS. Now, I think he has given you the greatest provocation in the world.—Can a man commit a more heinous offense against another than to fall in love with the same woman? Oh, by my soul! it is the most unpardonable breach of friendship.

ACRES. Breach of *friendship!* aye, aye; but I have no acquaintance with this man. I never saw him in my life.

SIR LUCIUS. That's no argument at all—he has the less right then to take such a liberty.

ACRES. 'Gad, that's true—I grow full of anger, Sir Lucius!—I fire apace! Odds hilts and blades! I find a man may have a deal of valor in him and not know it! But couldn't I contrive to have a little right of my side?

SIR LUCIUS. What the devil signifies *right,* when your *honor* is concerned? Do you think Achilles, or my little Alexander the Great, ever inquired where the right lay? No, by my soul, they drew their broad-swords and left the lazy sons of peace to settle the justice of it.

ACRES. Your words are a grenadier's march to my heart! I believe courage must be catching!—I certainly do feel a kind of valor rising, as it were—a kind of courage, as I may say.—Odds flints, pans, and triggers! I'll challenge him directly.

SIR LUCIUS. Ah, my little friend, if I had Blunderbuss Hall here, I could show you a range of ancestry in the old O'Trigger line that would furnish the New Room[10]—every one of whom had killed his man!—For though the mansion-house and dirty acres have slipped through my fingers, I thank God our honor and the family pictures are as fresh as ever.

ACRES. O Sir Lucius! I have had ancestors too!—every man of 'em colonel or captain in the militia!—Odds balls and barrels! say no more—I'm braced for it—my nerves are become catgut! my sinews wire! and my

heart pinchbeck![11] The thunder of your words has soured the milk of human kindness in my breast:—Zounds! as the man in the play says, "I could do such deeds!"

SIR LUCIUS. Come, come, there must be no passion at all in the case—these things should always be done civilly.

ACRES. I must be in a passion, Sir Lucius—I must be in a rage.—Dear Sir Lucius, let me be in a rage, if you love me. Come, here's pen and paper.—(*Sits down to write*) I would the ink were red!—Indite, I say, indite!—How shall I begin? Odds bullets and blades! I'll write a good *bold hand,* however.

SIR LUCIUS. Pray compose yourself.

ACRES. Come—now shall I begin with an oath? Do, Sir Lucius, let me begin with a "damme."

SIR LUCIUS. Pho! pho! do the thing *decently,* and like a Christian. Begin now—"Sir"!

ACRES. That's too civil by half.

SIR LUCIUS. "To prevent the confusion that might arise."

ACRES. Well—

SIR LUCIUS. "From our both addressing the same lady,"

ACRES. Aye, there's the reason—"same lady"—Well?

SIR LUCIUS. "I shall expect the honor of your company."

ACRES. Zounds! I'm not asking him to dinner.

SIR LUCIUS. Pray, be easy.

ACRES. Well then, "honor of your company."

SIR LUCIUS. "To settle our pretensions."

ACRES. Well.

SIR LUCIUS. Let me see—aye, King's-Mead-Fields will do—"in King's-Mead-Fields."

ACRES. So; that's done. Well, I'll fold it up presently; my own crest—a hand and dagger—shall be the seal.

SIR LUCIUS. You see now this little explanation will put a stop at once to all confusion or misunderstanding that might arise between you.

ACRES. Aye, we fight to prevent any misunderstanding.

SIR LUCIUS. Now, I'll leave you to fix your own time.—Take my advice, and you'll decide it this evening if you can; then let the

---

[10]The new assembly room, or ball room, which had been opened in 1771.

[11]An alloy of copper and zinc, named for its inventor, Pinchbeck, a London jeweler of the eighteenth century.

worst come of it, 'twill be off your mind to-morrow.

ACRES. Very true.

SIR LUCIUS. So I shall see nothing of you, unless it be by letter, till the evening. —I would do myself the honor to carry your message; but, to tell you a secret, I believe I shall have just such another affair on my own hands. There is a gay captain here who put a jest on me lately at the expense of my country, and I only want to fall in with the gentleman to call him out.

ACRES. By my valor, I should like to see you fight first! Odds life! I should like to see you kill him, if it was only to get a little lesson.

SIR LUCIUS. I shall be very proud of instructing you.—Well for the present—but remember now, when you meet your antagonist, do everything in a mild and agreeable manner.—Let your courage be as keen, but at the same time as polished as your sword.

[*Exeunt severally.*

ACT IV

SCENE I. ACRES' *Lodgings*

ACRES *and* DAVID

DAVID. Then, by the mass, sir! I would do no such thing—ne'er a St. Lucius O'Trigger in the kingdom should make me fight when I wa'n't so minded. Oons! what will the old lady say when she hears o't?

ACRES. Ah! David, if you had heard Sir Lucius!—Odds sparks and flames! he would have roused your valor.

DAVID. Not he, indeed. I hates such bloodthirsty cormorants. Look'ee, master; if you'd wanted a bout at boxing, quarter-staff, or short-staff, I should never be the man to bid you cry off; but for your curst sharps and snaps[1] I never knew any good come of 'em.

ACRES. But my *honor*, David—my *honor*! I must be very careful of my honor.

DAVID. Aye, by the mass! and I would be very careful of it; and I think in return my *honor* couldn't do less than to be very careful of *me*.

ACRES. Odds blades, David, no gentleman will ever risk the loss of his honor!

DAVID. I say then, it would be but civil in *honor* never to risk the loss of the *gentle-man*.—Look'ee, master, this *Honor* seems to

me to be a marvelous false friend—aye, truly, a very courtier-like servant. Put the case, I was a gentleman (which, thank God, no one can say of me); well, my honor makes me quarrel with another gentleman of my acquaintance.—So we fight. (Pleasant enough that!) Boh!—I kill him—(the more's my luck!) Now, pray who gets the profit of it? —why, my *honor*. But put the case that he kills me!—by the mass! I go to the worms and my honor whips over to my enemy.

ACRES. No, David—in that case, odds crowns and laurels! your honor follows you to the grave.

DAVID. Now, that's just the place where I could make a shift to do without it.

ACRES. Zounds! David, you are a coward!—It doesn't become my valor to listen to you.—What, shall I disgrace my ancestors? —Think of that, David—think what it would be to disgrace my ancestors!

DAVID. Under favor, the surest way of not disgracing them is to keep as long as you can out of their company. Look'ee, now, master; to go to them in such haste—with an ounce of lead in your brains—I should think might as well be let alone. Our ancestors are very good kind of folks, but they are the last people I should choose to have a visiting acquaintance with.

ACRES. But, David, now, you don't think there is such very, very, *very* great danger, hey?—Odds life, people often fight without any mischief done!

DAVID. By the mass, I think 'tis ten to one against you!—Oons! here to meet some lion-headed fellow, I warrant, with his damned double-barreled swords, and cut-and-thrust pistols! Lord, bless us! it makes me tremble to think o't—Those be such desperate, bloody-minded weapons! Well, I never could abide 'em!—from a child I never could fancy 'em!—I suppose there an't so merciless a beast in the world as your loaded pistol!

ACRES. Zounds! I *won't* be afraid! Odds fire and fury! you shan't make me afraid.— Here is the challenge, and I have sent for my dear friend Jack Absolute to carry it for me.

DAVID. Aye, i' the name of mischief, let *him* be the messenger.—For my part, I wouldn't lend a hand to it for the best horse in your stable. By the mass! it don't look like another letter! It is, as I may say, a designing and malicious-looking letter! and I warrant smells of gunpowder like a soldier's pouch!—Oons! I wouldn't swear it mayn't go off!

[1]Rapiers with sharpened points and pistols.

ACRES. Out, you poltroon! you ha'n't the valor of a grasshopper.

DAVID. Well, I say no more—'twill be sad news, to be sure, at Clod Hall!—but I ha' done. How Phillis will howl when she hears of it!—Aye, poor bitch, she little thinks what shooting her master's going after! And I warrant old Crop, who has carried your honor, field and road, these ten years, will curse the hour he was born.

(Whimpering)

ACRES. It won't do, David—I am determined to fight—so get along, you coward, while I'm in the mind.

Enter SERVANT

SERVANT. Captain Absolute, sir.

ACRES. Oh! show him up.

[*Exit* SERVANT.

DAVID. Well, Heaven send we be all alive this time to-morrow.

ACRES. What's that!—Don't provoke me, David!

DAVID. Good-bye, master.

(Whimpering)

ACRES. Get along, you cowardly, dastardly, croaking raven! [*Exit* DAVID.

Enter CAPTAIN ABSOLUTE

ABSOLUTE. What's the matter, Bob?

ACRES. A vile, sheep-hearted blockhead! If I hadn't the valor of St. George and the dragon to boot—

ABSOLUTE. But what did you want with me, Bob?

ACRES. Oh!—there—

(Gives him the challenge)

ABSOLUTE. "To Ensign Beverley."— *(Aside)* So—what's going on now?— *(Aloud)* Well, what's this?

ACRES. A challenge!

ABSOLUTE. Indeed! Why, you won't fight him, will you, Bob?

ACRES. Egad, but I will, Jack. Sir Lucius has wrought me to it. He has left me full of rage—and I'll fight this evening, that so much good passion mayn't be wasted.

ABSOLUTE. But what have I to do with this?

ACRES. Why, as I think you know something of this fellow, I want you to find him out for me and give him this mortal *defiance*.

ABSOLUTE. Well, give it to me, and trust me he gets it.

ACRES. Thank you, my dear friend, my dear Jack; but it is giving you a great deal of trouble.

ABSOLUTE. Not in the least—I beg you won't mention it. No trouble in the world, I assure you.

ACRES. You are very kind.—What it is to have a friend! You couldn't be my second, could you, Jack?

ABSOLUTE. Why no, Bob—not in *this* affair—it would not be quite so proper.

ACRES. Well, then, I must fix on my friend Sir Lucius. I shall have your good wishes, however, Jack?

ABSOLUTE. Whenever he meets you, believe me.

Enter SERVANT

SERVANT. Sir Anthony Absolute is below, inquiring for the captain.

ABSOLUTE. I'll come instantly.—*(Going)* Well, my little hero, success attend you.

ACRES. Stay—stay, Jack.—If Beverley should ask you what kind of a man your friend Acres is, do tell him I am a devil of a fellow—will you, Jack?

ABSOLUTE. To be sure I shall. I'll say you are a determined dog—hey, Bob?

ACRES. Aye, do, do—and if that frightens him, egad, perhaps he mayn't come. So tell him I generally kill a man a week; will you, Jack?

ABSOLUTE. I will, I will; I'll say you are called in the country "Fighting Bob."

ACRES. Right—right—'tis all to prevent mischief; for I don't want to take his life if I clear my honor.

ABSOLUTE. No!—that's very kind of you.

ACRES. Why, you don't wish me to kill him—do you, Jack?

ABSOLUTE. No, upon my soul, I do not. *(Going)* But "a devil of a fellow," hey?

ACRES. True, true;—but stay—stay, Jack! You may add, that you never saw me in such a rage before—a most devouring rage!

ABSOLUTE. I will, I will.

ACRES. Remember, Jack—a determined dog!

ABSOLUTE. Aye, aye—"Fighting Bob!"

[*Exeunt severally.*

SCENE II. MRS. MALAPROP'S *Lodgings*

MRS. MALAPROP *and* LYDIA

MRS. MALAPROP. Why, thou perverse one!—tell me what you can object to him! Isn't he a handsome man?—tell me that. A genteel man? a pretty figure of a man?

LYDIA. *(Aside)* She little thinks whom

she is praising!—(*Aloud*) So is Beverley, ma'am.

MRS. MALAPROP. No caparisons, miss, if you please. Caparisons don't become a young woman. No! Captain Absolute is indeed a fine gentleman!

LYDIA. (*Aside*) Aye, the Captain Absolute *you* have seen.

MRS. MALAPROP. Then he's *so* well bred —*so* full of alacrity and adulation!—and has *so much* to say for himself—in such good language, too! His physiognomy so grammatical! Then, his presence is so noble! I protest, when I saw him, I thought of what Hamlet says in the play:— "Hesperian curls—the front of *Job* himself! —An eye, like March, to threaten at command!—A station, like Harry Mercury, new—" Something about kissing—on a hill —however, the similitude struck me directly.[2]

LYDIA. (*Aside*) How enraged she'll be presently when she discovers her mistake!

Enter SERVANT

SERVANT. Sir Anthony and Captain Absolute are below, ma'am.

MRS. MALAPROP. Show them up here.— [*Exit* SERVANT.

Now, Lydia, I insist on your behaving as becomes a young woman. Show your good breeding, at least, though you have forgot your duty.

LYDIA. Madam, I have told you my resolution; I shall not only give him no encouragement, but I won't even speak to or look at him.

(*Flings herself into a chair, with her face from the door*)

Enter SIR ANTHONY *and* ABSOLUTE

SIR ANTHONY. Here we are, Mrs. Malaprop—come to mitigate the frowns of unrelenting beauty,—and difficulty enough I had to bring this fellow.—I don't know what's the matter, but if I hadn't held him by force, he'd have given me the slip.

MRS. MALAPROP. You have infinite trouble, Sir Anthony, in the affair. I am ashamed for the cause! (*Aside to her*) Lydia, Lydia! rise, I beseech you!—pay your respects!

SIR ANTHONY. I hope, madam, that Miss Languish has reflected on the worth of this

[2] *Hamlet*, III, iv, 56–59.

gentleman and the regard due to her aunt's choice and *my* alliance.—(*Aside to him*) Now, Jack, speak to her!

ABSOLUTE. (*Aside*) What the devil shall I do! (*Apart*) You see, sir, she won't even look at me whilst you are here. I knew she wouldn't! I told you so. Let me entreat you, sir, to leave us together!

(ABSOLUTE *seems to expostulate with his father*)

LYDIA. (*Aside*) I wonder I ha'n't heard my aunt exclaim yet! sure, she can't have looked at him!—Perhaps their regimentals are alike and she is something blind.

SIR ANTHONY. I say, sir, I won't stir a foot yet!

MRS. MALAPROP. I am sorry to say, Sir Anthony, that my affluence over my niece is very small.—(*Aside to her*) Turn round, Lydia; I blush for you!

SIR ANTHONY. May I not flatter myself that Miss Languish will assign what cause of dislike she can have to my son?—(*Aside to him*) Why don't you begin, Jack?— Speak, you puppy—speak!

MRS. MALAPROP. It is impossible, Sir Anthony, she can have any. She will not *say* she has.—(*Aside to her*) Answer, hussy! why don't you answer?

SIR ANTHONY. Then, madam, I trust that a childish and hasty predilection will be no bar to Jack's happiness.—(*Aside to him*) Zounds! sirrah! why don't you speak?

LYDIA (*Aside*) I think my lover seems as little inclined to conversation as myself.— How strangely blind my aunt must be!

ABSOLUTE. Hem! hem! madam—hem!— (ABSOLUTE *attempts to speak, then returns to* SIR ANTHONY) Faith! sir, I am so confounded!—and—so—so—confused!—I told you I should be so, sir—I knew it.—The— the—tremor of my passion entirely takes away my presence of mind.

SIR ANTHONY. But it don't take away your voice, fool, does it?—Go up, and speak to her directly!

(ABSOLUTE *makes signs to* MRS. MALAPROP *to leave them together*)

MRS. MALAPROP. Sir Anthony, shall we leave them together?—(*Aside to her*) Ah! you stubborn little vixen!

SIR ANTHONY. Not yet, ma'am, not yet! —(*Aside to him*) What the devil are you at? unlock your jaws, sirrah, or—

(ABSOLUTE *draws near* LYDIA)

ABSOLUTE. (*Aside*) Now Heav'n send she may be too sullen to look round!—I must disguise my voice.—(*Speaks in a low, hoarse tone*) Will not Miss Languish lend an ear to the mild accents of true love? Will not—

SIR ANTHONY. (*Apart*) What the devil ails the fellow? why don't you speak out?—not stand croaking like a frog in a quinsy!

ABSOLUTE. The—the—excess of my awe, and my—my—modesty quite choke me!

SIR ANTHONY. Ah! your *modesty* again!—I'll tell you what, Jack, if you don't speak out directly, and glibly too, I shall be in such a rage!—Mrs. Malaprop, I wish the lady would favor us with something more than a side-front.

(MRS. MALAPROP *seems to chide* LYDIA)

ABSOLUTE. So!—all will out, I see!—(*Goes up to* LYDIA, *speaks softly*) Be not surprised, my Lydia; suppress all surprise at present.

LYDIA. (*Aside*) Heav'ns! 'tis Beverley's voice! Sure he can't have imposed on Sir Anthony too!—(*Looks round by degrees, then starts up*) Is this possible!—my Beverley!—how can this be?—my Beverley?

ABSOLUTE. (*Aside*) Ah! 'tis all over.

SIR ANTHONY. Beverley!—the devil—Beverley!—What can the girl mean?—This is my son, Jack Absolute.

MRS. MALAPROP. For shame, hussy! for shame! your head runs so on that fellow that you have him always in your eyes! Beg Captain Absolute's pardon directly.

LYDIA. I see no Captain Absolute, but my loved Beverley!

SIR ANTHONY. Zounds! the girl's mad!—her brain's turned by reading.

MRS. MALAPROP. O' my conscience, I believe so!—What do you mean by Beverley, hussy? You saw Captain Absolute before to-day; there he is—your husband that shall be.

LYDIA. With all my soul, ma'am—when I refuse my Beverley—

SIR ANTHONY. Oh! she's as mad as Bedlam!—or has this fellow been playing us a rogue's trick?—Come here, sirrah; who the devil are you?

ABSOLUTE. Faith, sir, I am not quite clear myself; but I'll endeavor to recollect.

SIR ANTHONY. Are you my son or not?—answer for your mother, you dog, if you won't for me.

MRS. MALAPROP. Aye, sir, who are you?—O mercy! I begin to suspect!—

ABSOLUTE. (*Aside*) Ye Powers of impudence, befriend me!—Sir Anthony, most assuredly I am your wife's son; and that I sincerely believe myself to be *yours* also, I hope my duty has always shown.—Mrs. Malaprop, I am your most respectful admirer and shall be proud to add *affectionate nephew.*—I need not tell my Lydia that she sees her faithful Beverley who, knowing the singular generosity of her temper, assumed that name and a station which has proved a test of the most disinterested love, which he now hopes to enjoy in a more elevated character.

LYDIA. (*Sullenly*) So—there will be no elopement after all!

SIR ANTHONY. Upon my soul, Jack, thou art a very impudent fellow! To do you justice, I think I never saw a piece of more consummate assurance!

ABSOLUTE. Oh, you flatter me, sir—you compliment—'tis my *modesty,* you know, sir—my *modesty* that has stood in my way.

SIR ANTHONY. Well, I am glad you are not the dull, insensible varlet you pretended to be, however!—I'm glad you have made a fool of your father, you dog—I am. So this was your *penitence,* your *duty* and *obedience!*—I thought it was damned sudden!—"You never heard their names before," not you!—"What Languishes of Worcestershire," hey?—"if you could please me in the affair, 'twas all you desired!"—Ah! you dissembling villain!—What! (*Pointing to* LYDIA) "She squints, don't she?—a little red-haired girl!"—hey?—Why, you hypocritical young rascal!—I wonder you a'n't ashamed to hold up your head!

ABSOLUTE. 'Tis with difficulty, sir.—I *am* confused—very much confused, as you must perceive.

MRS. MALAPROP. O lud! Sir Anthony!—a new light breaks in upon me!—hey!—how! what! Captain, did *you* write the letters then?—What—I am to thank *you* for the elegant compilation of "an old weather-beaten she-dragon"—hey?—O mercy!—was it *you* that reflected on my parts of speech?

ABSOLUTE. Dear sir! my modesty will be overpowered at last if you don't assist me.—I shall certainly not be able to stand it!

SIR ANTHONY. Come, come, Mrs. Malaprop, we must forget and forgive;—odds life! matters have taken so clever a turn all of a sudden that I could find in my heart to be so good-humored! and so gallant!—hey, Mrs. Malaprop?

MRS. MALAPROP. Well, Sir Anthony, since *you* desire it, we will not anticipate the past;

—so mind, young people—our retrospection will be all to the future.

SIR ANTHONY. Come, we must leave them together; Mrs. Malaprop, they long to fly into each other's arms, I warrant!—Jack, isn't the *cheek* as I said, hey?—and the eye, you dog?—and the lip—hey? Come, Mrs. Malaprop, we'll not disturb their tenderness —theirs is the time of life for happiness!— (*Sings*) "Youth's the season made for joy"[3]—hey!—Odds life! I'm in such spirits,—I don't know what I couldn't do!— Permit me, ma'am—(*Gives his hand to* MRS. MALAPROP. *Sings*) Tol-de-rol—'gad, I should like to have a little fooling myself— Tol-de-rol! de-rol.

[*Exit singing, and handing* MRS. MALA-
PROP.

LYDIA *sits sullenly in her chair*

ABSOLUTE. (*Aside*) So much thought bodes me no good.—So grave, Lydia?

LYDIA. Sir!

ABSOLUTE. (*Aside*) So!—egad! I thought as much!—that damned monosyllable has froze me!—What, Lydia, now that we are as happy in our *friends' consent,* as in our *mutual vows*—

LYDIA. (*Peevishly*) *Friends' consent,* indeed!

ABSOLUTE. Come, come, we must lay aside some of our romance—a little *wealth* and *comfort* may be endured, after all. And for your fortune, the lawyers shall make such settlements as—

LYDIA. *Lawyers!* I *hate* lawyers!

ABSOLUTE. Nay then, we will not wait for their lingering forms, but instantly procure the license, and—

LYDIA. The *license!*—I *hate* license!

ABSOLUTE. O my love! *be* not so unkind! —(*Kneeling*) Thus let me entreat—

LYDIA. Pshaw!—what signifies kneeling when you know I *must* have you?

ABSOLUTE. (*Rising*) Nay, madam, there shall be no constraint upon your inclinations, I promise you.—If I have lost your *heart*— I resign the rest.—(*Aside*) 'Gad, I must try what a little *spirit* will do.

LYDIA. (*Rising*) Then, sir, let me tell you, the interest you had there was acquired by a mean, unmanly imposition, and deserves the punishment of fraud.—What, you have been treating *me* like a *child!*—humoring my

[3]The first line of a song in *The Beggar's Opera* (Act II), by John Gay.

romance! and laughing, I suppose, at your success!

ABSOLUTE. You wrong me, Lydia, you wrong me—only hear—

LYDIA. So, while *I* fondly imagined we were deceiving my relations, and flattered myself that I should outwit and incense them *all*—(*Walking about in heat*) behold! my hopes are to be crushed at once, by my aunt's consent and approbation—and *I* am *myself* the only dupe at last!—

ABSOLUTE. Nay, but hear me—

LYDIA. No, sir, you could not think that such paltry artifices could please me when the mask was thrown off! But I suppose since your tricks have made you secure of my *fortune,* you are little solicitous about my *affections.*—But here, sir, here is the picture—Beverley's picture! (*Taking a minia-ture from her bosom*) which I have worn night and day, in spite of threats and entreaties!—There, sir; (*Flings it to him*) and be assured I throw the original from my heart as easily!

ABSOLUTE. Nay, nay, ma'am, we will not differ as to that.—Here (*Taking out a pic-ture*), here is Miss Lydia Languish.—What a difference!—aye, *there* is the heav'nly, assenting smile that first gave soul and spirit to my hopes!—those are the lips which sealed a vow, as yet scarce dry in Cupid's calendar! and *there* the *half* resentful blush, that *would* have checked the ardor of my thanks!—Well, all that's past—all over indeed!—There, madam—in *beauty,* that copy is not equal to you, but in my mind its merit over the original, in being still the same, is such—that—I cannot find in my heart to *part with it.* (*Puts it up again*)

LYDIA. (*Softening*) 'Tis *your own* doing, sir—I, I, I suppose you are perfectly satisfied.

ABSOLUTE. Oh, most certainly—sure, now this is much better than being in love!— ha! ha! ha!—there's some spirit in *this!*— What signifies breaking some scores of solemn promises—half an hundred vows, under one's hand, with the marks of a dozen or two angels to witness—all that's of no consequence, you know. To be sure, people will say, "That miss don't know her own mind"—but never mind that.—Or, perhaps, they may be ill-natured enough to hint that the gentleman grew tired of the lady and forsook her—but don't let that fret you.

LYDIA. There is no bearing his insolence. (*Bursts into tears*)

Enter MRS. MALAPROP *and* SIR ANTHONY

MRS. MALAPROP. (*Entering*) Come, we must interrupt your billing and cooing a while.

LYDIA. (*Sobbing*) *This* is *worse* than your treachery and deceit, you base ingrate!

SIR ANTHONY. What the devil's the matter now?—Zounds! Mrs. Malaprop, this is the *oddest billing* and *cooing* I ever heard!—but what the deuce is the meaning of it?—I am quite astonished!

ABSOLUTE. Ask the lady, sir.

MRS. MALAPROP. O mercy!—I'm quite analyzed for my part!—Why, Lydia, what is the reason of this?

LYDIA. Ask the *gentleman,* ma'am.

SIR ANTHONY. Zounds! I shall be in a frenzy!—Why, Jack, you scoundrel, you are not come out to be anyone else, are you?

MRS. MALAPROP. Aye, sir—there's no more *trick,* is there?—you are not like Cerberus—*three* gentlemen at once, are you?

ABSOLUTE. You'll not let me speak.—I say the *lady* can account for *this* much better than I can.

LYDIA. Ma'am, you once commanded me never to think of Beverley again. *There* is the man—I now obey you; for from this moment I renounce him for ever.   [*Exit.*

MRS. MALAPROP. O mercy! and miracles! what a turn here is—Why sure, captain, you haven't behaved disrespectfully to my niece?

SIR ANTHONY. Ha! ha! ha!—ha! ha! ha! —now I see it. Ha! ha! ha!—now I see it —you have been too lively, Jack.

ABSOLUTE. Nay, sir, upon my word—

SIR ANTHONY. Come, no lying, Jack— I'm sure '*twas* so.

MRS. MALAPROP. O lud! Sir Anthony! —O fie, captain!

ABSOLUTE. Upon my soul, ma'am—

SIR ANTHONY. Come, no excuse, Jack; why, your father, you rogue, was so before you!—the blood of the Absolutes was always impatient.—Ha! ha! ha! poor little Lydia! why, you've frightened her, you dog, you have.

ABSOLUTE. By all that's good, sir—

SIR ANTHONY. Zounds! say no more, I tell you. Mrs. Malaprop shall make your peace. You must make his peace, Mrs. Malaprop; you must tell her 'tis Jack's way —tell her 'tis all our ways—it runs in the blood of our family! Come, get on, Jack. Ha! ha! ha!—Mrs. Malaprop—a young villain! (*Pushing him out*)

MRS. MALAPROP. O! Sir Anthony!—O fie, captain!   [*Exeunt severally.*

SCENE III. *The North Parade*

Enter SIR LUCIUS O'TRIGGER

SIR LUCIUS. I wonder where this Captain Absolute hides himself! Upon my conscience, these officers are always in one's way in love affairs!—I remember I might have married Lady Dorothy Carmine if it had not been for a little rogue of a major, who ran away with her before she could get a sight of me! And I wonder too what it is the ladies can see in them to be so fond of them—unless it be a touch of the old serpent in 'em, that makes the little creatures be caught, like vipers, with a bit of red cloth. Hah! isn't this the captain coming?—faith it is!—There is a probability of succeeding about that fellow, that is mighty provoking! Who the devil is he talking to?

(*Steps aside*)

Enter CAPTAIN ABSOLUTE

ABSOLUTE. To what fine purpose I have been plotting! a noble reward for all my schemes, upon my soul!—a little gipsy!—I did not think her romance could have made her so damned absurd either. 'Sdeath, I never was in a worse humor in my life!—I could cut my own throat or any other person's with the greatest pleasure in the world!

SIR LUCIUS. (*Aside*) Oh, faith! I'm in the luck of it. I never could have found him in a sweeter temper for my purpose—to be sure, I'm just come in the nick! Now to enter into conversation with him, and so quarrel genteelly. (SIR LUCIUS *goes up to* ABSOLUTE)—With regard to that matter, captain, I must beg leave to differ in opinion with you.

ABSOLUTE. Upon my word, then, you must be a very subtle disputant—because, sir, I happened just then to be giving no opinion at all.

SIR LUCIUS. That's no reason. For give me leave to tell you, a man may *think* an untruth as well as *speak* one.

ABSOLUTE. Very true, sir, but if a man never utters his thoughts, I should think they *might* stand a chance of escaping controversy.

SIR LUCIUS. Then, sir, you differ in opinion with me, which amounts to the same thing.

ABSOLUTE. Hark'ee, Sir Lucius: if I had not before known you to be a gentleman, upon my soul, I should not have discovered it at this interview; for what you can drive at, unless you mean to quarrel with me, I 5 cannot conceive!

SIR LUCIUS. I humbly thank you, sir, for the quickness of your apprehension—(*Bowing*) You have named the very thing I would be at.

ABSOLUTE. Very well, sir; I shall certainly not balk your inclinations.—But I should be glad you would please to explain your motives.

SIR LUCIUS. Pray, sir, be easy—the quar- 15 rel is a very pretty quarrel as it stands—we should only spoil it by trying to explain it.— However, your memory is very short, or you could not have forgot an affront you passed on me within this week. So no more, but 20 name your time and place.

ABSOLUTE. Well, sir, since you are so bent on it, the sooner the better; let it be this evening—here, by the Spring Gardens.—We shall scarcely be interrupted.

SIR LUCIUS. Faith! that same interruption in affairs of this nature shows very great ill-breeding. I don't know what's the reason, but in England, if a thing of this kind gets wind, people make such a pother that 30 a gentleman can never fight in peace and quietness. However, if it's the same to you, captain, I should take it as a particular kindness if you'd let us meet in King's-Mead-Fields, as a little business will call me there 35 about six o'clock and I may dispatch both matters at once.

ABSOLUTE. 'Tis the same to me exactly. A little after six, then, we will discuss this matter more seriously. 40

SIR LUCIUS. If you please, sir; there will be very pretty small-sword light, though it won't do for a long shot. So that matter's settled and my mind's at ease! [*Exit.*

Enter FAULKLAND *meeting* ABSOLUTE

ABSOLUTE. Well met—I was going to look for you. O Faulkland! all the demons of spite and disappointment have conspired against me! I'm so vexed that if I had not 50 the prospect of a resource in being knocked o' the head by and by, I should be scarce have spirits to tell you the cause.

FAULKLAND. What can you mean?—Has Lydia changed her mind?—I should have 55 thought her duty and inclination would now have pointed to the same object.

ABSOLUTE. Aye, just as the eyes do of a person who squints. When her *love-eye* was fixed on *me,* t'other—her eye of *duty*— was finely obliqued. But when duty bid her 5 point *that* the same way, off t'other turned on a swivel and secured its retreat with a frown!

FAULKLAND. But what's the resource you—

ABSOLUTE. Oh, to wind up the whole, a good-natured Irishman here has (*Mimicking* SIR LUCIUS) begged leave to have the pleasure of cutting my throat—and I mean to indulge him—that's all.

FAULKLAND. Prithee, be serious!

ABSOLUTE. 'Tis fact, upon my soul! Sir Lucius O'Trigger—you know him by sight —for some affront, which I am sure I never intended, has obliged me to meet him this evening at six o'clock. 'Tis on that account 20 I wished to see you—you must go with me.

FAULKLAND. Nay, there must be some mistake, sure.—Sir Lucius shall explain himself—and I dare say matters may be accommodated. But this evening did you say? I 25 wish it had been any other time.

ABSOLUTE. Why? there will be light enough; there will (as Sir Lucius says) "be very pretty small-sword light, though it won't do for a long shot." Confound his 30 long shots!

FAULKLAND. But I am myself a good deal ruffled by a difference I have had with Julia —my vile, tormenting temper has made me treat her so cruelly that I shall not be myself 35 till we are reconciled.

ABSOLUTE. By heav'ns, Faulkland, you don't deserve her!

Enter SERVANT, *gives* FAULKLAND *a letter*

FAULKLAND. Oh, Jack! this is from Julia! I dread to open it—I fear it may be to take a last leave—perhaps to bid me return her letters—and restore—Oh, how I suffer for 45 my folly!

ABSOLUTE. Here, let me see.—(*Takes the letter and opens it*) Aye, a final sentence indeed!—'tis all over with you, faith!

FAULKLAND. Nay, Jack, don't keep me in 50 suspense!

ABSOLUTE. Hear then—"As I am convinced that my dear Faulkland's own reflections have already upbraided him for his last unkindness to me, I will not add a word on 55 the subject. I wish to speak with you as soon as possible. Yours ever and truly, Julia." There's stubbornness and resentment for you!—(*Gives him the letter*) Why, man, you don't seem one whit happier at this!

FAULKLAND. Oh, yes, I am; but—but—

ABSOLUTE. Confound your *buts.*—You never hear anything that would make another man bless himself, but you immediately damn it with a *but.*

FAULKLAND. Now, Jack, as you are my friend, own honestly; don't you think there is something forward—something indelicate in this haste to forgive? Women should never sue for reconciliation; *that* should *always* come from us. *They* should retain their coldness till *wooed* to kindness; and their *pardon,* like their love, should "not unsought be won."[5]

ABSOLUTE. I have not patience to listen to you—thou'rt incorrigible! so say no more on the subject. I must go to settle a few matters. Let me see you before six—remember—at my lodgings.—A poor industrious devil like me, who have toiled and drudged and plotted to gain my ends, and am at last disappointed by other people's folly—may in pity be allowed to swear and grumble a little;—but a captious sceptic in love—a slave to fretfulness and whim—who has no difficulties but of *his own* creating —is a subject more fit for ridicule than compassion! [*Exit.*

FAULKLAND. I feel his reproaches!—yet I would not change this too exquisite nicety for the gross content with which *he* tramples on the thorns of love.—His engaging me in this duel has started an idea in my head which I will instantly pursue.—I'll use it as the touchstone of Julia's sincerity and disinterestedness. If her love prove pure and sterling ore, my name will rest on it with honor! and once I've stamped it there, I lay aside my doubts for ever. But if the dross of selfishness, the alloy of pride predominate, 'twill be best to leave her as a toy for some less cautious fool to sigh for! [*Exit.*

ACT V

SCENE I. JULIA'S *Dressing-Room*

JULIA, *sola*

JULIA. How this message has alarmed me! What dreadful accident can he mean? why such charge to be alone?—O Faulk-

[5]*Paradise Lost,* VIII, 502–503.

land!—how many unhappy moments!—how many tears, have you cost me!

Enter FAULKLAND, *muffled up in a riding-coat*

JULIA. What means this?—why this caution, Faulkland?

FAULKLAND. Alas! Julia, I am come to take a long farewell.

JULIA. Heav'ns! what do you mean?

FAULKLAND. You see before you a wretch whose life is forfeited. Nay, start not!— the infirmity of my temper has drawn all this misery on me.—I left you fretful and passionate—an untoward accident drew me into a quarrel—the event is, that I must fly this kingdom instantly. O Julia, had I been so fortunate as to have called you mine entirely before this mischance had fallen on me, I should not so deeply dread my banishment!—But no more of that—your heart and promise were given to one happy in friends, character, and station! They are not bound to wait upon a solitary, guilty exile.

JULIA. My soul is oppressed with sorrow at the *nature* of your misfortune. Had these adverse circumstances arisen from a less fatal cause, I should have felt strong comfort in the thought that I could *now* chase from your bosom every doubt of the warm sincerity of my love.—My heart has long known no other guardian—I now entrust my person to your honor—we will fly together. When safe from pursuit, my father's will may be fulfilled—and I receive a legal claim to be the partner of your sorrows and tenderest comforter. Then on the bosom of your wedded Julia, you may lull your keen regret to slumbering, while virtuous love, with a cherub's hand, shall smooth the brow of upbraiding thought, and pluck the thorn from compunction.

FAULKLAND. O Julia, I am bankrupt in gratitude! but the time is so pressing, it calls on you for so hasty a resolution.—Would you not wish some hours to weigh the advantages you forgo, and what little compensation poor Faulkland can make you beside his solitary love?

JULIA. I ask not a moment. No, Faulkland, I have loved you for yourself; and if I now, more than ever, prize the solemn engagement which so long has pledged us to each other, it is because it leaves no room for hard aspersions on my fame and puts the seal of duty to an act of love.—But let us not linger!—Perhaps this delay—

FAULKLAND. 'Twill be better I should not venture out again till dark.—Yet am I grieved to think what numberless distresses will press heavy on your gentle disposition!

JULIA. Perhaps your fortune may be forfeited by this unhappy act.—I know not whether 'tis so, but sure that alone can never make us unhappy. The little I have will be sufficient to *support* us; and *exile* never should be splendid.

FAULKLAND. Aye, but in such an abject state of life, my wounded pride perhaps may increase the natural fretfulness of my temper till I become a rude, morose companion, beyond your patience to endure. Perhaps the recollection of a deed my conscience cannot justify, may haunt me in such gloomy and unsocial fits that I shall hate the tenderness that would relieve me, break from your arms, and quarrel with your fondness!

JULIA. If your thoughts should assume so unhappy a bent, you will the more want some mild and affectionate spirit to watch over and console you—one who, by bearing *your* infirmities with gentleness and resignation, may teach you so to bear the evils of your fortune.

FAULKLAND. O Julia, I have proved you to the quick! and with this useless device I throw away all my doubts. How shall I plead to be forgiven this last unworthy effect of my restless, unsatisfied disposition?

JULIA. Has no such disaster happened as you related?

FAULKLAND. I am ashamed to own that it was pretended; yet in pity, Julia, do not kill me with resenting a fault which never can be repeated; but sealing, this once, my pardon, let me to-morrow, in the face of Heaven, receive my future guide and monitress and expiate my past folly by years of tender adoration.

JULIA. Hold, Faulkland!—that you are free from a crime which I before feared to name, Heaven knows how sincerely I rejoice!—These are tears of thankfulness for that! But that your cruel doubts should have urged you to an imposition that has wrung my heart, gives me now a pang more keen than I can express.

FAULKLAND. By heav'ns, Julia—

JULIA. Yet hear me.—My father loved you, Faulkland! and you preserved the life that tender parent gave me; in his presence I pledged my hand—*joyfully* pledged it— where before I had given my heart. When, soon after, I lost that parent, it seemed to me that Providence had, in Faulkland, shown me whither to transfer, without a pause, my grateful duty as well as my affection; hence I have been content to bear from you what pride and delicacy would have forbid me from another. I will not upbraid you by repeating how you have trifled with my sincerity—

FAULKLAND. I confess it all! yet hear—

JULIA. After such a year of trial, I might have flattered myself that I should not have been insulted with a new probation of my sincerity as cruel as unnecessary—a trick of such a nature, as to show me plainly that when I thought you loved me best, you even then regarded me as a mean dissembler—an artful, prudent hypocrite.

FAULKLAND. Never! never!

JULIA. I now see it is not in your nature to be content or confident in love. With this conviction, I never will be yours. While I had hopes that my persevering attention and unreproaching kindness might in time reform your temper, I should have been happy to have gained a dearer influence over you; but I will not furnish you with a licensed power to keep alive an incorrigible fault, at the expense of one who never would contend with you.

FAULKLAND. Nay, but Julia—by my soul and honor, if after this—

JULIA. But one word more.—As my faith has once been given to you, I never will barter it with another.—I shall pray for your happiness with the truest sincerity, and the dearest blessing I can ask of Heaven to send you will be to charm you from that unhappy temper which alone has prevented the performance of our solemn engagement.—All I request of *you* is, that you will yourself reflect upon this infirmity, and when you number up the many true delights it has deprived you of, let it not be your *least* regret, that it lost you the love of one who would have followed you in beggary through the world!   [*Exit.*

FAULKLAND. She's gone—for ever!— There was an awful resolution in her manner that riveted me to my place.—O fool!—dolt —barbarian! Cursed as I am with more imperfections than my fellow-wretches, kind Fortune sent a heaven-gifted cherub to my aid, and, like a ruffian, I have driven her from my side!—I must now haste to my appointment. Well my mind is tuned for such a scene. I shall wish only to become a principal in it, and reverse the tale my cursed folly put me upon forging here.—O

Love—tormenter—fiend!—whose influence, like the moon's, acting on men of dull souls, makes idiots of them, but meeting subtler spirits, betrays their course, and urges sensibility to madness! [*Exit.*

Enter MAID *and* LYDIA

MAID. My mistress, ma'am, I know, was here just now—perhaps she is only in the next room. [*Exit.*

LYDIA. Heigh-ho! Though he has used me so, this fellow runs strangely in my head. I believe one lecture from my grave cousin will make me recall him.

Enter JULIA

LYDIA. O Julia, I have come to you with such an appetite for consolation.—Lud! child, what's the matter with you? You have been crying!—I'll be hanged, if that Faulkland has not been tormenting you.

JULIA. You mistake the cause of my uneasiness. Something *has* flurried me a little—nothing that you can guess at.—(*Aside*) I would not accuse Faulkland to a sister!

LYDIA. Ah! whatever vexations you may have, I can assure you mine surpass them. You know who Beverley proves to be?

JULIA. I will now own to you, Lydia, that Mr. Faulkland had before informed me of the whole affair. Had young Absolute been the person you took him for, I should not have accepted your confidence on the subject without a serious endeavor to counteract your caprice.

LYDIA. So! then I see I have been deceived by every one! But I don't care—I'll never have him.

JULIA. Nay, Lydia—

LYDIA. Why, is it not provoking, when I thought we were coming to the prettiest distress imaginable, to find myself made a mere Smithfield[1] bargain of at last? There had I projected one of the most sentimental elopements—so becoming a disguise—so amiable a ladder of ropes!—conscious moon—four horses—Scotch parson[2]—with such surprise to Mrs. Malaprop—and such paragraphs in the newspapers!—Oh, I shall die with disappointment!

JULIA. I don't wonder at it!

LYDIA. Now—sad reverse!—what have I to expect but, after a deal of flimsy preparation with a bishop's license and my aunt's blessing, to go simpering up to the altar; or

perhaps be cried three times in a country-church, and have an unmannerly, fat clerk ask the consent of every butcher in the parish to join John Absolute and Lydia Languish, spinster! Oh, that I should live to hear myself called spinster!

JULIA. Melancholy, indeed!

LYDIA. How mortifying, to remember the dear delicious shifts I used to be put to, to gain half a minute's conversation with this fellow!—How often have I stole forth, in the coldest night in January, and found him in the garden, stuck like a dripping statue! There would he kneel to me in the snow, and sneeze and cough so pathetically—he shivering with cold, and I with apprehension! And while the freezing blast numbed our joints, how warmly would he press me to pity his flame, and glow with mutual ardor! —Ah, Julia, that was something like being in love.

JULIA. If I were in spirits, Lydia, I should chide you only by laughing heartily at you; but it suits more the situation of my mind at present earnestly to entreat you not to let a man who loves you with sincerity suffer that unhappiness from your *caprice,* which I know too well caprice can inflict.

LYDIA. O lud! what has brought my aunt here?

Enter MRS. MALAPROP, FAG, *and* DAVID

MRS. MALAPROP. So! so! here's fine work! —here's fine suicide, paracide, and salivation going on in the fields! and Sir Anthony not to be found to prevent the antistrophe!

JULIA. For Heaven's sake, madam, what's the meaning of this?

MRS. MALAPROP. That gentleman can tell you—'twas he enveloped the affair to me.

LYDIA. (*To* FAG) Do, sir, will you inform us?

FAG. Ma'am, I should hold myself very deficient in every requisite that forms the man of breeding if I delayed a moment to give all the information in my power to a lady so deeply interested in the affair as you are.

LYDIA. But quick!—quick, sir!

FAG. True, ma'am, as you say, one should be quick in divulging matters of this nature; for should we be tedious, perhaps while we are flourishing on the subject two or three lives may be lost!

LYDIA. O patience!—do, ma'am, for Heaven's sake! tell us what is the matter.

MRS. MALAPROP. Why, murder's the mat-

[1]Formerly the London cattle-market.
[2]Eloping couples frequently fled to Scotland.

ter! slaughter's the matter! killing's the matter!—but he can tell you the perpendiculars.

LYDIA. Then, prithee, sir, be brief.

FAG. Why, then, ma'am, as to murder—I cannot take upon me to say; and as to slaughter or man-slaughter, that will be as the jury finds it.

LYDIA. But who, sir—who are engaged in this?

FAG. Faith, ma'am, one is a young gentleman whom I should be very sorry anything was to happen to—a very pretty behaved gentleman! We have lived much together, and always on terms.

LYDIA. But who is this?—who? who? who?

FAG. My master, ma'am—my master—I speak of my master.

LYDIA. Heavens! What, Captain Absolute.

MRS. MALAPROP. Oh, to be sure, you are frightened now!

JULIA. But who are with him, sir?

FAG. As to the rest, ma'am, this gentleman can inform you better than I.

JULIA. (*To* DAVID) Do speak, friend.

DAVID. Look'ee, my lady—by the mass! there's mischief going on. Folks don't use to meet for amusement with firearms, firelocks, fire-engines, fire-screens, fire-office, and the devil knows what other crackers beside!—This, my lady, I say, has an angry savor.

JULIA. But who is there beside Captain Absolute, friend?

DAVID. My poor master—under favor for mentioning him first. You know me, my lady—I am David—and my master of course is, or *was,* Squire Acres.—Then comes Squire Faulkland.

JULIA. Do, ma'am, let us instantly endeavor to prevent mischief.

MRS. MALAPROP. O fie! it would be very inelegant in us; we should only participate things.

DAVID. Ah! do, Mrs. Aunt, save a few lives—they are desperately given, believe me.—Above all, there is that bloodthirsty Philistine, Sir Lucius O'Trigger.

MRS. MALAPROP. Sir Lucius O'Trigger? O mercy! have they drawn poor little dear Sir Lucius into the scrape?—Why, how you stand, girl! you have no more feeling than one of the Derbyshire putrefactions!

LYDIA. What are we to do, madam?

MRS. MALAPROP. Why, fly with the utmost felicity, to be sure, to prevent mischief!

—Here, friend, you can show us the place?

FAG. If you please, ma'am, I will conduct you.—David, do you look for Sir Anthony.

[*Exit* DAVID.

MRS. MALAPROP. Come, girls! this gentleman will exhort us.—Come, sir, you're our envoy—lead the way, and we'll precede.

FAG. Not a step before the ladies, for the world!

MRS. MALAPROP. You're sure you know the spot?

FAG. I think I can find it, ma'am; and one good thing is, we shall hear the report of the pistols as we draw near, so we can't well miss them;—never fear, ma'am, never fear.

[*Exeunt, he talking.*

SCENE II. *South Parade*

Enter ABSOLUTE, *putting his sword under his great-coat*

ABSOLUTE. A sword seen in the streets of Bath would raise as great an alarm as a mad dog.—How provoking this is in Faulkland! —never punctual! I shall be obliged to go without him at last.—Oh, the devil! here's Sir Anthony! How shall I escape him?

(*Muffles up his face, and takes a circle to go off*)

Enter SIR ANTHONY

SIR ANTHONY. How one may be deceived at a little distance! Only that I see he don't know me, I could have sworn that was Jack! —Hey! 'Gad's life! it is.—Why, Jack, you dog!—what are you afraid of? Hey—sure I'm right.—Why Jack, Jack Absolute!

(*Goes up to him*)

ABSOLUTE. Really, sir, you have the advantage of me. I don't remember ever to have had the honor—my name is Saunderson, at your service.

SIR ANTHONY. Sir, I beg your pardon— I took you—hey!—why, zounds! it is—Stay —(*Looks up to his face*) So, so—your humble servant, Mr. Saunderson! Why, you scoundrel, what tricks are you after now?

ABSOLUTE. Oh, a joke, sir, a joke! I came here on purpose to look for you, sir.

SIR ANTHONY. You did! well, I am glad you were so lucky. But what are you muffled up so for?—what's this for?—hey?

ABSOLUTE. 'Tis cool, sir, isn't it?—rather chilly somehow.—But I shall be late--I have a particular engagement.

SIR ANTHONY. Stay!—Why, I thought

you were looking for me!—Pray, Jack, where is't you are going?

ABSOLUTE. Going, sir?

SIR ANTHONY. Aye, where are you going?

ABSOLUTE. Where am I going?

SIR ANTHONY. You unmannerly puppy!

ABSOLUTE. I was going, sir, to—to—to—to Lydia—sir, to Lydia—to make matters up if I could—and I was looking for you, sir, to—to—

SIR ANTHONY. To go with you, I suppose.—Well, come along.

ABSOLUTE. Oh! zounds! no, sir, not for the world!—I wished to meet with you, sir, —to—to—to—You find it cool, I'm sure, sir —you'd better not stay out.

SIR ANTHONY. Cool!—not at all.—Well, Jack—and what will you say to Lydia?

ABSOLUTE. Oh, sir, beg her pardon, humor her—promise and vow; but I detain you, sir, —consider the cold air on your gout.

SIR ANTHONY. Oh, not at all!—not at all! I'm in no hurry.—Ah! Jack, you youngsters, when once you are wounded here. (*Putting his hand to* ABSOLUTE'S *breast*) Hey! what the deuce have you got here?

ABSOLUTE. Nothing, sir—nothing.

SIR ANTHONY. What's this?—here's something damned hard.

ABSOLUTE. Oh, trinkets, sir! trinkets!—a bauble for Lydia.

SIR ANTHONY. Nay, let me see your taste. —(*Pulls his coat open; the sword falls*) Trinkets! a bauble for Lydia!—zounds! sirrah, you are not going to cut her throat, are you?

ABSOLUTE. Ha! ha! ha!—I thought it would divert you, sir, though I didn't mean to tell you till afterwards.

SIR ANTHONY. You didn't?—Yes, this is a very diverting trinket, truly!

ABSOLUTE. Sir, I'll explain to you.—You know, sir, Lydia is romantic—dev'lish romantic, and very absurd of course. Now, sir, I intend, if she refuses to forgive me, to unsheath this sword, and swear I'll fall upon its point, and expire at her feet!

SIR ANTHONY. Fall upon fiddlestick's end!—why, I suppose it is the very thing that would please her.—Get along, you fool!

ABSOLUTE. Well, sir, you shall hear of my success—you shall hear.—"O Lydia!—forgive me, or this pointed steel"—says I.

SIR ANTHONY. "O booby! stab away and welcome"—says she.—Get along! and damn your trinkets! [*Exit* ABSOLUTE.

Enter DAVID, *running*

DAVID. Stop him! stop him! Murder! Thief! Fire!—Stop, fire! Stop, fire!—O Sir Anthony—call! call! bid 'em stop! Murder! Fire!

SIR ANTHONY. Fire! Murder!—Where?

DAVID. Oons! he's out of sight, and I'm out of breath for my part. O Sir Anthony, why didn't you stop him? why didn't you stop him?

SIR ANTHONY. Zounds! the fellow's mad! —Stop whom? stop Jack?

DAVID. Aye, the captain, sir!—there's murder and slaughter—

SIR ANTHONY. Murder?

DAVID. Aye, please you, Sir Anthony, there's all kinds of murder, all sorts of slaughter to be seen in the fields; there's fighting going on, sir—bloody sword-and-gun fighting.

SIR ANTHONY. Who are going to fight, dunce?

DAVID. Everybody that I know of, Sir Anthony—everybody is going to fight; my poor master, Sir Lucius O'Trigger, your son, the captain—

SIR ANTHONY. Oh, the dog! I see his tricks.—Do you know the place?

DAVID. King's-Mead-Fields.

SIR ANTHONY. You know the way?

DAVID. Not an inch; but I'll call the mayor—aldermen—constables—church-wardens—and beadles; we can't be too many to part them.

SIR ANTHONY. Come along—give me your shoulder! we'll get assistance as we go —the lying villain!—Well, I shall be in such a frenzy!—So—this was the history of his damned trinkets! I'll bauble him!

[*Exeunt.*

SCENE III. *King's-Mead-Fields*

Enter SIR LUCIUS *and* ACRES, *with pistols*

ACRES. By my valor! then, Sir Lucius, forty yards is a good distance. Odds levels and aims!—I say it is a good distance.

SIR LUCIUS. Is it for muskets or small field-pieces? Upon my conscience, Mr. Acres, you must leave those things to me.— Stay now—I'll show you.—(*Measures paces along the stage*) There now, that is a very pretty distance—a pretty gentleman's distance.

ACRES. Zounds! we might as well fight in a sentry-box! I tell you, Sir Lucius, the farther he is off, the cooler I shall take my aim.

SIR LUCIUS. Faith! then I suppose you would aim at him best of all if he was out of sight!

ACRES. No, Sir Lucius; but I should think forty, or eight and thirty yards—

SIR LUCIUS. Pho! pho! nonsense! three or four feet between the mouths of your pistols is as good as a mile.

ACRES. Odds bullets, no!—by my valor! there is no merit in killing him so near. Do, my dear Sir Lucius, let me bring him down at a long shot!—a long shot, Sir Lucius, if you love me!

SIR LUCIUS. Well—the gentleman's friend and I must settle that.—But tell me now, Mr. Acres; in case of an accident, is there any little will or commission I could execute for you?

ACRES. I am much obliged to you, Sir Lucius, but I don't understand—

SIR LUCIUS. Why, you may think there's no being shot at without a little risk—and if an unlucky bullet should carry a quietus with it—I say it will be no time then to be bothering you about family matters.

ACRES. A quietus!

SIR LUCIUS. For instance, now—if that should be the case—would you choose to be pickled and sent home?—or would it be the same to you to lie here in the Abbey? I'm told there is very snug lying in the Abbey.

ACRES. Pickled!—Snug lying in the Abbey!—Odds tremors! Sir Lucius, don't talk so!

SIR LUCIUS. I suppose, Mr. Acres, you never were engaged in an affair of this kind before?

ACRES. No, Sir Lucius, never before.

SIR LUCIUS. Ah! that's a pity!—there's nothing like being used to a thing. Pray now, how would you receive the gentleman's shot?

ACRES. Odds files!—I've practiced that—there, Sir Lucius—there. (*Puts himself in an attitude*) A side-front, hey? Odd! I'll make myself small enough; I'll stand edge-ways.

SIR LUCIUS. Now—you're quite out—for if you stand so when I take my aim—
(*Leveling at him*)

ACRES. Zounds! Sir Lucius—are you sure it is not cocked?

SIR LUCIUS. Never fear.

ACRES. But—but—you don't know—it may go off of its own head!

SIR LUCIUS. Pho! be easy.—Well, now if I hit you in the body, my bullet has a double chance—for if it misses a vital part of your right side—'twill be very hard if it don't succeed on the left!

ACRES. A vital part! Oh, my poor vitals!

SIR LUCIUS. But, there—fix yourself so —(*Placing him*) Let him see the broad-side of your full front—there!—now a ball or two may pass clean through your body, and never do any harm at all.

ACRES. Clean through me!—a ball or two clean through me!

SIR LUCIUS. Aye—may they—and it is much the genteelest attitude into the bargain.

ACRES. Look'ee! Sir Lucius—I'd just as lieve be shot in an awkward posture as a genteel one; so, by my valor! I will stand edge-ways.

SIR LUCIUS. (*Looking at his watch*) Sure they don't mean to disappoint us—Hah?— no, faith—I think I see them coming.

ACRES. Hey!—what!—coming?—

SIR LUCIUS. Aye.—Who are those yonder getting over the stile?

ACRES. There are two of them, indeed! —Well, let them come—hey, Sir Lucius?— we—we—we—we—won't run.

SIR LUCIUS. Run!

ACRES. No—I say—we *won't* run, by my valor!

SIR LUCIUS. What the devil's the matter with you?

ACRES. Nothing — nothing — my dear friend—my dear Sir Lucius—but I—I—I don't feel quite so bold, somehow, as I did.

SIR LUCIUS. O fie!—consider your honor.

ACRES. Aye—true—my honor. Do, Sir Lucius, edge in a word or two every now and then about my honor.

SIR LUCIUS. (*Looking*) Well, here they're coming.

ACRES. Sir Lucius—if I wa'n't with you, I should almost think I was afraid.—If my valor should leave me!—Valor will come and go.

SIR LUCIUS. Then pray keep it fast while you have it.

ACRES. Sir Lucius—I doubt it is going— yes—my valor is certainly going!—it is sneaking off!—I feel it oozing out as if it were at the palms of my hands!

SIR LUCIUS. Your honor—your honor!— Here they are.

ACRES. O mercy!—now—that I was safe

at Clod Hall! or could be shot before I was aware!

Enter Faulkland *and* Absolute

Sir Lucius. Gentlemen, your most obedient.—Hah!—what—Captain Absolute?—So, I suppose, sir, you are come here, just like myself—to do a kind office, first for your friend—then to proceed to business on your own account.

Acres. What, Jack!—my dear Jack!—my dear friend!

Absolute. Hark'ee, Bob, Beverley's at hand.

Sir Lucius. Well, Mr. Acres—I don't blame your saluting the gentleman civilly.—So, Mr. Beverley, (*To* Faulkland) if you'll choose your weapons, the captain and I will measure the ground.

Faulkland. *My* weapons, sir!

Acres. Odds life! Sir Lucius, I'm not going to fight Mr. Faulkland; these are my particular friends.

Sir Lucius. What, sir, did you not come here to fight Mr. Acres?

Faulkland. Not I, upon my word, sir.

Sir Lucius. Well, now, that's mighty provoking! But I hope, Mr. Faulkland, as there are three of us come on purpose for the game, you won't be so cantankerous as to spoil the party by sitting out.

Absolute. O pray, Faulkland, fight to oblige Sir Lucius.

Faulkland. Nay, if Mr. Acres is so bent on the matter—

Acres. No, no, Mr. Faulkland; I'll bear my disappointment like a Christian.—Look-'ee, Sir Lucius, there's no occasion at all for me to fight; and if it is the same to you, I'd as lieve let it alone.

Sir Lucius. Observe me, Mr. Acres—I must not be trifled with. You have certainly challenged somebody, and you came here to fight him. Now, if that gentleman is willing to represent him, I can't see, for my soul, why it isn't just the same thing.

Acres. Zounds,—Sir Lucius—I tell you, 'tis one Beverley I've challenged—a fellow, you see, that dare not show his face! If *he* were here, I'd make him give up his pretensions directly!

Absolute. Hold, Bob—let me set you right; there is no such man as Beverley in the case.—The person who assumed that name is before you; and as his pretensions are the same in both characters, he is ready to support them in whatever way you please.

Sir Lucius. Well, this is lucky.—Now you have an opportunity—

Acres. What, quarrel with my dear friend, Jack Absolute?—not if he were fifty Beverleys! Zounds! Sir Lucius, you would not have me be so unnatural.

Sir Lucius. Upon my conscience, Mr. Acres, your valor has *oozed* away with a vengeance!

Acres. Not in the least! Odds backs and abettors! I'll be your second with all my heart—and if you should get a quietus, you may command me entirely. I'll get you a "snug lying" in the "Abbey *here*"; or "pickle" you, and send you over to Blunderbuss Hall, or any of the kind, with the greatest pleasure.

Sir Lucius. Pho! pho! you are little better than a coward.

Acres. Mind, gentlemen, he calls me a *coward;* coward was the word, by my valor!

Sir Lucius. Well, sir?

Acres. Look'ee, Sir Lucius; 'tisn't that I mind the word coward—*coward* may be said in joke. But if you had called me a *poltroon,* odds daggers and balls—

Sir Lucius. Well, sir?

Acres. —I should have thought you a very ill-bred man.

Sir Lucius. Pho! you are beneath my notice.

Absolute. Nay, Sir Lucius, you can't have a better second than my friend Acres.—He is a most "determined dog"—called in the country "Fighting Bob."—He generally "kills a man a week"—don't you, Bob?

Acres. Aye—at home!

Sir Lucius. Well, then, captain, 'tis we must begin; so come out, my little counselor—(*Draws his sword*) and ask the gentleman whether he will resign the lady without forcing you to proceed against him.

Absolute. Come on then, sir (*Draws*); since you won't let it be an amicable suit, here's *my reply.*

Enter Sir Anthony, David, *and the*
Women

David. Knock 'em all down, sweet Sir Anthony; knock down my master in particular, and bind his hands over to their good behavior.

Sir Anthony. Put up, Jack, put up, or I shall be in a frenzy.—How came you in a duel, sir?

ABSOLUTE. Faith, sir, that gentleman can tell you better than I; 'twas he called on me, and you know, sir, I serve his Majesty.

SIR ANTHONY. Here's a pretty fellow; I catch him going to cut a man's throat, and he tells me he serves his Majesty!—Zounds! sirrah, then how durst you draw the King's sword against one of his subjects?

ABSOLUTE. Sir! I tell you, that gentleman called me out without explaining his reasons.

SIR ANTHONY. 'Gad!—Sir, how came you to call my son out without explaining your reasons!

SIR LUCIUS. Your son, sir, insulted me in a manner which my honor could not brook.

SIR ANTHONY. Zounds! Jack, how durst you insult the gentleman in a manner which his honor could not brook?

MRS. MALAPROP. Come, come, let's have no honor before ladies.—Captain Absolute, come here; how could you intimidate us so?—Here's Lydia has been terrified to death for you.

ABSOLUTE. For fear I should be killed or escape, ma'am?

MRS. MALAPROP. Nay, no delusions to the past—Lydia is convinced; speak, child.

SIR LUCIUS. With your leave, ma'am, I must put in a word here. I believe I could interpret the young lady's silence—Now mark—

LYDIA. What is it you mean, sir?

SIR LUCIUS. Come, come, Delia, we must be serious now—this is no time for trifling.

LYDIA. 'Tis true, sir; and your reproof bids me offer this gentleman my hand and solicit the return of his affections.

ABSOLUTE. Oh, my little angel, say you so?—Sir Lucius, I perceive there must be some mistake here; with regard to the affront which you affirm I have given you—I can only say that it could not have been intentional. And as you must be convinced that I should not fear to support a real injury—you shall now see that I am not ashamed to atone for an inadvertency. I ask your pardon. But for this lady, while honored with her approbation, I will support my claim against any man whatever.

SIR ANTHONY. Well said, Jack, and I'll stand by you, my boy.

ACRES. Mind, I give up all my claim—I make no pretensions to anything in the world; and if I can't get a wife without fighting for her, by my valor! I'll live a bachelor.

SIR LUCIUS. Captain, give me your hand —an affront handsomely acknowledged becomes an obligation; and as for the lady, if she chooses to deny her own handwriting here—(*Takes out letters*)

MRS. MALAPROP. Oh, he will dissolve my mystery!—Sir Lucius, perhaps there's some mistake; perhaps I can illuminate—

SIR LUCIUS. Pray, old gentlewoman, don't interfere where you have no business—Miss Languish, are you my Delia, or not?

LYDIA. Indeed, Sir Lucius, I am not.

(LYDIA *and* ABSOLUTE *walk aside*)

MRS. MALAPROP. Sir Lucius O'Trigger—ungrateful, as you are, I own the soft impeachment—pardon my blushes, I am Delia.

SIR LUCIUS. You Delia—pho! pho! be easy.

MRS. MALAPROP. Why, thou barbarous Vandyke—those letters are mine. When you are more sensible of my benignity, perhaps I may be brought to encourage your addresses.

SIR LUCIUS. Mrs. Malaprop, I am extremely sensible of your condescension, and whether you or Lucy have put this trick on me, I am equally beholden to you. And to show you I am not ungrateful, Captain Absolute, since you have taken that lady from me, I'll give you my Delia into the bargain.

ABSOLUTE. I am much obliged to you, Sir Lucius; but here's our friend, Fighting Bob, unprovided for.

SIR LUCIUS. Hah! little Valor!—here, will you make your fortune?

ACRES. Odds wrinkles! no!—But give me your hand, Sir Lucius, forget and forgive; but if ever I give you a chance of *pickling* me again, say Bob Acres is a dunce, that's all.

SIR ANTHONY. Come, Mrs. Malaprop, don't be cast down—you are in your bloom yet.

MRS. MALAPROP. O Sir Anthony—men are all barbarians.

(*All retire but* JULIA *and* FAULKLAND)

JULIA. (*Aside*) He seems dejected and unhappy—not sullen; there was some foundation, however, for the tale he told me. O woman! how true should be your judgment, when your resolution is so weak!

FAULKLAND. Julia!—How can I sue for what I so little deserve? I dare not presume —yet Hope is the child of Penitence.

JULIA. Oh! Faulkland, you have not been more faulty in your unkind treatment of me than I am now in wanting inclination to resent it. As my heart honestly bids me place my weakness to the account of love, I should be ungenerous not to admit the same plea for yours.

FAULKLAND. Now I shall be blessed indeed!

(SIR ANTHONY *comes forward*) 5
SIR ANTHONY. What's going on here?—So you have been quarreling too, I warrant. Come, Julia, I never interfered before, but let me have a hand in the matter at last.—All the faults I have ever seen in my friend 10 Faulkland seemed to proceed from what he calls the *delicacy* and *warmth* of his affection for you.—There, marry him directly, Julia; you'll find he'll mend surprisingly!

(*The rest come forward*) 15
SIR LUCIUS. Come, now, I hope there is no dissatisfied person but what is content; for as I have been disappointed myself, it will be very hard if I have not the satisfaction of seeing other people succeed better. 20

ACRES. You are right, Sir Lucius.—So, Jack, I wish you joy.—Mr. Faulkland, the same.—Ladies, come now; to show you I'm neither vexed nor angry, odds tabors and pipes! I'll order the fiddles in half an hour 25 to the New Rooms—and I insist on your all meeting me there.

SIR ANTHONY. 'Gad! sir, I like your spirit; and at night we single lads will drink a health to the young couples and a husband 30 to Mrs. Malaprop.

FAULKLAND. Our partners are stolen from us, Jack—I hope to be congratulated by each other—yours for having checked in time the errors of an ill-directed imagination, which 35 might have betrayed an innocent heart; and mine, for having, by her gentleness and candor, reformed the unhappy temper of one who by it made wretched whom he loved most and tortured the heart he ought to have 40 adored.

ABSOLUTE. Well, Jack,[3] we have both tasted the bitters, as well as the sweets of love—with this difference only, that *you* always prepared the bitter cup for yourself, 45 while I—

LYDIA. Was always obliged to *me* for it—hey, Mr. Modesty?—But come, no more of that—our happiness is now as unalloyed as general. 50

JULIA. Then let us study to preserve it so, and while Hope pictures to us a flattering scene of future bliss, let us deny its pencil those colors which are too bright to be lasting.—When hearts deserving happiness 55 would unite their fortunes, Virtue would

crown them with an unfading garland of modest, hurtless flowers; but ill-judging Passion will force the gaudier rose into the wreath, whose thorn offends them when its leaves are dropped!

[*Exeunt Omnes.*

EPILOGUE

BY THE AUTHOR

Ladies, for *you*—I heard our poet say—
He'd try to coax some *moral* from his play:
"One moral's plain"—cried I—"without more fuss;
Man's social happiness all rests on us;
Through all the drama—whether damned or not, 5
Love gilds the *scene,* and *women* guide the *plot.*
From ev'ry rank obedience is our due—
D'ye doubt?—The world's great stage shall prove it true."
The cit[1]—well skilled to shun domestic strife,
Will sup abroad;—but first—he'll ask his *wife:* 10
John Trot, his friend—for once, will do the same,
But then—he'll just "step home to tell my dame."
The surly squire—at noon resolves to rule
And half the day—zounds! madam is a fool!
Convinced at night, the vanquished victor says, 15
"Ah, Kate! you women have such coaxing ways."
The jolly toper chides each tardy blade,—
Till reeling Bacchus calls on Love for aid:
Then with each toast he sees fair bumpers swim,
And kisses Chloe on the sparkling brim! 20
Nay, I have heard that statesmen—great and wise—
Will *sometimes* counsel with a lady's eyes!
The servile suitors watch her various face, ⎫
She smiles preferment—or she frowns disgrace; ⎬
Curtsies a pension here—there nods a place. 25 ⎭
Nor with less awe, in scenes of humbler life,
Is *viewed* the *mistress,* or is *heard* the *wife.*
The poorest peasant of the poorest soil,

---

[3] I. e., Faulkland.

[1] Citizen.

The child of poverty, and heir to toil,
Early from radiant Love's impartial light   30
Steals one small spark, to cheer his world of
      night;
Dear spark!—that oft through winter's chill-
      ing woes
Is all the warmth his little cottage knows!
      The wandering tar, who not for *years* has
      pressed
The widowed partner of his *day* of rest,   35
On the cold deck—far from her arms re-
      moved,
Still hums the ditty which his Susan loved;
And while around the cadence rude is blown,
The boatswain whistles in a softer tone.
      The soldier, fairly proud of wounds and
      toil,   40
Pants for the *triumph* of his Nancy's smile!
But ere the battle should he list her cries
The lover trembles—and the hero dies!

That heart, by war and honor steeled to fear,
Droops on a sigh and sickens at a tear!   45
      But ye more cautious—ye nice judging
      few,
Who give to Beauty only Beauty's due,
Though friends to Love—*ye* view with deep
      regret
Our conquests marred, our triumphs incom-
      plete,
Till polished wit more lasting charms dis-
      close,   50
And Judgment fix the darts which Beauty
      throws!
In female breasts did Sense and Merit rule,
The lover's mind would ask no other school;
Shamed into sense—the scholars of our eyes,
Our beaux from *gallantry* would soon be
      wise;   55
Would gladly light, their homage to improve,
The lamp of knowledge at the torch of Love!

WILLIAM COWPER
1731-1800

Cowper was born on 15 November, 1731. His father was the Reverend John Cowper, Rector of Great Berkhampstead and Chaplain to George II; his mother was Ann Donne Cowper, probably a descendant of the poet and divine, John Donne. When he was seven years old Cowper was sent to a school kept by a Dr. Pitman, but after two years he had to withdraw on account of trouble with his eyes. Later, in 1741, he was sent to Westminster School, where he remained until 1748. Some of his schoolfellows were George Colman, Robert Lloyd, Charles Churchill, R. Cumberland, Warren Hastings, and Elijah Impey. The first three of these were among his close friends, as was also one of the masters, Vincent Bourne, whose poetry was later to exert a strong influence on that of his pupil. As late as 1781 Cowper wrote, "I love the memory of Vinny Bourne. I think him a better Latin poet than Tibullus, Propertius, Ausonius, or any of the writers in *his* way, except Ovid, and not at all inferior to *him*. . . . He was so good-natured, and so indolent, that I lost more than I got by him; for he made me as idle as himself. He was such a sloven, as if he had trusted to his genius as a cloak for everything that could disgust you in his person; and indeed in his writings he has almost made amends for all." Some months after he left Westminster Cowper was articled to a solicitor in London, where a fellow law-clerk was Edward Thurlow, later Lord Chancellor. Cowper says that while ostensibly studying the law he spent his days chiefly "in giggling and making giggle" with his two cousins, daughters of his uncle Ashley Cowper. With one of them, Theodora, he fell in love, but the girl's father would not permit an engagement. In 1752 Cowper went to live in the Middle Temple, and in 1754 he was called to the bar. He made no attempt, however, to practice the law, but lived rather aimlessly, doing some literary work and disporting himself with fellow-members of the Nonsense Club. In 1763 Cowper was nominated Clerk of the Journals of the House of Lords by his cousin Major Cowper,

who had the disposal of the office. For some years Cowper had been more or less subject to melancholy, and evidently at this time his mind was unable to stand excitement. Owing to some dispute over his nomination to the clerkship it was necessary for Cowper to appear before the bar of the House of Lords, and the prospect of this ordeal was too much for him. He broke down, made several attempts at suicide, and finally became insane, so that he had to be removed by his brother to an asylum, where he remained until June, 1765. Cowper's attacks of melancholy were apparently connected with religious emotions and fears which gradually increased in strength, and his madness took the form of a conviction that he was eternally damned in punishment for some sin. By the summer of 1765 he had completely recovered his sanity, but through the remainder of his life he was subject to attacks of deep melancholy which several times brought temporary returns of insanity; and during his last six or seven years he scarcely ever emerged from the black terrors conjured up by his troubled mind. Cowper spent the rest of his life in quiet country villages, living first at Huntingdon, then at Olney, later at Weston, and finally with his cousin John Johnson at East Dereham in Norfolk, where he died on 25 April, 1800, and where he was buried. During the greater number of these years Cowper was surrounded by good friends, without whose society, encouragement, and help his poetry never would have been written and his life, in all probability, would have been a complete wreck. Chief among these were Mrs. Unwin, from whom he was never separated from 1765 until her death in 1796, and whom he would have married had it not been for his third attack of madness (brought on, perhaps, by the mistaken religious zeal of his friend, the Rev. John Newton, early in 1773); Lady Austen who first met him in 1781, who became strongly attached to him for a time and probably wanted to marry him; and his cousin Lady Hesketh, sister of the Theodora Cowper whom he had loved in his youth.

After 1765 Cowper's mental health demanded that he have a settled occupation of some kind. The more busily he was occupied in some congenial pursuit the less was the danger of renewed insanity. Gardening served his turn, as did carpentry for a while, then drawing—he drew, he says, "many figures . . . which had, at least, the merit of being unparalleled by any production either of art or nature"—and finally poetry. He was turned to poetry by Mrs. Unwin, and he did some of his best work as the result of suggestions made by Lady Austen. He says himself, "I have no more right to the name of a poet than a maker of mouse-traps has to that of an engineer; but my little exploits in this way have at times amused me so much that I have often wished myself a good one. Such a talent in verse as mine is like a child's rattle—very entertaining to the trifler that uses it, and very disagreeable to all beside. But it has served to rid me of some melancholy moments, for I only take it up as a gentleman performer does his fiddle." And again, "Swift's darling motto was, *Vive la bagatelle*. . . . *La bagatelle* has no enemy in me, though it has neither so warm a friend nor so able a one as it had in him. If I trifle, and merely trifle, it is because I am reduced to it by necessity—a melancholy, that nothing else so effectually disperses, engages me sometimes in the arduous task of being merry by force. And, strange as it may seem, the most ludicrous lines I ever wrote have been written in the saddest mood, and, but for that saddest mood, perhaps had never been written at all. To say truth, it would be but a shocking vagary, should the mariners on board a ship buffeted by a terrible storm employ themselves in fiddling and dancing; yet sometimes much such a part act I." Nevertheless, writing thus for amusement and distraction often on subjects that came to him from others, Cowper "finished, and polished, and touched, and retouched, with the utmost care." And it has been well said of him that "no truer poet . . . ever wrote the English language. He did greater things than he knew. . . . Neither fancy, nor learning, nor philosophy came between him and his object. His creed does occasionally; his sympathetic tenderness always. Otherwise it is the thing itself, river, tree, or hill, that he gives us in naked simplicity. That simplicity was the central element in his character, and it is the secret both of what he confessed and of what he discovered. The perfectly simple can ask questions and reveal facts which no one else can reveal or ask. So it was with Cowper. He takes up his pen to amuse himself, to describe his walks, and his friends, and his garden, and his pets, and in the result finds himself, as it were by accident, a great poet, and a poet of a new order. He, more than anyone else, discovered that a man may be himself, and may tell the plain truth, and yet be a poet" (J. C. Bailey, Introduction to Cowper's *Poems*).

The Complete Poetical Works of William Cowper have been well edited by H. S. Milford (Oxford, 1905). The most complete and authoritative edition of *The Correspondence of William Cowper,* ed. Thomas Wright (London, 1904), is unfortunately marred by inaccuracies. An excellent and charming selection has been edited by Sir James George Frazer, *Letters of William Cowper* (2 vols., London, 1912). *William Cowper and the Eighteenth Century,* by Gilbert Thomas (1935), is a very good biographical and historical study. Lord David Cecil's life of Cowper, *The Stricken Deer* (1929), is agreeably written.

THE DIVERTING HISTORY OF JOHN GILPIN,

Showing How He Went Farther Than He Intended, and Came Safe Home Again[1]

John Gilpin was a citizen
  Of credit and renown,
A train-band captain eke was he
  Of famous London town.

John Gilpin's spouse said to her dear—   5
  Though wedded we have been

These twice ten tedious years, yet we
  No holiday have seen.

To-morrow is our wedding-day,
  And we will then repair   10
Unto the Bell at Edmonton
  All in a chaise and pair.

My sister, and my sister's child,
  Myself, and children three,
Will fill the chaise; so you must ride   15
  On horseback after we.

[1]First published anonymously in a newspaper (1782); later, having become popular, republished under Cowper's name in the same volume as *The Task* (1785).

He soon replied—I do admire
  Of woman kind but one,
And you are she, my dearest dear,
  Therefore it shall be done. 20

I am a linen-draper bold,
  As all the world doth know,
And my good friend the calender[2]
  Will lend his horse to go.

Quoth Mrs. Gilpin—That's well said; 25
  And, for that wine is dear,
We will be furnished with our own,
  Which is both bright and clear.

John Gilpin kissed his loving wife;
  O'erjoyed was he to find 30
That, though on pleasure she was bent,
  She had a frugal mind.

The morning came, the chaise was brought,
  But yet was not allowed
To drive up to the door, lest all 35
  Should say that she was proud.

So three doors off the chaise was stayed,
  Where they did all get in;
Six precious souls, and all agog
  To dash through thick and thin! 40

Smack went the whip, round went the
    wheels,
  Were never folk so glad,
The stones did rattle underneath,
  As if Cheapside were mad.

John Gilpin at his horse's side 45
  Seized fast the flowing mane,
And up he got, in haste to ride,
  But soon came down again;

For saddle-tree scarce reached had he,
  His journey to begin, 50
When, turning round his head, he saw
  Three customers come in.

So down he came; for loss of time,
  Although it grieved him sore,
Yet loss of pence, full well he knew, 55
  Would trouble him much more.

'Twas long before the customers
  Were suited to their mind,
When Betty screaming came down stairs—
  "The wine is left behind!" 60

Good lack! quoth he—yet bring it me,
  My leathern belt likewise,
In which I bear my trusty sword
  When I do exercise.

Now mistress Gilpin (careful soul!) 65
  Had two stone bottles found,
To hold the liquor that she loved,
  And keep it safe and sound.

Each bottle had a curling ear,
  Through which the belt he drew, 70
And hung a bottle on each side,
  To make his balance true.

Then, over all, that he might be
  Equipped from top to toe,
His long red cloak, well brushed and neat, 75
  He manfully did throw.

Now see him mounted once again
  Upon his nimble steed,
Full slowly pacing o'er the stones,
  With caution and good heed! 80

But, finding soon a smoother road
  Beneath his well-shod feet,
The snorting beast began to trot,
  Which galled him in his seat.

So, Fair and softly, John he cried, 85
  But John he cried in vain;
That trot became a gallop soon,
  In spite of curb and rein.

So stooping down, as needs he must
  Who cannot sit upright, 90
He grasped the mane with both his hands,
  And eke with all his might.

His horse, who never in that sort
  Had handled been before,
What thing upon his back had got 95
  Did wonder more and more.

Away went Gilpin, neck or nought;[3]
  Away went hat and wig!—
He little dreamt, when he set out,
  Of running such a rig![4] 100

The wind did blow, the cloak did fly,
  Like streamer long and gay,
Till, loop and button failing both,
  At last it flew away.

[2]One who rolls cloth.

[3]Ready for all risks.
[4]Of playing such pranks.

Then might all people well discern 105
  The bottles he had slung;
A bottle swinging at each side,
  As hath been said or sung.

The dogs did bark, the children screamed,
  Up flew the windows all; 110
And ev'ry soul cried out—Well done!
  As loud as he could bawl.

Away went Gilpin—who but he?
  His fame soon spread around—
He carries weight! he rides a race! 115
  'Tis for a thousand pound!

And still, as fast as he drew near,
  'Twas wonderful to view
How in a trice the turnpike-men
  Their gates wide open threw. 120

And now, as he went bowing down
  His reeking head full low,
The bottles twain behind his back
  Were shattered at a blow.

Down ran the wine into the road, 125
  Most piteous to be seen,
Which made his horse's flanks to smoke
  As they had basted been.

But still he seemed to carry weight,
  With leathern girdle braced; 130
For all might see the bottle-necks
  Still dangling at his waist.

Thus all through merry Islington
  These gambols he did play,
And till he came unto the Wash⁵ 135
  Of Edmonton so gay.

And there he threw the wash about
  On both sides of the way,
Just like unto a trundling mop,
  Or a wild goose at play. 140

At Edmonton his loving wife
  From the balcony spied
Her tender husband, wond'ring much
  To see how he did ride.

Stop, stop, John Gilpin!—Here's the house— 145
  They all at once did cry;
The dinner waits, and we are tir'd:
  Said Gilpin—So am I!

⁵Pool.

But yet his horse was not a whit
  Inclined to tarry there; 150
For why?—his owner had a house
  Full ten miles off, at Ware.

So like an arrow swift he flew,
  Shot by an archer strong;
So did he fly—which brings me to 155
  The middle of my song.

Away went Gilpin, out of breath,
  And sore against his will,
Till at his friend the calender's
  His horse at last stood still. 160

The calender, amazed to see
  His neighbor in such trim,
Laid down his pipe, flew to the gate,
  And thus accosted him:—

What news? what news? your tidings tell; 165
  Tell me you must and shall—
Say why bare-headed you are come,
  Or why you come at all?

Now Gilpin had a pleasant wit,
  And loved a timely joke; 170
And thus unto the calender
  In merry guise he spoke:—

I came because your horse would come;
  And, if I well forebode,
My hat and wig will soon be here— 175
  They are upon the road.

The calender, right glad to find
  His friend in merry pin,⁶
Returned him not a single word,
  But to the house went in; 180

Whence straight he came with hat and wig;
  A wig that flowed behind,
A hat not much the worse for wear,
  Each comely in its kind.

He held them up, and, in his turn, 185
  Thus showed his ready wit—
My head is twice as big as yours,
  They therefore needs must fit.

But let me scrape the dirt away
  That hangs upon your face; 190
And stop and eat, for well you may
  Be in a hungry case.

⁶Humor.

Away went Gilpin, neck or nought;
Away went hat and wig!—
He little dreamt, when he set out,
Of running such a rig!

Stop, stop, John Gilpin!—Here's the
house—
They all at once did cry;
The dinner waits, and we are tir'd:
Said Gilpin—So am I!

Ah, luckless speech, and bootless boast!
For which he paid full dear;
For, while he spake, a braying ass
Did sing most loud and clear.

And now the turnpike gates again
Flew open in short space;
The toll-men thinking, as before,
That Gilpin rode a race.

George Cruikshank (1792–1878) made six drawings for an edition of William Cowper's *Diverting History of John Gilpin* (1836). These were engraved on wood for reproduction in the book, and four are printed above. (Courtesy of the New York Public Library.) Thackeray, in his essay on Cruikshank, exclaimed over the famous artist's "amazing energetic fecundity." He worked like a demon, and illustrated nearly everything under the sun, including some of Dickens's books and the most famous novels of the eighteenth century. Thackeray has explained his success as well as anybody. "Living amongst the public," he wrote, Cruikshank "has a general wide-hearted sympathy with them, and laughs at what they laugh at; he has a kindly spirit of enjoyment, with not a morsel of mysticism in his composition; he pities and loves the poor, and jokes at the follies of the great, and addresses all in a perfectly sincere and manly way. He is greatly successful as a professional humorist because he is quite honest and shows that his heart is in his work."

WILLIE BREW'D A PECK O' MAUT

It is the moon, I ken her horn,
That's blinkin' in the lift sae hie.

TAM O' SHANTER

The landlady and Tam grew gracious,
Wi' favors secret, sweet, and precious.

JOHN ANDERSON MY JO

But now your brow is beld, John,
Your locks are like the snow.

DUNCAN GRAY

Duncan fleeched, and Duncan prayed;
Ha, ha, the wooing o't.

POEMS,

CHIEFLY IN THE

SCOTTISH DIALECT,

BY

ROBERT BURNS.

THE Simple Bard, unbroke by rules of Art,
He pours the wild effusions of the heart:
And if infpir'd, 'tis Nature's pow'rs infpire;
Her's all the melting thrill, and her's the kindling fire.

ANONYMOUS.

KILMARNOCK:
PRINTED BY JOHN WILSON.

M,DCC,LXXXVI.

The four illustrations on this page are taken from an early nineteenth-century edition of Burns's poetry—"The Entire Works of Robert Burns; with an Account of His Life, and a Criticism on His Writings. To Which are Prefixed, Some Observations on the Character and Condition of the Scottish Peasantry. By James Currie, M.D. Embellished with fourteen illustrations from Original Designs by Mr. Stewart." The title-page reproduced here is that of the Kilmarnock edition of Burns's poems (1786). Burns published this book to raise money for a voyage to Jamaica, where he hoped to be more successful in making a living than he had been in Scotland. He won instant fame, and for a second edition he was paid enough to enable him to remain in Scotland. (Courtesy of the New York Public Library.)

Said John—It is my wedding-day,
  And all the world would stare,
If wife should dine at Edmonton   195
  And I should dine at Ware!

So, turning to his horse, he said—
  I am in haste to dine;
'Twas for your pleasure you came here,
  You shall go back for mine.   200

Ah, luckless speech, and bootless boast!
  For which he paid full dear;
For, while he spake, a braying ass
  Did sing most loud and clear;

Whereat his horse did snort, as he   205
  Had heard a lion roar,
And galloped off with all his might,
  As he had done before.

Away went Gilpin, and away
  Went Gilpin's hat and wig!   210
He lost them sooner than at first—
  For why?—they were too big!

Now, mistress Gilpin, when she saw
  Her husband posting down
Into the country far away,   215
  She pulled out half a crown;[7]

And thus unto the youth she said
  That drove them to the Bell—
This shall be yours when you bring back
  My husband safe and well.   220

The youth did ride, and soon did meet
  John coming back amain;

Whom in a trice he tried to stop,
  By catching at his rein;

But, not performing what he meant,   225
  And gladly would have done,
The frighted steed he frighted more,
  And made him faster run.

Away went Gilpin, and away
  Went post-boy at his heels!—   230
The post-boy's horse right glad to miss
  The lumb'ring of the wheels.

Six gentlemen upon the road,
  Thus seeing Gilpin fly,
The post-boy scamp'ring in the rear,   235
  They raised the hue and cry:

Stop thief! stop thief!—a highwayman!
  Not one of them was mute;
And all and each that passed that way
  Did join in the pursuit.   240

And now the turnpike gates again
  Flew open in short space;
The toll-men thinking, as before,
  That Gilpin rode a race.

And so he did—and won it too!—   245
  For he got first to town;
Nor stopped till where he had got up
  He did again get down.

Now let us sing—Long live the king,
  And Gilpin long live he;   250
And, when he next doth ride abroad,
  May I be there to see!

THE TASK[1]

BOOK I

The Sofa

ARGUMENT OF THE FIRST BOOK.—Historical deduction of seats, from the stool to the Sofa —A School-boy's ramble—A walk in the country—The scene described—Rural sounds as well as sights delightful—Another walk— Mistake concerning the charms of solitude corrected—Colonnades commended—Alcove, and the view from it—The wilderness—The grove—The thresher—The necessity and the benefits of exercise—The works of nature

superior to, and in some instances inimitable by, art—The wearisomeness of what is commonly called a life of pleasure—Change of scene sometimes expedient—A common described, and the character of crazy Kate introduced—Gypsies—The blessings of civilized life—That state most favorable to virtue—

---

[7] A crown was worth five shillings.

[1] "The history of the following production is briefly this:—A lady, fond of blank verse, demanded a poem of that kind from the author, and gave him

the SOFA for a subject. He obeyed; and, having much leisure, connected another subject with it; and, pursuing the train of thought to which his situation and turn of mind led him, brought forth at length, instead of the trifle which he at first intended, a serious affair—a Volume!" (Cowper's "Advertisement," prefixed to the first edition of *The Task*.) The lady was Lady Austen, and Cowper began writing it probably in July, 1783. The complete poem, of which only the first book is here printed, consists of six books. It was published in 1785, in a volume containing also three shorter poems.

The South Sea islanders compassionated, but chiefly Omai—His present state of mind supposed—Civilized life friendly to virtue, but not great cities—Great cities, and London in particular, allowed their due praise, but censured—*Fête champêtre*—The book concludes with a reflection on the fatal effects of dissipation and effeminacy upon our public measures.

I sing the Sofa.   I, who lately sang
Truth, Hope, and Charity,[2] and touched with awe
The solemn chords, and with a trembling hand,
Escaped with pain from that advent'rous flight,
Now seek repose upon an humbler theme; 5
The theme though humble, yet august and proud
Th' occasion—for the Fair commands the song.
    Time was, when clothing sumptuous or for use,
Save their own painted skins, our sires had none.
As yet black breeches were not; satin smooth, 10
Or velvet soft, or plush with shaggy pile:
The hardy chief upon the rugged rock
Washed by the sea, or on the gravelly bank
Thrown up by wintry torrents roaring loud,
Fearless of wrong, reposed his weary strength. 15
Those barb'rous ages past, succeeded next
The birth-day of invention; weak at first,
Dull in design, and clumsy to perform.
Joint-stools were then created; on three legs
Upborne they stood.   Three legs upholding firm 20
A massy slab, in fashion square or round.
On such a stool immortal Alfred sat,
And swayed the scepter of his infant realms:
And such in ancient halls and mansions drear
May still be seen; but perforated sore, 25
And drilled in holes, the solid oak is found,
By worms voracious eating through and through.
    At length a generation more refined
Improved the simple plan; made three legs four,
Gave them a twisted form vermicular, 30
And o'er the seat, with plenteous wadding stuffed,
Induced a splendid cover, green and blue,

Yellow and red, of tap'stry richly wrought,
And woven close, or needle-work sublime.
There might ye see the peony spread wide, 35
The full-blown rose, the shepherd and his lass,
Lap-dog and lambkin with black staring eyes,
And parrots with twin cherries in their beak.
    Now came the cane from India, smooth and bright
With nature's varnish; severed into stripes 40
That interlaced each other, these supplied
Of texture firm a lattice-work, that braced
The new machine, and it became a chair.
But restless was the chair; the back erect
Distressed the weary loins, that felt no ease; 45
The slipp'ry seat betrayed the sliding part
That pressed it, and the feet hung dangling down,
Anxious in vain to find the distant floor.
These for the rich: the rest, whom fate had placed
In modest mediocrity, content 50
With base materials, sat on well-tanned hides,
Obdurate and unyielding, glassy smooth,
With here and there a tuft of crimson yarn,
Or scarlet crewel,[3] in the cushion fixed;
If cushion might be called, what harder seemed 55
Than the firm oak of which the frame was formed.
No want of timber then was felt or feared
In Albion's happy isle.   The lumber stood
Pond'rous and fixed by its own massy weight.
But elbows still were wanting; these, some say, 60
An alderman of Cripplegate contrived:
And some ascribe th' invention to a priest
Burly and big, and studious of his ease.
But, rude at first, and not with easy slope
Receding wide, they pressed against the ribs,
And bruised the side; and, elevated high, 66
Taught the raised shoulders to invade the ears.
Long time elapsed or e'er our rugged sires
Complained, though incommodiously pent in,
And ill at ease behind.   The ladies first 70
'Gan murmur, as became the softer sex.
Ingenious fancy, never better pleased
Than when employed t' accommodate the fair,
Heard the sweet moan with pity, and devised
The soft settee; one elbow at each end, 75
And in the midst an elbow it received,
United yet divided, twain at once.

---

[2]Titles of three of the pieces in Cowper's first volume of poems, published in 1782.

[3]Worsted yarn slackly twisted or, as here, knotted.

So sit two kings of Brentford[4] on one
   throne;
And so two citizens who take the air,
Close packed, and smiling, in a chaise and
   one.   80
But relaxation of the languid frame,
By soft recumbency of outstretched limbs,
Was bliss reserved for happier days. So
  slow
The growth of what is excellent; so hard
T' attain perfection in this nether world.   85
Thus first necessity invented stools,
Convenience next suggested elbow-chairs,
And luxury th' accomplished SOFA last.
   The nurse sleeps sweetly, hired to watch
   the sick,   89
Whom snoring she disturbs. As sweetly he,
Who quits the coach-box at the midnight
  hour
To sleep within the carriage more secure,
His legs depending at the open door.
Sweet sleep enjoys the curate in his desk,
The tedious rector drawling o'er his head; 95
And sweet the clerk below. But neither
  sleep
Of lazy nurse, who snores the sick man dead,
Nor his who quits the box at midnight hour
To slumber in the carriage more secure,
Nor sleep enjoyed by curate in his desk,   100
Nor yet the dozings of the clerk, are sweet,
Compared with the repose the SOFA yields.
   Oh, may I live exempted (while I live
Guiltless of pampered appetite obscene)
From pangs arthritic that infest the toe   105
Of libertine excess. The SOFA suits
The gouty limb, 'tis true; but gouty limb,
Though on a SOFA, may I never feel:
For I have loved the rural walk through
  lanes
Of grassy swarth, close cropped by nibbling
  sheep,   110
And skirted thick with intertexture firm
Of thorny boughs; have loved the rural walk
O'er hills, through valleys, and by rivers'
  brink,
E'er since a truant boy I passed my bounds
T' enjoy a ramble on the banks of Thames;
And still remember, nor without regret   116
Of hours that sorrow since has much en-
  deared,
How oft, my slice of pocket store consumed,
Still hung'ring, penniless and far from home,
I fed on scarlet hips and stony haws,   120

Or blushing crabs,[5] or berries, that emboss
The bramble, black as jet, or sloes[6] austere.
Hard fare! but such as boyish appetite
Disdains not; nor the palate, undepraved
By culinary arts, unsav'ry deems.   125
No SOFA then awaited my return;
Nor SOFA then I needed. Youth repairs
His wasted spirits quickly, by long toil
Incurring short fatigue; and, though our
  years
As life declines speed rapidly away,   130
And not a year but pilfers as he goes
Some youthful grace that age would gladly
  keep;
A tooth or auburn lock, and by degrees
Their length and color from the locks they
  spare;
Th' elastic spring of an unwearied foot 135
That mounts the stile with ease, or leaps the
  fence,
That play of lungs, inhaling and again
Respiring freely the fresh air, that makes
Swift pace or steep ascent no toil to me,
Mine have not pilfered yet; nor yet im-
  paired   140
My relish of fair prospect; scenes that
  soothed
Or charmed me young, no longer young, I
  find
Still soothing and of pow'r to charm me still.
And witness, dear companion of my walks,[7]
Whose arm this twentieth winter I perceive
Fast locked in mine, with pleasure such as
  love,   146
Confirmed by long experience of thy worth
And well-tried virtues, could alone inspire—
Witness a joy that thou hast doubled long.
Thou know'st my praise of nature most
  sincere,   150
And that my raptures are not conjured up
To serve occasions of poetic pomp,
But genuine, and art partner of them all.
How oft upon yon eminence our pace
Has slackened to a pause, and we have borne
The ruffling wind, scarce conscious that it
  blew,   156
While admiration, feeding at the eye,
And still unsated, dwelt upon the scene.
Thence with what pleasure have we just dis-
  cerned
The distant plow slow moving, and beside
His lab'ring team, that swerved not from
  the track,   161

---

[4]Characters who appear together on one throne in
the Duke of Buckingham's satiric drama, *The Rehearsal* (1671).

---

[5]Hip, ripened fruit of rosebush; haw, fruit of
hawthorn; crab, crab-apple.

[6]Fruit of the blackthorn.

[7]Mrs. Unwin.

ly swain diminished to a boy!
se, slow winding through a level

is meads with cattle sprinkled o'er,
the eye along its sinuous course 165
Delighted. There, fast rooted in his bank,
Stand, never overlooked, our fav'rite elms,
That screen the herdsman's solitary hut;
While far beyond, and overthwart the stream
That, as with molten glass, inlays the vale, 170
The sloping land recedes into the clouds;
Displaying on its varied side the grace
Of hedge-row beauties numberless, square tow'r,
Tall spire, from which the sound of cheerful bells
Just undulates upon the list'ning ear, 175
Groves, heaths, and smoking villages remote.
Scenes must be beautiful, which, daily viewed,
Please daily, and whose novelty survives
Long knowledge and the scrutiny of years.
Praise justly due to those that I describe.[8] 180
Nor rural sights alone, but rural sounds,
Exhilarate the spirit, and restore
The tone of languid nature. Mighty winds,
That sweep the skirt of some far-spreading wood
Of ancient growth, make music not unlike 185
The dash of ocean on his winding shore,
And lull the spirit while they fill the mind;
Unnumbered branches waving in the blast,
And all their leaves fast flutt'ring, all at once.
Nor less composure waits upon the roar 190
Of distant floods, or on the softer voice
Of neighb'ring fountain, or of rills that slip
Through the cleft rock, and, chiming as they fall
Upon loose pebbles, lose themselves at length
In matted grass, that with a livelier green 195
Betrays the secret of their silent course.
Nature inanimate employs sweet sounds,
But animated nature sweeter still,
To soothe and satisfy the human ear.
Ten thousand warblers cheer the day, and one 200
The livelong night: nor these alone, whose notes
Nice fingered art must emulate in vain,
But cawing rooks, and kites that swim sublime
In still repeated circles, screaming loud,

The jay, the pie,[9] and e'en the boding owl 205
That hails the rising moon, have charms for me.
Sounds inharmonious in themselves and harsh,
Yet heard in scenes where peace for ever reigns,
And only there, please highly for their sake.
Peace to the artist, whose ingenious thought 210
Devised the weather-house,[10] that useful toy!
Fearless of humid air and gathering rains,
Forth steps the man—an emblem of myself!
More delicate, his tim'rous mate retires.
When Winter soaks the fields, and female feet, 215
Too weak to struggle with tenacious clay,
Or ford the rivulets, are best at home,
The task of new discov'ries falls on me.
At such a season, and with such a charge,
Once went I forth: and found, till then unknown, 220
A cottage, whither oft we since repair:
'Tis perched upon the green-hill top, but, close
Environed with a ring of branching elms
That overhang the thatch, itself unseen,
Peeps at the vale below; so thick beset 225
With foliage of such dark redundant growth,
I called the low-roofed lodge the *peasant's nest.*
And, hidden as it is, and far remote
From such unpleasing sounds as haunt the ear
In village or in town, the bay of curs 230
Incessant, clinking hammers, grinding wheels,
And infants clam'rous whether pleased or pained,
Oft have I wished the peaceful covert mine.
Here, I have said, at least I should possess
The poet's treasure, silence, and indulge 235
The dreams of fancy, tranquil and secure.
Vain thought! the dweller in that still retreat
Dearly obtains the refuge it affords.
Its elevated site forbids the wretch
To drink sweet waters of the crystal well; 240
He dips his bowl into the weedy ditch,
And, heavy-laden, brings his bev'rage home,
Far-fetched and little worth; nor seldom waits,
Dependent on the baker's punctual call,

[9]Magpie.

[10]A substitute for the barometer, still occasionally to be seen. It is so contrived that the figure of a man comes forward when bad weather is to be expected, and that of a woman when good.

[8]The scenes described are those encountered in a walk from Olney to Weston.

To hear his creaking panniers at the door, 245
Angry and sad, and his last crust consumed.
So farewell envy of the *peasant's nest!*
If solitude make scant the means of life,
Society for me!—thou seeming sweet,
Be still a pleasing object in my view; 250
My visit still, but never mine abode.

Not distant far, a length of colonnade
Invites us: monument of ancient taste,
Now scorned, but worthy of a better fate.
Our fathers knew the value of a screen 255
From sultry suns; and, in their shaded walks
And long protracted bow'rs, enjoyed at noon
The gloom and coolness of declining day.
We bear our shades about us; self-deprived
Of other screen, the thin umbrella spread, 260
And range an Indian waste without a tree.
Thanks to Benevolus[11]—he spares me yet
These chestnuts ranged in corresponding
    lines;
And, though himself so polished, still re-
    prieves
The obsolete prolixity of shade. 265
    Descending now (but cautious, lest too
    fast)
A sudden steep, upon a rustic bridge
We pass a gulf, in which the willows dip
Their pendent boughs, stooping as if to drink.
Hence, ankle-deep in moss and flow'ry
    thyme, 270
We mount again, and feel at ev'ry step
Our foot half sunk in hillocks green and
    soft,
Raised by the mole, the miner of the soil.
He, not unlike the great ones of mankind,
Disfigures earth; and, plotting in the
    dark, 275
Toils much to earn a monumental pile,
That may record the mischiefs he has done.
    The summit gained, behold the proud
    alcove
That crowns it! yet not all its pride secures
The grand retreat from injuries impressed 280
By rural carvers, who with knives deface
The pannels, leaving an obscure, rude name,
In characters uncouth, and spelled amiss.
So strong the zeal t' immortalize himself 284
Beats in the breast of man, that e'en a few,
Few transient years, won from th' abyss
    abhorred
Of blank oblivion, seem a glorious prize,
And even to a clown.[12] Now roves the eye;
And, posted on this speculative height, 289
Exults in its command. The sheepfold here

[11]John Courtney Throckmorton, Esq., of Weston
Underwood (Cowper's note).
[12]Countryman.

Pours out its fleecy tenants o'er the glel.
At first, progressive as a stream, they seek
The middle field; but, scattered by degrees,
Each to his choice, soon whiten all the land.
There from the sunburned hay-field home-
    ward creeps 295
The loaded wain, while, lightened of its
    charge,
The wain that meets it passes swiftly by,
The boorish driver leaning o'er his team
Vocif'rous, and impatient of delay.
Nor less attractive is the woodland scene, 300
Diversified with trees of ev'ry growth,
Alike, yet various. Here the gray smooth
    trunks
Of ash, or lime, or beech, distinctly shine,
Within the twilight of their distant shades;
There, lost behind a rising ground, the wood
Seems sunk, and shortened to its topmost
    boughs. 306
No tree in all the grove but has its charms,
Though each its hue peculiar; paler some,
And of a wannish gray; the willow such,
And poplar, that with silver lines his leaf, 310
And ash far-stretching his umbrageous arm;
Of deeper green the elm; and deeper still,
Lord of the woods, the long-surviving oak.
Some glossy-leaved, and shining in the sun,
The maple, and the beech of oily nuts 315
Prolific, and the lime at dewy eve
Diffusing odors: nor unnoted pass
The sycamore, capricious in attire,
Now green, now tawny, and, ere autumn yet
Have changed the woods, in scarlet honors
    bright. 320
O'er these, but far beyond (a spacious map
Of hill and valley interposed between),
The Ouse, dividing the well-watered land,
Now glitters in the sun, and now retires,
As bashful, yet impatient to be seen. 325
    Hence the declivity is sharp and short,
And such the re-ascent; between them weeps
A little naiad her impov'rished urn
All summer long, which winter fills again.
The folded gates would bar my progress
    now, 330
But that the lord[14] of this enclosed demesne,
Communicative of the good he owns,
Admits me to a share; the guiltless eye
Commits no wrong, nor wastes what it en-
    joys.
Refreshing change! where now the blazing
    sun? 335
By short transition we have lost his glare,
And stepped at once into a cooler clime.
Ye fallen avenues! once more I mourn

[13]Field.   [14]Named in the last note but two.

Your fate unmerited, once more rejoice
That yet a remnant of your race survives. 340
How airy and how light the graceful arch,
Yet awful as the consecrated roof
Re-echoing pious anthems! while beneath
The checkered earth seems restless as a flood
Brushed by the wind. So sportive is the
  light   345
Shot through the boughs, it dances as they
  dance,
Shadow and sunshine intermingling quick,
And dark'ning and enlight'ning, as the leaves
Play wanton, ev'ry moment, ev'ry spot.
  And now, with nerves new-braced and
  spirits cheered,   350
We tread the wilderness, whose well-rolled
  walks,
With curvature of slow and easy sweep—
Deception innocent—give ample space
To narrow bounds. The grove receives us
  next;
Between the upright shafts of whose tall
  elms   355
We may discern the thresher at his task.
Thump after thump resounds the constant
  flail,
That seems to swing uncertain, and yet falls
Full on the destined ear. Wide flies the
  chaff;
The rustling straw sends up a frequent
  mist   360
Of atoms, sparkling in the noon-day beam.
Come hither, ye that press your beds of
  down
And sleep not: see him sweating o'er his
  bread
Before he eats it.—'Tis the primal curse,
But softened into mercy; made the pledge 365
Of cheerful days, and nights without a
  groan.
  By ceaseless action all that is subsists.
Constant rotation of th' unwearied wheel
That nature rides upon maintains her health,
Her beauty, her fertility. She dreads   370
An instant's pause, and lives but while she
  moves.
Its own revolvency upholds the world.
Winds from all quarters agitate the air,
And fit the limpid element for use,
Else noxious: oceans, rivers, lakes, and
  streams,   375
All feel the fresh'ning impulse, and are
  cleansed
By restless undulation: e'en the oak
Thrives by the rude concussion of the storm:
He seems indeed indignant, and to feel

Th' impression of the blast with proud dis-
  dain,   380
Frowning as if in his unconscious arm
He held the thunder: but the monarch owes
His firm stability to what he scorns—
More fixed below, the more disturbed above.
The law, by which all creatures else are
  bound,   385
Binds man the lord of all. Himself derives
No mean advantage from a kindred cause,
From strenuous toil his hours of sweetest
  ease.
The sedentary stretch their lazy length   389
When custom bids, but no refreshment find,
For none they need: the languid eye, the
  cheek
Deserted of its bloom, the flaccid, shrunk,
And withered muscle, and the vapid soul,
Reproach their owner with that love of rest
To which he forfeits e'en the rest he loves. 395
Not such th' alert and active. Measure life
By its true worth, the comforts it affords,
And theirs alone seems worthy of the name.
Good health and, its associate in most,
Good temper; spirits prompt to under-
  take,   400
And not soon spent, though in an arduous
  task;
The pow'rs of fancy and strong thought are
  theirs;
E'en age itself seems privileged in them
With clear exemption from its own defects.
A sparkling eye beneath a wrinkled front 405
The vet'ran shows, and, gracing a gray beard
With youthful smiles, descends toward the
  grave
Sprightly, and old almost without decay.
  Like a coy maiden, ease, when courted
  most,
Farthest retires—an idol, at whose shrine 410
Who oft'nest sacrifice are favored least.
The love of nature, and the scene she draws,
Is nature's dictate. Strange, there should be
  found,
Who, self-imprisoned in their proud saloons,
Renounce the odors of the open field   415
For the unscented fictions of the loom;
Who, satisfied with only penciled scenes,
Prefer to the performance of a God
Th' inferior wonders of an artist's hand!
Lovely indeed the mimic works of art;   420
But nature's works far lovelier. I admire—
None more admires—the painter's magic
  skill,
Who shows me that which I shall never see,
Conveys a distant country into mine,

And throws Italian light on English walls : 425
But imitative strokes can do no more
Than please the eye—sweet nature ev'ry
    sense.
The air salubrious of her lofty hills,
The cheering fragrance of her dewy vales,
And music of her woods—no works of
    man   430
May rival these; these all bespeak a pow'r
Peculiar, and exclusively her own.
Beneath the open sky she spreads the feast;
'Tis free to all—'tis ev'ry day renewed;
Who scorns it starves deservedly at home. 435
He does not scorn it, who, imprisoned long
In some unwholesome dungeon, and a prey
To sallow sickness, which the vapors, dank
And clammy, of his dark abode have bred,
Escapes at last to liberty and light :   440
His cheek recovers soon its healthful hue,
His eye relumines its extinguished fires,
He walks, he leaps, he runs—is winged with
    joy,
And riots in the sweets of ev'ry breeze.
He does not scorn it, who has long en-
    dured   445
A fever's agonies, and fed on drugs.
Nor yet the mariner, his blood inflamed
With acrid salts; his very heart athirst
To gaze at nature in her green array,
Upon the ship's tall side he stands, possessed
With visions prompted by intense desire : 451
Fair fields appear below, such as he left,
Far distant, such as he would die to find—
He seeks them headlong, and is seen no
    more.
    The spleen is seldom felt where Flora[15]
    reigns;   455
The low'ring eye, the petulance, the frown,
And sullen sadness, that o'ershade, distort,
And mar the face of beauty, when no cause
For such immeasurable woe appears,
These Flora banishes, and gives the fair 460
Sweet smiles, and bloom less transient than
    her own.
It is the constant revolution, stale
And tasteless, of the same repeated joys,
That palls and satiates, and makes languid
    life
A peddler's pack, that bows the bearer
    down.   465
Health suffers, and the spirits ebb; the heart
Recoils from its own choice—at the full
    feast
Is famished—finds no music in the song,
No smartness in the jest; and wonders why.
Yet thousands still desire to journey on. 470

---

[15]Goddess of flowers.

Though halt, and weary of the path they
    tread.
The paralytic, who can hold her cards,
But cannot play them, borrows a friend's
    hand
To deal and shuffle, to divide and sort,
Her mingled suits and sequences; and
    sits,   475
Spectatress both and spectacle, a sad
And silent cipher, while her proxy plays.
Others are dragged into the crowded room
Between supporters; and, once seated, sit,
Through downright inability to rise,   480
Till the stout bearers lift the corpse again.
These speak a loud memento. Yet e'en these
Themselves love life, and cling to it, as he
That overhangs a torrent to a twig.
They love it, and yet loathe it; fear to die, 485
Yet scorn the purposes for which they live.
Then wherefore not renounce them? No—
    the dread,
The slavish dread of solitude, that breeds
Reflection and remorse, the fear of shame,
And their invet'rate habits, all forbid.   490
    Whom call we gay? That honor has been
    long
The boast of mere pretenders to the name.
The innocent are gay—the lark is gay,
That dries his feathers, saturate with dew,
Beneath the rosy cloud, while yet the beams
Of day-spring overshoot his humble nest. 496
The peasant too, a witness of his song,
Himself a songster, is as gay as he.
But save me from the gayety of those
Whose headaches nail them to a noonday
    bed :   500
And save me too from theirs whose haggard
    eyes
Flash desperation, and betray their pangs
For property stripped off by cruel chance;
From gayety that fills the bones with pain,
The mouth with blasphemy, the heart with
    woe.   505
    The earth was made so various, that the
    mind
Of desultory man, studious of change,
And pleased with novelty, might be indulged.
Prospects, however lovely, may be seen
Till half their beauties fade; the weary sight,
Too well acquainted with their smiles, slides
    off,   511
Fastidious, seeking less familiar scenes.
Then snug enclosures in the sheltered vale,
Where frequent hedges intercept the eye,
Delight us; happy to renounce awhile, 515
Not senseless of its charms, what still we
    love,

That such short absence may endear it more.
Then forests, or the savage rock, may please,
That hides the sea-mew in his hollow clefts
Above the reach of man: his hoary head,   520
Conspicuous many a league, the mariner
Bound homeward, and in hope already there,
Greets with three cheers exulting. At his
    waist
A girdle of half-withered shrubs he shows,
And at his feet the baffled billows die.   525
The common, overgrown with fern, and
    rough
With prickly gorse, that, shapeless and de-
    formed,
And dang'rous to the touch, has yet its
    bloom,
And decks itself with ornaments of gold,   529
Yields no unpleasing ramble; there the turf
Smells fresh, and, rich in odorif'rous herbs
And fungous fruits of earth, regales the
    sense
With luxury of unexpected sweets.
    There often wanders one, whom better
        days
Saw better clad, in cloak of satin trimmed 535
With lace, and hat with splendid riband
    bound.
A serving maid was she, and fell in love
With one who left her, went to sea, and died.
Her fancy followed him through foaming
    waves
To distant shores; and she would sit and
    weep   540
At what a sailor suffers; fancy, too,
Delusive most where warmest wishes are,
Would oft anticipate his glad return,
And dream of transports she was not to
    know.
She heard the doleful tidings of his death—
And never smiled again. And now she
    roams   546
The dreary waste; there spends the livelong
    day,
And there, unless when charity forbids,
The livelong night. A tattered apron hides,
Worn as a cloak, and hardly hides, a
    gown   550
More tattered still; and both but ill conceal
A bosom heaved with never-ceasing sighs.
She begs an idle pin of all she meets,
And hoards them in her sleeve; but needful
    food,
Though pressed with hunger oft, or comelier
    clothes,   555
Though pinched with cold, asks never.—
    Kate is crazed.
    I see a column of slow-rising smoke

O'ertop the lofty wood that skirts the wild.
A vagabond and useless tribe there eat
Their miserable meal. A kettle, slung   560
Between two poles upon a stick transverse,
Receives the morsel—flesh obscene of dog,
Or vermin, or, at best, of cock purloined
From his accustomed perch. Hard-faring
    race!
They pick their fuel out of ev'ry hedge,   565
Which, kindled with dry leaves, just saves
    unquenched
The spark of life. The sportive wind blows
    wide
Their flutt'ring rags, and shows a tawny
    skin,
The vellum of the pedigree they claim.
Great skill have they in palmistry, and
    more   570
To conjure clean away the gold they touch,
Conveying worthless dross into its place;
Loud when they beg, dumb only when they
    steal.
Strange, that a creature rational, and cast
In human mold, should brutalize by choice
His nature; and, though capable of arts   576
By which the world might profit, and him-
    self,
Self-banished from society, prefer
Such squalid sloth to honorable toil!
Yet even these, though, feigning sickness oft,
They swathe the forehead, drag the limping
    limb,   581
And vex their flesh with artificial sores,
Can change their whine into a mirthful note
When safe occasion offers; and with dance,
And music of the bladder and the bag,   585
Beguile their woes, and make the woods re-
    sound.
Such health and gayety of heart enjoy
The houseless rovers of the sylvan world;
And, breathing wholesome air and wan-
    d'ring much,
Need other physic none to heal th' effects 590
Of loathsome diet, penury, and cold.
    Bless'd he, though undistinguished from
        the crowd
By wealth or dignity, who dwells secure,
Where man, by nature fierce, has laid aside
His fierceness, having learned, though slow
    to learn,   595
The manners and the arts of civil life.
His wants, indeed, are many; but supply
Is obvious, placed within the easy reach
Of temp'rate wishes and industrious hands.
Here virtue thrives as in her proper soil;   600
Not rude and surly, and beset with thorns,
And terrible to sight, as when she springs

(If e'er she spring spontaneous) in remote
And barb'rous climes, where violence pre-
vails,
And strength is lord of all; but gentle, kind,
By culture tamed, by liberty refreshed,   606
And all her fruits by radiant truth matured.
War and the chase engross the savage whole:
War followed for revenge, or to supplant
The envied tenants of some happier spot; 610
The chase for sustenance, precarious trust!
His hard condition with severe constraint
Binds all his faculties, forbids all growth
Of wisdom, proves a school in which he
learns
Sly circumvention, unrelenting hate,   615
Mean self-attachment, and scarce aught be-
side.
Thus fare the shiv'ring natives of the north,
And thus the rangers of the western world,
Where it advances far into the deep,
Towards th' antarctic. E'en the favored
isles   620
So lately found,[16] although the constant sun
Cheer all their seasons with a grateful smile,
Can boast but little virtue; and, inert
Through plenty, lose in morals what they
gain
In manners—victims of luxurious ease.   625
These therefore I can pity, placed remote
From all that science traces, art invents,
Or inspiration teaches; and enclosed
In boundless oceans, never to be passed
By navigators uninformed as they,   630
Or plowed perhaps by British bark again.
But, far beyond the rest, and with most
cause,
Thee, gentle savage![17] whom no love of thee
Or thine, but curiosity perhaps,
Or else vainglory, prompted us to draw   635
Forth from thy native bow'rs, to show thee
here
With what superior skill we can abuse
The gifts of providence, and squander life.
The dream is past; and thou hast found
again
Thy cocoas and bananas, palms and yams, 640
And homestall[18] thatched with leaves. But
hast thou found

[16]The Society and Friendly Islands.

[17]Omai, a native of Otaheite (Friendly Islands),
who was brought to England in 1774. He was received by George III, and aroused wide interest in
England. Dr. Johnson "was struck with the elegance of his behavior," and Sir Joshua Reynolds
painted him. Cowper's guess that he pined for the
refinements of England after his return to his native
island was correct.

[18]Homestead.

Their former charms? And, having seen
our state,
Our palaces, our ladies, and our pomp
Of equipage, our gardens, and our sports,
And heard our music; are thy simple friends,
Thy simple fare, and all thy plain delights 646
As dear to thee as once? And have thy joys
Lost nothing by comparison with ours?
Rude as thou art (for we returned thee rude
And ignorant, except of outward show),   650
I cannot think thee yet so dull of heart
And spiritless, as never to regret
Sweets tasted here, and left as soon as
known.
Methinks I see thee straying on the beach,
And asking of the surge that bathes thy foot
If ever it has washed our distant shore.   656
I see thee weep, and thine are honest tears,
A patriot's for his country: thou art sad
At thought of her forlorn and abject state,
From which no pow'r of thine can raise her
up.   660
Thus fancy paints thee, and, though apt to
err,
Perhaps errs little when she paints thee thus.
She tells me, too, that duly ev'ry morn
Thou climb'st the mountain top, with eager
eye
Exploring far and wide the wat'ry waste 665
For sight of ship from England. Ev'ry
speck
Seen in the dim horizon turns thee pale
With conflict of contending hopes and fears.
But comes at last the dull and dusky eve,
And sends thee to thy cabin, well-prepared
To dream all night of what the day denied.
Alas! expect it not. We found no bait   672
To tempt us in thy country. Doing good,
Disinterested good, is not our trade.   674
We travel far, 'tis true, but not for nought;
And must be bribed to compass earth again
By other hopes and richer fruits than yours.
But, though true worth and virtue in the
mild
And genial soil of cultivated life
Thrive most, and may perhaps thrive only
there,   680
Yet not in cities oft: in proud and gay
And gain-devoted cities. Thither flow,
As to a common and most noisome sew'r,
The dregs and feculence of ev'ry land.
In cities foul example on most minds   685
Begets its likeness. Rank abundance breeds
In gross and pampered cities sloth and lust,
And wantonness and gluttonous excess.
In cities vice is hidden with most ease,

Or seen with least reproach; and virtue,
     taught   690
By frequent lapse, can hope no triumph there
Beyond th' achievement of successful flight.
I do confess them nurs'ries of the arts,
In which they flourish most; where, in the
     beams
Of warm encouragement, and in the eye   695
Of public note, they reach their perfect size.
Such London is, by taste and wealth pro-
     claimed
The fairest capital of all the world,
By riot and incontinence the worst.
There, touched by Reynolds, a dull blank be-
     comes   700
A lucid mirror, in which nature sees
All her reflected features. Bacon[19] there
Gives more than female beauty to a stone,
And Chatham's eloquence to marble lips.
Nor does the chisel occupy alone   705
The pow'rs of sculpture, but the style as
     much;
Each province of her art her equal care.
With nice incision of her guided steel
She plows a brazen field, and clothes a soil
So sterile with what charms soe'er she will,
The richest scen'ry and the loveliest forms.
Where finds philosophy her eagle eye,   712
With which she gazes at yon burning disk
Undazzled, and detects and counts his spots?
In London. Where her implements exact,
With which she calculates, computes, and
     scans,   716
All distance, motion, magnitude, and now
Measures an atom, and now girds a world?
In London. Where has commerce such a
     mart,
So rich, so thronged, so drained, and so sup-
     plied,   720
As London—opulent, enlarged, and still
Increasing London? Babylon of old
Not more the glory of the earth than she,
A more accomplished world's chief glory
     now.
     She has her praise. Now mark a spot or
     two,   725
That so much beauty would do well to purge;
And show this queen of cities that so fair
May yet be foul; so witty, yet not wise.
It is not seemly, nor of good report,   729

That she is slack in discipline; more prompt
T' avenge than to prevent the breach of law:
That she is rigid in denouncing death
On petty robbers, and indulges life
And liberty, and oft-times honor too,
To peculators of the public gold: 735
That thieves at home must hang, but he that
     puts
Into his overgorged and bloated purse
The wealth of Indian provinces escapes.[20]
Nor is it well, nor can it come to good,
That, through profane and infidel contempt
Of holy writ, she has presumed t' annul 741
And abrogate, as roundly as she may,
The total ordinance and will of God;
Advancing fashion to the post of truth,
And cent'ring all authority in modes   745
And customs of her own, till sabbath rites
Have dwindled into unrespected forms,
And knees and hassocks are well-nigh di-
     vorced.
     God made the country, and man made the
     town.
What wonder then that health and virtue,
     gifts   750
That can alone make sweet the bitter draught
That life holds out to all, should most abound
And least be threatened in the fields and
     groves?
Possess ye, therefore, ye who, borne about
In chariots and sedans, know no fatigue 755
But that of idleness, and taste no scenes
But such as art contrives, possess ye still
Your element; there only can ye shine,
There only minds like yours can do no harm.
Our groves were planted to console at noon
The pensive wand'rer in their shades. At
     eve   761
The moonbeam, sliding softly in between
The sleeping leaves, is all the light they wish,
Birds warbling all the music. We can spare
The splendor of your lamps; they but eclipse
Our softer satellite. Your songs confound
Our more harmonious notes: the thrush de-
     parts   767
Scared, and th' offended nightingale is mute.
There is a public mischief in your mirth;
It plagues your country. Folly such as
     yours,   770
Graced with a sword, and worthier of a fan,
Has made, which enemies could ne'er have
     done,
Our arch of empire, steadfast but for you,
A mutilated structure, soon to fall.

---

[19]John Bacon (1740–1799), a sculptor. Among
his works are monuments of Chatham in the Guildhall and in Westminster Abbey. Bacon liked Cowper's first volume of poems and sent him a print of
his monument of Chatham.

[20]A thrust at Clive.

ON THE RECEIPT OF MY MOTHER'S PICTURE OUT OF NORFOLK[1]

The Gift of My Cousin Ann Bodham

Oh, that those lips had language! Life has passed
With me but roughly since I heard thee last.
Those lips are thine—thy own sweet smiles I see,
The same that oft in childhood solaced me;
Voice only fails, else, how distinct they say, 5
"Grieve not, my child, chase all thy fears away!"
The meek intelligence of those dear eyes
(Bless'd be the art that can immortalize,
The art that baffles time's tyrannic claim
To quench it) here shines on me still the same. 10
  Faithful remembrancer of one so dear,
O welcome guest, though unexpected here!
Who bidd'st me honor with an artless song,
Affectionate, a mother lost so long,
I will obey, not willingly alone, 15
But gladly, as the precept were her own;
And, while that face renews my filial grief,
Fancy shall weave a charm for my relief—
Shall steep me in Elysian reverie,
A momentary dream, that thou art she. 20
  My mother! when I learned that thou wast dead,
Say, wast thou conscious of the tears I shed?
Hovered thy spirit o'er thy sorrowing son,
Wretch even then, life's journey just begun?
Perhaps thou gav'st me, though unfelt,[2] a kiss; 25
Perhaps a tear, if souls can weep in bliss—
Ah, that maternal smile! it answers—Yes.
I heard the bell tolled on thy burial day,
I saw the hearse that bore thee slow away,
And, turning from my nurs'ry window, drew
A long, long sigh, and wept a last adieu! 31
But was it such?—It was.—Where thou art gone
Adieus and farewells are a sound unknown.
May I but meet thee on that peaceful shore,
The parting word shall pass my lips no more!

Thy maidens, grieved themselves at my concern, 36
Oft gave me promise of thy quick return.
What ardently I wished I long believed,
And, disappointed still, was still deceived;
By expectation every day beguiled, 40
Dupe of *to-morrow* even from a child.
Thus many a sad to-morrow came and went.
Till, all my stock of infant sorrow spent,
I learned at last submission to my lot;
But, though I less deplored thee, ne'er forgot.
  Where once we dwelt our name is heard no more, 46
Children not thine have trod my nurs'ry floor;
And where the gard'ner Robin, day by day,
Drew me to school along the public way,
Delighted with my bauble coach, and wrapped 50
In scarlet mantle warm, and velvet capped.
'Tis now become a history little known,
That once we called the past'ral house[3] our own.
Short-lived possession! but the record fair 54
That mem'ry keeps of all thy kindness there,
Still outlives many a storm that has effaced
A thousand other themes less deeply traced.
Thy nightly visits to my chamber made,
That thou might'st know me safe and warmly laid;
Thy morning bounties ere I left my home, 60
The biscuit, or confectionary plum;
The fragrant waters on my cheeks bestowed
By thy own hand, till fresh they shone and glowed;
All this, and more endearing still than all, 64
Thy constant flow of love, that knew no fall,
Ne'er roughened by those cataracts and brakes
That humor[4] interposed too often makes;
All this still legible in mem'ry's page,
And still to be so, to my latest age,
Adds joy to duty, makes me glad to pay 70
Such honors to thee as my numbers may;
Perhaps a frail memorial, but sincere,
Not scorned in heav'n, though little noticed here.
Could time, his flight reversed, restore the hours,
When, playing with thy vesture's tissued flow'rs, 75
The violet, the pink, and jessamine,
I pricked them into paper with a pin

---

[1] Written in February, 1790; published, without Cowper's knowledge or consent, in a small volume or pamphlet together with *The Dog and the Water Lily* in 1798. Anne Donne Bodham was the daughter of Roger Donne, the brother of Cowper's mother, and the wife of the Rev. Thomas Bodham. Cowper's mother died on 12 November, 1737.

[2] Some editions print "unseen." This is the first of several important variations between the text of 1798 and that of 1808 and later editions. Here and throughout the later readings have been adopted.

[3] The rectory of Great Berkhampstead, Hertfordshire, where Cowper was born.

[4] I. e., caprice.

(And thou wast happier than myself the
       while,
Would'st softly speak, and stroke my head
       and smile),   79
Could those few pleasant days again appear,
Might one wish bring them, would I wish
       them here?
I would not trust my heart—the dear delight
Seems so to be desired, perhaps I might.—
But no—what here we call our life is such,
So little to be loved, and thou so much,   85
That I should ill requite thee to constrain
Thy unbound spirit into bonds again.

       Thou, as a gallant bark from Albion's coast
(The storms all weathered and the ocean
       crossed)
Shoots into port at some well-havened isle, 90
Where spices breathe and brighter seasons
       smile,
There sits quiescent on the floods that show
Her beauteous form reflected clear below,
While airs impregnated with incense play
Around her, fanning light her streamers gay;
So thou, with sails how swift! hast reached
       the shore   96
"Where tempests never beat nor billows
       roar,"[5]
And thy loved consort on the dang'rous tide
Of life long since[6] has anchored by thy side.
But me, scarce hoping to attain that rest, 100
Always from port withheld, always dis-
       tressed—
Me howling blasts drive devious, tempest-
       tossed,
Sails ripped, seams op'ning wide, and com-
       pass lost,
And day by day some current's thwarting
       force
Sets me more distant from a prosp'rous
       course.   105
Yet, oh, the thought that thou art safe, and
       he!
That thought is joy, arrive what may to me.
My boast is not that I deduce my birth
From loins enthroned, and rulers of the
       earth;[7]
But higher far my proud pretensions rise—
The son of parents passed into the skies. 111
And now, farewell. Time unrevoked has
       run
His wonted course, yet what I wished is done.

----

[5] Inexactly quoted from Garth's *Dispensary*, III,
226. It should be, "Where billows never break,
nor tempests roar."

[6] Cowper's father died in 1756.

[7] Cowper's mother was descended by four different
lines from Henry III.

By contemplation's help, not sought in vain,
I seem t' have lived my childhood o'er again;
To have renewed the joys that once were
       mine,   116
Without the sin of violating thine:
And, while the wings of fancy still are free,
And I can view this mimic show of thee,
Time has but half succeeded in his theft— 120
Thyself removed, thy power to soothe me
       left.

TO MARY[1]

The twentieth year is well-nigh past
Since first our sky was overcast;
Ah, would that this might be the last,
              My Mary!

Thy spirits have a fainter flow,   5
I see thee daily weaker grow;
'Twas my distress that brought thee low,
              My Mary!

Thy needles, once a shining store,
For my sake restless heretofore,   10
Now rust disused and shine no more,
              My Mary!

For though thou gladly wouldst fulfill
The same kind office for me still,
Thy sight now seconds not thy will,   15
              My Mary!

But well thou playedst the housewife's part,
And all thy threads with magic art
Have wound themselves about this heart,
              My Mary!   20

Thy indistinct expressions seem
Like language uttered in a dream;[2]
Yet me they charm, whate'er the theme,
              My Mary!

Thy silver locks, once auburn bright,   25
Are still more lovely in my sight
Than golden beams of orient light,
              My Mary!

----

[1] Written in the fall of 1793; the last poem Cowper wrote at Weston. Published in 1803, with the
exception of the tenth stanza, which was first printed
in 1900. The poem is addressed to Mrs. Unwin,
and the reference in the first line is to 1773, when
Cowper's engagement to her was broken off because
of a return of his madness.

[2] Mrs. Unwin had suffered a paralytic stroke which
interfered with her speech.

For, could I view nor them nor thee,
What sight worth seeing could I see?   30
The sun would rise in vain for me,
   My Mary!

Partakers of thy sad decline,
Thy hands their little force resign;
Yet, gently pressed, press gently mine,   35
   My Mary!

And then I feel that still I hold
A richer store ten thousandfold
Than misers fancy in their gold,
   My Mary!   40

Such feebleness of limbs thou prov'st,
That now at every step thou mov'st
Upheld by two, yet still thou lov'st,
   My Mary!

And still to love, though pressed with ill,   45
In wintry age to feel no chill,
With me is to be lovely still,
   My Mary!

But ah! by constant heed I know,
How oft the sadness that I show   50
Transforms thy smiles to looks of woe,
   My Mary!

And should my future lot be cast
With much resemblance of the past,
Thy worn-out heart will break at last,   55
   My Mary!

THE CASTAWAY[1]

Obscurest night involved the sky,
 Th' Atlantic billows roared,
When such a destined wretch as I,
 Washed headlong from on board,
Of friends, of hope, of all bereft,   5
His floating home for ever left.

No braver chief could Albion boast
 Than he with whom he went,
Nor ever ship left Albion's coast,
 With warmer wishes sent.   10
He loved them both, but both in vain,
Nor him beheld, nor her again.

Not long beneath the whelming brine,
 Expert to swim, he lay;
Nor soon he felt his strength decline,   15
 Or courage die away;

[1]Written in 1799, a year before Cowper's death.
The source of the poem is an incident described in
Admiral George Anson's *Voyage Round the World*
(1748).

But waged with death a lasting strife,
Supported by despair of life.

He shouted: nor his friends had failed
 To check the vessel's course,   20
But so the furious blast prevailed,
 That, pitiless perforce,
They left their outcast mate behind,
And scudded still before the wind.

Some succor yet they could afford;   25
 And, such as storms allow,
The cask, the coop, the floated cord,
 Delayed not to bestow.
But he (they knew) nor ship, nor shore,
Whate'er they gave, should visit more.   30

Nor, cruel as it seemed, could he
 Their haste himself condemn,
Aware that flight, in such a sea,
 Alone could rescue them;
Yet bitter felt it still to die   35
Deserted, and his friends so nigh.

He long survives, who lives an hour
 In ocean, self-upheld;
And so long he, with unspent pow'r,
 His destiny repelled;   40
And ever, as the minutes flew,
Entreated help, or cried—Adieu!

At length, his transient respite past,
 His comrades, who before
Had heard his voice in ev'ry blast,   45
 Could catch the sound no more.
For then, by toil subdued, he drank
The stifling wave, and then he sank.

No poet wept him: but the page
 Of narrative sincere,   50
That tells his name, his worth, his age,
 Is wet with Anson's tear.
And tears by bards or heroes shed
Alike immortalize the dead.

I therefore purpose not, or dream,   55
 Descanting on his fate,
To give the melancholy theme
 A more enduring date:
But misery still delights to trace
Its 'semblance in another's case.   60

No voice divine the storm allayed,
 No light propitious shone;
When, snatched from all effectual aid,
 We perished, each alone:
But I beneath a rougher sea,   65
And whelmed in deeper gulfs than he.

LETTERS

I. To Joseph Hill[1]

Huntingdon, 3 July, 1765

Dear Joe,

Whatever you may think of the matter, it is no such easy thing to keep house for two people. A man cannot always live upon sheep's heads, and liver and lights,[2] like the lions in the Tower; and a joint of meat, in so small a family, is an endless encumbrance. My butcher's bill for last week amounted to four shillings and ten-pence. I set off with a leg of lamb, and was forced to give part of it away to my washerwoman. Then I made an experiment upon a sheep's heart, and that was too little. Next I put three pounds of beef into a pie, and this had like to have been too much, for it lasted three days, though my landlord was admitted to a share in it. Then as to small beer, I am puzzled to pieces about it. I have bought as much for a shilling as will serve us at least a month, and it is grown sour already. In short, I never knew how to pity poor housekeepers before; but now I cease to wonder at that politic cast which their occupation usually gives to their countenance, for it is really a matter full of perplexity.

I have received but one visit since here I came. I don't mean that I have refused any, but that only one has been offered. This was from my woollen-draper, a very healthy, wealthy, sensible, sponsible[3] man, and extremely civil. He has a cold bath, and has promised me a key of it, which I shall probably make use of in the winter. He has undertaken, too, to get me the *St. James's Chronicle* three times a-week, and to show me Hinchinbrook House,[4] and to do every service for me in his power; so that I did not exceed the truth, you see, when I spoke of his civility. Here is a card-assembly, and a dancing-assembly, and a horse-race, and a club, and a bowling-green, so that I am well off, you perceive, in point of diversion; especially as I shall go to 'em just as much as

I should if I lived a thousand miles off. But no matter for that; the spectator at a play is more entertained than the actor; and in real life it is much the same. You will say, perhaps, that if I never frequent these places, I shall not come within the description of a spectator; and you will say right. I have made a blunder, which shall be corrected in the next edition.

You are old dog at a bad tenant; witness all my uncle's and your mother's geese and gridirons. There is something so extremely impertinent in entering upon a man's premises, and using them without paying for 'em, that I could easily resent it if I would. But I rather choose to entertain myself with thinking how you will scour the man about, and worry him to death, if once you begin with him. Poor toad! I leave him entirely to your mercy.

My dear Joe, you desire me to write long letters.—I have neither matter enough, nor perseverance enough for the purpose. However, if you can but contrive to be tired of reading as soon as I am tired of writing, we shall find that short ones answer just as well; and, in my opinion, this is a very practicable measure.

My friend Colman[5] has had good fortune; I wish him better fortune still; which is, that he may make a right use of it. The tragedies of Lloyd and Bensley[6] are both very deep. If they are not of use to the surviving part of the society, it is their own fault.

I was debtor to Bensley seven pounds, or nine, I forget which. If you can find out his brother, you will do me a great favor if you will pay him for me; but do it at your leisure.—Yours and theirs,

W. C.

II. To Joseph Hill

Olney, 20 April, 1777

My dear Friend,

Thanks for a turbot, a lobster, and Captain Brydone,[7] a gentleman who relates his

---

[1] One of Cowper's most faithful friends. Hill was a lawyer in London.

[2] Lungs.   [3] Responsible.

[4] The seat of Oliver Cromwell's ancestors at Huntingdon.

[5] George Colman, manager of the Haymarket Theater.

[6] Friends who had recently died.

[7] Patrick Brydone (1741–1818), author of a book on Sicily and Malta.

travels so agreeably that he deserves always to travel with an agreeable companion. I have been reading Gray's *Works,* and think him the only poet since Shakespeare entitled to the character of sublime. Perhaps you will remember that I once had a different opinion of him. I was prejudiced. He did not belong to our Thursday society,[8] and was an Eton man, which lowered him prodigiously in our esteem. I once thought Swift's letters the best that could be written; but I like Gray's better. His humor, or his wit, or whatever it is to be called, is never ill-natured or offensive, and yet I think equally poignant with the Dean's.—I am, yours affectionately,

Wm. Cowper.

III. To William Unwin[9]

Olney, 31 October, 1779

My dear Friend,

I wrote my last letter merely to inform you that I had nothing to say; in answer to which you have said nothing. I admire the propriety of your conduct though I am a loser by it. I will endeavor to say something now, and shall hope for something in return.

I have been well entertained with Johnson's biographies,[10] for which I thank you: with one exception, and that a swingeing one, I think he has acquitted himself with his usual good sense and sufficiency. His treatment of Milton is unmerciful to the last degree. A pensioner is not likely to spare a republican; and the Doctor, in order, I suppose, to convince his royal patron of the sincerity of his monarchical principles, has belabored that great poet's character with the most industrious cruelty. As a man, he has hardly left him the shadow of one good quality. Churlishness in his private life, and a rancorous hatred of everything royal in his public, are the two colors with which he has smeared all the canvas. If he had

any virtues, they are not to be found in the Doctor's picture of him; and it is well for Milton that some sourness in his temper is the only vice with which his memory has been charged; it is evident enough that if his biographer could have discovered more, he would not have spared him. As a poet, he has treated him with severity enough, and has plucked one or two of the most beautiful feathers out of his muse's wing, and trampled them under his great foot. He has passed sentence of condemnation upon *Lycidas,* and has taken occasion, from that charming poem, to expose to ridicule (what is indeed ridiculous enough) the childish prattlement of pastoral compositions, as if *Lycidas* was the prototype and pattern of them all. The liveliness of the description, the sweetness of the numbers, the classical spirit of antiquity that prevails in it go for nothing. I am convinced, by the way, that he has no ear for poetical numbers, or that it was stopped by prejudice against the harmony of Milton's. Was there ever anything so delightful as the music of the *Paradise Lost?* It is like that of a fine organ; has the fullest and the deepest tones of majesty, with all the softness and elegance of the Dorian flute, variety without end and never equalled, unless perhaps by Virgil. Yet the Doctor has little or nothing to say upon this copious theme, but talks something about the unfitness of the English language for blank verse, and how apt it is, in the mouth of some readers, to degenerate into declamation. Oh! I could thresh his old jacket, till I made his pension jingle in his pocket.

I could talk a good while longer, but I have no room; our love attends yourself, Mrs. Unwin, and Miss Shuttleworth, not forgetting the two miniature pictures at your elbow.—Yours affectionately,

W. C.

IV. To Mrs. Newton[11]

Olney, 5 June, 1780

Dear Madam,

When I write to Mr. Newton, he answers me by letter; when I write to you, you an-

[8]The Nonsense Club, a society of young men who had attended the Westminster School. Cowper had been a member in London some twenty years before.

[9]Son of the Rev. Morley Unwin and Mary Unwin, in whose family Cowper had been living since 1765.

[10]Apparently the first volume, published in this year, of the work later called *The Lives of the English Poets.*

[11]Wife of the Rev. John Newton, vicar of Olney until 1779.

swer me in fish. I return you many thanks for the mackerel and lobster. They assured me in terms as intelligible as pen and ink could have spoken that you still remember Orchardside;[12] and though they never spoke in their lives, and it was still less to be expected from them that they should speak, being dead, they gave us an assurance of your affection that corresponds exactly with that which Mr. Newton expresses towards us in all his letters.—For my own part, I never in my life began a letter more at a venture than the present. It is possible that I may finish it, but perhaps more than probable that I shall not. I have had several indifferent nights, and the wind is easterly: two circumstances so unfavorable to me in all my occupations, but especially that of writing, that it was with the greatest difficulty I could even bring myself to attempt it.

You have never yet perhaps been made acquainted with the unfortunate Tom Freeman's misadventure. He and his wife, returning from Hanslope fair, were coming down Weston Lane: to wit, themselves, their horse, and their great wooden panniers, at ten o'clock at night. The horse, having a lively imagination and very weak nerves, fancied he either saw or heard something, but has never been able to say what. A sudden fright will impart activity, and a momentary vigor, even to lameness itself. Accordingly he started, and sprung from the middle of the road to the side of it, with such surprising alacrity that he dismounted the gingerbread baker and his gingerbread wife in a moment. Not contented with this effort, nor thinking himself yet out of danger, he proceeded as fast as he could to a full gallop, rushed against the gate at the bottom of the lane, and opened it for himself, without perceiving that there was any gate there. Still he galloped, and with a velocity and momentum continually increasing, till he arrived in Olney. I had been in bed about ten minutes when I heard the most uncommon and unaccountable noise that can be imagined. It was, in fact, occasioned by the clattering of tin patty-pans and a Dutch oven against the sides of the panniers.

Much gingerbread was picked up in the street, and Mr. Lucy's windows were broken all to pieces. Had this been all, it would have been a comedy, but we learned the next morning that the poor woman's collar-bone was broken, and she has hardly been able to resume her occupation since.

*   *   *

V. To Joseph Hill

Olney, 9 May, 1781

My dear Sir,

I am in the press,[13] and it is in vain to deny it. But how mysterious is the conveyance of intelligence from one end to the other of your great city!—Not many days since, except one man, and he but a little taller than yourself, all London was ignorant of it; for I do not suppose that the public prints have yet announced this most agreeable tidings, the title-page, which is the basis of the advertisement, having so lately reached the publisher; and now it is known to you, who live at least two miles distant from my confidant upon the occasion.

My labors are principally the production of the last winter: all indeed, except a few of the minor pieces. When I can find no other occupation, I think; and when I think, I am very apt to do it in rime. Hence it comes to pass that the season of the year which generally pinches off the flowers of poetry unfolds mine, such as they are, and crowns me with a winter garland. In this respect, therefore, I and my contemporary bards are by no means upon a par. They write when the delightful influences of fine weather, fine prospects, and a brisk motion of the animal spirits make poetry almost the language of nature; and I, when icicles depend from all the leaves of the Parnassian laurel, and when a reasonable man would as little expect to succeed in verse as to hear a blackbird whistle. This must be my apology to you for whatever want of fire and animation you may observe in what you will shortly have the perusal of. As to the public, if they like me not, there is no remedy. A

---

[12]The house in which Cowper and Mrs. Unwin lived at Olney.

[13]An allusion to the printing of his first volume, *Poems,* which did not actually appear until 1782.

friend will weigh and consider all disadvantages, and make as large allowances as an author can wish, and larger perhaps than he has any right to expect; but not so the world at large. Whatever they do not like they will not by any apology be persuaded to forgive, and it would be in vain to tell *them* that I wrote my verses in January, for they would immediately reply, "Why did not you write them in May?" a question that might puzzle a wiser head than we poets are generally blessed with.

W. C.

VI. To William Unwin

Olney, 23 May, 1781

My dear Friend,

If a writer's friends have need of patience, how much more the writer! Your desire to see my muse in public, and mine to gratify you, must both suffer the mortification of delay. I expected that my trumpeter would have informed the world by this time of all that is needful for them to know upon such an occasion; and that an advertising blast, blown through every newspaper, would have said—"The poet is coming!"—But man, especially man that writes verse, is born to disappointments, as surely as printers and booksellers are born to be the most dilatory and tedious of all creatures. The plain English of this magnificent preamble is that the season of publication is just elapsed, that the town is going into the country every day, and that my book cannot appear till they return, that is to say, not till next winter.

This misfortune, however, comes not without its attendant advantage; I shall now have, what I should not otherwise have had, an opportunity to correct the press myself, no small advantage upon any occasion, but especially important where poetry is concerned! A single *erratum* may knock out the brains of a whole passage, and that perhaps which of all others the unfortunate poet is the most proud of. Add to this that now and then there is to be found in a printing-house a presumptuous intermeddler, who will fancy himself a poet too and, what is still worse, a better than he that employs

him. The consequence is that with cobbling, and tinkering, and patching on here and there a shred of his own, he makes such a difference between the original and the copy that an author cannot know his own work again. Now as I choose to be responsible for nobody's dulness but my own, I am a little comforted when I reflect that it will be in my power to prevent all such impertinence; and yet not without your assistance. It will be quite necessary that the correspondence between me and Johnson should be carried on without the expense of postage, because proof sheets would make double or treble letters, which expense, as in every instance it must occur twice, first when the packet is sent, and again when it is returned, would be rather inconvenient to me, who, as you perceive, am forced to live by my wits, and to him who hopes to get a little matter no doubt by the same means. Half a dozen franks[14] therefore to me, and *totĭdem*[15] to him, will be singularly acceptable, if you can, without feeling it in any respect a trouble, procure them for me. * * *

My neckcloths being all worn out, I intend to wear stocks,[16] but not unless they are more fashionable than the former. In that case I shall be obliged to you if you will buy me a handsome stock-buckle for a very little money; for twenty or twenty-five shillings perhaps a second-hand affair may be purchased that will make a figure at Olney.

I am much obliged to you for your offer to support me in a translation of Bourne.[17] It is but seldom, however, and never except for my amusement, that I translate, because I find it disagreeable to work by another man's pattern; I should at least be sure to find it so in a business of any length. Again, *that* is epigrammatic and witty in Latin which would be perfectly insipid in English; and a translator of Bourne would frequently find himself obliged to supply what is called the turn, which is in fact the most difficult and the most expensive part of the whole

---

[14]Envelopes which, with their contents, might be posted free of charge.

[15]The same number.

[16]Neckcloths, apparently different in cut from ordinary ones.

[17]Vincent Bourne (1695–1747), the neo-Latin poet.

ition, and could not perhaps, in many
es, be done with any tolerable success.
atin poem is neat, elegant, and musical,
iough; but English readers are not so
easily satisfied. To quote myself, you will
find, in comparing "The Jackdaw"[18] with
the original, that I was obliged to sharpen a
point which, though smart enough in the
Latin, would in English have appeared as
plain and as blunt as the tag of a lace.[19] I
love the memory of Vinny Bourne. I think
him a better Latin poet than Tibullus, Propertius, Ausonius,[20] or any of the writers in
his way, except Ovid, and not at all inferior
to him. I love him too with a love of partiality, because he was usher of the fifth
form at Westminster when I passed through
it. He was so good-natured, and so indolent, that I lost more than I got by him; for
he made me as idle as himself. He was
such a sloven as if he had trusted to his
genius as a cloak for everything that could
disgust you in his person; and indeed in his
writings he has almost made amends for all.
His humor is entirely original; he can speak
of a magpie or a cat in terms so exquisitely
appropriated to the character he draws that
one would suppose him animated by the
spirit of the creature he describes. And
with all this drollery there is a mixture of
rational and even religious reflection at times,
and always an air of pleasantry, good-nature,
and humanity that makes him, in my mind,
one of the most amiable writers in the world.
It is not common to meet with an author who
can make you smile, and yet at nobody's
expense; who is always entertaining, and yet
always harmless; and who, though always
elegant and classical to a degree not always
found even in the classics themselves, charms
more by the simplicity and playfulness of
his ideas than by the neatness and purity of
his verse; yet such was poor Vinny. I remember seeing the Duke of Richmond set
fire to his greasy locks, and box his ears to
put it out again.

I am delighted with your project, but not
with the view I have of its success. If the
world would form its opinion of the clerical
character at large from yours in particular,
I have no doubt but the event would be as
prosperous as you could wish. But I suppose
there is not a member of either house[21] who
does not see within the circle of his own acquaintance a minister, perhaps many ministers, whose integrity would contribute but
little to the effect of such a bill. Here are
seven or eight in the neighborhood of Olney
who have shaken hands with sobriety, and
who would rather suppress the church, were
it not for the emoluments annexed, than discourage the sale of strong beer in a single
instance. Were I myself in Parliament, I
am not sure that I could favor your scheme.
Are there not to be found within five miles
of almost every neighborhood parsons who
would purchase well accustomed public-
houses, because they could secure them a
license, and patronize them when they had
done? I think no penalty would prevent the
abuse, on account of the difficulty of proof,
and that no ingenuity could guard against all
the possible abuses. To sum up all in few
words, the generality of the clergy, especially
within these last twenty or thirty years, have
worn their surcingles[22] so loose that I verily
believe no measure that proposed an accession of privilege to an order which the laity
retain but little respect for would meet with
the countenance of the legislature. You will
do me the justice to suppose that I do not say
these things to gratify a splenetic humor or
a censorious turn of mind; far from it,—it
may add, perhaps, to the severity of the foregoing observation to assert, but if it does, I
cannot help asserting, that I verily believe
them to be founded upon fact, and that I am
sure, partly from my own knowledge, and
partly from the report of those whose veracity I can depend upon, that, in this part of the
world at least, many of the most profligate
characters are the very men to whom the
morals and even the souls of others are entrusted; and I cannot suppose that the diocese of Lincoln, or this part of it in particular, is more unfortunate in that respect than
the rest of the kingdom.

---

[18]A translation Cowper had already made from a poem of Bourne's.

[19]Metal point at the end of a lace.

[20]Classical Latin poets, whose elegiac couplets Cowper compares with those of Bourne.

[21]House of Parliament.

[22]Belts worn around the cassocks of ministers.

Since I began to write long poems, I seem to turn up my nose at the idea of a short one. I have lately entered upon one which, if ever finished, cannot easily be comprised in much less than a thousand lines! But this must make part of a second publication, and be accompanied in due time by others not yet thought of; for it seems (which I did not know till the bookseller had occasion to tell me so) that single pieces stand no chance, and that nothing less than a volume will go down. You yourself afford me a proof of the certainty of this intelligence by sending me franks which nothing less than a volume can fill. I have accordingly sent you one, but am obliged to add that had the wind been in any other point of the compass, or, blowing as it does from the east, had it been less boisterous, you must have been contented with a much shorter letter; but the abridgement of every other occupation is very favorable to that of writing.

Our love attends all the family at Stock.[23]

I am glad I did not expect to hear from you by this post, for the boy has lost the bag in which your letter must have been enclosed —another reason for my prolixity!—Yours affectionately,

W. C.

VII. To William Unwin

Olney, 5 January, 1782

My dear Friend,

Did I allow myself to plead the common excuse of idle correspondents, and esteem it a sufficient reason for not writing that I have nothing to write about, I certainly should not write now. But I have so often found, on similar occasions, when a great penury of matter has seemed to threaten me with an utter impossibility of hatching a letter, that nothing is necessary but to put pen to paper, and go on, in order to conquer all difficulties, —that, availing myself of past experience, I now begin with a most assured persuasion that sooner or later, one idea naturally suggesting another, I shall come to a most prosperous conclusion.

In the last *Review,* I mean in the last but one, I saw Johnson's critique upon Prior and Pope. I am bound to acquiesce in his opinion of the latter because it has always been my own. I could never agree with those who preferred him to Dryden; nor with others (I have known such, and persons of taste and discernment too) who could not allow him to be a poet at all. He was certainly a mechanical maker of verses, and in every line he ever wrote we see indubitable marks of the most indefatigable industry and labor. Writers who find it necessary to make such strenuous and painful exertions are generally as phlegmatic as they are correct; but Pope was, in this respect, exempted from the common lot of authors of that class. With the unwearied application of a plodding Flemish painter, who draws a shrimp with the most minute exactness, he had all the genius of one of the first masters. Never, I believe, were such talents and such drudgery united. But I admire Dryden most, who has succeeded by mere dint of genius, and in spite of a laziness and carelessness almost peculiar to himself. His faults are numberless, but so are his beauties. His faults are those of a great man, and his beauties are such (at least sometimes) as Pope, with all his touching and retouching, could never equal. So far, therefore, I have no quarrel with Johnson. But I cannot subscribe to what he says of Prior. In the first place, though my memory may fail me, I do not recollect that he takes any notice of his *Solomon,*[24] in my mind the best poem, whether we consider the subject of it or the execution, that he ever wrote. In the next place, he condemns him for introducing Venus and Cupid into his love-verses, and concludes it impossible his passion could be sincere, because when he would express it he has recourse to fables. But when Prior wrote those deities were not so obsolete as now. His contemporary writers, and some that succeeded him, did not think them beneath their notice. Tibullus, in reality, disbelieved their existence as much as we do; yet Tibullus is allowed to be the prince of all poetical *inamoratos,* though he mentions them in almost every page. There is a fashion in these things, which the Doctor seems

---
[23]The place of which Unwin was rector.

[24]*Solomon on the Vanity of the World* (1718).

to have forgotten. But what shall we say of his old fusty-rusty remarks upon *Henry and Emma?*[25] I agree with him that morally considered both the knight and his lady are bad characters, and that each exhibits an example which ought not to be followed. The man dissembles in a way that would have justified the woman had she renounced him; and the woman resolves to follow him at the expense of delicacy, propriety, and even modesty itself. But when the critic calls it a dull dialogue, who but a critic will believe him? There are few readers of poetry of either sex, in this country, who cannot remember how that enchanting piece has bewitched them, who do not know that, instead of finding it tedious, they have been so delighted with the romantic turn of it as to have overlooked all its defects, and to have given it a consecrated place in their memories, without ever feeling it a burthen. I wonder almost that, as the Bacchanals served Orpheus, the boys and girls do not tear this husky, dry commentator limb from limb, in resentment of such an injury done to their darling poet. I admire Johnson as a man of great erudition and sense; but when he sets himself up for a judge of writers upon the subject of love, a passion which I suppose he never felt in his life, he might as well think himself qualified to pronounce upon a treatise on horsemanship, or the art of fortification. *   *   *

The next packet I receive will bring me, I imagine, the last proof sheet of my volume,[26] which will consist of about three hundred and fifty pages honestly printed. My public *entrée,* therefore, is not far distant.

Your mother joins with me in love to yourself and all at Stock. Yours, *mon ami,*[27]
Wm. Cowper

Had we known that the last cheeses were naught, we would not have sent you these. Your mother has, however, inquired for and found a better dairy, which she means shall furnish you with cheese another year.

---

[25]Modeled on *The Nut-Brown Maid,* a well-known ballad of the fifteenth century.

[26]The *Poems,* the printing of which is mentioned in letters V and VI.

[27]My friend.

VIII. To William Unwin

Olney, 18 November, *1782*

My dear William,

On the part of the poor, and on our part, be pleased to make acknowledgments, such as the occasion calls for, to our beneficent friend Mr. Smith.[28] I call him ours because, having experienced his kindness to myself in a former instance, and in the present his disinterested readiness to succor the distressed, my ambition will be satisfied with nothing less. He may depend upon the strictest secrecy; no creature shall hear him mentioned, either now or hereafter, as the person from whom we have received this bounty. But when I speak of him, or hear him spoken of by others, which sometimes happens, I shall not forget what is due to so rare a character. I wish, and your mother wishes it too, that he could sometimes take us in his way to Nottingham; he will find us happy to receive a person whom we must needs account it an honor to know. We shall exercise our best discretion in the disposal of the money; but in this town, where the Gospel has been preached so many years, where the people have been favored so long with laborious and conscientious ministers, it is not an easy thing to find those who make no profession of religion at all, and are yet proper objects of charity. The profane are so profane, so drunken, dissolute, and in every respect worthless that to make them partakers of his bounty would be to abuse it. We promise, however, that none shall touch it but such as are miserably poor, yet at the same time industrious and honest, two characters frequently united here, where the most watchful and unremitting labor will hardly procure them bread. We make none but the cheapest laces, and the price of them is fallen almost to nothing.

Thanks are due to yourself likewise, and are hereby accordingly rendered, for waiving your claim in behalf of your own parishioners. You are always with them, and they are always, at least some of them, the better

---

[28]Robert Smith (1752–1838), later Lord Carrington. As a member of Parliament he had frequently sent franks to Cowper.

for your residence among them. Olney is a populous place, inhabited chiefly by the half-starved and the ragged of the earth, and it is not possible for our small party and small ability to extend their operations so far as to be much felt among such numbers. Accept, therefore, your share of their gratitude, and be convinced that when they pray for a blessing upon those who have relieved their wants, He that answers that prayer, and when He answers it, will remember His servant at Stock.

I little thought, when I was writing the history of John Gilpin, that he would appear in print.[29]—I intended to laugh, and to make two or three others laugh, of whom you were one. But now all the world laughs, at least if they have the same relish for a tale ridiculous in itself, and quaintly told, as we have.—Well—they do not always laugh so innocently, or at so small an expense —for in a world like this, abounding with subjects for satire, and with satirical wits to mark them, a laugh that hurts nobody has at least the grace of novelty to recommend it. Swift's darling motto was *Vive la bagatelle*[30] —a good wish for a philosopher of his complexion, the greater part of whose wisdom, whencesoever it came, most certainly came not from above. *La bagatelle* has no enemy in me, though it has neither so warm a friend, nor so able a one, as it had in him. If I trifle, and merely trifle, it is because I am reduced to it by necessity—a melancholy that nothing else so effectually disperses engages me sometimes in the arduous task of being merry by force. And, strange as it may seem, the most ludicrous lines I ever wrote have been written in the saddest mood and, but for that saddest mood, perhaps had never been written at all. To say truth, it would be but a shocking vagary, should the mariners on board a ship buffeted by a terrible storm employ themselves in fiddling and dancing; yet sometimes much such a part act I. *   *   *

I hear from Mrs. Newton that some great persons have spoken with great approbation of a certain book.[31]—Who they are, and what they have said, I am to be told in a future letter. The Monthly Reviewers in the mean time have satisfied me well enough.—Yours, my dear William,

W. C.

IX. *To William Unwin*

Olney, 29 September, 1783

My dear William,

We are sorry that you and your household partake so largely of the ill effects of this unhealthy season. You are happy, however, in having hitherto escaped the epidemic fever which has prevailed much in this part of the kingdom, and carried many off. Your mother and I are well. After more than a fortnight's indisposition, which slight appellation is quite adequate to the description of all that I suffered, I am at length restored by a grain or two of emetic tartar. It is a tax I generally pay in autumn. By this time, I hope, a purer ether than we have seen for months, and these brighter suns than the summer had to boast, have cheered your spirits, and made your existence more comfortable. We are rational; but we are animal too, and therefore subject to the influences of the weather. The cattle in the fields show evident symptoms of lassitude and disgust in an unpleasant season, and we, their lords and masters, are constrained to sympathize with them; the only difference between us is that they know not the cause of their dejection, and we do,—but, for our humiliation, are equally at a loss to cure it. Upon this account I have sometimes wished myself a philosopher. How happy, in comparison with myself, does the sagacious investigator of nature seem, whose fancy is ever employed in the invention of *hypotheses,* and his reason in the support of them! While he is accounting for the origin of the winds, he has no leisure to attend to their influence upon himself; and while he considers what the sun is made of, forgets that he has not shone for a month. One project in-

---

[29]It had been published for the first time a few days before this, anonymously in a newspaper.

[30]Long live nonsense

[31]The *Poems* already mentioned in letters V, VI, and VII.

deed supplants another. The *vortices* of Descartes gave way to the gravitation of Newton, and this again is threatened by the electrical fluid of a modern. One generation blows bubbles, and the next breaks them. But in the meantime your philosopher is a happy man. He escapes a thousand inquietudes to which the indolent are subject, and finds his occupation, whether it be the pursuit of a butterfly or a demonstration, the wholesomest exercise in the world. As he proceeds, he applauds himself. His discoveries, though eventually perhaps they prove but dreams, are to him realities. The world gaze at him as he does at new phenomena in the heavens, and perhaps understand him as little. But this does not prevent their praises, nor at all disturb him in the enjoyment of that self-complacence to which his imaginary success entitles him. He wears his honors while he lives, and if another strips them off when he has been dead a century, it is no great matter; he can then make shift without them.

I have said a great deal upon this subject, and know not what it all amounts to. I did not intend a syllable of it when I began. But *currente calamo,*[32] I stumbled upon it. My end is to amuse myself and you. The former of these two points is secured. I shall be happy if I do not miss the latter.

By the way, what is your opinion of these air-balloons?[33] I am quite charmed with the discovery. Is it not possible (do you suppose) to convey such a quantity of inflammable air into the stomach and abdomen, that the philosopher, no longer gravitating to a center, shall ascend by his own comparative levity, and never stop till he has reached the medium exactly *in equilibrio* with himself? May he not by the help of a pasteboard rudder, attached to his posteriors, steer himself in that purer element with ease; and again by a slow and gradual discharge of his aerial contents, recover his former tendency to the earth, and descend without the smallest danger or inconvenience? These things are worth inquiry; and (I dare say) they will be inquired after as they deserve. The

pennae non homini datae[34] are likely to be less regretted than they were; and perhaps a flight of academicians and a covey of fine ladies may be no uncommon spectacle in the next generation. A letter which appeared in the public prints last week convinces me that the learned are not without hopes of some such improvement upon this discovery. The author is a sensible and ingenious man; and under a reasonable apprehension that the ignorant may feel themselves inclined to laugh upon a subject that affects himself with the utmost seriousness, with much good manners and management bespeaks their patience, suggesting many good consequences that may result from a course of experiments upon this machine, and amongst others, that it may be of use in ascertaining the shape of continents and islands, and the face of wide-extended and far distant countries: an end not to be hoped for, unless by these means of extraordinary elevation the human prospect may be immensely enlarged, and the philosopher, exalted to the skies, attain a view of the whole hemisphere at once. But whether he is to ascend by the mere inflation of his person, as hinted above, or whether in a sort of bandbox, supported upon balloons, is not yet apparent, nor (I suppose) even in his own idea perfectly decided.— Yours, my dear William,

W. C.

X. To John Newton[35]

Olney, 17 November, 1783

My dear Friend,

A parcel arrived last night, the contents of which shall be disposed of according to order. We thank Mrs. Newton (not from the teeth outwards) for the toothbrushes.

The country around us is much alarmed with apprehensions of fire. Two have happened since that of Olney: one at Hitchin, where the damage is said to amount to eleven thousand pounds, and another at a place not far from Hitchin, of which I have not learnt the name. Letters have been dropped at Bedford, threatening to burn the

---

[32] As the pen moved.

[33] Recently invented by two Frenchmen, the brothers Montgolfier.

[34] Wings not given to man.

[35] Vicar of Olney until 1779, and with Cowper the co-author of the *Olney Hymns* (1779).

town; and the inhabitants have been so intimidated as to have placed a guard in many parts of it several nights past. Some madman or some devil has broke loose, who it is to be hoped will pay dear for these effusions of his malignity. Since our conflagration here we have sent two women and a boy to the justice, for depredation; Sue Riviss, for stealing a piece of beef, which, in her excuse, she said she intended to take care of. This lady, whom you well remember, escaped for want of evidence; not that evidence was indeed wanting, but our men of Gotham judged it unnecessary to send it. With her went the woman I mentioned before, who, it seems, has made some sort of profession, but upon this occasion allowed herself a latitude of conduct rather inconsistent with it, having filled her apron with wearing apparel, which she likewise intended to take care of. She would have gone to the county gaol had Billy Raban, the baker's son, who prosecuted, insisted upon it; but he good-naturedly, though I think weakly, interposed in her favor, and begged her off. The young gentleman who accompanied these fair ones is the junior son of Molly Boswell. He had stolen some iron-work, the property of Griggs, the butcher. Being convicted, he was ordered to be whipt, which operation he underwent at the cart's tail, from the stone house to the high arch,[36] and back again. He seemed to show great fortitude, but it was all an imposition upon the public. The beadle who performed it had filled his left hand with red ochre, through which, after every stroke, he drew the lash of his whip, leaving the appearance of a wound upon the skin; but in reality not hurting him at all. This being perceived by Mr. Constable Handscomb, who followed the beadle, he applied his cane, without any such management or precaution, to the shoulders of the too merciful executioner. The scene immediately became more interesting. The beadle could by no means be prevailed upon to strike hard, which provoked the constable to strike harder; and this double flogging continued, till a lass of Silver End,[37] pitying the pitiful beadle thus suffering under the hands of the pitiless constable, joined the procession, and placing herself immediately behind the latter, seized him by his capillary club, and pulling him backwards by the same, slapt his face with a most Amazonian fury. This concatenation of events has taken up more of my paper than I intended it should, but I could not forbear to inform you how the beadle threshed the thief, the constable the beadle, and the lady the constable, and how the thief was the only person concerned who suffered nothing. Mr. Teedon[38] has been here, and is gone again. He came to thank me for an old pair of breeches. In answer to our inquiries after his health, he replied that he had a slow fever which made him take all possible care not to inflame his blood. I admitted his prudence, but in his particular instance could not very clearly discern the need of it. Pump water will not heat him much; and, to speak a little in his own style, more inebriating fluids are to him, I fancy, not very attainable. He brought us news, the truth of which, however, I do not vouch for, that the town of Bedford was actually on fire yesterday, and the flames not extinguished when the bearer of the tidings left it.

Swift observes, when he is giving his reasons why the preacher is elevated always above his hearers, that let the crowd be as great as it will below, there is always room enough overhead. If the French philosophers can carry their art of flying to the perfection they desire, the observation may be reversed; the crowd will be overhead, and they will have most room who stay below. I can assure you, however, upon my own experience, that this way of traveling is very delightful. I dreamt, a night or two since, that I drove myself through the upper regions in a balloon and pair, with the greatest ease and security. Having finished the tour I intended, I made a short turn, and, with one flourish of my whip, descended, my horses prancing and curveting with an infinite share of spirit, but without the least danger either to me or my vehicle. The time, we may suppose, is at hand, and seems to be prognosticated by my dream, when these airy excursions will be universal, when

---

[36]Local landmarks near the center of Olney.

[37]A street in Olney.

[38]A poor neighbor of Cowper's.

judges will fly the circuit, and bishops their visitations; and when the tour of Europe will be performed with much greater speed, and with equal advantage, by all who travel merely for the sake of having it to say, that they have made it.

I beg you will accept for yourself and yours our unfeigned love, and remember me affectionately to Mr. Bacon,[39] when you see him.—Yours, my dear friend,

Wm. Cowper

XI. To Joseph Johnson

Olney, *c.* December, 1784[40]

I DID not write the line that has been tampered with hastily, or without due attention to the construction of it; and what appeared to me its only merit is, in its present state, entirely annihilated.

I know that the ears of modern verse-writers are delicate to an excess, and their readers are as troubled with the squeamishness as themselves; so that if a line do not run as smooth as quicksilver, they are offended. A critic of the present day serves a poem as a cook serves a dead turkey, when she fastens the legs of it to a post, and draws out all the sinews. For this we may thank Pope; but unless we could imitate him in the closeness and compactness of his expression, as well as in the smoothness of his numbers, we had better drop the imitation, which serves no other purpose than to emasculate and weaken all we write. Give me a manly, rough line, with a deal of meaning in it, rather than a whole poem full of musical periods, that have nothing but their oily smoothness to recommend them.

I have said thus much, as I hinted in the beginning, because I have just finished a much longer poem[41] than the last, which our common friend will receive by the same messenger that has the charge of this letter. In that poem there are many lines which an ear so nice as the gentleman's who made the above-mentioned alteration would undoubtedly condemn; and yet (if I may be permitted to say it) they cannot be made smoother without being the worse for it. There is a roughness on a plum which nobody that understands fruit would rub off, though the plum would be much more polished without it. But lest I tire you, I will only add that I wish you to guard me from all such meddling; assuring you that I always write as smoothly as I can, but that I never did, never will, sacrifice the spirit or sense of a passage to the sound of it.

W. Cowper

XII. To John Newton

Olney, 24 September, 1785

My dear Friend,

I am sorry that an excursion which you would otherwise have found so agreeable was attended with so great a drawback upon its pleasures as Miss Cunningham's[42] illness must needs have been. Had she been able to bathe in the sea, it might have been of service to her; but I know her weakness and delicacy of habit to be such as did not encourage any very sanguine hopes that the regimen would suit her. I remember Southampton well, having spent much time there;[43] but though I was young, and had no objections on the score of conscience either to dancing or cards, I never was in the assembly-room in my life. I never was fond of company, and especially disliked it in the country. A walk to Netley Abbey, or to Freemantle, or to Redbridge, or a book by the fireside, had always more charms for me than any other amusement that the place afforded. I was also a sailor, and being of Sir Thomas Hesketh's[44] party, who was himself born one, was often pressed into the service. But though I gave myself an air, and wore trousers, I had no genuine right to that honor, disliking much to be occupied in great waters, unless in the finest weather.

---

[39]John Bacon, the sculptor, mentioned in *The Task*, I, 702–704.

[40]The date of this letter to Cowper's publisher is merely conjectural. It probably alludes to material included in the *Poems* of 1785.

[41]Probably *The Task*.

[42]Newton's niece.

[43]In 1752, when he was twenty-one.

[44]Later the husband of Cowper's cousin Harriet Cowper.

How they contrive to elude the wearisomeness that attends a sea life who take long voyages, you know better than I; but for my own part, I seldom have sailed so far as from Hampton River to Portsmouth without feeling the confinement irksome, and sometimes to a degree that was almost insupportable. There is a certain perverseness of which I believe all men have a share, but of which no man has a larger share than I;—I mean that temper, or humor, or whatever it is to be called, that indisposes us to a situation, though not unpleasant in itself, merely because we cannot get out of it. I could not endure the room in which I now write, were I conscious that the door were locked. In less than five minutes I should feel myself a prisoner, though I can spend hours in it, under an assurance that I may leave it when I please, without experiencing any tedium at all. It was for this reason, I suppose, that the yacht was always disagreeable to me. Could I have stepped out of it into a corn-field or a garden, I should have liked it well enough; but being surrounded with water, I was as much confined in it as if I had been surrounded by fire, and did not find that it made me any adequate compensation for such an abridgment of my liberty. I make little doubt but Noah was glad when he was enlarged from the ark; and we are sure that Jonah was, when he came out of the fish; and so was I to escape from the good sloop the *Harriet*.

In my last I wrote you word that Mr. Perry was given over by his friends, and pronounced a dead man by his physician. Just when I had reached the end of the foregoing paragraph, he came in. His errand hither was to bring two letters, which I enclose; one is to yourself, in which he will give you, I doubt not, such an account both of his body and mind as will make all that I might say upon those subjects superfluous. The only consequences of his illness seem to be that he looks a little pale, and that though always a most excellent man, he is still more angelic than he was. Illness sanctified is better than health. But I know a man who has been a sufferer by a worse illness than his, almost these fourteen years, and who at present is only the worse for it.

Mr. Scott[45] called upon us yesterday; he is much inclined to set up a Sunday School, if he can raise a fund for the purpose. Mr. Jones[46] has had one some time at Clifton, and Mr. Unwin writes me word that he has been thinking of nothing else day and night for a fortnight. It is a wholesome measure, that seems to bid fair to be pretty generally adopted, and for the good effects that it promises deserves well to be so. I know not, indeed, while the spread of the Gospel continues so limited as it is, how a reformation of manners in the lower class of mankind can be brought to pass, or by what other means the utter abolition of all principle among them, moral as well as religious, can possibly be prevented. Heathenish parents can only bring up heathenish children: an assertion nowhere oftener or more clearly illustrated than at Olney, where children seven years of age infest the streets every evening with curses and with songs to which it would be unseemly to give their proper epithet. Such urchins as these could not be so diabolically accomplished unless by the connivance of their parents. It is well, indeed, if in some instances their parents be not themselves their instructors. Judging by their proficiency, one can hardly suppose any other. It is, therefore, doubtless an act of the greatest charity to snatch them out of such hands before the inveteracy of the evil shall have made it desperate. Mr. Teedon, I should imagine, will be employed as a teacher, should this expedient be carried into effect. I know not, at least, that we have any other person among us so well qualified for the service. He is indisputably a Christian man, and miserably poor, whose revenues need improvement as much as any children in the world can possibly need instruction.

I understand that Mr. Jones is in London; it is possible that you may have seen him, and if you have, are better acquainted with his present intentions respecting Lord Peterborough than myself. We saw him, not long since, when he talked of resigning his office immediately; but I hear that he was

[45]Curate of Olney.
[46]Curate of Clifton Reynes, a mile from Olney.

afterwards otherwise advised, and repented of his purpose. I think it a great pity that he did. A thing that a man had better never have touched cannot too soon be relinquished. While his principal kept himself at a distance, his connection with him was less offensive; but now to all who interest themselves in his conduct as a minister of the Gospel it is an offence indeed. He seems aware of it, therefore, will soon abandon it.

Mrs. Unwin hopes that a hare, which she sent before Mrs. Newton went her journey, arrived safe. By this week's coach she also sent three fowls and a ham, with cabbages, of whose safe arrival she will likewise be glad to hear. She has long been troubled with a pain in her side, which we take to be of the spasmodic kind, but is otherwise well. She joins with me in love to yourself and Mrs. Newton, and to the young ladies; neither do we forget Sally Johnson.[47]—Believe me, my dear friend, with true affection, yours,

W. C.

Hannah desires me to give her duty to Miss Cunningham and to Miss Catlett.[48]

XIII. To Lady Hesketh[49]

Olney, 12 October, 1785

My dear Cousin,

It is no new thing with you to give pleasure; but I will venture to say that you do not often give more than you gave me this morning. When I came down to breakfast, and found upon the table a letter franked by my uncle,[50] and when opening that frank I found that it contained a letter from you, I said within myself—"This is just as it should be. We are all grown young again, and the days that I thought I should see no more are actually returned." You perceive, therefore, that you judged well when you conjectured that a line from you would not be disagreeable to me. It could

not be otherwise than, as in fact it proved, a most agreeable surprise, for I can truly boast of an affection for you that neither years nor interrupted intercourse have at all abated. I need only recollect how much I valued you once, and with how much cause, immediately to feel a revival of the same value, if that can be said to revive which at the most has only been dormant for want of employment; but I slander it when I say that it has slept. A thousand times have I recollected a thousand scenes, in which our two selves have formed the whole of the drama, with the greatest pleasure; at times, too, when I had no reason to suppose that I should ever hear from you again. I have laughed with you at the *Arabian Nights' Entertainments,* which afforded us, as you well know, a fund of merriment that deserves never to be forgot. I have walked with you to Netley Abbey, and have scrambled with you over hedges in every direction, and many other feats we have performed together upon the field of my remembrance, and all within these few years. Should I say within this twelvemonth, I should not transgress the truth. The hours that I have spent with you were among the pleasantest of my former days, and are therefore chronicled in my mind so deeply as to feel no erasure. Neither do I forget my poor friend, Sir Thomas. I should remember him, indeed, at any rate, on account of his personal kindness to myself; but the last testimony that he gave of his regard for you endears him to me still more. With his uncommon understanding (for with many peculiarities he had more sense than any of his acquaintance), and with his generous sensibilities, it was hardly possible that he should not distinguish you as he has done. As it was the last, so it was the best proof that he could give of a judgment that never deceived him when he would allow himself leisure to consult it.

You say that you have often heard of me; that puzzles me. I cannot imagine from what quarter, but it is no matter. I must tell you, however, my cousin, that your information has been a little defective. That I am happy in my situation is true; I live, and have lived these twenty years, with Mrs. Unwin, to whose affectionate care of me,

---

[47]Newton's maid.　[48]Newton's niece.

[49]Cowper's cousin, with whom he had not corresponded since 1767.

[50]Lady Hesketh's father, Ashley Cowper, who died in 1788 at the age of eighty-seven.

during the far greater part of that time, it is, under Providence, owing that I live at all. But I do not account myself happy in having been for thirteen of those years in a state of mind that has made all that care and atten- 5 tion necessary: an attention and a care that have injured her health, and which, had she not been uncommonly supported, must have brought her to the grave. But I will pass to another subject; it would be cruel to particu- 10 larize only to give pain; neither would I by any means give a sable hue to the first letter of a correspondence so unexpectedly re- newed.

I am delighted with what you tell me of 15 my uncle's good health. To enjoy any meas- ure of cheerfulness at so late a day is much; but to have that late day enlivened with the vivacity of youth is much more, and in these postdiluvian times a rarity indeed. Happy, 20 for the most part, are parents who have daughters. Daughters are not apt to outlive their natural affections, which a son has gen- erally survived, even before his boyish years are expired. I rejoice particularly in my 25 uncle's felicity, who has three female de- scendants from his little person, who leave him nothing to wish for upon that head.

My dear cousin, dejection of spirits, which, I suppose, may have prevented many a man 30 from becoming an author, made me one. I find constant employment necessary, and therefore take care to be constantly em- ployed. Manual occupations do not en- gage the mind sufficiently, as I know by ex- 35 perience, having tried many. But composi- tion, especially of verse, absorbs it wholly. I write, therefore, generally three hours in a morning, and in an evening I transcribe. I read also, but less than I write, for I must 40 have bodily exercise, and therefore never pass a day without it.

You ask me where I have been this sum- mer. I answer at Olney. Should you ask me where I spent the last seventeen sum- 45 mers, I should still answer, at Olney. Ay, and the winters also; I have seldom left it and, except when I attended my brother in his last illness, never, I believe, a fortnight together. 50

Adieu, my beloved cousin, I shall not al- ways be thus nimble in reply, but shall always have great pleasure in answering you when I can.—Yours, my dear friend and cousin,
W. C.

XIV. To William Unwin

Olney, c. 1786[51]

My dear William,

The fish happening to swim uppermost in my mind, I give it the precedence, and be- gin with returning our thanks for it, not for- getting the circumstance of free carriage. Upon the whole, I think this a handsomer way of acknowledging a present than to tuck it into a postscript.

I find the *Register* in all respects an enter- taining medley, but especially in this, that it has brought to my view some long-forgotten pieces of my own production;—I mean, by the way, two or three. These I have marked with my own initials, and you may be sure I found them peculiarly agreeable, as they had not only the grace of being mine, but that of novelty likewise to recommend them. It is at least twenty years since I saw them. You, I think, was never a dabbler in rime. I have been one ever since I was fourteen years of age, when I began with translating an elegy of Tibullus. I have no more right to the name of poet than a maker of mouse-traps has to that of an engineer; but my little ex- ploits in this way have at times amused me so much that I have often wished myself a good one. Such a talent in verse as mine is like a child's rattle,—very entertaining to the trifler that uses it, and very disagreeable to all beside. But it has served to rid me of some melancholy moments, for I only take it up as a gentleman performer does his fiddle. I have this peculiarity belonging to me as a rimist, that though I am charmed to a great degree with my own work, while it is on the anvil, I can seldom bear to look at it when it is once finished. The more I con- template it, the more it loses of its value, till I am at last quite disgusted with it. I then throw it by, take it up again perhaps ten years after, and am as much delighted with it as at first.

Few people have the art of being agreea-

―――――――――――――
[51]Date conjectural. Unwin died on 29 November, 1786.

ble when they talk of themselves; if you are not weary therefore by this time, you pay me a high compliment.

I dare say Miss Shuttleworth was much diverted with the conjecture of her friends. The true key to the pleasure she found at Olney was plain enough to be seen, but they chose to overlook it. She brought with her a disposition to be pleased, which whoever does is sure to find a visit agreeable, because they make it so.

Your mother joins me in affectionate remembrance to all your family.—Yours,

W. C.

We are obliged to little John for his P.S., and think his observation very just, but are a little doubtful about the exactness of his calculation.

XV. To Lady Hesketh

Weston Underwood,[52] 26 November, 1786

It is my birthday, my beloved cousin, and I determine to employ a part of it, that it may not be destitute of festivity, in writing to you. The dark, thick fog that has obscured it would have been a burthen to me at Olney, but here I have hardly attended to it. The neatness and snugness of our abode compensate all the dreariness of the season, and whether the ways are wet or dry, our house at least is always warm and commodious. Oh for you, my cousin, to partake these comforts with us! I will not begin already to tease you upon that subject, but Mrs. Unwin remembers to have heard from your own lips that you hate London in the spring. Perhaps therefore by that time you may be glad to escape from a scene which will be every day growing more disagreeable, that you may enjoy the comforts of the lodge. You well know that the best house has a desolate appearance unfurnished. This house accordingly, since it has been occupied by us and our *meubles,*[53] is as much superior to what it was when you saw it as you can imagine. The parlor is even elegant. When

I say that the parlor is elegant, I do not mean to insinuate that the study is not so. It is neat, warm, and silent, and a much better study than I deserve, if I do not produce in it an incomparable translation of Homer. I think every day of those lines of Milton, and congratulate myself on having obtained, before I am quite superannuated, what he seems not to have hoped for sooner:

> And may at length my weary age
> Find out the peaceful hermitage![54]

For if it is not an hermitage, at least it is a much better thing; and you must always understand, my dear, that when poets talk of cottages, hermitages, and such like things, they mean a house with six sashes in front, two comfortable parlors, a smart staircase, and three bedchambers of convenient dimensions; in short, exactly such a house as this.

The Throckmortons[55] continue the most obliging neighbors in the world. One morning last week they both went with me to the cliff;—a scene, my dear, in which you would delight beyond measure, but which you cannot visit except in the spring or autumn. The heat of summer and the clinging dirt of winter would destroy you. What is called the cliff is no cliff, nor at all like one, but a beautiful terrace, sloping gently down to the Ouse, and from the brow of which, though not lofty, you have a view of such a valley as makes that which you see from the hills near Olney, and which I have had the honor to celebrate, an affair of no consideration.

Wintry as the weather is, do not suspect that it confines me. I ramble daily, and every day change my ramble. Wherever I go, I find short grass under my feet; and when I have traveled perhaps five miles, come home with shoes not at all too dirty for a drawing-room. I was pacing yesterday under the elms that surround the field in which stands the great alcove,[56] when lifting my eyes I saw two black genteel figures bolt through a hedge into the path where I was

---

[52]Through the generosity of Lady Hesketh, Cowper and Mrs. Unwin were able to move to a more comfortable house at Weston Underwood, a short distance from Olney, in November, 1786.

[53]Furniture.

[54]*Il Penseroso,* 167–168.

[55]John Courtney Throckmorton and his wife, mentioned in the following paragraph. Throckmorton is the Benevolus of *The Task* (I, 262), and Cowper's landlord at Weston Underwood.

[56]See *The Task,* I, 278.

walking. You guess already who they were, and that they could be nobody but our neighbors. They had seen me from a hill at a distance, and had traversed a great turnip-field to get at me. You see therefore, my dear, that I am in some request. Alas! in too much request with some people. The verses of Cadwallader have found me at last.

I am charmed with your account of our little cousin[57] at Kensington. If the world does not spoil him hereafter, he will be a valuable man.—Good night, and may God bless thee.

W. C.

XVI. To Lady Hesketh

Weston Underwood, 27 November, 1787

IT IS the part of wisdom, my dearest cousin, to sit down contented under the demands of necessity, because they are such. I am sensible that you cannot in my uncle's present infirm state, and of which it is not possible to expect any considerable amendment, indulge either us or yourself with a journey to Weston. Yourself I say, both because I know it will give you pleasure to see *Causidice mi*[58] once more, especially in the comfortable abode where you have placed him, and because after so long an imprisonment in London you who love the country and have a taste for it would of course be glad to return to it. For my own part, to me it is ever new, and though I have now been an inhabitant of this village a twelvemonth, and have during the half of that time been at liberty to expatiate,[59] and to make discoveries, I am daily finding out fresh scenes and walks, which you would never be satisfied with enjoying;—some of them are unapproachable by you either on foot or in your carriage. Had you twenty toes (whereas I suppose you have but ten) you could not reach them; and coach wheels have never been seen there since the flood. Before it indeed (as Burnet says that the earth was then perfectly free from all inequalities in its surface) they might have been seen there every day. We have other walks both upon hilltops and in valleys beneath, some of which by the help of your carriage, and many of them without its help, would be always at your command.

On Monday morning last Sam[60] brought me word that there was a man in the kitchen who desired to speak with me. I ordered him in. A plain, decent, elderly figure made its appearance, and being desired to sit, spoke as follows: "Sir, I am clerk of the parish of All-Saints in Northampton, brother of Mr. Cox the upholsterer. It is customary for the person in my office to annex to a bill of mortality, which he publishes at Christmas, a copy of verses. You would do me a great favor, sir, if you would furnish me with one." To this I replied: "Mr. Cox, you have several men of genius in your town; why have you not applied to some of them? There is a namesake of yours in particular, Cox the statuary, who, every body knows, is a first-rate maker of verses. He surely is the man of all the world for your purpose." —"Alas! sir, I have heretofore borrowed help from him, but he is a gentleman of so much reading that the people of our town cannot understand him." I confess to you, my dear, I felt all the force of the compliment implied in this speech, and was almost ready to answer, "Perhaps, my good friend, they may find me unintelligible too for the same reason." But on asking him whether he had walked over to Weston on purpose to implore the assistance of my muse, and on his replying in the affirmative, I felt my mortified vanity a little consoled, and pitying the poor man's distress, which appeared to be considerable, promised to supply him. The waggon has accordingly gone this day to Northampton loaded in part with my effusions in the mortuary style. A fig for poets who write epitaphs upon individuals! I have written *one* that serves *two hundred* persons.

A few days since I received a second very obliging letter from Mr. Mackenzie.[61] He

[57]George Augustus Cowper (1776–1799), later fourth Earl of Cowper.

[58]My advocate (the name given Cowper by Lady Hesketh's husband).

[59]Walk about.

[60]Sam Roberts, Cowper's servant.

[61]Henry Mackenzie (1745–1831), author of *The Man of Feeling,* who contributed many papers to contemporary periodicals.

tells me that his own papers, which are by far, he is sorry to say, the most numerous, are marked V. I. Z. Accordingly, my dear, I am happy to find that I am engaged in a correspondence with Mr. Viz, a gentleman for whom I have always entertained the profoundest veneration. But the serious fact is that the papers distinguished by those signatures have ever pleased me most, and struck me as the work of a sensible man, who knows the world well, and has more of Addison's delicate humor than anybody.

A poor man begged food at the Hall lately. The cook gave him some vermicelli soup. He ladled it about sometime with the spoon, and then returned it to her, saying, "I am a poor man, it is true, and I am very hungry; but yet I cannot eat broth with maggots in it." Once more, my dear, a thousand thanks for your box full of good things, useful things, and beautiful things.—Yours ever,
W. C.

XVII. To Lady Hesketh

Weston Underwood, 19 December, 1787

SATURDAY, my dearest cousin, was a day of receipts. In the morning I received a box filled with an abundant variety of stationery ware, containing, in particular, a quantity of paper sufficient, well covered with good writing, to immortalize any man. I have nothing to do, therefore, but to cover it as aforesaid, and my name will never die. In the evening I received a smaller box, but still more welcome on account of its contents. It contained an almanac in red morocco, a pencil of a new invention, called an everlasting pencil, and a noble purse, with a noble gift in it, called a bank-note for twenty-five pounds. I need use no arguments to assure you, my cousin, that by the help of ditto note, we shall be able to fadge very comfortably till Christmas is turned, without having the least occasion to draw upon you. By the post yesterday—that is, Sunday morning—I received also a letter from Anonymous, giving me advice of the kind present which I have just particularized; in which letter allusion is made to a certain piece by me composed, entitled, I believe, *The Drop of Ink*. The only copy I ever

gave of that piece I gave to yourself. It is *possible,* therefore, that between you and Anonymous there may be some communication. If that should be the case, I will beg you just to signify to him, as opportunity may occur, the safe arrival of his most acceptable present, and my most grateful sense of it.

My toothache is in a great measure, that is to say almost entirely, removed; not by snipping my ears, as poor Lady Strange's ears were snipped, nor by any other chirurgical operation, except such as I could perform myself. The manner of it was as follows: we dined last Thursday at the Hall;[62] I sat down to table trembling lest the tooth, of which I told you in my last, should not only refuse its own office, but hinder all the rest. Accordingly, in less than five minutes, by a hideous dislocation of it I found myself not only in great pain, but under as absolute prohibition not only to eat, but to speak another word. Great emergencies sometimes meet the most effectual remedies. I resolved, if it were possible, then and there to draw it. This I effected so dexterously by a sudden twitch, and afterwards so dexterously conveyed it into my pocket, that no creature present, not even Mrs. Unwin, who sat facing me, was sensible either of my distress, or of the manner of my deliverance from it. I am poorer by one tooth than I was, but richer by the unimpeded use of all the rest.

When I lived in the Temple,[63] I was rather intimate with a son of the late Admiral Rowley and a younger brother of the present Admiral. Since I wrote to you last, I received a letter from him, in a very friendly and affectionate style. It accompanied half a dozen books which I had lent him five and twenty years ago, and which he apologized for having kept so long, telling me that they had been sent to him at Dublin by mistake; for at Dublin, it seems, he now resides. Reading my poems, he felt, he said, his friendship for me revive, and wrote accordingly. I have now, therefore, a correspondent in Ireland, another in Scotland, and

---

[62]The house of the Throckmortons.

[63]The London college of law, where Cowper had lived from 1752 to 1763.

a third in Wales. All this would be very diverting, had I a little more time to spare to them.

My dog,[64] my dear, is a spaniel. Till Miss Gunning begged him, he was the property of a farmer, and while he was their property had been accustomed to lie in the chimney corner, among the embers, till the hair was singed from his back, and till nothing was left of his tail but the gristle. Allowing for these disadvantages, he is really handsome; and when nature shall have furnished him with a new coat, a gift which, in consideration of the ragged condition of his old one, it is hoped she will not long delay, he will then be unrivalled in personal endowments by any dog in this country. He and my cat are excessively fond of each other, and play a thousand gambols together that it is impossible not to admire.

Know thou that from this time forth the post comes daily to Weston. This improvement is effected by an annual subscription of ten shillings. The Throcks[65] invited us to the measure, and we have acceded to it. Their servant will manage this concern for us at the Olney post office, and the subscription is to pay a man for stumping three times a week from Olney to Newport Pagnell, and back again.

Returning from my walk to-day, while I was passing by some small closes at the back of the town, I heard the voices of some persons extremely merry at the top of the hill. Advancing into the large field behind our house, I met there Mr. Throck, wife, and brother George. Combine in your imagination as large proportions as you can of earth and water intermingled so as to constitute what is commonly called mud, and you will have but an imperfect conception of the quantity that had attached itself to her petticoats; but she had half-boots, and laughed at her own figure. She told me that she had this morning transcribed sixteen pages of my Homer. I observed in reply that to write so much, and to gather all that dirt, was no bad morning's work, considering the shortness of the day at this season.—Yours, my dear,
W. C.

[64]Beau, who figures in several of Cowper's poems.
[65]Throckmortons.

XVIII. To Lady Hesketh

Weston Underwood, 3 March, 1788

ONE day last week Mrs. Unwin and I, having taken our morning walk and returning homeward through the wilderness, met the Throckmortons. A minute after we had met them, we heard the cry of hounds at no great distance, and mounting the broad stump of an elm which had been felled, and by the aid of which we were enabled to look over the wall, we saw them. They were all at that time in our orchard; presently we heard a terrier, belonging to Mrs. Throckmorton, which you may remember by the name of Fury, yelping with much vehemence, and saw her running through the thickets within a few yards of us at her utmost speed, as if in pursuit of something which we doubted not was the fox. Before we could reach the other end of the wilderness, the hounds entered also; and when we arrived at the gate which opens into the grove, there we found the whole weary cavalcade assembled. The huntsman, dismounting, begged leave to follow his hounds on foot, for he was sure, he said, that they had killed him: a conclusion which I suppose he drew from their profound silence. He was accordingly admitted, and with a sagacity that would not have dishonored the best hound in the world, pursuing precisely the same track which the fox and the dogs had taken, though he had never had a glimpse of either after their first entrance through the rails, arrived where he found the slaughtered prey. He soon produced dead reynard, and rejoined us in the grove with all his dogs about him. Having an opportunity to see a ceremony which I was pretty sure would never fall in my way again, I determined to stay and to notice all that passed with the most minute attention. The huntsman, having by the aid of a pitchfork lodged reynard on the arm of an elm, at the height of about nine feet from the ground, there left him for a considerable time. The gentlemen sat on their horses, contemplating the fox for which they had toiled so hard; and the hounds assembled at the foot of the tree, with faces not less expressive of the most rational delight, contemplated the same object. The huntsman remounted, cut off a foot, and threw it to the hounds;—one of them swallowed it whole like a bolus.[66] He then once more alighted, and drawing down the fox by the hinder legs, desired the people, who were by this time rather numerous, to open a lane for him to the right and left. He was instantly obeyed, when, throwing the fox to the distance of some yards, and screaming like a fiend, "tear him to pieces" —at least six times repeatedly, he consigned him over absolutely to the pack, who in a few minutes devoured him completely. Thus, my dear, as Virgil says, what none of the gods could have ventured to promise me, time itself, pursuing its accustomed course, has of its own accord presented me with. I have been in at the death of a fox, and you now know as much of the matter as I, who am as well informed as any sportsman in England.—Yours,

W. C.

XIX. To Mrs. King[67]

Weston Underwood, 11 October, 1788

My dear Madam,

You are perfectly secure from all danger of being overwhelmed with presents from me. It is not much that a poet can possibly have it in his power to give. When he has presented his own works, he may be supposed to have exhausted all means of donation. They are his only superfluity. There was a time, but that time was before I commenced writer for the press, when I amused myself in a way somewhat similar to yours; allowing, I mean, for the difference between masculine and female operations. The scissors and the needle are your chief implements; mine were the chisel and the saw. In those days you might have been in some danger of too plentiful a return for your favors. Tables, such as they were, and joint stools, such as never were, might have traveled to Pertenhall in most inconvenient abundance. But I have long since discontinued this practice, and many others which I found it necessary to adopt, that I might escape the worst of all evils, both in itself and in its consequences—an idle life. Many arts I have exercised with this view, for which nature never designed me, though among them were some in which I arrived at considerable proficiency by mere dint of the most heroic perseverance. There is not a 'squire in all this country who can boast of having made better squirrel-houses, hutches for rabbits, or bird-cages, than myself; and in the article of cabbage-nets I had no superior. I even had the hardiness to take in hand the pencil, and studied a whole year the art of drawing. Many figures were the fruit of my labors, which had at least the merit of being unparalleled by any production either of art or nature. But before the year was ended, I had occasion to wonder at the progress that may be made, in despite of natural deficiency, by dint alone of practice; for I actually produced three landscapes which a lady[68] thought worthy to be framed and glazed. I then judged it high time to exchange this occupation for another, lest, by any subsequent productions of inferior merit, I should forfeit the honor I had so fortunately acquired. But gardening was, of all employments, that in which I succeeded best, though even in this I did not suddenly attain perfection. I began with lettuces and cauliflowers; from them I proceeded to cucumbers; next to melons. I then purchased an orange-tree, to which, in due time, I added two or three myrtles. These served me day and night with employment during a severe winter. To defend them from the frost in a situation that exposed them to its severity cost me much ingenuity and much attendance. I contrived to give them a fire heat, and have waded night after night through the snow, with the bellows under my arm, just before going to bed, to give the latest possible puff to the embers, lest the frost should seize them before morning. Very minute beginnings have sometimes important consequences.

---

[66] Large pill.

[67] A lady who had begun a correspondence with Cowper a few months earlier, and whom he had not yet met. He had recently sent her the two volumes of his *Poems.*

[68] Lady Austen, who suggested the sofa as a subject for the poem which became *The Task.*

From nursing two or three little evergreens I became ambitious of a green-house, and accordingly built one; which, verse excepted, afforded me amusement for a longer time than any expedient of all the many to which I have fled for refuge from the misery of having nothing to do. When I left Olney for Weston, I could no longer have a green-house of my own; but in a neighbor's garden I find a better, of which the sole management is consigned to me.

I had need take care, when I begin a letter, that the subject with which I set off be of some importance; for before I can exhaust it, be it what it may, I have generally filled my paper. But self is a subject inexhaustible, which is the reason that though I have said little, and nothing, I am afraid, worth your hearing, I have only room to add that I am, my dear madam, most truly yours,

Wm. Cowper

Mrs. Unwin bids me present her best compliments, and say how much she shall be obliged to you for the receipt to make that most excellent cake which came hither in its native pan. There is no production of yours that will not be always most welcome at Weston.

XX. *To Lady Hesketh*

Weston Underwood, 26 June, 1791

MANY thanks, my cousin, for the bills, which arrived safe with all their accompaniments. Money is never unwelcome here, but at this time is especially welcome when servants' wages and house rent call for it. Mrs. Unwin enjoins me particularly to make you her affectionate acknowledgments both for the bonnet materials and for directions how to make the bonnet.

I am glad that Johnson[69] waited on you, and glad that he acquitted himself so well in your presence; glad too that he likes my prose, and filled with wonder that he likes my letters, because to him I have hardly sent any but letters of jobation.[70] I verily

believe that though a bookseller, he has in him the soul of a gentleman. Such strange combinations sometimes happen, and such a one may have happened in his instance. We shall see.

Johnny Higgins shall have his waistcoat to-morrow, together with a note in which I will tell him all that you say concerning his performance in the drawing way. Your gift will not be the less acceptable to him because, being in mourning, he cannot wear it at present. It is perfectly elegant, and he will always be, and will always have cause to be, proud of it. He mourns for his mother, who died about three weeks since, which, when I wrote last, I forgot to mention. You know, I believe, that she had ill health, and was subject to violent pains in her stomach. A fit of that sort seized her; she was attended by a nurse in the night, whom she ordered downstairs to get her some broth, and when the woman returned she was dead.

It gives us true pleasure that you interest yourself so much in the state of our turnpike. Learn then the present state of it. From Gayhurst to Weston the road is a gravel walk, but Weston itself is at present in a chaotic condition. About three weeks since they dug up the street and, having done so, left it. But it will not continue long in such disorder, and when you see it next you will find the village wonderfully improved. Already they have filled up two abominable ponds more fetid than any human nostrils could endure; they were to be found, as you must remember, one just under Farmer Archer's window, and the other a little beyond it. Covered drains are to be made wherever drains are wanted, and the causey[71] is to be new-laid. When all this is done and the road well graveled, we will hold our heads as high as any villagers in the kingdom. At the present time they are at work on the road from Weston to Olney. Olney is also itself in a state of beautification, and the road between Olney and Bedford is, I believe, nearly finished, but that I have never seen. The sooner you come to look at these things with your own eyes, the better.

---

[69]Joseph Johnson, Cowper's publisher.

[70]Reproof (from Job, who suffered the reproofs of his friends).

[71]Causeway.

I have hardly left myself room to tell you a story which yet I must tell, but as briefly as possible. While I reposed myself yesterday evening in the shop of Mr. Palmer,[72] lying at my length on the counter, a laboring man came in. He wanted a hat for his boy, and having bought one at two shillings, said he must have a handkerchief for himself, a silk one, to wear about his neck on Sundays. After much bargaining he suited himself with one at last for four shillings and sixpence. I liked the man's looks, and having just one shilling in my purse, I held it to him, saying: "Here, honest friend, here's something towards paying for your purchase!" He took the shilling and looked at me steadily for a long time, saying nothing. At last his surprise burst forth in these words—"I never saw such a gentleman in my life!" He then faced about, and was again for a long time silent; but at last, turning to me again, he said—"If I had known you had been so stout I would have had a better." Mr. Andrews told him that the cutting off would make no difference to him, and he might have a better if he pleased; so he took one at the price of five shillings, and went away all astonishment at my great bounty. I have learned since that he is a very worthy, industrious fellow, and has a mother between seventy and eighty, who walks every Sunday eight miles to hearing,[73] as they call it, and back again. This is another instance that my skill in physiognomy never deceives me.—Adieu, my dearest coz. With the love of all here, I remain ever thine,

Wm. Cowper

P.S.—Since I heard of Mrs. Madan's death I have thought much of her daughter Sally, and rejoice to hear that she is at last provided for.—We packed the drawings as well as we could, but the band-box was old and crazy, and was crushed, I suppose, in the hamper. I sent them that you might get them framed at your best leisure, for here we cannot frame them.

---

[72] In Olney.

[73] Attendance at preaching.

WILLIAM BLAKE

1757–1827

William Blake was born on 28 November, 1757, in London, where his father, James Blake, kept a hosier's shop. He received an elementary education, but the circumstances of his family made it necessary that he should early learn some trade. His father, perceiving that the boy's tastes ran in that direction, sent him at the age of ten to a teacher of drawing. Four years later he apprenticed him to the engraver Basire, with whom Blake remained until he was twenty. Then for a short time he was a member of the antique class of the Royal Academy, after which he set up as an engraver on his own account. The course of Blake's life was outwardly un-eventful. In August, 1782, he married Cather-ine Boucher, the daughter of a Richmond market-gardener. She was entirely uneducated —when she married she could not even read or write—but she proved a true helpmate to Blake, sustaining him with unshaken devotion through-out his life, and enabling him, despite their poverty, to do his own unrewarded work as artist and poet. In 1800 William Hayley was at work on a biography of his friend the poet Cowper, and he invited Blake to engrave the illustrations for this work. Blake accepted the invitation, and he and his wife removed from London to Felpham, and lived in the country near Hayley for several years. Save for this period, however, Blake's life was passed in London, where he worked in obscurity until his death on 12 August, 1827. His small earnings came chiefly from his work as an engraver, though he had a few friends who purchased his drawings and paintings. Among his more nota-ble achievements were his series of designs for Young's *Night Thoughts,* for Blair's *Grave,* for the Book of Job, for Dante's *Divine Comedy,* and the recently discovered designs for Gray's poems. Blake was, however, a poet as well as an artist, and to this fact we owe the existence of a series of books unique in the history of literature. For he himself published—if "pub-lishing" it can be called—all of his poems save those which remained in manuscript and those in his earliest volume (*Poetical Sketches,* 1783).

He inscribed the text, together with accompany-ing decorative designs, upon metal plates, to which he then applied acid which ate away the remaining surface. He thus obtained plates, similar in character to modern stereotype plates, from which he printed in the color which was to form the groundwork of the resulting page, and these pages were then tinted by hand, either by himself or by his wife. In this way Blake literally made his own books, and they were singularly beautiful. The process was, of course, both slow and expensive, and buyers were few, so that only a few copies of each of his books were made—copies which have become almost priceless. In this way were produced the two series of lyrics on which Blake's repu-tation as a poet now chiefly rests, *Songs of Innocence* (1789) and *Songs of Experience* (1794), as well as the longer poems, prophetic books, as he called them, in which he more directly expounded his peculiar system of thought in a symbolic language which is so much his own creation as to remain almost un-intelligible.

Fortunately one does not need to understand Blake's intricate and obscure symbolism in order to appreciate his shorter lyrics. Yet one should realize that Blake was a confident rebel against all the conventions of organized society. Quiet and blameless as was his outward life, still, in theory he permitted no concessions which might impair complete freedom of thought and action. In the name of freedom he made war alike upon civil law and the rational intellect, believing that the natural impulses of the human heart would lead us to better lives than external compulsion, and that the imagination is a surer guide to truth than reason or common sense. Blake was so confident of the truth of his in-tuitions that they took on sensible form and appeared to him as visions from the eternal, spiritual world from which, as he believed, we are more or less cut off by earthly life. "I assert, for myself, that I do not behold the out-ward creation, and that to me it is hindrance and not action. 'What!' it will be questioned, 'when the sun rises, do you not see a round disk of fire somewhat like a guinea?' Oh! no, no! I see an innumerable company of the heavenly host crying, 'Holy, holy, holy is the Lord God Almighty!' I question not my corporeal eye any more than I would question a window concerning a sight. I look through it, and not with it." Much of Blake's thought, no doubt, is the fruit, developing in an unusually positive personality, of his early acquaintance with the writings of Emanuel Swedenborg and of ideas imbibed in the days when he was associating, in the rooms of the bookseller Johnson, with Tom Paine and others sympathetic to the French Revolution. Blake became, indeed, the embodiment of practically everything that was contradictory to the spirit of the eighteenth century, and so foreshadowed much that was to be characteristic of the romantic movement. As the champion of the imagination against the reason he exclaimed, "To generalize is to be an idiot. To particularize is the great distinction of merit." And again he asserted, "Mere enthusiasm is the all in all." It is little wonder

that some, like Southey and Crabb Robinson, thought him mad. Yet the latter wrote, in his *Reminiscences:* "There is something in the madness of this man which interests me more than the sanity of Lord Byron or Walter Scott!"

The best edition of *The Writings of William Blake* is that of Geoffrey Keynes in three volumes (London, 1925); the same editor is also responsible for the less expensive one-volume *Poetry and Prose of William Blake* (London, 1927). Two of the most sensible biographies are Osbert Burdett's *William Blake,* in the "English Men of Letters" series (New York, 1926), and Mona Wilson's *Life of William Blake* (London, 1927). The philosophy underlying Blake's poetry has been notably, and with some differences, expounded by J. Foster Damon in *William Blake, His Philosophy and Symbols* (Boston, 1924), and by Milton O. Percival in *William Blake's Circle of Destiny* (New York, 1938). Basil de Selincourt's *William Blake* (London, 1909) is a sound introduction, including appreciative treatment of the poet's artistic work, with many illustrations.

TO WINTER [1]

"O winter! bar thine adamantine doors:
The north is thine; there hast thou built thy
    dark
Deep-founded habitation. Shake not thy
    roofs,
Nor bend thy pillars with thine iron car."

He hears me not, but o'er the yawning deep 5
Rides heavy; his storms are unchained,
    sheathèd
In ribbèd steel; I dare not lift mine eyes,
For he hath reared his scepter o'er the world.

Lo! now the direful monster, whose skin
    clings
To his strong bones, strides o'er the groan-
    ing rocks: 10
He withers all in silence, and in his hand
Unclothes the earth, and freezes up frail life.

He takes his seat upon the cliffs,—the mar-
    iner
Cries in vain. Poor little wretch, that deal'st
With storms!—till heaven smiles, and the
    monster   15
Is driv'n yelling to his caves beneath mount
    Hecla. [2]

[1] This and the four following poems are from *Poetical Sketches,* 1783.

[2] In southwestern Iceland.

SONG [3]

How sweet I roamed from field to field
And tasted all the summer's pride,
Till I the Prince of Love beheld
Who in the sunny beams did glide!

He showed me lilies for my hair,   5
And blushing roses for my brow;
He led me through his gardens fair
Where all his golden pleasures grow.

With sweet May dews my wings were wet,
And Phœbus fired my vocal rage;   10
He caught me in his silken net,
And shut me in his golden cage.

He loves to sit and hear me sing,
Then, laughing, sports and plays with me;
Then stretches out my golden wing,   15
And mocks my loss of liberty.

SONG

My silks and fine array,
My smiles and languished air,
By love are driv'n away;
And mournful lean Despair
Brings me yew to deck my grave;   5
Such end true lovers have.

[3] This poem is said to have been written before Blake was fourteen.

His face is fair as heav'n
When springing buds unfold;
O why to him was't giv'n
Whose heart is wintry cold?   10
His breast is love's all-worshiped tomb,
Where all love's pilgrims come.

Bring me an ax and spade,
Bring me a winding-sheet;
When I my grave have made   15
Let winds and tempests beat:
Then down I'll lie as cold as clay.
True love doth pass away!

MAD SONG

The wild winds weep,
And the night is a-cold;
Come hither, Sleep,
And my griefs unfold:
But lo! the morning peeps   5
Over the eastern steeps,
And the rustling beds of dawn
The earth do scorn.

Lo! to the vault
Of pavéd heaven,   10
With sorrow fraught
My notes are driven:
They strike the ear of night,
Make weep the eyes of day;
They make mad the roaring winds,   15
And with tempests play.

Like a fiend in a cloud,
With howling woe
After night I do crowd,
And with night will go;   20
I turn my back to the east
From whence comforts have increased;
For light doth seize my brain
With frantic pain.

TO THE MUSES

Whether on Ida's shady brow,
Or in the chambers of the East,
The chambers of the sun, that now
From ancient melody have ceased;

Whether in Heaven ye wander fair,   5
Or the green corners of the earth,
Or the blue regions of the air
Where the melodious winds have birth;

Whether on crystal rocks ye rove,
Beneath the bosom of the sea   10
Wand'ring in many a coral grove,
Fair Nine, forsaking Poetry!

How have you left the ancient love
That bards of old enjoyed in you!
The languid strings do scarcely move!   15
The sound is forced, the notes are few!

SONG FROM AN ISLAND IN THE MOON [4]

Hear then the pride and knowledge of a
   sailor!
His sprit sail, fore sail, main sail, and his
   mizen.
A poor frail man—God wot! I know none
   frailer,
I know no greater sinner than John Taylor.

INTRODUCTION TO SONGS OF INNOCENCE [5]

Piping down the valleys wild,
Piping songs of pleasant glee,
On a cloud I saw a child,
And he laughing said to me:

"Pipe a song about a Lamb!"   5
So I piped with merry cheer.
"Piper, pipe that song again;"
So I piped: he wept to hear.

"Drop thy pipe, thy happy pipe;
Sing thy songs of happy cheer:"   10
So I sang the same again,
While he wept with joy to hear.

"Piper, sit thee down and write
In a book, that all may read."
So he vanished from my sight,   15
And I plucked a hollow reed,

And I made a rural pen,
And I stained the water clear,
And I wrote my happy songs
Every child may joy to hear.   20

THE LAMB

Little Lamb, who made thee?
Dost thou know who made thee?
Gave thee life, and bid thee feed,
By the stream and o'er the mead;

[4] *An Island in the Moon* is a satirical sketch which Blake never completed. It was written probably in 1784, or shortly thereafter. It was first printed in full by E. J. Ellis in *The Real Blake*, 1907.

[5] This and the five following poems are from *Songs of Innocence*, 1789.

Gave thee clothing of delight,   5
Softest clothing, woolly, bright;
Gave thee such a tender voice,
Making all the vales rejoice?
 Little Lamb, who made thee?
 Dost thou know who made thee?   10

 Little Lamb, I'll tell thee,
 Little Lamb, I'll tell thee:
He is calléd by thy name,
For He calls Himself a Lamb,
He is meek, and He is mild;   15
He became a little child.
I a child, and thou a lamb,
We are calléd by His name.
 Little Lamb, God bless thee!
 Little Lamb, God bless thee!   20

INFANT JOY

 "I have no name:
 I am but two days old."
What shall I call thee?
 "I happy am,
 Joy is my name."   5
Sweet joy befall thee!

 Pretty Joy!
 Sweet Joy, but two days old.
 Sweet joy I call thee:
 Thou dost smile,   10
 I sing the while,
 Sweet joy befall thee!

THE LITTLE BLACK BOY

My mother bore me in the southern wild,
And I am black, but O! my soul is white;
White as an angel is the English child,
But I am black, as if bereaved of light.

My mother taught me underneath a tree,   5
And, sitting down before the heat of day,
She took me on her lap and kisséd me,
And, pointing to the east, began to say:

"Look on the rising sun,—there God does
 live,
And gives His light, and gives His heat
 away;   10
And flowers and trees and beasts and men
 receive
Comfort in morning, joy in the noonday.

"And we are put on earth a little space,
That we may learn to bear the beams of love;

And these black bodies and this sunburnt
 face   15
Is but a cloud, and like a shady grove.

"For when our souls have learned the heat
 to bear,
The cloud will vanish; we shall hear His
 voice,
Saying: 'Come out from the grove, My love
 and care,
And round My golden tent like lambs rejoice.'"   20

Thus did my mother say, and kisséd me;
And thus I say to little English boy.
When I from black and he from white cloud
 free,
And round the tent of God like lambs we joy,

I'll shade him from the heat, till he can bear
To lean in joy upon our Father's knee;   26
And then I'll stand and stroke his silver hair,
And be like him, and he will then love me.

A CRADLE SONG

Sweet dreams, form a shade
O'er my lovely infant's head;
Sweet dreams of pleasant streams
By happy, silent, moony beams.

Sweet sleep, with soft down   5
Weave thy brows an infant crown.
Sweet sleep, Angel mild,
Hover o'er my happy child.

Sweet smiles, in the night
Hover over my delight;   10
Sweet smiles, mother's smiles,
All the livelong night beguiles.

Sweet moans, dovelike sighs,
Chase not slumber from thy eyes.
Sweet moans, sweeter smiles,   15
All the dovelike moans beguiles.

Sleep, sleep, happy child,
All creation slept and smiled;
Sleep, sleep, happy sleep,
While o'er thee thy mother weep.   20

Sweet babe, in thy face
Holy image I can trace.
Sweet babe, once like thee,
Thy Maker lay and wept for me,

Wept for me, for thee, for all, 25
When He was an infant small.
Thou His image ever see,
Heavenly face that smiles on thee,

Smiles on thee, on me, on all;
Who became an infant small. 30
Infant smiles are His own smiles;
Heaven and earth to peace beguiles.

THE DIVINE IMAGE

To Mercy, Pity, Peace, and Love
All pray in their distress;
And to these virtues of delight
Return their thankfulness.

For Mercy, Pity, Peace, and Love 5
Is God, our Father dear,
And Mercy, Pity, Peace, and Love
Is man, His child and care.

For Mercy has a human heart,
Pity a human face, 10
And Love, the human form divine,
And Peace, the human dress.

Then every man, of every clime,
That prays in his distress,
Prays to the human form divine, 15
Love, Mercy, Pity, Peace.

And all must love the human form,
In heathen, Turk, or Jew;
Where Mercy, Love, and Pity dwell
There God is dwelling too. 20

THE FLY[6]

Little Fly,
Thy summer's play
My thoughtless hand
Has brushed away.

Am not I 5
A fly like thee?
Or art not thou
A man like me?

For I dance,
And drink, and sing, 10
Till some blind hand
Shall brush my wing.

[6]This and the four following poems are from
Songs of Experience, 1794.

If thought is life
And strength and breath,
And the want 15
Of thought is death;

Then am I
A happy fly,
If I live
Or if I die. 20

THE TIGER

Tiger! Tiger! burning bright
In the forests of the night,
What immortal hand or eye
Could frame thy fearful symmetry?

In what distant deeps or skies 5
Burnt the fire of thine eyes?
On what wings dare he aspire?
What the hand dare seize the fire?

And what shoulder, and what art,
Could twist the sinews of thy heart? 10
And when thy heart began to beat,
What dread hand? and what dread feet?

What the hammer? what the chain?
In what furnace was thy brain?
What the anvil? what dread grasp 15
Dare its deadly terrors clasp?

When the stars threw down their spears,
And watered heaven with their tears,
Did he smile his work to see?
Did he who made the Lamb make thee? 20

Tiger! Tiger! burning bright
In the forests of the night,
What immortal hand or eye
Dare frame thy fearful symmetry?

THE CLOD AND THE PEBBLE

"Love seeketh not itself to please,
Nor for itself hath any care,
But for another gives its ease,
And builds a Heaven in Hell's despair."

So sung a little Clod of Clay, 5
Trodden with the cattle's feet,
But a Pebble of the brook
Warbled out these meters meet:

"Love seeketh only Self to please,
To bind another to its delight,   10
Joys in another's loss of ease,
And builds a Hell in Heaven's despite."

A LITTLE BOY LOST

"Nought loves another as itself,
Nor venerates another so,
Nor is it possible to Thought
A greater than itself to know:

"And, Father, how can I love you   5
Or any of my brothers more?
I love you like the little bird
That picks up crumbs around the door."

The Priest sat by and heard the child,
In trembling zeal he seized his hair: 10
He led him by his little coat,
And all admired the priestly care.

And standing on the altar high,
"Lo! what a fiend is here," said he,
"One who sets reason up for judge   15
Of our most holy Mystery."

The weeping child could not be heard,
The weeping parents wept in vain;
They stripped him to his little shirt,
And bound him in an iron chain;   20

And burned him in a holy place,
Where many had been burned before:
The weeping parents wept in vain.
Are such things done on Albion's shore?

INFANT SORROW

My mother groaned, my father wept,
Into the dangerous world I leapt;
Helpless, naked, piping loud,
Like a fiend hid in a cloud.

Struggling in my father's hands,   5
Striving against my swaddling-bands,
Bound and weary, I thought best
To sulk upon my mother's breast.

STANZAS FROM MILTON[7]

And did those feet in ancient time
    Walk upon England's mountains green?
And was the holy Lamb of God
    On England's pleasant pastures seen?

And did the Countenance Divine   5
    Shine forth upon our clouded hills?
And was Jerusalem builded here
    Among these dark Satanic Mills?[8]

Bring me my bow of burning gold!
    Bring me my arrows of desire!   10
Bring me my spear! O clouds, unfold!
    Bring me my chariot of fire!

I will not cease from mental fight,
    Nor shall my sword sleep in my hand,
Till we have built Jerusalem   15
    In England's green and pleasant land.

[7]*Milton,* one of Blake's "prophetic books," was begun at some time between 1800 and 1803, though the plates from which it was printed were not completed until 1808 or 1809.

[8]Either the figurative mills of learning or the real mills of the industrial revolution.

ROBERT BURNS

1759–1796

The parents of Burns both came of yeoman stock. His father began life as a gardener and was later a small farmer, renting his land and toiling hard to wrest from it a bare living for himself and his family. Burns was born in the parish of Alloway, in Ayrshire, Scotland, on 25 January, 1759, in a small clay cottage which his father had built with his own hands. He was the oldest of seven children, all of whom, as fast as they grew sufficiently to do anything useful, had to share the hard, incessant labors of the farm. His father moved to Mount Oliphant in 1766, and then to a somewhat better farm at Lochlie in 1777, where the family remained until the death of the father in 1784. On these farms Burns grew to manhood, toiling like a galley slave, as he said, and yet managing to get the rudiments of an education and to do—for one in his circumstances at least—much reading. In a letter written in 1787 he says, "Though it cost the schoolmaster some thrashings, I made an excellent English scholar; and by the time I was ten or eleven years of age I was a critic in substantives, verbs, and particles. In my infant and boyish days, too, I owe much to an old woman who resided in the family, remarkable for her ignorance, credulity, and superstition. She had, I suppose, the largest collection in the country of tales and songs concerning devils, ghosts, fairies, brownies, witches, warlocks, spunkies, kelpies, elf-candles, dead-lights, wraiths, apparitions, cantraips, giants, enchanted towers, dragons and other trumpery. This cultivated the latent seeds of poetry; but had so strong an effect on my imagination that to this hour, in my nocturnal rambles, I sometimes keep a sharp lookout in suspicious places. . . . The first two books I ever read in private, and which gave me more pleasure than any two books I ever read since, were *The Life of Hannibal* and *The History of Sir William Wallace*. . . . What I know of ancient story was gathered from Salmon's and Guthrie's *Geographical Grammars;* and the ideas I had formed of modern manners of literature and criticism I got from the *Spectator*. These, with Pope's works, some plays of Shakespeare, Tull and Dickson *On Agriculture*, the *Pantheon*, Locke's *Essay on the Human Understanding*, Stackhouse's *History of the Bible*, Justice's *British Gardener's Directory*, Boyle's *Lectures*, Allan Ramsay's works, Taylor's *Scripture Doctrine of Original Sin, A Select Collection of English Songs,* and Hervey's *Meditations,* had formed the whole of my reading [when sixteen years old]. The collection of songs was my *vade mecum*. I pored over them, driving my cart or walking to labor, song by song, verse by verse, carefully noting the true, tender, or sublime from affectation and fustian. I am convinced I owe to this practice much of my critic-craft, such as it is. . . . The addition of two more authors to my library gave me great pleasure: Sterne and Mackenzie—*Tristram Shandy* and *The Man of Feeling*—were my bosom favorites. Poesy was still a darling walk for my mind, but it was only indulged in according to the humor of the hour. I had usually half a dozen or more pieces on hand; I took up one or other, as it suited the momentary tone of the mind, and dismissed the work as it bordered on fatigue. My passions, when once lighted up, raged like so many devils till they got vent in rime; and then the conning over my verses, like a spell, soothed all into quiet."

In 1781 Burns left the farm at Lochlie to try flax-dressing at Irvine. He did not prosper at this, but did learn the bad habits of loose companions he found in the town. He was a man of turbulent passions and weak will; and if his life was a life of song, he tended from this time more and more to unite with song the other two members of the famous triad. One of his friends at Irvine was a certain Richard Brown, who, said Burns, "was the only man I ever saw who was a greater fool than myself when Woman was the presiding star." After the death of their father in 1784 Burns and his brother Gilbert took Mossgiel farm, several miles from Lochlie. In the same year, too, Burns met Jean Armour, who later bore him a child, and whom he finally married in 1788. Things going badly on the farm, Burns resolved to emigrate to Jamaica; and it was in order to obtain money for his passage that he published a volume of his poems at Kilmarnock in 1786. The edition was soon sold, and its success led him to remain and bring out a second edition at Edinburgh in the following year. Burns was in that city through the winters of 1786–1787 and 1787–1788. There also his poems succeeded, netting him a profit of some £500, and attracting much social attention to himself. The latter was at first pleasing to him, but probably did him more harm than good, as he was disappointed in the hope of getting any substantial help from his new acquaintances and soon discovered that he was merely the object of a temporary curiosity. In 1788 he took a farm at Ellisland—chosen, it has been said, rather with a poet's than a farmer's eye—and settled there with Jean Armour. He found it impossible, however, to make a living from the land, and in 1789 took a position in the excise. In 1791 he gave up the farm and moved to the near-by town of Dumfries. During these years Burns wrote less and less as he drank more and more. He died, wrecked in both health and reputation by his habits, on 21 July, 1796.

Death came to Burns as a friend. His life was ruined, and his work as a poet was done. Principal Shairp has said, "At the basis of all his power lay absolute truthfulness, intense reality, truthfulness to the objects which he saw, truthfulness to himself as the seer of them." This the failures of his life did not prevent, and this, doubtless, is the secret of the permanence of his fame. His intensity and his truthfulness have made him for all time one of the greatest of lyric poets.

The standard edition is *The Poetry of Robert Burns,* ed. William E. Henley and Thomas F. Henderson (Edinburgh, 1896–1897); this also contains Henley's acute "Essay on the Life, Genius and Achievement of Burns." Burns's letters have been excellently edited by J. De-Lancey Ferguson (2 vols., Oxford, 1931). *The Life of Robert Burns* has been fully set forth by Catharine Carswell (London, 1930): and of more recent date is DeLancey Ferguson's *Pride and Passion: Robert Burns* (New York, 1939). Two well known studies by countrymen of the poet are Thomas Carlyle's "Burns," in vol. II of *Critical and Miscellaneous Essays,* and Robert Louis Stevenson's "Some Aspects of Robert Burns," in *Familiar Studies of Men and Books.* For a sympathetic, if unoriginal, interpretation see Franklyn B. Snyder, *Robert Burns: His Personality, His Reputation and His Art* (Toronto, 1936). The same author's *Life of Robert Burns* appeared in 1932, but has been largely superseded by Ferguson's study mentioned above.

MARY MORISON[1]

O Mary, at thy window be,
  It is the wished, the trysted hour!
Those smiles and glances let me see,
  That make the miser's treasure poor:
How blithely wad I bide the stoure,[2]   5
  A weary slave frae sun to sun,
Could I the rich reward secure,
  The lovely Mary Morison.

Yestreen,[3] when to the trembling string
  The dance gaed[4] thro' the lighted ha',
To thee my fancy took its wing,   11
  I sat, but neither heard nor saw:
Tho' this was fair, and that was braw,[5]
  And yon the toast of a' the town,
I sighed, and said amang them a',   15
  "Ye are na Mary Morison."

[1] Written in 1780 or 1781. From a statement by Gilbert Burns it has been inferred (perhaps wrongly) that the subject of this song was Elison Begbie.
[2] Would I bear the struggle.   [3] Last night.
[4] Went.   [5] Fine, handsome.

O Mary, canst thou wreck his peace,
  Wha for thy sake wad gladly die?
Or canst thou break that heart of his,
  Whase only faut is loving thee?   20
If love for love thou wilt na gie,[6]
  At least be pity to me shown!
A thought ungentle canna be
  The thought o' Mary Morison.

EPISTLE TO JOHN LAPRAIK, AN OLD SCOTTISH BARD[1]

While briers an' woodbines budding green,
An' paitricks scraichin' loud[2] at e'en,

[6] Not give.
[1] Written in the spring of 1785. Lapraik (1727–1807) was an Ayrshire poet who, until he lost all his means in 1772, possessed an estate near Muirkirk. Burns addressed two other epistles to him, both also written in 1785. The song referred to in the third stanza is Lapraik's *When I upon Thy Bosom Lean.*
[2] Partridges calling.

An' morning poussie whiddin'[3] seen,
    Inspire my Muse,
This freedom, in an unknown frien',   5
    I pray excuse.

On Fasten-een[4] we had a rockin',[5]
To ca' the crack[6] and weave our stockin';
And there was muckle[7] fun and jokin',
    Ye need na doubt;   10
At length we had a hearty yokin'[8]
    At "sang about."[9]

There was ae[10] sang, amang the rest,
Aboon[11] them a' it pleased me best,
That some kind husband had addressed   15
    To some sweet wife:
It thirled[12] the heart-strings thro' the breast,
    A' to the life.

I've scarce heard ought described sae weel,
What gen'rous, manly bosoms feel;   20
Thought I "Can this be Pope, or Steele,
    Or Beattie's wark?"
They tauld me 'twas an odd kind chiel[13]
    About Muirkirk.

It pat me fidgin' fain[14] to heart,   25
And sae about him there I spiered;[15]
Then a' that kenned[16] him round declared
    He had ingine,[17]
That nane excelled it, few cam near't,
    It was sae fine.   30

That, set him to a pint of ale,
An' either douce[18] or merry tale,
Or rimes an' sangs he'd made himsel,
    Or witty catches,[19]
'Tween Inverness and Teviotdale,   35
    He had few matches.

Then up I gat, an' swoor an aith,[20]
Tho' I should pawn my pleugh and graith,[21]
Or die a cadger pownie's[22] death,
    At some dyke-back,[23]   40
A pint an' gill I'd gie them baith
    To hear your crack.[24]

But, first an' foremost, I should tell,
Amaist[25] as soon as I could spell,
I to the crambo-jingle[26] fell;   45
    Tho' rude an' rough,
Yet crooning to a body's sel,
    Does weel eneugh.

I am nae poet, in a sense,
But just a rimer, like, by chance,   50
An' hae to learning nae pretense,
    Yet what the matter?
Whene'er my Muse does on me glance,
    I jingle at her.

Your critic-folk may cock their nose,   55
And say "How can you e'er propose,
You wha ken hardly verse frae prose,
    To mak a sang?"
But, by your leaves, my learned foes,
    Ye're maybe wrang.   60

What's a' your jargon o' your schools,
Your Latin names for horns[27] an' stools,
If honest nature made you fools,
    What sairs[28] your grammars?
Ye'd better ta'en up spades and shools,[29]   65
    Or knappin'-hammers.[30]

A set o' dull conceited hashes[31]
Confuse their brains in college classes!
They gang[32] in stirks,[33] and come out asses,
    Plain truth to speak;   70
An' syne[34] they think to climb Parnassus
    By dint o' Greek!

Gie me ae spark o' nature's fire,
That's a' the learning I desire;
Then tho' I drudge thro' dub[35] an' mire   75
    At pleugh or cart,
My Muse, though hamely in attire,
    May touch the heart.

O for a spunk[36] o' Allan's[37] glee,
Or Fergusson's,[38] the bauld an' slee,[39]   80
Or bright Lapraik's, my friend to be,
    If I can hit it!
That would be lear[40] eneugh for me,
    If I could get it.

---

[3]The hare scudding.
[4]Evening before Lent.   [5]Social meeting.
[6]To have a chat.   [7]Much.   [8]Set-to.
[9]I. e., each in turn sang a song.   [10]One.
[11]Above.   [12]Thrilled.   [13]Chap.
[14]Made me tingle with pleasure.
[15]Asked.   [16]Knew.   [17]Genius.
[18]Sober.   [19]Three-part songs, each sung in turn.
[20]Swore an oath.   [21]Plow and harness.
[22]Peddler's pony's.   [23]Behind a fence.   [24]Talk.

[25]Almost.
[26]Riming (Crambo is a game in which one has to supply a rime to a word given by another).
[27]Ink-horns (?).   [28]Serves.   [29]Shovels.
[30]Hammers for breaking stone.   [31]Fools.
[32]Go.   [33]Young bullocks.   [34]Then.
[35]Puddle.   [36]Spark.
[37]Allan Ramsay (1686–1738).
[38]Robert Ferguson (1750–1774).
[39]The bold and clever.   [40]Learning.

Now, sir, if ye hae friends enow,   85
Tho' real friends, I b'lieve, are few,
Yet, if your catalogue be fou,[41]
    I'se no[42] insist,
But gif ye want ae friend that's true,
    I'm on your list.   90

I winna blaw[43] about mysel,
As ill I like my fauts to tell;
But friends, an' folks that wish me well,
    They sometimes roose[44] me;
Tho' I maun[45] own, as mony still   95
    As far abuse me.

There's ae wee faut they whiles[46] lay to me,
I like the lasses—Gude[47] forgie me!
For mony a plack[48] they wheedle frae[49] me,
    At dance or fair;   100
Maybe some ither thing they gie me
    They weel can spare.

But Mauchline[50] race, or Mauchline fair,
I should be proud to meet you there;
We'se gie ae night's discharge to care,   105
    If we forgather,
An' hae a swap[51] o' rimin'-ware
    Wi' ane anither.

The four-gill chap, we'se gar[52] him clatter,
An' kirsen[53] him wi' reekin[54] water;   110
Syne we'll sit down an' tak our whitter,[55]
    To cheer our heart;
An' faith, we'se be acquainted better
    Before we part.

Awa, ye selfish warly[56] race,   115
Wha think that havins,[57] sense, an' grace,
E'en love an' friendship, should give place
    To catch-the-plack![58]
I dinna[59] like to see your face,
    Nor hear your crack.   120

But ye whom social pleasure charms,
Whose hearts the tide of kindness warms
Who hold your being on the terms,
    "Each aid the others,"
Come to my bowl, come to my arms,   125
    My friends, my brothers!

But to conclude my lang epistle,
As my auld pen's worn to the gristle;
Twa lines frae you wad gar me fissle,[60]
    Who am, most fervent,   130
While I can either sing, or whistle,
    Your friend and servant.

TO A LOUSE[1]

On Seeing One on a Lady's Bonnet at Church

Ha! wh'are ye gaun, ye crowlin' ferlie![2]
Your impudence protects you sairly:[3]
I canna say but ye strunt[4] rarely,
    Owre gauze and lace;
Tho' faith! I fear ye dine but sparely   5
    On sic a place.

Ye ugly, creepin', blastit wonner,[5]
Detested, shunned by saunt an' sinner!
How dare ye set your fit[6] upon her,
    Sae fine a lady?   10
Gae somewhere else, and seek your dinner
    On some poor body.

Swith,[7] in some beggar's haffet squattle;[8]
There ye may creep, and sprawl, and sprat-
    tle[9]
Wi'ither kindred jumping cattle,   15
    In shoals and nations;
Where horn nor bane[10] ne'er dare unsettle
    Your thick plantations.

Now haud[11] ye there, ye're out o' sight,
Below the fatt'rels,[12] snug an' tight;   20
Na, faith ye yet! ye'll no be right
    Till ye've got on it,
The very tapmost tow'ring height
    O' Miss's bonnet.

My sooth! right bauld ye set your nose out, 25
As plump and gray as onie grozet;[13]
O for some rank mercurial rozet,[14]
    Or fell red smeddum![15]
I'd gie you sic a hearty dose o't,
    Wad dress your droddum![16]   30

---

[41]Full. [42]I'll not. [43]I will not brag.
[44]Praise. [45]Must. [46]Sometimes. [47]God.
[48]Scotch coin of small value. [49]From.
[50]This town is not far from Mossgiel Farm. It is the town where Burns married Jean Armour.
[51]An exchange.
[52]The four-gill cup, we'll make. [53]Christen.
[54]Steaming. [55]Draught. [56]Worldly.
[57]Manners. [58]The hunt for coin. [59]Do not.

---

[60]Make me tingle.
[1]Written in 1786. [2]Crawling wonder.
[3]Greatly. [4]Strut. [5]Blasted wonder.
[6]Foot. [7]Quick, i e., "Off with you!"
[8]Temples sprawl. [9]Struggle.
[10]Comb nor poison. [11]Hold. [12]Ribbon-ends.
[13]Gooseberry. [14]Rosin. [15]Powder.
[16]Breech.

I wad na been surprised to spy
You on an auld wife's flannen toy;[17]
Or aiblins[18] some bit duddie[19] boy,
    On's wyliecoat;[20]
But Miss's fine Lunardi![21] fie,   35
    How daur ye do't?

O Jenny, dinna toss your head,
An' set your beauties a' abroad![22]
Ye little ken what curséd speed
    The blastie's makin'![23]   40
Thae[24] winks and finger-ends, I dread,
    Are notice takin'!

O wad some Pow'r the giftie[25] gie us
To see oursels as others see us!
It wad frae mony a blunder free us,   45
    And foolish notion:
What airs in dress an' gait wad lea'e us,
    And e'en devotion!

TO A MOUSE[1]

On Turning Her Up in Her Nest with the Plow

Wee, sleekit,[2] cow'rin', tim'rous beastie,
O what a panic's in thy breastie!
Thou need na start awa sae hasty,
    Wi' bickering brattle![3]
I wad be laith[4] to rin an' chase thee   5
    Wi' murd'ring pattle![5]

I'm truly sorry man's dominion
Has broken nature's social union,
An' justifies that ill opinion
    Which makes thee startle   10
At me, thy poor earth-born companion,
    An' fellow-mortal!

I doubt na, whyles,[6] but thou may thieve;
What then? poor beastie, thou maun live!
A daimen-icker in a thrave[7]   15
    'S a sma' request:
I'll get a blessin' wi' the lave,[8]
    And never miss't!

Thy wee bit housie, too, in ruin!
Its silly wa's the win's are strewin'!   20
An' naething, now, to big[9] a new ane,
    O' foggage green![10]
An' bleak December's winds ensuin',
    Baith snell[11] an' keen!

Thou saw the fields laid bare and waste,   25
An' weary winter comin' fast,
An' cozie here, beneath the blast,
    Thou thought to dwell,
Till crash! the cruel coulter[12] past
    Out-thro' thy cell.   30

That wee bit heap o' leaves an' stibble
Has cost thee mony a weary nibble!
Now thou's turned out, for a' thy trouble,
    But house or hald,[13]
To thole[14] the winter's sleety dribble,   35
    An' cranreuch[15] cauld!

But, Mousie, thou art no thy lane,[16]
In proving foresight may be vain:
The best laid schemes o' mice an' men
    Gang aft a-gley,[17]   40
An' lea'e us nought but grief an' pain
    For promised joy.

Still thou art blest compared wi' me!
The present only toucheth thee:
But oh! I backward cast my e'e   45
    On prospects drear!
An' forward tho' I canna see,
    I guess an' fear!

TO A MOUNTAIN DAISY[1]

On Turning One Down with the Plow

Wee modest crimson-tippéd flow'r,
Thou's met me in an evil hour;
For I maun crush amang the stoure[2]
    Thy slender stem:
To spare thee now is past my pow'r,   5
    Thou bonnie gem.

Alas! it's no thy neibor sweet,
The bonnie lark, companion meet,
Bending thee 'mang the dewy weet
    Wi' spreckled breast,   10
When upward springing, blithe, to greet
    The purpling east.

---

[17]Flannel head-dress.   [18]Maybe.
[19]Small ragged.   [20]Flannel vest.
[21]Bonnet, named after Lunardi, an aeronaut.
[22]Abroad.   [23]The blasted creature is making.
[24]Those.   [25]Small gift.
[1]Written in November, 1785.
[2]Sleek.   [3]Hurrying scamper.   [4]Loath.
[5]Plow-spade.   [6]Sometimes.
[7]An odd ear in 24 sheaves.   [8]With what's left.

[9]Build.   [10]Coarse grass.   [11]Both bitter.
[12]Cutter on plow to cut the sward.
[13]Without house or abode.   [14]Endure.
[15]Hoar-frost.   [16]Not alone.   [17]Go often astray.
[1]Written in April, 1786.   [2]Dust.

Cauld blew the bitter-biting north
Upon thy early humble birth;
Yet cheerfully thou glinted forth   15
    Amid the storm,
Scarce reared above the parent-earth
    Thy tender form.

The flaunting flow'rs our gardens yield
High shelt'ring woods and wa's[3] maun
    shield,
But thou, beneath the random bield[4]   21
    O' clod or stane,
Adorns the histie stibble-field,[5]
    Unseen, alane.

There, in thy scanty mantle clad,   25
Thy snawy bosom sun-ward spread,
Thou lifts thy unassuming head
    In humble guise;
But now the share uptears thy bed,
    And low thou lies!   30

Such is the fate of artless maid,
Sweet flow'ret of the rural shade,

By love's simplicity betrayed,
    And guileless trust,
Till she like thee, all soiled, is laid   35
    Low i' the dust.

Such is the fate of simple bard,
On life's rough ocean luckless starred:
Unskillful he to note the card
    Of prudent lore,   40
Till billows rage, and gales blow hard,
    And whelm him o'er!

Such fate to suffering worth is giv'n,
Who long with wants and woes has striv'n,
By human pride or cunning driv'n   45
    To mis'ry's brink,
Till wrenched of ev'ry stay but Heav'n,
    He, ruined, sink!

E'en thou who mourn'st the Daisy's fate,
That fate is thine—no distant date;   50
Stern Ruin's plowshare drives elate
    Full on thy bloom,
Till crushed beneath the furrow's weight
    Shall be thy doom!

THE COTTER'S SATURDAY NIGHT[1]

My loved, my honored, much respected
    friend!
No mercenary bard his homage pays:
With honest pride I scorn each selfish end,
    My dearest meed a friend's esteem and
    praise:
To you I sing, in simple Scottish lays,   5
The lowly train in life's sequestered scene;
    The native feelings strong, the guileless
    ways;
What Aiken in a cottage would have been—
Ah! tho' his worth unknown, far happier
    there, I ween.

November chill blaws loud wi' angry
    sough;[2]   10
    The short'ning winter-day is near a close;
The miry beasts retreating frae the pleugh;
    The black'ning trains o' craws[3] to their
    repose:

The toil-worn Cotter[4] frae his labor goes,
This night his weekly moil is at an end,   15
    Collects his spades, his mattocks, and his
    hoes,
Hoping the morn in ease and rest to spend,
And weary, o'er the moor, his course does
    hameward bend.

At length his lonely cot appears in view,
    Beneath the shelter of an agéd tree;   20
Th' expectant wee-things, toddlin', stacher[5]
    through
    To meet their Dad, wi' flichterin'[6] noise
    an' glee.
His wee bit ingie,[7] blinkin bonnilie,[8]
His clean hearth-stane, his thrifty wifie's
    smile,   24
    The lisping infant prattling on his knee,
Does a' his weary kiaugh[9] and care beguile,
An' makes him quite forget his labor an' his
    toil.

Belyve,[10] the elder bairns[11] come drapping
    in,
    At service out, amang the farmers roun';

---

[3]Walls.   [4]Shelter.   [5]Bare stubble-field.

[1]Written in November, 1785, or shortly thereafter. Burns used as a motto for this poem a stanza from Gray's *Elegy* ("Let not Ambition mock their useful toil," etc.), and addressed it to Robert Aiken (1739–1807), an Ayrshire solicitor. Aiken subscribed for 105 copies of the Kilmarnock edition of Burns's poems. The Spenserian stanza Burns borrowed, not from Spenser, whom he had not yet read at this time, but from Beattie, Shenstone, and Thomson.

[2]Wail.   [3]Crows.

---

[4]Cottager, peasant occupying a small holding.
[5]Totter.   [6]Fluttering.   [7]Fire-place.
[8]Shining prettily.   [9]Worry.   [10]Soon.
[11]Children.

Some ca'[12] the pleugh, some herd, some
  tentie rin[13]   30
A cannie[14] errand to a neibor town:[15]
Their eldest hope, their Jenny, woman-
  grown,
In youthfu' bloom, love sparkling in her e'e,
  Comes hame, perhaps to shew a braw[16]
  new gown,
Or deposite her sair-won penny-fee,[17]   35
To help her parents dear, if they in hardship
  be.

With joy unfeigned brothers and sisters
  meet,
  An' each for other's weelfare kindly
  spiers:[18]
The social hours, swift-winged, unnoticed
  fleet;
  Each tells the uncos[19] that he sees or
  hears;   40
  The parents, partial, eye their hopeful
  years;
Anticipation forward points the view.
  The mother, wi' her needle an' her sheers,
Gars auld claes look amaist[20] as weel's the
  new;
The father mixes a' wi' admonition due.   45

Their master's an' their mistress's command,
  The younkers a' are warnéd to obey;
An' mind their labors wi' an eydent[21] hand,
  An' ne'er, tho' out o' sight, to jauk[22] or
  play: 49
"And O! be sure to fear the Lord alway,
  An' mind your duty, duly, morn an' night!
  Lest in temptation's path ye gang astray,
Implore His counsel and assisting might:
They never sought in vain that sought the
  Lord aright!"   54

But hark! a rap comes gently to the door;
  Jenny, wha kens the meaning o' the same,
Tells how a neibor lad cam o'er the moor,
  To do some errands, and convoy her
  hame.
The wily mother sees the conscious flame
Sparkle in Jenny's e'e, and flush her cheek;
  Wi' heart-struck anxious care, inquires his
  name,   61
While Jenny hafflins[23] is afraid to speak;
Weel pleased the mother hears it's nae wild
  worthless rake.

Wi' kindly welcome, Jenny brings him ben;[24]
  A strappin' youth; he takes the mother's
  eye;   65
Blithe Jenny sees the visit's no ill ta'en;
  The father cracks[25] of horses, pleughs,
  and kye.[26]
  The youngster's artless heart o'erflows wi'
  joy,
But blate and laithfu',[27] scarce can weel be-
  have;
  The mother, wi' a woman's wiles, can spy
What makes the youth sae bashfu' an' sae
  grave;   71
Weel-pleased to think her bairn's respected
  like the lave.[28]

O happy love! where love like this is found;
  O heart-felt raptures! bliss beyond com-
  pare!
I've pacéd much this weary mortal round,
  And sage experience bids me this de-
  clare—   76
  "If Heaven a draught of heavenly pleas-
  ure spare,
One cordial in this melancholy vale,
  'Tis when a youthful, loving, modest pair
In other's arms breathe out the tender tale,
Beneath the milk-white thorn that scents the
  evening gale."   81

Is there, in human form, that bears a
  heart—
  A wretch, a villain, lost to love and
  truth—
That can, with studied, sly, ensnaring art,
  Betray sweet Jenny's unsuspecting
  youth?   85
  Curse on his perjured arts, dissembling
  smooth!
Are honor, virtue, conscience, all exiled?
  Is there no pity, no relenting ruth,
Points to the parents fondling o'er their
  child?
Then paints the ruined maid, and their dis-
  traction wild?   90

But now the supper crowns their simple
  board,
  The halesome parritch,[29] chief of Scotia's
  food:
The sowpe[30] their only hawkie[31] does afford,
  That 'yont the hallan[32] snugly chows her
  cood;

---

[12]Drive.   [13]Heedful run.   [14]Quiet.
[15]Farm-house, with its surrounding buildings.
[16]Fine.   [17]Hard-earned wages.   [18]Asks.
[19]Strange things.
[20]Makes old clothes look almost.
[21]Diligent.   [22]Trifle.   [23]Partly.

[24]In.   [25]Talks.   [26]Cows.
[27]Shy and bashful.   [28]Rest.
[29]Wholesome porridge.   [30]Milk.   [31]Cow.
[32]Beyond the wall.

The dame brings forth in complimental
    mood,   95
To grace the lad, her weel-hain'd kebbuck,
    fell;[33]
And aft he's pressed, and aft he ca's it
    good;
The frugal wifie, garrulous, will tell
How 'twas a towmond[34] auld sin' lint was i'
    the bell.[35]   99

The cheerfu' supper done, wi' serious face
    They round the ingle form a circle wide;
The sire turns o'er, wi' patriarchal grace,
    The big ha'-Bible,[36] ance his father's pride:
His bonnet rev'rently is laid aside,   104
His lyart haffets[37] wearing thin an' bare;
    Those strains that once did sweet in Zion
    glide—
He wales[38] a portion with judicious care,
And "Let us worship God!" he says with
    solemn air.

They chant their artless notes in simple
    guise;
    They tune their hearts, by far the noblest
    aim: 110
Perhaps *Dundee's* wild warbling measures
    rise,
    Or plaintive *Martyrs,* worthy of the name;
Or noble *Elgin*[39] beets[40] the heav'nward
    flame,
The sweetest far of Scotia's holy lays:
    Compared with these, Italian trills are
    tame;   115
The tickled ears no heartfelt raptures raise;
Nae unison hae they with our Creator's
    praise.

The priest-like father reads the sacred page,
    How Abram was the friend of God on
    high;
Or Moses bade eternal warfare wage   120
    With Amalek's ungracious progeny;
Or how the royal bard[41] did groaning lie
Beneath the stroke of Heaven's avenging ire;
    Or Job's pathetic plaint, and wailing cry;
Or rapt Isaiah's wild seraphic fire;   125
Or other holy seers that tune the sacred lyre.

Perhaps the Christian volume is the theme,
    How guiltless blood for guilty man was
    shed;
How He who bore in Heaven the second
    name
    Had not on earth whereon to lay His
    head;   130
How His first followers and servants sped;
The precepts sage they wrote to many a land:
    How he,[42] who lone in Patmos banishéd,
Saw in the sun a mighty angel stand,
And heard great Bab'lon's doom pronounced
    by Heaven's command.   135

Then kneeling down to Heaven's Eternal
    King
    The saint, the father, and the husband
    prays:
Hope "springs exulting on triumphant
    wing"[43]
    That thus they all shall meet in future
    days:
There ever bask in uncreated rays,   140
No more to sigh, or shed the bitter tear,
    Together hymning their Creator's praise,
In such society, yet still more dear;
While circling Time moves round in an
    eternal sphere.

Compared with this, how poor Religion's
    pride,   145
    In all the pomp of method and of art,
When men display to congregations wide
    Devotion's every grace, except the heart!
The Power, incensed, the pageant will de-
    sert,   149
The pompous strain, the sacerdotal stole;
    But haply, in some cottage far apart,
May hear, well pleased, the language of the
    soul;
And in His Book of Life the inmates poor
    enroll.

Then homeward all take off their several
    way;
    The youngling cottagers retire to rest: 155
The parent-pair their secret homage pay,
    And proffer up to Heav'n the warm re-
    quest,
    That He who stills the raven's clamorous
    nest,

---

[33]Her well-saved cheese, ripe.

[34]Twelve-month.   [35]Since flax was in flower.

[36]Hall-Bible ("So called from its original use in
the noble's hall, wherein the whole household assembled for religious services."—Henley and Henderson).

[37]Gray side-locks.   [38]Chooses.

[39]All sacred melodies.   [40]Fans.

[41]King David.

---

[42]John.

[43]Pope, *Windsor Forest,* l. 112, inexactly quoted.

And decks the lily fair in flowery pride,
  Would, in the way His wisdom sees the
    best,   160
For them and for their little ones provide;
But chiefly in their hearts with grace divine
    preside.

From scenes like these old Scotia's grandeur
    springs,
  That makes her loved at home, revered
    abroad:
Princes and lords are but the breath of
    kings,   165
  "An honest man's the noblest work of
    God;"[44]
And certes, in fair virtue's heavenly road,
The cottage leaves the palace far behind;
  What is a lordling's pomp? a cumbrous
    load,   169
Disguising oft the wretch of human kind,
Studied in arts of hell, in wickedness refined!

O Scotia! my dear, my native soil!
  For whom my warmest wish to Heaven is
    sent!
Long may thy hardy sons of rustic toil
  Be blest with health, and peace, and sweet
    content!   175
  And O may Heaven their simple lives
    prevent
From luxury's contagion, weak and vile;
  Then, howe'er crowns and coronets be
    rent,
A virtuous populace may rise the while,
And stand a wall of fire around their much-
    loved isle.   180

O Thou! who poured the patriotic tide
  That streamed thro' Wallace's[45] undaunted
    heart,
Who dared to nobly stem tyrannic pride,
  Or nobly die—the second glorious part,
  (The patriot's God, peculiarly thou art, 185
His friend, inspirer, guardian, and reward!)
  O never, never, Scotia's realm desert;
But still the patriot, and the patriot-bard,
In bright succession raise, her ornament and
    guard!

[44]Pope, *Essay on Man*, Epistle IV, l. 248.
[45]William Wallace (1274?–1305), the Scottish
national hero. Burns wrote in a letter: "The story
of Wallace poured a Scottish prejudice into my
veins which will boil along there till the floodgates
of life shut in eternal rest."

ADDRESS TO THE DEIL[1]

O Thou! whatever title suit thee,
Auld Hornie, Satan, Nick, or Clootie,[2]
Wha in yon cavern grim an' sootie,
      Closed under hatches,
Spairges[3] about the brunstane cootie,[4]   5
      To scaud[5] poor wretches!

Hear me, auld Hangie,[6] for a wee,[7]
An' let poor damnéd bodies be;
I'm sure sma' pleasure it can gie,
      E'en to a deil,   10
To skelp[8] an' scaud poor dogs like me,
      An' hear us squeal!

Great is thy pow'r, an' great thy fame:
Far kenned an' noted is thy name;
An', tho' yon lowin heugh's[9] thy hame,   15
      Thou travels far;
An' faith! thou's neither lag[10] nor lame,
      Nor blate nor scaur.[11]

Whyles[12] rangin' like a roarin' lion
For prey, a' holes an' corners tryin';   20
Whyles on the strong-winged tempest flyin',
      Tirlin' the kirks;[13]
Whyles, in the human bosom pryin',
      Unseen thou lurks.

I've heard my reverend grannie say,   25
In lanely glens ye like to stray;
Or, where auld ruined castles gray
      Nod to the moon,
Ye fright the nightly wand'rer's way,
      Wi' eldritch croon.[14]   30

When twilight did my grannie summon
To say her pray'rs, douce,[15] honest woman!
Aft yont[16] the dyke she's heard you bum-
    min',[17]
      Wi' eerie drone;[18]
Or, rustlin', thro' the boortrees[19] comin', 35
      Wi' heavy groan.

[1]Written at Mossgiel towards the end of 1785.
Burns used for a motto ll. 128–9 of *Paradise Lost*,
Bk. I:
"O Prince, O Chief of many thronéd Powers
That led the embattled Seraphim to war."
[2]Little hoof.   [3]Splashes.   [4]Brimstone tub.
[5]Scald.   [6]Old hangman.   [7]For a minute.
[8]Spank.   [9]Flaming hollow.   [10]Backward.
[11]Nor bashful nor timid.   [12]Sometimes.
[13]Uncovering the churches.   [14]Hideous groan.
[15]Grave.   [16]Beyond.   [17]Humming.
[18]With unearthly sound.   [19]Elder bushes.

Ae dreary windy winter night
The stars shot down wi' sklentin'[20] light,
Wi' you mysel I gat a fright
    Ayont the lough;[21]   40
Ye like a rash-buss[22] stood in sight
    Wi' waving sough.[23]

The cudgel in my nieve[24] did shake,
Each bristled hair stood like a stake,
When wi' an eldritch, stoor[25] "quaick,
  quaick,"
    Amang the springs,   46
Awa ye squattered like a drake
    On whistlin' wings.

Let warlocks[26] grim, an' withered hags,
Tell how wi' you on ragweed nags[27]   50
They skim the muirs,[28] an' dizzy crags
    Wi' wicked speed;
And in kirk-yards renew their leagues
    Owre howkit[29] dead.

Thence country wives, wi' toil an' pain,   55
May plunge an' plunge the kirn[30] in vain;
For oh! the yellow treasure's taen
    By witchin' skill;
An' dawtit twal-pint Hawkie's gane
    As yell's the bill.[31]   60

Thence mystic knots mak great abuse
On young guidmen,[32] fond, keen, an'
  crouse;[33]
When the best wark-lume[34] i' the house,
    By cantrip[35] wit,
Is instant made no worth a louse,   65
    Just at the bit.[36]

When thowes[37] dissolve the snawy hoord,
An' float the jinglin' icy-boord,[38]
Then water-kelpies[39] haunt the foord,
    By your direction,   70
An' 'nighted trav'lers are allured
    To their destruction.

An' aft your moss-traversing spunkies[40]
Decoy the wight that late an' drunk is:
The bleezin,[41] curst, mischievous monkies   75
    Delude his eyes,
Till in some miry slough he sunk is,
    Ne'er mair to rise.

When masons' mystic word an' grip
In storms an' tempests raise you up,   80
Some cock or cat your rage maun stop,[42]
    Or, strange to tell!
The youngest brither ye wad whip
    Aff straught to hell.

Lang syne,[43] in Eden's bonnie yard,   85
When youthfu' lovers first were paired,
And all the soul of love they shared,
    The raptured hour,
Sweet on the fragrant flow'ry swaird,
    In shady bow'r;   90

Then you, ye auld snick-drawing[44] dog!
Ye cam to Paradise incog,
An' played on man a curséd brogue,[45]
    (Black be you fa'![46])
An' gied the infant warld a shog,[47]   95
    'Maist ruined a'.

D'ye mind that day, when in a bizz,[48]
Wi' reekit[49] duds, an' reestit gizz,[50]
Ye did present your smoutie[51] phiz
    'Mang better folk,   100
An' sklented[52] on the man of Uz[53]
    Your spitefu' joke?

An' how ye gat him i' your thrall,
An' brak him out o' house an' hal',
While scabs an' blotches did him gall   105
    Wi' bitter claw,
An' lows'd[54] his ill-tongued wicked scawl,[55]
    Was warst ava?[56]

But a' your doings to rehearse,
Your wily snares an' fechtin'[57] fierce,   110
Sin' that day Michael did you pierce,
    Down to this time,
Wad ding a' Lallan tongue, or Erse,[58]
    In prose or rime.

---

[20]Slanting.   [21]Beyond the pond.

[22]Bush of rushes.   [23]Moan.

[24]Fist.   [25]With an hideous, harsh.   [26]Wizards.

[27]Ragwort stems;—the witch's steed, more usually a broomstick.

[28]Moors.   [29]Over dug-up.   [30]Churn.

[31]And the petted twelve-pint cow has gone as dry as the bull. (A Scottish pint is rather more than a quart.)

[32]Husbands.   [33]Bold.   [34]Tool.   [35]Magic.

[36]Just when most needed.   [37]Thaws.

[38]Surface of ice.

[39]Water-spirits, usually in the form of horses.

---

[40]Bog-traversing will-o'-the-wisps.   [41]Blazing.

[42]I. e., by being offered as a sacrifice.

[43]Long since.   [44]Intruding.   [45]Trick.

[46]Lot.   [47]Shock.   [48]Bustling haste.

[49]Smoky.   [50]Scorched wig.   [51]Smutty.

[52]Squinted.   [53]Job.   [54]Loosed.   [55]Scold.

[56]Of all.   [57]Fighting.

[58]Would surpass a Lowland tongue or Gaelic.

An' now, auld Cloots, I ken ye're thinkin', 115
A certain Bardie's rantin', drinkin',
Some luckless hour will send him linkin'[59]
      To your black pit;
But faith! he'll turn a corner jinkin',[60]
      An' cheat you yet. 120

But fare you weel, auld Nickie-ben!
O wad ye tak a thought an' men'!
Ye aiblins[61] might—I dinna ken—
      Still hae a stake:[62]
I'm wae[63] to think upo' yon den, 125
      E'en for your sake!

A BARD'S EPITAPH[1]

Is there a whim-inspiréd fool,
Owre fast for thought, owre hot for rule,
Owre blate[2] to seek, owre proud to snool,[3]
      Let him draw near;
And owre this grassy heap sing dool,[4] 5
      And drap a tear.

Is there a bard of rustic song,
Who, noteless, steals the crowds among,
That weekly this aréa throng,
      O, pass not by! 10
But, with a frater-feeling strong,
      Here heave a sigh.

Is there a man whose judgment clear,
Can others teach the course to steer,
Yet runs, himself, life's mad career, 15
      Wild as the wave;
Here pause—and, thro' the starting tear,
      Survey this grave.

The poor inhabitant below
Was quick to learn and wise to know, 20
And keenly felt the friendly glow,
      And softer flame;
But thoughtless follies laid him low,
      And stained his name!

Reader, attend! whether thy soul 25
Soars fancy flights beyond the pole,
Or darkling grubs this earthly hole,
      In low pursuit;
Know prudent cautious self-control
      Is wisdom's root. 30

---

[59]Hurrying.   [60]Dodging.   [61]Perhaps.
[62]Have something to gain.   [63]Sad.
[1]Written in 1786.   [2]Modest.   [3]Cringe.
[4]Woe.

ADDRESS TO THE UNCO GUID,[1] OR THE RIGIDLY RIGHTEOUS[2]

My son, these maxims make a rule,
  And lump them aye thegither:
The rigid righteous is a fool,
  The rigid wise anither:
The cleanest corn that e'er was dight,[3]
  May hae some pyles o' caff in,[4]
So ne'er a fellow-creature slight
  For random fits o' daffin.[5]
      —Solomon (Eccles., 7:16).

O ye wha are sae guid yoursel,
  Sae pious and sae holy,
Ye've nought to do but mark and tell
  Your neibor's fauts and folly!
Whase life is like a weel-gaun[6] mill, 5
  Supplied wi' store o' water:
The heapéd happer's[7] ebbing still,
  And still the clap[8] plays clatter:

Hear me, ye venerable core,[9]
  As counsel for poor mortals, 10
That frequent pass douce[10] Wisdom's door
  For glaikit[11] Folly's portals;
I, for their thoughtless careless sakes,
  Would here propone[12] defenses,—
Their donsie[13] tricks, their black mistakes, 15
  Their failings and mischances.

Ye see your state wi' theirs compared,
  And shudder at the niffer;[14]
But cast a moment's fair regard—
  What maks the mighty differ? 20
Discount what scant occasion gave,
  That purity ye pride in,
And (what's aft mair than a' the lave[15])
  Your better art o' hidin'.

Think, when your castigated pulse 25
  Gies now and then a wallop,
What ragings must his veins convulse,
  That still eternal gallop!
Wi' wind and tide fair i' your tail,
  Right on ye scud your sea-way; 30
But in the teeth o' baith to sail,
  It makes an unco leeway.

---

[1]Uncommonly good.
[2]Written in 1786.   [3]Winnowed.
[4]Grains of chaff in it.   [5]Larking.
[6]Well-going.   [7]Hopper.   [8]Clapper.
[9]Company.   [10]Staid.   [11]Giddy.   [12]Propose.
[13]Restive.   [14]Exchange.   [15]Rest.

See Social Life and Glee sit down,
  All joyous and unthinking,
Till, quite transmogrified,[16] they're grown 35
  Debauchery and Drinking:
O would they stay to calculate
  Th' eternal consequences;
Or—your more dreaded hell to state—
  Damnation of expenses! 40

Ye high, exalted, virtuous Dames,
  Tied up in godly laces,
Before ye gie poor Frailty names,
  Suppose a change o' cases;
A dear loved lad, convenience snug, 45
  A treacherous inclination—
But, let me whisper i' your lug,[17]
  Ye're aiblins[18] nae temptation.

Then gently scan your brother man,
  Still gentler sister woman; 50
Tho' they may gang a kennin[19] wrang,
  To step aside is human.
One point must still be greatly dark,
  The moving why they do it;
And just as lamely can ye mark 55
  How far perhaps they rue it.

Who made the heart, 'tis He alone
  Decidedly can try us;
He knows each chord, its various tone,
  Each spring, its various bias. 60
Then at the balance let's be mute,
  We never can adjust it;
What's done we partly may compute,
  But know not what's resisted.

JOHN ANDERSON MY JO[1]

John Anderson my jo,[2] John,
  When we were first acquent,
Your locks were like the raven,
  Your bonnie brow was brent;[3]
But now your brow is beld,[4] John, 5
  Your locks are like the snow;
But blessings on your frosty pow,[5]
  John Anderson, my jo.

John Anderson my jo, John,
  We clamb the hill thegither; 10
And mony a canty[6] day, John,
  We've had wi' ane anither:

Now we maun totter down, John.
  And hand in hand we'll go,
And sleep thegither at the foot, 15
  John Anderson, my jo.

THE LOVELY LASS OF INVERNESS[7]

The lovely lass o' Inverness,
  Nae joy nor pleasure can she see;
For e'en and morn she cries, alas!
  And aye the saut[8] tear blin's her e'e:
"Drumossie[9] moor, Drumossie day, 5
  A faefu' day it was to me;
For there I lost my father dear,
  My father dear, and brethren three.

"Their winding-sheet the bluidy[10] clay,
  Their graves are growing green to see; 10
And by them lies the dearest lad
  That ever blest a woman's e'e!
Now wae to thee, thou cruel lord,[11]
  A bluidy man I trow[12] thou be;
For mony a heart thou hast made sair,[13] 15
  That ne'er did wrang[14] to thine or thee.

A RED, RED ROSE[15]

My love is like a red, red rose
  That's newly sprung in June:
My love is like the melodie
  That's sweetly played in tune.

So fair art thou, my bonnie lass, 5
  So deep in love am I:
And I will love thee still, my dear,
  Till a' the seas gang[16] dry.

Till a' the seas gang dry, my dear,
  And the rocks melt wi' the sun: 10
And I will love thee still, my dear,
  While the sands o' life shall run.

And fare thee weel, my only love,
  And fare thee weel awhile!
And I will come again, my love, 15
  Tho' it were ten thousand mile.

---

[16]Transformed.   [17]Ear.   [18]Perhaps.
[19]Trifle.
[1]Written in 1788 or 1789.   [2]Sweetheart.
[3]Smooth.   [4]Bald.   [5]Head.   [6]Jolly.

[7]Written in 1794.   [8]Salt.
[9]I. e., Culloden. The poem commemorates the Battle of Culloden, fought on 16 April, 1746.
[10]Bloody.   [11]William, Duke of Cumberland.
[12]Believe.   [13]Sore.   [14]Wrong.
[15]Written probably in 1794.   [16]Go.

AULD LANG SYNE [17]

Should auld acquaintance be forgot,
  And never brought to min'?
Should auld acquaintance be forgot,
  And auld lang syne? [18]

CHORUS

    For auld lang syne, my dear,   5
      For auld lang syne,
    We'll tak a cup o' kindness yet,
      For auld lang syne.

And surely ye'll be your pint-stowp, [19]
  And surely I'll be mine;   10
And we'll tak a cup o' kindness yet
  For auld lang syne.

We twa hae run about the braes, [20]
  And pu'd [21] the gowans [22] fine,
But we've wandered mony a weary foot   15
  Sin' auld lang syne.

We twa hae paidled i' the burn, [23]
  From morning sun till dine; [24]
But seas between us braid hae roared
  Sin' auld lang syne.   20

And there's a hand, my trusty fiere, [25]
  And gie's a hand o' thine;
And we'll tak a right guid-willie waught, [26]
  For auld lang syne.

TAM GLEN [27]

My heart is breaking, dear Tittie, [28]
  Some counsel unto me come len',
To anger them a' is a pity;
  But what will I do wi' Tam Glen?

I'm thinking, wi' sic a braw [29] fellow,   5
  In poortith [30] I might mak a fen'; [31]
What care I in riches to wallow,
  If I maunna [32] marry Tam Glen?

There's Lowrie the laird o' Dumeller,
  "Guid-day to you," brute! he comes ben: [33]
He brags and he blaws o' his siller,   11
  But when will he dance like Tam Glen?

My minnie [34] does constantly deave [35] me,
  And bids me beware o' young men;
They flatter, she says, to deceive me;   15
  But wha can think sae o' Tam Glen?

My daddie says, gin [36] I'll forsake him,
  He'll gie me guid hunder marks [37] ten:
But, if it's ordained I maun take him,
  O wha will I get but Tam Glen?   20

Yestreen at the Valentines' dealing, [38]
  My heart to my mou gied a sten: [39]
For thrice I drew ane without failing,
  And thrice it was written, Tam Glen.

The last Halloween I was waukin'   25
  My droukit sark-sleeve, [40] as ye ken;
His likeness cam up the house stalkin'—
  And the very gray breeks [41] o' Tam Glen!

Come, counsel, dear Tittie, don't tarry;
  I'll gie you my bonnie black hen,   30
Gif ye will advise me to marry
  The lad I lo'e dearly, Tam Glen.

WILLIE BREWED A PECK O' MAUT [42]

O Willie brewed a peck o' maut,
  And Rob and Allan cam to see;
Three blither hearts, that lee-lang [43] night,
  Ye wad na found in Christendie.

---

[34]Mother.   [35]Deafen.   [36]If.
[37]Coins worth slightly more than 26 cents each.
[38]The custom was for the men and girls to pair off by drawing slips of paper with names written on them.
[39]To my mouth gave a spring.
[40]Was watching my drenched shirt-sleeve. ("You go out, one or more—for this is a social spell—to a south-running spring, or rivulet, where 'three lairds' lands meet,' and dip your left shirt-sleeve. Go to bed in sight of a fire, and hang your wet sleeve before it to dry. Lie awake; and, some time near midnight, an apparition, having the exact figure of the grand object in question [your future husband], will come and turn the sleeve, as if to dry the other side of it"—Burns's note to *Halloween*, stanza 24, l. 7).
[41]Breeches.
[42]Written in 1789. "The air is Masterton's; the song mine. The occasion of it was this:—Mr. Wm. Nicol of the High School, Edinburgh, during the autumn vacation being at Moffat, honest Allan (who was at that time on a visit to Dalswinton) and I went to pay Nicol a visit. We had such a joyous meeting that Mr. Masterton and I agreed, each in our own way, that we should celebrate the business" (Burns's note). Allan Masterton was appointed writing-master in the Edinburgh High School in the fall of 1789.
[43]Live-long.

---

[17]Written in 1788.
[18]I. e., old times.   [19]Pay for your three-pint measure.
[20]Hill-sides.   [21]Pulled.   [22]Daisies.
[23]Paddled in the brook.   [24]Dinner-time.
[25]Comrade.   [26]Hearty good-will draught.
[27]Written in 1788 or 1789.   [28]Sister.
[29]Such a fine.   [30]Poverty.   [31]Shift.
[32]Must not.   [33]In.

CHORUS

We are na fou,[44] we're no that fou,   5
    But just a drappie[45] in our e'e;
The cock may craw, the day may daw,
    And aye we'll taste the barley bree.[46]

Here are we met, three merry boys,
    Three merry boys, I trow, are we;   10
And mony a night we've merry been,
    And mony mae we hope to be!

It is the moon, I ken her horn,
    That's blinkin' in the lift[47] sae hie;
She shines sae bright to wyle[48] us hame,   15
    But, by my sooth! she'll wait a wee.

Wha first shall rise to gang awa,
    A cuckold, coward loun[49] is he!
Wha first beside his chair shall fa',
    He is the king among us three!   20

TO MARY IN HEAVEN [50]

Thou lingring star, with lessening ray,
    That lov'st to greet the early morn,
Again thou usherest in the day
    My Mary from my soul was torn.
O Mary! dear departed shade!   5
    Where is thy place of blissful rest?
Seest thou thy lover lowly laid?
    Hear'st thou the groans that rend his
        breast?

That sacred hour can I forget?
    Can I forget the hallowed grove,   10
Where by the winding Ayr we met,
    To live one day of parting love?

___

[44]Full.   [45]Small drop.

[46]Barley-brew. [47]Sky. [48]Entice. [49]Rogue.

[50]Written in the fall of 1789. Mary Campbell, the subject of this poem, is generally supposed to have died in the fall of 1788, though about her, her relations with Burns, and the time of her death there is some uncertainty. Burns wrote the following note about *My Highland Lassie, O:* "My 'Highland Lassie' was a warm-hearted, charming young creature as ever blessed a man with generous love. After a pretty long tract of the most ardent reciprocal attachment we met by appointment on the second Sunday of May, in a sequestered spot by the banks of Ayr, where we spent the day in taking farewell, before she should embark for the West Highlands to arrange matters for our projected change of life. At the close of the autumn following she crossed the sea to meet me at Greenock, where she had scarce landed when she was seized with a malignant fever, which hurried my dear girl to the grave in a few days, before I could even hear of her illness."

Eternity will not efface
    Those records dear of transports past;
Thy image at our last embrace—   15
    Ah! little thought we 'twas our last!

Ayr gurgling kissed his pebbled shore,
    O'erhung with wild woods, thickening
        green;
The fragrant birch, and hawthorn hoar,   19
    Twined amorous round the raptured scene.
The flowers sprang wanton to be pressed,
    The birds sang love on ev'ry spray,
Till too, too soon, the glowing west
    Proclaimed the speed of wingéd day.

Still o'er these scenes my memory wakes,   25
    And fondly broods with miser care!
Time but the impression deeper makes,
    As streams their channels deeper wear.
My Mary, dear departed shade!
    Where is thy place of blissful rest?   30
Seest thou thy lover lowly laid?
    Hear'st thou the groans that rend his
        breast?

SWEET AFTON [51]

Flow gently, sweet Afton, among thy green
        braes,[52]
Flow gently, I'll sing thee a song in thy
        praise;
My Mary's asleep by the murmuring stream,
Flow gently, sweet Afton, disturb not her
        dream.

Thou stock-dove whose echo resounds
        through the glen,   5
Ye wild whistling blackbirds in yon thorny
        den,
Thou green-crested lapwing, thy screaming
        forbear,
I charge you disturb not my slumbering fair.

How lofty, sweet Afton, thy neighboring
        hills,
Far marked with the courses of clear wind-
        ing rills;   10
There daily I wander as noon rises high,
My flocks and my Mary's sweet cot in my
        eye.

___

[51]Written, probably, early in 1789. There have been attempts to connect Mary Campbell with this poem, but Burns probably had no special person in mind. He stated that the poem was written as a compliment to the "small river Afton that flows into Nith, near New Cummock, which has some charming, wild, romantic scenery on its banks."

[52]Slopes.

How pleasant thy banks and green valleys below,
Where wild in the woodlands the primroses blow; 14
There oft as mild ev'ning weeps over the lea,
The sweet-scented birk[53] shades my Mary and me.

Thy crystal stream, Afton, how lovely it glides,
And winds by the cot where my Mary resides;

How wanton thy waters her snowy feet lave,
As gathering sweet flow'rets she stems thy clear wave. 20

Flow gently, sweet Afton, among thy green braes,
Flow gently, sweet river, the theme of my lays;
My Mary's asleep by the murmuring stream,
Flow gently, sweet Afton, disturb not her dream.

TAM O' SHANTER[1]
A Tale

When chapman billies[2] leave the street,
And drouthy[3] neibors neibors meet,
As markety-days are wearing late,
An' folk begin to tak the gate;[4]
While we sit bousing at the nappy,[5] 5
An' getting fou and unco[6] happy,
We think na on the lang Scots miles,[7]
The mosses, waters, slaps,[8] and styles,
That lie between us and our hame,
Where sits our sulky sullen dame, 10
Gathering her brows like gathering storm,
Nursing her wrath to keep it warm.
  This truth fand honest Tam o' Shanter,
As he frae Ayr ae night did canter—
(Auld Ayr, wham ne'er a town surpasses 15
For honest men and bonnie lasses).

O Tam! hadst thou but been sae wise
As ta'en thy ain wife Kate's advice!
She tauld thee weel thou was a skellum,[9]
A bletherin',[10] blusterin', drunken blellum;[11]
That frae November till October, 21
Ae market-day thou was na sober;
That ilka melder[12] wi' the miller
Thou sat as lang as thou had siller;
That every naig was ca'd[13] a shoe on, 25
The smith and thee gat roarin' fou on;
That at the Lord's house, even on Sunday,
Thou drank wi' Kirkton Jean till Monday.
She prophesied that, late or soon, 29
Thou would be found deep drowned in Doon;
Or catched wi' warlocks in the mirk[14]
By Alloway's auld haunted kirk.
  Ah, gentle dames! it gars me greet[15]
To think how mony counsels sweet,
How mony lengthened sage advices, 35
The husband frae the wife despises!
  But to our tale: Ae market night,
Tam had got planted unco right,
Fast by an ingle, bleezing finely,
Wi' reaming swats,[16] that drank divinely; 40
And at his elbow, Souter[17] Johnny,
His ancient, trusty, drouthy crony;
Tam lo'ed him like a very brither;
They had been fou for weeks thegither.
The night drave on wi' sangs and clatter, 45
And aye the ale was growing better:
The landlady and Tam grew gracious,
Wi' favors secret, sweet, and precious;
The souter tauld his queerest stories;
The landlord's laugh was ready chorus: 50
The storm without might rair and rustle,
Tam did na mind the storm a whistle.

---

[53]Birch.

[1]Written in 1790. Alloway Kirk is less than a mile south of Burns's birthplace. It fell into disuse after the annexation of the parish of Alloway to that of Ayr in 1690, and, when Burns wrote, it had long been ruinous. The old bridge over the Doon, which dates from the fifteenth century, stands about 200 yards to the south of the church. Burns had from his childhood heard witch-stories relating to Alloway Kirk, and *Tam o' Shanter* is based on one of them. It is said that Burns probably drew the suggestion of his hero from the character and adventures of Douglas Graham (1739–1811), a farmer noted for his convivial habits, and tenant of the farm of Shanter on the Carrick shore (Henley and Henderson, I, 437). Burns wrote to Mrs. Dunlop in 1791: "I look on *Tam o' Shanter* to be my standard performance in the poetical line. 'Tis true both the one [his new-born son] and the other discover a spice of roguish waggery that might perhaps be as well spared; but then they also show, in my opinion, a force of genius and a finishing polish that I despair of ever excelling."

[2]Peddler fellows.   [3]Thirsty.   [4]Road.
[5]Drinking ale.   [6]Getting full (drunk) and very.
[7]The Scottish mile was about an eighth longer than the English mile.
[8]The bogs, pools, gaps (in fences).

[9]Good-for-nothing.   [10]Chattering.   [11]Babbler.
[12]Every meal-grinding.   [13]Driven.
[14]Wizards in the dark.   [15]Makes me weep.
[16]Foaming new ale.   [17]Shoemaker.

Care, mad to see a man sae happy,
E'en drowned himsel amang the nappy.
As bees flee hame wi' lades o' treasure,   55
The minutes winged their way wi' pleasure;
Kings may be bless'd, but Tam was glorious,
O'er a' the ills o' life victorious!

But pleasures are like poppies spread—
You seize the flow'r, its bloom is shed;   60
Or like the snow falls in the river—
A moment white, then melts for ever;
Or like the borealis race,
That flit ere you can point their place;
Or like the rainbow's lovely form   65
Evanishing amid the storm.
Nae man can tether time nor tide;
The hour approaches Tam maun[18] ride;
That hour, o' night's black arch the keystane,
That dreary hour, he mounts his beast in;   70
And sic a night he taks the road in,
As ne'er poor sinner was abroad in.

The wind blew as 'twad blawn its last;
The rattling show'rs rose on the blast;   74
The speedy gleams the darkness swallowed;
Loud, deep, and lang, the thunder bellowed:
That night, a child might understand,
The Deil had business on his hand.

Weel mounted on his gray mare, Meg,
A better never lifted leg,   80
Tam skelpit[19] on thro' dub[20] and mire,
Despising wind, and rain, and fire;
Whiles[21] holding fast his gude blue bonnet;
Whiles crooning o'er some auld Scots sonnet;[22]
Whiles glow'ring round wi' prudent cares,   85
Lest bogles[23] catch him unawares.
Kirk-Alloway was drawing nigh,
Whare ghaists and houlets[24] nightly cry.

By this time he was cross the ford,
Where in the snaw the chapman smoor'd;[25]
And past the birks and meikle stane,[26]   91
Where drunken Charlie brak's neck-bane;
And thro' the whins,[27] and by the cairn,[28]
Where hunters fand the murdered bairn;[29]
And near the thorn, aboon[30] the well,   95
Where Mungo's mither hanged hersel.
Before him Doon pours all his floods;
The doubling storm roars thro' the woods;
The lightnings flash from pole to pole;
Near and more near the thunders roll: 100
When, glimmering thro' the groaning trees,
Kirk-Alloway seem'd in a bleeze;

Thro' ilka bore[31] the beams were glancing;
And loud resounded mirth and dancing.

Inspiring bold John Barleycorn!   105
What dangers thou canst make us scorn!
Wi' tippenny,[32] we fear nae evil;
Wi' usquebae,[33] we'll face the devil!
The swats sae reamed in Tammie's noddle,
Fair play, he cared na deils a boddle![34]   110
But Maggie stood right sair astonished,
Till, by the heel and hand admonished,
She ventured forward on the light;
And, vow! Tam saw an unco[35] sight!

Warlocks and witches in a dance!   115
Nae cotillon brent new[36] frae France,
But hornpipes, jigs, strathspeys, and reels,[37]
Put life and mettle in their heels.
A winnock-bunker[38] in the east,
There sat auld Nick, in shape o' beast—   120
A touzie tyke,[39] black, grim, and large!
To gie them music was his charge:
He screwed the pipes and gart them skirl,[40]
Till roof and rafters a' did dirl.[41]
Coffins stood round like open presses,   125
That shawed the dead in their last dresses;
And by some devilish cantraip[42] sleight
Each in its cauld hand held a light,
By which heroic Tam was able
To note upon the haly[43] table   130
A murderer's banes in gibbet-airns;[44]
Twa span-lang, wee, unchristened bairns;
A thief new-cutted frae the rape,[45]
Wi' his last gasp his gab[46] did gape;
Five tomahawks, wi' blude red rusted;   135
Five scymitars, wi' murder crusted;
A garter, which a babe had strangled;
A knife, a father's throat had mangled,
Whom his ain son o' life bereft—
The gray hairs yet stack to the heft;   140
Wi' mair of horrible and awfu',
Which even to name wad be unlawfu'.

As Tammie glowred,[47] amazed, and curious,
The mirth and fun grew fast and furious:
The piper loud and louder blew;   145
The dancers quick and quicker flew;
They reeled, they set, they crossed, they cleekit,[48]
Till ilka carlin swat and reekit,[49]

[18]Must.
[19]Clattered.   [20]Puddle.   [21]Now.   [22]Song.
[23]Bogies.   [24]Ghosts and owls.
[25]Peddler smothered.   [26]Birches and big stone.
[27]Furze.   [28]Pile of stones.   [29]Child.
[30]Above.

[31]Every chink.   [32]Ale.
[33]Whisky.   [34]Copper.   [35]Wonderful.
[36]Brand-new.   [37]Names of Scottish dances.
[38]Window-seat.   [39]Shaggy dog.
[40]Made them squeal.
[41]Ring.   [42]Magic.   [43]Holy.
[44]Bones in gibbet-irons.   [45]Rope.   [46]Mouth.
[47]Stared.   [48]Linked themselves.
[49]Till every old woman sweat and steamed.

And coost her duddies to the wark,[50]
And linkit at it in her sark![51] 150
   Now Tam, O Tam! had thae been queans,[52]
A' plump and strapping in their teens;
Their sarks, instead o' creeshie flannen,[53]
Been snaw-white seventeen hunder linen![54]
Thir breeks[55] o' mine, my only pair, 155
That ance were plush, o' gude blue hair,
I wad hae gi'en them off my hurdies,[56]
For ae blink o' the bonnie burdies.[57]
   But withered beldams, auld and droll,
Rigwoodie[58] hags wad spean[59] a foal, 160
Louping and flinging on a crummock,[60]
I wonder didna turn thy stomach.
   But Tam kent[61] what was what fu' braw-
     lie:[62]
There was ae winsome wench and walie[63]
That night enlisted in the core,[64] 165
Lang after kent on Carrick shore!
(For mony a beast to dead she shot,
And perished mony a bonnie boat,
And shook baith meikle corn and bear,[65]
And kept the country-side in fear.) 170
Her cutty[66] sark, o' Paisley harn,[67]
That while a lassie she had worn,
In longitude tho' sorely scanty,
It was her best, and she was vauntie.[68]
Ah! little kent thy reverend grannie 175
That sark she coft[69] for her wee Nannie
Wi' twa pund Scots[70] ('twas a' her riches)
Wad ever graced a dance of witches!
   But here my muse her wing maun cour;[71]
Sic flights are far beyond her pow'r— 180
To sing how Nannie lap and flang[72]
(A souple jade she was, and strang);
And how Tam stood, like ane bewitched,
And thought his very e'en enriched;
Even Satan glowred, and fidged[73] fu' fain, 185
And hotched[74] and blew wi' might and main:
Till first ae caper, syne anither,
Tam tint[75] his reason a' thegither,

And roars out, "Weel done, Cutty-sark!"
And in an instant all was dark! 190
And scarcely had he Maggie rallied,
When out the hellish legion sallied.
   As bees bizz out wi' angry fyke[76]
When plundering herds[77] assail their byke,[78]
As open pussie's mortal foes[79] 195
When, pop! she starts before their nose,
As eager runs the market-crowd,
When "Catch the thief!" resounds aloud,
So Maggie runs; the witches follow,
Wi' mony an eldritch skriech[80] and hol-
     low. 200
   Ah, Tam! ah, Tam! thou'll get thy fair-
     in'![81]
In hell they'll roast thee like a herrin'!
In vain thy Kate awaits thy comin'!
Kate soon will be a woefu' woman!
Now do thy speedy utmost, Meg, 205
And win the key-stane o' the brig:[82]
There at them thou thy tail may toss,
A running stream they darena cross.
But ere the key-stane she could make,
The fient[83] a tail she had to shake! 210
For Nannie, far before the rest,
Hard upon noble Maggie pressed,
And flew at Tam wi' furious ettle;[84]
But little wist[85] she Maggie's mettle!
Ae spring brought off her master hale, 215
But left behind her ain gray tail:
The carlin claught[86] her by the rump,
And left poor Maggie scarce a stump.
   Now, wha this tale o' truth shall read,
Each man and mother's son, take heed; 220
Whene'er to drink you are inclined,
Or cutty-sarks run in your mind,
Think! ye may buy the joys o'er dear;
Remember Tam o' Shanter's mare.

YE FLOWERY BANKS O' BONNIE DOON[1]

Ye flowery banks o' bonnie Doon,
   How can ye blume sae fair?
How can ye chant, ye little birds,
   And I sae fu' o' care?

---

[50]And cast off her clothes to the work.
[51]And tripped at it in her shirt.
[52]Had these been young women.
[53]Greasy flannel.
[54]I. e., fine linen, with 1700 threads to a width.
[55]These breeches.   [56]Hips.   [57]Maidens.
[58]*Probably* ancient, or lean.
[59]Wean (from disgust).
[60]Leaping and kicking on a staff.   [61]Knew.
[62]Full well.   [63]Choice.   [64]Company.
[65]Much wheat and barley.
[66]Short.   [67]Coarse linen.   [68]Proud.
[69]Bought.
[70]A pound Scots was only about 40 cents.
[71]Must stoop.   [72]Leaped and kicked.
[73]Fidgeted.   [74]Jerked.   [75]Lost.

[76]Fret.   [77]Herders of cattle.   [78]Hive.
[79]As the hare's mortal foes begin to bark.
[80]Unearthly screech.
[81]Literally, a present from a fair, but the word came to be used ironically (as it is here) for a beating.
[82]Bridge. "It is a well-known fact that witches, or any evil spirits, have no power to follow a poor wight any farther than the middle of the next running stream" (Burns's note).
[83]Devil.   [84]Aim.   [85]Knew.   [86]Seized.
[1]Written probably in 1791.

Thou'll break my heart, thou bonnie bird, 5
    That sings upon the bough;
Thou minds me o' the happy days,
    When my fause luve was true.

Thou'll break my heart, thou bonnie bird,
    That sings beside thy mate; 10
For sae I sat, and sae I sang,
    And wist[2] na o' my fate.

Aft hae I roved by bonnie Doon,
    To see the woodbine twine,
And ilka[3] bird sang o' its love, 15
    And sae did I o' mine.

Wi' lightsome heart I pu'd a rose
    Frae off its thorny tree:
And my fause luver staw[4] my rose,
    But left the thorn wi' me. 20

AE FOND KISS[5]

Ae fond kiss, and then we sever!
Ae fareweel, alas, for ever!
Deep in heart-wrung tears I'll pledge thee,
Warring sighs and groans I'll wage[6] thee.
Who shall say that fortune grieves him 5
While the star of hope she leaves him?
Me, nae cheerfu' twinkle lights me,
Dark despair around benights me.

I'll ne'er blame my partial fancy,
Naething could resist my Nancy; 10
But to see her was to love her,
Love but her, and love for ever.
Had we never loved sae kindly,
Had we never loved sae blindly,
Never met—or never parted— 15
We had ne'er been broken-hearted.

Fare thee weel, thou first and fairest!
Fare thee weel, thou best and dearest!
Thine be ilka[7] joy and treasure,
Peace, enjoyment, love, and pleasure. 20
Ae fond kiss, and then we sever;
Ae fareweel, alas, for ever!
Deep in heart-wrung tears I'll pledge thee,
Warring sighs and groans I'll wage thee.

---

[2]Knew.   [3]Every.   [4]Stole.
[5]Written in 1791.   [6]Pledge.   [7]Every.

DUNCAN GRAY[8]

Duncan Gray came here to woo,
    Ha, ha, the wooing o't,
On blithe Yule night[9] when we were fou,[10]
    Ha, ha, the wooing o't.
Maggie coost[11] her head fu' heigh, 5
Looked asklent and unco skeigh[12]
Gart[13] poor Duncan stand abeigh;[14]
    Ha, ha, the wooing o't.

Duncan fleeched,[15] and Duncan prayed;
    Ha, ha, the wooing o't, 10
Meg was deaf as Ailsa Craig,[16]
    Ha, ha, the wooing o't.
Duncan sighed baith out and in,
Grat[17] his e'en baith bleer't and blin',
Spak o' lowpin o'er a linn;[18] 15
    Ha, ha, the wooing o't.

Time and chance are but a tide,
    Ha, ha, the wooing o't,
Slighted love is sair to bide,[19]
    Ha, ha, the wooing o't. 20
Shall I, like a fool, quoth he,
For a haughty hizzie[20] die?
She may gae to—France for me!
    Ha, ha, the wooing o't.

How it comes let doctors tell, 25
    Ha, ha, the wooing o't,
Meg grew sick as he grew hale,
    Ha, ha, the wooing o't.
Something in her bosom wrings;
For relief a sigh she brings; 30
And O, her e'en they spak sic[21] things!
    Ha, ha, the wooing o't.

Duncan was a lad o' grace,
    Ha, ha, the wooing o't,
Maggie's was a piteous case, 35
    Ha, ha, the wooing o't.
Duncan couldna be her death,
Swelling pity smoored[22] his wrath;
Now they're crouse and cantie[23] baith!
    Ha, ha, the wooing o't. 40

---

[8]Written in 1792. The second or (as Henley and Henderson say) drawing-room set. Of the tune Burns wrote: *"Duncan Gray* is that kind of lighthorse gallop of an air which precludes sentiment. The ludicrous is its ruling feature."
[9]Christmas Eve.   [10]Drunk.   [11]Cast.
[12]Askance and very disdainful.   [13]Made.
[14]Off.   [15]Wheedled.
[16]A rocky islet in the Firth of Clyde, frequented by screaming sea-fowl.
[17]Wept.   [18]Leaping over a waterfall.
[19]Hard to endure.   [20]Young woman.   [21]Such.
[22]Smothered.   [23]Brisk and cheerful.

HIGHLAND MARY [24]

Ye banks and braes [25] and streams around
  The castle o' Montgomery,
Green be your woods, and fair your flowers,
  Your waters never drumlie! [26]
There summer first unfauld her robes,   5
  And there the langest tarry;
For there I took the last fareweel
  O' my sweet Highland Mary.

How sweetly bloomed the gay green birk, [27]
  How rich the hawthorn's blossom,   10
As underneath their fragrant shade
  I clasped her to my bosom!
The golden hours on angel wings
  Flew o'er me and my dearie;
For dear to me as light and life   15
  Was my sweet Highland Mary.

Wi' mony a vow, and locked embrace,
  Our parting was fu' tender;
And, pledging aft to meet again,
  We tore oursels asunder;   20
But oh! fell death's untimely frost,
  That nipped my flower sae early!
Now green's the sod, and cauld's the clay,
  That wraps my Highland Mary!

O pale, pale now, those rosy lips,   25
  I aft have kissed sae fondly!
And closed for aye the sparkling glance,
  That dwelt on me sae kindly!
And mold'ring now in silent dust,
  That heart that lo'ed me dearly!   30
But still within my bosom's core
  Shall live my Highland Mary.

SCOTS WHA HAE [28]

Scots, wha hae wi' Wallace bled,
Scots, wham Bruce has aften led,
Welcome to your gory bed,
  Or to victorie.

---

[24] Written in 1792. Concerning Mary Campbell, the subject of this song, see footnote on *To Mary in Heaven.*
[25] Slopes.   [26] Turbid.   [27] Birch.
[28] Written in 1793. There was a tradition that the air *Hey Tutti Taitti* was Robert Bruce's march at Bannockburn. Burns wrote: "This thought, in my solitary wanderings, roused me to a pitch of enthusiasm on the theme of liberty and independence, which I threw into a kind of Scottish ode, fitted to the air, that one might suppose to be the gallant royal Scot's address to his heroic followers on that eventful morning." The Battle of Bannockburn was fought on 24 June, 1314. The Scots under Bruce won a victory over Edward II and

Now's the day, and now's the hour;   5
See the front o' battle lour!
See approach proud Edward's power—
  Chains and slaverie!

Wha will be a traitor knave?
Wha can fill a coward's grave?   10
Wha sae base as be a slave?
  Let him turn and flee!

Wha for Scotland's king and law
Freedom's sword will strongly draw,
Freeman stand, or freeman fa'?   15
  Let him follow me!

By oppression's woes and pains!
By your sons in servile chains!
We will drain our dearest veins,
  But they shall be free!   20

Lay the proud usurpers low!
Tyrants fall in every foe!
Liberty's in every blow!
  Let us do or die!

IS THERE FOR HONEST POVERTY [29]

Is there, for honest poverty,
  That hangs his head, and a' that?
The coward-slave, we pass him by,
  We dare be poor for a' that!
    For a' that, and a' that,   5
      Our toils obscure, and a' that,
    The rank is but the guinea stamp;
      The man's the gowd [30] for a' that.

What tho' on hamely fare we dine,
  Wear hodden-gray, [31] and a' that?   10
Gie fools their silks, and knaves their wine
  A man's a man for a' that.
    For a' that, and a' that,
      Their tinsel show, and a' that,
    The honest man, tho' e'er sae poor,   15
      Is king o' men for a' that.

Ye see yon birkie, [32] ca'd a lord,
  Wha struts, and stares, and a' that;
Tho' hundreds worship at his word,
  He's but a coof [33] for a' that: 20

---

the English which secured the independence of Scotland until the union of the kingdoms in 1603. In the same letter from which the above sentence is quoted Burns also indicated that the French Revolution was in his mind when he was writing the poem.
[29] Written in 1793 or 1794.   [30] Gold.
[31] Coarse gray woolen cloth.   [32] Fellow.
[33] Fool.

For a' that, and a' that,
His ribband, star, and a' that,
The man of independent mind,
He looks and laughs at a' that.

A prince can mak a belted knight,   25
A marquis, duke, and a' that;
But an honest man's aboon[34] his might,
Guid faith he mauna fa[35] that!
For a' that, and a' that,
Their dignities, and a' that,   30
The pith o' sense, and pride o' worth,
Are higher rank than a' that.

Then let us pray that come it may,
As come it will for a' that,
That sense and worth, o'er a' the earth,   35
Shall bear the gree[36] and a' that;
For a' that, and a' that,
It's comin' yet for a' that,
That man to man, the world o'er,
Shall brithers be for a' that.   40

---

[34]Above.   [35]Must not lay claim to.
[36]Have the prize.

O, WERT THOU IN THE CAULD BLAST[37]

O, wert thou in the cauld blast
On yonder lea, on yonder lea,
My plaidie to the angry airt,[38]
I'd shelter thee, I'd shelter thee.
Or did misfortune's bitter storms   5
Around thee blaw, around thee blaw,
Thy bield[39] should be my bosom,
To share it a', to share it a'.

Or were I in the wildest waste,
Sae black and bare, sae black and bare,   10
The desert were a paradise,
If thou wert there, if thou wert there.
Or were I monarch o' the globe,
Wi' thee to reign, wi' thee to reign,
The brightest jewel in my crown   15
Wad be my queen, wad be my queen.

---

[37]Written in 1796, during Burns's last illness, in
honor of Jessie Lewars, who did much for him
and his family at that time.
[38]Quarter.   [39]Shelter.

WILLIAM WORDSWORTH

1770-1850

Wordsworth was born at Cockermouth in the county of Cumberland on 7 April, 1770. His early life was one of simplicity, almost of poverty, amid picturesque rural surroundings. His mother died when he was eight years old, and his father five years later. He attended the grammar school of Hawkshead, living as a boarder in the village, and thence passed in 1787 to St. John's College, Cambridge, two of his uncles providing the means necessary for his university education. He took his B. A. in 1791. Wordsworth was never a great reader, and he did not distinguish himself as a student. There may even have been a degree of wildness in his life during these years which it is still not usual to associate with the "Daddy Wordsworth"—to use Edward FitzGerald's phrase—perpetuated by the poet's earlier biographers. It is evident at any rate that, as he himself later said, he "was not for that hour, nor for that place," and that, while his strictly intellectual training was pursued somewhat listlessly at Cambridge, his heart was roused to fresh life in his vacations spent in the northern country known as the Lake District and, in the summer of 1790, in a walking tour through France and Switzerland. After he left Cambridge he spent some months in London and then went to France, where he remained until the beginning of 1793. There he was in close association with members of the revolutionary party, and at the same time he fell in love with a member of a royalist family, Marie-Anne Vallon, some four or five years his senior, who bore him a daughter in December, 1792. Reason exists for believing that Wordsworth later intended to marry the mother of his daughter, but he did not do so. On the other hand, as Professor G. M. Harper has said, "whatever, from a legal point of view, may have been the nature of the connection between Wordsworth and Marie-Anne Vallon, it was openly acknowledged and its consequences were honorably endured" (*Wordsworth's French Daughter*, p. 12).

Soon after his return to England in 1793

Wordsworth published *An Evening Walk* and *Descriptive Sketches*, and presently he became, at least partly by way of reaction from the excesses of the French Revolution, a disciple of William Godwin, an able man without common sense who for a short time was seriously regarded as the leader of English liberalism. His period of full allegiance to Godwin was, however, short, and also unhappy. He did not, in fact, really find himself until he became acquainted with Samuel Taylor Coleridge. In 1797 he went to live near Coleridge in Somersetshire. Coleridge was, as has been finely said, "one of those minds which startle other minds out of the *ordinariness* which so easily besets most men, and besets at fitful intervals even genius" (H. W. Garrod, *Wordsworth*, p. 139). By the beginning of his intimacy with Coleridge Wordsworth had finally wrung himself completely free of "that strong disease," as he calls it, of Godwinism, and it was during the years of his close association with Coleridge —that is to say, for about nine years following 1797—that he wrote practically all of his greatest poetry. In 1798 the two poets published *Lyrical Ballads* (the volume contained four poems by Coleridge). In 1798 and 1799 a large part of *The Prelude*, Wordsworth's long autobiographical poem, was written, and it was finished in 1805. In this period the fragment of *The Recluse* was written (1800) and part of *The Excursion*, including the episode concerning Margaret (1799). And at the end of this period was published *Poems in Two Volumes* (1807). This sums up the best of Wordsworth's poetry, and after 1807 he began to settle more and more deeply into that *ordinariness* to which he was, perhaps, naturally more prone than other men of equally great gifts.

Since 1795, when he had received a small legacy from Raisley Calvert which had freed him from dependence on his other relatives, Wordsworth had been living with his sister Dorothy—who also exerted a strong influence upon him. In 1798 Wordsworth and Dorothy and Coleridge had gone to spend some time in Germany; and in 1799 the Wordsworths took Dove Cottage, Grasmere, where they remained nine years. In 1802 Wordsworth married Mary Hutchinson. In 1813 he was given a government post, a sinecure, which greatly increased his income and enabled him to move to Rydal Mount, where he remained until his death. In the year following his appointment he published *The Excursion,* and in 1815 *The White Doe of Rylstone, Laodamia,* and other poems. In 1836–1837 a collected edition of his poems was published, in six volumes. In 1843 he was made poet laureate, in succession to Southey. He died on 23 April, 1850.

In the note concerning his *Ode, Intimations of Immortality from Recollections of Early Childhood,* which Wordsworth dictated to Miss Isabella Fenwick, he spoke of a difficulty he had had in childhood in admitting "the notion of death as a state applicable to my own being." This arose, he went on to say, "from a sense of the indomitableness of the Spirit within me," and from this it came about that "I was often unable to think of external things as having external existence, and I communed with all that I saw as something not apart from, but inherent in, my own immaterial nature. Many times while going to school have I grasped at a wall or tree to recall myself from this abyss of idealism to the reality. At that time I was afraid of such processes. In later periods of life I have deplored, as we have all reason to do, a subjugation of an opposite character. . . . To that dream-like vividness and splendor which invest objects of sight in childhood, every one, I believe, if he would look back, could bear testimony." It is hardly too much to say that this passage contains the key to Wordsworth's poetry. In his youth Wordsworth's animal sensibilities were strong. The life of the eye and ear was more to him than to other men. And while his richest and most vivid experiences came to him through the senses, at the same time they often carried him beyond sense to visions of an eternity not beyond the reach of man. From this Wordsworth inferred the natural goodness of the senses, and thus he was prepared for the influence of Rousseau and the French Revolution. To this faith in the life of the senses he returned after his period of subjection to Godwin, and in this faith much of his great poetry was written. In his great period he also attacked, with Coleridge's help, the question how one was to maintain one's spiritual life as one grew older and the impressions of the senses became less piercingly vivid.

To this question he found answers—we may read them in *The Character of the Happy Warrior* and the *Ode to Duty*—but evidently no answer that enabled him to maintain his own life on the exalted level of his great decade.

The *Lyrical Ballads* of 1798 mark, as is usually said, a new epoch in the history of English literature;—they definitely usher in the romantic movement. Among other things it is notable that these poems are largely concerned with the experiences of humble people living in the country and that their style has a simplicity and directness which marks a deliberate break with the artificial poetic diction of the eighteenth century. But the latter characteristic is not really separable from the substance of Wordsworth's poetry. What he wrote came from the depths of the man, and his style when at its best is simply the result of his effort to deal faithfully with his experience.

The best one-volume edition of his writings is *The Poetical Works of William Wordsworth,* ed. T. Hutchinson, in the series of "Oxford Standard Authors"; but the edition of the *Poems* by Nowell Charles Smith (3 vols., London, 1908) is admirable in every way and is easier to read. The letters of William and Dorothy Wordsworth have been definitively edited by Ernest de Selincourt (6 vols., Oxford, 1935–1939). Professor de Selincourt's edition of *The Prelude* (Oxford, 1926) presents this poem for the first time in print as Wordsworth originally wrote it, together with the much altered version published in 1850. Wordsworth's *Literary Criticism* has been conveniently edited by Nowell Smith (Oxford, 1905). An indispensable companion to Wordsworth studies is *The Journals of Dorothy Wordsworth,* ed. William Knight (2 vols., London, 1897). The standard biography is *William Wordsworth, His Life, Works, and Influence,* by George McLean Harper (2 vols., London, 1916; the revised edition in one volume, 1929, should not be used). *The Early Life of William Wordsworth,* by Émile Legouis (London, 1897; second ed. with corrections 1921), is a brilliant special study; and *The Later Wordsworth* by Edith C. Batho (Cambridge, 1933) also usefully supplements Professor Harper. The number of important books and articles about Wordsworth is very large. It is possible to mention here only two more books: C. H. Herford's excellent short biography, *Wordsworth* (London, 1930); and H. W. Garrod's *Wordsworth: Lectures and Essays* (Oxford, 1923; revised ed. 1927).

PREFACE TO THE SECOND EDITION OF
LYRICAL BALLADS[1]

THE first Volume of these Poems has already been submitted to general perusal. It was published as an experiment, which, I hoped, might be of some use to ascertain how far, by fitting to metrical arrangement a selection of the real language of men in a state of vivid sensation, that sort of pleasure and that quantity of pleasure may be imparted, which a Poet may rationally endeavor to impart.

I had formed no very inaccurate estimate of the probable effect of those Poems: I flattered myself that they who should be pleased with them would read them with more than common pleasure: and, on the other hand, I was well aware, that by those who should dislike them they would be read with more than common dislike. The result has differed from my expectation in this only, that a greater number have been pleased than I ventured to hope I should please.

Several of my Friends are anxious for the success of these Poems, from a belief that, if the views with which they were composed were indeed realized, a class of Poetry would be produced, well adapted to interest mankind permanently, and not unimportant in the quality and in the multiplicity of its moral relations: and on this account they have advised me to prefix a systematic defense of the theory upon which the Poems were written. But I was unwilling to undertake the task, knowing that on this occasion the reader would look coldly upon my arguments, since I might be suspected of having been principally influenced by the selfish and foolish hope of *reasoning* him into an approbation of these particular Poems: and I was still more unwilling to undertake the task, because adequately to display the opinions, and fully to enforce the arguments, would require a space wholly disproportionate to a preface. For, to treat the subject with the clearness and coherence of which it is susceptible, it would be necessary to give a full account of the present state of the public taste in this country, and to determine how far this taste is healthy or depraved; which, again, could not be determined without pointing out in what manner language and the human mind act and re-act on each other, and without retracing the revolutions, not of literature alone, but likewise of society itself. I have therefore altogether declined to enter regularly upon this defense; yet I am sensible that there would be something like impropriety in abruptly obtruding upon the Public, without a few words of introduction, Poems so materially different from those upon which general approbation is at present bestowed.

It is supposed that by the act of writing in verse an Author makes a formal engagement that he will gratify certain known habits of association; that he not only thus apprises the Reader that certain classes of ideas and expressions will be found in his book, but that others will be carefully excluded. This exponent or symbol held forth by metrical language must in different eras of literature have excited very different expectations: for example, in the age of Catullus, Terence, and Lucretius, and that of Statius or Claudian;[2] and in our own country, in the age of Shakespeare and Beaumont and Fletcher, and that of Donne and Cowley, or Dryden, or Pope. I will not take upon me to determine the exact import of the promise which, by the act of writing in verse, an Author in the present day makes to his reader; but it will undoubtedly appear to many persons that I have not fulfilled the terms of an engagement thus voluntarily contracted. They who have been accustomed to the gaudiness and inane phraseology of many modern writers, if they persist in reading this book to its conclusion, will, no doubt, frequently have to struggle with feelings of strangeness and awkwardness: they will look round for poetry, and

---

[1] The second edition of the *Lyrical Ballads,* with additions, was published in two volumes in 1800. The Preface which was then added was later revised and enlarged, and is here printed in its final form.

[2] The first three belong to the great period of Latin poetry, the latter two to a later age comparatively barren of high achievement.

will be induced to inquire by what species of courtesy these attempts can be permitted to assume that title. I hope, therefore, the reader will not censure me for attempting to state what I have proposed to myself to per-5 form; and also (as far as the limits of a preface will permit) to explain some of the chief reasons which have determined me in the choice of my purpose: that at least he may be spared any unpleasant feeling of dis-10 appointment, and that I myself may be protected from one of the most dishonorable accusations which can be brought against an Author; namely, that of an indolence which prevents him from endeavoring to ascertain 15 what is his duty, or, when his duty is ascertained, prevents him from performing it.

The principal object, then, proposed in these Poems, was to choose incidents and situations from common life, and to relate or 20 describe them throughout, as far as was possible, in a selection of language really used by men, and, at the same time, to throw over them a certain coloring of imagination, whereby ordinary things should be presented 25 to the mind in an unusual aspect; and further, and above all, to make these incidents and situations interesting by tracing in them, truly though not ostentatiously, the primary laws of our nature: chiefly, as far as regards 30 the manner in which we associate ideas in a state of excitement. Humble and rustic life was generally chosen, because in that condition the essential passions of the heart find a better soil in which they can attain their 35 maturity, are less under restraint, and speak a plainer and more emphatic language; because in that condition of life our elementary feelings co-exist in a state of greater simplicity, and, consequently, may be more ac-40 curately contemplated, and more forcibly communicated; because the manners of rural life germinate from those elementary feelings, and, from the necessary character of rural occupations, are more easily compre-45 hended, and are more durable; and, lastly, because in that condition the passions of men are incorporated with the beautiful and permanent forms of nature. The language, too, of these men has been adopted (purified in-50 deed from what appear to be its real defects, from all lasting and rational causes of dis-

like or disgust), because such men hourly communicate with the best objects from which the best part of language is originally derived; and because, from their rank in society and the sameness and narrow circle of their intercourse, being less under the influence of social vanity, they convey their feelings and notions in simple and unelaborated expressions. Accordingly, such a language, arising out of repeated experience and regular feelings, is a more permanent, and a far more philosophical language, than that which is frequently substituted for it by Poets, who think that they are conferring honor upon themselves and their art in proportion as they separate themselves from the sympathies of men, and indulge in arbitrary and capricious habits of expression, in order to furnish food for fickle tastes and fickle appetites of their own creation.[3]

I cannot, however, be insensible to the present outcry against the triviality and meanness, both of thought and language, which some of my contemporaries have occasionally introduced into their metrical compositions; and I acknowledge that this defect, where it exists, is more dishonorable to the Writer's own character than false refinement or arbitrary innovation, though I should contend at the same time that it is far less pernicious in the sum of its consequences. From such verses the Poems in these volumes will be found distinguished at least by one mark of difference, that each of them has a worthy *purpose.* Not that I always began to write with a distinct purpose formally conceived, but habits of meditation have, I trust, so prompted and regulated my feelings, that my descriptions of such objects as strongly excite those feelings will be found to carry along with them a *purpose.* If this opinion be erroneous, I can have little right to the name of a Poet. For all good poetry is the spontaneous overflow of powerful feelings: and though this be true, Poems to which any value can be attached were never produced on any variety of subjects but by a man who, being possessed of more than usual

---

[3]It is worth while here to observe that the affecting parts of Chaucer are almost always expressed in language pure and universally intelligible even to this day (Wordsworth's note).

organic sensibility, had also thought long and deeply. For our continued influxes of feeling are modified and directed by our thoughts, which are indeed the representatives of all our past feelings; and as, by contemplating the relation of these general representatives to each other, we discover what is really important to men, so, by the repetition and continuance of this act, our feelings will be connected with important subjects, till at length, if we be originally possessed of much sensibility, such habits of mind will be produced that, by obeying blindly and mechanically the impulses of those habits, we shall describe objects, and utter sentiments, of such a nature, and in such connection with each other, that the understanding of the Reader must necessarily be in some degree enlightened, and his affection strengthened and purified.

It has been said that each of these Poems has a purpose. Another circumstance must be mentioned which distinguishes these Poems from the popular Poetry of the day; it is this, that the feeling therein developed gives importance to the action and situation, and not the action and situation to the feeling.

A sense of false modesty shall not prevent me from asserting that the Reader's attention is pointed to this mark of distinction, far less for the sake of these particular Poems than from the general importance of the subject. The subject is indeed important! For the human mind is capable of being excited without the application of gross and violent stimulants; and he must have a very faint perception of its beauty and dignity who does not know this, and who does not further know that one being is elevated above another in proportion as he possesses this capability. It has therefore appeared to me, that to endeavor to produce or enlarge this capability is one of the best services in which, at any period, a Writer can be engaged; but this service, excellent at all times, is especially so at the present day. For a multitude of causes, unknown to former times, are now acting with a combined force to blunt the discriminating powers of the mind, and, unfitting it for all voluntary exertion, to reduce it to a state of almost savage torpor.

The most effective of these causes are the great national events which are daily taking place, and the increasing accumulation of men in cities, where the uniformity of their occupations produces a craving for extraordinary incident which the rapid communication of intelligence hourly gratifies. To this tendency of life and manners the literature and theatrical exhibitions of the country have conformed themselves. The invaluable works of our elder writers, I had almost said the works of Shakespeare and Milton, are driven into neglect by frantic novels, sickly and stupid German Tragedies, and deluges of idle and extravagant stories in verse.— When I think upon this degrading thirst after outrageous stimulation, I am almost ashamed to have spoken of the feeble endeavor made in these volumes to counteract it; and, reflecting upon the magnitude of the general evil, I should be oppressed with no dishonorable melancholy, had I not a deep impression of certain inherent and indestructible qualities of the human mind, and likewise of certain powers in the great and permanent objects that act upon it, which are equally inherent and indestructible; and were there not added to this impression a belief that the time is approaching when the evil will be systematically opposed by men of greater powers, and with far more distinguished success.

Having dwelt thus long on the subjects and aim of these Poems, I shall request the Reader's permission to apprise him of a few circumstances relating to their *style,* in order, among other reasons, that he may not censure me for not having performed what I never attempted. The Reader will find that personifications of abstract ideas rarely occur in these volumes, and are utterly rejected as an ordinary device to elevate the style and raise it above prose. My purpose was to imitate, and, as far as is possible, to adopt the very language of men; and assuredly such personifications do not make any natural or regular part of that language. They are, indeed, a figure of speech occasionally prompted by passion, and I have made use of them as such; but have endeavored utterly to reject them as a mechanical device of style, or as a family language which Writers in meter seem to lay claim to by prescription. I have wished to keep the Reader in the company of flesh and blood, persuaded that by so doing I shall interest him. Others who pursue a different track will interest him likewise; I do not interfere with their claim, but wish to prefer a claim of my own. There will also be found in these volumes little of what is usually called poetic diction; as much pains has been taken to avoid it as is ordinarily taken to produce it; this has been done for the reason already alleged, to bring my language near to the language of men; and further, because the pleasure which I have proposed to myself to impart is of a kind very different from that which is supposed by many persons to be the proper object of poetry. Without being culpably particular, I do not know how to give my Reader a more exact notion of the style in which it was my wish and intention to write, than by informing him that I have at all times endeavored to look steadily at my subject; consequently there is, I hope, in these Poems little falsehood of description, and my ideas are expressed in language fitted to their respective importance. Something must have been gained by this practice, as it is friendly to one property of all good poetry, namely, good sense: but it has necessarily cut me off from a large portion of phrases and figures of speech which from father to son have long been regarded as the common inheritance of Poets. I have also thought it expedient to restrict myself still further, having abstained from the use of many expressions, in themselves proper and beautiful, but which have been foolishly repeated by bad Poets, till such feelings of disgust are connected with them as it is scarcely possible by any art of association to overpower.

If in a poem there should be found a series of lines, or even a single line, in which the language, though naturally arranged, and according to the strict laws of meter, does not differ from that of prose, there is a numerous class of critics, who, when they stumble upon these prosaisms, as they call them, imagine that they have made a notable discovery, and exult over the Poet as over a man ignorant of his own profession. Now these men would establish a canon of criticism which the Reader will conclude he must utterly reject, if he wishes to be pleased with these volumes. And it would be a most easy task to prove to him that not only the language of a large portion of every good poem, even of the most elevated character, must necessarily, except with reference to the meter, in no respect differ from that of good prose, but likewise that some of the most interesting parts of the best poems will be found to be strictly the language of prose when prose is well written. The truth of this assertion might be demonstrated by innumerable passages from almost all the poetical writings, even of Milton himself. To illustrate the subject in a general manner, I will here adduce a short composition of Gray, who was at the head of those who, by their reasonings, have attempted to widen the space of separation betwixt Prose and Metrical composition,[4] and was more than any other man curiously elaborate in the structure of his own poetic diction.

In vain to me the smiling mornings shine,
And reddening Phoebus lifts his golden fire;
The birds in vain their amorous descant join,
Or cheerful fields resume their green attire.
These ears, alas! for other notes repine;
A different object do these eyes require;
My lonely anguish melts no heart but mine;
And in my breast the imperfect joys expire;
Yet morning smiles the busy race to cheer,
And new-born pleasure brings to happier men;
The fields to all their wonted tribute bear;
To warm their little loves the birds complain.
I fruitless mourn to him that cannot hear,
And weep the more because I weep in vain.[5]

It will easily be perceived, that the only part of this Sonnet which is of any value is the lines printed in Italics; it is equally obvious that, except in the rime and in the use of the single word "fruitless" for fruitlessly, which is so far a defect, the language of these lines does in no respect differ from that of prose.

By the foregoing quotation it has been shown that the language of Prose may yet be well adapted to Poetry; and it was previously asserted that a large portion of the language

[4]In the first volume of the present collection, see Gray's letter (no. VIII) on this subject.
[5]Gray's *Sonnet on the Death of Richard West.*

of every good poem can in no respect differ from that of good Prose. We will go further. It may be safely affirmed that there neither is, nor can be, any *essential* difference between the language of prose and metrical 5 composition. We are fond of tracing the resemblance between Poetry and Painting, and, accordingly, we call them Sisters: but where shall we find bonds of connection sufficiently strict to typify the affinity betwixt 10 metrical and prose composition? They both speak by and to the same organs; the bodies in which both of them are clothed may be said to be of the same substance, their affections are kindred, and almost identical, not 15 necessarily differing even in degree; Poetry[6] sheds no tears "such as Angels weep," but natural and human tears; she can boast of no celestial ichor[7] that distinguishes her vital juices from those of Prose; the same human 20 blood circulates through the veins of them both.

If it be affirmed that rime and metrical arrangement of themselves constitute a distinction which overturns what has just been 25 said on the strict affinity of metrical language with that of Prose, and paves the way for other artificial distinctions which the mind voluntarily admits, I answer that the language of such Poetry as is here recom- 30 mended is, as far as is possible, a selection of the language really spoken by men; that this selection, wherever it is made with true taste and feeling, will of itself form a distinction far greater than would at first be imagined, 35 and will entirely separate the composition from the vulgarity and meanness of ordinary life; and, if meter be superadded thereto, I believe that a dissimilitude will be produced altogether sufficient for the gratification of a 40 rational mind. What other distinction would

we have? Whence is it to come? And where is it to exist? Not, surely, where the Poet speaks through the mouths of his characters: it cannot be necessary here, either for elevation of style, or any of its supposed ornaments; for, if the Poet's subject be judiciously chosen, it will naturally, and upon fit occasion, lead him to passions, the language of which, if selected truly and judiciously, must necessarily be dignified and variegated, and alive with metaphors and figures. I forbear to speak of an incongruity which would shock the intelligent Reader, should the Poet interweave any foreign splendor of his own with that which the passion naturally suggests: it is sufficient to say that such addition is unnecessary. And, surely, it is more probable that those passages, which with propriety abound with metaphors and figures, will have their due effect if, upon other occasions where the passions are of a milder character, the style also be subdued and temperate.

But, as the pleasure which I hope to give by the Poems now presented to the Reader must depend entirely on just notions upon this subject, and as it is in itself of high importance to our taste and moral feelings, I cannot content myself with these detached remarks. And if, in what I am about to say, it shall appear to some that my labor is unnecessary, and that I am like a man fighting a battle without enemies, such persons may be reminded that, whatever be the language outwardly holden by men, a practical faith in the opinions which I am wishing to establish is almost unknown. If my conclusions are admitted, and carried as far as they must be carried if admitted at all, our judgments concerning the works of the greatest Poets, both ancient and modern, will be far different from what they are at present, both when we praise and when we censure: and our moral feelings influencing and influenced by these judgments will, I believe, be corrected and purified.

Taking up the subject, then, upon general grounds, let me ask, what is meant by the word Poet? What is a Poet? To whom does he address himself? And what language is to be expected from him?—He is a man speaking to men: a man, it is true, en-

---

[6] I here use the word "Poetry" (though against my own judgment) as opposed to the word Prose, and synonymous with metrical composition. But much confusion has been introduced into criticism by this contradistinction of Poetry and Prose, instead of the more philosophical one of Poetry and Matter of Fact, or Science. The only strict antithesis to Prose is Meter; nor is this, in truth, a *strict* antithesis, because lines and passages of meter so naturally occur in writing prose, that it would be scarcely possible to avoid them, even were it desirable (Wordsworth's note).

[7] An ethereal fluid that flows in the veins of the gods.

dowed with more lively sensibility, more enthusiasm and tenderness, who has a greater knowledge of human nature, and a more comprehensive soul, than are supposed to be common among mankind; a man pleased with his 5 own passions and volitions, and who rejoices more than other men in the spirit of life that is in him; delighting to contemplate similar volitions and passions as manifested in the goings-on of the Universe, and habitually 10 impelled to create them where he does not find them. To these qualities he has added a disposition to be affected more than any other men by absent things as if they were present; an ability of conjuring up in himself pas- 15 sions, which are indeed far from being the same as those produced by real events, yet (especially in those parts of the general sympathy which are pleasing and delightful) do more nearly resemble the passions produced 20 by real events than anything which, from the motions of their own minds merely, other men are accustomed to feel in themselves:— whence, and from practice, he has acquired a greater readiness and power in expressing 25 what he thinks and feels, and especially those thoughts and feelings which, by his own choice, or from the structure of his own mind, arise in him without immediate external excitement. 30

But whatever portion of this faculty we may suppose even the greatest Poet to possess, there cannot be a doubt that the language which it will suggest to him must often, in liveliness and truth, fall short of 35 that which is uttered by men in real life under the actual pressure of those passions, certain shadows of which the Poet thus produces, or feels to be produced, in himself.

However exalted a notion we would wish 40 to cherish of the character of a Poet, it is obvious that, while he describes and imitates passions, his employment is in some degree mechanical compared with the freedom and power of real and substantial action and suf- 45 fering. So that it will be the wish of the Poet to bring his feelings near to those of the persons whose feelings he describes, nay, for short spaces of time, perhaps, to let himself slip into an entire delusion, and even 50 confound and identify his own feelings with theirs; modifying only the language which is

thus suggested to him by a consideration that he describes for a particular purpose, that of giving pleasure. Here, then, he will apply the principle of selection which has been already insisted upon. He will depend upon this for removing what would otherwise be painful or disgusting in the passion; he will feel that there is no necessity to trick out or to elevate nature: and the more industriously he applies this principle the deeper will be his faith that no words, which *his* fancy or imagination can suggest, will be to be compared with those which are the emanations of reality and truth.

But it may be said by those who do not object to the general spirit of these remarks, that, as it is impossible for the Poet to produce upon all occasions language as exquisitely fitted for the passion as that which the real passion itself suggests, it is proper that he should consider himself as in the situation of a translator, who does not scruple to substitute excellences of another kind for those which are unattainable by him; and endeavors occasionally to surpass his original, in order to make some amends for the general inferiority to which he feels he must submit. But this would be to encourage idleness and unmanly despair. Further, it is the language of men who speak of what they do not understand; who talk of Poetry, as of a matter of amusement and idle pleasure; who will converse with us as gravely about a *taste* for Poetry, as they express it, as if it were a thing as indifferent as a taste for rope-dancing, or Frontiniac or Sherry. Aristotle, I have been told, has said that Poetry is the most philosophic of all writing:[8] it is so: its object is truth, not individual and local, but general and operative; not standing upon external testimony, but carried alive into the heart by passion; truth which is its own testimony, which gives competence and confidence to the tribunal to which it appeals, and receives them from the same tribunal. Poetry is the image of man and nature. The obstacles which stand in the way of the fidelity of the Biographer and Historian, and

---

[8] "Poetry is a more philosophical and a higher thing than history; for poetry tends to express the universal, history the particular" (Aristotle, *Poetics,* IX, 3).

of their consequent utility, are incalculably greater than those which are to be encountered by the Poet who comprehends the dignity of his art. The Poet writes under one restriction only, namely, the necessity of giv- [5] ing immediate pleasure to a human Being possessed of that information which may be expected from him, not as a lawyer, a physician, a mariner, an astronomer, or a natural philosopher, but as a Man. Except this one [10] restriction, there is no object standing between the Poet and the image of things; between this, and the Biographer and Historian, there are a thousand.

Nor let this necessity of producing im- [15] mediate pleasure be considered as a degradation of the Poet's art. It is far otherwise. It is an acknowledgment of the beauty of the universe, an acknowledgment the more sincere because not formal, but indirect; it is [20] a task light and easy to him who looks at the world in the spirit of love: further, it is a homage paid to the native and naked dignity of man, to the grand elementary principle of pleasure, by which he knows, and feels, and [25] lives, and moves. We have no sympathy but what is propagated by pleasure: I would not be misunderstood; but wherever we sympathize with pain, it will be found that the sympathy is produced and carried on [30] by subtle combinations with pleasure. We have no knowledge, that is, no general principles drawn from the contemplation of particular facts, but what has been built up by pleasure, and exists in us by pleasure alone. [35] The Man of science, the Chemist and Mathematician, whatever difficulties and disgusts they may have had to struggle with, know and feel this. However painful may be the objects with which the Anatomist's knowl- [40] edge is connected, he feels that his knowledge is pleasure; and where he has no pleasure he has no knowledge. What then does the Poet? He considers man and the objects that surround him as acting and re-acting [45] upon each other, so as to produce an infinite complexity of pain and pleasure; he considers man in his own nature and in his ordinary life as contemplating this with a certain quantity of immediate knowledge, with cer- [50] tain convictions, intuitions, and deductions, which from habit acquire the quality of intui-

tions; he considers him as looking upon this complex scene of ideas and sensations, and finding everywhere objects that immediately excite in him sympathies which, from the [5] necessities of his nature, are accompanied by an overbalance of enjoyment.

To this knowledge which all men carry about with them, and to these sympathies in which, without any other discipline than that [10] of our daily life, we are fitted to take delight, the Poet principally directs his attention. He considers man and nature as essentially adapted to each other, and the mind of man as naturally the mirror of the fairest and [15] most interesting properties of nature. And thus the Poet, prompted by this feeling of pleasure, which accompanies him through the whole course of his studies, converses with general nature, with affections akin to those [20] which, through labor and length of time, the Man of science has raised up in himself, by conversing with those particular parts of nature which are the objects of his studies. The knowledge both of the Poet and the [25] Man of science is pleasure; but the knowledge of the one cleaves to us as a necessary part of our existence, or natural and unalienable inheritance; the other is a personal and individual acquisition, slow to come to [30] us, and by no habitual and direct sympathy connecting us with our fellow-beings. The Man of science seeks truth as a remote and unknown benefactor; he cherishes and loves it in his solitude: the Poet, singing a song in [35] which all human beings join with him, rejoices in the presence of truth as our visible friend and hourly companion. Poetry is the breath and finer spirit of all knowledge; it is the impassioned expression which is in [40] the countenance of all Science. Emphatically may it be said of the Poet, as Shakespeare hath said of man, "that he looks before and after."[9] He is the rock of defense for human nature; an upholder and pre- [45] server, carrying everywhere with him relationship and love. In spite of difference of soil and climate, of language and manners, of laws and customs: in spite of things silently gone out of mind, and things vio- [50] lently destroyed; the Poet binds together by passion and knowledge the vast empire of

[9]*Hamlet.* IV, iv, 37.

human society, as it is spread over the whole earth and over all time. The objects of the Poet's thoughts are everywhere; though the eyes and senses of man are, it is true, his favorite guides, yet he will follow whereso- ⁵ ever he can find an atmosphere of sensation in which to move his wings. Poetry is the first and last of all knowledge—it is as immortal as the heart of man. If the labors of Men of science should ever create any ma- ¹⁰ terial revolution, direct or indirect, in our condition, and in the impressions which we habitually receive, the Poet will sleep then no more than at present; he will be ready to follow the steps of the Man of science, not ¹⁵ only in those general indirect effects, but he will be at his side, carrying sensation into the midst of the objects of the science itself. The remotest discoveries of the Chemist, the Botanist, or Mineralogist, will be as proper ²⁰ objects of the Poet's art as any upon which it can be employed, if the time should ever come when these things shall be familiar to us, and the relations under which they are contemplated by the followers of these re- ²⁵ spective sciences shall be manifestly and palpably material to us as enjoying and suffering beings. If the time should ever come when what is now called science, thus familiarized to men, shall be ready to put on, as it ³⁰ were, a form of flesh and blood, the Poet will lend his divine spirit to aid the transfiguration, and will welcome the Being thus produced as a dear and genuine inmate of the household of man.—It is not, then, to be ³⁵ supposed that any one, who holds that sublime notion of Poetry which I have attempted to convey, will break in upon the sanctity and truth of his pictures by transitory and accidental ornaments, and endeavor ⁴⁰ to excite admiration of himself by arts, the necessity of which must manifestly depend upon the assumed meanness of his subject.

What has been thus far said applies to Poetry in general, but especially to those parts ⁴⁵ of compositions where the Poet speaks through the mouths of his characters; and upon this point it appears to authorize the conclusion that there are few persons of good sense who would not allow that the dramatic ⁵⁰ parts of composition are defective in proportion as they deviate from the real language

of nature, and are colored by a diction of the Poet's own, either peculiar to him as an individual Poet or belonging simply to Poets in general; to a body of men who, from the circumstance of their compositions being in meter, it is expected will employ a particular language.

It is not, then, in the dramatic parts of composition that we look for this distinction of language; but still it may be proper and necessary where the Poet speaks to us in his own person and character. To this I answer by referring the Reader to the description before given of a Poet. Among the qualities there enumerated as principally conducing to form a Poet, is implied nothing differing in kind from other men, but only in degree. The sum of what was said is, that the Poet is chiefly distinguished from other men by a greater promptness to think and feel without immediate external excitement, and a greater power in expressing such thoughts and feelings as are produced in him in that manner. But these passions and thoughts and feelings are the general passions and thoughts and feelings of men. And with what are they connected? Undoubtedly with our moral sentiments and animal sensations, and with the causes which excite these; with the operations of the elements, and the appearances of the visible universe; with storm and sunshine, with the revolutions of the seasons, with cold and heat, with loss of friends and kindred, with injuries and resentments, gratitude and hope, with fear and sorrow. These, and the like, are the sensations and objects which the Poet describes, as they are the sensations of other men and the objects which interest them. The Poet thinks and feels in the spirit of human passions. How, then, can his language differ in any material degree from that of all other men who feel vividly and see clearly? It might be *proved* that it is impossible. But supposing that this were not the case, the Poet might then be allowed to use a peculiar language when expressing his feelings for his own gratification, or that of men like himself. But Poets do not write for Poets alone, but for men. Unless, therefore, we are advocates for that admiration which subsists upon ignorance, and that pleasure which arises from hearing what we do not understand, the Poet must descend from this supposed height; and, in order to excite rational sympathy, he must express himself as other men express themselves. To this it may be added, that while he is only selecting from the real language of men, or, which amounts to the same thing, composing accurately in the spirit of such selection, he is treading upon safe ground, and we know what we are to expect from him. Our feelings are the same with respect to meter; for, as it may be proper to remind the Reader, the distinction of meter is regular and uniform, and not, like that which is produced by what is usually called "poetic diction," arbitrary, and subject to infinite caprices upon which no calculation whatever can be made. In the one case, the Reader is utterly at the mercy of the Poet, respecting what imagery or diction he may choose to connect with the passion; whereas, in the other, the meter obeys certain laws, to which the Poet and Reader both willingly submit because they are certain, and because no interference is made by them with the passion but such as the concurring testimony of ages has shown to heighten and improve the pleasure which co-exists with it.

It will now be proper to answer an obvious question, namely, Why, professing these opinions, have I written in verse? To this, in addition to such answer as is included in what has been already said, I reply, in the first place, Because, however I may have restricted myself, there is still left open to me what confessedly constitutes the most valuable object of all writing, whether in prose or verse; the great and universal passions of men, the most general and interesting of their occupations, and the entire world of nature before me—to supply endless combinations of forms and imagery. Now, supposing for a moment that whatever is interesting in these objects may be as vividly described in prose, why should I be condemned for attempting to superadd to such description the charm which, by the consent of all nations, is acknowledged to exist in metrical language? To this, by such as are yet unconvinced, it may be answered that a very small part of the pleasure given by

Poetry depends upon the meter, and that it is injudicious to write in meter, unless it be accompanied with the other artificial distinctions of style with which meter is usually accompanied, and that, by such deviation, more will be lost from the shock which will thereby be given to the Reader's associations than will be counter-balanced by any pleasure which he can derive from the general power of numbers. In answer to those who still contend for the necessity of accompanying meter with certain appropriate colors of style in order to the accomplishment of its appropriate end, and who also, in my opinion, greatly underrate the power of meter in itself, it might, perhaps, as far as relates to these Volumes, have been almost sufficient to observe, that poems are extant, written upon more humble subjects, and in a still more naked and simple style, which have continued to give pleasure from generation to generation. Now, if nakedness and simplicity be a defect, the fact here mentioned affords a strong presumption that poems somewhat less naked and simple are capable of affording pleasure at the present day; and, what I wished *chiefly* to attempt, at present, was to justify myself for having written under the impression of this belief.

But various causes might be pointed out why, when the style is manly, and the subject of some importance, words metrically arranged will long continue to impart such a pleasure to mankind as he who proves the extent of that pleasure will be desirous to impart. The end of poetry is to produce excitement in co-existence with an over-balance of pleasure; but, by the supposition, excitement is an unusual and irregular state of the mind; ideas and feelings do not, in that state, succeed each other in accustomed order. If the words, however, by which this excitement is produced be in themselves powerful, or the images and feelings have an undue proportion of pain connected with them, there is some danger that the excitement may be carried beyond its proper bounds. Now the co-presence of something regular, something to which the mind has been accustomed in various moods and in a less excited state, cannot but have great efficacy in tempering and restraining the passion by an intertexture of ordinary feeling, and of feeling not strictly and necessarily connected with the passion. This is unquestionably true; and hence, though the opinion will at first appear paradoxical, from 5 the tendency of meter to divest language, in a certain degree, of its reality, and thus to throw a sort of half-consciousness of unsubstantial existence over the whole composition, there can be little doubt but that more 10 pathetic situations and sentiments, that is, those which have a greater proportion of pain connected with them, may be endured in metrical composition, especially in rime, than in prose. The meter of the old ballads 15 is very artless, yet they contain many passages which would illustrate this opinion; and, I hope, if the following poems be attentively perused, similar instances will be found in them. This opinion may be fur- 20 ther illustrated by appealing to the Reader's own experience of the reluctance with which he comes to the reperusal of the distressful parts of *Clarissa Harlowe,* or the *Gamester;*[10] while Shakespeare's writings, in the 25 most pathetic scenes, never act upon us, as pathetic, beyond the bounds of pleasure—an effect which, in a much greater degree than might at first be imagined, is to be ascribed to small, but continual and regular impulses 30 of pleasurable surprise from the metrical arrangement.—On the other hand (what it must be allowed will much more frequently happen), if the Poet's words should be incommensurate with the passion, and inada- 35 quate to raise the Reader to a height of desirable excitement, then (unless the Poet's choice of his meter has been grossly injudicious), in the feelings of pleasure which the Reader has been accustomed to connect 40 with meter in general, and in the feeling, whether cheerful or melancholy, which he has been accustomed to connect with that particular movement of meter, there will be found something which will greatly con- 45 tribute to impart passion to the words, and to effect the complex end which the Poet proposes to himself.

If I had undertaken a *systematic* defense

of the theory here maintained, it would have been my duty to develop the various causes upon which the pleasure received from metrical language depends. Among the chief of these causes is to be reckoned a principle which must be well known to those who have made any of the Arts the object of accurate reflection; namely, the pleasure which the mind derives from the perception of similitude in dissimilitude. This principle is the great spring of the activity of our minds, and their chief feeder. From this principle the direction of the sexual appetite, and all the passions connected with it, take their origin: it is the life of our ordinary conversation; and upon the accuracy with which similitude in dissimilitude, and dissimilitude in similitude, are perceived, depend our taste and our moral feelings. It would not be a useless employment to apply this principle to the consideration of meter, and to show that meter is hence enabled to afford much pleasure, and to point out in what manner that pleasure is produced. But my limits will 25 not permit me to enter upon this subject, and I must content myself with a general summary.

I have said that poetry is the spontaneous overflow of powerful feelings; it takes its 30 origin from emotion recollected in tranquillity; the emotion is contemplated till, by a species of re-action, the tranquillity gradually disappears, and an emotion, kindred to that which was before the subject of con- 35 templation, is gradually produced, and does itself actually exist in the mind. In this mood successful composition generally begins, and in a mood similar to this it is carried on; but the emotion, of whatever kind, 40 and in whatever degree, from various causes, is qualified by various pleasures, so that in describing any passions whatsoever, which are voluntarily described, the mind will, upon the whole, be in a state of enjoyment. 45 If Nature be thus cautious to preserve in a state of enjoyment a being so employed, the Poet ought to profit by the lesson held forth to him, and ought especially to take care that, whatever passions he communicates to his 50 Reader, those passions, if his Reader's mind be sound and vigorous, should always be accompanied with an over-balance of pleasure.

---

[10]The former a novel by Samuel Richardson, published in 1748; the latter a tragedy by Edward Moore, published in 1753.

Now the music of harmonious metrical language, the sense of difficulty overcome, and the blind association of pleasure which has been previously received from works of rime or meter of the same or similar construction, an indistinct perception perpetually renewed of language closely resembling that of real life, and yet, in the circumstance of meter, differing from it so widely—all these imperceptibly make up a complex feeling of delight, which is of the most important use in tempering the painful feeling always found intermingled with powerful descriptions of the deeper passions. This effect is always produced in pathetic and impassioned poetry; while, in lighter compositions, the ease and gracefulness with which the Poet manages his numbers are themselves confessedly a principal source of the gratification of the Reader. All that it is *necessary* to say, however, upon this subject, may be effected by affirming, what few persons will deny, that of two descriptions, either of passions, manners, or characters, each of them equally well executed, the one in prose and the other in verse, the verse will be read a hundred times where the prose is read once.

Having thus explained a few of my reasons for writing in verse, and why I have chosen subjects from common life, and endeavored to bring my language near to the real language of men, if I have been too minute in pleading my own cause, I have at the same time been treating a subject of general interest; and for this reason a few words shall be added with reference solely to these particular poems, and to some defects which will probably be found in them. I am sensible that my associations must have sometimes been particular instead of general, and that, consequently, giving to things a false importance, I may have sometimes written upon unworthy subjects; but I am less apprehensive on this account, than that my language may frequently have suffered from those arbitrary connections of feelings and ideas with particular words and phrases from which no man can altogether protect himself. Hence I have no doubt that, in some instances, feelings, even of the ludicrous, may be given to my Readers by expressions which appeared to me tender and pathetic.

Such faulty expressions, were I convinced they were faulty at present, and that they must necessarily continue to be so, I would willingly take all reasonable pains to correct. But it is dangerous to make these alterations on the simple authority of a few individuals, or even of certain classes of men; for where the understanding of an author is not convinced, or his feelings altered, this cannot be done without great injury to himself: for his own feelings are his stay and support; and, if he set them aside in one instance, he may be induced to repeat this act till his mind shall lose all confidence in itself, and become utterly debilitated. To this it may be added that the critic ought never to forget that he is himself exposed to the same errors as the Poet, and, perhaps, in a much greater degree: for there can be no presumption in saying of most readers that it is not probable they will be so well acquainted with the various stages of meaning through which words have passed, or with the fickleness of stability of the relations of particular ideas to each other; and, above all, since they are so much less interested in the subject, they may decide lightly and carelessly.

Long as the reader has been detained, I hope he will permit me to caution him against a mode of false criticism which has been applied to poetry, in which the language closely resembles that of life and nature. Such verses have been triumphed over in parodies, of which Dr. Johnson's stanza is a fair specimen:—

> I put my hat upon my head,
> And walked into the Strand,
> And there I met another man
> Whose hat was in his hand.

Immediately under these lines let us place one of the most justly-admired stanzas of the *Babes in the Wood*.[11]

> These pretty Babes with hand in hand
> Went wandering up and down;
> But never more they saw the Man
> Approaching from the Town.

In both these stanzas the words, and the order of the words, in no respect differ from the most unimpassioned conversation.

[11] A popular ballad of the sixteenth century.

There are words in both, for example, "the Strand," and "the Town," connected with none but the most familiar ideas; yet the one stanza we admit as admirable, and the other as a fair example of the superlatively con- 5 temptible. Whence arises this difference? Not from the meter, not from the language, not from the order of the words; but the *matter* expressed in Dr. Johnson's stanza is contemptible. The proper method of treat- 10 ing trivial and simple verses, to which Dr. Johnson's stanza would be a fair parallelism, is not to say, this is a bad kind of poetry, or, this is not poetry; but, this wants sense; it is neither interesting in itself, nor can *lead* 15 to anything interesting; the images neither originate in that sane state of feeling which arises out of thought, nor can excite thought or feeling in the Reader. This is the only sensible manner of dealing with such verses. 20 Why trouble yourself about the species till you have previously decided upon the genus? Why take pains to prove that an ape is not a Newton, when it is self-evident that he is not a man? 25

One request I must make of my Reader, which is, that in judging these Poems he would decide by his own feelings genuinely, and not by reflection upon what will prob- ably be the judgment of others. How com- 30 mon is it to hear a person say, I myself do not object to this style of composition, or this or that expression, but to such and such classes of people it will appear mean or ludi- crous! This mode of criticism, so destruc- 35 tive of all sound unadulterated judgment, is almost universal: let the Reader then abide, independently, by his own feelings, and, if he finds himself affected, let him not suffer such conjectures to interfere with his pleas- 40 ure.

If an Author, by any single composition, has impressed us with respect for his talents, it is useful to consider this as affording a presumption that on other occasions where 45 we have been displeased he, nevertheless, may not have written ill or absurdly; and fur- ther, to give him so much credit for this one composition as may induce us to review what has displeased us with more care than we 50 should otherwise have bestowed upon it. This is not only an act of justice, but, in our

decisions upon poetry especially, may con- duce, in a high degree, to the improvement of our own taste: for an *accurate* taste in poetry, and in all the other arts, as Sir Joshua Reynolds has observed, is an *acquired* tal- ent, which can only be produced by thought and a long-continued intercourse with the best models of composition. This is men- tioned, not with so ridiculous a purpose as to prevent the most inexperienced Reader from judging for himself (I have already said that I wish'him to judge for himself), but merely to temper the rashness of de- cision, and 'to suggest that, if Poetry be a subject on which much time has not been bestowed, the judgment may be erroneous; and that, in many cases, it necessarily will be so.

Nothing would, I know, have so effectu- ally contributed to further the end which I have in view, as to have shown of what kind the pleasure is, and how that pleasure is produced, which is confessedly produced by metrical composition essentially different from that which I have here endeavored to recommend: for the Reader will say that he has been pleased by such composition; and what more can be done for him? The power of any art is limited; and he will sus- pect that, if it be proposed to furnish him with new friends, that can be only upon con- dition of his abandoning his old friends. Besides, as I have said, the Reader is him- self conscious of the pleasure which he has received from such composition, composition to which he has peculiarly attached the en- dearing name of Poetry; and all men feel an habitual gratitude, and something of an honorable bigotry, for the objects which have long continued to please them: we not only wish to be pleased, but to be pleased in that particular way in which we have been ac- customed to be pleased. There is in these feelings enough to resist a host of argu- ments; and I should be the less able to com- bat them successfully, as I am willing to allow that, in order entirely to enjoy the Poetry which I am recommending, it would be necessary to give up much of what is ordinarily enjoyed. But would my limits have permitted me to point out how this pleasure is produced, many obstacles might have been removed, and the Reader assisted in perceiving that the powers of language are not so limited as he may suppose; and that it is possible for poetry to give other enjoyments, of a purer, more lasting, and 5 more exquisite nature. This part of the subject has not been altogether neglected, but it has not been so much my present aim to prove that the interest excited by some other kinds of poetry is less vivid, and less 10 worthy of the nobler powers of the mind, as to offer reasons for presuming that if my purpose were fulfilled, a species of poetry would be produced which is genuine poetry; in its nature well adapted to interest man- 15 kind permanently, and likewise important in the multiplicity and quality of its moral relations.

From what has been said, and from a perusal of the Poems, the Reader will be 20 able clearly to perceive the object which I had in view: he will determine how far it has been attained, and, what is a much more important question, whether it be worth attaining: and upon the decision of these two 25 questions will rest my claim to the approbation of the Public.

LINES

Left upon a Seat in a Yew-Tree, Which Stands near the Lake of Esthwaite, on a Desolate Part of the Shore, Commanding a Beautiful Prospect[1]

Nay, Traveler! rest. This lonely Yew-tree stands
Far from all human dwelling: what if here
No sparkling rivulet spread the verdant herb?
What if the bee love not these barren boughs?
Yet, if the wind breathe soft, the curling waves,   5
That break against the shore, shall lull thy mind
By one soft impulse saved from vacancy.
          Who he was
That piled these stones and with the mossy sod
First covered, and here taught this agéd Tree   10

---
[1]Begun in 1787; completed in 1795; published in 1798.

With its dark arms to form a circling bower,
I well remember.—He was one who owned
No common soul. In youth by science nursed,
And led by nature into a wild scene
Of lofty hopes, he to the world went forth 15
A favored Being, knowing no desire
Which genius did not hallow; 'gainst the taint
Of dissolute tongues, and jealousy, and hate,
And scorn,—against all enemies prepared,
All but neglect. The world, for so it thought,   20
Owed him no service; wherefore he at once
With indignation turned himself away,
And with the food of pride sustained his soul
In solitude.—Stranger! these bloomy boughs
Had charms for him; and here he loved to sit,   25
His only visitants a straggling sheep,
The stone-chat, or the glancing sand-piper:
And on these barren rocks, with fern and heath,
And juniper and thistle, sprinkled o'er,
Fixing his downcast eye, he many an hour 30
A morbid pleasure nourished, tracing here
An emblem of his own unfruitful life:
And, lifting up his head, he then would gaze
On the more distant scene,—how lovely 'tis
Thou seest,—and he would gaze till it became   35
Far lovelier, and his heart could not sustain
The beauty, still more beauteous! Nor, that time,
When nature had subdued him to herself,
Would he forget those Beings to whose minds,
Warm from the labors of benevolence,   40
The world, and human life, appeared a scene
Of kindred loveliness: then he would sigh,
Inly disturbed, to think that others felt
What he must never feel: and so, lost Man!
On visionary views would fancy feed,   45
Till his eye streamed with tears. In this deep vale
He died,—this seat his only monument.
If Thou be one whose heart the holy forms
Of young imagination have kept pure,
Stranger! henceforth be warned; and know that pride,   50
Howe'er disguised in its own majesty,
Is littleness; that he who feels contempt
For any living thing, hath faculties
Which he has never used; that thought with him
Is in its infancy. The man whose eye   55

Is ever on himself doth look on one,
The least of Nature's works, one who might
  move
The wise man to that scorn which wisdom
  holds
Unlawful, ever. O be wiser, Thou!
Instructed that true knowledge leads to love;
True dignity abides with him alone   61
Who, in the silent hour of inward thought,
Can still suspect, and still revere himself,
In lowliness of heart.

WE ARE SEVEN[1]

——A simple Child,
That lightly draws its breath,
And feels its life in every limb,
What should it know of death?[2]

I met a little cottage Girl: 5
She was eight years old, she said;
Her hair was thick with many a curl
That clustered round her head.

She had a rustic, woodland air,
And she was wildly clad: 10
Her eyes were fair, and very fair;
—Her beauty made me glad.

"Sisters and brothers, little Maid,
How many may you be?"
"How many?   Seven in all," she said,   15
And wondering looked at me.

"And where are they?   I pray you tell."
She answered, "Seven are we;
And two of us at Conway dwell,
And two are gone to sea.   20

"Two of us in the church-yard lie,
My sister and my brother;
And, in the church-yard cottage, I
Dwell near them with my mother."

"You say that two at Conway dwell,   25
And two are gone to sea,
Yet ye are seven!—I pray you tell,
Sweet Maid, how this may be."

Then did the little Maid reply,
"Seven boys and girls are we;   30
Two of us in the church-yard lie,
Beneath the church-yard tree."

"You run about, my little Maid,
Your limbs they are alive;

If two are in the church-yard laid,   35
Then ye are only five."

"Their graves are green, they may be seen,"
The little Maid replied,
"Twelve steps or more from my mother's
  door,
And they are side by side.   40

"My stockings there I often knit,
My kerchief there I hem;
And there upon the ground I sit,
And sing a song to them.

"And often after sunset, Sir,   45
When it is light and fair,
I take my little porringer,
And eat my supper there.

"The first that died was sister Jane;
In bed she moaning lay,   50
Till God released her of her pain;
And then she went away.

"So in the church-yard she was laid;
And, when the grass was dry,
Together round her grave we played,   55
My brother John and I.

"And when the ground was white with snow,
And I could run and slide,
My brother John was forced to go,
And he lies by her side."   60

"How many are you, then," said I,
"If they two are in heaven?"
Quick was the little Maid's reply,
"O Master! we are seven."

"But they are dead; those two are dead!   65
Their spirits are in heaven!"
'T was throwing words away; for still
The little Maid would have her will,
And said, "Nay, we are seven!"

ANECDOTE FOR FATHERS[1]

Showing How the Practice of Lying May Be Taught

I have a boy of five years old;
His face is fair and fresh to see;
His limbs are cast in beauty's mold,
And dearly he loves me.

---

[1]Composed in 1798; published in the same year.
[2]This stanza was written by Coleridge.

[1]Written and published in 1798. The child with
whom the poem is concerned was not Wordsworth's
own, but the son of a friend.

One morn we strolled on our dry walk,   5
Our quiet home all full in view,
And held such intermitted talk
As we are wont to do.

My thoughts on former pleasures ran;
I thought of Kilve's delightful shore,   10
Our pleasant home when spring began,
A long, long year before.

A day it was when I could bear
Some fond regrets to entertain;
With so much happiness to spare,   15
I could not feel a pain.

The green earth echoed to the feet
Of lambs that bounded through the glade,
From shade to sunshine, and as fleet
From sunshine back to shade.   20

Birds warbled round me—and each trace
Of inward sadness had its charm;
Kilve, thought I, was a favored place,
And so is Liswyn farm.

My boy beside me tripped, so slim   25
And graceful in his rustic dress!
And, as we talked, I questioned him,
In very idleness.

"Now tell me, had you rather be,"
I said, and took him by the arm,   30
"On Kilve's smooth shore, by the green sea,
Or here at Liswyn farm?"

In careless mood he looked at me,
While still I held him by the arm,
And said, "At Kilve I'd rather be   35
Than here at Liswyn farm."

"Now, little Edward, say why so:
My little Edward, tell me why."—
"I cannot tell, I do not know."—
"Why, this is strange," said I;   40

"For here are woods, hills smooth and warm:
There surely must some reason be
Why you would change sweet Liswyn farm
For Kilve by the green sea."

At this my boy hung down his head,   45
He blushed with shame, nor made reply;
And three times to the child I said,
"Why, Edward, tell me why?"

His head he raised—there was in sight,
It caught his eye, he saw it plain—   50
Upon the house-top, glittering bright,
A broad and gilded vane.

Then did the boy his tongue unlock,
And eased his mind with this reply:
"At Kilve there was no weather-cock;   55
And that's the reason why."

O dearest, dearest boy! my heart
For better lore would seldom yearn,
Could I but teach the hundredth part
Of what from thee I learn.   60

GOODY BLAKE AND HARRY GILL[1]

A True Story

Oh! what's the matter? what's the matter?
What is't that ails young Harry Gill?
That evermore his teeth they chatter,
Chatter, chatter, chatter still!
Of waistcoats Harry has no lack,   5
Good duffel[2] gray, and flannel fine;
He has a blanket on his back,
And coats enough to smother nine.

In March, December, and in July,
'Tis all the same with Harry Gill;   10
The neighbors tell, and tell you truly,
His teeth they chatter, chatter still.
At night, at morning, and at noon,
'Tis all the same with Harry Gill;
Beneath the sun, beneath the moon,   15
His teeth they chatter, chatter still!

Young Harry was a lusty drover,
And who so stout of limb as he?
His cheeks were red as ruddy clover;
His voice was like the voice of three.   20
Old Goody Blake was old and poor;
Ill fed she was, and thinly clad;
And any man who passed her door
Might see how poor a hut she had.

All day she spun in her poor dwelling: 25
And then her three hours' work at night,
Alas! 'twas hardly worth the telling,
It would not pay for candle-light.
Remote from sheltered village-green,
On a hill's northern side she dwelt,   30
Where from sea-blasts the hawthorns lean,
And hoary dews are slow to melt.

By the same fire to boil their pottage,
Two poor old Dames, as I have known,
Will often live in one small cottage;   35
But she, poor Woman! housed alone.

[1]Written and published in 1798.
[2]Coarse woolen cloth with thick nap.

'Twas well enough when summer came,
The long, warm, lightsome summer-day
Then at her door the *canty*[3] Dame
Would sit, as any linnet, gay.   40

But when the ice our streams did fetter,
Oh then how her old bones would shake!
You would have said, if you had met her,
'Twas a hard time for Goody Blake.
Her evenings then were dull and dead: 45
Sad case it was, as you may think,
For very cold to go to bed,
And then for cold not sleep a wink.

O joy for her! whene'er in winter
The winds at night had made a rout;   50
And scattered many a lusty splinter
And many a rotten bough about.
Yet never had she, well or sick,
As every man who knew her says,
A pile beforehand, turf or stick,   55
Enough to warm her for three days.

Now, when the frost was past enduring,
And made her poor old bones to ache,
Could any thing be more alluring
Than an old hedge to Goody Blake?   60
And, now and then, it must be said,
When her old bones were cold and chill,
She left her fire, or left her bed,
To seek the hedge of Harry Gill.

Now Harry he had long suspected   65
This trespass of old Goody Blake;
And vowed that she should be detected—
That he on her would vengeance take.
And oft from his warm fire he'd go,
And to the fields his road would take;   70
And there, at night, in frost and snow,
He watched to seize old Goody Blake.

And once, behind a rick of barley,
Thus looking out did Harry stand:
The moon was full and shining clearly,   75
And crisp with frost the stubble land.
—He hears a noise—he's all awake—
Again?—on tip-toe down the hill
He softly creeps—'tis Goody Blake;
She's at the hedge of Harry Gill!   80

Right glad was he when he beheld her:
Stick after stick did Goody pull:
He stood behind a bush of elder,
Till she had filled her apron full.
When with her load she turned about,   85
The by-way back again to take;
He started forward, with a shout,
And sprang upon poor Goody Blake.

[3]Cheerful.

And fiercely by the arm he took her,
And by the arm he held her fast,   90
And fiercely by the arm he shook her,
And cried, "I've caught you then at last!"
Then Goody, who had nothing said,
Her bundle from her lap let fall;
And, kneeling on the sticks, she prayed   95
To God that is the judge of all.

She prayed, her withered hand uprearing,
While Harry held her by the arm—
"God! who art never out of hearing,
O may he never more be warm!"   100
The cold, cold moon above her head,
Thus on her knees did Goody pray;
Young Harry heard what she had said:
And icy cold he turned away.

He went complaining all the morrow   105
That he was cold and very chill:
His face was gloom, his heart was sorrow,
Alas! that day for Harry Gill!
That day he wore a riding-coat,
But not a whit the warmer he: 110
Another was on Thursday brought,
And ere the Sabbath he had three.

'Twas all in vain, a useless matter,
And blankets were about him pinned;
Yet still his jaws and teeth they clatter,   115
Like a loose casement in the wind.
And Harry's flesh it fell away;
And all who see him say, 'tis plain,
That, live as long as live he may,
He never will be warm again.   120

No word to any man he utters,
A-bed or up, to young or old;
But ever to himself he mutters,
"Poor Harry Gill is very cold."
A-bed or up, by night or day;   125
His teeth they chatter, chatter still.
Now think, ye farmers all, I pray,
Of Goody Blake and Harry Gill!

SIMON LEE

The Old Huntsman; with an Incident in Which He Was Concerned[1]

In the sweet shire of Cardigan,
Not far from pleasant Ivor-hall,
An old Man dwells, a little man,—
'Tis said he once was tall.
Full five-and-thirty years he lived   5
A running huntsman merry;
And still the center of his cheek
Is red as a ripe cherry.

[1]Written and published in 1798.

No man like him the horn could sound,
And hill and valley rang with glee   10
When Echo bandied, round and round,
The halloo of Simon Lee.
In those proud days, he little cared
For husbandry or tillage;
To blither tasks did Simon rouse   15
The sleepers of the village.

He all the country could outrun,
Could leave both man and horse behind;
And often, ere the chase was done,
He reeled, and was stone-blind.   20
And still there's something in the world
At which his heart rejoices;
For when the chiming hounds are out,
He dearly loves their voices!

But, oh the heavy change!—bereft   25
Of health, strength, friends, and kindred, see!
Old Simon to the world is left
In liveried poverty.
His Master's dead,—and no one now
Dwells in the Hall of Ivor;   30
Men, dogs, and horses, all are dead;
He is the sole survivor.

And he is lean and he is sick;
His body, dwindled and awry,
Rests upon ankles swoln and thick;   35
His legs are thin and dry.
One prop he has, and only one,
His wife, an agéd woman,
Lives with him, near the waterfall,
Upon the village Common.   40

Beside their moss-grown hut of clay,
Not twenty paces from the door,
A scrap of land they have, but they
Are poorest of the poor.
This scrap of land he from the heath   45
Enclosed when he was stronger;
But what to them avails the land
Which he can till no longer?

Oft, working by her Husband's side,
Ruth does what Simon cannot do;   50
For she, with scanty cause for pride,
Is stouter of the two.
And, though you with your utmost skill
From labor could not wean them,
'Tis little, very little—all   55
That they can do between them.

Few months of life has he in store
As he to you will tell,
For still, the more he works, the more
Do his weak ankles swell.   60

My gentle Reader, I perceive
How patiently you've waited,
And now I fear that you expect
Some tale will be related.

O Reader! had you in your mind   65
Such stores as silent thought can bring,
O gentle Reader! you would find
A tale in every thing.
What more I have to say is short,
And you must kindly take it: 70
It is no tale; but, should you think,
Perhaps a tale you'll make it.

One summer-day I chanced to see
This old Man doing all he could
To unearth the root of an old tree,   75
A stump of rotten wood.
The mattock tottered in his hand;
So vain was his endeavor,
That at the root of the old tree
He might have worked for ever.   80

"You're overtasked, good Simon Lee,
Give me your tool," to him I said;
And at the word right gladly he
Received my proffered aid.
I struck, and with a single blow   85
The tangled root I severed,
At which the poor old Man so long
And vainly had endeavored.

The tears into his eyes were brought,
And thanks and praises seemed to run   90
So fast out of his heart, I thought
They never would have done.
—I've heard of hearts unkind, kind deeds
With coldness still returning;
Alas! the gratitude of men   95
Hath oftener left me mourning.

LINES WRITTEN IN EARLY SPRING[1]

I heard a thousand blended notes,
While in a grove I sat reclined,
In that sweet mood when pleasant thoughts
Bring sad thoughts to the mind.

To her fair works did Nature link   5
The human soul that through me ran;
And much it grieved my heart to think
What man has made of man.

Through primrose tufts, in that green bower
The periwinkle trailed its wreaths;   10
And 'tis my faith that every flower
Enjoys the air it breathes.

[1]Written and published in 1798.

The birds around me hopped and played,
Their thoughts I cannot measure:—
But the least motion which they made,   15
It seemed a thrill of pleasure.

The budding twigs spread out their fan,
To catch the breezy air;
And I must think, do all I can,
That there was pleasure there.   20

If this belief from heaven be sent,
If such be Nature's holy plan,
Have I not reason to lament
What man has made of man?

EXPOSTULATION AND REPLY[2]

"Why, William, on that old gray stone,
Thus for the length of half a day,
Why, William, sit you thus alone,
And dream your time away?

"Where are your books?—that light be-
queathed   5
To Beings else forlorn and blind!
Up! up! and drink the spirit breathed
From dead men to their kind.

"You look round on your Mother Earth,
As if she for no purpose bore you;   10
As if you were her first-born birth,
And none had lived before you!"

One morning thus, by Esthwaite lake,
When life was sweet, I knew not why,
To me my good friend Matthew spake,   15
And thus I made reply:

"The eye—it cannot choose but see;
We cannot bid the ear be still;
Our bodies feel, where'er they be,
Against or with our will.   20

"Nor less I deem that there are Powers
Which of themselves our minds impress;
That we can feed this mind of ours
In a wise passiveness.

"Think you, 'mid all this mighty sum   25
Of things for ever speaking,
That nothing of itself will come,
But we must still be seeking?

[2]Written and published in 1798. This poem and
the one which follows "arose out of conversation
with a friend who was somewhat unreasonably
attached to modern books of moral philosophy"
(Wordsworth, Preface to first edition of *Lyrical
Ballads*).

"—Then ask not wherefore, here, alone,
Conversing as I may,   30
I sit upon this old gray stone,
And dream my time away."

THE TABLES TURNED[3]
An Evening Scene on the Same Subject

Up! up! my Friend, and quit your books;
Or surely you'll grow double:
Up! up! my Friend, and clear your looks;
Why all this toil and trouble?

The sun, above the mountain's head,   5
A freshening luster mellow
Through all the long green fields has spread,
His first sweet evening yellow.

Books! 'tis a dull and endless strife:
Come, hear the woodland linnet,   10
How sweet his music! on my life,
There's more of wisdom in it.

And hark! how blithe the throstle sings!
He, too, is no mean preacher:
Come forth into the light of things,   15
Let Nature be your Teacher.

She has a world of ready wealth,
Our minds and hearts to bless—
Spontaneous wisdom breathed by health,
Truth breathed by cheerfulness.   20

One impulse from a vernal wood
May teach you more of man,
Of moral evil and of good,
Than all the sages can.

Sweet is the lore which Nature brings;   25
Our meddling intellect
Mis-shapes the beauteous forms of things:—
We murder to dissect.

Enough of Science and of Art;
Close up those barren leaves;   30
Come forth, and bring with you a heart
That watches and receives.

LINES
Composed a Few Miles above Tintern Abbey, on Revisiting the Banks of the Wye during a Tour. July 13, 1798[1]

Five years have passed; five summers, with
the length
Of five long winters! and again I hear

[3]Written and published in 1798.

[1]Published in 1798. "No poem of mine was
composed under circumstances more pleasant for

These waters, rolling from their mountain-
   springs
With a soft inland murmur.—Once again
Do I behold these steep and lofty cliffs,   5
That on a wild secluded scene impress
Thoughts of more deep seclusion; and con-
   nect
The landscape with the quiet of the sky.
The day is come when I again repose
Here, under this dark sycamore, and view 10
These plots of cottage-ground, these orchard-
   tufts,
Which at this season, with their unripe
   fruits,
Are clad in one green hue, and lose them-
   selves
'Mid groves and copses. Once again I see
These hedge-rows, hardly hedge-rows, little
   lines   15
Of sportive wood run wild: these pastoral
   farms,
Green to the very door; and wreaths of
   smoke
Sent up, in silence, from among the trees!
With some uncertain notice, as might seem
Of vagrant dwellers in the houseless
   woods   20
Or of some Hermit's cave, where by his fire
The hermit sits alone.
               These beauteous forms,
Through a long absence, have not been to me
As is a landscape to a blind man's eye:
But oft, in lonely rooms, and 'mid the din 25
Of towns and cities, I have owed to them
In hours of weariness, sensations sweet,
Felt in the blood, and felt along the heart;
And passing even into my purer mind,
With tranquil restoration:—feelings too 30
Of unremembered pleasure: such, perhaps,
As have no slight or trivial influence
On that best portion of a good man's life,
His little, nameless, unremembered acts
Of kindness and of love. Nor less, I
   trust,   35
To them I may have owed another gift,
Of aspect more sublime; that blessed mood,
In which the burthen of the mystery,
In which the heavy and the weary weight
Of all this unintelligible world,   40

---

me to remember than this. I began it upon leaving
Tintern, after crossing the Wye, and concluded it
just as I was entering Bristol in the evening, after
a ramble of four or five days, with my sister.
Not a line of it was altered, and not any part of
it written down till I reached Bristol" (Wordsworth, *Fenwick Note*). This great poem is of
the utmost importance for understanding the influence Wordsworth felt from nature.

Is lightened:—that serene and blessed mood,
In which the affections gently lead us on,—
Until, the breath of this corporeal frame
And even the motion of our human blood
Almost suspended, we are laid asleep   45
In body, and become a living soul:
While with an eye made quiet by the power
Of harmony, and the deep power of joy,
We see into the life of things.
                     If this
Be but a vain belief, yet, oh! how oft—   50
In darkness and amid the many shapes
Of joyless daylight; when the fretful stir
Unprofitable, and the fever of the world,
Have hung upon the beatings of my heart—
How oft, in spirit, have I turned to thee, 55
O sylvan Wye! thou wanderer through the
   woods,
How often has my spirit turned to thee!
   And now, with gleams of half-extinguished
   thought,
With many recognitions dim and faint,
And somewhat of a sad perplexity,   60
The picture of the mind revives again:
While here I stand, not only with the sense
Of present pleasure, but with pleasing
   thoughts
That in this moment there is life and food
For future years. And so I dare to hope, 65
Though changed, no doubt, from what I was
   when first
I came among these hills; when like a roe
I bounded o'er the mountains, by the sides
Of the deep rivers, and the lonely streams,
Wherever nature led: more like a man   70
Flying from something that he dreads, than
   one
Who sought the thing he loved. For nature
   then
(The coarser pleasures of my boyish days,
And their glad animal movements all gone
   by)
To me was all in all.—I cannot paint   75
What then I was. The sounding cataract
Haunted me like a passion; the tall rock,
The mountain, and the deep and gloomy
   wood,
Their colors and their forms, were then to
   me
An appetite; a feeling and a love,   80
That had no need of a remoter charm,
By thought supplied, nor any interest
Unborrowed from the eye.—That time is
   past,
And all its aching joys are now no more,
And all its dizzy raptures. Not for this 85
Faint I, nor mourn nor murmur; other gifts

Have followed; for such loss, I would be-
lieve,
Abundant recompense. For I have learned
To look on nature, not as in the hour
Of thoughtless youth; but hearing often-
times   90
The still, sad music of humanity,
Nor harsh nor grating, though of ample
power
To chasten and subdue.   And I have felt
A presence that disturbs me with the joy
Of elevated thoughts; a sense sublime   95
Of something far more deeply interfused,
Whose dwelling is the light of setting suns,
And the round ocean and the living air,
And the blue sky, and in the mind of man;
A motion and a spirit, that impels   100
All thinking things, all objects of all thought,
And rolls through all things.   Therefore am
I still
A lover of the meadows and the woods,
And mountains; and of all that we behold
From this green earth; of all the mighty
world   105
Of eye, and ear,—both what they half create,
And what perceive; well pleased to recognize
In nature and the language of the sense,
The anchor of my purest thoughts, the nurse,
The guide, the guardian of my heart, and
soul   110
Of all my moral being.
                              Nor perchance,
If I were not thus taught, should I the more
Suffer my genial spirits to decay:
For thou art with me here upon the banks
Of this fair river; thou my dearest Friend,
My dear, dear Friend;[2] and in thy voice I
catch   116
The language of my former heart, and read
My former pleasures in the shooting lights
Of thy wild eyes. Oh! yet a little while
May I behold in thee what I was once,   120
My dear, dear Sister! and this prayer I
make,
Knowing that Nature never did betray
The heart that loved her; 'tis her privilege,
Through all the years of this our life, to
lead
From joy to joy: for she can so inform   125
The mind that is within us, so impress
With quietness and beauty, and so feed
With lofty thoughts, that neither evil
tongues,
Rash judgments, nor the sneers of selfish
men,

---

[2]Dorothy Wordsworth.

Nor greetings where no kindness is, nor
all   130
The dreary intercourse of daily life,
Shall e'er prevail against us, or disturb
Our cheerful faith, that all which we behold
Is full of blessings.   Therefore let the moon
Shine on thee in thy solitary walk;   135
And let the misty mountain-winds be free
To blow against thee: and, in after years,
When these wild ecstasies shall be matured
Into a sober pleasure; when thy mind
Shall be a mansion for all lovely forms, 140
Thy memory be as a dwelling-place
For all sweet sounds and harmonies; oh!
then,
If solitude, or fear, or pain, or grief,
Should be thy portion, with what healing
thoughts
Of tender joy wilt thou remember me,   145
And these my exhortations! Nor, per-
chance—
If I should be where I no more can hear
Thy voice, nor catch from thy wild eyes
these gleams
Of past existence—wilt thou then forget
That on the banks of this delightful
stream   150
We stood together; and that I, so long
A worshiper of Nature, hither came
Unwearied in that service: rather say
With warmer love—oh! with far deeper zeal
Of holier love. Nor wilt thou then for-
get,   155
That after many wanderings, many years
Of absence, these steep woods and lofty
cliffs,
And this green pastoral landscape, were to
me
More dear, both for themselves and for thy
sake!

STRANGE FITS OF PAS-SION HAVE I KNOWN[1]

Strange fits of passion have I known:
And I will dare to tell,
But in the Lover's ear alone,
What once to me befell.

When she I loved looked every day   5
Fresh as a rose in June,
I to her cottage bent my way,
Beneath an evening-moon.

---

[1]Written in 1799; published in 1800. This poem
and the following four form a group known as the
"Lucy Poems." If Lucy was a real woman, there
seems to be little likelihood that she will ever be
identified.

Upon the moon I fixed my eye,
All over the wide lea;   10
With quickening pace my horse drew nigh
Those paths so dear to me.

And now we reached the orchard-plot;
And, as we climbed the hill,
The sinking moon to Lucy's cot   15
Came near, and nearer still.

In one of those sweet dreams I slept,
Kind nature's gentlest boon!
And all the while my eyes I kept
On the descending moon.   20

My horse moved on; hoof after hoof
He raised, and never stopped:
When down behind the cottage roof,
At once, the bright moon dropped.

What fond and wayward thoughts will slide
Into a Lover's head!   26
"O mercy!" to myself I cried,
"If Lucy should be dead!"

SHE DWELT AMONG THE UNTRODDEN WAYS[2]

She dwelt among the untrodden ways
  Beside the springs of Dove,
A Maid whom there were none to praise
  And very few to love:

A violet by a mossy stone   5
  Half hidden from the eye!
—Fair as a star, when only one
  Is shining in the sky.

She lived unknown, and few could know
  When Lucy ceased to be;   10
But she is in her grave, and, oh,
  The difference to me!

I TRAVELED AMONG UNKNOWN MEN[3]

I traveled among unknown men,
  In lands beyond the sea;
Nor, England! did I know till then
  What love I bore to thee.

'Tis past, that melancholy dream!   5
  Nor will I quit thy shore
A second time; for still I seem
  To love thee more and more.

[2]Written in 1799; published in 1800.
[3]Written in 1799; published in 1807.

Among thy mountains did I feel
  The joy of my desire;   10
And she I cherished turned her wheel
  Beside an English fire.

Thy mornings showed, thy nights concealed
  The bowers where Lucy played;
And thine too is the last green field   15
  That Lucy's eyes surveyed.

THREE YEARS SHE GREW IN SUN AND SHOWER[4]

Three years she grew in sun and shower,
Then Nature said, "A lovelier flower
On earth was never sown;
This Child I to myself will take;
She shall be mine, and I will make   5
A Lady of my own.

"Myself will to my darling be
Both law and impulse: and with me
The Girl, in rock and plain,
In earth and heaven, in glade and bower,   10
Shall feel an overseeing power
To kindle or restrain.

"She shall be sportive as the fawn
That wild with glee across the lawn,
Or up the mountain springs;   15
And hers shall be the breathing balm,
And hers the silence and the calm
Of mute insensate things.

"The floating clouds their state shall lend
To her; for her the willow bend;   20
Nor shall she fail to see
Even in the motions of the Storm
Grace that shall mold the Maiden's form
By silent sympathy.

"The stars of midnight shall be dear   25
To her; and she shall lean her ear
In many a secret place
Where rivulets dance their wayward round,
And beauty born of murmuring sound
Shall pass into her face.   30

"And vital feelings of delight
Shall rear her form to stately height,
Her virgin bosom swell;
Such thoughts to Lucy I will give
While she and I together live   35
Here in this happy dell."

[4]Written in 1799; published in 1800.

Thus Nature spake—The work was done—
How soon my Lucy's race was run!
She died, and left to me
This heath, this calm, and quiet scene;　40
The memory of what has been,
And never more will be.

A SLUMBER DID MY SPIRIT SEAL[5]

A slumber did my spirit seal;
　I had no human fears:
She seemed a thing that could not feel
　The touch of earthly years.

No motion has she now, no force;　5
　She neither hears nor sees;
Rolled round in earth's diurnal course,
　With rocks, and stones, and trees.

LUCY GRAY

or

Solitude[1]

Oft I had heard of Lucy Gray:
And, when I crossed the wild,
I chanced to see at break of day
The solitary child.

No mate, no comrade Lucy knew;　5
She dwelt on a wide moor,
—The sweetest thing that ever grew
Beside a human door!

You yet may spy the fawn at play,
The hare upon the green;　10
But the sweet face of Lucy Gray
Will never more be seen.

"To-night will be a stormy night—
You to the town must go;
And take a lantern, Child, to light　15
Your mother through the snow."

"That, Father! will I gladly do:
'Tis scarcely afternoon—
The minster-clock has just struck two,
And yonder is the moon!"　20

[5]Written in 1799; published in 1800.
[1]Written in 1799; published in 1800.

At this the Father raised his hook,
And snapped a faggot-band;
He plied his work;—and Lucy took
The lantern in her hand.

Not blither is the mountain roe:　25
With many a wanton stroke
Her feet disperse the powdery snow,
That rises up like smoke.

The storm came on before its time:
She wandered up and down;　30
And many a hill did Lucy climb:
But never reached the town.

The wretched parents all that night
Went shouting far and wide;
But there was neither sound nor sight　35
To serve them for a guide.

At day-break on a hill they stood
That overlooked the moor;
And thence they saw the bridge of wood,
A furlong from their door.　40

They wept—and, turning homeward, cried,
"In heaven we all shall meet;"
—When in the snow the mother spied
The print of Lucy's feet.

Then downwards from the steep hill's edge　45
They tracked the footmarks small;
And through the broken hawthorn hedge,
And by the long stone-wall;

And then an open field they crossed:
The marks were still the same;　50
They tracked them on, nor ever lost;
And to the bridge they came.

They followed from the snowy bank
Those footmarks, one by one,
Into the middle of the plank;　55
And further there were none!

—Yet some maintain that to this day
She is a living child;
That you may see sweet Lucy Gray
Upon the lonesome wild.　60

O'er rough and smooth she trips along,
And never looks behind;
And sings a solitary song
That whistles in the wind.

RUTH[1]

When Ruth was left half desolate,
Her Father took another Mate;
And Ruth, not seven years old,
A slighted child, at her own will
Went wandering over dale and hill,   5
In thoughtless freedom, bold.

And she had made a pipe of straw,
And music from that pipe could draw
Like sounds of winds and floods;
Had built a bower upon the green,   10
As if she from her birth had been
An infant of the woods.

Beneath her father's roof, alone
She seemed to live; her thoughts her own,
Herself her own delight;   15
Pleased with herself, nor sad, nor gay;
And, passing thus the live-long day,
She grew to woman's height.

There came a Youth from Georgia's shore—
A military casque he wore,   20
With splendid feathers dressed;
He brought them from the Cherokees;
The feathers nodded in the breeze,
And made a gallant crest.

From Indian blood you deem him sprung: 25
But no! he spake the English tongue,
And bore a soldier's name;
And, when America was free
From battle and from jeopardy,
He 'cross the ocean came.   30

With hues of genius on his cheek
In finest tones the Youth could speak:
—While he was yet a boy,
The moon, the glory of the sun,
And streams that murmur as they run,   35
Had been his dearest joy.

He was a lovely youth! I guess
The panther in the wilderness
Was not so fair as he;
And, when he chose to sport and play,   40
No dolphin ever was so gay
Upon the tropic sea.

Among the Indians he had fought,
And with him many tales he brought
Of pleasure and of fear;   45
Such tales as told to any maid
By such a Youth, in the green shade,
Were perilous to hear.

He told of girls—a happy rout!
Who quit their fold with dance and shout,   50
Their pleasant Indian town,
To gather strawberries all day long;
Returning with a choral song
When daylight is gone down.

He spake of plants that hourly change   55
Their blossoms, through a boundless range
Of intermingling hues;
With budding, fading, faded flowers
They stand the wonder of the bowers
From morn to evening dews.   60

He told of the magnolia, spread
High as a cloud, high over head!
The cypress and her spire;
—Of flowers that with one scarlet gleam
Cover a hundred leagues, and seem   65
To set the hills on fire.

The Youth of green savannahs spake,
And many an endless, endless lake,
With all its fairy crowds
Of islands, that together lie   70
As quietly as spots of sky
Among the evening clouds.

"How pleasant," then he said, "it were
A fisher or a hunter there,
In sunshine or in shade   75
To wander with an easy mind;
And build a household fire, and find
A home in every glade!

"What days and what bright years! Ah me!
Our life were life indeed, with thee   80
So passed in quiet bliss,
And all the while," said he, "to know
That we were in a world of woe,
On such an earth as this!"

And then he sometimes interwove   85
Fond thoughts about a father's love;
"For there," said he, "are spun
Around the heart such tender ties,
That our own children to our eyes
Are dearer than the sun.   90

"Sweet Ruth! and could you go with me
My helpmate in the woods to be,
Our shed at night to rear;
Or run, my own adopted bride,
A sylvan huntress at my side,   95
And drive the flying deer!

[1] Written in 1799; published in 1800.

"Belovéd Ruth!"—No more he said,
The wakeful Ruth at midnight shed
A solitary tear:
She thought again—and did agree   100
With him to sail across the sea,
And drive the flying deer.

"And now, as fitting is and right,
We in the church our faith will plight,
A husband and a wife."   105
Even so they did; and I may say
That to sweet Ruth that happy day
Was more than human life.

Through dream and vision did she sink,
Delighted all the while to think   110
That on those lonesome floods,
And green savannahs, she should share
His board with lawful joy, and bear
His name in the wild woods.

But, as you have before been told,   115
This Stripling, sportive, gay, and bold,
And, with his dancing crest,
So beautiful, through savage lands
Had roamed about, with vagrant bands
Of Indians in the West.   120

The wind, the tempest roaring high,
The tumult of a tropic sky,
Might well be dangerous food
For him, a Youth to whom was given
So much of earth—so much of heaven,   125
And such impetuous blood.

Whatever in those climes he found
Irregular in sight or sound
Did to his mind impart
A kindred impulse, seemed allied   130
To his own powers, and justified
The workings of his heart.

Nor less, to feed voluptuous thought,
The beauteous forms of nature wrought,
Fair trees and gorgeous flowers;   135
The breezes their own languor lent;
The stars had feelings, which they sent
Into those favored bowers.

Yet, in his worst pursuits I ween
That sometimes there did intervene   140
Pure hopes of high intent:
For passions linked to form so fair
And stately, needs must have their share
Of noble sentiment.

But ill he lived, much evil saw,   145
With men to whom no better law
Nor better life was known;
Deliberately, and undeceived,

Those wild men's vices he received,
And gave them back his own.   150

His genius and his moral frame
Were thus impaired, and he became
The slave of low desires:
A Man who without self-control
Would seek what the degraded soul   155
Unworthily admires.

And yet he with no feigned delight
Had wooed the Maiden, day and night
Had loved her, night and morn:
What could he less than love a Maid   160
Whose heart with so much nature played?
So kind and so forlorn!

Sometimes, most earnestly, he said,
"O Ruth! I have been worse than dead;
False thoughts, thoughts bold and vain,   165
Encompassed me on every side
When I, in confidence and pride,
Had crossed the Atlantic main.

"Before me shone a glorious world—
Fresh as a banner bright, unfurled   170
To music suddenly:
I looked upon those hills and plains,
And seemed as if let loose from chains,
To live at liberty.

"No more of this; for now, by thee   175
Dear Ruth! more happily set free
With nobler zeal I burn;
My soul from darkness is released,
Like the whole sky when to the east
The morning doth return."   180

Full soon that better mind was gone;
No hope, no wish remained, not one,—
They stirred him now no more;
New objects did new pleasure give,
And once again he wished to live   185
As lawless as before.

Meanwhile, as thus with him it fared,
They for the voyage were prepared,
And went to the sea-shore,
But, when they thither came, the Youth   190
Deserted his poor Bride, and Ruth
Could never find him more.

God help thee, Ruth!—Such pains she had,
That she in half a year was mad,
And in a prison housed;   195
And there, with many a doleful song
Made of wild words, her cup of wrong
She fearfully caroused.

Yet sometimes milder hours she knew,
Nor wanted sun, nor rain, nor dew,   200

Nor pastimes of the May;
—They all were with her in her cell;
And a clear brook with cheerful knell
Did o'er the pebbles play.

When Ruth three seasons thus had lain, 205
There came a respite to her pain;
She from her prison fled;
But of the Vagrant none took thought;
And where it liked her best she sought
Her shelter and her bread. 210

Among the fields she breathed again:
The master-current of her brain
Ran permanent and free;
And, coming to the Banks of Tone,[2]
There did she rest; and dwell alone 215
Under the greenwood tree.

The engines of her pain, the tools
That shaped her sorrow, rocks and pools,
And airs that gently stir
The vernal leaves—she loved them still; 220
Nor ever taxed them with the ill
Which had been done to her.

A Barn her *winter* bed supplies;
But, till the warmth of summer skies
And summer days is gone, 225
(And all do in this tale agree)
She sleeps beneath the greenwood tree,
And other home hath none.

²A stream which, like the Quantock Hills mentioned in l. 246 below, is in the immediate neighborhood of Alfoxden, where Wordsworth had lived a short time before the poem was composed.

An innocent life, yet far astray!
And Ruth will, long before her day, 230
Be broken down and old:
Sore aches she needs must have! but less
Of mind, than body's wretchedness,
From damp, and rain, and cold.

If she is pressed by want of food, 235
She from her dwelling in the wood
Repairs to a road-side;
And there she begs at one steep place
Where up and down with easy pace
The horsemen-travelers ride. 240

That oaten pipe of hers is mute,
Or thrown away; but with a flute
Her loneliness she cheers:
This flute, made of a hemlock stalk,
At evening in his homeward walk 245
The Quantock woodman hears.

I, too, have passed her on the hills
Setting her little water-mills
By spouts and fountains wild—
Such small machinery as she turned 250
Ere she had wept, ere she had mourned,
A young and happy Child!

Farewell! and when thy days are told,
Ill-fated Ruth, in hallowed mold
Thy corpse shall buried be, 255
For thee a funeral bell shall ring,
And all the congregation sing
A Christian psalm for thee.

MICHAEL[1]

A Pastoral Poem

If from the public way you turn your steps
Up the tumultuous brook of Greenhead
    Ghyll,[2]
You will suppose that with an upright path
Your feet must struggle; in such bold ascent

The pastoral mountains front you, face to
    face. 5
But, courage! for around that boisterous
    brook
The mountains have all opened out them-
    selves,
And made a hidden valley of their own.
No habitation can be seen; but they
Who journey thither find themselves alone 10
With a few sheep, with rocks and stones, and
    kites
That overhead are sailing in the sky.
It is in truth an utter solitude;

[1]Written and published in 1800. "Written at Town-end, Grasmere, about the same time as *The Brothers.* The Sheepfold, on which so much of the poem turns, remains, or rather the ruins of it. The character and circumstances of Luke were taken from a family to whom had belonged, many years before, the house we lived in at Town-end, along with some fields and woodlands on the eastern shore of Grasmere. The name of the Evening Star was not in fact given to this house, but to another on the same side of the valley, more to the north" (Wordsworth, *Fenwick Note*). Most of *Michael,* as the journal of Dorothy Wordsworth reveals, was actually written in the sheepfold. Wordsworth wrote to a friend: "I have attempted to give a picture of a man, of strong mind and

lively sensibility, agitated by two of the most powerful affections of the human heart: the parental affection and the love of property *(landed property),* including the feelings of inheritance, home, and personal and family independence."

[2]A ravine with a stream running through it.

Nor should I have made mention of this Dell
But for one object which you might pass
    by,   15
Might see and notice not. Beside the brook
Appears a straggling heap of unhewn stones!
And to that simple object appertains
A story—unenriched with strange events,
Yet not unfit, I deem, for the fireside,   20
Or for the summer shade. It was the first
Of those domestic tales that spake to me
Of shepherds, dwellers in the valleys, men
Whom I already loved; not verily
For their own sakes, but for the fields and
    hills   25
Where was their occupation and abode.
And hence this Tale, while I was yet a Boy
Careless of books, yet having felt the power
Of Nature, by the gentle agency
Of natural objects, led me on to feel   30
For passions that were not my own, and
    think
(At random and imperfectly indeed)
On man, the heart of man, and human life.
Therefore, although it be a history
Homely and rude, I will relate the same   35
For the delight of a few natural hearts;
And, with yet fonder feeling, for the sake
Of youthful Poets, who among these hills
Will be my second self when I am gone.

        Upon the forest-side in Grasmere Vale   40
There dwelt a Shepherd, Michael was his
    name;
An old man, stout of heart, and strong of
    limb.
His bodily frame had been from youth to
    age
Of an unusual strength: his mind was keen,
Intense, and frugal, apt for all affairs,   45
And in his shepherd's calling he was prompt
And watchful more than ordinary men.
Hence had he learned the meaning of all
    winds,
Of blasts of every tone; and oftentimes,   49
When others heeded not, He heard the South
Make subterraneous music, like the noise
Of bagpipers on distant Highland hills.
The Shepherd, at such warning, of his flock
Bethought him, and he to himself would say,
"The winds are now devising work for
    me!"   55
And, truly, at all times, the storm, that drives
The traveler to a shelter, summoned him
Up to the mountains: he had been alone
Amid the heart of many thousand mists,
That came to him, and left him, on the
    heights.   60

So lived he till his eightieth year was past.
And grossly that man errs, who should
    suppose
That the green valleys, and the streams and
    rocks,
Were things indifferent to the Shepherd's
    thoughts.
Fields, where with cheerful spirits he had
    breathed   65
The common air; hills, which with vigorous
    step
He had so often climbed; which had im-
    pressed
So many incidents upon his mind
Of hardship, skill or courage, joy or fear;
Which, like a book, preserved the memory 70
Of the dumb animals, whom he had saved,
Had fed or sheltered, linking to such acts
The certainty of honorable gain;
Those fields, those hills—what could they
    less? had laid
Strong hold on his affections, were to him 75
A pleasurable feeling of blind love,
The pleasure which there is in life itself.
    His days had not been passed in singleness.
His Helpmate was a comely matron, old—
Though younger than himself full twenty
    years.   80
She was a woman of a stirring life,
Whose heart was in her house: two wheels
    she had
Of antique form; this large, for spinning
    wool;
That small, for flax; and if one wheel had
    rest
It was because the other was at work.   85
The Pair had but one inmate in their house,
An only Child, who had been born to them
When Michael, telling o'er his years, began
To deem that he was old,—in shepherd's
    phrase,
With one foot in the grave. This only
    Son,   90
With two brave sheep-dogs tried in many a
    storm,
The one of an inestimable worth,
Made all their household. I may truly say,
That they were as a proverb in the vale
For endless industry. When day was gone, 95
And from their occupations out of doors
The Son and Father were come home, even
    then,
Their labor did not cease; unless when all
Turned to the cleanly supper-board, and
    there,
Each with a mess of pottage and skimmed
    milk,   100

Sat round the basket piled with oaten cakes,
And their plain home-made cheese. Yet
    when the meal
Was ended, Luke (for so the Son was
    named)
And his old Father both betook themselves
To such convenient work as might employ 105
Their hands by the fireside ; perhaps to card
Wool for the Housewife's spindle, or repair
Some injury done to sickle, flail, or scythe,
Or other implement of house or field.
    Down from the ceiling, by the chimney's
      edge, 110
That in our ancient uncouth country style
With huge and black projection overbrowed
Large space beneath, as duly as the light
Of day grew dim the Housewife hung a
    lamp ;
An agéd utensil, which had performed 115
Service beyond all others of its kind.
Early at evening did it burn—and late,
Surviving comrade of uncounted hours,
Which, going by from year to year, had
    found,
And left, the couple neither gay perhaps 120
Nor cheerful, yet with objects and with
    hopes,
Living a life of eager industry.
And now, when Luke had reached his eight-
    eenth year,
There by the light of this old lamp they sat,
Father and Son, while far into the night 125
The Housewife plied her own peculiar work,
Making the cottage through the silent hours
Murmur as with the sound of summer flies.
This light was famous in its neighborhood,
And was a public symbol of the life 130
That thrifty Pair had lived. For, as it
    chanced,
Their cottage on a plot of rising ground
Stood single, with large prospect, north and
    south,
High into Easedale,[3] up to Dunmail-Raise,[4]
And westward to the village near the lake ; 135
And from this constant light, so regular
And so far seen, the House itself, by all
Who dwelt within the limits of the vale,
Both old and young, was named the *Evening
Star*.
    Thus living on through such a length of
      years, 140
The Shepherd, if he loved himself, must
    needs
Have loved his Helpmate ; but to Michael's
    heart

[3]Near Grasmere.
[4]The pass on the way from Grasmere to Keswick.

This son of his old age was yet more dear—
Less from instinctive tenderness, the same
Fond spirit that blindly works in the blood
    of all— 145
Than that a child, more than all other gifts
That earth can offer to declining man,
Brings hope with it, and forward-looking
    thoughts,
And stirrings of inquietude, when they
By tendency of nature needs must fail. 150
Exceeding was the love he bare to him,
His heart and his heart's joy ! For often-
    times
Old Michael, while he was a babe in arms,
Had done him female service, not alone
For pastime and delight, as is the use 155
Of fathers, but with patient mind enforced
To acts of tenderness ; and he had rocked
His cradle, as with a woman's gentle hand.
    And, in a later time, ere yet the Boy
Had put on boy's attire, did Michael love, 160
Albeit of a stern unbending mind,
To have the Young-one in his sight, when he
Wrought in the field, or on his shepherd's
    stool
Sat with a fettered sheep before him stretched
Under the large old oak, that near his door 165
Stood single, and, from matchless depth of
    shade,
Chosen for the Shearer's covert from the
    sun,
Thence in our rustic dialect was called
The *Clipping Tree*, a name which yet it bears.
There, while they two were sitting in the
    shade, 170
With others round them, earnest all and
    blithe,
Would Michael exercise his heart with looks
Of fond correction and reproof bestowed
Upon the Child, if he disturbed the sheep
By catching at their legs, or with his shouts
Scared them, while they lay still beneath the
    shears. 176
    And when by Heaven's good grace the boy
      grew up
A healthy Lad, and carried in his cheek
Two steady roses that were five years old ;
Then Michael from a winter coppice cut 180
With his own hand a sapling, which he
    hooped
With iron, making it throughout in all
Due requisites a perfect shepherd's staff,
And gave it to the Boy ; wherewith equipped
He as a watchman oftentimes was placed 185
At gate or gap, to stem or turn the flock ;
And, to his office prematurely called,
There stood the urchin, as you will divine,

Something between a hindrance and a help;
And for this cause not always, I believe,   190
Receiving from his Father hire of praise;
Though nought was left undone which staff,
    or voice,
Or looks, or threatening gestures, could per-
    form.
    But soon as Luke, full ten years old, could
    stand
Against the mountain blasts; and to the
    heights,   195
Not fearing toil, nor length of weary ways,
He with his Father daily went, and they
Were as companions, why should I relate
That objects which the Shepherd loved be-
    fore
Were dearer now? that from the Boy there
    came   200
Feelings and emanations—things which were
Light to the sun and music to the wind;
And that the old Man's heart seemed born
    again?
    Thus in his Father's sight the Boy grew up:
And now, when he had reached his eighteenth
    year,   205
He was his comfort and his daily hope.
    While in this sort the simple household
    lived
From day to day, to Michael's ear there came
Distressful tidings. Long before the time
Of which I speak, the Shepherd had been
    bound   210
In surety for his brother's son, a man
Of an industrious life, and ample means;
But unforeseen misfortunes suddenly
Had pressed upon him; and old Michael now
Was summoned to discharge the forfeiture,
A grievous penalty, but little less   216
Than half his substance. This unlooked-for
    claim,
At the first hearing, for a moment took
More hope out of his life than he supposed
That any old man ever could have lost.   220
As soon as he had armed himself with
    strength
To look his trouble in the face, it seemed
The Shepherd's sole resource to sell at once
A portion of his patrimonial fields.   224
Such was his first resolve; he thought again,
And his heart failed him. "Isabel," said he,
Two evenings after he had heard the news,
"I have been toiling more than seventy years,
And in the open sunshine of God's love
Have we all lived; yet if these fields of
    ours   230
Should pass into a stranger's hand, I think
That I could not lie quiet in my grave.

Our lot is a hard lot; the sun himself
Has scarcely been more diligent than I;
And I have lived to be a fool at last   235
To my own family. An evil man
That was, and made an evil choice, if he
Were false to us; and if he were not false,
There are ten thousand to whom loss like this
Had been no sorrow. I forgive him;—
    but   240
'Twere better to be dumb than to talk thus.
    "When I began, my purpose was to speak
Of remedies and of a cheerful hope.
Our Luke shall leave us, Isabel; the land
Shall not go from us, and it shall be free;   245
He shall possess it, free as is the wind
That passes over it. We have, thou know'st,
Another kinsman—he will be our friend
In this distress. He is a prosperous man,
Thriving in trade—and Luke to him shall
    go,   250
And with his kinsman's help and his own
    thrift
He quickly will repair this loss, and then
He may return to us. If here he stay,
What can be done? Where every one is
    poor,
What can be gained?"
              At this the old Man paused,   255
And Isabel sat silent, for her mind
Was busy, looking back into past times.
There's Richard Bateman, thought she to
    herself,
He was a parish-boy—at the church-door
They made a gathering for him, shillings,
    pence,   260
And halfpennies, wherewith the neighbors
    bought
A basket, which they filled with peddler's
    wares;
And, with this basket on his arm, the lad
Went up to London, found a master there,
Who, out of many, chose the trusty boy   265
To go and overlook his merchandise
Beyond the seas; where he grew wondrous
    rich,
And left estates and monies to the poor.
And, at his birthplace, built a chapel, floored
With marble which he sent from foreign
    lands.   270
These thoughts, and many others of like sort,
Passed quickly through the mind of Isabel,
And her face brightened. The old Man was
    glad,
And thus resumed:—"Well, Isabel! this
    scheme
These two days has been meat and drink to
    me.   275

Far more than we have lost is left us yet.
—We have enough—I wish indeed that I
Were younger;—but this hope is a good
  hope.
—Make ready Luke's best garments, of the
  best   279
Buy for him more, and let us send him forth
To-morrow, or the next day, or to-night:
—If he *could* go, the Boy should go to-night."
  Here Michael ceased, and to the fields went
    forth
With a light heart. The Housewife for
  five days
Was restless morn and night, and all day
  long   285
Wrought on with her best fingers to prepare
Things needful for the journey of her son.
But Isabel was glad when Sunday came
To stop her in her work: for, when she lay
By Michael's side, she through the last two
  nights   290
Heard him, how he was troubled in his sleep:
And when they rose at morning she could see
That all his hopes were gone. That day at
  noon,
She said to Luke, while they two by them-
  selves   294
Were sitting at the door, "Thou must not go:
We have no other Child but thee to lose—
None to remember—do not go away,
For if thou leave thy Father he will die."
The Youth made answer with a jocund voice;
And Isabel, when she had told her fears, 300
Recovered heart. That evening her best fare
Did she bring forth, and all together sat
Like happy people round a Christmas fire.
  With daylight Isabel resumed her work;
And all the ensuing week the house appeared
As cheerful as a grove in Spring: at length 306
The expected letter from their kinsman
  came.
With kind assurances that he would do
His utmost for the welfare of the Boy;
To which, requests were added, that forth-
  with   310
He might be sent to him. Ten times or more
The letter was read over; Isabel
Went forth to show it to the neighbors
  round;
Nor was there at that time on English land
A prouder heart than Luke's. When Isabel
Had to her house returned, the old Man
  said,   316
"He shall depart to-morrow." To this word
The Housewife answered, talking much of
  things
Which, if at such short notice he should go,

Would surely be forgotten. But at length 320
She gave consent, and Michael was at ease.
  Near the tumultuous brook of Greenhead
    Ghyll,
In that deep valley, Michael had designed
To build a Sheepfold; and, before he heard
The tidings of his melancholy loss,   325
For this same purpose he had gathered up
A heap of stones, which by the streamlet's
  edge
Lay thrown together, ready for the work.
With Luke that evening thitherward he
  walked:
And soon as they had reached the place he
  stopped,   330
And thus the old Man spake to him:—"My
  Son,
To-morrow thou wilt leave me: with full
  heart
I look upon thee, for thou art the same
That wert a promise to me ere thy birth,
And all thy life hast been my daily joy. 335
I will relate to thee some little part
Of our two histories; 'twill do thee good
When thou art from me, even if I should
  touch
On things thou canst not know of.——After
  thou
First cam'st into the world—as oft befalls 340
To new-born infants—thou didst sleep away
Two days, and blessings from thy Father's
  tongue
Then fell upon thee. Day by day passed on,
And still I loved thee with increasing love.
Never to living ear came sweeter sounds 345
Than when I heard thee by our own fireside
First uttering, without words, a natural tune;
While thou, a feeding babe, didst in thy joy
Sing at thy Mother's breast. Month fol-
  lowed month,
And in the open fields my life was passed 350
And on the mountains; else I think that thou
Hadst been brought up upon thy Father's
  knees.
But we were playmates, Luke: among these
  hills,
As well thou knowest, in us the old and
  young
Have played together, nor with me didst
  thou   355
Lack any pleasure which a boy can know."
Luke had a manly heart; but at these words
He sobbed aloud. The old Man grasped his
  hand,
And said, "Nay, do not take it so—I see
That these are things of which I need not
  speak.   360

—Even to the utmost I have been to thee
A kind and a good Father: and herein
I but repay a gift which I myself
Received at others' hands; for, though now
    old
Beyond the common life of man, I still   365
Remember them who loved me in my youth.
Both of them sleep together: here they lived,
As all their Forefathers had done; and when
At length their time was come, they were not
    loath
To give their bodies to the family mold.   370
I wished that thou should'st live the life they
    lived:
But, 'tis a long time to look back, my Son,
And see so little gain from threescore years.
These fields were burthened when they came
    to me;
Till I was forty years of age, not more   375
Than half of my inheritance was mine.
I toiled and toiled; God blessed me in my
    work,
And till these three weeks past the land was
    free.
—It looks as if it never could endure   379
Another Master.   Heaven forgive me, Luke,
If I judge ill for thee, but it seems good
That thou should'st go."
                At this the old Man paused;
Then, pointing to the stones near which they
    stood,
Thus, after a short silence, he resumed: 384
"This was a work for us; and now, my Son,
It is a work for me.   But, lay one stone—
Here, lay it for me, Luke, with thine own
    hands.
Nay, Boy, be of good hope;—we both may
    live
To see a better day.   At eighty-four
I still am strong and hale;—do thou thy
    part;   390
I will do mine.—I will begin again
With many tasks that were resigned to thee:
Up to the heights, and in among the storms,
Will I without thee go again, and do
All works which I was wont to do alone,   395
Before I knew thy face.—Heaven bless thee,
    Boy!
Thy heart these two weeks has been beating
    fast
With many hopes; it should be so—yes—
    yes—
I knew that thou could'st never have a wish
To leave me, Luke: thou hast been bound to
    me   400
Only by links of love: when thou art gone,

What will be left to us!—But, I forget
My purposes.   Lay now the corner-stone,
As I requested; and hereafter, Luke,
When thou art gone away, should evil men   405
Be thy companions, think of me, my Son,
And of this moment; hither turn thy
    thoughts,
And God will strengthen thee: amid all fear
And all temptation, Luke, I pray that thou
May'st bear in mind the life thy Fathers
    lived,   410
Who, being innocent, did for that cause
Bestir them in good deeds.   Now, fare thee
    well—
When thou return'st, thou in this place wilt
    see
A work which is not here: a covenant
'Twill be between us; but, whatever fate   415
Befall thee, I shall love thee to the last,
And bear thy memory with me to the grave."
        The Shepherd ended here; and Luke
    stooped down,
And, as his Father had requested, laid
The first stone of the Sheepfold.   At the
    sight   420
The old Man's grief broke from him; to his
    heart
He pressed his Son, he kisséd him and wept:
And to the house together they returned.
—Hushed was that House in peace, or seem-
    ing peace,
Ere the night fell:—with morrow's dawn the
    Boy   425
Began his journey, and when he had reached
The public way, he put on a bold face;
And all the neighbors, as he passed their
    doors,
Came forth with wishes and with farewell
    prayers,
That followed him till he was out of sight.   430
    A good report did from their Kinsman
    come,
Of Luke and his well-doing: and the Boy
Wrote loving letters, full of wondrous news,
Which, as the Housewife phrased it, were
    throughout
"The prettiest letters that were ever seen."   435
Both parents read them with rejoicing hearts.
So, many months passed on: and once again
The Shepherd went about his daily work
With confident and cheerful thoughts; and
    now   439
Sometimes when he could find a leisure hour
He to that valley took his way, and there
Wrought at the Sheepfold.   Meantime Luke
    began
To slacken in his duty; and, at length,

He in the dissolute city gave himself
To evil courses: ignominy and shame   445
Fell on him, so that he was driven at last
To seek a hiding-place beyond the seas.

    There is a comfort in the strength of love;
'Twill make a thing endurable, which else
Would overset the brain, or break the heart:
I have conversed with more than one who
    well   451
Remember the old Man, and what he was
Years after he had heard this heavy news.
His bodily frame had been from youth to
    age
Of an unusual strength. Among the rocks 455
He went, and still looked up to sun and cloud,
And listened to the wind; and, as before,
Performed all kinds of labor for his sheep,
And for the land, his small inheritance.
And to that hollow dell from time to time 460
Did he repair, to build the Fold, of which
His flock had need. 'Tis not forgotten yet
The pity which was then in every heart
For the old Man—and 'tis believed by all
That many and many a day he thither went,
And never lifted up a single stone.   466
    There, by the Sheepfold, sometimes was he
    seen
Sitting alone, or with his faithful Dog,
Then old, beside him, lying at his feet.
The length of full seven years, from time to
    time, 470
He at the building of this Sheepfold wrought,
And left the work unfinished when he died.
Three years, or little more, did Isabel
Survive her Husband: at her death the estate
Was sold, and went into a stranger's hand. 475
The Cottage which was named the *Evening
Star*
Is gone—the plowshare has been through the
    ground
On which it stood; great changes have been
    wrought
In all the neighborhood:—yet the oak is left
That grew beside their door; and the remains
Of the unfinished Sheepfold may be seen 481
Beside the boisterous brook of Greenhead
    Ghyll.

TO A YOUNG LADY

Who Had Been Reproached for Taking Long Walks in the Country[1]

Dear Child of Nature, let them rail!
—There is a nest in a green dale,

[1]Written perhaps in 1801; printed in the *Morning Post*, 1802, and in the *Poems* of 1807.

A harbor and a hold;
Where thou, a Wife and Friend, shalt see
Thy own heart-stirring days, and be   5
A light to young and old.

There, healthy as a shepherd boy,
And treading among flowers of joy
Which at no season fade,
Thou, while thy babes around thee cling, 10
Shalt show us how divine a thing
A Woman may be made.

Thy thoughts and feelings shall not die,
Nor leave thee, when gray hairs are nigh,
A melancholy slave;   15
But an old age serene and bright,
And lovely as a Lapland night,
Shall lead thee to thy grave.

ALICE FELL

or

Poverty[2]

The post-boy drove with fierce career,
For threatening clouds the moon had
    drowned;
When, as we hurried on, my ear
Was smitten with a startling sound.

As if the wind blew many ways,   5
I heard the sound,—and more and more;
It seemed to follow with the chaise,
And still I heard it as before.

At length I to the boy called out;
He stopped his horses at the word,   10
But neither cry, nor voice, nor shout,
Nor aught else like it, could be heard.

The boy then smacked his whip, and fast
The horses scampered through the rain;
But, hearing soon upon the blast   15
The cry, I bade him halt again.

Forthwith alighting on the ground,
"Whence comes," said I, "this piteous
    moan?"
And there a little Girl I found,
Sitting behind the chaise, alone.   20

"My cloak!" no other word she spake,
But loud and bitterly she wept,
As if her innocent heart would break;
And down from off her seat she leapt.

[2]Written in 1802; published in 1807.

"What ails you, child?"—she sobbed, "Look
    here!"   25
I saw it in the wheel entangled
A weather-beaten rag as e'er
From any garden scare-crow dangled.

There, twisted between nave and spoke,
It hung, nor could at once be freed;   30
But our joint pains unloosed the cloak,
A miserable rag indeed!

"And whither are you going, child,
To-night along these lonesome ways?"
"To Durham," answered she, half wild— 35
"Then come with me into the chaise."

Insensible to all relief
Sat the poor girl, and forth did send
Sob after sob, as if her grief
Could never, never have an end.   40

"My child, in Durham do you dwell?"
She checked herself in her distress,
And said, "My name is Alice Fell;
I'm fatherless and motherless.

"And I to Durham, Sir, belong."   45
Again, as if the thought would choke
Her very heart, her grief grew strong;
And all was for her tattered cloak!

The chaise drove on; our journey's end
Was nigh; and, sitting by my side,   50
As if she had lost her only friend
She wept, nor would be pacified.

Up to the tavern-door we post;
Of Alice and her grief I told;
And I gave money to the host,   55
To buy a new cloak for the old.

"And let it be of duffel[3] gray,
As warm a cloak as man can sell!"
Proud creature was she the next day,
The little orphan, Alice Fell!   60

TO THE CUCKOO[4]

O blithe New-comer! I have heard,
I hear thee and rejoice.
O Cuckoo! shall I call thee Bird,
Or but a wandering Voice?

[3] Coarse woolen cloth with thick nap.
[4] Written in 1802; published in 1807.

While I am lying on the grass   5
Thy twofold shout I hear,
From hill to hill it seems to pass,
At once far off, and near.

Though babbling only to the Vale,
Of sunshine and of flowers,   10
Thou bringest unto me a tale
Of visionary hours.

Thrice welcome, darling of the Spring!
Even yet thou art to me
No bird, but an invisible thing,   15
A voice, a mystery;

The same whom in my school-boy days
I listened to; that Cry
Which made me look a thousand ways
In bush, and tree, and sky.   20

To seek thee did I often rove
Through woods and on the green;
And thou wert still a hope, a love;
Still longed for, never seen.

And I can listen to thee yet;   25
Can lie upon the plain
And listen, till I do beget
That golden time again.

O blessèd Bird! the earth we pace
Again appears to be   30
An unsubstantial, faery place;
That is fit home for Thee!

MY HEART LEAPS UP[5]

My heart leaps up when I behold
    A rainbow in the sky:
So was it when my life began;
So is it now I am a man;
So be it when I shall grow old,   5
    Or let me die!
The Child is father of the Man;
And I could wish my days to be
Bound each to each by natural piety.

[5] Written in 1802; published in 1807. Wordsworth wrote this poem immediately before beginning the *Ode on Intimations of Immortality;* and in early editions the last three lines of it appeared as a motto at the head of the longer poem.

RESOLUTION AND INDEPENDENCE [1]

I

There was a roaring in the wind all night;
The rain came heavily and fell in floods;
But now the sun is rising calm and bright;
The birds are singing in the distant woods;
Over his own sweet voice the Stock-dove
broods; 5
The Jay makes answer as the Magpie chatters;
And all the air is filled with pleasant noise of
waters.

II

All things that love the sun are out of doors;
The sky rejoices in the morning's birth;
The grass is bright with rain-drops;—on the
moors 10
The hare is running races in her mirth;
And with her feet she from the plashy earth
Raises a mist; that, glittering in the sun,
Runs with her all the way, wherever she doth
run.

III

I was a Traveler then upon the moor, 15
I saw the hare that raced about with joy;
I heard the woods and distant waters roar;
Or heard them not, as happy as a boy:
The pleasant season did my heart employ:
My old remembrances went from me wholly;
And all the ways of men, so vain and melancholy. 21

IV

But, as it sometimes chanceth, from the
might
Of joy in the minds that can no further go,
As high as we have mounted in delight
In our dejection do we sink as low; 25
To me that morning did it happen so;
And fears and fancies thick upon me came;
Dim sadness—and blind thoughts, I knew
not, nor could name.

V

I heard the sky-lark warbling in the sky;
And I bethought me of the playful hare: 30
Even such a happy Child of earth am I;
Even as these blissful creatures do I fare;
Far from the world I walk, and from all care;
But there may come another day to me— 34
Solitude, pain of heart, distress, and poverty.

VI

My whole life I have lived in pleasant
thought,
As if life's business were a summer mood;
As if all needful things would come unsought
To genial faith, still rich in genial good;
But how can He expect that others should 40
Build for him, sow for him, and at his call
Love him, who for himself will take no heed
at all?

VII

I thought of Chatterton, [2] the marvelous Boy,
The sleepless Soul that perished in his pride;
Of Him [3] who walked in glory and in joy 45
Following his plow, along the mountainside:
By our own spirits are we deified:
We Poets in our youth begin in gladness;
But thereof come in the end despondency and
madness.

VIII

Now, whether it were by peculiar grace, 50
A leading from above, a something given,
Yet it befell that, in this lonely place,
When I with these untoward thoughts had
striven,
Beside a pool bare to the eye of heaven
I saw a Man before me unawares: 55
The oldest man he seemed that ever wore
gray hairs.

IX

As a huge stone is sometimes seen to lie
Couched on the bald top of an eminence;
Wonder to all who do the same espy,
By what means it could thither come, and
whence; 60
So that it seems a thing endued with sense:
Like a sea-beast crawled forth, that on a shelf
Of rock or sand reposeth, there to sun itself;

---

[1] Written in 1802; published in 1807. "Written
at Town-end, Grasmere. This old Man I met a
few hundred yards from my cottage; and the
account of him is taken from his own mouth. I
was in the state of feeling described in the beginning of the poem, while crossing over Barton Fell
from Mr. Clarkson's, at the foot of Ullswater,
towards Askham. The image of the hare I then
observed on the ridge of the Fell" (Wordsworth,
Fenwick Note).

[2] Thomas Chatterton (1752–1770), who died by
his own hand.

[3] Robert Burns.

X

Such seemed this Man, not all alive nor dead,
Nor all asleep—in his extreme old age:— 65
His body was bent double, feet and head
Coming together in life's pilgrimage;
As if some dire constraint of pain, or rage
Of sickness felt by him in times long past,
A more than human weight upon his frame
    had cast.   70

XI

Himself he propped, limbs, body, and pale
    face,
Upon a long gray staff of shaven wood:
And, still as I drew near with gentle pace,
Upon the margin of that moorish flood
Motionless as a cloud the old Man stood, 75
That heareth not the loud winds when they
    call
And moveth all together, if it move at all.

XII

At length, himself unsettling, he the pond
Stirred with his staff, and fixedly did look
Upon the muddy water, which he conned, 80
As if he had been reading in a book:
And now a stranger's privilege I took;
And, drawing to his side, to him did say,
"This morning gives us promise of a glori-
    ous day."

XIII

A gentle answer did the old Man make,   85
In courteous speech which forth he slowly
    drew:
And him with further words I thus bespake,
"What occupation do you there pursue?
This is a lonesome place for one like you."
Ere he replied, a flash of mild surprise   90
Broke from the sable orbs of his yet-vivid
    eyes,

XIV

His words came feebly, from a feeble chest,
But each in solemn order followed each,
With something of a lofty utterance
    dressed—
Choice word and measured phrase, above the
    reach   95
Of ordinary men; a stately speech;
Such as grave Livers do in Scotland use,
Religious men, who give to God and man
    their dues.

XV

He told, that to these waters he had come
To gather leeches, being old and poor: 100
Employment hazardous and wearisome!
And he had many hardships to endure:
From pond to pond he roamed, from moor
    to moor;
Housing, with God's good help, by choice or
    chance,
And in this way he gained an honest main-
    tenance.   105

XVI

The old Man still stood talking by my side;
But now his voice to me was like a stream
Scarce heard; nor word from word could I
    divide;
And the whole body of the Man did seem
Like one whom I had met with in a
    dream;   110
Or like a man from some far region sent
To give me human strength, by apt admon-
    ishment.

XVII

My former thoughts returned: the fear that
    kills;
And hope that is unwilling to be fed;
Cold, pain, and labor, and all fleshly ills; 115
And mighty Poets in their misery dead.
—Perplexed, and longing to be comforted,
My question eagerly did I renew,
"How is it that you live, and what is it you
    do?"

XVIII

He with a smile did then his words re-
    peat;   120
And said, that, gathering leeches, far and
    wide
He traveled; stirring thus above his feet
The waters of the pools where they abide.
"Once I could meet with them on every side;
But they have dwindled long by slow decay;
Yet still I persevere, and find them where I
    may."   126

XIX

While he was talking thus, the lonely place.
The old Man's shape, and speech—all
    troubled me:
In my mind's eye I seemed to see him pace
About the weary moors continually,   130
Wandering about alone and silently.
While I these thoughts within myself pur-
    sued,
He, having made a pause, the same discourse
    renewed.

XX

And soon with this he other matter blended,
Cheerfully uttered, with demeanor kind,   135
But stately in the main; and, when he ended,
I could have laughed myself to scorn to find
In that decrepit Man so firm a mind.
"God," said I, "be my help and stay secure;
I'll think of the Leech-gatherer on the lonely
    moor!"   140

TO THE DAISY[1]

Bright Flower! whose home is everywhere,
Bold in maternal Nature's care,
And all the long year through the heir
    Of joy and sorrow;
Methinks that there abides in thee   5
Some concord with humanity,
Given to no other flower I see
    The forest thorough!

Is it that Man is soon depressed?
A thoughtless Thing! who, once unbless'd,   10
Does little on his memory rest,
    Or on his reason,
And Thou wouldst teach him how to find
A shelter under every wind,
A hope for times that are unkind   15
    And every season?

Thou wander'st the wide world about,
Unchecked by pride or scrupulous doubt,
With friends to greet thee, or without,
    Yet pleased and willing;   20
Meek, yielding to the occasion's call,
And all things suffering from all,
Thy function apostolical
    In peace fulfilling.

COMPOSED UPON WEST-MINSTER BRIDGE, SEP-TEMBER 3, 1802[2]

Earth has not anything to show more fair;
Dull would he be of soul who could pass by
A sight so touching in its majesty:
This City now doth, like a garment, wear
The beauty of the morning; silent, bare,   5
Ships, towers, domes, theaters, and temples
    lie
Open unto the fields, and to the sky;
All bright and glittering in the smokeless air.

Never did sun more beautifully steep
In his first splendor, valley, rock, or hill;   10
Ne'er saw I, never felt, a calm so deep!
The river glideth at his own sweet will:
Dear God! the very houses seem asleep;
And all that mighty heart is lying still!

IT IS A BEAUTEOUS EVENING, CALM AND FREE[3]

It is a beauteous evening, calm and free,
The holy time is quiet as a Nun
Breathless with adoration; the broad sun
Is sinking down in its tranquillity;
The gentleness of heaven broods o'er the
    Sea: 5
Listen! the mighty Being is awake,
And doth with his eternal motion make
A sound like thunder—everlastingly.
Dear Child![4] dear Girl! that walkest with me
    here,
If thou appear untouched by solemn thought,
Thy nature is not therefore less divine: 11
Thou liest in Abraham's bosom all the year,
And worship'st at the Temple's inner shrine,
God being with thee when we know it not.

COMPOSED BY THE SEA-SIDE, NEAR CALAIS, AUGUST, 1802[5]

Fair Star of evening, Splendor of the west,
Star of my Country!—on the horizon's brink
Thou hangest, stooping, as might seem, to
    sink
On England's bosom, yet well pleased to rest,
Meanwhile, and be to her a glorious crest   5
Conspicuous to the Nations.   Thou, I think,
Shouldst be my Country's emblem; and
    shouldst wink,
Bright Star! with laughter on her banners,
    dressed
In thy fresh beauty.   There! that dusky spot
Beneath thee, that is England; there she
    lies.   10
Blessings be on you both! one hope, one lot,
One life, one glory!—I, with many a fear
For my dear Country, many heartfelt sighs,
Among men who do not love her, linger here.

---

[1]Written in 1802; published in 1807.

[2]Really written on 31 July, 1802; published in 1807.

[3]Written in August, 1802; published in 1807.
[4]Wordsworth's French daughter, Caroline.
[5]Published in 1807.

ON THE EXTINCTION OF THE VENETIAN REPUBLIC [6]

Once did She hold the gorgeous east in fee;
And was the safeguard of the west: the
    worth
Of Venice did not fall below her birth,
Venice, the eldest Child of Liberty.
She was a maiden City, bright and free;   5
No guile seduced, no force could violate;
And, when she took unto herself a Mate,
She must espouse the everlasting Sea. [7]
And what if she had seen those glories fade,
Those titles vanish, and that strength decay;
Yet shall some tribute of regret be paid   11
When her long life hath reached its final day:
Men are we, and must grieve when even the
    Shade
Of that which once was great is passed away.

TO TOUSSAINT L'OUVERTURE [8]

Toussaint, the most unhappy man of men!
Whether the whistling Rustic tend his plow
Within thy hearing, or thy head be now
Pillowed in some deep dungeon's earless
    den;—
O miserable Chieftain! where and when   5
Wilt thou find patience? Yet die not; do
    thou
Wear rather in thy bonds a cheerful brow:
Though fallen thyself, never to rise again,
Live, and take comfort. Thou hast left be-
    hind
Powers that will work for thee; air, earth,
    and skies;   10

There's not a breathing of the common wind
That will forget thee; thou hast great allies;
Thy friends are exultations, agonies,
And love, and man's unconquerable mind.

SEPTEMBER, 1802. NEAR DOVER [9]

Inland, within a hollow vale, I stood;
And saw, while sea was calm and air was
    clear,
The coast of France—the coast of France
    how near!
Drawn almost into frightful neighborhood.
I shrunk; for verily the barrier flood   5
Was like a lake, or river bright and fair,
A span of waters; yet what power is there!
What mightiness for evil and for good!
Even so doth God protect us if we be
Virtuous and wise. Winds blow, and wat-
    ers roll,   10
Strength to the brave, and Power, and Deity;
Yet in themselves are nothing! One decree
Spake laws to *them,* and said that by the soul
Only, the Nations shall be great and free.

WRITTEN IN LONDON, SEPTEMBER, 1802 [10]

O friend! I know not which way I must
    look
For comfort, being, as I am, oppressed,
To think that now our life is only dressed
For show; mean handy-work of craftsman,
    cook,
Or groom!—We must run glittering like a
    brook   5
In the open sunshine, or we are unbless'd:
The wealthiest man among us is the best:
No grandeur now in nature or in book
Delights us. Rapine, avarice, expense,
This is idolatry; and these we adore: 10
Plain living and high thinking are no more:
The homely beauty of the good old cause
Is gone; our peace, our fearful innocence,
And pure religion breathing household laws.

LONDON, 1802 [11]

Milton! thou shouldst be living at this hour:
England hath need of thee: she is a fen
Of stagnant waters: altar, sword, and pen,
Fireside, the heroic wealth of hall and bower,

---

[6]Written in 1802; published in 1807. In the
thirteenth century Venice controlled a portion of
the Eastern Empire, and for a long time protected
Western Europe from the Turks. The city was
founded in the fifth century and had been independent for more than a thousand years when it
was conquered by Napoleon in 1797, and its territory divided between Austria and France.

[7]An allusion to the annual ceremony, dating from
the twelfth century, of marriage between Venice
and the Adriatic, in which the Doge threw a ring
into the sea.

[8]Written probably in August, 1802; published in
the *Morning Post* in 1803 and in the *Poems* of
1807. Toussaint was governor of St. Domingo and
leader of the African slaves freed by decree of
the French Convention in 1794. When Napoleon
published an edict reëstablishing slavery in St.
Domingo, Toussaint offered resistance, was arrested
and sent to France in June, 1802, and there died
in prison in April, 1803.

---

[9]Published in 1807.   [10]Published in 1807.
[11]Written in September, 1802; published in 1807.

Have forfeited their ancient English dower 5
Of inward happiness. We are selfish men;
Oh! raise us up, return to us again;
And give us manners, virtue, freedom, power.
Thy soul was like a Star, and dwelt apart;
Thou hadst a voice whose sound was like the
    sea: 10
Pure as the naked heavens, majestic, free,
So didst thou travel on life's common way,
In cheerful godliness; and yet thy heart
The lowliest duties on herself did lay.

GREAT MEN HAVE BEEN AMONG US [12]

Great men have been among us; hands that
    penned
And tongues that uttered wisdom—better
    none:
The later Sidney, Marvel, Harrington.
Young Vane,[13] and others who called Mil-
    ton friend. 4
These moralists could act and comprehend:
They knew how genuine glory was put on;
Taught us how rightfully a nation shone
In splendor: what strength was, that would
    not bend
But in magnanimous meekness. France, 'tis
    strange,
Hath brought forth no such souls as we had
    then. 10
Perpetual emptiness! unceasing change!
No single volume paramount, no code,
No master spirit, no determined road;
But equally a want of books and men!

IT IS NOT TO BE THOUGHT OF [14]

It is not to be thought of that the Flood
Of British freedom, which, to the open sea
Of the world's praise, from dark antiquity
Hath flowed, "with pomp of waters, unwith-
    stood,"[15]
Roused though it be full often to a mood 5
Which spurns the check of salutary bands,
That this most famous Stream in bogs and
    sands
Should perish; and to evil and to good

[12]Written in September, 1802; published in 1807.

[13]Algernon Sidney (1622?–1683), Andrew Marvell (1621–1678), James Harrington (1611–1677), and Sir Henry Vane (1612–1662).

[14]Written in 1802 or 1803; published in the latter year in the *Morning Post* and in the *Poems* of 1807.

[15]Samuel Daniel, *Civil War*, Bk. II, Stanza 7.

Be lost for ever. In our halls is hung
Armory of the invincible Knights of old: 10
We must be free or die, who speak the tongue
That Shakespeare spake; the faith and
    morals hold
Which Milton held.—In everything we are
    sprung
Of Earth's first blood, have titles manifold.

WHEN I HAVE BORNE IN MEMORY [16]

When I have borne in memory what has
    tamed
Great Nations, how ennobling thoughts de-
    part
When men change swords for ledgers, and
    desert
The student's bower for gold, some fears un-
    named
I had, my Country!—am I to be blamed? 5
Now, when I think of thee, and what thou
    art,
Verily, in the bottom of my heart,
Of those unfilial fears I am ashamed.
For dearly must we prize thee; we who find
In thee a bulwark for the cause of men: 10
And I by my affection was beguiled:
What wonder if a Poet now and then,
Among the many movements of his mind,
Felt for thee as a lover or a child!

THE GREEN LINNET [17]

Beneath these fruit-tree boughs that shed
Their snow-white blossoms on my head,
With brightest sunshine round me spread
    Of spring's unclouded weather,
In this sequestered nook how sweet 5
To sit upon my orchard-seat!
And birds and flowers once more to greet,
    My last year's friends together.

One have I marked, the happiest guest
In all this covert of the bless'd: 10
Hail to Thee, far above the rest
    In joy of voice and pinion!
Thou, Linnet! in thy green array,
Presiding Spirit here to-day,
Dost lead the revels of the May; 15
    And this is thy dominion.

[16]Written in 1802 or 1803; published in the latter year in the *Morning Post* and in the *Poems* of 1807.

[17]Written in 1803; published in 1807.

While birds, and butterflies, and flowers,
Make all one band of paramours,
Thou, ranging up and down the bowers,
  Art sole in thy employment: 20
A life, a Presence like the Air,
Scattering thy gladness without care,
Too bless'd with any one to pair;
  Thyself thy own enjoyment.

Amid yon tuft of hazel trees, 25
That twinkle to the gusty breeze,
Behold him perched in ecstasies,
  Yet seeming still to hover;
There! where the flutter of his wings
Upon his back and body flings 30
Shadows and sunny glimmerings,
  That cover him all over.

My dazzled sight he oft deceives,
A Brother of the dancing leaves;
Then flits, and from the cottage-eaves 35
  Pours forth his song in gushes;
As if by that exulting strain
He mocked and treated with disdain
The voiceless form he chose to feign,
  While fluttering in the bushes. 40

STEPPING WESTWARD[18]

"What, you are stepping westward?"—
  "Yea."
—'Twould be a *wildish* destiny,
If we, who thus together roam
In a strange Land, and far from home,
Were in this place the guests of Chance: 5
Yet who would stop, or fear to advance,
Though home or shelter he had none,
With such a sky to lead him on?

The dewy ground was dark and cold;
Behind, all gloomy to behold; 10
And stepping westward seemed to be
A kind of *heavenly* destiny:
I liked the greeting; 'twas a sound
Of something without place or bound;
And seemed to give me spiritual right 15
To travel through that region bright.

[18] Written between 1803 and 1805; published in 1807. "While my Fellow-traveler and I were walking by the side of Loch Ketterine, one fine evening after sunset, in our road to a Hut where, in the course of our Tour, we had been hospitably entertained some weeks before, we met, in one of the loneliest parts of that solitary region, two well-dressed Women, one of whom said to us, by way of greeting, 'What, you are stepping westward?'" (Wordsworth.) Wordsworth, Dorothy, and Coleridge went on a tour of Scotland in August, 1803, returning to Grasmere in the middle of October.

The voice was soft, and she who spake
Was walking by her native lake:
The salutation had to me
The very sound of courtesy: 20
Its power was felt; and while my eye
Was fixed upon the glowing Sky,
The echo of the voice enwrought
A human sweetness with the thought
Of traveling through the world that lay 25
Before me in my endless way.

TO A HIGHLAND GIRL

At Inversneyde, upon Loch Lomond[1]

Sweet Highland Girl, a very shower
Of beauty is thy earthly dower!
Twice seven consenting years have shed
Their utmost bounty on thy head:
And these gray rocks; that household
  lawn; 5
Those trees, a veil just half withdrawn;
This fall of water that doth make
A murmur near the silent lake;
This little bay; a quiet road
That holds in shelter thy Abode— 10
In truth together do ye seem
Like something fashioned in a dream;
Such Forms as from their covert peep
When earthly cares are laid asleep!
But, O fair Creature! in the light 15
Of common day, so heavenly bright,
I bless Thee, Vision as thou art,
I bless thee with a human heart;
God shield thee to thy latest years!
Thee, neither know I, nor thy peers; 20
And yet my eyes are filled with tears.
 With earnest feeling I shall pray
For thee when I am far away:
For never saw I mien, or face,
In which more plainly I could trace 25
Benignity and home-bred sense
Ripening in perfect innocence.
Here scattered, like a random seed,
Remote from men, Thou dost not need
The embarrassed look of shy distress, 30
And maidenly shamefacédness:
Thou wear'st upon thy forehead clear
The freedom of a Mountaineer:
A face with gladness overspread!
Soft smiles, by human kindness bred! 35
And seemliness complete, that sways
Thy courtesies, about thee plays;
With no restraint, but such as springs
From quick and eager visitings
Of thoughts that lie beyond the reach 40

[1] Written in 1803; published in 1807.

Of thy few words of English speech:
A bondage sweetly brooked, a strife
That gives thy gestures grace and life!
So have I, not unmoved in mind,   45
Seen birds of tempest-loving kind—
Thus beating up against the wind.
   What hand but would a garland cull
For thee who art so beautiful?
O happy pleasure! here to dwell
Beside thee in some heathy dell;   50
Adopt your homely ways, and dress,
A Shepherd, thou a Shepherdess!
But I could frame a wish for thee
More like a grave reality:
Thou art to me but as a wave   55
Of the wild sea; and I would have
Some claim upon thee, if I could,
Though but of common neighborhood.
What joy to hear thee, and to see!
Thy elder Brother I would be,   60
Thy Father—anything to thee!
   Now thanks to Heaven! that of its grace
Hath led me to this lovely place.
Joy have I had; and going hence
I bear away my recompense.   65
In spots like these it is we prize
Our Memory, feel that she hath eyes:
Then, why should I be loath to stir?
I feel this place was made for her;
To give new pleasure like the past,   70
Continued long as life shall last.
Nor am I loath, though pleased at heart,
Sweet Highland Girl! from thee to part:
For I, methinks, till I grow old,
As fair before me shall behold,   75
As I do now, the cabin small,
The lake, the bay, the waterfall;
And Thee, the Spirit of them all!

SHE WAS A PHANTOM OF DELIGHT [1]

She was a Phantom of delight
When first she gleamed upon my sight;
A lovely Apparition, sent
To be a moment's ornament;
Her eyes as stars of Twilight fair;   5
Like Twilight's, too, her dusky hair;
But all things else about her drawn
From May-time and the cheerful Dawn;
A dancing Shape, an Image gay,
To haunt, to startle, and waylay.   10

I saw her upon nearer view,
A Spirit, yet a Woman too!
Her household motions light and free,
And steps of virgin-liberty;
A countenance in which did meet   15
Sweet records, promises as sweet;
A Creature not too bright or good
For human nature's daily food;
For transient sorrows, simple wiles,   19
Praise, blame, love, kisses, tears, and smiles.

And now I see with eye serene
The very pulse of the machine;
A Being breathing thoughtful breath,
A Traveler between life and death;
The reason firm, the temperate will,   25
Endurance, foresight, strength, and skill;
A perfect Woman, nobly planned,
To warn, to comfort, and command;
And yet a Spirit still, and bright
With something of angelic light.   30

THE SOLITARY REAPER [2]

Behold her, single in the field,
Yon solitary Highland Lass!
Reaping and singing by herself;
Stop here, or gently pass!
Alone she cuts and binds the grain,   5
And sings a melancholy strain;
O listen! for the Vale profound
Is overflowing with the sound.

No Nightingale did ever chaunt
More welcome notes to weary bands   10
Of travelers in some shady haunt,
Among Arabian sands:
A voice so thrilling ne'er was heard
In spring-time from the Cuckoo-bird,
Breaking the silence of the seas   15
Among the farthest Hebrides.

Will no one tell me what she sings?—
Perhaps the plaintive numbers flow
For old, unhappy, far-off things,
And battles long ago: 20
Or is it some more humble lay,
Familiar matter of to-day?
Some natural sorrow, loss, or pain,
That has been, and may be again?

Whate'er the theme, the Maiden sang   25
As if her song could have no ending;
I saw her singing at her work,
And o'er the sickle bending;—

---

[1] Written in 1804; published in 1807. The subject of this poem is Mary Hutchinson, Wordsworth's wife.

[2] Written between 1803 and 1805; published in 1807.

I listened, motionless and still;
And, as I mounted up the hill   30
The music in my heart I bore,
Long after it was heard no more.

YARROW UNVISITED[1]

From Stirling castle we had seen
The mazy Forth unraveled;
Had trod the banks of Clyde, and Tay,
And with the Tweed had traveled;
And when we came to Clovenford,   5
Then said my *"winsome Marrow,"*[2]
"Whate'er betide, we'll turn aside,
And see the Braes[3] of Yarrow."

"Let Yarrow folk, *frae* Selkirk town,
Who have been buying, selling,   10
Go back to Yarrow, 'tis their own;
Each maiden to her dwelling!
On Yarrow's banks let herons feed,
Hares couch, and rabbits burrow!
But we will downward with the Tweed,   15
Nor turn aside to Yarrow.

"There's Galla Water, Leader Haughs,[4]
Both lying right before us;
And Dryborough, where with chiming
    Tweed
The lintwhites[5] sing in chorus;   20
There's pleasant Tiviot-dale, a land
Made blithe with plow and harrow:
Why throw away a needful day
To go in search of Yarrow?

"What's Yarrow but a river bare,   25
That glides the dark hills under?
There are a thousand such elsewhere
As worthy of your wonder."
—Strange words they seemed of slight and
    scorn;
My True-love sighed for sorrow;   30
And looked me in the face, to think
I thus could speak of Yarrow!

"Oh! green," said I, "are Yarrow's holms,
And sweet is Yarrow flowing!

Fair hangs the apple frae the rock,[6]   35
But we will leave it growing.
O'er hilly path, and open Strath,[7]
We'll wander Scotland thorough;
But, though so near, we will not turn
Into the dale of Yarrow.   40

"Let beeves and home-bred kine partake
The sweets of Burn-mill meadow;
The swan on still St. Mary's Lake[8]
Float double, swan and shadow!
We will not see them; will not go,   45
To-day, nor yet to-morrow,
Enough if in our hearts we know
There's such a place as Yarrow.

"Be Yarrow stream unseen, unknown!
It must, or we shall rue it: 50
We have a vision of our own;
Ah! why should we undo it?
The treasured dreams of times long past,
We'll keep them, winsome Marrow!
For when we're there, although 'tis fair, 55
'Twill be another Yarrow!

"If Care with freezing years should come,
And wondering seem but folly,—
Should we be loath to stir from home,
And yet be melancholy;   60
Should life be dull, and spirits low,
'Twill soothe us in our sorrow,
That earth has something yet to show,
The bonny holms of Yarrow!"

I WANDERED LONELY AS A CLOUD[1]

I wandered lonely as a cloud
That floats on high o'er vales and hills,
When all at once I saw a crowd,
A host, of golden daffodils;
Beside the lake, beneath the trees,   5
Fluttering and dancing in the breeze.

---

[1]Written in 1803; published in 1807.

[2]Partner, i. e., Dorothy Wordsworth. The words come from a ballad whose scene is laid upon the banks of the Yarrow.

[3]Slopes.

[4]The Gala flows into the Tweed near Abbotsford, and the Leader near Melrose. Haughs (holms) are low-lying lands, occasionally flooded.

[5]Linnets.

[6]This line is taken from the ballad called *The Braes of Yarrow* by Hamilton of Bangour—the ballad from which the quoted words in the first stanza also come.

[7]A valley through which a river flows.

[8]The body of water from which the Yarrow takes its rise.

[1]Written in 1804; published in 1807. "The two best lines in it are by Mary. The daffodils grew, and still grow, on the margin of Ullswater, and probably may be seen to this day as beautiful in the month of March, nodding their golden heads beside the dancing and foaming waves" (Wordsworth, *Fenwick Note*).

Continuous as the stars that shine
And twinkle on the milky way,
They stretched in never-ending line
Along the margin of a bay: 10
Ten thousand saw I at a glance,
Tossing their heads in sprightly dance.

The waves beside them danced; but they
Out-did the sparkling waves in glee:
A poet could not but be gay,   15
In such a jocund company:
I gazed—and gazed—but little thought
What wealth the show to me had brought:

For oft, when on my couch I lie
In vacant or in pensive mood,   20
They flash upon that inward eye
Which is the bliss of solitude;[2]
And then my heart with pleasure fills,
And dances with the daffodils.

THE SMALL CELANDINE[3]

There is a Flower, the lesser Celandine,
That shrinks, like many more, from cold and
    rain;
And, the first moment that the sun may
    shine,
Bright as the sun himself, 'tis out again!

When hailstones have been falling, swarm
    on swarm,   5
Or blasts the green field and the trees dis-
    tressed,
Oft have I seen it muffled up from harm,
In close self-shelter, like a Thing at rest.

But lately, one rough day, this Flower I
    passed
And recognized it, though an altered form, 10
Now standing forth an offering to the blast,
And buffeted at will by rain and storm.

I stopped, and said with inly-muttered voice,
"It doth not love the shower, nor seek the
    cold:
This neither is its courage nor its choice, 15
But its necessity in being old.

---

[2]This and the preceding line are those by "Mary"
—Mrs. Wordsworth.

[3]Written in 1804; published in 1807.

"The sunshine may not cheer it, nor the
    dew;
It cannot help itself in its decay;
Stiff in its members, withered, changed of
    hue."   19
And, in my spleen, I smiled that it was gray.

To be a Prodigal's Favorite—then, worse
    truth,
A Miser's Pensioner—behold our lot!
O Man, that from thy fair and shining youth
Age might but take the things Youth needed
    not!   24

ELEGIAC STANZAS

Suggested by a Picture of Peele Castle, in a Storm, Painted by Sir George Beaumont[1]

I was thy neighbor once, thou rugged Pile!
Four summer weeks I dwelt in sight of thee:[2]
I saw thee every day; and all the while
Thy Form was sleeping on a glassy sea.

So pure the sky, so quiet was the air!   5
So like, so very like, was day to day!
Whene'er I looked, thy Image still was there;
It trembled, but it never passed away.

How perfect was the calm! it seemed no
    sleep;
No mood, which season takes away, or
    brings:
I could have fancied that the mighty Deep
Was even the gentlest of all gentle Things.

Ah! *then,* if mine had been the Painter's
    hand,
To express what then I saw; and add the
    gleam,
The light that never was, on sea or land, 15
The consecration, and the Poet's dream;

I would have planted thee, thou hoary Pile
Amid a world how different from this!
Beside a sea that could not cease to smile;
On tranquil land, beneath a sky of bliss. 20

---

[1]Written in 1805; published in 1807. The Peele
Castle here referred to (there are two) is in Lancashire. Wordsworth's friend Beaumont painted
two pictures of the Castle, one of them intended
for Mrs. Wordsworth.

[2]A reference to a visit paid by Wordsworth
during a college vacation to his cousin, Mrs.
Barker, who lived at Rampside, not far from
Peele Castle.

Thou shouldst have seemed a treasure-house
   divine
Of peaceful years; a chronicle of heaven;—
Of all the sunbeams that did ever shine
The very sweetest had to thee been given.

A Picture had it been of lasting ease,   25
Elysian quiet, without toil or strife;
No motion but the moving tide, a breeze,
Or merely silent Nature's breathing life.

Such, in the fond illusion of my heart,
Such Picture would I at that time have
   made: 30
And seen the soul of truth in every part,
A steadfast peace that might not be betrayed.

So once it would have been,—'tis so no more;
I have submitted to a new control:
A power is gone, which nothing can re-
   store;   35
A deep distress hath humanized my Soul.[3]

Not for a moment could I now behold
A smiling sea, and be what I have been:
The feeling of my loss will ne'er be old;
This, which I know, I speak with mind se-
   rene.   40

Then, Beaumont, Friend! who would have
   been the Friend,
If he had lived, of Him whom I deplore,
This work, of thine I blame not, but com-
   mend;
This sea in anger, and that dismal shore.

O 'tis a passionate Work!—yet wise and
   well,   45
Well chosen is the spirit that is here;
That Hulk which labors in the deadly swell,
This rueful sky, this pageantry of fear!

And this huge Castle, standing here sublime,
I love to see the look with which it braves,   50
Cased in the unfeeling armor of old time,
The lightning, the fierce wind, and trampling
   waves.

Farewell, farewell the heart that lives alone,
Housed in a dream, at distance from the
   Kind!
Such happiness, wherever it be known,   55
Is to be pitied; for 'tis surely blind.

But welcome fortitude, and patient cheer,
And frequent sights of what is to be borne!
Such sights, or worse, as are before me
   here.—   59
Not without hope we suffer and we mourn.

✓ ODE TO DUTY[1]

Stern Daughter of the Voice of God!
O Duty! if that name thou love
Who art a light to guide, a rod
To check the erring, and reprove;
Thou, who art victory and law   5
When empty terrors overawe;
From vain temptations dost set free;
And calm'st the weary strife of frail human-
   ity!

There are who ask not if thine eye
Be on them; who, in love and truth,   10
Where no misgiving is, rely
Upon the genial sense of youth:
Glad Hearts! without reproach or blot;
Who do thy work, and know it not:
Oh! if through confidence misplaced   15
They fail, thy saving arms, dread Power!
   around them cast.

Serene will be our days and bright,
And happy will our nature be,
When love is an unerring light,
And joy its own security.   20
And they a blissful course may hold
Even now, who, not unwisely bold,
Live in the spirit of this creed;
Yet seek thy firm support, according to their
   need.

I, loving freedom, and untried;   25
No sport of every random gust,
Yet being to myself a guide,
Too blindly have reposed my trust:
And oft, when in my heart was heard
Thy timely mandate, I deferred   30
The task, in smoother walks to stray;
But thee I now would serve more strictly, if
   I may.

Through no disturbance of my soul,
Or strong compunction in me wrought,
I supplicate for thy control;   35
But in the quietness of thought:

[3]Wordsworth's brother, Captain John Wordsworth, went down with his ship, an East Indiaman,
off the Bill of Portland on 5 February, 1805.

[1]Written in 1805; published in 1807. "This ode
is on the model of Gray's *Ode to Adversity*"
(Wordsworth, *Fenwick Note*).

Me this unchartered freedom tires;
I feel the weight of chance-desires:
My hopes no more must change their name,
I long for a repose that ever is the same.[2] 40

Stern Lawgiver! yet thou dost wear
The Godhead's most benignant grace;
Nor know we anything so fair
As is the smile upon thy face:
Flowers laugh before thee on their beds 45
And fragrance in thy footing treads;
Thou dost preserve the stars from wrong;
And the most ancient heavens, through Thee,
    are fresh and strong.

To humbler functions, awful Power!
I call thee: I myself commend 50
Unto thy guidance from this hour;
Oh, let my weakness have an end!
Give unto me, made lowly wise,
The spirit of self-sacrifice;
The confidence of reason give; 55
And in the light of truth thy Bondman let
    me live!

CHARACTER OF THE HAPPY WARRIOR[1]

Who is the happy Warrior? Who is he
That every man in arms should wish to be?
—It is the generous Spirit, who, when
    brought

---

[2]In the edition of 1807 a stanza here followed which was omitted in all later editions:

Yet not the less would I throughout
Still act according to the voice
Of my own wish; and feel past doubt
That my submissiveness was choice:
Not seeking in the school of pride
For "precepts over dignified,"
Denial and restraint I prize
No farther than they breed a second Will more
    wise.

[1]Written in December, 1805, or January, 1806; published in 1807. "The course of the great war with the French naturally fixed one's attention upon the military character, and, to the honor of our country, there were many illustrious instances of the qualities that constitute its highest excellence. Lord Nelson carried most of the virtues that the trials he was exposed to in his department of the service necessarily call forth and sustain, if they do not produce the contrary vices. But his public life was stained with one great crime, so that though many passages of these lines were suggested by what was generally known as excellent in his conduct, I have not been able to connect his name with the poem as I could wish, or even to

---

Among the tasks of real life, hath wrought
Upon the plan that pleased his boyish
    thought: 5
Whose high endeavors are an inward light
That makes the path before him always
    bright:
Who, with a natural instinct to discern
What knowledge can perform, is diligent to
    learn;
Abides by this resolve, and stops not there, 10
But makes his moral being his prime care;
Who, doomed to go in company with Pain,
And Fear, and Bloodshed, miserable train!
Turns his necessity to glorious gain;
In face of these doth exercise a power 15
Which is our human nature's highest dower;
Controls them and subdues, transmutes, be-
    reaves
Of their bad influence, and their good re-
    ceives:
By objects, which might force the soul to
    abate
Her feeling, rendered more compassionate;
Is placable—because occasions rise 21
So often that demand such sacrifice;
More skillful in self-knowledge, even more
    pure,
As tempted more; more able to endure,
As more exposed to suffering and distress;
Thence, also, more alive to tenderness. 26
—'Tis he whose law is reason; who depends
Upon that law as on the best of friends;
Whence, in a state where men are tempted
    still
To evil for a guard against worse ill, 30
And what in quality or act is best
Doth seldom on a right foundation rest,
He labors good on good to fix, and owes
To virtue every triumph that he knows:
—Who, if he rise to station of command, 35
Rises by open means; and there will stand
On honorable terms, or else retire,
And in himself possess his own desire;
Who comprehends his trust, and to the same

---

think of him with satisfaction in reference to the idea of what a warrior ought to be. . . . I will add that many elements of the character here portrayed were found in my brother John, who perished by shipwreck" (Wordsworth, *Fenwick Note*). But in 1807, forty years earlier, Wordsworth had connected Nelson's name with this poem, in the following note: "The above Verses were written soon after tidings had been received of the death of Lord Nelson, which event directed the Author's thoughts to the subject. His respect for the memory of his great fellow-countryman induces him to mention this; though he is well aware that the Verses must suffer from any connection in the reader's mind with a name so illustrious."

Keeps faithful with a singleness of aim;   40
And therefore does not stoop, nor lie in wait
For wealth, or honors, or for worldly state;
Whom they must follow; on whose head
    must fall,
Like showers of manna, if they come at all:
Whose powers shed round him in the com-
    mon strife,   45
Or mild concerns of ordinary life,
A constant influence, a peculiar grace;
But who, if he be called upon to face
Some awful moment to which Heaven has
    joined
Great issues, good or bad for human kind,   50
Is happy as a Lover; and attired
With sudden brightness, like a Man inspired;
And, through the heat of conflict, keeps the
    law
In calmness made, and sees what he foresaw;
Or if an unexpected call succeed,   55
Come when it will, is equal to the need:
—He who, though thus endued as with a
    sense
And faculty for storm and turbulence,
Is yet a Soul whose master-bias leans
To homefelt pleasures and to gentle scenes;
Sweet images! which, wheresoe'er he be,   61
Are at his heart; and such fidelity
It is his darling passion to approve;
More brave for this, that he hath much to
    love:—
'Tis, finally, the Man, who, lifted high,   65
Conspicuous object in a Nation's eye,
Or left unthought-of in obscurity,—
Who, with a toward or untoward lot,
Prosperous or adverse, to his wish or not—
Plays, in the many games of life, that one   70
Where what he most doth value must be
    won:
Whom neither shape of danger can dismay,
Nor thought of tender happiness betray;
Who, not content that former worth stand
    fast,
Looks forward, persevering to the last,   75
From well to better, daily self-surpassed:
Who, whether praise of him must walk the
    earth
For ever, and to noble deeds give birth,
Or he must fall, to sleep without his fame,
And leave a dead unprofitable name—   80
Finds comfort in himself and in his cause;
And, while the mortal mist is gathering,
    draws
His breath in confidence of Heaven's ap-
    plause:
This is the Happy Warrior; this is He
That every Man in arms should wish to be.   85

A COMPLAINT [1]

There is a change—and I am poor;
Your love hath been, not long ago,
A fountain at my fond heart's door,
Whose only business was to flow;
And flow it did; not taking heed   5
Of its own bounty, or my need.

What happy moments did I count!
Bless'd was I then all bliss above!
Now, for that consecrated fount
Of murmuring, sparkling, living love,   10
What have I? shall I dare to tell?
A comfortless and hidden well.

A well of love—it may be deep—
I trust it is,—and never dry:
What matter? if the waters sleep   15
In silence and obscurity.
—Such change, and at the very door
Of my fond heart, hath made me poor.

NUNS FRET NOT AT THEIR CONVENT'S NARROW ROOM [2]

Nuns fret not at their convent's narrow
    room;
And hermits are contented with their cells;
And students with their pensive citadels; [3]
Maids at the wheel, the weaver at his loom,
Sit blithe and happy; bees that soar for
    bloom,   5
High as the highest Peak of Furness-fells, [4]
Will murmur by the hour in foxglove bells:
In truth the prison, into which we doom
Ourselves, no prison is: and hence for me,   9
In sundry moods, 'twas pastime to be bound
Within the Sonnet's scanty plot of ground;
Pleased if some Souls (for such there needs
    must be)
Who have felt the weight of too much lib-
    erty,
Should find brief solace there, as I have
    found.

---

[1] Written in 1806; published in 1807. "Suggested by a change in the manner of a friend" (Words-worth, *Fenwick Note*). The friend was probably Coleridge.

[2] Published in 1807.

[3] Retreats secure for uninterrupted thought.

[4] The hill country east of the Duddon, south of the Brathay, and west of Windermere.

PERSONAL TALK[5]

I

I am not One who much or oft delight
To season my fireside with personal talk,—
Of friends, who live within an easy walk,
Or neighbors, daily, weekly, in my sight:
And, for my chance-acquaintance, ladies
    bright,   5
Sons, mothers, maidens withering on the
    stalk,
These all wear out of me, like Forms, with
    chalk
Painted on rich men's floors, for one feast-
    night.
Better than such discourse doth silence long,
Long, barren silence, square with my desire;
To sit without emotion, hope, or aim,   11
In the loved presence of my cottage-fire,
And listen to the flapping of the flame,
Or kettle whispering its faint undersong.

II

"Yet life," you say, "is life; we have seen
    and see,
And with a living pleasure we describe;
And fits of sprightly malice do but bribe
The languid mind into activity.
Sound sense, and love itself, and mirth and
    glee   5
Are fostered by the comment and the gibe."
Even be it so; yet still among your tribe,
Our daily world's true Worldlings, rank not
    me!
Children are bless'd, and powerful; their
    world lies
More justly balanced; partly at their feet,   10
And part far from them:—sweetest melodies
Are those that are by distance made more
    sweet;
Whose mind is but the mind of his own eyes,
He is a Slave; the meanest we can meet!

III

Wings have we,—and as far as we can go,
We may find pleasure: wilderness and wood,
Blank ocean and mere sky, support that
    mood
Which with the lofty sanctifies the low.
Dreams, books, are each a world; and books,
    we know,   5
Are a substantial world, both pure and good:
Round these, with tendrils strong as flesh
    and blood,

Our pastime and our happiness will grow.
There find I personal themes, a plenteous
    store,
Matter wherein right voluble I am,   10
To which I listen with a ready ear;
Two shall be named, pre-eminently dear,—
The gentle Lady married to the Moor;[6]
And heavenly Una with her milk-white
    Lamb.[7]

IV

Nor can I not believe but that hereby
Great gains are mine; for thus I live remote
From evil-speaking; rancor, never sought,
Comes to me not; malignant truth, or lie.
Hence have I genial seasons, hence have I   5
Smooth passions, smooth discourse, and joy-
    ous thought:
And thus from day to day my little boat
Rocks in its harbor, lodging peaceably.
Blessings be with them—and eternal praise,
Who gave us nobler loves, and nobler cares—
The Poets, who on earth have made us heirs
Of truth and pure delight by heavenly lays!
Oh! might my name be numbered among
    theirs,   13
Then gladly would I end my mortal days.

THE WORLD IS TOO MUCH WITH US[8]

The world is too much with us; late and
    soon,
Getting and spending, we lay waste our
    powers:
Little we see in Nature that is ours;
We have given our hearts away, a sordid
    boon!
The Sea that bares her bosom to the moon; 5
The winds that will be howling at all hours,
And are up-gathered now like sleeping
    flowers;
For this, for everything, we are out of tune;
It moves us not.—Great God I'd rather be
A Pagan suckled in a creed outworn;   10
So might I, standing on this pleasant lea,
Have glimpses that would make me less
    forlorn;
Have sight of Proteus rising from the sea;
Or hear old Triton blow his wreathéd horn.

[5]Published in 1807.

[6]Desdemona, in *Othello*.
[7]Spenser, *Faerie Queene*, Bk. I.
[8]Published in 1807.

ODE

Intimations of Immortality from Recollections of Early Childhood[1]

The Child is father of the Man;
And I could wish my days to be
Bound each to each by natural piety.

I

There was a time when meadow, grove, and
    stream,
The earth, and every common sight,
        To me did seem
        Appareled in celestial light,
The glory and the freshness of a dream.   5
It is not now as it hath been of yore;—
        Turn wheresoe'er I may,
        By night or day,
The things which I have seen I now can see
    no more.

II

        The Rainbow comes and goes,   10
        And lovely is the Rose,
        The Moon doth with delight
Look round her when the heavens are bare,
        Waters on a starry night
        Are beautiful and fair;   15
    The sunshine is a glorious birth;
    But yet I know, where'er I go,
That there hath passed away a glory from
    the earth.

III

Now, while the birds thus sing a joyous song,
    And while the young lambs bound   20
        As to the tabor's[2] sound,
To me alone there came a thought of grief:
A timely utterance gave that thought relief,
        And I again am strong:
The cataracts blow their trumpets from the
    steep;   25
Nor more shall grief of mine the season
    wrong;[3]
I hear the Echoes through the mountains
    throng,
The Winds come to me from the fields of
    sleep,
        And all the earth is gay;
        Land and sea   30

Give themselves up to jollity,
        And with the heart of May
Doth every Beast keep holiday;—
        Thou Child of Joy,
Shout round me, let me hear thy shouts,
    thou happy Shepherd-boy!   35

IV

Ye blessed Creatures, I have heard the call
    Ye to each other make; I see
The heavens laugh with you in your jubilee;
        My heart is at your festival,
        My head hath its coronal,[4]   40
The fullness of your bliss, I feel—I feel it all.
        Oh evil day! if I were sullen
        While Earth herself is adorning
            This sweet May-morning,
        And the Children are culling   45
            On every side,
        In a thousand valleys far and wide,
Fresh flowers; while the sun shines warm,
And the Babe leaps up on his Mother's
    arm:—
    I hear, I hear, with joy I hear!   50
    —But there's a Tree, of many, one,
A single Field which I have looked upon,
Both of them speak of something that is
    gone:
        The Pansy at my feet
        Doth the same tale repeat: 55
Whither is fled the visionary gleam?
Where is it now, the glory and the dream?

V

Our birth is but a sleep and a forgetting:
The Soul that rises with us, our life's Star,
        Hath had elsewhere its setting,   60
            And cometh from afar:
        Not in entire forgetfulness,
        And not in utter nakedness,
But trailing clouds of glory do we come
        From God, who is our home: 65
Heaven lies about us in our infancy!
Shades of the prison-house begin to close
        Upon the growing Boy,
But He beholds the light, and whence it
    flows,
        He sees it in his joy;   70
The Youth, who daily farther from the east
    Must travel, still is Nature's Priest,

---

[1]Written in the years from 1803, or possibly 1802, to 1806; published in 1807. Concerning the meaning of this poem see the introductory note to Wordsworth's poems, above, where part of the *Fenwick Note* to the *Ode* is quoted.

[2]Small drum.   [3]I. e., by lack of sympathy.

[4]Garland.

In the upper picture Fonthill Abbey is shown in its romantic surroundings. It was built as a dwelling place by the novelist William Beckford (see page 11). The tower was so flimsily constructed that it promptly fell down. The picture is reproduced from *Picturesque Views of Noblemen's and Gentlemen's Seats,* engraved and published in 1812 by Robert Havell and Son. (Courtesy of the Metropolitan Museum of Art.) The lower picture is a view of Abbotsford (engraved by James Johnstone of Edinburgh in 1833), the mansion built at ruinous expense by Sir Walter Scott (see page 40). (Courtesy of the New York Public Library.)

The upper picture is a view of Rydal Water and Grasmere, drawn by George Pickering (1794–1857), a Yorkshire artist, and engraved by W. J. Cooke (1797–1865). Wordsworth went to live in this part of the Lake Country in 1799, residing at Dove Cottage, Grasmere. In 1813 he moved to Rydal Mount. The lower picture shows Westminster Bridge as it appeared when Wordsworth wrote his sonnet "Composed upon Westminster Bridge" (page 197). This was engraved by J. Walker in 1797 from a drawing by J. M. W. Turner (1775–1851), the landscape painter. (Courtesy of the Metropolitan Museum of Art.)

And by the vision splendid
Is on his way attended;
At length the Man perceives it die away,   75
And fade into the light of common day.

VI

Earth fills her lap with pleasures of her own;
Yearnings she hath in her own natural kind,
And, even with something of a Mother's
    mind,
    And no unworthy aim,   80
    The homely Nurse doth all she can
To make her Foster-child, her Inmate Man,
    Forget the glories he hath known,
And that imperial palace whence he came.

VII

Behold the Child among his new-born blisses,
A six years' Darling of a pigmy size!   86
See, where 'mid work of his own hand he
    lies,
Fretted by sallies of his mother's kisses,
With light upon him from his father's eyes!
See, at his feet, some little plan or chart,   90
Some fragment from his dream of human
    life,
Shaped by himself with newly-learned art;
    A wedding or a festival,
    A mourning or a funeral;
        And this hath now his heart,   95
    And unto this he frames his song:
        Then will he fit his tongue
To dialogues of business, love, or strife;
    But it will not be long
    Ere this be thrown aside,   100
    And with new joy and pride ·
The little Actor cons another part;
Filling from time to time his "humorous
    stage"[5]
With all the Persons, down to palsied Age,
That Life brings with her in her equipage; 105
    As if his whole vocation
    Were endless imitation.

VIII

Thou, whose exterior semblance doth belie
    Thy Soul's immensity;
Thou best Philosopher, who yet dost keep 110
Thy heritage, thou Eye among the blind,
That, deaf and silent, read'st the eternal
    deep,
Haunted for ever by the eternal mind,—
    Mighty Prophet! Seer bless'd!

---

[5]Moody stage. The allusion in these lines is to
the speech beginning "All the world's a stage," in
As You Like It, II, vii, 139–166.

On whom those truths do rest,   115
Which we are toiling all our lives to find,
In darkness lost, the darkness of the grave;
Thou, over whom thy Immortality
Broods like the Day, a Master o'er a Slave,
A Presence which is not to be put by;   120
Thou little Child, yet glorious in the might
Of heaven-born freedom on thy being's
    height,
Why with such earnest pains dost thou pro-
    voke
The years to bring the inevitable yoke,
Thus blindly with thy blessedness at strife?
Full soon thy Soul shall have her earthly
    freight,   126
And custom lie upon thee with a weight,
Heavy as frost, and deep almost as life!

IX

O joy! that in our embers
Is something that doth live,   130
That nature yet remembers
What was so fugitive!
The thought of our past years in me doth
    breed
Perpetual benediction: not indeed
For that which is most worthy to be bless'd—
Delight and liberty, the simple creed   136
Of Childhood, whether busy or at rest,
With new-fledged hope still fluttering in his
    breast:—
        Not for these I raise
        The song of thanks and praise;   140
    But for those obstinate questionings
    Of sense and outward things,
    Fallings from us, vanishings;
    Blank misgivings of a Creature
Moving about in worlds not realized,   145
High instincts before which our mortal Na-
    ture
Did tremble like a guilty Thing surprised:
        But for those first affections,
        Those shadowy recollections,
    Which, be they what they may,   150
Are yet the fountain light of all our day,
Are yet a master light of all our seeing;
    Uphold us, cherish, and have power to
    make
Our noisy years seem moments in the being
Of the eternal Silence: truths that wake, 155
        To perish never;
Which neither listlessness, nor mad endeavor,
        Nor Man nor Boy,
Nor all that is at enmity with joy,
Can utterly abolish or destroy!   160
        Hence in a season of calm weather

Though inland far we be,
Our Souls have sight of that immortal sea
Which brought us hither,
Can in a moment travel thither,   165
And see the Children sport upon the shore,
And hear the mighty waters rolling ever-
more.

X

Then sing, ye Birds, sing, sing a joyous song!
And let the young Lambs bound
As to the tabor's sound!   170
We in thought will join your throng,
Ye that pipe and ye that play,
Ye that through your hearts to-day
Feel the gladness of the May!
What though the radiance which was once so
bright   175
Be now for ever taken from my sight,
Though nothing can bring back the hour
Of splendor in the grass, of glory in the
flower;
We will grieve not, rather find
Strength in what remains behind;   180
In the primal sympathy
Which having been must ever be;
In the soothing thoughts that spring
Out of human suffering;
In the faith that looks through[6] death,   185
In years that bring the philosophic mind.

XI

And O, ye Fountains, Meadows, Hills, and
Groves,
Forebode not any severing of our loves!
Yet in my heart of hearts I feel your might;
I only have relinquished one delight   190
To live beneath your more habitual sway.
I love the Brooks which down their channels
fret,
Even more than when I tripped lightly as
they;
The innocent brightness of a new-born Day
Is lovely yet;   195
The Clouds that gather round the setting sun
Do take a sober coloring from an eye
That hath kept watch o'er man's mortality;
Another race hath been, and other palms are
won.   199
Thanks to the human heart by which we live,
Thanks to its tenderness, its joys, and fears,
To me the meanest flower that blows can
give
Thoughts that do often lie too deep for tears.

---

[6]Beyond.

THOUGHT OF A BRITON ON THE SUBJUGATION OF SWITZERLAND[1]

Two Voices are there; one is of the sea,
One of the mountains; each a mighty Voice:
In both from age to age thou didst rejoice,
They were thy chosen music, Liberty!
There came a Tyrant, and with holy glee   5
Thou fought'st against him; but hast vainly
striven:
Thou from thy Alpine holds at length art
driven,
Where not a torrent murmurs heard by thee.
Of one deep bliss thine ear hath been bereft:
Then cleave, O cleave to that which still is
left;   10
For, high-souled Maid, what sorrow would it
be
That Mountain floods should thunder as be-
fore,
And Ocean bellow from his rocky shore,
And neither awful Voice be heard by thee!

YARROW VISITED SEPTEMBER, 1814[2]

And is this—Yarrow?—*This* the Stream
Of which my fancy cherished,
So faithfully, a waking dream?
An image that hath perished!
O that some Minstrel's harp were near,   5
To utter notes of gladness,
And chase this silence from the air,
That fills my heart with sadness!

Yet why?—a silvery current flows
With uncontrolled meanderings;   10
Nor have these eyes by greener hills
Been soothed, in all my wanderings.

---

[1]Written probably in 1807, and published in the same year. Switzerland was conquered by France in 1798. By the time this sonnet was written Napoleon had made himself master of Europe, and England remained his only unconquered opponent.

[2]Written in 1814; published in 1815. "I seldom read or think of this poem without regretting that my dear Sister was not of the party [which included the Ettrick Shepherd, James Hogg], as she would have had so much delight in recalling the time when, traveling together in Scotland, we declined going in search of this celebrated stream, not altogether, I will frankly confess, for the reasons assigned in the poem on the occasion" (Wordsworth, *Fenwick Note*). See *Yarrow Unvisited*, above.

And, through her depths, Saint Mary's Lake
Is visibly delighted;
For not a feature of those hills   15
Is in the mirror slighted.

A blue sky bends o'er Yarrow vale,
Save where that pearly whiteness
Is round the rising sun diffused,
A tender hazy brightness;   20
Mild dawn of promise! that excludes
All profitless dejection;
Though not unwilling here to admit
A pensive recollection.

Where was it that the famous Flower   25
Of Yarrow Vale[3] lay bleeding?
His bed perchance was yon smooth mound
On which the herd is feeding:
And haply from this crystal pool,
Now peaceful as the morning,   30
The Water-wraith ascended thrice
And gave his doleful warning.

Delicious is the Lay that sings
The haunts of happy Lovers,
The path that leads them to the grove,   35
The leafy grove that covers:
And Pity sanctifies the Verse
That paints, by strength of sorrow,
The unconquerable strength of love;
Bear witness, rueful Yarrow!   40

But thou, that didst appear so fair
To fond imagination,
Dost rival in the light of day
Her delicate creation:
Meek loveliness is round thee spread,   45
A softness still and holy;
The grace of forest charms decayed,
And pastoral melancholy.

That region left, the vale unfolds
Rich groves of lofty stature,   50
With Yarrow winding through the pomp
Of cultivated nature;
And, rising from those lofty groves,
Behold a Ruin hoary!
The shattered front of Newark's Towers,[4]   55
Renowned in Border story.

Fair scenes for childhood's opening bloom,
For sportive youth to stray in;
For manhood to enjoy his strength;
And age to wear away in!   60
Yon cottage seems a bower of bliss,
A covert for protection
Of tender thoughts, that nestle there—
The brood of chaste affection.

How sweet, on this autumnal day,   65
The wild-wood fruits to gather,
And on my True-love's forehead plant
A crest of blooming heather!
And what if I enwreathed my own!
'Twere no offense to reason;   70
The sober Hills thus deck their brows
To meet the wintry season.

I see—but not by sight alone,
Loved Yarrow, have I won thee;
A ray of fancy still survives—   75
Her sunshine plays upon thee!
Thy ever-youthful waters keep
A course of lively pleasure;
And gladsome notes my lips can breathe,
Accordant to the measure.   80

The vapors linger round the Heights,
They melt, and soon must vanish;
One hour is theirs, nor more is mine—
Sad thought which I would banish,
But that I know, where'er I go,   85
Thy genuine image, Yarrow!
Will dwell with me—to heighten joy,
And cheer my mind in sorrow.

LAODAMIA[1]

"With sacrifice before the rising morn
Vows have I made by fruitless hope inspired;
And from the infernal Gods, 'mid shades
   forlorn
Of night, my slaughtered Lord have I re-
   quired:[2]
Celestial pity I again implore;—   5
Restore him to my sight—great Jove, re-
   store!"

---

[3]The "real" Flower of Yarrow was Mary Scott
of Dryhope, but Wordsworth's allusion is to
Logan's ballad, *The Braes of Yarrow*, in which
the lady laments her dead lover as the "flower of
Yarrow," and in which

   Thrice did the water-wraith ascend,
   And gave a doleful groan through Yarrow.

[4]About three miles from Selkirk.

[1]Written in 1814; published in 1815. "The incident of the trees growing and withering [men-
tioned in the concluding lines of the poem] put
the subject into my thoughts, and I wrote with the
hope of giving it a loftier tone than, so far as I
know, has been given to it by any of the Ancients
who have treated of it. It cost me more trouble
than almost anything of equal length I have ever
written" (Wordsworth, *Fenwick Note*).

[2]Requested.

So speaking, and by fervent love endowed
With faith, the Suppliant heavenward lifts
    her hands;
While, like the sun emerging from a cloud,
Her countenance brightens—and her eye ex-
    pands;   10
Her bosom heaves and spreads, her stature
    grows;
And she expects the issue in repose.

O terror! what hath she perceived?—O joy!
What doth she look on?—whom doth she
    behold?
Her Hero slain upon the beach of Troy?   15
His vital presence? his corporeal mold?
It is—if sense deceive her not—'tis He!
And a God leads him, wingéd Mercury!

Mild Hermes spake—and touched her with
    his wand
That calms all fear; "Such grace hath
    crowned thy prayer,   20
Laodamía! that at Jove's command
Thy Husband walks the paths of upper air:
He comes to tarry with thee three hours'
    space;
Accept the gift, behold him face to face!"

Forth sprang the impassioned Queen her
    Lord to clasp;   25
Again that consummation she essayed;
But unsubstantial Form eludes her grasp
As often as that eager grasp was made.
The Phantom parts—but parts to re-unite,
And re-assume his place before her sight.   30

"Protesiláus, lo! thy guide is gone!
Confirm, I pray, the vision with thy voice:
This is our palace,—yonder is thy throne;
Speak, and the floor thou tread'st on will
    rejoice.
Not to appal me have the gods bestowed   35
This precious boon; and blessed a sad abode."

"Great Jove, Laodamía! doth not leave
His gifts imperfect:—Specter though I be,
I am not sent to scare thee or deceive;
But in reward of thy fidelity.   40
And something also did my worth obtain;
For fearless virtue bringeth boundless gain.

"Thou knowest, the Delphic oracle foretold
That the first Greek who touched the Trojan
    strand
Should die; but me the threat could not with-
    hold: 45
A generous cause a victim did demand:

And forth I leaped upon the sandy plain;
A self-devoted chief—by Hector slain."

"Supreme of Heroes—bravest, noblest, best!
Thy matchless courage I bewail no more,   50
Which then, when tens of thousands were
    depressed
By doubt, propelled thee to the fatal shore;
Thou found'st—and I forgive thee—here
    thou art—
A nobler counselor than my poor heart.   54

"But thou, though capable of sternest deed,
Wert kind as resolute, and good as brave;
And he, whose power restores thee, hath
    decreed
Thou shouldst elude the malice of the grave:
Redundant are thy locks, thy lips as fair   59
As when their breath enriched Thessalian air.

"No Specter greets me,—no vain Shadow
    this;
Come, blooming Hero, place thee by my side!
Give, on this well-known couch, one nuptial
    kiss
To me, this day, a second time thy bride!"
Jove frowned in heaven: the conscious Par-
    cae[3] threw   65
Upon those roseate lips a Stygian hue.

"This visage tells thee that my doom is past:
Nor should the change be mourned, even if
    the joys
Of sense were able to return as fast
And surely as they vanish.   Earth destroys
Those raptures duly—Erebus[4] disdains: 71
Calm pleasures there abide—majestic pains.

"Be taught, O faithful Consort, to control
Rebellious passion: for the Gods approve
The depth, and not the tumult, of the soul;
A fervent, not ungovernable, love.   76
Thy transports moderate; and meekly mourn
When I depart, for brief is my sojourn—"

"Ah, wherefore?—Did not Hercules by force
Wrest from the guardian Monster of the
    tomb
Alcestis, a reanimated corse,   81
Given back to dwell on earth in vernal
    bloom?[5]
Medea's spells dispersed the weight of years,
And Aeson stood a youth 'mid youthful
    peers.[6]

---

[3]Fates.   [4]Hades.
[5]This is the theme of the *Alcestis* of Euripides.
[6]See Ovid, *Metamorphoses*, VII, 159–293.   Aeson
was the father of Jason.

"The Gods to us are merciful—and they 85
Yet further may relent: for mightier far
Than strength of nerve and sinew, or the
    sway
Of magic potent over sun and star,
Is love, though oft to agony distressed,
And though his favorite seat be feeble
    woman's breast. 90

"But if thou goest, I follow—" "Peace!"
    he said,—
She looked upon him and was calmed and
    cheered;
The ghastly color from his lips had fled;
In his deportment, shape, and mien, appeared
Elysian beauty, melancholy grace, 95
Brought from a pensive though a happy place.

He spake of love, such love as Spirits feel
In worlds whose course is equable and pure;
No fears to beat away—no strife to heal—
The past unsighed for, and the future
    sure; 100
Spake of heroic arts in graver mood
Revived, with finer harmony pursued;

Of all that is most beauteous—imaged there
In happier beauty; more pellucid streams,
An ampler ether, a diviner air, 105
And fields invested with purpureal gleams;
Climes which the sun, who sheds the brightest
    day
Earth knows, is all unworthy to survey.

Yet there the Soul shall enter which hath
    earned
That privilege by virtue.—"Ill," said he, 110
"The end of man's existence I discerned,
Who from ignoble games and revelry
Could draw, when we had parted, vain de-
    light,
While tears were thy best pastime, day and
    night; 114

"And while my youthful peers before my
    eyes
(Each hero following his peculiar bent)
Prepared themselves for glorious enterprise
By martial sports,—or, seated in the tent,
Chieftains and kings in council were de-
    tained;
What time the fleet at Aulis[7] lay enchained.

[7]A port in Boeotia. There the Greek fleet was
held until Iphigenia was sacrificed to appease
Artemis.

"The wished-for wind was given:—I then
    revolved 121
The oracle, upon the silent sea;
And, if no worthier led the way, resolved
That, of a thousand vessels, mine should be
The foremost prow in pressing to the
    strand,—
Mine the first blood that tinged the Trojan
    sand. 126

"Yet bitter, oft-times bitter, was the pang
When of thy loss I thought, belovéd Wife!
On thee too fondly did my memory hang,
And on the joys we shared in mortal life,—
The paths which we had trod—these foun-
    tains, flowers, 131
My new-planned cities, and unfinished tow-
    ers.

"But should suspense permit the Foe to cry,
'Behold they tremble!—haughty their array,
Yet of their number no one dares to die?' 135
In soul I swept the indignity away:
Old frailties then recurred:—but lofty
    thought,
In act embodied, my deliverance wrought.

"And Thou, though strong in love, art all too
    weak
In reason, in self-government too slow; 140
I counsel thee by fortitude to seek
Our bless'd re-union in the shades below.
The invisible world with thee hath sym-
    pathized;
Be thy affections raised and solemnized. 144

"Learn, by a mortal yearning, to ascend—
Seeking a higher object. Love was given,
Encouraged, sanctioned, chiefly for that end;
For this the passion to excess was driven—
That self might be annulled: her bondage
    prove 149
The fetters of a dream, opposed to love."——

Aloud she shrieked! for Hermes re-appears!
Round the dear Shade she would have clung
    —'tis vain:
The hours are past—too brief had they been
    years;
And him no mortal effort can detain:
Swift, toward the realms that know not
    earthly day, 155
He through the portal takes his silent way,
And on the palace-floor a lifeless corse She
    lay.

Thus, all in vain exhorted and reproved,
She perished; and, as for a willful crime, 159
By the just Gods whom no weak pity moved,
Was doomed to wear out her appointed time,
Apart from happy Ghosts, that gather flowers
Of blissful quiet 'mid unfading bowers.

—Yet tears to human suffering are due;
And mortal hopes defeated and o'er-
    thrown 165
Are mourned by man, and not by man alone,
As fondly he believes.—Upon the side
Of Hellespont (such faith was entertained)
A knot of spiry trees for ages grew 169
From out the tomb of him for whom she
    died;
And ever, when such stature they had gained
That Ilium's walls were subject to their view,
The trees' tall summits withered at the sight,
A constant interchange of growth and blight!

AFTER-THOUGHT, APPENDED TO *THE RIVER DUDDON* [1]

I thought of Thee, my partner and my guide,
As being passed away.—Vain sympathies!
For, backward, Duddon, as I cast my eyes,
I see what was, and is, and will abide; 4
Still glides the Stream, and shall for ever
    glide,
The Form remains, the Function never dies,
While we, the brave, the mighty, and the
    wise,
We Men, who in our morn of youth defied
The elements, must vanish,—be it so!
Enough, if something from our hands have
    power 10
To live, and act, and serve the future hour,
And if, as toward the silent tomb we go,
Through love, through hope, and faith's
    transcendent dower,
We feel that we are greater than we know.

MUTABILITY [2]

From low to high doth dissolution climb,
And sink from high to low, along a scale

Of awful notes, whose concord shall not fail;
A musical but melancholy chime,
Which they can hear who meddle not with
    crime, 5
Nor avarice, nor over-anxious care.
Truth fails not; but her outward forms that
    bear
The longest date do melt like frosty rime,
That in the morning whitened hill and plain
And is no more; drop like the tower sublime
Of yesterday, which royally did wear 11
His crown of weeds, but could not even
    sustain
Some casual shout that broke the silent air,
Or the unimaginable touch of Time.

INSIDE OF KING'S COLLEGE CHAPEL, CAMBRIDGE [3]

Tax not the royal Saint with vain expense,
With ill-matched aims the Architect who
    planned—
Albeit laboring for a scanty band
Of white robed Scholars only—this immense
And glorious Work of fine intelligence! 5
Give all thou canst; high Heaven rejects the
    lore
Of nicely-calculated less or more;
So deemed the man who fashioned for the
    sense
These lofty pillars, spread that branching
    roof
Self-poised, and scooped into ten thousand
    cells, 10
Where light and shade repose, where music
    dwells
Lingering—and wandering on as loath to die;
Like thoughts whose very sweetness yieldeth
    proof
That they were born for immortality.

THE SAME

What awful pérspective! while from our
    sight
With gradual stealth the lateral windows
    hide
Their Portraitures, their stone-work glim-
    mers, dyed
In the soft checkerings of a sleepy light.

[1] Published in 1820. This is the final sonnet of a series entitled *The River Duddon*. This stream rises on the borders of Westmoreland, Cumberland, and Lancashire, and flows between the latter two counties into the Irish Sea.

[2] This and the three following sonnets are from *Ecclesiastical Sonnets,* published in 1822. Most of the sonnets in the series were written in 1821.

[3] The College was founded (in 1441) and the chapel built by Henry VI, who was never actually canonized but who was worshiped as a martyr and saint. The scholars for whom the Chapel was built were clerks of St. Nicholas.

Martyr, or King, or sainted Eremite, 5
Whoe'er ye be, that thus, yourselves unseen,
Imbue your prison-bars with solemn sheen,
Shine on, until ye fade with coming Night!—
But, from the arms of silence—list! O list!
The music bursteth into second life; 10
The notes luxuriate, every stone is kissed
By sound, or ghost of sound, in mazy strife;
Heart-thrilling strains, that cast, before the eye
Of the devout, a veil of ecstasy!

CONTINUED

They dreamt not of a perishable home
Who thus could build.   Be mine, in hours of fear
Or groveling thought, to seek a refuge here;
Or through the aisles of Westminster[4] to roam:
Where bubbles burst, and folly's dancing foam 5
Melts, if it cross the threshold; where the wreath
Of awe-struck wisdom droops: or let my path
Lead to that younger Pile,[5] whose sky-like dome
Hath typified by reach of daring art
Infinity's embrace; whose guardian crest, 10
The silent Cross, among the stars shall spread
As now, when She hath also seen her breast
Filled with mementos, satiate with its part
Of grateful England's overflowing Dead.

TO —— [6]

O dearer far than light and life are dear,
Full oft our human foresight I deplore;
Trembling, through my unworthiness, with fear
That friends, by death disjoined, may meet no more!

Misgivings, hard to vanquish or control, 5
Mix with the day, and cross the hour of rest;
While all the future, for thy purer soul,
With "sober certainties"[7] of love is bless'd.

That sigh of thine, not meant for human ear,
Tells that these words thy humbleness offend;
Yet bear me up—else faltering in the rear 11
Of a steep march: support me to the end.

Peace settles where the intellect is meek,
And Love is dutiful in thought and deed;
Through Thee communion with that Love
I seek: 15
The faith Heaven strengthens where *he* molds the Creed.

TO A SKYLARK [8]

Ethereal minstrel! pilgrim of the sky!
Dost thou despise the earth where cares abound?
Or, while the wings aspire, are heart and eye
Both with thy nest upon the dewy ground?
Thy nest which thou canst drop into at will, 5
Those quivering wings composed, that music still!

Leave to the nightingale her shady wood;
A privacy of glorious light is thine;
Whence thou dost pour upon the world a flood
Of harmony, with instinct more divine; 10
Type of the wise who soar, but never roam;
True to the kindred points of Heaven and Home!

SCORN NOT THE SONNET [9]

Scorn not the Sonnet; Critic, you have frowned,
Mindless of its just honors; with this key
Shakespeare unlocked his heart; the melody
Of this small lute gave ease to Petrarch's wound;[10]
A thousand times this pipe did Tasso[11] sound; 5
With it Camöens[12] soothed in exile's grief;
The Sonnet glittered a gay myrtle leaf
Amid the cypress with which Dante crowned
His visionary brow: a glow-worm lamp,
It cheered mild Spenser, called from Faery-land 10

---

[4]Westminster Abbey.

[5]St. Paul's Cathedral, built in the seventeenth century by Sir Christopher Wren.

[6]Written in 1824; published in 1827. Addressed to Mrs. Wordsworth.

[7]*Comus*, l. 264.

[8]Written in 1825; published in 1827.

[9]Published in 1827.

[10]Italian humanist and poet (1304–1374), who wrote a series of love sonnets to Laura.

[11]Italian poet (1544–1595).

[12]Portuguese poet (1524–1580).

To struggle through dark ways; and, when a
    damp
Fell round the path of Milton, in his hand
The Thing became a trumpet; whence he
    blew
Soul-animating strains—alas, too few!

YARROW REVISITED[1]

The gallant Youth, who may have gained,
    Or seeks, a "winsome Marrow,"[2]
Was but an Infant in the lap
    When first I looked on Yarrow;
Once more, by Newark's Castle-gate   5
    Long left without a warder,
I stood, looked, listened, and with Thee,
    Great Minstrel of the Border!

Grave thoughts ruled wide on that sweet day,
    Their dignity installing   10
In gentle bosoms, while sere leaves
    Were on the bough, or falling;
But breezes played, and sunshine gleamed—
    The forest to embolden;
Reddened the fiery hues, and shot   15
    Transparence through the golden.

For busy thoughts the Stream flowed on
    In foamy agitation;
And slept in many a crystal pool
    For quiet contemplation: 20
No public and no private care
    The freeborn mind enthralling,
We made a day of happy hours,
    Our happy days recalling.

Brisk Youth appeared, the Morn of youth,   25
    With freaks of graceful folly,—
Life's temperate Noon, her sober Eve,
    Her Night not melancholy;
Past, present, future, all appeared
    In harmony united,   30
Like guests that meet, and some from far,
    By cordial love invited.

[1]Written in 1831; published in 1835. "In the
autumn of 1831, my daughter and I set off from
Rydal to visit Sir Walter Scott before his departure for Italy. . . . How sadly changed did I
find him from the man I had seen so healthy, gay,
and hopeful, a few years before. . . . On Tuesday
morning Sir Walter Scott accompanied us and
most of the party to Newark Castle on the Yarrow.
When we alighted from the carriages he walked
pretty stoutly, and had great pleasure in revisiting
those his favorite haunts. Of that occasion the
verses *Yarrow Revisited* are a memorial" (Wordsworth, *Fenwick Note*).

[2]See *Yarrow Unvisited* and *Yarrow Visited*,
above.

And if, as Yarrow, through the woods
    And down the meadow ranging,
Did meet us with unaltered face,   35
    Though we were changed and changing;
If, *then,* some natural shadows spread
    Our inward prospect over,
The soul's deep valley was not slow
    Its brightness to recover.   40

Eternal blessings on the Muse,
    And her divine employment!
The blameless Muse, who trains her Sons
    For hope and calm enjoyment;
Albeit sickness, lingering yet,   45
    Has o'er their pillow brooded;
And Care waylays their steps—a Sprite
    Not easily eluded.

For thee, O SCOTT! compelled to change
    Green Eildon-hill and Cheviot   50
For warm Vesuvio's vine-clad slopes;
    And leave thy Tweed and Tiviot
For mild Sorento's breezy waves;
    May classic Fancy, linking
With native Fancy her fresh aid,   55
    Preserve thy heart from sinking!

Oh! while they minister to thee,
    Each vying with the other,
May Health return to mellow Age
    With Strength, her venturous brother;   60
And Tiber, and each brook and rill
    Renowned in song and story,
With unimagined beauty shine,
    Nor lose one ray of glory!

For Thou, upon a hundred streams,   65
    By tales of love and sorrow,
Of faithful love, undaunted truth,
    Hast shed the power of Yarrow;
And streams unknown, hills yet unseen,
    Wherever they invite Thee,   70
At parent Nature's grateful call,
    With gladness must requite Thee.

A gracious welcome shall be thine,
    Such looks of love and honor
As thy own Yarrow gave to me   75
    When first I gazed upon her;
Beheld what I had feared to see,
    Unwilling to surrender
Dreams treasured up from early days,
    The holy and the tender.   80

And what, for this frail world, were all
    That mortals do or suffer,
Did no responsive harp, no pen,
    Memorial tribute offer?

Yea, what were mighty Nature's self?   85
  Her features, could they win us,
Unhelped by the poetic voice
  That hourly speaks within us?

Nor deem that localized Romance
  Plays false with our affections;   90
Unsanctifies our tears—made sport
  For fanciful dejections:
Ah, no! the visions of the past
  Sustain the heart in feeling
Life as she is—our changeful Life,   95
  With friends and kindred dealing.

Bear witness, Ye, whose thoughts that day
  In Yarrow's groves were centered;
Who through the silent portal arch
  Of moldering Newark entered;   100
And clomb the winding stair that once
  Too timidly was mounted
By the "last Minstrel,"[3] (not the last!)
  Ere he his Tale recounted.

Flow on for ever, Yarrow Stream!   105
  Fulfill thy pensive duty,
Well pleased that future Bards should chant
  For simple hearts thy beauty;
To dream-light dear while yet unseen,
  Dear to the common sunshine,   110
And dearer still, as now I feel,
  To memory's shadowy moonshine!

THE TROSACHS[1]

There's not a nook within this solemn Pass,
But were an apt confessional for One
Taught by his summer spent, his autumn
      gone,
That Life is but a tale of morning grass
Withered at eve.   From scenes of art which
      chase   5
That thought away, turn, and with watchful
      eyes

[3]See Scott's *Lay of the Last Minstrel*, ll. 31-32.
[1]Written in 1831; published in 1835 (No. vi of
the series entitled *Yarrow Revisited*). The Tros-
achs is a wooded valley in Perthshire.

Feed it 'mid Nature's old felicities,
Rocks, rivers, and smooth lakes more clear
      than glass
Untouched, unbreathed upon.   Thrice happy
      quest,
If from a golden perch of aspen spray   10
(October's workmanship to rival May)
The pensive warbler of the ruddy breast
That moral sweeten by a heaven-taught lay,
Lulling the year, with all its cares, to rest!

MOST SWEET IT IS WITH UNUPLIFTED EYES[2]

Most sweet it is with unuplifted eyes
To pace the ground, if path be there or none,
While a fair region round the traveler lies
Which he forbears again to look upon;
Pleased rather with some soft ideal scene, 5
The work of Fancy, or some happy tone
Of meditation, slipping in between
The beauty coming and the beauty gone.
If Thought and Love desert us, from that
      day
Let us break off all commerce with the Muse:
With Thought and Love companions of our
      way,   11
Whate'er the senses take or may refuse,
The Mind's internal heaven shall shed her
      dews
Of inspiration on the humblest lay.

IF THIS GREAT WORLD OF JOY AND PAIN[3]

If this great world of joy and pain
  Revolve in one sure track;
If freedom, set, will rise again,
  And virtue, flown, come back;
Woe to the purblind crew who fill   5
  The heart with each day's care;
Nor gain, from past or future, skill
  To bear, and to forbear!

[2]Written in 1833; published in 1835.
[3]Written in 1833; published in 1835.

SAMUEL TAYLOR COLERIDGE

1772-1834

Coleridge, the son of a clergyman of the Church of England, was born at Ottery St. Mary, in Devonshire, on 21 October, 1772. His early childhood clearly foreshadowed his later development. "I read," he says, speaking of his boyhood, "every book that came in my way without distinction; and my father was fond of me, and used to take me on his knee, and hold long conversations with me. I remember, when eight years old, walking with him one winter's evening from a farmer's house, a mile from Ottery; and he then told me the names of the stars, and how Jupiter was a thousand times larger than our world, and that the other twinkling stars were suns that had worlds rolling round them; and when I came home he showed me how they rolled round. I heard him with a profound delight and admiration, but without the least mixture of wonder or incredulity. For from my early reading of fairy tales and about genii, and the like, my mind had been habituated to *the Vast;* and I never regarded my *senses* in any way as the *criteria* of my belief. I regulated all my creeds by my conceptions, not by my sight, even at that age." Coleridge, in other words, was born with a sense of immaterial reality, and this he never lost. From 1782 until 1790 he was at Christ's Hospital, where began his lifelong friendship with Charles Lamb. And as Lamb later sketched his schoolfellow we see still the same Coleridge who as a boy of eight regulated his creeds by his conceptions, not by his sight: "Come back into memory, like as thou wert in the dayspring of thy fancies, with hope like a fiery column before thee—the dark pillar not yet turned—Samuel Taylor Coleridge—Logician, Metaphysician, Bard!—How have I seen the casual passer through the Cloisters stand still, entranced with admiration . . . to hear thee unfold, in thy deep and sweet intonations, the mysteries of Jamblichus, or Plotinus (for even in those years thou waxedst not pale at such philosophic draughts), or reciting Homer in his Greek, or Pindar—while the walls of the old Gray Friars re-echoed to the accents of the

inspired charity-boy!". From Christ's Hospital Coleridge proceeded to Jesus College, Cambridge. There he became a radical in politics and displayed ardor for the French Revolution, continued to read everything he could lay hands on—including notably Hartley's *Observations,* which converted him to necessitarianism for a time—accumulated debts, and suffered disappointment in love. Then after two years of Cambridge he suddenly enlisted in a regiment of dragoons, but found inside of four months that a soldier's life was not for him. Consequently he went back to Cambridge, but began also to plan, with Robert Southey, then a student at Oxford, the foundation of an ideal community along the banks of the Susquehanna in America. The plan, of course, fell through, but it did result in the marriage of Coleridge and Southey to the two Miss Frickers, who were to have been fellow-members of the American Pantisocracy. Coleridge's marriage proved unhappy. His would have been a difficult nature in any household, and it was doubtless the more so in one ill-provided with money. In later years he lived apart from his wife and children.

In 1795 Coleridge met Wordsworth, and at subsequent meetings each made a profound impression on the other. In 1797 they were much together, and there opened for both of them the period when their greatest poetry was written. In his *Biographia Literaria* Coleridge has written of these early days of friendship, and, at the same time, in his discussion of Wordsworth's poetry and poetical theory, has left us the best example we have of his critical genius and methods. He has also told how Wordsworth and he coöperated in writing the *Lyrical Ballads.* As he says, Wordsworth's industry proved greater than his, so that the book appeared in 1798 with only four poems by Coleridge—though one of these was *The Ancient Mariner,* a contribution sufficiently notable for its quality to atone for many failures in industry. In the same year Coleridge and Wordsworth went to Germany, the former to study philosophy, and to find in German Transcendentalism the confirmation of much of his own earlier thought. Philosophy and religion had always been major interests with Coleridge, and after 1800 his attention was more and more absorbed into the effort to lay a solid philosophic foundation for Christian belief. In the early years of the new century, however, he became the victim of opium, which in the course of time so undermined his health and character that he grew unfit for prolonged and steady work. To the end of his life he never ceased forming vast projects, and he apparently continued to believe that he was at least making progress towards the completion of his great philosophic reconstitution of Christianity; but neither this—the most famous unwritten book in English literature, as it has been called—nor other books ever saw the light. Some things were written, the essays composing *The Friend* (1809–1810), many articles for newspapers, *The Statesman's Manual* (1816), the *Biographia Literaria* (1817), *Aids to Reflection* (1825), *On the Constitution of the Church and State* (1830), and *The Confessions of an Inquiring Spirit* (not published until 1840), but these were fragments only in comparison with what Coleridge thought he could do, and in comparison with what he might have accomplished had he been more happily constituted.

In 1816 Coleridge was taken into the household of Dr. James Gillman of Highgate, and there he continued to live until his death on 25 July, 1834. Under Gillman's care he was partially cured of the opium habit, and his last years were years of comparative peace. They were also years in which Coleridge was regarded as little less than an oracle by a group of younger disciples who gathered round him at Highgate to hear his copious floods of extraordinary talk.

The *Complete Poetical Works of Samuel Taylor Coleridge* have been edited by Ernest Hartley Coleridge (Oxford, 1912), and the *Biographia Literaria* by J. Shawcross (Oxford, 1907). No complete edition of Coleridge's prose has ever been published, but *Coleridge's Shakespearean Criticism* has been collected and elaborately edited by T. M. Raysor (2 vols., Cambridge, Mass., 1930), and the same editor has also published *Coleridge's Miscellaneous Criticism* (Cambridge, Mass., 1936). An admirable selection from the whole range of Coleridge's writings—poetry, political journalism, notes, literary criticism, theological and philosophical fragments, table talk, and letters—is to be found in *Coleridge: Select Poetry and Prose,* ed. Stephen Potter (London, 1933). Coleridge's letters have been edited by E. H. Coleridge (2 vols., Boston, 1895), and a further selection by E. L. Griggs (2 vols., London, 1932). Sir Edmund K. Chambers has written a succinct biography, *Samuel Taylor Coleridge* (Oxford, 1938); and there has recently appeared the first volume of a much fuller account, Lawrence Hanson's *Life of Samuel Taylor Coleridge: The Early Years* (London, 1938). Of the aged Coleridge a well-known description appears in Thomas Carlyle's *Life of John Sterling,* Part I, Chapter 8. The process by which Coleridge's imagination converted his reading into poetry has been thoroughly studied by John L. Lowes in *The Road to Xanadu* (Boston, 1927; enlarged ed. 1930); more recently I. A. Richards has expounded the poet's aesthetic theories in *Coleridge on Imagination* (London, 1934). Unfortunately, books about Coleridge tend to be difficult, and Mr. Richards's book is no exception. Two which are helpful and less crabbed are: *Coleridge as Philosopher,* by John H. Muirhead (London, 1930), and *Coleridge and S. T. C.,* by Stephen Potter (London, 1935).

LOVE [1]

All thoughts, all passions, all delights,
Whatever stirs this mortal frame,
All are but ministers of Love,
    And feed his sacred flame.

Oft in my waking dreams do I   5
Live o'er again that happy hour,
When midway on the mount I lay,
    Beside the ruined tower.

The moonshine, stealing o'er the scene
Had blended with the lights of eve;   10
And she was there, my hope, my joy,
    My own dear Genevieve!

She leant against the arméd man,
The statue of the arméd knight;
She stood and listened to my lay,   15
    Amid the lingering light.

Few sorrows hath she of her own.
My hope! my joy! my Genevieve!
She loves me best, whene'er I sing
    The songs that make her grieve.   20

[1] First printed in 1799; written in that or the preceding year.

I played a soft and doleful air,
I sang an old and moving story—
An old rude song, that suited well
    That ruin wild and hoary.

She listened with a flitting blush,   25
With downcast eyes and modest grace;
For well she knew, I could not choose
    But gaze upon her face.

I told her of the Knight that wore
Upon his shield a burning brand;   30
And that for ten long years he wooed
    The Lady of the Land.

I told her how he pined: and ah!
The deep, the low, the pleading tone
With which I sang another's love,   35
    Interpreted my own.

She listened with a flitting blush,
With downcast eyes, and modest grace;
And she forgave me, that I gazed
    Too fondly on her face!   40

But when I told the cruel scorn
That crazed that bold and lovely Knight,
And that he crossed the mountain-woods,
    Nor rested day nor night;

That sometimes from the savage den,   45
And sometimes from the darksome shade,
And sometimes starting up at once,
    In green and sunny glade,—

There came and looked him in the face
An angel beautiful and bright;   50
And that he knew it was a Fiend,
    This miserable Knight!

And that unknowing what he did,
He leaped amid a murderous band,
And saved from outrage worse than death 55
    The Lady of the Land!

And how she wept, and clasped his knees;
And how she tended him in vain—
And ever strove to expiate
    The scorn that crazed his brain;—   60

And that she nursed him in a cave;
And how his madness went away,
When on the yellow forest-leaves
    A dying man he lay;—

His dying words—but when I reached   65
That tenderest strain of all the ditty,
My faltering voice and pausing harp
    Disturbed her soul with pity!

All impulses of soul and sense
Had thrilled my guileless Genevieve;   70
The music and the doleful tale,
    The rich and balmy eve;

And hopes, and fears that kindle hope,
An undistinguishable throng,
And gentle wishes long subdued,   75
    Subdued and cherished long!

She wept with pity and delight,
She blushed with love, and virgin-shame;
And like the murmur of a dream,
    I heard her breathe my name.   80

Her bosom heaved—she stepped aside,
As conscious of my look she stepped—
Then suddenly, with timorous eye
    She fled to me and wept.

She half enclosed me with her arms,   85
She pressed me with a meek embrace;
And bending back her head, looked up,
    And gazed upon my face.

'Twas partly love, and partly fear,
And partly 'twas a bashful art,   90
That I might rather feel, than see,
    The swelling of her heart.

I calmed her fears, and she was calm,
And told her love with virgin pride;
And so I won my Genevieve,   95
    My bright and beauteous Bride.

KUBLA KHAN[1]

In Xanadu did Kubla Khan
    A stately pleasure-dome decree:
Where Alph, the sacred river, ran
Through caverns measureless to man
    Down to a sunless sea.   5
So twice five miles of fertile ground
With walls and towers were girdled round:

[1] Written in 1797 or 1798; published in 1816. In a preface (written in the third person) Coleridge explains its composition: "In consequence of a slight indisposition an anodyne had been prescribed, from the effects of which he fell asleep in his chair at the moment that he was reading the following sentence, or words of the same substance, in *Purchas's Pilgrimage:* 'Here the Khan Kubla commanded a palace to be built, and a stately garden thereunto. And thus ten miles of fertile ground were enclosed with a wall.' The author continued for about three hours in a profound sleep, at least of the external senses, during which time he has the most vivid confidence that he could not have composed less than from two to three hundred lines; . . . On awaking he appeared

And here were gardens bright with sinuous rills
Where blossomed many an incense-bearing tree,
And here were forests ancient as the hills, 10
Enfolding sunny spots of greenery.

But oh! that deep romantic chasm which slanted
Down the green hill athwart a cedarn cover!
A savage place! as holy and enchanted
As e'er beneath a waning moon was haunted
By woman wailing for her demon-lover! 16
And from this chasm, with ceaseless turmoil seething,
As if this earth in fast thick pants were breathing,
A mighty fountain momently was forced,
Amid whose swift half-intermitted burst 20
Huge fragments vaulted like rebounding hail,
Or chaffy grain beneath the thresher's flail:
And 'mid these dancing rocks at once and ever
It flung up momently the sacred river.

Five miles meandering with a mazy motion 25
Through wood and dale the sacred river ran,
Then reached the caverns measureless to man,
And sank in tumult to a lifeless ocean:
And 'mid this tumult Kubla heard from far
Ancestral voices prophesying war! 30

The shadow of the dome of pleasure
Floated midway on the waves;
Where was heard the mingled measure
From the fountain and the caves.
It was a miracle of rare device, 35
A sunny pleasure-dome with caves of ice!

A damsel with a dulcimer
In a vision once I saw:
It was an Abyssinian maid,
And on her dulcimer she played, 40
Singing of Mount Abora.[2]
Could I revive within me
Her symphony and song,
To such a deep delight 'twould win me,
That with music loud and long, 45
I would build that dome in air,
That sunny dome! those caves of ice!
And all who heard should see them there,
And all should cry, Beware! Beware!
His flashing eyes, his floating hair! 50
Weave a circle round him thrice,
And close your eyes with holy dread,
For he on honey-dew hath fed,
And drunk the milk of Paradise.

---

to himself to have a distinct recollection of the whole, and, taking his pen, ink, and paper, instantly and eagerly wrote down the lines that are here preserved. At this moment he was unfortunately called out by a person on business . . . and detained by him above an hour, and on his return to his room found, to his no small surprise and mortification, that though he still retained some vague and dim recollection of the general purport of the vision, yet, with the exception of some eight or ten scattered lines and images, all the rest had passed away." Kubla Khan lived in the thirteenth century and was the founder of the Mongol dynasty in China. Khan, sometimes written Cham, is equivalent to "King." Xanadu (the form is Zaindu in *Purchas*) is a region in Tartary.

[2]Professor Lane Cooper has suggested that this is a variant of Amara, the name of a mountain in Abyssinia on which, according to tradition, there was a terrestrial paradise like that of the Khan Kubla.

THE RIME OF THE ANCIENT MARINER[1]
In Seven Parts

Facile credo, plures esse Naturas invisibiles quam visibiles in revum universitate. Sed horum omnium familiam quis nobis enarrabit, et gradus et cognationes et discrimina et singulorum munera? Quid agunt? quae loca habitant? Harum rerum notitiam semper ambivit ingenium humanum, nunquam attigit. Juvat, interea, non diffiteor, quandoque in animo, tanquam in tabula, majoris et melioris mundi imaginem contemplari: ne mens assuefacta hodiernae vitae minutiis se contrahat nimis et tota subsidat in pusillas cogitationes. Sede veritati interea invigilandum est, modusque servandus, ut certa ab incertis, diem a nocte, distinguamus.

T. BURNET: ARCHAEOL. PHIL., p. 68.

---

[1]Written 1797–1798; published 1798. Many changes were made for the 2nd edition of the *Lyrical Ballads,* 1800. The marginal gloss was added in 1815–1816, and was first published in *Sibylline Leaves,* 1817, when, also, the poem first appeared under Coleridge's name. In 1843 Wordsworth said that "much the greatest part of the story was Mr. Coleridge's invention," but that he had made certain suggestions, including the killing of the albatross as the crime which was wanted, to bring upon the Mariner the spectral persecution. Then and previously Wordsworth also said that he had contributed a few lines to the poem; and he told Alexander Dyce, in 1835 or 1836, that he had written one complete stanza (ll. 13–16).

The Latin motto from Thomas Burnet's *Arch-*

ARGUMENT

How a Ship having passed the Line[2] was driven by storms to the cold Country towards the South Pole; and how from thence she made her course to the tropical Latitude of the Great Pacific Ocean; and of the strange things that befell; and in what manner the Ancyent Marinere came back to his own Country.

PART I

It is an ancient Mariner,   An ancient
And he stoppeth one of three.   Mariner meet-
"By thy long gray beard and   eth three Gal-
    glittering eye,   lants bidden to
Now wherefore stopp'st thou   a wedding-
   me?   feast, and de-
   taineth one.

"The Bridegroom's doors are opened wide, 5
And I am next of kin;
The guests are met, the feast is set:
May'st hear the merry din."

He holds him with his skinny hand,
"There was a ship," quoth he.   10
"Hold off! unhand me, gray-beard loon!"
Eftsoons[3] his hand dropped he.

He holds him with his glittering   The Wedding-
   eye—   Guest is spell-
The Wedding-Guest stood still,   bound by the
And listens like a three years'   eye of the old
   child: seafaring man,
The Mariner hath his will.   and constrained to
   hear his tale.

The Wedding-Guest sat on a stone: 17
He cannot choose but hear;
And thus spake on that ancient man,
The bright-eyed Mariner.   20

------

aeologiae Philosophicae has been translated by Herbert Bates: "I find it easy to believe that in the universe the visible beings are outnumbered by the invisible. But who shall tell us the nature common to these, their rank, their kindreds, the signs by which they are distinguished, the gifts in which they excel? What is their task? Where is their abode? Close to full knowledge of these wonders, the mind of man has ever circled, nor ever attained the center. Meanwhile, I trust, it will give us profit to contemplate in the mind, as in a picture, the image of this other world, greater than ours and better, lest our minds, becoming wont to the petty details of daily life, be narrowed overmuch, and sink to paltry thoughts. We must, meanwhile, keep watch, with vigilance, toward truth, preserving temperance of judgment, that we distinguish things certain from things uncertain, day from night"

[2]Equator.   [3]At once.

"The ship was cheered, the harbor cleared,
Merrily did we drop
Below the kirk, below the hill,
Below the lighthouse top.   24

"The sun came up upon the left,   The Mariner
Out of the sea came he!   tells how the
And he shone bright, and on the   ship sailed
   right   southward with
Went down into the sea.   a good wind
   and fair
   weather till it
   reached the Line.

"Higher and higher every day,
Till over the mast at noon—"   30
The Wedding-Guest here beat his breast,
For he heard the loud bassoon.

The bride hath paced into the   The Wedding-
   hall,   Guest heareth
Red as a rose is she;   the bridal
Nodding their heads before her   music; but the
   goes   Mariner contin-
The merry minstrelsy.   ueth his tale.
     36

The Wedding-Guest he beat his breast,
Yet he cannot choose but hear;
And thus spake on that ancient man,
The bright-eyed Mariner.   40

"And now the Storm-blast came,   The ship
   and he   driven by a
Was tyrannous and strong: storm toward
He struck with his o'ertaking wings,   the south pole.
And chased us south along.

"With sloping masts and dipping prow,   45
As who pursued with yell and blow
Still treads the shadow of his foe,
And forward bends his head,
The ship drove fast, loud roared the blast,
And southward aye we fled.   50

"And now there came both mist and snow,
And it grew wondrous cold:
And ice, mast-high, came floating by,
As green as emerald.   54

"And through the drifts the   The land of ice,
   snowy clifts   and of fearful
Did send a dismal sheen: sounds where
Nor shapes of men nor beasts   no living thing
   we ken—   was to be seen.
The ice was all between.

"The ice was here, the ice was there,
The ice was all around: 60
It cracked and growled, and roared and
   howled,
Like noises in a swound![4]

[4]Swoon.

"At length did cross an Alba-
    tross,   *Till a great*
Thorough the fog it came;   *sea-bird,*
                            called the
As if it had been a Christian   *Albatross,*
    soul,   65   *came through*
                         the snow-fog,
We hailed it in God's name.   *and was re-*
                         ceived with
                         great joy and
                         hospitality.

"It ate the food it ne'er had eat,
And round and round it flew.
The ice did split with a thunder-fit;
The helmsman steered us through!   70

"And a good south wind sprung   *And lo! the*
    up behind;   *Albatross*
The Albatross did follow,   *proveth a bird*
                         of good omen,
And every day, for food or play,   *and followeth*
                         the ship as it
Came to the mariner's hollo!   *returned*
                         northward

"In mist or cloud, on mast or   *through fog*
    shroud,   75   *and floating ice.*
It perched for vespers nine;
Whiles all the night, through fog-smoke
    white,
Glimmered the white moon-shine."

"God save thee, ancient Mariner!   *The ancient*
From the fiends, that plague thee   *Mariner*
    thus!—   *inhospitably*
                         killeth the
Why look'st thou so?"—"With   *pious bird of*
    my cross-bow   81   *good omen.*
I shot the Albatross!"

PART II

"The Sun now rose upon the right:
Out of the sea came he,
Still hid in mist, and on the left   85
Went down into the sea.

"And the good south wind still blew behind,
But no sweet bird did follow,
Nor any day for food or play
Came to the mariner's hollo!   90

"And I had done a hellish thing,   *His shipmates*
And it would work 'em woe: *cry out against*
                         the ancient
For all averred, I had killed the   *Mariner, for*
    bird   *killing the bird*
That made the breeze to blow.   *of good luck.*
Ah wretch! said they, the bird to slay,   95
That made the breeze to blow!

"Nor dim nor red, like God's   *But when the*
    own head,   *fog cleared off*
The glorious Sun uprist: *they justify*
                         the same, and
Then all averred, I had killed   *thus make*
    the bird   *themselves ac-*
That brought the fog and mist.   *complices in the*
'Twas right, said they, such birds to slay,   *crime.*
That bring the fog and mist.   102

"The fair breeze blew, the white   *The fair breeze*
    foam flew,   *continues; the*
The furrow followed free;   *ship enters the*
                         Pacific Ocean,
We were the first that ever burst   *and sails north-*
                         ward, even till
Into that silent sea.   *it reaches the*
                         Line.

"Down dropped the breeze, the   *The ship hath*
    sails dropped down,   *been suddenly*
'Twas sad as sad could be;   *becalmed.*
And we did speak only to break
The silence of the sea!   110

"All in a hot and copper sky,
The bloody Sun, at noon,
Right up above the mast did stand,
No bigger than the Moon.

"Day after day, day after day,   115
We stuck, nor breath nor motion;
As idle as a painted ship
Upon a painted ocean.

"Water, water, everywhere,   *And the Alba-*
And all the boards did shrink;   *tross begins to*
                         be avenged.
Water, water, everywhere,   121
Nor any drop to drink.

"The very deep did rot: O Christ!
That ever this should be!
Yea, slimy things did crawl with legs   125
Upon the slimy sea.

"About, about, in reel and rout
The death-fires danced at night;
The water, like a witch's oils,
Burned green, and blue and white.   130

"And some in dreams assured   *A Spirit had*
    were   *followed them;*
Of the Spirit that plagued us so;   *one of the in-*
                         visible inhab-
Nine fathom deep he had fol-   *itants of this*
    lowed us   *planet, neither*
                         departed souls
From the land of mist and snow.   *nor angels; con-*
                         cerning whom
                         the learned Jew,
                         Josephus, and
the Platonic Constantinopolitan, Michael Psellus, may be con-
sulted. They are very numerous, and there is no climate or ele-
ment without one or more.

"And every tongue, through utter drought,
Was withered at the root;   136
We could not speak, no more   *The shipmates,*
    than if   *in their sore*
                         distress, would
We had been choked with soot.   *fain throw the*
                         whole guilt on
                         the ancient
"Ah! well-a-day! what evil looks   *Mariner: in*
Had I from old and young!   140   *sign whereof*
                         they hang the
Instead of the cross, the Alba-   *dead sea-bird*
    tross   *round his neck.*
About my neck was hung.

PART III

"There passed a weary time. Each throat
Was parched, and glazed each eye.
A weary time! a weary time!   145
How glazed each weary eye,
When looking westward, I be-   *The ancient*
held   *Mariner be-*
                                holdeth a sign
A something in the sky.   *in the element*
                                afar off.

"At first it seemed a little speck,
And then it seemed a mist;   150
It moved and moved, and took at last
A certain shape, I wist.⁵

"A speck, a mist, a shape, I wist!
And still it neared and neared:
As if it dodged a water-sprite,   155
It plunged and tacked and veered.

"With throats unslaked, with   *At its nearer*
   black lips baked,   *approach, it*
                                seemeth him to
We could nor laugh nor wail;   *be a ship; and*
                                at a dear ran-
Through utter drought all dumb *som he freeth*
   we stood!   *his speech from*
                                the bonds of
I bit my arm, I sucked the blood, *thirst.*
And cried, A sail! a sail!

"With throats unslaked, with black lips
   baked,   162
Agape they heard me call:
Gramercy! they for joy did grin,⁶
And all at once their breath   *A flash of joy;*
   drew in,   165
As they were drinking all.

"See! see! (I cried) she tacks   *And horror fol-*
   no more!   *lows. For can*
                                 it be a ship that
Hither to work us weal;   *comes onward*
                                 without wind or
Without a breeze, without a   *tide?*
   tide,
She steadies with upright keel!   170

"The western wave was all aflame,
The day was well nigh done!
Almost upon the western wave
Rested the broad bright Sun;
When that strange shape drove suddenly 175
Betwixt us and the Sun.

⁵Knew.

⁶"I took the thought of *grinning for joy* . . .
from my companion's remark to me, when we had
climbed to the top of Plinlimmon, and were nearly
dead with thirst. We could not speak from the
constriction, till we found a little puddle under a
stone. He said to me, 'You grinned like an idiot!'
He had done the same" (Coleridge, *Table Talk*, 31
May, 1830).

"And straight the Sun was   *It seemeth him*
   flecked with bars,   *but the skele-*
                              ton of a ship.
(Heaven's Mother send us
   grace!)
As if through a dungeon-grate he peered
With broad and burning face.   180

"Alas! (thought I, and my heart beat loud)
How fast she nears and nears! *And its ribs are*
                               seen as bars on
Are those *her* sails that glance *the face of the*
   in the Sun,   *setting Sun.*
Like restless gossameres?

"Are those *her* ribs through which the Sun
Did peer, as through a grate?   186
And is that Woman all her   *The Specter-*
   crew?   *Woman and her*
                               Death-mate, and
Is that a Death? and are there *no other on*
   two?   *board the*
                               skeleton-ship.
Is death that woman's mate?

"*Her* lips were red, *her* looks were free, 190
Her locks were yellow as gold: *Like vessel, like*
                                crew!
Her skin was as white as lep-
   rosy,
The Nightmare Life-in-Death was she,
Who thicks man's blood with cold.   194

"The naked hulk alongside   *Death and*
   came,   *Life-in-Death*
                                have diced for
And the twain were casting dice; *the ship's*
                                 crew, and she
'The game is done! I've won,   *(the latter)*
   I've won!'   *winneth the*
                                 ancient Mariner.
Quoth she, and whistles thrice.

"The Sun's rim dips; the stars *No twilight*
   rush out: *within the*
                                courts of the
At one stride comes the dark;   *Sun.*
With far-heard whisper, o'er the sea,   201
Off shot the specter-bark.

"We listened and looked side-   *At the rising of*
   ways up!   *the Moon,*
Fear at my heart, as at a cup,
My life-blood seemed to sip!   205
The stars were dim, and thick the night,
The steersman's face by his lamp gleamed
   white;
From the sails the dew did drip—
Till clomb above the eastern bar
The hornèd Moon with one bright star   210
Within the nether tip.

"One after one, by the star-   *One after an-*
   dogged Moon,   *other,*
Too quick for groan or sigh,
Each turned his face with a ghastly pang,
And cursed me with his eye.   215

"Four times fifty living men
(And I heard nor sigh nor
   groan),
With heavy thump, a lifeless lump,
They dropped down one by one. 219

His shipmates
drop down dead.

"The souls did from their bodies
   fly—
They fled to bliss or woe!
And every soul, it passed me by,
Like the whizz of my cross-bow!"

But Life-in-
Death begins
her work on
the ancient
Mariner.

PART IV

"I fear thee, ancient Mariner!
I fear thy skinny hand!
And thou art long, and lank, and
   brown,
As is the ribbed sea-sand.[7] 227

The Wedding-
Guest feareth
that a Spirit
is talking to
him.

"I fear thee and thy glittering eye,
And thy skinny hand, so brown."—
"Fear not, fear not, thou Wed-
   ding-Guest!
This body dropped not down.

But the ancient
Mariner assureth
him of his bod-
ily life, and pro-
ceedeth to re-
late his horrible
penance.

"Alone, alone, all, all alone,
Alone on a wide wide sea!
And never a saint took pity on
My soul in agony. 235

"The many men, so beautiful!
And they all dead did lie:
And a thousand thousand slimy
   things
Lived on; and so did I. 239

He despiseth the
creatures of the
calm,

"I looked upon the rotting sea,
And drew my eyes away;
I looked upon the rotting deck,
And there the dead men lay.

And envieth
that *they*
should live, and
so many lie
dead.

"I looked to heaven, and tried to pray;
But or ever a prayer had gushed, 245
A wicked whisper came, and made
My heart as dry as dust.

"I closed my lids, and kept them close,
And the balls like pulses beat;
For the sky and the sea, and the sea and the
   sky, 250
Lay like a load on my weary eye,
And the dead were at my feet.

[7]The last two lines of this stanza were contributed
by Wordsworth.

"The cold sweat melted from
   their limbs,
Nor rot nor reek did they:
The look with which they looked on me 255
Had never passed away.

But the curse
liveth for him
in the eye of
the dead men.

"An orphan's curse would drag to hell
A spirit from on high;
But oh! more horrible than that
Is the curse in a dead man's eye! 260
Seven days, seven nights, I saw that curse,
And yet I could not die.

"The moving Moon went up the
   sky,
And nowhere did abide:
Softly she was going up, 265
And a star or two beside—

In his loneli-
ness and fixed-
ness he
yearneth
towards the
journeying
Moon, and
the stars that
still sojourn,
yet still move
onward; and
everywhere
the blue sky
belongs to
them, and is
their ap-
pointed rest,
and their
native country
and their own
natural homes,
which they enter

"Her beams bemocked the sul-
   try main,
Like April hoar-frost spread;
But where the ship's huge
   shadow lay, 269
The charméd water burned al-
   way
A still and awful red.

unannounced, as lords that are certainly expected, and yet there
is a silent joy at their arrival.

"Beyond the shadow of the ship,
I watched the water-snakes:
They moved in tracks of shining
   white,
And when they reared, the elfish
   light 275
Fell off in hoary flakes.

By the light of
the Moon he
beholdeth God's
creatures of the
great calm.

"Within the shadow of the ship
I watched their rich attire:
Blue, glossy green, and velvet black,
They coiled and swam; and every track 280
Was a flash of golden fire.

"O happy living things! no
   tongue
Their beauty might declare:
A spring of love gushed from my heart, 284
And I blessed them unaware;
Sure my kind saint took pity on
   me,
And I blessed them unaware.

Their beauty
and their happi-
ness.

He blesseth
them in his
heart.
The spell be-
gins to break.

"The selfsame moment I could pray;
And from my neck so free
The Albatross fell off, and sank 290
Like lead into the sea."

PART V

"Oh sleep! it is a gentle thing,
Beloved from pole to pole!
To Mary Queen the praise be given!
She sent the gentle sleep from Heaven,   295
That slid into my soul.

"The silly[8] buckets on the deck,   *By grace of the*
That had so long remained,   *holy Mother,*
I dreamt that they were filled   *the ancient*
  with dew;   *Mariner is re-*
And when I awoke, it rained.   *freshed with rain.*

"My lips were wet, my throat was cold,   301
My garments all were dank;
Sure I had drunken in my dreams,
And still my body drank.

"I moved, and could not feel my limbs: 305
I was so light—almost
I thought that I had died in sleep,
And was a blessed ghost.

"And soon I heard a roaring   *He heareth*
  wind: *sounds and*
It did not come anear;   310   *seeth strange*
But with its sound it shook the   *sights and*
  sails,   *commotions in*
That were so thin and sere.   *the sky and the element.*

"The upper air burst into life!
And a hundred fire-flags sheen,[9]
To and fro they were hurried about!   315
And to and fro, and in and out,
The wan stars danced between.

"And the coming wind did roar more loud,
And the sails did sigh like sedge;[10]
And the rain poured down from one black
  cloud;   320
The Moon was at its edge.

"The thick black cloud was cleft, and still
The Moon was at its side:
Like waters shot from some high crag,
The lightning fell with never a jag,   325
A river steep and wide.

"The loud wind never reached   *The bodies of*
  the ship,   *the ship's crew*
Yet now the ship moved on!   *are inspired, and*
Beneath the lightning and the   *the ship moves*
  Moon   *on;*
The dead men gave a groan.   330

---

[8]What meaning Coleridge intended the word to
have here it is not easy to say. The buckets were
not fulfilling the purpose for which they were made:
perhaps he meant that this made them look "silly."
  [9]Bright.   [10]Swamp-grass.

"They groaned, they stirred, they all uprose,
Nor spake, nor moved their eyes;
It had been strange, even in a dream,
To have seen those dead men rise.

"The helmsman steered, the ship moved on;
Yet never a breeze up blew;   336
The mariners all 'gan work the ropes,
Where they were wont to do;
They raised their limbs like lifeless tools—
We were a ghastly crew.   340

"The body of my brother's son
Stood by me, knee to knee:
The body and I pulled at one rope,
But he said nought to me."   344

"I fear thee, ancient Mariner!"   *But not by the*
"Be calm, thou Wedding-Guest!   *souls of the*
'Twas not those souls that fled in   *men, nor by*
  pain,   *demons of earth*
Which to their corses came   *or middle air,*
  again,   *but by a*
But a troop of spirits blest: *blessed troop of*
  angelic spirits,
  sent down by
  the invocation
  of the guardian saint.

"For when it dawned—they dropped their
  arms,   350
And clustered round the mast;
Sweet sounds rose slowly through their
  mouths,
And from their bodies passed.

"Around, around, flew each sweet sound,
Then darted to the Sun;   355
Slowly the sounds come back again,
Now mixed, now one by one.

"Sometimes a-dropping from the sky
I heard the sky-lark sing;
Sometimes all little birds that are,   360
How they seemed to fill the sea and air
With their sweet jargoning!

"And now 'twas like all instruments,
Now like a lonely flute;
And now it is an angel's song,   365
That makes the heavens be mute.

"It ceased; yet still the sails made on
A pleasant noise till noon,
A noise like of a hidden brook
In the leafy month of June,   370
That to the sleeping woods all night
Singeth a quiet tune.

"Till noon we quietly sailed on,
Yet never a breeze did breathe:
Slowly and smoothly went the ship,   375
Moved onward from beneath.

"Under the keel nine fathom deep,
From the land of mist and snow,
The spirit slid; and it was he
That made the ship to go.   380
The sails at noon left off their tune,
And the ship stood still also.

The lonesome Spirit from the south-pole carries on the ship as far as the Line, in obedience to the angelic troop, but still requireth vengeance.

"The Sun, right up above the mast,
Had fixed her to the ocean;
But in a minute she 'gan stir,   385
With a short uneasy motion—
Backwards and forwards half her length,
With a short uneasy motion.

"Then like a pawing horse let go,
She made a sudden bound: 390
It flung the blood into my head,
And I fell down in a swound.

"How long in that same fit I lay,
I have not to declare,   394
But ere my living life returned,
I heard, and in my soul discerned
Two voices in the air.

The Polar Spirit's fellow-demons, the invisible inhabitants of the element, take part in his wrong; and two of them relate one to the other, that penance long

and heavy for the ancient Mariner hath been *accorded to the* Polar Spirit, who returneth southward.

"'Is it he?' quoth one, 'is this the man?
By Him who died on cross,
With his cruel bow he laid full low   400
The harmless Albatross.

"'The spirit who bideth by himself
In the land of mist and snow,
He loved the bird that loved the man
Who shot him with his bow.'   405

"The other was a softer voice,
As soft as honey-dew;
Quoth he, 'The man hath penance done,
And penance more will do.'

PART VI

First Voice

"'But tell me, tell me! speak again   410
Thy soft response renewing—
What makes that ship drive on so fast?
What is the ocean doing?'

Second Voice

"'Still as a slave before his lord,
The ocean hath no blast;   415
His great bright eye most silently
Up to the Moon is cast—

"'If he may know which way to go;
For she guides him, smooth or grim.
See, brother, see! how graciously   420
She looketh down on him.'

First Voice

"'But why drives on that ship so fast,
Without or wave or wind?'

The Mariner hath been cast into a trance; for the angelic power causeth the vessel to drive northward faster than human life could endure.

Second Voice

"'The air is cut away before,
And closes from behind.'

"'Fly, brother, fly! more high, more high!
Or we shall be belated: 427
For slow and slow that ship will go,
When the Mariner's trance is abated.'

"I woke, and we were sailing on
As in a gentle weather:
'Twas night, calm night, the moon was high;
The dead men stood together.

The supernatural motion is retarded; the Mariner awakes, and his penance begins anew.

"All stood together on the deck,
For a charnel-dungeon fitter: 435
All fixed on me their stony eyes,
That in the Moon did glitter.

"The pang, the curse, with which they died,
Had never passed away:
I could not draw my eyes from theirs,   440
Nor turn them up to pray.

"And now this spell was snapped: once more
I viewed the ocean green,
And looked far forth, yet little saw
Of what had else been seen—   445

The curse is finally expiated.

"Like one, that on a lonesome road
Doth walk in fear and dread,
And having once turned round, walks on,
And turns no more his head;
Because he knows, a frightful fiend   450
Doth close behind him tread.

"But soon there breathed a wind on me,
Nor sound nor motion made:
Its path was not upon the sea,
In ripple or in shade.   455

"It raised my hair, it fanned my cheek
Like a meadow-gale of spring—
It mingled strangely with my fears,
Yet it felt like a welcoming.

"Swiftly, swiftly flew the ship,   460
Yet she sailed softly too:
Sweetly, sweetly blew the breeze—
On me alone it blew.

"Oh! dream of joy! is this in-   *And the ancient*
deed   *Mariner behold-*
  eth his native
The light-house top I see?   465   *country.*
Is this the hill? is this the kirk?
Is this mine own countree?

"We drifted o'er the harbor-bar,
And I with sobs did pray—
O let me be awake, my God!   470
Or let me sleep alway.

"The harbor-bay was clear as glass,
So smoothly it was strewn!
And on the bay the moonlight lay,
And the shadow of the Moon.   475

"The rock shone bright, the kirk no less,
That stands above the rock:
The moonlight steeped in silentness
The steady weathercock.

"And the bay was white with silent light,   480
Till, rising from the same,
Full many shapes, that shadows   *The angelic*
were,   *spirits leave*
  the dead bodies,
In crimson colors came.

"A little distance from the prow   *And appear in*
  their own
Those crimson shadows were: *forms of light.*
I turned my eyes upon the deck—
Oh, Christ! what saw I there!   487

"Each corse lay flat, lifeless and flat,
And, by the holy rood![11]
A man all light, a seraph-man,   490
On every corse there stood.

"This seraph-band, each waved his hand:
It was a heavenly sight!
They stood as signals to the land,
Each one a lovely light;   495

"This seraph-band, each waved his hand,
No voice did they impart—
No voice; but oh! the silence sank
Like music on my heart.

"But soon I heard the dash of oars,   500
I heard the Pilot's cheer;
My head was turned perforce away,
And I saw a boat appear.

"The Pilot and the Pilot's boy,
I heard them coming fast: 505

[11]Cross.

Dear Lord in Heaven! it was a joy
The dead men could not blast.

"I saw a third—I heard his voice:
It is the Hermit good!
He singeth loud his godly hymns   510
That he makes in the wood.
He'll shrieve my soul,[12] he'll wash away
The Albatross's blood.

PART VII

"This Hermit good lives in that   *The Hermit of*
wood   *the Wood,*
Which slopes down to the sea.   515
How loudly his sweet voice he rears!
He loves to talk with marineres
That come from a far countree.

"He kneels at morn, and noon, and eve—
He hath a cushion plump: 520
It is the moss that wholly hides
The rotted old oak-stump.

"The skiff-boat neared: I heard them talk, ·
'Why, this is strange, I trow!
Where are those lights so many and fair,   525
That signal made but now?'

"'Strange, by my faith!' the   *Approacheth*
Hermit said—   *the ship*
  with wonder.
'And they answered not our cheer!
The planks look[13] warped! and see those
sails,
How thin they are and sere!   530
I never saw aught like to them,
Unless perchance it were

"'Brown skeletons of leaves that lag
My forest-brook along;
When the ivy-tod[14] is heavy with snow,   535
And the owlet whoops to the wolf below,
That eats the she-wolf's young.'

"'Dear Lord! it hath a fiendish look—
(The pilot made reply)
I am a-feared'—'Push on, push on!'   540
Said the Hermit cheerily.

"The boat came closer to the ship,
But I nor spake nor stirred;
The boat came close beneath the ship,
And straight a sound was heard.   545

[12]Hear my confession, assign penance, and absolve
me.

[13]In the edition of 1828 this was changed to
"looked," which was kept in the editions of 1829
and 1834.

[14]Ivy-bush.

"Under the water it rumbled on, *The ship sud-*
Still louder and more dread: *denly sinketh.*
It reached the ship, it split the bay;
The ship went down like lead. 549

"Stunned by that loud and *The ancient*
    dreadful sound, *Mariner is*
Which sky and ocean smote, *saved in the*
    Pilot's boat.
Like one that hath been seven days drowned,
My body lay afloat;
But swift as dreams, myself I found
Within the Pilot's boat. 555

"Upon the whirl, where sank the ship,
The boat spun round and round;
And all was still, save that the hill
Was telling of the sound.

"I moved my lips—the Pilot shrieked, 560
And fell down in a fit;
The holy Hermit raised his eyes,
And prayed where he did sit.

"I took the oars: the Pilot's boy,
Who now doth crazy go, 565
Laughed loud and long, and all the while
His eyes went to and fro.
'Ha! ha!' quoth he, 'full plain I see,
The Devil knows how to row.'

"And now, all in my own countree, 570
I stood on the firm land!
The Hermit stepped forth from the boat,
And scarcely he could stand.

"'O shrieve me, shrieve me, *The ancient*
    holy man!' 574 *Mariner*
The Hermit crossed his brow, *earnestly*
    entreateth the
'Say quick,' quoth he, 'I bid thee *Hermit to*
    say— *shrive him;*
    and the pen-
What manner of man art thou?' *ance of life*
    falls on him.

"Forthwith this frame of mine was wrenched
With a woeful agony,
Which forced me to begin my tale; 580
And then it left me free.

"Since then at an uncertain *And ever and*
    hour, *anon through-*
    out his future
That agony returns; *life an agony*
    constraineth
And till my ghastly tale is told, *him to travel*
This heart within me burns. *from land to*
    land,

"I pass, like night, from land to land; 586
I have strange power of speech;
That moment that his face I see,
I know the man that must hear me:
To him my tale I teach. 590

"What loud uproar bursts from that door!
The wedding-guests are there;
But in the garden-bower the bride
And bride-maids singing are;
And hark the little vesper bell, 595
Which biddeth me to prayer!

"O Wedding-Guest! this soul hath been
Alone on a wide, wide sea:
So lonely 'twas, that God himself
Scarce seeméd there to be. 600

"O sweeter than the marriage-feast,
'Tis sweeter far to me,
To walk together to the kirk
With a goodly company!—

"To walk together to the kirk, 605
And all together pray,
While each to his great Father bends,
Old men, and babes, and loving friends,
And youths and maidens gay! 609

"Farewell, farewell! but this I *And to teach by*
    tell *his own exam-*
    ple love and
To thee, thou Wedding-Guest! *reverence to all*
    things that God
He prayeth well, who loveth *made and*
    well *loveth.*
Both man and bird and beast.

"He prayeth best, who loveth best
All things both great and small; 615
For the dear God who loveth us,
He made and loveth all."

The Mariner, whose eye is bright,
Whose beard with age is hoar,
Is gone: and now the Wedding-Guest 620
Turned from the bridegroom's door.

He went like one that hath been stunned,
And is of sense forlorn:[15]
A sadder and a wiser man,
He rose the morrow morn.[16] 625

---

[15]Deprived.

[16]"Mrs. Barbauld once told me that she admired *The Ancient Mariner* very much, but that there were two faults in it—it was improbable, and had no moral. As for the probability, I owned that that might admit some question; but as to the want of a moral, I told her that in my own judgment the poem had too much; and that the only, or chief fault, if I might say so, was the obtrusion of the moral sentiment so openly on the reader as a principle or cause of action in a work of such pure imagination. It ought to have had no more moral than the *Arabian Nights'* tale of the merchant's sitting down to eat dates by the side of a well, and throwing the shells aside, and lo! a genie starts up, and says he *must* kill the aforesaid merchant, *because* one of the date shells had, it seems, put out the eye of the genie's son" (Coleridge, *Table Talk*, 31 May, 1830).

CHRISTABEL[1]

PART THE FIRST

'Tis the middle of night by the castle clock,
And the owls have awakened the crowing cock,
Tu—whit!—— Tu—whoo!
And hark, again! the crowing cock,
How drowsily it crew.　　5

Sir Leoline, the Baron rich,
Hath a toothless mastiff bitch;
From her kennel beneath the rock
She maketh answer to the clock,
Four for the quarters, and twelve for the hour;　　10
Ever and aye, by shine and shower,
Sixteen short howls, not over loud;
Some say, she sees my lady's shroud.

Is the night chilly and dark?
The night is chilly, but not dark.　　15
The thin gray cloud is spread on high,
It covers but not hides the sky.
The moon is behind, and at the full;
And yet she looks both small and dull.
The night is chill, the cloud is gray:　　20
'Tis a month before the month of May,
And the Spring comes slowly up this way.

The lovely lady, Christabel,
Whom her father loves so well,
What makes her in the wood so late,　　25
A furlong from the castle gate?
She had dreams all yesternight
Of her own betrothéd knight;
And she in the midnight wood will pray
For the weal of her lover that's far away.　　30

She stole along, she nothing spoke,
The sighs she heaved were soft and low,
And naught was green upon the oak
But moss and rarest mistletoe:
She kneels beneath the huge oak tree,　　35
And in silence prayeth she.

The lady sprang up suddenly,
The lovely lady, Christabel!
It moaned as near, as near can be,
But what it is she cannot tell.——　　40
On the other side it seems to be,
Of the huge, broad-breasted, old oak tree.

The night is chill; the forest bare;
Is it the wind that moaneth bleak?
There is not wind enough in the air　　45
To move away the ringlet curl
From the lovely lady's cheek—
There is not wind enough to twirl
The one red leaf, the last of its clan,
That dances as often as dance it can,　　50
Hanging so light, and hanging so high,
On the topmost twig that looks up at the sky.

Hush, beating heart of Christabel!
Jesu, Maria, shield her well!
She folded her arms beneath her cloak,　　55
And stole to the other side of the oak.
　　What sees she there?

There she sees a damsel bright,
Dressed in a silken robe of white,
That shadowy in the moonlight shone:　　60
The neck that made that white robe wan.
Her stately neck, and arms were bare;
Her blue-veined feet unsandaled were;
And wildly glittered here and there
The gems entangled in her hair.　　65
I guess, 'twas frightful there to see
A lady so richly clad as she—
Beautiful exceedingly!

"Mary mother, save me now!"
Said Christabel; "and who art thou?"　　70
The lady strange made answer meet,
And her voice was faint and sweet:—
"Have pity on my sore distress,
I scarce can speak for weariness:
Stretch forth thy hand, and have no fear!"　75
Said Christabel, "How camest thou here?"
And the lady, whose voice was faint and sweet,
Did thus pursue her answer meet:—

"My sire is of a noble line,
And my name is Geraldine:　　80
Five warriors seized me yestermorn,
Me, even me, a maid forlorn:
They choked my cries with force and fright,
And tied me on a palfrey white.
The palfrey was as fleet as wind,　　85
And they rode furiously behind.
They spurred amain, their steeds were white:
And once we crossed the shade of night
As sure as Heaven shall rescue me,
I have no thought what men they be;　　90
Nor do I know how long it is
(For I have lain entranced, I wis[2])

---

[1] The first part was written in 1797, the second in 1800, and the conclusion to the second part perhaps in 1801.　Published in 1816

[2] Think.

Since one, the tallest of the five,
Took me from the palfrey's back,
A weary woman, scarce alive. 95
Some muttered words his comrades spoke:
He placed me underneath this oak;
He swore they would return with haste;
Whither they went I cannot tell—
I thought I heard, some minutes past; 100
Sounds as of a castle bell.
Stretch forth thy hand," thus ended she,
"And help a wretched maid to flee."

Then Christabel stretched forth her hand,
And comforted fair Geraldine: 105
"O well, bright dame! may you command
The service of Sir Leoline;
And gladly our stout chivalry
Will he send forth, and friends withal,
To guide and guard you safe and free 110
Home to your noble father's hall."

She rose: and forth with steps they passed
That strove to be, and were not, fast.
Her gracious stars the lady bless'd,
And thus spake on sweet Christabel: 115
"All our household are at rest,
The hall as silent as the cell;
Sir Leoline is weak in health,
And may not well awakened be,
But we will move as if in stealth; 120
And I beseech your courtesy,
This night, to share your couch with me."

They crossed the moat, and Christabel
Took the key that fitted well;
A little door she opened straight, 125
All in the middle of the gate;
The gate that was ironed within and without,
Where an army in battle array had marched
    out.
The lady sank, belike through pain,
And Christabel with might and main 130
Lifted her up, a weary weight,
Over the threshold of the gate:[3]
Then the lady rose again,
And moved, as she were not in pain.

So free from danger, free from fear, 135
They crossed the court: right glad they were.
And Christabel devoutly cried
To the lady by her side,
"Praise we the Virgin all divine,
Who hath rescued thee from thy distress!"
"Alas, alas!" said Geraldine, 141

[3]The first intimation of Geraldine's real nature. It was formerly believed that evil spirits could not cross a Christian threshold. In the following stanza, again, Geraldine refuses to join in giving thanks to the Virgin Mary.

"I cannot speak for weariness."
So free from danger, free from fear,
They crossed the court: right glad they were.

Outside her kennel, the mastiff old 145
Lay fast asleep, in moonshine cold.
The mastiff old did not awake,
Yet she an angry moan did make![4]
And what can ail the mastiff bitch?
Never till now she uttered yell 150
Beneath the eye of Christabel.
Perhaps it is the owlet's scritch:
For what can ail the mastiff bitch?

They passed the hall, that echoes still,
Pass as lightly as you will! 155
The brands were flat, the brands were dying,
Amid their own white ashes lying;
But when the lady passed, there came
A tongue of light, a fit of flame;
And Christabel saw the lady's eye, 160
And nothing else saw she thereby,
Save the boss of the shield of Sir Leoline
    tall,
Which hung in a murky old niche in the
    wall.
"O softly tread," said Christabel,
"My father seldom sleepeth well." 165

Sweet Christabel her feet doth bare,
And jealous of the listening air
They steal their way from stair to stair,
Now in glimmer, and now in gloom,
And now they pass the Baron's room, 170
As still as death, with stifled breath!
And now have reached her chamber door;
And now doth Geraldine press down
The rushes of the chamber floor.

The moon shines dim in the open air, 175
And not a moonbeam enters here.
But they without its light can see
The chamber carved so curiously,
Carved with figures strange and sweet,
All made out of the carver's brain, 180
For a lady's chamber meet:
The lamp with twofold silver chain
Is fastened to an angel's feet.

The silver lamp burns dead and dim;
But Christabel the lamp will trim. 185
She trimmed the lamp, and made it bright,
And left it swinging to and fro,
While Geraldine, in wretched plight,
Sank down upon the floor below.

[4]Animals were formerly supposed to have a sense which warned them of the presence of spirits. In the following stanza even the fire feels Geraldine's presence.

"O weary lady, Geraldine,   190
I pray you, drink this cordial wine!
It is a wine of virtuous powers;
My mother made it of wild flowers."

"And will your mother pity me,
Who am a maiden most forlorn?"   195
Christabel answered—"Woe is me!
She died the hour that I was born.
I have heard the gray-haired friar tell
How on her death-bed she did say,
That she should hear the castle-bell   200
Strike twelve upon my wedding-day.
O mother dear! that thou wert here!"
"I would," said Geraldine, "she were!"
But soon with altered voice, said she—
"Off, wandering mother!   Peak and pine!
I have power to bid thee flee."   206
Alas! what ails poor Geraldine?
Why stares she with unsettled eye?
Can she the bodiless dead espy?
And why with hollow voice cries she,   210
"Off, woman, off! this hour is mine—
Though thou her guardian spirit be,
Off, woman, off! 'tis given to me."

Then Christabel knelt by the lady's side,
And raised to heaven her eyes so blue—   215
"Alas!" said she, "this ghastly ride—
Dear lady! it hath wildered you!"
The lady wiped her moist cold brow,
And faintly said, " 'Tis over now!"

Again the wild-flower wine she drank: 220
Her fair large eyes 'gan glitter bright,
And from the floor whereon she sank,
The lofty lady stood upright:
She was most beautiful to see,
Like a lady of a far countree.   225

And thus the lofty lady spake—
"All they who live in the upper sky,
Do love you, holy Christabel!
And you love them, and for their sake
And for the good which me befell,   230
Even I in my degree will try,
Fair maiden, to requite you well.
But now unrobe yourself; for I
Must pray, ere yet in bed I lie."

Quoth Christabel, "So let it be!"   235
And as the lady bade, did she.
Her gentle limbs did she undress,
And lay down in her loveliness.

But through her brain of weal and woe
So many thoughts moved to and fro,   240

That vain it were her lids to close;
So half-way from the bed she rose,
And on her elbow did recline
To look at the lady Geraldine.

Beneath the lamp the lady bowed,   245
And slowly rolled her eyes around;
Then drawing in her breath aloud,
Like one that shuddered, she unbound
The cincture from beneath her breast:
Her silken robe, and inner vest,   250
Dropped to her feet, and full in view,
Behold! her bosom and half her side——
A sight to dream of, not to tell!
O shield her! shield sweet Christabel!

Yet Geraldine nor speaks nor stirs;   255
Ah! what a stricken look was hers!
Deep from within she seems half-way
To lift some weight with sick assay,
And eyes the maid and seeks delay;
Then suddenly, as one defied,   260
Collects herself in scorn and pride,
And lay down by the Maiden's side!—
And in her arms the maid she took,
        Ah well-a-day!
And with low voice and doleful look   265
These words did say:
"In the touch of this bosom there worketh a
        spell,
Which is lord of thy utterance, Christabel!
Thou knowest to-night, and wilt know to-
        morrow,
This mark of my shame, this seal of my sor-
        row;   270
        But vainly thou warrest,
                For this is alone in
        Thy power to declare,
                That in the dim forest
        Thou heard'st a low moaning,   275
And found'st a bright lady, surpassingly
        fair;
And didst bring her home with thee in love
        and in charity,
To shield her and shelter her from the damp
        air."

THE CONCLUSION TO PART THE FIRST

It was a lovely sight to see
The lady Christabel, when she
Was praying at the old oak tree.
        Amid the jaggéd shadows
        Of mossy leafless boughs,   5
        Kneeling in the moonlight,
        To make her gentle vows;
Her slender palms together pressed,
Heaving sometimes on her breast;

Her face resigned to bliss or bale— 10
Her face, oh call it fair not pale,
And both blue eyes more bright than clear,
Each about to have a tear.

With open eyes (ah woe is me!)
Asleep, and dreaming fearfully, 15
Fearfully dreaming, yet, I wis,
Dreaming that alone, which is—
O sorrow and shame! Can this be she,
The lady, who knelt at the old oak tree?
And lo! the worker of these harms, 20
That holds the maiden in her arms,
Seems to slumber still and mild
As a mother with her child.

A star hath set, a star hath risen,
O Geraldine! since arms of thine 25
Have been the lovely lady's prison.
O Geraldine! one hour was thine—
Thou'st had thy will! By tairn⁵ and rill,
The night-birds all that hour were still.
But now they are jubilant anew, 30
From cliff and tower, tu—whoo! tu—whoo!
Tu—whoo! tu—whoo! from wood and fell!⁶

And see! the lady Christabel
Gathers herself from out her trance;
Her limbs relax, her countenance 35
Grows sad and soft; the smooth thin lids
Close o'er her eyes; and tears she sheds—
Large tears that leave the lashes bright!
And oft the while she seems to smile
As infants at a sudden light! 40

Yea, she doth smile, and she doth weep,
Like a youthful hermitess,
Beauteous in a wilderness,
Who, praying always, prays in sleep.
And, if she move unquietly, 45
Perchance, 'tis but the blood so free
Comes back and tingles in her feet.
No doubt, she hath a vision sweet.
What if her guardian spirit 'twere,
What if she knew her mother near? 50
But this she knows, in joys and woes,
That saints will aid if men will call:
For the blue sky bends over all!

PART THE SECOND

Each matin bell, the Baron saith,
Knells us back to a world of death.
These words Sir Leoline first said,
When he rose and found his lady dead:

⁵I. e., tarn, small mountain pool or lake.
⁶Mountain.

These words Sir Leoline will say 5
Many a morn to his dying day!

And hence the custom and law began
That still at dawn the sacristan,
Who duly pulls the heavy bell,
Five and forty beads must tell 10
Between each stroke—a warning knell,
Which not a soul can choose but hear
From Bratha Head to Wyndermere.⁷

Saith Bracy the bard, "So let it knell!
And let the drowsy sacristan 15
Still count as slowly as he can!
There is no lack of such, I ween,
As well fill up the space between.
In Langdale Pike and Witch's Lair,
And Dungeon-ghyll⁸ so foully rent, 20
With ropes of rock and bells of air
Three sinful sextons' ghosts are pent,
Who all give back, one after t'other,
The death-note to their living brother;
And oft too, by the knell offended, 25
Just as their one! two! three! is ended,
The devil mocks the doleful tale
With a merry peal from Borodale."

The air is still! through mist and cloud
That merry peal comes ringing loud; 30
And Geraldine shakes off her dread,
And rises lightly from the bed,
Puts on her silken vestments white,
And tricks her hair in lovely plight,⁹
And nothing doubting of her spell 35
Awakens the lady Christabel.
"Sleep you, sweet lady Christabel?
I trust that you have rested well."

And Christabel awoke and spied
The same who lay down by her side 40
O rather say, the same whom she
Raised up beneath the old oak tree!
Nay, fairer yet! and yet more fair!
For she belike hath drunken deep
Of all the blessedness of sleep! 45
And while she spake, her looks, her air
Such gentle thankfulness declare,
That (so it seemed) her girded vests
Grew tight beneath her heaving breasts.
"Sure I have sinned!" said Christabel, 50
"Now heaven be praised if all be well!"

⁷From the source of the river Brathay to Lake
Windermere, into which it flows. These and the
places subsequently mentioned are all in the Lake
Country.
⁸A ghyll is a ravine containing a stream.
⁹Plait.

And in low faltering tones, yet sweet,
Did she the lofty lady greet
With such perplexity of mind
As dreams too lively leave behind.   55

So quickly she rose, and quickly arrayed
Her maiden limbs, and having prayed
That He, who on the cross did groan,
Might wash away her sins unknown,
She forthwith led fair Geraldine   60
To meet her sire, Sir Leoline.

The lovely maid and the lady tall
Are pacing both into the hall,
And pacing on through page and groom,
Enter the Baron's presence-room.   65

The Baron rose, and while he pressed
His gentle daughter to his breast,
With cheerful wonder in his eyes
The lady Geraldine espies,
And gave such welcome to the same,   70
As might beseem so bright a dame!

But when he heard the lady's tale,
And when she told her father's name,
Why waxed Sir Leoline so pale,
Murmuring o'er the name again,   75
Lord Roland de Vaux of Tryermaine?

Alas! they had been friends in youth;
But whispering tongues can poison truth;
And constancy lives in realms above;
And life is thorny; and youth is vain;   80
And to be wroth with one we love
Doth work like madness in the brain.
And thus it chanced, as I divine,
With Roland and Sir Leoline.
Each spake words of high disdain   85
And insult to his heart's best brother:
They parted—ne'er to meet again!
But never either found another
To free the hollow heart from paining—
They stood aloof, the scars remaining,   90
Like cliffs which had been rent asunder;
A dreary sea now flows between:
But neither heat, nor frost, nor thunder,
Shall wholly do away, I ween,
The marks of that which once hath been.   95

Sir Leoline, a moment's space,
Stood gazing on the damsel's face:
And the youthful Lord of Tryermaine
Came back upon his heart again.

O then the Baron forgot his age,   100
His noble heart swelled high with rage;
He swore by the wounds in Jesu's side
He would proclaim it far and wide,
With trump and solemn heraldry,
That they, who thus had wronged the dame,
Were base as spotted infamy!   106
"And if they dare deny the same,
My herald shall appoint a week,
And let the recreant traitors seek
My tourney court—that there and then   110
I may dislodge their reptile souls
From the bodies and forms of men!"
He spake: his eye in lightning rolls!
For the lady was ruthlessly seized; and he
          kenned
In the beautiful lady the child of his friend!

And now the tears were on his face,   116
And fondly in his arms he took
Fair Geraldine, who met the embrace,
Prolonging it with joyous look.
Which when she viewed, a vision fell   120
Upon the soul of Christabel,
The vision of fear, the touch and pain!
She shrunk and shuddered, and saw again—
(Ah, woe is me! Was it for thee,
Thou gentle maid! such sights to see?)   125

Again she saw that bosom old,
Again she felt that bosom cold,
And drew in her breath with a hissing
          sound:
Whereat the Knight turned wildly round,
And nothing saw, but his own sweet maid   130
With eyes upraised, as one that prayed.

The touch, the sight, had passed away,
And in its stead that vision bless'd,
Which comforted her after-rest,
While in the lady's arms she lay,   135
Had put a rapture in her breast,
And on her lips and o'er her eyes
Spread smiles like light!
          With new surprise,
"What ails then my belovéd child?"
The Baron said.—His daughter mild   140
Made answer, "All will yet be well!"
I ween, she had no power to tell
Aught else: so mighty was the spell.

Yet he who saw this Geraldine
Had deemed her sure a thing divine.   145
Such sorrow with such grace she blended,
As if she feared she had offended
Sweet Christabel, that gentle maid!
And with such lowly tones she prayed

She might be sent without delay   150
Home to her father's mansion.
                              "Nay!
Nay, by my soul!" said Leoline.
"Ho! Bracy the bard, the charge be thine!
Go thou, with music sweet and loud,   154
And take two steeds with trappings proud,
And take the youth whom thou lov'st best
To bear thy harp, and learn thy song,
And clothe you both in solemn vest,
And over the mountains haste along,
Lest wandering folk, that are abroad,   160
Detain you on the valley road.

"And when he has crossed the Irthing flood,
My merry bard! he hastes, he hastes
Up Knorren Moor, through Halegarth
     Wood,
And reaches soon that castle good   165
Which stands and threatens Scotland's
     wastes.

"Bard Bracy! bard Bracy! your horses are
     fleet,
Ye must ride up the hall, your music so
     sweet,
More loud than your horses' echoing feet!
And loud and loud to Lord Roland call,   170
Thy daughter is safe in Langdale hall!
Thy beautiful daughter is safe and free—
Sir Leoline greets thee thus through me.
He bids thee come without delay
With all thy numerous array   175
And take thy lovely daughter home:
And he will meet thee on the way
With all his numerous array
White with their panting palfreys' foam:
And, by mine honor! I will say,   180
That I repent me of the day
When I spake words of fierce disdain
To Roland de Vaux of Tryermaine!—
—For since that evil hour hath flown,—
Many a summer's sun hath shone;   185
Yet ne'er found I a friend again
Like Roland de Vaux of Tryermaine."

The lady fell, and clasped his knees,
Her face upraised, her eyes o'erflowing;
And Bracy replied, with faltering voice,   190
His gracious hail on all bestowing:
"Thy words, thou sire of Christabel,
Are sweeter than my harp can tell;
Yet might I gain a boon of thee,
This day my journey should not be;   195
So strange a dream hath come to me,
That I had vowed with music loud

To clear yon wood from thing unbless'd,
Warned by a vision in my rest!
For in my sleep I saw that dove,   200
That gentle bird, whom thou dost love,
And call'st by thy own daughter's name—
Sir Leoline! I saw the same,
Fluttering, and uttering fearful moan,
Among the green herbs in the forest alone.
Which when I saw and when I heard,   206
I wondered what might ail the bird;
For nothing near it could I see,
Save the grass and green herbs underneath
     the old tree.

"And in my dream methought I went   210
To search out what might there be found;
And what the sweet bird's trouble meant,
That thus lay fluttering on the ground.
I went and peered, and could descry
No cause for her distressful cry;   215
But yet for her dear lady's sake
I stooped, methought, the dove to take,
When lo! I saw a bright green snake
Coiled around its wings and neck.
Green as the herbs on which it couched,   220
Close by the dove's its head it crouched;
And with the dove it heaves and stirs,
Swelling its neck as she swelled hers!
I woke; it was the midnight hour,
The clock was echoing in the tower;   225
But though my slumber was gone by,
This dream it would not pass away—
It seems to live upon my eye!
And thence I vowed this self-same day
With music strong and saintly song   230
To wander through the forest bare,
Lest aught unholy loiter there."

Thus Bracy said: the Baron, the while,
Half-listening heard him with a smile;
Then turned to Lady Geraldine,   235
His eyes made up of wonder and love;
And said in courtly accents fine,
"Sweet maid, Lord Roland's beauteous dove,
With arms more strong than harp or song,
Thy sire and I will crush the snake!"   240
He kissed her forehead as he spake,
And Geraldine in maiden wise
Casting down her large bright eyes,
With blushing cheek and courtesy fine
She turned her from Sir Leoline;   245
Softly gathering up her train,
That o'er her right arm fell again;
And folded her arms across her chest,
And couched her head upon her breast,
And looked askance at Christabel—   250
Jesu, Maria, shield her well!

A snake's small eye blinks dull and shy;
And the lady's eyes they shrunk in her head,
Each shrunk up to a serpent's eye,
And with somewhat of malice, and more of
      dread,   255
At Christabel she looked askance!——
One moment—and the sight was fled!
But Christabel in dizzy trance
Stumbling on the unsteady ground
Shuddered aloud, with a hissing sound;   260
And Geraldine again turned round,
And like a thing that sought relief,
Full of wonder and full of grief,
She rolled her large bright eyes divine
Wildly on Sir Leoline.   265

The maid, alas! her thoughts are gone,
She nothing sees—no sight but one!
The maid, devoid of guile and sin,
I know not how, in fearful wise,
So deeply had she drunken in   270
That look, those shrunken serpent eyes,
That all her features were resigned
To this sole image in her mind:
And passively did imitate
That look of dull and treacherous hate!   275
And thus she stood, in dizzy trance,
Still picturing that look askance
With forced unconscious sympathy
Full before her father's view——
As far as such a look could be   280
In eyes so innocent and blue!

And when the trance was o'er, the maid
Paused awhile, and inly prayed:
Then falling at the Baron's feet,
"By my mother's soul do I entreat   285
That thou this woman send away!"
She said: and more she could not say:
For what she knew she could not tell,
O'er-mastered by the mighty spell.

Why is thy cheek so wan and wild,   290
Sir Leoline? Thy only child
Lies at thy feet, thy joy, thy pride,
So fair, so innocent, so mild;
The same, for whom thy lady died!
O, by the pangs of her dear mother   295
Think thou no evil of thy child!
For her, and thee, and for no other,
She prayed the moment ere she died:
Prayed that the babe for whom she died,   299
Might prove her dear lord's joy and pride!
   That prayer her deadly pangs beguiled,
      Sir Leoline!
   And wouldst thou wrong thy only child,
      Her child and thine?

Within the Baron's heart and brain
If thoughts like these had any share,
They only swelled his rage and pain,   305
And did but work confusion there.
His heart was cleft with pain and rage,
His cheeks they quivered, his eyes were wild,
Dishonored thus in his old age;
Dishonored by his only child,   310
And all his hospitality
To the wronged daughter of his friend
By more than woman's jealousy
Brought thus to a disgraceful end——
He rolled his eye with stern regard   315
Upon the gentle minstrel bard,
And said in tones abrupt, austere—
"Why, Bracy! dost thou loiter here?
I bade thee hence!" The bard obeyed;
And turning from his own sweet maid,   320
The agéd knight, Sir Leoline,
Led forth the lady Geraldine!

THE CONCLUSION TO PART THE SECOND

A little child, a limber elf,
Singing, dancing to itself,
A fairy thing with red round cheeks,
That always finds, and never seeks,
Makes such a vision to the sight   5
As fills a father's eyes with light;
And pleasures flow in so thick and fast
Upon his heart, that he at last
Must needs express his love's excess
With words of unmeant bitterness.   10
Perhaps 'tis pretty to force together
Thoughts so all unlike each other;
To mutter and mock a broken charm,
To dally with wrong that does no harm.
Perhaps 'tis tender too and pretty   15
At each wild word to feel within
A sweet recoil of love and pity.
And what, if in a world of sin
(O sorrow and shame should this be true!)
Such giddiness of heart and brain   20
Comes seldom save from rage and pain,
So talks as it's most used to do.[10]

[10]Coleridge never finished *Christabel*, though he more than once insisted that he had "the whole plan entire from beginning to end" in his mind. James Gillman states that Coleridge outlined to his friends the conclusion of the story as follows: "The following relation was to have occupied a third and fourth canto, and to have closed the tale. Over the mountains, the Bard, as directed by Sir Leoline, hastes with his disciple; but in consequence of one of those inundations supposed to be common to this country, the spot only where the castle once stood is discovered—the edifice itself being washed away. He determines to return. Geraldine, being acquainted with all that is passing, like the weird sisters in Macbeth, vanishes. Reappearing, however,

HYMN BEFORE SUNRISE, IN THE VALE OF CHAMOUNI[1]

Hast thou a charm to stay the morning-star
In his steep course? So long he seems to
pause
On thy bald awful head, O sovran BLANC!
The Arve and Arveiron[2] at thy base
Rave ceaselessly; but thou, most awful
Form! 5
Risest from forth thy silent sea of pines,
How silently! Around thee and above
Deep is the air and dark, substantial, black,
An ebon mass: methinks thou piercest it,
As with a wedge! But when I look again, 10
It is thine own calm home, thy crystal shrine,
Thy habitation from eternity!
O dread and silent Mount! I gazed upon
thee,
Till thou, still present to the bodily sense,
Didst vanish from my thought: entranced in
prayer 15
I worshiped the Invisible alone.

---

she awaits the return of the Bard, exciting in the
meantime, by her wily arts, all the anger she could
rouse in the Baron's breast, as well as that jealousy
of which he is described to have been susceptible.
The old Bard and the youth at length arrive, and
therefore she can no longer personate the character
of Geraldine, the daughter of Lord Roland de Vaux,
but changes her appearance to that of the accepted
though absent lover of Christabel. Now ensues a
courtship most distressing to Christabel, who feels,
she knows not why, great disgust for her once favored knight. This coldness is very painful to the
Baron, who has no more conception than herself of
the supernatural transformation. She at last yields
to her father's entreaties, and consents to approach
the altar with this hated suitor. The real lover, returning, enters at this moment, and produces the
ring which she had once given him in sign of her
betrothment. Thus defeated, the supernatural being
Geraldine disappears. As predicted, the castle bell
tolls, the mother's voice is heard, and, to the exceeding great joy of the parties, the rightful marriage
takes place, after which follows a reconciliation and
explanation between the father and daughter."

[1]First printed in 1802. Chamouni is a valley,
about 14 miles in length, north of Mont Blanc. A
few months after Coleridge's death De Quincey
made it known (in an article in *Tait's Magazine*)
that Coleridge had never been to Chamouni, and
that the *Hymn* "is an expansion of a short poem in
stanzas upon the same subject by Frederica Brun,
a female poet of Germany. . . . The mere framework of the poem is exactly the same. . . . On the
other hand, by a judicious amplification of some
topics, and by its far deeper tone of lyrical enthusiasm, the dry bones of the German outline have
been created by Coleridge into the fullness of life.
It is not, therefore, a paraphrase, but a recast of
the original."

[2]Rivers rising at the foot of Mont Blanc.

Yet, like some sweet beguiling melody,
So sweet, we know not we are listening to it,
Thou, the meanwhile, wast blending with my
Thought,
Yea, with my Life and Life's own secret
joy: 20
Till the dilating Soul, enrapt, transfused,
Into the mighty vision passing—there
As in her natural form, swelled vast to
Heaven!

Awake, my soul! not only passive praise
Thou owest! not alone these swelling tears,
Mute thanks and secret ecstasy! Awake, 26
Voice of sweet song! Awake, my heart,
awake!
Green vales and icy cliffs, all join my hymn.

Thou first and chief, sole sovereign of the
Vale!
O struggling with the darkness all the night,
And visited all night by troops of stars, 31
Or when they climb the sky or when they
sink:
Companion of the morning-star at dawn,
Thyself Earth's rosy star, and of the dawn
Co-herald: wake, O wake, and utter
praise! 35
Who sank thy sunless pillars deep in Earth?
Who filled thy countenance with rosy light?
Who made thee parent of perpetual streams?

And you, ye five wild torrents fiercely
glad!
Who called you forth from night and utter
death, 40
From dark and icy caverns called you forth,
Down those precipitous, black, jaggéd rocks,
For ever shattered and the same for ever?
Who gave you your invulnerable life,
Your strength, your speed, your fury, and
your joy, 45
Unceasing thunder and eternal foam?
And who commanded (and the silence
came),
Here let the billows stiffen, and have rest?

Ye Ice-falls! ye that from the mountain's
brow
Adown enormous ravines slope amain— 50
Torrents, methinks, that heard a mighty
voice,
And stopped at once amid their maddest
plunge!
Motionless torrents! silent cataracts!
Who made you glorious as the Gates of
Heaven

Beneath the keen full moon? Who bade
  the sun   55
Clothe you with rainbows? Who, with liv-
  ing flowers
Of loveliest blue, spread garlands at your
  feet?—
GOD! let the torrents, like a shout of nations,
Answer! and let the ice-plains echo, GOD!
GOD! sing ye meadow-streams with glad-
  some voice!   60
Ye pine-groves, with your soft and soul-like
  sounds!
And they too have a voice, yon piles of snow,
And in their perilous fall shall thunder, GOD!

  Ye living flowers that skirt the eternal
    frost!
Ye wild goats sporting round the eagle's
  nest!   65
Ye eagles, play-mates of the mountain-
  storm!
Ye lightnings, the dread arrows of the
  clouds!
Ye signs and wonders of the element!
Utter forth God, and fill the hills with
  praise!

  Thou too, hoar Mount! with thy sky-
    pointing peaks,   70
Oft from whose feet the avalanche, unheard,
Shoots downward, glittering through the
  pure serene
Into the depth of clouds, that veil thy
  breast—
Thou too again, stupendous Mountain! thou
That as I raise my head, awhile bowed low 75
In adoration, upward from thy base
Slow traveling with dim eyes suffused with
  tears,
Solemnly seemest, like a vapory cloud,
To rise before me—Rise, O ever rise,   79
Rise like a cloud of incense from the Earth!
Thou kingly Spirit throned among the hills,
Thou dread ambassador from Earth to
  Heaven,
Great hierarch! tell thou the silent sky,
And tell the stars, and tell yon rising sun 84
Earth, with her thousand voices, praises GOD.

DEJECTION: AN ODE

Written April 4, 1802

Late, late yestreen I saw the new Moon,
  With the old Moon in her arms;
And I fear, I fear, my Master dear!
  We shall have a deadly storm.
      Ballad of Sir Patrick Spence.

I

Well! If the Bard was weather-wise, who
  made
The grand old ballad of Sir Patrick
  Spence,
This night, so tranquil now, will not go
  hence
Unroused by winds, that ply a busier trade
Than those which mold yon cloud in lazy
  flakes,   5
Or the dull sobbing draft, that moans and
  rakes
  Upon the strings of this Aeolian lute,[1]
  Which better far were mute.
For lo! the New-moon winter-bright!
And overspread with phantom light,   10
(With swimming phantom light o'erspread
But rimmed and circled by a silver thread)
I see the old Moon in her lap, foretelling
  The coming-on of rain and squally blast.
And oh! that even now the gust were swell-
  ing,   15
And the slant night-shower driving loud
  and fast!
Those sounds which oft have raised me,
  whilst they awed,
  And sent my soul abroad,
Might now perhaps their wonted impulse
  give,
Might startle this dull pain, and make it
  move and live!   20

II

A grief without a pang, void, dark, and
  drear,
A stifled, drowsy, unimpassioned grief,
Which finds no natural outlet, no relief,
  In word, or sigh, or tear—
O Lady![2] in this wan and heartless mood, 25
To other thoughts by yonder throstle wooed,
  All this long eve, so balmy and serene,
Have I been gazing on the western sky,
  And its peculiar tint of yellow green:
And still I gaze—and with how blank an eye!
And those thin clouds above, in flakes and
  bars,   31
That give away their motion to the stars;
Those stars, that glide behind them or be-
  tween,
Now sparkling, now bedimmed, but always
  seen:

---

[1]An Aeolian harp, a stringed instrument which
produced musical sounds when touched by the wind.

[2]"O Lady" reads "O William" in manuscript,
since the poem was originally offered to Wordsworth on the occasion of his marriage.

Yon crescent Moon, as fixed as if it grew 35
In its own cloudless, starless lake of blue;
I see them all so excellently fair,
I see, not feel, how beautiful they are!

III

My genial spirits fail;
  And what can these avail   40
To lift the smothering weight from off my
    breast?
  It were a vain endeavor,
  Though I should gaze for ever
On that green light that lingers in the west:
I may not hope from outward forms to win
The passion and the life, whose fountains
are within.   46

IV

O Lady! we receive but what we give,
And in our life alone does Nature live:
Ours is her wedding-garment, ours her
    shroud!
  And would we aught behold, of higher
    worth,   50
Than that inanimate cold world allowed
To the poor loveless ever-anxious crowd,
  Ah! from the soul itself must issue for
A light, a glory, a fair luminous cloud
    Enveloping the Earth—   55
And from the soul itself must there be sent
  A sweet and potent voice, of its own birth,
Of all sweet sounds the life and element!

V

O pure of heart! thou need'st not ask of me
What this strong music in the soul may be!
What, and wherein it doth exist,   61
This light, this glory, this fair luminous mist,
This beautiful and beauty-making power.
  Joy, virtuous Lady! Joy that ne'er was
    given,
Save to the pure, and in their purest hour, 65
Life, and Life's effluence, cloud at once and
    shower,
Joy, Lady! is the spirit and the power,
Which, wedding Nature to us, gives in
    dower
  A new Earth and new Heaven,   69
Undreamt of by the sensual and the proud—
Joy is the sweet, Joy the luminous cloud—
  We in ourselves rejoice!
And thence flows all that charms or ear or
    sight,
  All melodies the echoes of that voice,
All colors a suffusion from that light.   75

VI

There was a time when, though my path was
    rough,
  This joy within me dallied with distress,
And all misfortunes were but as the stuff
  Whence Fancy made me dreams of happi-
    ness:
For Hope grew round me, like the twining
    vine,   80
And fruits, and foliage, not my own, seemed
    mine.
But now afflictions bow me down to earth:
Nor care I that they rob me of my mirth;
  But oh! each visitation   84
Suspends what nature gave me at my birth,
  My shaping spirit of Imagination.
For not to think of what I needs must feel
  But to be still and patient, all I can;
And haply by abstruse research to steal   89
  From my own nature all the natural man—
This was my sole resource, my only plan:
Till that which suits a part infects the whole,
And now is almost grown the habit of my
    soul.

VII

Hence, viper thoughts, that coil around my
    mind,
  Reality's dark dream!   95
I turn from you, and listen to the wind,
  Which long has raved unnoticed. What
    a scream
Of agony by torture lengthened out
That lute sent forth! Thou Wind, that
    rav'st without,
  Bare crag, or mountain-tairn, or blasted
    tree,   100
Or pine-grove whither woodman never
    clomb,
Or lonely house, long held the witches' home,
  Methinks were fitter instruments for thee,
Mad Lutanist! who in this month of
    showers,
Of dark-brown gardens, and of peeping
    flowers,   105
Mak'st Devils' yule, with worse than wintry
    song,
The blossoms, buds, and timorous leaves
    among.
  Thou actor, perfect in all tragic sounds!
Thou mighty Poet, e'en to frenzy bold!
  What tell'st thou now about?   110
  'Tis of the rushing of an host in rout,
  With groans of trampled men, with smart-
    ing wounds—

At once they groan with pain, and shudder
　　with the cold!
But hush! there is a pause of deepest silence!
　　And all that noise, as of a rushing crowd,
With groans, and tremulous shudderings—
　　all is over——　　　　　　　　　　116
　　It tells another tale, with sounds less deep
　　　　and loud!
　　　　A tale of less affright,
　　　　And tempered with delight,
As Otway's[3] self had framed the tender
　　lay,——　　　　　　　　　120
　　　　'Tis of a little child
　　　　Upon a lonesome wild,
Not far from home, but she hath lost her
　　way:
And now moans low in bitter grief and fear,
And now screams loud, and hopes to make
　　her mother hear.　　　　　125

VIII

'Tis midnight, but small thoughts have I of
　　sleep:
Full seldom may my friend such vigils keep!
Visit her, gentle Sleep! with wings of heal-
　　ing,
　　And may this storm be but a mountain-
　　　　birth,
May all the stars hang bright above her
　　dwelling,　　　　　　　　130
　　Silent as though they watched the sleeping
　　　　Earth!
　　　　With light heart may she rise,
　　　　Gay fancy, cheerful eyes,
Joy lift her spirit, joy attune her voice;
To her may all things live, from pole to
　　pole,　　　　　　　　135
Their life the eddying of her living soul!
O simple spirit, guided from above,
Dear Lady! friend devoutest of my choice,
Thus mayest thou ever, evermore rejoice. 139

YOUTH AND AGE[1]

Verse, a breeze mid blossoms straying,
Where Hope clung feeding, like a bee—
Both were mine! Life went a-maying
　　With Nature, Hope, and Poesy,
　　　　When I was young!　　5

---

[3]Thomas Otway (1652–1685), the dramatist. In
the original version the allusion was made, not to
Otway, but to Wordsworth, whose *Lucy Gray* seems
to be described in the lines that follow.

[1]Begun in 1823; first printed (without the last
eleven lines) in 1828. The last eleven lines were
written, and published as a separate poem, in 1832.

When I was young?—Ah, woeful When!
Ah! for the change 'twixt Now and Then!
This breathing house not built with hands,
This body that does me grievous wrong,
O'er aery cliffs and glittering sands,　　10
How lightly then it flashed along:—
Like those trim skiffs, unknown of yore,
On winding lakes and rivers wide,
That ask no aid of sail or oar,
That fear no spite of wind or tide!　　15
Nought cared this body for wind or weather
When Youth and I lived in't together.

Flowers are lovely; Love is flower-like;
Friendship is a sheltering tree;
O! the joys, that came down shower-like, 20
Of Friendship, Love, and Liberty,
　　　　　　　　Ere I was old!

Ere I was old? Ah woeful Ere,
Which tells me, Youth's no longer here!
O Youth! for years so many and sweet,　25
'Tis known, that Thou and I were one,
I'll think it but a fond conceit—
It cannot be that Thou art gone!
Thy vesper-bell hath not yet tolled:—
And thou wert aye a masker bold!　　30
What strange disguise hast now put on,
To make believe, that thou art gone?
I see these locks in silvery slips,
This drooping gait, this altered size:
But Spring-tide blossoms on thy lips,　35
And tears take sunshine from thine eyes!
Life is but thought: so think I will
That Youth and I are house-mates still.

Dew-drops are the gems of morning,
But the tears of mournful eve!　　40
Where no hope is, life's a warning
That only serves to make us grieve,
　　　　　　　When we are old:

That only serves to make us grieve
With oft and tedious taking-leave,　　45
Like some poor nigh-related guest,
That may not rudely be dismissed;
Yet hath outstayed his welcome while,
And tells the jest without the smile.

WORK WITHOUT HOPE[2]

Lines Composed 21st February, 1825

All Nature seems at work. Slugs leave their
　　lair—
The bees are stirring—birds are on the
　　wing—
And Winter slumbering in the open air,

---

[2]First printed in 1828.

The range and quality of William Blake's work as an artist could only be exhibited from a much larger number of his designs than it is possible to reproduce here; but the three designs on this page do show the union of picture and text at which he aimed in his work as an illustrator. As a poet he is unique in the annals of English literature for having made his own books from start to finish, writing the poems, engraving them amidst symbolic designs and borders, printing them in colored ink and then tinting the designs by hand, and finally acting as his own publisher. Blake's books lose some of their unique quality in any reproduction, one obvious loss being their delicate coloring. Some idea of their appearance can be had, however, from the two pages above—the one at the upper left being the title page for *Songs of Innocence* (1789), and that at the upper right being the page containing "The Tiger" (page 139) in *Songs of Experience* (1794). Blake also made many designs to illustrate the writings of others—Dante's *Divine Comedy*, Milton's *Paradise Lost*, and Thomas Gray's poems, for example. The most famous and most successful of all these achievements was his series of elaborate and finely imagined symbolic engravings to illustrate the Book of Job, only completed towards the end of his life. At the left is reproduced one of the plates from this series. (Courtesy of the Metropolitan Museum of Art.)

. . . With my cross-bow
I shot the Albatross!

Water, water, everywhere
Nor any drop to drink.

The four illustrations for Coleridge's *Ancient Mariner* (page 221) here reproduced are the work of the French artist Gustave Doré (1832–1883). Doré won fame in the nineteenth century as a master of both macabre and sublime effects. He illustrated Dante's *Divine Comedy* and many other poems. (Courtesy of the Metropolitan Museum of Art.)

"The game is done! I've won, I've won!"
Quoth she, and whistles thrice.

The Mariner, whose eye is bright,
Whose beard with age is hoar, Is gone.

Wears on his smiling face a dream of
    Spring!
And I the while, the sole unbusy thing,   5
Nor honey make, nor pair, nor build, nor
    sing.

Yet well I ken the banks where amaranths
    blow,
Have traced the fount whence streams of
    nectar flow.

Bloom, O ye amaranths! bloom for whom ye
    may,
For me ye bloom not! Glide, rich streams,
    away!   10
With lips unbrightened, wreathless brow, I
    stroll:
And would you learn the spells that drowse
    my soul?
Work without Hope draws nectar in a sieve,
And Hope without an object cannot live.

BIOGRAPHIA LITERARIA;

or

Biographical Sketches of My Literary Life and Opinions (1817)

CHAPTER I

It has been my lot to have had my name introduced both in conversation, and in print, more frequently than I find it easy to explain, whether I consider the fewness, unimportance, and limited circulation of my writings, or the retirement and distance in which I have lived, both from the literary and political world. Most often it has been connected with some charge which I could not acknowledge, or some principle which I had never entertained. Nevertheless, had I had no other motive or incitement, the reader would not have been troubled with this exculpation. What my additional purposes were, will be seen in the following pages. It will be found that the least of what I have written concerns myself personally. I have used the narration chiefly for the purpose of giving a continuity to the work, in part for the sake of the miscellaneous reflections suggested to me by particular events, but still more as introductory to the statement of my principles in Politics, Religion, and Philosophy, and an application of the rules, deduced from philosophical principles, to poetry and criticism. But of the objects which I proposed to myself, it was not the least important to effect, as far as possible, a settlement of the long continued controversy concerning the true nature of poetic diction; and at the same time to define with the utmost impartiality the real *poetic* character of the poet[1] by whose writings this controversy was first kindled, and has been since fueled and fanned.

In 1794,[2] when I had barely passed the verge of manhood, I published a small volume of juvenile poems. They were received with a degree of favor which, young as I was, I well know was bestowed on them not so much for any positive merit, as because they were considered buds of hope, and promises of better works to come. The critics of that day, the most flattering, equally with the severest, concurred in objecting to them obscurity, a general turgidness of diction, and a profusion of new coined double epithets. The first is the fault which a writer is the least able to detect in his own compositions: and my mind was not then sufficiently disciplined to receive the authority of others, as a substitute for my own conviction. Satisfied that the thoughts, such as they were, could not have been expressed otherwise, or at least more perspicuously, I forgot to inquire, whether the thoughts themselves did not demand a degree of attention unsuitable to the nature and objects of poetry. This remark, however, applies chiefly, though not exclusively, to the *Religious Musings*. The remainder of the charge I admitted to its full extent, and not without sincere acknowledgments both to my private and public censors for their friendly admonitions. In the after editions, I pruned the double epithets with no sparing hand, and used my best efforts to tame the swell and glitter both of thought and diction; though in truth, these parasite plants of youthful poetry had insinuated themselves into my longer poems

[1] Wordsworth.

[2] A slip—really the spring of 1796. Coleridge's memory was treacherous, and there are other inaccuracies in the *Biographia Literaria*.

with such intricacy of union, that I was often obliged to omit disentangling the weed, from the fear of snapping the flower. From that period to the date of the present work I have published nothing, with my name, which could by any possibility have come before the board of anonymous criticism. Even the three or four poems printed with the works of a friend,[3] as far as they were censured at all, were charged with the same or similar defects, though I am persuaded not with equal justice—with an excess of ornament, in addition to strained and elaborate diction.[4] May I be permitted to add, that, even at the early period of my juvenile poems, I saw and admitted the superiority of an austerer and more natural style, with an insight not less clear than I at present possess. My judgment was stronger than were my powers of realizing its dictates; and the faults of my language, though indeed partly owing to a wrong choice of subjects, and the desire of giving a poetic coloring to abstract and metaphysical truths, in which a new world then seemed to open upon me, did yet, in part likewise, originate in unfeigned diffidence of my own comparative talent.— During several years of my youth and early manhood, I reverenced those who had re-introduced the manly simplicity of the Greek, and of our own elder poets, with such enthusiasm as made the hope seem presumptuous of writing successfully in the same style. Perhaps a similar process has happened to others; but my earliest poems were marked by an ease and simplicity, which I have studied, perhaps with inferior success, to impress on my later compositions.

At school I enjoyed the inestimable advantage of a very sensible, though at the same time, a very severe master. He[5] early molded my taste to the preference of Demosthenes to Cicero, of Homer and Theocritus

to Virgil, and again of Virgil to Ovid. He habituated me to compare Lucretius (in such extracts as I then read), Terence, and above all the chaster poems of Catullus, not only with the Roman poets of the, so called, silver and brazen ages; but with even those of the Augustan era: and on grounds of plain sense and universal logic to see and assert the superiority of the former in the truth and nativeness both of their thoughts and diction. At the same time that we were studying the Greek tragic poets, he made us read Shakespeare and Milton as lessons: and they were the lessons too, which required most time and trouble to *bring up*, so as to escape his censure. I learned from him that poetry, even that of the loftiest and, seemingly, that of the wildest odes, had a logic of its own, as severe as that of science; and more difficult, because more subtle, more complex, and dependent on more, and more fugitive causes. In the truly great poets, he would say, there is a reason assignable, not only for every word, but for the position of every word; and I well remember that, availing himself of the synonyms to the Homer of Didymus, he made us attempt to show, with regard to each, why it would not have answered the same purpose; and wherein consisted the peculiar fitness of the word in the original text.

In our own English compositions (at least for the last three years of our school education), he showed no mercy to phrase, metaphor, or image, unsupported by a sound sense, or where the same sense might have been conveyed with equal force and dignity in plainer words. *Lute, harp,* and *lyre, Muse, Muses,* and *inspirations, Pegasus, Parnassus,* and *Hippocrene* were all an abomination to him. In fancy I can almost hear him now, exclaiming "Harp? Harp? Lyre? Pen and ink, boy, you mean! Muse, boy, Muse? Your nurse's daughter, you mean! Pierian spring? Oh aye! the cloister-pump, I suppose!" Nay certain introductions, similes, and examples, were placed by name on a list of interdiction. Among the similes, there was, I remember, that of the manchineel fruit,[6] as suiting equally well

---

[3]Printed with Wordsworth's poems in *Lyrical Ballads,* 1798. Coleridge's poems in the volume were: *The Rime of the Ancient Mariner; The Nightingale, a Conversation Poem; The Foster-Mother's Tale;* and *The Dungeon.*

[4]See the criticisms on the *Ancient Mariner,* in the *Monthly* and *Critical Reviews* of the first volume of the *Lyrical Ballads* (Coleridge's note).

[5]The Rev. James Bowyer, many years Head Master of the Grammar School, Christ's Hospital (Coleridge's note).

[6]The manchineel is a West Indian tree with poisonous milky sap and acrid fruit.

with too many subjects; in which however it yielded the palm at once to the example of Alexander and Clytus, which was equally good and apt, whatever might be the theme. Was it ambition? Alexander and Clytus!— Flattery? Alexander and Clytus!—anger —drunkenness—pride—friendship—ingratitude—late repentance? Still, still Alexander and Clytus! At length, the praises of agriculture having been exemplified in the sagacious observation that, had Alexander been holding the plow, he would not have run his friend Clytus through with a spear, this tried and serviceable old friend was banished by public edict in *saecula saeculorum*.[7] I have sometimes ventured to think that a list of this kind, or an *index expurgatorius*[8] of certain well-known and ever-returning phrases, both introductory, and transitional, including a large assortment of modest egoisms, and flattering illeisms,[9] *etc., etc.,* might be hung up in our Law-Courts, and both Houses of Parliament, with great advantage to the public, as an important saving of national time, an incalculable relief to his Majesty's ministers, but above all, as insuring the thanks of country attorneys, and their clients, who have private bills to carry through the House.

Be this as it may, there was one custom of our master's which I cannot pass over in silence, because I think it imitable and worthy of imitation. He would often permit our exercises, under some pretext of want of time, to accumulate, till each lad had four or five to be looked over. Then placing the whole number abreast on his desk, he would ask the writer, why this or that sentence might not have found as appropriate a place under this or that other thesis: and if no satisfying answer could be returned, and two faults of the same kind were found in one exercise, the irrevocable verdict followed, the exercise was torn up, and another on the same subject to be produced, in addition to the tasks of the day. The reader will, I trust, excuse this tribute of recollection to a man whose severities, even now, not seldom furnish the dreams, by which the blind fancy would fain interpret to the mind the painful sensations of distempered sleep; but neither lessen nor dim the deep sense of my moral and intellectual obligations. He sent us to the University excellent Latin and Greek scholars, and tolerable Hebraists. Yet our classical knowledge was the least of the good gifts which we derived from his zealous and conscientious tutorage. He is now gone to his final reward, full of years, and full of honors, even of those honors which were dearest to his heart, as gratefully bestowed by that school, and still binding him to the interests of that school, in which he had been himself educated, and to which during his whole life he was a dedicated thing.

* * *

CHAPTER IV

* * * During the last year of my residence at Cambridge, I became acquainted with Mr. Wordsworth's first publication[1] entitled *Descriptive Sketches;* and seldom, if ever, was the emergence of an original poetic genius above the literary horizon more evidently announced. In the form, style, and manner of the whole poem, and in the structure of the particular lines and periods, there is an harshness and acerbity connected and combined with words and images all a-glow, which might recall those products of the vegetable world, where gorgeous blossoms rise out of the hard and thorny rind and shell, within which the rich fruit was elaborating. The language was not only peculiar and strong, but at times knotty and contorted, as by its own impatient strength; while the novelty and struggling crowd of images, acting in conjunction with the difficulties of the style, demanded always a greater closeness of attention, than poetry— at all events, than descriptive poetry—has a right to claim. It not seldom therefore justified the complaint of obscurity. In the following extract I have sometimes fancied that I saw an emblem of the poem itself, and of the author's genius as it was then displayed.—

'Tis storm; and hid in mist from hour to hour, All day the floods a deepening murmur pour;

---

[7]Forever. [8]List of prohibitions (as here used).

[9]Excessive use of the pronoun *he*, with reference either to another or to one's self in the 3rd person. Coleridge used this word also in *The Friend*, but apparently no one else has ever used it.

[1]Actually Wordsworth's second publication.

The sky is veiled, and every cheerful sight:
Dark is the region as with coming night;
And yet what frequent bursts of overpowering
　　　light!
Triumphant on the bosom of the storm,
Glances the fire-clad eagle's wheeling form;   5
Eastward, in long perspective glittering, shine
The wood-crowned cliffs that o'er the lake
　　　recline;
Wide o'er the Alps a hundred streams unfold,
At once to pillars turned that flame with gold;
Behind his sail the peasant strives to shun   10
The west, that burns like one dilated sun,
Where in a mighty crucible expire
The mountains, glowing hot, like coals of fire.

(The poetic Psyche, in its process to full
development, undergoes as many changes as   15
its Greek namesake, the butterfly.²) And it
is remarkable how soon genius clears and
purifies itself from the faults and errors of
its earliest products; faults which, in its
earliest compositions, are the more obtrusive   20
and confluent, because as heterogeneous elements, which had only a temporary use, they
constitute the very ferment, by which themselves are carried off.   Or we may compare
them to some diseases, which must work on   25
the humors, and be thrown out on the surface, in order to secure the patient from their
future recurrence. (I was in my twenty-
fourth year, when I had the happiness of
knowing Mr. Wordsworth personally, and   30
while memory lasts, I shall hardly forget
the sudden effect produced on my mind, by
his recitation of a manuscript poem, which
still remains unpublished, but of which the
stanza and tone of style were the same as   35
those of *The Female Vagrant,* as originally
printed in the first volume of the *Lyrical
Ballads.*) There was here no mark of strained
thought, or forced diction, no crowd or turbulence of imagery; and, as the poet hath   40
himself well described in his *Lines on revisit-*

ing the Wye,³ manly reflection and human
associations had given both variety, and an
additional interest to natural objects, which,
in the passion and appetite of the first love,
they had seemed to him neither to need nor
permit.) The occasional obscurities, which
had risen from an imperfect control over
the resources of his native language, had
almost wholly disappeared, together with
that worse defect of arbitrary and illogical
phrases, at once hackneyed and fantastic,
which hold so distinguished a place in the
technique of ordinary poetry, and will, more
or less, alloy the earlier poems of the truest
genius, unless the attention has been spe-
cifically directed to their worthlessness and
incongruity.⁴   I did not perceive anything
particular in the mere style of the poem
alluded to during its recitation, except indeed
such difference as was not separable from
the thought and manner; and the Spenserian
stanza, which always, more or less, recalls
to the reader's mind Spenser's own style,
would doubtless have authorized, in my then
opinion, a more frequent descent to the
phrases of ordinary life, than could without
an ill effect have been hazarded in the heroic
couplet. (It was not, however, the freedom
from false taste, whether as to common defects, or to those more properly his own,
which made so unusual an impression on my
feelings immediately, and subsequently on
my judgment.   It was the union of deep
feeling with profound thought; the fine

---

²The fact that, in Greek, Psyche is the common
name for the soul and the butterfly, is thus alluded
to in the following stanzas from an unpublished
poem of the author:

"The Butterfly the ancient Grecians made
　The soul's fair emblem, and its only name—
　But of the soul, escaped the slavish trade
　Of mortal life!   For in this earthly frame
　Ours is the reptile's lot, much toil, much blame,
　Manifold motions making little speed,
　And to deform and kill the things whereon we
　　　feed."

(Coleridge's note.)

³I. e., *Lines Composed a Few Miles above Tintern
Abbey.*
⁴Mr. Wordsworth, even in his two earliest, *The
Evening Walk* and the *Descriptive Sketches,* is more
free from this latter defect than most of the young
poets his contemporaries.   It may however be exemplified, together with the harsh and obscure construction, in which he more often offended, in the
following lines:—

" 'Mid stormy vapors ever driving by,
Where ospreys, cormorants, and herons cry;
Where hardly given the hopeless waste to cheer,
Denied the bread of life the foodful ear,
Dwindles the pear on autumn's latest spray,
And *apple sickens* pale in summer's ray;
*Ev'n here content has fixed her smiling reign
With independence, child of high disdain.*"

I hope, I need not say, that I have quoted these
lines for no other purpose than to make my meaning fully understood.   It is to be regretted that Mr.
Wordsworth has not republished these two poems
entire (Coleridge's note).

balance of truth in observing, with the imaginative faculty in modifying, the objects observed; and above all the original gift of spreading the tone, the atmosphere, and with it the depth and height of the ideal world around forms, incidents, and situations, of which, for the common view, custom had bedimmed all the luster, had dried up the sparkle and the dew drops. "To find no contradiction in the union of old and new; to contemplate the ANCIENT of days and all his works with feelings as fresh, as if all had then sprang forth at the first creative fiat; characterizes the mind that feels the riddle of the world, and may help to unravel it. To carry on the feelings of childhood into the powers of manhood; to combine the child's sense of wonder and novelty with the appearances, which every day for perhaps forty years had rendered familiar;

'With sun and moon and stars throughout the year,
And man and woman';

this is the character and privilege of genius, and one of the marks which distinguish genius from talents. (And therefore is it the prime merit of genius and its most unequivocal mode of manifestation, so to represent familiar objects as to awaken in the minds of others a kindred feeling concerning them and that freshness of sensation which is the constant accompaniment of mental, no less than of bodily, convalescence.) Who has not a thousand times seen snow fall on water? Who has not watched it with a new feeling, from the time that he has read Burns's comparison of sensual pleasure

'To snow that falls upon a river
A moment white—then gone for ever'![5]

In poems, equally as in philosophic disquisitions, genius produces the strongest impressions of novelty, while it rescues the most admitted truths from the impotence caused by the very circumstance of their universal admission. Truths of all others the most awful and mysterious, yet being at the same time of universal interest, are too often considered as *so* true, that they lose all the life and efficiency of truth, and lie bed-ridden in

the dormitory of the soul, side by side with the most despised and exploded errors."[6]

This excellence, which in all Mr. Wordsworth's writings is more or less predominant, and which constitutes the character of his mind, I no sooner felt, than I sought to understand. Repeated meditations led me first to suspect—and a more intimate analysis of the human faculties, their appropriate marks, functions, and effects, matured my conjecture into full conviction—that Fancy and Imagination were two distinct and widely different faculties, instead of being, according to the general belief, either two names with one meaning, or, at furthest, the lower and higher degree of one and the same power. It is not, I own, easy to conceive a more opposite translation of the Greek *phantasia* than the Latin *imaginatio;* but it is equally true that in all societies there exists an instinct of growth, a certain collective, unconscious good sense working progressively to desynomymize those words originally of the same meaning, which the conflux of dialects supplied to the more homogeneous languages, as the Greek and German: and which the same cause, joined with accidents of translation from original works of different countries, occasion in mixed languages like our own. The first and most important point to be proved is, that two conceptions perfectly distinct are confused under one and the same word, and —this done—to appropriate that word exclusively to one meaning, and the synonym, should there be one, to the other. But if— as will be often the case in the arts and sciences—no synonym exists, we must either invent or borrow a word. In the present instance the appropriation has already begun, and been legitimated in the derivative adjective: Milton had a highly *imaginative,* Cowley a very *fanciful* mind. If therefore I should succeed in establishing the actual existences of two faculties generally different, the nomenclature would be at once determined. To the faculty by which I had characterized Milton, we should confine the term *imagination;* while the other would be

---

[5] See *Tam O'Shanter,* ll. 59ff.

[6] Quoted (with omissions) from *The Friend,* No. 5. In a note Coleridge justifies quoting from an already-published work of his own.

contra-distinguished as *fancy.* Now were it once fully ascertained, that this division is no less grounded in nature than that of delirium from mania, or Otway's

Lutes, lobsters, seas of milk, and ships of amber,[7]

from Shakespeare's

What! have his daughters brought him to this pass?[8]

or from the preceding apostrophe to the elements; the theory of the fine arts, and of poetry in particular, could not, I thought, but derive some additional and important light. It would in its immediate effects furnish a torch of guidance to the philosophical critic; and ultimately to the poet himself. In energetic minds, truth soon changes by domestication into power; and from directing in the discrimination and appraisal of the product, becomes influencive in the production. To admire on principle, is the only way to imitate without loss of originality. * * *

CHAPTER XIV

DURING the first year that Mr. Wordsworth and I were neighbors, our conversations turned frequently on the two cardinal points of poetry, the power of exciting the sympathy of the reader by a faithful adherence to the truth of nature, and the power of giving the interest of novelty by the modifying colors of imagination. The sudden charm, which accidents of light and shade, which moon-light or sunset diffused over a known and familiar landscape, appeared to represent the practicability of combining both. These are the poetry of nature. (The thought suggested itself—to which of us I do not recollect—that a series of poems might be composed of two sorts. In the one, the incidents and agents were to be, in part at least, supernatural; and the excellence aimed at was to consist in the interesting of the affections by the dramatic truth of such emotions, as would naturally

accompany such situations, supposing them real.) And real in this sense they have been to every human being who, from whatever source of delusion, has at any time believed himself under supernatural agency. (For the second class, subjects were to be chosen from ordinary life; the characters and incidents were to be such as will be found in every village and its vicinity, where there is a meditative and feeling mind to seek after them, or to notice them, when they present themselves.)

(In this idea originated the plan of the *Lyrical Ballads;* in which it was agreed that my endeavors should be directed to persons and characters supernatural, or at least romantic; yet so as to transfer from our inward nature a human interest and a semblance of truth sufficient to procure for these shadows of imagination that willing suspension of disbelief for the moment, which constitutes poetic faith.) Mr. Wordsworth, on the other hand, was to propose to himself as his object, to give the charm of novelty to things of every day, and to excite a feeling analogous to the supernatural, by awakening the mind's attention from the lethargy of custom, and directing it to the loveliness and the wonders of the world before us; an inexhaustible treasure, but for which, in consequence of the film of familiarity and selfish solicitude, we have eyes, yet see not, ears that hear not, and hearts that neither feel nor understand.

With this view I wrote *The Ancient Mariner,* and was preparing among other poems, *The Dark Ladie,* and the *Christabel,* in which I should have more nearly realized my ideal than I had done in my first attempt. But Mr. Wordsworth's industry had proved so much more successful, and the number of his poems so much greater, that my compositions, instead of forming a balance, appeared rather an interpolation of heterogeneous matter. Mr. Wordsworth added two or three poems written in his own character, in the impassioned, lofty, and sustained diction which is characteristic of his genius. In this form the *Lyrical Ballads* were published; and were presented by him, as an experiment, whether subjects, which from their nature rejected the usual ornaments

---

[7]*Venice Preserved,* Act V. Otway wrote "laurels," *not* "lobsters."

[8]*Lear,* III, iv, 65.

and extra-colloquial style of poems in general, might not be so managed in the language of ordinary life as to produce the pleasurable interest, which it is the peculiar business of poetry to impart. To the second edition he added a preface of considerable length; in which, notwithstanding some passages of apparently a contrary import, he was understood to contend for the extension of this style to poetry of all kinds, and to reject as vicious and indefensible all phrases and forms of style that were not included in what he (unfortunately, I think, adopting an equivocal expression) called the language of real life. From this preface, prefixed to poems in which it was impossible to deny the presence of original genius, however mistaken its direction might be deemed, arose the whole long-continued controversy. For from the conjunction of perceived power with supposed heresy I explain the inveteracy and in some instances, I grieve to say, the acrimonious passions, with which the controversy has been conducted by the assailants.

Had Mr. Wordsworth's poems been the silly, the childish things, which they were for a long time described as being: had they been really distinguished from the compositions of other poets merely by meanness of language and inanity of thought; had they indeed contained nothing more than what is found in the parodies and pretended imitations of them; they must have sunk at once, a dead weight, into the slough of oblivion, and have dragged the preface along with them. But year after year increased the number of Mr. Wordsworth's admirers. They were found, too, not in the lower classes of the reading public, but chiefly among young men of strong sensibility and meditative minds; and their admiration (inflamed perhaps in some degree by opposition) was distinguished by its intensity, I might almost say, by its religious fervor. These facts, and the intellectual energy of the author, which was more or less consciously felt, where it was outwardly and even boisterously denied, meeting with sentiments of aversion to his opinions, and of alarm at their consequences, produced an eddy of criticism, which would of itself have borne up the poems by the violence with which it whirled them round and round. With many parts of this preface in the sense attributed to them and which the words undoubtedly seem to authorize, I never concurred; but on the contrary objected to them as erroneous in principle, and as contradictory (in appearance at least) both to other parts of the same preface, and to the author's own practice in the greater part of the poems themselves. Mr. Wordsworth in his recent collection has, I find, degraded this prefatory disquisition to the end of his second volume, to be read or not at the reader's choice. But he has not, as far as I can discover, announced any change in his poetic creed. At all events, considering it as the source of a controversy, in which I have been honored more than I deserve by the frequent conjunction of my name with his, I think it expedient to declare once for all, in what points I coincide with his opinions, and in what points I altogether differ. But in order to render myself intelligible I must previously, in as few words as possible, explain my views, first, of a Poem; and secondly, of Poetry itself, in kind, and in essence.

The office of philosophical disquisition consists in just distinction; while it is the privilege of the philosopher to preserve himself constantly aware that distinction is not division. In order to obtain adequate notions of any truth, we must intellectually separate its distinguishable parts; and this is the technical process of philosophy. But having so done, we must then restore them in our conceptions to the unity in which they actually co-exist; and this is the result of philosophy. A poem contains the same elements as a prose composition; the difference therefore must consist in a different combination of them, in consequence of a different object being proposed. According to the difference of the object will be the difference of the combination. It is possible that the object may be merely to facilitate the recollection of any given facts or observations by artificial arrangement; and the composition will be a poem, merely because it is distinguished from prose by meter, or by rime, or by both conjointly. In this the lowest sense, a man might attribute the name of a poem to the well-known enumeration of the days in the several months:

Thirty days hath September,
April, June, and November, etc.,

and others of the same class and purpose. And as a particular pleasure is found in anticipating the recurrence of sounds and quantities, all compositions that have this charm super-added, whatever be their contents, *may* be entitled poems.

So much for the superficial form. A difference of object and contents supplies an additional ground of distinction. The immediate purpose may be the communication of truths; either of truth absolute and demonstrable, as in works of science; or of facts experienced and recorded, as in history. Pleasure, and that of the highest and most permanent kind, may result from the attainment of the end; but it is not itself the immediate end. In other works the communication of pleasure may be the immediate purpose; and though truth, either moral or intellectual, ought to be the ultimate end, yet this will distinguish the character of the author, not the class to which the work belongs. Blest indeed is that state of society, in which the immediate purpose would be baffled by the perversion of the proper ultimate end; in which no charm of diction or imagery could exempt the *Bathyllus* even of an Anacreon, or the *Alexis* of Virgil, from disgust and aversion!

But the communication of pleasure may be the immediate object of a work not metrically composed; and that object may have been in a high degree attained, as in novels and romances. Would then the mere superaddition of meter, with or without rime, entitle these to the name of poems? The answer is, that nothing can permanently please, which does not contain in itself the reason why it is so, and not otherwise. If meter be superadded, all other parts must be made consonant with it. They must be such, as to justify the perpetual and distinct attention to each part, which an exact correspondent recurrence of accent and sound are calculated to excite. The final definition then, so deduced, may be thus worded: A poem is that species of composition, which is opposed to works of science, by proposing for its *immediate* object pleasure not truth; and from all other species—having *this* object in common with it—it is discriminated by proposing to itself such delight from the *whole*, as is compatible with a distinct gratification from each component *part*.

Controversy is not seldom excited in consequence of the disputants attaching each a different meaning to the same word; and in few instances has this been more striking than in disputes concerning the present subject. If a man chooses to call every composition a poem which is rime, or measure, or both, I must leave his opinion uncontroverted. The distinction is at least competent to characterize the writer's intention. If it were subjoined, that the whole is likewise entertaining or affecting, as a tale, or as a series of interesting reflections, I of course admit this as another fit ingredient of a poem, and an additional merit. But if the definition sought for be that of a *legitimate* poem, I answer, it must be one, the parts of which mutually support and explain each other; all in their proportion harmonizing with, and supporting the purpose and known influences of metrical arrangement. The philosophic critics of all ages coincide with the ultimate judgment of all countries, in equally denying the praises of a just poem, on the one hand, to a series of striking lines or distiches, each of which, absorbing the whole attention of the reader to itself, disjoins it from its context, and makes it a separate whole, instead of an harmonizing part; and on the other hand, to an unsustained composition, from which the reader collects rapidly the general result unattracted by the component parts. The reader should be carried forward, not merely or chiefly by the mechanical impulse of curiosity, or by a restless desire to arrive at the final solution; but by the pleasureable activity of mind excited by the attractions of the journey itself. Like the motion of a serpent, which the Egyptians made the emblem of intellectual power; or like the path of sound through the air;—at every step he pauses and half recedes, and from the retrogressive movement collects the force which again carries him onward. *Praecipi-*

tandus est liber spiritus,[1] says Petronius most happily. The epithet, *liber*, here balances the preceding verb; and it is not easy to conceive more meaning condensed in fewer words.

But if this should be admitted as a satisfactory character of a poem, we have still to seek for a definition of poetry. The writings of Plato, and Bishop Taylor,[2] and the *Theoria Sacra* of Burnet,[3] furnish undeniable proofs that poetry of the highest kind may exist without meter, and even without the contra-distinguishing objects of a poem. The first chapter of Isaiah—indeed a very large portion of the whole book—is poetry in the most emphatic sense; yet it would be not less irrational than strange to assert, that pleasure, and not truth was the immediate object of the prophet. In short, whatever specific import we attach to the word, Poetry, there will be found involved in it, as a necessary consequence, that a poem of any length neither can be, or ought to be, all poetry. Yet if an harmonious whole is to be produced, the remaining parts must be preserved *in keeping* with the poetry; and this can be no otherwise effected than by such a studied selection and artificial arrangement as will partake of *one*, though not a *peculiar* property of poetry. And this again can be no other than the property of exciting a more continuous and equal attention than the language of prose aims at, whether colloquial or written.

My own conclusions on the nature of poetry, in the strictest use of the word, have been in part anticipated in the preceding disquisition on the Fancy and Imagination. What is poetry? is so nearly the same question with, What is a poet? that the answer to the one is involved in the solution of the other. For it is a distinction resulting from the poetic genius itself, which sustains and modifies the images, thoughts, and emotions of the poet's own mind.

The poet, described in ideal perfection, brings the whole soul of man into activity, with the subordination of its faculties to each other according to their relative worth and dignity. He diffuses a tone and spirit of unity, that blends, and (as it were) *fuses*, each into each, by that synthetic and magical power, to which we have exclusively appropriated the name of Imagination. This power, first put in action by the will and understanding, and retained under their irremissive, though gentle and unnoticed, control (*laxis effertur habenis*)[4] reveals itself in the balance or reconciliation of opposite or discordant qualities: of sameness, with difference; of the general with the concrete; the idea with the image; the individual with the representative; the sense of novelty and freshness with old and familiar objects; a more than usual state of emotion with more than usual order; judgment ever awake and steady self-possession with enthusiasm and feeling profound or vehement; and while it blends and harmonizes the natural and the artificial, still subordinates art to nature; the manner to the matter; and our admiration of the poet to our sympathy with the poetry. "Doubtless," as Sir John Davies observes of the soul—and his words may with slight alteration be applied, and even more appropriately, to the poetic Imagination—

Doubtless this could not be, but that she turns
  Bodies to spirit by sublimation strange,
As fire converts to fire the things it burns,
  As we our food into our nature change.

From their gross matter she abstracts their
    forms,
  And draws a kind of quintessence from
    things;
Which to her proper nature she transforms,
  To bear them light on her celestial wings.

Thus does she, when from individual states
  She doth abstract the universal kinds;
Which then re-clothed in divers names and fates
  Steal access through our senses to our minds.[5]

Finally, Good Sense is the Body of poetic genius, Fancy its Drapery, Motion its Life,

---

[1] A free spirit must be urged forward (from the *Satyricon,* according to H. N. Coleridge's edition of 1847).

[2] Jeremy Taylor (1613–1667).

[3] Bishop Thomas Burnet (1635–1715), whose *Telluris Theoria Sacra* (1681–1689; English translation, 1684–1689) was a fanciful theory of the earth's structure. Wordsworth also knew the book.

[4] Driven with loosened reins.

[5] *Nosce Teipsum* (1599), Of the Soul of Man and the Immortality Thereof, Stanzas 8–10 of the section entitled "That it cannot be a Body." Coleridge has made numerous changes from Davies' text.

and Imagination the Soul that is everywhere, and in each; and forms all into one graceful and intelligent whole.

CHAPTER XVII

As FAR then as Mr. Wordsworth in his preface contended, and most ably contended, for a reformation in our poetic diction, as far as he has evinced the truth of passion, and the *dramatic* propriety of those figures and metaphors in the original poets, which, stripped of their justifying reasons, and converted into mere artifices of connection or ornament, constitute the characteristic falsity in the poetic style of the moderns; and as far as he has, with equal acuteness and clearness, pointed out the process by which this change was effected, and the resemblances between that state into which the reader's mind is thrown by the pleasurable confusion of thought from an unaccustomed train of words and images; and that state which is induced by the natural language of impassioned feeling; he undertook a useful task, and deserves all praise, both for the attempt and for the execution. The provocations to this remonstrance in behalf of truth and nature were still of perpetual recurrence before and after the publication of this preface. I cannot likewise but add, that the comparison of such poems of merit, as have been given to the public within the last ten or twelve years, with the majority of those produced previously to the appearance of that preface, leave no doubt on my mind, that Mr. Wordsworth is fully justified in believing his efforts to have been by no means ineffectual. Not only in the verses of those who have professed their admiration of his genius, but even of those who have distinguished themselves by hostility to his theory, and depreciation of his writings, are the impressions of his principles plainly visible. It is possible that with these principles others may have been blended, which are not equally evident; and some which are unsteady and subvertible from the narrowness or imperfection of their basis. But it is more than possible that these errors of defect or exaggeration, by kindling and feeding the controversy, may have conduced not only to the wider propagation of the accompanying truths, but that, by their frequent presentation to the mind in an excited state, they may have won for them a more permanent and practical result. A man will borrow a part from his opponent the more easily, if he feels himself justified in continuing to reject a part. While there remain important points in which he can still feel himself in the right, in which he still finds firm footing for continued resistance, he will gradually adopt those opinions which were the least remote from his own convictions, as not less congruous with his own theory than that which he reprobates. In like manner with a kind of instinctive prudence, he will abandon by little and little his weakest posts, till at length he seems to forget that they had ever belonged to him, or affects to consider them at most as accidental and "petty annexments," the removal of which leaves the citadel unhurt and unendangered.

My own differences from certain supposed parts of Mr. Wordsworth's theory ground themselves on the assumption that his words had been rightly interpreted, as purporting that the proper diction for poetry in general consists altogether in a language taken, with due exceptions, from the mouths of men in real life, a language which actually constitutes the natural conversation of men under the influence of natural feelings. My objection is, first, that in *any* sense this rule is applicable only to *certain* classes of poetry; secondly, that even to these classes it is not applicable, except in such a sense as hath never by any one (as far as I know or have read) been denied or doubted; and lastly, that as far as, and in that degree in which it is *practicable*, yet as a *rule* it is useless, if not injurious, and therefore either need not, or ought not to be practiced. The poet informs his reader that he had generally chosen *low and rustic* life; but not *as* low and rustic, or in order to repeat that pleasure of doubtful moral effect, which persons of elevated rank and of superior refinement oftentimes derive from a happy imitation of the rude unpolished manners and discourse of their inferiors. For the pleasure so derived may be traced to three exciting causes. The first is the naturalness, in *fact,* of the things represented. The second is the apparent naturalness of the representation, as raised and qualified by an imperceptible infusion of the author's own knowledge and talent, which infusion does, indeed, constitute it an imitation as distinguished from a mere copy. The third cause may be found in the reader's conscious feeling of his superiority awakened by the contrast presented to him; even as for the same purpose the kings and great barons of yore retained, sometimes actual clowns and fools, but more frequently shrewd and witty fellows in that character. These, however, were not Mr. Wordsworth's objects. *He* chose low and rustic life, "because in that condition the essential passions of the heart find a better soil, in which they can attain their maturity, are less under restraint, and speak a plainer and more emphatic language; because in that condition of life our elementary feelings coexist in a state of greater simplicity, and consequently may be more accurately contemplated, and more forcibly communicated; because the manners of rural life germinate from those elementary feelings; and from the necessary character of rural occupations are more easily comprehended, and are more durable; and lastly, because in that condition the passions of men are incorporated with the beautiful and permanent forms of nature."[1]

Now it is clear to me, that in the most interesting of the poems, in which the author is more or less dramatic, as *The Brothers, Michael, Ruth, The Mad Mother,* etc., the persons introduced are by no means taken from low or rustic life in the common acceptation of those words; and it is not less clear that the sentiments and language, as far as they can be conceived to have been really transferred from the minds and conversation of such persons, are attributable to causes and circumstances not necessarily connected with "their occupations and abode." The thoughts, feelings, language, and manners of the shepherd-farmers in the vales of Cumberland and Westmoreland, as far as they are actually adopted in those poems, may be accounted for from causes, which will and do produce the same results in every state of life, whether in town or country. As the two principal I rank that Independence, which raises a man above servitude, or daily toil for the profit of others, yet not above the necessity of industry and a frugal simplicity of domestic life; and the accompanying unambitious, but solid and religious, Education, which has rendered few books familiar, but the Bible, and the Liturgy or Hymn book. To this latter cause, indeed, which is so far accidental, that it is the blessing of particular countries and a particular age, not the product of particular places or employments, the poet owes the show of probability that his personages might really feel, think, and talk with any tolerable resemblance to his representation. It is an excellent remark of Dr. Henry More's, that "a man of confined education, but of good parts, by constant reading of the Bible will naturally form a more winning and commanding rhetoric than those that are learned: the intermixture of tongues and of artificial phrases debasing *their* style."[2]

It is, moreover, to be considered that to the formation of healthy feelings, and a reflecting mind, negations involve impediments not less formidable than sophistication and vicious intermixture. I am convinced, that for the human soul to prosper in rustic life a certain vantage-ground is prerequisite. It is not every man that is likely to be improved by a country life or by country labors. Education, or original sensibility, or both, must pre-exist, if the changes, forms, and incidents of nature are to prove a sufficient stimulant. And where these are not sufficient, the mind contracts and hardens by want of stimulants: and the man becomes selfish, sensual, gross, and hard-hearted. Let the management of the Poor Laws in Liverpool, Manchester, or Bristol be compared with the ordinary dispensation of the poor rates in agricultural villages, where the farmers are the overseers and guardians of the poor. If my own experience have not been particularly unfortunate, as well

[1] Preface to *Lyrical Ballads.*

[2] *Enthusiasmus Triumphatus,* Sec. XXXV (Coleridge's note). More (1614–1687) was one of the group known as the Cambridge Platonists. This book was published in 1656. Its sub-title is: "A Discourse of the Nature, Causes, Kinds, and Cure of Enthusiasm."

as that of the many respectable country clergymen with whom I have conversed on the subject, the result would engender more than scepticism concerning the desirable influences of low and rustic life in and for itself. Whatever may be concluded on the other side, from the stronger local attachments and enterprising spirit of the Swiss, and other mountaineers, applies to a particular mode of pastoral life, under forms of property that permit and beget manners truly republican, not to rustic life in general, or to the absence of artificial cultivation. On the contrary the mountaineers, whose manners have been so often eulogized, are in general better educated and greater readers than men of equal rank elsewhere. But where this is not the case, as among the peasantry of North Wales, the ancient mountains, with all their terrors and all their glories, are pictures to the blind, and music to the deaf.

I should not have entered so much into detail upon this passage, but here seems to be the point, to which all the lines of difference converge as to their source and center— I mean, as far as, and in whatever respect, my poetic creed *does* differ from the doctrines promulgated in this preface.—I adopt with full faith, the principle of Aristotle,[3] that poetry, as poetry, is essentially *ideal*, that it avoids and excludes all *accident;* that its apparent individualities of rank, character, or occupation must be representative of a class; and that the persons of poetry must be clothed with generic attributes, with the common attributes of the class: not with such as one gifted individual might possibly possess, but such as from his situation it is most probable before-hand that he would possess. If my premises are right and my deductions legitimate, it follows that there can be no poetic medium between the swains of Theocritus and those of an imaginary golden age.

The characters of the vicar and the shepherd-mariner in the poem of *The Brothers,* that of the shepherd of Green-head Ghyll in the *Michael,* have all the verisimilitude and representative quality that the purposes of poetry can require. They are

3 In the *Poetics,* IX, 1–4.

persons of a known and abiding class, and their manners and sentiments the natural product of circumstances common to the class. Take Michael for instance:

An old man stout of heart, and strong of limb,
His bodily frame had been from youth to age
Of an unusual strength: his mind was keen,
Intense, and frugal, apt for all affairs,
And in his shepherd's calling he was prompt
And watchful more than ordinary men.
Hence he had learned the meaning of all winds,
Of blasts of every tone; and oftentimes
When others heeded not, he heard the South
Make subterraneous music, like the noise
Of bagpipers on distant Highland hills.
The Shepherd, at such warning, of his flock
Bethought him, and he to himself would say,
"The winds are now devising work for me!"
And truly, at all times, the storm, that drives
The traveler to a shelter, summoned him
Up to the mountains: he had been alone
Amid the heart of many thousand mists,
That came to him and left him on the heights.
So lived he, until his eightieth year was past.
And grossly that man errs, who should suppose
That the green valleys, and the streams and rocks,
Were things indifferent to the Shepherd's thoughts.
Fields, where with cheerful spirits he had breathed
The common air; the hills, which he so oft
Had climbed with vigorous steps; which had impressed
So many incidents upon his mind
Of hardship, skill or courage, joy or fear;
Which, like a book, preserved the memory
Of the dumb animals, whom he had saved,
Had fed or sheltered, linking to such acts,
So grateful in themselves, the certainty
Of honorable gain; these fields, these hills
Which were his living being, even more
Than his own blood—what could they less? had laid
Strong hold on his affections, were to him
A pleasurable feeling of blind love,
The pleasure which there is in life itself.

On the other hand, in the poems which are pitched at a lower note, as the *Harry Gill,* and *The Idiot Boy,* the feelings are those of human nature in general; though the poet has judiciously laid the scene in the country, in order to place himself in the vicinity of interesting images, without the necessity of ascribing a sentimental perception of their beauty to the persons of his drama. In *The Idiot Boy,* indeed, the mother's character is not so much a real and native product of a "situation where the essential passions of the heart find a better soil, in which they can attain their maturity and speak a plainer and more emphatic language," as it is an impersonation of an instinct abandoned by judgment. Hence the two following charges seem to me not wholly groundless: at least, they are the only plausible objections, which I have heard to that fine poem. The one is, that the author has not, in the poem itself, taken sufficient care to preclude from the reader's fancy the disgusting images of ordinary morbid idiocy, which yet it was by no means his intention to represent. He was even by the "burr, burr, burr," uncounteracted by any preceding description of the boy's beauty, assisted in recalling them. The other is, that the idiocy of the boy is so evenly balanced by the folly of the mother, as to present to the general reader rather a laughable burlesque on the blindness of anile[4] dotage, than an analytic display of maternal affection in its ordinary workings.

In *The Thorn,* the poet himself acknowledges in a note the necessity of an introductory poem, in which he should have portrayed the character of the person from whom the words of the poem are supposed to proceed: a superstitious man moderately imaginative, of slow faculties and deep feelings, "a captain of a small trading vessel, for example, who, being past the middle age of life, had retired upon an annuity, or small independent income, to some village or country town of which he was not a native, or in which he had not been accustomed to live. Such men having nothing to do become credulous and talkative from indolence." But in a poem, still more in a lyric poem—and the Nurse in Shakespeare's *Romeo and Juliet* alone prevents me from extending the remark even to dramatic poetry, if indeed the Nurse itself can be deemed altogether a case in point—it is not possible to imitate truly a dull and garrulous discourser, without repeating the effects of dullness and garrulity. However this may be, I dare assert that the parts—and these form the far larger portion of the whole—which might as well or still better have proceeded from the poet's own imagination, and have been spoken in his own

[4]Old-womanish.

character, are those which have given, and which will continue to give, universal delight; and that the passages exclusively appropriate to the supposed narrator, such as the last couplet of the third stanza;[5] the seven last lines of the tenth;[6] and the five following stanzas, with the exception of the four admirable lines at the commencement of the fourteenth, are felt by many unprejudiced and unsophisticated hearts, as sudden and unpleasant sinkings from the height to which the poet had previously lifted them, and to which he again re-elevates both himself and his reader.

If then I am compelled to doubt the theory by which the choice of characters was to be directed, not only *a priori,* from grounds of reason, but both from the few instances in which the poet himself need be supposed to have been governed by it, and from the comparative inferiority of those instances; still more must I hesitate in my assent to the sentence which immediately follows the former citation; and which I can neither admit as particular fact, or as general rule. "The language, too, of these men is adopted (purified indeed from what appear to be its real defects, from all lasting and rational causes of dislike or disgust) because such men hourly communicate with the best objects from which the best part of language is originally derived; and because, from their rank in society and the sameness and narrow circle of their intercourse, being less under the action of social vanity, they convey their feelings and notions in simple and unelaborated expressions." To this I reply; that a rustic's language, purified from all provincialism and grossness, and so far reconstructed as to be made consistent with the rules of grammar—which are in essence no other than the laws of universal logic, applied

---

[5]"I've measured it from side to side:
'Tis three feet long, and two feet wide."

[6]"Nay, rack your brain—'tis all in vain,
I'll tell you everything I know;
But to the Thorn, and to the Pond
Which is a little step beyond,
I wish that you would go:
Perhaps, when you are at the place,
You something of her tale may trace."

(Coleridge also quotes the stanzas next mentioned, but these two passages sufficiently illustrate his criticism.)

to psychological materials—will not differ from the language of any other man of common sense, however learned or refined he may be, except as far as the notions, which the rustic has to convey, are fewer and more indiscriminate. This will become still clearer, if we add the consideration—equally important though less obvious—that the rustic, from the more imperfect development of his faculties, and from the lower state of their cultivation, aims almost solely to convey insulated facts, either those of his scanty experience or his traditional belief; while the educated man chiefly seeks to discover and express those connections of things, or those relative bearings of fact to fact, from which some more or less general law is deducible. For facts are valuable to a wise man, chiefly as they lead to the discovery of the indwelling law, which is the true being of things, the sole solution of their modes of existence, and in the knowledge of which consists our dignity and our power.

As little can I agree with the assertion, that from the objects with which the rustic hourly communicates the best part of language is formed. For first, if to communicate with an object implies such an acquaintance with it as renders it capable of being discriminately reflected on, the distinct knowledge of an uneducated rustic would furnish a very scanty vocabulary. The few things and modes of action requisite for his bodily conveniences would alone be individualized; while all the rest of nature would be expressed by a small number of confused general terms. Secondly, I deny that the words and combinations of words derived from the objects, with which the rustic is familiar, whether with distinct or confused knowledge, can be justly said to form the best part of language. It is more than probable that many classes of the brute creation possess discriminating sounds, by which they can convey to each other notices of such objects as concern their food, shelter, or safety. Yet we hesitate to call the aggregate of such sounds a language, otherwise than metaphorically. The best part of human language, properly so called, is derived from reflection on the acts of the mind itself. It is formed by a voluntary appropriation of fixed symbols to internal acts, to processes and results of imagination, the greater part of which have no place in the consciousness of uneducated man; though in civilized society, by imitation and passive remembrance of what they hear from their religious instructors and other superiors, the most uneducated share in the harvest which they neither sowed, nor reaped. If the history of the phrases in hourly currency among our peasants were traced, a person not previously aware of the fact would be surprised at finding so large a number, which three or four centuries ago were the exclusive property of the universities and the schools; and, at the commencement of the Reformation, had been transferred from the school to the pulpit, and thus gradually passed into common life. The extreme difficulty, and often the impossibility, of finding words for the simplest moral and intellectual processes of the languages of uncivilized tribes has proved perhaps the weightiest obstacle to the progress of our most zealous and adroit missionaries. Yet these tribes are surrounded by the same nature as our peasants are; but in still more impressive forms; and they are, moreover, obliged to particularize many more of them. When, therefore, Mr. Wordsworth adds, "accordingly, such a language"—meaning, as before, the language of rustic life purified from provincialism—"arising out of repeated experience and regular feelings, is a more permanent, and a far more philosophical language, than that which is frequently substituted for it by Poets, who think they are conferring honor upon themselves and their art in proportion as they indulge in arbitrary and capricious habits of expression"; it may be answered, that the language, which he has in view, can be attributed to rustics with no greater right, than the style of Hooker[7] or Bacon to Tom Brown[8] or Sir Roger L'Estrange.[9] Doubtless, if what is peculiar to each were omitted in each, the re-

---

[7]Richard Hooker (1554?–1600), author of the treatise *Of the Laws of Ecclesiastical Polity.*

[8]Born 1663, died 1704; translator of the *Comical Romance* of Scarron, and author of many burlesque pieces in prose and verse.

[9]Born *c.* 1617, died 1705; journalist, pamphleteer, author of controversial works remarkable chiefly for their scurrility.

sult must needs be the same. Further, that the poet, who uses an illogical diction, or a style fitted to excite only the low and changeable pleasure of wonder by means of groundless novelty, substitutes a language of folly and vanity, not for that of the rustic, but for that of good sense and natural feeling.

Here let me be permitted to remind the reader that the positions which I controvert are contained in the sentences—"a selection of the real language of men";—"the language of these men" (*i. e.,* men in low and rustic life) "I propose to myself to imitate, and, as far as is possible, to adopt the very language of men." "Between the language of prose and that of metrical composition, there neither is, nor can be, any essential difference." It is against these exclusively that my opposition is directed.

I object, in the very first instance, to an equivocation in the use of the word "real." Every man's language varies, according to the extent of his knowledge, the activity of his faculties, and the depth or quickness of his feelings. Every man's language has, first, its individualities; secondly, the common properties of the class to which he belongs; and thirdly, words and phrases of universal use. The language of Hooker, Bacon, Bishop Taylor, and Burke differs from the common language of the learned class only by the superior number and novelty of the thoughts and relations which they had to convey. The language of Algernon Sidney[10] differs not at all from that which every well-educated gentleman would wish to write, and (with due allowances for the undeliberateness, and less connected train, of thinking natural and proper to conversation) such as he would wish to talk. Neither one nor the other differ half as much from the general language of cultivated society, as the language of Mr. Wordsworth's homeliest composition differs from that of a common peasant. For "real" therefore, we must substitute ordinary, or *lingua communis*.[11] And this, we have proved, is no more to be found in the phraseology of low and rustic life than in that of any other class. Omit the peculiarities of each and the result of course must be common to all. And assuredly the omissions and changes to be made in the language of rustics, before it could be transferred to any species of poem, except the drama or other professed imitation, are at least as numerous and weighty, as would be required in adapting to the same purpose the ordinary language of tradesmen and manufacturers. Not to mention, that the language so highly extolled by Mr. Wordsworth varies in every county, nay in every village, according to the accidental character of the clergyman, the existence or non-existence of schools; or even, perhaps, as the exciseman, publican, or barber happen to be, or not to be, zealous politicians, and readers of the weekly newspaper *pro bono publico*.[12] Anterior to cultivation the *lingua communis* of every country, as Dante has well observed, exists everywhere in parts, and nowhere as a whole.

Neither is the case rendered at all more tenable by the addition of the words, "in a state of excitement." For the nature of a man's words, where he is strongly affected by joy, grief, or anger, must necessarily depend on the number and quality of the general truths, conceptions and images, and of the words expressing them, with which his mind had been previously stored. For the property of passion is not to create; but to set in increased activity. At least, whatever new connections of thoughts or images, or —which is equally, if not more than equally, the appropriate effect of strong excitement— whatever generalizations of truth or experience the heat of passions may produce; yet the terms of their conveyance must have preexisted in his former conversations, and are only collected and crowded together by the unusual stimulation. It is indeed very possible to adopt in a poem the unmeaning repetitions, habitual phrases, and other blank counters, which an unfurnished or confused understanding interposes at short intervals, in order to keep hold of his subject, which is still slipping from him, and to give him time for recollection; or, in mere aid of vacancy,

[10]Born *c.* 1622, beheaded for alleged treason 1683. He was active on the Puritan side in the Civil War, held office under Cromwell, and was an able political theorist, advocating the republican form of government.

[11]Common tongue.

[12]For the public good.

as in the scanty companies of a country stage the same player pops backwards and forwards, in order to prevent the appearance of empty spaces, in the procession of Macbeth, or Henry VIII. But what assistance to the poet, or ornament to the poem, these can supply, I am at a loss to conjecture. Nothing assuredly can differ either in origin or in mode more widely from the *apparent* tautologies of intense and turbulent feeling, in which the passion is greater and of longer endurance than to be exhausted or satisfied by a single representation of the image or incident exciting it. Such repetitions I admit to be a beauty of the highest kind; as illustrated by Mr. Wordsworth himself from the song of Deborah. "At her feet he bowed, he fell, he lay down: at her feet he bowed, he fell: where he bowed, there he fell down dead."[13]

CHAPTER XVIII

I CONCLUDE, therefore, that the attempt is impracticable; and that, were it not impracticable, it would still be useless. For the very power of making the selection implies the previous possession of the language selected. Or where can the poet have lived? And by what rules could he direct his choice, which would not have enabled him to select and arrange his words by the light of his own judgment? We do not adopt the language of a class by the mere adoption of such words exclusively, as that class would use, or at least understand; but likewise by following the *order,* in which the words of such men are wont to succeed each other. Now this order, in the intercourse of uneducated men, is distinguished from the diction of their superiors in knowledge and power, by the greater disjunction and separation in the component parts of that, whatever it be, which they wish to communicate. There is a want of that prospectiveness of mind, that surview, which enables a man to foresee the whole of what he is to convey, appertaining to any one point; and by this means so to subordinate and arrange the different parts according to their relative importance, as to convey it at once, and as an organized whole.

---

[13] Judges, 5:27.

Now I will take the first stanza on which I have chanced to open, in the *Lyrical Ballads.* It is one the most simple and the least peculiar in its language.

> In distant countries have I been,
> And yet I have not often seen
> A healthy man, a man full grown,
> Weep in the public roads, alone.
> But such a one, on English ground,
> And in the broad highway, I met;
> Along the broad highway he came,
> His cheeks with tears were wet:
> Sturdy he seemed, though he was sad;
> And in his arms a lamb he had.[1]

The words here are doubtless such as are current in all ranks of life; and of course not less so in the hamlet and cottage than in the shop, manufactory, college, or palace. But is this the *order,* in which the rustic would have placed the words? I am grievously deceived, if the following less compact mode of commencing the same tale be not a far more faithful copy. "I have been in a many parts, far and near, and I don't know that I ever saw before a man crying by himself in the public road; a grown man I mean, that was neither sick nor hurt," *etc., etc.* But when I turn to the following stanza in *The Thorn:*

> At all times of the day and night
> This wretched woman thither goes;
> And she is known to every star,
> And every wind that blows:
> And there, beside the Thorn, she sits,
> When the blue day-light's in the skies,
> And when the whirlwind's on the hill,
> Or frosty air is keen and still,
> And to herself she cries,
> Oh misery! Oh misery!
> Oh woe is me! Oh misery!

and compare this with the language of ordinary men; or with that which I can conceive at all likely to proceed, in real life, from such a narrator, as is supposed in the note to the poem; compare it either in the succession of the images or of the sentences; I am reminded of the sublime prayer and hymn of praise, which Milton, in opposition to an established liturgy, presents as a fair speci-

---

[1] This is the first stanza of Wordsworth's poem, *The Last of the Flock.*

men of common extemporary devotion, and such as we might expect to hear from every self-inspired minister of a conventicle! And I reflect with delight, how little a mere theory, though of his own workmanship, interferes with the processes of genuine imagination in a man of true poetic genius, who possesses, as Mr. Wordsworth, if ever man did, most assuredly does possess,

The Vision and the Faculty divine.[2]

*   *   *

[2]Wordsworth, *Excursion,* I, 79.

CHARLES LAMB

1775-1834

Lamb's father was a clerk and confidential servant of a barrister, and lived with his family in rooms in the Inner Temple, London, where Charles Lamb was born on 10 February, 1775, the youngest of seven children. Of these only two others survived childhood—John and Mary, who were respectively twelve and ten years older than Charles. In the Temple Lamb passed the first seven years of his life, and then, through the fortunate interest of one of the governors of Christ's Hospital, was admitted to that school, where he remained until he was fourteen. This was the sum of his formal education, which included a very fair knowledge of Latin and some knowledge of Greek. At Christ's Hospital, too, he formed several lasting friendships, perhaps the closest and certainly the most significant being that with Coleridge. Lamb was never blind to Coleridge's faults, small and large—he described him as an "archangel, a little damaged"—but, like most of Coleridge's other friends, he was deeply impressed by him; and when Coleridge died he wrote: "I feel how great a part he was of me. His great and dear spirit haunts me. I cannot think a thought, I cannot make a criticism on men or books, without an ineffectual turning and reference to him. He was the proof and touchstone of all my cogitations." After leaving Christ's Hospital Lamb obtained a minor post in the South Sea House, where his brother John was employed. A couple of years later, in 1792, he became a clerk in the employ of the East India Company—a position in which he faithfully served until 1825, when the directors of the company retired him on a pension. Thus Lamb's life was passed in London. In his childhood and youth he made occasional visits into the country in Hertfordshire, where his grandmother was housekeeper at Blakesware, a country home of the Plumer family; and there, possibly in the near-by village of Widford, he saw and fell in love with the "fair Alice" of *Dream Children,* whom he could not marry. Later in life, too, he spent some of his brief vacations in the country, but to London

he always returned with joy—"London," as he wrote to a Cambridge friend, "whose dirtiest drab-frequented alley, and her lowest-bowing tradesman, I would not·exchange for Skiddaw, Helvellyn, James, Walter, and the parson into the bargain. O! her lamps of a night! her rich goldsmiths, print-shops, toy-shops, mercers, hardware men, pastry-cooks, St. Paul's Church-Yard, the Strand, Exeter Change, Charing Cross, with the man *upon* a black horse! These are thy gods, O London! Ain't you mightily moped on the banks of the Cam? Had you not better come and set up here? You can't think what a difference. All the streets and pavements are pure gold, I warrant you. At least, I know an alchemy that turns her mud into that metal—a mind that loves to be at home in crowds."

Yet life in his beloved London was in one respect a never-ending tragedy to Lamb. There was a strain of insanity in his family which attacked him in the winter of 1795-1796. After it was over he could be merry enough about it, as he could so fortunately be merry over almost everything else. "My life," he wrote Coleridge, "has been somewhat diversified of late. The six weeks that finished last year and began this, your very humble servant spent very agreeably in a mad-house at Hoxton. I am got somewhat rational now, and don't bite any one. But mad I was!" Insanity never attacked Lamb again; but in September, 1796, his sister Mary suddenly became mad and, in Lamb's presence, stabbed their mother to death and wounded their father. Although she later recovered her sanity, she was still subject to recurrent fits of madness, and Lamb sacrificed his life to her welfare, becoming responsible for her and caring for her tenderly until his own death on 27 December, 1834.

In the earlier years of their life together the two were poor, and it was in the hope of increasing their income that Lamb published *A Tale of Rosamund Gray* in 1798. This, however, brought in very little money, and Lamb next attempted to write plays; but he could not get his tragedy, *John Woodvil,* accepted by any theatrical manager, while his comedy, *Mr. H.,* was hissed down as a failure on the first, and only, night of its performance at Drury Lane, Lamb himself joining in the hisses. Several years later William Godwin commissioned the Lambs to write a book for children, and this was immediately successful upon its publication in 1807. It was the *Tales from Shakespeare,* in which Mary did the comedies and Charles the tragedies. In the following year Lamb published his *Specimens of English Dramatic Poets Contemporary with Shakespeare,* which was a not unimportant manifesto of the English romantic movement, and in which Lamb finely exhibited his powers as a critic. But his most fully characteristic work was yet to come. This was the series of *Essays of Elia* contributed to the *London Magazine* in 1820–1822 and published as a book in 1823. A second series was published as the *Last Essays of Elia* in 1833. In these essays Lamb wrote at his ease in a style more intimately personal than had been usual with essayists before his day, and on topics which he freely chose for himself. No analysis is likely to succeed in disentangling their charms; for one reader it may lie chiefly in their quaint bookish flavor derived from Lamb's wide reading in seventeenth-century literature, for another it may lie in their vein of sensibility at once delicate and tender, and for still another it may lie in Lamb's odd, irrepressible humor. Yet the majority of Lamb's readers are probably content not to ask such questions; for of him it is truer than of most writers that there are no half-way measures—if one likes him at all one loves him.

E. V. Lucas is the editor of both *The Works of Charles and Mary Lamb* (7 vols., London, 1903–1905) and *The Letters of Charles Lamb, to Which Are Added Those of His Sister, Mary Lamb* (3 vols., London, 1935). Lucas is also the author of the standard *Life of Charles Lamb* in two volumes (London, 1905). A recent shorter biography is that by Alfred C. Ward, *The Frolic and the Gentle; a Centenary Study of Charles Lamb* (London, 1934); and Edmund Blunden has given an affectionate portrait in *Charles Lamb and His Contemporaries* (Cambridge, 1934). E. C. Johnson's *Lamb Always Elia* (London, 1935) contends that the essayist was not a thwarted man of action, but realized his potentialities in his writing. None of these books, however, has displaced Alfred Ainger's *Charles Lamb* ("English Men of Letters" series, 1882) as a sound and admirable introduction to the study of Elia.

THE TWO RACES OF MEN[1]

THE human species, according to the best theory I can form of it, is composed of two distinct races, *the men who borrow,* and *the men who lend.* To these two original diversities may be reduced all those impertinent classifications of Gothic and Celtic tribes, white men, black men, red men. All the dwellers upon earth, "Parthians, and Medes, and Elamites,"[2] flock hither, and do naturally fall in with one or other of these primary distinctions. The infinite superiority of the former, which I choose to designate as the *great race,* is discernible in their figure, port, and a certain instinctive sovereignty. The latter are born degraded. "He shall serve his brethren."[3] There is something in the air of one of this cast, lean and suspicious; contrasting with the open, trusting, generous manners of the other.

Observe who have been the greatest borrowers of all ages—Alcibiades[4]—Falstaff—Sir Richard Steele—our late incomparable Brinsley[5]—what a family likeness in all four!

What a careless, even deportment hath

---

[1] The first five of the essays here printed come from *Elia* (1823), the sixth and the *Popular Fallacies* from *The Last Essays of Elia* (1833). All of them were published in periodicals before being collected into books, the first six in the *London Magazine* and the *Popular Fallacies* in the *New Monthly Magazine.* Elia was the name of an Italian who had been a clerk in the South Sea House when Lamb was there (before 1792). Lamb explained why he began using this pseudonym in a letter to the publisher of the *London Magazine* concerning *The South Sea House* (the earliest of the Elia essays): "Having a brother now there, and doubting how he might relish certain descriptions in it, I clapped down the name of Elia to it, which passed off pretty well, for Elia himself added the function of an author to that of a scrivener, like myself. I went the other day (not having seen him [Elia] for a year) to laugh over with him at my usurpation of his name, and found him, alas! no more than a name, for he died of consumption eleven months ago, and I knew not of it. So the name has fairly devolved on me, I think; and 'tis all he has left me."

[2] Acts, 2:9.   [3] Genesis, 9:25.

[4] Athenian general, B. C. 450–404.

[5] Richard Brinsley Sheridan (1751–1816), playwright and wit.

your borrower! what rosy gills! what a beautiful reliance on Providence doth he manifest—taking no more thought than lilies![6] What contempt for money—accounting it (yours and mine especially) no better than dross! What a liberal confounding of those pedantic distinctions of *meum* and *tuum*![7] or rather, what a noble simplification of language (beyond Tooke[8]), resolving these supposed opposites into one clear, intelligible pronoun adjective!—What near approaches doth he make to the primitive *community*[9]— to the extent of one-half of the principle at least!—

He is the true taxer who "calleth all the world up to be taxed";[10] and the distance is as vast between him and *one of us,* as subsisted betwixt the Augustan Majesty and the poorest obolary Jew[11] that paid it tribute-pittance at Jerusalem!—His exactions, too, have such a cheerful, voluntary air! So far removed from your sour parochial or state-gatherers—those ink-horn varlets, who carry their want of welcome in their faces! He cometh to you with a smile, and troubleth you with no receipt; confining himself to no set season. Every day is his Candlemas,[12] or his Feast of Holy Michael. He applieth the *lene tormentum*[13] of a pleasant look to your purse—which to that gentle warmth expands her silken leaves, as naturally as the cloak of the traveler, for which sun and wind contended! He is the true Propontic[14] which never ebbeth! The sea which taketh handsomely at each man's hand. In vain the victim, whom he delighteth to honor, struggles with destiny; he is in the net. Lend therefore cheerfully, O man ordained to lend—that thou lose not in the end, with thy worldly penny, the reversion promised. Combine not preposterously in thine own person the penalties of Lazarus and of Dives![15]—but, when thou seest the proper authority coming, meet it smilingly, as it were half-way. Come, a handsome sacrifice! See how light *he* makes of it! Strain not courtesies with a noble enemy.

Reflections like the foregoing were forced upon my mind by the death of my old friend, Ralph Bigod,[16] Esq., who departed this life on Wednesday evening; dying, as he had lived, without much trouble. He boasted himself a descendant from mighty ancestors of that name, who heretofore held ducal dignities in this realm. In his actions and sentiments he belied not the stock to which he pretended. Early in life he found himself invested with ample revenues; which, with that noble disinterestedness which I have noticed as inherent in men of the *great race,* he took almost immediate measures entirely to dissipate and bring to nothing: for there is something revolting in the idea of a king holding a private purse; and the thoughts of Bigod were all regal. Thus furnished, by the very act of disfurnishment; getting rid of the cumbersome luggage of riches, more apt (as one sings)

To slacken virtue, and abate her edge,
Than prompt her to do aught may merit praise,[17]

he set forth, like some Alexander, upon his great enterprise, "borrowing and to borrow!"

In his periegesis,[18] or triumphant progress throughout this island, it has been calculated that he laid a tithe[19] part of the inhabitants under contribution. I reject this estimate as greatly exaggerated:—but having had the honor of accompanying my friend divers times, in his perambulations about this vast city, I own I was greatly struck at first with the prodigious number of faces we met, who claimed a sort of respectful acquaintance with us. He was one day so obliging as to explain the phenomenon. It seems, these were his tributaries; feeders of his exchequer; gentlemen, his good friends (as he

[6]St. Matthew, 6:28.   [7]Mine and thine.

[8]John Horne Tooke (1736–1812), politician and philologer, who published his philological theories in *The Diversions of Purley.*

[9]I. e., communism.   [10]St. Luke, 2:1.

[11]I. e., between the Emperor Augustus and the Jew who paid an obolus (about 3 cents).

[12]2nd February, a quarter-day, for the payment of rents, in Scotland. Michaelmas, 29 September, is an English quarter-day.

[13]Gentle stimulus.

[14]The Sea of Marmora, which has no tides.

[15]St. Luke, 16:19–31.

[16]I. e., John Fenwick, a friend of the Lambs who was usually in financial difficulties.

[17]*Paradise Regained,* II, 455–6.

[18]Journey round.   [19]Tenth.

was pleased to express himself), to whom he had occasionally been beholden for a loan. Their multitudes did in no way disconcert him. He rather took a pride in numbering them; and, with Comus, seemed pleased to be "stocked with so fair a herd."

With such sources, it was a wonder how he contrived to keep his treasury always empty. He did it by force of an aphorism, which he had often in his mouth, that "money kept longer than three days stinks." So he made use of it while it was fresh. A good part he drank away (for he was an excellent toss-pot), some he gave away, the rest he threw away, literally tossing and hurling it violently from him—as boys do burrs, or as if it had been infectious,—into ponds, or ditches, or deep holes,—inscrutable cavities of the earth;—or he would bury it (where he would never seek it again) by a river's side under some bank, which (he would facetiously observe) paid no interest—but out away from him it must go peremptorily, as Hagar's offspring[20] into the wilderness, while it was sweet. He never missed it. The streams were perennial which fed his fisc.[21] When new supplies became necessary, the first person that had the felicity to fall in with him, friend or stranger, was sure to contribute to the deficiency. For Bigod had an *undeniable* way with him. He had a cheerful, open exterior, a quick jovial eye, a bald forehead, just touched with gray (*cana fides*[22]). He anticipated no excuse, and found none. And, waiving for a while my theory as to the *great race,* I would put it to the most untheorizing reader, who may at times have disposable coin in his pocket, whether it is not more repugnant to the kindliness of his nature to refuse such a one as I am describing, than to say *no* to a poor petitionary rogue (your bastard borrower), who, by his mumping visnomy,[23] tells you that he expects nothing better; and, therefore, whose preconceived notions and expectations you do in reality so much less shock in the refusal.

When I think of this man; his fiery glow of heart; his swell of feeling; how magnificent, how *ideal* he was; how great at the midnight hour; and when I compare with him the companions with whom I have associated since, I grudge the saving of a few idle ducats,[24] and think that I am fallen into the society of *lenders,* and *little men.*

To one like Elia, whose treasures are rather cased in leather covers than closed in iron coffers, there is a class of alienators[25] more formidable than that which I have touched upon; I mean your *borrowers of books*—those mutilators of collections, spoilers of the symmetry of shelves, and creators of odd volumes. There is Comberbatch,[26] matchless in his depredations!

That foul gap in the bottom shelf facing you, like a great eye-tooth knocked out— (you are now with me in my little back study in Bloomsbury,[27] reader!)——with the huge Switzer-like[28] tomes on each side (like the Guildhall giants,[29] in their reformed posture, guardant of nothing) once held the tallest of my folios, *Opera Bonaventurae,*[30] choice and massy divinity, to which its two supporters (school[31] divinity also, but of a lesser caliber—Bellarmine,[32] and Holy Thomas[33]), showed but as dwarfs,—itself an Ascapart![34]—*that* Comberbatch abstracted upon the faith of a theory he holds, which is more easy, I confess, for me to suffer by than to refute, namely, that "the title to property in a book (my Bonaventure, for instance), is in exact ratio to the claimant's powers of understanding and appreciating the same." Should he go on acting upon this theory, which of our shelves is safe?

The slight vacuum in the left-hand case—

---

[20]Ishmael (Genesis, 21:9). [21]Purse.
[22]The gray hair of honor. *Cf. Aeneid,* I, 292.
[23]Begging physiognomy.

[24]Coins; originally, Italian coins.

[25]Takers of others' property.

[26]Coleridge, who when he enlisted in a regiment of dragoons assumed the name of Silas Titus Comberback.

[27]A section of London in which Lamb was *not* living when he wrote this.

[28]I. e., very large.

[29]Gog and Magog, Biblical giants whose statues are in the London Guildhall.

[30]The Works of St. Bonaventura.

[31]Scholastic. [32]Italian cardinal (1542-1621).

[33]St. Thomas Aquinas, 1227-1274.

[34]A giant thirty feet in height. He appears in *Bevis of Hampton.*

two shelves from the ceiling—scarcely distinguishable but by the quick eye of a loser——was whilom the commodious resting-place of Brown on Urn Burial.[35]   C. will hardly allege that he knows more about that treatise than I do, who introduced it to him, and was indeed the first (of the moderns) to discover its beauties—but so have I known a foolish lover to praise his mistress in the presence of a rival more qualified to carry her off than himself.—Just below, Dodsley's dramas[36] want their fourth volume, where Vittoria Corombona is! The remainder nine are as distasteful as Priam's refuse sons, when the Fates *borrowed* Hector. Here stood the Anatomy of Melancholy,[37] in sober state.—There loitered the Complete Angler,[38] quiet as in life, by some stream side.—In yonder nook, John Buncle,[39] a widower-volume, with "eyes closed," mourns his ravished mate.

One justice I must do my friend, that if he sometimes, like the sea, sweeps away a treasure, at another time, sea-like, he throws up as rich an equivalent to match it. I have a small under-collection of this nature (my friend's gatherings in his various calls), picked up, he has forgotten at what odd places, and deposited with as little memory at mine. I take in these orphans, the twice-deserted. These proselytes of the gate are welcome as the true Hebrews. There they stand in conjunction; natives, and naturalized. The latter seem as little disposed to inquire out their true lineage as I am.—I charge no warehouse-room for these deodands,[40] nor shall ever put myself to the ungentlemanly trouble of advertising a sale of them to pay expenses.

To lose a volume to C. carries some sense and meaning in it. You are sure that he will make one hearty meal on your viands,

if he can give no account of the platter after it. But what moved thee, wayward, spiteful K.,[41] to be so importunate to carry off with thee, in spite of tears and adjurations to thee to forbear, the Letters of that princely woman, the thrice noble Margaret Newcastle?[42]—knowing at the time, and knowing that I knew also, thou most assuredly wouldst never turn over one leaf of the illustrious folio:—what but the mere spirit of contradiction, and childish love of getting the better of thy friend?—Then, worst cut of all! to transport it with thee to the Gallican land—

Unworthy land to harbor such a sweetness,
A virtue in which all ennobling thoughts dwelt,
Pure thoughts, kind thoughts, high thoughts,
    her sex's wonder!

——hadst thou not thy play-books, and books of jests and fancies, about thee, to keep thee merry, even as thou keepest all companies with thy quips and mirthful tales?—Child of the Green-room, it was unkindly done of thee. Thy wife, too, that part-French, better-part-Englishwoman!—that *she* could fix upon no other treatise to bear away in kindly token of remembering us, than the works of Fulke Greville, Lord Brook[43]—of which no Frenchman, nor woman of France, Italy, or England, was ever by nature constituted to comprehend a tittle! *Was there not Zimmerman[44] on Solitude?*

Reader, if haply thou art blessed with a moderate collection, be shy of showing it; or if thy heart overfloweth to lend them, lend thy books; but let it be to such a one as S. T. C.—he will return them (generally anticipating the time appointed) with usury; enriched with annotations, tripling their value. I have had experience. Many are these precious MSS. of his—(in *matter* oftentimes, and almost in *quantity* not infrequently, vying with the originals)—in no

---

[35]Sir Thomas Browne's *Hydriotaphia, or Urn-Burial.*

[36]Robert Dodsley (1703–1764) edited a collection of plays, among which was John Webster's *The White Devil, or Vittoria Corombona* (1612).

[37]By Robert Burton (1577–1640).

[38]By Izaak Walton (1593–1683).

[39]By Thomas Amory (1691?–1788).

[40]In English law a thing which, having caused the death of a person, was forfeited to the Crown for pious uses.

[41]James Kenney (1780–1849), a dramatist, at this time living in France.

[42]The first Duchess of Newcastle (1624–1673).

[43]Lived 1554–1628, the friend and biographer of Sir Philip Sidney.

[44]Johann Georg von Zimmermann (1728–1795), a Swiss physician.

very clerkly hand—legible in my Daniel;[45] in old Burton; in Sir Thomas Browne; and those obstruser cogitations of the Greville, now, alas! wandering in Pagan lands.——I counsel thee, shut not thy heart, nor thy library, against S. T. C.

A CHAPTER ON EARS

I HAVE no ear.——

Mistake me not, reader,—nor imagine that I am by nature destitute of those exterior twin appendages, hanging ornaments, and (architecturally speaking) handsome volutes[1] to the human capital. Better my mother had never borne me.—I am, I think, rather delicately than copiously provided with those conduits; and I feel no disposition to envy the mule for his plenty, or the mole for her exactness, in those ingenious labyrinthine inlets—those indispensable side-intelligencers.

Neither have I incurred, nor done anything to incur, with Defoe, that hideous disfigurement, which constrained him to draw upon assurance—to feel "quite unabashed,"[2] and at ease upon that article. I was never, I thank my stars, in the pillory, nor, if I read them aright, is it within the compass of my destiny, that I ever should be.

When therefore I say that I have no ear, you will understand me to mean—*for music.* —To say that this heart never melted at the concourse of sweet sounds,[3] would be a foul self-libel.—*"Water parted from the sea"* never fails to move it strangely. So does *"In infancy."*[4] But they were used to be sung at her harpsichord (the old-fashioned instrument in vogue in those days) by a gentlewoman—the gentlest, sure, that ever merited the appellation—the sweetest—why should I hesitate to name Mrs. S——,[5] once the blooming Fanny Weatheral of the Temple—who had power to thrill the soul of Elia, small imp as he was even in his long coats; and to make him glow, tremble, and blush with a passion, that not faintly indicated the day-spring of that absorbing sentiment, which was afterwards destined to overwhelm and subdue his nature quite, for Alice W——n.[6]

I even think that *sentimentally* I am disposed to harmony. But *organically* I am incapable of a tune. I have been practicing *"God save the King"* all my life; whistling and humming of it over to myself in solitary corners; and am not yet arrived, they tell me, within many quavers of it. Yet hath the loyalty of Elia never been impeached.

I am not without suspicion that I have an undeveloped faculty of music within me. For, thrumming, in my wild way, on my friend A.'s[7] piano, the other morning, while he was engaged in an adjoining parlor,—on his return he was pleased to say, *"he thought it could not be the maid!"* On his first surprise at hearing the keys touched in somewhat an airy and masterful way, not dreaming of me, his suspicions had lighted on Jenny. But a grace, snatched from a superior refinement, soon convinced him that some being,—technically perhaps deficient, but higher informed from a principle common to all the fine arts,—had swayed the keys to a mood which Jenny, with all her (less cultivated) enthusiasm, could never have elicited from them. I mention this as a proof of my friend's penetration, and not with any view of disparaging Jenny.

Scientifically I could never be made to understand (yet have I taken some pains)

---

[45]Samuel Daniel (1562–1619).

[1]Spiral decorations on the tops of columns of the Ionic and Corinthian orders.

[2]On the first publication of this paper Lamb quoted in a note, from Pope's *Dunciad* (II, 147), "Earless on high stood unabashed Defoe." Defoe was pilloried for his tract, *The Shortest Way with the Dissenters,* but he never had his ears cropped.

[3]*Merchant of Venice,* V, i, 84.

[4]Both are songs from Arne's opera *Artaxerxes* (see Lamb's *My First Play*).

[5]Mrs. Spinkes. Nothing is known of her save her name.

[6]According to a key Lamb made for a fellow clerk at the East India House this name is Alice Winterton, but Lamb adds that the name is feigned. It has been suggested that Lamb means Ann Simmons, of Blenheims, near Blakesware; but Mr. E. V. Lucas thinks "that Alice W——n was more an abstraction around which now and then to group tender imaginings of what might have been than any tangible figure."

[7]Probably William Ayrton (1777–1818), musical critic and a friend of Lamb's.

what a note in music is; or how one note should differ from another. Much less in voices can I distinguish a soprano from a tenor. Only sometimes the thorough bass[8] I contrive to guess at, from its being super- eminently harsh and disagreeable. I tremble, however, for my misapplication of the simplest terms of *that* which I disclaim. While I profess my ignorance, I scarce know what to *say* I am ignorant of. I hate, perhaps, by misnomers. *Sostenuto* and *adagio*[9] stand in the like relation of obscurity to me; and *Sol, Fa, Mi, Re,*[10] is as conjuring as *Baralipton.*[11]

It is hard to stand alone—in an age like this,—(constituted to the quick and critical perception of all harmonious combinations, I verily believe, beyond all preceding ages, since Jubal tumbled upon the gamut[12])—to remain, as it were, singly unimpressible to the magic influences of an art which is said to have such an especial stroke at soothing, elevating, and refining the passions.—Yet rather than break the candid current of my confessions, I must avow to you that I have received a great deal more pain than pleasure from this so cried-up faculty.

I am constitutionally susceptible of noises. A carpenter's hammer, in a warm summer noon, will fret me into more than midsummer madness. But those unconnected, unset sounds are nothing to the measured malice of music. The ear is passive to those single strokes; willingly enduring stripes, while it hath no task to con.[13] To music it cannot be passive. It will strive—mine at least will— 'spite of its inaptitude, to thrid[14] the maze; like an unskilled eye painfully poring upon hieroglyphics. I have sat through an Italian Opera, till, for sheer pain, and inexplicable anguish, I have rushed out into the noisiest places of the crowded streets, to solace myself with sounds which I was not obliged to follow, and get rid of the distracting torment of endless, fruitless, barren attention! I take refuge in the unpretending assemblage

of honest, common-life sounds;—and the purgatory of the Enraged Musician[15] becomes my paradise.

I have sat at an Oratorio (that profanation of the purposes of the cheerful playhouse) watching the faces of the auditory in the pit (what a contrast to Hogarth's Laughing Audience!) immovable, or affecting some faint emotion—till (as some have said that our occupations in the next world will be but a shadow of what delighted us in this) I have imagined myself in some cold Theater in Hades, where some of the *forms* of the earthly one should be kept up, with none of the *enjoyment;* or like that—

———Party in a parlor,
All silent, and all DAMNED![16]

Above all, those insufferable concertos, and pieces of music, as they are called, do plague and embitter my apprehension.— Words are something; but to be exposed to an endless battery of mere sounds; to be long a dying, to lie stretched upon a rack of roses; to keep up languor by unintermitted effort; to pile honey upon sugar, and sugar upon honey, to an interminable tedious sweetness; to fill up sound with feeling, and strain ideas to keep pace with it; to gaze on empty frames, and be forced to make the pictures for yourself; to read a book, *all stops,*[17] and be obliged to supply the verbal matter; to invent extempore tragedies to answer to the vague gestures of an inexplicable rambling mime[18]—these are faint shadows of what I have undergone from a series of the ablest-executed pieces of this empty *instrumental music.*

I deny not, that in the opening of a concert, I have experienced something vastly lulling and agreeable:—afterwards followeth the languor, and the oppression. Like that disappointing book in Patmos;[19] or, like the comings on of melancholy, described by Bur-

---

[8]I. e., a bass voice. Lamb does not use the phrase in its technical sense.

[9]"Sustained" and "slow."   [10]Names of notes.

[11]I. e., as mysterious as an arbitrary term in logic.

[12]Musical scale. See Genesis, 4:21.

[13]To attend to.   [14]Thread.

[15]The allusion is to Hogarth's picture of a musician driven almost mad by street noises.

[16]Quoted from the first edition of Wordsworth's *Peter Bell.* The stanza containing these lines was omitted in later editions.

[17]All marks of punctuation, with no words.

[18]An actor playing a part without words.

[19]Revelation, 10:10.

ton,[20] doth music make her first insinuating approaches:—"Most pleasant it is to such as are melancholy given, to walk alone in some solitary grove, betwixt wood and water, by some brook side, and to meditate upon some delightsome and pleasant subject, which shall affect him most, *amabilis insania,* and *mentis gratissimus error.*[21] A most incomparable delight to build castles in the air, to go smiling to themselves, acting an infinite variety of parts, which they suppose, and strongly imagine, they act, or that they see done.—So delightsome these toys at first, they could spend whole days and nights without sleep, even whole years in such contemplations, and fantastical meditations, which are like so many dreams, and will hardly be drawn from them—winding and unwinding themselves as so many clocks, and still pleasing their humors, until at last the SCENE TURNS UPON A SUDDEN, and they being now habitated to such meditations, and solitary places, can endure no company, can think of nothing but harsh and distasteful subjects. Fear, sorrow, suspicion, *subrusticus pudor,*[22] discontent, cares, and weariness of life, surprise them on a sudden, and they can think of nothing else: continually suspecting, no sooner are their eyes open, but this infernal plague of melancholy seizeth on them, and terrifies their souls, representing some dismal object to their minds; which now, by no means, no labor, no persuasions, they can avoid, they cannot be rid of it, they cannot resist."

Something like this "SCENE-TURNING" I have experienced at the evening parties, at the house of my good Catholic friend *Nov*——[23] who, by the aid of a capital organ, himself the most finished of players, converts his drawing-room into a chapel, his week days into Sundays, and these latter into minor heavens.[24]

When my friend commences upon one of those solemn anthems, which peradventure struck upon my heedless ear, ramblings in the side aisles of the dim abbey,[25] some five and thirty years since, waking a new sense, and putting a soul of old religion into my young apprehension—(whether it be *that,* in which the psalmist, weary of the persecutions of bad men, wisheth to himself dove's wings—or *that other,* which with a like measure of sobriety and pathos, inquireth by what means the young man shall best cleanse his mind[26])—a holy calm pervadeth me.—I am for the time

——————rapt above earth,
And possess joys not promised at my birth.[27]

But when this master of the spell, not content to have laid a soul prostrate, goes on, in his power, to inflict more bliss than lies in her capacity to receive,—impatient to overcome her "earthly" with his "heavenly,"[28]—still pouring in, for protracted hours, fresh waves and fresh from the sea of sound, or from that inexhausted *German* ocean, above which, in triumphant progress, dolphin-seated,[29] ride those Arions *Haydn* and *Mozart,* with their attendant tritons,[30] *Bach, Beethoven,* and a countless tribe, whom to attempt to reckon up would but plunge me again in the deeps,—I stagger under the weight of harmony, reeling to and fro at my wit's end;—clouds, as of frankincense, oppress me—priests, altars, censers, dazzle before me—the genius of *his* religion hath me in her toils—a shadowy triple tiara invests the brow of my friend, late so naked, so ingenuous—he is Pope,—and by him sits, like as in the anomaly of dreams, a she-Pope too,—tri-coronated like himself!—I am converted, and yet a Protestant;—at once

[20]*Anatomy of Melancholy,* I, ii, ii, 6.

[21]"Delightful madness," and "most pleasing deception of the mind." (Both phrases come from Horace, *Odes* III, iv, 5, and *Epistles* II, ii, 140.)

[22]Awkward shyness (Cicero, *Ad. Fam.* V, xii).

[23]Vincent Novello (1781–1861), organist, father of Mrs. Cowden Clarke.

[24]I have been there, and still would go;
'Tis like a little heaven below.—*Dr. Watts.*
(Lamb's Note. From *Divine Songs for Children,* 28th Song.)

[25]Westminster Abbey.

[26]These anthems are based on Psalms LV and CXIX respectively.

[27]Quoted by Walton, *Compleat Angler,* I, iv.

[28]I Corinthians, 15:48.

[29]According to legend the Lesbian musician Arion, when threatened with death by sailors, so charmed a dolphin with his playing that the dolphin carried him on its back safely to land.

[30]Sea-gods, attendants of Neptune.

malleus hereticorum,[31] and myself grand heresiarch:[32] or three heresies center in my person:—I am Marcion, Ebion, and Cerinthus[33]—Gog and Magog[34]—what not?—till

[31]The heretics' hammer. The title was given to Johann Faber (1478–1541) because of his treatise, bearing the same title, against Luther.

[32]Leader in heresy.

[33]Heretics in the early days of Christianity.

[34]Unbelievers. See Revelation, 20:7–9.

the coming in of the friendly supper-tray dissipates the figment, and a draught of true Lutheran[35] beer (in which chiefly my friend shows himself no bigot) at once reconciles me to the rationalities of a purer faith; and restores to me the genuine unterrifying aspects of my pleasant-countenanced host and hostess.

[35]I. e., protestant.

DREAM-CHILDREN; A REVERIE[1]

CHILDREN love to listen to stories about their elders, when *they* were children; to stretch their imagination to the conception of a traditionary great-uncle or grandame, whom they never saw. It was in this spirit that my little ones crept about me the other evening to hear about their great-grandmother Field, who lived in a great house in Norfolk[2] (a hundred times bigger than that in which they and papa lived) which had been the scene—so at least it was generally believed in that part of the country—of the tragic incidents which they had lately become familiar with from the ballad of the Children in the Wood.[3] Certain it is that the whole story of the children and their cruel uncle was to be seen fairly carved out in wood upon the chimney-piece of the great hall, the whole story down to the Robin Redbreasts,[4] till a foolish rich person pulled it down to set up a marble one of modern invention in its stead, with no story upon it. Here Alice put out one of her dear mother's looks, too tender to be called upbraiding. Then I went on to say how religious and how good their great-grandmother Field was, how beloved and respected by everybody, though she was not indeed the mistress of this great house, but had only the charge of

[1]Lamb's brother John died on 26 October, 1821, and Lamb is believed to have begun this essay shortly afterwards, in a mood of reminiscence and reverie.

[2]The house is Blakesware, really in Hertfordshire, where Mary Field, Lamb's grandmother, was housekeeper.

[3]The scene of this legend is the county of Norfolk, a fact which may have induced Lamb to choose Norfolk in seeking to disguise the identity of Blakesware.

[4]Which, at the close of the ballad, cover with leaves the bodies of the murdered children.

it (and yet in some respects she might be said to be the mistress of it too) committed to her by the owner, who preferred living in a newer and more fashionable mansion which he had purchased somewhere in the adjoining county; but still she lived in it in a manner as if it had been her own, and kept up the dignity of the great house in a sort while she lived, which afterwards came to decay, and was nearly pulled down, and all its old ornaments stripped and carried away to the owner's other house, where they were set up, and looked as awkward as if some one were to carry away the old tombs they had seen lately at the Abbey, and stick them up in Lady C.'s tawdry gilt drawing-room. Here John smiled, as much as to say, "that would be foolish indeed." And then I told how, when she came to die, her funeral was attended by a concourse of all the poor, and some of the gentry too, of the neighborhood for many miles round, to show their respect for her memory, because she had been such a good and religious woman; so good indeed that she knew all the Psaltery[5] by heart, ay, and a great part of the Testament besides. Here little Alice spread her hands. Then I told what a tall, upright, graceful person their great-grandmother Field once was; and how in her youth she was esteemed the best dancer—here Alice's little right foot played an involuntary movement, till upon my looking grave, it desisted—the best dancer, I was saying, in the county, till a cruel disease, called a cancer, came, and bowed her down with pain; but it could never bend her good spirits, or make them stoop, but they were still upright, because she was so good and religious. Then I told

[5]Psalter, the Book of Psalms.

how she was used to sleep by herself in a lone chamber of the great lone house; and how she believed that an apparition of two infants was to be seen at midnight gliding up and down the great staircase near where she slept, but she said "those innocents would do her no harm"; and how frightened I used to be, though in those days I had my maid to sleep with me, because I was never half so good or religious as she—and yet I never saw the infants. Here John expanded all his eyebrows and tried to look courageous. Then I told how good she was to all her grandchildren, having us to the great house in the holidays, where I in particular used to spend many hours by myself, in gazing upon the old busts of the Twelve Caesars,[6] that had been Emperors of Rome, till the old marble heads would seem to live again, or I to be turned into marble with them; how I never could be tired with roaming about that huge mansion, with its vast empty rooms, with their worn-out hangings, fluttering tapestry, and carved oaken panels, with the gilding almost rubbed out—sometimes in the spacious old-fashioned gardens, which I had almost to myself, unless when now and then a solitary gardening man would cross me— and how the nectarines and peaches hung upon the walls, without my ever offering to pluck them, because they were forbidden fruit, unless now and then,—and because I had more pleasure in strolling about among the old melancholy-looking yew trees, or the firs, and picking up the red berries, and the fir apples,[7] which were good for nothing but to look at—or in lying about upon the fresh grass, with all the fine garden smells around me—or basking in the orangery, till I could almost fancy myself ripening too along with the oranges and the limes in that grateful warmth—or in watching the dace that darted to and fro in the fish-pond, at the bottom of the garden, with here and there a great sulky pike hanging midway down the water in silent state, as if it mocked at their impertinent friskings,—I had more pleasure in these busy-idle diversions than in all the sweet flavors of peaches, nectarines, oranges, and

such like common baits of children. Here John slily deposited back upon the plate a bunch of grapes, which, not unobserved by Alice, he had meditated dividing with her, and both seemed willing to relinquish them for the present as irrelevant. Then in somewhat a more heightened tone, I told how, though their great-grandmother Field loved all her grandchildren, yet in an especial manner she might be said to love their uncle, John L——,[8] because he was so handsome and spirited a youth, and a king to the rest of us; and, instead of moping about in solitary corners, like some of us, he would mount the most mettlesome horse he could get, when but an imp no bigger than themselves, and make it carry him half over the county in a morning, and join the hunters when there were any out—and yet he loved the old great house and gardens too, but had too much spirit to be always pent up within their boundaries—and how their uncle grew up to man's estate as brave as he was handsome, to the admiration of everybody, but of their great-grandmother Field most especially; and how he used to carry me upon his back when I was a lame-footed boy—for he was a good bit older than me—many a mile when I could not walk for pain;—and how in after life he became lame-footed too, and I did not always (I fear) make allowances enough for him when he was impatient, and in pain, nor remember sufficiently how considerate he had been to me when I was lame-footed; and how when he died, though he had not been dead an hour, it seemed as if he had died a great while ago, such a distance there is betwixt life and death; and how I bore his death as I thought pretty well at first, but afterwards it haunted and haunted me; and though I did not cry or take it to heart as some do, and as I think he would have done if I had died, yet I missed him all day long, and knew not till then how much I had loved him. I missed his kindness, and I missed his crossness, and wished him to be alive again, to be quarreling with him (for we quarreled sometimes), rather than not have him again, and was as uneasy without him, as he their poor uncle must have been when the doctor took off his

---

[6]The Roman Emperors from Julius Caesar to Domitian.

[7]Fir cones.

[8]Lamb's brother.

limb.[9] Here the children fell a crying, and asked if their little mourning which they had on was not for uncle John, and they looked up, and prayed me not to go on about their uncle, but to tell them some stories about their pretty dead mother. Then I told how for seven long years, in hope sometimes, sometimes in despair, yet persisting ever, I courted the fair Alice W——n;[10] and, as much as children could understand, I explained to them what coyness, and difficulty, and denial meant in maidens—when suddenly, turning to Alice, the soul of the first Alice looked out at her eyes with such a reality of re-presentment, that I became in doubt which of them stood there before me, or whose that bright hair was; and while I stood gazing, both the children gradually grew fainter to my view, receding, and still receding till nothing at last but two mournful features were seen in the uttermost distance, which, without speech, strangely impressed upon me the effects of speech; "We are not of Alice, nor of thee, nor are we children at all. The children of Alice call Bartrum[11] father. We are nothing; less than nothing, and dreams. We are only what might have been, and must wait upon the tedious shores of Lethe[12] millions of ages before we have existence, and a name"—and immediately awaking, I found myself quietly seated in my bachelor armchair, where I had fallen asleep, with the faithful Bridget[13] unchanged by my side—but John L. (or James Elia) was gone for ever.

[9]This, as far as is known, did not actually happen.

[10]Concerning this name see note to *A Chapter on Ears.*

[11]Ann Simmons married a Mr. Bartrum, or Bartram, a London pawnbroker.

[12]The river of forgetfulness, in Hades. In the *Aeneid* (VI, 703-751) Virgil tells how the soul, after many ages and after drinking of this river, returns to earth in a new body.

[13]Lamb's sister Mary, although in the *Essays of Elia* Bridget is spoken of as a cousin.

THE PRAISE OF CHIMNEY-SWEEPERS

I LIKE to meet a sweep—understand me—not a grown sweeper—old chimney-sweepers are by no means attractive—but one of those tender novices, blooming through their first nigritude,[1] the maternal washings not quite effaced from the cheek—such as come forth with the dawn, or somewhat earlier, with their little professional notes sounding like the *peep peep* of a young sparrow; or liker to the matin lark should I pronounce them, in their aerial ascents not seldom anticipating the sun-rise?

I have a kindly yearning toward these dim specks—poor blots—innocent blacknesses——

I reverence these young Africans of our own growth—these almost clergy imps, who sport their cloth[2] without assumption; and from their little pulpits (the tops of chimneys), in the nipping air of a December morning, preach a lesson of patience to mankind.

When a child, what a mysterious pleasure it was to witness their operation! to see a chit no bigger than one's self enter, one knew not by what process, into what seemed the *fauces Averni*[3]—to pursue him in imagination, as he went sounding on through so many dark stifling caverns, horrid shades!—to shudder with the idea that "now, surely, he must be lost for ever!"—to revive at hearing his feeble shout of discovered daylight—and then (O fullness of delight) running out of doors, to come just in time to see the sable phenomenon emerge in safety, the brandished weapon of his art victorious like some flag waved over a conquered citadel! I seem to remember having been told that a bad sweep was once left in a stack with his brush, to indicate which way the wind blew. It was an awful spectacle certainly; not much unlike the old stage direction in Macbeth,[4] where the "Apparition of a child crowned with a tree in his hand rises."

Reader, if thou meetest one of these small gentry in thy early rambles, it is good to give him a penny. It is better to give him twopence. If it be starving weather, and to the proper troubles of his hard occupation, a pair of kibed[5] heels (no unusual accompani-

[1]Blackness.   [2]The dress of their calling.

[3]The jaws of Hell (*Aeneid*, VI, 201).
[4]Act IV, sc. i.   [5]Afflicted with chilblains.

ment) be superadded, the demand on thy humanity will surely rise to a tester.[6]

There is a composition, the ground-work of which I have understood to be the sweet wood 'yclept[7] sassafras. This wood boiled down to a kind of tea, and tempered with an infusion of milk and sugar, hath to some tastes a delicacy beyond the China luxury. I know not how thy palate may relish it; for myself, with every deference to the judicious Mr. Read, who hath time out of mind kept open a shop (the only one he avers in London) for the vending of this "wholesome and pleasant beverage, on the south side of Fleet Street, as thou approachest Bridge Street—*the only Salopian house*,"[8]—I have never yet ventured to dip my own particular lip in a basin of his commended ingredients —a cautious premonition to the olfactories constantly whispering to me that my stomach must infallibly, with all due courtesy, decline it. Yet I have seen palates, otherwise not uninstructed in dietetical elegances, sup it up with avidity.

I know not by what particular conformation of the organ it happens, but I have always found that this composition is surprisingly gratifying to the palate of a young chimney-sweeper—whether the oily particles (sassafras is slightly oleaginous) do attenuate and soften the fuliginous[9] concretions, which are sometimes found (in dissections) to adhere to the roof of the mouth in these unfledged practitioners; or whether Nature, sensible that she had mingled too much of bitter wood[10] in the lot of these raw victims, caused to grow out of the earth her sassafras for a sweet lenitive[11]—but so it is, that no possible taste or odor to the senses of a young chimney-sweeper can convey a delicate excitement comparable to this mixture. Being penniless, they will yet hang their black heads over the ascending steam, to gratify one sense if possible, seemingly no less pleased than those domestic animals— cats—when they purr over a new-found sprig of valerian.[12] There is something more in these sympathies than philosophy can inculcate.

Now albeit Mr. Read boasteth, not without reason, that his is the *only Salopian house;* yet be it known to thee, reader—if thou art one who keepest what are called good hours, thou art haply ignorant of the fact—he hath a race of industrious imitators, who from stalls, and under open sky, dispense the same savory mess to humbler customers, at that dead time of the dawn, when (as extremes meet) the rake, reeling home from his midnight cups, and the hard-handed artisan leaving his bed to resume the premature labors of the day, jostle, not unfrequently to the manifest disconcerting of the former, for the honors of the pavement. It is the time when, in summer, between the expired and the not yet relumined kitchen fires, the kennels of our fair metropolis give forth their least satisfactory odors. The rake, who wisheth to dissipate his o'er-night vapors in more grateful coffee, curses the ungenial fume, as he passeth; but the artisan stops to taste, and blesses the fragrant breakfast.

This is *Saloop*—the precocious herb-woman's darling—the delight of the early gardener, who transports his smoking cabbages by break of day from Hammersmith to Covent Garden's famed piazzas[13]—the delight, and, oh I fear, too often the envy, of the unpennied sweep. Him shouldest thou haply encounter, with his dim visage pendent over the grateful steam, regale him with a sumptuous basin (it will cost thee but three halfpennies) and a slice of delicate bread and butter (an added halfpenny)—so may thy culinary fires, eased of the o'er-charged secretions from thy worse-placed hospitalities, curl up a lighter volume to the welkin[14] —so may the descending soot never taint thy costly well-ingredienced soups—nor the odious cry, quick-reaching from street to street, of the *fired chimney*, invite the rattling engines from ten adjacent parishes, to disturb for a casual scintillation[15] thy peace and pocket!

I am by nature extremely susceptible of

---

[6]Sixpence. [7]Called.
[8]Saloop was the name of this beverage, whence salopian.
[9]Sooty. [10]Wormwood.
[11]Softener of pain. [12]Or catnip.

[13]I. e., to London's fruit and flower market.
[14]Sky. [15]Eruption of sparks.

street affronts; the jeers and taunts of the populace; the low-bred triumph they display over the casual trip, or splashed stocking, of a gentleman. Yet can I endure the jocularity of a young sweep with something more than forgiveness.—In the last winter but one, pacing along Cheapside with my accustomed precipitation when I walk westward, a treacherous slide brought me upon my back in an instant. I scrambled up with pain and shame enough—yet outwardly trying to face it down, as if nothing had happened—when the roguish grin of one of these young wits encountered me. There he stood, pointing me out with his dusky finger to the mob, and to a poor woman (I suppose his mother) in particular, till the tears for the exquisiteness of the fun (so he thought it) worked themselves out at the corners of his poor red eyes, red from many a previous weeping, and soot-inflamed, yet twinkling through all with such a joy, snatched out of desolation, that Hogarth—— but Hogarth has got him already (how could he miss him?) in the March to Finchley, grinning at the pie-man——there he stood, as he stands in the picture, irremovable, as if the jest was to last for ever—with such a maximum of glee, and minimum of mischief, in his mirth—for the grin of a genuine sweep hath absolutely no malice in it— that I could have been content, if the honor of a gentleman might endure it, to have remained his butt and his mockery till midnight.

I am by theory obdurate to the seductiveness of what are called a fine set of teeth. Every pair of rosy lips (the ladies must pardon me) is a casket, presumably holding such jewels; but, methinks, they should take leave to "air" them as frugally as possible. The fine lady, or fine gentleman, who show me their teeth, show me bones. Yet must I confess, that from the mouth of a true sweep a display (even to ostentation) of those white and shining ossifications, strikes me as an agreeable anomaly in manners, and an allowable piece of foppery. It is, as when

A sable cloud
Turns forth her silver lining on the night.[16]

---

[16]Milton, *Comus*, 221–2.

It is like some remnant of gentry not quite extinct; a badge of better days; a hint of nobility:—and, doubtless, under the obscuring darkness and double night of their forlorn disguisement, oftentimes lurketh good blood, and gentle conditions, derived from lost ancestry, and a lapsed pedigree. The premature apprenticements of these tender victims give but too much encouragement, I fear, to clandestine, and almost infantile abductions; the seeds of civility and true courtesy, so often discernible in these young grafts (not otherwise to be accounted for), plainly hint at some forced adoptions; many noble Rachels[17] mourning for their children, even in our days, countenance the fact; the tales of fairy-spiriting may shadow a lamentable verity, and the recovery of the young Montagu[18] be but a solitary instance of good fortune, out of many irreparable and hopeless *defiliations*.[19]

In one of the state-beds at Arundel Castle,[20] a few years since—under a ducal canopy—(that seat of the Howards is an object of curiosity to visitors, chiefly for its beds, in which the late duke was especially a connoisseur)—encircled with curtains of delicatest crimson, with starry coronets inwoven—folded between a pair of sheets whiter and softer than the lap where Venus lulled Ascanius[21]—was discovered by chance, after all methods of search had failed, at noon-day, fast asleep, a lost chimneysweeper. The little creature, having somehow confounded his passage among the intricacies of those lordly chimneys, by some unknown aperture had alighted upon this magnificent chamber; and, tired with his tedious explorations, was unable to resist the delicious invitement to repose which he there saw exhibited; so, creeping between the sheets very quietly, laid his black head upon the pillow, and slept like a young Howard.

Such is the account given to the visitors

---

[17]Jeremiah, 31:15.

[18]Edward Wortley Montagu (1713–1776), son of Lady Mary Wortley Montagu, several times ran away from Westminster School and on one of these occasions became for a time a chimney-sweeper.

[19]Losses of sons.

[20]The Sussex seat of the Dukes of Norfolk.

[21]Ascanius was the son of Aeneas, whose mother was Venus.

at the Castle.——But I cannot help seeming to perceive a confirmation of what I have just hinted at in this story. A high instinct was at work in the case, or I am mistaken. Is it probable that a poor child of that description, with whatever weariness he might be visited, would have ventured, under such a penalty as he would be taught to expect, to uncover the sheets of a Duke's bed, and deliberately to lay himself down between them, when the rug, or the carpet, presented an obvious couch, still far above his pretensions—is this probable, I would ask, if the great power of nature, which I contend for, had not been manifested within him, prompting to the adventure? Doubtless this young nobleman (for such my mind misgives me that he must be) was allured by some memory, not amounting to full consciousness, of his condition in infancy, when he was used to be lapped by his mother, or his nurse, in just such sheets as he there found, into which he was but now creeping back as into his proper *incunabula*,[22] and resting-place.—By no other theory than by this sentiment of a pre-existent state (as I may call it), can I explain a deed so venturous, and, indeed, upon any other system, so indecorous, in this tender, but unseasonable, sleeper.

My pleasant friend JEM WHITE[23] was so impressed with a belief of metamorphoses like this frequently taking place, that in some sort to reverse the wrongs of fortune in these poor changelings, he instituted an annual feast of chimney-sweepers, at which it was his pleasure to officiate as host and waiter. It was a solemn supper held in Smithfield, upon the yearly return of the fair of St. Bartholomew.[24] Cards were issued a week before to the master-sweeps in and about the metropolis, confining the invitation to their younger fry. Now and then an elderly stripling would get in among us and be good-naturedly winked at; but our main body were infantry. One unfortunate wight, indeed, who relying upon his dusky suit, had intruded himself into our party, but by

tokens was providentially discovered in time to be no chimney-sweeper (all is not soot which looks so), was quoited[25] out of the presence with universal indignation, as not having on the wedding garment;[26] but in general the greatest harmony prevailed. The place chosen was a convenient spot among the pens, at the north side of the fair, not so far distant as to be impervious to the agreeable hubbub of that vanity;[27] but remote enough not to be obvious to the interruption of every gaping spectator in it. The guests assembled about seven. In those little temporary parlors three tables were spread with napery, not so fine as substantial, and at every board a comely hostess presided with her pan of hissing sausages. The nostrils of the young rogues dilated at the savor. JAMES WHITE, as head waiter, had charge of the first table; and myself, with our trusty companion BIGOD[28] ordinarily ministered to the other two. There was clambering and jostling, you may be sure, who should get at the first table—for Rochester[29] in his maddest days could not have done the humors of the scene with more spirit than my friend. After some general expression of thanks for the honor the company had done him, his inaugural ceremony was to clasp the greasy waist of old dame Ursula[30] (the fattest of the three), that stood frying and fretting, half-blessing, half-cursing "the gentleman," and imprint upon her chaste lips a tender salute, whereat the universal host would set up a shout that tore the concave, while hundreds of grinning teeth startled the night with their brightness.[31] O it was a pleasure to see the sable younkers[32] lick in the unctuous meat, with *his* more unctuous sayings—how he would fit the tit-bits to the puny mouths, reserving the lengthier links for the seniors—how he

---

[22]Cradle.

[23]James White (1775–1820), author of *Original Letters of Sir John Falstaff* (1796). He was a school-fellow of Lamb at Christ's Hospital.

[24]Held at Smithfield on 3 September until its abolition in the middle of the nineteenth century.

[25]Hurled.

[26]I. e., the garb of a sweep. See St. Matthew, 22:11.

[27]The word is used in allusion to Bunyan's Vanity Fair in *The Pilgrim's Progress*.

[28]John Fenwick, who is also mentioned in *The Two Races of Men.*

[29]The Earl of Rochester (1647–1680), a notorious rake.

[30]Lamb took this name from a character in Ben Jonson's *Bartholomew Fair.*

[31]Cf. *Paradise Lost*, I, 541.   [32]Youngsters.

would intercept a morsel even in the jaws of some young desperado, declaring it "must to the pan again to be browned, for it was not fit for a gentleman's eating"—how he would recommend this slice of white bread, or that piece of kissing-crust,[33] to a tender juvenile, advising them all to have a care of cracking their teeth, which were their best patrimony,—how genteelly he would deal about the small ale, as if it were wine, naming the brewer, and protesting, if it were not good he should lose their custom, with a special recommendation to wipe the lip before drinking. Then we had our toasts—"The King,"—the "Cloth,"[34]—which, whether they understood or not, was equally diverting and flattering;—and for a crowning sentiment, which never failed, "May the Brush supersede the Laurel!"[35] All these, and fifty

[33]The soft part of a loaf's crust, where loaves have touched each other in baking.

[34]I. e., the profession of chimney-sweepers.

[35]The brush is taken to be emblematic of the chimney-sweeper, as the laurel is emblematic of the poet.

other fancies, which were rather felt than comprehended by his guests, would he utter, standing upon tables, and prefacing every sentiment with a "Gentlemen, give me leave to propose so and so," which was a prodigious comfort to those young orphans; every now and then stuffing into his mouth (for it did not do to be squeamish on these occasions) indiscriminate pieces of those reeking sausages, which pleased them mightily, and was the savoriest part, you may believe, of the entertainment.

Golden lads and lasses must,
As chimney-sweepers, come to dust—[36]

JAMES WHITE is extinct, and with him these suppers have long ceased. He carried away with him half the fun of the world when he died—of my world at least. His old clients look for him among the pens; and, missing him, reproach the altered feast of St. Bartholomew, and the glory of Smithfield departed for ever.

[36]*Cymbeline*, IV, ii, 262–3.

A DISSERTATION UPON ROAST PIG

MANKIND, says a Chinese manuscript, which my friend M.[1] was obliging enough to read and explain to me, for the first seventy thousand ages ate their meat raw, clawing or biting it from the living animal, just as they do in Abyssinia to this day. This period is not obscurely hinted at by their great Confucius[2] in the second chapter of his Mundane Mutations, where he designates a kind of golden age by the term Cho-fang, literally the Cook's holiday. The manuscript goes on to say, that the art of roasting, or rather broiling (which I take to be the elder brother) was accidentally discovered in the manner following. The swine-herd, Ho-ti, having gone out into the woods one morning, as his manner was, to collect mast[3] for his hogs, left his cottage in the care of

[1]Thomas Manning (1772–1840), who spent some years in China. The central idea of this essay is a commonplace, but there is no reason for doubting Lamb's statement, here and in a letter to Bernard Barton, that he heard it from Manning.

[2]Chinese philosopher of the sixth century B.C. The reference is of Lamb's invention.

[3]Beech nuts.

his eldest son Bo-bo, a great lubberly boy, who being fond of playing with fire, as younkers of his age commonly are, let some sparks escape into a bundle of straw, which kindling quickly, spread the conflagration over every part of their poor mansion, till it was reduced to ashes. Together with the cottage (a sorry antediluvian makeshift of a building, you may think it), what was of much more importance, a fine litter of new-farrowed[4] pigs, no less than nine in number, perished. China pigs have been esteemed a luxury all over the East from the remotest periods that we read of. Bo-bo was in utmost consternation, as you may think, not so much for the sake of the tenement, which his father and he could easily build up again with a few dry branches, and the labor of an hour or two, at any time, as for the loss of the pigs. While he was thinking what he should say to his father, and wringing his hands over the smoking remnants of one of these untimely sufferers, an odor assailed his nostrils, unlike any scent which he had

[4]Newly born.

before experienced. What could it proceed from?—not from the burned cottage—he had smelt that smell before—indeed this was by no means the first accident of the kind which had occurred through the negligence of this unlucky young fire-brand. Much less did it resemble that of any known herb, weed, or flower. A premonitory moistening at the same time overflowed his nether lip. He knew not what to think. He next stooped down to feel the pig, if there were any signs of life in it. He burned his fingers, and to cool them he applied them in his booby fashion to his mouth. Some of the crumbs of the scorched skin had come away with his fingers, and for the first time in his life (in the world's life indeed, for before him no man had known it) he tasted—*crackling!* Again he felt and fumbled at the pig. It did not burn him so much now, still he licked his fingers from a sort of habit. The truth at length broke into his slow understanding, that it was the pig that smelt so, and the pig that tasted so delicious; and, surrendering himself up to the newborn pleasure, he fell to tearing up whole handfuls of the scorched skin with the flesh next it, and was cramming it down his throat in his beastly fashion, when his sire entered amid the smoking rafters, armed with retributory cudgel, and finding how affairs stood, began to rain blows upon the young rogue's shoulders, as thick as hailstones, which Bo-bo heeded not any more than if they had been flies. The tickling pleasure which he experienced in his lower regions, had rendered him quite callous to any inconveniences he might feel in those remote quarters. His father might lay on, but he could not beat him from his pig, till he had fairly made an end of it, when, becoming a little more sensible of his situation, something like the following dialogue ensued.

"You graceless whelp, what have you got there devouring? Is it not enough that you have burned me down three houses with your dog's tricks, and be hanged to you, but you must be eating fire, and I know not what—what have you got there, I say?"

"O, father, the pig, the pig, do come and taste how nice the burnt pig eats."

The ears of Ho-ti tingled with horror. He cursed his son, and he cursed himself that ever he should beget a son that should eat burnt pig.

Bo-bo, whose scent was wonderfully sharpened since morning, soon raked out another pig, and fairly rending it asunder, thrust the lesser half by main force into the fists of Ho-ti, still shouting out "Eat, eat, eat the burnt pig, father, only taste—O Lord,"—with such-like barbarous ejaculations, cramming all the while as if he would choke.

Ho-ti trembled in every joint while he grasped the abominable thing, wavering whether he should not put his son to death for an unnatural young monster, when the crackling scorching his fingers, as it had done his son's, and applying the same remedy to them, he in his turn tasted some of its flavor, which, make what sour mouths he would for a pretense, proved not altogether displeasing to him. In conclusion (for the manuscript here is a little tedious), both father and son fairly sat down to the mess, and never left off till they had despatched all that remained of the litter.

Bo-bo was strictly enjoined not to let the secret escape, for the neighbors would certainly have stoned them for a couple of abominable wretches, who could think of improving upon the good meat which God had sent them. Nevertheless, strange stories got about. It was observed that Ho-ti's cottage was burned down now more frequently than ever. Nothing but fires from this time forward. Some would break out in broad day, others in the night-time. As often as the sow farrowed, so sure was the house of Ho-ti to be in a blaze; and Ho-ti himself, which was the more remarkable, instead of chastising his son, seemed to grow more indulgent to him than ever. At length they were watched, the terrible mystery discovered, and father and son summoned to take their trial at Pekin, then an inconsiderable assize town.[5] Evidence was given, the obnoxious food itself produced in court, and verdict about to be pronounced, when the foreman of the jury begged that some of the burnt pig, of which the culprits stood

---

[5] In England the county town in which sessions of a superior court are held.

accused, might be handed into the box. He handled it, and they all handled it, and burning their fingers, as Bo-bo and his father had done before them, and nature prompting to each of them the same remedy, against the face of all the facts, and the clearest charge which judge had ever given,—to the surprise of the whole court, townsfolk, strangers, reporters, and all present—without leaving the box, or any manner of consultation whatever, they brought in a simultaneous verdict of Not Guilty.

The judge, who was a shrewd fellow, winked at the manifest iniquity of the decision: and, when the court was dismissed, went privily, and bought up all the pigs that could be had for love or money. In a few days his Lordship's town house was observed to be on fire. The thing took wing, and now there was nothing to be seen but fires in every direction. Fuel and pigs grew enormously dear all over the district. The insurance offices one and all shut up shop. People built slighter and slighter every day, until it was feared that the very science of architecture would in no long time be lost to the world. Thus this custom of firing the houses continued, till in process of time, says my manuscript, a sage arose, like our Locke,[6] who made a discovery, that the flesh of swine, or indeed of any other animal, might be cooked (*burnt,* as they called it) without the necessity of consuming a whole house to dress it. Then first began the rude form of a gridiron. Roasting by the string, or spit, came in a century or two later, I forget in whose dynasty. By such slow degrees, concludes the manuscript, do the most useful, and seemingly the most obvious arts, make their way among mankind.——

Without placing too implicit faith in the account above given, it must be agreed, that if a worthy pretext for so dangerous an experiment as setting houses on fire (especially in these days) could be assigned in favor of any culinary object, that pretext and excuse might be found in ROAST PIG.

Of all the delicacies in the whole *mundus edibilis,*[7] I will maintain it to be the most delicate—*princeps obsoniorum.*[8]

I speak not of your grown porkers—things between pig and pork—those hobbydehoys[9]—but a young and tender suckling—under a moon old—guiltless as yet of the sty—with no original speck of the *amor immunditiae,*[10] the hereditary failing of the first parent, yet manifest—his voice as yet not broken, but something between a childish treble, and a grumble—the mild forerunner, or *praeludium,*[11] of a grunt.

He must be roasted. I am not ignorant that our ancestors ate them seethed, or boiled —but what a sacrifice of the exterior tegument![12]

There is no flavor comparable, I will contend, to that of the crisp, tawny, well-watched, not over-roasted, *crackling*, as it is well called—the very teeth are invited to their share of the pleasure at this banquet in overcoming the coy, brittle resistance— with the adhesive oleaginous—O call it not fat—but an indefinable sweetness growing up to it—the tender blossoming of fat—fat cropped in the bud—taken in the shoot— in the first innocence—the cream and quintessence of the child-pig's yet pure food—— the lean, no lean, but a kind of animal manna[13] or, rather, fat and lean (if it must be so), so blended and running into each other, that both together make but one ambrosian[14] result, or common substance.

Behold him, while he is doing[15]—it seemeth rather a refreshing warmth, than a scorching heat, that he is so passive to. How equably he twirleth round the string![16]—Now he is just done. To see the extreme sensibility of that tender age, he hath wept out his pretty eyes—radiant jellies—shooting stars——[17]

See him in the dish, his second cradle, how meek he lieth!—wouldst thou have had this innocent grow up to the grossness and indocility which too often accompany maturer swinehood? Ten to one he would have

---

[6]English philosopher (1632–1704).
[7]World of eatables.   [8]King of dainties.

[9]Youths between boys and men.   [10]Love of dirt.
[11]Prelude.   [12]Skin.
[13]Animal food sent from heaven.   Concerning manna see Exodus, 16:14–15.
[14]In Greek mythology ambrosia was the food of the gods.
[15]Being cooked.
[16]By which he hangs while roasting.
[17]It was once believed that shooting stars left jellies where they fell.

proved a glutton, a sloven, an obstinate, disagreeable animal—wallowing in all manner of filthy conversation[18]—from these sins he is happily snatched away—

> Ere sin could blight, or sorrow fade,
> Death came with timely care—[19]

his memory is odoriferous—no clown curseth, while his stomach half rejecteth, the rank bacon—no coalheaver bolteth him in reeking sausages—he hath a fair sepulcher in the grateful stomach of the judicious epicure—and for such a tomb might be content to die.

He is the best of sapors.[20] Pine-apple is great. She is indeed almost too transcendent—a delight, if not sinful, yet so like to sinning, that really a tender-conscienced person would do well to pause—too ravishing for mortal taste, she woundeth and excoriateth[21] the lips that approach her—like lovers' kisses, she biteth—she is a pleasure bordering on pain from the fierceness and insanity of her relish—but she stoppeth at the palate—she meddleth not with the appetite[22]—and the coarsest hunger might barter her consistently for a mutton chop.

Pig—let me speak his praise—is no less provocative of the appetite, than he is satisfactory to the criticalness of the censorious palate. The strong man may batten[23] on him, and the weakling refuseth not his mild juices.

Unlike to mankind's mixed characters, a bundle of virtues and vices, inexplicably intertwisted, and not to be unraveled without hazard, he is—good throughout. No part of him is better or worse than another. He helpeth, as far as his little means extend, all around. He is the least envious[24] of banquets. He is all neighbors' fare.

I am one of those who freely and ungrudgingly impart a share of the good things of this life which fall to their lot (few as mine are in this kind) to a friend. I protest I take as great an interest in my friend's pleasures, his relishes, and proper satisfactions, as in mine own. "Presents," I often say, "endear Absents." Hares, pheasants, partridges, snipes, barn-door chickens (those "tame villatic fowl"[25]), capons, plovers, brawn,[26] barrels of oysters, I dispense as freely as I receive them. I love to taste them, as it were, upon the tongue of my friend. But a stop must be put somewhere. One would not, like Lear, "give everything."[27] I make my stand upon pig. Methinks it is an ingratitude to the Giver of all good flavors, to extra-domiciliate, or send out of the house, slightingly (under pretext of friendship, or I know not what), a blessing so particularly adapted, predestined, I may say, to my individual palate——It argues an insensibility.

I remember a touch of conscience in this kind at school. My good old aunt,[28] who never parted from me at the end of a holiday without stuffing a sweetmeat, or some nice thing, into my pocket, had dismissed me one evening with a smoking plum-cake, fresh from the oven. In my way to school (it was over London Bridge) a gray-headed old beggar saluted me (I have no doubt at this time of day that he was a counterfeit). I had no pence to console him with, and in the vanity of self-denial, and the very coxcombry of charity, school-boy-like, I made him a present of—the whole cake! I walked on a little, buoyed up, as one is on such occasions, with a sweet soothing of self-satisfaction; but before I had got to the end of the bridge, my better feelings returned, and I burst into tears, thinking how ungrateful I had been to my good aunt, to go and give her good gift away to a stranger that I had never seen before, and who might be a bad man for aught I knew; and then I thought of the pleasure my aunt would be taking in thinking that I—I myself, and not another—would eat her nice cake—and what should I say to her the next time I saw her—how naughty I was to part with her

---

[18]Ways of life.

[19]Coleridge, *Epitaph on an Infant.*

[20]Flavors.   [21]Takes the skin off.

[22]I. e., she gratifies the taste but does not satisfy the stomach.

[23]Feed.

[24]I. e., he gives no guest cause to envy another, for "he is—good throughout."

[25]Milton, *Samson Agonistes,* l. 1695.

[26]Boar's meat.   [27]*King Lear,* II, iv, 253.

[28]Probably Sarah Lamb, whom Lamb called Aunt Hetty.

pretty present—and the odor of that spicy cake came back upon my recollection, and the pleasure and the curiosity I had taken in seeing her make it, and her joy when she sent it to the oven, and how disappointed she would feel that I had never had a bit of it in my mouth at last—and I blamed my impertinent spirit of alms-giving, and out-of-place hypocrisy of goodness, and above all I wished never to see the face again of that insidious, good-for-nothing, old gray impostor.

Our ancestors were nice[29] in their method of sacrificing these tender victims. We read of pigs whipped to death with something of a shock, as we hear of any other obsolete custom. The age of discipline is gone by, or it would be curious to inquire (in a philosophical light merely) what effect this process might have towards intenerating and dulcifying[30] a substance, naturally so mild and dulcet as the flesh of young pigs. It looks like refining a violet.[31] Yet we should be cautious, while we condemn the inhumanity,

how we censure the wisdom of the practice. It might impart a gusto——

I remember an hypothesis, argued upon by the young students, when I was at St. Omer's,[32] and maintained with much learning and pleasantry on both sides, "Whether, supposing that the flavor of a pig who obtained his death by whipping (*per flagellationem extremam*) superadded a pleasure upon the palate of a man more intense than any possible suffering we can conceive in the animal, is man justified in using that method of putting the animal to death?" I forget the decision.

His sauce should be considered. Decidedly, a few bread crumbs, done up with his liver and brains, and a dash of mild sage. But, banish, dear Mrs. Cook, I beseech you, the whole onion tribe. Barbecue[33] your whole hogs to your palate, steep them in shalots,[34] stuff them out with plantations of the rank and guilty garlic; you cannot poison them, or make them stronger than they are—but consider, he is a weakling—a flower.

---

[29]Discriminating.   [30]Making tender and sweet.
[31]Cf. *King John*, IV, ii, 10–12.

[32]A Jesuit college for English youths, in France. Lamb, of course, was never there.
[33]To roast whole.   [34]Small onions.

THE SUPERANNUATED MAN[1]

*Sera tamen respexit
Libertas.*[2]   Virgil.

A clerk I was in London gay.
                    O'Keefe.[3]

IF PERADVENTURE, Reader, it has been thy lot to waste the golden years of thy life— thy shining youth—in the irksome confinement of an office; to have thy prison days prolonged through middle age down to decrepitude and silver hairs, without hope of release or respite; to have lived to forget that there are such things as holidays, or to remember them but as the prerogatives of childhood; then, and then only, will you be able to appreciate my deliverance.

It is now six and thirty years since I took my seat at the desk in Mincing Lane. Melancholy was the transition at fourteen from the abundant playtime, and the frequently intervening vacations of school days, to the eight, nine, and sometimes ten hours' a-day attendance at a counting-house. But time partially reconciles us to anything. I gradually became content—doggedly content, as wild animals in cages.

It is true I had my Sundays to myself; but Sundays, admirable as the institution of them is for purposes of worship, are for that very reason the very worst adapted for days of unbending and recreation. In particular, there is a gloom for me attendant upon a city Sunday, a weight in the air. I miss the cheerful cries of London, the music, and the ballad-singers—the buzz and stirring murmur of the streets. Those eternal bells depress me. The closed shops repel me. Prints, pictures, all the glittering and endless

---

[1]Lamb disguises his real employment, but in other respects this essay is substantially a record of fact.
[2]Liberty, though late, nevertheless visited me (from the first *Eclogue*, l. 27).
[3]John O'Keeffe (1747–1833), a writer of farces and comic operas. The song has also been attributed to George Colman.

succession of knacks and gewgaws, and ostentatiously displayed wares of tradesmen, which make a weekday saunter through the less busy parts of the metropolis so delightful—are shut out. No book-stalls deliciously to idle over—No busy faces to recreate the idle man who contemplates them ever passing by—the very face of business a charm by contrast to his temporary relaxation from it. Nothing to be seen but unhappy countenances—or half-happy at best —of emancipated 'prentices and little tradesfolks, with here and there a servant maid that has got leave to go out, who, slaving all the week, with the habit has lost almost the capacity of enjoying a free hour; and livelily expressing the hollowness of a day's pleasuring. The very strollers in the fields on that day looked anything but comfortable.

But besides Sundays I had a day at Easter, and a day at Christmas, with a full week in the summer to go and air myself in my native fields of Hertfordshire.[4] This last was a great indulgence; and the prospect of its recurrence, I believe, alone kept me up through the year, and made my durance tolerable. But when the week came round, did the glittering phantom of the distance keep touch with me? or rather was it not a series of seven uneasy days, spent in restless pursuit of pleasure, and a wearisome anxiety to find out how to make the most of them? Where was the quiet, where the promised rest? Before I had a taste of it, it was vanished. I was at the desk again, counting upon the fifty-one tedious weeks that must intervene before such another snatch would come. Still the prospect of its coming threw something of an illumination upon the darker side of my captivity. Without it, as I have said, I could scarcely have sustained my thraldom.

Independently of the rigors of attendance, I have ever been haunted with a sense (perhaps a mere caprice) of incapacity for business. This, during my latter years, had increased to such a degree that it was visible in all the lines of my countenance. My health and my good spirits flagged. I had

perpetually a dread of some crisis, to which I should be found unequal. Besides my daylight servitude, I served over again all night in my sleep, and would awake with terrors of imaginary false entries, errors in my accounts, and the like. I was fifty years of age, and no prospect of emancipation presented itself. I had grown to my desk, as it were; and the wood had entered into my soul.

My fellows in the office would sometimes rally me upon the trouble legible in my countenance; but I did not know that it had raised the suspicions of any of my employers, when on the 5th of last month, a day ever to be remembered by me, L——, the junior partner in the firm, calling me on one side, directly taxed me with my bad looks, and frankly inquired the cause of them. So taxed, I honestly made confession of my infirmity, and added that I was afraid I should eventually be obliged to resign his service. He spoke some words of course to hearten me, and there the matter rested. A whole week I remained laboring under the impression that I had acted imprudently in my disclosure; that I had foolishly given a handle against myself, and had been anticipating my own dismissal. A week passed in this manner, the most anxious one, I verily believe in my whole life, when on the evening of the 12th of April, just as I was about quitting my desk to go home (it might be about eight o'clock) I received an awful summons to attend the presence of the whole assembled firm in the formidable back parlor. I thought, now my time is surely come, I have done for myself, I am going to be told that they have no longer occasion for me. L——, I could see, smiled at the terror I was in, which was a little relief to me,— when to my utter astonishment B——, the eldest partner, began a formal harangue to me on the length of my services, my very meritorious conduct during the whole of the time (the deuce, thought I, how did he find out that? I protest I never had the confidence to think as much). He went on to descant[5] on the expediency of retiring at a certain time of life (how my heart panted!) and asking me a few questions as to the

---

[4] An exaggeration, as Lamb was born and brought up in London, though his mother and grandmother were natives of Hertfordshire.

[5] To discourse at large.

amount of my own property, of which I have a little, ended with a proposal, to which his three partners nodded a grave assent, that I should accept from the house, which I had served so well, a pension for life to the amount of two-thirds of my accustomed salary[6]—a magnificent offer! I do not know what I answered between surprise and gratitude, but it was understood that I accepted their proposal, and I was told that I was free from that hour to leave their service. I stammered out a bow, and at just ten minutes after eight I went home—for ever. This noble benefit—gratitude forbids me to conceal their names—I owe to the kindness of the most munificent firm in the world— the house of Boldero, Merryweather, Bosanquet, and Lacy.[7]

Esto Perpetua![8]

For the first day or two I felt stunned, overwhelmed. I could only apprehend my felicity; I was too confused to taste it sincerely. I wandered about, thinking I was happy, and knowing that I was not. I was in the condition of a prisoner in the Old Bastile, suddenly let loose after a forty years' confinement. I could scarce trust myself with myself. It was like passing out of Time into Eternity—for it is a sort of Eternity for a man to have his Time all to himself. It seemed to me that I had more time on my hands than I could ever manage. From a poor man, poor in Time, I was suddenly lifted up into a vast revenue; I could see no end of my possessions; I wanted some steward, or judicious bailiff, to manage my estates in Time for me. And here let me caution persons grown old in active business, not lightly, nor without weighing their own resources, to forgo their customary employment all at once, for there may be danger in it. I feel it by myself, but I know that my resources are sufficient; and now that those first giddy raptures have subsided, I have a quiet home-feeling of the blessedness of my condition. I am in no hurry. Having all holidays, I am as though I had none. If Time hung heavy upon me, I could walk it away; but I do *not* walk all day long, as I used to do in those old transient holidays, thirty miles a day, to make the most of them. If Time were troublesome, I could read it away, but I do *not* read in that violent measure, with which, having no Time my own but candlelight Time, I used to weary out my head and eye-sight in by-gone winters. I walk, read, or scribble (as now) just when the fit seizes me. I no longer hunt after pleasure; I let it come to me. I am like the man

—That's born, and has his years come to him,
In some green desert.[9]

"Years," you will say; "what is this superannuated simpleton calculating upon? He has already told us he is past fifty."

I have indeed lived nominally fifty years, but deduct out of them the hours which I have lived to other people, and not to myself, and you will find me still a young fellow. For *that* is the only true Time, which a man can properly call his own, that which he has all to himself; the rest, though in some sense he may be said to live it, is other people's time, not his. The remnant of my poor days, long or short, is at least multiplied for me threefold. My ten next years, if I stretch so far, will be as long as any preceding thirty. 'Tis a fair rule-of-three sum.

Among the strange fantasies which beset me at the commencement of my freedom, and of which all traces are not yet gone, one was, that a vast tract of time had intervened since I quitted the Counting House. I could not conceive of it as an affair of yesterday. The partners, and the clerks with whom I had for so many years, and for so many hours in each day of the year, been so closely associated—being suddenly removed from them—they seemed as dead to me. There is a fine passage, which may serve to illustrate this fancy, in a Tragedy[10]

---

[6]Lamb's salary was £730 the year. He was granted a pension of £450.

[7]Fictitious names, of course, standing for the directors of the East India Company.

[8]May it be eternal.

[9]Thomas Middleton, *Mayor of Queenborough*, I, i, 102–3.

[10]*The Vestal Virgin, or the Roman Ladies.* Howard was Dryden's brother-in-law and lived 1626–1698.

by Sir Robert Howard, speaking of a friend's death :—

——'Twas but just now he went away;
I have not since had time to shed a tear;
And yet the distance does the same appear
As if he had been a thousand years from me,
Time takes no measure in Eternity.

To dissipate this awkward feeling, I have been fain to go among them once or twice since; to visit my old desk-fellows—my co-brethren of the quill—that I had left below in the state militant. Not all the kindness with which they received me could quite restore to me that pleasant familiarity, which I had heretofore enjoyed among them. We cracked some of our old jokes, but methought they went off but faintly. My old desk; the peg where I hung my hat, were appropriated to another. I knew it must be, but I could not take it kindly. D——l take me if I did not feel some remorse—beast, if I had not,—at quitting my old compeers, the faithful partners of my toils for six and thirty years, that smoothed for me with their jokes and conundrums the ruggedness of my professional road. Had it been so rugged then after all? or was I a coward simply? Well, it is too late to repent; and I also know that these suggestions are a common fallacy of the mind on such occasions. But my heart smote me. I had violently broken the bands betwixt us. It was at least not courteous. I shall be some time before I get quite reconciled to the sep-aration. Farewell, old cronies, yet not for long, for again and again I will come among ye, if I shall have your leave. Fare-well, Ch——, dry, sarcastic, and friendly! Do——, mild, slow to move, and gentle-manly! Pl——,[11] officious to do, and to volunteer, good services!—and thou, thou dreary pile, fit mansion for a Gresham or a Whittington[12] of old, stately House of Mer-chants; with thy labyrinthine passages, and light-excluding, pent-up offices, where can-dles for one half the year supplied the place of the sun's light; unhealthy contributor to my weal, stern fosterer of my living, fare-well! In thee remain, and not in the ob-scure collection of some wandering book-seller, my "works!"[13] There let them rest, as I do from my labors, piled on thy massy shelves, more MSS. in folio than ever Aqui-nas left, and full as useful! My mantle I bequeath among ye.

A fortnight has passed since the date of my first communication. At that period I was approaching to tranquillity, but had not reached it. I boasted of a calm indeed, but it was comparative only. Something of the first flutter was left; an unsettling sense of novelty; the dazzle to weak eyes of unac-customed light. I missed my old chains, forsooth, as if they had been some necessary part of my apparel. I was a poor Car-thusian,[14] from strict cellular discipline sud-denly by some revolution returned upon the world. I am now as if I had never been other than my own master. It is natural to me to go where I please, to do what I please. I find myself at eleven o'clock in the day in Bond Street, and it seems to me that I have been sauntering there at that very hour for years past. I digress into Soho, to explore a book-stall. Methinks I have been thirty years a collector. There is nothing strange nor new in it. I find myself before a fine picture in the morning. Was it ever other-wise? What is become of Fish Street Hill? Where is Fenchurch Street? Stones of old Mincing Lane which I have worn with my daily pilgrimage for six and thirty years, to the footsteps of what toil-worn clerk are your everlasting flints now vocal? I indent the gayer flags of Pall Mall. It is 'Change time, and I am strangely among the Elgin marbles.[15] It was no hyperbole when I ventured to compare the change in my con-dition to a passing into another world. Time stands still in a manner to me. I have lost all distinction of season. I do not know the day of the week, or of the month. Each day used to be individually felt by me in its

---

[11]These are thought to be John Chambers, Henry Dodwell, and W. D. Plumely.

[12]Sir Thomas Gresham and Sir Richard Witting-ton.

[13]I. e., the ledgers which Lamb had filled with accounts. The 1570 edition of the works of St. Thomas Aquinas filled 17 folio volumes.

[14]I. e., a monk.

[15]They were brought to the British Museum in 1816.

reference to the foreign post days; in its distance from, or propinquity to the next Sunday. I had my Wednesday feelings, my Saturday nights' sensations. The genius of each day was upon me distinctly during the whole of it, affecting my appetite, spirits, *etc.* The phantom of the next day, with the dreary five to follow, sat as a load upon my poor Sabbath recreations. What charm has washed the Ethiop white?—What is gone of Black Monday? All days are the same. Sunday itself—that unfortunate failure of a holiday as it too often proved, what with my sense of its fugitiveness, and over-care to get the greatest quantity of pleasure out of it—is melted down into a week day. I can spare to go to church now, without grudging the huge cantle[16] which it used to seem to cut out of the holiday. I have Time for everything. I can visit a sick friend. I can interrupt the man of much occupation when he is busiest. I can insult over him with an invitation to take a day's pleasure with me to Windsor this fine May-morning. It is Lucretian pleasure[17] to behold the poor drudges, whom I have left behind in the world, carking and caring; like horses in a mill, drudging on in the same eternal round

—and what is it all for? A man can never have too much Time to himself, nor too little to do. Had I a little son, I would christen him NOTHING-TO-DO; he should do nothing. Man, I verily believe, is out of his element as long as he is operative. I am altogether for the life contemplative. Will no kindly earthquake come and swallow up those accursed cotton mills? Take me that lumber of a desk there, and bowl it down

As low as to the fiends.[18]

I am no longer —— ——, clerk to the firm of, *etc.* I am Retired Leisure. I am to be met with in trim gardens. I am already come to be known by my vacant face and careless gesture, perambulating at no fixed pace nor with any settled purpose. I walk about; not to and from. They tell me, a certain *cum dignitate*[19] air, that has been buried so long with my other good parts, has begun to shoot forth in my person. I grow into gentility perceptibly. When I take up a newspaper it is to read the state of the opera. *Opus operatum est.*[20] I have done all that I came into this world to do. I have worked taskwork, and have the rest of the day to myself.

[16]Slice.

[17]The allusion is to a famous passage at the beginning of Bk. II of Lucretius's *On the Nature of Things.* There is a paraphrase of the passage in Bacon's essay *Of Truth.*

[18]*Hamlet,* II, ii, 519.

[19]The allusion is to the phrase *otium cum dignitate,* ease with dignity.

[20]The work has been completed.

POPULAR FALLACIES

XIV

That We Should Rise with the Lark

At what precise minute that little airy musician doffs his night gear, and prepares to tune up his unseasonable matins, we are not naturalists enough to determine. But for a mere human gentleman—that has no orchestra business to call him from his warm bed to such preposterous exercises—we take ten, or half after ten (eleven, of course, during this Christmas solstice[1]), to be the very earliest hour, at which he can begin to think of abandoning his pillow. To think of it, we say; for to do it in earnest requires another half-hour's good consideration. Not but

there are pretty sun-risings, as we are told, and such like gawds,[2] abroad in the world, in summer time especially, some hours before what we have assigned; which a gentleman may see, as they say, only for getting up. But, having been tempted once or twice, in earlier life, to assist at those ceremonies, we confess our curiosity abated. We are no longer ambitious of being the sun's courtiers, to attend at his morning levees.[3] We hold the good hours of the dawn too sacred to waste them upon such observances; which have in them, besides, something Pagan and Persic.[4] To say truth, we never anticipated our usual hour, or got up with the

[1]Time when the sun is farthest north of the equator and seems to stand still in its course.

[2]Trifles.   [3]Receptions.

[4]Persian. The Persians formerly worshiped the sun.

sun (as 'tis called), to go a journey, or upon a foolish whole day's pleasuring, but we suffered for it all the long hours after in listlessness and headaches; Nature herself sufficiently declaring her sense of our presumption in aspiring to regulate our frail waking courses by the measures of that celestial and sleepless traveler. We deny not that there is something sprightly and vigorous, at the outset especially, in these break-of-day excursions. It is flattering to get the start of a lazy world; to conquer death by proxy in his image. But the seeds of sleep and mortality are in us; and we pay usually in strange qualms, before night falls, the penalty of the unnatural inversion. Therefore, while the busy part of mankind are fast huddling on their clothes, are already up and about their occupations, content to have swallowed their sleep by wholesale; we choose to linger a-bed, and digest our dreams. It is the very time to re-combine the wandering images, which night in a confused mass presented; to snatch them from forgetfulness; to shape, and mold them. Some people have no good of their dreams. Like fast feeders, they gulp them too grossly to taste them curiously. We love to chew the cud of a forgone vision; to collect the scattered rays of a brighter phantasm, or act over again, with firmer nerves, the sadder nocturnal tragedies; to drag into day-light a struggling and half-vanishing nightmare; to handle and examine the terrors, or the airy solaces. We have too much respect for these spiritual communications to let them go so lightly. We are not so stupid, or so careless, as that Imperial forgetter of his dreams,[5] that we should need a seer to remind us of the form of them. They seem to us to have as much significance as our waking concerns; or rather to import us more nearly, as more nearly we approach by years to the shadowy world, whither we are hastening. We have shaken hands with the world's business; we have done with it; we have discharged ourself of it. Why should we get up? we have neither suit to solicit, nor affairs to manage. The drama has shut in upon us at the fourth act. We have nothing here to expect, but in a short time a sick-bed, and a dismissal. We delight to anticipate death by such shadows as night affords. We are already half acquainted with ghosts. We were never much in the world. Disappointment early struck a dark veil between us and its dazzling illusions. Our spirits showed gray before our hairs. The mighty changes of the world already appear as but the vain stuff out of which dramas are composed. We have asked no more of life than what the mimic images in play-houses present us with. Even those types[6] have waxed fainter. Our clock appears to have struck. We are SUPERANNUATED. In this dearth of mundane · satisfaction, we contract politic alliances with shadows. It is good to have friends at court. The abstracted media of dreams seem no ill introduction to that spiritual presence, upon which, in no long time, we expect to be thrown. We are trying to know a little of the usages of that colony; to learn the language, and the faces we shall meet with there, that we may be the less awkward at our first coming among them. We willingly call a phantom our fellow, as knowing we shall soon be of their dark companionship. Therefore, we cherish dreams. We try to spell in them the alphabet of the invisible world; and think we know already, how it shall be with us. Those uncouth shapes, which, while we clung to flesh and blood, affrighted us, have become familiar. We feel attenuated into their meager essences, and have given the hand of halfway approach to incorporeal being. We once thought life to be something; but it has unaccountably fallen from us before its time. Therefore we choose to dally with visions. The sun has no purposes of ours to light us to. Why should we get up?

XV

That We Should Lie Down with the Lamb

WE COULD never quite understand the philosophy of this arrangement, or the wisdom of our ancestors in sending us for instruction to these woolly bedfellows. A sheep, when it is dark, has nothing to do but to shut his silly eyes, and sleep if he can.

---

[5]Nebuchadnezzar. See Daniel, 2.

[6]Images.

Man found out long sixes.[7]—Hail candle-light! without disparagement to sun or moon, the kindliest luminary of the three—if we may not rather style thee their radiant deputy, mild viceroy of the moon!—We love to read, talk, sit silent, eat, drink, sleep, by candle-light. They are everybody's sun and moon. This is our peculiar and household planet. Wanting it, what savage unsocial nights must our ancestors have spent, winter-ing in caves and unillumined fastnesses! They must have lain about and grumbled at one another in the dark. What repartees could have passed, when you must have felt about for a smile, and handled a neighbor's cheek to be sure that he understood it? This accounts for the seriousness of the elder poetry. It has a somber cast (try Hesiod or Ossian), derived from the tradition of those unlanterned nights. Jokes came in with candles. We wonder how they saw to pick up a pin, if they had any. How did they sup? what a melange[8] of chance carving they must have made of it!—here one had got the leg of a goat, when he wanted a horse's shoulder—there another had dipped his scooped palm in a kid-skin of wild honey, when he meditated right[9] mare's milk. There is neither good eating nor drinking in fresco.[10] Who, even in these civilized times, has never experienced this, when at some economic table he has commenced dining after dusk, and waited for the flavor till the lights came? The senses absolutely give and take reciprocally. Can you tell pork from veal in the dark? or distinguish Sherris from pure Malaga?[11] Take away the candle from the smoking man; by the glimmering of the left ashes, he knows that he is still smoking, but he knows it only by an inference; till the restored light, coming in aid of the ol-factories, reveals to both senses the full aroma. Then how he redoubles his puffs! how he burnishes!—There is absolutely no such thing as reading, but by a candle. We have tried the affectation of a book at noon-day in gardens, and in sultry arbors; but it was labor thrown away. Those gay motes in the beam come about you, hovering and teasing, like many coquettes, that will have you all to their self, and are jealous of your abstractions. By the midnight taper, the writer digests his meditations. By the same light, we must approach to their pe-rusal, if we would catch the flame, the odor. It is a mockery, all that is reported of the influential Phoebus. No true poem ever owed its birth to the sun's light. They are abstracted works—

Things that were born, when none but the still night,
And his dumb candle, saw his pinching throes.[12]

Marry, daylight—daylight might furnish the images, the crude material; but for the fine shapings, the true turning and filing (as mine author[13] hath it), they must be con-tent to hold their inspiration of the candle. The mild internal light, that reveals them, like fires on the domestic hearth, goes out in the sunshine. Night and silence call out the starry fancies. Milton's Morning Hymn in Paradise,[14] we would hold a good wager was penned at midnight, and Taylor's[15] rich description of a sunrise smells decidedly of the taper. Even ourselves, in these our humbler lucubrations, tune our best mea-sured cadences (Prose has her cadences) not unfrequently to the charm of the drowsier watchman, "blessing the doors"; or the wild sweeps of wind at midnight. Even now a loftier speculation than we have yet at-tempted, courts our endeavors. We would indite something about the Solar System.—*Betty, bring the candles.*

---

[7] Candles about eight inches in length, weighing six to the pound.

[8] Mixture.

[9] Real.

[10] Literally, "out of doors"; here equivalent to, "in darkness."

[11] Wines.

[12] Ben Jonson, *Poetaster,* "Apologetical Dialogue," 199–200.

[13] Ben Jonson, *To the Memory of my Beloved Master William Shakespeare,* 65–68.

[14] *Paradise Lost,* V, 153, and following lines.

[15] Jeremy Taylor (1613–1667), *Holy Dying,* Ch. I, S. iii, § 2.

LETTERS

I. To Samuel Taylor Coleridge

London, 27 September, 1796

My dearest friend—White[1] or some of my friends or the public papers by this time may have informed you of the terrible calamities that have fallen on our family. I will only give you the outlines. My poor dear, dearest sister in a fit of insanity has been the death of her own mother. I was at hand only time enough to snatch the knife out of her grasp. She is at present in a mad house, from whence I fear she must be moved to an hospital. God has preserved to me my senses,—I eat and drink and sleep, and have my judgment, I believe, very sound. My poor father was slightly wounded, and I am left to take care of him and my aunt. Mr. Norris of the blue-coat school[2] has been very kind to us, and we have no other friend, but thank God I am very calm and composed, and able to do the best that remains to do. Write,—as religious a letter as possible— but no mention of what is gone and done with;—with me the former things are passed away, and I have something more to do than[3] to feel——

> God almighty
> have us all in
> his keeping.———
>   C. Lamb

Mention nothing of poetry. I have destroyed every vestige of past vanities of that kind. Do as you please, but if you publish, publish mine (I give free leave) without name or initial, and never send me a book, I charge you; your[4] own judgment will convince you not to take notice of this yet to your dear wife.[5]—You look after your family,—I have my reason and strength left to take care of mine. I charge you don't think of coming to see me. Write. I will not see you if you come. God almighty love you and all of us——

II. To Samuel Taylor Coleridge

London, 17 October, 1796

My dearest friend, I grieve from my very soul to observe you in your plans of life veering about from this hope to the other, and settling nowhere. Is it an untoward fatality (speaking humanly) that does this for you, a stubborn irresistible concurrence of events? or lies the fault, as I fear it does, in your own mind? You seem to be taking up splendid schemes of fortune only to lay them down again, and your fortunes are an *ignis fatuus*[6] that has been conducting you, in thought, from Lancaster Court, Strand, to somewhere near Matlock, then jumping across to Dr. Somebody's whose son's tutor you were likely to be, and would to God the dancing demon *may* conduct you at last in peace and comfort to the "life and labors of a cottager."[7] You see, from the above awkward playfulness of fancy, that my spirits are not quite depressed; I should ill deserve God's blessings, which since the late terrible event have come down in mercy upon us, if I indulged regret or querulousness;—Mary continues serene and cheerful;—I have not by me a little letter she wrote to me, for, though I see her almost every day, yet we delight to write to one another (for we can scarce see each other but in company with some of the people of the house); I have not the letter by me but will quote from memory what she wrote in it. "I have no bad terrifying dreams. At midnight when I happen to awake, the nurse sleeping by the side of me, with the noise of the poor mad people around me, I have no fear. The spirit of my mother seems to descend, and smile upon me, and bid me live to enjoy the life and reason which the Almighty has given me;—I shall

---

[1]James White (1775–1820), Lamb's schoolfellow, who figures in *The Praise of Chimney-Sweepers.*

[2]Richard Norris of Christ's Hospital, the blue-coat or charity school Lamb had attended between the ages of seven and fourteen.

[3]Miswritten "that."

[4]Miswritten "you."

[5]Mrs. Coleridge had just become a mother.

---

[6]Will-o'-the-wisp.

[7]References, respectively, to Coleridge's plans to write for a London newspaper, to become a tutor at Matlock, to teach school at Derby on the suggestion of a Dr. Crompton, and to settle in a cottage at Nether Stowey (a plan which was soon realized).

see her again in heaven; she will then understand me better; my grandmother too will understand me better, and will then say no more, as she used to do, 'Polly, what are those poor crazy, moithered[8] brains of yours thinking of always?'"—Poor Mary, my mother indeed *never understood* her right. She loved her, as she loved us all, with a mother's love; but in opinion, in feeling, and sentiment, and disposition, bore so distant a resemblance to her daughter that she never understood her right, never could believe how much *she* loved her—but met her caresses, her protestations of filial affection, too frequently with coldness and repulse.—Still she was a good mother; God forbid I should think of her but *most* respectfully, *most* affectionately. Yet she would always love my brother[9] above Mary, who was not worthy of one tenth of that affection which Mary had a right to claim. But it is my sister's gratifying recollection that every act of duty and of love she could pay, every kindness (and I speak true when I say to the hurting of her health, and, most probably, in great part to the derangement of her senses) through a long course of infirmities and sickness, she could show her, *she ever did*. I will some day, as I promised, enlarge to you upon my sister's excellencies; 'twill seem like exaggeration; but I will do it. At present short letters suit my state of mind best. So take my kindest wishes for your comfort and establishment in life, and for Sara's[10] welfare and comforts with you. God love you; God love us all——

C. Lamb

III. To Robert Lloyd[11]

London, 13 November, 1798

Now 'tis Robert's turn.[12]

My dear Robert,

One passage in your letter a little displeased me. The rest was nothing but kind-

ness, which Robert's letters are ever brimful of. You say that "this world to you seems drained of all its sweets!" At first I had hoped you only meant to insinuate the high price of sugar! but I am afraid you meant more. O Robert, I don't know what you call sweet. Honey and the honeycomb, roses and violets, are yet in the earth. The sun and moon yet reign in heaven, and the lesser light keep up their pretty twinklings. Meats and drinks, sweet sights and sweet smells, a country walk, spring and autumn, follies and repentance, quarrels and reconcilements, have all a sweetness by turns. Good humor and good nature, friends at home that love you, and friends abroad that miss you, you possess all these things, and more innumerable, and these are all sweet things. You may extract honey from everything; do not go a-gathering after gall. The bees are wiser in their generation than the race of sonnet-writers and complainers, Bowles's and Charlotte Smiths,[13] and all that tribe, who can see no joys but what are past, and fill people's heads with notions of the unsatisfying nature of earthly comforts. I assure you I find this world a very pretty place. My kind love to all your sisters and to Thomas—he never writes to me—and tell Susanna I forgive her.

C. Lamb

IV. To Thomas Manning[14]

London, 1 March, 1800

I HOPE by this time you are prepared to say the *Falstaff's Letters*[15] are a bundle of the sharpest, queerest, profoundest humors of any these juice-drained latter times have spawned. I should have advertised you that the meaning is frequently hard to be got at; and so are the future guineas that now lie ripening and aurifying in the womb of some undiscovered Potosi;[16] but dig, dig, dig, dig,

---

[8]Worried.

[9]John Lamb, to whom reference is made in *Dream-Children*.

[10]Coleridge's wife.

[11]A young Quaker of Birmingham, not yet twenty years old.

[12]A hint, apparently added at the top of the letter before sealing.

[13]William Lisle Bowles (1762–1850), whose sonnets had had an early influence on Coleridge; Charlotte Smith (1749–1806), better known as a novelist than as a poetess

[14]One of Lamb's most intimate friends (1772–1840), at this time a private tutor at Cambridge.

[15]James White's *Original Letters of Sir John Falstaff* (1796).

[16]Fabulously wealthy mines in what is now Bolivia.

Manning! I set to with an unconquerable propulsion to write, and with a lamentable want of what to write. My private goings on are orderly as the movements of the spheres, and stale as their music to angels' ears. Public affairs—except as they touch upon me, and so turn into private, I cannot whip up my mind to feel any interest in. I grieve, indeed, that War and Nature and Mr. Pitt,[17] that hangs up in Lloyd's best parlor, should have conspired to call up three necessaries, simple commoners as our fathers knew them, into the upper house of luxuries: bread, and beer, and coals, Manning. But as to France and Frenchmen, and the Abbé Sieyès[18] and his constitutions, I cannot make these present times present to me. I read histories of the past, and I live in them; although, to abstract senses, they are far less momentous than the noises which keep Europe awake. I am reading Burnet's *Own Times.*[19] Did you ever read that garrulous, pleasant history? He tells his story like an old man past political service, bragging to his sons on winter evenings of the part he took in public transactions, when his "old cap was new." Full of scandal, which all true history is. No palliatives, but all the stark wickedness that actually gives the *momentum* to national actors: quite the prattle of age and out-lived importance, truth and sincerity staring out upon you perpetually in *alto relievo.*[20] Himself a party man—he makes you a party man. None of the damned philosophical Humeian indifference, so cold, and unnatural, and inhuman! None of the damned Gibbonian fine writing, so fine and composite.[21] None of Mr. Robertson's periods with three members. None of Mr. Roscoe's sage remarks, all so apposite, and coming in so

clever, lest the reader should have had the trouble of drawing an inference. Burnet's good old prattle I can bring present to my mind—I can make the revolution[22] present to me; the French Revolution, by a converse perversity in my nature, I fling as far *from* me. To quit this damned subject, and to relieve you from two or three dismal yawns, which I hear in spirit, I here conclude my more than commonly obtuse letter, dull up to the dulness of a Dutch commentator on Shakespeare.

My love to Lloyd and Sophia.[23]

C. L.

V. To William Wordsworth

London, 30 January, 1801

THANKS for your letter and present.[24] I had already borrowed your second volume. What most pleases me are the song of Lucy. . . .[25] "Simon's sickly daughter" in the *Sexton* made me *cry.* Next to these are the description of the continuous echoes in the story of Joanna's laugh,[26] where the mountains and all the scenery absolutely seem alive —and that fine Shakespearian character of the happy man in *The Brothers,*

——————that creeps about the fields,
Following his fancies by the hour, to bring
Tears down his cheek, or solitary smiles
Into his face, *until the Setting Sun*
Write Fool upon his forehead.

I will mention one more: the delicate and curious feeling in the wish for the Cumberland Beggar,[27] that he may have about him the melody of birds, although he hear them not. Here the mind knowingly passes a fiction upon herself, first substituting her own feelings for the Beggar's, and, in the same breath detecting the fallacy, will not part with the wish.—The *Poet's Epitaph* is dis-

---

[17] William Pitt the younger, head of the cabinet 1783–1801.

[18] Emmanuel Joseph Sieyès (1748–1836), a leading spirit in the French constitutional assembly of 1789.

[19] Gilbert Burnet's *History of My Own Time* (1723–1734).

[20] High relief.

[21] References to Hume's *History of England* (1754–1761) and Gibbon's *Decline and Fall of the Roman Empire* (1776–1778). Lamb goes on to mention the Scotch historian, William Robertson (1721–1793), and William Roscoe, whose *Life of Lorenzo de' Medici* had appeared in 1796.

[22] The Bloodless Revolution of 1688.

[23] Charles Lloyd, the brother of Robert Lloyd, and his wife.

[24] The second edition of the *Lyrical Ballads* (1800).

[25] Something is apparently omitted at this point. The Song of Lucy is probably "She Dwelt Among the Untrodden Ways."

[26] *Poems on the Naming of Places,* II.

[27] In *The Old Cumberland Beggar.*

figured to my taste by the vulgar satire upon parsons and lawyers in the beginning, and the coarse epithet of "pin point" in the sixth stanza. All the rest is eminently good, and your own. I will just add that it appears to me a fault in the *Beggar* that the instructions conveyed in it are too direct and like a lecture: they don't slide into the mind of the reader while he is imagining no such matter. An intelligent reader finds a sort of insult in being told, "I will teach you how to think upon this subject." This fault, if I am right, is in a ten-thousandth worse degree to be found in Sterne and many, many novelists and modern poets who continually put a sign-post up to show where you are to feel. They set out with assuming their readers to be stupid: very different from *Robinson Crusoe, The Vicar of Wakefield, Roderick Random,* and other beautiful bare narratives. There is implied an unwritten compact between author and reader: "I will tell you a story, and I suppose you will understand it." Modern novels, *St. Leon's*[28] and the like, are full of such flowers as these: "Let not my reader suppose," "Imagine, *if you can*"—modest!—*etc.*—I will here have done with praise and blame. I have written so much, only that you may not think I have passed over your book without observation.—I am sorry that Coleridge has christened his *Ancient Marinere* "a poet's reverie":—it is bad as Bottom the weaver's declaration[29] that he is not a lion but only the scenical representation of a lion. What new idea is gained by this title but one subversive of all credit, which the tale should force upon us, of its truth? For me, I was never so affected with any human tale. After first reading it, I was totally possessed with it for many days;—I dislike all the miraculous part of it, but the feelings of the man under the operation of such scenery dragged me along like Tom Piper's magic whistle. I totally differ from your idea that the Marinere should have had a character and profession. This is a beauty in *Gulliver's Travels,* where the

mind is kept in a placid state of little wonderments; but the Ancient Marinere undergoes such trials as overwhelm and bury all individuality or memory of what he was, like the state of a man in a bad dream, one terrible peculiarity of which is that all consciousness of personality is gone. Your other observation is, I think as well, a little unfounded: the Marinere from being conversant in supernatural events *has* acquired a supernatural and strange cast of *phrase,* eye, appearance, *etc.* which frighten the wedding guest. You will excuse my remarks, because I am hurt and vexed that you should think it necessary, with a prose apology, to open the eyes of dead men that cannot see. To sum up a general opinion of the second volume:—I do not feel any one poem in it so forcibly as *The Ancient Marinere, The Mad Mother,* and the *Lines at Tintern Abbey* in the first.—I could, too, have wished the critical preface had appeared in a separate treatise. All its dogmas are true and just, and most of them new, *as* criticism. But they associate a *diminishing* idea with the poems which follow, as having been written for *experiment* on the public taste, more than having sprung (as they must have done) from living and daily circumstances.—I am prolix, because I am gratified in the opportunity of writing to you, and I don't well know when to leave off.[30] I ought before this to have replied to your very kind invitation into Cumberland. With you and your sister I could gang[31] anywhere. But I am afraid whether I shall ever be able to afford so desperate a journey. Separate from the pleasure of your company, I don't much care if I never see a mountain in my life. I have passed all my days in London, until I have formed as many and intense local attachments as any of you mountaineers can have done with dead nature. The lighted shops of the Strand and Fleet Street, the innumerable trades, tradesmen and customers, coaches, waggons, playhouses, all the bustle and wickedness round about Covent Garden, the very women of the town, the watchmen,

---

[28]William Godwin's *St. Leon* (1799).
[29]The declaration is actually Snug the joiner's, although Bottom persuades him to make it *(Midsummer Night's Dream,* III, i, 33-42 and V, i, 217-224).

[30]This and the three sentences which precede it were suppressed by Wordsworth in early editions of Lamb's *Letters.*
[31]Go.

drunken scenes, rattles,—life awake, if you awake, at all hours of the night, the impossibility of being dull in Fleet Street, the crowds, the very dirt and mud, the sun shining upon houses and pavements, the print shops, the old-book stalls, parsons cheapening books, coffee houses, steams of soups from kitchens, the pantomimes, London itself a pantomime and a masquerade,—all these things work themselves into my mind and feed me, without a power of satiating me. The wonder of these sights impells me into nightwalks about her crowded streets, and I often shed tears in the motley Strand from fulness of joy at so much life.—All these emotions must be strange to you. So are your rural emotions to me. But consider, what must I have been doing all my life not to have lent great portions of my heart with usury to such scenes?—

My attachments are all local, purely local. I have no passion (or have had none since I was in love, and then it was the spurious engendering of poetry and books) to groves and valleys. The rooms where I was born, the furniture which has been before my eyes all my life, a book-case which has followed me about (like a faithful dog, only exceeding him in knowledge) wherever I have moved —old chairs, old tables, streets, squares where I have sunned myself, my old school, —these are my mistresses. Have I not enough without your mountains? I do not envy you. I should pity you, did I not know that the mind will make friends of anything. Your sun and moon and skies and hills and lakes affect me no more, or scarcely come to me in more venerable characters, than as a gilded room with tapestry and tapers, where I might live with handsome visible objects. I consider the clouds above me but as a roof, beautifully painted but unable to satisfy the mind, and at last, like the pictures of the apartment of a connoisseur, unable to afford him any longer a pleasure. So fading upon me, from disuse, have been the Beauties of Nature, as they have been confinedly called; so ever fresh and green and warm are all the inventions of men and assemblies of men in this great city. I should certainly have laughed with dear Joanna.

Give my kindest love, *and my sister's,* to D. and your*self* and a kiss from me to little Barbara Lewthwaite.[82]

C. Lamb

Thanks for liking my Play!![83]

VI. To Thomas Manning

London, 15 February, 1801

I HAD need be cautious henceforward what opinion I give of the *Lyrical Ballads.* All the North of England are in a turmoil. Cumberland and Westmoreland have already declared a state of war. I lately received from Wordsworth a copy of the second volume, accompanied by an acknowledgment of having received from me many months since a copy of a certain tragedy, with excuses for not having made any acknowledgment sooner, it being owing to an "almost insurmountable aversion from letter-writing." This letter I answered in due form and time, and enumerated several of the passages which had most affected me, adding, unfortunately, that no single piece had moved me so forcibly as the *Ancient Mariner, The Mad Mother,* or the *Lines at Tintern Abbey.* The post did not sleep a moment. I received almost instantaneously a long letter of four sweating pages from my Reluctant Letter-Writer, the purport of which was that he was sorry his second volume had not given me more pleasure (Devil a hint did I give that it had *not pleased me*), and "was compelled to wish that my range of sensibility was more extended, being obliged to believe that I should receive large influxes of happiness and happy thoughts" (I suppose from the *L. B.*)—with a deal of stuff about a certain Union of Tenderness and Imagination, which in the sense he used Imagination was not the characteristic of Shakespeare, but which Milton possessed in a degree far exceeding other poets: which Union, as the highest species of poetry, and chiefly deserving that name, "He was most proud to aspire to"; then illustrating the said Union by two quotations from his own second volume (which I had been so un-

---

[82]About whom Wordsworth wrote in *The Pet Lamb.*

[83]*John Woodvil,* of which Lamb had sent Wordsworth a manuscript copy.

fortunate as to miss). First specimen.—A father addresses his son:

When thou
First camest into the World, as it befalls
To new-born Infants, thou didst sleep away   5
Two days: and Blessings from Thy father's
    Tongue
Then fell upon thee.[34]

The lines were thus undermarked, and then followed: "This passage, as combining in an 10 extraordinary degree that Union of Imagination and Tenderness which I am speaking of, I consider as one of the best I ever wrote!"

Second specimen.—A youth, after years of 15 absence, revisits his native place, and thinks (as most people do) that there has been strange alteration in his absence:—

And that the rocks
And everlasting Hills themselves were 20 changed.[35]

You see both these are good poetry; but after one has been reading Shakespeare twenty of the best years of one's life, to have a fellow 25 start up, and prate about some unknown quality which Shakespeare possessed in a degree inferior to Milton and *somebody else!!* This was not to be *all* my castigation. Coleridge, who had not written to me some 30 months before, starts up from his bed of sickness to reprove me for my hardy presumption: four long pages, equally sweaty and more tedious, came from him, assuring me that, when the works of a man of true 35 genius such as W. undoubtedly was do not please me at first sight, I should suspect the fault to lie "in me and not in them," *etc., etc., etc., etc., etc.* What am I to do with such people? I certainly shall write them a very 40 merry letter. Writing to *you,* I may say that the second volume had no such pieces as the three I enumerated. It is full of original thinking and an observing mind, but it does not often make you laugh or cry.—It 45 too artfully aims at simplicity of expression. And you sometimes doubt if simplicity be not a cover for poverty. The best piece in it I will send you, being *short.* I have grievously offended my friends in the North by 50

declaring my undue preference; but I need not fear you:—

She dwelt among the untrodden ways
    Beside the Springs of Dove,
A maid whom there were few[36] to praise
    And very few to love.

A violet, by a mossy stone,
    Half hidden from the eye.
Fair as a star when only one
    Is shining in the sky.

She lived unknown; and few could know,
    When Lucy ceased to be.
But she is in the[37] grave, and oh!
    The difference to me.

This is choice and genuine, and so are many, many more. But one does not like to have 'em rammed down one's throat. "Pray take it—it's very good—let me help you—eat faster."

At length George Dyer's[38] first volume is come to a birth. One volume of three—subscribers being allowed by the prospectus to pay for all at once (though it's very doubtful if the rest ever come to anything, this having been already some years getting out). I paid two guineas for you and myself, which entitle us to the whole. I will send you your copy, if you are in a *great hurry.* Meantime you owe me a guinea.

George skipped about like a scorched pea at the receipt of so much cash. To give you a specimen of the beautiful absurdity of the notes, which defy imitation, take one: "Discrimination is not the *aim* of the present volume. It will be more strictly attended to in the next." One of the sonnets purports to have been written in Bedlam! This for a man to own!

The rest are addressed to Science, Genius, Melancholy—*etc., etc.*—two to the river Cam —an ode to the Nightingale; another to Howard, beginning: "Spirit of meek Philanthropy!" One is entitled *The Madman*— "being collected by the author from several madhouses." It begins: "Yes, yes,—'tis He!" A long poetical satire is addressed to

---

[34] *Michael* (339–343, slightly misquoted).
[35] *The Brothers* (98–99).

[36] Misquotation for "none."
[37] Misquotation for "her."
[38] A kindly eccentric (1755–1841), who was once nearly drowned when he stepped into the New River in a fit of abstraction.

"John Disney, D.D.—his wife and daughter!!!"

Now to my own affairs. I have not taken that thing[39] to Colman, but I have proceeded one step in the business. I have inquired his address, and am promised it in a few days. Meantime three acts and a half are finished galloping of a play on a Persian story which I must father in April. But far, very far, from *Antonio*[40] in composition. O Jephtha, Judge of Israel,[41] what a fool I was!

C. Lamb

VII. To Thomas Manning

London, 24 September, 1802

My dear Manning,

Since the date of my last letter I have been a traveler. A strong desire seized me of visiting remote regions. My first impulse was to go and see Paris. It was a trivial objection to my aspiring mind that I did not understand a word of the language, since I certainly intend some time in my life to see Paris, and equally certainly never intend to learn the language; therefore that could be no objection. However, I am very glad I did not go, because you had left Paris (I see) before I could have set out. I believe, Stoddart promising to go with me another year prevented that plan. My next scheme (for to my restless, ambitious mind London was become a bed of thorns) was to visit the far-famed Peak[42] in Derbyshire, where the Devil sits, they say, without breeches. *This* my purer mind rejected as indelicate. And my final resolve was a tour to the Lakes. I set out with Mary to Keswick, without giving Coleridge any notice; for my time, being precious, did not admit of it. He received us with all the hospitality in the world, and gave up his time to show us all the wonders of the country. He dwells upon a small hill by the side of Keswick, in a comfortable house, quite enveloped on all sides by a net of mountains: great floundering bears and monsters they seemed, all couchant[43] and asleep. We got in in the evening, traveling in a post-chaise from Penrith, in the midst of a gorgeous sunshine which transmuted all the mountains into colors, purple, *etc., etc.* We thought we had got into Fairy Land. But that went off (as it never came again—while we stayed we had no more fine sunsets); and we entered Coleridge's comfortable study just in the dusk, when the mountains were all dark with clouds upon their heads. Such an impression I never received from objects of sight before, nor do I suppose I can ever again. Glorious creatures, fine old fellows, Skiddaw,[44] *etc.,* I never shall forget ye, how ye lay about that night, like an intrenchment; gone to bed, as it seemed, for the night, but promising that ye were to be seen in the morning. Coleridge had got a blazing fire in his study; which is a large, antique, ill-shaped room, with an old-fashioned organ, never played upon, big enough for a church, shelves of scattered folios, an Aeolian harp,[45] and an old sofa, half-bed, *etc.,* and all looking out upon the last fading view of Skiddaw and his broad-breasted brethren: what a night! Here we stayed three full weeks, in which time I visited Wordsworth's cottage, where we stayed a day or two with the Clarksons[46] (good people and most hospitable, at whose house we tarried one day and night), and saw Lloyd. The Wordsworths were gone to Calais. They have since been in London and passed much time with us; he is now gone into Yorkshire to be married to a girl of small fortune,[47] but he is in expectation of augmenting his own in consequence of the death of Lord Lonsdale, who kept him out of his own in conformity with a plan my lord had taken up in early life of making everybody unhappy. So we have seen Keswick, Grasmere, Ambleside, Ullswater (where the Clarksons live), and a place at the other end

---

[39]Probably *John Woodvil*. George Colman was manager of the Haymarket Theater.

[40]A play of William Godwin's which had recently failed.

[41]*Hamlet,* II, ii, 342.

[42]A mountainous district in north central England.

[43]Lying down.

[44]A mountain in the neighborhood of Keswick.

[45]Stringed instrument on which the wind produces musical sounds.

[46]Thomas Clarkson (1760–1846) was the reformer responsible for the passing, in 1807, of an act making the slave-trade illegal in the British Empire.

[47]Wordsworth married Mary Hutchinson ten days after this letter was written.

of Ullswater—I forget the name—to which we traveled on a very sultry day, over the middle of Helvellyn.[48] We have clambered up to the top of Skiddaw, and I have waded up the bed of Lodore.[49] In fine, I have satisfied myself that there is such a thing as that which tourists call *romantic,* which I very much suspected before; they make such a spluttering about it, and toss their splendid epithets around them, till they give as dim a light as at four o'clock next morning the lamps do after an illumination. Mary was excessively tired when she got about half way up Skiddaw, but we came to a cold rill (than which nothing can be imagined more cold, running over cold stones), and with the reinforcement of a draught of cold water she surmounted it most manfully. Oh, its fine black head, and the bleak air atop of it, with a prospect of mountains all about, and about, making you giddy; and then Scotland afar off, and the border countries so famous in song and ballad! It was a day that will stand out like a mountain, I am sure, in my life. But I am returned (I have now been come home near three weeks—I was a month out), and you cannot conceive the degradation I felt at first, from being accustomed to wander free as air among mountains, and bathe in rivers without being controlled by any one, to come home and *work.* I felt very *little.* I had been dreaming I was a very great man. But that is going off, and I find I shall conform in time to that state of life to which it has pleased God to call me. Besides, after all, Fleet Street and the Strand are better places to live in for good and all than among Skiddaw. Still, I turn back to those great places where I wandered about, participating in their greatness. After all, I could not *live* in Skiddaw. I could spend a year—two, three years—among them, but I must have a prospect of seeing Fleet Street at the end of that time, or I should mope and pine away, I know. Still, Skiddaw is a fine creature. My habits are changing, I think, *i. e.* from drunk to sober. Whether I shall be happier or not remains to be proved. I

shall certainly be more happy in a morning; but whether I shall not sacrifice the fat, and the marrow, and the kidneys, *i. e.* the night, the glorious care-drowning night that heals all our wrongs, pours wine into our mortifications, changes the scene from indifferent and flat to bright and brilliant!—O Manning, if I should have formed a diabolical resolution, by the time you come to England, of not admitting any spirituous liquors into my house, will you be my guest on such shameworthy terms? Is life, with such limitations, worth trying? The truth is that my liquors bring a nest of friendly harpies about my house, who consume me. This is a pitiful tale to be read at St. Gothard; but it is just now nearest my heart. Fenwick[50] is a ruined man. He is hiding himself from his creditors, and has sent his wife and children into the country. Fell, my other drunken companion (that has been; *nam hic caestus artemque repono*[51]), is turned editor of a *Naval Chronicle.* Godwin[52] (with a pitiful, artificial wife) continues a steady friend, though the same facility does not remain of visiting him often. That bitch has detached Marshall from his house, Marshall the man who went to sleep when the *Ancient Mariner* was reading: the old, steady, unalterable friend of the Professor. Holcroft is not yet come to town. I expect to see him, and will deliver your message. How I hate *this part* of a letter. Things come crowding in to say, and no room for 'em. Some things are too little to be told, *i. e.* to have a preference; some are too big and circumstantial. Thanks for yours, which was most delicious. Would I had been with you, benighted, *etc.* I fear my head is turned with wandering. I shall never be the same acquiescent being. Farewell; write again quickly, for I shall not like

---

[48]A mountain in the neighborhood of Grasmere, where the Wordsworths had their cottage.

[49]A stream which forms a well-known cascade not far from Keswick.

[50]John Fenwick, the Bigod of Lamb's *Two Races of Men.*

[51]For here I give up my boxing gloves and the game *(Aeneid,* V, 484).

[52]William Godwin (1756–1836), radical thinker and author, referred to below as "the Professor." His second wife, of whom Lamb writes so feelingly, was the mother, by a former marriage, of Clare Clairmont and so the grandmother-to-be of Byron's child Allegra. Thomas Holcroft (1745–1809), one of the leading dramatists of the period, belonged to the same group as Godwin.

to hazard a letter, not knowing where the fates have carried you. Farewell, my dear fellow.

C. Lamb

VIII. To Thomas Manning

London, 19 February, 1803

My dear Manning,

The general scope of your letter afforded no indications of insanity, but some particular points raised a scruple. For God's sake don't think any more of "Independent Tartary." What have you to do among such Ethiopians? Is there no *lineal descendant* of Prester John?[53]

Is the chair empty? Is the sword unswayed?—depend upon't they'll never make you their king, as long as any branch of that great stock is remaining. I tremble for your Christianity. They'll certainly circumcise you. Read Sir John Mandeville's[54] travels to cure you, or come over to England. There is a Tartar-man now exhibiting at Exeter Change. Come and talk with him, and hear what he says first. Indeed, he is no very favorable specimen of his countrymen! But perhaps the best thing you can do is to *try* to get the idea out of your head. For this purpose repeat to yourself every night, after you have said your prayers, the words "Independent Tartary, Independent Tartary," two or three times, and associate with them the *idea of oblivion* ('tis Hartley's[55] method with obstinate memories), or say, "Independent, Independent, have I not already got an *Independence?*" That was a clever way of the old Puritans—pun-divinity. My dear friend, think what a sad pity it would be to bury such *parts* in heathen countries, among nasty, unconversable, horse-belching Tartar people! Some say they are cannibals; and then conceive a Tartar-fellow eating my friend, and adding the *cool malignity* of mustard and vinegar! I am afraid 'tis the reading of Chaucer has misled you; his foolish stories about Cambuscan and the ring, and the horse of brass.[56] Believe me, there's no such things; 'tis all the poet's *invention;* but if there were such *darling* things as old Chaucer sings, I would *up* behind you on the horse of brass, and frisk off for Prester John's country. But these are all tales; a horse of brass never flew and a king's daughter never talked with birds! The Tartars, really, are a cold, insipid, smouchy[57] set. You'll be sadly moped (if you are not eaten) among them. Pray *try* and cure yourself. Take hellebore[58] (the counsel is Horace's; 'twas none of my thought *originally*). Shave yourself oftener. Eat no saffron, for saffron-eaters contract a terrible Tartar-like yellow. Pray, to avoid the fiend. Eat nothing that gives the heartburn. *Shave the upper lip.* Go about like a European. Read no books of voyages (they're nothing but lies): only now and then a romance, to keep the fancy *under*. Above all, don't go to any sights of *wild beasts. That has been your ruin.* Accustom yourself to write familiar letters on common subjects to your friends in England, such as are of a moderate understanding. And think about common things more. There's your friend Holcroft, now, has written a play.[59] You used to be fond of the drama. Nobody went to see it. Notwithstanding this, with an audacity perfectly original, he faces the town down in a preface, that they *did like* it very much. I have heard a waspish punster say, "Sir, why did you not laugh at my jest?" But for a man boldly to face me out with, "Sir, I maintain it, you did laugh at my jest," is a little too much. I have seen H. but once. He spoke of you to me in honorable terms. H. seems to me to be drearily dull. Godwin is dull, but then he has a dash of affectation which smacks of the coxcomb, and your coxcombs are always agreeable. I supped last night with

---

[53]Lamb assumes that Manning intends to seize the throne of Prester John, the legendary King of Abyssinia. Manning was contemplating a long sojourn, which he subsequently made, in China.

[54]The ostensible author of a fourteenth-century book of travels to the East.

[55]David Hartley (1705–1757), a philosopher who advanced the theory that a human mind developed a moral or a religious sense through the association of ideas.

[56]See the Squire's tale in *The Canterbury Tales*.

[57]Word of uncertain meaning, perhaps "dirty" or "dishonest."

[58]A plant used as a cure for madness.

[59]*A Tale of Mystery* (1802).

Rickman,[60] and met a merry, *natural* captain, who pleases himself vastly with once having made a pun at Otaheite in the O. language. 'Tis the same man who said Shakespeare he liked, because he was so *much of the gentleman*. Rickman is a man "absolute in all numbers." I think I may one day bring you acquainted, if you do not go to Tartary first; for you'll never come back. Have a care, my dear friend, of anthropophagi! their stomachs are always craving. But if you do go among them[61] pray contrive to *stink* as soon as you can that you may not[61] hang a hand at the butcher's. 'Tis terrible to be weighed out for 5*d.* a pound. To sit at table (the reverse of fishes in Holland),[62] not as a guest, but as a meat.

God bless you; do come to England. Air and exercise may do great things. Talk with some minister. Why not your father? God dispose all for the best. I have discharged my duty.

Your sincere friend,

C. Lamb

IX. *Joint Letter to Louisa Martin*[63]

I. FROM MARY LAMB

London, 28 March, 1809

Dear Louisa,

I promised never to let a letter of yours remain unanswered one week; if I have exceeded the time a few days, you will not be surprised when I tell you we have been removing from our dear old dirty chambers into lodgings, which has been great labor and pain and grief to me. I had persuaded myself that I should be glad to quit them, but when the time came you cannot imagine what I felt, when they were clean swept out and I was about to lock the door and leave them.

We are in Hazlitt's[64] old lodgings and, I believe, must remain here at least two months before our new chambers are ready for us. Charles is now sitting by me writing to Manning. If you have any message to send him, now is your time to speak. Poor Holcroft died last Thursday. Mrs. Reynolds[65] is very ill. I am almost afraid she will never recover; her complaint seems to have fallen upon her lungs. Hazlitt has been in town and is just gone back again. His child is expected to die.

We were pleased to see by your specimen of law hand[66] that you have not quite forgotten old times, but we met with an instance yesterday of a still longer memory than yours. A Mr. Lloyd whom we have not seen since we lived at Islington dined with us; we had boiled pork and he waited some with the meat on his plate till Emily brought up the mustard, and he confessed afterwards that he could not eat his dinner because the mustard was in a different mustard pot to what he had been used to see at Islington.

Poor Nurse about a week before we left the Temple fell down and hurt her hip. She is now in the Westminster Infirmary and is not expected ever to be able to walk again. I think I have nothing but dismal news to send you.

We left the carpet, the beautiful carpet Sarah and you so much admired and which I hear you make frequent inquiries after in your letters to Hannah,[67] we left behind us with the deepest regret.

We have bought some very fine chairs and window curtains, and we intend almost to ruin ourselves in various other articles of expensive furniture—and we have hired a maid too. You will find strange alterations at your next holidays.

This is Wednesday, which I am very glad of, for it will make the place seem more like a home to me; at present I feel quite unsettled and unhomed.

---

[60]John Rickman (1771–1840), holder of various minor secretarial positions in the government. The captain whom Lamb met at his house was James Burney, a brother of the novelist Fanny Burney.

[61]Word not written, but conjectured to have been intended, by Lamb.

[62]An allusion to Marvell's couplet:

The fish ofttimes the burgher dispossessed
And sat not as a meat but as a guest.

[63]A young lady, fifteen or sixteen years old at this time, whom Lamb was in the habit of calling "Monkey."

[64]William Hazlitt (1778–1830), the essayist.

[65]Lamb's schoolmistress before he went to Christ's Hospital. Later in his life he gave her a small pension.

[66]Legal handwriting.

[67]Louisa Martin's sister.

2. FROM CHARLES LAMB

Mary is suddenly snatched away (not by death) and has left her letter open, which I am tempted to fill up. Some odd things have occurred since you went away. Dawe the painter has painted a picture of the Princess Charlotte of Wales which pleased the King so much that he knighted him. He is now Sir George Dawe. Mary has told you about Nurse. I was wishing her to die, and how lucky things turn out!

Hazlitt's child died of swallowing a bag of white paint, which the poor innocent thing mistook for sugar candy. It told its mother, just two hours before it died, that it did not like soft sugar candy, and so it came out, which was not before suspected. When it was opened several other things were found in it, particularly a small hearth brush, two golden pippins and a letter which I had written to Hazlitt from Bath. The letter had nothing remarkable in it. Martin Burney[68] has displeased his family by marrying. You know the person, Miss Winter, that used to come to work to our house. It was there they contrived to meet. We suspected nothing.

My brother John said in a public coffee house the other day that his brother Charles (meaning me) had the best heart of anybody he knew. An eminent merchant (in consequence) took it up very warmly and promised his interest at the next election of governors for Bartholomew Hospital[69] to make me a governor. Those institutions require humane people to have the superintendence of them. Why don't you mind your spelling better? In your last letter you spelt *finish, finnish,* with two *n's.* When you aren't quite sure of a word write it at full length on three sorts of paper, or as many, as you think it may be spelt, ways; then throw them up the chimney; the smoke will carry them up; and watch on the outside till they come down, and that that's most smoked is the right way of spelling it. They always do so in Wales. But their chimneys are lower.

Your sister Hannah spoke 34,750 words in twenty or twenty and one minutes last Saturday. There was a man with me who took them down: an amazing instance of the rapidity and volubility of some people's way of speaking.

3. FROM MARY LAMB

He has only left room for me to say I hope it is true that you do not show your friends' nonsensical letters to your governess.

I have not seen your mother since the moving day, nor Hannah for several weeks. Sarah seems to succeed admirably.

Let us hear from you soon. Farewell,
I am,
Yours affectionately,
M. Lamb

X. To Mrs. William Wordsworth

London, 18 February, 1818

(Mary shall send you all the *news,* which I find I have left out.)
My dear Mrs. Wordsworth,

I have repeatedly taken pen in hand to answer your kind letter. My sister should more properly have done it, but she having failed, I consider myself answerable for her debts. I am now trying to do it in the midst of commercial noises,[70] and with a quill which seems more ready to glide into arithmetical figures and names of goods, cassia, cardamoms, aloes, ginger, tea, than into kindly responses and friendly recollections.

The reason why I cannot write letters at home is that I am never alone. Plato's (I write to W. W. now), Plato's double animal parted never longed more[71] to be reciprocally reunited in the system of its first creation than I sometimes do to be but for a moment single and separate. Except my morning's walk to the office, which is like treading on sands of gold for that reason, I

---

[68]Son of Captain Burney and one of the best of Lamb's friends.
[69]The great public hospital of London.
[70]Lamb writes from the East India Company offices.
[71]Word not written, but probably intended, by Lamb. Plato's "double animal" is the explanation which Aristophanes, in Plato's *Symposium,* gave of love: each pair of lovers was originally one double body which Jove had split in two.

am never so. I cannot walk home from the office but some officious friend offers his damned unwelcome courtesies to accompany me. All the morning I am pestered. I could sit and gravely cast up sums in great books, or compare sum with sum, and write "paid" against this and "unp'd" against t'other, and yet reserve in some "corner of my mind" some darling thoughts all my own —faint memory of some passage in a book— or the tone of an absent friend's voice—a snatch of Miss Burrell's[72] singing—a gleam of Fanny Kelly's divine plain face.—The two operations might be going on at the same time without thwarting, as the sun's two mo- tions (earth's I mean), or as I sometimes turn round till I am giddy, in my back par- lor, while my sister is walking longitudinally in the front—or as the shoulder of veal twists round with the spit, while the smoke wreathes up the chimney;—but there are a set of amateurs of the belle lettres—the gay science—who come to me as a sort of ren- dezvous, putting questions of criticism, of British institutions, *Lalla Rookh's,*[73] etc., what Coleridge said at the lecture last night[74] —who have the form of reading men, but, for any possible use reading can be to them but to talk of, might as well have been Ante- Cadmeans born,[75] or have lain sucking out the sense of an Egyptian hieroglyph as long as the Pyramids will last before they should find it. These pests worrit me at business and in all intervals, perplexing my accounts, poisoning my little salutary warming-time at the fire, puzzling my paragraphs if I take a newspaper, cramming in between my own free thoughts and a column of figures which had come to an amicable compromise but for them. Their noise ended, one of them, as I said, accompanies me home lest I should be solitary for a moment; he at length takes his welcome leave at the door, up I go, mut- ton on table, hungry as hunter, hope to forget my cares and bury them in the agreeable

abstraction of mastication, knock at the door, in comes Mrs. Hazlitt, or M. Burney, or Morgan,[76] or Demogorgon, or my brother, or somebody, to prevent my eating alone, a process absolutely necessary to my poor wretched digestion. O the pleasure of eat- ing alone!—eating my dinner alone! let me think of it. But in they come, and make it absolutely necessary that I should open a bottle of orange—for my meat turns into stone when any one dines with me, if I have not wine—wine can mollify stones. Then *that* wine turns into acidity, acerbity, misan- thropy, a hatred of my interrupters (God bless 'em! I love some of 'em dearly), and with the hatred a still greater aversion to their going away. Bad is the dead sea they bring upon me, choaking and death-doing, but worse is the deader dry sand they leave me on if they go before bed time. "Come never," I would say to these spoilers of my dinner, "but if you come, never go." The fact is, this interruption does not happen very often, but every time it comes by sur- prise that present bane of my life, orange wine, with all its dreary, stifling conse- quences, follows. Evening company I should always like had I any mornings, but I am saturated with human faces (*divine* forsooth) and voices all the golden morn- ing, and five evenings in a week would be as much as I should covet to be in company; but I assure you that is a wonderful week in which I can get two, or one, to myself. I am never C. L. but always C. L. and Co.

He who thought it not good for a man to be alone, preserve me from the prodigious monstrosity of being never by myself. I forget bed time, but even there these sociable frogs clamber up to annoy me. Once a week, generally some singular evening that, being alone, I go to bed at the hour I ought always to be abed, just close to my bedroom window is the club room of a public house, where a set of singers, I take them to be chorus-singers of the two theaters[77] (it must be *both of them*), begin their orgies. They are a set of fellows (as I conceive) who be-

---

[72]Fanny Burrell, a popular singer. Fanny Kelly was the actress to whom Lamb wrote letter no. XI.

[73]Thomas Moore's *Lalla Rookh* had appeared in 1817.

[74]Coleridge was delivering a series of lectures on Shakespeare and poetry.

[75]Born before the time of Cadmus, who intro- duced letters.

[76]John Morgan, of whom Lamb writes in another letter that he "ate walnuts better than any man I ever knew."

[77]Drury Lane and Covent Garden.

ing limited by their talents to the burthen of the songs at the play houses, in revenge have got the common popular airs by Bishop[78] or some cheap composer arranged for choruses, that is, to be sung all in chorus. At least I never can catch any of the text of the plain song, nothing but the Babylonish choral howl at the tail on't. "That fury being quenched"—the howl I mean—a curseder burden succeeds, of shouts and clapping and knocking of the table. At length over-tasked nature drops under it and escapes for a few hours into the society of the sweet silent creatures of dreams, which go away with mocks and mows[79] at cockcrow. And then I think of the words Christabel's father used (bless me, I have dipt in the wrong ink) to say every morning by way of variety when he awoke—"Every knell, the Baron saith, Wakes us up to a world of death,"[80] or something like it. All I mean by this sense-less interrupted tale is that by my central situation I am a little over-companied. Not that I have any animosity against the good creatures that are so anxious to drive away the harpy solitude from me. I like 'em, and cards, and a cheerful glass, but I mean merely to give you an idea between office confinement and after-office society, how little time I can call my own. I mean only to draw a picture, not to make an inference. I would not, that I know of, have it other-wise. I only wish sometimes I could ex-change some of my faces and voices for the faces and voices which a late visitation brought most welcome and carried away leaving regret, but more pleasure, even a kind of gratitude at being so often favored with that kind northern visitation. My London faces and noises don't hear me—I mean no disrespect—or I should explain my-self that instead of their return 220 times a year and the return of W. W., *etc.,* 7 times in 104 weeks, some more equal distribution might be found. I have scarce room to put in Mary's kind love and my poor name.

Ch. Lamb

This to be read last.

W. H.[81] goes on lecturing against W. W. and making copious use of quotations from said W. W. to give zest to said lectures. S. T. C. is lecturing with success. I have not heard either him or H., but I dined with S. T. C. at Gilman's[82] a Sunday or two since and he was well and in good spirits. I mean to hear some of the course, but lectures are not much to my taste, whatever the lecturer may be. If *read,* they are dismal flat, and you can't think why you are brought together to hear a man read his works which you could read so much better at leisure yourself; if delivered extempore, I am always in pain lest the gift of utterance should suddenly fail the orator in the middle, as it did me at the dinner given in honor of me at the London Tavern. "Gentlemen," said I, and there I stopped,—the rest my feelings were under the necessity of supplying. Mrs. Wordsworth *will* go on, kindly haunting us with visions of seeing the Lakes once more, which never can be realized. Between us there is a great gulf—not of inexplicable moral antipathies and distances, I hope (as there seemed to be between me and that gen-tleman concerned in the Stamp Office that I so strangely coiled up from at Haydon's[83]). I think I had an instinct that he was the head of an office. I hate all such people—accountants, deputy accountants. The dear abstract notion of the East India Company, as long as she is unseen, is pretty, rather poetical; but as she makes herself manifest by the persons of such beasts, I loathe and detest her as the Scarlet What-do-you-call-her of Babylon. I thought, after abridging us of all our red-letter days, they had done their worst, but I was deceived in the length to which heads of offices, those true liberty-haters, can go. They are the tyrants, not Ferdinand, nor Nero:—by a decree past this

---

[78]Sir Henry Rowley Bishop, composer of "Home, Sweet Home."

[79]Derisive grimaces.

[80]Each matin bell, the Baron saith, Knells us back to a world of death. (*Christabel*, II, 1–2.)

[81]William Hazlitt, who was giving a course of lectures on the English poets.

[82]Dr. James Gilman, in whose household Coleridge spent the last eighteen years of his life.

[83]On that occasion a gentleman in the Stamp Office, a stranger, had asked Wordsworth if he did not think Milton was a great genius; and Lamb replied by chanting,

Diddle diddle dumpling, my son John Went to bed with his breeches on.

week they have abridged us of the immemorially observed custom of going at one o'clock of a Saturday, the little shadow of a holiday left us. Blast them. I speak it soberly. Dear W. W., be thankful for your liberty.

We have spent two very pleasant evenings lately with Mr. Monkhouse.

XI. To Fanny Kelly[84]

London, 9 July, 1819

Dear Miss Kelly,

If your bones[85] are not engaged on Monday night, will you favor us with the use of them? I know, if you can oblige us, you will make no bones of it; if you cannot, it shall break none betwixt us. We might ask somebody else, but we do not like the bones of any strange animal. We should be welcome to dear Mrs. Litson's, but then she is so plump there is no getting at them. I should prefer Miss Iver's—they must be ivory I take it for granted—but she is married to Mr. xxx, and become bone of his bone, consequently can have none of her own to dispose of. Well, it all comes to this,— if you can let us have them, you will, I dare say; if you cannot, God rest your bones. I am almost at the end of my bon-mots.

C. Lamb

XII. To Samuel Taylor Coleridge[86]

London, 9 March, 1822

Dear C.,

It gives me great satisfaction to hear that the pig turned out so well—they are interesting creatures at a certain age;—what a pity such buds should blow out into the maturity of rank bacon! You had all some of the crackling—and brain sauce;—did you remember to rub it with butter, and gently dredge it a little, just before the crisis? Did the eyes come away kindly with no Oedipean avulsion?[87] Was the crackling the color of the ripe pomegranate? Had you no complement of boiled neck of mutton before it, to blunt the edge of delicate desire? Did you flesh maiden teeth in it? Not that I sent the pig, or can form the remotest guess what part Owen[88] could play in the business. I never knew him give anything away in my life. He would not begin with strangers. I suspect the pig, after all, was meant for me; but at the unlucky juncture of time being absent, the present somehow went round to Highgate.[89] To confess an honest truth, a pig is one of those things I could never think of sending away. Teals, wigeons, snipes, barn-door fowl, ducks, geese—your tame villatic things[90]—Welsh mutton, collars of brawn, sturgeon fresh or pickled, your potted char, Swiss cheeses, French pies, early grapes, muscadines, I impart as freely unto my friends as to myself. They are but self-extended; but pardon me if I stop somewhere;—where the fine feeling of benevolence giveth a higher smack than the sensual rarity,—there my friends (or any good man) may command me; but pigs are pigs, and I myself therein am nearest to myself. Nay, I should think it an affront, an undervaluing done to Nature who bestowed such a boon upon me, if in a churlish mood I parted with the precious gift. One of the bitterest pangs of remorse I ever felt was when a child—when my kind old aunt had strained her pocket-strings to bestow a sixpenny whole plum-cake upon me. In my way home through the Borough I met a venerable old man, not a mendicant, but thereabouts—a look-beggar, not a verbal petitionist; and in the coxcombry of taught charity I gave away the cake to him. I walked on a little in all the pride of an Evangelical peacock, when of a sudden my old aunt's kindness crossed me—the sum it was to her—the pleasure she had a right to expect that I—not the old imposter—should

---

[84]The same actress to whose "divine plain face" Lamb had referred in the preceding letter. Eleven days after writing this lighthearted note he proposed marriage to her, but she felt compelled to reject the proposal.

[85]Free passes to the theater, made of bone.

[86]This letter is a first sketch of Lamb's *Dissertation upon Roast Pig.*

[87]When Oedipus learned that he had killed his father, Laius, King of Thebes, he put out his own eyes.

[88]Lamb's landlord.

[89]The Gilman household in which Coleridge was living.

[90]See the *Dissertation upon Roast Pig,* note 25, in this volume.

take in eating her cake—the cursed ingratitude by which, under the color of a Christian virtue, I had frustrated her cherished purpose. I sobbed, wept, and took it to heart so grievously that I think I never suffered the like—and I was right. It was a piece of unfeeling hypocrisy, and proved a lesson to me ever after. The cake has long been masticated, consigned to the dunghill with the ashes of that unseasonable pauper.

But when Providence, who is better to us all than our aunts, gives me a pig, remembering my temptation and my fall, I shall endeavor to act towards it more in the spirit of the donor's purpose.

Yours (short of pig) to command in everything,

C. L.

XIII. *To Peter George Patmore*[91]

Enfield,[92] June, 1827

Dear Patmore,

Excuse my anxiety—but how is Dash? (I should have asked if Mrs. Patmore kept her rules, and was improving—but Dash came uppermost. The order of our thoughts should be the order of our writing.) Goes he muzzled, or *aperto ore?*[93] Are his intellects sound, or does he wander a little in *his* conversation? You cannot be too careful to watch the first symptoms of incoherence. The first illogical snarl he makes, to St. Luke's with him! All the dogs here are going mad, if you believe the overseers; but I protest they seem to me very rational and collected. But nothing is so deceitful as mad people to those who are not used to them. Try him with hot water. If he won't lick it up, it is a sign he does not like it. Does his tail wag horizontally or perpendicularly? That has decided the fate of many dogs in Enfield. Is his general deportment cheerful? I mean when he is pleased—for otherwise there is no judging. You can't be too careful. Has he bit any of the children yet? If he has, have them shot, and keep *him* for curiosity, to see if it was the hydrophobia. They say all our army

in India had it at one time—but that was in *Hyder*-Ally's[94] time. Do you get paunch for him? Take care the sheep was sane. You might pull out his teeth (if he would let you), and then you need not mind if he were as mad as a bedlamite. It would be rather fun to see his odd ways. It might amuse Mrs. Patmore and the children. They'd have more sense than he! He'd be like a fool kept in the family, to keep the household in good humor with their own understanding. You might teach him the mad dance set to the mad howl. *Madge Owl-et* would be nothing to him. "My, how he capers!" One of the children speaks this.[95]

What I scratch out[96] is a German quotation from Lessing[97] on the bite of rabid animals; but, I remember, you don't read German. But Mrs. Patmore may, so I wish I had let it stand. The meaning in English is—"Avoid to approach an animal suspected of madness, as you would avoid fire or a precipice":—which I think is a sensible observation. The Germans are certainly profounder than we.

If the slightest suspicion arises in your breast that all is not right with him (Dash), muzzle him, and lead him in a string (common pack-thread will do; he don't care for twist) to Hood's,[98] his *quondam*[99] master, and he'll take him in at any time. You may mention your suspicion or not, as you like, or as you think it may wound or not Mr. H.'s feelings. Hood, I know, will wink at a few follies in Dash, in consideration of his former sense. Besides, Hood is deaf, and if you hinted anything, ten to one he would not hear you. Besides, you will have discharged your conscience, and laid the child at the right door, as they say.

We are dawdling our time away very idly and pleasantly, at a Mrs. Leishman's, Chace, Enfield, where, if you come a-hunting, we can give you cold meat and a tankard. Her husband is a tailor; but that, you know, does

---

[94]Ruler of Mysore in India, who fought the English in 1767–1769 and 1780–1782.

[95]This sentence is written in the margin.

[96]Three lines are erased just before this.

[97]Gotthold E. Lessing (1729–1781), German poet and critic.

[98]Thomas Hood (1799–1845), the poet.

[99]Former.

---

[91]Father of the poet Coventry Patmore. The latter was at this time a child of four years.

[92]A small town a few miles outside of London.

[93]With open mouth.

not make her one. I knew a jailor (which rimes), but his wife was a fine lady.

Let us hear from you respecting Mrs. Patmore's regimen. I send my love in a ——to Dash.

C. Lamb

Seriously, I wish you would call upon Hood when you are that way. He's a capital fellow. I sent him a couple of poems—one ordered by his wife, and written to order; and 'tis a week since, and I've not heard from him. I fear something is the matter. *Omitted within:*

Our kindest remembrance to Mrs. P.[100]

XIV. *To Louisa Holcroft*[101]

Enfield, 5 December, 1828

Dear Miss H.,

Mary, who never writes, bids me thank you for the handkerchief. I do not understand such work, but if I apprehend her rightly, she would have preferred blonde to white sarcenet for the trimming; but she did not wish me to tell you so. I only hint it for the next. We are sorry for the mess of illness you are involved in. Are you stout enough to be the general nurse? Who told you we should not be glad to see you on Sundays and all? Though we devote that day to its proper duties, as you know, yet you are come of a religious stock, and to you it is not irksome to join in our simple forms, where the heart is all. Your little *protégée* is well, and as yet honest, but she has no one to give her caps now.

Thus far I had written last night. You will see by my altered scrawl that I am not so well this morning. I got up with a fevered skin, and spots are come out all over me. Pray God it is not the measles. You did not let any of the children touch the seal with their little measly hands, did you? You should be careful when contagion is in the house. Pray God your letter may not have conveyed the disorder. Our poor postman looks flushed since. What a thing it would be to introduce a disease into a whole village! Yet so simple a thing as a letter has been known to convey a malady. I look at your note. I see it is wafered,[102] not sealed. That makes it more likely. Wafers are flour, and I've known a serious illness to be communicated in a piece of plum cake. I never had the measles. How my head throbs! You cannot be too cautious, dear Louisa, what you do under such a circum——

I am a little better than when I broke off at the last word. Your good sense will point out to you that the deficient syllables should be "stances." Circumstances. If I am incoherent, impute it to alarm. I will walk in the air——

I am not much refreshed. The air seemed hot and muggy. Somehow I feel quite irritable—there is no word in English—*à la variole;*—we have no phrase to answer it—smallpoxical comes the nearest. Maybe 'twas worse than the measles what Charles has. I will send for Mr. Asbury.[103]

I have seen the apothecary. He pronounces my complaint to be, as I feared, of the variola kind, but gives me hopes I shall not be much marked. I hope we shall get well together. But at my time of life it is attended with more hazards. Whatever becomes of me, I shall leave the world without a harsh thought of you. It was only a girlish imprudence. I am quite faint. Two pimples more came out within this last minute. Mary is crying. She looks red. So does Becky. I must go to bed.

Yours in constant pain,

C. L.

You will see by my will, if it comes to that—I bear you no ill w——. Oh!

XV. *To Dr. J. Vale Asbury*

Enfield, spring, 1830

Dear sir,

It is an observation of a wise man that "moderation is best in all things." I cannot agree with him "in liquor." There is a smoothness and oiliness in wine that makes it go down by a natural channel which I am

---

[100]All that follows Lamb's signature is written on the outside of the letter.

[101]Daughter of Thomas Holcroft. She was living with the large family of James Kenney, whom her mother had married after Holcroft's death.

[102]Fastened with an adhesive disk of dried paste.

[103]The Enfield doctor to whom the letter which follows is addressed.

positive was made for that descending. Else why does not wine choke us? could Nature have made that sloping lane not to facilitate the down-going? She does nothing in vain. You know that better than I. You know how often she has helped you at a dead lift, and how much better entitled she is to a fee than yourself sometimes, when you carry off the credit. Still there is something due to manners and customs, and I should apologize to you and Mrs. Asbury for being absolutely carried home upon a man's shoulders through Silver Street, up Parson's Lane, by the Chapels (which might have taught me better), and then to be deposited like a dead log at Gaffer Westwood's,[104] who, it seems, does not "insure" against intoxication. Not that the mode of conveyance is objectionable. On the contrary, it is more easy than a one-horse chaise. Ariel in *The Tempest* says

> On a Bat's back do I fly,
> After sunset[105] merrily.

Now I take it that Ariel must sometimes have stayed out late of nights. Indeed, he pretends that "where the bee sucks, there lurks he,"[106] as much as to say that his suction is as innocent as that little innocent (but damnably stinging when provoked) winged creature. But I take it that Ariel was fond of metheglin,[107] of which the bees are notorious brewers. But then you will say: What a shocking sight to see a middle-aged gentleman-and-a-half riding a gentleman's back up Parson's Lane at midnight. Exactly the time for that sort of conveyance, when nobody can see him, nobody but Heaven and his own conscience; now Heaven makes fools, and don't expect much from her own creation; and as for conscience, she and I have long since come to a compromise. I have given up false modesty, and she allows me to abate a little of the true. I like to be liked, but I don't care about being respected. I don't respect myself. But, as I was saying, I thought he would have let me down

just as we got to Lieutenant Barker's coal-shed (or emporium), but by a cunning jerk I eased myself, and righted my posture. I protest, I thought myself in a palanquin,[108] and never felt myself so grandly carried. It was a slave under me. There was I, all but my reason. And what is reason? and what is the loss of it? and how often in a day do we do without it, just as well? Reason is only counting, two and two makes four. And if on my passage home I thought it made five, what matter? Two and two will just make four, as it always did, before I took the finishing glass that did my business. My sister has begged me to write an apology to Mrs. A. and you for disgracing your party; now it does seem to me that I rather honored your party, for every one that was not drunk (and one or two of the ladies, I am sure, were not) must have been set off greatly in the contrast to me. I was the scapegoat: the soberer they seemed. By the way is magnesia good on these occasions? *iii pol: med: sum: ante noct: in rub: can:.*[109] I am no licentiate,[110] but know enough of simples to beg you to send me a draught after this model. But still you'll say (or the men and maids at your house will say) that it is not a seemly sight for an old gentleman to go home pick-a-back. Well, maybe it is not. But I have never studied grace. I take it to be a mere superficial accomplishment. I regard more the internal acquisitions. The great object after supper is to get home, and whether that is obtained in a horizontal posture or perpendicular (as foolish men and apes affect for dignity) I think is little to the purpose. The end is always greater than the means. Here I am, able to compose a sensible, rational apology, and what signifies how I got here? I have just sense enough to remember I was very happy last night, and to thank our kind host and hostess, and that's sense enough, I hope.

Charles Lamb

N.B.—What is good for a desperate headache? Why, patience and a determination

---

[104]Goodman Westwood, in whose house the Lambs were living at this time.

[105]Misquotation for "summer."

[106]Misquotation for "suck I."

[107]Beverage made of fermented honey and water.

[108]Covered litter.

[109]This mock prescription may have added to Dr. Asbury's enjoyment of Lamb's banter. Physicians today do not understand it.

[110]Licensed doctor.

not to mind being miserable all day long. And that I have made my mind up to.

So, here goes. It is better than not being alive at all, which I might have been, had your man toppled me down at Lieutenant Barker's coal-shed. My sister sends her sober compliments to Mrs. A. She is not much the worse.

Yours truly,

C. Lamb

XVI. *To Mrs. George Dyer*

Edmonton, 22 December, 1834[111]

Dear Mrs. Dyer,

I am very uneasy about a *book* which I either have lost or left at your house on

Thursday. It was the book I went out to fetch from Miss Buffam's, while the tripe was frying. It is called Phillip's *Theatrum Poetarum;*[112] but it is an English book. I think I left it in the parlor. It is Mr. Cary's[113] book, and I would not lose it for the world. Pray, if you find it, book it at the Swan, Snow Hill, by an Edmonton stage immediately, directed to Mr. Lamb, Church Street, Edmonton, or write to say you cannot find it. I am quite anxious about it. If it is lost, I shall never like tripe again.

With kindest love to Mr. Dyer and all,

Yours truly,

C. Lamb

---

[111] This is Lamb's last letter; on the same day he tripped and suffered the injury of which he died five days later.

[112] A small encyclopedia of English poets, compiled by Edward Phillips, Milton's nephew, and published in 1675.

[113] Henry F. Cary (1772–1844), translator of Dante's *Divine Comedy*.

GEORGE NOEL GORDON, LORD BYRON

1788-1824

One with Byron's ancestry could scarcely have escaped a passionate temperament and a turbulent life; Byron had both. His father, John Byron, was a "dazzlingly handsome and very dissipated guardsman" who came of a family many members of which had led wild lives. In his younger days he had eloped with and later married the Marchioness of Carmarthen, and on her death, shortly after the birth of their daughter Augusta, he had returned to England, badly in debt and avowedly on the lookout for a "Golden Dolly," to use Byron's phrase. He found her in the person of Catherine Gordon of Gight, whom he married in 1784 and then impoverished in the course of paying off his accumulated debts. She was a Scotch girl, not without intelligence, but provincial, capricious, and violent-tempered. "She is very amiable at a distance," her husband later wrote to his sister, "but I defy you and all the Apostles to live with her two months, for if anybody could live with her, it was me." To such parents Byron was born, in London, on 22 January, 1788. A little over three years later his father died in France, at the age of thirty-six, and Byron was left to be brought up solely by his mother. The two lived in Aberdeen until he was ten years old, the boy getting the beginnings of an education there, suffering from the ministrations of a shockingly bad nurse, and witnessing many a scene of violence caused by his mother's temper. In 1798 he became Lord Byron on the death of his grand-uncle at Newstead Abbey. He immediately grew worried because he could discern no change in his appearance now that he was a lord, and he long remained too conscious and too proud of his title. The estate which came to him with his peerage was in bad condition; and, though it yielded much more money than his mother had had even before her marriage, Byron was seldom free from financial difficulties, which were sometimes acute.

In the summer of 1798 Byron and his mother traveled south to Nottingham, and there and in the following year at London ineffectual efforts were made to cure the boy of the lameness with which he had been born. Byron, one is tempted to say, made the most of this lameness. Probably at times his pride did suffer from it, but he never let others forget it, and he apparently grew conscious that it added to the romantic interest of his otherwise strikingly handsome figure. From 1801 to 1805 he was at Harrow, whence he proceeded to Trinity College, Cambridge. There his career was, if not spectacular on a large scale, at least not without excitements and the beginnings of dissipation, love, and poetry. A volume of his poems (*Fugitive Pieces*) was privately printed in 1806, but all save two copies were destroyed by the author because one of the poems was harshly criticized for its viciousness. *Hours of Idleness* was published in 1807, and was seized on for castigation by the *Edinburgh Review*. This attack is chiefly notable because it aroused Byron's anger and led him to retaliate in an effective and immediately successful satire, *English Bards and Scotch Reviewers* (1809). Meanwhile he had left Cambridge in the summer of 1808 with an M. A. and had taken up residence at Newstead Abbey, which became the scene of events doubtless wild enough, though probably not so wild as rumor, and on occasion Byron himself, intimated. In the spring of 1809 he took his seat in the House of Lords, and later in the same year he left England for his Albanian tour, which lasted until 1811. On 3 May, 1810, he swam the Hellespont in one hour and ten minutes, an event which he is said never afterwards to have allowed his friends to forget.

In 1812, the year after his return to England, Byron published the first two cantos of *Childe Harold's Pilgrimage* and immediately found himself famous. Romantic interest in both the man and his poem became intense, and he was the social sensation of London. Sir Walter Scott had been finding the English public ready for the romantic tale in verse, and Byron now proceeded to outdo Scott—or at least for the time being to make him seem tame and spiritless by comparison—in what he had made his own field. With a rapid succession of exciting oriental tales (*The Giaour,* 1813; *The Bride of Abydos,* 1813; *The Corsair,* 1814; *Lara,* 1814) he kept up or even increased the interest which *Childe Harold* had aroused. He was beginning to achieve a more than British, a European renown when, at the height of his dazzling fame, he married Miss Anna Isabella Milbanke in January, 1815. In the following December a child, Augusta Ada, was born, and a little over a month afterwards Lady Byron left her husband, never to return. The marriage had proved a miserable failure. It is doubtful if any woman could have retained Byron's whole-hearted allegiance for long; certainly, at any rate, none did. He could not do without women or with them, and in this he was at least true to the attitude he took towards the whole life of the world in which he found himself. Moreover, Lady Byron's nature was of an unlikely sort to touch his feelings, while he was almost from the first extraordinarily brutal in his behavior towards her. She had, indeed, from many of his actions, come to doubt his sanity. Immediately after the separation ugly rumors about its crowning cause began to spread through society, and Byron suddenly found himself ostracized and reviled by the world—a world, he felt, at least no better than he was—which had recently paid lavish homage to him as its brightest star. Towards the end of April, 1816, he left England, to spend the remainder of his life on the Continent.

Byron went first to Geneva, where he spent some months and met Shelley for the first time. Each made a strong impression on the other, and their intercourse then, and later in Italy, was important for both of them. During this summer Byron took up *Childe Harold* again, and wrote the third canto. He also wrote *The Prisoner of Chillon* at this time and began *Manfred.* In the fall of 1816 he went down into Italy and settled at Venice. There he finished *Manfred,* wrote *The Lament of Tasso* (both in 1817), *Beppo,* and the fourth canto of *Childe Harold's Pilgrimage* (both in 1818). In 1819 he moved to Ravenna in order to be near the Countess Guiccioli, a young Italian girl with an aged husband. The latter at times gave Byron uncomfortable moments, but in the end proved dangerous to his pocketbook rather than to his person. In the same year the opening cantos of *Don Juan,* Byron's greatest poem, were published, further portions of which continued to appear until 1824. In following years

Byron wrote a number of dramatic poems—*Cain, Sardanapalus,* and *The Two Foscari* were published in 1821—and his satire, *The Vision of Judgment* (1822). At the same time he was growing restless in Italy. He had been interested in the cause of Italian freedom, but his interest now began to ebb with the failure of some enterprises which he had tried to assist, and his interest in the Guiccioli was also ebbing. He had some thoughts of going to "Bolivar's country," but finally decided to aid the Greeks in their fight against the Turks for independence. He sailed from Genoa in July, 1823, and proceeded to devote both his time and his money to the Greek cause, despite discouragement, hardships, and increasing illness. Finally he succumbed to a fever at Missolonghi, and died there on 19 April, 1824. Nothing, it has been said, so well became his life as the manner of its ending; and the man died, as he had lived and written, in a way that stirred the feeling and fired the imagination of Europe.

Byron in a sense courted rivalry with Napoleon in the romantic age when giants walked the earth, and he holds the stage securely still. Not preëminently a lyric poet in an age of great lyrics, he yet had a largeness and force which give weight to his disillusioned re-action from the European society and politics of his day, and keep alive the poems in which he voiced it. "You have so many '*divine*' poems," he exclaimed to his publisher, "is it nothing to have written a *human* one?" And while other poets were among the clouds, or at least among the mountains, Byron kept his station in the world and wrote, in *Don Juan,* the great epic of modern life.

The standard edition of Byron's *Works* is one in thirteen volumes (London, 1898–1904), in which the *Poetry* is edited by Ernest Hartley Coleridge and the *Letters and Journals* by Rowland E. Prothero (Lord Ernle). Two additional volumes of letters, edited by John Murray, appeared in 1922 under the title *Lord Byron's Correspondence.* The best one-volume edition of Byron's *Poetical Works* is that in the "Cambridge" series edited by Paul Elmer More. The best biography is Ethel Colburn Mayne's *Byron* (1912; revised edition 1924). Miss Mayne is also the author of *The Life and Letters of Lady Byron* (1929). S. C. Chew's *Byron in England: His Fame and After-Fame* (1924) is a useful history of English criticism of Byron and his writings. One of the best general essays on Byron is J. F. A. Pyre's "Byron in Our Day" (*Atlantic Monthly,* vol. XCIX, 1907, p. 542).

CHILDE HAROLD'S PILGRIMAGE [1]

CANTO III

Afin que cette application vous forçât de penser à autre chose; il n'y a en vérité de remède que celui-là et le temps.[2]
Lettre du Roi de Prusse à D'Alembert, Sept. 7, 1776.

I

Is thy face like thy mother's, my fair
   child!
ADA! sole daughter of my house and
   heart?[3]
When last I saw thy young blue eyes they
   smiled,
And then we parted,—not as now we part,
But with a hope.—
           Awaking with a start, 5
The waters heave around me; and on high
The winds lift up their voices: I depart,
Whither I know not, but the hour's gone
   by,
When Albion's lessening shores could grieve
   or glad mine eye.

2

Once more upon the waters! yet once
   more! 10
And the waves bound beneath me as a
   steed
That knows his rider. Welcome to their
   roar!
Swift be their guidance, wheresoe'er it
   lead!
Though the strained mast should quiver as
   a reed,

3

And the rent canvas fluttering strew the
   gale, 15
Still must I on; for I am as a weed,
Flung from the rock, on Ocean's foam to
   sail
Where'er the surge may sweep, the tempest's breath prevail.

In my youth's summer I did sing of One,[4]
The wandering outlaw of his own dark
   mind; 20
Again I seize the theme, then but begun,
And bear it with me, as the rushing wind
Bears the cloud onwards: in that Tale I
   find
The furrows of long thought, and dried-up
   tears, 24
Which, ebbing, leave a sterile track behind,
O'er which all heavily the journeying
   years
Plod the last sands of life,—where not a
   flower appears.

4

Since my young days of passion—joy, or
   pain,
Perchance my heart and harp have lost a
   string,
And both may jar: it may be, that in
   vain 30
I would essay as I have sung to sing.
Yet, though a dreary strain, to this I cling,
So that it wean me from the weary dream
Of selfish grief or gladness—so it fling
Forgetfulness around me—it shall seem 35
To me, though to none else, a not ungrateful
   theme.

5

He, who grown agèd in this world of woe,
In deeds, not years, piercing the depths of
   life, 38
So that no wonder waits him; nor below
Can love or sorrow, fame, ambition, strife,
Cut to his heart again with the keen knife
Of silent, sharp endurance: he can tell
Why thought seeks refuge in lone caves,
   yet rife
With airy images, and shapes which dwell
Still unimpaired, though old, in the soul's
   haunted cell. 45

---

[1] The first two cantos of *Childe Harold* were published in 1812. They tell of the travels of a disillusioned young man through Portugal, Spain, Albania, and Greece—what he saw and what he felt. Byron did not at the time continue the poem, but took it up again after his final departure from England in the spring of 1816. Canto III was written in Switzerland in May and June, 1816, and was published in the same year. Substantially the third and fourth cantos form a distinct poem. An external connection with the earlier cantos is maintained, but in the intervening years Byron had experienced much and suffered much, and now he speaks almost without disguise in his own person. The present canto tells of Byron's journey through Belgium and up the Rhine into Switzerland, description being mingled with reflective passages inspired by the scenes through which he passed.

[2] So that this employment may force you to think of something else; there is in truth no remedy save that and time.

[3] Byron never saw his daughter after she was five weeks old.

[4] I. e., Childe Harold.

6

'Tis to create, and in creating live
A being more intense that we endow
With form our fancy, gaining as we give
The life we image, even as I do now.
What am I? Nothing: but not so art
   thou,
Soul of my thought! with whom I traverse
   earth,   51
Invisible but gazing, as I glow
Mixed with thy spirit, blended with thy
   birth,
And feeling still with thee in my crushed
   feelings' dearth.

7

Yet must I think less wildly:—I *have*
   thought   55
Too long and darkly, till my brain became,
In its own eddy boiling and o'erwrought,
A whirling gulf of phantasy and flame:
And thus, untaught in youth my heart to
   tame,
My springs of life were poisoned. 'Tis
   too late!   60
Yet am I changed; though still enough the
   same
In strength to bear what time cannot
   abate,
And feed on bitter fruits without accusing
   Fate.

8

Something too much of this:—but now
   'tis past,
And the spell closes with its silent seal. 65
Long absent HAROLD re-appears at last;
He of the breast which fain no more would
   feel,
Wrung with the wounds which kill not,
   but ne'er heal;
Yet Time, who changes all, had altered
   him
In soul and aspect as in age: years steal 70
Fire from the mind as vigor from the limb;
And life's enchanted cup but sparkles near
   the brim.

9

His had been quaffed too quickly, and he
   found
The dregs were wormwood; but he filled
   again,
And from a purer fount, on holier ground,
And deemed its spring perpetual; but in
   vain!   76

Still round him clung invisibly a chain
Which galled for ever, fettering though
   unseen,
And heavy though it clanked not; worn
   with pain,
Which pined although it spoke not, and
   grew keen,   80
Entering with every step he took through
   many a scene.

10

Secure in guarded coldness, he had mixed
Again in fancied safety with his kind,
And deemed his spirit now so firmly fixed
And sheathed with an invulnerable mind, 85
That, if no joy, no sorrow lurked behind;
And he, as one, might 'midst the many
   stand
Unheeded, searching through the crowd to
   find
Fit speculation; such as in strange land
He found in wonder-works of God and Na-
   ture's hand.   90

11

But who can view the ripened rose, nor
   seek
To wear it? who can curiously behold
The smoothness and the sheen of beauty's
   cheek,
Nor feel the heart can never all grow old?
Who can contemplate Fame through
   clouds unfold   95
The star which rises o'er her steep, nor
   climb?
Harold, once more within the vortex,
   rolled
On with the giddy circle, chasing Time,
Yet with a nobler aim than in his youth's
   fond prime.

12

But soon he knew himself the most unfit
Of men to herd with Man; with whom he
   held   101
Little in common; untaught to submit
His thoughts to others, though his soul
   was quelled
In youth by his own thoughts; still un-
   compelled,   104
He would not yield dominion of his mind
To spirits against whom his own rebelled;
Proud though in desolation; which could
   find
A life within itself, to breathe without man-
   kind.

13

Where rose the mountains, there to him
were friends,
Where rolled the ocean, thereon was his
home,   110
Where a blue sky, and glowing clime, ex-
tends,
He had the passion and the power to roam;
The desert, forest, cavern, breaker's foam,
Were unto him companionship; they spake
A mutual language, clearer than the tome
Of his land's tongue, which he would oft
forsake   116
For Nature's pages glassed by sunbeams on
the lake.

14

Like the Chaldean, he could watch the
stars,
Till he had peopled them with beings
bright
As their own beams; and earth, and earth-
born jars,   120
And human frailties, were forgotten quite:
Could he have kept his spirit to that flight
He had been happy; but this clay will sink
Its spark immortal, envying it the light
To which it mounts, as if to break the link
That keeps us from yon heaven which woos
us to its brink.   126

15

But in Man's dwellings he became a thing
Restless and worn, and stern and weari-
some,
Drooped as a wild-born falcon with
clipped wing,
To whom the boundless air alone were
home: 130
Then came his fit again, which to o'ercome,
As eagerly the barred-up bird will beat
His breast and beak against his wiry dome
Till the blood tinge his plumage, so the
heat
Of his impeded soul would through his
bosom eat.   135

16

Self-exiled Harold wanders forth again,
With nought of hope left, but with less of
gloom,
The very knowledge that he lived in vain,
That all was over on this side the tomb,
Had made Despair a smilingness assume,

Which, though 'twere wild,—as on the
plundered wreck   141
When mariners would madly meet their
doom
With draughts intemperate on the sinking
deck,—
Did yet inspire a cheer, which he forbore to
check.

17

Stop!—for thy tread is on an Empire's
dust!   143
An Earthquake's spoil is sepulchered be-
low!
Is the spot marked with no colossal bust?
Nor column trophied for triumphal show?
None; but *the moral's truth* tells simpler
so.
As the ground was before, thus let it be;—
How that red rain hath made the harvest
grow!   151
And is this all the world has gained by
thee,
Thou first and last of fields! king-making
Victory?

18

And Harold stands upon this place of
skulls,
The grave of France, the deadly Water-
loo!   155
How in an hour the power which gave an-
nuls
Its gifts, transferring fame as fleeting too!
In "pride of place" here last the eagle[5]
flew,
Then tore with bloody talon the rent plain,
Pierced by the shaft of banded nations
through;   160
Ambition's life and labors all were vain;
He wears the shattered links of the world's
broken chain.

19

Fit retribution! Gaul may champ the bit
And foam in fetters;—but is Earth more
free?
Did nations combat to make *One* submit;
Or league to teach all kings true sover-
eignty?   166
What! shall reviving Thraldom again be
The patched-up idol of enlightened days?
Shall we, who struck the Lion down, shall
we

---

[5] Napoleon. *"Pride of place* is a term of falconry,
meaning the highest pitch of flight" (Byron's note).

Pay the Wolf homage? proffering lowly
　　gaze　　　　　　　　　　　　　170
And servile knees to thrones?　No; *prove*
　　before ye praise!

20

If not, o'er one fallen despot boast no
　　more!
In vain fair cheeks were furrowed with
　　hot tears
For Europe's flowers long rooted up be-
　　fore
The trampler of her vineyards; in vain,
　　years　　　　　　　　　　　　175
Of death, depopulation, bondage, fears,
Have all been borne, and broken by the
　　accord
Of roused-up millions; all that most en-
　　dears
Glory, is when the myrtle wreathes a
　　sword
Such as Harmodius[6] drew on Athens' tyrant
　　lord.　　　　　　　　　　　　180

21

There was a sound of revelry by night,
And Belgium's capital had gathered then
Her Beauty and her Chivalry, and bright
The lamps shone o'er fair women and
　　brave men;　　　　　　　　　184
A thousand hearts beat happily; and when
Music arose with its voluptuous swell,
Soft eyes looked love to eyes which spake
　　again,
And all went merry as a marriage bell;
But hush! hark! a deep sound strikes like a
　　rising knell!

22

Did ye not hear it?—No; 'twas but the
　　wind,　　　　　　　　　　　190
Or the car rattling o'er the stony street;
On with the dance! let joy be unconfined;
No sleep till morn, when Youth and
　　Pleasure meet
To chase the glowing Hours with flying
　　feet—
But hark!—that heavy sound breaks in
　　once more,　　　　　　　　　195
As if the clouds its echo would repeat;

And nearer, clearer, deadlier than before!
Arm! Arm! it is—it is—the cannon's open-
　　ing roar!

23

Within a windowed niche of that high hall
Sat Brunswick's fated chieftain;[7] he did
　　hear　　　　　　　　　　　　200
That sound the first amidst the festival,
And caught its tone with Death's pro-
　　phetic ear;
And when they smiled because he deemed
　　it near,
His heart more truly knew that peal too
　　well
Which stretched his father on a bloody
　　bier,　　　　　　　　　　　　205
And roused the vengeance blood alone
　　could quell;
He rushed into the field, and, foremost fight-
　　ing, fell.

24

Ah! then and there was hurrying to and
　　fro,
And gathering tears, and tremblings of
　　distress,
And cheeks all pale, which but an hour
　　ago　　　　　　　　　　　　210
Blushed at the praise of their own loveli-
　　ness;
And there were sudden partings, such as
　　press
The life from out young hearts, and chok-
　　ing sighs
Which ne'er might be repeated; who could
　　guess
If ever more should meet those mutual
　　eyes,　　　　　　　　　　　　215
Since upon night so sweet such awful morn
　　could rise!

25

And there was mounting in hot haste; the
　　steed,
The mustering squadron, and the clatter-
　　ing car,
Went pouring forward with impetuous
　　speed,
And swiftly forming in the ranks of
　　war;　　　　　　　　　　　　220
And the deep thunder peal on peal afar;
And near, the beat of the alarming drum
Roused up the soldier ere the morning
　　star;

---

[6]Harmodius and Aristogiton, concealing their
swords in branches of myrtle during a religious
festival, slew Hipparchus, who with his brother
Hippias tyrannically ruled Athens. After their
death and the later banishment of Hippias the two
were praised as martyred patriots.

[7]Frederick William, Duke of Brunswick.

While thronged the citizens with terror
dumb,
Or whispering, with white lips—"The foe!
they come! they come!"   225

26

And wild and high the "Cameron's gath-
ering"[8] rose!
The war-note of Lochiel, which Albyn's
hills
Have heard, and heard, too, have her
Saxon foes:—
How in the noon of night that pibroch
thrills,
Savage and shrill! But with the breath
which fills   230
Their mountain-pipe, so fill the mountain-
eers
With the fierce native daring which instills
The stirring memory of a thousand years,
And Evan's, Donald's fame rings in each
clansman's ears!

27

And Ardennes waves above them her
green leaves,   235
Dewy with nature's tear-drops as they
pass,
Grieving, if aught inanimate e'er grieves,
Over the unreturning brave,—alas!
Ere evening to be trodden like the grass
Which now beneath them, but above shall
grow   240
In its next verdure, when this fiery mass
Of living valor, rolling on the foe
And burning with high hope shall molder
cold and low.

28

Last noon beheld them full of lusty life,
Last eve in Beauty's circle proudly gay, 245
The midnight brought the signal-sound of
strife,
The morn the marshaling in arms,—the
day
Battle's magnificently stern array!
The thunder-clouds close o'er it, which
when rent
The earth is covered thick with other
clay,   250
Which her own clay shall cover, heaped
and pent,
Rider and horse,—friend, foe,—in one red
burial blent!

29

Their praise is hymned by loftier harps
than mine:
Yet one I would select from that proud
throng,
Partly because they blend me with his
line,   255
And partly that I did his sire some wrong,
And partly that bright names will hallow
song;
And his was of the bravest, and when
showered
The death-bolts deadliest the thinned files
along,
Even where the thickest of war's tempest
lowered,   260
They reached no nobler breast than thine,
young gallant Howard![9]

30

There have been tears and breaking hearts
for thee,
And mine were nothing had I such to give;
But when I stood beneath the fresh green
tree,
Which living waves where thou didst cease
to live,   265
And saw around me the wide field revive
With fruits and fertile promise, and the
Spring
Came forth her work of gladness to con-
trive,
With all her reckless birds upon the wing,
I turned from all she brought to those she
could not bring.   270

31

I turned to thee, to thousands, of whom
each
And one as all a ghastly gap did make
In his own kind and kindred, whom to
teach
Forgetfulness were mercy for their sake;
The Archangel's trump, not Glory's, must
awake   275
Those whom they thirst for; though the
sound of Fame
May for a moment soothe, it cannot slake
The fever of vain longing, and the name
So honored but assumes a stronger, bitterer
claim.

[8]The gathering-cry of the clan Cameron. The chief of the clan was called Lochiel because this was the name of his estate.

[9]Major Frederick Howard, Byron's second cousin. His father, the Earl of Carlisle, was Byron's guardian. Byron had given a satirical sketch of him in *English Bards and Scotch Reviewers*.

32

They mourn, but smile at length; and,
    smiling, mourn;   280
The tree will wither long before it fall;
The hull drives on, though mast and sail
    be torn;
The roof-tree sinks, but molders on the
    hall
In massy hoariness; the ruined wall
Stands when its wind-worn battlements
    are gone;   285
The bars survive the captive they enthrall;
The day drags through, though storms
    keep out the sun;
And thus the heart will break, yet brokenly
    live on:

33

Even as a broken mirror, which the glass
In every fragment multiplies; and makes
A thousand images of one that was,   291
The same, and still the more, the more it
    breaks;
And thus the heart will do which not for-
    sakes,
Living in shattered guise; and still, and
    cold,
And bloodless, with its sleepless sorrow
    aches,   295
Yet withers on till all without is old,
Showing no visible sign, for such things are
    untold.

34

There is a very life in our despair,
Vitality of poison,—a quick root
Which feeds these deadly branches; for it
    were   300
As nothing did we die; but Life will suit
Itself to Sorrow's most detested fruit,
Like to the apples on the Dead Sea's shore,
All ashes to the taste: Did man compute
Existence by enjoyment, and count o'er 305
Such hours 'gainst years of life,—say, would
    he name threescore?

35

The Psalmist numbered out the years of
    man:
They are enough; and if thy tale be *true*,
Thou, who didst grudge him even that
    fleeting span,
More than enough, thou fatal Water-
    loo!   310
Millions of tongues record thee, and anew
Their children's lips shall echo them, and
    say—

"Here, where the sword united nations
    drew,
Our countrymen were warring on that
    day!"
And this is much—and all—which will not
    pass away.   315

36

There sunk the greatest, nor the worst of
    men,[10]
Whose spirit, antithetically mixed,
One moment of the mightiest, and again
On little objects with like firmness fixed;
Extreme in all things! hadst thou been
    betwixt,   320
Thy throne had still been thine, or never
    been;
For daring made thy rise as fall: thou
    seek'st
Even now to re-assume the imperial mien,
And shake again the world, the Thunderer
    of the scene!

37

Conqueror and captive of the earth art
    thou!   325
She trembles at thee still, and thy wild
    name
Was ne'er more bruited in men's minds
    than now
That thou art nothing, save the jest of
    Fame,
Who wooed thee once, thy vassal, and be-
    came
The flatterer of thy fierceness, till thou
    wert   330
A god unto thyself; nor less the same
To the astounded kingdoms all inert,
Who deemed thee for a time whate'er thou
    didst assert.

38

Oh, more or less than man—in high or
    low,
Battling with nations, flying from the
    field;   335
Now making monarchs' necks thy foot-
    stool, now
More than thy meanest soldier taught to
    yield;
An empire thou couldst crush, command,
    rebuild,
But govern not thy pettiest passion, nor,
However deeply in men's spirits skilled, 340

---

[10]Napoleon.

Look through thine own, nor curb the lust
of war,
Nor learn that tempted Fate will leave the
loftiest star.

39

Yet well thy soul hath brooked the turning
tide
With that untaught innate philosophy,
Which, be it wisdom, coldness, or deep
pride,   345
Is gall and wormwood to an enemy.
When the whole host of hatred stood hard
by,
To watch and mock thee shrinking, thou
hast smiled
With a sedate and all-enduring eye;—
When Fortune fled her spoiled and favor-
ite child,   350
He stood unbowed beneath the ills upon him
piled.

40

Sager than in thy fortunes; for in them
Ambition steeled thee on too far to show
That just habitual scorn, which could con-
temn
Men and their thoughts; 'twas wise to feel,
not so   355
To wear it ever on thy lip and brow,
And spurn the instruments thou wert to
use
Till they were turned unto thine over-
throw:
'Tis but a worthless world to win or lose;
So hath it proved to thee, and all such lot
who choose.   360

41

If, like a tower upon a headland rock,
Thou hadst been made to stand or fall
alone,
Such scorn of man had helped to brave the
shock;
But men's thoughts were the steps which
paved thy throne,
Their admiration thy best weapon shone;
The part of Philip's son[11] was thine, not
then   366
(Unless aside thy purple had been
thrown)
Like stern Diogenes to mock at men;
For sceptered cynics earth were far too wide
a den.

---

[11]Alexander the Great.

42

But quiet to quick bosoms is a hell,   370
And *there* hath been thy bane; there is a
fire
And motion of the soul which will not
dwell
In its own narrow being, but aspire
Beyond the fitting medium of desire;
And, but once kindled, quenchless ever-
more,   375
Preys upon high adventure, nor can tire
Of aught but rest; a fever at the core,
Fatal to him who bears, to all who ever bore.

43

This makes the madmen who have made
men mad
By their contagion; Conquerors and
Kings,   380
Founders of sects and systems, to whom
add
Sophists, Bards, Statesmen, all unquiet
things
Which stir too strongly the soul's secret
springs,
And are themselves the fools to those they
fool;   384
Envied, yet how unenviable! what stings
Are theirs! One breast laid open were a
school
Which would unteach mankind the lust to
shine or rule:

44

Their breath is agitation, and their life
A storm whereon they ride, to sink at last,
And yet so nursed and bigoted to strife, 390
That should their days, surviving perils
past,
Melt to calm twilight, they feel overcast
With sorrow and supineness, and so die;
Even as a flame unfed, which runs to
waste
With its own flickering, or a sword laid
by,   395
Which eats into itself, and rusts ingloriously.

45

He who ascends to mountain-tops, shall
find
The loftiest peaks most wrapped in clouds
and snow;
He who surpasses or subdues mankind,
Must look down on the hate of those below.   400

Though high *above* the sun of glory glow,
And far *beneath* the earth and ocean
spread,
Round him are icy rocks, and loudly blow
Contending tempests on his naked head,
And thus reward the toils which to those
summits led.   405

46

Away with these! true Wisdom's world
will be
Within its own creation, or in thine,
Maternal Nature! for who teems like
thee,
Thus on the banks of thy majestic Rhine?
There Harold gazes on a work divine, 410
A blending of all beauties; streams and
dells,
Fruit, foliage, crag, wood, cornfield,
mountain, vine,
And chiefless castles breathing stern fare-
wells
From gray but leafy walls, where Ruin
greenly dwells.

47

And there they stand, as stands a lofty
mind,   415
Worn, but unstooping to the baser crowd,
All tenantless, save to the crannying wind,
Or holding dark communion with the
cloud.
There was a day when they were young
and proud;
Banners on high, and battles passed be-
low;   420
But they who fought are in a bloody
shroud,
And those which waved are shredless dust
ere now,
And the bleak battlements shall bear no fu-
ture blow.

48

Beneath these battlements, within those
walls,
Power dwelt amidst her passions; in proud
state   425
Each robber chief upheld his arméd halls,
Doing his evil will, nor less elate
Than mightier heroes of a longer date.
What want these outlaws conquerors
should have
But history's purchased page to call them
great?   430

A wider space, an ornamented grave?
Their hopes were not less warm, their souls
were full as brave.

49

In their baronial feuds and single fields,
What deeds of prowess unrecorded died!
And Love, which lent a blazon to their
shields,   435
With emblems well devised by amorous
pride,
Through all the mail of iron hearts would
glide;
But still their flame was fierceness, and
drew on
Keen contest and destruction near allied,
And many a tower for some fair mischief
won,   440
Saw the discolored Rhine beneath its ruin
run.

50

But Thou, exulting and abounding river!
Making thy waves a blessing as they flow
Through banks whose beauty would en-
dure for ever
Could man but leave thy bright creation
so,   445
Nor its fair promise from the surface mow
With the sharp scythe of conflict,—then
to see
Thy valley of sweet waters, were to know
Earth paved like Heaven; and to seem
such to me,
Even now what wants thy stream?—that it
should Lethe[12] be.   450

51

A thousand battles have assailed thy
banks,
But these and half their fame have passed
away,
And Slaughter heaped on high his weltering ranks;
Their very graves are gone, and what are
they?
Thy tide washed down the blood of yesterday,   455
And all was stainless, and on thy clear
stream
Glassed, with its dancing light, the sunny
ray;

---

[12]The river of forgetfulness. Were it Lethe,
Byron could drink of it and forget the past, his
own included.

But o'er the blackened memory's blighting
dream
Thy waves would vainly roll, all sweeping
as they seem.

52

Thus Harold inly said, and passed along,
Yet not insensible to all which here   461
Awoke the jocund birds to early song
In glens which might have made even
exile dear:
Though on his brow were graven lines
austere,
And tranquil sternness, which had ta'en
the place   465
Of feelings fiercer far but less severe,
Joy was not always absent from his face,
But o'er it in such scenes would steal with
transient trace.

53

Nor was all love shut from him, though
his days
Of passion had consumed themselves to
dust.   470
It is in vain that we would coldly gaze
On such as smile upon us; the heart must
Leap kindly back to kindness, though dis-
gust
Hath weaned it from all worldlings: thus
he felt,
For there was soft remembrance, and
sweet trust   475
In one fond breast,[13] to which his own
would melt,
And in its tenderer hour on that his bosom
dwelt.

54

And he had learned to love,—I know not
why,
For this in such as him seems strange of
mood,—
The helpless looks of blooming infancy, 480
Even in its earliest nurture; what subdued,
To change like this, a mind so far imbued
With scorn of man, it little boots to know,
But thus it was; and though in solitude
Small power the nipped affections have to
grow,   485
In him this glowed when all beside had
ceased to glow.

---

[13]In that of Byron's half-sister Augusta.

55

And there was one soft breast, as hath
been said,
Which unto his was bound by stronger
ties
Than the church links withal; and, though
unwed,
That love was pure, and, far above dis-
guise,   490
Had stood the test of mortal enmities
Still undivided, and cemented more
By peril, dreaded most in female eyes;
But this was firm, and from a foreign
shore
Well to that heart might his these absent
greetings pour!   495

I

The castled crag of Drachenfels[14]
Frowns o'er the wide and winding Rhine,
Whose breast of waters broadly swells
Between the banks which bear the vine,
And hills all rich with blossomed trees, 500
And fields which promise corn and wine,
And scattered cities crowning these,
Whose far white walls along them shine,
Have strewed a scene, which I should see
With double joy wert *thou* with me.   505

II

And peasant girls, with deep blue eyes,
And hands which offer early flowers,
Walk smiling o'er this paradise;
Above, the frequent feudal towers
Through green leaves lift their walls of
gray;   510
And many a rock which steeply lowers,
And noble arch in proud decay,
Look o'er this vale of vintage-bowers;
But one thing want these banks of
Rhine,—
Thy gentle hand to clasp in mine!   515

III

I send the lilies given to me;
Though long before thy hand they touch,
I know that they must withered be,
But yet reject them not as such;
For I have cherished them as dear,   520
Because they yet may meet thine eye,
And guide thy soul to mine even here,
When thou behold'st them drooping nigh,
And know'st them gathered by the Rhine,
And offered from my heart to thine!   525

---

[14]Dragon Rock. One of the Siebengebirge (Seven
Mountains) on the right bank of the Rhine between
Remagen and Bonn.

IV

The river nobly foams and flows,
The charm of this enchanted ground,
And all its thousand turns disclose
Some fresher beauty's varying round: 529
The haughtiest breast its wish might bound
Through life to dwell delighted here;
Nor could on earth a spot be found
To nature and to me so dear,
Could thy dear eyes in following mine   534
Still sweeten more these banks of Rhine!

56

By Coblentz, on a rise of gentle ground,
There is a small and simple pyramid,
Crowning the summit of the verdant
    mound;
Beneath its base are heroes' ashes hid,
Our enemy's—but let not that forbid   540
Honor to Marceau![15] o'er whose early
    tomb
Tears, big tears, gushed from the rough
    soldier's lid,
Lamenting and yet envying such a doom,
Falling for France, whose rights he battled
    to resume.

57

Brief, brave, and glorious was his young
    career,—   545
His mourners were two hosts, his friends
    and foes;
And fitly may the stranger lingering here
Pray for his gallant spirit's bright repose;
For he was Freedom's champion, one of
    those,
The few in number, who had not o'er-
    stepped   550
The charter to chastise which she bestows
On such as wield her weapons; he had kept
The whiteness of his soul, and thus men o'er
    him wept.

58

Here Ehrenbreitstein, [16] with her shattered
    wall
Black with the miner's blast, upon her
    height   555
Yet shows of what she was, when shell
    and ball
Rebounding idly on her strength did light:

---

[15]Soldier of revolutionary France who fell in battle in 1796, at the age of twenty-seven.

[16]A fortress on the Rhine opposite the mouth of the Moselle. The French captured it in 1799 and later destroyed it.

A tower of victory! from whence the
    flight
Of baffled foes was watched along the
    plain:
But Peace destroyed what War could never
    blight,   560
And laid those proud roofs bare to Sum-
    mer's rain—
On which the iron shower for years had
    poured in vain.

59

Adieu to thee, fair Rhine! How long de-
    lighted
The stranger fain would linger on his way!
Thine is a scene alike where souls
    united   565
Or lonely Contemplation thus might stray;
And could the ceaseless vultures cease to
    prey
On self-condemning bosoms, it were here,
Where Nature, nor too somber nor too
    gay,   569
Wild but not rude, awful yet not austere,
Is to the mellow Earth as Autumn to the
    year.

60

Adieu to thee again! a vain adieu!
There can be no farewell to scene like
    thine;
The mind is colored by thy every hue;
And if reluctantly the eyes resign   575
Their cherished gaze upon thee, lovely
    Rhine!
'Tis with the thankful glance of parting
    praise;
More mighty spots may rise, more glaring
    shine,
But none unite in one attaching maze
The brilliant, fair, and soft,—the glories of
    old days.   580

61

The negligently grand, the fruitful bloom
Of coming ripeness, the white city's sheen,
The rolling stream, the precipice's gloom,
The forest's growth, and Gothic walls be-
    tween,
The wild rocks shaped as they had turrets
    been,   585
In mockery of man's art; and these withal
A race of faces happy as the scene,
Whose fertile bounties here extend to all,
Still springing o'er thy banks, though Em-
    pires near them fall.   589

62

But these recede. Above me are the Alps,
The palaces of Nature, whose vast walls
Have pinnacled in clouds their snowy
    scalps,
And throned Eternity in icy halls   593
Of cold sublimity, where forms and falls
The avalanche—the thunderbolt of snow!
All that expands the spirit, yet appalls,
Gather around these summits, as to show
How Earth may pierce to Heaven, yet leave
    vain man below.

63

But ere these matchless heights I dare to
    scan,
There is a spot should not be passed in
    vain,—   600
Morat![17] the proud, the patriot field! where
    man
May gaze on ghastly trophies of the slain,
Nor blush for those who conquered on
    that plain;
Here Burgundy bequeathed his tombless
    host,
A bony heap, through ages to remain,   605
Themselves their monument;—the Stygian
    coast
Unsepulchered they roamed, and shrieked
    each wandering ghost.

64

While Waterloo with Cannæ's[18] carnage
    vies,
Morat and Marathon twin names shall
    stand;   609
They were true Glory's stainless victories,
Won by the unambitious heart and hand
Of a proud, brotherly, and civic band,
All unbought champions in no princely
    cause
Of vice-entailed Corruption; they no land
Doomed to bewail the blasphemy of laws
Making kings' rights divine, by some Dra-
    conic[19] clause.   616

65

By a lone wall a lonelier column rears
A gray and grief-worn aspect of old days;

'Tis the last remnant of the wreck of years,
And looks as with the wild-bewildered
    gaze
Of one to stone converted by amaze,   621
Yet still with consciousness; and there it
    stands
Making a marvel that it not decays,
When the coeval pride of human hands,
Leveled Adventicum,[20] hath strewed her sub-
    ject lands.   625

66

And there—oh! sweet and sacred be the
    name!—
Julia[21]—the daughter, the devoted—gave
Her youth to Heaven; her heart, beneath a
    claim
Nearest to Heaven's, broke o'er a father's
    grave.
Justice is sworn 'gainst tears, and hers
    would crave   630
The life she lived in; but the judge was
    just,
And then she died on him she could not
    save.
Their tomb was simple, and without a bust,
And held within their urn one mind, one
    heart, one dust.

67

But these are deeds which should not pass
    away,   635
And names that must not wither, though
    the earth
Forgets her empires with a just decay,
The enslavers and the enslaved, their death
    and birth;
The high, the mountain-majesty of worth
Should be, and shall, survivor of its
    woe,   640
And from its immortality look forth
In the sun's face, like yonder Alpine snow,
Imperishably pure beyond all things below.

68

Lake Leman[22] woos me with its crystal
    face,
The mirror where the stars and mountains
    view   645

---

[17]Name of a town and lake east of Neufchâtel;
the scene of a Swiss victory over Charles the Bold,
Duke of Burgundy, in 1476.

[18]Scene of a Roman defeat by Hannibal in the
Second Punic War.

[19]Draco was an Athenian, said to have been the
first to draw up a code of laws. This code has
become proverbial for its severity.

[20]Near Morat, capital of the Roman colony of
Helvetia.

[21]Julia Alpinula, a young Aventian priestess, died
soon after a vain endeavor to save her father,
condemned to death as a traitor by Aulus Caecina
(Byron's note).

[22]The Lake of Geneva.

The stillness of their aspect in each trace
Its clear depth yields of their far height
and hue:
There is too much of man here, to look
through
With a fit mind the might which I behold;
But soon in me shall Loneliness renew 650
Thoughts hid, but not less cherished than
of old,
Ere mingling with the herd had penned me
in their fold.

69

To fly from, need not be to hate, mankind:
All are not fit with them to stir and toil,
Nor is it discontent to keep the mind 655
Deep in its fountain, lest it overboil
In the hot throng, where we become the
spoil
Of our infection, till too late and long
We may deplore and struggle with the
coil,[23]
In wretched interchange of wrong for
wrong
Midst a contentious world, striving where
none are strong.   661

70

There, in a moment we may plunge our
years
In fatal penitence, and in the blight
Of our own soul turn all our blood to tears,
And color things to come with hues of
Night;   665
The race of life becomes a hopeless flight
To those that walk in darkness: on the sea
The boldest steer but where their ports
invite;
But there are wanderers o'er Eternity
Whose bark drives on and on, and anchored
ne'er shall be.   670

71

Is it not better, then, to be alone,
And love Earth only for its earthly sake?
By the blue rushing of the arrowy Rhone,
Or the pure bosom of its nursing lake,
Which feeds it as a mother who doth make
A fair but froward infant her own care, 676
Kissing its cries away as these awake;—
Is it not better thus our lives to wear,
Than join the crushing crowd, doomed to
inflict or bear?

---

[23]Trouble.

72

I live not in myself, but I become   680
Portion of that around me; and to me
High mountains are a feeling, but the hum
Of human cities torture: I can see
Nothing to loathe in nature, save to be
A link reluctant in a fleshly chain,   685
Classed among creatures, when the soul
can flee,
And with the sky, the peak, the heaving
plain
Of ocean, or the stars, mingle, and not in
vain.

73

And thus I am absorbed, and this is life:
I look upon the peopled desert past,   690
As on a place of agony and strife,
Where, for some sin, to sorrow I was cast,
To act and suffer, but remount at last
With a fresh pinion; which I feel to spring,
Though young, yet waxing vigorous as
the blast   695
Which it would cope with, on delighted
wing,
Spurning the clay-cold bonds which round
our being cling.

74

And when, at length, the mind shall be all
free
From what it hates in this degraded form,
Reft of its carnal life, save what shall
be   700
Existent happier in the fly and worm,—
When elements to elements conform,
And dust is as it should be, shall I not
Feel all I see, less dazzling, but more
warm?
The bodiless thought? the Spirit of each
spot?   705
Of which, even now, I share at times the
immortal lot?

75

Are not the mountains, waves, and skies,
a part
Of me and of my soul, as I of them?
Is not the love of these deep in my heart
With a pure passion? should I not contemn
All objects, if compared with these? and
stem   711
A tide of suffering, rather than forgo
Such feelings for the hard and worldly
phlegm

Of those whose eyes are only turned below,
Gazing upon the ground, with thoughts
     which dare not glow?   715

76

But this is not my theme; and I return
To that which is immediate, and require
Those who find contemplation in the urn,[24]
To look on One,[25] whose dust was once all
     fire,
A native of the land where I respire   720
The clear air for a while—a passing guest,
Where he became a being,—whose desire
Was to be glorious; 'twas a foolish quest,
The which to gain and keep, he sacrificed
     all rest.

77

Here the self-torturing sophist, wild Rous-
     seau,   725
The apostle of affliction, he who threw
Enchantment over passion, and from woe
Wrung overwhelming eloquence, first drew
The breath which made him wretched; yet
     he knew
How to make madness beautiful, and cast
O'er erring deeds and thoughts a heavenly
     hue   731
Of words, like sunbeams, dazzling as they
     passed
The eyes, which o'er them shed tears feelingly
     and fast.

78

His love was passion's essence:—as a tree
On fire by lightning, with ethereal flame 735
Kindled he was, and blasted; for to be
Thus, and enamored, were in him the
     same.
But his was not the love of living dame,
Nor of the dead who rise upon our dreams,
But of ideal beauty, which became   740
In him existence, and o'erflowing teems
Along his burning page, distempered though
     it seems.

79

This breathed itself to life in Julie,[26] *this*
Invested her with all that's wild and sweet;

This hallowed, too, the memorable kiss 745
Which every morn his fevered lip would
     greet,
From hers, who but with friendship his
     would meet;[27]
But to that gentle touch through brain and
     breast
Flashed the thrilled spirit's love-devouring
     heat;
In that absorbing sigh perchance more
     bless'd   750
Than vulgar minds may be with all they seek
     possessed.

80

His life was one long war with self-sought
     foes,
Or friends by him self-banished; for his
     mind
Had grown Suspicion's sanctuary, and
     chose,
For its own cruel sacrifice, the kind,   755
'Gainst whom he raged with fury strange
     and blind.
But he was frensied,—wherefore, who may
     know?
Since cause might be which skill could
     never find;
But he was frensied by disease or woe,
To that worst pitch of all, which wears a
     reasoning show.   760

81

For then he was inspired, and from him
     came,
As from the Pythian's mystic cave of yore,
Those oracles which set the world in flame,
Nor ceased to burn till kingdoms were no
     more:
Did he not this for France? which lay
     before   765
Bowed to the inborn tyranny of years?
Broken and trembling to the yoke she bore,
Till by the voice of him and his compeers
Roused up to too much wrath, which follows
     o'ergrown fears?

82

They made themselves a fearful monu-
     ment!
The wreck of old opinions—things which
     grew,   771

---

[24]Which contains the ashes of the dead.

[25]Jean Jacques Rousseau (1712–1778). He was
born at Geneva and spent his earliest years there.

[26]Heroine of Rousseau's novel, *Julie, ou la nou-
velle Héloïse.*

[27]This refers to the account in his *Confessions* of
his passion for the Comtesse d'Houdetot, and his
long walk every morning, for the sake of the
single kiss which was the common salutation of
French acquaintance (Byron's note).

Breathed from the birth of time: the veil
they rent,
And what behind it lay, all earth shall
view.
But good with ill they also overthrew,
Leaving but ruins, wherewith to rebuild 775
Upon the same foundation, and renew
Dungeons and thrones, which the same
hour refilled,
As heretofore, because ambition was self-
willed.

83

But this will not endure, nor be endured!
Mankind have felt their strength, and made
it felt. 780
They might have used it better, but, al-
lured
By their new vigor, sternly have they dealt
On one another; pity ceased to melt
With her once natural charities. But they,
Who in oppression's darkness caved had
dwelt, 785
They were not eagles, nourished with the
day;
What marvel then, at times, if they mistook
their prey?

84

What deep wounds ever closed without a
scar?
The heart's bleed longest, and but heal to
wear 789
That which disfigures it; and they who
war
With their own hopes, and have been vanquished, bear
Silence, but not submission: in his lair
Fixed Passion holds his breath, until the
hour
Which shall atone for years; none need
despair:
It came, it cometh, and will come,—the
power 795
To punish or forgive—in *one* we shall be
slower.

85

Clear, placid Leman! thy contrasted lake,
With the wild world I dwelt in, is a thing
Which warns me, with its stillness, to for-
sake 799
Earth's troubled waters for a purer spring.
This quiet sail is as a noiseless wing
To waft me from distraction; once I loved

Torn ocean's roar, but thy soft murmuring
Sounds sweet as if a Sister's voice reproved,
That I with stern delights should e'er have
been so moved. 805

86

It is the hush of night, and all between
Thy margin and the mountains, dusk, yet
clear,
Mellowed and mingling, yet distinctly seen,
Save darkened Jura, whose capped heights
appear
Precipitously steep; and drawing near, 810
There breathes a living fragrance from the
shore,
Of flowers yet fresh with childhood; on
the ear
Drops the light drip of the suspended oar,
Or chirps the grasshopper one good-night
carol more.

87

He is an evening reveler, who makes 815
His life an infancy, and sings his fill;
At intervals, some bird from out the brakes
Starts into voice a moment, then is still.
There seems a floating whisper on the hill,
But that is fancy, for the starlight dews 820
All silently their tears of love instill,
Weeping themselves away, till they infuse
Deep into Nature's breast the spirit of her
hues.

88

Ye stars! which are the poetry of heaven!
If in your bright leaves we would read the
fate 825
Of men and empires,—'tis to be forgiven,
That in our aspirations to be great,
Our destinies o'erleap their mortal state,
And claim a kindred with you; for ye are
A beauty and a mystery, and create 830
In us such love and reverence from afar,
That fortune, fame, power, life, have named
themselves a star.

89

All heaven and earth are still—though not
in sleep,
But breathless, as we grow when feeling
most;
And silent, as we stand in thoughts too
deep:— 835
All heaven and earth are still: From the
high host

Of stars, to the lulled lake and mountain-
   coast,
All is concentered in a life intense,
Where not a beam, nor air, nor leaf is lost,
But hath a part of being, and a sense   840
Of that which is of all Creator and defense.

90

Then stirs the feeling infinite, so felt
In solitude, where we are *least* alone;
A truth, which through our being then doth
   melt,
And purifies from self: it is a tone,   845
The soul and source of music, which makes
   known
Eternal harmony, and sheds a charm
Like to the fabled Cytherea's zone,[28]
Binding all things with beauty;—'twould
   disarm
The specter Death, had he substantial power
   to harm.   850

91

Not vainly did the early Persian make
His altar the high places, and the peak
Of earth-o'ergazing mountains, and thus
   take
A fit and unwalled temple, there to seek
The Spirit, in whose honor shrines are
   weak,
Upreared of human hands. Come, and
   compare   856
Columns and idol-dwellings, Goth or
   Greek,
With Nature's realms of worship, earth
   and air,
Nor fix on fond abodes to circumscribe thy
   pray'r!

92

The sky is changed!—and such a change!
   Oh night,   860
And storm, and darkness, ye are wondrous
   strong,
Yet lovely in your strength, as is the light
Of a dark eye in woman! Far along,
From peak to peak, the rattling crags
   among
Leaps the live thunder! Not from one
   lone cloud,   865
But every mountain now hath found a
   tongue,

[28]Aphrodite's girdle, which attracted love to its
wearer.

And Jura answers, through her misty
   shroud,
Back to the joyous Alps, who call to her
   aloud!

93

And this is in the night:—Most glorious
   night!   869
Thou wert not sent for slumber! let me be
A sharer in thy fierce and far delight,—
A portion of the tempest and of thee!
How the lit lake shines, a phosphoric sea,
And the big rain comes dancing to the
   earth!
And now again 'tis black,—and now, the
   glee   875
Of the loud hills shakes with its mountain-
   mirth,
As if they did rejoice o'er a young earth-
   quake's birth.

94

Now, where the swift Rhone cleaves his
   way between
Heights which appear as lovers who have
   parted   879
In hate, whose mining depths so intervene
That they can meet no more, though
   broken-hearted;
Though in their souls, which thus each
   other thwarted,
Love was the very root of the fond rage
Which blighted their life's bloom, and
   then departed:
Itself expired, but leaving them an age   885
Of years all winters,—war within themselves
   to wage.

95

Now, where the quick Rhone thus hath
   cleft his way,
The mightiest of the storms hath ta'en
   his stand:
For here, not one, but many, make their
   play,
And fling their thunder-bolts from hand
   to hand,   890
Flashing and cast around; of all the band,
The brightest through these parted hills
   hath forked
His lightnings,—as if he did understand,
That in such gaps as desolation worked,
There the hot shaft should blast whatever
   therein lurked.   895

96

Sky, mountains, river, winds, lake, light-
nings! ye!
With night, and clouds, and thunder, and
a soul
To make these felt and feeling, well may be
Things that have made me watchful; the
far roll
Of your departing voices, is the knoll[29] 900
Of what in me is sleepless,—if I rest.
But where of ye, O tempests! is the goal?
Are ye like those within the human breast?
Or do ye find, at length, like eagles, some
high nest?

97

Could I embody and unbosom now   905
That which is most within me,—could I
wreak
My thoughts upon expression, and thus
throw
Soul, heart, mind, passions, feelings, strong
or weak,
All that I would have sought, and all I
seek,
Bear, know, feel, and yet breathe—into
one word,   910
And that one word were Lightning, I
would speak;
But as it is, I live and die unheard,
With a most voiceless thought, sheathing it
as a sword.

98

The morn is up again, the dewy morn,
With breath all incense, and with cheek all
bloom,   915
Laughing the clouds away with playful
scorn,
And living as if earth contained no tomb,—
And glowing into day: we may resume
The march of our existence: and thus I,
Still on thy shores, fair Leman! may find
room   920
And food for meditation, nor pass by
Much, that may give us pause, if pondered
fittingly.

99

Clarens![30] sweet Clarens, birthplace of
deep Love!
Thine air is the young breath of passionate
thought;

[29]Knell.
[30]Village on the Lake of Geneva, the scene of
meetings of the lovers in Rousseau's *Julie.*

Thy trees take root in Love; the snows
above   925
The very Glaciers have his colors caught,
And sun-set into rose-hues sees them
wrought
By rays which sleep there lovingly: the
rocks,
The permanent crags, tell here of Love,
who sought   929
In them a refuge from the worldly shocks,
Which stir and sting the soul with hope that
woos, then mocks.

100

Clarens! by heavenly feet thy paths are
trod,—
Undying Love's, who here ascends a
throne
To which the steps are mountains; where
the god
Is a pervading life and light,—so shown 935
Not on those summits solely, nor alone
In the still cave and forest; o'er the flower
His eye is sparkling, and his breath hath
blown,
His soft and summer breath, whose tender
power
Passes the strength of storms in their most
desolate hour.   940

101

All things are here of *him;* from the black
pines,
Which are his shade on high, and the loud
roar
Of torrents, where he listeneth, to the vines
Which slope his green path downward to
the shore,
Where the bowed waters meet him, and
adore,   945
Kissing his feet with murmurs; and the
wood,
The covert of old trees, with trunks all
hoar,
But light leaves, young as joy, stands
where it stood,
Offering to him, and his, a populous solitude.

102

A populous solitude of bees and birds 950
And fairy-formed and many-colored
things,
Who worship him with notes more sweet
than words,
And innocently open their glad wings,

Fearless and full of life: the gush of springs,
And fall of lofty fountains, and the bend
Of stirring branches, and the bud which brings   956
The swiftest thought of beauty, here extend,
Mingling, and made by Love, unto one mighty end.

103

He who hath loved not, here would learn that lore,   959
And make his heart a spirit; he who knows
That tender mystery, will love the more;
For this is Love's recess, where vain men's woes,
And the world's waste, have driven him far from those,
For 'tis his nature to advance or die;   964
He stands not still, but or decays, or grows
Into a boundless blessing, which may vie
With the immortal lights, in its eternity!

104

'Twas not for fiction chose Rousseau this spot,
Peopling it with affections; but he found
It was the scene which Passion must allot
To the mind's purified beings; 'twas the ground   971
Where early Love his Psyche's zone unbound,
And hallowed it with loveliness: 'tis lone,
And wonderful, and deep, and hath a sound,
And sense, and sight of sweetness; here the Rhone   975
Hath spread himself a couch, the Alps have reared a throne.

105

Lausanne! and Ferney![31] ye have been the abodes
Of names which unto you bequeathed a name;
Mortals, who sought and found, by dangerous roads,
A path to perpetuity of fame: 980
They were gigantic minds, and their steep aim
Was, Titan-like, on daring doubts to pile

Thoughts which should call down thunder, and the flame
Of Heaven again assailed, if Heaven the while
On man and man's research could deign do more than smile.   985

106

The one[32] was fire and fickleness, a child
Most mutable in wishes, but in mind
A wit as various,—gay, grave, sage, or wild,—
Historian, bard, philosopher, combined;
He multiplied himself among mankind,   990
The Proteus of their talents: But his own
Breathed most in ridicule,—which, as the wind,
Blew where it listed, laying all things prone,—
Now to o'erthrow a fool, and now to shake a throne.

107

The other, deep and slow, exhausting thought,   995
And hiving wisdom with each studious year,
In meditation dwelt, with learning wrought,
And shaped his weapon with an edge severe,
Sapping a solemn creed with solemn sneer;
The lord of irony,—that master-spell,   1000
Which stung his foes to wrath, which grew from fear,
And doomed him to the zealot's ready Hell,
Which answers to all doubts so eloquently well.

108

Yet, peace be with their ashes,—for by them,
If merited, the penalty is paid;   1005
It is not ours to judge,—far less condemn;
The hour must come when such things shall be made
Known unto all, or hope and dread allayed
By slumber, on one pillow, in the dust,
Which, thus much we are sure, must lie decayed,   1010
And when it shall revive, as is our trust,
'Twill be to be forgiven, or suffer what is just.

---

[31]In the former Gibbon had lived, in the latter Voltaire.

[32]Voltaire.

109

But let me quit man's works, again to read
His Maker's, spread around me, and sus-
   pend   1014
This page, which from my reveries I feed,
Until it seems prolonging without end.
The clouds above me to the white Alps
   tend,
And I must pierce them, and survey what-
   e'er
May be permitted, as my steps I bend
To their most great and growing region,
   where   1020
The earth to her embrace compels the powers
   of air.

110

Italia, too! Italia! looking on thee,
Full flashes on the soul the light of ages,
Since the fierce Carthaginian almost won
   thee,
To the last halo of the chiefs and sages 1025
Who glorify thy consecrated pages;
Thou wert the throne and grave of em-
   pires; still,
The fount at which the panting mind as-
   suages
Her thirst of knowledge, quaffing there her
   fill,
Flows from the eternal source of Rome's im-
   perial hill.   1030

111

Thus far have I proceeded in a theme
Renewed with no kind auspices:—to feel
We are not what we have been, and to
   deem
We are not what we should be, and to steel
The heart against itself; and to conceal,
With a proud caution, love, or hate, or
   aught,—   1036
Passion or feeling, purpose, grief, or
   zeal,—
Which is the tyrant spirit of our thought,
Is a stern task of soul:—No matter,—it is
   taught.

112

And for these words, thus woven into
   song,
It may be that they are a harmless wile,—
The coloring of the scenes which fleet
   along,   1042
Which I would seize, in passing, to beguile
My breast, or that of others, for a while.

Fame is the thirst of youth, but I am not
So young as to regard men's frown or
   smile,
As loss or guerdon of a glorious lot; 1047
I stood and stand alone,—remembered or
   forgot.

113

I have not loved the world, nor the world
   me;
I have not flattered its rank breath, nor
   bowed   1050
To its idolatries a patient knee,
Nor coined my cheek to smiles, nor cried
   aloud
In worship of an echo; in the crowd
They could not deem me one of such; I
   stood
Among them, but not of them; in a shroud
Of thoughts which were not their thoughts,
   and still could,   1056
Had I not filed[33] my mind, which thus itself
   subdued.

114

I have not loved the world, nor the world
   me,—
But let us part fair foes; I do believe,
Though I have found them not, that there
   may be   1060
Words which are things, hopes which will
   not deceive,
And virtues which are merciful, nor weave
Snares for the failing; I would also deem
O'er others' griefs that some sincerely
   grieve;
That two, or one, are almost what they
   seem,   1065
That goodness is no name, and happiness no
   dream.

115

My daughter! with thy name this song be-
   gun;
My daughter! with thy name thus much
   shall end;
I see thee not, I hear thee not, but none
Can be so wrapped in thee; thou art the
   friend   1070
To whom the shadows of far years extend:
Albeit my brow thou never shouldst be-
   hold,
My voice shall with thy future visions
   blend,

[33]Defiled.

And reach into thy heart, when mine is
    cold,
A token and a tone, even from thy father's
    mold.   1075

116

To aid thy mind's development, to watch
Thy dawn of little joys, to sit and see
Almost thy very growth, to view thee
    catch
Knowledge of objects,—wonders yet to
    thee!
To hold thee lightly on a gentle knee,   1080
And print on thy soft cheek a parent's
    kiss,—
This, it should seem, was not reserved for
    me;
Yet this was in my nature: as it is,
I know not what is there, yet something like
to this.

117

Yet, though dull Hate as duty should be
    taught,   1085
I know that thou wilt love me; though my
    name
Should be shut from thee, as a spell still
    fraught
With desolation, and a broken claim:
Though the grave closed between us,—
    'twere the same,
I know that thou wilt love me; though to
    drain   1090
My blood from out thy being were an aim,
And an attainment,—all would be in
    vain,—
Still thou wouldst love me, still that more
    than life retain.

118

The child of love, though born in bitter-
    ness,   1094
And nurtured in convulsion! Of thy sire
These were the elements, and thine no less.
As yet such are around thee, but thy fire
Shall be more tempered, and thy hope far
    higher.
Sweet be thy cradled slumbers! O'er the
    sea
And from the mountains where I now re-
    spire,   1100
Fain would I waft such blessing upon
    thee,
As, with a sigh, I deem thou might'st have
    been to me!

MAID OF ATHENS, ERE WE PART[1]

Ζωή μου, σᾶς ἀγαπῶ.[2]

Maid of Athens, ere we part,
Give, oh give me back my heart!
Or, since that has left my breast,
Keep it now, and take the rest!   5
Hear my vow before I go,
Ζωή μου, σᾶς ἀγαπῶ.

By those tresses unconfined,
Wooed by each Aegean wind;
By those lids whose jetty fringe
Kiss thy soft cheeks' blooming tinge;   10
By those wild eyes like the roe,
Ζωή μου, σᾶς ἀγαπῶ.

By that lip I long to taste;
By that zone-encircled waist;
By all the token-flowers that tell   15
What words can never speak so well;
By love's alternate joy and woe,
Ζωή μου, σᾶς ἀγαπῶ.

Maid of Athens! I am gone:
Think of me, sweet! when alone.   20
Though I fly to Istambol,[3]
Athens holds my heart and soul:
Can I cease to love thee? No!
Ζωή μου, σᾶς ἀγαπῶ.

SHE WALKS IN BEAUTY[4]

I

She walks in beauty, like the night
    Of cloudless climes and starry skies;
And all that's best of dark and bright
    Meet in her aspect and her eyes:
Thus mellowed to that tender light   5
    Which heaven to gaudy day denies.

II

One shade the more, one ray the less,
    Had half impaired the nameless grace
Which waves in every raven tress,
    Or softly lightens o'er her face;   10
Where thoughts serenely sweet express
    How pure, how dear their dwelling-place.

[1]Written at Athens in 1810, published in 1812.
Supposed to have been addressed to Theresa Macri,
with whose mother Byron lodged while in Athens.
[2]My life, I love you.   [3]Constantinople.
[4]Written in 1814; published in 1815.

III

And on that cheek, and o'er that brow,
  So soft, so calm, yet eloquent,
The smiles that win, the tints that glow,   15
  But tell of days in goodness spent,
A mind at peace with all below,
  A heart whose love is innocent!

THE DESTRUCTION OF SENNACHERIB[5]

I

The Assyrian came down like the wolf on
  the fold,
And his cohorts were gleaming in purple and
  gold;
And the sheen of their spears was like stars
  on the sea,
When the blue wave rolls nightly on deep
  Galilee.

II

Like the leaves of the forest when Summer is
  green,   5
That host with their banners at sunset were
  seen:
Like the leaves of the forest when Autumn
  hath blown,
That host on the morrow lay withered and
  strown.

III

For the Angel of Death spread his wings on
  the blast,
And breathed in the face of the foe as he
  passed;   10
And the eyes of the sleepers waxed deadly
  and chill,
And their hearts but once heaved, and for
  ever grew still!

IV

And there lay the steed with his nostril all
  wide,
But through it there rolled not the breath of
  his pride;
And the foam of his gasping lay white on the
  turf,   15
And cold as the spray of the rock-beating
  surf.

V

And there lay the rider distorted and pale,
With the dew on his brow, and the rust on
  his mail:
And the tents were all silent, the banners
  alone,
The lances unlifted, the trumpet unblown. 20

VI

And the widows of Ashur[6] are loud in their
  wail,
And the idols are broke in the temple of
  Baal;
And the might of the Gentile, unsmote by the
  sword,
Hath melted like snow in the glance of the
  Lord!

WHEN WE TWO PARTED[7]

When we two parted
  In silence and tears,
Half broken-hearted
  To sever for years,
Pale grew thy cheek and cold,   5
  Colder thy kiss;
Truly that hour foretold
  Sorrow to this.

The dew of the morning
  Sunk chill on my brow—   10
It felt like the warning
  Of what I feel now.
Thy vows are all broken,
  And light is thy fame:
I hear thy name spoken,   15
  And share in its shame.

They name thee before me,
  A knell to mine ear;
A shudder comes o'er me—
  Why wert thou so dear?   20
They know not I knew thee,
  Who knew thee too well:—
Long, long shall I rue thee,
  Too deeply to tell.

In secret we met—   25
  In silence I grieve,
That thy heart could forget,
  Thy spirit deceive.

---

[5]Written and published in 1815. See 2 Kings, xviii–xix.

[6]Assyria.
[7]Written in 1808; published in 1816.

If I should meet thee
  After long years,   30
How should I greet thee?—
  With silence and tears.

STANZAS FOR MUSIC [8]

There's not a joy the world can give like that
  it takes away,
When the glow of early thought declines in
  feeling's dull decay;
'Tis not on youth's smooth cheek the blush
  alone, which fades so fast,
But the tender bloom of heart is gone, ere
  youth itself be past.

Then the few whose spirits float above the
  wreck of happiness   5
Are driven o'er the shoals of guilt or ocean
  of excess:
The magnet of their course is gone, or only
  points in vain
The shore to which their shivered sail shall
  never stretch again.

Then the mortal coldness of the soul like
  death itself comes down;
It cannot feel for others' woes, it dare not
  dream its own;   10
That heavy chill has frozen o'er the fountain
  of our tears,
And though the eye may sparkle still, 'tis
  where the ice appears.

Though wit may flash from fluent lips, and
  mirth distract the breast,
Through midnight hours that yield no more
  their former hope of rest;
'Tis but as ivy-leaves around the ruined turret wreath,   15
All green and wildly fresh without, but worn
  and gray beneath.

Oh could I feel as I have felt,—or be what I
  have been,
Or weep as I could once have wept o'er many
  a vanished scene;
As springs in deserts found seem sweet, all
  brackish though they be,
So, midst the withered waste of life, those
  tears would flow to me.   20

[8] Written in 1815; published in 1816.

STANZAS FOR MUSIC [9]

There be none of Beauty's daughters
  With a magic like thee;
And like music on the waters
  Is thy sweet voice to me:
When, as if its sound were causing   5
The charméd ocean's pausing,
The waves lie still and gleaming,
And the lulled winds seem dreaming:

And the midnight moon is weaving
  Her bright chain o'er the deep;   10
Whose breast is gently heaving,
  As an infant's asleep:
So the spirit bows before thee,
To listen and adore thee;
With a full but soft emotion,   15
Like the swell of Summer's ocean.

SONNET ON CHILLON [10]

Eternal Spirit of the chainless Mind!
  Brightest in dungeons, Liberty! thou art,
  For there thy habitation is the heart—
The heart which love of thee alone can bind;
And when thy sons to fetters are consigned—
  To fetters, and the damp vault's dayless
    gloom,   6
  Their country conquers with their martyr-
    dom,
And Freedom's fame finds wings on every
  wind.
Chillon! thy prison is a holy place,
  And thy sad floor an altar—for 'twas trod,
Until his very steps have left a trace   11
  Worn, as if thy cold pavement were a sod,
By Bonnivard! [11] May none those marks
  efface!
  For they appeal from tyranny to God.

[9] Written and published in 1816.

[10] This and the following poem were written in June, 1816, immediately after a visit with Shelley to the Castle of Chillon; published in the same year. The Castle is on the shore of the Lake of Geneva at the end farthest from the city of Geneva.

[11] A Swiss republican (1493–1570) who aided the Genevese in an attempt to free their city from the rule of the Duke of Savoy. He was imprisoned for six years at Chillon, four of which were spent in the cell Byron describes. At the time when Byron wrote his poem he knew little or nothing of the actual history of Bonnivard, so that Byron's "Prisoner" is largely an imaginary character.

THE PRISONER OF CHILLON

I

My hair is gray, but not with years,
   Nor grew it white
   In a single night,
As men's have grown from sudden fears:
My limbs are bowed, though not with toil, 5
   But rusted with a vile repose,
For they have been a dungeon's spoil,
   And mine has been the fate of those
To whom the goodly earth and air
Are banned, and barred—forbidden fare: 10
But this was for my father's faith
I suffered chains and courted death;
That father perished at the stake
For tenets he would not forsake;
And for the same his lineal race 15
In darkness found a dwelling-place;
We were seven—who now are one,
   Six in youth, and one in age,
Finished as they had begun,
   Proud of Persecution's rage; 20
One in fire, and two in field,
Their belief with blood have sealed,
Dying as their father died,
For the God their foes denied;
Three were in a dungeon cast, 25
Of whom this wreck is left the last.

II

There are seven pillars of Gothic mold,
In Chillon's dungeons deep and old,
There are seven columns, massy and gray,
Dim with a dull imprisoned ray, 30
A sunbeam which hath lost its way,
And through the crevice and the cleft
Of the thick wall is fallen and left;
Creeping o'er the floor so damp,
Like a marsh's meteor lamp: 35
And in each pillar there is a ring,
   And in each ring there is a chain;
That iron is a cankering thing,
   For in these limbs its teeth remain,
With marks that will not wear away, 40
Till I have done with this new day,
Which now is painful to these eyes,
Which have not seen the sun so rise
For years—I cannot count them o'er,
I lost their long and heavy score, 45
When my last brother drooped and died,
And I lay living by his side.

III

They chained us each to a column stone,
And we were three—yet, each alone;

We could not move a single pace, 50
We could not see each other's face,
But with that pale and livid light
That made us strangers in our sight:
And thus together—yet apart,
Fettered in hand, but joined in heart, 55
'Twas still some solace, in the dearth
Of the pure elements of earth,
To hearken to each other's speech,
And each turn comforter to each
With some new hope, or legend old, 60
Or song heroically bold;
But even these at length grew cold.
Our voices took a dreary tone,
An echo of the dungeon stone,
   A grating sound, not full and free, 65
   As they of yore were wont to be:
   It might be fancy, but to me
They never sounded like our own.

IV

I was the eldest of the three,
   And to uphold and cheer the rest 70
   I ought to do—and did my best—
And each did well in his degree.
   The youngest, whom my father loved,
Because our mother's brow was given
To him, with eyes as blue as heaven— 75
   For him my soul was sorely moved;
And truly might it be distressed
To see such bird in such a nest;
For he was beautiful as day—
   (When day was beautiful to me 80
   As to young eagles, being free)—
   A polar day, which will not see
A sunset till its summer's gone,
Its sleepless summer of long light,
The snow-clad offspring of the sun; 85
   And thus he was as pure and bright,
And in his natural spirit gay,
With tears for nought but others' ills,
And then they flowed like mountain rills,
Unless he could assuage the woe 90
Which he abhorred to view below.

V

The other was as pure of mind,
But formed to combat with his kind;
Strong in his frame, and of a mood
Which 'gainst the world in war had stood, 95
And perished in the foremost rank
   With joy:—but not in chains to pine:
His spirit withered with their clank,
   I saw it silently decline—
   And so perchance in sooth did mine: 100

But yet I forced it on to cheer
Those relics of a home so dear.
He was a hunter of the hills,
  Had followed there the deer and wolf;
  To him this dungeon was a gulf,   105
And fettered feet the worst of ills.

VI

  Lake Leman lies by Chillon's walls:
A thousand feet in depth below
Its massy waters meet and flow;
Thus much the fathom-line was sent   110
From Chillon's snow-white battlement,
  Which round about the wave enthralls:
A double dungeon wall and wave
Have made—and like a living grave
Below the surface of the lake   115
The dark vault lies wherein we lay:
We heard it ripple night and day;
  Sounding o'er our heads it knocked;
And I have felt the winter's spray
Wash through the bars when winds were
    high   120
And wanton in the happy sky;
  And then the very rock hath rocked,
  And I have felt it shake, unshocked,
Because I could have smiled to see
The death that would have set me free.   125

VII

I said my nearer brother pined,
I said his mighty heart declined,
He loathed and put away his food;
It was not that 'twas coarse and rude,
For we were used to hunter's fare,   130
And for the like had little care:
The milk drawn from the mountain goat
Was changed for water from the moat,
Our bread was such as captives' tears
Have moistened many a thousand years,   135
Since man first pent his fellow men
Like brutes within an iron den;
But what were these to us or him?
These wasted not his heart or limb;
My brother's soul was of that mold   140
Which in a palace had grown cold,
Had his free breathing been denied
The range of the steep mountain's side;
But why delay the truth?—he died.
I saw, and could not hold his head,   145
Nor reach his dying hand—nor dead,—
Though hard I strove, but strove in vain,
To rend and gnash my bonds in twain.
He died, and they unlocked his chain,
And scooped for him a shallow grave   150
Even from the cold earth of our cave.

I begged them as a boon to lay
His corse in dust whereon the day
Might shine—it was a foolish thought,
But then within my brain it wrought,   155
That even in death his freeborn breast
In such a dungeon could not rest.
I might have spared my idle prayer—
They coldly laughed, and laid him there:
The flat and turfless earth above   160
The being we so much did love;
His empty chain above it leant,
Such murder's fitting monument!

VIII

But he, the favorite and the flower,
Most cherished since his natal hour,   165
His mother's image in fair face,
The infant love of all his race,
His martyred father's dearest thought,
My latest care, for whom I sought
To hoard my life, that his might be   170
Less wretched now, and one day free;
He, too, who yet had held untired
A spirit natural or inspired—
He, too, was struck, and day by day
Was withered on the stalk away.   175
Oh, God! it is a fearful thing
To see the human soul take wing
In any shape, in any mood:
I've seen it rushing forth in blood,
I've seen it on the breaking ocean   180
Strive with a swoll'n convulsive motion,
I've seen the sick and ghastly bed
Of sin delirious with its dread;
But these were horrors—this was woe
Unmixed with such—but sure and slow: 185
He faded, and so calm and meek,
So softly worn, so sweetly weak,
So tearless, yet so tender, kind,
And grieved for those he left behind;
With all the while a cheek whose bloom   190
Was as a mockery of the tomb,
Whose tints as gently sunk away
As a departing rainbow's ray;
An eye of most transparent light,
That almost made the dungeon bright,   195
And not a word of murmur, not
A groan o'er his untimely lot,—
A little talk of better days,
A little hope my own to raise,
For I was sunk in silence—lost   200
In this last loss, of all the most;
And then the sighs he would suppress
Of fainting nature's feebleness,
More slowly drawn, grew less and less:
I listened, but I could not hear;   205
I called, for I was wild with fear;

I knew 'twas hopeless, but my dread
Would not be thus admonishéd;
I called, and thought I heard a sound—
I burst my chain with one strong bound,   210
And rushed to him:—I found him not,
I only stirred in this black spot,
I only lived, *I* only drew
The accurséd breath of dungeon-dew;
The last, the sole, the dearest link   215
Between me and the eternal brink,
Which bound me to my failing race,
Was broken in this fatal place.
One on the earth, and one beneath—
My brothers—both had ceased to breathe: 220
I took that hand which lay so still,
Alas! my own was full as chill;
I had not strength to stir, or strive,
But felt that I was still alive—
A frantic feeling, when we know   225
That what we love shall ne'er be so.
    I know not why
    I could not die,
I had no earthly hope but faith,
And that forbade a selfish death.   230

IX

What next befell me then and there
    I know not well—I never knew—
First came the loss of light, and air,
    And then of darkness too:
I had no thought, no feeling—none—   235
Among the stones I stood a stone,
And was, scarce conscious what I wist,
As shrubless crags within the mist;
For all was blank, and bleak, and gray;
It was not night, it was not day;   240
It was not even the dungeon-light
So hateful to my heavy sight,
But vacancy absorbing space,
And fixedness without a place;
There were no stars, no earth, no time,   245
No check, no change, no good, no crime,
But silence, and a stirless breath
Which neither was of life nor death;
A sea of stagnant idleness,
Blind, boundless, mute, and motionless!   250

X

A light broke in upon my brain,—
    It was the carol of a bird;
It ceased, and then it came again,
    The sweetest song ear ever heard,
And mine was thankful till my eyes   255
Ran over with the glad surprise,
And they that moment could not see
I was the mate of misery;

But then by dull degrees came back
My senses to their wonted track;   260
I saw the dungeon walls and floor
Close slowly round me as before,
I saw the glimmer of the sun
Creeping as it before had done,
But through the crevice where it came   265
That bird was perched, as fond and tame,
    And tamer than upon the tree;
A lovely bird, with azure wings,
And song that said a thousand things,
    And seemed to say them all for me!   270
I never saw its like before,
I ne'er shall see its likeness more:
It seemed like me to want a mate,
But was not half so desolate,
And it was come to love me when   275
None lived to love me so again,
And cheering from my dungeon's brink,
Had brought me back to feel and think.
I know not if it late were free,
    Or broke its cage to perch on mine,   280
But knowing well captivity,
    Sweet bird! I could not wish for thine!
Or if it were, in wingéd guise,
A visitant from Paradise;   284
For—Heaven forgive that thought! the while
Which made me both to weep and smile—
I sometimes deemed that it might be
My brother's soul come down to me;
But then at last away it flew,
And then 'twas mortal well I knew,   290
For he would never thus have flown,
And left me twice so doubly lone,
Lone as the corse within its shroud,
Lone as a solitary cloud,—
    A single cloud on a sunny day,   295
While all the rest of heaven is clear,
A frown upon the atmosphere,
That hath no business to appear
    When skies are blue, and earth is gay.

XI

A kind of change came in my fate,   300
My keepers grew compassionate;
I know not what had made them so,
They were inured to sights of woe,
But so it was:—my broken chain
With links unfastened did remain,   305
And it was liberty to stride
Along my cell from side to side,
And up and down, and then athwart,
And tread it over every part;
And round the pillars one by one,   310
Returning where my walk begun,
Avoiding only, as I trod,
My brothers' graves without a sod;

For if I thought with heedless tread
My step profaned their lowly bed, 315
My breath came gaspingly and thick,
And my crushed heart felt blind and sick.

XII

I made a footing in the wall,
It was not therefrom to escape,
For I had buried one and all 320
Who loved me in a human shape;
And the whole earth would henceforth be
A wider prison unto me:
No child, no sire, no kin had I,
No partner in my misery; 325
I thought of this, and I was glad,
For thought of them had[1] made me mad;
But I was curious to ascend
To my barred windows, and to bend
Once more, upon the mountains high, 330
The quiet of a loving eye.

XIII

I saw them, and they were the same,
They were not changed like me in frame;
I saw their thousand years of snow
On high—their wide long lake below, 335
And the blue Rhone in fullest flow;
I heard the torrents leap and gush
O'er channeled rock and broken bush;
I saw the white-walled distant town,
And whiter sails go skimming down; 340
And then there was a little isle,
Which in my very face did smile,
The only one in view;
A small green isle, it seemed no more,
Scarce broader than my dungeon floor, 345
But in it there were three tall trees,
And o'er it blew the mountain breeze,
And by it there were waters flowing,
And on it there were young flowers growing,
Of gentle breath and hue. 350
The fish swam by the castle wall,
And they seemed joyous each and all:
The eagle rode the rising blast,
Methought he never flew so fast
As then to me he seemed to fly; 355
And then new tears came in my eye,
And I felt troubled—and would fain
I had not left my recent chain;
And when I did descend again,
The darkness of my dim abode 360
Fell on me as a heavy load;
It was as is a new-dug grave,
Closing o'er one we sought to save,—

---

[1]Would have.

And yet my glance, too much oppressed,
Had almost need of such a rest. 365

XIV

It might be months, or years, or days,
I kept no count, I took no note,
I had no hope my eyes to raise,
And clear them of their dreary mote;
At last men came to set me free; 370
I asked not why, and recked not where;
It was at length the same to me,
Fettered or fetterless to be,
I learned to love despair.
And thus when they appeared at last, 375
And all my bonds aside were cast,
These heavy walls to me had grown
A hermitage—and all my own!
And half I felt as they were come
To tear me from a second home: 380
With spiders I had friendship made,
And watched them in their sullen trade,
Had seen the mice by moonlight play,
And why should I feel less than they?
We were all inmates of one place, 385
And I, the monarch of each race,
Had power to kill—yet, strange to tell!
In quiet we had learned to dwell;
My very chains and I grew friends,
So much a long communion tends 390
To make us what we are:—even I
Regained my freedom with a sigh.

TO THOMAS MOORE[1]

My boat is on the shore,
And my bark is on the sea;
But, before I go, Tom Moore,
Here's a double health to thee!

Here's a sigh to those who love me, 5
And a smile to those who hate;
And, whatever sky's above me,
Here's a heart for every fate.

Though the Ocean roar around me,
Yet it still shall bear me on; 10
Though a desert shall surround me,
It hath springs that may be won.

Were't the last drop in the well,
As I gasped upon the brink,
Ere my fainting spirit fell, 15
'Tis to thee that I would drink.

---

[1]Written in 1817 (the first stanza in 1816); published in 1821. This poem and the two following ones were all sent in letters to Thomas Moore (1779–1852), Irish poet and wit, and Byron's friend and biographer.

With that water, as this wine,
  The libation I would pour
Should be—peace with thine and mine,
  And a health to thee, Tom Moore.   20

SO WE'LL GO NO MORE A-ROVING[2]

So we'll go no more a-roving
  So late into the night,
Though the heart be still as loving,
  And the moon be still as bright.

For the sword outwears its sheath,   5
  And the soul wears out the breast,
And the heart must pause to breathe,
  And Love itself have rest.

Though the night was made for loving,
  And the day returns too soon,   10
Yet we'll go no more a-roving
  By the light of the moon.

[2]Written in 1817; published in 1830.

BEPPO:

A Venetian Story[1]

Rosalind. Farewell, Monsieur Traveler: Look you lisp, and wear strange suits: disable all the benefits of your own country; be out of love with your Nativity, and almost chide God for making you that countenance you are; or I will scarce think that you have swam in a *Gondola.*
—*As You Like It,* Act IV, Scene 1.

Annotation of the Commentators.

That is, been at Venice, which was much visited by the young English gentlemen of those times, and was then what Paris is now—the seat of all dissoluteness.—S. A.

[1]Written in the autumn of 1817; published in 1818. Byron's stimulus to the writing of *Beppo* came from the poem in *ottava rima* known as *Whistlecraft,* by John Hookham Frere, in which this writer attempted to imitate in English the tone and methods of Pulci and his Italian followers. At the time when he read *Whistlecraft* Byron knew little or nothing of Frere's models, but he at once divined the possibilities of this style of writing. He had found, in a word, a form of verse which enabled him to write as he talked, perfectly at his ease, unobstructed by conventions, free to express himself completely. The result was *Beppo, The Vision of Judgment,* and *Don Juan. Beppo* "is our best, almost our only comic story in verse since Chaucer wrote the tales of the Reeve and the Miller, the Friar and the Summoner. This is high praise, artistically, and Byron's slight, slight story, involved in endless digressions, may seem hardly to deserve it, yet Chaucer could not have bettered . . .

TO THOMAS MOORE[3]

What are you doing now,
  Oh Thomas Moore?
What are you doing now,
  Oh Thomas Moore?
Sighing or suing now,   5
Riming or wooing now,
Billing or cooing now,
  Which, Thomas Moore?

But the Carnival's coming,
  Oh Thomas Moore!   10
The Carnival's coming,
  Oh Thomas Moore!
Masking and humming,
Fifing and drumming,
Guitarring and strumming,   15
  Oh Thomas Moore!

[3]Written in December, 1816, and published in 1830.

I

'Tis known, at least it should be, that throughout
  All countries of the Catholic persuasion,
Some weeks before Shrove Tuesday comes about,[2]
The people take their fill of recreation,
And buy repentance, ere they grow devout, 5
  However high their rank, or low their station,
With fiddling, feasting, dancing, drinking, masking,
And other things which may be had for asking.

2

The moment night with dusky mantle covers
  The skies (and the more duskily the better),
The time less liked by husbands than by lovers   11
  Begins, and prudery flings aside her fetter;
And gayety on restless tiptoe hovers,
  Giggling with all the gallants who beset her;

the closing stanzas and Laura's welcome to her long-lost husband" (H. J. C. Grierson, Preface to *Poems of Lord Byron,* p. xii).

[2]I. e., in the period just preceding Lent.

And there are songs and quavers, roaring,
　　humming,   15
Guitars, and every other sort of strumming.

3

And there are dresses splendid, but fantasti-
　　cal,
　　Masks of all times and nations, Turks and
　　　　Jews,
And harlequins and clowns, with feats gym-
　　nastical,
　　Greeks, Romans, Yankee-doodles, and
　　　　Hindoos;   20
All kinds of dress, except the ecclesiastical,
　　All people, as their fancies hit, may choose,
But no one in these parts may quiz[3] the
　　clergy,—
Therefore take heed, ye Freethinkers! I
　　charge ye.

4

You'd better walk about begirt with briers, 25
　　Instead of coat and smallclothes,[4] than put
　　　　on
A single stitch reflecting upon friars,
　　Although you swore it only was in fun;
They'd haul you o'er the coals, and stir the
　　fires
　　Of Phlegethon[5] with every mother's son, 30
Nor say one mass to cool the caldron's bub-
　　ble
That boiled your bones, unless you paid them
　　double.

5

But saving this, you may put on whate'er 33
　　You like by way of doublet, cape, or cloak,
Such as in Monmouth-street,[6] or in Rag Fair,
　　Would rig you out in seriousness or joke;
And even in Italy such places are,
　　With prettier name in softer accents spoke,
For, bating Covent Garden, I can hit on
No place that's called "Piazza" in Great
　　Britain.   40

6

This feast is named the Carnival, which be-
　　ing
　　Interpreted, implies "farewell to flesh":
So called, because the name and thing agree-
　　ing,
　　Through Lent they live on fish both salt
　　　　and fresh.

But why they usher Lent with so much glee
　　in,   45
　　Is more than I can tell, although I guess
'Tis as we take a glass with friends at part-
　　ing,
　　In the stage-coach or packet, just at starting.

7

And thus they bid farewell to carnal dishes,
　　And solid meats, and highly spiced ra-
　　　　gouts,[7]   50
To live for forty days on ill-dressed fishes,
　　Because they have no sauces to their
　　　　stews;
A thing which causes many "poohs" and
　　"pishes,"
　　And several oaths (which would not suit
　　　　the Muse),
From travelers accustomed from a boy   55
To eat their salmon, at the least, with soy;[8]

8

And therefore humbly I would recommend
　　"The curious in fish-sauce," before they
　　　　cross
The sea, to bid their cook, or wife, or friend,
　　Walk or ride to the Strand, and buy in
　　　　gross   60
(Or if set out beforehand, these may send
　　By any means least liable to loss)
Ketchup, Soy, Chili-vinegar, and Harvey,
Or, by the Lord! a Lent will well nigh starve
　　ye;

9

That is to say, if your religion's Roman,   65
　　And you at Rome would do as Romans do,
According to the proverb,—although no man,
　　If foreign, is obliged to fast; and you,
If Protestant, or sickly, or a woman,
　　Would rather dine in sin on a ragout— 70
Dine and be d—d! I don't mean to be
　　coarse,
But that's the penalty, to say no worse.

10

Of all the places where the Carnival
　　Was most facetious in the days of yore,
For dance, and song, and serenade, and ball,
　　And masque, and mime, and mystery, and
　　　　more   76

---

[3]Ridicule.　　[4]Knee breeches.
[5]River of Hades containing fire instead of water.
[6]Noted throughout the eighteenth century as a place for the sale of second-hand clothes.

[7]Highly seasoned stew of meat with vegetables.
[8]Chinese and Japanese sauce for fish made from beans by long fermentation followed by long digestion in brine.

Than I have time to tell now, or at all,
  Venice the bell from every city bore,—[9]
And at the moment when I fix my story,
That sea-born city was in all her glory.   80

11

They've pretty faces yet, those same Venetians,
  Black eyes, arched brows, and sweet expressions still;
Such as of old were copied from the Grecians,
  In ancient arts by moderns mimicked ill;
And like so many Venuses of Titian's   85
  (The best's at Florence—see it, if ye will),
They look when leaning over the balcony,
Or stepped from out a picture by Giorgione,[10]

12

Whose tints are truth and beauty at their best;
  And when you to Manfrini's palace go,   90
That picture (however fine the rest)
  Is loveliest to my mind of all the show;
It may perhaps be also to *your* zest,
  And that's the cause I rime upon it so:
'Tis but a portrait of his son, and wife,   95
And self; but *such* a woman! Love in life!

13

Love in full life and length, not love ideal,
  No, nor ideal beauty, that fine name,
But something better still, so very real,
  That the sweet model must have been the same,   100
A thing that you would purchase, beg, or steal,
  Were't not impossible, besides a shame:
The face recalls some face, as 'twere with pain,
You once have seen, but ne'er will see again;

14

One of those forms which flit by us, when we   105
  Are young, and fix our eyes on every face;
And, oh! the loveliness at times we see
  In momentary gliding, the soft grace,

The youth, the bloom, the beauty which agree,
  In many a nameless being we retrace,   110
Whose course and home we knew not, nor shall know,
  Like the lost Pleiad seen no more below.[11]

15

I said that like a picture by Giorgione
  Venetian women were, and so they *are,*
Particularly seen from a balcony   115
  (For beauty's sometimes best set off afar),
And there, just like a heroine of Goldoni,[12]
  They peep from out the blind, or o'er the bar;
And truth to say, they're mostly very pretty,
And rather like to show it, more's the pity!   120

16

For glances beget ogles,[13] ogles sighs,
  Sighs wishes, wishes words, and words a letter,
Which flies on wings of light-heeled Mercuries,
  Who do such things because they know no better;
And then, God knows what mischief may arise,   125
  When love links two young people in one fetter,
Vile assignations, and adulterous beds,
Elopements, broken vows, and hearts, and heads.

17

Shakespeare described the sex in Desdemona
  As very fair, but yet suspect in fame,[14]   130
And to this day from Venice to Verona
  Such matters may be probably the same,
Except that since those times was never known a
  Husband whom mere suspicion could inflame
To suffocate a wife no more than twenty,   135
Because she had a "cavalier servente."[15]

---

[11]The seven Pleiads before being changed into stars were daughters of Atlas. When their metamorphosis took place one of them left her station in the heavens so that she might not behold the ruin of Troy, founded by her son.

[12]Italian playwright (1707–1793).

[13]Coquettish looks.

[14]See *Othello,* III, iii, 206–208.

[15]Literally, a serving cavalier; one attentive to a married woman.

---

[9]I. e., surpassed every other city.

[10]Venetian painter (1478–1511).

18

Their jealousy (if they are ever jealous)
  Is of a fair complexion altogether,
Not like that sooty devil of Othello's,   139
  Which smothers women in a bed of feather,
But worthier of these much more jolly fellows,
  When weary of the matrimonial tether
His head for such a wife no mortal bothers,
But takes at once another, or *another's*.

19

Didst ever see a Gondola? For fear   145
  You should not, I'll describe it you exactly:
'Tis a long covered boat that's common here,
  Carved at the prow, built lightly, but compactly,
Rowed by two rowers, each called "Gondolier,"
  It glides along the water looking blackly,
Just like a coffin clapped in a canoe,   151
  Where none can make out what you say or do.

20

And up and down the long canals they go,
  And under the Rialto[16] shoot along,
By night and day, all paces, swift or slow,   155
  And round the theaters, a sable throng,
They wait in their dusk livery of woe,—
  But not to them do woeful things belong,
For sometimes they contain a deal of fun,
Like mourning coaches when the funeral's done.   160

21

But to my story.—'Twas some years ago,
  It may be thirty, forty, more or less,
The Carnival was at its height, and so
  Were all kinds of buffoonery and dress;
A certain lady went to see the show,   165
  Her real name I know not, nor can guess,
And so we'll call her Laura, if you please,
Because it slips into my verse with ease.

22

She was not old, nor young, nor at the years
  Which certain people call a *"certain age,"*
Which yet the most uncertain age appears,   171
  Because I never heard, nor could engage

A person yet by prayers, or bribes, or tears,
  To name, define by speech, or write on page,
The period meant precisely by that word,—
Which surely is exceedingly absurd.   176

23

Laura was blooming still, had made the best
  Of time, and time returned the compliment,
And treated her genteelly, so that, dressed,
  She looked extremely well where'er she went;   180
A pretty woman is a welcome guest,
  And Laura's brow a frown had rarely bent;
Indeed, she shone all smiles, and seemed to flatter
Mankind with her black eyes for looking at her.

24

She was a married woman; 'tis convenient,
  Because in Christian countries 'tis a rule   186
To view their little slips with eyes more lenient;
  Whereas if single ladies play the fool
(Unless within the period intervenient
  A well-timed wedding makes the scandal cool),   190
I don't know how they ever can get over it,
Except they manage never to discover it.[17]

25

Her husband sailed upon the Adriatic,
  And made some voyages, too, in other seas,
And when he lay in quarantine for pratique[18]
  (A forty days' precaution 'gainst disease),
His wife would mount, at times, her highest attic,   197
  For thence she could discern the ship with ease:
He was a merchant trading to Aleppo,
His name Giuseppe, called more briefly, Beppo.   200

26

He was a man as dusky as a Spaniard,
  Sunburnt with travel, yet a portly figure;
Though colored, as it were, within a tanyard,
  He was a person both of sense and vigor—

---

[16]A bridge, as the word is here used; more properly the island to which the bridge leads, on which is situated the Exchange.

[17]Never to let it be known.

[18]A clean bill of health after quarantine.

A better seaman never yet did man yard; 205
   And she, although her manners showed no
     rigor,
Was deemed a woman of the strictest prin-
     ciple,
So much as to be thought almost invincible.

27

But several years elapsed since they had met;
   Some people thought the ship was lost, and
     some 210
That he had somehow blundered into debt,
   And did not like the thought of steering
     home;
And there were several offered any bet,
   Or that he would, or that he would not
     come; 214
For most men (till by losing rendered sager)
Will back their own opinions with a wager.

28

'Tis said that their last parting was pathetic,
   As partings often are, or ought to be,
And their presentiment was quite prophetic,
   That they should never more each other
     see 220
(A sort of morbid feeling, half poetic,
   Which I have known occur in two or
     three),
When kneeling on the shore upon her sad
     knee
He left this Adriatic Ariadne.[19]

29

And Laura waited long, and wept a little, 225
   And thought of wearing weeds, as well she
     might;
She almost lost all appetite for victual,
   And could not sleep with ease alone at
     night;
She deemed the window-frames and shutters
     brittle
Against a daring housebreaker or sprite, 230
And so she thought it prudent to connect her
With a vice-husband, *chiefly to protect her*.

30

She chose (and what is there they will not
     choose,
   If only you will but oppose their choice),

Till Beppo should return from his long
     cruise, 235
And bid once more her faithful heart re-
     joice,
A man some women like, and yet abuse—
   A coxcomb was he by the public voice;
A Count of wealth, they said, as well as
     quality,
And in his pleasures of great liberality. 240

31

And then he was a Count, and then he knew
   Music, and dancing, fiddling, French and
     Tuscan;
The last not easy, be it known to you,
   For few Italians speak the right Etruscan.
He was a critic upon operas, too, 245
   And knew all niceties of sock and
     buskin;[20]
And no Venetian audience could endure a
   Song, scene, or air, when he cried "secca-
     tura!"[21]

32

His "bravo" was decisive, for that sound
   Hushed "Academie"[22] sighed in silent
     awe; 250
The fiddlers trembled as he looked around,
   For fear of some false note's detected
     flaw;
The "prima donna's" tuneful heart would
     bound,
   Dreading the deep damnation of his
     "bah!"
Soprano, basso, even the contra-alto, 255
Wished him five fathom under the Rialto.

33

He patronized the Improvisatori,[23]
   Nay, could himself extemporize some
     stanzas,
Wrote rimes, sang songs, could also tell a
     story,
   Sold pictures, and was skillful in the
     dance as 260
Italians can be, though in this their glory
   Must surely yield the palm to that which
     France has;
In short, he was a perfect cavaliero,
And to his very valet seemed a hero. 264

---

[19]Ariadne, daughter of Minos, King of Crete, loved Theseus and gave him the thread which guided him out of the Cretan Labyrinth. After he had been thus aided, however, Theseus deserted her.

[20]Of the comic and tragic stage.

[21]I. e., "It's a bore."

[22]Academies, i. e., literary societies.

[23]Performers who recited or sang verses composed extemporaneously.

34

Then he was faithful too, as well as amorous;
  So that no sort of female could complain,
Although they're now and then a little
    clamorous,
  He never put the pretty souls in pain;
His heart was one of those which most
    enamor us,
  Wax to receive, and marble to retain: 270
He was a lover of the good old school,
Who still become more constant as they cool.

35

No wonder such accomplishments should
    turn   273
  A female head, however sage and steady—
With scarce a hope that Beppo could return,
  In law he was almost as good as dead, he
Nor sent, nor wrote, nor showed the least
    concern,
  And she had waited several years already;
And really if a man won't let us know
That he's alive, he's *dead*—or should be
    so.   280

36

Besides, within[24] the Alps, to every woman
  (Although, God knows, it is a grievous
    sin),
'Tis, I may say, permitted to have *two* men;
  I can't tell who first brought the custom in,
But "Cavalier Serventes" are quite common,
  And no one notices nor cares a pin;   286
And we may call this (not to say the worst)
A *second* marriage which corrupts the *first*.

37

The word was formerly a "Cicisbeo,"
  But *that* is now grown vulgar and in-
    decent;
The Spaniards call the person a *"Cortejo,"*[25]
  For the same mode subsists in Spain,
    though recent;   292
In short, it reaches from the Po to Teio,[26]
  And may perhaps at last be o'er the sea
    sent:
But Heaven preserve Old England from
    such courses!   295
Or what becomes of damage and divorces?

38

However, I still think, with all due deference
  To the fair *single* part of the creation,

[24]I. e., south of.
[25]This and *cicisbeo* are, as Byron says, synonymous with *cavalier servente.*
[26]Teijo, or Tykö, is in Finland.

That married ladies should preserve the
    preference
  In *tête-à-tête* or general conversation—300
And this I say without peculiar reference
  To England, France, or any other nation—
Because they know the world, and are at
    ease,
And being natural, naturally please.

39

'Tis true, your budding Miss is very charm-
    ing,   305
  But shy and awkward at first coming out,
So much alarmed, that she is quite alarming,
  All giggle, blush; half pertness, and half
    pout;
And glancing at *Mamma,* for fear there's
    harm in   309
  What you, she, it, or they, may be about,
The nursery still lisps out in all they utter—
Besides, they always smell of bread and but-
    ter.

40

But "Cavalier Servente" is the phrase
  Used in politest circles to express
This supernumerary slave, who stays   315
  Close to the lady as a part of dress,
Her word the only law which she obeys.
  His is no sinecure, as you may guess;
Coach, servants, gondola, he goes to call,
And carries fan and tippet,[27] gloves and
    shawl.   320

41

With all its sinful doings, I must say,
  That Italy's a pleasant place to me,
Who love to see the Sun shine every day,
  And vines (not nailed to walls) from tree
    to tree
Festooned, much like the back scene of a
    play,   325
  Or melodrame, which people flock to see,
When the first act is ended by a dance
In vineyards copied from the south of
    France.

42

I like on Autumn evenings to ride out,
  Without being forced to bid my groom be
    sure   330
My cloak is round his middle strapped about,
  Because the skies are not the most secure;

[27]Scarf for neck and shoulders.

I know too that, if stopped upon my route,
   Where the green alleys windingly allure,
Reeling with *grapes* red wagons choke the
   way,—   335
In England 'twould be dung, dust, or a dray.

43

I also like to dine on becaficas,[28]
   To see the Sun set, sure he'll rise to-
      morrow,
Not through a misty morning twinkling
   weak as
   A drunken man's dead eye in maudlin
      sorrow,
But with all Heaven t' himself; the day will
   break as   341
   Beauteous as cloudless, nor be forced to
      borrow
That sort of farthing candlelight which glim-
   mers
Where reeking London's smoky caldron sim-
   mers.

44

I love the language, that soft bastard Latin,
   Which melts like kisses from a female
      mouth,   346
And sounds as if it should be writ on satin,
   With syllables which breathe of the sweet
      South,
And gentle liquids gliding all so pat in,
   That not a single accent seems uncouth, 350
Like our harsh northern whistling, grunting
   guttural,
Which we're obliged to hiss, and spit, and
   sputter all.

45

I like the women too (forgive my folly),
   From the rich peasant cheek of ruddy
      bronze,
And large black eyes that flash on you a
   volley   355
Of rays that say a thousand things at once,
To the high dama's[29] brow, more melan-
   choly,
   But clear, and with a wild and liquid
      glance,
Heart on her lips, and soul within her eyes,
Soft as her clime, and sunny as her skies. 360

46

Eve of the land which still is Paradise!
   Italian beauty! didst thou not inspire

[28]Song birds, particularly the garden warbler.
[29]Lady's.

Raphael, who died in thy embrace, and vies
   With all we know of Heaven, or can de-
      sire,
In what he hath bequeathed us?—in what
   guise,   365
   Though flashing from the fervor of the
      lyre,
Would *words* describe thy past and present
   glow,
While yet Canova[30] can create below?

47

"England! with all thy faults I love thee
   still,"[31]
   I said at Calais, and have not forgot it; 370
I like to speak and lucubrate my fill;
   I like the government (but that is not it);
I like the freedom of the press and quill;
   I like the Habeas Corpus (when we've got
      it);
I like a parliamentary debate,   375
Particularly when 'tis not too late;

48

I like the taxes, when they're not too many;
   I like a seacoal fire, when not too dear;
I like a beef-steak, too, as well as any;
   Have no objection to a pot of beer; 380
I like the weather, when it is not rainy,
   That is, I like two months of every year;
And so God save the Regent,[32] Church, and
   King!
Which means that I like all and everything.

49

Our standing army, and disbanded sea-
   men,   385
   Poor's rate, Reform, my own, the nation's
      debt,
Our little riots just to show we're free men,
   Our trifling bankruptcies in the Gazette,
Our cloudy climate, and our chilly women,
   All these I can forgive, and those forget,
And greatly venerate our recent glories, 391
And wish they were not owing to the Tories.

50

But to my tale of Laura—for I find,—
   Digression is a sin, that by degrees
Becomes exceeding tedious to my mind, 395
   And, therefore, may the reader too dis-
      please—

[30]Italian sculptor (1757–1822).
[31]Cowper, *The Task,* Bk. II, l. 206.
[32]The Prince of Wales, who served as Regent
during the closing years of George III's life, and
who ascended the throne as George IV in 1820.

The gentle reader, who may wax unkind,
  And caring little for the author's ease,
Insist on knowing what he means, a hard
And hapless situation for a bard.   400

51

Oh, that I had the art of easy writing
  What should be easy reading! could I scale
Parnassus, where the Muses sit inditing
  Those pretty poems never known to fail,
How quickly would I print (the world delighting)   405
  A Grecian, Syrian, or *Assyrian* tale;
And sell you, mixed with western sentimentalism,
Some samples of the *finest Orientalism.*[33]

52

But I am but a nameless sort of person,
  (A broken Dandy lately on my travels[34])
And take for rime, to hook my rambling verse on,   411
  The first that Walker's Lexicon unravels,
And when I can't find that, I put a worse on,
  Not caring as I ought for critics' cavils;
I've half a mind to tumble down to prose, 415
But verse is more in fashion—so here goes!

53

The Count and Laura made their new arrangement,
  Which lasted, as arrangements sometimes do,
For half a dozen years without estrangement;
  They had their little differences, too;   420
Those jealous whiffs, which never any change meant;
  In such affairs there probably are few
Who have not had this pouting sort of squabble,
From sinners of high station to the rabble.

54

But, on the whole, they were a happy pair, 425
  As happy as unlawful love could make them;

The gentleman was fond, the lady fair,
  Their chains so slight, 'twas not worth while to break them;
The world beheld them with indulgent air;
  The pious only wished "the devil take them!"   430
He took them not; he very often waits,
And leaves old sinners to be young ones' baits.

55

But they were young: Oh! what without our youth
  Would love be! What would youth be without love!
Youth lends its joy, and sweetness, vigor, truth,   435
  Heart, soul, and all that seems as from above;
But, languishing with years, it grows uncouth—
  One of few things experience don't improve,
Which is, perhaps, the reason why old fellows
Are always so preposterously jealous.   440

56

It was the Carnival, as I have said
  Some six and thirty stanzas back, and so
Laura the usual preparations made,
  Which you do when your mind's made up to go
To-night to Mrs. Boehm's masquerade,[35] 445
  Spectator, or partaker in the show;
The only difference known between the cases
Is—*here,* we have six weeks of "varnished faces."[36]

57

Laura, when dressed, was (as I sang before)
  A pretty woman as was ever seen,   450
Fresh as the Angel o'er a new inn door,
  Or frontispiece of a new Magazine,
With all the fashions which the last month wore,
  Colored, and silver paper leaved between
That and the title-page, for fear the press 455
Should soil with parts of speech the parts of dress.

[33]This, of course, Byron had done immediately after the success of the first two cantos of *Childe Harold.*

[34]The allusion is to *Childe Harold.*

[35]This event was reported in the *Morning Chronicle* of 17 June, 1817. "On Monday evening this distinguished lady of the *haut ton* gave a splendid masquerade at her residence in St. James's Square," *etc.*

[36]I. e., of masking.

58

They went to the Ridotto;—'tis a hall
  Where people dance, and sup, and dance
    again;
Its proper name, perhaps, were a masked
    ball,
  But that's of no importance to my strain;
'Tis (on a smaller scale) like our Vaux-
    hall,   461
  Excepting that it can't be spoiled by rain;
The company is "mixed" (the phrase I quote
    is
  As much as saying they're below your
    notice);

59

For a "mixed company" implies that, save
  Yourself and friends, and half a hundred
    more,   466
Whom you may bow to without looking
    grave,
  The rest are but a vulgar set, the bore
Of public places, where they basely brave
  The fashionable stare of twenty score 470
Of well-bred persons, called *"The World"*;
    but I,
Although I know them, really don't know
    why.

60

This is the case in England; at least was
  During the dynasty of Dandies,[37] now
Perchance succeeded by some other class 475
  Of imitated imitators:—how
Irreparably soon decline, alas!
  The demagogues of fashion: all below
Is frail, how easily the world is lost
  By love, or war, and, now and then—by
    frost!   480

61

Crushed was Napoleon by the northern
    Thor,[38]
  Who knocked his army down with icy
    hammer,
Stopped by the *elements,* like a whaler, or
  A blundering novice in his new French
    grammar;
Good cause had he to doubt the chance of
    war,   485
  And as for Fortune—but I dare not d—n
    her,

---
[37]It extended from about 1813 to 1830. Cf. Bk.
III, chaps. ix–x, of Carlyle's *Sartor Resartus,* and
notes, below.
[38]I. e., in his Russian campaign and disastrous
winter retreat from Moscow.

Because, were I to ponder to infinity,
The more I should believe in her divinity.

62

She rules the present, past, and all to be yet,
  She gives us luck in lotteries, love, and
    marriage;   490
I cannot say that she's done much for me
    yet;
  Not that I mean her bounties to disparage,
We've not yet closed accounts, and we shall
    see yet
  How much she'll make amends for past
    miscarriage;
Meantime the Goddess I'll no more impor-
    tune,   495
Unless to thank her when she's made my
    fortune.

63

To turn,—and to return;—the devil take it!
  This story slips for ever through my
    fingers,
Because, just as the stanza likes to make it,
  It needs must be, and so it rather lingers:
This form of verse began, I can't well break
    it,   501
  But must keep time and tune like public
    singers;
But if I once get through my present meas-
    ure,
I'll take another when I'm next at leisure.

64

They went to the Ridotto ('tis a place 505
  To which I mean to go myself to-morrow,
Just to divert my thoughts a little space,
  Because I'm rather hippish,[39] and may
    borrow
Some spirits, guessing at what kind of face
  May lurk beneath each mask; and as my
    sorrow   510
Slackens its pace sometimes, I'll make, or
    find,
Something shall leave it half an hour be-
    hind).

65

Now Laura moves along the joyous crowd,
  Smiles in her eyes, and simpers on her
    lips;   514
To some she whispers, others speaks aloud;
  To some she curtsies, and to some she
    dips,

---
[39]Colloquial, for hypochondriac.

Complains of warmth, and this complaint
avowed,
  Her lover brings the lemonade, she sips;
She then surveys, condemns, but pities still
  Her dearest friends for being dressed so
    ill. 520

66

One has false curls, another too much paint,
  A third—where did she buy that frightful
    turban?
A fourth's so pale she fears she's going to
  faint,
  A fifth's look's vulgar, dowdyish, and sub-
    urban,
A sixth's white silk has got a yellow taint, 525
  A seventh's thin muslin surely will be her
    bane,
And lo! an eighth appears,—"I'll see no
  more!"
For fear, like Banquo's kings,[40] they reach a
  score.

67

Meantime, while she was thus at others gaz-
  ing,
  Others were leveling their looks at her;
She heard the men's half-whispered mode of
  praising, 531
  And, till 'twas done, determined not to
    stir;
The women only thought it quite amazing
  That, at her time of life, so many were
Admirers still,—but "Men are so debased, 535
Those brazen creatures always suit their
  taste."

68

For my part, now, I ne'er could understand
  Why naughty women—but I won't discuss
A thing which is a scandal to the land,
  I only don't see why it should be thus; 540
And if I were but in a gown and band,
  Just to entitle me to make a fuss,
I'd preach on this till Wilberforce and Ro-
  milly[41]
Should quote in their next speeches from my
  homily.

69

While Laura thus was seen, and seeing,
  smiling, 545

---

[40]*Macbeth*, IV, i.

[41]William Wilberforce (1759–1833), statesman
and supporter of the anti-slavery cause, and Sir
Samuel Romilly (1757–1818), philanthropist and
criminal-law reformer.

Talking, she knew not why, and cared not
  what,
So that her female friends, with envy broil-
  ing,
  Beheld her airs and triumph, and all that;
And well-dressed males still kept before her
  filing,
  And passing bowed and mingled with her
    chat; 550
More than the rest one person seemed to
  stare
With pertinacity that's rather rare.

70

He was a Turk, the color of mahogany;
  And Laura saw him, and at first was glad,
Because the Turks so much admire phi-
  logyny,[42] 555
  Although their usage of their wives is sad;
'Tis said they use no better than a dog any
  Poor woman, whom they purchase like a
    pad;[43]
They have a number, though they ne'er ex-
  hibit 'em,
Four wives by law, and concubines "ad libi-
  tum."[44] 560

71

They lock them up, and veil, and guard them
  daily,
  They scarcely can behold their male rela-
    tions,
So that their moments do not pass so gaily
  As is supposed the case with northern na-
    tions;
Confinement, too, must make them look
  quite palely; 565
  And as the Turks abhor long conversa-
    tions,
Their days are either passed in doing noth-
  ing,
Or bathing, nursing, making love, and cloth-
  ing.

72

They cannot read, and so don't lisp in criti-
  cism;
  Nor write, and so they don't affect the
    muse; 570
Were never caught in epigram or witticism,
  Have no romances, sermons, plays, re-
    views,—

---

[42]Fondness for women.

[43]An easy-paced horse.

[44]As many as they please.

In harams learning soon would make a pretty
schism,
But luckily these beauties are no
"Blues";[45]
No bustling *Botherby*[46] have they to show
'em 575
"That charming passage in the last new
poem":

73

No solemn, antique gentleman of rime,
Who having angled all his life for fame,
And getting but a nibble at a time,
Still fussily keeps fishing on, the same 580
Small "Triton of the minnows," the sublime
Of mediocrity, the furious tame,
The echo's echo, usher of the school
Of female wits, boy bards—in short, a fool!

74

A stalking oracle of awful phrase, 585
The approving *"Good!"* (by no means
GOOD in law),
Humming like flies around the newest blaze,
The bluest of bluebottles you e'er saw,
Teasing with blame, excruciating with praise,
Gorging the little fame he gets all raw, 590
Translating tongues he knows not even by
letter,
And sweating plays so middling, bad were
better.

75

One hates an author that's *all author,* fellows
In foolscap uniforms turned up with ink,
So very anxious, clever, fine, and jealous, 595
One don't know what to say to them, or
think,
Unless to puff them with a pair of bellows;
Of coxcombry's worst coxcombs e'en the
pink
Are preferable to these shreds of paper,
These unquenched snuffings of the midnight
taper. 600

76

Of these same we see several, and of others,
Men of the world, who know the world
like men,

Scott, Rogers,[47] Moore, and all the better
brothers,
Who think of something else besides the
pen;
But for the children of the "mighty
mother's," 605
The would-be wits, and can't-be gentle-
men,
I leave them to their daily "tea is ready,"
Smug coterie, and literary lady.

77

The poor dear Mussul*women*[48] whom I
mention
Have none of these instructive pleasant
people, 610
And *one* would seem to them a new inven-
tion,
Unknown as bells within a Turkish
steeple;
I think 'twould almost be worth while to
pension
(Though best-sown projects very often
reap ill)
A missionary author, just to preach 615
Our Christian usage of the parts of speech.

78

No chemistry for them unfolds her gases,
No metaphysics are let loose in lectures,
No circulating library amasses
Religious novels, moral tales, and stric-
tures 620
Upon the living manners, as they pass us;
No exhibition glares with annual pictures;
They stare not on the stars from out their
attics,
Nor deal (thank God for that!) in mathe-
matics. 624

79

Why I thank God for that is no great matter,
I have my reasons, you no doubt suppose,
And as, perhaps, they would not highly
flatter,
I'll keep them for my life (to come) in
prose;
I fear I have a little turn for satire, 629
And yet methinks the older that one grows
Inclines us more to laugh than scold, though
laughter
Leave us so doubly serious shortly after.

---

[45]Bluestockings, literary or learned ladies.

[46]This stands for William Sotheby (1757-1833),
a poet and patron of men of letters. Byron had
mentioned him with approbation in *English Bards
and Scotch Reviewers,* but later disliked him because he thought Sotheby had anonymously attacked
his poetry. His final conclusion about Sotheby,
however, was, "a good man, rimes well (if not
wisely); but is a bore."

[47]Samuel Rogers, banker and poet (1763-1855).
[48]Mahometan women.

80

Oh, mirth and innocence! Oh, milk and
    water!
Ye happy mixtures of more happy days!
In these sad centuries of sin and slaughter, 635
    Abominable Man no more allays
His thirst with such pure beverage. No
    matter,
    I love you both, and both shall have my
      praise: 638
Oh, for old Saturn's reign of sugar-
    candy![49]—
Meantime I drink to your return in brandy.

81

Our Laura's Turk still kept his eyes upon
    her,
    Less in the Mussulman than Christian
      way,
Which seems to say, "Madam, I do you
    honor,
    And while I please to stare, you'll please
      to stay."
Could staring win a woman, this had won
    her, 645
    But Laura could not thus be led astray;
She had stood fire too long and well, to
    boggle
Even at this stranger's most outlandish ogle.

82

The morning now was on the point of break-
    ing,
    A turn of time at which I would advise 650
Ladies who have been dancing, or partaking
    In any other kind of exercise,
To make their preparations for forsaking
    The ball-room ere the sun begins to rise,
Because when once the lamps and candles
    fail, 655
His blushes make them look a little pale.

83

I've seen some balls and revels in my time,
    And stayed them over for some silly
      reason,
And then I looked (I hope it was no crime)
    To see what lady best stood out the sea-
      son, 660
And though I've seen some thousands in
    their prime,

Lovely and pleasing, and who still may
    please on,
I never saw but one (the stars withdrawn)
Whose bloom could after dancing dare the
    dawn.

84

The name of this Aurora I'll not mention, 665
    Although I might, for she was nought to
      me
More than that patent work of God's inven-
    tion,
    A charming woman, whom we like to see;
But writing names would merit reprehension,
    Yet if you like to find out this fair *she,* 670
At the next London or Parisian ball
You still may mark her cheek out-blooming
    all.

85

Laura, who knew it would not do at all
    To meet the daylight after seven hours'
      sitting
Among three thousand people at a ball, 675
    To make her curtsey thought it right and
      fitting;
The Count was at her elbow with her shawl,
    And they the room were on the point of
      quitting,
When lo! those curséd gondoliers had got
Just in the very place where they *should
    not.* 680

86

In this they're like our coachmen, and the
    cause
    Is much the same—the crowd, and pull-
      ing, hauling,
With blasphemies enough to break their
    jaws,
    They make a never intermitted bawling.
At home, our Bow-street gemmen[50] keep the
    laws, 685
    And here a sentry stands within your call-
      ing;
But for all that, there is a deal of swearing,
And nauseous words past mentioning or
    bearing.

87

The Count and Laura found their boat at
    last,
    And homeward floated o'er the silent tide,
Discussing all the dances gone and past; 691
    The dancers and their dresses, too, be-
      side;

---

[49]Saturn (or Cornus) was a Titan and his reign,
which lasted until he was displaced by his son
Zeus, coincided with the Golden Age of innocence,
peace, and plenty.

[50]Cockney "gentlemen."

Some little scandals eke; but all aghast
    (As to their palace-stairs the rowers glide)
Sat Laura by the side of her adorer,   695
When lo! the Mussulman was there before
    her.

88

"Sir," said the Count, with brow exceeding
    grave,
    "Your unexpected presence here will
      make
It necessary for myself to crave   699
    Its import? But perhaps 'tis a mistake;
I hope it is so; and, at once to waive
    All compliment, I hope so for *your* sake;"
You understand my meaning, or you *shall*."
"Sir" (quoth the Turk), " 'tis no mistake at
    all:

89

"That lady is *my wife!*" Much wonder
    paints   705
    The lady's changing cheek, as well it
      might;
But where an Englishwoman sometimes
    faints,
    Italian females don't do so outright;
They only call a little on their saints,
    And then come to themselves, almost or
      quite;   710
Which saves much hartshorn, salts, and
    sprinkling faces,
And cutting stays, as usual in such cases.

90

She said,—what could she say? Why, not
    a word;
    But the Count courteously invited in
The stranger, much appeased by what he
    heard: 715
    "Such things, perhaps, we'd best discuss
      within,"
Said he; "don't let us make ourselves absurd
    In public, by a scene, nor raise a din,
For then the chief and only satisfaction
Will be much quizzing on the whole trans-
    action."   720

91

They entered, and for coffee called—it came,
    A beverage for Turks and Christians both,
Although the way they make it's not the
    same.
    Now Laura, much recovered, or less loath

To speak, cries "Beppo! what's your pagan
    name?   725
    Bless me! your beard is of amazing
      growth!
And how came you to keep away so long?
Are you not sensible 'twas very wrong?

92

"And are you *really, truly,* now a Turk?
    With any other women did you wive? 730
Is't true they use their fingers for a fork?
    Well, that's the prettiest shawl—as I'm
      alive!
You'll give it me? They say you eat no
    pork.
    And how so many years did you contrive
To—Bless me! did I ever? No, I never 735
Saw a man grown so yellow! How's your
    liver?

93

"Beppo! that beard of yours becomes you
    not;
    It shall be shaved before you're a day
      older:
Why do you wear it? Oh! I had for-
    got—
    Pray don't you think the weather here is
      colder?   740
How do I look? You sha'n't stir from this
    spot
    In that queer dress, for fear that some be-
      holder
Should find you out, and make the story
    known.
How short your hair is! Lord! how gray
    it's grown!"   744

94

What answer Beppo made to these demands
    Is more than I know. He was cast away
About where Troy stood once, and nothing
    stands;
    Became a slave of course, and for his pay
Had bread and bastinadoes, till some bands
    Of pirates landing in a neighboring bay,
He joined the rogues and prospered, and be-
    came   751
    A renegado of indifferent fame.

95

But he grew rich, and with his riches grew so
    Keen the desire to see his home again, 754
He thought himself in duty bound to do so,
    And not be always thieving on the main;[51]

[51]On the high seas.

Lonely he felt, at times, as Robin Crusoe,
  And so he hired a vessel come from Spain,
Bound for Corfu: she was a fine polacca,[52]
Manned with twelve hands, and laden with
    tobacco.   760

96

Himself, and much (Heaven knows how
    gotten!) cash,
  He then embarked, with risk of life and
    limb,
And got clear off, although the attempt was
    rash;
  He said that *Providence* protected him—
For my part, I say nothing—lest we clash 765
  In our opinions:—well, the ship was trim,
Set sail, and kept her reckoning fairly on,
Except three days of calm when off Cape
    Bonn.[53]

97

They reached the island, he transferred his
    lading   769
  And self and live stock to another bottom,
And passed for a true Turkey-merchant,
    trading
  With goods of various names, but I've
    forgot 'em.
However, he got off by this evading,
  Or else the people would perhaps have
    shot him;

---

[52]Three-masted merchant vessel of the Mediterranean.

[53]The northernmost point of Tunis.

And thus at Venice landed to reclaim   775
His wife, religion, house, and Christian
    name.

98

His wife received, the Patriarch re-baptized
    him
  (He made the church a present, by the
    way);
He then threw off the garments which dis-
    guised him,
  And borrowed the Count's smallclothes
    for a day: 780
His friends the more for his long absence
    prized him,
  Finding he'd wherewithal to make them
    gay,
With dinners, where he oft became the laugh
    of them,
  For stories—but *I* don't believe the half of
    them.   784

99

Whate'er his youth had suffered, his old age
  With wealth and talking made him some
    amends;
Though Laura sometimes put him in a rage,
  I've heard the Count and he were always
    friends.
My pen is at the bottom of a page,   789
  Which being finished, here the story ends:
'Tis to be wished it had been sooner done,
But stories somehow lengthen when begun.

DON JUAN[1]

CANTO III

The Isles of Greece

I

The isles of Greece, the isles of Greece!
   Where burning Sappho loved and sung,
Where grew the arts of war and peace,
   Where Delos rose, and Phoebus sprung![2]
Eternal summer gilds them yet,   5
But all, except their sun, is set.

II

The Scian and the Teian muse,[3]
   The hero's harp, the lover's lute,

Have found the fame your shores refuse:
   Their place of birth alone is mute   10
To sounds which echo further west
Than your sires' "Islands of the Blest."[4]

III

The mountains look on Marathon[5]—
   And Marathon looks on the sea;
And musing there an hour alone,   15
   I dreamed that Greece might still be free;
For standing on the Persians' grave,
I could not deem myself a slave.

IV

A king[6] sat on the rocky brow
   Which looks o'er sea-born Salamis;   20
And ships, by thousands, lay below,
   And men in nations;—all were his!
He counted them at break of day—
And when the sun set where were they?

V

And where are they? and where art thou, 25
   My country? On thy voiceless shore
The heroic lay is tuneless now—
   The heroic bosom beats no more!
And must thy lyre, so long divine,
Degenerate into hands like mine?   30

VI

'Tis something, in the dearth of fame,
   Though linked among a fettered race,
To feel at least a patriot's shame,
   Even as I sing, suffuse my face;
For what is left the poet here?   35
For Greeks a blush—for Greece a tear.

VII

Must *we* but weep o'er days more blest?
   Must *we* but blush?—Our fathers bled.
Earth! render back from out thy breast
   A remnant of our Spartan dead!   40
Of the three hundred grant but three,
To make a new Thermopylae![7]

[1]Written at intervals from 1818 to 1823 and published in 1819–1824, save for a fragment—the unfinished seventeenth canto—published in 1903. Byron took the name of his hero from a Spanish traditional story concerning the libertinism of one Don Juan Tenorio. But he took little more than the name, practically disregarding both the original Spanish dramatization of the story and the later French and Italian adaptations. When he had finished the first canto Byron wrote to Moore that his new poem was "meant to be a little quietly facetious upon everything." It was that—and more. For, as Byron went on, the work grew upon him and developed into a satirical picture of European aristocracy and politics. When he had completed the fifth canto he wrote to Murray, his publisher: "The 5th is so far from being the last of *D. J.* that it is hardly the beginning. I meant to take him the tour of Europe, with a proper mixture of siege, battle, and adventure, and to make him finish as Anacharsis Cloots in the French Revolution [who was executed in 1794]. To how many cantos this may extend, I know not, nor whether (even if I live) I shall complete it; but this was my notion: I meant to have him a Cavalier Servente in Italy, and a cause for a divorce in England, and a Sentimental "Werther-faced man" in Germany, so as to show the different ridicules of the society in each of those countries, and to have displayed him gradually *gâté* and *blasé* [growing tainted and dulled] as he grew older, as is natural. But I had not quite fixed whether to make him end in Hell, or in an unhappy marriage, not knowing which would be the severest. The Spanish tradition says Hell: but it is probably only an Allegory of the other state." In pursuance of this sufficiently elastic plan Byron wrote sixteen cantos, and had begun a seventeenth before he died, leaving the poem unfinished. The passages from the third and fourth cantos here printed are not sufficient to give any fair idea of the variety, the buoyancy, the largeness and force, and the human truth of *Don Juan*. They are justly famous passages, however, and within their limits may at least serve to illustrate some of the salient characteristics of the poem.

[2]Delos was said to have risen from the waves of the Aegean and to have been the birthplace of Phoebus Apollo.

[3]Homer, said to have been born on the island of Scio, and Anacreon, in Teos, Asia Minor.

[4]Mythical islands said to lie in the "Western Ocean," where those favored of the gods dwelt in happiness after death.

[5]The plain where the Greeks under Miltiades defeated the Persians (B. C. 490).

[6]Xerxes, King of Persia, whose fleet was defeated by the Greeks in the battle of Salamis (B. C. 480).

[7]The mountain pass where three hundred Spartans heroically opposed the advance of Xerxes' army (B. C. 480).

VIII

What, silent still? and silent all?
  Ah! no;—the voices of the dead
Sound like a distant torrent's fall,   45
  And answer, "Let one living head,
But one arise,—we come, we come!"
'Tis but the living who are dumb.

IX

In vain—in vain: strike other chords;
  Fill high the cup with Samian wine![8]   50
Leave battles to the Turkish hordes,
  And shed the blood of Scio's vine!
Hark! rising to the ignoble call—
How answers each bold Bacchanal!

X

You have the Pyrrhic dance as yet;   55
  Where is the Pyrrhic phalanx gone?[9]
Of two such lessons, why forget
  The nobler and the manlier one?
You have the letters Cadmus[10] gave—
Think ye he meant them for a slave?   60

XI

Fill high the bowl with Samian wine!
  We will not think of themes like these!
It made Anacreon's song divine:
  He served—but served Polycrates—
A tyrant; but our masters then   65
Were still, at least, our countrymen.

XII

The tyrant of the Chersonese
  Was freedom's best and bravest friend;
That tyrant was Miltiades!
  Oh! that the present hour would lend   70
Another despot of the kind!
Such chains as his were sure to bind.

XIII

Fill high the bowl with Samian wine!
  On Suli's rock, and Parga's shore,[11]
Exists the remnant of a line   75
  Such as the Doric mothers bore;
And there, perhaps, some seed is sown,
The Heracleidan blood[12] might own.

XIV

Trust not for freedom to the Franks—
  They have a king who buys and sells;   80
In native swords, and native ranks,
  The only hope of courage dwells:
But Turkish force, and Latin fraud,
Would break your shield, however broad.

XV

Fill high the bowl with Samian wine!   85
  Our virgins dance beneath the shade—
I see their glorious black eyes shine;
  But gazing on each glowing maid,
My own the burning tear-drop laves,
To think such breasts must suckle slaves.   90

XVI

Place me on Sunium's marbled steep,[13]
  Where nothing, save the waves and I,
May hear our mutual murmurs sweep;
  There, swan-like, let me sing and die:
A land of slaves shall ne'er be mine—   95
Dash down yon cup of Samian wine!

87

Thus sung, or would, or could, or should
    have sung,
  The modern Greek, in tolerable verse;[14]
If not like Orpheus quite, when Greece was
    young,
  Yet in these times he might have done
    much worse: 100
His strain displayed some feeling—right or
    wrong;
  And feeling, in a poet, is the source
Of others' feeling; but they are such liars,
And take all colors—like the hands of dyers.

88

But words are things, and a small drop of
    ink,
  Falling like dew, upon a thought, produces
That which makes thousands, perhaps mil-
    lions, think;   107
  'Tis strange, the shortest letter which man
    uses

---

[8]Anacreon, the poet of love and wine, lived at Samos.

[9]The former an ancient war dance, the latter a military formation used by Pyrrhus.

[10]A legendary figure reputed to have introduced the alphabet into Greece from Phoenicia.

[11]Places in Albania.

[12]The blood of Hercules.

[13]The promontory of Sunium, at the southern extremity of Attica.

[14]Juan, surviving shipwreck, had found himself on an island where lived Haidée, the daughter of a pirate, Lambro, who then was at sea. Juan and Haidée had fallen in love with each other and, supposing Lambro dead, were expending his treasures in feasting and revelry. One of Haidée's retinue was a poet, who is described in stanzas immediately preceding *The Isles of Greece*, and who "thus sung, or would, or could, or should have sung."

Instead of speech, may form a lasting link
  Of ages; to what straits old Time re-
    duces   110
Frail man, when paper—even a rag like this,
Survives himself, his tomb, and all that's
    his!

89

And when his bones are dust, his grave a
    blank,
  His station, generation, even his nation,
Become a thing, or nothing, save to rank 115
  In chronological commemoration,
Some dull MS. oblivion long has sank,
  Or graven stone found in a barrack's sta-
    tion
In digging the foundation of a closet,
May turn his name up, as a rare deposit. 120

90

And glory long has made the sages smile;
  'Tis something, nothing, words, illusion,
    wind—
Depending more upon the historian's style
Than on the name a person leaves behind:
Troy owes to Homer what whist owes to
    Hoyle:[15]   125
  The present century was growing blind
To the great Marlborough's skill in giving
    knocks,
Until his late Life by Archdeacon Coxe.[16]

91

Milton's the prince of poets—so we say;
  A little heavy, but no less divine: 130
An independent being in his day—
  Learned, pious, temperate in love and
    wine;
But his life falling into Johnson's way,[17]
  We're told this great high priest of all the
    Nine[18]
Was whipped at college—a harsh sire—odd
    spouse,   135
For the first Mrs. Milton left his house.

92

All these are, *certes,* entertaining facts,
  Like Shakespeare's stealing deer, Lord
    Bacon's bribes;

---

[15]Edmund Hoyle (1672-1769).

[16]William Coxe (1747-1828), published his *Life*
of the victor of Blenheim in 1817-1819.

[17]When Johnson was writing his *Lives of the
English Poets.*

[18]The Nine Muses.

Like Titus'[19] youth, and Caesar's earliest
    acts;
  Like Burns (whom Doctor Currie well
    describes);   140
Like Cromwell's pranks;—but although
    truth exacts
These amiable descriptions from the
    scribes,
As most essential to their hero's story,
They do not much contribute to his glory.

93

All are not moralists, like Southey, when 145
  He prated to the world of "Pantisoc-
    racy";[20]
Or Wordsworth unexcised, unhired, who
    then
  Seasoned his peddler poems with democ-
    racy;
Or Coleridge, long before his flighty pen
  Let to the Morning Post its aristocracy;150
When he and Southey, following the same
    path,
Espoused two partners (milliners of Bath).

94

Such names at present cut a convict figure,
  The very Botany Bay[21] in moral geog-
    raphy;
Their loyal treason, renegado rigor,   155
  Are good manure for their more bare
    biography;
Wordsworth's last quarto, by the way, is
    bigger
  Than any since the birthday of typog-
    raphy;
A drowsy, frowsy poem, called the "Excur-
    sion,"
Writ in a manner which is my aversion. 160

95

He there builds up a formidable dyke
  Between his own and others' intellect;
But Wordsworth's poem, and his followers,
    like
  Joanna Southcote's Shiloh[22] and her sect,

---

[19]Titus Vespasianus, who as a youth learned the
art of forgery.

[20]See the introductory note prefixed to Coleridge's
poems, above. Southey, Wordsworth, and Coleridge all were believers in democracy in their youth
but became more conservative in their views as they
grew older.

[21]Australian penal colony.

[22]She had prophesied that on 19 October, 1814, she
would give birth to a second Shilo, or Messiah.
This she failed to do, and shortly afterwards she
died of dropsy.

Are things which in this century don't strike
  The public mind,—so few are the elect; 166
And the new births of both their stale vir-
  ginities
Have proved but dropsies, taken for divin-
  ities.

96

But let me to my story: I must own,
  If I have any fault, it is digression, 170
Leaving my people to proceed alone,
  While I soliloquize beyond expression:
But these are my addresses from the throne,
  Which put off business to the ensuing ses-
    sion:
Forgetting each omission is a loss to 175
The world, not quite so great as Ariosto.

97

I know that what our neighbors call *"lon-
  gueurs,"*[23]
  (We've not so good a *word,* but have the
    thing,
In that complete perfection which insures
  An epic from Bob Southey every
    spring—) 180
Form not the true temptation which allures
  The reader; but 'twould not be hard to
    bring
Some fine examples of the *epopée,*[24]
To prove its grand ingredient is *ennui.*

98

We learn from Horace, "Homer sometimes
  sleeps";[25] 185
  We feel without him,—Wordsworth some-
    times wakes,—
To show with what complacency he creeps,
  With his dear *"Wagoners,"* around his
    lakes.
He wishes for "a boat" to sail the deeps—
  Of ocean?—No, of air; and then he makes
Another outcry for "a little boat,"[26] 191
And drivels seas to set it well afloat.

99

If he must fain sweep o'er the ethereal plain,
  And Pegasus runs restive in his "Wagon,"

Could he not beg the loan of Charles's
  Wain?[27] 195
  Or pray Medea for a single dragon?
Or if, too classic for his vulgar brain,
  He feared his neck to venture such a nag
    on,
And he must needs mount nearer to the
    moon,
Could not the blockhead ask for a balloon?200

100

"Peddlers,"[28] and "Boats," and "Wagons"!
  Oh! ye shades
  Of Pope and Dryden, are we come to
    this?
That trash of such sort not alone evades
  Contempt, but from the bathos' vast abyss
Floats scumlike uppermost, and these Jack
  Cades[29] 205
  Of sense and song above your graves may
    hiss—
The "little boatman" and his "Peter Bell"
Can sneer at him who drew "Achitophel"!

101

T' our tale.—The feast was over, the slaves
  gone,
  The dwarfs and dancing girls had all re-
    tired; 210
The Arab lore and poet's song were done,
  And every sound of revelry expired,
The lady and her lover, left alone,
  The rosy flood of twilight's sky ad-
    mired;—
Ave Maria! o'er the earth and sea, 215
That heavenliest hour of Heaven is worthiest
  thee!

102

Ave Maria! blesséd be the hour!
  The time, the clime, the spot, where I so
    oft
Have felt that moment in its fullest power
  Sink o'er the earth, so beautiful and
    soft, 220
While swung the deep bell in the distant
    tower,
  Or the faint dying day-hymn stole aloft,
And not a breath crept through the rosy air,
And yet the forest leaves seemed stirred with
  prayer.

[23]Tedious things.   [24]Epic poem.

[25]*Ars Poetica,* l. 359.

[26]See the opening stanza of *Peter Bell. The Wagoner* was a narrative poem of Wordsworth's, dealing with the inhabitants and landscape of the English Lake Country.

[27]Charles's wagon, the constellation also known as the Dipper.

[28]One of the most important figures in Wordsworth's *Excursion* is a peddler.

[29]Jack Cade was the leader of a popular rebellion in the fifteenth century.

103

Ave Maria! 'tis the hour of prayer!   225
　　Ave Maria! 'tis the hour of love!
Ave Maria! may our spirits dare
　　Look up to thine and to thy Son's above!
Ave Maria! oh that face so fair!
　　Those downcast eyes beneath the Almighty
　　　　Dove—   230
What though 'tis but a pictured image?—
　　strike—
That painting is no idol,—'tis too like.

104

Some kinder casuists are pleased to say,
　　In nameless print—that I have no devo-
　　　　tion;   234
But set those persons down with me to pray,
　　And you shall see who has the properest
　　　　notion
Of getting into heaven the shortest way;
　　My altars are the mountains and the ocean,
Earth, air, stars,—all that springs from the
　　great Whole,   239
Who hath produced, and will receive the soul.

105

Sweet hour of twilight!—in the solitude
　　Of the pine forest, and the silent shore
Which bounds Ravenna's immemorial wood,
　　Rooted where once the Adrian wave flowed
　　　　o'er,
To where the last Caesarean fortress
　　stood,   245
　　Evergreen forest! which Boccaccio's lore
And Dryden's lay[30] made haunted ground to
　　me,
How have I loved the twilight hour and thee!

106

The shrill cicalas, people of the pine,
　　Making their summer lives one ceaseless
　　　　song,   250
Were the sole echoes, save my steed's and
　　mine,
　　And vesper bell's that rose the boughs
　　　　along;
The specter huntsman of Onesti's[31] line,
　　His hell-dogs, and their chase, and the
　　　　fair throng
Which learned from this example not to
　　fly   255
From a true lover,—shadowed my mind's
　　eye.

---

[30]Dryden's *Theodore and Honoria* is an adaptation of the eighth tale of the fifth day of Boccaccio's *Decameron*.

[31]Dryden's Theodore is Boccaccio's Onesti.

107

Oh, Hesperus! thou bringest all good
　　things—
　　Home to the weary, to the hungry cheer,
To the young bird the parent's brooding
　　wings,   259
　　The welcome stall to the o'erlabored steer;
Whate'er of peace about our hearthstone
　　clings,
　　Whate'er our household gods protect of
　　　　dear,
Are gathered round us by thy look of rest;
Thou bring'st the child, too, to the mother's
　　breast.

108

Soft hour! which wakes the wish and melts
　　the heart   265
　　Of those who sail the seas, on the first day
When they from their sweet friends are torn
　　apart;
　　Or fills with love the pilgrim on his way
As the far bell of vesper makes him start,
　　Seeming to weep the dying day's decay; 270
Is this a fancy which our reason scorns?
Ah! surely nothing dies but something
　　mourns!

CANTO IV

12

"Whom the gods love die young" was said of
　　yore,[32]
　　And many deaths do they escape by this:
The death of friends, and that which slays
　　even more—
　　The death of friendship, love, youth, all
　　　　that is,
Except mere breath; and since the silent
　　shore   5
　　Awaits at last even those who longest miss
The old archer's shafts, perhaps the early
　　grave
Which men weep over may be meant to save.

13

Haidée and Juan thought not of the dead.
　　The heavens, and earth, and air, seemed
　　　　made for them: 10
They found no fault with Time, save that he
　　fled;
　　They saw not in themselves aught to con-
　　　　demn;

---

[32]The statement is found among the fragments of Menander, in Plautus's *Bacchides*, IV, vii, 18–19. and elsewhere.

Each was the other's mirror, and but read
  Joy sparkling in their dark eyes like a gem,
And knew such brightness was but the re-
  flection   15
Of their exchanging glances of affection.

14

The gentle pressure, and the thrilling touch,
  The least glance better understood than
    words,
Which still said all, and ne'er could say too
  much;
  A language, too, but like to that of birds, 20
Known but to them, at least appearing such
  As but to lovers a true sense affords;
Sweet playful phrases, which would seem
  absurd
To those who have ceased to hear such, or
  ne'er heard.

15

All these were theirs, for they were children
  still,   25
  And children still they should have ever
    been;
They were not made in the real world to fill
  A busy character in the dull scene,
But like two beings born from out a rill,
  A nymph and her belovéd, all unseen 30
To pass their lives in fountains and on
  flowers,
And never know the weight of human hours.

16

Moons changing had rolled on, and change-
  less found
  Those their bright rise had lighted to such
    joys   34
As rarely they beheld throughout their round;
  And these were not of the vain kind which
    cloys,
For theirs were buoyant spirits, never bound
  By the mere senses; and that which
    destroys
Most love, possession, unto them appeared
A thing which each endearment more en-
  deared.   40

17

Oh beautiful! and rare as beautiful!
  But theirs was love in which the mind de-
    lights
To lose itself, when the old world grows dull,
  And we are sick of its hack sounds and
    sights,   44

Intrigues, adventures of the common school,
  Its petty passions, marriages, and flights,
Where Hymen's torch but brands one strum-
  pet more,
Whose husband only knows her not a whore.

18

Hard words—harsh truth! a truth which
  many know.   49
  Enough.—The faithful and the fairy pair,
Who never found a single hour too slow,
  What was it made them thus exempt from
    care?
Young innate feelings all have felt below,
  Which perish in the rest, but in them were
Inherent—what we mortals call romantic, 55
And always envy, though we deem it frantic.

19

This is in others a factitious state,
  An opium dream of too much youth and
    reading,
But was in them their nature or their fate:
  No novels e'er had set their young hearts
    bleeding,   60
For Haidée's knowledge was by no means
  great,
  And Juan was a boy of saintly breeding;
So that there was no reason for their loves
More than for those of nightingales or doves.

20

They gazed upon the sunset; 'tis an hour 65
  Dear unto all, but dearest to *their* eyes,
For it had made them what they were: the
  power
  Of love had first o'erwhelmed them from
    such skies,
When happiness had been their only dower,
  And twilight saw them linked in passion's
    ties;   70
Charmed with each other, all things charmed
  that brought
The past still welcome as the present thought.

21

I know not why, but in that hour to-night,
  Even as they gazed, a sudden tremor came,
And swept, as 'twere, across their hearts'
  delight,   75
  Like the wind o'er a harp-string, or a
    flame,
When one is shook in sound, and one in sight.
  And thus some boding flashed through
    either frame,

And called from Juan's breast a faint low
　　sigh,
While one new tear arose in Haidée's eye. 80

22

That large black prophet eye seemed to dilate
　　And follow far the disappearing sun,
As if their last day of a happy date
　　With his broad, bright, and dropping orb
　　　were gone.
Juan gazed on her as to ask his fate— 85
　　He felt a grief, but knowing cause for
　　none,
His glance inquired of hers for some excuse
For feelings causeless, or at least abstruse.

23

She turned to him, and smiled, but in that
　　sort
　　Which makes not others smile ; then turned
　　aside : 90
Whatever feeling shook her, it seemed short,
　　And mastered by her wisdom or her pride ;
When Juan spoke, too—it might be in sport—
　　Of this their mutual feeling, she replied—
"If it should be so,—but—it cannot be— 95
Or I at least shall not survive to see."

24

Juan would question further, but she pressed
　　His lips to hers, and silenced them with
　　this,
And then dismissed the omen from her
　　breast,
　　Defying augury with that fond kiss ; 100
And no doubt of all methods 'tis the best :
　　Some people prefer wine—'tis not amiss ;
I have tried both ; so those who would a
　　part take
May choose between the headache and the
　　heartache.

25

One of the two, according to your choice, 105
　　Woman or wine, you'll have to undergo ;
Both maladies are taxes on our joys :
　　But which to choose, I really hardly know ;
And if I had to give a casting voice,
　　For both sides I could many reasons show,
And then decide, without great wrong to
　　either, 111
It were much better to have both than
　　neither.

26

Juan and Haidée gazed upon each other
　　With swimming looks of speechless ten-
　　derness,
Which mixed all feelings, friend, child, lover,
　　brother ; 115
　　All that the best can mingle and express
When two pure hearts are poured in one an-
　　other,
　　And love too much, and yet cannot love
　　less ;
But almost sanctify the sweet excess
By the immortal wish and power to bless. 120

27

Mixed in each other's arms, and heart in
　　heart,
　　Why did they not then die?—they had
　　lived too long
Should an hour come to bid them breathe
　　apart ;
　　Years could but bring them cruel things
　　or wrong ;
The world was not for them, nor the world's
　　art 125
　　For beings passionate as Sappho's song ;
Love was born *with* them, *in* them, so intense,
It was their very spirit—not a sense.

28

They should have lived together deep in
　　woods, 129
　　Unseen as sings the nightingale ; they were
Unfit to mix in these thick solitudes
　　Called social, haunts of hate, and vice, and
　　care ;
How lonely every freeborn creature broods !
　　The sweetest song-birds nestle in a pair ;
The eagle soars alone ; the gull and crow 135
Flock o'er their carrion, just like men below.

29

Now pillowed cheek to cheek, in loving sleep,
　　Haidée and Juan their siesta took,
A gentle slumber, but it was not deep,
　　For ever and anon a something shook 140
Juan, and shuddering o'er his frame would
　　creep ;
　　And Haidée's sweet lips murmured like a
　　brook
A wordless music, and her face so fair
Stirred with her dream, as rose-leaves with
　　the air.

30

Or as the stirring of a deep clear stream 145
　Within an Alpine hollow, when the wind
Walks o'er it, was she shaken by the dream,
　The mystical usurper of the mind—
O'erpowering us to be whate'er may seem
　Good to the soul which we no more can
　　bind: 150
Strange state of being! (for 'tis still to be)
Senseless to feel, and with sealed eyes to see.

31

She dreamed of being alone on the sea-shore,
　Chained to a rock; she knew not how, but
　　stir 154
She could not from the spot, and the loud
　　roar
　Grew, and each wave rose roughly, threat-
　　ening her;
And o'er her upper lip they seemed to pour,
　Until she sobbed for breath, and soon they
　　were
Foaming o'er her lone head, so fierce and
　　high—
Each broke to drown her, yet she could not
　　die. 160

32

Anon—she was released, and then she strayed
　O'er the sharp shingles with her bleeding
　　feet,
And stumbled almost every step she made;
　And something rolled before her in a sheet,
Which she must still pursue howe'er afraid:
　'Twas white and indistinct, nor stopped to
　　meet 166
Her glance nor grasp, for still she gazed and
　　grasped,
And ran, but it escaped her as she clasped.

33

The dream changed:—in a cave she stood, its
　　walls
　Were hung with marble icicles; the work
Of ages on its water-fretted halls, 171
　Where waves might wash, and seals might
　　breed and lurk;
Her hair was dripping, and the very balls
　Of her black eyes seemed turned to tears,
　　and mirk
The sharp rocks looked below each drop they
　　caught, 175
Which froze to marble as it fell,—she
　　thought.

34

And wet, and cold, and lifeless at her feet,
　Pale as the foam that frothed on his dead
　　brow,
Which she essayed in vain to clear (how
　　sweet
　Were once her cares, how idle seemed they
　　now!), 180
Lay Juan, nor could aught renew the beat
　Of his quenched heart; and the sea dirges
　　low
Rang in her sad ears like a mermaid's song,
And that brief dream appeared a life too
　　long.

35

And gazing on the dead, she thought his
　　face 185
　Faded, or altered into something new—
Like to her father's features, till each trace
　More like and like to Lambro's aspect
　　grew—
With all his keen worn look and Grecian
　　grace; 189
　And starting, she awoke, and what to view?
Oh! Powers of Heaven! what dark eye
　　meets she there?
'Tis—'tis her father's—fixed upon the pair!

36

Then shrieking, she arose, and shrieking fell,
　With joy and sorrow, hope and fear, to
　　see 194
Him whom she deemed a habitant where
　　dwell
　The ocean-buried, risen from death, to be
Perchance the death of one she loved too
　　well:
　Dear as her father had been to Haidée,
It was a moment of that awful kind—— 199
I have seen such—but must not call to mind.

37

Up Juan sprang to Haidée's bitter shriek,
　And caught her falling, and from off the
　　wall
Snatched down his saber, in hot haste to
　　wreak
　Vengeance on him who was the cause of
　　all:
Then Lambro, who till now forebore to
　　speak,
　Smiled scornfully, and said, "Within my
　　call, 206
A thousand scimitars await the word;
Put up, young man, put up your silly sword."

38

And Haidée clung around him; "Juan, 'tis—
  'Tis Lambro—'tis my father! Kneel with
  me— 210
He will forgive us—yes—it must be—yes.
  Oh! dearest father, in this agony
Of pleasure and of pain—even while I kiss
  Thy garment's hem with transport, can it
  be
That doubt should mingle with my filial
  joy? 215
Deal with me as thou wilt, but spare this
  boy."

39

High and inscrutable the old man stood,
  Calm in his voice, and calm within his
  eye—
Not always signs with him of calmest mood:
  He looked upon her, but gave no reply; 220
Then turned to Juan, in whose cheek the
  blood
  Oft came and went, as there resolved to
  die;
In arms, at least, he stood, in act to spring
On the first foe whom Lambro's call might
  bring.

40

"Young man, your sword"; so Lambro once
  more said: 225
  Juan replied, "Not while this arm is free."
The old man's cheek grew pale, but not with
  dread,
  And drawing from his belt a pistol, he
Replied, "Your blood be then on your own
  head."
  Then looked close at the flint, as if to
  see 230
'Twas fresh—for he had lately used the
  lock—
And next proceeded quietly to cock.

41

It has a strange quick jar upon the ear,
  That cocking of a pistol, when you know
A moment more will bring the sight to bear
  Upon your person, twelve yards off, or
  so; 236
A gentlemanly distance, not too near,
  If you have got a former friend for foe;
But after being fired at once or twice,
The ear becomes more Irish, and less nice. 240

42

Lambro presented, and one instant more
  Had stopped this Canto, and Don Juan's
  breath,
When Haidée threw herself her boy before;
  Stern as her sire: "On me," she cried, "let
  death
Descend—the fault is mine; this fatal shore
  He found—but sought not. I have
  pledged my faith; 246
I love him—I will die with him: I knew
Your nature's firmness—know your daugh-
  ter's too."

43

A minute past, and she had been all tears,
  And tenderness, and infancy; but now 250
She stood as one who championed human
  fears—
  Pale, statue-like, and stern, she wooed the
  blow;
And tall beyond her sex, and their compeers,
  She drew up to her height, as if to show
A fairer mark; and with a fixed eye scanned
Her father's face—but never stopped his
  hand. 256

44

He gazed on her, and she on him; 'twas
  strange
  How like they looked! the expression was
  the same;
Serenely savage, with a little change
  In the large dark eye's mutual-darted
  flame; 260
For she, too, was as one who could avenge,
  If cause should be—a lioness, though
  tame.
Her father's blood before her father's face
Boiled up, and proved her truly of his race.

45

I said they were alike, their features and 265
  Their stature, differing but in sex and
  years:
Even to the delicacy of their hand
There was resemblance, such as true blood
  wears;
And now to see them, thus divided, stand
  In fixed ferocity, when joyous tears 270
And sweet sensations should have welcomed
  both,
Shows what the passions are in their full
  growth.

46

The father paused a moment, then withdrew
  His weapon, and replaced it; but stood
    still,
And looking on her, as to look her through, 275
  "Not *I*," he said, "have sought this
    stranger's ill;
Not *I* have made this desolation: few
  Would bear such outrage, and forbear to
    kill;
But I must do my duty—how thou hast 279
Done thine, the present vouches for the past.

47

"Let him disarm, or, by my father's head,
  His own shall roll before you like a ball!"
He raised his whistle as the word he said,
  And blew; another answered to the call,
And rushing in disorderly, though led, 285
  And armed from boot to turban, one and
    all,
Some twenty of his train came, rank on rank;
He gave the word, "Arrest or slay the
    Frank."

48

Then, with a sudden movement, he withdrew
  His daughter; while compressed within his
    clasp, 290
'Twixt her and Juan interposed the crew;
  In vain she struggled in her father's
    grasp—
His arms were like a serpent's coil: then flew
  Upon their prey, as darts an angry asp,
The file of pirates—save the foremost,
  who 295
Had fallen, with his right shoulder half cut
  through.

49

The second had his cheek laid open; but
  The third, a wary, cool old sworder, took
The blows upon his cutlass, and then put 299
  His own well in; so well, ere you could
    look,
His man was floored, and helpless at his foot,
  With the blood running like a little brook
From two smart saber gashes, deep and red—
One on the arm, the other on the head.

50

And then they bound him where he fell, and
  bore 305
  Juan from the apartment; with a sign

Old Lambro bade them take him to the shore,
  Where lay some ships which were to sail
    at nine.
They laid him in a boat, and plied the oar
  Until they reached some galliots,[33] placed
    in line; 310
On board of one of these, and under hatches,
They stowed him, with strict orders to the
  watches.

51

The world is full of strange vicissitudes,
  And here was one exceedingly unpleasant:
A gentleman so rich in the world's goods, 315
  Handsome and young, enjoying all the
    present,
Just at the very time when he least broods
  On such a thing, is suddenly to sea sent,
Wounded and chained, so that he cannot
  move,
And all because a lady fell in love. 320

52

Here I must leave him, for I grow pathetic,
  Moved by the Chinese nymph of tears,
    green tea!
Than whom Casandra was not more pro-
    phetic;
  For if my pure libations exceed three,
I feel my heart become so sympathetic, 325
  That I must have recourse to black
    Bohea:[34]
'Tis pity wine should be so deleterious,
For tea and coffee leave us much more
  serious,

53

Unless when qualified with thee, Cogniac![35]
  Sweet Naïad of the Phlegethontic rill![36] 330
Ah! why the liver wilt thou thus attack,
  And make, like other nymphs, thy lovers
    ill?
I would take refuge in weak punch, but *rack*
  (In each sense[37] of the word), whene'er
    I fill
My mild and midnight beakers to the brim, 335
Wakes me next morning with its synonym.

---

[33]Small swift galleys.

[34]Another variety of tea.

[35]French brandy made from wine produced near
the town of Cognac.

[36]Phlegethon: a river of Hades containing fire instead of water.

[37]I. e., "punch" and "suffering."

54

I leave Don Juan for the present, safe—
   Not sound, poor fellow, but severely
      wounded;
Yet could his corporal pangs amount to half
   Of those with which his Haidée's bosom
      bounded!   340
She was not one to weep, and rave, and chafe,
   And then give way, subdued because sur-
      rounded;
Her mother was a Moorish maid from Fez,[38]
Where all is Eden, or a wilderness.

55

There the large olive rains its amber store 345
   In marble fonts; there grain, and flour,
      and fruit,
Gush from the earth until the land runs o'er;
   But there, too, many a poison-tree has root,
And midnight listens to the lion's roar,
   And long, long deserts scorch the camel's
      foot,   350
Or heaving whelm the helpless caravan;
And as the soil is, so the heart of man.

56

Afric is all the sun's, and as her earth
   Her human clay is kindled; full of power
For good or evil, burning from its birth, 355
   The Moorish blood partakes the planet's
      hour,
And like the soil beneath it will bring forth:
   Beauty and love were Haidée's mother's
      dower;
But her large dark eye showed deep Passion's
      force,
Though sleeping like a lion near a source. 360

57

Her daughter, tempered with a milder ray,
   Like summer clouds all silvery, smooth,
      and fair,
Till slowly charged with thunder they display
   Terror to earth, and tempest to the air,
Had held till now her soft and milky way; 365
   But overwrought with passion and despair,
The fire burst forth from her Numidian
      veins,
Even as the Simoom[39] sweeps the blasted
      plains.

[38] In Morocco.

[39] A dry, hot, violent, dust-laden wind.

58

The last sight which she saw was Juan's
      gore,
   And he himself o'ermastered and cut
      down;
His blood was running on the very floor 371
   Where late he trod, her beautiful, her own;
Thus much she viewed an instant and no
      more,—
   Her struggles ceased with one convulsive
      groan;
On her sire's arm, which until now scarce
      held   375
Her writhing, fell she like a cedar felled.

59

A vein had burst, and her sweet lips' pure
      dyes
   Were dabbled with the deep blood which
      ran o'er;
And her head drooped, as when the lily lies
   O'ercharged with rain: her summoned
      handmaids bore   380
Their lady to her couch with gushing eyes;
   Of herbs and cordials they produced their
      store,
But she defied all means they could employ,
Like one life could not hold, nor death de-
      stroy.

60

Days lay she in that state unchanged, though
      chill—   385
   With nothing livid, still her lips were red;
She had no pulse, but death seemed absent
      still;
   No hideous sign proclaimed her surely
      dead;
Corruption came not in each mind to kill
   All hope; to look upon her sweet face bred
New thoughts of life, for it seemed full of
      soul—   391
She had so much, earth could not claim the
      whole.

61

The ruling passion, such as marble shows
   When exquisitely chiseled, still lay there,
But fixed as marble's unchanged aspect
      throws
   O'er the fair Venus, but for ever fair; 396
O'er the Laocoön's all eternal throes,
   And ever-dying Gladiator's air,
Their energy like life forms all their fame,
Yet looks not life, for they are still the same.

62

She woke at length, but not as sleepers wake,
  Rather the dead, for life seemed something
  new,   402
A strange sensation which she must partake
  Perforce, since whatsoever met her view
Struck not on memory, though a heavy ache
  Lay at her heart, whose earliest beat still
  true   406
Brought back the sense of pain without the
  cause,
For, for a while, the furies made a pause.

63

She looked on many a face with vacant eye,
  On many a token without knowing what;
She saw them watch her without asking
  why,   411
  And recked not who around her pillow sat;
Not speechless, though she spoke not; not a
  sigh
  Relieved her thoughts; dull silence and
  quick chat
Were tried in vain by those who served; she
  gave   415
No sign, save breath, of having left the
  grave.

64

Her handmaids tended, but she heeded not;
  Her father watched, she turned her eyes
  away;
She recognized no being, and no spot,
  However dear or cherished in their
  day;   420
They changed from room to room, but all
  forgot,
  Gentle, but without memory she lay;
At length those eyes, which they would fain
  be weaning
Back to old thoughts, waxed full of fearful
  meaning.

65

And then a slave bethought her of a harp;   425
  The harper came, and tuned his instru-
  ment;
At the first notes, irregular and sharp,
  On him her flashing eyes a moment bent,
Then to the wall she turned as if to warp
  Her thoughts from sorrow through her
  heart re-sent;   430

And he began a long low island-song
Of ancient days, ere tyranny grew strong.

66

Anon her thin wan fingers beat the wall
  In time to his old tune; he changed the
  theme,
And sung of love; the fierce name struck
  through all   435
  Her recollection; on her flashed the dream
Of what she was, and is, if ye could call
  To be so being; in a gushing stream
The tears rushed forth from her o'erclouded
  brain,
Like mountain mists at length dissolved in
  rain.   440

67

Short solace, vain relief!—thought came too
  quick,
  And whirled her brain to madness; she
  arose
As one who ne'er had dwelt among the sick,
  And flew at all she met, as on her foes;
But no one ever heard her speak or shriek,   445
  Although her paroxysm drew towards its
  close;—
Hers was a frenzy which disdained to rave,
Even when they smote her, in the hope to
  save.

68

Yet she betrayed at times a gleam of sense;
  Nothing could make her meet her father's
  face,   450
Though on all other things with looks intense
  She gazed, but none she ever could retrace;
Food she refused, and raiment; no pretense
  Availed for either; neither change of place,
Nor time, nor skill, nor remedy, could give
  her   455
Senses to sleep—the power seemed gone for
  ever.

69

Twelve days and nights she withered thus;
  at last,
  Without a groan, or sigh, or glance, to
  show
A parting pang, the spirit from her passed:
  And they who watched her nearest could
  not know   460
The very instant, till the change that cast
  Her sweet face into shadow, dull and slow,

Glazed o'er her eyes—the beautiful, the black—
Oh! to possess such luster—and then lack!

70

She died, but not alone; she held, within, 465
 A second principle of life, which might
Have dawned a fair and sinless child of sin;
 But closed its little being without light,
And went down to the grave unborn, wherein
 Blossom and bough lie withered with one blight; 470
In vain the dews of Heaven descend above
The bleeding flower and blasted fruit of love.

71

Thus lived—thus died she; never more on her
 Shall sorrow light, or shame. She was not made
Through years or moons the inner weight to bear, 475
 Which colder hearts endure till they are laid
By age in earth: her days and pleasures were
 Brief, but delightful—such as had not stayed
Long with her destiny; but she sleeps well
By the sea-shore, whereon she loved to dwell.

72

That isle is now all desolate and bare, 481
 Its dwellings down, its tenants passed away;
None but her own and father's grave is there,
 And nothing outward tells of human clay;
Ye could not know where lies a thing so fair,
 No stone is there to show, no tongue to say,
What was; no dirge, except the hollow sea's,
Mourns o'er the beauty of the Cyclades.[40] 488

73

But many a Greek maid in a loving song
 Sighs o'er her name; and many an islander
With her sire's story makes the night less long;
 Valor was his, and beauty dwelt with her;
If she loved rashly, her life paid for wrong—
 A heavy price must all pay who thus err,
In some shape; let none think to fly the danger, 495
For soon or late Love is his own avenger.

[40] A group of islands in the Aegean, lying southeast of Attica.

ON THIS DAY I COMPLETE MY THIRTY-SIXTH YEAR[1]

'Tis time this heart should be unmoved,
 Since others it hath ceased to move:
Yet, though I cannot be beloved,
 Still let me love!

My days are in the yellow leaf; 5
 The flowers and fruits of love are gone;
The worm, the canker, and the grief
 Are mine alone!

The fire that on my bosom preys
 Is lone as some volcanic isle; 10
No torch is kindled at its blaze—
 A funeral pile.

The hope, the fear, the jealous care,
 The exalted portion of the pain
And power of love, I cannot share, 15
 But wear the chain.

But 'tis not *thus*—and 'tis not *here*—
 Such thoughts should shake my soul, nor *now*,
Where glory decks the hero's bier,
 Or binds his brow. 20

The sword, the banner, and the field,
 Glory and Greece, around me see!
The Spartan, borne upon his shield,[2]
 Was not more free.

Awake! (not Greece—she *is* awake!) 25
 Awake, my spirit! Think through *whom*
Thy life-blood tracks its parent lake,
 And then strike home!

Tread those reviving passions down,
 Unworthy manhood!—unto thee 30
Indifferent should the smile or frown
 Of beauty be.

If thou regrett'st thy youth, *why live?*
 The land of honorable death
Is here:—up to the field, and give 35
 Away thy breath!

Seek out—less often sought than found—
 A soldier's grave, for thee the best;
Then look around, and choose thy ground,
 And take thy rest. 40

[1] Written at Missolonghi on 22 January, 1824; published in the same year.
[2] Wounded or slain Spartans were borne from the field upon their shields.

PERCY BYSSHE SHELLEY
1792-1822

Shelley was born at Field Place, near Horsham, in Sussex, on 4 August, 1792, the eldest of the six children of Sir Timothy and Elizabeth Shelley. His childhood was sheltered and happy until, at the age of ten, he was placed in a school at Brentford, where his remarkable beauty and appearance of gentleness tempted his school-fellows to bully and torment him. There is reason for believing that his days here and later at Eton, where he was in residence from 1804 until 1810, were by no means wholly unhappy, and he made some friends at Eton. Nevertheless, he neither understood nor was understood by his school-fellows, and the strangeness of his temperament was more in evidence than his talents, with the result that he suffered much. A school-contemporary wrote, "I have seen him surrounded, hooted, baited like a maddened bull, and at this distance of time I seem to hear ringing in my ears the cry which Shelley was wont to utter in his paroxysm of revengeful anger." Imaginative, sensitive, overwrought, largely unguided, Shelley in effect retired as much as possible from the external world to one of his own. There he dreamed his own dreams, pursued studies not admitted to the curriculum, and read strange books—among them William Godwin's *Political Justice*. In the spring of 1810 he entered University College, Oxford. Here, of course, he had greater freedom than at Eton, and no wise guidance to direct his thoughts and activities, no critics even to stiffen with substance his eager scientific and philosophic inquiries. The result was that Shelley, already converted to Godwin's gospel of reason, after some study of Locke and Hume wrote a pamphlet on *The Necessity of Atheism*, grounding his conclusion on the contention that all knowledge must come through the senses. This pamphlet he proceeded to circulate among bishops, heads of colleges, and others, with the consequence that, about eleven months after his coming to Oxford, he was expelled. The event not unnaturally caused difficulties with his father, who was a kindly, well-intentioned country gentleman, not

without his perceptions—as is shown by a sentence from a letter to his solicitor, "This misguided young man courts persecution, and which to him would be a favor"—but totally unfitted to deal amicably with such a son. It was impossible that either should understand the other, and from this time Shelley's personal relations with his father practically ceased, though after a short interval Sir Timothy agreed to give him a small allowance. In August, 1811, Shelley eloped with Harriet Westbrook, the daughter of a well-to-do coffee-house keeper—an event which completed Shelley's estrangement from his father. He was nineteen at the time, and the girl sixteen. He had made her a convert to his political and philosophical radicalism, and he felt for her a master's enthusiasm for a willing disciple, and perhaps something more. She was in love with him, and made him believe that by marrying her he could rescue her from the tyranny exercised by her father.

A part of Shelley's strangeness was his habit of acting fully and immediately upon his convictions, whatever they were; and, in spite of experience, he believed that other people needed only to be told the saving truth in order to act on it. After his marriage he spent several years in wandering about, going to Ireland and to various places in England, attempting to advance the cause of freedom and of emancipation from outworn institutions by scattering incendiary literature among the people he met. During this period he learned that William Godwin was still alive and immediately got into communication with him, flattering him as the author of all his beliefs. In the spring of 1814 Shelley became definitely estranged from his wife, and the two finally separated in May. She had borne him one child and was about to bear him another. He, however, had fallen violently in love with Godwin's daughter Mary, and it was in accordance with the principles of all three that the existence of his wife should be no bar to his union with another; Godwin, Shelley, and Mary believed that marriage was an iniquitous institution, since love as well as everything else should be completely free. Accordingly in July, 1814, Shelley and Mary began living together. They were married, however, two years later, after Harriet had drowned herself in the Serpentine. It is not clear how far Shelley is to be blamed for his wife's suicide, but it is clear enough that his habit of acting instantly on his convictions was a force which no ordinary considerations of humanity towards others could have stopped. In 1814 he had gone to France with Mary Godwin; in 1816 he was in Switzerland, and during that summer spent much time with Byron there; in 1818 he again left England, this time not to return. The remaining years of his life were spent in Italy. He was at Naples and Venice in 1818 and 1819, at Rome in the latter year and in 1820, and at Pisa from 1820 until 1822. He was drowned while sailing in the Bay of Lerici on 8 July, 1822. When his body was found later, washed up on the shore, he had a volume of Sophocles in one pocket and a volume of Keats in another—the latter open with its covers turned back, as if he had suddenly thrust it there when the waters threatened to engulf him. He was buried in the Protestant cemetery at Rome.

When Shelley went to Italy he had already written much prose and poetry, but nearly all his greatest work was done during the last four years of his life. Then the fire of conviction which had intensely burned in him since boyhood broke forth into poetry which, for its union of metrical skill, ethereal imagination, and passionate ardor, has no equal in English literature. Much of this poetry, like much of the poet's life, is concerned with a Godwinian attack on the institutions which have given form to European society. But it is well to remember that some of Shelley's wisest critics consider him a follower, not only of Godwin, but of Plato. Although his debt to the revolutionary doctrines of his time is large and specific, he also responds to an older and more constructive teaching: the belief that happiness is

obtainable through spiritual regeneration. Shelley did not believe that men, or any class of men, are perfect; he came, in fact, to recognize that there is deep-seated evil in the human heart; but he held to his conviction that we are right to hope for a conversion to better things. It is this hope, regardless of the means proposed for realizing it, which makes *Prometheus Unbound* a noble and, to many, also a satisfying poem; and all of Shelley's finest poems have a relevant nobility.

The *Complete Works* of Shelley have been edited by Roger Ingpen and Walter E. Peck (10 vols., London, 1926–1930). This edition includes, in the last three volumes, Shelley's letters, with the exception of those discovered and edited by Leslie Hotson, in *Shelley's Lost Letters to Harriet* (Boston, 1930). Probably the best one-volume edition of Shelley's *Complete Poetical Works* is that edited by T. Hutchinson, with Introduction and Bibliographical Notes by Benjamin P. Kurtz ("Oxford Standard Editions," 1933). The standard biography is that by E. Dowden (2 vols., London, 1886), which has not been displaced by W. E. Peck's *Shelley* (2 vols., Boston, 1927). A famous (perhaps too famous) interpretation of the poet is Francis Thompson's *Shelley; an Essay* (*Dublin Review,* July, 1908; and London, 1909). H. N. Brailsford's *Shelley, Godwin, and Their Circle* ("Home University Library") is a good introduction; as is also, in a different kind, Carl H. Grabo's *Magic Plant; the Growth of Shelley's Thought* (Chapel Hill, 1936). A psychological analysis and apology has been attempted by Herbert Read in the title essay of his *In Defense of Shelley and Other Essays* (London, 1936); but a more convincing defense is C. S. Lewis's "Shelley, Dryden, and Mr. Eliot" in his *Rehabilitations and Other Essays* (Oxford, 1939). A. Clutton-Brock's *Shelley: The Man and the Poet* (London, 1910), and Mrs. Olwen Ward Campbell's *Shelley and the Unromantics* (London, 1924) are both readable, interesting, and valuable books.

HYMN TO INTELLECTUAL BEAUTY[1]

I

The awful shadow of some unseen Power
  Floats though unseen among us,—visiting
  This various world with as inconstant wing
As summer winds that creep from flower to
    flower,—
Like moonbeams that behind some piny
    mountain shower,   5
     It visits with inconstant glance
     Each human heart and countenance;
Like hues and harmonies of evening,—
     Like clouds in starlight widely
      spread,—
     Like memory of music fled,—   10
     Like aught that for its grace may be
Dear, and yet dearer for its mystery.

II

Spirit of BEAUTY, that dost consecrate
  With thine own hues all thou dost shine
    upon
  Of human thought or form,—where art
    thou gone?   15
Why dost thou pass away and leave our state,
This dim vast vale of tears, vacant and deso-
    late?
     Ask why the sunlight not for ever
     Weaves rainbows o'er yon mountain-
      river,
Why aught should fail and fade that once is
    shown,   20
     Why fear and dream and death and
      birth
     Cast on the daylight of this earth

[1] Written probably in Switzerland in the summer of 1816; published in the *Examiner* (edited by Leigh Hunt), January, 1817. By intellectual beauty Shelley means an immaterial form or archetype which is beauty itself. When we contemplate beautiful objects we get some notion, but only a partial, incomplete notion, of what beauty itself must be; for material objects, no matter how beautiful, always contain some flaws and are subject to change and decay. It is only when we are carried beyond the incomplete beauty of material objects that we are able to contemplate the idea of beauty itself. The conception is Platonic and the best commentary on this and other poems by Shelley is the speech of Diotima in Plato's *Symposium*. Shelley's Platonism, however, is frequently, if not always, combined with essentially modern ideas which are its negative. This is illustrated in the present poem by Shelley's hope that the spirit of beauty, could it be more securely possessed by men, would throw them back on themselves in a sudden access of universal brotherly love.

    Such gloom,—why man has such a
     scope
For love and hate, despondency and hope?

III

No voice from some sublimer world hath
    ever   25
  To sage or poet these responses given—
  Therefore the names of Demon, Ghost,
    and Heaven,
Remain the records of their vain endeavor,
Frail spells—whose uttered charm might not
    avail to sever,
     From all we hear and all we see,   30
     Doubt, chance, and mutability.
Thy light alone—like mist o'er mountains
    driven,
     Or music by the night-wind sent
     Through strings of some still instru-
      ment,   34
     Or moonlight on a midnight stream,
Gives grace and truth to life's unquiet dream.

IV

Love, Hope, and Self-esteem, like clouds de-
    part
  And come, for some uncertain moments
    lent.
Man were immortal, and omnipotent,
Didst thou, unknown and awful as thou art,
Keep with thy glorious train firm state within
    his heart.   41
     Thou messenger of sympathies,
     That wax and wane in lovers' eyes—
Thou—that to human thought art nourish-
    ment,
     Like darkness to a dying flame!   45
     Depart not as thy shadow came,
     Depart not—lest the grave should be,
Like life and fear, a dark reality.

V

While yet a boy I sought for ghosts, and sped
    Through many a listening chamber, cave
     and ruin,   50
    And starlight wood, with fearful steps
     pursuing
Hopes of high talk with the departed dead.
I called on poisonous names with which our
    youth is fed;
     I was not heard—I saw them not—
     When musing deeply on the lot   55
Of life, at that sweet time when winds are
    wooing

All vital things that wake to bring
    News of birds and blossoming,—
    Sudden, thy shadow fell on me;   59
I shrieked, and clasped my hands in ecstasy!

VI

I vowed that I would dedicate my powers
    To thee and thine—have I not kept the
        vow?
    With beating heart and streaming eyes,
        even now
I call the phantoms of a thousand hours
Each from his voiceless grave: they have in
        visioned bowers   65
    Of studious zeal or love's delight
    Outwatched with me the envious
        night—
They know that never joy illumed my brow
    Unlinked with hope that thou wouldst
        free
    This world from its dark slavery,   70
    That thou—O awful LOVELINESS,
Wouldst give whate'er these words cannot
    express.

VII

The day becomes more solemn and serene
    When noon is past—there is a harmony
    In autumn, and a luster in its sky,   75
Which through the summer is not heard or
        seen,
As if it could not be, as if it had not been!
    Thus let thy power, which like the
        truth
    Of nature on my passive youth
Descended, to my onward life supply   80
    Its calm—to one who worships thee,
    And every form containing thee,
    Whom, SPIRIT fair, thy spells did
        bind
To fear himself, and love all human kind.

OZYMANDIAS[1]

I met a traveler from an antique land
Who said: Two vast and trunkless legs of
    stone
Stand in the desert.   Near them, on the sand,
Half sunk, a shattered visage lies, whose
    frown,   4
And wrinkled lip, and sneer of cold com-
    mand,
Tell that its sculptor well those passions read

[1]Published in the *Examiner*, January, 1818.

Which yet survive, stamped on these lifeless
    things,
The hand that mocked them, and the heart
    that fed:[2]
And on the pedestal these words appear:
"My name is Ozymandias, King of Kings: 10
Look on my works, ye Mighty, and despair!"
Nothing beside remains.   Round the decay
Of that colossal wreck, boundless and bare
The lone and level sands stretch far away.

STANZAS

Written in Dejection, near Naples[3]

I

The sun is warm, the sky is clear,
    The waves are dancing fast and bright,
Blue isles and snowy mountains wear
    The purple noon's transparent might,
    The breath of the moist earth is light,   5
Around its unexpanded buds;
    Like many a voice of one delight,
The winds, the birds, the ocean floods,
The City's voice itself, is soft like Solitude's.

II

I see the Deep's untrampled floor   10
    With green and purple seaweeds
        strown;
I see the waves upon the shore,
    Like light dissolved in star-showers,
        thrown:
    I sit upon the sands alone,—
The lightning of the noontide ocean   15
    Is flashing round me, and a tone
Arises from its measured motion,
How sweet! did any heart now share in my
    emotion.

III

Alas! I have nor hope nor health,
    Nor peace within nor calm around,   20
Nor that content surpassing wealth
    The sage in meditation found,
    And walked with inward glory
        crowned—
Nor fame, nor power, nor love, nor leisure.
    Others I see whom these surround—25
Smiling they live, and call life pleasure;—
To me that cup has been dealt in another
        measure.

[2]The hand, i. e., of the sculptor, and the heart of
Ozymandias.
[3]Said by Mrs. Shelley to have been written in
December, 1818; published in 1824.

IV

Yet now despair itself is mild,
    Even as the winds and waters are;
I could lie down like a tired child,   30
    And weep away the life of care
Which I have borne and yet must bear,
    Till death like sleep might steal on me,
    And I might feel in the warm air
My cheek grow cold, and hear the sea   35
Breathe o'er my dying brain its last monotony.

V

Some might lament that I were cold,
    As I, when this sweet day is gone,
Which my lost heart, too soon grown old,
    Insults with this untimely moan;   40
    They might lament—for I am one
Whom men love not,—and yet regret,
    Unlike this day, which, when the sun
Shall on its stainless glory set,
Will linger, though enjoyed, like joy in
    memory yet.[4]   45

ENGLAND IN 1819[5]

An old, mad, blind, despised, and dying
    king,—[6]
Princes, the dregs of their dull race, who
    flow
Through public scorn,—mud from a muddy
    spring,—
Rulers who neither see, nor feel, nor know,
But leech-like to their fainting country cling,
Till they drop, blind in blood, without a
    blow,—   6
A people starved and stabbed in the untilled
    field,—
An army, which liberticide and prey
Makes as a two-edged sword to all who
    wield,—
Golden and sanguine laws which tempt and
    slay;   10
Religion Christless, Godless—a book sealed;
A Senate,—Time's worst statute unrepealed,—[7]

Are graves, from which a glorious Phantom[8]
    may
Burst, to illumine our tempestuous day.

ODE TO THE WEST WIND[1]

I

O Wild West Wind, thou breath of Autumn's being,
Thou, from whose unseen presence the leaves
    dead
Are driven, like ghosts from an enchanter
    fleeing,
Yellow, and black, and pale, and hectic red,
Pestilence-stricken multitudes: O thou,   5
Who chariotest to their dark wintry bed

The wingèd seeds, where they lie cold and
    low,
Each like a corpse within its grave, until
Thine azure sister of the Spring shall blow

Her clarion o'er the dreaming earth, and fill
(Driving sweet buds like flocks to feed in
    air)   11
With living hues and odors plain and hill:

Wild Spirit, which art moving everywhere;
Destroyer and preserver; hear, oh, hear!

II

Thou on whose stream, 'mid the steep sky's
    commotion,   15
Loose clouds like earth's decaying leaves are
    shed,
Shook from the tangled boughs of Heaven
    and Ocean,

Angels of rain and lightning: there are spread
On the blue surface of thine aëry surge,
Like the bright hair uplifted from the head 20

---

[8]Liberty.

[1]Written in 1819; published in 1820. "This poem
was conceived and chiefly written in a wood that
skirts the Arno, near Florence, and on a day when
that tempestuous wind, whose temperature is at
once mild and animating, was collecting the vapors
which pour down the autumnal rains. They began,
as I foresaw, at sunset with a violent tempest of
hail and rain, attended by that magnificent thunder
and lightning peculiar to the Cisalpine regions.
The phenomenon alluded to at the conclusion of the
third stanza is well known to naturalists. The
vegetation at the bottom of the sea, of rivers, and
of lakes, sympathizes with that of the land in the
change of seasons, and is consequently influenced by
the winds which announce it" (Shelley's note).

---

[4]This stanza may be paraphrased: Some might
lament my death, as I shall lament the passing of
this sweet day;—they might lament, but not with
joy, such as will surround the memory of this day.

[5]First published in 1839; presumably written in
1819.

[6]George III.

[7]The law imposing civil disabilities on Roman
Catholics.

Of some fierce Maenad,[2] even the dim verge
Of the horizon to the zenith's height,
The locks of the approaching storm.   Thou dirge

Of the dying year, to which this closing night
Will be the dome of a vast sepulcher,   25
Vaulted with all thy congregated might

Of vapors, from whose solid atmosphere
Black rain, and fire, and hail will burst: oh, hear!

III

Thou who didst waken from his summer dreams
The blue Mediterranean, where he lay,   30
Lulled by the coil of his crystálline streams,

Beside a pumice isle in Baiae's bay,[3]
And saw in sleep old palaces and towers
Quivering within the wave's intenser day,

All overgrown with azure moss and flow-
ers   35
So sweet, the sense faints picturing them!
Thou
For whose path the Atlantic's level powers

Cleave themselves into chasms, while far below
The sea-blooms and the oozy woods which
wear
The sapless foliage of the ocean, know   40

Thy voice, and suddenly grow gray with fear,
And tremble and despoil themselves: oh,
hear!

IV

If I were a dead leaf thou mightest bear;
If I were a swift cloud to fly with thee;   44
A wave to pant beneath thy power, and share

The impulse of thy strength, only less free
Than thou, O uncontrollable!   If even
I were as in my boyhood, and could be

The comrade of thy wanderings over Heaven,
As then, when to outstrip thy skyey speed   50
Scarce seemed a vision; I would ne'er have
striven

---

[2]Female attendant upon Bacchus.
[3]In Campania, Italy.

As thus with thee in prayer in my sore need.
Oh, lift me as a wave, a leaf, a cloud!
I fall upon the thorns of life!   I bleed!

A heavy weight of hours has chained and
bowed   55
One too like thee: tameless, and swift, and
proud.

V

Make me thy lyre, even as the forest is:
What if my leaves are falling like its own!
The tumult of thy mighty harmonies

Will take from both a deep, autumnal tone,
Sweet though in sadness.   Be thou, Spirit
fierce,   61
My spirit!   Be thou me, impetuous one!

Drive my dead thoughts over the universe
Like withered leaves to quicken a new birth!
And, by the incantation of this verse,   65

Scatter, as from an unextinguished hearth
Ashes and sparks, my words among man-
kind!
Be through my lips to unawakened earth

The trumpet of a prophecy!   O, Wind,   69
If Winter comes, can Spring be far behind?

THE INDIAN SERENADE [1]

I

I arise from dreams of thee
In the first sweet sleep of night,
When the winds are breathing low,
And the stars are shining bright:
I arise from dreams of thee,   5
And a spirit in my feet
Hath led me—who knows how?
To thy chamber window, Sweet!

II

The wandering airs they faint
On the dark, the silent stream—   10
The Champak[2] odors fail
Like sweet thoughts in a dream;
The nightingale's complaint,
It dies upon her heart;—
As I must on thine,   15
Oh, belovéd as thou art!

---

[1]Written in 1819; published in *The Liberal*, 1822.
[2]An East Indian tree related to the magnolia.

III

O lift me from the grass!
I die! I faint! I fail!
Let thy love in kisses rain
On my lips and eyelids pale. 20
My cheek is cold and white, alas!
My heart beats loud and fast;—
Oh! press it to thine own again,
Where it will break at last.

LOVE'S PHILOSOPHY[3]

I

The fountains mingle with the river
  And the rivers with the Ocean,
The winds of Heaven mix for ever
  With a sweet emotion;
Nothing in the world is single; 5
  All things by a law divine
In one spirit meet and mingle.
  Why not I with thine?—

II

See the mountains kiss high Heaven
  And the waves clasp one another; 10
No sister-flower would be forgiven
  If it disdained its brother;
And the sunlight clasps the earth
  And the moonbeams kiss the sea:
What is all this sweet work worth 15
  If thou kiss not me?

PROMETHEUS UNBOUND

Song of Asia[1]

My soul is an enchanted boat,
  Which, like a sleeping swan, doth float
Upon the silver waves of thy sweet singing;
  And thine doth like an angel sit
  Beside a helm conducting it, 5
Whilst all the winds with melody are ringing.
  It seems to float ever, for ever,
  Upon that many-winding river,
  Between mountains, woods, abysses,
  A paradise of wildernesses! 10
Till, like one in slumber bound,
Borne to the ocean, I float down, around,
Into a sea profound, of ever-spreading
    sound:

Meanwhile thy spirit lifts its pinions
  In music's most serene dominions; 15
Catching the winds that fan that happy
    heaven.
  And we sail on, away, afar,
  Without a course, without a star,
But, by the instinct of sweet music driven;
  Till through Elysian garden islets 20
  By thee, most beautiful of pilots,
  Where never mortal pinnace glided,
  The boat of my desire is guided:
Realm where the air we breathe is love,
Which in the winds and on the waves doth
    move, 25
Harmonizing this earth with what we feel
    above.

  We have passed Age's icy caves,
  And Manhood's dark and tossing waves,
And Youth's smooth ocean, smiling to be-
    tray:
  Beyond the glassy gulfs we flee 30
  Of shadow-peopled Infancy,
Through Death and Birth, to a diviner day;
  A paradise of vaulted bowers,
  Lit by downward-gazing flowers,
  And watery paths that wind between 35
  Wildernesses calm and green,
Peopled by shapes too bright to see,
And rest, having beheld; somewhat like thee;
Which walk upon the sea, and chant melodi-
    ously!

Song of Demogorgon[2]

This is the day, which down the void abysm
At the Earth-born's spell yawns for Heaven's
    despotism,
  And Conquest is dragged captive through
    the deep:
Love, from its awful throne of patient power
In the wise heart, from the last giddy hour 5
  Of dread endurance, from the slippery,
    steep,
And narrow verge of crag-like agony, springs
And folds over the world its healing wings.

Gentleness, Virtue, Wisdom, and Endurance,
These are the seals of that most firm assur-
    ance 10
  Which bars the pit over Destruction's
    strength;
And if, with infirm hand, Eternity,

---

[3] Written in 1819 and published by Hunt in *The Indicator* in the same year.

[1] Act II, scene v, ll. 72–110. Asia is a nymph of the ocean; she also symbolizes earthly love, and is ultimately married to the Titan, Prometheus. Here she is replying to a song sung by an invisible spirit.

[2] Act IV, ll. 554–578. Demogorgon is the embodiment of that eternal force which Shelley believed would in the end overthrow all tyrannies and redeem the universe.

Mother of many acts and hours, should free
   The serpent that would clasp her with his
     length;
These are the spells by which to reassume 15
An empire o'er the disentangled doom.

To suffer woes which Hope thinks infinite;
To forgive wrongs darker than death or
   night;
   To defy Power, which seems omnipotent;
To love, and bear; to hope till Hope creates 20
From its own wreck the thing it contem-
   plates;
   Neither to change, nor falter, nor repent;
This, like thy glory, Titan,[3] is to be
Good, great, and joyous, beautiful and free;
This is alone Life, Joy, Empire, and Vic-
   tory. 25

THE CLOUD[1]

I bring fresh showers for the thirsting
   flowers,
   From the seas and the streams;
I bear light shade for the leaves when laid
   In their noonday dreams.
From my wings are shaken the dews that
   waken 5
   The sweet buds every one,
When rocked to rest on their mother's breast,
   As she dances about the sun.
I wield the flail of the lashing hail,
   And whiten the green plains under, 10
And then again I dissolve it in rain,
   And laugh as I pass in thunder.

I sift the snow on the mountains below,
   And their great pines groan aghast;
And all the night 'tis my pillow white, 15
   While I sleep in the arms of the blast.
Sublime on the towers of my skyey bowers,
   Lightning my pilot sits;
In a cavern under is fettered the thunder,
   It struggles and howls at fits; 20
Over earth and ocean, with gentle motion,
   This pilot is guiding me,
Lured by the love of the genii that move
   In the depths of the purple sea;
Over the rills, and the crags, and the hills, 25
   Over the lakes and the plains,
Wherever he dreams, under mountain or
   stream,
   The Spirit he loves remains;

   [3]Prometheus.
   [1]Written and published in 1820.

And I all the while bask in Heaven's blue
   smile,
   Whilst he is dissolving in rains. 30

The sanguine Sunrise, with his meteor eyes,
   And his burning plumes outspread,
Leaps on the back of my sailing rack,
   When the morning star shines dead;
As on the jag of a mountain crag, 35
   Which an earthquake rocks and swings,
An eagle alit one moment may sit
   In the light of its golden wings.
And when Sunset may breathe, from the lit
   sea beneath,
   Its ardors of rest and of love, 40
And the crimson pall of eve may fall
   From the depth of Heaven above,
With wings folded I rest, on mine aëry nest,
   As still as a brooding dove.

That orbéd maiden with white fire laden, 45
   Whom mortals call the Moon,
Glides glimmering o'er my fleece-like floor,
   By the midnight breezes strewn;
And wherever the beat of her unseen feet,
   Which only the angels hear, 50
May have broken the woof of my tent's thin
   roof,
   The stars peep behind her and peer;
And I laugh to see them whirl and flee,
   Like a swarm of golden bees,
When I widen the rent in my wind-built tent,
   Till the calm rivers, lakes, and seas, 56
Like strips of the sky fallen through me on
   high,
   Are each paved with the moon and these.[2]

I bind the Sun's throne with a burning zone,
   And the Moon's with a girdle of pearl; 60
The volcanoes are dim, and the stars reel and
   swim,
   When the whirlwinds my banner unfurl.
From cape to cape, with a bridge-like shape,
   Over a torrent sea,
Sunbeam-proof, I hang like a roof,— 65
   The mountains its columns be.
The triumphal arch through which I march
   With hurricane, fire, and snow,
When the Powers of the air are chained to
   my chair,
   Is the million-colored bow; 70
The sphere-fire above its soft colors wove,
   While the moist Earth was laughing be-
     low.

   [2]The stars.

I am the daughter of Earth and Water,
  And the nursling of the Sky;
I pass through the pores of the ocean and
    shores;   75
  I change, but I cannot die.
For after the rain when with never a stain
  The pavilion of Heaven is bare,
And the winds and sunbeams with their con-
    vex gleams
  Build up the blue dome of air,   80
I silently laugh at my own cenotaph,[3]
  And out of the caverns of rain,
Like a child from the womb, like a ghost
    from the tomb,
  I arise and unbuild it again.

TO A SKYLARK[1]

Hail to thee, blithe Spirit!
  Bird thou never wert,
That from Heaven, or near it,
  Pourest thy full heart
In profuse strains of unpremeditated art.   5

Higher still and higher
  From the earth thou springest
Like a cloud of fire;
  The blue deep thou wingest,
And singing still dost soar, and soaring ever
    singest.   10

In the golden lightning
  Of the sunken sun,
O'er which clouds are bright'ning,
  Thou dost float and run;
Like an unbodied joy whose race is just be-
    gun.   15

The pale purple even
  Melts around thy flight:
Like a star of Heaven,
  In the broad daylight
Thou art unseen, but yet I hear thy shrill
    delight,   20

Keen as are the arrows
  Of that silver sphere,
Whose intense lamp narrows
  In the white dawn clear   24
Until we hardly see—we feel that it is there.

[3] I. e., the blue dome of air. A cenotaph is an
empty tomb, or a monument erected in honor of one
buried elsewhere.

[1] Written at Leghorn in 1820 and published in the
same year.

All the earth and air
  With thy voice is loud,
As, when night is bare,
  From one lonely cloud
The moon rains out her beams, and Heaven
    is overflowed.   30

What thou art we know not;
  What is most like thee?
From rainbow clouds there flow not
  Drops so bright to see
As from thy presence showers a rain of
    melody.   35

Like a Poet hidden
  In the light of thought,
Singing hymns unbidden,
  Till the world is wrought
To sympathy with hopes and fears it heeded
    not: 40

Like a high-born maiden
  In a palace-tower,
Soothing her love-laden
  Soul in secret hour
With music sweet as love, which overflows
    her bower: 45

Like a glow-worm golden
  In a dell of dew,
Scattering unbeholden
  Its aërial hue
Among the flowers and grass, which screen
    it from the view!   50

Like a rose embowered
  In its own green leaves,
By warm winds deflowered,
  Till the scent it gives
Makes faint with too much sweet those
    heavy-wingéd thieves: 55

Sound of vernal showers
  On the twinkling grass,
Rain-awakened flowers,
  All that ever was
Joyous, and clear, and fresh, thy music doth
    surpass: 60

Teach us, Sprite or Bird,
  What sweet thoughts are thine:
I have never heard
  Praise of love or wine   64
That panted forth a flood of rapture so divine.

Chorus Hymeneal,
  Or triumphal chant,
Matched with thine would be all
  But an empty vaunt,
A thing wherein we feel there is some hid-
  den want.   70

What objects are the fountains
  Of thy happy strain?
What fields, or waves, or mountains?
  What shapes of sky or plain?
What love of thine own kind? what ignorance
  of pain?   75

With thy clear keen joyance
  Languor cannot be:
Shadow of annoyance
  Never came near thee:
Thou lovest—but ne'er knew love's sad
  satiety.   80

Waking or asleep,
  Thou of death must deem
Things more true and deep
  Than we mortals dream,
Or how could thy notes flow in such a crystal
  stream?   85

We look before and after,
  And pine for what is not:
Our sincerest laughter
  With some pain is fraught;
Our sweetest songs are those that tell of
  saddest thought.   90

Yet if we could scorn
  Hate, and pride, and fear;
If we were things born
  Not to shed a tear,
I know not how thy joy we ever should come
  near.   95

Better than all measures
  Of delightful sound,
Better than all treasures
  That in books are found,
Thy skill to poet were, thou scorner of the
  ground!   100

Teach me half the gladness
  That thy brain must know,
Such harmonious madness
  From my lips would flow
The world should listen then—as I am listen-
  ing now.   105

ODE TO LIBERTY[1]

Yet, Freedom, yet, thy banner, torn but flying,
Streams like a thunder-storm against the wind.
                       —BYRON.

I

A glorious people vibrated again
  The lightning of the nations: Liberty
From heart to heart, from tower to tower,
  o'er Spain,
  Scattering contagious fire into the sky,
Gleamed. My soul spurned the chains of its
  dismay,   5
    And in the rapid plumes of song
    Clothed itself, sublime and strong
(As a young eagle soars the morning clouds
  among),
    Hovering in verse o'er its accustomed
    prey;
    Till from its station in the Heaven of
    fame   10
The Spirit's whirlwind rapped it, and the
  ray
  Of the remotest sphere of living flame
Which paves the void was from behind it
  flung,
  As foam from a ship's swiftness, when
  there came
A voice out of the deep: I will record the
  same.   15

II

"The Sun and the serenest Moon sprang
  forth:
    The burning stars of the abyss were
    hurled
    Into the depths of Heaven. The daedal[2]
    earth,
That island in the ocean of the world,
Hung in its cloud of all-sustaining air: 20
    But this divinest universe
    Was yet a chaos and a curse,
For thou[3] wert not: but, power from worst
  producing worse,
  The spirit of the beasts was kindled there,
    And of the birds, and of the watery
    forms,   25
  And there was war among them, and de-
  spair

---

[1]Written early in 1820 and published in the same year. The motto is from *Childe Harold*, IV, Stanza 98. The occasion of the poem was an uprising against absolutist government in Spain, which occurred early in 1820 and at the time appeared to be triumphing in Madrid.

[2]Curiously contrived or variously adorned.

[3]Liberty.

Within them, raging without truce or
    terms:
The bosom of their violated nurse
    Groaned, for beasts warred on beasts, and
        worms on worms,
    And men on men; each heart was as a hell
        of storms.   30

III

"Man, the imperial shape, then multiplied
    His generations under the pavilion
Of the Sun's throne: palace and pyramid,
    Temple and prison, to many a swarming
        million
Were, as to mountain-wolves their raggéd
        caves.   35
    This human living multitude
    Was savage, cunning, blind, and rude,
For thou wert not; but o'er the populous soli-
        tude,
    Like one fierce cloud over a waste of waves,
    Hung Tyranny; beneath, sat deified   40
The sister-pest,[4] congregator of slaves;
    Into the shadow of her pinions wide
Anarchs and priests, who feed on gold and
    blood
    Till with the stain their inmost souls are
        dyed,
Drove the astonished herds of men from
    every side.   45

IV

"The nodding promontories, and blue isles,
    And cloud-like mountains, and dividuous[5]
        waves
Of Greece, basked glorious in the open smiles
    Of favoring Heaven: from their enchanted
        caves
Prophetic echoes flung dim melody.   50
    On the unapprehensive wild,
    The vine, the corn, the olive mild,
Grew savage yet, to human use unreconciled;
    And, like unfolded flowers beneath the sea,
    Like the man's thought dark in the in-
        fant's brain,   55
    Like aught that is which wraps what is to
        be,
    Art's deathless dreams lay veiled by
        many a vein
Of Parian stone; and, yet a speechless child,
    Verse murmured, and Philosophy did
        strain
    Her lidless eyes for thee; when o'er the
        Aegean main   60

---

[4] I. e., religion.   [5] Dividing.

V

"Athens arose: a city such as vision
    Builds from the purple crags and silver
        towers
Of battlemented cloud, as in derision
    Of kingliest masonry: the ocean-floors
Pave it; the evening sky pavilions it;   65
    Its portals are inhabited
    By thunder-zonéd winds, each head
Within its cloudy wings with sun-fire gar-
       landed,—
    A divine work! Athens, diviner yet,
    Gleamed with its crest of columns, on
        the will   70
    Of man, as on a mount of diamond, set;[6]
    For thou wert, and thine all-creative
        skill
Peopled, with forms that mock the eternal
    dead
    In marble immortality, that hill[7]
    Which was thine earliest throne and latest
        oracle.   75

VI

"Within the surface of Time's fleeting river
    Its wrinkled image lies, as then it lay
Immovably unquiet, and for ever
    It trembles, but it cannot pass away!
The voices of thy bards and sages thunder 80
    With an earth-awakening blast
    Through the caverns of the past
(Religion veils her eyes; Oppression shrinks,
    aghast):
    A wingéd sound of joy, and love, and won-
        der,
    Which soars where Expectation never
        flew,   85
    Rending the veil of space and time asun-
        der!
    One ocean feeds the clouds, and streams,
        and dew;
One Sun illumines Heaven; one Spirit vast
    With life and love makes chaos ever new,
    As Athens doth the world with thy de-
        light renew.   90

VII

"Then Rome was, and from thy deep bosom
    fairest,
    Like a wolf-cub from a Cadmaean Mae-
        nad,[8]

---

[6] I. e., Athens was a state based on the will of its
citizens.
[7] The Acropolis.
[8] See Euripides., *Bacchae,* ll. 699–700. The Cad-

She drew the milk of greatness, though thy
dearest[9]
From that Elysian food was yet unweanéd;
And many a deed of terrible uprightness   95
    By thy sweet love was sanctified;
    And in thy smile, and by thy side,
Saintly Camillus[10] lived, and firm Atilius[11]
died.
But when tears stained thy robe of vestal
whiteness,   99
    And gold profaned thy Capitolian
throne,
    Thou didst desert, with spirit-wingéd light-
ness,
The senate of the tyrants: they sunk
prone
Slaves of one tyrant: Palatinus[12] sighed
    Faint echoes of Ionian song; that tone
    Thou didst delay to hear, lamenting to dis-
own.   105

VIII

"From what Hyrcanian[13] glen or frozen hill,
    Or piny promontory of the Arctic main,
Or utmost islet inaccessible,
Didst thou lament the ruin of thy reign,
Teaching the woods and waves, and desert
rocks,   110
    And every Naiad's ice-cold urn,
    To talk in echoes sad and stern
Of that sublimest lore which man had dared
unlearn?
    For neither didst thou watch the wizard
flocks
    Of the Scald's[14] dreams, nor haunt the
Druid's sleep.   115
What if the tears rained through thy shat-
tered locks
    Were quickly dried? for thou didst
groan, not weep,
When from its sea of death, to kill and burn,

---

maean Maenads are Theban followers of Bacchus,
and are described by Euripides as nursing young
wolves.
[9] Athens.
[10] A hero of republican Rome who defeated the
Gauls under Brennus in 390 B. C.
[11] Generally called Regulus. He was captured by
the Carthaginians but dissuaded the Senate from
concluding a peace that would have saved his life
(B. C. 250).
[12] One of the seven hills of Rome, on which was
the residence of Augustus and later emperors.
[13] Hyrcania was a region at the southeastern
corner of the Caspian Sea.
[14] A skald was a Scandinavian poet.

The Galilean serpent[15] forth did creep,
And made thy world an undistinguishable
heap.   120

IX

"A thousand years the Earth cried, 'Where
art thou?'
And then the shadow of thy cunning fell
On Saxon Alfred's[16] olive-cinctured brow:
And many a warrior-peopled citadel,
Like rocks which fire lifts out of the flat
deep,   125
    Arose in sacred Italy,
    Frowning o'er the tempestuous sea
Of kings, and priests, and slaves, in tower-
crowned majesty;
    That multitudinous anarchy did sweep
    And burst around their walls, like idle
foam,   130
Whilst from the human spirit's deepest
deep
    Strange melody with love and awe struck
dumb
Dissonant arms; and Art, which cannot die,
    With divine wand traced on our earthly
home
Fit imagery to pave Heaven's everlasting
dome.   135

X

"Thou huntress swifter than the Moon! thou
terror
    Of the world's wolves! thou bearer of the
quiver,
Whose sunlike shafts pierce tempest-wingéd
Error,
    As light may pierce the clouds when they
dissever
In the calm regions of the orient day!   140
    Luther caught thy wakening glance;
    Like lightning, from his leaden lance
Reflected, it dissolved the visions of the
trance
    In which, as in a tomb, the nations lay;
    And England's prophets hailed thee as
their queen,   145
In songs whose music cannot pass away,
    Though it must flow for ever: not un-
seen
Before the spirit-sighted countenance
    Of Milton didst thou pass, from the sad
scene
Beyond whose night he saw, with a dejected mien.   150

---

[15] Christianity.   [16] Alfred the Great.

XI

"The eager hours and unreluctant years
　As on a dawn-illumined mountain stood,
Trampling to silence their loud hopes and
　　fears,
　Darkening each other with their multitude,
And cried aloud, 'Liberty!'　Indignation　155
　　Answered Pity from her cave;
　　Death grew pale within the grave,
And Desolation howled to the destroyer,
　　Save!
　When like Heaven's Sun girt by the ex-
　　halation
　　Of its own glorious light, thou didst
　　　arise,　160
　Chasing thy foes from nation unto nation
　　Like shadows: as if day had cloven the
　　　skies
At dreaming midnight o'er the western wave,
　Men started, staggering with a glad sur-
　　prise,
　Under the lightnings of thine unfamiliar
　　eyes.　165

XII

"Thou Heaven of earth! what spells could
　　pall thee then
　In ominous eclipse? a thousand years
Bred from the slime of deep Oppression's
　　den,
　Dyed all thy liquid light with blood and
　　tears,
Till thy sweet stars could weep the stain
　　away;　170
　　How like Bacchanals of blood
　　Round France, the ghastly vintage,
　　stood
Destruction's sceptered slaves, and Folly's
　　mitered brood!
　When one,[17] like them, but mightier far
　　than they,
　　The Anarch of thine own bewildered
　　powers,　175
　Rose: armies mingled in obscure array,
　　Like clouds with clouds, darkening the
　　sacred bowers
Of serene Heaven.　He, by the past pursued,
　Rests with those dead, but unforgotten
　　hours,
　Whose ghosts scare victor kings in their
　　ancestral towers.　180

XIII

"England yet sleeps: was she not called of
　　old?

Spain calls her now, as with its thrilling
　　thunder
Vesuvius wakens Aetna, and the cold
　Snow-crags by its reply are cloven in
　　sunder:
O'er the lit waves every Aeolian isle[18]　185
　　From Pithecusa to Pelorus
　　Howls, and leaps, and glares in chorus:
They cry, 'Be dim; ye lamps of Heaven sus-
　　pended o'er us!'
　Her[19] chains are threads of gold, she need
　　but smile
　　And they dissolve; but Spain's were
　　links of steel,　190
　Till bit to dust by virtue's keenest file.
　　Twins of a single destiny! appeal
To the eternal years enthroned before us
　In the dim West; impress us from a seal,
　All ye have thought and done!　Time
　　cannot dare conceal.　195

XIV

"Tomb of Arminius[20] render up thy dead
　Till, like a standard from a watch-tower's
　　staff,
His soul may stream over the tyrant's head;
　Thy victory shall be his epitaph,
Wild Bacchanal of truth's mysterious wine,
　　King-deluded Germany,　201
　　His dead spirit lives in thee.
Why do we fear or hope? thou art already
　　free!
　And thou, lost Paradise of this divine
　　And glorious world! thou flowery wil-
　　derness!　205
　Thou island of eternity! thou shrine
　　Where Desolation, clothed with loveli-
　　ness,
Worships the thing thou wert!　O Italy,
　Gather thy blood into thy heart; repress
　The beasts who make their dens thy sacred
　　palaces.　210

XV

"Oh, that the free would stamp the impious
　　name
　Of King into the dust! or write it there,
So that this blot upon the page of fame
　Were as a serpent's path, which the light
　　air

---

[17]Napoleon.

[18]A group of islands northeast of Sicily.　Pithecusa is an island outside the Bay of Naples, and
Pelorus is a promontory northeast of Sicily.

[19]England's.

[20]He preserved the freedom of Germany in A. D. 9
by preventing the advance of the Romans beyond
the Rhine.

Erases, and the flat sands close behind! 215
    Ye the oracle have heard:
    Lift the victory-flashing sword,
And cut the snaky knots of this foul gor-
        dian[21] word,
    Which, weak itself as stubble, yet can
        bind
    Into a mass, irrefragably firm, 220
    The axes and the rods which awe man-
        kind;
    The sound has poison in it, 'tis the
        sperm
Of what makes life foul, cankerous, and
        abhorred;
    Disdain not thou, at thine appointed term,
    To set thine arméd heel on this reluctant
        worm. 225

XVI

"Oh, that the wise from their bright minds
        would kindle
    Such lamps within the dome of this dim
        world,
That the pale name of PRIEST might shrink
        and dwindle
Into the hell from which it first was hurled,
A scoff of impious pride from fiends im-
        pure; 230
    Till human thoughts might kneel alone,
    Each before the judgment-throne
Of its own aweless soul, or of the Power un-
        known!
    Oh, that the words which make the
        thoughts obscure
    From which they spring, as clouds of
        glimmering dew 235
From a white lake blot Heaven's blue por-
        traiture,
    Were stripped of their thin masks and
        various hue
And frowns and smiles and splendors not
        their own,
    Till in the nakedness of false and true
    They stand before their Lord, each to re-
        ceive its due! 240

XVII

'He who taught man to vanquish whatso-
        ever
Can be between the cradle and the grave
Crowned him the King of Life. Oh, vain
        endeavor!
If on his own high will, a willing slave,
He has enthroned the oppression and the
        oppressor. 245

---

[21] Intricate.

What if earth can clothe and feed
    Amplest millions at their need,
And power in thought be as the tree within
        the seed?
    Or what if Art, an ardent intercessor,
    Driving on fiery wings to Nature's
        throne, 250
Checks the great mother stooping to caress
        her,
    And cries: 'Give me, thy child, domin-
        ion
Over all height and depth'? if Life can breed
    New wants, and wealth from those who
        toil and groan,
    Rend of thy gifts and hers a thousandfold
        for one! 255

XVIII

"Come thou, but lead out of the inmost cave
    Of man's deep spirit, as the morning-star
Beckons the Sun from the Eoan wave,[22]
    Wisdom.   I hear the pennons of her car
Self-moving, like cloud charioted by flame.
    Comes she not, and come ye not, 261
    Rulers of eternal thought,
To judge, with solemn truth, life's ill-appor-
        tioned lot?
    Blind Love, and equal Justice, and the
        Fame
    Of what has been, the Hope of what
        will be? 265
O Liberty! if such could be thy name
    Wert thou disjoined from these, or they
        from thee:
If thine or theirs were treasures to be bought
    By blood or tears, have not the wise and
        free
    Wept tears, and blood like tears?"—The
        solemn harmony 270

XIX

Paused, and the Spirit of that mighty sing-
        ing
    To its abyss was suddenly withdrawn;
Then, as a wild swan, when sublimely wing-
        ing
    Its path athwart the thunder-smoke of
        dawn,
Sinks headlong through the aërial golden
        light 275
    On the heavy-sounding plain,
    When the bolt has pierced its brain;
As summer clouds dissolve, unburthened of
        their rain;

---

[22] The wave of dawn.

As a far taper fades with fading night,
　As a brief insect dies with dying
　　day,— 280
My song, its pinions disarrayed of might,
　Drooped; o'er it closed the echoes far
　　away
Of the great voice which did its flight sus-
　tain,
As waves which lately paved his watery way
Hiss round a drowner's head in their tem-
　pestuous play. 285

ODE TO NAPLES[1]

EPODE I α

I stood within the City disinterred;[2]
　And heard the autumnal leaves like light
　　footfalls
Of spirits passing through the streets; and
　heard
　The Mountain's[3] slumberous voice at
　　intervals
　　Thrill through those roofless halls; 5
The oracular thunder penetrating shook
　The listening soul in my suspended blood;
I felt that Earth out of her deep heart
　spoke—
　I felt, but heard not:—through white
　　columns glowed
　　The isle-sustaining ocean-flood, 10
A plane of light between two heavens of
　azure!
　Around me gleamed many a bright sepul-
　　cher
Of whose pure beauty, Time, as if his pleas-
　ure
Were to spare Death, had never made era-
　sure;
　But every living lineament was clear 15
　As in the sculptor's thought; and there
The wreaths of stony myrtle, ivy, and pine,
　Like winter leaves o'ergrown by molded
　　snow,
　　Seemed only not to move and grow
Because the crystal silence of the air 20

Weighed on their life; even as the Power
　divine
Which then lulled all things, brooded upon
　mine.

EPODE II α

　Then gentle winds arose
　With many a mingled close
Of wild Aeolian sound, and mountain-odors
　keen; 25
　And where the Baian ocean
　Welters with airlike motion,
Within, above, around its bowers of starry
　green,
Moving the sea-flowers in those purple
　caves,
　Even as the ever stormless atmosphere 30
　Floats o'er the Elysian realm,
It bore me, like an Angel, o'er the waves
　Of sunlight, whose swift pinnace of
　　dewy air
　No storm can overwhelm.
　I sailed, where ever flows 35
　Under the calm Serene
　A spirit of deep emotion
　From the unknown graves
　Of the dead Kings of Melody.[4]
Shadowy Aornos[5] darkened o'er the helm 40
The horizontal aether; Heaven stripped bare
Its depth over Elysium, where the prow
Made the invisible water white as snow;
From that Typhaean mount, Inarime,[6]
　There streamed a sunbright vapor, like the
　　standard 45
　Of some ethereal host;
　Whilst from all the coast,
Louder and louder, gathering round, there
　wandered
Over the oracular woods and divine sea
Prophesyings which grew articulate— 50
They seize me—I must speak them!—be
　they fate!

STROPHE I

Naples! thou Heart of men which ever pant-
　est
　Naked, beneath the lidless eye of Heaven!
Elysian City, which to calm enchantest
　The mutinous air and sea! they round
　　thee, even 55
　As sleep round Love, are driven!

---

[1]Written in August, 1820; published in 1824. "The author has connected many recollections of his visit to Pompeii and Baiae with the enthusiasm excited by the intelligence of the proclamation of a Constitutional Government at Naples. This has given a tinge of picturesque and descriptive imagery to the introductory Epodes which depicture these scenes, and some of the majestic feelings permanently connected with the scene of this animating event" (Shelley's note).

[2]Pompeii.　[3]Vesuvius.

[4]Homer and Virgil (Shelley's note).　[5]Hades
[6]An island northwest of the Bay of Naples containing a volcanic mountain under which Typhon was said to be buried.

Metropolis of a ruined Paradise
    Long lost, late won, and yet but half re-
        gained!
Bright Altar of the bloodless sacrifice,
    Which arméd Victory offers up un-
        stained   60
    To Love, the flower-enchained!
Thou which wert once, and then didst cease
      to be,
Now art, and henceforth ever shalt be, free,
If Hope, and Truth, and Justice can
      avail,—
    Hail, hail, all hail!   65

STROPHE II

Thou youngest giant birth
    Which from the groaning earth
Leap'st, clothed in armor of impenetrable
      scale!
    Last of the Intercessors!   69
Who 'gainst the Crowned Transgressors
Pleadest before God's love! Arrayed in
      Wisdom's mail,
    Wave thy lightning lance in mirth
    Nor let thy high heart fail,
Though from their hundred gates the leagued
      Oppressors
    With hurried legions move!   75
    Hail, hail, all hail!

ANTISTROPHE I α

What though Cimmerian Anarchs[7] dare
    .blaspheme
    Freedom and thee? thy shield is as a mir-
      ror
To make their blind slaves see, and with
      fierce gleam
    To turn his hungry sword upon the
      wearer;   80
      A new Actaeon's[8] error
Shall theirs have been—devoured by their
      own hounds!
Be thou like the imperial Basilisk[9]
Killing thy foe with unapparent wounds!
Gaze on Oppression, till at that dread risk
Aghast she pass from the Earth's disk: 86
Fear not, but gaze—for freemen mightier
      grow,
And slaves more feeble, gazing on their
      foe:—

If Hope, and Truth, and Justice may
    avail,
    Thou shalt be great—All hail!   90

ANTISTROPHE II α

From Freedom's form divine,
From Nature's inmost shrine,
Strip every impious gawd, rend Error veil
      by veil;
    O'er Ruin desolate,
    O'er Falsehood's fallen state,   95
Sit thou sublime, unawed; be the Destroyer
      pale!
    And equal laws be thine,
    And wingéd words let sail,
Freighted with truth even from the throne
      of God:
    That wealth, surviving fate,   100
    Be thine.—All hail!

ANTISTROPHE I β

Didst thou not start to hear Spain's thrilling
    paean
    From land to land re-echoed solemnly,
Till silence became music? From the
    Aeaean[10]
    To the cold Alps, eternal Italy   105
    Starts to hear thine! The Sea
Which paves the desert streets of Venice
    laughs
    In light and music; widowed Genoa wan
By moonlight spells ancestral epitaphs,
    Murmuring, "Where is Doria?"[11] fair Mi-
    lan,   110
    Within whose veins long ran
The viper's[12] palsying venom, lifts her heel
To bruise his head. The signal and the seal
    (If Hope and Truth and Justice can
    avail)
    Art thou of all these hopes.—O hail!   115

ANTISTROPHE II β

Florence! beneath the sun,
Of cities fairest one,
Blushes within her bower for Freedom's ex-
      pectation:
    From eyes of quenchless hope
    Rome tears the priestly cope,   120

---

[7]The Cimmerians, according to legend, dwelt in a
northern land of perpetual darkness.

[8]Actaeon was devoured by his own hounds after
he had seen Artemis bathing.

[9]A monster who could slay by merely looking at
its victim.

[10]The island of Circe (Shelley's note).

[11]Andrea Doria, an admiral who victoriously
fought, early in the sixteenth century, for the independence of Genoa.

[12]The viper was the armorial device of the Vis-
conti, tyrants of Milan (Shelley's note).

As ruling once by power, so now by admiration,—
  An athlete stripped to run
  From a remoter station
For the high prize lost on Philippi's shore:[13]—
  As then Hope, Truth, and Justice did avail, 125
  So now may Fraud and Wrong! O hail!

EPODE I β

Hear ye the march as of the Earth-born Forms[14]
Arrayed against the ever-living Gods?
The crash and darkness of a thousand storms
  Bursting their inaccessible abodes 130
  Of crags and thunder-clouds?
See ye the banners blazoned to the day,
  Inwrought with emblems of barbaric pride?
Dissonant threats kill Silence far away,
  The serene Heaven which wraps our Eden wide 135
  With iron light is dyed;
The Anarchs of the North[15] lead forth their legions
  Like Chaos o'er creation, uncreating;
An hundred tribes nourished on strange religions
  And lawless slaveries,—down the aërial regions 140
  Of the white Alps, desolating,
  Famished wolves that bide no waiting,
Blotting the glowing footsteps of old glory,
Trampling our columned cities into dust,
  Their dull and savage lust 145
  On Beauty's corse to sickness satiating—
They come! The fields they tread look black and hoary
With fire—from their red feet the streams run gory!

EPODE II β

Great Spirit, deepest Love!
  Which rulest and dost move 150
All things which live and are, within the Italian shore;
  Who spreadest Heaven around it,
  Whose woods, rocks, waves, surround it;

Who sittest in thy star, o'er Ocean's western floor;
Spirit of beauty! at whose soft command 155
  The sunbeams and the showers distil its foison[16]
  From the Earth's bosom chill;
Oh, bid those beams be each a blinding brand
  Of lightning! bid those showers be dews of poison!
  Bid the Earth's plenty kill! 160
  Bid thy bright Heaven above,
  Whilst light and darkness bound it,
  Be their tomb who planned
  To make it ours and thine!
Or, with thine harmonizing ardors fill 165
And raise thy sons, as o'er the prone horizon
Thy lamp feeds every twilight wave with fire—
Be man's high hope and unextinct desire
The instrument to work thy will divine!
  Then clouds from sunbeams, antelopes from leopards, 170
  And frowns and fears from thee,
  Would not more swiftly flee
Than Celtic wolves from the Ausonian[17] shepherds.—
  Whatever, Spirit, from thy starry shrine
  Thou yieldest or withholdest, oh, let be 175
  This city of thy worship ever free!

SONNET [1]

Ye hasten to the grave! What seek ye there,
Ye restless thoughts and busy purposes
Of the idle brain, which the world's livery wear?
O thou quick heart, which pantest to possess
All that pale Expectation feigneth fair! 5
Thou vainly curious mind which wouldest guess
Whence thou didst come, and whither thou must go,
And all that never yet was known would know—
Oh, whither hasten ye, that thus ye press,
With such swift feet life's green and pleasant path, 10
Seeking, alike from happiness and woe,
A refuge in the cavern of gray death?
O heart, and mind, and thoughts! what thing do you
Hope to inherit in the grave below?

---

[13]Brutus and Cassius at Philippi fought vainly for republican Rome against Octavius (42 B. C.).

[14]The Titans, sons of Earth, who warred on the gods.

[15]Austria and other countries.

[16]Plentiful harvest.   [17]Italian.

[1]Written in 1820; published by Leigh Hunt in 1823.

GOOD-NIGHT [2]

I

Good-night? ah! no; the hour is ill
  Which severs those it should unite;
Let us remain together still,
  Then it will be *good* night.

II

How can I call the lone night good,   5
  Though thy sweet wishes wing its flight?
Be it not said, thought, understood—
  Then it will be—*good* night.

III

To hearts which near each other move
  From evening close to morning light,   10
The night is good; because, my love,
  They never *say* good-night.

TO NIGHT [3]

I

Swiftly walk o'er the western wave,
    Spirit of Night!
Out of the misty eastern cave,
Where, all the long and lone daylight,
Thou wovest dreams of joy and fear,   5
Which make thee terrible and dear,—
    Swift be thy flight!

II

Wrap thy form in a mantle gray,
    Star-inwrought!
Blind with thine hair the eyes of Day;   10
Kiss her until she be wearied out,
Then wander o'er city, and sea, and land,
Touching all with thine opiate wand—
    Come, long-sought!

III

When I arose and saw the dawn,   15
    I sighed for thee;
When light rode high, and the dew was gone,
And noon lay heavy on flower and tree,
And the weary Day turned to his rest,
Lingering like an unloved guest,   20
    I sighed for thee.

IV

Thy brother Death came, and cried,
    Wouldst thou me?

Thy sweet child Sleep, the filmy-eyed,
Murmured like a noontide bee,   25
Shall I nestle near thy side?
Wouldst thou me?—And I replied,
    No, not thee!

V

Death will come when thou art dead,
    Soon, too soon—   30
Sleep will come when thou art fled;
Of neither would I ask the boon
I ask of thee, belovéd Night—
Swift be thine approaching flight,
    Come soon, soon!   35

TIME [4]

Unfathomable Sea! whose waves are years,
  Ocean of Time, whose waters of deep woe
Are brackish with the salt of human tears!
  Thou shoreless flood, which in thy ebb and
    flow
Claspest the limits of mortality,   5
And sick of prey, yet howling on for more,
Vomitest thy wrecks on its inhospitable
    shore;
  Treacherous in calm, and terrible in storm,
    Who shall put forth on thee,
    Unfathomable Sea?   10

TO —— [5]

Music, when soft voices die,
Vibrates in the memory—
Odors, when sweet violets sicken,
Live within the sense they quicken.

Rose leaves, when the rose is dead,   5
Are heaped for the belovéd's bed;
And so thy thoughts, when thou art gone,
Love itself shall slumber on.

SONG [6]

I

Rarely, rarely, comest thou,
  Spirit of Delight!
Wherefore hast thou left me now
  Many a day and night?
Many a weary night and day   5
'Tis since thou art fled away.

[2] Written in 1820; published by Hunt in 1822.
[3] Written in 1821; published in 1824.
[4] Written in 1821; published in 1824.
[5] Written in 1821; published in 1824.
[6] Written in 1821; published in 1824.

II

How shall ever one like me
 Win thee back again?
With the joyous and the free
 Thou wilt scoff at pain. 10
Spirit false! thou hast forgot
All but those who need thee not.

III

As a lizard with the shade
 Of a trembling leaf,
Thou with sorrow art dismayed; 15
 Even the sighs of grief
Reproach thee, that thou art not near,
And reproach thou wilt not hear.

IV

Let me set my mournful ditty
 To a merry measure; 20
Thou wilt never come for pity,
 Thou wilt come for pleasure;
Pity then will cut away
Those cruel wings, and thou wilt stay.

V

I love all that thou lovest, 25
 Spirit of Delight!
The fresh Earth in new leaves dressed,
 And the starry night;
Autumn evening, and the morn
When the golden mists are born. 30

VI

I love snow, and all the forms
 Of the radiant frost;
I love waves, and winds, and storms,
 Everything almost
Which is Nature's, and may be 35
Untainted by man's misery.

VII

I love tranquil solitude,
 And such society
As is quiet, wise, and good;
 Between thee and me 40
What difference? but thou dost possess
The things I seek, not love them less.

VIII

I love Love—though he has wings,
 And like light can flee,
But above all other things, 45
 Spirit, I love thee—
Thou art love and life! Oh, come,
Make once more my heart thy home.

MUTABILITY[7]

I

The flower that smiles to-day
 To-morrow dies;
All that we wish to stay
 Tempts and then flies.
What is this world's delight? 5
Lightning that mocks the night,
 Brief even as bright.

II

Virtue, how frail it is!
 Friendship how rare!
Love, how it sells poor bliss 10
 For proud despair!
But we, though soon they fall,
Survive their joy, and all
 Which ours we call.

III

Whilst skies are blue and bright, 15
 Whilst flowers are gay,
Whilst eyes that change ere night
 Make glad the day;
Whilst yet the calm hours creep,
Dream thou—and from thy sleep 20
 Then wake to weep.

POLITICAL GREATNESS[8]

Nor happiness, nor majesty, nor fame,
Nor peace, nor strength, nor skill in arms or
 arts,
Shepherd those herds whom tyranny makes
 tame;
Verse echoes not one beating of their hearts,
History is but the shadow of their shame, 5
Art veils her glass, or from the pageant starts
As to oblivion their blind millions fleet,
Staining that Heaven with obscene imagery
Of their own likeness. What are numbers
 knit
By force or custom? Man who man would
 be, 10
Must rule the empire of himself; in it
Must be supreme, establishing his throne
On vanquished will, quelling the anarchy
Of hopes and fears, being himself alone.

[7]Written in 1821; published in 1824.
[8]Written in 1821; published in 1824.

A LAMENT [9]

I

O world! O life! O time!
On whose last steps I climb,
   Trembling at that where I had stood before;
When will return the glory of your prime?
   No more—Oh, never more!   5

II

Out of the day and night
A joy has taken flight;
   Fresh spring, and summer, and winter hoar,
Move my faint heart with grief, but with delight
   No more—Oh, never more!   10

---

[9]Written in 1821; published in 1824.

TO —— [10]

I

One word is too often profaned
   For me to profane it,
One feeling too falsely disdained
   For thee to disdain it;
One hope is too like despair   5
   For prudence to smother,
And pity from thee more dear
   Than that from another.

II

I can give not what men call love,
   But wilt thou accept not   10
The worship the heart lifts above
   And the Heavens reject not,—
The desire of the moth for the star,
   Of the night for the morrow,
The devotion to something afar   15
   From the sphere of our sorrow?

---

[10]Written in 1821; published in 1824.

EPIPSYCHIDION [1]

Verses Addressed to the Noble and Unfortunate Lady, Emilia V——, Now Imprisoned in the Convent of ——

L'anima amante si slancia fuori del creato, e si crea nell' infinito un Mondo tutto per essa, diverso assai da questo oscuro e pauroso baratro. [2]

          —Her own words.

My song, I fear that thou wilt find but few
Who fitly shall conceive thy reasoning,
Of such hard matter dost thou entertain;
Whence, if by misadventure, chance should bring

Thee to base company (as chance may do),
Quite unaware of what thou dost contain,
I prithee, comfort thy sweet self again,
My last delight! tell them that they are dull,
And bid them own that thou art beautiful.

to a friend, "The person whom it celebrates was a cloud instead of a Juno; and poor Ixion starts from the Centaur that was the offspring of his own embrace. If you are curious, however, to hear what I am and have been, it will tell you something thereof. It is an idealized history of my own life and feelings. I think one is always in love with something or other; the error—I confess it is not easy for spirits cased in flesh and blood to avoid it —consists in seeking in a mortal image the likeness of what is, perhaps, eternal." In writing to another correspondent Shelley sought to veil the circumstances which had occasioned the poem: "The *Epipsychidion*," he wrote, "is a mystery; as to real flesh and blood, you know that I do not deal in these articles; you might as well go to a gin-shop for a leg of mutton, as expect anything human and earthly from me." He was, indeed, anxious to avoid gossip, and to this end published the poem anonymously, prefixing to it the "Advertisement" printed on the next page, in which he gives some account of the imaginary author.

[2]The soul of him who loves launches itself out of the created, and creates in the infinite a world for itself, and for itself alone, how different from this obscure and fearful den (Medwin's translation). These words come from an essay (*Il Vero Amore*, True Love) written by Emilia after reading Plato's *Symposium*.

---

[1]Written early in 1821 and published in the summer of the same year. The title is a Greek word coined by Shelley to convey the expression "this soul out of my soul," which occurs in the poem— i. e., this soul complementary to, or responsive to, my soul. The "noble and unfortunate lady" was Emilia Viviani, a young and beautiful Italian girl whose family had placed her against her will in the convent of St. Anna, near Pisa. When Shelley became acquainted with her and her story, she soon seemed to him "a type and symbol of what Goethe names 'the eternal feminine,' a type and symbol of all that is most radiant and divine in nature, all that is most remote and unattainable, yet ever to be pursued—the ideal of truth, beauty, and love. She was at once a living and breathing woman, young, lovely, ardent, afflicted, and the avator of the Ideal" (Dowden, *Life of Shelley*, II, 378). *Epipsychidion* is Shelley's expression of this feeling, which will be the better understood for a reading of Plato's *Symposium*. Shelley was quickly disillusioned about Emilia. He was soon writing of the poem

ADVERTISEMENT

THE Writer of the following lines died at Florence, as he was preparing for a voyage to one of the wildest of the Sporades, which he had bought, and where he had fitted up the ruins of an old building, and where it was his hope to have realized a scheme of life, suited perhaps to that happier and better world of which he is now an inhabitant, but hardly practicable in this. His life was singular; less on account of the romantic vicissitudes which diversified it, than the ideal tinge which it received from his own character and feelings. The present Poem, like the *Vita Nuova* of Dante, is sufficiently intelligible to a certain class of readers without a matter-of-fact history of the circumstances to which it relates; and to a certain other class it must ever remain incomprehensible, from a defect of a common organ of perception for the ideas of which it treats. Not but that *gran vergogna sarebbe a colui, che rimasse cosa sotto veste di figura, o di colore rettorico: e domandato non sapesse denudare le sue parole da cotal veste, in guisa che avessero verace intendimento.*[3]

The present poem appears to have been intended by the Writer as the dedication to some longer one. The stanza on the opposite page[4] is almost a literal translation from Dante's famous Canzone

Voi, ch' intendendo, il terzo ciel movete, etc.[5]

The presumptuous application of the concluding lines to his own composition will raise a smile at the expense of my unfortunate friend: be it a smile not of contempt, but pity.   S.

Sweet Spirit! Sister of that orphan one,[6]
Whose empire is the name[7] thou weepest on,

---

[3]Great were his shame who should rhyme anything under a garb of metaphor or rhetorical color, and then, being asked, should be incapable of stripping his words of this garb so that they might have a veritable meaning (From Dante's *Vita Nuova*, xxv, Rossetti's translation).

[4]I. e., the stanza here printed immediately above the "Advertisement."

[5]The first Canzone of the *Convito*. Shelley's stanza is a translation of its concluding lines.

[6]Mary Shelley. Her mother had died in giving birth to her.

[7]Shelley himself.

In my heart's temple I suspend to thee
These votive wreaths of withered memory.

Poor captive bird! who, from thy narrow cage,   5
Pourest such music, that it might assuage
The rugged hearts of those who prisoned thee,
Were they not deaf to all sweet melody;
This song shall be thy rose: its petals pale
Are dead, indeed, my adored Nightingale! 10
But soft and fragrant is the faded blossom,
And it has no thorn left to wound thy bosom.

High, spirit-wingéd Heart! who dost for ever
Beat thine unfeeling bars with vain endeavor,
Till those bright plumes of thought, in which arrayed   15
It over-soared this low and worldly shade,
Lie shattered; and thy panting, wounded breast
Stains with dear blood its unmaternal nest!
I weep vain tears: blood would less bitter be,
Yet poured forth gladlier, could it profit thee.   20

Seraph of Heaven! too gentle to be human,
Veiling beneath that radiant form of Woman
All that is insupportable in thee
Of light, and love, and immortality!
Sweet Benediction in the eternal Curse!   25
Veiled Glory of this lampless Universe!
Thou Moon beyond the clouds! Thou living Form
Among the Dead! Thou Star above the Storm!
Thou Wonder, and thou Beauty, and thou Terror!
Thou Harmony of Nature's art! Thou Mirror   30
In whom, as in the splendor of the Sun,
All shapes look glorious which thou gazest on!
Ay, even the dim words which obscure thee now
Flash, lightning-like, with unaccustomed glow;
I pray thee that thou blot from this sad song   35
All of its much mortality and wrong,
With those clear drops, which start like sacred dew

From the twin lights thy sweet soul darkens
    through,
Weeping, till sorrow becomes ecstasy:
Then smile on it, so that it may not die.   40

I never thought before my death to see
Youth's vision thus made perfect. Emily,
I love thee; though the world by no thin
    name
Will hide that love from its unvalued shame.
Would we two had been twins of the same
    mother!   45
Or, that the name my heart lent to another[8]
Could be a sister's bond for her and thee,
Blending two beams of one eternity!
Yet were one lawful and the other true,[9]
These names, though dear, could paint not,
    as is due,   50
How beyond refuge I am thine. Ah me!
I am not thine: I am a part of *thee.*

    Sweet Lamp! my moth-like Muse has
       burned its wings
Or, like a dying swan who soars and sings,
Young Love should teach Time, in his own
    gray style,   55
All that thou art. Art thou not void of
    guile,
A lovely soul formed to be blessed and bless?
A well of sealed and secret happiness,
Whose waters like blithe light and music
    are,
Vanquishing dissonance and gloom? A
    Star   60
Which moves not in the moving heavens,
    alone?
A Smile amid dark frowns? a gentle tone
Amid rude voices? a belovéd light?
A Solitude, a Refuge, a Delight?
A Lute, which those whom Love has taught
    to play   65
Make music on, to soothe the roughest day
And lull fond Grief asleep? a buried treas-
    ure?
A cradle of young thoughts of wingless
    pleasure?
A violet-shrouded grave of Woe?—I meas-
    ure
The world of fancies, seeking one like thee,
And find—alas! mine own infirmity.   71

    She met me, Stranger, upon life's rough
       way,
And lured me towards sweet Death; as
    Night by Day,

Winter by Spring, or Sorrow by swift Hope,
Let into light, life, peace. An antelope,   75
In the suspended impulse of its lightness,
Were less ethereally light: the brightness
Of her divinest presence trembles through
Her limbs, as underneath a cloud of dew
Embodied in the windless heaven of June   80
Amid the splendor-wingéd stars, the Moon
Burns, inextinguishably beautiful:
And from her lips, as from a hyacinth full
Of honey-dew, a liquid murmur drops,
Killing the sense with passion; sweet as
    stops   85
Of planetary music heard in trance.
In her mild lights the starry spirits dance,
The sunbeams of those wells which ever leap
Under the lightnings of the soul—too deep
For the brief fathom-line of thought or
    sense.   90
The glory of her being, issuing thence,
Stains the dead, blank, cold air with a warm
    shade
Of unentangled intermixture, made
By Love, of light and motion: one intense
Diffusion, one serene Omnipresence,   95
Whose flowing outlines mingle in their flow-
    ing,
Around her cheeks and utmost fingers
    glowing
With the unintermitted blood, which there
Quivers (as in a fleece of snow-like air
The crimson pulse of living morning
    quiver),   100
Continuously prolonged, and ending never,
Till they are lost, and in that Beauty furled
Which penetrates and clasps and fills the
    world;
Scarce visible from extreme loveliness.
Warm fragrance seems to fall from her light
    dress   105
And her loose hair; and where some heavy
    tress
The air of her own speed has disentwined,
The sweetness seems to satiate the faint
    wind;
And in the soul a wild odor is felt,
Beyond the sense, like fiery dews that melt 110
Into the bosom of a frozen bud.—
See where she stands! a mortal shape indued
With love and life and light and deity,
And motion which may change but cannot
    die;
An image of some bright Eternity;   115
A shadow of some golden dream; a Splendor
Leaving the third sphere pilotless;[10] a tender

---

[8]To Mary Shelley.

[9]I. e., wife and sister.

[10]In the Ptolemaic astronomy the third of the
concentric spheres surrounding the earth was that

Reflection of the eternal Moon of Love
Under whose motions life's dull billows
    move;
A Metaphor of Spring and Youth and Morn-
    ing; 120
A Vision like incarnate April, warning,
With smiles and tears, Frost the Anatomy[11]
Into his summer grave.
                Ah, woe is me!
What have I dared? where am I lifted? how
Shall I descend, and perish not? I know 125
That Love makes all things equal: I have
    heard
By mine own heart this joyous truth
    averred:
The spirit of the worm beneath the sod
In love and worship, blends itself with God.

Spouse! Sister! Angel! Pilot of the Fate[12]
Whose course has been so starless! O too
    late 131
Belovéd! O too soon adored, by me!
For in the fields of Immortality
My spirit should at first have worshiped
    thine,
A divine presence in a place divine; 135
Or should have moved beside it on this earth,
A shadow of that substance, from its birth;
But not as now:—I love thee; yes, I feel
That on the fountain of my heart a seal
Is set, to keep its waters pure and bright 140
For thee, since in those *tears* thou hast de-
    light.
We—are we not formed, as notes of music
    are,
For one another, though dissimilar;
Such difference without discord, as can
    make
Those sweetest sounds, in which all spirits
    shake 145
As trembling leaves in a continuous air?

Thy wisdom speaks in me, and bids me
    dare
Beacon the rocks on which high hearts are
    wrecked.
I never was attached to that great sect,
Whose doctrine is, that each one should
    select 150
Out of the crowd a mistress or a friend,
And all the rest, though fair and wise, com-
    mend
To cold oblivion, though it is in the code

Of modern morals, and the beaten road
Which those poor slaves with weary foot-
    steps tread, 155
Who travel to their home among the dead
By the broad highway of the world, and so
With one chained friend, perhaps a jealous
    foe,
The dreariest and the longest journey go.

True Love in this differs from gold and
    clay, 160
That to divide is not to take away.
Love is like understanding, that grows
    bright,
Gazing on many truths; 'tis like thy light,
Imagination! which from earth and sky,
And from the depths of human fantasy, 165
As from a thousand prisms and mirrors,
    fills
The Universe with glorious beams, and kills
Error, the worm, with many a sun-like arrow
Of its reverberated lightning. Narrow
The heart that loves, the brain that contem-
    plates, 170
The life that wears, the spirit that creates
One object, and one form, and builds thereby
A sepulcher for its eternity.

Mind from its object differs most in this:
Evil from good; misery from happiness; 175
The baser from the nobler; the impure
And frail, from what is clear and must en-
    dure.
If you divide suffering and dross, you may
Diminish till it is consumed away;
If you divide pleasure and love and thought,
Each part exceeds the whole; and we know
    not 181
How much, while any yet remains unshared,
Of pleasure may be gained, of sorrow
    spared:
This truth is that deep well, whence sages
    draw
The unenvied light of hope; the eternal law
By which those live, to whom this world of
    life 186
Is as a garden ravaged, and whose strife
Tills for the promise of a later birth
The wilderness of this Elysian earth.
There was a Being[13] whom my spirit oft 190
Met on its visioned wanderings, far aloft,
In the clear golden prime of my youth's
    dawn,
Upon the fairy isles of sunny lawn,

---

of Venus. Shelley implies that Venus has taken earthly form in Emilia, and in so doing has left her sphere pilotless.
[11]Frost the skeleton. [12]Shelley's fate.

---

[13]This Being is described in *Alastor*. See also the *Hymn to Intellectual Beauty*, above.

Amid the enchanted mountains, and the
  caves
Of divine sleep, and on the air-like waves 195
Of wonder-level dream, whose tremulous
  floor
Paved her light steps;—on an imagined
  shore,
Under the gray beak of some promontory
She met me, robed in such exceeding glory,
That I beheld her not. In solitudes   200
Her voice came to me through the whisper-
  ing woods,
And from the fountains, and the odors deep
Of flowers, which, like lips murmuring in
  their sleep
Of the sweet kisses which had lulled them
  there,
Breathed but of *her* to the enamored air ; 205
And from the breezes whether low or loud,
And from the rain of every passing cloud,
And from the singing of the summer-birds,
And from all sounds, all silence; in the
  words
Of antique verse and high romance,—in
  form,   210
Sound, color—in whatever checks that storm
Which with the shattered present chokes
  the past ;
And in that best philosophy, whose taste
Makes this cold common hell, our life, a
  doom
As glorious as a fiery martyrdom ;   215
Her Spirit was the harmony of truth.—

Then, from the caverns of my dreamy
  youth
I sprang, as one sandaled with plumes of
  fire,
And towards the lodestar of my one desire,
I flitted, like a dizzy moth, whose flight 220
Is as a dead leaf's in the owlet light,
When it would seek in Hesper's setting
  sphere[14]
A radiant death, a fiery sepulcher,
As if it were a lamp of earthly flame.—
But She, whom prayers or tears then could
  not tame,   225
Passed, like a God throned on a wingéd
  planet,
Whose burning plumes to tenfold swiftness
  fan it,
Into the dreary cone of our life's shade ;
And as a man with mighty loss dismayed,
I would have followed, though the grave be-
  tween   230

[14]In the Evening Star.

Yawned like a gulf whose specters are un-
  seen :
When a voice said :—"O thou of hearts the
  weakest,
The phantom is beside thee whom thou
  seekest."
Then I—"Where ?"—the world's echo an-
  swered "where ?"
And in that silence, and in my despair,   235
I questioned every tongueless wind that flew
Over my tower of mourning, if it knew
Whither 'twas fled, this soul out of my soul ;
And murmured names and spells which have
  control
Over the sightless[15] tyrants of our fate ;   240
But neither prayer nor verse could dissipate
The night which closed on her ; nor uncreate
That world within this Chaos, mine and me,
Of which she was the veiled Divinity,
The world I say of thoughts that worshiped
  her :   245
And therefore I went forth, with hope and
  fear
And every gentle passion sick to death,
Feeding my course with expectation's breath,
Into the wintry forest of our life ;
And struggling through its error with vain
  strife,   250
And stumbling in my weakness and my
  haste,
And half bewildered by new forms, I passed,
Seeking among those untaught foresters
If I could find one form resembling hers,
In which she might have masked herself
  from me.   255
There,—One, whose voice was venomed
  melody
Sat by a well, under blue nightshade bowers ;
The breath of her false mouth was like faint
  flowers,
Her touch was as electric poison,—flame
Out of her looks into my vitals came,   260
And from her living cheeks and bosom flew
A killing air, which pierced like honey-dew[16]
Into the core of my green heart, and lay
Upon its leaves ; until, as hair grown gray
O'er a young brow, they hid its unblown
  prime   265
With ruins of unseasonable time.

In many mortal forms I rashly sought
The shadow of that idol of my thought.
And some were fair—but beauty dies away :
Others were wise—but honeyed words be-
  tray :   270

[15]Invisible.
[16]Which blights the leaves on which it is formed.

And One was true—oh! why not true to me?
Then, as a hunted deer that could not flee,
I turned upon my thoughts, and stood at bay,
Wounded and weak and panting; the cold
　　day
Trembled, for pity of my strife and pain. 275
When, like a noonday dawn, there shone
　　again
Deliverance.　One[17] stood on my path who
　　seemed
As like the glorious shape which I had
　　dreamed
As is the Moon, whose changes ever run
Into themselves, to the eternal Sun;　280
The cold chaste Moon, the Queen of
　　Heaven's bright isles,
Who makes all beautiful on which she smiles,
That wandering shrine of soft yet icy flame
Which ever is transformed, yet still the same,
And warms not but illumines.　Young and
　　fair　285
As the descended Spirit of that sphere,
She hid me, as the Moon may hide the night
From its own darkness until all was bright
Between the Heaven and Earth of my calm
　　mind,
And, as a cloud charioted by the wind,　290
She led me to a cave in that wild place,
And sat beside me, with her downward face
Illumining my slumbers, like the Moon
Waxing and waning o'er Endymion.
And I was laid asleep, spirit and limb,　295
And all my being became bright or dim
As the Moon's image in a summer sea,
According as she smiled or frowned on me;
And there I lay, within a chaste cold bed:
Alas, I then was nor alive nor dead:—　300
For at her silver voice came Death and Life,
Unmindful each of their accustomed strife,
Masked like twin babes, a sister and a
　　brother,
The wandering hopes of one abandoned
　　mother,
And through the cavern without wings they
　　flew,　305
And cried "Away, he is not of our crew."
I wept, and though it be a dream, I weep.

What storms then shook the ocean of my
　　sleep,
Blotting that Moon, whose pale and waning
　　lips
Then shrank as in the sickness of eclipse;—
And how my soul was as a lampless sea,　311
And who was then its Tempest; and when
　　She,

[17]I. e., Mary Shelley.

The Planet of that hour, was quenched, what
　　frost
Crept o'er those waters, till from coast to
　　coast
The moving billows of my being fell　315
Into a death of ice, immovable;—
And then—what earthquakes made it gape
　　and split,
The white Moon smiling all the while on it,
These words conceal:—If not, each word
　　would be
The key of staunchless tears.　Weep not for
　　me!　320

At length, into the obscure Forest came
The Vision I had sought through grief and
　　shame.
Athwart that wintry wilderness of thorns
Flashed from her motion splendor like the
　　Morn's,
And from her presence life was radiated　325
Through the gray earth and branches bare
　　and dead;
So that her way was paved, and roofed above
With flowers as soft as thoughts of budding
　　love;
And music from her respiration spread
Like light,—all other sounds were pene-
　　trated　330
By the small, still, sweet spirit of that sound,
So that the savage winds hung mute around;
And odors warm and fresh fell from her
　　hair
Dissolving the dull cold in the frore air:
Soft as an Incarnation of the Sun,　335
When light is changed to love, this glorious
　　One
Floated into the cavern where I lay,
And called my Spirit, and the dreaming clay
Was lifted by the thing that dreamed below
As smoke by fire, and in her beauty's glow 340
I stood, and felt the dawn of my long night
Was penetrating me with living light:
I knew it was the Vision veiled from me
So many years—that it was Emily.

Twin Spheres of light who rule this pas-
　　sive Earth,[18]　345
This world of love, this *me*; and into birth
Awaken all its fruits and flowers, and dart
Magnetic might into its central heart;
And lift its billows and its mists, and guide
By everlasting laws, each wind and tide　350
To its fit cloud, and its appointed cave;
And lull its storms, each in the craggy grave
Which was its cradle, luring to faint bowers

[18]The Sun and Moon—Emilia and Mary.

The armies of the rainbow-wingéd showers;
And, as those married lights, which from the
    towers   355
Of Heaven look forth and fold the wandering
    globe
In liquid sleep and splendor, as a robe;
And all their many-mingled influence blend,
If equal, yet unlike, to one sweet end;—
So ye, bright regents, with alternate sway 360
Govern my sphere of being, night and day!
Thou, not disdaining even a borrowed might;
Thou, not eclipsing a remoter light;
And, through the shadow of the seasons
    three,
From Spring to Autumn's sere maturity, 365
Light it into the Winter of the tomb,
Where it may ripen to a brighter bloom.
Thou too, O Comet beautiful and fierce,[19]
Who drew the heart of this frail Universe
Towards thine own; till, wrecked in that
    convulsion,   370
Alternating attraction and repulsion,
Thine went astray and that was rent in
    twain;
Oh, float into our azure heaven again!
Be there Love's folding-star[20] at thy return;
The living Sun will feed thee from its
    urn   375
Of golden fire; the Moon will veil her horn
In thy last smiles; adoring Even and Morn
Will worship thee with incense of calm
    breath
And lights and shadows; as the star of Death
And Birth is worshiped by those sisters
    wild   380
Called Hope and Fear—upon the heart are
    piled
Their offerings,—of this sacrifice divine
A World shall be the altar.
                            Lady mine,
Scorn not these flowers of thought, the fad-
    ing birth
Which from its heart of hearts that plant
    puts forth   385
Whose fruit, made perfect by thy sunny
    eyes,
Will be as of the trees of Paradise.

The day is come, and thou wilt fly with me.
To whatsoe'er of dull mortality
Is mine, remain a vestal sister still;   390
To the intense, the deep, the imperishable,
Not mine but me, henceforth be thou united
Even as a bride, delighting and delighted.

---

[19]The person meant is not known, though various guesses have been made.
[20]Evening Star.

The hour is come:—the destined Star has
    risen
Which shall descend upon a vacant prison. 395
The walls are high, the gates are strong,
    thick set
The sentinels—but true Love never yet
Was thus constrained: it overleaps all fence:
Like lightning, with invisible violence
Piercing its continents;[21] like Heaven's free
    breath,   400
Which he who grasps can hold not: liker
    Death,
Who rides upon a thought, and makes his
    way
Through temple, tower, and palace, and the
    array
Of arms: more strength has Love than he or
    they;
For it can burst his charnel, and make
    free   405
The limbs in chains, the heart in agony,
The soul in dust and chaos.
                            Emily,
A ship is floating in the harbor now,
A wind is hovering o'er the mountain's brow;
There is a path on the sea's azure floor,   410
No keel has ever ploughed that path before;
The halcyons[22] brood around the foamless
    isles;
The treacherous Ocean has forsworn its
    wiles;
The merry mariners are bold and free:
Say, my heart's sister, wilt thou sail with
    me?   415
Our bark is as an albatross, whose nest
Is a far Eden of the purple East;
And we between her wings will sit, while
    Night,
And Day, and Storm, and Calm, pursue
    their flight,
Our ministers, along the boundless Sea,   420
Treading each other's heels, unheededly.
It is an isle under Ionian skies,
Beautiful as a wreck of Paradise,
And,—for the harbors are not safe and
    good,—
This land would have remained a solitude 425
But for some pastoral people native there,
Who from the Elysian, clear, and golden air
Draw the last spirit of the age of gold,
Simple and spirited; innocent and bold.
The blue Aegean girds this chosen home,   430
With ever-changing sound and light and
    foam,

---

[21]Receptacles.
[22]Kingfishers. It was fabled that they nested
upon the sea in winter, tranquilizing its waters.

Kissing the sifted sands, and caverns hoar;
And all the winds wandering along the shore
Undulate with the undulating tide:
There are thick woods where sylvan forms
    abide;   435
And many a fountain, rivulet, and pond,
As clear as elemental diamond, ·
Or serene morning air; and far beyond,
The mossy tracks made by the goats and deer
(Which the rough shepherd treads but once
    a year)   440
Pierce into glades, caverns, and bowers, and
    halls
Built round with ivy, which the waterfalls
Illuming, with sound that never fails
Accompany the noonday nightingales;
And all the place is peopled with sweet
    airs;   445
The light clear element which the isle wears
Is heavy with the scent of lemon-flowers,
Which floats like mist laden with unseen
    showers,
And falls upon the eyelids like faint sleep;
And from the moss violets and jonquils
    peep,   450
And dart their arrowy odor through the
    brain
Till you might faint with that delicious pain.
And every motion, odor, beam, and tone,
With that deep music is in unison:
Which is a soul within the soul—they
    seem   455
Like echoes of an antenatal dream.—
It is an isle 'twixt Heaven, Air, Earth, and
    Sea,
Cradled, and hung in clear tranquillity;
Bright as that wandering Eden Lucifer,[23]
Washed by the soft blue Oceans of young
    air.   460
It is a favored place. Famine or Blight,
Pestilence, War and Earthquake, never light
Upon its mountain-peaks; blind vultures,
    they
Sail onward far upon their fatal way:
The wingéd storms, chanting their thunder-
    psalm   465
To other lands, leave azure chasms of calm
Over this isle, or weep themselves in dew,
From which its fields and woods ever renew
Their green and golden immortality.
And from the sea there rise, and from the
    sky   470
There fall, clear exhalations, soft and bright,
Veil after veil, each hiding some delight,
Which Sun or Moon or zephyr draw aside,
Till the isle's beauty, like a naked bride

[23]The Morning Star.

Glowing at once with love and loveliness, 475
Blushes and trembles at its own excess:
Yet, like a buried lamp, a Soul no less
Burns in the heart of this delicious isle,
An atom of th' Eternal, whose own smile
Unfolds itself, and may be felt, not seen 480
O'er the gray rocks, blue waves, and forests
    green,
Filling their bare and void interstices.
But the chief marvel of the wilderness
Is a lone dwelling, built by whom or how
None of the rustic island-people know: 485
'Tis not a tower of strength, though with its
    height
It overtops the woods; but, for delight,
Some wise and tender Ocean-King, ere crime
Had been invented, in the world's young
    prime,
Reared it, a wonder of that simple time, 490
An envy of the isles, a pleasure-house
Made sacred to his sister and his spouse.
It scarce seems now a wreck of human art,
But, as it were Titanic; in the heart
Of Earth having assumed its form, then
    grown   495
Out of the mountains, from the living stone,
Lifting itself in caverns light and high:
For all the antique and learned imagery
Has been erased, and in the place of it
The ivy and the wild-vine interknit   500
The volumes of their many-twining stems;
Parasite flowers illume with dewy gems
The lampless halls, and when they fade, the
    sky
Peeps through their winter-woof of tracery
With moonlight patches, or star atoms
    keen,   505
Or fragments of the day's intense serene;—[24]
Working mosaic on their Parian floors.[25]
And, day and night, aloof, from the high
    towers
And terraces, the Earth and Ocean seem
To sleep in one another's arms, and dream 510
Of waves, flowers, clouds, woods, rocks, and
    all that we
Read in their smiles, and call reality.

This isle and house are mine, and I have
    vowed
Thee to be lady of the solitude.—
And I have fitted up some chambers there 515
Looking towards the golden Eastern air,
And level with the living winds, which flow
Like waves above the living waves below.—
I have sent books and music there, and all

[24]Calm brightness.
[25]Floors made of Parian marble.

Those instruments with which high Spirits call   520
The future from its cradle, and the past
Out of its grave, and make the present last
In thoughts and joys which sleep, but cannot die,
Folded within their own eternity.
Our simple life wants little, and true taste 525
Hires not the pale drudge Luxury, to waste
The scene it would adorn, and therefore still,
Nature with all her children haunts the hill.
The ring-dove, in the embowering ivy, yet
Keeps up her love-lament, and the owls flit 530
Round the evening tower, and the young stars glance
Between the quick bats in their twilight dance;
The spotted deer bask in the fresh moonlight
Before our gate, and the slow, silent night
Is measured by the pants of their calm sleep.   535
Be this our home in life, and when years heap
Their withered hours, like leaves, on our decay,
Let us become the overhanging day,
The living soul of this Elysian isle,
Conscious, inseparable, one.   Meanwhile 540
We two will rise, and sit, and walk together,
Under the roof of blue Ionian weather,
And wander in the meadows, or ascend
The mossy mountains, where the blue heavens bend
With lightest winds, to touch their paramour;   545
Or linger, where the pebble-paven shore,
Under the quick, faint kisses of the sea
Trembles and sparkles as with ecstasy,—
Possessing and possessed by all that is
Within that calm circumference of bliss, 550
And by each other, till to love and live
Be one:—or, at the noontide hour, arrive
Where some old cavern hoar seems yet to keep
The moonlight of the expired night asleep,
Through which the awakened day can never peep;   555
A veil for our seclusion, close as night's,
Where secure sleep may kill thine innocent lights;
Sleep, the fresh dew of languid love, the rain
Whose drops quench kisses till they burn again.
And we will talk, until thought's melody 560
Become too sweet for utterance, and it die
In words, to live again in looks, which dart
With thrilling tone into the voiceless heart,
Harmonizing silence without a sound.

Our breath shall intermix, our bosoms bound,   565
And our veins beat together; and our lips
With other eloquence than words, eclipse
The soul that burns between them, and the wells
Which boil under our being's inmost cells,
The fountains of our deepest life, shall be 570
Confused in Passion's golden purity,
As mountain-springs under the morning sun.
We shall become the same, we shall be one
Spirit within two frames, oh! wherefore two?
One passion in twin-hearts, which grows and grew,   575
Till like two meteors of expanding flame,
Those spheres instinct with it become the same,
Touch, mingle, are transfigured; ever still
Burning, yet ever inconsumable:
In one another's substance finding food,   580
Like flames too pure and light and unimbued
To nourish their bright lives with baser prey,
Which point to Heaven and cannot pass away:
One hope within two wills, one will beneath
Two overshadowing minds, one life, one death,   585
One Heaven, one Hell, one immortality,
And one annihilation.   Woe is me!
The wingéd words on which my soul would pierce
Into the height of Love's rare Universe,
Are chains of lead around its flight of fire—   590
I pant, I sink, I tremble, I expire!

———

Weak Verses, go, kneel at your Sovereign's feet,
And say:—"We are the masters of thy slave;
What wouldest thou with us and ours and thine?"
Then call your sisters from Oblivion's cave,   595
All singing loud: "Love's very pain is sweet,
But its reward is in the world divine
Which, if not here, it builds beyond the grave."
So shall ye live when I am there.   Then haste
Over the hearts of men, until ye meet   600
Marina, Vanna, Primus,[26] and the rest,
And bid them love each other and be blessed:
And leave the troop which errs, and which reproves,
And come and be my guest,—for I am Love's.

[26]Mary Shelley and two friends who cannot certainly be identified from these names.

ADONAIS[1]

An Elegy on the Death of John Keats, Author of Endymion, Hyperion, Etc.

Ἀστὴρ πρὶν μὲν ἔλαμπες ἐνὶ ζωοῖσιν Ἑῶος.   νῦν δὲ θανὼν
λάμπεις Ἔσπερος ἐν φθιμένοις.

—PLATO.[2]

PREFACE

Φάρμακον ἦλθε,Βίων, ποτὶ σὸν στόμα, φάρμακον εἶδες·
πῶς τευ τοῖς χείλεσσι ποτέδραμε, κοὐκ ἐγλυκάνθη;
τίς δὲ βροτὸς τοσσοῦτον ἀνάμερος, ἢ κεράσαι τοι,
ἢ δοῦναι λαλέοντι τὸ φάρμακον; ἔκφυγεν ᾠδάν.
                    —MOSCHUS, EPITAPH. BION.[3]

IT IS my intention to subjoin to the London edition of this poem a criticism upon the claims of its lamented object to be classed among the writers of the highest genius who have adorned our age. My known repugnance to the narrow principles of taste on which several of his earlier compositions were modeled proves at least that I am an impartial judge. I consider the fragment of *Hyperion* as second to nothing that was ever produced by a writer of the same years.

John Keats died at Rome of a consumption, in his twenty-fourth year, on the—— of—— 1821; and was buried in the romantic and lonely cemetery of the Protestants in that city, under the pyramid which is the tomb of Cestius, and the massy walls and towers, now moldering and desolate, which formed the circuit of ancient Rome. The cemetery is an open space among the ruins, covered in winter with violets and daisies. It might make one in love with death, to think that one should be buried in so sweet a place.

The genius of the lamented person to whose memory I have dedicated these unworthy verses was not less delicate and fragile than it was beautiful; and where cankerworms abound, what wonder if its young flower was blighted in the bud? The savage criticism on his *Endymion,* which appeared in the *Quarterly Review,* produced the most violent effect on his susceptible mind; the agitation thus originated ended in the rupture of a blood-vessel in the lungs; a rapid consumption ensued, and the succeeding acknowledgments from more candid critics of the true greatness of his powers were ineffectual to heal the wound thus wantonly inflicted.

It may be well said that these wretched men know not what they do. They scatter their insults and their slanders without heed as to whether the poisoned shaft lights on a heart made callous by many blows or one like Keats's composed of more penetrable stuff. One of their associates is, to my knowledge, a most base and unprincipled calumniator. As to *Endymion,* was it a poem, whatever might be its defects, to be treated contemptuously by those who had celebrated, with various degrees of complacency and panegyric, *Paris,* and *Woman,* and a *Syrian Tale,* and Mrs. Lefanu, and Mr. Barrett, and Mr. Howard Payne, and a long list of the illustrious obscure? Are these the men who in their venal good nature presumed to draw a parallel between the Rev.

[1] Written at Pisa during the early days of June, 1821, and published at Pisa in the middle of July in the same year. Part of the edition was sent to be sold in London, but there was, during Shelley's lifetime, no London edition such as is mentioned in the first sentence of the Preface. When he wrote the Preface Shelley did not know the exact time of Keats's death. He shared, too, the incorrect impression current at the time that adverse criticism had brought about Keats's illness. (Concerning this see the introductory note to Keats's poems, below.) Keats and Shelley had met each other at the house of Leigh Hunt, but had never seen much of each other. *Adonais* is not the result of a feeling of warm personal friendship so much as of Shelley's recognition of the similarity between his own life and that of Keats. While the poem was in progress he wrote: "I have been engaged these last days in composing a poem on the death of Keats, which will shortly be finished. . . . It is a highly wrought *piece of art,* and perhaps better in point of composition than anything I have written." The poem is modeled on the Greek pastoral elegy, and Shelley is particularly indebted to Bion's *Lament for Adonis* and Moschus's *Elegy on the Death of Bion.*

[2] Thou wert the morning star among the living,
    Ere thy fair light had fled;—
Now, having died, thou art as Hesperus, giving
    New splendor to the dead.
                    (Shelley's translation.)

[3] Poison came, Bion, to thy mouth—thou didst know poison. To such lips as thine did it come, and was not sweetened? What mortal was so cruel that could mix poison for thee, or who could give thee the venom that heard thy voice? Surely he had no music in his soul (Lang's translation).

Mr. Milman and Lord Byron? What gnat did they strain at here, after having swallowed all those camels? Against what woman taken in adultery dares the foremost of these literary prostitutes to cast his opprobious stone? Miserable man! you, one of the meanest, have wantonly defaced one of the noblest specimens of the workmanship of God. Nor shall it be your excuse, that, murderer as you are, you have spoken daggers, but used none.

The circumstances of the closing scene of poor Keats's life were not made known to me until the *Elegy* was ready for the press. I am given to understand that the wound which his sensitive spirit had received from the criticism of *Endymion* was exasperated by the bitter sense of unrequited benefits; the poor fellow seems to have been hooted from the stage of life, no less by those on whom he had wasted the promise of his genius, than those on whom he had lavished his fortune and his care. He was accompanied to Rome, and attended in his last illness by Mr. Severn, a young artist of the highest promise, who, I have been informed, "almost risked his own life, and sacrificed every prospect to unwearied attendance upon his dying friend." Had I known these circumstances before the completion of my poem, I should have been tempted to add my feeble tribute of applause to the more solid recompense which the virtuous man finds in the recollection of his own motives. Mr. Severn can dispense with a reward from "such stuff as dreams are made of." His conduct is a golden augury of the success of his future career—may the unextinguished Spirit of his illustrious friend animate the creations of his pencil, and plead against Oblivion for his name!

I

I weep for Adonais—he is dead!
Oh, weep for Adonais! though our tears
Thaw not the frost which binds so dear a
   head!
And thou, sad Hour, selected from all
   years
To mourn our loss, rouse thy obscure compeers,   5
And teach them thine own sorrow, say:
   "With me

Died Adonais; till the Future dares
Forget the Past, his fate and fame shall be
An echo and a light unto eternity!"

2

Where wert thou, mighty Mother, when
   he lay,   10
When thy Son lay, pierced by the shaft
   which flies
In darkness? where was lorn Urania[4]
When Adonais died? With veiléd eyes,
'Mid listening Echoes, in her Paradise
She sat, while one, with soft enamored
   breath,   15
Rekindled all the fading melodies,
With which, like flowers that mock the
   corse beneath,
He had adorned and hid the coming bulk of
   Death.

3

Oh, weep for Adonais—he is dead!
Wake, melancholy Mother, wake and
   weep!   20
Yet wherefore? Quench within their
   burning bed
Thy fiery tears, and let thy loud heart
   keep,
Like his, a mute and uncomplaining sleep;
For he is gone, where all things wise and
   fair
Descend;—oh, dream not that the amorous
   Deep   25
Will yet restore him to the vital air;
Death feeds on his mute voice, and laughs at
   our despair.

4

Most musical of mourners, weep again!
Lament anew, Urania!—he[5] died,
Who was the Sire of an immortal strain,   30
Blind, old, and lonely, when his country's
   pride,
The priest, the slave, and the liberticide,
Trampled and mocked with many a loathéd
   rite
Of lust and blood; he went, unterrified,
Into the gulf of death; but his clear Sprite
Yet reigns o'er the earth; the third[6] among
   the sons of light.   36

---

[4]The heavenly muse, to whom Milton appeals in *Paradise Lost;* or, more probably, the Uranian Aphrodite, spirit of heavenly love.
[5]Milton.
[6]The first and second, if one may judge from Shelley's *Defense of Poetry,* were Homer and Dante.

5

Most musical of mourners, weep anew!
Not all to that bright station dared to
climb;
And happier they their happiness who
knew,
Whose tapers yet burn through that night
of time   40
In which suns perished; others more sublime,
Struck by the envious wrath of man or
god,
Have sunk, extinct in their refulgent
prime;
And some yet live, treading the thorny
road,
Which leads, through toil and hate, to Fame's
serene abode.   45

6

But now, thy youngest, dearest one, has
perished—
The nursling of thy widowhood, who
grew,
Like a pale flower by some sad maiden
cherished,
And fed with true-love tears, instead of
dew;
Most musical of mourners, weep anew! 50
Thy extreme hope, the loveliest and the
last,
The bloom, whose petals, nipped before
they blew,
Died on the promise of the fruit, is waste;
The broken lily lies—the storm is overpast.

7

To that high Capital,[7] where kingly Death
Keeps his pale court in beauty and de-
cay,   56
He came; and bought, with price of purest
breath,
A grave among the eternal.—Come away!
Haste, while the vault of blue Italian day
Is yet his fitting charnel-roof! while still 60
He lies, as if in dewy sleep he lay;
Awake him not! surely he takes his fill
Of deep and liquid rest, forgetful of all ill.

8

He will awake no more, oh, never more!—
Within the twilight chamber spreads apace
The shadow of white Death, and at the
door   66
Invisible Corruption waits to trace

His extreme way to her dim dwelling-
place;
The eternal Hunger sits, but pity and awe
Soothe her pale rage, nor dares she to de-
face   70
So fair a prey, till darkness, and the law
Of change, shall o'er his sleep the mortal
curtain draw.

9

Oh, weep for Adonais!—The quick
Dreams,
The passion-wingéd Ministers of thought,
Who were his flocks, whom near the living
streams   75
Of his young spirit he fed, and whom he
taught
The love which was its music, wander
not,—
Wander no more, from kindling brain to
brain,
But droop there, whence they sprung; and
mourn their lot
Round the cold heart, where, after their
sweet pain,   80
They ne'er will gather strength, or find a
home again.

10

And one with trembling hands clasps his
cold head,
And fans him with her moonlight wings,
and cries;
"Our love, our hope, our sorrow, is not
dead;
See, on the silken fringe of his faint
eyes,   85
Like dew upon a sleeping flower, there lies
A tear some Dream has loosened from his
brain."
Lost Angel of a ruined Paradise!
She knew not 'twas her own; as with no
stain
She faded, like a cloud which had outwept its
rain.   90

11

One from a lucid urn of starry dew
Washed his light limbs as if embalming
them;
Another clipped her profuse locks, and
threw
The wreath upon him, like an anadem,[8]

---

[7] Rome.

[8] Garland.

Which frozen tears instead of pearls be-
gem;   95
Another in her willful grief would break
Her bow and wingéd reeds, as if to stem
A greater loss with one which was more
weak;
And dull the barbéd fire against his frozen
cheek.

12

Another Splendor on his mouth alit,   100
That mouth, whence it was wont to draw
the breath
Which gave it strength to pierce the
guarded wit,
And pass into the panting heart beneath
With lightning and with music: the damp
death
Quenched its caress upon his icy lips;   105
And, as a dying meteor stains a wreath
Of moonlight vapor, which the cold night
clips,[9]
It flushed through his pale limbs, and passed
to its eclipse.

13

And others came . . . Desires and Ado-
rations,
Wingéd Persuasions and veiled Destinies,
Splendors, and Glooms, and glimmering
Incarnations   111
Of hopes and fears, and twilight Phanta-
sies;
And Sorrow, with her family of Sighs,
And Pleasure, blind with tears, led by the
gleam
Of her own dying smile instead of eyes, 115
Came in slow pomp;—the moving pomp
might seem
Like pageantry of mist on an autumnal
stream.

14

All he had loved, and molded into thought,
From shape, and hue, and odor, and sweet
sound,
Lamented Adonais. Morning sought   120
Her eastern watch-tower, and her hair un-
bound,
Wet with the tears which should adorn
the ground,
Dimmed the aërial eyes that kindle day;
Afar the melancholy thunder moaned,

[9]Embraces.

Pale Ocean in unquiet slumber lay,   125
And the wild Winds flew round, sobbing in
their dismay.

15

Lost Echo sits amid the voiceless moun-
tains,
And feeds her grief with his remembered
lay,
And will no more reply to winds or foun-
tains,
Or amorous birds perched on the young
green spray,   130
Or herdsman's horn, or bell at closing day;
Since she can mimic not his lips, more dear
Than those for whose disdain she pined
away[10]
Into a shadow of all sounds:—a drear
Murmur, between their songs, is all the wood-
men hear.   135

16

Grief made the young Spring wild, and she
threw down
Her kindling buds, as if she Autumn were,
Or they dead leaves; since her delight is
flown,
For whom should she have waked the sul-
len year?
To Phoebus was not Hyacinth[11] so dear 140
Nor to himself Narcissus,[12] as to both
Thou, Adonais: wan they stand and sere
Amid the faint companions of their youth,
With dew all turned to tears; odor, to sigh-
ing ruth.

17

Thy spirit's sister, the lorn nightingale 145
Mourns not her mate with such melodious
pain;
Not so the eagle, who like thee could scale
Heaven, and could nourish in the sun's
domain
Her mighty youth with morning, doth com-
plain,
Soaring and screaming round her empty
nest,   150
As Albion wails for thee: the curse of Cain

[10]Than those of Narcissus, because of whose disdain she pined away, etc.

[11]A youth loved by Apollo, who changed him,
when he died, into a flower.

[12]After disdaining Echo and other nymphs, Narcissus was punished by falling in love with his own
reflected image. At his death he was changed into
a flower.

Light on his head who pierced thy innocent
  breast,[13]
And scared the angel soul that was its earthly
  guest!

18

Ah, woe is me! Winter is come and gone,
But grief returns with the revolving year;
The airs and streams renew their joyous
  tone; 156
The ants, the bees, the swallows reappear;
Fresh leaves and flowers deck the dead
  Season's bier;
The amorous birds now pair in every brake,
And build their mossy homes in field
  and brere;[14] 160
And the green lizard, and the golden snake,
Like unimprisoned flames, out of their trance
  awake.

19

Through wood and stream and field and
  hill and Ocean
A quickening life from the Earth's heart
  has burst
As it has ever done, with change and motion, 165
From the great morning of the world when
  first
God dawned on Chaos; in its stream immersed,
The lamps of Heaven flash with a softer
  light;
All baser things pant with life's sacred
  thirst;
Diffuse themselves; and spend in love's
  delight, 170
The beauty and the joy of their renewéd
  might.

20

The leprous corpse, touched by this spirit
  tender,
Exhales itself in flowers of gentle breath;
Like incarnations of the stars, when splendor
Is changed to fragrance, they illumine
  death 175
And mock the merry worm that wakes
  beneath;

---

[13]J. W. Croker, the author of the anonymous paper
on *Endymion* in the *Quarterly Review* which Shelley and other contemporaries believed to have been
the proximate cause of Keats's death.

[14]Brier.

Nought we know, dies. Shall that alone
  which knows
Be as a sword consumed before the sheath
By sightless[15] lightning?—the intense atom
  glows
A moment, then is quenched in a most cold
  repose. 180

21

Alas! that all we loved of him should be,
But for our grief, as if it had not been,
And grief itself be mortal! Woe is me!
Whence are we, and why are we? of what
  scene
The actors or spectators? Great and mean
Meet massed in death, who lends what life
  must borrow. 186
As long as skies are blue, and fields are
  green,
Evening must usher night, night urge the
  morrow,
Month follow month with woe, and year wake
  year to sorrow.

22

He will awake no more, oh, never more! 190
"Wake thou," cried Misery, "childless
  Mother, rise
Out of thy sleep, and slake, in thy heart's
  core,
A wound more fierce than his, with tears
  and sighs."
And all the Dreams that watched Urania's
  eyes, 194
And all the Echoes whom their sister's song
Had held in holy silence, cried: "Arise!"
Swift as a Thought by the snake Memory
  stung,
From her ambrosial rest the fading Splendor
  sprung.

23

She rose like an autumnal Night, that
  springs 199
Out of the East, and follows wild and drear
The golden Day, which, on eternal wings,
Even as a ghost abandoning a bier,
Had left the Earth a corpse. Sorrow and
  fear
So struck, so roused, so rapped Urania; 204
So saddened round her like an atmosphere
Of stormy mist; so swept her on her way
Even to the mournful place where Adonais
  lay.

---

[15]Invisible.

24

Out of her secret Paradise she sped,
Through camps and cities rough with
    stone, and steel,   209
And human hearts, which to her aery tread
Yielding not, wounded the invisible
Palms of her tender feet where'er they fell:
And barbéd tongues, and thoughts more
    sharp than they,
Rent the soft Form, they never could repel,
Whose sacred blood, like the young tears
    of May,   215
Paved with eternal flowers that undeserving
    way.

25

In the death-chamber for a moment Death,
Shamed by the presence of that living
    Might,
Blushed to annihilation, and the breath
Revisited those lips, and Life's pale
    light   220
Flashed through those limbs, so late her
    dear delight.
"Leave me not wild and drear and com-
    fortless,
As silent lightning leaves the starless night!
Leave me not!" cried Urania: her distress
Roused Death: Death rose and smiled, and
    met her vain caress.   225

26

"Stay yet.awhile! speak to me once again;
Kiss me, so long but as a kiss may live;
And in my heartless breast and burning
    brain
That word, that kiss, shall all thoughts else
    survive,   229
With food of saddest memory kept alive,
Now thou art dead, as if it were a part
Of thee, my Adonais! I would give
All that I am to be as thou now art!
But I am chained to Time, and cannot thence
    depart!

27

"O gentle child, beautiful as thou wert, 235
Why didst thou leave the trodden paths of
    men
Too soon, and with weak hands though
    mighty heart
Dare the unpastured dragon[16] in his den?
Defenseless as thou wert, oh, where was
    then

---

[16]The world of men.

Wisdom the mirrored shield, or scorn the
    spear?   240
Or hadst thou waited the full cycle, when
Thy spirit should have filled its crescent
    sphere,
The monsters of life's waste had fled from
    thee like deer.

28

"The herded wolves, bold only to pursue;
The obscene ravens, clamorous o'er the
    dead;   245
The vultures to the conqueror's banner true
Who feed where Desolation first has fed,
And whose wings rain contagion;—how
    they fled,
When, like Apollo, from his golden bow
The Pythian of the age[17] one arrow sped 250
And smiled!—The spoilers tempt no sec-
    ond blow,
They fawn on the proud feet that spurn them
    lying low.

29

"The sun comes forth, and many reptiles
    spawn;
He sets, and each ephemeral insect then
Is gathered into death without a dawn, 255
And the immortal stars awake again;
So it is in the world of living men:
A godlike mind soars forth, in its delight
Making earth bare and veiling heaven, and
    when
It sinks, the swarms that dimmed or shared
    its light   260
Leave to its kindred lamps the spirit's awful
    night."

30

Thus ceased she: and the mountain shep-
    herds came,
Their garlands sere, their magic mantles
    rent;
The Pilgrim of Eternity,[18] whose fame
Over his living head like Heaven is bent,
An early but enduring monument,   266
Came, veiling all the lightnings of his song
In sorrow; from her wilds Ierne sent
The sweetest lyrist of her saddest wrong,[19]
And Love taught Grief to fall like music from
    his tongue.   270

---

[17]Apollo was called the Pythian because he slew the Python. Shelley here applies the epithet to Byron, who attacked the reviewers in his satirical poem *English Bards and Scotch Reviewers.*

[18]Byron; so called because of *Childe Harold's Pilgrimage.* Cf. III, 70, 8, of *Childe Harold.*

[19]I. e., Ireland sent Thomas Moore.

31

Midst others of less note, came one frail Form,[20]
A phantom among men; companionless
As the last cloud of an expiring storm
Whose thunder is its knell; he, as I guess,
Had gazed on Nature's naked loveliness,
Actaeon-like,[21] and now he fled astray 276
With feeble steps o'er the world's wilderness,
And his own thoughts, along that rugged way,
Pursued, like raging hounds, their father and their prey.

32

A pardlike[22] Spirit beautiful and swift— 280
A Love in desolation masked;—a Power
Girt round with weakness;—it can scarce uplift
The weight of the superincumbent hour;
It is a dying lamp, a falling shower, 284
A breaking billow;—even whilst we speak
Is it not broken?   On the withering flower
The killing sun smiles brightly: on a cheek
The life can burn in blood, even while the heart may break.

33

His head was bound with pansies overblown,
And faded violets, white, and pied, and blue; 290
And a light spear topped with a cypress cone,
Round whose rude shaft dark ivy-tresses grew
Yet dripping with the forest's noonday dew,
Vibrated, as the ever-beating heart
Shook the weak hand that grasped it; of that crew 295
He came the last, neglected and apart;
A herd-abandoned deer struck by the hunter's dart.

34

All stood aloof, and at his partial moan[23]
Smiled through their tears; well knew that gentle band

Who in another's fate now wept his own, 300
As in the accents of an unknown land
He sung new sorrow; sad Urania scanned
The Stranger's mien, and murmured: "Who art thou?"
He answered not, but with a sudden hand
Made bare his branded and ensanguined brow, 305
Which was like Cain's or Christ's—oh! that it should be so!

35

What softer voice is hushed over the dead?
Athwart what brow is that dark mantle thrown?
What form leans sadly o'er the white death-bed,
In mockery of monumental stone, 310
The heavy heart heaving without a moan?
If it be He,[24] who, gentlest of the wise,
Taught, soothed, loved, honored the departed one,
Let me not vex, with inharmonious sighs,
The silence of that heart's accepted sacrifice.

36

Our Adonais has drunk poison—oh! 316
What deaf and viperous murderer could crown
Life's early cup with such a draught of woe?
The nameless worm[25] would now itself disown:
It felt, yet could escape, the magic tone 320
Whose prelude held all envy, hate, and wrong,
But what was howling in one breast alone,
Silent with expectation of the song,
Whose master's hand is cold, whose silver lyre unstrung. 324

37

Live thou, whose infamy is not thy fame!
Live! fear no heavier chastisement from me,
Thou noteless blot on a remembered name!
But be thyself, and know thyself to be!
And ever at thy season be thou free
To spill the venom when thy fangs o'erflow: 330
Remorse and Self-contempt shall cling to thee;

---

[20]Shelley.
[21]Actaeon was torn to pieces by his own hounds after he had seen Artemis bathing.
[22]Leopard-like.   [23]Fond.

[24]Leigh Hunt.
[25]The *Quarterly* reviewer; see note to stanza 17 above.

Hot Shame shall burn upon thy secret
    brow,
And like a beaten hound tremble thou shalt
    —as now.

38

Nor let us weep that our delight is fled
Far from these carrion kites that scream
    below;   335
He wakes or sleeps with the enduring dead;
Thou canst not soar where he is sitting
    now.—
Dust to the dust! but the pure spirit shall
    flow
Back to the burning fountain whence it
    came,
A portion of the Eternal, which must glow
Through time and change, unquenchably
    the same,   341
Whilst the cold embers choke the sordid
    hearth of shame.

39

Peace, peace! he is not dead, he doth not
    sleep—
He hath awakened from the dream of
    life—
'Tis we, who lost in stormy vision, keep
With phantoms an unprofitable strife, 346
And in mad trance, strike with our spirit's
    knife
Invulnerable nothings.— *We* decay
Like corpses in a charnel; fear and grief
Convulse us and consume us day by day,
And cold hopes swarm like worms within our
    living clay.   351

40

He has outsoared the shadow of our night;
Envy and calumny and hate and pain,
And that unrest which men miscall delight,
Can touch him not and torture not again;
From the contagion of the world's slow
    stain   356
He is secure, and now can never mourn
A heart grown cold, a head grown gray in
    vain;
Nor, when the spirit's self has ceased to
    burn,
With sparkless ashes load an unlamented urn.

41

He lives, he wakes—'tis Death is dead, not
    he;   361
Mourn not for Adonais.—Thou young
    Dawn,

Turn all thy dew to splendor, for from
    thee
The spirit thou lamentest is not gone;
Ye caverns and ye forests, cease to moan!
Cease, ye faint flowers and fountains, and
    thou Air,   366
Which like a mourning veil thy scarf hadst
    thrown
O'er the abandoned Earth, now leave it
    bare
Even to the joyous stars which smile on its
    despair!   369

42

He is made one with Nature: there is heard
His voice in all her music, from the moan
Of thunder, to the song of night's sweet
    bird;
He is a presence to be felt and known
In darkness and in light, from herb and
    stone,
Spreading itself where'er that Power may
    move   375
Which has withdrawn his being to its own;
Which wields the world with never-
    wearied love,
Sustains it from beneath, and kindles it
    above.

43

He is a portion of the loveliness
Which once he made more lovely: he doth
    bear   380
His part, while the one Spirit's plastic
    stress
Sweeps through the dull dense world, com-
    pelling there,
All new successions to the forms they
    wear;
Torturing th' unwilling dross that checks
    its flight   384
To its own like likeness, as each mass may
    bear;
And bursting in its beauty and its might
From trees and beasts and men into the
    Heaven's light.

44

The splendors of the firmament of time
May be eclipsed, but are extinguished not;
Like stars to their appointed height they
    climb,   390
And death is a low mist which cannot blot

The brightness it may veil.   When lofty
   thought
Lifts a young heart above its mortal lair,
And love and life contend in it, for what
Shall be its earthly doom, the dead live
   there   395
And move like winds of light on dark and
   stormy air.

45

The inheritors of unfulfilled renown
Rose from their thrones, built beyond mor-
   tal thought,
Far in the Unapparent.   Chatterton[26]
Rose pale,—his solemn agony had not   400
Yet faded from him; Sidney,[27] as he
   fought
And as he fell and as he lived and loved
Sublimely mild, a Spirit without spot,
Arose; and Lucan,[28] by his death ap-
   proved:
Oblivion as they rose shrank like a thing re-
   proved.   405

46

And many more, whose names on Earth
   are dark,
But whose transmitted effluence cannot die
So long as fire outlives the parent spark,
Rose, robed in dazzling immortality.
"Thou art become as one of us," they cry,
"It was for thee yon kingless sphere has
   long   411
Swung blind in unascended majesty,
Silent alone amid an Heaven of Song.
Assume thy wingéd throne, thou Vesper[29] of
   our throng!"

47

Who mourns for Adonais?   Oh, come
   forth,
Fond wretch! and know thyself and him
   aright.   416
Clasp with thy panting soul the pendulous
   Earth;
As from a center, dart thy spirit's light

[26]Thomas Chatterton (1752–1770), who died by
his own hand.

[27]Sir Philip Sidney (1554–1586), who died from
a wound received in battle.

[28]Roman poet (A. D. 39–65), who committed
suicide to escape execution commanded by Nero.

[29]Evening star.

Beyond all worlds, until its spacious might
Satiate the void circumference: then
   shrink
Even to a point within our day and night;
And keep thy heart light lest it make thee
   sink   422
When hope has kindled hope, and lured thee
   to the brink.

48

Or go to Rome, which is the sepulcher,
Oh, not of him, but of our joy: 'tis nought
That ages, empires, and religions there 426
Lie buried in the ravage they have
   wrought;
For such as he can lend,—they borrow not
Glory from those who made the world
   their prey;
And he is gathered to the kings of thought
Who waged contention with their time's
   decay,   431
And of the past are all that cannot pass away.

49

Go thou to Rome,—at once the Paradise,
The grave, the city, and the wilderness;
And where its wrecks like shattered moun-
   tains rise,   435
And flowering weeds, and fragrant copses
   dress
The bones of Desolation's nakedness
Pass, till the spirit of the spot shall lead
Thy footsteps to a slope of green access
Where, like an infant's smile, over the dead
A light of laughing flowers along the grass is
   spread;   441

50

And gray walls molder round, on which
   dull Time
Feeds, like slow fire upon a hoary brand;
And one keen pyramid[30] with wedge sub-
   lime,
Pavilioning the dust of him who plan-
   ned   445
This refuge for his memory, doth stand
Like flame transformed to marble; and be-
   neath,
A field is spread, on which a newer band
Have pitched in Heaven's smile their camp
   of death,
Welcoming him we lose with scarce extin-
   guished breath.   450

[30]The tomb of Cestius, overlooking the Protestant
Cemetery in which Keats is buried.

51

Here pause : these graves are all too young
  as yet
To have outgrown the sorrow which con-
  signed
Its charge to each ; and if the seal is set,
Here, on one fountain of a mourning mind,
Break it not thou ! too surely shalt thou
  find   455
Thine own well full, if thou returnest
  home,
Of tears and gall. From the world's bit-
  ter wind
Seek shelter in the shadow of the tomb.
What Adonais is, why fear we to become?

52

The One remains, the many change and
  pass ;   460
Heaven's light for ever shines, Earth's
  shadows fly ;
Life, like a dome of many-colored glass,
Stains the white radiance of Eternity,
Until Death tramples it to fragments.—
  Die,
If thou wouldst be with that which thou
  dost seek !   465
Follow where all is fled !—Rome's azure
  sky,
Flowers, ruins, statues, music, words, are
  weak
The glory they transfuse[31] with fitting truth
  to speak.

53

Why linger, why turn back, why shrink,
  my Heart?
Thy hopes are gone before : from all things
  here   470
They have departed ; thou shouldst now
  depart !
A light is passed from the revolving year,
And man, and woman ; and what still is
  dear
Attracts to crush, repels to make thee
  wither.
The soft sky smiles,—the low wind whis-
  pers near :   475
'Tis Adonais calls ! oh, hasten thither,
No more let Life divide what Death can join
  together.

[31]Instil

54

That Light whose smile kindles the Uni-
  verse,
That Beauty in which all things work and
  move,
That Benediction which the eclipsing Curse
Of birth can quench not, that sustaining
  Love   481
Which through the web of being blindly
  wove
By man and beast and earth and air and
  sea,
Burns bright or dim, as each are mirrors of
The fire for which all thirst ; now beams
  on me,   485
Consuming the last clouds of cold mortality.

55

The breath whose might I have invoked in
  song
Descends on me ; my spirit's bark is driven,
Far from the shore, far from the trembling
  throng
Whose sails were never to the tempest
  given ;   490
The massy earth and spheréd skies are
  riven !
I am borne darkly, fearfully, afar ;
Whilst, burning through the inmost veil of
  Heaven,
The soul of Adonais, like a star,
Beacons from the abode where the Eternal
  are.   495

HELLAS[1]

The Final Chorus

The world's great age begins anew,
  The golden years return,
The earth doth like a snake renew
  Her winter weeds outworn :
Heaven smiles, and faiths and empires gleam,
Like wrecks of a dissolving dream.   6

A brighter Hellas rears its mountains
  From waves serener far ;
A new Peneus[2] rolls his fountains
  Against the morning star.   10

[1]A lyrical drama, written in the autumn of 1821
and published in the spring of 1822 ; inspired by the
Greek war for independence, which Shelley thinks
of as ushering in a new Golden Age which will surpass the ancient glories of Greece. The opening
of the Final Chorus is reminiscent of Virgil's fourth
Eclogue.

[2]A river of Thessaly.

Where fairer Tempes[3] bloom, there sleep
Young Cyclads[4] on a sunnier deep.

A loftier Argo[5] cleaves the main,
    Fraught with a later prize;
Another Orpheus sings again,   15
    And loves, and weeps, and dies.
A new Ulysses leaves once more
Calypso[6] for his native shore.

Oh, write no more the tale of Troy,
    If earth Death's scroll must be!   20
Nor mix with Laian[7] rage the joy
    Which dawns upon the free:
Although a subtler Sphinx renew
Riddles of death Thebes never knew.

Another Athens shall arise,   25
    And to remoter time
Bequeath, like sunset to the skies,
    The splendor of its prime;
And leave, if nought so bright may live,
All earth can take or Heaven can give.   30

Saturn and Love their long repose
    Shall burst,[8] more bright and good
Than all who fell, than One who rose,
    Than many unsubdued:
Not gold, not blood, their altar dowers,   35
But votive tears and symbol flowers.

[3]The valley through which the Peneus flows.
[4]The Cyclades, islands in the Aegean Sea.
[5]The ship of Jason, in which the Golden Fleece was carried.
[6]The nymph who vainly sought to keep Ulysses on her island with her, though she promised him immortality if he would remain.
[7]The family of Laius, king of Thebes, was pursued by dreadful misfortunes. The son of Laius was Oedipus, who freed Thebes from the affliction of the Sphinx by answering her riddle correctly, but who unwittingly killed his father and married his mother.
[8]Saturn and Love were among the deities of a real or imaginary state of innocence and happiness. *All* those *who fell*, or the Gods of Greece, Asia, and Egypt; the *One who rose*, or Jesus Christ, at whose appearance the idols of the Pagan World were amerced of their worship; and *the many unsubdued,* or the monstrous objects of the idolatry of China, India, the Antarctic islands, and the native tribes of America, certainly have reigned over the understandings of men in conjunction or in succession, during periods in which all we know of evil has been in a state of portentous, and, until the revival of learning, perpetually increasing, activity. The Grecian gods seem indeed to have been personally more innocent, although it cannot be said, that as far as temperance and chastity are concerned, they gave so edifying an example as their successor. The sublime human character of Jesus Christ was deformed by an imputed identification

Oh, cease! must hate and death return?
    Cease! must men kill and die?
Cease! drain not to its dregs the urn
    Of bitter prophecy.   40
The world is weary of the past,
Oh, might it die or rest at last!

LINES: "WHEN THE LAMP IS SHATTERED" [1]

I

When the lamp is shattered
The light in the dust lies dead—
When the cloud is scattered
The rainbow's glory is shed.
    When the lute is broken,   5
Sweet tones are remembered not;
    When the lips have spoken,
Loved accents are soon forgot.

II

As music and splendor
Survive not the lamp and the lute,   10
    The heart's echoes render
No song when the spirit is mute:—
    No song but sad dirges,
Like the wind through a ruined cell,
    Or the mournful surges   15
That ring the dead seaman's knell.

III

When the hearts have once mingled
Love first leaves the well-built nest;
    The weak one is singled
To endure what it once possessed.   20
    O Love! who bewailest
The frailty of all things here,
    Why choose you the frailest
For your cradle, your home, and your bier?

IV

Its passions will rock thee   25
As the storms rock the ravens on high;
    Bright reason will mock thee,
Like the sun from a wintry sky.

with a Power, who tempted, betrayed, and punished the innocent beings who were called into existence by His sole will; and for the period of a thousand years, the spirit of this most just, wise, and benevolent of men has been propitiated with myriads of hecatombs of those who approached the nearest to His innocence and wisdom, sacrificed under every aggravation of atrocity and variety of torture. The horrors of the Mexican, the Peruvian, and the Indian superstitions are well known (Shelley's note).

[1]Written in 1822; published in 1824.

From thy nest every rafter
Will rot, and thine eagle home   30
   Leave thee naked to laughter,
When leaves fall and cold winds come.

TO JANE: THE INVITATION [1]

Best and brightest, come away!
Fairer far than this fair Day,
Which, like thee to those in sorrow,
Comes to bid a sweet good-morrow
To the rough Year just awake   5
In its cradle on the brake.
The brightest hour of unborn Spring,
Through the winter wandering,
Found, it seems, the halcyon Morn
To hoar February born.   10
Bending from Heaven, in azure mirth,
It kissed the forehead of the Earth,
And smiled upon the silent sea,
And bade the frozen streams be free,
And waked to music all their fountains,   15
And breathed upon the frozen mountains,
And like a prophetess of May
Strewed flowers upon the barren way,
Making the wintry world appear
Like one on whom thou smilest, dear.   20

Away, away, from men and towns,
To the wild wood and the downs—
To the silent wilderness
Where the soul need not repress
Its music, lest it should not find   25
An echo in another's mind,
While the touch of Nature's art
Harmonizes heart to heart.
I leave this notice on my door
For each accustomed visitor:—   30
"I am gone into the fields
To take what this sweet hour yields;—
Reflection, you may come to-morrow,
Sit by the fireside with Sorrow.—
You with unpaid bill, Despair,—   35
You, tiresome verse-reciter, Care,—
I will pay you in the grave,—
Death will listen to your stave.
Expectation too, be off!
To-day is for itself enough;   40
Hope, in pity mock not Woe
With smiles, nor follow where I go;
Long having lived on thy sweet food,
At length I find one moment's good

After long pain—with all your love,   45
This you never told me of."

Radiant Sister of the Day,
Awake! arise! and come away!
To the wild woods and the plains,
To the pools where winter rains   50
Image all their roof of leaves,
Where the pine its garland weaves
Of sapless green and ivy dun
Round stems that never kiss the sun;
Where the lawns and pastures be,   55
And the sandhills of the sea;—
Where the melting hoar-frost wets
The daisy-star that never sets,
And wind-flowers, and violets,
Which yet join not scent to hue,   60
Crown the pale year weak and new;
When the night is left behind
In the deep east, dun and blind,
And the blue noon is over us,
And the multitudinous   65
Billows murmur at our feet,
Where the earth and ocean meet,
And all things seem only one
In the universal sun.

WITH A GUITAR, TO JANE [1]

Ariel to Miranda:—Take
This slave of Music, for the sake
Of him who is the slave of thee,
And teach it all the harmony
In which thou canst, and only thou,   5
Make the delighted spirit glow,
Till joy denies itself again,
And, too intense, is turned to pain;
For by permission and command
Of thine own Prince Ferdinand,[2]   10
Poor Ariel sends this silent token
Of more than ever can be spoken;
Your guardian spirit, Ariel, who,
From life to life, must still pursue
Your happiness;—for thus alone   15
Can Ariel ever find his own.
From Prospero's enchanted cell,
As the mighty verses tell,
To the throne of Naples, he
Lit you o'er the trackless sea,   20
Flitting on, your prow before,
Like a living meteor.

---

[1] Written in 1822; published as part of another poem in 1824, and in its present form in 1839. While in Italy Shelley saw much of Jane Williams, to whom he addressed several poems.

[1] Written in 1822; published in the *Athenaeum* in 1832.

[2] Edward Williams, ostensibly Jane's husband. It is now known they had not actually been married, since she had not been divorced from her first husband.

When you die, the silent Moon,
In her interlunar swoon,
Is not sadder in her cell   25
Than deserted Ariel.
When you live again on earth,
Like an unseen star of birth,
Ariel guides you o'er the sea
Of life from your nativity.   30
Many changes have been run
Since Ferdinand and you begun
Your course of love, and Ariel still
Has tracked your steps, and served your will;
Now, in humbler, happier lot,   35
This is all remembered not;
And now, alas! the poor sprite is
Imprisoned, for some fault of his,
In a body like a grave;—
From you he only dares to crave,   40
For his service and his sorrow,
A smile to-day, a song-tomorrow.

The artist who this idol wrought,
To echo all harmonious thought,
Felled a tree, while on the steep 45
The woods were in their winter sleep,
Rocked in that repose divine
On the wind-swept Apennine;
And dreaming, some of Autumn past,
And some of Spring approaching fast, 50
And some of April buds and showers,
And some of songs in July bowers,
And all of love; and so this tree,—
O that such our death may be!—
Died in sleep, and felt no pain,   55
To live in happier form again:
From which, beneath Heaven's fairest star,
The artist wrought this loved Guitar,
And taught it justly to reply,
To all who question skillfully,   60
In language gentle as thine own;
Whispering in enamored tone

Sweet oracles of woods and dells,
And summer winds in sylvan cells;
For it had learned all harmonies   65
Of the plains and of the skies,
Of the forests and the mountains,
And the many-voicéd fountains;
The clearest echoes of the hills,
The softest notes of falling rills, 70
The melodies of birds and bees,
The murmuring of summer seas,
And pattering rain, and breathing dew,
And airs of evening; and it knew
That seldom-heard mysterious sound, 75
Which, driven on its diurnal round,
As it floats through boundless day,
Our world enkindles in its way.—
All this it knows, but will not tell
To those who cannot question well   80
The Spirit that inhabits it;
It talks according to the wit
Of its companions; and no more
Is heard than has been felt before,
By those who tempt it to betray   85
These secrets of an elder day:
But, sweetly as its answers will
Flatter hands of perfect skill,
It keeps its highest, holiest tone
For our belovéd Jane alone.   90

A DIRGE [1]

Rough wind, that moanest loud
  Grief too sad for song;
Wild wind, when sullen cloud
  Knells all the night long;
Sad storm, whose tears are vain,   5
Bare woods, whose branches strain,
Deep caves and dreary main,—
  Wail, for the world's wrong!

_____
[1] Written in 1822; published in 1824.

JOHN KEATS

1795-1821

Keats's father was stable-keeper at the Swan and Hoop Inn, Finsbury Pavement, London. He had married the daughter of the proprietor, and Keats was born there on 31 October, 1795. In 1803 the boy was sent to a good private school kept by the Rev. J. Clarke at Enfield. Here he attracted the attention of the junior master, Charles Cowden Clarke, and a relationship sprang up which extended beyond his period at the school and was of great use to him. Clarke later said that Keats, although during his last years at school an eager reader of history, fiction, and books of mythology, was also a sturdy, active youngster and a favorite amongst his school-fellows. In 1804 his father was killed by a fall from his horse, and in 1810 his mother—who in 1805 had married a second time and in the following year had separated from her husband—died of a consumption. Keats's guardians at once removed him from school and apprenticed him to a surgeon. His passion for reading did not leave him in his new work and surroundings, and he kept in touch with the Clarkes. It was in 1812 or 1813 that Cowden Clarke introduced him to the works of Spenser, reading to him Spenser's *Epithalamion* and lending him *The Faerie Queene*. A couple of years later it was also Clarke who introduced him to Chapman's *Homer,* which inspired the famous sonnet. Meanwhile Keats had in 1814 broken his apprenticeship and had gone to London to study medicine. Soon after this he began to write poetry, though continuing his medical studies. In 1816, through the instrumentality of Clarke, he met Leigh Hunt, a pleasant but superficial literary man and a champion of liberty. Hunt communicated his zeal for liberty to Keats and also encouraged the false taste evident in the young man's earlier poetry; but Hunt by his interest did much to stimulate his genius and introduced him to many of the literary men and artists of the time. Directly or indirectly through Hunt, Keats became acquainted with Benjamin Haydon—a mediocre artist but a man of fine taste who helped the poet to appreciate Greek sculpture—with J.

H. Reynolds, Shelley, Horace Smith, Hazlitt, C. Wentworth Dilke, Wordsworth, and others.

In 1817 Keats published his first volume, *Poems,* a volume which on the whole showed much immaturity and which was harshly criticized. This, however, hardly discouraged him, for his own critical faculty was developing and he saw many of his faults as clearly as did his critics. In 1816 when he had come of age he had determined to abandon medicine for poetry, and there is no sign that he ever wavered concerning the rightness of this decision. In 1818 he published *Endymion.* He was dissatisfied with it, but felt that it was as good a poem as he could then write, and that it was better to put it out of his reach by publication than to attempt to mend it. In a preface he said as much:—any reader of the poem "must soon perceive great inexperience, immaturity, and every error denoting a feverish attempt, rather than a deed accomplished." But despite this admission the poem was greeted with extreme abuse by the critics—abuse so extreme that at the time it was reputed to have been a cause of Keats's early death. This, as we now know, it was not. Keats's reaction to criticism can only be described as fine and manly. As for hostile critics, he wrote to his publisher several months after the appearance of the poem, "I begin to get a little acquainted with my own strength and weakness. Praise or blame has but a momentary effect on the man whose love of beauty in the abstract makes him a severe critic on his own works. My own domestic criticism has given me pain without comparison beyond what *Blackwood* or the *Quarterly* could possibly inflict—and also when I feel I am right, no external praise can give me such a glow as my own solitary reperception and ratification of what is fine. J. S. [the writer of a letter about the poem to the *Morning Chronicle*] is perfectly right in regard to the slip-shod *Endymion.* That it is so is no fault of mine. No! —though it may sound a little paradoxical. It is as good as I had power to make it—by myself. Had I been nervous about its being a perfect piece, and with that view asked advice, and trembled over every page, it would not have been written; for it is not in my nature to fumble—I will write independently.—I have written independently *without judgment*. I may write independently, and *with judgment,* hereafter. The Genius of Poetry must work out its own salvation in a man: It cannot be matured by law and precept, but by sensation and watchfulness in itself. That which is creative must create itself. In *Endymion* I leaped headlong into the sea, and thereby have become better acquainted with the soundings, the quicksands, and the rocks, than if I had stayed upon the green shore, and piped a silly pipe, and took tea and comfortable advice."

Already, indeed, before *Endymion* was published Keats was at work upon *Isabella* in the attempt to do something better. In the summer of 1818 he went with his friend Charles Brown on a walking tour through the Lake country to Scotland. After about six weeks of tramping he was compelled to return to London on account of throat trouble which had developed. This was the first warning sign of the illness which was to cut his life short. In the fall of the same year he met Fanny Brawne, a girl with whom he fell deeply in love. He was also during the fall of this year in constant attendance at the bedside of his brother Tom, who died of consumption in December. Early in 1819 Keats was at work on *Hyperion* and *The Eve of St. Agnes,* and during the spring and fall he wrote the greater number of his finest poems. In February, 1820, it became unmistakable that he had consumption. During the spring he saw the 1820 volume of his poems through the press, but from that time forward he was, and felt himself to be, a doomed man. His condition continually grew worse, and at the end of the summer he was warned that it would be fatal to him to spend another winter in England. He sailed for Naples in September, stayed there until November, and then went to Rome. He was, however, too ill for the Italian climate materially to help him, and he died on 23 February, 1821. He was buried in the Protestant cemetery at Rome, where Shelley's ashes were brought in the following year.

It has been remarked that, while Shelley wrote nearly all his greatest poetry in the period between his twenty-sixth year and the time of his death, Keats died at twenty-five, nor had he been a precocious youth. And yet, while Coleridge and Shelley were also pioneers in the nineteenth-century development of poetry, Sir

Herbert Grierson has said that "Keats has been, without any exception, the greatest influence in English poetry for a whole century. To his example and inspiration are due all the wonderful sensuous felicity, the splendor of exotic phrasing and harmony of Tennyson's 1842 volumes; the bold and varied experiments of Browning's *Bells and Pomegranates;* the curious subtleties of *The Blessed Damozel* and *The House of Life; The Defense of Guinevere* and *The Earthly Paradise; Poems and Ballads* and *Atalanta in Calydon.* If poetry be first and last a sensuous pleasure, then Keats and his successors are the greatest of our poets since Spenser, and the Marlowe of *Hero and Leander,* the Shakespeare of *Venus and Adonis* and the 'sugared sonnets'; as virtuosi of phrase and harmonies perhaps greater even than these' (Warton Lect. XI, Brit. Acad.). Of course poetry is not first and last a sensuous pleasure, but it is a part of Keats's greatness that, although he began his work wishing only to mirror in poetry the fine flower of exquisite sensation, he rapidly outgrew his starting-point and was unmistakably approaching a rich maturity when death cut him down. He "is a great poet, first of all because he had the supreme sensitiveness of a poet's imagination, and caught up the beauty about him as a lake takes color and shadow from the sky, partly because he was a born artist and studied with constant devotion the technique of his art, but also because he had a mind and spirit bent on applying to his art the searching test of hard thought and vital experience. We only read Keats aright when we learn from his own lips that he wrote, not for art's sake only, but for the sake of truth and for the sake of life" (E. de Selincourt, Warton Lect. XII, Brit. Acad.).

The best edition of *The Complete Works of John Keats* is edited by H. Buxton Forman (5 vols., Glasgow, 1900–1901). This contains Keats's letters which, however, have been re-edited with additions by Maurice Buxton Forman (Oxford, 1930; revised ed. 1935). The best edition of Keats's *Poems* is edited by E. de Selincourt (London, 1905; fifth ed. revised, 1926). The best biography is Sidney Colvin's *John Keats: His Life and Poetry, His Friends, Critics, and After-Fame* (New York, 1917; new ed. 1925). The much longer *John Keats* by Amy Lowell (Boston, 1925) contains new facts, but is not in general as sound a work as Colvin's biography. Elucidations and critical studies have multiplied of late years. Those most likely to be useful are: *The Mind of John Keats,* by Clarence DeWitt Thorpe (New

York, 1926) ; *Studies in Keats,* by John Middleton Murry (Oxford, 1930; second ed. with three new essays, 1939) ; *Keats's Craftsman-* *ship,* by M. R. Ridley (Oxford, 1933) ; and *The Evolution of Keats's Poetry,* by C. L. Finney (Cambridge, Mass., 1936).

SONNET [1]

Keen, fitful gusts are whisp'ring here and
  there
 Among the bushes, half leafless and dry ;
 The stars look very cold about the sky,
And I have many miles on foot to fare ;
Yet feel I little of the cold bleak air,   5
 Or of the dead leaves rustling drearily,
 Or of those silver lamps that burn on high,
Or of the distance from home's pleasant lair :
For I am brimful of the friendliness
 That in a little cottage I have found ; 10
Of fair-haired Milton's eloquent distress,
 And all his love for gentle Lycid [2] drowned ;
Of lovely Laura [3] in her light green dress,
 And faithful Petrarch gloriously crowned.

ON FIRST LOOKING INTO CHAPMAN'S HOMER [4]

Much have I traveled in the realms of gold,
 And many goodly states and kingdoms
  seen ;
 Round many western islands have I been
Which bards in fealty to Apollo hold.
Oft of one wide expanse had I been told, 5
 That deep-browed Homer ruled as his de-
  mesne :
 Yet did I never breathe its pure serene
Till I heard Chapman [5] speak out loud and
  bold :
Then felt I like some watcher of the skies
 When a new planet swims into his ken ; 10
Or like stout Cortez [6] when with eagle eyes
 He stared at the Pacific—and all his men
Looked at each other with a wild surmise—
 Silent, upon a peak in Darien.

---

[1] Written in 1816 after a visit to Leigh Hunt's cottage at Hampstead; published in 1817.

[2] *Lycidas.*

[3] The lady whose name Petrarch immortalized in the sonnets which record his love for her.

[4] Written in 1815; published in 1817.

[5] George Chapman (1559?–1634) published his translations of the *Iliad* and *Odyssey* 1598–1616.

[6] Either a conscious alteration or a slip, as it was really Balboa who discovered the Pacific.

ENDYMION [1]

BOOK I

Hymn to Pan

O thou, whose mighty palace roof doth
  hang
From jaggéd trunks, and overshadoweth
Eternal whispers, glooms, the birth, life,
  death
Of unseen flowers in heavy peacefulness ;
Who lov'st to see the hamadryads [2] dress 5
Their ruffled locks where meeting hazels
  darken ;
And through whole solemn hours dost sit,
  and hearken
The dreary melody of bedded reeds—
In desolate places, where dank moisture
  breeds
The pipy hemlock [3] to strange overgrowth, 10
Bethinking thee, how melancholy loath
Thou wast to lose fair Syrinx [4]—do thou
  now,
By thy love's milky brow !
By all the trembling mazes that she ran,
Hear us, great Pan !   15

O thou, for whose soul-soothing quiet,
  turtles [5]
Passion their voices cooingly 'mong myrtles,
What time thou wanderest at eventide
Through sunny meadows, that outskirt the
  side   19
Of thine enmosséd realms : O thou, to whom
Broad-leaved fig-trees even now foredoom
Their ripened fruitage ; yellow-girted bees
Their golden honeycombs ; our village leas
Their fairest-blossomed beans and poppied
  corn ; [6]
The chuckling linnet its five young unborn,

---

[1] Published in 1818. The *Hymn to Pan* forms ll. 232–306 of Bk. I and was written in the early summer of 1817. It is sung by those at the festival of Latmian shepherds with which *Endymion* opens.

[2] Tree-nymphs.

[3] A poisonous European plant with a hollow stem, like a pipe.

[4] A nymph who fled from Pan and, when she sought refuge in a river, was changed into a reed.

[5] Turtle-doves.

[6] Wheat intermingled with poppies.

To sing for thee; low-creeping strawber-
ries   26
Their summer coolness; pent-up butterflies[7]
Their freckled wings; yea, the fresh-budding
year
All its completions—be quickly near,   29
By every wind that nods the mountain pine,
O forester divine!

Thou, to whom every faun and satyr flies
For willing service; whether to surprise
The squatted hare while in half-sleeping fit;
'Or upward ragged precipices flit   35
To save poor lambkins from the eagle's maw;
Or by mysterious enticement draw
Bewildered shepherds to their path again;
Or to tread breathless round the frothy main,
And gather up all fancifulest shells   40
For thee to tumble into Naiads' cells,[8]
And, being hidden, laugh at their out-peep-
ing;
Or to delight thee with fantastic leaping,
The while they pelt each other on the crown
With silvery oak-apples, and fir-cones
brown—   45
By all the echoes that about thee ring,
Hear us, O satyr king!

O Hearkener to the loud-clapping shears,
While ever and anon to his shorn peers
A ram goes bleating: Winder of the horn, 50
When snouted wild-boars routing tender
corn
Anger our huntsmen: Breather round our
farms,
To keep off mildews, and all weather harms:
Strange ministrant of undescribéd sounds,
That come a-swooning over hollow grounds,
And wither drearily on barren moors: 56
Dread opener of the mysterious doors
Leading to universal knowledge—see,
Great son of Dryope,
The many that are come to pay their vows 60
With leaves about their brows!

Be still the unimaginable lodge
For solitary thinkings; such as dodge
Conception to the very bourn[9] of heaven,
Then leave the naked brain: be still the leaven
That, spreading in this dull and clodded
earth,   66
Gives it a touch ethereal—a new birth:
Be still a symbol of immensity;
A firmament reflected in a sea;

An element filling the space between;   70
An unknown—but no more: we humbly
screen
With uplift hands our foreheads, lowly bend-
ing,
And giving out a shout most heaven-rending,
Conjure thee to receive our humble Paean,[10]
Upon thy Mount Lycean![11]

BOOK IV

Song of the Indian Maid [12]

O Sorrow,
Why dost borrow
The natural hue of health, from vermeil[13]
lips?—
To give maiden blushes
To the white rose bushes?   5
Or is 't thy dewy hand the daisy tips?

O Sorrow,
Why dost borrow
The lustrous passion from a falcon-eye?—
To give the glow-worm light?   10
Or, on a moonless night,
To tinge, on siren shores, the salt sea-spry?[14]

O Sorrow,
Why dost borrow
The mellow ditties from a mourning
tongue?—   15
To give at evening pale
Unto the nightingale,
That thou mayst listen the cold dews among?

O Sorrow,
Why dost borrow   20
Heart's lightness from the merriment of
May?—
A lover would not tread
A cowslip on the head,
Though he should dance from eve till peep of
day—
Nor any drooping flower   25
Held sacred for thy bower,
Wherever he may sport himself and play.

[7]Chrysalises.

[8]The dwelling-places of nymphs of fresh-water
streams.

[9]Boundary.

[10]Hymn of praise.

[11]Pan was born on Lycaeus, a mountain in Arcadia.

[12]This song, or hymn, forms ll. 146–290 of Bk. IV.
It was written in the autumn of 1817. Endymion,
while searching vainly for Cynthia, whom he loves,
finds in the forest an Indian maiden who is bewail-
ing the loss of her lover and the emptiness of her
soul without love.

[13]Vermilion.

[14]Sea-spray.

To Sorrow
I bade good morrow,
And thought to leave her far away behind ; 30
But cheerly, cheerly,
She loves me dearly ;
She is so constant to me, and so kind :
I would deceive her
And so leave her,   35
But ah ! she is so constant and so kind.

Beneath my palm-trees, by the river side,
I sat a-weeping : in the whole world wide
There was no one to ask me why I wept—
And so I kept   40
Brimming the water-lily cups with tears
Cold as my fears.

Beneath my palm-trees, by the river side,
I sat a-weeping : what enamored bride,
Cheated by shadowy wooer from the clouds,
But hides and shrouds   46
Beneath dark palm-trees by a river side?

And as I sat, over the light blue hills
There came a noise of revelers : the rills
Into the wide stream came of purple hue— 50
'Twas Bacchus and his crew ![15]
The earnest trumpet spake, and silver thrills
From kissing cymbals made a merry din—
'Twas Bacchus and his kin !
Like to a moving vintage down they came, 55
Crowned with green leaves, and faces all on
    flame ;
All madly dancing through the pleasant val-
    ley,
    To scare thee, Melancholy !
O then, O then, thou wast a simple name !
And I forgot thee, as the berried holly   60
By shepherds is forgotten, when, in June,
Tall chestnuts keep away the sun and
    moon :—
    I rushed into the folly !

Within his car, aloft, young Bacchus stood,
Trifling his ivy-dart,[16] in dancing mood,   65
    With sidelong laughing ;
And little rills of crimson wine imbrued
His plump white arms, and shoulders, enough
    white
    For Venus' pearly bite ;

---

[15]The following description of the progress of
Bacchus is inspired by Titian's *Bacchus and Ariadne*,
a picture which is now in the National Gallery,
London.

[16]Playing with his thyrsus, or wand, which he
always carried.

And near him rode Silenus[17] on his ass,   70
Pelted with flowers as he on did pass
    Tipsily quaffing.

Whence came ye, merry Damsels ! whence
    came ye,
So many, and so many, and such glee ?
Why have ye left your bowers desolate,   75
    Your lutes, and gentler fate ?
"We follow Bacchus !   Bacchus on the wing,
    A-conquering !
Bacchus, young Bacchus ! good or ill betide,
We dance before him thorough kingdoms'
    wide :—   80
Come hither, lady fair, and joinéd be
    To our wild minstrelsy !"

Whence came ye, jolly Satyrs ! whence came
    ye,
So many, and so many, and such glee ?
Why have ye left your forest haunts, why
    left
    Your nuts in oak-tree cleft ?—   86
"For wine, for wine we left our kernel tree ;
For wine we left our heath, and yellow
    brooms,
    And cold mushrooms ;
For wine we follow Bacchus through the
    earth ;
Great god of breathless cups and chirping
    mirth !—   91
Come hither, lady fair, and joinéd be
    To our mad minstrelsy !"

Over wide streams and mountains great we
    went,
And, save when Bacchus kept his ivy tent, 95
Onward the tiger and the leopard pants,
    With Asian elephants :
Onward these myriads—with song and
    dance,
With zebras striped, and sleek Arabians'
    prance,
Web-footed alligators, crocodiles,   100
Bearing upon their scaly backs, in files,
Plump infant laughers mimicking the coil
Of seamen, and stout galley-rowers' toil :
With toying oars and silken sails they glide,
    Nor care for wind and tide.   105

Mounted on panthers' furs and lions' manes,
From rear to van they scour about the plains ;
A three days' journey in a moment done :
And always, at the rising of the sun,
About the wilds they hunt with spear and
    horn,   110
    On spleenful unicorn.

---

[17]The foster-father of Bacchus.

I saw Osirian[18] Egypt kneel adown
    Before the vine-wreath crown!
I saw parched Abyssinia rouse and sing
    To the silver cymbals' ring!   115
I saw the whelming vintage hotly pierce
    Old Tartary the fierce!
The kings of Ind their jewel-scepters vail,[19]
And from their treasures scatter pearléd
    hail;
Great Brahma from his mystic heaven
    groans,
    And all his priesthood moans,   121
Before young Bacchus' eye-wink turning
    pale.—
Into these regions came I, following him,
Sick-hearted, weary—so I took a whim
To stray away into these forests drear,   125
    Alone, without a peer:
And I have told thee all thou mayest hear.

    Young stranger!
    I've been a ranger
In search of pleasure throughout every
    clime;   130
    Alas, 'tis not for me!
    Bewitched I sure must be,
To lose in grieving all my maiden prime.

    Come then, Sorrow,
    Sweetest Sorrow!   135
Like an own babe I nurse thee on my breast:
    I thought to leave thee,
    And deceive thee,
But now of all the world I love thee best.

    There is not one,   140
    No, no, not one
But thee to comfort a poor lonely maid;
    Thou art her mother,
    And her brother,
Her playmate, and her wooer in the shade. 145

SONNET [1]

When I have fears that I may cease to be
    Before my pen has gleaned my teeming
        brain,
Before high-piléd books, in charact'ry,[2]
    Hold like rich garners the full-ripened
        grain;

When I behold, upon the night's starred
    face,   5
    Huge cloudy symbols of a high romance,
And think that I may never live to trace
    Their shadows, with the magic hand of
        chance;
And when I feel, fair creature of an hour,
    That I shall never look upon thee more, 10
Never have relish in the faery power
    Of unreflecting love;—then on the shore
Of the wide world I stand alone, and think,
Till Love and Fame to nothingness do sink.

FRAGMENT OF AN ODE TO MAIA, WRITTEN ON MAY DAY, 1818 [3]

Mother of Hermes! and still youthful Maia!
    May I sing to thee
As thou wast hymnéd on the shores of
    Baiae?[4]
    Or may I woo thee
In earlier Sicilian? or thy smiles   5
Seek as they once were sought, in Grecian
    isles,
By bards who died content on pleasant
    sward,
Leaving great verse unto a little clan?
O, give me their old vigor, and unheard
Save of the quiet primrose, and the span 10
    Of heaven and few ears,
Rounded by thee, my song should die away
    Content as theirs,
Rich in the simple worship of a day.

STANZAS [5]

In a drear-nighted December,
    Too happy, happy tree,
Thy branches ne'er remember
    Their green felicity:
The north cannot undo them,   5
    With a sleety whistle through them;
Nor frozen thawings glue them
    From budding at the prime.

---

[18] According to Keats's authority (Lemprière)
Osiris, a god worshiped by the Egyptians, corresponded to the Greek god Bacchus.

[19] Bend down.

[1] Written before 31 January, 1818; published in 1848.

[2] Writing.

---

[3] Published in 1848. Maia was the eldest and most beautiful of the seven sisters known as the Pleiads, and was a goddess of the spring.

[4] Baiae, near Naples, was famous for its situation and baths, and many wealthy Romans had country houses there. Keats thinks of the cult of Maia as extending from Roman times back to the days when Greek colonies were planted in Sicily and further back to earlier days in the Greek islands.

[5] Written in 1817 or 1818; published in 1829.

In a drear-nighted December,
Too happy, happy brook, 10
Thy bubblings ne'er remember
Apollo's summer look;
But with a sweet forgetting,
They stay their crystal fretting,
Never, never petting 15
About the frozen time.

Ah! would 'twere so with many
A gentle girl and boy!
But were there ever any
Writhed not at passéd joy? 20
To know the change and feel it,
When there is none to heal it,
Nor numbéd sense to steel it,
Was never said in rime.

FANCY[1]

Ever let the Fancy roam,
Pleasure never is at home:
At a touch sweet Pleasure melteth,
Like to bubbles when rain pelteth;
Then let wingéd Fancy wander 5
Through the thought still spread beyond her:
Open wide the mind's cage-door,
She'll dart forth, and cloudward soar.
O sweet Fancy! let her loose;
Summer's joys are spoilt by use, 10
And the enjoying of the Spring
Fades as does its blossoming:
Autumn's red-lipped fruitage too,
Blushing through the mist and dew,
Cloys with tasting: What do then? 15
Sit thee by the ingle,[2] when
The sear faggot blazes bright,
Spirit of a winter's night;
When the soundless earth is muffled,
And the cakéd snow is shuffled 20
From the plowboy's heavy shoon;[3]
When the Night doth meet the Noon
In a dark conspiracy
To banish Even from her sky.
Sit thee there, and send abroad, 25
With a mind self-overawed,
Fancy, high-commissioned:—send her!
She has vassals to attend her:
She will bring, in spite of frost,
Beauties that the earth hath lost; 30
She will bring thee, all together,
All delights of summer weather;
All the buds and bells of May,
From dewy sward or thorny spray;

All the heapéd Autumn's wealth, 35
With a still, mysterious stealth:
She will mix these pleasures up
Like three fit wines in a cup,
And thou shalt quoff it:—thou shalt hear
Distant harvest-carols clear; 40
Rustle of the reapéd corn;
Sweet birds antheming the morn:
And, in the same moment—hark!
'Tis the early April lark,
Or the rooks, with busy caw, 45
Foraging for sticks and straw.
Thou shalt, at one glance, behold
The daisy and the marigold;
White-plumed lilies, and the first
Hedge-grown primrose that hath burst; 50
Shaded hyacinth, alway
Sapphire queen of the mid-May;
And every leaf, and every flower
Pearléd with the self-same shower.
Thou shalt see the field-mouse peep 55
Meager from its celléd sleep;
And the snake all winter-thin
Cast on sunny bank its skin;
Freckled nest eggs thou shalt see
Hatching in the hawthorn-tree, 60
When the hen-bird's wing doth rest
Quiet on her mossy nest;
Then the hurry and alarm
When the bee-hive casts[4] its swarm;
Acorns ripe down-pattering, 65
While the autumn breezes sing.

Oh, sweet Fancy! let her loose;
Everything is spoilt by use:
Where's the cheek that doth not fade,
Too much gazed at? Where's the maid 70
Whose lip mature is ever new?
Where's the eye, however blue,
Doth not weary? Where's the face
One would meet in every place?
Where's the voice, however soft, 75
One would hear so very oft?
At a touch sweet Pleasure melteth
Like to bubbles when rain pelteth.
Let, then, wingéd Fancy find
Thee a mistress to thy mind: 80
Dulcet-eyed as Ceres' daughter,[5]
Ere the God of Torment taught her
How to frown and how to chide;
With a waist and with a side
White as Hebe's,[6] when her zone 85
Slipped its golden clasp, and down

---

[1]Written in 1818; published in 1820.
[2]Fireside.　[3]Shoes.

[4]Emits.
[5]Proserpine, who became the queen of Pluto, king of the underworld of shades.
[6]Jove's cup-bearer.

Fell her kirtle to her feet,
While she held the goblet sweet,
And Jove grew languid.—Break the mesh
Of the Fancy's silken leash; 90
Quickly break her prison-string,
And such joys as these she'll bring.
Let the wingéd Fancy roam,
Pleasure never is at home.

ODE[1]

Bards of Passion and of Mirth,
Ye have left your souls on earth!
Have ye souls in heaven too,
Double-lived in regions new?
Yes, and those of heaven commune 5
With the spheres of sun and moon;
With the noise of fountains wondrous,
And the parle[2] of voices thund'rous;
With the whisper of heaven's trees
And one another, in soft ease 10
Seated on Elysian lawns
Browsed by none but Dian's fawns;
Underneath large blue-bells tented,
Where the daisies are rose-scented,
And the rose herself has got 15
Perfume which on earth is not;
Where the nightingale doth sing
Not a senseless, trancéd thing,
But divine, melodious truth;
Philosophic numbers smooth; 20
Tales and golden histories
Of heaven and its mysteries.

Thus ye live on high, and then
On the earth ye live again;
And the souls ye left behind you 25
Teach us, here, the way to find you,
Where your other souls are joying
Never slumbered, never cloying.
Here, your earth-born souls still speak
To mortals, of their little week; 30
Of their sorrows and delights;
Of their passions and their spites;
Of their glory and their shame;
What doth strengthen and what maim.
Thus ye teach us, every day, 35
Wisdom, though fled far away.

Bards of Passion and of Mirth,
Ye have left your souls on earth!
Ye have souls in heaven too,
Double-lived in regions new! 40

LINES ON THE MERMAID TAVERN[3]

Souls of poets dead and gone,
What Elysium have ye known,
Happy field or mossy cavern,
Choicer than the Mermaid Tavern?
Have ye tippled drink more fine 5
Than mine host's Canary wine?
Or are fruits of Paradise
Sweeter than those dainty pies
Of venison? O generous food!
Dressed as though bold Robin Hood 10
Would, with his maid Marian,
Sup and bowse[4] from horn and can.

I have heard that on a day
Mine host's sign-board flew away,
Nobody knew whither, till 15
An Astrologer's old quill
To a sheepskin gave the story,—
Said he saw you in your glory,
Underneath a new-old sign
Sipping beverage divine, 20
And pledging with contented smack
The Mermaid in the Zodiac.[5]

Souls of poets dead and gone,
What Elysium have ye known,
Happy field or mossy cavern, 25
Choicer than the Mermaid Tavern?

ROBIN HOOD[1]

To a Friend

No! those days are gone away,
And their hours are old and gray,
And their minutes buried all
Under the down-trodden pall
Of the leaves of many years: 5
Many times have Winter's shears,

---

[1]Written in 1818; published in 1820. Keats wrote this in his copy of the plays of Beaumont and Fletcher, on the blank page preceding the tragicomedy entitled *The Fair Maid of the Inn*. The poem was, therefore, if not addressed to Beaumont and Fletcher, at least inspired by thought of their work.

[2]Speech.

[3]Written in 1818; published in 1820. The Mermaid Tavern, in Bread Street, Cheapside, was the favorite meeting-place of the chief men of letters at the close of the sixteenth century and in the early seventeenth.

[4]Drink. [5]I. e., in the heavens.

[1]Written early in 1818; published in 1820. The friend was John Hamilton Reynolds.

Frozen North, and chilling East,
Sounded tempests to the feast
Of the forest's whispering fleeces,[2]
Since men knew nor rent nor leases.   10

No, the bugle sounds no more,
And the twanging bow no more;
Silent is the ivory[3] shrill
Past the heath and up the hill;
There is no mid-forest laugh,   15
Where lone Echo gives the half
To some wight, amazed to hear
Jesting, deep in forest drear.

On the fairest time of June
You may go, with sun or moon,   20
Or the seven stars to light you,
Or the polar ray to right you;[4]
But you never may behold
Little John, or Robin bold:
Never one, of all the clan,   25
Thrumming on an empty can
Some old hunting ditty, while
He doth his green way beguile
To fair hostess Merriment,
Down beside the pasture Trent,[5]   30
For he left the merry tale,
Messenger for spicy ale.

---

[2] Leaves.   [3] Whistle.
[4] Or with Charles's Wain (the Dipper), or the North Star as your guide.
[5] The fields about the River Trent, which runs by Sherwood Forest.

Gone, the merry morris[6] din;
Gone, the song of Gamelyn;[7]
Gone, the tough-belted outlaw   35
Idling in the "grenè shawe";[8]
All are gone away and past!
And if Robin should be cast
Sudden from his turfé grave,
And if Marian should have   40
Once again her forest days,
She would weep, and he would craze;
He would swear, for all his oaks,
Fall'n beneath the dock-yard strokes,
Have rotted on the briny seas;   45
She would weep that her wild bees
Sang not to her—strange! that honey
Can't be got without hard money!

So it is; yet let us sing
Honor to the old bow-string!   50
Honor to the bugle-horn!
Honor to the woods unshorn!
Honor to the Lincoln green![9]
Honor to the archer keen!
Honor to tight little John,   55
And the horse he rode upon!
Honor to bold Robin Hood,
Sleeping in the underwood!
Honor to Maid Marian,
And to all the Sherwood clan!   60
Though their days have hurried by
Let us two a burden try.

---

[6] An outdoor dance in costume generally danced by five men and a boy who impersonated Maid Marian.
[7] Name of the hero of a tale of outlawry formerly attributed to Chaucer.
[8] Green wood.   [9] Green cloth dyed at Lincoln.

THE EVE OF ST. AGNES[1]

St. Agnes' Eve—ah, bitter chill it was!
The owl, for all his feathers, was a-cold;
The hare limped trembling through the frozen grass,
And silent was the flock in woolly fold;
Numb were the Beadsman's[2] fingers while he told   5
His rosary, and while his frosted breath,
Like pious incense from a censer old,

Seemed taking flight for heaven without a death,
Past the sweet Virgin's picture, while his prayer he saith.

His prayer he saith, this patient, holy man;
Then takes his lamp, and riseth from his knees,   11
And back returneth, meager, barefoot, wan,
Along the chapel aisle by slow degrees:
The sculptured dead, on each side, seem to freeze,
Emprisoned in black, purgatorial rails: 15
Knights, ladies, praying in dumb orat'ries,[8]

---

[1] Written early in 1819; published in 1820. The Eve of St. Agnes is 20 January. The subject may have been suggested to Keats by a passage in Burton's *Anatomy of Melancholy* (III, ii, 3, i), or by a popular pamphlet called *Mother Bunches Closet Newly Broken Open*, or merely by the words of a friend who had heard of the superstition that a girl who fasted on St. Agnes's Eve would dream of her future husband.
[2] Man paid to pray for his benefactor.

[8] Oratories, small chapels for prayer. The adjective is transferred from the statues to the place.

He passeth by; and his weak spirit fails
To think how they may ache in icy hoods and
mails.

Northward he turneth through a little
    door,
And scarce three steps, ere 'Music's golden
    tongue   20
Flattered to tears this agéd man and poor.
But no—already had his death-bell rung;
The joys of all his life were said and sung;
His was harsh penance on St. Agnes' Eve:
Another way he went, and soon among 25
Rough ashes sat he for his soul's reprieve,
And all night kept awake, for sinners' sake
    to grieve.

That ancient Beadsman heard the prelude
    soft;
And so it chanced, for many a door was
    wide,
From hurry to and fro. Soon, up aloft, 30
The silver, snarling trumpets 'gan to
    chide:
The level chambers, ready with their pride,
Were glowing to receive a thousand
    guests:
The carvéd angels, ever eager-eyed,
Stared, where upon their heads the cornice
    rests,   35
With hair blown back, and wings put cross-
    wise on their breasts.

At length burst in the argent revelry,
With plume, tiara, and all rich array,
Numerous as shadows haunting fairily
The brain, new-stuffed, in youth, with
    triumphs gay   40
Of old romance.   These let us wish away,
And turn, sole-thoughted, to one Lady
    there,
Whose heart had brooded, all that wintry
    day,
On love, and winged St. Agnes' saintly
    care,
As she had heard old dames full many times
    declare.   45

They told her how, upon St. Agnes' Eve,
Young virgins might have visions of de-
    light,
And soft adorings from their loves receive
Upon the honeyed middle of the night,
If ceremonies due they did aright;   50
As, supperless to bed they must retire,

And couch supine their beauties, lily
    white;
Nor look behind, nor sideways, but re-
    quire[4]
Of Heaven with upward eyes for all that
    they desire.[5]

Full of this whim was thoughtful Made-
    line: 55
The music, yearning like a God in pain,
She scarcely heard: her maiden eyes
    divine,
Fixed on the floor, saw many a sweeping
    train
Pass by—she heeded not at all: in vain
Came many a tiptoe, amorous cavalier, 60
And back retired; not cooled by high dis-
    dain,
But she saw not: her heart was other-
    where;
She sighed for Agnes' dreams, the sweetest
    of the year.

She danced along with vague, regardless
    eyes,
Anxious her lips, her breathing quick and
    short: 65
The hallowed hour was near at hand: she
    sighs
Amid the timbrels, and the thronged resort
    Of whisperers in anger or in sport;
'Mid looks of love, defiance, hate, and
    scorn,
Hoodwinked with fairy fancy; all
    amort,[6]   70
Save to St. Agnes and her lambs un-
    shorn,[7]
And all the bliss to be before to-morrow
    morn.

---

[4]Request.

[5]At this point one of the original manuscripts of
the poem contains the following stanza, helpful to
an understanding of what happens later, but apparently omitted from the printed text to satisfy the
scruples of the poet's friends:

'Twas said her future lord would there appear
Offering as sacrifice—all in the dream—
Delicious food even to her lips brought near:
Viands and wine and fruit and sugared cream,
To touch her palate with the fine extreme
Of relish: then soft music heard; and then
More pleasures followed in a dizzy stream
Palpable almost: then to wake again
Warm in the virgin morn, no weeping Magdalen.

[6]Deadened.

[7]St. Agnes was always pictured with lambs. On
the anniversary of her martyrdom two lambs are
blessed, then shorn, and the wool is spun and woven
by nuns.

So, purposing each moment to retire,
She lingered still.   Meantime, across the moors,
Had come young Porphyro,[8] with heart on fire   75
For Madeline.   Beside the portal doors,
Buttressed from moonlight, stands he, and implores
All saints to give him sight of Madeline,
But for one moment in the tedious hours,
That he might gaze and worship all unseen;
Perchance speak, kneel, touch, kiss—in sooth such things have been.   81

He ventures in: let no buzzed whisper tell;
All eyes be muffled, or a hundred swords
Will storm his heart, Love's fev'rous citadel:
For him, those chambers held barbarian hordes,   85
Hyena foemen, and hot-blooded lords,
Whose very dogs would execrations howl
Against his lineage; not one breast affords
Him any mercy in that mansion foul,
Save one old beldame, weak in body and in soul.   90

Ah, happy chance! the agéd creature came
Shuffling along with ivory-headed wand,
To where he stood, hid from the torch's flame,
Behind a broad hall-pillar, far beyond   94
The sound of merriment and chorus bland.
He startled her; but soon she knew his face,
And grasped his fingers in her palsied hand,
Saying, "Mercy, Porphyro! hie thee from this place;
They are all here to-night, the whole bloodthirsty race!

"Get hence! get hence! there's dwarfish Hildebrand;   100
He had a fever late, and in the fit
He curséd thee and thine, both house and land:
Then there's that old Lord Maurice, not a whit
More tame for his gray hairs—Alas me! flit!
Flit like a ghost away."—"Ah, Gossip dear,   105

We're safe enough; here in this arm-chair sit,
And tell me how"—"Good saints! not here, not here;
Follow me, child, or else these stones will be thy bier."   108

He followed through a lowly archéd way,
Brushing the cobwebs with his lofty plume,
And as she muttered "Well-a—well-a-day!"
He found him in a little moonlight room,
Pale, latticed, chill, and silent as a tomb.
"Now tell me where is Madeline," said he,
"O tell me, Angela, by the holy loom   115
Which none but secret sisterhood may see,
When they St. Agnes' wool are weaving piously."

"St. Agnes!   Ah! it is St. Agnes' Eve—
Yet men will murder upon holy days:
Thou must hold water in a witch's sieve,[9]
And be liege-lord of all the Elves and Fays
To venture so: it fills me with amaze   122
To see thee, Porphyro!—St. Agnes' Eve!
God's help! my lady fair the conjurer plays
This very night: good angels her deceive!
But let me laugh awhile,—I've mickle[10] time to grieve."   126

Feebly she laugheth in the languid moon,
While Porphyro upon her face doth look,
Like puzzled urchin on an agéd crone
Who keepeth closed a wondrous riddlebook,   130
As spectacled she sits in chimney nook.
But soon his eyes grew brilliant, when she told
His lady's purpose; and he scarce could brook
Tears, at the thought of those enchantments cold, ·
And Madeline asleep in lap of legends old. 135

Sudden a thought came like a full-blown rose,
Flushing his brow, and in his painéd heart
Made purple riot: then doth he propose
A stratagem, that makes the beldame start:
"A cruel man and impious thou art: 140
Sweet lady! let her pray, and sleep, and dream

---

[8]The hero, as one of Keats's manuscripts reveals, was originally named Lionel.

[9]Supposed to be a sign of supernatural power.
[10]Much.

Alone with her good angels, far apart
From wicked men like thee. Go, go! I
deem
Thou canst not surely be the same that thou
didst seem."

"I will not harm her, by all saints I swear,"
Quoth Porphyro: "O may I ne'er find
grace   146
When my weak voice shall whisper its last
prayer,
If one of her soft ringlets I displace,
Or look with ruffian passion in her face.
Good Angela, believe me, by these tears,
Or I will, even in a moment's space,   151
Awake, with horrid shout, my foemen's
ears,
And beard them, though they be more fanged
than wolves and bears."

"Ah! why wilt thou affright a feeble soul?
A poor, weak, palsy-stricken, churchyard
thing,   155
Whose passing-bell may ere the midnight
toll;
Whose prayers for thee, each morn and
evening,
Were never missed." Thus plaining, doth
she bring
A gentler speech from burning Porphyro;
So woeful, and of such deep sorrowing, 160
That Angela gives promise she will do
Whatever he shall wish, betide her weal or
woe.

Which was, to lead him, in close secrecy,
Even to Madeline's chamber, and there
hide
Him in a closet, of such privacy   165
That he might see her beauty unespied,
And win perhaps that night a peerless
bride,
While legioned fairies paced the coverlet,
And pale enchantment held her sleepy-
eyed.
Never on such a night have lovers met, 170
Since Merlin paid his Demon all the mon-
strous debt.[11]

"It shall be as thou wishest," said the
Dame:
"All cates[12] and dainties shall be stored
there

Quickly on this feast-night: by the tam-
bour-frame[13]
Her own lute thou wilt see: no time to
spare,   175
For I am slow and feeble, and scarce dare
On such a catering trust my dizzy head.
Wait here, my child, with patience; kneel
in prayer
The while. Ah! thou must needs the lady
wed,
Or may I never leave my grave among the
dead."   180

So saying, she hobbled off with busy fear.
The lover's endless minutes slowly passed;
The dame returned, and whispered in his
ear
To follow her; with agéd eyes aghast
From fright of dim espial. Safe at
last,   185
Through many a dusky gallery, they gain
The maiden's chamber, silken, hushed,
and chaste;
Where Porphyro took covert, pleased
amain.
His poor guide hurried back with agues in
her brain.

Her faltering hand upon the balustrade,
Old Angela was feeling for the stair,   191
When Madeline, St. Agnes' charméd-
maid,
Rose, like a missioned spirit, unaware:
With silver taper's light, and pious care,
She turned, and down the agéd gossip
led   195
To a safe level matting. Now prepare,
Young Porphyro, for gazing on that bed;
She comes, she comes again, like ring-dove
frayed[14] and fled.

Out went the taper as she hurried in; 199
Its little smoke, in pallid moonshine, died:
She closed the door, she panted, all akin
To spirits of the air, and visions wide:
No uttered syllable, or, woe betide!
But to her heart, her heart was voluble,
Paining with eloquence her balmy side; 205
As though a tongueless nightingale should
swell
Her throat in vain, and die, heart-stifled, in
her dell.

A casement high and triple-arched there
was,
All garlanded with carven imag'ries,

---

[11]According to one legend Merlin's father was a
demon, so that his "debt" to the demon was his
existence. He paid this when Vivien destroyed him
by means of a spell which he himself had taught her.

[12]Provisions.

[13]Double hoops for holding embroidery.

[14]Frightened.

Of fruits and flowers, and bunches of
    knot-grass,   210
And diamonded with panes of quaint de-
    vice,
Innumerable of stains and splendid dyes,
As are the tiger-moth's deep-damasked
    wings;
And in the midst, 'mong thousand herald-
    ries,
And twilight saints, and dim emblazon-
    ings,   215
A shielded scutcheon blushed with blood of
    queens and kings.

Full on this casement shone the wintry
    moon,
And threw warm gules[15] on Madeline's
    fair breast,
As down she knelt for Heaven's grace and
    boon;
Rose-bloom fell on her hands, together
    pressed,   220
And on her silver cross soft amethyst,
And on her hair a glory, like a saint:
She seemed a splendid angel, newly
    dressed,
Save wings, for heaven:—Porphyro grew
    faint:
She knelt, so pure a thing, so free from
    mortal taint.   225

Anon his heart revives: her vespers done,
Of all its wreathéd pearls her hair she
    frees;
Unclasps her warméd jewels one by one;
Loosens her fragrant bodice; by degrees
Her rich attire creeps rustling to her
    knees: 230
Half-hidden, like a mermaid in sea-weed,
Pensive awhile she dreams awake, and
    sees,
In fancy, fair St. Agnes in her bed,
But dares not look behind, or all the charm is
    fled.   234

Soon, trembling in her soft and chilly nest,
In sort of wakeful swoon, perplexed she
    lay,
Until the poppied warmth of sleep op-
    pressed
Her soothéd limbs, and soul fatigued
    away;
Flown, like a thought, until the morrow-
    day;   239
Blissfully havened both from joy and
    pain;

Clasped like a missal where swart Pay-
    nims pray;[16]
Blinded alike from sunshine and from
    rain,
As though a rose should shut, and be a bud
    again.

Stol'n to this paradise, and so entranced,
Porphyro gazed upon her empty dress, 245
And listened to her breathing, if it
    chanced
To wake into a slumberous tenderness;
Which when he heard, that minute did he
    bless,
And breathed himself: then from the
    closet crept,
Noiseless as fear in a wide wilderness, 250
And over the hushed carpet, silent,
    stepped,
And 'tween the curtains peeped, where, lo!
    —how fast she slept!

Then by the bedside, where the faded
    moon
Made a dim, silver twilight, soft he set 254
A table, and, half anguished, threw there-
    on
A cloth of woven crimson, gold, and jet:—
O for some drowsy Morphean amulet![17]
The boisterous, midnight, festive clarion,
The kettle-drum, and far-heard clarinet,
Affray his ears, though but in dying
    tone:—
The hall-door shuts again, and all the noise
    is gone.   261

And still she slept an azure-lidded sleep,
In blanchéd linen, smooth, and lavendered,
While he from forth the closet brought a
    heap
Of candied apple, quince, and plum, and
    gourd;   265
With jellies soother[18] than the creamy
    curd,
And lucent syrops, tinct[19] with cinnamon;
Manna and dates, in argosy[20] transferred
From Fez; and spicéd dainties, every one,
From silken Samarcand to cedared Lebanon.

These delicates he heaped with glowing
    hand   271
On golden dishes and in baskets bright

---

[15]Blood-red (heraldic term).

[16]As tightly closed as a Christian prayer-book in
a pagan land. (Keats originally wrote, "Shut like
a missal," etc.)

[17]Charm. Morpheus was the god of sleep

[18]Softer.   [19]Flavored.   [20]Merchant-ship.

Of wreathéd silver: sumptuous they stand
In the retiréd quiet of the night,
Filling the chilly room with perfume
    light.—   275
"And now, my love, my seraph fair,
    awake!
Thou art my heaven, and I thine eremite:[21]
Open thine eyes, for meek St. Agnes'
    sake,
Or I shall drowse beside thee, so my soul
    doth ache."   279

Thus whispering, his warm, unnervéd arm
Sank in her pillow. Shaded was her
    dream
By the dusk curtains:—'twas a midnight
    charm
Impossible to melt as icéd stream:
The lustrous salvers in the moonlight
    gleam;   284
Broad golden fringe upon the carpet lies:
It seemed he never, never could redeem
From such a steadfast spell his lady's
    eyes;
So mused awhile, entoiled in wooféd phan-
    tasies.[22]

Awakening up, he took her hollow lute,—
Tumultuous,—and, in chords that tender-
    est be,   290
He played an ancient ditty, long since
    mute,
In Provence called "La belle dame sans
    mercy":[23]
Close to her ear touching the melody;—
Wherewith disturbed, she uttered a soft
    moan:
He ceased—she panted quick—and sud-
    denly   295
Her blue affrayéd eyes wide open shone:
Upon his knees he sank, pale as smooth-
    sculptured stone.

Her eyes were open, but she still beheld,
Now wide awake, the vision of her sleep:
There was a painful change, that nigh ex-
    pelled   300
The blisses of her dream so pure and deep,
At which fair Madeline began to weep,

And moan forth witless words with many
    a sigh,
While still her gaze on Porphyro would
    keep;
Who knelt, with joinéd hands and piteous
    eye,   305
Fearing to move or speak, she looked so
    dreamingly.

"Ah, Porphyro!" said she, "but even now
Thy voice was at sweet tremble in mine
    ear,
Made tunable with every sweetest vow;
And those sad eyes were spiritual and
    clear:
How changed thou art! how pallid, chill,
    and drear!   311
Give me that voice again, my Porphyro,
Those looks immortal, those complainings
    dear!
Oh leave me not in this eternal woe,
For if thou diest, my Love, I know not where
    to go."   315

Beyond a mortal man impassioned far
At these voluptuous accents, he arose,
Ethereal, flushed, and like a throbbing star
Seen 'mid the sapphire heaven's deep re-
    pose;
Into her dream he melted, as the rose   320
Blendeth its odor with the violet,—[24]
Solution sweet: meantime the frost-wind
    blows
Like Love's alarum, pattering the sharp
    sleet
Against the window-panes; St. Agnes' moon
    hath set.

'Tis dark: quick pattereth the flaw-blown
    sleet: 325
"This is no dream, my bride, my Made-
    line!"
'Tis dark: the icéd gusts still rave and
    beat:
"No dream, alas! alas! and woe is mine!
Porphyro will leave me here to fade and
    pine.
Cruel! what traitor could thee hither
    bring?   330
I curse not, for my heart is lost in thine,

---

[21]Literally, hermit—i. e., here, consecrated servant.

[22]Fancies mingled together as are woven threads.

[23]The Beautiful Lady without Pity. The poem
is not of Provençal origin, but is by Alain Chartier,
court poet of Charles II of France. An English
translation of it was attributed to Chaucer, and
thus Keats happened to see the title.

[24]At this point some three stanzas, now lost, were
omitted from the printed text on the advice of
Keats's friends lest they "render the poem unfit
for ladies." Keats, though he yielded, said that
he did not want ladies to read his poetry, and that
he wrote for men.

Though thou forsakest a deceivéd thing;—
A dove forlorn and lost with sick unprunéd
  wing."

"My Madeline! sweet dreamer! lovely
  bride!
Say, may I be for aye thy vassal blest? 335
Thy beauty's shield, heart-shaped and
  vermeil-dyed?
Ah, silver shrine, here will I take my rest
After so many hours of toil and quest,
A famished pilgrim,—saved by miracle.
Though I have found, I will not rob thy
  nest,   340
Saving of thy sweet self; if thou think'st
  well
To trust, fair Madeline, to no rude infidel.

"Hark! 'tis an elfin storm from fairy land,
Of haggard seeming, but a boon indeed:
Arise—arise! the morning is at hand;—345
The bloated wassailers will never heed;—
Let us away, my love, with happy speed;
There are no ears to hear, or eyes to see,—
Drowned all in Rhenish and the sleepy
  mead.
Awake! arise! my love,[25] and fearless
  be,   350
For o'er the southern moors I have a home
  for thee."

She hurried at his words, beset with fears,
For there were sleeping dragons all
  around,
At glaring watch, perhaps, with ready
  spears—
Down the wide stairs a darkling way
  they found;   355
In all the house was heard no human
  sound.
A chain-drooped lamp was flickering by
  each door;
The arras, rich with horseman, hawk, and
  hound,
Fluttered in the besieging wind's uproar;
And the long carpets rose along the gusty
  floor.   360

They glide, like phantoms, into the wide
  hall;
Like phantoms to the iron porch they
  glide;

Where lay the Porter, in uneasy sprawl,
With a huge empty flagon by his side:
The wakeful bloodhound rose, and shook
  his hide,   365
But his sagacious eye an inmate owns:[26]
By one, and one, the bolts full easy
  slide:—
The chains lie silent on the footworn
  stones;
The key turns, and the door upon its hinges
  groans.

And they are gone: ay, ages long ago 370
These lovers fled away into the storm.
That night the Baron dreamed of many a
  woe,
And all his warrior-guests, with shade and
  form
Of witch, and demon, and large coffin-
  worm,
Were long be-nightmared. Angela the
  old
Died palsy-twitched, with meager face de-
  form;   376
The Beadsman, after thousand aves told,
For aye unsought-for slept among his ashes
  cold.

TO SLEEP[1]

O soft embalmer of the still midnight!
  Shutting, with careful fingers and benign,
Our gloom-pleased eyes, embowered from
    the light,
  Enshaded in forgetfulness divine;
O soothest Sleep! if so it please thee, close, 5
  In midst of this thine hymn, my willing
    eyes,
Or wait the amen, ere thy poppy throws
  Around my bed its lulling charities;
  Then save me, or the passéd day will
    shine
Upon my pillow, breeding many woes;   10
  Save me from curious conscience, that still
    lords
Its strength for darkness, burrowing like a
    mole;
  Turn the key deftly in the oiléd wards,[2]
And seal the hushéd casket of my soul.

---

[25]For "Awake! arise! my love" Keats originally
wrote, "Put on warm clothing, sweet."

[26]Recognizes.

[1]Written in 1819; published in 1848 (an early
draft was published in America, in the *Dial*, in
1843).

[2]Ridges on the inside of a lock.

LA BELLE DAME SANS MERCI[3]

O what can ail thee, knight-at-arms,
  Alone and palely loitering?
The sedge has withered from the lake,
  And no birds sing.

O what can ail thee, knight-at-arms,   5
  So haggard and so woe-begone?
The squirrel's granary is full,
  And the harvest's done.

I see a lily on thy brow
  With anguish moist and fever dew,   10
And on thy cheeks a fading rose
  Fast withereth too.

I met a lady in the meads,
  Full beautiful—a faery's child,
Her hair was long, her foot was light,   15
  And her eyes were wild.

I made a garland for her head,
  And bracelets too, and fragrant zone;[4]
She looked at me as she did love,
  And made sweet moan.   20

I set her on my pacing steed
  And nothing else saw all day long,
For sidelong would she bend, and sing
  A faery's song.

She found me roots of relish sweet,   25
  And honey wild, and manna dew,
And sure in language strange she said—
  "I love thee true!"

She took me to her elfin grot,
  And there she wept and sighed full sore, 30
And there I shut her wild, wild eyes
  With kisses four.

And there she lulléd me asleep,
  And there I dreamed—ah, woe betide!
The latest dream I ever dreamed   35
  On the cold hill side.

I saw pale kings, and princes too,
  Pale warriors, death-pale were they all;
They cried—"La Belle Dame sans Merci
  Thee hath in thrall!"   40

I saw their starved lips in the gloam,
  With horrid warning gapéd wide,
And I awoke and found me here,
  On the cold hill's side.

And this is why I sojourn here,   45
  Alone and palely loitering,
Though the sedge is withered from the lake,
  And no birds sing.

TWO SONNETS ON FAME[5]

I

Fame, like a wayward girl, will still be coy
  To those who woo her with too slavish
    knees,
But makes surrender to some thoughtless
  boy,
  And dotes the more upon a heart at ease;
She is a Gypsy will not speak to those   5
  Who have not learned to be content with-
    out her;
A Jilt, whose ear was never whispered close,
  Who thinks they scandal her who talk
    about her;
A very Gypsy is she, Nilus-born,[6]
  Sister-in-law to jealous Potiphar;   10
Ye love-sick Bards! repay her scorn for
  scorn;
  Ye Artists lovelorn! madmen that ye are!
Make your best bow to her and bid adieu,
Then, if she likes it, she will follow you.

II

"You cannot eat your cake and have it too."—
Proverb.

How fevered is the man, who cannot look
  Upon his mortal days with temperate
    blood,
Who vexes all the leaves of his life's book,
  And robs his fair name of its maiden-
    hood;
It is as if the rose should pluck herself,   5
  Or the ripe plum finger its misty bloom,
As if a Naiad, like a meddling elf,
  Should darken her pure grot with muddy
    gloom;
But the rose leaves herself upon the brier,
  For winds to kiss and grateful bees to
    feed,   10

[3]Written in the spring of 1819; published (by Leigh Hunt in the *Indicator*) in 1820. Two versions of the poem exist, the earlier of which is here printed. Keats owes the title—but nothing more than the title—to a poem by Alain Chartier.

[4]Girdle.

[5]Both sonnets were written in 1819 and published in 1848.

[6]Gypsies were formerly supposed to come from Egypt.

And the ripe plum still wears its dim attire;
  The undisturbéd lake has crystal space;
Why then should man, teasing the world
    for grace,
Spoil his salvation for a fierce miscreed?[7]

ODE TO A NIGHTIN-GALE[1]

My heart aches, and a drowsy numbness
    pains
  My sense, as though of hemlock[2] I had
    drunk,
Or emptied some dull opiate to the drains
  One minute past, and Lethe-wards had
    sunk:
'Tis not through envy of thy happy lot,   5
  But being too happy in thine happiness,—
    That thou, light-wingéd Dryad[3] of the
      trees,
        In some melodious plot
    Of beechen green, and shadows number-
      less,   9
      Singest of summer in full-throated ease.

O for a draught of vintage! that hath been
  Cooled a long age in the deep-delvéd earth,
Tasting of Flora[4] and the country-green,
  Dance, and Provençal song, and sunburnt
    mirth!
O for a beaker full of the warm South,   15
  Full of the true, the blushful Hippocrene,[5]
    With beaded bubbles winking at the
      brim,
        And purple-stainéd mouth;
    That I might drink, and leave the world
      unseen,
    And with thee fade away into the forest
      dim: 20

Fade far away, dissolve, and quite forget
  What thou among the leaves hast never
    known,
The weariness, the fever, and the fret
  Here, where men sit and hear each other
    groan;
Where palsy shakes a few, sad, last gray
    hairs,   25
  Where youth grows pale, and specter-
    thin, and dies;

───────

[7]Mistaken creed.
[1]Written in May, 1819; published in 1820.
[2]A poison.   [3]Tree-nymph.
[4]Goddess of flowers.
[5]Spring of the Muses on Mount Helicon.

Where but to think is to be full of sor-
    row
  And leaden-eyed despairs;
Where beauty cannot keep her lustrous
    eyes,
  Or new Love pine at them beyond to-
    morrow.   30

Away! away! for I will fly to thee,
  Not charioted by Bacchus and his pards,[6]
But on the viewless[7] wings of Poesy,
  Though the dull brain perplexes and re-
    tards:
Already with thee! tender is the night,   35
  And haply the Queen-Moon is on her
    throne,
    Clustered around by all her starry Fays;
      But here there is no light,
  Save what from heaven is with the breezes
    blown
  Through verdurous glooms and winding
    mossy ways.   40

I cannot see what flowers are at my feet,
  Nor what soft incense hangs upon the
    boughs,
But, in embalméd darkness, guess each
    sweet
  Wherewith the seasonable month endows
The grass, the thicket, and the fruit-tree
    wild;   45
  White hawthorn, and the pastoral eglan-
    tine;
    Fast-fading violets covered up in leaves;
      And mid-May's eldest child,
  The coming musk-rose, full of dewy wine,
  The murmurous haunt of flies on sum-
    mer eves.   50

Darkling I listen; and, for many a time
  I have been half in love with easeful
    Death,
Called him soft names in many a muséd
    rime,
  To take into the air my quiet breath,—
    Now more than ever seems it rich to
      die,   55
  To cease upon the midnight with no pain,
    While thou art pouring forth thy soul
      abroad
        In such an ecstasy!
  Still wouldst thou sing, and I have ears in
    vain—
    To thy high requiem become a sod.   60

───────

[6]Leopards.   [7]Invisible.

Thou wast not born for death, immortal
    Bird!
No hungry generations tread thee down;
The voice I hear this passing night was
    heard
In ancient days by emperor and clown:[8]
Perhaps the self-same song that found a
    path   65
    Through the sad heart of Ruth,[9] when,
        sick for home,
      She stood in tears amid the alien corn;
      The same that oft-times hath
Charmed magic casements, opening on the
    foam
    Of perilous seas, in faery lands for-
        lorn.   70

Forlorn! the very word is like a bell
    To toll me back from thee to my sole self.
Adieu! the fancy cannot cheat so well
    As she is famed to do, deceiving elf.
Adieu! adieu! thy plaintive anthem fades 75
    Past the near meadows, over the still
      stream,
      Up the hill-side; and now 'tis buried
        deep
    In the next valley-glades:
Was it a vision, or a waking dream?
    Fled is that music:—do I wake or
      sleep?   80

ODE ON A GRECIAN URN[1]

Thou still unravished bride of quietness,
    Thou foster-child of silence and slow
      time,
Sylvan historian, who canst thus express
    A flowery tale more sweetly than our
      rime:
What leaf-fringed legend haunts about thy
    shape   5
    Of deities or mortals, or of both,
      In Tempe or the dales of Arcady?[2]
What men or gods are these? What
    maidens loath?
What mad pursuit? What struggle to
    escape?
What pipes and timbrels? What wild ec-
    stasy?   10

[8]Peasant.   [9]See Ruth, 2.

[1]Written in February or March, 1819; published
in 1820.

[2]Tempe is a valley in Thessaly, Arcadia a mountainous region in the Peloponnese.

Heard melodies are sweet, but those unheard
    Are sweeter; therefore, ye soft pipes,
      play on;
Not to the sensual ear, but, more endeared,
    Pipe to the spirit ditties of no tone:
Fair youth, beneath the trees, thou canst not
    leave   15
    Thy song, nor ever can those trees be
      bare;
      Bold Lover, never, never canst thou
        kiss,
Though winning near the goal—yet, do not
    grieve;
    She cannot fade, though thou hast not
      thy bliss,
For ever wilt thou love, and she be fair! 20

Ah, happy, happy boughs! that cannot shed
    Your leaves, nor ever bid the Spring
      adieu;
And, happy melodist, unwearièd,
    For ever piping songs for ever new;
More happy love! more happy, happy love!25
    For ever warm and still to be enjoyed,
      For ever panting and for ever young;
All breathing human passion far above,
    That leaves a heart high-sorrowful and
      cloyed,
      A burning forehead, and a parching
      tongue.   30

Who are these coming to the sacrifice?
    To what green altar, O mysterious priest,
Lead'st thou that heifer lowing at the skies,
    And all her silken flanks with garlands
      dressed?
What little town by river or sea-shore, 35
    Or mountain-built with peaceful citadel,
      Is emptied of this folk, this pious morn?
And, little town, thy streets for evermore
    Will silent be; and not a soul to tell 39
      Why thou art desolate, can e'er return.

O Attic shape! Fair attitude! with brede[3]
    Of marble men and maidens overwrought,
With forest branches and the trodden weed;
    Thou, silent form, dost tease us out of
      thought
As doth eternity: Cold Pastoral!   45
    When old age shall this generation waste,
    Thou shalt remain, in midst of other
      woe
Than ours, a friend to man, to whom thou
    say'st,

[3]Embroidery.

"Beauty is truth, truth beauty,"—that is all
    Ye know on earth, and all ye need to
      know.   50

ODE TO PSYCHE[1]

O goddess! hear these tuneless numbers, wrung
    By sweet enforcement and remembrance dear,
And pardon that thy secrets should be sung
    Even into thine own soft-conchéd[2] ear:
Surely I dreamed to-day, or did I see   5
    The wingéd Psyche with awakened eyes?
I wandered in a forest thoughtlessly,
    And, on the sudden, fainting with surprise,
Saw two fair creatures, couchéd side by side
    In deepest grass, beneath the whispering roof   10
    Of leaves and trembled blossoms, where there ran
      A brooklet, scarce espied:

'Mid hushed, cool-rooted flowers, fragrant-eyed,
    Blue, silver-white, and budded Tyrian,[3]
They lay calm-breathing, on the bedded grass;   15
    Their arms embracéd, and their pinions too;
    Their lips touched not, but had not bade adieu,
As if disjoinéd by soft-handed slumber,
And ready still past kisses to outnumber
    At tender eye-dawn of aurorean love: 20
    The wingéd boy I knew;[4]
    But who wast thou, O happy, happy dove?
    His Psyche true!

---

[1] Written in the spring of 1819; published in 1820. Keats wrote in a letter, "You must recollect that Psyche was not embodied as a goddess before the time of Apuleius the Platonist, who lived after the Augustan age, and consequently the goddess was never worshiped or sacrificed to with any of the ancient fervor, and perhaps never thought of in the old religion—I am more orthodox than to let a heathen goddess be so neglected." In the same letter he said that this poem was the first with which he had taken "even moderate pains."

[2] Shaped like a shell.

[3] Crimson or purple.

[4] Cupid. The story of Cupid and Psyche may be read in Walter Pater's translation of Apuleius's version of it (in *Marius the Epicurean*) or in Robert Bridges' poem, *Eros and Psyche*.

O latest-born and loveliest vision far
    Of all Olympus' faded hierarchy!   25
Fairer than Phoebe's sapphire-regioned star,[5]
    Or Vesper, amorous glow-worm of the sky;[6]
Fairer than these, though temple thou hast none,
    Nor altar heaped with flowers;
Nor Virgin-choir to make delicious moan   30
    Upon the midnight hours;
No voice, no lute, no pipe, no incense sweet
    From chain-swung censer teeming;
No shrine, no grove, no oracle, no heat
    Of pale-mouthed prophet dreaming.   35

O brightest! though too late for antique vows,
    Too, too late for the fond believing lyre,
When holy were the haunted forest boughs,
    Holy the air, the water, and the fire;
Yet even in these days so far retired   40
    From happy pieties, thy lucent fans,[7]
    Fluttering among the faint Olympians,
I see, and sing, by my own eyes inspired.
So let me be thy choir, and make a moan
    Upon the midnight hours;   45
Thy voice, thy lute, thy pipe, thy incense sweet
    From swingéd censer teeming;
Thy shrine, thy grove, thy oracle, thy heat
    Of pale-mouthed prophet dreaming.

Yes, I will be thy priest, and build a fane[8]   50
    In some untrodden region of my mind,
Where branchéd thoughts, new-grown with pleasant pain,
    Instead of pines shall murmur in the wind:
Far, far around shall those dark-clustered trees
    Fledge the wild-ridged mountains steep by steep;   55
And there by zephyrs, streams, and birds, and bees,
    The moss-lain Dryads shall be lulled to sleep;
And in the midst of this wide quietness
A rosy sanctuary will I dress
With the wreathed trellis of a working brain,
    With buds, and bells, and stars without a name,   61
With all the gardener Fancy e'er could feign,
    Who breeding flowers, will never breed the same;

---

[5] The moon. Phoebe is Artemis.   [6] The Evening Star, Venus.

[7] Translucent wings.   [8] Temple.

And there shall be for thee all soft delight
  That shadowy thought can win,   65
A bright torch, and a casement ope at night,
  To let the warm Love in!

TO AUTUMN[1]

Season of mists and mellow fruitfulness,
  Close bosom-friend of the maturing sun;
Conspiring with him how to load and bless
    With fruit the vines that round the thatch-
      eaves run;
To bend with apples the mossed cottage-
      trees,   5
  And fill all fruit with ripeness to the core;
    To swell the gourd, and plump the hazel
      shells
  With a sweet kernel; to set budding more,
And still more, later flowers for the bees,
Until they think warm days will never cease,
    For Summer has o'er-brimmed their
      clammy cells.   11

Who hath not seen thee oft amid thy store?
  Sometimes whoever seeks abroad may find
Thee sitting careless on a granary floor,
  Thy hair soft-lifted by the winnowing
    wind;   15
Or on a half-reaped furrow sound asleep,
  Drowsed with the fumes of poppies, while
    thy hook
    Spares the next swath and all its twinéd
      flowers;
And sometimes like a gleaner thou dost keep
  Steady thy laden head across a brook; 20
Or by a cider-press, with patient look,
  Thou watchest the last oozings, hours
    by hours.

Where are the songs of Spring? Ay, where
    are they?
  Think not of them, thou hast thy music too,
While barréd clouds bloom the soft dying
    day,   25
  And touch the stubble-plains with rosy
    hue;
Then in a wailful choir, the small gnats
    mourn
  Among the river sallows,[2] borne aloft
    Or sinking as the light wind lives or
      dies;
And full-grown lambs loud bleat from hilly
    bourn;[3]   30

Hedge-crickets[4] sing; and now with treble
    soft
The redbreast whistles from a garden-
    croft;[5]
  And gathering swallows twitter in the
    skies.

ODE ON MELANCHOLY[1]

No, no, go not to Lethe,[2] neither twist
  Wolf's-bane, tight-rooted, for its poison-
    ous wine;
Nor suffer thy pale forehead to be kissed
  By nightshade, ruby grape of Proserpine;[3]
Make not your rosary of yew-berries,   5
  Nor let the beetle, nor the death-moth be
    Your mournful Psyche,[4] nor the downy
      owl
A partner in your sorrow's mysteries;
  For shade to shade will come too drowsily,
    And drown the wakeful anguish of the
      soul.   10

But when the melancholy fit shall fall
  Sudden from heaven like a weeping cloud,
That fosters the droop-headed flowers all,
  And hides the green hill in an April
    shroud;
Then glut thy sorrow on a morning rose, 15
  Or on the rainbow of the salt sand-wave,
    Or on the wealth of globéd peonies;
Or if thy mistress some rich anger shows,
  Emprison her soft hand, and let her rave,
    And feed deep, deep upon her peerless
      eyes.   20

She[5] dwells with Beauty—Beauty that must
    die;
  And Joy, whose hand is ever at his lips
Bidding adieu; and aching Pleasure nigh,
  Turning to poison while the bee-mouth sips:
Ay, in the very temple of Delight   25
  Veiled Melancholy has her sovran shrine,
    Though seen of none save him whose
      strenuous tongue
Can burst Joy's grape against his palate
    fine:
His soul shall taste the sadness of her might,
    And be among her cloudy trophies
      hung.   30

---

[1]Written in September, 1819; published in 1820.
[2]Willows.
[3]Literally, boundary, but the word can also mean, as here, domain.

[4]Grasshoppers.   [5]Garden-enclosure.
[1]Written in the spring of 1819; published in 1820.
[2]River of forgetfulness, in Hades.
[3]Queen of the lower world.
[4]The soul. Psyche was sometimes represented as a butterfly. Do not, says Keats, let insects who symbolize death represent your mournful soul.
[5]Melancholy.

LAMIA [1]

PART I

Upon a time, before the faery broods
Drove Nymph and Satyr from the prosperous
    woods,
Before King Oberon's bright diadem,
Scepter, and mantle, clasped with dewy gem,
Frighted away the Dryads and the Fauns 5
From rushes green, and brakes, and cow-
    slipped lawns,
The ever-smitten Hermes empty left
His golden throne, bent warm on amorous
    theft:
From high Olympus had he stolen light,
On this side of Jove's clouds, to escape the
    sight   10
Of his great summoner, and made retreat
Into a forest on the shores of Crete.
For somewhere in that sacred island dwelt
A nymph to whom all hooféd Satyrs knelt;
At whose white feet the languid Tritons
    poured   15
Pearls, while on land they withered and
    adored.
Fast by the springs where she to bathe was
    wont,
And in those meads where sometime she
    might haunt,

---

[1] Written in 1819 (finished apparently by 5 September); published in 1820. In a note appended to the poem on its first publication Keats gave his source, as follows: "Philostratus in his fourth book *de Vita Apollonii* [concerning the life of Apollonius], hath a memorable instance in this kind, which I may not omit, of one Menippus Lycius, a young man twenty-five years of age, that going betwixt Cenchreas and Corinth, met such a phantasm in the habit of a fair gentlewoman, which taking him by the hand, carried him home to her house, in the suburbs of Corinth, and told him she was a Phoenician by birth, and if he would tarry with her, he should hear her sing and play, and drink such wine as never any drank, and no man should molest him; but she, being fair and lovely, would live and die with him, that was fair and lovely to behold. The young man, a philosopher, otherwise staid and discreet, able to moderate his passions, though not this of love, tarried with her a while to his great content, and at last married her, to whose wedding, amongst other guests, came Apollonius; who, by some probable conjectures, found her out to be a serpent, a lamia; and that all her furniture was, like Tantalus' gold, described by Homer, no substance but mere illusions. When she saw herself described, she wept, and desired Apollonius to be silent, but he would not be moved, and thereupon she, plate, house, and all that was in it, vanished in an instant: many thousands took notice of this fact, for it was done in the midst of Greece" (Burton's *Anatomy of Melancholy*, III, ii, 1, i).

Were strewn rich gifts, unknown to any
    Muse,
Though Fancy's casket were unlocked to
    choose.   20
Ah, what a world of love was at her feet!
So Hermes thought, and a celestial heat
Burned from his wingéd heels to either ear,
That, from a whiteness as the lily clear,
Blushed into roses 'mid his golden hair,   25
Fallen in jealous curls about his shoulders
    bare.

From vale to vale, from wood to wood, he
    flew,
Breathing upon the flowers his passion new,
And wound with many a river to its head,
To find where this sweet nymph prepared her
    secret bed: 30
In vain; the sweet nymph might nowhere be
    found,
And so he rested on the lonely ground,
Pensive, and full of painful jealousies
Of the Wood-Gods, and even the very trees.
There as he stood, he heard a mournful
    voice,   35
Such as, once heard, in gentle heart destroys
All pain but pity; thus the lone voice spake:
"When from this wreathéd tomb shall I
    awake?
When move in a sweet body fit for life,   39
And love, and pleasure, and the ruddy strife
Of hearts and lips? Ah, miserable me!"
The God, dove-footed, glided silently
Round bush and tree, soft-brushing in his
    speed
The taller grasses and full-flowering weed,
Until he found a palpitating snake,   45
Bright and cirque-couchant,[2] in a dusky
    brake.

She was a gordian[3] shape of dazzling hue,
Vermilion-spotted, golden, green, and blue;
Striped like a zebra, freckled like a pard,
Eyed like a peacock, and all crimson-barred;
And full of silver moons, that, as she
    breathed,   51
Dissolved, or brighter shone, or inter-
    wreathed
Their lusters with the gloomier tapestries—
So rainbow-sided, touched with miseries,
She seemed, at once, some penanced lady
    elf,   55
Some demon's mistress, or the demon's self.

---

[2] Lying coiled.   [3] Knotted.

Upon her crest she wore a wannish fire
Sprinkled with stars, like Ariadne's tiar:[4]
Her head was serpent, but ah, bitter-sweet!
She had a woman's mouth with all its pearls
    complete;   60
For her eyes—what could such eyes do there
But weep and weep, that they were born so
    fair,
As Proserpine still weeps for her Sicilian
    air?
Her throat was serpent, but the words she
    spake
Came, as through bubbling honey, for Love's
    sake,   65
And thus; while Hermes on his pinions lay,
Like a stooped falcon ere he takes his prey:

"Fair Hermes, crowned with feathers,
    fluttering light,
I had a splendid dream of thee last night:
I saw thee sitting, on a throne of gold, 70
Among the Gods, upon Olympus old,
The only sad one; for thou didst not hear
The soft, lute-fingered Muses chaunting
    clear,
Nor even Apollo when he sang alone,
Deaf to his throbbing throat's long, long
    melodious moan.   75
I dreamed I saw thee, robed in purple flakes,
Break amorous through the clouds, as morn-
    ing breaks,
And, swiftly as a bright Phoebean dart,[5]
Strike for the Cretan isle; and here thou art!
Too gentle Hermes, hast thou found the
    maid?"
Whereat the star of Lethe[6] not delayed 81
His rosy eloquence, and thus inquired:
"Thou smooth-lipped serpent, surely high-
    inspired!
Thou beauteous wreath, with melancholy
    eyes,
Possess whatever bliss thou canst devise, 85
Telling me only where my nymph is fled—
Where she doth breathe!" "Bright planet,
    thou hast said,"
Returned the snake, "but seal with oaths,
    fair God!"
"I swear," said Hermes, "by my serpent rod,
And by thine eyes, and by thy starry crown!"
Light flew his earnest words, among the blos-
    soms blown.   91

Then thus again the brilliance feminine:
"Too frail of heart! for this lost nymph of
    thine,
Free as the air, invisibly she strays
About these thornless wilds; her pleasant
    days
She tastes unseen; unseen her nimble feet 96
Leave traces in the grass and flowers sweet:
From weary tendrils and bowed branches
    green
She plucks the fruit unseen, she bathes un-
    seen:
And by my power is her beauty veiled   100
To keep it unaffronted, unassailed
By the love-glances of unlovely eyes,
Of Satyrs, Fauns, and bleared Silenus'[7] sighs.
Pale grew her immortality, for woe
Of all these lovers, and she grievéd so   105
I took compassion on her, bade her steep
Her hair in weïrd syrops, that would keep
Her loveliness invisible, yet free
To wander as she loves, in liberty.   109
Thou shalt behold her, Hermes, thou alone,
If thou wilt, as thou swearest, grant my
    boon!"
Then, once again, the charméd God began
An oath, and through the serpent's ears it
    ran
Warm, tremulous, devout, psalterian.[8]
Ravished, she lifted her Circean head, 115
Blushed a live damask, and swift-lisping said,
"I was a woman, let me have once more
A woman's shape, and charming as before.
I love a youth of Corinth—O the bliss!
Give me my woman's form, and place me
    where he is.   120
Stoop, Hermes, let me breathe upon thy brow,
And thou shalt see thy sweet nymph even
    now."
The God on half-shut feathers sank serene,
She breathed upon his eyes, and swift was
    seen
Of both the guarded nymph near-smiling on
    the green.   125
It was no dream; or say a dream it was,
Real are the dreams of Gods, and smoothly
    pass
Their pleasures in a long immortal dream.
One warm, flushed moment, hovering, it
    might seem,
Dashed by the wood-nymph's beauty, so he
    burned;   130
Then, lighting on the printless verdure,
    turned

---

[4]Bacchus gave Ariadne a tiara, or crown, of seven
stars which after her death became a constellation.

[5]As one of Phoebus Apollo's arrows.

[6]Hermes is so called because it was one of his
duties to lead the souls of the dead to Hades.

[7]Foster-father of Bacchus.

[8]Musical.

To the swooned serpent, and with languid
    arm,
Delicate, put to proof the lithe Caducean
    charm.[9]
So done, upon the nymph his eyes he bent
Full of adoring tears and blandishment, 135
And towards her stepped: she, like a moon
    in wane,
Faded before him, cowered, nor could re-
    strain
Her fearful sobs, self-folding like a flower
That faints into itself at evening hour:
But the God fostering her chilléd hand, 140
She felt the warmth, her eyelids opened
    bland,
And, like new flowers at morning song of
    bees,
Bloomed, and gave up her honey to the lees.
Into the green-recesséd woods they flew;
Nor grew they pale, as mortal lovers do. 145

    Left to herself, the serpent now began
To change; her elfin blood in madness ran;
Her mouth foamed, and the grass, therewith
    besprent,[10]
Withered at dew so sweet and virulent; 149
Her eyes in torture fixed, and anguish drear,
Hot, glazed, and wide, with lid-lashes all sear,
Flashed phosphor and sharp sparks, without
    one cooling tear.
The colors all inflamed throughout her train,
She writhed about, convulsed with scarlet
    pain:
A deep volcanian yellow took the place 155
Of all her milder-mooného body's grace;
And, as the lava ravishes the mead,
Spoiled all her silver mail, and golden
    brede:[11]
Made gloom of all her frecklings, streaks, and
    bars, 159
Eclipsed her crescents, and licked up her
    stars:
So that, in moments few, she was undressed
Of all her sapphires, greens, and amethyst,
And rubious-argent: of all these bereft,
Nothing but pain and ugliness were left. 164
Still shone her crown; that vanished, also she
Melted and disappeared as suddenly;
And in the air, her new voice luting soft,
Cried, "Lycius! gentle Lycius!"—Borne aloft
With the bright mists about the mountains
    hoar
These words dissolved: Crete's forests heard
    no more. 170

Whither fled Lamia, now a lady bright,
A full-born beauty new and exquisite?
She fled into that valley they pass o'er
Who go to Corinth from Cenchreas' shore;
And rested at the foot of those wild hills, 175
The rugged founts of the Peraean rills,
And of that other ridge whose barren back
Stretches, with all its mist and cloudy rack,
South-westward to Cleone.   There she stood,
About a young bird's flutter from a wood, 180
Fair, on a sloping green of mossy tread,
By a clear pool, wherein she passionéd
To see herself escaped from so sore ills,
While her robes flaunted with the daffodils.

    Ah, happy Lycius!—for she was a maid 185
More beautiful than ever twisted braid,
Or sighed, or blushed, or on spring-flowered
    lea
Spread a green girtle to the minstrelsy:
A virgin purest lipped, yet in the lore 189
Of love deep learnéd to the red heart's core:
Not one hour old, yet of sciential brain
To unperplex bliss from its neighbor pain;
Define their pettish limits, and estrange
Their points of contact, and swift counter-
    change; 194
Intrigue with the specious chaos,[12] and dispart
Its most ambiguous atoms with sure art;
As though in Cupid's college she had spent
Sweet days a lovely graduate, still unshent,[13]
And kept his rosy terms in idle languishment.

    Why this fair creature chose so faerily 200
By the wayside to linger, we shall see;
But first 'tis fit to tell how she could muse
And dream, when in the serpent prison-house,
Of all she list, strange or magnificent: 204
How, ever, where she willed her spirit went;
Whether to faint Elysium, or where
Down through tress-lifting wayes the Ne-
    reids[14] fair
Wind into Thetis' bower by many a pearly
    stair;
Or where God Bacchus drains his cups
    divine,
Stretched out, at ease, beneath a glutinous
    pine; 210
Or where in Pluto's gardens palatine[15]
Mulciber's columns gleam in far piazzian
    line.[16]
And sometimes into cities she would send
Her dream, with feast and rioting to blend;

---

[9]Caduceus was the name of Hermes' wand.
[10]Sprinkled.   [11]Embroidery.

[12]The fair-appearing confusion of joy and pain.
[13]Yet unreproached.
[14]Sea-nymphs, sisters of Thetis.   [15]Palatial.
[16]Vulcan's columns gleam, forming covered walks.

And once, while among mortals dreaming thus,
She saw the young Corinthian Lycius   216
Charioting foremost in the envious race,
Like a young Jove with calm uneager face,
And fell into a swooning love of him.
Now on the moth-time of that evening dim 220
He would return that way, as well she knew,
To Corinth from the shore; for freshly blew
The eastern soft-wind, and his galley now
Grated the quay-stones with her brazen prow
In port Cenchreas, from Egina isle   225
Fresh anchored; whither he had been awhile
To sacrifice to Jove, whose temple there
Waits with high marble doors for blood and
     incense rare.
Jove heard his vows, and bettered his desire;
For by some freakful chance he made re-
     tire   230
From his companions, and set forth to walk,
Perhaps grown wearied of their Corinth talk:
Over the solitary hills he fared,
Thoughtless at first, but ere eve's star ap-
     peared
His phantasy was lost, where reason fades, 235
In the calmed twilight of Platonic shades.[17]
Lamia beheld him coming, near, more near—
Close to her passing, in indifference drear,
His silent sandals swept the mossy green;
So neighbored to him, and yet so unseen, 240
She stood: he passed, shut up in mysteries,
His mind wrapped like his mantle, while her
     eyes
Followed his steps, and her neck regal white
Turned—syllabling thus: "Ah, Lycius bright,
And will you leave me on the hills alone? 245
Lycius, look back! and be some pity shown."
He did; not with cold wonder, fearingly,
But Orpheus-like at an Eurydice;[18]
For so delicious were the words she sung,
It seemed he had loved them a whole summer
     long.   250
And soon his eyes had drunk her beauty up,
Leaving no drop in the bewildering cup,
And still the cup was full,—while he, afraid
Lest she should vanish ere his lip had paid
Due adoration, thus began to adore;   255
Her soft look growing coy, she saw his chain
     so sure:

"Leave thee alone! Look back! Ah, God-
     dess, see
Whether my eyes can ever turn from thee!
For pity do not this sad heart belie—
Even as thou vanishest so I shall die.   260
Stay! though a Naiad of the rivers, stay!
To thy far wishes will thy streams obey:
Stay! though the greenest woods be thy do-
     main,
Alone they can drink up the morning rain;
Though a descended Pleiad,[19] will not one 265
Of thine harmonious sisters keep in tune
Thy spheres, and as thy silver proxy shine?
So sweetly to these ravished ears of mine
Came thy sweet greeting, that if thou shouldst
     fade,
Thy memory will waste me to a shade:—270
For pity do not melt!" "If I should stay,"
Said Lamia, "here, upon this floor of clay,
And pain my steps upon these flowers too
     rough,
What canst thou say or do of charm enough
To dull the nice remembrance of my home?
Thou canst not ask me with thee here to
     roam   276
Over these hills and vales, where no joy is,—
Empty of immortality and bliss!
Thou art a scholar, Lycius, and must know
That finer spirits cannot breathe below   280
In human climes, and live. Alas! poor youth,
What taste of purer air hast thou to soothe
My essence? What serener palaces,
Where I may all my many senses please,
And by mysterious sleights a hundred thirsts
     appease?   285
It cannot be—adieu!" So said, she rose
Tiptoe, with white arms spread. He, sick to
     lose
The amorous promise of her lone complain,
Swooned, murmuring of love, and pale with
     pain.
The cruel lady, without any show   290
Of sorrow for her tender favorite's woe,
But rather, if her eyes could brighter be,
With brighter eyes and slow amenity,
Put her new lips to his, and gave afresh
The life she had so tangled in her mesh: 295
And as he from one trance was wakening
Into another, she began to sing,—
Happy in beauty, life, and love, and every-
     thing,—
A song of love, too sweet for earthly lyres,

[17]His thoughtless fancies disappeared while he considered the mysteries of Plato's philosophy.

[18]Orpheus succeeded in winning back his wife Eurydice from the world of shades on condition that as they returned to the world he would not look back to see her following him. He, however, so loved her that he could not forbear looking back—whereupon she vanished and returned to Hades.

[19]The Pleiads were seven sisters, changed into the constellation. The concentric spheres which, according to the old astronomy, surrounded the earth, were supposed to make music as they revolved.

While, like. held breath, the stars drew in their
    panting fires.   300
And then she whispered in such trembling
    tone
As those who, safe together met alone
For the first time through many anguished
    days,
Use other speech than looks; bidding him
    raise
His drooping head, and clear his soul of
    doubt,
For that she was a woman, and without 306
Any more subtle fluid in her veins
Than throbbing blood, and that the self-same
    pains
Inhabited her frail-strung heart as his.
And next she wondered how his eyes could
    miss   310
Her face so long in Corinth, where, she said,
She dwelt but half retired, and there had led
Days happy as the gold coin could invent
Without the aid of love; yet in content,
Till she saw him, as once she passed him by,
Where 'gainst a column he leaned thought-
    fully   316
At Venus' temple porch, 'mid baskets heaped
Of amorous herbs and flowers, newly reaped
Late on that eve, as 'twas the night before
The Adonian feast;[20] whereof she saw no
    more,
But wept alone those days,—for why should
    she adore?   321
Lycius from death awoke into amaze
To see her still, and singing so sweet lays;
Then from amaze into delight he fell
To hear her whisper woman's lore so well; 325
And every word she spake enticed him on
To unperplexed delight and pleasure known.
Let the mad poets say whate'er they please
Of the sweets of Faeries, Peris,[21] Goddesses,
There is not such a treat among them all— 330
Haunters of cavern, lake, and waterfall—
As a real woman, lineal indeed
From Pyrrha's pebbles[22] or old Adam's seed.
Thus gentle Lamia judged, and judged aright,
That Lycius could not love in half a fright, 335
So threw the goddess off, and won his heart
More pleasantly by playing woman's part,
With no more awe than what her beauty gave,

---

[20]Festival in honor of Adonis. He was a beautiful youth loved by Venus. When he was killed by
a wild boar she had him carried to Elysium.

[21]A Peri is, according to Persian fable, one descended from the fallen angels.

[22]After the flood Pyrrha and Deucalion, according to legend, cast stones behind them which sprang
up human beings, and so they re-peopled the world.

That, while it smote, still guaranteed to save.
Lycius to all made eloquent reply,   340
Marrying to every word a twin-born sigh;
And last, pointing to Corinth, asked her
    sweet,
If 'twas too far that night for her soft feet.
The way was short, for Lamia's eagerness
Made, by a spell, the triple league decrease
To a few paces; not at all surmised   346
By blinded Lycius, so in her comprised.
They passed the city gates, he knew not how,
So noiseless, and he never thought to know.

As men talk in a dream, so Corinth all, 350
Throughout her palaces imperial,
And all her populous streets and temples
    lewd,
Muttered, like tempest in the distance brewed,
To the wide-spreaded night above her towers.
Men, women, rich and poor, in the cool
    hours,   355
Shuffled their sandals o'er the pavement
    white,
Companioned or alone; while many a light
Flared, here and there, from wealthy festi-
    vals,
And threw their moving shadows on the
    walls,
Or found them clustered in the corniced
    shade   360
Of some arched temple door or dusky colon-
    nade.

Muffling his face, of greeting friends in
    fear,
Her fingers he pressed hard, as one came
    near
With curled gray beard, sharp eyes, and
    smooth bald crown,   364
Slow-stepped, and robed in philosophic
    gown:
Lycius shrank closer, as they met and passed,
Into his mantle, adding wings to haste,
While hurried Lamia trembled. "Ah," said
    he,
"Why do you shudder, love, so ruefully?
Why does your tender palm dissolve in
    dew?"—   370
"I'm wearied," said fair Lamia: "tell me who
Is that old man?   I cannot bring to mind
His features:—Lycius! wherefore did you
    blind
Yourself from his quick eyes?"   Lycius re-
    plied,
" 'Tis Apollonius sage, my trusty guide   375
And good instructor; but to-night he seems
The ghost of folly haunting my sweet
    dreams."

While yet he spake they had arrived before
A pillared porch, with lofty portal door,
Where hung a silver lamp, whose phosphor
    glow 380
Reflected in the slabbéd steps below,
Mild as a star in water; for so new
And so unsullied was the marble's hue,
So through the crystal polish, liquid fine,
Ran the dark veins, that none but feet divine
Could e'er have touched there. Sounds
    Aeolian[23] 386
Breathed from the hinges, as the ample span
Of the wide doors disclosed a place unknown
Some time to any, but those two alone,
And a few Persian mutes, who that same year
Were seen about the markets: none knew
    where 391
They could inhabit; the most curious
Were foiled, who watched to trace them to
    their house:
And but the flitter-wingéd verse[24] must tell,
For truth's sake, what woe afterwards befell,
'Twould humor many a heart to leave them
    thus 396
Shut from the busy world of more in-
    credulous.

PART II

Love in a hut, with water and a crust,
Is—Love, forgive us!—cinders, ashes, dust;
Love in a palace is perhaps at last
More grievous torment than a hermit's
    fast:—
That is a doubtful tale from faery land, 5
Hard for the non-elect to understand.
Had Lycius lived to hand his story down,
He might have given the moral a fresh frown,
Or clenched it quite: but too short was their
    bliss
To breed distrust and hate, that make the soft
    voice hiss. 10
Besides, there, nightly, with terrific glare,
Love, jealous grown of so complete a pair,
Hovered and buzzed his wings, with fearful
    roar,
Above the lintel of their chamber door,
And down the passage cast a glow upon the
    floor. 15

For all this came a ruin: side by side
They were enthronéd, in the eventide,
Upon a couch, near to a curtaining
Whose airy texture, from a golden string,

Floated into the room, and let appear 20
Unveiled the summer heaven, blue and clear,
Betwixt two marble shafts:—there they re-
    posed,
Where use had made it sweet, with eyelids
    closed,
Saving a tithe which love still open kept,
That they might see each other while they
    almost slept; 25
When from the slope side of a suburb hill,
Deafening the swallow's twitter, came a thrill
Of trumpets—Lycius started—the sounds
    fled,
But left a thought, a buzzing in his head.
For the first time, since first he harbored in 30
That purple-linéd palace of sweet sin,
His spirit passed beyond its golden bourn[1]
Into the noisy world almost forsworn.
The lady, ever watchful, penetrant,
Saw this with pain, so arguing a want 35
Of something more, more than her empery
Of joys; and she began to moan and sigh
Because he mused beyond her, knowing well
That but a moment's thought is passion's
    passing bell.
"Why do you sigh, fair creature?" whispered
    he: 40
"Why do you think?" returned she tenderly:
"You have deserted me; where am I now?
Not in your heart while care weighs on your
    brow:
No, no, you have dismissed me, and I go
From your breast houseless: ay, it must be
    so." 45
He answered, bending to her open eyes,
Where he was mirrored small in paradise,
"My silver planet, both of eve and morn!
Why will you plead yourself so sad forlorn,
While I am striving how to fill my heart 50
With deeper crimson and a double smart?
How to entangle, trammel up, and snare
Your soul in mine, and labyrinth you there
Like the hid scent in an unbudded rose? 54
Ay, a sweet kiss—you see your mighty woes.
My thoughts! shall I unveil them? Listen
    then!
What mortal hath a prize, that other men
May be confounded and abashed withal,
But lets it sometimes pace abroad majestical,
And triumph, as in thee I should rejoice 60
Amid the hoarse alarm of Corinth's voice.
Let my foes choke, and my friends shout
    afar,
While through the throngéd streets your
    bridal car

[23]Musical sounds.
[24]The verse winging its way like a bird.

[1]Domain.

Wheels round its dazzling spokes."—The
lady's cheek
Trembled; she nothing said, but, pale and
meek,   65
Arose and knelt before him, wept a rain
Of sorrows at his words; at last with pain
Beseeching him, the while his hand she
wrung,
To change his purpose. He thereat was
stung,
Perverse, with stronger fancy to reclaim   70
Her wild and timid nature to his aim;
Besides, for all his love, in self despite,
Against his better self, he took delight
Luxurious in her sorrows, soft and new.
His passion, cruel grown, took on a hue   75
Fierce and sanguineous as 'twas possible
In one whose brow had no dark veins to
swell.
Fine was the mitigated fury, like
Apollo's presence when in act to strike
The serpent—Ha, the serpent! certes, she 80
Was none. She burned, she loved the
tyranny,
And, all subdued, consented to the hour
When to the bridal he should lead his par-
amour.
Whispering in midnight silence, said the
youth,
"Sure some sweet name thou hast, though,
by my truth,   85
I have not asked it, ever thinking thee
Not mortal, but of heavenly progeny,
As still I do. Hast any mortal name,
Fit appellation for this dazzling frame?
Or friends or kinsfolk on the citied earth, 90
To share our marriage feast and nuptial
mirth?"
"I have no friends," said Lamia, "no, not
one;
My presence in wide Corinth hardly known:
My parents' bones are in their dusty urns 94
Sepulchered, where no kindled incense burns,
Seeing all their luckless race are dead save
me,
And I neglect the holy rite for thee.
Even as you list invite your many guests;
But if, as now it seems, your vision rests
With any pleasure on me, do not bid   100
Old Apollonius—from him keep me hid."
Lycius, perplexed at words so blind and
blank,
Made close inquiry; from whose touch she
shrank,
Feigning a sleep; and he to the dull shade
Of deep sleep in a moment was betrayed. 105

It was the custom then to bring away
The bride from home at blushing shut of day,
Veiled, in a chariot, heralded along
By strewn flowers, torches, and a marriage
song,
With other pageants: but this fair unknown
Had not a friend. So being left alone   111
(Lycius was gone to summon all his kin),
And knowing surely she could never win
His foolish heart from its mad pompousness,
She set herself, high-thoughted, how to dress
The misery in fit magnificence.   116
She did so, but 'tis doubtful how and whence
Came, and who were her subtle servitors.
About the halls, and to and from the doors,
There was a noise of wings, till in short space
The glowing banquet-room shone with wide-
archéd grace.   121
A haunting music, sole perhaps and lone
Supportress of the faery-roof, made moan
Throughout, as fearful the whole charm
might fade.
Fresh carvéd cedar, mimicking a glade 125
Of palm and plantain, met from either side,
High in the midst, in honor of the bride:
Two palms and then two plantains, and so on,
From either side their stems branched one to
one
All down the aiséd place; and beneath all 130
There ran a stream of lamps straight on
from wall to wall.
So canopied, lay an untasted feast
Teeming with odors. Lamia, regal dressed,
Silently paced about, and as she went,
In pale contented sort of discontent,   135
Missioned her viewless servants to enrich
The fretted splendor of each nook and niche.
Between the tree-stems, marbled plain at
first,
Came jasper panels; then anon there burst
Forth creeping imagery of slighter trees, 140
And with the larger wove in small intricacies.
Approving all, she faded at self-will,
And shut the chamber up, close, hushed and
still,
Complete and ready for the revels rude,
When dreadful guests would come to spoil
her solitude.   145

The day appeared, and all the gossip rout.
O senseless Lycius! Madman! wherefore
flout
The silent-blessing fate, warm cloistered
hours,
And show to common eyes these secret
bowers?

The herd approached; each guest, with busy
brain,   150
Arriving at the portal, gazed amain,
And entered marveling: for they knew the
street,
Remembered it from childhood all complete
Without a gap, yet ne'er before had seen
That royal porch, that high-built fair de-
mesne;[2]   155
So in they hurried all, mazed, curious and
keen;
Save one, who looked thereon with eye
severe,
And with calm-planted steps walked in aus-
tere;
'Twas Apollonius: something too he laughed,
As though some knotty problem, that had
daft[3]   160
His patient thought, had now begun to thaw
And solve and melt: 'twas just as he foresaw.

He met within the murmurous vestibule
His young disciple. " 'Tis no common rule,
Lycius," said he, "for uninvited guest   165
To force himself upon you, and infest
With an unbidden presence the bright throng
Of younger friends; yet must I do this
wrong,
And you forgive me." Lycius blushed, and
led
The old man through the inner doors broad-
spread;   170
With reconciling words and courteous mien
Turning into sweet milk the sophist's spleen.

Of wealthy luster was the banquet-room,
Filled with pervading brilliance and perfume:
Before each lucid panel fuming stood   175
A censer fed with myrrh and spicéd wood,
Each by a sacred tripod held aloft,
Whose slender feet wide-swerved upon the
soft
Wool-wooféd carpets: fifty wreaths of smoke
From fifty censers their light voyage took   180
To the high roof, still mimicked as they rose
Along the mirrored walls by twin-clouds
odorous.
Twelve spheréd tables by silk seats insphered,
High as the level of a man's breast reared
On libbard's[4] paws, upheld the heavy gold   185
Of cups and goblets, and the store thrice told
Of Ceres' horn,[5] and, in huge vessels, wine
Come from the gloomy tun[6] with merry shine.

Thus loaded with a feast the tables stood,   189
Each shrining in the midst the image of a
God.

When in an antechamber every guest
Had felt the cold full sponge to pleasure
pressed,
By ministering slaves, upon his hands and
feet,
And fragrant oils with ceremony meet   194
Poured on his hair, they all moved to the feast
In white robes, and themselves in order
placed
Around the silken couches, wondering
Whence all this mighty cost and blaze of
wealth could spring.

Soft went the music the soft air along,
While fluent Greek a voweled under-song   200
Kept up among the guests, discoursing low
At first, for scarcely was the wine at flow;
But when the happy vintage touched their
brains,
Louder they talk, and louder come the strains
Of powerful instruments:—the gorgeous
dyes,
The space, the splendor of the draperies,   206
The roof of awful richness, nectarous cheer,
Beautiful slaves, and Lamia's self, appear,
Now, when the wine has done its rosy deed,
And every soul from human trammels freed,
No more so strange; for merry wine, sweet
wine,   211
Will make Elysian shades not too fair, too
divine.
Soon was God Bacchus at meridian height;
Flushed were their cheeks, and bright eyes
double bright;
Garlands of every green and every scent   215
From vales deflowered or forest-trees branch-
rent,
In baskets of bright osiered gold[7] were
brought,
High as the handles heaped, to suit the
thought
Of every guest; that each, as he did please,
Might fancy-fit his brows, silk-pillowed at
his ease.   220

What wreath for Lamia? What for Ly-
cius?
What for the sage, old Apollonius?
Upon her aching forehead be there hung
The leaves of willow[8] and of adder's tongue;

---

[2]Dwelling.   [3]Eluded.   [4]Leopard's.

[5]Ceres was the goddess of harvests. The horn
was symbolic of plenty.

[6]Cask.

[7]Baskets of woven gold.

[8]The weeping-willow, symbolic of grief. "Adder's tongue" is the popular name for a certain
variety of fern.

And for the youth, quick, let us strip for him
The thyrsus,[9] that his watching eyes may
    swim   226
Into forgetfulness; and, for the sage,
Let spear-grass and the spiteful thistle wage
War on his temples. Do not all charms fly
At the mere touch of cold philosophy?   230
There was an awful rainbow once in heaven:
We know her woof, her texture; she is given
In the dull catalogue of common things.
Philosophy will clip an Angel's wings,
Conquer all mysteries by rule and line,   235
Empty the haunted air and gnoméd mine—
Unweave a rainbow, as it erewhile made
The tender-personed Lamia melt into a shade.

By her glad Lycius sitting, in chief place,
Scarce saw in all the room another face,   240
Till, checking his love trance, a cup he took
Full brimmed, and opposite sent forth a look
Cross the broad table, to beseech a glance
From his old teacher's wrinkled countenance,
And pledge him.   The bald-head philosopher
Had fixed his eye, without a twinkle or stir,
Full on the alarméd beauty of the bride,   247
Brow-beating her fair form and troubling her
    sweet pride.
Lycius then pressed her hand, with devout
    touch,
As pale it lay upon the rosy couch: 250
'Twas icy, and the cold ran through his veins;
Then sudden it grew hot, and all the pains
Of an unnatural heat shot to his heart.
"Lamia, what means this? Wherefore dost
    thou start?
Know'st thou that man?"   Poor Lamia an-
    swered not.   255
He gazed into her eyes, and not a jot
Owned they the lovelorn piteous appeal:
More, more he gazed: his human senses
    reel:
Some hungry spell that loveliness absorbs;
There was no recognition in those orbs.   260
"Lamia!" he cried—and no soft-toned reply.
The many heard, and the loud revelry
Grew hush; the stately music no more
    breathes;
The myrtle sickened in a thousand wreaths.
By faint degrees, voice, lute, and pleasure
    ceased;   265
A deadly silence step by step increased
Until it seemed a horrid presence there,
And not a man but felt the terror in his hair.
"Lamia!" he shrieked; and nothing but the
    shriek
With its sad echo did the silence break.   270

"Begone, foul dream!" he cried, gazing again
In the bride's face, where now no azure vein
Wandered on fair-spaced temples, no soft
    bloom
Misted the cheek, no passion to illume
The deep-recesséd vision:—all was blight;   275
Lamia, no longer fair, there sat, a deadly
    white.
"Shut, shut those juggling eyes, thou ruthless
    man!
Turn them aside, wretch! or the righteous
    ban
Of all the Gods, whose dreadful images
Here represent their shadowy presences,   280
May pierce them on the sudden with the thorn
Of painful blindness; leaving thee forlorn,
In trembling dotage to the feeblest fright
Of conscience, for their long-offended might,
For all thine impious proud-heart sophistries,
Unlawful magic, and enticing lies.   286
Corinthians! look upon that gray-beard
    wretch!
Mark how, possessed, his lashless eyelids
    stretch
Around his demon eyes!   Corinthians, see!
My sweet bride withers at their potency."   290
"Fool!" said the sophist, in an undertone
Gruff with contempt; which a death-nighing
    moan
From Lycius answered, as, heart-struck and
    lost,
He sank supine beside the aching ghost.
"Fool! Fool!" repeated he, while his eyes
    still   295
Relented not, nor moved; "from every ill
Of life have I preserved thee to this day,
And shall I see thee made a serpent's prey?"
Then Lamia breathed death-breath; the
    sophist's eye,   299
Like a sharp spear, went through her utterly,
Keen, cruel, perceant,[10] stinging: she, as well
As her weak hand could any meaning tell,
Motioned him to be silent; vainly so;
He looked and looked again a level—No!
"A serpent!" echoed he; no sooner said,   305
Than with a frightful scream she vanishéd;
And Lycius' arms were empty of delight,
As were his limbs of life, from that same
    night.
On the high couch he lay—his friends came
    round—   309
Supported him; no pulse or breath they
    found,
And in its marriage robe the heavy body
    wound.

_____
[9]A rod wreathed with ivy, the staff of Bacchus.

[10]Piercing.

SONNET[1]

Bright star! would I were steadfast as thou
    art—
    Not in lone splendor hung aloft the night,
And watching, with eternal lids apart,

Like Nature's patient, sleepless Eremite,[2]
The moving waters at their priestlike task 5
    Of pure ablution round earth's human
        shores,
Or gazing on the new soft fallen mask
    Of snow upon the mountains and the
        moors—
No—yet still steadfast, still unchangeable,
    Pillowed upon my fair love's ripening
        breast,   10
To feel for ever its soft fall and swell,
    Awake for ever in a sweet unrest,
Still, still to hear her tender-taken breath,
And so live ever—or else swoon to death.

[1] Believed to have been written in March, 1819; published in 1848. This was formerly thought to have been the last poem written by Keats, as he wrote the later (and until recently the only known) version of the sonnet after he had embarked for Italy, in September, 1820. This he wrote on a blank page, facing *A Lover's Complaint,* in a folio volume of Shakespeare which he gave to Severn, who accompanied him on his journey.

[2] Hermit.

THOMAS DE QUINCEY

1785-1859

Leslie Stephen wrote, in a sentence which he later removed from his essay in *Hours in a Library,* "For seventy-three years De Quincey had been carrying on an operation which for want of a better term we must describe as living, but which would be more fitly described by some mode of speech indicating an existence on the borders of dreamland and reality." Doubtless this is an exaggeration, yet undeniably it expresses the impression De Quincey makes, and always will make, on many people. The publication a generation ago of a full-length biography made De Quincey's life credible, if it did not make his nature comprehensible, but no amount of information or analysis can gloss over the fact that De Quincey in the flesh was one of the strangest creatures the world has known. He was born in Manchester, where his father was a merchant, on 15 August, 1785. Of his father, who died when Thomas was still a child, he never saw anything; and of his mother, who showed no signs of really understanding him, one is tempted to say he saw too much. He was a frail child, and in his earliest days, as in his later ones, he lived the life of a solitary. In 1796 his mother moved to Bath and placed Thomas at school there. Later he was sent to Winkfield School, in Wiltshire. He showed astonishing precocity, and at fifteen was ready to enter Oxford. Instead, however, he was sent to Manchester Grammar School to mark time for three years, so that he might gain a scholarship at Brasenose College. He strongly rebelled against this waste of time: "I ask," he wrote to his mother, "whether a person can be happy, or even simply easy, who is in a situation which deprives him of *health,* of *society,* of *amusement,* of *liberty,* of *congeniality of pursuits,* and which, to complete the precious picture, admits of no *variety.*" But his pleas were met with denial, so that in the end, in desperation, he ran away. His experiences he describes in his *Confessions.* In the spring of 1803 he was discovered by friends, brought home, and finally allowed to go to Oxford, where he entered Worcester College be-

cause of the smallness of his allowance. He came to be known in Oxford "as a strange being who associated with no one." He says himself: "For the first two years I compute that I did not utter one hundred words." It was at this time that he began the use of opium, though the first period of his great excesses did not come until his twenty-ninth year. At Oxford he extended his acquaintance with the Greek and Latin classics, studied Hebrew and German, and read widely in English literature. But he took no degree. Being displeased with the conduct of his examinations, in particular at not being allowed to answer questions in Greek, he simply disappeared, as he later did more than once on other occasions.

During several years after he left Oxford De Quincey led a rather wandering existence, becoming acquainted at one place or another with a number of literary people, among them Lamb, Coleridge, Wordsworth, and Southey. Wordsworth he regarded with peculiar veneration, and in 1809 he settled at Grasmere in the Lake Country in order to be near the Wordsworths. He did not, however, become really intimate with them, and in the course of time broke with them completely. It has been supposed that the break was at least partly caused by De Quincey's marriage in 1816 to Margaret Simpson, the daughter of a Westmoreland dalesman and a girl of a social station inferior to Mrs. Wordsworth's. However unsuited to him De Quincey's wife was—and it is practically impossible to imagine any woman who would have made him a suitable wife—she at least may be said to have put him in the way of beginning his literary career. For soon after his marriage he found his money exhausted, and he was compelled to turn from the reading of German literature and philosophy to productive work. It was in this way that he came to write, in 1821, the *Confessions of an English Opium-Eater* for the *London Magazine.* The work immediately aroused wide and keen interest, and De Quincey thereafter always found periodicals open for all that he could write. About

1830 he removed to Edinburgh, and maintained a home there for his family throughout the remainder of his life. He often even lived with his family, though he kept separate lodgings for himself in Edinburgh, and kept rooms for some years also in Glasgow, and perhaps elsewhere, for he was always likely to disappear suddenly for indefinite periods. The years of his worst opium-excesses were 1813, 1817, 1823, and 1844. After 1844, however, though he continued to drink laudanum until his death, he managed to keep the quantity within a moderate compass. During all this time he wrote voluminously for periodicals, though besides the *Confessions* he composed only two extended works, his romance, *Klosterheim* (1839), and his *Logic of Political Economy* (1844). Though we hear less of them in his later years, he frequently suffered from what he called "pecuniary embarrassments," not so much because his income was insufficient as because he was completely incapable of taking care of his money. He died in Edinburgh on 8 December, 1859. An acquaintance, J. R. Findlay, thus described his appearance as an old man: "He was a very little man (about five feet, three or four inches); his countenance the most remarkable for its intellectual attractiveness that I have ever seen. His features, though not regular, were aristocratically fine, and an air of delicate breeding pervaded the face. His forehead was unusually high, square, and compact. At first sight his face appeared boyishly fresh and smooth, with a sort of hectic glow upon it that contrasted strangely with the evident appearances of age in the grizzled hair and dim-looking eyes. The flush or bloom on the cheeks was, I have no doubt, an effect of his constant use of opium; and the apparent smoothness of the face disappeared upon examination."

De Quincey was, like Coleridge and Lamb, widely read in the great English prose writers of the first half of the seventeenth century, and this is one secret of the richness and majesty of his style. His biographer, A. H. Japp, has indicated the qualities of his mind which we find united in the *Confessions:* "De Quincey himself, in descanting on the dream-faculty, says, 'Habitually to dream magnificently, a man must have a constitutional determination to reverie.' In that sentence he announces the true law of all literature that comes under the order of pure fantasy. But in his case, in spite of the strength of the dream-element, we cannot proceed far till we discover that his determination to reverie was but the extreme projection of one phase of a phenomenal nature balancing its opposite. . . . He was skilled in the exercises of the analytic understanding—a logician exacting and precise—else his dreaming had never gained for him the eminence it has gained. Surely it is calculated to strike the most casual reader on a perusal of . . . the *Confessions,* that his power of following up sensational effects and tracing with absolute exactness the most delicately varying shades of experience, and recording them with conscientious precision, were as noticeable as were the dreams to which they served to give effect."

The standard edition of De Quincey's *Collected Writings* is edited by David Masson (14 vols., Edinburgh, 1889–1890; and later reprinted). Two good biographies have recently appeared: H. A. Eaton's *Thomas De Quincey* (Oxford, 1936) supplies a great deal of biographical material, while Edward Sackville-West's *Flame in Sunlight; the Life and Work of Thomas De Quincey* (London, 1936) makes a more critical approach to the essayist. *De Quincey,* by Malcolm Elwin (London, 1935), is a much briefer sketch. William Haller Bonner's *De Quincey at Work* (Buffalo, 1936) is interesting and illuminating. The *Selected Writings* of De Quincey, ed. Philip Van Doren Stern (New York, 1937), is another useful volume.

Passages from

CONFESSIONS OF AN ENGLISH OPIUM-EATER[1]

I

I HAVE often been asked how I came to be a regular opium-eater; and have suffered, very unjustly, in the opinion of my acquaint-ance, from being reputed to have brought upon myself all the sufferings which I shall have to record, by a long course of indulgence in this practice purely for the sake of creat-

[1] The *Confessions* were first published as a book in 1822. In 1856 De Quincey published, as part of a collected edition of his works, a greatly enlarged version. The text used in these selections is that of 1822, which has been generally preferred by critics and which there is some reason for believing that De Quincey himself preferred. Words inside square brackets replace dashes in the original edition.

ing an artificial state of pleasurable excitement. This, however, is a misrepresentation of my case. True it is, that for nearly ten years I did occasionally take opium for the sake of the exquisite pleasure it gave me; but, so long as I took it with this view, I was effectually protected from all material bad consequences by the necessity of interposing long intervals between the several acts of indulgence, in order to renew the pleasurable sensations. It was not for the purpose of creating pleasure, but of mitigating pain in the severest degree, that I first began to use opium as an article of daily diet. In the twenty-eighth year of my age, a most painful affection of the stomach, which I had first experienced about ten years before, attacked me in great strength. This affection had originally been caused by extremities of hunger, suffered in my boyish days. During the season of hope and redundant happiness which succeeded (that is, from eighteen to twenty-four) it had slumbered: for the three following years it had revived at intervals; and now, under unfavorable circumstances, from depression of spirits, it attacked me with a violence that yielded to no remedies but opium. As the youthful sufferings which first produced this derangement of the stomach were interesting in themselves and in the circumstances that attended them, I shall here briefly retrace them.

My father died when I was about seven years old, and left me to the care of four guardians. I was sent to various schools, great and small; and was very early distinguished for my classical attainments, especially for my knowledge of Greek. At thirteen I wrote Greek with ease; and at fifteen my command of that language was so great that I not only composed Greek verses in lyric meters, but could converse in Greek fluently, and without embarrassment—an accomplishment which I have not since met with in any scholar of my times, and which, in my case, was owing to the practice of daily reading off the newspapers into the best Greek I could furnish *extempore;* for the necessity of ransacking my memory and invention for all sorts and combinations of periphrastic expressions, as equivalents for modern ideas, images, relations of things,

etc., gave me a compass of diction which would never have been called out by a dull translation of moral essays, *etc.* "That boy," said one of my masters, pointing the attention of a stranger to me, "that boy could harangue an Athenian mob better than you or I could address an English one." He who honored me with this eulogy was a scholar, "and a ripe and good one,"[2] and, of all my tutors, was the only one whom I loved or reverenced. Unfortunately for me (and, as I afterwards learned, to this worthy man's great indignation), I was transferred to the care, first of a blockhead,[3] who was in a perpetual panic lest I should expose his ignorance; and, finally, to that of a respectable scholar,[4] at the head of a great school on an ancient foundation. This man had been appointed to his situation by [Brasenose] College, Oxford; and was a sound, well-built scholar, but (like most men whom I have known from that college) coarse, clumsy, and inelegant. A miserable contrast he presented, in my eyes, to the Etonian brilliancy of my favorite master; and, besides, he could not disguise from my hourly notice the poverty and meagerness of his understanding. It is a bad thing for a boy to be, and know himself, far beyond his tutors, whether in knowledge or in power of mind. This was the case, so far as regarded knowledge at least, not with myself only; for the two boys who jointly with myself composed the first form were better Grecians than the headmaster, though not more elegant scholars, nor at all more accustomed to sacrifice to the graces. When I first entered, I remember that we read Sophocles; and it was a constant matter of triumph to us, the learned triumvirate of the first form, to see our "Archididascalus"[5] (as he loved to be called) conning our lesson before we went up, and laying a regular train, with lexicon and grammar, for blowing up and blasting (as it were) any difficulties he found in the choruses; whilst *we* never condescended to open our books until the moment of going up, and

---

[2]Cf. *Henry VIII,* IV, ii, 51–52. The master was a Mr. Morgan, of Bath Grammar School.
[3]Mr. Spencer, of Winkfield School.
[4]Mr. Lawson, of Manchester Grammar School.
[5]Head-master (Greek).

were generally employed in writing epigrams upon his wig, or some such important matter. My two class-fellows were poor, and dependent for their future prospects at the university on the recommendation of the head-master; but I, who had a small patrimonial property, the income of which was sufficient to support me at college, wished to be sent thither immediately. I made earnest representations on the subject to my guardians but all to no purpose. One, who was more reasonable, and had more knowledge of the world than the rest, lived at a distance; two of the other three resigned all their authority into the hands of the fourth; and this fourth,[6] with whom I had to negotiate, was a worthy man in his way, but haughty, obstinate, and intolerant of all opposition to his will. After a certain number of letters and personal interviews, I found that I had nothing to hope for, not even a compromise of the matter, from my guardian: unconditional submission was what he demanded; and I prepared myself, therefore, for other measures. Summer was now coming on with hasty steps, and my seventeenth birthday was fast approaching; after which day I had sworn within myself that I would no longer be numbered amongst schoolboys. Money being what I chiefly wanted, I wrote to a woman of high rank,[7] who, though young herself, had known me from a child, and had latterly treated me with great distinction, requesting that she would "lend" me five guineas.[8] For upwards of a week no answer came; and I was beginning to despond, when, at length, a servant put into my hands a double letter, with a coronet on the seal. The letter was kind and obliging; the fair writer was on the sea-coast, and in that way the delay had arisen; she enclosed double of what I had asked, and good-naturedly hinted that if I should *never* repay her it would not absolutely ruin her. Now, then, I was prepared for my scheme: ten guineas, added to about two which I had remaining from my pocket money, seemed to me suffi-

cient for an indefinite length of time; and at that happy age, if no *definite* boundary can be assigned to one's power, the spirit of hope and pleasure makes it virtually infinite.

It is a just remark of Dr. Johnson's[9] (and, what cannot often be said of his remarks, it is a very feeling one) that we never do anything consciously for the last time (of things, that is, which we have long been in the habit of doing), without sadness of heart. This truth I felt deeply when I came to leave [Manchester], a place which I did not love, and where I had not been happy. On the evening before I left [Manchester] for ever, I grieved when the ancient and lofty school-room resounded with the evening service, performed for the last time in my hearing; and at night, when the muster-roll of names was called over, and mine (as usual) was called first, I stepped forward, and, passing the head-master, who was standing by, I bowed to him, and looked earnestly in his face, thinking to myself, "He is old and infirm, and in this world I shall not see him again." I was right; I never *did* see him again, nor ever shall. He looked at me complacently, smiled good-naturedly, returned my salutation (or rather my valediction), and we parted (though he knew it not) for ever. I could not reverence him intellectually; but he had been uniformly kind to me, and had allowed me many indulgences; and I grieved at the thought of the mortification I should inflict upon him.

The morning came, which was to launch me into the world, and from which my whole succeeding life has, in many important points, taken its coloring. I lodged in the head-master's house, and had been allowed, from my first entrance, the indulgence of a private room, which I used both as a sleeping room and as a study. At half after three I rose, and gazed with deep emotion at the ancient towers of [the Collegiate Church], "dressed in earliest light," and beginning to crimson with the radiant luster of a cloudless July morning. I was firm and immovable in my purpose, but yet agitated by anticipation of uncertain danger and troubles; and if I could have foreseen the hurricane

---

[6]The Rev. Samuel Hall, at one time De Quincey's tutor.

[7]Lady Carbery, a young friend of Mrs. De Quincey's, about ten years older than De Quincey.

[8]About $25.

[9]In the *Idler*, No. 103, with which the periodical ended.

and perfect hail-storm of affliction which soon fell upon me, well might I have been agitated. To this agitation the deep peace of the morning presented an affecting contrast, and in some degree a medicine. The silence was more profound than that of midnight: and to me the silence of a summer morning is more touching than all other silence, because, the light being broad and strong, as that of noon-day at other seasons of the year, it seems to differ from perfect day chiefly because man is not yet abroad; and thus the peace of nature, and of the innocent creatures of God, seems to be secure and deep, only so long as the presence of man, and his restless and unquiet spirit, are not there to trouble its sanctity. I dressed myself, took my hat and gloves, and lingered a little in the room. For the last year and a half this room had been my "pensive citadel":[10] here I had read and studied through all the hours of night: and, though true it was that for the latter part of this time I, who was framed for love and gentle affections, had lost my gayety and happiness, during the strife and fever of contention with my guardian; yet, on the other hand, as a boy so passionately fond of books, and dedicated to intellectual pursuits, I could not fail to have enjoyed many happy hours in the midst of general dejection. I wept as I looked round on the chair, hearth, writing-table, and other familiar objects, knowing too certainly that I looked upon them for the last time. Whilst I write this, it is eighteen years ago; and yet, at this moment, I see distinctly, as if it were yesterday, the lineaments and expressions of the object on which I fixed my parting gaze; it was a picture of the lovely ——,[11] which hung over the mantel-piece, the eyes and mouth of which were so beautiful, and the whole countenance so radiant with benignity and divine tranquillity, that I had a thousand times laid down my pen, or my book, to gather consolation from it, as a devotee from his patron saint. Whilst I was yet gazing upon it, the deep tones of

[the Collegiate Church] clock proclaimed that it was four o'clock. I went up to the picture, kissed it, and then gently walked out, and closed the door for ever!

*   *   *

So blended and intertwisted in this life are occasions of laughter and of tears, that I cannot yet recall, without smiling, an incident which occurred at that time, and which had nearly put a stop to the immediate execution of my plan. I had a trunk of immense weight; for, besides my clothes, it contained nearly all my library. The difficulty was to get this removed to a carrier's: my room was at an aërial elevation in the house, and (what was worse) the staircase which communicated with this angle of the building was accessible only by a gallery, which passed the head-master's chamberdoor. I was a favorite with all the servants; and knowing that any of them would screen me, and act confidentially, I communicated my embarrassment to a groom of the headmaster's. The groom swore he would do anything I wished; and, when the time arrived, went upstairs to bring the trunk down. This I feared was beyond the strength of any one man: however, the groom was a man

Of Atlantean shoulders, fit to bear
The weight of mightiest monarchies;[12]

and had a back as spacious as Salisbury Plain.[13] Accordingly he persisted in bringing down the trunk alone, whilst I stood waiting at the foot of the last flight, in anxiety for the event. For some time I heard him descending with slow and firm steps; but, unfortunately, from his trepidation, as he drew near the dangerous quarter, within a few steps of the gallery, his foot slipped; and the mighty burden, falling from his shoulders, gained such increase of impetus at each step of the descent, that, on reaching the bottom, it tumbled, or rather leaped, right across, with the noise of twenty devils, against the very bedroom door of the Archididascalus. My first thought was, that all was lost; and that my only chance for exe-

---

[10]From Wordsworth's sonnet, *Nuns Fret not at their Convent's Narrow Room,* l. 3.

[11]It was really a portrait of an unknown lady, according to a tradition in the school a copy from Vandyke.

[12]Milton, *Paradise Lost,* II, 306–7.

[13]In Wiltshire.

cuting a retreat was to sacrifice my baggage. However, on reflection, I determined to abide the issue. The groom was in the utmost alarm, both on his own account and on mine: but, in spite of this, so irresistibly had the sense of the ludicrous, in this unhappy *contretemps,*[14] taken possession of his fancy, that he sang out a long, loud, and canorous[15] peal of laughter, that might have wakened the Seven Sleepers.[16] At the sound of this resonant merriment, within the very ears of insulted authority, I could not myself forbear joining in it: subdued to this, not so much by the unhappy *étourderie*[17] of the trunk, as by the effect it had upon the groom. We both expected, as a matter of course, that Dr. [Lawson][18] would sally out of his room; for, in general, if but a mouse stirred, he sprang out like a mastiff from his kennel. Strange to say, however, on this occasion, when the noise of laughter had ceased, no sound, or rustling even, was to be heard in the bedroom. Dr. [Lawson] had a painful complaint, which, sometimes keeping him awake, made his sleep, perhaps, when it did come, the deeper. Gathering courage from the silence, the groom hoisted his burden again, and accomplished the remainder of his descent without accident. I waited until I saw the trunk placed on a wheelbarrow, and on its road to the carrier's: then, "with Providence my guide,"[19] I set off on foot, carrying a small parcel, with some articles of dress, under my arm: a favorite English poet in one pocket; and a small 12mo. volume, containing about nine plays of Euripides, in the other.

It had been my intention, originally, to proceed to Westmoreland, both from the love I bore to that county, and on other personal accounts.[20] Accident, however, gave a different direction to my wanderings, and I bent my steps towards North Wales.[21]

II

Soon after this,[22] I contrived, by means which I must omit for want of room,[23] to transfer myself to London. And now began the latter and fiercer stage of my long sufferings; without using a disproportionate expression, I might say, of my agony. For I now suffered, for upwards of sixteen weeks, the physical anguish of hunger in various degrees of intensity; but as bitter, perhaps, as ever any human being can have suffered who has survived it. I would not needlessly harass my reader's feelings by a detail of all that I endured; for extremities such as these, under any circumstances of heaviest misconduct or guilt, cannot be contemplated, even in description, without a rueful pity that is painful to the natural goodness of the human heart. Let it suffice, at least on this occasion, to say that a few fragments of bread from the breakfast-table of one individual[24] (who supposed me to be ill, but did not know of my being in utter want), and these at uncertain intervals, constituted my whole support. During the former part of my sufferings (that is, generally in Wales, and always for the first two months in London), I was houseless, and very seldom slept under a roof. To this constant exposure to the open air I ascribe it mainly that I did not sink under my torments. Latterly, however, when colder and more inclement weather came on, and when, from the length of my sufferings, I had begun to sink into a more languishing condition, it was, no doubt,

---

[14]Accident.   [15]Ringing.

[16]Christian youths of Ephesus who, according to legend, hid themselves in a cave during the persecution under Decius (A. D. 249–251) and slept there for several hundred years.

[17]Blunder.

[18]De Quincey explained in the edition of 1856 that he had created him a doctor in order "to evade too close an approach to the realities of the case, and consequently to personalities" which might have displeased others.

[19]Cf. the last four lines of *Paradise Lost.*

[20]He wished to see Wordsworth.

[21]De Quincey actually went first to Chester, where he saw some members of his family, and then journeyed into Wales.

[22]After a period of some days spent in Wales.

[23]He borrowed twelve guineas (about $60) from two lawyers whom he encountered in the Snowdon district.

[24]This was a Mr. Brunell, or Brown, to whom De Quincey had been referred by a money-lender named Dell. As De Quincey explains in a later passage of the *Confessions,* "he was one of those anomalous practitioners in lower departments of the law, who—what shall I say?—who, on prudential reasons, or from necessity, deny themselves all indulgence in the luxury of too delicate a conscience."

fortunate for me that the same person to whose breakfast-table I had access allowed me to sleep in a large, unoccupied house, of which he was tenant. Unoccupied, I call it, for there was no household or establishment in it; nor any furniture, indeed, except a table and a few chairs. But I found, on taking possession of my new quarters, that the house already contained one single inmate, a poor, friendless child, apparently ten years old; but she seemed hunger-bitten; and sufferings of that sort often make children look older than they are. From this forlorn child I learned that she had slept and lived there alone for some time before I came; and great joy the poor creature expressed, when she found that I was in future to be her companion through the hours of darkness. The house was large; and, from the want of furniture, the noise of the rats made a prodigious echoing on the spacious staircase and hall; and, amidst the real fleshly ills of cold, and, I fear, hunger, the forsaken child had found leisure to suffer still more (it appeared) from the self-created one of ghosts. I promised her protection against all ghosts whatsoever; but, alas! I could offer her no other assistance. We lay upon the floor, with a bundle of cursed law papers for a pillow, but with no other covering than a sort of large horseman's cloak; afterwards, however, we discovered, in a garret, an old sofa-cover, a small piece of rug, and some fragments of other articles, which added a little to our warmth. The poor child crept close to me for warmth, and for security against her ghostly enemies. When I was not more than usually ill, I took her into my arms, so that, in general, she was tolerably warm, and often slept when I could not; for, during the last two months of my sufferings, I slept much in the daytime, and was apt to fall into transient dozings at all hours. But my sleep distressed me more than my watching; for, besides the tumultuousness of my dreams (which were only not so awful as those which I shall have to describe hereafter as produced by opium) my sleep was never more than what is called *dog-sleep*; so that I could hear myself moaning, and was often, as it seemed to me, wakened suddenly by my own voice: and, about this time,

a hideous sensation began to haunt me as soon as I fell into a slumber, which has since returned upon me, at different periods of my life, namely, a sort of twitching (I know not where, but apparently about the region of the stomach), which compelled me violently to throw out my feet for the sake of relieving it. This sensation coming on as soon as I began to sleep, and the effort to relieve it constantly awaking me, at length I slept only from exhaustion; and, from increasing weakness (as I said before), I was constantly falling asleep, and constantly awaking. Meantime, the master of the house sometimes came in upon us suddenly, and very early; sometimes not till ten o'clock; sometimes not at all. He was in constant fear of bailiffs; improving on the plan of Cromwell, every night he slept in a different quarter of London;[25] and I observed that he never failed to examine, through a private window, the appearance of those who knocked at the door, before he would allow it to be opened. He breakfasted alone; indeed, his tea equipage would hardly have admitted of his hazarding an invitation to a second person, any more than the quantity of esculent *matériel*,[26] which, for the most part, was little more than a roll, or a few biscuits, which he had bought on his road from the place where he had slept. Or, if he *had* asked a party, as I once learnedly and facetiously observed to him, the several members of it must have *stood* in the relation to each other (not *sat* in any relation whatever) of succession, as the metaphysicians have it, and not of coexistence; in the relation of the parts of time, and not of the parts of space. During his breakfast, I generally contrived a reason for lounging in; and, with an air of as much indifference as I could assume, took up such fragments as he had left,—sometimes, indeed, there were none at all. In doing this, I committed no robbery except upon the man himself, who was thus obliged (I believe),

---

[25]De Quincey had perhaps read in Clarendon's *History of the Rebellion*, Bk. XV, the story that Cromwell became apprehensive of danger after the dissolution of his last Parliament, and "rarely lodged two nights together in one chamber, but had many furnished and prepared, to which his own key conveyed him."

[26]Edible substance.

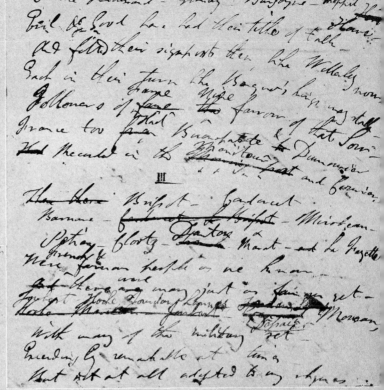

Above at the left is a miniature of Keats (now in the National Portrait Gallery, London) painted by Joseph Severn (1793–1879), and given to Fanny Brawne when Keats and Severn went to Italy. Below the portrait is the first page of the original autograph manuscript of Keats's *Endymion*. At the upper right is the autograph manuscript of two stanzas of Canto I of Byron's *Don Juan*. Beneath this is a miniature of Byron by an unknown artist. (Byron miniature and manuscript pages, courtesy of the Pierpont Morgan Library.)

The upper picture is a drawing of Byron attended by his Suliote Guards in Greece, where he went in 1823 to help the Greeks win independence. The drawing is by Robert Seymour (1800–1836), best known for his illustrations of Dickens's *Pickwick Papers*. (Courtesy of the Metropolitan Museum of Art.) The lower picture shows the burning of Shelley's body after he was drowned in the Bay of Lerici (July, 1822). At the right are Shelley's friends, Byron and E. J. Trelawny. Leigh Hunt is in the carriage close by the trees. The sketch was made on the spot by Trelawny's daughter. It is here reproduced from Trelawny's *Records of Shelley, Byron, and the Author* (1878). (Courtesy of the New York Public Library.)

now and then, to send out at noon for an extra biscuit; for, as to the poor child, *she* was never admitted into his study (if I may give that name to his chief depository of parchments, law writings, *etc.*); that room was to her the Bluebeard room of the house, being regularly locked on his departure to dinner, about six o'clock, which usually was his final departure for the night. Whether this child was an illegitimate daughter of Mr. [Brunell], or only a servant, I could not ascertain; she did not herself know; but certainly she was treated altogether as a menial servant. No sooner did Mr. [Brunell] make his appearance, than she went below stairs, brushed his shoes, coat, *etc.;* and, except when she was summoned to run an errand, she never emerged from the dismal Tartarus of the kitchens, *etc.,* to the upper air, until my welcome knock at night called up her little trembling footsteps to the front door. Of her life during the daytime, however, I knew little but what I gathered from her own account at night; for, as soon as the hours of business commenced, I saw that my absence would be acceptable; and, in general, therefore, I went off and sat in the parks, or elsewhere, until night-fall.

III

Whether desperate or not, however, the issue of the struggle in 1813 was what I have mentioned;[27] and from this date the reader is to consider me as a regular and confirmed opium-eater, of whom to ask whether on any particular day he had or had not taken opium, would be to ask whether his lungs had performed respiration, or the heart fulfilled its functions. You understand now, reader, what I am; and you are by this time aware, that no old gentleman, "with a snow-white beard," will have any chance of persuading me to surrender "the little golden receptacle of the pernicious drug."[28] No; I give notice to all, whether moralists or surgeons, that, whatever be their pretensions and skill in their respective lines of practice, they must not hope for any countenance from me, if they think to begin by any savage proposition for a Lent or Ramadan[29] of abstinence form opium. This, then, being all fully understood between us, we shall in future sail before the wind. Now, then, reader, from 1813, where all this time we have been sitting down and loitering, rise up, if you please, and walk forward about three years more. Now draw up the curtain, and you shall see me in a new character.

If any man, poor or rich, were to say that he would tell us what had been the happiest day in his life, and the why and the wherefore, I suppose that we should all cry out, Hear him! hear him! As to the happiest *day,* that must be very difficult for any wise man to name; because any event, that could occupy so distinguished a place in a man's retrospect of his life, or be entitled to have shed a special felicity on any one day, ought to be of such an enduring character as that (accidents apart) it should have continued to shed the same felicity, or one not distinguishably less, on many years together. To the happiest *lustrum,*[30] however, or even to the happiest *year,* it may be allowed to any man to point without discountenance from wisdom. This year, in my case, reader, was the one which we have now reached; though it stood, I confess, as a parenthesis between years of a gloomier character. It was a year of brilliant water (to speak after the manner of jewelers), set, as it were, and insulated, in the gloom and cloudy melancholy of opium. Strange as it may sound, I had a little before this time descended suddenly, and without any considerable effort,

[27]The section from which this passage is taken is preceded by one entitled "The Pleasures of Opium." In it De Quincey tells how he began taking opium when he was at Oxford—though he made his first purchase of it from a druggist in London—in 1804. He then goes on to state that he had continued to take a small quantity once a week until 1813, but that in this year he had suffered from "a most appalling irritation of the stomach" from which he had been able to find no relief except in daily doses of opium, and that his subsequent efforts to break off the habit had been unavailing.

[28]A reference to a preceding note in which De Quincey warns his readers not to believe statements about the harmful effects of opium made by Thomas Hope in a novel entitled *Anastasius* (published in 1819).

[29]Ninth month of the Mahometan year, each day of which is observed as a fast from dawn until sunset.

[30]Period of five years.

from three hundred and twenty grains of opium (that is, eight[31] thousand drops of laudanum) per day, to forty grains, or one-eighth part. Instantaneously, and as if by magic, the cloud of profoundest melancholy which rested upon my brain, like some black vapors that I have seen roll away from the summits of mountains, drew off in one day (νυχθημερον[32]); passed off with its murky banners as simultaneously as a ship that has been stranded, and is floated off by a spring tide,—

That moveth altogether, if it move at all.[33]

Now, then, I was again happy: I now took only one thousand drops of laudanum per day—and what was that? A latter spring had come to close up the season of youth: my brain performed its functions as healthily as ever before. I read Kant[34] again, and again I understood him, or fancied that I did. Again my feelings of pleasure expanded themselves to all around me; and if any man from Oxford or Cambridge, or from neither, had been announced to me in my unpretending cottage, I should have welcomed him with as sumptuous a reception as so poor a man could offer. Whatever else was wanting to a wise man's happiness, of laudanum I would have given him as much as he wished, and in a golden cup. And, by the way, now that I speak of giving laudanum away, I remember, about this time, a little incident, which I mention, because, trifling as it was, the reader will soon meet it again in my

[31]I here reckon twenty-five drops of laudanum as equivalent to one grain of opium, which, I believe, is the common estimate. However, as both may be considered variable quantities (the crude opium varying much in strength, and the tincture still more), I suppose that no infinitesimal accuracy can be had in such a calculation. Tea-spoons vary as much in size as opium in strength. Small ones hold about one hundred drops: so that eight thousand drops are about eighty times a tea-spoonful. The reader sees how much I kept within Doctor Buchan's indulgent allowance. (De Quincey's note. The allusion is to a pirated edition of Buchan's *Domestic Medicine* which De Quincey had seen, in which "the Doctor was made to say—'Be particularly careful never to take above 25 *ounces* of laudanum at once'; the true reading being probably 25 *drops*, which are held equal to about one grain of crude opium.")

[32]A night and a day.

[33]Wordsworth's *Resolution and Independence.*

[34]Immanuel Kant (1724–1804), the difficulty of whose writings has become proverbial.

dreams, which it influenced more fearfully than could be imagined. One day a Malay knocked at my door. What business a Malay could have to transact amongst English mountains, I cannot conjecture; but possibly he was on his road to a seaport about forty miles distant.

The servant who opened the door to him was a young girl[35] born and bred amongst the mountains, who had never seen an Asiatic dress of any sort: his turban, therefore, confounded her not a little; and as it turned out that his attainments in English were exactly of the same extent as hers in the Malay there seemed to be an impassable gulf fixed between all communication of ideas, if either party had happened to possess any. In this dilemma, the girl, recollecting the reputed learning of her master (and, doubtless, giving me credit for a knowledge of all the languages of the earth, besides, perhaps, a few of the lunar ones), came and gave me to understand that there was a sort of demon below, whom she clearly imagined that my art could exorcise from the house. I did not immediately go down; but when I did, the group which presented itself, arranged as it was by accident, though not very elaborate, took hold of my fancy and my eye in a way that none of the statuesque attitudes exhibited in the ballets at the opera-house, though so ostentatiously complex, had ever done. In a cottage kitchen, but paneled on the wall with dark wood that from age and rubbing resembled oak, and looking more like a rustic hall of entrance than a kitchen, stood the Malay, his turban and loose trousers of dingy white relieved upon the dark paneling; he had placed himself nearer to the girl than she seemed to relish, though her native spirit of mountain intrepidity contended with the feeling of simple awe which her countenance expressed, as she gazed upon the tiger-cat before her. And a more striking picture there could not be imagined than the beautiful English face of the girl, and its exquisite fairness, together with her erect and independent attitude, contrasted with the sallow and bilious skin of the Malay, enameled or veneered with mahogany by marine

[35]She was Barbara Lewthwaite, named in Wordsworth's *The Pet Lamb.*

air, his small, fierce, restless eyes, thin lips, slavish gestures, and adorations. Half hidden by the ferocious-looking Malay was a little child from a neighboring cottage, who had crept in after him, and was now in the act of reverting its head and gazing upwards at the turban and the fiery eyes beneath it, whilst with one hand he caught at the dress of the young woman for protection.

My knowledge of the oriental tongues is not remarkably extensive, being, indeed, confined to two words,—the Arabic word for barley, and the Turkish for opium (madjoon), which I have learned from *Anastasius.* And, as I had neither a Malay dictionary, nor even Adelung's *Mithridates,*[36] which might have helped me to a few words, I addressed him in some lines from the *Iliad,* considering that, of such languages as I possessed, Greek, in point of longitude, came geographically nearest to an oriental one. He worshiped me in a most devout manner, and replied in what I suppose was Malay. In this way I saved my reputation with my neighbors, for the Malay had no means of betraying the secret. He lay down upon the floor for about an hour, and then pursued his journey. On his departure, I presented him with a piece of opium. To him, as an orientalist, I concluded that opium must be familiar; and the expression of his face convinced me that it was. Nevertheless, I was struck with some little consternation when I saw him suddenly raise his hand to his mouth, and (in the school-boy phrase) bolt the whole, divided into three pieces, at one mouthful. The quantity was enough to kill three dragoons and their horses, and I felt some alarm for the poor creature; but what could be done? I had given him the opium in compassion for his solitary life, on recollecting that, if he had traveled on foot from London, it must be nearly three weeks since he could have exchanged a thought with any human being. I could not think of violating the laws of hospitality by having him seized and drenched with an emetic, and thus frightening him into a notion that we were going to sacrifice him to some English idol. No; there was clearly no help for it. He took his leave, and for some days I felt anxious; but, as I never heard of any Malay being found dead, I became convinced that he was used[37] to opium, and that I must have done him the service I designed, by giving him one night of respite from the pains of wandering.

This incident I have digressed to mention, because this Malay (partly from the picturesque exhibition he assisted to frame, partly from the anxiety I connected with his image for some days) fastened afterwards upon my dreams, and brought other Malays with him worse than himself, that ran "amuck"[38] at me, and led me into a world of troubles.—But to quit this episode, and to return to my intercalary[39] year of happiness. I have said already, that on a subject so important to us all as happiness, we should listen with pleasure to any man's experience or experiments, even though he were but a plowboy, who cannot be supposed to have plowed very deep in such an intractable soil as that of human pains and pleasures, or to have conducted his researches upon any very enlightened principles. But I, who have taken happiness, both in a solid and a liquid shape, both boiled and unboiled, both East India and Turkey—who have conducted my experiments upon this interesting subject with a sort of galvanic battery—and have, for the general benefit of the world, inoculated myself, as it were, with the poison

[36]A work on oriental languages named from the king of Pontus who, according to tradition, could speak the 22 dialects of his kingdom. The author was J. C. Adelung (1732–1806), a German philologer.

[37]This, however, is not a necessary conclusion; the varieties of effect produced by opium on different constitutions are infinite. A London magistrate (Harriott's *Struggles through Life,* vol. iii, p. 391, third edition) has recorded that on the first occasion of his trying laudanum for the gout, he took *forty* drops; the next night *sixty,* and on the fifth night *eighty,* without any effect whatever; and this at an advanced age. I have an anecdote from a country surgeon, however, which sinks Mr. Harriott's case into a trifle; and, in my projected medical treatise on opium, which I will publish, provided the College of Surgeons will pay me for enlightening their benighted understandings upon this subject, I will relate it; but it is far too good a story to be published gratis (De Quincey's note).

[38]See the common accounts, in any Eastern traveler or voyager, of the frantic excesses committed by Malays who have taken opium, or are reduced to desperation by ill luck at gambling (De Quincey's note).

[38]Interpolated.

of eight thousand drops of laudanum per day (just for the same reason as a French surgeon inoculated himself lately with cancer —an English one, twenty years ago, with plague—and a third, I know not of what nation,[40] with hydrophobia), *I,* it will be admitted, must surely know what happiness is, if anybody does. And therefore I will here lay down an analysis of happiness; and, as the most interesting mode of communicating it, I will give it, not didactically, but wrapped up and involved in a picture of one evening, as I spent every evening during the intercalary year when laudanum, though taken daily, was to me no more than the elixir of pleasure. This done, I shall quit the subject of happiness altogether, and pass to a very different one—the *pains of opium.*

Let there be a cottage, standing in a valley, eighteen miles from any town;[41] no spacious valley, but about two miles long by three-quarters of a mile in average width— the benefit of which provision is, that all the families resident within its circuit will compose, as it were, one larger household, per-

sonally familiar to your eye, and more or less interesting to your affections. Let the mountains be real mountains, between three and four thousand feet high, and the cottage a real cottage, not (as a witty author has it) "a cottage with a double coach-house";[42] let it be, in fact (for I must abide by the actual scene), a white cottage, embowered with flowering shrubs, so chosen as to unfold a succession of flowers upon the walls, and clustering around the windows, through all the months of spring, summer, and autumn —beginning, in fact, with May roses, and ending with jasmine. Let it, however, *not* be spring, nor summer, nor autumn—but winter, in his sternest shape. This is a most important point in the science of happiness. And I am surprised to see people overlook it, and think it matter of congratulation that winter is going, or, if coming, is not likely to be a severe one. On the contrary, I put up a petition annually for as much snow, hail, frost, or storm of one kind or other as the skies can possibly afford us. Surely everybody is aware of the divine pleasures which attend a winter fireside—candles at four o'clock, warm hearth-rugs, tea, a fair tea-maker, shutters closed, curtains flowing in ample draperies on the floor, whilst the wind and rain are raging audibly without,

And at the doors and windows seem to call,
As heaven and earth they would together mell;
Yet the least entrance find they none at all;
Whence sweeter grows our rest secure in massy
    hall.

Castle of Indolence.[43]

All these are items in the description of a winter evening which must surely be familiar to everybody born in a high latitude. And it is evident that most of these delicacies, like ice-cream, require a very low temperature of the atmosphere to produce them: they are fruits which cannot be ripened without weather stormy or inclement, in some way or other. I am not *"particular,"* as people say, whether it be snow, or black frost, or wind so strong that (as Mr. [Anti-Slavery Clarkson] says) "you may lean your back

[40] He also was English—a surgeon of Brighton— as De Quincey states in the edition of 1856.

[41] The cottage and the valley concerned in this description were not imaginary: the valley was the lovely one, *in those days,* of Grasmere; and the cottage was occupied for more than twenty years by myself, as immediate successor, in the year 1809, to Wordsworth. Looking to the limitation here laid down—*viz., in those days*—the reader will inquire in what way *Time* can have affected the beauty of Grasmere. Do the Westmoreland valleys turn gray-headed? O reader! this is a painful memento for some of us! Thirty years ago, a gang of Vandals (nameless, I thank heaven, to me), for the sake of building a mail-coach road that never would be wanted, carried, at a cost of £3000 to the defrauded parish, a horrid causeway of sheer granite masonry, for three-quarters of a mile, right through the loveliest succession of secret forest dells and sly recesses of the lake, margined by unrivaled ferns, amongst which was the *Osmunda regalis.* This sequestered angle of Grasmere is described by Wordsworth, as it unveiled itself on a September morning, in the exquisite poems on the "Naming of Places." From this also—*viz.,* this spot of ground, and this magnificent crest (the *Osmunda*)—was suggested that unique line, the finest independent line through all the records of verse,

"Or lady of the lake,
Sole-sitting by the shores of old romance."

Rightly, therefore, did I introduce this limitation. The Grasmere before and after this outrage were two different vales (De Quincey's note in the edition of 1856. The poem quoted from is IV in the *Poems on the Naming of Places*).

[42] Coleridge, in *The Devil's Thoughts.*

[43] By James Thomson. Canto I, stanza 43, quoted inexactly.

against it like a post." I can put up even with rain, provided that it rains cats and dogs; but something of the sort I must have; and, if I have it not, I think myself in a manner ill used: for why am I called on to pay so heavily for winter, in coals, and candles, and various privations that will occur even to gentlemen, if I am not to have the article good of its kind? No: a Canadian winter for my money: or a Russian one, where every man is but a co-proprietor with the north wind in the fee-simple[44] of his own ears. Indeed, so great an epicure am I in this matter, that I cannot relish a winter night fully, if it be much past St. Thomas's day,[45] and have degenerated into disgusting tendencies to vernal appearances;—no, it must be divided by a thick wall of dark nights from all return of light and sunshine. From the latter weeks of October to Christmas-eve, therefore, is the period during which happiness is in season, which, in my judgment, enters the room with the tea-tray; for tea, though ridiculed by those who are naturally of coarse nerves, or are become so from wine-drinking, and are not susceptible of influence from so refined a stimulant, will always be the favorite beverage of the intellectual; and, for my part, I would have joined Dr. Johnson in a *bellum inter-necinum*[46] against Jonas Hanway, or any other impious person who should presume to disparage it. But here, to save myself the trouble of too much verbal description, I will introduce a painter, and give him directions for the rest of the picture. Painters do not like white cottages, unless a good deal weather-stained, but, as the reader now understands that it is a winter night, his services will not be required except for the inside of the house.

Paint me, then, a room seventeen feet by twelve, and not more than seven and a half feet high. This, reader, is somewhat ambitiously styled, in my family, the drawing-room; but being contrived "a double debt to pay,"[47] it is also, and more justly, termed the library, for it happens that books are the only article of property in which I am richer than my neighbors. Of these I have about five thousand, collected gradually since my eighteenth year. Therefore, painter, put as many as you can into this room. Make it populous with books; and, furthermore, paint me a good fire, and furniture plain and modest, befitting the unpretending cottage of a scholar. And near the fire paint me a tea-table; and (as it is clear that no creature can come to see one, such a stormy night) place only two cups and saucers on the tea-tray; and, if you know how to paint such a thing symbolically, or otherwise, paint me an eternal tea-pot—eternal *à parte ante* and *à parte post;*[48] for I usually drink tea from eight o'clock at night to four o'clock in the morning. And, as it is very unpleasant to make tea, or to pour it out for one's self, paint me a lovely young woman, sitting at the table. Paint her arms like Aurora's, and her smiles like Hebe's;—but no, dear M[argaret],[49] not even in jest let me insinuate that thy power to illuminate my cottage rests upon a tenure so perishable as mere personal beauty; or that the witchcraft of angelic smiles lies within the empire of any earthly pencil. Pass, then, my good painter, to something more within its power; and the next article brought forward should naturally be myself—a picture of the Opium-eater, with his "little golden receptacle of the pernicious drug" lying beside him on the table. As to the opium, I have no objection to see a picture of *that,* though I would rather see the original; you may paint it, if you choose; but I apprize you that no "little" receptacle would, even in 1816, answer *my* purpose, who was at a distance from the "stately Pantheon,"[50] and all druggists (mortal or otherwise). No: you may as well paint the real receptacle, which was not of gold, but of glass, and as much like a wine-

---

[44] I. e., absolute ownership.   [45] 21 December.

[46] War to the death. Hanway, said to have been "the first man who ventured to walk the streets of London with an umbrella over his head," wrote an *Essay on Tea* (1756) which Dr. Johnson attacked in a review. Hanway angrily replied, and Dr. Johnson persisted in his defense of tea in a reply to the reply.

[47] Goldsmith, *The Deserted Village*, l. 229.

[48] From the times before and from the times to come.

[49] De Quincey's wife.

[50] A London concert hall, called stately by Wordsworth, near which was the druggist's shop in which De Quincey first purchased opium in 1804.

decanter as possible. Into this you may put a quart of ruby-colored laudanum; that, and a book of German metaphysics placed by its side, will sufficiently attest my being in the neighborhood; but as to myself, there I demur. I admit that, naturally, I ought to occupy the foreground of the picture; that being the hero of the piece, or (if you choose) the criminal at the bar, my body should be had into court. This seems reasonable; but why should I confess, on this point, to a painter? or why confess at all? If the public (into whose private ear I am confidentially whispering my confessions, and not into any painter's) should chance to have framed some agreeable picture for itself of the Opium-eater's exterior—should have ascribed to him, romantically, an elegant person, or a handsome face, why should I barbarously tear from it so pleasing a delusion—pleasing both to the public and to me? No: paint me, if at all, according to your own fancy; and, as a painter's fancy should teem with beautiful creations, I cannot fail, in that way, to be a gainer. And now, reader, we have run through all the ten categories of my condition, as it stood about 1816–1817, up to the middle of which latter year I judge myself to have been a happy man; and the elements of that happiness I have endeavored to place before you, in the above sketch of the interior of a scholar's library, in a cottage among the mountains, on a stormy winter evening.

But now farewell, a long farewell, to happiness, winter or summer! farewell to smiles and laughter! farewell to peace of mind! farewell to hope and to tranquil dreams, and to the blessed consolations of sleep! For more than three years and a half I am summoned away from these, I am now arrived at an Iliad of woes:[51] for I have now to record

THE PAINS OF OPIUM.

IV

I now pass[52] to what is the main subject of these latter confessions, to the history and journal of what took place in my dreams; for these were the immediate and proximate cause of my acutest suffering.

The first notice I had of any important change going on in this part of my physical economy, was from the reawakening of a state of eye generally incident to childhood, or exalted states of irritability. I know not whether my reader is aware that many children, perhaps most, have a power of painting, as it were, upon the darkness, all sorts of phantoms: in some that power is simply a mechanic affection[53] of the eye; others have a voluntary or a semi-voluntary power to dismiss or to summon them; or, as a child once said to me when I questioned him on this matter, "I can tell them to go, and they go; but sometimes they come when I don't tell them to come." Whereupon I told him that he had almost as unlimited a command over apparitions as a Roman centurion over his soldiers.—In the middle of 1817, I think it was, that this faculty became positively distressing to me: at night, when I lay awake in bed, vast processions passed along in mournful pomp; friezes of neverending stories, that to my feelings were as sad and solemn as if they were stories drawn from times before Oedipus or Priam, before Tyre, before Memphis. And, at the same time, a corresponding change took place in my dreams; a theater seemed suddenly opened and lighted up within my brain, which presented, nightly, spectacles of more than earthly splendor. And the four following facts may be mentioned, as noticeable at this time:

1. That, as the creative state of the eye increased, a sympathy seemed to arise between the waking and the dreaming states of the brain in one point—that whatsoever I happened to call up and to trace by a voluntary act upon the darkness was very apt to transfer itself to my dreams; so that I feared to exercise this faculty; for, as Midas turned all things to gold, that yet baffled his hopes and defrauded his human desires, so whatsoever things capable of being visually represented I did but think of in the darkness, immediately shaped themselves into phantoms of the eye; and, by a process apparently

---

[51]The allusion is to the opening lines of the *Iliad*.
[52]After statements showing the intellectual torpor to which the excessive use of opium reduced him.

[53]Property.

no less inevitable, when thus once traced in faint and visionary colors, like writings in sympathetic ink, they were drawn out, by the fierce chemistry of my dreams, into insufferable splendor that fretted my heart.

2. For this, and all other changes in my dreams, were accompanied by deep-seated anxiety and gloomy melancholy, such as are wholly incommunicable by words. I seemed every night to descend—not metaphorically, but literally to descend—into chasms and sunless abysses, depths below depths, from which it seemed hopeless that I could ever reascend. Nor did I, by waking, feel that I *had* reascended. This I do not dwell upon; because the state of gloom which attended these gorgeous spectacles, amounting at least to utter darkness, as of some suicidal despondency, cannot be approached by words.

3. The sense of space, and in the end the sense of time, were both powerfully affected. Buildings, landscapes, *etc.,* were exhibited in proportions so vast as the bodily eye is not fitted to receive. Space swelled, and was amplified to an extent of unutterable infinity. This, however, did not disturb me so much as the vast expansion of time. I sometimes seemed to have lived for seventy or one hundred years in one night; nay, sometimes had feelings representative of a millennium, passed in that time, or, however, of a duration far beyond the limits of any human experience.

4. The minutest incidents of childhood, or forgotten scenes of later years, were often revived. I could not be said to recollect them; for if I had been told of them when waking, I should not have been able to acknowledge them as parts of my past experience. But placed as they were before me, in dreams like intuitions, and clothed in all their evanescent circumstances and accompanying feelings, I *recognized* them instantaneously. I was once told by a near relative of mine,[54] that having in her childhood fallen into a river, and being on the very verge of death but for the critical assistance which reached her, she saw in a moment her whole life, in its minutest incidents, arrayed before her simultaneously

as in a mirror; and she had a faculty developed as suddenly for comprehending the whole and every part. This, from some opium experiences of mine, I can believe; I have, indeed, seen the same thing asserted twice in modern books, and accompanied by a remark which I am convinced is true, namely, that the dread book of account which the Scriptures speak of[55] is, in fact, the mind itself of each individual. Of this, at least, I feel assured, that there is no such thing as *forgetting* possible to the mind; a thousand accidents may and will interpose a veil between our present consciousness and the secret inscriptions on the mind; accidents of the same sort will also rend away this veil; but alike, whether veiled or unveiled, the inscription remains for ever; just as the stars seem to withdraw before the common light of day, whereas, in fact, we all know that it is the light which is drawn over them as a veil, and that they are waiting to be revealed, when the obscuring daylight shall have withdrawn.

Having noticed these four facts as memorably distinguishing my dreams from those of health, I shall now cite a case illustrative of the first fact; and shall then cite any others that I remember, either in their chronological order, or any other that may give them more effect as pictures to the reader.

I had been in youth, and even since, for occasional amusement, a great reader of Livy, whom I confess that I prefer, both for style and matter, to any other of the Roman historians; and I had often felt as most solemn and appalling sounds, and most emphatically representative of the majesty of the Roman people, the two words so often occurring in Livy—*Consul Romanus;* especially when the consul is introduced in his military character. I mean to say, that the words king, sultan, regent, *etc.,* or any other titles of those who embody in their own persons the collective majesty of a great people, had less power over my reverential feelings. I had also, though no great reader of history, made myself minutely and critically familiar with one period of English history, namely, the period of the Parliamentary War, having been attracted by the moral grandeur of

---

[54] It is said that the relative was De Quincey's mother.

[55] Cf. Revelation, 20:12.

some who figured in that day, and by the many interesting memoirs which survive those unquiet times. Both these parts of my lighter reading, having furnished me often with matter of reflection, now furnished me with matter for my dreams. Often I used to see, after painting upon the blank darkness a sort of rehearsal whilst waking, a crowd of ladies, and perhaps a festival, and dances. And I heard it said, or I said to myself, "These are English ladies from the unhappy times of Charles I. These are the wives and the daughters of those who met in peace, and sat at the same tables, and were allied by marriage or by blood; and yet, after a certain day in August, 1642,[56] never smiled upon each other again, nor met but in the field of battle; and at Marston Moor, at Newbury, or at Naseby, cut asunder all ties of love by the cruel saber, and washed away in blood the memory of ancient friendship." The ladies danced, and looked as lovely as the court of George IV. Yet I knew, even in my dream, that they had been in the grave for nearly two centuries. This pageant would suddenly dissolve; and, at a clapping of hands, would be heard the heart-quaking sound of *Consul Romanus;* and immediately came "sweeping by," in gorgeous paluda-ments,[57] Paulus, or Marius[58] girt round by a company of centurions, with the crimson tunic[59] hoisted on a spear, and followed by the *alalagmos*[60] of the Roman legions.

Many years ago, when I was looking over Piranesi's[61] *Antiquities of Rome,* Mr. Cole-ridge, who was standing by, described to me a set of plates by that artist, called his *Dreams,* and which record the scenery of his own visions during the delirium of a fever:

some of them (I describe only from memory of Mr. Coleridge's account) representing vast Gothic halls; on the floor of which stood all sorts of engines and machinery, wheels, cables, pulleys, levers, catapults, *etc., etc.,* expressive of enormous power put forth, and resistance overcome. Creeping along the sides of the walls, you perceived a staircase; and upon it, groping his way upwards, was Piranesi himself. Follow the stairs a little further, and you perceive it come to a sudden, abrupt termination, without any balustrade, and allowing no step onwards to him who had reached the extremity, except into the depths below. Whatever is to become of poor Piranesi, you suppose, at least, that his labors must in some way terminate here. But raise your eyes, and behold a second flight of stairs still higher; on which again Piranesi is perceived, but this time standing on the very brink of the abyss. Again elevate your eye, and a still more aërial flight of stairs is beheld; and again is poor Piranesi busy on his aspiring labors; and so on, until the unfinished stairs and Piranesi both are lost in the upper gloom of the hall. With the same power of endless growth and self-reproduction did my architecture proceed in dreams. In the early stage of my malady, the splendors of my dreams were indeed chiefly architectural; and I beheld such pomp of cities and palaces as was never yet beheld by the waking eye, unless in the clouds. From a great modern poet I cite part of a passage which describes, as an appearance actually beheld in the clouds, what in many of its circumstances I saw frequently in sleep:

The appearance, instantaneously disclosed
Was of a mighty city—boldly say
A wilderness of building, sinking far
And self-withdrawn into a wondrous depth,
Far sinking into splendor—without end!
Fabric it seemed of diamond, and of gold,
With alabaster domes, and silver spires,
And blazing terrace upon terrace, high
Uplifted; here. serene pavilions bright,
In avenues disposed; there towers begirt
With battlements that on their restless fronts
Bore stars—illumination of all gems!
By earthly nature had the effect been wrought
Upon the dark materials of the storm
Now pacified; on them, and on the coves,

[56]Charles I's standard, which gave the signal for the actual beginning of the English Civil War, was raised at Nottingham on 22 August, 1642.

[57]Military cloaks, worn by generals and their principal officers.

[58]Lucius Aemilius Paulus (died 160 B. C.), and Caius Marius (died 86 B. C.).

[59]The signal which announced a day of battle (De Quincey's note, edition of 1856).

[60]A word expressing collectively the gathering of the Roman war-cries—*Alála, Alála* (De Quincey's note, edition of 1856). Greek ἀ λαλ ή means war-cry.

[61]Italian engraver (died 1778). Piranesi never published a set of plates entitled *Dreams,* though some of his engravings depict imaginary edifices.

And mountain-steeps and summits, whereunto
The vapors had receded—taking there
Their station under a cerulean sky, etc.[62]

The sublime circumstance—"battlements
that on their *restless* fronts bore stars"—
might have been copied from my architectural dreams, for it often occurred. We
hear it reported of Dryden, and of Fuseli[63] in
modern times, that they thought proper to
eat raw meat for the sake of obtaining splendid dreams: how much better, for such a
purpose, to have eaten opium, which yet I
do not remember that any poet is recorded to
have done, except the dramatist Shadwell;[64]
and in ancient days, Homer is, I think, rightly
reputed to have known the virtues of opium.[65]

To my architecture succeeded dreams of
lakes and silvery expanses of water: these
haunted me so much, that I feared (though
possibly it will appear ludicrous to a medical
man) that some dropsical state or tendency
of the brain might thus be making itself (to
use a metaphysical word) *objective*,[66] and the
sentient organ *project* itself as its own object.

For two months I suffered greatly in my
head—a part of my bodily structure which
had hitherto been so clear from all touch or
taint of weakness (physically, I mean) that I
used to say of it, as the last Lord Orford[67]
said of his stomach, that it seemed likely to
survive the rest of my person. Till now I
had never felt headache even, or any the
slightest pain, except rheumatic pains caused
by my own folly. However, I got over this
attack, though it must have been verging on
something very dangerous.

The waters now changed their character—
from translucent lakes, shining like mirrors,
they now became seas and oceans. And
now came a tremendous change, which, unfolding itself slowly like a scroll, through
many months, promised an abiding torment;
and, in fact, never left me until the winding
up of my case. Hitherto the human face
had mixed often in my dreams, but not
despotically, nor with any special power of
tormenting. But now that which I have
called the tyranny of the human face began
to unfold itself. Perhaps some part of my
London life might be answerable for this.
Be that as it may, now it was that upon the
rocking waters of the ocean the human face
began to appear; the sea appeared paved with
innumerable faces, upturned to the heavens;
faces, imploring, wrathful, despairing, surged
upwards by thousands, by myriads, by
generations, by centuries: my agitation was
infinite, my mind tossed, and surged with
the ocean.

May, 1818.—The Malay had been a fearful enemy for months. I have been every
night, through his means, transported into
Asiatic scenes. I know not whether others
share in my feelings on this point; but I have
often thought that if I were compelled to
forgo England, and to live in China, and
among the Chinese manners and modes of life
and scenery, I should go mad. The causes
of my horror lie deep, and some of them
must be common to others. Southern Asia,
in general, is the seat of awful images and
associations. As the cradle of the human
race, it would alone have a dim and rever-

[62]Wordsworth, *The Excursion*, Bk. II, ll. 834-851.
De Quincey explains, in the edition of 1856, why he
did not in the first instance name Wordsworth:
"The year in which I wrote and published these
Confessions was 1821; and at that time the name of
Wordsworth, though beginning to emerge from the
dark cloud of scorn and contumely which had hitherto overshadowed it, was yet most imperfectly established. Not until ten years later was his greatness cheerfully and generally acknowledged. I,
therefore, as the very earliest (without one exception) of all who came forward, in the beginning of
his career, to honor and welcome him, shrank with
disgust from making any sentence of mine the occasion for an explosion of vulgar malice against him.
But the grandeur of the passage here cited inevitably spoke for itself; and he that would have been
most scornful on hearing the name of the poet
coupled with this epithet of 'great' could not but find
his malice intercepted, and himself cheated into cordial admiration, by the splendor of the verses."

[63]John Henry Fuseli (1741-1825), an artist of
Swiss extraction who passed most of his life in
England.

[64]Thomas Shadwell (1640-1692), Dryden's Mac
Flecknoe.

[65]The opinion is based on a passage in the *Odyssey*,
Bk. IV, where Helen is represented as giving Telemachus a potion which made him oblivious of his
sorrows.

[66]This word, so nearly unintelligible in 1821, so
intensely scholastic, and, consequently, when surrounded by familiar and vernacular words, so apparently pedantic, yet, on the other hand, so indispensable to accurate thinking, and to *wide* thinking,
has since 1821 become too common to need any
apology (De Quincey's note, edition of 1856).

[67]Horace Walpole (1717-1797).

ential feeling connected with it. But there are other reasons. No man can pretend that the wild, barbarous, and capricious superstitions of Africa, or of savage tribes elsewhere, affect him in the way that he is affected by the ancient, monumental, cruel, and elaborate religions of Indostan, *etc.* The mere antiquity of Asiatic things, of their institutions, histories, modes of faith, *etc.*, is so impressive, that to me the vast age of the race and name overpowers the sense of youth in the individual. A young Chinese seems to me an antediluvian man renewed. Even Englishmen, though not bred in any knowledge of such institutions, cannot but shudder at the mystic sublimity of *castes* that have flowed apart, and refused to mix, through such immemorial tracts of time; nor can any man fail to be awed by the names of the Ganges, or the Euphrates. It contributes much to these feelings that Southern Asia is, and has been for thousands of years, the part of the earth most swarming with human life, the great *officina gentium.*[68] Man is a weed in those regions. The vast empires, also, into which the enormous population of Asia has always been cast, give a further sublimity to the feelings associated with all oriental names or images. In China, over and above what it has in common with the rest of Southern Asia, I am terrified by the modes of life, by the manners, and the barrier of utter abhorrence, and want of sympathy, placed between us by feelings deeper than I can analyze. I could sooner live with lunatics, or brute animals. All this, and much more than I can say, or have time to say, the reader must enter into, before he can comprehend the unimaginable horror which these dreams of oriental imagery, and mythological tortures, impressed upon me. Under the connecting feeling of tropical heat and vertical sunlights, I brought together all creatures, birds, beasts, reptiles, all trees and plants, usages and appearances, that are found in all tropical regions, and assembled them together in China or Indostan. From kindred feelings, I soon brought Egypt and all her gods under the same law. I was stared at, hooted at, grinned at, chattered at, by monkeys, by

paroquets, by cockatoos. I ran into pagodas, and was fixed, for centuries, at the summit, or in secret rooms: I was the idol; I was the priest; I was worshiped; I was sacrificed. I fled from the wrath of Brama[69] through all the forests of Asia: Vishnu hated me; Seeva laid wait for me. I came suddenly upon Isis and Osiris;[70] I had done a deed, they said, which the ibis and the crocodile[71] trembled at. I was buried for a thousand years in stone coffins, with mummies and sphinxes, in narrow chambers at the heart of eternal pyramids. I was kissed, with cancerous kisses, by crocodiles; and laid, confounded with all unutterable slimy things, amongst reeds and Nilotic mud.[72]

I thus give the reader some slight abstraction of my oriental dreams, which always filled me with such amazement at the monstrous scenery, that horror seemed absorbed, for a while, in sheer astonishment. Sooner or later came a reflux of feeling that swallowed up the astonishment, and left me, not so much in terror, as in hatred and abomination of what I saw. Over every form, and threat, and punishment, and dim sightless incarceration, brooded a sense of eternity and infinity that drove me into an oppression as of madness. Into these dreams only, it was, with one or two slight exceptions, that any circumstances of physical horror entered. All before had been moral and spiritual terrors. But here the main agents were ugly birds, or snakes, or crocodiles, especially the last. The cursed crocodile became to me the object of more horror than almost all the rest. I was compelled to live with him; and (as was always the case, almost, in my dreams) for centuries. I escaped sometimes, and found myself in Chinese houses with cane tables, *etc.* All the feet of the tables, sofas, *etc.*, soon became instinct with life: the abominable head of the crocodile, and his leering eyes, looked out at me, multiplied into a thousand repetitions; and I stood loathing and fascinated. And so often did

---

[68]Workshop of races.

[69]Brahma, Vishnu, and Siva compose the Trinity of the Hindu religion of Brahmanism.

[70]Female and male deities, sister and brother, in Egyptian mythology.

[71]Both sacred animals to the Egyptians.

[72]I. e., mud of the Nile.

this hideous reptile haunt my dreams, that many times the very same dream was broken up in the very same way: I heard gentle voices speaking to me (I hear everything when I am sleeping), and instantly I awoke: it was broad noon, and my children were standing, hand in hand, at my bedside; come to show me their colored shoes, or new frocks, or to let me see them dressed for going out. I protest that so awful was the transition from the damned crocodile, and the other unutterable monsters and abortions of my dreams, to the sight of innocent *human* natures and of infancy, that, in the mighty and sudden revulsion of mind, I wept, and could not forbear it, as I kissed their faces.

V

As a final specimen, I cite one of a different character, from 1820.

The dream commenced with a music which now I often heard in dreams—a music of preparation and of awakening suspense; a music like the opening of the Coronation Anthem, and which, like *that,* gave the feeling of a vast march, of infinite cavalcades filing off, and the tread of innumerable armies. The morning was come of a mighty day—a day of crisis and of final hope for human nature, then suffering some mysterious eclipse, and laboring in some dread extremity. Somewhere, I knew not where— somehow, I knew not how—by some beings, I knew not whom—a battle, a strife, an agony, was conducting—was evolving like a great drama, or piece of music; with which my sympathy was the more insupportable from my confusion as to its place, its cause, its nature, and its possible issue. I, as is usual in dreams (where, of necessity, we make ourselves central to every movement), had the power, and yet had not the power, to decide it. I had the power, if I could raise myself, to will it; and yet again had not the power, for the weight of twenty Atlantics was upon me, or the oppression of inexpiable guilt. "Deeper than ever plummet sounded,"[73] I lay inactive. Then, like a chorus, the passion deepened. Some greater interest was at stake; some mightier cause than ever yet the sword had pleaded, or trumpet had proclaimed. Then came sudden alarms; hurryings to and fro; trepidations of innumerable fugitives, I knew not whether from the good cause or the bad; darkness and lights; tempest and human faces; and at last, with the sense that all was lost, female forms, and the features that were worth all the world to me, and but a moment allowed—and clasped hands, and heart-breaking partings, and then—everlasting farewells! and, with a sigh, such as the caves of hell sighed when the incestuous mother uttered the abhorred name of death,[74] the sound was reverberated—everlasting farewells! and again, and yet again reverberated—everlasting farewells!

And I awoke in struggles, and cried aloud —"I will sleep no more!"

[73] Cf. *The Tempest,* V, i, 56.
[74] Cf. *Paradise Lost,* Bk. II, 1. 746 and following lines.

SUSPIRIA DE PROFUNDIS

Being a Sequel to "The Confessions of an English Opium-Eater"[1]

LEVANA AND OUR LADIES OF SORROW

OFTENTIMES at Oxford I saw Levana in my dreams. I knew her by her Roman symbols. Who is Levana? Reader, that do not pretend to have leisure for very much scholarship, you will not be angry with me for telling you. Levana was the Roman goddess that performed for the new-born infant the earliest office of ennobling kindness —typical, by its mode, of that grandeur which belongs to man everywhere, and of that benignity in powers invisible which even in pagan worlds sometimes descends to sustain it. At the very moment of birth, just as the infant tasted for the first time the atmosphere of our troubled planet, it was laid on the ground. *That* might bear differ-

[1] The title means Breathings, or Sighs, from the Depths. *Levana* was first published in the June, 1845, issue of *Blackwood's Magazine.*

ent interpretations. But immediately, lest so grand a creature should grovel there for more than one instant, either the paternal hand, as proxy of the goddess Levana, or some near kinsman, as proxy for the father, raised it upright, bade it look erect as the king of all this world, and presented its forehead to the stars, saying, perhaps, in his heart, "Behold what is greater than yourselves!" This symbolic act represented the function of Levana. And that mysterious lady, who never revealed her face (except to me in dreams), but always acted by delegation, had her name from the Latin verb (as still it is the Italian verb) *levare,* to raise aloft.

This is the explanation of Levana. And hence it has arisen that some people have understood by Levana the tutelary power that controls the education of the nursery. She, that would not suffer at his birth even a prefigurative or mimic degradation for her awful ward, far less could be supposed to suffer the real degradation attaching to the non-development of his powers. She therefore watches over human education. Now, the word *edŭco,* with the penultimate short, was derived (by a process often exemplified in the crystallization of languages) from the word *edūco,* with the penultimate long. Whatsoever *edūces,* or develops, *educates.* By the education of Levana, therefore, is meant—not the poor machinery that moves by spelling-books and grammars, but that mighty system of central forces hidden in the deep bosom of human life, which by passion, by strife, by temptation, by the energies of resistance, works for ever upon children —resting not day or night, any more than the mighty wheel of day and night themselves, whose moments, like restless spokes, are glimmering[2] for ever as they revolve.

If, then, *these* are the ministries by which Levana works, how profoundly must she reverence the agencies of grief! But you, reader, think that children generally are not liable to grief such as mine. There are two senses in the word *generally*—the sense of Euclid, where it means *universally* (or in the whole extent of the *genus*), and a foolish sense of this word, where it means *usually.* Now, I am far from saying that children universally are capable of grief like mine. But there are more than you ever heard of who die of grief in this island of ours. I will tell you a common case. The rules of Eton require that a boy on the *foundation*[3] should be there twelve years: he is superannuated at eighteen, consequently he must come at six. Children torn away from mothers and sisters at that age not unfrequently die. I speak of what I know. The complaint is not entered by the registrar as grief, but *that* it is. Grief of that sort, and at that age, has killed more than ever have been counted amongst its martyrs.

Therefore it is that Levana often communes with the powers that shake man's heart; therefore it is that she dotes upon grief. "These ladies," said I softly to myself, on seeing the ministers with whom Levana was conversing, "these are the Sorrows, and they are three in number, as the *Graces* are three, who dress man's life with beauty; the *Parcae*[4] are three, who weave the dark arras[5] of man's life in their mysterious loom always with colors sad in part, sometimes angry with tragic crimson and black; the *Furies* are three, who visit with retributions called from the other side of the grave offenses that walk upon this; and once even the *Muses* were but three, who fit the harp, the trumpet, or the lute, to the great burdens of man's impassioned creations. These are the Sorrows, all three of whom I know."

---

[2] As I have never allowed myself to covet any man's ox nor his ass, nor anything that is his, still less would it become a philosopher to covet other people's images or metaphors. Here, therefore, I restore to Mr. Wordsworth this fine image of the revolving wheel and the glimmering spokes, as applied by him to the flying successions of day and night. I borrowed it for one moment in order to point my own sentence; which being done, the reader is witness that I now pay it back instantly by a note made for that sole purpose. On the same principle I often borrow their seals from young ladies, when closing my letters, because there is sure to be some tender sentiment upon them about "memory," or "hope," or "roses," or "reunion," and my correspondent must be a sad brute who is not touched by the eloquence of the seal, even if his taste is so bad that he remains deaf to mine (De Quincey's note).

[3] I. e., holding a scholarship, provided for in the college's original endowment.

[4] The Fates.

[5] Tapestry, originally tapestry made at Arras, France.

The last words I say *now;* but in Oxford I said, "one of whom I know, and the others too surely I *shall* know." For already, in my fervent youth, I saw (dimly relieved upon the dark background of my dreams) the imperfect lineaments of the awful Sisters.

These Sisters—by what name shall we call them? If I say simply, "The Sorrows," there will be a chance of mistaking the term; it might be understood of individual sorrow —separate cases of sorrow—whereas I want a term expressing the mighty abstractions that incarnate themselves in all individual sufferings of man's heart, and I wish to have these abstractions presented as impersonations—that is, as clothed with human attributes of life, and with functions pointing to flesh. Let us call them, therefore, *Our Ladies of Sorrow.*

I know them thoroughly, and have walked in all their kingdoms. Three sisters they are, of one mysterious household; and their paths are wide apart; but of their dominion there is no end. Them I saw often conversing with Levana, and sometimes about myself. Do they talk, then? O no! Mighty phantoms like these disdain the infirmities of language. They may utter voices through the organs of man when they dwell in human hearts, but amongst themselves is no voice nor sound; eternal silence reigns in *their* kingdoms. They spoke not as they talked with Levana; they whispered not; they sang not; though oftentimes methought they *might* have sung: for I upon earth had heard their mysteries oftentimes deciphered by harp and timbrel, by dulcimer and organ. Like God, whose servants they are, they utter their pleasure not by sounds that perish, or by words that go astray, but by signs in heaven, by changes on earth, by pulses in secret rivers, heraldries painted on darkness, and hieroglyphics written on the tablets of the brain. *They* wheeled in mazes; *I* spelled the steps. *They* telegraphed from afar; *I* read the signals. *They* conspired together; and on the mirrors of darkness *my* eye traced the plots. *Theirs* were the symbols; *mine* are the words.

What is it the Sisters are? What is it that they do? Let me describe their form and their presence, if form it were that still fluctuated in its outline, or presence it were that for ever advanced to the front or for ever receded amongst shades.

The eldest of the three is named *Mater Lachrymarum,* Our Lady of Tears. She it is that night and day raves and moans, calling for vanished faces. She stood in Rama, where a voice was heard of lamentation— Rachel weeping for her children, and refusing to be comforted.[6] She it was that stood in Bethlehem on the night when Herod's sword swept its nurseries of Innocents, and the little feet were stiffened for ever which, heard at times as they trotted along floors overhead, woke pulses of love in household hearts that were not unmarked in heaven. Her eyes are sweet and subtle, wild and sleepy, by turns; oftentimes rising to the clouds, oftentimes challenging the heavens. She wears a diadem round her head. And I knew by childish memories that she could go abroad upon the winds, when she heard the sobbing of litanies, or the thundering of organs, and when she beheld the mustering of summer clouds. This Sister, the elder, it is that carries keys more than papal at her girdle, which open every cottage and every palace. She, to my knowledge, sat all last summer by the bedside of the blind beggar, him that so often and so gladly I talked with, whose pious daughter, eight years old, with the sunny countenance, resisted the temptations of play and village mirth, to travel all day long on dusty roads with her afflicted father. For this did God send her a great reward. In the spring-time of the year, and whilst yet her own spring was budding, He recalled her to himself. But her blind father mourns for ever over *her;* still he dreams at midnight that the little guiding hand is locked within his own; and still he wakens to a darkness that is *now* within a second and a deeper darkness. This *Mater Lachrymarum* also has been sitting all this winter of 1844–5 within the bedchamber of the Czar, bringing before his eyes a daughter (not less pious) that vanished to God not less suddenly, and left behind her a darkness not less profound.[7]

[6]See Jeremiah, 31 :15, and St. Matthew, 2 :18.
[7]The Princess Alexandra, third daughter of the Czar Nicholas, died in August, 1844.

By the power of the keys it is that Our Lady of Tears glides, a ghostly intruder, into the chambers of sleepless men, sleepless women, sleepless children, from Ganges to the Nile, from Nile to Mississippi. And her, because she is the first-born of her house, and has the widest empire, let us honor with the title of "Madonna."

The second Sister is called *Mater Suspiriorum,* Our Lady of Sighs. She never scales the clouds, nor walks abroad upon the winds. She wears no diadem. And her eyes, if they were ever seen, would be neither sweet nor subtle; no man could read their story; they would be found filled with perishing dreams, and with wrecks of forgotten delirium. But she raises not her eyes; her head, on which sits a dilapidated turban, droops for ever, for ever fastens on the dust. She weeps not. She groans not. But she sighs inaudibly at intervals. Her sister, Madonna, is oftentimes stormy and frantic, raging in the highest against heaven, and demanding back her darlings. But Our Lady of Sighs never clamors, never defies, dreams not of rebellious aspirations. She is humble to abjectness. Hers is the meekness that belongs to the hopeless. Murmur she may, but it is in her sleep. Whisper she may, but it is to herself in the twilight. Mutter she does at times, but it is in solitary places that are desolate as she is desolate, in ruined cities, and when the sun has gone down to his rest. This Sister is the visitor of the Pariah, of the Jew, of the bondsman to the oar in the Mediterranean galleys; of the English criminal in Norfolk Island,[8] blotted out from the books of remembrance in sweet far-off England; of the baffled penitent reverting his eyes for ever upon a solitary grave, which to him seems the altar overthrown of some past and bloody sacrifice, on which altar no oblations can now be availing, whether towards pardon that he might implore, or towards reparation that he might attempt. Every slave that at noonday looks up to the tropical sun with timid reproach, as he points with one hand to the earth, our general mother, but for *him* a stepmother, as he points with the other hand to the Bible, our

general teacher, but against *him* sealed and sequestered;[9] every woman sitting in darkness, without love to shelter her head, or hope to illumine her solitude, because the heaven-born instincts kindling in her nature germs of holy affections, which God implanted in her womanly bosom, having been stifled by social necessities, now burn sullenly to waste, like sepulchral lamps amongst the ancients; every nun defrauded of her unreturning May-time by wicked kinsman, whom God will judge; every captive in every dungeon; all that are betrayed, and all that are rejected; outcasts by traditionary law, and children of *hereditary* disgrace—all these walk with Our Lady of Sighs. She also carries a key, but she needs it little. For her kingdom is chiefly amongst the tents of Shem,[10] and the houseless vagrant of every clime. Yet in the very highest ranks of man she finds chapels of her own; and even in glorious England there are some that, to the world, carry their heads as proudly as the reindeer, who yet secretly have received her mark upon their foreheads.

But the third Sister, who is also the youngest——! Hush! whisper whilst we talk of *her!* Her kingdom is not large, or else no flesh should live; but within that kingdom all power is hers. Her head, turreted like that of Cybele,[11] rises almost beyond the reach of sight. She droops not; and her eyes, rising so high, *might* be hidden by distance. But, being what they are, they cannot be hidden; through the treble veil of crape which she wears the fierce light of a blazing misery, that rests not for matins or for vespers,[12] for noon of day or noon of night, for ebbing or for flowing tide, may be read from the very ground. She is the defier of God. She also is the mother of lunacies, and the suggestress of suicides. Deep lie

---

[8] In the southern Pacific, east of Australia; formerly used by England as a penal settlement.

[9] This, the reader will be aware, applies chiefly to the cotton and tobacco States of North America; but not to them only: on which account I have not scrupled to figure the sun, which looks down upon slavery, as *tropical,*—no matter if strictly within the tropics, or simply so near to them as to produce a similar climate (De Quincey's note).

[10] See Genesis, 9:27.

[11] Nature goddess of the peoples of Asia Minor. She was pictured wearing a turreted diadem.

[12] For the religious offices of early morning or evening.

the roots of her power; but narrow is the nation that she rules. For she can approach only those in whom a profound nature has been upheaved by central convulsions; in whom the heart trembles and the brain rocks under conspiracies of tempest from without and tempest from within. Madonna moves with uncertain steps, fast or slow, but still with tragic grace. Our Lady of Sighs creeps timidly and stealthily. But this youngest Sister moves with incalculable motions, bounding, and with a tiger's leaps. She carries no key; for, though coming rarely amongst men, she storms all doors at which she is permitted to enter at all. And her name is *Mater Tenebrarum*—Our Lady of Darkness.

These were the *Semnai Theai* or Sublime Goddesses,[13] these were the *Eumenides* or Gracious Ladies (so called by antiquity in shuddering propitiation) of my Oxford dreams. Madonna spoke. She spoke by her mysterious hand. Touching my head, she beckoned to Our Lady of Sighs; and *what* she spoke, translated out of the signs which (except in dreams) no man reads, was this:

"Lo! here is he whom in childhood I dedicated to my altars. This is he that once I made my darling. Him I led astray, him I beguiled; and from heaven I stole away his young heart to mine. Through me did he become idolatrous; and through me it was, by languishing desires, that he worshiped the worm, and prayed to the wormy grave.

Holy was the grave to him; lovely was its darkness; saintly its corruption. Him, this young idolator, I have seasoned for thee, dear gentle Sister of Sighs! Do thou take him now to *thy* heart, and season him for our dreadful sister. And thou,"—turning to the *Mater Tenebrarum,* she said—"wicked sister, that temptest and hatest, do thou take him from *her.* See that thy scepter lie heavy on his head. Suffer not woman and her tenderness to sit near him in his darkness. Banish the frailties of hope, wither the relenting of love, scorch the fountains of tears, curse him as only *thou* canst curse. So shall he be accomplished in the furnace, so shall he see the things that ought *not* to be seen, sights that are abominable, and secrets that are unutterable. So shall he read elder truths, sad truths, grand truths, fearful truths. So shall he rise again *before* he dies. And so shall our commission be accomplished which from God we had—to plague his heart until we had unfolded the capacities of his spirit."[14]

---

[13]The word σεμνος is usually rendered *venerable* in dictionaries—not a very flattering epithet for females. But I am disposed to think that it comes nearest to our idea of the *sublime*—as near as a Greek word *could* come (De Quincey's note).

[14]The reader who wishes at all to understand the course of these Confessions ought not to pass over this dream-legend. There is no great wonder that a vision which occupied my waking thoughts in those years should reappear in my dreams. It was, in fact, a legend recurring in sleep, most of which I had myself silently written or sculptured in my daylight reveries. But its importance to the present Confessions is this, that it rehearses or prefigures their course. This FIRST part belongs to Madonna. The THIRD belongs to the "Mater Suspiriorum," and will be entitled *The Pariah Worlds.* The FOURTH, which terminates the work, belongs to the "Mater Tenebrarum," and will be entitled *The Kingdom of Darkness.* As to the SECOND, it is an interpolation requisite to the effect of the others, and will be explained in its proper place (De Quincey's note). The plan here somewhat vaguely outlined was never completed by De Quincey.

The Victorian Era and After, 1837–1914

In 1837 Alexandrina Victoria, the daughter of the fourth son of George III, succeeded her uncle, William IV, on the English throne. She was then eighteen years old, and she reigned over the British Isles and the overseas Empire until her death in 1901. She has given her name to an era of extraordinary development and expansion, but the word "Victorian" signifies above all a certain outlook and moral standard which the queen shared with the vast majority of her subjects during most of her reign. That moral outlook, furthermore, is the key to an orderly understanding of Victorian literature; for every writer in this era was strongly influenced by Victorianism, either by way of attraction or by way of repulsion. Hence we must, at the outset of our study of this period, clearly define Victorianism. In so doing, we may begin with the queen herself.

Victoria was not a remarkable person. Even as a young girl she had no beauty, though she was not without the charm which youth in itself gives, and she did have a clear musical voice. She was short, less than five feet in height, and as she grew older she became dumpy; but her demeanor is said to have been always graceful and dignified. She was, moreover, an accomplished horsewoman, and was fond of dancing and of games. She was "modern" in her love of fresh air. Her intelligence was middling. She had an exceptional memory, but otherwise her mental powers were those of the man in the street. Her artistic sense, too, was as little developed as that of the man

in the street, who is notoriously comfortable amidst tasteless and even ugly surroundings. She had a lively sense of the importance of her position, and took her responsibilities seriously; but her limitations can be judged from the fact that she never understood the social problems which were acute throughout her reign.

At the start, Victoria received invaluable instruction in the duties of her position from Viscount Melbourne, who was prime minister when she became queen. In 1840 she married her cousin Albert, son of the Duke of Saxe-Coburg-Gotha, who was both resourceful and astute. He became a useful adviser, and she regarded him with feelings approaching veneration, though she was not at all disposed to share her sovereignty with him. After his early death, from typhoid fever, in 1861, she virtually retired from public life for about ten years. During these years she became unpopular. After 1871, however, she grew popular again; and from about 1880 until the close of her reign she was fairly worshiped. In these years she was regarded as the living symbol of empire, though at the same time her actual power diminished.

From even so brief a sketch as this it is evident that Victoria was not a great dominating personality, bound to leave a mark on the nineteenth century. Her character was representative rather than masterful. She happened to possess, very largely, the mind and outlook of the middle class, at a time when that class, which had been slowly rising in importance for several generations, had finally attained a commanding position in the state. She was not a mere personification of the middle class, or of the manufacturing and trading portion of it, which was the part now dominant. She herself, for example, was not really prudish. But she did share some limitations of the new middle class. She upheld its narrow formal morality, its emphasis on the domestic virtues, its notion that many facts of life could be disposed of by shutting the eyes to them and not mentioning them, and its new standard, which was "respectability." She imposed severe rules on her court, but not on the nation, because the rules were for the most part already accepted by the nation. It cannot be said that anybody imposed them on the nation; they arose out of new conditions. The queen, then, can indeed reveal to us something of the nature of Victorianism, but if we are to see it completely and clearly in the light of its causes we must look beyond her to a set of conditions with the appearance of which she had nothing to do. By accident, the outlook and standards of the age were thoroughly congenial to her, with the consequence that she seemed to personify them; but she in no sense created them.

Expansion of Industry

It was said in the preceding chapter that the development of English life has continued, without any real break, from about the middle of the eighteenth century to the present, and that this continuous development has been determined by the progress of scientific discovery and by the applications of science in industry. It was also said that a revolutionary change in the processes of industry, brought about by the harnessing of steam power and by a succession of mechanical inventions, was well under way in the early years of the nineteenth century. The result was the rapid transformation of England from an agricultural to an industrial country, with much accompanying hardship and distress felt by laborers who found their work taken away from them by machines, and even by those who found employment under the new system, whether as machine tenders or as miners of coal and of iron ore.

This is not the place for facts and figures which attest the magnitude of the Industrial Revolution, nor for the discussion of economic theory. We must, however, understand the character of the change. And the first thing we have to notice is how inevitable it was, as soon as it became possible, and how impersonal. The initial cost of power-driven machinery was large, but the efficiency of the machinery was such that cloth and other commodities could be produced far more cheaply than by hand labor. The machine, therefore, could, in a real sense, dictate its own terms, and in fact it became the master both of its owners and of its attendants. Only if its conditions were met would it yield a profit, but the profits it could yield were enormous; because, throughout the nineteenth century, there seemed to be no limit to the world-wide demand for cheap consumable goods.

The market was capable of apparently endless expansion for several reasons. The population of the western world was increasing with extraordinary rapidity in the nineteenth century, from causes which are not entirely explicable, though probably the most important cause was simply the lowering of the rate of infant mortality through improved medical knowledge and practice. Wealth also was increasing, and many hundreds of thousands of families came into the market for increased purchases of necessities, and for comforts and luxuries, as quickly as old necessities or new comforts could be manufactured cheaply. Improved and cheapened transportation, in addition, obviously helped to widen the market as much as cheap production. With the appearance of railways and steamships the manufactured goods of England spread out over the whole world; for England was first in the field of industrial development, and scarcely began to feel the competition of other countries until towards the end of the nineteenth century.

One consequence was that money came rolling in. England prospered as never before. The flag followed trade to protect British interests, and the overseas empire grew as commerce expanded. Optimistic confidence rose high. After long ages of snail-like growth, the human race was finally entering into an era of magnificent progress and plenty, with God's own Englishmen directing everything and bringing the blessings of civilization to all the world. The temper engendered is well illustrated by the conclusion of a speech on foreign policy made by Viscount Palmerston in 1850. Palmerston was threatened with censure because he had taken the high-handed course of sending warships to Greece to enforce his demand for a settlement of the claims of a Jewish money-lender who, as a native of Gibraltar, was a British subject. He ended a triumphant defense of his "firm" policy with these resounding words:

As the Roman, in days of old, held himself free from indignity when he could say *Civis Romanus sum,* so also a British subject, in whatever land he may be, shall feel confident that the watchful eye and the strong arm of England will protect him against injustice and wrong.

The Plight of Laborers

Although the ascendancy of the machine was lifting England to a proud height as the wealthiest, strongest, and largest empire the world has ever known, it was at the same time producing misery. The hardship, already mentioned, which was brought about by the shift from home industry to the urban factory was not a small thing. But it was small in comparison with the appalling working conditions, in factories and in mines, to which laborers were subjected, and in comparison with the wretched living quarters in which the slaves of the new mechanized industry were housed. As long as the market for manufactured goods was expanding in the nineteenth century, labor-saving machinery did not really save labor; on the contrary, it increased the demand for laborers. The individual whose work was taken away from him by the machine was, it is true, faced with ruin and starvation, and repeatedly such persons took the desperate step of trying to smash up the hated machine. Presently, however, the increased demand for the machine-made article necessitated more and more machines, with the result that there was again employment, not only for the

man whose former work had vanished, but also for his wife, and his children. The far more serious trouble was that work in factory and in mine, when it was found, was so ill-paid, so confining, so ruinous to health and character, and often so monotonous and mechanical, that industrial workers were reduced to a state of misery impossible to describe in general terms. It seems unbelievable that human beings could have existed under such conditions as, for instance, young boys in coal mines were subjected to. It seems unbelievable that any men, for any purpose, could have subjected their fellow creatures—not only men and women, but very young children—to such degradation and suffering as was for many years almost universal.

Yet it should not be supposed that all employers were inhuman monsters. Undoubtedly some were. But in general the machine played the tune to which owner and employee alike danced. It owed its ascendancy entirely to the cheapness of its products, and all costs, including the cost of labor, had to be kept as low as possible. Moreover, there was a theory abroad which seemed to fit the facts and which was supposed to be, not a theory, but a branch of science. Economists regarded it as self-evident that the nature of business enterprise was to buy in the cheapest market and sell in the dearest. Labor was the laborer's commodity, that which he had to sell. In theory, the workingman was free to fix a price for his services and to try to get it. In theory, he was free to refuse his services unless he did receive his price—or, for that matter, to refuse his services at any price. The principle of *laissez-faire* applied to everybody—laborers as well as employers. Every man was to be free to do as he pleased with his own person and property, no one being as well qualified to look after a man's interests as that man himself. And it was assumed that the pursuit of a man's true interests could not bring him into conflict with his fellows, but would prove to be in the common interest of social well-being. This body of theory was espoused by the Utilitarians—the forward-looking social reformers of the early nineteenth century—and it logically led them to oppose all combinations, or unions, of workingmen.

Thus actually the laborer was helpless, and had to accept whatever was offered, or become a pauper, or starve. Employers found labor plentiful at wages far below the level of decent subsistence, with workdays of twelve hours or even more, in factories ill-lighted, unventilated, unsafe, and only less unsanitary than the vile holes in which families of workers were huddled together for sleep, feeding, and the brutal debauchery in which they sought forgetfulness of their troubles. Hence any employer who offered higher wages or better conditions than his competitors simply invited bankruptcy, as was demonstrated in a few cases. The truth is that the machine imposed conditions which no individual could resist, and offered rewards which no society could resist.

Machine-Made Men and Morals

We find, then, at the beginning of the Victorian era, a situation in which commercial shrewdness had become the essential quality needed for rising in the world. We find also a situation which was sharply dividing the nation in half, or which was, as Carlyle and Disraeli said, creating two nations, the rich and the poor. The former had no past, and the latter seemed to have no future. Both "nations" were bred from the slums of the manufacturing towns, and within the space of a few years were beginning to dominate English life. The familiar division of English society into lower, middle, and upper classes was beginning to be meaningless, and the long traditions of those classes began to seem shadowy and unsubstantial. The names lingered on as they do still, but the new realities could not be brought into any fruitful adjustment with the old names and the old standards. We must constantly remember, in the study of any aspect of human history, that generalizations are approximate, not absolute; but with this caution it can be said that the pressure of English and Christian culture had been in the direction of individualism, that encouragement had been given to the development of responsible personalities, with a keen sense of social duty, yet with strongly marked individual qualities, and above all with an ultimate standard of self-respect. The development of the science of mechanics with its applications in the field of industrial machinery spread a blight over the seedbeds of individualism.

The new poor were significantly called "hands." They could scarcely be called people. We have seen that they were in fact worse off than if they had really been slaves, because nobody was, even in theory, responsible for them. They were, as fully as the machines they tended, instruments of production; and to them the individualistic doctrine of *laissez-faire* was a cruel mockery. They were a brutalized herd, rapidly multiplying, utterly helpless and unimportant individually, and socially important only as a necessary evil for the sake of cheap goods. The only possibilities of improving their lot lay in their own collective action and in regulatory state action. Both possibilities involved the direct repudiation of individualism. Machinery, in other words, inexorably demanded from a large and increasing part of the population, and also from the state, a movement in opposition to what had been conceived as the goal of Western civilization.

The new rich were, as they apparently always are everywhere, without taste. But they were tasteless in ways almost too appalling to be credited, save by those who have themselves seen Victorian domestic architecture, Victorian furniture and bric-à-brac, Victorian wallpaper, pictures and picture frames, carpets, and window draperies. The fall from the exquisitely proportioned domestic architecture of the eighteenth century, the furniture of Chippendale and Hepplewhite, and the interior decoration of the brothers Adam is nothing less than frightful, and argues a kind of blindness and insensitiveness which tells its own story. One cannot learn everything, but one can learn much about people from their homes.

The Victorians were not at all indifferent to their surroundings. They really felt proud of their hideous flowered carpets, heavy plush draperies, haircloth sofas and chairs, moderator lamps, overmantels, ornate metal bedsteads, marble-topped tables, and antimacassars. These, and houses to hold them which were the worst monstrosities in the whole history of architecture, were what they toiled for, and spent large sums on. They felt, quite rightly, that a new age had dawned. What particularly distinguished it was mechanical inventiveness, which brought forth improvements in all household objects of use. The ugly Victorian fireplace really did throw out far more heat than its eighteenth-century predecessor. The moderator lamp really did give more and better light than its predecessors. These and other improvements encouraged the notion that the newest things made by the latest processes were the best. Those who had them were progressive in an age of progress, and had something to boast of.

The evidence, however, is overwhelming that industrial designers, in dressing up the household objects of the age, believed the public to want at all costs something which would show impressively, something which would instantly mark the owner as a man of substance surrounded by the luxury appropriate to his unrivaled prosperity. Tawdry ornamentation, glaring colors, sheer size and weight, and all manner of useless gewgaws were just right for such a purpose, provided the buyer was entirely without cultural background. Inventors were full of ideas for making things which seemed more expensive than they were—imitation stonework, imitation silver plate, imitation this, that, and the other. Yet at the same time there was much solid and honestly made stuff which was just as tasteless as the cheap imitation. The typical Victorian, one concludes, wanted something more than vulgar display if he could afford it, but was in any case determined to have the appearance.

And the truth is that the new rich had really no connection with the past and no standards except those afforded by a narrow religion. They did inherit the Wesleyan-Evangelical tradition of the preceding generation; and, what is more, many of them were sincerely as well as solemnly and ostentatiously religious. But the other-worldliness of the great religious revival of the eighteenth century, which connects it in spirit with the romantic literary movement, was radically inconsistent with conditions which now made commercial shrewdness the prime requisite for success in life, and which were causing civilization to be identified with bathtubs, spring cushions for chairs, patented ventilators, and all kinds of improved gadgets. Therefore religion was revised.

The revision was not, of course, carried out deliberately or consciously, but it was thorough. The man of business discovered, as had some earlier English Puritans, that certain virtues, heartily endorsed by Christian teachers, were profitable. He was much more likely to succeed in the battle of commerce if he took life seriously and kept himself unspotted by the sinful pleasures of the worldly or profligate. Abstinence from all forms of gambling, cautious moderation in drink if not teetotalism, and perfect fidelity to a lawful wife were restrictions which had their immediate reward. They really promoted health and wealth. So also the conviction that life was not an opportunity for enjoyment, but a solemn responsibility imposed by the Lord of Righteousness, encouraged whole-souled application to work. The cause of commerce was the cause of progressive civilization. Hence its earnest prosecution was a duty, in the performance of which a man could piously feel that he was justifying his existence. The proof lay in the fact that the more zealously he promoted national prosperity and the dissemination of the fruits of civilization, the more prosperous he himself was.

It is not easy to describe this or any form of self-delusion without the suspicion of irony. The fallacy is always obvious to everyone except those who are themselves guilty of it. The famous Victorian compromise under discussion is an example of what has been called "making the best of both worlds," or of hypocrisy. Yet historically it is a fact that many adopted this compromise in the sincere conviction that religion and their kind of worldliness were not inconsistent. They engaged in religious observances with zeal. The Victorian Sunday, indeed, has become notorious because of the rigor with which every form of secular activity was prohibited. It is true enough that the man of business who was almost fiercely religious all day on Sunday spent his energies, throughout the rest of the week, in the service of Mammon. But he was not guilty of the kind of inconsistency of which he has often been accused. For out of the compromise he had effected there had come a new standard of conduct which he followed equally on Sundays and weekdays. His aim was simply to be irreproachable at all times in the eyes of his associates.

So phrased, this aim looks its best; but even at its best it was negative, and was, besides, impossible of achievement. To try to be irreproachable was to have to ask continually, "What would Mrs. Grundy say?" That formidable censor, who had been invented by Thomas Morton (1764?–1838) in a comedy entitled *Speed the Plow* (1798), became the unseen tyrant of the Victorian era. In practice, her rule required men to reduce themselves to a norm of conventionality which banished individual taste and thought and action, and made them colorless units in a society standardized by fear. In practice, Mrs. Grundy required submission to scandalmongers, gossips, malicious detractors, or, in general, to the scum of the earth. She made most biological facts unmentionable, and, as an acute critic has said, thus inevitably made hypocrisy the one vice allowed to be respectable.

Respectability

Nothing is wholly new, and doubtless there have been hypocrites in all ages. Nevertheless, the Victorian era is the only one known to history in which the subhuman standard of "respectability" made a nation of hypocrites. And it did so then, because the new alignment of society, dictated by the machine, raised into dominance a set of men without culture, without traditions, without anything except money to account for their elevation. The machine finally disrupted a social order which had been decaying since the sixteenth century. But the new rich could not justify their position openly and solely by the fact that they had managed to get hold of money. The maintenance of order was vitally necessary, and for this purpose some better sanc-

tion for the ascendancy of the manufacturer and the trader had to be found, and found quickly. Furthermore, the sanction needed had to be one which any Tom, Dick, or Harry could achieve, or appear to achieve; and also one which the masses, no matter how ignorant or foolish, could understand. "Respectability" filled the bill. Any man who had the kind of shrewdness or cunning requisite for gathering in money was henceforth to appear deserving, because of his superior lack of independence, individuality, and distinction.

And even though an appreciable number of Victorian manufacturers and merchants were, as Ruskin declared his father to have been, men of sound integrity both in their private lives and in their business dealings, still, they could not redeem competitive trade from an element of ambiguity which was bound up with its very nature and was certain to spread corruption throughout the new ruling class. Men might say that in the development of manufacture and trade they were serving the cause of the national welfare, and that in conquering new markets abroad they were spreading the benefits of civilization amongst benighted peoples, and they might in both cases speak truly; yet at the same time they were reaping enormous profits from these services, and were growing rich by grinding the faces of the poor, reducing them, as we have seen, to a lower-than-animal level of existence, and by taking advantage of the elementary needs of the multitude. Often enough they created needs in order to profit from them. The art of salesmanship, someone has said, consists, not in selling a man what he wants, but in convincing him that he should want what you have to sell.

We can, therefore, see a natural affinity between the man of business and the sham standard of respectability. We can see, too, that in so far as men appeared to satisfy this sanction, they lost individuality and became standardized products of the industrial system. Thus the machine dehumanized both its slaves and their masters. And the lowering of man to the level of mechanical contrivances, and the spread of materialistic views, against which romantic writers had rebelled, continued with increased force. The triumph of man over nature, represented by mechanical invention, ministered to human pride and convenience alike, but the real triumph was won by materialism. The meaning of "civilization" had begun in the eighteenth century to be altered, and the new meaning was now taken for granted. Civilization was no longer thought of as the fruit of self-discipline, self-development, personal maturity, and hard-won wisdom. Not this kind of triumph over nature was now wanted, but the transformation of the material environment. In short, the march of civilization was to be measured by the march of industry. The whole change seems to be summed up in two sentences from the prospectus of the Rochdale Pioneers:

> The objects of this Society are the moral and intellectual advancement of its members. It provides them with groceries, butcher's meat, drapery goods, clothes and clogs.

The definition of "Victorianism" cannot be so neatly compressed into a few words, though essentially the word signifies the outlook and moral standard of the newly risen industrial class. Hence it has been identified particularly with respectability and hypocrisy, with abject conventionality, with prudery, and with materialistic worldliness. It might be called the spirit of pretense trying to sanctify itself by pious sentiment. But whatever else it was, it was a triumph of mechanics over man, of means over ends, of the herd over individuality, of vulgarity over taste, and of fear over honesty—all in the name of magnificent progress towards a democratic millennium.

Macaulay and Carlyle

Warning has been given in an earlier chapter that historical periods cannot be delimited with precision, and that, though they correspond to real changes, they represent no more than convenient approximations. We have already seen that Mrs. Grundy, who is inseparable from Victorianism and appears to be expressly designed for that era, actually started on her vile career in 1798. So also, Dr. Thomas Bowdler's *Family Shakespeare*, in which "those words and expressions were omitted which could not with propriety be read aloud in a family," and which is as characteristic of the era as Mrs. Grundy, was published in 1818. Other examples of Victorianism before 1837 could be given, and all would serve to emphasize the fact that Victoria lent her name and sanction to a point of view which she did nothing to create.

Nevertheless, 1837 is a significant dividing line between two literary eras. By that time the great romantic writers, and some who inspired them or led the way to their achievements, were all dead except Wordsworth, and all of Wordsworth's best work was done. Keats, Shelley, and Byron had died in the early 1820's, and also Mrs. Ann Radcliffe. Blake died in 1827, Hazlitt in 1830, Scott in 1832, Coleridge and Lamb in 1834, and Godwin in 1835. By 1837, too, a whole new generation of writers had appeared before the public. Macaulay had begun writing his brilliant essays for the *Edinburgh Review* as early as 1825. Carlyle had published his translations of German tales, his essay on Burns, and *Sartor Resartus*. Tennyson and his brother Charles had published their *Poems by Two Brothers* in 1827, and Tennyson had published additional poems in 1830 and 1832. Browning had published *Pauline* and *Paracelsus*. Cardinal Newman had published his *Arians of the Fourth Century* in 1833 and, in the same year, the first of the celebrated *Tracts for the Times*. Dickens also had begun publishing his *Sketches by Boz* in 1835. Furthermore, Sir Charles Lyell's *Principles of Geology* had appeared in 1830–1833, and Charles Darwin's *Narrative of the Surveying Voyages of H. M. S. Adventure and Beagle* in 1832–1836.

In 1837 Dickens published the *Pickwick Papers* and began publishing *Oliver Twist* in *Bentley's Miscellany,* where Thackeray's *The Professor* also appeared in this year. In the same year Thackeray's *Yellowplush Papers* were appearing in *Fraser's Magazine.* Browning's *Strafford* was published in 1837, and Carlyle's *French Revolution;* as were, in addition, the first volume of Newman's *Parochial Sermons,* Ruskin's "Poetry of Architecture," and Macaulay's essay on Bacon.

Clearly, with these names and books or essays, a new literary age, rich in variety and interest and brilliant in performance, has dawned. The age itself, we have been learning, was two-faced; and we could not have a clearer illustration of this cardinal fact than that afforded by the contrast between the two essayists and historians, Macaulay and Carlyle.

Macaulay, in his essay on Bacon, which is a tissue of falsification and flippancy, did at least contrive to reveal himself and some part of his own age when he wrote: "An acre in Middlesex is better than a principality in Utopia." He was an amiable materialist without knowing it, just as he was, until late in life, a pure Benthamite without knowing it, and as he was a child of the eighteenth-century Enlightenment without knowing it. He thought all religious opinions to be inherently unreasonable, but was Victorian in the dexterity with which he veiled this side of his worldliness. He was certainly not a conscious hypocrite. He was courageous, generous, high-principled, and personally independent. He was, too, incessantly and prodigiously active; and indeed his activity enables us to understand both his fame and his limitations. We hear of his impressiveness as a speaker in Parliament; and every reader of his essays or of his *History* has admired his ability to organize and dispose the material at his command. That material was usually, though not always, vast, because he was a voracious reader and apparently remembered everything he read. *But he never stopped to think.* Both Thomas Hobbes in the seventeenth century and Hazlitt in the nineteenth immodestly explained that if they had read more they might have thought less, and Macaulay bears them out. For all we can see, a great part of his reading was as idle and unprofitable as were the days of Addison's Clarinda or those of Dr. Johnson's Ned Drugget at his country lodgings.

Macaulay appears to have been born with his mind already made up; and it was made up to accept the beneficence of Whig liberalism and of industrial "progress." The inventions, the improvements, the growing trade, the hideous new cities of the midlands —none of these phenomena of his age suggested any question or doubt to him. He accepted them all unhesitatingly, enthusiastically, almost reverently, as evidences of the growth of civilization and the march of progress, led appropriately by Englishmen. One of the striking features of his *History* is the way in which he turns the England of 1685 into an occasion for singing the glories of his own time. In his justly famous third chapter, after pointing out that Manchester, Leeds, Sheffield, and Birmingham are rarely or never mentioned in historical accounts of the seventeenth century, he says that "within the memory of persons still living," they have "grown to a greatness which this generation contemplates with wonder and pride, not unaccompanied by awe and anxiety." He then shows how they have grown, materially, with every sign of pride and no sign of anxiety; and he continues:

These four chief seats of our great manufactures deserve especial mention. It would be tedious to enumerate all the populous and opulent hives of industry which, a hundred and fifty years ago, were hamlets without parish churches, or desolate moors, inhabited only by grouse and wild deer. Nor has the change been less signal in those outlets by which the products of the English looms and forges are poured forth over the whole world. At present Liverpool contains more than three hundred thousand inhabitants. The shipping registered at her port amounts to between four and five hundred thousand tons. Into her custom house has been repeatedly paid in one year a sum more than thrice as great as the whole income of the English crown in 1685. The receipts of her post office, even since the great reduction of the duty, exceed the sum which the postage of the whole kingdom yielded to the Duke of York. Her endless docks, quays, and warehouses are among the wonders of the world. . . . In the days of Charles II, Liverpool was described as a rising town which had recently made great advances, and which maintained a profitable intercourse with Ireland and with the sugar colonies. The customs had multiplied eightfold within sixteen years, and amounted to what was then considered as the immense sum of £15,000 annually. But the population can hardly have exceeded four thousand; the shipping was about fourteen hundred tons, less than the tonnage of a single modern

Indiaman of the first class; and the whole number of seamen belonging to the port cannot be estimated at more than two hundred. Such has been the progress of those towns where wealth is created and accumulated.

It is scarcely necessary, after quoting him, to underline the fact that Macaulay was dazzled by material development and physical growth, and considered that his statistical evidence was a complete proof of magnificent human progress. But we should realize how far he went. He insisted that machine-made goods were not only cheaper than handmade, but better in quality. He pointed out that the number of paupers, in relation to the total population, had decreased, between 1685 and his own day, from something near one-fourth to one-tenth or, in a good business year, less. He asserted, very truly, that there had been a large growth of humanitarian sentiment, and improvements in medicine. He was convinced that every class, from the lowest to the highest, had benefited enormously from the changes of the last century and a half, even though in justice he did admit "that the progress of civilization had diminished the physical comforts of a portion of the poorest class." In this admission he was not referring, however, as might be supposed, to little girls in factories or young boys in mines, or to any industrial employees. He shall again speak for himself:

It has already been mentioned that, before the Revolution [of 1688–1689], many thousands of square miles, now enclosed and cultivated, were marsh, forest, and heath. Of this wild land much was, by law, common, and much of what was not common by law was worth so little that the proprietors suffered it to be common in fact. In such a tract, squatters and trespassers were tolerated to an extent now unknown. The peasant who dwelt there could, at little or no charge, procure occasionally some palatable addition to his hard fare, and provide himself with fuel for the winter. He kept a flock of geese on what is now an orchard rich with apple blossoms. He snared wild fowl on the fen which has long since been drained and divided into corn fields and turnip fields. He cut turf among the furze bushes on the moor which is now a meadow bright with clover and renowned for butter and cheese. The progress

of agriculture and the increase of population necessarily deprived him of these privileges. But against this disadvantage a long list of advantages is to be set off.

We must remember that Macaulay was right in everything he said. He did not look through rose-colored spectacles. He based himself on fact; and the facts which impressed him were truly impressive. There *was* growth, there *was* improvement, there *was* a sudden and tremendous progress to contemplate and record. But there were two sides to the picture, and to one side he was blind. His fellow-historian, Carlyle, observing him once upon a time, thought to himself, indulgently, "Well, anyone can see that you are an honest, good sort of fellow, made out of oatmeal." But on another occasion Carlyle more harshly referred to his "essentially irremediable, commonplace nature"; and he was right. Macaulay said what could be said for his age, and spoke eloquently for all the irremediable, commonplace, solid men who were making England the home of a triumphant, vulgar materialism, never dreaming that they were accumulating gold (and heavy plush draperies, artificial flowers under glass, and the like) at the sacrifice of manhood, their own no less than that of their toiling slaves.

Carlyle, with fierce indignation, beheld the sacrifice; and poured out torrentially his contemptuous hatred of the new tyranny of the machine. He hated the impersonality of the machine, and perceived that his contemporaries were deluding themselves in fancying that it was an efficient servant. He saw, earlier than most men, that it was really a master, leading all England down to its own subhuman level of standardization. He was not content to look only at the material results of growing industry; he looked also at the processes, and was filled with pitying rage. When one sees the little children laboring for sixteen hours a day in Lancashire factories, he said, "inhaling at every breath a quantity of *fuzz,* falling asleep over their wheels, and roused again by the lash of thongs over their backs, or by the slap of 'billy-rollers' over their little crowns, one pauses with a kind of amazed horror, to ask if this be Earth, the place of Hope, or

Tophet, where hope never comes!" Whatever the gains, they were purchased too dearly at such a rate. And yet, he realized, the sheer inhumanity of machine production was not the worst evil which the system brought in. The utterly pernicious thing was the corruption of individualism, fostered by the economists of the day and enforced by the machine. This corrupted individualism bade men believe that they served the common welfare by buying in the cheapest market and selling in the dearest, and that their social obligations were met by cash payments, on their own terms, for such services as they could profitably use. No endurable human society could subsist, he was sure, on a basis of self-interest and cant, or on a system which was accumulating poverty in masses as fast as it was accumulating wealth.

Had Carlyle been the one-sided extremist that Macaulay was, and that he has sometimes been called, he might have written to more immediate practical purpose. He had extraordinary literary gifts, deep true feeling, piercing insight, and integrity. But just because he saw further and more truly than others, and was passionately determined to utter all that was in his heart without compromise or hindrance, he was unable to ally himself with any practical cause or existing movement or party, and was even unable in the end to offer his disciples a clear-cut coherent program. The English nation was destroying itself through unleashed selfishness and the confusion of means with ends—*that* he could see, and denounce; and he could see also that men must be brought back somehow to first principles. Like Coleridge (whom, however, he derided), he went to the German romantic philosophers for wisdom. He became convinced that reality is spiritual, and that man is a spirit with a hunger for reality which no material things can satisfy. He believed that the soul of man could be awakened to this truth and must respond to it, but that the darkness of misapprehension, unbelief, and despair in which men's souls were imprisoned could only be pierced by the living example, sympathy, and leadership of heroic characters capable of inspiring implicit confidence because they were worthy

of it. Thus he believed that every man has within him a spark of divinity, small and flickering in the vast majority, and overlaid with all manner of falsity, but burning brightly in a few men of uncorruptible honesty. The latter were the natural aristocracy of the race, born to lead and rule the weak majority, who under true leadership could rise to great heights of self-sacrificing devotion and work, but who without such leadership could only destroy themselves and society and civilization. The nexus of society was right social relations, which could not be founded on cash, but only on personal responsibility—the responsibility of the governor to the governed, and of the governed to the just governor. These considerations led Carlyle to look for guidance to medieval feudalism; and he ended, as Scott had, by idealizing the Middle Ages as a time when a truly organic society had been created.

The trouble, from the practical point of view, with Carlyle's gospel of social reform was that there was nothing in his own age to which it could be attached. He was emancipated from Christianity, and so was barred from giving his spiritual teaching a form which might have made it practically usable. He preached Consecration to Duty as a divine behest, and saw clearly that men can respond only to personal calls upon their energies; but he left shrouded in clouds of vagueness the vital question how the sense of duty is to be awakened and practically directed if Divinity is after all impersonal, inexpressible, intangible, or, to be candid, inane. Similarly Carlyle was emancipated from the cause of democracy and from every existing group or interest, because he saw fatal misdirection or falsehood wherever he turned. And his attempts to demonstrate his belief in the capacity of merely human powers for heroic leadership, from the history of the race, inspired interest but no confidence.

This is worth dwelling on, because the more one ponders Carlyle's search for wisdom, the more clearly one sees in him the prototype of later Victorian thought. The literature of the age, whatever form it took, became increasingly a protest, or a series of differing protests, against "Victorianism," and a series of attempts to find some way of stamping it out, as if it were a disease. And Carlyle is typical of those who were to follow him, who could see and denounce the disease, who could see some kind of cure, but who could not follow old methods and could not find new ones, or, at any rate, could not find successful new ones. To this generalization, however, there is an important exception.

Newman and the Oxford Movement

It should be clear from what has been said of Carlyle that his animating impulse was identical with the conviction or faith which was central in the Romantic Movement of the preceding generation. He based himself on the flaming heart, on the passions, on a dynamic, creative quality within man which could only be called divine, and which was a source of knowledge superior to the reasoning intellect. Thus he was, like his romantic predecessors, a ruthless opponent of "the mechanical philosophy" and a supporter of the authority of intuition; and he fought, like them, for the rights of personality against the threatened submergence of the individual in materialism, or in impersonal collectivisms which would make the individual the mere agent or instrument of "capital" or of "labor." He was, as has been said above, far more effective in denunciation than in construction, just because he was closely in touch with, and impressed by, the very "march of rational knowledge," or supposed knowledge, against which he opposed himself. He granted concessions to it, wanted to make terms with it, and came out with a "natural supernaturalism" which seemed to be neither natural nor supernatural, but just dyspepsia.

Of course, Carlyle's dyspepsia, about which he complained loudly and long, was stomachal; but what is here meant is that his attempt to accept both the conclusions of reason and the suggestions of intuition gave him, and others after him, a task beyond human powers of intellectual digestion, or synthesis. But there was another way open to those who were really convinced, as Carlyle was, of the spiritual nature and destiny of man, and a way which was bound sooner or

later to be taken, after the failures of romantic individualism and of Evangelical individualism to stem the rising flood of materialism and of impersonal forces. And it shows how far England had got away from historical, corporate Christianity, in the eighteenth century, that it was left for a small group of Oxford men in the 1830's to try to bring the Church of England into play as the divinely commissioned custodian of spiritual authority and guardian of the rights of personality.

Newman regarded John Keble as the leader of the attempt, but the world has given John Henry Newman himself the position of being the real leading force in the Oxford Movement, as it is called. It is impossible in this place to stop to characterize him, beyond saying that he was, in Carlyle's sense of the word, a man of truly heroic proportions, clear-headed, sincere, bold, uncompromising, and persistent; with a genius for persuasive utterance which made an indelible impression on all who heard him. He recognized that Southey, Wordsworth, Coleridge, and Walter Scott had done much to prepare the way for a revival of Christian faith; but what he and his companions set out to do was to remind their generation that the spiritual faith of Christians was founded, not on the subjective experience of individuals as the generations succeeded one another, but on an historical revelation. Both that revelation and the means of redemption had been entrusted to the Church Apostolic and Catholic, which was therefore a divine institution. Salvation from the body of this world could be attained, not by individual affirmation, but only through the Body and Blood of Christ within the Holy Catholic Church. The clergy of the Church of England, therefore, were not officers of the secular State, nor primarily moral teachers, but priests holding a supernatural office, without whose mediation the bridge between earth and Heaven could not be crossed.

The campaign of the Oxford men was conducted partly through a series of *Tracts for the Times*. Ninety tracts were published between 1833 and 1841, of which Newman wrote twenty-four, including the first and the last. There was nothing new in the doctrine advanced. Newman was simply trying to revive that conception of the Church as the English portion of the Church Universal which had been entertained by seventeenth-century Anglican divines; and to insist that spiritual life was not a purely individual matter, but properly a corporate act, for which there was a divinely instituted historical sanction. He was alarmed, indeed revolted, by the tendencies of the age which Carlyle flamingly denounced. The distinction between the two men here is a distinction without a difference. Newman saw chiefly the growing secularism of the times, and the trend towards trust in the reasoning intellect. Carlyle saw the growing inhumanity fostered by industrialism and endorsed by economic "science." Both saw, from different angles, the same ugly thing, and resolved to do what they could to combat it. Newman, furthermore, saw, amongst churchmen, exactly what he would also have seen had he looked beyond Oxford, had he looked as far as Carlyle, for example. He saw men getting nowhere by trying moderately to hold the balance between extremes in each of which they could see something desirable—trying, in other words, to make the best of both worlds.

Newman boldly took the course of combating entrenched worldliness by cleaving to entrenched other-worldliness. The Church of England had gone so far in the direction of Protestant individualism that his effort of revival was misunderstood and caused violent alarm. Finally, after the publication of *Tract Ninety,* he was severely condemned and in effect, as he felt, driven out of the Church. His effort had apparently failed. He himself, after painful deliberation, entered the Roman Catholic Church, and for some years practically disappeared from public view.

Time was to show, however, that both his Anglican career and his conversion to Rome were to have an abiding influence. His conception of the Anglican Church as a portion of the Church Catholic and Apostolic not only lived on, but became gradually stronger and finally dominant within that body. And after the publication of his *Apologia pro Vita Sua* in 1864, in which he vindicated

himself from an ugly accusation made by Charles Kingsley, and at the same time wrote one of the truly great books of the nineteenth century, he became again famous, and did much to bring Englishmen into friendly relations with the Roman Catholic Church. Thus throughout his career, in a world grown too large and too desperate for the isolated individual, he showed the way to a corporate spiritual life. He exerted, however, no direct influence on Victorian literature until towards the very end of the century. Not he, but Carlyle, is typical of the successive waves of reaction against Victorianism which were to give us, not all, but a great part of the literature of this era.

Tennyson and Browning

Beginning, as we have, with Macaulay, Carlyle, and Newman, we see that one change which has come with the 1830's is the predominance of prose. The compelling poetic impulse which fired the romantic writers and made their age a great period in the annals of English poetry was not destined to last. The Victorian age gave us much significant and beautiful poetry, it is true, but no poet of the first rank. Tennyson and Browning were the poetical giants of the era, and with the passage of time they have shrunk. They have by no means disappeared from view; and indeed some nine or ten poets of the last three-quarters of the nineteenth century have won for themselves permanent places, very probably, in English literature. Nevertheless, the age of Victoria was predominantly an age of prose. It is said nowadays that Tennyson's reputation, in particular, is suffering from a temporary reaction, and will rise again. But in so far as this reaction is one simply against Victorianism, it is noticeable that the reputations of Dickens, Thackeray, and Trollope all stand high today and perfectly secure. Trollope's novels went through a period of depreciation and neglect immediately after his death; readers, however, have long since returned to him and are standing by him devotedly. In so far, moreover, as there has been a reaction against Victorian "earnestness," it is noticeable that it has not diminished the reputations of Carlyle, Newman, Ruskin, or Arnold, all of them as earnest as Tennyson.

No, the fact is, account for it howsoever we may, that the greatest men of letters of the age were not poets, or not primarily poets. And though explanations of the fact do really explain it in part, we should remember that the most exhaustive analysis would still be confined to the prevailing conditions, the difficulties in the way, and would of necessity leave unanswered the question why the man to meet those conditions, to surmount those difficulties, did not appear. The age called aloud for satire, but after Byron the century had no effective satirist in verse. There were many attempts at poetic drama, but, as was said in the last chapter, none was fully successful; and most were downright failures. It is easy to see why there was no epic of industrial progress or of mercantile triumph. The people responsible for these developments could cause no poetic breast to swell with pride or joy. The breast of a Macaulay might swell, but his pride arose from material evidences of wealth and well-being, and he was only remotely aware of the human activities and human beings productive of nineteenth-century blessings. In addition, though Macaulay in his own personal qualities was a paragon, in his ability to see below the surface of personality he was an infant. Victorian life, Victorian people, and Victorian achievements, in short, were all unpoetical, and could give satisfaction only to unpoetical observers.

Tennyson was a born poet and mystic on the defensive. As a craftsman he was superb. In boyhood he had idolized Byron, but Keats was the romantic poet to whom he was closest in talent and from whom he learned most. He also learned much from a source closed to Keats, the Latin poetry of the Augustan age, especially Virgil's. The man who could write *The Lotos-Eaters* and *Ulysses* was an extraordinarily gifted virtuoso. In the case of many poets we cannot tell how far their art was deliberate and conscious. Tennyson's was entirely conscious, and under criticism he disciplined himself to subordinate the mere flow of beautifully modulated sound to his predetermined purpose. He never conquered entirely his tendency to write too much, to elaborate details, or even to drag them in, for their own sake, and to lose sense in pleasing sound and richly decorated language; but he did recognize his temptations, and fought against them. And no one in his century achieved finer lyrics in the elegiac vein which falls just short of the utmost intensity, or more perfect expressions of such moods as those of the two poems mentioned above.

But Tennyson wanted to be something more than a consummate and disinterested artist; he wanted to turn his art to a high purpose and rise to a place in the great tradition of poetry. He wanted, like Spenser, like Milton, like Wordsworth, to be a great teacher and a source of wisdom. He was encouraged into this kind of seriousness, no doubt, by the friends of his young manhood at Cambridge, but it is safe to suppose that he was very ready to be encouraged. And he and his friends were right to this extent: If he was to be more than an exquisite minor poet, if he was to write not simply for the pleasure of other poets as a pure artist, but for the world at large, he must concern himself with the world's interests and problems, and have something important, and wise, to say.

The trouble was that he did not have the inner confidence, the piercing insight, the prophetic inspiration, or whatever it takes to fill the role. His instinct really was to turn away from the world and build himself a Palace of Art, after Keats's example. But he knew, just as Keats had learned, that this would not do. Yet, when he dutifully faced the world, he became uncertain. For this one cannot blame him. We have seen that the Victorian world was complex and ambiguous. The world of 1784–1837 was only less so. And it was solely by what appears to be a bold decisiveness in selection and rejection that men like Blake, Wordsworth, Macaulay, and Newman made their way through conflicting evidence to some kind of understanding of life and its issues. But in truth they all, in their several ways, made a stand—for better, for worse—on the basis of what they were. They did select and reject, but we receive the impression that really some power or force acted through them, or, as we say, inspired them. And as a consequence they were thoroughly one thing and not another; and everything that they were appears in what they wrote.

But in Tennyson we encounter something quite different. He was not content to trust himself, for better, for worse. Significantly, he kept part of himself out of his poetry. We can catch glimpses, through the eyes of contemporaries, of a Tennyson we should not have suspected from anything he published. Thus he did not confront the world, in Carlylean fashion, to let the public make what it could out of him. Instead, he sought, after the fashion of Pope, to learn from the world and to adjust himself to the needs of the time. He was sensitive, in other words, to the charge that poets were mere dreamers who fled from reality and left practical men to do the world's hard work. Hence his own extraordinary talent for the expression of moods in lyrical and meditative verse was transformed into a temptation. But he did have confidence in his ability as a craftsman, provided he could adapt that ability to large purposes such as the Victorian public might gratefully appreciate. What was the most advanced opinion concerning religious faith? What seemed to be suggested as a next step in social progress? What was the meaning of industrial development? What attitude towards it ought one to take? What kind of example ought to be placed before the British public in the field of morals? These were not so much Tennyson's questions as questions of the age; and we discover him, as he asks, and conscientiously prepares answers, subduing himself to the experts, trying to re-form himself to meet public expectations, saying what the occasion seems to demand, attempting to absorb the age and distill out its finer essence. Men of science spoke admiringly of his knowledge of their discoveries; naturalists wondered at the exactness of his observation; the earliest advocates of women's rights had scarcely opened their mouths

when, lo, he was with them. He was one of the first to ride on a steam railway, and immediately got this new sign of progress into a poem. And so he continued—Alfred always up and coming, Alfred first on the spot.

He was no less resourceful and original in solving the technical problems of his craft. The most conspicuous was the question how to write a long poem when his talent was for short ones. *In Memoriam* was a brilliant solution, though others later were not completely successful. In general, however, as has been said above, he was a superb craftsman, and he got into difficulties only because he kept trying to exceed his limits.

His own age generously repaid him for his effort to become its spiritual voice. Our difficulty with him today, it has been suggested, would disappear if we could cast aside the pieces he wrote as the Poetical Department of the State, and then become acquainted with him as he really was. But there were not two Tennysons, one real and the other false. There was one Tennyson uncertain of himself, and yet trying, after the manner of every significant poet, to interpret experience. The attempt was very imperfectly successful because there were few points of contact between the springs of poetry within him and the life and thought of the time. Consequently he was at a loss for principles of interpretation and tended to accept the age at its own implicit valuation. Fitfully he rebelled, and then repented of his temerity; with the net result that, though poets may contemplate with admiring wonder his subtle and elaborate craftsmanship, others will look at him regretfully as one who did not fulfill his promise.

When we say that Browning as well as Tennyson has shrunk with the passage of time, we must recall what once was thought of him. Two years after his death a commentary on his poetry, written by a philosopher who attained eminence, was published, and ran through several editions. The philosopher was Sir Henry Jones, and this is how he spoke of Browning:

He is the high priest of our age, standing at the altar for us, and giving utterance to our

needs and aspirations, our fears and faith.
. . . It is because I thus regard Browning as
not merely a poet but a prophet, that I think
I am entitled to seek in him, as in Isaiah or
Aeschylus, a solution, or a help to the solution,
of the problems that press upon us when we reflect upon man, his place in the world and his
destiny.

No one today would dream of approaching
Browning in this spirit. No one today
wants his interpretation of experience any
more than Tennyson's. Tennyson, indeed,
achieved, in the way of interpretation, something more solid and durable than Browning's argumentative "religion," when he
wrote *Ulysses* and *In Memoriam.*

The latter poem pleased the Victorians
because they took it as the picture of a mind
open to all newest knowledge, to all difficulties and disturbing suspicions, and yet
bravely holding the ancient faith, not as a
triumph of faith over mind, but as the triumph of a mind seeing legitimate grounds
for faith even in the processes of free competition and of ruthless struggle which were
the ungodly realities both of the natural
world and of industrial society. These were
the fiery trials of goodness, through which
the race was slowly rising to a higher level.
Humanity had risen from the dust and was
still rising, which proved that there is a soul
of goodness towards which reality aspires,
and which somehow is converting us all into
itself. We can still be sure that immortality in Heaven is our destination; and we
can be the more sure for facing "honest
doubt." To the Victorians this was comforting and reassuring; and it was practical,
too, because it suggested that they had nothing to do except keep on fighting the good
fight, spreading the blessings of civilization,
and believing that Heaven was their destination. To a reader of our time *In Memoriam* conveys very different suggestions.
We see pictured in the poem a lonely and
frightened soul in an alien world, doubting,
clinging to hope, reasserting an old faith
which has no objective earthly support, because there appears to be nothing else possible except blank despair. Practically speaking, *In Memoriam* and *Ulysses* are Tennyson's only poems which look forward. The

rest look back to the romantic world
imagined by Keats, or else look out on the
Victorian world which has now become a
part of history. These two, however, point
onward to Clough and Arnold, and through
them to Hardy and Housman.

We cannot say as much for Browning's
"religion." It was very like the Victorian
notion of what Tennyson was saying in *In
Memoriam,* with the considerable difference
that Browning was hearty, cheerful, confident, and radiantly optimistic. He insisted
firmly that, because nearly all of his poems
were dramatic in character, his own personal
beliefs could not properly be inferred from
them. Nevertheless, every student of his
verse is agreed that he was more objective
in appearance than in reality, and that in
fact, to quote Sir Henry Jones once more,
we never escape

. . . the sense of the presence of the poet's
powerful personality, or of the great convictions
on which his life was based. Browning has, at
bottom, only one way of looking at the world
and one way of treating his objects; one point
of view and one artistic method. Nay, further,
he has one supreme interest, which he pursues
everywhere with a constancy shown by hardly
any other poet.

We will not err, then, in accepting the
famous song from *Pippa Passes* as an expression both of Browning's conviction and
of the buoyancy with which he held it:

> The year's at the spring
> And day's at the morn;
> Morning's at seven;
> The hillside's dew-pearled;
> The lark's on the wing;
> The snail's on the thorn:
> God's in his heaven—
> All's right with the world!

He was at great pains to prove that he did
not reach this cheerful conclusion by shutting his eyes to any difficulties. In the dramatic poem from which this song is quoted,
Pippa, a young Italian factory worker, starts
off early on the morning of her one annual
holiday, New Year's, to stare, as she sings,
at the houses of those she thinks happiest in
the village of Asolo. Inside one of those

houses an adulterous woman and her lover have just murdered the woman's husband; inside another an unscrupulous plot is being laid for the murder of Pippa herself; so different are the realities from her innocent guesses. Yet she, without knowing it, by her songs alters those realities, arousing the better selves of an evil and depraved generation.

Thus Browning does not hide, much less deny, the fact of evil, widely flourishing in the world. Indeed, he emphasizes it, and invites us to contemplate every kind of failure, depravity, viciousness, and even malignity. But from all his instances he draws the same conclusion: this world is the proving ground of virtue. Souls are made and developed by strife. Action is the law of our being, and practically any kind of activity is better than the dull not-being of the sluggard. Activity shows a man conscious of deficiency, and inspired by want or love of *something,* even though he may not have analysed correctly his real need. Without deficiency there would be no spur to effort for betterment. That we endeavor strenuously and fail is of no significance, because striving itself is the important thing. It is important not for its own sake, but as affording opportunity for the growth, through activity, of the spirit of love within us. Love is the spiritual principle animating all things—the soul of man, the earth, the universe. To be absorbed wholly by love of *something* is to fulfill one's nature and achieve perfect felicity. If one is a grammarian, for example, it may suffice to have a consuming desire to settle finally every question about the uses of a Greek particle. The world, therefore, with all its shortcomings, is simply the kind of world required for the manifestation of love. Evil itself is nothing positive or real, but only the condition of love.

Hence, Browning triumphantly concluded, we may well say "All's right with the world." And he went further. Apparently regarding traditional Christianity as a popular mythological equivalent of his own creed, he lent his support to it, though he himself found it incredible. Both English theologians and English disciples of the German philosopher, Georg Wilhelm Friedrich Hegel, were strengthened in their faiths by Browning. The student of English literature is inevitably struck by some articles in his creed which are reminiscent of the "atheist" Shelley, but above all by the fact that Browning reaches exactly the same point that Alexander Pope reached under the guidance of Shaftesbury and other deists, when he declared, in his *Essay on Man,* that "Whatever is, is right." And if Pope's optimism was frivolous and shallow, so was Browning's.

But Browning was thought to be profound, partly because his style was difficult, and partly because he did have a subtle and curious mind, with sufficient dramatic power to enable him to enter penetratingly into the most diverse and unusual characters and to depict them with incomparable verve and concentration. His style is not so difficult for us as it was for his earliest readers. The difficulties mostly arise, not from complexity of thought, but simply from incomplete or crabbed expression. Browning was an accomplished craftsman, able to write almost any kind of verse with brilliancy and ease, but he habitually wrote without much regard for the limitations of readers. Hence he sometimes presented riddles to the public; and intellectual or curiously learned people felt pleased with themselves when they had unraveled them. Not unnaturally, too, after they had worked hard for it, they felt they had got hold of something "choice." In reality, of course, the famous Browning style was a weakness.

The famous Browning gallery of dramatic portraits is something different. It is a triumph. By these studies of character, of personality revealed in crucial action or sketched perfectly in their own words, Browning lives, and deserves to live long. Most of them are not spoiled, many of them are not obviously touched, by the philosophy which inspired or justified them. They can be enjoyed without it, fortunately, and every one of them enlarges or enriches our understanding of human nature. A great part of the enduring strength and interest of English literature, from Chaucer, through Shakespeare, through the eighteenth-century novelists (of whom Jane Austen is properly one), comes from its wealth of living persons delineated with matchless penetration and vigor. Browning is one of the glories of this tradition, and he added to it not only a varied group of sharply drawn and keenly differentiated personalities of unfailing human interest, but also a distinctive method of portraiture, prophetic of the so-called psychological studies of character which later in the century were to give their chief interest to the works of some novelists.

Writing as a Form of Business

Browning himself, indeed, was almost a novelist in verse; and the fact suggests again what has already been said, that the Victorian age was not favorable to poetry, and placed those who would be poets in false positions, or else gave them tasks too difficult for human powers. There is a passage in Thackeray's *Pendennis* which shows how the wind was blowing. When Arthur Pendennis, after some escapades, goes to London and is living in chambers in the Temple with George Warrington, the latter suggests to him one day that he might refill his empty purse by writing. Pen modestly replies that he does not have Warrington's knowledge or powers. But Warrington thinks he has a natural gift, "a little of the real poetical fire." Pen then confesses:

"I *have* often thought I was a poet. I will be one—I think I am one, as you say so, though the world mayn't. Is it—is it the *Ariadne in Naxos* which you liked (I was only eighteen when I wrote it), or the Prize Poem?"

Warrington burst into a roar of laughter. "Why, you young goose," he yelled out—"of all the miserable weak rubbish I ever tried, *Ariadne in Naxos* is the most mawkish and disgusting. The Prize Poem is so pompous and feeble that I'm positively surprised, sir, it didn't get the medal. You don't suppose that you are a serious poet, do you, and are going to cut out Milton and Aeschylus? Are you setting up to be a Pindar, you absurd little tom-tit, and fancy you have the strength and pinion which the Theban eagles bear, sailing with supreme dominion through the azure fields of air? No, my boy, I think you can write a magazine article, and turn out a pretty copy of verses."

Writing was becoming a business. Signs of the change had begun to appear much earlier than the 1840's. Every teacher used to think it necessary to hail the career of Dr. Johnson as that of the first English man of letters who was able to earn his living by literary work without the support of a patron. The Doctor's famous letter to the Earl of Chesterfield, written on the eve of the publication of the *Dictionary,* has been flourished about as a noble declaration of literary independence. Since then, we used to be told, writers have been able, in manly fashion, to stand on their own feet and say what they felt or thought, under no servile compulsion to flatter noble lords or to advance the interest of a party. But this change, like many others, had its dubious side, as was clearly seen by Dr. Johnson's friend Goldsmith. In the fifty-first Letter of *The Citizen of the World,* Goldsmith made the bookseller, or publisher, who visited Lien Chi, say: "Others may pretend to direct the vulgar; but that is not my way; I always let the vulgar direct me."

The reading public was increasing rapidly in size as the eighteenth century drew to a close, and continued to grow as the nineteenth century advanced, until it embraced practically the whole population of such countries as England and the United States. The provision of reading matter for the growing market simultaneously became a business like any other, with possibilities of considerable profit. And those possibilities could most certainly be realized by the publishers who took the position of Goldsmith's bookseller. Hence, in practice, writers exchanged dependence on noble patrons for dependence on such creatures as he, and, through them, for dependence on the taste of the multitude.

The rise of a cheap press with the spread of reading, and the appearance of popular magazines and inexpensive newspapers, had been hopefully regarded by the friends of democracy. With the means now available, the multitude would be eager, it was thought, to fill its head with sound knowledge and to cultivate its taste by familiarity with the best literature. And in fact a few publishers acted on this confident prediction, and a few

...kens was fortunate in the first illustrators of his novels, and their ...ited humorous sketches have become integral parts of the *Pickwick ...ers, Oliver Twist, David Copperfield,* and the rest. The four above ...by Hablot K. Browne (1815–1882), who signed himself "Phiz," and ...one at the right is by George Cruikshank (1792–1878). (Courtesy ...he New York Public Library.) The picture at the upper left, from ...le Dorrit,* shows Little Dorrit, Edward Dorrit, and Flora Finching ...ing the Marshalsea Prison where Mr. Dorrit had been long held for ...t. The picture at the upper right shows Mr. Pickwick in Fleet ...on—where he had gone rather than pay the costs of a lawsuit— ...Sam Weller standing behind his chair. The turnkeys are ...iliarizing themselves with his appearance because at this time ...oners were not given uniforms. In the scene at the left center, Mr. ...kwick discovers Alfred Jingle in the Fleet. This filthy prison was ...lly demolished in the 1840's. The picture at the right center, from ...holas Nickleby,* exhibits the "foul appearance of dirt, disorder, and ...ase" at Dotheboys' Hall, a school conducted by the brutal and ...crupulous Mr. Wackford Squeers. Dickens's picture of Dotheboys' ...l was instrumental in effecting the disappearance of such schools. ...*Oliver Twist* he protested against another form of cruelty to chil-...n. Oliver, as a small orphan, was thrown into a workhouse, where ...was starved and beaten. In the picture at the right he has horrified ...rybody by "atrociously presuming to be hungry" and asking for more gruel.

CAPITAL AND LABOUR.

SUBSTANCE AND SHADOW.

When *Punch* was founded, in 1841, its editors promised to expose the social evils brought about by the Industrial Revolution (see pages 450 and 451). They showed courage and humanity by printing, in 1843, the series of cartoons from which two are here reproduced. (Courtesy of the New York Public Library.) The one above illustrated the following ironical comment: "Though there is much misery in the coal-mines, where the 'laborers are obliged to go on all-fours like dogs,' . . . a great deal of luxury results from it. The public mind has been . . . shocked by very offensive revelations of certain underground operations, carried on by an inferior race of human beings, employed in working the mines, but *Punch's* artist has endeavored to do away with the disagreeable impression, by showing the very refined and elegant result that happily arises from the labors of these inferior creatures." The cartoon at the left was also accompanied by an ironical explanation: "There are many silly dissatisfied people . . . who are continually urging upon Ministers the propriety of considering the wants of the pauper population, under the impression that it is as laudable to feed men as to shelter horses. . . . We conceive that Ministers have adopted the very best means to silence this unwarrantable outcry. They have considerately determined that, as they cannot afford to give hungry nakedness the *substance* which it covets, at least it shall have the *shadow*. The poor ask for bread, and the philanthropy of the State accords—an exhibition."

of those who did prospered. But, in general, literature sought the level of the multitude, instead of the multitude rising to the level of literature; no one for a long time has spoken, without ribald laughter, of the educational value of the newspaper or the cheap magazine or popular fiction. There have been, all along, some exceptions to the rule. We have seen that Walter Scott was an early one. He made commercial writing profitable by supplying a sound article, with no sacrifice of the enjoyment which readers had been deriving from shoddy romances. In this he had nothing to be ashamed of, yet it will be remembered that one reason for the anonymity of the Waverley Novels was the disrepute into which romance-writing had fallen under the direction of the vulgar.

Scott did nothing to change the tendency; and others after him protected themselves by anonymity while they took advantage of commercial demand to produce pot-boilers. George Warrington in Thackeray's novel did this, as Thackeray himself did in the early portion of his career. The pressure of the commercial market was for entertainment, and for fiction as the form of literary entertainment requiring the least effort from readers. But Warrington's advice to Arthur Pendennis shows that another kind of pressure was felt too. Mere poetry began to seem high-falutin—the kind of thing only a wild-eyed, long-haired eccentric, almost certainly deceived concerning his abilities, would waste his time on. The practical thing in verse (Pendennis wrote an excellent illustration of it a few days after his talk with Warrington) was a simple narrative or song flowing with obvious sentiment, with enough pathos to bring up a sympathetic moisture in the reader's eyes. Tennyson's efforts to reach a satisfactory adjustment with this situation drove him into falsity. Browning did not make the effort; though he did not rebel against the mid-Victorian outlook either, and consequently absorbed and expressed the optimism discussed above, with all the idiosyncrasy of a man writing as it were in a vacuum, or for private satisfaction, aided by no guidance or control from an audience.

The Novel after Scott

In the realm of fiction Scott, of course, had imitators, who helped to prove how exceptional he was. George Paine Rainsford James (1801–1860) is said to have written more than one hundred novels and romantic tales, all welcome when they were new, and all deservedly forgotten now. William Harrison Ainsworth (1805–1882) was also a prolific writer of romances, only a shade less ephemeral. But these and other writers of fiction, such as Pierce Egan (1772–1849), Captain Frederick Marryat (1792–1848), Samuel Lover (1797–1868), Charles Lever (1806–1872), Robert Smith Surtees (1803–1864), and Edward Bulwer (Lord Lytton, 1803–1873), serve to show that this form of literature was attaining, if it had not already by 1837 attained, the first place in popular esteem which it has ever since held.

The career of Bulwer Lytton exhibits clearly the development taking place. He began as a poet, and some of his verse was published as early as 1820. But he had a remarkable ability to divine changes in public taste just as they were occurring, and turned to the writing of novels with a strong Byronic flavor a few years later. His first two, *Falkland* (1827) and *Pelham* (1828), were about dandies—the type of dazzling and unscrupulous adventurer who flourished under the Prince Regent (later George IV). Benjamin Disraeli (1804–1881) barely contrived, in *Vivian Grey* (1826–1827), to anticipate him in this type of novel. Lord Lytton then turned, in *Paul Clifford* (1830) and *Eugene Aram* (1832), to tales of noble-hearted criminals, who were so presented as to excite sympathy for vicious deeds. A few years later he produced several historical romances under the inspiration of Walter Scott. Amongst these were *The Last Days of Pompeii* (1834) and *Rienzi, the Last of the Tribunes* (1835). At the end of the 1840's, when romances were growing out of date, he turned to the domestic novel in *The Caxtons* (1849). We need not pursue his long career further. He was in fact, whether consciously or not, a clever time-server who followed the market, in the spirit of Goldsmith's bookseller.

Charles Dickens

The first writer of fiction after Scott who proved able to meet the new conditions just discussed, and to triumph over them, was Dickens. From the point of view of contemporary popularity he was the most successful writer of the nineteenth century; and he can still today give more instant and irresistible pleasure to readers than any other writer of that century. It is easy to find fault with his novels on the score of exuberant expression which tended to become strained and rhetorical, careless construction, theatricalism, muddled thought, distortion of truth, sentimentalism, and perhaps much else. Nevertheless, Dickens's characters are *alive,* as are few others in all literature, and have a simple, yet rich and full humanity which appears in inimitable action and talk, and which has at the same time endeared them to readers and stamped them unforgettably on their minds. These characters were created with delight—Mrs. Sarah Gamp, Mr. Pecksniff, Uriah Heep, Mr. Micawber, Fagin, Bill Sikes and the Artful Dodger, the Cheeryble brothers, Harold Skimpole, Mrs. Jellyby, the Reverend Mr. Chadband, Thomas Gradgrind, Scrooge, Mr. and Mrs. Boffin, the Veneerings, Little Nell, Dick Swiveller, and Sam Weller, not to mention Mr. Pickwick himself or any of the others who gave their names to titles of the novels. Their creator laughed with them, cried with them, felt and acted with them, lived out their parts in his own person. It is not enough to say that he imagined them vividly. He was full of cheerful energy, confidence, humor, and instinctively humane feeling, with an unique power to project his own full-blooded vitality into his creations. He had no qualms, no sense of division within himself, at least in the earlier and most successful half of his career, and hence brought his complete powers into play, with the consequence that his characters and their world became indispensable to the whole reading public, learned and unlearned, cultivated and uncultivated, rich and poor, without distinction of background, class, religion, calling, or taste.

Dickens's world gets further away from us every day. Dickens's characters are, not all of them, but most of them, drawn from the lower middle class or from the ranks of working people or, in a few cases, from the underworld. It would be an exaggeration to say that Dickens transports us to the slums of a hundred years ago, but in general the scenes of his novels are depressing, or would be if we were actually placed in them ourselves, and often they are worse than depressing. The majority of the characters also would be, in real life, far indeed from the company we would choose, and many would be unbearable. We know what the real Mrs. Gamp must have been like, and the real Mr. Pecksniff. They must have been loathsome. How, then, did Dickens recommend these people and their surroundings to his own generation? And why are they still interesting today?

He took them as they were, and did not hide what they were. In fact he often emphasized their essential traits until his characters became classic types, definitive, monumental, immortal. This is one part of the answer to our questions. Dickens's genius enabled him to give his characters broadly representative qualities which lend them a human interest not only independent of time or place, but independent as well of the merely ugly or loathsome or painful elements of personality which, in real life, would often be so prominent as to obscure everything else in them. The unclean, scoundrelly, vile Mrs. Gamp, instead of appearing to be simply the unbearable blot on the face of humanity which her originals were a century ago, is transformed into the essence of grotesque vulgarity, and she and her sayings become the source of endless hearty laughter. Dickens's Mrs. Gamp is perhaps too hilariously amusing to be true. We may say that she never existed. But such criticism is felt to be irrelevant, because she is, in her own right, human, credible, and magnificent. Her creator, in transforming her into the essence of vulgarity, made bearable and indeed delightful by humor, has used hints derived from observation to paint an ideal portrait. Mrs. Gamp, Mr. Pecksniff, Mr. Micawber, and all the rest are humorous visions, just as is Shakespeare's Falstaff

They differ from everyday reality only in being more real, more richly, intensely, and amusingly human than their originals. The secret of Dickens's achievement lies in this— his power of idealization. The world seen through his eyes is transformed by his own inexhaustible heartiness, kindliness, and humor. It is transformed, yet in his masterpieces it is not essentially falsified.

This is why Dickens's characters instantly fixed themselves in the hearts and minds of the whole reading public when they were created, and why they have a perennial life and universal appeal. It matters not how distant and strange the England of a hundred years ago may become. Dickens has seen to it that his world will always be vivid and fresh, and in no need of historical explanation. Nor do we go to Dickens for the sake of history. We go to him for enjoyment of a kind sufficiently rare and hearty that for our own sakes we ought not to miss it; and when we have gone to him, we find our own humanity enlarged and refreshed.

Yet Dickens, aside from his genius, was emphatically a man of his own age, and could not have succeeded as he did had he felt any division between himself and his generation. He was not unconscious of the restrictions imposed on him by his public, but it never occurred to him to rebel against them. He accepted Victorian prudery, for example, quite as artists of other ages have accepted other conventions, and simply worked within it, and found he was not really hampered by it. He cordially agreed with his readers that literature should have a moral purpose; and occasionally he was drawn into falsehood as a consequence, but at any rate he was not in this false to his own convictions. He was, speaking generally, one with his readers; and it was this rather than any deliberate calculation which enabled him to give them what they wanted. At times he seemed to be engaged in commercial calculation; on more than one occasion he altered a book while it was appearing in monthly installments because sales were declining. But, while he was a shrewd man of business, his motive in these cases was not merely commercial. He sincerely felt that if readers were not interested he must be doing a poor job, and that if they were enthusiastic he must be doing well. His temperament was histrionic, and he had the same need of the audience's sympathy that actors on the stage have.

What we must remember, in considering this side of Dickens's nature, is that he might have made an excellent thing out of novel-writing, as a business, without giving the public one-half as much as he did in return for their money. He frankly accepted writing as a business, but brought a glorious gift to it, and put everything he had into his work. He did not, moreover, accept his age uncritically. He hated hypocrisy in all its forms, and religious fanaticism, special privilege, the law's delays, and a good deal else which he attacked satirically in his novels. On the whole, he stood with the reforming radicals of the 1830's and 1840's, and shared their belief in progress and their indifference to the past. He shared also their confused outlook, attacking on grounds of humanity those who permitted social injustice to flourish, but also attacking, as the friend of liberty, those who attempted reform by processes of governmental control. In later years he was influenced by Carlyle, who did nothing to help him out of this dilemma. Critics nowadays say that he got beyond his depth in meddling with economic and political problems, but the truth is that the problems of the age in these fields were beyond everybody's depth. And Dickens at any rate was always on the side of goodness, honor, justice, mercy—those values which, in so far as they can be kept aloft in a hostile world, make the difference between civilized humanity and brutish existence.

It has been impossible in this brief discussion to comment on any of Dickens's novels separately, but they form so important a part of Victorian literature that they should at least be named. They were preceded by two volumes of sketches in which Dickens discovered his powers: *Sketches by Boz* (1835–1836) and *The Posthumous Papers of the Pickwick Club* (1836–1837). The novels follow: *Oliver Twist* (1837–1838); *Nicholas Nickleby* (1838–1839); *Master Humphrey's Clock,* containing *The Old Curiosity Shop* and *Barnaby Rudge* (1840–

1841) ; *Martin Chuzzlewit* (1843–1844) ; *Dombey and Son* (1846–1848) ; *David Cop-perfield* (1849–1850) ; *Bleak House* (1852–1853) ; *Hard Times* (1854) ; *Little Dorrit* (1855–1857) ; *A Tale of Two Cities* (1859) ; *Great Expectations* (1860–1861) ; *Our Mutual Friend* (1864–1865) ; and *The Mystery of Edwin Drood* (1870), left unfinished, with the mystery unsolved, at the time of Dickens's death in 1870. Dickens wrote other books and short sketches, but the only one of these which will be mentioned here is *A Christmas Carol in Prose* (1843).

Thackeray and Trollope

Dickens was not alone in writing novels in the interest of reform. He began earliest, with *Oliver Twist,* but he soon had company. Benjamin Disraeli devoted to the problem of social injustice *Sybil* (1845), the second of the three novels in which he set forth his ideal of a Tory democracy. Mrs. Elizabeth Cleghorn Gaskell, who lived in the industrial city of Manchester, wrote from first-hand observation of the wretchedness of the factory-workers in *Mary Barton* (1848) and in other novels. Charles Kingsley, the Anglican clergyman whose false accusation against Newman occasioned the *Apologia pro Vita Sua,* attacked the evils of sweated labor and other wrongs against the working classes in *Alton Locke* (1850). Charlotte Brontë pictured at length the troubles of industrial workers in *Shirley* (1849). And there were others, all showing that by the middle of the century the English were becoming deeply concerned over the inhumanity of industrial "progress."

From the literary point of view, however, it is significant that Mrs. Gaskell is remembered, not for her novels of reform, but for her delightful idyl of village life, *Cranford* (1853), and for her classic *Life of Charlotte Brontë* (1857). And Charlotte Brontë is remembered, not as a chronicler of evils arising from industrialism, but as the author of *Jane Eyre* (1847), a novel which proved, as did Emily Brontë's *Wuthering Heights* (1847), that romantic passion and rebellion were still not only alive in England, but able to inspire creative art of a high order in a

family of genius living remote from the entrenched centers of Victorianism.

Thackeray, moreover, who was second only to Dickens in contemporary popularity, as he is second only to Dickens in genius and in continuing interest, made no contribution to the literature of reform. In some of his novels he was, like Dickens, a satirist; but the satire of both novelists lives because, like much of the satire of Swift and Addison, it transcends its immediate objects and has perennial and universal human relevance. Dickens and Thackeray are markedly different in ways which promptly strike the eye, and this obscures the fact that they have important resemblances also, and are really complementary to each other. Both were thorough Victorians, and honestly democratic, yet socially snobs, while they ridiculed snobbery in others. Both, furthermore, were nourished by the literature of the eighteenth century. Dickens's early reading was confined to a few books, but included the novels of Smollett, Fielding's *Tom Jones,* Goldsmith's *Vicar of Wakefield,* Steele's *Tatler,* Addison and Steele's *Spectator,* Johnson's *Idler,* Goldsmith's *Citizen of the World,* and *The Arabian Nights;* and these, practically speaking, comprise the literary influences which formed Dickens as a writer. Thackeray's reading was much wider. *Henry Esmond* (1852) proves that he knew and liked everything about the eighteenth century that a Victorian could understand. Yet the writers of that time from whom he learned most—Addison, Fielding, and Goldsmith—are amongst those who also nourished Dickens's mind and imagination. And both novelists carried on in their own time the work of their eighteenth-century predecessors in the humorous, satirical, and yet sympathetic delineation of manners and character, with a large infusion of sentimentalism to mitigate any uneasiness that might be caused by the satire, and with a great deal of moralizing.

Here the resemblances between the two end. They were as different in background, upbringing, and manner as were the fields to which they devoted their work. Dickens was self-made and almost uneducated. He worked his way up to fame from a shoe-blacking factory where he was employed as a boy, and the social scene he depicts is mostly that which he knew at first hand in his boyhood and youth. Thackeray's early life was very like that of Arthur Pendennis, in the novel called *The History of Pendennis* (1848–1850), except that Thackeray came of an Anglo-Indian family in easy circumstances, was born in India, and was sent back to England at the age of six for his education, which included some years at the Charterhouse and at Trinity College, Cambridge. His friends at Cambridge (which he left in 1830 without a degree) included Edward FitzGerald and Tennyson. Like Pendennis, he entered the Temple, ostensibly to study the law, but soon began to turn to account his natural gift for writing in order to fill an empty purse. Henceforth he wrote indefatigably, save for a period in the early 1830's when he settled in Paris with the intention, abandoned after a while, of becoming a painter.

Thackeray's writings are exceedingly large in volume and miscellaneous in character. As a professional man of letters he wrote reviews, parodies, ballads and other verse both humorous and pathetic, art criticism, journalistic correspondence, satirical burlesques, lectures on English writers and sovereigns of the eighteenth century (*The English Humorists,* 1853; and *The Four Georges,* 1860), essays (the most delightful of them are in *The Roundabout Papers,* 1863), Christmas books, tales, and, finally, the great novels on which his enduring fame rests. Two of these, *Pendennis* and *Henry Esmond,* have already been mentioned. The others are: *Vanity Fair* (1847–1848), *The Newcomes* (1853–1855), and *The Virginians* (1857–1859).

In three of the novels, *Vanity Fair, Pendennis,* and *The Newcomes,* Thackeray appears as the kindly yet ironical observer of contemporary society and as a moralist. The society pictured is that of the upper middle class and of the aristocracy, which he knew, inside and out, from his own observation. The other two novels are historical, but owe nothing to the example of Scott. All of the novels, indeed, are deliberately unromantic. *Vanity Fair* was described on its title-page as "a novel without a hero," and the description may fairly be extended to cover the other novels.

Thackeray aimed at realism, and hoped to better mankind by his social studies. But we do not value him today for his "philosophy" or for his moral reflections. As a thinker he was superficial and easy-going, and was unable to resolve the conflict between his sentimentalism and his penetrating insight into the game of life as it was actually being played around him. He saw through and disliked pretense and hypocrisy and selfish materialism, but was a very imperfectly emancipated Victorian, willing to close his eyes to the abyss of London worldliness after a single startled glance, and to enjoy worldly comforts while pacifying his conscience by saying a good word for virtue. His moral outlook can almost be summed up in some such imagined statement as this: "Alas, my dears, we live in a topsy-turvy world, where the wicked flourish at the expense of the virtuous; and, what is more, where the wicked are lively, clever, and interesting, and the virtuous are inactive, dull, and boring. Yet wickedness is ugly, and virtue, of course, is beautiful—never more beautiful than when in distress. Come, let us shed a tear for distressed virtue."

We value Thackeray, not for his invertebrate moral commonplaces, but for his extraordinary penetration and skill in characterization. He created a large group of persons who transcend their Victorian surroundings and loom before us as classic types, to be found in every generation and in every community. Mostly they are types of the "wicked" whom he knew and perfectly understood, and whom he liked while shaking his head disapprovingly at them. And he served, for their delineation, almost as a passive medium. "Once created," he said, "they lead me, and I follow where they direct. I have no idea where it all comes from. I have never seen the people I describe, nor heard the conversations I put down. I am often astonished myself to read it when I have got it on paper." This appears to be literally true; and once or twice Thackeray had the uncanny experience of meeting his creations in real life, faithful to his representation in every particular of appearance, dress, voice, gesture, and character, *after* he had published them to the world in one or another of his books. He could scarcely believe that they had thus stepped out of a novel into real life, but there they were. Thackeray, in other words, worked by a kind of instinct, which we may call a genius for the creation of living character in some of its perennial aspects. And this is the source both of his strength and of his weakness in his novels. The characters live, as few imagined characters ever have lived, and we can know them completely as we cannot really know anyone in daily life; yet at the same time Thackeray is never in control of the progress of his tales, and often fails to grasp the full meaning of the drama wherein they play their parts.

Thackeray, shortly before his death in 1863, was the first editor of *The Cornhill Magazine*. Amongst his contributors was Anthony Trollope (1815–1882), already known as the author of several of the novels in the series which eventually was called "The Chronicles of Barsetshire" (*The Warden,* 1855; *Barchester Towers,* 1857; *Doctor Thorne,* 1858; *Framley Parsonage,* 1861; *The Small House at Allington,* 1864; and *The Last Chronicle of Barset,* 1867). It is not possible here to do more than mention him and the most famous of his many novels, but he must be mentioned because, of all the novelists of the mid-Victorian time, he most faithfully delineated the manners and life of well-to-do people of the middle class. He had an unbounded admiration for Thackeray, and his aims were in general similar to Thackeray's, though his methods were his own and his novels are quite different from Thackeray's in construction, atmosphere, and effect. He was probably as successful as Thackeray in picturing enduring types, and he had some of Jane Austen's ability to make commonplace people interesting. He was a capable workman, and his novels today are not only eminently readable, but ring true, and strongly appeal to those who dislike affectation, pretentiousness, intensity, and bustling reform which, however well meant, too often leaves things, as Trollope thought, worse than they were.

Finally, just as Jane Austen shows us solid people going contentedly about their own business scarcely touched by the fervors of romanticism, so Trollope shows us other members of the same class a half-century later, busy with their own affairs, amusements, gossip, match-making, and the like, and mostly untouched by the great causes and changes which loom large on the page of history. A student does well to remember that while Carlyle was thundering against the age, and social reform was becoming a burning issue, and Charles Kingsley was trying to liberalize Christianity and to Christianize society with his Christian Socialism, Trollope's Bishop Proudie was troubled by a different kind of problem, and was praying God to "save him from being glad that his wife was dead."

The Widening Field of Science: The Doctrine of Evolution

The Victorian compromise which gave the appearance of stability to English society in the middle years of the nineteenth century was only a temporary makeshift. We may be grateful that it did give us Dickens, Thackeray, and Trollope; but it barely sufficed for their purposes, and was already breaking down by the time that Thackeray finished his work. The Victorians were gradually compelled to recognize that the individual's free pursuit of his own interests did not promote the welfare of society, and that no amount of personal respectability could resolve conflicts between self-interest and social interest. They were also compelled, by the end of the 1850's, to face the fact that the traditional religion which had served them as a basis for their moral standards was being shattered by the progress of science.

Even in the palmiest days of triumphant Victorianism, as it has been described earlier in this chapter, there was a strong undercurrent of mingled compassion and fear. Even under the rule of the stern unbending Tories, which had lasted until 1830, humanitarian sentiment had been strong enough to effect a number of social reforms. We think these beginnings timid and insignifi-

The Pall Mall Gazette

Pen hears himself in print

Mr. Joseph entangled

Virtue rewarded; A booth in Vanity Fair

On this page Thackeray appears as the illustrator of his own writings. He drew the two upper pictures to illustrate scenes in *Pendennis*, and the lower ones for *Vanity Fair*. His aptitude for drawing led him to study painting; but, despite study, his work as an illustrator remained amateurish. Charlotte Brontë extravagantly wrote: "Touched with his pencil, paper lives." We cannot echo this, though every reader of the novels must feel a lively interest in Thackeray's own representations of scenes in them. (The sketches are reproduced from first editions of the novels by courtesy of the New York Public Library.)

Above are reproduced pen-and-ink portraits of Leigh Hunt, Wordsworth, William Godwin, Coleridge, Lamb, and Scott. They are taken from a famous series made by Daniel Maclise (who sometimes signed himself "Alfred Croquis") for *Fraser's Magazine* during the period from 1830 to 1836. These portraits were deservedly popular, and were finally published in a book in 1871 (the year after Maclise's death), under the title *The Maclise Portrait Gallery*. Maclise also made, in 1834, a well-known drawing of "The Fraserians," including William Maginn (1793–1842) and Hugh Fraser, the founders, and "Barry Cornwall" (B. W. Procter), Southey, Coleridge, Carlyle, Harrison Ainsworth, and Thackeray. Maclise's artistic career was distinguished, and he enjoyed the intimate friendship of such celebrated writers as Thackeray and Dickens. (Courtesy of the New York Public Library.)

cant as we look back upon them, but we think so partly because historical understanding requires more study and patience than most of us are capable of, and also because it is easy to be wise after the event. The abolition of the slave trade in 1807 was not a small thing; the partial abolition of the pillory as an instrument of punishment, the abolition of flogging as a punishment for women, and the first Factory Act were not small things, even though the Factory Act was largely ineffective. And, in general, the plight of women and children in the factories and the plight of all industrial workers had only to become known in order to excite a wave of compassion and of insistent pressure for amelioration. Compassion was reinforced by fear when the workers showed signs of a rebellious attitude, and it began to be realized that industrialism was creating a very large class, sharply separated from the rest of the population, bound together by common grievances and a common interest, and perhaps able, if organized, to take possession of the state.

This is not the place in which to retell, even briefly, the story of the humanitarian and political reforms which thoroughly, though peacefully, effected a true revolution in England in the course of the nineteenth century and in the early years of the twentieth. It is essential, however, that we should understand the meaning and direction of this revolution. Every social reform was secured only by the sacrifice of some measure of personal liberty and only through the assumption, on the part of Government, of added power. The rights of individuals in their own property were progressively curtailed. Factory owners and tenement owners were compelled to meet standards of safety and of sanitation prescribed by Government. Government was both centralized and strengthened, and its sphere was immensely extended. At the same time the laborer lost independence by binding himself with his fellows in unions, wherein all were pledged to act together. The laborer made this sacrifice eagerly, of course, because he gained by it; nevertheless, he lost something valuable, whether or not he felt the loss. The whole movement was a march from

individualism towards collectivism, against the desires of the reforming Benthamites and their allies, simply because no other course was practicable if reform was to be secured. The nature of industrialism itself dictated the movement, in despite of theory, tradition, and desire.

The drift to collectivism was more or less disguised by a series of electoral reforms which gradually extended the franchise. The first electoral Reform Act, of 1832, chiefly benefited industrial employers. But later acts, of 1867, 1884, 1918, and 1928 extended voting rights to more and more people until, with the Act of 1928, all persons of twenty-one or over, both male and female, subject only to a residential qualification, became electors of parliamentary representatives. Thus by a transparent but indispensable fiction, the whole mass of the people were regarded as exercising absolute rule over themselves. In reality, each extension of the franchise rendered the influence of the individuals who possessed it more negligible, and increased the power of organized groups or parties. Hence the drift to collectivism was in fact reinforced by the progress of electoral reform.

This was the character of the peaceful democratic revolution which followed upon the application of mechanical science to industry. Nothing shows more clearly the fact that it was brought about by the pressure of new conditions and of humanitarian sentiment than this: successive reforms were not the achievement of any one political party. Both conservatives (as the Tories came to be called) and liberals passed reform acts. The liberals, indeed, were hampered in meeting the situation because they largely represented middle-class individualism; whereas the conservatives, under Benjamin Disraeli, effected for a time an alliance between the newly enfranchised industrial workers and the aristocracy against the middle class, and felt no objection to increasing collectivism.

But scientific research of every kind was encouraged by the triumphs of mechanical science, and the sciences of geology and biology in the middle years of the nineteenth century brought on another revolution.

This was a revolution in belief, which undermined Christianity, and in fact, for many persons, destroyed the validity of all religious faith. Sir Charles Lyell (1797–1875) struck the first blow with his *Principles of Geology* (1830–1833). And Robert Chambers (1802–1871), who was not himself a man of science but was an intelligent student of scientific discovery, did a great deal to prepare the public mind for the further course of the revolution in his *Vestiges of the Natural History of Creation* (1844). Lyell set forth evidence to show that the age of the earth must be far greater than would be supposed from the Bible, and also to show that geologic change, instead of being sudden or catastrophic, was gradual and regular, in accordance with discoverable laws. In the *Vestiges,* this lead and others were used as the basis for a picture of the earth and all that it inhabit, painted in terms of progressive development as the method of "creation." Thus the *Vestiges* prepared the way for Charles Darwin (1809–1892), who was seriously interested in it, and for Herbert Spencer (1820–1903), who scoffed at it. The crucial book, which brought the issue unescapably home, was Darwin's *Origin of Species* (1859).

As the issue presented itself to the public, the first question raised concerned the veracity of the account of the creation of the world and of man given in the Book of Genesis in the Old Testament. The traditional Christian view of this earth as the center of the created universe had long since been displaced by the heliocentric theory of Copernicus, and Christian faith had survived the shock. But the renewal of religious belief in the eighteenth century had been in part a revival of Protestant "Bible Christianity," and thousands of Englishmen in 1859 cherished the conviction that the whole Bible was the direct word of God, and therefore literally true throughout. These men and women had cried down the *Vestiges* of Chambers as an atheistical and blasphemous book because it impugned the Biblical story of the creation.

Now, however, Darwin in *The Origin of Species* went much further, and presented a wealth of indisputable evidence to show that animal species are not fixed, and that all known varieties of animal life are the product of a slow development from simpler forms, very few in number, and perhaps ultimately from a single form. Darwin showed also that new species are still continuing to appear, from the operation of natural causes. In short, he presented a picture which agreed with and supplemented that already suggested by the evidence from geology—a picture of the earth and of all the life upon its surface as a gradual evolution, or development, from a simple undifferentiated beginning, proceeding in accordance with natural laws, which adequately account for everything, without any necessity for postulating acts of special creation.

Darwin and Genesis could not be reconciled. Those who accepted Darwin's evidence as conclusive had to set down the Mosaic story of the creation as a fable. This in turn destroyed the notion that the Bible was inerrant, and enforced the view which Coleridge had advanced, that the Bible must be regarded as on the same plane with any other historical document. But, in addition, Darwin placed man amongst the animals, and in so doing seemed to destroy not only the hope of immortality but all of the values and moral standards derived from Christianity which hitherto had largely controlled men's thought about life, even when their acts were worldly.

It would be difficult to exaggerate the effect of the doctrine of evolution. As has been sketchily indicated above, it did not come before the world without preparation. Tennyson was in possession of substantial elements of the doctrine when he was writing *In Memoriam.* Darwin was not the only biologist engaged in gathering evidence. A younger contemporary, Alfred Russel Wallace (1823–1913), was reaching the same conclusions when *The Origin of Species* appeared. German scholars for some years had been critically examining the Bible as an historical document like any other, and had accumulated evidence to show that it was not infallible. Altogether there is reason to say that the theory of evolution and the conclusions it suggested were familiar to many educated men, and seemed to be necessary consequences of the progress of knowledge, by the time that *The Origin of Species* appeared. Nonetheless, the book, because it appeared to convert speculation that was in the air into science, caused a profound shock. A bitter and long-drawn-out controversy followed, in which the champions of orthodox religious belief did everything they could to discredit evolution. Darwin did not fight for his theory, but had a determined, skillful, and eloquent supporter in Thomas Henry Huxley (1825–1895), who engaged not only in popular exposition of the doctrine, but also in much destructive criticism of the Bible and of Christianity, and in attempts to formulate a new view of life based on science.

Disunion and Nonsense

The outcome of the controversy over evolution, we can see nowadays, was really at no time in doubt. Darwin's theory of the process contained difficulties which still remain problems not entirely solved. But the conception of evolution itself was supported by so much evidence, and almost at once proved so convenient a means of explaining many earthly phenomena, that it took firm possession of the modern mind. Christian apologists in the end had to accept it and revise their beliefs accordingly, or else suffer banishment from serious consideration. Because they did not promptly see this, but took a hostile position they could not maintain, they themselves helped to encourage a general belief amongst enlightened men that Christianity was finally exploded and that a substitute was the necessity of the hour.

The attitude and outlook which we have called Victorianism did not, of course, break asunder instantly under the impact of Darwinian evolution. Victorian respectability, prudery, and ugliness continued their course. The compromise through which men hoped to make the best of both worlds continued to appeal to many who did not realize that one world—the other-world of Christian faith—seemed to be relegated by the advances of science to the realm of fable. Yet from about 1860 a significant change did begin to take place. The old viewpoint did not disappear, to be replaced by a new, but the unity of outlook and purpose which had been the strength of Victorianism could no longer be maintained.

Henceforth an increasing number of challenging voices made themselves heard; and anyone who believed he knew the meaning of life, and how men should act, was sure of an audience. The consequence was division—no new thing in modern history, but now again increasing under new conditions. Groups with divergent beliefs and standards multiplied, cutting the nation into segments which communicated with one another only to a limited extent, and often only to exhibit misunderstanding and enmity. No English writer, in prose or verse, has spoken to the whole nation in the later nineteenth century or in the twentieth as Dickens and Thackeray did before 1860. Victorian earnestness persisted for some years despite increasing division, but it could not, and did not, hold out indefinitely before the spectacle of a dozen different prophets expounding a dozen conflicting "truths." And as early as 1865 at least one reader reacted to Ruskin's *Sesame and Lilies* in a manner which seems prophetic of the 1890's. Lady Rose Fane wrote to a friend: "I think the denunciations of *everything* in the Carlyle style are very amusing."

As a matter of fact the Victorians, early and late, welcomed amusement with enthusiasm, as a relief from their seriousness, and were occasionally amused even earlier than 1865 by overwrought or strained earnestness. In their unromantic way they liked humorous satire, burlesque or parody, and light verse as early as the 1830's. The greater part of Thackeray's early work falls into these categories, and Dickens's early popularity arose chiefly from his humor. Earnestness increased as disunion and conflict appeared, and at the same time humor turned into sheer nonsense. The masters of nonsense were the painter, Edward Lear (1812–1888), and the mathematician, Charles Lutwidge Dodgson (1832–1898), known to all the world as "Lewis Carroll." Lear had written limericks in the 1840's for the amusement of the grandchildren of the Earl of Derby; but his fame as a writer of nonsense verse which delighted grown people as well as children was a later growth, following the appearance of his *Nonsense Songs and Stories* and his *More Nonsense Songs* in 1871 and 1872. "Lewis Carroll's" *Alice in Wonderland* was published in 1865, and *Through the Looking Glass* followed in 1871.

Another master of nonsense, which in this case concealed a modicum of satire, was Sir William Schwenk Gilbert (1836–1911), who wrote during the sixties the poems which appeared in 1869 as the *Bab Ballads* (more of them were published in 1873). His lasting fame was won in following years by the series of comic operas for which perfect music was composed by Sir Arthur Sullivan (1842–1900). The best of them are: *Trial by Jury* (1875), *H. M. S. Pinafore* (1878), *The Pirates of Penzance* (1879), *Patience* (1881), *Iolanthe* (1882), *The Mikado* (1885), *Ruddigore* (1887), *The Yeomen of the Guard* (1888), and *The Gondoliers* (1889).

Belief in Progress

Nonsense was a relief from perplexity, not a solution. We must now glance at some solutions which were proposed. It is scarcely possible to make any general statement concerning the combined effect of scientific discovery and of historical criticism of the Bible. Some people were depressed and alarmed, others rejoiced, and still others soberly addressed themselves to the task of re-orientation. Those who rejoiced were not a united band. Some did so because they welcomed the personal freedom promised in the threatened destruction of Victorian standards. Others, however, were the heirs of eighteenth-century optimistic rationalism, and saw in the continuing advance of knowledge fresh evidence of the progress of humanity towards perfection.

The principal exponent of eighteenth-century notions of perfectibility, as transformed under the influence of the doctrine of evolution, was Herbert Spencer (1820–1903). In an early book entitled *Social Statics* (1851) he had pictured mankind as crying out, amidst disappointment and failure, "Give us a guide." He had been trained as an engineer, but had come to feel that he was pre-eminently qualified to serve mankind as a guide. And in this same book he announced that progress was not an accident, but a necessity. "The ultimate development of the ideal man is logically certain," he declared, "as certain as any conclusion in which we place the most implicit faith; for instance, that all men will die." Hence when *The Origin of Species* appeared eight years later, Spencer was ready for it, and especially ready for the note of optimism on which Darwin concluded the book. Darwin described evolution as a process of "natural selection" through which the "unfit" (those not satisfactorily adapted to their environment) perished and the "fittest" survived and propagated their kind, and he ended by saying: "As natural selection works solely by and for the good of each being, all corporeal and mental environments will tend to progress towards perfection."

Spencer leaped over difficulties, using, and perhaps seeing, only that which appeared to support what he already thought, and spent the remainder of his life in the construction, in many volumes, of his "Synthetic Philosophy," the keynote of which was the alleged "law" of nature whereby man, *of necessity,* progressed towards perfection. The volumes of the "Synthetic Philosophy" were never very widely read in England, but Spencer attained a formidable reputation as the expositor of a new interpretation of life supposed to be based on science. He therefore stands at the head of the modern believers in "progress." And his optimistic view of man as by nature a progressive animal became the leading article in the creed of a growing number in the later nineteenth century who found in humanitarianism a new religion.

The goal of this religion was not another world, to be shared by all elect spirits, but our own earth, ultimately to be transformed into a happy dwelling-place for some perfected future generation. The position of the intervening generations was that of workers in the vineyard. They were to find their satisfaction in the consciousness of work which was to bear glorious fruit for their children's children, or, more generally, in the consciousness that they were promoting social welfare. Their immortality was to be found in the reverent gratitude with which their memories would be cherished by the inheritors of better living conditions and better natures in the remote future, and also in the racial continuity of the "life-force" of which they were the temporary custodians and transmitters. It need scarcely be added that this substitute for traditional Christianity was often vaguely conceived and had many variations. Nevertheless, it became, towards the close of the nineteenth century, a strong force in both life and literature.

Matthew Arnold

The more immediate effect, however, of the unsettlement, if not destruction, of traditional belief, as we see it in the literature of the eighteen-sixties, seventies, and eighties, was not one of relief and optimistic exultation. There is no evidence that Matthew Arnold was seriously disturbed by any of the implications of the doctrine of evolution. It might or might not be true that man was descended from some arboreal ape-like creature, but the truth, whatever it was, did not strike him as of the first importance. It did not alter what man had become—a moral being with spiritual aspirations and a noble human history. He saw in history, religion, and art (more particularly in literature) the evidence of man's success in establishing life on a human level which answered to his abiding nature and distinctive capacities, with brutality always threatening the achievement, yet somehow kept down.

The loss of Christian faith in his own day seemed to him a calamity because he regarded Christianity as a "translation" into temporal and historical terms of eternal truths which could not be allowed to perish. Men had grounded their faith in a book, which was now coming to be understood as a fallible human record, written in terms of the credulities, the ignorance, of the times when the book was made. They had made claims for that book which it was impossible that any book should sustain. Discovering this, they were now in danger of throwing away both the book and the truth which it im-

perfectly expressed. Indeed, a generation was growing up ignorant of history and indifferent to it, and was being asked to contemplate with pride the new railways, the new steamships, all the new conveniences of life, and the freedom of Englishmen to say whatever they pleased, as if such things were the real achievements of civilization. Arnold saw these things for what they were. He labeled them all "machinery." By this he meant that they were means, not ends, and that judgment concerning them must depend on what they were used for. Liberty itself was to be valued in terms of its use. He saw the approach of a barbaric anarchy in which people were growing wild like weeds. He saw that into the hands of these raw and ignorant people were being placed instruments of incalculable power, not only all of the fruits of applied science in which his century was uniquely productive, but the control of the state itself.

Accordingly, Arnold felt that the state must assume both the position of positive moral leadership and the responsibility for education which formerly the church had held. The kind of education he wanted was liberal or humanistic in character. For his purposes a very little science would go a long way, because he desiderated primarily intimate contact between oncoming generations in their formative years and the great men of the past who have most clearly seen the highest reaches and the innermost recesses of human nature and have most vividly and beautifully expressed what they have seen. He wanted to open the eyes of youth to what man has been and can be, to the enduring values of life as discerned and illustrated by the genius of the race, and thus to form cultivated persons, capable themselves of seeing life steadily and of seeing it whole. The aim, in a word, was culture, to be got by maintaining continuity between the past and the present.

But Arnold did not think of the past after the manner of the undiscriminating antiquarian, who values whatever is old because it is old. He rather valued that which is itself timeless, though clothed in the garments of former ages. Hence he conceived the unceasing exercise of the informed critical spirit to be a vital part of civilized activity. And the true human use of liberty he took to be the practice of criticism.

Arnold himself has weathered the passage of time more successfully than any of his contemporaries. Others were more brilliant in various ways, but he saw more clearly than any of them the real problems of the age of democracy. The question was, and still is, whether or not democracy is compatible with civilization. In his poetry he illustrated what modernity has done to limit the creative spirit. He tried to write objectively in a way to satisfy his own critical standards, and found that he could only, with much labor, produce polished academic show-pieces. He could succeed no better with romantic fantasy. But when he was thus forced back into himself, he wrote a series of meditative poems which speak with the accents of reality, and classically express the moods of a spiritual being condemned to live in an age which mistakes bustling activity for achievement, gadgets for progress, distraction for happiness, and materialism for wisdom. He could not, however, rest satisfied with a passive role, and he discovered an outlet for his full powers when he turned to the criticism for which he was unusually qualified and which he rightly felt the age most needed.

The Novel in the Sixties, Seventies, and Eighties

The novel has continued to be the dominant form of imaginative literature, as was said above, from the time of Dickens's early triumphs to our own day. It has been, and still is, read with enjoyment by vast numbers of people who cannot read any other form of literature with interest. Its place in popular favor has been challenged by certain dramatists of recent times and by a couple of poets; but these writers, successful though they have been, have not dislodged the novel. As the public, however, has become more and more divided into groups with differing background, training, social experience, and outlook, the field of the popular novelist has been narrowed, individuality of expression or treatment has been discouraged, and fine discrimination, profundity in characterization,

and depth of insight have practically been forbidden. It early became evident also that a multitude of readers with elementary desires, little education, and no taste could be perfectly satisfied with mediocre work. The commercially successful novel, as a consequence, has tended to become a standardized product, like other articles manufactured for mass distribution; and it is almost a surprise that no one has yet invented a machine able to write it.

Hence from the sixties on, the average novel composed for the populace has had no place in literature. Yet it has had an effect on literature. It looks like literature, and is continually being mistaken for the real thing, sometimes for six months, or a year, or even longer. This has promoted confusion, and has helped to obscure the real thing when it has appeared. Certain other effects are more important. Because of the profits arising from success, writers of talent have been tempted into the field of the novel who would not voluntarily, or naturally, have taken to this form of art. Men with messages also— prophets, evangelists, and critics—have used the novel in order to reach a larger public than they could have reached through any other form of writing; and in this way the novel has become, in some of its developments, comparable to the soap-box from which humbler preachers and reformers have delivered their burning words in Hyde Park. Finally, born novelists of high artistic ability have been driven, by their contempt for the commercial article, into writing simply for their own satisfaction or for that of fellow-craftsmen, disregarding the stupid public or even feeling positive hostility to it; and this has contributed to divorce art not only from the public, but from life.

George Eliot

The unfortunate developments discussed above have continued to the present day, with some fantastic results, but their beginnings date from the sixties. In fact they are perceptible in the first novelist of power who appeared above the literary horizon after Trollope. Mary Ann Evans (1819–1880), who used the pseudonym "George Eliot," was a learned woman of extremely serious interests who, had she been born a man or had she been born in a later generation, would in all probability have become a scholar, or perhaps a moral philosopher. As it was, after translating a German life of Christ and another German theological work, and after writing critical articles for *The Westminster Review,* she turned to fiction, when in her late thirties, for the sake of money. It seemed clear from her first attempts (*Scenes of Clerical Life,* 1858) that she had a genius for it, and she won great fame from *Adam Bede* (1859), *The Mill on the Floss* (1860), and *Silas Marner* (1861). Enthusiastic readers have compared her with Thackeray to his disadvantage, but they have been forced to limit the comparison to her early novels and tales, just mentioned. For in her later novels George Eliot became a source of weariness and finally of boredom. And today, whatever critics may say in her honor, she is no longer read.

Moreover, we can easily see why, even though it may be agreed that present-day readers miss something genuine and fine in neglecting her. She was a deeply religious person, like Arnold; and like him she felt compelled to give up traditional Christian faith. There were many others in the same difficult situation; for example, Arnold's friend, Arthur Hugh Clough (1819–1861), who wrote poetry of some lasting interest, and the critic, and first editor of *The Dictionary of National Biography,* Leslie Stephen (1832–1904). Stephen had actually become a priest of the Church of England when he discovered that he had lost belief, and he then wrote in a notebook (at the beginning of 1865): "I now believe in nothing, to put it shortly; but I do not the less believe in morality, *etc., etc.* I mean to live and die like a gentleman if possible." None of these four reacted in exactly the same way to loss of belief, and they subsequently traveled divergent roads, but the other three could have made substantially Stephen's affirmation.

George Eliot set to work with much earnestness to try to build up new and independent foundations, chiefly psychological, for a morality learned in the Church, and

still cherished, though cut loose from its anchorage. This was a quite special purpose with which to burden the novel. The burden is least noticeable in her earliest books. But as time passed it grew heavier and heavier. Furthermore, it has long been clear that the task she undertook was hopeless, and that no "independent" morality can be identical with Christian morality.

In so far as George Eliot failed to give the world books of enduring vitality, despite all her genius, her sympathy and imaginative insight, it was not because she was concerned with morality. Dickens was concerned with morality, as was Thackeray, as was Shakespeare, as is any artist who deals with the stuff of human nature. But the great enduring artists in drama, in epic, in the novel, have been able to *assume* a standard of moral judgment accepted by them in common with their public, and have not used their stories as means for the fashioning, defining, or argumentative support of new moral positions. It was, of course, through no fault of theirs that George Eliot and her contemporaries and successors came at a time of unsettlement and perplexity, when the public was growing more and more divided, and when experimental attempts at some new adjustment or synthesis were inevitable. These conditions, nevertheless, made it equally inevitable that most of the literature of this period should have the limitations of transitional work.

George Meredith

We see evidences of the unsettlement and perplexities of the times in both the novels and the poems of George Meredith (1828–1909). He had extraordinary abilities. His novels sparkle with wit, which often rises to the plane of wisdom, and demonstrates the penetrating quality of his insight. He was not only brilliant but profound in characterization. Probably no reader of *The Egoist* (1879) has left it without feeling that he has been in the presence of genius. Yet every reader also feels that Meredith's reach exceeded his grasp, and that this— Browning to the contrary notwithstanding— is a fatal disadvantage, at least in a writer. He gave up Christianity more easily than

George Eliot, and clearly saw that this entailed not only a new outlook on life but also a new and different morality. Since man was now seen to be a product of natural forces, he deified Nature, and addressed the earth as our great Mother, and sought to show that all is well with us when we allow Nature to have free play, but that we come to grief when we disregard Nature or pit ourselves against her.

He himself came to grief, however, when he tried to be buoyantly natural. His mind was incisive, ironical, disillusioned, and detached. He stood aloof from common humanity in conscious superiority. Rightly or wrongly, he felt himself to be the poet of a new faith, and he turned to novels as a second best because he needed money. But in prose no less than in verse his relentlessly analytical mind drove him into dark corners which, his readers are tempted to suspect, were as dark to Meredith as they are to them. The effect, at any rate, is one of constant strain to track down meanings which are very elusive. Not unnaturally, the public, during the greater part of Meredith's life, failed to go to the bookstores and the circulating libraries in large numbers when he published a new novel. But small sales did not cause him to attempt to conciliate readers. Rather they drove him to write more and more for his own satisfaction, in implied contempt of popular judgment. In the end he won, like Browning, a considerable reputation as a writer, appreciation of whom was itself a sign of artistic and intellectual distinction.

Meredith deserved a better fate. What is said of him here is intended simply to show that even a man of his genius, cast loose on the sea of life and compelled to become his own guide, had too great a handicap for complete success. He seemed always to be reaching for a lucidity he could not achieve, because his professed creed was at odds with his own nature. Not only was the public becoming divided; the divided self was beginning to appear.

Samuel Butler

One of Meredith's contemporaries had perhaps a better fate than he deserved. This was Samuel Butler (1835–1902). His best-

known book, *The Way of All Flesh,* was not published until 1903, but he should be mentioned here because he belongs to the same generation as the other writers now under discussion, and because his emancipation from Christianity had the effect of a pleasurable release from intolerable bondage. Moreover, he wrote a great deal during the seventies, including a very characteristic satire entitled *Erewhon* (1872; the title is "Nowhere" spelled backwards, and the book is in the tradition of St. Thomas More's *Utopia*), and at that time began *The Way of All Flesh,* though it was not completed until much later. He was congenitally irreverent, skeptical, and self-confident. Mockery of whatever the world believed or esteemed was his delight, and he gaily attacked scholars, men of science, moralists, churches, tradition—everything. He was clever, and made palpable hits, but he had a method which lessens the admiration one might tend to feel for him as a fearless enemy of hypocrisy and delusion. His practice was systematically to turn everything upside down, and then to develop the inverted sentiment, thought, or theory in essay or treatise if he saw in it a possibility of shocking the public and if he felt he could make out a case for it. For example, he took Pope's line, "An honest man's the noblest work of God," and transformed it into "An honest God's the noblest work of man." This expressed his belief that men have created their gods by use of imagination, and in so doing have created idealized images of themselves.

He had only a fraction of the abilities of such a writer as Meredith, but he reached at one bound, with an undivided self, the iconoclastic, subversive attitude and wittily shocking style which was to become the fashion in the next generation, and which is still regarded in some quarters as of the essence of the modern emancipated spirit. Hence a few of his books, especially the two mentioned above, are still extremely interesting and still much read.

Thomas Hardy

The truest and finest artist of this period was Thomas Hardy (1840–1928), who also perceived more clearly than any of his slightly older contemporaries the real drift and meaning of the knowledge recently gained concerning the earth's past and concerning the natural history of man. There was only one word for it. That word was Disillusion. If the new knowledge and all its plain implications were to be accepted, man was stripped bare of every ground for optimistic faith, of every comforting hope, of every aspiration which for many centuries had given meaning and worth to earthly life. Life was transformed into a riddle whose solution was impossible, and there was but too much reason to fear that in fact the riddle was meaningless. Human reason itself now appeared to be only a power we have of making plausible excuses for believing what we instinctively want to believe and doing what we are instinctively compelled to do— a power, in other words, of self-justification, or of giving a good appearance to a bad business.

To such a desolating revelation there were only two possible reactions. One, by a species of accident, was classically expressed for the modern English-speaking world by Edward FitzGerald in his paraphrase of the *Rubáiyát* of Omar Khayyám (first published, oddly enough, in the same year as *The Origin of Species,* 1859). The counsels of Omar were those of despair "rationalized." Sink yourself, he advised, in forgetfulness, in the pleasant oblivion of instinctive enjoyments, breathing the odor of the rose, cooling your parched throat with draughts of wine; and cease from bothering your head over silly questions about yesterday and tomorrow:

> Ah, take the cash, and let the credit go,
> Nor heed the rumble of a distant drum.

The other possible reaction was to face despair steadily, with calm resignation, without cringing, without bitterness, but with no pretense that reality was one whit nearer "the heart's desire" than all human experience has shown it to be. This was Hardy's way, and in a half-dozen of his novels and in much of his poetry he transmuted his somber vision of life into the forms of enduring art. The world has agreed that he showed his powers much more fully and effectively in his novels

than in his verse. Indeed, in his power to depict the beauty of the Dorsetshire settings of his novels, and to connect those settings intimately and pervasively with the characters and fortunes of his actors, he not only achieved unity of atmosphere but proved himself to be one of the supreme imaginative artists of modern times. Finally, in comparison with his perfect integrity, the well-meant but futile "rationalizations" of his contemporaries and of some of his successors seem like the whistling of boys in the dark to keep their courage up.

John Ruskin

The first volume of Ruskin's *Modern Painters* appeared in 1843. The work had been undertaken as a defense and eulogy of the art of J. M. W. Turner (1775–1851). Ruskin felt that Turner was a supreme master; yet this master had been attacked by the critics of the day ever since about 1835 or 1836, when he had begun painting in the manner for which he is now famous, and which was prophetic of the impressionists. The charge against Turner was that his landscapes were not true to nature. Ruskin set out not only to refute the charge, but to correct what he came to regard as an appalling state of ignorance in England concerning the nature of art, its place in life, and the conditions under which art could be expected to flourish.

Thus Ruskin's first major work brought him into contact with an aspect of Victorianism which we today, thanks partly to Ruskin himself, find particularly depressing and discreditable. In the early part of this chapter the sheer ugliness of the Victorian home and its furnishings was discussed, and some explanation was attempted. Ruskin became a critic of the age as a consequence of his gradually deepening and widening conviction that art and life are inseparable. He found that Turner was not understood because the public had separated the two. The prevalent notion was that art was decoration, hence a luxury; and possession of a work of art, accordingly, was a sign that one could afford luxuries. A man would build a home and furnish it for comfort, and then add "art" here and there to the extent that he could, or wished to show that he could. A public building, too, would be designed for practical use, and then embellished for "grandeur" or ostentation. This viewpoint, in conjunction with other factors mentioned early in this chapter, produced the most hideous buildings and house-furnishings in the history of the western world, and paintings which were, to say the best, imitative, conventional, and lifeless. Grass and foliage, for example, were painted in shades of brown, because the greens used by the "old masters" had, under action of time and varnish, turned to brown.

Ruskin's studies and meditation brought him to the conviction that art is great only as it succeeds in revealing aspects of God, and can be expected only from a man who is good, sincere, and happy—who is, in other words, in a right relation to God, and able, through the spark of divinity he has kept alive in himself, to perceive the Divinity shining out of God's earth and God's creatures. The artist must, of course, have an artist's keen eye, and be master of brush or chisel; but no amount of technical ability and training can suffice without the nobility and integrity which enable the artist to see "the beauty of holiness" in concrete earthly forms. The mere imitation of natural objects is contemptible. The artist must see *through* the object and give *that* vision form. Hence, great art is an imaginative activity which, however, demands conventions because the great work of art is a symbolic expression of the divine principle of life abstracted from natural objects.

From the elaboration of these canons Ruskin was led to see that great art could not be expected from the England of the mid-nineteenth century because the kind of life fostered by industrialism was wholly adverse to the appearance of true artists and of a public able to appreciate them if they did appear. Witness Turner, and witness the failure of his own efforts in Turner's behalf! For, despite his eloquence and the beauty of his poetic style, he did not reach a large public, and was admired not for his conclusions, but for his skill as a "word painter" and "fine writer." Thus he was led, after

1860, under the guidance of Carlyle, to castigate the age for its Mammon-worship and to try to pulverize the political economists who, he thought, were encouraging the notion that the pursuit of wealth was the prime purpose of life. He vehemently assailed the materialism of the age, its social injustice, and its subjection of the workman to the conditions of profit-making. And, like Carlyle, he looked back to the Middle Ages as a time when conditions had been good. He praised Gothic architecture as the noble expression of sincere faith, produced by men who took pride in their work, and who worked, not for gain, but for the sake of giving appropriate, and hence beautiful, expression to their vision of divinity. Likewise he praised the medieval organization of society; for he was never democratic, but approved an hierarchical order in which every man should have his appointed place and work, for the good of the whole. Though not many paid any serious heed to his specific suggestions concerning social reform, it was during his later years of Carlylean denunciation that he finally gained great fame and an enormous public. Wider and wider agreement with his condemnation of industrial society was felt, and he came to be regarded with reverent awe as an arbiter of taste; but sober people dismissed him as a fantastic dreamer in his constructive plans for a better social order. It is a remarkable fact, however, that what he really proposed was a paternalistic government, with a large measure of state-capitalism, government-made work for the unemployed, old-age pensions, universal education, vocational guidance and training, fixed minimum wages in all fields of employment, and a good deal else which has a prophetic appearance.

Rossetti and the Pre-Raphaelite Brotherhood

In the late 1840's a group of young painters and poets formed the Pre-Raphaelite Brotherhood, in order to give concerted expression to their belief that English art could only be raised from sterile conventionalism to renewed life by a return to the naïve simplicity of medieval painters of the age before Raphael. They were not influenced by Ruskin, but their belief was close enough to his to arouse his sympathy; and he came to their support when they were attacked. Their leader was Dante Gabriel Rossetti, who succeeded better as a poet than as a painter, and illustrated their principles as fully in his verse as in his paintings. In fact, Rossetti had the qualities of a painter and the abilities of a poet. He sought in his ballads to tell a story for the story's sake, concerning himself not at all with the interpretation of events, but solely with the artistic effect of simplicity, dramatic conflict, and emotion. It was as if he were working on a picture which was to be drawn in with a few strong lines and then given sensuous warmth by the free use of rich colors. Again, in his sonnets he used the symbolic language of mysticism to express the passion of love, and not, as his medieval exemplars had done, the language of love as a symbol of mystical adoration.

W. B. Yeats has said that Rossetti did not care whether the earth moved around the sun or the sun moved around the earth. There was a great deal else that Rossetti did not care about. He did not so much revolt from the conventions and standards of the Victorians as simply turn his back on them, to step into the sensuous, romantic other-world of Keats. The Victorians could revel in ugliness and in all their earnest employments, and go their own way. Their works were no concern of his. In a world where everything seemed to be questionable if not already questioned, he felt free to devote himself wholly to beauty for beauty's own sake, that being the one thing entirely real to him.

Swinburne and William Morris

As we have noticed before, extremes provoke extremes; and Rossetti's implicit criticism of Victorianism was taken up by others and carried still further. Swinburne presently claimed the liberty to pursue beauty for beauty's sake in a manner outrageously shocking to Victorian moral feeling. He and Rossetti both were accused of sensuality; and sufficient pressure was brought to bear on Swinburne, as the open and flagrant offender, to curb him. Ruskin, however, though he deplored Swinburne's moral "corruption," defended him as he had defended Rossetti. When he was asked to protest against Swinburne's *Poems and Ballads* in 1866 he replied: "He is infinitely above me in all knowledge and power, and I should no more think of advising or criticizing him than of venturing to do it to Turner if he were alive again." Ruskin meant that Swinburne had the divine fire of creative genius and perfect mastery of a medium for its expression, and that this placed his work above criticism, as something to be accepted with devout gratitude. The suggestion is clear that the "revelation," or "aspect of God," was to be found in the quality of the artistry, and that the poet's subject-matter was to be accepted for the sake of his music and integral feeling.

Another poet who was nourished by Rossetti was William Morris (1834–1896), who proclaimed himself "the idle singer of an empty day," by which he meant that he wrote with no ulterior purpose. He sang because it gave him pleasure to make a melodious noise. He was a born craftsman, and was instinctively sympathetic to Ruskin's assertion that all work should be done in the spirit of the craftsman who loved his materials, respected them and their uses, and took pride in honest workmanship. He was the soul of enterprising activity, and set about making well-designed and soundly built furniture, good fabrics, wallpapers, finely printed books, stained glass, tapestries, and wrought metal pieces. In all this he was trying, under Ruskin's inspiration, to bring art and life together again, as they had been united in the Middle Ages. And the art which appealed to him and influenced all his work was medieval. He was influenced not only as a craftsman by Ruskin; he also, as a consequence of Ruskin's teaching and Carlyle's, became a socialist. His socialism found literary expression principally in two prose works, *A Dream of John Ball* (1888) and *News from Nowhere* (1890). The latter is an imaginative construction of the perfected social order of the future, delightful to read, but as unreal and unconvincing as are all other Utopias.

Walter Pater, the Aesthetic Movement, and Naturalistic Fiction

The legacy of the Romantic Movement in the Victorian era was carried by Carlyle, as we have just seen, to Ruskin. Rossetti then went back to Keats. And Rossetti and Swinburne between them rescued Blake from oblivion, and made him a strong influence on poets of the next generation. Through all of these writers, beginning with Blake, there is an unmistakable, though not deliberate or conscious, drift towards the doctrine of art for art's sake. In Carlyle and Ruskin the drift is no less definite than in the rest, though it is obscured by their humanitarianism and their advocacy of social "regimentation." It was observed when Carlyle was under discussion early in this chapter that he attempted to force together contradictory elements. The doctrine of work for work's sake, of performing with all one's might the duty immediately in front of one with no thought beyond it, which Carlyle preached, on the ground that man fulfills his nature only in throwing his whole self into dutiful action, was purely individualistic. It could in no way be brought into consistency with that absolute rule of the hero which he equally preached, on the ground that average human beings are incapable of deciding for themselves what is good for them and their fellows. Ruskin's confusion was similar. There was to be an imposed just order of society which would put every man in his proper place and keep him there. This would promote the general flowering of artistic genius because under these favorable conditions men could be sincere and throw themselves happily and whole-heartedly into their work. But when the great artist did appear, he was above all law!

Sooner or later the two members of this forced union were bound to separate. Complete personal independence is simply not compatible with dictatorship, no matter how benevolent. And already in Rossetti romantic individualism appears pure and undefiled, and takes the course which had earlier been suggested by both Blake and Keats— following art for art's sake. The meaning of this phrase was classically expressed by the French romantic poet and novelist, Théophile Gautier (1811–1872), who insisted that "the perfection of form is virtue." This view, that the artist is true to himself and his calling precisely to the extent that he is devoted to beauty, or perfection of form, and considers nothing save the achievement of such perfection in using any subject or theme which may stimulate his imagination, had indeed received explicit statement and exemplification in France before it was definitely recognized as an ideal in England. Yet it had in Blake and Keats an independent English beginning, and in Rossetti an independent English development, which prepared the way for influence from France. This influence was exerted chiefly by Gautier, Charles Baudelaire (1821–1867), and, in prose, Gustave Flaubert (1821–1880). Swinburne's *Poems and Ballads* of 1866 were permeated with the French ideal, and from this time on it became increasingly familiar in England, and was hailed by many very young people with enthusiasm.

One young person who became interested, and then convinced, and who happened to be both an Oxford scholar and a fastidious writer, was Walter Pater. He was sensitive, critical, and informed. The new lessons of exact science and of history seemed to him to give a new importance to the thought of those ancient Greek philosophers who had abandoned the search for anything enduring in our world, and had finally declared that all things are continually changing and dissolving into one another and that nothing, even for a moment, is fixed. Modern science, Pater thought, was on the way to confirm this ancient wisdom, and modern knowledge of many kinds all seemed to show that mankind's age-long search for certainties was futile. The "science," the philosophical "proofs," of one age always turned out in the next age to be delusion and error; and there was no reason to suppose one's own age any closer to absolute truth than the last age. Absolute truth was a will-o'-the-wisp—or lay in the disillusioned conclusion that nothing endures. What, then, is real? Nothing, Pater replied, except the momentary pleasures we receive through the senses. These are immediate and genuine, and while they

MR. MATTHEW ARNOLD.

ADMIT THAT HOMER SOMETIMES NODS, THAT POETS *DO* WRITE TRASH,
OUR BARD HAS WRITTEN "*BALDER DEAD*," AND ALSO BALDER-DASH

CHARLES ROBERT DARWIN, LL.D., F.R.S.

IN HIS *DESCENT OF MAN* HE BROUGHT HIS OWN SPECIES DOWN AS
LOW AS POSSIBLE—I.E., TO "A HAIRY QUADRUPED FURNISHED
WITH A TAIL AND POINTED EARS, AND PROBABLY ARBOREAL
IN ITS HABITS"—WHICH IS A REASON FOR THE VERY GENERAL
INTEREST IN A "FAMILY TREE." HE HAS LATELY BEEN
TURNING HIS ATTENTION TO THE "POLITIC WORM."

PROFESSOR HUXLEY, LL.D., F.R.S., L.S.D.,

PROFESSOR OF NATURAL HISTORY, NATURALIST, INSPECTOR OF
FISHERIES, ETC.

"There is more in heaven and earth, O ratio, than is dreamt of in
your philosophy "—(so perhaps he'll find it in the rivers).

ANTONIUS TROLLOPIUS.

AUTHOR OF THE *LAST CHRONICLES OF CHERB*.

"O Rare for Antony!"—SHAKESPEARE.

"FLOWERS OF "CULTURE"; OR, A SWINBURNE-JONES
CUTTING.

MR. NARCISSUS RUSKIN.

"WHO IS IT THAT SAYS MOST? WHICH CAN SAY MORE,
THAN THIS RICH PRAISE,—THAT YOU ALONE ARE YOU?"

Punch, the famous English weekly, has commanded the services of great illustrators and cartoonists ever since the first issue appeared in 1841. Sir John Tenniel (1820–1914), universally known for his illustrations of Lewis Carroll's *Alice in Wonderland* and *Through the Looking Glass*, joined the staff in 1850, and later succeeded John Leech (1817–1864) as *Punch's* chief cartoonist. Linley Sambourne (1844–1910) in turn succeeded Tenniel, but was on the staff for many years before Tenniel's retirement. He was affectionately known to his colleagues as "Sammy." Amongst his numerous satiric sketches were "Punch's Fancy Portraits." Seven of these, which appeared during 1880 and 1881, are reproduced on this page. (Courtesy of the New York Public Library.) His celebrated contemporaries did not fill "Sammy" with awe. The sketch of Arnold reflects the feeling aroused in many of his countrymen by Arnold's outspoken criticism; they returned his attitude of lofty contempt with interest. When the sketch of Darwin appeared, Samuel Butler (author of *Erewhon*) was complaining that the naturalist had become a British institution, and that anyone who attacked him was regarded very much as if he were defacing a national monument; but Sambourne shows that it was still possible to poke fun at Darwin, and at Huxley also. The cartoon of Wilde appeared upon the publication of his first volume, *Poems*, when Wilde was making himself notorious by parading about London in silk knee-breeches, with a sunflower in his hand, and with his hair undulating to his shoulders.

"O. W."

"O, I feel just as happy as a bright Sunflower
Lays of Christy Minstrelsy

Æsthete of Æsthetes !
What's in a name ?
The poet is WILDE,
But his poetry's tame.

Rebellion against Victorianism reached a climax in the so-called aesthetic movement of the 1880's and 1890's. Oscar Wilde was the flamboyant herald and brilliant playwright of the movement, and Aubrey Beardsley was its characteristic artist. Wilde's play, *Salomé*, was originally written in French (1893). When it was translated into English (1894), it was illustrated by Beardsley; and the picture at the left above shows Salomé bearing the head of John the Baptist. At the right above is a reproduction of Beardsley's drawing for the cover of the prospectus of *The Yellow Book*, which from 1894 to 1897 was the almost official organ of the movement. (Courtesy of the Metropolitan Museum of Art.) The scene below is Thomas Hardy's own sketch of the Downs of Wessex, which originally appeared in *Wessex Poems and Other Verses* (1898). (Courtesy of Harper and Brothers.)

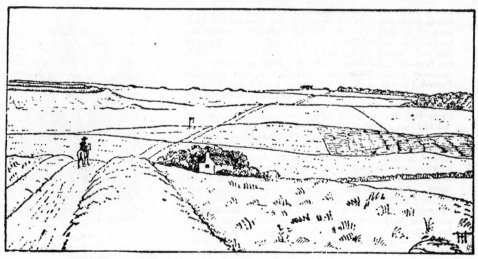

last are real, not absolutely, but relatively, to ourselves. What, then, is wisdom? Wisdom, he replied, consists in living as pleasurably as one can during the short time that the phosphorus, lime, carbon, water, and other substances of which a man consists hold together. There are, he added, differences in pleasures; some are more exquisite and intense than others, and it is these which, giving us a heightened sense of life, best enable us to make the most of our time. And "of such wisdom," he concluded, "the poetic passion, the desire of beauty, the love of art for its own sake, has most," because art frankly proposes "to give nothing but the highest quality to your moments as they pass, and simply for those moments' sake."

So Pater ended the celebrated "Conclusion" to his *Studies in the History of the Renaissance*. His counsel, like that of Fitz-Gerald's Omar, was the fruit of disillusion, but it was welcomed by readers still younger than he as authorization for a joyful release from duties, stuffy moral restraints, the whole stuffy Victorian outlook and attitude. Pater himself was austere, almost priest-like, the soul of discretion and tact, and a high-minded man. By publishing his meditations, however, he became the rather unwilling and troubled leader of the so-called aesthetic movement of the late nineteenth century. Oscar Wilde was the most prominent figure in that movement because he did everything humanly possible, by dress, manner, conversation, and printed work, to flaunt before the world his emancipation from all conventions; and then, with dramatic suddenness, he met what the conventional world thought to be his just fate. Wilde, however, was only one of many who all welcomed the doctrine of art for its own sake because it gave complete freedom to the artist to treat any subject he pleased in any way he pleased, and confined criticism to the one question whether or not perfection of form had been achieved. And it was inevitable that the first effort of these emancipated artists should be the eager exploration of just those aspects of life to which the Victorians had closed their eyes. Thus the final act of rebellion against Victorianism was an outburst of naughtiness— an orgy of unashamed and impudent literary and artistic treatment of forbidden subjects.

Wilde was the brilliant playwright of the movement. He wrote, indeed, poems, essays, tales, a novel, and was an all-round man of letters. But as a poet he was surpassed by Ernest Dowson, and as a critic by Arthur Symons. And the one man of high genius whom the movement turned up was Aubrey Beardsley, who was not, save incidentally, a writer at all, but a maker of pictures. *The Yellow Book,* which was from 1894 to 1897 the almost official organ of the movement, is as notable for its Beardsley illustrations (in its earlier numbers) as for any of its literary contributions.

Amongst the contributors to *The Yellow Book* was a writer of American birth, Henry James (1843–1916), who is not usually mentioned as a figure in the aesthetic movement. He was as little inclined to naughtiness as Pater, but as much interested in perfection of form as any writer associated with the movement, and far more successful in achieving it on a large scale than any other. It is not too much to say that, artistically, he won for himself a place above all other writers of fiction in English, and his novels have exerted an important influence on later writers.

Some of the tales in *The Yellow Book* were devoted to exposure of sordid aspects of life, with the evident aim of telling the worst in all its details. The motive seems to be almost vindictive, and suggests that the writers of these tales have used the new freedom of the artist, not to shock conventional readers by paradox and amoralism after the manner of the aesthetic writers, but rather to tell, with relentless emphasis, everything revolting and disgusting which illustrates the brute understructure of life. Here we have something closely related to the aesthetic movement, yet distinct from it. This art is realistic, but realism of a special kind. The word used to describe it is "naturalism." It stems from Flaubert's *Madame Bovary* (1856), which combines realism and aestheticism, and was developed in France by Émile Zola (1840–1902), who aspired to present through fiction a comprehensive picture of life as objective, impartial, and *complete* as if he were a man of science using every laboratory instrument of minute observation and analysis for a full and accurate description of the structure, characteristics, appearance, behavior, and affiliations of some animal organism. In practice this aim reduced itself in Zola's novels to a successful attempt to depict life's most cruel, debased, brutal aspects. Zola was the great "debunker," and as one-sided as the "debunker" usually is. Nevertheless, his aim was to construct a natural history of man under modern conditions of life, from which we get the descriptive adjective "naturalistic" to denote the kind of fiction he wrote. In England the foremost representative of Zolaesque naturalism in the 1880's was George Moore (1852–1933), whose *Mummer's Wife* (1884) and *Esther Waters* (1894), though they do not reach Zola's level of intensity, are impressive novels.

Romance and Imperialism

As we traverse the years after 1860, the impression derived from literature is that English life was disintegrating under the influence of disillusion. The old earnestness, confidence, and hearty enjoyment, all preserved magnificently in the pages of Dickens, were gone. In their place had come pessimism, decadence, immoralism, morbidity, and disunion. Literature was degenerating, Ruskin thought, into "pigs' flavoring of pigs' wash," and people were no better. Nobody any longer believed in anything that gave ground or impetus for disinterested effort, or had the nerve to face life courageously. If we should look further, at the realistic novels of George Gissing (1857–1903) for example, our impression that the human spirit was disheartened and faltering would be deepened.

Yet at the same time the outward condition of the English seemed more fortunate than that of any other people at any period of history. A century of unexampled material prosperity had made the nation wealthy beyond even Macaulay's rosiest anticipations. The British flag had followed trade to every corner of the world, and an empire had been created beside which that of Rome looked small, and on which the

sun never set. At home, though much remained to be done, much had been achieved in the correction of social injustice; and England, while clinging to the forms of ancient usage, was becoming in reality the most democratic country on earth. Abroad, subject peoples were, on the whole, exceedingly well governed, and much of the empire consisted of self-governing dominions bound together only by ties of mutual advantage and by common loyalty to the aging queen and empress. The one dark spot on the picture was England's tragic failure to solve the problem of Ireland. There were, besides, dissenting voices raised against imperialism, but there was no doubt, before 1900, that the nation as a whole was for it and took pride in it.

The explanation of this disparity between literature and life is to be found partly in what has already in this chapter been called the ambiguous character of Victorian expansion. England was raised to the very pinnacle of earthly power and greatness, but this end was accomplished by means which could appeal to no imagination or generous feeling. On the contrary, the means of mass-production, the things produced, and the methods of their distribution were all repellent to high-minded people. And though wealth increased, it was concentrated in so few hands, and was so ostentatiously and irresponsibly used, that no thinking person could honestly regard it as a sign of national greatness. The steady increase of machinery, too, and of impersonal organizations in the form of limited-liability companies, were dehumanizing in their influence. "Things were in the saddle, and rode mankind." On top of this, the science which had put things in the saddle had gone on to place man amongst the animals in a godless and perhaps meaningless world. There was unescapable reason for disillusion and for a feeling of helplessness in the face of blind forces. And the reason was most apparent to the educated man of talent who might, under different conditions, have become the voice of the nation.

There were, however, a few voices raised towards the end of the century to show, both in themselves and by the response they evoked, that the spirit of disillusion was not yet by any means universal. Robert Louis Stevenson spoke out for the joy of adventure and manly daring, and bade men see themselves once more in the mirror of bold human action and indomitable spirit triumphing over difficulties, instead of morbidly analyzing themselves and paralyzing their wills by self-pity. And though he wrote only for boys in *Treasure Island,* he showed himself a true inheritor of Walter Scott in his romances entitled *Kidnapped, The Master of Ballantrae,* and *Catriona.* He was, it should be added, thoroughly a man of his own day, emancipated from traditional beliefs, a conscious and mannered artist, and a student of the same French literature which was influencing some of his contemporaries very differently. The one significant divergence between him and those contemporaries, which can be seen in all his work—his essays and children's poems and travel narratives as well as his short stories and romances—lies in his invincible vitality.

Stevenson won a large public in his own day, and he is likely to be read longer than many of his contemporaries. Rudyard Kipling won an even larger public in the early part of his career, and he also is likely to be read longer than many of his and Stevenson's contemporaries, though from the first he provoked hostility in some quarters, and through the latter half of his life was condemned by every self-appointed spokesman for the welfare of mankind. Kipling was not, as a young man, a refined artist, and he perhaps never became a really masterly craftsman. But to this admission it must be added that he had superb energy and a ready command of humor, pathos, tenderness, and surprise, and an unusual power to catch the authentic flavor of certain types. His ballads concerning soldiers have had an universal appeal, and have been as popular amongst the soldiers themselves as elsewhere. Why, then, has it been long the fashion to condemn him? The reason is political. Kipling perceived a romantic glory in the far-flung empire, of which the English, who had taken it in their stride, had not been fully conscious. He made himself the panegyrist of imperialism at a time when it was being more and more questioned by liberals, and in so doing he took an unfashionable stand for "Law, Order, Duty an' Restraint, Obedience, Discipline."

What Kipling saw was the human side of the empire's growth and administration. He did not idealize Tommy Atkins or his officers, but he saw that they were *men.* They might seem like animals at play when there was no work to do. They could not stand up to the responsibilities of leisure and ease. But give them difficulty, hardship, danger, and they were transformed. They were built for action; and had courage, decision, endurance, and an unpretentious matter-of-fact heroism when they were in the presence of death. They never knew when they were beaten, but kept right on taking their beating until they exhausted the enemy from their sheer tenacity. Kipling was born in India, and went back there as a young man. He saw life at the frontier posts and elsewhere, and wrote from his own observation. He also visited other remote parts of the empire. He saw a handful of devoted civil servants preserving order and administering justice amongst hordes of savages who could have overpowered them in a moment, had they not been stayed by the instinctive respect they felt for character and integrity; and he saw that those barbaric tribesmen were far better off under a rule of firm simple justice than they had ever been when left to themselves.

When he finally settled in England, Kipling had fixed in his mind a vision of the Englishman as hero, bestowing order and justice on communities of inferior peoples throughout the world, making fair the wastelands of undeveloped continents, carrying the torch of civilization wherever he went. His observation told him it was all done through the force of disciplined yet rugged character. He studied English history, and saw the same lesson enforced in its pages. He came to believe that the Anglo-Saxon stock was superior to all others, and was born to lead the world. But this conviction arose from his acquaintance with the Englishman abroad and the Englishman of history. When he observed the "poor little street-bred people" of his own time who lived and worked at home, his confidence was shaken. They themselves needed a firm rule, a hard upbringing, reverence, a stern sense of responsibility; and he had dark forebodings lest, when a time of trial came for them, as he knew it inevitably would, they could no longer rise to its demands.

What Kipling failed to see was the growing belief at home that Tommy Atkins bled and died on foreign fields, and civil servants wasted their lives in fever-infested jungles, not for the sake of civilization, or any other more or less grand object, but solely for the enrichment of a few business men and financiers who had captured the government and enslaved the nation. These people, socialists or near-socialists for the most part, felt that Kipling was playing directly into the hands of the new plutocracy, which they hated and were determined to destroy. Kipling, it hardly needs to be said, was not in league with any betrayers of mankind. The trouble, rather, was that conditions had grown so complex that no one could any longer see life steadily and whole, and men of honest good will could find no common ground on which to stand.

The Irish Literary Revival

Three poets who were very widely read in the dozen years or so before the first World War were Kipling, A. E. Housman, and John Masefield. The popularity of Kipling and of Masefield is easy to understand. They both wrote, not for fellow poets or for critics or for some special group or clique, and not to advance some special technique, but to tell a story or sing a song of broad, elemental human appeal. And they both wanted to get away from literary language and delighted in colloquialism. Both of them managed to be direct, vivid, and forceful. Kipling, as we have seen, had a "message" to deliver, but it did not have to be accepted, or even understood, for hearty enjoyment. Masefield has been described as a successor of Kipling, but he had no "message," and probably none of the influences which can be discerned as entering into his work is very important.

He found an effective way in which to tell a good story, and used it half a dozen times, with minor variations, after the sensational success of *The Everlasting Mercy*. The popularity of A. E. Housman rests on significantly different grounds. Housman was full of that pessimistic sense of the futility of life which we have seen growing in the literature of the late nineteenth century, and he seemed to give compressed and classic expression to it. Obviously he was popular because an ever larger number of readers shared his outlook.

But none of these poets opened up any new prospect or stimulated further growth. If we did not look beyond them we might think of English poetry as coming to a helpless pause by about 1914 on two extremes as sharply opposed as can be imagined. In point of fact, however, a great quantity of other poetry was being written, and practically every possible position between those extremes was being held by somebody. The net result, in other words, of that increasing diversity of opinion and practice whose course we have been tracing, was that finally a kind of literary and intellectual freedom was being achieved wherein everyone was at liberty to think what he pleased and to write as he pleased, and could be sure of an audience. One of the consequences was a revival of Christian belief. Roman Catholicism gained many English converts in the 1890's and early years of the present century, and, moreover, found expression in distinguished prose and poetry. Francis Thompson's *Hound of Heaven* was no isolated achievement, but the forerunner of a new stream of Catholic English literature. It is only possible to mention, as among the most distinguished of these Catholic writers, Alice Meynell, G. K. Chesterton and Hilaire Belloc.

"Intellectual freedom" has an agreeable sound, but the reality back of it, at which we have been looking, was this: nobody could find any basis for belief which seemed unchallengeable to more than a small minority of the reading and thinking public. A man as recent as Matthew Arnold could say that reason, so it be true reason, must be "always and everywhere the same." Within a few years after his death, the next generation was deciding that philosophical reason was a fraud. Reason could make any view plausible, but could not prove a single one to be absolutely true. And science, for purposes of ultimate belief, was no better than reason. But man cannot exist in a state of blank unbelief. It is one of the conditions of conscious life that there be some end or purpose beyond itself towards which it can be directed. Further, a great many human beings not only desire certitude but are compelled by their nature somehow to achieve it.

These considerations explain the fact that in the late nineteenth century there was a marked revival of interest in mysticism. Mystical experience, or the testimony of mystics, was, in the case of some, the basis for their conversion to Catholic faith. For those brought up in the atmosphere of detached literary culture, there was the example of Blake. And Blake was eagerly studied, for his mysticism, about 1890, by two Irishmen, Edwin J. Ellis and William Butler Yeats (1865–1939), the latter of whom was to become a distinguished poet and poetic dramatist, and the leading figure in a remarkable growth of Irish national literature which was just beginning as Yeats reached manhood.

The stirrings of national feeling in Ireland were strong in Yeats's boyhood, and from 1880 on, the demand for home rule became formidable and at times violent. The political struggle, however, was only one part of a comprehensive nationalistic effort. The study of ancient Irish history was undertaken; Irish legends and folklore were collected; and an attempt was made to revive the use of Gaelic, the old Celtic language of the island. Yeats has told how, when he was only a youth, he began to dream of the possibility of uniting the Irish on the level of their best selves through "a national literature that made Ireland beautiful in the memory, and yet had been freed from provincialism by an exacting criticism." He himself came of a Protestant family, but had been deprived by Huxley and other scientists of Christian belief. He detested these men of science, wanted to believe every

report he could gather of supernatural visitations, and finally became, under the influence of Blake and others, a mystic. His mystical visions took the forms of shadowy figures out of Irish legendary lore; and, in effect, he thus made a species of religion out of the mythological stuff of Irish tradition.

This became the matter of his poetry. For the manner he went to the French symbolist poets, of whom Stéphane Mallarmé (1842–1898) was the leader. These poets were the inheritors of the romantic tendency to subjectivism. They sought to express their own feelings, their own sensations, with perfect fidelity. Their problem was made difficult by the fact that every human being is unique, and, in addition, has different feelings and sensations from moment to moment, even when the objects causing feeling and sensation remain the same. Language, however, as was observed when Blake was under discussion in the preceding chapter, is a generalized medium of communication. The symbolist poets derive their name from the fact that they, like the mystics, can only attain their aim of expression by the use of symbols which do not state, but suggest, their private momentary reactions or moods.

The reader's difficulty with this kind of poetry is exactly that which he has with Blake's prophetic books. The poet is writing about a private world in a private language, and would be no more unintelligible to most of us if he were writing in the language of the Zulus. Yeats escaped the worst possibilities, and achieved some beauties, because he dealt with symbols drawn from a mythology he did not himself invent. He was also drawn out into the world of social experience by his desire to participate practically in the creation of a new Irish literature. His most fruitful achievement was the founding of the Irish Literary Theater in Dublin which, after several years, was established permanently (in 1904) in the Abbey Theater. The most notable of the writers with whom Yeats was associated in this nationalist literary movement were George William Russell, who was a mystic also, and is known by the letters he used as a pseudonym ("A. E."); Lady Gregory, manager of the Theater, playwright, and collector of legends; John Millington Synge, the author of *The Playboy of the Western World* and other plays; and George Moore, who went to live in Dublin, made a nuisance of himself, and departed to write a malicious but very entertaining and informative account of his experience (*Hail and Farewell,* 1911–1913).

The Revival of Drama at the End of the Nineteenth Century

One important consequence of the new freedom being won by literary men in the 1880's was a revival of drama. As was remarked in the last chapter, the stage was kept alive in England from shortly after the beginning of the eighteenth century until towards the end of the nineteenth by a succession of great actors, the only dramatists of importance in that long stretch of time being Goldsmith and Sheridan. But now there was to be a change. Not only did Oscar Wilde, as we have noticed, write witty and successful comedies of manners in the early 1890's; and not only did Yeats, Lady Gregory, Synge, and others succeed in creating a new national drama in Ireland; at the same time a group of dramatists revivified the London stage by a succession of effective and significant plays which realistically depicted contemporary life and problems.

Two competent workmen who knew the secrets of stage effectiveness, and who began to breathe in the freer atmosphere of modern "emancipation" and to inject a measure of realism into their well-made plays, were the pioneers of this development. They were Sir Henry Arthur Jones (1851–1929) and Sir Arthur Wing Pinero (1855–1934). Jones's *Saints and Sinners* (1884) and *Breaking a Butterfly* (1885) were significant attempts to break away from mere conventionality and to achieve realistic effects. His later successful and important plays include *The Liars* (1897) and *Mrs. Dane's Defense* (1900). He himself thought his best play was *Michael and His Lost Angel* which, however, did not succeed when it was produced in 1896. Of Pinero's plays the following should be mentioned: *The Second Mrs. Tanqueray* (1893), *The Gay Lord Quex* (1899), *Iris* (1901), and *Mid-Channel* (1909).

Neither Jones nor Pinero, however, accomplished anything of the first importance except preparation of the way for others. And the great animating impulse to achievement came, not from them, but from the example of the Norwegian dramatist Henrik Ibsen (1828–1906), whose work began to be known and praised in England about 1890. Ibsen was realistic, thoughtful, serious, powerful, and emancipated. He tried to look at modern men and women as they are, to expose shams, and to attack moral standards which he thought outworn or vicious. He put on the stage social problems whose representation shocked conventional people, and he reached conclusions which equally shocked them. In this he was a reformer at a time when dissatisfaction with the established order of society was becoming acute. He aroused violent controversy, but won the enthusiastic approval of all those who felt that society had grown rotten through hypocrisy and injustice and must be remolded.

Chief amongst those in England who were fired by Ibsen's example was George Bernard Shaw (1856–   ). Shaw was an Irishman from Dublin who had become a socialist, had written some unsuccessful novels, and had turned to journalistic criticism for a living. In 1891 he published a small book entitled *The Quintessence of Ibsenism,* and in the following year he entered on his exciting dramatic career with a play called *Widowers' Houses,* in which he exposed evils connected with the profitable rental of tenements in slum districts.

Shaw's nature is closely akin to that of Samuel Butler, from whom he has learned a good deal. He is, like Butler, constitutionally paradoxical, irreverent, and iconoclastic; and he is at the same time more witty and more earnest than Butler. He has delighted in shocking and astonishing the public, and has often done so by the simple expedient of following ideas to their extreme logical conclusions. He has outraged sentiment, mocked at piety, torn patriotism to shreds, and, generally, shot up the existing state of things—and has been greeted with cheers.

His fellow socialists naturally have applauded his destructive sallies, but others who have by no means agreed with him have found his wit and his capacity for creating absurd situations irresistibly amusing, and his intellectual liveliness and zest exhilarating. His pose is that of an all-wise, infinitely superior being who looks at men with scorn, seeing nothing but stupidity, hypocrisy, and corruption in their lives, and declaring himself able (were he given the opportunity) to set everything right by altering their ideas, practices, and institutions. It may be regarded as one measure of his genius that this pose is not generally resented. But it has to be remembered also that this superior, detached, mocking attitude has become fashionable with the spread of modern disillusion. There have been, since the 1890's, thousands of people, mostly young, who could not successfully have ruled a village of a hundred souls for twenty-four hours, but who have imagined that they could set the whole world straight in a few months, if only they could liquidate the swine in high places and obtain unlimited control over the thoughts, activities, and purses of the populace. And to all these, of course, Shaw has been a delightful projection of themselves.

Further, Shaw's witty liquidation of the existing state of things is always subordinated to a constructive purpose, transparently well meant, whether or not it is practicable. The disillusioned generation which preceded him had no convictions and no earnestness. In general, we feel that any positive convictions are better than none; and it is invigorating to encounter a man who faces the facts and the future with cheerful confidence. Shaw's cure-all is the socialist state. He believes, with Herbert Spencer, that the race is progressing through evolution. And he has a religion—the worship of the Life-Force. He has appropriated this name to designate the beneficent creative power which he believes to be at work in the processes of evolution.

Shaw's plays are, by and large, a series of triumphs over the usual demands of successful drama. Action is reduced to a minimum, the plots are unimportant, and the characterization is elementary and often unconvinc-

ing. Everything is sacrificed in order to concentrate attention on brilliant dialogue in which the author's views are set forth. His earlier plays were published collectively in 1898 under the title *Plays, Pleasant and Unpleasant* (*Mrs. Warren's Profession, Candida, You Never Can Tell,* and others). Later plays are: *Man and Superman* (1903), *Fanny's First Play* (1911), *Pygmalion* (1912), *Heartbreak House* (1917), *Back to Methuselah* (1921), *Saint Joan* (1923), and *Too True to Be Good* (1932).

Other dramatists besides Shaw rose to deserved fame in the years between 1890 and 1914, though only their names can be mentioned here: Harley Granville-Barker, St. John Hankin, Somerset Maugham, John Galsworthy, and Sir James Barrie (*The Admirable Crichton,* 1902; *Peter Pan,* 1904; *What Every Woman Knows,* 1908; and *Dear Brutus,* 1917).

The Novel from 1890 to 1914

Neither the revival of dramatic activity in this period, nor any poetry, as has been said earlier, displaced the novel in popular favor, though the plays of Shaw, the poems of Kipling, and the narrative verse of Masefield all reached an exceedingly large public. The principal novelists who achieved fame in these years were Joseph Conrad (1857–1924), Herbert George Wells (1866–   ), Arnold Bennett (1867–1931), and John Galsworthy (1867–1933).

Conrad's position in English literature is unique. He was not only, like Henry James, of foreign birth; he was a Pole, born in the part of Poland held by Russia in the mid-nineteenth century. His education was French, and he could not even speak English until he was in his early twenties. He had an inborn love for the sea, and as a young man worked as a sailor on French merchant vessels. He joined an English ship after a year or so, and worked his way up until he obtained his master's certificate in 1885. Ten years later his health was so impaired that he had to give up the sea. He completed a novel on which he had been desultorily working, was surprised to find a publisher for it, and found at the same time that he had a new profession. The novel was *Almayer's Folly* (1895). It was followed by a long succession of books, mostly sea tales, which were welcomed with the highest praise by discerning critics and a small public, though Conrad did not become universally known and widely read until late in his career. Some of his books are: *The Outcast of the Islands* (1896), *The Nigger of the Narcissus* (1897), *Lord Jim* (1900), *Typhoon* (1903), *Nostromo* (1904), *The Secret Agent* (1907), *Under Western Eyes* (1911), and *The Arrow of Gold* (1919).

Conrad thought of himself as a pure artist, aiming only at perfection of form and fidelity in portraiture, and he believed this to be the reason for the small sales of his novels. "At a time when nothing that is not revolutionary can expect to attract much attention," he said, "I have not been revolutionary in my writings." Another reason, however, was that, though he had achieved mastery of the English language and shown a power to use it in his own way for rich effects, he himself remained foreign and difficult. His masters and affinities, in the art of fiction, were French and Russian. He loved methods of indirection, which seemed to him true to the inconclusiveness and indefiniteness of our knowledge of human beings, and which helped to emphasize his sense of the mystery of life. At the same time he was interested, not in action for its own sake, but in traits of character, in states of emotion, and especially in the tortuous ways in which impressions alter men. He was much preoccupied with misery; he felt that men's lives are formed, and often malformed, by forces which we cannot control and do not even understand; and consequently he was deeply and darkly pessimistic. This is perhaps enough to indicate that his novels had qualities of undogmatic reflectiveness which made heavy demands on readers. Their reward came in their contact with a really mature man of complete integrity, in his occasional pictures of human nature standing nobly against all odds, in his controlled intensity of vision, of realization, and in the beauty he revealed in places where we would not have thought to look for it.

H. G. Wells, like Dickens, made his own way up from the lower middle class. His father kept a small shop, and he himself as a youth was apprenticed to a druggist, and later became a clerk in a dry-goods shop. But he contrived to attend classes in the University of London, where he was a pupil of Huxley, and to enter the field of journalism, whence he ascended on the wings of imagination to fame. He is the great literary representative of all those in recent times who have been thrilled by the progress of science and of invention, and have fancied there is nothing that man cannot accomplish by setting his mind to it. The marvels of science stimulated his imagination, at the beginning of his career, to leap ahead into the future. He wrote vivid tales, fanciful but seemingly scientific, describing the end of the earth (*The Time Machine*, 1895), an invasion from Mars (*The War of the Worlds*, 1898), and other unlikely or exceedingly remote possibilities. In these books he showed unusual creative power, great vigor, and remarkable originality. From them he went on to depict real people in our present-day world, with equal vigor, a keen eye for comedy, and much feeling. His best novels are: *Kipps* (1905), *Tono-Bungay* (1909), *The History of Mr. Polly* (1910), *The New Machiavelli* (1911), *Marriage* (1912), and *Mr. Britling Sees It Through* (1916).

Wells's outlook and attitude are very similar to Bernard Shaw's. He sees things in somewhat different terms, but the differences between the two are those of detail, and not of great importance. He sees Stupidity as the ruling power on earth, and is confident that the scientifically trained intelligence, if given the opportunity, could in short order transform the earth, and make us all comfortable, peaceful, and happy. This cocksure confidence becomes more tiresome in Wells than in Shaw because it seems to be more intimately a part of Wells; but both of them may appear incredibly immature in outlook to a later generation.

Arnold Bennett, in his best novels, was a far more competent workman than Wells, and his books have real documentary value, as the records of detached and careful observation. He came from Staffordshire, knew the pottery district thoroughly, and never really succeeded in adding anything to what he had learned there as boy and youth. He has the solidity and the limitations of the middle-class mind, but the following novels are distinguished examples of realistic fiction: *The Old Wives' Tale* (1908), *Clayhanger* (1910), *Hilda Lessways* (1911), and *These Twain* (1916).

John Galsworthy was a finer artist than either Wells or Bennett, and more discerning, sensitive, and mature than these fellow novelists or Shaw. He was, like Shaw and Wells, a severe critic of English society, but there the resemblance almost stops, chiefly because of his truer and deeper feeling, his inner humanity, and his more comprehensive outlook. His general theme is the disintegra-tion of English society, and the powerlessness of the individual to stay a process which is really a failure of energy, of grasp, of constructive imagination, of will, of moral passion; and which has a startling resemblance to the decay of old age, the approach of death. His most important and impressive work is comprised in *The Forsyte Saga* (1922), a series of five novels, of which the earliest is *The Man of Property* (1906). The *Saga* was continued in a sixth novel, *A Modern Comedy* (1929). In these novels he recounts the history of a family in its several branches from 1886 to 1926, against the background of England's passage from mid-Victorian stability and prosperity to the perplexities, unsettlement, divisions, and decline of the years after the first World War.

THOMAS CARLYLE
1795–1881

Carlyle was born at Ecclefechan, Dumfries-shire, Scotland, on 4 December, 1795. His father was a stone-mason and a man of highly unusual character. "More remarkable man than my father," the son wrote, "I have never met in my journey through life; sterling sincerity in thought, word, and deed, most quiet, but capable of blazing into whirlwinds when needful, and such a flash of just insight and natural eloquence and emphasis, true to every feature of it, as I have never known in any other. . . . None of us will ever forget that bold, glowing style of his, flowing free from the untutored soul, full of metaphor, though he knew not what metaphor was, with all manner of potent words which he appropriated and applied with surprising accuracy." This characterization of his father helps us to see how Carlyle came to be the man he was, for sincerity was the touchstone by which the son later tried the world's great men, and the son's burning yet struggling utterance was clearly the development of a heritage. As a boy Carlyle received his first training in the village of his birth, and there showed such mental aptitude that his parents sent him to the Annan Grammar School in 1805. As he continued to show parts above the usual, his parents hoped that he might qualify himself for the ministry of the Scottish Kirk, and so in the fall of 1809 he walked the eighty miles from Ecclefechan to Edinburgh to enter the University. There he continued, as at Annan, to read widely, but with little or no guidance; he later called Edinburgh "the worst of all hitherto discovered universities," which means, as has been said, that he found no Fichte there to pierce the deep springs of idealism in his nature. Full self-discovery was only to come later, after painful enough wanderings. In 1814 he left the University and became the mathematical teacher at Annan Grammar School. Two years later he was appointed master of a school in Kirkcaldy, a position which he held until the fall of 1818. Meanwhile doubts had been growing in him about entrance into the ministry, and he had finally determined in 1817

that he could not do it—a decision severely disappointing to his parents but one which they accepted without remonstrance. After leaving Kirkcaldy Carlyle spent some time in Edinburgh, doing some writing and attempting to study the law; but the law too he found impossible as a career. And while he was thus uncertain about his future he was suffering physical anguish from dyspepsia, a curse which never left him, and spiritual anguish from the confused state of his beliefs. Unable to accept the simple Christianity of his mother, or any miraculously revealed religion, he yet reacted against the "mechanical philosophy" of the eighteenth century. He accepted the destructive work of Hume and Gibbon, whom he had been reading, but not their explicit or implied constructions—yet he knew of nothing with which to fill the void. It was at this juncture that he began the study of German, and presently found answers to his questions in the works of the transcendentalists, particularly in Jean Paul Richter and Fichte. In 1822 he began doing some writing for periodicals about his German discoveries, and from that year until 1824 he held a position as tutor in the Buller family. Meanwhile in 1821 he had met Jane Baillie Welsh, a brilliant girl to whom he was deeply attracted and whom he later married in 1826.

By this time Carlyle was definitely committed to literature as a career. He and his wife lived in Edinburgh until 1828, when they moved to Craigenputtock, a farm-house in Dumfriesshire, fifteen miles from anywhere. The loneliness of the place was disagreeable to Mrs. Carlyle; but the two lived there for six years, save for visits to London—when Carlyle became acquainted with John Stuart Mill and other men of letters —and to Edinburgh. During the earlier years of this period Carlyle fairly found himself, and managed to express in *Sartor Resartus* the chief ideas on which his later writings depend. In 1834 he moved to London and took the house in Cheyne Row, Chelsea, in which he lived throughout the remainder of his life. He was now at work upon his history of *The French Revolution.* Composition was always extraordinarily difficult for him, and while work was in progress he lived in anguish and despair. Mrs. Carlyle spoke, when a later work was being written, about living in "the valley of the shadow of Cromwell." But, as if this were not enough, when the first volume of *The French Revolution* was finished Carlyle suffered an additional grievous blow. He lent the manuscript of the volume to J. S. Mill, who lent it to Mrs. Taylor, whose maid burned it up. Carlyle had no notes, he was shattered by the pains the volume had cost him, he was hoping in despair only somehow to get the work *done,* whether it should be good or bad, and he was writing, besides, against time, as he had practically no money and was staking everything on this book. All that was fine in his nature, however, appeared in the gentleness with which he treated Mill; and, after several months of ineffectual effort, he heroically set to work and rewrote his volume. In January, 1837, the work was finished, and was published that year. Carlyle said to his wife, "I know not whether this book is worth anything, nor what the world will do with it, or misdo, or entirely forbear to do, as is likeliest; but this I could tell the world: You have not had for a hundred years any book that comes more direct and flamingly from the heart of a living man. Do what you like with it, you." The world bought, and read, and praised, and Carlyle's position as a writer was secure from this time. In the years from 1837 to 1840 he delivered several courses of lectures in London, one of which, *On Heroes, Hero-Worship, and the Heroic in History,* has been probably his most widely read book. During these years, he was also occupied in applying his ideas to contemporary political and social questions. He published *Chartism* in 1840 and *Past and Present* in 1843. In 1845 he published *Oliver Cromwell's Letters and Speeches,* in 1850 the *Latter-Day Pamphlets,* and in 1851 *The Life of John Sterling.* (Sterling was a disciple of Coleridge and a man of singularly winning personality who, before his untimely death, had attracted the interest and friendship of Carlyle.) From 1851 until 1865 he was at work upon his *History of Frederick the Great,*

which was published in six volumes, 1858–1865. In the latter year he was elected Lord Rector of Edinburgh University, where he delivered his inaugural address in April, 1866, less than three weeks before the sudden death of Mrs. Carlyle. His marriage had been, as is now known, one in name only; the domestic scene had often been stormy; and Mrs. Carlyle's death awoke in her husband bitter remorse for the wrongs which he began to feel he had done her. The remaining years of his life were full of honors from the outer world, full of sadness welling up from the world within. He died on 5 February, 1881, and was buried at Ecclefechan.

Sartor Resartus is the most fully expressive of Carlyle's writings, and it contains all the ideas which he variously developed in his other works. They are not many. "Belief in human freedom and in the 'infinite nature of Duty,' as the basis of religion; belief in the rule of the few wise and strong over the many weak and foolish, as the basis of government; belief in mutual sympathy, as the basis of society; belief in a spiritual interpretation of natural appearances, as the basis of philosophy; and, above all, belief in sincerity as the condition of all knowledge—these are the foundations upon which Carlyle built, and they will all be found well and truly laid in *Sartor*" (P. C. Parr, Introd. to *Sartor,* p. v.).

Carlyle's *Works* have been published in many editions; perhaps the best is the "Centenary Edition," ed. H. D. Traill (31 vols., London, 1897–1901). A good text of *Sartor Resartus* has been edited with an informative introduction and notes by Charles F. Harrold (New York, 1937). James Anthony Froude's *Thomas Carlyle* (London, 1882–1884) is inaccurate in detail but illuminating and a classic. David A. Wilson has written the fullest of more recent accounts, *The Life of Carlyle* (London, 1923–1934). For a general interpretation L. Cazamian's *Carlyle,* trans. E. K. Brown (New York, 1932), may be recommended. Valuable studies of special aspects of Carlyle are: Frederick W. Roe, *The Social Philosophy of Carlyle and Ruskin* (New York, 1921); Charles F. Harrold, *Carlyle and German Thought: 1819–1834* (New Haven, 1934); and Emory Neff, *Carlyle* (New York, 1932).

SARTOR RESARTUS[1]

BOOK I

CHAPTER I

Preliminary

CONSIDERING our present advanced state 5 of culture, and how the Torch of Science has now been brandished and borne about, with more or less effect, for five-thousand years and upwards; how, in these times especially, not only the Torch still burns, and perhaps 10 more fiercely than ever, but innumerable Rush-lights, and Sulphur-matches, kindled thereat, are also glancing in every direction, so that not the smallest cranny or doghole in Nature or Art can remain unilluminated,— 15 it might strike the reflective mind with some surprise that hitherto little or nothing of a fundamental character, whether in the way of Philosophy or History, has been written on the subject of Clothes. 20

Our Theory of Gravitation is as good as perfect: Lagrange,[2] it is well known, has proved that the Planetary System, on this scheme, will endure forever; Laplace,[3] still more cunningly, even guesses that it could 25 not have been made on any other scheme. Whereby, at least, our nautical Logbooks can be better kept; and water-transport of all kinds has grown more commodious. Of Geology and Geognosy[4] we know enough: 30 what with the labors of our Werners[5] and Huttons,[6] what with the ardent genius of their disciples, it has come about that now, to many a Royal Society, the Creation of a World is little more mysterious than the 35 cooking of a dumpling; concerning which last, indeed, there have been minds to whom

the question, *How the apples were got in,* presented difficulties.[7] Why mention our disquisitions on the Social Contract, on the Standard of Taste, on the Migrations of the Herring? Then, have we not a Doctrine of Rent, a Theory of Value; Philosophies of Language, of History, of Pottery, of Apparitions, of Intoxicating Liquors? Man's whole life and environment have been laid open and elucidated; scarcely a fragment or fiber of his Soul, Body, and Possessions, but has been probed, dissected, distilled, desiccated, and scientifically decomposed: our spiritual Faculties, of which it appears there are not a few, have their Stewarts,[8] Cousins,[9] Royer Collards:[10] every cellular, vascular, muscular Tissue glories in its Lawrences,[11] Majendies,[12] Bichâts.[13]

How, then, comes it, may the reflective mind repeat, that the grand Tissue of all Tissues, the only real Tissue, should have been quite overlooked by Science,—the vestural Tissue, namely, of woolen or other cloth; which Man's Soul wears as its outmost wrappage and overall; wherein his whole other Tissues are included and screened, his whole Faculties work, his whole Self lives, moves, and has its being? For if, now and then, some straggling, broken-winged thinker has cast an owl's-glance into this obscure region, the most have soared over it altogether heedless; regarding Clothes as a property, not an accident,[14] as quite natural and spontaneous, like the leaves of trees, like the

---

[1]First written in the fall of 1830; then revised and enlarged in the months from February until August, 1831. Printed in *Fraser's Magazine,* 1833–1834. First published as a book in America (Boston), 1836; first English edition, 1838. The title means, "the tailor patched." Diogenes Teufelsdröckh, author of the philosophy of clothes, is the tailor; Carlyle does the patching as his editor.

[2]French mathematician (1736–1813).

[3]French astronomer and mathematician (1749–1827). Carlyle saw him in Paris in 1824.

[4]Knowledge of the structure and materials of the earth.

[5]German mineralogist and geologist (1750–1817).

[6]British geologist (1726–1797).

[7]The question is asked by George III in *The Apple Dumplings and the King,* a poem by John Wolcot (Peter Pindar).

[8]Philosopher, professor at Edinburgh University (1753–1828).

[9]Philosopher and statesman (1792–1867).

[10]Philosopher, taught the doctrines of Thomas Reid (1763–1845).

[11]English surgeon and anatomist (1783–1867).

[12]French physiologist, one of the earliest vivisectors (1783–1855).

[13]French surgeon and physiologist (1771–1802).

[14]Terms used in logic. A "property" is an attribute which is inseparable from an object without altering its essential nature; an "accident" is an attribute which may be removed, or may be supposed removed, without altering an object's essence. In man the power of understanding speech is a property; his color is an accident.

plumage of birds. In all speculations they have tacitly figured man as a *Clothed Animal;* whereas he is by nature a *Naked Animal;* and only in certain circumstances, by purpose and device, masks himself in Clothes. Shakespeare says, we are creatures that look before and after:[15] the more surprising that we do not look round a little, and see what is passing under our very eyes.

But here, as in so many other cases, Germany, learned, indefatigable, deep-thinking Germany comes to our aid. It is, after all, a blessing that, in these revolutionary times, there should be one country where abstract Thought can still take shelter; that while the din and frenzy of Catholic Emancipations,[16] and Rotten Boroughs,[17] and Revolts of Paris,[18] deafen every French and every English ear, the German can stand peaceful on his scientific watch-tower; and, to the raging, struggling multitude here and elsewhere, solemnly, from hour to hour, with preparatory blast of cowhorn, emit his *Höret ihr Herren und lasset's Euch sagen;*[19] in other words, tell the Universe, which so often forgets that fact, what o'clock it really is. Not unfrequently the Germans have been blamed for an unprofitable diligence; as if they struck into devious courses, where nothing was to be had but the toil of a rough journey; as if, forsaking the gold-mines of finance and that political slaughter of fat oxen whereby a man himself grows fat, they were apt to run goose-hunting into regions of bilberries and crowberries, and be swallowed up at last in remote peat-bogs. Of that unwise science, which, as our Humorist expresses it,—

By geometric scale
Doth take the size of pots of ale;[20]

still more, of that altogether misdirected industry, which is seen vigorously thrashing mere straw, there can nothing defensive be said. In so far as the Germans are chargeable with such, let them take the consequence. Nevertheless be it remarked, that even a Russian steppe has tumuli and gold ornaments; also many a scene that looks desert and rockbound from the distance, will unfold itself, when visited, into rare valleys. Nay, in any case, would Criticism erect not only fingerposts and turnpikes, but spiked gates and impassable barriers, for the mind of man? It is written, "Many shall run to and fro, and knowledge shall be increased."[21] Surely the plain rule is, Let each considerate person have his way, and see what it will lead to. For not this man and that man, but all men make up mankind, and their united tasks the task of mankind. How often have we seen some such adventurous, and perhaps much-censured wanderer light on some out-lying, neglected, yet vitally momentous province; the hidden treasures of which he first discovered, and kept proclaiming till the general eye and effort were directed thither, and the conquest was completed;—thereby, in these his seemingly so aimless rambles, planting new standards, founding new habitable colonies, in the immeasurable circumambient realm of Nothingness and Night! Wise man was he who counseled that Speculation should have free course, and look fearlessly towards all the thirty-two points of the compass, whithersoever and howsoever it listed.

Perhaps it is proof of the stunted condition in which pure Science, especially pure moral Science, languishes among us English; and how our mercantile greatness, and invaluable Constitution, impressing a political or other immediately practical tendency on all English culture and endeavor, cramps the free flight of Thought,—that this, not Philosophy of Clothes, but recognition even that we have no such Philosophy, stands here for the first time published in our language. What English intellect could have chosen such a topic, or by chance stumbled on it? But for that same unshackled, and even sequestered condition of the German Learned, which permits and induces them to fish in all manner of

---

[15]*Hamlet,* IV, iv, 37.

[16]The bill removing civil disabilities from Roman Catholics was passed in 1829.

[17]Electoral districts having few or no voters. The Reform Bill of 1832 abolished 56 of these boroughs and gave representation in Parliament to other and populous districts which had had none.

[18]In the Three Days' Revolution of July, 1830, Charles X was expelled from the French throne and Louis-Philippe installed in his place.

[19]Listen, gentlemen, and let me tell you.

[20]Samuel Butler, *Hudibras.* Pt. I, canto i, ll. 121–122.

[21]Daniel, 12:4.

waters, with all manner of nets, it seems probable enough, this abstruse Inquiry might, in spite of the results it leads to, have continued dormant for indefinite periods. The Editor of these sheets, though otherwise 5 boasting himself a man of confirmed speculative habits, and perhaps discursive enough, is free to confess, that never, till these last months, did the above very plain considerations, on our total want of a Philosophy of 10 Clothes, occur to him; and then, by quite foreign suggestion. By the arrival, namely, of a new Book from Professor Teufelsdröckh[22] of Weissnichtwo;[23] treating expressly of this subject, and in a style which, 15 whether understood or not, could not even by the blindest be overlooked. In the present Editor's way of thought, this remarkable Treatise, with its Doctrines, whether as judicially acceded to, or judicially denied, has 20 not remained without effect.

"*Die Kleider, ihr Werden und Wirken* (Clothes, their Origin and Influence): *von Diog. Teufelsdröckh, J. U. D. etc. Stillschweigen und Co*[gnie].[24] *Weissnichtwo,* 25 *1831.*

"Here," says the *Weissnichtwo'sche Anzeiger*,[25] "comes a Volume of that extensive, close-printed, close-meditated sort, which, be it spoken with pride, is seen only in Ger- 30 many, perhaps only in Weissnichtwo. Issuing from the hitherto irreproachable Firm of Stillschweigen and Company, with every external furtherance, it is of such internal quality as to set Neglect at defiance." . . . 35 "A work," concludes the well-nigh enthusiastic Reviewer, "interesting alike to the antiquary, the historian, and the philosophic thinker; a masterpiece of boldness, lynx-eyed acuteness, and rugged independent Ger- 40 manism and Philanthropy (*derber Kerndeutschheit und Menschenliebe*); which will not, assuredly, pass current without opposition in high places; but must and will exalt the almost new name of Teufelsdröckh to 45 the first ranks of Philosophy, in our German Temple of Honor."

[22]Diogenes Teufelsdröckh means: God-born Devil's-dung.
[23]Know-not-where.
[24]Silence and Company. J. U. D. means: Doctor of Laws.
[25]Advertiser.

Mindful of old friendship, the distinguished Professor, in this the first blaze of his fame, which however does not dazzle him, sends hither a Presentation-copy of his Book; with compliments and encomiums which modesty forbids the present Editor to rehearse; yet without indicated wish or hope of any kind, except what may be implied in the concluding phrase: *Möchte es* (this remarkable Treatise) *auch im Brittischen Boden gedeihen!*[26]

CHAPTER IV
Characteristics

IT WERE a piece of vain flattery to pretend that this Work on Clothes entirely contents us; that it is not, like all works of genius, like the very Sun, which, though the highest published creation, or work of genius, has nevertheless black spots and troubled nebulosities amid its effulgence,—a mixture of insight, inspiration, with dullness, double-vision, and even utter blindness.

Without committing ourselves to those enthusiastic praises and prophesyings of the *Weissnichtwo'sche Anzeiger,* we admitted that the Book had in a high degree excited us to self-activity, which is the best effect of any book; that it had even operated changes in our way of thought; nay, that it promised to prove, as it were, the opening of a new mine-shaft, wherein the whole world of Speculation might henceforth dig to unknown depths. More especially it may now be declared that Professor Teufelsdröckh's acquirements, patience of research, philosophic and even poetic vigor, are here made indisputably manifest; and unhappily no less his prolixity and tortuosity and manifold ineptitude; that, on the whole, as in opening new mine-shafts is not unreasonable, there is much rubbish in his Book, though likewise specimens of almost invaluable ore. A paramount popularity in England we cannot promise him. Apart from the choice of such a topic as Clothes, too often the manner of treating it betokens in the Author a rusticity and academic seclusion, unblamable, indeed 50 inevitable in a German, but fatal to his success with our public.

[26]May it flourish also on British soil!

Of good society Teufelsdröckh appears to have seen little, or has mostly forgotten what he saw. He speaks-out with a strange plainness; calls many things by their mere dictionary names. To him the Upholsterer is no Pontiff, neither is any Drawing-room a Temple, were it never so begilt and overhung: "a whole immensity of Brussels carpets, and pier-glasses, and or-molu,"[1] as he himself expresses it, "cannot hide from me that such Drawing-room is simply a section of Infinite Space, where so many God-created Souls do for the time meet together." To Teufelsdröckh the highest Duchess is respectable, is venerable; but nowise for her pearl bracelets and Malines laces: in his eyes, the star[2] of a Lord is little less and little more than the broad button of Birmingham spelter[3] in a Clown's smock; "each is an implement," he says, "in its kind; a tag for *hooking-together;* and, for the rest, was dug from the earth, and hammered on a stithy before smith's fingers." Thus does the Professor look in men's faces with a strange impartiality, a strange scientific freedom; like a man unversed in the higher circles, like a man dropped thither from the Moon. Rightly considered, it is in this peculiarity, running through his whole system of thought, that all these shortcomings, over-shootings, and multiform perversities, take rise: if indeed they have not a second source, also natural enough, in his Transcendental Philosophies, and humor of looking at all Matter and Material things as Spirit;[4] whereby truly his case were but the more hopeless, the more lamentable.

To the Thinkers of this nation, however, of which class it is firmly believed there are individuals yet extant, we can safely recommend the Work: nay, who knows but among the fashionable ranks too, if it be true, as Teufelsdröckh maintains, that "within the most starched cravat there passes a windpipe and weasand, and under the thickliest embroidered waistcoat beats a heart,"—the force of that rapt earnestness may be felt, and here and there an arrow of the soul pierce through? In our wild Seer, shaggy, unkempt, like a Baptist living on locusts and wild honey,[5] there is an untutored energy, a silent, as it were unconscious, strength, which, except in the higher walks of Literature, must be rare. Many a deep glance, and often with unspeakable precision, has he cast into mysterious Nature, and the still more mysterious Life of Man. Wonderful it is with what cutting words, now and then, he severs asunder the confusion; shears down, were it furlongs deep, into the true center of the matter; and there not only hits the nail on the head, but with crushing force smites it home, and buries it.—On the other hand, let us be free to admit, he is the most unequal writer breathing. Often after some such feat, he will play truant for long pages, and go dawdling and dreaming, and mumbling and maundering the merest commonplaces, as if he were asleep with eyes open, which indeed he is.

Of his boundless Learning, and how all reading and literature in most known tongues from *Sanchoniathon*[6] to *Dr. Lingard,*[7] from your Oriental *Shasters,*[8] and *Talmuds,* and *Korans,* with Cassini's[9] *Siamese Tables,* and Laplace's *Mécanique Céleste,* down to *Robinson Crusoe* and the *Belfast Town and Country Almanack,* are familiar to him,—we shall say nothing: for unexampled as it is with us, to the Germans such universality of study passes without wonder, as a thing commendable, indeed, but natural, indispensable, and

---

[1] Gilded bronze used in decorating furniture.

[2] Part of the insignia of such orders as the Bath and the Garter is a jeweled ornament having the shape of a star.

[3] Zinc.

[4] The guiding principle of all Carlyle's ethical work is the principle of Fichte's speculation, that the world of experience is but the appearance or vesture of the divine idea or life; that in this divine life lie the springs of true poetry, of true science, and of true religion; and that he only has true life whose spirit is interpenetrated with the realities transcending empirical facts, who is willing to resign his own personality in the service of humanity, and who strives incessantly to work out the ideal that gives nobility and grandeur to human effort" (R. Adamson, *Fichte,* p. 79).

[5] St. Matthew, 3:1-6.

[6] The name of a supposed Phoenician writer whose works, real or pretended, were used by Philo Byblius in a Phoenician history, part of which is preserved in Eusebius.

[7] English Roman Catholic historian (1771-1851).

[8] Textbooks of Hindu laws and religion.

[9] The name of a family of French astronomers who long controlled the Paris Observatory.

there of course. A man that devotes his life to learning, shall he not be learned?

In respect of style our Author manifests the same genial capability, marred too often by the same rudeness, inequality, and appar- 5 ent want of intercourse with the higher classes. Occasionally, as above hinted, we find consummate vigor, a true inspiration; his burning thoughts step forth in fit burning words, like so many full-formed Minervas, 10 issuing amid flame and splendor from Jove's head; a rich, idiomatic diction, picturesque allusions, fiery poetic emphasis, or quaint tricksy turns; all the graces and terrors of a wild Imagination, wedded to the clearest In- 15 tellect, alternate in beautiful vicissitude. Were it not that sheer sleeping and sopo- rific passages; circumlocutions, repetitions, touches even of pure doting jargon, so often intervene! On the whole, Professor Teu- 20 felsdröckh is not a cultivated writer. Of his sentences perhaps not more than nine-tenths stand straight on their legs; the remainder are in quite angular attitudes, buttressed-up by props (of parentheses and dashes), and 25 ever with this or the other tagrag hanging from them; a few even sprawl-out helplessly on all sides, quite broken-backed and dis- membered. Nevertheless, in almost his very worst moods, there lies in him a singular 30 attraction. A wild tone pervades the whole utterance of the man, like its keynote and regulator; now screwing itself aloft as into the Song of Spirits, or else the shrill mockery of Fiends; now sinking in cadences, not with- 35 out melodious heartiness, though sometimes abrupt enough, into the common pitch, when we hear it only as a monotonous hum; of which hum the true character is extremely difficult to fix. Up to this hour we have 40 never fully satisfied ourselves whether it is a tone and hum of real Humor, which we reckon among the very highest qualities of genius, or some echo of mere Insanity and Inanity, which doubtless ranks below the 45 very lowest.

Under a like difficulty, in spite even of our personal intercourse, do we still lie with re- gard to the Professor's moral feeling. Gleams of an ethereal love burst forth from 50 him, soft wailings of infinite pity; he could clasp the whole Universe into his bosom, and

keep it warm; it seems as if under that rude exterior there dwelt a very seraph. Then again he is so sly and still, so imperturbably saturnine; shows such indifference, malign coolness towards all that men strive after; and ever with some half-visible wrinkle of a bitter sardonic humor, if indeed it be not mere stolid callousness,—that you look on him almost with a shudder, as on some in- carnate Mephistopheles,[10] to whom this great terrestrial and celestial Round, after all, were but some huge foolish Whirligig, where kings and beggars, and angels and demons, and stars and street-sweepings, were chaoti- cally whirled, in which only children could take interest. His look, as we mentioned, is probably the gravest ever seen: yet it is not of that cast-iron gravity frequent enough among our own Chancery suitors;[11] but rather the gravity as of some silent, high- encircled mountain-pool, perhaps the crater of an extinct volcano; into whose black deeps you fear to gaze: those eyes, those lights that sparkle in it, may indeed be reflexes of the heavenly Stars, but perhaps also glances from the region of Nether Fire!

Certainly a most involved, self-secluded, altogether enigmatic nature, this of Teufels- dröckh! Here, however, we gladly recall to mind that once we saw him laugh; once only, perhaps it was the first and last time in his life; but then such a peal of laughter, enough to have awakened the Seven Sleepers![12] It was of Jean Paul's[13] doing: some single billow in that vast World- Mahlstrom[14] of Humor, with its heaven- kissing coruscations, which is now, alas, all congealed in the frost of death! The large- bodied Poet and the small, both large enough in soul, sat talking miscellaneously together, the present Editor being privileged to listen; and now Paul, in his serious way, was giving one of those inimitable "Extra-harangues";

---

[10] An evil spirit, or devil. He appears in Mar- lowe's Doctor Faustus and Goethe's Faust.

[11] In Carlyle's day the English Court of Chancery was a place of almost infinite delays and red tape.

[12] Of Ephesus. (See note to De Quincey's Con- fessions, first passage.)

[13] Jean Paul Friedrich Richter (1763–1825), Ger- man humorist.

[14] A whirlpool in the Arctic Ocean near the coast of Norway.

and, as it chanced, On the Proposal for a *Cast-metal King:* gradually a light kindled in our Professor's eyes and face, a beaming, mantling, loveliest light; through those murky features, a radiant, ever-young Apollo looked; and he burst forth like the neighing of all Tattersall's,[15]—tears streaming down his cheeks, pipe held aloft, foot clutched into the air,—loud, long-continuing, uncontrollable; a laugh not of the face and diaphragm only, but of the whole man from head to heel. The present Editor, who laughed indeed, yet with measure, began to fear all was not right: however, Teufelsdröckh composed himself, and sank into his old stillness; on his inscrutable countenance there was, if anything, a slight look of shame; and Richter himself could not rouse him again. Readers who have any tincture of Psychology know how much is to be inferred from this; and that no man who has once heartily and wholly laughed can be altogether irreclaimably bad. How much lies in Laughter: the cipher-key, wherewith we decipher the whole man! Some men wear an everlasting barren simper; in the smile of others lies a cold glitter as of ice: the fewest are able to laugh, what can be called laughing, but only sniff and titter and snigger from the throat outwards; or at best, produce some whiffling husky cachinnation,[16] as if they were laughing through wool: of none such comes good. The man who cannot laugh is not only fit for treasons, stratagems, and spoils;[17] but his whole life is already a treason and a stratagem.

Considered as an Author, Herr Teufelsdröckh has one scarcely pardonable fault, doubtless his worst: an almost total want of arrangement. In this remarkable Volume, it is true, his adherence to the mere course of Time produces, through the Narrative portions, a certain show of outward method; but of true logical method and sequence there is too little. Apart from its multifarious sections and subdivisions, the Work naturally falls into two Parts; a Historical-Descriptive, and a Philosophical-Speculative: but falls, unhappily, by no firm line of demarcation; in that labyrinthic combination, each Part overlaps, and indents, and indeed runs quite through the other. Many sections are of a debatable rubric,[18] or even quite nondescript and unnameable; whereby the Book not only loses in accessibility, but too often distresses us like some mad banquet, wherein all courses had been confounded, and fish and flesh, soup and solid, oyster-sauce, lettuces, Rhine-wine and French mustard, were hurled into one huge tureen or trough, and the hungry Public invited to help itself. To bring what order we can out of this Chaos shall be part of our endeavor.

CHAPTER XI
Prospective

THE Philosophy of Clothes is now to all readers, as we predicted it would do, unfolding itself into new boundless expansions, of a cloudcapt, almost chimerical aspect, yet not without azure loomings in the far distance, and streaks as of an Elysian brightness; the highly questionable purport and promise of which is becoming more and more important for us to ascertain. Is that a real Elysian brightness, cries many a timid wayfarer, or the reflex of Pandemonian lava? Is it of a truth leading us into beatific Asphodel meadows, or the yellow-burning marl of a Hell-on-Earth?

Our Professor, like other Mystics, whether delirious or inspired, gives an Editor enough to do. Ever higher and dizzier are the heights he leads us to; more piercing, all-comprehending, all-confounding are his views and glances. For example, this of Nature being not an Aggregate but a Whole:

"Well sang the Hebrew Psalmist: 'If I take the wings of the morning and dwell in the uttermost parts of the universe, God is there.'[1] Thou thyself, O cultivated reader, who too probably art no Psalmist, but a Prosaist, knowing GOD only by tradition, knowest thou any corner of the world where at least FORCE is not? The drop which thou shakest from thy wet hand, rests not where

---

[15] A famous horse-market and stable in London.
[16] Immoderate laughter.
[17] *Merchant of Venice*, V, i, 85.

[18] Chapter or subject heading, written in red ink in early manuscripts.
[1] Psalms, 139:9, 10.

it falls, but tomorrow thou findest it swept away; already on the wings of the North-wind, it is nearing the Tropic of Cancer. How came it to evaporate, and not lie motion- 5 less? Thinkest thou there is ought motion-less; without Force, and utterly dead?

"As I rode through the Schwarzwald,[2] I said to myself: That little fire which glows star-like across the dark-growing (*nacht-ende*) moor, where the sooty smith bends 10 over his anvil, and thou hopest to replace thy lost horse-shoe,—is it a detached, sepa-rated speck, cut-off from the whole Universe; or indissolubly joined to the whole? Thou fool, that smithy-fire was (primarily) kindled 15 at the Sun; is fed by air that circulates from before Noah's Deluge, from beyond the Dog-star; therein, with Iron Force, and Coal Force, and the far stranger Force of Man, are cunning affinities and battles and vic- 20 tories of Force brought about; it is a little ganglion, or nervous center, in the great vital system of Immensity. Call it, if thou wilt, an unconscious Altar, kindled on the bosom of the All; whose iron sacrifice, whose iron 25 smoke and influence reach quite through the All; whose dingy Priest, not by word, yet by brain and sinew, preaches forth the mys-tery of Force; nay preaches forth (exoteri-cally enough) one little textlet from the Gos- 30 pel of Freedom, the Gospel of Man's Force, commanding, and one day to be all-commanding.

"Detached, separated! I say there is no such separation: nothing hitherto was ever 35 stranded, cast aside; but all, were it only a withered leaf, works together with all; is borne forward on the bottomless, shoreless flood of Action, and lives through perpetual metamorphoses. The withered leaf is not 40 dead and lost, there are Forces in it and around it, though working in inverse order; else how could it *rot?* Despise not the rag from which man makes Paper, or the litter from which the earth makes Corn.[3] Rightly 45 viewed no meanest object is insignificant; all objects are as windows, through which the philosophic eye looks into Infinitude itself."

Again, leaving that wondrous Schwarz- 50

wald Smithy-Altar, what vacant, high-sailing air-ships are these, and whither will they sail with us?

"All visible things are emblems; what thou seest is not there on its own account; strictly taken, is not there at all: Matter exists only spiritually, and to represent some Idea, and *body* it forth. Hence Clothes, as despicable as we think them, are so unspeakably sig-nificant. Clothes, from the King's mantle downwards, are emblematic, not of want only, but of a manifold cunning Victory over Want. On the other hand, all Emblematic things are properly Clothes, thought-woven or hand-woven: must not the Imagination weave Garments, visible Bodies, wherein the else invisible creations and inspirations of our Reason are, like Spirits, revealed, and first become all-powerful;—the rather if, as we often see, the Hand too aid her, and (by wool Clothes or otherwise) reveal such even to the outward eye?

"Men are properly said to be clothed with Authority, clothed with Beauty, with Curses, and the like. Nay, if you consider it, what is Man himself, and his whole terrestrial Life, but an Emblem; a Clothing or visible Garment for that divine ME of his, cast hither, like a light-particle, down from Heaven? Thus is he said also to be clothed with a Body.[4]

"Language is called the Garment of Thought: however, it should rather be, Lan-guage is the Flesh-Garment, the Body, of Thought. I said that imagination wove this Flesh-Garment; and does not she? Meta-phors are her stuff: examine Language; what, if you except some few primitive ele-ments (of natural sound), what is it all but Metaphors, recognized as such, or no longer recognized; still fluid and florid, or now solid-grown and colorless? If those same primitive elements are the osseous fixtures in the Flesh-Garment Language,—then are Metaphors its muscles and tissues and living integuments. An unmetaphorical style you shall in vain seek for: is not your very *Atten-tion* a *Stretching-to?*[5] The difference lies here: some styles are lean, adust,[6] wiry, the

[2]The Black Forest in Germany.
[3]Wheat.

[4]Cf. Job, 10:11.
[5]Latin: *ad tendere*, to *stretch* the neck *towards*.
[6]Scorched.

muscle itself seems osseous; some are even quite pallid, hunger-bitten and dead-looking; while others again glow in the flush of health and vigorous self-growth, sometimes (as in my own case) not without an apoplectic tendency. Moreover, there are sham Metaphors, which overhanging that same Thought's-Body (best naked), and deceptively bedizening, or bolstering it out, may be called its false stuffings, superfluous show-cloaks (*Putz-Mäntel*), and tawdry woolen rags: whereof he that runs and reads may gather whole hampers,—and burn them."

Than which paragraph on Metaphors did the reader ever chance to see a more surprisingly metaphorical? However, that is not our chief grievance; the Professor continues:

"Why multiply instances? It is written, the Heavens and the Earth shall fade away like a Vesture;[7] which indeed they are: the Time-vesture of the Eternal. Whatsoever sensibly exists, whatsoever represents Spirit to Spirit, is properly a Clothing, a suit of Raiment, put on for a season, and to be laid off. Thus in this one pregnant subject of CLOTHES, rightly understood, is included all that men have thought, dreamed, done, and been: the whole External Universe and what it holds is but Clothing, and the essence of all Science lies in the PHILOSOPHY OF CLOTHES."

Towards these dim infinitely-expanded regions, close-bordering on the impalpable Inane, it is not without apprehension, and perpetual difficulties, that the Editor sees himself journeying and struggling. Till lately a cheerful daystar of hope hung before him, in the expected Aid of Hofrath Heuschrecke;[8] which daystar, however, melts now, not into the red of morning, but into a vague, gray half-light, uncertain whether dawn of day or dusk of utter darkness. For the last week, these so-called Biographical Documents are in his hand. By the kindness of a Scottish Hamburg Merchant, whose name, known to the whole mercantile world, he must not mention; but whose honorable courtesy, now and often

before spontaneously manifested to him, a mere literary stranger, he cannot soon forget,—the bulky Weissnichtwo Packet, with all its Customhouse seals, foreign hieroglyphs, and miscellaneous tokens of Travel, arrived here in perfect safety, and free of cost. The reader shall now fancy with what hot haste it was broken up, with what breathless expectation glanced over; and, alas, with what unquiet disappointment it has, since then, been often thrown down, and again taken up.

Hofrath Heuschrecke, in a too long-winded Letter, full of compliments, Weissnichtwo politics, dinners, dining repartees, and other ephemeral trivialities, proceeds to remind us of what we knew well already: that however it may be with Metaphysics, and other abstract Science originating in the Head (*Verstand*) alone, no Life-Philosophy (*Lebensphilosophie*), such as this of Clothes pretends to be, which originates equally in the Character (*Gemüth*), and equally speaks thereto, can attain its significance till the Character itself is known and seen; "till the Author's View of the World (*Weltansicht*), and how he actively and passively came by such view, are clear: in short till a Biography of him has been philosophico-poetically written, and philosophico-poetically read." "Nay," adds he, "were the speculative scientific Truth even known, you still, in this inquiring age, ask yourself, Whence came it, and Why, and How?—and rest not, till, if no better may be, Fancy have shaped-out an answer; and either in the authentic lineaments of Fact, or the forged ones of Fiction, a complete picture and Genetical History of the Man and his spiritual Endeavor lies before you. But why," says the Hofrath, and indeed say we, "do I dilate on the uses of our Teufelsdröckh's Biography? The great Herr Minister von Goethe[9] has penetratingly remarked that 'Man is properly the *only* object that interests man': thus I too have noted, that in Weissnichtwo our whole conversation is little or nothing else but Biography or Auto-Biography; ever humano-anecdotical (*menschlich-anekdotisch*). Bi-

---

[7]St. Matthew, 4:4; see also Psalms, 102:25–27.

[8]Councilor Grasshopper (Teufelsdröckh's chief friend).

[9]Johann Wolfgang von Goethe (1749–1832), who was a cabinet-minister of the Duke of Weimar. The following quotation is from *Wilhelm Meister*

ography is by nature the most universally profitable, universally pleasant of all things: especially Biography of distinguished individuals.

"By this time, *mein Verehrtester* (my Most Esteemed)," continues he, with an eloquence which, unless the words be purloined from Teufelsdröckh, or some trick of his, as we suspect, is well-nigh unaccountable, "by this time you are fairly plunged (*vertieft*) in that mighty forest of Clothes-Philosophy; and looking round, as all readers do, with astonishment enough. Such portions and passages as you have already mastered, and brought to paper, could not but awaken a strange curiosity touching the mind they issued from; the perhaps unparalleled psychical mechanism, which manufactured such matter, and emitted it to the light of day. Had Teufelsdröckh also a father and mother; did he, at one time, wear drivel-bibs, and live on spoon-meat? Did he ever, in rapture and tears, clasp a friend's bosom to his; looks he also wistfully into the long burial-aisle of the Past, where only winds, and their low harsh moan, give inarticulate answer? Has he fought duels;—good Heaven! how did he comport himself when in Love? By what singular stair-steps, in short, and subterranean passages, and sloughs of Despair,[10] and steep Pisgah hills, has he reached this wonderful prophetic Hebron[11] (a true Old-Clothes Jewry) where he now dwells?

"To all these natural questions the voice of public History is as yet silent. Certain only that he has been, and is, a Pilgrim, and a Traveler from a far Country; more or less foot-sore and travel-soiled; has parted with road-companions; fallen among thieves, been poisoned by bad cookery, blistered with bugbites; nevertheless, at every stage (for they have let him pass), has had the Bill to discharge. But the whole particulars of his Route, his Weather-observations, the picturesque Sketches he took, though all regularly jotted down (in indelible sympathetic-ink[12] by an invisible interior Penman), are these nowhere forthcoming? Perhaps quite lost: one other leaf of that mighty Volume (of human Memory) left to fly abroad, unprinted, unpublished, unbound up, as waste paper; and to rot, the sport of rainy winds?

"No, *verehrtester Herr Herausgeber,*[13] in no wise! I here, by the unexampled favor you stand in with our Sage, send not a Biography only, but an Autobiography: at least the materials for such; wherefrom, if I misreckon not, your perspicacity will draw fullest insight: and so the whole Philosophy and Philosopher of Clothes will stand clear to the wondering eyes of England, nay thence, through America, through Hindostan, and the antipodal New Holland, finally conquer (*einnehmen*) great part of this terrestrial Planet!"

And now let the sympathizing reader judge of our feeling when, in place of this same Autobiography with "fullest insight," we find —Six considerable PAPER-BAGS, carefully sealed, and marked successively, in gilt China-ink, with the symbols of the Six southern Zodiacal Signs,[14] beginning at Libra; in the inside of which sealed Bags lie miscellaneous masses of Sheets, and oftener Shreds and Snips, written in Professor Teufelsdröckh's scarce legible *cursiv-schrift;*[15] and treating of all imaginable things under the Zodiac and above it, but of his own personal history only at rare intervals, and then in the most enigmatic manner.

Whole fascicles there are, wherein the Professor, or, as he here, speaking in the third person, calls himself, "the Wanderer," is not once named. Then again, amidst what seems to be a Metaphysico-theological Disquisition, "Detached Thoughts on the Steam-engine," or, "The continued Possibility of Prophecy," we shall meet with some quite private, not unimportant Biographical fact. On certain sheets stand Dreams, au-

---

[10]Cf. the Slough of Despond in Bunyan's *Pilgrim's Progress.*

[11]Pisgah was the mountain from which Moses viewed the Promised Land; Hebron, the residence of King David and burial place of the prophets.

[12]A fluid for invisible writing, to be made visible by pressing with a hot iron.

[13]Most esteemed Mr. Editor.

[14]Libra, Scorpio, Sagittarius, Capricornus, Aquarius, Pisces.

[15]A small running hand-writing.

thentic or not, while the circumjacent waking Actions are omitted. Anecdotes, oftenest without date of place or time, fly loosely on separate slips, like Sibylline leaves.[16] Interspersed also are long purely Autobiographical delineations; yet without connection, without recognizable coherence; so unimportant, so superfluously minute, they almost remind us of "P.P. Clerk of this Parish."[17] Thus does famine of intelligence alternate with waste. Selection, order, appears to be unknown to the Professor. In all Bags the same imbroglio; only perhaps in the Bag *Capricorn*, and those near it, the confusion a little worse confounded. Close by a rather eloquent Oration, "On receiving the Doctor's-Hat," lie wash-bills, marked *bezahlt* (settled). His Travels are indicated by the Street-Advertisements of the various cities he has visited; of which Street-Advertisements, in most living tongues, here is perhaps the completest collection extant.

So that if the Clothes-Volume itself was too like a Chaos, we have now instead of the solar Luminary that should still it, the airy Limbo which by intermixture will farther volatilize and discompose it! As we shall perhaps see it our duty ultimately to deposit these Six Paper-Bags in the British Museum, farther description, and all vituperation of them, may be spared. Biography or Autobiography of Teufelsdröckh there is, clearly enough, none to be gleaned here: at most some sketchy, shadowy fugitive likeness of him may, by unheard-of efforts, partly of intellect, partly of imagination, on the side of Editor and Reader, rise up between them. Only as a gaseous-chaotic Appendix to that aqueous-chaotic Volume can the contents of the Six Bags hover round us, and portions thereof be incorporated with our delineation of it.

Daily and nightly does the Editor sit (with green spectacles) deciphering these unimaginable Documents from their perplexed *cursiv-schrift;* collating them with the almost equally unimaginable Volume, which stands in legible print. Over such a universal medley of high and low, of hot, cold, moist and dry,[18] is he here struggling (by union of like with like, which is Method) to build a firm Bridge for British travelers. Never perhaps since our first Bridge-builders, Sin and Death, built that stupendous Arch from Hellgate to the Earth, did any Pontifex, or Pontiff, undertake such a task as the present Editor. For in this Arch too, leading, as we humbly presume, far otherwards than that grand primeval one, the materials are to be fished-up from the weltering deep, and down from the simmering air, here one mass, there another, and cunningly cemented, while the elements boil beneath: nor is there any supernatural force to do it with; but simply the Diligence and feeble thinking Faculty of an English Editor, endeavoring to evolve printed Creation out of a German printed and written Chaos, wherein, as he shoots to and fro in it, gathering, clutching, piecing the Why to the far-distant Wherefore, his whole Faculty and Self are like to be swallowed up.

Patiently, under these incessant toils and agitations, does the Editor, dismissing all anger, see his otherwise robust health declining; some fraction of his allotted natural sleep nightly leaving him, and little but an inflamed nervous-system to be looked for. What is the use of health, or of life, if not to do some work therewith? And what work nobler than transplanting foreign Thought into the barren domestic soil; except indeed planting Thought of your own, which the fewest are privileged to do? Wild as it looks, this Philosophy of Clothes, can we ever reach its real meaning, promises to reveal new-coming Eras, the first dim rudiments and already-budding germs of a nobler Era, in Universal History. Is not such a prize worth some striving? Forward with us, courageous reader; be it towards failure, or towards success! The latter thou sharest with us; the former also is not all our own.

---

[16] The answers of the Cumaean Sibyl to Aeneas were committed to leaves, to be blown about by the wind (*Aeneid*, VI).

[17] *Memoirs of P.P., Clerk of this Parish,* variously attributed to Pope, John Arbuthnot (1667–1735), and Swift.

[18] The four elements of which, according to ancient and medieval theory, the universe was composed. Here and in the allusion to the bridge built by Sin and Death Carlyle has in mind *Paradise Lost,* II, 890 ff.

BOOK II

CHAPTER VII

The Everlasting No

UNDER the strange nebulous envelopment, wherein our Professor has now shrouded himself, no doubt but his spiritual nature is nevertheless progressive, and growing: for how can the "Son of Time," in any case, stand still? We behold him, through those dim years, in a state of crisis, of transition: his mad Pilgrimings, and general solution into aimless Discontinuity, what is all this but a mad Fermentation; wherefrom, the fiercer it is, the clearer product will one day evolve itself?

Such transitions are ever full of pain: thus the Eagle when he molts is sickly; and, to attain his new beak, must harshly dash-off the old one upon rocks. What Stoicism soever our Wanderer, in his individual acts and motions, may affect, it is clear that there is a hot fever of anarchy and misery raging within; coruscations of which flash out: as, indeed, how could there be other? Have we not seen him disappointed, bemocked of Destiny, through long years? All that the young heart might desire and pray for has been denied; nay, as in the last worst instance, offered and then snatched away. Ever an "excellent Passivity"; but of useful, reasonable Activity, essential to the former as Food to Hunger, nothing granted: till at length, in this wild Pilgrimage, he must forcibly seize for himself an Activity, though useless, unreasonable. Alas, his cup of bitterness, which had been filling drop by drop, ever since that first "ruddy morning" in the Hinterschlag Gymnasium,[1] was at the very lip; and then with that poisondrop, of the Towgood-and-Blumine business,[2] it runs over, and even hisses over in a deluge of foam.

He himself says once, with more justice than originality: "Man is, properly speaking, based upon Hope, he has no other possession but Hope; this world of his is emphatically the 'Place of Hope.'" What, then, was our Professor's possession? We see him, for the present, quite shut-out from Hope; looking not into the golden orient, but vaguely all round into a dim copper firmament, pregnant with earthquake and tornado.

Alas, shut-out from Hope, in a deeper sense than we yet dream of! For, as he wanders wearisomely through this world, he has now lost all tidings of another and higher. Full of religion, or at least of religiosity, as our Friend has since exhibited himself, he hides not that, in those days, he was wholly irreligious: "Doubt had darkened into Unbelief," says he; "shade after shade goes grimly over your soul, till you have the fixed, starless, Tartarean black."[3] To such readers as have reflected, what can be called reflecting, on man's life, and happily discovered, in contradiction to much Profit-and-Loss Philosophy,[4] speculative and practical, that Soul is *not* synonymous with Stomach; who understand, therefore, in our Friend's words, "that, for man's well-being, Faith is properly the one thing needful; how, with it, Martyrs, otherwise weak, can cheerfully endure the shame and the cross; and without it, Worldlings puke-up their sick existence, by suicide, in the midst of luxury": to such it will be clear that, for a pure moral nature, the loss of his religious Belief was the loss of everything. Unhappy young man! All wounds, the crush of long-continued Destitution, the stab of false Friendship and of false Love, all wounds in thy so genial heart, would have healed again, had not its life-warmth been withdrawn. Well might he exclaim, in his wild way: "Is there no God, then; but at best an absentee God, sitting idle, ever since the first Sabbath, at the outside of his Universe, and *seeing* it go? Has the word Duty no meaning; is what we call Duty no divine Messenger and Guide, but a false earthly Phantasm, made-up of Desire and Fear, of emanations from the Gallows and from Doctor Graham's Celestial-Bed?[5] Happiness of

---

[1]The Smite-behind Grammar-School. Teufelsdröckh had seen a little dog, to whose tail the boys had tied a tin kettle, rush by on that morning, a symbol of what he himself was to suffer at the school.

[2]Towgood was a worldly young English friend of Teufelsdröckh, who married Blumine, the young lady whom Teufelsdröckh loved.

[3]Gloomy as Tartarus, the inner region of Hell.

[4]Utilitarianism, materialism.

[5]An elaborate bed supposed to cure sterility in married people, invented by the notorious quack doctor, James Graham (1745–94).

an approving Conscience! Did not Paul of Tarsus, whom admiring men have since named Saint, feel that *he* was 'the chief of sinners';[6] and Nero of Rome, jocund in spirit (*wohlgemuth*), spend much of his time in fiddling? Foolish Wordmonger and Motive-grinder,[7] who in thy Logic-mill hast an earthly mechanism for the Godlike itself, and wouldst fain grind me out Virtue from the husks of Pleasure,—I tell thee, Nay! To the unregenerate Prometheus Vinctus[8] of a man, it is ever the bitterest aggravation of his wretchedness that he is conscious of Virtue, that he feels himself the victim not of suffering only, but of injustice. What then? Is the heroic inspiration we name Virtue but some Passion; some bubble of the blood, bubbling in the direction others *profit* by? I know not: only this I know, If what thou namest Happiness be our true aim, then are we all astray. With Stupidity and sound Digestion man may front much. But what, in these dull unimaginative days, are the terrors of Conscience to the diseases of the Liver! Not on Morality, but on Cookery, let us build our stronghold: there brandishing our frying-pan, as censer, let us offer sweet incense to the Devil, and live at ease on the fat things *he* has provided for his Elect!"

Thus has the bewildered Wanderer to stand, as so many have done, shouting question after question into the Sibyl-cave of Destiny, and receive no Answer but an Echo. It is all a grim Desert, this once-fair world of his; wherein is heard only the howling of wild-beasts, or the shrieks of despairing, hate-filled men; and no Pillar of Cloud by day, and no Pillar of Fire by night,[9] any longer guides the Pilgrim. To such length has the spirit of Inquiry carried him. "But what boots it (*was thut's*)?" cries he: "it is but the common lot in this era. Not having come to spiritual majority prior to the *Siècle de Louis Quinze*,[10] and not being born purely a Loghead (*Dummkopf*), thou hadst no other outlook. The whole world is, like thee, sold to Unbelief; their old Temples of the Godhead, which for long have not been rainproof, crumble down; and men ask now: where is the Godhead; our eyes never saw him?"

Pitiful enough were it, for all these wild utterances, to call our Diogenes wicked. Unprofitable servants as we all are, perhaps at no era of his life was he more decisively the Servant of Goodness, the Servant of God, than even now when doubting God's existence. "One circumstance I note," says he: "after all the nameless woe that Inquiry, which for me, what it is not always, was genuine Love of Truth, had wrought me, I nevertheless still loved Truth, and would bate no jot of my allegiance to her. 'Truth!' I cried, 'though the Heavens crush me for following her: no Falsehood! though a whole celestial Lubberland were the price of Apostasy." In conduct it was the same. Had a divine Messenger from the clouds, or miraculous Handwriting on the wall, convincingly proclaimed to me *This thou shalt do*, with what passionate readiness, as I often thought, would I have done it, had it been leaping into the infernal Fire. Thus, in spite of all Motive-grinders, and Mechanical Profit-and-Loss Philosophies, with the sick ophthalmia and hallucination they had brought on, was the Infinite nature of Duty[11] still dimly present to me: living without God in the world, of God's light I was not utterly bereft; if my as yet sealed eyes, with their unspeakable longing, could nowhere see Him, nevertheless in my heart He was present, and His heaven-written Law still stood legible and sacred there."

Meanwhile, under all these tribulations, and temporal and spiritual destitutions, what must the Wanderer, in his silent soul, have endured! "The painfullest feeling," writes

---

[6]I Timothy, 1:15.

[7]An allusion to utilitarian philosophers like Jeremy Bentham (1748–1832), who believed that pleasure was the proper reward for virtue.

[8]*Prometheus Bound*, the title of Aeschylus's drama, representing the conflict of audacious genius with Fate.

[9]Cf. Exodus, 13:21.

[10]The age of Louis XV; i. e., the Age of Reason.

[11]That is, that duty is to be performed, not from considerations of reward and punishment—from space-time considerations—but from a conviction of the non-temporal, non-spatial (or absolute) good in performing it; also that the results of duty performed or neglected go on through endless time and infinite space (Charles F. Harrold).

he, "is that of your own Feebleness (*Un-kraft*); ever, as the English Milton says, to be weak is the true misery.[12] And yet of your Strength there is and can be no clear feeling, save by what you have prospered in, by what you have done. Between vague wavering Capability and fixed indubitable Performance, what a difference! A certain inarticulate Self-consciousness dwells dimly in us; which only our Works can render articulate and decisively discernible. Our Works are the mirror wherein the spirit first sees its natural lineaments. Hence, too, the folly of that impossible Precept, *Know thy-self*;[13] till it be translated into this partially possible one, *Know what thou canst work at*.

"But for me, so strangely unprosperous had I been, the net-result of my Workings amounted as yet simply to—Nothing. How then could I believe in my Strength, when there was as yet no mirror to see it in? Ever did this agitating, yet, as I now perceive, quite frivolous question, remain to me insolu-ble: Hast thou a certain Faculty, a certain Worth, such even as the most have not; or art thou the completest Dullard of these mod-ern times? Alas, the fearful Unbelief is unbelief in yourself; and how could I be-lieve? Had not my first, last Faith in my-self, when even to me the Heavens seemed laid open, and I dared to love, been all-too cruelly belied? The speculative Mystery of Life grew ever more mysterious to me: nei-ther in the practical Mystery had I made the slightest progress, but been everywhere buf-feted, foiled, and contemptuously cast out. A feeble unit in the middle of a threatening Infinitude, I seemed to have nothing given me but eyes, whereby to discern my own wretchedness. Invisible yet impenetrable walls, as of Enchantment, divided me from all living: was there, in the wide world, any true bosom I could press trustfully to mine? O Heaven, No, there was none! I kept a lock upon my lips: why should I speak much with that shifting variety of so-called Friends, in whose withered, vain and too-hungry souls Friendship was but an incredi-

ble tradition? In such cases, your resource is to talk little, and that little mostly from the Newspapers. Now when I look back, it was a strange isolation I then lived in. The men and women around me, even speaking with me, were but Figures; I had, practically, forgotten that they were alive, that they were not merely automatic. In the midst of their crowded streets and assemblages, I walked solitary; and (except as it was my own heart, not another's, that I kept devouring) savage also, as the tiger in his jungle. Some com-fort it would have been, could I, like a Faust, have fancied myself tempted and tormented of the Devil; for a Hell, as I imagine, with-out Life, though only diabolic Life, were more frightful: but in our age of Down-pulling and Disbelief, the very Devil has been pulled down, you cannot so much as be-lieve in a Devil. To me the Universe was all void of Life, of Purpose, of Volition, even of Hostility: it was one huge, dead, im-measurable Steam-engine, rolling on, in its dead indifference, to grind me limb from limb. O, the vast, gloomy, solitary Gol-gotha, and Mill of Death! Why was the Living banished thither companionless, con-scious? Why, if there is no Devil; nay, un-less the Devil is your God?"

A prey incessantly to such corrosions, might not, moreover, as the worst aggrava-tion to them, the iron constitution even of a Teufelsdröckh threaten to fail? We con-jecture that he has known sickness; and, in spite of his locomotive habits, perhaps sick-ness of the chronic sort. Hear this, for ex-ample: "How beautiful to die of broken-heart, on Paper! Quite another thing in practice; every window of your Feeling, even of your Intellect, as it were, begrimed and mud-bespattered, so that no pure ray can enter; a whole Drugshop in your inwards; the fordone soul drowning slowly in quag-mires of Disgust!"

Putting all which external and internal miseries together, may we not find in the fol-lowing sentences, quite in our Professor's still vein, significance enough? "From Suicide a certain aftershine (*Nachschein*) of Christianity withheld me: perhaps also a certain indolence of character; for, was not that a remedy I had at any time within

[12]*Paradise Lost,* i, 157.
[13]A maxim attributed to Solon, Socrates, Thales, etc.; inscribed over the portico of the temple at Delphi.

reach? Often, however, was there a question present to me: Should some one now, at the turning of that corner, blow thee suddenly out of Space, into the other World, or other No-world, by pistol-shot,—how were it? On which ground, too, I often, in sea-storms and sieged cities and other death-scenes, exhibited an imperturbability, which passed, falsely enough, for courage."

"So had it lasted," concludes the Wanderer, "so had it lasted, as in bitter protracted Death-agony, through long years. The heart within me, unvisited by any heavenly dew-drop was smoldering in sulphurous, slow-consuming fire. Almost since earliest memory I had shed no tear; or once only when I, murmuring half-audibly, recited Faust's Death-song, that wild *Selig der den er im Siegesglanze findet* (Happy whom *he* finds in Battle's splendor),[14] and thought that of this last Friend even I was not forsaken, that Destiny itself could not doom me not to die. Having no hope, neither had I any definite fear, were it of Man or of Devil: nay, I often felt as if it might be solacing, could the Arch-Devil himself, though in Tartarean terrors, but rise to me, that I might tell him a little of my mind. And yet, strangely enough, I lived in a continual, indefinite, pining fear; tremulous, pusillanimous, apprehensive of I knew not what; it seemed as if all things in the Heavens above and the Earth beneath would hurt me; as if the Heavens and the Earth were but boundless jaws of a devouring monster, wherein I, palpitating, waited to be devoured.

"Full of such humor, and perhaps the miserablest man in the whole French Capital or Suburbs, was I, one sultry Dog-day, after much perambulation, toiling along the dirty little *Rue Saint-Thomas de l'Enfer*,[15] among civic rubbish enough, in a close atmosphere, and over pavements hot as Nebuchadnezzar's Furnace;[16] whereby doubtless my spirits were little cheered; when, all at once, there rose a Thought in me, and I asked myself: 'What *art* thou afraid of? Wherefore, like a coward, dost thou forever pip and whimper, and go cowering and trembling? Despicable biped! what is the sum-total of the worst that lies before thee? Death? Well, Death; and say the pangs of Tophet too, and all that the Devil and Man may, will or can do against thee! Hast thou not a heart; canst thou not suffer whatsoever it be; and, as a Child of Freedom, though outcast, trample Tophet itself under thy feet, while it consumes thee? Let it come, then; I will meet it and defy it!' And as I so thought, there rushed like a stream of fire over my whole soul; and I shook base Fear away from me forever. I was strong, of unknown strength; a spirit, almost a god. Ever from that time, the temper of my misery was changed: not Fear or whining Sorrow was it, but Indignation and grim fire-eyed Defiance.

"Thus had the EVERLASTING No (*das ewige Nein*) pealed authoritatively through all the recesses of my Being, of my ME; and then was it that my whole ME stood up, in native God-created majesty, and with emphasis recorded its Protest. Such a Protest, the most important transaction in Life, may that same Indignation and Defiance, in a psychological point of view, be fitly called. The Everlasting No had said: 'Behold, thou art fatherless, outcast, and the Universe is mine (the Devil's)'; to which my whole Me now made answer: '*I* am not thine, but Free, and forever hate thee!'

"It is from this hour that I incline to date my Spiritual Newbirth, or Baphometic Fire-baptism;[17] perhaps I directly thereupon began to be a Man."

CHAPTER VIII

Center of Indifference

THOUGH, after this "Baphometic Fire-baptism" of his, our Wanderer signifies that his Unrest was but increased; as, indeed, "Indignation and Defiance," especially

---

[14] Adapted from Goethe's *Faust,* I, iv, 1573–1576.

[15] St. Thomas-of-Hell Street. Carlyle admitted that he himself had had Teufelsdröckh's experience, in Leith Walk, Edinburgh.

[16] Daniel, 3:19.

[17] A baptism of sudden, flame-like spiritual understanding (from Baffometus, an outcast who will receive such a baptism, in the novel of Zacharias Werner, *Die Söhne des Thals;* Baphomet was originally the name of an idol).

against things in general, are not the most peaceable inmates; yet can the Psychologist surmise that it was no longer a quite hopeless Unrest; that henceforth it had at least a fixed center to revolve round. For the fire-baptized soul, long so scathed and thunder-riven, here feels its own Freedom, which feeling is its Baphometic Baptism: the citadel of its whole kingdom it has thus gained by assault, and will keep inexpugnable; outwards from which the remaining dominions, not indeed without hard battling, will doubtless by degrees be conquered and pacificated. Under another figure, we might say, if in that great moment, in the *Rue Saint-Thomas de l'Enfer,* the old inward Satanic School[1] was not yet thrown out of doors, it received peremptory judicial notice to quit;—whereby, for the rest, its howl-chantings, Ernulphus-cursings,[2] and rebellious gnashings of teeth, might, in the meanwhile, become only the more tumultuous, and difficult to keep secret.

Accordingly, if we scrutinize these Pilgrimings well, there is perhaps discernible henceforth a certain incipient method in their madness. Not wholly as a Specter does Teufelsdröckh now storm through the world; at worst as a specter-fighting Man, nay who will one day be a Specter-queller. If pilgriming restlessly to so many "Saints' Wells,"[3] and ever without quenching of his thirst, he nevertheless finds little secular wells, whereby from time to time some alleviation is ministered. In a word, he is now, if not ceasing, yet intermitting to "eat his own heart"; and clutches round him outwardly on the NOT-ME for wholesomer food. Does not the following glimpse exhibit him in a much more natural state?

"Towns also and Cities, especially the ancient, I failed not to look upon with interest. How beautiful to see thereby, as through a long vista, into the remote Time; to have, as it were, an actual section of al- most the earliest Past brought safe into the Present, and set before your eyes! There, in that old City, was a live ember of Culinary Fire put down, say only two-thousand years ago; and there, burning more or less triumphantly, with such fuel as the region yielded, it has burnt, and still burns, and thou thyself seest the very smoke thereof. Ah! and the far more mysterious live ember of Vital Fire was then also put down there; and still miraculously burns and spreads; and the smoke and ashes thereof (in these Judgment-Halls and Churchyards), and its bellows-engines (in these Churches), thou still seest; and its flame, looking out from every kind countenance, and every hateful one, still warms thee or scorches thee.

"Of Man's Activity and Attainment the chief results are aeriform, mystic, and preserved in Tradition only: such are his Forms of Government, with the Authority they rest on; his Customs, or Fashions both of Cloth-habits and of Soul-habits; much more his collective stock of Handicrafts, the whole Faculty he has acquired of manipulating Nature: all these things, as indispensable and priceless as they are, cannot in any way be fixed under lock and key, but must flit, spirit-like, on impalpable vehicles, from Father to Son; if you demand sight of them, they are nowhere to be met with. Visible Plowmen and Hammermen there have been, ever from Cain and Tubalcain[4] downwards; but where does your accumulated Agricultural, Metallurgic, and other Manufacturing SKILL lie warehoused? It transmits itself on the atmospheric air, on the sun's rays (by Hearing and by Vision); it is a thing aeriform, impalpable, of quite spiritual sort. In like manner, ask me not, Where are the LAWS; where is the GOVERNMENT? In vain wilt thou go to Schönbrunn, to Downing Street, to the Palais Bourbon:[5] thou findest nothing there but brick or stone houses, and some bundles of Papers tied with tape. Where, then, is that same cunningly-devised almighty GOVERNMENT of theirs to be laid

---

[1] I. e., the psychological equivalent of the so-called Satanic School of English poetry: Byron, Shelley, and their followers.

[2] Ernulf was a mediaeval bishop of Rochester, whose curse is given in Sterne's *Tristram Shandy,* III, chapter xi.

[3] Wells dedicated to saints, whose patronage was supposed to give medicinal properties to the water.

[4] See Genesis, 4:1–22.

[5] Respectively, to the palace in Vienna where many early nineteenth-century treaties were signed, to the residence of the English Prime Minister in London, and to the building in Paris where the French Chamber of Deputies met.

hands on? Everywhere, yet nowhere: seen only in its works, this too is a thing aeriform, invisible; or if you will, mystic and miraculous. So spiritual (*geistig*) is our whole daily Life: all that we do springs out of Mystery, Spirit, invisible Force; only like a little Cloud-image, or Armida's Palace,[6] air-built, does the Actual body itself forth from the great mystic Deep.

"Visible and tangible products of the Past, again, I reckon-up to the extent of three. Cities, with their Cabinets and Arsenals; then tilled Fields, to either or to both of which divisions Roads with their Bridges, may belong; and thirdly——Books. In which third truly, the last invented, lies a worth far surpassing that of the two others. Wondrous indeed is the virtue of a true Book. Not like a dead city of stones, yearly crumbling, yearly needing repair; more like a tilled field, but then a spiritual field: like a spiritual tree, let me rather say, it stands from year to year, and from age to age (we have Books that already number some hundred-and-fifty human ages); and yearly comes its new produce of leaves (Commentaries, Deductions, Philosophical, Political Systems; or were it only Sermons, Pamphlets, Journalistic Essays), every one of which is talismanic and thaumaturgic, for it can persuade men. O thou who art able to write a Book, which once in the two centuries or oftener there is a man gifted to do, envy not him whom they name City-builder, and inexpressibly pity him whom they name Conqueror or City-burner! Thou too art a Conqueror and Victor; but of the true sort, namely over the Devil: thou too hast built what will outlast all marble and metal, and be a wonder-bringing City of the Mind, a Temple and Seminary and Prophetic Mount, whereto all kindreds of the Earth will pilgrim.—Fool! why journeyest thou wearisomely, in thy antiquarian fervor, to gaze on the stone pyramids of Geeza, or the clay ones of Sacchara?[7] These stand there, as I can tell thee, idle and inert, looking over the Desert, foolishly enough, for the last

three-thousand years: but canst thou not open thy Hebrew BIBLE, then, or even Luther's Version[8] thereof?"

No less satisfactory is his sudden appearance not in Battle, yet on some Battle-field; which, we soon gather, must be that of Wagram; so that here, for once, is a certain approximation to distinctiveness of date. Omitting much, let us impart what follows:

"Horrible enough! A whole Marchfeld[9] strewed with shell-splinters, cannon-shot, ruined tumbrels, and dead men and horses; stragglers still remaining not so much as buried. And those red mold heaps: ay, there lie the Shells of Men, out of which all the Life and Virtue has been blown; and now are they swept together, and crammed-down out of sight, like blown Egg-shells!—Did Nature, when she bade the Donau bring down his mold-cargoes from the Carinthian and Carpathian Heights, and spread them out here into the softest, richest level,—intend thee, O Marchfeld, for a corn-bearing Nursery, whereon her children might be nursed; or for a Cockpit, wherein they might the more commodiously be throttled and tattered? Were thy three broad Highways, meeting here from the ends of Europe, made for Ammunition-wagons, then? Were thy Wagrams and Stillfrieds but so many ready-built Casemates,[10] wherein the house of Hapsburg might batter with artillery, and with artillery be battered? König Ottokar, amid yonder hillocks, dies under Rodolf's truncheon; here Kaiser Franz falls a-swoon under Napoleon's: within which five centuries, to omit the others, how has thy breast, fair Plain, been defaced and defiled! The greensward is torn-up and trampled-down; man's fond care of it, his fruit-trees, hedgerows, and pleasant dwellings, blown away with gunpowder; and the kind seedfield lies a desolate, hideous Place of Sculls.—Nevertheless, Nature is at work; neither shall these

---

[6]The palace of an enchantress in Tasso's *Jerusalem Delivered*.

[7]The Pyramids of Ghizeh and Sakkara, near Cairo in Egypt.

[8]Luther's German translation of the Bible (1534-1535).

[9]A plain near Vienna, north of the Danube (Donau), where Ottokar, King of Bohemia, was slain by Rudolf of Hapsburg in the battle of Stillfried (or Stielfried) in 1278. In 1809, at Wagram in the same plain, Napoleon conquered the Hapsburgs.

[10]Fortress chambers.

Powder-Devilkins with their utmost devilry gainsay her: but all that gore and carnage will be shrouded-in, absorbed into manure; and next year the Marchfeld will be green, nay greener. Thrifty unwearied Nature, ever out of our great waste educing some little profit of thy own,—how dost thou, from the very carcass of the Killer, bring Life for the Living!

"What, speaking in quite unofficial language, is the net-purport and upshot of war? To my own knowledge, for example, there dwell and toil, in the British village of Dumdrudge,[11] usually some five-hundred souls. From these, by certain 'Natural Enemies' of the French, there are successively selected, during the French war, say thirty ablebodied men: Dumdrudge, at her own expense, has suckled and nursed them: she has, not without difficulty and sorrow, fed them up to manhood, and even trained them to crafts, so that one can weave, another build, another hammer, and the weakest can stand under thirty stone avoirdupois. Nevertheless, amid much weeping and swearing, they are selected; all dressed in red; and shipped away, at the public charges, some two-thousand miles, or say only to the south of Spain;[12] and fed there till wanted. And now to that same spot, in the south of Spain, are thirty similar French artisans, from a French Dumdrudge, in like manner wending: till at length, after infinite effort, the two parties come into actual juxtaposition; and Thirty stands fronting Thirty, each with a gun in his hand. Straightway the word 'Fire!' is given: and they blow the souls out of one another; and in place of sixty brisk useful craftsmen, the world has sixty dead carcasses, which it must bury, and anew shed tears for. Had these men any quarrel? Busy as the Devil is, not the smallest! They lived far enough apart; were the entirest strangers; nay, in so wide a Universe, there was even, unconsciously, by Commerce, some mutual helpfulness between them. How then? Simpleton! their Governors had fallen-out; and, instead of shooting one another, had the cunning to make these poor blockheads shoot.—Alas, so is it in Deutschland, and hitherto in all other lands; still as of old, 'what devilry soever Kings do, the Greeks must pay the piper!'[13]—In that fiction of the English Smollett,[14] it is true, the final Cessation of War is perhaps prophetically shadowed forth; where the two Natural Enemies, in person, take each a Tobaccopipe, filled with Brimstone; light the same, and smoke in one another's faces, till the weaker gives in: but from such predicted Peace-Era, what blood-filled trenches, and contentious centuries, may still divide us!"

Thus can the Professor, at least in lucid intervals, look away from his own sorrows, over the many-colored world, and pertinently enough note what is passing there. We may remark, indeed, that for the matter of spiritual culture, if for nothing else, perhaps few periods of his life were richer than this. Internally, there is the most momentous instructive Course of Practical Philosophy, with Experiments, going on; towards the right comprehension of which his Peripatetic[15] habits, favorable to Meditation, might help him rather than hinder. Externally, again, as he wanders to and fro, there are, if for the longing heart little substance, yet for the seeing eye sights enough: in these so boundless Travels of his, granting that the Satanic School was even partially kept down, what an incredible knowledge of our Planet, and its Inhabitants and their Works, that is to say, of all knowable things, might not Teufelsdröckh acquire!

"I have read in most Public Libraries," says he, "including those of Constantinople and Samarcand: in most Colleges, except the Chinese Mandarin ones, I have studied, or seen that there was no studying. Unknown Languages have I oftenest gathered from their natural repertory, the Air, by my organ of Hearing; Statistics, Geographics, Topographics came, through the Eye, almost of their own accord. The ways of Man, how he seeks food, and warmth, and protection

---

[11]Name invented by Carlyle for the typical English village of the time.

[12]To fight in the Peninsular War, 1808–1814.

[13]A free adaptation of Horace, *Epistles,* I, ii, 14.

[14]The Scotch novelist, Tobias Smollett (1721–1771), in *The Adventures of Ferdinand Count Fathom* (chapter xli).

[15]Itinerant. The followers of Aristotle were known as Peripatetics because his lectures were delivered on the walk.

for himself, in most regions, are ocularly known to me. Like the great Hadrian,[16] I meted-out much of the terraqueous Globe with a pair of Compasses that belonged to myself only.

"Of great Scenes why speak? Three summer days, I lingered reflecting, and even composing (*dichtete*), by the Pine-chasms of Vaucluse;[17] and in that clear Lakelet moistened my bread. I have sat under the Palm-trees of Tadmor;[18] smoked a pipe among the ruins of Babylon. The great Wall of China I have seen; and can testify that it is of gray brick, coped and covered with granite, and shows only second-rate masonry.—Great Events, also, have not I witnessed? Kings sweated-down (*ausgemergelt*) into Berlin-and-Milan Customhouse-Officers; the World well won, and the World well lost; oftener than once a hundred-thousand individuals shot (by each other) in one day. All kindreds and peoples and nations dashed together, and shifted and shoveled into heaps, that they might ferment there, and in time unite. The birthpangs of Democracy,[19] wherewith convulsed Europe was groaning in cries that reached Heaven, could not escape me.

"For great Men I have ever had the warmest predilection; and can perhaps boast that few such in this era have wholly escaped me. Great Men are the inspired (speaking and acting) Texts of that divine BOOK OF REVELATION, whereof a Chapter is completed from epoch to epoch, and by some named HISTORY; to which inspired Texts your numerous talented men, and your innumerable untalented men, are the better or worse exegetic Commentaries, and wagonload of too-stupid, heretical or orthodox, weekly Sermons. For my study, the inspired Texts themselves! Thus did not I, in very early days, having disguised me as tavern-waiter, stand behind the field-chairs, under that shady Tree at Treisnitz[20] by the Jena Highway; waiting upon the great Schiller and greater Goethe; and hearing what I have not forgotten. For——"

——But at this point the Editor recalls his principle of caution, some time ago laid down, and must suppress much. Let not the sacredness of Laureled, still more, of Crowned Heads, be tampered with. Should we, at a future day, find circumstances altered, and the time come for Publication, then may these glimpses into the privacy of the Illustrious be conceded; which for the present were little better than treacherous, perhaps traitorous Eavesdroppings. Of Lord Byron, therefore, of Pope Pius, Emperor Tarakwang,[21] and the "White Waterroses" (Chinese Carbonari[22]) with their mysteries, no notice here! Of Napoleon himself we shall only, glancing from afar, remark that Teufelsdröckh's relation to him seems to have been of very varied character. At first we find our poor Professor on the point of being shot as a spy; then taken into private conversation, even pinched on the ear, yet presented with no money; at last indignantly dismissed, almost thrown out of doors, as an "Ideologist." "He himself," says the Professor, "was among the completest Ideologists, at least Ideopraxists:[23] in the Idea (*in der Idee*) he lived, moved and fought. The man was a Divine Missionary, though unconscious of it; and preached, through the cannon's throat, that great doctrine, *La carrière ouverte aux talens*[24] (The Tools to him that can handle them), which is our ultimate Political Evangel, wherein alone can liberty lie. Madly enough he preached, it is true, as Enthusiasts and first Missionaries are wont, with imperfect utterance, amid much frothy rant; yet as articulately perhaps as the case admitted. Or call him, if you will, an American Backwoodsman, who had to fell unpenetrated forests, and battle with innumer-

---

[16]Emperor Hadrian (76–138) spent most of his reign traveling throughout the Roman Empire. The pair of compasses with which Teufelsdröckh similarly measures the globe are his two legs.

[17]A valley in southern France, famous as the home of Petrarch.

[18]Otherwise known as Palmyra, the City of Palms.

[19]Probably an allusion to the famous Three Days' Revolution in Paris, July 27–29, 1830, in which Charles X was overthrown.

[20]Triesnitz, near Jena in Germany.

[21]Pope Pius VII (Pope from 1800 to 1823) and the Chinese Emperor Tao Kuang (1781–1850).

[22]Secret revolutionaries.

[23]Those who put ideas into practice.

[24]Careers open to talents.

able wolves, and did not entirely forbear strong liquor, rioting, and even theft; whom, notwithstanding, the peaceful Sower will follow, and, as he cuts the boundless harvest, bless."

More legitimate and decisively authentic is Teufelsdröckh's appearance and emergence (we know not well whence) in the solitude of the North Cape, on that June Midnight. He has a "light-blue Spanish cloak" hanging round him, as his "most commodious, principal, indeed sole upper-garment"; and stands there, on the World-promontory, looking over the infinite Brine, like a little blue Belfry (as we figure), now motionless indeed, yet ready, if stirred, to ring quaintest changes.

"Silence as of death," writes he; "for Midnight, even in the Arctic latitudes, has its character: nothing but the granite cliffs ruddy-tinged, the peaceable gurgle of that slow-heaving Polar Ocean, over which in the utmost North the great Sun hangs low and lazy, as if he too were slumbering. Yet is his cloud-couch wrought of crimson and cloth-of-gold; yet does his light stream over the mirror of waters, like a tremulous fire-pillar, shooting downwards to the abyss, and hide itself under my feet. In such moments, Solitude also is invaluable; for who would speak, or be looked on, when behind him lies all Europe and Africa, fast asleep, except the watchmen; and before him the silent Immensity, and Palace of the Eternal, whereof our Sun is but a porch-lamp?

"Nevertheless, in this solemn moment comes a man, or monster, scrambling from among the rock-hollows; and, shaggy, huge as the Hyperborean[25] Bear, hails me in Russian speech: most probably, therefore, a Russian Smuggler. With courteous brevity, I signify my indifference to contraband trade, my humane intentions, yet strong wish to be private. In vain: the monster, counting doubtless on his superior stature, and minded to make sport for himself, or perhaps profit, were it with murder, continues to advance; ever assailing me with his importunate train-oil[26] breath; and now has advanced, till we stand both on the verge of the rock, the deep

Sea rippling greedily down below. What argument will avail? On the thick Hyperborean, cherubic reasoning, seraphic eloquence were lost. Prepared for such extremity, I, deftly enough, whisk aside one step; draw out, from my interior reservoirs, a sufficient Birmingham Horse-pistol, and say, 'Be so obliging as retire, Friend (*Er ziehe sich zurück, Freund*), and with promptitude!' This logic even the Hyperborean understands: fast enough, with apologetic, petitionary growl, he sidles off; and, except for suicidal as well as homicidal purposes, need not return.

"Such I hold to be the genuine use of Gunpowder: that it makes all men alike tall. Nay, if thou be cooler, cleverer than I, if thou have more *Mind,* though all but no *Body* whatever, then canst thou kill me first, and art the taller. Hereby, at last, is the Goliath powerless, and the David resistless; savage Animalism is nothing, inventive Spiritualism is all.

"With respect to Duels, indeed, I have my own ideas. Few things, in this so surprising world, strike me with more surprise. Two little visual Spectra of men, hovering with insecure enough cohesion in the midst of the UNFATHOMABLE, and to dissolve therein, at any rate, very soon,—make pause at the distance of twelve paces asunder; whirl round; and, simultaneously by the cunningest mechanism, explode one another into Dissolution; and off-hand become Air, and Non-extant! Deuce on it (*verdammt*), the little spitfires!—Nay, I think with old Hugo von Trimberg:[27] 'God must needs laugh outright, could such a thing be, to see his wondrous Manikins here below.' "

But amid these specialties, let us not forget the great generality, which is our chief quest here: How prospered the inner man of Teufelsdröckh under so much outward shifting? Does Legion[28] still lurk in him, though repressed; or has he exorcised that Devil's Brood? We can answer that the symptoms continue promising. Experience is the grand spiritual Doctor; and with him Teufelsdröckh has been long a patient, swal-

---

[25]Northern.   [26]Whale oil.

[27]Medieval moralist and poet (1260–1309).
[28]Cf. St. Mark, 5:9; St. Luke, 8:30.

lowing many a bitter bolus.[29] Unless our poor Friend belong to the numerous class of Incurables, which seems not likely, some cure will doubtless be effected. We should rather say that Legion, or the Satanic School, was now pretty well extirpated and cast out, but next to nothing introduced in its room; whereby the heart remains, for the while, in a quiet but no comfortable state.

"At length, after so much roasting," thus writes our Autobiographer, "I was what you might name calcined. Pray only that it be not rather, as is the more frequent issue, reduced to a *caput-mortuum!*[30] But in any case, by mere dint of practice, I had grown familiar with many things. Wretchedness was still wretched; but I could now partly see through it, and despise it. Which highest mortal, in this inane Existence, had I not found a Shadow-hunter, or Shadow-hunted; and, when I looked through his brave garnitures, miserable enough? Thy wishes have all been sniffed aside, thought I: but what, had they even been all granted! Did not the Boy Alexander weep because he had not two Planets to conquer; or a whole Solar System; or after that, a whole Universe? *Ach Gott,*[31] when I gazed into these Stars, have they not looked-down on me as if with pity, from their serene spaces; like Eyes glistening with heavenly tears over the little lot of man! Thousands of human generations, all as noisy as our own, have been swallowed-up of Time, and there remains no wreck[32] of them any more; and Arcturus and Orion and Sirius and the Pleiades are still shining in their courses, clear and young, as when the Shepherd first noted them in the plain of Shinar.[33] Pshaw! what is this paltry little Dog-cage[34] of an Earth; what art thou that sittest whining there? Thou art still Nothing, Nobody: true; but who, then, is Something, Somebody? For thee the Family of Man has no use; it rejects thee; thou art wholly as a dissevered limb: so be it; perhaps it is better so!"

Too-heavy-laden Teufelsdröckh! Yet surely his bands are loosening; one day he will hurl the burden far from him, and bound forth free and with a second youth.

"This," says our Professor, "was the CENTER OF INDIFFERENCE I had now reached; through which whoso travels from the Negative Pole to the Positive must necessarily pass."

CHAPTER IX
The Everlasting Yea

"TEMPTATIONS in the Wilderness!"[1] exclaims Teufelsdröckh: "Have we not all to be tried with such? Not so easily can the old Adam, lodged in us by birth, be dispossessed. Our Life is compassed round with Necessity; yet is the meaning of Life itself no other than Freedom, than Voluntary Force: thus have we a warfare; in the beginning, especially, a hard-fought battle. For the God-given mandate, *Work thou in Welldoing,* lies mysteriously written, in Promethean[2] Prophetic Characters, in our hearts; and leaves us no rest, night or day, till it be deciphered and obeyed; till it burn forth, in our conduct, a visible, acted Gospel of Freedom. And as the clay-given mandate, *Eat thou and be filled,* at the same time persuasively proclaims itself through every nerve,—must not there be a confusion, a contest, before the better Influence can become the upper?

"To me nothing seems more natural than the Son of Man, when such God-given mandate first prophetically stirs within him, and the Clay must now be vanquished or vanquish,—should be carried of the spirit into grim Solitudes, and there fronting the Tempter do grimmest battle with him; defiantly setting him at naught, till he yield and fly. Name it as we choose: with or without visible Devil, whether in the natural Desert of rocks and sands, or in the populous moral Desert of selfishness and baseness,— to such Temptation are we all called. Unhappy if we are not! Unhappy if we are but Half-men, in whom that divine handwriting has never blazed forth, all-subduing,

---

[29]Large pill.

[30]Literally, a death's head; also, a worthless residue.

[31]Good Heavens! [32]Wrack, ruin.

[33]Where the Tower of Babel was built (Genesis, 11:1–9).

[34]A wheel-like cage in which a dog was placed to turn the jack of a turnspit, and so roast the meat.

[1]St. Matthew, 4:1.

[2]Fire-bearing. Prometheus brought fire to men.

in true sun-splendor; but quivers dubiously amid meaner lights: or smolders, in dull pain, in darkness, under earthly vapors!—Our Wilderness is the wide World in an Atheistic Century; our Forty Days are long years of suffering and fasting: nevertheless, to these also comes an end. Yes, to me also was given, if not Victory, yet the consciousness of Battle, and the resolve to persevere therein while life or faculty is left. To me also, entangled in the enchanted forests, demon-peopled, doleful of sight and of sound, it was given, after weariest wanderings, to work out my way into the higher sunlight slopes—of that Mountain[3] which has no summit, or whose summit is in Heaven only!"

He says elsewhere, under a less ambitious figure; as figures are, once for all, natural to him: "Has not thy Life been that of most sufficient men (*tüchtigen Männer*) thou hast known in this generation? An outflush of foolish young Enthusiasm, like the first fallow-crop, wherein are as many weeds as valuable herbs: this all parched away, under the Droughts of practical and spiritual Un-belief, as Disappointment, in thought and act, often-repeated gave rise to Doubt, and Doubt gradually settled into Denial! If I have had a second-crop, and now see the perennial greensward, and sit under umbrageous ce-dars, which defy all Drought (and Doubt); herein too, be the Heavens praised, I am not without examples, and even exemplars."

So that, for Teufelsdröckh also, there has been a "glorious revolution":[4] these mad shadow-hunting and shadow-hunted Pilgrim-ings of his were but some purifying "Temptation in the Wilderness," before his apostolic work (such as it was) could begin; which Temptation is now happily over, and the Devil once more worsted! Was "that high moment in the *Rue de l'Enfer*," then, properly the turning-point of the battle; when the Fiend said, *Worship me, or be torn in shreds;* and was answered valiantly with an *Apage Satana?*[5]—singular Teufelsdröckh, would thou hadst told thy singular story in plain words! But it is fruitless to look there, in those Paper-bags, for such. Noth-ing but innuendoes, figurative crotchets: a typical Shadow, fitfully wavering, prophet-ico-satiric; no clear logical Picture. "How paint to the sensual eye," asks he once, "What passes in the Holy-of-Holies of Man's Soul; in what words, known to these pro-fane times, speak even afar-off of the un-speakable?" We ask in turn: Why perplex these times, profane as they are, with need-less obscurity, by omission and by commis-sion? Not mystical only is our Professor, but whimsical; and involves himself, now more than ever, in eye-bewildering *chiaro-scuro*.[6] Successive glimpses, here faithfully imparted, our more gifted readers must endeavor to combine for their own behoof.

He says: "The hot Harmattan wind[7] had raged itself out; its howl went silent within me; and the long-deafened soul could now hear. I paused in my wild wanderings; and sat me down to wait, and consider; for it was as if the hour of change drew nigh. I seemed to surrender, to renounce utterly, and say: Fly, then, false shadows of Hope; I will chase you no more, I will believe you no more. And ye too, haggard specters of Fear, I care not for you; ye too are all shadows and a lie. Let me rest here: for I am way-weary and life-weary; I will rest here, were it but to die: to die or to live is alike to me; alike insignificant."—And again: "Here, then, as I lay in that CENTER OF IN-DIFFERENCE; cast, doubtless by benignant upper Influence, into a healing sleep, the heavy dreams rolled gradually away, and I awoke to a new Heaven and a new Earth.[8] The first preliminary moral Act, Annihilation of Self (*Selbst-tödtung*), had been happily accomplished; and my mind's eyes were now unsealed, and its hands ungyved."[9]

Might we not also conjecture that the fol-lowing passage refers to his Locality, during this same "healing sleep"; that his Pilgrim-staff lies cast aside here, on "the high table-land"; and indeed that the repose is already taking wholesome effect on him? If it were

---

[3] Symbol of spiritual insight.

[4] Name generally given to the revolution which in 1688 replaced James II with William III and Mary II.

[5] Get thee hence, Satan! (Matthew, 4:8–10).

[6] Light and shade.

[7] Dry, dust-laden wind, at certain seasons blowing along the Atlantic coast of Africa from the interior.

[8] Cf. Revelation, 21:1.   [9] Unfettered.

not that the tone, in some parts, has more of riancy,[10] even of levity, than we could have expected! However, in Teufelsdröckh, there is always the strangest Dualism: light dancing, with guitar-music, will be going on in the forecourt, while by fits from within comes the faint whimpering of woe and wail. We transcribe the piece entire.

"Beautiful it was to sit there, as in my skyey Tent, musing and meditating; on the high table-land, in front of the Mountains; over me, as roof, the azure Dome, and around me, for walls, four azure-flowing curtains,— namely, of the Four azure Winds, on whose bottom-fringes also I have seen gilding. And then to fancy the fair Castles that stood sheltered in these Mountain hollows; with their green flower-lawns, and white dames and damosels, lovely enough: or better still, the straw-roofed Cottages, wherein stood many a Mother baking bread, with her children round her:—all hidden and protectingly folded-up in the valley-folds; yet there and alive, as sure as if I beheld them. Or to see, as well as fancy, the nine Towns and Villages, that lay round my mountain-seat, which, in still weather, were wont to speak to me (by their steeple-bells) with metal tongue: and, in almost all weather, proclaimed their vitality by repeated Smoke-clouds; whereon, as on a culinary horologe,[11] I might read the hour of the day. For it was the smoke of cookery, as kind housewives at morning, midday, eventide, were boiling their husbands' kettles; and ever a blue pillar rose up into the air, successively or simultaneously, from each of the nine, saying, as plainly as smoke could say: Such and such a meal is getting ready here. Not uninteresting! For you have the whole Borough, with all its love-makings and scandal-mongerings, contentions and contentments, as in miniature, and could cover it all with your hat.—If, in my wide Wayfarings, I had learned to look into the business of the World in its details, here perhaps was the place for combining it into general propositions, and deducing inferences therefrom.

"Often also could I see the black Tempest marching in anger through the Distance:

round some Schreckhorn,[12] as yet grim-blue, would the eddying vapor gather, and there tumultuously eddy, and flow down like a mad witch's hair; till, after a space, it vanished, and, in the clear sunbeam, your Schreckhorn stood smiling grim-white, for the vapor had held snow. How thou fermentest and elaboratest, in thy great fermenting-vat and laboratory of an Atmosphere, of a World, O Nature!—Or what is Nature? Ha! why do I not name thee God? Art not thou the 'Living Garment of God'? O Heavens, is it, in very deed, He, then, that ever speaks through thee; that lives and loves in thee, that lives and loves in me?

"Fore-shadows, call them rather fore-splendors, of that Truth, and Beginning of Truths, fell mysteriously over my soul. Sweeter than Dayspring to the Ship-wrecked in Nova Zembla;[13] ah, like the mother's voice to her little child that strays bewildered, weeping, in unknown tumults; like soft streamings of celestial music to my too-exasperated heart, came that Evangel. The Universe is not dead and demoniacal, a charnel-house with specters; but godlike, and my Father's!

"With other eyes, too, could I now look upon my fellow man: with an infinite Love, an infinite Pity. Poor, wandering, wayward man! Art thou not tried, and beaten with stripes, even as I am? Ever, whether thou bear the royal mantle or the beggar's gabardine, art thou not so weary, so heavy-laden; and thy Bed of Rest is but a Grave. O my Brother, my Brother, why cannot I shelter thee in my bosom, and wipe away all tears from thy eyes!—Truly, the din of many-voiced Life, which, in this solitude, with the mind's organ, I could hear, was no longer a maddening discord, but a melting one; like inarticulate cries, and sobbings of a dumb creature, which in the ear of Heaven are prayers. The poor Earth, with her poor joys, was now my needy Mother, not my cruel Stepdame; Man, with his so mad Wants and so mean Endeavors, had become the dearer to me; and even for his sufferings and his sins, I now first named him Brother.

---

[10]Laughableness.
[11]Clock.

[12]Peak of Terror. One of the principal summits of the Bernese Alps, in Switzerland.
[13]Island in the Arctic Ocean north of Russia.

Thus was I standing in the porch of that '*Sanctuary of Sorrow*';[14] by strange, steep ways had I too been guided thither; and ere long its sacred gates would open, and the '*Divine Depth of Sorrow*'[15] lie disclosed to me."

The Professor says, he here first got eye on the Knot that had been strangling him, and straightway could unfasten it, and was free. "A vain interminable controversy," writes he, "touching what is at present called Origin of Evil, or some such thing, arises in every soul, since the beginning of the world; and in every soul, that would pass from idle Suffering into actual Endeavoring, must first be put an end to. The most, in our time, have to go content with a simple, incomplete enough Suppression of this controversy; to a few some Solution of it is indispensable. In every new era, too, such Solution comes-out in different terms; and ever the Solution of the last era has become obsolete, and is found unserviceable. For it is man's nature to change his Dialect from century to century; he cannot help it though he would. The authentic *Church-Catechism* of our present century has not yet fallen into my hands: meanwhile, for my own private behoof, I attempt to elucidate the matter so. Man's Unhappiness, as I construe, comes of his Greatness; it is because there is an Infinite in him, which with all his cunning he cannot quite bury under the Finite. Will the whole Finance Ministers and Upholsterers and Confectioners of modern Europe undertake, in joint-stock company, to make one Shoeblack HAPPY? They cannot accomplish it, above an hour or two: for the Shoeblack also has a Soul quite other than his Stomach; and would require, if you consider it, for his permanent satisfaction and saturation, simply this allotment, no more, and no less: *God's infinite Universe altogether to himself,* therein to enjoy infinitely, and fill every wish as fast as it rose. Oceans of Hochheimer,[16] a Throat like that of Ophiuchus:[17] speak not of them; to the infinite Shoeblack they are as nothing. No sooner is your ocean filled, than he grumbles that it might have been of better vintage. Try him with half of a Universe, of an Omnipotence, he sets to quarreling with the proprietor of the other half, and declares himself the most maltreated of men.—Always there is a black spot in our sunshine: it is even, as I said, the *Shadow of Ourselves*.

"But the whim we have of Happiness is somewhat thus. By certain valuations, and averages, of our own striking, we come upon some sort of average terrestrial lot; this we fancy belongs to us by nature, and of indefeasible right. It is simple payment of our wages, of our deserts; requires neither thanks nor complaint; only such *overplus* as there may be do we account Happiness; any *deficit* again is Misery. Now consider that we have the valuation of our own deserts ourselves, and what a fund of Self-conceit there is in each of us,—do you wonder that the balance should so often dip the wrong way, and many a Blockhead cry: See there, what a payment; was ever worthy gentleman so used!—I tell thee, Blockhead, it all comes of thy Vanity; of what thou *fanciest* those same deserts of thine to be. Fancy that thou deservest to be hanged (as is most likely), thou wilt feel it happiness to be only shot: fancy that thou deservest to be hanged in a hair-halter, it will be a luxury to die in hemp.

"So true is it, what I then said, that *the Fraction of Life can be increased in value not so much by increasing your Numerator as by lessening your Denominator.* Nay, unless my Algebra deceive me, *Unity* itself divided by *Zero* will give *Infinity.* Make thy claim of wages a zero, then; thou hast the world under thy feet. Well did the Wisest of our time write: 'It is only with Renunciation (*Entsagen*) that Life, properly speaking, can be said to begin.'[18]

"I asked myself: What is this that, ever since earliest years, thou hast been fretting and fuming, and lamenting and self-

---

[14]The name of the hall into which Wilhelm Meister is to be taken to view the remaining murals representing the life of Christ; used here to denote a state of soul, later the state of the whole world (Charles F. Harrold).

[15]Christ's sorrow.

[16]A Rhine wine from Hochheim near Mainz.

[17]Evidently the throat of the serpent in the constellation of Ophiuchus.

[18]Adapted, rather than quoted, from Goethe's *Wilhelm Meister*.

tormenting, on account of? Say it in a word: is it not because thou art not HAPPY? Because the THOU (sweet gentleman) is not sufficiently honored, nourished, soft-bedded, and lovingly cared-for? Foolish soul! What Act of Legislature was there that *thou* shouldst be Happy? A little while ago thou hadst no right to *be* at all. What if thou wert born and predestined not to be Happy, but to be Unhappy! Art thou nothing other than a Vulture, then, that fliest through the Universe seeking after somewhat to *eat;* and shrieking dolefully because carrion enough is not given thee? Close thy *Byron;* open thy *Goethe."*

"Esleuchtet mir ein,[19] I see a glimpse of it!" cries he elsewhere: "there is in man a HIGHER than Love of Happiness: he can do without Happiness, and instead thereof find Blessedness! Was it not to preach-forth this same HIGHER that sages and martyrs, the Poet and the Priest, in all times, have spoken and suffered; bearing testimony, through life and through death, of the God-like that is in Man, and how in the Godlike only has he Strength and Freedom? Which God-inspired Doctrine art thou also honored to be taught; O Heavens! and broken with manifold merciful Afflictions, even till thou become contrite, and learn it! O, thank thy Destiny for these; thankfully bear what yet remain: thou hadst need of them; the Self in thee needed to be annihilated. By benignant fever-paroxysms is Life rooting out the deep-seated chronic Disease, and triumphs over Death. On the roaring billows of Time, thou art not engulfed, but borne aloft into the azure of Eternity. Love not Pleasure; love God. This is the EVERLASTING YEA, wherein all contradiction is solved: wherein whoso walks and works, it is well with him."

And again: "Small is it that thou canst trample the Earth with its injuries under thy feet, as old Greek Zeno[20] trained thee: thou canst love the Earth while it injures thee, and even because it injures thee; for this a Greater than Zeno was needed, and he too was sent. Knowest thou that *'Worship of Sorrow'?* The Temple thereof, founded some eighteen centuries ago, now lies in ruins, overgrown with jungle, the habitation of doleful creatures:[21] nevertheless, venture forward; in a low crypt, arched out of falling fragments, thou findest the Altar still there, and its sacred Lamp perennially burning."

Without pretending to comment on which strange utterances, the Editor will only remark, that there lies beside them much of a still more questionable character; unsuited to the general apprehension; nay wherein he himself does not see his way. Nebulous disquisitions on Religion, yet not without bursts of splendor; on the "perennial continuance of Inspiration"; on Prophecy; that there are "true Priests, as well as Baal-Priests,[22] in our own day": with more of the like sort. We select some fractions, by way of finish to this farrago.

"Cease, my much respected Herr von Voltaire,"[23] thus apostrophizes the Professor: "shut thy sweet voice; for the task appointed thee seems finished. Sufficiently hast thou demonstrated this proposition, considerable or otherwise: That the Mythus[24] of the Christian Religion looks not in the eighteenth century as it did in the eighth. Alas, were thy six-and-thirty quartos, and the six-and-thirty thousand other quartos and folios, and flying sheets or reams, printed before and since on the same subject, all needed to convince us of so little! But what next? Wilt thou help us to embody the divine Spirit of that Religion in a new Mythus, in a new vehicle and vesture, that our Souls, otherwise too like perishing, may live? What! thou hast no faculty in that kind? Only a torch for burning, no hammer for building? Take our thanks, then, and——thyself away.

"Meanwhile what are antiquated Mythuses to me? Or is the God present, felt in my own heart, a thing which Herr von Voltaire will dispute out of me; or dispute into me? To the *'Worship of Sorrow'* ascribe what origin and genesis thou pleasest, *has* not that

---

[19] An exclamation of Wilhelm Meister's.
[20] A Greek Stoic philosopher of the third century B. C.

[21] Cf. Isaiah, 13:21.   [22] False priests.
[23] François Marie Arouet (1694–1778), who for Carlyle typifies the skepticism of the eighteenth century.
[24] Myth.

Worship originated, and been generated; is it not *here?* Feel it in thy heart, and then say whether it is of God! This is Belief; all else is Opinion,—for which latter whoso will, let him worry and be worried."

"Neither," observes he elsewhere, "shall ye tear-out one another's eyes, struggling over 'Plenary Inspiration,'[25] and such-like: try rather to get a little even Partial Inspiration, each of you for himself. ONE BIBLE I know, of whose Plenary Inspiration doubt is not so much as possible; nay with my own eyes I saw the God's-Hand writing it: thereof all other Bibles are but Leaves,— say, in Picture-Writing to assist the weaker faculty."

Or, to give the wearied reader relief, and bring it to an end, let him take the following perhaps more intelligible passage:

"To me, in this our life," says the Professor, "which is an internecine warfare with the Time-spirit, other warfare seems questionable. Hast thou in any way a Contention with thy brother, I advise thee, think well what the meaning thereof is. If thou gauge it to the bottom, it is simply this: 'Fellow, see! thou art taking more than thy share of Happiness in the world, something from *my* share: which, by the Heavens, thou shalt not; nay I will fight thee rather.'— Alas, and the whole lot to be divided is such a beggarly matter, truly a 'feast of shells,' for the substance has been spilled out: not enough to quench one Appetite; and the collective human species clutching at them!— Can we not, in all such cases, rather say: 'Take it, thou too-ravenous individual; take that pitiful additional fraction of a share, which I reckoned mine, but which thou so wantest; take it with a blessing: would to Heaven I had enough for thee!'—If Fichte's *Wissenschaftslehre*[26] be, 'to a certain extent,

Applied Christianity,' surely to a still greater extent, so is this. We have here not a Whole Duty of Man,[27] yet a Half Duty, namely the Passive half: could we but do it, as we can demonstrate it!

"But indeed Conviction, were it never so excellent, is worthless till it convert itself into Conduct. Nay properly Conviction is not possible till then; inasmuch as all Speculation is by nature endless, formless, a vortex amid vortices: only by a felt indubitable certainty of Experience does it find any center to revolve round, and so fashion itself into a system. Most true is it, as a wise man teaches us, that 'Doubt of any sort cannot be removed except by Action.'[28] On which ground, too, let him who gropes painfully in darkness or uncertain light, and prays vehemently that the dawn may ripen into day, lay this other precept well to heart, which to me was of invaluable service: *'Do the Duty which lies nearest thee,'* which thou knowest to be a Duty! Thy second Duty will already have become clearer.

"May we not say, however, that the hour of Spiritual Enfranchisement is even this: When your Ideal World, wherein the whole man has been dimly struggling and inexpressibly languishing to work, becomes revealed, and thrown open; and you discover, with amazement enough, like the Lothario in *Wilhelm Meister,* that your 'America is here or nowhere'? The Situation that has not its Duty, its Ideal, was never yet occupied by man. Yes here, in this poor, miserable, hampered, despicable Actual, wherein thou even now standest, here or nowhere is thy Ideal: work it out therefrom; and working, believe, live, be free. Fool! the Ideal is in thyself, the impediment too is in thyself: thy Condition is but the stuff thou art to shape that same Ideal out of: what matters whether such stuff be of this sort or that, so the Form thou give it be heroic, be poetic? O thou that pinest in the imprisonment of the Actual, and criest bitterly to the gods for a kingdom wherein to rule and create,

---

[25] The theological doctrine of plenary inspiration, against which Voltaire was particularly violent, regards supernatural inspiration as extending to all subjects dealt with in the Bible, and therefore to be accepted as true and authoritative. Carlyle regarded Voltaire's attack as beside the point, since "Christianity, the worship of Sorrow," does not rest upon "miracles" and other "evidences," but has its verification "in mysterious, ineffaceable characters . . . written in the purest nature of man" (Charles F. Harrold).

[26] The Doctrine of Knowledge of the German philosopher, Johann Gottlieb Fichte (1762–1814).

[27] The title of an anonymous devotional work first published in 1658.

[28] This and the quotation in the following sentence are from Goethe's *Wilhelm Meister.*

know this of a truth: the thing thou seekest is already with thee, 'here or nowhere,' couldst thou only see!

"But it is with man's Soul as it was with Nature: the beginning of Creation is— Light.[29] Till the eye have vision, the whole members are in bonds. Divine moment, when over the tempest-tossed Soul, as once over the wild-weltering Chaos, it is spoken: Let there be Light! Ever to the greatest that has felt such moment, is it not miraculous and God-announcing; even as, under simpler figures, to the simplest and least. The mad primeval Discord is hushed; the rudely-jumbled conflicting elements bind themselves into separate Firmaments: deep silent rock-foundations are built beneath; and the skyey vault with its everlasting Luminaries above: instead of a dark wasteful Chaos, we have a blooming, fertile, heaven-encompassed World.

"I too could now say to myself: Be no longer a Chaos, but a World, or even World-kin. Produce! Produce! Were it but the pitifullest infinitesimal fraction of a Product, produce it, in God's name! 'Tis the utmost thou hast in thee: out with it, then. Up, up! Whatsoever thy hand findeth to do, do it with thy whole might. Work while it is called Today; for the Night cometh, wherein no man can work."[30]

BOOK III

CHAPTER VIII

Natural Supernaturalism

IT IS in his stupendous Section, headed *Natural Supernaturalism,* that the Professor first becomes a Seer; and, after long effort, such as we have witnessed, finally subdues under his feet this refractory Clothes-Philosophy, and takes victorious possession thereof. Phantasms enough he has had to struggle with; "Cloth-webs and Cob-webs," of Imperial Mantles, Superannuated Symbols, and what not: yet still did he courageously pierce through. Nay, worst of all,

two quite mysterious, world-embracing Phantasms, TIME and SPACE,[1] have ever hovered round him, perplexing and bewildering: but with these also he now resolutely grapples, these also he victoriously rends asunder. In a word, he has looked fixedly on Existence, till, one after the other, its earthly hulls and garnitures have all melted away; and now, to his rapt vision, the interior celestial Holy of Holies lies disclosed.

Here, therefore, properly it is that the Philosophy of Clothes attains to Transcendentalism;[2] this last leap, can we but clear it, takes us safe into the promised land, where *Palingenesia,*[3] in all senses, may be considered as beginning. "Courage, then!" may our Diogenes exclaim, with better right than Diogenes the First once did. This stupendous Section we, after long painful meditation, have found not to be unintelligible; but, on the contrary, to grow clear, nay radiant, and all-illuminating. Let the reader, turning on it what utmost force of speculative intellect is in him, do his part; as we, by judicious selection and adjustment, shall study to do ours:

"Deep has been, and is, the significance of Miracles," thus quietly begins the Professor; "far deeper perhaps than we imagine. Meanwhile, the question of questions were: What specially is a Miracle? To that Dutch King of Siam, an icicle had been a miracle;[4] whoso had carried with him an air-pump,

---

[29]Cf. Genesis, 1:3.

[30]Cf. Ecclesiastes, 9:10; John, 9:4.

[1]"Time and Space . . . are not external but internal entities: they have no outward existence; there is no Time and no Space *out* of the mind; they are mere *forms* of man's spiritual being, *laws* under which his thinking nature is constituted to act. This seems the hardest conclusion of all, but it is an important one with Kant; and is not given forth as a dogma but carefully deduced in his *Critik der Reinen Vernunft* with great precision and the strictest form of argument" (Carlyle, Essay on Novalis). In the present chapter, of course, Carlyle speaks rather as a poet and mystic than as a philosopher.

[2]"The Idealist . . . boasts that his Philosophy is Transcendental, that is 'ascending *beyond* the senses'; which, he asserts, *all* Philosophy, properly so-called, by its nature is and must be" (Carlyle, Essay on Novalis).

[3]New birth.

[4]"The Indian prince who refused to believe the first relations concerning the effects of frost reasoned justly" (Hume, *Inquiry concerning the Human Understanding,* Sec. x). In this and following paragraphs Carlyle has in mind Hume's discussion of miracles.

and vial of vitriolic ether, might have worked a miracle. To my Horse, again, who unhappily is still more unscientific, do not I work a miracle, and magical *'Open sesame!'*[5] every time I please to pay twopence, and open for him an impassable *Schlagbaum,* or shut Turnpike?

" 'But is not a real Miracle simply a violation of the Laws of Nature?' ask several. Whom I answer by this new question: What are the Laws of Nature? To me perhaps the rising of one from the dead were no violation of these Laws, but a confirmation; were some far deeper Law, now first penetrated into, and by Spiritual Force, even as the rest have all been, brought to bear on us with its Material Force.

"Here too may some inquire, not without astonishment: On what ground shall one, that can make Iron swim,[6] come and declare that therefore he can teach Religion? To us, truly, of the Nineteenth Century, such declaration were inept enough; which nevertheless to our fathers, of the First Century, was full of meaning.

" 'But is it not the deepest Law of Nature that she be constant?' cries an illuminated class: 'Is not the Machine of the Universe fixed to move by unalterable rules?' Probable enough, good friends: nay I, too, must believe that the God, whom ancient inspired men assert to be 'without variableness or shadow of turning,'[7] does indeed never change; that Nature, that the Universe, which no one whom it so pleases can be prevented from calling a Machine, does move by the most unalterable rules. And now of you, too, I make the old inquiry: What those same unalterable rules, forming the complete Statute-Book of Nature, may possibly be?

"They stand written in our Works of Science, say you; in the accumulated records of Man's Experience?—Was Man with his Experience present at the Creation, then, to see how it all went on? Have any deepest scientific individuals yet dived down to the foundations of the Universe, and gauged everything there? Did the Maker take them

into His counsel;[8] that they read His ground-plan of the incomprehensible All; and can say, This stands marked therein, and no more than this? Alas, not in anywise! These scientific individuals have been nowhere but where we also are; have seen some handbreadths deeper than we see into the Deep that is infinite, without bottom as without shore.

"Laplace's Book on the Stars, wherein he exhibits that certain Planets, with their Satellites, gyrate round our worthy Sun, at a rate and in a course, which, by greatest good fortune, he and the like of him have succeeded in detecting,—is to me as precious as to another. But is this what thou namest 'Mechanism of the Heavens,' and 'System of the World'; this, wherein Sirius and the Pleiades, and all Herschel's[9] Fifteen-thousand Suns per minute,[10] being left out, some paltry handful of Moons, and inert Balls, had been—looked at, nicknamed, and marked in the Zodiacal Way-bill; so that we can now prate of their Whereabout; their How, their Why, their What, being hid from us, as in the signless Inane?

"System of Nature! To the wisest man, wide as is his vision, Nature remains of quite *infinite* depth, of quite infinite expansion; and all Experience thereon limits itself to some few computed centuries and measured square-miles. The course of Nature's phases, on this our little fraction of a Planet, is partially known to us: but who knows what deeper courses these depend on; what infinitely larger Cycle (of causes) our little Epicycle[11] revolves on? To the Minnow every cranny and pebble, and quality and accident, of its little native Creek may have become familiar: but does the Minnow understand the Ocean Tides and periodic Currents, the Tradewinds, and Monsoons, and Moon's Eclipses; by all which the condition of its little Creek is regulated, and may, from time to time (*un*miraculously enough), be quite overset and reversed? Such a min-

---

[5]The magical words used to open the cave in the story of "Ali Baba and the Forty Thieves" in *The Arabian Nights.*

[6]2 Kings, 6:6.   [7]St. James, 1:17.

[8]See Job, 38:4–18.

[9]An English astronomer, of German birth (1738–1822).

[10]An astronomical minute, the sixtieth part of a degree.

[11]A circle whose center moves round in the circumference of a greater circle.

now is Man; his Creek this Planet Earth; his Ocean the immeasurable All; his Monsoons and periodic Currents the mysterious Course of Providence through Aeons of Aeons.

"We speak of the Volume of Nature: and truly a Volume it is,—whose Author and Writer is God. To read it! Dost thou, does man, so much as well know the Alphabet thereof? With its Words, Sentences, and grand descriptive Pages, poetical and philosophical, spread out through Solar Systems, and Thousands of Years, we shall not try thee. It is a Volume written in celestial hieroglyphs, in the true Sacred-writing; of which even Prophets are happy that they can read here a line and there a line. As for your Institutes, and Academies of Science, they strive bravely; and, from amid the thick-crowded, inextricably intertwisted hieroglyphic writing, pick out, by dexterous combinations, some Letters in the vulgar Character, and therefrom put together this and the other economic Recipe, of high avail in Practice. That Nature is more than some boundless Volume of such Recipes, or huge, well-nigh inexhaustible Domestic-Cookery Book, of which the whole secret will in this manner one day evolve itself, the fewest dream.

"Custom," continues the Professor, "doth make dotards of us all.[12] Consider well, thou wilt find that Custom is the greatest of Weavers; and weaves air-raiment for all the Spirits of the Universe; whereby indeed these dwell with us visibly, as ministering servants, in our houses and workshops; but their spiritual nature becomes, to the most, forever hidden. Philosophy complains that Custom has hoodwinked us, from the first; that we do everything by Custom, even Believe by it; that our very Axioms, let us boast of Free-thinking as we may, are oftenest simply such Beliefs as we have never heard questioned. Nay, what is Philosophy throughout but a continual battle against Custom; an ever-renewed effort to *transcend* the sphere of blind Custom, and so become Transcendental?

"Innumerable are the illusions and legerdemain-tricks of Custom: but of all these, perhaps the cleverest is her knack of persuading us that the Miraculous, by simple repetition, ceases to be Miraculous. True, it is by this means we live; for man must work as well as wonder: and herein is Custom so far a kind nurse, guiding him to his true benefit. But she is a fond foolish nurse, or rather we are false foolish nurslings, when, in our resting and reflecting hours, we prolong the same deception. Am I to view the Stupendous with stupid indifference, because I have seen it twice, or two-hundred, or two-million times? There is no reason in Nature or in Art why I should: unless, indeed, I am a mere Work-Machine, for whom the divine gift of Thought were no other than the terrestrial gift of Steam is to the Steam-engine; a power whereby cotton might be spun, and money and money's worth realized.

"Notable enough too, here as elsewhere, wilt thou find the potency of Names; which indeed are but one kind of such custom-woven, wonder-hiding Garments. Witchcraft, and all manner of Specter-work, and Demonology, we have now named Madness and Diseases of the Nerves. Seldom reflecting that still the new question comes upon us: What is Madness, what are Nerves? Ever, as before, does Madness remain a mysterious-terrific, altogether *infernal* boiling-up of the Nether Chaotic Deep, through this fair-painted Vision of Creation, which swims thereon, which we name the Real. Was Luther's Picture of the Devil[13] less a Reality, whether it were formed within the bodily eye, or without it? In every the wisest Soul lies a whole world of internal Madness, an authentic Demon-Empire; out of which, indeed, his world of Wisdom has been creatively built together, and now rests

---

[12] Cf. *Hamlet*, III, i, 83: "Thus conscience does make cowards of us all."

[13] "In the room of the Wartburg, where he sat translating the Bible, they still show you a black spot on the wall; the strange memorial of one of these conflicts. Luther sat translating one of the Psalms; he was worn-down with long labor, with sickness, abstinence from food: there rose before him some hideous indefinable Image, which he took for the Evil One to forbid his work. Luther started up, with fiend-defiance; flung the inkstand at the specter and it disappeared!" (Carlyle, *Heroes and Hero-Worship,* "The Hero as Priest.") Carlyle hardly answers the difficult question he raises.

there, as on its dark foundations does a habitable flowery Earth-rind.

"But deepest of all illusory Appearances, for hiding Wonder, as for many other ends, are your two grand fundamental world-enveloping Appearances, SPACE and TIME.[14] These, as spun and woven for us from before Birth itself, to clothe our celestial ME for dwelling here, and yet to blind it,—lie all-embracing, as the universal canvas, or warp and woof, whereby all minor Illusions, in this Phantasm Existence, weave and paint themselves. In vain, while here on Earth, shall you endeavor to strip them off; you can, at best, but rend them asunder for moments, and look through.

"Fortunatus had a wishing Hat, which when he put on, and wished himself Anywhere, behold he was There. By this means had Fortunatus triumphed over Space, he had annihilated Space;[15] for him there was no Where, but all was Here. Were a Hatter to establish himself, in the Wahngasse[16] of Weissnichtwo, and make felts of this sort for all mankind, what a world we should have of it! Still stranger, should, on the opposite side of the street, another Hatter establish himself; and, as his fellow-craftsman made Space-annihilating Hats, make Time-annihilating! Of both would I purchase, were it with my last groschen;[17] but chiefly of this latter. To clap-on your felt, and, simply by wishing that you were Any*where*, straightway to be *There!* Next to clap-on your other felt, and, simply by wishing that you were Any*when*, straightway to be *Then!* This were indeed the grander: shooting at will from the Fire-Creation of the World to its Fire-Consummation; here historically present in the First Century, conversing face to face with Paul and Seneca;[18] there prophetically in the Thirty-first, conversing also face to face with other Pauls and Senecas, who as yet stand hidden in the depth of that late Time!

"Or thinkest thou it were impossible, unimaginable? Is the Past annihilated, then, or only past; is the Future non-extant, or only future? Those mystic faculties of thine, Memory and Hope, already answer: already through those mystic avenues, thou the Earth-blinded summonest both Past and Future, and communest with them, though as yet darkly, and with mute beckonings. The curtains of Yesterday drop down, the curtains of Tomorrow roll up; but Yesterday and Tomorrow both *are*. Pierce through the Time-element, glance into the Eternal. Believe what thou findest written in the sanctuaries of Man's Soul, even as all Thinkers, in all ages, have devoutly read it there: that Time and Space are not God, but creations of God; that with God as it is a universal HERE, so is it an everlasting Now.

"And seest thou therein any glimpse of IMMORTALITY?—O Heaven! Is the white Tomb of our Loved One, who died from our arms, and had to be left behind us there, which rises in the distance, like a pale, mournfully receding Milestone, to tell how many toilsome uncheered miles we have journeyed on alone,—but a pale spectral Illusion! Is the lost Friend still mysteriously Here, even as we are Here mysteriously, with God! —Know of a truth that only the Time-shadows have perished, or are perishable; that the real Being of whatever was, and whatever is, and whatever will be, *is* even now and forever. This, should it unhappily seem new, thou mayest ponder at thy leisure; for the next twenty years, or the next twenty centuries: believe it thou must; understand it thou canst not.

"That the Thought-forms, Space and Time, wherein, once for all, we are sent into this Earth to live, should condition and determine our whole Practical reasonings, conceptions, and imagings or imaginings,— seems altogether fit, just, and unavoidable. But that they should, furthermore, usurp such sway over pure spiritual Meditation, and blind us to the wonder everywhere lying close on us, seems nowise so. Admit Space and Time to their due rank as Forms of

---

[14] See note at beginning of this chapter.

[15] Carlyle's instance illustrates the difficulty of triumphing over space, even in thought, as of course Fortunatus did not annihilate space; when he was "there" he was no longer "here." His quickness of movement has really nothing to do with the matter.

[16] Mad Street.

[17] German coin, worth about two cents (not used since 1876).

[18] They were contemporaries. Seneca (A. D. 4–65) was a Roman philosopher and tutor of Nero.

Thought; nay even, if thou wilt, to their quite undue rank of Realities: and consider, then, with thyself how their thin disguises hide from us the brightest God-effulgences! Thus, were it not miraculous, could I stretch forth my hand and clutch the Sun? Yet thou seest me daily stretch forth my hand and therewith clutch many a thing, and swing it hither and thither. Art thou a grown baby, then, to fancy that the Miracle lies in miles of distance, or in pounds avoirdupois of weight; and not to see that the true inexplicable God-revealing Miracle lies in this, that I can stretch forth my hand at all; that I have free Force to clutch aught therewith? Innumerable other of this sort are the deceptions, and wonder-hiding stupefactions, which Space practices on us.

"Still worse is it with regard to Time. Your grand anti-magician, and universal wonder-hider, is this same lying Time. Had we but the Time-annihilating Hat, to put on for once only, we should see ourselves in a World of Miracles, wherein all fabled or authentic Thaumaturgy, and feats of Magic, were outdone. But unhappily we have not such a Hat; and man, poor fool that he is, can seldom and scantily help himself without one.

"Were it not wonderful, for instance, had Orpheus,[19] or Amphion,[20] built the walls of Thebes by the mere sound of his Lyre? Yet tell me, Who built these walls of Weissnichtwo; summoning out all the sandstone rocks, to dance along from the *Steinbruch*[21] (now a huge Troglodyte[22] Chasm, with frightful green-mantled pools); and shape themselves into Doric and Ionic pillars, squared ashlar houses[23] and noble streets? Was it not the still higher Orpheus, or Orpheuses, who, in past centuries, by the divine Music of Wis-

dom, succeeded in civilizing Man? Our highest Orpheus walked in Judea, eighteen-hundred years ago: his sphere-melody, flowing in wild native tones, took captive the ravished souls of men; and, being of a truth sphere-melody, still flows and sounds, though now with thousandfold accompaniments, and rich symphonies, through all our hearts; and modulates, and divinely leads them. Is that a wonder, which happens in two hours; and does it cease to be wonderful if happening in two million? Not only was Thebes built by the music of an Orpheus; but without the music of some inspired Orpheus was no city ever built, no work that man glories in ever done.

"Sweep away the Illusion of Time; glance, if thou have eyes, from the near moving-cause to its far-distant Mover.[24] The stroke that came transmitted through a whole galaxy of elastic balls, was it less a stroke than if the last ball only had been struck, and sent flying? O, could I (with the Time-annihilating Hat) transport thee direct from the Beginnings to the Endings, how were thy eyesight unsealed, and thy heart set flaming in the Light-sea of celestial wonder! Then sawest thou that this fair Universe, were it in the meanest province thereof, is in very deed the star-domed City of God; that through every star, through every grass-blade, and most through every Living Soul, the glory of a present God still beams. But Nature, which is the Time-vesture of God, and reveals Him to the wise, hides Him from the foolish.

"Again, could anything be more miraculous than an actual authentic Ghost? The English Johnson longed, all his life, to see one; but could not, though he went to Cock Lane,[25] and thence to the church-vaults, and tapped on coffins. Foolish Doctor! Did he never, with the mind's eye as well as with the body's, look round him into that full tide of human Life he so loved; did he never so

---

[19]Son of Apollo and Calliope. He was Eurydice's husband and descended to Hades, charming its guardians by his music, to rescue her from death.

[20]Son of Zeus and Antiope. Mercury taught him to play on the lyre and, when he became King of Thebes, he charmed stones by his playing to move of their own accord to their places in the wall he was building.

[21]Stone-quarry.

[22]The Troglodytes were cave-dwellers of pre-historic times.

[23]Houses built of hewn stone.

[24]The First Cause, or God.

[25]The Cock Lane ghost (really a young girl who deceived the credulous) excited much attention in London in 1762. Dr. Johnson was always anxious for evidence for the supernatural, and took the stories about the ghost seriously enough to make an investigation, after which he concluded the girl to be an impostor.

much as look into Himself? The good Doctor was a Ghost, as actual and authentic as heart could wish; well-nigh a million of Ghosts were traveling the streets by his side. Once more I say, sweep away the illusion of Time; compress the threescore years into three minutes:[26] what else was he, what else are we? Are we not Spirits, that are shaped into a body, into an Appearance; and that fade away again into air and Invisibility? This is no metaphor, it is a simple scientific *fact;* we start out of Nothingness, take figure, and are Apparitions; round us, as round the veriest specter, is Eternity; and to Eternity minutes are as years and aeons. Come there not tones of Love and Faith, as from celestial harp-strings, like the Song of beautified Souls? And again, do not we squeak and gibber[27] (in our discordant, screech-owlish debatings and recriminatings); and glide bodeful, and feeble, and fearful; or uproar (*poltern*), and revel in our mad Dance of the Dead,—till the scent of the morning air summons us to our still Home; and dreamy Night becomes awake and Day? Where now is Alexander of Macedon: does the steel Host, that yelled in fierce battle-shouts at Issus and Arbela,[28] remain behind him; or have they all vanished utterly, even as perturbed Goblins must? Napoleon too, and his Moscow Retreats and Austerlitz Campaigns! Was it all other than the veriest Specter-hunt; which has now, with its howling tumult that made Night hideous, flitted away?—Ghosts! There are nigh a thousand-million walking the Earth openly at noontide; some half-hundred have vanished from it, some half-hundred have arisen in it, ere thy watch ticks once.

"O Heaven, it is mysterious, it is awful to consider that we not only carry each a future Ghost within him; but are, in very deed, Ghosts! These Limbs, whence had we them; this stormy Force; this life-blood with its burning Passion? They are dust and shadow; a Shadow-system gathered round our ME; wherein, through some moments or years, the Divine Essence is to be revealed in the Flesh. That warrior on his strong war-horse, fire flashes through his eyes; force dwells in his arm and heart: but warrior and war-horse are a vision; a revealed Force, nothing more. Stately they tread the Earth, as if it were a firm substance: fool! the Earth is but a film; it cracks in twain, and warrior and war-horse sink beyond plummet's sounding. Plummet's? Fantasy herself will not follow them. A little while ago, they were not; a little while, and they are not, their very ashes are not.

"So has it been from the beginning, so will it be to the end. Generation after generation takes to itself the Form of a Body; and forth-issuing from Cimmerian Night,[29] on Heaven's mission APPEARS. What Force and Fire is in each he expends: one grinding in the mill of Industry; one hunter-like climbing the giddy Alpine heights of Science; one madly dashed in pieces on the rocks of Strife, in war with his fellow:—and then the Heaven-sent is recalled; his earthly Vesture falls away, and soon even to Sense becomes a vanished Shadow. Thus, like some wild-flaming, wild-thundering train of Heaven's Artillery, does this mysterious MANKIND thunder and flame, in long-drawn, quick-succeeding grandeur, through the unknown Deep. Thus, like a God-created, fire-breathing Spirit-host, we emerge from the Inane; haste stormfully across the astonished Earth; then plunge again into the Inane. Earth's mountains are leveled, and her seas filled up, in our passage: can the Earth, which is but dead and a vision, resist Spirits which have reality and are alive? On the hardest adamant some footprint of us is stamped-in; the last Rear of the host will read traces of the earliest Van. But whence?—O Heaven, whither? Sense knows not; Faith knows not; only that it is through Mystery to Mystery, from God and to God.

> We *are such stuff*
> As Dreams are made of, and our little Life
> Is rounded with a sleep!"[30]

---

[26]This, of course, does not touch the problem, which is to conceive of time as non-existent.

[27]*Hamlet*, I, i, 116: "The sheeted dead did squeak and gibber in the Roman streets."

[28]Alexander the Great defeated Darius and the Persians in battles fought at these towns in Asia Minor (333 and 331 B. C.).

[29]The Cimmerians were a legendary people who dwelt in a land where the sun never shines.

[30]*Tempest*, IV. i, 156–158.

CHAPTER IX

Circumspective

HERE, then, arises the so momentous question: Have many British Readers actually arrived with us at the new promised country; is the Philosophy of Clothes now at last opening around them? Long and adventurous has the journey been: from those outmost vulgar, palpable Woolen Hulls of Man; through his wondrous Flesh-Garments, and his wondrous Social Garnitures; inwards to the Garments of his very Soul's Soul, to Time and Space themselves! And now does the spiritual, eternal Essence of Man, and of Mankind, bared of such wrappages, begin in any measure to reveal itself? Can many readers discern, as through a glass darkly, in huge wavering outlines, some primeval rudiments of Man's Being, what is changeable divided from what is unchangeable? Does that Earth-Spirit's speech in *Faust*,—

'Tis thus at the roaring Loom of Time I ply,
And weave for God the Garment thou seest
   Him by;[1]

or that other thousand-times repeated speech of the Magician, Shakespeare,—

And like the baseless fabric of this vision,
The cloudcapt Towers, the gorgeous Palaces,
The solemn Temples, the great Globe itself,
And all which it inherit, shall dissolve;
And like this unsubstantial pageant faded,
Leave not a wrack behind;[2]

begin to have some meaning for us? In a word, do we at length stand safe in the far region of Poetic Creation and Palingenesia, where that Phoenix Death-Birth of Human Society, and of all Human Things, appears possible, is seen to be inevitable?

---

[1]Goethe's *Faust*, I, 508–509. The whole passage, as quoted by Carlyle elsewhere in *Sartor*, is:

"In Being's floods, in Action's storm,
I walk and work, above, beneath,
Work and weave in endless motion!
   Birth and Death,
   An infinite ocean;
   A seizing and giving
   The fire of Living:
'Tis thus at the roaring Loom of Time I ply,
And weave for God the Garment thou seest
   Him by."
(Spoken by the Earth-Spirit.)
[2]*Tempest*, IV, i, 151–156.

Along this most insufficient, unheard-of Bridge, which the Editor, by Heaven's blessing, has now seen himself enabled to conclude if not complete, it cannot be his sober calculation, but only his fond hope, that many have traveled without accident. No firm arch, overspanning the Impassable with paved highway, could the Editor construct; only, as was said,[3] some zigzag series of rafts floating tumultuously thereon. Alas, and the leaps from raft to raft were too often of a breakneck character; the darkness, the nature of the element, all was against us!

Nevertheless, may not here and there one of a thousand, provided with a discursiveness of intellect rare in our day, have cleared the passage, in spite of all? Happy few! little band of Friends! be welcome, be of courage. By degrees, the eye grows accustomed to its new Whereabout; the hand can stretch itself forth to work there: it is in this grand and indeed highest work of Palingenesia that ye shall labor, each according to ability. New laborers will arrive; new Bridges will be built; nay, may not our own poor rope-and-raft Bridge, in your passings and repassings, be mended in many a point, till it grow quite firm, passable even for the halt?

Meanwhile, of the innumerable multitude that started with us, joyous and full of hope, where now is the innumerable remainder, whom we see no longer by our side? The most have recoiled, and stand gazing afar off, in unsympathetic astonishment, at our career: not a few, pressing forward with more courage, have missed footing, or leaped short; and now swim weltering in the Chaos-flood, some towards this shore, some towards that. To these also a helping hand should be held out; at least some word of encouragement be said.

Or, to speak without metaphor, with which mode of utterance Teufelsdröckh unhappily has somewhat infected us,—can it be hidden from the Editor that many a British reader sits reading quite bewildered in head, and afflicted rather than instructed by the present Work? Yes, long ago has many a British Reader been, as now, demanding with

---

[3]In Bk. I, chap. xi, "Prospective" (p. 503 of this volume).

something like a snarl: Whereto does all this lead; or what use is in it?

In the way of replenishing thy purse, or otherwise aiding thy digestive faculty, O British Reader, it leads to nothing, and there is no use in it; but rather the reverse, for it costs thee somewhat. Nevertheless, if through this unpromising Horn-gate,[4] Teufelsdröckh, and we by means of him, have led thee into the true Land of Dreams; and through the Clothes-screen, as through a magical *Pierre-Pertuis*,[5] thou lookest, even for moments, into the region of the Wonderful, and seest and feelest that thy daily life is girt with Wonder, and based on Wonder, and thy very blankets and breeches are Miracles,—then art thou profited beyond money's worth; and hast a thankfulness towards our Professor; nay, perhaps in many a literary Tea-circle wilt open thy kind lips, and audibly express that same.

Nay, further, art thou not too perhaps by this time made aware that all Symbols are properly Clothes; that all Forms whereby Spirit manifests itself to sense, whether outwardly or in the imagination, are Clothes; and thus not only the parchment Magna Charta,[6] which a Tailor was nigh cutting into measures, but the Pomp and Authority of Law, the sacredness of Majesty, and all inferior Worships (Worthships) are properly a Vesture and Raiment; and the Thirty-nine Articles[7] themselves are articles of wearing-apparel (for the Religious Idea)? In which case, must it not also be admitted that this Science of Clothes is a high one, and may with infinitely deeper study on thy part yield richer fruit: that it takes scientific rank beside Codification,[8] and Political Economy, and the Theory of the British Constitution;

nay rather, from its prophetic height looks down on all these, as on so many weaving-shops and spinning-mills, where the Vestures which *it* has to fashion, and consecrate and distribute, are, too often by haggard hungry operatives[9] who see no farther than their nose, mechanically woven and spun?

But omitting all this, much more all that concerns Natural Supernaturalism, and indeed whatever has reference to the Ulterior or Transcendental portion of the Science, or bears never so remotely on that promised Volume of the *Palingenesie der menschlichen Gesellschaft* (Newbirth of Society),—we humbly suggest that no province of Clothes-Philosophy, even the lowest, is without its direct value, but that innumerable inferences of a practical nature may be drawn therefrom. To say nothing of those pregnant considerations, ethical, political, symbolical, which crowd on the Clothes-Philosopher from the very threshold of his Science; nothing even of those "architectural ideas,"[10] which, as we have seen, lurk at the bottom of all Modes, and will one day, better unfolding themselves, lead to important revolutions,—let us glance for a moment, and with the faintest light of Clothes-Philosophy, on what may be called the Habilatory Class of our fellowmen. Here too overlooking, where so much were to be looked on, the million spinners, weavers, fullers, dyers, washers, and wringers, that puddle and muddle in their dark recesses, to make us Clothes, and die that we may live,—let us but turn the reader's attention upon two small divisions of mankind, who, like moths, may be regarded

[4]See *Aeneid*, VI, 893 ff.

[5]In the Bernese Alps; a natural opening in the rock between Tavannes and Sancboz.

[6]The Charter granted by King John at Runnymede, 15 June, 1215. The story Carlyle alludes to is that Sir Robert Cotton (1571–1631), the antiquary, one day found his tailor about to cut up the charter. Cotton bought the document, which is now in the British Museum.

[7]Articles of belief, in the Anglican Church.

[8]The process of reducing laws to a systematic body. The allusion is to Bentham, whose Utilitarianism was at the time dominant in English thought and a force in practical politics.

[9]Workers.

[10]"Neither in tailoring nor in legislating does man proceed by mere Accident, but the hand is ever guided on by mysterious operations of the mind. In all his Modes, and habilatory endeavors, an Architectural Idea will be found lurking; his Body and the Cloth are the site and materials whereon and whereby his beautiful edifice, of a Person, is to be built. Whether he flow gracefully out in folded mantles, based on light sandals; tower-up in high head-gear, from amid peaks, spangles, and bell-girdles; swell-out in starched ruffs, buckram stuffings, and monstrous tuberosities; or girth himself into separate sections, and front the world an Agglomeration of four limbs,—will depend on the nature of such architectural Idea: whether Grecian, Gothic, Later-Gothic or altogether Modern, and Parisian or Anglo-dandiacal" (*Sartor*, Bk. I, ch. v).

as Cloth-animals, creatures that live, move, and have their being in Cloth: we mean, Dandies[11] and Tailors.

In regard to both which small divisions it may be asserted without scruple, that the public feeling, unenlightened by Philosophy, is at fault; and even that the dictates of humanity are violated. As will perhaps abundantly appear to readers of the two following Chapters.

CHAPTER X
The Dandiacal Body

FIRST, touching Dandies, let us consider, with some scientific strictness, what a Dandy specially is. A Dandy is a Clothes-wearing Man, a Man whose trade, office, and existence consists in the wearing of Clothes. Every faculty of his soul, spirit, purse, and person is heroically consecrated to this one object, the wearing of Clothes wisely and well: so that as others dress to live, he lives to dress. The all-importance of Clothes, which a German Professor, of unequaled learning and acumen, writes his enormous Volume to demonstrate, has sprung up in the intellect of the Dandy without effort, like an instinct of genius; he is inspired with Cloth, a Poet of Cloth. What Teufelsdröckh would call a "Divine Idea of Cloth" is born with him; and this, like other such Ideas, will express itself outwardly, or wring his heart asunder with unutterable throes.

But, like a generous, creative enthusiast, he fearlessly makes his Idea an Action; shows himself in peculiar guise to mankind; walks forth, a witness and living Martyr to the eternal worth of Clothes. We called him a Poet: is not his body the (stuffed) parchment-skin whereon he writes, with cunning Huddersfield[1] dyes, a Sonnet to his mistress' eyebrow?[2] Say, rather, an Epos, and *Clotha Virumque cano,*[3] to the whole world, in Macaronic verses,[4] which he that runs may read. Nay, if you grant, what seems to be admissible, that the Dandy has a Thinking-principle in him, and some notions of Time and Space, is there not in this Life-devotedness to Cloth, in this so willing sacrifice of the Immortal to the Perishable, something (though in reverse order) of that blending and identification of Eternity with Time, which, as we have seen, constitutes the Prophetic character?

And now, for all this perennial Martyrdom, and Poesy, and even Prophecy, what is it that the Dandy asks in return? Solely, we may say, that you would recognize his existence; would admit him to be a living object; or even failing this, a visual object, or thing that will reflect rays of light. Your silver or your gold (beyond what the niggardly Law has already secured him) he solicits not; simply the glance of your eyes. Understand his mystic significance, or altogether miss and misinterpret it; do but look at him, and he is contented. May we not well cry shame on an ungrateful world, which refuses even this poor boon; which will waste its optic faculty on dried Crocodiles, and Siamese Twins; and over the domestic wonderful wonder of wonders, a live Dandy, glance with hasty indifference, and a scarcely concealed contempt! Him no Zoologist classes among the Mammalia, no Anatomist dissects with care: when did we see any injected Preparation of the Dandy in our Museums; any specimen of him preserved in spirits? Lord Herringbone may dress himself in a snuff-brown suit, with snuff-brown shirt and shoes: it skills[5] not; the undiscerning public, occupied with grosser wants, passes by regardless on the other side.

The age of Curiosity, like that of Chivalry, is indeed, properly speaking, gone. Yet perhaps only gone to sleep: for here arises the Clothes-Philosophy to resuscitate, strangely

---

[11]The period of the dandies in London society was from about 1813 to 1830.

[1]A town famous for the production of woolen goods.

[2]*As You Like It,* II, vii, 147–149:

"And then the lover
Sighing like a furnace, with a woeful ballad
Made to his mistress' eyebrow."

[3]The first line of the *Aeneid* begins, *Arma virumque cano.*

[4]Verses written in a mixture of Latin and vernacular words. Macaroni was also a name applied to English dandies in the latter half of the eighteenth century.

[5]Matters.

enough, both the one and the other! Should sound views of this Science come to prevail, the essential nature of the British Dandy, and the mystic significance that lies in him, cannot always remain hidden under laughable and lamentable hallucination. The following long Extract from Professor Teufelsdröckh may set the matter, if not in its true light, yet in the way towards such. It is to be regretted, however, that here, as so often elsewhere, the Professor's keen philosophic perspicacity is somewhat marred by a certain mixture of almost owlish purblindness, or else of some perverse, ineffectual, ironic tendency; our readers shall judge which:

"In these distracted times," writes he, "when the Religious Principle, driven out of most Churches, either lies unseen in the hearts of good men, looking and longing and silently working there towards some new Revelation; or else wanders homeless over the world, like a disembodied soul seeking its terrestrial organization,—into how many strange shapes, of Superstition and Fanaticism, does it not tentatively and errantly cast itself! The higher Enthusiasm of man's nature is for the while without Exponent; yet does it continue indestructible, unweariedly active, and work blindly in the great chaotic deep: thus Sect after Sect, and Church after Church, bodies itself forth, and melts again into new metamorphosis.

"Chiefly is this observable in England, which, as the wealthiest and worst-instructed of European nations, offers precisely the elements (of Heat, namely, and of Darkness), in which such moon-calves and monstrosities are best generated. Among the newer Sects of that country, one of the most notable, and closely connected with our present subject, is that of the *Dandies;* concerning which, what little information I have been able to procure may fitly stand here.

"It is true, certain of the English Journalists, men generally without sense for the Religious Principle, or judgment for its manifestations, speak, in their brief enigmatic notices, as if this were perhaps rather a Secular Sect, and not a Religious one; nevertheless, to the psychologic eye its devotional and even sacrificial character plainly enough reveals itself. Whether it belongs to the class of Fetish-worships, or of Hero-worships or Polytheisms, or to what other class, may in the present state of our intelligence remain undecided (*schweben*). A certain touch of Manicheism,[6] not indeed in the Gnostic[7] shape, is discernible enough: also (for human Error walks in a cycle, and reappears at intervals) a not-inconsiderable resemblance to that Superstition of the Athos Monks,[8] who by fasting from all nourishment, and looking intensely for a length of time into their own navels, came to discern therein the true Apocalypse of Nature, and Heaven Unveiled. To my own surmise, it appears as if this Dandiacal Sect were but a new modification, adapted to the new time, of that primeval Superstition, *Self-worship;* which Zerdusht,[9] Quangfoutchee,[10] Mohammed and others, strove rather to subordinate and restrain than to eradicate; and which only in the purer forms of Religion has been altogether rejected. Wherefore, if any one chooses to name it revived Ahrimanism,[11] or a new figure of Demon-worship, I have, so far as is yet visible, no objection.

"For the rest, these people, animated with the zeal of a new Sect, display courage and perseverance, and what force there is in man's nature, though never so enslaved. They affect great purity and separatism; distinguish themselves by a particular costume (whereof some notices were given in the earlier part of this Volume); likewise, so far as possible, by a particular speech (apparently some broken *Lingua-franca*,[12] or

[6]Recognition of two opposed powers in the world, manifesting themselves variously as light and darkness, good and evil, spirit and matter; so named from Mani, or Manes, a Persian.

[7]Because the Gnostics stressed the impurity of matter and the degradation of the body and so would have condemned the creed of the dandy.

[8]Mount Athos is in Macedonia. Monasteries have been there from earliest Christian times.

[9]Zarathustra, or Zoroaster, founder of the Persian religion which is called by his name.

[10]Confucius, an ethical teacher rather than the founder of a religion.

[11]Ahriman was the principle of darkness and evil in the dualism of Zoroaster.

[12]A bastard or hybrid language used by European travelers in the lands at the eastern end of the Mediterranean. Carlyle uses the term in allusion to the habit, fashionable at the time, of using many French terms in English speech.

English-French) ; and, on the whole, strive to maintain a true Nazarene[13] deportment, and keep themselves unspotted from the world.

"They have their Temples, whereof the chief, as the Jewish Temple did, stands in their metropolis; and is named *Almack's*,[14] a word of uncertain etymology. They worship principally by night; and have their Highpriests and Highpriestesses, who, however, do not continue for life. The rites, by some supposed to be of the Menadic[15] sort, or perhaps with an Eleusinian[16] or Cabiric[17] character, are held strictly secret. Nor are Sacred Books wanting to the Sect; these they call *Fashionable Novels:* however, the Canon is not completed, and some are canonical and others not.

"Of such Sacred Books I, not without expense, procured myself some samples; and in hope of true insight, and with the zeal which beseems an Inquirer into Clothes, set to interpret and study them. But wholly to no purpose: that tough faculty of reading, for which the world will not refuse me credit, was here for the first time foiled and set at naught. In vain that I summoned my whole energies (*mich weidlich anstrengte*), and did my very utmost; at the end of some short space, I was uniformly seized with not so much what I can call a drumming in my ears, as a kind of infinite, unsufferable, Jew's-harping and scrannel-piping[18] there; to which the frightfullest species of Magnetic[19] Sleep soon supervened. And if I strove to shake this way, and absolutely would not yield, there came a hitherto unfelt sensation, as of *Delirium Tremens,* and a melting into total deliquium :[20] till at last, by order of the Doctor, dreading ruin to my whole intellectual and bodily faculties, and a general breaking-up of the constitution, I reluctantly but determinedly forbore. Was there some miracle at work here; like those Fire-balls, and supernal and infernal prodigies, which, in the case of the Jewish Mysteries, have also more than once scared-back the Alien? Be this as it may, such failure on my part, after best efforts, must excuse the imperfection of this sketch; altogether incomplete, yet the completest I could give of a Sect too singular to be omitted.

"Loving my own life and senses as I do, no power shall induce me, as a private individual, to open another *Fashionable Novel.* But luckily, in this dilemma, comes a hand from the clouds; whereby if not victory, deliverance is held out to me. Round one of those Book-packages, which the *Still-schweigen'sche Buchhandlung*[21] is in the habit of importing from England, come, as is usual, various waste printed-sheets (*Maculaturblätter*), by way of interior wrappage: into these the Clothes-Philosopher, with a certain Mohammedan reverence even for waste-paper,[22] where curious knowledge will sometimes hover, disdains not to cast his eye. Readers may judge of his astonishment when on such a defaced stray-sheet, probably the outcast fraction of some English Periodical, such as they name *Magazine,* appears something like a Dissertation on this very subject of *Fashionable Novels!* It sets out, indeed, chiefly from a Secular point of view; directing itself, not without asperity, against some to me unknown individual named *Pelham,*[23] who seems to be a Mysta-gogue, and leading Teacher and Preacher of the Sect; so that, what indeed otherwise was not to be expected in such a fugitive fragmentary sheet, the true secret, the Religious physiognomy and physiology of the Dandiacal Body, is nowise laid fully open

---

[13]Native of Nazareth. Carlyle has probably confused the word with Nazarite, the name applied to a Jew living under certain strict vows.

[14]A famous club, or suite of assembly rooms, where fashionable people gathered.

[15]Belonging to the Maenads, female attendants on Bacchus.

[16]The Eleusinian mysteries were celebrated at Eleusis in Attica.

[17]The Cabiri were deities worshiped chiefly in Samothrace.

[18]See Milton, *Lycidas*, l. 124.   [19]Hypnotic.

[20]Liquefaction.

[21]Bookshop.

[22]"It is the custom of the Mahometans, if they see any printed or written paper on the ground, to take it up and lay it aside carefully, as not knowing but it may contain some piece of their Alcoran" —*Spectator*, No. 85 (MacMechan).

[23]The title of a novel by Bulwer Lytton, published 1828. Passages resembling those which here follow may be found particularly in Chapters 44 and 46.

there. Nevertheless scattered lights do from time to time sparkle out, whereby I have endeavored to profit. Nay, in one passage selected from the Prophecies, or Mythic Theogonies,[24] or whatever they are (for the style seems very mixed) of this Mystagogue, I find what appears to be a Confession of Faith, or Whole Duty of Man, according to the tenets of that Sect. Which Confession or Whole Duty, therefore, as proceeding from a source so authentic, I shall here arrange under Seven distinct Articles, and in very abridged shape lay before the German world; therewith taking leave of this matter. Observe also, that to avoid possibility of error, I, as far as may be, quote literally from the Original:

ARTICLES OF FAITH

1. Coats should have nothing of the triangle about them; at the same time, wrinkles behind should be carefully avoided.

2. The collar is a very important point: it should be low behind, and slightly rolled.

3. No license of fashion can allow a man of delicate taste to adopt the posterial luxuriance of a Hottentot.

4. There is safety in a swallow-tail.

5. The good sense of a gentleman is nowhere more finely developed than in his rings.

6. It is permitted to mankind, under certain restrictions, to wear white waistcoats.

7. The trousers must be exceedingly tight across the hips.

"All which Propositions I, for the present, content myself with modestly but peremptorily and irrevocably denying.

"In strange contrast with this Dandiacal Body stands another British Sect, originally, as I understand, of Ireland, where its chief seat still is; but known also in the main Island, and indeed everywhere rapidly spreading. As this Sect has hitherto emitted no Canonical Books, it remains to me in the same state of obscurity as the Dandiacal, which has published Books that the unassisted human faculties are inadequate to read. The members appear to be designated by a considerable diversity of names, according to their various places of establishment: in England they are generally called the *Drudge*

Sect; also, unphilosophically enough, the *White Negroes;* and, chiefly in scorn by those of other communions, the *Ragged-Beggar* Sect. In Scotland, again, I find them entitled *Hallanshakers,*[25] or the *Stook of Duds* Sect; any individual communicant is named *Stook of Duds* (that is, Shock of Rags), in allusion, doubtless, to their professional Costume. While in Ireland, which, as mentioned, is their grandparent hive, they go by a perplexing multiplicity of designations, such as *Bogtrotters, Redshanks, Ribbonmen, Cottiers, Peep-of-Day Boys, Babes of the Wood, Rockites, Poor-Slaves:*[26] which last, however, seems to be the primary and generic name; whereto, probably enough, the others are only subsidiary species, or slight varieties; or, at most, propagated offsets from the parent stem, whose minute subdivisions, and shades of difference, it were here loss of time to dwell on. Enough for us to understand, what seems indubitable, that the original Sect is that of the *Poor-Slaves;* whose doctrines, practices, and fundamental characteristics pervade and animate the whole Body, howsoever denominated or outwardly diversified.

"The precise speculative tenets of this Brotherhood: how the Universe, and Man, and Man's Life, picture themselves to the mind of an Irish Poor-Slave; with what feelings and opinions he looks forward on the Future, round on the Present, back on the Past, it were extremely difficult to specify. Something Monastic there appears to be in their Constitution: we find them bound by the two Monastic Vows, of Poverty and Obedience; which Vows, especially the former, it is said, they observe with great strictness; nay, as I have understood it, they are pledged, and be it by any solemn Nazarene ordination or not, irrevocably consecrated thereto, even *before* birth. That the third Monastic Vow, of Chastity, is rigidly enforced among them, I find no ground to conjecture.

"Furthermore, they appear to imitate the Dandiacal Sect in their grand principal of wearing a peculiar Costume. Of which

---

[24]Genealogies of the gods.

[25]Sturdy beggars.

[26]All names given to the poor and rebellious Irish in the early nineteenth century.

Irish Poor-Slave Costume no description will indeed be found in the present Volume; for this reason, that by the imperfect organ of Language it did not seem describable. Their raiment consists of innumerable skirts, lappets,[27] and irregular wings, of all cloths and of all colors; through the labyrinthic intricacies of which their bodies are introduced by some unknown process. It is fastened together by a multiplex combination of buttons, thrums,[28] and skewers; to which frequently is added a girdle of leather, of hempen or even of straw rope, round the loins. To straw rope, indeed, they seem partial, and often wear it by way of sandals. In head-dress they affect a certain freedom: hats with partial brim, without crown, or with only a loose, hinged, or valve crown; in the former case, they sometimes invert the hat, and wear it brim uppermost, like a University-cap, with what view is unknown.

"The name Poor-Slaves seems to indicate a Slavonic, Polish, or Russian origin: not so, however, the interior essence and spirit of their Superstition, which rather displays a Teutonic or Druidical character. One might fancy them worshipers of Hertha,[29] or the Earth: for they dig and affectionately work continually in her bosom; or else, shut-up in private Oratories,[30] meditate and manipulate the substances derived from her; seldom looking-up towards the Heavenly Luminaries, and then with comparative indifference. Like the Druids, on the other hand, they live in dark dwellings; often even breaking their glass-windows, where they find such, and stuffing them up with pieces of raiment, or other opaque substances, till the fit obscurity is restored. Again, like all followers of Nature-Worship, they are liable to out-breakings of an enthusiasm rising to ferocity; and burn men, if not in wicker idols, yet in sod cottages.

"In respect of diet, they have also their observances. All Poor-Slaves are Rhizophagous (or Root-eaters); a few are Ichthyophagous,[31] and use Salted Herrings: other animal food they abstain from; except indeed, with perhaps some strange inverted fragment of a Brahminical feeling, such animals as die a natural death.[32] Their universal sustenance is the root named Potato, cooked by fire alone; and generally without condiment or relish of any kind, save an unknown condiment named *Point,* into the meaning of which I have vainly inquired; the victual *Potatoes-and-Point*[33] not appearing, at least not with specific accuracy of description, in any European Cookery-Book whatever. For drink, they use, with an almost epigrammatic counterpoise of taste, Milk, which is the mildest of liquors, and *Potheen,*[34] which is the fiercest. This latter I have tasted, as well as the English *Blue-Ruin,* and the Scotch *Whisky,* analogous fluids used by the Sect in those countries: it evidently contains some form of alcohol, in the highest state of concentration, though disguised with acrid oils; and is, on the whole, the most pungent substance known to me,—indeed, a perfect liquid fire. In all their Religious Solemnities, Potheen is said to be an indispensable requisite, and largely consumed.

"An Irish Traveler, of perhaps common veracity, who presents himself under the to me unmeaning title of *The late John Bernard,* offers the following sketch[35] of a domestic establishment, the inmates whereof, though such is not stated expressly, appear to have been of that Faith. Thereby shall my German readers now behold an Irish Poor-Slave, as it were with their own eyes; and even see him at meat. Moreover, in the so precious waste-paper sheet above mentioned, I have found some corresponding picture of a Dandiacal Household, painted by that same Dandiacal Mystagogue, or Theogonist: this also, by way of counterpart and contrast, the world shall look into.

"First, therefore, of the Poor-Slave, who

---

[27] Folds.   [28] Loose threads.

[29] Germanic goddess of fertility, mentioned by Tacitus.

[30] I. e., factories.   [31] Fish-eating.

[32] The Brahmins do not permit themselves to kill any animals or insects.

[33] I. e., potatoes and nothing besides; bacon or herring, if there was any, being simply pointed at, not eaten, because there was not enough to go round.

[34] "Moonshine" whisky.

[35] Condensed from several paragraphs (Vol. I, pp. 348–350) in *Retrospections of the Stage* by John Bernard, published in 1830.

appears likewise to have been a species of Innkeeper. I quote from the original:

POOR-SLAVE HOUSEHOLD

The furniture of this Caravansera consisted of a large iron Pot, two oaken Tables, two Benches, two Chairs, and a Potheen Noggin.[36] There was a Loft above (attainable by a ladder), upon which the inmates slept; and the space below was divided by a hurdle into two Apartments; the one for their cow and pig, the other for themselves and guests. On entering the house we discovered the family, eleven in number, at dinner: the father sitting at the top, the mother at the bottom, the children on each side, of a large oaken Board, which was scooped-out in the middle, like a trough, to receive the contents of their Pot of Potatoes. Little holes were cut at equal distances to contain Salt; and a bowl of Milk stood on the table: all the luxuries of meat and beer, bread, knives, and dishes were dispensed with.

The Poor-Slave himself our Traveler found, as he says, broad-backed, black-browed, of great personal strength, and mouth from ear to ear. His Wife was a sun-browned but well-featured woman; and his young ones, bare and chubby, had the appetite of ravens. Of their Philosophical or Religious tenets or observances, no notice or hint.

"But now, secondly, of the Dandiacal Household; in which, truly, that often-mentional Mystagogue and inspired Penman himself has his abode:

DANDIACAL HOUSEHOLD

A Dressing-room splendidly furnished; violet-colored curtains, chairs and ottomans of the same hue. Two full-length Mirrors are placed, one on each side of a table, which supports the luxuries of the Toilet. Several Bottles of Perfumes, arranged in a peculiar fashion, stand upon a smaller table of mother-of-pearl: opposite to these are placed the appurtenances of Lavation richly wrought in frosted silver. A Wardrobe of Buhl[37] is on the left; the doors of which, being partly open, discover a profusion of Clothes; Shoes of a singularly small size monopolize the lower shelves. Fronting the wardrobe a door ajar gives some slight glimpse of a Bathroom. Folding-doors in the back-ground.—Enter the Author [our Theogonist in person] obsequiously preceded by a French Valet, in white silk Jacket and cambric Apron.[88]

"Such are the two Sects which, at this moment, divide the more unsettled portion of the British People; and agitate that ever-vexed country. To the eye of the political Seer, their mutual relation, pregnant with the elements of discord and hostility, is far from consoling. These two principals of Dandiacal Self-worship or Demon-worship, and Poor-Slavish or Drudgical Earth-worship, or whatever that same Drudgism may be, do as yet indeed manifest themselves under distant and nowise considerable shapes: nevertheless, in their roots and subterranean ramifications, they extend through the entire structure of Society, and work unweariedly in the secret depths of English national Existence; striving to separate and isolate it into two contradictory, uncommunicating masses.

"In numbers, and even individual strength, the Poor-Slaves or Drudges, it would seem, are hourly increasing. The Dandiacal, again, is by nature no proselytizing Sect; but it boasts of great hereditary resources, and is strong by union; whereas the Drudges, split into parties, have as yet no rallying-point; or at best only co-operate by means of partial secret affiliations. If, indeed, there were to arise a *Communion of Drudges,* as there is already a Communion of Saints, what strangest effects would follow therefrom! Dandyism as yet affects to look-down on Drudgism: but perhaps the hour of trial, when it will be practically seen which ought to look down, and which up, is not so distant.

"To me it seems probable that the two Sects will one day part England between them; each recruiting itself from the intermediate ranks, till there be none left to enlist on either side. Those Dandiacal Manicheans, with the host of Dandyizing Christians, will form one body: the Drudges, gathering round them whosoever is Drudgical, be he Christian or Infidel Pagan; sweeping-up likewise all manner of Utilitarians,

---

[36]Small mug.

[37]Cabinetwork inlaid with tortoise-shell or metal.

[88]Quoted, with a few minor changes, from the introduction to Bulwer Lytton's novel, *The Disowned* (1828).

Radicals, refractory Potwallopers,[39] and so forth, into their general mass, will form another. I could liken Dandyism and Drudgism to two bottomless boiling Whirlpools that had broken-out on opposite quarters of the firm land: as yet they appear only disquieted, foolishly bubbling wells, which man's art might cover-in; yet mark them, their diameter is daily widening: they are hollow Cones that boil-up from the infinite Deep, over which your firm land is but a thin crust or rind! Thus daily is the intermediate land crumbling-in, daily the empire of the two Buchan-Bullers[40] extending; till now there is but a foot-plank, a mere film of Land between them; this too is washed away: and then—we have the true Hell of Waters, and Noah's Deluge is outdeluged!

"Or better, I might call them two boundless, and indeed unexampled Electric Machines (turned by the 'Machinery of Society'), with batteries of opposite quality; Drudgism the Negative, Dandyism the Positive: one attracts hourly towards it and appropriates all the Positive Electricity of the nation (namely, the Money thereof); the other is equally busy with the Negative (that is to say the Hunger), which is equally potent. Hitherto you see only partial transient sparkles and sputters: but wait a little, till the entire nation is in an electric state; till your whole vital Electricity, no longer healthfully Neutral, is cut into two isolated portions of Positive and Negative (of Money and of Hunger); and stands there bottled-up in two World-Batteries! The stirring of a child's finger brings the two together; and then—What then? The Earth is but shivered into impalpable smoke by that Doom's-thunderpeal; the Sun misses one of his Planets in Space, and thenceforth there are no eclipses of the Moon.—Or better still, I might liken"——

Oh! enough, enough of likenings and similitudes; in excess of which, truly, it is hard to say whether Teufelsdröckh or ourselves sin the more.

We have often blamed him for a habit of wire-drawing and over-refining; from of old we have been familiar with his tendency to Mysticism and Religiosity, whereby in everything he was still scenting-out Religion: but never perhaps did these amaurosis-suffusions[41] so cloud and distort his otherwise most piercing vision, as in this of the *Dandiacal Body!* Or was there something of intended satire; is the Professor and Seer not quite the blinkard he affects to be? Of an ordinary mortal we should have decisively answered in the affirmative; but with a Teufelsdröckh there ever hovers some shade of doubt. In the meanwhile, if satire were actually intended, the case is little better. There are not wanting men who will answer: Does your Professor take us for simpletons? His irony has overshot itself; we see through it, and perhaps through him.

CHAPTER XI
Tailors

THUS, however, has our first Practical Inference from the Clothes-Philosophy, that which respects Dandies, been sufficiently drawn; and we come now to the second, concerning Tailors. On this latter our opinion happily quite coincides with that of Teufelsdröckh himself, as expressed in the concluding page of his Volume, to whom, therefore, we willingly give place. Let him speak his own last words, in his own way:

"Upwards of a century," says he, "must elapse, and still the bleeding fight of Freedom be fought, whoso is noblest perishing in the van, and thrones be hurled on altars like Pelion on Ossa,[1] and the Moloch[2] of Iniquity have his victims, and the Michael of Justice his martyrs, before Tailors can be admitted to their true prerogatives of manhood, and this last wound of suffering Humanity be closed.

[39] One who boils a pot, i. e., who prepares his own food. The name was applied to a certain class of voters in England before the passage of the Reform Bill of 1832—those who had resided in a borough for six months and had not been given poor-relief for twelve.

[40] The name of a well, or whirlpool enclosed in a rocky recess, six miles south of Peterhead on the Aberdeenshire coast.

[41] Amaurosis is a form of blindness.

[1] Mountains in Thessaly, the former of which the Titans were fabled to have piled on the latter in an effort to reach the abode of the gods.

[2] God of the Ammonites who was worshiped with human sacrifices.

"If aught in the history of the world's blindness could surprise us, here might we indeed pause and wonder. An idea has gone abroad, and fixed itself down into a wide-spreading rooted error, that Tailors are a distinct species in Physiology, not Men, but fractional Parts of a Man.[3] Call any one a *Schneider* (Cutter, Tailor), is it not, in our dislocated, hoodwinked, and indeed delirious condition of Society, equivalent to defying his perpetual fellest enmity? The epithet *schneidermässig* (tailor-like) betokens an otherwise unapproachable degree of pusil-lanimity: we introduce a *Tailor's-Melan-choly,*[4] more opprobrious than any Leprosy, into our Books of Medicine; and fable I know not what of his generating it by living on Cabbage. Why should I speak of Hans Sachs[5] (himself a Shoemaker, or kind of Leather-Tailor), with his *Schneider mit dem Panier?*[6] Why of Shakespeare, in his *Taming of the Shrew,* and elsewhere? Does it not stand on record that the English Queen Elizabeth, receiving a deputation of Eight-een Tailors, addressed them with a 'Good morning, gentlemen both!' Did not the same virago boast that she had a Cavalry Regiment, whereof neither horse nor man could be injured; her Regiment, namely, of Tailors on Mares? Thus everywhere is the falsehood taken for granted, and acted on as an indisputable fact.

"Nevertheless, need I put the question to any Physiologist, whether it is disputable or not? Seems it not at least presumable, that, under his Clothes, the Tailor has bones and viscera, and other muscles than the sarto-rius?[7] Which function of manhood is the Tailor not conjectured to perform? Can he not arrest for debt? Is he not in most countries a tax-paying animal?

"To no reader of this Volume can it be doubtful which conviction is mine. Nay if the fruit of these long vigils, and almost preternatural Inquiries, is not to perish ut-terly, the world will have approximated towards a higher Truth; and the doctrine, which Swift,[8] with the keen forecast of genius, dimly anticipated, will stand revealed in clear light: that the Tailor is not only a Man, but something of a Creator or Divinity. Of Franklin it was said, that 'he snatched the Thunder from Heaven and the Scepter from Kings':[9] but which is greater, I would ask, he that lends, or he that snatches? For, looking away from individual cases, and how a Man is by the Tailor new-created into a Nobleman, and clothed not only with Wool but with Dignity and a Mystic Do-minion,—is not the fair fabric of Society it-self, with all its royal mantles and pontifical stoles, whereby, from nakedness and dis-memberment, we are organized into Polities, into nations, and a whole co-operating Man-kind, the creation, as has here been often ir-refragably evinced, of the Tailor alone?— What too are all Poets and moral Teachers, but a species of Metaphorical Tailors? Touching which high Guild the greatest liv-ing Guild-brother has triumphantly asked us: 'Nay if thou wilt have it, who but the Poet first made Gods for men; brought them down to us; and raised us up to them?'[10]

"And this is he, whom sitting downcast, on the hard basis of his Shopboard, the world treats with contumely, as the ninth part of a man! Look up, thou much-injured one, look up with the kindling eye of hope, and pro-phetic bodings of a noble better time. Too long hast thou sat there, on crossed legs, wearing thy ankle-joints to horn; like some sacred Anchorite, or Catholic Fakir, doing penance, drawing down Heaven's richest blessings, for a world that scoffed at thee. Be of hope! Already streaks of blue peer through our clouds; the thick gloom of Ig-norance is rolling asunder, and it will be Day. Mankind will repay with interest their long-accumulated debt: the Anchorite that was scoffed at will be worshiped; the Fraction will become not an Integer only,

---

[3]According to a proverb of uncertain origin, "nine tailors make a man."

[4]See Lamb's essay *On the Melancholy of Tailors.* Lamb discusses the influence of cabbage.

[5]German poet and Meistersinger (1494–1576).

[6]Tailor with the Flag. In his song of this title Sachs tells how a tailor was frightened in a dream by a flag made of cloth he had stolen.

[7]A long muscle in the thigh.

[8]See *A Tale of a Tub,* Sec. II. This probably suggested to Carlyle the idea of writing a philoso-phy of clothes.

[9]The remark is ascribed to Turgot.

[10]From Goethe's *Wilhelm Meister.*

but a Square and Cube. With astonishment the world will recognize that the Tailor is its Hierophant and Hierarch, or even its God.

"As I stood in the Mosque of St. Sophia,[11] and looked upon these Four-and-Twenty Tailors, sewing and embroidering that rich Cloth, which the Sultan sends yearly for the Caaba of Mecca,[12] I thought within myself: How many other Unholies has your covering Art made holy, besides this Arabian Whinstone!

"Still more touching was it when, turning the corner of a lane, in the Scottish Town of Edinburgh, I came upon a Signpost, whereon stood written that such and such a one was 'Breeches-Maker to his Majesty'; and

stood painted the Effigies of a Pair of Leather Breeches, and between the knees these memorable words, SIC ITUR AD ASTRA.[13] Was not this the martyr prison-speech of a Tailor sighing indeed in bonds, yet sighing towards deliverance, and prophetically appealing to a better day? A day of justice, when the worth of Breeches would be revealed to man, and the Scissors become forever venerable.

"Neither, perhaps, may I now say, has his appeal been altogether in vain. It was in this high moment, when the soul, rent, as it were, and shed asunder, is open to inspiring influence, that I first conceived this Work on Clothes: the greatest I can ever hope to do; which has already, after long retardations, occupied, and will yet occupy, so large a section of my Life; and of which the Primary and simpler Portion may here find its conclusion."

---

[11]In Constantinople.

[12]The Caaba is a square building in the mosque at Mecca. In its northwest corner a black stone is let into the wall ("this Arabian whinstone") which is supposed to have been the original god of the natives of Mecca. This stone is an object of veneration for all Mahometans.

---

[13]Thus one goes to the stars—i. e., this is the way to immortality (*Aeneid*, IX, 641).

THOMAS BABINGTON, LORD
MACAULAY
1800–1859

Macaulay was born at the country-house of his father's brother-in-law, in Leicestershire, on 25 October (the anniversary of the battle of Agincourt), 1800. His first two years were passed in Birchin Lane, which runs between Cornhill and Lombard Street, in the very heart of the City of London, in a house which was also his father's place of business. His father, Zachary, was prosperous until late in life when, in order to devote all of his attention to philanthropic causes (chiefly the abolition of slavery), he entrusted the details of his business to an incompetent partner. At the end of Macaulay's second year his parents took a house in the High Street of Clapham, and there his boyhood was spent. From the age of three he read incessantly, and talked most remarkably in "book words," without, however, the slightest affectation. At seven he began a compendium of universal history, and at eight he wrote a treatise intended to convert the natives of Malabar to Christianity. He was neither a prig nor spoiled; "a more simple and natural child never lived, or a more lively and merry one"; he was simply extraordinary. And his memory was of a piece with his interests and development. In 1853 he was able to repeat a scrap from the "poet's corner" of a country newspaper of 1813 which he had never recalled in the interval. He thought that, if every copy had been lost, he could have reproduced in their entirety, from memory, both *Paradise Lost* and *The Pilgrim's Progress*. In 1812 he was sent to a school at Little Shelford, near Cambridge, and in 1818 he entered Trinity College, Cambridge. There he did not win honors commensurate with his abilities because mathematical studies were totally repugnant to him; but in the autumn of 1824 he was elected a fellow of Trinity (after two previous failures to win the post). He had already begun his literary career, by contributing an article (in 1823) to *Knight's Quarterly Magazine,* and he was presently asked to write for the *Edinburgh Review.* His first article for that quarterly—his essay

on Milton—appeared in August, 1825, and won him a secure place amongst its contributors, which he was to hold for twenty years, until absorption in his *History* forced him to abandon essay-writing. He became, in fact, the mainstay of the *Review,* quickly winning a great popular reputation by his lucid and brilliant compositions.

Meanwhile he was living with his family in London, was called to the bar in 1826, and in 1829 took chambers in Gray's Inn. It is said, however, that he never had more than one case to plead; and, indeed, his eyes were directed, not towards a legal, but towards a political career. He had left Cambridge a complete Whig, and throughout his life he remained "pretty much convinced that all but Whigs were fools." He entered Parliament in 1830, and soon made a profound impression on his colleagues, though he never became a finished orator or a ready debater, and was always physically clumsy—never, for example, learning how to tie his neckcloth properly and never being able to shave himself well. Shortly after 1830 the expiration of his fellowship and the loss of a public office he had held since 1828 reduced him to such straits that he had to sell the gold medals he had won as a student; but he contracted no debts, and in 1833 obtained the means to establish himself securely for the remainder of his life. For he was then offered a seat on the newly formed supreme council of India, with a salary of £10,000 the year for five years. He accepted the post and sailed for India with his sister Hannah in February, 1834, remaining there (chiefly at Calcutta) until 1838. During this time his industry was extraordinary; he played an active part in founding the educational system of India, and compiled, almost without help, the Indian criminal code and the code of criminal procedure. With his earnings he aided his father (who had in the 1820's lost all of his money) and secured for himself a comfortable income, which was increased by a legacy of £10,000 from an uncle. In the autumn of 1838 he traveled in Italy, and in the following spring began to work at his *History*.

But the rival attractions of politics soon turned him aside once more from literature, and during the greater part of the next fifteen years he sat in Parliament, and also held, for a time, a cabinet-post. In 1842 he published the *Lays of Ancient Rome,* and in 1843 his collected *Essays.* The latter he collected against his wish, because they had several times been reprinted in America and were being imported in large quantities into England. "I know," he said, "that these pieces are full of faults, and that their popularity has been very far beyond their merit. . . . Their natural life is only six weeks." And after their publication he wrote: "My collected reviews have succeeded well. . . . In spite, however, of the applause and of the profit, neither of which I despise, I am sorry that it had become necessary to republish these papers. There are few of them which I read with satisfaction." This should be remembered. The *Essays* have deserved their popularity, but they are very unequal, not so much in brilliancy, vivacity, and finish, as in adequacy to their subjects. They are not, as is often supposed, remarkable for wide or exact knowledge; and some of them are gravely misleading. The worst of them all, as practically every qualified judge has agreed, is the essay on Bacon; and of the essay on Milton Macaulay discerningly said that it contained scarcely a paragraph which did not demand revision.

Macaulay's powers, in fact, found their full scope only in his *History of England, from the Accession of James the Second;* and only in the *History* did he fully succeed in combining wide, deep, and accurate scholarship with his prodigious capacity to paint a life-like picture and tell a moving story. In 1841 he wrote: "I shall not be satisfied unless I produce something which shall for a few days supersede the last fashionable novel on the tables of young ladies." This he did; but, had it been his only aim, he could have achieved it more cheaply. It is his chief title to fame that "to extraordinary-fluency and facility he united patient, minute, and persistent diligence," which enabled him to produce the only literary work in the English language comparable to Gibbon's *Decline and Fall of the Roman Empire.* Detractors have characterized the *History* as a monument of Victorian Philistinism and as a piece of Whig propaganda; but neither charge has been helpful to the cause of just critical evaluation. No one, for example,

can read his account of the siege of Londonderry, in which he did for that city "what Thucydides had done for Plataea," without concluding that if this is Victorian Philistinism we want more of it. And Sir Charles Firth finally disposed of all that was serious in the other charge when he testified that "a close scrutiny of Macaulay's pages, while it made some defects and omissions more apparent, had increased, not diminished, his admiration for what Macaulay succeeded in doing."

The first two volumes of the *History* were published in December, 1848. In the following spring Macaulay delivered his address as Lord Rector of Glasgow University. In June he was offered the Regius Professorship of Modern History at Cambridge, but refused even to consider taking a post which offered him little in return for the sacrifice of his freedom, and which would have made the continuation of his *History* more difficult. But difficulties were to come, nevertheless; for in 1852 his health broke down in a serious failure of his heart, and thereafter he was practically an invalid. He grew twenty years older in a week, he said. However, he worked on as best he could, publishing his collected *Speeches* in 1854 to protect himself against a piratical edition, and publishing the third and fourth volumes of the *History* in December, 1855. The fifth volume he left not quite complete at his death, and it was not published until March, 1861. It carried the narrative to the death of William III (8 March, 1702). Meanwhile Macaulay had become Baron Macaulay of Rothley in 1857, and on 28 December, 1859, had died. He was buried in Westminster Abbey, in the poet's corner, at the foot of the statue of Addison.

The definitive edition of *The History of England, from the Accession of James the Second* has been edited by Sir Charles H. Firth (6 vols., London, 1913–1915); and the same scholar is also the author of an excellent *Commentary on Macaulay's History of England* (London, 1938). The best edition of Macaulay's *Critical and Historical Essays Contributed to The Edinburgh Review* is that edited by F. C. Montague (3 vols., London, 1903). The standard biography, which includes letters, is by Sir George Otto Trevelyan (London, 1876; and later editions). *Lord Macaulay, Victorian Liberal* (Norman, 1938) is a recent biography by Richmond C. Beatty. A shrewd and well-balanced study of Macaulay is included in Walter Bagehot's *Literary Studies,* ed. Richard H. Hutton (London, 1895), II, 1–43.

THE HISTORY OF ENGLAND

From the Accession of James the Second

CHAPTER XII[1]

*   *   *

THE voyage was safely and quietly performed; and, on the afternoon of the twelfth [5] of March, James landed in the harbor of Kinsale. By the Roman Catholic population he was received with shouts of unfeigned transport. The few Protestants who remained in that part of the country joined in [10] greeting him, and perhaps not insincerely. For, though an enemy of their religion, he was not an enemy of their nation; and they might reasonably hope that the worst king would show somewhat more respect for law [15] and property than had been shown by the Merry Boys and Rapparees.[2] The Vicar of Kinsale was among those who went to pay their duty: he was presented by the Bishop of Chester, and was not ungraciously re- [20] ceived.

James learned that his cause was prospering. In the three southern provinces of Ireland the Protestants were disarmed, and were so effectually bowed down by terror [25] that he had nothing to apprehend from them. In the North there was some show of resistance: but Hamilton was marching against the malcontents; and there was little doubt that they would easily be crushed. A day [30] was spent at Kinsale in putting the arms and ammunition out of reach of danger. Horses sufficient to carry a few travelers were with some difficulty procured; and, on the fourteenth of March, James proceeded to [35] Cork.

We should greatly err if we imagined that the road by which he entered that city bore any resemblance to the stately approach which strikes the traveler of the nineteenth [40] century with admiration. At present Cork,

though deformed by many miserable relics of a former age, holds no mean place among the ports of the empire. The shipping is more than half what the shipping of London was at the time of the Revolution. The customs exceed the whole revenue which the whole kingdom of Ireland, in the most peaceful and prosperous times, yielded to the Stuarts. The town is adorned by broad and well built streets, by fair gardens, by a Corinthian portico which would do honor to Palladio,[3] and by a Gothic college worthy to stand in the High Street of Oxford. In 1689, the city extended over about one tenth part of the space which it now covers, and was intersected by muddy streams, which have long been concealed by arches and buildings. A desolate marsh, in which the sportsman who pursued the waterfowl sank deep in water and mire at every step, covered the area now occupied by stately buildings, the palaces of great commercial societies. There was only a single street in which two wheeled carriages could pass each other. From this street diverged to right and left alleys squalid and noisome beyond the belief of those who have formed their notions of misery from the most miserable parts of Saint Giles's and Whitechapel.[4] One of these alleys, called, and, by comparison, justly called, Broad Lane, is about ten feet wide. From such places, now seats of hunger and pestilence, abandoned to the most wretched of mankind, the citizens poured forth to welcome James. He was received with military honors by Macarthy, who held the chief command in Munster.

It was impossible for the King to proceed immediately to Dublin; for the southern counties had been so completely laid waste by the banditti whom the priests had called to arms, that the means of locomotion were not easily to be procured. Horses had become rarities: in a large district there were

---

[1] The passage here printed comprises roughly the latter two-thirds of the chapter, and concerns the unavailing effort of James II (in 1689) to regain the English throne, with French aid, by leading a revolt in Ireland. Macaulay's notes, which throughout this passage contain merely references to his sources, have been omitted.

[2] Irregular Irish soldiers.

[3] Andrea Palladio, the Italian architect who gave his name to the Palladian school of neo-classical architecture.

[4] Sections of London.

only two carts; and those Avaux[5] pronounced good for nothing. Some days elapsed before the money which had been brought from France, though no very formidable mass, could be dragged over the few miles which separated Cork from Kinsale.

While the King and his Council were employed in trying to procure carriages and beasts, Tyrconnel[6] arrived from Dublin. He held encouraging language. The opposition of Enniskillen he seems to have thought deserving of little consideration. Londonderry, he said, was the only important post held by the Protestants; and even Londonderry would not, in his judgment, hold out many days.

At length James was able to leave Cork for the capital. On the road, the shrewd and observant Avaux made many remarks. The first part of the journey was through wild highlands, where it was not strange that there should be few traces of art and industry. But, from Kilkenny to the gates of Dublin, the path of the travelers lay over gently undulating ground rich with natural verdure. That fertile district should have been covered with flocks and herds, orchards and cornfields: but it was an untilled and unpeopled desert. Even in the towns the artisans were very few. Manufactured articles were hardly to be found, and if found could be procured only at immense prices. The envoy at first attributed the desolation which he saw on every side to the tyranny of the English colonists. In a very short time he was forced to change his opinion.

James received on his progress numerous marks of the goodwill of the peasantry; but marks such as, to men bred in the courts of France and England, had an uncouth and ominous appearance. Though very few laborers were seen at work in the fields, the road was lined by Rapparees armed with skeans,[7] stakes, and half pikes, who crowded to look upon the deliverer of their race. The highway along which he traveled presented the aspect of a street in which a fair is held. Pipers came forth to play before him in a style which was not exactly that of the French opera; and the villagers danced wildly to the music. Long frieze[8] mantles, resembling those which Spenser[9] had, a century before, described as meet beds for rebels and apt cloaks for thieves, were spread along the path which the cavalcade was to tread; and garlands, in which cabbage stalks supplied the place of laurels, were offered to the royal hand. The women insisted on kissing his Majesty; but it should seem that they bore little resemblance to their posterity; for this compliment was so distasteful to him that he ordered his retinue to keep them at a distance.

On the twenty-fourth of March he entered Dublin. That city was then, in extent and population, the second in the British isles. It contained between six and seven thousand houses, and probably above thirty thousand inhabitants. In wealth and beauty, however, Dublin was inferior to many English towns. Of the graceful and stately public buildings which now adorn both sides of the Liffey scarcely one had been even projected. The College,[10] a very different edifice from that which now stands on the same site, lay quite out of the city. The ground which is at present occupied by Leinster House and Charlemont House, by Sackville Street and Merrion Square, was open meadow. Most of the dwellings were built of timber, and have long given place to more substantial edifices. The Castle had in 1686 been almost uninhabitable. Clarendon had complained that he knew of no gentleman in Pall Mall who was not more conveniently and handsomely lodged than the Lord Lieutenant of Ireland. No public ceremony could be performed in a becoming manner under the Viceregal roof. Nay, in spite of constant

[5]The French ambassador who accompanied James on his expedition. He was an experienced and able diplomatist, though Macaulay adds that "of the difference between right and wrong he had no more notion than a brute. . . . Nothing that tended to promote the interest of the French monarchy seemed to him a crime."

[6]Richard Talbot, who came of a Norman family long settled in Ireland. In return for infamous services, James had made him Earl of Tyrconnel and, in 1687, Lord Deputy of Ireland. He was now the *de facto* ruler of a large portion of the island and, because it served his own ends, faithful to the cause of James.

[7]Daggers.   [8]Coarse woolen cloth.

[9]In his *View of the Present State of Ireland* (written 1596).

[10]Trinity College.

glazing and tiling, the rain perpetually drenched the apartments. Tyrconnel, since he became Lord Deputy, had erected a new building somewhat more commodious. To this building the King was conducted in state through the southern part of the city. Every exertion had been made to give an air of festivity and splendor to the district which he was to traverse. The streets, which were generally deep in mud, were strewn with gravel. Boughs and flowers were scattered over the path. Tapestry and arras hung from the windows of those who could afford to exhibit such finery. The poor supplied the place of rich stuffs with blankets and coverlids. In one place was stationed a troop of friars with a cross; in another a company of forty girls dressed in white and carrying nosegays. Pipers and harpers played "The King shall enjoy his own again." The Lord Deputy carried the sword of state before his master. The Judges, the Heralds, the Lord Mayor and Aldermen, appeared in all the pomp of office. Soldiers were drawn up on the right and left to keep the passages clear. A procession of twenty coaches belonging to public functionaries was mustered. Before the Castle gate, the King was met by the host under a canopy borne by four bishops of his church. At the sight he fell on his knees, and passed some time in devotion. He then rose and was conducted to the chapel of his palace, once—such are the vicissitudes of human things—the riding house of Henry Cromwell. A *Te Deum* was performed in honor of his Majesty's arrival. The next morning he held a Privy Council, discharged Chief Justice Keating from any further attendance at the board, ordered Avaux and Bishop Cartwright to be sworn in, and issued a proclamation convoking a Parliament to meet at Dublin on the seventh of May.

When the news that James had arrived in Ireland reached London, the sorrow and alarm were general, and were mingled with serious discontent. The multitude, not making sufficient allowance for the difficulties by which William was encompassed on every side, loudly blamed his neglect. To all the invectives of the ignorant and malicious he opposed, as was his wont, nothing but immutable gravity and the silence of profound disdain. But few minds had received from nature a temper so firm as his; and still fewer had undergone so long and so rigorous a discipline. The reproaches which had no power to shake his fortitude, tried from childhood upwards by both extremes of fortune, inflicted a deadly wound on a less resolute heart.

While all the coffeehouses were unanimously resolving that a fleet and army ought to have been long before sent to Dublin, and wondering how so renowned a politician as his Majesty could have been duped by Hamilton and Tyrconnel, a gentleman went down to the Temple Stairs, called a boat, and desired to be pulled to Greenwich. He took the cover of a letter from his pocket, scratched a few lines with a pencil, and laid the paper on the seat with some silver for his fare. As the boat passed under the dark central arch of London Bridge, he sprang into the water and disappeared. It was found that he had written these words: "My folly in undertaking what I could not execute hath done the King great prejudice which cannot be stopped—No easier way for me than this—May his undertaking prosper—May he have a blessing." There was no signature; but the body was soon found, and proved to be that of John Temple.[11] He was young and highly accomplished: he was heir to an honorable name; he was united to an amiable woman: he was possessed of an ample fortune; and he had in prospect the greatest honors of the state. It does not appear that the public had been at all aware to what an extent he was answerable for the policy which had brought so much obloquy on the government. The King, stern as he was, had far too great a heart to treat an error as a crime. He had just appointed the unfortunate young man Secretary at War; and the commission was actually preparing. It is not improbable that the cold magnanimity of the master was the very thing which made the remorse of the servant insupportable.

But, great as were the vexations which

---

[11] The son of Sir William Temple, Swift's patron. John Temple had persuaded King William to negotiate with Tyrconnel.

London in the 1840's is here delineated. The upper picture, engraved by Thomas Higham (1796–1844), is a "View of the Architectural Improvements in the Vicinity of the Bank, and the Mansion House." The latter (with pillared portico, towards the right) is the official residence of the Lord Mayor. The lower picture is from a series entitled *Original Views of London as It Is* (1842), lithographed by Thomas Shotter Boys (1803–1874). It shows Piccadilly, east of Bond Street. At the right is the Egyptian Hall, a popular museum. Napoleon's traveling carriage and Tom Thumb were exhibited here; and in 1842 Red Indians were being shown. Some of the people in the street are looking up at the two balloons, then a novelty. (Courtesy of the Metropolitan Museum of Art.)

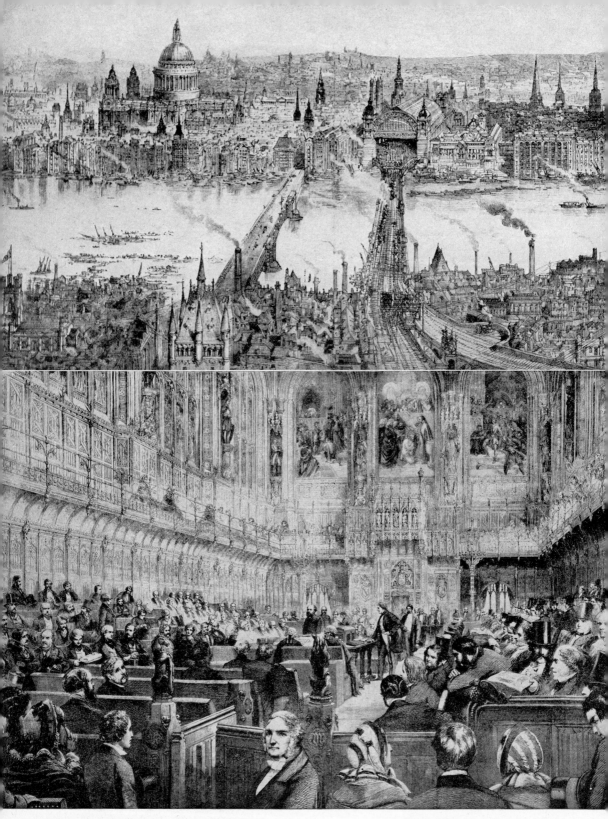

Across the top is a view of London published in the London *Graphic* (1 November, 1890). It is really the engraving of Claes Jan Visscher (1616; reproduced following page 256 in Volume I of this anthology) brought down to date. Practically nothing remains unchanged except the Tower of London (extreme right), and Southwark Cathedral on the lower side of the Thames. Amongst notable changes is the new St. Paul's Cathedral (extreme left) built by Sir Christopher Wren after the Great Fire of 1666. The lower picture at the left, from the *Illustrated London News*, shows the opening of Parliament early in 1859 in the House of Lords, the upper chamber

in the new Houses of Parliament built during the first twenty years of Victoria's reign. Sheridan,
Byron, and Macaulay were among the writers who were members of Parliament during the late
eighteenth and nineteenth centuries. The lower picture at the right, from the London *Graphic*,
shows the tower containing Big Ben, at one end of the new Parliamentary Buildings, and Westminster Abbey at the time of Queen Victoria's Golden Jubilee (21 June, 1887), with the Queen
just arriving for services in the Abbey. (The three pictures, from wood engravings published
in the periodicals mentioned, are reproduced by courtesy of the New York Public Library.)

The first "world's fair" was held in 1851 in Hyde Park, London, in the famous Crystal Palace, built of glass over an iron framework. Above are an exterior view and the interior of one transept, reproduced from contemporary paintings. (Courtesy of the New York Public Library.) After the exhibition, the Palace was pulled down and re-erected near Sydenham, where it remained until destroyed by fire (1936). Both building and exhibition were thought of as marvelous proofs of progress in 1851, but soon came to be regarded as the classic proof of Victorian lack of taste.

William had to undergo, those by which the temper of his father-in-law[12] was at this time tried were greater still. No court in Europe was distracted by more quarrels and intrigues than were to be found within the walls of Dublin Castle. The numerous petty cabals which sprang from the cupidity, the jealousy, and the malevolence of individuals scarcely deserve mention. But there was one cause of discord which has been too little noticed, and which is the key to much that has been thought mysterious in the history of those times.

Between English Jacobitism and Irish Jacobitism there was nothing in common. The English Jacobite was animated by a strong enthusiasm for the family of Stuart; and in his zeal for the interests of that family he too often forgot the interests of the state. Victory, peace, prosperity, seemed evils to the stanch nonjuror of our island if they tended to make usurpation popular and permanent. Defeat, bankruptcy, famine, invasion, were, in his view, public blessings, if they increased the chance of a restoration. He would rather have seen his country the last of the nations under James the Second or James the Third, than the mistress of the sea, the umpire between contending potentates, the seat of arts, the hive of industry, under a prince of the House of Nassau or of Brunswick.

The sentiments of the Irish Jacobite were very different, and, it must in candor be acknowledged, were of a nobler character. The fallen dynasty was nothing to him. He had not, like a Cheshire or Shropshire cavalier, been taught from his cradle to consider loyalty to that dynasty as the first duty of a Christian and a gentleman. All his family traditions, all the lessons taught him by his foster mother and by his priests, had been of a very different tendency. He had been brought up to regard the foreign sovereigns of his native land with the feeling with which the Jew regarded Caesar, with which the Scot regarded Edward the First, with which the Castilian regarded Joseph Bonaparte, with which the Pole regards the Autocrat of the Russias. It was the boast of the

high-born Milesian[13] that, from the twelfth century to the seventeenth, every generation of his family had been in arms against the English crown. His remote ancestors had contended with Fitzstephen and De Burgh. His great-grandfather had cloven down the soldiers of Elizabeth in the battle of the Blackwater. His grandfather had conspired with O'Donnel against James the First. His father had fought under Sir Phelim O'Neil against Charles the First. The confiscation of the family estate had been ratified by an Act of Charles the Second. No Puritan, who had been cited before the High Commission by Laud, who had charged by the side of Cromwell at Naseby, who had been prosecuted under the Conventicle Act, and who had been in hiding on account of the Rye House Plot, bore less affection to the House of Stuart than the O'Haras and Macmahons, on whose support the fortunes of that House now seemed to depend.

The fixed purpose of these men was to break the foreign yoke, to exterminate the Saxon colony, to sweep away the Protestant Church, and to restore the soil to its ancient proprietors. To obtain these ends they would without the smallest scruple have risen up against James; and to obtain these ends they rose up for him. The Irish Jacobites, therefore, were not at all desirous that he should again reign at Whitehall: for they were perfectly aware that a Sovereign of Ireland, who was also Sovereign of England, would not, and, even if he would, could not, long administer the government of the smaller and poorer kingdom in direct opposition to the feeling of the larger and richer. Their real wish was that the Crowns might be completely separated, and that their island might, whether with James or without James they cared little, form a distinct state under the powerful protection of France.

While one party in the Council at Dublin regarded James merely as a tool to be employed for achieving the deliverance of Ireland, another party regarded Ireland merely as a tool to be employed for effecting the

---

[12] James II. His daughter, Mary, had become the wife of William of Orange.

[13] Irishman (supposed to be descended from companions of Milesius, a legendary invader of Ireland).

restoration of James. To the English and Scotch lords and gentlemen who had accompanied him from Brest, the island in which they now sojourned was merely a stepping stone by which they were to reach Great Britain. They were still as much exiles as when they were at Saint Germains;[14] and indeed they thought Saint Germains a far more pleasant place of exile than Dublin Castle. They had no sympathy with the native population of the remote and half barbarous region to which a strange chance had led them. Nay, they were bound by common extraction and by common language to that colony which it was the chief object of the native population to root out. They had indeed, like the great body of their countrymen, always regarded the aboriginal Irish with very unjust contempt, as inferior to other European nations, not only in acquired knowledge, but in natural intelligence and courage; as born Gibeonites[15] who had been liberally treated, in being permitted to hew wood and to draw water for a wiser and mightier people. These politicians also thought—and here they were undoubtedly in the right—that, if their master's object was to recover the throne of England, it would be madness in him to give himself up to the guidance of the O's and the Macs who regarded England with mortal enmity. A law declaring the crown of Ireland independent, a law transferring miters, glebes, and tithes from the Protestant to the Roman Catholic Church, a law transferring ten millions of acres from Saxons to Celts, would doubtless be loudly applauded in Clare and Tipperary. But what would be the effect of such laws at Westminster? What at Oxford? It would be poor policy to alienate such men as Clarendon and Beaufort, Ken and Sherlock, in order to obtain the applause of the Rapparees of the Bog of Allen.

Thus the English and Irish factions in the Council at Dublin were engaged in a dispute which admitted of no compromise. Avaux meanwhile looked on that dispute from a point of view entirely his own. His object was neither the emancipation of Ireland nor the restoration of James, but the greatness of the French monarchy. In what way that object might be best attained was a very complicated problem. Undoubtedly a French statesman could not but wish for a counter-revolution in England. The effect of such a counter-revolution would be that the power which was the most formidable enemy of France would become her firmest ally, that William would sink into insignificance, and that the European coalition of which he was the chief would be dissolved. But what chance was there of such a counter-revolution? The English exiles indeed, after the fashion of exiles, confidently anticipated a speedy return to their country. James himself loudly boasted that his subjects on the other side of the water, though they had been misled for a moment by the specious names of religion, liberty, and property, were warmly attached to him, and would rally round him as soon as he appeared among them. But the wary envoy tried in vain to discover any foundation for these hopes. He could not find that they were warranted by any intelligence which had arrived from any part of Great Britain; and he was inclined to consider them as the mere daydreams of a feeble mind. He thought it unlikely that the usurper, whose ability and resolution he had, during an unintermitted conflict of ten years, learned to appreciate, would easily part with the great prize which had been won by such strenuous exertions and profound combinations. It was therefore necessary to consider what arrangements would be most beneficial to France, on the supposition that it proved impossible to dislodge William from England. And it was evident that, if William could not be dislodged from England, the arrangement most beneficial to France would be that which had been contemplated eighteen months before when James had no prospect of a male heir. Ireland must be severed from the English crown, purged of the English colonists, reunited to the Church of Rome, placed under the protection of the House of Bourbon, and made, in everything but name, a French province. In war, her resources would be absolutely at the command of her Lord Paramount. She would furnish his army with recruits. She would

[14] The court of the exiled Stuarts in France.
[15] Menials. Cf. Joshua, 9:27.

furnish his navy with fine harbors commanding all the great western outlets of the English trade. The strong national and religious antipathy with which her aboriginal population regarded the inhabitants of the neighboring island would be a sufficient guarantee for their fidelity to that government which could alone protect her against the Saxon.

On the whole, therefore, it appeared to Avaux that, of the two parties into which the Council at Dublin was divided, the Irish party was that which it was at present for the interest of France to support. He accordingly connected himself closely with the chiefs of that party, obtained from them the fullest avowals of all that they designed, and was soon able to report to his government that neither the gentry nor the common people were at all unwilling to become French.

The views of Louvois, incomparably the greatest statesman that France had produced since Richelieu, seem to have entirely agreed with those of Avaux. The best thing, Louvois wrote, that King James could do would be to forget that he had reigned in Great Britain, and to think only of putting Ireland into a good condition, and of establishing himself firmly there. Whether this were the true interest of the House of Stuart may be doubted. But it was undoubtedly the true interest of the House of Bourbon.

About the Scotch and English exiles, and especially about Melfort,[16] Avaux constantly expressed himself with an asperity hardly to have been expected from a man of so much sense and so much knowledge of the world. Melfort was in a singularly unfortunate position. He was a renegade: he was a mortal enemy of the liberties of his country: he was of a bad and tyrannical nature; and yet he was, in some sense, a patriot. The consequence was that he was more universally detested than any man of his time. For, while his apostasy and his arbitrary maxims of government made him the abhorrence of England and Scotland, his anxiety for the dignity and integrity of the empire made him the abhorrence of the Irish and of the French.

The first question to be decided was

whether James should remain at Dublin, or should put himself at the head of his army in Ulster. On this question the Irish and British factions joined battle. Reasons of no great weight were adduced on both sides; for neither party ventured to speak out. The point really in issue was whether the King should be in Irish or in British hands. If he remained at Dublin, it would be scarcely possible for him to withhold his assent from any bill presented to him by the Parliament which he had summoned to meet there. He would be forced to plunder, perhaps to attaint, innocent Protestant gentlemen and clergymen by hundreds; and he would thus do irreparable mischief to his cause on the other side of Saint George's Channel. If he repaired to Ulster, he would be within a few hours' sail of Great Britain. As soon as Londonderry had fallen, and it was universally supposed that the fall of Londonderry could not be long delayed, he might cross the sea with part of his forces, and land in Scotland, where his friends were supposed to be numerous. When he was once on British ground, and in the midst of British adherents, it would no longer be in the power of the Irish to extort his consent to their schemes of spoliation and revenge.

The discussions in the Council were long and warm. Tyrconnel, who had just been created a Duke, advised his master to stay at Dublin. Melfort exhorted his Majesty to set out for Ulster. Avaux exerted all his influence in support of Tyrconnel; but James, whose personal inclinations were naturally on the British side of the question, determined to follow the advice of Melfort. Avaux was deeply mortified. In his official letters he expressed with great acrimony his contempt for the King's character and understanding. On Tyrconnel, who had said that he despaired of the fortunes of James, and that the real question was between the King of France and the Prince of Orange, the ambassador pronounced what was meant to be a warm eulogy, but may perhaps be more properly called an invective. "If he were a born Frenchman he could not be more zealous for the interests of France." The conduct of Melfort, on the other hand, was the subject of an invective which much resem-

---

[16] John Drummond, Earl of Melfort (*d.* 1714).

bles eulogy: "He is neither a good Irishman nor a good Frenchman. All his affections are set on his own country."

Since the King was determined to go northward, Avaux did not choose to be left behind. The royal party set out, leaving Tyrconnel in charge at Dublin, and arrived at Charlemont on the thirteenth of April. The journey was a strange one. The country all along the road had been completely deserted by the industrious population, and laid waste by bands of robbers. "This," said one of the French officers, "is like traveling through the deserts of Arabia." Whatever effects the colonists had been able to remove were at Londonderry or Enniskillen. The rest had been stolen or destroyed. Avaux informed his court that he had not been able to get one truss of hay for his horses without sending five or six miles. No laborer dared bring anything for sale lest some marauder should lay hands on it by the way. The ambassador was put one night into a miserable taproom full of soldiers smoking, another night into a dismantled house without windows or shutters to keep out the rain. At Charlemont a bag of oatmeal was with great difficulty, and as a matter of favor, procured for the French legation. There was no wheaten bread, except at the table of the King, who had brought a little flour from Dublin, and to whom Avaux had lent a servant who knew how to bake. Those who were honored with an invitation to the royal table had their bread and wine measured out to them. Everybody else, however high in rank, ate horsecorn, and drank water or detestable beer, made with oats instead of barley, and flavored with some nameless herb as a substitute for hops. Yet report said that the country between Charlemont and Strabane was even more desolate than the country between Dublin and Charlemont. It was impossible to carry a large stock of provisions. The roads were so bad and the horses so weak, that the baggage wagons had all been left far behind. The chief officers of the army were consequently in want of necessaries; and the ill-humor which was the natural effect of these privations was increased by the insensibility of James, who seemed not to be aware that everybody about him was not perfectly comfortable.

On the fourteenth of April the King and his train proceeded to Omagh. The rain fell: the wind blew: the horses could scarcely make their way through the mud, and in the face of the storm; and the road was frequently intersected by torrents which might almost be called rivers. The travelers had to pass several fords where the water was breast high. Some of the party fainted from fatigue and hunger. All around lay a frightful wilderness. In a journey of forty miles Avaux counted only three miserable cabins. Everything else was rock, bog, and moor. When at length the travelers reached Omagh, they found it in ruins. The Protestants, who were the majority of the inhabitants, had abandoned it, leaving not a wisp of straw nor a cask of liquor. The windows had been broken: the chimneys had been beaten in: the very locks and bolts of the doors had been carried away.

Avaux had never ceased to press the King to return to Dublin; but these expostulations had hitherto produced no effect. The obstinacy of James, however, was an obstinacy which had nothing in common with manly resolution, and which, though proof to argument, was easily shaken by caprice. He received at Omagh, early on the sixteenth of April, letters which alarmed him. He learned that a strong body of Protestants was in arms at Strabane, and that English ships of war had been seen near the mouth of Lough Foyle. In one minute three messages were sent to summon Avaux to the ruinous chamber in which the royal bed had been prepared. There James, half dressed, and with the air of a man bewildered by some great shock, announced his resolution to hasten back instantly to Dublin. Avaux listened, wondered, and approved. Melfort seemed prostrated by despair. The travelers retraced their steps, and, late in the evening, got back to Charlemont. There the King received dispatches very different from those which had terrified him a few hours before. The Protestants who had assembled near Strabane had been attacked by Hamilton. Under a truehearted leader they would doubtless have stood their ground. But

Lundy, who commanded them, had told them that all was lost, had ordered them to shift for themselves, and had set them the example of flight. They had accordingly retired in confusion to Londonderry. The King's correspondents pronounced it to be impossible that Londonderry should hold out. His Majesty had only to appear before the gates; and they would instantly fly open. James now changed his mind again, blamed himself for having been persuaded to turn his face southward, and, though it was late in the evening, called for his horses. The horses were in miserable plight; but, weary and half starved as they were, they were saddled. Melfort, completely victorious, carried off his master to the camp. Avaux, after remonstrating to no purpose, declared that he was resolved to return to Dublin. It may be suspected that the extreme discomfort which he had undergone had something to do with this resolution. For complaints of that discomfort make up a large part of his letters; and, in truth, a life passed in the palaces of Italy, in the neat parlors and gardens of Holland, and in the luxurious pavilions which adorned the suburbs of Paris, was a bad preparation for the ruined hovels of Ulster. He gave, however, to his master a more weighty reason for refusing to proceed northward. The journey of James had been undertaken in opposition to the unanimous sense of the Irish, and had excited great alarm among them. They apprehended that he meant to quit them, and to make a descent on Scotland. They knew that, once landed in Great Britain, he would have neither the will nor the power to do those things which they most desired. Avaux, by refusing to proceed further, gave them an assurance that, whoever might betray them, France would be their constant friend.

While Avaux was on his way to Dublin, James hastened towards Londonderry. He found his army concentrated a few miles south of the city. The French generals who had sailed with him from Brest were in his train; and two of them, Rosen and Maumont, were placed over the head of Richard Hamilton. Rosen was a native of Livonia,[17] who had in early youth become a soldier of fortune, who had fought his way to distinction, and who, though utterly destitute of the graces and accomplishments characteristic of the Court of Versailles, was nevertheless high in favor there. His temper was savage: his manners were coarse: his language was a strange jargon compounded of various dialects of French and German. Even those who thought best of him, and who maintained that his rough exterior covered some good qualities, owned that his looks were against him, and that it would be unpleasant to meet such a figure in the dusk at the corner of a wood. The little that is known of Maumont is to his honor.

In the camp it was generally expected that Londonderry would fall without a blow. Rosen confidently predicted that the mere sight of the Irish army would terrify the garrison into submission. But Richard Hamilton, who knew the temper of the colonists better, had misgivings. The assailants were sure of one important ally within the walls. Lundy, the Governor, professed the Protestant religion, and had joined in proclaiming William and Mary; but he was in secret communication with the enemies of his Church and of the Sovereigns to whom he had sworn fealty. Some have suspected that he was a concealed Jacobite, and that he had affected to acquiesce in the Revolution only in order that he might be better able to assist in bringing about a Restoration: but it is probable that his conduct is rather to be attributed to faintheartedness and poverty of spirit than to zeal for any public cause. He seems to have thought resistance hopeless; and in truth, to a military eye, the defenses of Londonderry appeared contemptible. The fortifications consisted of a simple wall overgrown with grass and weeds: there was no ditch even before the gates: the drawbridges had long been neglected: the chains were rusty and could scarcely be used: the parapets and towers were built after a fashion which might well move disciples of Vauban[18] to laughter; and these feeble defenses were on almost every side commanded by heights. Indeed those who laid out the city had never

[17]Now a part of Latvia, USSR.

[18]Sébastien le Prestre, Marquis de Vauban (1638–1707), French military architect.

meant that it should be able to stand a regular siege, and had contented themselves with throwing up works sufficient to protect the inhabitants against a tumultuary attack of the Celtic peasantry. Avaux assured Louvois that a single French battalion would easily storm such a fastness. Even if the place should, notwithstanding all disadvantages, be able to repel a large army directed by the science and experience of generals who had served under Condé and Turenne,[19] hunger must soon bring the contest to an end. The stock of provisions was small; and the population had been swollen to seven or eight times the ordinary number by a multitude of colonists flying from the rage of the natives.

Lundy, therefore, from the time when the Irish army entered Ulster, seems to have given up all thought of serious resistance. He talked so despondingly that the citizens and his own soldiers murmured against him. He seemed, they said, to be bent on discouraging them. Meanwhile the enemy drew daily nearer and nearer; and it was known that James himself was coming to take the command of his forces.

Just at this moment a glimpse of hope appeared. On the fourteenth of April ships from England anchored in the bay. They had on board two regiments which had been sent, under the command of a Colonel named Cunningham, to reinforce the garrison. Cunningham and several of his officers went on shore and conferred with Lundy. Lundy dissuaded them from landing their men. The place, he said, could not hold out. To throw more troops into it would therefore be worse than useless: for the more numerous the garrison, the more prisoners would fall into the hands of the enemy. The best thing that the two regiments could do would be to sail back to England. He meant, he said, to withdraw himself privately; and the inhabitants must then try to make good terms for themselves.

He went through the form of holding a council of war; but from this council he excluded all those officers of the garrison whose

sentiments he knew to be different from his own. Some, who had ordinarily been summoned on such occasions, and who now came uninvited, were thrust out of the room. Whatever the Governor said was echoed by his creatures. Cunningham and Cunningham's companions could scarcely venture to oppose their opinion to that of a person whose local knowledge was necessarily far superior to theirs, and whom they were by their instructions directed to obey. One brave soldier murmured. "Understand this," he said, "to give up Londonderry is to give up Ireland." But his objections were contemptuously overruled. The meeting broke up. Cunningham and his officers returned to the ships, and made preparations for departing. Meanwhile Lundy privately sent a messenger to the headquarters of the enemy, with assurances that the city should be peaceably surrendered on the first summons.

But as soon as what had passed in the council of war was whispered about the streets, the spirit of the soldiers and citizens swelled up high and fierce against the dastardly and perfidious chief who had betrayed them. Many of his own officers declared that they no longer thought themselves bound to obey him. Voices were heard threatening, some that his brains should be blown out, some that he should be hanged on the walls. A deputation was sent to Cunningham imploring him to assume the command. He excused himself on the plausible ground that his orders were to take directions in all things from the Governor. Meanwhile it was rumored that the persons most in Lundy's confidence were stealing out of the town one by one. Long after dusk on the evening of the seventeenth it was found that the gates were open and that the keys had disappeared. The officers who made the discovery took on themselves to change the passwords and to double the guards. The night, however, passed over without any assault.

After some anxious hours the day broke. The Irish, with James at their head, were now within four miles of the city. A tumultuous council of the chief inhabitants was called. Some of them vehemently reproached the Governor to his face with his treachery. He had sold them, they cried,

---

[19]The Prince de Condé (1621–1686) and Henri de la Tour d'Auvergne, vicomte de Turenne (1611–1675), the two greatest French generals of the period.

to their deadliest enemy: he had refused admission to the force which good King William had sent to defend them. While the altercation was at the height, the sentinels who paced the ramparts announced that the vanguard of the hostile army was in sight. Lundy had given orders that there should be no firing; but his authority was at an end. Two gallant soldiers, Major Henry Baker and Captain Adam Murray, called the people to arms. They were assisted by the eloquence of an aged clergyman, George Walker, rector of the Parish of Donaghmore, who had, with many of his neighbors, taken refuge in Londonderry. The whole crowded city was moved by one impulse. Soldiers, gentlemen, yeomen, artisans, rushed to the walls and manned the guns. James, who, confident of success, had approached within a hundred yards of the southern gate, was received with a shout of "No surrender," and with a fire from the nearest bastion. An officer of his staff fell dead by his side. The King and his attendants made all haste to get out of reach of the cannon balls. Lundy, who was now in imminent danger of being torn limb from limb by those whom he had betrayed, hid himself in an inner chamber. There he lay during the day, and, with the generous and politic connivance of Murray and Walker, made his escape at night in the disguise of a porter. The part of the wall from which he let himself down is still pointed out; and people still living talk of having tasted the fruit of a pear tree which assisted him in his descent. His name is, to this day, held in execration by the Protestants of the North of Ireland; and his effigy is still annually hung and burned by them with marks of abhorrence similar to those which in England are appropriated to Guy Faux.

And now Londonderry was left destitute of all military and of all civil government. No man in the town had a right to command any other: the defenses were weak: the provisions were scanty: an incensed tyrant and a great army were at the gates. But within was that which has often, in desperate extremities, retrieved the fallen fortunes of nations. Betrayed, deserted, disorganized, unprovided with resources, begirt

with enemies, the noble city was still no easy conquest. Whatever an engineer might think of the strength of the ramparts, all that was most intelligent, most courageous, most high-spirited among the Englishry of Leinster and of Northern Ulster was crowded behind them. The number of men capable of bearing arms within the walls was seven thousand; and the whole world could not have furnished seven thousand men better qualified to meet a terrible emergency with clear judgment, dauntless valor, and stubborn patience. They were all zealous Protestants; and the Protestantism of the majority was tinged with Puritanism. They had much in common with that sober, resolute, and Godfearing class out of which Cromwell had formed his unconquerable army. But the peculiar situation in which they had been placed had developed in them some qualities which, in the mother country, might possibly have remained latent. The English inhabitants of Ireland were an aristocratic caste, which had been enabled, by superior civilization, by close union, by sleepless vigilance, by cool intrepidity, to keep in subjection a numerous and hostile population. Almost every one of them had been in some measure trained both to military and to political functions. Almost every one was familiar with the use of arms and was accustomed to bear a part in the administration of justice. It was remarked by contemporary writers that the colonists had something of the Castilian haughtiness of manner, though none of the Castilian indolence, that they spoke English with remarkable purity and correctness, and that they were, both as militiamen and as jurymen, superior to their kindred in the mother country. In all ages, men situated as the Anglo-Saxons in Ireland were situated have had peculiar vices and peculiar virtues, the vices and virtues of masters, as opposed to the vices and virtues of slaves. The member of a dominant race is, in his dealings with the subject race, seldom indeed fraudulent—for fraud is the resource of the weak—but imperious, insolent, and cruel. Towards his brethren, on the other hand, his conduct is generally just, kind, and even noble. His self-respect leads him to respect all who belong to his own order. His interest impels him to cultivate a good understanding with those whose prompt, strenuous, and courageous assistance may at any moment be necessary to preserve his property and life. It is a truth ever present to his mind that his own well-being depends on the ascendency of the class to which he belongs. His very selfishness therefore is sublimed into public spirit: and this public spirit is stimulated to fierce enthusiasm by sympathy, by the desire of applause, and by the dread of infamy. For the only opinion which he values is the opinion of his fellows; and in their opinion devotion to the common cause is the most sacred of duties. The character, thus formed, has two aspects. Seen on one side, it must be regarded by every well constituted mind with disapprobation. Seen on the other, it irresistibly extorts applause. The Spartan, smiting and spurning the wretched Helot, moves our disgust. But the same Spartan, calmly dressing his hair, and uttering his concise jests, on what he well knows to be his last day, in the pass of Thermopylae, is not to be contemplated without admiration. To a superficial observer it may seem strange that so much evil and so much good should be found together. But in truth the good and the evil, which at first sight appear almost incompatible, are closely connected, and have a common origin. It was because the Spartan had been taught to revere himself as one of a race of sovereigns, and to look down on all that was not Spartan as of an inferior species, that he had no fellow feeling for the miserable serfs who crouched before him, and that the thought of submitting to a foreign master, or of turning his back before an enemy, never, even in the last extremity, crossed his mind. Something of the same character, compounded of tyrant and hero, has been found in all nations which have domineered over more numerous nations. But it has nowhere in modern Europe shown itself so conspicuously as in Ireland. With what contempt, with what antipathy, the ruling minority in that country long regarded the subject majority may be best learned from the hateful laws which, within the memory of men still living, disgraced the Irish statute book. Those laws were at length annulled: but the spirit which had dictated them survived them, and even at this day sometimes breaks out in excesses pernicious to the commonwealth and dishonorable to the Protestant religion. Nevertheless it is impossible to deny that the English colonists have had, with too many of the faults, all the noblest virtues of a sovereign caste. The faults have, as was natural, been most offensively exhibited in times of prosperity and security: the virtues have been most resplendent in times of distress and peril; and never were those virtues more signally displayed than by the defenders of Londonderry, when their Governor had abandoned them, and when the camp of their mortal enemy was pitched before their walls.

No sooner had the first burst of the rage excited by the perfidy of Lundy spent itself than those whom he had betrayed proceeded, with a gravity and prudence worthy of the most renowned senates, to provide for the order and defense of the city. Two governors were elected, Baker and Walker. Baker took the chief military command. Walker's especial business was to preserve internal tranquillity, and to dole out supplies from the magazines. The inhabitants capable of bearing arms were distributed into eight regiments. Colonels, captains, and subordinate officers were appointed. In a few hours every man knew his post, and was ready to repair to it as soon as the beat of the drum was heard. That machinery, by which Oliver[20] had, in the preceding generation, kept up among his soldiers so stern and so pertinacious an enthusiasm, was again employed with not less complete success. Preaching and praying occupied a large part of every day. Eighteen clergymen of the Established Church and seven or eight nonconformist ministers were within the walls. They all exerted themselves indefatigably to rouse and sustain the spirit of the people. Among themselves there was for the time entire harmony. All disputes about church government, postures, ceremonies, were forgotten. The Bishop, having found that his lectures on passive obedience were derided even by the Episcopalians, had

[20]Oliver Cromwell.

withdrawn himself, first to Raphoe, and then to England, and was preaching in a chapel in London. On the other hand, a Scotch fanatic named Hewson, who had exhorted the Presbyterians not to ally themselves with such as refused to subscribe the Covenant, had sunk under the well merited disgust and scorn of the whole Protestant community. The aspect of the Cathedral was remarkable. Cannon were planted on the summit of the broad tower which has since given place to a tower of different proportions. Ammunition was stored in the vaults. In the choir the liturgy of the Anglican Church was read every morning. Every afternoon the Dissenters crowded to a simpler worship.

James had waited twenty-four hours, expecting, as it should seem, the performance of Lundy's promises; and in twenty-four hours the arrangements for the defense of Londonderry were complete. On the evening of the nineteenth of April, a trumpeter came to the southern gate, and asked whether the engagements into which the Governor had entered would be fulfilled. The answer was that the men who guarded these walls had nothing to do with the Governor's engagements, and were determined to resist to the last.

On the following day a messenger of higher rank was sent, Claude Hamilton, Lord Strabane, one of the few Roman Catholic peers of Ireland. Murray, who had been appointed to the command of one of the eight regiments into which the garrison was distributed, advanced from the gate to meet the flag of truce; and a short conference was held. Strabane had been authorized to make large promises. The citizens should have a free pardon for all that was past if they would submit to their lawful Sovereign. Murray himself should have a colonel's commission, and a thousand pounds in money. "The men of Londonderry," answered Murray, "have done nothing that requires a pardon, and own no Sovereign but King William and Queen Mary. It will not be safe for your lordship to stay longer, or to return on the same errand. Let me have the honor of seeing you through the lines."

James had been assured, and had fully expected, that the city would yield as soon as it was known that he was before the walls. Finding himself mistaken, he broke loose from the control of Melfort, and determined to return instantly to Dublin. Rosen accompanied the King. The direction of the siege was intrusted to Maumont. Richard Hamilton was second, and Pusignan third, in command.

The operations now commenced in earnest. The besiegers began by battering the town. It was soon on fire in several places. Roofs and upper stories of houses fell in, and crushed the inmates. During a short time the garrison, many of whom had never before seen the effect of a cannonade, seemed to be discomposed by the crash of chimneys, and by the heaps of ruin mingled with disfigured corpses. But familiarity with danger and horror produced in a few hours the natural effect. The spirit of the people rose so high that their chiefs thought it safe to act on the offensive. On the twenty-first of April a sally was made under the command of Murray. The Irish stood their ground resolutely; and a furious and bloody contest took place. Maumont, at the head of a body of cavalry, flew to the place where the fight was raging. He was struck in the head by a musket ball, and fell a corpse. The besiegers lost several other officers, and about two hundred men, before the colonists could be driven in. Murray escaped with difficulty. His horse was killed under him; and he was beset by enemies: but he was able to defend himself till some of his friends made a rush from the gate to his rescue, with old Walker at their head.

In consequence of the death of Maumont, Hamilton was once more commander of the Irish army. His exploits in that post did not raise his reputation. He was a fine gentleman and a brave soldier; but he had no pretensions to the character of a great general, and had never, in his life, seen a siege. Pusignan had more science and energy. But Pusignan survived Maumont little more than a fortnight. At four in the morning of the sixth of May, the garrison made another sally, took several flags, and killed many of the besiegers. Pusignan, fighting gallantly, was shot through the body. The wound was one which a skillful surgeon might have cured: but there was no such surgeon in the Irish camp; and the communication with Dublin was slow and irregular. The poor Frenchman died, complaining bitterly of the barbarous ignorance and negligence which had shortened his days. A medical man, who had been sent down express from the capital, arrived after the funeral. James, in consequence, as it should seem, of this disaster, established a daily post between Dublin Castle and Hamilton's headquarters. Even by this conveyance letters did not travel very expeditiously: for the couriers went on foot; and, from fear probably of the Enniskilleners, took a circuitous route from military post to military post.

May passed away: June arrived; and still Londonderry held out. There had been many sallies and skirmishes with various success: but, on the whole, the advantage had been with the garrison. Several officers of note had been carried prisoners into the city; and two French banners, torn after hard fighting from the besiegers, had been hung as trophies in the chancel of the Cathedral. It seemed that the siege must be turned into a blockade. But before the hope of reducing the town by main force was relinquished, it was determined to make a great effort. The point selected for assault was an outwork called Windmill Hill, which was not far from the southern gate. Religious stimulants were employed to animate the courage of the forlorn hope. Many volunteers bound themselves by oath to make their way into the works or to perish in the attempt. Captain Butler, son of the Lord Mountgarret, undertook to lead the sworn men to the attack. On the walls the colonists were drawn up in three ranks. The office of those who were behind was to load the muskets of those who were in front. The Irish came on boldly and with a fearful uproar, but after long and hard fighting were driven back. The women of Londonderry were seen amidst the thickest fire serving out water and ammunition to their husbands and brothers. In one place, where the wall was only seven feet high, Butler and some of his sworn men succeeded in reaching the top; but they were all killed or made prisoners. At length, after four hundred of the Irish had fallen, their chiefs ordered a retreat to be sounded.

Nothing was left but to try the effect of hunger. It was known that the stock of food in the city was but slender. Indeed it was thought strange that the supplies should have held out so long. Every precaution was now taken against the introduction of provisions. All the avenues leading to the city by land were closely guarded. On the south were encamped, along the left bank of the Foyle, the horsemen who had followed Lord Galmoy from the valley of the Barrow. Their chief was of all the Irish captains the most dreaded and the most abhorred by the Protestants. For he had disciplined his men with rare skill and care; and many frightful stories were told of his barbarity and perfidy. Long lines of tents, occupied by the infantry of Butler and O'Neil, of Lord Slane and Lord Gormanstown, by Nugent's Westmeath men, by Eustace's Kildare men, and by Cavanagh's Kerry men, extended northward till they again approached the water side. The river was fringed with forts and batteries which no vessel could pass without great peril. After some time it was determined to make the security still more complete by throwing a barricade across the stream, about a mile and a half below the city. Several boats full of stones were sunk. A row of stakes was driven into the bottom of the river. Large pieces of fir wood, strongly bound together, formed a boom which was more than a quarter of a mile in length, and which was firmly fastened to both shores, by cables a foot thick. A huge stone, to which the cable on the left bank was attached, was removed many years later, for the purpose of being polished and shaped into a column. But the intention was abandoned, and the rugged mass still lies, not many yards from its original site, amidst the shades which surround a pleasant country house named Boom Hall. Hard by is a well from which the besiegers drank. A little further off is a burial ground where they laid their slain, and where even in our own time the spade of the gardener has struck upon many skulls and thighbones at a short distance beneath the turf and flowers.

While these things were passing in the North, James was holding his court at Dublin. On his return thither from Londonderry he received intelligence that the French fleet, commanded by the Count of Chateau Renaud, had anchored in Bantry Bay, and had put on shore a large quantity of military stores and a supply of money. Herbert, who had just been sent to those seas with an English squadron for the purpose of intercepting the communications between Britanny and Ireland, learned where the enemy lay, and sailed into the bay with the intention of giving battle. But the wind was unfavorable to him: his force was greatly inferior to that which was opposed to him; and after some firing, which caused no serious loss to either side, he thought it prudent to stand out to sea, while the French retired into the recesses of the harbor. He steered for Scilly, where he expected to find reinforcements; and Chateau Renaud, content with the credit which he had acquired, and afraid of losing it if he stayed, hastened back to Brest, though earnestly entreated by James to come round to Dublin.

Both sides claimed the victory. The Commons at Westminster absurdly passed a vote of thanks to Herbert. James, not less absurdly, ordered bonfires to be lighted, and a *Te Deum* to be sung. But these marks of joy by no means satisfied Avaux, whose national vanity was too strong even for his characteristic prudence and politeness. He complained that James was so unjust and ungrateful as to attribute the result of the late action to the reluctance with which the English seamen fought against their rightful King and their old commander, and that his Majesty did not seem to be well pleased by being told that they were flying over the ocean pursued by the triumphant French. Dover, too, was a bad Frenchman. He seemed to take no pleasure in the defeat of his countrymen, and had been heard to say that the affair in Bantry Bay did not deserve to be called a battle.

On the day after the *Te Deum* had been sung at Dublin for this indecisive skirmish, the Parliament convoked by James assembled. The number of temporal peers of Ireland, when he arrived in that kingdom, was about a hundred. Of these only fourteen obeyed his summons. Of the fourteen, ten were Roman Catholics. By the reversing of old attainders, and by new creations, seventeen more Lords, all Roman Catholics, were introduced into the Upper House. The Protestant Bishops of Meath, Ossory, Cork, and Limerick, whether from a sincere conviction that they could not lawfully withhold their obedience even from a tyrant, or from a vain hope that the heart even of a tyrant might be softened by their patience, made their appearance in the midst of their mortal enemies.

The House of Commons consisted almost exclusively of Irishmen and Papists. With the writs the returning officers had received from Tyrconnel letters naming the persons whom he wished to see elected. The largest constituent bodies in the kingdom were at this time very small. For scarcely any but Roman Catholics dared to show their faces; and the Roman Catholic freeholders were then very few, not more, it is said, in some counties, than ten or twelve. Even in cities so considerable as Cork, Limerick, and Galway, the number of persons who, under the new Charters, were entitled to vote did not exceed twenty-four. About two hundred and fifty members took their seats. Of these only six were Protestants. The list of the names sufficiently indicates the religious and political temper of the assembly. Alone among the Irish parliaments of that age, this parliament was filled with Dermots and Geohagans, O'Neils and O'Donovans, Macmahons, Macnamaras, and Macgillicuddies. The lead was taken by a few men whose abilities had been improved by the study of the law, or by experience acquired in foreign countries. The Attorney General, Sir Richard Nagle, who represented the county of Cork, was allowed, even by Protestants, to be an acute and learned jurist. Francis Plowden, the Commissioner of Revenue, who sat for Bannow, and acted as chief minister of finance, was an Englishman, and, as he had been a principal agent of the Order of Jesuits in money matters, must be supposed to have been an excellent man of business.

Colonel Henry Luttrell, member for the county of Carlow, had served long in France, and had brought back to his native Ireland a sharpened intellect and polished manners, a flattering tongue, some skill in war, and much more skill in intrigue. His elder brother, Colonel Simon Luttrell, who was member for the county of Dublin, and military governor of the capital, had also resided in France, and, though inferior to Henry in parts and activity, made a highly distinguished figure among the adherents of James. The other member for the county of Dublin was Colonel Patrick Sarsfield. This gallant officer was regarded by the natives as one of themselves: for his ancestors on the paternal side, though originally English, were among those early colonists who were proverbially said to have become more Irish than Irishmen. His mother was of noble Celtic blood; and he was firmly attached to the old religion. He had inherited an estate of about two thousand a year, and was therefore one of the wealthiest Roman Catholics in the kingdom. His knowledge of courts and camps was such as few of his countrymen possessed. He had long borne a commission in the English Life Guards, had lived much about Whitehall, and had fought bravely under Monmouth on the Continent, and against Monmouth at Sedgemoor. He had, Avaux wrote, more personal influence than any man in Ireland, and was indeed a gentleman of eminent merit, brave, upright, honorable, careful of his men in quarters, and certain to be always found at their head in the day of battle. His intrepidity, his frankness, his boundless good nature, his stature, which far exceeded that of ordinary men, and the strength which he exerted in personal conflict, gained for him the affectionate admiration of the populace. It is remarkable that the Englishry generally respected him as a valiant, skillful, and generous enemy, and that, even in the most ribald farces which were performed by mountebanks in Smithfield,[21] he was always excepted from the disgraceful imputations which it was then the fashion to throw on the Irish nation.

But men like these were rare in the House of Commons which had met at Dublin. It is no reproach to the Irish nation, a nation which has since furnished its full proportion of eloquent and accomplished senators, to say that, of all the parliaments which have met in the British islands, Barebone's parliament[22] not excepted, the assembly convoked by James was the most deficient in all the qualities which a legislature should possess. The stern domination of a hostile caste had blighted the faculties of the Irish gentleman. If he was so fortunate as to have lands, he had generally passed his life on them, shooting, fishing, carousing, and making love among his vassals. If his estate had been confiscated, he had wandered about from bawn[23] to bawn, and from cabin to cabin, levying small contributions, and living at the expense of other men. He had never sat in the House of Commons: he had never even taken an active part at an election: he had never been a magistrate: scarcely ever had he been on a grand jury. He had therefore absolutely no experience of public affairs. The English squire of that age, though assuredly not a very profound or enlightened politician, was a statesman and a philosopher when compared with the Roman Catholic squire of Munster or Connaught.

The Parliaments of Ireland had then no fixed place of assembling. Indeed they met so seldom and broke up so speedily that it would hardly have been worth while to build and furnish a palace for their special use. It was not till the Hanoverian dynasty had been long on the throne, that a senate house which sustains a comparison with the finest compositions of Inigo Jones arose between the College and the Castle. In the seventeenth century there stood, on the spot where the portico and dome of the Four Courts now overlook the Liffey, an ancient building which had once been a convent of Dominican friars, but had since the Reformation been appropriated to the use of the legal profession, and bore the name of the King's Inns. There accommodation had been provided for the parliament. On the seventh

---

[21] A suburb of London.

[22] A Puritan assembly summoned by Cromwell in 1653; named after one of its members, Praise-God Barebone.

[23] Small fortified enclosure.

of May, James, dressed in royal robes and wearing a crown, took his seat on the throne in the House of Lords, and ordered the Commons to be summoned to the bar.

He then expressed his gratitude to the natives of Ireland for having adhered to his cause when the people of his other kingdoms had deserted him. His resolution to abolish all religious disabilities in all his dominions he declared to be unalterable. He invited the houses to take the Act of Settlement[24] into consideration, and to redress the injuries of which the old proprietors of the soil had reason to complain. He concluded by acknowledging in warm terms his obligations to the King of France.

When the royal speech had been pronounced, the Chancellor directed the Commons to repair to their chamber and to elect a Speaker. They chose the Attorney General Nagle; and the choice was approved by the King.

The Commons next passed resolutions expressing warm gratitude both to James and to Lewis.[25] Indeed it was proposed to send a deputation with an address to Avaux; but the Speaker pointed out the gross impropriety of such a step; and, on this occasion, his interference was successful. It was seldom however that the House was disposed to listen to reason. The debates were all rant and tumult. Judge Daly, a Roman Catholic, but an honest and able man, could not refrain from lamenting the indecency and folly with which the members of his Church carried on the work of legislation. Those gentlemen, he said, were not a Parliament: they were a mere rabble: they resembled nothing so much as the mob of fishermen and market gardeners, who, at Naples, yelled and threw up their caps in honor of Massaniello. It was painful to hear member after member talking wild nonsense about his own losses, and clamoring for an estate, when the lives of all and the independence of their common country were in peril. These words were spoken in private; but some talebearer repeated them to the Commons. A violent storm broke forth. Daly

was ordered to attend at the bar; and there was little doubt that he would be severely dealt with. But, just when he was at the door, one of the members rushed in, shouting, "Good news: Londonderry is taken." The whole House rose. All the hats were flung into the air. Three loud huzzas were raised. Every heart was softened by the happy tidings. Nobody would hear of punishment at such a moment. The order for Daly's attendance was discharged amidst cries of "No submission; no submission; we pardon him." In a few hours it was known that Londonderry held out as obstinately as ever. This transaction, in itself unimportant, deserves to be recorded, as showing how destitute that House of Commons was of the qualities which ought to be found in the great council of a kingdom. And this assembly, without experience, without gravity, and without temper, was now to legislate on questions which would have tasked to the utmost the capacity of the greatest statesmen.

One Act James induced them to pass which would have been most honorable to him and to them, if there were not abundant proofs that it was meant to be a dead letter. It was an Act purporting to grant entire liberty of conscience to all Christian sects. On this occasion a proclamation was put forth announcing in boastful language to the English people that their rightful King had now signally refuted those slanderers who had accused him of affecting zeal for religious liberty merely in order to serve a turn. If he were at heart inclined to persecution, would he not have persecuted the Irish Protestants? He did not want power. He did not want provocation. Yet at Dublin, where the members of his Church were the majority, as at Westminster, where they were a minority, he had firmly adhered to the principles laid down in his much maligned Declaration of Indulgence. Unfortunately for him, the same wind which carried his fair professions to England carried thither also evidence that his professions were insincere. A single law, worthy of Turgot[26] or of Franklin, seemed ludicrously

---

[24] The act by which the Cromwellian government in 1652 set aside ten Irish counties for new settlers.

[25] Louis XIV of France.

[26] Anne Robert Jaques Turgot (1727–1781), French financier and statesman.

out of place in the midst of a crowd of laws which would have disgraced Gardiner or Alva.[27]

A necessary preliminary to the vast work of spoliation and slaughter on which the legis- [5] lators of Dublin were bent, was an Act annulling the authority which the English Parliament, both as the supreme legislature and as the supreme Court of Appeal, had hitherto exercised over Ireland. This Act [10] was rapidly passed; and then followed, in quick succession, confiscations and proscriptions on a gigantic scale. The personal estates of absentees above the age of seventeen years were transferred to the King. [15] When lay property was thus invaded, it was not likely that the endowments which had been, in contravention of every sound principle, lavished on the Church of the minority would be spared. To reduce those endow- [20] ments, without prejudice to existing interests, would have been a reform worthy of a good prince and of a good parliament. But no such reform would satisfy the vindictive bigots who sat at the King's Inns. By one [25] sweeping Act, the greater part of the tithe was transferred from the Protestant to the Roman Catholic clergy; and the existing incumbents were left, without one farthing of compensation, to die of hunger. A Bill [30] repealing the Act of Settlement and transferring many thousands of square miles from Saxon to Celtic landlords was brought in and carried by acclamation.

Of legislation such as this it is impossible [35] to speak too severely: but for the legislators there are excuses which it is the duty of the historian to notice. They acted unmercifully, unjustly, unwisely. But it would be absurd to expect mercy, justice, or wisdom [40] from a class of men first abased by many years of oppression, and then maddened by the joy of a sudden deliverance, and armed with irresistible power. The representatives of the Irish nation were, with few excep- [45] tions, rude and ignorant. They had lived in a state of constant irritation. With aris-

tocratical sentiments they had been in a servile position. With the highest pride of blood, they had been exposed to daily affronts, such as might well have roused the choler of the humblest plebeian. In sight of the fields and castles which they regarded as their own, they had been glad to be invited by a peasant to partake of his whey and his potatoes. Those violent emotions of hatred and cupidity which the situation of the native gentleman could scarcely fail to call forth appeared to him under the specious guise of patriotism and piety. For his enemies were the enemies of his nation; and the same tyranny which had robbed him of his patrimony had robbed his Church of vast wealth bestowed on her by the devotion of an earlier age. How was power likely to be used by an uneducated and inexperienced man, agitated by strong desires and resentments which he mistook for sacred duties? And, when two or three hundred such men were brought together in one assembly, what was to be expected but that the passions which each had long nursed in silence would be at once matured into fearful vigor by the influence of sympathy?

Between James and his parliament there was little in common, except hatred of the Protestant religion. He was an Englishman. Superstition had not utterly extinguished all national feeling in his mind; and he could not but be displeased by the malevolence with which his Celtic supporters regarded the race from which he sprang. The range of his intellectual vision was small. Yet it was impossible that, having reigned in England, and looking constantly forward to the day when he should reign in England [40] once more, he should not take a wider view of politics than was taken by men who had no objects out of Ireland. The few Irish Protestants who still adhered to him, and the British nobles, both Protestant and Ro- [45] man Catholic, who had followed him into exile, implored him to restrain the violence of the rapacious and vindictive senate which he had convoked. They with peculiar earnestness implored him not to consent to the [50] repeal of the Act of Settlement. On what security, they asked, could any man invest his money or give a portion to his children,

---

[27]Stephen Gardiner (1483–1555), Bishop of Winchester, was leader of the extreme Catholic party in the reign of Mary I of England. The Duke of [50] Alva (1508–1583) was responsible for much of the Spanish oppression of the Netherlands in the sixteenth century.

if he could not rely on positive laws and on the uninterrupted possession of many years? The military adventurers among whom Cromwell portioned out the soil might perhaps be regarded as wrongdoers. But how large a part of their estates had passed, by fair purchase, into other hands! How much money had proprietors borrowed on mortgage, on statute merchant, on statute staple![28] How many capitalists had, trusting to legislative acts and to royal promises, come over from England, and bought land in Ulster and Leinster, without the least misgiving as to the title! What a sum had those capitalists expended, during a quarter of a century, in building, draining, inclosing, planting! The terms of the compromise which Charles the Second had sanctioned might not be in all respects just. But was one injustice to be redressed by committing another injustice more monstrous still? And what effect was likely to be produced in England by the cry of thousands of innocent English families whom an English king had doomed to ruin? The complaints of such a body of sufferers might delay, might prevent, the Restoration to which all loyal subjects were eagerly looking forward; and, even if his Majesty should, in spite of those complaints, be happily restored, he would to the end of his life feel the pernicious effects of the injustice which evil advisers were now urging him to commit. He would find that, in trying to quiet one set of malcontents, he had created another. As surely as he yielded to the clamor raised at Dublin for a repeal of the Act of Settlement, he would, from the day on which he returned to Westminster, be assailed by as loud and pertinacious a clamor for a repeal of that repeal. He could not but be aware that no English Parliament, however loyal, would permit such laws as were now passing through the Irish Parliament to stand. Had he made up his mind to take the part of Ireland against the universal sense of England? If so, to what could he look forward but another banishment and another deposition? Or would he, when he had recovered the greater kingdom, revoke the booms by which, in his distress,

he had purchased the help of the smaller? It might seem an insult to him even to suggest that he could harbor the thought of such unprincely, of such unmanly, perfidy. Yet what other course would be left to him? And was it not better for him to refuse unreasonable concessions now than to retract those concessions hereafter in a manner which must bring on him reproaches insupportable to a noble mind? His situation was doubtless embarrassing. Yet in this case, as in other cases, it would be found that the path of justice was the path of wisdom.

Though James had, in his speech at the opening of the session, declared against the Act of Settlement, he felt that these arguments were unanswerable. He held several conferences with the leading members of the House of Commons, and earnestly recommended moderation. But his exhortations irritated the passions which he wished to allay. Many of the native gentry held high and violent language. It was impudent, they said, to talk about the rights of purchasers. How could right spring out of wrong? People who chose to buy property acquired by injustice must take the consequences of their folly and cupidity. It was clear that the Lower House was altogether impracticable. James had, four years before, refused to make the smallest concession to the most obsequious parliament that has ever sat in England; and it might have been expected that the obstinacy, which he had never wanted when it was a vice, would not have failed him now when it would have been a virtue. During a short time he seemed determined to act justly. He even talked of dissolving the parliament. The chiefs of the old Celtic families, on the other hand, said publicly that, if he did not give them back their inheritance, they would not fight for his. His very soldiers railed on him in the streets of Dublin. At length he determined to go down himself to the House of Peers, not in his robes and crown, but in the garb in which he had been used to attend debates at Westminster, and personally to solicit the Lords to put some check on the violence of the Commons. But just as he was getting into his coach for this purpose he was stopped by Avaux. Avaux was as zealous as any

---

[28]According to the laws for trading and staple products.

Irishman for the bills which the Commons were urging forward. It was enough for him that those bills seemed likely to make the enmity between England and Ireland irreconcilable. His remonstrances induced James to abstain from openly opposing the repeal of the Act of Settlement. Still the unfortunate prince continued to cherish some faint hope that the law for which the Commons were so zealous would be rejected, or at least modified, by the Peers. Lord Granard, one of the few Protestant noblemen who sat in that parliament, exerted himself strenuously on the side of public faith and sound policy. The King sent him a message of thanks. "We Protestants," said Granard to Powis who brought the message, "are few in number. We can do little. His Majesty should try his influence with the Roman Catholics." "His Majesty," answered Powis with an oath, "dares not say what he thinks." A few days later James met Granard riding towards the parliament house. "Where are you going, my Lord?" said the King. "To enter my protest, Sir," answered Granard, "against the repeal of the Act of Settlement." "You are right," said the King; "but I am fallen into the hands of people who will ram that and much more down my throat."

James yielded to the will of the Commons; but the unfavorable impression which his short and feeble resistance had made upon them was not to be removed by his submission. They regarded him with profound distrust; they considered him as at heart an Englishman; and not a day passed without some indication of this feeling. They were in no haste to grant him a supply. One party among them planned an address urging him to dismiss Melfort as an enemy of their nation. Another party drew up a bill for deposing all the Protestant Bishops, even the four who were then actually sitting in Parliament. It was not without difficulty that Avaux and Tyrconnel, whose influence in the Lower House far exceeded the King's, could restrain the zeal of the majority.

It is remarkable that, while the King was losing the confidence and good will of the Irish Commons by faintly defending against them, in one quarter, the institution of property, he was himself, in another quarter, attacking that institution with a violence, if possible, more reckless than theirs. He soon found that no money came into his Exchequer. The cause was sufficiently obvious. Trade was at an end. Floating capital had been withdrawn in great masses from the island. Of the fixed capital much had been destroyed, and the rest was lying idle. Thousands of those Protestants who were the most industrious and intelligent part of the population had emigrated to England. Thousands had taken refuge in the places which still held out for William and Mary. Of the Roman Catholic peasantry who were in the vigor of life the majority had enlisted in the army or had joined gangs of plunderers. The poverty of the treasury was the necessary effect of the poverty of the country: public prosperity could be restored only by the restoration of private prosperity; and private prosperity could be restored only by years of peace and security. James was absurd enough to imagine that there was a more speedy and efficacious remedy. He could, he conceived, at once extricate himself from his financial difficulties by the simple process of calling a farthing a shilling. The right of coining was undoubtedly a flower of the prerogative; and, in his view, the right of coining included the right of debasing the coin. Pots, pans, knockers of doors, pieces of ordnance which had long been past use, were carried to the mint. In a short time lumps of base metal, nominally worth near a million sterling, intrinsically worth about a sixtieth part of that sum, were in circulation. A royal edict declared these pieces to be legal tender in all cases whatever. A mortgage for a thousand pounds was cleared off by a bag of counters made out of old kettles. The creditors who complained to the Court of Chancery were told by Fitton to take their money and be gone. But of all classes the tradesmen of Dublin, who were generally Protestants, were the greatest losers. At first, of course, they raised their demands: but the magistrates of the city took on themselves to meet this heretical machination by putting forth a tariff regulating prices. Any man who belonged to the caste now dominant might walk into a shop, lay on the counter a bit of brass worth threepence, and carry off goods to the value of half a guinea. Legal redress was out of the question. Indeed the sufferers thought themselves happy if, by the sacrifice of their stock in trade, they could redeem their limbs and their lives. There was not a baker's shop in the city round which twenty or thirty soldiers were not constantly prowling. Some persons who refused the base money were arrested by troopers and carried before the Provost Marshal, who cursed them, swore at them, locked them up in dark cells, and, by threatening to hang them at their own doors, soon overcame their resistance. Of all the plagues of that time none made a deeper or a more lasting impression on the minds of the Protestants of Dublin than the plague of the brass money. To the recollection of the confusion and misery which had been produced by James's coin must be in part ascribed the strenuous opposition which, thirty-five years later, large classes, firmly attached to the House of Hanover, offered to the government of George the First in the affair of Wood's patent.[29]

There can be no question that James, in thus altering, by his own authority, the terms of all the contracts in the kingdom, assumed a power which belonged only to the whole legislature. Yet the Commons did not remonstrate. There was no power, however unconstitutional, which they were not willing to concede to him, as long as he used it to crush and plunder the English population. On the other hand, they respected no prerogative, however ancient, however legitimate, however salutary, if they apprehended that he might use it to protect the race which they abhorred. They were not satisfied till they had extorted his reluctant consent to a portentous law, a law without a parallel in the history of civilized countries, the great Act of Attainder.

A list was framed containing between two and three thousand names. At the top was half the peerage of Ireland. Then came baronets, knights, clergymen, squires, merchants, yeomen, artisans, women, children. No investigation was made. Any member who wished to rid himself of a creditor, a rival, a private enemy, gave in the name to the clerk at the table, and it was generally inserted without discussion. The only debate of which any account has come down to us related to the Earl of Strafford. He had friends in the House who ventured to offer something in his favor. But a few words from Simon Luttrell settled the question. "I have," he said, "heard the King say some hard things of that lord." This was thought sufficient, and the name of Strafford stands fifth in the long table of the proscribed.

Days were fixed before which those whose names were on the list were required to surrender themselves to such justice as was then administered to English Protestants in Dublin. If a proscribed person was in Ireland, he must surrender himself by the tenth of August. If he had left Ireland since the fifth of November 1688, he must surrender himself by the first of September. If he had left Ireland before the fifth of November 1688, he must surrender himself by the first of October. If he failed to appear by the appointed day, he was to be hanged, drawn, and quartered without a trial, and his property was to be confiscated. It might be physically impossible for him to deliver himself up within the time fixed by the Act. He might be bedridden. He might be in the West Indies. He might be in prison. Indeed there notoriously were such cases. Among the attainted Lords was Mountjoy. He had been induced by the villainy of Tyrconnel to trust himself at Saint Germains: he had been thrown into the Bastile: he was still lying there; and the Irish parliament was not ashamed to enact that, unless he could, within a few weeks, make his escape from his cell, and present himself at Dublin, he should be put to death.

As it was not even pretended that there had been any inquiry into the guilt of those who were thus proscribed, as not a single one among them had been heard in his own defense, and as it was certain that it would be physically impossible for many of them to surrender themselves in time, it was clear that nothing but a large exercise of the royal prerogative of mercy could prevent the per-

[29]The occasion of Swift's *Drapier's Letters* (1724).

petration of iniquities so horrible that no precedent could be found for them even in the lamentable history of the troubles of Ireland. The Commons therefore determined that the royal prerogative of mercy should be limited. Several regulations were devised for the purpose of making the passing of pardons difficult and costly; and finally it was enacted that every pardon granted by his Majesty, after the end of November 1689, to any of the many hundreds of persons who had been sentenced to death without a trial, should be absolutely void and of none effect. Sir Richard Nagle came in state to the bar of the Lords and presented the bill with a speech worthy of the occasion. "Many of the persons here attainted," said he, "have been proved traitors by such evidence as satisfies us. As to the rest we have followed common fame."

With such reckless barbarity was the list framed that fanatical royalists, who were, at that very time, hazarding their property, their liberty, their lives, in the cause of James, were not secure from proscription. The most learned man of whom the Jacobite party could boast was Henry Dodwell, Camdenian Professor in the University of Oxford. In the cause of hereditary monarchy he shrank from no sacrifice and from no danger. It was about him that William uttered those memorable words: "He has set his heart on being a martyr; and I have set mine on disappointing him." But James was more cruel to friends than William to foes. Dodwell was a Protestant: he had some property in Connaught: these crimes were sufficient; and he was set down in the long roll of those who were doomed to the gallows and the quartering block.

That James would give his assent to a bill which took from him the power of pardoning, seemed to many persons impossible. He had, four years before, quarreled with the most loyal of parliaments rather than cede a prerogative which did not belong to him. It might, therefore, well be expected that he would now have struggled hard to retain a precious prerogative which had been enjoyed by his predecessors ever since the origin of the monarchy, and which even the Whigs allowed to be a power properly belonging to the Crown. The stern look and raised voice with which he had reprimanded the Tory gentlemen, who, in the language of profound reverence and fervent affection, implored him not to dispense with the laws, would now have been in place. He might also have seen that the right course was the wise course. Had he, on this great occasion, had the spirit to declare that he would not shed the blood of the innocent, and that, even as respected the guilty, he would not divest himself of the power of tempering judgment with mercy, he would have regained more hearts in England that he would have lost in Ireland. But it was ever his fate to resist where he should have yielded, and to yield where he should have resisted. The most wicked of all laws received his sanction; and it is but a very small extenuation of his guilt that his sanction was somewhat reluctantly given.

That nothing might be wanting to the completeness of this great crime, extreme care was taken to prevent the persons who were attainted from knowing that they were attainted, till the day of grace fixed in the Act was passed. The roll of names was not published, but kept carefully locked up in Fitton's closet. Some Protestants, who still adhered to the cause of James, but who were anxious to know whether any of their friends or relations had been proscribed, tried hard to obtain a sight of the list; but solicitation, remonstrance, even bribery, proved vain. Not a single copy got abroad, till it was too late for any of the thousands who had been condemned without a trial to obtain a pardon.

Towards the close of July James prorogued the Houses. They had sat more than ten weeks; and in that space of time they had proved most fully that, great as have been the evils which Protestant ascendency has produced in Ireland, the evils produced by Popish ascendency would have been greater still. That the colonists, when they had won the victory, grossly abused it, that their legislation was, during many years, unjust and tyrannical, is most true. But it is not less true that they never quite came up to the atrocious example set by their vanquished enemy during his short tenure of power.

Indeed, while James was loudly boasting that he had passed an Act granting entire liberty of conscience to all sects, a persecution as cruel as that of Languedoc was raging through all the provinces which owned his authority. It was said by those who wished to find an excuse for him that almost all the Protestants who still remained in Munster, Connaught, and Leinster were his enemies, and that it was not as schismatics, but as rebels in heart, who wanted only opportunity to become rebels in act, that he gave them up to be oppressed and despoiled; and to this excuse some weight might have been allowed if he had strenuously exerted himself to protect those few colonists, who, though firmly attached to the reformed religion, were still true to the doctrines of nonresistance and of indefeasible hereditary right. But even these devoted royalists found that their heresy was in his view a crime for which no services or sacrifices would atone. Three or four noblemen, members of the Anglican Church, who had welcomed him to Ireland, and had sat in his Parliament, represented to him that, if the rule which forbade any Protestant to possess any weapon were strictly enforced, their country houses would be at the mercy of the Rapparees, and obtained from him permission to keep arms sufficient for a few servants. But Avaux remonstrated. The indulgence, he said, was grossly abused: these Protestant lords were not to be trusted: they were turning their houses into fortresses: his Majesty would soon have reason to repent his goodness. These representations prevailed; and Roman Catholic troops were quartered in the suspected dwellings.

Still harder was the lot of those Protestant clergymen who continued to cling, with desperate fidelity, to the cause of the Lord's Anointed. Of all the Anglican divines the one who had the largest share of James's good graces seems to have been Cartwright. Whether Cartwright could long have continued to be a favorite without being an apostate may be doubted. He died a few weeks after his arrival in Ireland; and thenceforward his church had no one to plead her cause. Nevertheless a few of her prelates and priests continued for a time to teach what they had taught in the days of the Exclusion Bill.[30] But it was at the peril of life and limb that they exercised their functions. Every wearer of a cassock was a mark for the insults and outrages of soldiers and Rapparees. In the country his house was robbed, and he was fortunate if it was not burned over his head. He was hunted through the streets of Dublin with cries of "There goes the devil of a heretic." Sometimes he was knocked down: sometimes he was cudgeled. The rulers of the University of Dublin, trained in the Anglican doctrine of passive obedience, had greeted James on his first arrival at the Castle, and had been assured by him that he would protect them in the enjoyment of their property and their privileges. They were now, without any trial, without any accusation, thrust out of their house. The communion plate of the chapel, the books in the library, the very chairs and beds of the collegians were seized. Part of the building was turned into a magazine, part into a barrack, part into a prison. Simon Luttrell, who was Governor of the capital, was, with great difficulty and by powerful intercession, induced to let the ejected fellows and scholars depart in safety. He at length permitted them to remain at large, with this condition, that, on pain of death, no three of them should meet together. No Protestant divine suffered more hardships than Doctor William King, Dean of Saint Patrick's. He had been long distinguished by the fervor with which he had inculcated the duty of passively obeying even the worst rulers. At a later period, when he had published a defense of the Revolution, and had accepted a miter from the new government, he was reminded that he had invoked the divine vengeance of the usurpers, and had declared himself willing to die a hundred deaths rather than desert the cause of hereditary right. He had said that the true religion had often been strengthened by persecution, but could never be strengthened by rebellion; that it would be a glorious day for the Church of England when a whole cartload of her ministers should go to the gallows

[30]The bill (1679) to exclude James II, because he was a Catholic, from succeeding Charles II.

for the doctrine of nonresistance; and that his highest ambition was to be one of such a company. It is not improbable that, when he spoke thus, he felt as he spoke. But his principles, though they might perhaps have 5 held out against the severities and the promises of William, were not proof against the ingratitude of James. Human nature at last asserted its rights. After King had been repeatedly imprisoned by the government to 10 which he was devotedly attached, after he had been insulted and threatened in his own choir by the soldiers, after he had been interdicted from burying in his own churchyard, and from preaching in his own pulpit, after 15 he had narrowly escaped with life from a musketshot fired at him in the street, he began to think the Whig theory of government less unreasonable and unchristian than it had once appeared to him, and persuaded 20 himself that the oppressed Church might lawfully accept deliverance, if God should be pleased, by whatever means, to send it to her.

In no long time it appeared that James 25 would have done well to hearken to those counselors who had told him that the acts by which he was trying to make himself popular in one of his three kingdoms, would make him odious in the others. It was in 30 some sense fortunate for England that, after he had ceased to reign here, he continued during more than a year to reign in Ireland. The Revolution had been followed by a reaction of public feeling in his favor. That 35 reaction, if it had been suffered to proceed uninterrupted, might perhaps not have ceased till he was again King: but it was violently interrupted by himself. He would not suffer his people to forget: he would not suffer 40 them to hope: while they were trying to find excuses for his past errors, and to persuade themselves that he would not repeat these errors, he forced upon them, in their own despite, the conviction that he was 45 incorrigible, that the sharpest discipline of adversity had taught him nothing, and that, if they were weak enough to recall him, they would soon have to depose him again. It was in vain that the Jacobites put forth 50 pamphlets about the cruelty with which he had been treated by those who were nearest

to him in blood, about the imperious temper and uncourteous manners of William, about the favor shown to the Dutch, about the heavy taxes, about the suspension of the Habeas Corpus Act, about the dangers which threatened the Church from the enmity of Puritans and Latitudinarians. James refuted these pamphlets far more effectually than all the ablest and most eloquent Whig writers united could have done. Every week came the news that he had passed some new Act for robbing or murdering Protestants. Every colonist who succeeded in stealing across the sea from Leinster to Holyhead or Bristol, brought fearful reports of the tyranny under which his brethren groaned. What impression these reports made on the Protestants of our island may be easily inferred from the fact that they moved the indignation of Ronquillo, a Spaniard and a bigoted member of the Church of Rome. He informed his Court that, though the English laws against Popery might seem severe, they were so much mitigated by the prudence and humanity of the Government, that they caused no annoyance to quiet people; and he took upon himself to assure the Holy See that what a Roman Catholic suffered in London was nothing when compared with what a Protestant suffered in Ireland.

The fugitive Englishry found in England warm sympathy and munificent relief. Many were received into the houses of friends and kinsmen. Many were indebted for the means of subsistence to the liberality of strangers. Among those who bore a part in this work of mercy, none contributed more largely or less ostentatiously than the Queen. The House of Commons placed at the King's disposal fifteen thousand pounds for the relief of those refugees whose wants were most pressing, and requested him to give commissions in the army to those who were qualified for military employment. An Act was also passed enabling beneficed clergymen who had fled from Ireland to hold preferment in England. Yet the interest which the nation felt in these unfortunate guests was languid when compared with the interest excited by that portion of the Saxon colony which still maintained in Ulster a desperate conflict against overwhelming odds. On this subject scarcely one dissentient voice was to be heard in our island. Whigs, Tories, nay even those Jacobites in whom Jacobitism had not extinguished every patriotic sentiment, gloried in the glory of Enniskillen and Londonderry. The House of Commons was all of one mind. "This is no time to be counting cost," said honest Birch, who well remembered the way in which Oliver had made war on the Irish. "Are those brave fellows in Londonderry to be deserted? If we lose them will not all the world cry shame upon us? A boom across the river! Why have we not cut the boom in pieces? Are our brethren to perish almost in sight of England, within a few hours' voyage of our shores?" Howe, the most vehement man of one party, declared that the hearts of the people were set on Ireland. Seymour, the leader of the other party, declared that, though he had not taken part in setting up the new government, he should cordially support it in all that might be necessary for the preservation of Ireland. The Commons appointed a committee to inquire into the cause of the delays and miscarriages which had been all but fatal to the Englishry of Ulster. The officers to whose treachery or cowardice the public ascribed the calamities of Londonderry were put under arrest. Lundy was sent to the Tower, Cunningham to the Gate House. The agitation of the public mind was in some degree calmed by the announcement that, before the end of the summer, an army powerful enough to reëstablish the English ascendency in Ireland would be sent across Saint George's Channel, and that Schomberg would be the General. In the meantime an expedition which was thought to be sufficient for the relief of Londonderry was dispatched from Liverpool under the command of Kirke. The dogged obstinacy with which this man had, in spite of royal solicitations, adhered to his religion, and the part which he had taken in the Revolution, had perhaps entitled him to an amnesty for past crimes. But it is difficult to understand why the Government should have selected for a post of the highest importance an officer who was generally and justly hated, who had

never shown eminent talents for war, and who, both in Africa and in England, had notoriously tolerated among his soldiers a licentiousness, not only shocking to humanity, but also incompatible with discipline.

On the sixteenth of May, Kirke's troops embarked: on the twenty-second they sailed: but contrary winds made the passage slow, and forced the armament to stop long at the Isle of Man. Meanwhile the Protestants of Ulster were defending themselves with stubborn courage against a great superiority of force. The Enniskilleners had never ceased to wage a vigorous partisan war against the native population. Early in May they marched to encounter a large body of troops from Connaught, who had made an inroad into Donegal. The Irish were speedily routed, and fled to Sligo with the loss of a hundred and twenty men killed and sixty taken. Two small pieces of artillery and several horses fell into the hands of the conquerors. Elated by this success, the Enniskilleners soon invaded the county of Cavan, drove before them fifteen hundred of James's troops, took and destroyed the castle of Ballincarrig, reputed the strongest in that part of the kingdom, and carried off the pikes and muskets of the garrison. The next incursion was into Meath. Three thousand oxen and two thousand sheep were swept away and brought safe to the little island[31] in Lough Erne. These daring exploits spread terror even to the gates of Dublin. Colonel Hugh Sutherland was ordered to march against Enniskillen with a regiment of dragoons and two regiments of foot. He carried with him arms for the native peasantry; and many repaired to his standard. The Enniskilleners did not wait till he came into their neighborhood, but advanced to encounter him. He declined an action, and retreated, leaving his stores at Belturbet under the care of a detachment of three hundred soldiers. The Protestants attacked Belturbet with vigor, made their way into a lofty house which overlooked the town, and thence opened such a fire that in two hours the garrison surrendered. Seven hundred muskets, a great quantity of powder, many horses, many sacks of biscuits,

[31] I. e., Enniskillen.

many barrels of meal, were taken, and were sent to Enniskillen. The boats which brought these precious spoils were joyfully welcomed. The fear of hunger was removed. While the aboriginal population had, in many counties, altogether neglected the cultivation of the earth, in the expectation, it should seem, that marauding would prove an inexhaustible resource, the colonists, true to the provident and industrious character of their race, had, in the midst of war, not omitted carefully to till the soil in the neighborhood of their strongholds. The harvest was now not far remote; and, till the harvest, the food taken from the enemy would be amply sufficient.

Yet, in the midst of success and plenty, the Enniskilleners were tortured by a cruel anxiety for Londonderry. They were bound to the defenders of that city, not only by religious and national sympathy, but by common interest. For there could be no doubt that, if Londonderry fell, the whole Irish army would instantly march in irresistible force upon Lough Erne. Yet what could be done? Some brave men were for making a desperate attempt to relieve the besieged city; but the odds were too great. Detachments however were sent which infested the rear of the blockading army, cut off supplies, and, on one occasion, carried away the horses of three entire troops of cavalry. Still the line of posts which surrounded Londonderry by land remained unbroken. The river was still strictly closed and guarded. Within the walls the distress had become extreme. So early as the eighth of June horseflesh was almost the only meat which could be purchased; and of horseflesh the supply was scanty. It was necessary to make up the deficiency with tallow; and even tallow was doled out with a parsimonious hand.

On the fifteenth of June a gleam of hope appeared. The sentinels on the top of the Cathedral saw sails nine miles off in the bay of Lough Foyle. Thirty vessels of different sizes were counted. Signals were made from the steeples and returned from the mast heads, but were imperfectly understood on both sides. At last a messenger from the fleet eluded the Irish sentinels, dived under the boom, and informed the garrison that Kirke had arrived from England with troops, arms, ammunition, and provisions, to relieve the city.

In Londonderry expectation was at the height: but a few hours of feverish joy were followed by weeks of misery. Kirke thought it unsafe to make any attempt, either by land or by water, on the lines of the besiegers, and retired to the entrance of Lough Foyle, where, during several weeks, he lay inactive.

And now the pressure of famine became every day more severe. A strict search was made in all the recesses of all the houses of the city; and some provisions, which had been concealed in cellars by people who had since died or made their escape, were discovered and carried to the magazines. The stock of cannon balls was almost exhausted; and their place was supplied by brickbats coated with lead. Pestilence began, as usual, to make its appearance in the train of hunger. Fifteen officers died of fever in one day. The Governor Baker was among those who sank under the disease. His place was supplied by Colonel John Mitchelburne.

Meanwhile it was known at Dublin that Kirke and his squadron were on the coast of Ulster. The alarm was great at the Castle. Even before this news arrived, Avaux had given it as his opinion that Richard Hamilton was unequal to the difficulties of the situation. It had therefore been resolved that Rosen should take the chief command. He was now sent down with all speed.

On the nineteenth of June he arrived at the headquarters of the besieging army. At first he attempted to undermine the walls; but his plan was discovered; and he was compelled to abandon it after a sharp fight, in which more than a hundred of his men were slain. Then his fury rose to a strange pitch. He, an old soldier, a Marshal of France in expectancy, trained in the school of the greatest generals, accustomed, during many years, to scientific war, to be baffled by a mob of country gentlemen, farmers, shopkeepers, who were protected only by a wall which any good engineer would at once have pronounced untenable! He raved, he blasphemed, in a language of his own, made up of all the dialects spoken from the Baltic to the Atlantic. He would raze the city to the ground: he would spare no living thing; no, not the young girls; not the babies at the breast. As to the leaders, death was too light a punishment for them: he would rack them: he would roast them alive. In his rage he ordered a shell to be flung into the town with a letter containing a horrible menace. He would, he said, gather into one body all the Protestants who had remained at their homes between Charlemont and the sea, old men, women, children, many of them near in blood and affection to the defenders of Londonderry. No protection, whatever might be the authority by which it had been given, should be respected. The multitude thus brought together should be driven under the walls of Londonderry, and should there be starved to death in the sight of their countrymen, their friends, their kinsmen. This was no idle threat. Parties were instantly sent out in all directions to collect victims. At dawn, on the morning of the second of July, hundreds of Protestants, who were charged with no crime, who were incapable of bearing arms, and many of whom had protections granted by James, were dragged to the gates of the city. It was imagined that the piteous sight would quell the spirit of the colonists. But the only effect was to rouse that spirit to still greater energy. An order was immediately put forth that no man should utter the word Surrender on pain of death; and no man uttered that word. Several prisoners of high rank were in the town. Hitherto they had been well treated, and had received as good rations as were measured out to the garrison. They were now closely confined. A gallows was erected on one of the bastions; and a message was conveyed to Rosen, requesting him to send a confessor instantly to prepare his friends for death. The prisoners in great dismay wrote to the savage Livonian, but received no answer. They then addressed themselves to their countryman, Richard Hamilton. They were willing, they said, to shed their blood for their King; but they thought it hard to die the ignominious death of thieves in consequence of the barbarity of their own companions in arms. Hamilton, though a man of lax principles, was not cruel. He had been disgusted by the inhumanity of Rosen, but, being only second in command, could not venture to express publicly all that he thought. He however remonstrated strongly. Some Irish officers felt on this occasion as it was natural that brave men should feel, and declared, weeping with pity and indignation, that they should never cease to have in their ears the cries of the poor women and children who had been driven at the point of the pike to die of famine between the camp and the city. Rosen persisted during forty-eight hours. In that time many unhappy creatures perished: but Londonderry held out as resolutely as ever; and he saw that his crime was likely to produce nothing but hatred and obloquy. He at length gave way, and suffered the survivors to withdraw. The garrison then took down the gallows which had been erected on the bastion.

When the tidings of these events reached Dublin, James, though by no means prone to compassion, was startled by an atrocity of which the civil wars of England had furnished no example, and was displeased by learning that protections, given by his authority, and guaranteed by his honor, had been publicly declared to be nullities. He complained to the French ambassador, and said, with a warmth which the occasion fully justified, that Rosen was a barbarous Muscovite. Melfort could not refrain from adding that, if Rosen had been an Englishman, he would have been hanged. Avaux was utterly unable to understand this effeminate sensibility. In his opinion, nothing had been done that was at all reprehensible; and he had some difficulty in commanding himself when he heard the King and the secretary blame, in strong language, an act of wholesome severity. In truth the French ambassador and the French general were well paired. There was a great difference doubtless, in appearance and manner, between the handsome, graceful, and refined politician, whose dexterity and suavity had been renowned at the most polite courts of Europe, and the military adventurer, whose look and voice reminded all who came near him that he had been born in a half savage country, that he had risen from the ranks, and that he had once been sentenced to death for marauding. But the heart of the diplomatist was really even more callous than that of the soldier.

Rosen was recalled to Dublin; and Richard Hamilton was again left in the chief command. He tried gentler means than those which had brought so much reproach on his predecessor. No trick, no lie, which was thought likely to discourage the starving garrison was spared. One day a great shout was raised by the whole Irish camp. The defenders of Londonderry were soon informed that the army of James was rejoicing on account of the fall of Enniskillen. They were told that they had now no chance of being relieved, and were exhorted to save their lives by capitulating. They consented to negotiate. But what they asked was, that they should be permitted to depart armed and in military array, by land or by water at their choice. They demanded hostages for the exact fulfillment of these conditions, and insisted that the hostages should be sent on board of the fleet which lay in Lough Foyle. Such terms Hamilton durst not grant: the Governors would abate nothing: the treaty was broken off; and the conflict recommenced.

By this time July was far advanced; and the state of the city was, hour by hour, becoming more frightful. The number of the inhabitants had been thinned more by famine and disease than by the fire of the enemy. Yet that fire was sharper and more constant than ever. One of the gates was beaten in: one of the bastions was laid in ruins; but the breaches made by day were repaired by night with indefatigable activity. Every attack was still repelled. But the fighting men of the garrison were so much exhausted that they could scarcely keep their legs. Several of them, in the act of striking at the enemy, fell down from mere weakness. A very small quantity of grain remained, and was doled out by mouthfuls. The stock of salted hides was considerable, and by gnawing them the garrison appeased the rage of hunger. Dogs, fattened on the blood of the slain who lay unburied round the town, were luxuries which few could afford

to purchase. The price of a whelp's paw was five shillings and sixpence. Nine horses were still alive, and but barely alive. They were so lean that little meat was likely to be found upon them. It was, however, determined to slaughter them for food. The people perished so fast that it was impossible for the survivors to perform the rites of sepulture. There was scarcely a cellar in which some corpse was not decaying. Such was the extremity of distress, that the rats who came to feast in those hideous dens were eagerly hunted and greedily devoured. A small fish, caught in the river, was not to be purchased with money. The only price for which such a treasure could be obtained was some handfuls of oatmeal. Leprosies, such as strange and unwholesome diet engenders, made existence a constant torment. The whole city was poisoned by the stench exhaled from the bodies of the dead and of the half dead. That there should be fits of discontent and insubordination among men enduring such misery was inevitable. At one moment it was suspected that Walker had laid up somewhere a secret store of food, and was revelling in private, while he exhorted others to suffer resolutely for the good cause. His house was strictly examined: his innocence was fully proved: he regained his popularity; and the garrison, with death in near prospect, thronged to the cathedral to hear him preach, drank in his earnest eloquence with delight, and went forth from the house of God with haggard faces and tottering steps, but with spirit still unsubdued. There were, indeed, some secret plottings. A very few obscure traitors opened communications with the enemy. But it was necessary that all such dealings should be carefully concealed. None dared to utter publicly any words save words of defiance and stubborn resolution. Even in that extremity the general cry was "No surrender." And there were not wanting voices which, in low tones, added, "First the horses and hides; and then the prisoners; and then each other." It was afterwards related, half in jest, yet not without a horrible mixture of earnest, that a corpulent citizen, whose bulk presented a strange contrast to the skeletons which surrounded him, thought it expedient to conceal himself from the numerous eyes which followed him with cannibal looks whenever he appeared in the streets.

It was no slight aggravation of the sufferings of the garrison that all this time the English ships were seen far off in Lough Foyle. Communication between the fleet and the city was almost impossible. One diver who had attempted to pass the boom was drowned. Another was hanged. The language of signals was hardly intelligible. On the thirteenth of July, however, a piece of paper sewed up in a cloth button came to Walker's hands. It was a letter from Kirke, and contained assurances of speedy relief. But more than a fortnight of intense misery had since elapsed; and the hearts of the most sanguine were sick with deferred hope. By no art could the provisions which were left be made to hold out two days more.

Just at this time Kirke received from England a dispatch, which contained positive orders that Londonderry should be relieved. He accordingly determined to make an attempt which, as far as appears, he might have made, with at least an equally fair prospect of success, six weeks earlier.

Among the merchant ships which had come to Lough Foyle under his convoy was one called the Mountjoy. The master, Micaiah Browning, a native of Londonderry, had brought from England a large cargo of provisions. He had, it is said, repeatedly remonstrated against the inaction of the armament. He now eagerly volunteered to take the first risk of succoring his fellow citizens; and his offer was accepted. Andrew Douglas, master of the Phoenix, who had on board a great quantity of meal from Scotland, was willing to share the danger and the honor. The two merchantmen were to be escorted by the Dartmouth, a frigate of thirty-six guns, commanded by Captain John Leake, afterwards an admiral of great fame.

It was the twenty-eighth of July. The sun had just set: the evening sermon in the cathedral was over; and the heartbroken congregation had separated, when the sentinels on the tower saw the sails of three vessels coming up the Foyle. Soon there was a stir in the Irish camp. The besiegers were on the alert for miles along both shores. The ships were in extreme peril: for the river was low; and the only navigable channel ran very near to the left bank, where the headquarters of the enemy had been fixed, and where the batteries were most numerous. Leake performed his duty with a skill and spirit worthy of his noble profession, exposed his frigate to cover the merchantmen, and used his guns with great effect. At length the little squadron came to the place of peril. Then the Mountjoy took the lead, and went right at the boom. The huge barricade cracked and gave way: but the shock was such that the Mountjoy rebounded, and stuck in the mud. A yell of triumph rose from the banks: the Irish rushed to their boats, and were preparing to board; but the Dartmouth poured on them a well directed broadside, which threw them into disorder. Just then the Phoenix dashed at the breach which the Mountjoy had made, and was in a moment within the fence. Meantime the tide was rising fast. The Mountjoy began to move, and soon passed safe through the broken stakes and floating spars. But her brave master was no more. A shot from one of the batteries had struck him; and he died by the most enviable of all deaths, in sight of the city which was his birthplace, which was his home, and which had just been saved by his courage and self-devotion from the most frightful form of destruction. The night had closed in before the conflict at the boom began; but the flash of the guns was seen, and the noise heard, by the lean and ghastly multitude which covered the walls of the city. When the Mountjoy grounded, and when the shout of triumph rose from the Irish on both sides of the river, the hearts of the besieged died within them. One who endured the unutterable anguish of that moment has told us that they looked fearfully livid in each other's eyes. Even after the barricade had been passed, there was a terrible half hour of suspense. It was ten o'clock before the ships arrived at the quay. The whole population was there to welcome them. A screen made of casks filled with earth was hastily thrown up to protect the landing place from the batteries on the other side of the river; and then the work of unloading began. First were rolled on shore barrels containing six thousand bushels of meal. Then came great cheeses, casks of beef, flitches of bacon, kegs of butter, sacks of pease and biscuit, ankers[32] of brandy. Not many hours before, half a pound of tallow and three quarters of a pound of salted hide had been weighed out with niggardly care to every fighting man. The ration which each now received was three pounds of flour, two pounds of beef, and a pint of pease. It is easy to imagine with what tears grace was said over the suppers of that evening. There was little sleep on either side of the wall. The bonfires shone bright along the whole circuit of the ramparts. The Irish guns continued to roar all night; and all night the bells of the rescued city made answer to the Irish guns with a peal of joyous defiance. Through the three following days the batteries of the enemy continued to play. But, on the third night, flames were seen arising from the camp; and, when the first of August dawned, a line of smoking ruins marked the site lately occupied by the huts of the besiegers; and the citizens saw far off the long column of pikes and standards retreating up the left bank of the Foyle towards Strabane.

So ended this great siege, the most memorable in the annals of the British isles. It had lasted a hundred and five days. The garrison had been reduced from about seven thousand effective men to about three thousand. The loss of the besiegers cannot be precisely ascertained. Walker estimated it at eight thousand men. It is certain from the dispatches of Avaux that the regiments which returned from the blockade had been so much thinned that many of them were not more than two hundred strong. Of thirty-six French gunners who had superintended the cannonading, thirty-one had been killed or disabled. The means both of attack and of defense had undoubtedly been such as would have moved the great warriors of the Continent to laughter; and this is the very circumstance which gives so peculiar an interest to the history of the contest. It was a contest, not between engineers, but between nations; and the victory remained with the

nation which, though inferior in number, was superior in civilization, in capacity for self-government, and in stubbornness of resolution.

As soon as it was known that the Irish army had retired, a deputation from the city hastened to Lough Foyle, and invited Kirke to take the command. He came accompanied by a long train of officers, and was received in state by the two Governors, who delivered up to him the authority which, under the pressure of necessity, they had assumed. He remained only a few days; but he had time to show enough of the incurable vices of his character to disgust a population distinguished by austere morals and ardent public spirit. There was, however, no outbreak. The city was in the highest good humor. Such quantities of provisions had been landed from the fleet, that there was in every house a plenty never before known. A few days earlier a man had been glad to obtain for twenty pence a mouthful of carrion scraped from the bones of a starved horse. A pound of good beef was now sold for three halfpence. Meanwhile all hands were busied in removing corpses which had been thinly covered with earth, in filling up the holes which the shells had plowed in the ground, and in repairing the battered roofs of the houses. The recollection of past dangers and privations, and the consciousness of having deserved well of the English nation and of all Protestant Churches, swelled the hearts of the townspeople with honest pride. That pride grew stronger when they received from William a letter acknowledging, in the most affectionate language, the debt which he owed to the brave and trusty citizens of his good city. The whole population crowded to the Diamond to hear the royal epistle read. At the close all the guns on the ramparts sent forth a voice of joy: all the ships in the river made answer: barrels of ale were broken up; and the health of their Majesties was drunk with shouts and volleys of musketry.

Five generations have since passed away; and still the wall of Londonderry is to the Protestants of Ulster what the trophy of Marathon was to the Athenians. A lofty pillar, rising from a bastion which bore during

---

[32]Ten-gallon casks.

many weeks the heaviest fire of the enemy, is seen far up and far down the Foyle. On the summit is the statue of Walker, such as when, in the last and most terrible emergency, his eloquence roused the fainting courage of his brethren. In one hand he grasps a Bible. The other, pointing down the river, seems to direct the eyes of his famished audience to the English topmasts in the distant bay. Such a monument was well deserved: yet it was scarcely needed: for in truth the whole city is to this day a monument of the great deliverance. The wall is carefully preserved; nor would any plea of health or convenience be held by the inhabitants sufficient to justify the demolition of that sacred enclosure which, in the evil time, gave shelter to their race and their religion. The summit of the ramparts forms a pleasant walk. The bastions have been turned into little gardens. Here and there, among the shrubs and flowers, may be seen the old culverins which scattered bricks, cased with lead, among the Irish ranks. One antique gun, the gift of the Fishmongers of London, was distinguished, during the hundred and five memorable days, by the loudness of its report, and still bears the name of Roaring Meg. The cathedral is filled with relics and trophies. In the vestibule is a huge shell, one of many hundreds of shells which were thrown into the city. Over the altar are still seen the French flagstaves, taken by the garrison in a desperate sally. The white ensigns of the House of Bourbon have long been dust: but their place has been supplied by new banners, the work of the fairest hands of Ulster. The anniversary of the day on which the gates were closed, and the anniversary of the day on which the siege was raised, have been down to our own time celebrated by salutes, processions, banquets, and sermons: Lundy has been executed in effigy; and the sword, said by tradition to be that of Maumont, has, on great occasions, been carried in triumph. There is still a Walker Club and a Murray Club. The humble tombs of the Protestant captains have been carefully sought out, repaired, and embellished. It is impossible not to respect the sentiment which indicates itself by these tokens. It is a sentiment which belongs to the higher and purer part of human nature, and which adds not a little to the strength of states. A people which takes no pride in the noble achievements of remote ancestors will never achieve anything worthy to be remembered with pride by remote descendants. Yet it is impossible for the moralist or the statesman to look with unmixed complacency on the solemnities with which Londonderry commemorates her deliverance, and on the honors which she pays to those who saved her. Unhappily the animosities of her brave champions have descended with their glory. The faults which are ordinarily found in dominant castes and dominant sects have not seldom shown themselves without disguise at her festivities; and even with the expressions of pious gratitude which have resounded from her pulpits have too often been mingled words of wrath and defiance.

The Irish army which had retreated to Strabane remained there but a very short time. The spirit of the troops had been depressed by their recent failure, and was soon completely cowed by the news of a great disaster in another quarter.

Three weeks before this time the Duke of Berwick had gained an advantage over a detachment of the Enniskilleners, and had, by their own confession, killed or taken more than fifty of them. They were in hopes of obtaining some assistance from Kirke, to whom they had sent a deputation; and they still persisted in rejecting all terms offered by the enemy. It was therefore determined at Dublin that an attack should be made upon them from several quarters at once. Macarthy, who had been rewarded for his services in Munster with the title of Viscount Mountcashel, marched towards Lough Erne from the east with three regiments of foot, two regiments of dragoons, and some troops of cavalry. A considerable force, which lay encamped near the mouth of the river Drowes, was at the same time to advance from the west. The Duke of Berwick was to come from the north, with such horse and dragoons as could be spared from the army which was besieging Londonderry. The Enniskilleners were not fully apprised of the whole plan which had been laid for their destruction; but they knew that Macarthy was on the road with a force exceeding any which they could bring into the field. Their anxiety was in some degree relieved by the return of the deputation which they had sent to Kirke. Kirke could spare no soldiers; but he had sent some arms, some ammunition, and some experienced officers, of whom the chief were Colonel Wolseley and Lieutenant Colonel Berry. These officers had come by sea round the coast of Donegal, and had run up the Erne. On Sunday, the twenty-ninth of July, it was known that their boat was approaching the island of Enniskillen. The whole population, male and female, came to the shore to greet them. It was with difficulty that they made their way to the Castle through the crowds which hung on them, blessing God that dear old England had not quite forgotten the Englishmen who were upholding her cause against great odds in the heart of Ireland.

Wolseley seems to have been in every respect well qualified for his post. He was a stanch Protestant, had distinguished himself among the Yorkshiremen who rose up for the Prince of Orange and a free Parliament, and had, even before the landing of the Dutch army, proved his zeal for liberty and pure religion, by causing the Mayor of Scarborough who had made a speech in favor of King James, to be brought into the market place and well tossed there in a blanket. This vehement hatred of Popery was, in the estimation of the men of Enniskillen, the first of all the qualifications of a leader; and Wolseley had other and more important qualifications. Though himself regularly bred to war, he seems to have had a peculiar aptitude for the management of irregular troops. He had scarcely taken on himself the chief command when he received notice that Mountcashel had laid siege to the Castle of Crum. Crum was the frontier garrison of the Protestants of Fermanagh. The ruins of the old fortifications are now among the attractions of a beautiful pleasure-ground, situated on a woody promontory which overlooks Lough Erne. Wolseley determined to raise the siege. He sent Berry forward with such troops as could be instantly put in motion, and promised to follow speedily with a larger force.

Berry, after marching some miles, encountered thirteen companies of Macarthy's dragoons commanded by Anthony, the most brilliant and accomplished of all who bore the name of Hamilton, but much less successful as a soldier than as a courtier, a lover, and a writer. Hamilton's dragoons ran at the first fire: he was severely wounded; and his second in command was shot dead. Macarthy soon came up to support Hamilton; and at the same time Wolseley came up to support Berry. The hostile armies were now in presence of each other. Macarthy had above five thousand men and several pieces of artillery. The Enniskilleners were under three thousand; and they had marched in such haste that they had brought only one day's provisions. It was therefore absolutely necessary for them either to fight instantly or to retreat. Wolseley determined to consult the men; and this determination, which, in ordinary circumstances, would have been most unworthy of a general, was fully justified by the peculiar composition and temper of the little army, an army made up of gentlemen and yeomen fighting, not for pay, but for their lands, their wives, their children, and their God. The ranks were drawn up under arms; and the question was put, "Advance or Retreat?" The answer was an universal shout of "Advance." Wolseley gave out the word, "No Popery." It was received with loud applause. He instantly made his dispositions for an attack. As he approached, the enemy, to his great surprise, began to retire. The Enniskilleners were eager to pursue with all speed: but their commander, suspecting a snare, restrained their ardor, and positively forbade them to break their ranks. Thus one army retreated and the other followed, in good order, through the little town of Newton Butler. About a mile from that town the Irish faced about, and made a stand. Their position was well chosen. They were drawn up on a hill at the foot of which lay a deep bog. A narrow paved causeway which ran across the bog was the only road by which the cavalry of the Enniskilleners could advance; for on the right and left were pools, turf pits, and quagmires, which afforded no footing to horses. Macarthy placed his cannon in such a manner as to sweep this causeway.

Wolseley ordered his infantry to the attack. They struggled through the bog, made their way to firm ground, and rushed on the guns. There was then a short and desperate fight. The Irish cannoneers stood gallantly to their pieces till they were cut down to a man. The Enniskillen horse, no longer in danger of being mowed down by the fire of the artillery, came fast up the causeway. The Irish dragoons who had run away in the morning were smitten with another panic, and, without striking a blow, galloped from the field. The horse followed the example. Such was the terror of the fugitives that many of them spurred hard till their beasts fell down, and then continued to fly on foot, throwing away carbines, swords, and even coats as encumbrances. The infantry, seeing themselves deserted, flung down their pikes and muskets and ran for their lives. The conquerors now gave loose to that ferocity which has seldom failed to disgrace the civil wars of Ireland. The butchery was terrible. Near fifteen hundred of the vanquished were put to the sword. About five hundred more, in ignorance of the country, took a road which led to Lough Erne. The lake was before them: the enemy behind: they plunged into the waters and perished there. Macarthy, abandoned by his troops, rushed into the midst of the pursuers and very nearly found the death which he sought. He was wounded in several places: he was struck to the ground; and in another moment his brains would have been knocked out with the butt end of a musket, when he was recognized and saved. The colonists lost only twenty men killed and fifty wounded. They took four hundred prisoners, seven pieces of cannon, fourteen barrels of powder, all the drums and all the colors of the vanquished enemy.

The battle of Newton Butler was won on the third day after the boom thrown over the Foyle was broken. At Strabane the news met the Celtic army which was retreating from Londonderry. All was terror and confusion: the tents were struck: the military stores were flung by wagon loads into the waters of the Mourne; and the dismayed Irish, leaving many sick and wounded to the mercy of the victorious Protestants, fled to Omagh, and thence to Charlemont. Sarsfield, who commanded at Sligo, found it necessary to abandon that town, which was instantly occupied by a detachment of Kirke's troops. Dublin was in consternation. James dropped words which indicated an intention of flying to the Continent. Evil tidings indeed came fast upon him. Almost at the same time at which he learned that one of his armies had raised the siege of Londonderry, and that another had been routed at Newton Butler, he received intelligence scarcely less disheartening from Scotland. * * *

JOHN HENRY, CARDINAL NEWMAN

1801–1890

Newman was born in London on 21 February, 1801. His father was a banker and a man of cultivated interests; his mother a descendant of French Huguenots who had come to England after the revocation of the Edict of Nantes (1685). In his childhood he received religious training which may be described as a "modified Calvinism," and from an early time he was familiar with the Authorized Version of the Bible, but there is nothing in his ancestry or training which accounts for the strong sense of immaterial reality which he had even as a boy, and which contained the germs of his later development. As a child, he tells us, "I used to wish the Arabian Tales were true; my imagination ran on unknown influences, on magical powers, and talismans. . . . I thought life might be a dream, or I an Angel, and all this world a deception, my fellow-angels by a playful device concealing themselves from me, and deceiving me with the semblance of a material world." This was not a mere passing fancy with him, but an early manifestation of a conviction of immaterial reality which was later strengthened by such apparently diverse influences as the tales of Sir Walter Scott and the theological treatises of Thomas Scott, and which, deepened after his experience of "conversion" at fifteen, remained his abiding possession. He says that his religious studies at fifteen and in the years immediately following aided "in isolating me from the objects which surrounded me, in confirming me in my mistrust of the reality of material phenomena, and making me rest in the thought of two and two only supreme and luminously self-evident beings, myself and my Creator."

Newman received his secondary education at a school in Ealing, and went thence to Trinity College, Oxford, in 1816. He received his B.A. in 1820. In 1822 he was elected a Fellow of Oriel College, and two years later he was ordained a deacon in the Church of England. In 1825 he was ordained a priest and in the following year became one of the tutors of his college. About this time he also preached his first university sermon, and in 1828 he became vicar of St. Mary's Church, Oxford. This remained his outward position for a number of years. Newman's nature was closely akin to Coleridge's and Carlyle's. He heard the same inner voice that they heard, telling him of truths beyond the ken of rationalists and scientists. In his case this experience took the form of a living sense of the truth of Christianity very different from the largely formal professions of faith then usual in the Anglican Church outside of the evangelical party. Newman, moreover, saw with remarkable clearness the character and strength of the forces which were to oppose Christianity in the nineteenth century, and he consecrated his life to warfare against liberalism, as he called it, or rationalism. For this purpose he deemed it essential that the Anglican Church should be aroused from its lethargy and awakened to a full sense of the unbroken Christian tradition which it claimed to represent. This was the starting-point of the Oxford Movement, of which Newman was the leading spirit. He held that the "campaign" actually began with a sermon preached by John Keble in Oxford in 1833, a sermon in which an anti-clerical act of Parliament was termed an act of national apostasy. Keble's attack was quickly followed by the first of the famous series of ninety *Tracts for the Times*. In these pamphlets as well as in other ways Newman and his associates sought to emphasize the Catholic doctrines of the Anglican Church and to demonstrate that that Church was really the modern representative of Christianity as it had existed in earlier days before the degeneracy and corruption of the Roman Church had brought about the Reformation. In the course of his studies, however, Newman gradually became convinced that, despite the corruption and idolatry of Rome, the English Reformation had been an act of schism; and at the same time he had it forcibly borne in upon him that the Anglican Church would not follow him in his conclusion. The result was that in 1845 Newman himself went over to the Roman Catholic

Church. He had by this time become a national figure whose every movement was watched with deep interest and fear, and it is hardly too much to say that for a time the fate of the Church of England seemed to hang upon his actions.

In the early eighteen-fifties there was a movement on foot to establish a Catholic University in Dublin. In 1852, as a means of preparation for this, Newman delivered in Dublin a course of lectures *On the Scope and Nature of University Education,* later published with other papers as *The Idea of a University.* These lectures well illustrate the felicity of his prose style and have, in addition, been generally recognized as a classic statement of the meaning of a liberal education. From 1854 until 1858 Newman was Rector of the new Catholic University, but the enterprise was in the end a failure. His career in the Catholic Church was in fact outwardly a series of disappointments until late in his life, because he was misunderstood and distrusted by some of his ecclesiastical superiors. In addition he was, in the years after 1845, regarded with dislike by Englishmen in general because of the effort they felt he had made to destroy the Anglican Church. But in 1864 he was egregiously attacked by Charles Kingsley— "a popular writer, more remarkable for vigorous writing than vigorous thought"—who published an assertion that Newman had countenanced falsehood on the part of the Roman clergy. The latter immediately took advantage of this opportunity both to clear his name and to explain to the English public the development of his religious opinions. This he did in his *Apologia pro Vita Sua,* a justly famous book written with transparent candor and sincerity. In his old age Newman received honors both from England and from Rome which indicate the position he had attained as the greatest English religious leader of the nineteenth century. In 1877 he was elected an Honorary Fellow of Trinity College, Oxford, and in 1879 was created a cardinal of the Roman Catholic Church. He died on 11 August, 1890, and was buried at Rednal.

The Idea of a University Defined and Illustrated, in the standard authorized edition published by Longmans, Green and Co. (who also publish all of Newman's other writings), is made up of two volumes which originally appeared in 1852 (the "Nine Discourses") and in 1858 ("University Subjects"). The standard biography is *The Life and Letters of John Henry Cardinal Newman* by Wilfrid Ward (2 vols., London, 1912), which, however, does not supersede the earlier *Letters and Correspondence of J. H. Newman during His Life in the English Church,* ed. Anne Mozley (2 vols., London, 1891). Amongst recent biographies two may be recommended: J. Lewis May's *Cardinal Newman, a Study* (London, 1929), and Frank Leslie Cross's *John Henry Newman* (London, 1933). Paul Elmer More includes an acute interpretation of Newman in his *Shelburne Essays,* Eighth Series (Boston, 1913); and Geoffrey Faber gives a modern interpretation in his study of the Oxford Movement, *Oxford Apostles* (London, 1933).

THE IDEA OF A UNIVERSITY

DISCOURSE VI[1]

Liberal Knowledge Viewed in Relation to Learning

It were well if the English, like the Greek language, possessed some definite word to express, simply and generally, intellectual proficiency or perfection, such as "health," as used with reference to the animal frame, and "virtue," with reference to our moral nature. I am not able to find such a term;— talent, ability, genius, belong distinctly to

[1]The two Discourses here printed are given the numbers by which they are generally referred to, but they are taken from the revised edition of 1859 (where they are differently numbered), not from the first edition of 1852. They are reprinted with the permission of Messrs. Longmans, Green and Company, Newman's authorized publishers.

the raw material, which is the subject-matter, not to that excellence which is the result of exercise and training. When we turn, indeed, to the particular kinds of intellectual perfection, words are forthcoming for our purpose, as, for instance, judgment, taste, and skill; yet even these belong, for the most part, to powers or habits bearing upon practice or upon art, and not to any perfect condition of the intellect, considered in itself. Wisdom, again, which is a more comprehensive word than any other, certainly has a direct relation to conduct and to human life. Knowledge, indeed, and science express purely intellectual ideas, but still not a state or habit of the intellect; for knowledge, in its ordinary sense, is but one of its circumstances, denoting a possession or a faculty; and science has been appropriated to the subject-matter of the intellect, instead of belonging at present, as it ought to do, to the intellect itself. The consequence is that, on an occasion like this, many words are necessary, in order, first, to bring out and convey what surely is no difficult idea in itself—that of the cultivation of the intellect as an end; next, in order to recommend what surely is no unreasonable object; and lastly, to describe and make the mind realize the particular perfection in which that object consists. Every one knows practically what are the constituents of health or virtue; and every one recognizes health and virtue as ends to be pursued; it is otherwise with intellectual excellence, and this must be my excuse, if I seem to any one to be bestowing a good deal of labor on a preliminary matter.

In default of a recognized term, I have called the perfection or virtue of the intellect by the name of philosophy, philosophical knowledge, enlargement of mind, or illumination; terms which are not uncommonly given to it by writers of this day: but, whatever name we bestow on it, it is, I believe, as a matter of history, the business of a university to make this intellectual culture its direct scope, or to employ itself in the education of the intellect—just as the work of a hospital lies in healing the sick or wounded; of a riding or fencing school, or of a gymnasium, in exercising the limbs; of an almshouse, in aiding and solacing the old; of an orphanage, in protecting innocence; of a penitentiary, in restoring the guilty. I say a university, taken in its bare idea, and before we view it as an instrument of the Church, has this object and this mission; it contemplates neither moral impression nor mechanical production; it professes to exercise the mind neither in art nor in duty; its function is intellectual culture: here it may leave its scholars, and it has done its work when it has done as much as this. It educates the intellect to reason well in all matters, to reach out towards truth, and to grasp it.

This, I said in my foregoing Discourse, was the object of a university, viewed in itself, and apart from the Catholic Church,

or from the state, or from any other power which may use it; and I illustrated this in various ways. I said that the intellect must have an excellence of its own, for there was nothing which had not its specific good; that the word "educate" would not be used of intellectual culture, as it is used, had not the intellect had an end of its own; that, had it not such an end, there would be no meaning in calling certain intellectual exercises "liberal," in contrast with "useful," as is commonly done; that the very notion of a philosophical temper implied it, for it threw us back upon research and system as ends in themselves, distinct from effects and works of any kind; that a philosophical scheme of knowledge, or system of sciences, could not, from the nature of the case, issue in any one definite art or pursuit, as its end; and that, on the other hand, the discovery and contemplation of truth, to which research and systematizing led, were surely sufficient ends, though nothing beyond them were added, and that they had ever been accounted sufficient by mankind.

Here then I take up the subject; and having determined that the cultivation of the intellect is an end distinct and sufficient in itself, and that, so far as words go it is an enlargement or illumination, I proceed to inquire what this mental breadth, or power, or light, or philosophy consists in. A hospital heals a broken limb or cures a fever; what does an institution effect, which professes the health, not of the body, not of the soul, but of the intellect? What is this good, which in former times, as well as our own, has been found worth the notice, the appropriation, of the Catholic Church?

I have then to investigate, in the Discourses which follow, those qualities and characteristics of the intellect in which its cultivation issues or rather consists; and, with a view of assisting myself in this undertaking, I shall recur to certain questions which have already been touched upon. These questions are three: *viz.*, the relation of intellectual culture, first, to *mere* knowledge; secondly, to *professional* knowledge; and thirdly, to *religious* knowledge. In other words, are *acquirements* and *attainments* the scope of a university education? or *expertness in particular arts and pursuits?* or *moral and religious proficiency?* or something besides these three? These questions I shall examine in succession, with the purpose I 5 have mentioned; and I hope to be excused if, in this anxious undertaking, I am led to repeat what, either in these Discourses or elsewhere, I have already put upon paper. And first, of *mere knowledge,* or learning, 10 and its connection with intellectual illumination or philosophy.

I suppose the *primâ-facie*[2] view which the public at large would take of a university, considered as a place of education, is noth- 15 ing more or less than a place for acquiring a great deal of knowledge on a great many subjects. Memory is one of the first developed of the mental faculties; a boy's business when he goes to school is to learn, 20 that is, to store up things in his memory. For some years his intellect is little more than an instrument for taking in facts, or a receptacle for storing them; he welcomes them as fast as they come to him; he lives on 25 what is without; he has his eyes ever about him; he has a lively susceptibility of impressions; he imbibes information of every kind; and little does he make his own in a true sense of the word, living rather upon 30 his neighbors all around him. He has opinions, religious, political, and literary, and, for a boy, is very positive in them and sure about them; but he gets them from his schoolfellows, or his masters, or his parents, 35 as the case may be. Such as he is in his other relations, such also is he in his school exercises; his mind is observant, sharp, ready, retentive; he is almost passive in the acquisition of knowledge. I say this in 40 no disparagement of the idea of a clever boy. Geography, chronology, history, language, natural history, he heaps up the matter of these studies as treasures for a future day. It is the seven years of plenty with 45 him: he gathers in by handfuls, like the Egyptians, without counting; and though, as time goes on, there is exercise for his argumentative powers in the elements of mathematics, and for his taste in the poets 50 and orators, still, while at school, or at least,

till quite the last years of his time, he acquires, and little more; and when he is leaving for the university, he is mainly the creature of foreign influences and circumstances, and made up of accidents, homogeneous or not, as the case may be. Moreover, the moral habits, which are a boy's praise, encourage and assist this result; that is, diligence, assiduity, regularity, dispatch, persevering application; for these are the direct conditions of acquisition, and naturally lead to it. Acquirements, again, are emphatically producible, and at a moment; they are a something to show, both for master and scholar; an audience, even though ignorant themselves of the subjects of an examination, can comprehend when questions are answered and when they are not. Here again is a reason why mental culture should in the minds of men be identified with the acquisition of knowledge.

The same notion possesses the public mind, when it passes on from the thought of a school to that of a university: and with the best of reasons so far as this, that there is no true culture without acquirements, and that philosophy presupposes knowledge. It requires a great deal of reading, or a wide range of information, to warrant us in putting forth our opinions on any serious subject; and without such learning the most original mind may be able indeed to dazzle, to amuse, to refute, to perplex, but not to come to any useful result or any trustworthy conclusion. There are indeed persons who profess a different view of the matter, and even act upon it. Every now and then you will find a person of vigorous or fertile mind, who relies upon his own resources, despises all former authors, and gives the world, with the utmost fearlessness, his views upon religion, or history, or any other popular subject. And his works may sell for a while; he may get 45 a name in his day; but this will be all. His readers are sure to find in the long run that his doctrines are mere theories, and not the expression of facts, that they are chaff instead of bread, and then his popu- 50 larity drops as suddenly as it rose.

Knowledge, then, is the indispensable condition of expansion of mind, and the in-

---

[2]Superficial.

strument of attaining to it; this cannot be
denied, it is ever to be insisted on; I begin
with it as a first principle; however, the
very truth of it carries men too far, and
confirms to them the notion that it is the 5
whole of it. A narrow mind is thought to
be that which contains little knowledge;
and an enlarged mind, that which holds a
deal; and what seems to put the matter
beyond dispute is, the fact of the number 10
of studies which are pursued in a university,
by its very profession. Lectures are given
on every kind of subject; examinations are
held; prizes awarded. There are moral,
metaphysical, physical professors; profes- 15
sors of languages, of history, of mathematics,
of experimental science. Lists of questions
are published, wonderful for their range
and depth, variety and difficulty; treatises
are written, which carry upon their very 20
face the evidence of extensive reading or
multifarious information; what then is
wanted for mental culture to a person of
large reading and scientific attainments?
what is grasp of mind but acquirement? 25
where shall philosophical repose be found,
but in the consciousness and enjoyment of
large intellectual possessions?

And yet this notion is, I conceive, a
mistake, and my present business is to show 30
that it is one, and that the end of a liberal
education is not mere knowledge, or knowledge considered in its *matter;* and I shall
best attain my object by actually setting
down some cases, which will be generally 35
granted to be instances of the process of
enlightenment or enlargement of mind, and
others which are not, and thus, by the comparison, you will be able to judge for
yourselves, gentlemen, whether knowledge, 40
that is, acquirement, is after all the real
principle of the enlargement, or whether that
principle is not rather something beyond it.

For instance, let a person, whose experience has hitherto been confined to the more 45
calm and unpretending scenery of these
islands, whether here[3] or in England, go for
the first time into parts where physical
nature puts on her wilder and more awful
forms, whether at home or abroad, as into 50
mountainous districts; or let one, who has

[3] In Ireland.

ever lived in a quiet village, go for the first
time to a great metropolis—then I suppose
he will have a sensation which perhaps he
never had before. He has a feeling not in
addition or increase of former feelings, but
of something different in its nature. He
will perhaps be borne forward, and find for
a time that he has lost his bearings. He has
made a certain progress, and he has a consciousness of mental enlargement; he does
not stand where he did, he has a new center,
and a range of thoughts to which he was
before a stranger.

Again, the view of the heavens which the
telescope opens upon us, if allowed to fill
and possess the mind, may almost whirl it
round and make it dizzy. It brings in a
flood of ideas, and is rightly called an intellectual enlargement, whatever is meant by
the term.

And so again, the sight of beasts of prey
and other foreign animals, their strangeness,
the originality (if I may use the term) of
their forms and gestures and habits and
their variety and independence of each other,
throw us out of ourselves into another
creation, and as if under another Creator,
if I may so express the temptation which
may come on the mind. We seem to have
new faculties, or a new exercise for our
faculties, by this addition to our knowledge;
like a prisoner who, having been accustomed
to wear manacles or fetters, suddenly finds
his arms and legs free.

Hence physical science generally, in all
its departments, as bringing before us the
exuberant riches and resources, yet the orderly course, of the universe, elevates and
excites the student, and at first, I may say,
almost takes away his breath, while in time it
exercises a tranquilizing influence upon him.

Again, the study of history is said to
enlarge and enlighten the mind, and why?
because, as I conceive, it gives it a power
of judging of passing events, and of all
events, and a conscious superiority over
them which before it did not possess.

And in like manner, what is called seeing
the world, entering into active life, going
into society, traveling, gaining acquaintance
with the various classes of the community,
coming into contact with the principles and

modes of thought of various parties, interests, and races, their views, aims, habits, and manners, their religious creeds and forms of worship—gaining experience how various yet how alike men are, how low-minded, how bad, how opposed, yet how confident in their opinions; all this exerts a perceptible influence upon the mind, which it is impossible to mistake, be it good or be it bad, and is popularly called its enlargement.

And then again, the first time the mind comes across the arguments and speculations of unbelievers, and feels what a novel light they cast upon what he has hitherto accounted sacred; and still more, if it gives in to them and embraces them, and throws off as so much prejudice what it has hitherto held, and, as if waking from a dream, begins to realize to its imagination that there is now no such thing as law and the transgression of law, that sin is a phantom, and punishment a bugbear, that it is free to sin, free to enjoy the world and the flesh; and still further, when it does enjoy them, and reflects that it may think and hold just what it will, that "the world is all before it where to choose,"[4] and what system to build up as its own private persuasion; when this torrent of bad thoughts rushes over and inundates it, who will deny that the fruit of the tree of knowledge, or what the mind takes for knowledge, has made it one of the gods, with a sense of expansion and elevation—an intoxication in reality, still, so far as the subjective state of the mind goes, an illumination? Hence the fanaticism of individuals or nations, who suddenly cast off their Maker. Their eyes are opened, and, like the judgment-stricken king in the tragedy,[5] they see two suns, and a magic universe, out of which they look back upon their former state of faith and innocence with a sort of contempt and indignation, as if they were then but fools, and the dupes of imposture.

On the other hand, religion has its own enlargement, and an enlargement, not of

tumult, but of peace. It is often remarked of uneducated persons, who have hitherto thought little of the unseen world, that, on their turning to God, looking into themselves, regulating their hearts, reforming their conduct, and meditating on death and judgment, heaven and hell, they seem to become, in point of intellect, different beings from what they were. Before, they took things as they came, and thought no more of one thing than another. But now every event has a meaning; they have their own estimate of whatever happens to them; they are mindful of times and seasons, and compare the present with the past; and the world, no longer dull, monotonous, unprofitable, and hopeless, is a various and complicated drama, with parts and an object, and an awful moral.

Now from these instances, to which many more might be added, it is plain, first, that the communication of knowledge certainly is either a condition or the means of that sense of enlargement or enlightenment, of which at this day we hear so much in certain quarters: this cannot be denied; but next, it is equally plain, that such communication is not the whole of the process. The enlargement consists, not merely in the passive reception into the mind of a number of ideas hitherto unknown to it, but in the mind's energetic and simultaneous action upon and towards and among those new ideas, which are rushing in upon it. It is the action of a formative power, reducing to order and meaning the matter of our acquirements; it is a making the objects of our knowledge subjectively our own, or, to use a familiar word, it is a digestion of what we receive, into the substance of our previous state of thought; and without this no enlargement is said to follow. There is no enlargement, unless there be a comparison of ideas one with another, as they come before the mind, and a systematizing of them. We feel our minds to be growing and expanding *then,* when we not only learn, but refer what we learn to what we know already. It is not a mere addition to our knowledge which is the illumination; but the locomotion, the movement onwards, of that mental center, to which both what

---

[4] *Paradise Lost,* XII, 646.

[5] Pentheus of Thebes, in the *Bacchae* of Euripides. Pentheus speaks of seeming to see two suns in l. 918.

we know and what we are learning, the accumulating mass of our acquirements, gravitates. And therefore a truly great intellect, and recognized to be such by the common opinion of mankind, such as the intellect of Aristotle, or of St. Thomas,[6] or of Newton, or of Goethe (I purposely take instances within and without the Catholic pale, when I would speak of the intellect as such), is one which takes a connected view of old and new, past and present, far and near, and which has an insight into the influence of all these one on another; without which there is no whole, and no center. It possesses the knowledge, not only of things, but also of their mutual and true relations; knowledge, not merely considered as acquirement, but as philosophy.

Accordingly, when this analytical, distributive, harmonizing process is away, the mind experiences no enlargement, and is not reckoned as enlightened or comprehensive, whatever it may add to its knowledge. For instance, a great memory, as I have already said, does not make a philosopher, any more than a dictionary can be called a grammar. There are men who embrace in their minds a vast multitude of ideas, but with little sensibility about their real relations towards each other. These may be antiquarians, annalists, naturalists; they may be learned in the law; they may be versed in statistics; they are most useful in their own place; I should shrink from speaking disrespectfully of them; still, there is nothing in such attainments to guarantee the absence of narrowness of mind. If they are nothing more than well-read men, or men of information, they have not what specially deserves the name of culture of mind, or fulfills the type of liberal education.

In like manner we sometimes fall in with persons who have seen much of the world, and of the men who, in their day, have played a conspicuous part in it, but who generalize nothing, and have no observation, in the true sense of the word. They abound in information in detail, curious and entertaining, about men and things; and, having lived under the influence of no very clear or settled principles, religious or political, they speak of every one and everything, only as so many phenomena, which are complete in themselves, and lead to nothing, not discussing them, or teaching any truth, or instructing the hearer, but simply talking. No one would say that these persons, well informed as they are, had attained to any great culture of intellect or to philosophy.

The case is the same still more strikingly where the persons in question are beyond dispute men of inferior powers and deficient education. Perhaps they have been much in foreign countries, and they receive, in a passive, otiose, unfruitful way, the various facts which are forced upon them there. Seafaring men, for example, range from one end of the earth to the other; but the multiplicity of external objects which they have encountered forms no symmetrical and consistent picture upon their imagination; they see the tapestry of human life as it were on the wrong side, and it tells no story. They sleep, and they rise up, and they find themselves now in Europe, now in Asia; they see visions of great cities and wild regions; they are in the marts of commerce or amid the islands of the South; they gaze on Pompey's Pillar[7] or on the Andes; and nothing which meets them carries them forward or backward to any idea beyond itself. Nothing has a drift or relation; nothing has a history or a promise. Everything stands by itself, and comes and goes in its turn, like the shifting scenes of a show, which leave the spectator where he was. Perhaps you are near such a man on a particular occasion, and expect him to be shocked or perplexed at something which occurs; but one thing is much the same to him as another, or, if he is perplexed, it is as not knowing what to say, whether it is right to admire, or to ridicule, or to disapprove, while conscious that some expression of opinion is expected from him; for in fact he has no standard of judgment at all, and no landmarks to guide him to a conclusion. Such is mere acquisition, and, I repeat, no one would dream of calling it philosophy.

Instances such as these confirm, by the contrast, the conclusion I have already

[6] Aquinas (*c.* 1225–1274).

[7] Near Alexandria.

drawn from those which preceded them. That only is true enlargement of mind which is the power of viewing many things at once as one whole, of referring them severally to their true place in the universal system, of understanding their respective values, and determining their mutual dependence. Thus is that form of universal knowledge, of which I have on a former occasion spoken, set up in the individual intellect, and constitutes its perfection. Possessed of this real illumination, the mind never views any part of the extended subject-matter of knowledge without recollecting that it is but a part, or without the associations which spring from this recollection. It makes everything in some sort lead to everything else; it would communicate the image of the whole to every separate portion, till that whole becomes in imagination like a spirit, everywhere pervading and penetrating its component parts, and giving them one definite meaning. Just as our bodily organs, when mentioned, recall their function in the body, as the word "creation" suggests the Creator, and "subjects" a sovereign, so, in the mind of the philosopher, as we are abstractedly conceiving of him, the elements of the physical and moral world, sciences, arts, pursuits, ranks, offices, events, opinions, individualities, are all viewed as one, with correlative functions, and as gradually by successive combinations converging, one and all, to the true center.

To have even a portion of this illuminative reason and true philosophy is the highest state to which nature can aspire, in the way of intellect; it puts the mind above the influences of chance and necessity, above anxiety, suspense, tumult, and superstition, which are the portion of the many. Men, whose minds are possessed with some one object, take exaggerated views of its importance, are feverish in the pursuit of it, make it the measure of things which are utterly foreign to it, and are startled and despond if it happens to fail them. They are ever in alarm or in transport. Those on the other hand who have no object or principle whatever to hold by, lose their way, every step they take. They are thrown out, and do not know what to think or say, at every fresh juncture; they have no view of persons, or occurrences, or facts, which come suddenly upon them, and they hang upon the opinion of others, for want of internal resources. But the intellect, which has been disciplined to the perfection of its powers, which knows, and thinks while it knows, which has learned to leaven the dense mass of facts and events with the elastic force of reason, such an intellect cannot be partial, cannot be exclusive, cannot be impetuous, cannot be at a loss, cannot but be patient, collected, and majestically calm, because it discerns the end in every beginning, the origin in every end, the law in every interruption, the limit in each delay; because it ever knows where it stands, and how its path lies from one point to another. It is the τετράγωνος of the Peripatetic,[8] and has the *nil admirari*[9] of the Stoic—

Felix qui potuit rerum cognoscere causas,
Atque metus omnes, et inexorabile fatum
Subjecit pedibus, strepitumque Acherontis
  avari.[10]

There are men who, when in difficulties, originate at the moment vast ideas or dazzling projects; who, under the influence of excitement, are able to cast a light, almost as if from inspiration, on a subject or course of action which comes before them; who have a sudden presence of mind equal to any emergency, rising with the occasion, and an undaunted magnanimous bearing, and an energy and keenness which is but made intense by opposition. This is genius, this is heroism; it is the exhibition of a natural gift, which no culture can teach, at which no institution can aim; here, on the contrary, we are concerned, not with mere nature, but with training and teaching. That perfection of the intellect, which is the result of education, and its *beau ideal,* to be imparted to individuals in their respective

---

[8] The four-square man of Aristotle (see *Nicomachean Ethics,* I, x, 11), who was called the Peripatetic because, according to tradition, he walked about in the Lyceum while lecturing to his pupils.

[9] To wonder at nothing (Horace, *Epistles,* I, vi, 1).

[10] Happy is he who is able to know the sequences of things, and thus triumphs over all fear, and inexorable fate, and the roar of greedy Acheron (Virgil, *Georgics,* II, 490–492).

measures, is the clear, calm, accurate vision and comprehension of all things, as far as the finite mind can embrace them, each in its place, and with its own characteristics upon it. It is almost prophetic from its knowledge of history; it is almost heart-searching from its knowledge of human nature; it has almost supernatural charity from its freedom from littleness and preju-dice; it has almost the repose of faith, because nothing can startle it; it has almost the beauty and harmony of heavenly con-templation, so intimate is it with the eternal order of things and the music of the spheres.

And now, if I may take for granted that the true and adequate end of intellectual training and of a university is not learning or acquirement, but rather, is thought or reason exercised upon knowledge, or what may be called philosophy, I shall be in a position to explain the various mistakes which at the present day beset the subject of university education.

I say then, if we would improve the in-tellect, first of all, we must ascend: we cannot gain real knowledge on a level; we must generalize, we must reduce to method, we must have a grasp of principles, and group and shape our acquisitions by them. It matters not whether our field of operation be wide or limited; in every case, to com-mand it, is to mount above it. Who has not felt the irritation of mind and impa-tience created by a deep, rich country, visited for the first time, with winding lanes, and high hedges, and green steeps, and tangled woods, and everything smiling indeed, but in a maze? The same feeling comes upon us in a strange city, when we have no map of its streets. Hence you hear of prac-ticed travelers, when they first come into a place, mounting some high hill or church tower, by way of reconnoitering its neigh-borhood. In like manner you must be above your knowledge, gentlemen, not under it, or it will oppress you; and the more you have of it the greater will be the load. The learning of a Salmasius[11] or a Burman,[12]

unless you are its master, will be your tyrant. *Imperat aut servit;*[13] if you can wield it with a strong arm, it is a great weapon; otherwise,

Vis consili expers
Mole ruit sua.[14]

You will be overwhelmed, like Tarpeia,[15] by the heavy wealth which you have exacted from tributary generations.

Instances abound; there are authors who are as pointless as they are inexhaustible in their literary resources. They measure knowledge by bulk, as it lies in the rude block, without symmetry, without design. How many commentators are there on the Classics, how many on Holy Scripture, from whom we rise up, wondering at the learning which has passed before us, and wondering why it passed! How many writers are there of ecclesiastical history, such as Mos-heim or Du Pin,[16] who, breaking up their subject into details, destroy its life, and defraud us of the whole by their anxiety about the parts! The sermons, again, of the English divines in the seventeenth cen-tury, how often are they mere repertories of miscellaneous and officious learning! Of course Catholics also may read without thinking; and in their case, equally as with Protestants, it holds good, that that knowl-edge of theirs is unworthy of the name, knowledge which they have not thought through, and thought out. Such readers are only possessed by their knowledge, and not possessed of it; nay, in matter of fact they are often even carried away by it, without any volition of their own. Recol-lect, the memory can tyrannize as well as the imagination. Derangement, I believe, has been considered as a loss of control over the sequence of ideas. The mind, once set in motion, is henceforth deprived of the power of initiation, and becomes the victim

---

[11]Dutch classical scholar (1588–1653), professor at Leyden.

[12]Also a Dutch scholar (1668–1741), professor at Utrecht and Leyden.

[13]It either commands or serves (said of money, Horace, *Epistles,* I, x, 48).

[14]Force without discretion falls of its own weight (Horace, *Odes,* III, iv, 65).

[15]She betrayed the Roman citadel on the Capitoline Hill to the Sabines, in return for what they wore on their arms. What she wanted was their bracelets, but instead they cast their shields on her and crushed her to death.

[16]The former a German Protestant (1694–1755), the latter a Frenchman (1783–1865).

of a train of associations, one thought suggesting another, in the way of cause and effect, as if by a mechanical process, or some physical necessity. No one, who has had experience of men of studious habits, but must recognize the existence of a parallel phenomenon in the case of those who have over-stimulated the memory. In such persons reason acts almost as feebly and as impotently as in the madman; once fairly started on any subject whatever, they have no power of self-control; they passively endure the succession of impulses which are evolved out of the original exciting cause; they are passed on from one idea to another and go steadily forward, plodding along one line of thought in spite of the amplest concessions of the hearer, or wandering from it in endless digression in spite of his remonstrances. Now, if, as is very certain, no one would envy the madman the glow and originality of his conceptions, why must we extol the cultivation of that intellect, which is the prey, not indeed of barren fancies but of barren facts, of random intrusions from without, though not of morbid imaginations from within? And in thus speaking, I am not denying that a strong and ready memory is in itself a real treasure; I am not disparaging a well-stored mind, though it be nothing besides, provided it be sober, any more than I would despise a bookseller's shop: it is of great value to others, even when not so to the owner. Nor am I banishing, far from it, the possessors of deep and multifarious learning from my ideal university; they adorn it in the eyes of men; I do but say that they constitute no type of the results at which it aims; that it is no great gain to the intellect to have enlarged the memory at the expense of faculties which are indisputably higher.

Nor indeed am I supposing that there is any great danger, at least in this day, of over-education; the danger is on the other side. I will tell you, gentlemen, what has been the practical error of the last twenty years—not to load the memory of the student with a mass of undigested knowledge, but to attempt so much that nothing has been really effected, to teach so many things, that nothing has properly been learned at all. It has been the error of distracting and enfeebling the mind by an unmeaning profusion of subjects; of implying that a smattering in a dozen branches of study was not shallowness, which it really is, but enlargement; of considering an acquaintance with the learned names of things and persons, and the possession of clever duodecimos, and attendance on eloquent lecturers, and membership with scientific institutions, and the sight of the experiments of a platform and the specimens of a museum, that all this was not dissipation of mind, but progress. All things now are to be learned at once, not first one thing, then another, not one well but many badly. Learning is to be without exertion, without attention, without toil; without grounding, without advance, without finishing. There is to be nothing individual in it; and this, forsooth, is the wonder of the age. What the steam-engine does with matter, the printing-press is to do with mind; it is to act mechanically, and the population is to be passively, almost unconsciously enlightened, by the mere multiplication and dissemination of volumes. Whether it be the schoolboy, or the schoolgirl, or the youth at college, or the mechanic in the town, or the politician in the senate, all have been the victims in one way or other of this most preposterous and pernicious of delusions. Wise men have lifted up their voices in vain; and at length, lest their own institutions should be outshone and should disappear in the folly of the hour, they have been obliged, as far as was conscientiously possible, to humor a spirit which they could not withstand, and make temporizing concessions at which they could not but inwardly smile.

Now I must guard, gentlemen, against any possible misconception of my meaning. Let me frankly declare then, that I have no fear at all of the education of the people: the more education they have the better, so that it is really education. Next, as to the cheap publication of scientific and literary works, which is now in vogue, I consider it a great advantage, convenience, and gain; that is, to those to whom education has given a capacity for using them. Further,

I consider such innocent recreations as science and literature are able to furnish will be a very fit occupation of the thoughts and the leisure of young persons, and may be made the means of keeping them from bad employments and bad companions. Moreover, as to that superficial acquaintance with chemistry, and geology, and astronomy, and political economy, and modern history, and biography, and other branches of knowledge, which periodical literature and occasional lectures and scientific institutions diffuse through the community, I think it a graceful accomplishment, and a suitable, nay, in this day a necessary accomplishment, in the case of educated men. Nor, lastly, am I disparaging or discouraging the thorough acquisition of any one of these studies, or denying that, as far as it goes, such thorough acquisition is a real education of the mind. All I say is, call things by their right names, and do not confuse together ideas which are essentially different. A thorough knowledge of one science and a superficial acquaintance with many, are not the same thing; a smattering of a hundred things or a memory for detail, is not a philosophical or comprehensive view. Recreations are not education; accomplishments are not education. Do not say, the people must be educated, when, after all, you only mean amused, refreshed, soothed, put into good spirits and good humor, or kept from vicious excesses. I do not say that such amusements, such occupations of mind, are not a great gain; but they are not education. You may as well call drawing and fencing education, as a general knowledge of botany or conchology. Stuffing birds or playing stringed instruments is an elegant pastime, and a resource to the idle, but it is not education; it does not form or cultivate the intellect. Education is a high word; it is the preparation for knowledge, and it is the imparting of knowledge in proportion to that preparation. We require intellectual eyes to know withal, as bodily eyes for sight. We need both objects and organs intellectual; we cannot gain them without setting about it; we cannot gain them in our sleep or by haphazard. The best telescope does not dispense with eyes; the printing-press or the lecture room will assist us greatly, but we must be true to ourselves, we must be parties in the work. A university is, according to the usual designation, an *alma mater,* knowing her children one by one, not a foundry, or a mint, or a treadmill.

I protest to you, gentlemen, that if I had to choose between a so-called university which dispensed with residence and tutorial superintendence, and gave its degrees to any person who passed an examination in a wide range of subjects, and a university which had no professors or examinations at all, but merely brought a number of young men together for three or four years, and then sent them away as the University of Oxford is said to have done some sixty years since, if I were asked which of these two methods was the better discipline of the intellect—mind, I do not say which is *morally* the better, for it is plain that compulsory study must be a good and idleness an intolerable mischief—but if I must determine which of the two courses was the more successful in training, molding, enlarging the mind, which sent out men the more fitted for their secular duties, which produced better public men, men of the world, men whose names would descend to posterity, I have no hesitation in giving the preference to that university which did nothing, over that which exacted of its members an acquaintance with every science under the sun. And, paradox as this may seem, still if results be the test of systems, the influence of the public schools and colleges of England, in the course of the last century, at least will bear out one side of the contrast as I have drawn it. What would come, on the other hand, of the ideal systems of education which have fascinated the imagination of this age, could they ever take effect, and whether they would not produce a generation frivolous, narrow-minded, and resourceless, intellectually considered, is a fair subject for debate, but so far is certain, that the universities and scholastic establishments to which I refer, and which did little more than bring together first boys and then youths in large numbers, these institutions, with miserable deformities on the side of morals, with a hollow profession of Christianity, and a heathen code of ethics—I say, at least they can boast of a succession of heroes and statesmen, of literary men and philosophers, of men conspicuous for great natural virtues, for habits of business, for knowledge of life, for practical judgment, for cultivated tastes, for accomplishments, who have made England what it is—able to subdue the earth, able to domineer over Catholics.

How is this to be explained? I suppose as follows: When a multitude of young persons, keen, open-hearted, sympathetic, and observant, as young persons are, come together and freely mix with each other, they are sure to learn one from another, even if there be no one to teach them; the conversation of all is a series of lectures to each, and they gain for themselves new ideas and views, fresh matter of thought, and distinct principles for judging and acting, day by day. An infant has to learn the meaning of the information which its senses convey to it, and this seems to be its employment. It fancies all that the eye presents to it to be close to it, till it actually learns the contrary, and thus by practice does it ascertain the relations and uses of those first elements of knowledge which are necessary for its animal existence. A parallel teaching is necessary for our social being, and it is secured by a large school or a college, and this effect may be fairly called in its own department an enlargement of mind. It is seeing the world on a small field with little trouble; for the pupils or students come from very different places, and with widely different notions, and there is much to generalize, much to adjust, much to eliminate, there are inter-relations to be defined, and conventional rules to be established, in the process, by which the whole assemblage is molded together, and gains one tone and one character. Let it be clearly understood, I repeat it, that I am not taking into account moral or religious considerations; I am but saying that that youthful community will constitute a whole, it will embody a specific idea, it will represent a doctrine, it will administer a code of conduct, and it will furnish principles of thought and action. It will give birth to a living teaching, which in course of time will take the shape of a self-perpetuating tradition, or a *genius loci,*[17] as it is sometimes called, which haunts the home where it has been born, and which imbues and forms, more or less, and one by one, every individual who is successively brought under its shadow. Thus it is that, independent of direct instruction on the part of superiors, there is a sort of self-education in the academic institutions of protestant England; a characteristic tone of thought, a recognized standard of judgment is found in them, which, as developed in the individual who is submitted to it, becomes a twofold source of strength to him, both from the distinct stamp it impresses on his mind, and from the bond of union which it creates between him and others—effects which are shared by the authorities of the place, for they themselves have been educated in it, and at all times are exposed to the influence of its moral atmosphere. Here then is a real teaching, whatever be its standards and principles, true or false; and it at least tends towards cultivation of the intellect; it at least recognizes that knowledge is something more than a sort of passive reception of scraps and details; it is a something, and it does a something, which never will issue from the most strenuous efforts of a set of teachers, with no mutual sympathies and no intercommunion, of a set of examiners with no opinions which they dare profess, and with no common principles, who are teaching or questioning a set of youths who do not know them, and do not know each other, on a large number of subjects, different in kind, and connected by no wide philosophy, three times a week, or three times a year, or once in three years, in chill lecture-rooms or on a pompous anniversary.

Nay, self-education in any shape, in the most restricted sense, is preferable to a system of teaching which, professing so much, really does so little for the mind. Shut your college gates against the votary of knowledge, throw him back upon the searchings and the efforts of his own mind; he will gain by being spared an entrance into your Babel. Few indeed there are who

[17] Spirit of the place.

can dispense with the stimulus and support of instructors, or will do anything at all, if left to themselves. And fewer still (though such great minds are to be found) who will not, from such unassisted attempts, contract a self-reliance and a self-esteem, which are not only moral evils, but serious hindrances to the attainment of truth. And next to none, perhaps, or none, who will not be reminded from time to time of the disadvantage under which they lie, by their imperfect grounding, by the breaks, deficiencies, and irregularities of their knowledge, by the eccentricity of opinion and the confusion of principle which they exhibit. They will be too often ignorant of what every one knows and takes for granted, of that multitude of small truths which fall upon the mind like dust, impalpable and ever accumulating; they may be unable to converse, they may argue perversely, they may pride themselves on their worst paradoxes or their grossest truisms, they may be full of their own mode of viewing things, unwilling to be put out of their way, slow to enter into the minds of others;—but, with these and whatever other liabilities upon their heads, they are likely to have more thought, more mind, more philosophy, more true enlargement, than those earnest but ill-used persons who are forced to load their minds with a score of subjects against an examination, who have too much on their hands to indulge themselves in thinking or investigation, who devour premise and conclusion together with indiscriminate greediness, who hold whole sciences on faith, and commit demonstrations to memory, and who too often, as might be expected, when their period of education is passed, throw up all they have learned in disgust, having gained nothing really by their anxious labors, except perhaps the habit of application.

Yet such is the better specimen of the fruit of that ambitious system which has of late years been making way among us: for its result on ordinary minds, and on the common run of students, is less satisfactory still; they leave their place of education simply dissipated and relaxed by the multiplicity of subjects, which they have never really mastered, and so shallow as not even to know their shallowness. How much better, I say, is it for the active and thoughtful intellect, where such is to be found, to eschew the college and the university altogether, than to submit to a drudgery so ignoble, a mockery so contumelious! How much more profitable for the independent mind, after the mere rudiments of education, to range through a library at random, taking down books as they meet him, and pursuing the trains of thought which his mother wit suggests! How much healthier to wander into the fields, and there with the exiled prince to find "tongues in the trees, books in the running brooks!"[18] How much more genuine an education is that of the poor boy in the poem[19]—a poem, whether in conception or in execution, one of the most touching in our language—who, not in the wide world, but ranging day by day around his widowed mother's home, "a dexterous gleaner" in a narrow field, and with only such slender outfit

> . "as the village school and books a few
> Supplied,"

contrived from the beach, and the quay, and the fisher's boat, and the inn's fireside, and the tradesman's shop, and the shepherd's walk, and the smuggler's hut, and the mossy moor, and the screaming gulls, and the restless waves, to fashion for himself a philosophy and a poetry of his own!

But in a large subject I am exceeding my necessary limits. Gentlemen, I must conclude abruptly; and postpone any summing up of my argument, should that be necessary, to another day.

DISCOURSE VII

Liberal Knowledge Viewed in Relation to Professional

I HAVE been insisting, in my two preceding Discourses, first, on the cultivation of the intellect, as an end which may reasonably

---

[18] See *As You Like It*, II, i, 16.

[19] Crabbe's *Tales of the Hall* [Book IV]. This Poem, let me say, I read on its first publication, above thirty years ago, with extreme delight, and have never lost my love of it; and on taking it up lately found I was even more touched by it than heretofore. A work which can please in youth and age seems to fulfill (in logical language) the *accidental definition* of a Classic (Newman's note).

be pursued for its own sake; and next, on the nature of that cultivation, or what that cultivation consists in. Truth of whatever kind is the proper object of the intellect; its cultivation then lies in fitting it to apprehend 5 and contemplate truth. Now the intellect in its present state, with exceptions which need not here be specified, does not discern truth intuitively, or as a whole. We know, not by a direct and simple vision, not at a 10 glance, but, as it were, by piecemeal and accumulation, by a mental process, by going round an object, by the comparison, the combination, the mutual correction, the continual adaptation, of many partial notions, 15 by the joint application and concentration upon it of many faculties and exercises of mind. Such a union and concert of the intellectual powers, such an enlargement and development, such a comprehensiveness, is 20 necessarily a matter of training. And again, such a training is a matter of rule; it is not mere application, however exemplary, which introduces the mind to truth, nor the reading many books, nor the getting up 25 many subjects, nor the witnessing many experiments, nor the attending many lectures. All this is short of enough; a man may have done it all, yet be lingering in the vestibule of knowledge: he may not realize what his 30 mouth utters; he may not see with his mental eye what confronts him; he may have no grasp of things as they are; or at least he may have no power at all of advancing one step forward of himself, in consequence 35 of what he has already acquired, no power of discriminating between truth and falsehood, of sifting out the grains of truth from the mass, of arranging things according to their real value, and, if I may use 40 the phrase, of building up ideas. Such a power is the result of a scientific formation of mind; it is an acquired faculty of judgment, of clear-sightedness, of sagacity, of wisdom, of philosophical reach of mind, and 45 of intellectual self-possession and repose— qualities which do not come of mere acquirement. The bodily eye, the organ for apprehending material objects, is provided by nature; the eye of the mind, of which the 50 object is truth, is the work of discipline and habit.

This process of training, by which the intellect, instead of being formed or sacrificed to some particular or accidental purpose, some specific trade or profession, or 5 study or science, is disciplined for its own sake, for the perception of its own proper object, and for its own highest culture, is called liberal education; and though there is no one in whom it is carried as far as is 10 conceivable, or whose intellect would be a pattern of what intellects should be made, yet there is scarcely any one but may gain an idea of what real training is, and at least look towards it, and make its true scope 15 and result, not something else, his standard of excellence; and numbers there are who may submit themselves to it, and secure it to themselves in good measure. And to set forth the right standard, and to train according to it, and to help forward all students towards it according to their various capacities, this I conceive to be the business of a university.

Now this is what some great men are very slow to allow; they insist that education should be confined to some particular and narrow end, and should issue in some definite work, which can be weighed and measured. They argue as if everything, as well 30 as every person, had its price; and that where there has been a great outlay, they have a right to expect a return in kind. This they call making education and instruction "useful," and "utility" becomes their watchword. 35 With a fundamental principle of this nature, they very naturally go on to ask, what there is to show for the expense of a university; what is the real worth in the market of the article called "a liberal education," 40 on the supposition that it does not teach us definitely how to advance our manufactures, or to improve our lands, or to better our civil economy; or again, if it does not at once make this man a lawyer, 45 that an engineer, and that a surgeon; or at least if it does not lead to discoveries in chemistry, astronomy, geology, magnetism, and science of every kind.

This question, as might have been expected, has been keenly debated in the present age, and formed one main subject of the controversy, to which I referred in the

Introduction to the present Discourses, as having been sustained in the first decade of this century by a celebrated Northern Review[1] on the one hand, and defenders of the University of Oxford on the other. Hardly had the authorities of that ancient seat of learning, waking from their long neglect, set on foot a plan for the education of the youth committed to them, than the representatives of science and literature in the city, which has sometimes been called the Northern Athens,[2] remonstrated with their gravest arguments and their most brilliant satire, against the direction and shape which the reform was taking. Nothing would content them, but that the University should be set to rights on the basis of the philosophy of utility; a philosophy, as they seem to have thought, which needed but to be proclaimed in order to be embraced. In truth, they were little aware of the depth and force of the principles on which the authorities academical were proceeding, and, this being so, it was not to be expected that they would be allowed to walk at leisure over the field of controversy which they had selected. Accordingly they were encountered in behalf of the university by two men of great name in influence in their day, of very different minds, but united, as by collegiate ties, so in the clear-sighted and large view which they took of the whole subject of liberal education; and the defense thus provided for the Oxford studies has kept its ground to this day.

Let me be allowed to devote a few words to the memory of distinguished persons, under the shadow of whose name I once lived, and by whose doctrine I am now profiting. In the heart of Oxford there is a small plot of ground, hemmed in by public thoroughfares, which has been the possession and the home of one society for above five hundred years. In the old time of Boniface the Eighth and John the Twenty-second, in the age of Scotus and Occam and Dante,[3] before Wiclif or Huss had kindled those miserable fires which are still raging to the ruin of the highest interests of man, an unfortunate king of England, Edward the Second,[4] flying from the field of Bannockburn, is said to have made a vow to the Blessed Virgin to found a religious house in her honor, if he got back in safety. Prompted and aided by his almoner, he decided on placing this house in the city of Alfred; and the Image of our Lady, which is opposite its entrance-gate, is the token of the vow and its fulfillment to this day. King and almoner have long been in the dust, and strangers have entered into their inheritance, and their creed has been forgotten, and their holy rites disowned; but day by day a memento is still made in the holy Sacrifice by at least one Catholic priest, once a member of that college, for the souls of those Catholic benefactors who fed him there for so many years.[5] The visitor, whose curiosity has been excited by its present fame, gazes perhaps with something of disappointment on a collection of buildings which have with them so few of the circumstances of dignity or wealth. Broad quadrangles, high halls and chambers, ornamented cloisters, stately walks, or umbrageous gardens, a throng of students, ample revenues, or a glorious history, none of these things were the portion of that old Catholic foundation; nothing in short which to the common eye sixty years ago would have given tokens of what it was to be. But it had at that time a spirit working within it, which enabled its inmates to do, amid its seeming insignificance, what no other body in the place could equal; not a very abstruse gift of extraordinary boast, but a rare one, the honest purpose to administer the trust committed to them in such a way as their conscience pointed out as best. So, whereas the Colleges of Oxford are self-electing bodies, the fellows in each perpetually filling up for themselves the vacancies which occur in their number, the members of this foundation determined, at a time when, either from evil custom or

---

[1] The *Edinburgh Review*.   [2] Edinburgh.

[3] I. e., towards the close of the Middle Age, in the opening years of the fourteenth century. Boniface and John were popes, Scotus and Occam scholastic philosophers. Wiclif and Huss contributed to bring about the Protestant Reformation.

[4] Born in 1284, reigned from 1307, murdered in 1327. The Battle of Bannockburn was fought in 1314. Edward founded Oriel College.

[5] Newman's allusion is, of course, to himself.

from ancient statute, such a thing was not known elsewhere, to throw open their fellowships to the competition of all comers, and, in the choice of associates henceforth, to cast to the winds every personal motive and feeling, family connection, and friendship, and patronage, and political interest, and local claim, and prejudice, and party jealousy, and to elect solely on public and patriotic grounds. Nay, with a remarkable independence of mind, they resolved that even the table of honors, awarded to literary merit by the University in its new system of examination for degrees, should not fetter their judgment as electors; but that at all risks, and whatever criticism it might cause, and whatever odium they might incur, they would select the men, whoever they were, to be children of their founder, whom they thought in their consciences to be most likely from their intellectual and moral qualities to please him, if (as they expressed it) he were still upon earth, most likely to do honor to his College, most likely to promote the objects which they believed he had at heart. Such persons did not promise to be the disciples of a low utilitarianism; and consequently, as their collegiate reform synchronized with that reform of the academical body, in which they bore a principal part, it was not unnatural that, when the storm broke upon the University from the North, their *alma mater,* whom they loved, should have found her first defenders within the walls of that small College, which had first put itself into a condition to be her champion.

These defenders, gentlemen, I have said, were two, of whom the more distinguished was the late Dr. Copleston, then a Fellow of the College, successively its Provost, and Protestant Bishop of Llandaff. In that society, which owes so much to him, his name lives, and ever will live, for the distinction which his talents bestowed on it, for the academical importance to which he raised it, for the generosity of spirit, the liberality of sentiment, and the kindness of heart, with which he adorned it, and which even those who had least sympathy with some aspects of his mind and character could not but admire and love. Men come to

their meridian at various periods of their lives; the last years of the eminent person I am speaking of were given to duties which, I am told, have been the means of endearing him to numbers, but which afforded no scope for that peculiar vigor and keenness of mind which enabled him, when a young man, single-handed, with easy gallantry, to encounter and overthrow the charge of three giants of the North combined against him.[6] I believe I am right in saying that, in the progress of the controversy, the most scientific, the most critical, and the most witty, of that literary company, all of them now, as he himself, removed from this visible scene, Professor Playfair, Lord Jeffrey, and the Rev. Sydney Smith, threw together their several efforts into one article of their review, in order to crush and pound to dust the audacious controvertist who had come out against them in defense of his own institutions. To have even contended with such men was a sufficient voucher for his ability, even before we open his pamphlets, and have actual evidence of the good sense, the spirit, the scholar-like taste, and the purity of style, by which they are distinguished.

He was supported in the controversy, on the same general principles, but with more of method and distinctness, and, I will add, with greater force and beauty and perfection, both of thought and of language, by the other distinguished writer, to whom I have already referred, Mr. Davison; who, though not so well known to the world in his day, has left more behind him than the Provost of Oriel, to make his name remembered by posterity. This thoughtful man, who was the admired and intimate friend of a very remarkable person, whom, whether he wish it or not, numbers revere and love as the first author of the subsequent movement in the Protestant Church towards Catholicism,[7] this grave and philosophical writer, whose works I can never look into without sighing that such a man was lost to the Catholic Church, as

---

[6] Newman alludes to Copleston's activity in church restoration in Wales.

[7] Mr. Keble, Vicar of Hursley, late Fellow of Oriel, and Professor of Poetry in the University of Oxford (Newman's note).

Dr. Butler[8] before him, by some early bias or some fault of self-education—he, in a review of work by Mr. Edgeworth on Professional Education, which attracted a good deal of attention in its day, goes leisurely over the same ground, which had already been rapidly traversed by Dr. Copleston, and, though professedly employed upon Mr. Edgeworth, is really replying to the northern critic who had brought that writer's work into notice, and to a far greater author than either of them, who in a past age had argued on the same side.[9]

The author to whom I allude is no other than Locke.[10] That celebrated philosopher has preceded the Edinburgh Reviewers in condemning the ordinary subjects in which boys are instructed at school, on the ground that they are not needed by them in after life; and before quoting what his disciples have said in the present century, I will refer to a few passages of the master. " 'Tis matter of astonishment," he says in his work on education, "that men of quality and parts should suffer themselves to be so far misled by custom and implicit faith. Reason, if consulted with, would advise, that their children's time should be spent in acquiring what might be useful to them, when they come to be men, rather than that their heads should be stuffed with a deal of trash, a great part whereof they usually never do ('tis certain they never need to) think on again as long as they live; and so much of it as does stick by them they are only the worse for."

And so again, speaking of verse-making, he says: "I know not what reason a father can have to wish his son a poet, who does not desire him to bid defiance to all other callings and business; which is not yet the worst of the case; for, if he proves a successful rimer, and gets once the reputation of a wit, I desire it to be considered, what company and places he is likely to spend his time in, nay, and estate too; for it is very seldom seen that any one discovers mines of gold or silver in Parnassus. 'Tis a pleasant air but a barren soil."

In another passage he distinctly limits utility in education to its bearing on the future profession or trade of the pupil, that is, he scorns the idea of any education of the intellect, simply as such. "Can there be anything more ridiculous," he asks, "than that a father should waste his own money, and his son's time, in setting him to learn the Roman language, when at the same time he designs him for a trade, wherein he, having no use of Latin, fails not to forget that little which he brought from school, and which 'tis ten to one he abhors for the ill-usage it procured him? Could it be believed, unless we have everywhere amongst us examples of it, that a child should be forced to learn the rudiments of language, which he is never to use in the course of life that he is designed to, and neglect all the while the writing a good hand, and casting accounts, which are of great advantage in all conditions of life, and to most trades indispensably necessary?"[11] Nothing of course can be more absurd than to neglect in education those matters which are necessary for a boy's future calling; but the tone of Locke's remarks evidently implies more than this, and is condemnatory of any teaching which tends to the general cultivation of the mind.

Now to turn to his modern disciples. The study of the classics has been made the basis of the Oxford education, in the reforms which I have spoken of, and the Edinburgh Reviewers protested, after the manner of Locke, that no good could come of a system which was not based upon the principle of utility.

---

[8]Bishop Joseph Butler (1692–1752), author of the *Analogy of Religion.*

[9]Edgeworth's *Essays on Professional Education* were reviewed in the *Edinburgh* in October, 1809 (Vol. XV, p. 40), and the review was made the occasion for an attack on Oxford for its neglect of "useful knowledge." In 1810 Copleston answered the *Edinburgh* in a pamphlet entitled *A Reply to the Calumnies of the Edinburgh Review against Oxford.* Copleston also published a *Second Reply* and a *Third Reply* in this and the following year. Meanwhile in April, 1810, the *Edinburgh* (XVI, 158) published a reply to Copleston, which Newman believed to have been written by Playfair, Jeffrey, and Sydney Smith. Davison's paper on Edgeworth's *Essays* was published in the *Quarterly Review* for October, 1811 (VI, 166).

[10]John Locke (1632–1704), author of the *Essay Concerning the Human Understanding.*

[11]These quotations are from Locke's tract *Of Education,* Sections 94, 174, and 164.

"Classical literature," they said, "is the great object at Oxford. Many minds, so employed, have produced many works and much fame in that department; but if all liberal arts and sciences, useful to human life, had been taught there, if some had dedicated themselves to chemistry, some to mathematics, some to experimental philosophy, and if every attainment had been honored in the mixed ratio of its difficulty and utility, the system of such a university would have been much more valuable, but the splendor of its name something less."

Utility may be made the end of education, in two respects: either as regards the individual educated, or the community at large. In which light do these writers regard it? in the latter. So far they differ from Locke, for they consider the advancement of science as the supreme and real end of a university. This is brought into view in the sentences which follow.

"When a university has been doing useless things for a long time, it appears at first degrading to them to be useful. A set of lectures on political economy would be discouraged in Oxford, probably despised, probably not permitted. To discuss the inclosure of commons, and to dwell upon imports and exports, to come so near to common life, would seem to be undignified and contemptible. In the same manner, the Parr or the Bentley[12] of the day would be scandalized, in a university, to be put on a level with the discoverer of a neutral salt; and yet, what other measure is there of dignity in intellectual labor but usefulness? And what ought the term university to mean, but a place where every science is taught which is liberal, and at the same time useful to mankind? Nothing would so much tend to bring classical literature within proper bounds as a steady and invariable appeal to utility in our appreciation of all human knowledge. . . . Looking always to real utility as our guide, we should see, with equal pleasure, a studious and inquisitive mind arranging the productions of nature, investigating the qualities of bodies, or mastering the difficulties of the learned languages. We should not care whether he

[12]Classical scholars.

was chemist, naturalist, or scholar, because we know it to be as necessary that matter should be studied and subdued to the use of man, as that taste should be gratified, and imagination inflamed."

Such then is the enunciation, as far as words go, of the theory of utility in education; and both on its own account, and for the sake of the able men who have advocated it, it has a claim on the attention of those whose principles I am here representing. Certainly it is specious to contend that nothing is worth pursuing but what is useful; and that life is not long enough to expend upon interesting, or curious, or brilliant trifles. Nay, in one sense, I will grant it is more than specious, it is true; but, if so, how do I propose directly to meet the objection? Why, gentlemen, I have really met it already, *viz.*, in laying down that intellectual culture is its own end; for what has its end in itself, has its use in itself also. I say, if a liberal education consists in the culture of the intellect, and if that culture be in itself a good, here, without going further, is an answer to Locke's question; for if a healthy body is a good in itself, why is not a healthy intellect? and if a college of physicians is a useful institution, because it contemplates bodily health, why is not an academical body, though it were simply and solely engaged in imparting vigor and beauty and grasp to the intellectual portion of our nature? And the Reviewers I am quoting seem to allow this in their better moments, in a passage which, putting aside the question of its justice in fact, is sound and true in the principles to which it appeals:—

The present state of classical education [they say] cultivates the imagination a great deal too much, and other habits of mind a great deal too little, and trains up many young men in a style of elegant imbecility, utterly unworthy of the talents with which nature has endowed them. . . . The matter of fact is, that a classical scholar of twenty-three or twenty-four is a man principally conversant with works of imagination. His feelings are quick, his fancy lively, and his taste good. Talents for speculation and original inquiry he has none, nor has he formed the invaluable habit of pushing things up to their first principles, or of collecting dry and unamusing facts as the materials for reasoning. All the solid and masculine parts of his understanding are left wholly without cultivation; he hates the pain of thinking, and suspects every man whose boldness and originality call upon him to defend his opinions and prove his assertions.

Now, I am not at present concerned with the specific question of classical education; else I might reasonably question the justice of calling an intellectual discipline, which embraces the study of Aristotle, Thucydides, and Tacitus, which involves scholarship and antiquities, imaginative; still so far I readily grant, that the cultivation of the "understanding," of a "talent for speculation and original inquiry," and of "the habit of pushing things up to their first principles," is a principal portion of a good or liberal education. If then the Reviewers consider such cultivation the characteristic of a useful education, as they seem to do in the foregoing passage, it follows that what they mean by "useful" is just what I mean by "good" or "liberal": and Locke's question becomes a verbal one. Whether youths are to be taught Latin or verse-making will depend on the fact, whether these studies tend to mental culture; but, however this is determined, so far is clear, that in that mental culture consists what I have called a liberal or non-professional, and what the Reviewers call a useful education.

This is the obvious answer which may be made to those who urge upon us the claims of utility in our plans of education; but I am not going to leave the subject here: I mean to take a wider view of it. Let us take "useful," as Locke takes it, in its proper and popular sense, and then we enter upon a large field of thought, to which I cannot do justice in one Discourse, though to-day's is all the space that I can give to it. I say, let us take "useful" to mean, not what is simply good, but what tends to good, or is the instrument of good; and in this sense also, gentlemen, I will show you how a liberal education is truly and fully a useful, though it be not a professional education. "Good" indeed means one thing, and "useful" means another; but I lay it down as a principle, which will save us a great deal

of anxiety, that, though the useful is not always good, the good is always useful. Good is not only good, but reproductive of good; this is one of its attributes; nothing is excellent, beautiful, perfect, desirable for its own sake, but it overflows, and spreads the likeness of itself all around itself. Good is prolific; it is not only good to the eye, but to the taste; it not only attracts us, but it communicates itself; it excites first our admiration and love, then our desire and our gratitude, and that, in proportion to its intenseness and fullness in particular instances. A great good will impart great good. If then the intellect is so excellent a portion of us, and its cultivation so excellent, it is not only beautiful, perfect, admirable, and noble in itself, but in a true and high sense it must be useful to the possessor and to all around him; not useful in any low, mechanical, mercantile sense, but as diffusing good, or as a blessing, or a gift, or power, or a treasure, first to the owner, then through him to the world. I say then, if a liberal education be good, it must necessarily be useful too.

You will see what I mean by the parallel of bodily health. Health is a good in itself, though nothing came of it, and is especially worth seeking and cherishing; yet, after all, the blessings which attend its presence are so great, while they are so close to it and so redound back upon it and encircle it, that we never think of it except as useful as well as good, and praise and prize it for what it does, as well as for what it is, though at the same time we cannot point out any definite and distinct work or production which it can be said to effect. And so as regards intellectual culture, I am far from denying utility in this large sense as the end of education, when I lay it down, that the culture of the intellect is a good in itself and its own end; I do not exclude from the idea of intellectual culture what it cannot but be, from the very nature of things; I only deny that we must be able to point out, before we have any right to call it useful, some art, or business, or profession, or trade, or work as resulting from it, and as its real and complete end. The parallel is exact:—As the body may be sacrificed to some manual or other toil, whether moderate or oppressive, so may the intellect be devoted to some specific profession; and I do not call *this* the culture of the intellect. Again, as some member or organ of the body may be inordinately used and developed, so may memory, or imagination, or the reasoning faculty; and *this* again is not intellectual culture. On the other hand, as the body may be tended, cherished, and exercised with a simple view to its general health, so may the intellect also be generally exercised in order to its perfect state; and this *is* its cultivation.

Again, as health ought to precede labor of the body, and as a man in health can do what an unhealthy man cannot do, and as of this health the properties are strength, energy, agility, graceful carriage and action, manual dexterity, and endurance of fatigue, so in like manner general culture of mind is the best aid to professional and scientific study, and educated men can do what illiterate cannot; and the man who has learned to think and to reason and to compare and to discriminate and to analyze, who has refined his taste, and formed his judgment, and sharpened his mental vision, will not indeed at once be a lawyer, or a pleader, or an orator, or a statesman, or a physician, or a good landlord, or a man of business, or a soldier, or an engineer, or a chemist, or a geologist, or an antiquarian, but he will be placed in that state of intellect in which he can take up any one of the sciences or callings I have referred to, or any other for which he has a taste or special talent, with an ease, a grace, a versatility, and a success, to which another is a stranger. In this sense then, and as yet I have said but a very few words on a large subject, mental culture is emphatically useful.

If then I am arguing, and shall argue, against professional or scientific knowledge as the sufficient end of a university education, let me not be supposed, gentlemen, to be disrespectful towards particular studies, or arts, or vocations, and those who are engaged in them. In saying that law or medicine is not the end of a university course, I do not mean to imply that the university does not teach law or medicine.

What indeed can it teach at all, if it does not teach something particular? It teaches *all* knowledge by teaching all branches of knowledge, and in no other way. I do but say that there will be this distinction as regards a professor of law, or of medicine, or of geology, or of political economy, in a university and out of it, that out of a university he is in danger of being absorbed and narrowed by his pursuit and of giving lectures which are the lectures of nothing more than a lawyer, physician, geologist, or political economist; whereas in a university he will just know where he and his science stand, he has come to it, as it were, from a height, he has taken a survey of all knowledge, he is kept from extravagance by the very rivalry of other studies, he has gained from them a special illumination and largeness of mind and freedom and self-possession, and he treats his own in consequence with a philosophy and a resource, which belongs not to the study itself, but to his liberal education.

This then is how I should solve the fallacy, for so I must call it, by which Locke and his disciples would frighten us from cultivating the intellect, under the notion that no education is useful which does not teach us some temporal calling, or some mechanical art, or some physical secret. I say that a cultivated intellect, because it is a good in itself, brings with it a power and a grace to every work and occupation which it undertakes, and enables us to be more useful, and to a greater number. There is a duty we owe to human society as such, to the state to which we belong, to the sphere in which we move, to the individuals towards whom we are variously related, and whom we successively encounter in life; and that philosophical or liberal education, as I have called it, which is the proper function of a university, if it refuses the foremost place to professional interests, does but postpone them to the formation of the citizen, and while it subserves the larger interests of philanthropy, prepares also for the successful prosecution of those merely personal objects which at first sight it seems to disparage.

And now, gentlemen, I wish to be allowed

to enforce in detail what I have been saying by some extracts from the writings to which I have already alluded, and to which I am so greatly indebted:

It is an undisputed maxim in political economy [says Dr. Copleston] that the separation of professions and the division of labor tend to the perfection of every· art, to the wealth of nations, to the general comfort and well-being of the community. This principle of division is in some instances pursued so far as to excite the wonder of people to whose notice it is for the first time pointed out. There is no saying to what extent it may not be carried; and the more the powers of each individual are concentrated in one employment, the greater skill and quickness will he naturally display in performing it. But, while he thus contributes more effectually to the accumulation of national wealth, he becomes himself more and more degraded as a rational being. In proportion as his sphere of action is narrowed his mental powers and habits become contracted; and he resembles a subordinate part of some powerful machinery, useful in its place, but insignificant and worthless out of it. If it be necessary, as it is beyond all question necessary, that society should be split into divisions and subdivisions, in order that its several duties may be well performed, yet we must be careful not to yield up ourselves wholly and exclusively to the guidance of this system; we must observe what its evils are, and we should modify and restrain it, by bringing into action other principles, which may serve as a check and counterpoise to the main force.

There can be no doubt that every art is improved by confining the professor of it to that single study. But, although the art itself is advanced by this concentration of mind in its service, the individual who is confined to it goes back. The advantage of the community is nearly in an inverse ratio with his own.

Society itself requires some other contribution from each individual, besides the particular duties of his profession. And, if no such liberal intercourse be established, it is the common failing of human nature, to be engrossed with petty views and interests, to underrate the importance of all in which we are not concerned, and to carry our partial notions into cases where they are inapplicable, to act, in short, as so many unconnected units, displacing and repelling one another.

In the cultivation of literature is found that common link, which, among the higher and middling departments of life, unites the jarring sects and subdivisions into one interest, which supplies common topics, and kindles common feelings, unmixed with those narrow prejudices with which all professions are more or less infected. The knowledge, too, which is thus acquired, expands and enlarges the mind, excites its faculties, and calls those limbs and muscles into freer exercise which, by too constant use in one direction, not only acquire an illiberal air, but are apt also to lose somewhat of their native play and energy. And thus, without directly qualifying a man for any of the employments of life, it enriches and ennobles all. Without teaching him the peculiar business of any one office or calling, it enables him to act his part in each of them with better grace and more elevated carriage; and, if happily planned and conducted, is a main ingredient in that complete and generous education which fits a man "to perform justly, skillfully, and magnanimously, all the offices, both private and public, of peace and war."[13]

The view of liberal education, advocated in these extracts, is expanded by Mr. Davison in the essay to which I have already referred. He lays more stress on the "usefulness" of 5 liberal education in the larger sense of the word than his predecessor in the controversy. Instead of arguing that the utility of knowledge to the individual varies inversely with its utility to the public, he 10 chiefly employs himself on the suggestions contained in Dr. Copleston's last sentences. He shows, first, that a liberal education is something far higher, even in the scale of utility, than what is commonly called a use- 15 ful education, and next, that it is necessary or useful for the purposes even of that professional education which commonly engrosses the title of useful. The former of these two theses he recommends to us in an 20 argument from which the following passages are selected:

It is to take a very contracted view of life [he says] to think with great anxiety how persons may be educated to superior skill in their department, comparatively neglecting or excluding the more liberal and enlarged cultivation. In his (Mr. Edgeworth's) system, the value of every attainment is to be measured by its subserviency to a calling. The spe-

[13]*Vid.* Milton on Education (Newman's note).

cific duties of that calling are exalted at the cost of those free and independent tastes and virtues which come in to sustain the common relations of society, and raise the individual in them. In short, a man is to be usurped by his profession. He is to be clothed in its garb from head to foot. His virtues, his science, and his ideas are all to be put into a gown or uniform, and the whole man to be shaped, pressed, and stiffened, in the exact mold of his technical character. Any interloping accomplishments or a faculty which cannot be taken into public pay, if they are to be indulged in him at all, must creep along under the cloak of his more serviceable privileged merits. Such is the state of perfection to which the spirit and general tendency of this system would lead us.

But the professional character is not the only one which a person engaged in a profession has to support. He is not always upon duty. There are services he owes, which are neither parochial, nor forensic, nor military, nor to be described by any such epithet of civil regulation, and yet are in nowise inferior to those that bear these authoritative titles; inferior neither in their intrinsic value, nor their moral import, nor their impression upon society. As a friend, as a companion, as a citizen at large; in the connections of domestic life; in the improvement and embellishment of his leisure, he has a sphere of action, revolving, if you please, within the sphere of his profession, but not clashing with it; in which if he can show none of the advantages of an improved understanding, whatever may be his skill or proficiency in the other, he is no more than an ill-educated man.

There is a certain faculty in which all nations of any refinement are great practitioners. It is not taught at school or college as a distinct science; though it deserves that what is taught there should be made to have some reference to it; nor is it endowed at all by the public; everybody being obliged to exercise it for himself in person, which he does to the best of his skill. But in nothing is there a greater difference than in the manner of doing it. The advocates of professional learning will smile when we tell them that this same faculty which we would have encouraged, is simply that of speaking good sense in English, without fee or reward in common conversation. They will smile when we lay some stress upon it; but in reality it is no such trifle as they imagine. Look into the huts of savages, and see, for there is nothing to listen to, the dismal blank

of their stupid hours of silence; their professional avocations of war and hunting are over; and, having nothing to do, they have nothing to say. Turn to improved life, and you find conversation in all its forms the medium of something more than an idle pleasure; indeed, a very active agent in circulating and forming the opinions, tastes, and feelings of a whole people. It makes of itself a considerable affair. Its topics are the most promiscuous—all those which do not belong to any particular province. As for its power and influence, we may fairly say that it is of just the same consequence to a man's immediate society, how he talks, as how he acts. Now of all those who furnish their share to rational conversation, a mere adept in his own art is universally admitted to be the worst. The sterility and uninstructiveness of such a person's social hours are quite proverbial. Or if he escape being dull, it is only by launching into ill-timed, learned loquacity. We do not desire of him lectures or speeches; and he has nothing else to give. Among benches he may be powerful, but seated on a chair he is quite another person. On the other hand, we may affirm, that one of the best companions is a man who, to the accuracy and research of a profession, has joined a free excursive acquaintance with various learning, and caught from it the spirit of general observation.

Having thus shown that a liberal education is a real benefit to the subjects of it, as members of society, in the various duties and circumstances and accidents of life, he 5 goes on, in the next place, to show that, over and above those direct services which might fairly be expected of it, it actually subserves the discharge of those particular functions, and the pursuit of those particular advantages, which are connected with professional 10 exertion, and to which professional education is directed:

We admit [he observes] that when a person makes a business of one pursuit, he is in the right way to eminence in it; and that divided attention will rarely give excellence in many. But our assent will go no further. For, to think that the way to prepare a person for excelling in any one pursuit (and that is the only point in hand), is to fetter his early studies, and cramp the first development of his mind, by a reference to the exigencies of that pursuit barely, is a very different notion, and one which, we apprehend, deserves to be exploded rather than received. Possibly a few of the abstract insulated kinds of learning might be approached in that way. The exceptions to be made are very few, and need not be recited. But for the acquisition of professional and practical ability such maxims are death to it. The main ingredients of that ability are requisite knowledge and cultivated faculties; but, of the two, the latter is by far the chief. A man of well-improved faculties has the command of another's knowledge. A man without them, has not the command of his own.

Of the intellectual powers, the judgment is that which takes the foremost lead in life. How to form it to the two habits it ought to possess, of exactness and vigor, is the problem. It would be ignorant presumption so much as to hint at any routine of method by which these qualities may with certainty be imparted to every or any understanding. Still, however, we may safely lay it down that they are not to be got "by a gatherer of simples," but are the combined essence and extracts of many different things, drawn from much varied reading and discipline, first, and observation afterwards. For if there be a single intelligible point on this head, it is that a man who has been trained to think upon one subject or for one subject only, will never be a good judge even in that one; whereas the enlargement of his circle gives him increased knowledge and power in a rapidly increasing ratio. So much do ideas act, not as solitary units, but by grouping and combination; and so clearly do all the things that fall within the proper province of the same faculty of the mind, intertwine with and support each other. Judgment lives as it were by comparison and discrimination. Can it be doubted, then, whether the range and extent of that assemblage of things upon which it is practiced in its first essays are of use to its power?

To open our way a little further on this matter, we will define what we mean by the power of judgment; and then try to ascertain among what kind of studies the improvement of it may be expected at all.

Judgment does not stand here for a certain homely, useful quality of intellect, that guards a person from committing mistakes to the injury of his fortunes or common reputation; but for that master-principle of business, literature, and talent, which gives him strength in any subject he chooses to grapple with, and enables him to seize the strong point in it. Whether this definition be metaphysically correct or not, it comes home to the substance of our inquiry.

It describes the power that every one desires to possess when he comes to act in a profession, or elsewhere; and corresponds with our best idea of a cultivated mind.

Next, it will not be denied, that in order to do any good to the judgment, the mind must be employed upon such subjects as come within the cognizance of that faculty, and give some real exercise to its perceptions. Here we have a rule of selection by which the different parts of learning may be classed for our purpose. Those which belong to the province of the judgment are religion (in its evidences and interpretation), ethics, history, eloquence, poetry, theories of general speculation, the fine arts, and works of wit. Great as the variety of these large divisions of learning may appear, they are all held in union by two capital principles of connection. First, they are all quarried out of one and the same great subject of man's moral, social, and feeling nature. And secondly, they are all under the control (more or less strict) of the same power of moral reason.

If these studies [he continues] be such as give a direct play and exercise to the faculty of the judgment, then they are the true basis of education for the active and inventive powers, whether destined for a profession or any other use. Miscellaneous as the assemblage may appear, of history, eloquence, poetry, ethics, *etc.*, blended together, they will all conspire in an union of effect. They are necessary mutually to explain and interpret each other. The knowledge derived from them all will amalgamate, and the habits of a mind versed and practiced in them by turns will join to produce a richer vein of thought and of more general and practical application than could be obtained of any single one, as the fusion of the metals into Corinthian brass gave the artist his most ductile and perfect material. Might we venture to imitate an author (whom indeed it is much safer to take as an authority than to attempt to copy), Lord Bacon, in some of his concise illustrations of the comparative utility of the different studies,[14] we should say that history would give fullness, moral philosophy strength, and poetry elevation to the understanding. Such in reality is the natural force and tendency of the studies; but there are few minds susceptible enough to derive from them any sort of virtue adequate to those high expressions. We must be contented therefore to lower our panegyric to this, that a person cannot avoid receiving some infusion and tincture, at least, of those several qualities, from

---

[14] See Bacon's essay, *Of Studies.*

that course of diversified reading. One thing is unquestionable, that the elements of general reason are not to be found fully and truly expressed in any one kind of study; and that he who would wish to know her idiom, must read it in many books.

If different studies are useful for aiding, they are still more useful for correcting each other; for as they have their particular merits severally, so they have their defects, and the most extensive acquaintance with one can produce only an intellect either too flashy or too jejune, or infected with some other fault of confined reading. History, for example, shows things as they are, that is, the morals and interests of men disfigured and perverted by all their imperfections of passion, folly, and ambition; philosophy strips the picture too much; poetry adorns it too much; the concentrated lights of the three correct the false peculiar coloring of each, and show us the truth. The right mode of thinking upon it is to be had from them taken all together, as every one must know who has seen their united contributions of thought and feeling expressed in the masculine sentiment of our immortal statesman, Mr. Burke,[15] whose eloquence is inferior only to his more admirable wisdom. If any mind improved like his, is to be our instructor, we must go to the fountain head of things as he did, and study not his works but his method; by the one we may become feeble imitators, by the other arrive at some ability of our own. But, as all biography assures us, he, and every other able thinker, has been formed, not by a parsimonious admeasurement of studies to some definite future object (which is Mr. Edgeworth's maxim), but by taking a wide and liberal compass, and thinking a great deal on many subjects with no better end in view than because the exercise was one which made them more rational and intelligent beings.

But I must bring these extracts to an end. To-day I have confined myself to saying that that training of the intellect, which is best for the individual himself, best enables him to discharge his duties to society. The philosopher, indeed, and the man of the world differ in their very notion, but the methods by which they are respectively formed are pretty much the same. The philosopher has the same command of matters of thought, which the true citizen and gentleman has of matters of business and conduct. If then a practical end must be assigned to a university course, I say it is that of training good members of society. Its art is the art of social life, and its end is fitness for the world. It neither confines its views to particular professions on the one hand, nor creates heroes or inspires genius on the other. Works indeed of genius fall under no art; heroic minds come under no rule; a university is not a birthplace of poets or of immortal authors, of founders of schools, leaders of colonies, or conquerors of nations. It does not promise a generation of Aristotles or Newtons, of Napoleons or Washingtons, of Raphaels or Shakespeares, though such miracles of nature it has before now contained within its precincts. Nor is it content on the other hand with forming the critic or the experimentalist, the economist or the engineer, though such too it includes within its scope. But a university training is the great ordinary means to a great but ordinary end; it aims at raising the intellectual tone of society, at cultivating the public mind, at purifying the national taste, at supplying true principles to popular enthusiasm and fixed aims to popular aspiration, at giving enlargement and sobriety to the ideas of the age, at facilitating the exercise of political power, and refining the intercourse of private life. It is the education which gives a man a clear conscious view of his own opinions and judgments, a truth in developing them, an eloquence in expressing them, and a force in urging them. It teaches him to see things as they are, to go right to the point, to disentangle a skein of thought, to detect what is sophistical, and to discard what is irrelevant. It prepares him to fill any post with credit, and to master any subject with facility. It shows him how to accommodate himself to others, how to throw himself into their state of mind, how to bring before them his own, how to influence them, how to come to an understanding with them, how to bear with them. He is at home in any society, he has common ground with every class; he knows when to speak and when to be silent; he is able to converse, he is able to listen; he can ask a question pertinently, and gain a lesson sea-

---

[15]Edmund Burke (1729-1797).

sonably, when he has nothing to impart himself; he is ever ready, yet never in the way; he is a pleasant companion, and a comrade you can depend upon; he knows when to be serious and when to trifle, and he has a sure tact which enables him to trifle with gracefulness and to be serious with effect. He has the repose of a mind which lives in itself, while it lives in the world, and which has resources for its happiness at home when it cannot go abroad. He has a gift which serves him in public, and supports him in retirement, without which good fortune is but vulgar, and with which failure and disappointment have a charm. The art which tends to make a man all this, is in the object which it pursues as useful as the art of wealth or the art of health, though it is less susceptible of method, and less tangible, less certain, less complete in its result.

ALFRED, LORD TENNYSON
1809-1892

Tennyson's father was a clergyman, and his mother the daughter of a clergyman. To them were born twelve children, one of whom died in infancy. Their fourth child was Alfred, who was born at Somersby, in Lincolnshire, on 6 August, 1809. Somersby was at that time a village of less than a hundred inhabitants, and the children of the Rev. George Tennyson had a country upbringing. The rectory and the garden, the surrounding fen country, and the Lincolnshire farmers—all these made a deep impression upon Alfred and remained abiding influences upon which later experiences were, so to say, grafted. When he was eight years old he was sent to the grammar school at Louth, about ten miles north of Somersby. There he spent more than three years, miserable years which he hated at the time and hated afterwards in memory so deeply that he would never revisit the school. It is said that he was bullied both by a brutal schoolmaster and by his schoolfellows. At the end of this period he went back to Somersby and completed his preparation for the university under his father's guidance. At the same time he was writing poetry, had indeed been writing more or less poetry from early childhood. "The first poetry that moved me," he later said, "was my own at five years old." To this influence others succeeded, that of Scott, and then Byron's. When Byron died in 1824, Tennyson later said, "I thought everything was over and finished for every one—that nothing else mattered. I remember I walked out alone and carved 'Byron is dead' into the sandstone." And in 1827 Tennyson published with his brother Charles his first volume, *Poems by Two Brothers.* Early in the following year the two brothers went up to Cambridge, where they entered Trinity College. Tennyson probably never felt quite at home in Cambridge; yet the friendships he made there had a deep influence upon him. He became a member of a group known as "The Apostles," a band "of Platonico-Wordsworthian-Coleridgean-anti-utilitarians," as one of their number afterwards called them; and these morally earnest, theologically liberal

young men did much to convince Tennyson that as a poet it was his office not merely to give pleasure to his readers but to become the spiritual guide of his age. Moreover, one of the "Apostles" was Arthur Henry Hallam, son of the historian, an apparently brilliant young man, who became Tennyson's closest friend, with results that markedly colored both his life and his poetry. Meanwhile poetry continued to be written. In 1829 Tennyson won the Chancellor's Medal with a blank-verse piece called *Timbuctoo,* and in 1830 he published his second volume, *Poems Chiefly Lyrical.* In 1831 he left Cambridge without being able to secure a degree. In December, 1832 (the volume is dated 1833), he published more verse, under the title *Poems.* This volume and that of 1830 contained some of the work by which Tennyson is still best known, but there were few to perceive that a great poet had made his appearance. Not only so, but, at least partly because of injudicious praise given the *Poems* by Hallam and other young friends, this volume was seized on for destruction by Lockhart, who published a merciless attack on it in the *Quarterly Review.* Tennyson was always extremely sensitive to criticism, and in his later years would never tolerate it even from his closest friends. So severely wounded was he by Lockhart's article that he did not publish another volume for ten years—years spent in study, writing, and the careful revision of those of his earlier poems which he wished to republish.

In September, 1833, Hallam died suddenly in Vienna, causing Tennyson the greatest sorrow of his life. He almost immediately began writing the "Elegies" which gradually grew in number until they were finally published under the title *In Memoriam A. H. H.* in 1850. Eight years before, in 1842, he had published *English Idyls,* which had at once been recognized as an important volume and had given him a secure place in the world of letters. In 1845 he had been granted a pension, and in 1847 he had published *The Princess.* At length in 1850 he felt able to marry Emily Sellwood, to whom he had been engaged for some thirteen years. In the same year he was appointed, in succession to Wordsworth, poet laureate. His position as the great poet of the age was now secure, and during the remainder of his long life all, or nearly all, that he wrote contributed to the steady growth of his almost fabulous reputation amongst his contemporaries. Shortly after his marriage he acquired Farringford, on the Isle of Wight. In 1852 was published the *Ode on the Death of the Duke of Wellington,* in 1855 *Maud,* and in 1859 the first group of *Idyls of the King.* More *Idyls* were published in 1869 and in 1872. In 1864 *Enoch Arden* was published. Shortly before 1870 Tennyson built Aldworth, near Haslemere, in Surrey, and thenceforth his time was divided between his new home and Farringford. In 1875 he published *Queen Mary,* the first of some half-dozen plays which he wrote. In January, 1884, he was created Baron of Aldworth and Farringford, an honor which he is said to have accepted reluctantly and only "for the sake of literature," but an honor, too, which not unfairly indicates the exalted position he had attained in the eyes of the whole English-speaking world. He was by this time an old man, but he continued to the last to write and publish poetry which not only maintained but even added to his reputation. He died on 6 October, 1892, and was buried in Westminster Abbey.

Tennyson was in a peculiar sense the poet of his age. In his pages we read its littleness and its greatness—its religious doubts and insecure faith, its moral primness, its muddled politics, its ugly all-enveloping industrialism, its confidence in human progress and in the worth of individual endeavor, its pride of achievement, its active sense of a great past to be lived up to, and its noble—if perhaps too emotional and thoughtless—patriotism. Yet at the same time Tennyson was curiously different from his age. One who knows only the legendary Tennyson comes with some surprise on Sir Edmund Gosse's description of him as "a gaunt, black, touzled man, rough in speech, brooding like an old gypsy over his inch of clay pipe stuffed with

shag and sucking in port wine with gusto"—a description confirmed by Carlyle's portrait: "A fine, large-featured, dim-eyed, bronze-colored, shaggy-headed man is Alfred: dusty, smoky, free and easy: who swims, outwardly and inwardly, with great composure in an articulate element as of tranquil chaos and tobacco smoke; great now and then when he does emerge; a most restful, brotherly, solid-hearted man." The truth is that Tennyson's was a complex, if not divided, nature. He was a great public and civic figure, the almost official Victorian guide through life's mazes, but he was also a serious, subtle, painstaking craftsman in verse; and he was at bottom a heavy-hearted mystic, anxious to be alone with his moods, and never perhaps so truly himself as in the purely lyric portions of his poetry.

The standard authorized edition of Tennyson's *Poems* is one annotated by Tennyson himself and edited by his son Hallam, Lord Tennyson (9 vols., London, 1898–1899; and later reprinted). The most easily available one-volume edition is that in the series of "Cambridge" poets, ed. W. J. Rolfe (Boston, 1898); but this edition does not contain all the poetry published after 1880, and it contains only a selection from *Poems by Two Brothers.* Hallam, Lord Tennyson's memoir of his father (London, 1897), is a standard biography; Arthur C. Benson's *Alfred Tennyson* (London, 1904) is also a valuable portrait. Thomas R. Lounsbury's *Life and Times of Tennyson* (New Haven, 1915) unfortunately covers only the period from 1809 to 1850. In his *Tennyson, Aspects of His Life, Character and Poetry* (New York, 1923) Harold G. Nicolson emphasizes Tennyson's importance as a lyric rather than as a didactic poet. A. C. Bradley's *Commentary on Tennyson's In Memoriam* (London, 1901; but revised in later editions through 1915) and Morton Luce's *Handbook to the Works of Alfred Lord Tennyson* (London, 1910) are standard works of reference. For Tennyson's intellectual background see D. C. Somervell, *English Thought in the Nineteenth Century* (London, 1929).

THE POET [1]

The poet in a golden clime was born,
  With golden stars above;
Dowered with the hate of hate, the scorn of
    scorn,
    The love of love.

He saw through life and death, through good
    and ill,   5
  He saw through his own soul.
The marvel of the everlasting will,
    An open scroll,

---

[1] Published in 1830. Tennyson frequently revised his poems as they were reprinted in successive editions, but the dates appended to those here printed are in general simply those of first publication.

Before him lay; with echoing feet he threaded
    The secretest walks of fame: 10
The viewless² arrows of his thoughts were
       headed
    And winged with flame,

Like Indian reeds blown from his silver
      tongue,
    And of so fierce a flight,
From Calpe³ unto Caucasus they sung,   15
    Filling with light

And vagrant melodies the winds which bore
    Them earthward till they lit;
Then, like the arrow-seeds of the field flower,
    The fruitful wit   20

Cleaving took root and springing forth anew
    Where'er they fell, behold,
Like to the mother plant in semblance, grew
    A flower all gold,

And bravely furnished all abroad to fling   25
    The wingéd shafts of truth,
To throng with stately blooms the breathing
      spring
    Of Hope and Youth.

So many minds did gird their orbs with
      beams,
    Though one did fling the fire;   30
Heaven flowed upon the soul in many dreams
    Of high desire.

Thus truth was multiplied on truth, the world
    Like one great garden showed,
And through the wreaths of floating dark
      upcurled,   35
    Rare sunrise flowed.

And Freedom reared in that august sunrise
    Her beautiful bold brow,
When rites and forms before his burning
      eyes
    Melted like snow.   40

There was no blood upon her maiden robes
    Sunned by those orient skies;
But round about the circles of the globes
    Of her keen eyes

And in her raiment's hem was traced in flame
    WISDOM, a name to shake   46
All evil dreams of power—a sacred name.
    And when she spake,

---

²Invisible.   ³Gibraltar.

Her words did gather thunder as they ran,
    And as the lightning to the thunder   50
Which follows it, riving the spirit of man,
    Making earth wonder,

So was their meaning to her words. No
      sword
    Of wrath her right arm whirled,   54
But one poor poet's scroll, and with *his* word
    She shook the world.

THE LADY OF
SHALOTT¹

PART I

On either side the river lie
Long fields of barley and of rye,
That clothe the wold² and meet the sky;
And through the field the road runs by
    To many-towered Camelot;³   5
And up and down the people go,
Gazing where the lilies blow
Round an island there below,
    The island of Shalott.⁴

Willows whiten, aspens quiver,   10
Little breezes dusk and shiver
Through the wave that runs for ever
By the island in the river
    Flowing down to Camelot.
Four gray walls, and four gray towers,   15
Overlook a space of flowers,
And the silent isle imbowers
    The Lady of Shalott.

By the margin, willow-veiled,
Slide the heavy barges trailed   20
By slow horses; and unhailed
The shallop flitteth silken-sailed
    Skimming down to Camelot:
But who hath seen her wave her hand?
Or at the casement seen her stand?   25
Or is she known in all the land,
    The Lady of Shalott?

Only reapers, reaping early
In among the bearded barley,

---

¹Published in 1832. Tennyson's earliest handling
of a theme from Arthurian legend. When he later
wrote *Lancelot and Elaine* he adopted a different
version of the story he tells here.

²Open country.

³The legendary city where King Arthur held his
court, commonly supposed to be in Cornwall.

⁴In Malory (*Morte d'Arthur*, Bk. XVIII) this
word is Astolat. An Italian version of the story
of Elaine is said to have suggested Tennyson's
poem, which would account for the form Shalott.

Hear a song that echoes cheerly   30
From the river winding clearly,
    Down to towered Camelot;
And by the moon the reaper weary,
Piling sheaves in uplands airy,
Listening, whispers " 'Tis the fairy   35
    Lady of Shalott."

PART II

There she weaves by night and day
A magic web with colors gay.
She has heard a whisper say,
A curse is on her if she stay   40
    To look down to Camelot.
She knows not what the curse may be,
And so she weaveth steadily,
And little other care hath she,
    The Lady of Shalott.   45

And moving through a mirror clear
That hangs before her all the year,
Shadows of the world appear.
There she sees the highway near
    Winding down to Camelot;   50
There the river eddy whirls,
And there the surly village-churls,
And the red cloaks of market girls,
    Pass onward from Shalott.

Sometimes a troop of damsels glad,   55
An abbot on an ambling pad,[5]
Sometimes a curly shepherd-lad,
Or long-haired page in crimson clad,
    Goes by to towered Camelot;
And sometimes through the mirror blue 60
The knights come riding two and two:
She hath no loyal knight and true,
    The Lady of Shalott.

But in her web she still delights
To weave the mirror's magic sights,   65
For often through the silent nights
A funeral, with plumes and lights
    And music, went to Camelot;
Or when the moon was overhead,
Came two young lovers lately wed: 70
"I am half sick of shadows," said
    The Lady of Shalott.

PART III

A bow-shot from her bower-eaves,
He rode between the barley-sheaves,
The sun came dazzling through the leaves, 75
And flamed upon the brazen greaves
    Of bold Sir Lancelot.

[5]Easy-paced horse.

A red-cross knight for ever kneeled
To a lady in his shield,
That sparkled on the yellow field,   80
    Beside remote Shalott.

The gemmy bridle glittered free,
Like to some branch of stars we see
Hung in the golden Galaxy.[6]
The bridle bells rang merrily   85
    As he rode down to Camelot;
And from his blazoned baldric slung
A mighty silver bugle hung,
And as he rode his armor rung,
    Beside remote Shalott.   90

All in the blue unclouded weather
Thick-jeweled shone the saddle-leather,
The helmet and the helmet-feather
Burned like one burning flame together,
    As he rode down to Camelot;   95
As often through the purple night,
Below the starry clusters bright,
Some bearded. meteor, trailing light,
    Moves over still Shalott.

His broad clear brow in sunlight glowed; 100
On burnished hooves his war-horse trode;
From underneath his helmet flowed
His coal-black curls as on he rode,
    As he rode down to Camelot.
From the bank and from the river   105
He flashed into the crystal mirror,
"Tirra lirra," by the river
    Sang Sir Lancelot.

She left the web, she left the loom,
She made three paces through the room, 110
She saw the water-lily bloom,
She saw the helmet and the plume,
    She looked down to Camelot.
Out flew the web and floated wide;
The mirror cracked from side to side;   115
"The curse is come upon me," cried
    The Lady of Shalott.

PART IV

In the stormy east-wind straining,
The pale yellow woods were waning,   119
The broad stream in his banks complaining,
Heavily the low sky raining
    Over towered Camelot;
Down she came and found a boat
Beneath a willow left afloat,
And round about the prow she wrote   125
    The Lady of Shalott.

[6]The Milky Way.

And down the river's dim expanse
Like some bold seër in a trance,
Seeing all his own mischance—
With a glassy countenance   130
    Did she look to Camelot.
And at the closing of the day
She loosed the chain, and down she lay;
The broad stream bore her far away,
    The Lady of Shalott.   135

Lying, robed in snowy white
That loosely flew to left and right—
The leaves upon her falling light—
Through the noises of the night
    She floated down to Camelot;   140
And as the boat-head wound along
The willowy hills and fields among,
They heard her singing her last song,
    The Lady of Shalott.

Heard a carol, mournful, holy   145
Chanted loudly, chanted lowly,
Till her blood was frozen slowly,
And her eyes were darkened wholly,
    Turned to towered Camelot.

For ere she reached upon the tide   150
The first house by the water-side,
Singing in her song she died,
    The Lady of Shalott.

Under tower and balcony,
By garden-wall and gallery,   155
A gleaming shape she floated by,
Dead-pale between the houses high,
    Silent into Camelot.
Out upon the wharfs they came,
Knight and burgher, lord and dame,   160
And round the prow they read her name,
    The Lady of Shalott.

Who is this? and what is here?
And in the lighted palace near
Died the sound of royal cheer;   165
And they crossed themselves for fear,
    All the knights at Camelot:
But Lancelot mused a little space;
He said, "She has a lovely face;
God in his mercy lend her grace,   170
    The Lady of Shalott."

OENONE[1]

There lies a vale in Ida, lovelier
Than all the valleys of Ionian hills.
The swimming vapor slopes athwart the glen,
Puts forth an arm, and creeps from pine to
    pine,
And loiters, slowly drawn.   On either hand 5
The lawns and meadow-ledges midway down
Hang rich in flowers, and far below them
    roars
The long brook falling through the cloven
    ravine
In cataract after cataract to the sea.

---

[1]Published in 1832. Oenone was the daughter of
a river-god, and the wife of Paris, son of King
Priam of Troy. Paris was asked to judge which
of the three goddesses, Hera, Pallas Athena, and
Aphrodite, was the fairest, and each tried to influence his judgment in her own favor by offering him
a reward. Aphrodite said she would give him the
most beautiful of women for a wife, whereupon
Paris immediately judged her the fairest of the
goddesses. Under Aphrodite's care he then left
Oenone and sailed for Sparta, whence he bore away
Helen to Troy, thus bringing about the Trojan war.
Ida is the name of a mountain range forming the
southern boundary of the territory of Troas, or
Ilium. It was in these mountains that Paris was
brought up by shepherds, having been abandoned
there as a baby after his mother dreamed that he
would bring ruin on Troy. Gargarus is the name
of one of the highest peaks of Ida.

Behind the valley topmost Gargarus   10
Stands up and takes the morning; but in
    front
The gorges, opening wide apart, reveal
Troas and Ilion's columned citadel,
The crown of Troas.
        Hither came at noon
Mournful Oenone, wandering forlorn   15
Of Paris, once her playmate on the hills.
Her cheek had lost the rose, and round her
    neck
Floated her hair or seemed to float in rest.
She, leaning on a fragment twined with vine,
Sang to the stillness, till the mountain-
    shade   20
Sloped downward to her seat from the upper
    cliff.

"O mother Ida, many fountained Ida,
Dear mother Ida, harken ere I die.
For now the noonday quiet holds the hill;
The grasshopper is silent in the grass;   25
The lizard, with his shadow on the stone,
Rests like a shadow, and the winds are dead.
The purple flower droops, the golden bee
Is lily-cradled; I alone awake.
My eyes are full of tears, my heart of love, 30
My heart is breaking, and my eyes are dim,
And I am all aweary of my life.

"O mother Ida, many-fountained Ida,
Dear mother Ida, harken ere I die.
Hear me, O earth, hear me, O hills, O
   caves   35
That house the cold crowned snake! O
   mountain brooks,
I am the daughter of a River-God,
Hear me, for I will speak, and build up all
My sorrow with my song, as yonder walls
Rose slowly to a music slowly breathed, 40
A cloud that gathered shape;[2] for it may be
That, while I speak of it, a little while
My heart may wander from its deeper woe.

"O mother Ida, many-fountained Ida,
Dear mother Ida, harken ere I die.   45
I waited underneath the dawning hills;
Aloft the mountain lawn was dewy-dark,
And dewy dark aloft the mountain pine.
Beautiful Paris, evil-hearted Paris,
Leading a jet-black goat white-horned,
   white-hooved,   50
Came up from reedy Simois[3] all alone.

"O mother Ida, harken ere I die.
Far-off the torrent called me from the cleft;
Far up the solitary morning smote
The streaks of virgin snow.   With down-
   dropped eyes   55
I sat alone; white-breasted like a star
Fronting the dawn he moved; a leopard skin
Drooped from his shoulder, but his sunny
   hair
Clustered about his temples like a God's;
And his cheek brightened as the foam-bow
   brightens   60
When the wind blows the foam, and all my
   heart
Went forth to embrace him coming ere he
   came.

"Dear mother Ida, harken ere I die.
He smiled, and opening out his milk-white
   palm
Disclosed a fruit of pure Hesperian gold,[4] 65
That smelt ambrosially, and while I looked
And listened, the full-flowing river of speech
Came down upon my heart:
    "'My own Oenone,
Beautiful-browed Oenone, my own soul,
Behold this fruit, whose gleaming rind in-
   graven   70

"For the most fair," would seem to **award**
   it thine,
As lovelier than whatever Oread[5] haunt
The knolls of Ida, loveliest in all grace
Of movement, and the charm of married
   brows.'

"Dear mother Ida, harken ere I die.   75
He pressed the blossom of his lips to mine,
And added, 'This was upon the board,
When all the full-faced presence of the Gods
Ranged in the halls of Peleus; whereupon
Rose feud, with question unto whom 'twere
   due;   80
But light-foot Iris[6] brought it yester-eve,
Delivering, that to me, by common voice
Elected umpire, Herë comes to-day,
Pallas and Aphrodite, claiming each   84
This meed of fairest.   Thou, within the cave
Behind yon whispering tuft of oldest pine,
Mayst well behold them unbeheld, unheard
Hear all, and see thy Paris judge of Gods.'

"Dear mother Ida, harken ere I die.
It was the deep midnoon; one silvery cloud 90
Had lost his way between the piny sides
Of this long glen.   Then to the bower they
   came,
Naked they came to that smooth-swarded
   bower,
And at their feet the crocus brake like fire,
Violet, amaracus, and asphodel,[7]   95
Lotos and lilies; and a wind arose,
And overhead the wandering ivy and vine,
This way and that, in many a wild festoon
Ran riot, garlanding the gnarléd boughs
With bunch and berry and flower through
   and through.   100

"O mother Ida, harken ere I die.
On the tree-tops a crested peacock lit,
And o'er him flowed a golden cloud, and
   leaned
Upon him, slowly dropping fragrant dew. 104
Then first I heard the voice of her to whom
Coming through heaven, like a light that
   grows
Larger and clearer, with one mind the Gods
Rise up for reverence.   She to Paris made
Proffer of royal power, ample rule
Unquestioned, overflowing revenue   110
Wherewith to embellish state, 'from many a
   vale

---

[2]The walls of Troy were said to have arisen in obedience to Apollo's music.
[3]A stream which rises on Mount Ida.
[4]A golden apple like those which grew in the gardens of the Hesperides.

[5]Mountain-nymph.   [6]Messenger of the gods.
[7]Amaracus is the modern marjoram; asphodel is a lily-shaped plant.

And river-sundered champaign clothed with
  corn,
Or labored mine undrainable of ore.   113
Honor,' she said, 'and homage, tax and toll,
From many an inland town and haven large,
Mast-thronged beneath her shadowing cita-
  del
In glassy bays among her tallest towers.'

"O mother Ida, harken ere I die.
Still she spake on and still she spake of
  power,
'Which in all action is the end of all;   120
Power fitted to the season; wisdom-bred
And throned of wisdom—from all neighbor
  crowns
Alliance and allegiance, till thy hand
Fail from the scepter-staff.   Such boon from
  me,
From me, heaven's queen, Paris, to thee
  king-born,   125
A shepherd all thy life but yet king-born,
Should come most welcome, seeing men, in
  power
Only, are likest Gods, who have attained
Rest in a happy place and quiet seats
Above the thunder, with undying bliss   130
In knowledge of their own supremacy.'

"Dear mother Ida, harken ere I die.
She ceased, and Paris held the costly fruit
Out at arm's-length, so much the thought of
  power   134
Flattered his spirit; but Pallas where she
  stood
Somewhat apart, her clear and bared limbs
O'erthwarted with the brazen-headed spear
Upon her pearly shoulder leaning cold,   138
The while, above, her full and earnest eye
Over her snow-cold breast and angry cheek
Kept watch, waiting decision, made reply:
'Self-reverence, self-knowledge, self-control,
These three alone lead life to sovereign
  power.
Yet not for power (power of herself   144
Would come uncalled for) but to live by law,
Acting the law we live by without fear;
And, because right is right, to follow right
Were wisdom in the scorn of consequence.'

"Dear mother Ida, harken ere I die.
Again she said: 'I woo thee not with gifts. 150
Sequel of guerdon could not alter me
To fairer.   Judge thou me by what I am,
So shalt thou find me fairest.
                          Yet, indeed,
If gazing on divinity disrobed

Thy mortal eyes are frail to judge of fair, 155
Unbiased by self-profit, O, rest thee sure
That I shall love thee well and cleave to thee,
So that my vigor, wedded to thy blood,
Shall strike within thy pulses, like a God's,
To push thee forward through a life of
  shocks,
Dangers, and deeds, until endurance grow 161
Sinewed with action, and the full-grown will,
Circled through all experiences, pure law,
Commeasure[8] perfect freedom.'
                          "Here she ceased,
And Paris pondered, and I cried, 'O Paris, 165
Give it to Pallas!' but he heard me not,
Or hearing would not hear me, woe is me!

"O mother Ida, many-fountained Ida,
Dear mother Ida, harken ere I die.
Idalian[9] Aphrodite beautiful,   170
Fresh as the foam, new-bathed in Paphian
  wells,
With rosy slender fingers backward drew
From her warm brows and bosom her deep
  hair
Ambrosial, golden round her lucid throat 174
And shoulder; from the violets her light foot
Shone rosy-white, and o'er her rounded form
Between the shadows of the vine-bunches
Floated the glowing sunlights, as she moved.

"Dear mother Ida, harken ere I die.
She with a subtle smile in her mild eyes,   180
The herald of her triumph, drawing nigh
Half-whispered in his ear, 'I promise thee
The fairest and most loving wife in Greece.'
She spoke and laughed; I shut my sight for
  fear;
But when I looked, Paris had raised his arm,
And I beheld great Herë's angry eyes,   186
As she withdrew into the golden cloud,
And I was left alone within the bower;
And from that time to this I am alone,
And I shall be alone until I die.   190

"Yet, mother Ida, harken ere I die.
Fairest—why fairest wife? am I not fair?
My love hath told me so a thousand times.
Methinks I must be fair, for yesterday,   194
When I passed by, a wild and wanton pard,[10]
Eyed like the evening star, with playful tail
Crouched fawning in the weed.   Most lov-
  ing is she?
Ah me, my mountain shepherd, that my arms

[8]Be equal in measure to.
[9]Idalium and Paphos were towns in Cyprus where
Aphrodite was specially worshiped.
[10]Leopard.

Were wound about thee, and my hot lips
    pressed   199
Close, close to thine in that quick-falling dew
Of fruitful kisses, thick as autumn rains
Flash in the pools of whirling Simois!

"O mother, hear me yet before I die.
They[11] came, they cut away my tallest pines,
My tall dark pines, that plumed the craggy
    ledge   205
High over the blue gorge, and all between
The snowy peak and snow-white cataract
Fostered the callow eaglet—from beneath
Whose thick mysterious boughs in the dark
    morn   209
The panther's roar came muffled, while I sat
Low in the valley.   Never, never more
Shall lone Oenone see the morning mist
Sweep through them; never see them over-
    laid
With narrow moonlit slips of silver cloud,
Between the loud stream and the trembling
    stars.   215

"O mother, hear me yet before I die.
I wish that somewhere in the ruined folds,
Among the fragments tumbled from the
    glens,
Or the dry thickets, I could meet with her
The Abominable,[12] that uninvited came   220
Into the fair Peleïan banquet-hall,
And cast the golden fruit upon the board,
And bred this change; that I might speak my
    mind,
And tell her to her face how much I hate
Her presence, hated both of Gods and
    men.   225

"O mother, hear me yet before I die.
Hath he not sworn his love a thousand times,
In this green valley, under this green hill,
Even on this hand, and sitting on this stone?
Sealed it with kisses? watered it with tears?

[11]Shipwrights, who cut down the pines to make
ships for Paris's journey to Sparta.

[12]Eris, goddess of strife.

O happy tears, and how unlike to these!   231
O happy heaven, how canst thou see my
    face?
O happy earth, how canst thou bear my
    weight?
O death, death, death, thou ever-floating
    cloud,
There are enough unhappy on this earth,   235
Pass by the happy souls, that love to live;
I pray thee, pass before my light of life,
And shadow all my soul, that I may die.
Thou weighest heavy on the heart within,
Weigh heavy on my eyelids; let me die.   240

"O mother, hear me yet before I die.
I will not die alone, for fiery thoughts
Do shape themselves within me, more and
    more,
Whereof I catch the issue, as I hear
Dead sounds at night come from the inmost
    hills,   245
Like footsteps upon wool.   I dimly see
My far-off doubtful purpose, as a mother
Conjectures of the features of her child
Ere it is born.   Her child!—a shudder
    comes
Across me: never child be born of me,   250
Unblest, to vex me with his father's eyes!

"O mother, hear me yet before I die.
Hear me, O earth.   I will not die alone,
Lest their shrill happy laughter come to me
Walking the cold and starless road of death
Uncomforted, leaving my ancient love   256
With the Greek woman.   I will rise and go
Down into Troy, and ere the stars come
    forth
Talk with the wild Cassandra,[13] for she says
A fire dances before her, and a sound   260
Rings ever in her ears of arméd men.
What this may be I know not, but I know
That, wheresoe'er I am by night and day,
All earth and air seem only burning fire."

[13]Daughter of Priam, who predicted the destruction of Troy but was thought to be mad.

THE PALACE OF ART[1]

I built my soul a lordly pleasure-house,
  Wherein at ease for aye to dwell.
I said, "O Soul, make merry and carouse,
  Dear soul, for all is well."

A huge crag-platform, smooth as burnished
      brass,   5
  I chose. The rangéd ramparts bright
From level meadow-bases of deep grass
  Suddenly scaled the light.

Thereon I built it firm. Of ledge or shelf
  The rock rose clear, or winding stair. 10
My soul would live alone unto herself
  In her high palace there.

And "while the world runs round and
    round," I said,
  "Reign thou apart, a quiet king,
Still as, while Saturn whirls, his steadfast
    shade   15
  Sleeps on his luminous ring."

To which my soul made answer readily:
  "Trust me, in bliss I shall abide
In this great mansion, that is built for me,
  So royal-rich and wide."   20

. . . . .

Four courts I made, East, West and South
    and North,
  In each a squaréd lawn, wherefrom
The golden gorge[2] of dragons spouted forth
  A flood of fountain-foam.

And round the cool green courts there ran a
    row   25
  Of cloisters, branched like mighty woods,
Echoing all night to that sonorous flow
  Of spouted fountain-floods;

And round the roofs a gilded gallery
  That lent broad verge to distant lands, 30
Far as the wild swan wings, to where the sky
  Dipped down to sea and sands.

From those four jets four currents in one
    swell
  Across the mountain streamed below
In misty folds, that floating as they fell 35
  Lit up a torrent-bow.

And high on every peak a statue seemed
  To hang on tiptoe, tossing up
A cloud of incense of all odor steamed
  From out a golden cup.   40

So that she thought, "And who shall gaze
    upon
  My palace with unblinded eyes,
While this great bow will waver in the sun,
  And that sweet incense rise?"

For that sweet incense rose and never failed,
  And, while day sank or mounted higher, 46
The light aerial gallery, golden-railed,
  Burned like a fringe of fire.

Likewise the deep-set windows, stained and
    traced,
  Would seem slow-flaming crimson fires 50
From shadowed grots of arches interlaced,
  And tipped with frost-like spires.

. . . . .

Full of long-sounding corridors it was,
  That over-vaulted grateful gloom,
Through which the livelong day my soul did
    pass,   55
  Well-pleased, from room to room.

Full of great rooms and small the palace
    stood,
  All various, each a perfect whole
From living Nature, fit for every mood
  And change of my still soul. 60

For some were hung with arras green and
    blue,
  Showing a gaudy summer-morn,
Where with puffed cheek the belted hunter
    blew
  His wreathéd bugle-horn.

---

[1]Published in 1832, but much altered in later editions. Tennyson prefixed to the poem the following explanation:

  I send you here a sort of allegory
  (For you will understand it), of a soul,
  A sinful soul possessed of many gifts,
  A spacious garden full of flowering weeds,
  A glorious Devil, large in heart and brain,
  That did love Beauty only (Beauty seen
  In all varieties of mold and mind)
  And Knowledge for its beauty; or if Good,
  Good only for its beauty, seeing not
  That Beauty, Good, and Knowledge are three
    sisters
  That dote upon each other, friends to man,
  Living together under the same roof,
  And never can be sundered without tears.
  And he that shuts Love out, in turn shall be
  Shut out from Love, and on her threshold lie
  Howling in outer darkness. Not for this
  Was common clay ta'en from the common
    earth,
  Molded by God, and tempered with the tears
  Of angels to the perfect shape of man.

[2]Throat.

One seemed all dark and red—a tract of
    sand,   65
And some one pacing there alone,
Who paced for ever in a glimmering land,
    Lit with a low large moon.

One showed an iron coast and angry waves.
    You seemed to hear them climb and fall 70
And roar rock-thwarted under bellowing
    caves,
    Beneath the windy wall.

And one, a full-fed river winding slow
    By herds upon an endless plain,
The ragged rims of thunder brooding low 75
    With shadow-streaks of rain.

And one, the reapers at their sultry toil.
    In front they bound the sheaves.   Behind
Were realms of upland, prodigal in oil,
    And hoary to the wind.[3]   80

And one a foreground black with stones and
    slags;
Beyond, a line of heights; and higher
All barred with long white cloud the scorn-
    ful crags;
    And highest, snow and fire.

And one, an English home—gray twilight
    poured   85
On dewy pastures, dewy trees,
Softer than sleep—all things in order stored,
    A haunt of ancient Peace.

Nor these alone, but every landscape fair,
    As fit for every mood of mind,   90
Or gay, or grave, or sweet, or stern, was
    there,
    Not less than truth designed.

.   .   .   .   .

Or the maid-mother by a crucifix,
    In tracts of pasture sunny-warm,
Beneath branch-work of costly sardonyx[4] 95
    Sat smiling, babe in arm.

Or in a clear-walled city on the sea,
    Near gilded organ-pipes, her hair
Wound with white roses, slept Saint Cecily;[5]
    An angel looked at her.   100

---

[3] I. e., the whitish underside of the olive leaves
turned up by the wind.

[4] Ornamental patterns of a yellow and white polished stone.

[5] St. Cecilia was said to have invented the organ.

Or thronging all one porch of Paradise
    A group of Houris[6] bowed to see
The dying Islamite, with hands and eyes
    That said, We wait for thee.

Or mythic Uther's deeply-wounded son[7] 105
    In some fair space of sloping greens
Lay, dozing in the vale of Avalon,
    And watched by weeping queens.

Or hollowing one hand against his ear,
    To list a foot-fall, ere he saw   110
The wood-nymph, stayed the Ausonian
    King[8] to hear
    Of wisdom and of law.

Or over hills with peaky tops engrailed,
    And many a tract of palm and rice,
The throne of Indian Cama[9] slowly sailed 115
    A summer fanned with spice.

Or sweet Europa's mantle blew unclasped,
    From off her shoulder backward borne;
From one hand drooped a crocus; one hand
    grasped
    The mild bull's golden horn.[10]   120

Or else flushed Ganymede, his rosy thigh
    Half-buried in the eagle's down,
Sole as a flying star shot through the sky
    Above the pillared town.[11]

Nor these alone; but every legend fair 125
    Which the supreme Caucasian mind
Carved out of Nature for itself was there,
    Not less than life designed.

.   .   .   .   .

Then in the towers I placed great bells that
    swung,
Moved of themselves, with silver sound;
And with choice paintings of wise men I
    hung   131
    The royal dais round.

---

[6] The virgins who, according to the Koran, attend
upon the faithful Mahometan in Paradise.

[7] King Arthur. Tennyson tells the story of his
death in *The Passing of Arthur*.

[8] Numa, legislator and second king of Rome, was
said to have been instructed in the art of government by the wood-nymph Egeria.

[9] The god of love in Hindu mythology.

[10] Europa while gathering flowers was carried off
by Zeus under the form of a bull.

[11] Ganymede was carried off by the eagle of Zeus
to become Zeus's cup-bearer.

For there was Milton like a seraph strong,
    Beside him Shakespeare bland and mild;
And there the world-worn Dante grasped his
        song,   135
    And somewhat grimly smiled.

And there the Ionian father of the rest;[12]
    A million wrinkles carved his skin;
A hundred winters snowed upon his breast,
    From cheek and throat and chin.   140

Above, the fair hall-ceiling stately-set
    Many an arch high up did lift,
And angels rising and descending met
    With interchange of gift.

Below was all mosaic choicely planned   145
    With cycles of the human tale
Of this wide world, the times of every land
    So wrought they will not fail.

The people here, a beast of burden slow,
    Toiled onward, pricked with goads and
        stings;   150
Here played, a tiger, rolling to and fro
    The heads and crowns of kings;

Here rose, an athlete, strong to break or bind
    All force in bonds that might endure,
And here once more like some sick man de-
        clined,   155
    And trusted any cure.

But over these she trod; and those great bells
    Began to chime. She took her throne;
She sat betwixt the shining oriels,
    To sing her songs alone.   160

And through the topmost oriels' colored flame
    Two godlike faces gazed below;
Plato the wise, and large-browed Verulam,[13]
    The first of those who know.

And all those names that in their motion
       were   165
Full-welling fountain-heads of change,
Betwixt the slender shafts were blazoned
       fair
    In diverse raiment strange;

Through which the lights, rose, amber, emer-
       ald, blue,
    Flushed in her temples and her eyes,   170

And from her lips, as morn from Memnon,[14]
       drew
    Rivers of melodies.

No nightingale delighteth to prolong
    Her low preamble all alone,
More than my soul to hear her echoed song
    Throb through the ribbéd stone;   176

Singing and murmuring in her feastful
       mirth,
    Joying to feel herself alive,
Lord over Nature, lord of the visible earth,
    Lord of the senses five;   180

Communing with herself: "All these are
       mine,
    And let the world have peace or wars,
'Tis one to me." She—when young night
       divine
    Crowned dying day with stars,

Making sweet close of his delicious toils—185
    Lit light in wreaths and anadems,[15]
And pure quintessences of precious oils
    In hollowed moons of gems,

To mimic heaven; and clapped her hands
       and cried,
    "I marvel if my still delight   190
In this great house so royal-rich and wide
    Be flattered to the height.

"O all things fair to sate my various eyes!
    O shapes and hues that please me well!
O silent faces of the Great and Wise,   195
    My Gods, with whom I dwell!

"O Godlike isolation which art mine,
    I can but count thee perfect gain,
What time I watch the darkening droves of
       swine
    That range on yonder plain.   200

"In filthy sloughs they roll a prurient skin,
    They graze and wallow, breed and sleep;
And oft some brainless devil enters in,
    And drives them to the deep."[16]

Then of the moral instinct would she prate
    And of the rising from the dead,   206
As hers by right of full-accomplished Fate;
    And at the last she said:

---

[12]Homer.

[13]Francis Bacon. The following line translates
the epithet Dante applies to Aristotle (*Inferno*, iv,
131).

[14]A colossal Egyptian statue (really of Ameno-
phis) which was said to give forth a musical sound
when first struck by the rays of the rising sun.

[15]In lamps arranged like wreaths and garlands.

[16]See St. Mark, 5:13.

"I take possession of man's mind and deed.
  I care not what the sects may brawl. 210
I sit as God holding no form of creed,
  But contemplating all."

    .   .   .   .   .

Full oft the riddle of the painful earth
  Flashed through her as she sat alone,
Yet not the less held she her solemn mirth,
  And intellectual throne. 216

And so she throve and prospered; so three
    years
She prospered; on the fourth she fell,
Like Herod, when the shout was in his ears,
  Struck through with pangs of hell.[17]

Lest she should fall and perish utterly, 221
  God, before whom ever lie bare
The abysmal deeps of personality,
  Plagued her with sore despair.

When she would think, where'er she turned
    her sight 225
  The airy hand confusion wrought,
Wrote, "Mene, mene,"[18] and divided quite
  The kingdom of her thought.

Deep dread and loathing of her solitude
  Fell on her, from which mood was born
Scorn of herself; again, from out that mood
  Laughter at her self-scorn. 232

"What! is not this my place of strength," she
    said,
  "My spacious mansion built for me,
Whereof the strong foundation-stones were
    laid 235
  Since my first memory?"

But in dark corners of her palace stood
  Uncertain shapes; and unawares
On white-eyed phantasms weeping tears of
    blood,
  And horrible nightmares, 240

And hollow shades enclosing hearts of flame,
  And, with dim-fretted[19] foreheads all,
On corpses three-months-old at noon she
    came,
  That stood against the wall.

A spot of dull stagnation, without light 245
  Or power of movement, seemed my soul,
Mid onward-sloping motions infinite
  Making for one sure goal;

---

[17]See Acts, 12:21–23.
[18]See the account of Belshazzar's feast, Daniel, 5.
[19]Worm-eaten (Tennyson's explanation).

A still salt pool, locked in with bars of sand,
  Left on the shore, that hears all night 250
The plunging seas draw backward from the
    land
  Their moon-led waters white;

A star that with the choral starry dance
  Joined not, but stood, and standing saw
The hollow orb of moving Circumstance 255
  Rolled round by one fixed law.

Back on herself her serpent pride had curled
  "No voice," she shrieked in that lone hall,
"No voice breaks through the stillness of this
    world;
  One deep, deep silence all!" 260

She, moldering with the dull earth's molder-
    ing sod,
  Inwrapped tenfold in slothful shame,
Lay there exiléd from eternal God,
  Lost to her place and name;

And death and life she hated equally, 265
  And nothing saw, for her despair,
But dreadful time, dreadful eternity,
  No comfort anywhere;

Remaining utterly confused with fears,
  And ever worse with growing time, 270
And ever unrelieved by dismal tears,
  And all alone in crime.

Shut up as in a crumbling tomb, girt round
  With blackness as a solid wall,
Far off she seemed to hear the dully sound
  Of human footsteps fall: 276

As in strange lands a traveler walking slow,
  In doubt and great perplexity,
A little before moonrise hears the low
  Moan of an unknown sea; 280

And knows not if it be thunder, or a sound
  Of rocks thrown down, or one deep cry
Of great wild beasts; then thinketh, "I have
    found
  A new land, but I die."

She howled aloud, "I am on fire within. 285
  There comes no murmur of reply.
What is it that will take away my sin,
  And save me lest I die?"

So when four years were wholly finished,
  She threw her royal robes away. 290
"Make me a cottage in the vale," she said,
  "Where I may mourn and pray.

"Yet pull not down my palace towers, that are
  So lightly, beautifully built;
Perchance I may return with others there 295
  When I have purged my guilt."

THE LOTOS-EATERS[1]

"Courage!" he[2] said, and pointed toward the land,
"This mounting wave will roll us shoreward soon."
In the afternoon they came unto a land
In which it seeméd always afternoon.
All round the coast the languid air did swoon, 5
Breathing like one that hath a weary dream.
Full-faced above the valley stood the moon;
And, like a downward smoke, the slender stream
Along the cliff to fall and pause and fall did seem.

A land of streams! some, like a downward smoke, 10
Slow-dropping veils of thinnest lawn, did go;
And some through wavering lights and shadows broke,
Rolling a slumbrous sheet of foam below.
They saw the gleaming river seaward flow
From the inner land; far off, three mountain-tops, 15
Three silent pinnacles of agéd snow,
Stood sunset-flushed; and, dewed with showery drops,
Up-clomb the shadowy pine above the woven copse.

The charméd sunset lingered low adown
In the red West; through mountain clefts the dale 20
Was seen far inland, and the yellow down
Bordered with palm, and many a winding vale
And meadow, set with slender galingale;[3]
A land where all things always seemed the same!
And round about the keel with faces pale, 25
Dark faces pale against that rosy flame,
The mild-eyed melancholy Lotos-eaters came.

[1]Published in 1832. The land of the lotos-eaters was visited by Ulysses, and Tennyson drew the framework of his poem from the *Odyssey*, IX, 82–97. The lotos referred to is an African plant, sometimes called the Cyrenean lotos.

[2]Ulysses. [3]Plant with an aromatic root.

Branches they bore of that enchanted stem,
Laden with flower and fruit, whereof they gave
To each, but whoso did receive of them 30
And taste, to him the gushing of the wave
Far far away did seem to mourn and rave
On alien shores; and if his fellow spake,
His voice was thin, as voices from the grave;
And deep-asleep he seemed, yet all awake, 35
And music in his ears his beating heart did make.

They sat them down upon the yellow sand,
Between the sun and moon upon the shore;
And sweet it was to dream of Fatherland,
Of child, and wife, and slave; but evermore 40
Most wearied seemed the sea, weary the oar,
Weary the wandering fields of barren foam.
Then some one said, "We will return no more";
And all at once they sang, "Our island home
Is far beyond the wave; we will no longer roam." 45

CHORIC SONG

I

THERE is sweet music here that softer falls
Than petals from blown roses on the grass,
Or night-dews on still waters between walls
Of shadowy granite, in a gleaming pass;
Music that gentlier on the spirit lies, 5
Than tired eyelids upon tired eyes;
Music that brings sweet sleep down from the blissful skies.
Here are cool mosses deep,
And through the moss the ivies creep,
And in the stream the long-leaved flowers weep, 10
And from the craggy ledge the poppy hangs in sleep.

II

Why are we weighed upon with heaviness,
And utterly consumed with sharp distress,
While all things else have rest from weariness?
All things have rest: why should we toil alone,
We only toil, who are the first of things, 16
And make perpetual moan,
Still from one sorrow to another thrown;
Nor ever fold our wings,
And cease from wanderings, 20
Nor steep our brows in slumber's holy balm;
Nor hearken what the inner spirit sings,

"There is no joy but calm!"—
Why should we only toil, the roof and crown
　　of things?

III

Lo! in the middle of the wood,　　25
The folded leaf is wooed from out the bud
With winds upon the branch, and there
Grows green and broad, and takes no care,
Sun-steeped at noon, and in the moon
Nightly dew-fed; and turning yellow　　30
Falls, and floats adown the air.
Lo! sweetened with the summer light,
The full-juiced apple, waxing over-mellow,
Drops in a silent autumn night.
All its allotted length of days　　35
The flower ripens in its place,
Ripens and fades, and falls, and hath no toil,
Fast-rooted in the fruitful soil.

IV

Hateful is the dark-blue sky,
Vaulted o'er the dark-blue sea.　　40
Death is the end of life; ah, why
Should life all labor be?
Let us alone. Time driveth onward fast,
And in a little while our lips are dumb.
Let us alone. What is it that will last?　　45
All things are taken from us, and become
Portions and parcels of the dreadful past.
Let us alone. What pleasure can we have
To war with evil? Is there any peace
In ever climbing up the climbing wave?　　50
All things have rest, and ripen toward the
　　grave
In silence—ripen, fall, and cease:
Give us long rest or death, dark death, or
　　dreamful ease.

V

How sweet it were, hearing the downward
　　stream,
With half-shut eyes ever to seem　　55
Falling asleep in a half-dream!
To dream and dream, like yonder amber
　　light,
Which will not leave the myrrh-bush on the
　　height;
To hear each other's whispered speech;
Eating the Lotos day by day,　　60
To watch the crisping ripples on the beach,
And tender curving lines of creamy spray;
To lend our hearts and spirits wholly
To the influence of mild-minded melancholy;
To muse and brood and live again in memory,
With those old faces of our infancy　　66

Heaped over with a mound of grass,
Two handfuls of white dust, shut in an urn
　　of brass!

VI

Dear is the memory of our wedded lives,
And dear the last embraces of our wives　　70
And their warm tears; but all hath suffered
　　change;
For surely now our household hearths are
　　cold,
Our sons inherit us, our looks are strange,
And we should come like ghosts to trouble
　　joy.
Or else the island princes over-bold　　75
Have eat our substance, and the minstrel
　　sings
Before them of the ten years' war in Troy,
And our great deeds, as half-forgotten things.
Is there confusion in the little isle?
Let what is broken so remain.　　80
The Gods are hard to reconcile;
'Tis hard to settle order once again.
There *is* confusion worse than death,
Trouble on trouble, pain on pain,
Long labor unto agéd breath,　　85
Sore task to hearts worn out by many wars
And eyes grown dim with gazing on the pilot-
　　stars.

VII

But, propped on beds of amaranth and moly,[4]
How sweet—while warm airs lull us, blow-
　　ing lowly—
With half-dropped eyelid still,　　90
Beneath a heaven dark and holy,
To watch the long bright river drawing
　　slowly
His waters from the purple hill—
To hear the dewy echoes calling
From cave to cave through the thick-twined
　　vine—　　95
To watch the emerald-colored water falling
Through many a woven acanthus-wreath[5]
　　divine!
Only to hear and see the far-off sparkling
　　brine,
Only to hear were sweet, stretched out be-
　　neath the pine.

---

[4]Amaranth was a fabled unfading flower; moly a
fabled plant with black root and milk-white flower
given by Hermes to Ulysses to protect him from the
draught of Circe (*Odyssey*, x, 305).

[5]Acanthus is a plant with pendant leaves, reproduced on the capitals of Corinthian columns.

VIII

The Lotos blooms below the barren peak, 100
The Lotos blows by every winding creek;
All day the wind breathes low with mellower
    tone;
Through every hollow cave and alley lone
Round and round the spicy downs the yellow
    Lotos-dust is blown.
We have had enough of action, and of motion
    we, 105
Rolled to starboard, rolled to larboard, when
    the surge was seething free,
Where the wallowing monster spouted his
    foam-fountains in the sea.
Let us swear an oath, and keep it with an
    equal mind,
In the hollow Lotos-land to live and lie re-
    clined
On the hills like Gods together, careless of
    mankind. 110
For they lie beside their nectar, and the bolts
    are hurled
Far below them in the valleys, and the clouds
    are lightly curled
Round their golden houses, girdled with the
    gleaming world;
Where they smile in secret, looking over
    wasted lands,
Blight and famine, plague and earthquake,
    roaring deeps and fiery sands, 115
Clanging fights, and flaming towns, and sink-
    ing ships, and praying hands.
But they smile, they find a music centered
    in a doleful song
Steaming up, a lamentation and an ancient
    tale of wrong,
Like a tale of little meaning though the words
    are strong;
Chanted from an ill-used race of men that
    cleave the soil, 120
Sow the seed, and reap the harvest with en-
    during toil,
Storing yearly little dues of wheat, and wine
    and oil;
Till they perish and they suffer—some, 'tis
    whispered—down in hell
Suffer endless anguish, others in Elysian
    valleys dwell,
Resting weary limbs at last on beds of as-
    phodel. 125
Surely, surely, slumber is more sweet than
    toil, the shore
Than labor in the deep mid-ocean, wind and
    wave and oar;
O, rest ye, brother mariners, we will not
    wander more.

YOU ASK ME, WHY, THOUGH ILL AT EASE [1]

You ask me, why, though ill at ease,
    Within this region I subsist,
    Whose spirits falter in the mist,
And languish for the purple seas.

It is the land that freemen till, 5
    That sober-suited Freedom chose,
    The land, where girt with friends or foes
A man may speak the thing he will;

A land of settled government,
    A land of just and old renown,
    Where Freedom slowly broadens down 10
From precedent to precedent;

Where faction seldom gathers head,
    But, by degrees to fullness wrought,
    The strength of some diffusive thought 15
Hath time and space to work and spread.

Should banded unions persecute
    Opinion, and induce a time
    When single thought is civil crime,
And individual freedom mute, 20

Though power should make from land to land
    The name of Britain trebly great—
    Though every channel of the State
Should fill and choke with golden sand—

Yet waft me from the harbor-mouth, 25
    Wild wind! I seek a warmer sky,
    And I will see before I die
The palms and temples of the South.

ULYSSES [1]

It little profits that an idle king,
By this still hearth, among these barren crags,
Matched with an aged wife, I mete[2] and dole
Unequal laws unto a savage race,
That hoard, and sleep, and feed, and know
    not me. 5
I cannot rest from travel; I will drink
Life to the lees. All times I have enjoyed
Greatly, have suffered greatly, both with
    those

---

[1]Published in 1842.

[1]Published in 1842. This imagined speech of
Ulysses (essentially modern in character) after his
return to Ithaca and Penelope (his "aged wife")
was suggested to Tennyson, not by Homer, but by
Dante's *Inferno*, xxvi, 90–142.

[2]Measure.

That loved me, and alone; on shore, and
    when
Through scudding drifts the rainy Hyades[3] 10
Vexed the dim sea. I am become a name;
For always roaming with a hungry heart
Much have I seen and known,—cities of men
And manners, climates, councils, govern-
    ments,
Myself not least, but honored of them all,—
And drunk delight of battle with my peers, 16
Far on the ringing plains of windy Troy.
I am a part of[4] all that I have met;
Yet all experience is an arch wherethrough
Gleams that untraveled world whose margin
    fades   20
For ever and for ever when I move.
How dull it is to pause, to make an end,
To rust unburnished, not to shine in use!
As though to breathe were life! Life piled
    on life
Were all too little, and of one to me   25
Little remains; but every hour is saved
From that eternal silence, something more,
A bringer of new things; and vile it were
For some three suns to store and hoard my-
    self,
And this gray spirit yearning in desire   30
To follow knowledge like a sinking star,
Beyond the utmost bound of human thought.
    This is my son, mine own Telemachus,
To whom I leave the scepter and the isle,—
Well-loved of me, discerning to fulfil   35
This labor, by slow prudence to make mild
A rugged people, and through soft degrees
Subdue them to the useful and the good.
Most blameless is he, centered in the sphere
Of common duties, decent not to fail   40
In offices of tenderness, and pay
Meet adoration to my household gods,
When I am gone. He works his work, I
    mine.
    There lies the port; the vessel puffs her
    sail;
There gloom the dark, broad seas. My
    mariners,   45
Souls that have toiled, and wrought, and
    thought with me,—
That ever with a frolic welcome took
The thunder and the sunshine, and opposed
Free hearts, free foreheads,—you and I are
    old;
Old age hath yet his honor and his toil.   50
Death closes all; but something ere the end,

Some work of noble note, may yet be done,
Not unbecoming men that strove with Gods.
The lights begin to twinkle from the rocks;
The long day wanes; the slow moon climbs;
    the deep   55
Moans round with many voices. Come, my
    friends.
'Tis not too late to seek a newer world.
Push off, and sitting well in order smite
The sounding furrows; for my purpose holds
To sail beyond the sunset, and the baths   60
Of all the western stars, until I die.
It may be that the gulfs will wash us down;
It may be we shall touch the Happy Isles,
And see the great Achilles, whom we knew.
Though much is taken, much abides; and
    though   65
We are not now that strength which in old
    days
Moved earth and heaven, that which we are,
    we are,—
One equal temper of heroic hearts,
Made weak by time and fate, but strong in
    will
To strive, to seek, to find, and not to yield. 70

TITHONUS[1]

The woods decay, the woods decay and fall,
The vapors weep their burthen to the ground,
Man comes and tills the field and lies beneath,
And after many a summer dies the swan.
Me only cruel immortality   5
Consumes; I wither slowly in thine arms,
Here at the quiet limit of the world,
A white-haired shadow roaming like a dream
The ever-silent spaces of the East,
Far-folded mists, and gleaming halls of
    morn.   10
    Alas! for this gray shadow, once a man—
So glorious in his beauty and thy choice,
Who madest him thy chosen, that he seemed
To his great heart none other than a God!
I asked thee, "Give me immortality."   15
Then didst thou grant mine asking with a
    smile,
Like wealthy men who care not how they
    give.

---

[3] A group of seven stars whose rising and setting were anciently believed to be accompanied by much rain.

[4] I. e., I am known by.

[1] Published in 1860. The story of this poem is to be found in the Homeric *Hymn to Aphrodite*, 218–239. Tithonus was loved by Aurora, goddess of dawn, who made him immortal at his request. He, however, had neglected to ask for the perpetuation of his youth, so that he grew slowly older and more decrepit until he finally asked the goddess for death. As she could not give him death, she changed him into a grasshopper.

But thy strong Hours[2] indignant worked
    their wills,
And beat me down and marred and wasted
    me,
And though they could not end me, left me
    maimed   20
To dwell in presence of immortal youth,
Immortal age beside immortal youth,
And all I was in ashes. Can thy love,
Thy beauty, make amends, though even now,
Close over us, the silver star, thy guide, 25
Shines in those tremulous eyes that fill with
    tears
To hear me? Let me go; take back thy gift.
Why should a man desire in any way
To vary from the kindly race of men,
Or pass beyond the goal of ordinance   30
Where all should pause, as is most meet for
    all?
  A soft air fans the cloud apart; there
    comes
A glimpse of that dark world where I was
    born.
Once more the old mysterious glimmer steals
From thy pure brows, and from thy shoul-
    ders pure,   35
And bosom beating with a heart renewed.
Thy cheek begins to redden through the
    gloom,
Thy sweet eyes brighten slowly close to mine,
Ere yet they blind the stars, and the wild
    team[3]
Which love thee, yearning for thy yoke, arise,
And shake the darkness from their loosened
    manes,   41
And beat the twilight into flakes of fire.
  Lo! ever thus thou growest beautiful
In silence, then before thine answer given
Departest, and thy tears are on my cheek. 45

Why wilt thou ever scare me with thy
    tears,
And make me tremble lest a saying learnt,
In days far-off, on that dark earth, be true?
"The Gods themselves cannot recall their
    gifts."
  Ay me! ay me! with what another heart 50
In days far-off, and with what other eyes
I used to watch—if I be he that watched—
The lucid outline forming round thee; saw
The dim curls kindle into sunny rings;
Changed with thy mystic change, and felt
    my blood   55
Glow with the glow that slowly crimsoned all
Thy presence and thy portals, while I lay,
Mouth, forehead, eyelids, growing dewy-
    warm
With kisses balmier than half-opening buds
Of April, and could hear the lips that
    kissed   60
Whispering I knew not what of wild and
    sweet,
Like that strange song I heard Apollo sing,
While Ilion like a mist rose into towers.[4]
  Yet hold me not for ever in thine East;
How can my nature longer mix with thine? 65
Coldly thy rosy shadows bathe me, cold
Are all thy lights, and cold my wrinkled feet
Upon thy glimmering thresholds, when the
    steam
Floats up from those dim fields about the
    homes
Of happy men that have the power to die, 70
And grassy barrows of the happier dead.
Release me, and restore me to the ground.
Thou seest all things, thou wilt see my grave;
Thou wilt renew thy beauty morn by morn,
I earth in earth forget these empty courts, 75
And thee returning on thy silver wheels.

---

[2]Goddesses of the seasons.
[3]The horses which drew Dawn's chariot.

[4]The walls of Ilion, or Troy, were said to have
arisen in obedience to Apollo's music.

LOCKSLEY HALL[1]

Comrades, leave me here a little, while as yet
    'tis early morn;
Leave me here and when you want me, sound
    upon the bugle-horn.

'Tis the place, and all around it, as of old, the
    curlews[2] call,
Dreary gleams about the moorland flying
    over Locksley Hall;

Locksley Hall, that in the distance overlooks
    the sandy tracts,   5
And the hollow ocean-ridges roaring into
    cataracts.

Many a night from yonder ivied casement,
    ere I went to rest,
Did I look on great Orion[3] sloping slowly to
    the west.

---

[1]Published in 1842.   [2]Birds of the snipe family.

[3]The constellation.

Many a night I saw the Pleiads,[4] rising
through the mellow shade,
Glitter like a swarm of fireflies tangled in a
silver braid. 10

Here about the beach I wandered, nourishing
a youth sublime
With the fairy tales of science, and the long
result of time;

When the centuries behind me like a fruitful
land reposed;
When I clung to all the present for the
promise that it closed;

When I dipped into the future far as human
eye could see, 15
Saw the vision of the world and all the
wonder that would be.—

In the spring a fuller crimson comes upon
the robin's breast;
In the spring the wanton lapwing gets himself another crest;

In the spring a livelier iris changes on the
burnished dove;
In the spring a young man's fancy lightly
turns to thoughts of love. 20

Then her cheek was pale and thinner than
should be for one so young,
And her eyes on all my motions with a mute
observance hung.

And I said, "My cousin Amy, speak, and
speak the truth to me,
Trust me, cousin, all the current of my being
sets to thee."

On her pallid cheek and forehead came a
color and a light, 25
As I have seen the rosy red flushing in the
northern night.

And she turned—her bosom shaken with a
sudden storm of sighs—
All the spirit deeply dawning in the dark of
hazel eyes—

Saying, "I have hid my feelings, fearing they
should do me wrong";
Saying, "Dost thou love me, cousin?" weeping, "I have loved thee long." 30

Love took up the glass of Time, and turned
it in his glowing hands;
Every moment, lightly shaken, ran itself in
golden sands.

[4] A group of stars.

Love took up the harp of Life, and smote on
all the chords with might;
Smote the chord of Self, that, trembling,
passed in music out of sight.

Many a morning on the moorland did we
hear the copses ring, 35
And her whisper thronged my pulses with
the fullness of the spring.

Many an evening by the waters did we watch
the stately ships,
And our spirits rushed together at the touching of the lips.

O my cousin, shallow-hearted! O my Amy,
mine no more!
O the dreary, dreary moorland! O the barren, barren shore! 40

Falser than all fancy fathoms, falser than all
songs have sung,
Puppet to a father's threat, and servile to a
shrewish tongue!

Is it well to wish thee happy?—having known
me—to decline
On a range of lower feelings and a narrower
heart than mine!

Yet it shall be; thou shalt lower to his level
day by day, 45
What is fine within thee growing coarse to
sympathize with clay.

As the husband is, the wife is; thou art mated
with a clown,[5]
And the grossness of his nature will have
weight to drag thee down.

He will hold thee, when his passion shall have
spent its novel force,
Something better than his dog, a little dearer
than his horse. 50

What is this? his eyes are heavy; think not
they are glazed with wine.
Go to him, it is thy duty; kiss him, take his
hand in thine.

It may be my lord is weary, that his brain is
overwrought;
Soothe him with thy finer fancies, touch him
with thy lighter thought.

He will answer to the purpose, easy things to
understand— 55
Better thou wert dead before me, though I
slew thee with my hand!

[5] Countryman.

Better thou and I were lying, hidden from the
    heart's disgrace,
Rolled in one another's arms, and silent in a
    last embrace.

Cursed be the social wants that sin against
    the strength of youth!
Cursed be the social lies that warp us from
    the living truth!   60

Cursed be the sickly forms that err from
    honest Nature's rule!
Cursed be the gold that gilds the straitened
    forehead of the fool!

Well—'tis well that I should bluster!—Hadst
    thou less unworthy proved—
Would to God—for I had loved thee more
    than ever wife was loved.

Am I mad, that I should cherish that which
    bears but bitter fruit?   65
I will pluck it from my bosom, though my
    heart be at the root.

Never, though my mortal summers to such
    length of years should come
As the many-wintered crow that leads the
    clanging rookery home.

Where is comfort? in division of the records
    of the mind?
Can I part her from herself, and love her, as
    I knew her, kind?   70

I remember one that perished; sweetly did
    she speak and move;
Such a one do I remember, whom to look at
    was to love.

Can I think of her as dead, and love her for
    the love she bore?
No—she never loved me truly; love is love
    for evermore.

Comfort? comfort scorned of devils![6] this is
    truth the poet[7] sings,   75
That a sorrow's crown of sorrow is remem-
    bering happier things.

Drug thy memories, lest thou learn it, lest
    thy heart be put to proof,
In the dead unhappy night, and when the
    rain is on the roof.

Like a dog, he hunts in dreams, and thou art
    staring at the wall,
Where the dying night-lamp flickers, and the
    shadows rise and fall.   80

[6]The allusion is to *Paradise Lost*, Bks. I and II.
[7]Dante, *Inferno*. v, 121-123.

Then a hand shall pass before thee, pointing
    to his drunken sleep,
To thy widowed marriage-pillows, to the
    tears that thou wilt weep.

Thou shalt hear the "Never, never," whis-
    pered by the phantom years,
And a song from out the distance in the
    ringing of thine ears;

And an eye shall vex thee, looking ancient
    kindness on thy pain.   85
Turn thee, turn thee on thy pillow; get thee
    to thy rest again.

Nay, but Nature brings thee solace; for a
    tender voice will cry.
'Tis a purer life than thine, a lip to drain thy
    trouble dry.

Baby lips will laugh me down; my latest rival
    brings thee rest.
Baby fingers, waxen touches, press me from
    the mother's breast.   90

O, the child too clothes the father with a
    dearness not his due.
Half is thine and half is his; it will be worthy
    of the two.

O, I see thee old and formal, fitted to thy
    petty part,
With a little hoard of maxims preaching
    down a daughter's heart.

"They were dangerous guides the feelings—
    she herself was not exempt—   95
Truly, she herself had suffered"—Perish in
    thy self-contempt!

Overlive it—lower yet—be happy! wherefore
    should I care?
I myself must mix with action, lest I wither
    by despair.

What is that which I should turn to, lighting
    upon days like these?
Every door is barred with gold, and opens
    but to golden keys.   100

Every gate is thronged with suitors, all the
    markets overflow.
I have but an angry fancy; what is that which
    I should do?

I had been content to perish, falling on the
    foeman's ground,
When the ranks are rolled in vapor, and the
    winds are laid with sound.

But the jingling of the guinea helps the hurt
  that Honor feels,   105
And the nations do but murmur, snarling at
  each other's heels.

Can I but relive in sadness? I will turn that
  earlier page.
Hide me from my deep emotion, O thou
  wondrous Mother-Age!

Make me feel the wild pulsation that I felt
  before the strife,
When I heard my days before me, and the
  tumult of my life;   110

Yearning for the large excitement that the
  coming years would yield,
Eager-hearted as a boy when first he leaves
  his father's field,

And at night along the dusky highway near
  and nearer drawn,
Sees in heaven the light of London flaring
  like a dreary dawn;

And his spirit leaps within him to be gone
  before him then,   115
Underneath the light he looks at, in among
  the throngs of men;

Men, my brothers, men the workers, ever
  reaping something new;
That which they have done but earnest of the
  things that they shall do.

For I dipped into the future, far as human
  eye could see,
Saw the Vision of the world, and all the
  wonder that would be;   120

Saw the heavens fill with commerce, argosies
  of magic sails,
Pilots of the purple twilight, dropping down
  with costly bales;

Heard the heavens fill with shouting, and
  there rained a ghastly dew
From the nations' airy navies grappling in
  the central blue;

Far along the world-wide whisper of the
  south-wind rushing warm,   125
With the standards of the peoples plunging
  through the thunder-storm;

Till the war-drum throbbed no longer, and
  the battle-flags were furled
In the Parliament of man, the Federation of
  the world.

There the common sense of most shall hold a
  fretful realm in awe,
And the kindly earth shall slumber, lapped
  in universal law.   130

So I triumphed ere my passion sweeping
  through me left me dry,
Left me with the palsied heart, and left me
  with the jaundiced eye;

Eye, to which all order festers, all things here
  are out of joint.
Science moves, but slowly, slowly, creeping
  on from point to point;

Slowly comes a hungry people, as a lion,
  creeping nigher,   135
Glares at one that nods and winks behind a
  slowly-dying fire.

Yet I doubt not through the ages one increasing purpose runs,
And the thoughts of men are widened with
  the process of the suns.

What is that to him that reaps not harvest
  of his youthful joys,
Though the deep heart of existence beat for
  ever like a boy's?   140

Knowledge comes, but wisdom lingers, and I
  linger on the shore,
And the individual withers, and the world is
  more and more.

Knowledge comes, but wisdom lingers, and
  he bears a laden breast,
Full of sad experience, moving toward the
  stillness of his rest.

Hark, my merry comrades call me, sounding
  on the bugle-horn,   145
They to whom my foolish passion were a
  target for their scorn.

Shall it not be scorn to me to harp on such
  a moldered string?
I am shamed through all my nature to have
  loved so slight a thing.

Weakness to be wroth with weakness! woman's pleasure, woman's pain—
Nature made them blinder motions bounded
  in a shallower brain.   150

Woman is the lesser man, and all thy passions, matched with mine,
Are as moonlight unto sunlight, and as water
  unto wine—

Here at least, where nature sickens, nothing.
    Ah, for some retreat
Deep in yonder shining Orient, where my
    life began to beat,

Where in wild Mahratta-battle[8] fell my
    father evil-starred;— 155
I was left a trampled orphan, and a selfish
    uncle's ward.

Or to burst all links of habit—there to wan-
    der far away,
On from island unto island at the gateways
    of the day.

Larger constellations burning, mellow moons
    and happy skies,
Breadths of tropic shade and palms in cluster,
    knots of Paradise. 160

Never comes the trader, never floats an Euro-
    pean flag,
Slides the bird o'er lustrous woodland, swings
    the trailer from the crag;

Droops the heavy-blossomed bower, hangs
    the heavy-fruited tree—
Summer isles of Eden lying in dark-purple
    spheres of sea.

There methinks would be enjoyment more
    than in this march of mind, 165
In the steamship, in the railway, in the
    thoughts that shake mankind.

There the passions cramped no longer shall
    have scope and breathing space;
I will take some savage woman, she shall rear
    my dusky race.

Iron-jointed, supple-sinewed, they shall dive,
    and they shall run,
Catch the wild goat by the hair, and hurl
    their lances in the sun; 170

Whistle back the parrot's call, and leap the
    rainbows of the brooks,
Not with blinded eyesight poring over mis-
    erable books—

Fool, again the dream, the fancy! but I *know*
    my words are wild,
But I count the gray barbarian lower than
    the Christian child.

[8]The Mahrattas are a Hindu people.

I, to herd with narrow foreheads, vacant of
    our glorious gains, 175
Like a beast with lower pleasures, like a
    beast with lower pains!

Mated with a squalid savage—what to me
    were sun or clime?
I the heir of all the ages, in the foremost files
    of time—

I that rather held it better men should perish
    one by one,
Than that earth should stand at gaze like
    Joshua's moon in Ajalon![9] 180

Not in vain the distance beacons. Forward,
    forward, let us range,
Let the great world spin for ever down the
    ringing grooves of change.[10]

Through the shadow of the globe we sweep
    into the younger day;
Better fifty years of Europe than a cycle of
    Cathay.[11]

Mother-Age,—for mine I knew not,—help
    me as when life begun; 185
Rift the hills, and roll the waters, flash the
    lightnings, weigh the sun.

O, I see the crescent promise of my spirit
    hath not set.
Ancient founts of inspiration well through
    all my fancy yet.

Howsoever these things be, a long farewell to
    Locksley Hall!
Now for me the woods may wither, now for
    me the roof-tree fall. 190

Comes a vapor from the margin, blackening
    over heath and holt,
Cramming all the blast before it, in its breast
    a thunderbolt.

Let it fall on Locksley Hall, with rain or
    hail or fire or snow;
For the mighty wind arises, roaring seaward,
    and I go.

[9]See Joshua, 10:12–13.
[10]Tennyson explained that when he rode on the
first train from Liverpool to Manchester in 1830 he
supposed that the wheels ran in grooves, and so used
the word in this line.
[11]China.

BREAK, BREAK, BREAK [1]

Break, break, break,
　On thy cold gray stones, O Sea!
And I would that my tongue could utter
　The thoughts that arise in me.

O well for the fisherman's boy,　　5
　That he shouts with his sister at play!
O well for the sailor lad,
　That he sings in his boat on the bay!

And the stately ships go on
　To their haven under the hill;　　10
But O for the touch of a vanished hand,
　And the sound of a voice that is still!

Break, break, break,
　At the foot of thy crags, O Sea!
But the tender grace of a day that is dead 15
　Will never come back to me.

SONGS FROM
THE PRINCESS [1]

I

The splendor falls on castle walls
　And snowy summits old in story;
The long light shakes across the lakes,
　And the wild cataract leaps in glory.
Blow, bugle, blow, set the wild echoes
　flying,　　5
Blow, bugle; answer, echoes, dying, dying,
　dying.

O hark, O hear! how thin and clear,
　And thinner, clearer, farther going!
O sweet and far from cliff and scar [2]
　The horns of Elfland faintly blowing! 10
Blow, let us hear the purple glens replying,
Blow, bugle; answer, echoes, dying, dying,
　dying.

O love, they die in yon rich sky,
　They faint on hill or field or river
Our echoes roll from soul to soul,　　15
　And grow for ever and for ever.

---

[1] Published in 1842. One of Tennyson's first attempts to express his grief over the death of A. H. Hallam.

[1] Published in 1847. The first of these songs was, however, added in 1848, and the third in 1850.

[2] Crag.

Blow, bugle, blow, set the wild echoes flying,
And answer, echoes, answer, dying, dying,
　dying.

II

Tears, idle tears, I know not what they
　mean,
Tears from the depth of some divine despair
Rise in the heart, and gather to the eyes,
In looking on the happy autumn-fields,
And thinking of the days that are no more. 5

Fresh as the first beam glittering on a sail,
That brings our friends up from the under-
　world,
Sad as the last which reddens over one
That sinks with all we love below the verge;
So sad, so fresh, the days that are no more. 10

Ah, sad and strange as in dark summer
　dawns
The earliest pipe of half-awakened birds
To dying ears, when unto dying eyes
The casement slowly grows a glimmering
　square;　　14
So sad, so strange, the days that are no more.

Dear as remembered kisses after death,
And sweet as those by hopeless fancy feigned
On lips that are for others; deep as love,
Deep as first love, and wild with all regret,
O Death in Life, the days that are no more! 20

III

Home they brought her warrior dead;
　She nor swooned nor uttered cry.
All her maidens, watching, said,
　"She must weep or she will die."

Then they praised him, soft and low,　　5
　Called him worthy to be loved,
Truest friend and noblest foe;
　Yet she neither spoke nor moved.

Stole a maiden from her place,
　Lightly to the warrior stepped,　　10
Took the face-cloth from the face;
　Yet she neither moved nor wept.

Rose a nurse of ninety years,
　Set his child upon her knee—
Like summer tempest came her tears— 15
　"Sweet my child, I live for thee."

IN MEMORIAM A. H. H.[1]

Strong Son of God, immortal Love,
  Whom we, that have not seen thy face,
  By faith, and faith alone, embrace
Believing where we cannot prove;

Thine are these orbs of light and shade; 5
  Thou madest Life in man and brute;
  Thou madest Death; and lo, thy foot
Is on the skull which thou hast made.

Thou wilt not leave us in the dust:
  Thou madest man, he knows not why, 10
  He thinks he was not made to die;
And thou hast made him: thou art just.

Thou seemest human and divine,
  The highest, holiest, manhood, thou.
  Our wills are ours, we know not how; 15
Our wills are ours, to make them thine.

Our little systems have their day;
  They have their day and cease to be;
  They are but broken lights of thee,
And thou, O Lord, art more than they. 20

We have but faith: we cannot know,
  For knowledge is of things we see;
  And yet we trust it comes from thee,
A beam in darkness: let it grow.

Let knowledge grow from more to more, 25
  But more of reverence in us dwell;
  That mind and soul, according well,
May make one music as before,

But vaster. We are fools and slight;
  We mock thee when we do not fear: 30
  But help thy foolish ones to bear;
Help thy vain worlds to bear thy light.

Forgive what seemed my sin in me,
  What seemed my worth since I began;
  For merit lives from man to man, 35
And not from man, O Lord, to thee.

Forgive my grief for one removed,
  Thy creature, whom I found so fair.
  I trust he lives in thee, and there
I find him worthier to be loved. 40

Forgive these wild and wandering cries,
  Confusions of a wasted youth;
  Forgive them where they fail in truth,
And in thy wisdom make me wise.

[1]Published in 1850. The poems were gradually written in the period between the death of Arthur Henry Hallam on 15 September, 1833, and the date of publication. At the time of his death Hallam was engaged to Tennyson's sister Emily. His body was brought to England by sea (he had died in Vienna) and was buried at Clevedon, on the Bristol Channel, on 3 January, 1834. Clevedon Court was the residence of Hallam's maternal grandfather. Tennyson says: "It must be remembered that this is a poem, *not* an actual biography. . . . The different moods of sorrow as in a drama are dramatically given, and my conviction that fear, doubts, and suffering will find answer and relief only through Faith in a God of Love. 'I' is not always the author speaking of himself, but the voice of the human race speaking through him." Tennyson also says: "The sections were written at many different places, and as the phases of our intercourse came to my memory and suggested them. I did not write them with any view of weaving them into a whole, or for publication, until I found that I had written so many." This circumstance of the poem's composition has given room for differences of opinion concerning the period of time covered in it. Some, imagining that Tennyson wrote, as it were, an historical record of his grief, and connecting allusions in the sections with actual happenings, hold that the period covered by the poem is 1833–1842. More probably, however, the internal chronology of the poem is independent of the actual order of events, and the period of time covered is not quite three years. The following table indicates the chronology, the Christmas sections marking the major divisions of the poem:

Section	XI,	Early Autumn, 1833.
	XV,	Later Autumn.
	XXVIII–XXX,	Christmas, 1833.
	XXXVIII–XXXIX,	Spring.
	LXXII,	First Anniversary, September, 1834.
	LXXVIII,	Christmas, 1834.
	LXXXIII,	Delaying Spring.
	LXXXVI,	
	LXXXVIII,	Spring.
	LXXXIX, XCV,	
	XCVIII,	Summer.
	XCIX,	Second Anniversary.
	CIV, CV,	Christmas, 1835.
	CVI,	New Year's Day.
	CVII,	Winter.
	CXV, CXVI,	Spring.

Tennyson sometimes referred to *In Memoriam* as "The Way of the Soul"; it is "a journey from the first stupor and confusion of grief, through a growing acquiescence often disturbed by the recurrence of pain, to an almost unclouded peace and joy. The anguish of wounded love passes into the triumph of love over sorrow, time, and death. The soul, at first, almost sunk in the feeling of loss, finds itself at last freed from regret and yet strengthened in affection. It pines no longer for the vanished hand and silent voice; it is filled with the consciousness of union with the spirit. The world, which once seemed to it a mere echo of its sorrow, has become the abode of that immortal Love, at once divine and human, which includes the living and the dead" (A. C. Bradley, *Commentary*, p. 27, from which the above table has also been adapted).

I

I held it truth, with him[2] who sings
  To one clear harp in divers tones,
  That men may rise on stepping-stones
Of their dead selves to higher things.

But who shall so forecast the years   5
  And find in loss a gain to match?
  Or reach a hand through time to catch
The far-off interest of tears?

Let Love clasp Grief lest both be drowned,
  Let darkness keep her raven gloss.   10
  Ah, sweeter to be drunk with loss,
To dance with Death, to beat the ground,

Than that the victor Hours should scorn
  The long result of love, and boast,
  "Behold the man that loved and lost,   15
But all he was is overworn."

II

Old yew, which graspest at the stones
  That name the underlying dead,
  Thy fibers net the dreamless head,
Thy roots are wrapped about the bones.

The seasons bring the flower again,   5
  And bring the firstling to the flock;
  And in the dusk of thee the clock
Beats out the little lives of men.

O, not for thee the glow, the bloom,
  Who changest not in any gale,   10
  Nor branding summer suns avail
To touch thy thousand years of gloom;

And gazing on thee, sullen tree,
  Sick for thy stubborn hardihood,
  I seem to fail from out my blood   15
And grow incorporate into thee.

III

O Sorrow, cruel fellowship,
  O Priestess in the vaults of Death,
  O sweet and bitter in a breath,
What whispers from thy lying lip?

"The stars," she whispers, "blindly run;   5
  A web is woven across the sky;
  From out waste places comes a cry,
And murmurs from the dying sun;

---

[2]Tennyson thought, in 1880, that his allusion was
to Goethe.

"And all the phantom, Nature, stands—
  With all the music in her tone,   10
  A hollow echo of my own,—
A hollow form with empty hands."

And shall I take a thing so blind,
  Embrace her as my natural good;
  Or crush her, like a vice of blood,   15
Upon the threshold of the mind?

IV

To Sleep I give my powers away;
  My will is bondsman to the dark;
  I sit within a helmless bark,
And with my heart I muse and say:

O heart, how fares it with thee now,   5
  That thou shouldst fail from thy desire,
  Who scarcely darest to inquire,
"What is it makes me beat so low?"

Something it is which thou hast lost,
  Some pleasure from thine early years.   10
  Break, thou deep vase of chilling tears,
That grief hath shaken into frost!

Such clouds of nameless trouble cross
  All night below the darkened eyes;
  With morning wakes the will, and cries,   15
"Thou shalt not be the fool of loss."

V

I sometimes hold it half a sin
  To put in words the grief I feel;
  For words, like Nature, half reveal
And half conceal the Soul within.

But, for the unquiet heart and brain,   5
  A use in measured language lies;
  The sad mechanic exercise,
Like dull narcotics, numbing pain.

In words, like weeds, I'll wrap me o'er,
  Like coarsest clothes against the cold;   10
  But that large grief which these enfold
Is given in outline and no more.

VI

One writes, that "other friends remain,"
  That "loss is common to the race"—
  And common is the commonplace,
And vacant chaff well meant for grain.

That loss is common would not make   5
  My own less bitter, rather more.
  Too common! Never morning wore
To evening, but some heart did break.

O father, wheresoe'er thou be,
   Who pledgest now thy gallant son,   10
   A shot, ere half thy draught be done,
Hath stilled the life that beat from thee.

O mother, praying God will save
   Thy sailor,—while thy head is bowed,
   His heavy-shotted hammock-shroud   15
Drops in his vast and wandering grave.

Ye know no more than I who wrought
   At that last hour to please him well;
   Who mused on all I had to tell,   19
And something written, something thought;

Expecting still his advent home;
   And ever met him on his way
   With wishes, thinking, "here to-day,"
Or "here to-morrow will he come."

O, somewhere, meek, unconscious dove,   25
   That sittest ranging golden hair;
   And glad to find thyself so fair,
Poor child, that waitest for thy love!

For now her father's chimney glows
   In expectation of a guest;   30
   And thinking "this will please him best,"
She takes a riband or a rose:

For he will see them on to-night;
   And with the thought her color burns;
   And, having left the glass, she turns   35
Once more to set a ringlet right;

And, even when she turned, the curse
   Had fallen, and her future lord
   Was drowned in passing through the ford,
Or killed in falling from his horse.   40

O, what to her shall be the end?
   And what to me remains of good?
   To her perpetual maidenhood,
And unto me no second friend.

VII

Dark house,[3] by which once more I stand
   Here in the long unlovely street,
   Doors, where my heart was used to beat
So quickly, waiting for a hand,

A hand that can be clasped no more—   5
   Behold me, for I cannot sleep,
   And like a guilty thing I creep
At earliest morning to the door.

---

[3]In which Hallam lived, in London.

He is not here; but far away
   The noise of life begins again,   10
   And ghastly through the drizzling rain
On the bald street breaks the blank day.

VIII

A happy lover who has come
   To look on her that loves him well,
   Who 'lights and rings the gateway bell,
And learns her gone and far from home;

He saddens, all the magic light   5
   Dies off at once from bower and hall,
   And all the place is dark, and all
The chambers emptied of delight:

So find I every pleasant spot
   In which we two were wont to meet,   10
   The field, the chamber, and the street,
For all is dark where thou art not.

Yet as that other, wandering there
   In those deserted walks, may find
   A flower beat with rain and wind,   15
Which once she fostered up with care;

So seems it in my deep regret,
   O my forsaken heart, with thee
   And this poor flower of poesy
Which, little cared for, fades not yet.   20

But since it pleased a vanished eye,
   I go to plant it on his tomb,
   That if it can it there may bloom,
Or, dying, there at least may die.

IX

Fair ship, that from the Italian shore[4]
   Sailest the placid ocean-plains
   With my lost Arthur's loved remains,
Spread thy full wings, and waft him o'er.

So draw him home to those that mourn   5
   In vain; a favorable speed
   Ruffle thy mirrored mast, and lead
Through prosperous floods his holy urn.

All night no ruder air perplex
   Thy sliding keel, till Phosphor,[5] bright   10
   As our pure love, through early light
Shall glimmer on the dewy decks.

---

[4]Hallam's body was brought to England by sea, from Trieste.

[5]The morning star.

Sphere all your lights around, above;
  Sleep, gentle heavens, before the prow;
  Sleep, gentle winds, as he sleeps now,   15
My friend, the brother of my love;

My Arthur, whom I shall not see
  Till all my widowed race be run;
  Dear as the mother to the son,
More than my brothers are to me.   20

X

I hear the noise about thy keel;
  I hear the bell struck in the night;
  I see the cabin-window bright;
I see the sailor at the wheel.

Thou bring'st the sailor to his wife,   5
  And traveled men from foreign lands;
  And letters unto trembling hands;
And, thy dark freight, a vanished life.

So bring him; we have idle dreams;
  This look of quiet flatters thus   10
  Our home-bred fancies. O, to us,
The fools of habit, sweeter seems

To rest beneath the clover sod,
  That takes the sunshine and the rains,
  Or where the kneeling hamlet drains   15
The chalice of the grapes of God;

Than if with thee the roaring wells
  Should gulf him fathom-deep in brine,
  And hands so often clasped in mine,
Should toss with tangle and with shells.   20

XI

Calm is the morn without a sound,
  Calm as to suit a calmer grief,
  And only through the faded leaf
The chestnut pattering to the ground;

Calm and deep peace on this high wold,[6]   5
  And on these dews that drench the furze,
  And all the silvery gossamers
That twinkle into green and gold;

Calm and still light on yon great plain
  That sweeps with all its autumn bowers,   10
  And crowded farms and lessening towers,
To mingle with the bounding main;[7]

Calm and deep peace in this wide air,
  These leaves that redden to the fall,
  And in my heart, if calm at all,   15
If any calm, a calm despair;

---

[6] Open country.   [7] Limiting sea.

Calm on the seas, and silver sleep,
  And waves that sway themselves in rest,
  And dead calm in that noble breast
Which heaves but with the heaving deep.   20

XII

Lo, as a dove when up she springs
  To bear through heaven a tale of woe,
  Some dolorous message knit below
The wild pulsation of her wings;

Like her I go, I cannot stay;   5
  I leave this mortal ark behind,
  A weight of nerves without a mind,
And leave the cliffs, and haste away

O'er ocean-mirrors rounded large,
  And reach the glow of southern skies,   10
  And see the sails at distance rise,
And linger weeping on the marge,

And saying, "Comes he thus, my friend?
  Is this the end of all my care?"
  And circle moaning in the air,   15
"Is this the end? Is this the end?"

And forward dart again, and play
  About the prow, and back return
  To where the body sits, and learn
That I have been an hour away.   20

XIII

Tears of the widower, when he sees
  A late-lost form that sleep reveals,
  And moves his doubtful arms, and feels
Her place is empty, fall like these;

Which weep a loss for ever new,   5
  A void where heart on heart reposed;
  And, where warm hands have pressed and
    closed,
Silence, till I be silent too;

Which weep the comrade of my choice,
  An awful thought, a life removed,   10
  The human-hearted man I loved,
A Spirit, not a breathing voice.

Come, Time, and teach me, many years,
  I do not suffer in a dream;
  For now so strange do these things seem,   15
Mine eyes have leisure for their tears,

My fancies time to rise on wing,
  And glance about the approaching sails,
  As though they brought but merchants'
    bales,
And not the burthen that they bring.   20

XIV

If one should bring me this report,
　That thou hadst touched the land to-day,
　And I went down unto the quay,
And found thee lying in the port;

And standing, muffled round with woe,　5
　Should see thy passengers in rank
　Come stepping lightly down the plank,
And beckoning unto those they know;

And if along with these should come
　The man I held as half-divine,　10
　Should strike a sudden hand in mine,
And ask a thousand things of home;

And I should tell him all my pain,
　And how my life had drooped of late,
　And he should sorrow o'er my state　15
And marvel what possessed my brain;

And I perceived no touch of change,
　No hint of death in all his frame,
　But found him all in all the same,
I should not feel it to be strange.　20

XV

To-night the winds begin to rise
　And roar from yonder dropping day;
　The last red leaf is whirled away,
The rooks are blown about the skies;

The forest cracked, the waters curled,　5
　The cattle huddled on the lea;
　And wildly dash'd on tower and tree
The sunbeam strikes along the world:

And but for fancies, which aver
　That all thy motions gently pass　10
　Athwart a plane of molten glass,[8]
I scarce could brook the strain and stir

That makes the barren branches loud;
　And but for fear it is not so,
　The wild unrest that lives in woe　15
Would dote and pore on yonder cloud

That rises upward always higher,
　And onward drags a laboring breast,
　And topples round the dreary west,
A looming bastion fringed with fire.　20

XVI

What words are these have fallen from me?
　Can calm despair and wild unrest
　Be tenants of a single breast,
Or Sorrow such a changeling be?

[8] Across a calm sea.

Or doth she only seem to take　5
　The touch of change in calm or storm,
　But knows no more of transient form
In her deep self, than some dead lake

That holds the shadow of a lark
　Hung in the shadow of a heaven?　10
　Or has the shock, so harshly given,
Confused me like the unhappy bark

That strikes by night a craggy shelf,
　And staggers blindly ere she sink?
　And stunned me from my power to think　15
And all my knowledge of myself;

And made me that delirious man
　Whose fancy fuses old and new,
　And flashes into false and true,
And mingles all without a plan?　20

XVII

Thou comest, much wept for; such a breeze
　Compelled thy canvas, and my prayer
　Was as the whisper of an air
To breathe thee over lonely seas.

For I in spirit saw thee move　5
　Through circles of the bounding sky,
　Week after week; the days go by;
Come quick, thou bringest all I love.

Henceforth, wherever thou mayst roam,
　My blessing, like a line of light,　10
　Is on the waters day and night,
And like a beacon guards thee home.

So may whatever tempest mars
　Mid-ocean spare thee, sacred bark,
　And balmy drops in summer dark　15
Slide from the bosom of the stars;

So kind an office hath been done,
　Such precious relics brought by thee,
　The dust of him I shall not see
Till all my widowed race be run.　20

XVIII

'Tis well; 'tis something; we may stand
　Where he in English earth is laid,
　And from his ashes may be made
The violet of his native land.

'Tis little; but it looks in truth　5
　As if the quiet bones were blest
　Among familiar names to rest
And in the places of his youth.

Come then, pure hands, and bear the head
  That sleeps or wears the mask of sleep, 10
  And come, whatever loves to weep,
And hear the ritual of the dead.

Ah yet, even yet, if this might be,
  I, falling on his faithful heart,
  Would breathing through his lips impart 15
The life that almost dies in me;

That dies not, but endures with pain,
  And slowly forms the firmer mind,
  Treasuring the look it cannot find,
The words that are not heard again. 20

XIX

The Danube to the Severn gave
  The darkened heart that beat no more;
  They laid him by the pleasant shore,
And in the hearing of the wave.[9]

There twice a day the Severn fills; 5
  The salt sea-water passes by,
  And hushes half the babbling Wye,
And makes a silence in the hills.

The Wye is hushed nor moved along,
  And hushed my deepest grief of all, 10
  When filled with tears that cannot fall,
I brim with sorrow drowning song.

The tide flows down, the wave again
  Is vocal in its wooded walls;
  My deeper anguish also falls, 15
And I can speak a little then.

XX

The lesser griefs that may be said,
  That breathe a thousand tender vows,
  Are but as servants in a house
Where lies the master newly dead;

Who speak their feeling as it is, 5
  And weep the fullness from the mind.
  "It will be hard," they say, "to find
Another service such as this."

My lighter moods are like to these,
  That out of words a comfort win; 10
  But there are other griefs within,
And tears that at their fountain freeze;

For by the hearth the children sit
  Cold in that atmosphere of death,
  And scarce endure to draw the breath, 15
Or like to noiseless phantoms flit;

[9]Clevedon Churchyard is near the point where the
Severn River flows into Bristol Channel.

But open cónverse is there none,
  So much the vital spirits sink
  To see the vacant chair, and think,
"How good! how kind! and he is gone." 20

XXI

I sing to him that rests below,
  And, since the grasses round me wave,
  I take the grasses of the grave,
And make them pipes whereon to blow.

The traveler hears me now and then, 5
  And sometimes harshly will he speak:
  "This fellow would make weakness weak,
And melt the waxen hearts of men."

Another answers: "Let him be,
  He loves to make parade of pain, 10
  That with his piping he may gain
The praise that comes to constancy."

A third is wroth: "Is this an hour
  For private sorrow's barren song,
  When more and more the people throng 15
The chairs and thrones of civil power?

"A time to sicken and to swoon,
  When Science reaches forth her arms
  To feel from world to world, and charms
Her secret from the latest moon?" 20

Behold, ye speak an idle thing;
  Ye never knew the sacred dust.
  I do but sing because I must,
And pipe but as the linnets sing;

And one is glad; her note is gay, 25
  For now her little ones have ranged;
  And one is sad; her note is changed,
Because her brood is stolen away.

XXII

The páth by which we twain did go,
  Which led by tracts that pleased us well,
  Through four sweet years arose and fell,
From flower to flower, from snow to snow;

And we with singing cheered the way, 5
  And, crowned with all the season lent,
  From April on to April went,
And glad at heart from May to May.

But where the path we walked began
  To slant the fifth autumnal slope, 10
  As we descended following Hope,
There sat the Shadow feared of man;

Who broke our fair companionship,
  And spread his mantle dark and cold,
  And wrapped thee formless in the fold, 15
And dulled the murmur on thy lip,

And bore thee where I could not see
  Nor follow, though I walk in haste,
  And think that somewhere in the waste
The Shadow sits and waits for me. 20

XXIII

Now, sometimes in my sorrow shut,
  Or breaking into song by fits,
  Alone, alone, to where he sits,
The Shadow cloaked from head to foot,[10]

Who keeps the keys of all the creeds, 5
  I wander, often falling lame,
  And looking back to whence I came,
Or on to where the pathway leads;

And crying, How changed from where it ran
  Through lands where not a leaf was dumb,
  But all the lavish hills would hum 11
The murmur of a happy Pan;

When each by turns was guide to each,
  And Fancy light from Fancy caught,
  And Thought leapt out to wed with
    Thought 15
Ere Thought could wed itself with Speech,

And all we met was fair and good,
  And all was good that Time could bring,
  And all the secret of the Spring
Moved in the chambers of the blood; 20

And many an old philosophy
  On Argive heights divinely sang,
  And round us all the thicket rang
To many a flute of Arcady.[11]

XXIV

And was the day of my delight
  As pure and perfect as I say?
  The very source and fount of day
Is dashed with wandering isles of night.

If all was good and fair we met, 5
  This earth had been the Paradise
  It never looked to human eyes
Since our first sun arose and set.

And is it that the haze of grief
  Makes former gladness loom so great? 10
  The lowness of the present state,
That sets the past in this relief?

[10]Death.

[11]The allusion is to Greek philosophy and poetry.

Or that the past will always win
  A glory from its being far,
  And orb into the perfect star 15
We saw not when we moved therein?

XXV

I know that this was Life,—the track
  Whereon with equal feet we fared;
  And then, as now, the day prepared
The daily burden for the back.

But this it was that made me move 5
  As light as carrier-birds in air;
  I loved the weight I had to bear,
Because it needed help of Love;

Nor could I weary, heart or limb,
  When mighty Love would cleave in
    twain 10
  The lading of a single pain,
And part it, giving half to him.

XXVI

Still onward winds the dreary way;
  I with it, for I long to prove
  No lapse of moons can canker Love,
Whatever fickle tongues may say.

And if that eye which watches guilt 5
  And goodness, and hath power to see
  Within the green the moldered tree,
And towers fallen as soon as built—

O, if indeed that eye foresee
  Or see—in Him is no before— 10
  In more of life true life no more
And Love the indifference to be,

Then might I find, ere yet the morn
  Breaks hither over Indian seas,
  That Shadow waiting with the keys, 15
To shroud me from my proper scorn.

XXVII

I envy not in any moods
  The captive void of noble rage,
  The linnet born within the cage,
That never knew the summer woods;

I envy not the beast that takes 5
  His license in the field of time,
  Unfettered by the sense of crime,
To whom a conscience never wakes;

Nor, what may count itself as blest,
  The heart that never plighted troth 10
  But stagnates in the weeds of sloth;
Nor any want-begotten rest.

I hold it true, whate'er befall;
　I feel it, when I sorrow most;
　'Tis better to have loved and lost   15
Than never to have loved at all.

XXVIII

The time draws near the birth of Christ.
　The moon is hid, the night is still;
　The Christmas bells from hill to hill
Answer each other in the mist.

Four voices of four hamlets round,   5
　From far and near, on mead and moor,
　Swell out and fail, as if a door
Were shut between me and the sound;

Each voice four changes on the wind,
　That now dilate, and now decrease,   10
　Peace and goodwill, goodwill and peace,
Peace and goodwill, to all mankind.

This year I slept and woke with pain,
　I almost wished no more to wake,
　And that my hold on life would break   15
Before I heard those bells again;

But they my troubled spirit rule,
　For they controlled me when a boy;
　They bring me sorrow touched with joy,
The merry, merry bells of Yule.   20

XXIX

With such compelling cause to grieve
　As daily vexes household peace,
　And chains regret to his decease,
How dare we keep our Christmas-eve,

Which brings no more a welcome guest   5
　To enrich the threshold of the night
　With showered largess of delight
In dance and song and game and jest?

Yet go, and while the holly boughs
　Entwine the cold baptismal font,   10
　Make one wreath more for Use and Wont,
That guard the portals of the house;

Old sisters of a day gone by,
　Gray nurses, loving nothing new—
　Why should they miss their yearly due   15
Before their time? They too will die.

XXX

With trembling fingers did we weave
　The holly round the Christmas hearth;
　A rainy cloud possessed the earth,
And sadly fell our Christmas-eve.

At our old pastimes in the hall   5
　We gamboled, making vain pretense
　Of gladness, with an awful sense
Of one mute Shadow watching all.

We paused: the winds were in the beech;
　We heard them sweep the winter land;   10
　And in a circle hand-in-hand
Sat silent, looking each at each.

Then echo-like our voices rang;
　We sung, though every eye was dim,
　A merry song we sang with him   15
Last year; impetuously we sang.

We ceased; a gentler feeling crept
　Upon us: surely rest is meet.
　"They rest," we said, "their sleep is
　　sweet,"
And silence followed, and we wept.   20

Our voices took a higher range;
　Once more we sang: "They do not die
　Nor lose their mortal sympathy,
Nor change to us, although they change;

"Rapt from the fickle and the frail   25
　With gathered power, yet the same,
　Pierces the keen seraphic flame
From orb to orb, from veil to veil."

Rise, happy morn, rise, holy morn,
　Draw forth the cheerful day from night: 30
　O Father, touch the east, and light
The light that shone when Hope was born.

XXXI

When Lazarus left his charnel-cave,
　And home to Mary's house returned,
　Was this demanded—if he yearned
To hear her weeping by his grave?

"Where wert thou, brother, those four days?"
　There lives no record of reply,   6
　Which telling what it is to die
Had surely added praise to praise.

From every house the neighbors met,
　The streets were filled with joyful sound, 10
　A solemn gladness even crowned
The purple brows of Olivet.

Behold a man raised up by Christ!
　The rest remaineth unrevealed;
　He told it not, or something sealed   15
The lips of that Evangelist.[12]

---

[12] St. John 11:1–44.

XXXII

Her eyes[13] are homes of silent prayer,
  Nor other thought her mind admits
  But, he was dead, and there he sits,
And he that brought him back is there.

Then one deep love doth supersede   5
  All other, when her ardent gaze
  Roves from the living brother's face,
And rests upon the Life indeed.

All subtle thought, all curious fears,
  Borne down by gladness so complete, 10
  She bows, she bathes the Savior's feet
With costly spikenard and with tears.

Thrice blest whose lives are faithful prayers,
  Whose loves in higher love endure;
  What souls possess themselves so pure, 15
Or is there blessedness like theirs?

XXXIII

O thou that after toil and storm
  Mayst seem to have reached a purer air,
  Whose faith has center everywhere,
Nor cares to fix itself to form,

Leave thou thy sister when she prays   5
  Her early heaven, her happy views;
  Nor thou with shadowed hint confuse
A life that leads melodious days.

Her faith through form is pure as thine,
  Her hands are quicker unto good. 10
  O, sacred be the flesh and blood
To which she links a truth divine!

See thou, that countest reason ripe
  In holding by the law within,
  Thou fail not in a world of sin, 15
And even for want of such a type.

XXXIV

My own dim life should teach me this,
  That life shall live for evermore,
  Else earth is darkness at the core,
And dust and ashes all that is;

This round of green, this orb of flame,   5
  Fantastic beauty; such as lurks
  In some wild poet, when he works
Without a conscience or an aim.

What then were God to such as I?
  'Twere hardly worth my while to choose 10
  Of things all mortal, or to use
A little patience ere I die;

[13]The eyes of Mary, the sister of Lazarus.

'Twere best at once to sink to peace,
  Like birds the charming serpent draws
  To drop head-foremost in the jaws 15
Of vacant darkness and to cease.

XXXV

Yet if some voice that man could trust
  Should murmur from the narrow house,
  "The cheeks drop in, the body bows;
Man dies, nor is there hope in dust;"

Might I not say? "Yet even here,   5
  But for one hour, O Love, I strive
  To keep so sweet a thing alive."
But I should turn mine ears and hear

The moanings of the homeless sea,
  The sound of streams that swift or slow 10
  Draw down Aeonian[14] hills, and sow
The dust of continents to be;

And Love would answer with a sigh,
  "The sound of that forgetful shore
  Will change my sweetness more and
    more, 15
Half-dead to know that I shall die."

O me, what profits it to put
  An idle case? If Death were seen
  At first as Death, Love had not been,
Or been in narrowest working shut, 20

Mere fellowship of sluggish moods,
  Or in his coarsest Satyr-shape
  Had bruised the herb and crushed the
    grape,
And basked and battened[15] in the woods.

XXXVI

Though truths in manhood darkly join,
  Deep-seated in our mystic frame,
  We yield all blessing to the name
Of Him that made them current coin;

For Wisdom dealt with mortal powers,   5
  Where truth in closest words shall fail,
  When truth embodied in a tale
Shall enter in at lowly doors.

And so the Word had breath, and wrought
  With human hands the creed of creeds 10
  In loveliness of perfect deeds,
More strong than all poetic thought;

[14]Everlasting.   [15]Fed.

Which he may read that binds the sheaf,
  Or builds the house, or digs the grave,
  And those wild eyes that watch the wave 15
In roarings round the coral reef.

XXXVII

Urania[16] speaks with darkened brow:
  "Thou pratest here where thou art least;
  This faith has many a purer priest,
And many an abler voice than thou.

"Go down beside thy native rill,   5
  On thy Parnassus[17] set thy feet,
  And hear thy laurel whisper sweet
About the ledges of the hill."

And my Melpomene[18] replies,
  A touch of shame upon her cheek: 10
  "I am not worthy even to speak
Of thy prevailing mysteries;

"For I am but an earthly Muse,
  And owning but a little art
  To lull with song an aching heart,   15
And render human love his dues;

"But brooding on the dear one dead,
  And all he said of things divine,—
  And dear to me as sacred wine
To dying lips is all he said,—   20

"I murmured, as I came along,
  Of comfort clasped in truth revealed,
  And loitered in the master's field,
And darkened sanctities with song."

XXXVIII

With weary steps I loiter on,
  Though always under altered skies
  The purple from the distance dies,
My prospect and horizon gone.

No joy the blowing season gives,   5
  The herald melodies of spring,
  But in the songs I love to sing
A doubtful gleam of solace lives.

If any care for what is here
  Survive in spirits rendered free,   10
  Then are these songs I sing of thee
Not all ungrateful to thine ear.

[16]The heavenly muse, who reproves the poet for touching on revealed truth.
[17]The hill sacred to Apollo and the muses. The laurel, with which poets were crowned, grows on its slopes.
[18]Muse of tragedy, in this instance of elegy.

XXXIX

Old warder of these buried bones,
  And answering now my random stroke
  With fruitful cloud and living smoke,
Dark yew, that graspest at the stones

And dippest toward the dreamless head,   5
  To thee too comes the golden hour
  When flower is feeling after flower;
But Sorrow,—fixed upon the dead,

And darkening the dark graves of men,—
  What whispered from her lying lips?   10
  Thy gloom is kindled at the tips,
And passes into gloom again.

XL

Could we forget the widowed hour
  And look on Spirits breathed away,
  As on a maiden in the day
When first she wears her orange-flower!

When crowned with blessing she doth rise 5
  To take her latest leave of home,
  And hopes and light regrets that come
Make April of her tender eyes;

And doubtful joys the father move,
  And tears are on the mother's face,   10
  As parting with a long embrace
She enters other realms of love;

Her office there to rear, to teach,
  Becoming as is meet and fit
  A link among the days, to knit   15
The generations each with each;

And, doubtless, unto thee is given
  A life that bears immortal fruit
  In those great offices that suit
The full-grown energies of heaven.   20

Ay me, the difference I discern!
  How often shall her old fireside
  Be cheered with tidings of the bride,
How often she herself return,

And tell them all they would have told,   25
  And bring her babe, and make her boast,
  Till even those that missed her most
Shall count new things as dear as old;

But thou and I have shaken hands,
  Till growing winters lay me low;   30
  My paths are in the fields I know,
And thine in undiscovered lands.

XLI

Thy spirit ere our fatal loss
  Did ever rise from high to higher,
  As mounts the heavenward altar-fire,
As flies the lighter through the gross.

But thou art turned to something strange,   5
  And I have lost the links that bound
  Thy changes; here upon the ground,
No more partaker of thy change.

Deep folly! yet that this could be—
  That I could wing my will with might   10
  To leap the grades of life and light,
And flash at once, my friend, to thee!

For though my nature rarely yields
  To that vague fear implied in death,
  Nor shudders at the gulfs beneath,   15
The howlings from forgotten fields;

Yet oft when sundown skirts the moor
  An inner trouble I behold,
  A spectral doubt which makes me cold,
That I shall be thy mate no more,   20

Though following with an upward mind
  The wonders that have come to thee,
  Through all the secular to-be,[19]
But ever more a life behind.

XLII

I vex my heart with fancies dim.
  He still outstripped me in the race;
  It was but unity of place
That made me dream I ranked with him.

And so may Place retain us still,   5
  And he the much-beloved again,
  A lord of large experience, train
To riper growth the mind and will;

And what delights can equal those
  That stir the spirit's inner deeps,   10
  When one that loves, but knows not, reaps
A truth from one that loves and knows?

XLIII

If Sleep and Death be truly one,
  And every spirit's folded bloom
  Through all its intervital gloom
In some long trance should slumber on;

Unconscious of the sliding hour,   5
  Bare of the body, might it last,
  And silent traces of the past
Be all the color of the flower:

[19]Through all the ages of the future.

So then were nothing lost to man;
  So that still garden of the souls   10
  In many a figured leaf enrolls
The total world since life began;

And love will last as pure and whole
  As when he loved me here in Time,
  And at the spiritual prime[20]   15
Rewaken with the dawning soul.

XLIV

How fares it with the happy dead?
  For here the man is more and more;
  But he forgets the days before
God shut the doorways of his head.[21]

The days have vanished, tone and tint,   5
  And yet perhaps the hoarding sense
  Gives out at times—he knows not
    whence—
A little flash, a mystic hint;

And in the long harmonious years—
  If Death so taste Lethean[22] springs—   10
  May some dim touch of earthly things
Surprise thee ranging with thy peers.

If such a dreamy touch should fall,
  O, turn thee round, resolve the doubt;
  My guardian angel will speak out   15
In that high place, and tell thee all.

XLV

The baby new to earth and sky,
  What time his tender palm is pressed
  Against the circle of the breast,
Has never thought that "this is I";

But as he grows he gathers much,   5
  And learns the use of "I" and "me,"
  And finds "I am not what I see,
And other than the things I touch."

[20]Dawn.

[21]The dead after this life may have no remembrance of life, like the living babe who forgets the time before the sutures of the skull are closed; yet the living babe grows in knowledge, and though the remembrance of his earliest days has vanished, yet with his increasing knowledge there comes a dreamy vision of what has been; it may be so with the dead; if so, resolve my doubts, *etc.* (Tennyson's note). The notion that Brahma enters the body through one of the sutures of the skull is found in the *Upanishads*, and Tennyson may have known this.

[22]Lethe was a river in Hades, the taste of whose waters brought forgetfulness.

So rounds he to a separate mind
　From whence clear memory may begin,　10
　As through the frame that binds him in
His isolation grows defined.

This use may lie in blood and breath,
　Which else were fruitless of their due,
　Had man to learn himself anew　15
Beyond the second birth of death.

XLVI

We ranging down this lower track,
　The path we came by, thorn and flower,
　Is shadowed by the growing hour,
Lest life should fail in looking back.

So be it: there no shade can last　5
　In that deep dawn behind the tomb,
　But clear from marge to marge shall bloom
The eternal landscape of the past;

A lifelong tract of time revealed,
　The fruitful hours of still increase;　10
　Days ordered in a wealthy peace,
And those five years its richest field.

O love, thy province were not large,
　A bounded field, nor stretching far;
　Look also, Love, a brooding star,　15
A rosy warmth from marge to marge.

XLVII

That each, who seems a separate whole,
　Should move his rounds, and fusing all
　The skirts of self again, should fall
Remerging in the general Soul,

Is faith as vague as all unsweet.　5
　Eternal form shall still divide
　The eternal soul from all beside;
And I shall know him when we meet;

And we shall sit at endless feast,
　Enjoying each the other's good.　10
　What vaster dream can hit the mood
Of Love on earth?　He seeks at least

Upon the last and sharpest height,
　Before the spirits fade away,
　Some landing-place, to clasp and say,　15
"Farewell!　We lose ourselves in light."

XLVIII

If these brief lays, of Sorrow born,
　Were taken to be such as closed
　Grave doubts and answers here proposed,
Then these were such as men might scorn.

Her care is not to part and prove;　5
　She takes, when harsher moods remit,
　What slender shade of doubt may flit,
And makes it vassal unto love;

And hence, indeed, she sports with words,
　But better serves a wholesome law,　10
　And holds it sin and shame to draw
The deepest measure from the chords;

Nor dare she trust a larger lay,
　But rather loosens from the lip
　Short swallow-flights of song, that dip　15
Their wings in tears, and skim away.

XLIX

From art, from nature, from the schools,
　Let random influences glance,
　Like light in many a shivered lance
That breaks about the dappled pools.

The lightest wave of thought shall lisp,　5
　The fancy's tenderest eddy wreathe,
　The slightest air of song shall breathe
To make the sullen surface crisp.[23]

And look thy look, and go thy way,
　But blame not thou the winds that make　10
　The seeming-wanton ripple break,
The tender-penciled shadow play.

Beneath all fancied hopes and fears
　Ay me, the sorrow deepens down,
　Whose muffled motions blindly drown　15
The bases of my life in tears.

L

Be near me when my light is low,
　When the blood creeps, and the nerves
　　prick
　And tingle; and the heart is sick,
And all the wheels of being slow.

Be near me when the sensuous frame　5
　Is racked with pangs that conquer trust;
　And Time, a maniac scattering dust,
And Life, a Fury slinging flame.

Be near me when my faith is dry,
　And men the flies of latter spring,　10
　That lay their eggs, and sting and sing
And weave their petty cells and die.

Be near me when I fade away,
　To point the term of human strife,
　And on the low dark verge of life　15
The twilight of eternal day.

---

[23]Rippled.

LI

Do we indeed desire the dead
    Should still be near us at our side?
    Is there no baseness we would hide?
No inner vileness that we dread?

Shall he for whose applause I strove,   5
    I had such reverence for his blame,
    See with clear eye some hidden shame
And I be lessened in his love?

I wrong the grave with fears untrue.
    Shall love be blamed for want of faith?   10
    There must be wisdom with great Death;
The dead shall look me through and through.

Be near us when we climb or fall;
    Ye watch, like God, the rolling hours
    With larger other eyes than ours,   15
To make allowance for us all.

LII

I cannot love thee as I ought,
    For love reflects the thing beloved;
    My words are only words, and moved
Upon the topmost froth of thought.

"Yet blame not thou thy plaintive song,"   5
    The Spirit of true love replied;
    "Thou canst not move me from thy side,
Nor human frailty do me wrong.

"What keeps a spirit wholly true
    To that ideal which he bears?   10
    What record? not the sinless years
That breathed beneath the Syrian blue,[24]

"So fret not, like an idle girl,
    That life is dashed with flecks of sin.
    Abide; thy wealth is gathered in,   15
When Time hath sundered shell from pearl."

LIII

How many a father have I seen,
    A sober man, among his boys,
    Whose youth was full of foolish noise,
Who wears his manhood hale and green;

And dare we to this fancy give,[25]   5
    That had the wild oat not been sown,
    The soil, left barren, scarce had grown
The grain by which a man may live?

[24]Not even the record of the life of Jesus.
[25]Yield.

Or, if we held the doctrine sound
    For life outliving heats of youth,   10
    Yet who would preach it as a truth
To those that eddy round and round?

Hold thou the good, define it well;
    For fear divine Philosophy
    Should push beyond her mark, and be   15
Procuress to the Lords of Hell.

LIV

O, yet we trust that somehow good
    Will be the final goal of ill,
    To pangs of nature, sins of will,
Defects of doubt, and taints of blood;

That nothing walks with aimless feet;   5
    That not one life shall be destroyed,
    Or cast as rubbish to the void,
When God hath made the pile complete;

That not a worm is cloven in vain;
    That not a moth with vain desire   10
    Is shriveled in a fruitless fire,
Or but subserves another's gain.

Behold, we know not anything;
    I can but trust that good shall fall
    At last—far off—at last, to all,   15
And every winter change to spring.

So runs my dream; but what am I?
    An infant crying in the night;
    An infant crying for the light,
And with no language but a cry.   20

LV

The wish, that of the living whole
    No life may fail beyond the grave,
    Derives it not from what we have
The likest God within the soul?

Are God and Nature then at strife,   5
    That Nature lends such evil dreams?
    So careful of the type she seems,
So careless of the single life,

That I, considering everywhere
    Her secret meaning in her deeds,
    And finding that of fifty seeds   10
She often brings but one to bear,

I falter where I firmly trod,
    And falling with my weight of cares
    Upon the great world's altar-stairs   15
That slope through darkness up to God,

I stretch lame hands of faith, and grope,
  And gather dust and chaff, and call
  To what I feel is Lord of all,
And faintly trust the larger hope.   20

LVI

"So careful of the type?" but no.
  From scarpèd cliff and quarried stone
  She cries, "A thousand types are gone;
I care for nothing, all shall go.

"Thou makest thine appeal to me: 5
  I bring to life, I bring to death;
  The spirit does but mean the breath:
I know no more." And he, shall he,

Man, her last work, who seemed so fair,
  Such splendid purpose in his eyes,   10
  Who rolled the psalm to wintry skies,
Who built him fanes of fruitless prayer,

Who trusted God was love indeed
  And love Creation's final law—
  Though Nature, red in tooth and claw   15
With ravine, shrieked against his creed—

Who loved, who suffered countless ills,
  Who battled for the True, the Just,
  Be blown about the desert dust,
Or sealed within the iron hills?   20

No more? A monster then, a dream,
  A discord. Dragons of the prime,[26]
  That tare each other in their slime,
Were mellow music matched with him.

O life as futile, then, as frail!   25
  O for thy voice to soothe and bless!
  What hope of answer, or redress?
Behind the veil, behind the veil.

LVII

Peace; come away: the song of woe
  Is after all an earthly song.
  Peace; come away: we do him wrong
To sing so wildly: let us go.

Come; let us go: your cheeks are pale;   5
  But half my life I leave behind.
  Methinks my friend is richly shrined;
But I shall pass, my work will fail.

Yet in these ears, till hearing dies,
  One set slow bell will seem to toll   10
  The passing of the sweetest soul
That ever looked with human eyes.

[26] Prehistoric monsters.

I hear it now, and o'er and o'er,
  Eternal greetings to the dead;
  And "Ave, Ave, Ave," said,   15
"Adieu, adieu," for evermore.

LVIII

In those sad words I took farewell.
  Like echoes in sepulchral halls,
  As drop by drop the water falls
In vaults and catacombs, they fell;

And, falling, idly broke the peace   5
  Of hearts that beat from day to day,
  Half-conscious of their dying clay,
And those cold crypts where they shall cease.

The high Muse answered: "Wherefore grieve
  Thy brethren with a fruitless tear?   10
  Abide a little longer here,
And thou shalt take a nobler leave."

LIX

O Sorrow, wilt thou live with me
  No casual mistress, but a wife,
  My bosom-friend and half of life;
As I confess it needs must be?

O Sorrow, wilt thou rule my blood,   5
  Be sometimes lovely like a bride,
  And put thy harsher moods aside,
If thou wilt have me wise and good?

My centered passion cannot move,
  Nor will it lessen from to-day;   10
  But I'll have leave at times to play
As with the creature of my love;

And set thee forth, for thou art mine,
  With so much hope for years to come,
  That, howsoe'er I know thee, some   15
Could hardly tell what name were thine.

LX

He passed, a soul of nobler tone;
  My spirit loved and loves him yet,
  Like some poor girl whose heart is set
On one whose rank exceeds her own.

He mixing with his proper sphere,   5
  She finds the baseness of her lot,
  Half jealous of she knows not what,
And envying all that meet him there.

The little village looks forlorn;
  She sighs amid her narrow days,   10
  Moving about the household ways,
In that dark house where she was born.

The foolish neighbors come and go,
    And tease her till the day draws by;
    At night she weeps, "How vain am I!   15
How should he love a thing so low?"

LXI

If, in thy second state sublime,
    Thy ransomed reason change replies
    With all the circle of the wise,
The perfect flower of human time;

And if thou cast thine eyes below,   5
    How dimly charactered and slight,
    How dwarfed a growth of cold and night,
How blanched with darkness must I grow!

Yet turn thee to the doubtful shore,
    Where thy first form was made a man; 10
    I loved thee, Spirit, and love, nor can
The soul of Shakespeare love thee more.

LXII

Though if an eye that's downward cast
    Could make thee somewhat blench or fail,
    Then be my love an idle tale
And fading legend of the past;

And thou, as one that once declined,   5
    When he was little more than boy,
    On some unworthy heart with joy,
But lives to wed an equal mind,

And breathes a novel world, the while
    His other passion wholly dies,   10
    Or in the light of deeper eyes
Is matter for a flying smile.

LXIII

Yet pity, for a horse o'er-driven,
    And love in which my hound has part,
    Can hang no weight upon my heart
In its assumptions up to heaven;

And I am so much more than these,   5
    As thou, perchance, art more than I,
    And yet I spare them sympathy,
And I would set their pains at ease.

So mayst thou watch me where I weep,
    As, unto vaster motions bound,   10
    The circuits of thine orbit round
A higher height, a deeper deep.

LXIV

Dost thou look back on what hath been,
    As some divinely gifted man,
    Whose life in low estate began
And on a simple village green;

Who breaks his birth's invidious bar,   5
    And grasps the skirts of happy chance,
    And breasts the blows of circumstance,
And grapples with his evil star;

Who makes by force his merit known
    And lives to clutch the golden keys,   10
    To mold a mighty state's decrees,
And shape the whisper of the throne;

And moving up from high to higher,
    Becomes on Fortune's crowning slope
    The pillar of a people's hope,   15
The center of a world's desire;

Yet feels, as in a pensive dream,
    When all his active powers are still,
    A distant dearness in the hill,
A secret sweetness in the stream,   20

The limit of his narrower fate,
    While yet beside its vocal springs
    He played at counselors and kings,
With one that was his earliest mate;

Who plows with pain his native lea   25
    And reaps the labor of his hands,
    Or in the furrow musing stands:
"Does my old friend remember me?"

LXV

Sweet soul, do with me as thou wilt;
    I lull a fancy trouble-tossed
    With "Love's too precious to be lost
A little grain shall not be spilt."

And in that solace can I sing,   5
    Till out of painful phases wrought
    There flutters up a happy thought,
Self-balanced on a lightsome wing;

Since we deserved the name of friends,
    And thine effect so lives in me,   10
    A part of mine may live in thee
And move thee on to noble ends.

LXVI

You thought my heart too far diseased;
    You wonder when my fancies play
    To find me gay among the gay,
Like one with any trifle pleased.

The shade by which my life was crossed,   5
  Which makes a desert in the mind,
  Has made me kindly with my kind,
And like to him whose sight is lost;

Whose feet are guided through the land,
  Whose jest among his friends is free,   10
  Who takes the children on his knee,
And winds their curls about his hand.

He plays with threads, he beats his chair
  For pastime, dreaming of the sky;
  His inner day can never die,   15
His night of loss is always there.

LXVII

When on my bed the moonlight falls,
  I know that in thy place of rest
  By that broad water of the west
There comes a glory on the walls:

Thy marble bright in dark appears,   5
  As slowly steals a silver flame
  Along the letters of thy name,
And o'er the number of thy years.

The mystic glory swims away,
  From off my bed the moonlight dies;   10
  And closing eaves of wearied eyes
I sleep till dusk is dipped in gray;

And then I know the mist is drawn
  A lucid veil from coast to coast,
  And in the dark church like a ghost   15
Thy tablet glimmers in the dawn.

LXVIII

When in the down I sink my head,
  Sleep, Death's twin-brother, times my
    breath;
  Sleep, Death's twin-brother, knows not
    Death,
Nor can I dream of thee as dead.

I walk as ere I walked forlorn,   5
  When all our path was fresh with dew,
  And all the bugle breezes blew
Reveillée to the breaking morn.

But what is this? I turn about,
  I find a trouble in thine eye,   10
  Which makes me sad I know not why,
Nor can my dream resolve the doubt;

But ere the lark hath left the lea
  I wake, and I discern the truth;
  It is the trouble of my youth   15
That foolish sleep transfers to thee.

LXIX

I dreamed there would be Spring no more,
  That Nature's ancient power was lost;
  The streets were black with smoke and
    frost,
They chattered trifles at the door;

I wandered from the noisy town,   5
  I found a wood with thorny boughs;
  I took the thorns to bind my brows,
I wore them like a civic crown;

I met with scoffs, I met with scorns
  From youth and babe and hoary hairs: 10
  They called me in the public squares
The fool that wears a crown of thorns.

They called me fool, they called me child:
  I found an angel of the night;
  The voice was low, the look was bright: 15
He looked upon my crown and smiled.

He reached the glory of a hand,
  That seemed to touch it into leaf;
  The voice was not the voice of grief,
The words were hard to understand.   20

LXX

I cannot see the features right,
  When on the gloom I strive to paint
  The face I know; the hues are faint
And mix with hollow masks of night;

Cloud-towers by ghostly masons wrought,   5
  A gulf that ever shuts and gapes,
  A hand that points, and palléd shapes
In shadowy thoroughfares of thought;

And crowds that stream from yawning doors,
  And shoals of puckered faces drive;   10
  Dark bulks that tumble half alive,
And lazy lengths on boundless shores:

Till all at once beyond the will
  I hear a wizard music roll,
  And through a lattice on the soul   15
Looks thy fair face and makes it still.

LXXI

Sleep, kinsman thou to death and trance
  And madness, thou hast forged at last
  A night-long present of the past
In which we went through summer France.[27]

---

[27]Tennyson and Hallam had traveled through
France in the summer of 1830.

Hadst thou such credit with the soul? 5
  Then bring an opiate trebly strong,
  Drug down the blindfold sense of wrong,
That so my pleasure may be whole;

While now we talk as once we talked
  Of men and minds, the dust of change, 10
  The days that grow to something strange,
In walking as of old we walked

Beside the river's wooded reach,
  The fortress, and the mountain ridge,
  The cataract flashing from the bridge, 15
The breaker breaking on the beach.

LXXII

Risest thou thus, dim dawn, again,
  And howlest, issuing out of night,
  With blasts that blow the poplar white,
And lash with storm the streaming pane?

Day, when my crowned estate begun 5
  To pine in that reverse of doom,[28]
  Which sickened every living bloom,
And blurred the splendor of the sun;

Who usherest in the dolorous hour
  With thy quick tears that make the rose 10
  Pull sideways, and the daisy close
Her crimson fringes to the shower;

Who mightst have heaved a windless flame
  Up the deep East, or, whispering, played
  A checker-work of beam and shade 15
Along the hills, yet looked the same,

As wan, as chill, as wild as now;
  Day, marked as with some hideous crime,
  When the dark hand struck down through
    time,
And canceled nature's best: but thou, 20

Lift as thou mayst thy burthened brows
  Through clouds that drench the morning
    star,
  And whirl the ungarnered sheaf afar,
And sow the sky with flying boughs,

And up thy vault with roaring sound 25
  Climb thy thick moon, disastrous day;
  Touch thy dull goal of joyless gray,
And hide thy shame beneath the ground.

----

[28]In Hallam's death.

LXXIII

So many worlds, so much to do,
  So little done, such things to be,
  How know I what had need of thee,
For thou wert strong as thou wert true?

The fame is quenched that I foresaw, 5
  The head hath missed an earthly wreath:
  I curse not Nature, no, nor Death;
For nothing is that errs from law.

We pass; the path that each man trod
  Is dim, or will be dim, with weeds. 10
  What fame is left for human deeds
In endless age? It rests with God.

O hollow wraith of dying fame,
  Fade wholly, while the soul exults,
  And self-infolds the large results 15
Of force that would have forged a name.

LXXIV

As sometimes in a dead man's face,
  To those that watch it more and more,
  A likeness, hardly seen before,
Comes out—to some one of his race;

So, dearest, now thy brows are cold, 5
  I see thee what thou art, and know
  Thy likeness to the wise below,
Thy kindred with the great of old.

But there is more than I can see,
  And what I see I leave unsaid, 10
  Nor speak it, knowing Death has made
His darkness beautiful with thee.

LXXV

I leave thy praises unexpressed
  In verse that brings myself relief,
  And by the measure of my grief
I leave thy greatness to be guessed.

What practice howsoe'er expert 5
  In fitting aptest words to things,
  Or voice the richest-toned that sings,
Hath power to give thee as thou wert?

I care not in these fading days
  To raise a cry that lasts not long, 10
  And round thee with the breeze of song
To stir a little dust of praise.

Thy leaf has perished in the green,
  And, while we breathe beneath the sun,
  The world which credits what is done 15
Is cold to all that might have been.

So here shall silence guard thy fame;
  But somewhere, out of human view,
  Whate'er thy hands are set to do
Is wrought with tumult of acclaim.   20

LXXVI

Take wings of fancy, and ascend,
  And in a moment set thy face
  Where all the starry heavens of space
Are sharpened to a needle's end;[29]

Take wings of foresight; lighten through   5
  The secular abyss[30] to come,
  And lo, thy deepest lays are dumb
Before the moldering of a yew;

And if the matin songs, that woke
  The darkness of our planet, last,   10
  Thine own shall wither in the vast,
Ere half the lifetime of an oak.

Ere these have clothed their branchy bowers
  With fifty Mays, thy songs are vain;
  And what are they when these remain   15
The ruined shells of hollow towers?

LXXVII

What hope is here for modern rime
  To him who turns a musing eye
  On songs, and deeds, and lives, that lie
Foreshortened in the tract of time?

These mortal lullabies of pain   5
  May bind a book, may line a box,
  May serve to curl a maiden's locks;
Or when a thousand moons shall wane

A man upon a stall may find,
  And, passing, turn the page that tells   10
  A grief, then changed to something else,
Sung by a long-forgotten mind.

But what of that?   My darkened ways
  Shall ring with music all the same;
  To breathe my loss is more than fame,   15
To utter love more sweet than praise.

LXXVIII

Again at Christmas did we weave
  The holly round the Christmas hearth;
  The silent snow possessed the earth,
And calmly fell our Christmas-eve.

The yule-clog[31] sparkled keen with frost,   5
  No wing of wind the region swept,
  But over all things brooding slept
The quiet sense of something lost.

As in the winters left behind,
  Again our ancient games had place,   10
  The mimic picture's breathing grace,
And dance and song and hoodman-blind.

Who showed a token of distress?
  No single tear, no mark of pain—
  O sorrow, then can sorrow wane?   15
O grief, can grief be changed to less?

O last regret, regret can die!
  No—mixed with all this mystic frame,
  Her deep relations are the same,
But with long use her tears are dry.   20

LXXIX

"More than my brothers are to me,"—
  Let this not vex thee,[32] noble heart!
  I know thee of what force thou art
To hold the costliest love in fee.

But thou and I are one in kind,   5
  As molded like in Nature's mint;
  And hill and wood and field did print
The same sweet forms in either mind.

For us the same cold streamlet curled
  Through all his eddying coves, the same   10
  All winds that roam the twilight came
In whispers of the beauteous world.

At one dear knee we proffered vows,
  One lesson from one book we learned,
  Ere childhood's flaxen ringlet turned   15
To black and brown on kindred brows.

And so my wealth resembles thine,
  But he was rich where I was poor,
  And he supplied my want the more
As his unlikeness fitted mine.   20

LXXX

If any vague desire should rise,
  That holy Death ere Arthur died
  Had moved me kindly from his side,
And dropped the dust on tearless eyes;

---

[29]So distant in void space that all our firmament would appear to be a needle-point thence (Tennyson's note).

[30]The abyss of the ages.

[31]Log.

[32]Charles, Tennyson's brother. The line within quotation-marks is the last line of Section IX.

Then fancy shapes, as fancy can,   5
  The grief my loss in him had wrought,
  A grief as deep as life or thought,
But stayed in peace with God and man.

I make a picture in the brain;
  I hear the sentence that he speaks;   10
  He bears the burthen of the weeks,
But turns his burthen into gain.

His credit thus shall set me free;
  And, influence-rich to soothe and save,
  Unused example from the grave   15
Reach out dead hands to comfort me.

LXXXI

Could I have said while he was here,
  "My love shall now no further range;
  There cannot come a mellower change,
For now is love mature in ear"?

Love, then, had hope of richer store: 5
  What end is here to my complaint?
  This haunting whisper makes me faint,
"More years had made me love thee more."

But Death returns an answer sweet:
  "My sudden frost was sudden gain,   10
  And gave all ripeness to the grain
It might have drawn from after-heat."

LXXXII

I wage not any feud with Death
  For changes wrought on form and face;
  No lower life that earth's embrace
May breed with him can fright my faith.

Eternal process moving on,   5
  From state to state the spirit walks;
  And these are but the shattered stalks,
Or ruined chrysalis of one.

Nor blame I Death, because he bare
  The use of virtue out of earth;   10
  I know transplanted human worth
Will bloom to profit, otherwhere.

For this alone on Death I wreak
  The wrath that garners in my heart:
  He put our lives so far apart   15
We cannot hear each other speak.

LXXXIII

Dip down upon the northern shore,
  O sweet new-year delaying long;
  Thou doest expectant Nature wrong;
Delaying long, delay no more.

What stays thee from the clouded noons,   5
  Thy sweetness from its proper place?
  Can trouble live with April days,
Or sadness in the summer moons?

Bring orchis, bring the foxglove spire,
  The little speedwell's darling blue,   10
  Deep tulips dashed with fiery dew,
Laburnums, dropping-wells of fire.

O thou, new-year, delaying long,
  Delayest the sorrow in my blood,
  That longs to burst a frozen bud   15
And flood a fresher throat with song.

LXXXIV

When I contemplate all alone
  The life that had been thine below,
  And fix my thoughts on all the glow
To which thy crescent would have grown,

I see thee sitting crowned with good,   5
  A central warmth diffusing bliss
  In glance and smile, and clasp and kiss,
On all the branches of thy blood;

Thy blood, my friend, and partly mine;
  For now the day was drawing on,   10
  When thou shouldst link thy life with one
Of mine own house,[33] and boys of thine

Had babbled "Uncle" on my knee;
  But that remorseless iron hour
  Made cypress of her orange flower,   15
Despair of hope, and earth of thee.

I seem to meet their least desire,
  To clap their cheeks, to call them mine.
  I see their unborn faces shine
Beside the never-lighted fire.   20

I see myself an honored guest,
  Thy partner in the flowery walk
  Of letters, genial table-talk,
Or deep dispute, and graceful jest;

While now thy prosperous labor fills   25
  The lips of men with honest praise,
  And sun by sun the happy days
Descend below the golden hills

With promise of a morn as fair;
  And all the train of bounteous hours   30
  Conduct, by paths of growing powers,
To reverence and the silver hair;

[33]Emily, Tennyson's sister.

Till slowly worn her earthly robe,
　Her lavish mission richly wrought,
　Leaving great legacies of thought,   35
Thy spirit should fail from off the globe;

What time mine own might also flee,
　As linked with thine in love and fate,
　And, hovering o'er the dolorous strait
To the other shore, involved in thee,   40

Arrive at last the blessèd goal,
　And He that died in Holy Land
　Would reach us out the shining hand,
And take us as a single soul.

What reed was that on which I leant?   45
　Ah, backward fancy, wherefore wake
　The old bitterness again, and break
The low beginnings of content?

LXXXV[34]

This truth came borne with bier and pall,
　I felt it, when I sorrowed most,
　'Tis better to have loved and lost,
Than never to have loved at all—

O true in word, and tried in deed,   5
　Demanding, so to bring relief
　To this which is our common grief,
What kind of life is that I lead;

And whether trust in things above
　Be dimmed of sorrow, or sustained;   10
　And whether love for him have drained
My capabilities of love;

Your words have virtue such as draws
　A faithful answer from the breast,
　Through light reproaches, half expressed,
And loyal unto kindly laws.   16

My blood an even tenor kept,
　Till on mine ear this message falls,
　That in Vienna's fatal walls
God's finger touched him, and he slept.   20

The great Intelligences fair
　That range above our mortal state,
　In circle round the blessèd gate,
Received and gave him welcome there;

And led him through the blissful climes,   25
　And showed him in the fountain fresh
　All knowledge that the sons of flesh
Shall gather in the cycled times.

---

[34]This section is addressed to Edmund Lushington, whose marriage to Tennyson's sister Cecilia is celebrated in the Epilogue which concludes *In Memoriam.*

But I remained, whose hopes were dim,
　Whose life, whose thoughts were little
　　worth,   30
　To wander on a darkened earth,
Where all things round me breathed of him.

O friendship, equal-poised control,
　O heart, with kindliest motion warm,
　O sacred essence, other form,   35
O solemn ghost, O crownèd soul!

Yet none could better know than I,
　How much of act at human hands
　The sense of human will demands
By which we dare to live or die.   40

Whatever way my days decline,
　I felt and feel, though left alone,
　His being working in mine own,
The footsteps of his life in mine;

A life that all the Muses decked   45
　With gifts of grace, that might express
　All-comprehensive tenderness,
All-subtilizing intellect:

And so my passion hath not swerved
　To works of weakness, but I find   50
　An image comforting the mind,
And in my grief a strength reserved.

Likewise the imaginative woe,
　That loved to handle spiritual strife,
　Diffused the shock through all my life,   55
But in the present broke the blow.

My pulses therefore beat again
　For other friends that once I met;
　Nor can it suit me to forget
The mighty hopes that make us men.   60

I woo your love: I count it crime
　To mourn for any overmuch;
　I, the divided half of such
A friendship as had mastered Time;

Which masters Time indeed, and is   65
　Eternal, separate from fears.
　The all-assuming months and years
Can take no part away from this;

But Summer on the steaming floods,
　And Spring that swells the narrow brooks,
　And Autumn, with a noise of rooks,   71
That gather in the waning woods,

And every pulse of wind and wave
　Recalls, in change of light or gloom,
　My old affection of the tomb,   75
And my prime passion in the grave.

My old affection of the tomb,
  A part of stillness, yearns to speak:
  "Arise, and get thee forth and seek
A friendship for the years to come.   80

"I watch thee from the quiet shore;
  Thy spirit up to mine can reach;
  But in dear words of human speech
We two communicate no more."

And I, "Can clouds of nature stain   85
  The starry clearness of the free?
  How is it? Canst thou feel for me
Some painless sympathy with pain?"

And lightly does the whisper fall:
  " 'Tis hard for thee to fathom this;   90
  I triumph in conclusive bliss,
And that serene result of all."

So hold I commerce with the dead;
  Or so methinks the dead would say;
  Or so shall grief with symbols play   95
And pining life be fancy-fed.

Now looking to some settled end,
  That these things pass, and I shall prove
  A meeting somewhere, love with love,
I crave your pardon, O my friend;   100

If not so fresh, with love as true,
  I, clasping brother-hands, aver
  I could not, if I would, transfer
The whole I felt for him to you.

For which be they that hold apart   105
  The promise of the golden hours?
  First love, first friendship, equal powers,
That marry with the virgin heart.

Still mine, that cannot but deplore,
  That beats within a lonely place,   110
  That yet remembers his embrace,
But at his footstep leaps no more,

My heart, though widowed, may not rest
  Quite in the love of what is gone,
  But seeks to beat in time with one   115
That warms another living breast.

Ah, take the imperfect gift I bring,
  Knowing the primrose yet is dear,
  The primrose of the later year,
As not unlike to that of Spring.   120

LXXXVI

Sweet after showers, ambrosial air,
  That rollest from the gorgeous gloom
  Of evening over brake and bloom
And meadow, slowly breathing bare

The round of space, and rapt below   5
  Through all the dewy tasseled wood,
  And shadowing down the hornéd[35] flood
In ripples, fan my brows and blow

The fever from my cheek, and sigh
  The full new life that feeds thy breath   10
  Throughout my frame, till Doubt and Death,
Ill brethren, let the fancy fly

From belt to belt of crimson seas
  On leagues of odor streaming far,
  To where in yonder orient star   15
A hundred spirits whisper "Peace."

LXXXVII

I passed beside the reverend walls
  In which of old I wore the gown;
  I roved at random through the town,
And saw the tumult of the halls;

And heard once more in college fanes   5
  The storm their high-built organs make,
  And thunder-music, rolling, shake
The prophet blazoned on the panes;

And caught once more the distant shout,
  The measured pulse of racing oars   10
  Among the willows; paced the shores
And many a bridge, and all about

The same gray flats again, and felt
  The same, but not the same; and last
  Up that long walk of limes I passed   15
To see the rooms in which he dwelt.

Another name was on the door.
  I lingered; all within was noise
  Of songs, and clapping hands, and boys
That crashed the glass and beat the floor;   20

Where once we held debate, a band
  Of youthful friends, on mind and art,
  And labor, and the changing mart,
And all the framework of the land;

When one would aim an arrow fair,   25
  But send it slackly from the string;
  And one would pierce an outer ring,
And one an inner, here and there;

---

[35]Winding.

And last the master-bowman, he,
  Would cleave the mark. A willing ear 30
We lent him. Who but hung to hear
The rapt oration flowing free

From point to point, with power and grace
  And music in the bounds of law,
  To those conclusions when we saw 35
The God within him light his face,

And seem to lift the form, and glow
  In azure orbits heavenly-wise;
  And over those ethereal eyes
The bar of Michael Angelo?[36] 40

LXXXVIII

Wild bird,[37] whose warble, liquid sweet,
  Rings Eden through the budded quicks,[38]
  O tell me where the senses mix,
O tell me where the passions meet,

Whence radiate: fierce extremes employ 5
  Thy spirits in the darkening leaf,
  And in the midmost heart of grief
Thy passion clasps a secret joy;

And I—my harp would prelude woe—
  I cannot all command the strings; 10
  The glory of the sum of things
Will flash along the chords and go.

LXXXIX

Witch-elms that counterchange[39] the floor
  Of this flat lawn with dusk and bright;
  And thou, with all thy breadth and height
Of foliage, towering sycamore;

How often, hither wandering down, 5
  My Arthur found your shadows fair,
  And shook to all the liberal air
The dust and din and steam of town!

He brought an eye for all he saw;
  He mixed in all our simple sports; 10
  They pleased him, fresh from brawling courts
And dusty purlieus of the law.

---

[36]These lines I wrote from what Arthur Hallam said after reading of the prominent ridge of bone over the eyes of Michael Angelo: "Alfred, look over my eyes; surely I have the bar of Michael Angelo!" (Tennyson.)

[37]Presumably the nightingale.

[38]Hedge-rows formed of living shrubs or small trees.

[39]Checker.

O joy to him in this retreat,
  Immantled in ambrosial dark,
  To drink the cooler air, and mark 15
The landscape winking through the heat!

O sound to rout the brood of cares,
  The sweep of scythe in morning dew,
  The gust that round the garden flew,
And tumbled half the mellowing pears! 20

O bliss, when all in circle drawn
  About him, heart and ear were fed
  To hear him, as he lay and read
The Tuscan poets on the lawn!

Or in the all-golden afternoon 25
  A guest, or happy sister, sung,
  Or here she brought the harp and flung
A ballad to the brightening moon.

Nor less it pleased in livelier moods,
  Beyond the bounding hill to stray, 30
  And break the livelong summer day
With banquet in the distant woods;

Whereat we glanced from theme to theme,
  Discussed the books to love or hate,
  Or touched the changes of the state, 35
Or threaded some Socratic dream;

But if I praised the busy town,
  He loved to rail against it still,
  For "ground in yonder social mill
We rub each other's angles down, 40

"And merge," he said, "in form and gloss
  The picturesque of man and man."
  We talked: the stream beneath us ran,
The wine-flask lying couched in moss,

Or cooled within the glooming wave; 45
  And last, returning from afar,
  Before the crimson-circled star
Had fallen into her father's grave,[40]

And brushing ankle-deep in flowers,
  We heard behind the woodbine veil 50
  The milk that bubbled in the pail,
And buzzings of the honeyed hours.

XC

He tasted love with half his mind,
  Nor ever drank the inviolate spring
  Where nighest heaven, who first could fling
This bitter seed among mankind:

---

[40]Before Venus, the evening star, had dipped into the sunset. The planets, according to Laplace, were evolved from the sun (Tennyson).

That could the dead, whose dying eyes   5
  Were closed with wail, resume their life,
  They would but find in child and wife
An iron welcome when they rise.

'Twas well, indeed, when warm with wine,
  To pledge them with a kindly tear,   10
  To talk then o'er, to wish them here,
To count their memories half divine;

But if they came who passed away,
  Behold their brides in other hands;
  The hard heir strides about their lands, 15
And will not yield them for a day.

Yea, though their sons were none of these,
  Not less the yet-loved sire would make
  Confusion worse than death, and shake
The pillars of domestic peace.   20

Ah, dear, but come thou back to me!
  Whatever change the years have wrought,
  I find not yet one lonely thought
That cries against my wish for thee.

XCI

When rosy plumelets tuft the larch,
  And rarely pipes the mounted thrush,
  Or underneath the barren bush
Flits by the sea-blue bird of March;[41]

Come, wear the form by which I know   5
  Thy spirit in time among thy peers:
  The hope of unaccomplished years
Be large and lucid round thy brow.

When summer's hourly-mellowing change
  May breathe, with many roses sweet,   10
  Upon the thousand waves of wheat
That ripple round the lowly grange,

Come; not in watches of the night,
  But where the sunbeam broodeth warm,
  Come, beauteous in thine after form, 15
And like a finer light in light.

XCII

If any vision should reveal
  Thy likeness, I might count it vain
  As but the canker of the brain;
Yea, though it spake and made appeal

To chances where our lots were cast   5
  Together in the days behind,
  I might but say, I hear a wind
Of memory murmuring the past.

---

[41]The kingfisher.

Yea, though it spake and bared to view
  A fact within the coming year;   10
  And though the months, revolving near,
Should prove the phantom-warning true,

They might not seem thy prophecies,
  But spiritual presentiments,
  And such refraction of events   15
As often rises ere they rise.

XCIII

I shall not see thee. Dare I say
  No spirit ever brake the band
  That stays him from the native land
Where first he walked when clasped in clay?

No visual shade of some one lost,   5
  But he, the Spirit himself, may come
  Where all the nerve of sense is numb,
Spirit to Spirit, Ghost to Ghost.

O, therefore from thy sightless range
  With gods in unconjectured bliss,   10
  O, from the distance of the abyss
Of tenfold-complicated change,

Descend, and touch, and enter; hear
  The wish too strong for words to name,
  That in this blindness of the frame 15
My Ghost may feel that thine is near.

XCIV

How pure at heart and sound in head,
  With what divine affections bold
  Should be the man whose thought would hold
An hour's communion with the dead.

In vain shalt thou, or any, call   5
  The spirits from their golden day,
  Except, like them, thou too canst say,
My spirit is at peace with all.

They haunt the silence of the breast,
  Imaginations calm and fair,   10
  The memory like a cloudless air,
The conscience as a sea at rest;

But when the heart is full of din,
  And doubt beside the portal waits,
  They can but listen at the gates, 15
And hear the household jar within.

XCV

By night we lingered on the lawn,
  For underfoot the herb was dry;
  And genial warmth; and o'er the sky
The silvery haze of summer drawn:

And calm that let the tapers burn   5
  Unwavering: not a cricket chirred;
  The brook alone far-off was heard,
And on the board the fluttering urn.

And bats went round in fragrant skies,
  And wheeled or lit the filmy shapes[42]   10
  That haunt the dusk, with ermine capes
And woolly breasts and beaded eyes;

While now we sang old songs that pealed
  From knoll to knoll, where, couched at
    ease,
  The white kine glimmered, and the trees 15
Laid their dark arms about the field.

But when those others, one by one,
  Withdrew themselves from me and night,
  And in the house light after light
Went out, and I was all alone,   20

A hunger seized my heart; I read
  Of that glad year which once had been,
  In those fallen leaves which kept their
    green,
The noble letters of the dead.

And strangely on the silence broke   25
  The silent-speaking words, and strange
  Was love's dumb cry defying change
To test his worth; and strangely spoke

The faith, the vigor, bold to dwell
  On doubts that drive the coward back, 30
  And keen through wordy snares to track
Suggestion to her inmost cell.

So word by word, and line by line,
  The dead man touched me from the past,
  And all at once it seemed at last   35
The living soul was flashed on mine,

And mine in this was wound, and whirled
  About empyreal heights of thought,
  And came on that which is, and caught
The deep pulsations of the world,   40

Aeonian music measuring out
  The steps of Time—the shocks of
    Chance—
  The blows of Death. At length my trance
Was canceled, stricken through with doubt.

Vague words! but ah, how hard to frame 45
  In matter-molded forms of speech,
  Or even for intellect to reach
Through memory that which I became;

[42]Night moths (Tennyson).

Till now the doubtful dusk revealed
  The knolls once more where, couched at
    ease,   50
  The white kine glimmered, and the trees
Laid their dark arms about the field;

And sucked from out the distant gloom
  A breeze began to tremble o'er
  The large leaves of the sycamore,   55
And fluctuate all the still perfume,

And gathering freshlier overhead,
  Rocked the full-foliaged elms, and swung
  The heavy-folded rose, and flung
The lilies to and fro, and said,   60

"The dawn, the dawn," and died away;
  And East and West, without a breath,
  Mixed their dim lights, like life and death,
To broaden into boundless day.

XCVI

You say, but with no touch of scorn,
  Sweet-hearted, you, whose light-blue eyes
  Are tender over drowning flies,
You tell me, doubt is Devil-born.

I know not: one indeed I knew   5
  In many a subtle question versed,
  Who touched a jarring lyre at first,
But ever strove to make it true;

Perplexed in faith, but pure in deeds,
  At last he beat his music out.   10
  There lives more faith in honest doubt,
Believe me, than in half the creeds.

He fought his doubts and gathered strength,
  He would not make his judgment blind,
  He faced the specters of the mind   15
And laid them; thus he came at length

To find a stronger faith his own,
  And Power was with him in the night,
  Which makes the darkness and the light,
And dwells not in the light alone,   20

But in the darkness and the cloud,
  As over Sinaï's peaks of old,
  While Israel made their gods of gold,
Although the trumpet blew so loud.[43]

XCVII

My love has talked with rocks and trees;
  He finds on misty mountain-ground
  His own vast shadow glory-crowned;
He sees himself in all he sees.

[43]See Exodus. 19 and 22.

Two partners of a married life— 5
  I looked on these and thought of thee
  In vastness and in mystery,
And of my spirit as of a wife.

These two—they dwelt with eye on eye,
  Their hearts of old have beat in tune, 10
  Their meetings made December June,
Their every parting was to die.

Their love has never passed away;
  The days she never can forget
  Are earnest that he loves her yet, 15
Whate'er the faithless people say.

Her life is lone, he sits apart;
  He loves her yet, she will not weep,
  Though rapt in matters dark and deep
He seems to slight her simple heart. 20

He thrids[44] the labyrinth of the mind,
  He reads the secret of the star,
  He seems so near and yet so far,
He looks so cold: she thinks him kind.

She keeps the gift of years before, 25
  A withered violet is her bliss;
  She knows not what his greatness is,
For that, for all, she loves him more.

For him she plays, to him she sings
  Of early faith and plighted vows; 30
  She knows but matters of the house,
And he, he knows a thousand things.

Her faith is fixed and cannot move,
  She darkly feels him great and wise,
  She dwells on him with faithful eyes, 35
"I cannot understand; I love."

XCVIII

You leave us:[45] you will see the Rhine,
  And those fair hills I sailed below,
  When I was there with him; and go
By summer belts of wheat and vine

To where he breathed his latest breath, 5
  That city. All her splendor seems
  No livelier than the wisp that gleams
On Lethe in the eyes of Death.

Let her great Danube rolling fair
  Enwind her isles, unmarked of me; 10
  I have not seen, I will not see
Vienna; rather dream that there,

A treble darkness, Evil haunts
  The birth, the bridal; friend from friend
  Is oftener parted, fathers bend 15
Above more graves, a thousand wants

Gnarr[46] at the heels of men, and prey
  By each cold hearth, and sadness flings
  Her shadow on the blaze of kings.
And yet myself have heard him say, 20

That not in any mother town
  With statelier progress to and fro
  The double tides of chariots flow
By park and suburb under brown

Of lustier leaves; nor more content, 25
  He told me, lives in any crowd,
  When all is gay with lamps, and loud
With sport and song, in booth and tent,

Imperial halls, or open plain;
  And wheels the circled dance, and breaks
  The rocket molten into flakes 31
Of crimson or in emerald rain.

XCIX

Risest thou thus, dim dawn, again,
  So loud with voices of the birds,
  So thick with lowings of the herds,
Day, when I lost the flower of men;

Who tremblest through thy darkling red 5
  On yon swollen brook that bubbles fast
  By meadows breathing of the past,
And woodlands holy to the dead;

Who murmurest in the foliaged eaves
  A song that slights the coming care, 10
  And Autumn laying here and there
A fiery finger on the leaves;

Who wakenest with thy balmy breath
  To myriads on the genial earth,
  Memories of bridal, or of birth, 15
And unto myriads more, of death.

O, wheresoever those may be,
  Betwixt the slumber of the poles,
  To-day they count as kindred souls;
They know me not, but mourn with me. 20

C[47]

I climb the hill: from end to end
  Of all the landscape underneath,
  I find no place that does not breathe
Some gracious memory of my friend;

[44]Threads.

[45]Charles Tennyson and his bride, who on their
marriage-tour visited Vienna.

[46]Snarl.

[47]This and the two following sections were occasioned by the removal of the Tennysons from
Somersby.

No gray old grange, or lonely fold,   5
  Or low morass and whispering reed,
  Or simple stile from mead to mead,
Or sheepwalk up the windy wold;

Nor hoary knoll of ash and haw
  That hears the latest linnet trill,   10
  Nor quarry trenched along the hill
And haunted by the wrangling daw;

Nor runlet tinkling from the rock;
  Nor pastoral rivulet that swerves
  To left and right through meadowy curves,
That feeds the mothers of the flock;   16

But each has pleased a kindred eye,
  And each reflects a kindlier day;
  And, leaving these, to pass away,
I think once more he seems to die.   20

CI

Unwatched, the garden bough shall sway,
  The tender blossom flutter down,
  Unloved, that beech will gather brown,
This maple burn itself away;

Unloved, the sunflower, shining fair,   5
  Ray round with flames her disk of seed,
  And many a rose-carnation feed
With summer spice the humming air;

Unloved, by many a sandy bar,
  The brook shall babble down the plain,   10
  At noon or when the Lesser Wain
Is twisting round the polar star;

Uncared for, gird the windy grove,
  And flood the haunts of hern and crake,
  Or into silver arrows break   15
The sailing moon in creek and cove;

Till from the garden and the wild
  A fresh association blow,
  And year by year the landscape grow
Familiar to the stranger's child;   20

As year by year the laborer tills
  His wonted glebe, or lops the glades,
  And year by year our memory fades
From all the circle of the hills.

CII

We leave the well-belovéd place
  Where first we gazed upon the sky;
  The roofs that heard our earliest cry
Will shelter one of stranger race.

We go, but ere we go from home,   5
  As down the garden-walks I move,
  Two spirits of a diverse love
Contend for loving masterdom.

One whispers, "Here thy boyhood sung
  Long since its matin song, and heard   10
  The low love-language of the bird
In native hazels tassel-hung."

The other answers, "Yea, but here
  Thy feet have strayed in after hours
  With thy lost friend among the bowers,   15
And this hath made them trebly dear."

These two have striven half the day,
  And each prefers his separate claim,
  Poor rivals in a losing game,
That will not yield each other way.   20

I turn to go; my feet are set
  To leave the pleasant fields and farms;
  They[48] mix in one another's arms
To one pure image of regret.

CIII

On that last night before we went
  From out the doors where I was bred,
  I dreamed a vision of the dead,
Which left my after-morn content.

Methought I dwelt within a hall,   5
  And maidens[49] with me; distant hills
  From hidden summits fed with rills
A river sliding by the wall.

The hall with harp and carol rang.
  They sang of what is wise and good   10
  And graceful.   In the center stood
A statue veiled, to which they sang;

And which, though veiled, was known to me,
  The shape of him I loved, and love
  For ever.   Then flew in a dove   15
And brought a summons from the sea;[50]

And when they learned that I must go,
  They wept and wailed, but led the way
  To where a little shallop lay
At anchor in the flood below;   20

[48]The rivals of the preceding stanza.

[49]They are the muses, poetry, arts—all that made life beautiful here, which we hope will pass with us beyond the grave (Tennyson). Tennyson also stated that the "hidden summits" of the following line and the "river" of the last line of the stanza mean, respectively, "the divine" and "life."

[50]Eternity (Tennyson).

And on by many a level mead,
  And shadowing bluff that made the banks,
  We glided winding under ranks
Of iris and the golden reed;

And still as vaster grew the shore[51]   25
  And rolled the floods in grander space,
  The maidens gathered strength and grace
And presence, lordlier than before;

And I myself, who sat apart
  And watched them, waxed in every limb;
  I felt the thews of Anakim,[52]   31
The pulses of a Titan's heart;

As one would sing the death of war,
  And one would chant the history
  Of that great race which is to be,   35
And one the shaping of a star;[53]

Until the forward-creeping tides
  Began to foam, and we to draw
  From deep to deep, to where we saw
A great ship lift her shining sides.   40

The man we loved was there on deck,
  But thrice as large as man he bent
  To greet us. Up the side I went,
And fell in silence on his neck;

Whereat those maidens with one mind   45
  Bewailed their lot; I did them wrong:
  "We served thee here," they said, "so long,
And wilt thou leave us now behind?"

So rapt I was, they could not win
  An answer from my lips, but he   50
  Replying, "Enter likewise ye
And go with us": they entered in.

And while the wind began to sweep
  A music out of sheet and shroud,
  We steered her toward a crimson cloud   55
That landlike slept along the deep.

CIV

The time draws near the birth of Christ;
  The moon is hid, the night is still;
  A single church below the hill
Is pealing, folded in the mist.

---

[51]The progress of the Age (Tennyson).
[52]Giants (see Deuteronomy, 9:2).
[53]The great hopes of humanity and science (Tennyson).

A single peal of bells below,   5
  That wakens at this hour of rest
  A single murmur in the breast,
That these are not the bells I know.

Like strangers' voices here they sound,
  In lands where not a memory strays,   10
  Nor landmark breathes of other days,
But all is new unhallowed ground.

CV

To-night ungathered let us leave
  This laurel, let this holly stand:
  We live within the stranger's land,
And strangely falls our Christmas-eve.

Our father's dust is left alone   5
  And silent under other snows:
  There in due time the woodbine blows,
The violet comes, but we are gone.

No more shall wayward grief abuse
  The genial hour with mask and mime;   10
  For change of place, like growth of time,
Has broke the bond of dying use.

Let cares that petty shadows cast,
  By which our lives are chiefly proved,
  A little spare the night I loved,   15
And hold it solemn to the past.

But let no footstep beat the floor,
  Nor bowl of wassail mantle warm;
  For who would keep an ancient form   19
Through which the spirit breathes no more?

Be neither song, nor game, nor feast;
  Nor harp be touched, nor flute be blown;
  No dance, no motion, save alone
What lightens in the lucid East

Of rising worlds by yonder wood.   25
  Long sleeps the summer in the seed;
  Run out your measured arcs, and lead
The closing cycle rich in good.

CVI

Ring out, wild bells, to the wild sky,
  The flying cloud, the frosty light:
  The year is dying in the night;
Ring out, wild bells, and let him die.

Ring out the old, ring in the new,   5
  Ring, happy bells, across the snow:
  The year is going, let him go;
Ring out the false, ring in the true.

Ring out the grief that saps the mind,
  For those that here we see no more;   10
  Ring out the feud of rich and poor,
Ring in redress to all mankind.

Ring out a slowly dying cause,
  And ancient forms of party strife;
  Ring in the nobler modes of life,   15
With sweeter manners, purer laws.

Ring out the want, the care, the sin,
  The faithless coldness of the times;
  Ring out, ring out my mournful rimes,
But ring the fuller minstrel in.   20

Ring out false pride in place of blood,
  The civil slander and the spite;
  Ring in the love of truth and right,
Ring in the common love of good.

Ring out old shapes of foul disease;   25
  Ring out the narrowing lust of gold;
  Ring out the thousand wars of old,
Ring in the thousand years of peace.

Ring in the valiant man and free,
  The larger heart, the kindlier hand;   30
  Ring out the darkness of the land,
Ring in the Christ that is to be.

CVII

It is the day when he was born,[54]
  A bitter day that early sank
  Behind a purple-frosty bank
Of vapor, leaving night forlorn.

The time admits not flowers or leaves   5
  To deck the banquet. Fiercely flies
  The blast of North and East, and ice
Makes daggers at the sharpened eaves,

And bristles all the brakes and thorns
  To yon hard crescent, as she hangs   10
  Above the wood which grides[55] and clangs
Its leafless ribs and iron horns

Together, in the drifts that pass
  To darken on the rolling brine
  That breaks the coast. But fetch the wine,
Arrange the board and grim the glass;   16

Bring in great logs and let them lie,
  To make a solid core of heat;
  Be cheerful-minded, talk and treat
Of all things even as he were by;   20

---

[54]Hallam's birthday, 1 February.   [55]Scrapes.

We keep the day. With festal cheer,
  With books and music, surely we
  Will drink to him, whate'er he be,
And sing the songs he loved to hear.

CVIII

I will not shut me from my kind,
  And, lest I stiffen into stone,
  I will not eat my heart alone,
Nor feed with sighs a passing wind:

What profit lies in barren faith,   5
  And vacant yearning, though with might
  To scale the heaven's highest height,
Or dive below the wells of death?

What find I in the highest place,
  But mine own phantom chanting hymns?
  And on the depths of death there swims   11
The reflex of a human face.

I'll rather take what fruit may be
  Of sorrow under human skies:
  'Tis held that sorrow makes us wise,   15
Whatever wisdom sleep with thee.

CIX

Heart-affluence in discursive talk
  From household fountains never dry;
  The critic clearness of an eye
That saw through all the Muses' walk;

Seraphic intellect and force   5
  To seize and throw the doubts of man;
  Impassioned logic, which outran
The hearer in its fiery course;

High nature amorous of the good,
  But touched with no ascetic gloom;   10
  And passion pure in snowy bloom
Through all the years of April blood;

A love of freedom rarely felt,
  Of freedom in her regal seat
  Of England; not the schoolboy heat,   15
The blind hysterics of the Celt;

And manhood fused with female grace
  In such a sort, the child would twine
  A trustful hand, unasked, in thine,
And find his comfort in thy face;   20

All these have been and thee mine eyes
  Have looked on: if they looked in vain,
  My shame is greater who remain,
Nor let thy wisdom make me wise.

CX

Thy converse drew us with delight,
  The men of rathe[56] and riper years;
  The feeble soul, a haunt of fears,
Forgot his weakness in thy sight.

On thee the loyal-hearted hung,   5
  The proud was half disarmed of pride,
  Nor cared the serpent at thy side[57]
To flicker with his double tongue.

The stern were mild when thou wert by,
  The flippant put himself to school   10
  And heard thee, and the brazen fool
Was softened, and he knew not why;

While I, thy nearest, sat apart,
  And felt thy triumph was as mine;
  And loved them more, that they were thine,
The graceful tact, the Christian art;   16

Nor mine the sweetness or the skill,
  But mine the love that will not tire,
  And, born of love, the vague desire
That spurs an imitative will.   20

CXI

The churl in spirit, up or down
  Along the scale of ranks, through all,
  To him who grasps a golden ball,
By blood a king, at heart a clown,—[58]

The churl in spirit, howe'er he veil   5
  His want in forms for fashion's sake,
  Will let his coltish nature break
At seasons through the gilded pale;

For who can always act? but he,
  To whom a thousand memories call,   10
  Not being less but more than all
The gentleness he seemed to be,

Best seemed the thing he was, and joined
  Each office of the social hour
  To noble manners, as the flower   15
And native growth of noble mind;

Nor ever narrowness or spite,
  Or villain fancy fleeting by,
  Drew in the expression of an eye
Where God and Nature met in light;   20

[56]Early.
[57]The envious and venomous slanderer.
[58]Peasant.

And thus he bore without abuse
  The grand old name of gentleman,
  Defamed by every charlatan,
And soiled with all ignoble use.

CXII

High wisdom holds my wisdom less,
  That I, who gaze with temperate eyes
  On glorious insufficiencies,
Set light by narrower perfectness.

But thou, that fillest all the room   5
  Of all my love, art reason why
  I seem to cast a careless eye
On souls, the lesser lords of doom.[59]

For what wert thou? some novel power
  Sprang up for ever at a touch,   10
  And hope could never hope too much,
In watching thee from hour to hour,

Large elements in order brought,
  And tracts of calm from tempest made,
  And world-wide fluctuation swayed   15
In vassal tides that followed thought.

CXIII

'Tis held that sorrow makes us wise;
  Yet how much wisdom sleeps with thee
  Which not alone had guided me,
But served the seasons that may rise;

For can I doubt, who knew thee keen   5
  In intellect, with force and skill
  To strive, to fashion, to fulfill—
I doubt not what thou wouldst have been:

A life in civic action warm,
  A soul on highest mission sent,   10
  A potent voice of Parliament,
A pillar steadfast in the storm,

Should licensed boldness gather force,
  Becoming, when the time has birth,
  A lever to uplift the earth   15
And roll it in another course,

With thousand shocks that come and go,
  With agonies, with energies,
  With overthrowings, and with cries,
And undulations to and fro.   20

[59]Those that have free will but less intellect (Tennyson).

CXIV

Who loves not Knowledge? Who shall rail
  Against her beauty? May she mix
  With men and prosper! Who shall fix
Her pillars? Let her work prevail.

But on her forehead sits a fire;   5
  She sets her forward countenance
  And leaps into the future chance,
Submitting all things to desire.

Half-grown as yet, a child, and vain—
  She cannot fight the fear of death.   10
  What is she, cut from love and faith,
But some wild Pallas[60] from the brain

Of demons? fiery-hot to burst
  All barriers in her onward race
  For power. Let her know her place;   15
She is the second, not the first.

A higher hand must make her mild,
  If all be not in vain, and guide
  Her footsteps, moving side by side
With Wisdom, like the younger child;   20

For she is earthly of the mind,
  But Wisdom heavenly of the soul.
  O friend, who camest to thy goal
So early, leaving me behind,

I would the great world grew like thee,   25
  Who grewest not alone in power
  And knowledge, but by year and hour
In reverence and in charity.

CXV

Now fades the last long streak of snow,
  Now burgeons every maze of quick[61]
  About the flowering squares,[62] and thick
By ashen roots the violets blow.

Now rings the woodland loud and long,   5
  The distance takes a lovelier hue,
  And drowned in yonder living blue
The lark becomes a sightless song.

Now dance the lights on lawn and lea,
  The flocks are whiter down the vale,   10
  And milkier every milky sail
On winding stream or distant sea;

Where now the seamew pipes, or dives
  In yonder greening gleam, and fly
  The happy birds, that change their sky   15
To build and brood, that live their lives

From land to land; and in my breast
  Spring wakens too, and my regret
  Becomes an April violet,
And buds and blossoms like the rest.   20

CXVI

Is it, then, regret for buried time
  The keenlier in sweet April wakes,
  And meets the year, and gives and takes
The colors of the crescent prime?[63]

Not all: the songs, the stirring air,   5
  The life re-orient out of dust,
  Cry through the sense to hearten trust
In that which made the world so fair.

Not all regret: the face will shine
  Upon me, while I muse alone,   10
  And that dear voice, I once have known,
Still speak to me of me and mine.

Yet less of sorrow lives in me
  For days of happy commune dead,
  Less yearning for the friendship fled   15
Than some strong bond which is to be.

CXVII

O days and hours, your work is this,
  To hold me from my proper place,
  A little while from his embrace,
For fuller gain of after bliss;

That out of distance might ensue   5
  Desire of nearness doubly sweet,
  And unto meeting, when we meet,
Delight a hundredfold accrue,

For every grain of sand that runs,[64]
  And every span of shade that steals,   10
  And every kiss of toothéd wheels,[65]
And all the courses of the suns.

CXVIII

Contemplate all this work of Time,
  The giant laboring in his youth;
  Nor dream of human love and truth,
As dying Nature's earth and lime;

But trust that those we call the dead   5
  Are breathers of an ampler day
  For ever nobler ends. They say,
The solid earth whereon we tread

---

[60]Pallas Athena sprang full-grown and full-armed
from the head of Zeus.
  [61]Hedge.   [62]Fields.

[63]Spring.
  [64]In allusion to the hour-glass.
  [65]The wheels of a clock.

In tracts of fluent heat began,
    And grew to seeming-random forms,   10
    The seeming prey of cyclic storms,
Till at the last arose the man;

Who throve and branched from clime to
    clime,
    The herald of a higher race,
    And of himself in higher place,   15
If so he type this work of time

Within himself, from more to more;
    Or, crowned with attributes of woe
    Like glories, move his course, and show
That life is not as idle ore,   20

But iron dug from central gloom,
    And heated hot with burning fears,
    And dipped in baths of hissing tears,
And battered with the shocks of doom

To shape and use. Arise and fly   25
    The reeling Faun, the sensual feast;
    Move upward, working out the beast,
And let the ape and tiger die.

CXIX

Doors, where my heart was used to beat
    So quickly, not as one that weeps
    I come once more; the city sleeps;
I smell the meadow in the street;

I hear a chirp of birds; I see   5
    Betwixt the black fronts long-withdrawn
    A light-blue lane of early dawn,
And think of early days and thee,

And bless thee, for thy lips are bland,
    And bright the friendship of thine eye; 10
    And in my thoughts with scarce a sigh
I take the pressure of thine hand.

CXX

I trust I have not wasted breath:
    I think we are not wholly brain,
    Magnetic mockeries; not in vain,
Like Paul with beasts,[66] I fought with Death;

Not only cunning casts in clay: 5
    Let Science prove we are, and then
    What matters Science unto men,
At least to me? I would not stay.

Let him, the wiser man who springs
    Hereafter, up from childhood shape   10
    His action like the greater ape,
But I was *born* to other things.

[66] I Corinthians, 15:32.

CXXI

Sad Hesper[67] o'er the buried sun
    And ready, thou, to die with him,
    Thou watchest all things ever dim
And dimmer, and a glory done.

The team is loosened from the wain,   5
    The boat is drawn upon the shore;
    Thou listenest to the closing door,
And life is darkened in the brain.

Bright Phosphor, fresher for the night,
    By thee the world's great work is heard 10
    Beginning, and the wakeful bird;
Behind thee comes the greater light.

The market boat is on the stream,
    And voices hail it from the brink;
    Thou hear'st the village hammer clink, 15
And see'st the moving of the team.

Sweet Hesper-Phosphor, double name
    For what is one, the first, the last,
    Thou, like my present and my past,
Thy place is changed; thou art the same. 20

CXXII

O, wast thou with me, dearest, then,
    While I rose up against my doom,
    And yearned to burst the folded gloom,
To bare the eternal heavens again,

To feel once more, in placid awe,   5
    The strong imagination roll
    A sphere of stars about my soul,
In all her motion one with law?

If thou wert with me, and the grave
    Divide us not, be with me now,   10
    And enter in at breast and brow,
Till all my blood, a fuller wave,

Be quickened with a livelier breath,
    And like an inconsiderate boy,
    As in the former flash of joy, 15
I slip the thoughts of life and death;

[67] Hesper, the evening star, which follows the setting sun and watches the fading light and ending life of day, is also Phosphor, the morning star, which precedes the sun and sees the dawn of light and life. They are the same "planet of Love" (*Maud*), which does but change its place. And so the poet's past and present are in substance one thing (Love), which has merely changed its place in becoming present instead of past (A. C. Bradley).

And all the breeze of Fancy blows,
  And every dewdrop paints a bow,[68]
  The wizard lightnings deeply glow,
And every thought breaks out a rose.   20

CXXIII

There rolls the deep where grew the tree.
  O earth, what changes hast thou seen!
  There where the long street roars hath been
The stillness of the central sea.

The hills are shadows, and they flow   5
  From form to form, and nothing stands;
  They melt like mist, the solid lands,
Like clouds they shape themselves and go.

But in my spirit will I dwell,
  And dream my dream, and hold it true;   10
  For though my lips may breathe adieu,
I cannot think the thing farewell.

CXXIV

That which we dare invoke to bless;
  Our dearest faith; our ghastliest doubt;
  He, They, One, All; within, without;[69]
The Power in darkness, whom we guess,—

I found Him not in world or sun,   5
  Or eagle's wing, or insect's eye,
  Nor through the questions men may try,
The petty cobwebs we have spun.

If e'er when faith had fallen asleep,
  I heard a voice, "believe no more,"   10
  And heard an ever-breaking shore
That tumbled in the Godless deep,

A warmth within the breast would melt
  The freezing reason's colder part,
  And like a man in wrath the heart   15
Stood up and answered, "I have felt."

No, like a child in doubt and fear:
  But that blind clamor made me wise;
  Then was I as a child that cries,
But, crying, knows his father near;   20

And what I am beheld again
  What is, and no man understands;
  And out of darkness came the hands
That reach through nature, molding men.

---

[68]Rainbow.

[69]The Deity, however imagined to exist, whether as conceived by the theist, the polytheist, the monist, or the pantheist, or as inside us or outside us.

CXXV

Whatever I have said or sung,
  Some bitter notes my harp would give,
  Yea, though there often seemed to live
A contradiction on the tongue,

Yet Hope had never lost her youth,   5
  She did but look through dimmer eyes;
  Or Love but played with gracious lies,
Because he felt so fixed in truth;

And if the song were full of care,
  He breathed the spirit of the song;   10
  And if the words were sweet and strong
He set his royal signet there;

Abiding with me till I sail
  To seek thee on the mystic deeps,
  And this electric force, that keeps   15
A thousand pulses dancing, fail.

CXXVI

Love is and was my lord and king,
  And in his presence I attend
  To hear the tidings of my friend,
Which every hour his couriers bring.

Love is and was my king and lord,   5
  And will be, though as yet I keep
  Within the court on earth, and sleep
Encompassed by his faithful guard,

And hear at times a sentinel
  Who moves about from place to place,   10
  And whispers to the worlds of space,
In the deep night, that all is well.

CXXVII

And all is well, though faith and form
  Be sundered in the night of fear;
  Well roars the storm to those that hear
A deeper voice across the storm,

Proclaiming social truth shall spread,   5
  And justice, even though thrice again
  The red fool-fury of the Seine[70]
Should pile her barricades with dead.

But ill for him that wears a crown,
  And him, the lazar, in his rags!   10
  They tremble, the sustaining crags;
The spires of ice are toppled down,

And molten up, the roar in flood;
  The fortress crashes from on high,
  The brute earth lightens to the sky,   15
And the great Aeon[71] sinks in blood,

---

[70]The violent revolutions in France.

[71]The modern age.

And compassed by the fires of hell;
  While thou, dear spirit, happy star,
  O'erlook'st the tumult from afar,
And smilest, knowing all is well.   20

CXXVIII

The love that rose on stronger wings,
  Unpalsied when he met with Death,
  Is comrade of the lesser faith
That sees the course of human things.

No doubt vast eddies in the flood   5
  Of onward time shall yet be made,
  And thronéd races may degrade;[72]
Yet, O ye mysteries of good,

Wild Hours that fly with Hope and Fear,
  If all your office had to do   10
  With old results that look like new—
If this were all your mission here,

To draw, to sheathe a useless sword,
  To fool the crowd with glorious lies,
  To cleave a creed in sects and cries,   15
To change the bearing of a word,

To shift an arbitrary power,
  To cramp the student at his desk,
  To make old bareness picturesque
And tuft with grass a feudal tower,   20

Why, then my scorn might well descend
  On you and yours.   I see in part
  That all, as in some piece of art,
Is toil coöperant to an end.

CXXIX

Dear friend, far off, my lost desire,
  So far, so near in woe and weal,
  O loved the most, when most I feel
There is a lower and a higher;

Known and unknown, human, divine;   5
  Sweet human hand and lips and eye;
  Dear heavenly friend that canst not die,
Mine, mine, for ever, ever mine;

Strange friend, past, present, and to be;
  Loved deeplier, darklier understood;   10
  Behold, I dream a dream of good,
And mingle all the world with thee.

CXXX

Thy voice is on the rolling air;
  I hear thee where the waters run;
  Thou standest in the rising sun,
And in the setting thou art fair.

[72]And races now highest may degenerate.

What art thou then?   I cannot guess;   5
  But though I seem in star and flower
  To feel thee some diffusive power,
I do not therefore love thee less.

My love involves the love before;
  My love is vaster passion now;   10
  Though mix'd with God and Nature thou,
I seem to love thee more and more.

Far off thou art, but ever nigh;
  I have thee still, and I rejoice;
  I prosper, circled with thy voice;   15
I shall not lose thee though I die.

CXXXI

O living will that shalt endure
  When all that seems shall suffer shock,
  Rise in the spiritual rock,[73]
Flow through our deeds and make them pure,

That we may lift from out of dust   5
  A voice as unto him that hears,
  A cry above the conquered years
To one that with us works, and trust,

With faith that comes of self-control,
  The truths that never can be proved   10
  Until we close with all we loved,
And all we flow from, soul in soul.

_____

O true and tried, so well and long,[74]
  Demand not thou a marriage lay;
  In that it is thy marriage day
Is music more than any song.

Nor have I felt so much of bliss   5
  Since first he told me that he loved
  A daughter of our house, nor proved
Since that dark day a day like this;

Though I since then have numbered o'er
  Some thrice three years;[75] they went and
    came,   10
  Remade the blood and changed the frame,
And yet is love not less, but more;

[73]I Corinthians, 10:4.

[74]This Epilogue is an epithalamium written to celebrate the marriage of Edmund Lushington to Tennyson's sister Cecilia in 1842. Tennyson said of *In Memoriam:* "It begins with a funeral and ends with a marriage—begins with death and ends in promise of a new life—a sort of *Divine Comedy,* cheerful at the close."

[75]In making this statement Tennyson violates the internal chronology of the poem elsewhere maintained.

No longer caring to embalm
  In dying songs a dead regret,
  But like a statue solid-set,   15
And molded in colossal calm.

Regret is dead, but love is more
  Than in the summers that are flown,
  For I myself with these have grown
To something greater than before;   20

Which makes appear the songs I made
  As echoes out of weaker times,
  As half but idle brawling rimes,
The sport of random sun and shade.

But where is she, the bridal flower,   25
  That must be made a wife ere noon?
  She enters, glowing like the moon
Of Eden on its bridal bower.

On me she bends her blissful eyes
  And then on thee; they meet thy look   30
  And brighten like the star that shook
Betwixt the palms of Paradise.

Oh, when her life was yet in bud,
  He[76] too foretold the perfect rose.
  For thee she grew, for thee she grows   35
For ever, and as fair as good.

And thou art worthy, full of power;
  As gentle; liberal-minded, great,
  Consistent; wearing all that weight
Of learning lightly like a flower.[77]   40

But now set out: the noon is near,
  And I must give away the bride;
  She fears not, or with thee beside
And me behind her, will not fear.

For I that danced her on my knee,   45
  That watched her on her nurse's arm,
  That shielded all her life from harm,
At last must part with her to thee;

Now waiting to be made a wife,
  Her feet, my darling, on the dead;   50
  Their pensive tablets round her head,
And the most living words of life

Breathed in her ear. The ring is on,
  The "Wilt thou?" answered, and again
  The "Wilt thou?" asked, till out of twain
Her sweet "I will" has made you one.   56

---

[76]Hallam.
[77]Lushington was a classical scholar, who became
Professor of Greek at Glasgow.

Now sign your names, which shall be read,
  Mute symbols of a joyful morn,
  By village eyes as yet unborn.
The names are signed, and overhead   60

Begins the clash and clang that tells
  The joy to every wandering breeze;
  The blind wall rocks, and on the trees
The dead leaf trembles to the bells.

O happy hour, and happier hours   65
  Await them. Many a merry face
  Salutes them—maidens of the place,
That pelt us in the porch with flowers.

O happy hour, behold the bride
  With him to whom her hand I gave.   70
  They leave the porch, they pass the grave
That has to-day its sunny side.

To-day the grave is bright for me,
  For them the light of life increased,
  Who stay to share the morning feast,   75
Who rest to-night beside the sea.

Let all my genial spirits advance
  To meet and greet a whiter sun;
  My drooping memory will not shun
The foaming grape of eastern France.   80

It circles round, and fancy plays,
  And hearts are warmed and faces bloom,
  As drinking health to bride and groom
We wish them store of happy days.

Nor count me all to blame if I   85
  Conjecture of a stiller guest,
  Perchance, perchance, among the rest,
And, though in silence, wishing joy.

But they must go, the time draws on,
  And those white-favored horses wait;   90
  They rise, but linger; it is late;
Farewell, we kiss, and they are gone.

A shade falls on us like the dark
  From little cloudlets on the grass,
  But sweeps away as out we pass   95
To range the woods, to roam the park,

Discussing how their courtship grew.
  And talk of others that are wed,
  And how she looked, and what he said,
And back we come at fall of dew.   100

Again the feast, the speech, the glee,
  The shade of passing thought, the wealth
  Of words and wit, the double health,
The crowning cup, the three-times-three,

And last the dance;—till I retire.   105
  Dumb is that tower which spake so loud,
  And high in heaven the streaming cloud,
And on the downs a rising fire:

And rise, O moon, from yonder down,
  Till over down and over dale   110
  All night the shining vapor sail
And pass the silent-lighted town,

The white-faced halls, the glancing rills,
  And catch at every mountain head,
  And o'er the friths[78] that branch and
    spread   115
Their sleeping silver through the hills;

And touch with shade the bridal doors,
  With tender gloom the roof, the wall;
  And breaking let the splendor fall
To spangle all the happy shores   120

By which they rest, and ocean sounds,
  And, star and system rolling past,
  A soul shall draw from out the vast
And strike his being into bounds,

And, moved through life of lower phase,   125
  Result in man, be born and think,
  And act and love, a closer link
Betwixt us and the crowning race

Of those that, eye to eye, shall look
  On knowledge; under whose command   130
  Is Earth and Earth's, and in their hand
Is Nature like an open book;

No longer half-akin to brute,
  For all we thought and loved and did,
  And hoped, and suffered, is but seed   135
Of what in them is flower and fruit;

Whereof the man that with me trod
  This planet was a noble type
  Appearing ere the times were ripe,
That friend of mine who lives in God,   140

That God, which ever lives and loves,
  One God, one law, one element,
  And one far-off divine event,
To which the whole creation moves.

---

[78]Firths, arms of the sea.

THE CHARGE OF THE LIGHT BRIGADE[1]

I

Half a league, half a league,
Half a league onward,
All in the valley of Death
  Rode the six hundred.
"Forward, the Light Brigade!   5
Charge for the guns!" he said.
Into the valley of Death
  Rode the six hundred.

II

"Forward, the Light Brigade!"
Was there a man dismayed?   10
Not though the soldier knew
  Some one had blundered.
Theirs not to make reply,
Theirs not to reason why,
Theirs but to do and die.   15
Into the valley of Death
  Rode the six hundred.

III

Cannon to right of them,
Cannon to left of them,
Cannon in front of them   20
  Volleyed and thundered;
Stormed at with shot and shell,
Boldly they rode and well,
Into the jaws of Death,
Into the mouth of hell   25
  Rode the six hundred.

IV

Flashed all their sabers bare,
Flashed as they turned in air
Sab'ring the gunners there,
Charging an army, while   30
  All the world wondered.
Plunged in the battery-smoke
Right through the line they broke;
Cossack and Russian
Reeled from the saber-stroke   35
  Shattered and sundered.
Then they rode back, but not,
  Not the six hundred.

V

Cannon to right of them,
Cannon to left of them,   40
Cannon behind them
  Volleyed and thundered;

---

[1]Published in December, 1854. The charge occurred in the Battle of Balaclava, 1854, an engagement of the Crimean War.

Stormed at with shot and shell,
While horse and hero fell,
They that had fought so well   45
Came through the jaws of Death,
Back from the mouth of hell,
All that was left of them,
    Left of six hundred.

VI

When can their glory fade?   50
O the wild charge they made!
    All the world wondered.
Honor the charge they made!
Honor the Light Brigade,
    Noble six hundred!   55

COME INTO THE GARDEN[1]

I

Come into the garden, Maud,
    For the black bat, night, has flown,
Come into the garden, Maud,
    I am here at the gate alone;
And the woodbine spices are wafted abroad,
    And the musk of the rose is blown.   6

II

For a breeze of morning moves,
    And the planet of Love is on high,
Beginning to faint in the light that she loves
    On a bed of daffodil sky,   10
To faint in the light of the sun she loves,
    To faint in his light, and to die.

III

All night have the roses heard
    The flute, violin, bassoon;
All night has the casement jessamine stirred
    To the dancers dancing in tune;   16
Till a silence fell with the waking bird,
    And a hush with the setting moon.

IV

I said to the lily, "There is but one,
    With whom she has heart to be gay.   20
When will the dancers leave her alone?
    She is weary of dance and play."
Now half to the setting moon are gone,
    And half to the rising day;
Low on the sand and loud on the stone   25
    The last wheel echoes away.

---

[1]From *Maud*, published in 1855.

V

I said to the rose, "The brief night goes
    In babble and revel and wine.
O young lord-lover, what sighs are those,
    For one that will never be thine?   30
But mine, but mine," so I sware to the rose,
    "For ever and ever, mine."

VI

And the soul of the rose went into my blood
    As the music clashed in the hall;
And long by the garden lake I stood,   35
    For I heard your rivulet fall
From the lake to the meadow and on to the
        wood,
    Our wood, that is dearer than all;

VII

From the meadow your walks have left so
        sweet
    That whenever a March-wind sighs   40
He sets the jewel-print of your feet
    In violets blue as your eyes,
To the woody hollows in which we meet
    And the valleys of Paradise.

VIII

The slender acacia would not shake   45
    One long milk-bloom on the tree;
The white lake-blossom fell into the lake
    As the pimpernel dozed on the lea;
But the rose was awake all night for your
        sake,
    Knowing your promise to me;   50
The lilies and roses were all awake,
    They sighed for the dawn and thee.

IX

Queen rose of the rosebud garden of girls,
    Come hither, the dances are done,
In gloss of satin and glimmer of pearls,   55
    Queen lily and rose in one;
Shine out, little head, sunning over with curls,
    To the flowers, and be their sun.

X

There has fallen a splendid tear
    From the passion-flower at the gate.   60
She is coming, my dove, my dear;
    She is coming, my life, my fate.
The red rose cries, "She is near, she is near";
    And the white rose weeps, "She is late";
The larkspur listens, "I hear, I hear";   65
    And the lily whispers, "I wait."

XI

She is coming, my own, my sweet;
  Were it ever so airy a tread,
My heart would hear her and beat,
  Were it earth in an earthy bed; 70
My dust would hear her and beat,
  Had I lain for a century dead,
Would start and tremble under her feet,
  And blossom in purple and red.

MILTON [1]

(*Alcaics*)

O mighty-mouthed inventor of harmonies,
O skilled to sing of Time or Eternity,
  God-gifted organ-voice of England,
    Milton, a name to resound for ages;
Whose Titan angels, Gabriel, Abdiel, 5
Starred from Jehovah's gorgeous armories,
  Tower, as the deep-domed empyrean
    Rings to the roar of an angel onset!
Me rather all that bowery loneliness,
The brooks of Eden mazily murmuring, 10
  And bloom profuse and cedar arches
    Charm, as a wanderer out in ocean,
Where some refulgent sunset of India
Streams o'er a rich ambrosial ocean isle,
  And crimson-hued the stately palm-woods
    Whisper in odorous heights of even. 16

NORTHERN FARMER, OLD STYLE [1]

I

Wheer 'asta beän saw long and meä liggin'[2]
  'ere aloän?
Noorse? thoort nowt o' a noorse; whoy, Doctor's abeän an' agoän;
Says that I moänt 'a naw moor aäle, but I
  beänt a fool;
Git ma my aäle, fur I beänt a-gawin' to
  breäk my rule.

II

Doctors, they knaws nowt, fur a says what's
  nawways true; 5
Naw soort o' koind o' use to saäy the things
  that a do.

---

[1]Published in December, 1863. One of several attempts made by Tennyson to reproduce in English the effect of classical meters.

[1]Published in 1864. The dialect is the rustic speech of Lincolnshire, where Tennyson was born and brought up.

[2]Lying.

I've 'ed my point o' aäle ivry noight sin' I
  beän 'ere.
An' I've 'ed my quart ivry market-noight for
  foorty year.

III

Parson's a beän loikewoise, an' a sittin' ere o'
  my bed.
"The Amoighty's a taäkin o' you[3] to 'issén,[4]
  my friend," a said, 10
An' a towd ma my sins, an' 's toithe[5] were
  due, an' I gied it in hond;
I done moy duty boy 'um, as I 'a done boy
  the lond.

IV

Larn'd a ma' beä.[6] I reckons I 'annot sa
  mooch to larn.
But a cast oop,[7] thot a did, 'bout Bessy
  Marris's barne.[8]
Thaw a knaws I hallus voäted wi' Squoire
  an' choorch an' staäte, 15
An' i' the woost o' toimes I wur niver agin
  the raäte.[9]

V

An' I hallus coom'd to 's choorch afoor moy
  Sally wur deäd,
An' 'eärd 'um a bummin'[10] awaäy loike a
  buzzard-clock[11] ower my 'eäd,
An' I niver knaw'd whot a meän'd but I
  thowt a 'ad summut to saäy,
An' I thowt a said whot a owt to 'a said, an'
  I coom'd awaäy. 20

VI

Bessy Marris's barne! tha knaws she laäid
  it to meä.
Mowt a beän, mayhap, for she wur a bad un,
  sheä.
'Siver,[12] I kep 'um, I kep 'um, my lass, tha
  mun understond;
I done moy duty boy 'um, as I 'a done boy
  the lond.

VII

But Parson a cooms an' a goäs, an' a says
  it eäsy an' freeä: 25
"The Amoighty 's a taäkin o' you to 'issén,
  my friend," says 'eä.
I weänt saäy men be loiars, thaw summun
  said it in 'aäste;
But 'e reäds wonn sarmin a weeäk, an' I 'a
  stubb'd[13] Thurnaby waäste.

---

[3]*ou* as in hour.   [4]Himself.   [5]Tithe.
[6]He may be.   [7]Confessed.   [8]Child.
[9]Tax for relief of the poor.   [10]Buzzing.
[11]Cockchafer.   [12]Howsoever.
[13]Dug out the tree-roots.

VIII

D' ya moind the waäste, my lass? naw, naw,
　　tha was not born then;
Theer wur a boggle[14] in it, I often 'eärd 'um,
　　mysén;　　　　　　　　　　　　　　　30
Moäst loike a butter-bump,[15] fur I 'eärd 'um
　　about an' about,
But I stubb'd 'um oop wi' the lot, an' raäved
　　an' rembled 'um out.[16]

IX

Keäper's[17] it wur; fo' they fun 'um theer
　　a-laäid of 'is faäce
Down i' the woild 'enemies[18] afoor I coom'd
　　to the plaäce.
Noäks or Thimbleby—toäner[19] 'ed shot 'um
　　as deäd as a naäil.　　　　　　　　　35
Noäks wur 'ang'd for it oop at 'soize[20]—but
　　git ma my aäle.

X

Dubbut looök at the waäste; theer warn't not
　　feeäd for a cow;
Nowt at all but bracken an' fuzz,[21] an' looök
　　at it now—
Warn't worth nowt a haäcre, an' now theer's
　　lots o' feeäd,
Fourscoor yows[22] upon it, an' some on it
　　down i' seeäd.[23]　　　　　　　　　40

XI

Nobbut a bit on it's left, an' I meän'd to 'a
　　stubb'd it at fall,
Done it ta-year[24] I meän'd, an' runn'd plow
　　thruff it an' all,
If Godamoighty an' parson 'ud nobbut let
　　ma aloän,—
Meä, wi' haäte hoonderd haäcre o' Squoire's,
　　an' lond o' my oän.

XII

Do Godamoighty knaw what a 's doing
　　a-taäkin' o' meä?　　　　　　　　　45
I beänt wonn as saws 'ere a beän an' yonder
　　a peä;
An' Squoire 'ull be sa mad an' all—a' dear,
　　a' dear!
And I 'a managed for Squoire coom Michael-
　　mas thutty year.

XIII

A mowt 'a taäen owd Joänes, as 'ant not a
　　'aäpoth[25] o' sense,
Or a mowt 'a taäen young Robins—a niver
　　mended a fence;　　　　　　　　　50
But Godamoighty a moost taäke meä an'
　　taäke ma now,
Wi' aäf the cows to cauve an' Thurnaby
　　hoälms[26] to plow!

XIV

Looök 'ow quoloty[27] smoiles when they seeäs
　　ma a passin' boy,
Says to thessén,[28] naw doubt, "What a man a
　　beä sewer-loy!"[29]
Fur they knaws what I beän to Squoire sin'
　　fust a coom'd to the 'All;　　　　　55
I done moy duty by Squoire an' I done moy
　　duty boy hall.

XV

Squoire's i' Lunnon, an' summun I reckons
　　'ull 'a to wroite,
For whoä's to howd the lond ater meä thot
　　muddles ma quoit;
Sartin-sewer I beä thot a weänt niver give it
　　to Joänes,
Naw, nor a moänt to Robins—a niver rem-
　　bles the stoäns.　　　　　　　　　60

XVI

But summun 'ull come ater meä mayhap wi'
　　'is kittle o' steäm[30]
Huzzin' an' maäzin'[31] the blessed feälds wi'
　　the divil's oän teäm.
Sin' I mun doy I mun doy, thaw loife they
　　says is sweet,
But sin' I mun doy I mun doy, for I couldn
　　abeär to see it.

XVII

What atta stannin' theer fur, an' doesn bring
　　ma the aäle?　　　　　　　　　　65
Doctor's a 'toättler,[32] lass, an a's hallus i' the
　　owd taäle;[33]
I weänt breäk rules fur Doctor, a knaws
　　naw moor nor a floy;
Git ma my aäle, I tell tha, an' if I mun doy
　　I mun doy.

---

[14]Goblin.　　[15]Bittern.
[16]Tore him up and threw him out.
[17]I. e., it was the ghost of the game-keeper.
[18]Anemones.　　[19]One or the other.
[20]The assizes.　　[21]Furze.　　[22]Ewes.　　[23]Clover
[24]This year.

[25]Halfpennyworth.
[26]Holms, flat land near a river.
[27]The gentry (quality).　　[28]Themselves.
[29]Surely.　　[30]Steam-engine.
[31]Buzzing and amazing.　　[32]Teetotaler.
[33]He is always at the old story.

IDYLS OF THE KING[1]

The Passing of Arthur

That story which the bold Sir Bedivere,
First made and latest left of all the knights,
Told, when the man was no more than a voice
In the white winter of his age, to those
With whom he dwelt, new faces, other minds. 5

For on their march to westward, Bedivere,
Who slowly paced among the slumbering host,
Heard in his tent the moanings of the King:

"I found Him in the shining of the stars,
I marked Him in the flowering of His fields,
But in His ways with men I find Him not. 11
I waged His wars, and now I pass and die.
O me! for why is all around us here
As if some lesser god had made the world,
But had not force to shape it as he would, 15
Till the High God behold it from beyond,
And enter it, and make it beautiful?
Or else as if the world were wholly fair,
But that these eyes of men are dense and dim,
And have not power to see it as it is— 20
Perchance, because we see not to the close;—
For I, being simple, thought to work His will,
And have but stricken with the sword in vain,
And all whereon I leaned in wife and friend
Is traitor to my peace, and all my realm 25
Reels back into the beast, and is no more.
My God, thou hast forgotten me in my death!
Nay—God my Christ—I pass but shall not die."

Then, ere that last weird battle in the west,
There came on Arthur sleeping, Gawain killed 30
In Lancelot's war, the ghost of Gawain blown
Along a wandering wind, and past his ear
Went shrilling: "Hollow, hollow all delight!
Hail, King! to-morrow thou shalt pass away.
Farewell! there is an isle of rest for thee. 35
And I am blown along a wandering wind,
And hollow, hollow, hollow all delight!"
And fainter onward, like wild birds that change
Their season in the night and wail their way
From cloud to cloud, down the long wind the dream 40
Shrilled; but in going mingled with dim cries
Far in the moonlit haze among the hills,
As of some lonely city sacked by night,
When all is lost, and wife and child with wail
Pass to new lords; and Arthur woke and called: 45
"Who spake? A dream. O, light upon the wind,
Thine, Gawain, was the voice—are these dim cries
Thine? or doth all that haunts the waste and wild
Mourn, knowing it will go along with me?"

This heard the bold Sir Bedivere and spake: 50
"O me, my King, let pass whatever will,
Elves, and the harmless glamour of the field;
But in their stead thy name and glory cling
To all high places like a golden cloud
For ever; but as yet thou shalt not pass. 55
Light was Gawain in life, and light in death
Is Gawain, for the ghost is as the man;
And care not thou for dreams from him, but rise—
I hear the steps of Modred in the west,
And with him many of thy people, and knights 60
Once thine, whom thou hast loved, but grosser grown
Than heathen, spitting at their vows and thee.
Right well in heart they know thee for the King.
Arise, go forth and conquer as of old."

Then spake King Arthur to Sir Bedivere:
"Far other is this battle in the west 66

[1]The *Idyls of the King* are twelve in number. In 1859 four were published: "Enid" (in 1884 divided into two Idyls, which in 1888 were finally entitled "The Marriage of Geraint" and "Geraint and Enid"), "Merlin and Vivien," "Lancelot and Elaine," and "Guinevere." In 1869 four more were published: "The Coming of Arthur," "The Holy Grail," "Pelleas and Ettarre," and "The Passing of Arthur." In the last-named Idyl Tennyson incorporated his *Morte d'Arthur* which had been published in 1842 and had been written by 1835. In 1871 "The Last Tournament" was published, in 1872 "Gareth and Lynette," and in 1885 "Balin and Balan," which completed the series. "The Passing of Arthur" is the last of the Idyls as finally arranged, and is based on the narrative in Malory's *Morte d'Arthur*, Bk. XXI.

Whereto we move than when we strove in
   youth,
And brake the petty kings, and fought with
   Rome,
Or thrust the heathen from the Roman wall,
And shook him through the north. Ill doom
   is mine   70
To war against my people and my knights.
The king who fights his people fights himself.
And they my knights, who loved me once, the
   stroke
That strikes them dead is as my death to me.
Yet let us hence, and find or feel a way   75
Through this blind haze which, ever since I
   saw
One[2] lying in the dust at Almesbury,
Hath folded in the passes of the world."

   Then rose the King and moved his host by
      night,
And ever pushed Sir Modred, league by
   league,   80
Back to the sunset bound of Lyonnesse[3]—
A land of old upheaven from the abyss
By fire, to sink into the abyss again;
Where fragments of forgotten peoples dwelt,
And the long mountains ended in a coast   85
Of ever-shifting sand, and far away
The phantom circle of a moaning sea.
There the pursuer could pursue no more,
And he that fled no further fly the King;
And there, that day when the great light of
   heaven   90
Burned at his lowest in the rolling year,
On the waste sand by the waste sea they
   closed.
Nor ever yet had Arthur fought a fight
Like this last, dim, weird battle of the west.
A death-white mist slept over sand and sea,
Whereof the chill, to him who breathed it,
   drew   96
Down with his blood, till all his heart was
   cold
With formless fear; and even on Arthur fell
Confusion, since he saw not whom he fought.
For friend and foe were shadows in the mist,
And friend slew friend not knowing whom
   he slew;   101
And some had visions out of golden youth,
And some beheld the faces of old ghosts
Look in upon the battle; and in the mist
Was many a noble deed, many a base,   105

---

[2]Guinevere, who had entered a nunnery at Almesbury.

[3]Supposed to have been a country (now covered by the sea) uniting the Scilly Islands with western Cornwall.

And chance and craft and strength in single
   fights,
And ever and anon with host to host
Shocks, and the splintering spear, the hard
   mail hewn,
Shield-breakings, and the clash of brands,
   the crash
Of battle-axes on shattered helms, and
   shrieks   110
After the Christ, of those who falling down
Looked up for heaven, and only saw the
   mist;
And shouts of heathen and the traitor
   knights,
Oaths, insult, filth, and monstrous blasphe-
   mies,
Sweat, writhings, anguish, laboring of the
   lungs   115
In that close mist, and cryings for the light,
Moans of the dying, and voices of the dead.

   Last, as by some one death-bed after wail
Of suffering, silence follows, or through
   death
Or death-like swoon, thus over all that shore,
Save for some whisper of the seething seas,
A dead hush fell; but when the dolorous
   day   122
Grew drearier toward twilight falling, came
A bitter wind, clear from the north, and blew
The mist aside, and with that wind the tide
Rose, and the pale King glanced across the
   field   126
Of battle. But no man was moving there;
Nor any cry of Christian heard thereon,
Nor yet of heathen; only the wan wave
Brake in among dead faces, to and fro   130
Swaying the helpless hands, and up and
   down
Tumbling the hollow helmets of the fallen,
And shivered brands that once had fought
   with Rome,
And rolling far along the gloomy shores
The voice of days of old and days to be.   135

   Then spake King Arthur to Sir Bedivere,
And whiter than the mist that all day long
Had held the field of battle was the King:

   "Hearest thou this great voice that shakes
      the world,
And wastes the narrow realm whereon we
   move,   140
And beats upon the faces of the dead,
My dead, as though they had not died for
   me?—
O Bedivere, for on my heart hath fallen

Confusion, till I know not what I am,
Nor whence I am, nor whether I be king; 145
Behold, I seem but king among the dead."

Then spake the bold Sir Bedivere: "My
    king!
King everywhere! and so the dead have
    kings,
There also will I worship thee as king.
Yet still thy life is whole, and still I live 150
Who love thee; but who hates thee, he that
    brought
The heathen back among us, yonder stands,
Modred, unharmed, the traitor of thine
    house."

Then spake the King: "My house hath
    been my doom.
But call not thou this traitor of my house 155
Who hath but dwelt beneath one roof with
    me.
My house are rather they who sware my
    vows,
Yea, even while they brake them, owned me
    king.
And well for thee, saying my dark hour,
When all the purport of my throne hath
    failed, 160
That quick or dead thou holdest me for king.
King am I, whatsoever be their cry;
And one last act of kinghood shalt thou see
Yet, ere I pass." And uttering this the King
Made at the man. Then Modred smote his
    liege 165
Hard on that helm which many a heathen
    sword
Had beaten thin; while Arthur at one blow,
Striking the last stroke with Excalibur,
Slew him, and, all but slain himself, he fell.

So all day long the noise of battle rolled 170
Among the mountains by the winter sea,
Until King Arthur's Table, man by man,
Had fallen in Lyonnesse about their lord,
King Arthur; then, because his wound was
    deep,
The bold Sir Bedivere uplifted him, 175
And bore him to a chapel nigh the field,
A broken chancel with a broken cross,
That stood on a dark strait of barren land.
On one side lay the Ocean, and on one
Lay a great water, and the moon was full. 180

Then spake King Arthur to Sir Bedivere:
"The sequel of to-day unsolders all
The goodliest fellowship of famous knights

Whereof this world holds record. Such a
    sleep
They sleep—the men I loved. I think that
    we 185
Shall never more, at any future time,
Delight our souls with talk of knightly deeds,
Walking about the gardens and the halls
Of Camelot, as in the days that were.
I perish by this people which I made,— 190
Though Merlin sware that I should come
    again
To rule once more—but let what will be be,
I am so deeply smitten through the helm
That without help I cannot last till morn.
Thou therefore take my brand Excalibur, 195
Which was my pride; for thou rememberest
    how
In those old days, one summer noon, an arm
Rose up from out the bosom of the lake,
Clothed in white samite,[4] mystic, wonderful,
Holding the sword—and how I rowed across
And took it, and have worn it, like a king; 201
And, wheresoever I am sung or told
In aftertime, this also shall be known.
But now delay not; take Excalibur,
And fling him far into the middle mere;[5] 205
Watch what thou seest, and lightly bring me
    word."

To him replied the bold Sir Bedivere:
"It is not meet, Sir King, to leave thee thus,
Aidless, alone, and smitten through the
    helm—
A little thing may harm a wounded man; 210
Yet I thy hest will all perform at full,
Watch what I see, and lightly bring thee
    word."

So saying, from the ruined shrine he
    stepped,
And in the moon athwart the place of tombs,
Where lay the mighty bones of ancient men,
Old knights, and over them the sea-wind
    sang 216
Shrill, chill, with flakes of foam. He, step-
    ping down
By zigzag paths and juts of pointed rock,
Came on the shining levels of the lake.

There drew he forth the brand Excalibur,
And o'er him, drawing it, the winter moon,
Brightening the skirts of a long cloud, ran
    forth 222
And sparkled keen with frost against the
    hilt;

---

[4]Heavy silk cloth, generally interwoven with gold
[5]Lake—the "great water" mentioned above.

For all the haft twinkled with diamond
    sparks,
Myriads of topaz-lights, and jacinth-work 225
Of subtlest jewelry.   He gazed so long
That both his eyes were dazzled as he stood,
This way and that dividing the swift mind,
In act to throw; but at the last it seemed
Better to leave Excalibur concealed   230
There in the many-knotted water-flags,
That whistled stiff and dry about the marge.
So strode he back slow to the wounded King.

Then spake King Arthur to Sir Bedivere:
"Hast thou performed my mission which I
    gave?   235
What is it thou hast seen? or what hast
    heard?"

And answer made the bold Sir Bedivere:
"I heard the ripple washing in the reeds,
And the wild water lapping on the crag."

To whom replied King Arthur, faint and
    pale: 240
"Thou hast betrayed thy nature and thy
    name,
Not rendering true answer, as beseemed
Thy fealty, nor like a noble knight;
For surer sign had followed, either hand,
Or voice, or else a motion of the mere.   245
This is a shameful thing for men to lie.
Yet now, I charge thee, quickly go again,
As thou art lief and dear, and do the thing
I bade thee, watch, and lightly bring me
    word."   249

Then went Sir Bedivere the second time
Across the ridge, and paced beside the mere,
Counting the dewy pebbles, fixed in thought;
But when he saw the wonder of the hilt,
How curiously and strangely chased, he
    smote
His palms together, and he cried aloud: 255

"And if indeed I cast the brand away,
Surely a precious thing, one worthy note,
Should thus be lost for ever from the earth,
Which might have pleased the eyes of many
    men.
What good should follow this, if this were
    done?   260
What harm, undone?   Deep harm to disobey,
Seeing obedience is the bond of rule.
Were it well to obey then, if a king demand
An act unprofitable, against himself?
The King is sick, and knows not what he
    does.   265

What record or what relic of my lord
Should be to aftertime, but empty breath
And rumors of a doubt? But were this kept,
Stored in some treasure-house of mighty
    kings,
Some one might show it at a joust of arms,
Saying: 'King Arthur's sword, Excalibur, 271
Wrought by the lonely Maiden of the Lake.
Nine years she wrought it, sitting in the
    deeps
Upon the hidden bases of the hills.'
So might some old man speak in the after-
    time   275
To all the people, winning reverence.
But now much honor and much fame were
    lost."

So spake he, clouded with his own conceit,[6]
And hid Excalibur the second time,
And so strode back slow to the wounded
    King.   280

Then spoke King Arthur, breathing heav-
    ily:
"What is it thou hast seen? or what hast
    heard?"

And answer made the bold Sir Bedivere:
"I heard the water lapping on the crag,
And the long ripple washing in the reeds." 285

To whom replied King Arthur, much in
    wrath:
"Ah miserable, and unkind, untrue,
Unknightly, traitor-hearted!   Woe is me!
Authority forgets a dying king,
Laid widowed of the power in his eye   290
That bowed the will. I see thee what thou
    art,
For thou, the latest-left of all my knights,
In whom should meet the offices of all,
Thou wouldst betray me for the precious
    hilt;
Either from lust of gold, or like a girl   295
Valuing the giddy pleasure of the eyes.
Yet, for a man may fail in duty twice,
And the third time may prosper, get thee
    hence;
But, if thou spare to fling Excalibur,
I will arise and slay thee with my hands." 300

Then quickly rose Sir Bedivere, and ran,
And, leaping down the ridges lightly, plunged
Among the bulrush beds, and clutched the
    sword,

[6]Fancy.

And strongly wheeled and threw it. The great brand 304
Made lightnings in the splendor of the moon,
And flashing round and round, and whirled in an arch,
Shot like a streamer of the northern morn,
Seen where the moving isles of winter shock
By night, with noises of the Northern Sea.
So flashed and fell the brand Excalibur; 310
But ere he dipped the surface, rose an arm
Clothed in white samite, mystic, wonderful,
And caught him by the hilt, and brandished him
Three times, and drew him under in the mere.
And lightly went the other to the King. 315

Then spoke King Arthur, drawing thicker breath:
"Now see I by thine eyes that this is done.
Speak out; what is it thou hast heard, or seen?"

And answer made the bold Sir Bedivere:
"Sir King, I closed mine eyelids, lest the gems 320
Should blind my purpose, for I never saw,
Nor shall see, here or elsewhere, till I die,
Not though I live three lives of mortal men,
So great a miracle as yonder hilt.
Then with both hands I flung him, wheeling him; 325
But when I looked again, behold an arm,
Clothed in white samite, mystic, wonderful,
That caught him by the hilt, and brandished him
Three times, and drew him under in the mere."

And answer made King Arthur, breathing hard: 330
"My end draws nigh; 'tis time that I were gone.
Make broad thy shoulders to receive my weight,
And bear me to the margin; yet I fear
My wound hath taken cold, and I shall die."

So saying, from the pavement he half rose,
Slowly, with pain, reclining on his arm, 336
And looking wistfully with wide blue eyes
As in a picture. Him Sir Bedivere
Remorsefully regarded through his tears,
And would have spoken, but he found not words; 340
Then took with care, and kneeling on one knee,

O'er both his shoulders drew the languid hands,
And rising bore him through the place of tombs.

But, as he walked, King Arthur panted hard,
Like one that feels a nightmare on his bed 345
When all the house is mute. So sighed the King,
Muttering and murmuring at his ear,
"Quick, quick!
I fear it is too late, and I shall die."
But the other swiftly strode from ridge to ridge,
Clothed with his breath, and looking, as he walked, 350
Larger than human on the frozen hills.
He heard the deep behind him, and a cry
Before. His own thought drove him like a goad.
Dry clashed his harness in the icy caves
And barren chasms, and all to left and right
The bare black cliff clanged round him, as he based 356
His feet on juts of slippery crag that rang
Sharp-smitten with the dint of arméd heels—
And on a sudden, lo, the level lake,
And the long glories of the winter moon! 360

Then saw they how there hove a dusky barge,
Dark as a funeral scarf from stem to stern,
Beneath them; and descending they were ware
That all the decks were dense with stately forms,
Black-stoled, black-hooded, like a dream—by these 365
Three queens with crowns of gold—and from them rose
A cry that shivered to the tingling stars,
And, as it were one voice, an agony
Of lamentation, like a wind that shrills
All night in a waste land, where no one comes, 370
Or hath come, since the making of the world.

Then murmured Arthur, "Place me in the barge."
So to the barge they came. There those three queens
Put forth their hands, and took the King, and wept.
But she that rose the tallest of them all 375
And fairest laid his head upon her lap,

And loosed the shattered casque,[7] and chafed
   his hands,
And called him by his name, complaining
   loud,
And dropping bitter tears against a brow
Striped with dark blood; for all his face was
   white   380
And colorless, and like the withered moon
Smote by the fresh beam of the springing
   east;
And all his greaves and cuisses[8] dashed with
   drops
Of onset; and the light and lustrous curls—
That made his forehead like a rising sun 385
High from the dais-throne—were parched
   with dust,
Or, clotted into points and hanging loose,
Mixed with the knightly growth that fringed
   his lips.
So like a shattered column lay the King; 389
Not like that Arthur who, with lance in rest,
From spur to plume a star of tournament,
Shot through the lists at Camelot, and
   charged
Before the eyes of ladies and of kings.

Then loudly cried the bold Sir Bedivere:
"Ah! my Lord Arthur, whither shall I go?
Where shall I hide my forehead and my
   eyes?   396
For now I see the true old times are dead,
When every morning brought a noble chance,
And every chance brought out a noble knight.
Such times have been not since the light
   that led   400
The holy Elders with the gift of myrrh.[9]
But now the whole Round Table is dissolved
Which was an image of the mighty world;[10]
And I, the last, go forth companionless,
And the days darken round me, and the
   years,   405
Among new men, strange faces, other
   minds."

And slowly answered Arthur from the
   barge:
"The old order changeth, yielding place to
   new,
And God fulfills himself in many ways,
Lest one good custom should corrupt the
   world.   410
Comfort thyself; what comfort is in me?

[7]Helmet.

[8]Armor for the leg below the knee, and armor for
the thigh.

[9]See St. Matthew, 2:11.

[10]According to Malory, "Merlin made the Round
Table in tokening of the roundness of the world."

I have lived my life, and that which I have
   done
May He within himself make pure! but thou,
If thou shouldst never see my face again,
Pray for my soul. More things are wrought
   by prayer   415
Than this world dreams of. Wherefore, let
   thy voice
Rise like a fountain for me night and day.
For what are men better than sheep or goats
That nourish a blind life within the brain,
If, knowing God, they lift not hands of
   prayer   420
Both for themselves and those who call them
   friend?
For so the whole round earth is every way
Bound by gold chains about the feet of God.
But now farewell. I am going a long way
With these thou seest—if indeed I go—   425
For all my mind is clouded with a doubt—
To the island-valley of Avilion;[11]
Where falls not hail, or rain, or any snow,
Nor ever wind blows loudly; but it lies
Deep-meadowed, happy, fair with orchard
   lawns   430
And bowery hollows crowned with summer
   sea,
Where I will heal me of my grievous
   wound."

So said he, and the barge with oar and sail
Moved from the brink, like some full-
   breasted swan
That, fluting a wild carol ere her death,   435
Ruffles her pure cold plume, and takes the
   flood
With swarthy webs. Long stood Sir Bedi-
   vere
Revolving many memories, till the hull
Looked one black dot against the verge of
   dawn,
And on the mere the wailing died away.   440

But when that moan had passed for evermore,
The stillness of the dead world's winter dawn
Amazed him, and he groaned, "The King is
   gone."
And therewithal came on him the weird
   rime,
"From the great deep to the great deep he
   goes."[12]   445

Whereat he slowly turned and slowly
   clomb

[11]Avalon, home of spirits of the departed.

[12]Merlin's song when Arthur was born.

The last hard footstep of that iron crag,
Thence marked the black hull moving yet,
   and cried:
"He passes to be king among the dead,
And after healing of his grievous wound 450
He comes again; but—if he come no more—
O me, be yon dark queens in yon black boat,
Who shrieked and wailed, the three whereat
   we gazed
On that high day, when, clothed with living
   light,
They stood before his throne in silence,
   friends 455
Of Arthur, who should help him at his
   need?"

Then from the dawn it seemed there came,
   but faint
As from beyond the limit of the world,
Like the last echo born of a great cry,
Sounds, as if some fair city were one voice
Around a king returning from his wars. 461

Thereat once more he moved about, and
   clomb
Even to the highest he could climb, and saw,
Straining his eyes beneath an arch of hand,
Or thought he saw, the speck that bare the
   King, 465
Down that long water opening on the deep
Somewhere far off, pass on and on, and go
From less to less and vanish into light.
And the new sun rose bringing the new year.

FLOWER IN THE CRANNIED WALL[1]

Flower in the crannied wall,
I pluck you out of the crannies,
I hold you here, root and all, in my hand,
Little flower—but *if* I could understand
What you are, root and all, and all in all, 5
I should know what God and man is.

THE REVENGE[1]

A Ballad of the Fleet

I

At Flores in the Azores Sir Richard Grenville lay,
And a pinnace, like a fluttered bird, came
   flying from far away:

[1]Published in 1869.

[2]Published in 1878. According to Sir Walter
Raleigh—whose account of the fight is the basis of

"Spanish ships of war at sea! we have
   sighted fifty-three!"
Then sware Lord Thomas Howard: " 'Fore
   God I am no coward;
But I cannot meet them here, for my ships
   are out of gear, 5
And the half my men are sick. I must fly,
   but follow quick.
We are six ships of the line; can we fight
   with fifty-three?"

II

Then spake Sir Richard Grenville: "I know
   you are no coward;
You fly them for a moment to fight with
   them again.
But I've ninety men and more that are lying
   sick ashore. 10
I should count myself the coward if I left
   them, my Lord Howard,
To these Inquisition dogs and the devildoms
   of Spain."

III

So Lord Howard passed away with five ships
   of war that day,
Till he melted like a cloud in the silent sum-
   mer heaven;
But Sir Richard bore in hand all his sick
   men from the land 15
Very carefully and slow,
Men of Bideford in Devon,
And we laid them on the ballast down below;
For we brought them all aboard,
And they blessed him in their pain, that they
   were not left to Spain, 20
To the thumb-screw and the stake, for the
   glory of the Lord.

IV

He had only a hundred seamen to work the
   ship and to fight,
And he sailed away from Flores till the
   Spaniard came in sight,
With his huge sea-castles heaving upon the
   weather bow.
"Shall we fight or shall we fly? 25
Good Sir Richard, tell us now,
For to fight is but to die!
There'll be little of us left by the time this
   sun be set."

Tennyson's poem—the engagement took place on the
afternoon of 10 September, 1591. The English
fleet, under the command of Howard, had sailed to
the Azores to intercept Spanish treasure-ships on
their way from America.

And Sir Richard said again: "We be all good
English men.
Let us bang these dogs of Seville, the chil-
dren of the devil,   30
For I never turned my back upon Don or
devil yet."

V

Sir Richard spoke and he laughed, and we
roared a hurrah, and so
The little *Revenge* ran on sheer into the heart
of the foe,
With her hundred fighters on deck, and her
ninety sick below;
For half of their fleet to the right and half
to the left were seen,   35
And the little *Revenge* ran on through the
long sea-lane between.

VI

Thousands of their soldiers looked down
from their decks and laughed,
Thousands of their seamen made mock at
the mad little craft
Running on and on, till delayed
By their mountain-like *San Philip* that, of
fifteen hundred tons,   40
And up-shadowing high above us with her
yawning tiers of guns,
Took the breath from our sails, and we
stayed.

VII

And while now the great *San Philip* hung
above us like a cloud
Whence the thunderbolt will fall
Long and loud,   45
Four galleons drew away
From the Spanish fleet that day,
And two upon the larboard and two upon the
starboard lay,
And the battle-thunder broke from them all.

VIII

But anon the great *San Philip,* she bethought
herself and went,   50
Having that within her womb that had left
her ill content;
And the rest they came aboard us, and they
fought us hand to hand,
For a dozen times they came with their pikes
and musketeers,
And a dozen times we shook 'em off as a dog
that shakes his ears
When he leaps from the water to the land. 55

IX

And the sun went down, and the stars came
out far over the summer sea,
But never a moment ceased the fight of the
one and the fifty-three.
Ship after ship, the whole night long, their
high-built galleons came,
Ship after ship, the whole night long, with her
battle-thunder and flame;
Ship after ship, the whole night long, drew
back with her dead and her shame.   60
For some were sunk and many were shattered, and so could fight us no more—
God of battles, was ever a battle like this in
the world before?

X

For he said, "Fight on! fight on!"
Though his vessel was all but a wreck;
And it chanced that, when half of the short
summer night was gone,   65
With a grisly wound to be dressed he had left
the deck,
But a bullet struck him that was dressing it
suddenly dead,
And himself he was wounded again in the
side and the head,
And he said, "Fight on! fight on!"

XI

And the night went down, and the sun smiled
out far over the summer sea,   70
And the Spanish fleet with broken sides lay
round us all in a ring;
But they dared not touch us again, for they
feared that we still could sting,
So they watched what the end would be.
And we had not fought them in vain,
But in perilous plight were we,   75
Seeing forty of our poor hundred were slain,
And half of the rest of us maimed for life
In the crash of the cannonades and the des-
perate strife;
And the sick men down in the hold were
most of them stark and cold,
And the pikes were all broken or bent, and
the powder was all of it spent;   80
And the masts and the rigging were lying
over the side;
But Sir Richard cried in his English pride:
"We have fought such a fight for a day and
a night
As may never be fought again!
We have won great glory, my men!   85
And a day less or more

At sea or ashore,
We die—does it matter when?
Sink me the ship, Master Gunner—sink her,
    split her in twain!
Fall into the hands of God, not into the
    hands of Spain!"   90

XII

And the gunner said, "Ay, ay," but the sea-
    men made reply:
"We have children, we have wives,
And the Lord hath spared our lives.
We will make the Spaniard promise, if we
    yield, to let us go;
We shall live to fight again and to strike an-
    other blow."   95
And the lion there lay dying, and they yielded
    to the foe.

XIII

And the stately Spanish men to their flagship
    bore him then,
Where they laid him by the mast, old Sir
    Richard caught at last,
And they praised him to his face with their
    courtly foreign grace;
But he rose upon their decks, and he cried:
"I have fought for Queen and Faith like a
    valiant man and true;   101
I have only done my duty as a man is bound
    to do.
With a joyful spirit I Sir Richard Grenville
    die!"
And he fell upon their decks, and he died.

XIV

And they stared at the dead that had been so
    valiant and true,   105
And had holden the power and glory of Spain
    so cheap
That he dared her with one little ship and his
    English few;
Was he devil or man? He was devil for
    aught they knew,
But they sank his body with honor down into
    the deep,
And they manned the *Revenge* with a swar-
    thier alien crew,   110
And away she sailed with her loss and longed
    for her own;
When a wind from the lands they had ruined
    awoke from sleep,
And the water began to heave and the
    weather to moan,
And or ever that evening ended a great gale
    blew,

And a wave like the wave that is raised by an
    earthquake grew,   115
Till it smote on their hulls and their sails and
    their masts and their flags,
And the whole sea plunged and fell on the
    shot-shattered navy of Spain,
And the little *Revenge* herself went down by
    the island crags
To be lost evermore in the main.

TO VIRGIL[1]

Written at the Request of the Mantuans for the Nineteenth Centenary of Virgil's Death

I

Roman Virgil, thou that singest
    Ilion's lofty temples robed in fire,
Ilion falling, Rome arising,
    wars, and filial faith, and Dido's pyre;

II

Landscape-lover, lord of language
    more than he that sang the "Works
    and Days,"[2]
All the chosen coin of fancy
    flashing out from many a golden
    phrase;

III

Thou that singest wheat and woodland,
    tilth and vineyard, hive and horse and
    herd;   5
All the charm of all the Muses
    often flowering in a lonely word;

IV

Poet of the happy Tityrus[3]
    piping underneath his beechen bowers;
Poet of the poet-satyr[4]
    whom the laughing shepherd bound
    with flowers;

V

Chanter of the Pollio,[5] glorying
    in the blissful years again to be,
Summers of the snakeless meadow,
    unlaborious earth and oarless sea;   10

---

[1]Published in November, 1882.   [2]Hesiod.
[3]A shepherd in Virgil's first Eclogue.
[4]Silenus, *Eclogue VI.*   [5]*Eclogue IV.*

VI

Thou that seest Universal
     Nature moved by Universal Mind;[6]
Thou majestic in thy sadness
     at the doubtful doom of human kind;

VII

Light among the vanished ages;
     star that gildest yet this phantom
          shore;
Golden branch amid the shadows,[7]
     kings and realms that pass to rise no
          more;

VIII

Now thy Forum roars no longer,
     fallen every purple Caesar's dome— 15
Though thine ocean-roll of rhythm
     sound for ever of Imperial Rome—

IX

Now the Rome of slaves hath perished,
     and the Rome of freemen holds her
          place,
I, from out the Northern Island
     sundered once from all the human
          race,[8]

---

[6]See *Aeneid*, VI, 727.
[7]See *Aeneid*, VI, 208.   [8]See *Eclogue*, I, 67.

X

I salute thee, Mantovano,[9]
     I that loved thee since my day began,
Wielder of the stateliest measure
     ever molded by the lips of man.   20

CROSSING THE BAR[1]

Sunset and evening star,
     And one clear call for me!
And may there be no moaning of the bar,
     When I put out to sea,

But such a tide as moving seems asleep,   5
     Too full for sound and foam,
When that which drew from out the bound-
          less deep
     Turns again home.

Twilight and evening bell,
     And after that the dark!   10
And may there be no sadness of farewell,
     When I embark;

For though from out our bourn[2] of Time and
          Place
     The flood may bear me far,
I hope to see my Pilot face to face   15
     When I have crossed the bar.

---

[9]I. e., Mantuan. Virgil was born at Mantua.
[1]Published in 1889. Tennyson wished this poem
to be placed at the end of all editions of his poems.
[2]Boundary.

ROBERT BROWNING

1812-1889

Browning's father was a clerk in the Bank of England who lived in Camberwell, a suburb of London in the early nineteenth century. He was a man in easy circumstances and of unusual culture, interested in art, in music, and in literature. He had a good collection of pictures and a large library containing many curious and out-of-the-way books. In Camberwell Browning was born on 7 May, 1812. His education was almost entirely derived from his parents and the influences of his home. Occasionally he attended near-by schools, and occasionally, when he made it plain that conventional methods of education were not for him, he had a private tutor at home; but his formal training was decidedly irregular. He was enrolled in the University of London, but spent only a short time in university studies and made no attempt to take a degree. All this does not mean that Browning was an idle and ignorant youth; on the contrary, he was very early a man of wide and curious learning, with a cultivated taste in both painting and music. But it means that what he learned came from the influences of his home, from the encouragement of his parents, from reading in his father's library, and from the cultivated friends of his family. He early began the writing of verse and early fell under the influence of Shelley. His first published poem, *Pauline*, which appeared in 1833 when he was twenty, shows this influence strongly. *Pauline* made no impression on the public; but Browning's next poem, *Paracelsus*, published in 1835, while it attracted only a few readers, gained for its author the attention or friendship of a number of men of letters. Among these were Wordsworth, Landor, Leigh Hunt, and Dickens.

Paracelsus also attracted the attention of the actor-manager Macready, and led him to ask the poet for a play. As a result Browning wrote *Strafford*, which was acted at the Covent Garden Theater in 1837 and published in the same year. He had dramatic genius, as was evident from *Paracelsus*, and it was natural both for him and for Macready to suppose that he could succeed with plays; yet it is unfortunate that he was led to expend as much time as he did on the effort.

Strafford, while it was not a complete failure, had only a very qualified success. Nevertheless, Browning went on to write other plays, hoping for a better result, producing work which shows powerfully some of the elements of dramatic genius, and yet not writing one play which could hold the stage with complete success. This was true even of *A Blot in the 'Scutcheon* (1843), the best of the half-dozen or more plays he wrote and one which evoked the enthusiastic praise of Dickens. The truth would seem to be that Browning, knowing that he had dramatic genius, did not yet know his limitations, and needed his eight years' trial of play-writing in order to help him to the discovery of the form of poetry which he was soon to make peculiarly his own and in which he did his best work with all his powers in free play. Not all of his time during these years, however, was spent upon "regular" drama. In 1841 he published *Pippa Passes*, a series of dramatic scenes, which contains poetry that can scarcely be overpraised and at least one scene, the incident of Ottima and Sebald, of tremendous power. And in the late eighteen-thirties he had been working on another long poem into which he put the fruit of much study and for the sake of which he had made his first visit to Italy. This poem, however, *Sordello*, published in 1840, was a worse failure than were the plays. Largely because of its obscure style it disappointed Browning's friends and alienated from him for many years the general reading public. But two years later, with the publication of *Dramatic Lyrics*, he showed that he was beginning to find his true work; and this and *Dramatic Romances and Lyrics*, published in 1845, contained some of his finest poems.

About this time Browning became acquainted with Elizabeth Barrett, herself a gifted writer of poetry, conducted with her a correspondence which has become famous, finally met her and talked with her, and in 1846 married her despite the violent opposition of her father. Partly on account of her delicate health and partly because of difficulties with her father, the Brownings went to Italy and settled in Florence, where they remained until Mrs. Browning's death in 1861. During this period Browning published *Christmas Eve and Easter Day* (1850) and *Men and Women* (1855), the latter volume containing some of the best and most widely liked of all his poems. After Mrs. Browning's death he returned to England and for some years spent much time in London. In 1864 he published *Dramatis Personae,* and in 1868–1869 his longest work and, in the opinion of many, his greatest, *The Ring and the Book,* a series of poems founded on an account which he had accidentally found of a Roman murder trial of the seventeenth century. In later years Browning published much, including several translations of Greek plays; but as he grew older his style became more difficult and harsh, and a certain waywardness or indifference to the legitimate demands of readers, perhaps always to some extent apparent in his work, increased. The consequence is that much, if not most, of his latest work is inferior to the work of his best years and is no longer widely read. Browning died in his son's house at Venice on 12 December, 1889, and was buried in Westminster Abbey.

The form of poetry which Browning, as was said above, made peculiarly his own is commonly known as the dramatic monologue—a kind of poem in which some person speaks to another, or to others, self-revealingly, either narrating an incident or telling the story of his life, but in any case laying bare his soul through what he says. This form of poem gave Browning full scope for his dramatic genius without making apparent his limitations. It enabled him to exercise his dramatic imagination in the creation of a single character and a single scene without calling upon him for a large constructive ability which he did not have. It was the happiest of discoveries; here was a kind of poem apparently designed expressly for him, and he proceeded to put into it all that he had of rich imagination, deep insight, tender or delicate feeling, and curious learning. He even, when he came to

write a long poem, cast *The Ring and the Book* in this form, making it a series of monologues in which the characters of his story and several spectators each tells the story in his own way. This was an extraordinary experiment, bound to result, as it did, in some unevenness of execution and interest, but resulting also in the greatest of his achievements in the dramatic delineation of character.

The best edition of Browning is the "Centenary Edition" ed. F. G. Kenyon (*Works,* 10 vols., London, 1912). The best one-volume edition, containing some poems first published in 1914 besides all poems in the edition just mentioned, is that edited by A. Birrell (New York, 1915). *The Letters of Robert Browning and Elizabeth Barrett Browning, 1845–1846* (London, 1899) is the most important collection which has been published. *The Life of Robert Browning* by H. W. Griffin and H. C. Minchin (London, 1910; later revised) is the standard biography. Other good or useful books are: *Robert Browning* by G. K. Chesterton ("English Men of Letters" series, 1903); *Robert Browning* by C. H. Herford (London, 1905); *A Commentary upon Browning's "The Ring and the Book"* by A. K. Cook (London, 1920); *Browning as a Philosophical and Religious Teacher* by Henry Jones (Glasgow, 1891; revised ed. 1892); *Browning's Parleyings; The Autobiography of a Mind* by William Clyde DeVane (New Haven, 1927); and *A Browning Handbook* by W. C. DeVane (New York, 1935)—a model of its kind and indispensable. Finally three essays should be mentioned: Walter Bagehot's "Wordsworth, Tennyson, and Browning; or Pure, Ornate, and Grotesque Art," in *Literary Studies,* ed. Richard H. Hutton (London, 1895), II, 326–381; George Santayana's "The Poetry of Barbarism," in *Interpretations of Poetry and Religion* (New York, 1900); and D. C. Somervell's "The Reputation of Robert Browning," in *Essays and Studies by Members of the English Association,* Vol. XV (Oxford, 1929).

CAVALIER TUNES[1]

I. Marching Along

Kentish Sir Byng stood for his King,
Bidding the crop-headed Parliament swing:
And, pressing a troop unable to stoop

And see the rogues flourish and honest folk droop,
Marched them along, fifty-score strong,   5
Great-hearted gentlemen, singing this song.

God for King Charles! Pym and such carles[2]
To the Devil that prompts 'em their treasonous parles!

[1]Published in 1842, the bicentenary of the beginning of the English Civil Wars which supplied Browning's subject.

[2]Churls.

Cavaliers, up! Lips from the cup,　9
Hands from the pasty, nor bite take nor sup
Till you're—
　　Cho.—Marching along, fifty-score strong,
　　　　Great-hearted gentlemen, singing
　　　　this song.

Hampden to hell, and his obsequies' knell.
Serve Hazelrig, Fiennes, and young Harry[3]
as well!
England, good cheer! Rupert[4] is near!　15
Kentish and loyalists, keep we not here,
　　Cho.—Marching along, fifty-score strong,
　　　　Great-hearted gentlemen, singing
　　　　this song?

Then, God for King Charles! Pym and his
snarls
To the Devil that pricks on such pestilent
carles!　20
Hold by the right, you double your might;
So, onward to Nottingham,[5] fresh for the
fight,
　　Cho.—Marching along, fifty-score strong,
　　　　Great-hearted gentlemen, singing
　　　　this song!

II. Give a Rouse

King Charles, and who'll do him right now?
King Charles, and who's ripe for fight now?
Give a rouse: here's, in hell's despite now,
King Charles!

Who gave me the goods that went since?　5
Who raised me the house that sank once?
Who helped me to gold I spent since?
Who found me in wine you drank once?
　　Cho.—King Charles, and who'll do him
　　　　right now?
　　　　King Charles, and who's ripe for
　　　　fight now?　10
　　　　Give a rouse: here's, in hell's
　　　　despite now,
　　　　King Charles!

To whom used my boy George quaff else,
By the old fool's side that begot him?
For whom did he cheer and laugh else,　15
While Noll's[6] damned troopers shot him?

Cho.—King Charles, and who'll do him
　　　right now?
　　　King Charles, and who's ripe for
　　　fight now?
　　　Give a rouse: here's, in hell's
　　　despite now,
　　　King Charles!　20

III. Boot and Saddle

Boot, saddle, to horse, and away!
Rescue my castle before the hot day
Brightens to blue from its silvery gray.
　　Cho.—Boot, saddle, to horse, and away!

Ride past the suburbs, asleep as you'd say;　5
Many's the friend there, will listen and pray
"God's luck to gallants that strike up the
lay—
　　Cho.—Boot, saddle, to horse, and away!"

Forty miles off, like a roebuck at bay,
Flouts Castle Brancepeth the Roundheads'
array:　10
Who laughs, "Good fellows ere this, by my
fay,
　　Cho.—Boot, saddle, to horse, and away!"

Who? My wife Gertrude; that, honest and
gay,
Laughs when you talk of surrendering,
"Nay!　14
I've better counselors; what counsel they?
　　Cho.—Boot, saddle, to horse, and away!"

MY LAST DUCHESS[1]

Ferrara

That's my last Duchess painted on the wall,
Looking as if she were alive. I call
That piece a wonder, now: Fra Pandolf's[2]
hands
Worked busily a day, and there she stands.
Will't please you sit and look at her? I
said　5
"Fra Pandolf" by design, for never read
Strangers like you that pictured countenance,
The depth and passion of its earnest glance,

---

[3]Sir Henry Vane the younger.
[4]Prince Rupert, cousin of Charles I, under whom
he served as general.
[5]Here Charles I's standard was raised in 1642.
[6]Cromwell's.

[1]Published in 1842. Ferrara is a town in northern
Italy. The character and story of the Duke may be
founded on those of a real, sixteenth century Duke
of Ferrara.
[2]Fra means brother. Pandolf is an imaginary
artist—and monk—of the Renaissance.

But to myself they turned (since none puts by
The curtain I have drawn for you, but I)   10
And seemed as they would ask me, if they durst,
How such a glance came there; so, not the first
Are you to turn and ask thus. Sir, 't was not
Her husband's presence only, called that spot
Of joy into the Duchess' cheek: perhaps   15
Fra Pandolf chanced to say, "Her mantle laps
Over my lady's wrist too much," or "Paint
Must never hope to reproduce the faint
Half-flush that dies along her throat": such stuff   19
Was courtesy, she thought, and cause enough
For calling up that spot of joy. She had
A heart—how shall I say?—too soon made glad,
Too easily impressed: she liked whate'er
She looked on, and her looks went everywhere.
Sir, 'twas all one! My favor at her breast,
The dropping of the daylight in the West,   26
The bough of cherries some officious fool
Broke in the orchard for her, the white mule
She rode with round the terrace—all and each
Would draw from her alike the approving speech,   30
Or blush, at least. She thanked men,—good! but thanked
Somehow—I know not how—as if she ranked
My gift of a nine-hundred-years-old name
With anybody's gift. Who'd stoop to blame
This sort of trifling? Even had you skill   35
In speech—(which I have not)—to make your will
Quite clear to such an one, and say, "Just this
Or that in you disgusts me; here you miss,
Or there exceed the mark"—and if she let
Herself be lessoned so, nor plainly set   40
Her wits to yours, forsooth, and made excuse,
—E'en then would be some stooping; and I choose
Never to stoop. Oh sir, she smiled, no doubt,
Whene'er I passed her; but who passed without
Much the same smile? This grew; I gave commands;   45
Then all smiles stopped together. There she stands

As if alive. Will 't please you rise? We'll meet
The company below, then. I repeat
The Count your master's known munificence
Is ample warrant that no just pretense   50
Of mine for dowry will be disallowed;
Though his fair daughter's self, as I avowed
At starting, is my object. Nay, we'll go
Together down, sir. Notice Neptune, though,
Taming a sea-horse, thought a rarity,   55
Which Claus of Innsbruck[3] cast in bronze for me!

SOLILOQUY OF THE SPANISH CLOISTER[1]

Gr-r-r—there go, my heart's abhorrence!
    Water your damned flower-pots, do!
If hate killed men, Brother Lawrence,
    God's blood, would not mine kill you!
What? your myrtle-bush wants trimming?   5
    Oh, that rose has prior claims—
Needs its leaden vase filled brimming?
    Hell dry you up with its flames!

At the meal we sit together:
    Salve tibi![2] I must hear   10
Wise talk of the kind of weather,
    Sort of season, time of year:
Not a plenteous cork-crop: scarcely
    Dare we hope oak-galls,[3] I doubt:
What's the Latin name for "parsley"?   15
    What's the Greek name for Swine's Snout?

Whew! We'll have our platter burnished,
    Laid with care on our own shelf!
With a fire-new spoon we're furnished,
    And a goblet for ourself,   20
Rinsed like something sacrificial
    Ere 'tis fit to touch our chaps—
Marked with L for our initial!
    (He-he! There his lily snaps!)

Saint, forsooth! While brown Dolores   25
    Squats outside the Convent bank
With Sanchicha, telling stories,
    Steeping tresses in the tank,
Blue-black, lustrous, thick like horsehairs,
    —Can't I see his dead eye glow,   30
Bright as 'twere a Barbary corsair's?
    (That is, if he'd let it show!)

[3]Like Pandolf, an imaginary artist.
[1]Published in 1842. [2]Save you! (a salutation).
[3]Excrescences, made on oak trees by insects, used in manufacturing ink.

When he finishes refection,
  Knife and fork he never lays
Cross-wise, to my recollection,   35
  As do I, in Jesu's praise.
I the Trinity illustrate,
  Drinking watered orange-pulp—
In three sips the Arian[4] frustrate;
  While he drains his at one gulp.   40

Oh, those melons! If he's able
  We're to have a feast! so nice!
One goes to the Abbot's table,
  All of us get each a slice.
How go on your flowers? None double?   45
  Not one fruit-sort can you spy?
Strange!—And I, too, at such trouble
  Keep them close-nipped on the sly!

There's a great text in Galatians,[5]
  Once you trip on it, entails   50
Twenty-nine distinct damnations,
  One sure, if another fails:
If I trip him just a-dying,
  Sure of heaven as sure can be,
Spin him round and send him flying   55
  Off to hell, a Manichee?[6]

Or, my scrofulous French novel
  On gray paper with blunt type!
Simply glance at it, you grovel
  Hand and foot in Belial's gripe: 60
If I double down its pages
  At the woeful sixteenth print,
When he gathers his greengages,
  Ope a sieve and slip it in't?

Or, there's Satan!—one might venture   65
  Pledge one's soul to him, yet leave
Such a flaw in the indenture
  As he'd miss till, past retrieve,
Blasted lay that rose-acacia
  We're so proud of! *Hy, Zy, Hine*[7] . . .   70
'St, there's Vespers! *Plena gratiâ,*
  Ave, Virgo![8] Gr-r-r—you swine!

---

[4]One who holds with Arius (A. D. 256–336) that
Christ is a created being, inferior to God the Father
in nature and dignity.

[5]Probably Galations 5:19–21.

[6]Follower of the Persian Manes who maintained
the existence of two supreme principles, light
(good) and darkness (evil).

[7]Sounds perhaps echoing the vesper bell.

[8]Hail, Virgin, full of grace!

CRISTINA[1]

She should never have looked at me
  If she meant I should not love her!
There are plenty . . . men, you call such,
  I suppose . . . she may discover
All her soul to, if she pleases,   5
  And yet leave much as she found them:
But I'm not so, and she knew it
  When she fixed me, glancing round them.

What? To fix me thus meant nothing?
  But I can't tell (there's my weakness)   10
What her look said!—no vile cant, sure,
  About "need to strew the bleakness
Of some lone shore with its pearl-seed,
  That the sea feels"—no "strange yearning
That such souls have, most to lavish   15
  Where there's chance of least returning."

Oh, we're sunk enough here, God knows!
  But not quite so sunk that moments,
Sure though seldom, are denied us,
  When the spirit's true endowments   20
Stand out plainly from its false ones,
  And apprise it if pursuing
Or the right way or the wrong way,
  To its triumph or undoing.

There are flashes struck from midnights,   25
  There are fire-flames noondays kindle,
Whereby piled-up honors perish,
  Whereby swollen ambitions dwindle,
While just this or that poor impulse,
  Which for once had play unstifled,   30
Seems the sole work of a lifetime,
  That away the rest have trifled.

Doubt you if, in some such moment,
  As she fixed me, she felt clearly,
Ages past the soul existed,   35
  Here an age 'tis resting merely,
And hence fleets again for ages,
  While the true end, sole and single,
It stops here for is, this love-way,
  With some other soul to mingle?   40

Else it loses what it lived for,
  And eternally must lose it;
Better ends may be in prospect,
  Deeper blisses (if you choose it),

---

[1]Published in 1842. The title was suggested by
Maria Christina of Naples (1806–1878), who in
1829 became the fourth wife of the aged King
Ferdinand VII of Spain and who, after his death
in 1833, ruled that country for eight years as regent.
She was a coquette of dissolute life.

But this life's end and this love-bliss   45
  Have been lost here.   Doubt you whether
This she felt as, looking at me,
  Mine and her souls rushed together?

Oh, observe!   Of course, next moment,
  The world's honors, in derision,   50
Trampled out the light for ever:
  Never fear but there's provision
Of the devil's to quench knowledge
  Lest we walk the earth in rapture!
—Making those who catch God's secret   55
  Just so much more prize their capture!

Such am I: the secret's mine now!
  She has lost me, I have gained her;
Her soul's mine: and thus, grown perfect,
  I shall pass my life's remainder.   ·   60
Life will just hold out the proving
  Both our powers, alone and blended:
And then, come the next life quickly!
  This world's use will have been ended.

HOW THEY BROUGHT THE GOOD NEWS FROM GHENT TO AIX[1]

I sprang to the stirrup, and Joris, and he;
I galloped, Dirck galloped, we galloped all
    three;
"Good speed!" cried the watch, as the gate-
    bolts undrew;
"Speed!" echoed the wall to us galloping
    through;
Behind shut the postern, the lights sank to
    rest,   5
And into the midnight we galloped abreast.

Not a word to each other; we kept the great
    pace
Neck by neck, stride by stride, never chang-
    ing our place;
I turned in my saddle and made its girths
    tight,
Then shortened each stirrup, and set the
    pique[2] right,   10
Rebuckled the cheek-strap, chained slacker
    the bit,
Nor galloped less steadily Roland a whit.

'Twas moonset at starting; but while we
    drew near

---

[1]Published in 1845. Browning had no particular
historical incident in mind and only a vague idea of
Flemish geography: Roland covers about 120 miles.
[2]Peak.

Lokeren, the cocks crew and twilight dawned
    clear;
At Boom, a great yellow star came out to
    see;   15
At Düffeld, 'twas morning as plain as could
    be;
And from Mecheln church-steeple we heard
    the half-chime,
So Joris broke silence with, "Yet there is
    time!"

At Aershot, up leaped of a sudden the sun,
And against him the cattle stood black every
    one,   20
To stare through the mist at us galloping
    past,
And I saw my stout galloper Roland at last,
With resolute shoulders, each butting away
The haze, as some bluff river headland its
    spray:

And his low head and crest, just one sharp
    ear bent back   25
For my voice, and the other pricked out on
    his track;
And one eye's black intelligence,—ever that
    glance
O'er its white edge at me, his own master,
    askance!
And the thick heavy spume-flakes which aye
    and anon
His fierce lips shook upwards in galloping
    on.   30

By Hasselt, Dirck groaned; and cried Joris,
    "Stay spur!
Your Roos galloped bravely, the fault's not
    in her,
We'll remember at Aix"—for one heard the
    quick wheeze
Of her chest, saw the stretched neck and
    staggering knees,
And sunk tail, and horrible heave of the
    flank,   35
As down on her haunches she shuddered and
    sank.

So, we were left galloping, Joris and I,
Past Looz and past Tongres, no cloud in the
    sky;
The broad sun above laughed a pitiless laugh,
'Neath our feet broke the brittle bright
    stubble like chaff;   40
Till over by Dalhem a dome-spire sprang
    white,
And "Gallop," gasped Joris, "for Aix is in
    sight!"

"How they'll greet us!"—and all in a moment his roan
Rolled neck and croup over, lay dead as a stone;
And there was my Roland to bear. the whole weight 45
Of the news which alone could save Aix from her fate,
With his nostrils like pits full of blood to the brim,
And with circles of red for his eye-sockets' rim.

Then I cast loose my buffcoat, each holster let fall,
Shook off both my jack-boots, let go belt and all, 50
Stood up in the stirrup, leaned, patted his ear,
Called my Roland his pet-name, my horse without peer;
Clapped my hands, laughed and sang, any noise, bad or good,
Till at length into Aix Roland galloped and stood.

And all I remember is—friends flocking round 55
As I sat with his head 'twixt my knees on the ground;
And no voice but was praising this Roland of mine,
As I poured down his throat our last measure of wine,
Which (the burgesses voted by common consent)
Was no more than his due who brought good news from Ghent. 60

PICTOR IGNOTUS[1]

Florence, 15—

I could have painted pictures like that youth's
Ye praise so. How my soul springs up!
No bar
Stayed me—ah, thought which saddens while it soothes!
—Never did fate forbid me, star by star,
To outburst on your night with all my gift 5
Of fires from God: nor would my flesh have shrunk
From seconding my soul, with eyes uplift
And wide to heaven, or, straight like thunder, sunk

___
[1] Published in 1845.

To the center, of an instant; or around
Turned calmly and inquisitive, to scan 10
The license and the limit, space and bound,
Allow to truth made visible in man.
And, like that youth ye praise so, all I saw,
Over the canvas could my hand have flung,
Each face obedient to its passion's law, 15
Each passion clear proclaimed without a tongue;
Whether Hope rose at once in all the blood,
A-tiptoe for the blessing of embrace,
Or Rapture drooped the eyes, as when her brood
Pull down the nesting dove's heart to its place; 20
Or Confidence lit swift the forehead up,
And locked the mouth fast, like a castle braved,—
O human faces, hath it spilt, my cup?
What did ye give me that I have not saved?
Nor will I say I have not dreamed (how well!) 25
Of going—I, in each new picture,—forth,
As, making new hearts beat and bosoms swell,
To Pope or Kaiser, East, West, South, or North,
Bound for the calmly satisfied great State,
Or glad aspiring little burgh, it went, 30
Flowers cast upon the car which bore the freight,
Through old streets named afresh from the event,
Till it reached home, where learned age should greet
My face, and youth, the star not yet distinct
Above his hair, lie learning at my feet!— 35
Oh, thus to live, I and my picture, linked
With love about, and praise, till life should end,
And then not go to heaven, but linger here,
Here on my earth, earth's every man my friend,—
The thought grew frightful, 'twas so wildly dear! 40
But a voice changed it. Glimpses of such sights
Have scared me, like the revels through a door
Of some strange house of idols at its rites!
This world seemed not the world it was before:
Mixed with my loving trusting ones, there trooped 45

. . . Who summoned those cold faces that begun
To press on me and judge me? Though I stooped
Shrinking, as from the soldiery a nun,
They drew me forth, and spite of me . . . enough!
These buy and sell our pictures, take and give, 50
Count them for garniture and household-stuff,
And where they live needs must our pictures live
And see their faces, listen to their prate,
Partakers of their daily pettiness,
Discussed of,—"This I love, or this I hate, 55
This likes me more, and this affects me less!"
Wherefore I chose my portion. If at whiles
My heart sinks, as monotonous I paint
These endless cloisters and eternal aisles
With the same series, Virgin, Babe and Saint, 60
With the same cold calm beautiful regard,—
At least no merchant traffics in my heart;
The sanctuary's gloom at least shall ward
Vain tongues from where my pictures stand apart:
Only prayer breaks the silence of the shrine
While, blackening in the daily candle-smoke, 66
They moulder on the damp wall's travertine,
'Mid echoes the light foot never woke.
So, die my pictures! surely, gently die!
O youth, men praise so,—holds their praise its worth? 70
Blown harshly, keeps the trump its golden cry?
Tastes sweet the water with such specks of earth?

THE LOST LEADER [1]

Just for a handful of silver he left us,
Just for a riband to stick in his coat—
Found the one gift of which fortune bereft us,
Lost all the others she lets us devote;

They, with the gold to give, doled him out silver, 5
So much was theirs who so little allowed:
How all our copper had gone for his service!
Rags—were they purple, his heart had been proud!
We that had loved him so, followed him, honored him,
Lived in his mild and magnificent eye, 10
Learned his great language, caught his clear accents,
Made him our pattern to live and to die!
Shakespeare was of us, Milton was for us,
Burns, Shelley, were with us,—they watch from their graves!
He alone breaks from the van and the freemen, 15
—He alone sinks to the rear and the slaves!
We shall march prospering,—not through his presence;
Songs may inspirit us,—not from his lyre;
Deeds will be done,—while he boasts his quiescence,
Still bidding crouch whom the rest bade aspire: 20
Blot out his name, then, record one lost soul more,
One task more declined, one more foot-path untrod,
One more devils'-triumph and sorrow for angels,
One wrong more to man, one more insult to God!
Life's night begins: let him never come back to us! 25
There would be doubt, hesitation and pain,

---

[1] Published in 1845. Browning was often asked if Wordsworth was the subject of this poem. The following letter, written to A. B. Grosart on 24 February, 1875, is one of his replies:
"DEAR MR. GROSART,—I have been asked the question you now address me with, and as duly answered it, I can't remember how many times; there is no sort of objection to one more assurance or rather confession, on my part, that I *did* in my hasty youth presume to use the great and venerated personality of Wordsworth as a sort of painter's model; one from which this or the other particular feature may be selected and turned to account; had I intended more, above all, such a boldness as portraying the entire man, I should not have talked about 'handfuls of silver and bits of ribbon.' These never influenced the change of politics in the great poet, whose defection, nevertheless, accompanied as it was by a regular face-about of his special party, was to my juvenile apprehension, and even mature consideration, an event to deplore. But just as in the tapestry on my wall I can recognize figures which have *struck out* a fancy, on occasion, that though truly enough thus derived, yet would be preposterous as a copy, so, though I dare not deny the original of my little poem, I altogether refuse to have it considered as the 'very effigies' of such a moral and intellectual superiority.
"Faithfully yours,
"ROBERT BROWNING."
In 1845, however, Browning's "handful of silver" and "riband" could only be interpreted as references to Wordsworth's recent acceptance of a pension and the laureateship.

Forced praise on our part—the glimmer of
    twilight,
  Never glad confident morning again!
Best fight on well, for we taught him—strike
    gallantly,
  Menace our heart ere we master his own;
Then let him receive the new knowledge and
    wait us,   31
  Pardoned in heaven, the first by the throne!

HOME THOUGHTS FROM ABROAD[2]

Oh, to be in England
Now that April's there,
And whoever wakes in England
Sees, some morning, unaware,
That the lowest boughs and the brush-wood
    sheaf   5
Round the elm-tree bole are in tiny leaf,
While the chaffinch sings on the orchard
    bough
In England—now!

And after April, when May follows,
And the whitethroat builds, and all the swal-
    lows!   10
Hark, where my blossomed pear-tree in the
    hedge
Leans to the field and scatters on the clover
Blossoms and dewdrops—at the bent spray's
    edge—
That's the wise thrush; he sings each song
    twice over,
Lest you should think he never could recap-
    ture   15
The first fine careless rapture!
And though the fields look rough with hoary
    dew,
All will be gay when noontide wakes anew
The buttercups, the little children's dower
—Far brighter than this gaudy melon-
    flower!   20

THE BISHOP ORDERS HIS TOMB AT SAINT PRAXED'S CHURCH[1]

Rome, 15—

Vanity, saith the preacher, vanity!
Draw round my bed: is Anselm keeping
    back?

[2]Published in 1845.

[1]Published in 1845. In October, 1844, Browning had visited the church of S. Prassede in Rome; but apparently he did not have the life of any individual bishop in mind when he wrote.

Nephews—sons mine . . . ah God, I know
    not! Well—
She, men would have to be your mother once,
Old Gandolf envied me, so fair she was!   5
What's done is done, and she is dead beside,
Dead long ago, and I am Bishop since,
And as she died so must we die ourselves,
And thence ye may perceive the world's a
    dream.
Life, how and what is it? As here I lie   10
In this state-chamber, dying by degrees,
Hours and long hours in the dead night, I ask
"Do I live, am I dead?" Peace, peace seems
    all.
Saint Praxed's ever was the church for
    peace;
And so, about this tomb of mine. I fought
With tooth and nail to save my niche, ye
    know: 16
—Old Gandolf cozened me, despite my care;
Shrewd was that snatch from out the cor-
    ner South
He graced his carrion with, God curse the
    same!
Yet still my niche is not so cramped but
    thence   20
One sees the pulpit o' the epistle-side,[2]
And somewhat of the choir, those silent seats,
And up into the aery dome where live
The angels, and a sunbeam's sure to lurk:
And I shall fill my slab of basalt there,   25
And 'neath my tabernacle take my rest,
With those nine columns round me, two and
    two,
The odd one at my feet where Anselm
    stands:
Peach-blossom marble all, the rare, the ripe
As fresh-poured red wine of a mighty pulse.
—Old Gandolf with his paltry onion-stone,
Put me where I may look at him! True
    peach,   32
Rosy and flawless: how I earned the prize!
Draw close: that conflagration of my church
—What then? So much was saved if aught
    were missed!   35
My sons, ye would not be my death? Go dig
The white-grape vineyard where the oil-press
    stood,
Drop water gently till the surface sink,
And if ye find . . . Ah God, I know not,
    I! . . .
Bedded in store of rotten fig-leaves soft,   40
And corded up in a tight olive-frail,[3]

[2]The right or south side of the altar, the side on which a passage from the apostolical epistles is read in the communion service.

[3]Olive-basket.

Some lump, ah God, of *lapis lazuli,*
Big as a Jew's head cut off at the nape,
Blue as a vein o'er the Madonna's breast . . .
Sons, all have I bequeathed you, villas, all, 45
That brave Frascati villa with its bath,
So, let the blue lump poise between my knees,
Like God the Father's globe on both his
    hands
Ye worship in the Jesu Church so gay,
For Gandolf shall not choose but see and
    burst! 50
Swift as a weaver's shuttle fleet our years:
Man goeth to the grave, and where is he?
Did I say basalt for my slab, sons?   Black—
'Twas ever antique-black I meant!   How
    else
Shall we contrast my frieze to come be-
    neath? 55
The bas-relief in bronze ye promised me,
Those Pans and Nymphs ye wot of, and per-
    chance
Some tripod, thyrsus,[4] with a vase or so,
The Savior at his sermon on the mount,
Saint Praxed in a glory, and one Pan 60
Ready to twitch the Nymph's last garment
    off
And Moses with the tables . . . but I know
Ye mark me not!   What do they whisper
    thee,
Child of my bowels, Anselm?   Ah, ye hope
To revel down my villas while I gasp 65
Bricked o'er with beggar's moldy travertine
Which Gandolf from his tomb-top chuckles
    at!
Nay, boys, ye love me—all of jasper, then!
'Tis jasper ye stand pledged to, lest I grieve
My bath must needs be left behind, alas! 70
One block, pure green as a pistachio-nut,
There's plenty jasper somewhere in the
    world—
And have I not Saint Praxed's ear to pray
Horses for ye, and brown Greek manu-
    scripts,
And mistresses with great smooth marbly
    limbs? 75
—That's if ye carve my epitaph aright,
Choice Latin, picked phrase, Tully's[5] every
    word,
No gaudy ware like Gandolf's second line—
Tully, my masters?   Ulpian[6] serves his need!
And then how I shall lie through centuries, 80
And hear the blessed mutter of the mass,

And see God made and eaten all day long,
And feel the steady candle-flame, and taste
Good   strong   thick   stupefying   incense-
    smoke!
For as I lie here, hours of the dead night, 85
Dying in state and by such slow degrees,
I fold my arms as if they clasped a crook,
And stretch my feet forth straight as stone
    can point,
And let the bedclothes, for a mortcloth,[7] drop
Into great laps and folds of sculptor's-work:
And as yon tapers dwindle, and strange
    thoughts 91
Grow, with a certain humming in my ears,
About the life before I lived this life,
And this life too, popes, cardinals and
    priests,
Saint Praxed at his sermon on the mount, 95
Your tall pale mother with her talking eyes,
And new found agate urns as fresh as day,
And marble's language, Latin pure, discreet,
—Aha, ELUCESCEBAT[8] quoth our friend?
No Tully, said I, Ulpian at the best! 100
Evil and brief hath been my pilgrimage.
All *lapis,* all, sons!   Else I give the Pope
My villas!   Will ye ever eat my heart?
Ever your eyes were as a lizard's quick,
They glitter like your mother's for my soul,
Or ye would heighten my impoverished
    frieze, 106
Piece out its starved design, and fill my vase
With grapes, and add a visor and a Term,[9]
And to the tripod ye would tie a lynx
That in his struggle throws the thyrsus down,
To comfort me on my entablature 111
Whereon I am to lie till I must ask
"Do I live, am I dead?"   There, leave me,
    there!
For ye have stabbed me with ingratitude
To death—ye wish it—God, ye wish it!
    Stone— 115
Gritstone,   a-crumble!   Clammy   squares
    which sweat
As if the corpse they keep were oozing
    through—
And no more *lapis* to delight the world!
Well, go!   I bless ye.   Fewer tapers there,
But in a row: and, going, turn your backs 120
—Ay, like departing altar-ministrants,
And leave me in my church, the church for
    peace,
That I may watch at leisure if he leers—
Old Gandolf—at me, from his onion-stone,
As still he envied me, so fair she was! 125

----

[4]Staff borne by Bacchus and his followers.
[5]Cicero's.
[6]Domitius Ulpianus, Latin legal writer of the
third century A. D.

[7]Funeral pall.   [8]He shone.
[9]Antique boundary post with carved head.

MEETING AT NIGHT[1]

The gray sea and the long black land;
And the yellow half-moon large and low;
And the startled little waves that leap
In fiery ringlets from their sleep,
As I gain the cove with pushing prow,   5
And quench its speed i' the slushy sand.

Then a mile of warm sea-scented beach;
Three fields to cross till a farm appears;
A tap at the pane, the quick sharp scratch
And blue spurt of a lighted match,   10
And a voice less loud, through its joys and
    fears,
Than the two hearts beating each to each!

PARTING AT MORNING[2]

Round the cape of a sudden came the sea,
And the sun looked over the mountain's rim:
And straight was a path of gold for him,[3]
And the need of a world of men for me.

LOVE AMONG THE RUINS[4]

Where the quiet-colored end of evening
    smiles
    Miles and miles
On the solitary pastures where our sheep
    Half-asleep
Tinkle homeward through the twilight, stray
    or stop   5
    As they crop—
Was the site once of a city great and gay,
    (So they say)
Of our country's very capital, its prince
    Ages since   10
Held his court in, gathered councils, wielding
    far
    Peace or war.

Now,—the country does not even boast a
    tree,
    As you see,
To distinguish slopes of verdure, certain rills
    From the hills   16
Intersect and give a name to (else they run
    Into one),

Where the domed and daring palace shot its
    spires
    Up like fires   20
O'er the hundred-gated circuit of a wall
    Bounding all,
Made of marble, men might march on nor be
    pressed,
    Twelve abreast.

And such plenty and perfection, see, of grass
    Never was!   26
Such a carpet as, this summer-time, o'er-
    spreads
    And embeds
Every vestige of the city, guessed alone,
    Stock or stone—   30
Where a multitude of men breathed joy and
    woe
    Long ago;
Lust of glory pricked their hearts up, dread
    of shame
    Struck them tame;
And that glory and that shame alike, the gold
    Bought and sold.   36

Now,—the single little turret that remains
    On the plains,
By the caper overrooted, by the gourd
    Overscored,   40
While the patching houseleek's head of blos-
    som winks
    Through the chinks—
Marks the basement whence a tower in
    ancient time
    Sprang sublime,
And a burning ring, all round, the chariots
    traced   45
    As they raced,
And the monarch and his minions and his
    dames
    Viewed the games.

And I know, while thus the quiet-colored eve
    Smiles to leave   50
To their folding, all our many-tinkling fleece
    In such peace,
And the slopes and rills in undistinguished
    gray
    Melt away—
That a girl with eager eyes and yellow hair 55
    Waits me there
In the turret whence the charioteers caught
    soul
    For the goal,
When the king looked, where she looks now,
    breathless, dumb
    Till I come.   60

---

[1]Published in 1845.
[2]Published in 1845.   [3]The sun.
[4]Published in 1855.

But he looked upon the city, every side,
    Far and wide,
All the mountains topped with temples, all
    the glades'
    Colonnades,
All the causeys,[5] bridges, aqueducts,—and
    then,   65
    All the men!
When I do come, she will speak not, she will
    stand,
    Either hand
On my shoulder, give her eyes the first em-
    brace
    Of my face,   70
Ere we rush, ere we extinguish sight and
    speech
    Each on each.

In one year they sent a million fighters forth
    South and North,
And they built their gods a brazen pillar high
    As the sky,   76
Yet reserved a thousand chariots in full
    force—
    Gold, of course.
Oh heart! oh blood that freezes, blood that
    burns!
    Earth's returns   80
For whole centuries of folly, noise and sin!
    Shut them in
With their triumphs and their glories and the
    rest!
    Love is best.

UP AT A VILLA—DOWN IN THE CITY[1]

(As Distinguished by an Italian Person of Quality)

Had I but plenty of money, money enough
    and to spare,
The house for me, no doubt, were a house in
    the city-square;
Ah, such a life, such a life, as one leads at
    the window there!
Something to see, by Bacchus, something to
    hear, at least!
There, the whole day long, one's life is a per-
    fect feast;   5
While up at a villa one lives, I maintain it,
    no more than a beast.

Well now, look at our villa! stuck like the
    horn of a bull

---

[5]Causeways.

[1]Published in 1855. The city is probably Siena,
in a villa outside of which the Brownings lived in
the autumn of 1850.

Just on a mountain-edge as bare as the crea-
    ture's skull,
Save a mere shag of a bush with hardly a
    leaf to pull!
—I scratch my own, sometimes, to see if the
    hair's turned wool.   10

But the city, oh the city—the square with
    the houses!   Why?
They are stone-faced, white as a curd, there's
    something to take the eye!
Houses in four straight lines, not a single
    front awry;
You watch who crosses and gossips, who
    saunters, who hurries by;
Green blinds, as a matter of course, to draw
    when the sun gets high;   15
And the shops with fanciful signs which are
    painted properly.

What of a villa? Though winter be over in
    March by rights,
'Tis May perhaps ere the snow shall have
    withered well off the heights:
You've the brown plowed land before, where
    the oxen steam and wheeze,
And the hills over-smoked behind by the
    faint gray olive-trees.   20

Is it better in May, I ask you? You've sum-
    mer all at once;
In a day he leaps complete with a few strong
    April suns.
'Mid the sharp short emerald wheat, scarce
    risen three fingers well,
The wild tulip, at end of its tube, blows out
    its great red bell
Like a thin clear bubble of blood, for the
    children to pick and sell.   25

Is it ever hot in the square? There's a
    fountain to spout and splash!
In the shade it sings and springs; in the shine
    such foambows flash
On the horses with curling fish-tails, that
    prance and paddle and pash
Round the lady atop in her conch—fifty
    gazers do not abash,
Though all that she wears is some weeds
    round her waist in a sort of sash.   30

All the year long at the villa, nothing to see
    though you linger,
Except yon cypress that points like death's
    lean lifted forefinger.
Some think fireflies pretty, when they mix i'
    the corn and mingle,

Or thrid[2] the stinking hemp till the stalks of
it seem a-tingle.
Late August or early September, the stun-
ning cicala is shrill,   35
And the bees keep their tiresome whine
round the resinous firs on the hill.
Enough of the seasons,—I spare you the
months of the fever and chill.

Ere you open your eyes in the city, the
blessed church-bells begin:
No sooner the bells leave off than the diligence rattles in:
You get the pick of the news, and it costs you
never a pin.   40
By and by there's the traveling doctor gives
pills, lets blood, draws teeth;
Or the Pulcinello-trumpet[3] breaks up the
market beneath.
At the post-office such a scene-picture—the
new play, piping hot!
And a notice how, only this morning, three
liberal thieves[4] were shot.
Above it, behold the Archbishop's most
fatherly of rebukes,   45
And beneath, with his crown and his lion,
some little new law of the Duke's!
Or a sonnet with flowery marge, to the Rev-
erend Don So-and-so,
Who is[5] Dante, Boccaccio, Petrarca, Saint
Jerome, and Cicero,

---

[2]Thread.

[3]The trumpet announcing a Punch-and-Judy
show.

[4]I. e., those executed were republicans, and
"thieves" indicates the "person of quality's" attitude
towards those whose politics differed from his.

[5]I. e., rivals.

"And moreover," (the sonnet goes riming)
"the skirts of Saint Paul has reached,
Having preached us those six Lent-lectures
more unctuous than ever he preached."
Noon strikes,—here sweeps the procession!
our Lady borne smiling and smart   51
With a pink gauze gown all spangles, and
seven swords stuck in her heart![6]
Bang-whang-whang goes the drum, *tootle-te-
tootle* the fife;
No keeping one's haunches still: it's the
greatest pleasure in life.

But bless you, it's dear—it's dear! fowls,
wine, at double the rate.   55
They have clapped a new tax upon salt, and
what oil pays passing the gate[7]
It's a horror to think of. And so, the villa
for me, not the city!
Beggars can scarcely be choosers: but still—
ah, the pity, the pity!
Look, two and two go the priests, then the
monks with cowls and sandals,
And the penitents dressed in white shirts,
a-holding the yellow candles;   60
One, he carries a flag up straight, and another a cross with handles,
And the Duke's guard brings up the rear, for
the better prevention of scandals:
Bang-whang-whang goes the drum, *tootle-te-
tootle* the fife.
Oh, a day in the city-square, there is no such
pleasure in life!

---

[6]The swords symbolize the Seven Sorrows of our
Lady—the Virgin Mary.

[7]I. e., what tax has to be paid when it is brought
into the city.

FRA LIPPO LIPPI[1]

I am poor brother Lippo, by your leave!
You need not clap your torches to my face.
Zooks, what's to blame? you think you see
a monk!
What, 'tis past midnight, and you go the
rounds,
And here you catch me at an alley's end   5
Where sportive ladies leave their doors ajar?
The Carmine's[2] my cloister: hunt it up,
Do,—harry out, if you must show your zeal,
Whatever rat, there, haps on his wrong hole,
And nip each softling of a wee white mouse,

Weke, weke, that's crept to keep him com-
pany!
Aha, you know your betters! Then, you'll
take
Your hand away that's fiddling on my throat,
And please to know me likewise. Who am
I?
Why, one, sir, who is lodging with a friend 15
Three streets off—he's a certain . . . how
d'ye call?
Master—a . . . Cosimo of the Medici,[3]
I' the house that caps the corner. Boh! you
were best!

---

[1]Published in 1855. Filippo Lippi's life (1406?–
1469) is to be found in Vasari's *Lives of the
Painters.*

[2]The monastery of the friars Del Carmine.

[3]Cosimo de' Medici (1389–1464), who built "the
house that caps the corner" in 1430. The time of the
poem is between that year and 1432, when Fra
Lippo left his monastery.

Remember and tell me, the day you're
    hanged,
How you affected such a gullet's-gripe!   20
But you, sir, it concerns you that your knaves
Pick up a manner nor discredit you:
Zooks, are we pilchards, that they sweep the
    streets
And count fair prize what comes into their
    net?
He's Judas to a tittle, that man is!   25
Just such a face! Why, sir, you make
    amends.
Lord, I'm not angry! Bid your hangdogs go
Drink out this quarter-florin to the health
Of the munificent House that harbors me
(And many more beside, lads! more beside!)
And all's come square again. I'd like his
    face—   31
His, elbowing on his comrade in the door
With the pike and lantern,—for the slave
    that holds
John Baptist's head a-dangle by the hair
With one hand ("Look you, now," as who
    should say)   35
And his weapon in the other, yet unwiped!
It's not your chance to have a bit of chalk,
A wood-coal or the like? or you should see!
Yes, I'm the painter, since you style me so.
What, brother Lippo's doings, up and down,
You know them and they take you? Like
    enough!   41
I saw the proper twinkle in your eye—
'Tell you, I liked your looks at very first.
Let's sit and set things straight now, hip to
    haunch.
Here's spring come, and the nights one
    makes up bands   45
To roam the town and sing out carnival,
And I've been three weeks shut within my
    mew,
A-painting for the great man, saints and
    saints
And saints again. I could not paint all night—
Ouf! I leaned out of window for fresh air.   50
There came a hurry of feet and little feet,
A sweep of lute-strings, laughs, and whifts
    of song,—
Flower o' the broom,
Take away love, and our earth is a tomb!
Flower o' the quince,   55
I let Lisa go, and what good in life since?
Flower o' the thyme[4]—and so on. Round
    they went.
Scarce had they turned the corner when a
    titter

[4]This and the following flower-songs are modeled
on the *stornelli* sung by the peasants of Tuscany.

Like the skipping of rabbits by moonlight,—
    three slim shapes,
And a face that looked up . . . zooks, sir,
    flesh and blood,   60
That's all I'm made of! Into shreds it went,
Curtain and counterpane and coverlet,
All the bed-furniture—a dozen knots,
There was a ladder! Down I let myself,
Hands and feet, scrambling somehow, and so
    dropped,   65
And after them. I came up with the fun
Hard by Saint Laurence,[5] hail fellow, well
    met,—
Flower o' the rose,
If I've been merry, what matter who knows?
And so as I was stealing back again   70
To get to bed and have a bit of sleep
Ere I rise up to-morrow and go work
On Jerome knocking at his poor old breast
With his great round stone to subdue the
    flesh,
You snap me of the sudden. Ah, I see!   75
Though your eye twinkles still, you shake
    your head—
Mine's shaved—a monk, you say—the sting's
    in that!
If Master Cosimo announced himself,
Mum's the word naturally; but a monk!
Come, what am I a beast for? tell us, now!
I was a baby when my mother died   81
And father died and left me in the street.
I starved there, God knows how, a year or
    two
On fig-skins, melon-parings, rinds and
    shucks,
Refuse and rubbish. One fine frosty day,   85
My stomach being empty as your hat,
The wind doubled me up and down I went.
Old Aunt Lapaccia trussed me with one hand
(Its fellow was a stinger as I knew),
And so along the wall, over the bridge,   90
By the straight cut to the convent. Six words
    there, ·
While I stood munching my first bread that
    month:
"So, boy, you're minded," quoth the good
    fat father,
Wiping his own mouth, 'twas refection-
    time,—
"To quit this very miserable world?   95
Will you renounce" . . . "the mouthful of
    bread?" thought I;
By no means! Brief, they made a monk of
    me;
I did renounce the world, its pride and greed,
Palace, farm, villa, shop, and banking-house,

[5]The church of San Lorenzo.

Trash, such as these poor devils of Medici
Have given their hearts to—all at eight years
   old.   101
Well, sir, I found in time, you may be sure,
'Twas not for nothing—the good bellyful,
The warm serge and the rope that goes all
   round,
And day-long blessèd idleness beside!   105
"Let's see what the urchin's fit for"—that
   came next.
Not overmuch their way, I must confess.
Such a to-do! They tried me with their
   books;
Lord, they'd have taught me Latin in pure
   waste!
Flower o' the clove,   110
All the Latin I construe is "amo," I love!
But, mind you, when a boy starves in the
   streets
Eight years together, as my fortune was,
Watching folk's faces to know who will fling
The bit of half-stripped grape-bunch he
   desires,   115
And who will curse or kick him for his
   pains,—
Which gentleman processional and fine,
Holding a candle to the Sacrament,
Will wink and let him lift a plate and catch
The droppings of the wax to sell again,   120
Or holla for the Eight[6] and have him
   whipped,—
How say I?—nay, which dog bites, which
   lets drop
His bone from the heap of offal in the
   street,—
Why, soul and sense of him grow sharp alike,
He learns the look of things, and none the
   less   125
For admonition from the hunger-pinch.
I had a store of such remarks, be sure,
Which, after I found leisure, turned to use.
I drew men's faces on my copy-books,
Scrawled them within the antiphonary's[7]
   marge,   130
Joined legs and arms to the long music-notes,
Found eyes and nose and chin for A's and
   B's,
And made a string of pictures of the world
Betwixt the ins and outs of verb and noun,
On the wall, the bench, the door. The
   monks looked black.   135
"Nay," quoth the Prior, "turn him out, d'ye
   say?
In no wise. Lose a crow and catch a lark.
What if at last we get our man of parts,

[6]The magistrates who governed Florence.

[7]The Roman service-book.

We Carmelites, like those Camaldolese
And Preaching Friars,[8] to do our church up
   fine   140
And put the front on it that ought to be!"
And hereupon he bade me daub away.
Thank you! my head being crammed, the
   walls a blank,
Never was such prompt disemburdening.
First, every sort of monk, the black and
   white,   145
I drew them, fat and lean: then, folk at
   church,
From good old gossips waiting to confess
Their cribs[9] of barrel-droppings, candle-
   ends,—
To the breathless fellow at the altar-foot,
Fresh from his murder, safe and sitting
   there   150
With the little children round him in a row
Of admiration, half for his beard and half
For that white anger of his victim's son
Shaking a fist at him with one fierce arm,
Signing himself with the other because of
   Christ   155
(Whose sad face on the cross sees only this
After the passion of a thousand years)
Till some poor girl, her apron o'er her head,
(Which the intense eyes looked through)
   came at eve
On tiptoe, said a word, dropped in a loaf, 160
Her pair of earrings and a bunch of flowers
(The brute took growling), prayed, and so
   was gone.
I painted all, then cried " 'Tis ask and have;
Choose, for more's ready!"—laid the ladder
   flat,   164
And showed my covered bit of cloister-wall.
The monks closed in a circle and praised loud
Till checked, taught what to see and not to
   see,
Being simple bodies,—"That's the very man!
Look at the boy who stoops to pat the dog!
That woman's like the Prior's niece who
   comes   170
To care about his asthma: it's the life!"
But there my triumph's straw-fire flared and
   funked;
Their betters took their turn to see and say:
The Prior and the learnèd pulled a face
And stopped all that in no time. "How?
   what's here?   175
Quite from the mark of painting, bless us all!
Faces, arms, legs, and bodies like the true
As much as pea and pea! it's devil's-game!
Your business is not to catch men with show,
With homage to the perishable clay,   180

[8]The Dominicans.   [9]Petty thefts.

But lift them over it, ignore it all,
Make them forget there's such a thing as
flesh.
Your business is to paint the souls of men—
Man's soul, and it's a fire, smoke . . . no, it's
not . . . 184
It's vapor done up like a new-born babe—
(In that shape when you die it leaves your
mouth)
It's . . . well, what matters talking, it's the
soul!
Give us no more of body than shows soul!
Here's Giotto,[10] with his Saint a-praising
God,
That sets us praising,—why not stop with
him? 190
Why put all thoughts of praise out of our
head
With wonder at lines, colors, and what not?
Paint the soul, never mind the legs and arms!
Rub all out, try at it a second time.
Oh, that white smallish female with the
breasts, 195
She's just my niece . . . Herodias,[11] I would
say,—
Who went and danced and got men's heads
cut off!
Have it all out!" Now, is this sense, I ask?
A fine way to paint soul, by painting body
So ill, the eye can't stop there, must go fur-
ther 200
And can't fare worse! Thus, yellow does
for white
When what you put for yellow's simply
black,
And any sort of meaning looks intense
When all beside itself means and looks
naught.
Why can't a painter lift each foot in turn, 205
Left foot and right foot, go a double step,
Make his flesh liker and his soul more like,
Both in their order? Take the prettiest face,
The Prior's niece . . . patron-saint—is it so
pretty 209
You can't discover if it means hope, fear,
Sorrow or joy? won't beauty go with these?
Suppose I've made her eyes all right and
blue,
Can't I take breath and try to add life's flash,
And then add soul and heighten them three-
fold?
Or say there's beauty with no soul at all—215
(I never saw it—put the case the same—)
If you get simple beauty and naught else,
You get about the best thing God invents:

That's somewhat: and you'll find the soul
you have missed,
Within yourself, when you return him
thanks. 220
"Rub all out!" Well, well, there's my life, in
short,
And so the thing has gone on ever since.
I'm grown a man no doubt, I've broken
bonds:
You should not take a fellow eight years
old 224
And make him swear to never kiss the girls.
I'm my own master, paint now as I please—
Having a friend, you see, in the Corner-
house![12]
Lord, it's fast holding by the rings in front—
Those great rings serve more purposes than
just
To plant a flag in, or tie up a horse! 230
And yet the old schooling sticks, the old
grave eyes
Are peeping o'er my shoulder as I work,
The heads shake still—"It's art's decline, my
son!
You're not of the true painter, great and
old;
Brother Angelico's[13] the man, you'll find; 235
Brother Lorenzo stands his single peer:
Fag on at flesh, you'll never make the third!"
Flower o' the pine,
You keep your mistr . . . manners, and I'll
stick to mine!
I'm not the third, then: bless us, they must
know! 240
Don't you think they're the likeliest to know,
They with their Latin? So, I swallow my
rage,
Clench my teeth, suck my lips in tight, and
paint
To please them—sometimes do and some-
times don't;
For, doing most, there's pretty sure to come
A turn, some warm eve finds me at my
saints— 246
A laugh, a cry, the business of the world—
(*Flower o' the peach,*
Death for us all, and his own life for each!)
And my whole soul revolves, the cup runs
over, 250
The world and life's too big to pass for a
dream,

---

[10] Architect and painter (1266–1337).
[11] See St. Matthew, 14:6–11.

[12] I. e., in the Medici Palace.
[13] Fra Angelico (1387–1455) was a religious painter, painting the soul and not minding the legs and arms. He is said to have fasted and prayed before painting, and to have painted some of his pictures while kneeling. Lorenzo Monaco (the monk) was a painter of the Camaldolese.

And I do these wild things in sheer despite,
And play the fooleries you catch me at,
In pure rage! The old mill-horse, out at
   grass   254
After hard years, throws up his stiff heels so,
Although the miller does not preach to him
The only good of grass is to make chaff.
What would men have? Do they like grass
   or no—
May they or mayn't they? all I want's the
   thing
Settled for ever one way. As it is,   260
You tell too many lies and hurt yourself:
You don't like what you only like too much,
You do like what, if given you at your word,
You find abundantly detestable.
For me, I think I speak as I was taught; 265
I always see the garden and God there
A-making man's wife: and, my lesson
   learned,
The value and significance of flesh,
I can't unlearn ten minutes afterwards.

You understand me: I'm a beast, I know.
But see, now—why, I see as certainly 271
As that the morning-star's about to shine,
What will hap some day. We've a youngster
   here
Comes to our convent, studies what I do,
Slouches and stares and lets no atom drop:
His name is Guidi[14]—he'll not mind the
   monks—   276
They call him Hulking Tom, he lets them
   talk—
He picks my practice up—he'll paint apace,
I hope so—though I never live so long, 279
I know what's sure to follow. You be judge!
You speak no Latin more than I, belike;
However, you're my man, you've seen the
   world
—The beauty and the wonder and the power,
The shapes of things, their colors, lights and
   shades,
Changes, surprises,—and God made it all!
—For what? Do you feel thankful, ay or
   no,   286
For this fair town's face, yonder river's
   line,
The mountain round it and the sky above,
Much more the figures of man, woman,
   child,
These are the frame to? What's it all
   about?   290
To be passed over, despised? or dwelt upon,

Wondered at? oh, this last of course!—you
   say.
But why not do as well as say,—paint these
Just as they are, careless what comes of it?
God's works—paint any one, and count it
   crime   295
To let a truth slip. Don't object, "His
   works
Are here already; nature is complete:
Suppose you reproduce her—(which you
   can't)
There's no advantage! you must beat her,
   then."
For, don't you mark? we're made so that
   we love   300
First when we see them painted, things we
   have passed
Perhaps a hundred times nor cared to see;
And so they are better, painted—better to us,
Which is the same thing. Art was given for
   that;
God uses us to help each other so,   305
Lending our minds out. Have you noticed,
   now,
Your cullion's[15] hanging face? A bit of
   chalk,
And trust me but you should, though! How
   much more,
If I drew higher things with the same truth!
That were to take the Prior's pulpit-place,
Interpret God to all of you! Oh, oh,   311
It makes me mad to see what men shall do
And we in our graves! This world's no blot
   for us,
Nor blank; it means intensely, and means
   good: 314
To find its meaning is my meat and drink.
"Ay, but you don't so instigate to prayer!"
Strikes in the Prior: "when your meaning's
   plain
It does not say to folk—remember matins,
Or, mind you fast next Friday!" Why, for
   this
What need of art at all? A skull and bones,
Two bits of stick nailed crosswise, or, what's
   best,   321
A bell to chime the hour with, does as well.
I painted a Saint Laurence six months since
At Prato, splashed the fresco in fine style:
"How looks my painting, now the scaffold's
   down?"   325
I ask a brother: "Hugely," he returns—
"Already not one phiz of your three slaves
Who turn the Deacon off his toasted side,[16]

---

[14]Tommaso Guidi, called Masaccio (1401–1428). Browning for the sake of his point reverses the historical relationship between him and Fra Lippo.

[15]Rascal's.

[16]St. Laurence suffered martyrdom by being burned on a gridiron

But's scratched and prodded to our heart's
content,
The pious people have so eased their own 330
With coming to say prayers there in a rage:
We get on fast to see the bricks beneath.
Expect another job this time next year,
For pity and religion grow i' the crowd—
Your painting serves its purpose!" Hang the
fools!   335

—That is—you'll not mistake an idle word
Spoke in a huff by a poor monk, God wot,
Tasting the air this spicy night which turns
The unaccustomed head like Chianti wine!
Oh, the church knows! don't misreport me,
now!   340
It's natural a poor monk out of bounds
Should have his apt word to excuse himself:
And hearken how I plot to make amends.
I have bethought me: I shall paint a piece
. . . There's for you! Give me six
months, then go, see   345
Something in Sant' Ambrogio's! Bless the
nuns!
They want a cast o' my office. I shall paint[17]
God in the midst, Madonna and her babe,
Ringed by a bowery, flowery angel-brood,
Lilies and vestments and white faces, sweet
As puff on puff of grated orris-root   351
When ladies crowd to Church at midsummer.
And then i' the front, of course a saint or
two—
Saint John, because he saves the Florentines,
Saint Ambrose, who puts down in black and
white   355
The convent's friends and gives them a long
day,
And Job, I must have him there past mis-
take,
The man of Uz (and Us without the z,
Painters who need his patience). Well, all
these
Secured at their devotion, up shall come   360
Out of a corner when you least expect,
As one by a dark stair into a great light,
Music and talking, who but Lippo! I!—
Mazed, motionless, and moonstruck—I'm the
the man!
Back I shrink—what is this I see and hear?
I, caught up with my monk's-things by mis-
take,   366
My old serge gown and rope that goes all
round,
I, in this presence, this pure company!

Where's a hole, where's a corner for escape?
Then steps a sweet angelic slip of a thing 370
Forward, puts out a soft palm—"Not so
fast!"
—Addresses the celestial presence, "nay—
He made you and devised you, after all,
Though he's none of you! Could Saint John
there draw—
His camel-hair make up a painting-brush?
We come to brother Lippo for all that,   376
Iste perfecit opus!"[18]   So, all smile—
I shuffle sideways with my blushing face
Under the cover of a hundred wings
Thrown like a spread of kirtles when you're
gay   380
And play hot cockles, all the doors being shut,
Till, wholly unexpected, in there pops
The hothead husband! Thus I scuttle off
To some safe bench behind, not letting go
The palm of her, the little lily thing   385
That spoke the good word for me in the nick,
Like the Prior's niece . . . Saint Lucy, I
would say.
And so all's saved for me, and for the church
A pretty picture gained. Go, six months
hence!
Your hand, sir, and good-by: no lights, no
lights!   390
The street's hushed, and I know my own way
back,
Don't fear me! There's the gray beginning.
Zooks!

M Y   S T A R [1]

All that I know
  Of a certain star
Is, it can throw
  (Like the angled spar[2])
Now a dart of red,   5
  Now a dart of blue;
Till my friends have said
  They would fain see, too,
My star that dartles the red and the blue!
Then it stops like a bird; like a flower, hangs
furled: 10
  They must solace themselves with the
Saturn above it.
What matter to me if their star is a world?
  Mine has opened its soul to me; therefore
I love it.

[17]The picture described is known as "The Coronation of the Virgin." It is now in the Accademia
delle Belle Arti at Florence.

[18]This man made the picture (work). The words
appear in the picture, on a scroll running from the
speaker towards Fra Lippo.

[1]Published in 1855. The star undoubtedly symbolizes Mrs. Browning.

[2]Piece of crystalline mineral with an angular surface.

"CHILDE ROLAND TO THE DARK TOWER CAME"[1]

See Edgar's Song in "Lear"

My first thought was, he lied in every word,
  That hoary cripple, with malicious eye
  Askance to watch the working of his lie
On mine, and mouth scarce able to afford
Suppression of the glee, that pursed and
    scored   5
  Its edge, at one more victim gained
    thereby.

What else should he be set for, with his
    staff?
  What, save to waylay with his lies, ensnare
All travelers who might find him posted
    there
And ask the road? I guessed what skull-
    like laugh   10
Would break, what crutch 'gin write my
    epitaph
  For pastime in the dusty thoroughfare,

If at his counsel I should turn aside
  Into that ominous tract which, all agree,
  Hides the Dark Tower. Yet acquiesc-
    ingly   15
I did turn as he pointed: neither pride
Nor hope rekindling at the end descried,
  So much as gladness that some end might
    be.

For, what with my whole world-wide wan-
    dering,
  What with my search drawn out through
    years, my hope   20
  Dwindled into a ghost not fit to cope
With that obstreperous joy success would
    bring,—
I hardly tried now to rebuke the spring
  My heart made, finding failure in its scope.

As when a sick man very near to death   25
  Seems dead indeed, and feels begin and
    end
  The tears, and takes the farewell of each
    friend,
And hears one bid the other go, draw breath
Freelier outside, ("since all is o'er," he
    saith,
  "And the blow fallen no grieving can
    amend;")   30

While some discuss if near the other graves
  Be room enough for this, and when a day
  Suits best for carrying the corpse away,
With care about the banners, scarves and
    staves:
And still the man hears all, and only craves
  He may not shame such tender love and
    stay.   36

Thus, I had so long suffered in this quest,
  Heard failure prophesied so oft, been writ
  So many times among "The Band"—to
    wit,
The knights who to the Dark Tower's search
    addressed   40
Their steps—that just to fail as they, seemed
    best,
  And all the doubt was now—should I be
    fit?

So, quiet as despair, I turned from him,
  That hateful cripple, out of his highway
  Into the path he pointed. All the day   45
Had been a dreary one at best, and dim
Was settling to its close, yet shot one grim
  Red leer to see the plain catch its estray.

For mark! no sooner was I fairly found
  Pledged to the plain, after a pace or two, 50
  Than, pausing to throw backward a last
    view
O'er the safe road, 'twas gone; gray plain
    all round:
Nothing but plain to the horizon's bound.
  I might go on; naught else remained to do.

So, on I went. I think I never saw   55
  Such starved ignoble nature; nothing
    throve:
  For flowers—as well expect a cedar grove!
But cockle, spurge, according to their law
Might propagate their kind, with none to
    awe,
  You'd think: a burr had been a treasure
    trove.   60

[1]Published in 1855. The title, as Browning explains in the sub-heading, is quoted from *King Lear*
(III, iv, 187); "Childe" is a title of gentility.

The details of the landscape were derived from
Gerard de Lairesse's *Art of Painting,* an English
translation of which Browning had read as a child.
He composed the whole poem in one day, and later
said that he was conscious of no allegorical intention in writing it, and that it came upon him as a
kind of dream.

No! penury, inertness and grimace,
    In some strange sort, were the land's por-
        tion. "See
    Or shut your eyes," said Nature peevishly,
"It nothing skills:[2] I cannot help my case:
'Tis the Last Judgment's fire must cure this
        place,   65
    Calcine its clods and set my prisoners
        free."

If there pushed any ragged thistle-stalk
    Above its mates, the head was chopped;
        the bents[3]
    Were jealous else. What made those
        holes and rents
In the dock's harsh swarth leaves, bruised
        as to balk   70
All hope of greenness? 'tis a brute must
        walk
    Pashing their life out, with a brute's in-
        tents.

As for the grass, it grew as scant as hair
    In leprosy; thin dry blades pricked the
        mud
    Which underneath looked kneaded up
        with blood.   75
One stiff blind horse, his every bone a-stare,
Stood stupefied, however he came there:
    Thrust out past service from the devil's
        stud!

Alive? he might be dead for aught I know,
    With that red gaunt and colloped[4] neck
        a-strain,   80
    And shut eyes underneath the rusty mane;
Seldom went such grotesqueness with such
        woe;
    I never saw a brute I hated so;
    He must be wicked to deserve such pain.

I shut my eyes and turned them on my heart.
    As a man calls for wine before he fights,
    I asked one draught of earlier, happier
        sights,   87
Ere fitly I could hope to play my part.
Think first, fight afterwards—the soldier's
        art:
    One taste of the old time sets all to
        rights.   90

Not it! I fancied Cuthbert's reddening face
    Beneath its garniture of curly gold,
    Dear fellow, till I almost felt him fold
An arm in mine to fix me to the place,

That way he used. Alas, one night's dis-
        grace!   95
    Out went my heart's new fire and left it
        cold.

Giles then, the soul of honor—there he stands
    Frank as ten years ago when knighted
        first.
    What honest man should dare (he said) he
        durst.
Good—but the scene shifts—faugh! what
        hangman hands   100
Pin to his breast a parchment? His own
        bands
    Read it. Poor traitor, spit upon and curst!

Better this present than a past like that;
    Back therefore to my darkening path
        again!
    No sound, no sight as far as eye could
        strain.   105
Will the night send a howlet or a bat?
I asked: when something on the dismal flat
    Came to arrest my thoughts and change
        their train.

A sudden little river crossed my path
    As unexpected as a serpent comes.   110
    No sluggish tide congenial to the glooms;
This, as it frothed by, might have been a bath
For the fiend's glowing hoof—to see the
        wrath
    Of its black eddy bespate[5] with flakes and
        spumes.

So petty yet so spiteful! All along,   115
    Low scrubby alders kneeled down over it;
    Drenched willows flung them headlong in
        a fit
Of mute despair, a suicidal throng:
The river which had done them all the wrong,
    Whate'er that was, rolled by, deterred no
        whit.   120

Which, while I forded,—good saints, how I
        feared
    To set my foot upon a dead man's cheek,
    Each step, or feel the spear I thrust to
        seek
For hollows, tangled in his hair or beard!
—It may have been a water-rat I speared, 125
    But, ugh! it sounded like a baby's shriek.

Glad was I when I reached the other bank.
    Now for a better country. Vain presage!
    Who were the strugglers, what war did
        they wage,

---

²Avails.   ³Grasses.   ⁴Wrinkled.

⁵Spattered.

Whose savage trample thus could pad the
    dank   130
Soil to a plash? Toads in a poisoned tank,
    Or wild cats in a red-hot iron cage—

The fight must so have seemed in that fell
    cirque.
    What penned them there, with all the plain
    to choose?   134
No footprint leading in that horrid mews,[6]
None out of it.   Mad brewage set to work
Their brains, no doubt, like galley-slaves the
    Turk
    Pits for his pastime, Christians against
    Jews.

And more than that—a furlong on—why,
    there!
    What bad use was that engine for, that
    wheel,   140
    Or brake, not wheel—that harrow fit to
    reel
Men's bodies out like silk? with all the air
Of Tophet's[7] tool, on earth left unaware,
    Or brought to sharpen its rusty teeth of
    steel.

Then came a bit of stubbed ground, once a
    wood,   145
    Next a marsh, it would seem, and now
    mere earth
    Desperate and done with: (so a fool finds
    mirth,
Makes a thing and then mars it, till his mood
Changes and off he goes!) within a rood—
    Bog, clay and rubble, sand and stark black
    dearth.   150

Now blotches rankling, colored gay and grim,
    Now patches where some leanness of the
    soil's
    Broke into moss or substances like boils;
Then came some palsied oak, a cleft in him
Like a distorted mouth that splits its rim   155
    Gaping at death, and dies while it recoils.

And just as far as ever from the end!
    Naught in the distance but the evening,
    naught
    To point my footstep further! At the
    thought,   159
A great black bird, Apollyon's[8] bosom-friend,
Sailed past, nor beat his wide wing dragon-
    penned[9]
    That brushed my cap—perchance the guide
    I sought.

For, looking up, aware I somehow grew,
    'Spite of the dusk, the plain had given
    place
    All round to mountains—with such name
    to grace   165
Mere ugly heights and heaps now stolen in
    view.
How thus they had surprised me,—solve it,
    you!
    How to get from them was no clearer case.

Yet half I seemed to recognize some trick
    Of mischief happened to me, God knows
    when—   170
    In a bad dream perhaps. Here ended,
    then,
Progress this way.   When, in the very nick
Of giving up, one time more, came a click
    As when a trap shuts—you're inside the
    den!

Burningly it came on me all at once,   175
    This was the place! those two hills on the
    right,
    Crouched like two bulls locked horn in
    horn in fight;
While to the left, a tall scalped mountain . . .
    Dunce,
Dotard, a-dozing at the very nonce,[10]
    After a life spent training for the sight! 180

What in the midst lay but the Tower itself?
    The round squat turret, blind as the fool's
    heart,
    Built of brown stone, without a counter-
    part
In the whole world.   The tempest's mocking
    elf   184
Points to the shipman thus the unseen shelf
    He strikes on, only when the timbers start.

Not see? because of night perhaps?—why,
    day
    Came back again for that! before it left,
    The dying sunset kindled through a cleft:
The hills, like giants at a hunting, lay,   190
Chin upon hand, to see the game at bay,—
    "Now stab and end the creature—to the
    heft!"

Not hear? when noise was everywhere! it
    tolled
    Increasing like a bell.   Names in my ears,
    Of all the lost adventurers my peers,— 195
How such a one was strong, and such was
    bold,

---

[6]Stable.   [7]Hell's.   [8]The Devil's.
[9]Dragon-winged.

[10]At the very moment.

And such was fortunate, yet each of old
   Lost, lost! one moment knelled the woe of
     years.

There they stood, ranged along the hillsides,
     met
   To view the last of me, a living frame   200
For one more picture! in a sheet of flame
I saw them and I knew them all.   And yet
Dauntless the slug-horn[11] to my lips I set,
   And blew.   *"Childe Roland to the Dark
     Tower came."*

RESPECTABILITY [1]

Dear, had the world in its caprice
   Deigned to proclaim "I know you both,
   Have recognized your plighted troth,
Am sponsor for you: live in peace!"—
How many precious months and years   5
   Of youth had passed, that speed so fast,
   Before we found it out at last,
The world, and what it fears!

---

[11]Apparently, trumpet (Browning, like Chatterton,
does not use *slughorn* correctly: it really means
slogan).
[1]Published in 1855.

How much of priceless life were spent
   With men that every virtue decks,   10
   And women models of their sex,
Society's true ornament,—
Ere we dared wander, nights like this,
   Through wind and rain, and watch the
     Seine,
   And feel the Boulevard break again   15
To warmth and light and bliss!

I know! the world proscribes not love;
   Allows my finger to caress
   Your lips' contour and downiness,
Provided it supply a glove.   20
The world's good word!—the Institute!
   Guizot receives Montalembert![2]
   Eh? Down the court three lampions[3]
     flare:
Put forward your best foot!

---

[2]The glove is the body of accepted social conventions.   The French Institute symbolizes the rewards
of conventionality.   Guizot, although a constitutional royalist who hated the liberalism of Montalembert, welcomed him into the Institute.
[3]Small lamps.

THE STATUE AND THE BUST [1]

There's a palace in Florence, the world knows
     well,
And a statue watches it from the square,[2]
And this story of both do our townsmen tell.

Ages ago, a lady there,
At the farthest window facing the East   5
Asked, "Who rides by with the royal air?"

The bridesmaids' prattle around her ceased;
She leaned forth, one on either hand;
They saw how the blush of the bride in-
     creased—

They felt by its beats her heart expand—   10
As one at each ear and both in a breath
Whispered, "The Great-Duke Ferdinand."

That selfsame instant, underneath,
The Duke rode past in his idle way,
Empty and fine like a swordless sheath.   15

Gay he rode, with a friend as gay,
Till he threw his head back—"Who is she?"
—"A bride the Riccardi brings home to-day."

---

[1]Published in 1855.   The following inquiry was
once sent to an American newspaper:
"1.   When, how, and where did it happen?
Browning's divine vagueness lets one gather only
that the lady's husband was a Riccardi.   2.   Who
was the lady? who the duke?   3.   The magnificent
house wherein Florence lodges her préfet is known
to all Florentine ball-goers as the Palazzo Riccardi.
It was bought by the Riccardi from the Medici in
1659.   From none of its windows did the lady gaze
at her more than royal lover.   From what window,
then, if from any?   Are the statue and the bust
still in their original positions?"
   These questions were found by Mr. Thomas J.
Wise, who sent them to Browning.   He received
from Browning the following reply, written on 8
January, 1887:
   "DEAR MR. WISE,—I have seldom met with such
a strange inability to understand what seems the
plainest matter possible: 'ball-goers' are probably
not history-readers, but any guide-book would confirm what is sufficiently stated in the poem.   I will
append a note or two, however.   1.   'This story
the townsmen tell;' 'when, how, and where.' con-

stitutes the subject of the poem.   2.   The lady was
the wife of Riccardi; and the duke, Ferdinand,
just as the poem says.   3.   As it was built by, and
inhabited by, the Medici till sold, long after, to
the Riccardi, it was not from the duke's palace, but
a window in that of the Riccardi, that the lady
gazed at her lover riding by.   The statue is still in
its place, looking at the window under which 'now
is the empty shrine.'   Can anything be clearer?
My 'vagueness' leaves what to be 'gathered' when
all these things are put down in black and white?
Oh, 'ball-goers'!"
   [2]The Piazza della Annunziata.   The statue is of
the Grand Duke Ferdinand I (1549–1608).

Hair in heaps lay heavily
Over a pale brow spirit-pure—   20
Carved like the heart of the coal-black tree,

Crisped like a war-steed's encolure—[8]
And vainly sought to dissemble her eyes
Of the blackest black our eyes endure,

And lo, a blade for a knight's emprise   25
Filled the fine empty sheath of a man,—
The Duke grew straightway brave and wise.

He looked at her, as a lover can;
She looked at him, as one who awakes:
The past was a sleep, and her life began.   30

Now, love so ordered for both their sakes,
A feast was held that selfsame night
In the pile which the mighty shadow makes.[4]

(For Via Larga is three-parts light,
But the palace overshadows one,   35
Because of a crime, which may God requite!

To Florence and God the wrong was done,
Through the first republic's murder there
By Cosimo[5] and his curséd son.)

The Duke (with the statue's face in the
    square)   40
Turned in the midst of his multitude
At the bright approach of the bridal pair.

Face to face the lovers stood
A single minute and no more,
While the bridegroom bent as a man sub-
    dued—   45

Bowed till his bonnet brushed the floor—
For the Duke on the lady a kiss conferred,
As the courtly custom was of yore.

In a minute can lovers exchange a word?
If a word did pass, which I do not think,   50
Only one out of a thousand heard.

That was the bridegroom. At day's brink
He and his bride were alone at last
In a bed chamber by a taper's blink.

Calmly he said that her lot was cast,   55
That the door she had passed was shut on her
Till the final catafalk[6] repassed.

[8]Neck and shoulders.

[4]The Palace of Ferdinand.

[5]Cosimo de' Medici (1389–1464). Through him Florence prospered, while its republican government was undermined. He built the palace later occupied by Ferdinand.

[6]Funeral canopy.

The world meanwhile, its noise and stir,
Through a certain window facing the East
She could watch like a convent's chronicler.

Since passing the door might lead to a feast,
And a feast might lead to so much beside,   62
He, of many evils, chose the least.

"Freely I choose too," said the bride—
"Your window and its world suffice,"   65
Replied the tongue, while the heart replied—

"If I spend the night with that devil twice,
May his window serve as my loop of hell
Whence a damned soul looks on paradise!

"I fly to the Duke who loves me well,   70
Sit by his side and laugh at sorrow
Ere I count another ave-bell.

" 'Tis only the coat of a page to borrow,
And tie my hair in a horse-boy's trim,
And I save my soul—but not to-morrow"—

(She checked herself and her eye grew dim)
"My father tarries to bless my state: 77
I must keep it one day more for him.

"Is one day more so long to wait?
Moreover the Duke rides past, I know;   80
We shall see each other, sure as fate."

She turned on her side and slept. Just so!
So we resolve on a thing and sleep:
So did the lady, ages ago.

That night the Duke said, "Dear or cheap
As the cost of this cup of bliss may prove   86
To body or soul, I will drain it deep."

And on the morrow, bold with love,
He beckoned the bridegroom (close on call,
As his duty bade, by the Duke's alcove)   90

And smiled " 'Twas a very funeral,
Your lady will think, this feast of ours,—
A shame to efface, whate'er befall!

"What if we break from the Arno bowers,
And try if Petraja,[7] cool and green,   95
Cure last night's fault with this morning's
    flowers?"

The bridegroom, not a thought to be seen
On his steady brow and quiet mouth,
Said, "Too much favor for me so mean!

[7]Outside of Florence. The Arno is a river flowing through Florence.

"But, alas! my lady leaves the South;[8]   100
Each wind that comes from the Apennine
Is a menace to her tender youth:

"Nor a way exists, the wise opine,
If she quits her palace twice this year,
To avert the flower of life's decline."   105

Quoth the Duke, "A sage and a kindly fear.
Moreover Petraja is cold this spring:
Be our feast to-night as usual here!"

And then to himself—"Which night shall
       bring
Thy bride to her lover's embraces, fool—   110
Or I am the fool, and thou art the king!

"Yet my passion must wait a night, nor
       cool—
For to-night the Envoy arrives from France
Whose heart I unlock with thyself, my tool.

"I need thee still and might miss perchance.
To-day is not wholly lost, beside,   116
With its hope of my lady's countenance:

"For I ride—what should I do but ride?
And passing her palace, if I list,
May glance at its window—well betide!"   120

So said, so done: nor the lady missed
One ray that broke from the ardent brow,
Nor a curl of the lips where the spirit kissed.

Be sure that each renewed the vow,
No morrow's sun should arise and set   125
And leave them then as it left them now.

But next day passed, and next day yet,
With still fresh cause to wait one day more
Ere each leaped over the parapet.

And still, as love's brief morning wore,   130
With a gentle start, half smile, half sigh,
They found love not as it seemed before.

They thought it would work infallibly,
But not in despite of heaven and earth:
The rose would blow when the storm passed
       by.   135

Meantime they could profit in winter's dearth
By store of fruits that supplant the rose:
The world and its ways have a certain worth:

And to press a point while these oppose
Were simple[9] policy; better wait: 140
We lose no friends and we gain no foes.

Meantime, worse fates than a lover's fate,
Who daily may ride and pass and look
Where his lady watches behind the grate!

And she—she watched the square like a book
Holding one picture and only one,   146
Which daily to find she undertook:

When the picture was reached the book was
       done,
And she turned from the picture at night to
       scheme
Of tearing it out for herself next sun.   150

So weeks grew months, years; gleam by
       gleam
The glory dropped from their youth and love,
And both perceived they had dreamed a
       dream;

Which hovered as dreams do, still above:
But who can take a dream for a truth?   155
Oh, hide our eyes from the next remove!

One day as the lady saw her youth
Depart, and the silver thread that streaked
Her hair, and, worn by the serpent's tooth,

The brow so puckered, the chin so peaked,—
And wondered who the woman was,   161
Hollow-eyed and haggard-cheeked,

Fronting her silent in the glass—
"Summon here," she suddenly said,
"Before the rest of my old self pass,   165

"Him, the Carver, a hand to aid,
Who fashions the clay no love will change,
And fixes a beauty never to fade.

"Let Robbia's craft[10] so apt and strange
Arrest the remains of young and fair,   170
And rivet them while the seasons range.

"Make me a face on the window there,
Waiting as ever, mute the while,
My love to pass below in the square!

[9]Silly.

[10]Robbia is not here the name of the artist (the
last famous Robbia had died in 1566), but is applied to the kind of work done by the Robbias—
terra-cotta relief work covered with enamel.

[8]I. e., is from the South. Apennine is the mountain range amidst which Florence is situated.

"And let me think that it may beguile 175
Dreary days which the dead must spend
Down in their darkness under the aisle,

"To say, 'What matters it at the end?
I did no more while my heart was warm
Than does that image, my pale-faced friend.'

"Where is the use of the lip's red charm, 181
The heaven of hair, the pride of the brow,
And the blood that blues the inside arm—

"Unless we turn, as the soul knows how,
The earthly gift to an end divine? 185
A lady of clay is as good, I trow."

But long ere Robbia's cornice, fine,
With flowers and fruits which leaves enlace.
Was set where now is the empty shrine—

(And, leaning out of a bright blue space, 190
As a ghost might lean from a chink of sky,
The passionate pale lady's face—

Eying ever, with earnest eye
And quick-turned neck at its breathless
    stretch,
Some one who ever is passing by—) 195

The Duke had sighed like the simplest wretch
In Florence, "Youth—my dream escapes!
Will its record stay?" And he bade them
    fetch

Some subtle molder of brazen shapes—
"Can the soul, the will, die out of a man 200
Ere his body find the grave that gapes?

"John of Douay shall effect my plan,
Set me on horseback here aloft,
Alive, as the crafty sculptor can,

"In the very square I have crossed so oft:
That men may admire, when future suns 206
Shall touch the eyes to a purpose soft,

"While the mouth and the brow stay brave in
    bronze—
Admire and say, 'When he was alive
How he would take his pleasure once!' 210

"And it shall go hard but I contrive
To listen the while, and laugh in my tomb
At idleness which aspires to strive."

So! While these wait the trump of doom,
How do their spirits pass, I wonder, 215
Nights and days in the narrow room?

Still, I suppose, they sit and ponder
What a gift life was, ages ago,
Six steps out of the chapel yonder.

Only they see not God, I know, 220
Nor all that chivalry of his,
The soldier-saints who, row on row,

Burn upward each to his point of bliss—
Since, the end of life being manifest,
He had burned his way through the world to
    this. 225

I hear you reproach, "But delay was best,
For their end was a crime."—Oh, a crime
    will do
As well, I reply, to serve for a test,

As a virtue golden through and through,
Sufficient to vindicate itself 230
And prove its worth at a moment's view!

Must a game be played for the sake of pelf?
Where a button goes, 'twere an epigram
To offer the stamp of the very Guelph.[11]

The true has no value beyond the sham: 235
As well the counter as coin, I submit,
When your table's a hat, and your prize, a
    dram.

Stake your counter as boldly every whit,
Venture as warily, use the same skill,
Do your best, whether winning or losing it,

If you chose to play!—is my principle. 241
Let a man contend to the uttermost
For his life's set prize, be it what it will!

The counter our lovers staked was lost
As surely as if it were lawful coin: 245
And the sin I impute to each frustrate ghost

Is—the unlit lamp and the ungirt loin,
Though the end in sight was a vice, I say.
You of the virtue (we issue join)
How strive you? *De te, fabula!*[12] 250

[11]Where a button will pass as readily as real
money ("the stamp of the very Guelph") it would
be absurd ("an epigram," i. e., a matter for satire)
to use the latter.

[12]The story concerns you.

THE LAST RIDE TOGETHER[1]

I said—Then, dearest, since 'tis so,
Since now at length my fate I know,
Since nothing all my love avails,
Since all, my life seemed meant for, fails,
    Since this was written and needs must
    be— 5
My whole heart rises up to bless
Your name in pride and thankfulness!
Take back the hope you gave,—I claim
Only a memory of the same,
—And this beside, if you will not blame, 10
    Your leave for one more last ride with me.

My mistress bent that brow of hers;
Those deep dark eyes where pride demurs
When pity would be softening through,
Fixed me a breathing-while or two 15
    With life or death in the balance: right!
The blood replenished me again;
My last thought was at least not vain:
I and my mistress, side by side
Shall be together, breathe and ride, 20
So, one day more am I deified.
    Who knows but the world may end to-
    night?

Hush! if you saw some western cloud
All billowy-bosomed, over-bowed
By many benedictions—sun's 25
And moon's and evening-star's at once—
    And so, you, looking and loving best,
Conscious grew, your passion drew
Cloud, sunset, moonrise, star-shine too,
Down on you, near and yet more near, 30
Till flesh must fade for heaven was here!—
Thus leant she and lingered—joy and fear!
    Thus lay she a moment on my breast.

Then we began to ride. My soul
Smoothed itself out, a long-cramped scroll 35
Freshening and fluttering in the wind.
Past hopes already lay behind.
    What need to strive with a life awry?
Had I said that, had I done this,
So might I gain, so might I miss. 40
Might she have loved me? just as well
She might have hated, who can tell!
Where had I been now if the worst befell?
    And here we are riding, she and I.

Fail I alone, in words and deeds? 45
Why, all men strive, and who succeeds?

We rode; it seemed my spirit flew,
Saw other regions, cities new,
    As the world rushed by on either side.
I thought,—All labor, yet no less 50
Bear up beneath their unsuccess.
Look at the end of work, contrast
The petty done, the undone vast,
This present of theirs with the hopeful past!
    I hoped she would love me; here we ride. 55

What hand and brain went ever paired?
What heart alike conceived and dared?
What act proved all its thought had been?
What will but felt the fleshly screen?
    We ride and I see her bosom heave. 60
There's many a crown for who can reach.
Ten lines,[2] a statesman's life in each!
The flag stuck on a heap of bones,
A soldier's doing! what atones?
They scratch his name on the Abbey-stones.[3]
    My riding is better, by their leave. 66

What does it all mean, poet? Well,
Your brains beat into rhythm, you tell
What we felt only; you expressed
You hold things beautiful the best, 70
    And place them in rime so, side by side.
'Tis something, nay 'tis much: but then,
Have you yourself what's best for men?
Are you—poor, sick, old ere your time—
Nearer one whit your own sublime 75
Than we who never have turned a rime?
    Sing, riding's a joy! For me, I ride.

And you, great sculptor—so, you gave
A score of years to Art, her slave,
And that's your Venus, whence we turn 80
To yonder girl that fords the burn![4]
    You acquiesce, and shall I repine?
What, man of music, you grown gray
With notes and nothing else to say,
Is this your sole praise from a friend, 85
"Greatly his opera's strains intend,
But in music we know how fashions end!"
    I gave my youth; but we ride, in fine.

Who knows what's fit for us? Had fate
Proposed bliss here should sublimate 90
My being—had I signed the bond—
Still one must lead some life beyond,
    Have a bliss to die with, dim-descried.

---

[1] Published in 1855.

[2] I. e., of history.   [3] At Westminster.
[4] Brook.

This foot once planted on the goal,
This glory-garland round my soul,　95
Could I descry such? Try and test!
I sink back shuddering from the quest.
Earth being so good, would heaven seem
　　best?
　Now, heaven and she are beyond this ride.

And yet—she has not spoke so long!　100
What if heaven be that, fair and strong
At life's best, with our eyes upturned
Whither life's flower is first discerned,
　We, fixed so, ever should so abide?
What if we still ride on, we two,　105
With life for ever old yet new,
Changed not in kind but in degree,
The instant made eternity,—
And heaven just prove that I and she
　Ride, ride together, for ever ride?　110

THE PATRIOT[1]

An Old Story

It was roses, roses, all the way,
　With myrtle mixed in my path like mad:
The house-roofs seemed to heave and sway,
　The church-spires flamed, such flags they
　　had,
A year ago on this very day.　5

---

[1]Published in 1855.

The air broke into a mist with bells,
　The old walls rocked with the crowd and
　　cries.
Had I said, "Good folk, mere noise repels—
　But give me your sun from yonder skies!"
They had answered "And afterward, what
　else?"　10

Alack, it was I who leaped at the sun
　To give it my loving friends to keep!
Naught man could do, have I left undone:
　And you see my harvest, what I reap
This very day, now a year is run.　15

There's nobody on the house-tops now—
　Just a palsied few at the windows set,
For the best of the sight is, all allow,
　At the Shambles' Gate—or, better yet,
By the very scaffold's foot, I trow.　20

I go in the rain, and, more than needs,
　A rope cuts both my wrists behind;
And I think, by the feel, my forehead bleeds,
　For they fling, whoever has a mind,
Stones at me for my year's misdeeds.　25

Thus I entered, and thus I go!
　In triumphs, people have dropped down
　　dead.
"Paid by the world, what dost thou owe
　Me?"—God might question; now instead,
'Tis God shall repay: I am safer so.　30

ANDREA DEL SARTO[1]

Called "The Faultless Painter"

But do not let us quarrel any more,
No, my Lucrezia; bear with me for once:
Sit down and all shall happen as you wish.
You turn your face, but does it bring your
　heart?
I'll work then for your friend's friend, never
　fear,　5
Treat his own subject after his own way,
Fix his own time, accept too his own price,
And shut the money into this small hand
When next it takes mine. Will it? tenderly?
Oh, I'll content him,—but to-morrow, Love!
I often am much wearier than you think,　11
This evening more than usual, and it seems
As if—forgive now—should you let me sit
Here by the window with your hand in mine

And look a half-hour forth on Fiesole,[2]　15
Both of one mind, as married people use,
Quietly, quietly the evening through,
I might get up to-morrow to my work
Cheerful and fresh as ever. Let us try.
To-morrow, how you shall be glad for this!
Your soft hand is a woman of itself,　21
And mine the man's bared breast she curls
　inside.
Don't count the time lost, neither; you must
　serve
For each of the five pictures we require:
It saves a model. So! keep looking so—　25
My serpentining beauty, rounds on rounds!
—How could you ever prick those perfect
　ears,
Even to put the pearl there! oh, so sweet—

---

[1]Published in 1855. Andrea's life (1486-1531) is to be found in the *Lives of the Painters,* by Giorgio Vasari, one of Andrea's pupils.

[2]A small town about three miles west of Florence.

My face, my moon, my everybody's moon,
Which everybody looks on and calls his, 30
And, I suppose, is looked on by in turn,
While she looks—no one's: very dear, no
less.
You smile? why, there's my picture ready
made,
There's what we painters call our harmony!
A common grayness silvers everything,— 35
All in a twilight, you and I alike
—You, at the point of your first pride in me
(That's gone you know),—but I, at every
point;
My youth, my hope, my art, being all toned
down
To yonder sober pleasant Fiesole. 40
There's the bell clinking from the chapel-top;
That length of convent-wall across the way
Holds the trees safer, huddled more inside;
The last monk leaves the garden; days de-
crease,
And autumn grows, autumn in everything. 45
Eh? the whole seems to fall into a shape
As if I saw alike my work and self
And all that I was born to be and do,
A twilight-piece. Love, we are in God's
hand.
How strange now looks the life he makes us
lead; 50
So free we seem, so fettered fast we are!
I feel he laid the fetter: let it lie!
This chamber for example—turn your
head—
All that's behind us! You don't understand
Nor care to understand about my art, 55
But you can hear at least when people speak:
And that cartoon, the second from the door
—It is the thing, Love! so such thing should
be—
Behold Madonna!—I am bold to say.
I can do with my pencil what I know, 60
What I see, what at bottom of my heart
I wish for, if I ever wish so deep—
Do easily, too—when I say, perfectly,
I do not boast, perhaps: yourself are judge,
Who listened to the Legate's talk last week,
And just as much they used to say in France.
At any rate 'tis easy, all of it! 67
No sketches first, no studies, that's long past:
I do what many dream of all their lives,
—Dream? strive to do, and agonize to do, 70
And fail in doing. I could count twenty such
On twice your fingers, and not leave this
town,
Who strive—you don't know how the others
strive
To paint a little thing like that you smeared

Carelessly passing with your robes afloat,—
Yet do much less, so much less, Someone
says, 76
(I know his name, no matter)—so much less!
Well, less is more, Lucrezia: I am judged.
There burns a truer light of God in them,
In their vexed beating stuffed and stopped-up
brain, 80
Heart, or whate'er else, than goes on to
prompt
This low-pulsed forthright craftsman's hand
of mine.
Their works drop groundward, but them-
selves, I know,
Reach many a time a heaven that's shut to me,
Enter and take their place there sure enough,
Though they come back and cannot tell the
world. 86
My works are nearer heaven, but I sit here.
The sudden blood of these men! at a word—
Praise them, it boils, or blame them, it boils
too.
I, painting from myself and to myself, 90
Know what I do, am unmoved by men's
blame
Or their praise either. Somebody remarks
Morello's outline[3] there is wrongly traced,
His hue mistaken; what of that? or else,
Rightly traced and well ordered; what of
that? 95
Speak as they please, what does the mountain
care?
Ah, but a man's reach should exceed his
grasp,
Or what's a heaven for? All is silver-gray
Placid and perfect with my art: the worse!
I know both what I want and what might
gain, 100
And yet how profitless to know, to sigh
"Had I been two, another and myself,
Our head would have o'erlooked the world!"
No doubt.
Yonder's a work now, of that famous youth
The Urbinate[4] who died five years ago. 105
('Tis copied, George Vasari sent it me.)
Well, I can fancy how he did it all,
Pouring his soul, with kings and popes to see,
Reaching, that heaven might so replenish
him, 109
Above and through his art—for it gives way;
That arm is wrongly put—and there again—
A fault to pardon in the drawing's lines,
Its body, so to speak: its soul is right,

---

[3]Morello is a mountain of the Apennines, north
of Florence.

[4]Raphael (1483–1520), who was born at Urbino.

He means right—that, a child may under-
stand.
Still, what an arm! and I could alter it: 115
But all the play, the insight and the stretch—
Out of me, out of me! And wherefore out?
Had you enjoined them on me, given me soul,
We might have risen to Rafael, I and you!
Nay, Love, you did give all I asked, I think—
More than I merit, yes, by many times. 121
But had you—oh, with the same perfect
brow,
And perfect eyes, and more than perfect
mouth,
And the low voice my soul hears, as a bird
The fowler's pipe, and follows to the snare—
Had you, with these the same, but brought
a mind! 126
Some women do so. Had the mouth there
urged,
"God and the glory! never care for gain.
The present by the future, what is that?
Live for fame, side by side with Agnolo![5] 130
Rafael is waiting: up to God, all three!"
I might have done it for you. So it seems:
Perhaps not. All is as God overrules.
Beside, incentives come from the soul's self;
The rest avail not. Why do I need you? 135
What wife had Rafael, or has Agnolo?
In this world, who can do a thing, will not;
And who would do it, cannot, I perceive:
Yet the will's somewhat—somewhat, too, the
power— 139
And thus we half-men struggle. At the end,
God, I conclude, compensates, punishes.
'Tis safer for me, if the award be strict,
That I am something underrated here,
Poor this long while, despised, to speak the
truth.
I dared not, do you know, leave home all day,
For fear of chancing on the Paris lords. 146
The best is when they pass and look aside;
But they speak sometimes; I must bear it all.
Well may they speak! That Francis,[6] that
first time,
And that long festal year at Fontainebleau!
I surely then could sometimes leave the
ground, 151
Put on the glory, Rafael's daily wear,
In that humane great monarch's golden
look,—
One finger in his beard or twisted curl
Over his mouth's good mark that made the
smile, 155

---

[5]Michael Angelo (1475-1564).
[6]King Francis I of France, Andrea's patron.
Fontainebleau is a town near Paris, where is situated the royal palace in which Andrea worked.

One arm about my shoulder, round my neck,
The jingle of his gold chain in my ear,
I painting proudly with his breath on me,
All his court round him, seeing with his eyes,
Such frank French eyes, and such a fire of
souls 160
Profuse, my hand kept plying by those
hearts,—
And, best of all, this, this, this face beyond,
This in the background, waiting on my work,
To crown the issue with a last reward!
A good time, was it not, my kingly days? 165
And had you not grown restless . . . but I
know—
'Tis done and past; 'twas right, my instinct
said;
Too live the life grew, golden and not gray,
And I'm the weak-eyed bat no sun should
tempt
Out of the grange whose four walls make his
world. 170
How could it end in any other way?
You called me, and I came home to your
heart.
The triumph was—to reach and stay there;
since
I reached it ere the triumph, what is lost?
Let my hands frame your face in your hair's
gold, 175
You beautiful Lucrezia that are mine!
"Rafael did this, Andrea painted that;
The Roman's is the better when you pray,
But still the other's Virgin was his wife"—
Men will excuse me. I am glad to judge 180
Both pictures in your presence; clearer grows
My better fortune, I resolve to think.
For, do you know, Lucrezia, as God lives,
Said one day Agnolo, his very self,
To Rafael . . . I have known it all these
years . . . 185
(When the young man was flaming out his
thoughts
Upon a palace-wall for Rome to see,
Too lifted up in heart because of it)
"Friend, there's a certain sorry little scrub
Goes up and down our Florence, none cares
how, 190
Who, were he set to plan and execute
As you are, pricked on by your popes and
kings,
Would bring the sweat into that brow of
yours!"
To Rafael's!—And indeed the arm is wrong.
I hardly dare . . . yet, only you to see,
Give the chalk here—quick, thus the line
should go! 196
Ay, but the soul! he's Rafael! rub it out!

Still, all I care for, if he spoke the truth,
(What he? why, who but Michel Agnolo?)
Do you forget already words like those?) 200
If really there was such a chance, so lost,—
Is, whether you're—not grateful—but more
    pleased.
Well, let me think so. And you smile in-
    deed!
This hour has been an hour! Another smile?
If you would sit thus by me every night 205
I should work better, do you comprehend?
I mean that I should earn more, give you
    more.
See, it is settled dusk now; there's a star;
Morello's gone, the watch-lights show the
    wall,
The cue-owls[7] speak the name we call them
    by. 210
Come from the window, love,—come in, at
    last,
Inside the melancholy little house
We built to be so gay with. God is just.
King Francis may forgive me: oft at nights
When I look up from painting, eyes tired
    out, 215
The walls become illumined, brick from brick
Distinct, instead of mortar, fierce bright gold,
That gold of his I did cement them with!
Let us but love each other. Must you go?
That Cousin here again? he waits outside? 220
Must see you—you, and not with me? Those
    loans?
More gaming debts to pay? you smiled for
    that?
Well, let smiles buy me! have you more to
    spend?
While hand and eye and something of a heart
Are left me, work's my ware, and what's it
    worth? 225
I'll pay my fancy. Only let me sit
The gray remainder of the evening out,
Idle, you call it, and muse perfectly
How I could paint, were I but back in France,
One picture, just one more—the Virgin's
    face, 230
Not yours this time! I want you at my side
To hear them—that is, Michel Agnolo—
Judge all I do and tell you of its worth.
Will you? To-morrow, satisfy your friend.
I take the subjects for his corridor, 235
Finish the portrait out of hand—there, there,
And throw him in another thing or two
If he demurs; the whole should prove enough
To pay for this same Cousin's freak. Be-
    side,

[7]The scops owl, whose cry sounds like Italian *ciù.*

What's better and what's all I care about, 240
Get you the thirteen scudi[8] for the ruff!
Love, does that please you? Ah, but what
    does he,
The Cousin! what does he to please you
    more?

I am grown peaceful as old age to-night.
I regret little, I would change still less. 245
Since there my past life lies, why alter it?
The very wrong to Francis!—it is true
I took his coin, was tempted and complied,
And built this house and sinned, and all is
    said.
My father and my mother died of want. 250
Well, had I riches of my own? you see
How one gets rich! Let each one bear his
    lot.
They were born poor, lived poor, and poor
    they died:
And I have labored somewhat in my time
And not been paid profusely. Some good
    son 255
Paint my two hundred pictures—let him try!
No doubt, there's something strikes a balance.
    Yes,
You loved me quite enough, it seems to-night.
This must suffice me here. What would one
    have?
In heaven, perhaps, new chances, one more
    chance— 260
Four great walls in the New Jerusalem,
Meted on each side by the angel's reed,
For Leonard,[9] Rafael, Agnolo and me
To cover—the three first without a wife, 264
While I have mine! So—still they overcome
Because there's still Lucrezia,—as I choose.

Again the Cousin's whistle! Go, my Love.

"DE GUSTIBUS——"[1]

Your ghost will walk, you lover of trees,
    (If our loves remain)
    In an English lane,
By a cornfield-side a-flutter with poppies.
Hark, those two in the hazel coppice— 5
A boy and a girl, if the good fates please,
    Making love, say,—
    The happier they!
Draw yourself up from the light of the moon,
And let them pass, as they will too soon, 10
    With the beanflowers' boon,

[8]Coins worth about 97 cents.
[9]Leonardo da Vinci (1452–1519).
[1]Published in 1855. The title is an abbreviation
of the Latin proverb: *de gustibus non est disputan-
dum,* there's no disputing tastes.

And the blackbird's tune,
And May, and June!

What I love best in all the world
Is a castle, precipice-encurled, 15
In a gash of the wind-grieved Apennine.
Or look for me, old fellow of mine,
(If I get my head from out the mouth
O' the grave, and loose my spirit's bands,
And come again to the land of lands)— 20
In a sea-side house to the farther South,
Where the baked cicala[2] dies of drought,
And one sharp tree—'tis a cypress—stands,
By the many hundred years red-rusted,
Rough iron-spiked, ripe fruit-o'ercrusted, 25
My sentinel to guard the sands
To the water's edge. For, what expands
Before the house, but the great opaque
Blue breadth of sea without a break?
While, in the house, forever crumbles 30
Some fragment of the frescoed walls,
From blisters where a scorpion sprawls.
A girl bare-footed brings, and tumbles
Down on the pavement, green-flesh melons,
And says there's news to-day—the king[3] 35
Was shot at, touched in the liver-wing,[4]
Goes with his Bourbon arm in a sling:
—She hopes they have not caught the felons.
Italy, my Italy!
Queen Mary's[5] saying serves for me— 40
  (When fortune's malice
    Lost her Calais)
Open my heart and you will see
Graved inside of it, "Italy."
Such lovers old are I and she: 45
So it always was, so shall ever be!

A GRAMMARIAN'S FUNERAL[1]

Shortly after the Revival of Learning in Europe

Let us begin and carry up this corpse,
  Singing together.
Leave we the common crofts, the vulgar
    thorpes[2]
  Each in its tether

[2]Cicada.

[3]Undoubtedly Ferdinand II, Bourbon ruler of the Two Sicilies.

[4]The right arm (since the liver of a fowl lies under the right wing).

[5]Mary Tudor, who lost Calais to the French in 1558.

[1]Published in 1855.

[2]The common farms, the vulgar villages.

Sleeping safe on the bosom of the plain, 5
  Cared-for till cock-crow:
Look out if yonder be not day again
  Rimming the rock-row!
That's the appropriate country; there, man's
    thought,
  Rarer, intenser, 10
Self-gathered for an outbreak, as it ought,
  Chafes in the censer.
Leave we the unlettered plain its herd and
    crop;
  Seek we sepulture
On a tall mountain, cited to the top, 15
  Crowded with culture!
All the peaks soar, but one the rest excels;
  Clouds overcome it;
No! yonder sparkle is the citadel's
  Circling its summit. 20
Thither our path lies; wind we up the
    heights;
  Wait ye the warning?
Our low life was the level's and the night's;
  He's for the morning.
Step to a tune, square chests, erect each head,
  'Ware the beholders! 26
This is our master, famous, calm and dead,
  Borne on our shoulders.

Sleep, crop and herd! sleep, darkling thorpe
    and croft,
  Safe from the weather! 30
He, whom we convoy to his grave aloft,
  Singing together,
He was a man born with thy face and throat,
  Lyric Apollo!
Long he lived nameless: how should Spring
    take note 35
  Winter would follow?
Till lo, the little touch, and youth was gone!
  Cramped and diminished,
Moaned he, "New measures, other feet anon!
  My dance is finished"? 40
No, that's the world's way: (keep the moun-
    tain-side,
  Make for the city!)
He knew the signal, and stepped on with
    pride
  Over men's pity;
Left play for work, and grappled with the
    world 45
  Bent on escaping:
"What's in the scroll," quoth he, "thou
    keepest furled?
  Show me their shaping,
Theirs who most studied man, the bard and
    sage,—
  Give!"—So, he gowned him, 50

Straight got by heart that book to its last
    page:
    Learned, we found him.
Yea, but we found him bald too, eyes like
    lead,
    Accents uncertain:
"Time to taste life," another would have said,
    "Up with the curtain!"   56
This man said rather, "Actual life comes
    next?
    Patience a moment!
Grant I have mastered learning's crabbed
    text,
    Still there's the comment.   60
Let me know all! Prate not of most or least,
    Painful or easy!
Even to the crumbs I'd fain eat up the feast,
    Ay, nor feel queasy."
Oh, such a life as he resolved to live,   65
    When he had learned it,
When he had gathered all books had to give!
    Sooner, he spurned it.
Imagine the whole, then execute the parts—
    Fancy the fabric   70
Quite, ere you build, ere steel strike fire from
    quartz,
    Ere mortar dab brick!

(Here's the town-gate reached: there's the
    market-place
    Gaping before us.)
Yea, this in him was the peculiar grace   75
    (Hearten our chorus!)
That before living he'd learn how to live—
    No end to learning:
Earn the means first—God surely will con-
    trive
    Use for our earning.   80
Others mistrust and say, "But time escapes:
    Live now or never!"
He said, "What's time? Leave Now for dogs
    and apes!
    Man has Forever."
Back to his book then: deeper drooped his
    head: 85
    Calculus[3] racked him:
Leaden before, his eyes grew dross of lead:
    Tussis[4] attacked him.
"Now, master, take a little rest!"—not he!
    (Caution redoubled,   90
Step two abreast, the way winds narrowly!)
    Not a whit troubled,
Back to his studies, fresher than at first,
    Fierce as a dragon
He (soul-hydroptic[5] with a sacred thirst) 95
    Sucked at the flagon.

[3]The stone.   [4]A cough.   [5]Soul-thirsty.

Oh, if we draw a circle premature,
    Heedless of far gain,
Greedy for quick returns of profit, sure
    Bad is our bargain!   100
Was it not great? did not he throw on God,
    (He loves the burthen)—
God's task to make the heavenly period
    Perfect the earthen?
Did not he magnify the mind, show clear 105
    Just what it all meant?
He would not discount life, as fools do here,
    Paid by instalment.
He ventured neck or nothing—heaven's
    success
    Found, or earth's failure: 110
"Wilt thou trust death or not?" He an-
    swered "Yes!
    Hence with life's pale lure!"
That low man seeks a little thing to do,
    Sees it and does it:
This high man, with a great thing to pursue,
    Dies ere he knows it.   116
That low man goes on adding one to one,
    His hundred's soon hit:
This high man, aiming at a million,
    Misses an unit.   120
That, has the world here—should he need the
    next,
    Let the world mind him!
This, throws himself on God, and unper-
    plexed
    Seeking shall find him.
So, with the throttling hands of death at
    strife,
    Ground he at grammar;   126
Still, through the rattle, parts of speech were
    rife;
    While he could stammer
He settled *Hoti's* business—let it be!—
    Properly based *Oun*—   130
Gave us the doctrine of the enclitic *De*[6]
    Dead from the waist down.

[6]These are Greek particles, meaning respectively
that, therefore, and *towards.* Concerning the last
Browning wrote to the London *Daily News* on 20
November, 1874: "In a clever article this morning
you speak of 'the doctrine of enclitic De'—'which,
with all deference to Mr. Browning, in point of
fact does not exist.' No, not to Mr. Browning:
but pray defer to Herr Buttmann, whose fifth list
of 'enclitics' ends with 'the inseparable *De*'—or to
Curtius, whose fifth list ends also with '*De* (meaning *"towards"* and as a demonstrative appendage).'
That this is not to be confounded with the accentu-
ated '*De*, meaning *but*' was the doctrine' which the
Grammarian bequeathed to those capable of receiving it."

Well, here's the platform, here's the proper
place:
   Hail to your purlieus,
All ye highfliers of the feathered race, 135
   Swallows and curlews!
Here's the top-peak; the multitude below
   Live, for they can, there:
This man decided not to Live but Know—
   Bury this man there? 140
Here—here's his place, where meteors shoot,
clouds form,
   Lightnings are loosened,
Stars come and go! Let joy break with the
storm,
   Peace let the dew send!
Lofty designs must close in like effects: 145
   Loftily lying,
Leave him—still loftier than the world sus-
pects,
   Living and dying.

ABT VOGLER [1]

(*After He Has Been Extemporizing upon the Musical Instrument of His Invention*)

Would that the structure brave, the manifold music I build,
   Bidding my organ obey, calling its keys
to their work,
Claiming each slave of the sound, at a touch,
as when Solomon willed
   Armies of angels that soar, legions of
demons that lurk,
Man, brute, reptile, fly,—alien of end and
of aim, 5
   Adverse, each from the other heaven-high,
hell-deep removed,—
Should rush into sight at once as he named
the ineffable Name,
   And pile him a palace straight, to pleasure
the princess he loved! [2]

Would it might tarry like his, the beautiful
building of mine,
   This which my keys in a crowd pressed
and importuned to raise! 10

Ah, one and all, how they helped, would dispart now and now combine,
   Zealous to hasten the work, heighten their
master his praise!
And one would bury his brow with a blind
plunge down to hell,
   Burrow awhile and build, broad on the
roots of things,
Then up again swim into sight, having based
me my palace well, 15
   Founded it, fearless of flame, flat on the
nether springs.

And another would mount and march, like
the excellent minion he was,
   Ay, another and yet another, one crowd
but with many a crest,
Raising my rampired [3] walls of gold as transparent as glass,
   Eager to do and die, yield each his place to
the rest: 20
For higher still and higher (as a runner tips
with fire,
   When a great illumination surprises a
festal night—
Outlining round and round Rome's dome [4]
from space to spire)
   Up, the pinnacled glory reached, and the
pride of my soul was in sight.

In sight? Not half! for it seemed, it was
certain, to match man's birth, 25
   Nature in turn conceived, obeying an impulse as I;
And the emulous heaven yearned down,
made effort to reach the earth,
   As the earth had done her best, in my
passion, to scale the sky:
Novel splendors burst forth, grew familiar
and dwelt with mine,
   Not a point nor peak but found and fixed
its wandering star; 30
Meteor-moons, balls of blaze: and they did
not pale nor pine,
   For earth had attained to heaven, there
was no more near nor far.

Nay more; for there wanted not who walked
in the glare and glow,
   Presences [5] plain in the place; or, fresh
from the Protoplast, [6]
Furnished for ages to come, when a kindlier
wind should blow, 35

---

[1] Published in 1864. George Joseph Vogler
(1749-1814), organist and composer, was a native
of Würzburg. He invented an instrument called
the Orchestrion—a compact organ with four key-
boards of five octaves each and a pedal-board of
thirty-six keys. Vogler was a Catholic priest—
hence Browning's "Abt."

[2] Jewish legend gave Solomon such powers as this.
"The ineffable Name" is the unspeakable name of
God.

[3] Protected with a rampart.
[4] St. Peter's.   [5] Spirits.
[6] The thing first formed, as a model to be imitated.

Lured now to begin and live, in a house to
their liking at last;
Or else the wonderful Dead who have passed
through the body and gone,
But were back once more to breathe in an
old world worth their new:
What never had been, was now; what was,
as it shall be anon;
And what is,—shall I say, matched both?
for I was made perfect too.   40

All through my keys that gave their sounds
to a wish of my soul,
All through my soul that praised as its wish
flowed visibly forth,
All through music and me!   For think, had I
painted the whole,
Why, there it had stood, to see, nor the
process so wonder-worth:
Had I written the same, made verse—still,
effect proceeds from cause,   45
Ye know why the forms are fair, ye hear
how the tale is told;
It is all triumphant art, but art in obedience
to laws,
Painter and poet are proud in the artist-list
enrolled:—

But here is the finger of God, a flash of the
will that can,
Existent behind all laws, that made them
and, lo, they are!   50
And I know not if, save in this, such gift be
allowed to man,
That out of three sounds he frame, not a
fourth sound, but a star.
Consider it well: each tone of our scale in
itself is naught:
It is everywhere in the world—loud, soft,
and all is said:
Give it to me to use!   I mix it with two in
my thought: 55
And, there!   Ye have heard and seen:
consider and bow the head!

Well, it is gone at last, the palace of music I
reared;
Gone! and the good tears start, the praises
that come too slow;
For one is assured at first, one scarce can say
that he feared,
That he even gave it a thought, the gone
thing was to go.   60
Never to be again!   But many more of the
kind
As good, nay, better perchance · is this
your comfort to me?

To me, who must be saved because I cling
with my mind
To the same, same self, same love, same
God: ay, what was, shall be.

Therefore to whom turn I but to Thee, the
ineffable Name?   65
Builder and maker, Thou, of houses not
made with hands!
What, have fear of change from Thee who
art ever the same?
Doubt that Thy power can fill the heart
that Thy power expands?
There shall never be one lost good!   What
was, shall live as before;
The evil is null, is naught, is silence implying sound;   70
What was good shall be good, with, for evil,
so much good more;
On the earth the broken arcs; in the heaven
a perfect round.

All we have willed or hoped or dreamed of
good shall exist;
Not its semblance, but itself; no beauty,
nor good, nor power
Whose voice has gone forth, but each survives for the melodist   75
When eternity affirms the conception of
an hour.
The high that proved too high, the heroic for
earth too hard,
The passion that left the ground to lose
itself in the sky,
Are music sent up to God by the lover and
the bard;
Enough that he heard it once: we shall
hear it by and by.   80

And what is our failure here but a triumph's
evidence
For the fullness of the days?   Have we
withered or agonized?
Why else was the pause prolonged but that
singing might issue thence?
Why rushed the discords in, but that
harmony should be prized?
Sorrow is hard to bear, and doubt is slow to
clear,   85
Each sufferer says his say, his scheme of
the weal and woe:
But God has a few of us whom he whispers
in the ear;
The rest may reason and welcome: 'tis
we musicians know.

Well, it is earth with me; silence resumes her
    reign:
I will be patient and proud, and soberly
    acquiesce.   90
Give me the keys. I feel for the common
    chord[7] again,
    Sliding by semitones, till I sink to the
      minor,—yes,
And I blunt it into a ninth,[8] and I stand on
    alien ground,
    Surveying awhile the heights I rolled from
      into the deep;
Which, hark, I have dared and done, for my
    resting-place is found,   95
    The C Major[9] of this life: so, now I will
      try to sleep.

RABBI BEN EZRA [1]

Grow old along with me!
The best is yet to be,
The last of life, for which the first was made:
Our times are in His hand
Who saith, "A whole I planned,   5
Youth shows but half; trust God: see all,
    nor be afraid!"

Not that, amassing flowers,
Youth sighed, "Which rose make ours,
Which lily leave and then as best recall?"
Not that, admiring stars,   10
It yearned, "Nor Jove, nor Mars;
Mine be some figured flame which blends,
    transcends them all!"

Not for such hopes and fears
Annulling youth's brief years,
Do I remonstrate: folly wide the mark!   15
Rather I prize the doubt
Low kinds exist without,
Finished and finite clods, untroubled by a
    spark.

---

[7] A fundamental tone with its major (4 semi-tones) or minor (3 semitones) third, and a perfect fifth (7 semitones) above it.

[8] Either an interval containing an octave and two semitones (major) or one containing an octave and one semitone (minor).

[9] This scale contains no sharps or flats.

[1] Published in 1864. Abenezra, or Ibn Ezra (1092–1167), was one of the most distinguished Jewish learned men of the Middle Age, and attained eminence as philosopher, astronomer, physician, and poet, and particularly as grammarian and commentator. Browning derived much in this poem from his works, though his own views coincided largely with Ibn Ezra's teaching. It is also probable that *Rabbi Ben Ezra* was written as a reply to the philosophy advanced by Edward Fitz-Gerald in *The Rubáiyát of Omar Khayyám* (1859).

Poor vaunt of life indeed,
Were man but formed to feed   20
On joy, to solely seek and find and feast:
Such feasting ended, then
As sure an end to men;
Irks care the crop full bird? Frets doubt
    the maw-crammed beast?

Rejoice we are allied   25
To That which doth provide
And not partake, effect, and not receive!
A spark disturbs our clod;
Nearer we hold of God
Who gives, than of His tribes that take, I
    must believe.   30

Then, welcome each rebuff
That turns earth's smoothness rough,
Each sting that bids nor sit nor stand but go!
Be our joys three-parts pain!
Strive, and hold cheap the strain;   35
Learn, nor account the pang; dare, never
    grudge the throe!

For thence,—a paradox
Which comforts while it mocks,—
Shall life succeed in that it seems to fail:
What I aspired to be,   40
And was not, comforts me:
A brute I might have been, but would not
    sink i' the scale.

What is he but a brute
Whose flesh has soul to suit,
Whose spirit works lest arms and legs want
    play?   45
To man, propose this test—
Thy body at its best,
How far can that project thy soul on its lone
    way?

Yet gifts should prove their use:
I own the Past profuse   50
Of power each side, perfection every turn:
Eyes, ears took in their dole,
Brain treasured up the whole;
Should not the heart beat once "How good to
    live and learn"?

Not once beat "Praise be thine!   55
I see the whole design,
I, who saw power, see now Love perfect too:
Perfect I call Thy plan:
Thanks that I was a man!
Maker, remake, complete,—I trust what
    Thou shalt do!"   60

For pleasant is this flesh;
Our soul, in its rose-mesh
Pulled ever to the earth, still yearns for rest:
Would we some prize might hold
To match those manifold   65
Possessions of the brute,—gain most, as we
    did best!

Let us not always say,
"Spite of this flesh to-day
I strove, made head, gained ground upon the
    whole!"
As the bird wings and sings,   70
Let us cry, "All good things
Are ours, nor soul helps flesh more, now,
    than flesh helps soul!"

Therefore I summon age
To grant youth's heritage,
Life's struggle having so far reached its
    term: 75
Thence shall I pass, approved
A man, for aye removed
From the developed brute; a God though in
    the germ.

And I shall thereupon
Take rest, ere I be gone   80
Once more on my adventure brave and new:
Fearless and unperplexed,
When I wage battle next,
What weapons to select, what armor to in-
    due.[2]

Youth ended, I shall try   85
My gain or loss thereby;
Leave the fire ashes, what survives is gold:
And I shall weigh the same,
Give life its praise or blame:
Young, all lay in dispute; I shall know, being
    old.   90

For note, when evening shuts,
A certain moment cuts
The deed off, calls the glory from the gray:
A whisper from the west
Shoots—"Add this to the rest,   95
Take it and try its worth: here dies another
    day."

So, still within this life,
Though lifted o'er its strife,
Let me discern, compare, pronounce at last,
"This rage was right i' the main,   100
That acquiescence vain:
The Future I may face now I have proved
    the Past."

[2] To put on.

For more is not reserved
To man, with soul just nerved
To act to-morrow what he learns to-day: 105
Here, work enough to watch
The Master work, and catch
Hints of the proper craft, tricks of the
    tool's true play.

As it was better, youth
Should strive, through acts uncouth,   110
Toward making, than repose on aught found
    made:
So, better, age, exempt
From strife, should know, than tempt
Further. Thou waitedst age: wait death nor
    be afraid!

Enough now, if the Right   115
And Good and Infinite
Be named here, as thou callest thy hand
    thine own,
With knowledge absolute,
Subject to no dispute
From fools that crowded youth, nor let thee
    feel alone.   120

Be there, for once and all,
Severed great minds from small,
Announced to each his station in the Past!
Was I, the world arraigned,
Were they, my soul disdained,   125
Right? Let age speak the truth and give
    us peace at last!

Now, who shall arbitrate?
Ten men love what I hate,
Shun what I follow, slight what I receive;
Ten, who in ears and eyes   130
Match me: we all surmise,
They this thing, and I that: whom shall my
    soul believe?

Not on the vulgar mass
Called "work," must sentence pass,
Things done, that took the eye and had the
    price;   135
O'er which, from level stand,
The low world laid its hand,
Found straightway to its mind, could value
    in a trice:

But all, the world's coarse thumb
And finger failed to plumb,   140
So passed in making up the main account;
All instincts immature,
All purposes unsure,
That weighed not as his work, yet swelled
    the man's amount:

Thoughts hardly to be packed 145
Into a narrow act,
Fancies that broke through language and
  escaped;
All I could never be,
All, men ignored in me,
This, I was worth to God, whose wheel the
  pitcher shaped. 150

Ay, note that Potter's wheel,[3]
That metaphor! and feel
Why time spins fast, why passive lies our
  clay,—
Thou, to whom fools propound,
When the wine makes its round, 155
"Since life fleets, all is change; the Past gone,
  seize to-day!"

Fool! All that is, at all,
Lasts ever, past recall;
Earth changes, but thy soul and God stand
  sure:
What entered into thee, 160
That was, is, and shall be:
Time's wheel runs back or stops: Potter and
  clay endure.

He fixed thee 'mid this dance
Of plastic circumstance,
This Present, thou, forsooth, wouldst fain
  arrest: 165
Machinery just meant
To give thy soul its bent,
Try thee and turn thee forth, sufficiently im-
  pressed.

What though the earlier grooves,
Which ran the laughing loves 170
Around thy base, no longer pause and press;
What though, about thy rim,
Skull-things in order grim
Grow out, in graver mood, obey the sterner
  stress?

Look not thou down but up! 175
To uses of a cup,
The festal board, lamp's flash and trumpet's
  peal,
The new wine's foaming flow,
The Master's lips aglow!
Thou, heaven's consummate cup, what needst
  thou with earth's wheel? 180

But I need, now as then,
Thee, God, who moldest men;
And since, not even while the whirl was
  worst,
Did I—to the wheel of life
With shapes and colors rife, 185
Bound dizzily—mistake my end, to slake Thy
  thirst:

So, take and use Thy work:
Amend what flaws may lurk,
What strain o' the stuff, what warpings past
  the aim!
My times be in Thy hand! 190
Perfect the cup as planned!
Let age approve of youth, and death com-
  plete the same!

CALIBAN UPON SETEBOS
Or
Natural Theology in the Island[1]

"Thou thoughtest that I was altogether such
  an one as thyself."

['Will[2] sprawl, now that the heat of day is
  best,
Flat on his belly in the pit's much mire,

With elbows wide, fists clenched to prop his
  chin.
And, while he kicks both feet in the cool
  slush,
And feels about his spine small eft-things[3]
  course, 5
Run in and out each arm, and make him
  laugh:
And while above his head a pompion-plant,[4]
Coating the cave-top as a brow its eye,

[3]See Isaiah, 64:8; also Jeremiah, 18:1-6.

[1]Published in 1864. Caliban is the savage slave of Shakespeare's *Tempest*. Setebos was a Patagonian god whom Shakespeare—reading of him in an Elizabethan narrative of travel—made the god worshiped by Caliban's mother (dam). As Browning's motto (from Psalms, 1:21) indicates, Caliban's theological reflections constitute a commentary upon crudely anthropomorphic conceptions of the Deity.

[2]I. e., he will. Caliban's imperfect speech in-

cludes use of the third person when he is speaking of himself. The brackets around this and a later section of the poem are Browning's.

[3]Lizard-like animals.

[4]A vine of the pumpkin family.

Creeps down to touch and tickle hair and
 beard,
And now a flower drops with a bee inside, 10
And now a fruit to snap at, catch and
 crunch,—
He looks out o'er yon sea which sunbeams
 cross
And recross till they weave a spider-web
(Meshes of fire, some great fish breaks at
 times),
And talks to his own self, howe'er he please,
Touching that other, whom his dam called
 God. 16
Because to talk about Him, vexes—ha,
Could He but know! and time to vex is now,
When talk is safer than in winter-time.
Moreover Prosper and Miranda sleep 20
In confidence he drudges at their task,
And it is good to cheat the pair, and gibe,
Letting the rank tongue blossom into
 speech.]

Setebos, Setebos, and Setebos!
'Thinketh, He dwelleth i' the cold o' the
 moon. 25

'Thinketh He made it, with the sun to match,
But not the stars; the stars came otherwise;
Only made clouds, winds, meteors, such as
 that:
Also this isle, what lives and grows thereon,
And snaky sea which rounds and ends the
 same. 30

'Thinketh, it came of being ill at ease:
He hated that He cannot change His cold,
Nor cure its ache. 'Hath spied an icy fish
That longed to 'scape the rock-stream where
 she lived,
And thaw herself within the lukewarm brine
O' the lazy sea her stream thrusts far amid,
A crystal spike 'twixt two warm walls of
 wave; 37
Only, she ever sickened, found repulse
At the other kind of water, not her life
(Green-dense and dim-delicious, bred o' the
 sun), 40
Flounced back from bliss she was not born to
 breathe,
And in her old bounds buried her despair,
Hating and loving warmth alike: so He.

'Thinketh, He made thereat the sun, this
 isle,
Trees and the fowls here, beast and creeping
 thing. 45
Yon otter, sleek-wet, black, lithe as a leech;

Yon auk, one fire-eye in a ball of foam,
That floats and feeds; a certain badger
 brown
He hath watched hunt with that slant white-
 wedge eye
By moonlight; and the pie[5] with the long
 tongue 50
That pricks deep into oakwarts[6] for a worm,
And says a plain word when she finds her
 prize,
But will not eat the ants; the ants them-
 selves
That build a wall of seeds and settled stalks
About their hole—He made all these and
 more, 55
Made all we see, and us, in spite: how else?
He could not, Himself, make a second self
To be His mate; as well have made Himself:
He would not make what He mislikes or
 slights,
An eyesore to Him, or not worth His pains:
But did, in envy, listlessness or sport, 61
Make what Himself would fain, in a manner,
 be—
Weaker in most points, stronger in a few,
Worthy, and yet mere playthings all the
 while,
Things He admires and mocks too,—that is
 it. 65
Because, so brave, so better though they be,
It nothing skills if He begin to plague.
Look now, I melt a gourd-fruit into mash,
Add honeycomb and pods, I have perceived,
Which bite like finches when they bill and
 kiss,— 70
Then, when froth rises bladdery, drink up
 all,
Quick, quick, till maggots scamper through
 my brain;
Last, throw me on my back i' the seeded
 thyme,
And wanton, wishing I were born a bird.
Put case, unable to be what I wish, 75
I yet could make a live bird out of clay:
Would not I take clay, pinch my Caliban
Able to fly?—for, there, see, he hath wings,
And great comb like the hoopoe's to admire,
And there, a sting to do his foes offense, 80
There, and I will that he begin to live,
Fly to yon rock-top, nip me off the horns
Of grigs[7] high up that make the merry din,
Saucy through their veined wings, and mind
 me not.

———

[5] The magpie.
[6] Swellings on oaktrees, caused by insects.
[7] Crickets or grasshoppers.

In which feat, if his leg snapped, brittle clay,
And he lay stupid-like,—why, I should
   laugh; 86
And if he, spying me, should fall to weep,
Beseech me to be good, repair his wrong,
Bid his poor leg smart less or grow again,—
Well, as the chance were, this might take or
   else 90
Not take my fancy: I might hear his cry,
And give the manikin three sound legs for
   one,
Or pluck the other off, leave him like an egg,
And lessoned he was mine and merely clay.
Were this no pleasure, lying in the thyme, 95
Drinking the mash, with brain become alive,
Making and marring clay at will? So He.

'Thinketh, such shows nor right nor wrong
   in Him,
Nor kind, nor cruel: He is strong and Lord.
'Am strong myself compared to yonder crabs
That march now from the mountain to the
   sea; 101
'Let twenty pass, and stone the twenty-first,
Loving not, hating not, just choosing so.
'Say, the first straggler that boasts purple
   spots
Shall join the file, one pincer twisted off; 105
'Say, this bruised fellow shall receive a
   worm,
And two worms he whose nippers end in
   red;
As it likes me each time, I do: so He.

Well then, 'supposeth He is good i' the main,
Placable if His mind and ways were guessed,
But rougher than His handiwork, be sure!
Oh, He hath made things worthier than
   Himself, 112
And envieth that, so helped, such things do
   more
Than He who made them! What consoles
   but this?
That they, unless through Him, do naught at
   all, 115
And must submit: what other use in things?
'Hath cut a pipe of pithless elder-joint
That, blown through, gives exact the scream
   o' the jay
When from her wing you twitch the feathers
   blue:
Sound this, and little birds that hate the jay
Flock within stone's throw, glad their foe is
   hurt: 121
But case such pipe could prattle and boast
   forsooth,
"I catch the birds, I am the crafty thing,

I make the cry my maker cannot make
With his great round mouth; he must blow
   through mine!" 125
Would not I smash it with my foot? So He.

But wherefore rough, why cold and ill at
   ease?
Aha, that is a question! Ask, for that,
What knows,—the something over Setebos
That made Him, or He, may be, found and
   fought, 130
Worsted, drove off and did to nothing, per-
   chance.
There may be something quiet o'er His head,
Out of His reach, that feels nor joy nor
   grief,
Since both derive from weakness in some
   way.
I joy because the quails come; would not
   joy 135
Could I bring quails here when I have a
   mind:
This Quiet, all it hath a mind to, doth.
'Esteemeth stars the outposts of its couch,
But never spends much thought nor care
   that way.
It may look up, work up,—the worse for
   those 140
It works on! 'Careth but for Setebos
The many-handed as a cuttle-fish,
Who, making Himself feared through what
   He does,
Looks up, first, and perceives he cannot soar
To what is quiet and hath happy life; 145
Next looks down here, and out of very spite
Makes this a bauble-world to ape yon real,
These good things to match those as hips[8]
   do grapes.
'Tis solace making baubles, ay, and sport.
Himself peeped late, eyed Prosper at his
   books 150
Careless and lofty, lord now of the isle:
Vexed, 'stitched a book of broad leaves,
   arrow-shaped,
Wrote thereon, he knows what, prodigious
   words;
Has peeled a wand and called it by a name;
Weareth at whiles for an enchanter's robe 155
The eyed skin of a supple oncelot;[9]
And hath an ounce sleeker than youngling
   mole,
A four-legged serpent he makes cower and
   couch,

---

[8]The ripened fruit of the wild rosebush.

[9]A small leopard-like animal (diminutive of
ounce in following line).

Now snarl, now hold its breath and mind his eye,
And saith she is Miranda and my wife: 160
'Keeps for his Ariel a tall pouch-bill crane
He bids go wade for fish and straight disgorge;
Also a sea-beast, lumpish, which he snared,
Blinded the eyes of, and brought somewhat tame,
And split its toe-webs, and now pens the drudge
In a hole o' the rock and calls him Caliban; 165
A bitter heart that bides its time and bites.
'Plays thus at being Prosper in a way,
Taketh his mirth with make-believes: so He.

His dam held that the Quiet made all things
Which Setebos vexed only; 'holds not so. 171
Who made them weak, meant weakness He might vex.
Had He meant other, while His hand was in,
Why not make horny eyes no thorn could prick,
Or plate my scalp with bone against the snow, 175
Or overscale my flesh 'neath joint and joint,
Like an orc's[10] armor? Ay,—so spoil His sport!
He is the One now: only He doth all.

'Saith, He may like, perchance, what profits Him.
Ay, himself loves what does him good; but why? 180
'Gets good no otherwise. This blinded beast
Loves whoso places flesh-meat on his nose,
But, had he eyes, would want no help, but hate
Or love, just as it liked him: He hath eyes.
Also it pleaseth Setebos to work, 185
Use all His hands, and exercise much craft,
By no means for the love of what is worked.
'Tasteth, himself, no finer good i' the world
When all goes right, in this safe summertime,
And he wants little, hungers, aches not much, 190
Than trying what to do with wit and strength.
'Falls to make something: 'piled yon pile of turfs,
And squared and stuck there squares of soft white chalk,
And, with a fish-tooth, scratched a moon on each,
And set up endwise certain spikes of tree, 195

And crowned the whole with a sloth's[11] skull a-top,
Found dead i' the woods, too hard for one to kill.
No use at all i' the work, for work's sole sake;
'Shall some day knock it down again: so He.

'Saith He is terrible: watch His feats in proof!
One hurricane will spoil six good months' hope. 200
He hath a spite against me, that I know,
Just as He favors Prosper, who knows why?
So it is, all the same, as well I find.
'Wove wattles[12] half the winter, fenced them firm 205
With stone and stake to stop she-tortoises
Crawling to lay their eggs here: well, one wave,
Feeling the foot of Him upon its neck,
Gaped as a snake does, lolled out its large tongue,
And licked the whole labor flat: so much for spite. 210

'Saw a ball flame down late (yonder it lies)
Where, half an hour before, I slept i' the shade:
Often they scatter sparkles: there is force!
'Dug up a newt He may have envied once
And turned to stone, shut up inside a stone.
Please Him and hinder this?—What Prosper does? 216
Aha, if He would tell me how! Not He!
There is the sport: discover how or die!
All need not die, for of the things o' the isle
Some flee afar, some dive, some run up trees; 220
Those at His mercy,—why, they please Him most
When . . . when . . . well, never try the same way twice!
Repeat what act has pleased, He may grow wroth.
You must not know His ways, and play Him off,
Sure of the issue. 'Doth the like himself: 225
'Spareth a squirrel that it nothing fears
But steals the nut from underneath my thumb,
And when I threat, bites stoutly in defense:
'Spareth an urchin that contrariwise,

[10] A sea monster.

[11] A slow-moving arboreal mammal, akin to the ant-eater.

[12] Twigs.

Curls up into a ball, pretending death   230
For fright at my approach: the two ways
  please.
But what would move my choler more than
  this,
That either creature counted on its life
To-morrow and next day and all days to
  come,
Saying, forsooth, in the inmost of its heart,
"Because he did so yesterday with me,   236
And otherwise with such another brute,
So must he do henceforth and always."—
  Ay?
Would teach the reasoning couple what
  "must" means!
'Doth as he likes, or wherefore Lord? So
He.   240

'Conceiveth all things will continue thus,
And we shall have to live in fear of Him
So long as He lives, keeps His strength: no
  change,
If He have done His best, make no new
  world
To please Him more, so leave off watching
  this,—   245
If He surprise not even the Quiet's self
Some strange day,—or, suppose, grow into it
As grubs grow butterflies: else, here we are,
And there is He, and nowhere help at all.

'Believeth with the life, the pain shall stop.
His dam held different, that after death 251
He both plagued enemies and feasted
  friends:
Idly! He doth His worst in this our life,
Giving just respite lest we die through pain,
Saving last pain for worst,—with which, an
  end.   255
Meanwhile, the best way to escape His ire
Is, not to seem too happy. 'Sees, himself,
Yonder two flies, with purple films and pink,
Bask on the pompion-bell above: kills both.
'Sees two black painful beetles roll their ball
On head and tail as if to save their lives: 261
Moves them the stick away they strive to
  clear.

Even so, 'would have Him misconceive, sup-
  pose
This Caliban strives hard and ails no less,
And always, above all else, envies Him; 265
Wherefore he mainly dances on dark nights,
Moans in the sun, gets under holes to laugh,
And never speaks his mind save housed as
  now:
Outside, 'groans, curses. If He caught me
  here,

O'erheard this speech, and asked "What
  chucklest at?"   270
'Would, to appease Him, cut a finger off,
Or of my three kid yearlings burn the best,
Or let the toothsome apples rot on tree,
Or push my tame beast for the orc to taste:
While myself lit a fire, and made a song 275
And sung it, *"What I hate, be consecrate*
To celebrate Thee and Thy state, no mate
For Thee; what see for envy in poor me?"
Hoping the while, since evils sometimes
  mend,
Warts rub away and sores are cured with
  slime,   280
That some strange day, will either the Quiet
  catch
And conquer Setebos, or likelier He
Decrepit may doze, doze, as good as die.

[What, what? A curtain o'er the world at
  once!
Crickets stop hissing; not a bird—or, yes, 285
There scuds His raven that has told Him all!
It was fool's play, this prattling! Ha!
  The wind
Shoulders the pillared dust, death's house o'
  the move,
And fast invading fires begin! White
  blaze—
A tree's head snaps—and there, there, there,
  there, there,   290
His thunder follows! Fool to gibe at Him!
Lo! 'Lieth flat and loveth Setebos!
'Maketh his teeth meet through his upper lip,
Will let those quails fly, will not eat this
  month
One little mess of whelks,[13] so he may
  'scape!]   295

PROSPICE[1]

Fear death?—to feel the fog in my throat,
  The mist in my face,
When the snows begin; and the blasts denote
  I am nearing the place,
The power of the night, the press of the
  storm,   5
  The post of the foe;
Where he stands, the Arch Fear in a visible
  form,
  Yet the strong man must go:
For the journey is done and the summit
  attained,
  And the barriers fall,   10

[13]Mollusks.

[1]Published in 1864; written in 1861 not long after
Mrs. Browning's death. The title means, Look
forward.

Though a battle's to fight ere the guerdon be
    gained,
    The reward of it all.
I was ever a fighter, so—one fight more,
    The best and the last!
I would hate that death bandaged my eyes,
    and forebore,   15
    And bade me creep past.
No! let me taste the whole of it, fare like my
    peers
    The heroes of old,
Bear the brunt, in a minute pay glad life's
    arrears
    Of pain, darkness and cold.   20
For sudden the worst turns the best to the
    brave,
    The black minute's at end,
And the elements' rage, the fiend-voices that
    rave,
    Shall dwindle, shall blend,
Shall change, shall become first a peace out
    of pain,   25
    Then a light, then thy breast,
O thou soul of my soul! I shall clasp thee
    again,
    And with God be the rest!

NEVER THE TIME AND THE PLACE [2]

Never the time and the place
    And the loved one all together!
This path—how soft to pace!
    This May—what magic weather!
Where is the loved one's face?   5
In a dream that loved one's face meets mine,
    But the house is narrow, the place is bleak
Where, outside, rain and wind combine
    With a furtive ear, if I strive to speak,
    With a hostile eye at my flushing cheek, 10
With a malice that marks each word, each
    sign!
O enemy sly and serpentine,
    Uncoil thee from the waking man!
    Do I hold the Past
    Thus firm and fast   15
Yet doubt if the Future hold I can?
This path so soft to pace shall lead
Through the magic of May to herself in-
    deed!
Or narrow if needs the house must be,
    Outside are the storms and strangers:
    we—   20
Oh, close, safe, warm sleep I and she,
    —I and she!

_____
[2]Published in 1883, twenty-two years after Mrs.
Browning's death.

WHY I AM A LIBERAL [3]

"Why?"   Because all I haply can and do,
    All that I am now, all I hope to be,—
    Whence comes it save from fortune set-
        ting free
Body and soul the purpose to pursue,
God traced for both? If fetters, not a few,
    Of prejudice, convention, fall from me,   6
    These shall I bid men—each in his degree
Also God-guided—bear, and gaily, too?

But little do or can the best of us:
    That little is achieved through Liberty. 10
Who, then dares hold, emancipated thus,
    His fellows shall continue bound? Not I,
Who live, love, labor freely, nor discuss
    A brother's right to freedom. That is
    "Why."

EPILOGUE [4]

At the midnight in the silence of the sleep-
    time,
    When you set your fancies free,
Will they pass to where—by death, fools
    think, imprisoned—
Low he lies who once so loved you, whom
    you loved so,
            —Pity me?   5

Oh to love so, be so loved, yet so mistaken!
    What had I on earth to do
With the slothful, with the mawkish, the
    unmanly?
Like the aimless, helpless, hopeless, did I
    drivel
            —Being—who?   10

One who never turned his back but marched
    breast forward,
    Never doubted clouds would break,
Never dreamed, though right were worsted,
    wrong would triumph,
Held we fall to rise, are baffled to fight better,
            Sleep to wake.   15

No, at noonday in the bustle of man's work-
    time
    Greet the unseen[5] with a cheer!
Bid him forward, breast and back as either
    should be,
"Strive and thrive!" cry "Speed,—fight on,
    fare ever
            There as here!"   20

_____
[3]Published in 1885 in *Why I am a Liberal*, a
book to which various leading liberals contributed
explanations of their doctrines.
[4]Published in 1889. The poem concludes *Aso-
lando*, the last volume Browning published.
[5]Browning when he is dead.

EDWARD FITZGERALD
1809–1883

FitzGerald's father was John Purcell, the son of a wealthy Irish doctor, who had married his first cousin, Mary Frances FitzGerald, and who, on the death of her father, took the name and arms of FitzGerald. Edward was the seventh of their eight children, and was born at Bredfield House, near Woodbridge, Suffolk, on 31 March, 1809. In 1821 he was sent to King Edward the Sixth's Grammar School at Bury St. Edmonds. He entered Trinity College, Cambridge, in 1826, and took his degree in 1830. At school had begun what was to be a life-long friendship with James Spedding, the editor, biographer, and wholehearted defender of Francis Bacon. At Cambridge a similar friendship with Thackeray was formed. The Tennysons, Charles, Frederic, and Alfred, were also college contemporaries, but he did not know them until later. The greater part of Fitz-Gerald's life was passed in the county of his birth. He was not pressed by his family to enter any profession, and apparently never even thought of doing so. He had an allowance from his father until the latter's bankruptcy, and thereafter from his mother—her estates not being involved—until her death, after which he enjoyed a large income. For some of his relatives he felt a true affection, but got along well with all of them by dint of meeting them very seldom. At Cambridge he had formed large plans for literary work; but after his departure he drifted promptly into a vague, easy, indeterminate way of life which lasted, not entirely to his content, yet not without its sufficient rewards, until his death. In 1837, feeling a need for a place of his own, he took a thatched lodge on property belonging to his family. "Here, with Shakespeare's bust in a recess, with a cat, a dog, and a parrot called 'Beauty Bob,' he began what he called a very pleasant Robinson Crusoe sort of life. He was waited upon by an old couple, John Faiers, a laborer on the estate, a Waterloo veteran, and Mrs. Faiers, a red-armed, vain, and snuff-taking lady, with a flower-trimmed bonnet. FitzGerald installed his books and pictures in the cottage. The place

was a scene of desperate confusion. There were books everywhere; pictures on easels; music, pipes, sticks lying on tables or on the piano. A barrel of beer provided the means of simple conviviality. Here FitzGerald would sit, unkempt and unshaven, in dressing-gown and slippers, or moon about in the garden. He strolled about the neighborhood, calling on his friends; sometimes, but rarely, he went to church, noting the toadstools that grew in the chancel; and led a thoroughly indolent life," though still with dreams of literary achievement.

This picture, drawn by A. C. Benson, is typical, and may stand for FitzGerald's way of life from this time on, though as he grew older he grew somewhat more eccentric, withdrew himself further and further from the world and society, and became more convinced than ever of the futility of earthly existence—without, however, losing his interest in literature and in his own occasional and modest achievements, and without ceasing to carry on correspondence with dear friends. The two closest to him at the time of Benson's picture were George Crabbe, son of the poet (who liked his father for everything except his poetry), and Bernard Barton, a Quaker poet of Woodbridge and friend of Charles Lamb. When Barton died, Fitz-Gerald undertook to see that his daughter, Lucy, was provided for, and ended by marrying her (November, 1856). It was, as he seems himself to have suspected, a wretchedly mistaken venture; and after a few months the two separated, without ill-feeling, Lucy receiving through the remainder of her life a liberal allowance from him. Meanwhile FitzGerald had published *Euphranor* (1851), a dialogue in the Platonic manner, in which he sought to define the well-balanced man; *Polonius: A Collection of Wise Saws and Modern Instances* (1852); and *Six Dramas of Calderon Freely Translated* (1853). The last was the only book which he published with his own name attached to it—and he did so in this instance only to help distinguish his book from another volume of translations from Calderon which was published almost simultaneously. His modesty, his detachment, his concern for the work rather than for his own reputation, all contributed to his determined anonymity; but, in addition, he had an actual dislike for his own name. He had "some unpleasant associations with it," he said. Later he printed other translations—all, like the one upon which his fame now securely rests, free adaptations rather than faithful renderings, aimed to catch the spirit rather than the letter, in a form pleasing to English readers. He owed his acquaintance with Persian literature to his friend E. B. Cowell, later a professor at Cambridge, and found the quatrains of Omar Khayyám peculiarly congenial to his own temper—so much so, in fact, that he drifted almost unawares into the attempt to make an English poem of them. The first edition of the *Rubáiyát* was printed in 1859. Other editions, much changed, appeared in 1868, 1872, and 1879.

During all these years FitzGerald's quiet life went on with little change. Very rarely he saw friends from a distance. Carlyle had visited him in 1855, and had never afterwards lost touch with this "lonely, shy, kind-hearted man," as he called him. In 1876 Tennyson visited him, and on this occasion his host told the great man that it would have been better for his reputation had he ceased to write poetry after 1842— but their old friendship was not broken. Fitz-Gerald was then living in his own house, Little Grange, which he had owned since 1864, but which he apparently objected to occupying—as he was only forced to inhabit it after he had been ejected from lodgings in Woodbridge, and

had found other lodgings uncomfortable. The reason for his ejection was characteristic. His landlord, named Berry, became engaged to a widow. FitzGerald did not like the impending change, and remarked that "old Berry would now have to be called 'Old Gooseberry.'" The widow heard of this, and punished the offender by compelling his ejection. He had still some years to live, dying suddenly on 14 June, 1883, while on a visit to the grandson of the poet Crabbe, at Merton Rectory, in Norfolk. In 1889 his friend W. Aldis Wright published FitzGerald's *Letters and Literary Remains* in three volumes, and thus gave him a new claim to remembrance;—for, if he very properly remains best known for his singularly happy rendering of the *Rubáiyát*, he has become only less well known as one of the most delightful letter-writers England has had.

The Variorum and Definitive Edition of the Poetical and Prose Writings of Edward Fitz-Gerald is edited by George Bentham and includes an Introduction by Edmund Gosse (7 vols., New York, 1902–1903). Most of the published letters may be found in the following volumes: *Letters and Literary Remains of Edward FitzGerald,* ed. William Aldis Wright (London, 1889; the letters were reprinted separately with additions in 2 vols., 1894); *Letters of Edward FitzGerald to Fanny Kemble, 1871–1883,* ed. William Aldis Wright (London, 1895); and *More Letters of Edward FitzGerald* (London, 1901). Arthur C. Benson's *Edward FitzGerald* in the "English Men of Letters" series (London, 1905) is a charming biography.

RUBÁIYÁT OF OMAR KHAYYÁM[1]

(1859)

I

Wake! For the Sun, who scattered into flight
The Stars before him from the field of Night,
   Drives Night along with them from heav'n, and strikes
The Sultán's turret with a shaft of light.

II

Before the phantom of False Morning[2] died,   5
Methought a Voice within the Tavern cried:
   "When all the temple is prepared within,
Why nods the drowsy worshiper outside?"

---

[1] The poem is here printed in its final form (4th ed., 1879). Omar Khayyám lived during the last half of the 11th century and the earlier years of the 12th. He was a philosopher and a man of science, and during the later years of his life was the astronomer-royal at the court of the Turkish sultan then ruling in Persia. He aided at this time in reforming the calendar. His extant quatrains are about 1200 in number, though not all of these may really come from his hand. Those qualified to

judge say that FitzGerald's poem reproduces very exactly the spirit of Omar's verse; but it is not, in the sense of the word now usual, a translation. Great liberties are taken in rearranging, combining, compressing, and omitting Omar's quatrains, so as to permit the composition of an English poem of moderate length having the connection between its parts, the organic structure, which Western readers expect.

[2] A transient light on the horizon about an hour before the true dawn; a well-known phenomenon in the East. (FitzGerald.)

III

And, as the cock crew, those who stood before
The Tavern shouted: "Open, then, the door!
  You know how little while we have to stay, 11
And, once departed, may return no more."

IV

Now the New Year[3] reviving old desires,
The thoughtful soul to solitude retires,
  Where the WHITE HAND OF MOSES[4] on the bough 15
Puts out, and Jesus from the ground suspires.[5]

V

Iram[6] indeed is gone with all his Rose,
And Jamshyd's Sev'n-ringed Cup[7] where no one knows:
  But still a ruby kindles in the vine,
And many a garden by the water blows. 20

VI

And David's lips are locked; but in divine
High-piping Pehlevi,[8] with "Wine! Wine! Wine!
  Red Wine!"—the Nightingale cries to the Rose
That sallow cheek of hers to incarnadine.

VII

Come, fill the cup, and in the fire of spring 25
Your winter-garment of repentance fling:
  The Bird of Time has but a little way
To flutter—and the Bird is on the wing.

VIII

Whether at Naishápúr or Babylon,
Whether the Cup with sweet or bitter run, 30
  The Wine of Life keeps oozing drop by drop,
The Leaves of Life keep falling one by one.

[3]Beginning on 21 March.

[4]See Exodus, iv, 6. (The expression here denotes the white blossoms of the spring.)

[5]Breathes. (The Persians conceived the healing power of Jesus to reside in his breath.)

[6]A royal garden now sunk somewhere in the sands of Arabia. (FitzGerald.)

[7]It was typical of the 7 heavens, 7 planets, 7 seas, *etc.*, and was a divining cup. (FitzGerald.) Jamshyd: an ancient legendary king of Persia.

[8]The old heroic Sanskrit of Persia. (FitzGerald.) The people's language changes with the generations, while the nightingale's song remains ever the same

IX

Each morn a thousand roses brings, you say:
Yes, but where leaves the rose of yesterday?
  And this first summer month that brings the rose 35
Shall take Jamshyd and Kaikobád away.

X

Well, let it take them! What have we to do
With Kaikobád the Great, or Kaikhosrú?
  Let Zál and Rustum[9] bluster as they will,
Or Hátim call to supper—heed not you. 40

XI

With me along the strip of herbage strown
That just divides the desert from the sown,
  Where name of Slave and Sultán is forgot—
And peace to Mahmúd[10] on his golden throne!

XII

A book of verses underneath the bough, 45
A jug of wine, a loaf of bread—and Thou
  Beside me singing in the wilderness—
Oh, wilderness were Paradise enow!

XIII

Some for the glories of this world; and some
Sigh for the Prophet's[11] Paradise to come; 50
  Ah, take the cash, and let the credit go,
Nor heed the rumble of a distant drum![12]

XIV

Look to the blowing Rose about us—"Lo,
Laughing," she says, "into the world I blow,
  At once the silken tassel of my purse 55
Tear, and its treasure[13] on the garden throw."

XV

And those who husbanded the golden grain,
And those who flung it to the winds like rain,
  Alike to no such aureate earth are turned
As, buried once, men want dug up again. 60

[9]The Hercules of Persia. Zál was his father. Hátim, a well-known type of oriental generosity (FitzGerald).

[10]The earliest ruler of Persia to call himself sultan (*c.* 975).

[11]Mahomet's.

[12]Beaten outside a palace (FitzGerald).

[13]The rose's golden center (FitzGerald).

XVI

The worldly hope men set their hearts upon
Turns ashes—or it prospers; and anon,
  Like snow upon the desert's dusty face,
Lighting a little hour or two—is gone.

XVII

Think, in this battered Caravanserai   65
Whose portals are altérnate Night and Day,
  How Sultán after Sultán with his pomp
Abode his destined hour, and went his way.

XVIII

They say the lion and the lizard keep
The Courts where Jamshyd gloried and
    drank deep: 70
And Bahrám,[14] that great Hunter—the wild
    ass
Stamps o'er his head, but cannot break his
    sleep.

XIX

I sometimes think that never blows so red
The rose as where some buried Caesar bled;
  That every hyacinth the garden wears   75
Dropped in her lap from some once lovely
    head.

XX

And this reviving herb whose tender green
Fledges[15] the river-lip on which we lean—
  Ah, lean upon it lightly! for who knows
From what once lovely lip it springs unseen!

XXI

Ah, my Belovéd, fill the cup that clears   81
To-DAY of past regrets and future fears:
  To-morrow! —Why, to-morrow I may be
Myself with yesterday's Sev'n Thousand
    Years.[16]

XXII

For some we loved, the loveliest and the best
That from his vintage rolling Time hath
    pressed,   86
  Have drunk their Cup a round or two
    before,
And one by one crept silently to rest.

————
[14]A Sassanid ruler of Persia, who sank in a swamp
while hunting.
[15]Adorns as with feathers.
[16]A thousand years to each planet (FitzGerald).

XXIII

And we that now make merry in the room
They left, and Summer dresses in new
    bloom,   90
  Ourselves, must we beneath the couch of
    earth
Descend—ourselves to make a couch—for
    whom?

XXIV

Ah, make the most of what we yet may
    spend,
Before we too into the dust descend.
  Dust into dust, and under dust to lie, 95
Sans[17] wine, sans song, sans singer, and—
    sans end!

XXV

Alike for those who for TO-DAY prepare,
And those that after some TO-MORROW stare,
  A Muezzín[18] from the Tower of Darkness
    cries,
"Fools! your reward is neither here nor
    there."   100

XXVI

Why, all the Saints and Sages who discussed
Of the Two Worlds so wisely—they are
    thrust
  Like foolish prophets forth: their words
    to scorn
Are scattered, and their mouths are stopped
    with dust.

XXVII

Myself when young did eagerly frequent 105
Doctor and saint, and heard great argument
  About it and about: but evermore
Came out by the same door where in I went.

XXVIII

With them the seed of Wisdom did I sow,
And with mine own hand wrought to make it
    grow;   110
  And this was all the harvest that I reaped:
"I came like water, and like wind I go."

XXIX

Into this Universe, and *Why* not knowing
Nor *Whence,* like water willy-nilly flowing;
  And out of it, as wind along the waste, 115
I know not *Whither,* willy-nilly blowing.

————
[17]Without.
[18]One who calls Mahometans to prayer.

XXX

What, without asking, hither hurried *Whence?*
And, without asking, *Whither* hurried hence?
Oh, many a cup of this forbidden wine
Must drown the memory of that insolence!

XXXI

Up from Earth's center through the Seventh Gate 121
I rose, and on the throne of Saturn[19] sate,
And many a knot unraveled by the road,
But not the Master-knot of Human Fate.

XXXII

There was the door to which I found no key;
There was the veil through which I might not see: 126
Some little talk awhile of ME and THEE[20]
There was—and then no more of THEE and ME.

XXXIII

Earth could not answer; nor the seas that mourn
In flowing purple, of their Lord forlorn; 130
Nor rolling Heaven, with all his Signs revealed
And hidden by the sleeve of Night and Morn.

XXXIV

Then of the THEE IN ME who works behind
The Veil, I lifted up my hands to find
A lamp amid the Darkness; and I heard,
As from Without: "THE ME WITHIN THEE BLIND!" 136

XXXV

Then to the lip of this poor earthen urn
I leaned, the Secret of my Life to learn:
And lip to lip it murmured: "While you live,
Drink!—for, once dead, you never shall return." 140

XXXVI

I think the vessel, that with fugitive
Articulation answered, once did live,
And drink; and ah! the passive lip I kissed,
How many kisses might it take—and give!

XXXVII

For I remember stopping by the way 145
To watch a Potter thumping his wet Clay:
And with its all-obliterated tongue
It murmured: "Gently, Brother, gently, pray!"[21]

XXXVIII

And has not such a story from of old
Down Man's successive generations rolled
Of such a clod of saturated earth 151
Cast by the Maker into human mold?

XXXIX

And not a drop that from our cups we throw
For Earth to drink of,[22] but may steal below
To quench the fire of anguish in some eye
There hidden—far beneath, and long ago. 156

XL

As then the Tulip, for her morning sup
Of heav'nly vintage, from the soil looks up,
Do you devoutly do the like, till Heav'n
To Earth invert you—like an empty Cup. 160

XLI

Perplexed no more with Human or Divine,
To-morrow's tangle to the winds resign,
And lose your fingers in the tresses of
The cypress-slender minister of wine. 164

XLII

And if the wine you drink, the lip you press,
End in what All begins and ends in—Yes:
Think then you are *To-day* what *Yesterday*
You were—*To-morrow* you shall not be less.

XLIII

So when that Angel of the Darker Drink
At last shall find you by the river-brink, 170
And, offering his cup, invite your soul
Forth to your lips to quaff—you shall not shrink.

XLIV

Why, if the Soul can fling the dust aside,
And naked on the air of Heaven ride,
Were't not a shame—were't not a shame for him 175
In this clay carcase crippled to abide?

[19]Lord of the seventh heaven (FitzGerald).

[20]Some dividual existence or personality distinct from the Whole (FitzGerald).

[21]The clay from which the bowl is made was once man (FitzGerald).

[22]The custom of throwing a little wine on the ground before drinking still continues in Persia, and perhaps generally in the East (FitzGerald).

XLV

'Tis but a tent where takes his one day's rest
A sultán to the realm of Death addressed:
   The Sultán rises, and the dark Ferrásh[23]
Strikes and prepares it for another Guest.   180

XLVI

And fear not lest Existence closing your
Account, and mine, should know the like no
   more:
   The Eternal Sákí[24] from that bowl has
   poured
Millions of bubbles like us, and will pour.

XLVII

When You and I behind the Veil are past,   185
Oh, but the long, long while the World shall
   last,
   Which of our coming and departure heeds
As the Sea's self should heed a pebble-cast.

XLVIII

A moment's halt—a momentary taste   189
Of BEING from the Well amid the Waste—
   And lo! the phantom Caravan has reached
The NOTHING it set out from . . . Oh,
   make haste!

XLIX

Would you that spangle of Existence spend
About THE SECRET—quick about it, Friend!
   A hair perhaps divides the False and
   True—
And upon what, prithee, may life depend?

L

A hair perhaps divides the False and True:
Yes; and a single Alif[25] were the clue—
   Could you but find it—to the Treasure-
   house,
And peradventure to THE MASTER too;   200

LI

Whose secret Presence, through Creation's
   veins
Running, quicksilver-like eludes your pains;
   Taking all shapes from Máh to Máhi;[26]
   and
They change and perish all—but He remains;

LII

A moment guessed—then back behind the
   fold   205

[23]Servant.   [24]Wine-bearer.
[25]Letter A, represented by a single stroke.
[26]From Fish to Moon (FitzGerald).

Immersed of darkness round the Drama
   rolled
   Which, for the pastime of Eternity,
He doth Himself contrive, enact, behold.

LIII

But if in vain, down on the stubborn floor
Of Earth, and up to Heav'n's unopening
   door,
   You gaze *To-day*, while You are You—
   how then   211
To-morrow, when You shall be You no
   more?

LIV

Waste not your hour; nor, in the vain pursuit
Of This and That endeavor and dispute:
   Better be jocund with the fruitful grape   215
Than sadden after none, or bitter, fruit.

LV

You know, my Friends, with what a brave
   carouse
I made a second marriage in my house;
   Divorced old barren Reason from my bed,
And took the Daughter of the Vine to spouse.

LVI

For "Is" and "Is-NOT" though with rule and
   line,   221
And "UP-AND-DOWN" by Logic, I define,
   Of all that one should care to fathom, I
Was never deep in anything but—Wine.

LVII

Ah, but my Computations, people say,   225
Reduced the Year to better reckoning?—
   Nay,
   'Twas only striking from the Calendar
Unborn To-morrow, and dead Yesterday.

LVIII

And lately, by the Tavern Door agape,
Came shining through the dusk an Angel
   Shape   230
   Bearing a vessel on his shoulder; and
He bid me taste of it; and 'twas—the Grape!

LIX

The Grape that can with Logic absolute
The two-and-seventy jarring sects[27] confute,
   The sovereign Alchemist that in a trice   235
Life's leaden metal into gold transmute;

[27]The 72 religions supposed to divide the world
(FitzGerald).

LX

The mighty Mahmúd, Allah-breathing Lord,
That all the misbelieving and black horde[28]
Of Fears and Sorrows that infest the Soul
Scatters before him with his whirlwind
    sword.   240

LXI

Why, be this Juice the growth of God, who
    dare
Blaspheme the twisted tendril as a snare?
    A blessing, we should use it, should we
    not?
And if a curse—why, then, Who set it there?

LXII

I must abjure the balm of life, I must,   245
Scared by some After-reckoning ta'en on
    trust,
    Or lured with hope of some diviner drink
To fill the Cup—when crumbled into dust!

LXIII

Oh, threats of Hell and hopes of Paradise!
One thing at least is certain,—*This* Life flies;
    One thing is certain and the rest is lies; 251
The flower that once has blown for ever dies.

LXIV

Strange, is it not? that of the myriads who
Before us passed the door of Darkness
    through,
    Not one returns to tell us of the Road,   255
Which to discover we must travel too.

LXV

The revelations of Devout and Learn'd
Who rose before us, and as prophets burned,
    Are all but stories which, awoke from
    sleep,
They told their comrades, and to sleep re-
    turned.   260

LXVI

I sent my Soul through the Invisible,
Some letter of that After-life to spell:
    And by and by my Soul returned to me,
And answered, "I myself am Heav'n and
    Hell"—

LXVII

Heav'n but the vision of fulfilled desire,   265
And Hell the shadow from a soul on fire,

[28]Alluding to Sultan Mahmúd's conquest of India
and its dark people (FitzGerald).

    Cast on the Darkness into which Our-
    selves,
So late emerged from, shall so soon expire.

LXVIII

We are no other than a moving row
Of magic shadow-shapes that come and go
    Round with the Sun-illumined Lantern
    held   271
In midnight by the Master of the Show;

LXIX

But helpless Pieces of the game He plays
Upon this checker-board of nights and days;
    Hither and thither moves, and checks, and
    slays,   275
And one by one back in the closet lays.

LXX

The ball no question makes of Ayes and
    Noes,
But here or there, as strikes the player, goes;
    And He that tossed you down into the
    field,
He knows about it all—HE knows—HE
    . knows!   280

LXXI

The Moving Finger writes; and, having writ,
Moves on: nor all your piety nor wit
    Shall lure it back to cancel half a line;
Nor all your tears wash out a word of it.

LXXII

And that inverted bowl they call the Sky, 285
Whereunder crawling cooped we live and die,
    Lift not your hands to *It* for help—for It
As impotently moves as you or I.

LXXIII

With Earth's first clay they did the last man
    knead,   289
And there of the last harvest sowed the seed;
    And the first morning of Creation wrote
What the last dawn of reckoning shall read.

LXXIV

YESTERDAY *This* Day's Madness did prepare,
TO-MORROW's silence, triumph, or despair:
    Drink! for you know not whence you came,
    nor why;   295
Drink! for you know not why you go, nor
    where.

LXXV

I tell you this :—When, started from the goal,
Over the flaming shoulders of the Foal
  Of Heav'n, Parwín and Mushtarí[29] they
    flung,
In my predestined plot of Dust and Soul	300

LXXVI

The Vine had struck a fiber ; which about
If clings my Being—let the Dervish flout :
  Of my base metal may be filed a key
That shall unlock the Door he howls without.

LXXVII

And this I know: whether the one True
    Light	305
Kindle to Love, or wrath-consume me quite,
  One flash of It within the Tavern caught
Better than in the Temple lost outright.

LXXVIII

What ! out of senseless Nothing to provoke
A conscious Something to resent the yoke	310
  Of unpermitted pleasure, under pain
Of everlasting penalties, if broke !

LXXIX

What ! from his helpless creature be repaid
Pure gold for what he lent him dross-
    allayed—
  Sue for a debt he never did contract,	315
And cannot answer—Oh, the sorry trade !

LXXX

Oh Thou, who didst with pitfall and with
    gin[30]
Beset the road I was to wander in,
  Thou wilt not with predestined evil round
Enmesh, and then impute my fall to sin !	320

LXXXI

Oh Thou, who Man of baser Earth didst
    make,
And ev'n with Paradise devise the Snake :
  For all the sin wherewith the face of Man
Is blackened—Man's forgiveness give—and
    take !

*   *   *

---

[29]The Pleiads and Jupiter (FitzGerald).
[30]Snare.

LXXXII

As under cover of departing day	325
Slunk hunger-stricken Ramazán[31] away,
  Once more within the Potter's house alone
I stood, surrounded by the shapes of clay :

LXXXIII

Shapes of all sorts and sizes, great and small,
That stood along the floor and by the wall ;	330
  And some loquacious vessels were ; and
    some
Listened perhaps, but never talked at all.

LXXXIV

Said one among them : "Surely not in vain
My substance of the common earth was ta'en
  And to this figure molded, to be broke,	335
Or trampled back to shapeless earth again."

LXXXV

Then said a second : "Ne'er a peevish boy
Would break the bowl from which he drank
    in joy ;
  And He that with his hand the vessel made
Will surely not in after wrath destroy."	340

LXXXVI

After a momentary silence spake
Some vessel of a more ungainly make :
  "They sneer at me for leaning all awry—
What ! did the hand, then, of the Potter
    shake ?"

LXXXVII

Whereat some one of the loquacious lot—	345
I think a Súfi[32] pipkin—waxing hot :
  "All this of Pot and Potter—Tell me, then,
Who is the Potter, pray, and who the Pot ?"

LXXXVIII

"Why," said another, "some there are who
    tell
Of one who threatens he will toss to Hell	350
  The luckless Pots he marred in making—
    Pish !
He's a Good Fellow, and 'twill all be well."

LXXXIX

"Well," murmured one, "let whoso make or
    buy,
My clay with long oblivion is gone dry :
  But fill me with the old familiar Juice,	355
Methinks I might recover by and by."

---

[31]The month for fasting.	[32]A pantheist.

XC

So while the vessels one by one were speak-
 ing,
The little Moon[33] looked in that all were
 seeking;
  And then they jogged each other:
 "Brother! Brother!
Now for the Porter's shoulder-knot[34] a-
 creaking!" 360

*   *   *

XCI

Ah, with the Grape my fading life provide;
And wash the body whence the life has died,
  And lay me, shrouded in the living Leaf,
By some not unfrequented garden-side—

XCII

That ev'n my buried ashes such a snare 365
Of vintage shall fling up into the air
  As not a True-believer passing by
But shall be overtaken unaware.

XCIII

Indeed, the Idols I have loved so long
Have done my credit in this World much
 wrong: 370
  Have drowned my glory in a shallow cup,
And sold my reputation for a song.

XCIV

Indeed, indeed, repentance oft before
I swore—but was I sober when I swore?
  And then, and then came Spring, and rose-
 in-hand 375
My threadbare penitence apieces tore.

XCV

And much as Wine has played the Infidel,
And robbed me of my robe of Honor—Well,
  I wonder often what the vintners buy
One half so precious as the stuff they sell. 380

[33]Signalizing the end of Ramazán.
[34]Used for carrying jars of wine.

XCVI

Yet ah, that Spring should vanish with the
 rose!
That Youth's sweet-scented manuscript
 should close!
  The nightingale that in the branches sang,
Ah whence, and whither flown again, who
 knows!

XCVII

Would but the Desert of the Fountain yield
One glimpse—if dimly, yet indeed, re-
 vealed— 386
  To which the fainting Traveler might
 spring,
As springs the trampled herbage of the field!

XCVIII

Would but some wingéd angel, ere too late,
Arrest the yet unfolded Roll of Fate, 390
  And make the stern Recorder otherwise
Enregister, or quite obliterate!

XCIX

Ah Love! could you and I with Him conspire
To grasp this sorry Scheme of Things entire,
  Would not we shatter it to bits—and then
Remold it nearer to the Heart's desire! 396

*   *   *

C

Yon rising Moon that looks for us again—
How oft hereafter will she wax and wane;
  How oft hereafter rising look for us
Through this same garden—and for *one* in
 vain! 400

CI

And when like her, oh Sákí, you shall pass
Among the guests star-scattered on the grass,
  And in your joyous errand reach the spot
Where I made one—turn down an empty
 glass!

TAMAM[35]

[35]The end.

LETTERS

I. To Bernard Barton[1]

London, April, 1838

Dear sir,

  John[2] who is going down into Suffolk, 5
will, I hope, take this letter and despatch it
to you properly. I write more on account of
this opportunity than of anything I have to
say: for I am very heavy indeed with a kind
of influenza, which has blocked up most of my
senses, and put a wet blanket over my brains.
This state of head has not been improved
by trying to get through a new book much
in fashion—Carlyle's *French Revolution*[3]

[1]A Quaker poet whose daughter FitzGerald later
married.
[2]FitzGerald's brother.
[3]First published the year before.

—written in a German style. An English-man writes of French Revolutions in a German style. People say the book is very deep; but it appears to me that the meaning *seems* deep from lying under mystical language. There is no repose, nor equable movement in it: all cut up into short sentences half reflective, half narrative, so that one labors through it as vessels do through what is called a short sea—small, contrary-going waves caused by shallows, and straits, and meeting tides, *etc.* I like to sail before the wind over the surface of an even-rolling eloquence, like that of Bacon or the *Opium-Eater.*[4] There is also pleasant fresh-water sailing with such writers as Addison. Is there any *pond*-sailing in literature? that is, drowsy, slow, and of small compass? Perhaps we may say, some sermons. But this is only conjecture. Certainly Jeremy Taylor[5] rolls along as majestically as any of them. We have had Alfred Tennyson here, very droll, and very wayward; and much sitting up of nights till two and three in the morning with pipes in our mouths, at which good hour we would get Alfred to give us some of his magic music, which he does between growling and smoking; and so to bed. All this has not cured my influenza as you may imagine; but these hours shall be remembered long after the influenza is forgotten.

I have bought scarce any new books or prints; and am not sorry to see that I want so little more. One large purchase I have made, however, the *Biographie Universelle,* 53 octavo volumes. It contains everything, and is the very best thing of its kind, and so referred to by all historians, *etc.* Surely nothing is more pleasant than, when some name crosses one, to go and get acquainted with the owner of the name; and this *Biographie* really has found places for people whom one would have thought almost too small for so comprehensive a work—which sounds like a solecism, or bull, does it not?

Now I must finish my letter; and a very

stupid one it is. Here is a sentence of Warburton's[6] that, I think, is very wittily expressed; though why I put it in here is not very discoverable. "The Church, like the Ark of Noah, is worth saving: not for the sake of the unclean beasts that almost filled it, and probably made most noise and clamor in it, but for the little corner of rationality that was as much distressed by the stink within as by the tempest without." Is it not good? It is out of his letters, and the best thing in them. It is also the best thing in mine.

With kind remembrances to Miss Barton, believe me, yours very affectionately,

E. FitzGerald

II. To John Allen[7]

Beccles, 28 April, 1839

My dear Allen,

Some one from this house is going to London; and I will try and write you some lines now in half an hour before dinner; I am going out for the evening to my old lady who teaches me the names of the stars, and other chaste information. You see, Master John Allen, that if I do not come to London (and I have no thought of going yet) and you will not write, there is likely to be an end of our communication: not, by the way, that I am never to go to London again, but not just yet. Here I live with tolerable content, perhaps with as much as most people arrive at, and what, if one were properly grateful, one would perhaps call perfect happiness. Here is a glorious sunshiny day: all the morning I read about Nero in Tacitus, lying at full length on a bench in the garden, a nightingale singing, and some red anemones eyeing the sun manfully not far off. A funny mixture all this: Nero, and the delicacy of Spring; all very human, however. Then at half past one lunch on Cambridge cream cheese; then a ride over hill and dale; then spudding up some weeds from the grass; and

---

[4] De Quincey's *Confessions of an Opium-Eater* had made its first appearance in 1821.

[5] Author of *Holy Living* (1650) and *Holy Dying* (1651).

[6] William Warburton (1698–1779), scholar and ecclesiastic. FitzGerald quotes from Letter XLVI in *Letters from an Eminent Prelate to one of his Friends.*

[7] A friend with whom FitzGerald had become acquainted when an undergraduate at Cambridge, ten years earlier.

then coming in, I sit down to write to you, my sister winding red worsted from the back of a chair, and the most delightful little girl in the world chattering incessantly. So runs the world away. You think I live in Epicurean ease; but this happens to be a jolly day; one isn't always well, or tolerably good, the weather is not always clear, nor nightingales singing, nor Tacitus full of pleasant atrocity. But such as life is, I believe I have got hold of a good end of it. . . .[8]

Give my love to Thackeray from your upper window across the street. So he has lost a little child: and moreover has been sorry to do so. Well, good-bye, my dear John Allen: "Auld Lang Syne." My kind regards to your lady.

> Down to the vale this water steers,
>   How merrily it goes:
> 'Twill murmur on a thousand years,
>   And flow as now it flows.[9]

E. F. G.

III. To Frederic Tennyson[10]

London, 16 January, 1841

Dear Frederic,

I have just concluded, with all the throes of imprudent pleasure, the purchase of a large picture by Constable,[11] of which, if I can continue in the mood, I will enclose you a sketch. It is very good; but how you and Morton would abuse it! Yet this, being a sketch, escapes some of Constable's faults, and might escape some of your censures. The trees are not splashed with that white sky-mud, which (according to Constable's theory) the earth scatters up with her wheels in traveling so briskly round the sun; and there is a dash and felicity in the execution that gives one a thrill of good digestion in one's room, and the thought of which makes one inclined to jump over the children's heads in the streets. But if you could see my great enormous Venetian picture you would be extonished. Does the thought ever strike you, when looking at pictures in a house, that you are to run and jump at one, and go right through it into some behind-scene world on the other side, as harlequins do? A steady portrait especially invites one to do so; the quietude of it ironically tempts one to outrage it; one feels it would close again over the panel, like water, as if nothing had happened. That portrait of Spedding,[12] for instance, which Laurence has given me: not swords, nor cannon, nor all the Bulls of Bashan butting it, could, I feel sure, discompose that venerable forehead. No wonder that no hair can grow at such an altitude; no wonder his view of Bacon's virtue is so rarefied that the common consciences of men cannot endure it. Thackeray and I occasionally amuse ourselves with the idea of Spedding's forehead; we find it somehow or other in all things, just peering out of all things; you see it in a milestone, Thackeray says. He also draws the forehead rising with a sober light over Mont Blanc, and reflected in the lake of Geneva. We have great laughing over this. The forehead is at present in Pembrokeshire, I believe, or Glamorganshire, or Mommothshire: it is hard to say which. It has gone to spend its Christmas there.

This,[13] you see, is a sketch of my illustrious new purchase. The two animals in the water are cows; that on the bank a dog; and that in the glade of the wood a man or woman as you may choose. I can't say my drawing gives you much idea of my picture, except as to the composition of it; and even that depends on the color and disposition of light and shade. The effect of the light breaking under the trees is very beautiful in the original; but this can only be given in water-colors on thick paper, where one can scratch out the lights. One would fancy that Constable had been looking at that fine picture of Gainsborough's in the

---

[8] Dots here and at other places indicate omissions by FitzGerald's editor, William Aldis Wright.

[9] Wordsworth's *Fountain*, ll. 21–24.

[10] An elder brother of Alfred Tennyson and himself a poet of distinction.

[11] John Constable (1776–1837), an English landscape painter whose theories about light had a decisive influence on French art.

[12] James Spedding (1808–1881), a scholar chiefly known for his monumental edition of Francis Bacon's *Works* and *Life and Letters*. The giver of Spedding's portrait was the painter, Samuel Laurence.

[13] A water-color sketch of Constable's picture, included in the letter at this point.

National[14]: "The Watering Place"; which is superior, in my mind, to all the Claudes there. But this is perhaps because I am an Englishman and not an Italian.

IV. To Bernard Barton

London, 21 February, 1842

I HAVE just got home a new coat for my Constable, which coat cost 33 shillings: just the same price as I gave for a Chesterfield wrapper (as it is called) for myself some weeks ago. People told me I was not improved by my Chesterfield wrapper; and I am vext to see how little my Constable is improved by his coat of cloth of gold. But I have been told what is the use of a frame lately; only as it requires nice explanation I shall leave it till I see you. Don't you wish me to buy that little evening piece I told you of? worth a dozen of your Paul Veroneses[15] put together.

When I rate you (as you call it) about showing my verses, letters, *etc.*, you know in what spirit I rate you: thanking you all the time for your generous intention of praising me. It would be very hard, and not desirable, to make you understand why my mama need not have heard the verses; but it is a very little matter; so no more of it. As to my doing anything else in that way, I know that I could write volume after volume as well as others of the mob of gentlemen who write with ease; but I think unless a man can do better, he had best not do at all; I have not the strong inward call, nor cruel-sweet pangs of parturition, that prove the birth of anything bigger than a mouse. With you the case is different, who have so long been a follower of the muse, and who have had a kindly, sober, English, wholesome, religious spirit within you that has communicated kindred warmth to many honest souls. Such a creature as Augusta—John's wife—a true lady, was very fond of your poems; and I think that is no mean praise, a good assurance that you have not written in vain.

I am a man of taste, of whom there are hundreds born every year; only that less easy circumstances than mine at present are compel them to one calling, that calling perhaps a mechanical one, which overlies all their other and naturally perhaps more energetic impulses. As to an occasional copy of verses, there are few men who have leisure to read, and are possessed of any music in their souls, who are not capable of versifying on some ten or twelve occasions during their natural lives, at a proper conjunction of the stars. There is no harm in taking advantage of such occasions.

This letter-writing fit (one must suppose) can but happen once in one's life, though I hope you and I shall live to have many a little bargain for pictures. But I hold communion with Suffolk through you. In this big London all full of intellect and pleasure and business I feel pleasure in dipping down into the country, and rubbing my hand over the cool dew upon the pastures, as it were. I know very few people here, and care for fewer; I believe I should like to live in a small house just outside a pleasant English town all the days of my life, making myself useful in a humble way, reading my books, and playing a rubber of whist at night. But England cannot expect long such a reign of inward quiet as to suffer men to dwell so easily to themselves. But time will tell us:

Come what come may,
Time and the Hour runs through the roughest day.[16]

It is hard to give you so long a letter, so dull an one, and written in so cramped a hand, to read in this hardworking part of your week. But you can read a bit at odd times, you know; or none at all. Anyhow 'tis time to have done. I am going to walk with Lusia.[17] So farewell.

P.S. I always direct to you as "Mr. Barton" because I know not if Quakers ought to endure squiredom. How I long to show you my Constable!

Pray let me know how Mr. Jenney is. I think that we shall get down to Suffolk the end of next week.

---

[14]The National Gallery in London. Thomas Gainsborough (1727–1788) was an English painter of portraits and landscapes; Claude Lorraine (1600–1682), a French landscape painter.

[15]Works by the Italian artist, Paolo Veronese (1528–1588).

[16]*Macbeth*, I, iii, 146–147.

[17]FitzGerald's sister, Andalusia.

V. To Frederic Tennyson

Woodbridge, 8 December, 1844

My dear Frederic,

What is a poor devil to do? You tell me [5] quite truly that my letters have not two ideas in them, and yet you tell me to write my two ideas as soon as I can. So indeed it is so far easy to write down one's two ideas, if they are not very abstruse ones; but then [10] what the devil encouragement is it to a poor fellow to expose his nakedness so? All I can say is to say again that, if you lived in this place, you would not write so long a letter as you have done, full of capital de- [15] scription and all good things; though without any compliment I am sure you would write a better than I shall. But you see the original fault in me is that I choose to be in such a place as this at all; that argues cer- [20] tainly a talent for dullness which no situation nor intercourse of men could much improve. It is true; I really do like to sit in this doleful place with a good fire, a cat and dog on the rug, and an old woman in the kitchen. [25] This is all my livestock. The house is yet damp as last year; and the great event of this winter is my putting up a trough round the eaves to carry off the wet. There was discussion whether the trough should be of iron [30] or zinc: iron dear and lasting; zinc the reverse. It was decided for iron; and accordingly iron is put up.

Why should I not live in London and see the world? you say. Why then *I* say as be- [35] fore, I don't like it. I think the dullness of country people is better than the impudence of Londoners; and the fresh cold and wet of our clay fields better than a fog that stinks *per se*;[18] and this room of mine, clean at all [40] events, better than a dirty room in Charlotte St. If you, Morton, and Alfred, were more in London, I should be there more; but now there is but Spedding and Allen whom I care a straw about. I have written two notes [45] to Alfred to ask him just to notify his existence to me; but you know he is obstinate on that point. I heard from Carlyle that he (Alfred) had passed an evening at Chelsea[19]

much to C's delight, who has opened the gates of his Valhalla to let Alfred in. Thackeray is at Malta, where I am told he means to winter. . . .

As I have no people to tell you of, so have I very few books, and know nothing of what is stirring in the literary world. I have read the life of Arnold of Rugby,[20] who was a noble fellow; and the letters of Burke, which do not add to, or detract from, what I knew and liked in him before. I am meditating to begin Thucydides one day, perhaps this winter. . . .

Old Seneca, I have no doubt, was a great humbug in deed, and his books have plenty of it in word; but he had got together a vast deal of what was not humbug from others; and, as far as I see, the old philosophers are available now as much as two thousand years back. Perhaps you will think that is not saying much. Don't suppose I think it good philosophy in myself to keep here out of the world, and sport a gentle Epicurism; I do not; I only follow something of a natural inclination, and know not if I could do better under a more complex system. It is very smooth sailing hitherto down here. No velvet waistcoat and ever-lustrous pumps to be considered; no *bon mots* got up; no information necessary. There is a pipe for the parsons to smoke, and quite as much *bon mots*, literature, and philosophy as they care for without any trouble at all. If we could but feed our poor! It is now the eighth of December; it has blown a most desperate east wind, all razors, a wind like one of those knives one sees at shops in London, with 365 blades all drawn and pointed; the wheat is all sown; the fallows cannot be plowed. What are all the poor folks to do during the winter? And they persist in having the same enormous families they used to do; a woman came to me two days ago who had seventeen children! What farmers are to employ all these? What landlord can find room for them? The Law of Generation must be repealed. The London press does nothing but rail at us poor country folks for our cruelty.

---

[18]Of itself.

[19]The part of London in which Carlyle lived.

[20]Thomas Arnold, father of Matthew Arnold and headmaster of Rugby. FitzGerald refers to Arthur Stanley's *Life of Dr. Arnold* and Edmund Burke's *Correspondence 1744–1797*, both published in 1844.

I am glad they do so; for there is much to be set right. But I want to know if the editor of the *Times* is more attentive to his devils,[21] their wives and families, than our squires and squiresses and parsons are to their fellow parishioners. *Punch* also assumes a tone of virtuous satire, from the mouth of Mr. Douglas Jerrold! It is easy to sit in arm chairs at a club in Pall Mall and rail on the stupidity and brutality of those in High Suffolk.

Come, I have got more than two ideas into this sheet; but I don't know if you won't dislike them worse than mere nothing. But I was determined to fill my letter. Yes, you are to know that I slept at Woodbridge last night, went to church there this morning, where every one sat with a purple nose, and heard a dismal well-meant sermon; and the organ blew us out with one grand idea at all events, one of old Handel's coronation anthems; that I dined early, also in Woodbridge; and walked up here with a tremendous east wind blowing sleet in my face from over the German Sea,[22] that I found your letter when I entered my room; and reading it through, determined to spin you off a sheet incontinently, and lo! here it is! Now or never! I shall now have my tea in, and read over your letter again while at it. You are quite right in saying that Gravesend[23] excursions with you do me good. When did I doubt it? I remember them with great pleasure; few of my travels so much so. I like a short journey in good company; and I like you all the better for your Englishman's humors. One doesn't find such things in London; something more like it here in the country, where every one, with whatever natural stock of intellect endowed, at least grows up his own way, and flings his branches about him, not stretched on the espalier of London dinner-table company.

P. S. Next morning. Snow over the ground. We have our wonders of inundation in Suffolk also, I can tell you. For three weeks ago such floods came that an old woman was carried off as she was retiring from a beer house about 9 p.m., and drowned. She was probably half seas over before she left the beer house.

And three nights ago I looked out at about ten o'clock at night, before going to bed. It seemed perfectly still; frosty, and the stars shining bright. I heard a continuous moaning sound, which I knew to be, not that of an infant exposed, or female ravished, but of the sea, more than ten miles off! What little wind there was carried to us the murmurs of the waves circulating round these coasts so far over a flat country. But people here think that this sound so heard is not from the waves that break, but a kind of prophetic voice from the body of the sea itself, announcing great gales. Sure enough we have got them, however heralded. Now I say that all this shows that we in this Suffolk are not so completely given over to prose and turnips as some would have us. I always said that being near the sea, and being able to catch a glimpse of it from the tops of hills, and of houses, redeemed Suffolk from dullness; and at all events that our turnip fields, dull in themselves, were at least set all round with an undeniably poetic element. And so I see Arnold says; he enumerates five inland counties as the only parts of England for which nothing could be said in praise. Not that I agree with him there neither; I cannot allow the valley of the Ouse, about which some of my pleasantest recollections hang, to be without its great charm. W. Browne, whom you despised, is married, and I shall see but little of him for the future. I have laid by my rod and line by the willows of the Ouse for ever. "He is married and cannot come." This change is the true meaning of those verses,

> Friend after friend departs;
> Who has not lost a friend?[24]

and so on. If I were conscious of being stedfast and good-humored enough, I would marry to-morrow. But a humorist is best by himself.

---

[21] The errand boys in his printing office.
[22] The North Sea.
[23] A port on the Thames a few miles east of London.

[24] From a poem called *Friends* by James Montgomery (1771–1854).

VI. To E. B. Cowell[25]

Beccles, 27 April, 1859

My dear Cowell,

Above is the address you had better direct to in future. I have had a great loss. W. Browne was fallen upon and half crushed by his horse near three months ago; and though the doctors kept giving hopes while he lay patiently for two months in a condition no one else could have borne for a fortnight, at last they could do no more, nor Nature neither; and he sunk. I went to see him before he died—the comely spirited boy I had known first seven and twenty years ago lying all shattered, and death in his face and voice. . . .

Well, this is so; and there is no more to be said about it. It is one of the things that reconcile me to my own stupid decline of life—to the crazy state of the world—Well—no more about it.

I sent you poor Omar,[26] who has his kind of consolation for all these things. I doubt you will regret you ever introduced him to me. And yet you would have me print the original, with many worse things than I have translated. The bird epic[27] might be finished at once; but *cul bono?*[28] No one cares for such things; and there are doubtless so many better things to care about. I hardly know why I print any of these things, which nobody buys; and I scarce now see the few I give them to. But when one has done one's best, and is sure that that best is better than so many will take pains to do, though far from the best that *might be done,* one likes to make an end of the matter by print. I suppose very few people have ever taken such pains in translation as I have, though certainly not to be literal. But at all cost, a thing must *live:* with a transfusion of one's own worse life if one can't retain the original's better. Better a live sparrow than a stuffed eagle. I shall be very well pleased to see the new MS. of Omar. I shall *one day* (if I live) print the *Birds,* and a strange experiment on old Calderon's two great plays;[29] and then shut up shop in the poetic line. Adieu. Give my love to the lady; and believe me yours very truly

E. F. G.

You see where those Persepolitan verses come from. I wonder you were not startled with the meter, though maimed a bit.

VII. To George Crabbe[30]

Woodbridge, 31 January, 1862

Dear George,

Thank you always for your invitations to Merton: why don't I go there? as well as to London, *etc.* Ah, why! You know, I hope, that you will always be welcome to my seedy home. Board here, bed at the Bull. But I am (as for the last ten years) looking out for a house, and indeed have gone so far as to have (though without my asking for it) a plan of alterations drawn up for a wretched little house (where Mr. Reynolds, once parson here, used to live), at the end of Seckford Street. But, little as I want, I doubt this would be almost too little, with scarce a scrap of garden ground. I had even thoughts of that house where Mr. Causton once lived at foot of the Bredfield Sandhill—do you remember? which has a bit of garden, and might be altered to my use. But the house lies low in a corner where one can't get out except one way—up the hill—and into the town by those *Ship-meadows,* whereas Seckford Street is high and dry, and leads out to Farlingay, Ipswich Road, *etc.* But all the better houses are occupied by dowagers like myself: the Miss Tolls, Mrs. Pulham, the Miss Silvers, and Billy Whincupp; and none of them will die, or otherwise migrate, for love or money; so here I go floun-

---

[25] A student of Oriental languages who later became Professor of Sanskrit at Cambridge.

[26] I. e., a copy of *The Rubáiyát,* which had just been published for the first time.

[27] The abridged translation, called *The Bird Parliament,* of Attar's *Mantik-ut-Tair.* The translation remained in manuscript until after FitzGerald's death.

[28] To what good?

[29] Probably *The Mighty Magician* and *Such Stuff as Dreams Are Made of,* which FitzGerald published in 1865 (in addition to the six plays of the Spanish dramatist which he had already translated).

[30] Rector of Merton, grandson of the George Crabbe who wrote *The Village* and *Tales of the Hall.*

dering on and teasing everybody without any progress at all. I wish you were here, or could give me any advice from where you are; for I am so certain to blunder in all I do that I quite lose heart to decide. I do really want, however, to get into a house of my own with my own servants (where and with whom, of course, I shan't do half as well as here), and this for several reasons. Do not forget me in case you hear of any likely housekeeper or servant, though I can't yet engage the former because I have no house for her to keep. But a good maid-servant I would almost undertake here, pay-ing her instead of Mrs. Berry's doing so, who hires at 1s. a week such a slut as even I cannot put up with. We are now, I hope, getting rid of the third since I have been here, and I yesterday went to see another at Hasketon. Also, if when you are at Nor-wich you should see any pretty and quaint furniture, I should be glad to hear of it, and would even go to Norwich if you knew of a place where such things were in plenty. When I took my niece to London in Novem-ber, I went to the Baker Street Bazaar; but spent what time and money I had in the new Chinese Department, where I bought a heap of things which, however, have chiefly gone in presents. I, however, like Oriental things: their quaint shapes, fine colors, and musky sandal-wood scents; and, though I do not so much look at these things individually, yet their presence in the room creates a cheerful-ness which is good as one grows old, blind, deaf, and dull. A little time in London would soon set one up in such things; but I don't care to go there, and perhaps it is as well to have to pick up such things now and then only.

I have not yet hung up my pictures, which are now got back to the room they were outed from; but the truth is they look so much better on the floor. I have cleaned and put a thick coat of varnish on the secre-tary; this fills up some cracks, though it makes him a little too glossy. Laurence was delighted with my hideous larger Span-ish woman, which is certainly Velasquez,[31] he says; I have turpentined her, which (as I have learned from Mr. Churchyard) will

freshen up old varnish, and so do better than overlaying a new coat of *that*. But what do you think of my impudence in actually rubbing down my Titian landscape! which Mr. C. was frightened to think of my doing, but says it is certainly improved, now it's done. I will not have green skies at any price. . . .

I should like some of the old light cane chairs such as one used to see in old inns, watering places, *etc.* Do keep me and my wants of this kind in your eye, as you have an eye for such things, and may not be un-amused at thus keeping it open.

Here is a stupendous letter, all about my-self. You seem too engaged, or too little inclined, to write much; and indeed I can't expect other people to repay me with such coin as my own idleness can spare so easily. I am reading a book of almost as dull letters as my own: the second series of Mrs. De-lany,[32] five thick volumes of five hundred pages apiece of almost the poorest twaddle, and often very vulgar twaddle, from the very greatest people to one another.

VIII. To E. B. Cowell

Woodbridge, 5 August, 1863

My dear Cowell,

I don't hear from you; I rather think you are deterred by those *Birds* which I asked you to print (in my last letter) with some correction, *etc.,* of your own, and which you have not found time or inclination to get done. But don't let anything of this sort prevent your writing to me now and then; no one can be more utterly indifferent than I am whether those *Birds* are printed or not; and I suppose I distinctly told you *not* to put yourself to any trouble. Indeed I dare say I should only be bored with the copies when they were printed; for I don't know a soul here who would care for the thing if it were ten times as well done as I have done it, nor do I care for translation or original, myself. Oh dear, when I do look into Homer, Dante, and Virgil, Aeschylus,

---

[31]Spanish portrait painter (1599–1660).

[32]Mrs. Mary Delany (1700–1788), whose *Auto-biography and Correspondence* was published 1861-1862.

Shakespeare, *etc.,* those Orientals look—silly! Don't resent my saying so. *Don't they?* I am now a good deal[33] about in a new boat I have built, and thought (as Johnson took Cocker's *Arithmetic* with him on travel, because he shouldn't exhaust it[34]) so I would take Dante and Homer with me, instead of Mudie's books,[35] which I read through directly. I took Dante by way of slow digestion, not having looked at him for some years; but I am glad to find I relish him as much as ever; he atones[36] with the sea, as, you know, does the *Odyssey*—these are the men!

I am just returned in my ship from Holland—where I stayed—two days!—and was so glad to rush away home after being imprisoned in a sluggish un-sweet canal in Rotterdam; and after tearing about to Amsterdam, The Hague, *etc.,* to see things which were neither new nor remarkable to me though I had never seen them before—except in pictures, which represent to you the places as well as if you went there, without the trouble of going. I am sure wiser men, with keener *out*sight and *in*sight, would see what no pictures could give; but this, I know, is always the case with me; this is my last voyage abroad, I believe; unless I go to see Raffaelle's Madonna at Dresden, which no other picture can represent than itself, unless Dante's Beatrice.

I don't think you ever told me if you had got, or read, Spedding's two first volumes of Bacon.[37] My opinion is not the least altered of the case; and (as I anticipated) Spedding has brooded over his egg so long he has rather addled it. Thompson told me that the very papers he adduces to clear Bacon in Essex's business[38] rather go against him. I haven't seen any notice of the book in any review but *Fraser,* where Donne (of

course) was convinced, *etc.,* and I hear that even the wise old Spedding is *mortified* that he has awakened so little interest for his hero. You know his mortification would not be on *his own* score. His last letter to me (some months ago) seemed to indicate that he could scarce lift up his pen to go on —he had as yet, he said, written nothing of volumes three and four. But I suppose he *will* in time. I say this life of his wasted on a vain work is a tragedy pathetic as *Antigone* or *Iphigenia.*[39] Of Tennyson I hear but little; and I have ceased to look forward to any future work of his. Thackeray seems dumb as a gorged blackbird too: all growing old!

I have lost my sister Kerrich, the only one of my family I much cared for, or who much cared for me.

But (not to dwell on what cannot be helped, and to which my talking of all growing old led me) I see in last week's *Athenaeum* great praise of a new volume of poems by Jean Ingelow.[40] The reviewer talks of a "new poet," *etc.,* quite unaware that some dozen years ago the "new poet" published a volume (as you may remember) with as distinct indications of sweet, fresh, and original genius as anything he adduces from this second volume. I remember writing a sort of review, when about you at Bramford, which I sent to Mitford, to try and give the book a little move; but Mitford had just quitted the *Gentleman's Magazine,* and I tore up my paper. Your Elizabeth knows (I think) all about this lady; who, I suppose, is connected with Lincolnshire, for the reviewer speaks of some of the poems as relating to that coast—shipwrecks, *etc.* I was told that Tennyson was writing a sort of Lincolnshire idyll: I will bet on Miss Ingelow now; he should never have left his old county, and gone up to be suffocated by London adulation. He has lost that which caused the long roll of the Lincolnshire wave to reverberate in the measure of *Locksley Hall.* Don't believe that I rejoice like a dastard in what I believe to be the decay of a great man; my sorrow has been

---

[33]Word omitted, but probably intended, by Fitz-Gerald.

[34]See Boswell's *Journal of a Tour to the Hebrides* under 31 August, 1773.

[35]Books in the lending library founded by Charles Mudie in 1842.

[36]Harmonizes.

[37]Spedding's *Life and Letters of Bacon* began to appear in 1861.

[38]Bacon contributed evidence which led to the execution of the Earl of Essex in 1601.

[39]Tragedies by Sophocles and Euripides respectively.

[40]A popular poetess (1820–1897).

so much about it that (for one reason) I have the less cared to meet him of late years, having nothing to say in sincere praise. Nor do I mean that his decay is all owing to London, *etc.* He is growing old, and I don't believe much in the fine arts thriving on an old tree; I can't think Milton's *Paradise Lost* so good as his *Allegro, etc.*; one feels the strain of the pump all through; only Shakespeare—the exception to all rule—struck out Macbeth at past fifty.[41]

By the way, there is a new—and the best —edition of *Him* coming out, edited by two men (fellows[42]) of Cambridge. Just the text, with the various readings of folio and quartos, scarce any notes, but suggestions of alterations from Pope, Theobald, Coleridge, *etc.,* and—Spedding; who (as I told him twenty years ago) should have done the work these two men are doing. He also says they are well doing about *half* what is wanted to be done. He should—for he could—have done all; and one frontispiece portrait would have served for author and editor.

Come—here is a long letter—and (as I read it over) with more *go* than usually attends my old pen now. Let it inspire you to answer; never mind the *Birds;*—which really suggests to me one of Dante's beautiful lines which made me *cry* the other day at sea.

Mentre che gli occhi per la fronda verde
Ficcava io così, come far suole
Chi dietro all' uccellin la vita perde,
Lo più che Padre mi dicea, *etc.*[48]

IX. To George Crabbe

Woodbridge, 12 January, 1864

My dear George,

. . . Have we exchanged a word about Thackeray since his death? I am quite surprised to see how I sit moping about him; to be sure, I keep reading his books. Oh, the *Newcomes* are fine! And now I have got hold of *Pendennis,* and seem to like that much more than when I first read it. I keep hearing him say so much of it; and really think I shall hear his step up the stairs to this lodging as in old Charlotte Street thirty years ago. Really, a great figure has sunk under earth.

X. To W. F. Pollock[44]

1869

My dear Pollock,

I meant to have thanked you for your first long, and capital, letter, even had it not been followed by that of yesterday. You think to mystify a poor country man? Well, it is all capital fooling. Do, pray when you have an idle half-hour, send me any such letters. I cannot return them in kind, *you* know as *I* know: I have not the material, nor the wit to work it. That is quite true.

I have not seen Forster's *Landor,*[45] not caring much for either party. Foster seems to me a genuine cockney, be-heroing Goldsmith, Landor, *etc., à outrance.*[46] I remember so well his being red-hot in admiration of Coventry Patmore's[47] first poems: "By God, they came up to Tennyson's," *etc.* Talking of Tennyson, by the way, I had the curiosity to ask Carlyle (in my yearly letter) what he thought of Browning's *Book.*[48] I dare say you have heard him talk on the subject. He writes to me: "I have read—insisted on reading—Browning's *Book.* It is full of talent, energy, and effort, but actually without *backbone* or basis of common-sense. I think it among the absurdest books ever written by a gifted man."

Such is the opinion of all the men I know, whose opinion is certainly worth as much as the newspaper critics'. Then why don't some of you step out into the newspapers

---

[41]Shakespeare cannot have been much more than forty when he wrote *Macbeth.*

[42]One of them William Aldis Wright, who became a friend of FitzGerald's and eventually edited his letters.

[43]"While I was fixing my eyes upon the green leafage, just as he who wastes his life following the little bird is wont to do, my more than Father said to me . . ." (*Divina Commedia,* Purgatorio, xxiii, 1–4, translation of Charles Eliot Norton).

[44]Sir William F. Pollock (1815–1888), lawyer and translator of Dante.

[45]John Forster's *Life of Walter Savage Landor* (1869).

[46]To excess.

[47]Best known for his long work in praise of married love, *The Angel in the House* (1854–1862).

[48]*The Ring and the Book* (1868–1869).

and magazines, and tell the truth of the case? Why does not Venables? Stephen? Pollock? I am sure I would if I could; but I have not the faculty. I can only say, "I do not like you, Doctor Fell,"[49] but there I stop —knowing I'm right. If Browning were half as great as they say, he would himself write to disclaim any approximation to Tennyson. . . .

XI. To W. F. Pollock

Woodbridge, 29 April, 1870

My dear Pollock,

Though you are now, I suppose, getting into the thick of the London season, yet (as we used to sing in Bunn's days) "You will remember me!" Which reminds me that I have bought and have been looking over the first twelve volumes of *Punch,* only for the sake of recovering some of Thackeray's first papers there, which I remember his doing when I was staying with him in what we used to call *Joram* Street. There is not much that one would wish others to recognise for his so far as 1847, when my set ends, and when Thackeray had launched *Vanity Fair.* It is curious to me how slowly, and then how suddenly, he got to that. Some people say that *Barry Lyndon* and others were as good as his best; I never could read them, only his Irish and part of his Paris sketch-books. There is a good ballad about King Canute in some papers called *Miss Tickletoby on English Literature,* in one of the early *Punches.* I remembered the side of the page, *etc.,* as it lay on the Joram breakfast table. By the bye of that again, you may (if you like) borrow of Donne some MS. extracts of letters from Morton, who used to be with us then. The best part of the letters I cut out and sent under Thackeray's auspices to *Blackwood,* hoping to get £10 for Morton, who was always wanting it, you know. *Blackwood* only lost the papers, as Thackeray was not then great man enough

to command obedience. But even the remainder was too good to be lost; so I copied out scraps, and you can read them if you will—taking all care of them! They will repay you the trouble of deciphering, I am sure. It is a pity they cannot go into some magazine that others may read; but I have no interest in magazine quarters.

By the bye again, I read a very nice paper on the French and English stage, by Mrs. Pollock I am told. Please to make her proud and happy by such a royal approval.

Laurence has been down with me, he wishing, and I wishing him, to paint a sketch of my grand lugger man[50] from a photograph which he admired. So captain and painter met at my château in Easter Week. But all ended in nothing. First day nothing done; second day all that was done effaced; third day much the same, the light all amiss, previous measurements incorrect; and after four days the captain was obliged to return to his business, and the painter also to his, carrying with him what he himself pronounced a failure. I had told him to come and do his hastiest and worst (which I think best), but he will prepare grounds, paint by stages, *etc.,* and so he seems to me to muddle all. I fancy he should stick to crayons: he can draw, but he never could, never can, and never will color. He was very pleasant (sometimes a little prosy), and sat wondering at and studying the captain, who for stately simplicity of soul and body is fit company for Phidias himself. But the weather was cross; so it is now—"beastly," as old Alfred used to say. I read in the *Athenaeum* how a Mr. Austin calls him "School Miss Alfred," as Lord Lytton did twenty years ago.[51] All this comes of people only remembering A. T.'s later works, forgetting *Locksley Hall, Vision of Sin, Sleeping Palace, Oak, Waterproof,* and all the English pastorals in the two volumes of 1842. Do they

---

[49] I do not love thee, Dr. Fell,
The reason why I cannot tell.

(Thomas Brown's epigram on Dr. John Fell, a seventeenth-century ecclesiastic and friend of the Oxford University Press.)

[50] A sea captain whom FitzGerald greatly admired, in whose fishing business he was a partner, and whom he employed to sail his lugger.

[51] Alfred Austin, who was, ironically, to succeed Tennyson in the laureateship, did not actually call the older poet "School Miss Alfred," the name applied to him by Bulwer Lytton in *The New Timon* (1846). But Austin's *Poetry of the Period* did place Tennyson in the third rank.

smack of the School Miss? But when King Arthur was identified with Prince Albert, and all so moral and artistic, and ballads about "my little one, my pretty one sleeps,"[52] and then it was all over with him.

Do you—can you—read Morris, who (Cowell tells me) almost shares the throne with Browning? *Ter conatus eram*[53] with *Jason*—as with *Book and Ring*. No Go. *Will Waterproof* shall survive them all.

Yours ever,

E. Browning-proof.

The weather is still desperate: cold N. E. winds, clouds as if charged with snow and thunder at once, trees scarcely venturing into leaf, flowers nipped in the bud, forlorn nightingales, *etc.* I am just going off to Lowestoft, where my business is to be settled —that is, of parting company with the fishing trade—the last hobby I was ever to have in this world, and now I am to be dismounted.

I scarce know what has made me write such a lot; a little better written would have been better for you if not for me.

XII. To Samuel Laurence

Woodbridge, 4 July, 1874

My dear Laurence,

. . . I am (for a wonder) going out on a few days' visit. . . . And, once out, I meditate a run to Edinburgh, only to see where Sir Walter Scott lived and wrote about. But as I have meditated this great enterprise for these thirty years, it may perhaps now end again in meditation only. . . .

I am just finishing Forster's Dickens:[54] very good, I think; only, he has no very nice perception of character, I think, or chooses not to let his readers into it. But there is enough to show that Dickens was a very noble fellow as well as a very wonderful one. . . . I, for one, worship Dickens, in spite of Carlyle and the critics; and wish to see his Gadshill[55] as I wished to see Shakespeare's Stratford and Scott's Abbotsford. One must love the man for that.

XIII. To W. F. Pollock

Woodbridge, 23 July, 1874

BUT I did get to Abbotsford, and was rejoiced to find it was not at all cockney, not a castle, but only in the half-castellated style of heaps of other houses in Scotland; the grounds simply and broadly laid out before the windows, down to a field, down to the Tweed, with the woods which he left so little now well aloft and flourishing, and I was glad. I could not find my way to Maida's grave in the garden, with its false quantity,

Ad jănuam Domini, etc.[56]

which the Whigs and critics taunted Scott with, and Lockhart[57] had done it. "You know I don't care a curse about what I write,"[58] nor about what was imputed to him. In this, surely like Shakespeare; as also in other respects. I will worship him in spite of Gurlyle, who sent me an ugly autotype of Knox[59] whom I was to worship instead.

Then I went to see Jedburgh Abbey, in a half-ruined corner of which he lies entombed—Lockhart beside him—a beautiful place, with his own Tweed still running close by, and his Eildon Hills looking on. The man who drove me about showed me a hill which Sir Walter was very fond of visiting, from which he could see over the Border, *etc.* This hill is between Abbotsford and Jedburgh; and when his coach horses, who drew his hearse, got there, to that hill, they could scarce be got on.

My mission to Scotland was done; but some civil, pleasant people whom I met at

---

[52]The refrain of the lyric "Sweet and Low," at the end of the Second Part of *The Princess*.

[53]Three times had I attempted. William Morris's *Life and Death of Jason* had appeared in 1867.

[54]John Forster's *Life of Charles Dickens* (1872–1874).

[55]The town in which Dickens lived in his later years. Abbotsford is the country estate which belonged to Scott.

[56]To the door of the Lord, etc.—the first *a* in *januam* is naturally long in quantity, not short as the meter requires.

[57]John Lockhart (1794–1854), son-in-law and biographer of Scott.

[58]Letters to Lockhart, 15 January, 1826.

[59]John Knox (1505–1572), the Scotch reformer.

Abbotsford made me go with them (under Cook's guidance) to the Trossachs, Katrine, Lomond,[60] *etc.,* which I did not care at all about; but it only took a day. After which I came in a day to London, rather glad to be in my old flat land again, with a sight of my old sea as we came along.

* * *

XIV. To Charles Eliot Norton[61]

Woodbridge, 23 January, 1876

My dear sir,

. . . I suppose you may see one of the Carlyle medallions; and you can judge better of the likeness than I, who have not been to Chelsea, and hardly out of Suffolk, these fifteen years and more. I dare say it is like him; but his profile is not his best phase. In two notes dictated by him since that business he has not adverted to it; I think he must be a little ashamed of it, though it would not do to say so in return, I suppose. And yet I think he might have declined the honors of a life of "heroism." I have no doubt he would have played a brave man's part if called on; but, meanwhile, he has only sat pretty comfortably at Chelsea, scolding all the world for not being heroic, and not always very precise in telling them how. He has, however, been so far heroic as to be always independent, whether of wealth, rank, and coteries of all sorts: nay, apt to fly in the face of some who courted him. I suppose he is changed, or subdued, at eighty; but up to the last ten years he seemed to me just the same as when I first knew him five and thirty years ago. What a fortune he might have made by showing himself as a lecturer, as Thackeray and Dickens did; I don't mean they did it for vanity, but to make money, and that to spend generously. Carlyle did indeed lecture near forty years ago before he was a lion to be shown, and when he had but few readers. I heard his *Heroes*[62] which now seems to me one of his best books. He looked very handsome then, with his black hair, fine eyes, and a sort of crucified expression.

I know, of course, (in books) several of those you name in your letter: Longfellow, whom I may say I love, and so (I see) can't call him *Mister;* and Emerson whom I admire, for I don't feel that I know the philosopher so well as the poet; and Mr. Lowell's *Among My Books* is among mine. I also have always much liked, I think rather loved, O. W. Holmes. I scarce know why I could never take to that man of true genius, Hawthorne. There is a little of my confession of faith about your countrymen, and I should say mine, if I were not more Irish than English.

XV. To Charles Eliot Norton

Woodbridge, 7 February, 1876

My dear sir,

I will not look on the book[63] you have sent me as any return for the booklet I sent you, but as a free and kindly gift. I really don't know that you could have sent me a better. I have read it with more continuous attention and gratification than I now usually feel, and always (as Lamb suggested) well disposed to say grace after reading.

Seeing what Mr. Lowell has done for Dante, Rousseau, *etc.,* one does not wish him to be limited in his subjects; but I do wish he would do for English writers what Sainte Beuve has done for French. Mr. Lowell so far goes along with him as to give so much of each writer's life as may illustrate his writings; he has more humor (in which alone I fancy S. B. somewhat wanting), more extensive reading, I suppose, and a power of metaphorical illustration which (if I may say so) seems to me to want only a little reserve in its use: as was the case perhaps with Hazlitt.[64] But Mr. Lowell is not biased by Hazlitt's—(by anybody's, so far as I see)—party or personal prejudices; and altogether seems to me the man most fitted to do this good work, where it has not

---

[60]The Trossachs is a wooded valley, Katrine and Lomond are lakes, in the most beautiful part of the Scotch highlands.

[61]The American critic and teacher (1827–1908).

[62]*Heroes, Hero-Worship, and the Heroic in History* (1841).

[63]Apparently Lowell's *Among My Books,* Second Series, published in this year.

[64]William Hazlitt (1778–1830), the essayist.

(as with Carlyle's *Johnson*) been done, for good and all, before. Of course, one only wants the great men, in their kind: Chaucer, Pope (Dryden being done[65]), and perhaps some of the *minora sidera*[66] clustered together, as Hazlitt has done them. Perhaps all this will come forth in some future series even now gathering in Mr. Lowell's head. However that may be, this present series will make me return to some whom I have not [10] lately looked up. Dante's face I have not seen these ten years, only his back on my book shelf. What Mr. Lowell says of him recalled to me what Tennyson said to me some thirty-five or forty years ago. We [15] were stopping before a shop in Regent Street where were two figures of Dante and Goethe. I (I suppose) said, "What is there in old Dante's face that is missing in Goethe's?" And Tennyson (whose profile [20] then had certainly a remarkable likeness to Dante's) said: "The Divine." Then Milton; I don't think I've read him these forty years; the whole scheme of the poem, and certain parts of it, looming as grand as anything in [25] my memory; but I never could read ten lines together without stumbling at some pedantry that tipped me at once out of Paradise, or even Hell, into the schoolroom, worse than either. Tennyson again used to say that [30] the two grandest of all similes were those of the ships hanging in the air, and "the gunpowder one," which he used slowly and grimly to enact, in the days that are no more. He certainly then thought Milton the sub- [35] limest of all the gang; his diction modeled on Virgil, as perhaps Dante's.

Spencer I never could get on with, and (spite of Mr. Lowell's good word) shall still content myself with such delightful quota- [40] tions from him as one lights upon here and there: the last from Mr. Lowell.

Then, old "Daddy Wordsworth," as he was sometimes called, I am afraid, from my christening:[67] he is now, I suppose, passing [45] under the eclipse consequent on the glory which followed his obscure rise. I remember fifty years ago at our Cambridge, when the battle was fighting for him by the few

against the many of us who laughed at *Louisa in the Shade, etc.* His brother[68] was then Master of Trinity College, like all Wordsworths (unless the drowned sailor) pompous and priggish. He used to drawl [5] out the chapel responses so that we called him the "Mēēserable Sinner" and his brother the "Meeserable Poet." Poor fun enough; but I never can forgive the Lakers all who first despised, and then patronized "Walter [10] Scott," as they loftily called him; and he, dear, noble fellow, thought they were quite justified. Well, your Emerson has done him far more justice than his own countryman Carlyle, who won't allow him to be a hero [15] in any way, but sets up such a cantankerous, narrow-minded bigot as John Knox in his stead. I did go to worship at Abbotsford, as to Stratford on Avon; and saw that it was good to have so done. If you, if Mr. Lowell, [20] have not lately read it, pray read Lockhart's account of his journey to Douglas Dale on (I think) July 18 or 19, 1831.[69] It is a piece of tragedy, even to the muttering thunder, like the *Lammermuir,* which does [25] not look very small beside *Peter Bell* and Co.

My dear sir, this is a desperate letter; and that last sentence will lead to another dirty little story about my Daddy; to which you must listen or I should feel like the fine lady [30] in one of Vanbrugh's[70] plays, "Oh my God, that you won't listen to a woman of quality when her heart is bursting with malice!" And perhaps you on the other side of the Great Water may be amused with a little of [35] your Old Granny's gossip.

Well then: about 1826, or 7, Professor Airy (now our Astronomer Royal) and his brother William called on the Daddy at Rydal.[71] In the course of conversation [40] Daddy mentioned that sometimes when genteel parties came to visit him, he contrived to

---

[65]In the First Series of *Among My Books* (1870).

[66]Lesser stars.

[67]I. e., my christening of him.

[68]Christopher Wordsworth. The drowned sailor was John Wordsworth, whose character contributed many elements to *The Happy Warrior.*

[69]The account in Lockhart's *Life of Scott,* of an occasion on which Sir Walter, who had not many months to live, showed more emotion than was usual with him. FitzGerald alludes to Scott's *Bride of Lammermoor* and Wordsworth's *Peter Bell.*

[70]Sir John Vanbrugh (1664–1726), author of *The Relapse* and *The Provoked Wife.*

[71]Wordsworth's home during his later years.

slip out of the room, and down the garden walk to where "the party's" traveling carriage stood. This carriage he would look into to see what books they carried with them; and he observed it was generally "Walter Scott's." It was Airy's brother (a very veracious man, and an admirer of Wordsworth, but, to be sure, more of Sir Walter) who told me this. It is this conceit that diminishes Wordsworth's stature among us, in spite of the mountain mists he lived among. Also, a stinginess; not like Sir Walter in that! I remember Hartley Coleridge telling us at Ambleside how Professor Wilson and some one else (H. C. himself perhaps) stole a leg of mutton from Wordsworth's larder for the fun of the thing.

Here then is a long letter of Old World gossip from the old home. I hope it won't tire you out; it need not, you know.

P. S. By way of something better from the Old World, I post you Hazlitt's own copy of his *English Poets,* with a few of his marks for another edition in it. If you like to keep it, pray do; if you like better to give it to Hazlitt's successor, Mr. Lowell, do that from yourself.

XVI. To Fanny Kemble[72]

Lowestoft, 24 October, 1876

Dear Mrs. Kemble,

Little—nothing—as I have to write, I am nevertheless beginning to write to you from this old lodging of mine, from which I think our correspondence chiefly began—ten years ago. I am in the same room, the same dull sea moaning before me, the same wind screaming through the windows; so I take up the same old story. My lugger was then about building; she has passed into other hands now; I see her from time to time bouncing into harbor, with her "244" on her bows. Her captain and I have parted; I thought he did very wrongly—drink, among other things; but he did not think he did wrong: a different morality from ours—that, indeed, of Carlyle's ancient sea kings. I saw him a few days ago in his house, with wife and children, looking, as always, too big for his house, but always grand, polite, and unlike anybody else. I was noticing the many flies in the room;—"Poor things," he said, "it is the warmth of our stove makes them alive." When Tennyson was with me, whose portrait hangs in my house in company with those of Thackeray and this man (the three greatest men I have known), I thought that both Tennyson and Thackeray were inferior to him in respect of thinking of themselves. When Tennyson was telling me of how *The Quarterly* abused him (humorously too), and desirous of knowing why one did not care for his later works, *etc.,* I thought that if he had lived an active life, as Scott and Shakespeare, or even ridden, shot, drunk, and played the devil, as Byron, he would have done much more, and talked about it much less. "You know," said Scott to Lockhart, "that I don't care a curse about what I write," and one sees he did not. I don't believe it was far otherwise with Shakespeare. Even old Wordsworth, wrapt up in his mountain mists, and proud as he was, was above all this vain disquietude; proud, not vain, was he; and that a great man (as Dante) has some right to be—but not to care what the coteries say. What a rigmarole!

Donne[73] scarce ever writes to me (Twalmley the Great), and if he do not write to you, depend upon it he thinks he has nothing worth sending over the Atlantic. I heard from Mowbray quite lately that his father was very well.

Yes: you told me in a previous letter that you were coming to England after Christmas. I shall not be up to going to London to see you, with all your company about you; perhaps (don't think me very impudent!) you may come down, if we live till summer, to my Woodbridge château, and there talk over some old things.

I make a kind of summer in my room here with Boccaccio. What a mercy that one can return with a relish to these books! As Don Quixote can only be read in Spanish, so I

---

[72]The great actress (1809-1893), to whom Fitz-Gerald wrote a large number of his later letters.

[73]W. B. Donne, an old friend who had become licenser of plays. Twalmley was the inventor of a new kind of laundry iron, who therefore introduced himself as "the Great" (Boswell's *Life of Johnson,* under 1783).

fancy Boccaccio only in his Italian; and yet one is used to fancy that poetry is the mainly untranslatable thing. How prettily innocent are the ladies, who, after telling very loose stories, finish with *"E così Iddio faccia noi* [5] *godere del nostro amore,"*[74] *etc.;* sometimes, *"Domeneddio,"* more affectionately.

Anyhow, these ladies are better than the accursed Eastern Question;[75] of which I have determined to read, and, if possible, [10] here, no more till the one question be settled of peace or war. If war, I am told I may lose some £5000 in Russian bankruptcy; but I can truly say I would give that, and more, to ensure peace and good will among men at [15] this time. Oh, the apes we are! I must retire to my Montaigne—whom, by the way, I remember reading here when the lugger was building! Oh, the apes, *etc.* But there was A Man in all that business still, who is [20] so now, somewhat tarnished.—And I am yours as then sincerely

E. F. G.

XVII.   To W. F. Pollock

Lowestoft, 22 September, 1878

My dear Pollock,

You will scarce thank me for a letter in [30] pencil; perhaps you would thank me less if I used the steel pen, which is my other resource. You could very well dispense with a letter altogether; and yet I believe it is pleasant to get one when abroad.

I dare say I may have told you what Tennyson said of the Sistine Child,[76] which he then knew only by engraving. He first thought the expression of his face (as also the attitude) almost too solemn, even for the [40] Christ within. But some time after, when A. T. was married, and had a son, he told me that Raffaelle was all right; that no man's face was so solemn as a child's, full of wonder. He said one morning that he watched [45] his babe "worshipping the sunbeam on the bedpost and curtain." I risk telling you this again for the sake of the holy ground you are now standing on.

Which reminds me also of a remark of Béranger's[77] not out of place. He says God forgot to give Raffaelle to Greece, and made a *joli cadeau*[78] of him to the Church of Rome.

I brought here some volumes of Lever's[79] *Cornelius O'Dowd* essays, very much better reading than Addison, I think. Also some of Sainte Beuve's better than either. A sentence in *O'Dowd* reminded me of your distrust of civil service examinations: "You could not find a worse pointer than the poodle which would pick you out all the letters of the alphabet." And is not this pretty good of the world we live in? "You ask me if I am going to 'the masquerade.' I am at it: *Circumspice!*"[80]

So I pick out and point to other men's game, this Sunday morning, when the sun makes the sea shine, and a strong head wind [25] drives the ships with shortened sail across it. Last night I was with some sailors at the inn; some one came in who said there was a schooner with five feet of water in her in the roads; and off they went to see if anything beside water could be got out of her. But, as you say, one mustn't be epigrammatic and clever. Just before grog and pipe, the band had played some German waltzes, a bit of Verdi, Rossini's *Cujus Animan,*[81] [35] and a capital sailors' tramp-chorus from Wagner, all delightful to me, on the pier: how much better than all the dreary oratorios going on all the week at Norwich, Elijah, St. Peter, St. Paul, Eli, *etc.* There will be an oratorio for every saint and prophet; which reminds me of my last story. Voltaire had an especial grudge against Habakkuk. Some one proved to him that he had misrepresented facts in Habakkuk's history. *"C'est égal,"* [45] says V.; *Habakkuk était capable de tout."*[82]

---

[74]"And so may God make us enjoy our love" (*"noi"* omitted by FitzGerald). *Domeneddio* is a variant of *Iddio* (God).

[75]The unrest preceding the Russo-Turkish War of 1877–1878.

[76]The Christ Child in Raphael's *Sistine Madonna* at Dresden, where Pollock was evidently stopping at the moment.

[77]Pierre Jean de Béranger (1780–1857), the French poet.

[78]A nice gift.

[79]Charles Lever (1806–1872), author of *Charles O'Malley.*

[80]Look about you.   [81]*Whose Soul.*

[82]"It's all the same," says Voltaire; "Habakkuk was capable of anything."

Cornewall Lewis, who (like most other Whigs) had no humor, yet tells this: I wonder if it will reach Dresden.

XVIII. To Charles Eliot Norton

Woodbridge, 13 March, 1881

My dear Norton,

I send you along with this letter Part II of *Oedipus*,[83] with some corrections or suggestions which I have been obliged to make in pencil, because of the paper blotting under the lightest penwork, and, along with it, a preliminary letter, which I believe I told you of also, addressed to your initial; for I did not wish to compromise you even with yourself in such a business. I know you will like it probably more than it deserves, and excuse its inroads on the original, though you may, and probably will, think I might better have left it alone, or followed it more faithfully. As to those students you tell me of who are meditating, or by this time may have accomplisht, their representation, they could only look on me as a blasphemer. . . .

It seems almost wrong or unreasonable of me to be talking thus of myself and my little doings, when not only Carlyle has departed from us, but one, not so illustrious in genius, but certainly not less wise, my dear old friend of sixty years, James Spedding, whose name you will know as connected with Lord Bacon. To re-edit his *Works,* which did not want any such re-edition, and to vindicate his character, which could not be cleared, did this Spedding sacrifice forty years which he

might well have given to accomplish much greater things; Shakespeare, for one. But Spedding had no sort of ambition, and liked to be kept at one long work which he knew would not glorify himself. He was the wisest man I have known: not the less so for plenty of the boy in him, a great sense of humor, a Socrates in life and in death, which he faced with all serenity so long as consciousness lasted. I suppose something of him will reach America, I mean, of his death, run over by a cab and dying in St. George's Hospital, to which he was taken, and from which he could not be removed home alive. I believe that had Carlyle been alive, and but as well as he was three months ago, he would have insisted on being carried to the Hospital to see his friend, whom he respected as he did few others. I have just got the Carlyle *Reminiscences,*[84] which will take me some little time to read, impatient as I may be to read them. What I have read is of a stuff we can scarce find in any other autobiographer; whether his editor, Froude, has done quite well in publishing them as they are, and so soon, is another matter. Carlyle's niece thinks, not quite. She sent me a pipe her uncle had used, for memorial. I had asked her for the bowl, and an inch of stem, of one of the clay pipes such as I had smoked with him under that little old pear tree in his Chelsea garden many an evening. But she sent me a small meerschaum which Lady Ashburton had given him, and which he used when from home.

---

[83]FitzGerald's translation of the *Oedipus the King* and *Oedipus at Colonus* of Sophocles.

[84]The first of several autobiographical volumes, edited by James Anthony Froude. The frankness of the work caused much indignation.

JOHN RUSKIN

1819–1900

Ruskin's father was a wine-merchant dealing in sherry. He was a Scotchman, a man of unusual practical ability and of considerable fortune, with conventional views, but possessed of fine taste. He married his first cousin, a woman of great power, with a harsh and deeply religious nature. To them John Ruskin, their only child, was born in London on 8 February, 1819. Few youths have been so completely and so long subjected to the influences of their homes as was Ruskin, and something of the general character of his early years may be gathered from the brief autobiographical passages printed below. After a somewhat irregular course of preparation he entered Christ Church, Oxford, at the age of eighteen, as a gentleman-commoner. His work there was interrupted by bad health which forced him to spend a year and a half abroad, chiefly in Italy. He took his B.A. in May, 1842, receiving an honorary fourth class both in classics and in mathematics. His parents had expected him to become a clergyman, and he disappointed them by refusing either to take holy orders or to enter the sherry trade. What he was to do was not yet perhaps entirely clear to himself, yet he had been since boyhood persistently training himself for writing. Nearly every day since his seventh year he had been writing poetry, and his exercises in prose composition had begun almost as early. Likewise he had been from youth an enthusiastic lover of the landscape art of J. M. W. Turner, convinced as he was that Turner alone of contemporary artists saw nature truly and painted what he saw; and at the age of seventeen he had written an eloquent, impassioned essay in defense of Turner against adverse criticism. Now, his academic career concluded and his future at least negatively determined, he settled down in the autumn and winter of 1842 to the writing of "Turner and the Ancients," as he at first intended to entitle his book. The title was later changed to *Modern Painters,* and the volume was published anonymously in 1843. It caused a sensation in both the artistic and literary worlds, and it was almost immediately recognized that a new master had appeared. Ruskin was, indeed, by his successive volumes to work a veritable revolution in taste and to rise to a position of authority as an art-critic unexampled in England. What he did, said William Morris, was "to let a flood of daylight into the cloud of sham-twaddle which was once the whole substance of art-criticism." And he did this with an assurance, an eloquence, a wealth of ingenious illustration, and a splendor of language which fairly swept many contemporaries off their feet. The basis of his work, moreover, was exceedingly simple. He preached in his own way essentially the great lesson of Carlyle, by whom he was much influenced;—he preached that better than all things else in the world is truth. He asked of artists only that they should submit themselves, humbly and obediently, to the truth of nature, and told them that in this way, and in this way alone, they could discover the highest inspiration and learn how to use their pencils and their brushes in the noble fashion of the master.

Ruskin was twenty-four when the first volume of *Modern Painters* was published; despite his manifest genius and his thoughtfulness above his years, he obviously had some things yet to learn. As new chapters in the history of art were opened up to him by travel and study the original plan of *Modern Painters* was changed and expanded, and in addition Ruskin was more than once drawn aside into other work, with the result that the fifth and final volume did not appear until 1860. In the intervening years occurred his unhappy marriage to Euphemia Chalmers Gray, which took place in April, 1848, and which was a few years later annulled on the petition of Mrs. Ruskin. In those years, too, he wrote *The Seven Lamps of Architecture* (1849) —Truth, Beauty, Power, Sacrifice, Obedience, Labor, Memory—in which he did for the art of building what he had already done for painting, and *The Stones of Venice* (1851–1853), which is, so to say, a practical amplification of the *Seven Lamps,* applying its doctrine to the defense of Gothic architecture.

From the first Ruskin's art-criticism was a consideration of the conditions under which great works of art may come into being, and from the first Ruskin regarded the good, the true, and the beautiful as ultimately one in their nature. In other words, he taught that beauty is at bottom the concomitant or outgrowth of a right and true system of values, and that ugliness consequently must be the expression of a wrong or low or false system of values. And as he went on with his work he saw more and more clearly that this conviction implied that only a good man could be a great artist. Thus it was that the *Seven Lamps* was written to show, as he later explained, "that certain right states of temper and moral feeling were the magic powers by which all good architecture without exception had been produced. *The Stones of Venice* had, from beginning to end, no other aim than to show that the Gothic architecture of Venice had arisen out of, and indicated in all its features, a state of pure national faith and of domestic virtue; and that its Renaissance architecture had arisen out of, and in all its features indicated, a state of concealed national infidelity and of domestic corruption." This, then, is the secret of his transition in middle life from the rôle of art-critic to that of social reformer. The two are ordinarily thought of as very different activities, but in Ruskin the social reformer grew naturally, indeed inevitably, out of the art-critic, and to separate them from each other is in his case to misunderstand both. From the late eighteen-fifties until the close of his active life he gave himself increasingly to social work, and wrote, and spent his money, in the effort to arouse the upper classes to a sense of their responsibilities and to help the poor to rise out of the misery and ugliness which surrounded them. Some of the books which preserve the writings of this period are *Unto this Last, Munera Pulveris, Time and Tide, Fors Clavigera, Sesame and Lilies,* and *The Crown of Wild Olive.* In these

Ruskin no doubt often wrote rashly, as was indeed his habit in all his work, and he aroused bitter feeling which at the moment seemed to go far towards destroying the reputation he had previously built up for himself. Time has, however, been remarkably on Ruskin's side, and it is today an astonishing and illuminating thing to count up for one's self the number of his one-time social heresies which have since become accepted commonplaces.

In his later life Ruskin was for some years the Slade Professor of Fine Art at Oxford, where his lectures drew very large audiences. After his retirement from Oxford he wrote those autobiographical sketches which were published under the title *Praeterita.* He died on 20 January, 1900. He had once said: "Life without industry is guilt, and industry without art is brutality." This sentence sums up better than could any other words the meaning of all his work.

The standard edition, never likely to be superseded, of the complete *Works* of Ruskin is the "Library Edition," ed. E. T. Cook and Alexander Wedderburn (39 vols., London, 1903–1912). The standard biography is *The Life of John Ruskin* by E. T. Cook (2 vols., London, 1911). *Selections and Essays by John Ruskin,* ed. F. W. Roe ("Modern Student's Library," 1918) is a good and useful book of selections. Biographical and critical studies of Ruskin are numerous, and only a few can be mentioned: *John Ruskin, Social Reformer,* by J. A. Hobson (London, 1898); *John Ruskin* by Mrs. Meynell (New York, 1900); *John Ruskin* by Frederic Harrison ("English Men of Letters" series, 1902); *Ruskin, A Study in Personality,* by A. C. Benson (New York, 1911); *The Exquisite Tragedy, An Intimate Life of John Ruskin,* by Amabel Williams-Ellis (New York, 1929); *John Ruskin, An Introduction to Further Study of His Life and Work,* by R. H. Wilenski (London, 1933); and *Ruskin* by Gerald Crow ("Great Lives" series, 1936).

PRAETERITA

Early Reading and Summer Travel[1]

I AM, and my father was before me, a violent Tory of the old school;—Walter Scott's

[1] *Praeterita* (things gone by) was published in chapters at irregular intervals from 1885 to 1889. This passage is from vol. I, chap. i, which consists of slightly revised passages from *Fors Clavigera,* written 1871–1875.

school, that is to say, and Homer's. I name these two out of the numberless great Tory writers, because they were my own two masters. I had Walter Scott's novels, and the *Iliad* (Pope's translation), for constant reading when I was a child, on week-days: on Sunday, their effect was tempered by *Robinson Crusoe* and the *Pilgrim's Progress;* my mother having it deeply in her heart to make an evangelical clergyman of me. Fortunately, I had an aunt more evangelical than my mother; and my aunt gave me cold mutton for Sunday's dinner, which—as I much preferred it hot—greatly diminished the influence of the *Pilgrim's Progress;* and the end of the matter was, that I got all the noble imaginative teaching of Defoe and Bunyan, and yet—am not an evangelical clergyman.

I had, however, still better teaching than theirs, and that compulsorily, and every day of the week.

Walter Scott and Pope's Homer were reading of my own election, and my mother forced me, by steady daily toil, to learn long chapters of the Bible by heart; as well as to read it every syllable through, aloud, hard names and all, from Genesis to the Apocalypse, about once a year: and to that discipline—patient, accurate, and resolute—I owe, not only a knowledge of the book, which I find occasionally serviceable, but much of my general power of taking pains, and the best part of my taste in literature. From Walter Scott's novels I might easily, as I grew older, have fallen to other people's novels; and Pope might, perhaps, have led me to take Johnson's English, or Gibbon's, as types of language; but once knowing the 32nd of Deuteronomy, the 119th Psalm, the 15th of 1st Corinthians, the Sermon on the Mount, and most of the Apocalypse, every syllable by heart, and having always a way of thinking with myself what words meant, it was not possible for me, even in the foolishest times of youth, to write entirely superficial or formal English; and the affectation of trying to write like Hooker and George Herbert was the most innocent I could have fallen into.

From my own chosen masters, then, Scott and Homer, I learned the Toryism which my best after-thought has only served to confirm.

That is to say, a most sincere love of kings, and dislike of everybody who attempted to disobey them. Only, both by Homer and Scott, I was taught strange ideas about kings, which I find for the present much obsolete; for, I perceived that both the author of the *Iliad* and the author of *Waver-*

ley made their kings, or king-loving persons, do harder work than anybody else. Tydides or Idomeneus always killed twenty Trojans to other people's one, and Redgauntlet speared more salmon than any of the Solway fishermen;[2] and—which was particularly a subject of admiration to me—I observed that they not only did more, but in proportion to their doings *got* less, than other people—nay, that the best of them were even ready to govern for nothing! and let their followers divide any quantity of spoil or profit. Of late it has seemed to me that the idea of a king has become exactly the contrary of this, and that it has been supposed the duty of superior persons generally to govern less, and get more, than anybody else. So that it was, perhaps, quite as well that in those early days my contemplation of existent kingship was a very distant one.

The aunt who gave me cold mutton on Sundays was my father's sister: she lived at Bridge-end, in the town of Perth, and had a garden full of gooseberry-bushes, sloping down to the Tay, with a door opening to the water, which ran past it, clear-brown over the pebbles three or four feet deep; swift-eddying,—an infinite thing for a child to look down into.

My father began business as a wine-merchant, with no capital, and a considerable amount of debts bequeathed him by my grandfather. He accepted the bequest, and paid them all before he began to lay by anything for himself,—for which his best friends called him a fool, and I, without expressing any opinion as to his wisdom, which I knew in such matters to be at least equal to mine, have written on the granite slab over his grave that he was "an entirely honest merchant." As days went on he was able to take a house in Hunter Street, Brunswick Square, No. 54 (the windows of it, fortunately for me, commanded a view of a marvelous iron post, out of which the water-carts were filled through beautiful little trap-doors, by pipes like boa-constrictors; and I was never weary of contemplating that mystery, and the de-

---

[2] For Diomed (son of Tydeus) see such a passage in Pope's *Iliad* as **x**, 560; for Idomeneus, xiii, 457. For Redgauntlet see Letter 4 of Scott's novel of the same name.

licious dripping consequent); and as years went on, and I came to be four or five years old, he could command a postchaise and pair for two months in the summer, by help of which, with my mother and me, he went the round of his country customers (who liked to see the principal of the house his own traveler); so that, at a jog-trot pace, and through the panoramic opening of the four windows of a postchaise, made more panoramic still to me because my seat was a little bracket in front (for we used to hire the chaise regularly for the two months out of Long Acre, and so could have it bracketed and pocketed as we liked), I saw all the highroads, and most of the cross ones, of England and Wales; and great part of lowland Scotland, as far as Perth, where every other year we spent the whole summer: and I used to read the *Abbot* at Kinross, and the *Monastery* in Glen Farg, which I confused with "Glendearg," and thought that the White Lady had as certainly lived by the streamlet in that glen of the Ochils, as the Queen of Scots in the island of Loch Leven.

To my farther great benefit, as I grew older, I thus saw nearly all the noblemen's houses in England; in reverent and healthy delight of uncovetous admiration,—perceiving, as soon as I could perceive any political truth at all, that it was probably much happier to live in a small house, and have Warwick Castle to be astonished at, than to live in Warwick Castle and have nothing to be astonished at; but that, at all events, it would not make Brunswick Square in the least more pleasantly habitable, to pull Warwick Castle down. And at this day, though I have kind invitations enough to visit America, I could not, even for a couple of months, live in a country so miserable as to possess no castles.

Nevertheless, having formed my notion of kinghood chiefly from the FitzJames of the *Lady of the Lake,* and of noblesse from the Douglas there, and the Douglas in *Marmion,* a painful wonder soon arose in my child-mind, why the castles should now be always empty. Tantallon was there; but no Archibald of Angus:—Stirling, but no Knight of Snowdoun. The galleries and gardens of England were beautiful to see—but his Lordship and her Ladyship were always in town, said the housekeepers and gardeners. Deep yearning took hold of me for a kind of "Restoration," which I began slowly to feel that Charles the Second had not altogether effected, though I always wore a gilded oak-apple very piously in my button-hole on the 29th of May. It seemed to me that Charles the Second's Restoration had been, as compared with the Restoration I wanted, much as that gilded oak-apple to a real apple. And as I grew wiser, the desire for sweet pippins instead of bitter ones, and Living Kings instead of dead ones, appeared to me rational as well as romantic; and gradually it has become the main purpose of my life to grow pippins, and its chief hope, to see Kings.

Daily Life at Herne Hill[1]

WHEN I was about four years old my father found himself able to buy the lease of a house on Herne Hill, a rustic eminence four miles south of the "Standard in Cornhill";[2] of which the leafy seclusion remains, in all essential points of character, unchanged to this day: certain Gothic splendors, lately indulged in by our wealthier neighbors, being the only serious innovations; and these are so graciously concealed by the fine trees of their grounds, that the passing viator[3] remains unappalled by them; and I can still walk up and down the piece of road between the Fox tavern and the Herne Hill station, imagining myself four years old.

Our house was the northernmost of a group which stand accurately on the top or dome of the hill, where the ground is for a small space level, as the snows are (I understand), on the dome of Mont Blanc; presently falling, however, in what may be, in the London clay formation, considered a precipitous slope, to our valley of Chamouni

---

[1]From vol. I, chap. ii, the greater part of which consists of slightly revised passages from *Fors Clavigera,* written 1873–1875.

[2]A standard was a lofty structure containing a vertical conduit pipe with spouts and taps for supplying water to the public. This one, built in 1582, stood near the junction of Cornhill with Leadenhall Street.

[3]Traveler.

(or of Dulwich) on the east; and with' a softer descent into Cold Harbor-lane on the west: on the south, no less beautifully declining to the dale of the Effra (doubtless shortened from Effrena, signifying the "Unbridled" river; recently, I regret to say, bricked over for the convenience of Mr. Biffin, chemist, and others); while on the north, prolonged indeed with slight depression some half mile or so, and receiving, in the parish of Lambeth, the chivalric title of "Champion Hill," it plunges down at last to efface itself in the plains of Peckham, and the rural barbarism of Goose Green.

The group, of which our house was the quarter, consisted of two precisely similar partner-couples of houses, gardens and all to match; still the two highest blocks of buildings seen from Norwood on the crest of the ridge; so that the house itself, three-stories, with garrets above, commanded, in those comparatively smokeless days, a very notable view from its garret windows, of the Norwood hills on one side, and the winter sunrise over them; and of the valley of the Thames on the other, with Windsor telescopically clear in the distance, and Harrow, conspicuous always in fine weather to open vision against the summer sunset. It had front and back garden in sufficient proportion to its size; the front, richly set with old evergreens, and well-grown lilac and laburnum; the back, seventy yards long by twenty wide, renowned over all the hill for its pears and apples, which had been chosen with extreme care by our predecessor (shame on me to forget the name of a man to whom I owe so much!)—and possessing also a strong old mulberry tree, a tall white-heart cherry tree, a black Kentish one, and an almost unbroken hedge, all round, of alternate gooseberry and currant bush; decked, in due season (for the ground was wholly beneficent), with magical splendor of abundant fruit: fresh green, soft amber, and rough-bristled crimson bending the spinous branches; clustered pearl and pendent ruby joyfully discoverable under the large leaves that looked like vine.

The differences of primal importance which I observed between the nature of this garden, and that of Eden, as I had imagined it, were, that, in this one, *all* the fruit was

forbidden; and there were no companionable beasts: in other respects the little domain answered every purpose of Paradise to me; and the climate, in that cycle of our years, allowed me to pass most of my life in it. My mother never gave me more to learn than she knew I could easily get learned, if I set myself honestly to work, by twelve o'clock. She never allowed anything to disturb me when my task was set; if it was not said rightly by twelve o'clock, I was kept in till I knew it, and in general, even when Latin Grammar came to supplement the Psalms, I was my own master for at least an hour before half-past one dinner, and for the rest of the afternoon.

My mother, herself finding her chief personal pleasure in her flowers, was often planting or pruning beside me, at least if I chose to stay beside *her*. I never thought of doing anything behind her back which I would not have done before her face; and her presence was therefore no restraint to me; but, also, no particular pleasure, for, from having always been left so much alone, I had generally my own little affairs to see after; and, on the whole, by the time I was seven years old, was already getting too independent, mentally, even of my father and mother; and, having nobody else to be dependent upon, began to lead a very small, perky, contented, conceited, Cock-Robinson-Crusoe sort of life, in the central point which it appeared to me (as it must naturally appear to geometrical animals) that I occupied in the universe.

This was partly the fault of my father's modesty; and partly of his pride. He had so much more confidence in my mother's judgment as to such matters than in his own, that he never ventured even to help, much less to cross her, in the conduct of my education; on the other hand, in the fixed purpose of making an ecclesiastical gentleman of me, with the superfinest of manners, and access to the highest circles of fleshly and spiritual society, the visits to Croydon, where I entirely loved my aunt,[4] and young baker-cousins, became rarer and more rare: the society of our neighbors on the hill could not be had without

---

[4]The sister of Ruskin's mother, who married a baker in Croydon named Richardson.

breaking up our regular and sweetly selfish manner of living; and on the whole, I had nothing animate to care for, in a childish way, but myself, some nests of ants, which the gardener would never leave undisturbed for me, and a sociable bird or two; though I never had the sense of perseverance to make one really tame. But that was partly because, if ever I managed to bring one to be the least trustful of me, the cats got it.

Under these circumstances, what powers of imagination I possessed, either fastened themselves on inanimate things—the sky, the leaves, and pebbles, observable within the walls of Eden—or caught at any opportunity of flight into regions of romance, compatible with the objective realities of existence in the nineteenth century, within a mile and a quarter of Camberwell Green.

Herein my father, happily, though with no definite intention other than of pleasing me, when he found he could do so without infringing any of my mother's rules, became my guide. I was particularly fond of watching him shave; and was always allowed to come into his room in the morning (under the one in which I am now writing), to be the motionless witness of that operation. Over his dressing-table hung one of his own water-color drawings, made under the teaching of the elder Nasmyth; I believe, at the High School of Edinburgh. It was done in the early manner of tinting, which, just about the time when my father was at the High School, Dr. Munro[5] was teaching Turner; namely, in gray under-tints of Prussian blue and British ink, washed with warm color afterward on the lights. It represented Conway Castle, with its Frith, and, in the foreground, a cottage, a fisherman, and a boat at the water's edge.

When my father had finished shaving, he always told me a story about this picture. The custom began without any initial purpose of his, in consequence of my troublesome curiosity whether the fisherman lived in the cottage, and where he was going to in the boat. It being settled, for peace' sake,

that he *did* live in the cottage, and was going in the boat to fish near the castle, the plot of the drama afterward gradually thickened; and became, I believe, involved with that of the tragedy of *Douglas,* and of the *Castle Specter,*[6] in both of which pieces my father had performed in private theatricals, before my mother, and a select Edinburgh audience, when he was a boy of sixteen, and she, at grave twenty, a model housekeeper, and very scornful and religiously suspicious of theatricals. But she was never weary of telling me, in later years, how beautiful my father looked in his Highland dress, with the high black feathers.

In the afternoons, when my father returned (always punctually) from his business, he dined, at half-past four, in the front parlor, my mother sitting beside him to hear the events of the day, and give counsel and encouragement with respect to the same;—chiefly the last, for my father was apt to be vexed if orders for sherry fell the least short of their due standard, even for a day or two. I was never present at this time, however, and only avouch what I relate by hearsay and probable conjecture; for between four and six it would have been a grave misdemeanor in me if I so much as approached the parlor door. After that, in summer time, we were all in the garden as long as the day lasted; tea under the white-heart cherry tree; or in winter and rough weather, at six o'clock in the drawing-room,—I having my cup of milk, and slice of bread-and-butter, in a little recess, with a table in front of it, wholly sacred to me; and in which I remained in the evenings as an Idol in a niche, while my mother knitted, and my father read to her, —and to me, so far as I chose to listen.

The series of the Waverley novels, then drawing towards its close, was still the chief source of delight in all households caring for literature; and I can no more recollect the time when I did not know them than when I did not know the Bible; but I have still a vivid remembrance of my father's intense expression of sorrow mixed with scorn, as he threw down *Count Robert of Paris,* after

---

[5] Thomas Munro (1759–1833), a physician and an early patron of J. M. W. Turner (1775–1851), the landscape artist, who was responsible for Ruskin's beginning *Modern Painters.*

[6] The former by John Home (published in 1757), the latter by M. G. ("Monk") Lewis, played at Drury Lane Theater in 1798.

reading three or four pages; and knew that the life of Scott was ended: the scorn being a very complex and bitter feeling in him,— partly, indeed, of the book itself, but chiefly of the wretches who were tormenting and selling the wrecked intellect, and not a little, deep down, of the subtle dishonesty which had essentially caused the ruin. My father never could forgive Scott his concealment of the Ballantyne partnership.

Such being the salutary pleasures of Herne Hill, I have next with deeper gratitude to chronicle what I owe to my mother for the resolutely consistent lessons which so exercised me in the Scriptures as to make every word of them familiar to my ear in habitual music,—yet in that familarity reverenced, as transcending all thought, and ordaining all conduct.

This she effected, not by her own sayings or personal authority; but simply by compelling me to read the book thoroughly, for myself. As soon as I was able to read with fluency, she began a course of Bible work with me, which never ceased till I went to Oxford. She read alternate verses with me, watching, at first, every intonation of my voice, and correcting the false ones, till she made me understand the verse, if within my reach, rightly, and energetically. It might be beyond me altogether; that she did not care about; but she made sure that as soon as I got hold of it at all, I should get hold of it by the right end.

In this way she began with the first verse of Genesis, and went straight through, to the last verse of the Apocalypse; hard names, numbers, Levitical law, and all; and began again at Genesis the next day. If a name was hard, the better the exercise in pronunciation,—if the chapter was tiresome, the better lesson in patience,—if loathsome, the better lesson in faith that there was some use in its being so outspoken. After our chapters (from two to three a day, according to their length, the first thing after breakfast, and no interruption from servants allowed,— none from visitors, who either joined in the reading or had to stay upstairs,—and none from any visitings or excursions, except real traveling), I had to learn a few verses by heart, or repeat, to make sure I had not lost,

something of what was already known; and, with the chapters thus gradually possessed from the first word to the last, 1 had to learn the whole body of the fine old Scottish paraphrases, which are good, melodious, and forceful verse; and to which, together with the Bible itself, I owe the first cultivation of my ear in sound.

It is strange that of all the pieces of the Bible which my mother thus taught me, that which cost me most to learn, and which was, to my child's mind, chiefly repulsive—the 119th Psalm—has now become of all the most precious to me, in its overflowing and glorious passion of love for the Law of God, in opposition to the abuse of it by modern preachers of what they imagine to be His gospel.

But it is only by deliberate effort that I recall the long morning hours of toil, as regular as sunrise,—toil on both sides equal— by which, year after year, my mother forced me to learn these paraphrases, and chapters (the eighth of 1st Kings being one—try it, good reader, in a leisure hour!), allowing not so much as a syllable to be missed or misplaced; while every sentence was required to be said over and over again till she was satisfied with the accent of it. I recollect a struggle between us of about three weeks, concerning the accent of the "of" in the lines

Shall any following spring revive
The ashes of the urn?[7]—

I insisting, partly in childish obstinacy, and partly in true instinct for rhythm (being wholly careless on the subject both of urns and their contents), on reciting it with an accented *of*. It was not, I say, till after three weeks' labor, that my mother got the accent lightened on the "of" and laid on the ashes, to her mind. But had it taken three years she would have done it, having once undertaken to do it. And, assuredly, had she not done it,—well, there's no knowing what would have happened; but I'm very thankful she *did*.

I have just opened my oldest (in use) Bible,—a small, closely, and very neatly printed volume it is, printed in Edinburgh by

[7]By John Logan, in one of the *Scottish Church Paraphrases*.

Sir D. Hunter Blair and J. Bruce, Printers of the King's Most Excellent Majesty, in 1816. Yellow, now, with age; and flexible, but not unclean, with much use; except that the lower corners of the pages at 8th of 1st 5 Kings, and 32nd Deuteronomy, are worn somewhat thin and dark, the learning of these two chapters having cost me much pains. My mother's list of the chapters with which, thus learned, she established my 10 soul in life, has just fallen out of it. I will take what indulgence the incurious reader can give me, for printing the list thus accidentally occurrent :—

Exodus,	chapters	15th and 20th.
2 Samuel,	"	1st, from 17th verse to end.
1 Kings,	"	8th.

Psalms,	chapters	23rd, 32nd, 90th, 91st, 103rd, 112th, 119th, 139th.
Proverbs,	"	2nd, 3rd, 8th, 12th.
Isaiah,	"	58th.
Matthew,	"	5th, 6th, 7th.
Acts,	"	26th.
1 Corinthians,	"	13th, 15th.
James,	"	4th.
Revelation,	"	5th, 6th.

And, truly, though I have picked up the elements of a little further knowledge—in mathematics, meteorology, and the like, in after life,—and owe not a little to the teach-15 ing of many people, this maternal installation of my mind in that property of chapters I count very confidently the most precious, and, on the whole, the one *essential* part of all my education.

MODERN PAINTERS

Definition of Greatness in Art[1]

In the 15th Lecture of Sir Joshua Reynolds,[2] incidental notice is taken of the distinction between those excellences in the 5 painter which belong to him *as such,* and those which belong to him in common with all men of intellect, the general and exalted powers of which art is the evidence and expression, not the subject. But the distinc-10 tion is not there dwelt upon as it should be, for it is owing to the slight attention ordinarily paid to it, that criticism is open to every form of coxcombry, and liable to every phase of error. It is a distinction on which 15 depend all sound judgment of the rank of the artist, and all just appreciation of the dignity of art.

Painting, or art generally, as such, with all its technicalities, difficulties, and particular 20 ends, is nothing but a noble and expressive language, invaluable as the vehicle of thought, but by itself nothing. He who has learned what is commonly considered the whole art of painting, that is, the art of representing any natural object faithfully, has as yet only learned the language by which his thoughts are to be expressed. He has 5 done just as much towards being that which we ought to respect as a great painter, as a man who has learned how to express himself grammatically and melodiously has towards being a great poet. The language is, in-10 deed, more difficult of acquirement in the one case than in the other, and possesses more power of delighting the sense, while it speaks to the intellect ; but it is, nevertheless, nothing more than language, and all those 15 excellences which are peculiar to the painter as such, are merely what rhythm, melody, precision, and force are in the words of the orator and the poet, necessary to their greatness, but not the tests of their greatness. It 20 is not by the mode of representing and saying, but by what is represented and said, that the respective greatness either of the painter or the writer is to be finally determined.

Speaking with strict propriety, therefore, 25 we should call a man a great painter only as he excelled in precision and force in the language of lines, and a great versifier, as he excelled in precision and force in the language of words. A great poet would then be a

---

[1]Vol. I (published in 1843), part I, section 1, chapter 2.

[2]During his presidency of the Royal Academy Reynolds delivered a series of lectures, or discourses as they are usually called (1769–1790).

term strictly, and in precisely the same sense, applicable to both, if warranted by the character of the images or thoughts which each in their respective languages conveyed.

Take, for instance, one of the most perfect poems or pictures (I use the words as synonymous) which modern times have seen: —the "Old Shepherd's Chief-mourner."[3] Here the exquisite execution of the glossy and crisp hair of the dog, the bright sharp touching of the green bough beside it, the clear[4] painting of the wood of the coffin and the folds of the blanket, are language— language clear and expressive in the highest degree. But the close pressure of the dog's breast against the wood, the convulsive clinging of the paws, which has dragged the blanket off the trestle, the total powerlessness of the head laid, close and motionless, upon its folds, the fixed and tearful fall of the eye in its utter hopelessness, the rigidity of repose which marks that there has been no motion nor change in the trance of agony since the last blow was struck on the coffin-lid, the quietness and gloom of the chamber, the spectacles marking the place where the Bible was last closed, indicating how lonely has been the life, how unwatched the departure, of him who is now laid solitary in his sleep; —these are all thoughts—thoughts by which the picture is separated at once from hundreds of equal merit, as far as mere painting goes, by which it ranks as a work of high art, and stamps its author, not as the neat imitator of the texture of a skin, or the fold of a drapery, but as the Man of Mind.

It is not, however, always easy, either in painting or literature, to determine where the influence of language stops, and where that of thought begins. Many thoughts are so dependent upon the language in which they are clothed, that they would lose half their beauty if otherwise expressed. But the highest thoughts are those which are least dependent on language, and the dignity of any composition, and praise to which it is entitled, are in exact proportion to its inde-

pendency of language or expression. A composition is indeed usually most perfect, when to such intrinsic dignity is added all that expression can do to attract and adorn; but in every case of supreme excellence this all becomes as nothing. We are more gratified by the simplest lines or words which can suggest the idea in its own naked beauty, than by the robe and the gem which conceal while they decorate; we are better pleased to feel by their absence how little they could bestow, than by their presence how much they can destroy.

There is therefore a distinction to be made between what is ornamental in language and what is expressive. That part of it which is necessary to the embodying and conveying of the thought is worthy of respect and attention as necessary to excellence, though not the test of it. But that part of it which is decorative has little more to do with the intrinsic excellence of the picture than the frame or the varnishing of it. And this caution in distinguishing between the ornamental and the expressive is peculiarly necessary in painting: for in the language of words it is nearly impossible for that which is not expressive to be beautiful, except by mere rhythm or melody, any sacrifice to which is immediately stigmatized as error. But the beauty of mere language in painting is not only very attractive and entertaining to the spectator, but requires for its attainment no small exertion of mind and devotion of time by the artist. Hence, in art, men have frequently fancied that they were becoming rhetoricians and poets when they were only learning to speak melodiously, and the judge has over and over again advanced to the honor of authors those who were never more than ornamental writing-masters.

Most pictures of the Dutch school, for instance, excepting always those of Rubens, Vandyke, and Rembrandt, are ostentatious exhibitions of the artist's power of speech, the clear and vigorous elocution of useless and senseless words; while the early efforts of Cimabue[5] and Giotto[6] are the burning messages of prophecy, delivered by the stam-

---

[3] By Sir Edwin Landseer, now in the Victoria and Albert South Kensington Museum.

[4] "Clear" is printed in all the editions, and so is retained here, but Ruskin originally wrote "clever" and probably never detected the misprint.

[5] Florentine painter (1240?–1302?).

[6] Florentine painter and architect (1276?–1337?).

mering lips of infants. It is not by ranking the former as more than mechanics, or the latter as less than artists, that the taste of the multitude, always awake to the lowest pleasures which art can bestow, and blunt to the highest, is to be formed or elevated. It must be the part of the judicious critic carefully to distinguish what is language, and what is thought, and to rank and praise pictures chiefly for the latter, considering the former as a totally inferior excellence, and one which cannot be compared with nor weighed against thought in any way or in any degree whatsoever. The picture which has the nobler and more numerous ideas, however awkwardly expressed, is a greater and a better picture than that which has the less noble and less numerous ideas, however beautifully expressed. No weight, nor mass, nor beauty of execution, can outweigh one grain or fragment of thought. Three pen-strokes of Raffaelle are a greater and a better picture than the most finished work that ever Carlo Dolci[7] polished into inanity. A finished work of a great artist is only better than its sketch, if the sources of pleasure belonging to color and realization—valuable in themselves—are so employed as to increase the impressiveness of the thought. But if one atom of thought has vanished, all color, all finish, all execution, all ornament, are too dearly bought. Nothing but thought can pay for thought, and the instant that the increasing refinement or finish of the picture begins to be paid for by the loss of the faintest shadow of an idea, that instant all refinement or finish is an excrescence and a deformity.

Yet although in all our speculations on art, language is thus to be distinguished from, and held subordinate to, that which it conveys, we must still remember that there are certain ideas inherent in language itself, and that, strictly speaking, every pleasure connected with art has in it some reference to the intellect. The mere sensual pleasure of the eye, received from the most brilliant piece of coloring, is as nothing to that which it receives from a crystal prism, except as it depends on our perception of a certain meaning and intended arrangement of color,

which has been the subject of intellect. Nay, the term idea, according to Locke's[8] definition of it, will extend even to the sensual impressions themselves as far as they are "things which the mind occupies itself about in thinking"; that is, not as they are felt by the eye only, but as they are received by the mind through the eye. So that, if I say that the greatest picture is that which conveys to the mind of the spectator the greatest number of the greatest ideas, I have a definition which will include as subjects of comparison every pleasure which art is capable of conveying. If I were to say, on the contrary, that the best picture was that which most closely imitated nature, I should assume that art could only please by imitating nature; and I should cast out of the pale of criticism those parts of works of art which are not imitative, that is to say, intrinsic beauties of color and form, and those works of art wholly, which, like the Arabesques of Raffaelle in the Loggias,[9] are not imitative at all. Now, I want a definition of art wide enough to include all its varieties of aim. I do not say, therefore, that the art is greatest which gives most pleasure, because perhaps there is some art whose end is to teach, and not to please. I do not say that the art is greatest which teaches us most, because perhaps there is some art whose end is to please, and not to teach. I do not say that the art is greatest which imitates best, because perhaps there is some art whose end is to create and not to imitate. But I say that the art is greatest which conveys to the mind of the spectator, by any means whatsoever, the greatest number of the greatest ideas; and I call an idea great in proportion as it is received by a higher faculty of the mind, and as it more fully occupies, and in occupying, exercises and exalts, the faculty by which it is received.

If this, then, be the definition of great art, that of a great artist naturally follows. He is the greatest artist who has embodied, in the sum of his works, the greatest number of the greatest ideas.

---

[7] Tuscan painter (1616–1686).

[8] John Locke (1632–1704). The following quotation comes from Bk. II, chap. i, of the *Essay Concerning Human Understanding*.

[9] Of the Vatican, Rome.

La Riccia[1]

THERE is, in the first room of the National Gallery, a landscape attributed to Gaspar Poussin,[2] called sometimes Aricia, sometimes Le or La Riccia, according to the fancy of catalogue printers. Whether it can be supposed to resemble the ancient Aricia, now La Riccia, close to Albano, I will not take upon me to determine, seeing that most of the towns of these old masters are quite as like one place as another; but, at any rate, it is a town on a hill, wooded with two-and-thirty bushes, of very uniform size, and possessing about the same number of leaves each. These bushes are all painted in with one dull opaque brown, becoming very slightly greenish toward the lights, and discover in one place a bit of rock, which of course would in nature have been cool and gray beside the lustrous hues of foliage, and which, therefore, being moreover completely in shade, is consistently and scientifically painted of a very clear, pretty, and positive brick red, the only thing like color in the picture. The foreground is a piece of road which, in order to make allowance for its greater nearness, for its being completely in light, and, it may be presumed, for the quantity of vegetation usually present on carriage-roads, is given in a very cool green gray; and the truth of the picture is completed by a number of dots in the sky on the right, with a stalk to them, of a sober and similar brown.[3]

Not long ago, I was slowly descending this very bit of carriage-road, the first turn after you leave Albano, not a little impeded by the worthy successors of the ancient prototypes of Veiento.[4] It had been wild weather when I left Rome, and all across the Campagna the clouds were sweeping in sulphurous blue, with a clap of thunder or two, and breaking gleams of sun along the Claudian aqueduct lighting up the infinity of its arches like the bridge of chaos. But as I climbed the long slope of the Alban Mount, the storm swept finally to the north, and the noble outline of the domes of Albano, and graceful darkness of its ilex grove rose against pure streaks of alternate blue and amber; the upper sky gradually flushing through the last fragments of rain-cloud in deep palpitating azure, half ether and half dew. The noonday sun came slanting down the rocky slopes of La Riccia, and their masses of entangled and tall foliage, whose autumnal tints were mixed with the wet verdure of a thousand evergreens, were penetrated with it as with rain. I cannot call it color, it was conflagration. Purple, and crimson, and scarlet, like the curtains of God's tabernacle, the rejoicing trees sank into the valley in showers of light, every separate leaf quivering with buoyant and burning life; each, as it turned to reflect or to transmit the sunbeam, first a torch and then an emerald. Far up into the recesses of the valley, the green vistas arched like the hollows of mighty waves of some crystalline sea, with the arbutus flowers dashed along their flanks for foam, and silver flakes of orange spray tossed into the air around them, breaking over the gray walls of rock into a thousand separate stars, fading and kindling alternately as the weak wind lifted and let them fall. Every glade of grass burned like the golden floor of heaven, opening in sudden gleams as the foliage broke and closed above it, as sheet-lightning opens in a cloud at sunset; the motionless masses of dark rock—dark though flushed with scarlet lichen, casting their quiet shadows across its restless radiance, the fountain underneath them filling its marble hollow with blue mist and fitful sound; and over all, the multitudinous bars of amber and rose, the sacred clouds that have no darkness, and only exist to illumine, were seen in fathomless intervals between the solemn and orbed repose of the stone pines, passing to lose themselves in the last, white, blinding luster of the measureless line where the Campagna melted into the blaze of the sea.

---

[1] Volume I, part II, section 2, from chapter 2, "Of Truth of Color."

[2] French landscape painter (1613–1675), brother-in-law and pupil of the more famous Nicolas Poussin.

[3] It should be said that this picture was very dirty when Ruskin wrote the first volume of *Modern Painters*. In 1880 it was cleaned and varnished.

[4] I. e., by beggars (Ruskin refers to a passage in Juvenal—*Sat.*, IV, 116—where, however, it is one Catullus, and not Veiento, who is described as fit only to beg alms on the Arician road).

Of the Pathetic Fallacy[1]

GERMAN dullness, and English affectation, have of late much multiplied among us the use of two of the most objectionable words that were ever coined by the troublesomeness of metaphysicians,—namely, "Objective" and "Subjective."

No words can be more exquisitely, and in all points, useless; and I merely speak of them that I may, at once and forever, get them out of my way, and out of my reader's. But to get that done, they must be explained.

The word "Blue," say certain philosophers, means the sensation of color which the human eye receives in looking at the open sky, or at a bell-gentian.

Now, say they farther, as this sensation can only be felt when the eye is turned to the object, and as, therefore, no such sensation is produced by the object when nobody looks at it, therefore the thing, when it is not looked at, is not blue; and thus (say they) there are many qualities of things which depend as much on something else as on themselves. To be sweet, a thing must have a taster; it is only sweet while it is being tasted, and if the tongue had not the capacity of taste, then the sugar would not have the quality of sweetness.

And then they agree that the qualities of things which thus depend upon our perception of them, and upon our human nature as affected by them, shall be called Subjective; and the qualities of things which they always have, irrespective of any other nature, as roundness or squareness, shall be called Objective.

From these ingenious views the step is very easy to a farther opinion, that it does not much matter what things are in themselves, but only what they are to us; and that the only real truth of them is their appearance to, or effect upon, us. From which position, with a hearty desire for mystification, and much egotism, selfishness, shallowness, and impertinence, a philosopher may easily go so far as to believe, and say, that everything in the world depends upon his seeing or thinking of it, and that nothing, therefore, exists but what he sees or thinks of.

Now, to get rid of all these ambiguities and troublesome words at once, be it observed that the word "Blue" does *not* mean the *sensation* caused by a gentian on the human eye; but it means the *power* of producing that sensation: and this power is always there, in the thing, whether we are there to experience it or not, and would remain there though there were not left a man on the face of the earth. Precisely in the same way gunpowder has a power of exploding. It will not explode if you put no match to it. But it has always the power of so exploding, and is therefore called an explosive compound, which it very positively and assuredly is, whatever philosophy may say to the contrary.

In like manner, a gentian does not produce the sensation of blueness, if you don't look at it. But it has always the power of doing so; its particles being everlastingly so arranged by its Maker. And, therefore, the gentian and the sky are always verily blue, whatever philosophy may say to the contrary; and if you do not see them blue when you look at them, it is not their fault, but yours.[2]

Hence I would say to these philosophers: If, instead of using the sonorous phrase, "It is objectively so," you will use the plain old phrase, "It *is* so," and if instead of the sonorous phrase, "It is subjectively so," you will say, in plain old English, "It does so," or "It seems so to me," you will, on the whole, be more intelligible to your fellow-creatures; and besides, if you find that a thing which generally "does so" to other people (as a gentian looks blue to most men), does *not* so to you, on any particular occasion, you will not fall into the impertinence of saying, that the thing is not so, or did not so, but you will

---

[1]Vol. III (published in 1856), part IV, chap. 12.

[2]It is quite true, that in all qualities involving sensation, there may be a doubt whether different people receive the same sensation from the same thing . . . ; but, though this makes such facts not distinctly explicable, it does not alter the facts themselves. I derive a certain sensation, which I call sweetness, from sugar. That is a fact. Another person feels a sensation, which *he* also calls sweetness, from sugar. That is also a fact. The sugar's power to produce these two sensations, which we suppose to be, and which are, in all probability, very nearly the same in both of us, and, on the whole, in the human race, is its sweetness (Ruskin's note).

say simply (what you will be all the better for speedily finding out), that something is the matter with you. If you find that you cannot explode the gunpowder, you will not declare that all gunpowder is subjective, and all explosion imaginary, but you will simply suspect and declare yourself to be an ill-made match. Which, on the whole, though there may be a distant chance of a mistake about it, is, nevertheless, the wisest conclu- 10 sion you can come to until further experiment.

Now, therefore, putting these tiresome and absurd words quite out of our way, we may go on at our ease to examine the point 15 in question,—namely, the difference between the ordinary, proper, and true appearances of things to us; and the extraordinary, or false appearances, when we are under the influence of emotion, or contemplative fancy; 20 false appearances, I say, as being entirely unconnected with any real power or character in the object, and only imputed to it by us.

For instance—

The spendthrift crocus, bursting through the mold
Naked and shivering, with his cup of gold.[3]

This is very beautiful, and yet very untrue. The crocus is not a spendthrift, but a 30 hardy plant; its yellow is not gold, but saffron. How is it that we enjoy so much the having it put into our heads that it is anything else than a plain crocus?

It is an important question. For, through- 35 out our past reasonings about art, we have always found that nothing could be good or useful, or ultimately pleasurable, which was untrue. But here is something pleasurable in written poetry, which is nevertheless un- 40 true. And what is more, if we think over our favorite poetry, we shall find it full of this kind of fallacy, and that we like it all the more for being so.

It will appear also, on consideration of the 45 matter, that this fallacy is of two principal kinds. Either, as in this case of the crocus, it is the fallacy of wilful fancy, which involves no real expectation that it will be believed; or else it is a fallacy caused by an 50 excited state of the feelings, making us, for

[3] From Oliver Wendell Holmes's *Astraea* (1850).

the time, more or less irrational. Of the cheating of the fancy we shall have to speak presently; but, in this chapter, I want to examine the nature of the other error, that which the mind admits when affected strongly by emotion. Thus, for instance, in *Alton Locke*,[4]—

They rowed her in across the rolling foam—
The cruel, crawling foam.

The foam is not cruel, neither does it crawl. The state of mind which attributes to it these characters of a living creature is one in which the reason is unhinged by grief. All violent feelings have the same effect. They produce in us a falseness in all our impressions of external things, which I would generally characterize as the "pathetic fallacy."

Now we are in the habit of considering this fallacy as eminently a character of poetical description, and the temper of mind in which we allow it, as one eminently poetical, because passionate. But I believe, if we look well into the matter, that we shall find the greatest poets do not often admit this kind of falseness,—that it is only the second order of poets who much delight in it.[5]

[4] Charles Kingsley's novel (1850). The quotation is from a song in chap. xxvi.

[5] I admit two orders of poets, but no third; and by these two orders I mean the creative (Shakespeare, Homer, Dante), and Reflective or Perceptive (Wordsworth, Keats, Tennyson). But both of these must be *first*-rate in their range, though their range is different; and with poetry second-rate in *quality* no one ought to be allowed to trouble mankind. There is quite enough of the best,—much more than we can ever read or enjoy in the length of a life; and it is a literal wrong or sin in any person to encumber us with inferior work. I have no patience with apologies made by young pseudo-poets, "that they believe there is *some* good in what they have written: that they hope to do better in time," etc. *Some* good! If there is not *all* good, there is no good. If they ever hope to do better, why do they trouble us now? Let them rather courageously burn all they have done, and wait for the better days. There are few men, ordinarily educated, who in moments of strong feeling could not strike out a poetical thought, and afterwards polish it so as to be presentable. But men of sense know better than so to waste their time; and those who sincerely love poetry, know the touch of the master's hand on the chords too well to fumble among them after him. Nay, more than this, all inferior poetry is an injury to the good, inasmuch as it takes away the freshness of rimes, blunders upon and gives a wretched commonalty to good thoughts; and, in general, adds

Thus, when Dante describes the spirits falling from the bank of Acheron "as dead leaves flutter from a bough,"[6] he gives the most perfect image possible of their utter lightness, feebleness, passiveness, and scattering agony of despair, without, however, for an instant losing his own clear perception that *these* are souls, and *those* are leaves; he makes no confusion of one with the other. But when Coleridge speaks of

The one red leaf, the last of its clan,
That dances as often as dance it can,[7]

he has a morbid, that is to say, a so far false, idea about the leaf; he fancies a life in it, and will, which there are not; confuses its powerlessness with choice, its fading death with merriment, and the wind that shakes it with music. Here, however, there is some beauty, even in the morbid passage; but take an instance in Homer and Pope. Without the knowledge of Ulysses, Elpenor, his youngest follower, has fallen from an upper chamber in the Circean palace, and has been left dead, unmissed by his leader or companions, in the haste of their departure. They cross the sea to the Cimmerian land; and Ulysses summons the shades from Tartarus. The first which appears is that of the lost Elpenor. Ulysses, amazed, and in exactly the spirit of bitter and terrified lightness which is seen in Hamlet,[8] addresses the spirit with the simple, startled words:—

"Elpenor! How camest thou under the shadowy darkness? Hast thou come faster on foot than I in my black ship?"[9]

Which Pope renders thus:—

O, say, what angry power Elpenor led
To glide in shades, and wander with the dead?

How could thy soul, by realms and seas disjoined,
Outfly the nimble sail, and leave the lagging wind?

I sincerely hope the reader finds no pleasure here, either in the nimbleness of the sail, or the laziness of the wind! And yet how is it that these conceits are so painful now, when they have been pleasant to us in the other instances?

For a very simple reason. They are not a *pathetic* fallacy at all, for they are put into the mouth of the wrong passion—a passion which never could possibly have spoken them —agonized curiosity. Ulysses wants to know the facts of the matter; and the very last thing his mind could do at the moment would be to pause, or suggest in any wise what was *not* a fact. The delay in the first three lines, and conceit in the last, jar upon us instantly like the most frightful discord in music. No poet of true imaginative power could possibly have written the passage.[10]

Therefore we see that the spirit of truth must guide us in some sort, even in our enjoyment of fallacy. Coleridge's fallacy has no discord in it, but Pope's has set our teeth on edge. Without farther questioning, I will endeavor to state the main bearings of this matter.

The temperament which admits the pathetic fallacy, is, as I said above, that of a mind and body in some sort too weak to deal fully with what is before them or upon them; borne away, or overclouded, or overdazzled by emotion; and it is a more or less noble state, according to the force of the emotion which has induced it. For it is no credit to a man that he is not morbid or inaccurate

---

to the weight of human weariness in a most woeful and culpable manner. There are few thoughts likely to come across ordinary men, which have not already been expressed by greater men in the best possible way; and it is a wiser, more generous, more noble thing to remember and point out the perfect words, than to invent poorer ones, wherewith to encumber temporarily the world (Ruskin's note).

[6]*Inferno,* iii, 112.

[7]*Christabel,* Part I, 49–50.

[8]"Well said, old mole! canst work i' the ground so fast?" (Ruskin's note.) From *Hamlet,* I, v, 162.

[9]*Odyssey,* xi, 56–57.

[10]It is worth while comparing the way a similar question is put by the exquisite sincerity of Keats:—

"He wept, and his bright tears
Went trickling down the golden bow he held.
Thus, with half-shut, suffuséd eyes, he stood;
While from beneath some cumbrous boughs hard by
With solemn step an awful goddess came,
And there was purport in her looks for him,
Which he with eager guess began to read
Perplexed, the while melodiously he said,
'*How camest thou over the unfooted sea?*'"
(Ruskin's note; quotation from *Hyperion,* III, 42–50.)

in his perceptions, when he has no strength of feeling to warp them; and it is in general a sign of higher capacity and stand in the ranks of being, that the emotions should be strong enough to vanquish, partly, the in- tellect, and make it believe what they choose. But it is still a grander condition when the intellect also rises, till it is strong enough to assert its rule against, or together with, the utmost efforts of the passions; and the whole man stands in an iron glow, white hot, per- haps, but still strong, and in no wise evapo- rating; even if he melts, losing none of his weight.

So, then, we have the three ranks: the man who perceives rightly, because he does not feel, and to whom the primrose is very ac- curately the primrose, because he does not love it. Then, secondly, the man who per- ceives wrongly, because he feels, and to whom the primrose is anything else than a primrose: a star, or a sun, or a fairy's shield, or a forsaken maiden. And then, lastly, there is the man who perceives rightly in spite of his feelings, and to whom the prim- rose is forever nothing else than itself—a little flower apprehended in the very plain and leafy fact of it, whatever and how many soever the associations and passions may be that crowd around it. And, in general, these three classes may be rated in compara- tive order, as the men who are not poets at all, and the poets of the second order, and the poets of the first; only however great a man may be, there are always some subjects which *ought* to throw him off his balance; some, by which his poor human capacity of thought should be conquered, and brought into the inaccurate and vague state of per- ception, so that the language of the highest inspiration becomes broken, obscure, and wild in metaphor, resembling that of the weaker man, overborne by weaker things.

And thus, in full, there are four classes: the men who feel nothing, and therefore see truly; the men who feel strongly, think weakly, and see untruly (second order of poets); the men who feel strongly, think strongly, and see truly (first order of poets); and the men who, strong as human creatures can be, are yet submitted to influences stronger than they, and see in a sort untruly,

because what they see is inconceivably above them. This last is the usual condition of prophetic inspiration.

I separate these classes, in order that their character may be clearly understood; but of course they are united each to the other by imperceptible transitions, and the same mind, according to the influences to which it is subjected, passes at different times into the various states. Still, the difference between the great and less man is, on the whole, chiefly in this point of *alterability*. That is to say, the one knows too much, and per- ceives and feels too much of the past and future, and of all things beside and around that which immediately affects him, to be in any wise shaken by it. His mind is made up; his thoughts have an accustomed cur- rent; his ways are steadfast; it is not this or that new sight which will at once unbalance him. He is tender to impression at the sur- face, like a rock with deep moss upon it; but there is too much mass of him to be moved. The smaller man, with the same degree of sensibility, is at once carried off his feet; he wants to do something he did not want to do before; he views all the universe in a new light through his tears; he is gay or enthusi- astic, melancholy or passionate, as things come and go to him. Therefore the high creative poet might even be thought, to a great extent, impassive (as shallow people think Dante stern), receiving indeed all feel- ings to the full, but having a great center of reflection and knowledge in which he stands serene, and watches the feeling, as it were, from afar off.

Dante, in his most intense moods, has en- tire command of himself, and can look around calmly, at all moments, for the image or the word that will best tell what he sees to the upper or lower world. But Keats and Tennyson, and the poets of the second order, are generally themselves subdued by the feelings under which they write, or, at least, write as choosing to be so; and there- fore admit certain expressions and modes of thought which are in some sort diseased or false.

Now so long as we see that the *feeling* is true, we pardon, or are even pleased by, the confessed fallacy of sight which it induces:

we are pleased, for instance, with those lines of Kingsley's above quoted, not because they fallaciously describe foam, but because they faithfully describe sorrow. But the moment the mind of the speaker becomes cold, that moment every such expression becomes untrue, as being forever untrue in the external facts. And there is no greater baseness in literature than the habit of using these metaphorical expressions in cool blood. An inspired writer, in full impetuosity of passion, may speak wisely and truly of "raging waves of the sea foaming out their own shame";[11] but it is only the basest writer who cannot speak of the sea without talking of "raging waves," "remorseless floods," "ravenous billows," etc.; and it is one of the signs of the highest power in a writer to check all such habits of thought, and to keep his eyes fixed firmly on the *pure fact,* out of which if any feeling comes to him or his reader, he knows it must be a true one.

To keep to the waves, I forget who it is who represents a man in despair desiring that his body may be cast into the sea,

Whose changing mound, and foam that passed
    away,
Might mock the eye that questioned where I lay.

Observe, there is not here a single false, or even overcharged, expression. "Mound" of the sea wave is perfectly simple and true; "changing" is as familiar as may be; "foam that passed away," strictly literal; and the whole line descriptive of the reality with a degree of accuracy which I know not any other verse, in the range of poetry, that altogether equals. For most people have not a distinct idea of the clumsiness and massiveness of a large wave. The word "wave" is used too generally of ripples and breakers, and bendings in light drapery or grass: it does not by itself convey a perfect image. But the word "mound" is heavy, large, dark, definite; there is no mistaking the kind of wave meant, nor missing the sight of it. Then the term "changing" has a peculiar force also. Most people think of waves as rising and falling. But if they look at the sea carefully, they will perceive that the waves do not rise and fall. They change.

Change both place and form, but they do not fall; one wave goes on, and on, and still on; now lower, now higher, now tossing its mane like a horse, now building itself together like a wall, now shaking, now steady, but still the same wave, till at last it seems struck by something, and changes, one knows not how, —becomes another wave.

The close of the line insists on this image, and paints it still more perfectly,—"foam that passed away." Not merely melting, disappearing, but passing on, out of sight, on the career of the wave. Then, having put the absolute ocean fact as far as he may before our eyes, the poet leaves us to feel about it as we may, and to trace for ourselves the opposite fact,—the image of the green mounds that do not change, and the white and written stones that do not pass away; and thence to follow out also the associated images of the calm life with the quiet grave, and the despairing life with the fading foam—

Let no man move his bones.
As for Samaria, her king is cut off like the foam upon the water.[12]

But nothing of this is actually told or pointed out, and the expressions, as they stand, are perfectly severe and accurate, utterly uninfluenced by the firmly governed emotion of the writer. Even the word "mock" is hardly an exception, as it may stand merely for "deceive" or "defeat," without implying any impersonation of the waves.

It may be well, perhaps, to give one or two more instances to show the peculiar dignity possessed by all passages, which thus limit their expression to the pure fact, and leave the hearer to gather what he can from it. Here is a notable one from the *Iliad.* Helen, looking from the Scaean gate of Troy over the Grecian host, and telling Priam the names of its captains, says at last:—

I see all the other dark-eyed Greeks; but two I cannot see,—Castor and Pollux,—whom one mother bore with me. Have they not followed from fair Lacedaemon, or have they in-

---

[11] Jude, 13.

[12] II Kings, 23:18; Hosea, 10:7.

deed come in their sea-wandering ships, but now will not enter into the battle of men, fearing the shame and the scorn that is in Me?

Then Homer :—

So she spoke. But them, already, the life-giving earth possessed, there in Lacedaemon, in the dear fatherland.[13]

Note, here, the high poetical truth carried to the extreme. The poet has to speak of the earth in sadness, but he will not let that sadness affect or change his thoughts of it. No; though Castor and Pollux be dead, yet the earth is our mother still, fruitful, life-giving. These are the facts of the thing. I see nothing else than these. Make what you will of them.

Take another very notable instance from Casimir de la Vigne's terrible ballad, "La Toilette de Constance." I must quote a few lines out of it here and there, to enable the reader who has not the book by him, to understand its close.

"Vite, Anna! vite; au miroir!
　　Plus vite, Anna. L'heure s'avance,
Et je vais au bal ce soir
　　Chez l'ambassadeur de France.

"Y pensez-vous? ils sont fanés, ces noeuds;
　Ils sont d'hier; mon Dieu, comme tout passe!
Que du réseau qui retient mes cheveux
　Les glands d'azur retombent avec grâce.
Plus haut! Plus bas! Vous ne comprenez
　　rien!
Que sur mon front ce saphir étincelle:
Vous me piquez, maladroite. Ah, c'est bien,
Bien,—chère Anna! Je t'aime, je suis belle!

"Vite, j'en crois mon miroir,
　　Et mon coeur bat d'espérance.
Vite, Anna, je vais ce soir
　　Chez l'ambassadeur de France.

"Celui qu'en vain je voudrais oublier . . .
　　(Anna, ma robe) il y sera, j'espère.
　　(Ah, fi! profane, est-ce là mon collier?
Quoi! ces grains d'or bénits par le Saint-
　　Père!)

Il y sera; Dieu, s'il pressait ma main,
　　En y pensant à peine je respire:
Frère Anselmo doit m'entendre demain,
　　Comment ferai-je, Anna, pour tout lui
　　dire? . . .

"Vite! un coup d'œil au miroir,
　　Le dernier. ——J'ai l'assurance
Qu'on va m'adorer ce soir
　　Chez l'ambassadeur de France."

"Près du foyer, Constance s'admirait.
　　Dieu! sur sa robe il vole une étincelle!
Au feu! Courez! Quand l'espoir l'enivrait,
　　Tout perdre ainsi! Quoi! Mourir,—et si
　　belle!
L'horrible feu ronge avec volupté
　　Ses bras, son sein, et l'entoure, et s'élève,
Et sans pitié dévore sa beauté,
　　Ses dix-huit ans, hélas, et son doux rêve!

"Adieu, bal, plaisir, amour!
　　On se dit, "Pauvre Constance."
Et l'on dansa, jusqu'au jour,
　　Chez l'ambassadeur de France.[14]

---

[13]*Iliad*, III, 234-245. In the manuscript Ruskin notes "the insurpassably tender irony in the epithet —'life-giving earth'—of the grave"; and he goes on to compare the passage with Thackeray's ironic revelation of the death of George Osborne (*Vanity Fair*, chapter xxxii).

[14]From the *Oeuvres Posthumes* (1855) of the French poet Casimir Delavigne (1793-1843). Three stanzas with their refrains are omitted after the second stanza. The passage quoted may be translated as follows: "'Quick, Anna! quick; to the mirror! Quicker, Anna. The time draws near, and this evening I go to the ball at the house of the French Ambassador.—Do you know, these knots are drooping; they are yesterday's; Heavens, how all things pass! Let the blue tassels fall gracefully from the net that holds my hair. Higher! Lower! You understand nothing! Let this sapphire sparkle on my forehead. You prick me, clumsy. Ah, that's fine, fine, dear Anna! I love you, I'm beautiful.—Quick, I believe my mirror, and my heart beats with hope. Quick, Anna, this evening I go to the house of the French Ambassador.—The one I vainly hoped I should forget . . . (Anna, my gown) he will be there, I hope. (Ah, fie! profane one, is that my necklace? What! these gold beads blessed by the Holy Father!) He will be there; Heavens, if he presses my hand, thinking of that I can hardly breathe: Brother Anselm is to hear me in confession tomorrow; what shall I do, Anna, tell him all? . . . —Quick! A glance at the mirror, the last. I am sure that this evening I am going to be adored at the house of the French Ambassador'—Near the hearth, Constance was pleased with herself. Heavens! a spark flew on her gown! Fire! Run! While drunk with hope, to lose all in this way! What! To die,—and so beautiful! The horrible fire gnawed voluptuously at her arms, her breast, and surrounded her, and arose, and without pity devoured her beauty, her eighteen years, alas, and her sweet dream!—Adieu, ball, pleasure, love! People say, 'Poor Constance.' And they dance, until dawn, at the house of the French Ambassador."

The picture above is the "Scene on the French Coast with an English Ship of War Stranded," painted by J. M. W. Turner (1775–1851) in 1831. It is often given the shorter title of "The Wreck." It hangs in the New York Public Library, and is a good example of the treatment of scenery which aroused critical hostility to Turner in the 1830's and brought Ruskin to his defense (in *Modern Painters*, the first volume of which appeared in 1843). At the right is the portrait of Ruskin as a young man painted by Sir John Everett Millais (1829–1896). (Courtesy of University Prints.) In *Pre-Raphaelitism* (1851) Ruskin compared Turner and Millais, remarking of the latter that he "sees everything, small and large, with almost the same clearness: mountains and grasshoppers alike; the leaves on the branches; the veins in the pebbles; the bubbles in the stream; but he can remember nothing, and invent nothing." Turner on the contrary, he said, "beholds the entire scene in broad, soft masses of the true gradation; and the very feebleness of his sight is in some sort an advantage to him, in making him more sensible of the aërial mystery of distance, and hiding from him the multitudes of circumstances which it would have been impossible for him to represent." Five years later Ruskin was able to look at the paintings of Millais with more detachment; and he then expressed the opinion that Millais might "be destined to surpass all that has been done in figure painting, as Turner did all past landscape."

Victorian sentimentalism was concentrated on the home, and in the upper picture domestic affections and domestic life are idealized in a characteristically Victorian fashion. The picture is entitled "The Breakfast Table," and was painted in 1838 by Thomas Webster (1800–1886), who devoted his talent for many years to the treatment of sentimental scenes. The lower picture is a sketch of Queen Victoria's favorite daughter, the Princess Beatrice, in her private room at Osborne (then a royal residence, in the Isle of Wight), shortly before her marriage in 1885. The room is a perfect example of Victorian lack of taste in household furniture and decoration. The over-mantel in particular, with its collection of ornamental objects, the fringed drapery tacked to the mantel, and, at the right, the elaborate whatnot and the long heavy window-curtain are unmistakably and uniquely Victorian. (Courtesy of the New York Public Library.)

Yes, that is the fact of it. Right or wrong, the poet does not say. What you may think about it, he does not know. He has nothing to do with that. There lie the ashes of the dead girl in her chamber. There they danced, till the morning, at the Ambassador's of France. Make what you will of it.

If the reader will look through the ballad, of which I have quoted only about the third part, he will find that there is not, from beginning to end of it, a single poetical (so called) expression, except in one stanza. The girl speaks as simple prose as may be; there is not a word she would not have actually used as she was dressing. The poet stands by, impassive as a statue, recording her words just as they come. At last the doom seizes her, and in the very presence of death, for an instant, his own emotions conquer him. He records no longer the facts only, but the facts as they seem to him. The fire gnaws with *voluptuousness—without pity*. It is soon past. The fate is fixed forever; and he retires into his pale and crystalline atmosphere of truth. He closes all with the calm veracity,

> They said, "Poor Constance!"

Now in this there is the exact type of the consummate poetical temperament. For, be it clearly and constantly remembered, that the greatness of a poet depends upon the two faculties, acuteness of feeling, and command of it. A poet is great, first in proportion to the strength of his passion, and then, that strength being granted, in proportion to his government of it; there being, however, always a point beyond which it would be inhuman and monstrous if he pushed this government, and, therefore, a point at which all feverish and wild fancy becomes just and true. Thus the destruction of the kingdom of Assyria cannot be contemplated firmly by a prophet of Israel. The fact is too great, too wonderful. It overthrows him, dashes him into a confused element of dreams. All the world is, to his stunned thought, full of strange voices. "Yea, the fir-trees rejoice at thee, and the cedars of Lebanon, saying, 'Since thou art gone down to the grave, no feller is come up against

us.' "[15] So, still more, the thought of the presence of Deity cannot be borne without this great astonishment. "The mountains and the hills shall break forth before you into singing, and all the trees of the field shall clap their hands."[16]

But by how much this feeling is noble when it is justified by the strength of its cause, by so much it is ignoble when there is not cause enough for it; and beyond all other ignobleness is the mere affectation of it, in hardness of heart. Simply bad writing may almost always, as above noticed, be known by its adoption of these fanciful metaphorical expressions as a sort of current coin; yet there is even a worse, at least a more harmful condition of writing than this, in which such expressions are not ignorantly and feelinglessly caught up, but, by some master, skilful in handling, yet insincere, deliberately wrought out with chill and studied fancy; as if we should try to make an old lava-stream look red-hot again, by covering it with dead leaves, or white-hot, with hoar-frost.

When Young is lost in veneration, as he dwells on the character of a truly good and holy man, he permits himself for a moment to be overborne by the feeling so far as to exclaim—

> Where shall I find him? angels, tell me where.
> You know him; he is near you; point him out.
> Shall I see glories beaming from his brow,
> Or trace his footsteps by the rising flowers?[17]

This emotion has a worthy cause, and is thus true and right. But now hear the cold-hearted Pope say to a shepherd girl—

> Where'er you walk, cool gales shall fan the glade;
> Trees, where you sit, shall crowd into a shade.
>   . . .
> Your praise the birds shall chant in every grove,
> And winds shall waft it to the powers above.
> But would you sing, and rival Orpheus' strain,
> The wondering forests soon should dance again;
> The moving mountains hear the powerful call,
> And headlong streams hang, listening, in their fall.[18]

[15]Isaiah, 14 :8.   [16]Isaiah, 55 :12.
[17]Edward Young's *Night Thoughts*, II, 345–348.
[18]*Pastorals*, "Summer," ll. 73–74, 79–84.

This is not, nor could it for a moment be mistaken for, the language of passion. It is simple falsehood, uttered by hypocrisy; definite absurdity, rooted in affectation, and coldly asserted in the teeth of nature and fact. Passion will indeed go far in deceiving itself; but it must be a strong passion, not the simple wish of a lover to tempt his mistress to sing. Compare a very closely parallel passage in Wordsworth, in which the lover has lost his mistress:

> Three years had Barbara in her grave been laid,
> When thus his moan he made:—
>
> "Oh, move, thou cottage, from behind yon oak,
>   Or let the ancient tree uprooted lie,
> That in some other way yon smoke
>   May mount into the sky. . . .
> If still behind yon pine-tree's ragged bough,
>   Headlong, the waterfall must come,
>   Oh, let it, then, be dumb—
> Be anything, sweet stream, but that which thou
>   art now."[19]

Here is a cottage to be moved, if not a mountain, and a waterfall to be silent, if it is not to hang listening: but with what different relation to the mind that contemplates them! Here, in the extremity of its agony, the soul cries out wildly for relief, which at the same moment it partly knows to be impossible, but partly believes possible, in a vague impression that a miracle *might* be wrought to give relief even to a less sore distress,—that nature is kind, and God is kind, and that grief is strong: it knows not well what *is* possible to such grief. To silence a stream, to move a cottage wall,—one might think it could do as much as that!

I believe these instances are enough to illustrate the main point I insist upon, respecting the pathetic fallacy,—that so far as it *is* a fallacy, it is always the sign of a morbid state of mind, and comparatively of a weak one. Even in the most inspired prophet it is a sign of the incapacity of his human sight or thought to bear what has been revealed to it. In ordinary poetry, if it is found in the thoughts of the poet himself, it is at once a sign of his belonging to the inferior school; if in the thoughts of the characters imagined by him, it is right or wrong according to the genuineness of the emotion from which it springs; always, however, implying necessarily *some* degree of weakness in the character.

Take two most exquisite instances from master hands. The Jessy of Shenstone, and the Ellen of Wordsworth, have both been betrayed and deserted. Jessy, in the course of her most touching complaint, says:

> If through the garden's flowery tribes I stray,
>   Where bloom the jasmines that could once allure,
> "Hope not to find delight in us," they say,
>   "For we are spotless, Jessy; we are pure."[20]

Compare with this some of the words of Ellen:

> "Ah, why," said Ellen, sighing to herself,
> "Why do not words, and kiss, and solemn pledge,
> And nature, that is kind in woman's breast,
> And reason, that in man is wise and good,
> And fear of Him Who is a righteous Judge,—
> Why do not these prevail for human life,
> To keep two hearts together, that began
> Their springtime with one love, and that have need
> Of mutual pity and forgiveness sweet
> To grant, or be received; while that poor bird—
> O, come and hear him! Thou who hast to me
> Been faithless, hear him;—though a lowly creature,
> One of God's simple children that yet know not
> The Universal Parent, *how* he sings!
> As if he wished the firmament of heaven
> Should listen, and give back to him the voice
> Of his triumphant constancy and love;
> The proclamation that he makes, how far
> His darkness doth transcend our fickle light."[21]

The perfection of both these passages, as far as regards truth and tenderness of imagination in the two poets, is quite insuperable. But of the two characters imagined, Jessy is weaker than Ellen, exactly in so far as something appears to her to be in nature which is not. The flowers do not really reproach her. God meant them to comfort

---

[19] Inexactly quoted from "'Tis said, that some have died for love," ll. 11–16, 33–36.

[20] Elegy xxvi, ll. 61–64.
[21] *The Excursion*, VI, 869–887.

her, not to taunt her; they would do so if she saw them rightly.

Ellen, on the other hand, is quite above the slightest erring emotion. There is not the barest film of fallacy in all her thoughts. 5 She reasons as calmly as if she did not feel. And, although the singing of the bird suggests to her the idea of its desiring to be heard in heaven, she does not for an instant admit any veracity in the thought. "As if," 10 she says,—"I know he means nothing of the kind; but it does verily seem as if." The reader will find, by examining the rest of the poem, that Ellen's character is throughout consistent in this clear though passionate 15 strength.[22]

It then being, I hope, now made clear to the reader in all respects that the pathetic fallacy is powerful only so far as it is pathetic, feeble so far as it is fallacious, and, 20 therefore, that the dominion of Truth is entire, over this, as over every other natural and just state of the human mind, we may go on to the subject[23] for the dealing with which this prefatory inquiry became nec- 25 essary; and why necessary, we shall see forthwith.

Of Modern Landscape[1]

WE TURN our eyes, therefore, as boldly and as quickly as may be, from these serene fields and skies of medieval art,[2] to the most characteristic examples of modern landscape.

---

[22]I cannot quit this subject without giving two more instances, both exquisite, of the pathetic fallacy, which I have just come upon in *Maud*:—

"For a great speculation had failed;
And ever he muttered and maddened, and ever
  wanned with despair;
And out he walked, when the wind like a broken
  worldling wailed,
And the *flying gold of the ruined woodlands
  drove through the air.*"
"There has fallen a splendid tear
  From the passion-flower at the gate.
*The red rose cries, 'She is near, she is near!'
  And the white rose weeps, 'She is late.'
The larkspur listens, 'I hear, I hear!'
  And the lily whispers, 'I wait.'*"

(Ruskin's note; quotations from Tennyson's *Maud*, Part I, i, 3 and xxii, 10.)
[23]The subject of landscape.
[1]Volume III, part IV, from chapter 16.
[2]The preceding chapter is entitled "Of Medieval Landscape."

And, I believe, the first thing that will strike us, or that ought to strike us, is their *cloudiness*.

Out of perfect light and motionless air, we find ourselves on a sudden brought under somber skies, and into drifting wind; and, with fickle sunbeams flashing in our face, or utterly drenched with sweep of rain, we are reduced to track the changes of the shadows on the grass, or watch the rents of twilight through angry cloud. And we find that whereas all the pleasure of the medieval was in *stability, definiteness,* and *luminousness,* we are expected to rejoice in darkness, and triumph in mutability; to lay the foundation of happiness in things which momentarily change or fade; and to expect the utmost satisfaction and instruction from what it is impossible to arrest, and difficult to comprehend.

We find, however, together with this general delight in breeze and darkness, much attention to the real form of clouds, and careful drawing of effects of mist; so that the appearance of objects, as seen through it, becomes a subject of science with us; and the faithful representation of that appearance is made of primal importance, under the name of aërial perspective. The aspects of sunset and sunrise, with all their attendant phenomena of cloud and mist, are watchfully delineated; and in ordinary daylight landscape, the sky is considered of so much importance, that a principal mass of foliage, or a whole foreground, is unhesitatingly thrown into shade merely to bring out the form of a white cloud. So that, if a general and characteristic name were needed for modern landscape art, none better could be invented than "the service of clouds."

And this name would, unfortunately, be characteristic of our art in more ways than one. In the last chapter, I said that all the Greeks spoke kindly about the clouds, except Aristophanes; and he, I am sorry to say (since his report is so unfavorable), is the only Greek who had studied them attentively. He tells us, first, that they are "great goddesses to idle men"; then, that they are "mistresses of disputings, and logic, and monstrosities, and noisy chattering"; declares that whoso believes in their divinity must first disbelieve in Jupiter, and place supreme power in the hands of an unknown god "Whirlwind"; and, finally, he displays their influence over the mind of one of their disciples, in his sudden desire "to speak in- [5] geniously concerning smoke."[3]

There is, I fear, an infinite truth in this Aristophanic judgment applied to our modern cloud-worship. Assuredly, much of the love of mystery in our romances, our poetry, [10] our art, and, above all, in our metaphysics, must come under that definition so long ago given by the great Greek, "speaking ingeniously concerning smoke." And much of the instinct, which, partially developed in [15] painting, may be now seen throughout every mode of exertion of mind,—the easily encouraged doubt, easily excited curiosity, habitual agitation, and delight in the changing and the marvelous, as opposed to the old [20] quiet serenity of social custom and religious faith,—is again deeply defined in those few words, the "dethroning of Jupiter," the "coronation of the whirlwind."

Nor of whirlwind merely, but also of [25] darkness or ignorance respecting all stable facts. That darkening of the foreground to bring out the white cloud, is, in one aspect of it, a type of the subjection of all plain and positive fact, to what is uncertain and [30] unintelligible. And, as we examine farther into the matter, we shall be struck by another great difference between the old and modern landscape, namely, that in the old no one ever thought of drawing anything but as well *as* [35] *he could.* That might not be *well,* as we have seen in the case of rocks; but it was as well as he *could,* and always distinctly. Leaf, or stone, or animal, or man, it was equally drawn with care and clearness, and [40] its essential characters shown. If it was an oak tree, the acorns were drawn; if a flint pebble, its veins were drawn; if an arm of the sea, its fish were drawn; if a group of figures, their faces and dresses were drawn [45] —to the very last subtlety of expression and end of thread that could be got into the space, far off or near. But now our ingenuity is all "concerning smoke." Nothing is truly drawn but that; all else is vague, slight, [50]

imperfect; got with as little pains as possible. You examine your closest foreground, and find no leaves; your largest oak, and find no acorns; your human figure, and find a spot of red paint instead of a face; and in all this, again and again, the Aristophanic words come true, and the clouds seem to be "great goddesses to idle men."

The next thing that will strike us, after this love of clouds, is the love of liberty. Whereas the medieval was always shutting himself into castles, and behind fosses, and drawing brickwork neatly, and beds of flowers primly, our painters delight in getting to the open fields and moors; abhor all hedges and moats; never paint anything but freegrowing trees, and rivers gliding "at their own sweet will";[4] eschew formality down to the smallest detail; break and displace the brickwork which the medieval would have carefully cemented; leave unpruned the thickets he would have delicately trimmed; and, carrying the love of liberty even to license, and the love of wildness even to ruin, take pleasure at last in every aspect of age and desolation which emancipates the objects of nature from the government of men;—on the castle wall displacing its tapestry with ivy, and spreading, through the garden, the bramble for the rose.

Connected with this love of liberty we find a singular manifestation of love of mountains, and see our painters traversing the wildest places of the globe in order to obtain subjects with craggy foregrounds and purple distances. Some few of them remain content with pollards and flat land; but these are always men of third-rate order; and the leading masters, while they do not reject the beauty of the low grounds, reserve their highest powers to paint Alpine peaks or Italian promontories. And it is eminently noticeable, also, that this pleasure in the mountains is never mingled with fear, or tempered by a spirit of meditation, as with the medieval; but is always free and fearless, brightly exhilarating, and wholly unreflective; so that the painter feels that his mountain foreground may be more consistently animated by a sportsman than a hermit; and

---

[3] See the *Clouds* of Aristophanes, ll. 316–318, 320, and 360.

[4] Wordsworth, sonnet *Composed upon Westminster Bridge, 3 September, 1802,* l. 12.

our modern society in general goes to the mountains, not to fast, but to feast, and leaves their glaciers covered with chicken-bones and eggshells.

Connected with this want of any sense of solemnity in mountain scenery, is a general profanity of temper in regarding all the rest of nature; that is to say, a total absence of faith in the presence of any deity therein. Whereas the medieval never painted a cloud, but with the purpose of placing an angel in it; and a Greek never entered a wood without expecting to meet a god in it; *we* should think the appearance of an angel in the cloud wholly unnatural, and should be seriously surprised by meeting a god anywhere. Our chief ideas about the wood are connected with poaching. We have no belief that the clouds contain more than so many inches of rain or hail, and from our ponds and ditches expect nothing more divine than ducks and watercresses.

Finally: connected with this profanity of temper is a strong tendency to deny the sacred element of color, and make our boast in blackness. For though occasionally glaring or violent, modern color is on the whole eminently somber, tending continually to gray or brown, and by many of our best painters consistently falsified, with a confessed pride in what they call chaste or subdued tints; so that, whereas a medieval paints his sky bright blue and his foreground bright green, gilds the towers of his castles, and clothes his figures with purple and white, we paint our sky gray, our foreground black, and our foliage brown, and think that enough is sacrificed to the sun in admitting the dangerous brightness of a scarlet cloak or a blue jacket.

These, I believe, are the principal points which would strike us instantly, if we were to be brought suddenly into an exhibition of modern landscapes out of a room filled with medieval work. It is evident that there are both evil and good in this change; but how much evil, or how much good, we can only estimate by considering, as in the former divisions of our inquiry, what are the real roots of the habits of mind which have caused them.

And first, it is evident that the title "Dark Ages," given to the medieval centuries, is, respecting art, wholly inapplicable. They were, on the contrary, the bright ages; ours are the dark ones. I do not mean metaphysically, but literally. They were the ages of gold; ours are the ages of umber.

This is partly mere mistake in us; we build brown brick walls, and wear brown coats, because we have been blunderingly taught to do so, and go on doing so mechanically. There is, however, also some cause for the change in our own tempers. On the whole, these are much *sadder* ages than the early ones; not sadder in a noble and deep way, but in a dim wearied way,—the way of ennui, and jaded intellect, and uncomfortableness of soul and body. The Middle Ages had their wars and agonies, but also intense delights. Their gold was dashed with blood; but ours is sprinkled with dust. Their life was inwoven with white and purple: ours is one seamless stuff of brown. Not that we are without apparent festivity, but festivity more or less forced, mistaken, embittered, incomplete—not of the heart. How wonderfully, since Shakespeare's time, have we lost the power of laughing at bad jests! The very finish of our wit belies our gayety.

The profoundest reason of this darkness of heart is, I believe, our want of faith. There never yet was a generation of men (savage or civilized) who, taken as a body, so woefully fulfilled the words "having no hope, and without God in the world,"[5] as the present civilized European race. A Red Indian or Otaheitan[6] savage has more sense of a divine existence round him, or government over him, than the plurality of refined Londoners and Parisians: and those among us who may in some sense be said to believe, are divided almost without exception into two broad classes, Romanist and Puritan; who, but for the interference of the unbelieving portions of society, would, either of them, reduce the other sect as speedily as possible to ashes; the Romanist having always done so whenever he could, from the beginning of their separation, and the Puri-

[5]Ephesians, 2:12.
[6]Otaheite (Tahiti) is the largest of the Society Islands, in the South Pacific.

tan at this time holding himself in complacent expectation of the destruction of Rome by volcanic fire. Such division as this between persons nominally of one religion, that is to say, believing in the same God, and the same Revelation, cannot but become a stumbling-block of the gravest kind to all thoughtful and far-sighted men,—a stumbling-block which they can only surmount under the most favorable circumstances of early educa-tion. Hence, nearly all our powerful men in this age of the world are unbelievers; the best of them in doubt and misery; the worst in reckless defiance; the plurality, in plod-ding hesitation, doing, as well as they can, what practical work lies ready to their hands. Most of our scientific men are in this last class: our popular authors either set them-selves definitely against all religious form, pleading for simple truth and benevolence (Thackeray, Dickens), or give themselves up to bitter and fruitless statement of facts (De Balzac), or surface-painting (Scott), or careless blasphemy, sad or smiling (Byron, Béranger). Our earnest poets and deepest thinkers are doubtful and indignant (Tenny-son, Carlyle); one or two, anchored, indeed, but anxious or weeping (Wordsworth, Mrs. Browning); and of these two, the first is not so sure of his anchor, but that now and then it drags with him, even to make him cry out,—

Great God, I had rather be
A Pagan suckled in some creed outworn;
So might I, standing on this pleasant lea,
Have glimpses that would make me less forlorn.[7]

In politics, religion is now a name; in art, a hypocrisy or affectation. Over German religious pictures the inscription, "See how Pious I am," can be read at a glance by any clear-sighted person. Over French and Eng-lish religious pictures the inscription, "See how Impious I am," is equally legible. All sincere and modest art is, among us, pro-fane.[8]

This faithlessness operates among us ac-cording to our tempers, producing either sad-ness or levity, and being the ultimate root alike of our discontents and of our wanton-nesses. It is marvelous how full of con-tradiction it makes us: we are first dull, and seek for wild and lonely places because we have no heart for the garden; presently we recover our spirits, and build an assembly-room among the mountains, because we have no reverence for the desert. I do not know if there be game on Sinai, but I am always expecting to hear of some one's shooting over it.[9]

There is, however, another, and a more in-nocent root of our delight in wild scenery.

All the Renaissance principles of art tended, as I have before often explained, to the setting Beauty above Truth, and seeking for it always at the expense of truth. And the proper punishment of such pursuit—the punishment which all the laws of the uni-verse rendered inevitable—was, that those who thus pursued beauty should wholly lose sight of beauty. All the thinkers of the age, as we saw previously, declared that it did not exist. The age seconded their efforts, and banished beauty, so far as human effort could succeed in doing so, from the face of the earth, and the form of man. To powder the hair, to patch the cheek, to hoop the body, to buckle the foot, were all part and parcel of the same system which reduced streets to brick walls, and pictures to brown stains. One desert of Ugliness was extended before the eyes of mankind; and their pursuit of the beautiful, so recklessly continued, received unexpected consummation in high-heeled shoes and periwigs,—Gower Street, and Gas-par Poussin.

Reaction from this state was inevitable, if any true life was left in the races of man-kind; and, accordingly, though still forced, by rule and fashion, to the producing and wearing all that is ugly, men steal out, half-ashamed of themselves for doing so, to the fields and mountains; and, finding among these the color, and liberty, and variety, and power, which are for ever grateful to them, delight in these to an extent never before

---

[7] Sonnet beginning "The world is too much with us; late and soon," ll. 9–12.

[8] Pre-Raphaelitism, of course, excepted, which is a new phase of art, in no wise considered in this chapter. Blake was sincere, but full of wild creeds, and somewhat diseased in brain (Ruskin's note).

[9] Ruskin's expectation was soon fulfilled; see his description of a drawing by J. F. Lewis, *Academy Notes,* 1856.

known; rejoice in all the wildest shattering of the mountain side, as an opposition to Gower Street, gaze in a rapt manner at sunsets and sunrises, to see there the blue, and gold, and purple, which glow for them no longer on knight's armor or temple porch; and gather with care out of the fields, into their blotted herbaria, the flowers which the five orders of architecture have banished from their doors and casements.

The absence of care for personal beauty, which is another great characteristic of the age, adds to this feeling in a twofold way: first, by turning all reverent thoughts away from human nature; and making us think of men as ridiculous or ugly creatures, getting through the world as well as they can, and spoiling it in doing so; not ruling it in a kingly way and crowning all its loveliness. In the Middle Ages hardly anything but vice could be caricatured, because virtue was always visibly and personally noble: now virtue itself is apt to inhabit such poor human bodies, that no aspect of it is invulnerable to jest; and for all fairness we have to seek to the flowers; for all sublimity, to the hills.

The same want of care operates, in another way, by lowering the standard of health, increasing the susceptibility to nervous or sentimental impressions, and thus adding to the other powers of nature over us whatever charm may be felt in her fostering the melancholy fancies of brooding idleness.

It is not, however, only to existing inanimate nature that our want of beauty in person and dress has driven us. The imagination of it, as it was seen in our ancestors, haunts us continually; and while we yield to the present fashions, or act in accordance with the dullest modern principles of economy and utility, we look fondly back to the manners of the ages of chivalry, and delight in painting, to the fancy, the fashions we pretend to despise, and the splendors we think it wise to abandon. The furniture and personages of our romance are sought, when the writer desires to please most easily, in the centuries which we profess to have surpassed in everything; the art which takes us into the present times is considered as both daring and degraded; and while the weakest words please us, and are regarded as poetry, which

recall the manners of our forefathers, or of strangers, it is only as familiar and vulgar that we accept the description of our own.

In this we are wholly different from all the races that preceded us. All other nations have regarded their ancestors with reverence as saints or heroes; but have nevertheless thought their own deeds and ways of life the fitting subjects for their arts of painting or of verse. We, on the contrary, regard our ancestors as foolish and wicked, but yet find our chief artistic pleasures in descriptions of their ways of life.

The Greeks and medievals honored, but did not imitate their forefathers; we imitate, but do not honor.

With this romantic love of beauty, forced to seek in history, and in external nature, the satisfaction it cannot find in ordinary life, we mingle a more rational passion, the due and just result of newly awakened powers of attention. Whatever may first lead us to the scrutiny of natural objects, that scrutiny never fails of its reward. Unquestionably they are intended to be regarded by us with both reverence and delight; and every hour we give to them renders their beauty more apparent, and their interest more engrossing. Natural science—which can hardly be considered to have existed before modern times—rendering our knowledge fruitful in accumulation, and exquisite in accuracy, has acted for good or evil, according to the temper of the mind which received it; and though it has hardened the faithlessness of the dull and proud, has shown new grounds for reverence to hearts which were thoughtful and humble. The neglect of the art of war, while it has somewhat weakened and deformed the body,[10] has given us leisure and opportunity for studies to which, before, time and space were equally wanting; lives which once were early wasted on the battlefield are now passed usefully in the study; nations which exhausted themselves in an-

---

[10] Of course this is meant only of the modern citizen or country gentleman, as compared with a citizen of Sparta or old Florence. I leave it to others to say whether the "neglect of the *art* of war" may or may not, in a yet more fatal sense, be predicated of the English nation. War *without* art, we seem, with God's help, able still to wage nobly (Ruskin's note). The "war *without* art" was the Crimean War.

nual warfare now dispute with each other the discovery of new planets;[11] and the serene philosopher dissects the plants, and analyzes the dust, of lands which were of old only traversed by the knight in hasty march, or by the borderer in heedless rapine.

The elements of progress and decline being thus strangely mingled in the modern mind, we might beforehand anticipate that one of the notable characters of our art would be its inconsistency; that efforts would be made in every direction, and arrested by every conceivable cause and manner of failure; that in all we did, it would become next to impossible to distinguish accurately the grounds for praise or for regret; that all previous canons of practice and methods of thought would be gradually overthrown, and criticism continually defied by successes which no one had expected, and sentiments which no one could define.

Accordingly, while, in our inquiries into Greek and medieval art, I was able to describe, in general terms, what all men did or felt, I find now many characters in many men; some, it seems to me, founded on the inferior and evanescent principles of modernism, on its recklessness, impatience, or faithlessness; others founded on its science, its new affection for nature, its love of openness and liberty. And among all these characters, good or evil, I see that some, remaining to us from old or transitional periods, do not properly belong to us, and will soon fade away, and others, though not yet distinctly developed, are yet properly our own, and likely to grow forward into greater strength.

For instance: our reprobation of bright color is, I think, for the most part, mere affectation, and must soon be done away with. Vulgarity, dullness, or impiety, will indeed always express themselves through art in brown and gray, as in Rembrandt, Caravaggio,[12] and Salvator;[13] but we are not wholly vulgar, dull, or impious; nor, as moderns, are we necessarily obliged to continue so in any wise. Our greatest men, whether sad or gay, still delight, like the great men of all ages, in brilliant hues. The coloring of Scott and Byron is full and pure; that of Keats and Tennyson rich even to excess. Our practical failures in coloring are merely the necessary consequences of our prolonged want of practice during the periods of Renaissance affectation and ignorance; and the only durable difference between old and modern coloring, is the acceptance of certain hues, by the modern, which please him by expressing that melancholy peculiar to his more reflective or sentimental character, and the greater variety of them necessary to express his greater science.

Again: if we ever become wise enough to dress consistently and gracefully, to make health a principal object in education, and to render our streets beautiful with art, the external charm of past history will in great measure disappear. There is no essential reason, because we live after the fatal seventeenth century, that we should never again be able to confess interest in sculpture, or see brightness in embroidery; nor, because now we choose to make the night deadly with our pleasures, and the day with our labors, prolonging the dance till dawn, and the toil to twilight, that we should never again learn how rightly to employ the sacred trusts of strength, beauty, and time. Whatever external charm attaches itself to the past, would then be seen in proper subordination to the brightness of present life; and the elements of romance would exist, in the earlier ages, only in the attraction which must generally belong to whatever is unfamiliar; in the reverence which a noble nation always pays to its ancestors; and in the enchanted light which races, like individuals, must perceive in looking back to the days of their childhood.

Again: the peculiar levity with which natural scenery is regarded by a large number of modern minds cannot be considered as entirely characteristic of the age, inasmuch as it never can belong to its greatest intellects. Men of any high mental power must be serious, whether in ancient or modern days; a certain degree of reverence for fair scenery is found in all our great writers without exception,—even the one who has made us

---

[11]The allusion is to France and England. In each country several minor planets were discovered independently during the years 1854–1856.

[12]Italian painter (1569–1609).

[13]Salvator Rosa (1615?–1673), Neapolitan painter, musician, and satirical poet.

laugh oftenest, taking us to the valley of Chamouni, and to the sea beach, there to give peace after suffering, and change revenge into pity.[14] It is only the dull, the uneducated, or the worldly, whom it is painful to meet on the hillsides; and levity, as a ruling character, cannot be ascribed to the whole nation, but only to its holiday-making apprentices, and its House of Commons.

We need not, therefore, expect to find any single poet or painter representing the entire group of powers, weaknesses, and inconsistent instincts which govern or confuse our modern life. But we may expect that in the man who seems to be given by Providence as the type of the age (as Homer and Dante were given, as the types of classical and medieval mind), we shall find whatever is fruitful and substantial to be completely present, together with those of our weaknesses, which are indeed nationally characteristic, and compatible with general greatness of mind, just as the weak love of fences, and dislike of mountains, were found compatible with Dante's greatness in other respects.

Farther: as the admiration of mankind is found, in our times, to have in great part passed from men to mountains, and from human emotion to natural phenomena, we may anticipate that the great strength of art will also be warped in this direction; with this notable result for us, that whereas the greatest painters or painter of classical and medieval periods, being wholly devoted to the representation of humanity, furnished us with but little to examine in landscape, the greatest painters or painter of modern times will in all probability be devoted to landscape principally; and farther, because in representing human emotion words surpass painting, but in representing natural scenery painting surpasses words, we may anticipate also that the painter and poet (for convenience' sake I here• use the words in opposition) will somewhat change their relations of rank in illustrating the mind of the age; that the painter will become of more importance, the poet of less; and that the relations between the men who are the types and first-fruits of the age in word and work, —namely, Scott and Turner,—will be, in many curious respects, different from those between Homer and Phidias, or Dante and Giotto.

THE STONES OF VENICE

St. Mark's[1]

"AND so Barnabas took Mark, and sailed unto Cyprus." If as the shores of Asia lessened upon his sight, the spirit of prophecy had entered into the heart of the weak disciple who had turned back when his hand was on the plough, and who had been judged, by the chiefest of Christ's captains, unworthy thenceforward to go forth with him to the work,[2] how wonderful would he have thought it, that by the lion symbol in future ages he was to be represented among men! how woeful, that the war-cry of his name should so often reanimate the rage of the soldier, on those very plains where he himself had failed in the courage of the Chris-

tian, and so often dye with fruitless blood that very Cypriot Sea, over whose waves, in repentance and shame, he was following the Son of Consolation!

That the Venetians possessed themselves of his body in the ninth century, there appears no sufficient reason to doubt, nor that it was principally in consequence of their having done so, that they chose him for their patron saint. There exists, however, a tradition that before he went into Egypt he had founded the church at Aquileia, and was thus in some sort the first bishop of the Venetian isles and people. I believe that this tradition stands on nearly as good grounds as that of St. Peter having been the first bishop of Rome; but, as usual, it is enriched by various later additions and embellishments, much resembling the stories told respecting the church of· Murano. Thus we find it recorded by the Santo Padre who compiled the *Vite de' Santi spettanti alle Chiese di*

---

[14] See *David Copperfield,* chaps. lv and lviii (Ruskin's note).

[1] Vol. II (published in 1853) entitled "The Sea-Stories," from chapter 4.

[2] Acts, 13:13; 15:38, 39 (Ruskin's note).

Venezia,[3] that "St. Mark having seen the people of Aquileia well grounded in religion, and being called to Rome by St. Peter, before setting off took with him the holy bishop Hermagoras, and went in a small boat to the marshes of Venice. There were at that period some houses built upon a certain high bank called Rialto, and the boat being driven by the wind was anchored in a marshy place, when St. Mark, snatched into ecstasy, heard the voice of an angel saying to him: 'Peace be to thee, Mark; here shall thy body rest.'" The angel goes on to foretell the building of *una stupenda, ne più veduta Città;*[4] but the fable is hardly ingenious enough to deserve farther relation.

But whether St. Mark was first bishop of Aquileia or not, St. Theodore was the first patron of the city; nor can he yet be considered as having entirely abdicated his early right, as his statue, standing on a crocodile, still companions the winged lion on the opposing pillar of the piazzetta. A church erected to this Saint is said to have occupied, before the ninth century, the site of St. Mark's; and the traveler, dazzled by the brilliancy of the great square, ought not to leave it without endeavoring to imagine its aspect in that early time, when it was a green field, cloister-like and quiet, divided by a small canal, with a line of trees on each side; and extending between the two churches of St. Theodore and St. Geminian, as the little piazza of Torcello lies between its "palazzo" and cathedral.

But in the year 813, when the seat of government was finally removed to the Rialto, a Ducal Palace, built on the spot where the present one stands, with a Ducal Chapel beside it, gave a very different character to the Square of St. Mark; and fifteen years later, the acquisition of the body of the Saint, and its deposition in the Ducal Chapel, perhaps not yet completed, occasioned the investiture of that Chapel with all possible splendor. St. Theodore was deposed from his patronship, and his church destroyed, to make room for the aggrandizement of the one attached

to the Ducal Palace, and thenceforward known as "St. Mark's."

This first church was however destroyed by fire, when the Ducal Palace was burned in the revolt against Candiano, in 976. It was partly rebuilt by his successor, Pietro Orseolo, on a larger scale; and, with the assistance of Byzantine architects, the fabric was carried on under successive Doges for nearly a hundred years; the main building being completed in 1071, but its incrustation with marble not till considerably later. It was consecrated on the 8th of October, 1085, according to Sansovino and the author of the *Chiesa Ducale di S. Marco,*[5] in 1094 according to Lazari, but certainly between 1084 and 1096, those years being the limits of the reign of Vital Falier; I incline to the supposition that it was soon after his accession to the throne in 1085, though Sansovino writes, by mistake, Ordelafo instead of Vital Falier. But, at all events, before the close of the eleventh century the great consecration of the church took place. It was again injured by fire in 1106, but repaired; and from that time to the fall of Venice there was probably no Doge who did not in some slight degree embellish or alter the fabric, so that few parts of it can be pronounced boldly to be of any given date. Two periods of interference are, however, notable above the rest: the first, that in which the Gothic school had superseded the Byzantine towards the close of the fourteenth century, when the pinnacles, upper archivolts, and window traceries were added to the exterior, and the great screen, with various chapels and tabernacle-work, to the interior; the second, when the Renaissance school superseded the Gothic, and the pupils of Titian and Tintoret substituted, over one-half of the church, their own compositions for the Greek mosaics with which it was originally decorated; happily, though with no good-will, having left enough to enable us to imagine and lament what they destroyed. Of this irreparable loss we shall have more to say hereafter; meantime, I wish only to fix in the reader's mind the succession of periods of alterations as firmly and simply as possible.

We have seen that the main body of the

---

[3] By the Holy Father who compiled the *Lives of the Patron Saints of the Venetian Churches* (Ruskin gives the reference: Venice, 1761, I, 126).

[4] A wonderful city, never before seen.

[5] Ducal church of St. Mark.

church may be broadly stated to be of the eleventh century, the Gothic additions of the fourteenth, and the restored mosaics of the seventeenth. There is no difficulty in distinguishing at a glance the Gothic portions from the Byzantine; but there is considerable difficulty in ascertaining how long, during the course of the twelfth and thirteenth centuries, additions were made to the Byzantine church, which cannot be easily distinguished from the work of the eleventh century, being purposely executed in the same manner. Two of the most important pieces of evidence on this point are, a mosaic in the south transept, and another over the northern door of the façade; the first representing the interior, the second the exterior, of the ancient church.

It has just been stated that the existing building was consecrated by the Doge Vital Falier. A peculiar solemnity was given to that act of consecration, in the minds of the Venetian people, by what appears to have been one of the best arranged and most successful impostures ever attempted by the clergy of the Romish Church. The body of St. Mark had, without doubt, perished in the conflagration of 976; but the revenues of the church depended too much upon the devotion excited by these relics to permit the confession of their loss. The following is the account given by Corner, and believed to this day by the Venetians, of the pretended miracle by which it was concealed.

"After the repairs undertaken by the Doge Orseolo, the place in which the body of the holy Evangelist rested had been altogether forgotten; so that the Doge Vital Falier was entirely ignorant of the place of the venerable deposit. This was no light affliction, not only to the pious Doge, but to all the citizens and people; so that at last, moved by confidence in the Divine mercy, they determined to implore, with prayer and fasting, the manifestation of so great a treasure, which did not now depend upon any human effort. A general fast being therefore proclaimed, and a solemn procession appointed for the 25th day of June, while the people assembled in the church interceded with God in fervent prayers for the desired boon, they beheld, with as much amazement as joy, a

slight shaking in the marbles of a pillar (near the place where the altar of the Cross is now), which, presently falling to the earth, exposed to the view of the rejoicing people the chest of bronze in which the body of the Evangelist was laid."

Of the main facts of this tale there is no doubt. They were embellished afterward, as usual, by many fanciful traditions; as, for instance, that, when the sarcophagus was discovered, St. Mark extended his hand out of it, with a gold ring on one of the fingers which he permitted a noble of the Dolfin family to remove; and a quaint and delightful story was further invented of this ring, which I shall not repeat here, as it is now as well known as any tale of the Arabian Nights.[6] But the fast and the discovery of the coffin, by whatever means effected, are facts; and they are recorded in one of the best-preserved mosaics of the south transept, executed very certainly not long after the event had taken place, closely resembling in its treatment that of the Bayeux tapestry,[7] and showing, in a conventional manner, the interior of the church, as it then was, filled by the people, first in prayer, then in thanksgiving, the pillar standing open before them, and the Doge, in the midst of them, distinguished by his crimson bonnet embroidered with gold, but more unmistakably by the inscription "Dux" over his head, as uniformly is the case in the Bayeux tapestry, and most other pictorial works of the period. The church is, of course, rudely represented, and the two upper stories of it reduced to a small scale in order to form a background to the figures; one of those bold pieces of picture history which we in our pride of perspective, and a thousand things besides, never dare attempt.[8] We should have put in a column or two, of the real or perspective

---

[6] The story tells of the miraculous intervention of St. Mark, with St. George and St. Nicholas, to save Venice from destruction by a great storm in 1340. It is translated in Mrs. Jameson's *Sacred and Legendary Art*.

[7] A representation of episodes in the conquest of England by William of Normandy, dating probably from early in the twelfth century. It is in the Public Library of Bayeux.

[8] I leave this exceedingly ill-written sentence, trusting the reader will think I write better now (Ruskin's note, added in 1879).

size, and subdued it into a vague background: the old workman crushed the church together that he might get it all in, up to the cupolas; and has, therefore, left us some useful notes of its ancient form, though any one who is familiar with the method of drawing employed at the period will not push the evidence too far. The two pulpits are there, however, as they are at this day, and the fringe of mosaic flowerwork which then encompassed the whole church, but which modern restorers have destroyed, all but one fragment still left in the south aisle. There is no attempt to represent the other mosaics on the roof, the scale being too small to admit of their being represented with any success; but some at least of those mosaics had been executed at that period, and their absence in the representation of the entire church is especially to be observed, in order to show that we must not trust to any negative evidence in such works. M. Lazari has rashly concluded that the central archivolt of St. Mark's *must* be posterior to the year 1205, because it does not appear in the representation of the exterior of the church over the northern door;[9] but he justly observes that this mosaic (which is the other piece of evidence we possess respecting the ancient form of the building) cannot itself be earlier than 1205, since it represents the bronze horses which were brought from Constantinople in that year. And this one fact renders it very difficult to speak with confidence respecting the date of any part of the exterior of St. Mark's; for we have above seen that it was consecrated in the eleventh century, and yet here is one of its most important exterior decorations assuredly retouched, if not entirely added, in the thirteenth, although its style would have led us to suppose it had been an original part of the fabric. However, for all our purposes, it will be enough for the reader to remember that the earliest parts of the building belong to the eleventh, twelfth, and first part of the thirteenth century; the Gothic portions to the fourteenth; some of the altars and embellishments to the fifteenth and sixteenth; and the modern portion of the mosaics to the seventeenth.

This, however, I only wish him to recollect in order that I may speak generally of the Byzantine architecture of St. Mark's, without leading him to suppose the whole church to have been built and decorated by Greek artists. Its later portions, with the single exception of the seventeenth century mosaics, have been so dexterously accommodated to the original fabric that the general effect is still that of a Byzantine building; and I shall not, except when it is absolutely necessary, direct attention to the discordant points, or weary the reader with anatomical criticism. Whatever in St. Mark's arrests the eye, or affects the feelings, is either Byzantine, or has been modified by Byzantine influence; and our inquiry into its architectural merits need not therefore be disturbed by the anxieties of antiquarianism, or arrested by the obscurities of chronology.

And now I wish that the reader, before I bring him into St. Mark's Place, would imagine himself for a little time in a quiet English cathedral town, and walk with me to the west front of its cathedral.[10] Let us go together up the more retired street, at the end of which we can see the pinnacles of one of the towers, and then through the low gray gateway, with its battlemented top and small latticed window in the center, into the inner private-looking road or close, where nothing goes in but the carts of the tradesmen who supply the bishop and the chapter, and where there are little shaven grass-plots, fenced in by neat rails, before old-fashioned groups of somewhat diminutive and excessively trim houses, with little oriel and bay windows jutting out here and there, and deep wooden cornices and eaves painted cream color and white, and small porches to their doors in the shape of cockle-shells, or little, crooked, thick, indescribable wooden gables warped a little on one side; and so forward till we come to larger houses, also old-fashioned, but of red brick, and with garden behind them, and fruit walls, which show here and there, among the nectarines, the vestiges of an old cloister arch or shaft, and looking in front on the cathedral square itself, laid out

[9]In 1879 Ruskin added the note: "He is right, however."

[10]Some have identified this English cathedral with Canterbury, others with Salisbury. Ruskin, however, meant his description to be generic.

in rigid divisions of smooth grass and gravel walk, yet not uncheerful, especially on the sunny side, where the canon's children are walking with their nursery maids. And so, taking care not to tread on the grass, we will go along the straight walk to the west front, and there stand for a time, looking up at its deep-pointed porches and the dark places between their pillars where there were statues once, and where the fragments, here and there, of a stately figure are still left, which has in it the likeness of a king, perhaps indeed a king on earth, perhaps a saintly king long ago in heaven; and so higher and higher up to the great moldering wall of rugged sculpture and confused arcades, shattered, and gray, and grisly with heads of dragons and mocking fiends, worn by the rain and swirling winds into yet unseemlier shape, and colored on their stony scales by the deep russet-orange lichen,[11] melancholy gold; and so, higher still, to the bleak towers, so far above that the eye loses itself among the bosses of their traceries, though they are rude and strong, and only sees like a drift of eddying black points, now closing, now scattering, and now settling suddenly into invisible places among the bosses and flowers, the crowd of restless birds that fill the whole square with that strange clangor of theirs, so harsh and yet so soothing, like the cries of birds on a solitary coast between the cliffs and sea.

Think for a little while of that scene, and the meaning of all its small formalisms, mixed with its serene sublimity. Estimate its secluded, continuous, drowsy felicities, and its evidence of the sense and steady performance of such kind of duties as can be regulated by the cathedral clock; and weigh the influence of those dark towers on all who have passed through the lonely square at their feet for centuries, and on all who have seen them rising far away over the wooded plain, or catching on their square masses the last rays of the sunset, when the city at their feet was indicated only by the mist at the bend of the river. And then let us quickly recollect that we are in Venice, and land at the extremity of the Calle Lunga San Moisè, which may be considered as there answering to the secluded street that led us to our English cathedral gateway.[12]

We find ourselves in a paved alley, some seven feet wide where it is widest, full of people, and resonant with cries of itinerant salesmen,—a shriek in their beginning, and dying away into a kind of brazen ringing, all the worse for its confinement between the high houses of the passage along which we have to make our way. Over head, an inextricable confusion of rugged shutters, and iron balconies and chimney flues, pushed out on brackets to save room, and arched windows with projecting sills of Istrian stone, and gleams of green leaves here and there where a fig-tree branch escapes over a lower wall from some inner cortile,[13] leading the eye up to the narrow stream of blue sky high over all. On each side, a row of shops, as densely set as may be, occupying, in fact, intervals between the square stone shafts, about eight feet high, which carry the first floors: intervals of which one is narrow and serves as a door; the other is, in the more respectable shops, wainscoted to the height of the counter and glazed above, but in those of the poorer tradesmen left open to the ground, and the wares laid on benches and tables in the open air, the light in all cases entering at the front only, and fading away in a few feet from the threshold into a gloom which the eye from without cannot penetrate, but which is generally broken by a ray or two from a feeble lamp at the back of the shop, suspended before a print of the Virgin. The less pious shopkeeper sometimes leaves his lamp unlighted, and is contented with a penny print; the more religious one has his print colored and set in a little shrine with a gilded or figured fringe, with perhaps a faded flower or two on each side, and his lamp burning brilliantly. Here, at the fruiterer's, where the dark-green watermelons

---

[11]Alas! all this was described from things now never to be seen more. Read, for "the great moldering wall," and the context of four lines, "the beautiful new parapet by Mr. Scott, with a gross of kings sent down from Kensington" (Ruskin's note, added in 1879). Sir Gilbert Scott restored a number of cathedrals. The restoration of Salisbury was begun in 1862 and 60 new statues were placed on its west front.

[12]The Venetian street has been widened and re named since this was written.

[13]Courtyard.

are heaped upon the counter like cannon balls, the Madonna has a tabernacle of fresh laurel leaves; but the pewterer next door has let his lamp out, and there is nothing to be seen in his shop but the dull gleam of the studded patterns on the copper pans, hanging from his roof in the darkness. Next comes a *Vendita Frittole e Liquori*,[14] where the Virgin, enthroned in a very humble manner beside a tallow candle on a back shelf, presides over certain ambrosial morsels of a nature too ambiguous to be defined or enumerated. But a few steps farther on, at the regular wine-shop of the calle, where we are offered *Vino Nostrani a Soldi* 28.32, the Madonna is in great glory, enthroned above ten or a dozen large red casks of three-year-old vintage, and flanked by goodly ranks of bottles of Maraschino, and two crimson lamps; and for the evening, when the gondoliers will come to drink out, under her auspices, the money they have gained during the day, she will have a whole chandelier.

A yard or two farther, we pass the hostelry of the Black Eagle, and glancing as we pass through the square door of marble, deeply molded, in the outer wall, we see the shadows of its pergola of vines resting on an ancient well, with a pointed shield carved on its side; and so presently emerge on the bridge and Campo San Moisè, whence to the entrance into St. Mark's Place, called the Bocca di Piazza (mouth of the square), the Venetian character is nearly destroyed, first by the frightful façade of San Moisè, which we will pause at another time to examine,[15] and then by the modernizing of the shops as they near the piazza, and the mingling with the lower Venetian populace of lounging groups of English and Austrians. We will push fast through them into the shadow of the pillars at the end of the Bocca di Piazza, and then we forget them all; for between those pillars there opens a great light, and, in the midst of it, as we advance slowly, the vast tower of St. Mark seems to lift itself visibly forth from the level field of checkered stones; and, on each side, the countless arches prolong themselves into ranged symmetry, as if the rugged and irregular

houses that pressed together above us in the dark alley had been struck back into sudden obedience and lovely order, and all their rude casements and broken walls had been transformed into arches charged with goodly sculpture, and fluted shafts of delicate stone.

And well may they fall back, for beyond those troops of ordered arches there rises a vision out of the earth, and all the great square seems to have opened from it in a kind of awe, that we may see it far away;— a multitude of pillars and white domes, clustered into a long low pyramid of colored light; a treasure-heap, it seems, partly of gold, and partly of opal and mother-of-pearl, hollowed beneath into five great vaulted porches, ceiled with fair mosaic, and beset with sculpture of alabaster, clear as amber and delicate as ivory,—sculpture fantastic and involved, of palm leaves and lilies, and grapes and pomegranates, and birds clinging and fluttering among the branches, all twined together into an endless network of buds and plumes; and, in the midst of it, the solemn forms of angels, sceptered, and robed to the feet, and leaning to each other across the gates, their figures indistinct among the gleaming of the golden ground through the leaves beside them, interrupted and dim, like the morning light as it faded back among the branches of Eden, when first its gates were angel-guarded long ago. And round the walls of the porches there are set pillars of variegated stones, jasper and porphyry, and deep-green serpentine spotted with flakes of snow, and marbles, that half refuse and half yield to the sunshine, Cleopatra-like, "their bluest veins to kiss"[16]— the shadow, as it steals back from them, revealing line after line of azure undulation, as a receding tide leaves the waved sand; their capitals rich with interwoven tracery, rooted knots of herbage, and drifting leaves of acanthus and vine, and mystical signs, all beginning and ending in the Cross; and above them, in the broad archivolts, a continuous chain of language and of life— angels, and the signs of heaven, and the labors of men, each in its appointed season upon the earth; and above these, another range of glittering pinnacles, mixed with

---

[14]Fritter and Liquor Shop.

[15]See vol. III, chap. 3.

[16]*Antony and Cleopatra*, II, v, 29.

white arches edged with scarlet flowers—a confusion of delight, amidst which the breasts of the Greek horses are seen blazing in their breadth of golden strength, and the St. Mark's lion, lifted on a blue field covered with stars, until at last, as if in ecstasy, the crests of the arches break into a marble foam, and toss themselves far into the blue sky in flashes and wreaths of sculptured spray, as if the breakers on the Lido shore had been frost-bound before they fell, and the sea-nymphs had inlaid them with coral and amethyst.

Between that grim cathedral of England and this, what an interval! There is a type of it in the very birds that haunt them; for, instead of the restless crowd, hoarse-voiced and sable-winged, drifting on the bleak upper air, the St. Mark's porches are full of doves, that nestle among the marble foliage, and mingle the soft iridescense of their living plumes, changing at every motion, with the tints, hardly less lovely, that have stood unchanged for seven hundred years.

And what effect has this splendor on those who pass beneath it? You may walk from sunrise to sunset, to and fro, before the gateway of St. Mark's, and you will not see an eye lifted to it, nor a countenance brightened by it. Priest and layman, soldier and civilian, rich and poor, pass by it alike regardlessly. Up to the very recesses of the porches, the meanest tradesmen of the city push their counters; nay, the foundations of its pillars are themselves the seats—not "of them that sell doves"[17] for sacrifice, but of the vendors of toys and caricatures. Round the whole square in front of the church there is almost a continuous line of cafés, where the idle Venetians of the middle classes lounge, and read empty journals; in its center the Austrian bands play during the time of vespers, their martial music jarring with the organ notes,—the march drowning the miserere, and the sullen crowd thickening round them,—a crowd, which, if it had its will, would stiletto every soldier that pipes to it.[18] And in the recesses of the porches all day long, knots of men of the lowest classes, unemployed and listless, lie basking in the sun like lizards; and unregarded children,—every heavy glance of their young eyes full of desperation and stony depravity, and their throats hoarse with cursing,—gamble, and fight, and snarl, and sleep, hour after hour, clashing their bruised centesimi[19] upon the marble ledges of the church porch. And the images of Christ and His angels look down upon it continually.

That we may not enter the church out of the midst of the horror of this, let us turn aside under the portico which looks across the sea, and passing round within the two massive pillars brought from St. Jean d'Acre, we shall find the gate of the Baptistery; let us enter there. The heavy door closes behind us instantly, and the light and the turbulence of the Piazzetta are together shut out by it.

We are in a low vaulted room; vaulted, not with arches but with small cupolas starred with gold, and checkered with gloomy figures: in the center is a bronze font charged with rich bas-reliefs, a small figure of the Baptist standing above it in a single ray of light that glances across the narrow room, dying as it falls from a window high in the wall, and the first thing that it strikes, and the only thing that it strikes brightly, is a tomb. We hardly know if it be a tomb indeed; for it is like a narrow couch set beside the window, low-roofed and curtained, so that it might seem, but that it is some height above the pavement, to have been drawn towards the window, that the sleeper might be wakened early;—only there are two angels, who have drawn the curtain back, and are looking down upon him. Let us look also, and thank that gentle light that rests upon his forehead for ever, and dies away upon his breast.

The face is of a man in middle life, but there are two deep furrows right across the forehead, dividing it like the foundations of a tower: the height of it above is bound by the fillet of the ducal cap. The rest of the features are singularly small and delicate, the lips sharp, perhaps the sharpness of death being added to that of the natural lines; but there is a sweet smile upon them, and a deep

[17]St. Matthew, 21:12; St. John, 2:16.

[18]This was written before 1866, when Venice was surrendered by Austria to the new Kingdom of Italy.

[19]Small coins, normally worth about one-fifth of a cent.

serenity upon the whole countenance. The roof of the canopy above has been blue, filled with stars; beneath, in the center of the tomb on which the figure rests, is a seated figure of the Virgin, and the border of it all around is of flowers and soft leaves, growing rich and deep, as if in a field in summer.

It is the Doge Andrea Dandolo, a man early great among the great of Venice; and early lost. She chose him for her king in his 36th year; he died ten years later, leaving behind him that history to which we owe half of what we know of her former fortunes.[20]

Look round at the room in which he lies. The floor of it is of rich mosaic, encompassed by a low seat of red marble, and its walls are of alabaster, but worn and shattered, and darkly stained with age, almost a ruin,—in places the slabs of marble have fallen away altogether, and the rugged brickwork is seen through the rents, but all beautiful; the ravaging fissures fretting their way among the islands and channeled zones of the alabaster, and the time-stains on its translucent masses darkened into fields of rich golden brown, like the color of seaweed when the sun strikes on it through deep sea. The light fades away into the recess of the chamber towards the altar, and the eye can hardly trace the lines of the bas-relief behind it of the baptism of Christ: but on the vaulting of the roof the figures are distinct, and there are seen upon it two great circles, one surrounded by the "Principalities and powers in heavenly places,"[21] of which Milton has expressed the ancient division in the single massy line,

Thrones, Dominations, Princedoms, Virtues, Powers,[22]

and around the other, the Apostles; Christ the center of both: and upon the walls, again and again repeated, the gaunt figure of the Baptist, in every circumstance of his life and death; and the streams of the Jordan running down between their cloven rocks; the ax laid to the root of a fruitless tree that springs up on their shore. "Every tree that bringeth not forth good fruit shall be hewn down, and cast into the fire."[23] Yes, verily: to be baptized with fire, or to be cast therein; it is the choice set before all men. The march-notes still murmur through the grated window, and mingle with the sounding in our ears of the sentence of judgment, which the old Greek has written on the Baptistery wall. Venice has made her choice.

He who lies under that stony canopy would have taught her another choice, in his day, if she would have listened to him; but he and his counsels have long been forgotten by her, and the dust lies upon his lips.

Through the heavy door whose bronze network closes the place of his rest, let us enter the church itself. It is lost in still deeper twilight, to which the eye must be accustomed for some moments before the form of the building can be traced; and then there opens before us a vast cave, hewn out into the form of a Cross, and divided into shadowy aisles by many pillars. Round the domes of its roof the light enters only through narrow apertures like large stars; and here and there a ray or two from some faraway casement wanders into the darkness, and casts a narrow phosphoric stream upon the waves of marble that heave and fall in a thousand colors along the floor. What else there is of light is from torches, or silver lamps, burning ceaselessly in the recesses of the chapels; the roof sheeted with gold, and the polished walls covered with alabaster, give back at every curve and angle some feeble gleaming to the flames; and the glories round the heads of the sculptured saints flash out upon us as we pass them, and sink again into the gloom. Under foot and over head, a continual succession of crowded imagery, one picture passing into another, as in a dream; forms beautiful and terrible mixed together; dragons and serpents, and ravening beasts of prey, and graceful birds that in the midst of them drink from running fountains and feed from vases of crystal; the passions and the pleasures of human life symbolized together, and the mystery of its redemption; for the mazes of interwoven lines and changeful pictures lead always at last to the Cross, lifted and carved in every place and upon every stone; sometimes with

---

[20]The *Venetian Chronicle of Andrea Dandolo*. He reigned from 1343 to 1354.

[21]See Ephesians, 3:10.   [22]*Paradise Lost*, v, 601.

[23]St. Matthew, 3:10.

the serpent of eternity wrapped round it, sometimes with doves beneath its arms, and sweet herbage growing forth from its feet; but conspicuous most of all on the great rood that crosses the church before the altar, raised in bright blazonry against the shadow of the apse. And although in the recesses of the aisles and chapels, when the mist of the incense hangs heavily, we may see continually a figure traced in faint lines upon their marble, a woman standing with her eyes raised to heaven, and the inscription above her, "Mother of God," she is not here[24] the presiding deity. It is the Cross that is first seen, and always, burning in the center of the temple; and every dome and hollow of its roof has the figure of Christ in the utmost height of it, raised in power, or returning in judgment.

Nor is this interior without effect on the minds of the people. At every hour of the day there are groups collected before the various shrines, and solitary worshipers scattered through the darker places of the church, evidently in prayer both deep and reverent, and, for the most part, profoundly sorrowful. The devotees at the greater number of the renowned shrines of Romanism may be seen murmuring their appointed prayers with wandering eyes and unengaged gestures; but the step of the stranger does not disturb those who kneel on the pavement of St. Mark's; and hardly a moment passes, from early morning to sunset, in which we may not see some half-veiled figure enter beneath the Arabian porch, cast itself into long abasement on the floor of the temple, and then rising slowly with more confirmed step, and with a passionate kiss and clasp of the arms given to the feet of the crucifix, by which the lamps burn always in the northern aisle, leave the church, as if comforted.

But we must not hastily conclude from this that the nobler characters of the building have at present any influence in fostering a devotional spirit. There is distress enough in Venice to bring many to their knees, without excitement from external imagery; and whatever there may be in the temper of the worship offered in St. Mark's more than can be accounted for by reference to the unhappy circumstances of the city, is assuredly not owing either to the beauty of its architecture or to the impressiveness of the Scripture histories embodied in its mosaics. That it has a peculiar effect, however slight, on the popular mind, may perhaps be safely conjectured from the number of worshipers which it attracts, while the churches of St. Paul and the Frari, larger in size and more central in position, are left comparatively empty.[25] But this effect is altogether to be ascribed to its richer assemblage of those sources of influence which address themselves to the commonest instincts of the human mind, and which, in all ages and countries, have been more or less employed in the support of superstition. Darkness and mystery; confused recesses of building; artificial light employed in small quantity, but maintained with a constancy which seems to give it a kind of sacredness; preciousness of material easily comprehended by the vulgar eye; close air loaded with a sweet and peculiar odor associated only with religious services, solemn music, and tangible idols or images having popular legends attached to them,—these, the stage properties of superstition, which have been from the beginning of the world, and must be to the end of it, employed by all nations, whether openly savage or nominally civilized, to produce a false awe in minds incapable of apprehending the true nature of the Deity, are assembled in St. Mark's to a degree, as far as I know, unexampled in any other European church. The arts of the Magus[26] and the Brahmin are exhausted in the animation of a paralyzed Christianity; and the popular sentiment which these arts excite is to be regarded by us with no more respect than we should have considered ourselves justified in rendering to the devotion of the worshipers at Eleusis, Ellora, or Edfou.[27]

---

[24]There is an implied reference to the church of San Donato at Murano, described in the preceding chapter, in which the Virgin is "the presiding deity."

[25]The mere warmth of St. Mark's in winter, which is much greater than that of the other two churches above named, must, however, be taken into consideration, as one of the most efficient causes of its being then more frequented (Ruskin's note).

[26]Member of the ancient Persian priestly class.

[27]Ellora is in Hyderabad, India; Edfou in upper Egypt.

UNTO THIS LAST

The Roots of Honor[1]

AMONG the delusions which at different periods have possessed themselves of the minds of large masses of the human race, perhaps the most curious—certainly the least creditable—is the modern *soi-disant*[2] science of political economy, based on the idea that an advantageous code of social action may be determined irrespectively of the influence of social affection.

Of course, as in the instances of alchemy, astrology, witchcraft, and other such popular creeds, political economy has a plausible idea at the root of it. "The social affections," says the economist, "are accidental and disturbing elements in human nature; but avarice and the desire of progress are constant elements. Let us eliminate the inconstants, and, considering the human being merely as a covetous machine, examine by what laws of labor, purchase, and sale, the greatest accumulative result in wealth is obtainable. Those laws once determined, it will be for each individual afterwards to introduce as much of the disturbing affectionate element as he chooses, and to determine for himself the result on the new conditions supposed."

This would be a perfectly logical and successful method of analysis, if the accidentals afterward to be introduced were of the same nature as the powers first examined. Supposing a body in motion to be influenced by constant and inconstant forces, it is usually the simplest way of examining its course to trace it first under the persistent conditions, and afterwards introduce the causes of variation. But the disturbing elements in the social problem are not of the same nature as the constant ones: they alter the essence of the creature under examination the moment they are added; they operate, not mathematically, but chemically, introducing conditions which render all our previous knowledge unavailable. We made learned experiments upon pure nitrogen, and have convinced ourselves that it is a very manageable gas: but, behold! the thing which we have practically to deal with is its chloride; and this, the moment we touch it on our established principles, sends us and our apparatus through the ceiling.

Observe, I neither impugn nor doubt the conclusion of the science if its terms are accepted. I am simply uninterested in them, as I should be in those of a science of gymnastics which assumed that men had no skeletons. It might be shown, on that supposition, that it would be advantageous to roll the students up into pellets, flatten them into cakes, or stretch them into cables; and that when these results were effected, the reinsertion of the skeleton would be attended with various inconveniences to their constitution. The reasoning might be admirable, the conclusions true, and the science deficient only in applicability. Modern political economy stands on a precisely similar basis. Assuming, not that the human being has no skeleton, but that it is all skeleton, it founds an ossifiant[3] theory of progress on this negation of a soul; and having shown the utmost that may be made of bones, and constructed a number of interesting geometrical figures with death's-head and humeri,[4] successfully proves the inconvenience of the reappearance of a soul among these corpuscular structures. I do not deny the truth of this theory: I simply deny its applicability to the present phase of the world.

This inapplicability has been curiously manifested during the embarrassment caused by the late strikes of our workmen.[5] Here occurs one of the simplest cases, in a pertinent and positive form, of the first vital problem which political economy has to deal with (the relation between employer and employed); and, at a severe crisis, when lives in multitudes and wealth in masses are at stake, the political economists are helpless—practically mute: no demonstrable solution

---

[1] The four essays composing *Unto This Last* were published in the *Cornhill Magazine* in 1860 and as a book in 1862. *The Roots of Honor* is the first essay in the volume.

[2] Would-be.

[3] Bone-making.   [4] Armbones.

[5] The reference is particularly to a builders' strike in the autumn of 1859.

of the difficulty can be given by them, such as may convince or calm the opposing parties. Obstinately the masters take one view of the matter; obstinately the operatives[6] another; and no political science can set them at one.

It would be strange if it could, it being not by "science" of any kind that men were ever intended to be set at one. Disputant after disputant vainly tries to show that the interests of the masters are, or are not, antagonistic to those of the men: none of the pleaders ever seeming to remember that it does not absolutely or always follow that the persons must be antagonistic because their interests are. If there is only a crust of bread in the house, and mother and children are starving, their interests are not the same. If the mother eats it, the children want it; if the children eat it, the mother must go hungry to her work. Yet it does not necessarily follow that there will be "antagonism" between them, that they will fight for the crust, and that the mother, being strongest, will get it, and eat it. Neither, in any other case, whatever the relations of the persons may be, can it be assumed for certain that, because their interests are diverse, they must necessarily regard each other with hostility, and use violence or cunning to obtain the advantage.

Even if this were so, and it were as just as it is convenient to consider men as actuated by no other moral influences than those which affect rats or swine, the logical conditions of the question are still indeterminable. It can never be shown generally either that the interests of master and laborer are alike, or that they are opposed; for, according to circumstances, they may be either. It is, indeed, always the interest of both that the work should be rightly done, and a just price obtained for it; but, in the division of profits, the gain of the one may or may not be the loss of the other. It is not the master's interest to pay wages so low as to leave the men sickly and depressed, nor the workman's interest to be paid high wages if the smallness of the master's profit hinders him from enlarging his business, or conducting it in a safe and liberal way. A stoker ought

[6] Workers.

not to desire high pay if the company is too poor to keep the engine-wheels in repair.

And the varieties of circumstance which influence these reciprocal interests are so endless, that all endeavor to deduce rules of action from balance of expediency is in vain. And it is meant to be in vain. For no human actions ever were intended by the Maker of men to be guided by balances of expediency, but by balances of justice. He has therefore rendered all endeavors to determine expediency futile for evermore. No man ever knew, or can know, what will be the ultimate result to himself, or to others, of any given line of conduct. But every man may know, and most of us do know, what is a just and unjust act. And all of us may know also, that the consequences of justice will be ultimately the best possible, both to others and ourselves, though we can neither say what *is* best, or how it is likely to come to pass.

I have said balances of justice, meaning, in the term justice, to include affection,— such affection as one man *owes* to another. All right relations between master and operative, and all their best interests, ultimately depend on these.

We shall find the best and simplest illustration of the relations of master and operative in the position of domestic servants.

We will suppose that the master of a household desires only to get as much work out of his servants as he can, at the rate of wages he gives. He never allows them to be idle; feeds them as poorly and lodges them as ill as they will endure, and in all things pushes his requirements to the exact point beyond which he cannot go without forcing the servant to leave him. In doing this, there is no violation on his part of what is commonly called "justice." He agrees with the domestic for his whole time and service, and takes them;—the limits of hardship in treatment being fixed by the practice of other masters in his neighborhood; that is to say, by the current rate of wages for domestic labor. If the servant can get a better place, he is free to take one, and the master can only tell what is the real market value of his labor, by requiring as much as he will give.

This is the politico-economical view of the case, according to the doctors of that science; who assert that by this procedure the greatest average of work will be obtained from the servant, and therefore the greatest bene- 5 fit to the community, and through the community, by reversion, to the servant himself.

That, however, is not so. It would be so if the servant were an engine of which the motive power was steam, magnetism, gravi- 10 tation, or any other agent of calculable force. But he being, on the contrary, an engine whose motive power is a Soul, the force of this very peculiar agent, as an unknown quantity, enters into all the political econo- 15 mist's equations, without his knowledge, and falsifies every one of their results. The largest quantity of work will not be done by this curious engine for pay, or under pressure, or by help of any kind of fuel 20 which may be supplied by the chaldron. It will be done only when the motive force, that is to say, the will or spirit of the creature, is brought to its greatest strength by its own proper fuel: namely, by the affections. 25

It may indeed happen, and does happen often, that if the master is a man of sense and energy, a large quantity of material work may be done under mechanical pressure, enforced by strong will and guided by 30 wise method; also it may happen, and does happen often, that if the master is indolent and weak (however good-natured), a very small quantity of work, and that bad, may be produced by the servant's undirected 35 strength, and contemptuous gratitude. But the universal law of the matter is that, assuming any given quantity of energy and sense in master and servant, the greatest material result obtainable by them will be, 40 not through antagonism to each other, but through affection for each other; and that, if the master, instead of endeavoring to get as much work as possible from the servant, seeks rather to render his appointed and nec- 45 essary work beneficial to him, and to forward his interests in all just and wholesome ways, the real amount of work ultimately done, or of good rendered, by the person so cared for, will indeed be the greatest possible. 50

Observe, I say, "of good rendered," for a servant's work is not necessarily or always the best thing he can give his master. But good of all kinds, whether in material service, in protective watchfulness of his master's interest and credit, or in joyful readiness to seize unexpected and irregular occasions of help.

Nor is this one whit less generally true because indulgence will be frequently abused, and kindness met with ingratitude. For the servant who, gently treated, is ungrateful, treated ungently, will be revengeful; and the man who is dishonest to a liberal master will be injurious to an unjust one.

In any case, and with any person, this unselfish treatment will produce the most effective return. Observe, I am here considering the affections wholly as a motive power; not at all as things in themselves desirable or noble, or in any other way abstractedly good. I look at them simply as an anomalous force, rendering every one of the ordinary political economist's calculations nugatory; while, even if he desired to introduce this new element into his estimates, he has no power of dealing with it; for the affections only become a true motive power when they ignore every other motive and condition of political economy. Treat the servant kindly, with the idea of turning his gratitude to account, and you will get, as you deserve, no gratitude, nor any value for your kindness; but treat him kindly without any economical purpose, and all economical purposes will be answered; in this, as in all other matters, whosoever will save his life shall lose it, whoso loses it shall find it.[7]

---

[7]The difference between the two modes of treatment, and between their effective material results, may be seen very accurately by a comparison of the relations of Esther and Charlie in *Bleak House* with those of Miss Brass and the Marchioness in *Master Humphrey's Clock.*

The essential value and truth of Dickens's writings have been unwisely lost sight of by many thoughtful persons, merely because he presents his truth with some color of caricature. Unwisely, because Dickens's caricature, though often gross, is never mistaken. Allowing for his manner of telling them, the things he tells us are always true. I wish that he could think it right to limit his brilliant exaggeration to works written only for public amusement; and when he takes up a subject of high national importance, such as that which he handled in *Hard Times,* that he would use severer and more accurate analysis. The usefulness of that work (to my mind, in several respects the greatest he has written) is with many persons seriously

The next clearest and simplest example of relation between master and operative is that which exists between the commander of a regiment and his men.

Supposing the officer only desires to apply the rules of discipline so as, with least trouble to himself, to make the regiment most effective, he will not be able, by any rules or administration of rules, on this selfish principle, to develop the full strength of his subordinates. If a man of sense and firmness, he may, as in the former instance, produce a better result than would be obtained by the irregular kindness of a weak officer; but let the sense and firmness be the same in both cases, and assuredly the officer who has the most direct personal relations with his men, the most care for their interests, and the most value for their lives, will develop their effective strength, through their affection for his own person, and trust in his character, to a degree wholly unattainable by other means. This law applies still more stringently as the numbers concerned are larger: a charge may often be successful, though the men dislike their officers; a battle has rarely been won, unless they loved their general.

Passing from these simple examples to the more complicated relations existing between a manufacturer and his workmen, we are met first by certain curious difficulties, resulting, apparently, from a harder and colder state of moral elements. It is easy to imagine an enthusiastic affection existing among soldiers for the colonel. Not so easy to imagine an enthusiastic affection among cotton-spinners for the proprietor of the mill. A body of men associated for purposes of

robbery (as a Highland clan in ancient times) shall be animated by perfect affection, and every member of it be ready to lay down his life for the life of his chief. But a band of men associated for purposes of legal production and accumulation is usually animated, it appears, by no such emotions, and none of them are in anywise willing to give his life for the life of his chief. Not only are we met by this apparent anomaly, in moral matters, but by others connected with it, in administration of system. For a servant or a soldier is engaged at a definite rate of wages, for a definite period; but a workman at a rate of wages variable according to the demand for labor, and with the risk of being at any time thrown out of his situation by chances of trade. Now, as, under these contingencies, no action of the affections can take place, but only an explosive action of *dis*affections, two points offer themselves for consideration in the matter.

The first—How far the rate of wages may be so regulated as not to vary with the demand for labor.

The second—How far it is possible that bodies of workmen may be engaged and maintained at such fixed rate of wages (whatever the state of trade may be), without enlarging or diminishing their number, so as to give them permanent interest in the establishment with which they are connected, like that of the domestic servants in an old family, or an *esprit de corps,* like that of the soldiers in a crack regiment.

The first question is, I say, how far it may be possible to fix the rate of wages, irrespectively of the demand for labor.

Perhaps one of the most curious facts in the history of human error is the denial by the common political economist of the possibility of thus regulating wages; while, for all the important, and much of the unimportant, labor, on the earth, wages are already so regulated.

We do not sell our prime-ministership by Dutch auction; nor, on the decease of a bishop, whatever may be the general advantages of simony, do we (yet) offer his diocese to the clergyman who will take the episcopacy at the lowest contract. We (with exquisite sagacity of political economy!) do

diminished because Mr. Bounderby is a dramatic monster, instead of a characteristic example of a worldly master; and Stephen Blackpool a dramatic perfection, instead of a characteristic example of an honest workman. But let us not lose the use of Dickens's wit and insight, because he chooses to speak in a circle of stage fire. He is entirely right in his main drift and purpose in every book he has written; and all of them, but especially *Hard Times,* should be studied with close and earnest care by persons interested in social questions. They will find much that is partial, and, because partial, apparently unjust; but if they examine all the evidence on the other side, which Dickens seems to overlook, it will appear, after all their trouble, that his view was the finally right one, grossly and sharply told (Ruskin's note).

indeed sell commissions; but not openly, generalships: sick, we do not inquire for a physician who takes less than a guinea; litigious, we never think of reducing six-and-eightpence to four-and-sixpence; caught in a shower, we do not canvass the cabmen, to find one who values his driving at less than sixpence a mile.

It is true that in all these cases there is, and in every conceivable case there must be, ultimate reference to the presumed difficulty of the work, or number of candidates for the office. If it were thought that the labor necessary to make a good physician would be gone through by a sufficient number of students with the prospect of only half-guinea fees, public consent would soon withdraw the unnecessary half-guinea. In this ultimate sense, the price of labor is indeed always regulated by the demand for it; but, so far as the practical and immediate administration of the matter is regarded, the best labor always has been, and is, as *all* labor ought to be, paid by an invariable standard.

"What!" the reader perhaps answers amazedly: "pay good and bad workmen alike?"

Certainly. The difference between one prelate's sermons and his successor's—or between one physician's opinion and another's —is far greater, as respects the qualities of mind involved, and far more important in result to you personally, than the difference between good and bad laying of bricks (though that is greater than most people suppose). Yet you pay with equal fee, contentedly, the good and bad workmen upon your soul, and the good and bad workmen upon your body; much more may you pay, contentedly, with equal fees, the good and bad workmen upon your house.

"Nay, but I choose my physician and (?) my clergyman, thus indicating my sense of the quality of their work." By all means, also, choose your bricklayer; that is the proper reward of the good workman, to be "chosen." The natural and right system respecting all labor is, that it should be paid at a fixed rate, but the good workman employed, and the bad workman unemployed. The false, unnatural, and destructive system is when the bad workman is allowed to offer his work at half-price, and either take the place of the good, or force him by his competition to work for an inadequate sum.

This equality of wages, then, being the first object towards which we have to discover the directest available road; the second is, as above stated, that of maintaining constant numbers of workmen in employment, whatever may be the accidental demand for the article they produce.

I believe the sudden and extensive inequalities of demand, which necessarily arise in the mercantile operations of an active nation, constitute the only essential difficulty which has to be overcome in a just organization of labor.

The subject opens into too many branches to admit of being investigated in a paper of this kind; but the following general facts bearing on it may be noted.

The wages which enable any workman to live are necessarily higher, if his work is liable to intermission, than if it is assured and continuous; and however severe the struggle for work may become, the general law will always hold, that men must get more daily pay if, on the average, they can only calculate on work three days a week than they would require if they were sure of work six days a week. Supposing that a man cannot live on less than a shilling a day, his seven shillings he must get, either for three days' violent work, or six days' deliberate work. The tendency of all modern mercantile operations is to throw both wages and trade into the form of a lottery, and to make the workman's pay depend on intermittent exertion, and the principal's profit on dexterously used chance.

In what partial degree, I repeat, this may be necessary in consequence of the activities of modern trade, I do not here investigate; contenting myself with the fact that in its fatalest aspects it is assuredly unnecessary, and results merely from love of gambling on the part of the masters, and from ignorance and sensuality in the men. The masters cannot bear to let any opportunity of gain escape them, and frantically rush at every gap and breach in the walls of Fortune, raging to be rich, and affronting, with impatient covetousness, every risk of ruin, while the men prefer three days of violent labor, and three days of drunkenness, to six days of moderate work and wise rest. There is no way in which a principal, who really desires to help his workmen, may do it more effectually than by checking these disorderly habits both in himself and them; keeping his own business operations on a scale which will enable him to pursue them securely, not yielding to temptations of precarious gain; and at the same time, leading his workmen into regular habits of labor and life, either by inducing them rather to take low wages, in the form of a fixed salary, than high wages, subject to the chance of their being thrown out of work; or, if this be impossible, by discouraging the system of violent exertion for nominally high day wages, and leading the men to take lower pay for more regular labor.

In effecting any radical changes of this kind, doubtless there would be great inconvenience and loss incurred by all the originators of the movement. That which can be done with perfect convenience and without loss, is not always the thing that most needs to be done, or which we are most imperatively required to do.

I have already alluded to the difference hitherto existing between regiments of men associated for purposes of violence, and for purposes of manufacture; in that the former appear capable of self-sacrifice—the latter, not; which singular fact is the real reason of the general lowness of estimate in which the profession of commerce is held, as compared with that of arms. Philosophically, it does not, at first sight, appear reasonable (many writers have endeavored to prove it unreasonable) that a peaceable and rational person, whose trade is buying and selling, should be held in less honor than an unpeaceable and often irrational person, whose trade is slaying. Nevertheless, the consent of mankind has always, in spite of the philosophers, given precedence to the soldier.

And this is right.

For the soldier's trade, verily and essentially, is not slaying, but being slain. This, without well knowing its own meaning, the world honors it for. A bravo's trade is slaying; but the world has never respected bravos more than merchants: the reason it honors the soldier is, because he holds his life at the service of the State. Reckless he may be—fond of pleasure or of adventure—all kinds of bye-motives and mean impulses may have determined the choice of his profession, and may affect (to all appearance exclusively) his daily conduct in it; but our estimate of him is based on this ultimate fact—of which we are well assured—that put him in a fortress breach, with all the pleasures of the world behind him, and only death and his duty in front of him, he will keep his face to the front; and he knows that his choice may be put to him at any moment—and has beforehand taken his part—virtually takes such part continually—does, in reality, die daily.[8]

Not less is the respect we pay to the lawyer and physician, founded ultimately on their self-sacrifice. Whatever the learning or acuteness of a great lawyer, our chief respect for him depends on our belief that, set in a judge's seat, he will strive to judge justly, come of it what may. Could we suppose that he would take bribes, and use his acuteness and legal knowledge to give plausibility to iniquitous decisions, no degree of intellect would win for him our respect. Nothing will win it, short of our tacit conviction, that in all important acts of his life justice is first with him; his own interest, second.

In the case of a physician, the ground of the honor we render him is clearer still. Whatever his science, we would shrink from him in horror if we found him regard his patients merely as subjects to experiment upon; much more, if we found that, receiving bribes from persons interested in their deaths, he was using his best skill to give poison in the mask of medicine.

Finally, the principle holds with utmost clearness as it respects clergymen. No goodness of disposition will excuse want of science in a physician, or of shrewdness in an advocate; but a clergyman, even though his power of intellect be small, is respected on the presumed ground of his unselfishness and serviceableness.

---

[8] See I Corinthians, 15:31.

Now, there can be no question but that the tact, foresight, decision, and other mental powers, required for the successful management of a large mercantile concern, if not such as could be compared with those of a great lawyer, general, or divine, would at least match the general conditions of mind required in the subordinate officers of a ship, or of a regiment, or in the curate of a country parish. If, therefore, all the efficient members of the so-called liberal professions are still, somehow, in public estimate of honor, preferred before the head of a commercial firm, the reason must lie deeper than in the measurement of their several powers of mind.

And the essential reason for such preference will be found to lie in the fact that the merchant is presumed to act always selfishly. His work may be very necessary to the community; but the motive of it is understood to be wholly personal. The merchant's first object in all his dealings must be (the public believe) to get as much for himself, and leave as little to his neighbor (or customer) as possible. Enforcing this upon him, by political statute, as the necessary principle of his action; recommending it to him on all occasions, and themselves reciprocally adopting it; proclaiming vociferously, for law of the universe, that a buyer's function is to cheapen, and a seller's to cheat,—the public, nevertheless, involuntarily condemn the man of commerce for his compliance with their own statement, and stamp him forever as belonging to an inferior grade of human personality.

This they will find, eventually, they must give up doing. They must not cease to condemn selfishness; but they will have to discover a kind of commerce which is not exclusively selfish. Or, rather, they will have to discover that there never was, or can be, any other kind of commerce; that this which they have called commerce was not commerce at all, but cozening; and that a true merchant differs as much from a merchant according to laws of modern political economy, as the hero of the *Excursion* from Autolycus.[9] They will find that commerce

is an occupation which gentlemen will every day see more need to engage in, rather than in the businesses of talking to men, or slaying them; that, in true commerce, as in true preaching, or true fighting, it is necessary to admit the idea of occasional voluntary loss; —that sixpences have to be lost, as well as lives, under a sense of duty; that the market may have its martyrdoms as well as the pulpit; and trade its heroisms as well as war.

May have—in the final issue, must have— and only has not had yet, because men of heroic temper have always been misguided in their youth into other fields; not recognizing what is in our days, perhaps, the most important of all fields; so that, while many a zealous person loses his life in trying to teach the form of a gospel, very few will lose a hundred pounds in showing the practice of one.

The fact is, that people never have had clearly explained to them the true functions of a merchant with respect to other people. I should like the reader to be very clear about this.

Five great intellectual professions, relating to daily necessities of life, have hitherto existed—three[10] exist necessarily, in every civilized nation:

The Soldier's profession is to *defend* it.

The Pastor's to *teach* it.

The Physician's to *keep it in health.*

The Lawyer's to *enforce justice* in it.

The Merchant's to *provide* for it.

And the duty of all these men is, on due occasion, to *die* for it.

"On due occasion," namely:—

The Soldier, rather than leave his post in battle.

The Physician, rather than leave his post in plague.

The Pastor, rather than teach Falsehood.

The Lawyer, rather than countenance Injustice.

The Merchant—what is *his* "due occasion" of death?

It is the main question for the merchant,

---

[9] The hero of Wordsworth's *Excursion* is a high-minded peddler, known as the Wanderer. Autolycus,

in Shakespeare's *Winter's Tale,* is, as he calls himself, "a snapper-up of unconsidered trifles," a sneak thief, who on occasion assumes the part of a peddler.

[10] The professions of the pastor, the physician, and the merchant.

as for all of us. For, truly, the man who does not know when to die, does not know how to live.

Observe, the merchant's function (or manufacturer's, for in the broad sense in which it is here used the word must be understood to include both) is to provide for the nation. It is no more his function to get profit for himself out of that provision than it is a clergyman's function to get his stipend. This stipend is a due and necessary adjunct, but not the object of his life, if he be a true clergyman, any more than his fee (or honorarium) is the object of life to a true physician. Neither is his fee the object of life to a true merchant. All three, if true men, have a work to be done irrespective of fee—to be done even at any cost, or for quite the contrary of fee; the pastor's function being to teach, the physician's to heal, and the merchant's, as I have said, to provide. That is to say, he has to understand to their very root the qualities of the thing he deals in, and the means of obtaining or producing it; and he has to apply all his sagacity and energy to the producing or obtaining it in perfect state, and distributing it at the cheapest possible price where it is most needed.

And because the production or obtaining of any commodity involves necessarily the agency of many lives and hands, the merchant becomes in the course of his business the master and governor of large masses of men in a more direct, though less confessed way, than a military officer or pastor; so that on him falls, in great part, the responsibility for the kind of life they lead: and it becomes his duty, not only to be always considering how to produce what he sells, in the purest and cheapest forms, but how to make the various employments involved in the production, or transference of it, most beneficial to the men employed.

And as into these two functions, requiring for their right exercise the highest intelligence, as well as patience, kindness, and tact, the merchant is bound to put all his energy, so for their just discharge he is bound, as soldier or physician is bound, to give up, if need be, his life, in such way as it may be demanded of him. Two main points he has in his providing function to maintain: first, his engagements (faithfulness to engagements being the real root of all possibilities, in commerce); and, secondly, the perfectness and purity of the thing provided; so that, rather than fail in any engagement, or consent to any deterioration, adulteration, or unjust and exorbitant price of that which he provides, he is bound to meet fearlessly any form of distress, poverty, or labor, which may, through maintenance of these points, come upon him.

Again: in his office as governor of the men employed by him, the merchant or manufacturer is invested with a distinctly paternal authority and responsibility. In most cases, a youth entering a commercial establishment is withdrawn altogether from home influence; his master must become his father, else he has, for practical and constant help, no father at hand: in all cases the master's authority, together with the general tone and atmosphere of his business, and the character of the men with whom the youth is compelled in the course of it to associate, have more immediate and pressing weight than the home influence, and will usually neutralize it either for good or evil; so that the only means which the master has of doing justice to the men employed by him is to ask himself sternly whether he is dealing with such subordinate as he would with his own son, if compelled by circumstances to take such a position.

Supposing the captain of a frigate saw it right, or were by any chance obliged, to place his own son in the position of a common sailor: as he would then treat his son, he is bound always to treat every one of the men under him. So, also, supposing the master of a manufactory saw it right, or were by any chance obliged, to place his own son in the position of an ordinary workman; as he would then treat his son, he is bound always to treat every one of his men. This is the only effective, true, or practical RULE which can be given on this point of political economy.

And as the captain of a ship is bound to be the last man to leave his ship in case of wreck, and to share his last crust with the sailors in case of famine, so the manufacturer, in any commercial crisis or distress, is bound to take the suffering of it with his men, and even to take more of it for himself than he allows his men to feel; as a father would in a famine, shipwreck, or battle, sacrifice himself for his son.

All which sounds very strange: the only real strangeness in the matter being, nevertheless, that it should so sound. For all this is true, and that not partially nor theoretically, but everlastingly and practically; all other doctrine than this respecting matters political being false in premises, absurd in deduction, and impossible in practice, consistently with any progressive state of national life; all the life which we now possess as a nation showing itself in the resolute denial and scorn, by a few strong minds and faithful hearts, of the economic principles taught to our multitudes, which principles, so far as accepted, lead straight to national destruction. Respecting the modes and forms of destruction to which they lead, and, on the other hand, respecting the farther practical working of true polity, I hope to reason farther in a following paper.

FORS CLAVIGERA

Companionship[1]

As I am now often asked, in private letters, the constitution of St. George's Company, and cannot, hitherto, refer, in answer, to any clear summary of it, I will try to write such a summary in this number of *Fors,* that it may henceforward be sent to inquirers as alone sufficiently explanatory.

The St. George's Company is a society established to carry out certain charitable objects, towards which it invites, and thankfully will receive, help from any persons caring to give it, either in money, labor, or any kind of gift. But the Company itself consists of persons who agree in certain general principles of action, and objects of pursuit, and who can, therefore, act together in effective and constant unison.

These objects of pursuit are, in brief terms, the health, wealth, and long life of the British nation: the Company having thus devoted itself, in the conviction that the British nation is at present unhealthy, poor, and likely to perish, as a power, from the face of the earth. They accordingly propose to themselves the general medicining, enriching, and preserving in political strength, of the population of these islands; they themselves numbering at present, in their ranks, about thirty persons—none of them rich, several of them sick, and the leader of them, at all events, not likely to live long.

Whether the nation be healthy, or in unwholesome degradation of body and mind; wealthy, or in continual and shameful distress; strong, or in rapid decline of political power and authority,—the reader will find debated throughout the various contents of the preceding five volumes of *Fors.* But there is one public fact, which cannot be debated—that the nation is in debt. And the St. George's Company do practically make it their *first,* though not their principal, object, to bring *that* state of things to an end; and to establish, instead of a National Debt, a National Store. (See the last line of the fifth page of the first letter of the series, published 1st January, 1871, and the eleventh, and twenty-seventh, letters, throughout.)

That very few readers of *this* page have any notion, at this moment, what a National Debt is, or can conceive what a National Store should be, is one of many evil consequences of the lies which, under the title of "Political Economy," have been taught by the ill-educated, and mostly dishonest, commercial men who at present govern the press of the country.

I have again and again stated the truth in both these matters, but must try once more to do it, emphatically and intelligibly.

A "civilized nation" in modern Europe consists, in broad terms, of (A) a mass of half-taught, discontented, and mostly penniless populace, calling itself the people; of (B) a thing which it calls a government,

---

[1] *Fors Clavigera* was a collection of letters to the workmen of Great Britain, published 1871–1884; *Companionship,* the sixty-seventh letter, published in Vol. VI (1876). Ruskin explained the title of the series as follows: *Fors* combines in its meaning Force, Fortitude, and Fortune; *Clavigera* is equivalent to the Nail-Bearer, the Club-Bearer, and the Key-Bearer (*Fors,* letter 2).

meaning an apparatus for collecting and spending money; and (C) a small number of capitalists, many of them rogues, and most of them stupid persons, who have no idea of any object of human existence other than money-making, gambling, or champagne-bibbing. A certain quantity of literary men, saying anything they can get paid to say,—of clergymen, saying anything they have been taught to say,—of natural philosophers, saying anything that comes into their heads,—and of nobility, saying nothing at all, combine in disguising the action, and perfecting the disorganization, of the mass; but with respect to practical business, the civilized nation consists broadly of mob, money-collecting machine, and capitalist.

Now when the civilized mob wants to spend money for any profitless or mischievous purposes,—fireworks, illuminations, battles, driving about from place to place, or what not,—being itself penniless, it sets its money-collecting machine to borrow the sum needful for these amusements from the civilized capitalist.

The civilized capitalist lends the money, on condition that, through the money-collecting machine, he may tax the civilized mob thenceforward forever. The civilized mob spends the money forthwith, in gunpowder, infernal machines,[2] masquerade dresses, new boulevards, or anything else it has set its idiotic mind on for the moment; and appoints its money-collecting machine to collect a daily tax from its children, and children's children, to be paid to the capitalists from whom it had received the accommodation, thenceforward forever.

That is the nature of a National Debt.

In order to understand that of a National Store, my readers must first consider what any store whatever, serviceable to human beings, consists of. A store properly means a collection of useful things. Literally, it signifies only a quantity,—or much of *anything*. But the heap of broken bottles which, I hear, is accumulating under the principal cliff of Snowdon,[3] through the contributions of tourists from the summit, is not properly to be called a store; though a bin full of old

wine is. Neither is a heap of cannon-balls a store;[4] though a heap of potatoes is. Neither is a cellar full of gunpowder a store; though a cellar full of coals is. A store is, for squirrels, of nuts; for bees, of honey; for men, of food, clothes, fuel, or pretty things, such as toys or jewels,—and, for educated persons, of books and pictures.

And the possession of such a store by the nation would signify, that there were no taxes to pay; that everybody had clothes enough, and some stuff laid by for next year; that everybody had food enough, and plenty of salted pork, pickled walnuts, potted shrimps, or other conserves, in the cupboard; that everybody had jewels enough, and some of the biggest laid by, in treasuries and museums; and, of persons caring for such things, that everybody had as many books and pictures as they could read or look at; with quantities of the highest quality besides, in easily accessible public libraries and galleries.

Now the wretches who have, at present, the teaching of the people in their hands, through the public press, tell them that it is not "practical" to attempt to bring about this state of things;—and that their government, or money-collecting machine, must not buy wine, potatoes, jewels, or pictures for them; but *must* buy iron plates two feet thick, gunpowder, and red tape. And this popular instruction is given, you will find, in the end, by persons who know that they could not get a percentage themselves (without the public's coming to know it) on buying potatoes or pictures; but *can* get it, and a large one, on manufacturing iron, on committing wholesale murder, or on tying up papers with red tape.

Now the St. George's Company propose to themselves,—and, if the God they believe in, lives, will assuredly succeed in their proposition,—to put an end to this rascally and inhuman state of things, and bring about an honest and human state of them, instead. And they have already actually begun the accumulation of a National Store of good

[2]Machines for producing harmful explosions.
[3]A mountain in Wales.

[4]They may serve for the *defense* of the store, of course;—so may the broken bottles, stuck on the top of a wall. But the lock of your cupboard is not the contents of it (Ruskin's note).

and useful things; by the collection and administration of which, they are not themselves to derive any gain whatsoever, but the Nation only.

We are, therefore, at present, as I said at first, a company established for a charitable purpose; the object of charity being the entire body of the British nation, now paying taxes to cheating capitalists. But we hope to include, finally, in our ranks a large number of the people themselves, and to make quite a different sort of people of them, carrying out our company's laws, to the abolition of many existing interests, and in abrogation of many existing arrangements.

And the laws which we hope thus to see accepted are none of them new; but have been already recommended by all wise men, and practised by all truly prosperous states; nor is there anything whatever new in the modes of administration proposed;—and especially be it noted, there is nothing of the present leader's fancies, in any part or character of the scheme—which is merely the application, to our nationally diseased thoughts and practices, of the direct precepts of the true sages of past time, who are every one of them in harmony concerning all that is necessary for men to do, feel, and know.

And we hope to establish these laws, not by violence, but by obeying them ourselves, to the extent of which existing circumstances admit; and so gradually showing the advantage of them, and making them acceptable to others. Not that, for the enforcement of some of them (the abolition of all manufactures that make the air unwholesome, for instance), we shall hesitate to use the strong hand, when once our hands are strong. But we shall not begin by street riots to throw down our neighbor's chimneys, or break his machinery;—though what we shall *end* in doing—God knows, not I,—but I have my own thoughts concerning it; not at present needing exposition.

The Companions, for the most part, will remain exactly in the condition of life they held before entering the Society; but they will direct all their powers, and some part of their revenues, in that condition, to the advance of its interests. We hold it shortsighted and ruinous policy to form separate institutions, or attempt the sudden establishment of new systems of labor. Every one of us must use the advantages he now possesses, whatever they may be, and contend with the difficulties arising out of his present position, gradually modifying it, as he can, into conformity with the laws which the Society desires may be ultimately observed by all its members.

The first of our conditions of Companionship is Honesty. We are a company of honest persons, vowing to have no fellowship with dishonest ones. Persons who do not know the meaning of the word "Honesty," or who would in anywise, for selfish convenience, tolerate any manner of cheating or lying, either in others or themselves, we class indiscriminately with the self-conscious rogues, for whom we have more respect; and our separation from all such is to be quite manifest and unmistakable. We do not go into monasteries,—we seek no freedom of conscience in foreign lands,—we profess no severities of asceticism at home. We simply refuse to have any dealings with rogues, whether at home or abroad.

I repeat, for this must be strictly understood, we are a company of honest persons; and will add to ourselves none but persons of that quality. We, for our own part, entirely decline to live by passing bad half-crowns, by selling bad goods, or by lying as to their relative quality. And we hold only such communication with persons guilty of such practices, as we should with any other manner of thieves or liars.

It will follow that anything gravely said by a Companion of St. George may be, without investigation, believed; and anything sold by one, without scrutiny, bought for what it is said to be,—of which recovery of old principles of human speech and commerce, no words can set forth the infinitude of beneficial consequences, when it is once brought about among a discernible and every day increasing body of persons.

The second condition of Companionship is the resolution, so far as we have ability, to earn our own living with our own hands; and not to allow, much less compel, other people to work for us: this duty being of double force,—first, as necessary to our own health and honor; but much more, as striking home at the ghastly universal crime of modern society,—stealing the laborer's bread from him (making him work, that is to say, for ours, as well as his own), and then abusing and despising him for the degradation of character which his perpetual toil involves; deliberately, in many cases, refusing to encourage him in economy, that we may have him at our mercy to grind in the mill; always selling as much gin and beer to him as we can persuade him to swill, at the rate of twentypence for twopence worth (see Letter 27), to fill our own pockets; and teaching him pious catechisms, that we may keep him our quiet slave.

We cannot, at present, all obey this great law concerning labor, however willing we may be; for we may not, in the condition of life in which we have been brought up, have been taught any manual labor by which we now could make a living. I myself, the present Master of the Society, cannot obey this, its second main law; but then I am only a makeshift Master, taking the place till somebody more fit for it be found. Sir Walter Scott's life, in the full strength of it at Ashestiel, and early at Abbotsford, with his literary work done by ten, or at latest twelve in the morning; and the rest of the day spent in useful work with Tom Purdie in his woods, is a model of wise moral management of mind and body, for men of true literary power; but I had neither the country training of body, nor have the natural strength of brain, which can reach this ideal in anywise. Sir Walter wrote as a stream flows; but I do all my brainwork like a wrung sponge, and am tired out, and good for nothing, after it. Sir Walter was in the open air, farm-bred, and playing with lambs, while I was a poor little Cockney wretch, playing, in a dark London nursery, with a bunch of keys. I do the best I can, and know what ought to be: and that is all the Company really need of me. I would fain, at this moment, both for pleasure and duty's sake, be cutting the dead stems out of my wood, or learning to build a dry stone wall under my good mason, Mr. Usher,[5] than

writing these institutes of St. George; but the institutes are needed, and must be written by me, since there is nobody else to write them.

Anyone, therefore, may be a Companion of St. George who sincerely does what they can, to make themselves useful, and earn their daily bread by their own labor: and some forms of intellectual or artistic labor, inconsistent (as a musician's) with other manual labor, are accepted by the Society as useful; provided they be truly undertaken for the good and help of all; and that the intellectual laborer ask no more pay than any other workman. A scholar can generally live on less food than a plowman, and there is no conceivable reason why he should have more.[6] And if he be a false-hearted scholar, or a bad painter or fiddler, there is infinite reason why he should have less. My readers may have been surprised at the instant and eager assertion, as of a leading principle, in the first of these letters (January '71), that people cannot live by art. But I spoke swiftly, because the attempt so to live is among the worst possible ways they can take of injurious begging. There are a few, a very few persons born in each generation, whose words are worth hearing, whose art is worth seeing. These born few will preach, or sing, or paint, in spite of you; they will starve like grasshoppers, rather than stop singing; and even if you don't choose to listen, it is charitable to throw them some crumbs to keep them alive. But the people who take to writing or painting as a means of livelihood, because they think it genteel, are just by so much more contemptible than common beggars, in that they are noisy and offensive beggars. I am quite willing to pay for keeping our poor vagabonds in the workhouse; but not to pay them for grinding or-

---

[5] It was of Mr. Usher, when he made his mark instead of writing his name, that Ruskin said, warmly shaking his hand, "Now I know I have an honest man to deal with."

[6] Again, I have more myself—but that is because I have been ill-bred; and I shall be most thankful to take less, as soon as other people cease to be paid for doing nothing. People cry out upon me for asking ten shillings for a year's *Fors;* but never object to Mr. Barber's paying his clerk a guinea for opening his study door to me five times, charging the same to St. George's account (Ruskin's note).

gans outside my door, defacing the streets with bills and caricatures, tempting young girls to read rubbishy novels, or deceiving the whole nation to its ruin, in a thousand leagues square of dirtily printed falsehood, every morning at breakfast. Whatever in literature, art, or religion, is done for money, is poisonous itself; and doubly deadly, in preventing the hearing or seeing of the noble literature and art which have been done for love and truth. If people cannot make their bread by honest labor, let them at least make no noise about the streets; but hold their tongues, and hold out their idle hands humbly; and they shall be fed kindly.

Then the third condition of Companionship is, that, after we have done as much manual work as will earn our food, we all of us discipline ourselves, our children, and anyone else willing to be taught, in all the branches of honorable knowledge and graceful art attainable by us. Having honestly obtained our meat and drink, and having sufficiently eaten and drunken, we proceed, during the rest of the day, to seek after things better than meat and drink; and to provide for the nobler necessities of what, in ancient days, Englishmen used to call their souls.

To this end, we shall, as we increase in numbers, establish such churches and schools as may best guide religious feeling, and diffuse the love of sound learning and prudent art. And when I set myself first to the work of forming the Society, I was induced to do so chiefly by the consciousness that the balanced unison of artistic sensibility with scientific faculty, which enabled me at once to love Giotto, and learn from Galileo, gave me singular advantages for a work of this kind. More particularly, the course of study through which, after being trained in the severest schools of Protestant divinity, I became acquainted with the mythology of Greece, and legends of Rome, in their most vivid power over the believing minds of both nations, permits me now to accept with freedom and respect the concurrence of a wider range of persons holding different views on religious subjects, than any other scholar I know, at the present day, in England, would feel himself secure in the hope of reconciling to a common duty, and in uncontested elements of faith.

The scheme, and elementary means, of this common education, I am now occupied in arranging and choosing as I best may. In especial, I have set myself to write three grammars—of geology, botany, and zoology, —which will contain nothing but indisputable facts in those three branches of proper human learning; and which, if I live a little longer, will embrace as many facts as any ordinary schoolboy or schoolgirl need be taught. In these three grammars (*Deucalion, Proserpina,* and *Love's Meinie*)[7] I shall accept every aid that sensible and earnest men of science can spare me, towards the task of popular education: and I hope to keep thankful records of the names of the persons who are making true discoveries in any of these sciences, and of the dates of such discovery, which shall be unassailably trustworthy as far as they extend. I hope also to be able to choose, and in some degree provide, a body of popular literature of entirely serviceable quality. Of some of the most precious books needed, I am preparing, with the help of my friends, new editions, for a common possession in all our school libraries.

If I have powers fitted for this task (and I should not have attempted it but in conviction that I have), they are owing mainly to this one condition of my life, that, from my youth up, I have been seeking the fame, and honoring the work, of others;—never my own. I first was driven into literature that I might defend the fame of Turner;[8] since that day I have been explaining the power, or proclaiming the praise, of Tintoret,—of Luini,—of Carpaccio,—of Botticelli,[9]—of Carlyle;—never thinking for an instant of myself: and sacrificing what little faculty, and large pleasure, I had in painting, either from nature or noble art, that, if possible, I might bring others to see what I

---

[7]*Deucalion: Collected Studies of the Lapse of Waves and Life of Stones* (1875–1883); *Proserpina: Studies of Wayside Flowers* (1875–1886); and *Love's Meinie: Lectures on Greek and English Birds* (1873–1881).

[8]Joseph M. W. Turner (1775–1851), the landscape painter, in defense of whom Ruskin began *Modern Painters.*

[9]Four Italian painters of the Renaissance.

rejoiced in, and understand what I had deciphered. There has been no heroism in this, nor virtue;—but only, as far as I am myself concerned, quaint ordering of Fate; but the result is, that I *have* at last obtained an instinct of impartial and reverent judgment, which sternly fits me for this final work, to which, if to anything, I was appointed.

And for the right doing of it, and for all future work of the same kind, requiring to be done for the Society by other persons, it is absolutely needful that the person charged with it should be implicitly trusted, and accurately obeyed by the Companions, in all matters necessary to the working of the Society. He cannot lose his time in contention or persuasion; he must act undisturbedly, or his mind will not suffice for its toil; and with concurrence of all the Society's power, or half their power will be wasted, and the whole perverted, by hesitation, and opposition. His authority over them must correspond precisely, in the war against the poverty and vice of the State, to that of a Roman Dictator, in his war against its external enemies.

Of a Roman *"Dictator,"* I say, observe; not a Roman *"Emperor."* It is not the command of private will, but the dictation of necessary law, which the Society obeys:— only, the obedience must be absolute, and without question; faithful to the uttermost, —that is to say, trusting to the uttermost. The practice of faith and obedience to some of our fellow-creatures is the alphabet by which we learn the higher obedience to heaven; and it is not only needful to the prosperity of all noble united action, but essential to the happiness of all noble living spirits.

I have not, in my past letters, much noticed this condition of the Society's work; because its explanation will involve that of our religious creed to the full; and its enforcement must be in the very teeth of the mad-dog's creed of modernism, "I will not be dictated to," which contains the essence of all diabolical error. For, in sum, the moral scale is raised exactly according to the degree and motive of obedience. To be disobedient through temptation, is human sin; but to be disobedient for the sake of disobedience,

fiendish sin. To be obedient for the sake of success in conduct, is human virtue; but to be obedient for the sake of obedience, angelic virtue.

The constitution of the Society is to be, therefore, that of an aristocracy electing an absolute chief (as the Senate of Rome their Dictator, or the Senate of Venice their Doge), who is to be entirely responsible for the conduct of the Society's affairs; to appoint its principal officers, and to grant or refuse admission to candidates for Companionship. But he is liable to deposition at any moment, by a vote of the majority of the Companions; and is to have no control over the property of the Society, but through the Trustees in whom that property is vested.

And now, for farther explanation of the details of our constitution and design, I must refer the reader to the *Fors* for March of this year;[10] and, if he desires to pursue his inquiry, to the 8th, 9th, 11th, 17th, and 19th Letters of the previous series. These state clearly what we propose to do, and how: but for defence of our principles, the entire series of Letters must be studied; and that with quiet attention, for not a word of them has been written but with purpose. Some parts of the plan are confessedly unexplained, and others obscurely hinted at; nor do I choose to say how much of this indistinctness has been intentional. But I am well assured that if any patient and candid person cares to understand the book, and master its contents, he may do so with less pains than would be required for the reading of any ordinary philosophical treatise on equally important subjects.

Only readers should be clearly aware of one peculiarity in the manner of my writing in *Fors,* which might otherwise much mislead them:—namely, that if they will enclose in brackets with their pen, passages of evident irony, all the rest of the book is written with absolute seriousness and literalness of meaning. The violence, or grotesque aspect, of a statement may seem as if I were mocking; but this comes mainly of my endeavor to bring the absolute truth out into pure crystalline structure, unmodified by disguise of custom, or obscurity of language; for the

[10]Letter 63.

result of that process is continually to reduce the facts into a form so contrary, if theoretical, to our ordinary impressions, and so contrary, if moral, to our ordinary practice, that the straightforward statement of them looks like a jest. But every such apparent jest will be found, if you think of it, a pure, very dreadful, and utterly imperious veracity.

With this understanding, the following series of aphorisms contain the gist of the book, and may serve to facilitate the arrangement of its incidental matter.

(1) Any form of government will work, provided the governors are real, and the people obey them; and none will work, if the governors are unreal, or the people disobedient. If you mean to have logs for kings, no quantity of liberty in choice of the wood will be of any profit to you:—nor will the wisest or best governor be able to serve you, if you mean to discuss his orders instead of obeying them. Read carefully on this matter Letter 13, §§ 7, 8.

(2) The first duty of government is to see that the people have food, fuel, and clothes. The second, that they have means of moral and intellectual education.

(3) Food, fuel, and clothes can only be got out of the ground, or sea, by muscular labor; and no man has any business to have any, unless he has done, if able, the muscular work necessary to produce his portion, or to render (as the labor of a surgeon or a physician renders) equivalent benefit to life. It indeed saves both toil and time that one man should dig, another bake, and another tan; but the digger, baker, and tanner are alike bound to do their equal day's duty; and the business of the government is to see that they have done it, before it gives any one of them their dinner.

(4) While the daily teaching of God's truth, doing of His justice, and heroic bearing of His sword, are to be required of every human soul according to its ability, the mercenary professions of preaching, lawgiving, and fighting must be entirely abolished.

(5) Scholars, painters, and musicians may be advisedly kept, on due pittance, to instruct or amuse the laborer after, or at, his work; provided the duty be severely restricted to those who have high special gifts of voice, touch, and imagination;[11] and that the possessors of these melodious lips, light-fingered hands, and lively brains, do resolutely undergo the normal discipline necessary to ensure their skill; the people whom they are to please, understanding, always, that they cannot employ these tricksy artists without working double-tides[12] themselves, to provide them with beef and ale.

(6) The duty of the government, as regards the distribution of its work, is to attend first to the wants of the most necessitous; therefore, to take particular charge of the back streets of every town; leaving the fine ones, more or less, according to their finery, to take care of themselves. And it is the duty of magistrates, and other persons in authority, but especially of all bishops, to know thoroughly the numbers, means of subsistence, and modes of life of the poorest persons in the community, and to be sure that *they* at least are virtuous and comfortable; for if poor persons be not virtuous, after all the wholesome discipline of poverty, what must be the state of the rich, under their perilous trials and temptations?[13]—but, on the other hand, if the poor are made comfortable and good, the rich have a fair chance of entering the kingdom of heaven also, if they choose to live honorably and decently.

(7) Since all are to be made to labor for their living, and it is not possible to labor without materials and tools, these must be

---

[11]Such limitation being secured by the severity of the required education in the public schools of art, and thought; and by the high standard of examination fixed before granting license of exhibition, in the public theaters, or picture galleries (Ruskin's note).

[12]Double times.

[13]Here is just an instance of what might at first seem to be a jest; but is a serious and straightforward corollary from the eternally true fact stated by St. Paul to Timothy [I Timothy, 6:9]: "They that will be rich fall into temptation and a snare, and into many foolish lusts, which drown men in destruction and perdition"; and by Horace:

"Quanto quisque sibi plura negaverit
Ab Dis plura feret." [*Odes*, III, xvi, 21–22.]

The passage might at first be thought inconsistent with what is said above of the "degradation" which perpetual toil involves. But toil and poverty are two different things. Poverty ennobles, and secures; toil degrades, and endangers. We are all bound to fulfill our task; but happy only if we can also enter into our rest (Ruskin's note).

Above are portraits of four celebrated Victorians. At the upper left is John Henry Newman, from a lithograph by J. A. Vinter published in 1850. At the upper right is Thomas Carlyle, as painted in 1837 (the year in which his *French Revolution* appeared) by Count Alfred D'Orsay (1801–1852). D'Orsay is better known as a dandy of the Regency period than as an artist, but he made interesting portraits of several men of letters. Below at the left is Tennyson as a young man, painted by Samuel Laurence (1812–1884). Carlyle thought Tennyson "one of the finest-looking men in the world." At the right below is a pencil drawing of Robert Browning made in July, 1837, by the Comte Amédée de Ripert Monclar, a close friend of Browning at this time. When he met Browning and Mrs. Browning in Rome in 1854, he pleased the latter by assuring her that her husband "was not changed for the intermediate years." (Newman, Carlyle, Browning, courtesy of the New York Public Library. Laurence's "Tennyson" is in the National Portrait Gallery, London.)

On this page are reproduced four plates from a book which, as William Ivins, Jr., of the Metropolitan Museum writes, "will always be remembered among the greater triumphs of English art." The book is Tennyson's *Poems,* published by Moxon in 1857. Its illustrations were made by three members of the Pre-Raphaelite Brotherhood: D. G. Rossetti, W. Holman Hunt, and John Everett Millais. The two designs above, for "The Lady of Shalott" (page 598), are by Hunt (at the left) and Rossetti (at the right). At the left below is Rossetti's illustration for "The Palace of Art" (page 603); and at the right below is an illustration by Millais for "Locksley Hall" (page 613). (Courtesy of the New York Public Library.)

provided by the government, for all persons, in the necessary quantities. If bricks are to be made, clay and straw must be provided; if sheep are to be kept, grass; if coats are to be made, cloth; if oakum to be picked, oakum. All these raw materials, with the tools for working them, must be provided by the government, at first, free of cost to the laborer, the value of them being returned to them as the first-fruits of his toil; and no pawnbrokers or usurers may be allowed to live by lending sea to fishermen, air to fowlers, land to farmers, crooks to shepherds, or bellows to smiths.

(8) When the lands and seas belonging to any nation are all properly divided, cultivated, and fished, its population cannot be increased, except by importing food in exchange for useless articles,—that is to say, by living as the toy-manufacturers of some independent nation, which can both feed itself, and afford to buy toys besides. But no nation can long exist in this servile state. It must either emigrate, and form colonies to assist in cultivating the land which feeds it, or become entirely slavish and debased. The moment any nation begins to import food,[14] its political power and moral worth are ended.

(9) All the food, clothing, and fuel required by men, can be produced by the labor of their own arms on the earth and sea; all food is appointed to be so produced, and *must* be so produced, at their peril. If instead of taking the quantity of exercise made necessary to their bodies by God, in the work appointed by God, they take it in hunting or shooting, they become ignorant, irreligious, and finally insane, and seek to live by fighting as well as by hunting; whence the type of Nimrod, in the circle of the Hell-towers, which I desired you to study in Dante.[15] If they do not take exercise at all, they become sensual, and insane in worse ways. *And it is physically impossible that true religious knowledge, or pure morality, should exist among any classes of a nation who do not work with their hands for their bread.* Read Letter 11 carefully.

(10) The use of machinery[16] in agriculture throws a certain number of persons out of wholesome employment, who must thenceforward either do nothing, or mischief. The use of machinery in art destroys the national intellect; and, finally, renders all luxury impossible. All machinery needful in ordinary life to supplement human or animal labor may be moved by wind or water: while steam, or any modes of *heat-power,* may only be employed justifiably under extreme or special conditions of need; as for speed on main lines of communication, and for raising water from great depths, or other such work beyond human strength.

(11) No true luxury, wealth, or religion is possible to dirty persons; nor is it decent or human to attempt to compass any temporal prosperity whatever by the sacrifice of cleanliness. The speedy abolition of all abolishable filth is the first process of education;[17] the principles of which I state in the second group of aphorisms following.

(12) All education must be moral first; intellectual secondarily. Intellectual, before—(much more without)—moral education, is, in completeness, impossible; and in incompleteness, a calamity.

(13) Moral education begins in making the creature to be educated, clean, and obedient. This must be done thoroughly, and at any cost, and with any kind of compulsion rendered necessary by the nature of the animal, be it dog, child, or man.

---

[14] It may always import such food as its climate cannot produce, in exchange for such food as it can; it may buy oranges with corn, or pepper with cheese. But not with articles that do not support life. Separate *cities* may honorably produce salable art; Limoges its enamel, Sheffield its whittle; but a *nation* must not live on enamel or whittles (Ruskin's note). "Whittles" are large knives.—Ruskin in a later memorandum wrote that this note needed to be expanded.

[15] *Inferno,* xxxi, 40–45.

[16] Foolish people are continually quibbling and stupefying themselves about the word "machine." Briefly, any instrument is a machine so far as its action is, in any particular, or moment, beyond the control of the human hand. A violin, a pencil, and a plow, are tools, not machines. A grinding organ, or a windmill, is a machine, not a tool: often the two are combined; thus a lathe is a machine, and the workman's chisel, used at it, a tool (Ruskin's note).

[17] The ghastly squalor of the once lovely fields of Dulwich, trampled into mud, and strewn with rags and paper by the filthy London population, bred in cigar smoke, which is attracted by the Crystal Palace, would alone neutralize all possible gentlemanly education in the district (Ruskin's note).

(14) Moral education consists next in making the creature practically serviceable to other creatures, according to the nature and extent of his own capacities; taking care that these be healthily developed in such service. It may be a question how long, and to what extent, boys and girls of fine race may be allowed to run in the paddock before they are broken; but assuredly the sooner they are put to such work as they are able for, the better. Moral education is summed when the creature has been made to do its work with delight, and thoroughly; but this cannot be until some degree of intellectual education has been given also.

(15) Intellectual education consists in giving the creature the faculties of admiration, hope, and love.

These are to be taught by the study of beautiful Nature; the sight and history of noble persons; and the setting forth of noble objects of action.

(16) Since all noble persons hitherto existent in the world have trusted in the government of it by a supreme Spirit, and in that trust, or faith, have performed all their great actions, the history of these persons will finally mean the history of their faith; and the sum of intellectual education will be the separation of what is inhuman, in such faiths, and therefore perishing, from what is human, and, for human creatures, eternally true.

These sixteen aphorisms contain, as plainly as I can speak it, the substance of what I have hitherto taught, and am now purposed to enforce practice of, as far as I am able. It is no business of mine to think about possibilities;—any day, any moment, may raise up someone to take the carrying forward of the plan out of my hands, or to furnish me with larger means of prosecuting it; meantime, neither hastening nor slackening, I shall go on doing what I can, with the people, few or many, who are ready to help me.

Such help (to conclude with what simplest practical direction I can) may be given me by any persons interested in my plans, mainly by sending me money; secondly, by acting out as much as they agree with of the directions for private life given in *Fors;* and thirdly, by promulgating and recommending such principles. If they wish to do more than this, and to become actual members of the Company, they must write to me, giving a short and clear account of their past lives, and present circumstances. I then examine them on such points as seem to me necessary; and if I accept them, I inscribe their names in the roll, at Corpus Christi College,[18] with two of our masters for witnesses. This roll of the Company is written, hitherto, on the blank leaves of an eleventh-century MS. of the Gospels, always kept in my rooms; and would enable the Trustees, in case of my death, at once to consult the Companions respecting the disposition of the Society's property. As to the legal tenure of that property, I have taken counsel with my lawyer-friends till I am tired; and, as will be seen by the statement in the second page of the Correspondence,[19] I purpose henceforward to leave all such legal arrangements to the discretion of the Companions themselves.

---

[18] The Oxford college in which Ruskin was living at this time.

[19] The correspondence department published after each letter of *Fors*.

MATTHEW ARNOLD

1822–1888

Arnold was born at Laleham, in Middlesex, on 24 December, 1822. His father, Thomas Arnold, later became famous as the head-master of Rugby School; and the son, widely as his thought came to diverge from his father's, never ceased to feel the influence of the simple and powerful personality who, by his work at Rugby, transformed English public-school life. Arnold was sent first to his father's school, the Wykehamist College of Winchester, but after a year there was brought to Rugby, where he remained four years, until, in 1841, he went up to Balliol College, Oxford, with a classical scholarship. He took his B. A. in 1845. He failed to secure a first class, but nevertheless was soon elected a fellow of Oriel College. This opened up to him the possibility of an academic career; but, deeply as Arnold loved Oxford throughout his life, he seems never seriously to have considered remaining there; and one feels that he was right if he thought that his nature demanded the contacts of a larger world and could ill brook the small restraints of academic life. In 1847 he became a private secretary to Lord Lansdowne, who was then President of the Privy Council. Four years later Arnold was appointed an inspector of schools. He took this post, as he many years later told an audience of teachers, not because he liked the work or indeed at first knew anything about it, but in order to be able to marry. And shortly thereafter he was married to Miss Frances Lucy Wightman, who made a home for him which during the remainder of his life was his chief resource and stay. Arnold never grew to like—as who could have grown to like?—the incessant drudgery of his educational post; but he soon came to see the importance of his work and to value his position for the influence it gave him in improving education. His post also gave him various opportunities for travel on the Continent, and enabled him to publish some of the best and wisest writing on education that the nineteenth century saw. He remained an inspector of schools until within a few years of his death on 15 April, 1888.

It is a severe loss to literature that Arnold was thus compelled to earn his living; for the greater part of his literary work had to be done in time stolen, so to say, from his official duties. That he accomplished as much as he did in untoward circumstances fairly indicates that he would have been able to do much more had he ever been given the opportunity. He began his literary career as a poet, publishing *The Strayed Reveler and Other Poems* anonymously in 1849, and three years later, also anonymously, *Empedocles on Etna and Other Poems.* Both volumes were soon withdrawn from sale because of Arnold's dissatisfaction with some of the pieces they contained. In 1853 and 1855, however, the greater number of the earlier poems were re-issued, together with some new ones, among the latter *Sohrab and Rustum* and *The Scholar Gypsy. Merope,* a dramatic poem, was published in 1858, and *New Poems* in 1867. Meanwhile Arnold had been elected Professor of Poetry at Oxford in 1857, a post which he held, as was then possible, for two terms, until 1867. The duties of this position turned his attention definitely to criticism, and from the early eighteen-sixties his work was almost exclusively critical; he wrote little or no poetry after 1867. His lectures *On Translating Homer* were published in 1861, *Essays in Criticism* in 1865, and *Celtic Literature* in 1867. In a famous and often disputed phrase Arnold defined poetry as a "criticism of life." It is a phrase which, at any rate, may stand for the poetry which he valued most highly, and it may stand, too, for his own critical work. Like Ruskin, Arnold was unable to consider artistic excellence as a thing separable from the common life of men, and like Ruskin he was inevitably drawn on from the consideration of art to consideration of the social and moral problems raised by industrial democracies. His major contributions to the discussion of these questions are contained in *Culture and Anarchy* (1869), *St. Paul and Protestantism* (1870), *Friendship's Garland* (1871), *Literature and Dogma* (1873), *God and the Bible* (1875), *Mixed Essays*

(1879), and *Irish Essays* (1882). The *Discourses in America* (1885) were delivered in a lecture-tour of the United States in the winter of 1883–1884.

In a letter to his mother written in 1869 Arnold says: "My poems represent, on the whole, the main movement of mind of the last quarter of a century, and thus they will probably have their day as people become conscious to themselves of what that movement of mind is, and interested in the literary productions which reflect it. It might be fairly urged that I have less poetical sentiment than Tennyson, and less intellectual vigor and abundance than Browning; yet, because I have perhaps more of a fusion of the two than either of them, and have more regularly applied that fusion to the main line of modern development, I am likely enough to have my turn, as they have had theirs." The passage of years has served to show that Arnold's verdict on his own poetry was essentially just. His verse has never been widely popular, but it securely holds, and will long hold, the attention of thoughtful people. Likewise his criticism, whether one can agree with all his conclusions or not, will long be read for its persuasive charm, its ease and urbanity, its combined lightness and sureness of touch, and its honest good faith always showing beneath the surface of Arnold's playfulness.

Properly speaking, no collected edition of Arnold's writings has ever been published. A uniformly and finely printed edition of the volumes by Arnold which Macmillan and Co., of London, had published appeared in 1903, with the general title of *Works,* but this was seriously incomplete. Lists of Arnold's books will be found in several of the volumes mentioned below. A convenient one-volume edition of Arnold's *Poems* is published by the Oxford University Press with Introduction by Sir Arthur Quiller-Couch (1906, and later editions).

A new edition in the series of "Oxford Standard Authors" has been announced, under the editorship of C. B. Tinker and H. F. Lowry (who have also in preparation a commentary on Arnold's poems); and a definitive complete edition of the poems is being prepared for the Oxford Press by Sir Edmund Chambers. An excellent, though unattractively printed, selection from Arnold's prose, *Representative Essays,* has been edited by E. K. Brown (New York, 1936); and *Culture and Anarchy* has been notably edited by J. Dover Wilson (Cambridge, 1932). A selection from Arnold's *Note Books* was published in 1902 (a new edition, presumably complete, is in preparation). Arnold's *Letters,* ed. George W. E. Russell, were published in two volumes in 1895. Additional letters have since been published, the most important being *The Letters of Matthew Arnold to Arthur Hugh Clough,* ed. H. F. Lowry (London, 1932). It was Arnold's wish that no biography of him should be written, but his friend G. W. E. Russell after editing the *Letters* wrote an account of the effect Arnold produced "on the thought and action of his age" (*Matthew Arnold,* in the series of "Literary Lives," 1904) which has permanent value. The best appreciative and critical introduction to Arnold, with many long quotations from his verse and prose, is Stuart P. Sherman's *Matthew Arnold, How to Know Him* (Indianapolis, 1917). *Matthew Arnold* by Lionel Trilling (New York, 1939) is a thorough critical study, too long, but scholarly, intelligent, and illuminating. Critical essays concerning Arnold are numerous, and only three books containing such essays can be mentioned here: *Three Studies in Literature* by Lewis E. Gates (New York, 1899); *Poetry and the Criticism of Life* by H. W. Garrod (Cambridge, Mass., 1931); and *The Use of Poetry and the Use of Criticism* by T. S. Eliot (London, 1933).

THE FUNCTION OF CRITICISM AT THE PRESENT TIME[1]

MANY objections have been made to a proposition which, in some remarks of mine on translating Homer, I ventured to put forth; a proposition about criticism, and its importance at the present day. I said: "Of the literature of France and Germany, as of the intellect of Europe in general, the main effort, for now many years, has been a critical effort; the endeavor, in all branches of knowledge, theology, philosophy, history, art, science, to see the object as in itself it really is."[2] I added, that owing to the operation in

[1]The initial essay in *Essays in Criticism,* 1865. It had previously been published in the *National Review,* November, 1864.

[2]This and the following quotation are from the conclusion of the second lecture in Arnold's *On Translating Homer.*

English literature of certain causes, "almost the last thing for which one would come to English literature is just that very thing which now Europe most desires,—criticism"; and that the power and value of English literature was thereby impaired. More than one rejoinder declared that the importance I here assigned to criticism was excessive, and asserted the inherent superiority of the creative effort of the human spirit over its critical effort. And the other day, having been led by an excellent notice of Wordsworth[3] published in the *North British Review,* to turn again to his biography, I found in the words of this great man, whom I, for one, must always listen to with the profoundest respect, a sentence passed on the critic's business, which seems to justify every possible disparagement of it. Wordsworth says in one of his letters:

The writers in these publications [the Reviews], while they prosecute their inglorious employment, can not be supposed to be in a state of mind very favorable for being affected by the finer influences of a thing so pure as genuine poetry.

And a trustworthy reporter of his conversation quotes a more elaborate judgment to the same effect:

Wordsworth holds the critical power very low, infinitely lower than the inventive; and he said to-day that if the quantity of time consumed in writing critiques on the works of others were given to original composition, of whatever kind it might be, it would be much better employed; it would make a man find out sooner his own level, and it would do infinitely less mischief. A false or malicious criticism may do much injury to the minds of others; a

---

[3]I cannot help thinking that a practice, common in England during the last century, and still followed in France, of printing a notice of this kind, —a notice by a competent critic,—to serve as an introduction to an eminent author's works, might be revived among us with advantage. To introduce all succeeding editions of Wordsworth, Mr. Shairp's notice (it is permitted, I hope, to mention his name) might, it seems to me, excellently serve; it is written from the point of view of an admirer, nay, of a disciple, and that is right; but then the disciple must be also, as in this case he is, a critic, a man of letters, not, as too often happens, some relation or friend with no qualification for his task except affection for his author (Arnold's note). John Campbell Shairp was Professor of Poetry at Oxford from 1877 to 1887.

stupid invention, either in prose or verse, is quite harmless.

It is almost too much to expect of poor human nature, that a man capable of producing some effect in one line of literature, should, for the greater good of society, voluntarily doom himself to impotence and obscurity in another. Still less is this to be expected from men addicted to the composition of the "false or malicious criticism," of which Wordsworth speaks. However, everybody would admit that a false or malicious criticism had better never have been written. Everybody, too, would be willing to admit, as a general proposition, that the critical faculty is lower than the inventive.

But is it true that criticism is really, in itself, a baneful and injurious employment; is it true that all time given to writing critiques on the works of others would be much better employed if it were given to original composition, of whatever kind this may be? Is it true that Johnson had better have gone on producing more *Irenes*[4] instead of writing his *Lives of the Poets;* nay, is it certain that Wordsworth himself was better employed in making his Ecclesiastical Sonnets, than when he made his celebrated Preface,[5] so full of criticism, and criticism of the works of others? Wordsworth was himself a great critic, and it is to be sincerely regretted that he has not left us more criticism; Goethe was one of the greatest of critics, and we may sincerely congratulate ourselves that he has left us so much criticism. Without wasting time over the exaggeration which Wordsworth's judgment on criticism clearly contains, or over an attempt to trace the causes,—not difficult I think to be traced,—which may have led Wordsworth to this exaggeration, a critic may with advantage seize an occasion for trying his own conscience, and for asking himself of what real service, at any given moment, the practice of criticism either is, or may be made, to his own mind and spirit, and to the minds and spirits of others.

---

[4]*Irene,* Dr. Johnson's only play, is a classical tragedy. It ran for nine nights at Drury Lane Theater in 1749.

[5]The Preface to the second edition of *Lyrical Ballads* (1800)

The critical power is of lower rank than the creative. True; but in assenting to this proposition, one or two things are to be kept in mind. It is undeniable that the exercise of a creative power, that a free creative activity, is the true function of man; it is proved to be so by man's finding in it his true happiness. But it is undeniable, also, that men may have the sense of exercising this free creative activity in other ways than in producing great works of literature or art; if it were not so, all but a very few men would be shut out from the true happiness of all men; they may have it in well-doing, they may have it in learning, they may have it even in criticizing. This is one thing to be kept in mind. Another is, that the exercise of the creative power in the production of great works of literature or art, however high this exercise of it may rank, is not at all epochs and under all conditions possible; and that therefore labor may be vainly spent in attempting it, which might with more fruit be used in preparing for it, in rendering it possible. This creative power works with elements, with materials; what if it has not those materials, those elements, ready for its use? In that case it must surely wait till they are ready. Now in literature,—I will limit myself to literature, for it is about literature that the question arises,—the elements with which the creative power works are ideas; the best ideas, on every matter which literature touches, current at the time; at any rate we may lay it down as certain that in modern literature no manifestation of the creative power not working with these can be very important or fruitful. And I say *current* at the time, not merely accessible at the time; for creative literary genius does not principally show itself in discovering new ideas; that is rather the business of the philosopher: the grand work of literary genius is a work of synthesis and exposition, not of analysis and discovery; its gift lies in the faculty of being happily inspired by a certain intellectual and spiritual atmosphere, by a certain order of ideas, when it finds itself in them; of dealing divinely with these ideas, presenting them in the most effective and attractive combinations,—making beautiful works with them, in short. But it must have

the atmosphere, it must find itself amidst the order of ideas, in order to work freely; and these it is not so easy to command. This is why great creative epochs in literature are so rare; this is why there is so much that is unsatisfactory in the productions of many men of real genius; because for the creation of a master-work of literature two powers must concur, the power of the man and the power of the moment, and the man is not enough without the moment; the creative power has, for its happy exercise, appointed elements, and those elements are not in its own control.

Nay, they are more within the control of the critical power. It is the business of the critical power, as I said in the words already quoted, "in all branches of knowledge, theology, philosophy, history, art, science, to see the object as in itself it really is." Thus it tends, at last, to make an intellectual situation of which the creative power can profitably avail itself. It tends to establish an order of ideas, if not absolutely true, yet true by comparison with that which it displaces; to make the best ideas prevail. Presently these new ideas reach society, the touch of truth is the touch of life, and there is a stir and growth everywhere; out of this stir and growth come the creative epochs of literature.

Or, to narrow our range, and quit these considerations of the general march of genius and of society, considerations which are apt to become too abstract and impalpable,—every one can see that a poet, for instance, ought to know life and the world before dealing with them in poetry; and life and the world being, in modern times, very complex things, the creation of a modern poet, to be worth much, implies a great critical effort behind it; else it must be a comparatively poor, barren, and short-lived affair. This is why Byron's poetry had so little endurance in it, and Goethe's so much; both Byron and Goethe had a great productive power, but Goethe's was nourished by a great critical effort providing the true materials for it, and Byron's was not; Goethe knew life and the world, the poet's necessary subjects, much more comprehensively and thoroughly than Byron. He knew a great deal more of them, and he knew them much more as they really are.

It has long seemed to me that the burst of creative activity in our literature, through the first quarter of this century, had about it, in fact, something premature; and that from this cause its productions are doomed, most of them, in spite of the sanguine hopes which accompanied and do still accompany them, to prove hardly more lasting than the productions of far less splendid epochs. And this prematureness comes from its having proceeded without having its proper data, without sufficient materials to work with. In other words, the English poetry of the first quarter of this century, with plenty of energy, plenty of creative force, did not know enough. This makes Byron so empty of matter, Shelley so incoherent, Wordsworth even, profound as he is, yet so wanting in completeness and variety. Wordsworth cared little for books, and disparaged Goethe. I admire Wordsworth, as he is, so much that I cannot wish him different; and it is vain, no doubt, to imagine such a man different from what he is, to suppose that he could have been different; but surely the one thing wanting to make Wordsworth an even greater poet than he is,—his thought richer, and his influence of wider application,—was that he should have read more books, among them, no doubt, those of that Goethe whom he disparaged without reading him.

But to speak of books and reading may easily lead to a misunderstanding here. It was not really books and reading that lacked to our poetry, at this epoch; Shelley had plenty of reading, Coleridge had immense reading. Pindar and Sophocles—as we all say so glibly, and often with so little discernment of the real import of what we are saying—had not many books; Shakespeare was no deep reader. True; but in the Greece of Pindar and Sophocles,[6] in the England of Shakespeare, the poet lived in a current of ideas in the highest degree animating and nourishing to the creative power; society was, in the fullest measure, permeated by fresh thought, intelligent and alive; and this state of things is the true basis for the creative power's exercise,—in this it finds its data,

_____
[6] I. e., Greece in the fifth century B. C.

its materials, truly ready for its hand; all the books and reading in the world are only valuable as they are helps to this. Even when this does not actually exist, books and reading may enable a man to construct a kind of semblance of it in his own mind, a world of knowledge and intelligence in which he may live and work: this is by no means an equivalent, to the artist, for the nationally diffused life and thought of the epochs of Sophocles or Shakespeare, but, besides that it may be a means of preparation for such epochs, it does really constitute, if many share in it, a quickening and sustaining atmosphere of great value. Such an atmosphere the many-sided learning and the long and widely-combined critical effort of Germany formed for Goethe, when he lived and worked. There was no national glow of life and thought there, as in the Athens of Pericles, or the England of Elizabeth. That was the poet's weakness. But there was a sort of equivalent for it in the complete culture and unfettered thinking of a large body of Germans. That was his strength. In the England of the first quarter of this century, there was neither a national glow of life and thought, such as we had in the age of Elizabeth, nor yet a culture and a force of learning and criticism, such as were to be found in Germany. Therefore the creative power of poetry wanted, for success in the highest sense, materials and a basis; a thorough interpretation of the world was necessarily denied to it.

At first sight it seems strange that out of the immense stir of the French Revolution and its age should not have come a crop of works of genius equal to that which came out of the stir of the great productive time of Greece, or out of that of the Renaissance, with its powerful episode the Reformation. But the truth is that the stir of the French Revolution took a character which essentially distinguished it from such movements as these. These were, in the main, disinterestedly intellectual and spiritual movements; movements in which the human spirit looked for its satisfaction in itself and in the increased play of its own activity: the French Revolution took a political, practical character. The movement which went on in

France under the old *régime,* from 1700 to 1789, was far more really akin than that of the Revolution itself to the movement of the Renaissance; the France of Voltaire and Rousseau told far more powerfully upon the mind of Europe than the France of the Revolution. Goethe reproached this last expressly with having "thrown quiet culture back." Nay, and the true key to how much in our Byron, even in our Wordsworth, is this!—that they had their source in a great movement of feeling, not in a great movement of mind. The French Revolution, however,—that object of so much blind love and so much blind hatred,—found undoubtedly its motive-power in the intelligence of men and not in their practical sense;—this is what distinguishes it from the English Revolution of Charles the First's time; this is what makes it a more spiritual event than our Revolution, an event of much more powerful and world-wide interest, though practically less successful;—it appeals to an order of ideas which are universal, certain, permanent. 1789 asked of a thing, Is it rational? 1642 asked of a thing, Is it legal? or, when it went furthest, Is it according to conscience? This is the English fashion; a fashion to be treated, within its own sphere, with the highest respect; for its success, within its own sphere, has been prodigious. But what is law in one place, is not law in another; what is law here to-day, is not law even here to-morrow; and as for conscience, what is binding on one man's conscience is not binding on another's; the old woman who threw her stool at the head of the surpliced minister in St. Giles's Church at Edinburgh[7] obeyed an impulse to which millions of the human race may be permitted to remain strangers. But the prescriptions of reason are absolute, unchanging, of universal validity; *to count by tens is the easiest way of counting,*—that is a proposition of which every one, from here to the Antipodes, feels the force; at least, I should say so, if we did not live in a country where it is not impossible that any morning we may

find a letter in the *Times* declaring that a decimal coinage is an absurdity. That a whole nation should have been penetrated with an enthusiasm for pure reason, and with an ardent zeal for making its prescriptions triumph, is a very remarkable thing, when we consider how little of mind, or anything so worthy and quickening as mind, comes into the motives which alone, in general, impel great masses of men. In spite of the extravagant direction given to this enthusiasm, in spite of the crimes and follies in which it lost itself, the French Revolution derives from the force, truth, and universality of the ideas which it took for its law, and from the passion with which it could inspire a multitude for these ideas, a unique and still living power; it is—it will probably long remain—the greatest, the most animating event in history. And, as no sincere passion for the things of the mind, even though it turn out in many respects an unfortunate passion, is ever quite thrown away and quite barren of good, France has reaped from hers one fruit, the natural and legitimate fruit, though not precisely the grand fruit she expected; she is the country in Europe where *the people* is most alive.

But the mania for giving an immediate political and practical application to all these fine ideas of the reason was fatal. Here an Englishman is in his element: on this theme we can all go on for hours. And all we are in the habit of saying on it has undoubtedly a great deal of truth. Ideas cannot be too much prized in and for themselves, cannot be too much lived with; but to transport them abruptly into the world of politics and practice, violently to revolutionize this world to their bidding,—that is quite another thing. There is the world of ideas and there is the world of practice; the French are often for suppressing the one and the English the other; but neither is to be suppressed. A member of the House of Commons said to me the other day: "That a thing is an anomaly, I consider to be no objection to it whatever." I venture to think he was wrong; that a thing is an anomaly *is* an objection to it, but absolutely and in the sphere of ideas: it is not necessarily, under such and such circumstances, or at such and such

[7]The story to which Arnold alludes is apocryphal, but had its origin in riotous actions which took place in the church on Sunday, 23 July, 1637, when Archbishop Laud's Liturgy was introduced there.

a moment, an objection to it in the sphere of politics and practice. Joubert[8] has said beautifully: *C'est la force et le droit qui règlent toutes choses dans le monde; la force en attendant le droit.* (Force and right are 5 the governors of this world; force till right is ready.) *Force till right is ready;* and till right is ready, force, the existing order of things, is justified, is the legitimate ruler. But right is something moral, and implies 10 inward recognition, free assent of the will; we are not ready for right,—*right*, so far as we are concerned, *is not ready*,—until we have attained this sense of seeing it and willing it. The way in which for us it may 15 change and transform force, the existing order of things, and become, in its turn, the legitimate ruler of the world, will depend on the way in which, when our time comes, we see it and will it. Therefore for other peo- 20 ple enamored of their own newly discerned right, to attempt to impose it upon us as ours, and violently to substitute their right for our force, is an act of tyranny, and to be resisted. It sets at nought the second great 25 half of our maxim, *force till right is ready.* This was the grand error of the French Revolution; and its movement of ideas, by quitting the intellectual sphere and rushing furiously into the political sphere, ran, in- 30 deed, a prodigious and memorable course, but produced no such intellectual fruit as the movement of ideas of the Renaissance, and created, in opposition to itself, what I may call an *epoch of concentration.* The great 35 force of that epoch of concentration was England; and the great voice of that epoch of concentration was Burke. It is the fashion to treat Burke's writings on the French Revolution as superannuated and 40 conquered by the event; as the eloquent but unphilosophical tirades of bigotry and prejudice. I will not deny that they are often disfigured by the violence and passion of the moment, and that in some directions Burke's 45 view was bounded, and his observation therefore at fault; but on the whole, and for those who can make the needful corrections, what distinguishes these writings is their profound,

permanent, fruitful, philosophical truth; they contain the true philosophy of an epoch of concentration, dissipate the heavy atmosphere which its own nature is apt to engender round it, and make its resistance rational instead of mechanical.

But Burke is so great because, almost alone in England, he brings thought to bear upon politics, he saturates politics with thought; it is his accident that his ideas were at the service of an epoch of concentration, not of an epoch of expansion; it is his characteristic that he so lived by ideas, and had such a source of them welling up within him, that he could float even an epoch of concentration and English Tory politics with them. It does not hurt him that Dr. Price[9] and the Liberals were enraged with him; it does not even hurt him that George the Third and the Tories were enchanted with him. His greatness is that he lived in a world which neither English Liberalism nor English Toryism is apt to enter;—the world of ideas, not the world of catchwords and party habits. So far is it from being really true of him that he "to party gave up what was meant for mankind,"[10] that at the very end of his fierce struggle with the French Revolution, after all his invectives against its false pretensions, hollowness, and madness, with his sincere conviction of its mischievousness, he can close a memorandum on the best means of combating it, some of the last pages he ever wrote,[11]—the *Thoughts on French Affairs,* in December, 1791,—with these striking words:

The evil is stated, in my opinion, as it exists. The remedy must be where power, wisdom, and information, I hope, are more united with good intentions than they can be with me. I have done with this subject, I believe, forever. It has given me many anxious moments for the last two years. *If a great change is to be made in human affairs, the minds of men will be fitted to it; the general opinions and feelings will draw that way. Every fear, every hope will*

---

[8]Joseph Joubert (1754–1824), French moralist and man of letters. The seventh essay in Arnold's *Essays in Criticism* is devoted to him.

[9]Richard Price (1723–1791), a Unitarian minister, a moralist, and an advocate of civil and religious liberty.

[10]From Goldsmith's *Retaliation*, l. 32.

[11]Arnold is here in error. Burke wrote his *Letter to a Noble Lord* and his *Letters on a Regicide Peace* in 1796 (he died in 1797).

*forwrd it; and then they who persist in oppos-
ing this mighty current in human affairs, will
appear rather to resist the decrees of Providence
itself, than the mere designs of men. They
will not be resolute and firm, but perverse and
obstinate.*

That return of Burke upon himself has always seemed to me one of the finest things
in English literature, or indeed in any
literature. That is what I call living by
ideas; when one side of a question has long
had your earnest support, when all your
feelings are engaged, when you hear all
round you no language but one, when your
party talks this language like a steam-engine
and can imagine no other,—still to be able
to think, still to be irresistibly carried, if so
it be, by the current of thought to the opposite
side of the question, and, like Balaam,[12] to be
unable to speak of anything *but what the
Lord has put in your mouth.* I know noth-
!ng more striking, and I must add that I
know nothing more un-English.

For the Englishman in general is like my
friend the Member of Parliament, and believes, point-blank, that for a thing to be an
anomaly is absolutely no objection to it
whatever. He is like the Lord Auckland[13]
of Burke's day, who, in a memorandum on
the French Revolution, talks of "certain
miscreants, assuming the name of philosophers, who have presumed themselves
capable of establishing a new system of
society." The Englishman has been called
a political animal, and he values what is political and practical so much that ideas easily
become objects of dislike in his eyes, and
thinkers "miscreants," because ideas and
thinkers have rashly meddled with politics
and practice. This would be all very well
if the dislike and neglect confined themselves to ideas transported out of their own
sphere, and meddling rashly with practice;
but they are inevitably extended to ideas as
such, and to the whole life of intelligence;
practice is everything, a free play of the
mind is nothing. The notion of the free
play of the mind upon all subjects being a
pleasure in itself, being an object of desire,

being an essential provider of elements without which a nation's spirit, whatever compen-
sations it may have for them, must, in the
long run, die of inanition, hardly enters into
an Englishman's thoughts. It is noticeable
that the word *curiosity,* which in other languages is used in a good sense, to mean, as a
high and fine quality of man's nature, just
this disinterested love of a free play of the
mind on all subjects, for its own sake,—it is
noticeable, I say, that this word has in our
language no sense of the kind, no sense but a
rather bad and disparaging one. But
criticism, real criticism, is essentially the
exercise of this very quality; it obeys an instinct prompting it to try to know the best
that is known and thought in the world,
irrespectively of practice, politics, and everything of the kind; and to value knowledge
and thought as they approach this best, without the intrusion of any other considerations
whatever. This is an instinct for which
there is, I think, little original sympathy in
the practical English nature, and what there
was of it has undergone a long benumbing
period of blight and suppression in the epoch
of concentration which followed the French
Revolution.

But epochs of concentration cannot well
endure for ever; epochs of expansion, in the
due course of things, follow them. Such an
epoch of expansion seems to be opening in
this country. In the first place all danger of
a hostile forcible pressure of foreign ideas
upon our practice has long disappeared; like
the traveler in the fable,[14] therefore, we begin
to wear our cloak a little more loosely.
Then, with a long peace, the ideas of Europe
steal gradually and amicably in, and mingle,
though in infinitesimally small quantities at
a time, with our own notions. Then, too,
in spite of all that is said about the absorbing
and brutalizing influence of our passionate
material progress, it seems to me indisputable
that this progress is likely, though not certain,
to lead in the end to an apparition of intellectual life; and that man, after he has made
himself perfectly comfortable and has now
to determine what to do with himself next,

---

[12]See Numbers, 22:38.

[13]William Eden (1744–1814), raised to the peerage
in 1789.

[14]Of Aesop. The fable tells of a contest between
the North Wind and the Sun as to which would
first strip a man of his clothes.

may begin to remember that he has a mind, and that the mind may be made the source of great pleasure. I grant it is mainly the privilege of faith, at present, to discern this end to our railways, our business, and our fortune-making; but we shall see if, here as elsewhere, faith is not in the end the true prophet. Our ease, our traveling, and our unbounded liberty to hold just as hard and securely as we please to the practice to which our notions have given birth, all tend to beget an inclination to deal a little more freely with these notions themselves, to canvass them a little, to penetrate a little into their real nature. Flutterings of curiosity, in the foreign sense of the word, appear amongst us, and it is in these that criticism must look to find its account. Criticism first; a time of true creative activity, perhaps,—which, as I have said, must inevitably be preceded amongst us by a time of criticism,—hereafter, when criticism has done its work.

It is of the last importance that English criticism should clearly discern what rule for its course, in order to avail itself of the field now opening to it, and to produce fruit for the future, it ought to take. The rule may be summed up in one word,—*disinterestedness*. And how is criticism to show disinterestedness? By keeping aloof from practice; by resolutely following the law of its own nature, which is to be a free play of the mind on all subjects which it touches; by steadily refusing to lend itself to any of those ulterior, political, practical considerations about ideas which plenty of people will be sure to attach to them, which perhaps ought often to be attached to them, which in this country at any rate are certain to be attached to them quite sufficiently, but which criticism has really nothing to do with. Its business is, as I have said, simply to know the best that is known and thought in the world, and by in its turn making this known, to create a current of true and fresh ideas. Its business is to do this with inflexible honesty, with due ability; but its business is to do no more, and to leave alone all questions of practical consequences and applications, questions which will never fail to have due prominence given to them. Else criticism, besides being really false to its own nature,

merely continues in the old rut which it has hitherto followed in this country, and will certainly miss the chance now given to it. For what is at present the bane of criticism in this country? It is that practical considerations cling to it and stifle it; it subserves interests not its own; our organs of criticism are organs of men and parties having practical ends to serve, and with them those practical ends are the first thing and the play of mind the second; so much play of mind as is compatible with the prosecution of those practical ends is all that is wanted. An organ like the *Revue des Deux Mondes,* having for its main function to understand and utter the best that is known and thought in the world, existing, it may be said, as just an organ for a free play of the mind, we have not; but we have the *Edinburgh Review,* existing as an organ of the old Whigs, and for as much play of mind as may suit its being that; we have the *Quarterly Review,* existing as an organ of the Tories, and for as much play of mind as may suit its being that; we have the *British Quarterly Review,* existing as an organ of the political Dissenters, and for as much play of mind as may suit its being that; we have the *Times,* existing as an organ of the common, satisfied, well-to-do Englishman, and for as much play of mind as may suit its being that. And so on through all the various fractions, political and religious, of our society; every fraction has, as such, its organ of criticism, but the notion of combining all fractions in the common pleasure of a free disinterested play of mind meets with no favor. Directly this play of mind wants to have more scope, and to forget the pressure of practical considerations a little, it is checked, it is made to feel the chain; we saw this the other day in the extinction, so much to be regretted, of the *Home and Foreign Review;* perhaps in no organ of criticism in this country was there so much knowledge, so much play of mind; but these could not save it: the *Dublin Review* subordinates play of mind to the practical business of English and Irish Catholicism, and lives. It must needs be that men should act in sects and parties, that each of these sects and parties should have its organ, and should make this organ subserve the interests of its action; but it would be well, too, that there should be a criticism, not the minister of these interests, not their enemy, but absolutely and entirely independent of them. No other criticism will ever attain any real authority or make any real way towards its end,—the creating a current of true and fresh ideas.

It is because criticism has so little kept in the pure intellectual sphere, has so little detached itself from practice, has been so directly polemical and controversial, that it has so ill accomplished, in this country, its best spiritual work; which is to keep man from a self-satisfaction which is retarding and vulgarizing, to lead him towards perfection, by making his mind dwell upon what is excellent in itself, and the absolute beauty and fitness of things. A polemical practical criticism makes men blind even to the ideal imperfection of their practice, makes them willingly assert its ideal perfection, in order the better to secure it against attack; and clearly this is narrowing and baneful for them. If they were reassured on the practical side, speculative considerations of ideal perfection they might be brought to entertain, and their spiritual horizon would thus gradually widen. Mr. Adderley[15] says to the Warwickshire farmers:

Talk of the improvement of breed! Why, the race we ourselves represent, the men and women, the old Anglo-Saxon race, are the best breed in the whole world. . . . The absence of a too enervating climate, too unclouded skies, and a too luxurious nature, has produced so vigorous a race of people, and has rendered us so superior to all the world.

Mr. Roebuck[16] says to the Sheffield cutlers:

I look around me and ask what is the state of England? Is not property safe? Is not every man able to say what he likes? Can you not walk from one end of England to the other in perfect security? I ask you whether, the world over or in past history, there is anything like it? Nothing. I pray that our unrivaled happiness may last.

Now obviously there is a peril for poor human nature in words and thoughts of such exuberant self-satisfaction, until we find ourselves safe in the streets of the Celestial City.

*Das wenige verschwindet leicht dem Blicke
Der vorwärts sieht, wie viel noch übrig bleibt*[17]

says Goethe; the little that is done seems nothing when we look forward and see how much we have yet to do. Clearly this is a better line of reflection for weak humanity, so long as it remains on this earthly field of labor and trial. But neither Mr. Adderley nor Mr. Roebuck is by nature inaccessible to considerations of this sort. They only lose sight of them owing to the controversial life we all lead, and the practical form which all speculation takes with us. They have in view opponents whose aim is not ideal, but practical; and in their zeal to uphold their own practice against these innovators, they go so far as even to attribute to this practice an ideal perfection. Somebody has been wanting to introduce a six-pound franchise,[18] or to abolish church-rates,[19] or to collect agricultural statistics by force, or to diminish local self-government. How natural, in reply to such proposals, very likely improper or ill-timed, to go a little beyond the mark, and to say stoutly, "Such a race of people as we stand, so superior to all the world! The old Anglo-Saxon race, the best breed in the whole world! I pray that our unrivaled happiness may last! I ask you whether, the world over or in past history, there is anything like it!" And so long as criticism answers this dithyramb by insisting that the old Anglo-Saxon race would be still more superior to all others if it had no church-rates, or that our unrivaled happiness would last yet longer with a six-pound franchise, so long will the strain, "The best breed in the whole world!" swell louder and louder, everything ideal and refining will be

---

[15]Charles Bowyer Adderley (1814–1905), first Baron Norton, a Tory statesman.

[16]The Right Hon. J. A. Roebuck (1801–1879), barrister and politician.

[17]*Iphigenie auf Tauris,* I, ii, 91–92. Arnold translates the lines in the concluding portion of the sentence.

[18]I. e., widen the franchise, which at this time was restricted to occupants of premises worth not less than £10 the year.

[19]Taxes levied on assessed property in a parish for the maintenance of the church.

lost out of sight, and both the assailed and their critics will remain in a sphere, to say the truth, perfectly unvital, a sphere in which spiritual progression is impossible. But let criticism leave church-rates and the franchise alone, and in the most candid spirit, without a single lurking thought of practical innovation, confront with our dithyramb this paragraph on which I stumbled in a newspaper soon after reading Mr. Roebuck:

A shocking child murder has just been committed at Nottingham. A girl named Wragg left the workhouse there on Saturday morning with her young illegitimate child. The child was soon afterwards found dead on Mapperly Hills, having been strangled. Wragg is in custody.

Nothing but that; but, in juxtaposition with the absolute eulogies of Mr. Adderley and Mr. Roebuck, how eloquent, how suggestive are those few lines! "Our old Anglo-Saxon breed, the best in the whole world!"—how much that is harsh and ill-favored there is in this best! *Wragg!* If we are to talk of ideal perfection, of "the best in the whole world," has any one reflected what a touch of grossness in our race, what an original shortcoming in the more delicate spiritual perceptions, is shown by the natural growth amongst us of such hideous names,—Higginbottom, Stiggins, Bugg! In Ionia and Attica they were luckier in this respect than "the best race in the world"; by the Ilissus[20] there was no Wragg, poor thing! And "our unrivaled happiness";— what an element of grimness, bareness, and hideousness mixes with it and blurs it; the workhouse, the dismal Mapperly Hills,—how dismal those who have seen them will remember;—the gloom, the smoke, the cold, the strangled illegitimate child! "I ask you whether the world over, or in past history, there is anything like it?" Perhaps not, one is inclined to answer; but at any rate, in that case, the world is very much to be pitied. And the final touch,—short, bleak, and inhuman: *Wragg is in custody.* The sex lost in the confusion of our unrivaled happiness; or (shall I say?) the superfluous Christian

[20]A river adjacent to Athens.

name lopped off by the straight-forward vigor of our old Anglo-Saxon breed! There is profit for the spirit in such contrasts as this; criticism serves the cause of perfection by establishing them. By eluding sterile conflict, by refusing to remain in the sphere where alone narrow and relative conceptions have any worth and validity, criticism may diminish its momentary importance, but only in this way has it a chance of gaining admittance for those wider and more perfect conceptions to which all its duty is really owed. Mr. Roebuck will have a poor opinion of an adversary who replies to his defiant songs of triumph only by murmuring under his breath, *Wragg is in custody;* but in no other way will these songs of triumph be induced gradually to moderate themselves, to get rid of what in them is excessive and offensive, and to fall into a softer and truer key.

It will be said that it is a very subtle and indirect action which I am thus prescribing for criticism, and that by embracing in this manner the Indian virtue of detachment and abandoning the sphere of practical life, it condemns itself to a slow and obscure work. Slow and obscure it may be, but it is the only proper work of criticism. The mass of mankind will never have any ardent zeal for seeing things as they are; very inadequate ideas will always satisfy them. On these inadequate ideas reposes, and must repose, the general practice of the world. That is as much as saying that whoever sets himself to see things as they are will find himself one of a very small circle; but it is only by this small circle resolutely doing its own work that adequate ideas will ever get current at all. The rush and roar of practical life will always have a dizzying and attracting effect upon the most collected spectator, and tend to draw him into its vortex; most of all will this be the case where that life is so powerful as it is in England. But it is only by remaining collected, and refusing to lend himself to the point of view of the practical man, that the critic can do the practical man any service; and it is only by the greatest sincerity in pursuing his own course, and by at last convincing even the practical man of his sincerity, that he can escape misunderstandings which perpetually threaten him.

For the practical man is not apt for fine distinctions, and yet in these distinctions truth and the highest culture greatly find 5 their account. But it is not easy to lead a practical man—unless you reassure him as to your practical intentions, you have no chance of leading him—to see that a thing which he has always been used to look at 10 from one side only, which he greatly values, and which, looked at from that side, more than deserves, perhaps, all the prizing and admiring which he bestows upon it,—that this thing, looked at from another side, may ap- 15 pear much less beneficent and beautiful, and yet retain all its claims to our practical allegiance. Where shall we find language innocent enough, how shall we make the spotless purity of our intentions evident enough, 20 to enable us to say to the political Englishman that the British Constitution itself, which, seen from the practical side, looks such a magnificent organ of progress and virtue, seen from the speculative side,—with its com- 25 promises, its love of facts, its horror of theory, its studied avoidance of clear thoughts,—that, seen from this side, our august Constitution sometimes looks,—forgive me, shade of Lord Somers![21]—a colos- 30 sal machine for the manufacture of Philistines?[22] How is Cobbett[23] to say this and not be misunderstood, blackened as he is with the smoke of a lifelong conflict in the field of political practice? how is Mr. Carlyle to say 35 it and not be misunderstood, after his furious raid into this field with his *Latter-Day Pamphlets?* how is Mr. Ruskin, after his pugnacious political economy? I say, the critic must keep out of the region of immediate 40 practice in the political, social, humanitarian sphere, if he wants to make a beginning for that more free speculative treatment of things, which may perhaps one day make its benefits felt even in this sphere, but in a 45 natural and thence irresistible manner.

Do what he will, however, the critic will still remain exposed to frequent misunderstandings, and nowhere so much as in this country. For here people are particularly indisposed even to comprehend that without this free disinterested treatment of things, truth and the highest culture are out of the question. So immersed are they in practical life, so accustomed to take all their notions from this life and its processes, that they are apt to think that truth and culture themselves can be reached by the processes of this life, and that it is an impertinent singularity to think of reaching them in any other. "We are all *terrae filii*,"[24] cries their eloquent advocate; "all Philistines together. Away with the notion of proceeding by any other course than the course dear to the Philistines; let us have a social movement, let us organize and combine a party to pursue truth and new thought, let us call it *the liberal party,* and let us all stick to each other, and back each other up. Let us have no nonsense about independent criticism, and intellectual delicacy, and the few and the many; don't let us trouble ourselves about foreign thought; we shall invent the whole thing for ourselves as we go along: if one of us speaks well, applaud him; if one of us speaks ill, applaud him too; we are all in the same movement, we are all liberals, we are all in pursuit of truth." In this way the pursuit of truth becomes really a social, practical, pleasurable affair, almost requiring a chairman, a secretary, and advertisements; with the excitement of an occasional scandal, with a little resistance to give the happy sense of difficulty overcome; but, in general, plenty of bustle and very little thought. To act is so easy, as Goethe says; to think is so hard! It is true that the critic has many temptations to go with the stream, to make one of the party of movement, one of these *terrae filii;* it seems ungracious to refuse to be a *terrae filius,* when so many excellent people are; but the critic's duty is to refuse, or, if resistance is vain, at least to cry with Obermann: *Périssons en résistant.*[25]

---

[21]John, Baron Somers (1651–1716), Lord Chancellor. He was a member of the Convention Parliament in 1689.

[22]Arnold's term for the solid, respectable, unenlightened middle class.

[23]William Cobbett (1762–1835), essayist and politician.

[24]Children of earth—i. e., "nobodies."

[25]Let us perish resisting. *Obermann* is the title of a series of letters written by Étienne Pivert de Senancour (1770–1846), published at Paris in 1804.

How serious a matter is it to try and resist, I had ample opportunity of experiencing when I ventured some time ago to criticize the celebrated first volume of Bishop Colenso.[26] The echoes of the storm which was then raised I still, from time to time, hear grumbling round me. That storm arose out of a misunderstanding almost inevitable. It is a result of no little culture to attain to a clear perception that science and religion are two wholly different things; the multitude will for ever confuse them, but happily that is of no great real importance, for while the multitude imagines itself to live by its false science, it does really live by its true religion. Dr. Colenso, however, in his first volume did all he could to strengthen the confusion,[27] and to make it dangerous. He did this with the best intentions, I freely admit, and with the most candid ignorance that this was the natural effect of what he was doing; but, says Joubert, "Ignorance, which in matters of morals extenuates the crime, is itself, in intellectual matters, a crime of the first order." I criticized Bishop Colenso's speculative confusion. Immediately there was a cry raised: "What is this? here is a liberal attacking a liberal. Do not you belong to the movement? are not you a friend of truth? Is not Bishop Colenso in pursuit of truth? then speak with proper respect of his book. Dr. Stanley[28] is another friend of truth, and you speak with proper respect of his book; why make these invidious differences? both books are excellent, admirable, liberal; Bishop Colenso's perhaps the most so, because it is the boldest, and will have the best practical consequences for the liberal cause. Do you want to encourage to the attack of a brother liberal his, and your, and our implacable enemies, the *Church and State Review* or the *Record*,—the High Church rhinoceros and the Evangelical hyena? Be silent, therefore; or rather speak, speak as loud as ever you can, and go into ecstasies over the eighty and odd pigeons."[29]

But criticism cannot follow this coarse and indiscriminate method. It is unfortunately possible for a man in pursuit of truth to write a book which reposes upon a false conception. Even the practical consequences of a book are to genuine criticism no recommendation of it, if the book is, in the highest sense, blundering. I see that a lady who herself, too, is in pursuit of truth, and who writes with great ability, but a little too much, perhaps, under the influence of the practical spirit of the English liberal movement, classes Bishop Colenso's book and M. Renan's[30] together, in her survey of the religious state of Europe,[31] as facts of the same order, works, both of them, of "great importance"; "great ability, power, and skill"; Bishop Colenso's, perhaps the most powerful; at least, Miss Cobbe gives special expression to her gratitude that to Bishop Colenso "has been given the strength to grasp, and the courage to teach, truths of such deep import." In the same way, more than one popular writer has compared him to Luther. Now

---

[26] So sincere is my dislike to all personal attack and controversy, that I abstain from reprinting, at this distance of time from the occasion which called them forth, the essays in which I criticized Dr. Colenso's book [the first volume of his examination of the *Pentateuch*]; I feel bound, however, after all that has passed, to make here a final declaration of my sincere impenitence for having published them. Nay, I cannot forbear repeating yet once more, for his benefit and that of his readers, this sentence from my original remarks upon him: *There is truth of science and truth of religion; truth of science does not become truth of religion till it is made religious.* And I will add: Let us have all the science there is from the men of science; from the men of religion let us have religion (Arnold's note). J. W. Colenso (1814–1883) endeavored to show that the Pentateuch was largely unhistorical and that much of the legislation attributed to Moses was really centuries later in date.

[27] It has been said I make it "a crime against literary criticism and the higher culture to attempt to inform the ignorant." Need I point out that the ignorant are not informed by being confirmed in a confusion? (Arnold's note.)

[28] Arthur Penrhyn Stanley (1815–1881), Dean of Westminster Abbey, who was a supporter of Colenso. "His book" is entitled *Lectures on the History of the Jewish Church* (1863–1865).

[29] Colenso in commenting on Leviticus, 10:16, 20, had written: "The very pigeons to be brought as sin-offerings for the birth of children would have averaged according to the story more than 250 a day; and each priest would have had to eat daily more than 80 for his own portion 'in the most holy place'!"

[30] The *Vie de Jésus* (1863) by Ernest Renan (1823–1892).

[31] *Broken Lights* (1864) by Frances Power Cobbe (1822–1904).

it is just this kind of false estimate which the critical spirit is, it seems to me, bound to resist. It is really the strongest possible proof of the low ebb at which, in England, the critical spirit is, that while the critical hit [5] in the religious literature of Germany is Dr. Strauss's[32] book, in that of France M. Renan's book, the book of Bishop Colenso is the critical hit in the religious literature of England.[33] Bishop Colenso's book reposes [10] on a total misconception of the essential elements of the religious problem, as that problem is now presented for solution. To criticism, therefore, which seeks to have the best that is known and thought on this problem, it [15] is, however well meant, of no importance whatever. M. Renan's book attempts a new synthesis of the elements furnished to us by the Four Gospels. It attempts, in my opinion, a synthesis, perhaps premature, per- [20] haps impossible, certainly not successful. Up to the present time, at any rate, we must acquiesce in Fleury's sentence on such recastings of the Gospel-story: *Quiconque s'imagine la pouvoir mieux écrire, ne l'entend* [25] *pas.*[34] M. Renan had himself passed by anticipation a like sentence on his own work, when he said: "If a new presentation of the character of Jesus were offered to me, I would not have it; its very clearness would [30] be, in my opinion, the best proof of its insufficiency." His friends may with perfect justice rejoin that at the sight of the Holy Land, and of the actual scene of the Gospel-story, all the current of M. Renan's thoughts [35] may have naturally changed, and a new casting of that story irresistibly suggested itself to him; and that this is just a case for applying Cicero's maxim: Change of mind is not inconsistency—*nemo doctus unquam muta-* [40] *tionem consilii inconstantiam dixit esse.*[35] Nevertheless, for criticism, M. Renan's first

thought must still be the truer one, as long as his new casting so fails more fully to commend itself, more fully (to use Coleridge's happy phrase about the Bible) to *find* us.[36] Still M. Renan's attempt is, for criticism, of the most real interest and importance, since, with all its difficulty, a fresh synthesis of the New Testament *data,*—not a making war on them, in Voltaire's fashion, not a leaving them out of mind, in the world's fashion, but the putting a new construction upon them, the taking them from under the old, adoptive, traditional, unspiritual point of view and placing them under a new one,—is the very essence of the religious problem, as now presented; and only by efforts in this direction can it receive a solution.

Again, in the same spirit in which she judges Bishop Colenso, Miss Cobbe, like so many earnest liberals of our practical race, both here and in America, herself sets vigorously about a positive reconstruction of religion, about making a religion of the future out of hand, or at least setting about making it; we must not rest, she and they are always thinking and saying, in negative criticism, we must be creative and constructive; hence we have such works as her recent *Religious Duty,* and works still more considerable, perhaps, by others, which will be in everyone's mind. These works often have much ability; they often spring out of sincere convictions, and a sincere wish to do good; and they sometimes, perhaps, do good. Their fault is (if I may be permitted to say so) one which they have in common with the British College of Health, in the New Road. Every one knows the British College of Health; it is that building with the lion and the statue of the Goddess Hygeia[37] before it; at least, I am sure about the lion, though I am not absolutely certain about the Goddess Hygeia. This building does credit, perhaps, to the resources of Dr. [45] Morrison[38] and his disciples; but it falls a good deal short of one's idea of what a British College of Health ought to be. In England, where we hate public interference

---

[32]*Leben Jesu* (1835) by David Friedrich Strauss (1808–1874).

[33]It should be said that there was more of feeling than of logic in Arnold's attitude towards Colenso, that his work was of real importance, and that his chief conclusions are now generally accepted.

[34]Whoever imagines that he could write it better does not understand it. From the Preface to the *Ecclesiastical History* (1691) of Claude Fleury (1640–1723).

[35]*Letters to Atticus,* xvi, 7, 3.

---

[36]See *Confessions of an Inquiring Spirit,* Letter L.
[37]The goddess of health.
[38]James Morrison (1770–1840)

and love individual enterprise, we have a whole crop of places like the British College of Health; the grand name without the grand thing. Unluckily, creditable to individual enterprise as they are, they tend to impair our taste by making us forget what more grandiose, noble, or beautiful character properly belongs to a public institution. The same may be said of the religions of the future of Miss Cobbe and others. Creditable, like the British College of Health, to the resources of their authors, they yet tend to make us forget what more grandiose, noble, or beautiful character properly belongs to religious constructions. The historic religions, with all their faults, have had this; it certainly belongs to the religious sentiment, when it truly flowers, to have this; and we impoverish our spirit if we allow a religion of the future without it. What then is the duty of criticism here? To take the practical point of view, to applaud the liberal movement and all its works,—its New Road religions of the future into the bargain,—for their general utility's sake? By no means; but to be perpetually dissatisfied with these works, while they perpetually fall short of a high and perfect ideal.

For criticism, these are elementary laws; but they never can be popular, and in this country they have been very little followed, and one meets with immense obstacles in following them. That is a reason for asserting them again and again. Criticism must maintain its independence of the practical spirit and its aims. Even with well-meant efforts of the practical spirit it must express dissatisfaction, if in the sphere of the ideal they seem impoverishing and limiting. It must not hurry on to the goal because of its practical importance. It must be patient, and know how to wait; and flexible, and know how to attach itself to things and how to withdraw from them. It must be apt to study and praise elements that for the fullness of spiritual perfection are wanted, even though they belong to a power which in the practical sphere may be maleficent. It must be apt to discern the spiritual shortcomings or illusions of powers that in the practical sphere may be beneficent. And this without any notion of favoring or injuring, in the practical sphere, one power or the other; without any notion of playing off, in this sphere, one power against the other. When one looks, for instance, at the English Divorce Court,—an institution which perhaps has its practical conveniences, but which in the ideal sphere is so hideous; an institution which neither makes divorce impossible nor makes it decent, which allows a man to get rid of his wife, or a wife of her husband, but makes them drag one another first, for the public edification, through a mire of unutterable infamy,—when one looks at this charming institution, I say, with its crowded benches, its newspaper-reports, and its money-compensations, this institution in which the gross unregenerate British Philistine has indeed stamped an image of himself,—one may be permitted to find the marriage-theory of Catholicism refreshing and elevating. Or when Protestantism, in virtue of its supposed rational and intellectual origin, gives the law to criticism too magisterially, criticism may and must remind it that its pretensions, in this respect, are illusive and do it harm; that the Reformation was a moral rather than an intellectual event; that Luther's theory of grace no more exactly reflects the mind of the spirit than Bossuet's philosophy of history reflects it; and that there is no more antecedent probability of the Bishop of Durham's stock of ideas being agreeable to perfect reason than of Pope Pius the Ninth's. But criticism will not on that account forget the achievements of Protestantism in the practical and moral sphere; nor that, even in the intellectual sphere, Protestantism, though in a blind and stumbling manner, carried forward the Renaissance, while Catholicism threw itself violently across its path.

I lately heard a man of thought and energy contrasting the want of ardor and movement which he now found amongst young men in this country with what he remembered in his own youth, twenty years ago. "What reformers we were then!" he exclaimed; "what a zeal we had! how we canvassed every institution in Church and State, and were prepared to remodel them all on first principles!" He was inclined to regret, as a spiritual flagging, the lull which he saw. I am disposed rather to regard it as a pause in which the turn to a new mode of spiritual progress is being accomplished. Everything was long seen, by the young and ardent amongst us, in inseparable connection with politics and practical life; we have pretty well exhausted the benefits of seeing things in this connection, we have got all that can be got by so seeing them. Let us try a more disinterested mode of seeing them; let us betake ourselves more to the serener life of the mind and spirit. This life, too, may have its excesses and dangers; but they are not for us at present. Let us think of quietly enlarging our stock of true and fresh ideas, and not, as soon as we get an idea or half an idea, be running out with it into the street, and trying to make it rule there. Our ideas will, in the end, shape the world all the better for maturing a little. Perhaps in fifty years' time it will in the English House of Commons be an objection to an institution that it is an anomaly, and my friend the Member of Parliament will shudder in his grave. But let us in the meanwhile rather endeavor that in twenty years' time it may, in English literature, be an objection to a proposition that it is absurd. That will be a change so vast, that the imagination almost fails to grasp it. *Ab integro saeclorum nàscitur ordo*.[39]

If I have insisted so much on the course which criticism must take where politics and religion are concerned, it is because, where these burning matters are in question, it is most likely to go astray. I have wished, above all, to insist on the attitude which criticism should adopt towards everything; on its right tone and temper of mind. Then comes the question as to the subject-matter which criticism should most seek. Here, in general, its course is determined for it by the idea which is the law of its being; the idea of a disinterested endeavor to learn and propagate the best that is known and thought in the world, and thus to establish a current of fresh and true ideas. By the very nature of things, as England is not all the world, much of the best that is known and thought in the world cannot be of English growth, must be for-

eign; by the nature of things, again, it is just this that we are least likely to know, while English thought is streaming in upon us from all sides and takes excellent care that we shall not be ignorant of its existence; the English critic, therefore, must dwell much on foreign thought, and with particular heed on any part of it, which, while significant and fruitful in itself, is for any reason specially likely to escape him. Again, judging is often spoken of as the critic's one business; and so in some sense it is; but the judgment which almost insensibly forms itself in a fair and clear mind, along with fresh knowledge, is the valuable one; and thus knowledge, and ever fresh knowledge, must be the critic's great concern for himself; and it is by communicating fresh knowledge, and letting his own judgment pass along with it,—but insensibly, and in the second place not the first, as a sort of companion and clue, not as an abstract lawgiver,—that he will generally do most good to his readers. Sometimes, no doubt, for the sake of establishing an author's place in literature, and his relation to a central standard (and if this is not done, how are we to get at our *best in the world?*), criticism may have to deal with a subject-matter so familiar that fresh knowledge is out of the question, and then it must be all judgment; an enunciation and detailed application of principles. Here the great safeguard is never to let oneself become abstract, always to retain an intimate and lively consciousness of the truth of what one is saying, and, the moment this fails us, to be sure that something is wrong. Still, under all circumstances, this mere judgment and application of principles is, in itself, not the most satisfactory work to the critic; like mathematics, it is tautological, and cannot well give us, like fresh learning, the sense of creative activity.

But stop, some one will say; all this talk is of no practical use to us whatever; this criticism of yours is not what we have in our minds when we speak of criticism; when we speak of critics and criticism, we mean critics and criticism of the current English literature of the day; when you offer to tell criticism its function, it is to this criticism that we expect you to address yourself. I am sorry for

[39] The cycle of the ages is born anew (Virgil, *Eclogue* IV, 5).

it, for I am afraid I must disappoint these expectations. I am bound by my own definition of criticism: *a disinterested endeavor to learn and propagate the best that is known and thought in the world.* How much of current English literature comes into this "best that is known and thought in the world"? Not very much, I fear; certainly less, at this moment, than of the current literature of France or Germany. Well, then, am I to alter my definition of criticism, in order to meet the requirements of a number of practising English critics, who, after all, are free in their choice of a business? That would be making criticism lend itself just to one of those alien practical considerations, which, I have said, are so fatal to it. One may say, indeed, to those who have to deal with the mass—so much better disregarded —of current English literature, that they may at all events endeavor, in dealing with this, to try it, so far as they can, by the standard of the best that is known and thought in the world; one may say, that to get anywhere near this standard, every critic should try and possess one great literature, at least, besides his own; and the more unlike his own, the better. But, after all, the criticism I am really concerned with,—the criticism which alone can much help us for the future, the criticism which, throughout Europe, is at the present day meant, when so much stress is laid on the importance of criticism and the critical spirit,—is a criticism which regards Europe as being, for intellectual and spiritual purposes, one great confederation, bound to a joint action and working to a common result; and whose members have, for their proper outfit, a knowledge of Greek, Roman, and Eastern antiquity, and of one another. Special, local, and temporary advantages being put out of account, that modern nation will in the intellectual and spiritual sphere make most progress, which most thoroughly carries out this programme. And what is that but saying that we too, all of us, as individuals, the more thoroughly we carry it out, shall make the more progress?

There is so much inviting us!—what are we to take? what will nourish us in growth towards perfection? That is the question which, with the immense field of life and of literature lying before him, the critic has to answer; for himself first, and afterwards for others. In this idea of the critic's business the essays brought together in the following pages[40] have had their origin; in this idea, widely different as are their subjects, they have, perhaps, their unity.

I conclude with what I said at the beginning: to have the sense of creative activity is the great happiness and the great proof of being alive, and it is not denied to criticism to have it; but then criticism must be sincere, simple, flexible, ardent, ever widening its knowledge. Then it may have, in no contemptible measure, a joyful sense of creative activity; a sense which a man of insight and conscience will prefer to what he might derive from a poor, starved, fragmentary, inadequate creation. And at some epochs no other creation is possible.

Still, in full measure, the sense of creative activity belongs only to genuine creation; in literature we must never forget that. But what true man of letters ever can forget it? It is no such common matter for a gifted nature to come into possession of a current of true and living ideas, and to produce amidst the inspiration of them, that we are likely to underrate it. The epochs of Aeschylus and Shakespeare make us feel their pre-eminence. In an epoch like those is, no doubt, the true life of a literature; there is the promised land, towards which criticism can only beckon. That promised land it will not be ours to enter, and we shall die in the wilderness: but to have desired to enter it, to have saluted it from afar, is already, perhaps, the best distinction among contemporaries; it will certainly be the best title to esteem with posterity.

[40] I. e., in *Essays in Criticism.*

SWEETNESS AND LIGHT[1]

THE disparagers of culture make its motive curiosity; sometimes, indeed, they make its motive mere exclusiveness and vanity. The culture which is supposed to plume itself on a smattering of Greek and Latin is a culture which is begotten by nothing so intellectual as curiosity; it is valued either out of sheer vanity and ignorance or else as an engine of social and class distinction, separating its holder, like a badge or title, from other people who have not got it. No serious man would call this *culture,* or attach any value to it, as culture, at all. To find the real ground for the very different estimate which serious people will set upon culture, we must find some motive for culture in the terms of which may lie a real ambiguity; and such a motive the word *curiosity* gives us.

I have before now pointed out that we English do not, like the foreigners, use this word in a good sense as well as in a bad sense. With us the word is always used in a somewhat disapproving sense. A liberal and intelligent eagerness about the things of the mind may be meant by a foreigner when he speaks of curiosity, but with us the word always conveys a certain notion of frivolous and unedifying activity. In the *Quarterly Review,* some little time ago, was an estimate of the celebrated French critic, M. Sainte-Beuve,[2] and a very inadequate estimate it in my judgment was. And its inadequacy consisted chiefly in this: that in our English way it left out of sight the double sense really involved in the word *curiosity,* thinking enough was said to stamp M. Sainte-Beuve with blame if it was said that he was impelled in his operations as a critic by curiosity, and omitting either to perceive that M. Sainte-Beuve himself, and many other people with him, would consider that this was praiseworthy and not blame-worthy, or to point out why it ought really to be accounted worthy of blame and not of praise. For as there is a curiosity about intellectual matters which is futile, and merely a disease, so there is certainly a curiosity,—a desire after the things of the mind simply for their own sakes and for the pleasure of seeing them as they are,—which is, in an intelligent being, natural and laudable. Nay, and the very desire to see things as they are implies a balance and regulation of mind which is not often attained without fruitful effort, and which is the very opposite of the blind and diseased impulse of mind which is what we mean to blame when we blame curiosity. Montesquieu[3] says: "The first motive which ought to impel us to study is the desire to augment the excellence of our nature, and to render an intelligent being yet more intelligent." This is the true ground to assign for the genuine scientific passion, however manifested, and for culture, viewed simply as a fruit of this passion; and it is a worthy ground, even though we let the term *curiosity* stand to describe it.

But there is of culture another view, in which not solely the scientific passion, the sheer desire to see things as they are, natural and proper in an intelligent being, appears as the ground of it. There is a view in which all the love of our neighbor, the impulses towards action, help, and beneficence, the desire for removing human error, clearing human confusion, and diminishing human misery, the noble aspiration to leave the world better and happier than we found it,—motives eminently such as are called social,—come in as part of the grounds of culture, and the main and pre-eminent part. Culture is then properly described not as having its origin in curiosity, but as having its origin in the love of perfection; it is *a study of perfection.* It moves by the force, not merely or primarily of the scientific passion for pure knowledge, but also of the moral and social passion for doing good. As, in the first view of it, we took for its worthy motto Montesquieu's words: "To

---

[1] The initial essay in *Culture and Anarchy,* 1869. In 1867 Arnold had delivered it as his last lecture as Professor of Poetry at Oxford, and in the same year it had been published in the *Cornhill Magazine;* the original title of the essay was *Culture and Its Enemies.*

[2] Charles A. Sainte-Beuve (1804–1869), author of the *Causeries du Lundi.*

[3] Charles L. de Secondat de Montesquieu (1689–1755), author of the *De l'Esprit des Lois.*

render an intelligent being yet more intelligent!" so, in the second view of it, there is no better motto which it can have than these words of Bishop Wilson:[4] "To make reason and the will of God prevail!"

Only, whereas the passion for doing good is apt to be overhasty in determining what reason and the will of God say, because its turn is for acting rather than thinking and it wants to be beginning to act; and whereas it is apt to take its own conceptions, which proceed from its own state of development and share in all the imperfections and immaturities of this, for a basis of action; what distinguishes culture is, that it is possessed by the scientific passion as well as by the passion of doing good; that it demands worthy notions of reason and the will of God, and does not readily suffer its own crude conceptions to substitute themselves for them. And knowing that no action or institution can be salutary and stable which is not based on reason and the will of God, it is not so bent on acting and instituting, even with the great aim of diminishing human error and misery ever before its thoughts, but that it can remember that acting and instituting are of little use, unless we know how and what we ought to act and to institute.

This culture is more interesting and more far-reaching than that other, which is founded solely on the scientific passion for knowing. But it needs times of faith and ardor, times when the intellectual horizon is opening and widening all round us, to flourish in. And is not the close and bounded intellectual horizon within which we have long lived and moved now lifting up, and are not new lights finding free passage to shine in upon us? For a long time there was no passage for them to make their way in upon us, and then it was of no use to think of adapting the world's action to them. Where was the hope of making reason and the will of God prevail among people who had a routine which they had christened reason and the will of God, in which they were inextricably bound, and beyond which they had no power of looking? But now the iron force of adhesion to the old routine,—social, political, religious,—has wonderfully yielded; the iron force of exclusion of all which is new has wonderfully yielded. The danger now is, not that people should obstinately refuse to allow anything but their old routine to pass for reason and the will of God, but either that they should allow some novelty or other to pass for these too easily, or else that they should underrate the importance of them altogether, and think it enough to follow action for its own sake, without troubling themselves to make reason and the will of God prevail therein. Now, then, is the moment for culture to be of service, culture which believes in making reason and the will of God prevail, believes in perfection, is the study and pursuit of perfection, and is no longer debarred, by a rigid invincible exclusion of whatever is new, from getting acceptance for its ideas, simply because they are new.

The moment this view of culture is seized, the moment it is regarded not solely as the endeavor to see things as they are, to draw towards a knowledge of the universal order which seems to be intended and aimed at in the world, and which it is a man's happiness to go along with or his misery to go counter to,—to learn, in short, the will of God,—the moment, I say, culture is considered not merely as the endeavor to *see* and *learn* this, but as the endeavor, also, to make it *prevail,* the moral, social, and beneficent character of culture becomes manifest. The mere endeavor to see and learn the truth for our own personal satisfaction is indeed a commencement for making it prevail, a preparing the way for this, which always serves this, and is wrongly, therefore, stamped with blame absolutely in itself and not only in its caricature and degeneration. But perhaps it has got stamped with blame, and disparaged with the dubious title of curiosity, because in comparison with this wider endeavor of such great and plain utility it looks selfish, petty, and unprofitable.

And religion, the greatest and most important of the efforts by which the human race has manifested its impulse to perfect itself,—religion, that voice of the deepest human experience,—does not only enjoin

⁴Thomas Wilson (1663–1755), Bishop of Sodor and Man.

and sanction the aim which is the great aim of culture, the aim of setting ourselves to ascertain what perfection is and to make it prevail; but also, in determining generally in what human perfection consists, religion comes to a conclusion identical with that which culture,—culture seeking the determination of this question through *all* the voices of human experience which have been heard upon it, of art, science, poetry, philosophy, history, as well as of religion, in order to give a greater fulness and certainty to its solution,—likewise reaches. Religion says: *The kingdom of God is within you;* and culture, in like manner, places human perfection in an *internal* condition, in the growth and predominance of our humanity proper, as distinguished from our animality. It places it in the ever-increasing efficacy and in the general harmonious expansion of those gifts of thought and feeling, which make the peculiar dignity, wealth, and happiness of human nature. As I have said on a former occasion: "It is in making endless additions to itself, in the endless expansion of its powers, in endless growth in wisdom and beauty, that the spirit of the human race finds its ideal. To reach this ideal, culture is an indispensable aid, and that is the true value of culture." Not a having and a resting, but a growing and a becoming, is the character of perfection as culture conceives it; and here, too, it coincides with religion.

And because men are all members of one great whole, and the sympathy which is in human nature will not allow one member to be indifferent to the rest or to have a perfect welfare independent of the rest, the expansion of our humanity, to suit the idea of perfection which culture forms, must be a *general* expansion. Perfection, as culture conceives it, is not possible while the individual remains isolated. The individual is required, under pain of being stunted and enfeebled in his own development if he disobeys, to carry others along with him in his march towards perfection, to be continually doing all he can to enlarge and increase the volume of the human stream sweeping thitherward. And here, once more, culture lays on us the same obligation as religion, which says, as Bishop Wilson has admirably put it,

that "to promote the kingdom of God is to increase and hasten one's own happiness."

But, finally, perfection,—as culture from a thorough disinterested study of human nature and human experience learns to conceive it,—is a harmonious expansion of *all* the powers which make the beauty and worth of human nature, and is not consistent with the over-development of any one power at the expense of the rest. Here culture goes beyond religion as religion is generally conceived by us.

If culture, then, is a study of perfection, and of harmonious perfection, general perfection, and perfection which consists in becoming something rather than in having something, in an inward condition of the mind and spirit, not in an outward set of circumstances,—it is clear that culture, instead of being the frivolous and useless thing which Mr. Bright, and Mr. Frederic Harrison,[5] and many other Liberals are apt to call it, has a very important function to fulfil for mankind. And this function is particularly important in our modern world, of which the whole civilization is, to a much greater degree than the civilization of Greece and Rome, mechanical and external, and tends constantly to become more so. But above all in our own country has culture a weighty part to perform, because here that mechanical character, which civilization tends to take everywhere, is shown in the most eminent degree. Indeed nearly all the characters of perfection, as culture teaches us to fix them, meet in this country with some powerful tendency which thwarts them and sets them at defiance. The idea of perfection as an *inward* condition of the mind and spirit is at variance with the mechanical and material civilization in esteem with us, and nowhere, as I have said, so much in esteem as with us. The idea of perfection as a *general* expansion of the human family is at variance with our strong individualism, our hatred of all limits to the unrestrained swing

---

[5]The Quaker, John Bright (1811–1889), was one of the leading middle-class liberals of his time, a manufacturer, a member of Parliament, and a member of several cabinets. Frederic Harrison (1831–1923) was a writer who devoted much of his energy to the propagation of the positivistic philosophy of Auguste Comte.

of the individual's personality, our maxim of "every man for himself." Above all, the idea of perfection as a *harmonious* expansion of human nature is at variance with our want of flexibility, with our inaptitude for seeing more than one side of a thing, with our intense energetic absorption in the particular pursuit we happen to be following. So culture has a rough task to achieve in this country. Its preachers have, and are likely long to have, a hard time of it, and they will much oftener be regarded, for a great while to come, as elegant or spurious Jeremiahs than as friends and benefactors. That, however, will not prevent their doing in the end good service if they persevere. And, meanwhile, the mode of action they have to pursue, and the sort of habits they must fight against, ought to be made quite clear for every one to see, who may be willing to look at the matter attentively and dispassionately.

Faith in machinery is, I said, our besetting danger; often in machinery most absurdly disproportioned to the end which this machinery, if it is to do any good at all, is to serve; but always in machinery, as if it had a value in and for itself. What is freedom but machinery? what is population but machinery? what is coal but machinery? what are railroads but machinery? what is wealth but machinery? what are, even, religious organizations but machinery? Now almost every voice in England is accustomed to speak of these things as if they were precious ends in themselves, and therefore had some of the characters of perfection indisputably joined to them. I have before now noticed Mr. Roebuck's[6] stock argument for proving the greatness and happiness of England as she is, and for quite stopping the mouths of all gainsayers. Mr. Roebuck is never weary of reiterating this argument of his, so I do not know why I should be weary of noticing it. "May not every man in England say what he likes?"—Mr. Roebuck perpetually asks; and that, he thinks, is quite sufficient, and when every man may say what he likes, our aspirations ought to be satisfied. But the aspirations of culture, which is the study of perfection, are not satisfied, unless

what men say, when they may say what they like, is worth saying,—has good in it, and more good than bad. In the same way the *Times*,[7] replying to some foreign strictures on the dress, looks, and behavior of the English abroad, urges that the English ideal is that every one should be free to do and look just as he likes. But culture indefatigably tries, not to make what each raw person may like the rule by which he fashions himself; but to draw ever nearer to a sense of what is indeed beautiful, graceful, and becoming, and to get the raw person to like that.

And in the same way with respect to railroads and coal. Every one must have observed the strange language current during the late discussions as to the possible failure of our supplies of coal. Our coal, thousands of people were saying, is the real basis of our national greatness; if our coal runs short, there is an end of the greatness of England. But what *is* greatness?—culture makes us ask. Greatness is a spiritual condition worthy to excite love, interest, and admiration; and the outward proof of possessing greatness is that we excite love, interest, and admiration. If England were swallowed up by the sea to-morrow, which of the two, a hundred years hence, would most excite the love, interest, and admiration of mankind,—would most, therefore, show the evidences of having possessed greatness,—the England of the last twenty years, or the England of Elizabeth, of a time of splendid spiritual effort, but when our coal, and our industrial operations depending on coal, were very little developed? Well, then, what an unsound habit of mind it must be which makes us talk of things like coal or iron as constituting the greatness of England, and how salutary a friend is culture, bent on seeing things as they are, and thus dissipating delusions of this kind and fixing standards of perfection that are real!

Wealth, again, that end to which our prodigious works for material advantage are directed,—the commonest of commonplaces tells us how men are always apt to regard wealth as a precious end in itself; and certainly they have never been so apt thus to

---

[6]See Arnold's *Function of Criticism at the Present Time*, note 16.

[7]The London *Times*, the most authoritative English newspaper.

regard it as they are in England at the present time. Never did people believe anything more firmly than nine Englishmen out of ten at the present day believe that our greatness and welfare are proved by our being so very rich. Now, the use of culture is that it helps us, by means of its spiritual standard of perfection, to regard wealth as but machinery, and not only to say as a matter of words that we regard wealth as but machinery, but really to perceive and feel that it is so. If it were not for this purging effect wrought upon our minds by culture, the whole world, the future as well as the present, would inevitably belong to the Philistines. The people who believe most that our greatness and welfare are proved by our being very rich, and who most give their lives and thoughts to becoming rich, are just the very people whom we call Philistines. Culture says: "Consider these people, then, their way of life, their habits, their manners, the very tones of their voice; look at them attentively; observe the literature they read, the things which give them pleasure, the words which come forth out of their mouths, the thoughts which make the furniture of their minds: would any amount of wealth be worth having with the condition that one was to become just like these people by having it?" And thus culture begets a dissatisfaction which is of the highest possible value in stemming the common tide of men's thoughts in a wealthy and industrial community, and which saves the future, as one may hope, from being vulgarized, even if it cannot save the present.

Population, again, and bodily health and vigor, are things which are nowhere treated in such an unintelligent, misleading, exaggerated way as in England. Both are really machinery; yet how many people all around us do we see rest in them and fail to look beyond them! Why, one has heard people, fresh from reading certain articles of the *Times* on the Registrar-General's returns of marriages and births in this country, who would talk of our large English families in quite a solemn strain, as if they had something in itself beautiful, elevating, and meritorious in them; as if the British Philistine would have only to present himself before the Great Judge with his twelve children, in order to be received among the sheep as a matter of right!

But bodily health and vigor, it may be said, are not to be classed with wealth and population as mere machinery; they have a more real and essential value. True; but only as they are more intimately connected with a perfect spiritual condition than wealth or population are. The moment we disjoin them from the idea of a perfect spiritual condition, and pursue them, as we do pursue them, for their own sake and as ends in themselves, our worship of them becomes as mere worship of machinery, as our worship of wealth or population, and as unintelligent and vulgarizing a worship as that is. Every one with anything like an adequate idea of human perfection has distinctly marked this subordination to higher and spiritual ends of the cultivation of bodily vigor and activity. "Bodily exercise profiteth little; but godliness is profitable unto all things," says the author of the Epistle to Timothy.[8] And the utilitarian Franklin says just as explicitly:— "Eat and drink such an exact quantity as suits the constitution of thy body, *in reference to the services of the mind.*" But the point of view of culture, keeping the mark of human perfection simply and broadly in view, and not assigning to this perfection, as religion or utilitarianism assigns to it, a special and limited character, this point of view, I say, of culture is best given by these words of Epictetus:[9]—"It is a sign of ἀφυΐα," says he,—that is, of a nature not finely tempered, —"to give yourselves up to things which relate to the body; to make, for instance, a great fuss about exercise, a great fuss about eating, a great fuss about drinking, a great fuss about walking, a great fuss about riding. All these things ought to be done merely by the way: the formation of the spirit and character must be our real concern." This is admirable; and, indeed, the Greek word εὐφυΐα, a finely tempered nature, gives exactly the notion of perfection as culture brings us to conceive it: a harmonious perfection, a perfection in which the characters of beauty and intelligence are both

---

[8] I Timothy, 4:8.

[9] The Stoic philosopher of the first century A. D.

present, which unites "the two noblest of things,"—as Swift, who of one of the two, at any rate, had himself all too little, most happily calls them in his *Battle of the Books,*—"the two noblest of things, *sweetness and light.*" The εὐφυής is the man who tends towards sweetness and light; the ἀφυής, on the other hand, is our Philistine. The immense spiritual significance of the Greeks is due to their having been inspired with this central and happy idea of the essential character of human perfection; and Mr. Bright's misconception of culture, as a smattering of Greek and Latin, comes itself, after all, from this wonderful significance of the Greeks having affected the very machinery of our education, and is in itself a kind of homage to it.

In thus making sweetness and light to be characters of perfection, culture is of like spirit with poetry, follows one law with poetry. Far more than on our freedom, our population, and our industrialism, many amongst us rely upon our religious organizations to save us. I have called religion a yet more important manifestation of human nature than poetry, because it has worked on a broader scale for perfection, and with greater masses of men. But the idea of beauty and of a human nature perfect on all its sides, which is the dominant idea of poetry, is a true and invaluable idea, though it has not yet had the success that the idea of conquering the obvious faults of our animality, and of a human nature perfect on the moral side,—which is the dominant idea of religion,—has been enabled to have; and it is destined, adding to itself the religious idea of a devout energy, to transform and govern the other.

The best art and poetry of the Greeks, in which religion and poetry are one, in which the idea of beauty and of a human nature perfect on all sides adds to itself a religious and devout energy, and works in the strength of that, is on this account of such surpassing interest and instructiveness for us, though it was,—as, having regard to the human race in general, and, indeed, having regard to the Greeks themselves, we must own,—a premature attempt, an attempt which for success needed the moral and religious fiber in humanity to be more braced and developed than it had yet been. But Greece did not err in having the idea of beauty, harmony, and complete human perfection, so present and paramount. It is impossible to have this idea too present and paramount; only, the moral fiber must be braced too. And we, because we have braced the moral fiber, are not on that account in the right way, if at the same time the idea of beauty, harmony, and complete human perfection, is wanting or misapprehended amongst us; and evidently it *is* wanting or misapprehended at present. And when we rely as we do on our religious organizations, which in themselves do not and cannot give us this idea, and think we have done enough if we make them spread and prevail, then, I say, we fall into our common fault of overvaluing machinery.

Nothing is more common than for people to confound the inward peace and satisfaction which follows the subduing of the obvious faults of our animality with what I may call absolute inward peace and satisfaction,—the peace and satisfaction which are reached as we draw near to complete spiritual perfection, and not merely to moral perfection, or rather to relative moral perfection. No people in the world have done more and struggled more to attain this relative moral perfection than our English race has. For no people in the world has the command to *resist the devil,* to *overcome the wicked one,* in the nearest and most obvious sense of those words, had such a pressing force and reality. And we have had our reward, not only in the great worldly prosperity which our obedience to this command has brought us, but also, and far more, in great inward peace and satisfaction. But to me few things are more pathetic than to see people, on the strength of the inward peace and satisfaction which their rudimentary efforts towards perfection have brought them, employ, concerning their incomplete perfection and the religious organizations within which they have found it, language which properly applies only to complete perfection, and is a far-off echo of the human soul's prophecy of it. Religion itself, I need hardly say, supplies them in abundance with this grand language. And very freely do they use it; yet it is really the severest possible criticism of such an incomplete perfection as alone we have yet reached through our religious organizations.

The impulse of the English race towards moral development and self-conquest has nowhere so powerfully manifested itself as in Puritanism. Nowhere has Puritanism found so adequate an expression as in the religious organization of the Independents.[10] The modern Independents have a newspaper, the *Nonconformist,* written with great sincerity and ability. The motto, the standard, the profession of faith which this organ of theirs carries aloft, is: "The Dissidence of Dissent and the Protestantism of the Protestant religion." There is sweetness and light, and an ideal of complete harmonious human perfection! One need not go to culture and poetry to find language to judge it. Religion, with its instinct for perfection, supplies language to judge it, language, too, which is in our mouths every day. "Finally, be of one mind, united in feeling," says St. Peter.[11] There is an ideal which judges the Puritan ideal: "The Dissidence of Dissent and the Protestantism of the Protestant religion!" And religious organizations like this are what people believe in, rest in, would give their lives for! Such, I say, is the wonderful virtue of even the beginnings of perfection, of having conquered even the plain faults of our animality, that the religious organization which has helped us to do it can seem to us something precious, salutary, and to be propagated, even when it wears such a brand of imperfection on its forehead as this. And men have got such a habit of giving to the language of religion a special application, of making it a mere jargon, that for the condemnation which religion itself passes on the shortcomings of their religious organizations they have no ear; they are sure to cheat themselves and to explain this condemnation away. They can only be reached by the criticism which culture, like poetry, speaking a language not to be sophisticated, and resolutely testing these organizations by the ideal of a human perfection complete on all sides, applies to them.

But men of culture and poetry, it will be

said, are again and again failing, and failing conspicuously, in the necessary first stage to a harmonious perfection, in the subduing of the great obvious faults of our animality, which it is the glory of these religious organizations to have helped us to subdue. True, they do often so fail. They have often been without the virtues as well as the faults of the Puritan; it has been one of their dangers that they so felt the Puritan's faults that they too much neglected the practice of his virtues. I will not, however, exculpate them at the Puritan's expense. They have often failed in morality, and morality is indispensable. And they have been punished for their failure, as the Puritan has been rewarded for his performance. They have been punished wherein they erred; but their ideal of beauty, of sweetness and light, and a human nature complete on all its sides, remains the true ideal of perfection still; just as the Puritan's ideal of perfection remains narrow and inadequate, although for what he did well he has been richly rewarded. Notwithstanding the mighty results of the Pilgrim Fathers' voyage, they and their standard of perfection are rightly judged when we figure to ourselves Shakespeare or Virgil,— souls in whom sweetness and light, and all that in human nature is most humane, were eminent,—accompanying them on their voyage, and think what intolerable company Shakespeare and Virgil would have found them! In the same way let us judge the religious organizations which we see all around us. Do not let us deny the good and the happiness which they have accomplished; but do not let us fail to see clearly that their idea of human perfection is narrow and inadequate, and that the Dissidence of Dissent and the Protestantism of the Protestant religion will never bring humanity to its true goal. As I said with regard to wealth: Let us look at the life of those who live in and for it,—so I say with regard to the religious organizations. Look at the life imaged in such a newspaper as the *Nonconformist,*—a life of jealousy of the Establishment,[12] disputes, tea-meetings, openings of chapels, sermons; and then think of it as an ideal of a human life completing

---

[10] Congregationalists. [11] I Peter, 3:8.

[12] The ecclesiastical system of the Church of England, established by law.

itself on all sides, and aspiring with all its organs after sweetness, light, and perfection!

Another newspaper, representing, like the *Nonconformist,* one of the religious organizations of this country, was a short time 5 ago giving an account of the crowd at Epsom on the Derby day, and of all the vice and hideousness which was to be seen in that crowd; and then the writer turned suddenly round upon Professor Huxley,[13] and asked 10 him how he proposed to cure all this vice and hideousness without religion. I confess I felt disposed to ask the asker this question: and how do you propose to cure it with such a religion as yours? How is the ideal of 15 a life so unlovely, so unattractive, so incomplete, so narrow, so far removed from a true and satisfying ideal of human perfection, as is the life of your religious organization as you yourself reflect it, to conquer and trans- 20 form all this vice and hideousness? Indeed, the strongest plea for the study of perfection as pursued by culture, the clearest proof of the actual inadequacy of the idea of perfection held by the religious organizations,—ex- 25 pressing, as I have said, the most widespread effort which the human race has yet made after perfection,—is to be found in the state of our life and society with these in possession of it, and having been in possession of it 30 I know not how many hundred years. We are all of us included in some religious organization or other; we all call ourselves, in the sublime and aspiring language of religion which I have before noticed, *children* 35 *of God.* Children of God;—it is an immense pretension!—and how are we to justify it? By the works which we do, and the words which we speak. And the work which we collective children of God do, our 40 grand center of life, our *city* which we have builded for us to dwell in, is London! London, with its unutterable external hideousness, and with its internal canker of *publice egestas, privatim opulentia,*[14]—to use the 45 words which Sallust puts into Cato's mouth about Rome,—unequaled in the world! The word, again, which we children of God speak, the voice which most hits our collective thought, the newspaper with the largest circulation in England, nay, with the largest circulation in the whole world, is the *Daily Telegraph!* I say that when our religious organizations,—which I admit to express the most considerable effort after perfection that our race has yet made,—land us in no better result than this, it is high time to examine carefully their idea of perfection, to see whether it does not leave out of account sides and forces of human nature which we might turn to great use; whether it would not be more operative if it were more complete. And I say that the English reliance on our religious organizations and on their ideas of human perfection just as they stand, is like our reliance on freedom, on muscular Christianity, on population, on coal, on wealth,—mere belief in machinery, and unfruitful; and that it is wholesomely counteracted by culture, bent on seeing things as they are, and on drawing the human race onwards to a more complete, a harmonious perfection.

Culture, however, shows its single-minded love of perfection, its desire simply to make reason and the will of God prevail, its freedom from fanaticism, by its attitude towards all this machinery, even while it insists that it *is* machinery. Fanatics, seeing the mischief men do themselves by their blind belief in some machinery or other,—whether it is wealth and industrialism, or whether it is the cultivation of bodily strength and activity, or whether it is a political organization,—or whether it is a religious organization,—oppose with might and main the tendency to this or that political and religious organization, or to games and athletic exercises, or to wealth and industrialism, and try violently to stop it. But the flexibility which sweetness and light give, and which is one of the rewards of culture pursued in good faith, enables a man to see that a tendency may be necessary, and even, as a preparation for something in the 50 future, salutary, and yet that the generations or individuals who obey this tendency are sacrificed to it, that they fall short of the hope of

---

[13]Thomas Henry Huxley (1825–1895), the English writer who did most to popularize the ideas of the new science in Arnold's time.

[14]Public poverty, private wealth. Quoted from the *Bellum Catilinarium* (chap. 56) of Sallust, the Roman historian of the first century B. C.; the words were used by Marcus Porcius Cato (Cato Uticensis) in a speech.

perfection by following it; and that its mischiefs are to be criticized, lest it should take too firm a hold and last after it has served its purpose.

Mr. Gladstone[15] well pointed out, in a speech at Paris,—and others have pointed out the same thing,—how necessary is the present great movement towards wealth and industrialism, in order to lay broad foundations of material well-being for the society of the future. The worst of these justifications is, that they are generally addressed to the very people engaged, body and soul, in the movement in question; at all events, that they are always seized with the greatest avidity by these people, and taken by them as quite justifying their life; and that thus they tend to harden them in their sins. Now, culture admits the necessity of the movement towards fortune-making and exaggerated industrialism, readily allows that the future may derive benefit from it; but insists, at the same time, that the passing generations of industrialists,—forming, for the most part, the stout main body of Philistinism,—are sacrificed to it. In the same way, the result of all the games and sports which occupy the passing generation of boys and young men may be the establishment of a better and sounder physical type for the future to work with. Culture does not set itself against the games and sports; it congratulates the future, and hopes it will make a good use of its improved physical basis; but it points out that our passing generation of boys and young men is, meantime, sacrificed. Puritanism was perhaps necessary to develop the moral fiber of the English race, Nonconformity to break the yoke of ecclesiastical domination over men's minds and to prepare the way for freedom of thought in the distant future; still, culture points out that the harmonious perfection of generations of Puritans and Nonconformists has been, in consequence, sacrificed. Freedom of speech may be necessary for the society of the future, but the young lions of the *Daily Telegraph* in the meanwhile are sacrificed. A voice for every man in his country's government may be necessary for the society of the future, but meanwhile Mr. Beales and Mr. Bradlaugh[16] are sacrificed.

Oxford, the Oxford of the past, has many faults; and she has heavily paid for them in defeat, in isolation, in want of hold upon the modern world. Yet we in Oxford, brought up amidst the beauty and sweetness of that beautiful place, have not failed to seize one truth,—the truth that beauty and sweetness are essential characters of a complete human perfection. When I insist on this, I am all in the faith and tradition of Oxford. I say boldly that this our sentiment for beauty and sweetness, our sentiment against hideousness and rawness, has been at the bottom of our attachment to so many beaten causes, of our opposition to so many triumphant movements. And the sentiment is true, and has never been wholly defeated, and has shown its power even in its defeat. We have not won our political battles, we have not carried our main points, we have not stopped our adversaries' advance, we have not marched victoriously with the modern world; but we have told silently upon the mind of the country, we have prepared currents of feeling which sap our adversaries' position when it seems gained, we have kept up our own communications with the future. Look at the course of the great movement which shook Oxford to its center some thirty years ago![17] It was directed, as any one who reads Dr. Newman's *Apology* may see, against what in one word may be called "Liberalism." Liberalism prevailed; it was the appointed force to do the work of the hour; it was necessary, it was inevitable that it should prevail. The Oxford movement was broken, it failed; our wrecks are scattered on every shore:—

Quae regio in terris nostri non plena laboris?[18]

---

[15]William Ewart Gladstone (1809–1898), several times prime minister.

[16]Edmond Beales (1803–1881), president of the Reform League, which advocated manhood suffrage; Charles Bradlaugh (1833–1891), who claimed and eventually succeeded in obtaining the right to sit in Parliament without taking an oath on the Bible.

[17]The Oxford Movement (1833–1845), an effort to return to the forms and doctrines of traditional Anglicanism. The most important member of the Movement, Newman, ultimately became a Roman Catholic; his *Apologia pro Vita Sua* (1864) was an explanation and defense of the steps in his conversion.

[18]What region of the earth is not filled with the story of our troubles? (*Aeneid,* I, 460.)

But what was it, this liberalism, as Dr. Newman saw it, and as it really broke the Oxford movement? It was the great middle-class liberalism, which had for the cardinal points of its belief the Reform Bill of 1832, and local self-government, in politics; in the social sphere, free-trade, unrestricted competition, and the making of large industrial fortunes; in the religious sphere, the Dissidence of Dissent and the Protestantism of the Protestant religion. I do not say that other and more intelligent forces than this were not opposed to the Oxford movement: but this was the force which really beat it; this was the force which Dr. Newman felt himself fighting with; this was the force which till only the other day seemed to be the paramount force in this country, and to be in possession of the future; this was the force whose achievements fill Mr. Lowe[19] with such inexpressible admiration, and whose rule he was so horror-struck to see threatened. And where is this great force of Philistinism now? It is thrust into the second rank, it is become a power of yesterday, it has lost the future. A new power has suddenly appeared, a power which it is impossible yet to judge fully, but which is certainly a wholly different force from middle-class liberalism; different in its cardinal points of belief, different in its tendencies in every sphere. It loves and admires neither the legislation of middle-class Parliaments, nor the local self-government of middle-class vestries, nor the unrestricted competition of middle-class industrialists, nor the dissidence of middle-class Dissent and the Protestantism of middle-class Protestant religion. I am not now praising this new force, or saying that its own ideals are better; all I say is, that they are wholly different. And who will estimate how much the currents of feeling created by Dr. Newman's movement, the keen desire for beauty and sweetness which it nourished, the deep aversion it manifested to the hardness and vulgarity of middle-class liberalism, the strong light it turned on the hideous and grotesque illusions of middle-class Protestantism,—who will estimate how much all these contributed to swell the tide of secret dissatisfaction which has mined the ground under the self-confident liberalism of the last thirty years, and has prepared the way for its sudden collapse and supersession? It is in this manner that the sentiment of Oxford for beauty and sweetness conquers, and in this manner long may it continue to conquer!

In this manner it works to the same end as culture, and there is plenty of work for it yet to do. I have said that the new and more democratic force which is now superseding our old middle-class liberalism cannot yet be rightly judged. It has its main tendencies still to form. We hear promises of its giving us administrative reform, law reform, reform of education, and I know not what; but those promises come rather from its advocates, wishing to make a good plea for it and to justify it for superseding middle-class liberalism, than from clear tendencies which it has itself yet developed. But meanwhile it has plenty of well-intentioned friends against whom culture may with advantage continue to uphold steadily its ideal of human perfection; that this is *an inward spiritual activity, having for its characters increased sweetness, increased light, increased life, increased sympathy.* Mr. Bright, who has a foot in both worlds, the world of middle-class liberalism and the world of democracy, but who brings most of his ideas from the world of middle-class liberalism in which he was bred, always inclines to inculcate that faith in machinery to which, as we have seen, Englishmen are so prone, and which has been the bane of middle-class liberalism. He complains with a sorrowful indignation of people who "appear to have no proper estimate of the value of the franchise"; he leads his disciples to believe—what the Englishman is always too ready to believe,—that the having a vote, like the having a large family, or a large business, or large muscles, has in itself some edifying and perfecting effect upon human nature. Or else he cries out to the democracy,—"the men," as he calls them, "upon whose shoulders the greatness of England rests,"—he cries out to them: "See what you have done! I look over this country and

---

[19]Robert Lowe, later Lord Sherbrooke, leader of the Liberals who broke from their own party in 1866 when it proposed further reforms of a democratic character.

see the cities you have built, the railroads you have made, the manufactures you have produced, the cargoes which freight the ships of the greatest mercantile navy the world has ever seen! I see that you have converted by [5] your labors what was once a wilderness, these islands, into a fruitful garden; I know that you have created this wealth, and are a nation whose name is a word of power throughout all the world." Why, this is just the very [10] style of laudation with which Mr. Roebuck or Mr. Lowe debauches the minds of the middle classes, and makes such Philistines of them. It is the same fashion of teaching a man to value himself not on what he *is,* not [15] on his progress in sweetness and light, but on the number of the railroads he has constructed, or the bigness of the tabernacle he has built. Only the middle classes are told they have done it all with their energy, self- [20] reliance, and capital, and the democracy are told they have done it all with their hands and sinews. But teaching the democracy to put its trust in achievements of this kind is merely training them to be Philistines to take [25] the place of the Philistines whom they are superseding; and they, too, like the middle class, will be encouraged to sit down at the banquet of the future without having on a wedding garment, and nothing excellent can [30] then come from them. Those who know their besetting faults, those who have watched them and listened to them, or those who will read the instructive account recently given of them by one of themselves, the [35] *Journeyman Engineer,* will agree that the idea which culture sets before us of perfection,—an increased spiritual activity, having for its characters increased sweetness, increased light, increased life, increased sym- [40] pathy,—is an idea which the new democracy needs far more than the idea of the blessedness of the franchise, or the wonderfulness of its own industrial performances.

Other well-meaning friends of this new [45] power are for leading it, not in the old ruts of middle-class Philistinism, but in ways which are naturally alluring to the feet of democracy, though in this country they are novel and untried ways. I may call them [50] the ways of Jacobinism.[20] Violent indigna-

tion with the past, abstract systems of renovation applied wholesale, a new doctrine drawn up in black and white for elaborating down to the very smallest details a rational society for the future,—these are the ways of Jacobinism. Mr. Frederic Harrison and other disciples of Comte,[21]—one of them, Mr. Congreve, is an old friend of mine, and I am glad to have an opportunity of publicly expressing my respect for his talents and character,—are among the friends of democracy who are for leading it in paths of this kind. Mr. Frederic Harrison is very hostile to culture, and from a natural enough motive; for culture is the eternal opponent of the two things which are the signal marks of Jacobinism,—its fierceness, and its addiction to an abstract system. Culture is always assigning to system-makers and systems a smaller share in the bent of human destiny than their friends like. A current in people's minds sets towards new ideas; people are dissatisfied with their old narrow stock of Philistine ideas, Anglo-Saxon ideas, or any other; and some man, some Bentham[22] or Comte, who has the real merit of having early and strongly felt and helped the new current, but who brings plenty of narrowness and mistakes of his own into his feeling and help of it, is credited with being the author of the whole current, the fit person to be entrusted with its regulation and to guide the human race.

The excellent German historian of the mythology of Rome, Preller,[23] relating the introduction at Rome under the Tarquins of the worship of Apollo, the god of light, healing, and reconciliation, will have us observe that it was not so much the Tarquins who brought to Rome the new worship of Apollo, as a current in the mind of the Roman people which set powerfully at that time towards a new worship of this kind, and away from the old run of Latin and Sabine religious

---

[20] The ultra-democratic principles of the Jacobins, a political society influential during the French Revolution.

[21] Auguste Comte (1798–1857), the French philosopher, author of the system of positivism, which replaces religion and metaphysics with the ideals of sociological ethics.

[22] Jeremy Bentham (1748–1832), the English utilitarian philosopher.

[23] Ludwig Preller (1809–1861), author of *Römische Mythologie.*

ideas. In a similar way, culture directs our attention to the natural current there is in human affairs, and to its continual working, and will not let us rivet our faith upon any one man and his doings. It makes us see not only his good side, but also how much in him was of necessity limited and transient; nay, it even feels a pleasure, a sense of an increased freedom and of an ampler future, in so doing.

I remember, when I was under the influence of a mind to which I feel the greatest obligations, the mind of a man who was the very incarnation of sanity and clear sense, a man the most considerable, it seems to me, whom America has yet produced,—Benjamin Franklin,—I remember the relief with which, after long feeling the sway of Franklin's imperturbable common-sense, I came upon a project of his for a new version of the Book of Job, to replace the old version, the style of which, says Franklin, has become obsolete, and thence less agreeable. "I give," he continues, "a few verses, which may serve as a sample of the kind of version I would recommend." We all recollect the famous verse in our translation: "Then Satan answered the Lord and said: 'Doth Job fear God for nought?'" Franklin makes this: "Does your Majesty imagine that Job's good conduct is the effect of mere personal attachment and affection?" I well remember how, when first I read that, I drew a deep breath of relief and said to myself: "After all, there is a stretch of humanity beyond Franklin's victorious good sense!"[24] So, after hearing Bentham cried loudly up as the renovator of modern society, and Bentham's mind and ideas proposed as the rulers of our future, I open the *Deontology*. There I read: "While Xenophon was writing his history and Euclid teaching geometry, Socrates and Plato were talking nonsense under pretense of talking wisdom and morality. This morality of theirs consisted in words; this wisdom of theirs was the denial of matters known to every man's experience." From the moment of reading that, I am delivered from the bondage of Bentham! the fanaticism of his adherents can touch me no longer. I feel the

inadequacy of his mind and ideas for supplying the rule of human society, for perfection.

Culture tends always thus to deal with the men of a system, of disciples, of a school; with men like Comte, or the late Mr. Buckle, or Mr. Mill.[25] However much it may find to admire in these personages, or in some of them, it nevertheless remembers the text: "Be not ye called Rabbi!" and it soon passes on from any Rabbi. But Jacobinism loves a Rabbi; it does not want to pass on from its Rabbi in pursuit of a future and still unreached perfection; it wants its Rabbi and his ideas to stand for perfection, that they may with the more authority recast the world; and for Jacobinism, therefore, culture,— eternally passing onwards and seeking,—is an impertinence and an offence. But culture, just because it resists this tendency of Jacobinism to impose on us a man with limitations and errors of his own along with the true ideas of which he is the organ, really does the world and Jacobinism itself a service.

So, too, Jacobinism, in its fierce hatred of the past and of those whom it makes liable for the sins of the past, cannot away with the inexhaustible indulgence proper to culture, the consideration of circumstances, the severe judgment of actions joined to the merciful judgment of persons. "The man of culture is in politics," cries Mr. Frederic Harrison, "one of the poorest mortals alive!" Mr. Frederic Harrison wants to be doing business, and he complains that the man of culture stops him with a "turn for small fault-finding, love of selfish ease, and indecision in action." Of what use is culture, he asks, except for "a critic of new books or a professor of *belles lettres?*" Why, it is of use because, in presence of the fierce exasperation which breathes, or rather, I may say, hisses through the whole production in which Mr. Frederic Harrison asks that question, it reminds us that the perfection of human nature is sweetness and light. It is of use, because, like religion,—that other effort after perfection,—it testifies that,

---

[24]Arnold fails to realize that in the passage to which he refers Franklin is joking.

[25]Henry Thomas Buckle (1821–1862), author of a *History of Civilization in England;* John Stuart Mill (1806–1873), during the early part of his life a follower of Bentham's utilitarian philosophy.

where bitter envying and strife are, there is confusion and every evil work.

The pursuit of perfection, then, is the pursuit of sweetness and light.[26] He who works for sweetness and light, works to make reason and the will of God prevail. He who works for machinery, he who works for hatred, works only for confusion. Culture looks beyond machinery, culture hates hatred; culture has one great passion, the passion for sweetness and light. It has one even yet greater!—the passion for making them *prevail*. It is not satisfied till we *all* come to a perfect man; it knows that the sweetness and light of the few must be imperfect until the raw and unkindled masses of humanity are touched with sweetness and light. If I have not shrunk from saying that we must work for sweetness and light, so neither have I shrunk from saying that we must have a broad basis, must have sweetness and light for as many as possible. Again and again I have insisted how those are the happy moments of humanity, how those are the marking epochs of a people's life, how those are the flowering times for literature and art and all the creative power of genius, when there is a *national* glow of life and thought, when the whole of society is in the fullest measure permeated by thought, sensible to beauty, intelligent and alive. Only it must be *real* thought and *real* beauty; *real* sweetness and *real* light. Plenty of

people will try to give the masses, as they call them, an intellectual food prepared and adapted in the way they think proper for the actual condition of the masses. The ordinary popular literature is an example of this way of working on the masses. Plenty of people will try to indoctrinate the masses with the set of ideas and judgments constituting the creed of their own profession or party. Our religious and political organizations give an example of this way of working on the masses. I condemn neither way; but culture works differently. It does not try to teach down to the level of inferior classes; it does not try to win them for this or that sect of its own, with ready-made judgments and watchwords. It seeks to do away with classes; to make the best that has been thought and known in the world current everywhere; to make all men live in an atmosphere of sweetness and light, where they may use ideas, as it uses them itself, freely, —nourished, and not bound by them.

This is the *social idea;* and the men of culture are the true apostles of equality. The great men of culture are those who have had a passion for diffusing, for making prevail, for carrying from one end of society to the other, the best knowledge, the best ideas of their time; who have labored to divest knowledge of all that was harsh, uncouth, difficult, abstract, professional, exclusive; to humanize it, to make it efficient outside the clique of the cultivated and learned, yet still remaining the *best* knowledge and thought of the time, and a true source, therefore, of sweetness and light. Such a man was Abelard[27] in the Middle Ages, in spite of all his imperfections; and thence the boundless emotion and enthusiasm which Abelard excited. Such were Lessing and Herder[28] in Germany, at the end of the last century; and their services to Germany were in this way inestimably precious. Generations will pass, and literary monuments will accumulate, and works far more perfect than the works of Lessing and Herder will be produced in Germany; and yet the names of these two men

---

[26]At this point in earlier versions Arnold had added:

"On this, the last occasion that I am to speak from this place, I have permitted myself, in justifying culture and in enforcing the reasons for it, to keep chiefly on ground where I am at one with the central instinct and sympathy of Oxford. The pursuit of perfection is the pursuit of sweetness and light. Oxford has worked with all the best of her nature for sweetness, for beauty, and I have allowed myself today chiefly to insist on sweetness, on beauty, as necessary characters of perfection. Light, too, is a necessary character of perfection; Oxford must not suffer herself to forget that! At other times during my passage in this chair I have not failed to remind her, so far as my feeble voice availed, that light is a necessary character of perfection. I never shall cease, so long as anywhere my voice finds any utterance, to insist on the need of light as well as of sweetness. Today I have spoken most of that which Oxford has loved most. But he who works for sweetness, works in the end for light also; he who works for light works in the end for sweetness also."

---

[27]The medieval thinker (1079–1142).

[28]Gotthold E. Lessing (1729–1781), critic and dramatist; Johann G. Herder (1744–1803), critic and poet.

will fill a German with a reverence and enthusiasm such as the names of the most gifted masters will hardly awaken. And why? Because they *humanized* knowledge; because they broadened the basis of life and intelligence; because they worked powerfully to diffuse sweetness and light, to make reason and the will of God prevail. With Saint Augustine they said: "Let us not leave thee alone to make in the secret of thy knowledge, as thou didst before the creation of the firmament, the division of light from darkness;

let the children of thy spirit, placed in their firmament, make their light shine upon the earth, mark the division of night and day, and announce the revolution of the times; for the old order is passed, and the new arises; the night is spent, the day is come forth; and thou shalt crown the year with thy blessing, when thou shalt send forth laborers into thy harvest sown by other hands than theirs; when thou shalt send forth new laborers to new seed-times, whereof the harvest shall be not yet."

WORDSWORTH[1]

I REMEMBER hearing Lord Macaulay say, after Wordsworth's death, when subscriptions were being collected to found a memorial of him, that ten years earlier more money could have been raised in Cambridge alone, to do honor to Wordsworth, than was now raised all through the country. Lord Macaulay had, as we know, his own heightened and telling way of putting things, and we must always make allowance for it. But probably it is true that Wordsworth has never, either before or since, been so accepted and popular, so established in possession of the minds of all who profess to care for poetry, as he was between the years 1830 and 1840, and at Cambridge. From the very first, no doubt, he had his believers and witnesses. But I have myself heard him declare that, for he knew not how many years, his poetry had never brought him in enough to buy his shoe-strings. The poetry-reading public was very slow to recognize him, and was very easily drawn away from him. Scott effaced him with this public, Byron effaced him.

The death of Byron seemed, however, to make an opening for Wordsworth. Scott, who had for some time ceased to produce poetry himself, and stood before the public as a great novelist; Scott, too genuine himself not to feel the profound genuineness of Wordsworth, and with an instinctive recogni-

tion of his firm hold on nature and of his local truth, always admired him sincerely. and praised him generously. The influence of Coleridge upon young men of ability was then powerful, and was still gathering strength; this influence told entirely in favor of Wordsworth's poetry. Cambridge was a place where Coleridge's influence had great action, and where Wordsworth's poetry, therefore, flourished especially. But even amongst the general public its sale grew large, the eminence of its author was widely recognized, and Rydal Mount[2] became an object of pilgrimage. I remember Wordsworth relating how one of the pilgrims, a clergyman, asked him if he had ever written anything besides the *Guide to the Lakes*.[3] Yes, he answered modestly, he had written verses. Not every pilgrim was a reader, but the vogue was established, and the stream of pilgrims came.

Mr. Tennyson's decisive appearance dates from 1842. One cannot say that he effaced Wordsworth as Scott and Byron had effaced him. The poetry of Wordsworth had been so long before the public, the suffrage of good judges was so steady and so strong in its favor, that by 1842 the verdict of posterity, one may almost say, had been already pronounced, and Wordsworth's English fame was secure. But the vogue, the ear and applause of the great body of poetry-readers,

---

[1]The fifth essay in *Essays in Criticism*, Second Series (1888). *Wordsworth* had been published in *Macmillan's Magazine*, July, 1879, and in the same year used as the preface to an anthology of Wordsworth's poems.

[2]Wordsworth's home during the second half of his life.

[3]Wordsworth's prose *Topographical Description of the Country of the Lakes* (1810), later called a *Guide through the Lakes*.

never quite thoroughly perhaps his, he gradually lost more and more, and Mr. Tennyson gained them. Mr. Tennyson drew to himself, and away from Wordsworth, the poetry-reading public, and the new genera-tions. Even in 1850, when Wordsworth died, this diminution of popularity was visible, and occasioned the remark of Lord Macaulay which I quoted at starting.

The diminution has continued. The influ-ence of Coleridge has waned, and Words-worth's poetry can no longer draw succor from this ally. The poetry has not, how-ever, wanted eulogists; and it may be said to have brought its eulogists luck, for al-most every one who has praised Words-worth's poetry has praised it well. But the public has remained cold, or, at least, unde-termined. Even the abundance of Mr. Palgrave's[4] fine and skilfully chosen speci-mens of Wordsworth, in the *Golden Treas-ury,* surprised many readers, and gave offence to not a few. To tenth-rate critics and compilers, for whom any violent shock to the public taste would be a temerity not to be risked, it is still quite permissible to speak of Wordsworth's poetry, not only with ignorance, but with impertinence. On the Continent he is almost unknown.

I cannot think, then, that Wordsworth has, up to this time, at all obtained his deserts. "Glory," said M. Renan the other day, "glory after all is the thing which has the best chance of not being altogether vanity."[5] Words-worth was a homely[6] man, and himself would

---

[4]Francis Palgrave (1824–1897).

[5]Ernest Renan (1823–1892), the French writer. In the original version of this essay Arnold con-tinued:

"And when M. Renan presents himself to the French Academy,—the only authentic dispensers, he says, of glory, of 'this grand light,'—he presents himself supported by M. Victor Hugo, his 'dear and illustrious master,' a poet irradiated with it; a poet 'whose genius has throughout our century struck the hour for us, has given body to every one of our dreams, wings to every one of our thoughts.' Yet probably not twenty people in that magnificent as-semblage, all coruscating with the beams of the 'grand light,' had ever even heard of Wordsworth's name. And it is quite impossible for us to esteem recognition by the French Academy, or by the French nation, or by any single nation or institution, as so decisive a title to glory as M. Renan supposes it."

[6]Unpretentious.

certainly never have thought of talking of glory as that which, after all, has the best chance of not being altogether vanity. Yet we may well allow that few things are less vain than *real* glory. Let us conceive of the whole group of civilized nations as being, for intellectual and spiritual purposes, one great confederation, bound to a joint action and working towards a common result; a confederation whose members have a due knowledge both of the past, out of which they all proceed, and of one another. This was the ideal of Goethe, and it is an ideal which will impose itself upon the thoughts of our modern societies more and more. Then to be recognized by the verdict of such a con-federation as a master, or even as a seriously and eminently worthy workman, in one's own line of intellectual or spiritual activity, is indeed glory; a glory which it would be difficult to rate too highly. For what could be more beneficent, more salutary? The world is forwarded by having its attention fixed on the best things; and here is a tri-bunal, free from all suspicion of national and provincial partiality, putting a stamp on the best things, and recommending them for general honor and acceptance. A nation, again, is furthered by recognition of its real gifts and successes; it is encouraged to de-velop them further. And here is an honest verdict, telling us which of our supposed successes are really, in the judgment of the great impartial world, and not in our own private judgment only, successes, and which are not.

It is so easy to feel pride and satisfaction in one's own things, so hard to make sure that one is right in feeling it! We have a great empire. But so had Nebuchadnezzar. We extol the "unrivaled happiness" of our national civilization. But then comes a can-did friend, and remarks that our upper class is materialized, our middle class vulgarized, and our lower class brutalized. We are proud of our painting, our music. But we find that in the judgment of other people our painting is questionable, and our music non-existent. We are proud of our men of science. And here it turns out that the world is with us; we find that in the judg-ment of other people, too, Newton among the dead, and Mr. Darwin among the living, hold as high a place as they hold in our national opinion.

Finally, we are proud of our poets and poetry. Now poetry is nothing less than 5 the most perfect speech of man, that in which he comes nearest to being able to utter the truth. It is no small thing, therefore, to succeed eminently in poetry. And so much is required for duly estimating success here, 10 that about poetry it is perhaps hardest to arrive at a sure general verdict, and takes longest. Meanwhile, our own conviction of the superiority of our national poets is not decisive, is almost certain to be mingled, as 15 we see constantly in English eulogy of Shakespeare, with much of provincial infatuation. And we know what was the opinion current amongst our neighbors the French—people of taste, acuteness, and quick 20 literary tact—not a hundred years ago, about our great poets. The old *Biographie Universelle* notices the pretension of the English to a place for their poets among the chief poets of the world, and says that this is a 25 pretension which to no one but an Englishman can ever seem admissible. And the scornful, disparaging things said by foreigners about Shakespeare and Milton, and about our national over-estimate of them, have 30 been often quoted, and will be in every one's remembrance.

A great change has taken place, and Shakespeare is now generally recognized, even in France, as one of the greatest of poets. 35 Yes, some anti-Gallican cynic will say, the French rank him with Corneille and with Victor Hugo! But let me have the pleasure of quoting a sentence about Shakespeare, which I met with by accident not long ago in 40 the *Correspondant,* a French review which not a dozen English people, I suppose, look at. The writer is praising Shakespeare's prose. With Shakespeare, he says, "prose comes in whenever the subject, being more 45 familiar, is unsuited to the majestic English iambic." And he goes on: "Shakespeare is the king of poetic rhythm and style, as well as the king of the realm of thought; along with his dazzling prose, Shakespeare has 50 succeeded in giving us the most varied, the most harmonious verse which has ever

sounded upon the human ear since the verse of the Greeks." M. Henry Cochin,[7] the writer of this sentence, deserves our gratitude for it; it would not be easy to praise Shakespeare, in a single sentence, more justly. And when a foreigner and a Frenchman writes thus of Shakespeare, and when Goethe says of Milton, in whom there was so much to repel Goethe rather than to attract him, that "nothing has been ever done so entirely in the sense of the Greeks as *Samson Agonistes,*" and that "Milton is in very truth a poet whom we must treat with all reverence," then we understand what constitutes a European recognition of poets and poetry as contradistinguished from a merely national recognition, and that in favor both of Milton and of Shakespeare the judgment of the high court of appeal has finally gone.[8]

---

[7] Later well known as a student of Italian literature (1854-1926).

[8] In the original version Arnold adds:
"Or again judgment may go the other way. Byron has had an immense reputation, not in England only but on the Continent. M. Taine, in his history of English literature, takes Byron as seriously as he takes Shakespeare. Byron is the supreme and incomparable expression of the English genius after eight centuries of preparation, he is the one single contemporary author who has *atteint à la cime,* 'reached the summit.' *Manfred* is the twin brother of *Faust.* But then M. Schérer strikes in with his words of truth and soberness. Remarking that 'Byron is one of our French superstitions,' he points out how Byron's talent is oratorical rather than poetical; he points out how to high and serious art, art impersonal and disinterested, Byron never could rise; and how the man in Byron, finally, is even less sincere than the poet. And by this we may perceive that we have not in Byron what we have in Milton and Shakespeare,—a poetical reputation which time and the authentic judgment of mankind will certainly accept and consecrate.

"So excellent a writer and critic as M. Renan sees in M. Victor Hugo, a 'beloved and illustrious master whose voice has throughout our century struck the hour for us.' Of these 'strikings of the hour' by the voice of M. Victor Hugo, none certainly was more resonant, none was hailed with more passionate applause by his friends than *Hernani.* It is called for again, made to strike over again; we have the privilege of hearing it strike in London. And still there is no lack of applause to this work of a talent 'combining,' says Théophile Gautier, 'the qualities of Corneille and of Shakespeare.' But I open by chance a little volume, the conversations of Goethe with the Chancellor Von Müller. There I come upon this short sentence: 'Goethe said *Hernani* was an absurd composition.' *Hernani sei eine absurde Composition.* So speaks this great foreign witness; a German, certainly, but a German favorable to French literature and to France, 'to which' said he 'I owe so much of my culture!' So speaks

I come back to M. Renan's praise of glory, from which I started. Yes, real glory is a most serious thing, glory authenticated by the Amphictyonic Court[9] of final appeal, definitive glory. And even for poets and poetry, long and difficult as may be the process of arriving at the right award, the right award comes at last, the definitive glory rests where it is deserved. Every establishment of such a real glory is good and wholesome for mankind at large, good and wholesome for the nation which produced the poet crowned with it. To the poet himself it can seldom do harm; for he, poor man, is in his grave, probably, long before his glory crowns him.

Wordsworth has been in his grave for some thirty years, and certainly his lovers and admirers cannot flatter themselves that this great and steady light of glory as yet shines over him. He is not fully recognized at home; he is not recognized at all abroad. Yet I firmly believe that the poetical performance of Wordsworth is, after that of Shakespeare and Milton, of which all the world now recognizes the worth, undoubtedly the most considerable in our language from the Elizabethan age to the present time. Chaucer is anterior; and on other grounds, too, he cannot well be brought into the comparison. But taking the roll of our chief poetical names, besides Shakespeare and Milton, from the age of Elizabeth downwards, and going through it,—Spenser, Dryden, Pope, Gray, Goldsmith, Cowper, Burns, Coleridge, Scott, Campbell,[10] Moore,[11] Byron, Shelley, Keats (I mention those only who are dead),—I think it certain that Wordsworth's name deserves to stand, and will finally stand, above them all. Several of the poets named have gifts and excellences which Wordsworth has not. But taking the performance of each as a whole, I say that Wordsworth seems to me to have left a body of poetical work superior in power, in interest, in the qualities which give enduring freshness, to that which any one of the others has left.

But this is not enough to say. I think it certain, further, that if we take the chief poetical names of the Continent since the death of Molière, and, omitting Goethe, confront the remaining names with that of Wordsworth, the result is the same. Let us take Klopstock, Lessing, Schiller, Uhland, Rückert, and Heine for Germany; Filicaia, Alfieri, Manzoni, and Leopardi for Italy; Racine, Boileau, Voltaire, André Chenier, Béranger, Lamartine, Musset, M. Victor Hugo (he has been so long celebrated that although he still lives I may be permitted to name him) for France. Several of these, again, have evidently gifts and excellences to which Wordsworth can make no pretension. But in real poetical achievement it seems to me indubitable that to Wordsworth, here again, belongs the palm. It seems to me that Wordsworth has left behind him a body of poetical work which wears, and will wear, better on the whole than the performance of any one of these personages, so far more brilliant and celebrated, most of them, than the homely poet of Rydal. Wordsworth's performance in poetry is on the whole, in power, in interest, in the qualities which give enduring freshness, superior to theirs.

This is a high claim to make for Wordsworth. But if it is a just claim, if Wordsworth's place among the poets who have appeared in the last two or three centuries is after Shakespeare, Molière, Milton, Goethe, indeed, but before all the rest, then in time Wordsworth will have his due. We shall recognize him in his place, as we recognize Shakespeare and Milton; and not only we ourselves shall recognize him, but he will be recognized by Europe also. Meanwhile, those who recognize him already may do well, perhaps, to ask themselves whether there are not in the case of Wordsworth certain special obstacles which hinder or delay his due recognition by others, and whether these obstacles are not in some measure removable.

The *Excursion* and the *Prelude,* his poems of greatest bulk, are by no means Words-

---

Goethe, the critic who above all others may count as European and whose judgment on the value of a work of modern poetry is the judgment which will, we may be almost sure, at last prevail generally."

[9]A court, in ancient Greece, composed of representatives from various states.

[10]Thomas Campbell (1777-1844), author of *Lord Ullin's Daughter.*

[11]Thomas Moore (1779-1852), author of *Lalla Rookh.*

worth's best work. His best work is in his shorter pieces, and many indeed are there of these which are of first-rate excellence. But in his seven volumes the pieces of high merit are mingled with a mass of pieces very inferior to them; so inferior to them that it seems wonderful how the same poet should have produced both. Shakespeare frequently has lines and passages in a strain quite false, and which are entirely unworthy of him. But one can imagine his smiling if one could meet him in the Elysian Fields and tell him so; smiling and replying that he knew it perfectly well himself, and what did it matter? But with Wordsworth the case is different. Work altogether inferior, work quite uninspired, flat and dull, is produced by him with evident unconsciousness of its defects, and he presents it to us with the same faith and seriousness as his best work. Now a drama or an epic fill the mind, and one does not look beyond them; but in a collection of short pieces the impression made by one piece requires to be continued and sustained by the piece following. In reading Wordsworth the impression made by one of his fine pieces is too often dulled and spoiled by a very inferior piece coming after it.

Wordsworth composed verses during a space of some sixty years; and it is no exaggeration to say that within one single decade of those years, between 1798 and 1808, almost all his really first-rate work was produced. A mass of inferior work remains, work done before and after this golden prime, imbedding the first-rate work and clogging it, obstructing our approach to it, chilling, not unfrequently, the high-wrought mood with which we leave it. To be recognized far and wide as a great poet, to be possible and receivable as a classic, Wordsworth needs to be relieved of a great deal of the poetical baggage which now encumbers him. To administer this relief is indispensable, unless he is to continue to be a poet for the few only,—a poet valued far below his real worth by the world.

There is another thing. Wordsworth classified his poems not according to any commonly received plan of arrangement, but according to a scheme of mental physiology. He has poems of the fancy, poems of the imagination, poems of sentiment and reflection, and so on. His categories are ingenious but far-fetched, and the result of his employment of them is unsatisfactory. Poems are separated one from another which possess a kinship of subject or of treatment far more vital and deep than the supposed unity of mental origin, which was Wordsworth's reason for joining them with others.

The tact of the Greeks in matters of this kind was infallible. We may rely upon it that we shall not improve upon the classification adopted by the Greeks for kinds of poetry; that their categories of epic, dramatic, lyric, and so forth, have a natural propriety, and should be adhered to. It may sometimes seem doubtful to which of two categories a poem belongs; whether this or that poem is to be called, for instance, narrative or lyric, lyric or elegiac. But there is to be found in every good poem a strain, a predominant note, which determines the poem as belonging to one of these kinds rather than the other; and here is the best proof of the value of the classification, and of the advantage of adhering to it. Wordsworth's poems will never produce their due effect until they are freed from their present artificial arrangement, and grouped more naturally.

Disengaged from the quantity of inferior work which now obscures them, the best poems of Wordsworth, I hear many people say, would indeed stand out in great beauty, but they would prove to be very few in number, scarcely more than half a dozen. I maintain, on the other hand, that what strikes me with admiration, what establishes in my opinion Wordsworth's superiority, is the great and ample body of powerful work which remains to him, even after all his inferior work has been cleared away. He gives us so much to rest upon, so much which communicates his spirit and engages ours!

This is of very great importance. If it were a comparison of single pieces, or of three or four pieces, by each poet, I do not say that Wordsworth would stand decisively above Gray, or Burns, or Coleridge, or Keats, or Manzoni, or Heine. It is in his ampler body of powerful work that I find his superiority. His good work itself, his work which counts, is not all of it, of course, of equal value. Some kinds of poetry are in themselves lower kinds than others. The ballad kind is a lower kind; the didactic kind, still more, is a lower kind. Poetry of this latter sort counts, too, sometimes, by its biographical interest partly, not by its poetical interest pure and simple; but then this can only be when the poet producing it has the power and importance of Wordsworth, a power and importance which he assuredly did not establish by such didactic poetry alone. Altogether, it is, I say, by the great body of powerful and significant work which remains to him, after every reduction and deduction has been made, that Wordsworth's superiority is proved.

To exhibit this body of Wordsworth's best work, to clear away obstructions from around it, and to let it speak for itself, is what every lover of Wordsworth should desire. Until this has been done, Wordsworth, whom we, to whom he is dear, all of us know and feel to be so great a poet, has not had a fair chance before the world. When once it has been done, he will make his way best, not by our advocacy of him, but by his own worth and power. We may safely leave him to make his way thus, we who believe that a superior worth and power in poetry finds in mankind a sense responsive to it and disposed at last to recognize it. Yet at the outset, before he has been duly known and recognized, we may do Wordsworth a service, perhaps, by indicating in what his superior power and worth will be found to consist, and in what it will not.

Long ago, in speaking of Homer, I said that the noble and profound application of ideas to life is the most essential part of poetic greatness. I said that a great poet receives his distinctive character of superiority from his application, under the conditions immutably fixed by the laws of poetic beauty and poetic truth, from his application, I say, to his subject, whatever it may be, of the ideas

On man, on nature, and on human life,[12]

which he has acquired for himself. The line quoted is Wordsworth's own; and his

superiority arises from his powerful use, in his best pieces, his powerful application to his subject, of ideas "on man, on nature, and on human life."

Voltaire, with his signal acuteness, most truly remarked that "no nation has treated in poetry moral ideas with more energy and depth than the English nation." And he adds: "There, it seems to me, is the great merit of the English poets." Voltaire does not mean, by "treating in poetry moral ideas," the composing moral and didactic poems;—that brings us but a very little way in poetry. He means just the same thing as was meant when I spoke above "of the noble and profound application of ideas to life"; and he means the application of these ideas under the conditions fixed for us by the laws of poetic beauty and poetic truth. If it is said that to call these ideas *moral* ideas is to introduce a strong and injurious limitation, I answer that it is to do nothing of the kind, because moral ideas are really so main a part of human life. The question, *how to live,* is itself a moral idea; and it is the question which most interests every man, and with which, in some way or other, he is perpetually occupied. A large sense is of course to be given to the term *moral*. Whatever bears upon the question, "how to live," comes under it.

Nor love thy life, nor hate; but, what thou liv'st, Live well; how long or short, permit to heaven.[13]

In those fine lines Milton utters, as every one at once perceives, a moral idea. Yes, but so too, when Keats consoles the forward-bending lover on the Grecian Urn, the lover arrested and presented in immortal relief by the sculptor's hand before he can kiss, with the line,

For ever wilt thou love, and she be fair—[14]

he utters a moral idea. When Shakespeare says, that

> We are such stuff
> As dreams are made of, and our little life
> Is rounded with a sleep,[15]

he utters a moral idea.

[12]*The Recluse,* I, i, 754.

[13]*Paradise Lost,* XI, 553–554.
[14]*Ode on a Grecian Urn,* l. 20.
[15]*The Tempest,* IV, i, 156–158.

Voltaire was right in thinking that the energetic and profound treatment of moral ideas, in this large sense, is what distinguishes the English poetry. He sincerely meant praise, not dispraise or hint of limitation; and they err who suppose that poetic limitation is a necessary consequence of the fact, the fact being granted as Voltaire states it. If what distinguishes the greatest poets is their powerful and profound application of ideas to life, which surely no good critic will deny, then to prefix to the term *ideas* here the term *moral* makes hardly any difference, because human life itself is in so preponderating a degree moral.

It is important, therefore, to hold fast to this: that poetry is at bottom a criticism of life; that the greatness of a poet lies in his powerful and beautiful application of ideas to life,—to the question: How to live. Morals are often treated in a narrow and false fashion; they are bound up with systems of thought and belief which have had their day; they are fallen into the hands of pedants and professional dealers; they grow tiresome to some of us. We find attraction, at times, even in a poetry of revolt against them; in a poetry which might take for its motto Omar Khayam's words: "Let us make up in the tavern for the time which we have wasted in the mosque."[16] Or we find attractions in a poetry indifferent to them; in a poetry where the contents may be what they will, but where the form is studied and exquisite. We delude ourselves in either case; and the best cure for our delusion is to let our minds rest upon that great and inexhaustible word *life*, until we learn to enter into its meaning. A poetry of revolt against moral ideas is a poetry of revolt against *life;* a poetry of indifference towards moral ideas is a poetry of indifference towards *life*.

Epictetus[17] had a happy figure for things like the play of the senses, or literary form and finish, or argumentative ingenuity, in comparison with "the best and master thing" for us, as he called it, the concern, how to live. Some people were afraid of them, he said, or they disliked and undervalued them.

Such people were wrong; they were unthankful or cowardly. But the things might also be over-prized, and treated as final when they are not. They bear to life the relation which inns bear to home. "As if a man, journeying home, and finding a nice inn on the road, and liking it, were to stay for ever at the inn! Man, thou hast forgotten thine object; thy journey was not *to* this, but *through* this. 'But this inn is taking.' And how many other inns, too, are taking, and how many fields and meadows! but as places of passage merely. You have an object, which is this: to get home, to do your duty to your family, friends, and fellow-countrymen, to attain inward freedom, serenity, happiness, contentment. Style takes your fancy, arguing takes your fancy, and you forget your home and want to make your abode with them and to stay with them, on the plea that they are taking. Who denies that they are taking? but as places of passage, as inns. And when I say this, you suppose me to be attacking the care for style, the care for argument. I am not; I attack by resting in them, the not looking to the end which is beyond them."

Now, when we come across a poet like Théophile Gautier,[18] we have a poet who has taken up his abode at an inn, and never got farther. There may be inducements to this or that one of us, at this or that moment, to find delight in him, to cleave to him; but after all, we do not change the truth about him,—we only stay ourselves in his inn along with him. And when we come across a poet like Wordsworth, who sings

Of truth, of grandeur, beauty, love and hope,
And melancholy fear subdued by faith,
Of blessed consolations in distress,
Of moral strength and intellectual power,
Of joy in widest commonalty spread—[19]

then we have a poet intent on "the best and master thing," and who prosecutes his journey home. We say, for brevity's sake, that he deals with *life,* because he deals with that in which life really consists. This is what Voltaire means to praise in the English poets,—this dealing with what is really life. But always it is the mark of the greatest

---

[16] See FitzGerald's *Rubáiyát of Omar Khayyám*, ll. 307–308.
[17] The Stoic philosopher of the first century A. D.
[18] French Romantic poet and novelist (1811–1872).
[19] *The Recluse,* I, i, 767–771.

poets that they deal with it; and to say that the English poets are remarkable for dealing with it, is only another way of saying, what is true, that in poetry the English genius has especially shown its power.

Wordsworth deals with it, and his greatness lies in his dealing with it so powerfully. I have named a number of celebrated poets above all of whom he, in my opinion, deserves to be placed. He is to be placed above poets like Voltaire, Dryden, Pope, Lessing, Schiller, because these famous personages, with a thousand gifts and merits, never, or scarcely ever, attain the distinctive accent and utterance of the high and genuine poets—

Quique pii vates et Phoebo digna locuti,[20]

at all. Burns, Keats, Heine, not to speak of others in our list, have this accent;—who can doubt it? And at the same time they have treasures of humor, felicity, passion, for which in Wordsworth we shall look in vain. Where, then, is Wordsworth's superiority? It is here; he deals with more of *life* than they do; he deals with *life,* as a whole, more powerfully.

No Wordsworthian will doubt this. Nay, the fervent Wordsworthian will add, as Mr. Leslie Stephen[21] does, that Wordsworth's poetry is precious because his philosophy is sound; that his "ethical system is as distinctive and capable of exposition as Bishop Butler's";[22] that his poetry is informed by ideas which "fall spontaneously into a scientific system of thought." But we must be on our guard against the Wordsworthians, if we want to secure for Wordsworth his due rank as a poet. The Wordsworthians are apt to praise him for the wrong things, and to lay far too much stress upon what they call his philosophy. His poetry is the reality, his philosophy,—so far, at least, as it may put on the form and habit of "a scientific system of thought," and the more that it puts them on,—is the illusion. Perhaps we shall

one day learn to make this proposition general, and to say: Poetry is the reality, philosophy the illusion. But in Wordsworth's case, at any rate, we cannot do him justice until we dismiss his formal philosophy.

The *Excursion* abounds with philosophy, and therefore the *Excursion* is to the Wordsworthian what it never can be to the disinterested lover of poetry,—a satisfactory work. "Duty exists," says Wordsworth, in the *Excursion;* and then he proceeds thus—

. . . Immutably survive,
For our support, the measures and the forms,
Which an abstract Intelligence supplies,
Whose kingdom is, where time and space are not.[23]

And the Wordsworthian is delighted, and thinks that here is a sweet union of philosophy and poetry. But the disinterested lover of poetry will feel that the lines carry us really not a step farther than the proposition which they would interpret; that they are a tissue of elevated but abstract verbiage, alien to the very nature of poetry.

Or let us come direct to the center of Wordsworth's philosophy, as "an ethical system, as distinctive and capable of systematical exposition as Bishop Butler's"—

. . . One adequate support
For the calamities of mortal life
Exists, one only;—an assured belief
That the procession of our fate, howe'er
Sad or disturbed, is ordered by a Being
Of infinite benevolence and power;
Whose everlasting purposes embrace
All accidents, converting them to good.[24]

That is doctrine such as we hear in church too, religious and philosophic doctrine; and the attached Wordsworthian loves passages of such doctrine, and brings them forward in proof of his poet's excellence. But however true the doctrine may be, it has, as here presented, none of the characters of *poetic* truth, the kind of truth which we require from a poet, and in which Wordsworth is really strong.

Even the "intimations" of the famous Ode, those corner-stones of the supposed philosophic system of Wordsworth,—the idea of the high instincts and affections coming out

---

[20]All reverent poets, who speak things worthy of Apollo.

[21]Sir Leslie Stephen (1832–1904), author of a *History of English Thought in the Eighteenth Century* and *Hours in a Library.*

[22]Bishop Joseph Butler (1692–1752), author of the *Analogy of Religion.*

[23]*The Excursion,* IV, 73–76.

[24]*The Excursion,* IV, 10–17.

in childhood, testifying of a divine home recently left, and fading away as our life proceeds,—this idea, of undeniable beauty as a play of fancy, has itself not the character of poetic truth of the best kind; it has no real solidity. The instinct of delight in Nature and her beauty had no doubt extraordinary strength in Wordsworth himself as a child. But to say that universally this instinct is mighty in childhood, and tends to die away afterwards, is to say what is extremely doubtful. In many people, perhaps with the majority of educated persons, the love of nature is nearly imperceptible at ten years old, but strong and operative at thirty. In general we may say of these high instincts of early childhood, the base of the alleged systematic philosophy of Wordsworth, what Thucydides says of the early achievements of the Greek race: "It is impossible to speak with certainty of what is so remote; but from all that we can really investigate, I should say that they were no very great things."[25]

Finally, the "scientific system of thought" in Wordsworth gives us at last such poetry as this, which the devout Wordsworthian accepts—

O for the coming of that glorious time
When, prizing knowledge as her noblest wealth
And best protection, this Imperial Realm,
While she exacts allegiance, shall admit
An obligation, on her part, to *teach*
Them who are born to serve her and obey;
Binding herself by statute to secure,
For all the children whom her soil maintains,
The rudiments of letters, and inform
The mind with moral and religious truth.[26]

Wordsworth calls Voltaire dull, and surely the production of these un-Voltairian lines must have been imposed on him as a judgment! One can hear them being quoted at a Social Science Congress; one can call up the whole scene. A great room in one of our dismal provincial towns; dusty air and jaded afternoon daylight; benches full of men with bald heads and women in spectacles; an orator lifting up his face from a manuscript written within and without to declaim these lines of Wordsworth; and in the soul of any poor child of nature who may have wandered in thither, an unutterable sense of lamentation, and mourning, and woe!

"But turn we," as Wordsworth says, "from these bold, bad men,"[27] the haunters of Social Science Congresses. And let us be on our guard, too, against the exhibitors and extollers of a "scientific system of thought" in Wordsworth's poetry. The poetry will never been seen aright while they thus exhibit it. The cause of its greatness is simple, and may be told quite simply. Wordsworth's poetry is great because of the extraordinary power with which Wordsworth feels the joy offered to us in nature, the joy offered to us in the simple primary affections and duties; and because of the extraordinary power with which, in case after case, he shows us this joy, and renders it so as to make us share it.

The source of joy from which he thus draws is the truest and most unfailing source of joy accessible to man. It is also accessible universally. Wordsworth brings us word, therefore, according to his own strong and characteristic line, he brings us word

Of joy in widest commonalty spread.

Here is an immense advantage for a poet. Wordsworth tells of what all seek, and tells of it at its truest and best source, and yet a source where all may go and draw for it.

Nevertheless, we are not to suppose that everything is precious which Wordsworth, standing even at this perennial and beautiful source, may give us. Wordsworthians are apt to talk as if it must be. They will speak with the same reverence of *The Sailor's Mother,* for example, as of *Lucy Gray.* They do their master harm by such lack of discrimination. *Lucy Gray* is a beautiful success; *The Sailor's Mother* is a failure. To give aright what he wishes to give, to interpret and render successfully, is not always within Wordsworth's own command. It is within no poet's command; here is the part of the Muse, the inspiration, the God, the "not ourselves." In Wordsworth's case, the accident, for so it may almost be called, of inspiration, is of peculiar importance. No poet, perhaps, is so evidently filled with

---

[25] *History of the Peloponnesian War,* I, i.
[26] *The Excursion,* IX, 293–302.
[27] *To the Lady Fleming,* I, 81.

a new and sacred energy when the inspiration is upon him; no poet, when it fails him, is so left "weak as is a breaking wave." I remember hearing him say that "Goethe's poetry was not inevitable enough." The remark is striking and true; no line in Goethe, as Goethe said himself, but its maker knew well how it came there. Wordsworth is right, Goethe's poetry is not inevitable; not inevitable enough. But Wordsworth's poetry, when he is at his best, is inevitable, as inevitable as Nature herself. It might seem that Nature not only gave him the matter for his poem, but wrote his poem for him. He has no style. He was too conversant with Milton not to catch at times his master's manner, and he has fine Miltonic lines; but he has no assured poetic style of his own, like Milton. When he seeks to have a style he falls into ponderosity and pomposity. In the *Excursion* we have his style, as an artistic product of his own creation; and although Jeffrey completely failed to recognize Wordsworth's real greatness, he was yet not wrong in saying of the *Excursion,* as a work of poetic style: "This will never do." And yet magical as is that power, which Wordsworth has not, of assured and possessed poetic style, he has something which is an equivalent for it.

Every one who has any sense for these things feels the subtle turn, the heightening, which is given to a poet's verse by his genius for style. We can feel it in the

After life's fitful fever, he sleeps well—[28]

of Shakespeare; in the

... though fall'n on evil days,
On evil days though fall'n, and evil tongues—[29]

of Milton. It is the incomparable charm of Milton's power of poetic style which gives such worth to *Paradise Regained,* and makes a great poem of a work in which Milton's imagination does not soar high. Wordsworth has in constant possession, and at command, no style of this kind; but he had too poetic a nature, and had read the great poets too well, not to catch, as I have already remarked,

something of it occasionally. We find it not only in his Miltonic lines; we find it in such a phrase as this, where the manner is his own, not Milton's—

the fierce confederate storm
Of sorrow barricadoed evermore
Within the walls of cities;

although even here, perhaps, the power of style which is undeniable, is more properly that of eloquent prose than the subtle heightening and change wrought by genuine poetic style. It is style, again, and the elevation given by style, which chiefly makes the effectiveness of *Laodameia.* Still the right sort of verse to choose from Wordsworth, if we are to seize his true and most characteristic form of expression, is a line like this from *Michael*—

And never lifted up a single stone.[30]

There is nothing subtle in it, no heightening, no study of poetic style, strictly so called, at all; yet it is expression of the highest and most truly expressive kind.

Wordsworth owed much to Burns, and a style of perfect plainness, relying for effect solely on the weight and force of that which with entire fidelity it utters, Burns could show him.

The poor inhabitant below
Was quick to learn and wise to know,
And keenly felt the friendly glow
   And softer flame;
But thoughtless follies laid him low
And stained his name.[31]

Every one will be conscious of a likeness here to Wordsworth; and if Wordsworth did great things with this nobly plain manner, we must remember, what indeed he himself would always have been forward to acknowledge, that Burns used it before him.

Still Wordsworth's use of it has something unique and unmatchable. Nature herself seems, I say, to take the pen out of his hand, and to write for him with her own bare, sheer, penetrating power. This arises from two causes; from the profound sincereness with which Wordsworth feels his subject, and also from the profoundly sincere and

[28]*Macbeth,* III, ii, 23.
[29]*Paradise Lost,* VII, 25–26.

[30]*Michael,* l. 466.
[31]Burns's *Bard's Epitaph,* ll. 19–24.

natural character of his subject itself. He can and will treat such a subject with nothing but the most plain, first-hand, almost austere naturalness. His expression may often be called bald, as, for instance, in the poem of *Resolution and Independence;* but it is bald as the bare mountain tops are bald, with a baldness which is full of grandeur.

Wherever we meet with the successful balance, in Wordsworth, of profound truth of subject with profound truth of execution, he is unique. His best poems are those which most perfectly exhibit this balance. I have a warm admiration for *Laodameia* and for the great *Ode;* but if I am to tell the very truth, I find *Laodameia* not wholly free from something artificial, and the great *Ode* not wholly free from something declamatory. If I had to pick out poems of a kind most perfectly to show Wordsworth's unique power, I should rather choose poems such as *Michael, The Fountain, The Highland Reaper.* And poems with the peculiar and unique beauty which distinguishes these, Wordsworth produced in considerable number; besides very many other poems of which the worth, although not so rare as the worth of these, is still exceedingly high.

On the whole, then, as I said at the beginning, not only is Wordsworth eminent by reason of the goodness of his best work, but he is eminent also by reason of the great body of good work which he has left to us. With the ancients I will not compare him. In many respects the ancients are far above us, and yet there is something that we demand which they can never give. Leaving the ancients, let us come to the poets and poetry of Christendom. Dante, Shakespeare, Molière, Milton, Goethe, are altogether larger and more splendid luminaries in the poetical heaven than Wordsworth. But I know not where else, among the moderns, we are to find his superiors.

To disengage the poems which show his power, and to present them to the English-speaking public and to the world, is the object of this volume.[32] I by no means say

that it contains all which in Wordsworth's poems is interesting. Except in the case of *Margaret,* a story composed separately from the rest of the *Excursion,* and which belongs to a different part of England, I have not ventured on detaching portions of poems, or on giving any piece otherwise than as Wordsworth himself gave it. But under the conditions imposed by this reserve, the volume contains, I think, everything, or nearly everything, which may best serve him with the majority of lovers of poetry, nothing which may disserve him.

I have spoken lightly of Wordsworthians; and if we are to get Wordsworth recognized by the public and by the world, we must recommend him not in the spirit of a clique, but in the spirit of disinterested lovers of poetry. But I am a Wordsworthian myself. I can read with pleasure and edification *Peter Bell,* and the whole series of *Ecclesiastical Sonnets,* and the address to Mr. Wilkinson's spade,[33] and even the *Thanksgiving Ode;*—everything of Wordsworth, I think, except *Vaudracour and Julia.* It is not for nothing that one has been brought up in the veneration of a man so truly worthy of homage; that one has seen him and heard him, lived in his neighborhood, and been familiar with his country. No Wordsworthian has a tenderer affection for this pure and sage master than I, or is less really offended by his defects. But Wordsworth is something more than the pure and sage master of a small band of devoted followers, and we ought not to rest satisfied until he is seen to be what he is. He is one of the very chief glories of English Poetry; and by nothing is England so glorious as by her poetry. Let us lay aside every weight which hinders our getting him recognized as this, and let our one study be to bring to pass, as widely as possible and as truly as possible, his own word concerning his poems: "They will co-operate with the benign tendencies in human nature and society, and will, in their degree, be efficacious in making men wiser, better, and happier."

---

[32]The collection of Wordsworth's poems to which the present essay served as a preface in 1879.

[33]*To the Spade of a Friend,* which begins: "Spade! with which Wilkinson hath tilled his lands," etc.

TO A FRIEND [1]

Who prop, thou ask'st, in these bad days,
    my mind?—
He[2] much, the old man, who, clearest-souled
    of men,
Saw The Wide Prospect,[3] and the Asian
    Fen,
And Tmolus hill,[4] and Smyrna bay, though
    blind.
Much he,[5] whose friendship I not long since
    won,   5
That halting slave, who in Nicopolis
Taught Arrian, when Vespasian's brutal son[6]
Cleared Rome of what most shamed him.
    But be his[7]
My special thanks, whose even-balanced soul
From first youth tested up to extreme old
    age,   10
Business could not make dull, nor passion
    wild;
Who saw life steadily, and saw it whole;
The mellow glory of the Attic stage,
Singer of sweet Colonus, and its child.

SHAKESPEARE

Others abide our question. Thou art free.
We ask and ask—Thou smilest and art still,
Out-topping knowledge. For the loftiest
    hill,
Who to the stars uncrowns his majesty,
Planting his steadfast footsteps in the sea, 5
Making the heaven of heavens his dwelling-
    place,
Spares but the cloudy border of his base
To the foiled searching of mortality;
And thou, who didst the stars and sunbeams
    know,
Self-schooled, self-scanned, self-honored,
    self-secure,   10

[1] Published, as were also the two following sonnets, in 1849.

[2] Homer.

[3] Europe (Εὐρώπη, *the wide prospect*) probably describes the appearance of the European coast to the Greeks on the coast of Asia Minor opposite. The name Asia, again, comes, it has been thought, from the muddy fens of the rivers of Asia Minor such as the Cayster or Maeander, which struck the imagination of the Greeks living near them (Arnold's note).

[4] A mountain range near Smyrna, which is one of the cities that claimed to be Homer's birthplace.

[5] Epictetus, the Stoic.

[6] Domitian, who banished the philosophers from Rome in A. D. 89.

[7] Sophocles's, who was born at Colonus, which he described in his tragedy *Oedipus at Colonus.*

Didst walk on earth unguessed at.—Better
    so!
All pains the immortal spirit must endure,
All weakness which impairs, all griefs which
    bow,
Find their sole speech in that victorious brow.

IN HARMONY WITH NATURE
To a Preacher

"In harmony with Nature?" Restless fool,
Who with such heat dost preach what were
    to thee,
When true, the last impossibility—
To be like Nature strong, like Nature cool!
Know, man hath all which Nature hath, but
    more,   5
And in that *more* lie all his hopes of good.
Nature is cruel, man is sick of blood;
Nature is stubborn, man would fain adore;
Nature is fickle, man hath need of rest;
Nature forgives no debt, and fears no grave;
Man would be mild, and with safe conscience
    blest.   11
Man must begin, know this, where Nature
    ends;
Nature and man can never be fast friends.
Fool, if thou canst not pass her, rest her
    slave!

REQUIESCAT [1]

Strew on her roses, roses,
    And never a spray of yew!
In quiet she reposes:
    Ah, would that I did too!

Her mirth the world required;   5
    She bathed it in smiles of glee.
But her heart was tired, tired,
    And now they let her be.

Her life was turning, turning,
    In mazes of heat and sound.   10
But for peace her soul was yearning,
    And now peace laps her round.

Her cabined, ample spirit,
    It fluttered and failed for breath.
To-night it doth inherit   15
    The vasty hall of death.

[1] Published in 1853.

RESIGNATION[1]

To Fausta

"To die be given us, or attain!
Fierce work it were, to do again."
So pilgrims, bound for Mecca, prayed
At burning noon; so warriors said,
Scarfed with the cross, who watched the
    miles   5
Of dust which wreathed their struggling files
Down Lydian mountains; so, when snows
Round Alpine summits, eddying, rose,
The Goth, bound Rome-wards; so the Hun,
Crouched on his saddle, while the sun   10
Went lurid down o'er flooded plains
Through which the groaning Danube strains
To the drear Euxine;—so pray all,
Whom labors, self-ordained, enthrall;
Because they to themselves propose   15
On this side the all-common close
A goal which, gained, may give repose.
So pray they.; and to stand again
Where they stood once, to them were pain;
Pain to thread back and to renew   20
Past straits, and currents long steered
    through.

But milder natures, and more free—
Whom an unblamed serenity
Hath freed from passions, and the state
Of struggle these necessitate;   25
Whom schooling of the stubborn mind
Hath made, or birth hath found, resigned—
These mourn not, that their goings pay
Obedience to the passing day.
These claim not every laughing Hour   30
For handmaid to their striding power;
Each in her turn, with torch upreared,
To await their march; and when appeared,
Through the cold gloom, with measured race,
To usher for a destined space   35
(Her own sweet errands all forgone)
The too imperious traveler on.
These, Fausta, ask not this; nor thou,
Time's chafing prisoner, ask it now!

We left, just ten years since, you say,   40
That wayside inn we left to-day.[2]
Our jovial host, as forth we fare,
Shouts greeting from his easy chair.

High on a bank our leader stands,
Reviews and ranks his motley bands,   45
Makes clear our goal to every eye—
The valley's western boundary.
A gate swings to! our tide hath flowed
Already from the silent road.
The valley-pastures, one by one,   50
Are threaded, quiet in the sun;
And now beyond the rude stone bridge
Slopes gracious up the western ridge.
Its woody border, and the last
Of its dark upland farms is past—   55
Cool farms, with open-lying stores,
Under their burnished sycamores;
All past! and through the trees we glide,
Emerging on the green hill-side.
There climbing hangs, a far-seen sign,   60
Our wavering, many-colored line;
There winds, upstreaming slowly still
Over the summit of the hill.
And now, in front, behold outspread
Those upper regions we must tread!   65
Mild hollows, and clear heathy swells,
The cheerful silence of the fells.[3]
Some two hours' march with serious air,
Through the deep noontide heats we fare;
The red-grouse, springing at our sound,   70
Skims, now and then, the shining ground;
No life, save his and ours, intrudes
Upon these breathless solitudes.
Oh joy! again the farms appear.
Cool shade is there, and rustic cheer;   75
There springs the brook will guide us down,
Bright comrade, to the noisy town.
Lingering, we follow down; we gain
The town, the highway, and the plain
And many a mile of dusty way,   80
Parched and road-worn, we made that day;
But, Fausta, I remember well,
That as the balmy darkness fell
We bathed our hands with speechless glee,
That night, in the wide-glimmering sea.   85

Once more we tread this self-same road,
Fausta, which ten years since we trod;
Alone we tread it, you and I,
Ghosts of that boisterous company.
Here, where the brook shines, near its head,
In its clear, shallow, turf-fringed bed;   91
Here, whence the eye first sees, far down,
Capped with faint smoke, the noisy town;
Here sit we, and again unroll,
Though slowly, the familiar whole.   95

---

[1] Published in 1849.

[2] Those who have been long familiar with the English Lake Country will find no difficulty in recalling, from the description in the text, the roadside inn at Wythburn on the descent from Dunmail Raise towards Keswick; its sedentary landlord of thirty years ago, and the passage over the Wythburn Fells to Watendlath (Arnold's note).

---

[3] Mountains.

The solemn wastes of heathy hill
Sleep in the July sunshine still;
The self-same shadows now, as then,
Play through this grassy upland glen;
The loose dark stones on the green way 100
Lie strewn, it seems, where then they lay;
On this mild bank above the stream,
(You crush them!) the blue gentians gleam.
Still this wild brook, the rushes cool,
The sailing foam, the shining pool! 105
These are not changed; and we, you say,
Are scarce more changed, in truth, than they.

The gypsies, whom we met below,
They, too, have long roamed to and fro;
They ramble, leaving, where they pass, 110
Their fragments on the cumbered grass.
And often to some kindly place
Chance guides the migratory race,
Where, though long wanderings intervene,
They recognize a former scene. 115
The dingy tents are pitched; the fires
Give to the wind their wavering spires;
In dark knots crouch round the wild flame
Their children, as when first they came;
They see their shackled beasts again 120
Move, browsing, up the gray-walled lane.
Signs are not wanting, which might raise
The ghost in them of former days—
Signs are not wanting, if they would;
Suggestions to disquietude. 125
For them, for all, time's busy touch,
While it mends little, troubles much.
Their joints grow stiffer—but the year
Runs his old round of dubious cheer;
Chilly they grow—yet winds in March, 130
Still, sharp as ever, freeze and parch;
They must live still—and yet, God knows,
Crowded and keen the country grows;
It seems as if, in their decay,
The law grew stronger every day. 135
So might they reason, so compare,
Fausta, times past with times that are.
But no!—they rubbed through yesterday
In their hereditary way,
And they will rub through, if they can, 140
To-morrow on the self-same plan,
Till death arrive to supersede,
For them, vicissitude and need.

The poet, to whose mighty heart
Heaven doth a quicker pulse impart, 145
Subdues that energy to scan
Not his own course, but that of man.
Though he move mountains, though his day
Be passed on the proud heights of sway,
Though he hath loosed a thousand chains, 150
Though he hath borne immortal pains,

Action and suffering though he know—
He hath not lived, if he lives so.
He sees, in some great-historied land,
A ruler of the people stand, 155
Sees his strong thought in fiery flood
Roll through the heaving multitude,
Exults—yet for no moment's space
Envies the all-regarded place.
Beautiful eyes meet his—and he 160
Bears to admire uncravingly;
They pass—he, mingled with the crowd,
Is in their far-off triumphs proud.
From some high station he looks down,
At sunset, on a populous town; 165
Surveys each happy group, which fleets,
Toil ended, through the shining streets,
Each with some errand of its own—
And does not say, "I am alone."
He sees the gentle stir of birth 170
When morning purifies the earth;
He leans upon a gate and sees
The pastures, and the quiet trees.
Low woody hill, with gracious bound,
Folds the still valley almost round; 175
The cuckoo, loud on some high lawn,
Is answered from the depth of dawn;
In the hedge straggling to the stream,
Pale, dew-drenched, half-shut roses gleam;
But, where the farther side slopes down, 180
He sees the drowsy new-waked clown
In his white quaint-embroidered frock
Make, whistling, towards his mist-wreathed
  flock—
Slowly, behind the heavy tread,
The wet, flowered grass heaves up its head.
Leaned on his gate, he gazes—tears 186
Are in his eyes, and in his ears
The murmur of a thousand years.
Before him he sees life unroll,
A placid and continuous whole— 190
That general life, which does not cease,
Whose secret is not joy, but peace;
That life, whose dumb wish is not missed
If birth proceeds, if things subsist;
The life of plants, and stones, and rain, 195
The life he craves—if not in vain
Fate gave, what chance shall not control,
His sad lucidity of soul.

You listen—but that wandering smile,
Fausta, betrays you cold the while! 200
Your eyes pursue the bells of foam
Washed, eddying, from this bank, their home.
"Those gypsies," so your thoughts I scan,
"Are less, the poet more, than man.
They feel not, though they move and see; 205
Deeply the poet feels; but he

Breathes, when he will, immortal air,
Where Orpheus and where Homer are.
In the day's life, whose iron round
Hems us all in, he is not bound;   210
He leaves his kind, o'erleaps their pen,
And flees the common life of men.
He escapes thence, but we abide—
Not deep the poet sees, but wide."

The world in which we live and move   215
Outlasts aversion, outlasts love,
Outlasts each effort, interest, hope,
Remorse, grief, joy;—and were the scope
Of these affections wider made,
Man still would see, and see dismayed,   220
Beyond his passion's widest range,
Far regions of eternal change.
Nay, and since death, which wipes out man,
Finds him with many an unsolved plan,
With much unknown, and much untried,   225
Wonder not dead, and thirst not dried,
Still gazing on the ever full
Eternal mundane spectacle—
This world in which we draw our breath,
In some sense, Fausta, outlasts death.   230

Blame thou not, therefore, him who dares
Judge vain beforehand human cares;
Whose natural insight can discern
What through experience others learn;
Who needs not love and power, to know   235
Love transient, power an unreal show;
Who treads at ease life's uncheered ways—
Him blame not, Fausta, rather praise!
Rather thyself for some aim pray
Nobler than this, to fill the day;   240
Rather that heart, which burns in thee,
Ask, not to amuse, but to set free;
Be passionate hopes not ill resigned
For quiet, and a fearless mind.
And though fate grudge to thee and me   245
The poet's rapt security,
Yet they, believe me, who await
No gifts from chance, have conquered fate;
They, winning room to see and hear,
And to men's business not too near,   250
Through clouds of individual strife
Draw homeward to the general life.
Like leaves by suns not yet uncurled;
To the wise, foolish; to the world,
Weak;—yet not weak, I might reply,   255
Not foolish, Fausta, in His eye,
To whom each moment in its race,
Crowd as we will its neutral space,
Is but a quiet watershed
Whence, equally, the seas of life and death
       are fed.   260

Enough, we live!—and if a life,
With large results so little rife,
Though bearable, seem hardly worth
This pomp of worlds, this pain of birth;
Yet, Fausta, the mute turf we tread,   265
The solemn hills around us spread,
This stream which falls incessantly,
The strange-scrawled rocks, the lonely sky,
If I might lend their life a voice,
Seem to bear rather than rejoice.   270
And even could the intemperate prayer
Man iterates, while these forbear,
For movement, for an ampler sphere,
Pierce Fate's impenetrable ear;
Not milder is the general lot   275
Because our spirits have forgot,
In action's dizzying eddy whirled,
The something that infects the world.

THE FORSAKEN MERMAN[1]

Come, dear children, let us away;
Down and away below!
Now my brothers call from the bay,
Now the great winds shoreward blow,
Now the salt tides seaward flow;   5
Now the wild white horses play,
Champ and chafe and toss in the spray.
Children dear, let us away!
This way, this way!

Call her once before you go—   10
Call once yet!
In a voice that she will know:
"Margaret! Margaret!"
Children's voices should be dear
(Call once more) to a mother's ear;   15
Children's voices, wild with pain—
Surely she will come again!
Call her once and come away;
This way, this way!
"Mother dear, we cannot stay!   20
The wild white horses foam and fret."
Margaret! Margaret!

Come, dear children, come away down;
Call no more!
One last look at the white-walled town,   25
And the little gray church on the windy
       shore;
Then come down!
She will not come though you call all day;
Come away, come away!

---

[1]Published in 1849.

Children dear, was it yesterday   30
We heard the sweet bells over the bay?
In the caverns where we lay,
Through the surf and through the swell,
The far-off sound of a silver bell?
Sand-strewn caverns, cool and deep,   35
Where the winds are all asleep;
Where the spent lights quiver and gleam,
Where the salt weed sways in the stream,
Where the sea-beasts, ranged all round,
Feed in the ooze of their pasture-ground;   40
Where the sea-snakes coil and twine,
Dry their mail and bask in the brine;
Where great whales come sailing by,
Sail and sail, with unshut eye,
Round the world for ever and aye?   45
When did music come this way?
Children dear, was it yesterday?

Children dear, was it yesterday
(Call yet once) that she went away?
Once she sat with you and me,   50
On a red gold throne in the heart of the sea,
And the youngest sat on her knee.
She combed its bright hair, and she tended it
    well,
When down swung the sound of a far-off
    bell.
She sighed, she looked up through the clear
    green sea;   55
She said: "I must go, for my kinsfolk pray
In the little gray church on the shore to-day.
'Twill be Easter-time in the world—ah me!
And I lose my poor soul, Merman! here with
    thee."
I said: "Go up, dear heart, through the
    waves;   60
Say thy prayer, and come back to the kind
    sea-caves!"
She smiled, she went up through the surf in
    the bay.
Children dear, was it yesterday?

Children dear, were we long alone?   64
"The sea grows stormy, the little ones moan;
Long prayers," I said, "in the world they
    say;
Come!" I said; and we rose through the surf
    in the bay.
We went up the beach, by the sandy down
Where the sea-stocks bloom, to the white-
    walled town;
Through the narrow paved streets, where all
    was still,   70
To the little gray church on the windy hill.
From the church came a murmur of folk at
    their prayers,

But we stood without in the cold blowing
    airs.
We climbed on the graves, on the stones
    worn with rains,
And we gazed up the aisle through the small
    leaded panes.   75
She sat by the pillar; we saw her clear:
"Margaret, hist! come quick, we are here!
Dear heart," I said, "we are long alone;
The sea grows stormy, the little ones moan."
But, ah, she gave me never a look,   80
For her eyes were sealed to the holy book!
Loud prays the priest; shut stands the door.
Come away, children, call no more!
Come away, come down, call no more!

Down, down, down!   85
Down to the depths of the sea!
She sits at her wheel in the humming town,
Singing most joyfully.
Hark what she sings: "O joy, O joy,
For the humming street, and the child with
    its toy!   90
For the priest, and the bell, and the holy
    well;
For the wheel where I spun,
And the blessèd light of the sun!"
And so she sings her fill,
Singing most joyfully,   95
Till the spindle falls from her hand,
And the whizzing wheel stands still.
She steals to the window, and looks at the
    sand,
And over the sand at the sea;
And her eyes are set in a stare;   100
And anon there breaks a sigh,
And anon there drops a tear,
From a sorrow-clouded eye,
And a heart sorrow-laden,
A long, long sigh;   105
For the cold strange eyes of a little Mer-
    maiden
And the gleam of her golden hair.

Come away, away children;
Come children, come down!
The hoarse wind blows coldly;   110
Lights shine in the town.
She will start from her slumber
When gusts shake the door;
She will hear the winds howling,
Will hear the waves roar.   115
We shall see, while above us
The waves roar and whirl,
A ceiling of amber,
A pavement of pearl.

Singing: "Here came a mortal, 120
But faithless was she!
And alone dwell for ever
The kings of the sea."
But, children, at midnight,
When soft the winds blow, 125
When clear falls the moonlight,
When spring-tides are low;
When sweet airs come seaward
From heaths starred with broom,
And high rocks throw mildly 130
On the blanched sands a gloom;

Up the still, glistening beaches,
Up the creeks we will hie,
Over banks of bright seaweed
The ebb-tide leaves dry. 135
We will gaze, from the sand-hills,
At the white, sleeping town;
At the church on the hill-side—
And then come back down.
Singing: "There dwells a loved one, 140
But cruel is she!
She left lonely for ever
The kings of the sea."

SWITZERLAND[1]

1. Meeting

Again I see my bliss at hand,
The town, the lake are here;
My Marguerite smiles upon the strand,
Unaltered with the year.

I know that graceful figure fair, 5
That cheek of languid hue;
I know that soft, enkerchiefed hair,
And those sweet eyes of blue.

Again I spring to make my choice;
Again in tones of ire 10
I hear a God's tremendous voice:
"Be counseled, and retire."

Ye guiding Powers who join and part,
What would ye have with me?
Ah, warn some more ambitious heart, 15
And let the peaceful be!

2. Parting

Ye storm-winds of Autumn!
Who rush by, who shake
The window, and ruffle
The gleam-lighted lake;
Who cross to the hill-side 5
Thin-sprinkled with farms,
Where the high woods strip sadly
Their yellowing arms—
Ye are bound for the mountains!
Ah! with you let me go 10
Where your cold, distant barrier,
The vast range of snow,

Through the loose clouds lifts dimly
Its white peaks in air—
How deep is their stillness! 15
Ah, would I were there!

But on the stairs what voice is this I hear,
Buoyant as morning, and as morning clear?
Say, has some wet bird-haunted English
lawn
Lent it the music of its trees at dawn? 20
Or was it from some sun-flecked mountain-
brook
That the sweet voice its upland clearness
took?
Ah! it comes nearer—
Sweet notes, this way!

Hark! fast by the window 25
The rushing winds go,
To the ice-cumbered gorges,
The vast seas of snow!
There the torrents drive upward
Their rock-strangled hum; 30
There the avalanche thunders
The hoarse torrent dumb.
—I come, O ye mountains!
Ye torrents, I come!

But who is this, by the half-opened door, 35
Whose figure casts a shadow on the floor?
The sweet blue eyes—the soft, ash-colored
hair—
The cheeks that still their gentle paleness
wear—
The lovely lips, with their arch smile that
tells
The unconquered joy in which her spirit
dwells— 40
Ah! they bend nearer—
Sweet lips, this way!

[1] The general title was given to this group of
poems in 1853, though some of them were published
in 1852. The third poem was published in 1869, the
fourth in 1857, and the seventh in 1867, though it
was not made a member of this group until 1869.
A final change in arrangement brought the group to
its present form in 1885.

Hark!   The wind rushes past us!
Ah! with that let me go
To the clear, waning hill-side,   45
Unspotted by snow,
There to watch, o'er the sunk vale,
The frore mountain-wall,
Where the niched snow-bed sprays down
Its powdery fall.   50
There its dusky blue clusters
The aconite² spreads;
There the pines slope, the cloud-strips
Hung soft in their heads.
No life but, at moments,   55
The mountain-bee's hum.
—I come, O ye mountains!
Ye pine-woods, I come!

Forgive me! forgive me!
    Ah, Marguerite, fain   60
Would these arms reach to clasp thee!
    But see! 'tis in vain.

In the void air, towards thee,
    My stretched arms are cast;
But a sea rolls between us—   65
    Our different past!

To the lips, ah! of others
    Those lips have been pressed,
And others, ere I was;
    Were strained to that breast;   70

Far, far from each other
    Our spirits have grown;
And what heart knows another?
    Ah! who knows his own?

Blow, ye winds! lift me with you!   75
    I come to the wild.
Fold closely, O Nature!
    Thine arms round thy child.

To thee only God granted
    A heart ever new—   80
To all always open,
    To all always true.

Ah! calm me, restore me;
    And dry up my tears
On thy high mountain-platforms,   85
    Where morn first appears;

Where the white mists, for ever,
    Are spread and upfurled—
In the stir of the forces
    Whence issued the world.   90

---

²The flower, monkshood.

3. A Farewell

My horse's feet beside the lake,
Where sweet the unbroken moonbeams lay,
Sent echoes through the night to wake
Each glistening strand, each heath-fringed
    bay.

The poplar avenue was passed,   5
And the roofed bridge that spans the stream;
Up the steep street I hurried fast,
Led by thy taper's starlike beam.

I came!   I saw thee rise!—the blood
Poured flushing to thy languid cheek.   10
Locked in each other's arms we stood,
In tears, with hearts too full to speak.

Days flew;—ah, soon I could discern
A trouble in thine altered air!
Thy hand lay languidly in mine,   15
Thy cheek was grave, thy speech grew rare.

I blame thee not!—this heart, I know,
To be long loved was never framed;
For something in its depths doth glow
Too strange, too restless, too untamed.   20

And women—things that live and move
Mined by the fever of the soul—
They seek to find in those they love
Stern strength, and promise of control.

They ask not kindness, gentle ways—   25
These they themselves have tried and known;
They ask a soul which never sways
With the blind gusts that shake their own.

I too have felt the load I bore
In a too strong emotion's sway;   30
I too have wished, no woman more,
This starting, feverish heart away.

I too have longed for trenchant force,
And will like a dividing spear;   34
Have praised the keen, unscrupulous course,
Which knows no doubt, which feels no fear.

But in the world I learned, what there
Thou too wilt surely one day prove,
That will, that energy, though rare,
Are yet far, far less rare than love.   40

Go, then!—till time and fate impress
This truth on thee, be mine no more!
They will!—for thou, I feel, not less
Than I, wast destined to this lore.

We school our manners, act our parts— 45
But He, who sees us through and through,
Knows that the bent of both our hearts
Was to be gentle, tranquil, true.

And though we wear out life, alas!
Distracted as a homeless wind, 50
In beating where we must not pass,
In seeking what we shall not find;

Yet we shall one day gain, life past,
Clear prospect o'er our being's whole;
Shall see ourselves, and learn at last 55
Our true affinities of soul.

We shall not then deny a course
To every thought the mass ignore;
We shall not then call hardness force,
Nor lightness wisdom any more. 60

Then, in the eternal Father's smile,
Our soothed, encouraged souls will dare
To seem as free from pride and guile,
As good, as generous, as they are.

Then we shall know our friends!—though much 65
Will have been lost—the help in strife,
The thousand sweet, still joys of such
As hand in hand face earthly life—

Though these be lost, there will be yet
A sympathy august and pure; 70
Ennobled by a vast regret,
And by contrition sealed thrice sure.

And we, whose ways were unlike here,
May then more neighboring courses ply;
May to each other be brought near, 75
And greet across infinity.

How sweet, unreached by earthly jars,
My sister! to maintain with thee
The hush among the shining stars,
The calm upon the moonlit sea! 80

How sweet to feel, on the boon air,
All our unquiet pulses cease!
To feel that nothing can impair
The gentleness, the thirst for peace—

The gentleness too rudely hurled 85
On this wild earth of hate and fear;
The thirst for peace a raving world
Would never let us satiate here.

4. Isolation. To Marguerite

We were apart; yet, day by day,
I bade my heart more constant be.
I bade it keep the world away,
And grow a home for only thee;
Nor feared but thy love likewise grew, 5
Like mine, each day, more tried, more true.

The fault was grave! I might have known
What far too soon, alas! I learned—
The heart can bind itself alone,
And faith may oft be unreturned. 10
Self-swayed our feelings ebb and swell—
Thou lov'st no more;—Farewell! Farewell!

Farewell!—and thou, thou lonely heart,
Which never yet without remorse
Even for a moment didst depart 15
From thy remote and spheréd course
To haunt the place where passions reign—
Back to thy solitude again!

Back! with the conscious thrill of shame
Which Luna[3] felt, that summer night, 20
Flash through her pure immortal frame,
When she forsook the starry height
To hang over Endymion's sleep
Upon the pine-grown Latmian steep.

Yet she, chaste queen, had never proved 25
How vain a thing is mortal love,
Wandering in Heaven, far removed.
But thou hast long had place to prove
This truth—to prove, and make thine own:
"Thou hast been, shalt be, art, alone." 30

Or, if not quite alone, yet they
Which touch thee are unmating things—
Ocean and clouds and night and day;
Lorn autumns and triumphant springs;
And life, and others' joy and pain, 35
And love, if love, of happier men.

Of happier men—for they, at least,
Have *dreamed* two human hearts might blend
In one, and were through faith released
From isolation without end 40
Prolonged; nor knew, although not less
Alone than thou, their loneliness.

5. To Marguerite—Continued

Yes! in the sea of life enisled,
With echoing straits between us thrown,
Dotting the shoreless watery wild,
We mortal millions live *alone*.
The islands feel the enclasping flow, 5
And then their endless bounds they know.

[3] Artemis.

But when the moon their hollows lights,
And they are swept by balms of spring,
And in their glens, on starry nights,
The nightingales divinely sing;　　10
And lovely notes, from shore to shore,
Across the sounds and channels pour—

Oh! then a longing like despair
Is to their farthest caverns sent;
For surely once, they feel, we were　　15
Parts of a single continent!
Now round us spreads the watery plain—
Oh might our marges meet again!

Who ordered, that their longing's fire
Should be, as soon as kindled, cooled?　　20
Who renders vain their deep desire?—
A God, a God their severance ruled!
And bade betwixt their shores to be
The unplumbed, salt, estranging sea.

6. Absence

In this fair stranger's eyes of gray
Thine eyes, my love! I see.
I shiver; for the passing day
Had borne me far from thee.

This is the curse of life! that not　　5
A nobler, calmer train
Of wiser thoughts and feelings blot
Our passions from our brain;

But each day brings its petty dust
Our soon-choked souls to fill,　　10
And we forget because we must
And not because we will.

I struggle towards the light; and ye,
Once-longed-for storms of love!
If with the light ye cannot be,　　15
I bear that ye remove.

I struggle towards the light—but oh,
While yet the night is chill,
Upon time's barren, stormy flow,
Stay with me, Marguerite, still!　　20

7. The Terrace at Berne

(COMPOSED TEN YEARS AFTER THE
PRECEDING)

Ten years!—and to my waking eye
Once more the roofs of Berne appear;
The rocky banks, the terrace high,
The stream!—and do I linger here?

The clouds are on the Oberland,　　5
The Jungfrau snows look faint and far;
But bright are those green fields at hand,
And through those fields comes down the
　　Aar,

And from the blue twin-lakes it comes,
Flows by the town, the churchyard fair;　　10
And 'neath the garden-walk it hums,
The house!—and is my Marguerite there?

Ah, shall I see thee, while a flush
Of startled pleasure floods thy brow,
Quick through the oleanders brush,　　15
And clap thy hands, and cry: " 'Tis thou!"

Or hast thou long since wandered back,
Daughter of France! to France, thy home;
And flitted down the flowery track
Where feet like thine too lightly come?　　20

Doth riotous laughter now replace
Thy smile; and rouge, with stony glare,
Thy cheeks' soft hue; and fluttering lace
The kerchief that enwound thy hair?

Or is it over?—art thou dead?—　　25
Dead!—and no warning shiver ran
Across my heart, to say thy thread
Of life was cut, and closed thy span!

Could from earth's ways that figure slight
Be lost, and I not feel 'twas so?　　30
Of that fresh voice the gay delight
Fail from earth's air, and I not know?

Or shall I find thee still, but changed,
But not the Marguerite of thy prime?
With all thy being re-arranged,　　35
Passed through the crucible of time;

With spirit vanished, beauty waned,
And hardly yet a glance, a tone,
A gesture—anything—retained
Of all that was my Marguerite's own?　　40

I will not know! For wherefore try,
To things by mortal course that live,
A shadowy durability,
For which they were not meant, to give?

Like driftwood spars, which meet and pass
Upon the boundless ocean-plain,　　46
So on the sea of life, alas!
Man meets man—meets, and quits again.

I knew it when my life was young;
I feel it still, now youth is o'er.   50
—The mists are on the mountain hung,
And Marguerite I shall see no more.

PHILOMELA[1]

Hark! ah, the nightingale—
The tawny-throated!
Hark, from that moonlit cedar what a burst!
What triumph! hark!—what pain!

O wanderer from a Grecian shore,   5
Still, after many years, in distant lands,
Still nourishing in thy bewildered brain
That wild, unquenched, deep-sunken, old-
    world pain—
Say, will it never heal?
And can this fragrant lawn   10
With its cool trees, and night,
And the sweet, tranquil Thames,
And moonshine, and the dew,
To thy racked heart and brain
Afford no balm?   15

Dost thou to-night behold
Here, through the moonlight on this English
    grass,
The unfriendly palace in the Thracian wild?
Dost thou again peruse
With hot cheeks and seared eyes   20
The too clear web, and thy dumb sister's
    shame?
Dost thou once more assay
Thy flight, and feel come over thee,
Poor fugitive, the feathery change
Once more, and once more seem to make re-
    sound   25
With love and hate, triumph and agony,
Lone Daulis, and the high Cephissian vale?
Listen, Eugenia—
How thick the bursts come crowding through
    the leaves!
Again—thou hearest?   30
Eternal Passion!
Eternal Pain!

[1]Philomela was violated by her brother-in-law,
Tereus, King of Daulis, who thereafter cut out her
tongue so that she might not betray the deed. She,
however, made it known to her sister Procne,
Tereus's wife, by weaving words into a robe ("the
too clear web"). Procne killed her son, gave his
body as food to his father, and fled with Philomela.
When Tereus pursued them, and they prayed for
deliverance, the gods changed them into birds—
Philomela into a nightingale. In the poem (published in 1853), Arnold reverses the positions of
Philomela and Procne.

DOVER BEACH[2]

The sea is calm to-night.
The tide is full, the moon lies fair
Upon the straits;—on the French coast the
    light
Gleams and is gone; the cliffs of England
    stand,
Glimmering and vast, out in the tranquil
    bay.   5
Come to the window, sweet is the night-air!
Only, from the long line of spray
Where the sea meets the moon-blanched land,
Listen! you hear the grating roar
Of pebbles which the waves draw back, and
    fling,   10
At their return, up the high strand,
Begin, and cease, and then again begin,
With tremulous cadence slow, and bring
The eternal note of sadness in.

Sophocles long ago   15
Heard it on the Aegean, and it brought
Into his mind the turbid ebb and flow
Of human misery; we
Find also in the sound a thought,
Hearing it by this distant northern sea.   20

The Sea of Faith
Was once, too, at the full, and round earth's
    shore
Lay like the folds of a bright girdle furled.
But now I only hear
Its melancholy, long, withdrawing roar,   25
Retreating, to the breath
Of the night-wind, down the vast edges
    drear
And naked shingles[3] of the world.

Ah, love, let us be true
To one another! for the world, which seems
To lie before us like a land of dreams,   31
So various, so beautiful, so new,
Hath really neither joy, nor love, nor light,
Nor certitude, nor peace, nor help for pain;
And we are here as on a darkling plain   35
Swept with confused alarms of struggle and
    flight,
Where ignorant armies clash by night.

SELF-DEPENDENCE[4]

Weary of myself, and sick of asking
What I am, and what I ought to be,
At this vessel's prow I stand, which bears me
Forwards, forwards, o'er the star-lit sea.

[2]Published in 1867.   [3]Pebbly shores.
[4]Published in 1852.

And a look of passionate desire   5
O'er the sea and to the stars I send:
"Ye who from my childhood up have calmed me,
Calm me, ah, compose me to the end!"

"Ah, once more," I cried, "ye stars, ye waters,
On my heart your mighty charm renew;   10
Still, still let me, as I gaze upon you,
Feel my soul becoming vast like you!"

From the intense, clear, star-sown vault of heaven,
Over the lit sea's unquiet way,
In the rustling night-air came the answer: 15
"Wouldst thou *be* as these are? *Live* as they.

"Unaffrighted by the silence round them,
Undistracted by the sights they see,
These demand not that the things without them
Yield them love, amusement, sympathy.   20

"And with joy the stars perform their shining,
And the sea its long moon-silvered roll;
For self-poised they live, nor pine with noting
All the fever of some differing soul.

"Bounded by themselves, and unregardful   25
In what state God's other works may be,
In their own tasks all their powers pouring,
These attain the mighty life you see."

O air-born voice! long since, severely clear,
A cry like thine in my own heart I hear: 30
"Resolve to be thyself; and know that he,
Who finds himself, loses his misery!"

MORALITY[5]

We cannot kindle when we will
The fire which in the heart resides;
The spirit bloweth and is still,
In mystery our soul abides.
  But tasks in hours of insight willed   5
  Can be through hours of gloom fulfilled.

With aching hands and bleeding feet
We dig and heap, lay stone on stone;
We bear the burden and the heat
Of the long day, and wish 'twere done.   10
  Not till the hours of light return,
  All we have built do we discern.

[5]Published in 1852.

Then, when the clouds are off the soul,
When thou dost bask in Nature's eye,
Ask, how *she* viewed thy self-control,   15
Thy struggling, tasked morality—
  Nature, whose free, light, cheerful air,
  Oft made thee, in thy gloom, despair.

And she, whose censure thou dost dread,
Whose eye thou wast afraid to seek,   21
See, on her face a glow is spread,
A strong emotion on her cheek!
  "Ah, child!" she cries, "that strife divine,
  Whence was it, for it is not mine?

"There is no effort on *my* brow—   25
I do not strive, I do not weep;
I rush with the swift spheres and glow
In joy, and when I will, I sleep.
  Yet that severe, that earnest air,
  I saw, I felt it once—but where?   30

"I knew not yet the gauge of time,
Nor wore the manacles of space;
I felt it in some other clime,
I saw it in some other place.
  'Twas when the heavenly house I trod,   35
  And lay upon the breast of God."

THE BURIED LIFE[1]

Light flows our war of mocking words, and yet,
Behold, with tears mine eyes are wet!
I feel a nameless sadness o'er me roll.
Yes, yes, we know that we can jest,
We know, we know that we can smile!   5
But there's a something in this breast,
To which thy light words bring no rest,
And thy gay smiles no anodyne.
Give me thy hand, and hush awhile,
And turn those limpid eyes on mine,   10
And let me read there, love! thy inmost soul.

Alas! is even love too weak
To unlock the heart, and let it speak?
Are even lovers powerless to reveal
To one another what indeed they feel?   15
I knew the mass of men concealed
Their thoughts, for fear that if revealed
They would by other men be met
With blank indifference, or with blame reproved;
I knew they lived and moved   20
Tricked in disguises, alien to the rest
Of men, and alien to themselves—and yet
The same heart beats in every human breast!

[1]Published in 1852.

But we, my love!—doth a like spell benumb
Our hearts, our voices?—must we too be
    dumb? 25

Ah! well for us, if even we,
Even for a moment, can get free
Our heart, and have our lips unchained;
For that which seals them hath been deep-
    ordained!

Fate, which foresaw 30
How frivolous a baby man would be—
By what distractions he would be possessed,
How he would pour himself in every strife,
And well-nigh change his own identity—
That it might keep from his capricious play
His genuine self, and force him to obey 36
Even in his own despite his being's law,
Bade through the deep recesses of our breast
The unregarded river of our life
Pursue with indiscernible flow its way; 40
And that we should not see
The buried stream, and seem to be
Eddying at large in blind uncertainty,
Though driving on with it eternally.

But often, in the world's most crowded
    streets, 45
But often, in the din of strife,
There rises an unspeakable desire
After the knowledge of our buried life;
A thirst to spend our fire and restless force
In tracking out our true, original course; 50
A longing to inquire
Into the mystery of this heart which beats
So wild, so deep in us—to know
Whence our lives come and where they go.
And many a man in his own breast then
    delves, 55
But deep enough, alas! none ever mines.
And we have been on many thousand lines,[2]
And we have shown, on each, spirit and
    power;
But hardly have we, for one little hour,
Been on our own line, have we been our-
    selves— 60
Hardly had skill to utter one of all
The nameless feelings that course through
    our breast,
But they course on for ever unexpressed.
And long we try in vain to speak and act
Our hidden self, and what we say and do 65
Is eloquent, is well—but 'tis not true!
And then we will no more be racked
With inward striving, and demand
Of all the thousand nothings of the hour
Their stupefying power; 70

[2] Appointed tasks.

Ah yes, and they benumb us at our call!
Yet still, from time to time, vague and for-
    lorn,
From the soul's subterranean depth upborne
As from an infinitely distant land,
Come airs, and floating echoes, and convey
A melancholy into all our day. 76

Only—but this is rare—
When a belovéd hand is laid in ours,
When, jaded with the rush and glare
Of the interminable hours, 80
Our eyes can in another's eyes read clear,
When our world-deafened ear
Is by the tones of a loved voice caressed—
A bolt is shot back somewhere in our breast,
And a lost pulse of feeling stirs again. 85
The eye sinks inward, and the heart lies
    plain,
And what we mean, we say, and what we
    would, we know.
A man becomes aware of his life's flow,
And hears its winding murmur; and he sees
The meadows where it glides, the sun, the
    breeze. 90

And there arrives a lull in the hot race
Wherein he doth for ever chase
That flying and elusive shadow, rest.
An air of coolness plays upon his face,
And an unwonted calm pervades his breast.
And then he thinks he knows 96
The hills where his life rose,
And the sea where it goes.

THE FUTURE[1]

A wanderer is man from his birth.
He was born in a ship
On the breast of the river of Time;
Brimming with wonder and joy
He spreads out his arms to the light, 5
Rivets his gaze on the banks of the stream.

As what he sees is, so have his thoughts been.
Whether he wakes,
Where the snowy mountainous pass,
Echoing the screams of the eagles, 10
Hems in its gorges the bed
Of the new-born clear-flowing stream;
Whether he first sees light
Where the river in gleaming rings
Sluggishly winds through the plain; 15
Whether in sound of the swallowing sea—
As is the world on the banks,
So is the mind of the man.

[1] Published in 1852.

Vainly does each, as he glides,
Fable and dream   20
Of the lands which the river of Time
Had left ere he woke on its breast,
Or shall reach when his eyes have been
      closed.
Only the tract where he sails
He wots of; only the thoughts,   25
Raised by the objects he passes, are his.

Who can see the green earth any more
As she was by the sources of Time?
Who imagines her fields as they lay
In the sunshine, unworn by the plow?   30
Who thinks as they thought,
The tribes who then roamed on her breast,
Her vigorous, primitive sons?

What girl
Now reads in her bosom as clear   35
As Rebekah read, when she sat
At eve by the palm-shaded well?[2]
Who guards in her breast
As deep, as pellucid a spring
Of feeling, as tranquil, as sure?   40

What bard,
At the height of his vision, can deem
Of God, of the world, of the soul,
With a plainness as near,
As flashing as Moses felt   45
When he lay in the night by his flock
On the starlit Arabian waste?[3]
Can rise and obey
The beck of the Spirit like him?

This tract which the river of Time   50
Now flows through with us, is the plain.

---

[2]See Genesis, 24.   [3]See Exodus, 3.

Gone is the calm of its earlier shore.
Bordered by cities and hoarse
With a thousand cries is its stream.
And we on its breast, our minds   55
Are confused as the cries which we hear,
Changing and shot as the sights which we see.

And we say that repose has fled
For ever the course of the river of Time.
That cities will crowd to its edge   60
In a blacker, incessanter line;
That the din will be more on its banks,
Denser the trade on its stream,
Flatter the plain where it flows,
Fiercer the sun overhead.   65
That never will those on its breast
See an ennobling sight,
Drink of the feeling of quiet again.

But what was before us we know not,
And we know not what shall succeed.   70

Haply, the river of Time—
As it grows, as the towns on its marge
Fling their wavering lights
On a wider, statelier stream—
May acquire, if not the calm   75
Of its early mountainous shore,
Yet a solemn peace of its own.
And the width of the waters, the hush
Of the gray expanse where he floats,   79
Freshening its current and spotted with foam
As it draws to the Ocean, may strike
Peace to the soul of the man on its breast—
As the pale waste widens around him,
As the banks fade dimmer away,
As the stars come out, and the night-wind   85
Brings up the stream
Murmurs and scents of the infinite sea.

THE SCHOLAR-GYPSY[1]

Go, for they call you, shepherd, from the hill;
   Go, shepherd, and untie the wattled cotes![2]

No longer leave thy wistful flock unfed,
   Nor let thy bawling fellows rack their
         throats,
   Nor the cropped herbage shoot another
         head.   5
   But when the fields are still,

---

[1]"There was very lately a lad in the University of Oxford, who was by his poverty forced to leave his studies there; and at last to join himself to a company of vagabond gypsies. Among these extravagant people, by the insinuating subtlety of his carriage, he quickly got so much of their love and esteem as that they discovered to him their mystery. After he had been a pretty while exercised in the trade, there chanced to ride by a couple of scholars, who had formerly been of his acquaintance. They quickly spied out their old friend among the gypsies; and he gave them an account of the necessity which drove him to that kind of life, and told them that the people he went with were not such impostors as they were taken for, but that they had a traditional kind of learning among them, and could do wonders by the power of imagination, their fancy binding that of others; that himself had learned much of their art, and when he had compassed the whole secret, he intended, he said, to leave their company, and give the world an account of what he had learned."—Glanvil, *Vanity of Dogmatizing*, 1661 (Arnold's note). The poem was published in 1853.

[2]Sheep-folds.

And the tired men and dogs all gone to rest,
And only the white sheep are sometimes
seen
Cross and recross the strips of moon-
blanched green, 9
Come, shepherd, and again begin the quest!

Here, where the reaper was at work of late—
In this high field's dark corner, where he
leaves
His coat, his basket, and his earthen
cruse,
And in the sun all morning binds the
sheaves,
Then here, at noon, comes back his
stores to use— 15
Here will I sit and wait,
While to my ear from uplands far away
The bleating of the folded flocks is
borne,
With distant cries of reapers in the
corn—
All the live murmur of a summer's day. 20

Screened is this nook o'er the high, half-
reaped field,
And here till sun-down, shepherd! will I
be.
Through the thick corn the scarlet pop-
pies peep,
And round green roots and yellowing
stalks I see
Pale pink convolvulus in tendrils creep;
And air-swept lindens yield 26
Their scent, and rustle down their per-
fumed showers
Of bloom on the bent grass where I am
laid,
And bower me from the August sun
with shade;
And the eye travels down to Oxford's
towers. 30

And near me on the grass lies Glanvil's
book—
Come, let me read the oft-read tale again!
The story of the Oxford scholar poor,
Of pregnant parts and quick inventive
brain,
Who, tired of knocking at preferment's
door,[3] 35
One summer morn forsook
His friends, and went to learn the gypsy-
lore,
And roamed the world with that wild
brotherhood,

[3] I. e., of trying to secure a post in the Church.

And came, as most men deemed, to little
good,
But came to Oxford and his friends no
more. 40

But once, years after, in the country lanes,
Two scholars, whom at college erst he
knew,
Met him, and of his way of life in-
quired;
Whereat he answered, that the gypsy-
crew,
His mates, had arts to rule as they de-
sired 45
The workings of men's brains,
And they can bind them to what thoughts
they will.
"And I," he said, "the secret of their
art,
When fully learned, will to the world
impart;
But it needs heaven-sent moments for this
skill." 50

This said, he left them, and returned no
more.—
But rumors hung about the country-side,
That the lost Scholar long was seen to
stray,
Seen by rare glimpses, pensive and tongue-
tied,
In hat of antique shape, and cloak of
gray, 55
The same the gypsies wore.
Shepherds had met him on the Hurst in
spring;
At some lone alehouse in the Berkshire
moors,
On the warm ingle-bench, the smock-
frocked boors
Had found him seated at their entering, 60

But, 'mid their drink and clatter, he would
fly.
And I myself seem half to know thy looks,
And put the shepherds, wanderer! on
thy trace;
And boys who in lone wheatfields scare the
rooks
I ask if thou hast passed their quiet
place; 65
Or in my boat I lie
Moored to the cool bank in the summer
heats,
'Mid wide grass meadows which the sun-
shine fills,

And watch the warm, green-muffled
    Cumner hills,
And wonder if thou haunt'st their shy re-
    treats.   70

For most, I know, thou lov'st retired ground!
    Thee at the ferry Oxford riders blithe,
      Returning home on summer nights, have
        met
Crossing the stripling Thames at Bab-lock-
    hithe,
      Trailing in the cool stream thy fingers
        wet,   75
        As the punt's rope chops round;
And leaning backward in a pensive dream,
    And fostering in thy lap a heap of
      flowers
    Plucked in shy fields and distant Wych-
      wood[4] bowers,
And thine eyes resting on the moonlit
    stream.   80

And then they land, and thou art seen no
    more!—
    Maidens, who from the distant hamlets
      come
    To dance around the Fyfield elm in May,
Oft through the darkening fields have seen
    thee roam,
    Or cross a stile into the public way. 85
      Oft thou hast given them store
Of flowers—the frail-leafed, white anem-
    one,
    Dark bluebells drenched with dews of
      summer eves,
    And purple orchises with spotted
      leaves—
But none hath words she can report of
    thee.   90

And, above Godstow Bridge, when hay-time's
    here
In June, and many a scythe in sunshine
    flames,
    Men who through those wide fields of
      breezy grass
    Where black-winged swallows haunt the
      glittering Thames,
      To bathe in the abandoned lasher[5] pass,
      Have often passed thee near 96
    Sitting upon the river bank o'ergrown;
      Marked thine outlandish garb, thy figure
      spare,

[4] A forest about ten miles from Oxford.
[5] The pool below a dam.

Thy dark vague eyes, and soft ab-
    stracted air—
But, when they came from bathing, thou
    wast gone!   100

At some lone homestead in the Cumner hills,
    Where at her open door the housewife
      darns,
    Thou hast been seen, or hanging on a
      gate
To watch the threshers in the mossy barns.
    Children, who early range these slopes
      and late 105
      For cresses from the rills,
Have known thee eying, all an April-day,
    The springing pastures and the feeding
      kine;
    And marked thee, when the stars come
      out and shine,
Through the long dewy grass move slow
    away.   110

In autumn, on the skirts of Bagley wood—
    Where most the gypsies by the turf-edged
      way
    Pitch their smoked tents, and every bush
      you see
With scarlet patches tagged and shreds of
    gray,
    Above the forest ground called Thes-
      saly— 115
      The blackbird, picking food,
Sees thee, nor stops his meal, nor fears at
    all;
    So often has he known thee past him
      stray,
    Rapt, twirling in thy hand a withered
      spray,
And waiting for the spark from heaven to
    fall.   120

And once, in winter, on the causeway chill
    Where home through flooded fields foot-
      travelers go,
    Have I not passed thee on the wooden
      bridge,
Wrapped in thy cloak and battling with the
    snow,
    Thy face tow'rd Hinksey and its wintry
      ridge? 125
      And thou hast climbed the hill
And gained the white brow of the Cumner
    range;
    Turned once to watch, while thick the
      snowflakes fall,

The line of festal light in Christ-Church
hall[6]—
Then sought thy straw in some sequestered
grange.   130

But what—I dream! Two hundred years
are flown
Since first thy story ran through Oxford
halls,
And the grave Glanvil did the tale in-
scribe
That thou wert wandered from the stu-
dious walls
To learn strange arts, and join a gypsy-
tribe;   135
And thou from earth art gone
Long since, and in some quiet churchyard
laid—
Some country-nook, where o'er thy un-
known grave
Tall grasses and white flowering nettles
wave,   139
Under a dark, red-fruited yew-tree's shade.

—No, no, thou hast not felt the lapse of
hours!
For what wears out the life of mortal
men?
'Tis that from change to change their
being rolls;
'Tis that repeated shocks, again, again,
Exhaust the energy of strongest souls
And numb the elastic powers.   146
Till having used our nerves with bliss and
teen,[7]
And tired upon a thousand schemes our
wit,
To the just-pausing Genius[8] we remit
Our worn-out life, and are—what we have
been.   150

Thou hast not lived, why should'st thou per-
ish, so?
Thou hadst *one* aim, *one* business, *one* de-
sire;
Else wert thou long since numbered with
the dead!
Else hadst thou spent, like other men, thy
fire!
The generations of thy peers are fled, 155
And we ourselves shall go;

But thou possessest an immortal lot,
And we imagine thee exempt from age
And living as thou liv'st on Glanvil's
page,
Because thou hadst—what we, alas! have
not.   160

For early didst thou leave the world, with
powers
Fresh, undiverted to the world without,
Firm to their mark, not spent on other
things;
Free from the sick fatigue, the languid
doubt,
Which much to have tried, in much been
baffled, brings.   165
O life unlike to ours!
Who fluctuate idly without term or scope,
Of whom each strives, nor knows for
what he strives,
And each half lives a hundred different
lives;
Who wait like thee, but not, like thee, in
hope.   170

Thou waitest for the spark from heaven! and
we,
Light half-believers of our casual creeds,
Who never deeply felt, nor clearly
willed,
Whose insight never has borne fruit in
deeds,
Whose vague resolves never have been
fulfilled;   175
For whom each year we see
Breeds new beginnings, disappointments
new;
Who hesitate and falter life away,
And lose to-morrow the ground won
to-day—
Ah! do not we, wanderer! await it too? 180

Yes, we await it!—but it still delays,
And then we suffer! and amongst us one,[9]
Who most has suffered, takes dejectedly
His seat upon the intellectual throne;
And all his store of sad experience he 185
Lays bare of wretched days;

---

[6]The hall of the college of that name, Oxford.
[7]Suffering. [8]Spirit attendant on an individual.

[9]Whether or not Arnold had in mind some contemporary is not known. Carlyle has been suggested and, with much greater plausibility, Tennyson.

Tells us his misery's birth and growth and
    signs,
    And how the dying spark of hope was
        fed,
    And how the breast was soothed, and
        how the head,
    And all his hourly varied anodynes.   190

This for our wisest! and we others pine,
    And wish the long unhappy dream would
        end,
    And waive all claim to bliss, and try to
        bear;
    With close-lipped patience for our only
        friend,
    Sad patience, too near neighbor to de-
        spair—   195
    But none has hope like thine!
Thou through the fields and through the
    woods dost stray,
    Roaming the country-side, a truant boy,
    Nursing thy project in unclouded joy,
    And every doubt long blown by time
        away.   200

O born in days when wits were fresh and
    clear,
    And life ran gayly as the sparkling
        Thames;
    Before this strange disease of modern
        life,
    With its sick hurry, its divided aims,
    Its heads o'ertaxed, its palsied hearts,
        was rife—   205
    Fly hence, our contact fear!
Still fly, plunge deeper in the bowering
    wood!
    Averse, as Dido did with gesture stern
    From her false friend's approach in
        Hades turn,[10]
Wave us away, and keep thy solitude!   210

Still nursing the unconquerable hope,
    Still clutching the inviolable shade,
    With a free, onward impulse brushing
        through,
    By night, the silvered branches of the
        glade—
    Far on the forest skirts, where none
        pursue,   215
    On some mild pastoral slope
Emerge, and resting on the moonlit pales
Freshen thy flowers as in former years

With dew, or listen with enchanted ears,
From the dark dingles, to the nightingales!

But fly our paths, our feverish contact fly!   221
    For strong the infection of our mental
        strife,
    Which, though it gives no bliss, yet spoils
        for rest;
    And we should win thee from thy own
        fair life,
    Like us distracted, and like us unblest.
        Soon, soon thy cheer would die,   226
    Thy hopes grow timorous, and unfixed
        thy powers,
    And thy clear aims be cross and shift-
        ing made;
    And then thy glad perennial youth would
        fade,
    Fade, and grow old at last, and die like
        ours.   230

Then fly our greetings, fly our speech and
    smiles!
    —As some grave Tyrian trader, from the
        sea,
    Described at sunrise an emerging prow
Lifting the cool-haired creepers stealthily,
    The fringes of a southward-facing brow
        Among the Aegean isles;   236
And saw the merry Grecian coaster come,
    Freighted with amber grapes, and Chian
        wine,
    Green, bursting figs, and tunnies[11]
        steeped in brine—
    And knew the intruders on his ancient
        home,   240

The young light-hearted masters of the
    waves—
    And snatched his rudder, and shook out
        more sail;
    And day and night held on indignantly
O'er the blue Midland[12] waters with the
    gale,
    Betwixt the Syrtes[13] and soft Sicily,   245
        To where the Atlantic raves
Outside the western straits; and unbent
    sails
    There, where down cloudy cliffs, through
        sheets of foam,
    Shy traffickers, the dark Iberians[14]
        come;   249
And on the beach undid his corded bales.

---

[10]The "false friend" was Aeneas; see *Aeneid*, VI,
469.

[11]A large oceanic fish.   [12]Mediterranean.
[13]Shoals off the north coast of Africa.
[14]Inhabitants of the Spanish peninsula.

THYRSIS[1]

A Monody: To Commemorate The Author's Friend, Arthur Hugh Clough, Who Died at Florence, 1861

How changed is here each spot man makes
    or fills!
In the two Hinkseys nothing keeps the
    same;
    The village street its haunted mansion
      lacks,
And from the sign is gone Sibylla's name,
    And from the roofs the twisted chimney-
      stacks—   5
      Are ye too changed, ye hills?
See, 'tis no foot of unfamiliar men
    To-night from Oxford up your pathway
      strays!
Here came I often, often, in old days—
Thyrsis and I; we still had Thyrsis then. 10

Runs it not here, the track by Childsworth
    Farm,
    Past the high wood, to where the elm-tree
      crowns
    The hill behind whose ridge the sunset
      flames?
The signal-elm, that looks on Ilsley Downs,
    The Vale, the three lone weirs,[2] the
      youthful Thames?—   15
      This winter-eve is warm,
Humid the air! leafless, yet soft as spring,
    The tender purple spray on copse and
      briers!
And that sweet city with her dreaming
    spires
She needs not June for beauty's heighten-
    ing,   20

Lovely all times she lies, lovely to-night!—
    Only, methinks, some loss of habit's power
    Befalls me wandering through this up-
      land dim.
Once passed I blindfold here, at any hour;
    Now seldom come I, since I came with
      him.   25
      That single elm-tree bright
Against the west—I miss it! is it gone?
    We prized it dearly; while it stood, we
      said,
    Our friend, the Gypsy-Scholar, was not
      dead;

While the tree lived, he in these fields lived
    on.   30

Too rare, too rare, grow now my visits here.
    But once I knew each field, each flower,
      each stick;
    And with the country-folk acquaintance
      made
By barn in threshing-time, by new-built
    rick.
Here, too, our shepherd-pipes we first
    assayed.   35
      Ah me! this many a year
My pipe is lost, my shepherd's holiday!
    Needs must I lose them, needs with
      heavy heart
    Into the world and wave of men depart;
But Thyrsis of his own will went away. 40

It irked him to be here, he could not rest.[3]
    He loved each simple joy the country
      yields,
    He loved his mates; but yet he could not
      keep,
For that a shadow lowered on the fields,
    Here with the shepherds and the silly
      sheep.   45
      Some life of men unblest
He knew, which made him droop, and
    filled his head.
    He went; his piping took a troubled
      sound
    Of storms that rage outside our happy
      ground;   49
He could not wait their passing, he is dead.

So, some tempestuous morn in early June,
    When the year's primal burst of bloom is
      o'er,
    Before the roses and the longest day—
When garden-walks and all the grassy
    floor
    With blossoms red and white of fallen
      May   55
      And chestnut-flowers are strewn—

---

[1]Throughout this poem there is reference to the preceding piece, *The Scholar-Gypsy* (Arnold's note). The poem was published in 1867.

[2]Dams.

[3]Clough, who was, like Arnold, a Fellow of Oriel College, left Oxford in 1848, dissatisfied with his work there and uneasy, because of religious questionings, about professing conformity to the Anglican Church, as an Oxford tutor then had to do. He tried several other kinds of work in following years.

So have I heard the cuckoo's parting cry,
   From the wet field, through the vexed
      garden-trees,
   Come with the volleying rain and tossing
      breeze:
The bloom is gone, and with the bloom
      go I!   60

Too quick despairer, wherefore wilt thou go?
   Soon will the high Midsummer pomps
      come on,
   Soon will the musk carnations break and
      swell,
   Soon shall we have gold-dusted snap-
      dragon,
   Sweet-William with its homely cottage-
      smell,   65
      And stocks in fragrant blow;[4]
Roses that down the alleys shine afar,
   And open, jasmine-muffled lattices,
   And groups under the dreaming garden-
      trees,   •
   And the full moon, and the white evening-
      star.   70

He hearkens not! light comer, he is flown!
   What matters it? next year he will return,
      And we shall have him in the sweet
         spring-days,
   With whitening hedges, and uncrumpling
      fern,
   And blue-bells trembling by the forest-
      ways,   75
      And scent of hay new-mown.
   But Thyrsis never more we swains shall
      see;
      See him come back, and cut a smoother
         reed,
      And blow a strain the world at last shall
         heed—
   For Time, not Corydon, hath conquered
      thee.[5]   80

Alack, for Corydon no rival now!—
   But when Sicilian shepherds lost a mate,
      Some good survivor with his flute would
         go,
   Piping a ditty sad for Bion's[6] fate;
      And cross the unpermitted ferry's
         flow   85
      And relax Pluto's brow,

And make leap up with joy the beautous
      head
   Of Proserpine, among whose crownéd
      hair
   Are flowers first opened on Sicilian air,[7]
And flute his friend, like Orpheus, from
      the dead.   90

O easy access to the hearer's grace,
   When Dorian shepherds sang to Proser-
      pine!
   For she herself had trod Sicilian fields,
   She knew the Dorian water's gush divine,
      She knew each lily white which Enna
         yields,   95
      Each rose with blushing face;
   She loved the Dorian pipe, the Dorian
      strain.
   But ah, of our poor Thames she never
      heard!
   Her foot the Cumner cowslips never
      stirred;
   And we should tease her with our plaint in
      vain!   100

Well! wind-dispersed and vain the words will
      be,
   Yet, Thyrsis, let me give my grief its hour
      In the old haunt, and find our tree-
         topped hill!
   Who, if not I, for questing here hath
      power?
   I know the wood which hides the daf-
      fodil,   105
      I know the Fyfield tree,
 I know what white, what purple fritillaries[8]
   The grassy harvest of the river-fields,
   Above by Ensham, down by Sandford,
      yields,
   And what sedged brooks are Thames's trib-
      utaries;   110

I know these slopes; who knows them if not
      I?—
   But many a dingle on the loved hill-side,
      With thorns once studded, old, white-
         blossomed trees,
   Where thick the cowslips grew, and far
      descried
      High towered the spikes of purple or-
         chises,   115
      Hath since our day put by

---

[4] Bloom.

[5] Corydon is the winner in a verse-contest with Thyrsis in Virgil's *Eclogue* VII.

[6] Sicilian poet upon whose death Moschus wrote an elegy.

[7] Pluto carried off Proserpine, seizing her while she was gathering flowers at Enna in Sicily, to be his queen of the lower world.

[8] A bell-shaped flower which grows in fields bordering the Thames.

The coronals of that forgotten time,
Down each green bank hath gone the
plowboy's team,
And only in the hidden brookside gleam
Primroses, orphans of the flowery prime.[9]

Where is the girl, who by the boatman's
door,   121
Above the locks, above the boating throng,
Unmoored our skiff when through the
Wytham flats,
Red loosestrife[10] and blond meadow-sweet
among,
And darting swallows and light water-
gnats,   125
We tracked the shy Thames shore?
Where are the mowers, who, as the tiny
swell
Of our boat passing heaved the river-
grass,
Stood with suspended scythe to see us
pass?—
They all are gone, and thou art gone as
well!   130

Yes, thou art gone! and round me too the
night
In ever-nearing circle weaves her shade.
I see her veil draw soft across the day,
I feel her slowly chilling breath invade
The cheek grown thin, the brown hair
sprent[11] with gray;   135
I feel her finger light
Laid pausefully upon life's headlong
train;—
The foot less prompt to meet the morn-
ing dew,
The heart less bounding at emotion new,
And hope, once crushed, less quick to
spring again.   140

And long the way appears, which seemed so
short
To the less practiced eye of sanguine
youth;
And high the mountain-tops, in cloudy
air,
The mountain-tops where is the throne of
Truth,
Tops in life's morning-sun so bright and
bare!   145
Unbreachable the fort

Of the long-battered world uplifts its
wall;
And strange and vain the earthly turmoil grows,
And near and real the charm of thy repose,
And night as welcome as a friend would
fall.   150

But hush! the upland hath a sudden loss
Of quiet!—Look, adown the dusk hillside,
A troop of Oxford hunters going home,
As in old days, jovial and talking, ride!
From hunting with the Berkshire hounds
they come.   155
Quick! let me fly, and cross
Into yon farther field!—'Tis done; and see,
Backed by the sunset, which doth glorify
The orange and pale violet evening-sky,
Bare on its lonely ridge, the Tree! the
Tree!   160

I take the omen! Eve lets down her veil,
The white fog creeps from bush to bush
about,
The west unflushes, the high stars grow
bright,
And in the scattered farms the lights come
out.
I cannot reach the signal-tree to-night,
Yet, happy omen, hail!   166
Hear it from thy broad lucent Arno-vale[12]
(For there thine earth-forgetting eye-
lids keep
The morningless and unawakening sleep
Under the florey oleanders pale),   170

Hear it, O Thyrsis, still our tree is there!—
Ah, vain! These English fields, this up-
land dim,
These brambles pale with mist engar-
landed,
That lone, sky-pointing tree, are not for
him;
To a boon southern country he is fled,
And now in happier air,   176
Wandering with the great Mother's[13] train
divine
(And purer or more subtle soul than
thee,
I trow, the mighty Mother doth not see)
Within a folding of the Apennine,   180

<hr>

[9]Spring. [10]A flowering plant.
[11]Sprinkled.

[12]The Arno flows through Florence.
[13]Rhea, mother of the gods.

Thou hearest the immortal chants of old!—
  Putting his sickle to the perilous grain
    In the hot cornfield of the Phrygian
      king,
  For thee the Lityerses-song again
    Young Daphnis with his silver voice
      doth sing;[14]   185
      Sings his Sicilian fold,
  His sheep, his hapless love, his blinded
      eyes—
  And how a call celestial round him rang,
  And heavenward from the fountain-
      brink he sprang,
  And all the marvel of the golden skies. 190

There thou art gone, and me thou leavest
    here
  Sole in these fields! yet will I not despair.
  Despair I will not, while I yet descry
  'Neath the mild canopy of English air
    That lonely tree against the western sky.
      Still, still these slopes, 'tis clear, 196
  Our Gypsy-Scholar haunts, outliving thee!
    Fields where soft sheep from cages pull
      the hay,
    Woods with anemones in flower till
      May,
  Know him a wanderer still; then why not
    me? 200

A fugitive and gracious light he seeks,
  Shy to illumine; and I seek it too.
    This does not come with houses or with
      gold,
  With place, with honor, and a flattering
      crew;
  'Tis not in the world's market bought
    and sold— 205
      But the smooth-slipping weeks

[14]Daphnis, the ideal Sicilian shepherd of Greek pastoral poetry, was said to have followed into Phrygia his mistress Piplea, who had been carried off by robbers, and to have found her in the power of the king of Phrygia, Lityerses. Lityerses used to make strangers try a contest with him in reaping corn, and to put them to death if he overcame them. Hercules arrived in time to save Daphnis, took upon himself the reaping-contest with Lityerses, overcame him, and slew him. The Lityerses-song connected with this tradition was, like the Linus-song, one of the early plaintive strains of Greek popular poetry, and used to be sung by corn-reapers. Other traditions represented Daphnis as beloved by a nymph who exacted from him an oath to love no one else. He fell in love with a princess, and was struck blind by the jealous nymph. Mercury, who was his father, raised him to Heaven, and made a fountain spring up in the place from which he ascended. At this fountain the Sicilians offered yearly sacrifices (Arnold's note).

Drop by, and leave its seeker still untired;
  Out of the heed of mortals he is gone,
  He wends unfollowed, he must house
    alone; 209
  Yet on he fares, by his own heart inspired.

Thou too, O Thyrsis, on like quest wast
    bound;
  Thou wanderedst with me for a little hour!
    Men gave thee nothing; but this happy
      quest,
  If men esteemed thee feeble, gave thee
      power,
  If men procured thee trouble, gave thee
    rest. 215
      And this rude Cumner ground,
  Its fir-topped Hurst, its farms, its quiet
    fields,
  Here cam'st thou in thy jocund youthful
    time,
  Here was thine height of strength, thy
      golden prime! 219
  And still the haunt beloved a virtue yields.

What though the music of thy rustic flute
  Kept not for long its happy, country tone;
    Lost it too soon, and learned a stormy
      note
  Of men contention-tossed, of men who
      groan,
    Which tasked thy pipe too sore, and
      tired thy throat— 225
      It failed, and thou wast mute!
  Yet hadst thou alway visions of our light,
    And long with men of care thou couldst
      not stay,
    And soon thy foot resumed its wander-
      ing way, 229
  Left human haunt, and on alone till night.

Too rare, too rare, grow now my visits here!
  'Mid city-noise, not, as with thee of yore,
    Thyrsis! in reach of sheep-bells is my
      home.
  —Then through the great town's harsh,
      heart-wearying roar,
    Let in thy voice a whisper often come,
      To chase fatigue and fear: 236
Why faintest thou? I wandered till I died.
Roam on! The light we sought is shin-
    ing still.
    Dost thou ask proof? Our tree yet
      crowns the hill, 239
Our Scholar travels yet the loved hill-side.

RUGBY CHAPEL [1]
November, 1857

Coldly, sadly descends
The autumn-evening.   The field
Strewn with its dank yellow drifts
Of withered leaves, and the elms,
Fade into dimness apace,   5
Silent;—hardly a shout
From a few boys late at their play!
The lights come out in the street,
In the school-room windows;—but cold,
Solemn, unlighted, austere,   10
Through the gathering darkness, arise
The chapel-walls, in whose bound
Thou, my father! art laid.

There thou dost lie, in the gloom
Of the autumn evening.   But ah!   15
That word, *gloom,* to my mind
Brings thee back, in the light
Of thy radiant vigor, again;
In the gloom of November we passed
Days not dark at thy side;   20
Seasons impaired not the ray
Of thy buoyant cheerfulness clear.
Such thou wast! and I stand
In the autumn evening, and think
Of bygone autumns with thee.   25

Fifteen years have gone round
Since thou arosest to tread,
In the summer-morning, the road
Of death, at a call unforeseen,
Sudden.   For fifteen years,   30
We who till then in thy shade
Rested as under the boughs
Of a mighty oak, have endured
Sunshine and rain as we might,
Bare, unshaded, alone,   35
Lacking the shelter of thee.

O strong soul, by what shore
Tarriest thou now? For that force,
Surely, has not been left vain!
Somewhere, surely, afar,   40
In the sounding labor-house vast
Of being, is practiced that strength,
Zealous, beneficent, firm!

Yes, in some far-shining sphere,
Conscious or not of the past,   45
Still thou performest the word
Of the Spirit in whom thou dost live—

Prompt, unwearied, as here!
Still thou upraisest with zeal
The humble good from the ground,   50
Sternly repressest the bad!
Still, like a trumpet, dost rouse
Those who with half-open eyes
Tread the border-land dim
'Twixt vice and virtue; reviv'st,   55
Succorest!—this was thy work,
This was thy life upon earth.

What is the course of the life
Of mortal men on the earth?—
Most men eddy about   60
Here and there—eat and drink,
Chatter and love and hate,
Gather and squander, are raised
Aloft, are hurled in the dust,
Striving blindly, achieving   65
Nothing; and then they die—
Perish;—and no one asks
Who or what they have been,
More than he asks what waves,
In the moonlit solitudes mild   70
Of the midmost Ocean, have swelled,
Foamed for a moment, and gone.

And there are some, whom a thirst
Ardent, unquenchable, fires,
Not with the crowd to be spent,   75
Not without aim to go round
In an eddy of purposeless dust,
Effort unmeaning and vain.
Ah yes! some of us strive
Not without action to die   80
Fruitless, but something to snatch
From dull oblivion, nor all
Glut the devouring grave!
We, we have chosen our path—
Path to a clear-purposed goal,   85
Path of advance!—but it leads
A long, steep journey, through sunk
Gorges, o'er mountains in snow.
Cheerful, with friends, we set forth—
Then, on the height, comes the storm.   90
Thunder crashes from rock
To rock, the cataracts reply,
Lightnings dazzle our eyes.
Roaring torrents have breached
The track, the stream-bed descends   95
In the place where the wayfarer once
Planted his footstep—the spray
Boils o'er its borders! aloft
The unseen snow-beds dislodge

[1]Published in 1867. Arnold's father, Thomas Arnold, died on 12 June, 1842, and was buried in Rugby Chapel.

Their hanging ruin; alas,   100
Havoc is made in our train!
Friends, who set forth at our side,
Falter, are lost in the storm.
We, we only are left!
With frowning foreheads, with lips   105
Sternly compressed, we strain on,
On—and at nightfall at last
Come to the end of our way,
To the lonely inn 'mid the rocks;
Where the gaunt and taciturn host   110
Stands on the threshold, the wind
Shaking his thin white hairs—
Holds his lantern to scan
Our storm-beat figures, and asks:
Whom in our party we bring?   115
Whom we have left in the snow?

Sadly we answer: We bring
Only ourselves! we lost
Sight of the rest in the storm.
Hardly ourselves we fought through,   120
Stripped, without friends, as we are.
Friends, companions, and train,
The avalanche swept from our side.

But thou wouldst not *alone*
Be saved, my father! *alone*   125
Conquer and come to thy goal,
Leaving the rest in the wild.
We were weary, and we
Fearful, and we in our march
Fain to drop down and to die.   130
Still thou turnedst, and still
Beckonedst the trembler, and still
Gavest the weary thy hand.

If, in the paths of the world,
Stones might have wounded thy feet,   135
Toil or dejection have tried
Thy spirit, of that we saw
Nothing—to us thou wast still
Cheerful, and helpful, and firm!
Therefore to thee it was given   140
Many to save with thyself;
And, at the end of thy day,
O faithful shepherd! to come,
Bringing thy sheep in thy hand.

And through thee I believe   145
In the noble and great who are gone;
Pure souls honored and blest
By former ages, who else—
Such, so soulless, so poor,
Is the race of men whom I see—   150
Seemed but a dream of the heart,
Seemed but a cry of desire.
Yes! I believe that there lived

Others like thee in the past,
Not like the men of the crowd   155
Who all round me to-day
Bluster or cringe, and make life
Hideous, and arid, and vile;
But souls tempered with fire,
Fervent, heroic, and good,   160
Helpers and friends of mankind.

Servants of God!—or sons
Shall I not call you? because
Not as servants ye knew
Your Father's innermost mind,   165
His, who unwillingly sees
One of his little ones lost—
Yours is the praise, if mankind
Hath not as yet in its march
Fainted, and fallen, and died!   170

See! In the rocks of the world
Marches the host of mankind,
A feeble, wavering line.
Where are they tending?—A God
Marshaled them, gave them their goal.   175
Ah, but the way is so long!
Years they have been in the wild!
Sore thirst plagues them; the rocks,
Rising all round, overawe;
Factions divide them, their host   180
Theatens to break, to dissolve.
—Ah! keep, keep them combined!
Else, of the myriads who fill
That army, not one shall arrive;
Sole they shall stray; in the rocks   185
Stagger for ever in vain,
Die one by one in the waste.

Then, in such hour of need
Of your fainting, dispirited race,
Ye, like angels, appear,   190
Radiant with ardor divine!
Beacons of hope, ye appear!
Languor is not in your heart,
Weakness is not in your word,
Weariness not on your brow.   195
Ye alight in our van! at your voice,
Panic, despair, flee away.
Ye move through the ranks, recall
The stragglers, refresh the outworn,
Praise, re-inspire the brave!   200
Order, courage, return.
Eyes rekindling, and prayers,
Follow your steps as ye go.
Ye fill up the gaps in our files,
Strengthen the wavering line,   205
Stablish, continue our march,
On, to the bound of the waste,
On, to the City of God.

STANZAS FROM THE GRANDE CHARTREUSE[1]

Through Alpine meadows soft-suffused
With rain, where thick the crocus blows,
Past the dark forges long disused,
The mule-track from Saint Laurent goes.
The bridge is crossed, and slow we ride, 5
Through forest, up the mountain-side.

The autumnal evening darkens round,
The wind is up, and drives the rain;
While, hark! far down, with strangled sound
Doth the Dead Guier's stream complain 10
Where that wet smoke, among the woods,
Over his boiling caldron broods.

Swift rush the spectral vapors white
Past limestone scars with ragged pines,
Showing—then blotting from our sight!—
Halt—through the cloud-drift something
    shines! 16
High in the valley, wet and drear,
The huts of Courrerie appear.

Strike leftward! cries our guide; and higher
Mounts up the stony forest-way. 20
At last the encircling trees retire;
Look! through the showery twilight gray
What pointed roofs are these advance?—
A palace of the Kings of France?

Approach, for what we seek is here!
Alight, and sparely sup, and wait 25
For rest in this outbuilding near;
Then cross the sward and reach that gate.
Knock; pass the wicket!   Thou art come
To the Carthusians' world-famed home. 30

The silent courts, where night and day
Into their stone-carved basins cold
The splashing icy fountains play—
The humid corridors behold!
Where, ghostlike in the deepening night, 35
Cowled forms brush by in gleaming white.

The chapel, where no organ's peal
Invests the stern and naked prayer—
With penitential cries they kneel
And wrestle; rising then, with bare 40
And white uplifted faces stand,
Passing the Host from hand to hand;

Each takes, and then his visage wan
Is buried in his cowl once more.

The cells!—the suffering Son of Man 45
Upon the wall—the knee-worn floor—
And where they sleep, that wooden bed,
Which shall their coffin be, when dead!

The library, where tract and tome
Not to feed priestly pride are there, 50
To hymn the conquering march of Rome,
Nor yet to amuse, as ours are!
They paint of souls the inner strife,
Their drops of blood, their death in life.

The garden, overgrown—yet mild, 55
See, fragrant herbs are flowering there!
Strong children of the Alpine wild
Whose culture is the brethren's care;
Of human tasks their only one,
And cheerful works beneath the sun. 60

Those halls, too, destined to contain
Each its own pilgrim-host of old,[2]
From England, Germany, or Spain—
All are before me!   I behold
The House, the Brotherhood austere! 65
—And what am I, that I am here?

For rigorous teachers seized my youth,
And purged its faith, and trimmed its fire,
Showed me the high, white star of Truth,
There bade me gaze, and there aspire. 70
Even now their whispers pierce the gloom:
What dost thou in this living tomb?

Forgive me, masters of the mind!
At whose behest I long ago
So much unlearned, so much resigned— 75
I come not here to be your foe!
I seek these anchorites, not in ruth,
To curse and to deny your truth;

Not as their friend, or child, I speak!
But as, on some far northern strand, 80
Thinking of his own Gods, a Greek
In pity and mournful awe might stand
Before some fallen Runic stone—
For both were faiths, and both are gone.

Wandering between two worlds, one dead, 85
The other powerless to be born,
With nowhere yet to rest my head,
Like these, on earth I wait forlorn.
Their faith, my tears, the world deride—
I come to shed them at their side. 90

---

[1] Published in 1855. The Grande Chartreuse is the chief monastery of the Carthusian monks, founded in the eleventh century.   It is situated in the Alps of southeastern France.

[2] Carthusian monks on pilgrimage.

Oh, hide me in your gloom profound,
Ye solemn seats of holy pain!
Take me, cowled forms, and fence me round,
Till I possess my soul again;
Till free my thoughts before me roll,   95
Not chafed by hourly false control!

For the world cries your faith is now
But a dead time's exploded dream;
My melancholy, sciolists[3] say,
Is a passed mode, an outworn theme—   100
As if the world had ever had
A faith, or sciolists been sad!

Ah, if it *be* passed, take away,
At least, the restlessness, the pain;
Be man henceforth no more a prey   105
To these out-dated stings again!
The nobleness of grief is gone—
Ah, leave us not the fret alone!

But—if you cannot give us ease—
Last of the race of them who grieve   110
Here leave us to die out with these
Last of the people who believe!
Silent, while years engrave the brow;
Silent—the best are silent now.

Achilles ponders in his tent,[4]   115
The kings of modern thought are dumb;
Silent they are, though not content,
And wait to see the future come.
They have the grief men had of yore,
But they contend and cry no more.   120

Our fathers watered with their tears
This sea of time whereon we sail,
Their voices were in all men's ears
Who passed within their puissant hail.
Still the same ocean round us raves,   125
But we stand mute, and watch the waves.

For what availed it, all the noise
And outcry of the former men?—
Say, have their sons achieved more joys,
Say, is life lighter now than then?   130
The sufferers died, they left their pain—
The pangs which tortured them remain.

What helps it now, that Byron bore,
With haughty scorn which mocked the smart,
Through Europe to the Aetolian shore[5]   135
The pageant of his bleeding heart?
That thousands counted every groan,
And Europe made his woe her own?

What boots it, Shelley! that the breeze
Carried thy lovely wail away,   140
Musical through Italian trees
Which fringe thy soft blue Speezian bay?[6]
Inheritors of thy distress
Have restless hearts one throb the less?

Or are we easier, to have read,   145
O Obermann![7] the sad, stern page,
Which tells us how thou hidd'st thy head
From the fierce tempest of thine age
In the lone brakes of Fontainebleau,
Or chalets near the Alpine snow?   150

Ye slumber in your silent grave!—
The world, which for an idle day
Grace to your mood of sadness gave,
Long since hath flung her weeds away.
The eternal trifler breaks your spell;   155
But we—we learned your lore too well!

Years hence, perhaps, may dawn an age,
More fortunate, alas! than we,
Which without hardness will be sage,
And gay without frivolity.   160
Sons of the world, oh, speed those years;
But, while we wait, allow our tears!

Allow them!   We admire with awe
The exulting thunder of your race;
You give the universe your law,   165
You triumph over time and space!
Your pride of life, your tireless powers,
We laud them, but they are not ours.

We are like children reared in shade
Beneath some old-world abbey wall,   170
Forgotten in a forest-glade,
And secret from the eyes of all.
Deep, deep the greenwood round them waves,
Their abbey, and its close[8] of graves!

But, where the road runs near the stream,   175
Oft through the trees they catch a glance
Of passing troops in the sun's beam—
Pennon, and plume, and flashing lance!
Forth to the world those soldiers fare,
To life, to cities, and to war!   180

And through the wood, another way,
Faint bugle-notes from far are borne,
Where hunters gather, staghounds bay,
Round some fair forest-lodge at morn.
Gay dames are there, in sylvan green;   185
Laughter and cries—those notes between!

[6]Shelley's last days were spent on the shores of the Gulf of Spezzia, in northwestern Italy.
[7]Étienne Pivert de Senancour (1770–1846), whose book is entitled *Obermann*.
[8]Enclosed plot.

[3]Smatterers.   [4]*Iliad,* Bk. I.   [5]Grecian shore.

The banners flashing through the trees
Make their blood dance and chain their eyes,
That bugle-music on the breeze
Arrests them with a charmed surprise. 190
Banner by turns and bugle woo:
Ye shy recluses, follow too!

O children, what do ye reply?—
"Action and pleasure, will ye roam
Through these secluded dells to cry 195
And call us?—but too late ye come!
Too late for us your call ye blow,
Whose bent was taken long ago.

"Long since we pace this shadowed nave;
We watch those yellow tapers shine, 200
Emblems of hope over the grave,
In the high altar's depth divine;
The organ carries to our ear
Its accents of another sphere.

"Fenced early in this cloistral round 205
Of reverie, of shade, of prayer,
How should we grow in other ground?
How can we flower in foreign air?
—Pass, banners, pass, and bugles, cease;
And leave our desert to its peace!" 210

DANTE GABRIEL ROSSETTI

1828–1882

Rossetti was the eldest son of Gabriele Rossetti and Mary Lavinia Polidori, and was born in London on 12 May, 1828. Gabriele was a native of the Kingdom of Naples, where he had been Curator of Antiquities in the Naples Museum, but he had had to flee from that country because of his share in the insurrectionary movements of 1820 and 1821. He had come to England in 1824, where he was for many years Professor of Italian in King's College, London. The environment of his home early stimulated Dante Gabriel Rossetti's powers, and he was writing poetry at the age of five or six. At nine he began attending lectures at King's College, where he remained until he was fourteen. This was the extent of his formal education, though extensive reading done at home was of great importance in his development. When he left King's College in 1842 he determined that painting was to be his profession, and for the next six years he studied drawing at Cary's Drawing Academy and in the antique class of the Royal Academy. In this work he did not make remarkable progress, partly because then, as later, he was impatient for great results and tended to neglect the slow and tiresome drudgery necessary for a thorough foundation in drawing. He also began in this period the writing of poetry, some of his translations from Dante and his contemporaries being made as early as 1845, and several of his most remarkable poems, notably *The Blessed Damozel,* being written about 1847. In 1848 Rossetti applied to Ford Madox Brown for instruction, and this proved a momentous step. Through Brown he was introduced to a group of young men who were feeling their way to a new movement in art, resolving to abandon the conventionalities inherited from the eighteenth century and to revive the detailed elaboration and mystical interpretation of nature that characterized early medieval art. The best known of these are Woolner, Holman Hunt, and Millais, and they formed themselves, with Brown, Rossetti, and others, into the so-called Pre-Raphaelite Brotherhood. The literary mani-

festo of the group was the *Germ,* four numbers of which appeared in 1850 under the editorship of William Michael Rossetti, a younger brother of Dante Gabriel. In this *The Blessed Damozel* was printed, as was also *Hand and Soul,* the only imaginative work in prose which D. G. Rossetti ever completed. About this time he fell in love with Elizabeth Eleanor Siddal, a milliner's assistant who was the daughter of a Sheffield cutler. He became engaged to her probably in 1851, and she served then and later as a model for many of his pictures; but he did not marry her until May, 1860, both because of his scanty means and because of her uncertain, delicate health. For several years his income was increased by Ruskin, who not only defended the aims of the Pre-Raphaelite painters but made an arrangement, which lasted until after 1861, to purchase Rossetti's pictures. Ruskin also stood the expense of the publication of Rossetti's translations from the *Early Italian Poets* (in later editions entitled *Dante and His Circle*) in 1861. Another friend who was at this time useful to him was Sir Edward Burne-Jones, who introduced him to Swinburne, William Morris, and others, at Oxford.

When Rossetti married in 1860 it was obvious that his wife could not live long, because of the consumption which had attacked her. She died, however, even sooner than anyone expected, in February, 1862, from an overdose of laudanum taken to relieve neuralgia. Rossetti characteristically expressed his grief by burying with her the manuscripts of his unpublished poems. And there they remained until the fall of 1869, when he consented to their disinterment. His *Collected Poems* were published in the following year and immediately secured for him a great reputation. The remainder of his life, however, was a prolonged tragedy, owing to his addiction to the habit of taking chloral. This, in combination with his weak health, produced mental aberrations which made his life painful both to himself and to his friends. He continued at times, nevertheless, his work as a painter, and in the last years of his life wrote two of his greatest poems, the *White Ship* and the *King's Tragedy*. These and other poems were published under the title *Ballads and Sonnets* in 1881. In the following year he died at Birchington, near Margate, on 10 April.

Rossetti was, as Ruskin said, "the chief intellectual force in the establishment of the Modern Romantic School in England." This he was, alike in the fine arts and in poetry. In the latter his chief followers were William Morris and Swinburne. This school voiced a reaction in its own lesser, sensuous way from the materialism and ugliness of the growing industrial civilization of England, just as the earlier romantic writers of the beginning of the century had reacted against the skeptical rationalism of the eighteenth century.

The standard edition of Rossetti's *Works* is edited by William Michael Rossetti (London, 1911; this is a revised and enlarged edition in one volume, superseding the *Collected Works* in two volumes, ed. W. M. R., 1886). All of the poems published in Rossetti's life-time, together with selections from his posthumously published verse and his translations, and *Hand and Soul* have been excellently edited by Paull F. Baum in a volume in the "Doubleday-Doran Series in Literature" (1937). The standard biography is *Dante Gabriel Rossetti: His Family Letters, with a Memoir*, by W. M. Rossetti (2 vols., London, 1895; Vol. I contains the *Memoir*, Vol. II the *Letters*). A. C. Benson's *Rossetti* ("English Men of Letters" series, 1904) is a very good short life; more recent is Evelyn Waugh's *Rossetti: His Life and Works* (London, 1928). H. C. Marillier's *Dante Gabriel Rossetti: An Illustrated Memorial of His Life and Art* (London, 1899) is indispensable for the study of Rossetti's drawings and paintings. A. C. Swinburne's essay on Rossetti's poems is to be found in his *Essays and Studies* (London, 1875); and there is an essay by Walter Pater in *Appreciations* (London, 1889). Robert Buchanan's provocative attack on Rossetti, *The Fleshly School of Poetry and Other Phenomena of the Day* (London, 1872), has been reprinted in Albert Mordell's *Notorious Literary Attacks* (New York, 1926).

SISTER HELEN[1]

"Why did you melt your waxen man,
　　　　Sister Helen?
To-day is the third since you began."
"The time was long, yet the time ran,
　　　　Little brother."　　　　5
　　　(*O Mother, Mary Mother,*
Three days to-day, between Hell and Heaven!)

"But if you have done your work aright,
　　　　Sister Helen,
You'll let me play, for you said I might." 10
"Be very still in your play to-night,
　　　　Little brother."
　　　(*O Mother, Mary Mother,*
Third night, to-night, between Hell and Heaven!)

"You said it must melt ere vesper-bell, 15
　　　　Sister Helen;
If now it be molten, all is well."
"Even so,—nay, peace! you cannot tell,
　　　　Little brother."
　　　(*O Mother, Mary Mother,*　　20
O what is this, between Hell and Heaven?)

"Oh the waxen knave was plump to-day,
　　　　Sister Helen;
How like dead folk he has dropped away!"
"Nay now, of the dead what can you say, 25
　　　　Little brother?"
　　　(*O Mother, Mary Mother,*
What of the dead, between Hell and Heaven?)

"See, see, the sunken pile of wood,
　　　　Sister Helen,　　　　30
Shines through the thinned wax red as blood!"
"Nay now, when looked you yet on blood,
　　　　Little brother?"
　　　(*O Mother, Mary Mother,*　　34
How pale she is, between Hell and Heaven!)

"Now close your eyes, for they're sick and sore,
　　　　Sister Helen,
And I'll play without the gallery door."
"Aye, let me rest,—I'll lie on the floor,
　　　　Little brother."　　　　40
　　　(*O Mother, Mary Mother,*
What rest to-night, between Hell and Heaven?)

---

[1] Published in 1853. The poem is founded on the belief, long and widely held, that if a wax or clay image were roasted the person whose name it bore would be melted or dried away by continual sickness.

"Here high up in the balcony,
        Sister Helen,
The moon flies face to face with me." 45
"Aye, look and say whatever you see,
        Little brother."
      (*O Mother, Mary Mother,*
What sight to-night, between Hell and
    Heaven?)

"Outside it's merry in the wind's wake, 50
        Sister Helen;
In the shaken trees the chill stars shake."
"Hush, heard you a horse-tread, as you
    spake,
        Little brother?"
      (*O Mother, Mary Mother,* 55
What sound to-night, between Hell and
    Heaven?)

"I hear a horse-tread, and I see,
        Sister Helen,
Three horsemen that ride terribly."
"Little brother, whence come the three, 60
        Little brother?"
      (*O Mother, Mary Mother,*
Whence should they come, between Hell and
    Heaven?)

"They come by the hill-verge from Boyne
    Bar,
        Sister Helen, 65
And one draws nigh, but two are afar."
"Look, look, do you know them who they are,
        Little brother?"
      (*O Mother, Mary Mother,*
Who should they be between Hell and
    Heaven?) 70

"Oh, it's Keith of Eastholm rides so fast,
        Sister Helen,
For I know the white mane on the blast."
"The hour has come, has come at last,
        Little brother!" 75
      (*O Mother, Mary Mother,*
Her hour at last, between Hell and Heaven!)

"He has made a sign and called Halloo!
        Sister Helen,
And he says that he would speak with you."
"Oh tell him I fear the frozen dew, 81
        Little brother."
      (*O Mother, Mary Mother,*
Why laughs she thus, between Hell and
    Heaven?)

"The wind is loud, but I hear him cry, 85
        Sister Helen,
That Keith of Ewern's like to die."
"And he and thou, and thou and I,
        Little brother."
      (*O Mother, Mary Mother,* 90
And they and we, between Hell and
    Heaven!)

"Three days ago, on his marriage-morn,
        Sister Helen,
He sickened, and lies since then forlorn."
"For bridegroom's side is the bride a thorn,
        Little brother?" 96
      (*O Mother, Mary Mother,*
Cold bridal cheer, between Hell and
    Heaven!)

"Three days and nights he has lain abed,
        Sister Helen, 100
And he prays in torment to be dead."
"The thing may chance, if he have prayed,
        Little brother!"
      (*O Mother, Mary Mother,*
If he have prayed, between Hell and
    Heaven!) 105

"But he has not ceased to cry to-day,
        Sister Helen,
That you should take your curse away."
"*My* prayer was heard,—he need but pray,
        Little brother!" 110
      (*O Mother, Mary Mother,*
Shall God not hear, between Hell and
    Heaven?)

"But he says, till you take back your ban,[2]
        Sister Helen,
His soul would pass, yet never can." 115
"Nay then, shall I slay a living man,
        Little brother?"
      (*O Mother, Mary Mother,*
A living soul, between Hell and Heaven!)

"But he calls for ever on your name, 120
        Sister Helen,
And says that he melts before a flame."
"My heart for his pleasure fared the same,
        Little brother."
      (*O Mother, Mary Mother,* 125
Fire at the heart, between Hell and Heaven!)

---

[2] Curse.

"Here's Keith of Westholm riding fast,
        Sister Helen,
For I know the white plume on the blast."
"The hour, the sweet hour I forecast, 130
        Little brother!"
    (*O Mother, Mary Mother,*
Is the hour sweet, between Hell and
Heaven?)

"He stops to speak, and he stills his horse,
        Sister Helen; 135
But his words are drowned in the wind's
    course."
"Nay hear, nay hear, you must hear perforce,
        Little brother!"
    (*O Mother, Mary Mother,*
What word now heard, between Hell and
Heaven?) 140

"Oh he says that Keith of Ewern's cry,
        Sister Helen,
Is ever to see you ere he die."
"In all that his soul sees, there am I,
        Little brother!" 145
    (*O Mother, Mary Mother,*
The soul's one sight, between Hell and
Heaven!)

"He sends a ring and a broken coin,[3]
        Sister Helen,
And bids you mind the banks of Boyne." 150
"What else he broke will he ever join,
        Little brother?"
    (*O Mother, Mary Mother,*
No, never joined, between Hell and
Heaven!)

"He yields you these and craves full fain, 155
        Sister Helen,
You pardon him in his mortal pain."
"What else he took will he give again,
        Little brother?"
    (*O Mother, Mary Mother,* 160
Not twice to give, between Hell and
Heaven!)

"He calls your name in an agony,
        Sister Helen,
That even dead Love must weep to see."
"Hate, born of Love, is blind as he, 165
        Little brother!"
    (*O Mother, Mary Mother,*
Love turned to hate, between Hell and
Heaven!)

---

[3]The two had broken a coin, each keeping half as
a pledge.

"Oh it's Keith of Keith now that rides fast,
        Sister Helen, 170
For I know the white hair on the blast."
"The short short hour will soon be past,
        Little brother!"
    (*O Mother, Mary Mother,*
Will soon be past, between Hell and
Heaven!) 175

"He looks at me and he tries to speak,
        Sister Helen,
But oh! his voice is sad and weak!"
"What here should the mighty Baron seek,
        Little brother?" 180
    (*O Mother, Mary Mother,*
Is this the end, between Hell and Heaven?)

"Oh his son still cries, if you forgive,
        Sister Helen,
The body dies but the soul shall live." 185
"Fire shall forgive me as I forgive,
        Little brother!"
    (*O Mother, Mary Mother,*
As she forgives, between Hell and Heaven!)

"Oh he prays you, as his heart would rive, 190
        Sister Helen,
To save his dear son's soul alive."
"Fire cannot slay it, it shall thrive,
        Little brother!"
    (*O Mother, Mary Mother,* 195
Alas, alas, between Hell and Heaven!)

"He cries to you, kneeling in the road,
        Sister Helen,
To go with him for the love of God!"
"The way is long to his son's abode, 200
        Little brother."
    (*O Mother, Mary Mother,*
The way is long, between Hell and
Heaven!)

"A lady's here, by a dark steed brought,
        Sister Helen, 205
So darkly clad, I saw her not."
"See her now or never see aught,
        Little brother!"
    (*O Mother, Mary Mother,*
What more to see, between Hell and
Heaven?) 210

"Her hood falls back, and the moon shines
    fair,
        Sister Helen,
On the Lady of Ewern's golden hair."

"Blest hour of my power and her despair,
   Little brother!" 215
  (*O Mother, Mary Mother,*
Hour blest and banned, between Hell and
Heaven!)

"Pale, pale her cheeks, that in pride did glow,
   Sister Helen,
'Neath the bridal-wreath three days ago." 220
"One morn for pride and three days for woe,
   Little brother!"
  (*O Mother, Mary Mother,*
Three days, three nights, between Hell and
Heaven!)

"Her clasped hands stretch from her bending
  head, 225
   Sister Helen;
With the loud wind's wail her sobs are wed."
"What wedding-strains hath her bridal-bed,
   Little brother?"
  (*O Mother, Mary Mother,* 230
What strain but death's, between Hell and
Heaven!)

"She may not speak, she sinks in a swoon,
   Sister Helen,—
She lifts her lips and gasps on the moon."
"Oh! might I but hear her soul's blithe tune,
   Little brother!" 236
  (*O Mother, Mary Mother,*
Her woe's dumb cry, between Hell and
Heaven!)

"They've caught her to Westholm's saddle-
  bow,
   Sister Helen, 240
And her moonlit hair gleams white in its
  flow."
"Let it turn whiter than winter snow,
   Little brother!"
  (*O Mother, Mary Mother,*
Woe-withered gold, between Hell and
Heaven!) 245

"O Sister Helen, you heard the bell,
   Sister Helen!
More loud than the vesper-chime it fell."
"No vesper-chime, but a dying knell,
   Little brother!" 250
  (*O Mother, Mary Mother,*
His dying knell, between Hell and Heaven!)

"Alas! but I fear the heavy sound,
   Sister Helen;
Is it in the sky or in the ground?" 255
"Say, have they turned their horses round,
   Little brother?"
  (*O Mother, Mary Mother,*
What would she more, between Hell and
Heaven?)

"They have raised the old man from his knee,
   Sister Helen, 261
And they ride in silence hastily."
"More fast the naked soul doth flee,
   Little brother!"
  (*O Mother, Mary Mother,* 265
The naked soul, between Hell and Heaven!)

"Flank to flank are the three steeds gone,
   Sister Helen,
But the lady's dark steed goes alone."
"And lonely her bridegroom's soul hath
  flown, 270
   Little brother."
  (*O Mother, Mary Mother,*
The lonely ghost, between Hell and
Heaven!)

"Oh the wind is sad in the iron chill,
   Sister Helen, 275
And weary sad they look by the hill."
"But he and I are sadder still,
   Little brother!"
  (*O Mother, Mary Mother,* 279
Most sad of all, between Hell and Heaven!)

"See, see, the wax has dropped from its
  place,
   Sister Helen,
And the flames are winning up apace!"
"Yet here they burn but for a space,
   Little brother!" 285
  (*O Mother, Mary Mother,*
Here for a space, between Hell and
Heaven!)

"Ah! what white thing at the door has
  crossed,
   Sister Helen?
Ah! what is this that sighs in the frost?" 290
"A soul that's lost as mine is lost,
   Little brother!"
  (*O Mother, Mary Mother,*
Lost, lost, all lost, between Hell and
Heaven!)

THE HOUSE OF LIFE[1]
A Sonnet-Sequence

A sonnet is a moment's monument,—
  Memorial from the Soul's eternity
  To one dead deathless hour.   Look that it
    be,
Whether for lustral rite or dire portent,
Of its own arduous fullness reverent: 5
  Carve it in ivory or in ebony,
  As Day or Night may rule; and let Time
    see
Its flowering crest impearled and orient.

A Sonnet is a coin: its face reveals
  The soul,—its converse, to what Power 'tis
    due :—   10
Whether for tribute to the august appeals
  Of Life, or dower in Love's high retinue,
It serve; or, 'mid the dark wharf's cavernous
    breath,
In Charon's[2] palm it pay the toll to Death.

PART I—YOUTH AND CHANGE
4. *Lovesight*

When do I see thee most, belovéd one?
  When in the light the spirits of mine eyes
  Before thy face, their altar, solemnize
The worship of that Love through thee made
    known?
Or when in the dusk hours (we two alone),   5
  Close-kissed and eloquent of still replies
  Thy twilight-hidden glimmering visage
    lies,
And my soul only sees thy soul its own?

O love, my love! if I no more should see   9
Thyself, nor on the earth the shadow of thee,
  Nor image of thine eyes in any spring,—
How then should sound upon Life's darken-
    ing slope
The ground-whirl of the perished leaves of
    Hope,
  The wind of Death's imperishable wing?

5. *Heart's Hope*

By what word's power, the key of paths un-
    trod,
  Shall I the difficult deeps of Love explore,
  Till parted waves of Song yield up the
    shore
Even as that sea which Israel crossed dry-
    shod?[3]
For lo! in some poor rhythmic period,   5
  Lady, I fain would tell how evermore
  Thy soul I know not from thy body, nor
Thee from myself, neither our love from
    God.

Yea, in God's name, and Love's, and thine,
    would I
Draw from one loving heart such evidence
As to all hearts all things shall signify;   11
  Tender as dawn's first hill-fire, and intense
  As instantaneous penetrating sense,
In Spring's birth-hour, of other Springs gone
    by.

19. *Silent Noon*

Your hands lie open in the long fresh
    grass,—
  The finger-points look through like rosy
    blooms:
  Your eyes smile peace. The pasture
    gleams and glooms
'Neath billowing skies that scatter and amass.
All round our nest, far as the eye can pass, 5
  Are golden kingcup-fields with silver edge
  Where the cow-parsley skirts the haw-
    thorn-hedge.
'Tis visible silence, still as the hour-glass.

Deep in the sun-searched growths the dragon-
    fly
Hangs like a blue thread loosened from the
    sky;—   10
  So this winged hour is dropped to us from
    above.
Oh! clasp we to our hearts, for deathless
    dower,
This close-companioned inarticulate hour
  When twofold silence was the song of love.

---

[1] Published in its final form in 1881. Rossetti began writing the sonnets as early as 1848. They
were chiefly inspired by Elizabeth Siddal. The title
of the sequence was drawn from the astrological
division of the heavens into twelve "houses," the
first and greatest of which was the "house of life."

[2] The ferryman of the lower world, who for a
coin conveyed the souls of the dead across the rivers
Styx and Acheron.

[3] Exodus, 14:15–31.

21. *Love-Sweetness*

Sweet dimness of her loosened hair's down-
    fall
  About thy face; her sweet hands round thy
    head
  In gracious fostering union garlanded;
Her tremulous smiles; her glances' sweet re-
    call
Of love; her murmuring sighs memorial;   5
  Her mouth's culled sweetness by thy kisses
    shed
  On cheeks and neck and eyelids, and so led
Back to her mouth which answers there for
    all :—

What sweeter than these things, except the
    thing
  In lacking which all these would lose their
    sweet :—   10
  The confident heart's still fervor: the
    swift beat
And soft subsidence of the spirit's wing,
Then when it feels, in cloud-girt wayfaring,
  The breath of kindred plumes against its
    feet?

22. *Heart's Haven*

Sometimes she is a child within mine arms,
  Cowering beneath dark wings that love
    must chase,—
  With still tears showering and averted
    face,
Inexplicably filled with faint alarms:
And oft from mine own spirit's hurtling
    harms   5
  I crave the refuge of her deep embrace,—
  Against all ills the fortified strong place
And sweet reserve of sovereign counter-
    charms.

And Love, our light at night and shade at
    noon,   9
  Lulls us to rest with songs, and turns away
  All shafts of shelterless tumultuous day.
Like the moon's growth, his face gleams
    through his tune;
And as soft waters warble to the moon,
  Our answering spirits chime one rounde-
    lay.

25. *Winged Hours*

Each hour until we meet is as a bird
  That wings from far his gradual way along
  The rustling covert of my soul,—his song
Still loudlier trilled through leaves more
    deeply stirred:

But at the hour of meeting, a clear word   5
  Is every note he sings, in Love's own
    tongue;
  Yet, Love, thou know'st the sweet strain
    suffers wrong,
Full oft through our contending joys un-
    heard.

What of that hour at last, when for her sake
  No wing may fly to me nor song may flow;
  When, wandering round my life unleaved,
    I know   11
The bloodied feathers scattered in the brake,[4]
And think how she, far from me, with like
    eyes
Sees through the untuneful bough the wing-
    less skies?

26. *Mid-Rapture*

Thou lovely and beloved, thou my love;
  Whose kiss seems still the first; whose
    summoning eyes,
  Even now, as for our love-world's new
    sunrise,
Shed very dawn; whose voice, attuned above
All modulation of the deep-bowered dove,   5
  Is like a hand laid softly on the soul;
  Whose hand is like a sweet voice to control
Those worn tired brows it hath the keeping
    of :—

What word can answer to thy word,—what
    gaze
  To thine, which now absorbs within its
    sphere   10
  My worshiping face, till I am mirrored
    there
Light-circled in a heaven of deep-drawn
    rays?
What clasp, what kiss mine inmost heart can
    prove,
O lovely and belovéd, O my love?

27. *Heart's Compass*

Sometimes thou seem'st not as thyself alone,
  But as the meaning of all things that are;
  A breathless wonder, shadowing forth afar
Some heavenly solstice hushed and halcyon;[5]
  Whose unstirred lips are music's visible
    tone;   5
  Whose eyes the sun-gate of the soul unbar,
  Being of its furthest fires oracular ;—
The evident heart of all life sown and mown.

---

[4]Thicket.   [5]Calm.

Even such Love is; and is not thy name
    Love?
  Yea, by thy hand the Love-god rends apart
  All gathering clouds of Night's ambiguous
    art;   11
Flings them far down, and sets thine eyes
    above;
And simply, as some gage of flower or glove,
  Stakes with a smile the world against thy
    heart.

34. *The Dark Glass*

Not I myself know all my love for thee:
  How should I reach so far, who cannot
    weigh
  To-morrow's dower by gage of yesterday?
Shall birth and death, and all dark names that
    be
As doors and windows bared to some loud
    sea,   5
  Lash deaf mine ears and blind my face
    with spray;
  And shall my sense pierce love,—the last
    relay
And ultimate outpost of eternity?

Lo! what am I to Love, the lord of all?
  One murmuring shell he gathers from the
    sand,—   10
  One little heart-flame sheltered in his hand.
Yet through thine eyes he grants me clearest
    call
And veriest touch of powers primordial
  That any hour-girt life may understand.

36. *Life-in-Love*

Not in thy body is thy life at all,
  But in this lady's lips and hands and eyes;
  Through these she yields thee life that
    vivifies
What else were sorrow's servant and death's
    thrall.
Look on thyself without her, and recall   5
  The waste remembrance and forlorn sur-
    mise
  That lived but in a dead-drawn breath of
    sighs
O'er vanished hours and hours eventual.

Even so much life hath the poor tress of
    hair
  Which, stored apart, is all love hath to
    show   10
  For heart-beats and for fire-heats long
    ago;

Even so much life endures unknown, even
    where,
'Mid change the changeless night environeth,
Lies all that golden hair undimmed in death.

55. *Stillborn Love*

The hour which might have been yet might
    not be,
  Which man's and woman's heart conceived
    and bore
  Yet whereof life was barren,—on what
    shore
Bides it the breaking of Time's weary sea?
Bondchild of all consummate joys set free, 5
  It somewhere sighs and serves, and mute
    before
  The house of Love, hears through the
    echoing door
His hours elect in choral consonancy.

But lo! what wedded souls now hand in hand
Together tread at last the immortal strand 10
  With eyes where burning memory lights
    love home?
Lo! how the little outcast hour has turned
And leaped to them and in their faces
    yearned:—
  "I am your child: O Parents, ye have
    come!"

56, 57, 58. *True Woman*

I. HERSELF

To be a sweetness more desired than Spring;
  A bodily beauty more acceptable
  Than the wild rose-tree's arch that crowns
    the fell;[6]
To be an essence more environing[7]
Than wine's drained juice; a music ravishing
  More than the passionate pulse of Philo-
    mel;[8]—   6
  To be all this 'neath one soft bosom's swell
That is the flower of life:—how strange a
    thing!

How strange a thing to be what Man can
    know
  But as a sacred secret! Heaven's own
    screen   10
Hides her soul's purest depth and loveliest
    glow;
  Closely withheld, as all things most un-
    seen,—

---

[6]Moor.   [7]Pervading.   [8]The nightingale.

The wave-bowered pearl,—the heart-
　shaped seal of green
That flecks the snowdrop underneath the
　snow.

II. HER LOVE

She loves him; for her infinite soul is Love,
　And he her lodestar. Passion in her is
A glass facing his fire, where the bright
　bliss
Is mirrored, and the heat returned. Yet
　move
That glass, a stranger's amorous flame to
　prove,　　　　　　　　　　　　5
And it shall turn, by instant contraries,
Ice to the moon; where her pure fire to his
For whom it burns, clings close i' the heart's
　alcove.

Lo! they are one. With wifely breast to
　breast
　And circling arms, she welcomes all com-
　mand　　　　　　　　　　　　10
　Of love,—her soul to answering ardors
　fanned:
Yet as morn springs or twilight sinks to rest,
Ah! who shall say she deems not loveliest
The hour of sisterly sweet hand-in-hand?

III. HER HEAVEN

If to grow old in Heaven is to grow young,
　(As the Seer[9] saw and said), then blest
　were he
　With youth for evermore, whose heaven
　should be
True Woman, she whom these weak notes
　have sung.
Here and hereafter,—choir-strains of her
　tongue,—　　　　　　　　　　5
　Sky-spaces of her eyes,—sweet signs that
　flee
About her soul's immediate sanctuary,—
Where Paradise all uttermost worlds among.

The sunrise blooms and withers on the hill
　Like any hillflower; and the noblest troth
　Dies here to dust. Yet shall Heaven's
　promise clothe　　　　　　　　11
Even yet those lovers who have cherished
　still
This test for love:—in every kiss sealed fast
To feel the first kiss and forebode the last.

　　　―――――――――
　　[9] Swedenborg

PART II—CHANGE AND FATE

63. *Inclusiveness*

The changing guests, each in different mood,
　Sit at the roadside table and arise:
　And every life among them in likewise
Is a soul's board set daily with new food.
What man has bent o'er his son's sleep, to
　brood　　　　　　　　　　　　5
　How that face shall watch his when cold it
　lies?—
　Or thought, as his own mother kissed his
　eyes,
Of what her kiss was when his father
　wooed?

May not this ancient room thou sitt'st in
　dwell
　In separate living souls for joy or pain?　10
　Nay, all its corners may be painted plain
Where Heaven shows pictures of some life
　spent well,
　And may be stamped, a memory all in vain
Upon the sight of lidless eyes in Hell.

65. *Known in Vain*

As two whose love, first foolish, widening
　scope,
　Knows suddenly, to music high and soft,
　The Holy of holies; who because they
　scoffed
Are now amazed with shame, nor dare to
　cope
With the whole truth aloud, lest heaven
　should ope;　　　　　　　　　5
　Yet, at their meetings, laugh not as they
　laughed
　In speech; nor speak, at length; but sitting
　oft
Together, within hopeless sight of hope
For hours are silent:—So it happeneth
　When Work and Will awake too late, to
　gaze　　　　　　　　　　　　10
After their life sailed by, and hold their
　breath.
　Ah! who shall dare to search through what
　sad maze
　Thenceforth their incommunicable ways
Follow the desultory feet of Death?

66. *The Heart of the Night*

From child to youth; from youth to arduous
　man;
　From lethargy to fever of the heart;

From faithful life to dream-dowered days
    apart;
From trust to doubt; from doubt to brink of
    ban;[10]—
Thus much of change in one swift cycle ran 5
    Till now. Alas, the soul!—how soon
        must she
Accept her primal immortality,—
The flesh resume its dust whence it began?

O Lord of work and peace! O Lord of life!
    O Lord, the awful Lord of will! though
        late, 10
      Even yet renew this soul with duteous
        breath;
That when the peace is garnered in from
    strife,
    The work retrieved, the will regenerate,
      This soul may see thy face, O Lord of
        death!

67. *The Landmark*

Was *that* the landmark? What,—the fool-
    ish well
    Whose wave, low down, I did not stoop to
      drink,
    But sat and flung the pebbles from its brink
In sport to send its imaged skies pell-mell,
(And mine own image, had I noted well!)—
    Was that my point of turning?—I had
      thought 6
    The stations of my course should rise un-
      sought,
As altar-stone or ensigned citadel.

But lo! the path is missed, I must go back,
    And thirst to drink when next I reach the
      spring 10
Which once I stained, which since may have
    grown black.
    Yet though no light be left nor bird now
      sing
    As here I turn, I'll thank God, hastening,
That the same goal is still on the same track.

71, 72, 73. *The Choice*

I

Eat thou and drink; to-morrow thou shalt
    die.
    Surely the earth, that's wise being very old,
    Needs not our help. Then loose me, love,
      and hold
Thy sultry hair up from my face; that I

---

[10]Curse.

May pour for thee this golden wine, brim-
    high, 5
Till round the glass thy fingers glow like
    gold.
We'll drown all hours: thy song, while
    hours are tolled,
Shall leap, as fountains veil the changing sky.

Now kiss, and think that there are really
    those,
    My own high-bosomed beauty, who in-
      crease 10
      Vain gold, vain lore, and yet might
      choose our way!
    Through many years they toil; then on
    a day
They die not,—for their life was death,—
    but cease;
And round their narrow lips the mold falls
    close.

II

Watch thou and fear; to-morrow thou shalt
    die.
    Or art thou sure thou shalt have time for
      death?
Is not the day which God's word promiseth
To come man knows not when? In yonder
    sky,
Now while we speak, the sun speeds forth:
    can I 5
Or thou assure him of his goal? God's
    breath
Even at this moment haply quickeneth
The air to a flame; till spirits, always nigh
Though screened and hid, shall walk the day-
    light here.
    And dost thou prate of all that man shall
    do? 10
    Canst thou, who hast but plagues, pre-
    sume to be
    Glad in his gladness that comes after
    thee?
Will *his* strength slay *thy* worm in Hell?
    Go to:
Cover thy countenance, and watch, and fear.

III

Think thou and act; to-morrow thou shalt
    die.
    Outstretched in the sun's warmth upon the
    shore,
    Thou say'st: "Man's measured path is all
    gone o'er:
Up all his years, steeply, with strain and sigh,

Man clomb until he touched the truth; and I,
　Even I, am he whom it was destined for."
　How should this be? Art thou then so
　　much more　　　　　　　　　　　　7
Than they who sowed, that thou shouldst
　reap thereby?

Nay, come up hither. From this wave-
　washed mound
Unto the furthest flood-brim look with me;
Then reach on with thy thought till it be
　drowned.　　　　　　　　　　　　11
　Miles and miles distant though the last
　　line be,
And though thy soul sail leagues and leagues
　beyond,—
　Still, leagues beyond those leagues, there
　　is more sea.

82.　*Hoarded Joy*

I said: "Nay, pluck not,—let the first fruit
　be:
　Even as thou sayest, it is sweet and red,
　But let it ripen still. The tree's bent
　　head
Sees in the stream its own fecundity
And bides the day of fullness. Shall not we
　At the sun's hour that day possess the
　　shade,　　　　　　　　　　　　6
　And claim our fruit before its ripeness
　　fade,
And eat it from the branch and praise the
　tree?"

I say: "Alas! our fruit hath wooed the sun
　Too long,—'tis fallen and floats adown
　　the stream.　　　　　　　　　　10
Lo, the last clusters! Pluck them every one,
　And let us sup with summer; ere the gleam
Of autumn set the year's pent sorrow free,
And the woods wail like echoes from the
　sea."

85.　*Vain Virtues*

What is the sorriest thing that enters Hell?
　None of the sins,—but this and that fair
　　deed
　Which a soul's sin at length could super-
　　sede.
These yet are virgins, whom death's timely
　knell
Might once have sainted; whom the fiends
　compel　　　　　　　　　　　　5

Together now, in snake-bound shuddering
　sheaves
Of anguish, while the pit's pollution leaves
Their refuse maidenhood abominable.

Night sucks them down, the tribute of the
　pit,
　Whose names, half entered in the book of
　　Life,　　　　　　　　　　　　10
　　Were God's desire at noon. And as
　　　their hair
And eyes sink last, the Torturer deigns no
　whit
To gaze, but, yearning, waits his destined
　wife,
　The Sin still blithe on earth that sent
　　them there.

86.　*Lost Days*

The lost days of my life until to-day,
　What were they, could I see them on the
　　street
　Lie as they fell? Would they be ears of
　　wheat
Sown once for food but trodden into clay?
Or golden coins squandered and still to pay?
　Or drops of blood dabbling the guilty feet?
　Or such spilt water as in dreams must
　　cheat　　　　　　　　　　　　7
The undying throats of Hell, athirst alway?

I do not see them here; but after death
　God knows I know the faces I shall see, 10
Each one a murdered self, with low last
　breath.
　"I am thyself,—what hast thou done to
　　me?"
"And I—and I—thyself" (lo! each one
　saith)
　"And thou thyself to all eternity!"

97.　*A Superscription*

Look in my face; my name is Might-have-
　been;
　I am also called No-more, Too-late, Fare-
　　well;
　Unto thine ear I hold the dead-sea shell
Cast up thy Life's foam-fretted feet be-
　tween;
Unto thine eyes the glass where that is seen 5
　Which had Life's form and Love's, but by
　　my spell
　Is now a shaken shadow intolerable,
Of ultimate things unuttered the frail screen.

Mark me, how still I am! But should there
 dart
  One moment through thy soul the soft
   surprise   10
  Of that winged Peace which lulls the
   breath of sighs,—
Then shalt thou see me smile, and turn apart
Thy visage to mine ambush at thy heart
  Sleepless with cold commemorative eyes.

101. *The One Hope*

When vain desire at last and vain regret
  Go hand in hand to death, and all is vain,
  What shall assuage the unforgotten pain
And teach the unforgetful to forget?
Shall Peace be still a sunk stream long un-
 met,—   5
  Or may the soul at once in a green plain
  Stoop through the spray of some sweet
   life-fountain
And cull the dew-drenched flowering amulet?

Ah! when the wan soul in that golden air
  Between the scriptured petals softly blown
  Peers breathless for the gift of grace un-
   known,—   11
Ah! let none other alien spell soe'er
But only the one Hope's one name be
 there,—
  Not less nor more, but even that word
   alone.

MY SISTER'S SLEEP[1]

She fell asleep on Christmas Eve.
  At length the long-ungranted shade
  Of weary eyelids overweighed
The pain nought else might yet relieve.

Our mother, who had leaned all day   5
  Over the bed from chime to chime,
  Then raised herself for the first time,
And as she sat her down, did pray.

Her little work-table was spread
  With work to finish. For the glare   10
  Made by her candle, she had care
To work some distance from the bed.

Without, there was a cold moon up,
  Of winter radiance sheer and thin;
  The hollow halo it was in   15
Was like an icy crystal cup.

Through the small room, with subtle sound
  Of flame, by vents the fireshine drove
  And reddened. In its dim alcove
The mirror shed a clearness round.   20

I had been sitting up some nights,
  And my tired mind felt weak and blank;
  Like a sharp strengthening wine it drank
The stillness and the broken lights.

Twelve struck. That sound, by dwindling
 years   25
  Heard in each hour, crept off; and then
  The ruffled silence spread again,
Like water that a pebble stirs.

Our mother rose from where she sat:
  Her needles, as she laid them down,   30
  Met lightly, and her silken gown
Settled: no other noise than that.

"Glory unto the Newly Born!"
  So, as said angels, she did say;
  Because we were in Christmas Day,   35
Though it would still be long till morn.

Just then in the room over us
  There was a pushing back of chairs,
  As some who had sat unawares
So late, now heard the hour, and rose.   40

With anxious softly-stepping haste
  Our mother went where Margaret lay,
  Fearing the sounds o'erhead—should they
Have broken her long watched-for rest!

She stooped an instant, calm, and turned;   45
  But suddenly turned back again;
  And all her features seemed in pain
With woe, and her eyes gazed and yearned.

For my part, I but hid my face,
  And held my breath, and spoke no word:
  There was none spoken; but I heard   51
The silence for a little space.

Our mother bowed herself and wept:
  And both my arms fell, and I said,
  "God knows I knew that she was dead."   55
And there, all white, my sister slept.

Then kneeling, upon Christmas morn
  A little after twelve o'clock,
  We said, ere the first quarter struck,
"Christ's blessing on the newly born!"   60

[1]This and the three following poems were written
not later than 1850.

THE BLESSED DAMOZEL

The blesséd damozel leaned out
  From the gold bar of Heaven;
Her eyes were deeper than the depth
  Of waters stilled at even;
She had three lilies in her hand,   5
  And the stars in her hair were seven.

Her robe, ungirt from clasp to hem,
  No wrought flowers did adorn,
But a white rose of Mary's gift,
  For service meetly worn;   10
Her hair that lay along her back
  Was yellow like ripe corn.

Herseemed she scarce had been a day
  One of God's choristers;
The wonder was not yet quite gone   15
  From that still look of hers;
Albeit, to them she left, her day
  Had counted as ten years.

(To one, it is ten years of years.
  . . . Yet now, and in this place,   20
Surely she leaned o'er me—her hair
  Fell all about my face. . . .
Nothing: the autumn-fall of leaves.
  The whole year sets apace.)

It was the rampart of God's house   25
  That she was standing on;
By God built over the sheer depth
  The which is Space begun;
So high, that looking downward thence
  She scarce could see the sun.   30

It lies in Heaven, across the flood,
  Of ether, as a bridge.
Beneath, the tides of day and night
  With flame and darkness ridge
The void, as low as where this earth   35
  Spins like a fretful midge.

Around her, lovers, newly met
  'Mid deathless love's acclaims,
Spoke evermore among themselves
  Their heart-remembered names;   40
And the souls mounting up to God
  Went by her like thin flames.

And still she bowed herself and stooped
  Out of the circling charm;
Until her bosom must have made   45
  The bar she leaned on warm,
And the lilies lay as if asleep
  Along her bended arm.

From the fixed place of Heaven she saw
  Time like a pulse shake fierce   50
Through all the worlds. Her gaze still
    strove
  Within the gulf to pierce
Its path; and now she spoke as when
  The stars sang in their spheres.

The sun was gone now; the curled moon   55
  Was like a little feather
Fluttering far down the gulf; and now
  She spoke through the still weather.
Her voice was like the voice the stars
  Had when they sang together.   60

(Ah sweet! Even now, in that bird's song,
  Strove not her accents there,
Fain to be hearkened? When those bells
  Possessed the mid-day air,
Strove not her steps to reach my side   65
  Down all the echoing stair?)

"I wish that he were come to me,
  For he will come," she said.
"Have I not prayed in Heaven?—on earth,
  Lord, Lord, has he not prayed?   70
Are not two prayers a perfect strength?
  And shall I feel afraid?

"When round his head the aureole clings,
  And he is clothed in white,
I'll take his hand and go with him   75
  To the deep wells of light;
As unto a stream we will step down,
  And bathe there in God's sight.

"We two will stand beside that shrine,
  Occult, withheld, untrod,   80
Whose lamps are stirred continually
  With prayer sent up to God;
And see our old prayers, granted, melt
  Each like a little cloud.

"We two will lie i' the shadow of   85
  That living mystic tree
Within whose secret growth the Dove
  Is sometimes felt to be,
While every leaf that His plumes touch
  Saith His Name audibly.   90

"And I myself will teach to him,
  I myself, lying so,
The songs I sing here; which his voice
  Shall pause in, hushed and slow,
And find some knowledge at each pause,   95
  Or some new thing to know."

(Alas! we two, we two, thou say'st!
   Yea, one wast thou with me
That once of old. But shall God lift
   To endless unity   100
The soul whose likeness with thy soul
   Was but its love for thee?)

"We two," she said, "will seek the groves
   Where the lady Mary is,
With her five handmaidens, whose names 105
   Are five sweet symphonies,
Cecily, Gertrude, Magdalene,
   Margaret and Rosalys.

"Circlewise sit they, with bound locks
   And foreheads garlanded;   110
Into the fine cloth white like flame
   Weaving the golden thread,
To fashion the birth-robes for them
   Who are just born, being dead.

"He shall fear, haply, and be dumb: 115
   Then will I lay my cheek
To his, and tell about our love,
   Not once abashed or weak:
And the dear Mother will approve
   My pride, and let me speak.   120

"Herself shall bring us, hand in hand,
   To Him round whom all souls
Kneel, the clear-ranged unnumbered heads
   Bowed with their aureoles:
And angels meeting us shall sing   125
   To their citherns and citoles.[1]

"There will I ask of Christ the Lord
   Thus much for him and me:—
Only to live as once on earth
   With Love,—only to be,   130
As then awhile, for ever now
   Together, I and he."

She gazed and listened and then said,
   Less sad of speech than mild,—
"All this is when he comes." She ceased. 135
   The light thrilled towards her, filled
With angels in strong level flight.
   Her eyes prayed, and she smiled.

(I saw her smile.) But soon their path
   Was vague in distant spheres: 140
And then she cast her arms along
   The golden barriers,
And laid her face between her hands,
   And wept. (I heard her tears.)

---

[1]Stringed musical instruments.

THE SEA-LIMITS

Consider the sea's listless chime:
   Time's self it is, made audible,—
   The murmur of the earth's own shell.
Secret continuance sublime
   Is the sea's end: our sight may pass 5
   No furlong further. Since time was,
This sound hath told the lapse of time.

No quiet, which is death's,—it hath
   The mournfulness of ancient life,
   Enduring always at dull strife.   10
As the world's heart of rest and wrath,
   Its painful pulse is in the sands.
   Last utterly, the whole sky stands,
Gray and not known, along its path.

Listen alone beside the sea,   15
   Listen alone among the woods;
   Those voices of twin solitudes
Shall have one sound alike to thee:
   Hark where the murmurs of thronged men
   Surge and sink back and surge again,— 20
Still the one voice of wave and tree.

Gather a shell from the strown beach
   And listen at its lips: they sigh
   The same desire and mystery,
The echo of the whole sea's speech.   25
   And all mankind is thus at heart
   Not anything but what thou art:
And Earth, Sea, Man, are all in each.

SUDDEN LIGHT

I have been here before,
   But when or how I cannot tell:
I know the grass beyond the door,
   The sweet keen smell,
The sighing sound, the lights around the
     shore.   5

You have been mine before,—
   How long ago I may not know:
But just when at that swallow's soar
   Your neck turned so,
Some veil did fall,—I knew it all of yore. 10

Has this been thus before?
   And shall not thus time's eddying flight
Still with our lives our love restore
   In death's despite,
And day and night yield one delight once
     more?   15

THE CLOUD CONFINES

The day is dark and the night
  To him that would search their heart;
  No lips of cloud that will part
Nor morning song in the light:
  Only, gazing alone,   5
  To him wild shadows are shown,
  Deep under deep unknown
And height above unknown height.
    Still we say as we go,—
    "Strange to think by the way,   10
    Whatever there is to know,
    That shall we know one day."

The Past is over and fled;
  Named new, we name it the old;
  Thereof some tale hath been told,   15
But no word comes from the dead;
  Whether at all they be,
  Or whether as bond or free,
  Or whether they too were we,
Or by what spell they have sped.   20
    Still we say as we go,—
    "Strange to think by the way,
    Whatever there is to know,
    That shall we know one day."

What of the heart of hate   25
  That beats in thy breast, O Time?—
  Red strife from the furthest prime,
And anguish of fierce debate;
  War that shatters her slain,
  And peace that grinds them as grain, 30
  And eyes fixed ever in vain
On the pitiless eyes of Fate.
    Still we say as we go,—
    "Strange to think by the way,
    Whatever there is to know,   35
    That shall we know one day."

What of the heart of love
  That bleeds in thy breast, O Man?—
  Thy kisses snatched 'neath the ban
Of fangs that mock them above;   40
  Thy bells prolonged unto knells,
  Thy hope that a breath dispels,
  Thy bitter forlorn farewells
And the empty echoes thereof?

    Still we say as we go,—   45
    "Strange to think by the way,
    Whatever there is to know,
    That shall we know one day."

The sky leans dumb on the sea,
  Aweary with all its wings;   50
  And oh! the song the sea sings
Is dark everlastingly.
  Our past is clean forgot,
  Our present is and is not,
  Our future's a sealed seedplot,   55
And what betwixt them are we?—
    We who say as we go,—
    "Strange to think by the way,
    Whatever there is to know,
    That shall we know one day."   60

THREE SHADOWS

I looked and saw your eyes
  In the shadow of your hair
As a traveler sees the stream
  In the shadow of the wood;
And I said, "My faint heart sighs   5
  Ah me! to linger there,
To drink deep and to dream
  In that sweet solitude."

I looked and saw your heart
  In the shadow of your eyes,   10
As a seeker sees the gold
  In the shadow of the stream;
And I said, "Ah me! what art
  Should win the immortal prize,
Whose want must make life cold   15
  And Heaven a hollow dream?"

I looked and saw your love
  In the shadow of your heart,
As a diver sees the pearl
  In the shadow of the sea;   20
And I murmured, not above
  My breath, but all apart,—
"Ah! you can love, true girl,
  And is your love for me?"

WALTER PATER

1839–1894

Walter Horatio Pater was born at Shadwell, in East London, on 4 August, 1839. His father, who was a physician, died so early that in later life Pater could scarcely remember him. At his death the family moved to a house in Chase Side, Enfield, where they remained some fourteen or fifteen years. Pater received his earliest education at a school in Enfield, and at fourteen proceeded to King's School, Canterbury. There he led a happy life—to some extent portrayed in *Emerald Uthwart*—despite his complete indifference to outdoor games. He did creditable work at school, but was not precocious in his development, though as a youth he shadowed forth his manhood by living much alone and exhibiting a meditative and serious disposition. Just before he left school he came upon Ruskin's *Modern Painters,* and fell abruptly under the influence of that book. In June, 1858, Pater entered Queen's College, Oxford, with a scholarship from his Canterbury school. In 1862 he took his B. A. with a second class in classics. He had long intended to take holy orders, but had later abandoned the idea, and for a time he now read with private pupils. In 1863 he was elected a member of the "Old Mortality," an essay society whose membership then included T. H. Green, H. Nettleship, J. Bryce, Edward Caird, and I. Bywater; and through this society Pater also became acquainted with Swinburne. In 1864 he was elected a fellow of Brasenose College, and at once went into residence there. He held his fellowship and his rooms at Brasenose through the remainder of his life, though in later years he also maintained, with his sisters, a house in Oxford, and, for a brief period, one in London. He generally spent his long vacations in Germany or northern France, and in 1865 he went to Italy with his friend C. L. Shadwell. In 1882 he also spent the winter in Rome. Save for these journeys and the publication of his essays and books Pater's life was uneventful. He was attacked by rheumatic fever in June, 1894, and died suddenly on the following 30 July. He was buried in the cemetery of St. Giles, Oxford.

Pater may be termed the philosopher of the modern or neo-romantic school of Rossetti, Swinburne, and Morris. He sought to think through what they felt and expressed in poetry and art. He saw that their attitude towards life coincided with what, one might contend, was the great lesson of modern philosophy and science in their progress away from ancient and medieval confidence in the ability of human reason to penetrate reality, and in their conclusion that the intellectual life of man is bounded by the impressions of the senses. He concluded that if the sole stuff of life is sense-impressions, Rossetti and his followers were right in their implication that life is fundamentally a problem in aesthetics. Consequently Pater attempted to found an aesthetic criticism in a series of studies and imaginary portraits, the more important of which are contained in *Studies in the History of the Renaissance* (1873), *Imaginary Portraits* (1887), and *Appreciations* (1889). His lectures on *Plato and Platonism* (1893) are in reality, though less obviously, an effort in the same kind. And his longest and most carefully wrought work, *Marius the Epicurean* (1885)—to which he gave six years of sustained labor—contains his full exposition, in a form at once literary and meditative, of his aesthetic Epicureanism. Pater's work taken as a whole thus has an important historical interest, and, in addition, his books are full of the rare charm and rightness of a very distinguished and finely cultivated mind. His readers are inevitably struck by his humanity, by the unobtrusiveness of his scholarship, by his never-failing good taste, and by his gift—amounting to genius—for the precise expression of his meaning.

The standard edition of Pater's writings is the "Library Edition" (10 vols., London, 1910). Pieces not included in this edition are to be found in *Uncollected Essays* (Portland, Maine, 1903) and in *Sketches and Reviews,* ed. A. Mordell (New York, 1919). The best edition of *Marius the Epicurean* is edited by Joseph Sagmaster (Garden City, N. Y., 1935). The fullest biography is *The Life of Walter Pater* by Thomas Wright (2 vols., London, 1907), but this is an uncritical work, expanded by the inclusion of trivial details and dubious conjectures, and is to be used with caution. The best biographical and critical study is A. C. Benson's *Walter Pater* ("English Men of Letters" series, 1906). Ferris Greenslet's shorter and slighter *Walter Pater* (New York, 1903) is also a good introduction. Finally three essays on Pater should be mentioned—those in Edward Dowden's *Essays Modern and Elizabethan* (London, 1910), in P. E. More's *The Drift of Romanticism* ("Shelburne Essays," Eighth Series, Boston, 1913), and in T. S. Eliot's *Selected Essays, 1917–1932* (London, 1932).

STUDIES IN THE HISTORY OF THE RENAISSANCE

Conclusion[1]

Λέγει που Ἡράκλειτος ὅτι πάντα χωρεῖ καὶ οὐδὲν μένει.[2]

To REGARD all things and principles of things as inconstant modes or fashions has more and more become the tendency of modern thought. Let us begin with that which is without—our physical life. Fix upon it in one of its more exquisite intervals, the moment, for instance, of delicious recoil from the flood of water in summer heat. What is the whole physical life in that moment but a combination of natural elements to which science gives their names? But those elements, phosphorus and lime and delicate fibers, are present not in the human body alone: we detect them in places most remote from it. Our physical life is a perpetual motion of them—the passage of the blood, the waste and repairing of the lenses of the eye, the modification of the tissues of the brain under every ray of light and sound—processes which science reduces to simpler and more elementary forces. Like the elements of which we are composed, the action of these forces extends beyond us: it rusts iron and ripens corn. Far out on every side of us those elements are broadcast, driven in many currents; and birth and gesture[3] and death and the springing of violets from the grave are but a few out of ten thousand resultant combinations. That clear, perpetual outline of face and limb is but an image of ours, under which we group them—a design in a web, the actual threads of which pass out beyond it. This at least of flamelike our life has, that it is but the concurrence, renewed from moment to moment, of forces parting sooner or later on their ways.

Or if we begin with the inward world of thought and feeling, the whirlpool is still more rapid, the flame more eager and devouring. There is no longer the gradual darkening of the eye, the gradual fading of color from the wall—movements of the shore-side, where the water flows down indeed, though in apparent rest—but the race of the midstream, a drift of momentary acts of sight and passion and thought. At first sight experience seems to bury us under a flood of external objects, pressing upon us with a sharp and importunate reality, calling us out of ourselves in a thousand forms of action. But when reflection begins to play upon those objects they are dissipated under its influence; the cohesive force seems suspended like some trick of magic; each object is loosed into a group of impressions—color, odor, texture—in the mind of the observer. And if we continue to dwell in thought on this world, not of objects in the solidity with which language invests them, but of impressions, unstable, flickering, inconsistent, which burn and are extinguished with our consciousness of them, it contracts still further: the whole scope of observation is dwarfed

[1] Written in 1868 and printed at the end of *Studies in the History of the Renaissance* in 1873. It was omitted from the second edition of that book (1877), but restored in the third edition (1888) with the following note: "This brief *Conclusion* was omitted in the second edition of this book, as I conceived it might possibly mislead some of those young men into whose hands it might fall. On the whole, I have thought it best to reprint it here, with some slight changes which bring it closer to my original meaning. I have dealt more fully in *Marius the Epicurean* with the thoughts suggested by it."

[2] Heraclitus says that all things give way and nothing remains (Plato, *Cratylus*).

[3] Bearing, behavior.

into the narrow chamber of the individual mind. Experience, already reduced to a group of impressions, is ringed round for each one of us by that thick wall of personality through which no real voice has ever pierced on its way to us, or from us to that which we can only conjecture to be without. Every one of those impressions is the impression of the individual in his isolation, each mind keeping as a solitary prisoner its own dream of a world. Analysis goes a step farther still, and assures us that those impressions of the individual mind to which, for each one of us, experience dwindles down, are in perpetual flight; that each of them is limited by time, and that as time is infinitely divisible, each of them is infinitely divisible also, all that is actual in it being a single moment, gone while we try to apprehend it, of which it may ever be more truly said that it has ceased to be than that it is. To such a tremulous wisp constantly reforming itself on the stream, to a single sharp impression, with a sense in it, a relic more or less fleeting, of such moments gone by, what is real in our life fines itself down. It is with this movement, with the passage and dissolution of impressions, images, sensations, that analysis leaves off—that continual vanishing away, that strange, perpetual weaving and unweaving of ourselves.

Philosophiren, says Novalis, *ist dephlegmatisiren vivificiren.*[4] The service of philosophy, of speculative culture, towards the human spirit, is to rouse, to startle it to a life of constant and eager observation. Every moment some form grows perfect in hand or face; some tone on the hills or the sea is choicer than the rest; some mood of passion or insight or intellectual excitement is irresistibly real and attractive to us,—for that moment only. Not the fruit of experience, but experience itself, is the end. A counted number of pulses only is given to us of a variegated, dramatic life. How may we see in them all that is to be seen in them by the finest senses? How shall we pass most swiftly from point to point, and be present always at the focus where the greatest num-

ber of vital forces unite in their purest energy?

To burn always with this hard, gemlike flame, to maintain this ecstasy, is success in life. In a sense it might even be said that our failure is to form habits: for, after all, habit is relative to a stereotyped world, and meantime it is only the roughness of the eye that makes any two persons, things, situations, seem alike. While all melts under our feet, we may well grasp at any exquisite passion, or any contribution to knowledge that seems by a lifted horizon to set the spirit free for a moment, or any stirring of the senses, strange dyes, strange colors, and curious odors, or work of the artist's hands, or the face of one's friend. Not to discriminate every moment some passionate attitude in those about us, and in the very brilliancy of their gifts some tragic dividing of forces on their ways, is, on this short day of frost and sun, to sleep before evening. With this sense of the splendor of our experience and of its awful brevity, gathering all we are into one desperate effort to see and touch, we shall hardly have time to make theories about the things we see and touch. What we have to do is to be for ever curiously testing new opinions and courting new impressions, never acquiescing in a facile orthodoxy of Comte, or of Hegel,[5] or of our own. Philosophical theories or ideas, as points of view, instruments of criticism, may help us to gather up what might otherwise pass unregarded by us. "Philosophy is the microscope of thought." The theory or idea or system which requires of us the sacrifice of any part of this experience, in consideration of some interest into which we cannot enter, or some abstract theory we have not identified with ourselves, or of what is only conventional, has no real claim upon us.

One of the most beautiful passages of Rousseau is that in the sixth book of the *Confessions* where he describes the awakening in him of the literary sense. An undefinable taint of death had clung always about him, and now in early manhood he believed

---

[4] To be a philosopher is to rid one's self of inertia, to become alive. (Novalis was the pseudonym of Friedrich von Hardenberg, 1772–1801.)

[5] The French thinker, Auguste Comte (1798–1857), and the German, Georg W. F. Hegel (1770–1831). Both were founders of philosophical systems.

himself smitten by mortal disease. He asked himself how he might make as much as possible of the interval that remained; and he was not biased by anything in his previous life when he decided that it must be by intellectual excitement, which he found just then in the clear, fresh writings of Voltaire. Well! we are all *condamnés,* as Victor Hugo says: we are all under sentence of death but with a sort of indefinite reprieve—*les hommes sont tous condamnés à mort avec des sursis indéfinis:* we have an interval, and then our place knows us no more. Some spend this interval in listlessness, some in high passions, the wisest, at least among "the children of this world," in art and song. For our one chance lies in expanding that interval, in getting as many pulsations as possible into the given time. Great passions may give us this quickened sense of life, ecstasy and sorrow of love, the various forms of enthusiastic activity, disinterested or otherwise, which come naturally to many of us. Only be sure it is passion—that it does yield you this fruit of a quickened, multiplied consciousness. Of such wisdom, the poetic passion, the desire of beauty, the love of art for its own sake, has most. For art comes to you proposing frankly to give nothing but the highest quality to your moments as they pass, and simply for those moments' sake.

STYLE [1]

SINCE all progress of mind consists for the most part in differentiation, in the resolution of an obscure and complex object into its component aspects, it is surely the stupidest of losses to confuse things which right reason has put asunder, to lose the sense of achieved distinctions, the distinction between poetry and prose, for instance, or, to speak more exactly, between the laws and characteristic excellences of verse and prose composition. On the other hand, those who have dwelt most emphatically on the distinction between prose and verse, prose and poetry, may sometimes have been tempted to limit the proper functions of prose too narrowly; and this again is at least false economy, as being, in effect, the renunciation of a certain means or faculty, in a world where after all we must needs make the most of things. Critical efforts to limit art *a priori,* [2] by anticipations regarding the natural incapacity of the material with which this or that artist works, as the sculptor with solid form, or the prose-writer with the ordinary language of men, are always liable to be discredited by the facts of artistic production; and while prose is actually found to be a colored thing with Bacon, picturesque with Livy and Carlyle, musical with Cicero and Newman, mystical and intimate with Plato and Michelet [3] and Sir Thomas Browne, exalted or florid, it may be, with Milton and Taylor, [4] it will be useless to protest that it can be nothing at all, except something very tamely and narrowly confined to mainly practical ends—a kind of "good round-hand"; as useless as the protest that poetry might not touch prosaic subjects as with Wordsworth, or an abstruse matter as with Browning, or treat contemporary life nobly as with Tennyson. In subordination to one essential beauty in all good literary style, in all literature as a fine art, as there are many beauties of poetry so the beauties of prose are many, and it is the business of criticism to estimate them as such; as it is good in the criticism of verse to look for those hard, logical, and quasi-prosaic excellences which that too has, or needs. To find in the poem, amid the flowers, the allusions, the mixed perspectives, of *Lycidas* for instance, the thought, the logical structure:—how wholesome! how delightful! as to identify in prose what we call the poetry, the imaginative power, not treating it as out of place and a kind of vagrant intruder, but by way of an estimate of its rights, that is, of its achieved powers, there.

Dryden, with the characteristic instinct of his age, loved to emphasize the distinction

---

[1] The initial essay in *Appreciations, with an Essay on Style* (1889).

[2] Prior to experience.

[3] Jules Michelet (1798–1874), French historian.

[4] Jeremy Taylor (1613–1667), Bishop of Dromore author of *Holy Living* and *Holy Dying.*

between poetry and prose, the protest against their confusion with each other, coming with somewhat diminished effect from one whose poetry was so prosaic. In truth, his sense of prosaic excellence affected his verse rather than his prose, which is not only fervid, richly figured, poetic, as we say, but vitiated, all unconsciously, by many a scanning line. Setting up correctness, that humble merit of prose, as the central literary excellence, he is really a less correct writer than he may seem, still with an imperfect mastery of the relative pronoun. It might have been foreseen that, in the rotations of mind, the province of poetry in prose would find its assertor; and, a century after Dryden, amid very different intellectual needs, and with the need therefore of great modifications in literary form, the range of the poetic force in literature was effectively enlarged by Wordsworth. The true distinction between prose and poetry he regarded as the almost technical or accidental one of the absence or presence of metrical beauty, or say! metrical restraint; and for him the opposition came to be between verse and prose of course; but, as the essential dichotomy[5] in this matter, between imaginative and unimaginative writing, parallel to De Quincey's distinction between "the literature of power and the literature of knowledge," in the former of which the composer gives us not fact, but his peculiar sense of fact, whether past or present.

Dismissing then, under sanction of Wordsworth, that harsher opposition of poetry to prose, as savoring in fact of the arbitrary psychology of the last century, and with it the prejudice that there can be but one only beauty of prose style, I propose here to point out certain qualities of all literature as a fine art, which, if they apply to the literature of fact, apply still more to the literature of the imaginative sense of fact, while they apply indifferently to verse and prose, so far as either is really imaginative —certain conditions of true art in both alike, which conditions may also contain in them the secret of the proper discrimination and guardianship of the peculiar excellencies of either.

The line between fact and something quite different from external fact is, indeed, hard to draw. In Pascal,[6] for instance, in the persuasive writers generally, how difficult to define the point where, from time to time, argument which, if it is to be worth anything at all, must consist of facts or groups of facts, becomes a pleading—a theorem no longer, but essentially an appeal to the reader to catch the writer's spirit, to think with him, if one can or will—an expression no longer of fact but of his sense of it, his peculiar intuition of a world, prospective, or discerned below the faulty conditions of the present, in either case changed somewhat from the actual world. In science, on the other hand, in history so far as it conforms to scientific rule, we have a literary domain where the imagination may be thought to be always an intruder. And as, in all science, the functions of literature reduce themselves eventually to the transcribing of fact, so all the excellences of literary form in regard to science are reducible to various kinds of painstaking; this good quality being involved in all "skilled work" whatever, in the drafting of an act of parliament, as in sewing. Yet here again, the writer's sense of fact, in history especially, and in all those complex subjects which do but lie on the borders of science, will still take the place of fact, in various degrees. Your historian, for instance, with absolutely truthful intention, amid the multitude of facts presented to him must needs select, and in selecting assert something of his own humor, something that comes not of the world without but of a vision within. So Gibbon molds his unwieldy material to a preconceived view. Livy, Tacitus, Michelet, moving full of poignant sensibility amid the records of the past, each, after his own sense, modifies— who can tell where and to what degree?— and becomes something else than a transcriber; each, as he thus modifies, passing into the domain of art proper. For just in proportion as the writer's aim, consciously or unconsciously, comes to be the transcribing, not of the world, not of mere fact, but of his sense of it, he becomes an artist, his

---

[5]Division into two parts.

[6]Blaise Pascal (1623–1662), French mathematician, thinker, and mystic.

work *fine* art; and good art (as I hope ultimately to show) in proportion to the truth of his presentment of that sense; as in those humbler or plainer functions of literature also, truth—truth to bare fact, there— is the essence of such artistic quality as they may have. Truth! there can be no merit, no craft at all, without that. And further, all beauty is in the long run only *fineness* of truth, or what we call expression, the finer accommodation of speech to that vision within.

—The transcript of his sense of fact rather than the fact, as being preferable, pleasanter, more beautiful to the writer himself. In literature, as in every other product of human skill, in the molding of a bell or a platter for instance, wherever this sense asserts itself, wherever the producer so modifies his work as, over and above its primary use or intention, to make it pleasing (to himself, of course, in the first instance) there, "fine" as opposed to merely serviceable art, exists. Literary art, that is, like all art which is in any way imitative or reproductive of fact—form, or color, or incident—is the representation of such fact as connected with soul, of a specific personality, in its preferences, its volition and power.

Such is the matter of imaginative or artistic literature—this transcript, not of mere fact, but of fact in its infinite variety, as modified by human preference in all its infinitely varied forms. It will be good literary art not because it is brilliant or sober, or rich, or impulsive, or severe, but just in proportion as its representation of that sense, that soul-fact, is true, verse being only one department of such literature, and imaginative prose, it may be thought, being the special art of the modern world. That imaginative prose should be the special and opportune art of the modern world results from two important facts about the latter: first, the chaotic variety and complexity of its interests, making the intellectual issue, the really master currents of the present time incalculable—a condition of mind little susceptible of the restraint proper to verse form, so that the most characteristic verse of the nineteenth century has been lawless verse; and secondly, an all-pervading natural-

ism, a curiosity about everything whatever as it really is, involving a certain humility of attitude, cognate to what must, after all, be the less ambitious form of literature. And prose thus asserting itself as the special and privileged artistic faculty of the present day, will be, however critics may try to narrow its scope, as varied in its excellence as humanity itself reflecting on the facts of its latest experience—an instrument of many stops, meditative, observant, descriptive, eloquent, analytic, plaintive, fervid. Its beauties will be not exclusively "pedestrian": it will exert, in due measure, all the varied charms of poetry, down to the rhythm which, as in Cicero, or Michelet, or Newman, at their best, gives its musical value to every syllable.[7]

The literary artist is of necessity a scholar, and in what he proposes to do will have in mind, first of all, the scholar and the scholarly conscience—the male conscience in this matter, as we must think it, under a system of education which still to so large an extent limits real scholarship to men. In his self-criticism, he supposes always that sort of reader who will go (full of eyes) warily, considerately, though without consideration for him, over the ground which the female conscience traverses so lightly, so amiably. For the material in which he works is no more a creation of his own than the sculptor's marble. Product of a myriad various minds and contending tongues, compact of obscure and minute association, a language has its own abundant and often recondite laws, in the habitual and summary recognition of which scholarship consists. A writer, full of a matter he is before all things anxious to express, may think of those laws, the limitations of vocabulary, structure, and the like, as a restriction, but if a real artist will find in them an opportunity. His punctilious

---

[7]Mr. Saintsbury, in his *Specimens of English Prose, from Malory to Macaulay,* has succeeded in tracing, through successive English prose-writers, the tradition of that severer beauty in them, of which this admirable scholar of our literature is known to be a lover. *English Prose, from Mandeville to Thackeray,* more recently "chosen and edited" by a younger scholar, Mr. Arthur Galton, of New College, Oxford, a lover of our literature at once enthusiastic and discreet, aims at a more various illustration of the eloquent powers of English prose, and is a delightful companion (Pater's note).

observance of the proprieties of his medium will diffuse through all he writes a general air of sensibility, of refined usage. *Exclusiones debitae naturae*—the exclusions, or rejections, which nature demands—we know how large a part these play, according to Bacon, in the science of nature. In a somewhat changed sense, we might say that the art of the scholar is summed up in the observance of those rejections demanded by the nature of his medium, the material he must use. Alive to the value of an atmosphere in which every term finds its utmost degree of expression, and with all the jealousy of a lover of words, he will resist a constant tendency on the part of the majority of those who use them to efface the distinctions of language, the facility of writers often reinforcing in this respect the work of the vulgar. He will feel the obligation not of the laws only, but of those affinities, avoidances, those mere preferences, of his language, which through the associations of literary history have become a part of its nature, prescribing the rejection of many a neology,[8] many a license, many a gipsy phrase which might present itself as actually expressive. His appeal, again, is to the scholar, who has great experience in literature, and will show no favor to short-cuts, or hackneyed illustration, or an affectation of learning designed for the unlearned. Hence a contention, a sense of self-restraint and renunciation, having for the susceptible reader the effect of a challenge for minute consideration; the attention of the writer, in every minutest detail, being a pledge that it is worth the reader's while to be attentive to, that the writer is dealing scrupulously with his instrument, and therefore, indirectly, with the reader himself also, that he has the science of the instrument he plays on, perhaps, after all, with a freedom which in such case will be the freedom of a master.

For meanwhile, braced only by those restraints, he is really vindicating his liberty in the making of a vocabulary, an entire system of composition, for himself, his own true manner; and when we speak of the manner of a true master we mean what is essential in his art. Pedantry being only the scholar-ship of *le cuistre*[9] (we have no English equivalent) he is no pedant, and does but show his intelligence of the rules of language in his freedoms with it, addition or expansion, which like the spontaneities of manner in a well-bred person will still further illustrate good taste.—The right vocabulary! Translators have not invariably seen how all-important that is in the work of translation, driving for the most part at idiom or construction; whereas, if the original be first-rate, one's first care should be with its elementary particles, Plato, for instance, being often reproducible by an exact following, with no variation in structure, of word after word, as the pencil follows a drawing under tracing-paper, so only each word or syllable be not of false color, to change my illustration a little.

Well! that is because any writer worth translating at all has winnowed and searched through his vocabulary, is conscious of the words he would select in systematic reading of a dictionary, and still more of the words he would reject were the dictionary other than Johnson's;[10] and doing this with his peculiar sense of the world ever in view, in search of an instrument for the adequate expression of that, he begets a vocabulary faithful to the coloring of his own spirit, and in the strictest sense original. That living authority which language needs lies, in truth, in its scholars, who recognizing always that every language possesses a genius, a very fastidious genius, of its own, expand at once and purify its very elements, which must needs change along with the changing thoughts of living people. Ninety years ago, for instance, great mental force, certainly, was needed by Wordsworth, to break through the consecrated poetic associations of a century, and speak the language that was his, that was to become in a measure the language of the next generation. But he did it with the tact of a scholar also. English, for a quarter of a century past, has been assimilating the phraseology of pictorial art; for half a century, the phraseology of the great

---

[8]Neologism; innovation in language.

[9]The fag, or drudge.

[10]An allusion to the personal characteristics evident in many of the definitions given by Samuel Johnson in his *English Dictionary*.

German metaphysical movement of eighty years ago; in part also the language of mystical theology: and none but pedants will regret a great consequent increase of its resources. For many years to come its enterprise may well lie in the naturalization of the vocabulary of science, so only it be under the eye of a sensitive scholarship—in a liberal naturalization of the ideas of science too, for after all the chief stimulus of good style is to possess a full, rich, complex matter to grapple with. The literary artist, therefore, will be well aware of physical science; science also attaining, in its turn, its true literary ideal. And then, as the scholar is nothing without the historic sense, he will be apt to restore not really obsolete or really worn-out words, but the finer edge of words still in use: *ascertain, communicate, discover*—words like these it has been part of our "business" to misuse. And still, as language was made for man, he will be no authority for correctnesses which, limiting freedom of utterance, were yet but accidents in their origin; as if one vowed not to say *"its,"* which ought to have been in Shakespeare; *"his"* and *"hers,"* for inanimate objects, being but a barbarous and really inexpressive survival. Yet we have known many things like this. Racy Saxon monosyllables, close to us as touch and sight, he will intermix readily with those long, savorsome, Latin words, rich in "second intention." In this late day certainly, no critical process can be conducted reasonably without eclecticism. Of such eclecticism we have a justifying example in one of the first poets of our time. How illustrative of monosyllabic effect, of sonorous Latin, of the phraseology of science, of metaphysic, of colloquialism even, are the writings of Tennyson; yet with what a fine, fastidious scholarship throughout!

A scholar writing for the scholarly, he will of course leave something to the willing intelligence of his reader. "To go preach to the first passer-by," says Montaigne, "to become tutor to the ignorance of the first I meet, is a thing I abhor"; a thing, in fact, naturally distressing to the scholar, who will therefore ever be shy of offering uncomplimentary assistance to the reader's wit. To really strenuous minds there is a pleasurable stimulus in the challenge for a continuous effort on their part, to be rewarded by securer and more intimate grasp of the author's sense. Self-restraint, a skilful economy of means, *ascêsis,*[11] that too has a beauty of its own; and for the reader supposed there will be an aesthetic satisfaction in that frugal closeness of style which makes the most of a word, in the exaction from every sentence of a precise relief, in the just spacing out of word to thought, in the logically filled space connected always with the delightful sense of difficulty overcome.

Different classes of persons, at different times, make, of course, very various demands upon literature. Still, scholars, I suppose, and not only scholars, but all disinterested lovers of books, will always look to it, as to all other fine art, for a refuge, a sort of cloistral refuge, from a certain vulgarity in the actual world. A perfect poem like *Lycidas,* a perfect fiction like *Esmond,* the perfect handling of a theory like Newman's *Idea of a University,* has for them something of the uses of a religious "retreat." Here, then, with a view to the central need of a select few, those "men of a finer thread" who have formed and maintain the literary ideal, everything, every component element, will have undergone exact trial, and, above all, there will be no uncharacteristic or tarnished or vulgar decoration, permissible ornament being for the most part structural, or necessary. As the painter in his picture, so the artist in his book, aims at the production by honorable artifice of a peculiar atmosphere. "The artist," says Schiller, "may be known rather by what he *omits"*; and in literature, too, the true artist may be best recognized by his tact of omission. For to the grave reader words too are grave; and the ornamental word, the figure, the accessory form or color or reference, is rarely content to die to thought precisely at the right moment, but will inevitably linger awhile, stirring a long "brain-wave" behind it of perhaps quite alien associations.

Just there, it may be, is the detrimental tendency of the sort of scholarly attentiveness of mind I am recommending. But the

---

[11] A Greek word, literally meaning "exercise, training."

true artist allows for it. He will remember that, as the very word ornament indicates what is in itself non-essential, so the "one beauty" of all literary style is of its very essence, and independent, in prose and verse alike, of all removable decoration; that it may exist in its fullest luster, as in Flaubert's[12] *Madame Bovary,* for instance, or in Stendhal's[13] *Le Rouge et Le Noir,* in a composition utterly unadorned, with hardly a single suggestion of visibly beautiful things. Parallel, allusion, the allusive way generally, the flowers in the garden:—he knows the narcotic force of these upon the negligent intelligence to which any *diversion,* literally, is welcome, any vagrant intruder, because one can go wandering away with it from the immediate subject. Jealous, if he have a really quickening motive within, of all that does not hold directly to that, of the facile, the otiose, he will never depart from the strictly pedestrian process, unless he gains a ponderable something thereby. Even assured of its congruity, he will still question its serviceableness. Is it worth while, can we afford, to attend to just that, to just that figure or literary reference, just then?—Surplusage! he will dread that, as the runner on his muscles.[14] For in truth all art does but consist in the removal of surplusage, from the last finish of the gem-engraver blowing away the last particle of invisible dust, back to the earliest divination of the finished work to be, lying somewhere, according to Michelangelo's fancy, in the rough-hewn block of stone.

And what applies to figure or flower must be understood of all other accidental or removable ornaments of writing whatever; and not of specific ornament only, but of all that latent color and imagery which language as such carries in it. A lover of words for their own sake, to whom nothing about them is unimportant, a minute and constant observer of their physiognomy, he will be on the alert not only for obviously mixed metaphors of course, but for the metaphor that is mixed in all our speech, though a rapid use may involve no cognition of it. Currently recognizing the incident, the color, the physical elements or particles in words like *absorb, consider, extract,* to take the first that occur, he will avail himself of them, as further adding to the resources of expression. The elementary particles of language will be realized as color and light and shade through his scholarly living in the full sense of them. Still opposing the constant degradation of language by those who use it carelessly, he will not treat colored glass as if it were clear; and while half the world is using figure unconsciously, will be fully aware not only of all that latent figurative texture in speech, but of the vague, lazy, half-formed personification—a rhetoric, depressing, and worse than nothing, because it has no really rhetorical motive—which plays so large a part there, and, as in the case of more ostentatious ornament, scrupulously exact of it, from syllable to syllable, its precise value.

So far I have been speaking of certain conditions of the literary art arising out of the medium or material in or upon which it works, the essential qualities of language and its aptitudes for contingent ornamentation, matters which define scholarship as science and good taste respectively. They are both subservient to a more intimate quality of good style: more intimate, as coming nearer to the artist himself. The otiose, the facile, surplusage: why are these abhorrent to the true literary artist, except because, in literary as in all other art, structure is all-important, felt, or painfully missed, everywhere?—that architectural conception of work, which foresees the end in the beginning and never loses sight of it, and in every part is conscious of all the rest, till the last sentence does but, with undiminished vigor, unfold and justify the first—a condition of literary art, which, in contradistinction to another quality of the artist himself, to be spoken of later, I shall call the necessity of *mind* in style.

An acute philosophical writer, the late Dean Mansel[15] (a writer whose works illustrate the literary beauty there may be in closeness, and with obvious repression or economy of a

---

[12]Gustave Flaubert (1821–1880), French novelist, whose *Madame Bovary* appeared in 1856.

[13]Pseudonym for Henri Beyle (1783–1842), French novelist, whose *Le Rouge et le noir* appeared in 1831.

[14]I. e., as the runner will dread surplusage on his muscles.

[15]Henry L. Mansel (1820–1871), metaphysician and Dean of St. Paul's.

fine rhetorical gift) wrote a book, of fascinating precision in a very obscure subject, to show that all the technical laws of logic are but means of securing, in each and all of its apprehensions, the unity, the strict identity with itself, of the apprehending mind. All the laws of good writing aim at a similar unity or identity of the mind in all the processes by which the word is associated to its import. The term is right, and has its essential beauty, when it becomes, in a manner, what it signifies, as with the names of simple sensations. To give the phrase, the sentence, the structural member, the entire composition, song, or essay, a similar unity with its subject and with itself:—style is in the right way when it tends towards that. All depends upon the original unity, the vital wholeness and identity, of the initiatory apprehension or view. So much is true of all art, which therefore requires always its logic, its comprehensive reason—insight, foresight, retrospect, in simultaneous action —true, most of all, of the literary art, as being of all the arts most closely cognate to the abstract intelligence. Such logical coherency may be evidenced not merely in the lines of composition as a whole, but in the choice of a single word, while it by no means interferes with, but may even prescribe, much variety, in the building of the sentence for instance, or in the manner, argumentative, descriptive, discursive, of this or that part or member of the entire design. The blithe, crisp sentence, decisive as a child's expression of its needs, may alternate with the long-contending, victoriously intricate sentence; the sentence, born with the integrity of a single word, relieving the sort of sentence in which, if you look closely, you can see much contrivance, much adjustment, to bring a highly qualified matter into compass at one view. For the literary architecture, if it is to be rich and expressive, involves not only foresight of the end in the beginning, but also development or growth of design, in the process of execution, with many irregularities, surprises, and afterthoughts; the contingent as well as the necessary being subsumed under the unity of the whole. As truly, to the lack of such architectural design, of a single, almost visual, image, vigorously informing an entire, per-

haps very intricate, composition, which shall be austere, ornate, argumentative, fanciful, yet true from first to last to that vision within, may be attributed those weaknesses of conscious or unconscious repetition of word, phrase, motive, or member of the whole matter, indicating, as Flaubert was aware, an original structure in thought not organically complete. With such foresight, the actual conclusion will most often get itself written out of hand, before, in the more obvious sense, the work is finished. With some strong and leading sense of the world, the tight hold of which secures true *composition* and not mere loose accretion, the literary artist, I suppose, goes on considerately, setting joint to joint, sustained by yet restraining the productive ardor, retracing the negligences of his first sketch, repeating his steps only that he may give the reader a sense of secure and restful progress, readjusting mere assonances even, that they may soothe the reader, or at least not interrupt him on his way; and then, somewhere before the end comes, is burdened, inspired, with his conclusion, and betimes delivered of it, leaving off, not in weariness and because he finds *himself* at an end, but in all the freshness of volition. His work now structurally complete, with all the accumulating effect of secondary shades of meaning, he finishes the whole up to the just proportion of that antepenultimate[16] conclusion, and all becomes expressive. The house he has built is rather a body he has informed. And so it happens, to its greater credit, that the better interest even of a narrative to be recounted, a story to be told, will often be in its second reading. And though there are instances of great writers who have been no artists, an unconscious tact sometimes directing work in which we may detect, very pleasurably, many of the effects of conscious art, yet one of the greatest pleasures of really good prose literature is in the critical tracing out of that conscious artistic structure, and the pervading sense of it as we read. Yet of poetic literature too; for, in truth, the kind of constructive intelligence here supposed is one of the forms of the imagination.

That is the special function of mind, in

---

[16]Third to the last.

style. Mind and soul:—hard to ascertain philosophically, the distinction is real enough practically, for they often interfere, are sometimes in conflict, with each other. Blake, in the last century, is an instance of preponderating soul, embarrassed, at a loss, in an era of preponderating mind. As a quality of style, at all events, soul is a fact, in certain writers—the way they have of absorbing language, of attracting it into the peculiar spirit they are of, with a subtlety which makes the actual result seem like some inexplicable inspiration. By mind, the literary artist reaches us, through static and objective indications of design in his work, legible to all. By soul, he reaches us, somewhat capriciously perhaps, one and not another, through vagrant sympathy and a kind of immediate contact. Mind we cannot choose but approve where we recognize it; soul may repel us, not because we misunderstand it. The way in which theological interests sometimes avail themselves of language is perhaps the best illustration of the force I mean to indicate generally in literature, by the word *soul*. Ardent religious persuasion may exist, may make its way, without finding any equivalent heat in language: or, again, it may enkindle words to various degrees, and when it really takes hold of them doubles its force. Religious history presents many remarkable instances in which, through no mere phrase-worship, an unconscious literary tact has, for the sensitive, laid open a privileged pathway from one to another. "The altar-fire," people say, "has touched those lips!" The Vulgate, the English Bible, the English Prayer-Book, the writings of Swedenborg,[17] the Tracts for the Times:[18]—there, we have instances of widely different and largely diffused phrases of religious feeling in operation as soul in style. But something of the same kind acts with similar power in certain writers of quite another than theological literature, on behalf of some wholly personal and peculiar sense of theirs. Most easily

illustrated by theological literature, this quality lends to profane writers a kind of religious influence. At their best, these writers become, as we say sometimes, "prophets"; such character depending on the effect not merely of their matter, but of their matter as allied to, in "electric affinity" with, peculiar form, and working in all cases by an immediate sympathetic contact, on which account it is that it may be called soul, as opposed to mind, in style. And this too is a faculty of choosing and rejecting what is congruous or otherwise, with a drift towards unity—unity of atmosphere here, as there of design—soul securing color (or perfume, might we say?) as mind secures form, the latter being essentially finite, the former vague or infinite, as the influence of a living person is practically infinite. There are some to whom nothing has any real interest, or real meaning, except as operative in a given person; and it is they who best appreciate the quality of soul in literary art. They seem to know a *person,* in a book, and make way by intuition: yet, although they thus enjoy the completeness of a personal information, it is still a characteristic of soul, in this sense of the word, that it does but suggest what can never be uttered, not as being different from, or more obscure than, what actually gets said, but as containing that plenary substance of which there is only one phase or facet in what is there expressed.

If all high things have their martyrs, Gustave Flaubert might perhaps rank as the martyr of literary style. In his printed correspondence, a curious series of letters, written in his twenty-fifth year, records what seems to have been his one other passion—a series of letters which, with its fine casuistries, its firmly repressed anguish, its tone of harmonious gray, and the sense of disillusion in which the whole matter ends, might have been, a few slight changes supposed, one of his own fictions. Writing to Madame X.[19] certainly he does display, by "taking thought" mainly, by constant and delicate pondering, as in his love for literature, a heart really moved, but still more, and as the pledge of that emotion, a loyalty to his work. Madame

[17]Emanuel Swedenborg (1688–1772), Swedish scientist and mystic.

[18]The series of ninety tracts written in the interest of the Oxford Movement, of which John Henry Newman was a guiding spirit, between 1833 and 1841.

[19]In reality a certain Madame Colet, to whom Flaubert wrote letters in 1846.

X., too, is a literary artist, and the best gifts he can send her are precepts of perfection in art, counsels for the effectual pursuit of that better love. In his love-letters it is the pains and pleasures of art he insists on, its solaces: he communicates secrets, reproves, encourages, with a view to that. Whether the lady was dissatisfied with such divided or indirect service, the reader is not enabled to see; but sees that, on Flaubert's part at least, a living person could be no rival of what was, from first to last, his leading passion, a somewhat solitary and exclusive one.

I must scold you [he writes] for one thing, which shocks, scandalizes me, the small concern, namely, you show for art just now. As regards glory be it so: there, I approve. But for art!— the one thing in life that is good and real—can you compare with it an earthly love?—prefer the adoration of a relative beauty to the *cultus*[20] of the true beauty? Well! I tell you the truth. That is the one thing good in me: the one thing I have, to me estimable. For yourself, you blend with the beautiful a heap of alien things, the useful, the agreeable, what not?—

The only way not to be unhappy is to shut yourself up in art, and count everything else as nothing. Pride takes the place of all beside when it is established on a large basis. Work! God wills it. That, it seems to me, is clear.—

I am reading over again the *Aeneid,* certain verses of which I repeat to myself to satiety. There are phrases there which stay in one's head, by which I find myself beset, as with those musical airs which are for ever returning, and cause you pain, you love them so much. I observe that I no longer laugh much, and am no longer depressed. I am ripe. You talk of my serenity, and envy me. It may well surprise you. Sick, irritated, the prey a thousand times a day of cruel pain, I continue my labor like a true working-man, who, with sleeves turned up, in the sweat of his brow, beats away at his anvil, never troubling himself whether it rains or blows, for hail or thunder. I was not like that formerly. The change has taken place naturally, though my will has counted for something in the matter.—

Those who write in good style are sometimes accused of a neglect of ideas, and of the moral end, as if the end of the physician were something else than healing, of the painter than painting—as if the end of art were not, before all else, the beautiful.

[20]Cult.

What, then, did Flaubert understand by beauty, in the art he pursued with so much fervor, with so much self-command? Let us hear a sympathetic commentator:[21]—

Possessed of an absolute belief that there exists but one way of expressing one thing, one word to call it by, one adjective to qualify, one verb to animate it, he gave himself to superhuman labor for the discovery, in every phrase, of that word, that verb, that epithet. In this way, he believed in some mysterious harmony of expression, and when a true word seemed to him to lack euphony still went on seeking another, with invincible patience, certain that he had not yet got hold of the *unique* word. . . . A thousand preoccupations would beset him at the same moment, always with this desperate certitude fixed in his spirit: Among all the expressions in the world, all forms and turns of expression, there is but *one*—one form, one mode—to express what I want to say.

The one word for the one thing, the one thought, amid the multitude of words, terms, that might just do: the problem of style was there!—the unique word, phrase, sentence, paragraph, essay, or song, absolutely proper to the single mental presentation or vision within. In that perfect justice, over and above the many contingent and removable beauties with which beautiful style may charm us, but which it can exist without, independent of them yet dexterously availing itself of them, omnipresent in good work, in function at every point, from single epithets to the rhythm of a whole book, lay the specific, indispensable, very intellectual, beauty of literature, the possibility of which constitutes it a fine art.

One seems to detect the influence of a philosophic idea there, the idea of a natural economy, of some pre-existent adaptation, between a relative, somewhere in the world of thought, and its correlative, somewhere in the world of language—both alike, rather, somewhere in the mind of the artist, desiderative, expectant, inventive—meeting each other with the readiness of "soul and body reunited," in Blake's rapturous design; and, in

[21]Guy de Maupassant, Flaubert's literary follower, in an introduction to the *Lettres de Gustave Flaubert à George Sand.*

fact, Flaubert was fond of giving his theory philosophical expression.—

There are no beautiful thoughts [he would say] without beautiful forms, and conversely. As it is impossible to extract from a physical 5 body the qualities which really constitute it— color, extension, and the like—without reducing it to a hollow abstraction, in a word, without destroying it; just so it is impossible to detach the form from the idea, for the idea only exists 10 by virtue of the form.

All the recognized flowers, the removable ornaments of literature (including harmony and ease in reading aloud, very carefully considered by him) counted certainly; for these 15 too are part of the actual value of what one says. But still, after all, with Flaubert, the search, the unwearied research, was not for the smooth, or winsome, or forcible word, as such, as with false Ciceronians,[22] but quite 20 simply and honestly, for the word's adjustment to its meaning. The first condition of this must be, of course, to know yourself, to have ascertained your own sense exactly. Then, if we suppose an artist, he says to the 25 reader,—I want you to see precisely what I see. Into the mind sensitive to "form," a flood of random sounds, colors, incidents, is ever penetrating from the world without, to become, by sympathetic selection, a part of 30 its very structure, and, in turn, the visible vesture and expression of that other world it sees so steadily within, nay, already with a partial conformity thereto, to be refined, enlarged, corrected, at a hundred points; and 35 it is just there, just at those doubtful points that the function of style, as tact or taste, intervenes. The unique term will come more quickly to one than another, at one time than another, according also to the kind of matter 40 in question. Quickness and slowness, ease and closeness alike, have nothing to do with the artistic character of the true word found at last. As there is a charm of ease, so there is also a special charm in the signs of dis- 45 covery, of effort and contention towards a due end, as so often with Flaubert himself— in the style which has been pliant, as only obstinate, durable metal can be, to the inherent perplexities and recusancy of a cer- 50 tain difficult thought.

_____
[22]Imitators of the style of Cicero.

If Flaubert had not told us, perhaps we should never have guessed how tardy and painful his own procedure really was, and after reading his confession may think that his almost endless hesitation had much to do with diseased nerves. Often, perhaps, the felicity supposed will be the product of a happier, a more exuberant nature than Flaubert's. Aggravated, certainly, by a morbid physical condition, that anxiety in "seeking the phrase," which gathered all the other small *ennuis* of a really quiet existence into a kind of battle, was connected with his life-long contention against facile poetry, facile art—art, facile and flimsy; and what constitutes the true artist is not the slowness or quickness of the process, but the absolute success of the result. As with those laborers in the parable,[23] the prize is independent of the mere length of the actual day's work. "You talk," he writes, odd, trying lover, to Madame X.—

You talk of the exclusiveness of my literary tastes. That might have enabled you to divine what kind of a person I am in the matter of love. I grow so hard to please as a literary artist, that I am driven to despair. I shall end by not writing another line.

"Happy," he cries, in a moment of discouragement at that patient labor, which for him, certainly, was the condition of a great success—

Happy those who have no doubts of themselves! who lengthen out, as the pen runs on, all that flows forth from their brains. As for me, I hesitate, I disappoint myself, turn round upon myself in despite: my taste is augmented in proportion as my natural vigor decreases, and I afflict my soul over some dubious word out of all proportion to the pleasure I get from a whole page of good writing. One would have to live two centuries to attain a true idea of any matter whatever. What Buffon[24] said is a big blasphemy: genius is not long-continued patience. Still, there is some truth in the statement, and more than people think, especially as regards our own day. Art! art! art! bitter deception! phantom that glows with light, only to lead one on to destruction.

_____
[23]St. Matthew, 20:1–16.
[24]Georges L. L. de Buffon (1707–1788), French naturalist.

Again—

I am growing so peevish about my writing. I am like a man whose ear is true but who plays falsely on the violin: his fingers refuse to reproduce precisely those sounds of which he has the inward sense. Then the tears come rolling down from the poor scraper's eyes and the bow falls from his hand.

Coming slowly or quickly, when it comes, as it came with so much labor of mind, but also with so much luster, to Gustave Flaubert, this discovery of the word will be, like all artistic success and felicity, incapable of strict analysis: effect of an intuitive condition of mind, it must be recognized by like intuition on the part of the reader, and a sort of immediate sense. In every one of those masterly sentences of Flaubert there was, below all mere contrivance, shaping and afterthought, by some happy instantaneous concourse of the various faculties of the mind with each other, the exact apprehension of what was *needed* to carry the meaning. And that it fits with absolute justice will be a judgment of immediate sense in the appreciative reader. We all feel this in what may be called inspired translation. Well! all language involves translation from inward to outward. In literature, as in all forms of art, there are the absolute and the merely relative or accessory beauties; and precisely in that exact proportion of the term to its purpose is the absolute beauty of style, prose or verse. All the good qualities, the beauties, of verse also, are such, only as precise expression.

In the highest as in the lowliest literature, then, the one indispensable beauty is, after all, truth:—truth to bare fact in the latter, as to some personal sense of fact, diverted somewhat from men's ordinary sense of it, in the former; truth there as accuracy, truth here as expression, that finest and most intimate form of truth, the *vraie vérité*.[25] And what an eclectic principle this really is! employing for its one sole purpose—that absolute accordance of expression to idea—all other literary beauties and excellences whatever: how many kinds of style it covers, explains, justifies, and at the same time safeguards!

[25]Truth itself.

Scott's facility, Flaubert's deeply pondered evocation of "the phrase," are equally good art. Say what you have to say, what you have a will to say, in the simplest, the most direct and exact manner possible, with no surplusage:—there, is the justification of the sentence so fortunately born, "entire, smooth, and round," that it needs no punctuation, and also (that is the point!) of the most elaborate period, if it be right in its elaboration. Here is the office of ornament: here also the purpose of restraint in ornament. As the exponent of truth, that austerity (the beauty, the function, of which in literature Flaubert understood so well) becomes not the correctness or purism of the mere scholar, but a security against the otiose, a jealous exclusion of what does not really tell towards the pursuit of relief, of life and vigor in the portraiture of one's sense. License again, the making free with rule, if it be indeed, as people fancy, a habit of genius, flinging aside or transforming all that opposes the liberty of beautiful production, will be but faith to one's own meaning. The seeming baldness of *Le Rouge et Le Noir* is nothing in itself; the wild ornament of *Les Misérables* is nothing in itself; and the restraint of Flaubert, amid a real natural opulence, only redoubled beauty—the phrase so large and so precise at the same time, hard as bronze, in service to the more perfect adaptation of words to their matter. Afterthoughts, retouchings, finish, will be of profit only so far as they too really serve to bring out the original, initiative, generative, sense in them.

In this way, according to the well-known saying, "The style is the man," complex or simple, in his individuality, his plenary sense of what he really has to say, his sense of the world; all cautions regarding style arising out of so many natural scruples as to the medium through which alone he can expose that inward sense of things, the purity of this medium, its laws or tricks of refraction: nothing is to be left there which might give conveyance to any matter save that. Style in all its varieties, reserved or opulent, terse, abundant, musical, stimulant, academic, so long as each is really characteristic or expressive, finds thus its justification, the sumptuous good taste of Cicero being as

truly the man himself, and not another, justified, yet insured inalienably to him, thereby,
as would have been his portrait by Raffaelle,
in full consular splendor, on his ivory chair.

A relegation, you may say perhaps—a
relegation of style to the subjectivity, the
mere caprice, of the individual, which must
soon transform it into mannerism. Not so!
since there is, under the conditions supposed,
for those elements of the man, for every
lineament of the vision within, the one word,
the one acceptable word, recognizable by the
sensitive, by others "who have intelligence"
in the matter, as absolutely as ever anything
can be in the evanescent and delicate region
of human language. The style, the manner,
would be the man, not in his unreasoned and
really uncharacteristic caprices, involuntary
or affected, but in absolutely sincere apprehension of what is most real to him. But let
us hear our French guide[26] again.—

Styles [says Flaubert's commentator], *Styles,*
as so many peculiar molds, each of which bears
the mark of a particular writer, who is to pour
into it the whole content of his ideas, were no
part of his theory. What he believed in was
Style: that is to say, a certain absolute and
unique manner of expressing a thing, in all its
intensity and color. For him the *form* was the
work itself. As in living creatures, the blood,
nourishing the body, determines its very contour and external aspect, just so, to his mind,
the *matter,* the basis, in a work of art, imposed,
necessarily, the unique, the just expression, the
measure, the rhythm—the *form* in all its characteristics.

If the style be the man, in all the color and
intensity of a veritable apprehension, it will
be in a real sense "impersonal."

I said, thinking of books like Victor
Hugo's *Les Misérables,* that prose literature
was the characteristic art of the nineteenth
century, as others, thinking of its triumphs
since the youth of Bach,[27] have assigned that
place to music. Music and prose literature

[26]De Maupassant.

[27]Johann Sebastian Bach (1685–1750), the father
of German music.

are, in one sense, the opposite terms of art;
the art of literature presenting to the imagination, through the intelligence, a range of
interests, as free and various as those which
music presents to it through sense. And certainly the tendency of what has been here
said is to bring literature too under those
conditions, by conformity to which music
takes rank as the typically perfect art. If
music be the ideal of all art whatever, precisely because in music it is impossible to distinguish the form from the substance or matter, the subject from the expression, then,
literature, by finding its specific excellence in
the absolute correspondence of the term to
its import, will be but fulfilling the condition
of all artistic quality in things everywhere,
of all good art.

Good art, but not necessarily great art; the
distinction between great art and good art depending immediately, as regards literature at
all events, not on its form, but on the matter.
Thackeray's *Esmond,* surely, is greater art
than *Vanity Fair,* by the greater dignity of its
interests. It is on the quality of the matter
it informs or controls, its compass, its variety,
its alliance to great ends, or the depth of
the note of revolt, or the largeness of hope in
it, that the greatness of literary art depends,
as *The Divine Comedy, Paradise Lost, Les
Misérables, The English Bible,* are great art.
Given the conditions I have tried to explain
as constituting good art;—then, if it be devoted further to the increase of men's happiness, to the redemption of the oppressed,
or the enlargement of our sympathies with
each other, or to such presentment of new or
old truth about ourselves and our relation to
the world as may ennoble and fortify us in
our sojourn here, or immediately, as with
Dante, to the glory of God, it will be also
great art; if, over and above those qualities I
summed up as mind and soul—that color
and mystic perfume, and that reasonable
structure, it has something of the soul of
humanity in it, and finds its logical, its architectural place, in the great structure of
human life.

POSTSCRIPT[1]

THE words, *classical* and *romantic,* although, like many other critical expressions, sometimes abused by those who have understood them too vaguely or too absolutely, yet define two real tendencies in the history of art and literature. Used in an exaggerated sense, to express a greater opposition between those tendencies than really exists, they have at times tended to divide people of taste into opposite camps. But in that *House Beautiful,*[2] which the creative minds of all generations—the artists and those who have treated life in the spirit of art—are always building together, for the refreshment of the human spirit, these oppositions cease; and the *Interpreter* of the *House Beautiful,* the true aesthetic critic, uses these divisions, only so far as they enable him to enter into the peculiarities of the objects with which he has to do. The term *classical,* fixed, as it is, to a well-defined literature, and a well-defined group in art, is clear, indeed; but then it has often been used in a hard, and merely scholastic sense, by the praisers of what is old and accustomed, at the expense of what is new, by critics who would never have discovered for themselves the charm of any work, whether new or old, who value what is old, in art or literature, for its accessories, and chiefly for the conventional authority that has gathered about it—people who would never really have been made glad by any Venus fresh-risen from the sea, and who praise the Venus of old Greece and Rome, only because they fancy her grown now into something staid and tame.

And as the term, *classical,* has been used in a too absolute, and therefore in a misleading sense, so the term, *romantic,* has been used much too vaguely, in various accidental senses. The sense in which Scott is called a romantic writer is chiefly this; that, in opposition to the literary tradition of the last century, he loved strange adventure, and

sought it in the Middle Age. Much later, in a Yorkshire village, the spirit of romanticism bore a more really characteristic fruit in the work of a young girl, Emily Brontë, the romance of *Wuthering Heights;* the figures of Hareton Earnshaw, of Catherine Linton, and of Heathcliffe—tearing open Catherine's grave, removing one side of her coffin, that he may really lie beside her in death—figures so passionate, yet woven on a background of delicately beautiful, moorland scenery, being typical examples of that spirit. In Germany, again, that spirit is shown less in Tieck,[3] its professional representative, than in Meinhold, the author of *Sidonia the Sorceress* and the *Amber-Witch.* In Germany and France, within the last hundred years, the term has been used to describe a particular school of writers; and, consequently, when Heine criticizes the *Romantic School* in Germany—that movement which culminated in Goethe's *Goetz von Berlichingen;* or when Théophile Gautier[4] criticizes the romantic movement in France, where, indeed, it bore its most characteristic fruits, and its play is hardly yet over—where, by a certain audacity, or *bizarrerie*[5] of motive, united with faultless literary execution, it still shows itself in imaginative literature—they use the word, with an exact sense of special artistic qualities, indeed; but use it, nevertheless, with a limited application to the manifestation of those qualities at a particular period. But the romantic spirit is, in reality, an ever-present, an enduring principle, in the artistic temperament; and the qualities of thought and style which that, and other similar uses of the word *romantic* really indicate, are indeed but symptoms of a very continuous and widely working influence.

Though the words *classical* and *romantic,* then, have acquired an almost technical meaning, in application to certain developments of German and French taste, yet this is but one variation of an old opposition, which

---

[1]Published with the title *Romanticism* in *Macmillan's Magazine,* November, 1876. In 1889 reprinted with its present title as the final essay in *Appreciations, with an Essay on Style.*

[2]Visited by Christian in the *Pilgrim's Progress* of Bunyan.

[3]Ludwig Tieck (1773–1853), the dramatist. Wilhelm Meinhold (1797–1851) was a novelist.

[4]French poet and novelist (1811–1872).

[5]Extravagance.

may be traced from the very beginning of the formation of European art and literature. From the first formation of anything like a standard of taste in these things, the restless curiosity of their more eager lovers necessarily made itself felt, in the craving for new motives, new subjects of interest, new modifications of style. Hence, the opposition between the classicists and the romanticists—between the adherents, in the culture of beauty, of the principles of liberty, and authority, respectively—of strength, and order or what the Greeks called κοσμιότης.[6]

Sainte-Beuve,[7] in the third volume of the *Causeries du Lundi,* has discussed the question, *What is meant by a classic?* It was a question he was well fitted to answer, having himself lived through many phases of taste, and having been in earlier life an enthusiastic member of the romantic school: he was also a great master of that sort of "philosophy of literature," which delights in tracing traditions in it, and the way in which various phases of thought and sentiment maintain themselves, through successive modifications, from epoch to epoch. His aim, then, is to give the word *classic* a wider and, as he says, a more generous sense than it commonly bears, to make it expressly *grandiose et flottant;*[8] and, in doing this, he develops, in a masterly manner, those qualities of measure, purity, temperance, of which it is the especial function of classical art and literature, whatever meaning, narrower or wider, we attach to the term, to take care.

The charm, therefore, of what is classical, in art or literature, is that of the well-known tale, to which we can, nevertheless, listen over and over again, because it is told so well. To the absolute beauty of its artistic form, is added the accidental, tranquil, charm of familiarity. There are times, indeed, at which these charms fail to work on our spirits at all, because they fail to excite us. "Romanticism," says Stendhal,[9] "is the art of presenting to people the literary works which,

in the actual state of their habits and beliefs, are capable of giving them the greatest possible pleasure; *classicism,* on the contrary, of presenting them with that which gave the greatest possible pleasure to their grandfathers." But then, beneath all changes of habits and beliefs, our love of that mere abstract proportion—of music—which what is classical in literature possesses, still maintains itself in the best of us, and what pleased our grandparents may at least tranquilize us. The "classic" comes to us out of the cool and quiet of other times, as the measure of what a long experience has shown will at least never displease us. And in the classical literature of Greece and Rome, as in the classics of the last century, the essentially classical element is that quality of order in beauty, which they possess, indeed, in a pre-eminent degree, and which impresses some minds to the exclusion of everything else in them.

It is the addition of strangeness to beauty, that constitutes the romantic character in art; and the desire of beauty being a fixed element in every artistic organization, it is the addition of curiosity to this desire of beauty, that constitutes the romantic temper. Curiosity and the desire of beauty, have each their place in art, as in all true criticism. When one's curiosity is deficient, when one is not eager enough for new impressions, and new pleasures, one is liable to value mere academical proprieties too highly, to be satisfied with worn-out or conventional types, with the insipid ornament of Racine, or the prettiness of that later Greek sculpture, which passed so long for true Hellenic work; to miss those places where the handiwork of nature, or of the artist, has been most cunning; to find the most stimulating products of art a mere irritation. And when one's curiosity is in excess; when it overbalances the desire of beauty, then one is liable to value in works of art what is inartistic in them; to be satisfied with what is exaggerated in art, with productions like some of those of the romantic school in Germany; not to distinguish, jealously enough, between what is admirably done, and what is done not quite so well, in the writings, for instance, of Jean Paul.[10] And if I had to give instances

---

[6] Decorum.

[7] Charles A. Sainte-Beuve (1804–1869), French critic and poet.

[8] Large and general.

[9] Henri Beyle (1783–1842), the French novelist who went by the pen-name of Stendhal.

[10] Jean Paul Richter (1763–1825).

of these defects, then I should say, that Pope, in common with the age of literature to which he belonged, had too little curiosity, so that there is always a certain insipidity in the effect of his work, exquisite as it is; and, coming down to our own time, that Balzac had an excess of curiosity—curiosity not duly tempered with the desire of beauty.

But, however falsely those two tendencies may be opposed by critics, or exaggerated by artists themselves, they are tendencies really at work at all times in art, molding it, with the balance sometimes a little on one side, sometimes a little on the other, generating, respectively, as the balance inclines on this side or that, two principles, two traditions, in art, and in literature so far as it partakes of the spirit of art. If there is a great over-balance of curiosity, then, we have the grotesque in art: if the union of strangeness and beauty, under very difficult and complex conditions, be a successful one, if the union be entire, then the resultant beauty is very exquisite, very attractive. With a passionate care for beauty, the romantic spirit refuses to have it, unless the condition of strangeness be first fulfilled. Its desire is for a beauty born of unlikely elements, by a profound alchemy, by a difficult initiation, by the charm which wrings it even out of terrible things; and a trace of distortion, of the grotesque, may perhaps linger, as an additional element of expression, about its ultimate grace. Its eager, excited spirit will have strength, the grotesque, first of all—the trees shrieking as you tear off the leaves; for Jean Valjean,[11] the long years of convict life; for Redgauntlet,[12] the quicksands of Solway Moss; then, incorporate with this strangeness, and intensified by restraint, as much sweetness, as much beauty, as is compatible with that. *Énergique, frais, et dispos*—these, according to Sainte-Beuve, are the characteristics of a genuine classic—*les ouvrages anciens ne sont pas classiques parce qu'ils sont vieux, mais parce qu'ils sont énergiques, frais, et dispos.*[13] Energy, freshness, intelligent and

masterly disposition:—these are characteristics of Victor Hugo when his alchemy is complete, in certain figures, like Marius and Cosette, in certain scenes, like that in the opening of *Les Travailleurs de la Mer,* where Déruchette writes the name of *Gilliatt* in the snow, on Christmas morning; but always there is a certain note of strangeness discernible there, as well.

The essential elements, then, of the romantic spirit are curiosity and the love of beauty; and it is only as an illustration of these qualities, that it seeks the Middle Age, because, in the overcharged atmosphere of the Middle Age, there are unworked sources of romantic effect, of a strange beauty, to be won, by strong imagination, out of things unlikely or remote.

Few, probably, now read Madame de Staël's *De l'Allemagne,* though it has its interest, the interest which never quite fades out of work really touched with the enthusiasm of the spiritual adventurer, the pioneer in culture. It was published in 1810, to introduce to French readers a new school of writers—the romantic school, from beyond the Rhine; and it was followed, twenty-three years later, by Heine's *Romantische Schule,* as at once a supplement and a correction. Both these books, then, connect romanticism with Germany, with the names especially of Goethe and Tieck; and, to many English readers, the idea of romanticism is still inseparably connected with Germany—that Germany which, in its quaint old towns, under the spire of Strasburg or the towers of Heidelberg, was always listening in rapt inaction to the melodious, fascinating voices of the Middle Age, and which, now that it has got Strasburg back again,[14] has, I suppose, almost ceased to exist. But neither Germany, with its Goethe and Tieck, nor England, with its Byron and Scott, is nearly so representative of the romantic temper as France, with Murger,[15] and Gautier, and Victor Hugo. It is in French literature that its most characteristic expression is to be found; and that, as most closely derivative, historically, from

---

[11]In Victor Hugo's *Les Misérables.*

[12]In Scott's *Redgauntlet.*

[13]Ancient literature is not classical because it is old, but because it is spirited, fresh, and well-ordered.

[14]In 1870.

[15]Henri Murger (1822-1861), author of the novel *Scènes de la Vie de Bohème* from which was made the opera *La Bohème.*

such peculiar conditions, as ever reinforce it to the utmost.

For, although temperament has much to do with the generation of the romantic spirit, and although this spirit, with its curiosity, its thirst for a curious beauty, may be always traceable in excellent art (traceable even in Sophocles), yet ·still, in a limited sense, it may be said to be a product of special epochs. Outbreaks of this spirit, that is, come naturally with particular periods—times, when, in men's approaches towards art and poetry, curiosity may be noticed to take the lead, when men come to art and poetry, with a deep thirst for intellectual excitement, after a long *ennui,* or in reaction against the strain of outward, practical things: in the later Middle Age, for instance; so that medieval poetry, centering in Dante, is often opposed to Greek and Roman poetry, as romantic poetry to the classical. What the romanticism of Dante is, may be estimated, if we compare the lines in which Virgil describes the hazel-wood, from whose broken twigs flows the blood of Polydorus, not without the expression of a real shudder at the ghastly incident, with the whole canto of the *Inferno,* into which Dante has expanded them, beautifying and softening it, meanwhile, by a sentiment of profound pity. And it is especially in that period of intellectual disturbance, immediately preceding Dante, amid which the romance languages define themselves at last, that this temper is manifested. Here, in the literature of Provence, the very name of *romanticism* is stamped with its true signification: here we have indeed a romantic world, grotesque even, in the strength of its passions, almost insane in its curious expression of them, drawing all things into its sphere, making the birds, nay! lifeless things, its voices and messengers, yet so penetrated with the desire for beauty and sweetness, that it begets a wholly new species of poetry, in which the *Renaissance* may be said to begin. The last century was pre-eminently a classical age, an age in which, for art and literature, the element of a comely order was in the ascendant; which, passing away, left a hard battle to be fought between the classical and the romantic schools. Yet, it is in the heart of this century, of Goldsmith and Stot-

hard,[16] of Watteau and the *Siècle de Louis XIV*[17]—in one of its central, if not most characteristic figures, in Rousseau—that the modern or French romanticism really originates. But, what in the eighteenth century is but an exceptional phenomenon, breaking through its fair reserve and discretion only at rare intervals, is the habitual guise of the nineteenth, breaking through it perpetually, with a feverishness, an incomprehensible straining and excitement, which all experience to some degree, but yearning also, in the genuine children of the romantic school, to be *énergique, frais, et dispos*—for those qualities of energy, freshness, comely order; and often, in Murger, in Gautier, in Victor Hugo, for instance, with singular felicity attaining them.

It is in the terrible tragedy of Rousseau, in fact, that French romanticism, with much else, begins: reading his *Confessions* we seem actually to assist at the birth of this new, strong spirit in the French mind. The wildness which has shocked so many, and the fascination which has influenced almost every one, in the squalid, yet eloquent figure, we see and hear so clearly in that book, wandering under the apple-blossoms and among the vines of Neuchâtel or Vevey actually give it the quality of a very successful romantic invention. His strangeness or distortion, his profound subjectivity, his passionateness— the *cor laceratum*[18]—Rousseau makes all men in love with these. *Je ne suis fait comme aucun de ceux que j'ai sus. Mais si je ne vaux pas mieux, au moins je suis autre.*—"I am not made like any one else I have ever known: yet, if I am not better, at least I am different." These words, from the first page of the *Confessions,* anticipate all the Werthers, Renés, Obermanns,[19] of the last hundred years. For Rousseau did but anticipate a trouble in the spirit of the whole world; and thirty years afterwards, what in him was a peculiarity, became part of the general consciousness. A storm was coming: Rousseau, with others, felt it in the

---

[16]Thomas Stothard (1755-1834), English painter and illustrator.
[17]By Voltaire. [18]Torn heart.
[19]*The Sorrows of Werther,* by Goethe; *René,* by Chateaubriand; *Obermann,* by Senancour.

air, and they helped to bring it down: they introduced a disturbing element into French literature, then so trim and formal, like our own literature of the age of Queen Anne.

In 1815 the storm had come and gone, but had left, in the spirit of "young France," the *ennui* of an immense disillusion, In the last chapter of Edgar Quinet's *Révolution Française,* a work itself full of irony, of disillusion, he distinguishes two books, Senancour's *Obermann* and Chateaubriand's *Génie du Christianisme,* as characteristic of the first decade of the present century. In those two books we detect already the disease and the cure—in *Obermann* the irony, refined into a plaintive philosophy of "indifference"—in Chauteaubriand's *Génie du Christianisme,* the refuge from a tarnished actual present, a present of disillusion, into a world of strength and beauty in the Middle Age, as at an earlier period—in *René* and *Atala*—into the free play of them in savage life. It is to minds in this spiritual situation, weary of the present, but yearning for the spectacle of beauty and strength, that the works of French romanticism appeal. They set a positive value on the intense, the exceptional; and a certain distortion is sometimes noticeable in them, as in conceptions like Victor Hugo's *Quasimodo,* or *Gwynplaine,*[20] something of a terrible grotesque, of the *macabre,* as the French themselves call it; though always combined with perfect literary execution, as in Gautier's *La Morte Amoureuse,* or the scene of the "maimed" burial-rites of the player, dead of the frost, in his *Capitaine Fracasse*—true "flowers of the yew." It becomes grim humor in Victor Hugo's combat of Gilliatt with the devil-fish, or the incident, with all its ghastly comedy drawn out at length, of the great gun detached from its fastenings on shipboard, in *Quatre-Vingt-Treize* (perhaps the most terrible of all the accidents that can happen by sea) and in the entire episode, in that book, of the *Convention.* Not less surely does it reach a genuine pathos; for the habit of noting and distinguishing one's own intimate passages of sentiment makes one sympathetic, begetting,

as it must, the power of entering, by all sorts of finer ways, into the intimate recesses of other minds; so that pity is another quality of romanticism, both Victor Hugo and Gautier being great lovers of animals, and charming writers about them, and Murger being unrivaled in the pathos of his *Scènes de la Vie de Jeunesse.* Penetrating so finely into all situations which appeal to pity, above all, into the special or exceptional phases of such feeling, the romantic humor is not afraid of the quaintness or singularity of its circumstances or expression, pity, indeed, being of the essence of humor; so that Victor Hugo does but turn his romanticism into practice, in his hunger and thirst after practical *Justice!*—a justice which shall no longer wrong children, or animals, for instance, by ignoring in a stupid, mere breadth of view, minute facts about them. Yet the romanticists are antinomian, too, sometimes, because the love of energy and beauty, of distinction in passion, tended naturally to become a little *bizarre,* plunging into the Middle Age, into the secrets of old Italian story. *Are we in the Inferno?*—we are tempted to ask, wondering at something malign in so much beauty. For over all a care for the refreshment of the human spirit by fine art manifests itself, a predominant sense of literary charm, so that, in their search for the secret of exquisite expression, the romantic school went back to the forgotten world of early French poetry, and literature itself became the most delicate of the arts—like "goldsmith's work," says Sainte-Beuve, of Bertrand's *Gaspard de la Nuit*—and that peculiarly French gift, the gift of exquisite speech, *argute loqui,*[21] attained in them a perfection which it had never seen before.

Stendhal, a writer whom I have already quoted, and of whom English readers might well know much more than they do, stands between the earlier and later growths of the romantic spirit. His novels are rich in romantic quality; and his other writings— partly criticism, partly personal reminiscences —are a very curious and interesting illustration of the needs out of which romanticism arose. In his book on *Racine and Shakespeare,* Stendhal argues that all good art was

---

[20]Characters in *Notre Dame de Paris* and *L'Homme Qui Rit,* respectively.

[21]To speak subtly.

romantic in its day; and this is perhaps true in Stendhal's sense. That little treatise, full of "dry light" and fertile ideas, was published in the year 1823, and its object is to defend an entire independence and liberty in the choice and treatment of subject, both in art and literature, against those who upheld the exclusive authority of precedent. In pleading the cause of romanticism, therefore, it is the novelty, both of form and of motive, in writings like the *Hernani* of Victor Hugo (which soon followed it, raising a storm of criticism) that he is chiefly concerned to justify. To be interesting and really stimulating, to keep us from yawning even, art and literature must follow the subtle movements of that nimbly-shifting *Time-Spirit,* or *Zeit-Geist,* understood by French not less than by German criticism, which is always modifying men's taste, as it modifies their manners and their pleasures. This, he contends, is what all great workmen had always understood. Dante, Shakespeare, Molière, had exercised an absolute independence in their choice of subject and treatment. To turn always with that ever-changing spirit, yet to retain the flavor of what was admirably done in past generations, in the classics, as we say —is the problem of true romanticism. "Dante," he observes, "was pre-eminently the romantic poet. He adored Virgil, yet he wrote the *Divine Comedy,* with the episode of Ugolino, which is as unlike the Aeneid as can possibly be. And those who thus obey the fundamental principle of romanticism, one by one become classical, and are joined to that ever-increasing common league, formed by men of all countries, to approach nearer and nearer to perfection."

Romanticism, then, although it has its epochs, is in its essential characteristics rather a spirit which shows itself at all times, in various degrees, in individual workmen and their work, and the amount of which criticism has to estimate in them taken one by one, than the peculiarity of a time or a school. Depending on the varying proportion of curiosity and the desire of beauty, natural tendencies of the artistic spirit at all times, it must always be partly a matter of individual temperament. The eighteenth century in England has been regarded as almost exclusively a classical period; yet William Blake, a type of so much which breaks through what are conventionally thought the influences of that century, is still a noticeable phenomenon in it, and the reaction in favor of naturalism in poetry begins in that century, early. There are, thus, the born romanticists and the born classicists. There are the born classicists who start with *form,* to whose minds the comeliness of the old, immemorial, well-recognized types in art and literature, have revealed themselves impressively; who will entertain no matter which will not go easily and flexibly into them; whose work aspires only to be a variation upon, or study from, the older masters. "'Tis art's decline, my son!"[22] they are always saying, to the progressive element in their own generation; to those who care for that which in fifty years' time every one will be caring for. On the other hand, there are the born romanticists, who start with an original, untried *matter,* still in fusion; who conceive this vividly, and hold by it as the essence of their work; who, by the very vividness and heat of their conception, purge away, sooner or later, all that is not organically appropriate to it, till the whole effect adjusts itself in clear, orderly, proportionate form; which form, after a very little time, becomes classical in its turn.

The romantic or classical character of a picture, a poem, a literary work, depends, then, on the balance of certain qualities in it; and in this sense, a very real distinction may be drawn between good classical and good romantic work. But all critical terms are relative; and there is at least a valuable suggestion in that theory of Stendhal's, that all good art was romantic in its day. In the beauties of Homer and Pheidias, quiet as they now seem, there must have been, for those who confronted them for the first time, excitement and surprise, the sudden, unforeseen satisfaction of the desire of beauty. Yet the *Odyssey,* with its marvelous adventure, is more romantic than the *Iliad,* which nevertheless contains, among many other romantic episodes, that of the immortal horses of Achilles, who weep at the death of Patroclus. Aeschylus is more romantic than Sophocles,

[22]Browning, *Fra Lippo Lippi,* 233.

whose *Philoctetes,* were it written now, might figure, for the strangeness of its motive and the perfectness of its execution, as typically romantic; while, of Euripides, it may be said, that his method in writing his plays is to sacrifice readily almost everything else, so that he may attain the fullness of a single romantic effect. These two tendencies, indeed, might be applied as a measure or standard, all through Greek and Roman art and poetry, with very illuminating results; and for an analyst of the romantic principle in art, no exercise would be more profitable, than to walk through the collection of classical antiquities at the Louvre, or the British Museum, or to examine some representative collection of Greek coins, and note how the element of curiosity, of the love of strangeness, insinuates itself into classical design, and record the effects of the romantic spirit there, the traces of struggle, of the grotesque even, though over-balanced here by sweetness; as in the sculpture of Chartres and Rheims, the real sweetness of mind in the sculptor is often overbalanced by the grotesque, by the rudeness of his strength.

Classicism, then, means for Stendhal, for that younger enthusiastic band of French writers whose unconscious method he formulated into principles, the reign of what is pedantic, conventional, and narrowly academical in art; for him, all good art is romantic. To Sainte-Beuve, who understands the term in a more liberal sense, it is the characteristic of certain epochs, of certain spirits in every epoch, not given to the exercise of original imagination, but rather to the working out of refinements of manner on some authorized matter; and who bring to their perfection, in this way, the elements of sanity, of order and beauty in manner. In general criticism, again, it means the spirit of Greece and Rome, of some phases in literature and art that may seem of equal authority with Greece and Rome, the age of Louis the Fourteenth, the age of Johnson; though this is at best an uncritical use of the term, because in Greek and Roman work there are typical examples of the romantic spirit. But explain the terms as we may, in application to particular epochs, there are these two elements always recognizable; united in per-

fect art—in Sophocles, in Dante, in the highest work of Goethe, though not always absolutely balanced there; and these two elements may be not inappropriately termed the classical and romantic tendencies.

Material for the artist, motives of inspiration, are not yet exhausted: our curious, complex, aspiring age still abounds in subjects for aesthetic manipulation by the literary as well as by other forms of art. For the literary art, at all events, the problem just now is, to induce order upon the contorted, proportionless accumulation of our knowledge and experience, our science and history, our hopes and disillusion, and, in effecting this, to do consciously what has been done hitherto for the most part too unconsciously, to write our English language as the Latins wrote theirs, as the French write, as scholars should write. Appealing, as he may, to precedent in this matter, the scholar will still remember that if "the style is the man" it is also the age: that the nineteenth century too will be found to have had its style, justified by necessity—a style very different, alike from the baldness of an impossible "Queen Anne" revival, and an incorrect, incondite exuberance, after the mode of Elizabeth: that we can only return to either at the price of an impoverishment of form or matter, or both, although, an intellectually rich age such as ours being necessarily an eclectic one, we may well cultivate some of the excellences of literary types so different as those: that in literature as in other matters it is well to unite as many diverse elements as may be: that the individual writer or artist, certainly, is to be estimated by the number of graces he combines, and his power of interpenetrating them in a given work. To discriminate schools, of art, of literature, is, of course, part of the obvious business of literary criticism: but, in the work of literary production, it is easy to be overmuch occupied concerning them. For, in truth, the legitimate contention is, not of one age or school of literary art against another, but of all successive schools alike, against the stupidity which is dead to the substance, and the vulgarity which is dead to form.

THE CHILD IN THE HOUSE[1]

As FLORIAN DELEAL walked, one hot afternoon, he overtook by the wayside a poor aged man, and, as he seemed weary with the road, helped him on with the burden which he carried, a certain distance. And as the man told his story, it chanced that he named the place, a little place in the neighborhood of a great city, where Florian had passed his earliest years, but which he had never since seen, and, the story told, went forward on his journey comforted. And that night, like a reward for his pity, a dream of that place came to Florian, a dream which did for him the office of the finer sort of memory, bringing its object to mind with a great clearness, yet, as sometimes happens in dreams, raised a little above itself, and above ordinary retrospect. The true aspect of the place, especially of the house there in which he had lived as a child, the fashion of its doors, its hearths, its windows, the very scent upon the air of it, was with him in sleep for a season; only, with tints more musically blent on wall and floor, and some finer light and shadow running in and out along its curves and angles, and with all its little carvings daintier. He awoke with a sigh at the thought of almost thirty years which lay between him and that place, yet with a flutter of pleasure still within him at the fair light, as if it were a smile, upon it. And it happened that this accident of his dream was just the thing needed for the beginning of a certain design he then had in view, the noting, namely, of some things in the story of his spirit—in that process of brain-building by which we are, each one of us, what we are. With the image of the place so clear and favorable upon him, he fell to thinking of himself therein, and how his thoughts had grown up to him. In that half-spiritualized house he could watch the better, over again, the gradual expansion of the soul which had come to be there—of which indeed, through the law which makes the material objects about them so large an element in children's lives, it had actually become a part; inward and outward being woven through and through each other into one inextricable texture—half, tint and trace and accident of homely color and form, from the wood and the bricks; half, mere soul-stuff, floated thither from who knows how far. In the house and garden of his dream he saw a child moving, and could divide the main streams at least of the winds that had played on him, and study so the first stage in that mental journey.

The *old house,* as when Florian talked of it afterwards he always called it (as all children do, who can recollect a change of home, soon enough but not too soon to mark a period in their lives), really was an old house; and an element of French descent in its inmates—descent from Watteau, the old court-painter, one of whose gallant pieces still hung in one of the rooms—might explain, together with some other things, a noticeable trimness and comely whiteness about everything there—the curtains, the couches, the paint on the walls with which the light and shadow played so delicately; might explain also the tolerance of the great poplar in the garden, a tree most often despised by English people, but which French people love, having observed a certain fresh way its leaves have of dealing with the wind, making it sound, in never so slight a stirring of the air, like running water.

The old-fashioned, low wainscoting went round the rooms, and up the staircase with carved balusters and shadowy angles, landing half-way up at a broad window, with a swallow's nest below the sill, and the blossom of an old pear-tree showing across it in late April, against the blue, below which the perfumed juice of the find of fallen fruit in autumn was so fresh. At the next turning came the closet which held on its deep shelves the best china. Little angel faces and reedy flutings stood out round the fireplace of the children's room. And on the top of the house, above the large attic, where the white mice ran in the twilight—an infinite, unexplored wonderland of childish treasures, glass beads, empty scent-bottles still sweet, thrum[2]

[1]Published in *Macmillan's Magazine,* August, 1878, with the title, "Imaginary Portrait. The Child in the House." Reprinted in *Miscellaneous Studies* (1895).

[2]Waste thread.

of colored silks, among its lumber—a flat space of roof, railed round, gave a view of the neighboring steeples; for the house, as I said, stood near a great city, which sent up heavenwards, over the twisting weather-vanes, not seldom, its beds of rolling cloud and smoke, touched with storm or sunshine. But the child of whom I am writing did not hate the fog because of the crimson lights which fell from it sometimes upon the chimneys, and the whites which gleamed through its openings, on summer mornings, on turret or pavement. For it is false to suppose that a child's sense of beauty is dependent on any choiceness or special fineness, in the objects which present themselves to it, though this indeed comes to be the rule with most of us in later life; earlier, in some degree, we see inwardly; and the child finds for itself, and with unstinted delight, a difference for the sense, in those whites and reds through the smoke on very homely buildings, and in the gold of the dandelions at the road-side, just beyond the houses, where not a handful of earth is virgin and untouched, in the lack of better ministries to its desire of beauty.

This house then stood not far beyond the gloom and rumors of the town, among high garden-wall, bright all summer-time with Golden-rod, and brown-and-golden Wall-flower—*Flos Parietis,* as the children's Latin-reading father taught them to call it, while he was with them. Tracing back the threads of his complex spiritual habit, as he was used in after years to do, Florian found that he owed to the place many tones of sentiment afterwards customary with him, certain inward lights under which things most naturally presented themselves to him. The coming and going of travelers to the town along the way, the shadow of the streets, the sudden breath of the neighboring gardens, the singular brightness of bright weather there, its singular darknesses which linked themselves in his mind to certain engraved illustrations in the old big Bible at home, the coolness of the dark, cavernous shops round the great church, with its giddy winding stair up to the pigeons and the bells—a citadel of peace in the heart of the trouble—all this acted on his childish fancy, so that ever afterwards the like aspects and incidents never failed to throw him into a well-recognized imaginative mood, seeming actually to have become a part of the texture of his mind. Also, Florian could trace home to this point a pervading preference in himself for a kind of comeliness and dignity, an *urbanity* literally, in modes of life, which he connected with the pale people of towns, and which made him susceptible to a kind of exquisite satisfaction in the trimness and well-considered grace of certain things and persons he afterwards met with, here and there, in his way through the world.

So the child of whom I am writing lived on there quietly; things without thus ministering to him, as he sat daily at the window with the birdcage hanging below it, and his mother taught him to read, wondering at the ease with which he learned, and at the quickness of his memory. The perfume of the little flowers of the lime-tree fell through the air upon them like rain; while time seemed to move ever more slowly to the murmur of the bees in it, till it almost stood still on June afternoons. How insignificant, at the moment, seem the influences of the sensible things which are tossed and fall and lie about us, so, or so, in the environment of early childhood. How indelibly, as we afterwards discover, they affect us; with what capricious attractions and associations they figure themselves on the white paper, the smooth wax, of our ingenuous souls, as "with lead in the rock for ever,"[3] giving form and feature, and as it were assigned house-room in our memory, to early experiences of feeling and thought, which abide with us ever afterwards, thus, and not otherwise. The realities and passions, the rumors of the greater world without, steal in upon us, each by its own special little passage-way, through the wall of custom about us; and never afterwards quite detach themselves from this or that accident, or trick, in the mode of their first entrance to us. Our susceptibilities, the discovery of our powers, manifold experiences—our various experiences of the coming and going of bodily pain, for instance—belong to this or the other well-remembered place in the material habitation—that little white room with the window

---

[3] Job. 19:24.

across which the heavy blossoms could beat so peevishly in the wind, with just that particular catch or throb, such a sense of teasing in it, on gusty mornings; and the early habitation thus gradually becomes a sort of material shrine or sanctuary of sentiment; a system of visible symbolism interweaves itself through all our thoughts and passions; and irresistibly, little shapes, voices, accidents—the angle at which the sun in the morning fell on the pillow—become parts of the great chain wherewith we are bound.

Thus far, for Florian, what all this had determined was a peculiarly strong sense of home—so forcible a motive with all of us—prompting to us our customary love of the earth, and the larger part of our fear of death, that revulsion we have from it, as from something strange, untried, unfriendly; though life-long imprisonment, they tell you, and final banishment from home is a thing bitterer still; the looking forward to but a short space, a mere childish *goûter*[4] and dessert of it, before the end, being so great a resource of effort to pilgrims and wayfarers, and the soldier in distant quarters, and lending, in lack of that, some power of solace to the thought of sleep in the home churchyard, at least—dead cheek by dead cheek, and with the rain soaking in upon one from above.

So powerful is this instinct, and yet accidents like those I have been speaking of so mechanically determine it; its essence being indeed the early familiar, as constituting our ideal, or typical conception, of rest and security. Out of so many possible conditions, just this for you and that for me, brings ever the unmistakable realization of the delightful *chez soi;*[5] this for the Englishman, for me and you, with the closely-drawn white curtain and the shaded lamp; that, quite other, for the wandering Arab, who folds his tent every morning, and makes his sleeping-place among haunted ruins, or in old tombs.

With Florian then the sense of home became singularly intense, his good fortune being that the special character of his home was in itself so essentially home-like. As after many wanderings I have come to fancy that some parts of Surrey and Kent are, for

Englishmen, the true landscape, true home-counties, by right, partly, of a certain earthy warmth in the yellow of the sand below their gorse-bushes, and of a certain gray-blue mist after rain, in the hollows of the hills there, welcome to fatigued eyes, and never seem farther south; so I think that the sort of house I have described, with precisely those proportions of red-brick and green, and with a just perceptible monotony in the subdued order of it, for its distinguishing note, is for Englishmen at least typically home-like. And so for Florian that general human instinct was reinforced by this special home-likeness in the place his wandering soul had happened to light on, as, in the second degree, its body and earthly tabernacle; the sense of harmony between his soul and its physical environment became, for a time at least, like perfectly played music, and the life led there singularly tranquil and filled with a curious sense of self-possession. The love of security, of an habitually undisputed standing-ground or sleeping-place, came to count for much in the generation and correcting of his thoughts, and afterwards as a salutary principle of restraint in all his wanderings of spirit. The wistful yearning towards home, in absence from it, as the shadows of evening deepened, and he followed in thought what was doing there from hour to hour, interpreted to him much of a yearning and regret he experienced afterwards, towards he knew not what, out of strange ways of feeling and thought in which, from time to time, his spirit found itself alone; and in the tears shed in such absences there seemed always to be some soul-subduing foretaste of what his last tears might be.

And the sense of security could hardly have been deeper, the quiet of the child's soul being one with the quiet of its home, a place "inclosed" and "sealed." But upon this assured place, upon the child's assured soul which resembled it, there came floating in from the larger world without, as at windows left ajar unknowingly, or over the high garden walls, two streams of impressions, the sentiments of beauty and pain—recognitions of the visible, tangible, audible loveliness of things, as a very real and somewhat tyrannous element in them—and of the sorrow of

[4]Luncheon.

[5]Homelikeness (literally, at one's home).

the world, of grown people and children and animals, as a thing not to be put by in them. From this point he could trace two predominant processes of mental change in him —the growth of an almost diseased sensibility to the spectacle of suffering, and, parallel with this, the rapid growth of a certain capacity of fascination by bright color and choice form—the sweet curvings, for instance, of the lips of those who seemed to him comely persons, modulated in such delicate unison to the things they said or sang,— marking early the activity in him of a more than customary sensuousness, "the lust of the eye," as the Preacher[6] says, which might lead him, one day, how far! Could he have foreseen the weariness of the way! In music sometimes the two sorts of impressions came together, and he would weep, to the surprise of older people. Tears of joy too the child knew, also to older people's surprise; real tears, once, of relief from long-strung, childish expectation, when he found returned at evening, with new roses in her cheeks, the little sister who had been to a place where there was a wood, and brought back for him a treasure of fallen acorns, and black crow's feathers, and his peace at finding her again near him mingled all night with some intimate sense of the distant forest, the rumor of its breezes, with the glossy blackbirds aslant and the branches lifted in them, and of the perfect nicety of the little cups that fell. So those two elementary apprehensions of the tenderness and of the color in things grew apace in him, and were seen by him afterwards to send their roots back into the beginnings of life.

Let me note first some of the occasions of his recognition of the element of pain in things—incidents, now and again, which seemed suddenly to awake in him the whole force of that sentiment which Goethe has called the *Weltschmerz,* and in which the concentrated sorrow of the world seemed suddenly to lie heavy upon him. A book lay in an old book-case, of which he cared to remember one picture—a woman sitting, with hands bound behind her, the dress, the cap, the hair, folded with a simplicity which touched him strangely, as if not by her own hands, but with some ambiguous care of the hands of others—Queen Marie Antoinette, on her way to execution—we all remember David's[7] drawing, meant merely to make her ridiculous. The face that had been so high had learned to be mute and resistless; but out of its very resistlessness, seemed now to call on men to have pity, and forbear; and he took note of that, as he closed the book, as a thing to look at again, if he should at any time find himself tempted to be cruel. Again, he would never quite forget the appeal in the small sister's face, in the garden under the lilacs, terrified at a spider lighted on her sleeve. He could trace back to the look then noted a certain mercy he conceived always for people in fear, even of little things, which seemed to make him, though but for a moment capable of almost any sacrifice of himself. Impressible, susceptible persons, indeed, who had had their sorrows, lived about him; and this sensibility was due in part to the tacit influence of their presence, enforcing upon him habitually the fact that there are those who pass their days, as a matter of course, in a sort of "going quietly." Most poignantly of all he could recall, in unfading minutest circumstance, the cry on the stair, sounding bitterly through the house, and struck into his soul for ever, of an aged woman, his father's sister, come now to announce his death in distant India; how it seemed to make the aged woman like a child again; and, he knew not why, but this fancy was full of pity to him. There were the little sorrows of the dumb animals too—of the white angora, with a dark tail like an ermine's, and a face like a flower, who fell into a lingering sickness, and became quite delicately human in its valetudinarianism, and came to have a hundred different expressions of voice—how it grew worse and worse, till it began to feel the light too much for it, and at last, after one wild morning of pain, the little soul flickered away from the body, quite worn to death already, and now but feebly retaining it.

---

[6] Ecclesiastes. There are several passages which might have suggested the quoted phrase to Pater, but its words are his own.

[7] Jacques Louis David (1748–1825), court-painter to Louis XVI, supporter of the Revolution, and court-painter to Napoleon.

So he wanted another pet; and as there were starlings about the place, which could be taught to speak, one of them was caught, and he meant to treat it kindly; but in the night its young ones could be heard crying after it, and the responsive cry of the mother-bird towards them; and at last, with the first light, though not till after some debate with himself, he went down and opened the cage, and saw a sharp bound of the prisoner up to her nestlings; and therewith came the sense of remorse,—that he too was become an accomplice in moving, to the limit of his small power, the springs and handles of that great machine in things, constructed so ingeniously to play pain-fugues on the delicate nerve-work of living creatures.

I have remarked how, in the process of our brain-building, as the house of thought in which we live gets itself together, like some airy bird's-nest of floating thistle-down and chance straws, compact at last, little accidents have their consequence; and thus it happened that, as he walked one evening, a garden gate, usually closed, stood open; and lo! within, a great red hawthorn in full flower, embossing heavily the bleached and twisted trunk and branches, so aged that there were but a few green leaves thereon—a plumage of tender, crimson fire out of the heart of the dry wood. The perfume of the tree had now and again reached him, in the currents of the wind, over the wall, and he had wondered what might be behind it, and was now allowed to fill his arms with the flowers—flowers enough for all the old blue-china pots along the chimney-piece, making *fête* in the children's room. Was it some periodic moment in the expansion of soul within him, or mere trick of heat in the heavily-laden summer air? But the beauty of the thing struck home to him feverishly; and in dreams all night he loitered along a magic roadway of crimson flowers, which seemed to open ruddily in thick, fresh masses about his feet, and fill softly all the little hollows in the banks on either side. Always afterwards summer by summer, as the flowers came on, the blossom of the red hawthorn still seemed to him absolutely the reddest of all things; and the goodly crimson, still alive in the works of old Venetian masters or old Flemish tapestries, called out always from afar the recollection of the flame in those perishing little petals, as it pulsed gradually out of them, kept long in the drawers of an old cabinet. Also then, for the first time, he seemed to experience a passionateness in his relation to fair outward objects, an inexplicable excitement in their presence, which disturbed him, and from which he half longed to be free. A touch of regret or desire mingled all night with the remembered presence of the red flowers, and their perfume in the darkness about him; and the longing for some undivined entire possession of them was the beginning of a revelation to him, growing ever clearer, with the coming of the gracious summer guise of fields and trees and persons in each succeeding year, of a certain, at times seemingly exclusive, predominance in his interests, of beautiful physical things, a kind of tyranny of the senses over him.

In later years he came upon philosophies which occupied him much in the estimate of the proportion of the sensuous and the ideal elements in human knowledge, the relative parts they bear in it; and, in his intellectual scheme, was led to assign very little to the abstract thought, and much to its sensible vehicle or occasion. Such metaphysical speculation did but reinforce what was instinctive in his way of receiving the world, and for him, everywhere, that sensible vehicle or occasion became, perhaps only too surely, the necessary concomitant of any perception of things, real enough to be of any weight or reckoning, in his house of thought. There were times when he could think of the necessity he was under of associating all thoughts to touch and sight, as a sympathetic link between himself and actual, feeling, living objects; a protest in favor of real men and women against mere gray, unreal abstractions; and he remembered gratefully how the Christian religion, hardly less than the religion of the ancient Greeks, translating so much of its spiritual verity into things that may be seen, condescends in part to sanction this infirmity, if so it be, of our human existence, wherein the world of sense is so much with us, and welcomed this thought as a kind of keeper and sentinel over his soul therein. But certainly, he came more and more to be unable to care for, or think of soul but as in an actual body, or of any world but that wherein are water and trees, and where men and women look, so or so, and press actual hands. It was the trick even his pity learned, fastening those who suffered in anywise to his affections by a kind of sensible attachments. He would think of Julian, fallen into incurable sickness, as spoiled in the sweet blossom of his skin like pale amber, and his honey-like hair; of Cecil, early dead, as cut off from the lilies, from golden summer days, from women's voices; and then what comforted him a little was the thought of the turning of the child's flesh to violets in the turf above him. And thinking of the very poor, it was not the things which most men care most for that he yearned to give them; but fairer roses, perhaps, and power to taste quite as they will, at their ease and not task-burdened, a certain desirable, clear light in the new morning, through which sometimes he had noticed them, quite unconscious of it, on their way to their early toil.

So he yielded himself to these things, to be played upon by them like a musical instrument, and began to note with deepening watchfulness, but always with some puzzled, unutterable longing in his enjoyment, the phases of the seasons and of the growing or waning day, down even to the shadowy changes wrought on bare wall or ceiling—the light cast up from the snow, bringing out their darkest angles; the brown light in the cloud, which meant rain; that almost too austere clearness, in the protracted light of the lengthening day, before warm weather began, as if it lingered but to make a severer workday, with the school-books opened earlier and later; that beam of June sunshine, at last, as he lay awake before the time, a way of gold-dust across the darkness; all the humming, the freshness, the perfume of the garden seemed to lie upon it—and coming in one afternoon in September, along the red gravel walk, to look for a basket of yellow crab-apples left in the cool, old parlor, he remembered it the more, and how the colors struck upon him, because a wasp in one bitten apple stung him, and he felt the passion of sudden, severe pain. For this too brought its curious reflections; and,

in relief from it, he would wonder over it— how it had then been with him—puzzled at the depth of the charm or spell over him, which lay, for a little while at least, in the mere absence of pain; once, especially, when an older boy taught him to make flowers of sealing-wax, and he had burned his hand badly at the lighted taper, and been unable to sleep. He remembered that also afterwards, as a sort of typical thing—a white vision of heat about him, clinging closely, through the languid scent of the ointments put upon the place to make it well.

Also, as he felt this pressure upon him of the sensible world, then, as often afterwards, there would come another sort of curious questioning how the last impressions of the eye and ear might happen to him, how they would find him—the scent of the last flower, the soft yellowness of the last morning, the last recognition of some object of affection, hand or voice; it could not be but that the latest look of the eyes, before their final closing, would be strangely vivid; one would go with the hot tears, the cry, the touch of the wistful bystander, impressed how deeply on one! or would it be, perhaps, a mere frail retiring of all things, great or little, away from one, into a level distance?

For with this desire of physical beauty mingled itself early the fear of death—the fear of death intensified by the desire of beauty. Hitherto he had never gazed upon dead faces, as sometimes, afterwards, at the *Morgue* in Paris, or in that fair cemetery at Munich, where all the dead must go and lie in state before burial, behind glass windows, among the flowers and incense and holy candles—the aged clergy with their sacred ornaments, the young men in their dancing-shoes and spotless white linen—after which visits, those waxen resistless faces would always live with him for many days, making the broadest sunshine sickly. The child had heard indeed of the death of his father, and how, in the Indian station, a fever had taken him, so that though not in action he had yet died as a soldier; and hearing of the "resurrection of the just,"[8] he could think of him as still abroad in the world, somehow, for his protection—a grand, though perhaps rather

[8]St. Luke, 14:14.

terrible figure, in beautiful soldier's things, like the figure in the picture of Joshua's Vision in the Bible[9]—and of that, round which the mourners moved so softly, and afterwards with such solemn singing, as but a worn-out garment left at a deserted lodging. So it was, until on a summer day he walked with his mother through a fair churchyard. In a bright dress he rambled among the graves, in the gay weather, and so came, in one corner, upon an open grave for a child—a dark space on the brilliant grass—the black mold lying heaped up round it, weighing down the little jeweled branches of the dwarf rose-bushes in flower. And therewith came, full-grown, never wholly to leave him, with the certainty that even children do sometimes die, the physical horror of death, with its wholly selfish recoil from the association of lower forms of life, and the suffocating weight above. No benign, grave figure in beautiful soldier's things any longer abroad in the world for his protection! only a few poor, piteous bones; and above them, possibly, a certain sort of figure he hoped not to see. For sitting one day in the garden below an open window, he heard people talking, and could not but listen, how, in a sleepless hour, a sick woman had seen one of the dead sitting beside her, come to call her hence; and from the broken talk evolved with much clearness the notion that not all those dead people had really departed to the churchyard, nor were quite so motionless as they looked, but led a secret, half-fugitive life in their old homes, quite free by night, though sometimes visible in the day, dodging from room to room, with no great good will towards those who shared the place with them. All night the figure sat beside him in the reveries of his broken sleep, and was not quite gone in the morning—an odd, irreconcilable new member of the household, making the sweet familiar chambers unfriendly and suspect by its uncertain presence. He could have hated the dead he had pitied so, for being thus. Afterwards he came to think of those poor, home-returning ghosts, which all men have fancied to themselves—the *revenants*—pathetically, as crying, or beating with vain

hands at the doors, as the wind came, their cries distinguishable in it as a wilder inner note. But, always making death more unfamiliar still, that old experience would ever, from time to time, return to him; even in the living he sometimes caught its likeness; at any time or place, in a moment, the faint atmosphere of the chamber of death would be breathed around him, and the image with the bound chin, the quaint smile, the straight, stiff feet, shed itself across the air upon the bright carpet, amid the gayest company, or happiest communing with himself.

To most children the somber questionings to which impressions like these attach themselves, if they come at all, are actually suggested by religious books, which therefore they often regard with much secret distaste; and dismiss, as far as possible, from their habitual thoughts as a too depressing element in life. To Florian such impressions, these misgivings as to the ultimate tendency of the years, of the relationship between life and death, had been suggested spontaneously in the natural course of his mental growth by a strong innate sense for the soberer tones in things, further strengthened by actual circumstances; and religious sentiment, that system of biblical ideas in which he had been brought up, presented itself to him as a thing that might soften and dignify, and light up as with a "lively hope,"[10] a melancholy already deeply settled in him. So he yielded himself easily to religious impressions, and with a kind of mystical appetite for sacred things; the more as they came to him through a saintly person who loved him tenderly, and believed that this early pre-occupation with them already marked the child out for a saint. He began to love, for their own sakes, church lights, holy days, all that belonged to the comely order of the sanctuary, the secrets of its white linen, and holy vessels, and fonts of pure water; and its hieratic purity and simplicity became the type of something he desired always to have about him in actual life. He pored over the pictures in religious books, and knew by heart the exact mode in which the wrestling angel grasped Jacob, how Jacob looked in his mysterious sleep, how the bells and pomegranates were

---

[9] Joshua, 5:13-14.

[10] I Peter, 1:3.

attached to the hem of Aaron's vestment, [11] sounding sweetly as he glided over the turf of the holy place. His way of conceiving religion came then to be in effect what it ever afterwards remained—a sacred history indeed, but still more a sacred ideal, a transcendent version or representation, under intenser and more expressive light and shade, of human life and its familiar or exceptional incidents, birth, death, marriage, youth, age, tears, joy, rest, sleep, waking—a mirror, towards which men might turn away their eyes from vanity and dullness, and see themselves therein as angels, with their daily meat and drink, even, become a kind of sacred transaction—a complementary strain or burden,[12] applied to our every-day existence, whereby the stray snatches of music in it re-set themselves, and fall into the scheme of some higher and more consistent harmony. A place adumbrated itself in his thoughts, wherein those sacred personalities, which are at once the reflex and the pattern of our nobler phases of life, housed themselves; and this region in his intellectual scheme all subsequent experience did but tend still further to realize and define. Some ideal, hieratic persons he would always need to occupy it and keep a warmth there. And he could hardly understand those who felt no such need at all, finding themselves quite happy without such heavenly companionship, and sacred double of their life, beside them.

Thus a constant substitution of the typical for the actual took place in his thoughts. Angels might be met by the way, under English elm or beech-tree; mere messengers seemed like angels, bound on celestial errands; a deep mysticity brooded over real meetings and partings; marriages were made in heaven; and deaths also, with hands of angels thereupon, to bear soul and body quietly asunder, each to its appointed rest. All the acts and accidents of daily life borrowed a sacred color and significance; the very colors of things became themselves weighty with meanings like the sacred stuffs of Moses' tabernacle,[13] full of penitence or peace. Sentiment, congruous in the first instance only with those divine transactions, the deep effu-

sive unction of the House of Bethany, was assumed as the due attitude for the reception of our every-day existence; and for a time he walked through the world in a sustained, not unpleasurable awe, generated by the habitual recognition, beside every circumstance and event of life, of its celestial correspondent.

Sensibility—the desire of physical beauty —a strange biblical awe, which made any reference to the unseen act on him like solemn music—these qualities the child took away with him, when, at about the age of twelve years, he left the old house, and was taken to live in another place. He had never left home before, and, anticipating much from this change, had long dreamed over it, jealously counting the days till the time fixed for departure should come; had been a little careless about others even, in his strong desire for it—when Lewis fell sick, for instance, and they must wait still two days longer. At last the morning came, very fine; and all things—the very pavement with its dust, at the roadside—seemed to have a white, pearl-like luster in them. They were to travel by a favorite road on which he had often walked a certain distance, and on one of those two prisoner days, when Lewis was sick, had walked farther than ever before, in his great desire to reach the new place. They had started and gone a little way when a pet bird was found to have been left behind, and must even now—so it presented itself to him—have already all the appealing fierceness and wild self-pity at heart of one left by others to perish of hunger in a closed house; and he returned to fetch it, himself in hardly less stormy distress. But as he passed in search of it from room to room, lying so pale, with a look of meekness in their denudation, and at last through that little, stripped white room, the aspect of the place touched him like the face of one dead; and a clinging back towards it came over him, so intense that he knew it would last long, and spoiling all his pleasure in the realization of a thing so eagerly anticipated. And so, with the bird found, but himself in an agony of homesickness, thus capriciously sprung up within him, he was driven quickly away, far into the rural distance, so fondly speculated on, of that favorite country-road.

[11]Genesis, 32:24; 28:11; Exodus, 28:33.
[12]Bass under-part. [13]Exodus, 26.

ROBERT LOUIS STEVENSON

1850–1894

Stevenson was born in Edinburgh on 13 November, 1850. He was the only child of his parents, and his health was infirm from the beginning of his life. Through his boyhood and youth he suffered from frequent bronchial affections and acute nervous excitability, and was thus prevented from getting much regular or continuous schooling. From 1862 until 1867 he spent a large amount of time in travel on the Continent. In the latter year he entered Edinburgh University and for several years attended classes there with such regularity as his health permitted. He read widely, but did not give much attention to routine college studies. He came of a family of distinguished engineers and was expected to follow this profession. Some of his university studies were directed to this end, but in 1871 it was agreed that his health would not allow of his becoming an engineer. He accordingly turned to the study of the law, albeit in a desultory fashion, and was called to the bar in 1875; but he never attempted to practice. Outwardly his life had been hitherto, and was still to be for several years, that of a semi-invalid and idler; but in reality Stevenson was attempting with the utmost industry to learn the art of writing. And in 1876 the fruits of his industry began to appear, in the shape of a series of essays contributed to the *Cornhill Magazine*. Two years later his first book was published, *An Inland Voyage,* an account of a canoe-trip in Belgium and France. A few critical readers, such as Leslie Stephen, promptly recognized Stevenson's promise, perceiving that he "aimed at, and often achieved, those qualities of sustained precision, lucidity, and grace of style which are characteristic of the best French prose, but in English rare in the extreme. He had known how to stamp all he wrote with the impress of a vivid personal charm; had shown himself a master of the apt and animated phrase; and whether in tale or parable, essay or wayside musing, had touched on vital points of experience and feeling with the observation and insight of a true poet and humorist" (S. Colvin,

D. N. B.). Nevertheless, he did not win a large audience until, in 1882, several years had passed, and then only with a story written for boys, *Treasure Island.*

Meanwhile Stevenson had met in France Mrs. Fanny Osbourne, an American woman then separated from her husband. In 1878 she went to California, and in the following year Stevenson determined to follow her. The journey was exceedingly hard on him and would probably have cost him his life had it not been for the careful nursing of Mrs. Osbourne. By 1880 she had secured a divorce from her husband and was married to Stevenson, who took her back to his home in Scotland in August of that year. She herself had delicate health, but she proved a perfect companion for him and was through the remainder of his life his devoted nurse;—his nurse, for Stevenson never won his battle against consumption, but only delayed the end while he continued despite all ills to write, and write, and write. For several years he continued to seek health, or at least a respite from his disease, at various places in Europe, and then in 1887 sailed for America on the same quest. He spent the winter of 1887–1888 at Saranac Lake in the Adirondacks. In the following June he sailed from San Francisco on a voyage among the island groups of the South Sea; and there he established himself in Samoa, where he remained until his death on 4 December, 1894.

Stevenson's life was one of heroic endeavor in the face of constant illness, with the threat of death ever hovering above him. A few of his many books, in addition to those mentioned above, are: *Travels with a Donkey* (1879), *Virginibus Puerisque* (1881), *Familiar Studies of Men and Books* (1882), *The New Arabian Nights* (1882), *Kidnapped* (1886), *Memories and Portraits* (1887), *The Master of Ballantrae* (1889), and *Across the Plains* (1892).

There are several collected editions of Stevenson's writings. The "Pentland Edition" (20 vols., London, 1906–1907) contains bibliographical notes by E. Gosse. The "Swanston Edition" (25 vols., 1911–1912) contains an Introduction by Andrew Lang. Most easily accessible are the volumes of the "Biographical Edition." Stevenson's *Letters* have been edited by Sidney Colvin (the last ed., 4 vols., London, 1911, is the fullest). The standard biography is by Stevenson's cousin, Graham Balfour (2 vols., London, 1901; later reprinted in one vol.). New matter is presented and important questions are raised in *Robert Louis Stevenson, A Critical Biography,* by John A. Steuart (2 vols., Boston, 1924), and in the same writer's *The*

Cap of Youth, Being the Love-Romance of Robert Louis Stevenson (Philadelphia, 1927). An instructive critical study, *Robert Louis Stevenson* (London, 1914; new ed. 1923), has been written by Frank Swinnerton. The following three books may also be found useful: *An Intimate Portrait of R. L. S.* by Lloyd Osbourne (New York, 1924); *Robert Louis Stevenson* by G. K. Chesterton (New York, 1928), which is entertaining; and *Presbyterian Pirate, A Portrait of Stevenson,* by Doris N. Dalglish (Oxford, 1937).

AN APOLOGY FOR IDLERS[1]

BOSWELL: We grow weary when idle.

JOHNSON: That is, sir, because others being busy, we want company; but if we were all idle, there would be no growing weary; we should all entertain one another.[2]

JUST now, when every one is bound, under pain of a decree in absence convicting them of *lèse*-respectability, to enter on some lucrative profession, and labor therein with something not far short of enthusiasm, a cry from the opposite party who are content when they have enough, and like to look on and enjoy in the meanwhile, savors a little of bravado and gasconade. And yet this should not be. Idleness so called, which does not consist in doing nothing, but in doing a great deal not recognized in the dogmatic formularies of the ruling class, has as good a right to state its position as industry itself. It is admitted that the presence of people who refuse to enter in the great handicap race for sixpenny pieces, is at once an insult and a disenchantment for those who do. A fine fellow (as we see so many) takes his determination, votes for the sixpences, and in the emphatic Americanism, "goes for" them. And while such an one is plowing distressfully up the road, it is not hard to understand his resentment, when he perceives cool persons in the meadows by the wayside, lying with a handkerchief over their ears and a glass at their elbow. Alexander is touched in a very delicate place by the disregard of Diogenes. Where was the glory of having taken Rome for these tumultuous barbarians, who poured into the Senate house, and found the Fathers sitting silent and unmoved by their success? It is a sore thing to have labored along and scaled the arduous hilltops, and when all is done, find humanity indifferent to your achievement. Hence physicists condemn the unphysical; financiers have only a superficial toleration for those who know little of stocks; literary persons despise the unlettered; and people of all pursuits combine to disparage those who have none.

But though this is one difficulty of the subject, it is not the greatest. You could not be put in prison for speaking against industry, but you can be sent to Coventry[3] for speaking like a fool. The greatest difficulty with most subjects is to do them well; therefore, please to remember this is an apology. It is certain that much may be judiciously argued in favor of diligence; only there is something to be said against it, and that is what, on the present occasion, I have to say. To state one argument is not necessarily to be deaf to all others, and that a man has written a book of travels in Montenegro, is no reason why he should never have been to Richmond.

It is surely beyond a doubt that people should be a good deal idle in youth. For though here and there a Lord Macaulay may escape from school honors with all his wits

---

[1] Published in 1877; reprinted in the volume entitled *Virginibus Puerisque.* This essay, the three following ones, and the selections from *A Child's Garden of Verses* and *Underwoods* by Stevenson are here reprinted with the permission of Charles Scribner's Sons.

[2] Boswell's *Johnson* (Hill's edition, N. Y.), II, 113.

[3] You can be excluded from the society of which you are a member.

about him, most boys pay so dear for their medals that they never afterward have a shot in their locker, and begin the world bankrupt. And the same holds true during all the time a lad is educating himself, or suffering others 5 to educate him. It must have been a very foolish old gentleman who addressed Johnson at Oxford in these words: "Young man, ply your book diligently now, and acquire a stock of knowledge; for when years come 10 upon you, you will find that poring upon books will be but an irksome task." The old gentleman seems to have been unaware that many other things besides reading grow irksome, and not a few become impossible, by 15 the time a man has to use spectacles and cannot walk without a stick. Books are good enough in their own way, but they are a mighty bloodless substitute for life. It seems a pity to sit, like the Lady of Shalott, 20 peering into a mirror, with your back turned on all the bustle and glamour of reality. And if a man reads very hard, as the old anecdote reminds us, he will have little time for thoughts. 25

If you look back on your own education, I am sure it will not be the full, vivid, instructive hours of truantry that you regret; you would rather cancel some lack-luster periods between sleep and waking in the class. For 30 my own part, I have attended a good many lectures in my time. I still remember that the spinning of a top is a case of Kinetic Stability. I still remember that Emphyteusis[4] is not a disease, nor Stillicide[5] a 35 crime. But though I would not willingly part with such scraps of science, I do not set the same store by them as by certain other odds and ends that I came by in the open street while I was playing truant. This is 40 not the moment to dilate on that mighty place of education, which was the favorite school of Dickens and of Balzac, and turns out yearly many inglorious masters in the Science of the Aspects of Life. Suffice it to 45 say this: if a lad does not learn in the streets,

---

[4] A kind of conditional grant of a right to the possession and enjoyment of land.

[5] A continual falling or succession of drops. In Roman law, the right to have rain from one's roof drop on another's land or roof, or the right to refuse to allow rain from another's roof to drop on one's own land or roof.

it is because he has no faculty of learning. Nor is the truant always in the streets, for if he prefers, he may go out by the gardened suburbs into the country. He may pitch on some tuft of lilacs over a burn,[6] and smoke innumerable pipes to the tune of the water on the stones. A bird will sing in the thicket. And there he may fall into a vein of kindly thought, and see things in a new perspective. Why, if this be not education, what is? We may conceive Mr. Worldly Wiseman accosting such an one, and the conversation that should thereupon ensue:

"How now, young fellow, what dost thou here?"

"Truly, sir, I take mine ease."

"Is not this the hour of the class? and should'st thou not be plying thy Book with diligence, to the end thou mayest obtain knowledge?"

"Nay, but thus also I followed after Learning, by your leave."

"Learning, quotha! After what fashion, I pray thee? Is it mathematics?"

"No, to be sure."

"Is it metaphysics?"

"Nor that."

"Is it some language?"

"Nay, it is no language."

"Is it a trade?"

"Nor a trade neither."

"Why, then, what is't?"

"Indeed, sir, as a time may soon come for me to go upon Pilgrimage, I am desirous to note what is commonly done by persons in my case, and where are the ugliest Sloughs and Thickets on the Road; as also, what manner of Staff is of the best service. Moreover, I lie here, by this water, to learn by root-of-heart a lesson which my master teaches me to call Peace, or Contentment."

Hereupon Mr. Worldly Wiseman was much commoved with passion, and shaking his cane with a very threatful countenance, broke forth upon this wise: "Learning, quotha!" said he; "I would have all such rogues scourged by the Hangman!"

And so he would go his way, ruffling out his cravat with a crackle of starch, like a turkey when it spread its feathers.

Now this, of Mr. Wiseman's, is the com-

---

[6] Brook.

mon opinion. A fact is not called a fact, but a piece of gossip, if it does not fall into one of your scholastic categories. An inquiry must be in some acknowledged direction, with a name to go by; or else you are not in- 5 quiring at all, only lounging; and the work-house is too good for you. It is supposed that all knowledge is at the bottom of a well, or the far end of a telescope. Sainte-Beuve,[7] as he grew older, came to regard all ex- 10 perience as a single great book, in which to study for a few years ere we go hence; and it seemed all one to him whether you should read in Chapter xx, which is the differential calculus, or in Chapter xxxix, which is hear- 15 ing the band play in the gardens. As a matter of fact, an intelligent person, looking out of his eyes and hearkening in his ears, with a smile on his face all the time, will get more true education than many another in a 20 life of heroic vigils. There is certainly some chill and arid knowledge to be found upon the summits of formal and laborious science; but it is all round about you, and for the trouble of looking, that you will 25 acquire the warm and palpitating facts of life. While others are filling their memory with a lumber of words, one-half of which they will forget before the week be out, your truant may learn some really useful art: to play the 30 fiddle, to know a good cigar, or to speak with ease and opportunity to all varieties of men. Many who have "plied their book diligently," and know all about some one branch or another of accepted lore, come out 35 of the study with an ancient and owl-like demeanor, and prove dry, stockish, and dyspeptic in all the better and brighter parts of life. Many make a large fortune, who remain underbred and pathetically stupid 40 to the last. And meantime there goes the idler, who began life along with them—by your leave, a different picture. He has had time to take care of his health and his spirits; he has been a great deal in the open 45 air, which is the most salutary of all things for both body and mind; and if he has never read the great Book in very recondite places, he has dipped into it and skimmed it over to excellent purpose. Might not the 50

student afford some Hebrew roots, and the business man some of his half-crowns, for a share of the idler's knowledge of life at large, and Art of Living? Nay, and the idler has another and more important quality than these. I mean his wisdom. He who has much looked on at the childish satisfaction of other people in their hobbies, will regard his own with only a very ironical indulgence. He will not be heard among the dogmatists. He will have a great and cool allowance for all sorts of people and opinions. If he finds no out-of-the-way truths, he will identify himself with no very burning falsehood. His way takes him along a by-road, not much 15 frequented, but very even and pleasant, which is called Commonplace Lane, and leads to the Belvedere[8] of Common-sense. Thence he shall command an agreeable, if no very noble prospect; and while others behold the East 20 and West, the Devil and the Sunrise, he will be contentedly aware of a sort of morning hour upon all sublunary things, with an army of shadows running speedily and in many different directions into the great daylight of 25 Eternity. The shadows and the generations, the shrill doctors and the plangent wars, go by into ultimate silence and emptiness; but underneath all this, a man may see, out of the Belvedere windows, much green and peace- 30 ful landscape; many firelit parlors; good people laughing, drinking, and making love as they did before the Flood or the French Revolution; and the old shepherd telling his tale under the hawthorn. 35

Extreme *busyness,* whether at school or college, kirk or market, is a symptom of deficent vitality; and a faculty for idleness implies a catholic appetite and a strong sense of personal identity. There is a sort of 40 dead-alive, hackneyed people about, who are scarcely conscious of living except in the exercise of some conventional occupation. Bring these fellows into the country, or set them aboard ship, and you will see how they 45 pine for their desk or their study. They have no curiosity; they cannot give themselves over to random provocations; they do not take pleasure in the exercise of their faculties for its own sake; and unless Ne- 50 cessity lays about them with a stick, they

---

[7]Charles A. Sainte-Beuve (1804–1869), French critic and poet.

[8]A building commanding a fine prospect.

will even stand still. It is no good speaking to such folk: they *cannot* be idle, their nature is not generous enough; and they pass those hours in a sort of coma, which are not dedicated to furious moiling in the gold-mill. When they do not require to go to the office, when they are not hungry and have no mind to drink, the whole breathing world is a blank to them. If they have to wait an hour or so for a train, they fall into a stupid trance with their eyes open. To see them, you would suppose there was nothing to look at and no one to speak with; you would imagine they were paralyzed or alienated;[9] and yet very possibly they are hard workers in their own way, and have good eyesight for a flaw in a deed or a turn of the market. They have been to school and college, but all the time they had their eye on the medal; they have gone about in the world and mixed with clever people, but all the time they were thinking of their own affairs. As if a man's soul were not too small to begin with, they have dwarfed and narrowed theirs by a life of all work and no play; until here they are at forty, with a listless attention, a mind vacant of all material of amusement, and not one thought to rub against another while they wait for the train. Before he was breeched, he might have clambered on the boxes; when he was twenty, he would have stared at the girls; but now the pipe is smoked out, the snuffbox empty, and my gentleman sits bolt upright upon a bench, with lamentable eyes. This does not appeal to me as being Success in Life.

But it is not only the person himself who suffers from his busy habits, but his wife and children, his friends and relations, and down to the very people he sits with in a railway carriage or an omnibus. Perpetual devotion to what a man calls his business is only to be sustained by perpetual neglect of many other things. And it is not by any means certain that a man's business is the most important thing he has to do. To an impartial estimate it will seem clear that many of the wisest, most virtuous, and most beneficent parts that are to be played upon the Theater of Life are filled by gratuitous performers, and pass, among the world at large, as phases of idleness. For in that Theater, not only the walking gentlemen, singing chambermaids, and diligent fiddlers in the orchestra, but those who look on and clap their hands from the benches, do really play a part and fulfill important offices towards the general result. You are no doubt very dependent on the care of your lawyer and stockbroker, of the guards and signalmen who convey you rapidly from place to place, and the policemen who walk the streets for your protection; but is there not a thought of gratitude in your heart for certain other benefactors who set you smiling when they fall in your way, or season your dinner with good company? Colonel Newcome helped to lose his friend's money; Fred Bayham had an ugly trick of borrowing shirts; and yet they were better people to fall among than Mr. Barnes.[10] And though Falstaff was neither sober nor very honest, I think I could name one or two long-faced Barabbases[11] whom the world could better have done without. Hazlitt mentions that he was more sensible of obligation to Northcote,[12] who had never done him anything he could call a service, than to his whole circle of ostentatious friends; for he thought a good companion emphatically the greatest benefactor. I know there are people in the world who cannot feel grateful unless the favor has been done them at the cost of pain and difficulty. But this is a churlish disposition. A man may send you six sheets of letter-paper covered with the most entertaining gossip, or you may pass half an hour pleasantly, perhaps profitably, over an article of his; do you think the service would be greater, if he had made the manuscript in his heart's blood, like a compact with the devil? Do you really fancy you should be more beholden to your correspondent, if he had been damning you all the while for your importunity? Pleasures are more beneficial than duties because, like the quality of mercy, they are not strained,[13]

---

[9]Mentally deranged.

[10]Characters in Thackeray's *Newcomes*.

[11]Falstaff appears in *Henry IV, I* and *II,* and in *The Merry Wives of Windsor.* Barabbas was the robber whose freedom, instead of that of Jesus, the Jews demanded of Pilate.

[12]James Northcote (1746–1831), painter and writer.

[13]See *The Merchant of Venice,* IV, i, 184.

and they are twice blest. There must always be two to a kiss, and there may be a score in a jest; but wherever there is an element of sacrifice, the favor is conferred with pain, and, among generous people, received with confusion. There is no duty we so much underrate as the duty of being happy. By being happy, we sow anonymous benefits upon the world, which remain unknown even to ourselves, or when they are disclosed, surprise nobody so much as the benefactor. The other day, a ragged, barefoot boy ran down the street after a marble, with so jolly an air that he set everyone he passed into a good-humor; one of these persons, who had been delivered from more than usually black thoughts, stopped the little fellow and gave him some money with this remark: "You see what sometimes comes of looking pleased." If he had looked pleased before, he had now to look both pleased and mystified. For my part, I justify this encouragement of smiling rather than tearful children; I do not wish to pay for tears anywhere but upon the stage; but I am prepared to deal largely in the opposite commodity. A happy man or woman is a better thing to find than a five-pound note. He or she is a radiating focus of good-will; and their entrance into a room is as though another candle had been lighted. We need not care whether they could prove the forty-seventh proposition;[14] they do a better thing than that, they practically demonstrate the great Theorem of the Livableness of Life. Consequently, if a person cannot be happy without remaining idle, idle he should remain. It is a revolutionary precept; but thanks to hunger and the workhouse, one not easily to be abused; and within practical limits, it is one of the most incontestable truths in the whole Body of Morality. Look at one of your industrious fellows for a moment, I beseech you. He sows hurry and reaps indigestion; he puts a vast deal of activity out to interest, and receives a large measure of nervous derangement in return. Either he absents himself entirely from all fellowship, and lives a recluse in a garret, with carpet slippers and a leaden inkpot; or he comes

among people swiftly and bitterly, in a contraction of his whole nervous system, to discharge some temper before he returns to work. I do not care how much or how well he works, this fellow is an evil feature in other people's lives. They would be happier if he were dead. They could easier do without his services in the Circumlocution Office,[15] than they can tolerate his fractious spirits. He poisons life at the well-head. It is better to be beggared out of hand by a scapegrace nephew, than daily hag-ridden by a peevish uncle.

And what, in God's name, is all this pother about? For what cause do they embitter their own and other people's lives? That a man should publish three or thirty articles a year, that he should finish or not finish his great allegorical picture, are questions of little interest to the world. The ranks of life are full; and although a thousand fall, there are always some to go into the breach. When they told Joan of Arc she should be at home minding women's work, she answered there were plenty to spin and wash. And so, even with your own rare gifts! When nature is "so careless of the single life,"[16] why should we coddle ourselves into the fancy that our own is of exceptional importance? Suppose Shakespeare had been knocked on the head some dark night in Sir Thomas Lucy's preserves,[17] the world would have wagged on better or worse, the pitcher gone to the well, the scythe to the corn, and the student to his book; and no one been any the wiser of the loss. There are not many works extant, if you look the alternative all over, which are worth the price of a pound of tobacco to a man of limited means. This is a sobering reflection for the proudest of our earthly vanities. Even a tobacconist may, upon consideration, find no great cause for personal vainglory in the phrase; for although tobacco is an admirable sedative, the qualities necessary for retailing it are neither rare nor precious in themselves. Alas and alas! you may take it how you will,

---

[14]Of Bk. I, Euclid's *Elements*—the Pythagorean theorem.

[15]See Dickens's *Little Dorrit*.

[16]Tennyson, *In Memoriam*, LV, 8.

[17]The game preserves in the neighborhood of Stratford, where, according to an apocryphal story, young Shakespeare was caught poaching.

but the services of no single individual are indispensable. Atlas[18] was just a gentleman with a protracted nightmare! And yet you see merchants who go and labor themselves into a great fortune and thence into the bankruptcy court; scribblers who keep scribbling at little articles until their temper is a cross to all who come about them, as though Pharaoh should set the Israelites to make a pin instead of a pyramid; and fine young men who work themselves into a decline, and are driven off in a hearse with white plumes upon it. Would you not suppose these persons had been whispered, by the Master of the Ceremonies, the promise of some momentous destiny? and that this lukewarm bullet on which they play their farces was the bull's eye and center-point of all the universe? And yet it is not so. The ends for which they gave away their priceless youth, for all they know, may be chimerical or hurtful; the glory and riches they expect may never come, or may find them indifferent; and they and the world they inhabit are so inconsiderable that the mind freezes at the thought.

AES TRIPLEX[1]

THE changes wrought by death are in themselves so sharp and final, and so terrible and melancholy in their consequences, that the thing stands alone in man's experience, and has no parallel upon earth. It outdoes all other accidents because it is the last of them. Sometimes it leaps suddenly upon its victims like a Thug;[2] sometimes it lays a regular siege and creeps upon their citadel during a score of years. And when the business is done, there is sore havoc made in other people's lives, and a pin knocked out by which many subsidiary friendships hung together. There are empty chairs, solitary walks, and single beds at night. Again, in taking away our friends, death does not take them away utterly, but leaves behind a mocking, tragical, and soon intolerable residue, which must be hurriedly concealed. Hence a whole chapter of sights and customs striking to the mind, from the pyramids of Egypt to the gibbets and dule trees[3] of mediaeval Europe. The poorest persons have a bit of pageant going toward the tomb; memorial stones are set up over the least memorable; and, in order to preserve some show of respect for what remains of our old loves and friendships, we must accompany it with much grimly ludicrous ceremonial, and the hired undertaker parades before the door. All this, and much more of the same sort, accompanied by the eloquence of poets, has gone a great way to put humanity in error; nay, in many philosophies the error has been embodied and laid down with every circumstance of logic; although in real life the bustle and swiftness, in leaving people little time to think, have not left them time enough to go dangerously wrong in practice.

As a matter of fact, although few things are spoken of with more fearful whisperings than this prospect of death, few have less influence on conduct under healthy circumstances. We have all heard of cities in South America built upon the side of fiery mountains, and how, even in this tremendous[4] neighborhood, the inhabitants are not a jot more impressed by the solemnity of mortal conditions than if they were delving gardens in the greenest corner of England. There are serenades and suppers and much gallantry among the myrtles overhead; and meanwhile the foundation shudders underfoot, the bowels of the mountain growl, and at any moment living ruin may leap sky-high into the moonlight, and tumble man and his merry-making in the dust. In the eyes of very young people, and very dull old ones, there is something indescribably reckless and desperate in such a picture. It seems not credible that respectable married people, with umbrellas, should find appetite for a bit of

---

[18]Who supported the world on his head.

[1]Published in *Virginibus Puerisque* (1881). *Aes Triplex* may be translated Triple Bronze and is borrowed from Horace (*Odes*, I, iii, 9), who writes that "Oak and triple bronze must have girt the breast of him who first committed his frail bark to the angry sea" (translation of C. E. Bennett).

[2]One of an association of professional murderers in India.

[3]Trees of sorrow.

[4]Horrible.

supper within quite a long distance of a fiery mountain; ordinary life begins to smell of high-handed debauch when it is carried on so close to a catastrophe; and even cheese and salad, it seems, could hardly be relished in such circumstances without something like a defiance of the Creator. It should be a place for nobody but hermits dwelling in prayer and maceration, or mere born-devils drowning care in a perpetual carouse.

And yet, when one comes to think upon it calmly, the situation of these South American citizens forms only a very pale figure for the state of ordinary mankind. This world itself, traveling blindly and swiftly in over-crowded space, among a million other worlds traveling blindly and swiftly in contrary directions, may very well come by a knock that would set it into explosion like a penny squib. And what, pathologically looked at, is the human body with all its organs, but a mere bagful of petards?[5] The least of these is as dangerous to the whole economy as the ship's powder-magazine to the ship; and with every breath we breathe, and every meal we eat, we are putting one or more of them in peril. If we clung as devotedly as some philosophers pretend we do to the abstract idea of life, or were half as frightened as they make out we are, for the subversive accident that ends it all, the trumpets might sound by the hour and no one would follow them into battle—the blue peter might fly at the truck;[6] but who would climb into a sea going ship? Think (if these philosophers were right) with what a preparation of spirit we should affront the daily peril of the dinner-table: a deadlier spot than any battle-field in history, where the far greater proportion of our ancestors have miserably left their bones! What woman would ever be lured into marriage, so much more dangerous than the wildest sea? And what would it be to grow old? For, after a certain distance, every step we take in life we find the ice growing thinner below our feet, and all around us and behind us we see our contemporaries going through. By the time a man gets well into the seventies, his continued existence is a mere miracle; and when he lays

his old bones in bed for the night, there is an overwhelming probability that he will never see the day. Do the old men mind it, as a matter of fact? Why, no. They were never merrier; they have their grog at night, and tell the raciest stories; they hear of the death of people about their own age, or even younger, not as if it was a grisly warning, but with a simple childlike pleasure at having outlived some one else; and when a draught might puff them out like a guttering candle, or a bit of a stumble shatter them like so much glass, their old hearts keep sound and unaffrighted, and they go on, bubbling with laughter, through years of man's age compared to which the valley at Balaclava[7] was as safe and peaceful as a village cricket-green on Sunday. It may fairly be questioned (if we look to the peril only) whether it was a much more daring feat for Curtius[8] to plunge into the gulf, than for any old gentleman of ninety to doff his clothes and clamber into bed.

Indeed, it is a memorable subject for consideration, with what unconcern and gaiety mankind pricks on along the Valley of the Shadow of Death. The whole way is one wilderness of snares, and the end of it, for those who fear the last pinch, is irrevocable ruin. And yet we go spinning through it all, like a party for the Derby.[9] Perhaps the reader remembers one of the humorous devices of the deified Caligula:[10] how he encouraged a vast concourse of holiday-makers on to his bridge over Baiae bay; and when they were in the height of their enjoyment, turned loose the Praetorian guards among the company, and had them tossed into the sea. This is no bad miniature of the dealings of nature with the transitory race of man. Only, what a checkered picnic we have of it, even while it lasts! and into what great waters, not to be crossed by any swimmer,

---

[5] Firecrackers.

[6] The flag for departure might fly at the masthead.

[7] The battle, fought in 1854 during the Crimean War, in which an English brigade was by mistake thrown against a much larger force of Russians and annihilated.

[8] Mettus Curtius, who according to legend saved Rome in B. C. 362 by jumping into a chasm which had opened in the Forum.

[9] The annual horse-race run at Epsom.

[10] Roman emperor (A. D. 37–41) and madman. Baiae was a resort on the Bay of Naples; the Praetorians, the imperial bodyguard.

God's pale Praetorian throws us over in the end!

We live the time that a match flickers; we pop the cork of a ginger-beer bottle, and the earthquake swallows us on the instant. Is it not odd, is it not incongruous, is it not, in the highest sense of human speech, incredible, that we should think so highly of the ginger-beer, and regard so little the devouring earthquake? The love of Life and the fear of Death are two famous phrases that grow harder to understand the more we think about them. It is a well-known fact that an immense proportion of boat accidents would never happen if people held the sheet[11] in their hands instead of making it fast; and yet, unless it be some martinet of a professional mariner or some landsman with shattered nerves, every one of God's creatures makes it fast. A strange instance of man's unconcern and brazen boldness in the face of death!

We confound ourselves with metaphysical phrases, which we import into daily talk with noble inappropriateness. We have no idea of what death is, apart from its circumstances and some of its consequences to others; and although we have some experience of living, there is not a man on earth who has flown so high into abstraction as to have any practical guess at the meaning of the word *life*. All literature, from Job and Omar Khayyám to Thomas Carlyle or Walt Whitman, is but an attempt to look upon the human state with such largeness of view as shall enable us to rise from the consideration of living to the Definition of Life. And our sages give us about the best satisfaction in their power when they say that it is a vapor, or a show, or made of the same stuff with dreams. Philosophy, in its more rigid sense, has been at the same work for ages; and after a myriad bald heads have wagged over the problem, and piles of words have been heaped one upon another into dry and cloudy volumes without end, philosophy has the honor of laying before us, with modest pride, her contribution toward the subject: that life is a Permanent Possibility of Sensation. Truly a fine result! A man may very well love beef, or hunting, or a woman; but surely, surely, not a Permanent Possibility of Sensa-

tion! He may be afraid of a precipice, or a dentist, or a large enemy with a club, or even an undertaker's man; but not certainly of abstract death. We may trick with the word *life* in its dozen senses until we are weary of tricking; we may argue in terms of all the philosophies on earth, but one fact remains true throughout—that we do not love life, in the sense that we are greatly preoccupied about its conservation—that we do not, properly speaking, love life at all, but living. Into the views of the least careful there will enter some degree of providence; no man's eyes are fixed entirely on the passing hour; but although we have some anticipation of good health, good weather, wine, active employment, love, and self-approval, the sum of these anticipations does not amount to anything like a general view of life's possibilities and issues; nor are those who cherish them most vividly, at all the most scrupulous of their personal safety. To be deeply interested in the accidents of our existence, to enjoy keenly the mixed texture of human experience, rather leads a man to disregard precautions, and risk his neck against a straw. For surely the love of living is stronger in an Alpine climber roping over a peril, or a hunter riding merrily at a stiff fence, than in a creature who lives upon a diet and walks a measured distance in the interest of his constitution.

There is a great deal of very vile nonsense talked upon both sides of the matter: tearing[12] divines reducing life to the dimensions of a mere funeral procession, so short as to be hardly decent; and melancholy unbelievers yearning for the tomb as if it were a world too far away. Both sides must feel a little ashamed of their performances now and again when they draw in their chairs to dinner. Indeed, a good meal and a bottle of wine is an answer to most standard works upon the question. When a man's heart warms to his viands, he forgets a great deal of sophistry, and soars into a rosy zone of contemplation. Death may be knocking at the door, like the Commander's statue;[13] we

[11] Rope controlling the angle of a sail.

[12] Ranting.

[13] In the Spanish legend: the funereal statue of the Commander, whose daughter Don Juan has ravished, visits the seducer and delivers him over to devils.

have something else in hand, thank God, and let him knock. Passing bells are ringing all the world over. All the world over, and every hour, some one is parting company with all his aches and ecstasies. For us also the trap is laid. But we are so fond of life that we have no leisure to entertain the terror of death. It is a honeymoon with us all through, and none of the longest. Small blame to us if we give our whole hearts to this glowing bride of ours, to the appetites, to honor, to the hungry curiosity of the mind, to the pleasure of the eyes in nature, and the pride of our own nimble bodies.

We all of us appreciate the sensations; but as for caring about the Permanence of the Possibility, a man's head is generally very bald, and his senses very dull, before he comes to that. Whether we regard life as a lane leading to a dead wall—a mere bag's end, as the French say—or whether we think of it as a vestibule or gymnasium, where we wait our turn and prepare our faculties for some more noble destiny; whether we thunder in a pulpit, or pule in little atheistic poetry-books, about its vanity and brevity; whether we look justly for years of health and vigor, or are about to mount into a Bath chair,[14] as a step toward the hearse; in each and all of these views and situations there is but one conclusion possible: that a man should stop his ears against paralyzing terror, and run the race that is set before him with a single mind. No one surely could have recoiled with more heartache and terror from the thought of death than our respected lexicographer;[15] and yet we know how little it affected his conduct, how wisely and boldly he walked, and in what a fresh and lively vein he spoke of life. Already an old man, he ventured on his Highland tour; and his heart, bound with triple brass, did not recoil before twenty-seven individual cups of tea. As courage and intelligence are the two qualities best worth a good man's cultivation, so it is the first part of intelligence to recognize our precarious estate in life, and the first part of courage to be not at all abashed before the fact. A frank and somewhat headlong carriage, not looking too anxiously before, not

[14]Invalid's chair on wheels.
[15]Samuel Johnson.

dallying in maudlin regret over the past, stamps the man who is well armored for this world.

And not only well armored for himself, but a good friend and a good citizen to boot. We do not go to cowards for tender dealing; there is nothing so cruel as panic; the man who has least fear for his own carcass, has most time to consider others. That eminent chemist who took his walks abroad in tin shoes, and subsisted wholly upon tepid milk, had all his work cut out for him in considerate dealings with his own digestion. So soon as prudence has begun to grow up in the brain, like a dismal fungus, it finds its first expression in a paralysis of generous acts. The victim begins to shrink spiritually; he develops a fancy for parlors with a regulated temperature, and takes his morality on the principle of tin shoes and tepid milk. The care of one important body or soul becomes so engrossing, that all the noises of the outer world begin to come thin and faint into the parlor with the regulated temperature; and the tin shoes go equally forward over blood and rain. To be overwise is to ossify; and the scruple-monger ends by standing stock-still. Now the man who has his heart on his sleeve, and a good whirling weathercock of a brain, who reckons his life as a thing to be dashingly used and cheerfully hazarded, makes a very different acquaintance of the world, keeps all his pulses going true and fast, and gathers impetus as he runs, until, if he be running toward anything better than wildfire, he may shoot up and become a constellation in the end. Lord, look after his health; Lord, have a care of his soul, says he; and he has at the key of the position, and swashes through incongruity and peril toward his aim. Death is on all sides of him with pointed batteries, as he is on all sides of all of us; unfortunate surprises gird him round; mim-mouthed friends and relations hold up their hands in quite a little elegiacal synod about his path: and what cares he for all this? Being a true lover of living, a fellow with something pushing and spontaneous in his inside, he must, like any other soldier, in any other stirring, deadly warfare, push on at his best pace until he touch the goal. "A peerage or Westminster Abbey!" cried

Nelson in his bright, boyish, heroic manner. These are great incentives; not for any of these, but for the plain satisfaction of living, of being about their business in some sort or other, do the brave, serviceable men of every nation tread down the nettle danger, and pass flyingly over all the stumbling-blocks of prudence. Think of the heroism of Johnson, think of that superb indifference to mortal limitation that set him upon his dictionary, and carried him through triumphantly until the end! Who, if he were wisely considerate of things at large, would ever embark upon any work much more considerable than a halfpenny post card? Who would project a serial novel, after Thackeray and Dickens had each fallen in mid-course?[16] Who would find heart enough to begin to live, if he dallied with the consideration of death?

And, after all, what sorry and pitiful quibbling all this is! To forego all the issues of living in a parlor with the regulated temperature—as if that were not to die a hundred times over, and for ten years at a stretch! As if it were not to die in one's own lifetime, and without even the sad immunities of death! As if it were not to die, and yet be the patient spectators of our own pitiable change! The Permanent Possibility is preserved, but the sensations carefully held at arm's length, as if one kept a photographic plate in a dark chamber. It is better to lose health like a spendthrift than to waste it like a miser. It is better to live and be done with it, than to die daily in the sickroom. By all means begin your folio; even if the doctor does not give you a year, even if he hesitates

about a month, make one brave push and see what can be accomplished in a week. It is not only in finished undertakings that we ought to honor useful labor. A spirit goes out of the man who means execution, which outlives the most untimely ending. All who have meant good work with their whole hearts, have done good work, although they may die before they have the time to sign it. Every heart that has beat strong and cheerfully has left a hopeful impulse behind it in the world, and bettered the tradition of mankind. And even if death catch people, like an open pitfall, and in mid-career, laying out vast projects, and planning monstrous foundations, flushed with hope, and their mouths full of boastful language, they should be at once tripped up and silenced: is there not something brave and spirited in such a termination? and does not life go down with a better grace, foaming in full body over a precipice, than miserably straggling to an end in sandy deltas? When the Greeks made their fine saying that those whom the gods love die young, I cannot help believing they had this sort of death also in their eye. For surely, at whatever age it overtake the man, this is to die young. Death has not been suffered to take so much as an illusion from his heart. In the hot-fit of life, a-tiptoe on the highest point of being, he passes at a bound on to the other side. The noise of the mallet and chisel is scarcely quenched, the trumpets are hardly done blowing, when, trailing with him clouds of glory, this happy-starred, full-blooded spirit shoots into the spiritual land.

A GOSSIP ON ROMANCE[1]

IN ANYTHING fit to be called by the name of reading, the process itself should be absorbing and voluptuous; we should gloat over a book, be rapt clean out of ourselves, and rise from the perusal, our mind filled with the busiest, kaleidoscopic dance of

images, incapable of sleep or of continuous thought. The words, if the book be eloquent, should run thenceforward in our ears like the noise of breakers, and the story, if it be a story, repeat itself in a thousand colored pictures to the eye. It was for this last pleasure that we read so closely, and loved our books so dearly, in the bright, troubled period of boyhood. Eloquence and thought, character and conversation, were but obstacles to brush aside as we dug blithely after a certain sort of incident, like a pig for truffles. For my

[16]Thackeray died without finishing *Denis Duval;* Dickens left *Edwin Drood* incomplete. In the same way, Stevenson himself did not live to complete his masterpiece, *Weir of Hermiston.*

[1]Published in 1882; reprinted in the volume entitled *Memories and Portraits.*

part, I liked a story to begin with an old wayside inn where, "towards the close of the year 17—," several gentlemen in three-cocked hats were playing bowls. A friend of mine preferred the Malabar coast in a storm, with a ship beating to windward, and a scowling fellow of herculean proportions striding along the beach; he, to be sure, was a pirate. This was further afield than my home-keeping fancy loved to travel, and designed altogether for a larger canvas than the tales that I affected. Give me a highwayman and I was full to the brim; a Jacobite would do, but the highwayman was my favorite dish. I can still hear that merry clatter of the hoofs along the moonlit lane; night and the coming of the day are still related in my mind with the doings of John Rann or Jerry Abershaw;[2] and the words "postchaise," the "great North road," "ostler," and "nag" still sound in my ears like poetry. One and all, at least, and each with his particular fancy, we read story-books in childhood, not for eloquence or character or thought, but for some quality of the brute incident. That quality was not mere bloodshed or wonder. Although each of these was welcome in its place, the charm for the sake of which we read depended on something different from either. My elders used to read novels aloud; and I can still remember four different passages which I heard, before I was ten, with the same keen and lasting pleasure. One I discovered long afterwards to be the admirable opening of *What Will He Do With It:*[3] it was no wonder I was pleased with that. The other three still remain unidentified. One is a little vague; it was about a dark, tall house at night, and people groping on the stairs by the light that escaped from the open door of a sick-room. In another, a lover left a ball, and went walking in a cool, dewy park, whence he could watch the lighted windows and the figures of the dancers as they moved. This was the most sentimental impression I think I had yet received, for a child is somewhat deaf to the sentimental. In the last, a poet, who had been tragically wrangling with his wife, walked forth on the sea-beach on a tempestuous night and witnessed the horrors of a wreck.[4] Different as they are, all these early favorites have a common note—they have all a touch of the romantic.

Drama is the poetry of conduct, romance the poetry of circumstance. The pleasure that we take in life is of two sorts—the active and the passive. Now we are conscious of a great command over our destiny; anon we are lifted up by circumstance, as by a breaking wave, and dashed we know not how into the future. Now we are pleased by our conduct, anon merely pleased by our surroundings. It would be hard to say which of these modes of satisfaction is the more effective, but the latter is surely the more constant. Conduct is three parts of life, they say; but I think they put it high. There is a vast deal in life and letters both which is not immoral, but simply a-moral; which either does not regard the human will at all, or deals with it in obvious and healthy relations; where the interest turns, not upon what a man shall choose to do, but on how he manages to do it; not on the passionate slips and hesitations of the conscience, but on the problems of the body and of the practical intelligence, in clean, open-air adventure, the shock of arms or the diplomacy of life. With such material as this it is impossible to build a play, for the serious theater exists solely on moral grounds, and is a standing proof of the dissemination of the human conscience. But it is possible to build, upon this ground, the most joyous of verses, and the most lively, beautiful, and buoyant tales.

One thing in life calls for another; there is a fitness in events and places. The sight of a pleasant arbor puts it in our mind to sit there. One place suggests work, another idleness, a third early rising and long rambles in the dew. The effect of night, of any flowing water, of lighted cities, of the peep of day, of ships, of the open ocean, calls up in the mind an army of anonymous desires and pleasures. Something, we feel, should happen; we know not what, yet we proceed in quest of it. And many of the happiest hours of life fleet by us in this vain attendance on the genius of the place and moment. It is thus that tracts of young fir, and low rocks

---

[2] Highway robbers.

[3] By Bulwer Lytton, published in 1858.

[4] Since traced by many obliging correspondents to the gallery of Charles Kingsley (Stevenson's note).

that reach into deep soundings, particularly torture and delight me. Something must have happened in such places, and perhaps ages back, to members of my race; and when I was a child I tried in vain to invent appropriate games for them, as I still try, just as vainly, to fit them with the proper story. Some places speak distinctly. Certain dank gardens cry aloud for a murder; certain old houses demand to be haunted; certain coasts are set apart for shipwreck. Other spots again seem to abide their destiny, suggestive and impenetrable, "miching mallecho."[5] The inn at Burford Bridge, with its arbors and green garden and silent, eddying river— though it is known already as the place where Keats wrote some of his *Endymion* and Nelson parted from his Emma[6]—still seems to wait the coming of the appropriate legend. Within these ivied walls, behind these old green shutters, some further business smolders, waiting for its hour. The old Hawes Inn at the Queen's Ferry makes a similar call upon my fancy. There it stands, apart from the town, beside the pier, in a climate of its own, half inland, half marine— in front, the ferry bubbling with the tide and the guardship swinging to her anchor; behind, the old garden with the trees. Americans seek it already for the sake of Lovel and Oldbuck, who dined there at the beginning of the *Antiquary*.[7] But you need not tell me—that is not all; there is some story, unrecorded or not yet complete, which must express the meaning of that inn more fully. So it is with names and faces; so it is with incidents that are idle and inconclusive in themselves, and yet seem like the beginning of some quaint romance, which the all-careless author leaves untold. How many of these romances have we not seen determine at their birth; how many people have met us with a look of meaning in their eye, and sunk at once into trivial acquaintances; to how many places have we not drawn near, with express intimations—"here my destiny awaits me"—and we have but dined there and passed on! I have lived both at the Hawes

and Burford in a perpetual flutter, on the heels, as it seemed, of some adventure that should justify the place; but though the feeling had me to bed at night and called me again at morning in one unbroken round of pleasure and suspense, nothing befell me in either worth remark. The man or the hour had not yet come; but some day, I think, a boat shall put off from the Queen's Ferry, fraught with a dear cargo, and some frosty night a horseman, on a tragic errand, rattle with his whip upon the green shutters of the inn at Burford.[8]

Now, this is one of the natural appetites with which any lively literature has to count. The desire for knowledge, I had almost added the desire for meat, is not more deeply seated than this demand for fit and striking incident. The dullest of clowns tells, or tries to tell, himself a story, as the feeblest of children uses inventions in his play; and even as the imaginative grown person, joining in the game, at once enriches it with many delightful circumstances, the great creative writer shows us the realization and the apotheosis of the day-dreams of common men. His stories may be nourished with the realities of life, but their true mark is to satisfy the nameless longings of the reader, and to obey the ideal laws of the day-dream. The right kind of thing should fall out in the right kind of place; the right kind of thing should follow; and not only the characters talk aptly and think naturally, but all the circumstances in a tale answer one to another like notes in music. The threads of a story come from time to time together and make a picture in the web; the characters fall from time to time into some attitude to each other or to nature, which stamps the story home like an illustration. Crusoe recoiling from the footprint, Achilles shouting over against the Trojans, Ulysses bending the great bow, Christian running with his fingers in his ears,[9] these are each culminating moments in the legend, and each has been printed on the mind's eye for ever. Other things we may

---

[5] Sneaking mischief (*Hamlet*, III, ii, 147).

[6] Lady Hamilton (1761–1815), Lord Nelson's mistress.

[7] Scott's novel (1816).

[8] Since the above was written I have tried to launch the boat with my own hands in *Kidnapped*. Some day, perhaps, I may try a rattle at the shutters (Stevenson's note).

[9] In *Robinson Crusoe*, the *Iliad*, the *Odyssey*, and the *Pilgrim's Progress* respectively.

forget; we may forget the words, although they are beautiful; we may forget the author's comment, although perhaps it was ingenious and true; but these epoch-making scenes, which put the last mark of truth upon a story and fill up, at one blow, our capacity for sympathetic pleasure, we so adopt into the very bosom of our mind that neither time nor tide can efface or weaken the impression. This, then, is the plastic part of literature: to embody character, thought, or emotion in some act or attitude that shall be remarkably striking to the mind's eye. This is the highest and hardest thing to do in words; the thing which, once accomplished, equally delights the schoolboy and the sage, and makes, in its own right, the quality of epics. Compared with this, all other purposes in literature, except the purely lyrical or the purely philosophic, are bastard in nature, facile of execution, and feeble in result. It is one thing to write about the inn at Burford, or to describe scenery with the word-painters; it is quite another to seize on the heart of the suggestion and make a country famous with a legend. It is one thing to remark and to dissect, with the most cutting logic, the complications of life, and of the human spirit; it is quite another to give them body and blood in the story of Ajax[10] or of Hamlet. The first is literature, but the second is something besides, for it is likewise art.

English people of the present day are apt, I know not why, to look somewhat down on incident, and reserve their admiration for the clink of teaspoons and the accents of the curate. It is thought clever to write a novel with no story at all, or at least with a very dull one. Reduced even to the lowest terms, a certain interest can be communicated by the art of narrative; a sense of human kinship stirred; and a kind of monotonous fitness, comparable to the words and air of *Sandy's Mull,* preserved among the infinitesimal occurrences recorded. Some people work, in this manner, with even a strong touch. Mr. Trollope's inimitable clergymen naturally arise to the mind in this connection. But even Mr. Trollope does not confine himself to chronicling small beer. Mr. Crawley's collision with the Bishop's wife, Mr. Melnette

dallying in the deserted banquet-room,[11] are typical incidents, epically conceived, fitly embodying a crisis. Or again look at Thackeray. If Rawdon Crawley's blow were not delivered, *Vanity Fair* would cease to be a work of art. That scene is the chief ganglion of the tale; and the discharge of energy from Rawdon's fist is the reward and consolation of the reader. The end of *Esmond* is a yet wider excursion from the author's customary fields; the scene at Castlewood is pure Dumas; the great and wily English borrower has here borrowed from the great, unblushing French thief; as usual, he has borrowed admirably well, and the breaking of the sword rounds off the best of all his books with a manly, martial note. But perhaps nothing can more strongly illustrate the necessity for marking incident than to compare the living fame of *Robinson Crusoe* with the discredit of *Clarissa Harlowe.*[12] *Clarissa* is a book of a far more startling import, worked out, on a great canvas, with inimitable courage and unflagging art. It contains wit, character, passion, plot, conversations full of spirit and insight, letters sparkling with unstrained humanity; and if the death of the heroine be somewhat frigid and artificial, the last days of the hero strike the only note of what we now call Byronism, between the Elizabethans and Byron himself. And yet a little story of a shipwrecked sailor, with not a tenth part of the style nor a thousandth part of the wisdom, exploring none of the arcana of humanity and deprived of the perennial interest of love, goes on from edition to edition, ever young, while *Clarissa* lies upon the shelves unread. A friend of mine, a Welsh blacksmith, was twenty-five years old and could neither read nor write, when he heard a chapter of *Robinson* read aloud in a farm kitchen. Up to that moment he had sat content, huddled in his ignorance, but he left that farm another man. There were day-dreams, it appeared, divine day-dreams, written and printed and bound, and to be bought for money and enjoyed at pleasure. Down he sat that day, painfully learned to read Welsh, and returned to borrow the book.

[10] A tragedy of the same name by Sophocles.

[11] In *The Last Chronicle of Barset* and in *The Way We Live Now,* respectively.

[12] By Samuel Richardson, published in 1747–1748.

It had been lost, nor could he find another copy but one that was in English. Down he sat once more, learned English, and at length, and with entire delight, read *Robinson*. It is like the story of a love-chase. If he had heard a letter from *Clarissa*, would he have been fired with the same chivalrous ardor? I wonder. Yet *Clarissa* has every quality that can be shown in prose, one alone excepted—pictorial or picture-making romance. While *Robinson* depends, for the most part and with the overwhelming majority of its readers, on the charm of circumstance.

In the highest achievements of the art of words, the dramatic and the pictorial, the moral and romantic interest, rise and fall together by a common and organic law. Situation is animated with passion, passion clothed upon with situation. Neither exists for itself, but each inheres indissolubly with the other. This is high art; and not only the highest art possible in words, but the highest art of all, since it combines the greatest mass and diversity of the elements of truth and pleasure. Such are epics, and the few prose tales that have the epic weight. But as from a school of works, aping the creative, incident and romance are ruthlessly discarded, so may character and drama be omitted or subordinated to romance. There is one book, for example, more generally loved than Shakespeare, that captivates in childhood, and still delights in age—I mean the *Arabian Nights* —where you shall look in vain for moral or for intellectual interest. No human face or voice greets us among that wooden crowd of kings and genies, sorcerers and beggarmen. Adventure, on the most naked terms, furnishes forth the entertainment and is found enough. Dumas approaches perhaps nearest of any modern to these Arabian authors in the purely material charm of some of his romances. The early part of *Monte Cristo,* down to the finding of the treasure, is a piece of perfect story-telling; the man never breathed who shared these moving incidents without a tremor; and yet Faria is a thing of packthread and Dantès little more than a name. The sequel is one long-drawn error, gloomy, bloody, unnatural, and dull; but as for these early chapters, I do not believe there is another volume extant where you can

breathe the same unmingled atmosphere of romance. It is very thin and light, to be sure, as on a high mountain; but it is brisk and clear and sunny in proportion. I saw the other day, with envy, an old, and a very clever lady setting forth on a second or third voyage into *Monte Cristo*. Here are stories which powerfully affect the reader, which can be reperused at any age, and where the characters are no more than puppets. The bony fist of the showman visibly propels them; their springs are an open secret; their faces are of wood, their bellies filled with bran; and yet we thrillingly partake of their adventures. And the point may be illustrated still further. The last interview between Lucy and Richard Feverel[13] is pure drama; more than that, it is the strongest scene, since Shakespeare, in the English tongue. Their first meeting by the river, on the other hand, is pure romance; it has nothing to do with character; it might happen to any other boy and maiden, and be none the less delightful for the change. And yet I think he would be a bold man who should choose between these passages. Thus, in the same book, we may have two scenes, each capital in its order: in the one, human passion, deep calling unto deep, shall utter its genuine voice; in the second, according circumstances, like instruments in tune, shall build up a trivial but desirable incident, such as we love to prefigure for ourselves; and in the end, in spite of the critics, we may hesitate to give the preference to either. The one may ask more genius—I do not say it does; but at least the other dwells as clearly in the memory.

True romantic art, again, makes a romance of all things. It reaches into the highest abstraction of the ideal; it does not refuse the most pedestrian realism. *Robinson Crusoe* is as realistic as it is romantic: both qualities are pushed to an extreme, and neither suffers. Nor does romance depend upon the material importance of the incidents. To deal with strong and deadly elements, banditti, pirates, war and murder, is to conjure with great names, and, in the event of failure, to double the disgrace. The arrival of Haydn and Consuelo at the Canon's villa[14] is a very

---

[13] In George Meredith's *Ordeal of Richard Feverel*
[14] In George Sand's *Consuelo*.

trifling incident; yet we may read a dozen boisterous stories from beginning to end, and not receive so fresh and stirring an impression of adventure. It was the scene of Crusoe at the wreck, if I remember rightly, that so bewitched my blacksmith. Nor is the fact surprising. Every single article the castaway recovers from the hulk is "a joy for ever"[15] to the man who reads of them. They are the things that should be found, and the bare enumeration stirs the blood. I found a glimmer of the same interest the other day in a new book, *The Sailor's Sweetheart,* by Mr. Clark Russell. The whole business of the brig *Morning Star* is very rightly felt and spiritedly written; but the clothes, the books and the money satisfy the reader's mind like things to eat. We are dealing here with the old cut-and-dry, legitimate interest of treasure trove. But even treasure trove can be made dull. There are few people who have not groaned under the plethora of goods that fell to the lot of the *Swiss Family Robinson,*[16] that dreary family. They found article after article, creature after creature, from milk kine to pieces of ordnance, a whole consignment; but no informing taste had presided over the selection, there was no smack or relish in the invoice; and these riches left the fancy cold. The box of goods in Verne's *Mysterious Island* is another case in point; there was no gusto and no glamour about that; it might have come from a shop. But the two hundred and seventy-eight Australian sovereigns on board the *Morning Star* fell upon me like a surprise that I had expected; whole vistas of secondary stories, besides the one in hand, radiated forth from that discovery, as they radiate from a striking particular in life; and I was made for the moment as happy as a reader has the right to be.

To come at all at the nature of this quality of romance, we must bear in mind the peculiarity of our attitude to any art. No art produces illusion; in the theater we never forget that we are in the theater; and while we read a story, we sit wavering between two minds, now merely clapping our hands at the merit of the performance, now condescending to take an active part in fancy with the characters. This last is the triumph of romantic story-telling: when the reader consciously plays at being the hero, the scene is a good scene. Now, in character-studies the pleasure that we take is critical; we watch, we approve, we smile at incongruities, we are moved to sudden heats of sympathy with courage, suffering, or virtue. But the characters are still themselves, they are not us; the more clearly they are depicted, the more widely do they stand away from us, the more imperiously do they thrust us back into our place as a spectator. I cannot identify myself with Rawdon Crawley or with Eugène de Rastignac,[17] for I have scarce a hope or fear in common with them. It is not character but incident that woos us out of our reserve. Something happens as we desire to have it happen to ourselves; some situation, that we have long dallied with in fancy, is realized in the story with enticing and appropriate details. Then we forget the characters; then we push the hero aside; then we plunge into the tale in our own person and bathe in fresh experience; and then, and then only, do we say we have been reading a romance. It is not only pleasurable things that we imagine in our day-dreams; there are lights in which we are willing to contemplate even the idea of our own death; ways in which it seems as if it would amuse us to be cheated, wounded, or calumniated. It is thus possible to construct a story, even of tragic import, in which every incident, detail, and trick of circumstance shall be welcome to the reader's thoughts. Fiction is to the grown man what play is to the child; it is there that he changes the atmosphere and tenor of his life; and when the game so chimes with his fancy that he can join in it with all his heart, when it pleases him with every turn, when he loves to recall it and dwells upon its recollection with entire delight, fiction is called romance.

Walter Scott is out and away the king of the romantics. *The Lady of the Lake* has no indisputable claim to be a poem beyond the

---

[15]Keats, *Endymion,* I, 1.

[16]By Johann R. Wyss (1781–1830), a Swiss professor.

[17]In Thackeray's *Vanity Fair* and in Balzac's *Père Goriot* and other stories, respectively.

inherent fitness and desirability of the tale. It is just such a story as a man would make up for himself, walking, in the best health and temper, through just such scenes as it is laid in. Hence it is that a charm dwells undefinable among these slovenly verses, as the unseen cuckoo fills the mountains with his note; hence, even after we have flung the book aside, the scenery and adventures remain present to the mind, a new and green possession, not unworthy of that beautiful name, *The Lady of the Lake,* or that direct, romantic opening,—one of the most spirited and poetical in literature,—"The stag at eve had drunk his fill." The same strength and the same weaknesses adorn and disfigure the novels. In that ill-written, ragged book, *The Pirate,* the figure of Cleveland—cast up by the sea on the resounding foreland of Dunrossness—moving, with the blood on his hands and the Spanish words on his tongue, among the simple islanders—singing a serenade under the window of his Shetland mistress—is conceived in the very highest manner of romantic invention. The words of his song, "Through groves of palm," sung in such a scene and by such a lover, clench, as in a nutshell, the emphatic contrast upon which the tale is built. In *Guy Mannering,* again, every incident is delightful to the imagination; and the scene when Harry Bertram lands at Ellangowan is a model instance of romantic method.

" 'I remember the tune well,' he says, 'though I cannot guess what should at present so strongly recall it to my memory.' He took his flageolet from his pocket and played a simple melody. Apparently the tune awoke the corresponding associations of a damsel. . . . She immediately took up the song—

" 'Are these the links of Forth, she said;
    Or are they the crooks of Dee,
    Or the bonny woods of Warroch Head
    That I so fain would see?'

" 'By heaven!' said Bertram, 'it is the very ballad.' "

On this quotation two remarks fall to be made. First, as an instance of modern feeling for romance, this famous touch of the flageolet and the old song is selected by Miss Braddon[18] for omission. Miss Braddon's idea of a story, like Mrs. Todgers's idea of a wooden leg, were something strange to have expounded. As a matter of personal experience, Meg's appearance to old Mr. Bertram on the road, the ruins of Derncleugh, the scene of the flageolet, and the Dominie's recognition of Harry, are the four strong notes that continue to ring in the mind after the book is laid aside. The second point is still more curious. The reader will observe a mark of excision in the passage as quoted by me. Well, here is how it runs in the original: "A damsel, who, close behind a fine spring about half-way down the descent, and which had once supplied the castle with water, was engaged in bleaching linen." A man who gave in such copy would be discharged from the staff of a daily paper. Scott has forgotten to prepare the reader for the presence of the "damsel"; he has forgotten to mention the spring and its relation to the ruin; and now, face to face with his omission, instead of trying back and starting fair, crams all this matter, tail foremost, into a single shambling sentence. It is not merely bad English, or bad style; it is abominably bad narrative besides.

Certainly the contrast is remarkable; and it is one that throws a strong light upon the subject of this paper. For here we have a man of the finest creative instinct touching with perfect certainty and charm the romantic junctures of his story; and we find him utterly careless, almost, it would seem, incapable, in the technical matter of style, and not only frequently weak, but frequently wrong in points of drama. In character parts, indeed, and particularly in the Scotch, he was delicate, strong, and truthful; but the trite, obliterated features of too many of his heroes have already wearied two generations of readers. At times his characters will speak with something far beyond propriety with a true heroic note; but on the next page they will be wading wearily forward with an ungrammatical and undramatic rigmarole of words. The man who could conceive and write the character of Elspeth of the Craig-

[18]Mary Elizabeth Braddon (Mrs. John Maxwell, 1837-1915), a novelist. Mrs. Todgers appears in Dickens's *Martin Chuzzlewit.*

burnfoot,[19] as Scott has conceived and written it, had not only splendid romantic, but splendid tragic gifts. How comes it, then, that he could so often fob us off with languid, inarticulate twaddle?

It seems to me that the explanation is to be found in the very quality of his surprising merits. As his books are play to the reader, so were they play to him. He conjured up the romantic with delight, but he had hardly patience to describe it. He was a great day-dreamer, a seer of fit and beautiful and humorous visions, but hardly a great artist; hardly, in the manful sense, an artist at all. He pleased himself, and so he pleases us. Of the pleasures of his art he tasted fully; but of its toils and vigils and distresses never man knew less. A great romantic—an idle child.

FATHER DAMIEN[1]

An Open Letter to the Reverend Dr. Hyde of Honolulu

Sydney, February 25, 1890.

SIR,—It may probably occur to you that we have met, and visited, and conversed; on my side, with interest. You may remember that you have done me several courtesies, for which I was prepared to be grateful. But there are duties which come before gratitude, and offenses which justly divide friends, far more acquaintances. Your letter to the Reverend H. B. Gage is a document, which, in my sight, if you had filled me with bread when I was starving, if you had sat up to nurse my father when he lay a-dying, would yet absolve me from the bonds of gratitude. You know enough, doubtless, of the process of canonization to be aware that, a hundred years after the death of Damien, there will appear a man charged with the painful office of the *devil's advocate*. After that noble brother of mine, and of all frail clay, shall have lain a century at rest, one shall accuse, one defend him. The circumstance is unusual that the devil's advocate should be a volunteer, should be a member of a sect immediately rival, and should make haste to take upon himself his ugly office ere the bones are cold; unusual, and of a taste which I shall leave my readers free to qualify; unusual, and to me inspiring. If I have at all learned the trade of using words to convey truth and to arouse emotion, you have at last furnished me with a subject. For it is in the interest of all mankind and the cause of public decency in every quarter of the world, not only that Damien should be righted, but that you and your letter should be displayed at length, in their true colors, to the public eye.

To do this properly, I must begin by quoting you at large: I shall then proceed to criticize your utterance from several points of view, divine and human, in the course of which I shall attempt to draw again and with more specification the character of the dead saint whom it has pleased you to vilify: so much being done, I shall say farewell to you for ever.

Honolulu, August 2, 1889.

REV. H. B. GAGE.

Dear Brother,—In answer to your inquiries about Father Damien, I can only reply that we who knew the man are surprised at the extravagant newspaper laudations, as if he was a most saintly philanthropist. The simple truth is, he was a coarse, dirty man, headstrong and bigoted. He was not sent to Molokai, but went there without orders; did not stay at the leper settlement (before he became one himself), but circulated freely over the whole island (less than half the island is devoted to the lepers), and he

---

[19]In the *Antiquary*.

[1]Printed at Sydney, Australia, in 1890, at Stevenson's expense; reprinted in the volume entitled *Lay Morals and Other Papers*. In 1889 Stevenson was at Honolulu and visited the leper settlement on Molokai (one of the Hawaiian Islands), there learning at first hand what he tells about Joseph Damien de Veuster (1840–1889), the Belgian priest who devoted his life to the lepers. Later Stevenson learned of Dr. Hyde's letter through a statement in a newspaper to the effect that the publication of the letter had caused the abandonment of a project to erect a monument to Damien's memory. "I'll not believe it," he said, "unless I see it with my own eyes; for it is too damnable for belief." When, however, he presently reached Sydney, Stevenson did see Dr. Hyde's published letter and the same day wrote his reply. "I knew," he said, "I was writing a libel; I thought he [Hyde] would bring an action; I made sure I should be ruined; I asked leave of my gallant family, and the sense that I was signing away all I possessed kept me up to high-water mark, and made me feel every insult heroic."

came often to Honolulu. He had no hand in the reforms and improvements inaugurated, which were the work of our Board of Health, as occasion required and means were provided. He was not a pure man in his relations with women, and the leprosy of which he died should be attributed to his vices and carelessness. Others have done much for the lepers, our own ministers, the government physicians, and so forth, but never with the Catholic idea of meriting eternal life.—Yours, *etc.*,

C. M. Hyde.[2]

To deal fitly with a letter so extraordinary, I must draw at the outset on my private knowledge of the signatory and his sect. It may offend others; scarcely you, who have been so busy to collect, so bold to publish, gossip on your rivals. And this is perhaps the moment when I may best explain to you the character of what you are to read: I conceive you as a man quite beyond and below the reticences of civility: with what measure you mete, with that shall it be measured you again; with you, at last, I rejoice to feel the button off the foil and to plunge home. And if in aught that I shall say I should offend others, your colleagues, whom I respect and remember with affection, I can but offer them my regret; I am not free, I am inspired by the consideration of interests far more large; and such pain as can be inflicted by anything from me must be indeed trifling when compared with the pain with which they read your letter. It is not the hangman, but the criminal, that brings dishonor on the house.

You belong, sir, to a sect—I believe my sect, and that in which my ancestors labored —which has enjoyed, and partly failed to utilize, an exceptional advantage in the islands of Hawaii. The first missionaries came; they found the land already self-purged of its old and bloody faith; they were embraced, almost on their arrival, with enthusiasm; what troubles they supported came far more from whites than from Hawaiians; and to these last they stood (in a rough figure) in the shoes of God. This is not the place to enter into the degree or causes of their failure, such as it is. One element alone is pertinent, and must here be plainly dealt with. In the course of their evangelical calling, they—or too many of them— grew rich. It may be news to you that the houses of missionaries are a cause of mocking on the streets of Honolulu. It will at least be news to you, that when I returned your civil visit, the driver of my cab commented on the size, the taste, and the comfort of your home. It would have been news certainly to myself, had any one told me that afternoon that I should live to drag such matter into print. But you see, sir, how you degrade better men to your own level; and it is needful that those who are to judge betwixt you and me, betwixt Damien and the devil's advocate, should understand your letter to have been penned in a house which could raise, and that very justly, the envy and the comments of the passers-by. I think (to employ a phrase of yours which I admire) it "should be attributed" to you that you have never visited the scene of Damien's life and death. If you had, and had recalled it, and looked about your pleasant rooms, even your pen perhaps would have been stayed.

Your sect (and remember, as far as any sect avows me, it is mine) has not done ill in a worldly sense in the Hawaiian Kingdom. When calamity befell their innocent parishioners, when leprosy descended and took root in the Eight Islands, a *quid pro quo*[3] was to be looked for. To that prosperous mission, and to you, as one of its adornments, God had sent at last an opportunity. I know I am touching here upon a nerve acutely sensitive. I know that others of your colleagues look back on the inertia of your Church, and the intrusive and decisive heroism of Damien, with something almost to be called remorse. I am sure it is so with yourself; I am persuaded your letter was inspired by a certain envy, not essentially ignoble, and the one human trait to be espied in that performance. You were thinking of the lost chance, the past day; of that which should have been conceived and was not; of the service due and not rendered. *Time was,* said the voice in your ear, in your pleasant room, as you sat raging and writing; and if the words written were base

[2]From the Sydney *Presbyterian*, October 26, 1889 (Stevenson's note).

[3]A fair return.

beyond parallel, the rage, I am happy to repeat—it is the only compliment I shall pay you—the rage was almost virtuous. But, sir, when we have failed, and another has succeeded; when we have stood by, and another has stepped in; when we sit and grow bulky in our charming mansions, and a plain, uncouth peasant steps into the battle, under the eyes of God, and succors the afflicted, and consoles the dying, and is himself afflicted in his turn, and dies upon the field of honor—the battle cannot be retrieved as your unhappy irritation has suggested. It is a lost battle, and lost for ever. One thing remained to you in your defeat—some rags of common honor; and these you have made haste to cast away.

Common honor; not the honor of having done anything right, but the honor of not having done aught conspicuously foul; the honor of the inert: that was what remained to you. We are not all expected to be Damiens; a man may conceive his duty more narrowly, he may love his comforts better; and none will cast a stone at him for that. But will a gentleman of your reverend profession allow me an example from the fields of gallantry? When two gentlemen compete for the favor of a lady, and the one succeeds and the other is rejected, and (as will sometimes happen) matter damaging to the successful rival's credit reaches the ear of the defeated, it is held by plain men of no pretensions that his mouth is, in the circumstance, almost necessarily closed. Your Church and Damien's were in Hawaii upon a rivalry to do well: to help, to edify, to set divine examples. You having (in one huge instance) failed, and Damien succeeded, I marvel it should not have occurred to you that you were doomed to silence; that when you had been outstripped in that high rivalry, and sat inglorious in the midst of your well-being, in your pleasant room—and Damien, crowned with glories and horrors, toiled and rotted in that pigsty of his under the cliffs of Kalawao—you, the elect who would not, were the last man on earth to collect and propagate gossip on the volunteer who would and did.

I think I see you—for I try to see you in the flesh as I write these sentences—I think

I see you leap at the word pigsty, a hyperbolical expression at the best. "He had no hand in the reforms," he was "a coarse, dirty man"; these were your own words; and you may think it possible that I am come to support you with fresh evidence. In a sense, it is even so. Damien has been too much depicted with a conventional halo and conventional features; so drawn by men who perhaps had not the eye to remark or the pen to express the individual; or who perhaps were only blinded and silenced by generous admiration, such as I partly envy for myself—such as you, if your soul were enlightened, would envy on your bended knees. It is the least defect of such a method of portraiture that it makes the path easy for the devil's advocate, and leaves for the misuse of the slanderer a considerable field of truth. For the truth that is suppressed by friends is the readiest weapon of the enemy. The world, in your despite, may perhaps owe you something, if your letter be the means of substituting once for all a credible likeness for a wax abstraction. For, if that world at all remember you, on the day when Damien of Molokai shall be named Saint, it will be in virtue of one work: your letter to the Reverend H. B. Gage.

You may ask on what authority I speak. It was my inclement destiny to become acquainted, not with Damien, but with Dr. Hyde. When I visited the lazaretto Damien was already in his resting grave. But such information as I have, I gathered on the spot in conversation with those who knew him well and long: some indeed who revered his memory; but others who had sparred and wrangled with him, who beheld him with no halo, who perhaps regarded him with small respect, and through whose unprepared and scarcely partial communications the plain, human features of the man shone on me convincingly. These gave me what knowledge I possess; and I learned it in that scene where it could be most completely and sensitively understood—Kalawao, which you have never visited, about which you have never so much as endeavored to inform yourself: for, brief as your letter is, you have found the means to stumble into that confession. *"Less than one-half* of the island," you say, "is devoted to the lepers." Molokai—"*Molokai ahina,*" the "gray," lofty, and most desolate island— along all its northern side plunges a front of precipice into a sea of unusual profundity. This range of cliff is, from east to west, the 5 true end and frontier of the island. Only in one spot there projects into the ocean a cer- tain triangular and rugged down, grassy, stony, windy, and rising in the midst into a hill with a dead crater : the whole bearing to 10 the cliff that overhangs it somewhat the same relation as a bracket to a wall. With this hint you will now be able to pick out the leper station on a map; you will be able to judge how much of Molokai is thus cut off between 15 the surf and precipice, whether less than a half, or less than a quarter, or a fifth, or a tenth—or say, a twentieth; and the next time you burst into print you will be in a position to share with us the issue of your calcula- 20 tions.

I imagine you to be one of those persons who talk with cheerfulness of that place which oxen and wainropes could not drag you to behold. You, who do not even know 25 its situation on the map, probably denounce sensational descriptions, stretching your limbs the while in your pleasant parlor on Beretania Street. When I was pulled ashore there one early morning, there sat with me 30 in the boat two sisters, bidding farewell (in humble imitation of Damien) to the lights and joys of human life. One of these wept silently; I could not withhold myself from joining her. Had you been there, it is my 35 belief that nature would have triumphed even in you; and as the boat drew but a little nearer, and you beheld the stairs crowded with abominable deformations of our com- mon manhood, and saw yourself landing in 40 the midst of such a population as only now and then surrounds us in the horror of a nightmare—what a haggard eye you would have rolled over your reluctant shoulder towards the house on Beretania Street! 45 Had you gone on; had you found every fourth face a blot upon the landscape; had you visited the hospital and seen the butt- ends of human beings lying there almost un- recognizable, but still breathing, still think- 50 ing, still remembering; you would have un- derstood that life in the lazaretto is an or-

deal from which the nerves of a man's spirit shrink, even as his eye quails under the brightness of the sun; you would have felt it was (even to-day) a pitiful place to visit and a hell to dwell in. It is not the fear of pos- sible infection. That seems a little thing when compared with the pain, the pity, and the disgust of the visitor's surroundings, and the atmosphere of affliction, disease, and physical disgrace in which he breathes. I do not think I am a man more than usually timid; but I never recall the days and nights I spent upon that island promontory (eight days and seven nights), without heartfelt thankfulness that I am somewhere else. I find in my diary that I speak of my stay as a "grinding experience": I have once jotted in the margin, *"Harrowing* is the word"; and when the *Mokolii* bore me at last towards the outer world, I kept repeating to myself, with a new conception of their pregnancy, those simple words of the song—

" 'Tis the most distressful country that ever yet was seen."

And observe : that which I saw and suffered from was a settlement purged, bettered, beautified; the new village built, the hospital and the Bishop-Home excellently arranged; the sisters, the doctor, and the missionaries, all indefatigable in their noble tasks. It was a different place when Damien came there, and made his great renunciation, and slept that first night under a tree amidst his rotting brethren: alone with pestilence; and looking forward (with what courage, with what pitiful sinkings of dread, God only knows) to a lifetime of dressing sores and stumps.

You will say, perhaps, I am too sensitive, that sights as painful abound in cancer hos- pitals and are confronted daily by doctors and nurses. I have long learned to admire and envy the doctors and the nurses. But there is no cancer hospital so large and populous as Kalawao and Kalaupapa; and in such a matter every fresh case, like every inch of length in the pipe of an organ, deepens the note of the impression; for what daunts the onlooker is that monstrous sum of human suffering by which he stands sur- rounded. Lastly, no doctor or nurse is called upon to enter once for all the doors of that gehenna; they do not say farewell, they need not abandon hope, on its sad threshold; they but go for a time to their high calling, and can look forward as they go to relief, to recreation, and to rest. But Damien shut to with his own hand the doors of his own sepulcher.

I shall now extract three passages from my diary at Kalawao:

A. Damien is dead and already somewhat ungratefully remembered in the field of his labors and sufferings. "He was a good man, but very officious," says one. Another tells me he had fallen (as other priests so easily do) into something of the ways and habits of thought of a Kanaka;[4] but he had the wit to recognize the fact, and the good sense to laugh at [over] it. A plain man it seems he was; I cannot find he was a popular.

B. After Ragsdale's death [Ragsdale was a famous Luna, or overseer, of the unruly settlement] there followed a brief term of office by Father Damien which served only to publish the weakness of that noble man. He was rough in his ways, and he had no control. Authority was relaxed; Damien's life was threatened, and he was soon eager to resign.

C. Of Damien I begin to have an idea. He seems to have been a man of the peasant class, certainly of the peasant type: shrewd; ignorant and bigoted, yet with an open mind, and capable of receiving and digesting a reproof if it were bluntly administered; superbly generous in the least thing as well as in the greatest, and as ready to give his last shirt (although not without human grumbling) as he had been to sacrifice his life; essentially indiscreet and officious, which made him a troublesome colleague; domineering in all his ways, which made him incurably unpopular with the Kanakas, but yet destitute of real authority, so that his boys laughed at him and he must carry out his wishes by the means of bribes. He learned to have a mania for doctoring; and set up the Kanakas against the remedies of his regular rivals: perhaps (if anything matter at all in the treatment of such a disease) the worst thing that he did, and certainly the easiest. The best and worst of the man appear very plainly in his dealings with Mr. Chapman's money; he had originally laid it out [intended to lay it out] entirely for the benefit of Catholics, and even so not wisely,

[4] The name given to the aboriginal inhabitants of the Hawaiian Islands.

but after a long, plain talk, he admitted his error fully and revised the list. The sad state of the boys' home is in part the result of his lack of control; in part, of his own slovenly ways and false ideas of hygiene. Brother officials used to call it "Damien's Chinatown." "Well," they would say, "your Chinatown keeps growing." And he would laugh with perfect good-nature, and adhere to his errors with perfect obstinacy. So much I have gathered of truth about this plain, noble human brother and father of ours; his imperfections are the traits of his face, by which we know him for our fellow; his martyrdom and his example nothing can lessen or annul; and only a person here on the spot can properly appreciate their greatness.

I have set down these private passages, as you perceive, without correction; thanks to you, the public has them in their bluntness. They are almost a list of the man's faults, for it is rather these that I was seeking: with his virtues, with the heroic profile of his life, I and the world were already sufficiently acquainted. I was besides a little suspicious of Catholic testimony; in no ill sense, but merely because Damien's admirers and disciples were the least likely to be critical. I know you will be more suspicious still; and the facts set down above were one and all collected from the lips of Protestants who had opposed the father in his life. Yet I am strangely deceived, or they build up the image of a man, with all his weaknesses, essentially heroic, and alive with rugged honesty, generosity, and mirth.

Take it for what it is, rough private jottings of the worst sides of Damien's character, collected from the lips of those who had labored with and (in your own phrase) "knew the man";—though I question whether Damien would have said that he knew you. Take it, and observe with wonder how well you were served by your gossips, how ill by your intelligence and sympathy; in how many points of fact we are at one, and how widely our appreciations vary. There is something wrong here; either with you or me. It is possible, for instance, that you, who seem to have so many ears in Kalawao, had heard of the affair of Mr. Chapman's money, and were singly struck by Damien's intended wrong-doing. I was struck with that also, and set it fairly down;

but I was struck much more by the fact that he had the honesty of mind to be convinced. I may here tell you that it was a long business; that one of his colleagues sat with him late into the night, multiplying arguments and accusations; that the father listened as usual with "perfect good-nature and perfect obstinacy"; but at the last when he was persuaded,—"Yes," said he, "I am very much obliged to you; you have done me a service; it would have been a theft." There are many (not Catholics merely) who require their heroes and saints to be infallible; to these the story will be painful; not to the true lovers, patrons, and servants of mankind.

And I take it, this is a type of our division; that you are one of those who have an eye for faults and failures; that you take a pleasure to find and publish them; and that, having found them, you make haste to forget the overvailing virtues and the real success which had alone introduced them to your knowledge. It is a dangerous frame of mind. That you may understand how dangerous, and into what a situation it has already brought you, we will (if you please) go hand-in-hand through the different phrases of your letter, and candidly examine each from the point of view of its truth, its appositeness, and its charity.

Damien was *coarse*.

It is very possible. You make us sorry for the lepers who had only a coarse old peasant for their friend and father. But you, who were so refined, why were you not there, to cheer them with the lights of culture? Or may I remind you that we have some reason to doubt if John the Baptist were genteel; and in the case of Peter, on whose career you doubtless dwell approvingly in the pulpit, no doubt at all he was a "coarse, headstrong" fisherman! Yet even in our Protestant Bibles Peter is called Saint.

Damien was *dirty*.

He was. Think of the poor lepers annoyed with this dirty comrade! But the clean Dr. Hyde was at his food in a fine house.

Damien was *headstrong*.

I believe you are right again; and I thank God for his strong head and heart.

Damien was *bigoted*.

I am not fond of bigots myself, because they are not fond of me. But what is meant by bigotry, that we should regard it as a blemish in a priest? Damien believed his own religion with the simplicity of a peasant or a child; as I would I could suppose that you do. For this, I wonder at him some way off; and had that been his only character, should have avoided him in life. But the point of interest in Damien, which has caused him to be so much talked about and made him at last the subject of your pen and mine, was that, in him, his bigotry, his intense and narrow faith, wrought potently for good, and strengthened him to be one of the world's heroes and exemplars.

Damien *was not sent to Molokai, but went there without orders.*

Is this a misreading? or do you really mean the words for blame? I have heard Christ, in the pulpits of our Church, held up for imitation on the ground that His sacrifice was voluntary. Does Dr. Hyde think otherwise?

Damien *did not stay at the settlement, etc.*

It is true he was allowed many indulgences. Am I to understand that you blame the father for profiting by these, or the officers for granting them? In either case, it is a mighty Spartan standard to issue from the house on Beretania Street; and I am convinced you will find yourself with few supporters.

Damien *had no hand in the reforms, etc.*

I think even you will admit that I have already been frank in my description of the man I am defending; but before I take you up upon this head, I will be franker still, and tell you that perhaps nowhere in the world can a man taste a more pleasurable sense of contrast than when he passes from Damien's "Chinatown" at Kalawao to the beautiful Bishop-Home at Kalaupapa. At this point, in my desire to make all fair for you, I will break my rule and adduce Catholic testimony. Here is a passage from my diary about my visit to the Chinatown, from which you will see how it is (even now) regarded by its own officials: "We went round all the dormitories, refectories, *etc.*—dark and dingy 5 enough, with a superficial cleanliness, which he" [Mr. Dutton, the lay brother] "did not seek to defend. 'It is almost decent,' said he; 'the sisters will make that all right when we get them here.'" And yet I gathered it 10 was already better since Damien was dead, and far better than when he was there alone and had his own (not always excellent) way. I have now come far enough to meet you on a common ground of fact; and I tell you 15 that, to a mind not prejudiced by jealousy, all the reforms of the lazaretto, and even those which he most vigorously opposed, are properly the work of Damien. They are the evidence of his success; they are what his 20 heroism provoked from the reluctant and the careless. Many were before him in the field; Mr. Meyer, for instance, of whose faithful work we hear too little: there have been many since; and some had more worldly 25 wisdom, though none had more devotion, than our saint. Before his day, even you will confess, they had effected little. It was his part, by one striking act of martyrdom, to direct all men's eyes on that distressful coun- 30 try. At a blow, and with the price of his life, he made the place illustrious and pub- lic. And that, if you will consider largely, was the one reform needful; pregnant of all that should succeed. It brought money; it 35 brought (best individual addition of them all) the sisters; it brought supervision, for public opinion and public interest landed with the man at Kalawao. If ever any man brought reforms, and died to bring them, it 40 was he. There is not a clean cup or towel in the Bishop-Home, but dirty Damien washed it.

Damien *was not a pure man in his relations* 45 *with women, etc.*

How do you know that? Is this the na- ture of the conversation in that house on Beretania Street which the cabman envied, driving past?—racy details of the misconduct 50 of the poor peasant priest, toiling under the cliffs of Molokai?

Many have visited the station before me; they seem not to have heard the rumor. When I was there I heard many shocking tales, for my informants were men speaking with the plainness of the laity; and I heard plenty of complaints of Damien. Why was this never mentioned? and how came it to you in the retirement of your clerical parlor?

But I must not even seem to deceive you. This scandal, when I read it in your letter, was not new to me. I had heard it once be- fore; and I must tell you how. There came to Samoa a man from Honolulu; he, in a public-house on the beach, volunteered the statement that Damien had "contracted the disease from having connection with the female lepers"; and I find a joy in telling you how the report was welcomed in a public- house. A man sprang to his feet; I am not at liberty to give his name, but from what I heard I doubt if you would care to have him to dinner in Beretania Street. "You mis- erable little ——" (here is a word I dare not print, it would so shock your ears). "You miserable little——," he cried, "if the story were a thousand times true, can't you see you are a million times a lower —— for daring to repeat it?" I wish it could be told of you that when the report reached you in your house, perhaps after family worship, you had found in your soul enough holy anger to receive it with the same expressions: ay, even with that one which I dare not print; it would not need to have been blotted away, like Uncle Toby's oath,[5] by the tears of the recording angel; it would have been counted to you for your brightest righteous- ness. But you have deliberately chosen the part of the man from Honolulu, and you have played it with improvements of your own. The man from Honolulu—miserable, leering creature—communicated the tale to a rude knot of beach-combing drinkers in a public-house, where (I will so far agree with your temperance opinions) man is not always at his noblest; and the man from Honolulu had himself been drinking—drinking, we may charitably fancy, to excess. It was to your "Dear Brother, the Reverend H. B. Gage," that you chose to communicate the sickening story; and the blue ribbon which

[5]In Laurence Sterne's *Tristram Shandy.*

adorns your portly bosom forbids me to allow you the extenuating plea that you were drunk when it was done. Your "dear brother"—a brother indeed—made haste to deliver up your letter (as a means of grace, perhaps) to the religious papers; where, after many months, I found and read and wondered at it; and whence I have now reproduced it for the wonder of others. And you and your dear brother have, by this cycle of operations, built up a contrast very edifying to examine in detail. The man whom you would not care to have to dinner, on the one side; on the other, the Reverend Dr. Hyde and the Reverend H. B. Gage: the Apia bar-room, the Honolulu manse.

But I fear you scarce appreciate how you appear to your fellow-men; and to bring it home to you, I will suppose your story to be true. I will suppose—and God forgive me for supposing it—that Damien faltered and stumbled in his narrow path of duty; I will suppose that, in the horror of his isolation, perhaps in the fever of incipient disease, he, who was doing so much more than he had sworn, failed in the letter of his priestly oath

—he, who was so much a better man than either you or me, who did what we have never dreamed of daring—he too tasted of our common frailty. "O, Iago, the pity of it!"[6] The least tender should be moved to tears; the most incredulous to prayer. And all that you could do was to pen your letter to the Reverend H. B. Gage!

Is it growing at all clear to you what a picture you have drawn of your own heart? I will try yet once again to make it clearer. You had a father: suppose this tale were about him, and some informant brought it to you, proof in hand: I am not making too high an estimate of your emotional nature when I suppose you would regret the circumstance? that you would feel the tale of frailty the more keenly since it shamed the author of your days? and that the last thing you would do would be to publish it in the religious press? Well, the man who tried to do what Damien did, is my father, and the father of the man in the Apia bar, and the father of all who love goodness; and he was your father too, if God had given you grace to see it.

A CHILD'S GARDEN OF VERSES[1]

I. Bed in Summer

In winter I get up at night
And dress by yellow candle-light.
In summer, quite the other way,
I have to go to bed by day.

I have to go to bed and see
The birds still hopping on the tree,
Or hear the grown-up people's feet,
Still going past me in the street.

And does it not seem hard to you,
When all the sky is clear and blue,
And I should like so much to play,
To have to go to bed by day?

II. A Thought

It is very nice to think
The world is full of meat and drink,
With little children saying grace
In every Christian kind of place.

IV. Young Night Thought

All night long and every night,
When my mama puts out the light,
I see the people marching by,
As plain as day, before my eye.

Armies and emperors and kings,
All carrying different kinds of things,
And marching in so grand a way,
You never saw the like by day.

So fine a show was never seen
At the great circus of the green;
For every kind of beast and man
Is marching in that caravan.

At first they move a little slow,
But still the faster on they go,
And still beside them close I keep
Until we reach the town of Sleep.

---

[1]Published in 1885.

[6]*Othello*, IV, i, 207.

V. Whole Duty of Children

A child should always say what's true
And speak when he is spoken to,
And behave mannerly at table;
At least as far as he is able.

XVI. The Land of Counterpane

When I was sick and lay a-bed,
I had two pillows at my head,
And all my toys beside me lay
To keep me happy all the day.

And sometimes for an hour or so   5
I watched my leaden soldiers go,
With different uniforms and drills,
Among the bed-clothes, through the hills;

And sometimes sent my ships in fleets
All up and down among the sheets;   10
Or brought my trees and houses out,
And planted cities all about.

I was the giant great and still
That sits upon the pillow-hill,
And sees before him, dale and plain,   15
The pleasant land of counterpane.

XVIII. My Shadow

I have a little shadow that goes in and out
    with me,
And what can be the use of him is more than
    I can see.
He is very, very like me from the heels up to
    the head;
And I see him jump before me, when I jump
    into my bed.

The funniest thing about him is the way he
    likes to grow—   5
Not at all like proper children, which is
    always very slow;
For he sometimes shoots up taller like an
    india-rubber ball,
And he sometimes gets so little that there's
    none of him at all.

He hasn't got a notion of how children ought
    to play,
And can only make a fool of me in every
    sort of way.   10
He stays so close beside me, he's a coward
    you can see;
I'd think shame to stick to nursie as that
    shadow sticks to me!

One morning, very early, before the sun was
    up,
I rose and found the shining dew on every
    buttercup;
But my lazy little shadow, like an arrant
    sleepy-head,   15
Had stayed at home behind me and was fast
    asleep in bed.

XXIII. The Cow

The friendly cow all red and white,
    I love with all my heart:
She gives me cream with all her might,
    To eat with apple-tart.

She wanders lowing here and there,   5
    And yet she cannot stray,
All in the pleasant open air,
    The pleasant light of day;

And blown by all the winds that pass
    And wet with all the showers,   10
She walks among the meadow grass
    And eats the meadow flowers.

XXIV. Happy Thought

The world is so full of a number of things,
I'm sure we should all be as happy as kings.

XXVIII. Foreign Children

Little Indian, Sioux or Crow,
Little frosty Eskimo,
Little Turk or Japanee,
O! don't you wish that you were me?

You have seen the scarlet trees   5
And the lions over seas;
You have eaten ostrich eggs,
And turned the turtles off their legs.

Such a life is very fine,
But it's not so nice as mine: 10
You must often, as you trod,
Have wearied *not* to be abroad.

You have curious things to eat,
I am fed on proper meat;
You must dwell beyond the foam,   15
But I am safe and live at home.
    Little Indian, Sioux or Crow,
    Little frosty Eskimo,
    Little Turk or Japanee,
O! don't you wish that you were me?   20

UNDERWOODS[1]

BOOK I

XXI. Requiem

Under the wide and starry sky,
Dig the grave and let me lie.
Glad did I live and gladly die,
   And I laid me down with a will.

This be the verse you grave for me: 5
Here he lies where he longed to be;
Home is the sailor, home from sea,
   And the hunter home from the hill.

XXII. The Celestial Surgeon

If I have faltered more or less
In my great task of happiness;
If I have moved among my race
And shown no glorious morning face;

[1]Published in 1887.

If beams from happy human eyes   5
Have moved me not; if morning skies,
Books, and my food, and summer rain
Knocked on my sullen heart in vain:—
Lord, thy most pointed pleasure take
And stab my spirit broad awake;   10
Or, Lord, if too obdurate I,
Choose thou, before that spirit die,
A piercing pain, a killing sin,
And to my dead heart run them in!

BOOK III

XXI

I have trod the upward and the downward
   slope
I have endured and done in days before;
I have longed for all, and bid farewell to
   hope;
And I have lived and loved, and closed the
   door.

ALGERNON CHARLES SWINBURNE

1837-1909

Swinburne was born in London on 5 April, 1837, the eldest child of Admiral Charles Henry Swinburne and the Lady Jane Henrietta, daughter of the third Earl of Ashburnham. It is said that Swinburne's features and something of his mental character were inherited from his mother, who was a woman of unusual accomplishment and widely read in foreign literature. His paternal grandfather, Sir John Edward Swinburne, sixth baronet of Capheaton, Northumberland, who had been born and brought up in France, and who in habits, dress, and modes of thought resembled a French nobleman of the *ancien régime,* exercised a strong influence over his grandson's youth. The boy was brought up in the Isle of Wight, and from his earliest years was trained by his grandfather and mother in French and Italian. In 1849 he was sent to Eton, where he proceeded to read enormously, devouring everything he could lay his hands on, particularly in the fields of lyric poetry and the Elizabethan drama. By the time he was fourteen many of his life-long partialities and prejudices were fully formed; at that time he was immersed in Shelley, Keats, Landor, the *Orlando Furioso,* and the tragedies of Corneille, and already he was indifferent to Horace, disliked Racine, and hated Euripides. In 1853 Swinburne left Eton under something of a cloud, because of his rebellious attitude towards one or more of his teachers. There was then some talk in his family of preparing him for the army, but the project was abandoned because of his shortness and slightness, to his own lifelong regret. In January, 1856, he entered Balliol College, Oxford. After his first year there his high-church proclivities melted away, and he became, what he remained, a nihilist in religion and a republican. He kept his terms regularly at Oxford until 1858, after which he was there less regularly; and he finally left the University without a degree in the fall of 1859. He was a brilliant though self-willed student, and his attainments in Greek were remarkable; but Benjamin Jowett, who long remained his warm friend, advised his leaving Oxford be-

cause of irregular ways of life into which he was drifting.

Late in 1860 Swinburne's first book was published, *The Queen Mother and Rosamond,* containing two plays. It passed at the time entirely unnoticed both by reviewers and by the public, and it is said that not a single copy was sold until some years afterwards. In the years immediately following he began to indulge in those "excitements of London life" which were long to arouse the fears of his friends, when he could not be kept away from them, and which played havoc with his health. Early in 1864 he went abroad for the longest journey of his life, traveling through France to Italy, where he saw his idol, Landor, then in his ninetieth year. In April, 1865, Swinburne's second book, *Atalanta in Calydon,* was published. The magnificent verse of this play did not go unappreciated, and the book became, indeed, the literary sensation of the year. At the end of 1865 a fourth play was published, *Chastelard,* which also was successful, though it was regarded by a section of the public as an immoral performance. Suspicion concerning his morals was electrified into certainty by the publication in the following year of *Poems and Ballads.* So violent and universal were the attacks on this book that after a few months it was withdrawn from sale by its publisher. The pressure of friends rather than any change of mind or heart kept Swinburne thereafter from offending British sensibilities in the same way. The pressure of friends, however, did not prevent him from continuing disastrously to indulge in the "excitements of London life," until finally in 1879 Theodore Watts-Dunton removed the poet to his own house, The Pines, Putney, where he slowly recovered his health and where he lived in the closest retirement until his death from pneumonia on 10 April, 1909. In the years after 1866 Swinburne continued to write voluminously, both plays and lyric poems, and he also published from time to time a number of critical studies written in dithyrambic prose. Among his volumes are: *Songs before Sunrise*

(1871), *Bothwell, a Tragedy* (1874), *Songs of Two Nations* (1875), *Erechtheus* (1876), *Poems and Ballads, Second Series* (1878), *Mary Stuart, a Tragedy* (1881), *Tristram of Lyonesse, and Other Poems* (1882), *A Century of Roundels* (1883), *Poems and Ballads, Third Series* (1889), *Astrophel and Other Poems* (1894), *The Tale of Balen* (1896), and *A Channel Passage, and Other Poems* (1904). His critical studies include: *William Blake* (1868), *George Chapman* (1875), *Essays and Studies* (1875), *A Study of Shakespeare* (1880), *A Study of Victor Hugo* (1886), *A Study of Ben Jonson* (1889), and *The Age of Shakespeare* (1908).

Swinburne in an essay on *Wordsworth and Byron* wrote, "It would be an absolute waste of time, for one who assumes it as indisputable, to enter into controversy with one who holds it as disputable, that the two primary and essential qualities of poetry are imagination and harmony; that where these qualities are wanting there can be no poetry, properly so called; and that where these qualities are perceptible in the highest degree, there, even though they should be unaccompanied and unsupported by any other great quality whatever—even though the ethi-

cal or critical faculty should be conspicuous by its absence—there, and only there, is the best and highest poetry." This definition of poetry is at least useful to indicate the qualities for which Swinburne's own verse is pre-eminent. Whether or not he had the highest poetical imagination may be a question, but there can be no doubt about his lyrical fervor and his unparalleled mastery of the rhythmical possibilities of the language.

The standard edition of Swinburne is the "Bonchurch Edition" of *The Complete Works,* ed. Sir Edmund Gosse and Thomas James Wise (20 vols., London, 1925–1927). Vol. 18 of this edition contains *Letters;* Vol. 19, the standard biography by Gosse; and Vol. 20, a bibliography by Wise. There is a volume of *Selections from Swinburne,* ed. William O. Raymond (New York, 1925). Harold Nicolson's *Swinburne* ("English Men of Letters" series, 1926) is a good brief introduction. The following more detailed critical studies are valuable: *Swinburne* by Samuel C. Chew (Boston, 1929); *Swinburne, A Literary Biography* by Georges Lafourcade (London, 1932); and *Swinburne's Literary Career and Fame* by Clyde Kenneth Hyder (Durham, N. C., 1933).

CHORUSES FROM
ATALANTA IN CALYDON[1]

I

When the hounds of spring are on winter's
    traces,
  The mother of months[2] in meadow or
    plain
Fills the shadows and windy places
  With lisp of leaves and ripple of rain;
And the brown bright nightingale amorous 5
Is half assuaged for Itylus,[3]
For the Thracian ships and the foreign faces,
  The tongueless vigil, and all the pain.

Come with bows bent and with emptying of
    quivers,
  Maiden most perfect, lady of light,   10
With a noise of winds and many rivers,
  With a clamor of waters, and with might;
Bind on thy sandals, O thou most fleet,
Over the splendor and speed of thy feet;

For the faint east quickens, the wan west
    shivers,   15
  Round the feet of the day and the feet of
    the night.

Where shall we find her, how shall we sing
    to her,
  Fold our hands round her knees, and cling?
O that man's heart were as fire and could
    spring to her,
  Fire, or the strength of the streams that
    spring!   20
For the stars and the winds are unto her
As raiment, as songs of the harp-player;
For the risen stars and the fallen cling to her,
  And the southwest-wind and the west-
    wind sing.

For winter's rains and ruins are over,   25
  And all the season of snows and sins;
The days dividing lover and lover,
  The light that loses, the night that wins;
And time remembered is grief forgotten,
And frosts are slain and flowers begotten,   30
And in green underwood and cover
  Blossom by blossom the spring begins.

---

[1] The following poems are reprinted from their collected edition of Swinburne's poems, in six volumes, by permission of Harper and Brothers.

[2] The moon, Artemis.

[3] See note to Arnold's *Philomela* above. Itylus was the son of Procne, the nephew of Philomela (the nightingale).

The full streams feed on flower of rushes,
　Ripe grasses trammel a traveling foot,
The faint fresh flame of the young year
　　flushes　　　　35
　From leaf to flower and flower to fruit;
And fruit and leaf are as gold and fire,
And the oat is heard above the lyre,
And the hooféd heel of a satyr crushes
　The chestnut-husk at the chestnut-root. 40

And Pan by noon and Bacchus by night,
　Fleeter of foot than the fleet-foot kid,
Follows with dancing and fills with delight
　The Maenad and the Bassarid;[4]
And soft as lips that laugh and hide　　45
The laughing leaves of the trees divide,
And screen from seeing and leave in sight
　The god pursuing, the maiden hid.
The ivy falls with the Bacchanal's hair
　Over her eyebrows hiding her eyes;　　50
The wild vine slipping down leaves bare
　Her bright breast shortening into sighs;
The wild vine slips with the weight of its
　　leaves,
But the berried ivy catches and cleaves
To the limbs that glitter, the feet that scare 55
　The wolf that follows, the fawn that flies.

II

Before the beginning of years
　There came to the making of man
Time, with a gift of tears;
　Grief, with a glass that ran;
Pleasure, with pain for leaven;　　　5
　Summer, with flowers that fell;
Remembrance fallen from heaven,
　And madness risen from hell;
Strength without hands to smite;
　Love that endures for a breath:　　10
Night, the shadow of light,
　And life, the shadow of death.

And the high gods took in hand
　Fire, and the falling of tears,
And a measure of sliding sand　　15
　From under the feet of the years;
And froth and drift of the sea;
　And dust of the laboring earth;
And bodies of things to be
　In the houses of death and of birth;　20
And wrought with weeping and laughter,
　And fashioned with loathing and love,
With life before and after
　And death beneath and above,

---

[4]Bacchantes, worshipers of Bacchus.

For a day and a night and a morrow,　　25
　That his strength might endure for a span
With travail and heavy sorrow,
　The holy spirit of man.

From the winds of the north and the south
　They gathered as unto strife;　　30
They breathed upon his mouth,
　They filled his body with life;
Eyesight and speech they wrought
　For the veils of the soul therein,
A time for labor and thought,　　35
　A time to serve and to sin;
They gave him light in his ways,
　And love, and a space for delight,
And beauty and length of days,
　And night, and sleep in the night.　　40
His speech is a burning fire;
　With his lips he travaileth;
In his heart is a blind desire,
　In his eyes foreknowledge of death;
He weaves, and is clothed with derision;　45
　Sows, and he shall not reap;
His life is a watch or a vision
　Between a sleep and a sleep.

III

We have seen thee, O Love, thou art fair;
　thou art goodly, O Love;
Thy wings make light in the air as the wings
　of a dove.
Thy feet are as winds that divide the stream
　of the sea;
Earth is thy covering to hide thee, the gar-
　ment of thee.
Thou art swift and subtle and blind as a
　flame of fire;　　5
Before thee the laughter, behind thee the
　tears of desire;
And twain go forth beside thee, a man with
　a maid;
Her eyes are the eyes of a bride whom de-
　light makes afraid;
As the breath in the buds that stir is her
　bridal breath:
But Fate is the name of her; and his name
　is Death.　　10

For an evil blossom was born
　Of sea-foam and the frothing of blood,
　　Blood-red and bitter of fruit,
　　　And the seed of it laughter and tears,
And the leaves of it madness and scorn;　15
　A bitter flower from the bud,
　　Sprung of the sea without root,
　　　Sprung without graft from the years.

The weft of the world was untorn
  That is woven of the day on the night, 20
  The hair of the hours was not white
Nor the raiment of time overworn,
  When a wonder, a world's delight,
A perilous goddess was born;
  And the waves of the sea as she came 25
Clove, and the foam at her feet,
  Fawning, rejoiced to bring forth
  A fleshly blossom, a flame
Filling the heavens with heat
  To the cold white ends of the north. 30

And in air the clamorous birds,
  And men upon earth that hear
Sweet articulate words
  Sweetly divided apart,
  And in shallow and channel and mere 35
The rapid and footless herds,
  Rejoiced, being foolish of heart.

For all they said upon earth,
  She is fair, she is white like a dove,
  And the life of the world in her breath 40
Breathes, and is born at her birth;
  For they knew thee for mother of love,
  And knew thee not mother of death.

What hadst thou to do being born,
  Mother, when winds were at ease, 45
As a flower of the springtime of corn,
  A flower of the foam of the seas?
For bitter thou wast from thy birth,
  Aphrodite, a mother of strife;
For before thee some rest was on earth, 50
  A little respite from tears,
  A little pleasure of life;
For life was not then as thou art,
  But as one that waxeth in years
Sweet-spoken, a fruitful wife; 55
  Earth had no thorn, and desire
No sting, neither death any dart;
  What hadst thou to do among these,
  Thou, clothed with a burning fire,
Thou, girt with sorrow of heart, 60
  Thou, sprung of the seed of the seas
As an ear from a seed of corn,
  As a brand plucked forth of a pyre,
As a ray shed forth of the morn,
  For division of soul and disease, 65
For a dart and a sting and a thorn?
What ailed thee then to be born?

Was there not evil enough,
  Mother, and anguish on earth
Born with a man at his birth, 70
Wastes underfoot, and above

Storm out of heaven, and dearth
Shaken down from the shining thereof,
  Wrecks from afar overseas
And peril of shallow and firth, 75
  And tears that spring and increase
In the barren places of mirth,
That thou, having wings as a dove,
  Being girt with desire for a girth,
  That thou must come after these, 80
That thou must lay on him love?

Thou shouldst not so have been born:
  But death should have risen with thee,
  Mother, and visible fear,
  Grief, and the wringing of hands, 85
And noise of many that mourn;
  The smitten bosom, the knee
  Bowed, and in each man's ear
  A cry as of perishing lands,
A moan as of people in prison, 90
  A tumult of infinite griefs;
  And thunder of storm on the sands,
  And wailing of waves on the shore;
And under thee newly arisen
  Loud shoals and shipwrecking reefs, 95
  Fierce air and violent light;
  Sail rent and sundering oar,
  Darkness, and noises of night;
Clashing of streams in the sea,
  Wave against wave as a sword, 100
  Clamor of currents, and foam;
  Rains making ruin on earth,
  Winds that wax ravenous and roam
As wolves in a wolfish horde;
Fruits growing faint in the tree, 105
  And blind things dead in their birth;
  Famine, and blighting of corn,
When thy time was come to be born.

All these we know of; but thee
  Who shall discern or declare? 110
In the uttermost ends of the sea
  The light of thine eyelids and hair,
  The light of thy bosom as fire
  Between the wheel of the sun
And the flying flames of the air? 115
  Wilt thou turn thee not yet nor have pity,
But abide with despair and desire
  And the crying of armies undone,
  Lamentation of one with another
  And breaking of city by city; 120
The dividing of friend against friend,
  The severing of brother and brother;
Wilt thou utterly bring to an end?
  Have mercy, mother!

For against all men from of old   125
  Thou hast set thine hand as a curse,
    And cast out gods from their places.
      These things are spoken of thee.
Strong kings and goodly with gold
  Thou hast found out arrows to pierce,   130
    And made their kingdoms and races
      As dust and surf of the sea.
All these, overburdened with woes
  And with length of their days waxen weak,
    Thou slewest; and sentest moreover   135
      Upon Tyro[5] an evil thing,
Rent hair and a fetter and blows
  Making bloody the flower of the cheek,
    Though she lay by a god as a lover,   139
      Though fair, and the seed of a king.
For of old, being full of thy fire,
  She endured not longer to wear
    On her bosom a saffron vest,
      On her shoulder an ashwood quiver;
Being mixed and made one through desire
  With Enipeus, and all her hair   146
    Made moist with his mouth, and her
      breast
        Filled full of the foam of the river.

ITYLUS [1]

Swallow, my sister, O sister swallow,
  How can thine heart be full of the spring?
    A thousand summers are over and dead.
What hast thou found in the spring to fol-
      low?
    What hast thou found in thine heart to
      sing?   5
      What wilt thou do when the summer is
        shed?

O swallow sister, O fair swift swallow,
  Why wilt thou fly after spring to the south,
    The soft south whither thine heart is
      set?
Shall not the grief of the old time follow? 10
  Shall not the song thereof cleave to thy
      mouth?
    Hast thou forgotten ere I forget?

---

[5]The wife of Cretheus. She was loved by Enipeus, Macedonian river-god.

[1]This and the four following poems are from *Poems and Ballads,* First Series (1866). Concerning Itylus see notes above to the first chorus from *Atalanta in Calydon* and to Arnold's *Philomela.* It is Philomela, the nightingale, not Procne, her "sister swallow" and the mother of Itylus, who here laments the slain boy.

Sister, my sister, O fleet sweet swallow,
  Thy way is long to the sun and the south;
    But I, fulfilled of my heart's desire,   15
Shedding my song upon height, upon hollow,
  From tawny body and sweet small mouth
    Feed the heart of the night with fire.

I the nightingale all spring through,
  O swallow, sister, O changing swallow,   20
    All spring through till the spring be
      done,
Clothed with the light of the night on the
      dew,
    Sing, while the hours and the wild birds
      follow,
      Take flight and follow and find the sun.

Sister, my sister, O soft light swallow,   25
  Though all things feast in the spring's
      guest-chamber,
    How hast thou heart to be glad thereof
      yet?
For where thou fliest I shall not follow,
  Till life forget and death remember,
    Till thou remember and I forget.   30

Swallow, my sister, O singing swallow,
  I know not how thou hast heart to sing.
    Hast thou the heart? is it all past over?
Thy lord the summer is good to follow,
  And fair the feet of thy lover the spring:
    But what wilt thou say to the spring thy
      lover?   36

O swallow, sister, O fleeting swallow,
  My heart in me is a molten ember
    And over my head the waves have met.
But thou wouldst tarry or I would follow,   40
  Could I forget or thou remember,
    Couldst thou remember and I forget.

O sweet stray sister, O shifting swallow,
  The heart's division divideth us.
    Thy heart is light as a leaf of a tree;   45
But mine goes forth among sea-gulfs hollow
  To the place of the slaying of Itylus,
    The feast of Daulis, the Thracian sea.

O swallow, sister, O rapid swallow,
  I pray thee sing not a little space.   50
    Are not the roofs and the lintels wet?
The woven web that was plain to follow,
  The small slain body, the flowerlike face,
    Can I remember if thou forget?

O sister, sister, thy first-begotten! 55
 The hands that cling and the feet that
  follow,
  The voice of the child's blood crying yet:
*Who hath remembered me? who hath for-
  gotten?*
 Thou hast forgotten, O summer swallow,
  But the world shall end when I forget. 60

SATIA TE SANGUINE [1]

If you loved me ever so little,
 I could bear the bonds that gall,
I could dream the bonds were brittle;
 You do not love me at all.

O beautiful lips, O bosom 5
 More white than the moon's and warm,
A sterile, a ruinous blossom
 Is blown your way in a storm.

As the lost white feverish limbs
 Of the Lesbian Sappho, adrift 10
In foam where the sea-weed swims,
 Swam loose for the streams to lift,

My heart swims blind in a sea
 That stuns me; swims to and fro,
And gathers to windward and lee 15
 Lamentation, and mourning, and woe.

A broken, an emptied boat,
 Sea saps it, winds blow apart,
Sick and adrift and afloat,
 The barren waif of a heart. 20

Where, when the gods would be cruel,
 Do they go for a torture? where
Plant thorns, set pain like a jewel?
 Ah, not in the flesh, not there!

The racks of earth and the rods 25
 Are weak as foam on the sands;
In the heart is the prey for gods,
 Who crucify hearts, not hands.

Mere pangs corrode and consume,
 Dead when life dies in the brain; 30
In the infinite spirit is room
 For the pulse of an infinite pain.

I wish you were dead, my dear;
 I would give you, had I to give,
Some death too bitter to fear; 35
 It is better to die than live.

[1]Satiate thyself with blood.

I wish you were stricken of thunder
 And burnt with a bright flame through,
Consumed and cloven in sunder,
 I dead at your feet like you. 40

If I could but know after all,
 I might cease to hunger and ache,
Though your heart were ever so small,
 If it were not a stone or a snake.

You are crueler, you that we love, 45
 Than hatred, hunger, or death;
You have eyes and breasts like a dove,
 And you kill men's hearts with a breath.

As plague in a poisonous city
 Insults and exults on her dead, 50
So you, when pallid for pity
 Comes love, and fawns to be fed.

As a tame beast writhes and wheedles,
 He fawns to be fed with wiles;
You carve him a cross of needles, 55
 And whet them sharp as your smiles.

He is patient of thorn and whip,
 He is dumb under ax or dart;
You suck with a sleepy red lip
 The wet red wounds in his heart. 60

You thrill as his pulses dwindle,
 You brighten and warm as he bleeds,
With insatiable eyes that kindle
 And insatiable mouth that feeds.

Your hands nailed love to the tree, 65
 You stripped him, scourged him with rods,
And drowned him deep in the sea
 That hides the dead and their gods.

And for all this, die will he not;
 There is no man sees him but I; 70
You came and went and forgot;
 I hope he will some day die.

A MATCH

If love were what the rose is,
 And I were like the leaf,
Our lives would grow together
In sad or singing weather,
Blown fields or flowerful closes, 5
 Green pleasure or gray grief;
If love were what the rose is,
 And I were like the leaf.

If I were what the words are,
  And love were like the tune,   10
With double sound and single
Delight our lips would mingle,
With kisses glad as birds are
  That get sweet rain at noon;
If I were what the words are,   15
  And love were like the tune.

If you were life, my darling,
  And I your love were death,
We'd shine and snow together
  Ere March made sweet the weather   20
With daffodil and starling
  And hours of fruitful breath;
If you were life, my darling,
  And I your love were death.

If you were thrall to sorrow,   25
  And I were page to joy,
We'd play for lives and seasons
With loving looks and treasons
And tears of night and morrow
  And laughs of maid and boy;   30
If you were thrall to sorrow,
  And I were page to joy.

If you were April's lady,
  And I were lord in May,
We'd throw with leaves for hours   35
And draw for days with flowers,
Till day like night were shady
  And night were bright like day;
If you were April's lady,
  And I were lord in May.   40

If you were queen of pleasure,
  And I were king of pain,
We'd hunt down love together,
Pluck out his flying-feather,
And teach his feet a measure,   45
  And find his mouth a rein;
If you were queen of pleasure,
  And I were king of pain.

THE GARDEN OF PROSERPINE[1]

Here, where the world is quiet;
  Here, where all trouble seems
Dead winds' and spent waves' riot
  In doubtful dreams of dreams;
I watch the green field growing   5
For reaping folk and sowing,
For harvest-time and mowing,
  A sleepy world of streams.

---

[1]Proserpine was the wife of Pluto and queen of the lower world.

I am tired of tears and laughter,
  And men that laugh and weep;   10
Of what may come hereafter
  For men that sow to reap:
I am weary of days and hours,
Blown buds of barren flowers,
Desires and dreams and powers   15
  And everything but sleep.

Here life has death for neighbor,
  And far from eye or ear
Wan waves and wet winds labor,
  Weak ships and spirits steer;   20
They drive adrift, and whither
They wot not who make thither;
But no such winds blow hither,
  And no such things grow here.

No growth of moor or coppice,   25
  No heather-flower or vine,
But bloomless buds of poppies,
  Green grapes of Proserpine,
Pale beds of blowing rushes
Where no leaf blooms or blushes   30
Save this whereout she crushes
  For dead men deadly wine.

Pale, without name or number,
  In fruitless fields of corn,
They bow themselves and slumber   35
  All night till light is born;
And like a soul belated,
In hell and heaven unmated,
By cloud and mist abated
  Comes out of darkness morn.   40

Though one were strong as seven,
  He too with death shall dwell,
Nor wake with wings in heaven,
  Nor weep for pains in hell;
Though one were fair as roses,   45
His beauty clouds and closes;
And well though love reposes,
  In the end it is not well.

Pale, beyond porch and portal,
  Crowned with calm leaves, she stands   50
Who gathers all things mortal
  With cold immortal hands;
Her languid lips are sweeter
Than love's who fears to greet her
To men that mix and meet her   55
  From many times and lands.

She waits for each and other,
  She waits for all men born;
Forgets the earth her mother,[2]
  The life of fruits and corn;   60

---

[2]Her mother was Demeter, goddess of the earth.

And spring and seed and swallow
Take wing for her and follow
Where summer song rings hollow
    And flowers are put to scorn.

There go the loves that wither,   65
    The old loves with wearier wings;
And all dead years draw thither,
    And all disastrous things;
Dead dreams of days forsaken,
Blind buds that snows have shaken,   70
Wild leaves that winds have taken,
    Red strays of ruined springs.

We are not sure of sorrow,
    And joy was never sure;
To-day will die to-morrow;   75
    Time stoops to no man's lure;
And love, grown faint and fretful,
With lips but half regretful
Sighs, and with eyes forgetful
    Weeps that no loves endure.   80

From too much love of living,
    From hope and fear set free,
We thank with brief thanksgiving
    Whatever gods may be
That no life lives for ever;   85
That dead men rise up never;
That even the weariest river
    Winds somewhere safe to sea.

Then star nor sun shall waken,
    Nor any change of light: 90
Nor sound of waters shaken,
    Nor any sound or sight:
Nor wintry leaves nor vernal,
Nor days nor things diurnal;
Only the sleep eternal   95
    In an eternal night.

AN INTERLUDE

In the greenest growth of the Maytime,
    I rode where the woods were wet,
Between the dawn and the daytime;
    The spring was glad that we met.

There was something the season wanted,   5
    Though the ways and the woods smelt
        sweet;
The breath at your lips that panted,
    The pulse of the grass at your feet.

You came, and the sun came after,
    And the green grew golden above;   10

And the flag-flowers lightened with laughter,
    And the meadow-sweet shook with love.

Your feet in the full-grown grasses
    Moved soft as a weak wind blows;
You passed me as April passes,   15
    With face made out of a rose.

By the stream where the stems were slender,
    Your bright foot paused at the sedge;
It might be to watch the tender
    Light leaves in the springtime hedge,   20

On boughs that the sweet month blanches
    With flowery frost of May:
It might be a bird in the branches,
    It might be a thorn in the way.

I waited to watch you linger   25
    With foot drawn back from the dew,
Till a sunbeam straight like a finger
    Struck sharp through the leaves at you.

And a bird overhead sang *Follow,*
    And a bird to the right sang *Here;*   30
And the arch of the leaves was hollow,
    And the meaning of May was clear.

I saw where the sun's hand pointed,
    I knew what the bird's note said;
By the dawn and the dewfall anointed,   35
    You were queen by the gold on your head.

As the glimpse of a burnt-out ember
    Recalls a regret of the sun,
I remember, forget, and remember
    What Love saw done and undone.   40

I remember the way we parted,
    The day and the way we met;
You hoped we were both broken-hearted,
    And knew we should both forget.

And May with her world in flower   45
    Seemed still to murmur and smile
As you murmured and smiled for an hour;
    I saw you turn at the stile.

A hand like a white wood-blossom
    You lifted, and waved, and passed,   50
With head hung down to the bosom,
    And pale, as it seemed, at last.

And the best and the worst of this is
    That neither is most to blame
If you've forgotten my kisses   55
    And I've forgotten your name.

HERTHA[1]

I am that which began;
    Out of me the years roll;
Out of me God and man;
    I am equal and whole;
God changes, and man, and the form of them
        bodily; I am the soul.   5

    Before ever land was,
    Before ever the sea,
    Or soft hair of the grass,
    Or fair limbs of the tree,
Or the flesh-colored fruit of my branches, I
        was, and thy soul was in me.   10

    First life on my sources
    First drifted and swam;
    Out of me are the forces
    That save it or damn;
Out of me man and woman, and wild-beast
        and bird; before God was, I am.   15

    Beside or above me
    Nought is there to go;
    Love or unlove me,
    Unknow me or know,
I am that which unloves me and loves; I am
        stricken, and I am the blow.   20

    I the mark that is missed
    And the arrows that miss,
    I the mouth that is kissed
    And the breath in the kiss,
The search, and the sought, and the seeker,
        the soul and the body that is.   25

    I am that thing which blesses
    My spirit elate;
    That which caresses
    With hands uncreate
My limbs unbegotten that measure the length
        of the measure of fate.   30

    But what things dost thou now,
    Looking Godward, to cry
    "I am I, thou art thou,
    I am low, thou art high"?
I am thou, whom thou seekest to find him;
        find thou but thyself, thou art I.   35

    I the grain and the furrow,
    The plow-cloven clod
    And the plowshare drawn thorough,
    The germ and the sod,
The deed and the doer, the seed and the
        sower, the dust which is God.   40

    Hast thou known how I fashioned thee,
    Child, underground?
    Fire that impassioned thee,
    Iron that bound,
Dim changes of water, what thing of all these
        hast thou known of or found?   45

    Canst thou say in thine heart
    Thou hast seen with thine eyes
    With what cunning of art
    Thou wast wrought in what wise,
By what force of what stuff thou wast
        shapen, and shown on my breast to the
        skies?   50

    Who hath given, who hath sold it thee,
    Knowledge of me?
    Hath the wilderness told it thee?
    Hast thou learned of the sea?
Hast thou communed in spirit with night?
        have the winds taken counsel with
        thee?   55

    Have I set such a star
    To show light on thy brow
    That thou sawest from afar
    What I show to thee now?
Have ye spoken as brethren together, the sun
        and the mountains and thou?   60

    What is here, dost thou know it?
    What was, hast thou known?
    Prophet nor poet
    Nor tripod nor throne[2]
Nor spirit nor flesh can make answer, but
        only thy mother alone.   65

    Mother, not maker,
    Born, and not made;
    Though her children forsake her,
    Allured or afraid,   69
Praying prayers to the God of their fashion,
        she stirs not for all that have prayed.

    A creed is a rod,
    And a crown is of night;
    But this thing is God,
    To be man with thy might,
To grow straight in the strength of thy spirit,
        and live out thy life as the light.   75

---

[1] This and the two following poems are from
Songs before Sunrise. Hertha (of Nerthus) was
the Germanic earth-mother, goddess of fertility and
growing things. Swinburne himself said, "Of all I
have done, I rate *Hertha* highest as a single piece,
finding in it the most of lyric force and music combined with the most of condensed and clarified
thought."

[2] I. e., nor priest nor king.

I am in thee to save thee,
　As my soul in thee saith;
Give thou as I gave thee,
　Thy life-blood and breath,
Green leaves of thy labor, white flowers of
　　thy thought, and red fruit of thy
　　death.　　80

Be the ways of thy giving
　As mine were to thee;
The free life of thy living,
　Be the gift of it free;
Not as servant to lord, nor as master to
　　slave, shalt thou give thee to me.　　85

O children of banishment,
　Souls overcast,
Were the lights ye see vanish meant
　Alway to last,
Ye would know not the sun overshining the
　　shadows and stars overpast.　　90

I that saw where ye trod
　The dim paths of the night
Set the shadow called God
　In your skies to give light;
But the morning of manhood is risen, and the
　　shadowless soul is in sight.　　95

The tree many-rooted
　That swells to the sky
With frondage³ red-fruited,
　The life-tree am I;
In the buds of your lives is the sap of my
　　leaves: ye shall live and not die.　　100

But the Gods of your fashion
　That take and that give,
In their pity and passion
　That scourge and forgive,
They are worms that are bred in the bark that
　　falls off; they shall die and not live.　105

My own blood is what stanches
　The wounds in my bark;
Stars caught in my branches
　Make day of the dark,
And are worshiped as suns till the sunrise
　　shall tread out their fires as a spark.　110

Where dead ages hide under
　The live roots of the tree,
In my darkness the thunder
　Makes utterance of me;
In the clash of my boughs with each other ye
　　hear the waves sound of the sea.　　115

³Foliage.

That noise is of Time,
　As his feathers are spread
And his feet set to climb
　Through the boughs overhead,　　119
And my foliage rings round him and rustles,
　and branches are bent with his tread.

The storm-winds of ages
　Blow through me and cease,
The war-wind that rages,
　The spring-wind of peace,
Ere the breath of them roughen my tresses,
　ere one of my blossoms increase.　125

All sounds of all changes,
　All shadows and lights
On the world's mountain-ranges
　And stream-riven heights,
Whose tongue is the wind's tongue and lan-
　guage of storm-clouds on earth-
　shaking nights;　　130

All forms of all faces,
　All works of all hands
In unsearchable places
　Of time-stricken lands,
All death and all life, and all reigns and all
　ruins, drop through me as sands.　135

Though sore be my burden
　And more than ye know,
And my growth have no guerdon
　But only to grow,
Yet I fail not of growing for lightnings
　above me or deathworms below.　　140

These too have their part in me,
　As I too in these;
Such fire is at heart in me,
　Such sap is this tree's,
Which hath in it all sounds and all secrets of
　infinite lands and of seas.　145

In the spring-colored hours
　When my mind was as May's,
There brake forth of me flowers
　By centuries of days,
Strong blossoms with perfume of manhood,
　shot out from my spirit as rays.　150

And the sound of them springing
　And smell of their shoots
Were as warmth and sweet singing
　And strength to my roots;　154
And the lives of my children made perfect
　with freedom of soul were my fruits.

I bid you but be;
    I have need not of prayer;
    I have need of you free
        As your mouths of mine air;
That my heart may be greater within me,
    beholding the fruits of me fair.   160

More fair than strange fruit is
    Of faiths ye espouse;
In me only the root is
    That blooms in your boughs;
Behold now your God that ye made you, to
    feed him with faith of your vows. 165

In the darkening and whitening
    Abysses adored,
With dayspring and lightning
    For lamp and for sword,
God thunders in heaven, and his angels are
    red with the wrath of the Lord.   170

O my sons, O too dutiful
    Toward Gods not of me,
Was not I enough beautiful?
    Was it hard to be free?
For behold, I am with you, am in you and of
    you; look forth now and see.   175

Lo, winged with world's wonders,
    With miracles shod,
With the fires of his thunders
    For raiment and rod,
God trembles in heaven, and his angels are
    white with the terror of God.   180

For his twilight is come on him,
    His anguish is here;
And his spirits gaze dumb on him,
    Grown gray from his fear;
And his hour taketh hold on him stricken, the
    last of his infinite year.   185

Thought made him and breaks him,
    Truth slays and forgives;
But to you, as time takes him,
    This new thing it gives,
Even love, the beloved Republic, that feeds
    upon freedom and lives.   190

For truth only is living,
    Truth only is whole,
And the love of his giving
    Man's polestar and pole;
Man, pulse of my center, and fruit of my
    body, and seed of my soul.   195

One birth of my bosom;
    One beam of mine eye;
One topmost blossom
    That scales the sky;
Man, equal and one with me, man that is
    made of me, man that is I.   200

TO WALT WHITMAN IN AMERICA

Send but a song oversea for us,
    Heart of their hearts who are free,
Heart of their singer, to be for us
    More than our singing can be;
Ours, in the tempest at error,   5
With no light but the twilight of terror;
    Send us a song oversea!

Sweet-smelling of pine-leaves and grasses,
    And blown as a tree through and through
With the winds of the keen mountain-passes,
    And tender as sun-smitten dew;   11
Sharp-tongued as the winter that shakes
The wastes of your limitless lakes,
    Wide-eyed as the sea-line's blue.

O strong-winged soul with prophetic   15
    Lips hot with the bloodbeats of song,
With tremor of heartstrings magnetic,
    With thoughts as thunders in throng,
With consonant ardors of chords
That pierce men's souls as with swords   20
    And hale them hearing along,

Make us too music, to be with us
    As a word from a world's heart warm,
To sail the dark as a sea with us,
    Full-sailed, outsinging the storm,   25
A song to put fire in our ears
Whose burning shall burn up tears,
    Whose sign bid battle reform;

A note in the ranks of a clarion,
    A word in the wind of cheer,   30
To consume as with lightning the carrion
    That makes time foul for us here;
In the air that our dead things infest
A blast of the breath of the west,
    Till east way as west way is clear.   35

Out of the sun beyond sunset,
    From the evening whence morning shall be,
With the rollers in measureless onset,
    With the van of the storming sea,
With the world-wide wind, with the breath 40
That breaks ships driven upon death,
    With the passion of all things free,

With the sea-steeds footless and frantic,
    White myriads for death to bestride
In the charge of the ruining Atlantic   45
    Where deaths by regiments ride,
With clouds and clamors of waters,
With a long note shriller than slaughter's
    On the furrowless fields world-wide.

With terror, with ardor and wonder,   50
    With the soul of the season that wakes
When the weight of a whole year's thunder
    In the tidestream of autumn breaks,
Let the flight of the wide-winged word
Come over, come in and be heard,   55
    Take form and fire for our sakes.

For a continent bloodless with travail
    Here toils and brawls as it can,
And the web of it who shall unravel
    Of all that peer on the plan;   60
Would fain grow men, but they grow not,
And fain be free, but they know not
    One name for freedom and man?

One name, not twain for division;
    One thing, not twain, from the birth;   65
Spirit and substance and vision,
    Worth more than worship is worth;
Unbeheld, unadored, undivined,
The cause, the center, the mind,
    The secret and sense of the earth.   70

Here as a weakling in irons,
    Here as a weanling in bands,
As a prey that the stake-net environs,
    Our life that we looked for stands;
And the man-child naked and dear,   75
Democracy, turns on us here
    Eyes trembling with tremulous hands.

It sees not what season shall bring to it
    Sweet fruit of its bitter desire;
Few voices it hears yet sing to it,   80
    Few pulses of hearts reaspire;
Foresees not time, nor forehears
The noises of imminent years,
    Earthquake, and thunder, and fire:

When crowned and weaponed and curbless   85
    It shall walk without helm or shield
The bare burnt furrows and herbless
    Of war's last flame-stricken field,
Till godlike, equal with time,
It stand in the sun sublime,   90
    In the godhead of man revealed.

Round your people and over them
    Light like raiment is drawn,
Close as a garment to cover them
    Wrought not of mail nor of lawn;   95
Here, with hope hardly to wear,
Naked nations and bare
    Swim, sink, strike out for the dawn.

Chains are here, and a prison,
    Kings, and subjects, and shame,   100
If the God upon you be arisen,
    How should our songs be the same?
How, in confusion of change,
How shall we sing, in a strange
    Land, songs praising his name?   105

God is buried and dead to us,
    Even the spirit of earth,
Freedom; so have they said to us,
    Some with mocking and mirth,
Some with heartbreak and tears;   110
And a God without eyes, without ears,
    Who shall sing of him, dead in the birth?

The earth-God Freedom, the lonely
    Face lightening, the footprint unshod,
Not as one man crucified only   115
    Nor scourged with but one life's rod;
The soul that is substance of nations,
Reincarnate with fresh generations;
    The great god Man, which is God.

But in weariest of years and obscurest   120
    Doth it live not at heart of all things,
The one God and one spirit, a purest
    Life, fed from unstanchable springs?
Within love, within hatred it is,
And its seed in the stripe as the kiss,   125
    And in slaves is the germ, and in kings.

Freedom we call it, for holier
    Name of the soul's there is none;
Surlier it labors, if slowlier,
    Than the meters of star or of sun;   130
Slowlier than life into breath,
Surelier than time into death,
    It moves till its labor be done.

Till the motion be done and the measure
    Circling through season and clime,   135
Slumber and sorrow and pleasure,
    Vision of virtue and crime;
Till consummate with conquering eyes,
A soul disembodied, it rise
    From the body transfigured of time.   140

Till it rise and remain and take station
　With the stars of the worlds that rejoice;
Till the voice of its heart's exultation
　Be as theirs an invariable voice;
By no discord of evil estranged, 145
By no pause, by no breach in it changed,
　By no clash in the chord of its choice.

It is one with the world's generations,
　With the spirit, the star, and the sod; 149
With the kingless and king-stricken nations,
　With the cross, and the chain, and the rod;
The most high, the most secret, most lonely,
The earth-soul Freedom, that only
　Lives, and that only is God. 154

THE OBLATION

Ask nothing more of me, sweet;
　All I can give you I give.
　Heart of my heart, were it more,
More would be laid at your feet:
　Love that should help you to live, 5
　Song that should spur you to soar.

All things were nothing to give
　Once to have sense of you more,
　Touch you and taste of you, sweet,
Think you and breathe you and live, 10
　Swept of your wings as they soar,
　Trodden by chance of your feet.

I that have love and no more
　Give you but love of you, sweet:
　He that hath more, let him give; 15
He that hath wings, let him soar;
　Mine is the heart at your feet
　Here, that must love you to live.

A FORSAKEN GARDEN[1]

In a coign of the cliff between lowland and
　　highland,
　At the sea-down's edge between windward
　　and lee,
Walled round with rocks as an inland island,
　The ghost of a garden fronts the sea.
A girdle of brushwood and thorn encloses 5
　The steep square slope of the blossomless
　　bed
Where the weeds that grew green from the
　　graves of its roses
　　Now lie dead.

---

[1]This and the two following poems are from
Poems and Ballads, Second Series (1878).

The fields fall southward, abrupt and broken,
　To the low last edge of the long lone land.
If a step should sound or a word be spoken,
　Would a ghost not rise at the strange
　　guest's hand? 12
So long have the gray bare walks lain guest-
　　less,
　Through branches and briers if a man
　　make way,
He shall find no life but the sea-wind's, rest-
　　less 15
　　Night and day.

The dense hard passage is blind and stifled
　That crawls by a track none turn to climb
To the strait waste place that the years have
　　rifled
　Of all but the thorns that are touched not
　　of time. 20
The thorns he spares when the rose is taken;
　The rocks are left when he wastes the
　　plain.
The wind that wanders, the weeds wind-
　　shaken,
　　These remain.

Not a flower to be pressed of the foot that
　　falls not; 25
　As the heart of a dead man the seed-plots
　　are dry;
From a thicket of thorns whence the night-
　　ingale calls not,
　Could she call, there were never a rose to
　　reply.
Over the meadows that blossom and wither
　Rings but the note of a sea-bird's song; 30
Only the sun and the rain come hither
　　All year long.

The sun burns sere and the rain dishevels
　One gaunt bleak blossom of scentless
　　breath.
Only the wind here hovers and revels 35
　In a round where life seems barren as
　　death.
Here there was laughing of old, there was
　　weeping,
　Haply, of lovers none ever will know,
Whose eyes went seaward a hundred sleep-
　　ing
　　Years ago. 40

Heart handfast in heart as they stood, "Look
　　thither,"
　Did he whisper? "look forth from the
　　flowers to the sea;

For the foam-flowers endure when the rose-
blossoms wither,
  And men that love lightly may die—but
    we?"
And the same wind sang and the same waves
whitened, 45
And or ever the garden's last petals were
shed,
In the lips that had whispered, the eyes that
had lightened,
  Love was dead.

Or they loved their life through, and then
went whither?
  And were one to the end—but what end
    who knows? 50
Love deep as the sea as a rose must wither,
  As the rose-red seaweed that mocks the
    rose.
Shall the dead take thought for the dead to
love them?
  What love was ever as deep as a grave?
They are loveless now as the grass above
them 55
  Or the wave.

All are at one now, roses and lovers,
  Not known of the cliffs and the fields and
    the sea.
Not a breath of the time that has been hovers
  In the air now soft with a summer to be. 60
Not a breath shall there sweeten the seasons
hereafter

Of the flowers or the lovers that laugh now
or weep,
When as they that are free now of weeping
and laughter
  We shall sleep.

Here death may deal not again for ever; 65
  Here change may come not till all change
    end.
From the graves they have made they shall
rise up never,
  Who have left nought living to ravage and
    rend.
Earth, stones, and thorns of the wild ground
growing,
  While the sun and the rain live, these shall
    be: 70
Till a last wind's breath upon all these blow-
ing
  Roll the sea.

Till the slow sea rise and the sheer cliff
crumble,
  Till terrace and meadow the deep gulfs
    drink,
Till the strength of the waves of the high
tides humble 75
  The fields that lessen, the rocks that shrink,
Here now in his triumph where all things
falter,
  Stretched out on the spoils that his own
    hand spread,
As a god self-slain on his own strange altar,
  Death lies dead. 80

AVE ATQUE VALE[1]

In Memory of Charles Baudelaire

Nous devrions pourtant lui porter quelques
* fleurs;*
Les morts, les pauvres morts, ont de grandes
* douleurs,*
Et quand Octobre souffle, émondeur des vieux
* arbres,*
Son vent mélancolique à l'entour de leur
* marbres,*
Certe, ils doivent trouver les vivants bien in-
* grats.*[2]
              —Les Fleurs du Mal.

I

Shall I strew on thee rose or rue or laurel,
  Brother, on this that was the veil of
    thee?
  Or quiet sea-flower molded by the sea,

Or simplest growth of meadow-sweet or
sorrel,
  Such as the summer-sleepy Dryads[3]
    weave, 5
  Waked up by snow-soft sudden rains at
    eve?
Or wilt thou rather, as on earth before,
  Half-faded fiery blossoms, pale with
    heat
  And full of bitter summer, but more
    sweet
To thee than gleanings of a northern shore
  Trod by no tropic feet? 11

---

[1] Hail and Farewell. Charles Baudelaire, author
of the *Fleurs du Mal,* died in 1867.

[2] These lines from Baudelaire may be translated:

Yet we should bear him a few flowers; the dead,
the poor dead, have great sorrows, and when October, pruner of ancient trees, breathes its sad wind
about their tombs, certainly they must deem the
living very thankless.

[3] Wood-nymphs.

II

For always thee the fervid languid glories
 Allured of heavier suns in mightier
  skies;
 Thine ears knew all the wandering
  watery sighs
Where the sea sobs round Lesbian promon-
  tories,   15
 The barren kiss of piteous wave to wave
 That knows not where is that Leucadian
  grave
Which hides too deep the supreme head of
  song.[4]
 Ah, salt and sterile as her kisses were,
 The wild sea winds her and the green
  gulfs bear   20
Hither and thither, and vex and work her
  wrong,
 Blind gods that cannot spare.

III

Thou sawest, in thine old singing season,
  brother,
 Secrets and sorrows unbeheld of us:
 Fierce loves, and lovely leaf-buds poison-
  ous   25
Bare to thy subtler eye, but for none other
 Blowing by night in some unbreathed-in
  clime;
 The hidden harvest of luxurious time,
Sin without shape, and pleasure without
  speech;
 And where strange dreams in a tumul-
  tuous sleep   30
 Make the shut eyes of stricken spirits
  weep;
And with each face thou sawest the shadow
  on each,
 Seeing as men sow men reap.

IV

O sleepless heart and somber soul unsleeping,
 That were athirst for sleep and no more
  life   35
 And no more love, for peace and no
  more strife!
Now the dim gods of death have in their
  keeping
 Spirit and body and all the springs of
  song,
 Is it well now where love can do no
  wrong,

Where stingless pleasure has no foam or
  fang   40
 Behind the unopening closure of her
  lips?
 Is it not well where soul from body
  slips
And fresh from bone divides without a pang
 As dew from flower-bell drips?

V

It is enough; the end and the beginning 45
 Are one thing to thee, who art past the
  end.
 O hand unclasped of unbeholden friend,
For thee no fruits to pluck, no palms for win-
  ning,
 No triumph and no labor and no lust, 49
 Only dead yew-leaves and a little dust.
O quiet eyes wherein the light saith nought,
 Whereto the day is dumb, nor any night
 With obscure finger silences your sight,
Nor in your speech the sudden soul speaks
  thought,
 Sleep, and have sleep for light.   55

VI

Now all strange hours and all strange loves
  are over,
 Dreams and desires and somber songs
  and sweet,
 Hast thou found place at the great knees
  and feet
Of some pale Titan-woman like a lover,
 Such as thy vision here solicited,[5] 60
 Under the shadow of her fair vast head,
The deep division of prodigious breasts,
 The solemn slope of mighty limbs asleep,
 The weight of awful tresses that still
  keep
The savor and shade of old-world pine-
  forests   65
 Where the wet hill-winds weep?

VII

Hast thou found any likeness for thy vision?
 O gardener of strange flowers, what
  bud, what bloom,
 Hast thou found sown, what gathered in
  the gloom?
What of despair, of rapture, of derision, 70
 What of life is there, what of ill or
  good?
 Are the fruits gray like dust or bright
  like blood?

---

[4] Sappho, who was born on the island of Lesbos and was said to have cast herself into the sea from the Leucadian promontory.

[5] See Baudelaire's *La Géante*.

Does the dim ground grow any seed of ours,
    The faint fields quicken any terrene
        root,
    In low lands where the sun and moon
        are mute   75
And all the stars keep silence? Are there
    flowers
    At all, or any fruit?

VIII

Alas, but though my flying song flies after,
    O sweet strange elder singer, thy more
        fleet
    Singing, and footprints of thy fleeter
        feet,
Some dim derision of mysterious laughter 81
    From the blind tongueless warders of
        the dead,
    Some gainless glimpse of Proserpine's
        veiled head,
Some little sound of unregarded tears
    Wept by effaced unprofitable eyes,   85
    And from pale mouths some cadence of
        dead sighs—
These only, these the hearkening spirit hears,
    Sees only such things rise.

IX

Thou art far too far for wings of words to
    follow,
    Far too far off for thought or any
        prayer.   90
    What ails us with thee, who art wind
        and air?
What ails us gazing where all seen is hollow?
    Yet with some fancy, yet with some
        desire,
    Dreams pursue death as winds a flying
        fire,
Our dreams pursue our dead and do not find.
    Still, and more swift than they, the thin
        flame flies,   96
    The low light fails us in elusive skies,
Still the foiled earnest ear is deaf, and blind
    Are still the eluded eyes.

X

Not thee, O never thee, in all time's changes,
    Not thee, but this the sound of thy sad
        soul,   101
    The shadow of thy swift spirit, this shut
        scroll
I lay my hand on, and not death estranges
    My spirit from communion of thy
        song—

These memories and these melodies that
    throng   105
Veiled porches of a Muse funereal—
    These I salute, these touch, these clasp
        and fold
    As though a hand were in my hand to
        hold,
Or through mine ears a mourning musical
    Of many mourners rolled.   110

XI

I among these, I also, in such station
    As when the pyre was charred, and piled
        the sods,
    And offering to the dead made, and
        their gods,
The old mourners had, standing to make
    libation,
    I stand, and to the gods and to the dead
    Do reverence without prayer or praise,
        and shed   116
Offering to these unknown, the gods of
    gloom,
    And what of honey and spice my seed-
        lands bear,
    And what I may of fruits in this chilled
        air,
And lay, Orestes-like,[6] across the tomb   120
    A curl of severed hair.

XII

But by no hand nor any treason stricken,
    Not like the low-lying head of Him, the
        King,[7]
    The flame that made of Troy a ruinous
        thing,
Thou liest, and on this dust no tears could
    quicken   125
    There fall no tears like theirs that all
        men hear
    Fall tear by sweet imperishable tear
Down the opening leaves of holy poets'
    pages.
    Thee not Orestes, not Electra mourns;
    But bending us-ward with memorial
        urns   130
The most high Muses that fulfill all ages
    Weep, and our God's heart yearns.

XIII

For, sparing of his sacred strength, not often
    Among us darkling here the lord of light
    Makes manifest his music and his might
In hearts that open and in lips that soften 136

---

[6]See Aeschylus, *Choëphorae,* 4–8. [7]Agamemnon.

With the soft flame and heat of songs
    that shine.
Thy lips indeed he touched with bitter
    wine,
And nourished them indeed with bitter
    bread;
    Yet surely from his hand thy soul's food
      came,   140
    The fire that scarred thy spirit at his
      flame
Was lighted, and thine hungering heart he
    fed
    Who feeds our hearts with fame.

XIV

Therefore he too now at thy soul's sunsetting,
    God of all suns and songs, he too bends
      down   145
    To mix his laurel with thy cypress
      crown,
And save thy dust from blame and from for-
    getting.
    Therefore he too, seeing all thou wert
      and art,
    Compassionate, with sad and sacred
      heart,
Mourns thee of many his children the last
    dead,   150
    And hallows with strange tears and alien
      sighs
    Thine unmelodious mouth and sunless
      eyes,
And over thine irrevocable head
    Sheds light from the under skies.

XV

And one weeps with him in the ways
    Lethean,   155
    And stains with tears her changing
      bosom chill:
    That obscure Venus of the hollow hill,[8]
That thing transformed which was the
    Cytherean,
    With lips that lost their Grecian laugh
      divine
    Long since, and face no more called
      Erycine;[9]   160
A ghost, a bitter and luxurious god.

---

[8] The Venus of medieval legend, fabled to hold her
court in the recesses of the Venusberg, or Hörsel-
berg, in central Germany.

[9] So called because there was a temple to Aphrodite Urania (the goddess of heavenly love) at Eryx,
in Sicily.

Thee also with fair flesh and singing
    spell
Did she, a sad and second prey, compel
Into the footless places once more trod,
    And shadows hot from hell.   165

XVI

And now no sacred staff shall break in blos-
    som,[10]
    No choral salutation lure to light
    A spirit sick with perfume and sweet
      night
And love's tired eyes and hands and barren
    bosom.
    There is no help for these things; none
      to mend   170
    And none to mar; not all our songs, O
      friend,
Will make death clear or make life durable.
    Howbeit with rose and ivy and wild
      vine
    And with wild notes about this dust of
      thine
At least I fill the place where white dreams
    dwell   175
    And wreathe an unseen shrine.

XVII

Sleep; and if life was bitter to thee, pardon,
    If sweet, give thanks; thou hast no more
      to live;
    And to give thanks is good, and to for-
      give.
Out of the mystic and the mournful garden
    Where all day through thine hands in
      barren braid   181
    Wove the sick flowers of secrecy and
      shade,
Green buds of sorrow and sin, and remnants
    gray,
    Sweet-smelling, pale with poison, san-
      guine-hearted,
    Passions that sprang from sleep and
      thoughts that started,   185
Shall death not bring us all as thee one day
    Among the days departed?

XVIII

For thee, O now a silent soul, my brother,
    Take at my hands this garland, and
      farewell.

---

[10] Tannhäuser's pilgrimage in search of absolution. See note 7 on p. 949 below.

Thin is the leaf, and chill the wintry
   smell,   190
And chill the solemn earth, a fatal mother,
   With sadder than the Niobean[11] womb,
   And in the hollow of her breasts a tomb.
Content thee, howsoe'er, whose days are
   done;
   There lies not any troublous thing be-
     fore,   195
   Nor sight nor sound to war against thee
     more,
For whom all winds are quiet as the sun,
   All waters as the shore.

A BALLAD OF
FRANÇOIS VILLON[1]

Prince of All Ballad-Makers

Bird of the bitter bright grey golden morn
   Scarce risen upon the dusk of dolorous
     years,
First of us all and sweetest singer born
   Whose far shrill note the world of new
     men hears
   Cleave the cold shuddering shade as twi-
     light clears;   5
When song new-born put off the old world's
   attire
And felt its tune on her changed lips expire,
   Writ foremost on the roll of them that
     came
Fresh girt for service of the latter lyre,
   Villon, our sad bad glad mad brother's
     name!   10

Alas the joy, the sorrow, and the scorn,
   That clothed thy life with hopes and sins
     and fears,
And gave thee stones for bread and tares for
   corn
   And plume-plucked gaol-birds for thy
     starveling peers
Till death clipt close their flight with
   shameful shears;   15
Till shifts came short and loves were hard
   to hire,
When lilt of song nor twitch of twangling
   wire

Could buy thee bread or kisses; when light
   fame
Spurned like a ball and haled through brake
   and briar,
   Villon, our sad bad glad mad brother's
     name!   20

Poor splendid wings so frayed and soiled
   and torn!
   Poor kind wild eyes so dashed with light
     quick tears!
Poor perfect voice, most blithe when most
   forlorn,
   That rings athwart the sea whence no
     man steers
   Like joy-bells crossed with death-bells in
     our ears!   25
What far delight has cooled the fierce desire
That like some ravenous bird was strong to
   tire
   On that frail flesh and soul consumed with
     flame,
But left more sweet than roses to respire,
   Villon, our sad bad glad mad brother's
     name?   30

ENVOI

Prince of sweet songs made out of tears and
   fire,
A harlot was thy nurse, a God thy sire;
   Shame soiled thy song, and song assoiled
     thy shame.
But from thy feet now death has washed the
   mire,
Love reads out first at head of all our quire,
   Villon, our sad bad glad mad brother's
     name.   *36*

FIRST FOOTSTEPS[1]

A little way, more soft and sweet
   Than fields aflower with May,
A babe's feet, venturing, scarce complete
   A little way.

Eyes full of dawning day   5
Look up for mother's eyes to meet,
   Too blithe for song to say.

---

[11]Niobe, with fourteen children, boasted of her
superiority to the goddess Latona, with her two,
whereupon all of Niobe's children were slain.

[1]The French lyric poet of the fifteenth century.

[1]This and the following poem are from *A Century of Roundels.* The roundel, or rondel, is a
French lyric form having but two rimes. It commonly has fourteen lines, of which the first two are
repeated as the seventh and eighth and as the thirteenth and fourteenth.

Glad as the golden spring to greet
  Its first live leaflet's play,
Love, laughing, leads the little feet   10
  A little way.

THE ROUNDEL

A roundel is wrought as a ring or a star-
  bright sphere,
With craft of delight and with cunning of
  sound unsought,
That the heart of the hearer may smile if to
  pleasure his ear
    A roundel is wrought.

Its jewel of music is carven of all or of
  aught—   5
Love, laughter, or mourning—remembrance
  of rapture or fear—
That fancy may fashion to hang in the ear
  of thought.

As a bird's quick song runs round, and the
  hearts in us hear
Pause answer to pause, and again the same
  strain caught,
So moves the device whence, round as a pearl
  or tear,   10
    A roundel is wrought.

ON THE DEATHS OF THOMAS CARLYLE AND GEORGE ELIOT [1]

Two souls diverse out of our human sight
  Pass, followed one with love and each with
    wonder:
  The stormy sophist with his mouth of
    thunder,
Clothed with loud words and mantled in the
  might
Of darkness and magnificence of night;   5
  And one whose eye could smite the night
    in sunder,
  Searching if light or no light were there-
    under,
And found in love of loving-kindness light.
Duty divine and Thought with eyes of fire
Still following Righteousness with deep de-
  sire   10
  Shone sole and stern before her and above,
Sure stars and sole to steer by; but more
  sweet
Shone lower the loveliest lamp for earthly
  feet,
  The light of little children, and their love.

[1] From *Tristram of Lyonesse and Other Poems.* George Eliot died near the end of 1880, Carlyle near the beginning of 1881.

OSCAR WILDE

1854-1900

Oscar Fingal O'Flahertie Wills Wilde was born in Dublin on 16 October, 1854. Although he had some Anglo-Saxon blood, his ancestry was predominantly Celtic. His father, Sir William Wilde, enjoyed a European reputation as an eye and ear doctor, and Lady Wilde, or "Speranza" as she signed herself, had intellectual pretensions; nevertheless it is generally agreed that his parents set the boy an unfortunate example of domestic shabbiness and laxity. In 1864 he was sent to the Portora Royal School at Enniskillen, whence he proceeded to Trinity College, Dublin, in 1871. At Trinity he distinguished himself in classics; and his tutor, John P. Mahaffy, in the preface to his *Social Life in Greece from Homer to Menander* (1874), acknowledged an obligation to his pupil for improvements and corrections. It was only natural that Wilde should continue his education at Oxford, where he secured a scholarship at Magdalen College in the autumn of 1874. His career at the University was marked by a deliberate aesthetic dandyism, cultivated in response partly to personal taste and partly to the doctrines of Walter Pater; from this time on, in fact, Pater's philosophy was to have a strong influence on the younger writer. In 1877 Wilde visited Greece under the expert guidance of Mahaffy, and in the following year he won the Newdigate Prize with his poem "Ravenna," the fruit of two visits to Italy. By the time he left Oxford his writing had already won him some fame; in 1881 he published his first volume, *Poems,* at his own expense; but he was now faced with the necessity of earning his living as a man of letters in London. In order to secure notoriety he made public appearances in silk knee-breeches, a sunflower or green carnation in his hand and his long hair undulating to his shoulders. This form of self-advertisement soon began to defeat itself, as Wilde became aware during a lecture tour of the United States in 1882. Although the aesthetic pose remained, he gradually gave over the attempt to scandalize his contemporaries

and sought rather to win them by the brilliance of his wit. In 1884 he married Constance Lloyd, a young lady of means, by whom he later had two sons; and he settled down to a productive decade of literary work. In addition to much of a purely journalistic character he wrote: *The Soul of Man under Socialism* (1891), a humanitarian tract; *The Happy Prince and Other Tales* (1888) and *A House of Pomegranates* (1891), stories for children; *The Portrait of Mr. W. H.* (1889), an excursion into Shakespearian scholarship; *The Picture of Dorian Gray* (1891), and *Lord Arthur Savile's Crime and Other Stories* (1891), sophisticated fiction; *Intentions* (1891), a volume of essays on art; *Salomé* (in French, 1893), an erotic drama; finally a series of comedies dealing with London society, *Lady Windermere's Fan* (acted 1892), *A Woman of No Importance* (acted 1893), *The Importance of Being Earnest* (acted 1895), and *An Ideal Husband* (acted 1895). With these brilliant plays Wilde reached the height of his career, and then, just in the moment of his greatest popularity, he fell from grace. Relying on his literary fame to defend him, he instituted an action for libel against the eighth Marquis of Queensberry, who had accused him of sexual immorality. Unfortunately Queensberry's lawyer was able to establish the truth of the accusation, and Wilde not only failed to win his case but was eventually tried and convicted of gross indecency. He served two years of hard labor at Reading Gaol (1895–1897). Towards the end of his imprisonment he was allowed the use of writing materials and recorded his feelings of penitence and self-justification in a long letter, later published with the the title *De Profundis.* Immediately on being freed he went to northern France; there in the village of Berneval he wrote his finest poem, *The Ballad of Reading Gaol.* But after the *Ballad* had been written an inherent weakness of will, as well as the sense of his own degradation, made it impossible for him to do more. Impoverished and without purpose, he spent the next few years wandering hopelessly from place to place in Italy and France. He died at Paris on 30 November, 1900.

At Oxford Wilde seems to have momentarily undergone the influence of Ruskin, but from the first he can only have been a rebel against Ruskin's doctrine that truth and a system of moral values underlie good art. Wilde believed that art was, not an outgrowth of reality or of moral values, but actually the source of whatever values the rest of life might happen to possess. "I treated art as the supreme reality and life as a mere mode of fiction," he remarks in *De Profundis;* indeed he and his followers, the Aesthetes as they were called derisively, asserted not only the independence but the supreme importance of the artistic ego. Most of what Wilde himself wrote is the counterpart if not the deliberate embodiment of this creed. His poems, with the great exception of *The Ballad of Reading Gaol,* have only a tenuous connection with any life beyond that of art; he imitates a hundred other poets—the Greek and Latin Classics, Dante, Milton, Shakespeare, the French Symbolists—but he imitates only the superficial aspects of their craft, and he fails to establish a fruitful contact with the reality either of the past or of the contemporary world. The same limitation appears in a far more fortunate shape when we turn to his comedies. *The Importance of Being Earnest* is not a picture of London society as it really existed at the end of the nineteenth century, or of human life at any period; and the play fails to produce a sense of dramatic reality, because it is without serious characterization or logical structure. The plot, in fact, is hardly more than another of the author's jests. All that has made *The Importance of Being Earnest* a universal favorite, all the gay, nonsensical brilliance which makes it one of the most amusing of English comedies, whether it is read or seen upon the stage, issues wholly from the wit and temperament of Wilde himself. His play is a final, perfected version of his own conversation. It illustrates the success, and the limits to the success, with which he could apply his theory that the artist was a self-sufficient being.

Wilde's writings have been published in several collected editions. One, entitled *The Complete Works,* with introductions to the several volumes by various authors, was published in 12 volumes, New York, 1923. Robert H. Sherard is the author of a too laudatory and partisan *Life of Oscar Wilde* (London, 1906); and in *Oscar Wilde, His Life and Confessions* (New York, 1918; revised ed. 1930) Frank Harris emphasizes and elaborates the sensational aspects of his subject, although much that he reports may be true. A better balanced study than either of these is Boris L. Brasol's *Oscar Wilde, the Man, the Artist, the Martyr* (New York, 1938). *Oscar Wilde Discovers America* by Lloyd Lewis and H. J. Smith (New York, 1936) is amusing. For a critical interpretation of Wilde's work, see *Oscar Wilde* by Arthur Ransome (London, 1913); and for discussion chiefly of Wilde's plays, see Archibald Henderson, *Interpreters of Life* (New York, 1911), pp. 35–103. Holbrook Jackson's *The Eighteen-Nineties* (London, 1913) furnishes an excellent picture of the literary scene at the time of Wilde's success and downfall; and Osbert Burdett's *The Beardsley Period* (London, 1925) is a distinguished critical study of the 1890's.

HELAS! [1]

To drift with every passion till my soul
Is a stringed lute on which all winds can play,
Is it for this that I have given away
Mine ancient wisdom, and austere control?
Methinks my life is a twice-written scroll 5
Scrawled over on some boyish holiday
With idle songs for pipe and virelay,[2]
Which do but mar the secret of the whole.
Surely there was a time I might have trod
The sunlit heights, and from life's dissonance

Struck one clear chord to reach the ears of
    God: 11
Is that time dead? lo! with a little rod
I did but touch the honey of romance—
And must I lose a soul's inheritance?

AMOR INTELLEC-
TUALIS [3]

Oft have we trod the vales of Castaly[4]
  And heard sweet notes of sylvan music
    blown
  From antique reeds to common folk un-
    known:

---

[1] This and the following sonnet were published in *Poems,* 1881.

[2] A song or short lyric piece, usually written in interlocking stanzas, each limited to two rime sounds.

[3] Intellectual Love.

[4] Castalia was a fountain on Mt. Parnassus, sacred to Apollo and the Muses.

And often launched our bark upon that sea
Which the nine Muses hold in empery,   5
    And plowed free furrows through the
        wave and foam,
    Nor spread reluctant sail for more safe
        home
Till we had freighted well our argosy.
Of which despoiléd treasures these remain,
    Sordello's passion, and the honied line   10
Of young Endymion, lordly Tamburlaine
    Driving his pampered jades, and, more
        than these,
The seven-fold vision of the Florentine,[5]
    And grave-browed Milton's solemn har-
        monies.

FANTAISIES DÉCO-
RATIVES [6]

I. LE PANNEAU

Under the rose-tree's dancing shade
    There stands a little ivory girl,
    Pulling the leaves of pink and pearl
With pale green nails of polished jade.

The red leaves fall upon the mold,   5
    The white leaves flutter, one by one,
    Down to a blue bowl where the sun,
Like a great dragon, writhes in gold.

The white leaves float upon the air,
    The red leaves flutter idly down,   10
    Some fall upon her yellow gown,
And some upon her raven hair.

She takes an amber lute and sings,
    And as she sings a silver crane
    Begins his scarlet neck to strain,   15
And flap his burnished metal wings.

She takes a lute of amber bright,
    And from the thicket where he lies
    Her lover, with his almond eyes,
Watches her movements in delight.   20

And now she gives a cry of fear,
    And tiny tears begin to start:
    A thorn has wounded with its dart
The pink-veined sea-shell of her ear.

And now she laughs a merry note: 25
    There has fallen a petal of the rose
    Just where the yellow satin shows
The blue-veined flower of her throat.

With pale green nails of polished jade,
    Pulling the leaves of pink and pearl,   30
    There stands a little ivory girl
Under the rose-tree's dancing shade.

II. LES BALLONS

Against these turbid turquoise skies
    The light and luminous balloons
    Dip and drift like satin moons,
Drift like silken butterflies;

Reel with every windy gust,   5
    Rise and reel like dancing girls,
    Float like transparent pearls,
Fall and float like silver dust.

Now to the low leaves they cling,
    Each with coy fantastic pose,   10
    Each a petal of a rose
Straining at a gossamer string.

Then to the tall trees they climb,
    Like thin globes of amethyst,
    Wandering opals keeping tryst   15
With the rubies of the lime.

SYMPHONY IN YELLOW [7]

An omnibus across the bridge
    Crawls like a yellow butterfly,
    And, here and there, a passer-by
Shows like a little restless midge.

Big barges full of yellow hay   5
    Are moved against the shadowy wharf,
    And, like a yellow silken scarf,
The thick fog hangs along the quay.

The yellow leaves begin to fade
    And flutter from the Temple[8] elms,   10
    And at my feet the pale green Thames
Lies like a rod of rippled jade.

---

[5]Allusions to Browning's *Sordello*, Keats's *Endymion*, Marlowe's *Tamburlaine*, and (apparently) Dante's *Divine Comedy*.

[6]First published in *The Lady's Pictorial*, Christmas, 1887. The title may be translated *Decorative Fantasies*; the title of I, *The Panel*; the title of II, *The Balloons*.

---

[7]First published in the *Centennial Magazine* (of Sydney, Australia), February, 1889.

[8]The London legal collegiate societies.

THE BALLAD OF READING GAOL[1]

In Memoriam C. T. W.: Sometime Trooper of the Royal Horse Guards.
Obiit H. M. Prison, Reading, Berkshire, July 7th, 1896.

I

He did not wear his scarlet coat,
  For blood and wine are red,
And blood and wine were on his hands
  When they found him with the dead,
The poor dead woman whom he loved,   5
  And murdered in her bed.

He walked amongst the Trial Men
  In a suit of shabby gray;
A cricket cap was on his head,
  And his step seemed light and gay;   10
But I never saw a man who looked
  So wistfully at the day.

I never saw a man who looked
  With such a wistful eye
Upon that little tent of blue   15
  Which prisoners call the sky,
And at every drifting cloud that went
  With sails of silver by.

I walked, with other souls in pain,
  Within another ring,   20
And was wondering if the man had done
  A great or little thing,
When a voice behind me whispered low,
  "That fellow's got to swing."

Dear Christ! the very prison walls   25
  Suddenly seemed to reel,
And the sky above my head became
  Like a casque of scorching steel;
And, though I was a soul in pain,
  My pain I could not feel.   30

I only knew what hunted thought
  Quickened his step, and why
He looked upon the garish day
  With such a wistful eye;
The man had killed the thing he loved,   35
  And so he had to die.

Yet each man kills the thing he loves,
  By each let this be heard,
Some do it with a bitter look,
  Some with a flattering word,   40

The coward does it with a kiss,
  The brave man with a sword!

Some kill their love when they are young,
  And some when they are old;
Some strangle with the hands of Lust,   45
  Some with the hands of Gold:
The kindest use a knife, because
  The dead so soon grow cold.

Some love too little, some too long,
  Some sell, and others buy;   50
Some do the deed with many tears,
  And some without a sigh:
For each man kills the thing he loves,
  Yet each man does not die.

He does not die a death of shame   55
  On a day of dark disgrace,
Nor have a noose about his neck,
  Nor a cloth upon his face,
Nor drop feet foremost through the floor
  Into an empty space.   60

He does not sit with silent men
  Who watch him night and day;
Who watch him when he tries to weep,
  And when he tries to pray;
Who watch him lest himself should rob   65
  The prison of its prey.

He does not wake at dawn to see
  Dread figures throng his room,
The shivering Chaplain robed in white,
  The Sheriff stern with gloom,   70
And the Governor all in shiny black,
  With the yellow face of Doom.

He does not rise in piteous haste
  To put on convict-clothes,
While some coarse-mouthed Doctor gloats,
  and notes   75
  Each new and nerve-twitched pose,
Fingering a watch whose little ticks
  Are like horrible hammer-blows.

He does not know that sickening thirst
  That sands one's throat, before   80
The hangman with his gardener's gloves
  Slips through the padded door,
And binds one with three leathern thongs,
  That the throat may thirst no more.

[1]First published in 1898. The "C. T. W." to
whose memory the poem is dedicated was Charles
T. Wooldridge, who was executed for the murder
of his wife.

He does not bend his head to hear 85
  The Burial Office read,
Nor while the terror of his soul
  Tells him he is not dead,
Cross his own coffin, as he moves
  Into the hideous shed. 90

He does not stare upon the air
  Through a little roof of glass:
He does not pray with lips of clay
  For his agony to pass;
Nor feel upon his shuddering cheek 95
  The kiss of Caiaphas.

II

Six weeks our guardsman walked the yard,
  In the suit of shabby gray:
His cricket cap was on his head,
  And his step seemed light and gay,
But I never saw a man who looked 5
  So wistfully at the day.

I never saw a man who looked
  With such a wistful eye
Upon that little tent of blue
  Which prisoners call the sky, 10
And at every wandering cloud that trailed
  Its raveled fleeces by.

He did not wring his hands, as do
  Those witless men who dare
To try to rear the changeling Hope 15
  In the cave of black Despair:
He only looked upon the sun,
  And drank the morning air.

He did not wring his hands nor weep,
  Nor did he peek or pine, 20
But he drank the air as though it held
  Some healthful anodyne;
With open mouth he drank the sun
  As though it had been wine!

And I and all the souls in pain, 25
  Who tramped the other ring,
Forgot if we ourselves had done
  A great or little thing,
And watched with gaze of dull amaze
  The man who had to swing. 30

And strange it was to see him pass
  With a step so light and gay,
And strange it was to see him look
  So wistfully at the day,
And strange it was to think that he 35
  Had such a debt to pay.

For oak and elm have pleasant leaves
  That in the spring-time shoot:
But grim to see is the gallows-tree,
  With its adder-bitten root, 40
And, green or dry, a man must die
  Before it bears its fruit!

The loftiest place is that seat of grace
  For which all worldlings try:
But who would stand in hempen band 45
  Upon a scaffold high,
And through a murderer's collar take
  His last look at the sky?

It is sweet to dance to violins
  When Love and Life are fair: 50
To dance to flutes, to dance to lutes
  Is delicate and rare:
But it is not sweet with nimble feet
  To dance upon the air!

So with curious eyes and sick surmise 55
  We watched him day by day,
And wondered if each one of us
  Would end the self-same way,
For none can tell to what red Hell
  His sightless soul may stray. 60

At last the dead man walked no more
  Amongst the Trial Men,
And I knew that he was standing up
  In the black dock's dreadful pen,
And that never would I see his face 65
  In God's sweet world again.

Like two doomed ships that pass in storm
  We had crossed each other's way:
But we made no sign, we said no word,
  We had no word to say; 70
For we did not meet in the holy night,
  But in the shameful day.

A prison wall was round us both,
  Two outcast men we were:
The world had thrust us from its heart, 75
  And God from out His care:
And the iron gin that waits for Sin
  Had caught us in its snare.

III

In Debtors' Yard the stones are hard,
  And the dripping wall is high,
So it was there he took the air
  Beneath the leaden sky,
And by each side a Warder walked, 5
  For fear the man might die.

Or else he sat with those who watched
 His anguish night and day;
Who watched him when he rose to weep,
 And when he crouched to pray; 10
Who watched him lest himself should rob
 Their scaffold of its prey.

The Governor was strong upon
 The Regulations Act:
The Doctor said that Death was but 15
 A scientific fact:
And twice a day the Chaplain called,
 And left a little tract.

And twice a day he smoked his pipe,
 And drank his quart of beer: 20
His soul was resolute, and held
 No hiding-place for fear;
He often said that he was glad
 The hangman's hands were near.

But why he said so strange a thing 25
 No Warder dared to ask:
For he to whom a watcher's doom
 Is given as his task,
Must set a lock upon his lips,
 And make his face a mask. 30

Or else he might be moved, and try
 To comfort or console:
And what should Human Pity do
 Pent up in Murderer's Hole?
What word of grace in such a place 35
 Could help a brother's soul?

With slouch and swing around the ring
 We trod the Fools' Parade!
We did not care: we knew we were
 The Devil's Own Brigade: 40
And shaven head and feet of lead
 Make a merry masquerade.

We tore the tarry rope to shreds
 With blunt and bleeding nails;
We rubbed the doors, and scrubbed the floors,
 And cleaned the shining rails: 46
And, rank by rank, we soaped the plank,
 And clattered with the pails.

We sewed the sacks, we broke the stones,
 We turned the dusty drill: 50
We banged the tins, and bawled the hymns,
 And sweated on the mill:
But in the heart of every man
 Terror was lying still.

So still it lay that every day 55
 Crawled like a weed-clogged wave:
And we forgot the bitter lot
 That waits for fool and knave,
Till once, as we tramped in from work,
 We passed an open grave. 60

With yawning mouth the yellow hole
 Gaped for a living thing;
The very mud cried out for blood
 To the thirsty asphalt ring:
And we knew that ere one dawn grew fair 65
 Some prisoner had to swing.

Right in we went, with soul intent
 On Death and Dread and Doom:
The hangman, with his little bag,
 Went shuffling through the gloom: 70
And each man trembled as he crept
 Into his numbered tomb.

That night the empty corridors
 Were full of forms of Fear,
And up and down the iron town 75
 Stole feet we could not hear,
And through the bars that hide the stars
 White faces seemed to peer.

He lay as one who lies and dreams
 In a pleasant meadow-land, 80
The watchers watched him as he slept,
 And could not understand
How one could sleep so sweet a sleep
 With a hangman close at hand.

But there is no sleep when men must weep 85
 Who never yet have wept:
So we—the fool, the fraud, the knave—
 That endless vigil kept,
And through each brain on hands of pain
 Another's terror crept. 90

Alas! it is a fearful thing
 To feel another's guilt!
For, right within, the sword of Sin
 Pierced to its poisoned hilt,
And as molten lead were the tears we shed 95
 For the blood we had not spilt.

The Warders with their shoes of felt
 Crept by each padlocked door,
And peeped and saw, with eyes of awe,
 Gray figures on the floor, 100
And wondered why men knelt to pray
 Who never prayed before.

All through the night we knelt and prayed,
  Mad mourners of a corse!
The troubled plumes of midnight were   105
  The plumes upon a hearse:
And bitter wine upon a sponge
  Was the savor of Remorse.

The gray cock crew, the red cock crew,
  But never came the day: 110
And crooked shapes of Terror crouched,
  In the corners where we lay:
And each evil sprite that walks by night
  Before us seemed to play.

They glided past, they glided fast,   115
  Like travelers through a mist:
They mocked the moon in a rigadoon[2]
  Of delicate turn and twist,
And with formal pace and loathsome grace
  The phantoms kept their tryst.   120

With mop and mow,[3] we saw them go,
  Slim shadows hand in hand:
About, about, in ghostly rout
  They trod a saraband:[4]
And the damned grotesques made arabesques,
  Like the wind upon the sand!   126

With the pirouettes of marionettes,
  They tripped on pointed tread:
But with flutes of Fear they filled the ear,
  As their grisly masque they led,   130
And loud they sang, and long they sang,
  For they sang to wake the dead.

"Oho!" they cried, *"The world is wide,*
  But fettered limbs go lame!
And once, or twice, to throw the dice   135
  Is a gentlemanly game,
But he does not win who plays with Sin
  In the secret House of Shame."

No things of air these antics were,
  That frolicked with such glee: 140
To men whose lives were held in gyves[5]
  And whose feet might not go free,
Ah! wounds of Christ! they were living
    things,
  Most terrible to see.

Around, around, they waltzed and wound; 145
  Some wheeled in smirking pairs;
With the mincing step of a demirep[6]
  Some sidled up the stairs:

----

[2]A complicated dance.   [3]With grimaces.
[4]A slow and stately dance.   [5]Shackles.
[6]An adventuress.

And with subtle sneer, and fawning leer,
  Each helped us at our prayers.   150

The morning wind began to moan,
  But still the night went on:
Through its giant loom the web of gloom
  Crept till each thread was spun:
And, as we prayed, we grew afraid   155
  Of the Justice of the Sun.

The moaning wind went wandering round
  The weeping prison-wall:
Till like a wheel of turning steel
  We felt the minutes crawl: 160
O moaning wind! what had we done
  To have such a seneschal?

At last I saw the shadowed bars,
  Like a lattice wrought in lead,
Move right across the whitewashed wall 165
  That faced my three-plank bed,
And I knew that somewhere in the world
  God's dreadful dawn was red.

At six o'clock we cleaned our cells,
  At seven all was still,   170
But the sough and swing of a mighty wing
  The prison seemed to fill,
For the Lord of Death with icy breath
  Had entered in to kill.

He did not pass in purple pomp,   175
  Nor ride a moon-white steed.
Three yards of cord and a sliding board
  Are all the gallows' need:
So with rope of shame the Herald came
  To do the secret deed.   180

We were as men who through a fen
  Of filthy darkness grope:
We did not dare to breathe a prayer,
  Or to give our anguish scope:
Something was dead in each of us,   185
  And what was dead was Hope.

For Man's grim Justice goes its way,
  And will not swerve aside:
It slays the weak, it slays the strong,
  It has a deadly stride: 190
With iron heel it slays the strong,
  The monstrous parricide!

We waited for the stroke of eight:
  Each tongue was thick with thirst:
For the stroke of eight is the stroke of Fate
  That makes a man accursed,   196
And Fate will use a running noose
  For the best man and the worst.

We had no other thing to do,
    Save to wait for the sign to come :   200
So, like things of stone in a valley lone,
    Quiet we sat and dumb :
But each man's heart beat thick and quick,
    Like a madman on a drum !

With sudden shock the prison-clock   205
    Smote on the shivering air,
And from all the gaol rose up a wail
    Of impotent despair,
Like the sound that frightened marshes hear
    From some leper in his lair.   210

And as one sees most fearful things
    In the crystal of a dream,
We saw the greasy hempen rope
    Hooked to the blackened beam,
And heard the prayer the hangman's snare
    Strangled into a scream.   216

And all the woe that moved him so
    That he gave that bitter cry,
And the wild regrets, and the bloody sweats,
    None knew so well as I :　 220
For he who lives more lives than one
    More deaths than one must die.

IV

There is no chapel on the day
    On which they hang a man :
The Chaplain's heart is far too sick,
    Or his face is far too wan,
Or there is that written in his eyes   5
    Which none should look upon.

So they kept us close till nigh on noon,
    And then they rang the bell,
And the Warders with their jingling keys
    Opened each listening cell,   10
And down the iron stair we tramped,
    Each from his separate Hell.

Out into God's sweet air we went,
    But not in wonted way,
For this man's face was white with fear,   15
    And that man's face was gray,
And I never saw sad men who looked
    So wistfully at the day.

I never saw sad men who looked
    With such a wistful eye   20
Upon that little tent of blue
    We prisoners called the sky,
And at every careless cloud that passed
    In happy freedom by.

But there were those amongst us all   25
    Who walked with downcast head,
And knew that, had each got his due,
    They should have died instead :
He had but killed a thing that lived,
    Whilst they had killed the dead.   30

For he who sins a second time
    Wakes a dead soul to pain,
And draws it from its spotted shroud,
    And makes it bleed again,
And makes it bleed great gouts of blood,   35
    And makes it bleed in vain !

Like ape or clown, in monstrous garb
    With crooked arrows starred,
Silently we went round and round
    The slippery asphalt yard ;   40
Silently we went round and round,
    And no man spoke a word.

Silently we went round and round,
    And through each hollow mind
The Memory of dreadful things   45
    Rushed like a dreadful wind,
And Horror stalked before each man,
    And Terror crept behind.

The Warders strutted up and down,
    And kept their herd of brutes,   50
Their uniforms were spick and span,
    And they wore their Sunday suits,
But we knew the work they had been at,
    By the quicklime on their boots.

For where a grave had opened wide,   55
    There was no grave at all :
Only a stretch of mud and sand
    By the hideous prison-wall,
And a little heap of burning lime,
    That the man should have his pall.   60

For he has a pall, this wretched man,
    Such as few men can claim :
Deep down below a prison-yard,
    Naked for greater shame,
He lies, with fetters on each foot,   65
    Wrapt in a sheet of flame !

And all the while the burning lime
    Eats flesh and bone away,
It eats the brittle bone by night,
    And the soft flesh by day,   70
It eats the flesh and bone by turns,
    But it eats the heart alway.

For three long years they will not sow
  Or root or seedling there:
For three long years the unbless'd spot   75
  Will sterile be and bare,
And look upon the wondering sky
  With unreproachful stare.

They think a murderer's heart would taint
  Each simple seed they sow.   80
It is not true! God's kindly earth
  Is kindlier than men know,
And the red rose would but blow more red,
  The white rose whiter blow.

Out of his mouth a red, red rose!   85
  Out of his heart a white!
For who can say by what strange way,
  Christ brings His will to light,
Since the barren staff the pilgrim bore
  Bloomed in the great Pope's sight?[7]   90

But neither milk-white rose nor red
  May bloom in prison-air;
The shard, the pebble, and the flint,
  Are what they give us there:
For flowers have been known to heal   95
  A common man's despair.

So never will wine-red rose or white,
  Petal by petal, fall
On that stretch of mud and sand that lies
  By the hideous prison-wall,   100
To tell the men who tramp the yard
  That God's Son died for all.

Yet though the hideous prison-wall
  Still hems him round and round,
And a spirit may not walk by night   105
  That is with fetters bound,
And a spirit may but weep that lies
  In such unholy ground,

He is at peace—this wretched man—
  At peace, or will be soon: 110
There is no thing to make him mad,
  Nor does Terror walk at noon,
For the lampless Earth in which he lies
  Has neither Sun nor Moon.

They hanged him as a beast is hanged: 115
  They did not even toll

---

[7]After living with Venus for seven years, Tannhäuser went on a pilgrimage to Rome to seek absolution from the Pope. His Holiness replied that it was as impossible for Tannhäuser to be forgiven as for his pilgrim staff to blossom. Three days later, after the sinner had gone off in despair, his staff (left in Rome) began to blossom. Then the Pope sent for him, but he had returned to Venus.

A requiem that might have brought
  Rest to his startled soul,
But hurriedly they took him out.
  And hid him in a hole.   120

They stripped him of his canvas clothes,
  And gave him to the flies:
They mocked the swollen purple throat,
  And the stark and staring eyes:
And with laughter loud they heaped the
    shroud   125
  In which their convict lies.

The Chaplain would not kneel to pray
  By his dishonored grave:
Nor mark it with that blessed Cross
  That Christ for sinners gave,   130
Because the man was one of those
  Whom Christ came down to save.

Yet all is well; he has but passed
  To Life's appointed bourne:[8]
And alien tears will fill for him   135
  Pity's long-broken urn,
For his mourners will be outcast men,
  And outcasts always mourn.

V

I know not whether Laws be right,
  Or whether Laws be wrong;
All that we know who lie in gaol
  Is that the wall is strong;
And that each day is like a year,   5
  A year whose days are long.

But this I know, that every Law
  That men have made for Man,
Since first Man took his brother's life,
  And the sad world began,   10
But straws[9] the wheat and saves the chaff
  With a most evil fan.

This too I know—and wise it were
  If each could know the same—
That every prison that men build   15
  Is built with bricks of shame,
And bound with bars lest Christ should see
  How men their brothers maim.

With bars they blur the gracious moon,
  And blind the goodly sun: 20
And they do well to hide their Hell,
  For in it things are done
That Son of God nor son of Man
  Ever should look upon!

---

[8]Destination.   [9]Throws away like straw.

The vilest deeds like poison weeds   25
  Bloom well in prison-air:
It is only what is good in Man
  That wastes and withers there:
Pale Anguish keeps the heavy gate,
  And the Warder is Despair.   30

For they starve the little frightened child
  Till it weeps both night and day:
And they scourge the weak, and flog the fool,
  And gibe the old and gray,
And some grow mad, and all grow bad,   35
  And none a word may say.

Each narrow cell in which we dwell
  Is a foul and dark latrine,
And the fetid breath of living Death
  Chokes up each grated screen,   40
And all, but Lust, is turned to dust
  In Humanity's machine.

The brackish water that we drink
  Creeps with a loathsome slime,
And the bitter bread they weigh in scales   45
  Is full of chalk and lime,
And Sleep will not lie down, but walks
  Wild-eyed, and cries to Time.

But though lean Hunger and green Thirst
  Like asp with adder fight,   50
We have little care of prison fare,
  For what chills and kills outright
Is that every stone one lifts by day
  Becomes one's heart by night.

With midnight always in one's heart,   55
  And twilight in one's cell,
We turn the crank, or tear the rope,
  Each in his separate Hell,
And the silence is more awful far
  Than the sound of a brazen bell.   60

And never a human voice comes near
  To speak a gentle word:
And the eye that watches through the door
  Is pitiless and hard:
And by all forgot, we rot and rot,   65
  With soul and body marred.

And thus we rust Life's iron chain
  Degraded and alone:
And some men curse, and some men weep,
  And some men make no moan: 70
But God's eternal Laws are kind
  And break the heart of stone.

And every human heart that breaks,
  In prison-cell or yard,
Is as that broken box that gave   75
  Its treasure to the Lord,
And filled the unclean leper's house
  With the scent of costliest nard.[10]

Ah! happy they whose hearts can break
  And peace of pardon win!   80
How else may man make straight his plan
  And cleanse his soul from Sin?
How else but through a broken heart
  May Lord Christ enter in?

And he of the swollen purple throat,   85
  And the stark and staring eyes,
Waits for the holy hands that took
  The Thief to Paradise;
And a broken and a contrite heart
  The Lord will not despise.   90

The man in red who reads the Law
  Gave him three weeks of life,
Three little weeks in which to heal
  His soul of his soul's strife,
And cleanse from every blot of blood   95
  The hand that held the knife.

And with tears of blood he cleansed the hand,
  The hand that held the steel:
For only blood can wipe out blood,
  And only tears can heal: 100
And the crimson stain that was of Cain
  Became Christ's snow-white seal.

VI

In Reading gaol by Reading town
  There is a pit of shame,
And in it lies a wretched man
  Eaten by teeth of flame,
In a burning winding-sheet he lies,   5
  And his grave has got no name.

And there, till Christ call forth the dead,
  In silence let him lie:
No need to waste the foolish tear,
  Or heave the windy sigh: 10
The man had killed the thing he loved,
  And so he had to die.

And all men kill the thing they love,
  By all let this be heard,
Some do it with a bitter look,   15
  Some with a flattering word,
The coward does it with a kiss,
  The brave man with a sword!

[10]An allusion to the story of Lazarus (St. John
11).

THE IMPORTANCE OF BEING EARNEST[1]

THE PERSONS OF THE PLAY

JOHN WORTHING, J.P.[2]
ALGERNON MONCRIEFF
REV. CANON CHASUBLE, D.D.
MERRIMAN, *Butler*
LANE, *Manservant*
LADY BRACKNELL
HON. GWENDOLEN FAIRFAX
CECILY CARDEW
MISS PRISM, *Governess*

THE SCENES OF THE PLAY

ACT I. *Algernon Moncrieff's Flat in Half-Moon Street, W.*[3]
ACT II. *The Garden at the Manor House, Woolton*
ACT. III. *Drawing room at the Manor House, Woolton*

TIME: *The Present*

ACT I

SCENE

Morning room in ALGERNON'S *flat in Half-Moon Street. The room is luxuriously and artistically furnished. The sound of a piano is heard in the adjoining room.*

LANE *is arranging afternoon tea on the table, and after the music has ceased,* ALGERNON *enters.*

ALGERNON. Did you hear what I was playing, Lane?

LANE. I didn't think it polite to listen, sir.

ALGERNON. I'm sorry for that, for your sake. I don't play accurately—anyone can play accurately—but I play with wonderful expression. As far as the piano is concerned, sentiment is my forte. I keep science for Life.

LANE. Yes, sir.

ALGERNON. And, speaking of the science of Life, have you got the cucumber sandwiches cut for Lady Bracknell?

LANE. Yes, sir. [*Hands them on a salver.*

ALGERNON. [*Inspects them, takes two, and sits down on the sofa.*] Oh! . . . by the way, Lane, I see from your book that on

Thursday night, when Lord Shoreman and Mr. Worthing were dining with me, eight bottles of champagne are entered as having been consumed.

5 LANE. Yes, sir; eight bottles and a pint.

ALGERNON. Why is it that at a bachelor's establishment the servants invariably drink the champagne? I ask merely for information.

10 LANE. I attribute it to the superior quality of the wine, sir. I have often observed that in married households the champagne is rarely of a first-rate brand.

ALGERNON. Good heavens! Is marriage 15 so demoralizing as that?

LANE. I believe it *is* a very pleasant state, sir. I have had very little experience of it myself up to the present. I have only been married once. That was in consequence of a 20 misunderstanding between myself and a young person.

ALGERNON. [*Languidly.*] I don't know that I am much interested in your family life, Lane.

25 LANE. No, sir; it is not a very interesting subject. I never think of it myself.

ALGERNON. Very natural, I am sure. That will do, Lane, thank you.

LANE. Thank you, sir. [LANE *goes out.*

30 ALGERNON. Lane's views on marriage seem somewhat lax. Really, if the lower orders don't set us a good example, what on earth is the use of them? They seem, as a class, to have absolutely no sense of moral 35 responsibility.

Enter LANE.

LANE. Mr. Ernest Worthing.

Enter JACK.

[LANE *goes out.*

ALGERNON. How are you, my dear Ernest? What brings you up to town?

45 JACK. Oh, pleasure, pleasure! What else should bring one anywhere? Eating as usual, I see, Algy!

ALGERNON. [*Stiffly.*] I believe it is customary in good society to take some slight re-50 freshment at five o'clock. Where have you been since last Thursday?

JACK. [*Sitting down on the sofa.*] In the country.

ALGERNON. What on earth do you do 55 there?

---

[1]This play was produced in 1895; published in 1899.

[2]Justice of the Peace.

[3]The western postal district of London (a fashionable quarter).

JACK. [*Pulling off his gloves.*] When one is in town one amuses oneself. When one is in the country one amuses other people. It is excessively boring.

ALGERNON. And who are the people you amuse?

JACK. [*Airily.*] Oh, neighbors, neighbors.

ALGERNON. Got nice neighbors in your part of Shropshire?

JACK. Perfectly horrid! Never speak to one of them.

ALGERNON. How immensely you must amuse them! [*Goes over and takes sandwich.*] By the way, Shropshire is your county, is it not?

JACK. Eh? Shropshire? Yes, of course. Hallo! Why all these cups? Why cucumber sandwiches? Why such reckless extravagance in one so young? Who is coming to tea?

ALGERNON. Oh! merely Aunt Augusta and Gwendolen.

JACK. How perfectly delightful!

ALGERNON. Yes, that is all very well; but I am afraid Aunt Augusta won't quite approve of your being here.

JACK. May I ask why?

ALGERNON. My dear fellow, the way you flirt with Gwendolen is perfectly disgraceful. It is almost as bad as the way Gwendolen flirts with you.

JACK. I am in love with Gwendolen. I have come up to town expressly to propose to her.

ALGERNON. I thought you had come up for pleasure? . . . I call that business.

JACK. How utterly unromantic you are!

ALGERNON. I really don't see anything romantic in proposing. It is very romantic to be in love. But there is nothing romantic about a definite proposal. Why, one may be accepted. One usually is, I believe. Then the excitement is all over. The very essence of romance is uncertainty. If ever I get married, I'll certainly try to forget the fact.

JACK. I have no doubt about that, dear Algy. The Divorce Court was specially invented for people whose memories are so curiously constituted.

ALGERNON. Oh! there is no use speculating on that subject. Divorces are made in Heaven—— [JACK *puts out his hand to take a sandwich.* ALGERNON *at once interferes.*] Please don't touch the cucumber sandwiches. They are ordered specially for Aunt Augusta.   [*Takes one and eats it.*

JACK. Well, you have been eating them all the time.

ALGERNON. That is quite a different matter. She is my aunt. [*Takes plate from below.*] Have some bread and butter. The bread and butter is for Gwendolen. Gwendolen is devoted to bread and butter.

JACK. [*Advancing to table and helping himself.*] And very good bread and butter it is too.

ALGERNON. Well, my dear fellow, you need not eat as if you were going to eat it all. You behave as if you were married to her already. You are not married to her already, and I don't think you ever will be.

JACK. Why on earth do you say that?

ALGERNON. Well, in the first place girls never marry the men they flirt with. Girls don't think it right.

JACK. Oh, that is nonsense!

ALGERNON. It isn't. It is a great truth. It accounts for the extraordinary number of bachelors that one sees all over the place. In the second place, I don't give my consent.

JACK. Your consent!

ALGERNON. My dear fellow, Gwendolen is my first cousin. And before I allow you to marry her, you will have to clear up the whole question of Cecily.   [*Rings bell.*

JACK. Cecily! What on earth do you mean? What do you mean, Algy, by Cecily! I don't know anyone of the name of Cecily.

Enter LANE.

ALGERNON. Bring me that cigarette case Mr. Worthing left in the smoking room the last time he dined here.

LANE. Yes, sir.   [LANE *goes out.*

JACK. Do you mean to say you have had my cigarette case all this time? I wish to goodness you had let me know. I have been writing frantic letters to Scotland Yard about it. I was very nearly offering a large reward.

ALGERNON. Well, I wish you would offer one. I happen to be more than usually hard up.

JACK. There is no good offering a large reward now that the thing is found.

Enter LANE *with the cigarette case on a salver.* ALGERNON *takes it at once.* LANE *goes out.*

ALGERNON. I think that is rather mean of you, Ernest, I must say. [*Opens case and examines it.*] However, it makes no matter, for, now that I look at the inscription inside, I find that the thing isn't yours after all.

JACK. Of course it's mine. [*Moving to him.*] You have seen me with it a hundred times, and you have no right whatsoever to read what is written inside. It is a very ungentlemanly thing to read a private cigarette case.

ALGERNON. Oh! it is absurd to have a hard and fast rule about what one should read and what one shouldn't. More than half of modern culture depends on what one shouldn't read.

JACK. I am quite aware of the fact, and I don't propose to discuss modern culture. It isn't the sort of thing one should talk of in private. I simply want my cigarette case back.

ALGERNON. Yes; but this isn't your cigarette case. This cigarette case is a present from someone of the name of Cecily, and you said you didn't know anyone of that name.

JACK. Well, if you want to know, Cecily happens to be my aunt.

ALGERNON. Your aunt!

JACK. Yes. Charming old lady she is, too. Lives at Tunbridge Wells. Just give it back to me, Algy.

ALGERNON. [*Retreating to back of sofa.*] But why does she call herself little Cecily if she is your aunt and lives at Tunbridge Wells? [*Reading.*] "From little Cecily with her fondest love."

JACK. [*Moving to sofa and kneeling upon it.*] My dear fellow, what on earth is there in that? Some aunts are tall, some aunts are not tall. That is a matter that surely an aunt may be allowed to decide for herself. You seem to think that every aunt should be exactly like your aunt! That is absurd! For Heaven's sake give me back my cigarette case.

[*Follows* ALGERNON *round the room.*

ALGERNON. Yes. But why does your aunt call you her uncle? "From little Cecily, with her fondest love to her dear Uncle Jack." There is no objection, I admit, to an aunt being a small aunt, but why an aunt, no matter what her size may be, should call her own nephew her uncle, I can't quite make out. Besides, your name isn't Jack at all; it is Ernest.

JACK. It isn't Ernest; it's Jack.

ALGERNON. You have always told me it was Ernest. I have introduced you to everyone as Ernest. You answer to the name of Ernest. You look as if your name was Ernest. You are the most earnest-looking person I ever saw in my life. It is perfectly absurd your saying that your name isn't Ernest. It's on your cards. Here is one of them. [*Taking it from case.*] "Mr. Ernest Worthing, B. 4, The Albany." I'll keep this as a proof that your name is Ernest if ever you attempt to deny it to me, or to Gwendolen, or to anyone else.

[*Puts the card in his pocket.*

JACK. Well, my name is Ernest in town and Jack in the country, and the cigarette case was given to me in the country.

ALGERNON. Yes, but that does not account for the fact that your small Aunt Cecily, who lives at Tunbridge Wells, calls you her dear uncle. Come, old boy, you had much better have the thing out at once.

JACK. My dear Algy, you talk exactly as if you were a dentist. It is very vulgar to talk like a dentist when one isn't a dentist. It produces a false impression.

ALGERNON. Well, that is exactly what dentists always do. Now, go on! Tell me the whole thing. I may mention that I have always suspected you of being a confirmed and secret Bunburyist; and I am quite sure of it now.

JACK. Bunburyist? What on earth do you mean by a Bunburyist?

ALGERNON. I'll reveal to you the meaning of that incomparable expression as soon as you are kind enough to inform me why you are Ernest in town and Jack in the country.

JACK. Well, produce my cigarette case first.

ALGERNON. Here it is. [*Hands cigarette case.*] Now produce your explanation, and pray make it improbable. [*Sits on sofa.*

JACK. My dear fellow, there is nothing improbable about my explanation at all. In fact it's perfectly ordinary. Old Mr. Thomas Cardew, who adopted me when I was a little boy, made me in his will guardian to his grand-daughter, Miss Cecily Cardew. Cecily, who addresses me as her uncle from motives of respect that you could not possibly appreciate, lives at my place in the country under the charge of her admirable governess, Miss Prism.

ALGERNON. Where is that place in the country, by the way?

JACK. That is nothing to you, dear boy. You are not going to be invited. . . . I may tell you candidly that the place is not in Shropshire.

ALGERNON. I suspected that, my dear fellow! I have Bunburyed all over Shropshire on two separate occasions. Now, go on.

Why are you Ernest in town and Jack in the country?

JACK. My dear Algy, I don't know whether you will be able to understand my real motives. You are hardly serious enough. When one is placed in the position of guardian, one has to adopt a very high moral tone on all subjects. It's one's duty to do so. And as a high moral tone can hardly be said to conduce very much to either one's health or one's happiness, in order to get up to town I have always pretended to have a younger brother of the name of Ernest, who lives in the Albany, and gets into the most dreadful scrapes. That, my dear Algy, is the whole truth pure and simple.

ALGERNON. The truth is rarely pure and never simple. Modern life would be very tedious if it were either, and modern literature a complete impossibility!

JACK. That wouldn't be at all a bad thing.

ALGERNON. Literary criticism is not your forte, my dear fellow. Don't try it. You should leave that to people who haven't been at a University. They do it so well in the daily papers. What you really are is a Bunburyist. I was quite right in saying you were a Bunburyist. You are one of the most advanced Bunburyists I know.

JACK. What on earth do you mean?

ALGERNON. You have invented a very useful younger brother called Ernest, in order that you may be able to come up to town as often as you like. I have invented an invaluable permanent invalid called Bunbury, in order that I may be able to go down into the country whenever I choose. Bunbury is perfectly invaluable. If it wasn't for Bunbury's extraordinary bad health, for instance, I wouldn't be able to dine with you at Willis's to-night, for I have been really engaged to Aunt Augusta for more than a week.

JACK. I haven't asked you to dine with me anywhere to-night.

ALGERNON. I know. You are absurdly careless about sending out invitations. It is very foolish of you. Nothing annoys people so much as not receiving invitations.

JACK. You had much better dine with your Aunt Augusta.

ALGERNON. I haven't the smallest intention of doing anything of the kind. To begin with, I dined there on Monday, and once a week is quite enough to dine with one's own relations. In the second place, whenever I do dine there I am always treated as a member of the family, and sent down with either no woman at all, or two. In the third place, I know perfectly well whom she will place me next to, tonight. She will place me next Mary Farquhar, who always flirts with her own husband across the dinner table. That is not very pleasant. Indeed, it is not even decent . . . and that sort of thing is enormously on the increase. The amount of women in London who flirt with their own husbands is perfectly scandalous. It looks so bad. It is simply washing one's clean linen in public. Besides, now that I know you to be a confirmed Bunburyist, I naturally want to talk to you about Bunburying. I want to tell you the rules.

JACK. I'm not a Bunburyist at all. If Gwendolen accepts me, I am going to kill my brother, indeed I think I'll kill him in any case. Cecily is a little too much interested in him. It is rather a bore. So I am going to get rid of Ernest. And I strongly advise you to do the same with Mr. . . . with your invalid friend who has the absurd name.

ALGERNON. Nothing will induce me to part with Bunbury, and if you ever get married, which seems to me extremely problematic, you will be very glad to know Bunbury. A man who marries without knowing Bunbury has a very tedious time of it.

JACK. That is nonsense. If I marry a charming girl like Gwendolen, and she is the only girl I ever saw in my life that I would marry, I certainly won't want to know Bunbury.

ALGERNON. Then your wife will. You don't seem to realize, that in married life three is company and two is none.

JACK. [*Sententiously.*] That, my dear young friend, is the theory that the corrupt French Drama has been propounding for the last fifty years.

ALGERNON. Yes; and that the happy English home has proved in half the time.

JACK. For heaven's sake, don't try to be cynical. It's perfectly easy to be cynical.

ALGERNON. My dear fellow, it isn't easy to be anything nowadays. There's such a lot of beastly competition about. [*The sound of an electric bell is heard.*] Ah! that must be Aunt Augusta. Only relatives, or creditors, ever ring in that Wagnerian manner. Now, if I get her out of the way for ten minutes, so that you can have an opportunity for proposing to Gwendolen, may I dine with you to-night at Willis's?

JACK. I suppose so, if you want to.

ALGERNON. Yes, but you must be serious about it. I hate people who are not serious about meals. It is so shallow of them.

Enter LANE.

LANE. Lady Bracknell and Miss Fairfax. [ALGERNON *goes forward to meet them.*

Enter LADY BRACKNELL *and* GWENDOLEN.

LADY BRACKNELL. Good afternoon, dear Algernon, I hope you are behaving very well.

ALGERNON. I'm feeling very well, Aunt Augusta.

LADY BRACKNELL. That's not quite the same thing. In fact the two things rarely go together.

[*Sees* JACK *and bows to him with icy coldness.*

ALGERNON. [*To* GWENDOLEN.] Dear me, you are smart!

GWENDOLEN. I am always smart! Aren't I, Mr. Worthing?

JACK. You're quite perfect, Miss Fairfax.

GWENDOLEN. Oh! I hope I am not that. It would leave no room for developments, and I intend to develop in many directions.

[GWENDOLEN *and* JACK *sit down together in the corner.*

LADY BRACKNELL. I'm sorry if we are a little late, Algernon, but I was obliged to call on dear Lady Harbury. I hadn't been there since her poor husband's death. I never saw a woman so altered; she looks quite twenty years younger. And now I'll have a cup of tea, and one of those nice cucumber sandwiches you promised me.

ALGERNON. Certainly, Aunt Augusta.

[*Goes over to tea table.*

LADY BRACKNELL. Won't you come and sit here, Gwendolen?

GWENDOLEN. Thanks, mamma, I'm quite comfortable where I am.

ALGERNON. [*Picking up empty plate in horror.*] Good heavens! Lane! Why are there no cucumber sandwiches? I ordered them specially.

LANE. [*Gravely.*] There were no cucumbers in the market this morning, sir. I went down twice.

ALGERNON. No cucumbers!

LANE. No, sir. Not even for ready money.

ALGERNON. That will do, Lane, thank you.

LANE. Thank you, sir. [*Goes out.*

ALGERNON. I am greatly distressed, Aunt Augusta, about there being no cucumbers, not even for ready money.

LADY BRACKNELL. It really makes no matter, Algernon. I had some crumpets' with Lady Harbury, who seems to me to be living entirely for pleasure now.

ALGERNON. I hear her hair has turned quite gold from grief.

LADY BRACKNELL. It certainly has changed its color. From what cause I, of course, cannot say. [ALGERNON *crosses and hands tea.*] Thank you. I've quite a treat for you to-night, Algernon. I am going to send you down with Mary Farquhar. She is such a nice woman, and so attentive to her husband. It's delightful to watch them.

ALGERNON. I am afraid, Aunt Augusta, I shall have to give up the pleasure of dining with you tonight after all.

LADY BRACKNELL. [*Frowning.*] I hope not, Algernon. It would put my table completely out. Your uncle would have to dine upstairs. Fortunately he is accustomed to that.

ALGERNON. It is a great bore, and, I need hardly say, a terrible disappointment to me, but the fact is I have just had a telegram to say that my poor friend Bunbury is very ill again. [*Exchanges glances with* JACK.] They seem to think I should be with him.

LADY BRACKNELL. It is very strange. This Mr. Bunbury seems to suffer from curiously bad health.

ALGERNON. Yes; poor Bunbury is a dreadful invalid.

LADY BRACKNELL. Well, I must say, Algernon, that I think it is high time that Mr. Bunbury made up his mind whether he was going to live or to die. This shilly-shallying with the question is absurd. Nor do I in any way approve of the modern sympathy with invalids. I consider it morbid. Illness of any kind is hardly a thing to be encouraged in others. Health is the primary duty of life. I am always telling that to your poor uncle, but he never seems to take much notice . . . as far as any improvement in his ailments goes. I should be much obliged if you would ask Mr. Bunbury, from me, to be kind enough not to have a relapse on Saturday, for I rely on you to arrange my music for me. It is my last reception, and one wants something that will encourage conversation, particularly at the end of the season when every one has practically said whatever they had to say, which, in most cases, was probably not much.

ALGERNON. I'll speak to Bunbury, Aunt

'Thin griddle cakes.

Augusta, if he is still conscious, and I think I can promise you he'll be all right by Saturday. Of course the music is a great difficulty. You see, if one plays good music, people don't listen, and if one plays bad music, people don't talk. But I'll run over the program I've drawn out, if you will kindly come into the next room for a moment.

LADY BRACKNELL. Thank you, Algernon. It is very thoughtful of you. [*Rising, and following* ALGERNON.] I'm sure the programme will be delightful, after a few expurgations. French songs I cannot possibly allow. People always seem to think that they are improper, and either look shocked, which is vulgar, or laugh, which is worse. But German sounds a thoroughly respectable language, and indeed, I believe is so. Gwendolen, you will accompany me.

GWENDOLEN. Certainly, mamma.

[LADY BRACKNELL *and* ALGERNON *go into the music room,* GWENDOLEN *remains behind.*

JACK. Charming day it has been, Miss Fairfax.

GWENDOLEN. Pray don't talk to me about the weather, Mr. Worthing. Whenever people talk to me about the weather, I always feel quite certain that they mean something else. And that makes me so nervous.

JACK. I do mean something else.

GWENDOLEN. I thought so. In fact, I am never wrong.

JACK. And I would like to be allowed to take advantage of Lady Bracknell's temporary absence . . .

GWENDOLEN. I would certainly advise you to do so. Mamma has a way of coming back suddenly into a room that I have often had to speak to her about.

JACK. [*Nervously.*] Miss Fairfax, ever since I met you I have admired you more than any girl . . . I have ever met since . . . I met you.

GWENDOLEN. Yes, I am quite aware of the fact. And I often wish that in public, at any rate, you had been more demonstrative. For me you have always had an irresistible fascination. Even before I met you I was far from indifferent to you. [JACK *looks at her in amazement.*] We live, as I hope you know, Mr. Worthing, in an age of ideals. The fact is constantly mentioned in the more expensive monthly magazines, and has reached the provincial pulpits I am told: and my ideal has always been to love some one of the name of Ernest. There is something in that name that inspires absolute confidence. The moment Algernon first mentioned to me that he had a friend called Ernest, I knew I was destined to love you.

JACK. You really love me, Gwendolen?

GWENDOLEN. Passionately!

JACK. Darling! You don't know how happy you've made me.

GWENDOLEN. My own Ernest!

JACK. But you don't really mean to say that you couldn't love me if my name wasn't Ernest?

GWENDOLEN. But your name is Ernest.

JACK. Yes, I know it is. But supposing it was something else? Do you mean to say you couldn't love me then?

GWENDOLEN. [*Glibly.*] Ah! that is clearly a metaphysical speculation, and like most metaphysical speculations has very little reference at all to the actual facts of real life, as we know them.

JACK. Personally, darling, to speak quite candidly, I don't much care about the name of Ernest. . . . I don't think the name suits me at all.

GWENDOLEN. It suits you perfectly. It is a divine name. It has a music of its own. It produces vibrations.

JACK. Well, really, Gwendolen, I must say that I think there are lots of other much nicer names. I think Jack, for instance, a charming name.

GWENDOLEN. Jack? . . . No, there is very little music in the name Jack, if any at all, indeed. It does not thrill. It produces absolutely no vibrations. . . . I have known several Jacks, and they all, without exception, were more than usually plain. Besides, Jack is a notorious domesticity for John! And I pity any woman who is married to a man called John. She would probably never be allowed to know the entrancing pleasure of a single moment's solitude. The only really safe name is Ernest.

JACK. Gwendolen, I must get christened at once—I mean we must get married at once. There is no time to be lost.

GWENDOLEN. Married, Mr. Worthing?

JACK. [*Astounded.*] Well . . . surely. You know that I love you, and you led me to believe, Miss Fairfax, that you were not absolutely indifferent to me.

GWENDOLEN. I adore you. But you haven't proposed to me yet. Nothing has been said at all about marriage. The subject has not even been touched on.

JACK. Well . . . may I propose to you now?

GWENDOLEN. I think it would be an admirable opportunity. And to spare you any possible disappointment, Mr. Worthing, I think it only fair to tell you quite frankly beforehand that I am fully determined to accept you.

JACK. Gwendolen!

GWENDOLEN. Yes, Mr. Worthing, what have you got to say to me?

JACK. You know what I have got to say to you.

GWENDOLEN. Yes, but you don't say it.

JACK. Gwendolen, will you marry me? [*Goes on his knees.*

GWENDOLEN. Of course I will, darling. How long you have been about it! I am afraid you have had very little experience in how to propose.

JACK. My own one, I have never loved anyone in the world but you.

GWENDOLEN. Yes, but men often propose for practice. I know my brother Gerald does. All my girl-friends tell me so. What wonderfully blue eyes you have, Ernest! They are quite, quite blue. I hope you will always look at me just like that, especially when there are other people present.

Enter LADY BRACKNELL.

LADY BRACKNELL. Mr. Worthing! Rise, sir, from this semi-recumbent posture. It is most indecorous.

GWENDOLEN. Mamma! [*He tries to rise; she restrains him.*] I must beg you to retire. This is no place for you. Besides, Mr. Worthing has not quite finished yet.

LADY BRACKNELL. Finished what, may I ask?

GWENDOLEN. I am engaged to Mr. Worthing, mamma.

[*They rise together.*

LADY BRACKNELL. Pardon me, you are not engaged to anyone. When you do become engaged to someone, I, or your father, should his health permit him, will inform you of the fact. An engagement should come on a young girl as a surprise, pleasant or unpleasant, as the case may be. It is hardly a matter that she could be allowed to arrange for herself. . . . And now I have a few questions to put to you, Mr. Worthing. While I am making these inquiries, you, Gwendolen, will wait for me below in the carriage.

GWENDOLEN. [*Reproachfully.*] Mamma!

LADY BRACKNELL. In the carriage, Gwendolen! [GWENDOLEN *goes to the door. She and* JACK *blow kisses to each other behind* LADY BRACKNELL'S *back.* LADY BRACKNELL *looks vaguely about as if she could not understand what the noise was. Finally turns round.*] Gwendolen, the carriage!

GWENDOLEN. Yes, mamma.

[*Goes out, looking back at* JACK.

LADY BRACKNELL. [*Sitting down.*] You can take a seat, Mr. Worthing.

[*Looks in her pocket for notebook and pencil.*

JACK. Thank you, Lady Bracknell, I prefer standing.

LADY BRACKNELL. [*Pencil and notebook in hand.*] I feel bound to tell you that you are not down on my list of eligible young men, although I have the same list as the dear Duchess of Bolton has. We work together, in fact. However, I am quite ready to enter your name, should your answers be what a really affectionate mother requires. Do you smoke?

JACK. Well, yes, I must admit I smoke.

LADY BRACKNELL. I am glad to hear it. A man should always have an occupation of some kind. There are far too many idle men in London as it is. How old are you?

JACK. Twenty-nine.

LADY BRACKNELL. A very good age to be married at. I have always been of opinion that a man who desires to get married should know either everything or nothing. Which do you know?

JACK. [*After some hesitation.*] I know nothing, Lady Bracknell.

LADY BRACKNELL. I am pleased to hear it. I do not approve of anything that tampers with natural ignorance. Ignorance is like a delicate exotic fruit; touch it and the bloom is gone. The whole theory of modern education is radically unsound. Fortunately in England, at any rate, education produces no effect whatsoever. If it did, it would prove a serious danger to the upper classes, and probably lead to acts of violence in Grosvenor Square. What is your income?

JACK. Between seven and eight thousand a year.

LADY BRACKNELL. [*Makes a note in her book.*] In land, or in investments?

JACK. In investments, chiefly.

LADY BRACKNELL. That is satisfactory. What between the duties expected of one during one's lifetime, and the duties exacted from one after one's death, land has ceased to be either a profit or a pleasure. It gives one position, and prevents one from keeping it up. That's all that can be said about land. 5

JACK. I have a country house with some land, of course, attached to it, about fifteen hundred acres, I believe; but I don't depend on that for my real income. In fact, as far as I can make out, the poachers are the only 10 people who make anything out of it.

LADY BRACKNELL. A country house! How many bedrooms? Well, that point can be cleared up afterwards. You have a town house, I hope? A girl with a simple, un- 15 spoiled nature, like Gwendolen, could hardly be expected to reside in the country.

JACK. Well, I own a house in Belgrave Square,[5] but it is let by the year to Lady Bloxham. Of course, I can get it back when- 20 ever I like, at six months' notice.

LADY BRACKNELL. Lady Bloxham? I don't know her.

JACK. Oh, she goes about very little. She is a lady considerably advanced in years. 25

LADY BRACKNELL. Ah, nowadays that is no guarantee of respectability of character. What number in Belgrave Square?

JACK. 149.

LADY BRACKNELL. [*Shaking her head.*] 30 The unfashionable side. I thought there was something. However, that could easily be altered.

JACK. Do you mean the fashion, or the side?

LADY BRACKNELL. [*Sternly.*] Both, if · 35 necessary, I presume. What are your politics?

JACK. Well, I am afraid I really have none. I am a Liberal Unionist.[6]

LADY BRACKNELL. Oh, they count as 40 Tories. They dine with us. Or come in the evening, at any rate. Now to minor matters. Are your parents living?

JACK. I have lost both my parents.

LADY BRACKNELL. Both? . . . That 45 looks like carelessness. Who was your father? He was evidently a man of some wealth. Was he born in what the Radical papers call the purple of commerce, or did he 50 rise from the ranks of the aristocracy?

JACK. I am afraid I really don't know. The fact is, Lady Bracknell, I said I had lost

---

[5] One of the most fashionable residential parts of London.

[6] A member of the Liberal party who sided with the Conservatives in opposing Irish home rule.

---

my parents. It would be nearer the truth to say that my parents seem to have lost me. . . . I don't actually know who I am by birth. I was . . . well, I was found.

LADY BRACKNELL. Found!

JACK. The late Mr. Thomas Cardew, an old gentleman of a very charitable and kindly disposition, found me, and gave me the name of Worthing, because he happened to have a first-class ticket for Worthing in his pocket at the time. Worthing is a place in Sussex. It is a seaside resort.

LADY BRACKNELL. Where did the charitable gentleman who had a first-class ticket for this seaside resort find you?

JACK. [*Gravely.*] In a handbag.

LADY BRACKNELL. A handbag?

JACK. [*Very seriously.*] Yes, Lady Bracknell. I was in a handbag—a somewhat large, black leather handbag, with handles to it—an ordinary handbag in fact.

LADY BRACKNELL. In what locality did this Mr. James, or Thomas, Cardew come across this ordinary handbag?

JACK. In the cloakroom at Victoria Station. It was given to him in mistake for his own.

LADY BRACKNELL. The cloakroom at Victoria Station?

JACK. Yes. The Brighton line.

LADY BRACKNELL. The line is immaterial. Mr. Worthing, I confess I feel somewhat bewildered by what you have just told me. To be born, or at any rate, bred in a handbag, whether it had handles or not, seems to me to display a contempt for the ordinary decencies of family life that reminds one of the worst excesses of the French Revolution. And I presume you know what that unfortunate movement led to? As for the particular locality in which the handbag was found, a cloakroom at a railway station might serve to conceal a social indiscretion—has probably, indeed, been used for that purpose before now—but it could hardly be regarded as an assured basis for a recognized position in good society.

JACK. May I ask you then what you would advise me to do? I need hardly say I would do anything in the world to ensure Gwendolen's happiness.

LADY BRACKNELL. I would strongly advise you, Mr. Worthing, to try and acquire some relations as soon as possible, and to make a definite effort to produce at any rate one parent, of either sex, before the season is quite over.

JACK. Well, I don't see how I could possibly manage to do that. I can produce the handbag at any moment. It is in my dressing room at home. I really think that should satisfy you, Lady Bracknell.

LADY BRACKNELL. Me, sir! What has it to do with me? You can hardly imagine that I and Lord Bracknell would dream of allowing our only daughter—a girl brought up with the utmost care—to marry into a cloakroom, and form an alliance with a parcel? Good morning, Mr. Worthing!

[LADY BRACKNELL *sweeps out in majestic indignation.*

JACK. Good morning! [ALGERNON, *from the other room, strikes up the Wedding March.* JACK *looks perfectly furious, and goes to the door.*] For goodness' sake don't play that ghastly tune, Algy! How idiotic you are!

The music stops, and ALGERNON *enters cheerily.*

ALGERNON. Didn't it go off all right, old boy? You don't mean to say Gwendolen refused you? I know it is a way she has. She is always refusing people. I think it is most ill-natured of her.

JACK. Oh, Gwendolen is as right as a trivet.[7] As far as she is concerned, we are engaged. Her mother is perfectly unbearable. Never met such a Gorgon. . . . I don't really know what a Gorgon is like, but J am quite sure that Lady Bracknell is one. In any case, she is a monster, without being a myth, which is rather unfair. . . . I beg your pardon, Algy, I suppose I shouldn't talk about your own aunt in that way before you.

ALGERNON. My dear boy, I love hearing my relations abused. It is the only thing that makes me put up with them at all. Relations are simply a tedious pack of people, who haven't got the remotest knowledge of how to live, nor the smallest instinct about when to die.

JACK. Oh, that is nonsense!

ALGERNON. It isn't!

JACK. Well, I won't argue about the matter. You always want to argue about things.

ALGERNON. That is exactly what things were originally made for.

JACK. Upon my word, if I thought that, I'd shoot myself. . . . [*A pause.*] You don't think there is any chance of Gwendolen becoming like her mother in about a hundred and fifty years, do you, Algy?

ALGERNON. All women become like their mothers. That is their tragedy. No man does. That's his.

JACK. Is that clever?

ALGERNON. It is perfectly phrased! and quite as true as any observation in civilized life should be.

JACK. I am sick to death of cleverness. Everybody is clever nowadays. You can't go anywhere without meeting clever people. The thing has become an absolute public nuisance. I wish to goodness we had a few fools left.

ALGERNON. We have.

JACK. I should extremely like to meet them. What do they talk about?

ALGERNON. The fools? Oh! about the clever people, of course.

JACK. What fools!

ALGERNON. By the way, did you tell Gwendolen the truth about your being Ernest in town, and Jack in the country?

JACK. [*In a very patronizing manner.*] My dear fellow, the truth isn't quite the sort of thing one tells to a nice, sweet, refined girl. What extraordinary ideas you have about the way to behave to a woman!

ALGERNON. The only way to behave to a woman is to make love to her, if she is pretty, and to someone else, if she is plain.

JACK. Oh, that is nonsense!

ALGERNON. What about your brother? What about the profligate Ernest?

JACK. Oh, before the end of the week I shall have got rid of him. I'll say he died in Paris of apoplexy. Lots of people die of apoplexy, quite suddenly, don't they?

ALGERNON. Yes, but it's hereditary, my dear fellow. It's a sort of thing that runs in families. You had much better say a severe chill.

JACK. You are sure a severe chill isn't hereditary, or anything of that kind?

ALGERNON. Of course it isn't!

JACK. Very well, then. My poor brother Ernest is carried off suddenly, in Paris, by a severe chill. That gets rid of him.

ALGERNON. But I thought you said that . . . Miss Cardew was a little too much interested in your poor brother Ernest? Won't she feel his loss a good deal?

JACK. Oh, that is all right. Cecily is not a silly romantic girl, I am glad to say. She has got a capital appetite, goes long walks, and pays no attention at all to her lessons.

ALGERNON. I would rather like to see Cecily.

---

[7]As right as a tripod; thoroughly right.

JACK. I will take very good care you never do. She is excessively pretty, and she is only just eighteen.

ALGERNON. Have you told Gwendolen yet that you have an excessively pretty ward who is only just eighteen?

JACK. Oh! one doesn't blurt these things out to people. Cecily and Gwendolen are perfectly certain to be extremely great friends. I'll bet you anything you like that half an hour after they have met, they will be calling each other sister.

ALGERNON. Women only do that when they have called each other a lot of other things first. Now, my dear boy, if we want to get a good table at Willis's, we really must go and dress. Do you know it is nearly seven?

JACK. [*Irritably.*] Oh! it always is nearly seven.

ALGERNON. Well, I'm hungry.

JACK. I never knew you when you weren't. . . .

ALGERNON. What shall we do after dinner? Go to a theater?

JACK. Oh, no! I loathe listening.

ALGERNON. Well, let us go to the club?

JACK. Oh, no! I hate talking.

ALGERNON. Well, we might trot round to the Empire at ten?

JACK. Oh, no! I can't bear looking at things. It is so silly.

ALGERNON. Well, what shall we do?

JACK. Nothing!

ALGERNON. It is awfully hard work doing nothing. However, I don't mind hard work where there is no definite object of any kind.

Enter LANE.

LANE. Miss Fairfax.

Enter GWENDOLEN. LANE *goes out.*

ALGERNON. Gwendolen, upon my word!

GWENDOLEN. Algy, kindly turn your back. I have something very particular to say to Mr. Worthing.

ALGERNON. Really, Gwendolen, I don't think I can allow this at all.

GWENDOLEN. Algy, you always adopt a strictly immoral attitude towards life. You are not quite old enough to do that.

[ALGERNON *retires to the fireplace.*

JACK. My own darling!

GWENDOLEN. Ernest, we may never be married. From the expression on mamma's face I fear we never shall. Few parents nowadays pay any regard to what their children say to them. The old-fashioned respect for the young is fast dying out. Whatever influence I ever had over mamma, I lost at the age of three. But although she may prevent us from becoming man and wife, and I may marry someone else, and marry often, nothing that she can possibly do can alter my eternal devotion to you.

JACK. Dear Gwendolen!

GWENDOLEN. The story of your romantic origin, as related to me by mamma, with unpleasing comments, has naturally stirred the deeper fibers of my nature. Your Christian name has an irresistible fascination. The simplicity of your character makes you exquisitely incomprehensible to me. Your town address at the Albany I have. What is your address in the country?

JACK. The Manor House, Woolton, Hertfordshire.

[ALGERNON, *who has been carefully listening, smiles to himself, and writes the address on his shirt cuff. Then picks up the Railway Guide.*

GWENDOLEN. There is a good postal service, I suppose? It may be necessary to do something desperate. That of course will require serious consideration. I will communicate with you daily.

JACK. My own one!

GWENDOLEN. How long do you remain in town?

JACK. Till Monday.

GWENDOLEN. Good! Algy, you may turn round now.

ALGERNON. Thanks, I've turned round already.

GWENDOLEN. You may also ring the bell.

JACK. You will let me see you to your carriage, my own darling?

GWENDOLEN. Certainly.

JACK. [*To* LANE, *who now enters.*] I will see Miss Fairfax out.

LANE. Yes, sir.

[JACK *and* GWENDOLEN *go off.*

[LANE *presents several letters on a salver to* ALGERNON. *It is to be surmised that they are bills, as* ALGERNON, *after looking at the envelopes, tears them up.*

ALGERNON. A glass of sherry, Lane.

LANE. Yes, sir.

ALGERNON. Tomorrow, Lane, I'm going Bunburying.

LANE. Yes, sir.

ALGERNON. I shall probably not be back till Monday. You can put up my dress clothes, my smoking jacket, and all the Bunbury suits . . .

LANE. Yes, sir.   [*Handing sherry.*

ALGERNON. I hope tomorrow will be a fine day, Lane.

LANE. It never is, sir.

ALGERNON. Lane, you're a perfect pessimist.

LANE. I do my best to give satisfaction, sir.

Enter JACK. LANE *goes off.*

JACK. There's a sensible, intellectual girl! the only girl I ever cared for in my life. [ALGERNON *is laughing immoderately.*] What on earth are you so amused at?

ALGERNON. Oh, I'm a little anxious about poor Bunbury, that is all.

JACK. If you don't take care, your friend Bunbury will get you into a serious scrape some day.

ALGERNON. I love scrapes. They are the only things that are never serious.

JACK. Oh, that's nonsense, Algy. You never talk anything but nonsense.

ALGERNON. Nobody ever does.

[JACK *looks indignantly at him, and leaves the room.* ALGERNON *lights a cigarette, reads his shirt cuff, and smiles.*

ACT-DROP

ACT II

SCENE

Garden at the Manor House. A flight of gray stone steps leads up to the house. The garden, an old-fashioned one, full of roses. Time of year, July. Basket chairs, and a table covered with books, are set under a large yew tree.

MISS PRISM *discovered seated at the table.* CECILY *is at the back watering flowers.*

MISS PRISM. [*Calling.*] Cecily, Cecily! Surely such a utilitarian occupation as the watering of flowers is rather Moulton's duty than yours? Especially at a moment when intellectual pleasures await you. Your German grammar is on the table. Pray open it at page fifteen. We will repeat yesterday's lesson.

CECILY. [*Coming over very slowly.*] But I don't like German. It isn't at all a becoming language. I know perfectly well that I look quite plain after my German lesson.

MISS PRISM. Child, you know how anxious your guardian is that you should improve yourself in every way. He laid particular stress on your German, as he was leaving for town yesterday. Indeed, he always lays stress on your German when he is leaving for town.

CECILY. Dear Uncle Jack is so very serious! Sometimes he is so serious that I think he cannot be quite well.

MISS PRISM. [*Drawing herself up.*] Your guardian enjoys the best of health, and his gravity of demeanor is especially to be commended in one so comparatively young as he is. I know no one who has a higher sense of duty and responsibility.

CECILY. I suppose that is why he often looks a little bored when we three are together.

MISS PRISM. Cecily! I am surprised at you. Mr. Worthing has many troubles in his life. Idle merriment and triviality would be out of place in his conversation. You must remember his constant anxiety about that unfortunate young man, his brother.

CECILY. I wish Uncle Jack would allow that unfortunate young man, his brother, to come down here sometimes. We might have a good influence over him, Miss Prism. I am sure you certainly would. You know German, and geology, and things of that kind influence a man very much.

[CECILY *begins to write in her diary.*

MISS PRISM. [*Shaking her head.*] I do not think that even I could produce any effect on a character that according to his own brother's admission is irretrievably weak and vacillating. Indeed I am not sure that I would desire to reclaim him. I am not in favor of this modern mania for turning bad people into good people at a moment's notice. As a man sows so let him reap. You must put away your diary, Cecily. I really don't see why you should keep a diary at all.

CECILY. I keep a diary in order to enter the wonderful secrets of my life. If I didn't write them down I should probably forget all about them.

MISS PRISM. Memory, my dear Cecily, is the diary that we all carry about with us.

CECILY. Yes, but it usually chronicles the things that have never happened, and couldn't possibly have happened. I believe that Memory is responsible for nearly all the three-volume novels that Mudie[1] sends us.

MISS PRISM. Do not speak slightingly of the three-volume novel, Cecily. I wrote one myself in earlier days.

CECILY. Did you really, Miss Prism?

[1] A lending library, chiefly of contemporary books.

How wonderfully clever you are! I hope it did not end happily? I don't like novels that end happily. They depress me so much.

MISS PRISM. The good ended happily, and the bad unhappily. That is what Fiction means.

CECILY. I suppose so. But it seems very unfair. And was your novel ever published?

MISS PRISM. Alas! no. The manuscript unfortunately was abandoned. I use the word in the sense of lost or mislaid. To your work, child, these speculations are profitless.

CECILY. [*Smiling.*] But I see dear Dr. Chasuble coming up through the garden.

MISS PRISM. [*Rising and advancing.*] Dr. Chasuble! This is indeed a pleasure.

Enter CANON CHASUBLE.

CHASUBLE. And how are we this morning? Miss Prism, you are, I trust, well?

CECILY. Miss Prism has just been complaining of a slight headache. I think it would do her so much good to have a short stroll with you in the Park, Dr. Chasuble.

MISS PRISM. Cecily, I have not mentioned anything about a headache.

CECILY. No, dear Miss Prism, I know that, but I felt instinctively that you had a headache. Indeed I was thinking about that, and not about my German lesson, when the Rector came in.

CHASUBLE. I hope, Cecily, you are not inattentive.

CECILY. Oh, I am afraid I am.

CHASUBLE. That is strange. Were I fortunate enough to be Miss Prism's pupil, I would hang upon her lips. [MISS PRISM *glares.*] I spoke metaphorically.—My metaphor was drawn from bees. Ahem! Mr. Worthing, I suppose, has not returned from town yet?

MISS PRISM. We do not expect him till Monday afternoon.

CHASUBLE. Ah yes, he usually likes to spend his Sunday in London. He is not one of those whose sole aim is enjoyment, as, by all accounts, that unfortunate young man his brother seems to be. But I must not disturb Egeria[2] and her pupil any longer.

MISS PRISM. Egeria? My name is Laetitia, Doctor.

CHASUBLE. [*Bowing.*] A classical allusion merely, drawn from the Pagan authors. I shall see you both no doubt at Evensong?

MISS PRISM. I think, dear Doctor, I will

[2]The nymph who, according to classical legend, gave counsel to Numa, King of Rome.

have a stroll with you. I find I have a headache after all, and a walk might do it good.

CHASUBLE. With pleasure, Miss Prism, with pleasure. We might go as far as the schools and back.

MISS PRISM. That would be delightful. Cecily, you will read your Political Economy in my absence. The chapter on the Fall of the Rupee you may omit. It is somewhat too sensational. Even these metallic problems have their melodramatic side. [*Goes down the garden with* DR. CHASUBLE.

CECILY. [*Picks up books and throws them back on table.*] Horrid Political Economy! Horrid Geography! Horrid, horrid German!

Enter MERRIMAN *with a card on a salver.*

MERRIMAN. Mr. Ernest Worthing has just driven over from the station. He has brought his luggage with him.

CECILY. [*Takes the card and reads it.*] "Mr. Ernest Worthing, B. 4, The Albany, W." Uncle Jack's brother! Did you tell him Mr. Worthing was in town?

MERRIMAN. Yes, Miss. He seemed very much disappointed. I mentioned that you and Miss Prism were in the garden. He said he was anxious to speak to you privately for a moment.

CECILY. Ask Mr. Ernest Worthing to come here. I suppose you had better talk to the housekeeper about a room for him.

MERRIMAN. Yes, Miss.

[MERRIMAN *goes off.*

CECILY. I have never met any really wicked person before. I feel rather frightened. I am so afraid he will look just like everyone else. He does!

Enter ALGERNON, *very gay and debonair.*

ALGERNON. [*Raising his hat.*] You are my little cousin Cecily, I'm sure.

CECILY. You are under some strange mistake. I am not little. In fact, I believe I am more than usually tall for my age. [ALGERNON *is rather taken aback.*] But I am your cousin Cecily. You, I see from your card, are Uncle Jack's brother, my cousin Ernest, my wicked cousin Ernest.

ALGERNON. Oh! I am not really wicked at all, cousin Cecily. You mustn't think that I am wicked.

CECILY. If you are not, then you have certainly been deceiving us all in a very inexcusable manner. I hope you have not been leading a double life, pretending to be wicked and being really good all the time. That would be hypocrisy.

ALGERNON. [*Looks at her in amazement.*] Oh! Of course I have been rather reckless.

CECILY. I am glad to hear it.

ALGERNON. In fact, now you mention the subject, I have been very bad in my own small way.

CECILY. I don't think you should be so proud of that, though I am sure it must have been very pleasant.

ALGERNON. It is much pleasanter being here with you.

CECILY. I can't understand how you are here at all. Uncle Jack won't be back till Monday afternoon.

ALGERNON. That is a great disappointment. I am obliged to go up by the first train on Monday morning. I have a business appointment that I am anxious . . . to miss.

CECILY. Couldn't you miss it anywhere but in London?

ALGERNON. No: the appointment is in London.

CECILY. Well, I know of course, how important it is not to keep a business engagement, if one wants to retain any sense of the beauty of life, but still I think you had better wait till Uncle Jack arrives. I know he wants to speak to you about your emigrating.

ALGERNON. About my what?

CECILY. Your emigrating. He has gone up to buy your outfit.

ALGERNON. I certainly wouldn't let Jack buy my outfit. He has no taste in neckties at all.

CECILY. I don't think you will require neckties. Uncle Jack is sending you to Australia.

ALGERNON. Australia! I'd sooner die.

CECILY. Well, he said at dinner on Wednesday night, that you would have to choose between this world, the next world, and Australia.

ALGERNON. Oh, well! The accounts I have received of Australia and the next world are not particularly encouraging. This world is good enough for me, cousin Cecily.

CECILY. Yes, but are you good enough for it?

ALGERNON. I'm afraid I'm not that. That is why I want you to reform me. You might make that your mission, if you don't mind, cousin Cecily.

CECILY. I'm afraid I've no time, this afternoon.

ALGERNON. Well, would you mind my reforming myself this afternoon?

CECILY. It is rather Quixotic of you. But I think you should try.

ALGERNON. I will. I feel better already.

CECILY. You are looking a little worse.

ALGERNON. That is because I am hungry.

CECILY. How thoughtless of me. I should have remembered that when one is going to lead an entirely new life, one requires regular and wholesome meals. Won't you come in?

ALGERNON. Thank you. Might I have a buttonhole first? I never have any appetite unless I have a buttonhole first.

CECILY. A Maréchal Niel? [*Picks up scissors.*

ALGERNON. No, I'd sooner have a pink rose.

CECILY. Why? [*Cuts a flower.*

ALGERNON. Because you are like a pink rose, cousin Cecily.

CECILY. I don't think it can be right for you to talk to me like that. Miss Prism never says such things to me.

ALGERNON. Then Miss Prism is a short-sighted old lady. [CECILY *puts the rose in his buttonhole.*] You are the prettiest girl I ever saw.

CECILY. Miss Prism says that all good looks are a snare.

ALGERNON. They are a snare that every sensible man would like to be caught in.

CECILY. Oh, I don't think I would care to catch a sensible man. I shouldn't know what to talk to him about.

[*They pass into the house.* MISS PRISM *and* DR. CHASUBLE *return.*

MISS PRISM. You are too much alone, dear Dr. Chasuble. You should get married. A misanthrope I can understand—a womanthrope, never!

CHASUBLE. [*With a scholar's shudder.*] Believe me, I do not deserve so neologistic a phrase. The precept as well as the practice of the Primitive Church was distinctly against matrimony.

MISS PRISM. [*Sententiously.*] That is obviously the reason why the Primitive Church has not lasted up to the present day. And you do not seem to realize, dear Doctor, that by persistently remaining single, a man converts himself into a permanent public temptation. Men should be more careful; this very celibacy leads weaker vessels astray.

CHASUBLE. But is a man not equally attractive when married?

Miss Prism. No married man is ever attractive except to his wife.

Chasuble. And often, I've been told, not even to her.

Miss Prism. That depends on the intellectual sympathies of the woman. Maturity can always be depended on. Ripeness can be trusted. Young women are green. [Dr. Chasuble *starts.*] I spoke horticulturally. My metaphor was drawn from fruits. But where is Cecily?

Chasuble. Perhaps she followed us to the schools.

Enter Jack *slowly from the back of the garden. He is dressed in the deepest mourning, with crape hatband and black gloves.*

Miss Prism. Mr. Worthing!

Chasuble. Mr. Worthing?

Miss Prism. This is indeed a surprise. We did not look for you till Monday afternoon.

Jack. [*Shakes* Miss Prism's *hand in a tragic manner.*] I have returned sooner than I expected. Dr. Chasuble, I hope you are well?

Chasuble. Dear Mr. Worthing, I trust this garb of woe does not betoken some terrible calamity?

Jack. My brother.

Miss Prism. More shameful debts and extravagance?

Chasuble. Still leading his life of pleasure?

Jack. [*Shaking his head.*] Dead!

Chasuble. Your brother Ernest dead?

Jack. Quite dead.

Miss Prism. What a lesson for him! I trust he will profit by it.

Chasuble. Mr. Worthing, I offer you my sincere condolence. You have at least the consolation of knowing that you were always the most generous and forgiving of brothers.

Jack. Poor Ernest! He had many faults, but it is a sad, sad blow.

Chasuble. Very sad indeed. Were you with him at the end?

Jack. No. He died abroad; in Paris, in fact. I had a telegram last night from the manager of the Grand Hotel.

Chasuble. Was the cause of death mentioned?

Jack. A severe chill, it seems.

Miss Prism. As a man sows, so shall he reap.

Chasuble. [*Raising his hand.*] Charity, dear Miss Prism, charity! None of us are perfect. I myself am peculiarly susceptible to draughts. Will the interment take place here?

Jack. No. He seemed to have expressed a desire to be buried in Paris.

Chasuble. In Paris! [*Shakes his head.*] I fear that hardly points to any very serious state of mind at the last. You would no doubt wish me to make some slight allusion to this tragic domestic affliction next Sunday. [Jack *presses his hand convulsively.*] My sermon on the meaning of the manna in the wilderness can be adapted to almost any occasion, joyful, or, as in the present case, distressing. [*All sigh.*] I have preached it at harvest celebrations, christenings, confirmations, on days of humiliation and festal days. The last time I delivered it was in the Cathedral, as a charity sermon on behalf of the Society for the Prevention of Discontent among the Upper Orders. The Bishop, who was present, was much struck by some of the analogies I drew.

Jack. Ah! that reminds me, you mentioned christenings, I think, Dr. Chasuble? I suppose you know how to christen all right? [Dr. Chasuble *looks astounded.*] I mean, of course, you are continually christening, aren't you?

Miss Prism. It is, I regret to say, one of the Rector's most constant duties in this parish. I have often spoken to the poorer classes on the subject. But they don't seem to know what thrift is.

Chasuble. But is there any particular infant in whom you are interested, Mr. Worthing? Your brother was, I believe, unmarried, was he not?

Jack. Oh yes.

Miss Prism. [*Bitterly.*] People who live entirely for pleasure usually are.

Jack. But it is not for any child, dear Doctor. I am very fond of children. No! the fact is, I would like to be christened myself, this afternoon, if you have nothing better to do.

Chasuble. But surely, Mr. Worthing, you have been christened already?

Jack. I don't remember anything about it.

Chasuble. But have you any grave doubts on the subject?

Jack. I certainly intend to have. Of course I don't know if the thing would bother you in any way, or if you think I am a little too old now.

Chasuble. Not at all. The sprinkling, and, indeed, the immersion of adults is a perfectly canonical practice.

JACK. Immersion!

CHASUBLE. You need have no apprehensions. Sprinkling is all that is necessary, or indeed I think advisable. Our weather is so changeable. At what hour would you wish the ceremony performed?

JACK. Oh, I might trot round about five if that would suit you.

CHASUBLE. Perfectly, perfectly! In fact I have two similar ceremonies to perform at that time. A case of twins that occurred recently in one of the outlying cottages on your own estate. Poor Jenkins the carter, a most hard-working man.

JACK. Oh! I don't see much fun in being christened along with other babies. It would be childish. Would half-past five do?

CHASUBLE. Admirably! A d m i r a b l y ! [*Takes out watch.*] And now, dear Mr. Worthing, I will not intrude any longer into a house of sorrow. I would merely beg you not to be too much bowed down by grief. What seem to us bitter trials are often blessings in disguise.

MISS PRISM. This seems to me a blessing of an extremely obvious kind.

Enter CECILY *from the house.*

CECILY. Uncle Jack! Oh, I am pleased to see you back. But what horrid clothes you have got on! Do go and change them.

MISS PRISM. Cecily!

CHASUBLE. My child! my child!

[CECILY *goes towards* JACK; *he kisses her brow in a melancholy manner.*

CECILY. What is the matter, Uncle Jack? Do look happy! You look as if you had toothache, and I have got such a surprise for you. Who do you think is in the dining room? Your brother!

JACK. Who?

CECILY. Your brother Ernest. He arrived about half an hour ago.

JACK. What nonsense! I haven't got a brother.

CECILY. Oh, don't say that. However badly he may have behaved to you in the past he is still your brother. You couldn't be so heartless as to disown him. I'll tell him to come out. And you will shake hands with him, won't you, Uncle Jack?

[*Runs back into the house.*

CHASUBLE. These are very joyful tidings.

MISS PRISM. After we had all been resigned to his loss, his sudden return seems to me peculiarly distressing.

JACK. My brother is in the dining room?

I don't know what it all means. I think it is perfectly absurd.

Enter ALGERNON *and* CECILY *hand in hand. They come slowly up to* JACK.

JACK. Good heavens!

[*Motions* ALGERNON *away.*

ALGERNON. Brother John, I have come down from town to tell you that I am very sorry for all the trouble I have given you, and that I intend to lead a better life in the future.

[JACK *glares at him and does not take his hand.*

CECILY. Uncle Jack, you are not going to refuse your own brother's hand?

JACK. Nothing will induce me to take his hand. I think his coming down here disgraceful. He knows perfectly well why.

CECILY. Uncle Jack, do be nice. There is some good in everyone. Ernest has just been telling me about his poor invalid friend Mr. Bunbury whom he goes to visit so often. And surely there must be much good in one who is kind to an invalid, and leaves the pleasures of London to sit by a bed of pain.

JACK. Oh! he has been talking about Bunbury, has he?

CECILY. Yes, he has told me all about poor Mr. Bunbury, and his terrible state of health.

JACK. Bunbury! Well, I won't have him talk to you about Bunbury or about anything else. It is enough to drive one perfectly frantic.

ALGERNON. Of course I admit that the faults were all on my side. But I must say that I think that Brother John's coldness to me is peculiarly painful. I expected a more enthusiastic welcome, especially considering it is the first time I have come here.

CECILY. Uncle Jack, if you don't shake hands with Ernest I will never forgive you.

JACK. Never forgive me?

CECILY. Never, never, never!

JACK. Well, this is the last time I shall ever do it.

[*Shakes hands with* ALGERNON *and glares.*

CHASUBLE. It's pleasant, is it not, to see so perfect a reconciliation? I think we might leave the two brothers together.

MISS PRISM. Cecily, you will come with us.

CECILY. Certainly, Miss Prism. My little task of reconciliation is over.

CHASUBLE. You have done a beautiful action today, dear child.

MISS PRISM. We must not be premature in our judgments.

CECILY. I feel very happy.

[*They all go off except* JACK *and* ALGERNON.

JACK. You young scoundrel, Algy, you must get out of this place as soon as possible. I don't allow any Bunburying here.

Enter MERRIMAN.

MERRIMAN. I have put Mr. Ernest's things in the room next to yours, sir. I suppose that is all right?

JACK. What?

MERRIMAN. Mr. Ernest's luggage, sir. I have unpacked it and put it in the room next to your own.

JACK. His luggage?

MERRIMAN. Yes, sir. Three portmanteaus, a dressing case, two hatboxes, and a large luncheon basket.

ALGERNON. I am afraid I can't stay more than a week this time.

JACK. Merriman, order the dogcart at once. Mr. Ernest has been suddenly called back to town.

MERRIMAN. Yes, sir.

[*Goes back into the house.*

ALGERNON. What a fearful liar you are, Jack! I have not been called back to town at all.

JACK. Yes, you have.

ALGERNON. I haven't heard anyone call me.

JACK. Your duty as a gentleman calls you back.

ALGERNON. My duty as a gentleman has never interfered with my pleasures in the smallest degree.

JACK. I can quite understand that.

ALGERNON. Well, Cecily is a darling.

JACK. You are not to talk of Miss Cardew like that. I don't like it.

ALGERNON. Well, I don't like your clothes. You look perfectly ridiculous in them. Why on earth don't you go up and change? It is perfectly childish to be in deep mourning for a man who is actually staying for a whole week with you in your house as a guest. I call it grotesque.

JACK. You are certainly not staying with me for a whole week as a guest or anything else. You have got to leave . . . by the four-five train.

ALGERNON. I certainly won't leave you so long as you are in mourning. It would be most unfriendly. If I were in mourning you would stay with me, I suppose. I should think it very unkind if you didn't.

JACK. Well, will you go if I change my clothes?

ALGERNON. Yes, if you are not too long. I never saw anybody take so long to dress, and with such little result.

JACK. Well, at any rate, that is better than being always overdressed as you are.

ALGERNON. If I am occasionally a little overdressed, I make up for it by being always immensely overeducated.

JACK. Your vanity is ridiculous, your conduct an outrage, and your presence in my garden utterly absurd. However, you have got to catch the four-five, and I hope you will have a pleasant journey back to town. This Bunburying, as you call it, has not been a great success for you. [*Goes into the house.*

ALGERNON. I think it has been a great success. I'm in love with Cecily, and that is everything.

Enter CECILY *at the back of the garden. She picks up the can and begins to water the flowers.*

But I must see her before I go, and make arrangements for another Bunbury. Ah, there she is.

CECILY. Oh, I merely came back to water the roses. I thought you were with Uncle Jack.

ALGERNON. He's gone to order the dogcart for me.

CECILY. Oh, is he going to take you for a nice drive?

ALGERNON. He's going to send me away.

CECILY. Then have we got to part?

ALGERNON. I am afraid so. It's a very painful parting.

CECILY. It is always painful to part from people whom one has known for a very brief space of time. The absence of old friends one can endure with equanimity. But even a momentary separation from anyone to whom one has just been introduced is almost unbearable.

ALGERNON. Thank you.

Enter MERRIMAN.

MERRIMAN. The dogcart is at the door, sir.

[ALGERNON *looks appealingly at* CECILY.

CECILY. It can wait, Merriman . . . for . . . five minutes.

MERRIMAN. Yes, Miss.

[*Exit* MERRIMAN.

ALGERNON. I hope, Cecily, I shall not offend you if I state quite frankly and openly that you seem to me to be in every way the visible personification of absolute perfection.

CECILY. I think your frankness does you great credit, Ernest. If you will allow me I will copy your remarks into my diary.

[*Goes over to table and begins writing in diary.*

ALGERNON. Do you really keep a diary? I'd give anything to look at it. May I?

CECILY. Oh, no! [*Puts her hand over it.*] You see, it is simply a very young girl's record of her own thoughts and impressions and consequently meant for publication. When it appears in volume form I hope you will order a copy. But pray, Ernest, don't stop. I delight in taking down from dictation. I have reached "absolute perfection." You can go on. I am quite ready for more.

ALGERNON. [*Somewhat taken aback.*] Ahem! Ahem!

CECILY. Oh, don't cough, Ernest. When one is dictating one should speak fluently and not cough. Besides, I don't know how to spell a cough.

[*Writes as* ALGERNON *speaks.*

ALGERNON. [*Speaking very rapidly.*] Cecily, ever since I first looked upon your wonderful and incomparable beauty, I have dared to love you wildly, passionately, devotedly, hopelessly.

CECILY. I don't think that you should tell me that you love me wildly, passionately, devotedly, hopelessly. Hopelessly doesn't seem to make much sense, does it?

ALGERNON. Cecily!

Enter MERRIMAN.

MERRIMAN. The dogcart is waiting, sir.

ALGERNON. Tell it to come round next week, at the same hour.

MERRIMAN. [*Looks at* CECILY, *who makes no sign.*] Yes, sir.

[MERRIMAN *retires.*

CECILY. Uncle Jack would be very much annoyed if he knew you were staying on till next week, at the same hour.

ALGERNON. Oh, I don't care about Jack. I don't care for anybody in the whole world but you. I love you, Cecily. You will marry me, won't you?

CECILY. You silly boy! Of course! Why, we have been engaged for the last three months.

ALGERNON. For the last three months?

CECILY. Yes, it will be exactly three months on Thursday.

ALGERNON. But how did we become engaged?

CECILY. Well, ever since dear Uncle Jack first confessed to us that he had a younger brother who was very wicked and bad, you of course have formed the chief topic of conversation between myself and Miss Prism. And of course a man who is much talked about is always very attractive. One feels there must be something in him, after all. I daresay it was foolish of me, but I fell in love with you, Ernest.

ALGERNON. Darling! And when was the engagement actually settled?

CECILY. On the 14th of February last. Worn out by your entire ignorance of my existence, I determined to end the matter one way or the other, and after a long struggle with myself I accepted you under this dear old tree here. The next day I bought this little ring in your name, and this is the little bangle with the true lovers' knot I promised you always to wear.

ALGERNON. Did I give you this? It's very pretty, isn't it?

CECILY. Yes, you've wonderfully good taste, Ernest. It's the excuse I've always given for your leading such a bad life. And this is the box in which I keep all your dear letters.

[*Kneels at table, opens box, and produces letters tied up with blue ribbon.*

ALGERNON. My letters! But my own sweet Cecily, I have never written you any letters.

CECILY. You need hardly remind me of that, Ernest. I remember only too well that I was forced to write your letters for you. I wrote always three times a week, and sometimes oftener.

ALGERNON. Oh, do let me read them, Cecily?

CECILY. Oh, I couldn't possibly. They would make you far too conceited. [*Replaces box.*] The three you wrote me after I had broken off the engagement are so beautiful, and so badly spelled, that even now I can hardly read them without crying a little.

ALGERNON. But was our engagement ever broken off?

CECILY. Of course it was. On the 22nd of last March. You can see the entry if you like. [*Shows diary.*] "To-day I broke off my engagement with Ernest. I feel it is better to do so. The weather still continues charming."

ALGERNON. But why on earth did you break it off? What had I done? I had done nothing at all. Cecily, I am very much hurt indeed to hear you broke it off. Particularly when the weather was so charming.

CECILY. It would hardly have been a really serious engagement if it hadn't been broken off at least once. But I forgave you before the week was out.

ALGERNON. [*Crossing to her, and kneeling.*] What a perfect angel you are, Cecily!

CECILY. You dear romantic boy! [*He kisses her, she puts her fingers through his hair.*] I hope your hair curls naturally, does it?

ALGERNON. Yes, darling, with a little help from others.

CECILY. I am so glad.

ALGERNON. You'll never break off our engagement again, Cecily?

CECILY. I don't think I could break it off now that I have actually met you. Besides, of course, there is the question of your name.

ALGERNON. Yes, of course. [*Nervously.*]

CECILY. You must not laugh at me, darling, but it had always been a girlish dream of mine to love someone whose name was Ernest. [ALGERNON *rises,* CECILY *also.*] There is something in that name that seems to inspire absolute confidence. I pity any poor married woman whose husband is not called Ernest.

ALGERNON. But, my dear child, do you mean to say you could not love me if I had some other name?

CECILY. But what name?

ALGERNON. Oh, any name you like—Algernon—for instance . . .

CECILY. But I don't like the name of Algernon.

ALGERNON. Well, my own dear, sweet, loving little darling, I really can't see why you should object to the name of Algernon. It is not at all a bad name. In fact, it is rather an aristocratic name. Half of the chaps who get into the Bankruptcy Court are called Algernon. But seriously, Cecily . . . [*Moving to her.*] . . . if my name was Algy, couldn't you love me?

CECILY. [*Rising.*] I might respect you, Ernest, I might admire your character, but I fear that I should not be able to give you my undivided attention.

ALGERNON. Ahem! Cecily! [*Picking up hat.*] Your Rector here is, I suppose, thoroughly experienced in the practice of all the rites and ceremonials of the Church?

CECILY. Oh, yes. Dr. Chasuble is a most learned man. He has never written a single

book, so you can imagine how much he knows.

ALGERNON. I must see him at once on a most important christening—I mean on most important business.

CECILY. Oh!

ALGERNON. I shan't be away more than half an hour.

CECILY. Considering that we have been engaged since February the 14th, and that I only met you today for the first time, I think it is rather hard that you should leave me for so long a period as half an hour. Couldn't you make it twenty minutes?

ALGERNON. I'll be back in no time.

[*Kisses her and rushes down the garden.*

CECILY. What an impetuous boy he is! I like his hair so much. I must enter his proposal in my diary.

Enter MERRIMAN.

MERRIMAN. A Miss Fairfax has just called to see Mr. Worthing. On very important business Miss Fairfax states.

CECILY. Isn't Mr. Worthing in his library?

MERRIMAN. Mr. Worthing went over in the direction of the Rectory some time ago.

CECILY. Pray ask the lady to come out here; Mr. Worthing is sure to be back soon. And you can bring tea.

MERRIMAN. Yes, Miss. [*Goes out.*

CECILY. Miss Fairfax! I suppose one of the many good elderly women who are associated with Uncle Jack in some of his philanthropic work in London. I don't quite like women who are interested in philanthropic work. I think it is so forward of them.

Enter MERRIMAN.

MERRIMAN. Miss Fairfax.

Enter GWENDOLEN.

[*Exit* MERRIMAN.

CECILY. [*Advancing to meet her.*] Pray let me introduce myself to you. My name is Cecily Cardew.

GWENDOLEN. Cecily Cardew? [*Moving to her and shaking hands.*] What a very sweet name! Something tells me that we are going to be great friends. I like you already more than I can say. My first impressions of people are never wrong.

CECILY. How nice of you to like me so much after we have known each other such a comparatively short time. Pray sit down.

GWENDOLEN. [*Still standing up.*] I may call you Cecily, may I not?

CECILY. With pleasure!

GWENDOLEN. And you will always call me Gwendolen, won't you?

CECILY. If you wish.

GWENDOLEN. Then that is all quite settled, is it not?

CECILY. I hope so.

[*A pause. They both sit down together.*

GWENDOLEN. Perhaps this might be a favorable opportunity for my mentioning who I am. My father is Lord Bracknell. You have never heard of papa, I suppose?

CECILY. I don't think so.

GWENDOLEN. Outside of the family circle, papa, I am glad to say, is entirely unknown. I think that is quite as it should be. The home seems to me to be the proper sphere for the man. And certainly once a man begins to neglect his domestic duties he becomes painfully effeminate, does he not? And I don't like that. It makes men so very attractive. Cecily, mamma, whose views on education are remarkably strict, has brought me up to be extremely short-sighted; it is part of her system; so do you mind my looking at you through my glasses?

CECILY. Oh! not at all, Gwendolen. I am very fond of being looked at.

GWENDOLEN. [*After examining* CECILY *carefully through a lorgnette.*] You are here on a short visit I suppose.

CECILY. Oh no! I live here.

GWENDOLEN. [*Severely.*] Really? Your mother, no doubt, or some female relative of advanced years, resides here also?

CECILY. Oh no! I have no mother, nor, in fact, any relations.

GWENDOLEN. Indeed?

CECILY. My dear guardian, with the assistance of Miss Prism, has the arduous task of looking after me.

GWENDOLEN. Your guardian?

CECILY. Yes, I am Mr. Worthing's ward.

GWENDOLEN. Oh! It is strange he never mentioned to me that he had a ward. How secretive of him! He grows more interesting hourly. I am not sure, however, that the news inspires me with feelings of unmixed delight. [*Rising and going to her.*] I am very fond of you, Cecily; I have liked you ever since I met you! But I am bound to state that now that I know that you are Mr. Worthing's ward, I cannot help expressing a wish you were—well just a little older than you seem to be—and not quite so very alluring in appearance. In fact, if I may speak candidly——

CECILY. Pray do! I think that whenever one has anything unpleasant to say, one should always be quite candid.

GWENDOLEN. Well, to speak with perfect candor, Cecily, I wish that you were fully forty-two, and more than usually plain for your age. Ernest has a strong upright nature. He is the very soul of truth and honor. Disloyalty would be as impossible to him as deception. But even men of the noblest possible moral character are extremely susceptible to the influence of the physical charms of others. Modern, no less than Ancient History, supplies us with many most painful examples of what I refer to. If it were not so, indeed, History would be quite unreadable.

CECILY. I beg your pardon, Gwendolen, did you say Ernest?

GWENDOLEN. Yes.

CECILY. Oh, but it is not Mr. Ernest Worthing who is my guardian. It is his brother—his elder brother.

GWENDOLEN. [*Sitting down again.*] Ernest never mentioned to me that he had a brother.

CECILY. I am sorry to say they have not been on good terms for a long time.

GWENDOLEN. Ah! that accounts for it. And now that I think of it I have never heard any man mention his brother. The subject seems distasteful to most men. Cecily, you have lifted a load from my mind. I was growing almost anxious. It would have been terrible if any cloud had come across a friendship like ours, would it not? Of course you are quite, quite sure that it is not Mr. Ernest Worthing who is your guardian?

CECILY. Quite sure. [*A pause.*] In fact, I am going to be his.

GWENDOLEN. [*Inquiringly.*] I beg your pardon?

CECILY. [*Rather shy and confidingly.*] Dearest Gwendolen, there is no reason why I should make a secret of it to you. Our little county newspaper is sure to chronicle the fact next week. Mr. Ernest Worthing and I are engaged to be married.

GWENDOLEN. [*Quite politely, rising.*] My darling Cecily, I think there must be some slight error. Mr. Ernest Worthing is engaged to me. The announcement will appear in the *Morning Post* on Saturday at the latest.

CECILY. [*Very politely, rising.*] I am afraid you must be under some misconception. Ernest proposed to me exactly ten minutes ago. [*Shows diary.*

GWENDOLEN. [*Examines diary through her lorgnette carefully.*] It is certainly very curious, for he asked me to be his wife yesterday afternoon at 5.30. If you would care to verify the incident, pray do so. [*Produces diary of her own.*] I never travel without my diary. One should always have something sensational to read in the train. I am so sorry, dear Cecily, if it is any disappointment to you, but I am afraid *I* have the prior claim.

CECILY. It would distress me more than I can tell you, dear Gwendolen, if it caused you any mental or physical anguish, but I feel bound to point out that since Ernest proposed to you he clearly has changed his mind.

GWENDOLEN. [*Meditatively.*] If the poor fellow has been entrapped into any foolish promise I shall consider it my duty to rescue him at once, and with a firm hand.

CECILY. [*Thoughtfully and sadly.*] Whatever unfortunate entanglement my dear boy may have got into, I will never reproach him with it after we are married.

GWENDOLEN. Do you allude to me, Miss Cardew, as an entanglement? You are presumptuous. On an occasion of this kind it becomes more than a moral duty to speak one's mind. It becomes a pleasure.

CECILY. Do you suggest, Miss Fairfax, that I entrapped Ernest into an engagement? How dare you? This is no time for wearing the shallow mask of manners. When I see a spade I call it a spade.

GWENDOLEN. [*Satirically.*] I am glad to say that I have never seen a spade. It is obvious that our social spheres have been widely different.

Enter MERRIMAN, *followed by the footman. He carries a salver, tablecloth, and plate stand.* CECILY *is about to retort. The presence of the servants exercises a restraining influence, under which both girls chafe.*

MERRIMAN. Shall I lay tea here as usual, Miss?

CECILY. [*Sternly, in a calm voice.*] Yes, as usual.

[MERRIMAN *begins to clear table and lay cloth. A long pause.* CECILY *and* GWENDOLEN *glare at each other.*

GWENDOLEN. Are there many interesting walks in the vicinity, Miss Cardew?

CECILY. Oh! yes! a great many. From the top of one of the hills quite close one can see five counties.

GWENDOLEN. Five counties! I don't think I should like that; I hate crowds.

CECILY. [*Sweetly.*] I suppose that is why you live in town?

[GWENDOLEN *bites her lip, and beats her foot nervously with her parasol.*

GWENDOLEN. [*Looking round.*] Quite a well-kept garden this is, Miss Cardew.

CECILY. So glad you like it, Miss Fairfax.

GWENDOLEN. I had no idea there were any flowers in the country.

CECILY. Oh, flowers are as common here, Miss Fairfax, as people are in London.

GWENDOLEN. Personally I cannot understand how anybody manages to exist in the country, if anybody who is anybody does. The country always bores me to death.

CECILY. Ah! This is what the newspapers call agricultural depression, is it not? I believe the aristocracy are suffering very much from it just at present. It is almost an epidemic amongst them, I have been told. May I offer you some tea, Miss Fairfax?

GWENDOLEN. [*With elaborate politeness.*] Thank you. [*Aside.*] Detestable girl! But I require tea!

CECILY. [*Sweetly.*] Sugar?

GWENDOLEN. [*Superciliously.*] No, thank you. Sugar is not fashionable any more.

[CECILY *looks angrily at her, takes up the tongs and puts four lumps of sugar into the cup.*

CECILY. [*Severely.*] Cake or bread and butter?

GWENDOLEN. [*In a bored manner.*] Bread and butter, please. Cake is rarely seen at the best houses nowadays.

CECILY. [*Cuts a very large slice of cake, and puts it on the tray.*] Hand that to Miss Fairfax.

[MERRIMAN *does so, and goes out with footman.* GWENDOLEN *drinks the tea and makes a grimace. Puts down cup at once, reaches out her hand to the bread and butter, looks at it, and finds it is cake. Rises in indignation.*

GWENDOLEN. You have filled my tea with lumps of sugar, and though I asked most distinctly for bread and butter, you have given me cake. I am known for the gentleness of my disposition, and the extraordinary sweetness of my nature, but I warn you, Miss Cardew, you may go too far.

CECILY. [*Rising.*] To save my poor, innocent, trusting boy from the machinations of any other girl there are no lengths to which I would not go.

GWENDOLEN. From the moment I saw you I distrusted you. I felt that you were false and deceitful. I am never deceived in such 5 matters. My first impressions of people are invariably right.

CECILY. It seems to me, Miss Fairfax, that I am trespassing on your valuable time. No doubt you have many other calls of a similar 10 character to make in the neighborhood.

Enter JACK.

GWENDOLEN. [*Catching sight of him.*] Ernest! My own Ernest!

JACK. Gwendolen! Darling!

[*Offers to kiss her.*

GWENDOLEN. [*Drawing back.*] A moment! May I ask if you are engaged to be married to this young lady? 20

[*Points to* CECILY.

JACK. [*Laughing.*] To dear little Cecily! Of course not! What could have put such an idea into your pretty little head?

GWENDOLEN. Thank you. You may! 25

[*Offers her cheek.*

CECILY. [*Very sweetly.*] I knew there must be some misunderstanding, Miss Fairfax. The gentleman whose arm is at present round your waist is my dear guardian, Mr. 30 John Worthing.

GWENDOLEN. I beg your pardon?

CECILY. This is Uncle Jack.

GWENDOLEN. [*Receding.*] Jack! Oh!

Enter ALGERNON.

CECILY. Here is Ernest.

ALGERNON. [*Goes straight over to* CECILY *without noticing anyone else.*] My own love!

[*Offers to kiss her.* 40

CECILY. [*Drawing back.*] A moment, Ernest! May I ask you—are you engaged to be married to this young lady?

ALGERNON. [*Looking round.*] To what young lady? Good heavens! Gwendolen! 45

CECILY. Yes! to good heavens, Gwendolen, I mean to Gwendolen.

ALGERNON. [*Laughing.*] Of course not! What could have put such an idea into your pretty little head? 50

CECILY. Thank you. [*Presenting her cheek to be kissed.*] You may.

[ALGERNON *kisses her.*

GWENDOLEN. I felt there was some slight error, Miss Cardew. The gentleman who is 55 now embracing you is my cousin, Mr. Algernon Moncrieff.

CECILY. [*Breaking away from* ALGERNON.] Algernon Moncrieff! Oh!

[*The two girls move towards each other and put their arms round each other's waists as if for protection.*

CECILY. Are you called Algernon?

ALGERNON. I cannot deny it.

CECILY. Oh!

GWENDOLEN. Is your name really John?

JACK. [*Standing rather proudly.*] I could deny it if I liked. I could deny anything if I liked. But my name certainly is John. It has been John for years.

CECILY. [*To* GWENDOLEN.] A gross deception has been practised on both of us. 15

GWENDOLEN. My poor wounded Cecily!

CECILY. My sweet wronged Gwendolen.

GWENDOLEN. [*Slowly and seriously.*] You will call me sister, will you not?

[*They embrace.* JACK *and* ALGERNON 20 *groan and walk up and down.*

CECILY. [*Rather brightly.*] There is just one question I would like to be allowed to ask my guardian.

GWENDOLEN. An admirable idea! Mr. Worthing, there is just one question I would like to be permitted to put to you. Where is your brother Ernest? We are both engaged to be married to your brother Ernest, so it is a matter of some importance to us to know where your brother Ernest is at present.

JACK. [*Slowly and hesitatingly.*] Gwendolen—Cecily—it is very painful for me to be forced to speak the truth. It is the first 35 time in my life that I have ever been reduced to such a painful position, and I am really quite inexperienced in doing anything of the kind. However, I will tell you quite frankly that I have no brother Ernest. I have no 40 brother at all. I never had a brother in my life, and I certainly have not the smallest intention of ever having one in the future.

CECILY. [*Surprised.*] No brother at all?

JACK. [*Cheerily.*] None!

GWENDOLEN. [*Severely.*] Had you never a brother of any kind?

JACK. [*Pleasantly.*] Never. Not even of any kind.

GWENDOLEN. I am afraid it is quite clear, 50 Cecily, that neither of us is engaged to be married to anyone.

CECILY. It is not a very pleasant position for a young girl suddenly to find herself in. Is it?

GWENDOLEN. Let us go into the house. They will hardly venture to come after us there.

CECILY. No, men are so cowardly, aren't they?

[*They retire into the house with scornful looks.*

JACK. This ghastly state of things is what you call Bunburying, I suppose?

ALGERNON. Yes, and a perfectly wonderful Bunbury it is. The most wonderful Bunbury I have ever had in my life.

JACK. Well, you've no right whatsoever to Bunbury here.

ALGERNON. That is absurd. One has a right to Bunbury anywhere one chooses. Every serious Bunburyist knows that.

JACK. Serious Bunburyist! Good heavens!

ALGERNON. Well, one must be serious about something, if one wants to have any amusement in life. I happen to be serious about Bunburying. What on earth you are serious about I haven't got the remotest idea. About everything, I should fancy. You have such an absolutely trivial nature.

JACK. Well, the only small satisfaction I have in the whole of this wretched business is that your friend Bunbury is quite exploded. You won't be able to run down to the country quite so often as you used to do, dear Algy. And a very good thing too.

ALGERNON. Your brother is a little off color, isn't he, dear Jack? You won't be able to disappear to London quite so frequently as your wicked custom was. And not a bad thing either.

JACK. As for your conduct towards Miss Cardew, I must say that your taking in a sweet, simple, innocent girl like that is quite inexcusable. To say nothing of the fact that she is my ward.

ALGERNON. I can see no possible defense at all for your deceiving a brilliant, clever, thoroughly experienced young lady like Miss Fairfax. To say nothing of the fact that she is my cousin.

JACK. I wanted to be engaged to Gwendolen, that is all. I love her.

ALGERNON. Well, I simply wanted to be engaged to Cecily. I adore her.

JACK. There is certainly no chance of your marrying Miss Cardew.

ALGERNON. I don't think there is much likelihood, Jack, of you and Miss Fairfax being united.

JACK. Well, that is no business of yours.

ALGERNON. If it was my business, I wouldn't talk about it. [*Begins to eat muffins.*] It is very vulgar to talk about one's business. Only people like stockbrokers do that, and then merely at dinner parties.

JACK. How you can sit there, calmly eating muffins when we are in this horrible trouble, I can't make out. You seem to me to be perfectly heartless.

ALGERNON. Well, I can't eat muffins in an agitated manner. The butter would probably get on my cuffs. One should always eat muffins quite calmly. It is the only way to eat them.

JACK. I say it's perfectly heartless your eating muffins at all, under the circumstances.

ALGERNON. When I am in trouble, eating is the only thing that consoles me. Indeed, when I am in really great trouble, as anyone who knows me intimately will tell you, I refuse everything except food and drink. At the present moment I am eating muffins because I am unhappy. Besides, I am particularly fond of muffins. [*Rising.*

JACK. [*Rising.*] Well, that is no reason why you should eat them all in that greedy way. [*Takes muffins from* ALGERNON.

ALGERNON. [*Offering tea-cake.*] I wish you would have tea-cake instead. I don't like tea-cake.

JACK. Good heavens! I suppose a man may eat his own muffins in his own garden.

ALGERNON. But you have just said it was perfectly heartless to eat muffins.

JACK. I said it was perfectly heartless of you, under the circumstances. That is a very different thing.

ALGERNON. That may be. But the muffins are the same.

[*He seizes the muffin dish from* JACK.

JACK. Algy, I wish to goodness you would go.

ALGERNON. You can't possibly ask me to go without having some dinner. It's absurd. I never go without my dinner. No one ever does, except vegetarians and people like that. Besides I have just made arrangements with Dr. Chasuble to be christened at a quarter to six under the name of Ernest.

JACK. My dear fellow, the sooner you give up that nonsense the better. I made arrangements this morning with Dr. Chasuble to be christened myself at 5.30, and I naturally will take the name of Ernest. Gwendolen would wish it. We can't both be christened Ernest. It's absurd. Besides, I have a perfect right to be christened if I like. There is no evidence at all that I ever have been christened by anybody. I should think it extremely probable I never was, and so does Dr. Chasuble. It is entirely different in your case. You have been christened already.

ALGERNON. Yes, but I have not been christened for years.

JACK. Yes, but you have been christened. That is the important thing.

ALGERNON. Quite so. So I know my constitution can stand it. If you are not quite sure about your ever having been christened, I must say I think it rather dangerous your venturing on it now. It might make you very unwell. You can hardly have forgotten that someone very closely connected with you was very nearly carried off this week in Paris by a severe chill.

JACK. Yes, but you said yourself that a severe chill was not hereditary.

ALGERNON. It usen't to be, I know—but I dare say it is now. Science is always making wonderful improvements in things.

JACK. [*Picking up the muffin dish.*] Oh, that is nonsense; you are always talking nonsense.

ALGERNON. Jack, you are at the muffins again! I wish you wouldn't. There are only two left. [*Takes them.*] I told you I was particularly fond of muffins.

JACK. But I hate tea-cake.

ALGERNON. Why on earth then do you allow tea-cake to be served up for your guests? What ideas you have of hospitality!

JACK. Algernon! I have already told you to go. I don't want you here. Why don't you go!

ALGERNON. I haven't quite finished my tea yet! and there is still one muffin left.

[JACK *groans, and sinks into a chair.* ALGERNON *still continues eating.*

ACT-DROP

ACT III

SCENE

Morning room at the Manor House.

GWENDOLEN *and* CECILY *are at the window, looking out into the garden.*

GWENDOLEN. The fact that they did not follow us at once into the house, as anyone else would have done, seems to me to show that they have some sense of shame left.

CECILY. They have been eating muffins. That looks like repentance.

GWENDOLEN. [*After a pause.*] They don't seem to notice us at all. Couldn't you cough?

CECILY. But I haven't got a cough.

GWENDOLEN. They're looking at us. What effrontery!

CECILY. They're approaching. That's very forward of them.

GWENDOLEN. Let us preserve a dignified silence.

CECILY. Certainly. It's the only thing to do now.

Enter JACK *followed by* ALGERNON. *They whistle some dreadful popular air from a British Opera.*

GWENDOLEN. This dignified silence seems to produce an unpleasant effect.

CECILY. A most distasteful one.

GWENDOLEN. But we will not be the first to speak.

CECILY. Certainly not.

GWENDOLEN. Mr. Worthing, I have something very particular to ask you. Much depends on your reply.

CECILY. Gwendolen, your common sense is invaluable. Mr. Moncrieff, kindly answer me the following question. Why did you pretend to be my guardian's brother?

ALGERNON. In order that I might have an opportunity of meeting you.

CECILY. [*To* GWENDOLEN.] That certainly seems a satisfactory explanation, does it not?

GWENDOLEN. Yes, dear, if you can believe him.

CECILY. I don't. But that does not affect the wonderful beauty of his answer.

GWENDOLEN. True. In matters of grave importance, style, not sincerity is the vital thing. Mr. Worthing, what explanation can you offer to me for pretending to have a brother? Was it in order that you might have an opportunity of coming up to town to see me as often as possible?

JACK. Can you doubt it, Miss Fairfax?

GWENDOLEN. I have the gravest doubts upon the subject. But I intend to crush them. This is not the moment for German skepticism. [*Moving to* CECILY.] Their explanations appear to be quite satisfactory, especially Mr. Worthing's. That seems to me to have the stamp of truth upon it.

CECILY. I am more than content with what Mr. Moncrieff said. His voice alone inspires one with absolute credulity.

GWENDOLEN. Then you think we should forgive them?

CECILY. Yes. I mean no.

GWENDOLEN. True! I had forgotten. There are principles at stake that one cannot surrender. Which of us should tell them? The task is not a pleasant one.

CECILY. Could we not both speak at the same time?

GWENDOLEN. An excellent idea! I nearly always speak at the same time as other people. Will you take the time from me?

CECILY. Certainly

[GWENDOLEN *beats time with uplifted finger.*

GWENDOLEN AND CECILY. [*Speaking together.*] Your Christian names are still an insuperable barrier. That is all!

JACK AND ALGERNON. [*Speaking together.*] Our Christian names! Is that all? But we are going to be christened this afternoon.

GWENDOLEN. [*To* JACK.] For my sake you are prepared to do this terrible thing?

JACK. I am.

CECILY. [*To* ALGERNON.] To please me you are ready to face this fearful ordeal?

ALGERNON. I am!

GWENDOLEN. How absurd to talk of the equality of the sexes! Where questions of self-sacrifice are concerned, men are infinitely beyond us.

JACK. We are.

[*Clasps hands with* ALGERNON.

CECILY. They have moments of physical courage of which we women know absolutely nothing.

GWENDOLEN. [*To* JACK.] Darling!

ALGERNON. [*To* CECILY.] Darling! [*They fall into each other's arms.*

Enter MERRIMAN. *When he enters he coughs loudly, seeing the situation.*

MERRIMAN. Ahem! Ahem! Lady Bracknell!

JACK. Good heavens!

Enter LADY BRACKNELL. *The couples separate in alarm.*

[*Exit* MERRIMAN.

LADY BRACKNELL. Gwendolen! What does this mean?

GWENDOLEN. Merely that I am engaged to be married to Mr. Worthing, mamma.

LADY BRACKNELL. Come here. Sit down. Sit down immediately. Hesitation of any kind is a sign of mental decay in the young, of physical weakness in the old. [*Turns to* JACK.] Apprised, sir, of my daughter's sudden flight by her trusty maid, whose confidence I purchased by means of a small coin, I followed her at once by a luggage train. Her unhappy father is, I am glad to say, under the impression that she is attending a more than usually lengthy lecture by the University Extension Scheme on the Influence of a Permanent Income on Thought. I do not propose to undeceive him. Indeed I have never undeceived him on any question. I would consider it wrong. But of course, you will clearly understand that all communication between yourself and my daughter must cease immediately from this moment. On this point, as indeed on all points, I am firm.

JACK. I am engaged to be married to Gwendolen, Lady Bracknell!

LADY BRACKNELL. You are nothing of the kind, sir. And now as regards Algernon! . . . Algernon!

ALGERNON. Yes, Aunt Augusta.

LADY BRACKNELL. May I ask if it is in this house that your invalid friend Mr. Bunbury resides?

ALGERNON. [*Stammering.*] Oh! No! Bunbury doesn't live here. Bunbury is somewhere else at present. In fact, Bunbury is dead.

LADY BRACKNELL. Dead! When did Mr. Bunbury die? His death must have been extremely sudden.

ALGERNON. [*Airily.*] Oh! I killed Bunbury this afternoon. I mean poor Bunbury died this afternoon.

LADY BRACKNELL. What did he die of?

ALGERNON. Bunbury? Oh, he was quite exploded.

LADY BRACKNELL. Exploded! Was he the victim of a revolutionary outrage? I was not aware that Mr. Bunbury was interested in social legislation. If so, he is well punished for his morbidity.

ALGERNON. My dear Aunt Augusta, I mean he was found out! The doctors found out that Bunbury could not live, that is what I mean—so Bunbury died.

LADY BRACKNELL. He seems to have had great confidence in the opinion of his physicians. I am glad, however, that he made up his mind at the last to some definite course of action, and acted under the proper medical advice. And now that we have finally got rid of this Mr. Bunbury, may I ask, Mr. Worthing, who is that young person whose hand my nephew Algernon is now holding in what seems to me a peculiarly unnecessary manner?

JACK. That lady is Miss Cecily Cardew, my ward.

[LADY BRACKNELL *bows coldly to* CECILY.

ALGERNON. I am engaged to be married to Cecily, Aunt Augusta.

LADY BRACKNELL. I beg your pardon?

CECILY. Mr. Moncrieff and I are engaged to be married, Lady Bracknell.

LADY BRACKNELL. [*With a shiver, crossing to the sofa and sitting down.*] I do not know whether there is anything peculiarly exciting in the air of this particular part of Hertfordshire, but the number of engagements that go on seems to me considerably above the proper average that statistics have laid down for our guidance. I think some preliminary inquiry on my part would not be out of place. Mr. Worthing, is Miss Cardew at all connected with any of the larger railway stations in London? I merely desire information. Until yesterday I had no idea that there were any families or persons whose origin was a Terminus.

[JACK *looks perfectly furious, but restrains himself.*

JACK. [*In a clear, cold voice.*] Miss Cardew is the granddaughter of the late Mr. Thomas Cardew of 149 Belgrave Square, S.W.;[1] Gervase Park, Dorking, Surrey; and The Sporran, Fifeshire, N.B.[2]

LADY BRACKNELL. That sounds not unsatisfactory. Three addresses always inspire confidence, even in tradesmen. But what proof have I of their authenticity?

JACK. I have carefully preserved the Court Guides of the period. They are open to your inspection, Lady Bracknell.

LADY BRACKNELL. [*Grimly.*] I have known strange errors in that publication.

JACK. Miss Cardew's family solicitors are Messrs. Markby, Markby, and Markby.

LADY BRACKNELL. Markby, Markby, and Markby? A firm of the very highest position in their profession. Indeed I am told that one of the Mr. Markbys is occasionally to be seen at dinner parties. So far I am satisfied.

JACK. [*Very irritably.*] How extremely kind of you, Lady Bracknell! I have also in my possession, you will be pleased to hear, certificates of Miss Cardew's birth, baptism, whooping cough, registration, vaccination, confirmation, and the measles; both the German and the English variety.

LADY BRACKNELL. Ah! A life crowded with incident, I see; though perhaps somewhat too exciting for a young girl. I am not myself in favor of premature experiences. [*Rises, looks at her watch.*] Gwendolen! the time approaches for our departure. We have not a moment to lose. As a matter of form, Mr. Worthing, I had better ask you if Miss Cardew has any little fortune?

JACK. Oh! about a hundred and thirty thousand pounds in the Funds.[3] That is all. Goodby, Lady Bracknell. So pleased to have seen you.

LADY BRACKNELL. [*Sitting down again.*] A moment, Mr. Worthing. A hundred and thirty thousand pounds! And in the Funds! Miss Cardew seems to me a most attractive young lady, now that I look at her. Few girls of the present day have any really solid qualities, any of the qualities that last, and improve with time. We live, I regret to say, in an age of surfaces. [*To* CECILY.] Come over here, dear. [CECILY *goes across.*] Pretty child! your dress is sadly simple, and your hair seems almost as Nature might have left it. But we can soon alter all that. A thoroughly experienced French maid produces a really marvelous result in a very brief space of time. I remember recommending one to young Lady Lancing, and after three months her own husband did not know her.

JACK. [*Aside.*] And after six months nobody knew her.

LADY BRACKNELL. [*Glares at* JACK *for a few moments. Then bends, with a practised smile, to* CECILY.] Kindly turn round, sweet child. [CECILY *turns completely round.*] No, the side view is what I want. [CECILY *presents her profile.*] Yes, quite as I expected. There are distinct social possibilities in your profile. The two weak points in our age are its want of principle and its want of profile. The chin a little higher, dear. Style largely depends on the way the chin is worn. They are worn very high, just at present. Algernon!

ALGERNON. Yes, Aunt Augusta!

LADY BRACKNELL. There are distinct social possibilities in Miss Cardew's profile.

ALGERNON. Cecily is the sweetest, dearest, prettiest girl in the whole world. And I don't care twopence about social possibilities.

LADY BRACKNELL. Never speak disrespectfully of Society, Algernon. Only people who can't get into it do that. [*To*

---

[1]The southwestern postal district of London.

[2]North Britain (Scotland).

[3]Government bonds, the most desirable form of investment.

CECILY.] Dear child, of course you know that Algernon has nothing but his debts to depend upon. But I do not approve of mercenary marriages. When I married Lord Bracknell I had no fortune of any kind. But I never dreamed for a moment of allowing that to stand in my way. Well, I suppose I must give my consent.

ALGERNON. Thank you, Aunt Augusta.

LADY BRACKNELL. Cecily, you may kiss me!

CECILY. [*Kisses her.*] Thank you, Lady Bracknell.

LADY BRACKNELL. You may also address me as Aunt Augusta for the future.

CECILY. Thank you, Aunt Augusta.

LADY BRACKNELL. The marriage, I think, had better take place quite soon.

ALGERNON. Thank you, Aunt Augusta.

CECILY. Thank you, Aunt Augusta.

LADY BRACKNELL. To speak frankly, I am not in favor of long engagements. They give people the opportunity of finding out each other's character before marriage, which I think is never advisable.

JACK. I beg your pardon for interrupting you, Lady Bracknell, but this engagement is quite out of the question. I am Miss Cardew's guardian, and she cannot marry without my consent until she comes of age. That consent I absolutely decline to give.

LADY BRACKNELL. Upon what grounds may I ask? Algernon is an extremely, I may almost say an ostentatiously, eligible young man. He has nothing, but he looks everything. What more can one desire?

JACK. It pains me very much to have to speak frankly to you, Lady Bracknell, about your nephew, but the fact is that I do not approve at all of his moral character. I suspect him of being untruthful.

[ALGERNON *and* CECILY *look at him in indignant amazement.*

LADY BRACKNELL. Untruthful! My nephew Algernon? Impossible! He is an Oxonian.[4]

JACK. I fear there can be no possible doubt about the matter. This afternoon, during my temporary absence in London on an important question of romance, he obtained admission to my house by means of the false pretense of being my brother. Under an assumed name he drank, I've just been informed by my butler, an entire pint bottle of my Perrier-Jouet, Brut, '89; a wine I was specially reserving for myself. Continuing

[4] Graduate of Oxford.

his disgraceful deception, he succeeded in the course of the afternoon in alienating the affections of my only ward. He subsequently stayed to tea, and devoured every single muffin. And what makes his conduct all the more heartless is, that he was perfectly well aware from the first that I have no brother, that I never had a brother, and that I don't intend to have a brother, not even of any kind. I distinctly told him so myself yesterday afternoon.

LADY BRACKNELL. Ahem! Mr. Worthing, after careful consideration I have decided entirely to overlook my nephew's conduct to you.

JACK. That is very generous of you, Lady Bracknell. My own decision, however, is unalterable. I decline to give my consent.

LADY BRACKNELL. [*To* CECILY.] Come here, sweet child. [CECILY *goes over.*] How old are you, dear?

CECILY. Well, I am really only eighteen, but I always admit to twenty when I go to evening parties.

LADY BRACKNELL. You are perfectly right in making some slight alteration. Indeed, no woman should ever be quite accurate about her age. It looks so calculating. . . . [*In a meditative manner.*] Eighteen, but admitting to twenty at evening parties. Well, it will not be very long before you are of age and free from the restraints of tutelage. So I don't think your guardian's consent is, after all, a matter of any importance.

JACK. Pray excuse me, Lady Bracknell, for interrupting you again, but it is only fair to tell you that according to the terms of her grandfather's will Miss Cardew does not come legally of age till she is thirty-five.

LADY BRACKNELL. That does not seem to me to be a grave objection. Thirty-five is a very attractive age. London society is full of women of the very highest birth who have, of their own free choice, remained thirty-five for years. Lady Dumbleton is an instance in point. To my own knowledge she has been thirty-five ever since she arrived at the age of forty, which was many years ago now. I see no reason why our dear Cecily should not be even still more attractive at the age you mention than she is at present. There will be a large accumulation of property.

CECILY. Algy, could you wait for me till I was thirty-five?

ALGERNON. Of course I could, Cecily. You know I could.

CECILY. Yes. I felt it instinctively, but I

couldn't wait all that time. I hate waiting even five minutes for anybody. It always makes me rather cross. I am not punctual myself, I know, but I do like punctuality in others, and waiting, even to be married, is quite out of the question.

ALGERNON. Then what is to be done, Cecily?

CECILY. I don't know, Mr. Moncrieff.

LADY BRACKNELL. My dear Mr. Worthing, as Miss Cardew states positively that she cannot wait till she is thirty-five—a remark which I am bound to say seems to me to show a somewhat impatient nature—I would beg of you to reconsider your decision.

JACK. But my dear Lady Bracknell, the matter is entirely in your own hands. The moment you consent to my marriage with Gwendolen, I will most gladly allow your nephew to form an alliance with my ward.

LADY BRACKNELL. [*Rising and drawing herself up.*] You must be quite aware that what you propose is out of the question.

JACK. Then a passionate celibacy is all that any of us can look forward to.

LADY BRACKNELL. That is not the destiny I propose for Gwendolen. Algernon, of course, can choose for himself. [*Pulls out her watch.*] Come, dear, [GWENDOLEN *rises*] we have already missed five, if not six, trains. To miss any more might expose us to comment on the platform.

Enter DR. CHASUBLE.

CHASUBLE. Everything is quite ready for the christenings.

LADY BRACKNELL. The christenings, sir! Is not that somewhat premature?

CHASUBLE. [*Looking rather puzzled, and pointing to* JACK *and* ALGERNON.] Both these gentlemen have expressed a desire for immediate baptism.

LADY BRACKNELL. At their age? The idea is grotesque and irreligious! Algernon, I forbid you to be baptized. I will not hear of such excesses. Lord Bracknell would be highly displeased if he learned that that was the way in which you wasted your time and money.

CHASUBLE. Am I to understand then that there are to be no christenings at all this afternoon?

JACK. I don't think that, as things are now, it would be of much practical value to either of us, Dr. Chasuble.

CHASUBLE. I am grieved to hear such sentiments from you, Mr. Worthing. They savor of the heretical views of the Anabaptists, views that I have completely refuted in four of my unpublished sermons. However, as your present mood seems to be one peculiarly secular, I will return to the church at once. Indeed, I have just been informed by the pew-opener that for the last hour and a half Miss Prism has been waiting for me in the vestry.

LADY BRACKNELL. [*Starting.*] Miss Prism! Did I hear you mention a Miss Prism?

CHASUBLE. Yes, Lady Bracknell. I am on my way to join her.

LADY BRACKNELL. Pray allow me to detain you for a moment. This matter may prove to be one of vital importance to Lord Bracknell and myself. Is this Miss Prism a female of repellent aspect, remotely connected with education?

CHASUBLE. [*Somewhat indignantly.*] She is the most cultivated of ladies, and the very picture of respectability.

LADY BRACKNELL. It is obviously the same person. May I ask what position she holds in your household?

CHASUBLE. [*Severely.*] I am a celibate, madam.

JACK. [*Interposing.*] Miss Prism, Lady Bracknell, has been for the last three years Miss Cardew's esteemed governess and valued companion.

LADY BRACKNELL. In spite of what I hear of her, I must see her at once. Let her be sent for.

CHASUBLE. [*Looking off.*] She approaches; she is nigh.

Enter MISS PRISM *hurriedly.*

MISS PRISM. I was told you expected me in the vestry, dear Canon. I have been waiting for you there for an hour and three quarters.

[*Catches sight of* LADY BRACKNELL *who has fixed her with a stony glare.* MISS PRISM *grows pale and quails. She looks anxiously round as if desirous to escape.* LADY BRACKNELL. [*In a severe, judicial voice.*] Prism! [MISS PRISM *bows her head in shame.*] Come here, Prism! [MISS PRISM *approaches in a humble manner.*] Prism! Where is that baby? [*General consternation. The* CANON *starts back in horror.* ALGERNON *and* JACK *pretend to be anxious to shield* CECILY *and* GWENDOLEN *from hearing the details of a terrible public scandal.*] Twenty-eight years ago, Prism, you left Lord Bracknell's house, Number 104, Upper Grosvenor Street, in charge of a perambulator that contained a baby, of the male sex. You never returned. A few weeks later, through the elaborate investigations of the Metropolitan police, the perambulator was discovered at midnight, standing by itself in a remote corner of Bayswater. It contained the manuscript of a three-volume novel of more than usually revolting sentimentality. [MISS PRISM *starts in involuntary indignation.*] But the baby was not there! [*Everyone looks at* MISS PRISM.] Prism! Where is that baby? [*A pause.*]

MISS PRISM. Lady Bracknell, I admit with shame that I do not know. I only wish I did. The plain facts of the case are these. On the morning of the day you mention, a day that is for ever branded on my memory, I prepared as usual to take the baby out in its perambulator. I had also with me a somewhat old, but capacious handbag in which I had intended to place the manuscript of a work of fiction that I had written during my few unoccupied hours. In a moment of mental abstraction, for which I never can forgive myself, I deposited the manuscript in the basinette, and placed the baby in the handbag.

JACK. [*Who has been listening attentively.*] But where did you deposit the handbag?

MISS PRISM. Do not ask me, Mr. Worthing.

JACK. Miss Prism, this is a matter of no small importance to me. I insist on knowing where you deposited the handbag that contained that infant.

MISS PRISM. I left it in the cloakroom of one of the larger railway stations in London.

JACK. What railway station?

MISS PRISM. [*Quite crushed.*] Victoria. The Brighton line.

[*Sinks into a chair.*

JACK. I must retire to my room for a moment. Gwendolen, wait here for me.

GWENDOLEN. If you are not too long, I will wait here for you all my life.

[*Exit* JACK *in great excitement.*

CHASUBLE. What do you think this means, Lady Bracknell?

LADY BRACKNELL. I dare not even suspect, Dr. Chasuble. I need hardly tell you that in families of high position strange coincidences are not supposed to occur. They are hardly considered the thing.

[*Noises heard overhead as if someone was throwing trunks about. Everyone looks up.*

CECILY. Uncle Jack seems strangely agitated.

CHASUBLE. Your guardian has a very emotional nature.

LADY BRACKNELL. This noise is extremely unpleasant. It sounds as if he was having an argument. I dislike arguments of any kind. They are always vulgar, and often convincing.

CHASUBLE. [*Looking up.*] It has stopped now.

[*The noise is redoubled.*

LADY BRACKNELL. I wish he would arrive at some conclusion.

GWENDOLEN. This suspense is terrible. I hope it will last.

Enter JACK *with a handbag of black leather in his hand.*

JACK. [*Rushing over to* MISS PRISM.] Is this the handbag, Miss Prism? Examine it carefully before you speak. The happiness of more than one life depends on your answer.

MISS PRISM. [*Calmly.*] It seems to be mine. Yes, here is the injury it received through the upsetting of a Gower Street omnibus in younger and happier days. Here is the stain on the lining caused by the explosion of a temperance beverage, an incident that occurred at Leamington. And here, on the lock, are my initials. I had forgotten that in an extravagant mood I had had them placed there. The bag is undoubtedly mine. I am delighted to have it so unexpectedly restored to me. It has been a great inconvenience being without it all these years.

JACK. [*In a pathetic voice.*] Miss Prism, more is restored to you than this handbag. I was the baby you placed in it.

MISS PRISM. [*Amazed.*] You?

JACK. [*Embracing her.*] Yes . . . mother!

MISS PRISM. [*Recoiling in indignant astonishment.*] Mr. Worthing! I am unmarried!

JACK. Unmarried! I do not deny that is a serious blow. But after all, who has the right to cast a stone against one who has suffered? Cannot repentance wipe out an act of folly? Why should there be one law for men, and another for women? Mother, I forgive you. [*Tries to embrace her again.*

MISS PRISM. [*Still more indignant.*] Mr. Worthing, there is some error. [*Pointing to*

LADY BRACKNELL.] There is the lady who can tell you who you really are.

JACK. [*After a pause.*] Lady Bracknell, I hate to seem inquisitive, but would you kindly inform me who I am?

LADY BRACKNELL. I am afraid that the news I have to give you will not altogether please you. You are the son of my poor sister, Mrs. Moncrieff, and consequently Algernon's elder brother.

JACK. Algy's elder brother! Then I have a brother after all. I knew I had a brother! I always said I had a brother! Cecily—how could you have ever doubted that I had a brother? [*Seizes hold of* ALGERNON.] Dr. Chasuble, my unfortunate brother. Miss Prism, my unfortunate brother. Gwendolen, my unfortunate brother. Algy, you young scoundrel, you will have to treat me with more respect in the future. You have never behaved to me like a brother in all your life.

ALGERNON. Well, not till today, old boy, I admit. I did my best, however, though I was out of practice. [*Shakes hands.*

GWENDOLEN. [*To* JACK.] My own! But what own are you? What is your Christian name, now that you have become someone else?

JACK. Good heavens! . . . I had quite forgotten that point. Your decision on the subject of my name is irrevocable, I suppose?

GWENDOLEN. I never change, except in my affections.

CECILY. What a noble nature you have, Gwendolen!

JACK. Then the question had better be cleared up at once. Aunt Augusta, a moment. At the time when Miss Prism left me in the handbag, had I been christened already?

LADY BRACKNELL. Every luxury that money could buy, including christening, had been lavished on you by your fond and doting parents.

JACK. Then I was christened! That is settled. Now, what name was I given? Let me know the worst.

LADY BRACKNELL. Being the eldest son you were naturally christened after your father.

JACK. [*Irritably.*] Yes, but what was my father's Christian name?

LADY BRACKNELL. [*Meditatively.*] I cannot at the present moment recall what the General's Christian name was. But I have no doubt he had one. He was eccentric, I admit. But only in later years. And that was the result of the Indian climate, and marriage, and indigestion, and other things of that kind.

JACK. Algy! Can't you recollect what our father's Christian name was?

ALGERNON. My dear boy, we were never even on speaking terms. He died before I was a year old.

JACK. His name would appear in the Army Lists of the period, I suppose, Aunt Augusta?

LADY BRACKNELL. The General was essentially a man of peace, except in his domestic life. But I have no doubt his name would appear in any military directory.

JACK. The Army Lists of the last forty years are here. These delightful records should have been my constant study. [*Rushes to bookcase and tears the books out.*] M. Generals . . . Mallam, Maxbohm, Magley, what ghastly names they have— Markby, Migsby, Mobbs, Moncrieff! Lieutenant 1840, Captain, Lieutenant-Colonel, Colonel, General 1869, Christian names, Ernest John. [*Puts book very quietly down and speaks quite calmly.*] I always told you, Gwendolen, my name was Ernest, didn't I? Well, it is Ernest after all. I mean it naturally is Ernest.

LADY BRACKNELL. Yes, I remember now that the General was called Ernest. I knew I had some particular reason for disliking the name.

GWENDOLEN. Ernest! My own Ernest! I felt from the first that you could have no other name!

JACK. Gwendolen, it is a terrible thing for a man to find out suddenly that all his life he has been speaking nothing but the truth. Can you forgive me?

GWENDOLEN. I can. For I feel that you are sure to change.

JACK. My own one!

CHASUBLE. [*To* MISS PRISM.] Laetitia! [*Embraces her.*

MISS PRISM. [*Enthusiastically.*] Frederick! At last!

ALGERNON. Cecily! [*Embraces her.*] At last!

JACK. Gwendolen! [*Embraces her.*] At last!

LADY BRACKNELL. My nephew, you seem to be displaying signs of triviality.

JACK. On the contrary, Aunt Augusta, I've now realized for the first time in my life the vital Importance of Being Earnest.

CURTAIN

FRANCIS THOMPSON

1859–1907

Thompson was born at Preston on 16 December, 1859. His parents were converts to the Roman Catholic Church, and the boy was sent in 1870 to Ushaw College to receive a classical education—a first step towards preparation for the priesthood. He was studious and devoted to the Church; but he was also frail, shy, and wayward. When he was seventeen his father deemed it best for him to undertake the study of medicine (he himself was a homeopathic physician), and sent him to Owens College, Manchester, for that purpose. Thompson went, but disliked medical study and apparently made little effort to succeed. He read much, especially in Blake, Aeschylus, and De Quincey, but at the end of six years had failed three times to pass his examinations for a medical degree. Reproaches not unnaturally followed and might, with anyone less completely unfitted for the world than Thompson, have led to a declaration for a literary career and to some measure of understanding. He, however, simply turned away from his family and sought the nearest way to independence in whatever humble employment he might find. In November, 1885, he went to London, where he drifted to the lowest conceivable stage of poverty, aided in his course by laudanum, to which he had fallen a victim when attacked by neuralgia. For a time he was reduced to sleeping in the open, to earning a few pennies by selling matches or by fetching cabs, to receiving aid (like De Quincey) from a girl of the street who pitied him, and to securing from a charitable bootmaker paper on which he might try to compose a poem or two. In 1888 he sent two poems and an essay to *Merry England,* a periodical edited by Wilfrid Meynell. They were accepted and published; and thus began—not without difficulties arising from the poet's elusiveness and utterly disorganized way of life—a relationship which changed the face of the world for Thompson and made possible all of his later work. Laudanum and poverty had wrecked his health; but Meynell and his wife, Alice, cared for him sympathetically, restored him in strength, brought his opium-eating under control, encouraged him to write, and generally made themselves his good angels. During the 1890's he published three volumes of verse (*Poems,* 1893; *Sister Songs,* 1895; and *New Poems,* 1897), and during the remainder of his life he wrote much for the critical reviews. He died from tuberculosis on 13 November, 1907.

From the beginning he had enthusiastic admirers, and the fineness of his poetic gift is now everywhere recognized. Of *The Hound of Heaven* no less than 50,000 copies were sold during the three years following his death. Of his prose essay, *Shelley* (posthumously published in 1908, though written some twenty years earlier), George Wyndham wrote, with perhaps mistaken but infectious enthusiasm: "It is the most important contribution to pure letters written in English during the last twenty years." Despite difficulties which he gives his readers, despite his involved language and strange words, his willfulness, his seeming remoteness, his subtle and sometimes confused thought, Thompson's poetry is likely to live because it answers finely to a deep and perennial need. "To be the poet of the return to Nature," he wrote, "is somewhat; but I would be the poet of the return to God."

The standard edition is *The Works of Francis Thompson,* ed. Wilfrid Meynell (3 vols., London, 1913). The title is somewhat misleading; all of Thompson's poetry is collected in Vols. I and II (since reprinted in one vol. in the series of "Oxford Standard Authors," 1937), but not all of his prose is included in Vol. III (his *Life of St. Ignatius Loyola,* for example, being excluded). The standard *Life of Francis Thompson* is that by Everard Meynell (London, 1913; revised ed. 1926). A full-length interpretation of Thompson as a religious poet has been written by R. L. Mégroz, *Francis Thompson: the Poet of Earth in Heaven; a Study in Poetic Mysticism and the Evolution of Love-Poetry* (London, 1927).

THE HOUND OF HEAVEN[1]

I fled Him, down the nights and down the
    days;
  I fled Him, down the arches of the years;
I fled Him, down the labyrinthine ways
    Of my own mind; and in the mist of tears
I hid from Him, and under running laughter.
      Up vistaed hopes, I sped;   6
      And shot, precipitated,
  Adown Titanic glooms of chasméd fears,
From those strong Feet that followed, fol-
    lowed after.
      But with unhurrying chase,   10
      And unperturbéd pace,
Deliberate speed, majestic instancy,
      They beat—and a Voice beat
      More instant than the Feet:
"All things betray thee, who betrayest Me."

      I pleaded, outlaw-wise,   16
By many a hearted casement, curtained red,
  Trellised with intertwining charities;
(For, though I knew His love Who followéd,
    Yet was I sore adread   20
Lest, having Him, I must have naught be-
    side).
But, if one little casement parted wide,
  The gust of His approach would clash it
    to.
  Fear wist not to evade, as Love wist to
    pursue.
Across the margent of the world I fled,   25
  And troubled the gold gateways of the
    stars,
  Smiting for shelter on their clangéd bars;
    Fretted to dulcet jars
And silvern chatter the pale ports o' the
    moon.
I said to Dawn, Be sudden—to Eve, Be soon:
  With thy young skyey blossoms heap me
    over   31
    From this tremendous Lover—
Float thy vague veil about me, lest He see!
  I tempted all His servitors, but to find
My own betrayal in their constancy,   35
In faith to Him their fickleness to me,
  Their traitorous trueness, and their loyal
    deceit.
To all swift things for swiftness did I sue;
  Clung to the whistling mane of every wind.
      But whether they swept, smoothly
      fleet,   40

      The long savannahs of the blue;
      Or whether, thunder-driven,
  They clanged His chariot 'thwart a
    heaven
Plashy with flying lightnings round the spurn
    o' their feet:
  Fear wist not to evade as Love wist to
    pursue.   45
      Still with unhurrying chase,
      And unperturbéd pace,
Deliberate speed, majestic instancy,
      Came on the following Feet,
      And a Voice above their beat: 50
"Naught shelters thee, who wilt not shelter
    Me."

I sought no more that after which I strayed
    In face of man or maid;
But still within the little children's eyes
    Seems something, something that replies,
They at least are for me, surely for me!   56
I turned me to them very wistfully;
But just as their young eyes grew sudden fair
    With dawning answers there,
Their angel plucked them from me by the
    hair.   60
"Come then, ye other children, Nature's,—
    share
With me" (said I) "your delicate fellowship;
    Let me greet you lip to lip,
    Let me twine with you caresses,
      Wantoning   65
  With our Lady-Mother's[2] vagrant
    tresses;
      Banqueting
  With her in her wind-walled palace,
  Underneath her azured daïs;
Quaffing, as your taintless way is,   70
    From a chalice
Lucent-weeping out of the dayspring."
    So it was done:
I in their delicate fellowship was one—
Drew the bolt of Nature's secrecies.   75
  I knew all the swift importings
  On the willful face of skies;
  I knew how the clouds arise
  Spuméd of the wild sea-snortings—
    All that's born or dies,   80
  Rose and drooped with; made them
    shapers
Of mine own moods, or wailful or divine;
  With them joyed and was bereaven.
    I was heavy with the even,

---

[1]Written in 1889 or 1890; published in *Poems*,
1893.

[2]I. e., Nature's.

When she lit her glimmering tapers   85
    Round the day's dead sanctities;
I laughed in the morning's eyes.
I triumphed and I saddened with all weather:
    Heaven and I wept together,
And its sweet tears were salt with mortal
    mine;   90
Against the red throb of its sunset-heart
    I laid my own to beat,
    And share commingling heat.
But not by that, by that, was eased my human
    smart;
In vain my tears were wet on Heaven's gray
    cheek.   95
For ah! we know not what each other says,
    These things and I: in sound *I* speak—
Their sound is but their stir, they speak by
    silences.
Nature, poor stepdame, cannot slake my
    drouth;
    Let her, if she would owe[3] me,   100
Drop yon blue bosom-veil of sky, and show
    me
    The breasts o' her tenderness:
Never did any milk of hers once bless
    My thirsting mouth.
Nigh and nigh draws the chase,   105
    With unperturbéd pace,
Deliberate speed, majestic instancy,
    And past those noiséd Feet
    A Voice comes yet more fleet—
"Lo! naught contents thee, who content'st not
    Me."   110

Naked I wait Thy love's uplifted stroke!
My harness piece by piece Thou hast hewn
    from me,
    And smitten me to my knee:
    I am defenseless utterly.
    I slept, methinks, and woke,   115
And, slowly gazing, find me stripped in sleep.
In the rash lustihead of my young powers,
    I shook the pillaring hours
And pulled my life upon me;[4] grimed with
    smears,   119
I stand amid the dust o' the mounded years—
My mangled youth lies dead beneath the heap.
My days have crackled and gone up in smoke,
Have puffed and burst as sun-starts on a
    stream.
    Yea, faileth now even dream
The dreamer, and the lute the lutanist;   125
Even the linked fantasies, in whose blossomy
    twist

---

[3]Own.

[4]In allusion to Samson (Judges, 16:29–30).

I swung the earth a trinket at my wrist,
Are yielding—cords of all too weak account
For earth, with heavy griefs so overplussed.
    Ah! is Thy love indeed   130
A weed, albeit an amaranthine weed,
Suffering no flowers except its own to
    mount?
    Ah! must—
    Designer infinite!—
Ah! must Thou char the wood ere Thou canst
    limn with it?   135
My freshness spent its wavering shower i' the
    dust;
And now my heart is as a broken fount,
Wherein tear-drippings stagnate, spilt down
    ever
    From the dank thoughts that shiver
Upon the sighful branches of my mind.   140
    Such is: what is to be?
The pulp so bitter, how shall taste the rind?
I dimly guess what Time in mist confounds;
Yet ever and anon a trumpet sounds
From the hid battlements of Eternity: 145
Those shaken mists a space unsettle, then
Round the half-glimpséd turrets slowly wash
    again.
    But not ere him who summoneth
    I first have seen, enwound
With glooming robes purpureal, cypress-
    crowned: 150
His name I know, and what his trumpet saith.
Whether man's heart or life it be which yields
    Thee harvest, must Thy harvest fields
    Be dunged with rotten death?

    Now of that long pursuit   155
    Comes on at hand the bruit;
That Voice is round me like a bursting sea:
    "And is thy earth so marred,
    Shattered in shard on shard?
Lo, all things fly thee, for thou fliest Me!   160
    Strange, piteous, futile thing!
Wherefore should any set thee love apart?
Seeing none but I makes much of naught"
    (He said),
"And human love needs human meriting:
    How hast thou merited—   165
Of all man's clotted clay the dingiest clot?
    Alack, thou knowest not
How little worthy of any love thou art!
Whom wilt thou find to love ignoble thee,
    Save Me, save only Me?   170
All which I took from thee I did but take,
    Not for thy harms,
But just that thou might'st seek it in My
    arms.
    All which thy child's mistake

Fancies as lost, I have stored for thee at
    home: 175
  Rise, clasp My hand, and come!"

  Halts by me that footfall:
  Is my gloom, after all,

Shade of His hand, outstretched caress-
    ingly?—
  "Ah, fondest, blindest, weakest,   180
  I am He Whom thou seekest!
Thou dravest love from thee, who dravest
  Me."

THOMAS HARDY

1840–1928

Thomas Hardy was born in Dorsetshire, in the country, about three miles from Dorchester, on 2 June, 1840. He received his earlier education from his mother and from Dorchester schools. From 1856 until 1861 he was the pupil of an ecclesiastical architect of the same place, John Hicks. As a part of his work Hardy sketched and measured many old country churches since pulled down or altered. During a portion of this period he also read Latin and Greek with a fellow-pupil and did other reading not related to his architectural studies. In 1862 he went to London and studied Gothic architecture under Sir A. Blomfield until 1867. During these years he also attended some classes at King's College. While his studies were being pursued to their completion there were already indications of the course which Hardy's life was actually to take, for he had begun to write verse as early as 1860, and he continued to do so throughout his years in London. In 1867 he moved from London to Weymouth, where he practiced his profession of architecture. It is said that a promising career was opening up before him, but that he early experienced a disillusion the like of which a thoughtful man can hardly escape on entering any profession. He learned, as he writes in *Desperate Remedies*, that "those who get rich need have no skill at all as artists.—What need they have?—A certain kind of energy which men with any fondness for art possess very seldom indeed—an earnestness in making acquaintances, and a love for using them. They give their whole attention to the art of dining out, after mastering a few rudimentary facts to serve up in conversation." Probably this discovery increased Hardy's determination to cultivate another mode of expression, and, finding no publisher for the verse he had written, he turned for a time to prose and wrote a novel, *The Poor Man and the Lady*. It was submitted to Chapman and Hall, and was rejected, with good advice, by their reader, George Meredith.

Fortunately Hardy, though he learned that it took "a judicious omission of your real thoughts to make a novel popular," proceeded to write *Desperate Remedies,* which was published, anon-

ymously and at his own expense, in 1871. *Under the Greenwood Tree or the Mellstock Quire* was published, also anonymously, in 1872, and in the following year *A Pair of Blue Eyes,* over Hardy's name. This novel was successful enough to warrant his abandonment of architecture, and after 1873 his time was given entirely to literature. In 1885 he built the house on the outskirts of Dorchester, Max Gate, which remained his home until his death on 11 January, 1928. Immediately after his death conflicting demands were made concerning the disposition of the remains—demands which necessitated a compromise. His heart was taken out and placed in the grave of his first wife, in Stinsford churchyard, while the rest of the body was cremated and buried in the poet's corner in Westminster Abbey.

His novels, in addition to those already mentioned, are: *Far from the Madding Crowd* (1874), *The Hand of Ethelberta* (1876), *The Return of the Native* (1878), *The Trumpet-Major* (1879), *A Laodicean* (1881), *Two on a Tower* (1882), *The Life and Death of the Mayor of Casterbridge* (1885), *The Woodlanders* (1887), *Tess of the D'Urbervilles* (1891), *Jude the Obscure* (1895), and *The Well-Beloved* (1897). Hardy also published several volumes of tales. His first collection of verse, *Wessex Poems,* written from 1865 onwards, was published in 1898. Other volumes are: *Poems of the Past and the Present* (1901), *The Dynasts,* an epic-drama of the war with Napoleon (1903–1908), *Time's Laughing-Stocks and Other Verses* (1909), *Satires of Circumstance* (1914), *Moments of Vision* (1917), *Late Lyrics and Earlier* (1922), *The Famous Tragedy of the Queen of Cornwall at Tintagel in Lyonnesse* (1923), *Human Shows; Far Phantasies; Songs, and Trifles* (1925), and *Winter Words in Various Moods and Meters* (1928).

Although some of Hardy's novels and poems have been bitterly criticized both for their frankness of speech and for the pessimistic outlook on life which they exhibit, still their author's pre-eminent position in English literature of the last half-century was long ago universally acknowledged, and Hardy's old age was full of many distinguished testimonies to his greatness of achievement. One of these was the Order of Merit, bestowed on him in 1910. As for his frankness, or truthfulness in speaking of things as they are, the time came some years ago when this began to be recognized as something to commend. But concerning his pessimism questions may long remain. They arise not from the fact that Hardy depicted life as a frustration of man's higher aims and nobler qualities, for this tragic fact is the theme of much of the world's greatest literature. But the questions arise because of the peculiar character of his view, which seems to rob us of our very humanity. His outlook, in truth, was determined by the scientific thought dominant in the latter half of the nineteenth century, or was at least in full consonance with it. According to the view of science man was merely a complex mechanism, tossed into the air like a bubble by accident, and there the helpless victim of forces which he could neither understand nor control. This view of life Hardy tempered with certain inconsistencies inevitable in lifting it from the region of abstract theory to the concrete portrayal of recognizable human beings, and this is fortunate; for he was a born tragic artist and the master of an austere style appropriate to this high theme, whereas, of course, on a basis of mechanistic determinism life loses even its tragedy in the abyss of illusion which is the sole stuff of consciousness.

Of the several collected editions of Hardy's writings the "Wessex Edition" (London, 1912)

should be regarded as the standard and definitive one. To the original 20 volumes others have been added containing works first published or first collected since 1912. A substantial portion of Hardy's first novel, which had been rejected by publishers, has been recovered from an obscure periodical and edited by Carl J. Weber (*An Indiscretion in the Life of an Heiress,* Baltimore, 1935). The Macmillan Co., New York, publishes a one-volume collected edition of Hardy's poems, and also a one-volume edition of *The Dynasts.* A small volume of *Selected Poems* is included in the "Golden Treasury" series (London, 1916). An unauthorized collection of Hardy's minor prose has been published under the title *Life and Art,* ed. E. Brennecke, Jr. (New York, 1925). The standard biography is by Hardy's wife, Florence Emily Hardy: *The Early Life of Thomas Hardy, 1840–1891* (New York, 1928), and *The Later Years of Thomas Hardy, 1892–1928* (New York, 1930). *Thomas Hardy* by William R. Rutland (London and Glasgow, 1938) is a brief sketch. Critical studies of Hardy are numerous and only a few can be mentioned: *The Art of Thomas Hardy* by Lionel Johnson (London, 1894; republished with additions, 1922); *Thomas Hardy, A Critical Study,* by Lascelles Abercrombie (London, 1912); *Thomas Hardy: A Study of the Wessex Novels,* by H. C. Duffin (Manchester, 1916; later reissued with additions); *Thomas Hardy, Poet and Novelist,* by Samuel C. Chew (New York, 1921; revised ed. 1928); and *Thomas Hardy, A Critical Study,* by A. Macdowall (London, 1931).

THE WITHERED ARM[1]

I. A Lorn Milkmaid

IT WAS an eighty-cow dairy, and the troop of milkers, regular and supernumerary, were all at work; for, though the time of year was as yet but early April, the feed lay entirely in water-meadows, and the cows were "in full pail." The hour was about six in the evening, and three-fourths of the large, red, rectangular animals having been finished off, there was opportunity for a little conversation.

"He do bring home his bride tomorrow, I hear. They've come as far as Anglebury today."

The voice seemed to proceed from the belly

of the cow called Cherry, but the speaker was a milking-woman, whose face was buried in the flank of that motionless beast.

"Hav' anybody seen her?" said another.

There was a negative response from the first. "Though they say she's a rosy-cheeked, tisty-tosty little body enough," she added; and as the milkmaid spoke she turned her face so that she could glance past her cow's tail to the other side of the barton,[2] where a thin, fading woman of thirty milked somewhat apart from the rest.

"Years younger than he, they say," continued the second, with also a glance of reflectiveness in the same direction.

"How old do you call him, then?"

---

[1]Published in 1888; reprinted from *Wessex Tales* by permission of Harper and Brothers.

[2]Farmyard.

"Thirty or so."

"More like forty," broke in an old milkman near, in a long white pinafore or "wropper," and with the brim of his hat tied down, so that he looked like a woman. " 'A was born before our Great Weir[3] was builded, and I hadn't man's wages when I laved[4] water there."

The discussion waxed so warm that the purr of the milk streams became jerky, till a voice from another cow's belly cried with authority, "Now then, what the Turk do it matter to us about Farmer Lodge's age, or Farmer Lodge's new mis'ess? I shall have to pay him nine pound a year for the rent of every one of these milchers, whatever his age or hers. Get on with your work, or 'twill be dark afore we have done. The evening is pinking in[5] a'ready." This speaker was the dairyman himself, by whom the milkmaids and men were employed.

Nothing more was said publicly about Farmer Lodge's wedding, but the first woman murmured under her cow to her next neighbor, " 'Tis hard for *she*," signifying the thin worn milkmaid aforesaid.

"O no," said the second. "He ha'n't spoke to Rhoda Brook for years."

When the milking was done they washed their pails and hung them on a many-forked stand made as usual of the peeled limb of an oak-tree, set upright in the earth, and resembling a colossal antlered horn. The majority then dispersed in various directions homeward. The thin woman who had not spoken was joined by a boy of twelve or thereabout, and the twain went away up the field also.

Their course lay apart from that of the others, to a lonely spot high above the water-meads, and not far from the border of Egdon Heath, whose dark countenance was visible in the distance as they drew nigh to their home.

"They've just been saying down in barton that your father brings his young wife home from Anglebury to-morrow," the woman observed. "I shall want to send you for a few things to market, and you'll be pretty sure to meet 'em."

"Yes, mother," said the boy. "Is father married then?"

---
[3] Dam.　　[4] Drew.　　[5] Drawing in.

"Yes. . . . You can give her a look, and tell me what she's like, if you do see her."

"Yes, mother."

"If she's dark or fair, and if she's tall—as tall as I. And if she seems like a woman who has ever worked for a living, or one that has been always well off, and has never done anything, and shows marks of the lady on her, as I expect she do."

"Yes."

They crept up the hill in the twilight and entered the cottage. It was built of mud-walls, the surface of which had been washed by many rains into channels and depressions that left none of the original flat face visible; while here and there in the thatch above a rafter showed like a bone protruding through the skin.

She was kneeling down in the chimney-corner, before two pieces of turf laid together with the heather inwards, blowing at the red-hot ashes with her breath till the turves flamed. The radiance lit her pale cheek, and made her dark eyes, that had once been handsome, seem handsome anew. "Yes," she resumed, "see if she is dark or fair, and if you can, notice if her hands be white; if not, see if they look as though she had ever done housework, or are milker's hands like mine."

The boy again promised, inattentively this time, his mother not observing that he was cutting a notch with his pocket-knife in the beech-backed chair.

II. The Young Wife

THE road from Anglebury to Holmstoke is in general level; but there is one place where a sharp ascent breaks its monotony. Farmers homeward-bound from the former market-town, who trot all the rest of the way, walk their horses up this short incline.

The next evening while the sun was yet bright a handsome new gig, with a lemon-colored body and red wheels, was spinning westward along the level highway at the heels of a powerful mare. The driver was a yeoman in the prime of life, cleanly shaven like an actor, his face being toned to that bluish-vermilion hue which so often graces a thriving farmer's features when returning home after successful dealings in the town. Beside him sat a woman, many years his junior—almost, indeed, a girl. Her face too was fresh in color, but it was of a totally different quality—soft and evanescent, like the light under a heap of rose-petals.

Few people traveled this way, for it was not a main road; and the long white riband of gravel that stretched before them was empty, save of one small scarce-moving speck, which presently resolved itself into the figure of a boy, who was creeping on at a snail's pace, and continually looking behind him—the heavy bundle he carried being some excuse for, if not the reason of, his dilatoriness. When the bouncing gig-party slowed at the bottom of the incline above mentioned, the pedestrian was only a few yards in front. Supporting the large bundle by putting one hand on his hip, he turned and looked straight at the farmer's wife as though he would read her through and through, pacing along abreast of the horse.

The low sun was full in her face, rendering every feature, shade, and contour distinct, from the curve of her little nostril to the color of her eyes. The farmer, though he seemed annoyed at the boy's persistent presence, did not order him to get out of the way; and thus the lad preceded them, his hard gaze never leaving her, till they reached the top of the ascent, when the farmer trotted on with relief in his lineaments—having taken no outward notice of the boy whatever.

"How that poor lad stared at me!" said the young wife.

"Yes, dear; I saw that he did."

"He is one of the village, I suppose?"

"One of the neighborhood. I think he lives with his mother a mile or two off."

"He knows who we are, no doubt?"

"O yes. You must expect to be stared at just at first, my pretty Gertrude."

"I do,—though I think the poor boy may have looked at us in the hope we might relieve him of his heavy load, rather than from curiosity."

"O no," said her husband off-handedly. "These country lads will carry a hundred-weight once they get it on their backs; besides his pack had more size than weight in it. Now, then, another mile and I shall be able to

show you our house in the distance—if it is not too dark before we get there." The wheels spun round, and particles flew from their periphery as before, till a white house of ample dimensions revealed itself, with farm-buildings and ricks at the back.

Meanwhile the boy had quickened his pace, and turning up a by-lane some mile and a half short of the white farmstead, ascended towards the leaner pastures, and so on to the cottage of his mother.

She had reached home after her day's milking at the outlying dairy, and was washing cabbage at the doorway in the declining light. "Hold up the net a moment," she said, without preface, as the boy came up.

He flung down his bundle, held the edge of the cabbage-net, and as she filled its meshes with the dripping leaves she went on, "Well, did you see her?"

"Yes; quite plain."

"Is she ladylike?"

"Yes; and more. A lady complete."

"Is she young?"

"Well, she's growed up, and her ways be quite a woman's."

"Of course. What color is her hair and face?"

"Her hair is lightish, and her face as comely as a live doll's."

"Her eyes, then, are not dark like mine?"

"No—of a bluish turn, and her mouth is very nice and red; and when she smiles, her teeth show white."

"Is she tall?" said the woman sharply.

"I couldn't see. She was sitting down."

"Then do you go to Holmstoke church to-morrow morning: she's sure to be there. Go early and notice her walking in, and come home and tell me if she's taller than I."

"Very well, mother. But why don't you go and see for yourself?"

"*I* go to see her! I wouldn't look up at her if she were to pass my window this instant. She was with Mr. Lodge, of course. What did he say or do?"

"Just the same as usual."

"Took no notice of you?"

"None."

Next day the mother put a clean shirt on the boy, and started him off for Holmstoke church. He reached the ancient little pile when the door was just being opened, and he was the first to enter. Taking his seat by the font, he watched all the parishioners file in. The well-to-do Farmer Lodge came nearly last; and his young wife, who accompanied him, walked up the aisle with the shyness natural to a modest woman who had appeared thus for the first time. As all other eyes were fixed upon her, the youth's stare was not noticed now.

When he reached home his mother said, "Well?" before he had entered the room.

"She is not tall. She is rather short," he replied.

"Ah!" said his mother, with satisfaction.

"But she's very pretty—very. In fact, she's lovely." The youthful freshness of the yeoman's wife had evidently made an impression even on the somewhat hard nature of the boy.

"That's all I want to hear," said his mother quickly. "Now, spread the table-cloth. The hare you wired is very tender; but mind that nobody catches you.—You've never told me what sort of hands she had."

"I have never seen 'em. She never took off her gloves."

"What did she wear this morning?"

"A white bonnet and a silver-colored gownd. It whewed and whistled so loud when it rubbed against the pews that the lady colored up more than ever for very shame at the noise, and pulled it in to keep it from touching; but when she pushed into her seat, it whewed more than ever. Mr. Lodge, he seemed pleased, and his waistcoat stuck out, and his great golden seals hung like a lord's; but she seemed to wish her noisy gownd anywhere but on her."

"Not she! However, that will do now."

These descriptions of the newly-married couple were continued from time to time by the boy at his mother's request, after any chance encounter he had had with them. But Rhoda Brook, though she might easily have seen young Mrs. Lodge for herself by walking a couple of miles, would never attempt an excursion towards the quarter where the farmhouse lay. Neither did she, at the daily milking in the dairyman's yard on Lodge's outlying second farm, ever speak on the subject of the recent marriage. The dairyman, who rented the cows of Lodge, and knew perfectly the tall milkmaid's history, with manly kindliness always kept the gossip in the cow-barton from annoying Rhoda. But the atmosphere thereabout was full of the subject during the first days of Mrs. Lodge's arrival; and from her boy's description and the casual words of the other milkers, Rhoda Brook could raise a mental image of the unconscious Mrs. Lodge that was realistic as a photograph.

III. A Vision

ONE night, two or three weeks after the bridal return, when the boy was gone to bed, Rhoda sat a long time over the turf ashes that she had raked out in front of her to extinguish them. She contemplated so intently the new wife, as presented to her in her mind's eye over the embers, that she forgot the lapse of time. At last, wearied with her day's work, she too retired.

But the figure which had occupied her so much during this and the previous days was not to be banished at night. For the first time Gertrude Lodge visited the supplanted woman in her dreams. Rhoda Brook dreamed—since her assertion that she really saw, before falling asleep, was not to be believed—that the young wife, in the pale silk dress and white bonnet, but with features shockingly distorted, and wrinkled as by age, was sitting upon her chest as she lay. The pressure of Mrs. Lodge's person grew heavier; the blue eyes peered cruelly into her face; and then the figure thrust forward its left hand mockingly, so as to make the wedding-ring it wore glitter in Rhoda's eyes. Maddened mentally, and nearly suffocated by pressure, the sleeper struggled; the incubus,[1] still regarding her, withdrew to the foot of the bed, only, however, to come forward by degrees, resume her seat, and flash her left hand as before.

Gasping for breath, Rhoda, in a last desperate effort, swung out her right hand, seized the confronting specter by its obtrusive left arm, and whirled it backward to the floor, starting up herself as she did so with a low cry.

---

[1]Oppressive spirit in a nightmare.

"O, merciful heaven!" she cried, sitting on the edge of the bed in a cold sweat; "that was not a dream—she was here!"

She could feel her antagonist's arm within her grasp even now—the very flesh and bone of it, as it seemed. She looked on the floor whither she had whirled the specter, but there was nothing to be seen.

Rhoda Brook slept no more that night, and when she went milking at the next dawn they noticed how pale and haggard she looked. The milk that she drew quivered into the pail; her hand had not calmed even yet, and still retained the feel of the arm. She came home to breakfast as wearily as if it had been supper-time.

"What was that noise in your chimmer, mother, last night?" said her son. "You fell off the bed, surely?"

"Did you hear anything fall? At what time?"

"Just when the clock struck two."

She could not explain, and when the meal was done went silently about her household work, the boy assisting her, for he hated going afield on the farms, and she indulged his reluctance. Between eleven and twelve the garden-gate clicked, and she lifted her eyes to the window. At the bottom of the garden, within the gate, stood the woman of her vision. Rhoda seemed transfixed.

"Ah, she said she would come!" exclaimed the boy, also observing her.

"Said so—when? How does she know us?"

"I have seen and spoken to her. I talked to her yesterday."

"I told you," said the mother, flushing indignantly, "never to speak to anybody in that house, or go near the place."

"I did not speak to her till she spoke to me. And I did not go near the place. I met her in the road."

"What did you tell her?"

"Nothing. She said, 'Are you the poor boy who had to bring the heavy load from market?' And she looked at my boots, and said they would not keep my feet dry if it came on wet, because they were so cracked. I told her I lived with my mother, and we had enough to do to keep ourselves, and that's how it was; and she said then, 'I'll come and bring you some better boots, and see your mother.' She gives away things to other folks in the meads besides us."

Mrs. Lodge was by this time close to the door—not in her silk, as Rhoda had dreamt of in the bed-chamber, but in a morning hat, and gown of common light material, which became her better than silk. On her arm she carried a basket.

The impression remaining from the night's experience was still strong. Brook had almost expected to see the wrinkles, the scorn, and the cruelty on her visitor's face. She would have escaped an interview, had escape been possible. There was, however, no backdoor to the cottage, and in an instant the boy had lifted the latch to Mrs. Lodge's gentle knock.

"I see I have come to the right house," said she, glancing at the lad, and smiling. "But I was not sure till you opened the door."

The figure and action were those of the phantom; but her voice was so indescribably sweet, her glance so winning, her smile so tender, so unlike that of Rhoda's midnight visitant, that the latter could hardly believe the evidence of her senses. She was truly glad that she had not hidden away in sheer aversion, as she had been inclined to do. In her basket Mrs. Lodge brought the pair of boots that she had promised to the boy, and other useful articles.

At these proofs of a kindly feeling towards her and hers Rhoda's heart reproached her bitterly. This innocent young thing should have her blessing and not her curse. When she left them a light seemed gone from the dwelling. Two days later she came again to know if the boots fitted; and less than a fortnight after that paid Rhoda another call. On this occasion the boy was absent.

"I walk a good deal," said Mrs. Lodge, "and your house is the nearest outside our own parish. I hope you are well. You don't look quite well."

Rhoda said she was well enough; and, indeed, though the paler of the two, there was more of the strength that endures in her well-defined features and large frame than in the soft-cheeked young woman before her. The conversation became quite confidential as regarded their powers and weaknesses; and when Mrs. Lodge was leaving, Rhoda said, "I hope you will find this air agree with you, ma'am, and not suffer from the damp of the water meads."

The younger one replied that there was not much doubt of it, her general health being usually good. "Though, now you remind me," she added, "I have one little ailment which puzzles me. It is nothing serious, but I cannot make it out."

She uncovered her left hand and arm; and their outline confronted Rhoda's gaze as the exact original of the limb she had beheld and seized in her dream. Upon the pink round surface of the arm were faint marks of an unhealthy color, as if produced by a rough grasp. Rhoda's eyes became riveted on the discolorations; she fancied that she discerned in them the shape of her own four fingers.

"How did it happen?" she said mechanically.

"I cannot tell," replied Mrs. Lodge, shaking her head. "One night when I was sound asleep, dreaming I was away in some strange place, a pain suddenly shot into my arm there, and was so keen as to awaken me. I must have struck it in the daytime, I suppose, though I don't remember doing so." She added, laughing, "I tell my dear husband that it looks just as if he had flown into a rage and struck me there. O, I daresay it will soon disappear."

"Ha, ha! Yes. . . . On what night did it come?"

Mrs. Lodge considered, and said it would be a fortnight ago on the morrow. "When I awoke I could not remember where I was," she added, "till the clock striking two reminded me."

She had named the night and the hour of Rhoda's spectral encounter, and Brook felt like a guilty thing. The artless disclosure startled her; she did not reason on the freaks of coincidence; and all the scenery of that ghastly night returned with double vividness to her mind.

"O, can it be," she said to herself, when her visitor had departed, "that I exercise a malignant power over people against my own will?" She knew that she had been slily called a witch since her fall; but never having understood why that particular stigma had

been attached to her, it had passed disregarded. Could this be the explanation, and had such things as this ever happened before?

IV. A Suggestion

THE summer drew on, and Rhoda Brook almost dreaded to meet Mrs. Lodge again, notwithstanding that her feeling for the young wife amounted well-nigh to affection. Something in her own individuality seemed to convict Rhoda of crime. Yet a fatality sometimes would direct the steps of the latter to the outskirts of Holmstoke whenever she left her house for any other purpose than her daily work; and hence it happened that their next encounter was out of doors. Rhoda could not avoid the subject which had so mystified her, and after the first few words she stammered, "I hope your—arm is well again, ma'am?" She had perceived with consternation that Gertrude Lodge carried her left arm stiffly.

"No; it is not quite well. Indeed it is no better at all; it is rather worse. It pains me dreadfully sometimes."

"Perhaps you had better go to a doctor, ma'am."

She replied that she had already seen a doctor. Her husband had insisted upon her going to one. But the surgeon had not seemed to understand the afflicted limb at all; he had told her to bathe it in hot water, and she had bathed it, but the treatment had done no good.

"Will you let me see it?" said the milkwoman.

Mrs. Lodge pushed up her sleeve and disclosed the place, which was a few inches above the wrist. As soon as Rhoda Brook saw it, she could hardly preserve her composure. There was nothing of the nature of a wound, but the arm at that point had a shriveled look, and the outline of the four fingers appeared more distinct than at the former time. Moreover, she fancied that they were imprinted in precisely the relative position of her clutch upon the arm in the trance; the first finger towards Gertrude's wrist, and the fourth towards her elbow.

What the impress resembled seemed to have struck Gertrude herself since their last meeting. "It looks almost like finger-marks," she said; adding with a faint laugh, "my husband says it is as if some witch, or the devil himself, had taken hold of me there, and blasted the flesh."

Rhoda shivered. "That's fancy," she said hurriedly. "I wouldn't mind it, if I were you."

"I shouldn't so much mind it," said the younger, with hesitation, "if—if I hadn't a notion that it makes my husband—dislike me—no, love me less. Men think so much of personal appearance."

"Some do—he for one."

"Yes; and he was very proud of mine, at first."

"Keep your arm covered from his sight."

"Ah—he knows the disfigurement is there!" She tried to hide the tears that filled her eyes.

"Well, ma'am, I earnestly hope it will go away soon."

And so the milkwoman's mind was chained anew to the subject by a horrid sort of spell as she returned home. The sense of having been guilty of an act of malignity increased, affect as she might to ridicule her superstition. In her secret heart Rhoda did not altogether object to a slight diminution of her successor's beauty, by whatever means it had come about; but she did not wish to inflict upon her physical pain. For though this pretty young woman had rendered impossible any reparation which Lodge might have made Rhoda for his past conduct, everything like resentment at the unconscious usurpation had quite passed away from the elder's mind.

If the sweet and kindly Gertrude Lodge only knew of the dream-scene in the bed-chamber, what would she think? Not to inform her of it seemed treachery in the presence of her friendliness; but tell she could not of her own accord—neither could she devise a remedy.

She mused upon the matter the greater part of the night; and the next day, after the morning milking, set out to obtain another glimpse of Gertrude Lodge if she could, being held to her by a gruesome fascination. By watching the house from a distance the milkmaid was presently able to discern the farmer's wife in a ride she was taking alone —probably to join her husband in some distant field. Mrs. Lodge perceived her, and cantered in her direction.

"Good morning, Rhoda!" Gertrude said, when she had come up. "I was going to call."

Rhoda noticed that Mrs. Lodge held the reins with some difficulty.

"I hope—the bad arm," said Rhoda.

"They tell me there is possibly one way by which I might be able to find out the cause, and so perhaps the cure, of it," replied the other anxiously. "It is by going to some clever man over in Egdon Heath. They did not know if he was still alive—and I cannot remember his name at this moment; but they said that you knew more of his movements than anybody else hereabout, and could tell me if he were still to be consulted. Dear me—what was his name? But you know."

"Not Conjuror Trendle?" said her thin companion, turning pale.

"Trendle—yes. Is he alive?"

"I believe so," said Rhoda, with reluctance.

"Why do you call him conjuror?"

"Well—they say—they used to say he was a—he had powers other folks have not."

"O, how could my people be so superstitious as to recommend a man of that sort! I thought they meant some medical man. I shall think no more of him."

Rhoda looked relieved, and Mrs. Lodge rode on. The milkwoman had inwardly seen, from the moment she heard of her having been mentioned as a reference for this man, that there must exist a sarcastic feeling among the work-folk that a sorceress would know the whereabouts of the exorcist. They suspected her, then. A short time ago this would have given no concern to a woman of her common-sense. But she had a haunting reason to be superstitious now; and she had been seized with sudden dread that this Conjuror Trendle might name her as the malignant influence which was blasting the fair person of Gertrude, and so lead her friend to hate her for ever, and to treat her as some fiend in human shape.

But all was not over. Two days after, a shadow intruded into the window-pattern thrown on Rhoda Brook's floor by the afternoon sun. The woman opened the door at once, almost breathlessly.

"Are you alone?" said Gertrude. She seemed to be no less harassed and anxious than Brook herself.

"Yes," said Rhoda.

"The place on my arm seems worse, and troubles me!" the young farmer's wife went on. "It is so mysterious! I do hope it will not be an incurable wound. I have again been thinking of what they said about Conjuror Trendle. I don't really believe in such men, but I should not mind just visiting him, from curiosity—though on no account must my husband know. Is it far to where he lives?"

"Yes—five miles," said Rhoda backwardly. "In the heart of Egdon."

"Well, I should have to walk. Could not you go with me to show me the way—say to-morrow afternoon?"

"O, not I; that is——," the milkwoman murmured, with a start of dismay. Again the dread seized her that something to do with her fierce act in the dream might be revealed, and her character in the eyes of the most useful friend she had ever had be ruined irretrievably.

Mrs. Lodge urged, and Rhoda finally assented, though with much misgiving. Sad as the journey would be to her, she could not conscientiously stand in the way of a possible remedy for her patron's strange affliction. It was agreed that, to escape suspicion of their mystic intent, they should meet at the edge of the heath at the corner of a plantation which was visible from the spot where they now stood.

V. Conjuror Trendle

By the next afternoon Rhoda would have done anything to escape this inquiry. But she had promised to go. Moreover, there was a horrid fascination at times in becoming instrumental in throwing such possible light on her own character as would reveal her to be something greater in the occult world than she had ever herself suspected.

She started just before the time of day mentioned between them, and half-an-hour's brisk walking brought her to the south-eastern extension of the Egdon tract of country, where the fir plantation was. A slight figure, cloaked and veiled, was already there. Rhoda recognized, almost with a shudder, that Mrs. Lodge bore her left arm in a sling.

They hardly spoke to each other, and immediately set out on their climb into the interior of this solemn country, which stood high above the rich alluvial soil they had left half-an-hour before. It was a long walk; thick clouds made the atmosphere dark, though it was as yet only early afternoon; and the wind howled dismally over the slopes of the heath—not improbably the same heath which had witnessed the agony of the Wessex King Ina, presented to after-ages as Lear. Gertrude Lodge talked most, Rhoda replying with monosyllabic preoccupation. She had a strange dislike to walking on the side of her companion where hung the afflicted arm, moving round to the other when inadvertently near it. Much heather had been brushed by their feet when they descended upon a cart-track, beside which stood the house of the man they sought.

He did not profess his remedial practices openly, or care anything about their continuance, his direct interests being those of a dealer in furze, turf, "sharp[1] sand," and other local products. Indeed, he affected not to believe largely in his own powers, and when warts that had been shown him for cure miraculously disappeared—which it must be owned they infallibly did—he would say lightly, "O, I only drink a glass of grog upon 'em at your expense—perhaps it's all chance," and immediately turn the subject.

He was at home when they arrived, having in fact seen them descending into his valley. He was a gray-bearded man, with a reddish face, and he looked singularly at Rhoda the first moment he beheld her. Mrs. Lodge told him her errand; and then with words of self-disparagement he examined her arm.

"Medicine can't cure it," he said promptly. " 'Tis the work of an enemy."

Rhoda shrank into herself, and drew back.

"An enemy? What enemy?" asked Mrs. Lodge.

He shook his head. "That's best known to yourself," he said. "If you like, I can show

---

[1] Hard; angular: **gritty**.

the person to you, though I shall not myself know who it is. I can do no more; and don't wish to do that."

She pressed him; on which he told Rhoda to wait outside where she stood, and took 5 Mrs. Lodge into the room. It opened immediately from the door; and, as the latter remained ajar, Rhoda Brook could see the proceedings without taking part in them. He brought a tumbler from the dresser, 10 nearly filled it with water, and fetching an egg, prepared it in some private way; after which he broke it on the edge of the glass, so that the white went in and the yolk remained. As it was getting gloomy, he took 15 the glass and its contents to the window, and told Gertrude to watch the mixture closely. They leant over the table together, and the milkwoman could see the opaline hue of the egg-fluid changing form as it sank in the 20 water, but she was not near enough to define the shape that it assumed.

"Do you catch the likeness of any face or figure as you look?" demanded the conjuror of the young woman.

She murmured a reply, in tones so low as to be inaudible to Rhoda, and continued to gaze intently into the glass. Rhoda turned, and walked a few steps away.

When Mrs. Lodge came out, and her face 30 was met by the light, it appeared exceedingly pale—as pale as Rhoda's—against the sad dun shades of the upland's garniture. Trendle shut the door behind her, and they at once started homeward together. But 35 Rhoda perceived that her companion had quite changed.

"Did he charge much?" she asked tentatively.

"O no—nothing. He would not take a 40 farthing," said Gertrude.

"And what did you see?" inquired Rhoda.

"Nothing I—care to speak of." The constraint in her manner was remarkable; her face was so rigid as to wear an oldened as- 45 pect, faintly suggestive of the face in Rhoda's bed-chamber.

"Was it you who first proposed coming here?" Mrs. Lodge suddenly inquired, after a long pause. "How very odd, if you did!" 50

"No. But I am not sorry we have come, all things considered," she replied. For the

first time a sense of triumph possessed her, and she did not altogether deplore that the young thing at her side should learn that their lives had been antagonized by other influences than their own.

The subject was no more alluded to during the long and dreary walk home. But in some way or other a story was whispered about the many-dairied lowland that winter that Mrs. Lodge's gradual loss of the use of her left arm was owing to her being "overlooked"[2] by Rhoda Brook. The latter kept her own counsel about the incubus, but her face grew sadder and thinner; and in the spring she and her boy disappeared from the neighborhood of Holmstoke.

VI. A Second Attempt

HALF a dozen years passed away, and Mr. and Mrs. Lodge's married experience sank into prosiness, and worse. The farmer was usually gloomy and silent: the woman whom he had wooed for her grace and beauty was contorted and disfigured in the left limb; moreover, she had brought him no child, which rendered it likely that he would be the last of a family who had occupied that valley for some two hundred years. He thought of Rhoda Brook and her son; and feared this might be a judgment from heaven upon him.

The once blithe-hearted and enlightened Gertrude was changing into an irritable, superstitious woman, whose whole time was given to experimenting upon her ailment with every quack remedy she came across. She was honestly attached to her husband, and was ever secretly hoping against hope to win back his heart again by regaining some at least of her personal beauty. Hence it arose that her closet was lined with bottles, packets, and ointment-pots of every description—nay, bunches of mystic herbs, charms, and books of necromancy, which in her schoolgirl time she would have ridiculed as folly.

"Damned if you won't poison yourself with these apothecary messes and witch mixtures some time or other," said her husband, when his eye chanced to fall upon the multitudinous array.

---

[2]Bewitched.

She did not reply, but turned her sad, soft glance upon him in such heart-swollen reproach that he looked sorry for his words, and added, "I only meant it for your good, you know, Gertrude."

"I'll clear out the whole lot, and destroy them," said she huskily, "and try such remedies no more!"

"You want somebody to cheer you," he observed. "I once thought of adopting a boy; but he is too old now. And he is gone away I don't know where."

She guessed to whom he alluded; for Rhoda Brook's story had in the course of years become known to her; though not a word had ever passed between her husband and herself on the subject. Neither had she ever spoken to him of her visit to Conjuror Trendle, and of what was revealed to her, or she thought was revealed to her, by that solitary heathman.

She was now five-and-twenty; but she seemed older. "Six years of marriage, and only a few months of love," she sometimes whispered to herself. And then she thought of the apparent cause, and said, with a tragic glance at her withering limb, "If I could only again be as I was when he first saw me!"

She obediently destroyed her nostrums and charms; but there remained a hankering wish to try something else—some other sort of cure altogether. She had never revisited Trendle since she had been conducted to the house of the solitary by Rhoda against her will; but it now suddenly occurred to Gertrude that she would, in a last desperate effort at deliverance from this seeming curse, again seek out the man, if he yet lived. He was entitled to a certain credence, for the indistinct form he had raised in the glass had undoubtedly resembled the only woman in the world who—as she now knew, though not then—could have a reason for bearing her ill-will. The visit should be paid.

This time she went alone, though she nearly got lost on the heath, and roamed a considerable distance out of her way. Trendle's house was reached at last, however: he was not indoors, and instead of waiting at the cottage, she went to where his bent figure was pointed out to her at work a long way off. Trendle remembered her, and laying down the handful of furze-roots which he was gathering and throwing into a heap, he offered to accompany her in her homeward direction, as the distance was considerable and the days were short. So they walked together, his head bowed nearly to the earth, and his form of a color with it.

"You can send away warts and other excrescences, I know," she said; "why can't you send away this?" And the arm was uncovered.

"You think too much of my powers!" said Trendle; "and I am old and weak now, too. No, no; it is too much for me to attempt in my own person. What have ye tried?"

She named to him some of the hundred medicaments and counterspells which she had adopted from time to time. He shook his head.

"Some were good enough," he said approvingly; "but not many of them for such as this. This is of the nature of a blight, not of the nature of a wound; and if you ever do throw it off, it will be all at once."

"If I only could!"

"There is only one chance of doing it known to me. It has never failed in kindred afflictions,—that I can declare. But it is hard to carry out, and especially for a woman."

"Tell me!" said she.

"You must touch with the limb the neck of a man who's been hanged."

She started a little at the image he had raised.

"Before he's cold—just after he's cut down," continued the conjuror impassively.

"How can that do good?"

"It will turn the blood and change the constitution. But, as I say, to do it is hard. You must go to the jail when there's a hanging, and wait for him when he's brought off the gallows. Lots have done it, though perhaps not such pretty women as you. I used to send dozens for skin complaints. But that was in former times. The last I sent was in '13—near twelve years ago."

He had no more to tell her; and, when he had put her into a straight track homeward, turned and left her, refusing all money as at first.

VII. A Ride

THE communication sank deep into Gertrude's mind. Her nature was rather a timid one; and probably of all remedies that the white[1] wizard could have suggested there was not one which would have filled her with so much aversion as this, not to speak of the immense obstacles in the way of its adoption.

Casterbridge, the county-town, was a dozen or fifteen miles off; and though in those days, when men were executed for horse-stealing, arson, and burglary, an assize seldom passed without a hanging, it was not likely that she could get access to the body of the criminal unaided. And the fear of her husband's anger made her reluctant to breathe a word of Trendle's suggestion to him or to anybody about him.

She did nothing for months, and patiently bore her disfigurement as before. But her woman's nature, craving for renewed love, through the medium of renewed beauty (she was but twenty-five), was ever stimulating her to try what, at any rate, could hardly do her any harm. "What came by a spell will go by a spell surely," she would say. Whenever her imagination pictured the act she shrank in terror from the possibility of it: then the words of the conjuror, "It will turn your blood," were seen to be capable of a scientific no less than a ghastly interpretation; the mastering desire returned, and urged her on again.

There was at this time but one county paper, and that her husband only occasionally borrowed. But old-fashioned days had old-fashioned means, and news was extensively conveyed by word of mouth from market to market, or from fair to fair, so that, whenever such an event as an execution was about to take place, few within a radius of twenty miles were ignorant of the coming sight; and, so far as Holmstoke was concerned, some enthusiasts had been known to walk all the way to Casterbridge and back in one day, solely to witness the spectacle. The next assizes were in March; and when Gertrude Lodge heard that they had been held, she inquired stealthily at the inn as to the result, as soon as she could find opportunity.

She was, however, too late. The time at which the sentences were to be carried out had arrived, and to make the journey and obtain admission at such short notice required at least her husband's assistance. She dared not tell him, for she had found by delicate experiment that these smoldering village beliefs made him furious if mentioned, partly because he half entertained them himself. It was therefore necessary to wait for another opportunity.

Her determination received a fillip from learning that two epileptic children had attended from this very village of Holmstoke many years before with beneficial results, though the experiment had been strongly condemned by the neighboring clergy. April, May, June, passed; and it is no overstatement to say that by the end of the last-named month Gertrude well-nigh longed for the death of a fellow-creature. Instead of her formal prayers each night, her unconscious prayer was, "O Lord, hang some guilty or innocent person soon!"

This time she made earlier inquiries, and was altogether more systematic in her proceedings. Moreover, the season was summer, between the haymaking and the harvest, and in the leisure thus afforded him her husband had been holiday-taking away from home.

The assizes were in July, and she went to the inn as before. There was to be one execution—only one—for arson.

Her greatest problem was not how to get to Casterbridge, but what means she should adopt for obtaining admission to the jail. Though access for such purposes had formerly never been denied, the custom had fallen into desuetude; and in contemplating her possible difficulties, she was again almost driven to fall back upon her husband. But, on sounding him about the assizes, he was so uncommunicative, so more than usually cold, that she did not proceed, and decided that whatever she did she would do alone.

Fortune, obdurate hitherto, showed her unexpected favor. On the Thursday before the Saturday fixed for the execution, Lodge remarked to her that he was going away from

---

[1]Beneficent, as opposed to a black, or maleficent, wizard.

home for another day or two on business at a fair, and that he was sorry he could not take her with him.

She exhibited on this occasion so much readiness to stay at home that he looked at her in surprise. Time had been when she would have shown deep disappointment at the loss of such a jaunt. However, he lapsed into his usual taciturnity, and on the day named left Holmstoke.

It was now her turn. She at first had thought of driving, but on reflection held that driving would not do, since it would necessitate her keeping to the turnpike-road, and so increase by tenfold the risk of her ghastly errand being found out. She decided to ride, and avoid the beaten track, notwithstanding that in her husband's stables there was no animal just at present which by any stretch of imagination could be considered a lady's mount, in spite of his promise before marriage to always keep a mare for her. He had, however, many cart-horses, fine ones of their kind; and among the rest was a serviceable creature, an equine Amazon, with a back as broad as a sofa, on which Gertrude had occasionally taken an airing when unwell. This horse she chose.

On Friday afternoon one of the men brought it round. She was dressed, and before going down looked at her shriveled arm. "Ah!" she said to it, "if it had not been for you this terrible ordeal would have been saved me!"

When strapping up the bundle in which she carried a few articles of clothing, she took occasion to say to the servant, "I take these in case I should not get back to-night from the person I am going to visit. Don't be alarmed if I am not in by ten, and close up the house as usual. I shall be at home to-morrow for certain." She meant then to tell her husband privately: the deed accomplished was not like the deed projected. He would almost certainly forgive her.

And then the pretty palpitating Gertrude Lodge went from her husband's homestead; but though her goal was Casterbridge she did not take the direct route thither through Stickleford. Her cunning course at first was in precisely the opposite direction. As soon as she was out of sight, however, she turned to the left, by a road which led into Egdon, and on entering the heath wheeled round, and set out in the true course, due westerly. A more private way down the county could not be imagined; and as to direction, she had merely to keep her horse's head to a point a little to the right of the sun. She knew that she would light upon a furze-cutter or cottager of some sort from time to time, from whom she might correct her bearing.

Though the date was comparatively recent, Egdon was much less fragmentary in character than now. The attempts—successful and otherwise—at cultivation on the lower slopes, which intrude and break up the original heath into small detached heaths, had not been carried far; Enclosure Acts[2] had not taken effect, and the banks and fences which now exclude the cattle of those villagers who formerly enjoyed rights of commonage[3] thereon, and the carts of those who had turbary privileges[4] which kept them in firing all the year round, were not erected. Gertrude, therefore, rode along with no other obstacles than the prickly furze-bushes, the mats of heather, the white water-courses, and the natural steeps and declivities of the ground.

Her horse was sure, if heavy-footed and slow, and though a draught animal, was easy-paced; had it been otherwise, she was not a woman who could have ventured to ride over such a bit of country with a half-dead arm. It was therefore nearly eight o'clock when she drew rein to breathe her bearer on the last outlying high point of heath-land towards Casterbridge, previous to leaving Egdon for the cultivated valleys.

She halted before a pool called Rushy-pond, flanked by the ends of two hedges; a railing ran through the center of the pond, dividing it in half. Over the railing she saw the low green country; over the green trees the roofs of the town; over the roofs a white flat façade, denoting the entrance to the county jail. On the roof of this front specks

---

[2] Acts of Parliament to permit enclosing as private land particular tracts which had previously been used by whole communities.

[3] Use in common, particularly for pasturage.

[4] Privileges to cut turf.

were moving about; they seemed to be work-men erecting something. Her flesh crept. She descended slowly, and was soon amid corn-fields and pastures. In another half-hour, when it was almost dusk, Gertrude reached the White Hart, the first inn of the town on that side.

Little surprise was excited by her arrival; farmers' wives rode on horseback then more than they do now; though, for that matter, Mrs. Lodge was not imagined to be a wife at all; the innkeeper supposed her some harum-scarum young woman who had come to at-tend "hang-fair" next day. Neither her husband nor herself ever dealt in Caster-bridge market, so that she was unknown. While dismounting she beheld a crowd of boys standing at the door of a harness-maker's shop just above the inn, looking in-side it with deep interest.

"What is going on there?" she asked of the ostler.

"Making the rope for to-morrow."

She throbbed responsively, and contracted her arm.

"'Tis sold by the inch afterwards," the man continued. "I could get you a bit, miss, for nothing, if you'd like?"

She hastily repudiated any such wish, all the more from a curious creeping feeling that the condemned wretch's destiny was becom-ing interwoven with her own; and having en-gaged a room for the night, sat down to think.

Up to this time she had formed but the vaguest notions about her means of obtaining access to the prison. The words of the cunning-man returned to her mind. He had implied that she should use her beauty, im-paired though it was, as a pass-key. In her inexperience she knew little about jail func-tionaries; she had heard of a high-sheriff and an under-sheriff, but dimly only. She knew, however, that there must be a hangman, and to the hangman she determined to apply.

VIII. *A Water-side Hermit*

AT THIS date, and for several years after, there was a hangman to almost every jail. Gertrude found, on inquiry, that the Caster-bridge official dwelt in a lonely cottage by a deep slow river flowing under the cliff on which the prison buildings were situate—the stream being the self-same one, though she did not know it, which watered the Stickle-ford and Holmstoke meads lower down in its course.

Having changed her dress, and before she had eaten or drunk—for she could not take her ease till she had ascertained some par-ticulars—Gertrude pursued her way by a path along the water-side to the cottage in-dicated. Passing thus the outskirts of the jail, she discerned on the level roof over the gateway three rectangular lines against the sky, where the specks had been moving in her distant view; she recognized what the erection was, and passed quickly on. An-other hundred yards brought her to the ex-ecutioner's house, which a boy pointed out. It stood close to the same stream, and was hard by a weir, the waters of which emitted a steady roar.

While she stood hesitating the door opened, and an old man came forth shading a candle with one hand. Locking the door on the outside, he turned to a flight of wooden steps fixed against the end of the cottage, and began to ascend them, this be-ing evidently the staircase to his bedroom. Gertrude hastened forward, but by the time she reached the foot of the ladder he was at the top. She called to him loudly enough to be heard above the roar of the weir; he looked down and said, "What d'ye want here?"

"To speak to you a minute."

The candle-light, such as it was, fell upon her imploring, pale, upturned face, and Davies (as the hangman was called) backed down the ladder. "I was just going to bed," he said; "'Early to bed and early to rise,' but I don't mind stopping a minute for such a one as you. Come into house." He reopened the door, and preceded her to the room within.

The implements of his daily work, which was that of a jobbing gardener, stood in a corner, and seeing probably that she looked rural, he said, "If you want me to undertake country work I can't come, for I never leave Casterbridge for gentle nor simple—not I. My real calling is officer of justice," he added formally.

"Yes, yes! That's it. To-morrow!"

"Ah! I thought so. Well, what's the matter about that? 'Tis no use to come here about the knot—folks do come continually, but I tell 'em one knot is as merciful as another if ye keep it under the ear. Is the unfortunate man a relation; or, I should say, perhaps" (looking at her dress) "a person who's been in your employ?"

"No. What time is the execution?"

"The same as usual—twelve o'clock, or as soon after as the London mail-coach gets in. We always wait for that, in case of a reprieve."

"O—a reprieve—I hope not!" she said involuntarily.

"Well,—hee, hee!—as a matter of business, so do I! But still, if ever a young fellow deserved to be let off, this one does; only just turned eighteen, and only present by chance when the rick was fired. Howsomever, there's not much risk of it, as they are obliged to make an example of him, there having been so much destruction of property that way lately."

"I mean," she explained, "that I want to touch him for a charm, a cure of an affliction, by the advice of a man who has proved the virtue of the remedy."

"O yes, miss! Now I understand. I've had such people come in past years. But it didn't strike me that you looked of a sort to require blood-turning. What's the complaint? The wrong kind for this, I'll be bound."

"My arm." She reluctantly showed the withered skin.

"Ah!—'tis all a-scram!" said the hangman, examining it.

"Yes," said she.

"Well," he continued, with interest, "that *is* the class o' subject, I'm bound to admit! I like the look of the wownd; it is truly as suitable for the cure as any I ever saw. 'Twas a knowing-man that sent 'ee, whoever he was."

"You can contrive for me all that's necessary?" she said breathlessly.

"You should really have gone to the governor of the jail, and your doctor with 'ee, and given your name and address—that's how it used to be done, if I recollect. Still, perhaps, I can manage it for a trifling fee."

"O, thank you! I would rather do it this way, as I should like it kept private."

"Lover not to know, eh?"

"No—husband."

"Aha! Very well. I'll get 'ee a touch of the corpse."

"Where is it now?" she said, shuddering.

"It?—*he,* you mean; he's living yet. Just inside that little small winder up there in the glum." He signified the jail on the cliff above.

She thought of her husband and her friends. "Yes, of course," she said; "and how am I to proceed?"

He took her to the door. "Now, do you be waiting at the little wicket in the wall, that you'll find up there in the lane, not later than one o'clock. I will open it from the inside, as I shan't come home to dinner till he's cut down. Good-night. Be punctual; and if you don't want anybody to know 'ee, wear a veil. Ah—once I had such a daughter as you!"

She went away, and climbed the path above, to assure herself that she would be able to find the wicket next day. Its outline was soon visible to her—a narrow opening in the outer wall of the prison precincts. The steep was so great that, having reached the wicket, she stopped a moment to breathe; and, looking back upon the water-side cot, saw the hangman again ascending his outdoor staircase. He entered the loft or chamber to which it led, and in a few minutes extinguished his light.

The town clock struck ten, and she returned to the White Hart as she had come.

IX. A Rencounter

It was one o'clock on Saturday. Gertrude Lodge, having been admitted to the jail as above described, was sitting in a waiting-room within the second gate, which stood under a classic archway of ashlar,[1] then comparatively modern, and bearing the inscription, "COVNTY JAIL: 1793." This had been the façade she saw from the heath the day before. Near at hand was a passage to the roof on which the gallows stood.

---

[1] Masonry of square hewn stones.

The town was thronged, and the market suspended; but Gertrude had seen scarcely a soul. Having kept her room till the hour of the appointment, she had proceeded to the spot by a way which avoided the open space below the cliff where the spectators had gathered; but she could, even now, hear the multitudinous babble of their voices, out of which rose at intervals the hoarse croak of a single voice uttering the words, "Last dying speech and confession!" There had been no reprieve, and the execution was over; but the crowd still waited to see the body taken down.

Soon the persistent woman heard a trampling overhead, then a hand beckoned to her, and, following directions, she went out and crossed the inner paved court beyond the gatehouse, her knees trembling so that she could scarcely walk. One of her arms was out of its sleeve, and only covered by her shawl.

On the spot at which she had now arrived were two trestles, and before she could think of their purpose she heard heavy feet descending stairs somewhere at her back. Turn her head she would not, or could not, and, rigid in this position, she was conscious of a rough coffin passing her shoulder, borne by four men. It was open, and in it lay the body of a young man, wearing the smockfrock of a rustic, and fustian breeches. The corpse had been thrown into the coffin so hastily that the skirt of the smockfrock was hanging over. The burden was temporarily deposited on the trestles.

By this time the young woman's state was such that a gray mist seemed to float before her eyes, on account of which, and the veil she wore, she could scarcely discern anything: it was as though she had nearly died, but was held up by a sort of galvanism.[2]

"Now!" said a voice close at hand, and she was just conscious that the word had been addressed to her.

By a last strenuous effort she advanced, at the same time hearing persons approaching behind her. She bared her poor curst arm; and Davies, uncovering the face of the corpse, took Gertrude's hand, and held it so that her arm lay across the dead man's neck,

[2]Electric current.

upon a line the color of an unripe blackberry, which surrounded it.

Gertrude shrieked: "the turn o' the blood," predicted by the conjuror, had taken place. But at that moment a second shriek rent the air of the enclosure: it was not Gertrude's, and its effect upon her was to make her start round.

Immediately behind her stood Rhoda Brook, her face drawn, and her eyes red with weeping. Behind Rhoda stood Gertrude's own husband; his countenance lined, his eyes dim, but without a tear.

"D—n you! what are you doing here?" he said hoarsely.

"Hussy—to come between us and our child now!" cried Rhoda. "This is the meaning of what Satan showed me in the vision! You are like her at last!" And clutching the bare arm of the younger woman, she pulled her unresistingly back against the wall. Immediately Brook had loosened her hold the fragile young Gertrude slid down against the feet of her husband. When he lifted her up she was unconscious.

The mere sight of the twain had been enough to suggest to her that the dead young man was Rhoda's son. At that time the relatives of an executed convict had the privilege of claiming the body for burial, if they chose to do so; and it was for this purpose that Lodge was awaiting the inquest with Rhoda. He had been summoned by her as soon as the young man was taken in the crime, and at different times since; and he had attended in court during the trial. This was the "holiday" he had been indulging in of late. The two wretched parents had wished to avoid exposure; and hence had come themselves for the body, a wagon and sheet for its conveyance and covering being in waiting outside.

Gertrude's case was so serious that it was deemed advisable to call to her the surgeon who was at hand. She was taken out of the jail into the town; but she never reached home alive. Her delicate vitality, sapped perhaps by the paralyzed arm, collapsed under the double shock that followed the severe strain, physical and mental, to which she had subjected herself during the previous twenty-four hours. Her blood had been "turned" indeed—too far. Her death took place in the town three days after.

Her husband was never seen in Casterbridge again; once only in the old market-place at Anglebury, which he had so much frequented, and very seldom in public anywhere. Burdened at first with moodiness and remorse, he eventually changed for the better, and appeared as a chastened and thoughtful man. Soon after attending the funeral of his poor young wife he took steps towards giving up the farms in Holmstoke and the adjoining parish, and, having sold every head of his stock, he went away to Port-Bredy, at the other end of the county, living there in solitary lodgings till his death two years later of a painless decline. It was then found that he had bequeathed the whole of his not inconsiderable property to a reformatory for boys, subject to the payment of a small annuity to Rhoda Brook, if she could be found to claim it.

For some time she could not be found; but eventually she reappeared in her old parish,—absolutely refusing, however, to have anything to do with the provision made for her. Her monotonous milking at the dairy was resumed, and followed for many long years, till her form became bent, and her once abundant dark hair white and worn away at the forehead—perhaps by long pressure against the cows. Here, sometimes, those who knew her experiences would stand and observe her, and wonder what somber thoughts were beating inside that impassive, wrinkled brow, to the rhythm of the alternating milk-streams.

HAP [1]

If but some vengeful god would call to me
From up the sky, and laugh: "Thou suffering
    thing,
Know that thy sorrow is my ecstasy,
That thy love's loss is my hate's profiting!"

Then would I bear it, clench myself, and die,
Steeled by the sense of ire unmerited;   6
Half-ease in that a Powerfuller than I
Had willed and meted me the tears I shed.

[1] The following poems are reprinted with the permission of The Macmillan Company. *Hap* and the three following pieces are from *Wessex Poems and Other Verses* (1898).

But not so. How arrives it joy lies slain,
And why unblooms the best hope ever sown?
—Crass Casualty obstructs the sun and rain,
And dicing Time for gladness casts a
    moan. . . .   12
These purblind Doomsters had as readily
    strown
Blisses about my pilgrimage as pain.

HER DEATH AND AFTER

The summons was urgent: and forth I
    went—
By the way of the Western Wall, so drear
On that winter night, and sought a gate,
     Where one, by Fate,
     Lay dying that I held dear.   5

And there, as I paused by her tenement,
And the trees shed on me their rime and hoar,
I thought of the man who had left her lone—
     Him who made her his own
     When I loved her, long before.   10

The rooms within had the piteous shine
That home-things wear when there's aught
    amiss;
From the stairway floated the rise and fall
     Of an infant's call,   14
     Whose birth had brought her to this.

Her life was the price she would pay for that
    whine—
For a child by the man she did not love.
"But let that rest for ever," I said,
     And bent my tread
     To the bedchamber above.   20

She took my hand in her thin white own,
And smiled her thanks—though nigh too
    weak—
And made them a sign to leave us there,
     Then faltered, ere
     She could bring herself to speak.   25

"Just to see you—before I go—he'll condone
Such a natural thing now my time's not
    much—
When Death is so near it hustles hence
     All passioned sense
     Between woman and man as such!   30

"My husband is absent. As heretofore
The City detains him. But, in truth,
He has not been kind. . . . I will speak no
    blame,
     But—the child is lame;
     O, I pray she may reach his ruth!   35

"Forgive past days—I can say no more—
Maybe had we wed you would now re-
pine! . . .
But I treated you ill. I was punished.
Farewell!
    —Truth shall I tell?   39
Would the child were yours and mine!

"As a wife I was true. But, such my unease
That, could I insert a deed back in Time,
I'd make her yours, to secure your care;
    And the scandal bear,
And the penalty for the crime!"   45

—When I had left, and the swinging trees
Rang above me, as lauding her candid say,
Another was I. Her words were enough:
    Came smooth, came rough,
I felt I could live my day.   50

Next night she died; and her obsequies
In the Field of Tombs where the earthworks
frowned
Had her husband's heed. His tendance
spent,
    I often went
And pondered by her mound.   55

All that year and the next year whiled,
And I still went thitherward in the gloam;
But the Town forgot her and her nook,
    And her husband took
Another Love to his home.   60

And the rumor flew that the lame lone child
Whom she wished for its safety child of
mine,
Was treated ill when offspring came
    Of the new-made dame,
And marked a more vigorous line.   65

A smarter grief within me wrought
Than even at loss of her so dear
That the being whose soul my soul suffused
    Had a child ill-used,
While I dared not interfere!   70

One eve as I stood at my spot of thought
In the white-stoned Garth,[1] brooding thus
her wrong,
Her husband neared; and to shun his nod
    By her hallowed sod
I went from the tombs among   75

[1]Enclosure.

To the Cirque of the Gladiators which
faced—
That haggard mark of Imperial Rome,
Whose Pagan echoes mock the chime
    Of our Christian time
From its hollows of chalk and loam. 80

The sun's gold touch was scarce displaced
From the vast Arena where men once bled,
When her husband followed; bowed; half-
passed
    With lip upcast;
Then halting sullenly said: 85

"It is noised that you visit my first wife's
tomb.
Now, I gave her an honored name to bear
While living, when dead. So I've claim to
ask
    By what right you task
My patience by vigiling there?   90

"There's decency even in death, I assume;
Preserve it, sir, and keep away;
For the mother of my first-born you
    Show mind undue!
—Sir, I've nothing more to say."   95

A desperate stroke discerned I then—
God pardon—or pardon not—the lie;
She had sighed that she wished (lest the child
should pine
    Of slights) 'twere mine,
So I said: "But the father I.   100

"That you thought it yours is the way of
men;
But I won her troth long ere your day:
You learned how, in dying, she summoned
me?
    'Twas in fealty.
—Sir, I've nothing more to say,   105

"Save that, if you'll hand me my little maid,
I'll take her, and rear her, and spare you toil.
Think it more than a friendly act none can;
    I'm a lonely man,
While you've a large pot to boil.   110

"If not, and you'll put it to ball or blade—
To-night, to-morrow night, anywhen—
I'll meet you here. . . . But think of it,
    And in season fit
Let me hear from you again."   115

—Well, I went away, hoping; but nought I
　　heard
Of my stroke for the child, till there greeted
　　me
A little voice that one day came
　　　　To my window-frame
And babbled innocently:　　　　　120

"My father who's not my own, sends word
I'm to stay here, sir, where I belong!"
Next a writing came: "Since the child was
　　the fruit
　　　　Of your lawless suit,
　　Pray take her, to right a wrong." 125

And I did. And I gave the child my love,
And the child loved me, and estranged us
　　none.
But compunctions loomed; for I'd harmed
　　the dead
　　　　By what I said
For the good of the living one. 　　130

—Yet though, God wot, I am sinner enough,
And unworthy the woman who drew me so,
Perhaps this wrong for her darling's good
　　　　She forgives, or would,
　　If only she could know! 　　　　135

NATURE'S QUESTION-ING

When I look forth at dawning, pool,
　　Field, flock, and lonely tree,
　　All seem to gaze at me
Like chastened children sitting silent in a
　　school;

Their faces dulled, constrained, and worn,
　　As though the master's ways 　　6
　　Through the long teaching days
Had cowed them till their early zest was
　　overborne.

Upon them stirs in lippings mere
　　(As if once clear in call, 　　10
　　But now scarce breathed at all)—
"We wonder, ever wonder, why we find us
　　here!

"Has some Vast Imbecility,
　　Mighty to build and blend,
　　But impotent to tend, 　　15
Framed us in jest, and left us now to haz-
　　ardry?

"Or come we of an Automaton
　　Unconscious of our pains? . . .
　　Or are we live remains
Of Godhead dying downwards, brain and eye
　　now gone? 　　　　20

"Or is it that some high Plan betides,
　　As yet not understood,
　　Of Evil stormed by Good,
We the Forlorn Hope over which Achieve-
　　ment strides?"

Thus things around. No answerer I. . . .
　　Meanwhile the winds, and rains, 　　26
　　And Earth's old glooms and pains
Are still the same, and Life and Death are
　　neighbors nigh.

THE SLOW NATURE
(*An Incident of Froom Valley*)

"Thy husband—poor, poor Heart!—is dead!
　　Dead, out by Moreford Rise;
A bull escaped the barton-shed,[1]
　　Gored him, and there he lies!"

—"Ha, ha—go away! 'Tis a tale, methink.
　　Thou joker Kit!" laughed she. 　　6
"I've known thee many a year, Kit Twink,
　　And ever hast thou fooled me!"

—"But, Mistress Damon—I can swear
　　Thy goodman John is dead! 　　10
And soon th'lt hear their feet who bear
　　His body to his bed."

So unwontedly sad was the merry man's
　　face—
　　That face which had long deceived—
That she gazed and gazed; and then could
　　trace 　　　　15
　　The truth there; and she believed.

She laid a hand on the dresser-ledge,
　　And scanned far Egdon-side;
And stood; and you heard the wind-swept
　　sedge
　　And the rippling Froom; till she cried: 20

"O my chamber's untidied, unmade my bed,
　　Though the day has begun to wear!
'What a slovenly hussif!'[2] it will be said,
　　When they all go up my stair!"

[1] Farmyard-shed.　　[2] Housewife.

She disappeared; and the joker stood   25
    Depressed by his neighbor's doom,
And amazed that a wife struck to widowhood
    Thought first of her unkempt room.

But a fortnight thence she could take no food,
    And she pined in a slow decay;   30
While Kit soon lost his mournful mood
    And laughed in his ancient way.

GOD-FORGOTTEN [1]

I towered far, and lo! I stood within
    The presence of the Lord Most High,
Sent thither by the sons of Earth, to win
    Some answer to their cry.

—"The Earth, sayest thou?   The Human
    race?   5
By Me created?   Sad its lot?
Nay: I have no remembrance of such place:
    Such world I fashioned not."—

—"O Lord, forgive me when I say
Thou spakest the word that made it all."—
"The Earth of men—let me bethink me. . .
    Yea!   11
    I dimly do recall

"Some tiny sphere I built long back
(Mid millions of such shapes of mine)
So named. . . It perished, surely—not a
    wrack   15
    Remaining, or a sign?

"It lost my interest from the first,
    My aims therefore succeeding ill;
Haply it died of doing as it durst?"—
    "Lord, it existeth still."   20

"Dark, then, its life!   For not a cry
    Of aught it bears do I now hear;
Of its own act the threads were snapped
    whereby
    Its plaints had reached mine ear.

"It used to ask for gifts of good,   25
    Till came its severance, self-entailed,
When sudden silence on that side ensued,
    And has till now prevailed.

"All other orbs have kept in touch;
    Their voicings reach me speedily: 30
Thy people took upon them overmuch
    In sundering them from me!

[1] This and the following two pieces are from
Poems of the Past and the Present (1901).

"And it is strange—though sad enough—
Earth's race should think that one whose
    call
Frames, daily, shining spheres of flawless
    stuff   35
    Must heed their tainted ball! . . .

"But sayest it is by pangs distraught,
    And strife, and silent suffering?—
Sore grieved am I that injury should be
    wrought
    Even on so poor a thing!   40

"Thou shouldst have learned that *Not to
    Mend*
For Me could mean but *Not to Know:*
Hence, Messengers! and straightway put an
    end
    To what men undergo." . . .

Homing at dawn, I thought to see   45
One of the Messengers standing by.
—Oh, childish thought! . . . Yet often it
    comes to me
    When trouble hovers nigh.

ON A FINE MORNING

Whence comes Solace?—Not from seeing
What is doing, suffering, being,
Not from noting Life's conditions,
Nor from heeding Time's monitions;
    But in cleaving to the Dream,   5
    And in gazing at the gleam
    Whereby gray things golden seem.

Thus do I this heyday, holding
Shadows but as lights unfolding,
As no specious show this moment   10
With its iris-hued embowment;
    But as nothing other than
    Part of a benignant plan;
    Proof that earth was made for man.

THE WELL-BELOVED

I went by star and planet shine
    Towards the dear one's home
At Kingsbere, there to make her mine
    When the next sun upclomb.

I edged the ancient hill and wood   5
    Beside the Ikling Way,
Nigh where the Pagan temple stood
    In the world's earlier day.

And as I quick and quicker walked
    On gravel and on green,   10
I sang to sky, and tree, or talked
    Of her I called my queen.

—"O faultless is her dainty form,
    And luminous her mind;
She is the God-created norm   15
    Of perfect womankind!"

A shape whereon one star-blink gleamed
    Slid softly by my side,
A woman's; and her motion seemed
    The motion of my bride.   20

And yet methought she'd drawn erstwhile
    Out from the ancient leaze,[2]
Where once were pile and peristyle
    For men's idolatries.

—"O maiden lithe and lone, what may   25
    Thy name and lineage be
Who so resemblest by this ray
    My darling?—Art thou she?"

The Shape: "Thy bride remains within
    Her father's grange and grove."   30
—"Thou speakest rightly," I broke in,
    "Thou art not she I love."

—"Nay: though thy bride remains inside
    Her father's walls," said she,
"The one most dear is with thee here,   35
    For thou dost love but me."

Then I: "But she, my only choice,
    Is now at Kingsbere Grove?"
Again her soft mysterious voice:
    "I am thy only Love."   40

Thus still she vouched, and still I said,
    "O sprite, that cannot be!" . . .
It was as if my bosom bled,
    So much she troubled me.

The sprite resumed: "Thou hast transferred
    To her dull form awhile   46
My beauty, fame, and deed, and word,
    My gestures and my smile.

"O fatuous man, this truth infer,
    Brides are not what they seem;   50
Thou lovest what thou dreamest her;
    I am thy very dream!"

_____
[2]Meadow-land, or common.

—"O then," I answered miserably,
    Speaking as scarce I knew,
"My loved one, I must wed with thee   55
    If what thou sayest be true!"

She, proudly, thinning in the gloom:
    "Though, since troth-plight began,
I have ever stood as bride to groom,
    I wed no mortal man!"   60

Thereat she vanished by the lane
    Adjoining Kingsbere town,
Near where, men say, once stood the Fane
    To Venus, on the Down.

—When I arrived and met my bride   65
    Her look was pinched and thin,
As if her soul had shrunk and died,
    And left a waste within.

THE CURATE'S
KINDNESS[1]

A Workhouse Irony

I

I thought they'd be strangers aroun' me,
    But she's to be there!
Let me jump out o' wagon and go back and
        drown me
    At Pummery or Ten-Hatches Weir.

II

I thought: "Well, I've come to the Union—
    The workhouse at last—   6
After honest hard work all the week, and
        Communion
    O' Zundays, these fifty years past.

III

" 'Tis hard; but," I thought, "never mind it:
    There's gain in the end: 10
And when I get used to the place I shall find
        it
    A home, and may find there a friend.

IV

"Life there will be better than t'other,
    For peace is assured.
*The men in one wing and their wives in an-
        other*   15
    Is strictly the rule of the Board."

_____
[1]This and the following five poems are from
Time's Laughingstocks and Other Verses (1909).

V

Just then one young Pa'son arriving
  Steps up out of breath
To the side o' the wagon wherein we were
    driving
  To Union; and calls out and saith: 20

VI

"Old folks, that harsh order is altered,
  Be not sick of heart!
The Guardians they poohed and they pished
    and they paltered
  When urged not to keep you apart.

VII

"'It is wrong,' I maintained, 'to divide them,
  Near forty years wed.'   26
'Very well, sir. We promised, then, they
    shall abide them
  In one wing together,' they said."

VIII

Then I sank—knew 'twas quite a foredone
    thing
  That misery should be   30
To the end! . . . To get freed of her there
    was the one thing
  Had made the change welcome to me.

IX

To go there was ending but badly;
  'Twas shame and 'twas pain;
"But anyhow," thought I, "thereby I shall
    gladly   35
  Get free of this forty years' chain."

X

I thought they'd be strangers aroun' me,
  But she's to be there!
Let me jump out o' wagon and go back and
    drown me
  At Pummery or Ten-Hatches Weir.   40

THE DAWN AFTER THE DANCE

Here is your parents' dwelling with its cur-
    tained windows telling
Of no thought of us within it or of our ar-
    rival here;
Their slumbers have been normal after one
    day more of formal
Matrimonial commonplace and household
    life's mechanic gear.

I would be candid willingly, but dawn draws
    on so chillingly   5
As to render further cheerlessness intolerable
    now,
So I will not stand endeavoring to declare a
    day for severing,
But will clasp you just as always—just the
    olden love avow.

Through serene and surly weather we have
    walked the ways together,
And this long night's dance this year's end
    eve now finishes the spell;   10
Yet we dreamed us but beginning a sweet
    sempiternal spinning
Of a cord we have spun to breaking—too in-
    temperately, too well.

Yes; last night we danced I know, Dear, as
    we did that year ago, Dear,
When a new strange bond between our days
    was formed, and felt, and heard;
Would that dancing were the worst thing
    from the latest to the first thing   15
That the faded year can charge us with; but
    what avails a word!

That which makes man's love the lighter and
    the woman's burn no brighter
Came to pass with us inevitably while slipped
    the shortening year. . . .
And there stands your father's dwelling with
    its blind bleak windows telling
That the vows of man and maid are frail as
    filmy gossamere.   20

MISCONCEPTION

I busied myself to find a sure
  Snug hermitage
That should preserve my Love secure
  From the world's rage;
Where no unseemly saturnals,[1]   5
  Or strident traffic-roars,
Or hum of intervolved cabals
  Should echo at her doors.

I labored that the diurnal spin
  Of vanities   10
Should not contrive to suck her in
  By dark degrees,
And cunningly operate to blur
  Sweet teachings I had begun;
And then I went full-heart to her   15
  To expound the glad deeds done.

[1]Periods of unrestrained license and revelry (from
the Roman holiday of Saturn, held in December).

She looked at me, and said thereto
　　With a pitying smile,
"And *this* is what has busied you
　　So long a while? 　　　　　　　　20
O poor exhausted one, I see
　　You have worn you old and thin
For naught! Those moils you fear for me
　　I find most pleasure in!"

THE HOMECOMING

Gruffly growled the wind on Toller down-
　　land broad and bare,
And lonesome was the house, and dark; and
　　few came there.

"Now don't ye rub your eyes so red; we're
　　home and have no cares;
Here's a skimmer-cake for supper, peckled
　　onions, and some pears;
I've got a little keg o' summat strong, too,
　　under stairs: 　　　　　　　　5
—What, slight your husband's victuals?
　　Other brides can tackle theirs!"

The wind of winter mooed and mouthed
　　their chimney like a horn,
And round the house and past the house 'twas
　　leafless and lorn,

"But my dear and tender poppet,[2] then, how
　　came ye to agree
In Ivel church this morning? Sure, there-
　　right you married me!" 　　　　10
—"Hoo-hoo!—I don't know—I forgot how
　　strange and far 'twould be,
An' I wish I was at home again with dear
　　daddee!"

Gruffly growled the wind on Toller downland
　　broad and bare,
And lonesome was the house and dark; and
　　few came there.

"I didn't think such furniture as this was all
　　you'd own, 　　　　　　　　15
And great black beams for ceiling, and a floor
　　o' wretched stone,
And nasty pewter platters, horrid forks of
　　steel and bone,
And a monstrous crock in chimney. 'Twas
　　to me quite unbeknown!"

Rattle rattle went the door; down flapped a
　　cloud of smoke,
As shifting north the wicked wind assayed a
　　smarter stroke. 　　　　　20

---

[2]Doll; dainty person; darling.

"Now sit ye by the fire, poppet; put yourself
　　at ease:
And keep your little thumb out of your
　　mouth, dear, please!
And I'll sing to 'ee a pretty song of lovely
　　flowers and bees,
And happy lovers taking walks within a
　　grove o' trees."

Gruffly growled the wind on Toller Down, so
　　bleak and bare, 　　　　　25
And lonesome was the house, and dark; and
　　few came there.

"Now, don't ye gnaw your handkercher;
　　'twill hurt your little tongue,
And if you do feel spitish, 'tis because ye
　　are over young;
But you'll be getting older, like us all, ere
　　very long,
And you'll see me as I am—a man who never
　　did 'ee wrong." 　　　　　30

Straight from Whit'sheet Hill to Benvill
　　Lane the blusters pass,
Hitting hedges, milestones, handposts, trees,
　　and tufts of grass.

"Well, had I only known, my dear, that this
　　was how you'd be,
I'd have married her of riper years that was
　　so fond of me.
But since I can't, I've half a mind to run
　　away to sea, 　　　　　　35
And leave 'ee to go barefoot to your d——d
　　daddee!"

Up one wall and down the other—past each
　　window-pane—
Prance the gusts, and then away down Crim-
　　mercrock's long lane.

"I—I—don't know what to say to 't, since
　　your wife I've vowed to be;
And as 'tis done, I s'pose here I must bide—
　　poor me! 　　　　　　　40
Aye—as you are ki-ki-kind, I'll try to live
　　along with 'ee,
Although I'd fain have stayed at home with
　　dear daddee!"

Gruffly growled the wind on Toller Down, so
　　bleak and bare,
And lonesome was the house and dark; and
　　few came there.

"That's right, my Heart! And though on
　　haunted Toller Down we be, 　　45
And the wind swears things in chimley, we'll
　　to supper merrily!"

So don't ye tap your shoe so pettish-like; but
    smile at me,
And ye'll soon forget to sock and sigh for
    dear daddee!"

TO SINCERITY

O sweet sincerity!—
Where modern methods be
What scope for thine and thee?

Life may be sad past saying,
Its greens for ever graying,   5
Its faiths to dust decaying;

And youth may have foreknown it,
And riper seasons shown it,
But custom cries: "Disown it:

"Say ye rejoice, though grieving,   10
Believe, while unbelieving,
Behold, without perceiving!"

—Yet, would men look at true things,
And unilluded view things,
And count to bear undue things,   15

The real might mend the seeming,
Facts better their foredeeming,
And Life its disesteeming.

GEORGE MEREDITH

(1828–1909)

Forty years back, when much had place
That since has perished out of mind,
I heard that voice and saw that face.

He spoke as one afoot will wind
A morning horn ere men awake;   5
His note was trenchant, turning kind.

He was of those whose wit can shake
And riddle to the very core
The counterfeits that Time will break . . .

Of late, when we two met once more,   10
The luminous countenance and rare
Shone just as forty years before.

So that, when now all tongues declare
His shape unseen by his green hill,[1]
I scarce believe he sits not there.   15

No matter. Further and further still
Through the world's vaporous vitiate air
His words wing on—as live words will.

[1] Box Hill, Surrey, where his home was.

THE FACE AT THE CASEMENT[1]

If ever joy leave
An abiding sting of sorrow,
So befell it on the morrow
    Of that May eve. . . .

The traveled sun dropped   5
To the north-west, low and lower,
The pony's trot grew slower,
    Until we stopped.

"This cozy house just by
I must call at for a minute,   10
A sick man lies within it
    Who soon will die.

"He wished to—marry me,
So I am bound, when I drive near him,
To inquire, if but to cheer him,   15
    How he may be."

A message was sent in,
And wordlessly we waited,
Till someone came and stated
    The bulletin.   20

And that the sufferer said,
For her call no words could thank her;
As his angel he must rank her
    Till life's spark fled.

Slowly we drove away,   25
When I turned my head, although not
Called to: why I turned I know not
    Even to this day:

And lo, there in my view
Pressed against an upper lattice   30
Was a white face, gazing at us
    As we withdrew.

And well did I divine
It to be the man's there dying,
Who but lately had been sighing   35
    For her pledged mine.

Then I deigned a deed of hell;
It was done before I knew it;
What devil made me do it
    I cannot tell!   40

Yes, while he gazed above,
I put my arm about her
That he might see, nor doubt her
    My plighted Love.

[1] This and the following three poems are from
Satires of Circumstance. Lyrics and Reveries
(1914).

The pale face vanished quick,　　　45
As if blasted, from the casement,
And my shame and self-abasement
　　Began their prick.

And they prick on, ceaselessly,
For that stab in Love's fierce fashion　　50
Which, unfired by lover's passion,
　　Was foreign to me.

She smiled at my caress,
But why came the soft embowment
Of her shoulder at that moment　　　55
　　She did not guess.

Long long years has he lain
In thy garth,[2] O sad Saint Cleather:
What tears there, bared to weather,
　　Will cleanse that stain!　　　60

Love is long-suffering, brave,
Sweet, prompt, precious as a jewel;
But jealousy is cruel,
　　Cruel as the grave!

LOST LOVE

I play my sweet old airs—
　　The airs he knew
　　When our love was true—
But he does not balk
　　His determined walk,　　　5
And passes up the stairs.

I sing my songs once more,
　　And presently hear
　　His footstep near
As if it would stay;　　　10
　　But he goes his way,
And shuts a distant door.

So I wait for another morn,
　　And another night
　　In this soul-sick blight;　　　15
And I wonder much
　　As I sit, why such
A woman as I was born!

AH, ARE YOU DIGGING ON MY GRAVE?

"Ah, are you digging on my grave
　　My loved one?—planting rue?"
—"No: yesterday he went to wed
One of the brightest wealth has bred.
It cannot hurt her now, he said,　　5
　　'That I should not be true.'"

"Then who is digging on my grave?
　　My nearest dearest kin?"
—"Ah, no: they sit and think, 'What use!
What good will planting flowers produce?　　10
No tendance of her mound can loose
　　Her spirit from Death's gin.'"

"But someone digs upon my grave?
　　My enemy?—prodding sly?"
—"Nay: when she heard you had passed the
　　Gate　　　15
That shuts on all flesh soon or late,
She thought you no more worth her hate,
　　And cares not where you lie."

"Then, who is digging on my grave?
　　Say—since I have not guessed!"　　20
—"Oh it is I, my mistress dear,
Your little dog, who still lives near,
And much I hope my movements here
　　Have not disturbed your rest?"

"Ah, yes! *You* dig upon my grave . . .　25
　　Why flashed it not on me
That one true heart was left behind!
What feeling do we ever find
To equal among human kind
　　A dog's fidelity!"　　　30

"Mistress, I dug upon your grave
　　To bury a bone, in case
I should be hungry near this spot
When passing on my daily trot.
I am sorry, but I quite forgot　　　35
　　It was your resting-place."

THE SWEET HUSSY

In his early days he was quite surprised
When she told him she was compromised
By meetings and lingerings at his whim,
And thinking not of herself but him;
While she lifted orbs aggrieved and round　5
That scandal should so soon abound
(As she had raised them to nine or ten
Of antecedent nice young men):
And in remorse he thought with a sigh,
How good she is, and how bad am I!—　　10
It was years before he understood
That she was the wicked one—he the good.

YOU WERE THE SORT THAT MEN FORGET[1]

You were the sort that men forget;
　　Though I—not yet!—
Perhaps not ever. Your slighted weakness
　　Adds to the strength of my regret!

---

[2] Yard.

[1] This and the following poems are from *Moments of Vision and Miscellaneous Verses* (1918).

You'd not the art—you never had   5
  For good or bad—
To make men see how sweet your meaning,
Which, visible, had charmed them glad.

You would, by words inept let fall,
  Offend them all,   10
Even if they saw your warm devotion
Would hold your life's blood at their call.

You lacked the eye to understand
  Those friends offhand
Whose mode was crude, though whose dim
    purport   15
Outpriced the courtesies of the bland.

I am now the only being who
  Remembers you
It may be.   What a waste that Nature
Grudged soul so dear the art its due!   20

TO THE MOON

"What have you looked at, Moon,
  In your time,
Now long past your prime?"
"O, I have looked at, often looked at
  Sweet, sublime,   5
Sore things, shudderful, night and noon
  In my time."

"What have you mused on, Moon,
  In your day,
So aloof, so far away?"   10
"O, I have mused on, often mused on
  Growth, decay,
Nations alive, dead, mad, aswoon,
  In my day!"

"Have you much wondered, Moon,   15
  On your rounds,
Self-wrapt, beyond Earth's bounds?"
"Yea, I have wondered, often wondered
  At the sounds
Reaching me of the human tune   20
  On my rounds."

"What do you think of it, Moon,
  As you go?
Is Life much or no?"
"O, I think of it, often think of it   25
  As a show
God ought surely to shut up soon,
  As I go."

THE STATUE OF LIBERTY

This statue of Liberty, busy man,
  Here erect in the city square,
I have watched while your scrubbings, this
    early morning,
  Strangely wistful,
  And half tristful,   5
Have turned her from foul to fair;

With your bucket of water, and mop, and
    brush,
  Bringing her out of the grime
That has smeared her during the smokes of
    winter
  With such glumness   10
  In her dumbness,
And aged her before her time.

You have washed her down with motherly
    care—
  Head, shoulders, arm, and foot,
To the very hem of the robes that drape
    her—   15
  All expertly
  And alertly,
Till a long stream, black with soot,

Flows over the pavement to the road,
  And her shape looms pure as snow: 20
I read you are hired by the City guardians—
  May be yearly,
  Or once merely—
To treat the statues so?

"Oh, I'm not hired by the Councilmen   25
  To cleanse the statues here.
I do this one as a self-willed duty,
  Not as paid to,
  Or at all made to,
But because the doing is dear."   30

Ah, then I hail you brother and friend!
  Liberty's knight divine.
What you have done would have been my
    doing,
  Yea, most verily,
  Well, and thoroughly,   35
Had but your courage been mine!

"Oh I care not for Liberty's mold,
  Liberty charms not me;
What's Freedom but an idler's vision,
  Vain, pernicious,   40
  Often vicious,
Of things that cannot be!

"Memory it is that brings me to this—
Of a daughter—my one sweet own.
She grew a famous carver's model,　　　45
　　One of the fairest
　　And of the rarest:—
　　She sat for the figure as shown.

"But alas, she died in this distant place
　　Before I was warned to betake　　50
Myself to her side! . . . And in love of my
　　　darling,
　　In love of the fame of her,
　　And the good name of her,
　　I do this for her sake."

Answer I gave not.　Of that form　　55
　　The carver was I at his side;
His child, my model, held so saintly,
　　Grand in feature,
　　Gross in nature,
　　In the dens of vice had died.　　60

LIFE LAUGHS ONWARD

Rambling I looked for an old abode
Where, years back, one had lived I knew;
Its site a dwelling duly showed,
　　But it was new.

I went where, not so long ago,　　　5
The sod had riven two breasts asunder;
Daisies throve gayly there, as though
　　No grave were under.

I walked along a terrace where
Loud children gamboled in the sun;　　10
The figure that had once sat there
　　Was missed by none.

Life laughed and moved on unsubdued,
I saw that Old succumbed to Young:
'Twas well.　My too regretful mood　　15
　　Died on my tongue.

RUDYARD KIPLING

1865-1936

Rudyard Kipling was born on 30 December, 1865, at Bombay, India, where his father held a professorship in a school of art established by the British government. Both of Rudyard's grandfathers were Wesleyan ministers; on the mother's side he was also a cousin of Stanley Baldwin and a nephew, by marriage, of Sir Edward Burne-Jones, the Pre-Raphaelite painter. At the age of six he was taken to England, where his parents, on their return to India, left him to be brought up in an evangelical household; but the advantages of climate and instruction which it was intended that this measure should give the child were offset by the bigotry and unkindness of the people with whom he lived; he was happy only while spending vacations at the Grange, the home of Burne-Jones. In 1878 Kipling was transferred to an excellent boarding school then recently set up near Bideford—the United Services College—largely filled with the sons of army officers of small means; the four years spent here he later recorded in *Stalky and Co.* The school was as close as he ever came to an academic education, for in 1882, at the age of sixteen, he returned to India to become a journalist, first at Bombay and later at Allahabad; in this employment he gained a thorough knowledge of Indian life and entered upon a literary career. From material contributed to newspapers he collected a book of poems, *Departmental Ditties* (1886); another in prose, *Plain Tales from the Hills* (1888); and several small paperbound volumes which were sold at stalls in the Indian railway stations. The success of his books induced the ambitious young writer to abandon colonial journalism; although he was only twenty-three when he reached London in 1889, his reputation had preceded him; he was received as a man of letters who had already made his mark.

During the next few years Kipling wrote *The Light That Failed* and *Barrack-Room Ballads;* with his earnings he was able to travel extensively in various parts of the British Empire; and in 1892 he married Caroline Bal-

estier, the sister of an American friend of his who had recently died. The young couple settled in the United States, not far from Brattleboro, Vermont; here, on a piece of hillside land, they built a large house which they intended to make their permanent home; here Kipling wrote the two *Jungle Books* and *Captains Courageous;* here, unfortunately, he entered into a quarrel with Beatty Balestier, a devil-may-care brother-in-law. In 1896, after a meeting which left him with the impression that Balestier had threatened his life, Kipling instituted legal proceedings; but the publicity which attended the first hearing was so repugnant to him that he dropped the case and abruptly left Vermont, never to return. The defeat which he had suffered at the hands of his American relative undoubtedly explains some of his later bitterness against the "frank, brutal decivilization" of the United States. After 1896 he and his wife established themselves in England, eventually purchasing a seventeenth-century stone farmhouse, called Bateman's, at Burwash in Sussex; they usually passed the summer months near Cape Town in South Africa, where they were neighbors of Cecil Rhodes. In a journalistic capacity Kipling saw some of the fighting in the Boer War (1899–1902); henceforth he neglected no opportunity to defend both the aims and the methods of British imperialism. A son, one of several children, was killed early in the Great War. From the beginning of the century until his death on 18 January, 1936, Kipling's life was chiefly distinguished by his success as a man of letters. He received the Nobel Prize for literature in 1907. Of his later books the most important are *Kim* (1901), *Just So Stories* (1902), *Traffics and Discoveries* (1904), *Puck of Pook's Hill* (1906), and *Rewards and Fairies* (1910).

When Kipling speaks of Browning's Fra Lippo Lippi as "a not too remote . . . ancestor of mine," he is acknowledging the naturalism, or desire to give a bold, unvarnished picture of the natural world, which characterizes much of his own work. With this self-assertive masculinity he combines another element which was equally fitted to make him popular: an ability to express the democratic and imperialistic ideals of the generation of Anglo-Saxons for which he wrote. "When to Kipling's instinctive utterance of the popular needs are added his wit and dramatic power, his skill in telling a story, his mastery of the clinging epithet, his pulsating language and sturdy rhythms, it is easy to understand his immense vogue. The limitations that debar him from ranking with the truly great poets of England and the world are again inherent in the people for whom he writes—limitations which the master singers were able to transcend while still retaining the strength of the national character. . . . Righteousness that rules in the hurly-burly of a contentious life, he knows and celebrates; but of that other spirit that turns from the passion and toil of existence as from a wasteful illusion, and whose eyes are set on solitude and a triumph of peace beyond earthly victories, there is in Kipling hardly a breath" (Paul Elmer More, *Shelburne Essays,* Second Series, p. 112).

In 1937 Macmillan and Co., Ltd., London, began publication of the "Sussex Edition" of Kipling's *Complete Works in Prose and Verse,* 35 vols. This may remain the definitive edition, but it is too expensive for most readers and even for most public or university libraries. Kipling's books are published in the U. S. by Doubleday, Doran and Co. The best edition of the poems is *Rudyard Kipling's Verse, Inclusive Edition, 1885–1932* (New York, 1934). Kipling himself supplies the best sketch of his life in the autobiographical fragment *Something of Myself for My Friends Known and Unknown* (New York, 1937); for the years which he spent in the United States this must be supplemented with Frederic F. Van de Water's *Rudyard Kipling's Vermont Feud* (New York, 1937).

Three helpful books may be mentioned: *A Handbook to the Poetry of Rudyard Kipling,* by Ralph Durand (New York, 1914); *Rudyard Kipling, A Critical Study,* by Holbrook Jackson (London, 1914); and *Rudyard Kipling; A study in Literature and Political Ideas,* by Edward B. Shanks (London, 1940). In recent years more essays or studies concerning Kipling have been written by foreign critics than by Englishmen or Americans. One of the best of these has been translated—see *Prophets and Poets* by André Maurois (New York, 1935). There is a useful essay by Lionel Stevenson, "The Ideas in Kipling's Poetry," in *The University of Toronto Quarterly* (Vol. I, 1932).

TOMLINSON[1]

1891

Now Tomlinson gave up the ghost in his
    house in Berkeley Square,
And a Spirit came to his bedside and gripped
    him by the hair—
A Spirit gripped him by the hair and carried
    him far away,
Till he heard as the roar of a rain-fed ford
    the roar of the Milky Way:
Till he heard the roar of the Milky Way die
    down and drone and cease,   5
And they came to the Gate within the Wall
    where Peter holds the keys.
"Stand up, stand up now, Tomlinson, and
    answer loud and high
The good that ye did for the sake of men or
    ever ye came to die—
The good that ye did for the sake of men on
    little earth so lone!"
And the naked soul of Tomlinson grew white
    as a rain-washed bone.   10

---

[1]This and the following six poems are reprinted by permission of Mrs. Kipling and of Doubleday, Doran and Company.

"Oh I have a friend on earth," he said, "that
    was my priest and guide,
And well would he answer all for me if he
    were at my side."
—"For that ye strove in neighbor-love it shall
    be written fair,
But now ye wait at Heaven's Gate and not in
    Berkeley Square:
Though we called your friend from his bed
    this night, he could not speak for you, 15
For the race is run by one and one and never
    by two and two."
Then Tomlinson looked up and down, and
    little gain was there,
For the naked stars grinned overhead, and he
    saw that his soul was bare.
The Wind that blows between the Worlds, it
    cut him like a knife,
And Tomlinson took up the tale and spoke of
    his good in life.   20
"O this I have read in a book," he said, "and
    that was told to me,
And this I have thought that another man
    thought of a Prince in Muscovy."
The good souls flocked like homing doves and
    bade him clear the path,

And Peter twirled the jangling Keys in weariness and wrath.
"Ye have read, ye have heard, ye have thought," he said, "and the tale is yet to run: 25
By the worth of the body that once ye had, give answer—what ha' ye done?"
Then Tomlinson looked back and forth, and little good it bore,
For the darkness stayed at his shoulder-blade and Heaven's Gate before :—
"O this I have felt, and this I have guessed, and this I have heard men say,
And this they wrote that another man wrote of a carl[2] in Norroway."   30
"Ye have read, ye have felt, ye have guessed, good lack! Ye have hampered Heaven's Gate;
There's little room between the stars in idleness to prate!
O none may reach by hired speech of neighbor, priest, and kin
Through borrowed deed to God's good meed that lies so fair within;
Get hence, get hence to the Lord of Wrong, for the doom has yet to run,   35
And . . . the faith that ye share with Berkeley Square uphold you, Tomlinson!"

.   .   .   .

The Spirit gripped him by the hair, and sun by sun they fell
Till they came to the belt of Naughty Stars that rim the mouth of Hell.
The first are red with pride and wrath, the next are white with pain,
But the third are black with clinkered sins[3] that cannot burn again :   40
They may hold their path, they may leave their path, with never a soul to mark,
They may burn or freeze, but they must not cease in the Scorn of the Outer Dark.
The Wind that blows between the Worlds, it nipped him to the bone,
And he yearned to the flare of Hell-gate there as the light of his own hearthstone.
The Devil he sat behind the bars, where the desperate legions drew,   45
But he caught the hasting Tomlinson and would not let him through.
"Wot ye the price of good pit-coal that I must pay?" said he,
"That ye rank yoursel' so fit for Hell and ask no leave of me?

---

[2] A base fellow.

[3] Sins left over like slag from burned coal.

I am all o'er-sib[4] to Adam's breed that ye should give me scorn,
For I strove with God for your First Father the day that he was born.   50
Sit down, sit down upon the slag, and answer loud and high
The harm that ye did to the Sons of Men or ever you came to die."
And Tomlinson looked up and up, and saw against the night
The belly of a tortured star blood-red in Hell-Mouth light;
And Tomlinson looked down and down, and saw beneath his feet   55
The frontlet of a tortured star milk-white in Hell-Mouth heat.
"O I had a love on earth," said he, "that kissed me to my fall;
And if ye would call my love to me I know she would answer all."
—"All that ye did in love forbid it shall be written fair,
But now ye wait at Hell-Mouth Gate and not in Berkeley Square :   60
Though we whistled your love from her bed to-night, I trow she would not run,
For the sin ye do by two and two ye must pay for one by one!"
The Wind that blows between the Worlds, it cut him like a knife,
And Tomlinson took up the tale and spake of his sins in life :—
"Once I ha' laughed at the power of Love and twice at the grip of the Grave,   65
And thrice I ha' patted my God on the head that men might call me brave."
The Devil he blew on a brandered soul and set it aside to cool :—
"Do ye think I would waste my good pit-coal on the hide of a brain-sick fool?
I see no worth in the hobnailed mirth or the jolthead jest ye did
That I should waken my gentlemen that are sleeping three on a grid."   70
Then Tomlinson looked back and forth, and there was little grace.
For Hell-Gate filled the houseless soul with the Fear of Naked Space.
"Nay, this I ha' heard," quo' Tomlinson, "and this was noised abroad,
And this I ha' got from a Belgian book on the word of a dead French lord."
—"Ye ha' heard, ye ha' read, ye ha' got, good lack! and the tale begins afresh—   75
Have ye sinned one sin for the pride o' the eye or the sinful lust of the flesh?"

---

[4] All too closely akin.

Then Tomlinson he gripped the bars and
    yammered, "Let me in—
"For I mind that I borrowed my neighbor's
    wife to sin the deadly sin."
The Devil he grinned behind the bars, and
    banked the fires high:
"Did ye read of that sin in a book?" said he;
    and Tomlinson said, "Ay!"   80
The Devil he blew upon his nails, and the
    little devils ran,
And he said: "Go husk this whimpering thief
    that comes in the guise of a man:
Winnow him out 'twixt star and star, and
    sieve his proper worth:
There's sore decline in Adam's line if this be
    spawn of earth."
Empusa's[5] crew, so naked-new they may not
    face the fire,   85
But weep that they bin too small to sin to the
    height of their desire,
Over the coal they chased the Soul, and
    racked it all abroad,
As children rifle a caddis-case or the raven's
    foolish hoard
And back they came with the tattered Thing,
    as children after play,
And they said: "The soul that he got from
    God he has bartered clean away.   90
We have threshed a stook[6] of print and book,
    and winnowed a chattering wind,
And many a soul wherefrom he stole, but his
    we cannot find.
We have handled him, we have dandled him,
    we have seared him to the bone,
And Sire, if tooth and nail show truth he has
    no soul of his own."
The Devil he bowed his head on his breast
    and rumbled deep and low:—   95
"I'm all o'er-sib to Adam's breed that I
    should bid him go.
Yet close we lie, and deep we lie, and if I
    gave him place,
My gentlemen that are so proud would flout
    me to my face;
They'd call my house a common stews and
    me a careless host,
And—I would not anger my gentlemen for
    the sake of a shiftless ghost."   100
The Devil he looked at the mangled Soul that
    prayed to feel the flame,
And he thought of Holy Charity, but he
    thought of his own good name:—
"Now ye could haste my coal to waste, and
    sit ye down to fry.

Did ye think of that theft for yourself?" said
    he; and Tomlinson said, "Ay!"
The Devil he blew an outward breath, for his
    heart was free from care:—   105
"Ye have scarce the soul of a louse," he said,
    "but the roots of sin are there.
And for that sin should ye come in were I the
    lord alone.
But sinful pride has rule inside—ay, mightier
    than my own.
Honor and Wit, fore-damned they sit, to each
    his Priest and Whore;
Nay scarce I dare myself go there, and you
    they'd torture sore.   110
Ye are neither spirit nor spirk," he said; "ye
    are neither book nor brute—
Go, get ye back to the flesh again for the sake
    of Man's repute.
I'm all o'er-sib to Adam's breed that I should
    mock your pain,
But look that ye win to worthier sin ere ye
    come back again.
Get hence, the hearse is at your door—the
    grim black stallions wait—   115
They bear your clay to place to-day. Speed,
    lest ye come too late!
Go back to Earth with a lip unsealed—go
    back with an open eye,
And carry my word to the Sons of Men or
    ever ye come to die:
That the sin they do by two and two they
    must pay for one by one,
And . . . the God that you took from a printed
    book be with you, Tomlinson!"   120

TOMMY[1]

I went into a public-'ouse to get a pint o' beer,
The publican 'e up an' sez, "We serve no red-
    coats here."
The girls be'ind the bar they laughed an'
    giggled fit to die,
I outs into the street again an' to myself sez I:
    O it's Tommy this, an' Tommy that, an'
    "Tommy, go away";   5
    But it's "Thank you, Mister Atkins," when
    the band begins to play—
    The band begins to play, my boys, the band
    begins to play,
    O it's "Thank you, Mister Atkins," when
    the band begins to play.

I went into a theater as sober as could be,
They gave a drunk civilian room, but 'adn't
    none for me;   10

---

[5] In classical mythology a monstrous creature,
reputed to devour human beings.
[6] Shock.

[1] This and the three following poems were published in *Barrack-Room Ballads* (1892).

They sent me to the gallery or round the
    music-'alls,
But when it comes to fightin', Lord! they'll
    shove me in the stalls!
    For it's Tommy this, an' Tommy that, an'
      "Tommy, wait outside";
    But it's "Special train for Atkins" when
      the trooper's on the tide—
    The troopship's on the tide, my boys, the
      troopship's on the tide,   15
    O it's "Special Train for Atkins" when the
      trooper's on the tide.

Yes, makin' mock o' uniforms that guard you
    while you sleep
Is cheaper than them uniforms, an' they're
    starvation cheap;
An' hustlin' drunken soldiers when they're
    goin' large a bit
Is five times better business the paradin' in
    full kit.   20
    Then it's Tommy this, an' Tommy that, an'
      "Tommy, 'ow's yer soul?"
    But it's "Thin red line of 'eroes" when the
      drums begin to roll—
    The drums begin to roll, my boys, the
      drums begin to roll,
    O it's "Thin red line of 'eroes" when the
      drums begin to roll.

We aren't no thin red 'eroes, nor we aren't no
    blackguards too,   25
But single men in barricks, most remarkable
    like you;
An' if sometimes our conduck isn't all your
    fancy paints;
Why, single men in barricks don't grow into
    plaster saints;
    While it's Tommy this, an' Tommy that,
      an' "Tommy, fall be'ind,"
    But it's "Please to walk in front, sir," when
      there's trouble in the wind,   30
    There's trouble in the wind, my boys,
      there's trouble in the wind,
    O it's "Please to walk in front, sir," when
      there's trouble in the wind.

You talk o' better food for us, an' schools, an'
    fires, an' all:
We'll wait for extry rations if you treat us
    rational.
Don't mess about the cook-room slops, but
    prove it to our face   35
The Widow's Uniform is not the soldier-
    man's disgrace.

For it's Tommy this, an' Tommy that, an'
    "Chuck him out, the brute!"
But it's "Savior of 'is country" when the
    guns begin to shoot;
An' it's Tommy this, an' Tommy that, an'
    anything you please;
An' Tommy ain't a bloomin' fool—you bet
    that Tommy sees!   40

"FUZZY-WUZZY"

(*Sudan Expeditionary Force*)

We've fought with many men acrost the seas,
    An' some of 'em was brave an' some was
      not:
The Paythan an' the Zulu an' Burmese;
    But the Fuzzy was the finest o' the lot.
We never got a ha'porth's[1] change of 'im: 5
    'E squatted in the scrub an' 'ocked our
      'orses,[2]
'E cut our sentries up at Sua*kim,*
    An' 'e played the cat an' banjo with our
      forces.
    So 'ere's *to* you, Fuzzy-Wuzzy, at your
      'ome in the Sudan;
    You're a pore benighted 'eathen but a
      first-class fightin' man;   10
    We gives you your certificate, an' if you
      want it signed
    We'll come an' 'ave a romp with you
      whenever you're inclined.

We took our chanst among the Kyber 'ills,
    The Boers knocked us silly at a mile,
The Burman give us Irriwaddy chills,   15
    An' a Zulu *impi*[3] dished us up in style:
But all we ever got from such as they
    Was pop to what the Fuzzy made us
      swaller;
We 'eld our bloomin' own, the papers say,
    But man for man the Fuzzy knocked us
      'oller.   20
    Then 'ere's *to* you, Fuzzy-Wuzzy, an'
      the missis and the kid;
    Our orders was to break you, an' of
      course we went an' did.
    We sloshed you with Martinis, an' it
      wasn't 'ardly fair;
    But for all the odds agin' you, Fuzzy-
      Wuz, you broke the square.

---

[1] A halfpenny worth's.

[2] Cut the tendons in the hocks, or joints in the
middle of the hind legs, of our horses.

[3] Body of warriors.

'E 'asn't got no papers of 'is own,　25
'E 'asn't got no medals nor rewards,
So *we* must certify the skill 'e's shown,
In usin' of 'is long two-'anded swords:
When 'e's 'oppin' in an' out among the bush
　With 'is coffin-'eaded shield an' shovel-
　　spear,　30
An 'appy day with Fuzzy on the rush
　Will last an 'ealthy Tommy for a year.
　　So 'ere's *to* you, Fuzzy-Wuzzy, an' your
　　　friends which are no more,
　　If we 'adn't lost some messmates we
　　　would 'elp you to deplore.
　　But give an' take's the gospel, an' we'll
　　　call the bargain fair,　35
　　For if you 'ave lost more than us, you
　　　crumpled up the square!

'E rushes at the smoke when we let drive,
　An', before we know, 'e's 'ackin' at our
　　'ead;
'E's all 'ot sand an' ginger when alive,
　An' 'e's generally shammin' when 'e's dead.
'E's a daisy, 'e's a ducky, 'e's a lamb!　41
'E's a injia-rubber idiot on the spree,
'E's the on'y thing that doesn't give a damn
　For a Regiment o' British Infantree!
　　So 'ere's *to* you, Fuzzy-Wuzzy, at your
　　　'ome in the Sudan;　45
　　You're a pore benighted 'eathen but a
　　　first-class fightin' man;
　　An' 'ere's *to* you, Fuzzy-Wuzzy, with
　　　your 'ayrick 'ead of 'air—
　　You big black boundin' beggar—for you
　　　broke a British square!

GUNGA DIN

You may talk o' gin and beer
When you're quartered safe out 'ere,
An' you're sent to penny-fights an' Aldershot
　it;
But when it comes to slaughter
You will do your work on water,　5
An' you'll lick the bloomin' boots of 'im that's
　got it.
Now in Injia's sunny clime,
　Where I used to spend my time
A-servin' of 'Er Majesty the Queen,
Of all them blackfaced crew　10
　The finest man I knew
Was our regimental bhisti,[1] Gunga Din.

---

[1]Water-carrier.

He was "Din! Din! Din!
You limpin' lump o' brick-dust, **Gunga
　Din!**
　Hi! Slippy *hitherao!*　15
　Water, get it!　*Panee lao*[2]
You squidgy-nosed old idol, Gunga Din."

The uniform 'e wore
Was nothin' much before,
An' rather less than 'arf o' that be'ind,　20
For a piece o' twisty rag
An' a goatskin water-bag
Was all the field-equipment 'e could find.
When the sweatin' troop-train lay
In a sidin' through the day,　25
Where the 'eat would make your bloomin'
　eyebrows crawl,
We shouted "Harry By!"[3]
Till our throats were bricky-dry,
Then we wopped 'im 'cause 'e couldn't serve
　us all.
　　It was "Din! Din! Din!　30
　You 'eathen, where the mischief 'ave you
　　been?
　　You put some *juldee*[4] in it
　　Or I'll *marrow*[5] you this minute
　If you don't fill up my helmet, Gunga
　　Din!"

'E would dot an' carry one　35
Till the longest day was done;
An' 'e didn't seem to know the use o' fear.
If we charged or broke or cut,
You could bet your bloomin' nut,
'E'd be waitin' fifty paces right flank rear.　40
With 'is mussick[6] on 'is back,
'E would skip with our attack,
An' watch us till the bugles made "Retire"
An' for all 'is dirty 'ide
'E was white, clear white, inside　45
When 'e went to tend the wounded under
　fire!
　　It was "Din! Din! Din!"
　With the bullets kickin' dust-spots on the
　　green
　　When the cartridges ran out,
　　You could hear the front ranks shout,　50
　"Hi! ammunition-mules an' Gunga Din!"

I sha'n't forget the night
When I dropped be'ind the fight
With a bullet where my belt-plate should 'a'
　been.

---

[2]Bring water quickly.　[3]O Brother!
[4]Be quick.　[5]Hit you.　[6]Water-skin.

I was chokin' mad with thirst, 55
An' the man that spied me first
Was our good old grinnin', gruntin' Gunga
Din.
'E lifted up my 'ead,
An' he plugged me where I bled,
An' 'e guv me 'arf-a-pint o' water green. 60
It was crawlin' and it stunk,
But of all the drinks I've drunk,
I'm gratefullest to one from Gunga Din.
It was "Din! Din! Din!
'Ere's a beggar with a bullet through 'is
spleen; 65
'E's chawin' up the ground,
An' 'e's kickin' all around:
For Gawd's sake git the water, Gunga
Din!"

'E carried me away
To where a dooli[7] lay, 70
An' a bullet came an' drilled the beggar clean.
'E put me safe inside,
An' just before 'e died,
"I 'ope you liked your drink," sez Gunga Din.
So I'll meet 'im later on 75
At the place where 'e is gone—
Where it's always double drill and no canteen.
'E'll be squattin' on the coals
Givin' drink to poor damned souls,
An' I'll get a swig in hell from Gunga Din! 80
Yes, Din! Din! Din!
You Lazarushian-leather Gunga Din!
Though I've belted you and flayed you,
By the livin' Gawd that made you,
You're a better man than I am, Gunga
Din! 85

MANDALAY[1]

By the old Moulmein[2] Pagoda, lookin' east-
ward to the sea,
There's a Burma girl a-settin', and I know
she thinks o' me;
For the wind is in the palm-trees, and the
temple-bells they say:
"Come you back, you British soldier; come
you back to Mandalay!"
Come you back to Mandalay, 5
Where the old Flotilla lay:

---

[7]Litter used in carrying wounded.

[1]Mandalay is the capital of Upper Burma, whose
ruler, Theebaw, provoked hostilities with the British
in 1885. As a result of the expedition sent against
him his country was annexed to India in the following year.

[2]Moulmein and Rangoon are seaports in Lower
Burma.

Can't you 'ear their paddles chunkin'
from Rangoon to Mandalay?
On the road to Mandalay,
Where the flyin'-fishes play,
An' the dawn comes up like thunder
outer China 'crost the Bay! 10

'Er petticoat was yaller an' 'er little cap was
green,
An' 'er name was Supi-yaw-lat—jes' the
same as Theebaw's Queen,
An' I seed her first a-smokin' of a whackin'
white cheroot,
An' a-wastin' Christian kisses on an 'eathen
idol's foot:
Bloomin' idol made o' mud— 15
Wot they called the Great Gawd
Budd—
Plucky lot she cared for idols when
I kissed 'er where she stud!
On the road to Mandalay . . .

When the mist was on the rice-fields an' the
sun was droppin' slow,
She'd git 'er little banjo an' she'd sing
"*Kulla-lo-lo!*" 20
With 'er arm upon my shoulder an' 'er cheek
agin my cheek
We useter watch the steamers an' the *hathis*
pilin' teak.
Elephints a-pilin' teak
In the sludgy, squdgy creek,
Where the silence 'ung that 'eavy
you was 'arf afraid to speak! 25
On the road to Mandalay . . .

But that's all shove be'ind me—long ago an'
fur away,
An' there ain't no 'busses runnin' from the
Bank to Mandalay;
An' I'm learnin' 'ere in London what the ten-
year soldier tells:
"If you've 'eard the East a-callin', you won't
never 'eed naught else." 30
No! you won't 'eed nothin' else
But them spicy garlic smells,
An' the sunshine an' the palm-trees
an' the tinkly temple-bells;
On the road to Mandalay . . .

I am sick o' wastin' leather on these gritty
pavin'-stones, 35
An' the blasted Henglish drizzle wakes the
fever in my bones;
'Tho' I walks with fifty 'ousemaids outer
Chelsea to the Strand,
An' they talks a lot o' lovin', but wot do they
understand?

Beefy face an' grubby 'and—
Law! wot do they understand? 40
I've a neater, sweeter maiden in a
　　cleaner, greener land!
On the road to Mandalay . . .

Ship me somewheres east of Suez, where the
　　best is like the worst,
Where there aren't no Ten Commandments
　　an' a man can raise a thirst;
For the temple-bells are callin', an' it's there
　　that I would be— 45
By the old Moulmein Pagoda, looking lazy at
　　the sea;
　　　　On the road to Mandalay,
　　　　Where the old Flotilla lay,
　　　　With our sick beneath the awnings
　　　　　　when we went to Mandalay!
　　　　On the road to Mandalay, 50
　　　　Where the flyin'-fishes play,
　　　　An' the dawn comes up like thunder
　　　　　　outer China 'crost the Bay!

RECESSIONAL

1897

God of our fathers, known of old,
　　Lord of our far-flung battle-line,
Beneath whose awful Hand we hold
　　Dominion over palm and pine—
Lord God of Hosts, be with us yet, 5
Lest we forget—lest we forget!

The tumult and the shouting dies;
　　The Captains and the Kings depart:
Still stands Thine ancient sacrifice,
　　An humble and a contrite heart. 10
Lord God of Hosts, be with us yet,
Lest we forget—lest we forget!

Far-called, our navies melt away;
　　On dune and headland sinks the fire:
Lo, all our pomp of yesterday 15
　　Is one with Nineveh and Tyre!
Judge of the Nations, spare us yet,
Lest we forget—lest we forget!

If, drunk with sight of power, we loose
　　Wild tongues that have not Thee in awe, 20
Such boastings as the Gentiles use,
　　Or lesser breeds without the Law—
Lord God of Hosts, be with us yet,
Lest we forget—lest we forget!

For heathen heart that puts her trust 25
　　In reeking tube and iron shard,[1]
All valiant dust that builds on dust,
　　And guarding, calls not Thee to guard,
For frantic boast and foolish word—
Thy mercy on Thy People, Lord! 30

WHEN 'OMER SMOTE 'IS BLOOMIN' LYRE

When 'Omer smote 'is bloomin' lyre,
　　He'd 'eard men sing by land an' sea;
An' what he thought 'e might require,
　　'E went an' took—the same as me!

The market-girls an' fishermen, 5
　　The shepherds an' the sailors, too,
They 'eard old songs turn up again,
　　But kep' it quiet—same as you!

They knew 'e stole; 'e knew they knowed.
　　They didn't tell, nor make a fuss, 10
But winked at 'Omer down the road,
　　An' 'e winked back—the same as us!

[1] In gun and bullet.

ALFRED EDWARD HOUSMAN

1859-1936

Not Shropshire, as it might be supposed, but Worcestershire was the county in which A. E. Housman was born on 26 March, 1859. He was the eldest of seven children, and the others remembered his affectionate leadership long after he had left them. He received his early education at the near-by Bromsgrove School, where he showed unusual ability both as a student and as a versifier. After winning most of the prizes for which he was eligible in his last year at the school, he entered St. John's College, Oxford, in the autumn of 1877. Everything promised well for his career at the University, and the letters written home at the beginning of his residence there show that he was happy and interested in a variety of subjects; but a gloomy reticence seems later to have settled upon him. At the same time he began to concentrate on the study of Greek and Latin poetry, neglecting less attractive curricular requirements. In 1881, when faced with Greats, the examinations on which all depended, he was able to answer half of the questions brilliantly, but failed to write any answers for the questions in history and philosophy which he knew he could not answer well. As a result he did not receive a degree. For a short time he taught at Bromsgrove and then, from 1882 to 1892, served as a clerk in Her Majesty's Patent Office in London.

This has been called Housman's period in purgatory: acutely sensitive though he was over his academic failure, he courageously and conscientiously went on with his study of classical, and in particular of Latin, poetry, publishing papers which soon established his reputation as a scholar. After another examination he had no trouble in securing a pass degree from Oxford; and in 1892, when an appointment to a professorship of Latin was to be made at University College, London, a number of Continental as well as English scholars gave him testimonials of their high regard for his abilities. Housman was appointed to the position and held it until 1911, when he accepted the more honorable Kennedy Professorship of Latin at Cambridge University. While teaching in London and Cambridge he published editions of Manilius (1903–1920), of Juvenal (1905), and of Lucan (1926), all distinguished by the acrimony with which he criticized the work of less able editors. He became a fellow of Trinity College, Cambridge, and an honorary fellow of St. John's College, Oxford. Before his death on 30 April, 1936, he was likewise offered various other honors, but these he declined, largely, it appears, because he mistrusted the judgment of his fellow men: "You should be welcome to praise me," he once wrote, "if you did not praise one another."

The same fastidious and self-denying pride is evident when we turn to his poetry. The two volumes he published during his lifetime, *A Shropshire Lad* (1896) and *Last Poems* (1922), contain no more than a hundred and five lyrics; and before he died he arranged to have published only such other of his verses as were not inferior in quality to these. Housman's poetry, although it may remind us of Hardy's in its tone and outlook, is written with a scrupulous artistry unknown to Hardy. And even the tone and outlook of Housman's poetry were probably determined as much by his selective, fastidious temperament as by other circumstances. If he suffered from feelings of the deepest despair, he was also a generous and affectionate man who enjoyed good drink and merry talk, who had a musical laugh for his friends, and who frequently entertained them by writing nonsense verses; but he did not allow the lighter, more amiable side of his nature to dilute the pessimism of the work for which he wished to be remembered. He believed that life was essentially a hopeless, humiliating experience, and what he believed to be the essential truth he expressed without compromise or qualification. This intense sincerity, as well as the painstaking art with which it is joined, gives to his best lyrics a finality which is rare in modern writing. Housman is apt to be dogmatic when he expresses himself in prose, and in his poetry some readers may feel that his bitter fatalism is similarly arbitrary; but for the immediate purposes of lyric poetry his limitations are on the whole a source of strength. No other English poet of the early twentieth century is likely to have a more enduring fame, and Housman's fame is necessarily dependent on his peculiar ability to concentrate his powers.

In addition to *A Shropshire Lad* and *Last Poems* a student of Housman should be familiar with *More Poems* (London, 1936) and with the two addresses, the *Introductory Lecture, 1892* (Cambridge, 1937) and *The Name*

and *Nature of Poetry* (Cambridge, 1933). The fullest biographical study is Laurence Housman's *A. E. H.: Some Poems, Some Letters and a Personal Memoir by His Brother* (London, 1937); but with this should be consulted *Alfred Edward Housman* (Bromsgrove, 1936), a group of short essays by various friends, and A. S. F. Gow's *A. E. Housman* (Cambridge, 1936), a judicious summary of Housman's academic career. A long-promised book about Housman by his friend and publisher, Grant Richards, should be of interest when it appears.

A SHROPSHIRE LAD[1]

I. 1887

From Clee to heaven the beacon burns,
  The shires have seen it plain,
From north and south the sign returns
  And beacons burn again.

Look left, look right, the hills are bright, 5
  The dales are light between,
Because 'tis fifty years to-night
  That God has saved the Queen.

Now, when the flame they watch not towers
  About the soil they trod, 10
Lads, we'll remember friends of ours
  Who shared the work with God.

To skies that knit their heartstrings right,
  To fields that bred them brave,
The saviors come not home to-night: 15
  Themselves they could not save.

It dawns in Asia, tombstones show
  And Shropshire names are read;
And the Nile spills his overflow
  Beside the Severn's dead. 20

We pledge in peace by farm and town
  The Queen they served in war,
And fire the beacons up and down
  The land they perished for.

"God save the Queen" we living sing, 25
  From height to height 'tis heard;
And with the rest your voices ring,
  Lads of the Fifty-third.

Oh, God will save her, fear you not:
  Be you the men you've been, 30
Get you the sons your father got,
  And God will save the Queen.

II

Loveliest of trees, the cherry now
Is hung with bloom along the bough,
And stands about the woodland ride
Wearing white for Eastertide.

Now, of my threescore years and ten, 5
Twenty will not come again,
And take from seventy springs a score,
It only leaves me fifty more.

And since to look at things in bloom
Fifty springs are little room, 10
About the woodlands I will go
To see the cherry hung with snow.

IV. REVEILLE

Wake: the silver dusk returning
  Up the beach of darkness brims,
And the ship of sunrise burning
  Strands upon the eastern rims.

Wake: the vaulted shadow shatters, 5
  Trampled to the floor it spanned,
And the tent of night in tatters
  Straws[2] the sky-pavilioned land.

Up, lad, up, 'tis late for lying:
  Hear the drums of morning play; 10
Hark, the empty highways crying
  "Who'll beyond the hills away?"

---

[1] Published in 1896.

[2] Strews.

Towns and countries woo together,
　Forelands beacon, belfries call;
Never lad that trod on leather　　　15
　Lived to feast his heart with all.

Up, lad: thews that lie and cumber
　Sunlit pallets never thrive;
Morns abed and daylight slumber
　Were not meant for man alive.　　20

Clay lies still, but blood's a rover;
　Breath's a ware that will not keep.
Up, lad: when the journey's over
　There'll be time enough to sleep.

VIII

"Farewell to barn and stack and tree,
　Farewell to Severn shore.
Terence, look your last at me,
　For I come home no more.

"The sun burns on the half-mown hill,　　5
　By now the blood is dried;
And Maurice amongst the hay lies still
　And my knife is in his side.

"My mother thinks us long away;
　'Tis time the field were mown.　　10
She had two sons at rising day,
　To-night she'll be alone.

"And here's a bloody hand to shake,
　And oh, man, here's good-bye;
We'll sweat no more on scythe and rake,　　15
　My bloody hands and I.

"I wish you strength to bring you pride,
　And a love to keep you clean,
And I wish you luck, come Lammastide,
　At racing on the green.　　20

"Long for me the rick will wait,
　And long will wait the fold,
And long will stand the empty plate,
　And dinner will be cold."

XI

On your midnight pallet lying,
　Listen, and undo the door:
Lads that waste the night in sighing
　In the dark should sigh no more;
Night should ease a lover's sorrow;　　5
Therefore, since I go to-morrow,
　Pity me before.

In the land to which I travel,
　The far dwelling, let me say—
Once, if here the couch is gravel,　　10
　In a kinder bed I lay,
And the breast the darnel smothers
Rested once upon another's
　When it was not clay.

XVIII

Oh, when I was in love with you,
　Then I was clean and brave,
And miles around the wonder grew
　How well did I behave.

And now the fancy passes by,　　5
　And nothing will remain,
And miles around they'll say that I
　Am quite myself again.

XIX.　TO AN ATHLETE DYING YOUNG

The time you won your town the race
We chaired you through the market-place;
Man and boy stood cheering by,
And home we brought you shoulder-high.

To-day, the road all runners come,　　5
Shoulder-high we bring you home,
And set you at your threshold down,
Townsman of a stiller town.

Smart lad, to slip betimes away
From fields where glory does not stay　　10
And early though the laurel grows
It withers quicker than the rose.

Eyes the shady night has shut
Cannot see the record cut,
And silence sounds no worse than cheers　　15
After earth has stopped the ears:

Now you will not swell the rout
Of lads that wore their honors out,
Runners whom renown outran
And the name died before the man.　　20

So set, before its echoes fade,
The fleet foot on the sill of shade,
And hold to the low lintel up
The still-defended challenge-cup.

And round that early-laureled head　　25
Will flock to gaze the strengthless dead,
And find unwithered on its curls
The garland briefer than a girl's.

XXVII

"Is my team plowing,
　That I used to drive
And hear the harness jingle
　When I was man alive?"

Ay, the horses trample,　　　　　　5
　The harness jingles now;
No change though you lie under
　The land you used to plow.

"Is football playing
　Along the river shore,　　　　　　10
With lads to chase the leather,
　Now I stand up no more?"

Ay, the ball is flying,
　The lads play heart and soul;
The goal stands up, the keeper　　　15
　Stands up to keep the goal.

"Is my girl happy,
　That I thought hard to leave,
And has she tired of weeping
　As she lies down at eve?"　　　　　20

Ay, she lies down lightly,
　She lies not down to weep:
Your girl is well contented.
　Be still, my lad, and sleep.

"Is my friend hearty,　　　　　　25
　Now I am thin and pine,
And has he found to sleep in
　A better bed than mine?"

Yes, lad, I lie easy,
　I lie as lads would choose;　　　　30
I cheer a dead man's sweetheart,
　Never ask me whose.

XXXIV. THE NEW MISTRESS

*"Oh, sick I am to see you, will you never let
　me be?*
*You may be good for something but you are
　not good for me.*
*Oh, go where you are wanted, for you are
　not wanted here."*
And that was all the farewell when I parted
　from my dear.

"I will go where I am wanted, to a lady born
　and bred　　　　　　　　　　　　5
Who will dress me free for nothing in a uni-
　form of red;

She will not be sick to see me if I only keep
　it clean:
I will go where I am wanted for a soldier of
　the Queen.

"I will go where I am wanted, for the ser-
　geant does not mind;
He may be sick to see me but he treats me
　very kind:　　　　　　　　　　　10
He gives me beer and breakfast and a ribbon
　for my cap,
And I never knew a sweetheart spend her
　money on a chap.

"I will go where I am wanted, where there's
　room for one or two,
And the men are none too many for the work
　there is to do;
Where the standing line wears thinner and
　the dropping dead lie thick;　　　15
And the enemies of England they shall see
　me and be sick."

XL

Into my heart an air that kills
　From yon far country blows:
What are those blue remembered hills,
　What spires, what farms are those?

That is the land of lost content,　　　5
　I see it shining plain,
The happy highways where I went
　And cannot come again.

XLIV

Shot? so quick, so clean an ending?
　Oh that was right, lad, that was brave:
Yours was not an ill for mending,
　'Twas best to take it to the grave.

Oh you had forethought, you could reason,　5
　And saw your road and where it led,
And early wise and brave in season
　Put the pistol to your head.

Oh soon, and better so than later
　After long disgrace and scorn,　　　10
You shot dead the household traitor,
　The soul that should not have been born.

Right you guessed the rising morrow
　And scorned to tread the mire you must:
Dust's your wages, son of sorrow,　　　15
　But men may come to worse than dust.

Souls undone, undoing others,—
    Long time since the tale began.
You would not live to wrong your brothers:
    Oh lad, you died as fits a man. 20

Now to your grave shall friend and stranger
    With ruth and some with envy come:
Undishonored, clear of danger,
    Clean of guilt, pass hence and home.

Turn safe to rest, no dreams, no waking; 25
    And here, man, here's the wreath I've
      made:
'Tis not a gift that's worth the taking,
    But wear it and it will not fade.

XLVII. THE CARPENTER'S SON

"Here the hangman stops his cart:
Now the best of friends must part.
Fare you well, for ill fare I:
Live, lads, and I will die.

"Oh, at home had I but stayed 5
'Prenticed to my father's trade,
Had I stuck to plane and adze,
I had not been lost, my lads.

"Then I might have built perhaps
Gallow-trees for other chaps, 10
Never dangled on my own,
Had I but left ill alone.

"Now, you see, they hang me high,
And the people passing by
Stop to shake their fists and curse; 15
So 'tis come from ill to worse.

"Here hang I, and right and left
Two poor fellows hang for theft:
All the same's the luck we prove,
Though the midmost hangs for love. 20

"Comrades all, that stand and gaze,
Walk henceforth in other ways;
See my neck and save your own:
Comrades all, leave ill alone.

"Make some day a decent end, 25
Shrewder fellows than your friend.
Fare you well, for ill fare I:
Live, lads, and I will die."

XLVIII

Be still, my soul, be still; the arms you bear
    are brittle,
    Earth and high heaven are fixed of old and
      founded strong.

Think rather,—call to thought, if now you
    grieve a little,
    The days when we had rest, O soul, for
      they were long.

Men loved unkindness then, but lightless in
    the quarry 5
    I slept and saw not; tears fell down, I did
      not mourn;
Sweat ran and blood sprang out and I was
    never sorry:
    Then it was well with me, in days ere I was
      born.

Now, and I muse for why and never find the
    reason,
    I pace the earth, and drink the air, and feel
      the sun. 10
Be still, be still, my soul; it is but for a
    season:
    Let us endure an hour and see injustice
      done.

Aye, look: high heaven and earth ail from the
    prime foundation;
    All thoughts to rive the heart are here, and
      all are vain:
Horror and scorn and hate and fear and in-
    dignation— 15
    Oh why did I awake? when shall I sleep
      again?

XLIX

Think no more, lad; laugh, be jolly:
    Why should men make haste to die?
Empty heads and tongues a-talking
Make the rough road easy walking,
And the feather pate of folly 5
    Bears the falling sky.

Oh, 'tis jesting, dancing, drinking
    Spins the heavy world around.
If young hearts were not so clever,
Oh, they would be young for ever: 10
Think no more; 'tis only thinking
    Lays lads underground.

LIV

With rue my heart is laden
    For golden friends I had,
For many a rose-lipt maiden
    And many a lightfoot lad.

By brooks too broad for leaping 3
    The lightfoot boys are laid;
The rose-lipt girls are sleeping
    In fields where roses fade.

LXII

"Terence, this is stupid stuff:
You eat your victuals fast enough;
There can't be much amiss, 'tis clear,
To see the rate you drink your beer.
But oh, good Lord, the verse you make,   5
It gives a chap the belly-ache.
The cow, the old cow, she is dead;
It sleeps well, the horned head:
We poor lads, 'tis our turn now
To hear such tunes as killed the cow.   10
Pretty friendship 'tis to rime
Your friends to death before their time
Moping melancholy mad:
Come, pipe a tune to dance to, lad."

Why, if 'tis dancing you would be,   15
There's brisker pipes than poetry.
Say, for what were hop-yards meant,
Or why was Burton built on Trent?[8]
Oh many a peer of England brews
Livelier liquor than the Muse,   20
And malt does more than Milton can
To justify God's ways to man.
Ale, man, ale's the stuff to drink
For fellows whom it hurts to think:
Look into the pewter pot   25
To see the world as the world's not.
And faith, 'tis pleasant till 'tis past:
The mischief is that 'twill not last.
Oh I have been to Ludlow fair
And left my necktie God knows where,   30
And carried half way home, or near,
Pints and quarts of Ludlow beer:
Then the world seemed none so bad,
And I myself a sterling lad;
And down in lovely muck I've lain,   35
Happy till I woke again.
Then I saw the morning sky:
Heigho, the tale was all a lie;
The world, it was the old world yet,
I was I, my things were wet,   40
And nothing now remained to do
But begin the game anew.

Therefore, since the world has still
Much good, but much less good than ill,
And while the sun and moon endure   45
Luck's a chance, but trouble's sure,
I'd face it as a wise man would,
And train for ill and not for good.
'Tis true, the stuff I bring for sale
Is not so brisk a brew as ale: 50
Out of a stem that scored the hand
I wrung it in a weary land.

[8] Burton upon Trent is a town famous for the manufacture of beer.

But take it: if the smack is sour,
The better for the embittered hour;
It should do good to heart and head   55
When your soul is in my soul's stead;
And I will friend you, if I may
In the dark and cloudy day.

There was a king reigned in the East:
There, when kings will sit to feast,   60
They get their fill before they think
With poisoned meat and poisoned drink.
He gathered all that springs to birth
From the many-venomed earth;
First a little, thence to more,   65
He sampled all her killing store;
And easy, smiling, seasoned sound,
Sate the king when healths went round.
They put arsenic in his meat
And stared aghast to watch him eat;   70
They poured strychnine in his cup
And shook to see him drink it up:
They shook, they stared as white's their shirt:
Them it was their poison hurt.
—I tell the tale that I heard told.   75
Mithridates, he died old.

LAST POEMS[1]

VII

In valleys green and still
  Where lovers wander maying
They hear from over hill
  A music playing.

Behind the drum and fife,   5
  Past hawthornwood and hollow,
Through earth and out of life
  The soldiers follow.

The soldier's is the trade:
  In any wind or weather   10
He steals the heart of maid
  And man together.

The lover and his lass
  Beneath the hawthorn lying
Have heard the soldiers pass,   15
  And both are sighing.

And down the distance they
  With dying note and swelling
Walk the resounding way
  To the still dwelling.   20

[1] Published in 1922. The following selections from *Last Poems* are reprinted by permission of Henry Holt and Company, publishers.

IX

The chestnut casts his flambeaux, and the
flowers
    Stream from the hawthorn on the wind
away,
The doors clap to, the pane is blind with
showers.
    Pass me the can, lad; there's an end of
May.

There's one spoilt spring to scant our mortal
lot,   5
    One season ruined of our little store.
May will be fine next year as like as not:
    Oh, aye, but then we shall be twenty-four.

We for a certainty are not the first
    Have sat in taverns while the tempest
hurled   10
Their hopeful plans to emptiness, and cursed
    Whatever brute and blackguard made the
world.

It is in truth iniquity on high
    To cheat our sentenced souls of aught they
crave,
And mar the merriment as you and I   15
    Fare on our long fool's-errand to the
grave.

Iniquity it is; but pass the can.
    My lad, no pair of kings our mothers bore;
Our only portion is the estate of man:
    We want the moon, but we shall get no
more.   20

If here to-day the cloud of thunder lours
    To-morrow it will hie on far behests;

The flesh will grieve on other bones than ours
    Soon, and the soul will mourn in other
breasts.

The troubles of our proud and angry dust 25
    Are from eternity, and shall not fail.
Bear them we can, and if we can we must.
    Shoulder the sky, my lad, and drink your
ale.

XI

Yonder see the morning blink:
    The sun is up, and up must I,
To wash and dress and eat and drink
And look at things and talk and think
    And work, and God knows why.   5

Oh often have I washed and dressed
    And what's to show for all my pain?
Let me lie abed and rest:
Ten thousand times I've done my best
    And all's to do again.   10

MORE POEMS

THEY SAY MY VERSE IS SAD[1]

They say my verse is sad: no wonder;
    Its narrow measure spans
Tears of eternity, and sorrow,
    Not mine, but man's.

This is for all ill-treated fellows   5
    Unborn and unbegot,
For them to read when they're in trouble
    And I am not.

<hr>

[1] From *More Poems* (1936), published by Alfred
A. Knopf. Reprinted by permission.

JOHN MASEFIELD

1878-

John Masefield was born at Ledbury, Herefordshire, on 1 June, 1878. Both his mother and his father, a solicitor, died while he was still very young; and his aunt, under whose care he was then placed, sent him to the local Ledbury school. Here he showed an early taste for Scott's narrative poetry and Macaulay's *Lays of Ancient Rome;* the boy himself became a proficient story-teller and composed poems in his head, although he did not write them down. Unfortunately, from the standpoint of his guardians, he also developed a taste for tramping long distances through the countryside. In order to curb this bold spirit they indentured him, at the age of fourteen, to a merchant ship. Three of his most impressionable years were spent at sea as a common sailor. Masefield endured this harsh life successfully, but towards the end of his sixteenth year he decided to leave it because it prevented him from reading and writing. In April, 1895, he landed in New York with five dollars and his clothes. He proceeded to make his living doing odd jobs along the waterfront; for four months he was employed in a saloon, and for nearly two years in a carpet factory. What is equally important, he was able to buy and had time to read the most memorable English authors, beginning with Chaucer. When he returned from New York to London in 1897 he had definitely fixed on a literary career.

Masefield's first volume of poetry, *Salt-Water Ballads,* was published in England in 1902, and the book is said to have dazzled readers with its daring and realism. From that time on Masefield's career was marked by a long series of literary triumphs: *A Mainsail Haul* (1905), prose stories of the sea; *Captain Margaret* (1908), *Multitude and Solitude* (1909), *Sard Harker* (1924), and *Odtaa* (1926), all novels; *The Tragedy of Nan* (1909), a drama of English country life; *The Everlasting Mercy* (1911), *The Widow in the Bye Street* (1912), *Dauber* (1913), and *The Daffodil Fields* (1913), long narrative poems

dealing with humble people; *Gallipoli* (1916), an account of one of the campaigns in the World War; *Lollingdon Downs* (1917), Masefield's most important volume of lyrics; *Reynard the Fox* (1919) and *Right Royal* (1920), narrative poems dealing respectively with fox-hunting and horse-racing; *Shakespeare and the Spiritual Life* (1924), a series of lectures; and *With the Living Voice* (1925), an address on the relationship of poet to people. In 1930 Masefield became poet laureate in succession to Robert Bridges. In 1935 the Order of Merit was bestowed on him. For many years he made his home at Boar's Hill, Oxford; but even the neighborhood of the University has begun to suffer from the stress of modern life, and he has since removed to the remoter countryside of Worcestershire.

Although *Salt-Water Ballads* appeared to be a volume of great originality in 1903, it is now clear that much of it echoed the realistic style of Kipling. In the same way the more romantic lyrics which Masefield later added to the same collection echo the style of the Irish poets, John M. Synge and William Butler Yeats. But valuable as these contemporary models may once have been for him, Masefield only found himself when he turned to an older tradition and drew upon a deeper experience of English life. "The Everlasting Mercy," he has explained, "began to form images in my mind early in the morning of a fine day in May, 1911. I had risen very early and had gone out into the morning with a friend who had to ride to catch a train some miles away. On our way down a lane in the freshness and brightness of the dew we saw coming towards us, up a slope in a field close to us, a plow team of noble horses followed by the advancing breaking wave of red clay thrust aside by the share. The plowman was like Piers Plowman or Chaucer's plowman, a staid, elderly, honest, and most kindly man whom we had long known and respected. The beauty and nobility of this sight moved me profoundly all day long." This genuine native inspiration, combining a calm, Chaucerian sense of the realities with a note of religious exaltation, gives *The Everlasting Mercy* a place by itself among the works of Masefield. It not only marks a turning point in the development of his poetry; it is also, with the possible exception of *Dauber,* a finer and a more powerful poem than any he has written before or since.

Masefield's *Collected Poems* (London, 1932) includes all those in the present anthology. For accounts of the poet's life see *John Masefield,* a brochure published by The Macmillan Company (New York, 1930), and Rica Brenner, *Ten Modern Poets* (New York, 1930), pp. 225–252. For a critical summary of all except the most recent works see W. H. Hamilton, *John Masefield, A Popular Study* (London, 1922; revised ed. 1925). A. E. Dubois has written an interesting critical attack, "The Cult of Beauty: A Study of John Masefield," in *Publications of the Modern Language Association* for December, 1930 (Vol. XLV). Reference may also be made to *John Masefield* by Gilbert O. Thomas (1932).

CARGOES[1]

Quinquireme of Nineveh from distant Ophir,[2]
Rowing home to haven in sunny Palestine,
With a cargo of ivory,
And apes and peacocks,
Sandalwood, cedarwood, and sweet white wine.　　　　5

Stately Spanish galleon coming from the Isthmus,
Dipping through the Tropics by the palm-green shores,
With a cargo of diamonds,
Emeralds, amethysts,
Topazes, and cinnamon, and gold moidores.[3]　　　10

Dirty British coaster with a salt-caked smoke stack,
Butting through the Channel in the mad March days,
With a cargo of Tyne coal,
Road-rails, pig-lead,
Firewood, iron-ware, and cheap tin trays. 15

CAPTAIN STRATTON'S FANCY

Oh some are fond of red wine, and some are fond of white,
And some are all for dancing by the pale moonlight;

But rum alone's the tipple, and the heart's delight
Of the old bold mate of Henry Morgan.[4]

Oh some are fond of Spanish wine, and some are fond of French,　　　5
And some'll swallow tay and stuff fit only for a wench;
But I'm for right Jamaica till I roll beneath the bench,
Says the old bold mate of Henry Morgan.

Oh some are for the lily, and some are for the rose,
But I am for the sugar-cane that in Jamaica grows;　　　10
For it's that that makes the bonny drink to warm my copper nose,
Says the old bold mate of Henry Morgan.

Oh some are fond of fiddles, and a song well sung,
And some are all for music for to lilt upon the tongue;
But mouths were made for tankards, and for sucking at the bung,　　　15
Says the old bold mate of Henry Morgan.

Oh some are fond of dancing, and some are fond of dice,
And some are all for red lips, and pretty lasses' eyes;
But a right Jamaica puncheon[5] is a finer prize
To the old bold mate of Henry Morgan. 20

---

[1] This and the following five poems are reprinted by permission of The Macmillan Company, publishers, and of Mr. Masefield.

[2] The place, probably in southeastern Arabia, from which the ships of King Solomon brought gold and precious stones (I Kings, 10:11).

[3] Portuguese coins.

[4] Sir Henry Morgan (1635–1688), who was at one time leader of the West Indian buccaneers, but was later knighted by Charles II and sent to Jamaica as lieutenant-governor.

[5] Cask of Jamaica rum.

Oh some that's good and godly ones they hold
    that it's a sin
To troll[6] the jolly bowl around, and let the
    dollars spin;
But I'm for toleration and for drinking at the
    inn,
    Says the old bold mate of Henry Morgan.

Oh some are sad and wretched folk that go in
    silken suits,   25
And there's a mort[7] of wicked rogues that
    live in good reputes;
So I'm for drinking honestly, and dying in
    my boots,
    Like an old bold mate of Henry Morgan.

THE WEST WIND

It's a warm wind, the west wind, full of birds'
    cries;
I never hear the west wind but tears are in
    my eyes.
For it comes from the west lands, the old
    brown hills,
And April's in the west wind, and daffodils.

It's a fine land, the west land, for hearts as
    tired as mine,   5
Apple orchards blossom there, and the air's
    like wine.
There is cool green grass there, where men
    may lie at rest,
And the thrushes are in song there, fluting
    from the nest.

"Will you not come home, brother? you have
    been long away,
It's April, and blossom time, and white is the
    spray;   10
And bright is the sun, brother, and warm is
    the rain,—
Will you not come home, brother, home to us
    again?

"The young corn is green, brother, where the
    rabbits run,
It's blue sky, and white clouds, and warm
    rain and sun.
It's song to a man's soul, brother, fire to a
    man's brain,   15
To hear the wild bees and see the merry
    spring again.

---

[6]Pass.   [7]Great number.

"Larks are singing in the west, brother,
    above the green wheat,
So will ye not come home, brother, and rest
    your tired feet?
I've a balm for bruised hearts, brother, sleep
    for aching eyes,"
Says the warm wind, the west wind, full of
    birds' cries.   20

It's the white road westwards is the road I
    must tread
To the green grass, the cool grass, and rest
    for heart and head,
To the violets and the brown brooks and the
    thrushes' song,
In the fine land, the west land, the land where
    I belong.

C. L. M.

In the dark womb where I began
My mother's life made me a man.
Through all the months of human birth
Her beauty fed my common earth.
I cannot see, nor breathe, nor stir,
But through the death of some of her.

Down in the darkness of the grave
She cannot see the life she gave.
For all her love, she cannot tell
Whether I use it ill or well,   10
Nor knock at dusty doors to find
Her beauty dusty in the mind.

If the grave's gates could be undone,
She would not know her little son,
I am so grown. If we should meet   15
She would pass by me in the street,
Unless my soul's face let her see
My sense of what she did for me.

What have I done to keep in mind
My debt to her and womankind?   20
What woman's happier life repays
Her for those months of wretched days?
For all my mouthless body leeched
Ere Birth's releasing hell was reached?

What have I done, or tried, or said   25
In thanks to that dear woman dead?
Men triumph over women still,
Men trample women's right at will,
And man's lust roves the world untamed.

O grave, keep shut lest I be shamed.   30

THE EVERLASTING MERCY[1]

Thy place is biggyd[2] above the sterrys cleer,
Noon erthely paleys wrouhte in so statly wyse,
Com on my freend, my brothir moost enteer,
For the I offryd my blood in sacrifise.
JOHN LYDGATE.

From '41 to '51
I was my folk's contrary son;
I bit my father's hand right through
And broke my mother's heart in two.
I sometimes go without my dinner 5
Now that I know the times I've gi'n her.

From '51 to '61
I cut my teeth and took to fun.
I learned what not to be afraid of
And what stuff women's lips are made of; 10
I learned with what a rosy feeling
Good ale makes floors seem like the ceiling,
And how the moon gives shiny light
To lads as roll home singing by't.
My blood did leap, my flesh did revel, 15
Saul Kane was tokened to the devil.

From '61 to '67
I lived in disbelief of Heaven.
I drunk, I fought, I poached, I whored,
I did despite unto the Lord. 20
I cursed, 'would make a man look pale,
And nineteen times I went to jail.

Now, friends, observe and look upon me,
Mark how the Lord took pity on me.
By Dead Man's Thorn, while setting wires, 25
Who should come up but Billy Myers,
A friend of mine, who used to be
As black as sprig of hell as me,
With whom I'd planned, to save encroachin',
Which fields and coverts each should poach
in. 30
Now when he saw me set my snare,
He tells me "Get to hell from there.
This field is mine," he says, "by right;
If you poach here, there'll be a fight.
Out now," he says, "and leave your wire; 35
It's mine."
          "It ain't."
               "You put."[3]
                    "You liar."
"You closhy put."
"You bloody liar."
"This is my field."
"This is my wire." 40

"I'm ruler here."
"You ain't."
"I am."
"I'll fight you for it."
"Right, by damn. 45
Not now, though, I've a-sprained my thumb,
We'll fight after the harvest hum[4]
And Silas Jones, that bookie[5] wide,
Will make a purse five pounds a side."
Those were the words, that was the place 50
By which God brought me into grace.

On Wood Top Field the peewits go
Mewing and wheeling ever so;
And like the shaking of a timbrel[6]
Cackles the laughter of the whimbrel.[7] 55
In the old quarry-pit they say
Head-keeper Pike was made away.
He walks, head-keeper Pike, for harm,
He taps the windows of the farm;
The blood drips from his broken chin, 60
He taps and begs to be let in.
On Wood Top, nights, I've shaked to hark
The peewits wambling[8] in the dark
Lest in the dark the old man might
Creep up to me to beg a light. 65

But Wood Top grass is short and sweet
And springy to a boxer's feet;
At harvest hum the moon so bright
Did shine on Wood Top for the fight.

When Bill was stripped down to his bends[9] 70
I thought how long we two'd been friends,
And in my mind, about that wire,
I thought "He's right, I am a liar.
As sure as skilly's[10] made in prison
The right to poach that copse is his'n. 75
I'll have no luck to-night," thinks I.
"I'm fighting to defend a lie.
And this moonshiny evening's fun
Is worse than aught I've ever done."
And thinking that way my heart bled so 80
I almost stept to Bill and said so.
And now Bill's dead I would be glad
If I could only think I had.
But no. I put the thought away
For fear of what my friends would say. 85
They'd backed me, see? O Lord, the sin
Done for the things there's money in.

[1] Published in *The English Review,* in the issue
dated October, 1911.
[2] Built. [3] Lout.

[4] Home.
[5] Bookmaker; professional betting-man.
[6] Tambourine. [7] Small bird of the curlew species.
[8] Staggering.
[9] Bands. [10] A thin porridge or soup.

The stakes were drove, the ropes were
    hitched,
Into the ring my hat I pitched.
My corner faced the Squire's park   90
Just where the fir trees make it dark;
The place where I begun poor Nell
Upon the woman's road to hell.
I thought of't, sitting in my corner
After the time-keep struck his warner   95
(Two brandy flasks, for fear of noise,
Clinked out the time to us two boys).
And while my seconds chafed and gloved me
I thought of Nell's eyes when she loved me,
And wondered how my tot would end,   100
First Nell cast off and now my friend;
And in the moonlight dim and wan
I knew quite well my luck was gone;
And looking round I felt a spite
At all who'd come to see me fight;   105
The five and forty human faces
Inflamed by drink and going to races,
Faces of men who'd never been
Merry or true or live or clean;
Who'd never felt the boxer's trim   110
Of brain divinely knit to limb,
Nor felt the whole live body go
One tingling health from top to toe;
Nor took a punch nor given a swing,
But just soaked deady round the ring   115
Until their brains and bloods were foul
Enough to make their throttles[11] howl,
While we whom Jesus died to teach
Fought round on round, three minutes each.
And thinking that, you'll understand   120
I thought, "I'll go and take Bill's hand.
I'll up and say the fault was mine,
He shan't make play for these here swine."
And then I thought that that was silly,
They'd think I was afraid of Billy;   125
They'd think (I thought it, God forgive me)
I funked the hiding Bill could give me.
And that thought made me mad and hot.
"Think that, will they? Well, they shall not.
They shan't think that. I will not. I'm   130
Damned if I will. I will not."
    Time!

From the beginning of the bout
My luck was gone, my hand was out.
Right from the start Bill called the play,
But I was quick and kept away   135
Till the fourth round, when work got mixed,
And then I knew Bill had me fixed.
My hand was out, why, Heaven knows;
Bill punched me when and where he chose.

Through two more rounds we quartered[12]
    wide,   140
And all the time my hands seemed tied;
Bill punched me when and where he pleased.
The cheering from my backers eased,
But every punch I heard a yell
Of "That's the style, Bill, give him hell."   145
No one for me, but Jimmy's light
"Straight left! Straight left!" and "Watch
    his right."

I don't know how a boxer goes
When all his body hums from blows;
I know I seemed to rock and spin,   150
I don't know how I saved my chin;
I know I thought my only friend
Was that clinked flask at each round's end
When my two seconds, Ed and Jimmy,
Had sixty seconds help to gimme.   155

But in the ninth, with pain and knocks
I stopped: I couldn't fight nor box.
Bill missed his swing, the light was tricky,
But I went down, and stayed down, dicky.[13]

"Get up," cried Jim. I said, "I will."   160
Then all the gang yelled, "Out him, Bill.
Out him." Bill rushed . . . and Clink,
    Clink, Clink.
Time! and Jim's knee, and rum to drink.
And round the ring there ran a titter:
"Saved by the call, the bloody quitter."   165

They drove (a dodge that never fails)
A pin beneath my finger nails.
They poured what seemed a running beck[14]
Of cold spring water down my neck;
Jim with a lancet quick as flies   170
Lowered the swellings round my eyes.
They sluiced my legs and fanned my face
Through all that blessed minute's grace;
They gave my calves a thorough kneading,
They salved my cuts and stopped the bleed-   175
    ing.
A gulp of liquor dulled the pain,
And then the two flasks clinked again.

Time!
        There was Bill as grim as death,
He rushed, I clinched, to get more breath,
And breath I got, though Billy bats   180
Some stinging short-arms in my slats.
And when we broke, as I foresaw,
He swung his right in for the jaw.
I stopped it on my shoulder bone,
And at the shock I heard Bill groan—   185

---

[11]Throats.

[12]Ranged.   [13]Shaky.   [14]Brook.

A little groan or moan or grunt
As though I'd hit his wind a bunt.[15]
At that, I clinched, and while we clinched,
His old time right arm dig was flinched,
And when we broke he hit me light   190
As though he didn't trust his right,
He flapped me somehow with his wrist
As though he couldn't use his fist,
And when he hit he winced with pain.
I thought, "Your sprained thumb's crocked[16]
   again."   195
So I got strength and Bill gave ground,
And that round was an easy round.

During the wait my Jimmy said,
"What's making Billy fight so dead?
He's all to pieces.   Is he blown?"   200
"His thumb's out."
"No?   Then it's your own.
It's all your own, but don't be rash—
He's got the goods if you've got cash,
And what one hand can do he'll do,   205
Be careful this next round or two."

Time.   There was Bill, and I felt sick
That luck should play so mean a trick
And give me leave to knock him out
After he'd plainly won the bout.   210
But by the way the man came at me
He made it plain he meant to bat me;
If you'd a seen the way he come
You wouldn't think he'd crocked a thumb.
With all his skill and all his might   215
He clipped me dizzy left and right;
The Lord knows what the effort cost,
But he was mad to think he'd lost,
And knowing nothing else could save him
He didn't care what pain it gave him.   220
He called the music and the dance
For five rounds more and gave no chance.

Try to imagine if you can
The kind of manhood in the man,
And if you'd like to feel his pain   225
You sprain your thumb and hit the sprain.
And hit it hard, with all your power
On something hard for half-an-hour,
While someone thumps you black and blue,
And then you'll know what Billy knew.   230
Bill took that pain without a sound
Till halfway through the eighteenth round,
And then I sent him down and out,
And Silas said, "Kane wins the bout."

When Bill came to, you understand,   235
I ripped the mitten from my hand

---

[15]Knock.   [16]Cracked (?).

And went across to ask Bill shake.
My limbs were all one pain and ache,
I was so weary and so sore
I don't think I'd a stood much more.   240
Bill in his corner bathed his thumb,
Buttoned his shirt and glowered glum.
"I'll never shake your hand," he said.
"I'd rather see my children dead.
I've been about and had some fun with
   you,   245
But you're a liar and I've done with you.
You've knocked me out, you didn't beat me;
Look out the next time that you meet me,
There'll be no friend to watch the clock for
   you
And no convenient thumb to crock for you,
And I'll take care, with much delight,   251
You'll get what you'd a got to-night;
That puts my meaning clear, I guess,
Now get to hell; I want to dress."

I dressed.   My backers one and all   255
Said, "Well done you," or "Good old Saul."
"Saul is a wonder and a fly[17] 'un,
What'll you have, Saul, at the Lion?"
With merry oaths they helped me down
The stony wood path to the town.   260

The moonlight shone on Cabbage Walk,
It made the limestone look like chalk.
It was too late for any people,
Twelve struck as we went by the steeple.
A dog barked, and an owl was calling,   265
The squire's brook was still a-falling,
The carved heads on the church looked down
On "Russell, Blacksmith of this Town,"
And all the graves of all the ghosts
Who rise on Christmas Eve in hosts   270
To dance and carol in festivity
For joy of Jesus Christ's Nativity
(Bell-ringer Dawe and his two sons
Beheld 'em from the bell-tower once),
Two and two about about   275
Singing the end of Advent out,
Dwindling down to windlestraws[18]
When the glittering peacock craws,
As craw the glittering peacock should
When Christ's own star comes over the wood.
Lamb of the sky come out of fold   281
Wandering windy heavens cold.
So they shone and sang till twelve
When all the bells ring out of theirselve.
Rang a peal for Christmas morn,   285
Glory, men, for Christ is born.

All the old monks' singing places
Glimmered quick with flitting faces,

---

[17]Knowing.   [18]Withered stalks of grass.

Singing anthems, singing hymns
Under carven cherubims.   290
Ringer Dawe aloft could mark
Faces at the window dark
Crowding, crowding, row on row,
Till all the Church began to glow.
The chapel glowed, the nave, the choir,   295
All the faces became fire
Below the eastern window high
To see Christ's star come up the sky.
Then they lifted hands and turned,
And all their lifted fingers burned, ·   300
Burned like the golden altar tallows,
Burned like a troop of God's own Hallows,[19]
Bringing to mind the burning time
When all the bells will rock and chime
And burning saints on burning horses   305
Will sweep the planets from their courses
And loose the stars to burn up night.
Lord, give us eyes to bear the light.

We all went quiet down the Scallenge
Lest Police Inspector Drew should challenge.
But 'Spector Drew was sleeping sweet,   311
His head upon a charges sheet,
Under the gas jet flaring full,
Snorting and snoring like a bull,
His bull cheeks puffed, his bull lips blowing,
His ugly yellow front teeth showing.   316
Just as we peeped we saw him fumble
And scratch his head, and shift, and mumble.

Down in the lane so thin and dark
The tan-yards stank of bitter bark, .   320
The curate's pigeons gave a flutter,
A cat went courting down the gutter,
And none else stirred a foot or feather.
The houses put their heads together,
Talking, perhaps, so dark and sly,   325
Of all the folk they'd seen go by,
Children, and men and women, merry all,
Who'd some day pass that way to burial.
It was all dark, but at the turning
The Lion had a window burning.   330
So in we went and up the stairs,
Treading as still as cats and hares.
The way the stairs creaked made you wonder
If dead men's bones were hidden under.
At head of stairs upon the landing   335
A woman with a lamp was standing;
She greet each gent at head of stairs
With "Step in, gents, and take your chairs.
The punch'll come when kettle bubble,
But don't make noise or there'll be trouble."
'Twas Doxy Jane, a bouncing girl   341
With eyes all sparks and hair all curl,

[19]Saints.

And cheeks all red and lips all coal,
And thirst for men instead of soul.
She's trod her pathway to the fire.   345
Old Rivers had his nephew by her.

I step aside from Tom and Jimmy
To find if she'd a kiss to gimme.
I blew out lamp 'fore she could speak.
She said, "If you ain't got a cheek,"   350
And then beside me in the dim,
"Did he beat you or you beat him?"
"Why, I beat him" (though that was wrong).
She said, "You must be turble strong.
I'd be afraid you'd beat me, too."   355
"You'd not," I said, "I wouldn't do."
"Never?"
"No, never."
"Never?"
"No."   360
"O Saul.   Here's missus.   Let me go."
It wasn't missus, so I didn't,
Whether I mid do or I midn't,
Until she'd promised we should meet
Next evening, six, at top of street,   365
When we could have a quiet talk
On that low wall up Worcester Walk.
And while we whispered there together
I give her silver for a feather
And felt a drunkenness like wine   370
And shut out Christ in husks and swine.
I felt the dart strike through my liver.
God punish me for't and forgive her.

Each one could be a Jesus mild,
Each one has been a little child,   375
A little child with laughing look,
A lovely white unwritten book;
A book that God will take, my friend,
As each goes out at journey's end.
The Lord Who gave us Earth and Heaven
Takes that as thanks for all He's given.   381
The book he lent is given back
All blotted red and smutted black.

"Open the door," said Jim, "and call."
Jane gasped "They'll see me.   Loose me,
            Saul."   385
She pushed me by, and ducked downstair
With half the pins out of her hair.
I went inside the lit room rollen
Her scented handkerchief I'd stolen.
"What would you fancy, Saul?" they said.
"A gin punch hot and then to bed."   391
"Jane, fetch the punch bowl to the gemmen;
And mind you don't put too much lemon.
Our good friend Saul has had a fight of it,
Now smoke up, boys, and make a night of it."

The room was full of men and stink 396
Of bad cigars and heavy drink.
Riley was nodding to the floor
And gurgling as he wanted more.
His mouth was wide, his face was pale, 400
His swollen face was sweating ale;
And one of those assembled Greeks[20]
Had corked black crosses on his cheeks.
Thomas was having words with Goss,
He "wouldn't pay, the fight was cross." 405
And Goss told Tom that "cross or no,
The bets go as the verdicts go,
By all I've ever heard or read of.
So pay, or else I'll knock your head off."
Jim Gurvil said his smutty say 410
About a girl down Bye Street way,
And how the girl from Froggatt's circus
Died giving birth in Wewent work'us.
And Dick told how the Dymock wench
Bore twins, poor thing, on Dog Hill bench;
And how he'd owned to one in Court 416
And how Judge made him sorry for't.

Jack set a jew's harp twanging drily;
"Gimme another cup," said Riley.
A dozen more were in their glories 420
With laughs and smokes and smutty stories;
And Jimmy joked and took his sup
And sang his song of "Up, come up."
Jane brought the bowl of stewing gin
And poured the egg and lemon in, 425
And whisked it up and served it out
While bawdy questions went about.
Jack chucked her chin, and Jim accost her
With bits out of the "Maid of Gloster."
And fifteen arms went round her waist. 430
(And then men ask, Are Barmaids chaste?)

O young men, pray to be kept whole
From bringing down a weaker soul.
Your minute's joy so meet in doin'
May be the woman's door to ruin; 435
The door to wandering up and down,
A painted whore at half a crown.
The bright mind fouled, the beauty gay
All eaten out and fallen away,
By drunken days and weary tramps 440
From pub to pub by city lamps
Till men despise the game they started
Till health and beauty are departed,
And in a slum the reeking hag
Mumbles[21] a crust with toothy jag, 445
Or gets the river's help to end
The life too wrecked for man to mend.

We spat and smoked and took our swipe[22]
Till Silas up and tap his pipe,

---

[20]Sharpers.   [21]Chews.   [22]Beer.

And begged us all to pay attention 450
Because he'd several things to mention.
We'd seen the fight (Hear, hear. That's
     you);
But still one task remained to do,
That task was his, he didn't shun it,
To give the purse to him as won it. 455
With this remark, from start to out
He'd never seen a brisker bout.
There was the purse. At that he'd leave it.
Let Kane come forward to receive it.

I took the purse and hemmed and bowed, 460
And called for gin punch for the crowd;
And when the second bowl was done,
I called, "Let's have another one."
Si's wife come in and sipped and sipped
(As women will) till she was pipped. 465
And Si hit Dicky Twot a clouter
Because he put his arm about her;
But after Si got overtasked
She sat and kissed whoever asked.
My Doxy Jane was splashed by this, 470
I took her on my knee to kiss.
And Tom cried out, "O damn the gin;
Why can't we all have women in?
Bess Evans, now, or Sister Polly,
Or those two housemaids at the Folly? 475
Let someone nip[23] to Biddy Price's,
They'd all come in a brace of trices.
Rose Davies, Sue, and Betsy Perks;
One man, one girl, and damn all Turks."
But, no. "More gin," they cried; "Come
     on. 480
We'll have the girls in when it's gone."
So round the gin went, hot and heady,
Hot Hollands punch on top of deady.[24]

Hot Hollands punch on top of stout[25]
Puts madness in and wisdom out. 485
From drunken man to drunken man
The drunken madness raged and ran.
"I'm climber Joe who climbed the spire."
"You're climber Joe the bloody liar."
"Who says I lie?"   "I do."
                         "You lie, 490
I climbed the spire and had a fly."
"I'm French Suzanne, the Circus Dancer,
I'm going to dance a bloody Lancer."[26]
"If I'd my rights I'm Squire's heir."
"By rights I'd be a millionaire." 495
"By rights I'd be the lord of you,
But Farmer Scriggins had his do,

---

[23]Run.   [24]Gin.   [25]Strong, bitter beer.
[26]A kind of dance.

He done me, so I've had to hoove it,
I've got it all wrote down to prove it.
And one of these dark winter nights   500
He'll learn I mean to have my rights;
I'll bloody him a bloody fix,
I'll bloody burn his bloody ricks."

From three long hours of gin and smokes,
And two girls' breath and fifteen blokes,   505
A warmish night, and windows shut,
The room stank like a fox's gut.
The heat and smell and drinking deep
Began to stun the gang to sleep.
Some fell downstairs to sleep on the mat,   510
Some snored it sodden where they sat.
Dick Twot had lost a tooth and wept,
But all the drunken others slept.
Jane slept beside me in the chair,
And I got up; I wanted air.   515

I opened window wide and leaned
Out of that pigstye of the fiend
And felt a cool wind go like grace
About the sleeping market-place.
The clock struck three, and sweetly, slowly,
The bells chimed Holy, Holy, Holy;   521
And in a second's pause there fell
The cold note of the chapel bell,
And then a cock crew, flapping wings,
And summat made me think of things.   525
How long those ticking clocks had gone
From church and chapel, on and on,
Ticking the time out, ticking slow
To men and girls who'd come and go,
And how they ticked in belfry dark   530
When half the town was bishop's park,
And how they'd rung a chime full tilt
The night after the church was built,
And how that night was Lambert's Feast,
The night I'd fought and been a beast.   535
And how a change had come.   And then
I thought, "You tick to different men."

What with the fight and what with drinking
And being awake alone there thinking,
My mind began to carp and tetter,[27]   540
"If this life's all, the beasts are better."
And then I thought, "I wish I'd seen
The many towns this town has been;
I wish I knew if they'd a-got
A kind of summat we've a-not,   545
If them as built the church so fair
Were half the chaps folk say they were;
For they'd the skill to draw their plan,
And skill's a joy to any man;
And they'd the strength, not skill alone,   550

To build it beautiful in stone;
And strength and skill together thus
O, they were happier men than us.

"But if they were, they had to die
The same as every one and I.   555
And no one lives again, but dies,
And all the bright goes out of eyes,
And all the skill goes out of hands,
And all the wise brain understands,
And all the beauty, all the power   560
Is cut down like a withered flower.
In all the show from birth to rest
I give the poor dumb cattle best."

I wondered, then, why life should be,
And what would be the end of me   565
When youth and health and strength were
          gone
And cold old age came creeping on?
A keeper's gun?   The Union[28] ward?
Or that new quod[29] at Hereford?
And looking round I felt disgust   570
At all the nights of drink and lust,
And all the looks of all the swine
Who'd said that they were friends of mine;
And yet I knew, when morning came,
The morning would be just the same,   575
For I'd have drinks and Jane would meet me
And drunken Silas Jones would greet me,
And I'd risk quod and keeper's gun
Till all the silly game was done.
"For parson chaps are mad, supposin'   580
A chap can change the road he's chosen."
And then the Devil whispered, "Saul,
Why should you want to live at all?
Why fret and sweat and try to mend?
It's all the same thing in the end.   585
But when it's done," he said, "it's ended.
Why stand it, since it can't be mended?"
And in my heart I heard him plain,
"Throw yourself down and end it, Kane."

"Why not?" said I.   "Why not?   But no.
I won't.   I never had my go.   591
I've not had all the world can give.
Death by and by, but first I'll live.
The world owes me my time of times,
And that time's coming now, by crimes."   595

A madness took me then.   I felt
I'd like to hit the world a belt.
I felt that I could fly through air,
A screaming star with blazing hair,
A rushing comet, crackling, numbing   600
The folk with fear of judgment coming,

[27]Grow irritated (as with a skin disease).

[28]Workhouse.   [29]Prison.

A 'Lijah in a fiery car,
Coming to tell folk what they are.

"That's what I'll do," I shouted loud,
"I'll tell this sanctimonious crowd   605
This town of window peeping, prying,
Maligning, peering, hinting, lying,
Male and female human blots
Who would, but daren't be, whores and sots,
That they're so steeped in petty vice   610
That they're less excellent than lice,
That they're so soaked in petty virtue
That touching one of them will dirt you,
Dirt you with the stain of mean
Cheating trade and going between,   615
Pinching, starving, scraping, hoarding,
Spying through the chinks of boarding
To see if Sue, the prentice lean,
Dares to touch the margarine.
Fawning, cringing, oiling boots,   620
Raging in the crowd's pursuits,
Flinging stones at all the Stephens,[30]
Standing firm with all the evens,
Making hell for all the odd,
All the lonely ones of God,   625
Those poor lonely ones who find
Dogs more mild than human kind.
For dogs," I said, "are nobles born
To most of you, you cockled corn.[31]
I've known dogs to leave their dinner,   630
Nosing a kind heart in a sinner.
Poor old Crafty wagged his tail
The day I first came home from jail.
When all my folk, so primly clad,
Glowered black and thought me mad,   635
And muttered how they'd been respected,
While I was what they'd all expected.
(I've thought of that old dog for years,
And of how near I come to tears.)

But you, you minds of bread and cheese,   640
Are less divine than that dog's fleas.
You suck blood from kindly friends,
And kill them when it serves your ends.
Double traitors, double black,
Stabbing only in the back,   645
Stabbing with the knives you borrow
From the friends you bring to sorrow.
You stab all that's true and strong,
Truth and strength you say are wrong,
Meek and mild, and sweet and creeping,   650
Repeating, canting, cadging,[32] peeping,
That's the art and that's the life
To win a man his neighbor's wife.

All that's good and all that's true,
You kill that, so I'll kill you."   655

At that I tore my clothes in shreds
And hurled them on the window leads;
I flung my boots through both the winders
And knocked the glass to little flinders;   659
The punch bowl and the tumblers followed,
And then I seized the lamps and holloed,
And down the stairs, and tore back bolts,
As mad as twenty blooded colts;
And out into the street I pass,
As mad as two-year-olds at grass,   665
A naked madman waving grand
A blazing lamp in either hand.
I yelled like twenty drunken sailors,
"The devil's come among the tailors."
A blaze of flame behind me streamed,   670
And then I clashed the lamps and screamed
"I'm Satan, newly come from hell."
And then I spied the fire bell.

I've been a ringer, so I know
How best to make a big bell go.   675
So on to bell-rope swift I swoop,
And stick my one foot in the loop
And heave a down-swig[33] till I groan,
"Awake, you swine, you devil's own."
I made the fire-bell awake,   680
I felt the bell-rope throb and shake;
I felt the air mingle and clang
And beat the walls a muffled bang,
And stifle back and boom and bay
Like muffled peals on Boxing Day,[34]   685
And then surge up and gather shape,
And spread great pinions and escape;
And each great bird of clanging shrieks
O Fire! Fire, from iron beaks.
My shoulders cracked to send around   690
Those shrieking birds made out of sound
With news of fire in their bills.
(They heard 'em plain beyond Wall Hills.)

Up go the winders, out come heads,
I heard the springs go creak in beds;   695
But still I heave and sweat and tire,
And still the clang goes "Fire, Fire!"
"Where is it, then? Who is it, there?
You ringer, stop, and tell us where."
"Run round and let the Captain know."   700
"It must be bad, he's ringing so."
"It's in the town, I see the flame;
Look there! Look there, how red it came."

---

[30]Stephen was the apostle whose faith in Christ led to his being stoned to death for blasphemy.
[31]Weedy wheat.   [32]Begging.

[33]A downward pull.
[34]The first weekday after Christmas, when presents are given to servants, postmen, etc.

"Where is it, then? O stop the bell."
I stopped and called: "It's fire of hell;   705
And this is Sodom and Gomorrah,
And now I'll burn you up, begorra."

By this the firemen were mustering,
The half-dressed stable men were flustering,
Backing the horses out of stalls   710
While this man swears and that man bawls,
"Don't take th' old mare. Back, Toby, back.
Back, Lincoln. Where's the fire, Jack?"
"Damned if I know. Out Preston way."
"No. It's at Chancey's Pitch, they say."   715
"It's sixteen ricks at Pauntley burnt."
"You back old Darby out, I durn't."
They ran the big red engine out,
And put 'em to with damn and shout.
And then they start to raise the shire,   720
"Who brought the news, and where's the
    fire?"
They'd moonlight, lamps, and gas to light
    'em.
I give a screech-owl's screech to fright 'em,
And snatch from underneath their noses
The nozzles of the fire hoses.   725
"I am the fire. Back, stand back,
Or else I'll fetch your skulls a crack;
D'you see these copper nozzles here?
They weigh ten pounds apiece, my dear;
I'm fire of hell come up this minute   730
To burn this town, and all that's in it.
To burn you dead and burn you clean,
You cogwheels in a stopped machine,
You hearts of snakes, and brains of pigeons,
You dead devout of dead religions,   735
You offspring of the hen and ass,
By Pilate ruled, and Caiaphas.
Now your account is totted.[35] Learn
Hell's flames are loose and you shall burn."

At that I leaped and screamed and ran,   740
I heard their cries go, "Catch him, man."
"Who was it?" "Down him." "Out him,
    Ern."
"Duck him at pump, we'll see who'll burn."
A policeman clutched, a fireman clutched,
A dozen others snatched and touched.   745
"By God, he's stripped down to his buff."[36]
"By God, we'll make him warm enough."
"After him." "Catch him." "Out him."[37]

    "Scrob[38] him."
"We'll give him hell." "By God, we'll mob
    him."

"We'll duck him, scrout[39] him, flog him,
    fratch[40] him."   750
"All right," I said. "But first you'll catch
    him."

The men who don't know to the root
The joy of being swift of foot,
Have never known divine and fresh
The glory of the gift of flesh,   755
Nor felt the feet exult, nor gone
Along a dim road, on and on,
Knowing again the bursting glows,
The mating hare in April knows,
Who tingles to the pads with mirth   760
At being the swiftest thing on earth.
O, if you want to know delight,
Run naked in an autumn night,
And laugh, as I laughed then, to find
A running rabble drop behind,   765
And whang, on every door you pass,
Two copper nozzles, tipped with brass,
And doubly whang at every turning,
And yell, "All hell's let loose, and burning."

I beat my brass and shouted fire   770
At doors of parson, lawyer, squire,
At all three doors I threshed and slammed
And yelled aloud that they were damned.
I clodded squire's glass with turves
Because he spring-gunned his preserves.   775
Through parson's glass my nozzle swishes
Because he stood for loaves and fishes,
But parson's glass I spared a tittle.
He gave me a orange once when little,
And he who gives a child a treat   780
Makes joy-bells ring in Heaven's street,
And he who gives a child a home
Builds palaces in Kingdom come,
And she who gives a baby birth
Brings Savior Christ again to Earth,   785
For life is joy, and mind is fruit,
And body's precious earth and root.
But lawyer's glass—well, never mind,
Th' old Adam's strong in me, I find.
God pardon man, and may God's son   790
Forgive the evil things I've done.

What more? By Dirty Lane I crept
Back to the Lion, where I slept.
The raging madness hot and floodin'
Boiled itself out and left me sudden,   795
Left me worn out with sick and cold,
Aching as though I'd all grown old;
So there I lay, and there they found me
On door-mat, with a curtain round me.

---

[35] Added up.
[36] Bare skin.   [37] Knock him out.   [38] Scratch him.
[39] Scratch.   [40] Scold.

Si took my heels and Jane my head 800
And laughed, and carried me to bed.
And from the neighboring street they reskied
My boots and trousers, coat and weskit;
They bath-bricked[41] both the nozzles bright
To be mementos of the night, 805
And knowing what I should awake with
They flanneled me a quart to slake with,
And sat and shook till half past two
Expecting Police Inspector Drew.

I woke and drank, and went to meat 810
In clothes still dirty from the street.
Down in the bar I heard 'em tell
How someone rang the fire bell,
And how th' inspector's search had thriven,
And how five pounds reward was given. 815
And Shepherd Boyce, of Marley, glad us
By saying it was blokes from mad'us,
Or two young rips[42] lodged at the Prince
Whom none had seen nor heard of since,
Or that young blade from Worcester Walk
(You know how country people talk). 821
Young Joe the ostler come in sad,
He said th'old mare had bit his dad.
He said there'd come a blazing screeching
Daft Bible-prophet chap a-preaching, 825
Had put th'old mare in such a taking
She'd thought the bloody earth was quaking.
And others come and spread a tale
Of cut-throats out of Gloucester jail,
And how we needed extra cops 830
With all them Welsh come picking hops;
With drunken Welsh in all our sheds
We might be murdered in our beds.

By all accounts, both men and wives
Had had the scare up of their lives. 835

I ate and drank and gathered strength,
And stretched along the bench full length,
Or crossed to window seat to pat
Black Silas Jones's little cat.
At four I called, "You devil's own, 840
The second trumpet shall be blown.
The second trump, the second blast;
Hell's flames are loosed, and judgment's
    passed.
Too late for mercy now.   Take warning.
I'm death and hell and Judgment morning."
I hurled the bench into the settle, 846
I banged the table on the kettle,
I sent Joe's quart of cider spinning.
"Lo, here begins my second inning."
Each bottle, mug, and jug and pot 850
I smashed to crocks in half a tot;

[41]Bathed in a preparation for cleaning metal.
[42]Rakes.

And Joe, and Si, and Nick, and Percy
I rolled together topsy versy.
And as I ran I heard 'em call,
"Now damn to hell, what's gone with Saul?"

Out into street I ran uproarious 856
The devil dancing in me glorious.
And as I ran I yell and shriek
"Come on, now, turn the other cheek."
Across the way by almshouse pump 860
I see old puffing parson stump.
Old parson, red-eyed as a ferret
From nightly wrestlings with the spirit;
I ran across, and barred his path.
His turkey gills went red as wrath 865
And then he froze, as parsons can.
"The police will deal with you, my man."
"Not yet," said I, "not yet they won't;
And now you'll hear me, like or don't.
The English Church both is and was 870
A subsidy of Caiaphas.
I don't believe in Prayer nor Bible,
They're lies all through, and you're a libel,
A libel on the Devil's plan
When first he miscreated man. 875
You mumble through a formal code
To get which martyrs burned and glowed.

"I look on martyrs as mistakes,
But still they burned for it at stakes;
Your only fire's the jolly fire 880
Where you can guzzle port with Squire,
And back and praise his damned opinions
About his temporal dominions.
You let him give the man who digs,
A filthy hut unfit for pigs, 885
Without a well, without a drain,
With mossy thatch that lets in rain,
Without a 'lotment,[43] 'less he rent it,
And never meat, unless he scent it,
But weekly doles of 'leven shilling 890
To make a grown man strong and willing,
To do the hardest work on earth
And feed his wife when she gives birth,
And feed his little children's bones.
I tell you, man, the Devil groans. 895
With all your main and all your might
You back what is against what's right;
You let the Squire do things like these,
You back him in't and give him ease,
You take his hand, and drink his wine, 900
And he's a hog, but you're a swine.
For you take gold to teach God's ways
And teach man how to sing God's praise.
And now I'll tell you what you teach
In downright honest English speech. 905

[43]A small portion of land for his own use.

"You teach the ground-down starving man
That Squire's greed's Jehovah's plan.
You get his learning circumvented
Lest it should make him discontented
(Better a brutal, starving nation   910
Than men with thoughts above their station),
You let him neither read nor think,
You goad his wretched soul to drink
And then to jail, the drunken boor;
O sad intemperance of the poor.   915
You starve his soul till it's rapscallion,
Then blame his flesh for being stallion.
You send your wife around to paint
The golden glories of 'restraint.'
How moral exercise bewild'rin'   920
Would soon result in fewer children.
You work a day in Squire's fields
And see what sweet restraint it yields,
A woman's day at turnip picking,
Your heart's too fat for plow or ricking.   925

"And you whom luck taught French and
        Greek
Have purple flaps on either cheek,
A stately house, and time for knowledge,
And gold to send your sons to college,
That pleasant place, where getting learning
Is also key to money earning.   931
But quite your damndest want of grace
Is what you do to save your face;
The way you sit astride the gates
By padding wages out of rates;[44]   935
Your Christmas gifts of shoddy blankets
That every working soul may thank its
Loving parson, loving squire
Through whom he can't afford a fire.
Your well-packed bench, your prison pen,   940
To keep them something less than men;
Your friendly clubs to help 'em bury,
Your charities of midwifery.
Your bidding children duck and cap
To them who give them workhouse pap.   945
O, what you are, and what you preach,
And what you do, and what you teach
Is not God's Word, nor honest schism,
But Devil's cant and pauperism."

By this time many folk had gathered   950
To listen to me while I blathered;
I said my piece, and when I'd said it,
I'll do old purple parson credit,
He sunk (as sometimes parsons can)
His coat's excuses[45] in the man.   955
"You think that Squire and I are kings
Who made the existing state of things,

[44] Assessments on property, used to relieve the poor.

[45] Excuses for his profession.

And made it ill. I answer, No,
States are not made, nor patched; they grow,
Grow slow through centuries of pain   960
And grow correctly in the main,
But only grow by certain laws
Of certain bits in certain jaws.
You want to doctor that. Let be.
You cannot patch a growing tree.   965
Put these two words beneath your hat,
These two: securus judicat.[46]
The social states of human kinds
Are made by multitudes of minds,
And after multitudes of years   970
A little human growth appears
Worth having, even to the soul
Who sees most plain it's not the whole.

"This state is dull and evil, both,
I keep it in the path of growth;   975
You think the Church an outworn fetter;
Kane, keep it, till you've built a better.
And keep the existing social state;
I quite agree it's out of date,
One does too much, another shirks,   980
Unjust, I grant; but still . . . it works.
To get the whole world out of bed
And washed, and dressed, and warmed, and
        fed,
To work, and back to bed again,
Believe me, Saul, costs worlds of pain.   985
Then, as to whether true or sham
That book of Christ, Whose priest I am;
The Bible is a lie, say you,
Where do you stand, suppose it true?
Good-bye. But if you've more to say,   990
My doors are open night and day.
Meanwhile, my friend, 'twould be no sin
To mix more water in your gin.
We're neither saints nor Philip Sidneys,
But mortal men with mortal kidneys."   995

He took his snuff, and wheezed a greeting,
And waddled off to mothers' meeting;
I hung my head upon my chest,
I give old purple parson best.
For while the Plow tips round the Pole   1000
The trained mind outs the upright soul,
As Jesus said the trained mind might,
Being wiser than the sons of light,
But trained men's minds are spread so thin
They let all sorts of darkness in;   1005
Whatever light man finds they doubt it
They love, not light, but talk about it.

But parson'd proved to people's eyes
That I was drunk, and he was wise;

[46] The man who is untroubled judges.

And people grinned and women tittered, 1010
And little children mocked and twittered.
So, blazing mad, I stalked to bar
To show how noble drunkards are,
And guzzled spirits like a beast,
To show contempt for Church and priest, 1015
Until, by six, my wits went round
Like hungry pigs in parish pound.
At half past six, rememb'ring Jane,
I staggered into street again
With mind made up (or primed with gin)
To bash the cop who'd run me in; 1021
For well I knew I'd have to cock up
My legs that night inside the lock-up,
And it was my most fixed intent
To have a fight before I went. 1025
Our Fates are strange, and no one knows his;
Our lovely Savior Christ disposes.

Jane wasn't where we'd planned, the jade.
She'd thought me drunk and hadn't stayed.
So I went up the Walk to look for her 1030
And lingered by the little brook for her,
And dowsed my face, and drank at spring,
And watched two wild duck on the wing.
The moon come pale, the wind come cool,
A big pike leapt in Lower Pool, 1035
The peacock screamed, the clouds were strak-
ing,[47]
My cut cheek felt the weather breaking;
An orange sunset waned and thinned
Foretelling rain and western wind, ·
And while I watched I heard distinct 1040
The metals on the railway clinked.
The blood-edged clouds were all in tatters,
The sky and earth seemed mad as hatters;
They had a death look, wild and odd,
Of something dark foretold by God. 1045
And seeing it so, I felt so shaken
I wouldn't keep the road I'd taken,
But wandered back towards the inn
Resolved to brace myself with gin.
And as I walked, I said, "It's strange, 1050
There's Death let loose to-night, and
Change."

In Cabbage Walk I made a haul
Of two big pears from lawyer's wall,
And, munching one, I took the lane
Back into Market-place again. 1055
Lamp-lighter Dick had passed the turning.
And all the Homend lamps were burning.
The windows shone, the shops were busy,
But that strange Heaven made me dizzy.
The sky had all God's warning writ 1060
In bloody marks all over it,

[47]Streaking.

And over all I thought there was
A ghastly light besides the gas.
The Devil's tasks and Devil's rages
Were giving me the Devil's wages. 1065

In Market-place it's always light,
The big shop windows make it bright;
And in the press of people buying
I spied a little fellow crying
Because his mother'd gone inside 1070
And left him there, and so he cried.
And mother'd beat him when she found him,
And mother's whip would curl right round
him,
And mother'd say he'd done't to crost her,
Though there being crowds about he'd lost
her. 1075

Lord, give to men who are old and rougher
The things that little children suffer,
And let keep bright and undefiled
The young years of the little child.
I pat his head at edge of street 1080
And gi'm my second pear to eat.
Right under lamp, I pat his head,
"I'll stay till mother come," I said,
And stay I did, and joked and talked,
And shoppers wondered as they walked. 1085
"There's that Saul Kane, the drunken blag-
gard,
Talking to little Jimmy Jaggard.
The drunken blaggard reeks of drink."
"Whatever will his mother think?"
"Wherever has his mother gone? 1090
Nip round to Mrs. Jaggard's, John,
And say her Jimmy's out again,
In Market place, with boozer Kane."
"When he come out to-day he staggered.
O, Jimmy Jaggard, Jimmy Jaggard." 1095
"His mother's gone inside to bargain,
Run in and tell her, Polly Margin,
And tell her poacher Kane is tipsy
And selling Jimmy to a gipsy."
"Run in to Mrs. Jaggard, Ellen, 1100
Or else, dear knows, there'll be no tellin',
And don't dare leave yer till you've fount her,
You'll find her at the linen counter."
I told a tale, to Jim's delight,
Of where the tom-cats go by night, 1105
And how when moonlight come they went
Among the chimneys black and bent,
From roof to roof, from house to house,
With little baskets full of mouse
All red and white, both joint and chop 1110
Like meat out of a butcher's shop;
Then all along the wall they creep
And everyone is fast asleep,

And honey-hunting moths go by,
And by the bread-batch[48] crickets cry;   1115
Then on they hurry, never waiting
To lawyer's backyard cellar grating
Where Jaggard's cat, with clever paw,
Unhooks a broke-brick's secret door;
Then down into the cellar black,   1120
Across the wood slug's slimy track,
Into an old cask's quiet hollow,
Where they've got seats for what's to follow;
Then each tom-cat lights little candles,
And O, the stories and the scandals,   1125
And O, the songs and Christmas carols,
And O, the milk from little barrels.
They light a fire fit for roasting
(And how good mouse-meat smells when
        toasting),
Then down they sit to merry feast   1130
While moon goes west and sun comes east.

Sometimes they make so merry there
Old lawyer come to head of stair
To 'fend with fist and poker took firm
His parchments channeled by the bookworm,
And all his deeds, and all his packs   1136
Of withered ink and sealing wax;
And there he stands, with candle raised,
And listens like a man amazed,
Or like a ghost a man stands dumb at,   1140
He says, "Hush! Hush! I'm sure there's
        summat."
He hears outside the brown owl call,
He hears the death-tick tap the wall,
The gnawing of the wainscot mouse,
The creaking up and down the house,   1145
The unhooked window's hinges ranging,
The sounds that say the wind is changing.
At last he turns, and shakes his head,
"It's nothing, I'll go back to bed."

And just then Mrs. Jaggard came   1150
To view and end her Jimmy's shame.

She made one rush and gi'm a bat
And shook him like a dog a rat.
"I can't turn round but what you're straying.
I'll give you tales and gipsy playing.   1155
I'll give you wand'ring off like this
And listening to whatever 'tis,
You'll laugh the little side of the can,
You'll have the whip for this, my man;
And not a bite of meat nor bread   1160
You'll touch before you go to bed.
Some day you'll break your mother's heart,
After God knows she's done her part,
Working her arms off day and night

Trying to keep your collars white.   1165
Look at your face, too, in the street.
What dirty filth've you found to eat?
Now don't you blubber here, boy, or
I'll give you sum't to blubber for."
She snatched him off from where we stand
And knocked the pear-core from his hand,
And looked at me, "You Devil's limb,   1172
How dare you talk to Jaggard's Jim;
You drunken, poaching, boozing brute, you,
If Jaggard was a man he'd shoot you."   1175
She glared all this, but didn't speak,
She gasped, white hollows in her cheek;
Jimmy was writhing, screaming wild,
The shoppers thought I'd killed the child.

I had to speak, so I begun.   1180
"You'd oughtn't beat your little son;
He did no harm, but seeing him there
I talked to him and gi'm a pear;
I'm sure the poor child meant no wrong,
It's all my fault he stayed so long,   1185
He'd not have stayed, mum, I'll be bound
If I'd not chanced to come around.
It's all my fault he stayed, not his.
I kept him here, that's how it is."
"Oh! And how dare you, then?" says she,
"How dare you tempt my boy from me?   1191
How dare you do't, you drunken swine,
Is he your child or is he mine?
A drunken sot they've had the beak[49] to,
Has got his dirty whores to speak to,   1195
His dirty mates with whom he drink,
Not little children, one would think.
Look on him, there," she says, "look on him
And smell the stinking gin upon him,
The lowest sot, the drunk'nest liar,   1200
The dirtiest dog in all the shire:
Nice friends for any woman's son
After ten years, and all she's done.

"For I've had eight, and buried five,
And only three are left alive.   1205
I've given them all we could afford.
I've taught them all to fear the Lord.
They've had the best we had to give,
The only three the Lord let live.

"For Minnie whom I loved the worst   1210
Died mad in childbed with her first.
And John and Mary died of measles,
And Rob was drownded at the Teasels.
And little Nan, dear little sweet,
A cart run over in the street;   1215
Her little shift was all one stain,
I prayed God put her out of pain.

---

[48] Quantity of dough, or bread, for one baking.

[49] Magistrate.

And all the rest are gone or going
The road to hell, and there's no knowing
For all I've done and all I've made them 1220
I'd better not have overlaid[50] them.
For Susan went the ways of shame
The time the 'till'ry regiment came,
And t'have her child without a father
I think I'd have her buried rather. 1225
And Dicky boozes, God forgimme,
And now't's to be the same with Jimmy.
And all I've done and all I've bore
Has made a drunkard and a whore,
A bastard boy who wasn't meant, 1230
And Jimmy gwine where Dicky went;
For Dick began the self-same way
And my old hairs are going gray,
And my poor man's a withered knee,
And all the burden falls on me. 1235

"I've washed eight little children's limbs,
I've taught eight little souls their hymns,
I've risen sick and lain down pinched
And borne it all and never flinched;
But to see him, the town's disgrace, 1240
With God's commandments broke in's face,
Who never worked, not he, nor earned,
Nor will do till the seas are burned,
Who never did since he was whole
A hand's turn for a human soul, 1245
But poached and stole and gone with women,
And swilled down gin enough to swim in,
To see him only lift one finger
To make my little Jimmy linger.
In spite of all his mother's prayers, 1250
And all her ten long years of cares,
And all her broken spirit's cry
That drunkard's finger puts them by,
And Jimmy turns. And now I see
That just as Dick was, Jim will be, 1255
And all my life will have been vain.
I might have spared myself the pain,
And done the world a blessed riddance
If I'd a drowned 'em all like kittens.
And he the sot, so strong and proud, 1260
Who'd make white shirts of's mother's
    shroud,
He laughs now, it's a joke to him,
Though it's the gates of hell to Jim.

"I've had my heart burnt out like coal,
And drops of blood wrung from my soul 1265
Day in, day out, in pain and tears,
For five and twenty wretched years;
And he, he's ate the fat and sweet,
And loafed and spat at top of street,

And drunk and leched from day till morrow,
And never known a moment's sorrow. 1271
He come out drunk from th' inn to look
The day my little Nan was took;
He sat there drinking, glad and gay,
The night my girl was led astray; 1275
He praised my Dick for singing well,
The night Dick took the road to hell;
And when my corpse goes stiff and blind,
Leaving four helpless souls behind,
He will be there still, drunk and strong. 1280
It do seem hard.   It do seem wrong.
But 'Woe to him by whom the offence,'
Says our Lord Jesus' Testaments.
Whatever seems, God doth not slumber
Though he lets pass times without number.
He'll come with trump to call his own, 1286
And this world's way'll be overthrown.
He'll come with glory and with fire
To cast great darkness on the liar,
To burn the drunkard and the treacher,[51] 1290
And do his judgment on the lecher,
To glorify the spirits' faces
Of those whose ways were stony places,
Who chose with Ruth the better part;
O Lord, I see Thee as Thou art, 1295
O God, the fiery four-edged sword,
The thunder of the wrath outpoured,
The fiery four-faced creatures burning,
And all the four-faced wheels all turning,
Coming with trump and fiery saint. 1300
Jim, take me home, I'm turning faint."
They went, and some cried, "Good old sod."
"She put it to him straight, by God."

Summat she was, or looked, or said,
Went home and made me hang my head. 1305
I slunk away into the night
Knowing deep down that she was right.
I'd often heard religious ranters,
And put them down as windy canters,
But this old mother made me see 1310
The harm I done by being me.
Being both strong and given to sin
I 'tracted weaker vessels in.
So back to bar to get more drink,
I didn't dare begin to think, 1315
And there were drinks and drunken singing,
As though this life were dice for flinging;
Dice to be flung, and nothing furder,
And Christ's blood just another murder.
"Come on, drinks round, salue,[52] drink
    hearty, 1320
Now, Jane, the punch-bowl for the party.
If any here won't drink with me
I'll knock his bloody eyes out.   See?

---

[50]Smothered.

[51]Deceiver.   [52]Salutations.

Come on, cigars round, rum for mine,
Sing us a smutty song, some swine." 1325
But though the drinks and songs went round
That thought remained, it was not drowned.
And when I'd rise to get a light
I'd think, "What's come to me to-night?"

There's always crowds when drinks are
    standing. 1330
The house doors slammed along the landing,
The rising wind was gusty yet,
And those who came in late were wet;
And all my body's nerves were snappin'
With sense of summat 'bout to happen, 1335
And music seemed to come and go
And seven lights danced in a row.
There used to be a custom then,
Miss Bourne, the Friend, went round at ten
To all the pubs in all the place, 1340
To bring the drunkards' souls to grace;
Some sulked, of course, and some were
    stirred,
But none give her a dirty word.
A tall pale woman, grey and bent,
Folk said of her that she was sent. 1345
She wore Friends' clothes, and women
    smiled,
But she'd a heart just like a child.
She come to us near closing time
When we were at some smutty rime,
And I was mad, and ripe for fun; 1350
I wouldn't a minded what I done.
So when she come so prim and grey
I pound the bar and sing, "Hooray,
Here's Quaker come to bless and kiss us,
Come, have a gin and bitters, missus. 1355
Or may be Quaker girls so prim
Would rather start a bloody hymn.
Now Dick, oblige. A hymn, you swine,
Pipe up the 'Officer of the Line,'
A song to make one's belly ache, 1360
Or 'Nell and Roger at the Wake,'
Or that sweet song, the talk in town,
'The lady fair and Abel Brown.'
'O, who's that knocking at the door,'
Miss Bourne'll play the music score." 1365
The men stood dumb as cattle are,
They grinned, but thought I'd gone too far,
There come a hush and no one break it,
They wondered how Miss Bourne would
    take it.
She up to me with black eyes wide, 1370
She looked as though her spirit cried;
She took my tumbler from the bar
Beside where all the matches are
And poured it out upon the floor dust,
Among the fag-ends, spit and sawdust. 1375

"Saul Kane," she said "when next you drink,
Do me the gentleness to think
That every drop of drink accursed
Makes Christ within you die of thirst,
That every dirty word you say 1380
Is one more flint upon His way,
Another thorn about His head,
Another mock by where He tread,
Another nail, another cross.
All that you are is that Christ's loss." 1385
The clock run down and struck a chime
And Mrs. Si said, "Closing time."

The wet was pelting on the pane
And something broke inside my brain,
I heard the rain drip from the gutters 1390
And Silas putting up the shutters,
While one by one the drinkers went;
I got a glimpse of what it meant,
How she and I had stood before
In some old town by some old door 1395
Waiting intent while someone knocked
Before the door for ever locked;
She was so white that I was scared,
A gas jet, turned the wrong way, flared,
And Silas snapped the bars in place. 1400
Miss Bourne stood white and searched my
    face.
When Silas done, with ends of tunes
He 'gan a gathering the spittoons,
His wife primmed lips and took the till.
Miss Bourne stood still and I stood still, 1405
And "Tick. Slow. Tick. Slow" went the
    clock.
She said, "He waits until you knock."
She turned at that and went out swift,
Si grinned and winked, his missus sniffed.

I heard her clang the Lion door, 1410
I marked a drink-drop roll to floor;
It took up scraps of sawdust, furry,
And crinkled on, a half inch, blurry;
A drop from my last glass of gin;
And someone waiting to come in, 1415
A hand upon the door latch gropen
Knocking the man inside to open.
I know the very words I said,
They bayed like bloodhounds in my head.
"The water's going out to sea 1420
And there's a great moon calling me;
But there's a great sun calls the moon,
And all God's bells will carol soon
For joy and glory and delight
Of someone coming home to-night." 1425

Out into darkness, out to night,
My flaring heart gave plenty light,

So wild it was there was no knowing
Whether the clouds or stars were blowing;
Blown chimney pots and folk blown blind,
And puddles glimmering like my mind,   1431
And chinking glass from windows banging,
And inn signs swung like people hanging,
And in my heart the drink unpriced,
The burning cataracts of Christ.   1435

I did not think, I did not strive,
The deep peace burnt my me alive;
The bolted door had broken in,
I knew that I had done with sin.
I knew that Christ had given me birth   1440
To brother all the souls on earth,
And every bird and every beast
Should share the crumbs broke at the feast.

O glory of the lighted mind.
How dead I'd been, how dumb, how blind.
The station brook, to my new eyes,   1446
Was babbling out of Paradise,
The waters rushing from the rain
Were singing Christ has risen again.
I thought all earthly creatures knelt   1450
From rapture of the joy I felt.
The narrow station-wall's brick ledge,
The wild hop withering in the hedge,
The lights in huntsman's upper storey
Were parts of an eternal glory,   1455
Were God's eternal garden flowers.
I stood in bliss at this for hours.

O glory of the lighted soul.
The dawn came up on Bradlow Knoll,
The dawn with glittering on the grasses, 1460
The dawn which pass and never passes.

"It's dawn," I said, "And chimney's smok-
     ing,
And all the blessed fields are soaking.
It's dawn, and there's an engine shunting;
And hounds, for huntsman's going hunting.
It's dawn, and I must wander north   1466
Along the road Christ led me forth."

So up the road I wander slow
Past where the snowdrops used to grow
With celandines in early springs,   1470
When rainbows were triumphant things
And dew so bright and flowers so glad,
Eternal joy to lass and lad.
And past the lovely brook I paced,
The brook whose source I never traced, 1475
The brook, the one of two which rise
In my green dream in Paradise,

In wells where heavenly buckets clink
To give God's wandering thirsty drink
By those clean cots of carven stone   1480
Where the clear water sings alone.
Then down, past that white-blossomed pond,
And past the chestnut trees beyond,
And past the bridge the fishers knew,
Where yellow flag flowers once grew,   1485
Where we'd go gathering cops[53] of clover,
In sunny June times long since over.
O clover-cops half white, half red,
O beauty from beyond the dead.
O blossom, key. to earth and heaven,   1490
O souls that Christ has new forgiven.

Then down the hill to gipsies' pitch
By where the brook clucks in the ditch.
A gipsy's camp was in the copse,
Three felted tents, with beehive tops,   1495
And round black marks where fires had
     been,
And one old wagon painted green,
And three ribbed horses wrenching grass,
And three wild boys to watch me pass,
And one old woman by the fire   1500
Hulking[54] a rabbit warm from wire.
I loved to see the horses bait.
I felt I walked at Heaven's gate,
That Heaven's gate was opened wide
Yet still the gipsies camped outside.   1505
The waste souls will prefer the wild,
Long after life is meek and mild.
Perhaps when man has entered in
His perfect city free from sin,
The campers will come past the walls   1510
With old lame horses full of galls,
And wagons hung about with withies,
And burning coke in tinker's stithies,
And see the golden town, and choose,
And think the wild too good to lose.   1515
And camp outside, as these camped then
With wonder at the entering men.
So past, and past the stone heap white
That dewberry trailers hid from sight,
And down the field so full of springs,   1520
Where mewing peewits clap their wings,
And past the trap made for the mill
Into the field below the hill.
There was a mist along the stream,
A wet mist, dim, like in a dream;   1525
I heard the heavy breath of cows,
And waterdrops from th'alder boughs;
And eels, or snakes, in dripping grass,
Whipping aside to let me pass.
The gate was backed against the ryme[55] 1530
To pass the cows at milking time.

---

[53]Tops.   [54]Disemboweling.   [55]Rim(?).

And by the gate as I went out
A moldwarp[56] rooted earth wi's snout.
A few steps up the Callows' Lane
Brought me above the mist again,   1535
The two great fields arose like death
Above the mists of human breath.

All earthly things that blessed morning
Were everlasting joy and warning.
The gate was Jesus' way made plain,   1540
The mole was Satan foiled again,
Black blinded Satan snouting way
Along the red of Adam's clay;
The mist was error and damnation,
The lane the road unto salvation.   1545
Out of the mist into the light,
O blessed gift of inner sight.
The past was faded like a dream;
There come the jingling of a team,
A plowman's voice, a clink of chain,   1550
Slow hoofs, and harness under strain.
Up the slow slope a team came bowing,
Old Callow at his autumn plowing,
Old Callow, stooped above the hales,[57]
Plowing the stubble into wales.[58]   1555
His grave eyes looking straight ahead,
Shearing a long straight furrow red;
His plow-foot high to give it earth
To bring new food for men to birth.
O wet red swath of earth laid bare,   1560
O truth, O strength, O gleaming share,[59]
O patient eyes that watch the goal,
O plowman of the sinner's soul.
O Jesus, drive the colter deep
To plow my living man from sleep.   1565

Slow up the hill the plow team plod,
Old Callow at the task of God,
Helped by man's wit, helped by the brute,
Turning a stubborn clay to fruit,
His eyes forever on some sign   1570
To help him plow a perfect line.
At top of rise the plow team stopped,
The fore-horse bent his head and cropped.
Then the chains chack,[60] the brasses jingle,
The lean reins gather through the cringle,[61]
The figures move against the sky,   1576
The clay wave breaks as they go by.
I kneeled there in the muddy fallow,
I knew that Christ was there with Callow,
That Christ was standing there with me,   1580
That Christ had taught me what to be,
That I should plow, and as I plowed
My Savior Christ would sing aloud,
And as I drove the clods apart

Christ would be plowing in my heart,   1585
Through rest-harrow[62] and bitter roots,
Through all my bad life's rotten fruits.

O Christ who holds the open gate,
O Christ who drives the furrow straight,
O Christ, the plow, O Christ, the laughter
Of holy white birds flying after,   1591
Lo, all my heart's field red and torn,
And Thou wilt bring the young green corn,
The young green corn divinely springing,
The young green corn forever singing;   1595
And when the field is fresh and fair
Thy blessed feet shall glitter there,
And we will walk the weeded field,
And tell the golden harvest's yield,
The corn that makes the holy bread   1600
By which the soul of man is fed,
The holy bread, the food unpriced,
Thy everlasting mercy, Christ.

The share will jar on many a stone,
Thou wilt not let me stand alone;   1605
And I shall feel (thou wilt not fail),
Thy hand on mine upon the hale.
Near Bullen Bank, on Gloucester Road,
Thy everlasting mercy showed
The plowman patient on the hill   1610
Forever there, forever still,
Plowing the hill with steady yoke
Of pine-trees lightning-struck and broke.
I've marked the May Hill plowman stay
There on his hill, day after day   1615
Driving his team against the sky,
While men and women live and die.
And now and then he seems to stoop
To clear the colter with the scoop,
Or touch an ox to haw or gee[63]   1620
While Severn stream goes out to sea.
The sea with all her ships and sails,
And that great smoky port in Wales,
And Gloucester tower bright i' the sun,
All know that patient wandering one.   1625
And sometimes when they burn the leaves
The bonfires' smoking trails and heaves,
And girt red flamë twink and twire[64]
As though he plowed the hill afire.
And in men's hearts in many lands   1630
A spiritual plowman stands
Forever waiting, waiting now,
The heart's "Put in, man, zook the plow."

By this the sun was all one glitter,
The little birds were all in twitter;   1635

---

[56]Mole.   [57]Handles of a plow.   [58]Ridges.
[59]Plowshare.   [60]Snap into place.   [61]Ring.

[62]A field shrub.
[63]Left or right.   [64]Peer (figuratively).

Out of a tuft a little lark
Went higher up than I could mark,
His little throat was all one thirst
To sing until his heart should burst
To sing aloft in golden light   1640
His song from blue air out of sight.
The mist drove by, and now the cows
Came plodding up to milking house.
Followed by Frank, the Callows' cowman,
Who whistled "Adam was a plowman."   1645
There come such cawing from the rooks,
Such running chuck[65] from little brooks,
One thought it March, just budding green,
With hedgerows full of celandine.
An otter 'out of stream and played,   1650
Two hares come loping up and stayed;
Wide-eyed and tender-eared but bold.
Sheep bleated up by Penny's fold.
I heard a partridge covey call,
The morning sun was bright on all.   1655
Down the long slope the plow team drove
The tossing rooks arose and hove.
A stone struck on the share. A word
Came to the team. The red earth stirred.

I crossed the hedge by shooter's gap,   1660
I hitched my boxer's belt a strap,
I jumped the ditch and crossed the fallow:
I took the hales from farmer Callow.

How swift the summer goes,
Forget-me-not, pink, rose.   1665
The young grass when I started
And now the hay is carted,
And now my song is ended,
And all the summer spended;
The blackbird's second brood   1670
Routs beech leaves in the wood;
The pink and rose have speeded,
Forget-me-not has seeded.
Only the winds that blew,
The rain that makes things new,   1675
The earth that hides things old,
And blessings manifold.

O lovely lily clean,
O lily springing green,

[65]Running with direct impact.

O lily bursting white,   1680
Dear lily of delight,
Spring in my heart agen
That I may flower to men.

ON GROWING OLD

Be with me Beauty for the fire is dying,
My dog and I are old, too old for roving,
Man, whose young passion sets the spindrift
    flying
Is soon too lame to march, too cold for loving.

I take the book and gather to the fire,   5
Turning old yellow leaves; minute by minute,
The clock ticks to my heart; a withered wire
Moves a thin ghost of music in the spinet.

I cannot sail your seas, I cannot wander,
Your cornland, nor your hill-land nor your
    valleys,   10
Ever again, nor share the battle yonder
Where the young knight the broken squadron
    rallies.

Only stay quiet while my mind remembers
The beauty of fire from the beauty of embers.

Beauty, have pity, for the strong have power
The rich their wealth, the beautiful their
    grace   16
Summer of man its sunlight and its flower
Spring of man all April in a face.

Only, as in the jostling in the Strand,
Where the mob thrusts or loiters or is loud 20
The beggar with the saucer in his hand
Asks only a penny from the passing crowd.

So, from this glittering world with all its
    fashion
Its fire and play of men, its stir, its march,
Let me have wisdom, Beauty, wisdom and
    passion,   25
Bread to the soul, rain where the summers
    parch.

Give me but these, and though the darkness
    close
Even the night will blossom as the rose.

VII

The Present Time, 1914–

WHEN Great Britain declared war on Germany on 4 August, 1914, following Germany's declarations of war against Russia on 1 August and against France on 3 August, and her immediate violation of the neutrality of Belgium, the whole English-speaking world was inexpressibly shocked. Many in England, as well as in the United States, could scarcely believe their eyes and ears, and were too horrified to think. The distinguished liberal statesman, Lord Morley, resigned his cabinet post and retired to private life in an ecstasy of unthinking horror. Nearly everybody felt that at any rate the war would be short. But the first battle of the Marne, in September, destroyed the Germans' hope for swift crushing victory on their western front, and Earl Kitchener warned the English that they were in for a long desperate fight that might last several years. Slowly it began to dawn on the public mind that a life-or-death struggle for world domination was under way between rival economies and opposed "ideologies." No country in any part of the world could be indifferent to the outcome, and gradually almost every country was forced to take sides. Woodrow Wilson, then President of the United States, formulated the most appealing interpretation of the conflict. England, France, and their allies, he declared, were fighting to make the world safe for democracy; and he led the United States into battle on their side to assist in this purpose.

The letters written by Henry James from the summer of 1914 until his death early in 1916 form a singularly illuminating record of the immediate impact of the war on a man of acute intelligence and sound feeling. James, of course, was American-born, but had made his home in England ever since the end of 1876, and wrote his war letters from there. On 31 July, just before the declarations above-mentioned, he wrote to a friend:

What one first feels one's self uttering is the intense unthinkability of anything so blank and so infamous in an age that we have been living in and taking for our own as if it were of a high refinement of civilization—in spite of all conscious incongruities; finding it after all carrying this abomination in its blood, finding this to have been what it *meant* all the while, is like suddenly having to recognize in one's family circle or group of best friends a band of murderers, swindlers, and villains. It makes us wonder whom in the world we are now to live with; and even if, with everything publicly and internationally so given away, we can live, or want to live at all. . . . Almost the worst thing is that the dreadfulness, all of it, *may* become interesting—to the blight and ruin of our poor dear old cherished source of interest, and in spite of one's resentment at having to live in such a way. With it all, too, is the terrible sense that the people of this country may well—by some awful brutal justice—be going to get something bad for the exhibition that has gone on so long of their huge materialized stupidity and vulgarity.

On 1 October he still found the war "a huge nightmare and a huge unspeakability," but, he added,

That isn't my last word or my last *sense*. This great country has found, and is still more finding, certain parts of herself again that had seemed for long a good deal lost. But here they are now—magnificent; and we haven't yet seen a quarter of them.

As time went on, he continued to be heartened by multiplying evidence that

England is not a whit less sound, less fundamentally sane, than she ever was, but in fact ever so much *finer* and inwardly wiser, and has been appointed by the gods to find herself again, without more delay, in some of those aspects and on some of those sides that she had allowed to get too much overlaid and encrusted. She is doing this in the grand manner, and I can only say that I find the spectacle really splendid to assist at.

In the summer of 1915 James, partly to underline his opinion of those Americans who appeared to be shocked "at everything that is not a reiterated blandishment and slobberation of Germany," of "the enemy, damn his soul to hell," became at last a British subject. He did not live to hail the entry of the United States into a conflict which he regarded simply as a defense of civilization and decency against unspeakably brutal barbarism.

On the whole, James's view of the war was that of educated English-speaking people everywhere. A small minority were less surprised than he, because they had seen that English domination of the earth was bound sooner or later to be challenged, and had realized that Germany was preparing to strike for a big place in the sun. Members of another minority were actually pleased to see exhausting conflict spreading everywhere because they had grown bitterly critical of modern industrial civilization, and hoped it might destroy itself. Still others had become converted to pacifism, and preferred personal ignomiiny and national disaster to military service. In general, however, the English believed they were upholding the cause of decency against brutality, and hoped

that victory would bring in a new era, characterized by growing democracy, growing social justice, and the peaceful co-operation of free peoples. Under the stress of emergency a species of unity, incomplete and imperfect but sufficient for the immediate purpose, was thus achieved. The basis of unity was broad enough to draw in many of the critics of the existing order of society, James amongst them, who imagined that not only a new order but also a regenerate spirit capable of sustaining that order would be the significant outcome of the war.

Victory was won; and from that instant it began to appear that the varied interests demanding consideration from those who were to reconstruct the political framework of a large part of the world could not be reconciled with one another. It is not possible here to enter into any discussion of the problems confronting the peacemakers, or to ask how well qualified they were for their task. They have been strongly condemned. Certainly they could not have satisfied everybody; but it became evident as time passed that they had satisfied practically nobody, and that their partition of European territory, if not also of colonial territory, was an impracticable makeshift. It may be that no group of men could have grasped and solved all of the complex questions which were placed before the statesmen of 1918. This possibility has scarcely been discussed, and perhaps cannot usefully be discussed for another half-century or more; yet it is worth bearing in mind because already it is evident that the critics of the treaty-makers were no more clearheaded or practical than those whom they criticized.

The hard fact which emerged, and which is important for us, is that no magic change of any kind was effected by all the fighting and the costly victory. Men in the 1920's found themselves living in the same old world as that which existed before the war, different only in that it was considerably the worse for wear. No new and better era had dawned. The same old politicians were running the show in much the old way. The old abuses, inequalities, and pretenses were not abolished. Every cause of social division and disintegration which had arisen before the war returned to plague humanity again, with the consequence that the survivors of the conflict who had been held in line by false promises and false hopes now sank into a state of angry disillusion and despair.

Those who most warmly professed themselves to be the true friends of humanity could see only a single ray of light amidst the encircling gloom. It shone in Russia, the one country, it was believed, in which through a bold revolution the people themselves had come into their own. Full-fledged converts to communism were not numerous in England, and as time passed their cause became negligible as a political threat. Nevertheless, communism remained the only source of inspiration and basis of positive belief accessible to many readers and some writers during the 1920's and 1930's. And as events gradually proved that the USSR was moving away from communism, and as the word itself simultaneously fell into disrepute, socialism, broadly or vaguely conceived as an ultimate ideal, retained the power to inspire positive assent and literary effort.

In general, however, recent English literature expresses more clearly and emphatically than anything else a radical unbelief. Even when writers are heading towards positive affirmations they dwell so long and so feelingly upon all that they disbelieve, dislike, or condemn, and present their beliefs so tentatively, if not confusedly, that they in effect swell the chorus of skepticism. Yet here we have to make a distinction. The perfect skeptic, if he anywhere exists, is perfectly silent, and at least makes no contribution to literature. Stephen Spender (1909–), in his critical study entitled *The Destructive Element,* speaks of our time as one "without belief," though his book is wholly concerned with contemporary beliefs. E. M. Forster, asked what he believes, replies: "I do not believe in Belief. But this is an age of faith, and there are so many militant creeds that, in self-defense, one has to formulate a creed of one's own." Both Spender and Forster are looking at the same scene; but one sees our civilization as "decaying, and in some ways barbaric," because it is "without faith," while the other confidently asserts that civilization and faith

are incompatible, and boasts that he is on the side of civilization in adopting as his motto "Lord, I disbelieve—help thou my unbelief."

Obviously these two distinguished writers have one thing in common, and only one. They both dislike intensely our present civilization and think it self-evident that it is going from bad to worse. But their reasons are diametrically different, because they have differing positive beliefs, and each sees present conditions in terms of his own beliefs, and sees, moreover, only a part of a very complex whole.

From this typical illustration several conclusions may fairly be drawn. For whatever reasons, contemporary civilization does not give the imaginative artist any material to work with except by way of satirical attack. Contemplating man as he now is, and man's works, the artist is filled with loathing, contempt, or despair. A delusory appearance of all-dissolving skepticism is created because modern civilization is attacked from every angle, and because there is no semblance of union amongst the artists, who also freely attack one another's positive beliefs. The picture we get is rather one of disintegration into chaos than of consistent skepticism, and this is exactly what both Spender and Forster have in mind. When Spender and others speak of the present age as one without faith or without convictions, they mean that there is no commonly held belief which binds modern society together in unity of outlook and effort. And when Forster and others term this an age of faith they mean, as Forster makes clear for himself, an age of faiths, of militant contradictory competing faiths, all seeking the allegiance of those whom the decay of old beliefs has left bewildered and without direction.

This is very much the situation that had existed before the war of 1914–1918. The war did not mark the beginning of a new era in literature any more than it marked new beginnings in other fields. The postwar literature of England is simply a further development of positions taken up before the war. This is not to say that it presents nothing new, but only that the directions it has followed, in some cases to their extreme limits, are not themselves new. This is not to say, either, that the war had no influence on literature. It did in fact have a direct and immediate influence in the field of poetry; and, as time passed, the war's effects on the national life and temper were duly reflected in fiction.

War-Born Poetry

The war's immediate action on poetry can best be understood in terms of the position of poetry in England in the earliest years of the present century. Briefly, those years were far less favorable to poetry than the Victorian era had been; and that era, we may recall, derives its literary distinction and importance more from its prose than from its gallery of poets. The "coming poet" of the decade ending in 1914 was, in the opinion not only of readers but of some critics, Alfred Noyes (1880–   ). He showed much skill and facility in the composition of narratives in verse. His tales had all the marks of poetry which were then familiar to the general public, and were almost as easy to read and as interesting as the ephemeral novels of the day. And, in the lack of anyone better, he was regarded as a poet, until John Masefield (1878–   ) blasted his way to public attention with *The Everlasting Mercy*.

Noyes was a belated Victorian, able to go where others had worn a path, but without any significant originative powers. A number of his contemporaries were trying, just before the war, to write poetry of one kind or another which might strike a universal note and yet be neither an echo nor a radical departure from tradition. Wilfrid Wilson Gibson (1878–   ), for example, after some early work imitative of Tennyson, began to develop a style of his own, appropriate to the realistic treatment of the lives of poor folk, countrymen, miners, and the like. Humanitarianism was a legacy of the eighteenth century which had weathered the changes and storms of the nineteenth, and seemed to be gathering strength from the break-up of traditional religion. Wilfrid Gibson sought reality and substance by picturing some of the ugly consequences of modern specialization and industrialism, through which he appealed to the sentiment of humanity.

One sufficient trouble with this effort was that Gibson had neither the creative energy nor the freshness of vision to lift his work above the level of conscientious good intention. He attracted some notice because he was getting away from mere decorative prettiness and sentimental idealization, and was trying to find springs of poetry in the common lot of man in our day. Whether or not the attempt was misguided it may not be possible to determine; but at any rate neither Gibson nor others were conspicuously successful in making it.

Some critics and imaginative writers, however, felt that poetry in England had reached the end of known roads, and that the work of Noyes and his like proved it. And Gibson's kind of attempt to strike a fresh poetic spring was not the only one made. Walter John de la Mare (1873–   ), for instance, found it possible as a man to retain or to recapture the simplicity, the direct vision, the playfulness, the unconscious mingling of reality and fantasy, and the delightful inconsequence of a gifted child. He wrote books for children, and childlike poetry for men, in which he explored and vivified a world of imaginative delicacy and beauty which seems to hover on the edge of day-to-day reality. It is our own world and it is not. It is not a dream world, but rather our own world seen through eyes innocent of all our adult problems and our adult knowledge, and eyes consequently open to some mysteries and ghostly visitations which we are accustomed to dismiss incredulously.

Walter de la Mare's imaginative power is unusual, and his books have deserved the warm welcome they have received; nevertheless, he solved the poetic problem, not by facing "this very world which is the world of all of us," but by gracefully escaping to that other world, so like ours, yet so different, where children of all ages lead free lives. He stands ready to welcome us to that world when we are on holiday; but we cannot live there any more than we can live in the dream-world of Keats, or in the imaginative worlds to which Swinburne and William Morris escaped.

Should we look further at the poetry which was appearing just before the war, we should find little that is different in essential character from that at which we have just glanced; and we should be only the more fully justified in concluding that though there was a desire for poetry, and though a good many men of talent were trying to find some way of writing it, even modest success was beyond the reach of all save a few who deliberately turned their backs on the age and escaped, whether to the immemorial calm of a remote countryside or to some fairy world of the detached imagination.

None, however, could escape the war. It brought men back from all their many separate fields of activity and thought and aspiration, from pleasant retreats of the imagination, from selfish amusements, from baffling uncertainties, and placed them face to face with elementary and dreadful realities. Whatever England meant to them individually and to their fellows, or could again mean, depended now on their willingness to fight. The emergency did draw them, as Henry James saw, into unity of conviction, feeling, and action; and forced upon many of them a self-searching or self-recollection which can best be described as a process of getting down to rock bottom. Men stirred to their depths, shocked into sincerity, certain of one thing if of nothing else, and living in unison with their fellows, were in a situation to write true poetry, were there any amongst them born poets. A large number of them did write poetry, and a small part of what they wrote turned out to be the real thing. That none of it was "great" signifies only that no "great" poet happened to be about at the time. There is a kind of truth in the proposition that what men can do is dependent on antecedent and surrounding conditions; and this element of truth is always tempting us to believe that conditions "produce" men and works of art. But we cannot be too often reminded that such a rationalization of the data of history is the height of folly. There was nothing inevitable in the appearance of Wordsworth at the beginning of the nineteenth century, and nothing inevitable in the absence of anyone of equal genius in the early years of the twentieth.

The situation just described did promote sincerity and genuineness, and some sincere and genuine poems were written, notably by Julian Grenfell (1888–1915), Wilfred Owen (1893–1918), Siegfried Sassoon (1886–   ), and Rupert Brooke (1887–1915). None of these except Sassoon survived the war, and it is futile to conjecture how the other three might have developed. The poems of Brooke were received everywhere as the work of a young man of genius, and his fate inevitably suggested comparisons with Sir Philip Sidney. Today, however, Brooke's reputation has shrunk to very modest proportions; and of all the war-born poetry only a few pieces by Wilfred Owen seem still to possess any enduring vitality. Owen was profoundly moved, not by the immediate situation of England, or by patriotism, or by any heroic exploits comparable to that of the Light Brigade in the Crimean war, but by the pity of the sacrifices war demanded:

If in some smothering dreams, you too could pace
Behind the wagon that we flung him in,
And watch the white eyes writhing in his face,
His hanging face, like a devil's sick of sin;
If you could hear, at every jolt, the blood
Come gargling from the froth-corrupted lungs
Bitter as the end
Of vile, incurable sores on innocent tongues,—
My friend, you would not tell with such high zest
To children ardent for some desperate glory,
The old Lie: Dulce et decorum est
Pro patria mori.

Such poetry as this gained an added significance in the years of disillusion after 1918; but, in general, the war's stimulus to the poetic impulse was of so special a kind that it could not be turned to further account, once the war was over. The old, rather fumbling, rather ineffectual efforts to prove that poetry could still be written in modern England were renewed; and it was again demonstrated that a good many Englishmen could write a good many kinds of verse with some distinction, and that there was public interest in what they could do. There was, however, no new life stirring in the veins of these singing gentlemen, and there would be little indeed to say about English poetry since 1918 were it not for the achievements of two American-born writers who have lived and worked abroad, and who became, in the second decade of this century, the sources of a fresh poetic movement in England.

The Imagists and Ezra Pound

Ezra Loomis Pound (1885–   ) and Thomas Stearns Eliot (1888–   ), who between them have inaugurated a distinctive period of English poetry, impress on us forcibly the growing power of America in Europe. In a general way, doubtless, most of us are aware of the fact. We know that the inspiring aim of the leaders of the USSR has been the Americanization of Russia. The progressive Americanization of England has long been a subject of comment on both sides of the Atlantic. But the American influence which is recognized and talked of comes mostly from the fields of industry and commerce, and, where English is spoken, from expressive locutions. We are not equally aware that the literary influence of the United States on Europe began early, with Fenimore Cooper (1789–1851), rose to high importance with Edgar Allan Poe (1809–1849), Walt Whitman (1819–1892), and Henry James (1843–1916), and remains important today.

We are accustomed, indeed, to think of the United States, in the fields of art, literature, and ideas, in very different terms. We know that a good deal of our own literature is not much more than a feeble and belated echo of the literature of Europe. We often hear it said that what Europe is beginning to think and to do now, America will be thinking and doing fifteen or twenty years hence. And Ezra Pound, when he explained his departure from the United States in 1908, wrote contemptuously of our diluted and derivative ideas. Whenever some brilliant person in Europe discards a set of ideas, Pound wrote, or happens to be in need of money,

. . . he refrigerates the ideas into a book. And the London reviewers and journalists review it, and absorb some of the ideas and dilute them to ten per cent of the original force. And the American Press dilutes the result to ten per cent of the derivative strength, and the American public gets the "hogwash." And if you try to talk on any such exotic matters with Americans, you get the hogwash.

The consequence, Pound added, is that those who have a vital interest in the arts sooner or later leave the country, as he did. He remained, however, unmistakably American; and embodied in his literary work American characteristics which make him an example of the continuing literary influence of the United States on Europe, even though his departure from this country was an act of repudiation.

Henry James more urbanely but no less decisively repudiated the United States when he made his home on the other side of the Atlantic; but the critics both of James and of T. S. Eliot have clearly shown that these writers remained fundamentally American. The fact may be considered more curious than important; yet the case of James, Pound, and Eliot usefully reminds us that English literature of every age, including the present, has been no isolated phenomenon, but rather a fusion of native elements with others drawn from abroad.

When Pound left the United States, he abandoned at the same time a design of obtaining the degree of Ph.D. and of entering into a professorial career, and turned instead to poetry. He had at that time some knowledge of French, Italian, and Spanish, and immediately plunged into a study of the twelfth-century poetry of Provence because he regarded an acquaintance with this poetry as an indispensable foundation for the understanding of later European versification. As the years have passed, Pound has added to his linguistic achievements. His friends say that he is now the master of no less than eight languages, though his enemies assert that he is guilty of egregious mistakes whenever he attempts to use any of them. It seems probable that he is a gifted linguist, but not a scholarly one. In any case, he has worked long and hard to gain skill in versification and in the use of words. In his earliest poems he could not help echoing the language and rhythms of Swinburne, of Ernest Dowson (1867–1900), of Browning.

and of W. B. Yeats. He struggled manfully to break through "the crust of dead English" which, he thought, was hindering the poets of his generation, and to achieve a style based on living speech, which should be direct and economical, in the sense that neither his words nor his rhythms should say or imply anything except what he himself wanted to say. His verse, for example, was not to suggest Swinburne by its movement, when its words and statements were not Swinburnian. He wanted a concentrated effect, with all his material freed from adventitious or inappropriate associations and completely under his control for his purposes.

In 1909 Pound was in London, and came into contact there with Thomas Ernest Hulme (1883–1917) and with a small group who were gathered round Hulme and engaged with him in discussion and experimentation looking towards the development of a new technique of poetry. Hulme was a turbulent willful man, interested in both philosophy and the arts, and remarkable alike for his keen insight and for his power to stimulate intellectual and artistic activity in those around him. He was not an original or a systematic thinker, and as a poet he was almost negligible. Nevertheless, he was a born leader, and he helped Pound and others to take the all-important first step on the way towards the distinctive poetry of our time.

What Hulme was saying when Pound became acquainted with him was that the romantic outlook on life was mistaken and immoral, and that the romantic poets had imposed on the modern world an empty high-flown rhetoric and a vagueness in the use of words which passed for "elevation" though it really promoted the degeneracy of taste. He regarded the nineteenth-century "religion of humanity," faith in progress, and liberal utopianism as the revealing climax of romanticism, and pointed out that the romantic writers had simply transferred the attributes of divinity from God to man, and given up the Heaven of traditional Christianity only to project into the future a Heaven on earth. Hence he called romanticism "spilt religion." Belief in God and in heavenly existence he took to be as

inseparable from humanity as hunger and thirst. The latter, however, remind us daily that man is a limited, imperfect, and temporal creature for whom infinity and perfection are ends unattainable on this earth. The falsehood of which romanticism was guilty was that of confounding this world with the next, and so of introducing a species of confusion which had led inevitably to exasperation, perversion, and frustration. Moreover, Hulme felt that in the early years of the present century the romantic era was drawing to an inglorious but blessed end, and that the time had come for what he called a new classicism.

As a practical means for bringing in a new classical poetry, Hulme thought there was everything to be said for a definite, even though limited aim. He concentrated his effort, in fact, upon a single point. He thought the romantic poets had blurred and then falsified reality by pretending to see infinity in a grain of sand, eternity in a flower, and so on. They had tried to see things, not as they are, but as they wished to see them. This wishful distortion of reality suggested the first step towards reform. The true poet, Hulme insisted, must engage in disinterested contemplation, and must find a kind of interest in what he sees sufficient to force him into the attempt to describe accurately the impression made through his senses. Perfect faithfulness in the expression of just that perception which may actually, for a moment, transfix one's whole being, with nothing added, and with not a word, not a syllable, more or less than may be needed for accurate notation—this should be the ideal of the true poet. Both the object perceived and the emotion felt by the poet were to be regarded as matters of indifference:

It doesn't matter an atom that the emotion produced is not of dignified vagueness, but on the contrary amusing; the point is that exactly the same activity is at work as in the highest verse. That is the avoidance of conventional language in order to get the exact curve of the thing. . . . It isn't the scale or kind of emotion produced that decides, but this one fact: Is there any real zest in it? Did the poet have an actually realized visual object before him in which he delighted? It doesn't matter if it were a lady's shoe or the starry heavens.

Unconventional language is a prime necessity because familiar locutions have acquired general meanings and convey only what is common in all experience. Often enough, long familiarity with certain words and stock comparisons so dulls a reader's attention that a poem conveys no definite or fresh impression. The words call up only colorless and lifeless abstractions. With these the reader may feel comfortably at ease, just as a man is at ease in a pair of old slippers; for neither the old familiar words nor the old familiar slippers rouse one from indolent somnolence to open-eyed, excited attention. But the one justifying reason for poetry, the one basis for distinguishing true poetry from worthless verse, Hulme thought, is the poet's ability to discover something unique, something not hitherto seen or felt exactly as he sees or feels it, and to express this unique impression so faithfully as to evoke in the reader precisely the poet's own discovery in its every shade of differentiation and with its particular certifying physical sensation.

Thus every poet, Hulme continued, must create his own language and rhythm, absolutely peculiar to himself, as did Shakespeare, as did Keats, as did Rossetti. When we read these poets, when we read any genuine poet, our reward lies in our enlarged and heightened consciousness, secured through their discoveries and through their invention of fresh techniques for the full communication of them. We could not have made their discoveries, but they have enabled us to share them and in so doing have conferred on us a more abundant life.

The practical conclusion which Hulme drew from these considerations was that the true poet in the year 1909, should, by way of discipline and of making a start, attempt the accurate translation of distinct images into words. It appears that Pound, by the time he met Hulme, was well on the way to the same conclusion for much the same reasons. During the next few years he gradually assumed the leadership of a small group con- sisting principally of F. S. Flint (1885–), Richard Aldington (1892–), and the American poet H. D. (Hilda Doo- little, 1886–). In 1912, when he pub- lished five of Hulme's poems, he gave the group a name, "Les Imagistes." In the spring of 1913 they announced three prin- ciples on which they were agreed:

(1) Direct treatment of the "thing" whether subjective or objective.
(2) To use absolutely no word that does not contribute to the presentation.
(3) As regards rhythm: to compose in the sequence of the musical phrase, not in the sequence of a metronome.

Early in 1914 *Des Imagistes: An Anthology* appeared under Pound's editorship, contain- ing poems by himself, Flint, H. D., Alding- ton, and several others, including Amy Lowell (1874–1925). Perhaps the most famous example of imagist poetry is Pound's "In a Station of the Metro":

The apparition of these faces in the crowd;
Petals on a wet, black bough.

Obviously, if anything of much sig- nificance was to issue from an effort of which this poem is the classic illustration, the effort could not stop with pure imagism. And it did not. Nevertheless, it is essential to dwell on what the imagists were trying to do, and why they were trying to do it, in order to understand the whole poetical de- velopment which followed from their experi- ments. It is also essential to notice that de- spite Hulme's detestation of romantic poetry, he and the imagists ended by embrac- ing an aim which placed them in a close re- lationship with the so-called Symbolist poets of nineteenth-century France. We en- countered these poets in the preceding chap- ter in our brief discussion of W. B. Yeats, and it was there said that the Symbolists were the inheritors of the romantic tendency to subjectivism and that their leader was Stéphane Mallarmé (1842–1898).

Symbolist Poetry

The problem of the serious artist in their day, as the Symbolists conceived it, was the invention of some means of suggesting to the reader or of evoking in him the precise state of inward being of the poet at a given moment. To this point they had been driven by successive waves of disillusion. We should be able to understand the situation as they saw it from our study of the progress of disillusion in England in the nineteenth century. Their artistic aim was faithfulness to reality; but, as one kind of certainty after another was destroyed, they were pushed back to momentary states of being as the sole absolute realities left to them. These were their very own, inalienable, and directly present—yet not, of course, directly communicable.

If you are out of doors and observe to your companion, "The sky is blue today," and he replies, "Uh-huh," you have successfully used language for communication, but how far have you got? The two of you have agreed on a word which covers an indefinitely large variety of blues. If you try to discriminate more precisely, you will find that any qualifying words you can employ will still fall short of exact description. If your companion had happened to be unusually impressed by the quality of the blueness and had tried to suggest his emotional response by replying, "Yeah, blue as blazes!" he also would have communicated only a fraction of the reality immediately present to him, and any comparison he could have hit on would still have fallen short of suggesting precisely his state of feeling. In the end, both of you, confronted by the simplest problem it is possible to think of, would have to recognize that, beyond a quickly reached limit, you were stumped.

It is conceivable, however, that if one took a different line of approach, one might achieve a lucky hit on another level, or plane, of communication. There is a celebrated poem by John Donne, "The Ecstasy," in which we see two persons so united that it is obviously inadequate to say they understand each other. They go further and deeper. Yet they do not exchange a word; they get entirely off the plane of the intellect, or of intelligible discourse. They are under a spell, and somehow through their clasped hands they meet so perfectly that each not only sees into, but actually *becomes*

the other. Now this is exactly the kind of union that the Symbolist poets were impelled to try to achieve by literary means. They were forced into the attempt because they had lost belief in everything except their own states of being; and of these states they became keenly aware in proportion as they appeared to be unique. But you cannot even partially describe that which is unique; you can only label it. "Gold" is a perfectly arbitrary collocation of sounds and letters. It is intelligible when seen or pronounced solely because we have been taught to accept it as signifying a "something" which has known relations with other "somethings" all of which together form an orderly whole. Gold is describable only to the extent that it is not unique.

The problem of the Symbolist poets, therefore, was to achieve through words an aim for which the language of intelligible discourse is not designed. It is a fact of experience that those human beings who live most fully are the men and women who rise to calls which stretch their capacities to the utmost. The endeavor of the Symbolists has been regarded in this light. Arthur Symons (1865–   ), for example, in his book, *The Symbolist Movement,* wrote:

> To evoke by some elaborate, instantaneous magic of language, without the formality of an after all impossible description; to be, rather than to express: that is what Mallarmé has consistently, and from the first, sought in verse and prose. To say that he has found what he sought is impossible; but (is it possible to avoid saying?) how heroic a search, and what marvelous discoveries by the way!

It has also been said of the Symbolists, however, that to succeed they needed to become wizards and speak the language of incantation. And certainly it is true that only the successful use of sound, of images, of rhythms, for casting a spell over the reader, and so inducing in him a state of being identical with that of the writer, could fulfill their purpose.

Pound's "In a Station of the Metro" is not only a perfect imagist poem but also a simple and elementary example of evocation. But probably even this poem is something of a mystery to those who have not read

Pound's explanation of its origin. He writes:

Three years ago in Paris I got out of a "metro" train at La Concorde, and saw suddenly a beautiful face, and then another and another, and then a beautiful child's face, and then another beautiful woman, and I tried all that day to find words for what this had meant to me, and I could not find any words that seemed to me worthy, or as lovely as that sudden emotion. And that evening I found suddenly the expression, not in speech but in little splotches of color. It was just that—a "pattern" or hardly a pattern if by pattern you mean something with a "repeat" in it. But it was a word, the beginning, for me, of a new language in color.

Pound goes on to say that he then "wrote a thirty-line poem, and destroyed it because it was what we call work of the second intensity." Six months later he found himself able to write a fifteen-line poem about the faces; and finally after a year he produced the two-line masterpiece quoted above. If "In a Station of the Metro" needs this commentary, or at any rate gains interest from it, the difficulties of the poetical sorcerer may fairly be judged to be very great. What are we to make of the following poem, for which Pound's early studies and years of discipline as an imagist prepared the way? It is entitled "Concava Vallis":

The wire-like bands of color involute mount
    from my fingers;
I have wrapped the wind round your shoulders
And the molten metal of your shoulders
    bends into the turn of the wind,
AOI!
The whirling tissue of light
    is woven and grows solid beneath us;
The sea-clear sapphire of air, the sea-dark
    clarity,
    stretches both sea-cliff and ocean.

Unless these lines throw a spell over the reader, "Concava Vallis" is a complete failure. It cannot properly be called obscure or difficult, because it has no core of meaning or thought which patient study might reveal. Only Pound himself could tell the world out of what "state of being" the poem issued; and, even if he did take the public into his confidence concerning "Concava Vallis" and other similar pieces

he has published, these poems would remain failures. Much of the world's finest literature which is worth handing on from one generation to another requires explanatory comment, and patient study, but all successful literature is self-contained at least in the sense that study will reveal what the author has been driving at. "Concava Vallis" and other modern poems fall into a different category. In these poems the author is talking, muttering, or singing to himself in a private language, or private adaptation of our language, about nobody knows what. In some instances not even the poet himself knows about what he sings. He obeys a "voice," coming, as he believes or hopes, from something deeper within him than conscious thought or feeling.

But when we term these poems "failures" we are, in the case of Pound at any rate, called to account by no less an authority than T. S. Eliot, who regards Pound as a figure of unique importance. The following statements make plain the reason for his opinion:

No one living has practiced the art of verse with such austerity and devotion; and no one living has practiced it with more success. . . . A man who devises new rhythms is a man who extends and refines our sensibility; and that is not merely a matter of "technique." . . . He has enabled a few persons, including myself, to improve their verse sense; so that he has improved poetry through other men as well as by himself. I cannot think of anyone writing verse, of our generation and the next, whose verse (if any good) has not been improved by the study of Pound's. His poetry is an inexhaustible reference book of verse form. There is, in fact, no one else to study. . . . I confess that I am seldom interested in what he is saying, but only in the way he says it.

Pound, this is to say, is the inventor of new harmonies; and nothing claimed for him by Eliot is inconsistent with the conclusion that an unintelligible poem is an unsuccessful poem. It may be the notation of a new music; and accordingly it may have the value, for other poets, that Eliot asserts it has, but this is a quite special and restricted value. We are, indeed, forced to conclude that a poet such as Pound addresses himself only to those absorbedly interested in the tricks of the trade, or, in other words, to fellow craftsmen who are primarily concerned with problems of technique. And that Pound is a pure craftsman is further suggested by this fact: some of his poems do have meaning, and from them we discover that his thought is commonplace and his emotion immature. Their interest lies, just as Eliot says, not in what Pound is telling us but only in the manner of the telling.

Consequently, if we are to form any judgment concerning Pound's importance as a poet, we must look beyond him to the other men through whom he is said to have improved poetry. He has given others something new to work with; and the instrument is in fact so new that it has not been possible to describe it and account for it briefly. The question raised, however, is what others have been able to do with it.

T. S. Eliot and the Poets of the Next Generation

By universal consent, T. S. Eliot is the foremost poet of our time. He began to write verse in 1908 or 1909, when he was twenty or twenty-one, in a style which, he says, was "directly drawn" from his study of the French poet Jules Laforgue (1860–1887) "together with the later Elizabethan drama." It was only afterwards that he came under the influence of Ezra Pound. But though he made an independent beginning, he discovered in Pound such kinship of technical purpose that he perforce swore allegiance to him, as we have seen, and went on to admit that in his own poems he has very often followed Pound's lead. Eliot, then, if anyone, should show us to what uses the poetic style developed by Pound can be put.

Eliot's first small volume of poems, *Prufrock and Other Observations,* was published in 1917, though some of the pieces had appeared earlier in magazines. This book was followed in 1920 by another small collection, and in 1922 by *The Waste Land,* a poem in five parts running in all to four hundred and thirty-three lines, with an appendix containing notes. *The Waste Land* established Eliot's position, is generally re-garded as the only important long poem of the last quarter of a century, and stands between two distinct periods in its author's poetical career. Not many poems have subsequently appeared, and the total quantity of Eliot's verse is small.

One reason for this meagerness of output will be instantly apparent to anyone who has attempted to read one of Eliot's poems. All of them carry on their surface the signs of immense labor. It is possible to consider them as a concentrated deposit from wide and incessant reading in several literatures, ancient and modern; so rich are they in allusions, echoes, and quotations, all used by Eliot for his own purposes, but still presenting the effect of a learned pasticcio. Even this, however, is not the most obvious sign of labor. For the first characteristic of these poems to strike the reader is the artificiality of their style. It is a curious fact that we are enabled to believe what Eliot says about the many years of hard work lying back of Pound's developed technique rather by Eliot's own use of that technique than by Pound's.

This, however, can be explained. The technique, we have learned, was devised for the purpose of suggestion. The effort to express faithfully the poet's whole unique inward "state of being," when raised to a high intensity under some stimulus, necessitated the abandonment of communication on the level of intelligible discourse, and the resort to symbols intended by a kind of magic to suggest the aforesaid "state of being" to the reader, or to evoke it in him. The difficulty in this was that in the attempt to avoid sacrificing his individuality the poet might sacrifice not only intelligibility but communication itself. We have observed that Pound, in such a poem as "Concava Vallis," might as well have used gibberish; and it may be added that the effect would have been less bewildering had he done so. But Pound was doomed to failure because he really had nothing to say. He had impressions, but no meanings which the impressions were to symbolize. There is a truth embedded in Hulme's assertion that it makes no difference what the subject of a poem may be, that a good poem may be written about a lady's shoe just as well as about the starry heavens. There is truth, probably, in everything said by serious apologists for the strange forms assumed by modern literature and painting. Nevertheless, nothing urged in disparagement of the notion that some subjects are more "poetical" than others or more important, and nothing urged concerning the limitations of intelligible discourse, in the least undermines the elementary fact that the fine arts use mediums of communication—sounds, words, pictures—and use them for the purpose of communication between artist and public. Moreover, communication is not possible without something to communicate; and for significant communication the artist must have something significant to say. A poem about a lady's shoe can be good only if the shoe has suggested something worth saying which the poet succeeds in saying well.

Now the difference between Pound and Eliot is not only that Eliot really has something to say, and something which significantly carries on and deepens the late Victorian criticism of modern industrial civilization, but also that he has a capacity for profound, serious, and sustained feeling. The consequence is that he uses the new technique of suggestion for a moving and significant purpose. His symbolic utterance is charged through and through with a weight of feeling which is successfully communicated. Even the most bewildered reader can see that Eliot's poems are written by a man who has suffered disillusion and is oppressed by a sense of the futility of life, but who is not willing to accept blank negation as the sum of wisdom. The reader will see this more readily if he is familiar with Matthew Arnold, but cannot help seeing it in any case. He will, however, be struck by the fact that though disillusion and the sense of futility are, so to speak, the common property of the present age, Eliot has made them his own by the quality of his experience of them. The reader cannot help seeing, in addition, that Eliot speaks the common, indeed the vulgar, language of the present moment, and seems determined to make the kind of poetry (if any) that it will make, rather than sacrifice one iota of directly observed or experienced reality to previously existing notions of the "poetic" subject or "poetic" treatment.

Beyond these perceptions, however, the average reader is not likely to advance. It is a question, indeed, how much further he is really expected to advance. Eliot believes that poetry does not need to be understood in order to be enjoyed, and has complained because readers insist on puzzling their heads "for a kind of 'meaning' which is not there, and is not meant to be there." But since Eliot *does* communicate *something,* his readers are predisposed to believe that there *is* a purpose which controls his choice and arrangement of words, allusions, statements, and that there must be a meaning to be discovered, whether of the kind they are used to or not. Hence the more difficult one of Eliot's poems is, the more readily will a reader allow that many years of hard work must have been required for the development of a technique for saying what can only be said, apparently, in riddles.

Nevertheless, though Eliot thus induces a sympathetic attitude in readers, the fact remains that he does speak in riddles and is found baffling. The defenders of his poetry assure us that readers are inevitably baffled, simply because every new technical invention requires a new kind of response from readers, which they can only make successfully as they slowly learn what is expected of them. Readers are asked to remember that at first the new way of writing brought in by Wordsworth and Coleridge seemed as clear as mud to the public, and that these poets had to wait for appreciative understanding until the public grew accustomed to their style. Accordingly, Eliot's defenders attempt to hasten the education of the contemporary public by composing commentaries on his poems, though these explanations, they insist, should not be necessary, and are not needed by really intelligent readers. But these *unneeded* explanations, surprisingly enough, differ from one another, and prove that even the all-wise commentators are baffled. Eliot has remarked upon the number of differing interpretations of *The Waste Land* which seem to be possible, and from what he says it begins to appear that some at least of his poems are in the nature of blank checks which anyone may fill in to suit himself.

Evidently, then, we are confronted by a kind of poetry which is different from anything hitherto known, or at any rate different from anything known since the days of magical incantations, spells, and the like. And nobody can safely say whether or not it may be profitable to puzzle our heads over it. But we can and should understand that though this poetry is "different," it does not, as its composers and defenders think, inaugurate a new literary era. The comparison with Wordsworth and Coleridge is misleading. Pound and Eliot are not pioneers in at all the sense that the romantic poets were. They are the last descendants of the romantic rebels. The stages of the development from the 1790's to Eliot have been set forth in the preceding chapter and in our discussion of Pound. The evidence is full, clear, and conclusive. The romantic poets were fighting for individualism, and brought in subjectivism. We have seen how, under pressure from the progress of science and historical knowledge, later poets were pushed into a more and more reckless individualism and a narrowed but intensified subjectivism, which at length issued in the doctrine of art for art's sake, or, as it might usefully be called, art for the artist's sake. It was then that the central artistic problem became one of exact self-expression, and then that the perverse passion for being "different" at all costs appeared in full bloom. The most exotic flowers were the Symbolist poems of France, which became the inspiration of Pound and Eliot.

The continuity of this development was obscured by Hulme, in his acute attack on Romanticism and his plea for anti-romantic poetry. But in reality, as we have noticed, he merely led the way from one part of the romantic legacy to another. He was unable to lead poetry away from subjective individualism. Imagist poets simply tried to make symbols, or images, out of subjective impressions. We are witnessing, consequently, not the first blossoms of a new literary era in the work of Pound and Eliot and their successors, but the extreme con-

sequences, and perhaps dying struggles, of an old impulse. Pound is unmistakably a child of the days of art for art's sake, and has of late years been a fish out of water. Eliot, if the figure may be continued, is a flying fish, better able to breathe air, but native to the stream of art for art's sake. As has been emphasized above, he does have something to say; yet, in order to make a reputation as a poet under modern conditions, he had to write in the fashionable manner interesting to fellow poets, *and primarily for them.* *The Waste Land* has been praised with enthusiasm for just the qualities which make it unintelligible and unreadable, because these qualities also make it a classic example of the modern manner. It has something of the character of a nightmare; and if it lives beyond our time it can scarcely be remembered as anything save one of the curiosities of literature. It has, in fact, been acclaimed by an admiring critic of Eliot for its "rich disorganization"—precisely the quality which reduces it to the position of an historical document. As such, it may have importance. It may stand as a symbol of artistic helplessness in a period of social and cultural disintegration.

Unfortunately, if "rich disorganization," ambiguity, bewildering tricks of style, recondite allusions, private jokes recognizable only by the writer's intimate friends, and other marks of artistic helplessness and ineptitude are wanted, they can be supplied rather easily, without going as far as the Surrealists have gone in looking to insane asylums for the literary masterpieces of the future. The young poets of the last ten years—William Empson (1906–   ), W. H. Auden (1907–   ), C. Day Lewis (1904–   ), Stephen Spender (1909–   ), Ronald Bottrall, (1906–   ), Dylan Thomas (1914–   ), Louis MacNeice (1907–   ), and others—mostly have something to say, because mostly they are communists or socialists. One of them even affirms boldly that "what a book is actually about is far more important" than it has been fashionable to admit for a generation or more. Another assures us that "the intellectual"—"rightly," he thinks—has begun to assume that it is "no longer his vocation to sit face inwards in a corner weaving from his own intestines a spider's web of private fantasy." Despite these sound affirmations, however, the poets just mentioned have inherited the stylistic canons of a generation committed to individualism and subjectivism in art, and so have gone on writing verse which is mostly private and unintelligible. However difficult the first descent into a state of "rich disorganization" may have been, these young poets of today have found it easy to follow the path already marked out for them.

Meanwhile Eliot himself has quietly accepted some of the limitations on artistic freedom and expression imposed by the demands of intelligibility. His talent from the beginning was perceived to be dramatic, and of late years he has wanted to write for the public stage. He projected an "Aristophanic melodrama" in colloquial language and music-hall verse, but never got beyond two fragments which he published, first in a periodical, and then, in 1933, in a small book, under the title *Sweeney Agonistes*. The preoccupation with murder which inspired this abortive experiment stayed with him, and reappeared as the theme of the verse-play entitled *The Family Reunion* (1939). In the years between *Sweeney* and *The Family Reunion* he wrote the choruses for a pageant play entitled *The Rock* (1934), and a play concerning the martyrdom of St. Thomas Becket (*Murder in the Cathedral*, 1935), which was performed in Canterbury Cathedral and later had a successful run on the stage. None of this dramatic work is of the first order of excellence; yet it is all genuinely impressive, and gives ground for the belief that at length Eliot has found a way out of the blind alley into which he helped to lead modern writers and in which he won a dubious and disquieting distinction. Hope for modern poetry, as far as can now be seen, depends on the success with which the guidance given in Eliot's dramatic work may be followed.

Drama since 1914

The plays of Bernard Shaw were noticed in the preceding chapter. John Galsworthy was also briefly noticed there; as were other writers who, though they have continued to be leading figures in English literature in the years since the first World War, attained fame and an established position before 1914. In the present chapter, though we have to glance back of 1914 for origins and affiliations, we are directly concerned only with writers who first won public attention after 1914.

In the early years of the present century the revival of dramatic activity had assumed large proportions and was an important feature of the literary scene; but in the years following the war the promise of that revival was not fulfilled. Dramatic activity has continued, and new men of talent—perhaps one or two of extraordinary talent—have appeared. Nothing, however, has been produced which seems destined to long life; and nothing has been produced which, whether or not it may endure, seems to mark an epoch as do, for example, some of the plays of Shaw.

The most important new playwrights of the 1920's and 1930's are Sean O'Casey (1884–), James Bridie (1888–), Noel Pierce Coward (1899–), Wystan Hugh Auden (1907–) and Christopher Isherwood (1904–), Stephen Spender (1909–), and T. S. Eliot (1888–) whose plays have already been mentioned. O'Casey was born and brought up in Dublin, and is a self-made man. He did not learn to read until he was twelve, and as a youth and young man he was employed as an unskilled laborer. The Abbey Theater in Dublin produced his first play, *The Shadow of a Gunman,* in 1923. This was followed by his very successful *Juno and the Paycock* (published 1925) and by his tragedy, *The Plow and the Stars* (1926). In these plays he showed himself to be a born dramatist. He used the speech of the common people of Dublin with a fine sense for style, and, through his powerful imagination, achieved extraordinary tragic and comic effects. He seemed to be entering on a really great career. But in subsequent plays he was betrayed by the vogue of expressionism, of which we have discussed one variety in Symbolist poetry, into experiments in so-called direct communication, with unfortunate consequences. In these plays, as in many Symbolist poems, the attempt to achieve complete and direct expression has defeated itself, and has proved once again that the artist who tries to say more than is humanly possible within the limits of intelligible communication only invites the disaster of appearing to say nothing, or of appearing to say very little and to say that little in a clumsy, roundabout way.

The plays of James Bridie show intelligence and critical power, and are somewhat more clearly within the bounds of literature than those of St. John Ervine (1883–   ), R. C. Sherriff (1896–   ), or John William van Druten (1901–   ); though about this there is room for difference of opinion, or argument. On the subject of Noel Coward, however, there is universal agreement, yet very little understanding. He is a sign of the times. Something of a case can be made for regarding him as the inheritor of a tradition. The revival of comedy for which Oscar Wilde was responsible in the 1890's was not entirely snuffed out by the discredit into which the aesthetic movement fell after Wilde's conviction and imprisonment, and by the passion for social reform which took possession of the stage in the early twentieth century. Sophisticated comedies of manners continued to be written by William Somerset Maugham (1874–   ); and from him Coward may have derived hints. But what is important in Coward is not so much his literary affiliations as his genius for catching the lighter side of the disillusioned temper of society in the 1920's.

The critics very properly and severely say that Coward is only capable of presenting trivial people engaged in trivial activities. They probably do not give him sufficient credit for the skill and finish with which he does work that seems to them insignificant. But, though it may be freely conceded that he is not "great" or "deep," it is at least true that his plays have value as social documents. The characters in Coward's *Private Lives* (1930) are emancipated from the framework of conventions and beliefs which, though weakened before the war, continued to give direction and consistency to social life. Ever since the eighteenth century there

has been a great deal of hopeful talk, as we have seen in earlier chapters, about the good to be expected from such emancipation. *Private Lives* is a faithful presentment of what happened, in countless instances, when the war and its aftermath finally shattered social sanctions. The picture is heightened, and on the surface it is amusing; but the truth is not obscured. The facts are simply allowed to speak for themselves. And what we observe is that average people set free, and thrown back on the immemorial realities stored up in the deep reservoir of the "unconscious," become infantile anarchists. Average people are not better and larger than the conventions which formerly held them in chains; they are smaller and worse. Corruption did not attack them through hated social institutions; they corrupted everything entrusted to them, while blaming everything and everybody except themselves.

It is immaterial whether or not Coward himself draws any such conclusion. He is regarded as a "commercial artist," and may be, so far as his conscious aims go, little more than a skilled contriver of sure-fire stage effects. His work is, none the less, a portent, and does more to explain the revolt against modern civilization now spreading through the world than do the writings of many of those engaged in forwarding rebellion.

The only other dramatic activity of serious interest in recent years is the attempt which has been made to bring poetic plays back to the modern stage. T. S. Eliot's share in this attempt has already been discussed. W. H. Auden has written, with the same purpose, *The Dance of Death* (1933), and, in partnership with Christopher Isherwood, *The Dog beneath the Skin* (1935) and *The Ascent of F6* (1936). These plays are full of tricks, and of not much else. Expressionism achieves a ludicrous effect in *The Ascent of F6:* when the leader of the exploring party finally reaches the mountain's summit, he discovers his mother there, and this precious scene is intended to show that the leader's heroic, disinterested endeavors and exemplary sentiments are merely disguises, and that in reality he is just the victim of a mother-complex.

The dramatic outlook is not perceptibly brightened by such puerilities. The cause of the poetic play, however, has received sound and impressive support not only from T. S. Eliot, but also from Stephen Spender, whose *Trial of a Judge* (1938) is a treatment of the struggle for social justice. In this play Spender has succeeded in giving concrete embodiment to one problem connected with that struggle and in creating, in the figure of the judge, a finely imagined symbol of contemporary human aspiration. He has true dramatic power, a solid grasp on moral realities, and a poetic style adequate to the needs of his play. It cannot be said of him, any more than it can of Eliot, that he has produced a play of the first order of excellence; and it remains to be seen what both men may be able to do in the future, if the condition of the world permits them to do anything. Both have proved, however, that poetic plays bearing on contemporary problems can successfully be written, and that such plays will attract a large public; and they have done this in the face of a widespread opinion that the thing was impossible.

Fiction since 1914

Prose fiction continues to be the most popular form of literary art, as it was during the greater part of the nineteenth century and the early years of the twentieth. Accordingly, the number of writers in this field is very large; and the variety in the kinds of fiction offered to the public is so great as to be bewildering. To name all, or even the greater number, of the novelists and story-tellers who have attracted wide public attention in the last twenty-five years would be to reduce this part of the present chapter to a mere catalogue. Hence selection, though hazardous when we are concerned with contemporaries or very recent writers, is imperative.

Some preliminary generalizations, however, are possible. Everything said in the preceding chapter (p. 476) about the effect on fiction of its popularity remains true today. Some observers think that the general level of artistic competence has risen as time has passed; and it is true that very many novels with a life-expectancy of from six months to two years are nowadays well constructed and well written, and might, on these grounds, put to shame a novel by Dickens or Thackeray. It is true also that members of the reading public demand good workmanship of certain kinds. The slow start usually made by Scott, the artless intrusions of Thackeray into his tales, and the wordiness of Thackeray and other Victorian novelists would all be thought intolerable in a novel of the present day. But this does not mean that fiction readers have gone so far as to pore over novels for the sake of the art displayed in their composition. The generality of readers want what they have always wanted—action, and plenty of it—and are still willing to tolerate any amount of poor workmanship for the sake of a rousing, swiftly moving story about definitely characterized people. No amount of painstaking or subtle art will compensate for absence of plot, or for the dissolution of personality and human values which can result from the analytic treatment of character.

It so happens, however, that some of the most discussed and most admired developments in the realm of fiction since 1914 have caused the element of plot to shrink away to nothing or almost to nothing, and have caused character practically to disappear in a maze of distinctions, uncertainties, complexities, and delusions. Modern psychology has made everybody conscious of the "unconscious." That dark area of the mind, we are now told, is the important part. Thence issue all the forces which really direct our activities and shape our lives. The conscious part of the mind is comparatively negligible and extremely deceptive. Its role, in fact, is merely to put as good a face as possible on the commands of the "unconscious" which we must obey, or to hide realities we do not like, and to devise means to ends which we must try to achieve whether we consciously disapprove or approve of them. This, of course, is a grossly inadequate account of the "unconscious"; but it may suffice to show why the modern novelist tends to lose himself in the intricacies of characterization, without ever getting to the point of forming a plot. It also gives us one reason why novelists have become more and more immersed in technical problems: the new conception of man's inner workings demands new methods of presentation which tax to the utmost the artist's ingenuity.

But there is another reason for the contemporary novelist's concern over technique. The conditions which brought about the development of Symbolist poetry were, of course, conditions which every kind of artist has had to face, whatever his medium. And writers of fiction have turned to expressionism for the same reasons that poets have: as a means of breaking new ground in the development of their art and as, at the same time, a means of leaping over the difficulty created by the modern chaos of conflicting beliefs and standards.

How an elaborate and subtle new technique of communication could be expected to take the place of beliefs and standards common to a writer and his readers requires a word of explanation. There is a saying by a Frenchman that "to understand all is to forgive all." It is possible that if we could be enabled to see *completely* some momentary act, or some word spoken, that if we could see everything that had led up to it and everything that followed from it, and how the same act or word would have had a different meaning in any other circumstances or coming from any other person, and also how inevitably it fitted into its own particular context, we might begin to see that act or word assuming fateful proportions, no matter how insignificant it was in itself. The act, the word, would acquire a meaning and interest derived entirely from its own relations, without any dependence on the reader's beliefs and standards. Thus, if we knew all, an apparent moral offense might turn out to be an act of heroism, given a particular kind of person "guilty" of it in certain circumstances. But, more than this, we might see that *no* act can be labeled or valued as one thing or another in itself. Everything done or said is relative to some person in his particular circumstances. Hence it is, in the last resort, impossible to say simply that murder is a crime. Nothing is necessarily anything, and anything whatever may be good, bad, important, or unimportant.

Everything derives its meaning, not from itself, but from its particular context, background, past and future.

In these considerations, which could be indefinitely enlarged, we have the basis for experimental efforts to devise a kind of fiction complete in itself, in the sense that it does not assume any beliefs or standards shared by writer and reader, and demands nothing of the reader except an open mind. What the reader is to think and feel, in other words, is determined wholly by the particular set of references and relations established within a given piece of fiction, and the significance attached to events and words holds good solely for that one given piece of fiction. The author invites you, when you open his book, to enter a self-contained world, where everything is to be seen and felt and understood in terms of the unique mind of the principal character (or minds of several principal characters), as that mind has been formed by circumstances which, however commonplace or trivial in themselves, take their meaning and value from the peculiar context into which they enter, and which they in turn alter. The given piece of fiction is, in short, one of Henry James's famous "special cases," to be established by the author, and to be accepted on its own terms. It is not an instance, an example; it is itself alone, unlike any other case. And the plausibility, the interest, the relative "truth" of such a piece of fiction will depend wholly on the author's mastery of a technique of full, direct expression.

Both the problem and the solution in terms of technical invention, we see, have an obvious likeness to the Symbolist poet's problem and solution. And just as the poetry of Pound and Eliot and their followers was shown to be "different" but not something new, so the most revolutionary fiction of our time is also "different" rather than new. In England Henry James (1843–1916) was its pioneer, and his example has had more influence on subsequent English fiction than the work of all other English novelists of the nineteenth century put together. James learned most from Flaubert (1821–1880) and, from amongst the Russians whom every modern English novelist has studied, from

Ivan Turgenev (1818–1883); but his remarkable distillation from the whole body of Continental fiction of the last century was a species of romantic fable. These fables, chiefly the work of his later years, were "romantic" in the same sense as were the other productions of the aesthetic movement. James was incomparably the finest artist of the movement, and his later novels and tales have a moral significance which places them on a plane of insight not dreamed of by his contemporaries, but they also have this in common with other "aesthetic" literature: they exhibit James turning away from the world around him to create imaginatively a self-contained private world which he enjoys for its own sake, and his enjoyment of which he aims to communicate by the fullness and exactness of his transcription, inventing for the purpose a new technique. Further, James became so absorbed in technical problems, in his attempt to achieve perfection of texture, tone, and pattern for the sake of complete realization, or communication through words, that he in effect practiced the art in fiction for its own sake.

In so doing, however, James buried what he had to say to the world in a form which can be read with appreciative understanding and delight only by fellow craftsmen and a small group of specially disciplined critics. He produced a series of masterpieces, but, as Stephen Spender says in *The Destructive Element,* they are "long, excellent and unreadable masterpieces." Moreover, though they are the starting-point of something different in fiction from anything produced in the past, they are really, like Symbolist poetry, a development out of romantic individualism; and in them, it must be added, we see individualism driven into a corner.

Though James was the pioneer showing the way to the revolutionary fiction of recent years, other influences have not been unimportant. Modern psychology has already been mentioned. Amongst literary influences the almost interminable *A la Recherche du Temps Perdu* (1913–1927) of Marcel Proust (1871–1922) must be mentioned. The general title of the masterly English translation by C. K. Scott Moncrieff (1889–1930) is *Remembrance of Things Past.*

Practically speaking, the eight large volumes in which this monumental fiction is comprised were Proust's life-work. Proust had no faith in anything, and the theme of his book, in so far as it has one, appears to be his progressive abandonment of even the semblance of belief in the aristocratic doctrine of *noblesse oblige.* Yet, as one of the novelist's approving critics says,

The total effect is not one of chaos or of despair, because the work itself is beautiful even if the material which composes it is not, and in that fact lies the key to the secret [of the book's unity, despite its variety and apparent disconnectedness]. Proust's greatest invention was the invention of a form, of a method by means of which events could be arranged in a pattern having a formal beauty and a formal meaning capable of replacing the beauty and the meaning lost to those who, like himself, had no moral or religious faith capable of giving them any other kind. (J. W. Krutch, Introduction to the edition of *Remembrance of Things Past* published by Random House.)

This sufficiently places the book for our purpose and accounts for its influence. Nevertheless, though Proust is justly acclaimed for his extraordinary technical skill and though his book has aroused widespread curiosity both as a modern masterpiece and as a treatment of a repellent (and therefore interesting) subject, it is doubtful if many persons have been able to read it through. We are told that a publisher to whom the earliest section was submitted, rejected the manuscript, saying that he could not understand why a man should use thirty pages to describe how he tossed about on his bed before going to sleep. But it is not merely the inordinate length to which Proust draws out everything that deters readers; it is, even more, precisely the fact emphasized in the above-quoted passage—the fact that Proust's private world is not interesting or significant in itself, but only for the sake of the art with which it is recaptured and re-created in multitudinous words.

The central fact, then, concerning fiction in recent years is that the novel began, before 1914, to be valued for the sake of the art with which it might be written; and that from the moment when technique took the center of the stage the "advanced" novel's appeal was narrowed down to the novelist's fellow technicians, to a fringe of would-be technicians and of critics, and to the kind of reader who prides himself on being smartly up-to-date and familiar with the very latest thing. The novel, in short, became esoteric, the novelist writing for his peers, or simply for his own satisfaction. And this was a logical, if not inevitable, development brought on by the disintegration of modern society. It proceeded to its extreme limit in the 1920's and 1930's.

James Joyce

In two books by James Augustine Aloysius Joyce (1882–　） fiction written for the sake of art appears to have reached the extreme limit humanly possible in this kind. The books are the far-famed *Ulysses* (1922) and *Finnegans Wake* (1939). These are not Joyce's only books. In 1907 he published thirty-six short poems under the title *Chamber Music,* and in 1914, after vexatious negotiations and delays, a volume of short stories entitled *Dubliners.* Two years later there appeared an autobiographical narrative thinly disguised as fiction (*A Portrait of the Artist as a Young Man*), and in 1918 a play called *Exiles.* A further volume of poems, *Pomes Penyeach,* was published in 1927.

All of these books are important for the study of Joyce, and they are all mentioned here because Joyce himself is widely regarded as the only British imaginative writer of the very first importance who has come before the public in our time. He was born in Dublin and brought up there, receiving his education in Catholic institutions. His parents were of the shabby-genteel class, and their household arrangements grew shabbier every year as Joyce's father gradually sank in the world. Their son was sensitive, highly strung, self-important, and venomous as a rattlesnake when his hostility was aroused. As a youth he gave up a design of entering the Jesuit Order, and also renounced Christian belief. Other renunciations followed. He found he had no feeling of loyalty to home or fatherland or friends. Indeed, one receives the impression that he

has used other people who have come in his way, in so far as he could, but that, as he reached maturity, he became confirmed in the attitude of regarding nothing except himself as real, or important, or even useful save as means to his own ends. He became arrogant in proportion as he grew self-absorbed, and as a consequence he was disliked and scorned, and was laughed at for his boastfulness.

Joyce regarded his progressive disillusion as the increase of freedom, and it became his aim to achieve complete personal detachment for the sake of unfettered artistic creation. From boyhood he had loved words for their own sake, as if they were things having an existence and properties of their own independently of their use to denote meanings. He now wanted to work out a purely personal and individual aesthetic as a preparation for using words in a new way, which was to be uniquely his own way. To gain isolation he spent some months in Paris in the winter of 1902–1903, in dreadful poverty. He was called back to Dublin in the spring of 1903 by the fatal illness of his mother; but in October, 1904, he left Ireland again, this time with a wife to support, and has never returned except for one or two brief visits. He taught languages, chiefly at Trieste, until 1914; then lived in Zurich, Switzerland, during the war, which he regarded as a mischievous interference with his artistic life; and has since made his home in Paris.

Though he has lived an expatriate, the one home of Joyce's imagination has been Ireland. There is no evidence that his surroundings since his youth and young manhood have made any impression on him. His work suggests that his life in the world ceased with his retreat to the Continent, and that from then on he has contemplated and used only his early self. His first experimental poems and stories were objective, but as he withdrew into himself he found that he himself was his own best subject. The modern writer, driven back into fullness of self-expression as an aim, has inevitably tended to make his books from fragments of autobiography, however disguised; and Joyce has been no exception to the rule. He had left

Dublin determined to show the scoffers that they were wrong and to prove that he did amount to something. He had predicted that in ten years he would shame the skeptics by publishing a masterpiece. His notion of a masterpiece was a composition that would go further in the way of "revelation" than anyone else had dared to go or would dream of going, the masterliness appearing in the art with which words were made to serve the purpose of relentless self-exploitation.

The *Portrait* was the outcome. In it we see the progress of Stephen Dedalus, who is Joyce, from boyhood to young manhood, his emancipation from beliefs, and the formation of his decision "to discover the mode of life or art whereby his spirit could express itself in unfettered freedom." When it was finished, the book seemed to Joyce a prelude to his promised masterpiece rather than the real right thing itself. If readers thought the *Portrait* a work of genius, let them wait; they hadn't seen nothin' yet—he would show 'em, he would blister their eyes and bowl them clean over. There was nobody like Joyce, and the world was going to find that out, and worship at his feet. What he projected was a continuation of the *Portrait,* in which Stephen was to appear as hero.

As he got to work, however, his conception of what he might accomplish broadened out. The real subject remained Joyce— Joyce the impartial, all-comprehending spectator of mankind in all ages and places, sitting impassive and aloof, embracing and transcending all limited, ephemeral, conflicting beliefs and values, and creating, in "unfettered freedom," by a supreme triumph of imaginative insight and of artistic skill, the finally perfect picture of Man as he truly is and always has been. But the form had to be altered to fit this conception of the real subject, and autobiographical narrative was abandoned. Stephen remained, but remained only as one of three characters, who were to be presented, inside and out, as they went through a normal day's existence. This is the framework of *Ulysses,* as the book was in the end called, for a reason which will presently be mentioned. The scene is Dublin. The story begins at 8:00 A.M. on 16 June, 1904, and ends at 2:00 A.M.

on the following day. The reader not only sees Stephen, and the principal character, Leopold Bloom, and his wife Marion Bloom, as they go about their business through the day and into the night, but also follows their thoughts and even the inarticulate "stream of consciousness" lying below and around their explicit thoughts. This fullness of presentation requires many words. *Ulysses* runs to nearly eight hundred closely printed pages in the definitive edition published at Hamburg in 1932. Joyce takes nothing for granted, and from the completeness of his transcription of one day's events succeeds in presenting the whole personality of each of the characters.

There is one respect in which no one can be found in the field of English literature to compare with Joyce except Jonathan Swift. Swift and Joyce are alike in that both will go to any staggering length to achieve their object. Stopping at nothing, Joyce has written in *Ulysses* what have been called "swell dirty passages" which have excited considerable interest. Even this source of interest, however, could not prevent *Ulysses* as a whole from being extremely boring, because of the lack of plot and action and the absence of significant human qualities in the characters, were it not for two features of the book yet to be discussed.

In the first place, we know that every novelist, every imaginative creator of character, assumes the privilege and responsibilities of omniscience. He enters into his characters, as we say, and knows more about them than anyone can learn about actual human beings from mere closeness of observation. If he is anxious to preserve verisimilitude, he endeavors to obscure his privileged position, and tends to accept approximately the limitations of the dramatist, who makes his characters reveal themselves through their own action and speech, with some help from the comment of a chorus or of other actors. Joyce, however, goes to the opposite extreme, takes the bull by the horns, and boldly thrusts the novelist's superhuman omniscience in the face of the reader. His most telling instrument of revelation is the so-called interior monologue, in which he puts into words the inarticulate wanderings of the mind when conscious control is relaxed and the "unconscious" rises dimly like some object half-perceived, or less than half-perceived, through a dense fog. There is not really any human interest in such revelation. It might possess scientific interest if it were not the product of deliberate artifice. The interest it does have is purely artistic. The "interior monologue" in Joyce's hands is a marvel of virtuosity. He attempts the impossible, and so nearly succeeds that fellow-artists, themselves engaged in trying to make language do more than it is capable of doing, and hence aware of all the difficulties overcome, hail his achievement as "magical."

This interest possessed by *Ulysses* is wholly technical and professional. It is aroused, not by the stuff of the "unconscious" used, which is from this point of view a matter of indifference, but entirely by the way it is used, by the technique employed to bring the inarticulate "unconscious" out into the open. And the second feature of the book which gives it interest also gives it a kind of interest wholly technical and professional in character, arising, as it does, from the virtuosity of the artist. Joyce wanted to present Mr. and Mrs. Bloom unsentimentally and nakedly, but this was only the beginning of what he aimed to do. He wanted, in addition, without sacrificing their individualities, to insist constantly throughout his book that in Bloom and his wife, and, generally, in the normal course of Dublin life, we can see all Mankind and all Life in all times and places. He undertook to achieve this further purpose through suggestion, by a complex symbolism. He chose as his chief point of reference the *Odyssey* of Homer. Leopold Bloom, underneath the surface, is Ulysses all over again (and hence the title of Joyce's novel). Further, Joyce's *Ulysses* falls into eighteen parts which correspond to the eighteen principal episodes of the *Odyssey,* the relationship being indicated by covert allusion and the method of treatment. Still further, these parts of *Ulysses* are each governed as to treatment by one of the arts of mankind, and for each a different technique of presentation is adopted, and each has its own symbol. Finally, many of the episodes also are allusively related to parts of the human body, and some of them to colors. Thus the episode in *Ulysses* which corresponds to the Aeolus episode of the *Odyssey* has for its art, rhetoric; for its technique, progress through argument of the kind known in logic as the enthymeme; for its symbol, "Editor"; for its part of the body, lungs; and for its color, red. Even more symbolism of varying kinds pervades the book; for example, in a hospital scene where a woman gives birth to a child, growth is symbolized by passages which reflect the development of English prose style from earliest times to the present.

For those who like the game of spotting the allusion, *Ulysses* has almost inexhaustible possibilities and many very sporting hazards. And every solution enables a player to think how clever he is, and also how preternaturally clever Joyce was. The real and serious interest of the symbolism, however, is purely aesthetic, and lies in the technical means employed by Joyce for tying all his allusions firmly into the texture of his primary material, and also in the endless variety of his symbolic methodology.

Ulysses, evidently, is a composition of wonderful virtuosity, of kinds which cannot be fully understood and appreciated by more than a few hundred people, and not even by them without careful and prolonged study. If art, or technique, has a value in and for itself, independently of its material and of any purpose beyond itself, *Ulysses* occupies a high place amongst human achievements. And that Joyce is a man of genius of a kind nobody would deny. But his genius is of a valuable kind only if art cultivated in a vacuum, for its own sake, is valuable. For none of his elaborate and laborious efforts to convince us that everything is identical with everything else has the slightest value, save as a warning. After he is through, Bloom remains Bloom and not Ulysses, and Ulysses remains Ulysses and not Bloom. The attempt to find a slimy lowest common denominator in which we are to see what is "real" in both Bloom and Ulysses is as puerile as Auden's thoughtless, empty joke at the expense of the explorer who discovers his mother atop the mountain. The warning Joyce gives is that individualism in modern art has gone up a blind alley. Technique is not a substitute for wisdom or even sense. Joyce's tortured language and maze of symbols express only himself—a self deliberately disunited from humanity for the sake of "unfettered freedom." But the consequence of that disunion is a species of dehumanization. The would-be Olympian spectator, from his height, finds humanity to be a race of dirty maudlin insects; the dirty maudlin insects find him to be over-ingenious and empty. The contrast here between Swift and Joyce is as marked as the resemblance mentioned above, and very illuminating.

Of *Finnegans Wake,* at which Joyce worked for sixteen years, little need be said, except that it carries still further Joyce's retreat into himself in pursuit of a wholly individual or "unfettered" medium of expression. In six hundred and twenty-six large pages he puts into words the dreams of a public-house keeper of Dublin during a single night's sleep. There are some very curious features of these dreams, as one scarcely need say, and there are isolated passages which are wonderfully expressive. Joyce proves himself even more ingenious than one could have supposed from *Ulysses,* and, it must be said, even more puerile. If language was tortured in *Ulysses,* it is crucified in *Finnegans Wake.* The consequence is that a large part of the book is practically unintelligible; and it is not conceivable that anyone except Joyce will ever know fully what he has been saying. At times words are twisted in simple ways for merely "cute" effects: "Vamp, vamp, vamp, the girls are merchand." But in general Joyce is speaking in a really private language, with what he calls "holusbolus authoritativeness," to himself alone. He has finally left this world for another, fashioned according to his own specifications, as Blake did, and it seems likely that the world will leave him in undisturbed possession of his dream.

Virginia Woolf

Joyce has not stood alone in his attempt to withdraw the novel from the world of action and to center it in the dimly lighted inner field of his characters' half-conscious reveries or dreams. He was preceded by Dorothy M. Richardson (Mrs. Alan Odle), who began to use the so-called stream-of-consciousness technique in the first book of her interminable *Pilgrimage,* written before the outbreak of the first World War, though not published until 1915, under the title *Pointed Roofs.* She has gone on to write book after book, using the same technique, publishing them as separate volumes with titles of their own, though they all are successive parts of *Pilgrimage.* This work has one resemblance (and only one) to Laurence Sterne's *Tristram Shandy,* in that there seems to be no reason why it should not continue indefinitely, stopping only with the author's death. Dorothy Richardson employs the stream-of-consciousness technique with competence, and her work interests other novelists, who have praised it but have not succeeded in arousing any public interest in it.

The case is different with Virginia Woolf (Mrs. Leonard Woolf, 1882–), the brilliant and keenly intelligent daughter of Leslie Stephen, the distinguished critic of literature and thought mentioned in the preceding chapter. Her earliest novels—the first, *The Voyage Out,* appeared in 1915— proved that she was a talented writer with acute perceptions and a sound imagination. She was, perhaps from the first, dissatisfied with the sociological novels then in fashion, and with the naturalistic attempts to make novels having the value of scientific documents from crude "slices of life." She thought Wells, Bennett, and Galsworthy materialistic and superficial; and was impressed, like many others, with the power of Russian writers of fiction—particularly Feodor Dostoevsky (1821–1881) and Anton Chekhov, or Tchehov (1860–1904)—to penetrate below the surface of life and lay bare the innermost souls of their characters. But she was apparently at a loss for some practicable way of going and doing likewise until she read the earliest work of Dorothy Richardson and some portions of Joyce's *Ulysses* which were printed in a periodical before the publication of the complete book. When she saw *Ulysses* in its entirety she felt compelled to pronounce it "a memorable catastrophe—immense in daring, terrific in disaster"—though she thought Joyce was on the right track.

After some experimentation, she wrote several novels in which she used the "stream-of-consciousness" technique (*Mrs. Dalloway,* 1925, and *To the Lighthouse,* 1927), and in which she has been accused of watering down and popularizing Joyce. The truth seems to be rather that she is just as courageous and just as independent as Joyce in using any material and any artistic method which she considers essential to her own purpose, but that she sees life differently and is a more competent artist. She has not, however, been able to make the so-called psychological novel popular, any more than has any other writer from Henry James on. And in *The Waves* (1931) it began to appear that she would in the end be no better able than others to overcome the difficulties which beset the artist in an age when there are no significant convictions shared alike by writers and the mass of common readers.

The Realm of Fantasy

Artist and prophet, artist and philosopher, artist and discoverer or inventor—any of these combinations is possible, as are still others. Hence no useful generalization concerning artists can be free from important exceptions. Nevertheless, it is an historical fact that much of the world's greatest art has come into being in ages when the patterns of social life and belief seemed to be fixed, or rather *were* for the time being fixed, and when artists were, as a consequence, freed to do their best in the way of giving classic form to that which was accepted alike by them and by their public. The romantic literature of the early nineteenth century was, as we have seen, a literature of protest and revolt, and it achieved both significance and beauty, and is, therefore, an exception to what has just been said. Yet it is not wholly an exception. The greater part of that literature has been a subject of acrimonious controversy for two generations because it raised questions which it could not answer and which we today still cannot answer; because, too, it implanted the notion that freedom

in itself is a good thing, for its own sake, and encouraged that disintegration of society whose disastrous progress we have traced into our own time.

Growing disunion produced, and has continued steadily in our time to produce, a crop of prophets or philosophers who were imperfect artists, and a crop of empty artists trying to disguise or brazen out their emptiness in the name of "pure" art. The pressure of the times on artists trying to escape this dilemma has, we have seen, forced them back upon themselves—forced them into reliance upon a purely personal or individual scale of values. Thus has arisen the paradox of self-expression as the aim of art, which has logically reached its apogee in kinds of writing which have no significance to anyone except the writer himself, alone in his strictly private world. In spite of herself, Virginia Woolf has in her successive books progressed towards this goal. But there is a way of escape, peculiarly tempting in desperate and disrupted times, for artists who feel that they are not prophets or philosophers and who are reluctant to withdraw completely from the world. There is the realm of fantasy, the realm of possibilities half-believed in, or of impossibilities not believed in at all but liked—the immemorially congenial realm of the *Arabian Nights' Entertainments.*

Virginia Woolf escaped into this realm, though not leaving all her serious preoccupations behind, in *Orlando* (1928). Her readers found a halfhearted escape rather bewildering, and in her next novel she returned to the serious and difficult job of wrestling with the "interior monologue." But other writers of our time, a numerous band, have gone over to the realm of fantasy, pure or mischievously adulterated, and have succeeded in being entertaining. Probably the most sensitive artist of them all is Sylvia Townsend Warner (1893–   ), whose *Lolly Willowes* (1926) deserves a place amongst the minor classics of English literature. None of her other books is quite so successful, though all are written in a beautiful restrained English and with a perfect sense for tone.

Others who have entered the realm of

fantasy, to make their homes there or for temporary relief, are: Arthur Machen (1863–); Algernon Blackwood (1869–); Forrest Reid (1876–); James Stephens (1882–), *The Crock of Gold,* 1912; Theodore Francis Powys (1875–), *Mr. Weston's Good Wine,* 1928; David Garnett (1892–), *Lady into Fox,* 1922; and E. M. Forster (1879–), in some of his stories in *The Celestial Omnibus,* 1911, and in *The Eternal Moment,* 1928.

Satire: Aldous Huxley

It might have been expected that the access of disillusion following the war years 1914–1918 would have conduced to a wave of satiric writing, but it did not. Several of the later plays of Bernard Shaw have shown the effect of the war and the postwar years on his inveterately satiric spirit; and Wyndham Lewis (1886–), in his buoyant and irrepressible way, has announced himself as the leader of a new age of satire, and has written several satirical novels, most notably *The Apes of God* (1930), to show how to be satiric in a modern way. But, in general, disillusion has thrown poets and novelists back into themselves in those experiments in self-expression which have been discussed at length in the present chapter. And the fact is that for effective satire, as for other forms of successful art, there must be points of reference which readers and writers accept, or which writers can take for granted in readers. This, however, as we have seen, is just what has been less and less the case in recent years.

Nevertheless, there have appeared since 1918 several writers who have given direct expression to angry or bitter complaint against the times and in whose books there are satirical elements. One of these writers is Richard Aldington (1892–), whose *Death of a Hero* (1929) outraged conventional patriotic sentiment in its picture of the state of mind of a returned soldier, who had held himself together through the horrors of war but could not face the horrors of peace, and preferred death. The book is hysterical; yet it is a truthful reflection of the feelings of many who fought in the war

and who later concluded that only a completely rotten society could have brought them up in ignorance of life's realities and sent them out to be slaughtered.

In *Death of a Hero* and in several subsequent novels, however, Aldington exhibits very little of the spirit of satire. He is merely angry because life is hard and the times are bad. Significantly, in *All Men Are Enemies* (1933), he concludes that this world is no place for sensitive souls, and pictures a battered artist and his battered companion agreeing to retire from it to nurse their dreams and grievances in isolation.

Aldous Leonard Huxley (1894–), who is a grandson of Thomas Henry Huxley and a grand-nephew of Matthew Arnold, has been mistaken for a satirist with more reason than can be found in the case of Aldington. His method is genuinely satirical in such novels as *Antic Hay* (1923) and *Point Counter Point* (1928); and in *Brave New World* (1932) he has, with little art but with much vivacity and humor, sketched a satirical caricature of the collectivist Utopia towards which science and industry are leading the way. He is altogether a more considerable figure than Aldington because he is more enlightened, more thoughtful, more completely disillusioned, and yet more resilient; but he is at bottom no more a satirist than Aldington. He is, rather, a moralist, who began life by rejecting everything in the name of an illusory freedom. And to his principal early rejections he remains constant. Like almost every modern English imaginative writer, he rejects not only traditional Christianity, but the outlook on life and scale of values enshrined in Christianity; yet at the same time he rejects the worldly alternative—belief in progress through science—towards which modern men have hopefully turned. His earlier novels made up, by clear implication, a comprehensive indictment of our age. They fall this side of true greatness because he is a very imperfect artist and seems to be incapable of deep feeling. They also fall short of satire because there appears to be nothing substantial in terms of which the indictment is drawn up.

Huxley seemed in the 1920's to be content

with the exposure of hypocrisy, and seemed to see nothing in human life except that and vulgar, sensual worldliness. He adopted some of the fashionable tricks of technique which have been mentioned in this chapter, not because the books he was writing demanded them, but apparently just to be in the swim. This strongly suggested that what he was saying also was said, not in the way of even imperfect satire, but rather as a journalistic report: "Ladies and Gentlemen, my generation, looking at the world with open eyes, has discovered that everything is the bunk. The human race is composed of swine. Those who do not admit it, and especially those who have been running the show, are hypocrites as well."

As was said in the early part of the present chapter, a conclusion of approximately this drift was reached in the 1920's by many sophisticated and immature people; and Huxley, becoming one of their representative voices, produced novels which, in catching the mood and thought of the time, have some value as social documents. The conclusion that "everything is the bunk" except swinishness is the verdict of immaturity, if for no other reason, because no one can live by it, as Huxley's later novels themselves show. In *Eyeless in Gaza* (1936) and *After Many a Summer Dies the Swan* (1940), and also in a critical inquiry entitled *Ends and Means* (1937), he has traveled very far from his earlier position and has, in fact, become a believer in a kind of non-Christian mysticism. Moreover, he has himself pointed out that his earlier insistence on the meaninglessness of everything was only a stage in his growth towards maturity, and not a point at which one could stop.

Huxley's development prompts two reflections. In the first place, his relatively immature books have seemed more impressive to readers than his mature ones. There are more reasons for this than can be mentioned here, but one reason is of particular importance to us. The "philosophy of meaninglessness" gives formal expression to a situation which no one in his senses wants to stay in or believes he can stay in, but out of which no one in our time has been able to show a clear way. The situation has been produced by that destruction of old beliefs and standards which seemed to be finally accomplished in the nineteenth century, by the subsequent disintegration of society, and by our contemporary disenchantment with the worldly gospel of progress through science. The gospel of meaninglessness is a confession of collapse and failure, and a signal for a fresh start. Everybody in his senses wants to make the fresh start, and there have been many in the last two generations—the later Huxley amongst them—who have offered to show the way. But there is no agreement amongst them, and they cannot all be right, and consequently the suggestion is irresistible that none of them is right. And we remain where we were. Some believe that we are helplessly witnessing the death of a civilization.

In the second place, Huxley's development is symbolic of the times in that his books are a series of more or less uncertain and provisional experiments. They can be regarded as a set of bulletins from a laboratory, recording stages in the prosecution of a prolonged piece of research. They enable us to follow an interesting personal growth. They show us a promising artist forced by the times to become a philosopher and finally becoming a prophet, while his art suffers. For he cannot be everything at once, and he has grown to personal maturity at the expense of art; just as others in our time have become artistic virtuosos at the expense of their humanity. But we do not have to be content with half-books when we turn from contemporary literature to Homer or Dante or Shakespeare.

D. H. Lawrence

David Herbert Lawrence (1885–1930) and Huxley were intimate friends. Huxley modeled from him a character in one of his novels, and Lawrence was not pleased; but the friendship held fast, and in 1932 Huxley edited *The Letters of D. H. Lawrence* with an Introduction which is the best critical explanation of the novelist and poet that has been published. The *Letters* themselves constitute an invaluable and profoundly interesting record. Indeed, the large volume containing them is Lawrence's best book, and probably the only one of his many productions which can be counted on to outlast the age and remain permanently fresh, illuminating, and treasurable. For Lawrence was a man of genius—perhaps the only Englishman of genius, in the full sense of the word, who has appeared in the British Isles in our time—yet he wrote no book which at all satisfyingly embodies his genius.

He arrested the attention of the discerning from the beginning of his career (he had published three novels and one volume of poems before 1914), and roused their hopes. Almost continuously through the last dozen years of his life he was surrounded by small bands of disciples who really looked on him as a new Redeemer come to lead the human race once more out of the wilderness. And he was continually writing; for he was impelled in spite of himself to try to give imaginative form—or, we may say, living reality—to the intense convictions which possessed him and endowed him with energy. Nevertheless, though he was primarily an artist, he remained to the end a very imperfect one; and it can be said of his novels, tales, and poems, as it was said of Huxley's books, that they are a series of more or less uncertain and provisional experiments.

Some have thought of Lawrence as primarily an evangelist or prophet, becoming an awkward artist for the sake of spreading his gospel. And he *was* a prophet, an inspired man, faithful at any cost to his intuitive certainties. He was, in a sense, the creature or servant of "firm persuasions," and was firmly persuaded that his intuitions sprang from a kind of primordial stuff far within, deeper than his conscious self and truer. In fact his intuitions came, he believed, directly from the universal principle of life itself. Herein lay his greatness. The kind of certitude he felt has, in some historical periods, been widespread, and has on occasion supported very odd or trivial conceits. There is no telling what some human being somewhere may not be firmly persuaded of —that the moon is made of green cheese, for example. Nevertheless, though humanity cannot accept every daemonic voice at its own valuation, we owe an incalculable debt to inspired seers and prophets; and in some instances we owe that debt because of what they have been, even though we do not know how to take what they have said.

Lawrence may have belonged to this race within the human race. Those who came into personal contact with him felt that he did, as was said above. And we can at least partly see why—from his letters better than from his books. Yet it is a mistake to suppose that he was only an artist secondarily, for the sake of his "message." He was, rather, a man comparable to William Blake, and has been instructively compared with Blake by several critics. His failures as an artist, moreover, though they were not at all of the same kind as Blake's, arose from the same cause. Both men wrote as the spirit dictated. Lawrence once confessed that he had got halfway through the writing of a novel without yet knowing what it was about. We are told that he never revised anything; if he thought he had not got a novel right, he sat down and wrote the whole thing out afresh. The imperfect art of some mystics has been valued more highly by succeeding generations than the finished and polished compositions of the men who have been masters of technique and of nothing else. And it has been highly valued because, however lamely, it did really translate into terms of the imagination some fragments of mystical wisdom. We have to ask, then, what were Lawrence's intuitive certainties, and whether he was wise beyond the common measure?

He was a mystic not only in our time but of our time. He was romantic in exactly the same sense that Blake was, but more than a century later. He had the benefit, if benefit it was, of knowing what modern psychology could tell him of the "unconscious." And though he was perhaps fanatically independent, and fully shared, in the twentieth century, Blake's disdain of the scientific intellect, he felt the pressure of the times and was a materialist in his mysticism. He could not believe that life is a spiritual principle which takes on material form; rather he believed that matter itself is living, in accordance with a true wisdom dark to us because our temporary lease of individuality and consciousness separates us off, deceptively, from the springs of our being. He therefore valued any experience in which a human being could be lifted out of himself and plunged into direct shuddering contact with that dark "otherness," as he called it, lying below consciousness and individuality, and really Real.

This is a species of denial of the wisdom of this world. It is not easy, however, to assess it. If one turns to Lawrence's efforts to express his conviction imaginatively, the most notorious and also the most explicit example is *Lady Chatterley's Lover* (1928) —a painful book which seems positively to invite misunderstanding. And, whatever bearing the fact may have on our estimate of Lawrence, the fact is that we can discover much better the quality and nature of his certitude from some of his letters than from any of his imaginative writings. There is in particular a letter he wrote as early as June, 1914, which places his central intuition in a clear light. He was answering a question about one of his novels:

Somehow that which is physic—non-human in humanity—is more interesting to me than the old-fashioned human element, which causes one to conceive a character in a certain moral scheme and make him consistent. The certain moral scheme is what I object to. In Turgenev, and in Tolstoi, and in Dostoevsky, the moral scheme into which all the characters fit . . . is dull, old, dead. When Marinetti [author of a manifesto concerning "Futurism"] writes: "It is the solidity of a blade of steel that is interesting by itself, that is, the incomprehending and inhuman alliance of its molecules in resistance to, let us say, a bullet. The heat of a piece of wood or iron is in fact more passionate, for us, than the laughter or tears of a woman"—then I know what he means. He is stupid, as an artist, for contrasting the heat of the iron and the laugh of the woman. Because what is interesting in the laugh of the woman is the same as the binding of the molecules of steel or their action in heat: it is the inhuman will, call it physiology, that fascinates me. I don't so much care for what the woman *feels*, in the ordinary usage of the word. That presumes an *ego* to feel with. I only care about what the woman *is* —what she IS—inhumanly, physiologically, materially—according to the use of the word: but for me, what she *is* as a phenomenon (or as representing some greater, inhuman will), in-

stead of what she feels according to the human conception. . . . You mustn't look in my novel for the old stable *ego* of the character. There is another *ego*, according to whose action the individual is unrecognizable, and passes through, as it were, allotropic states which it needs a deeper sense than any we've been used to exercise, to discover are states of the same single radically unchanged element.

Whether this be a new wisdom or a new folly, it is subversive. And Lawrence's revolt is strikingly and significantly different from that of his romantic predecessors of the nineteenth century. They rose in the name of our humanity against materialism, mechanism, and standardization; and even though their rebellion was unavailing, and unavailing in part because of their own failures, they nobly succeeded in reminding their generation and succeeding generations that man is a being with mysterious potentialities beyond the reach of a machine, and that no man should be used, like a machine, simply as a means to the ends of others. But Lawrence sees our humanity as a delusion. The conscious part of human nature, he believes, draws an obscuring veil over Reality, and even makes us engage unwittingly and wrongly in a conflict with Reality. He wants to give up the struggle, resign his separateness, and identify himself with some primal, undifferentiated, impersonal stuff which is the Reality alike of undiscerning stones and of men. Not even James Joyce is a more uncompromising individualist than Lawrence was in his life and art, yet Lawrence could see what he yearned for only as a dissolution into unconscious matter. T. S. Eliot has said that Lawrence's books strike him as those of a very sick man. But the sickness, if he is right, is widespread today; for it should be clear that Lawrence only bears witness, in his own way, to that progressive disintegration—of society, of beliefs and standards, of character, and of form in art—which has been a central feature of our times.

Popular Fiction

Many people look with incredulity on the evidences of cultural decay and death which recent literature presents; and point out, correctly, that in no earlier age of the Western world have so many men of talent been engaged in writing, and that, in fact, our time is producing a rich and varied literature amidst a perfect ferment of ideas and of artistic experimentation. There is indeed a positively embarrassing wealth of matter for the literary historian. Despite the length of this chapter, it has been impossible even to glance at such a keenly intelligent and artistically accomplished writer of short stories as Katherine Mansfield (1888–1923), or at such a novelist as Edward Morgan Forster (1879–), whose *A Passage to India* (1924) was a remarkable achievement deserving the very highest praise; and there are many others—Sir Hugh Seymour Walpole (1884–), for example—who would demand attention in any really comprehensive account of present-day English literature.

But it is not merely space which forbids us from going on and on. There was once a little boy who could not see the forest for the trees, and we all suffer from the same kind of difficulty when contemplating that which immediately surrounds us. Our only hope of getting a clear view of the distinguishing characteristics of very recent English literature has lain in selection and concentration. Otherwise, as was said earlier in the chapter, the handling of the subject would have been brought down to the level of a catalogue. We have now examined those writers in whose work we can most clearly see the ferment of ideas and of artistic experiment; and we can see, for one thing, that the process of fermentation has, against its historical background, a quite different significance from that which the workers in the vineyard themselves ascribe to it. There is, unfortunately, compelling reason to remember that fermentation is, after all, not a process of growth, but one of decay.

The truth is, moreover, that the recent literature most discussed and most praised by all the knowing critics is not understood and not read by the public. The reading public will not read verse or prose which is trying vainly to be "symphonic" or "polyphonic." Those members of the public who have a taste for symphonies prefer the genuine article, as presented by a good orchestra, and are to be complimented upon their discrimination. And similarly the reading public wants fiction which *is* fiction, with plot and action, as was remarked on an earlier page. That public prefers, also, in character study, what is human in humanity, just "the old-fashioned human element" that D. H. Lawrence rejected in favor of what Huxley calls "violent monotony and intense indistinctness."

Accordingly, in this age of independent and revolutionary writing, the public too has been showing some manly independence and has been carrying on a revolution of its own. It has turned to detective stories and dramatized biography. The detective story, one devoted reader of that species has acutely remarked, is the only form of contemporary fiction in which a murder is still a murder, and burglary (whatever the reasons, whatever the ancestry, family relationships, personal circumstances, idiosyncrasies, and what-not of the burglar and his victim) is still burglary and a crime, and so on. Hence, however elementary its treatment may be, the detective story at least is grounded firmly in the world we really live in, and all recognizable meaning is not refined away by subtle analysis. It may be sensational, improbable, infantile, fancy, or decked out in paste jewels; still, it does have a sound core of distinct meaning—and it flourishes, as every publisher and every proprietor of every lending library knows. And for those who are interested in what is human in humanity, the modern interpretative biography does very satisfyingly that which our "advanced" novelists have left behind them in their downhill "progress."

CHRONOLOGICAL OUTLINE

Political, Social, Religious		Literary, Philosophical
	1717–1797	Horace Walpole.
	1724–1804	Kant.
	1729–1797	Edmund Burke.
	1731–1800	William Cowper.
	1737–1794	Edward Gibbon.
	1740–1795	James Boswell.
	1748–1832	Jeremy Bentham.
Charles James Fox.	1749–1806	
	1749–1832	Goethe.
	1751–1816	Richard Brinsley Sheridan.
	1754–1832	George Crabbe.
	1757–1827	William Blake.
	1759–1796	Robert Burns.
	1759–1805	Schiller.
Reign of George III.	1760–1820	
	1768–1848	Chateaubriand.
	1770–1850	William Wordsworth.
	1771–1832	Sir Walter Scott.
	1772–1834	Samuel Taylor Coleridge.
	1774–1843	Robert Southey.
	1775	Sheridan's *Rivals* performed.
	1775–1817	Jane Austen.
	1775–1834	Charles Lamb.
	1775–1864	Walter Savage Landor.
	1777	Sheridan's *School for Scandal* performed.
	1778–1830	William Hazlitt.
	1782	Cowper's *Poems* and *Diverting History of John Gilpin*.
	1783	Blake's *Poetical Sketches*.
William Pitt the younger at the head of the cabinet.	1783–1801	
	1784–1859	Leigh Hunt.
	1785	Boswell's *Journal of a Tour to the Hebrides*.
		Cowper's *Poems* (including *The Task*).
	1785–1790	Thomas Warton poet laureate.
	1785–1859	Thomas De Quincey.
	1785–1873	Manzoni.
	1786	William Beckford's *Vathek* (English translation from original French).
		Burns's *Poems* (published at Kilmarnock).

POLITICAL, SOCIAL, RELIGIOUS		LITERARY, PHILOSOPHICAL
American Constitution signed.	1787	Goethe's *Iphigenie auf Tauris.*
Society for the Abolition of the Slave-trade founded (under William Wilberforce).		
Trial of Warren Hastings.	1788–1795	
	1788–1824	George Noel Gordon, Lord Byron.
Fall of the Bastille (beginning of the French Revolution).	1789	Blake's *Songs of Innocence.*
		William Lisle Bowles's *Fourteen Sonnets.*
		Gilbert White's *Natural History of Selborne.*
	1789–1792	Erasmus Darwin's *Botanic Garden.*
	1790	Blake's *Marriage of Heaven and Hell.*
		Burke's *Reflections on the French Revolution.*
		Ann Radcliffe's *Sicilian Romance.*
		Wordsworth's first visit to the Continent.
		Goethe's *Faust* (first published version).
	1790–1813	Henry James Pye poet laureate.
	1791	Boswell's *Life of Johnson.*
		Cowper's translation of the *Iliad* and the *Odyssey.*
	1791–1792	Thomas Paine's *Rights of Man.*
	1791–1793	Wordsworth's second visit to the Continent.
	1792	Thomas Holcroft's *Anna St. Ives.*
		Mary Wollstonecraft's *Rights of Woman.*
		Arthur Young's *Travels in France.*
	1792–1822	Percy Bysshe Shelley.
Louis XVI executed.	1793	William Godwin's *Political Justice.*
England enters the first coalition against France.		Wordsworth's *Evening Walk* and *Descriptive Sketches.*
Reign of Terror in France.	1793–1794	
Fall of Robespierre.	1794	William Godwin's *Caleb Williams.*
		Ann Radcliffe's *Mysteries of Udolpho.*
		Blake's *Songs of Experience.*
		Thomas Paine's *Age of Reason* (Part II, 1795; Part III, 1811).
	1795	Matthew Lewis's *Monk.*
		First meeting of Wordsworth and Coleridge.
	1795–1796	Goethe's *Wilhelm Meister.*
	1795–1821	John Keats.
	1795–1881	Thomas Carlyle.
Napoleon's Italian campaign.	1796	Gibbon's *Memoirs* (ed. Earl of Sheffield) published.
		William Roscoe's *Life of Lorenzo de' Medici.*
		Scott's *William and Helen* (translation of Bürger's *Leonore*).
	1797	Coleridge's *Kubla Khan* written.
	1797–1801	Coleridge's *Christabel* written.
	1797–1856	Heine.
Battle of the Nile.	1798	Landor's *Gebir.*
		Malthus's *Essay on Population.*

POLITICAL, SOCIAL, RELIGIOUS		LITERARY, PHILOSOPHICAL
	1798	Wordsworth and Coleridge's *Lyrical Ballads*.
		Wordsworth and Coleridge go to Germany.
	1798–1805	Wordsworth's *Prelude* written.
	1798–1828	Dorothy Wordsworth's *Journals* written.
	1798–1837	Leopardi.
Napoleon First Consul.	1799–1804	
Parliamentary Union of England and Ireland.	1800	Maria Edgeworth's *Castle Rackrent*.
		Wordsworth and Coleridge's *Lyrical Ballads* (second edition, with Preface).
	1800–1859	Thomas Babington, Lord Macaulay.
	1801	Chateaubriand's *Atala*.
		Southey's *Thalaba*.
	1801–1890	John Henry, Cardinal Newman.
Peace of Amiens.	1802	Chateaubriand's *Génie du Christianisme*.
		Edinburgh Review founded.
		Minstrelsy of the Scottish Border (ed. Scott).
	1802–1885	Victor Hugo.
War with France renewed.	1803	Jane Porter's *Thaddeus of Warsaw*.
	1803–1873	Edward Bulwer, Lord Lytton.
	1803–1882	Emerson.
	1804–1869	Sainte-Beuve.
Benjamin Disraeli, Earl of Beaconsfield.	1804–1881	
Battles of Austerlitz and Trafalgar.	1805	Scott's *Lay of the Last Minstrel*.
	1805–1812	Henry Cary's translation of the *Divina Commedia*.
Ministry of All the Talents.	1806–1807	
	1806–1861	Elizabeth Barrett Browning.
	1806–1873	John Stuart Mill.
Abolition of the slave trade.	1807	Byron's *Hours of Idleness*.
		Charles and Mary Lamb's *Tales from Shakespeare*.
		Wordsworth's *Poems in Two Volumes*.
	1808	Scott's *Marmion*.
		Lamb's *Specimens of the English Dramatic Poets*.
		August Wilhelm von Schlegel's lectures on Shakespeare.
Peninsular Campaign.	1808–1814	
	1808–1832	Goethe's *Faust*.
	1809	Thomas Campbell's *Gertrude of Wyoming and Other Poems*.
		Byron's *English Bards and Scotch Reviewers*.
		Hannah More's *Coelebs in Search of a Wife*.
		Quarterly Review founded.
	1809–1810	Coleridge's *Friend*.
	1809–1882	Charles Darwin.
	1809–1883	Edward FitzGerald.
	1809–1892	Alfred, Lord Tennyson.

POLITICAL, SOCIAL, RELIGIOUS		LITERARY, PHILOSOPHICAL
William Ewart Gladstone.	1809–1898	
	1810	Coleridge's lectures on Shakespeare (first published 1849).
		Crabbe's *Borough*.
		Jane Porter's *Scottish Chiefs*.
		Scott's *Lady of the Lake*.
	1811	Jane Austen's *Sense and Sensibility*.
Regency of Prince of Wales (later George IV).	1811–1820	
	1811–1833	Goethe's *Dichtung und Wahrheit*.
	1811–1863	William Makepeace Thackeray.
Napoleon's Russian campaign.	1812	
War with the United States.	1812–1815	
	1812–1816	Hegel's *Logic*.
	1812–1818	Byron's *Childe Harold*.
	1812–1870	Charles Dickens.
	1812–1889	Robert Browning.
Battle of Leipsic.	1813	Robert Owen's *New View of Society*.
		Shelley's *Queen Mab*.
		Southey's *Life of Nelson*.
		Jane Austen's *Pride and Prejudice*.
	1813–1843	Southey poet laureate.
Napoleon's abdication.	1814	Jane Austen's *Mansfield Park*.
		Scott's *Waverley*.
		Wordsworth's *Excursion*.
		Shelley's departure from England to the Continent.
Congress of Vienna.	1814–1815	
Return of Napoleon from Elba.	1815	Scott's *Guy Mannering*.
Battle of Waterloo.		Wordsworth's *White Doe of Rylstone*.
	1815–1882	Anthony Trollope.
	1816	Jane Austen's *Emma*.
		Byron's departure from England to the Continent.
		Coleridge's *Christabel* and *Kubla Khan* published.
		Leigh Hunt's *Story of Rimini*.
		Shelley's *Alastor*.
	1816–1855	Charlotte Brontë.
	1817	Byron's *Manfred*.
		Thomas Moore's *Lalla Rookh*.
		Coleridge's *Biographia Literaria* and *Sibylline Leaves*.
		Shelley's *Laon and Cythna* (*Revolt of Islam*).
		Keats's *Poems*.
		Hazlitt's *Characters of Shakespeare's Plays*.
		Blackwood's Magazine founded.
		David Ricardo's *Principles of Political Economy and Taxation*.
	1818	Byron's *Beppo*.
		Keats's *Endymion*.
		Mary Shelley's *Frankenstein*.
		Attack on Keats in the *Quarterly Review*.

POLITICAL, SOCIAL, RELIGIOUS		LITERARY, PHILOSOPHICAL
	1818	Jane Austen's *Northanger Abbey* and *Persuasion*.
		Thomas Love Peacock's *Nightmare Abbey*.
		Scott's *Heart of Midlothian*.
		Hazlitt's *Lectures on the English Poets*.
	1818–1848	Emily Brontë.
Peterloo Massacre.	1819	Scott's *Ivanhoe*.
		Crabbe's *Tales of the Hall*.
		Shelley's *Cenci*.
		Schopenhauer's *World as Will and Idea*.
	1819–1824	Byron's *Don Juan*.
	1819–1861	Arthur Hugh Clough.
	1819–1875	Charles Kingsley.
	1819–1880	Mary Ann Evans (George Eliot).
	1819–1900	John Ruskin.
	1820	Keats's *Lamia, Isabella, The Eve of St. Agnes, Hyperion, and Other Poems*.
		Shelley's *Prometheus Unbound*.
		John Clare's *Poems Descriptive of Rural Life*.
		Lamartine's *Méditations Poétiques*.
Reign of George IV.	1820–1830	
	1820–1903	Herbert Spencer.
	1821	Scott's *Kenilworth*.
		Shelley's *Adonais* and *Epipsychidion*.
		Southey's *Vision of Judgment*.
	1821–1880	Flaubert.
	1821–1881	Dostoevsky.
	1822	Byron's *Vision of Judgment*.
		De Quincey's *Confessions of an English Opium-Eater* (first version).
	1822–1888	Matthew Arnold.
	1823	Lamb's *Essays of Elia*.
		Scott's *Quentin Durward*.
	1824	Carlyle's translation of Goethe's *Wilhelm Meister*.
	1824–1829	Landor's *Imaginary Conversations*.
	1824–1832	Mary Mitford's *Our Village*.
Completion of the first railroad line in England.	1825	Coleridge's *Aids to Reflection*.
		Macaulay's *Milton*.
	1825–1895	Thomas Henry Huxley.
	1827	De Quincey's *Murder as One of the Fine Arts*.
		Heine's *Buch der Lieder*.
		John Keble's *Christian Year*.
Catholic Emancipation Act.	1828	Bulwer Lytton's *Pelham*.
		Carlyle's *Burns*.
	1828–1882	Dante Gabriel Rossetti.
	1828–1909	George Meredith.
	1828–1910	Tolstoy.
	1829	William Cobbett's *Advice to Young Men*.
July Revolution in France.	1830	William Cobbett's *Rural Rides* published.
		Hugo's *Hernani*.
		Tennyson's *Poems, Chiefly Lyrical*.

POLITICAL, SOCIAL, RELIGIOUS		LITERARY, PHILOSOPHICAL
	1830	Attack on Tennyson in the *Quarterly Review*.
	1830–1833	Sir Charles Lyell's *Principles of Geology*.
Reign of William IV.	1830–1837	
	1830–1894	Christina Rossetti.
	1831	Macaulay's *Samuel Johnson* and *Boswell*.
Reform Bill passed.	1832	Bulwer Lytton's *Eugene Aram*.
		Tennyson's *Poems*.
Factory Acts.	1833	Death of Arthur Hallam.
		Lamb's *Last Essays of Elia*.
		Browning's *Pauline*.
		Newman's *Arians of the Fourth Century*.
	1833–1834	Carlyle's *Sartor Resartus* published in *Fraser's Magazine*.
	1833–1841	*Tracts for the Times* (by Newman and others).
Oxford Movement.	1833–1845	
	1833–1850	Tennyson's *In Memoriam* written.
Poor Law.	1834	Sir Henry Taylor's *Philip van Artevelde*.
		Frederick Marryat's *Peter Simple* and *Jacob Faithful*.
		Bulwer Lytton's *Last Days of Pompeii*.
	1834–1896	William Morris.
	1835	Browning's *Paracelsus*.
		Bulwer Lytton's *Rienzi*.
		Vigny's *Chatterton*.
	1835–1902	Samuel Butler.
	1835–1907	Carducci.
	1836	Carlyle's *Sartor Resartus* published as a book (in Boston, U. S. A.).
		Emerson's *Nature*.
		Dickens's *Pickwick Papers* and *Sketches by Boz*.
	1836–1838	John Lockhart's *Life of Scott*.
	1837	Carlyle's *French Revolution*.
	1837–1838	Dickens's *Oliver Twist*.
Reign of Victoria.	1837–1901	
	1837–1909	Algernon Charles Swinburne.
Chartist Movement.	1838–1848	
	1839	William Harrison Ainsworth's *Jack Sheppard*.
		De Quincey's *Klosterheim*.
Opium War.	1839–1842	
	1839–1894	Walter Pater.
	1840	Browning's *Sordello*.
		Poe's *Tales of the Grotesque and Arabesque*.
		Shelley's *Letters and Miscellaneous Prose* (including the *Defense of Poetry*) published.
	1840–1847	Richard Barham's *Ingolsby Legends*.
	1840–1928	Thomas Hardy.

POLITICAL, SOCIAL, RELIGIOUS		LITERARY, PHILOSOPHICAL
	1841	Browning's *Pippa Passes*.
		Carlyle's *Heroes and Hero-Worship*.
		Charles J. Lever's *Charles O'Malley*.
		Macaulay's *Warren Hastings*.
		Newman's *Tract XC*.
	1841–1922	William Henry Hudson.
	1842	Browning's *Dramatic Lyrics*.
		Macaulay's *Lays of Ancient Rome*.
		Tennyson's *Poems*.
	1843	Carlyle's *Past and Present*.
		Thomas Hood's *Song of the Shirt* (in *Punch*).
		Macaulay's *Essays* (first authorized collection).
	1843–1850	Wordsworth poet laureate.
	1843–1860	Ruskin's *Modern Painters*.
	1843–1916	Henry James.
Opening of the first co-operative shop in Rochdale.	1844	William Barnes's *Poems of Rural Life*.
		Disraeli's *Coningsby*.
		Dumas's *Three Musketeers*.
		Alexander Kinglake's *Eothen*.
	1844–1889	Gerard Manley Hopkins (*Poems* first published 1918).
	1844–1930	Robert Bridges.
	1845	Carlyle's *Oliver Cromwell's Letters and Speeches*.
		Dickens's *Cricket on the Hearth*.
		Newman's entry into the Roman Catholic Church.
Corn Laws repealed.	1846	Marriage of Elizabeth Barrett and Robert Browning.
		Poems of the Brontë sisters.
		Bulwer Lytton's *New Timon*.
	1846–1856	George Grote's *History of Greece*.
	1847	C. Brontë's *Jane Eyre*.
		E. Brontë's *Wuthering Heights*.
		Tennyson's *Princess*.
	1847–1848	Thackeray's *Vanity Fair*.
	1848	Clough's *Bothie of Toper-na-Fuosich*.
		Elizabeth Gaskell's *Mary Barton*.
	1848–1850	Thackeray's *Pendennis*.
	1848–1861	Macaulay's *History of England, from the Accession of James the Second*.
	1849	Arnold's *Strayed Reveler and Other Poems*.
		Ruskin's *Seven Lamps of Architecture*.
	1849–1850	Dickens's *David Copperfield*.
	1850	E. B. Browning's *Sonnets from the Portuguese*.
		Browning's *Christmas Eve and Easter Day*.
		Carlyle's *Latter Day Pamphlets*.
		Emerson's *Representative Men*.
		The Germ (Rossetti and others).
		Hawthorne's *Scarlet Letter*.
		Kingsley's *Alton Locke*.

POLITICAL, SOCIAL, RELIGIOUS		LITERARY, PHILOSOPHICAL
	1850	Tennyson's *In Memoriam* published.
		Wordsworth's *Prelude* published.
	1850–1892	Tennyson poet laureate.
	1850–1894	Robert Louis Stevenson.
Great Exhibition at the Crystal Palace.	1851	Thomas Lovell Beddoes's *Death's Jest Book.*
Coup d'État of Louis Napoleon (Napoleon III).		George Borrow's *Lavengro.*
		Carlyle's *Life of John Sterling.*
		FitzGerald's *Euphranor.*
		Melville's *Moby Dick.*
	1851–1853	Ruskin's *Stones of Venice.*
	1852	Arnold's *Empedocles on Etna and Other Poems.*
		Newman's lectures *On the Scope and Nature of University Education.*
		Thackeray's *Henry Esmond.*
	1852–1853	Dickens's *Bleak House.*
	1852–1933	George Moore.
	1853	Arnold's *Poems* (including *The Scholar Gypsy*).
		C. Brontë's *Villette.*
		Elizabeth Gaskell's *Cranford.*
		Kingsley's *Hypatia.*
		Landor's *Last Fruit off an Old Tree.*
		Thackeray's *English Humorists* published.
	1853–1855	Thackeray's *Newcomes.*
	1853–1856	
Crimean War.	1853–1902	
Cecil John Rhodes.	1854	Dickens's *Hard Times.*
		Thoreau's *Walden.*
	1854–1862	Coventry Patmore's *Angel in the House.*
	1854–1900	Oscar Wilde.
	1855	Browning's *Men and Women.*
		Kingsley's *Westward Ho.*
		Spencer's *Principles of Psychology.*
		Tennyson's *Maud.*
		Trollope's *Warden.*
		Whitman's *Leaves of Grass.*
Second Chinese War.	1855–1860	
	1856	Dinah Mulock's *John Halifax, Gentleman.*
		De Quincey's *Confessions of an English Opium-Eater* (enlarged edition).
		The Oxford and Cambridge Magazine (Morris and others).
	1856–1870	James Anthony Froude's *History of England.*
	1856–	George Bernard Shaw.
	1857	Henry Thomas Buckle's *History of Civilization in England.*
		E. B. Browning's *Aurora Leigh.*
		Flaubert's *Madame Bovary.*
		Thomas Hughes's *Tom Brown's School Days.*
		Trollope's *Barchester Towers.*

Sepoy Mutiny.	1857–1858	
	1857–1903	George Gissing.
	1857–1924	Joseph Conrad.
	1858	Eliot's *Scenes of Clerical Life.*
		Morris's *Defense of Guinevere.*
	1858–1865	Carlyle's *Frederick the Great.*
	1859	Darwin's *Origin of Species.*
		Dickens's *Tale of Two Cities.*
		FitzGerald's *Rubáiyát of Omar Khay-yám* (first edition).
		Meredith's *Ordeal of Richard Feverel.*
		Mill's *On Liberty.*
		Eliot's *Adam Bede.*
		Newman's *Idea of a University.*
Unification of Italy.	1859–1871	
	1859–1880	David Masson's *Life of Milton.*
	1859–1885	Tennyson's *Idyls of the King.*
	1859–1907	Francis Thompson.
	1859–1936	Alfred E. Housman.
	1860	Wilkie Collins's *Woman in White.*
		Eliot's *Mill on the Floss.*
	1860–1937	James M. Barrie.
Death of Prince Albert.	1861	Arnold's *On Translating Homer.*
		Eliot's *Silas Marner.*
		Reade's *Cloister and the Hearth.*
American Civil War.	1861–1865	
	1861–1874	James Spedding's *Life and Letters of Francis Bacon.*
	1862	Meredith's *Modern Love and Other Poems.*
		C. Rossetti's *Goblin Market and Other Poems.*
		Ruskin's *Unto This Last.*
		Spencer's *First Principles.*
		Turgenev's *Fathers and Sons.*
	1863	Eliot's *Romola.*
		Huxley's *Man's Place in Nature.*
		Kingsley's *Water Babies.*
		Renan's *Vie de Jésus.*
	1863–1864	Taine's *Histoire de la Littérature Anglaise.*
	1864	Browning's *Dramatis Personae.*
		Newman's *Apologia pro Vita Sua.*
		Tennyson's *Enoch Arden.*
	1865	Arnold's *Essays in Criticism* (First Series).
		Lewis Carroll's (Charles L. Dodgson's) *Alice's Adventures in Wonderland.*
		Swinburne's *Atalanta in Calydon.*
	1865–1868	Ruskin's *Sesame and Lilies.*
	1865–1872	Tolstoy's *War and Peace.*
	1865–1936	Rudyard Kipling.
	1865–1939	William Butler Yeats.
	1866	Dostoevsky's *Crime and Punishment.*
		Ruskin's *Crown of Wild Olive.*

POLITICAL, SOCIAL, RELIGIOUS		LITERARY, PHILOSOPHICAL
	1866	Swinburne's *Poems and Ballads* (First Series).
	1866–	Herbert George Wells.
Factory Acts.	1867	Arnold's *New Poems* (including *Thyrsis*).
Reform Act.		Bagehot's *English Constitution*.
		Morris's *Life and Death of Jason*.
		Thomas William Robertson's *Caste* acted.
	1867–1905	Marx and Engels's *Kapital*.
	1867–1933	John Galsworthy.
	1868	Wilkie Collins's *Moonstone*.
		FitzGerald's *Rubáiyát of Omar Khayyám* (second and much altered edition).
	1868–1869	Browning's *Ring and the Book*.
	1868–1870	Morris's *Earthly Paradise*.
Gladstone head of the cabinet.	1868–1874	
Suez Canal opened.	1869	Arnold's *Culture and Anarchy*.
		William Edward Lecky's *History of European Morals*.
		Richard D. Blackmore's *Lorna Doone*.
		Clough's *Dipsychus*.
Elementary Education Act.	1870	Rossetti's *Collected Poems*.
		Huxley's *Lay Sermons*.
Franco-Prussian War.	1870–1871	
Abolition of the religious tests at Oxford and Cambridge.	1871	Robert Buchanan's *Fleshly School of Poetry* (magazine article attacking Rossetti).
		Darwin's *Descent of Man*.
		Swinburne's *Songs before Sunrise*.
		Benjamin Jowett's translation of Plato's *Dialogues*.
	1871–1872	Eliot's *Middlemarch*.
	1871–1884	Ruskin's *Fors Clavigera*.
	1871–1909	John Millington Synge.
	1871–1922	Marcel Proust.
Act providing for the use of the Australian ballot.	1872	Butler's *Erewhon*.
		Hardy's *Under the Greenwood Tree*.
	1873	Arnold's *Literature and Dogma*.
		John Stuart Mill's *Autobiography*.
		Pater's *Studies in the History of the Renaissance*.
	1874	Hardy's *Far from the Madding Crowd*.
		James Thomson's *City of Dreadful Night*.
Disraeli head of the cabinet.	1874–1880	
Employers' and Workmen's Act.	1875	
	1875–1876	Tolstoy's *Anna Karenina*.
	1875–	Thomas Mann.
	1876	Bridges' *Growth of Love*.
		Sir Leslie Stephen's *English Thought in the Eighteenth Century*.
	1877	James's *American*.
Congress of Berlin.	1878	Hardy's *Return of the Native*.
		Lecky's *History of England in the Eighteenth Century*.

POLITICAL, SOCIAL, RELIGIOUS		LITERARY, PHILOSOPHICAL
	1878	Swinburne's *Poems and Ballads* (Second Series).
	1878–	John Masefield.
	1879	Edwin Arnold's *Light of Asia*.
		Walter Bagehot's *Literary Studies*.
		Ibsen's *Doll's House*.
		Meredith's *Egoist*.
	1880	Dostoevsky's *Brothers Karamazov*.
		Wilfred Scawen Blunt's *Love Sonnets of Proteus*.
		Gissing's *Workers in the Dawn*.
		Lewis Wallace's *Ben Hur*.
	1881	Ibsen's *Ghosts*.
		James's *Portrait of a Lady*.
		Rossetti's *Ballads and Sonnets*.
		Stevenson's *Virginibus Puerisque*.
		Wilde's *Poems*.
Triple Alliance.	1882	Stevenson's *New Arabian Nights* and *Treasure Island*.
	1882–	James Joyce.
	1883	Richard Jefferies's *Story of My Heart*.
Fall of Khartoum.	1885	Sir William Gilbert and Sir Arthur Sullivan's *Mikado*.
		Meredith's *Diana of the Crossways*.
		Pater's *Marius the Epicurean*.
		Stevenson's *Child's Garden of Verses*.
	1885–1889	Ruskin's *Praeterita*.
	1885–1930	David Herbert Lawrence.
	1886	Kipling's *Departmental Ditties*.
		Hardy's *Mayor of Casterbridge*.
		Stevenson's *Doctor Jekyll and Mr. Hyde* and *Kidnapped*.
		Tennyson's *Locksley Hall Sixty Years After*.
	1888	Arnold's *Essays in Criticism* (Second Series).
		Charles Montagu Doughty's *Travels in Arabia Deserta*.
		Hardy's *Wessex Tales*.
		Kipling's *Soldiers Three*.
		Mrs. Humphry Ward's *Robert Elsmere*.
	1888–1935	Thomas Edward Lawrence.
	1888–	Thomas Stearns Eliot.
	1889	Browning's *Asolando*.
		FitzGerald's *Letters and Literary Remains*.
		Pater's *Appreciations*.
		Stevenson's *Master of Ballantrae*.
		Yeats's *Wanderings of Oisin and Other Poems*.
Fall of Bismarck.	1890	Sir James George Frazer's *Golden Bough* (first edition; later much enlarged).
		Sir William Watson's *Wordsworth's Grave*.
	1890–	Aldous Huxley.

POLITICAL, SOCIAL, RELIGIOUS		LITERARY, PHILOSOPHICAL
	1891	Barrie's *Little Minister.*
		Gissing's *New Grub Street.*
		Hardy's *Tess of the D'Urbervilles.*
		Morris's *News from Nowhere.*
		Wilde's *House of Pomegranates, Picture of Dorian Gray,* and *Intentions.*
	1892	Kipling's *Barrack-Room Ballads.*
		Wilde's *Lady Windermere's Fan* acted.
	1892–1896	Austen Dobson's *Eighteenth-Century Vignettes.*
	1893	Anatole France's *La Rôtisserie de la Reine Pedauque.*
		William Ernest Henley's *London Voluntaries.*
		Sir Arthur Pinero's *Second Mrs. Tanqueray* acted.
		Pater's *Plato and Platonism.*
		Thompson's *Poems* (including *The Hound of Heaven*).
Dreyfus Trial.	1894	John Davidson's *Ballads and Songs.*
		Kipling's *Jungle Book.*
		George Moore's *Esther Waters.*
	1894–1897	*The Yellow Book* (Aubrey Beardsley and others).
	1895	Stephen Crane's *Red Badge of Courage.*
		Hardy's *Jude the Obscure.*
		Lionel Johnson's *Poems.*
		Wilde's *Importance of Being Earnest* acted.
	1896	Housman's *Shropshire Lad.*
		Stevenson's *Weir of Hermiston.*
	1896–1913	Alfred Austin poet laureate.
Diamond Jubilee of Queen Victoria.	1897	Conrad's *Nigger of the Narcissus.*
		Henry Arthur Jones's *Liars.*
		Meredith's *Essay on Comedy.*
	1898	Hardy's *Wessex Poems.*
		Maurice Hewlett's *Forest Lovers.*
		James's *Two Magics* (including *The Turn of the Screw*).
		Shaw's *Plays: Pleasant and Unpleasant.*
		Wilde's *Ballad of Reading Gaol.*
Boxer Uprising.	1899–1900	
Boer War.	1899–1902	
	1900	Conrad's *Lord Jim.*
	1901	Kipling's *Kim.*
		Shaw's *Three Plays for Puritans.*
Reign of Edward VII.	1901–1910	
	1902	Conrad's *Youth.*
		James's *Wings of the Dove.*
		Mann's *Buddenbrooks.*
		Masefield's *Saltwater Ballads.*
	1903	Chekhov's *Cherry Orchard.*
		John, Viscount Morley's *Life of William Ewart Gladstone.*
		Butler's *Way of All Flesh.*

	POLITICAL, SOCIAL, RELIGIOUS		LITERARY, PHILOSOPHICAL
		1903	Gissing's *Private Papers of Henry Ryecroft.*
			James's *Ambassadors.*
			Shaw's *Man and Superman.*
	Entente Cordiale between France and Britain.	1903–1908	Hardy's *Dynasts.*
		1904	Barrie's *Peter Pan.*
			Conrad's *Nostromo.*
			Hudson's *Green Mansions.*
			James's *Golden Bowl.*
		1905	Ernest Dowson's *Poems.*
			Synge's *Riders to the Sea.*
	Algeciras Crisis.	1905–1906	George Santayana's *Life of Reason.*
		1906	Kipling's *Puck of Pook's Hill.*
		1906–1922	Galsworthy's *Forsyte Saga.*
	Triple Entente.	1907	Sir John E. E. Dalberg, Lord Acton's *History of Freedom.*
			Synge's *Playboy of the Western World.*
		1908	Arnold Bennett's *Old Wives' Tale.*
			Anatole France's *Penguin Island.*
			Sir Arthur W. Pinero's *Thunderbolt.*
	Lloyd George's budget.	1909	Galsworthy's *Justice.*
			Lady Augusta Gregory's *Seven Short Plays.*
			H. G. Wells's *Tono Bungay.*
		1910	Arnold Bennett's *Clayhanger.*
			Alfred Noyes's *Collected Poems.*
	Reign of George V.	1910–1936	
	Agadir Crisis.	1911	Max Beerbohm's *Zuleika Dobson.*
			Rupert Brooke's *Poems.*
			Masefield's *Everlasting Mercy.*
			H. G. Wells's *New Machiavelli.*
			Yeats's *Celtic Twilight.*
		1911–1913	Moore's *Hail and Farewell.*
		1912	Max Beerbohm's *Christmas Garland.*
			Walter De la Mare's *Listeners.*
			Masefield's *Widow in the Bye Street.*
			James Stephens's *Crock of Gold.*
		1913	D. H. Lawrence's *Sons and Lovers.*
			Masefield's *Dauber.*
		1913–1925	Proust's *À la Recherche du Temps Perdu.*
		1913–1930	Bridges poet laureate.
	Assassination of Archduke Ferdinand at Sarajevo.	1914	Hardy's *Satires of Circumstance.*
	World War.		Joyce's *Dubliners.*
		1914–1918	

Index of Historical and Critical Introductions

Index of Authors, Titles, and First Lines of Poems

Names of authors are printed in CAPITALS, and titles are printed in *italics*. Titles beginning with
"A," "An," or "The" are indexed under their second words. In cases where the title of a poem is
identical with its first line, or with the initial portion of it, the title only is indexed.